ADVANCES IN NEURAL INFORMATION PROCESSING SYSTEMS 12

ADVANCES IN NEURAL INFORMATION PROCESSING SYSTEMS

Published by Morgan-Kaufmann

NIPS-1
Advances in Neural Information Processing Systems 1: Proceedings of the 1988 Conference,
David S. Touretzky, ed., 1989.

NIPS-2
Advances in Neural Information Processing Systems 2: Proceedings of the 1989 Conference,
David S. Touretzky, ed., 1990.

NIPS-3
Advances in Neural Information Processing Systems 3: Proceedings of the 1990 Conference,
Richard Lippmann, John E. Moody and David S. Touretzky, eds., 1991.

NIPS-4
Advances in Neural Information Processing Systems 4: Proceedings of the 1991 Conference,
John E. Moody, Stephen J. Hanson and Richard P. Lippmann, eds., 1992.

NIPS-5
Advances in Neural Information Processing Systems 5: Proceedings of the 1992 Conference,
Stephen J. Hanson, Jack D. Cowan and C. Lee Giles, eds., 1993.

NIPS-6
Advances in Neural Information Processing Systems 6: Proceedings of the 1993 Conference,
Jack D. Cowan, Gerald Tesauro and Joshua Alspector, eds., 1994.

Published by The MIT Press

NIPS-7
Advances in Neural Information Processing Systems 7: Proceedings of the 1994 Conference,
Gerald Tesauro, David S. Touretzky and Todd K. Leen, eds., 1995.

NIPS-8
Advances in Neural Information Processing Systems 8: Proceedings of the 1995 Conference,
David S. Touretzky, Michael C. Mozer and Michael E. Hasselmo, eds., 1996.

NIPS-9
Advances in Neural Information Processing Systems 9: Proceedings of the 1996 Conference,
Michael C. Mozer, Michael I. Jordan and Thomas Petsche, eds., 1997.

NIPS-10
Advances in Neural Information Processing Systems 10: Proceedings of the 1997 Conference,
Michael I. Jordan, Michael J. Kearns and Sara A. Solla, eds., 1998.

NIPS-11
Advances in Neural Information Processing Systems 11: Proceedings of the 1998 Conference,
Michael S. Kearns, Sara A. Solla and David A. Cohn, eds., 1999.

NIPS-12
Advances in Neural Information Processing Systems 12: Proceedings of the 1999 Conference,
Sara A. Solla, Todd K. Leen and Klaus-Robert Müller, eds., 2000.

ADVANCES IN NEURAL INFORMATION PROCESSING SYSTEMS 12

Proceedings of the 1999 Conference

edited by
Sara A. Solla, Todd K. Leen and Klaus-Robert Müller

A Bradford Book
The MIT Press
Cambridge, Massachusetts
London, England

© 2000 Massachusetts Institute of Technology

All rights reserved. No part of this book may be reproduced in any form by any electronic or mechanical means (including photocopying, recording or information storage and retrieval) without permission in writing from the publisher.

This book was printed and bound in the United States of America.

ISSN: 1049-5258
ISBN: 0-262-19450-3

Contents

Preface xiii

NIPS Committees xv

Reviewers xvii

Part I Cognitive Science

Recognizing Evoked Potentials in a Virtual Environment,
Jessica D. Bayliss and Dana H. Ballard 3

A Neurodynamical Approach to Visual Attention, Gustavo Deco and Josef Zihl . . . 10

*Effects of Spatial and Temporal Contiguity on the Acquisition of Spatial
Information,* Thea B. Ghiselli-Crippa and Paul W. Munro 17

Acquisition in Autoshaping, Sham Kakade and Peter Dayan 24

Robust Recognition of Noisy and Superimposed Patterns via Selective Attention,
Soo-Young Lee and Michael C. Mozer 31

Perceptual Organization Based on Temporal Dynamics,
Xiuwen Liu and DeLiang L. Wang 38

Information Factorization in Connectionist Models of Perception,
Javier R. Movellan and James L. McClelland 45

Graded Grammaticality in Prediction Fractal Machines,
Shan Parfitt, Peter Tiño and Georg Dorffner 52

Rules and Similarity in Concept Learning, Joshua B. Tenenbaum 59

Evolving Learnable Languages, Bradley Tonkes, Alan Blair and Janet Wiles 66

Learning Statistically Neutral Tasks without Expert Guidance,
Ton Weijters, Antal van den Bosch and Eric Postma 73

A Generative Model for Attractor Dynamics,
Richard S. Zemel and Michael C. Mozer 80

Part II Neuroscience

Recurrent Cortical Competition: Strengthen or Weaken?,
Péter Adorján, Lars Schwabe, Christian Piepenbrock and Klaus Obermayer 89

Effective Learning Requires Neuronal Remodeling of Hebbian Synapses,
Gal Chechik, Isaac Meilijson and Eytan Ruppin 96

Wiring Optimization in the Brain, Dmitri B. Chklovskii and Charles F. Stevens . . 103

Optimal Sizes of Dendritic and Axonal Arbors, Dmitri B. Chklovskii 108

Neural Representation of Multi-Dimensional Stimuli,
Christian W. Eurich, Stefan D. Wilke and Helmut Schwegler 115

Spiking Boltzmann Machines, Geoffrey E. Hinton and Andrew D. Brown 122

Distributed Synchrony of Spiking Neurons in a Hebbian Cell Assembly,
David Horn, Nir Levy, Isaac Meilijson and Eytan Ruppin 129

Can V1 Mechanisms Account for Figure-Ground and Medial Axis Effects?,
Zhaoping Li 136

Channel Noise in Excitable Neural Membranes,
Amit Manwani, Peter N. Steinmetz and Christof Koch 143

LTD Facilitates Learning in a Noisy Environment,
Paul W. Munro and Gerardina Hernandez 150

Memory Capacity of Linear vs. Nonlinear Models of Dendritic Integration,
Panayiota Poirazi and Bartlett W. Mel 157

Predictive Sequence Learning in Recurrent Neocortical Circuits,
Rajesh P. N. Rao and Terrence J. Sejnowski 164

*A Recurrent Model of the Interaction Between Prefrontal and Inferotemporal
Cortex in Delay Tasks,* Alfonso Renart, Nestor Parga and Edmund T. Rolls 171

Information Capacity and Robustness of Stochastic Neuron Models,
Elad Schneidman, Idan Segev and Naftali Tishby 178

*An MEG Study of Response Latency and Variability in the Human Visual System
During a Visual-Motor Integration Task,* Akaysha C. Tang,
Barak A. Pearlmutter, Tim A. Hely, Michael Zibulevsky and Michael P. Weisend . 185

Population Decoding Based on an Unfaithful Model,
Si Wu, Hiroyuki Nakahara, Noboru Murata and Shun-ichi Amari 192

Spike-based Learning Rules and Stabilization of Persistent Neural Activity,
Xiaohui Xie and H. Sebastian Seung 199

Part III Theory

A Variational Baysian Framework for Graphical Models, Hagai Attias 209

Model Selection in Clustering by Uniform Convergence Bounds,
Joachim M. Buhmann and Marcus Held 216

Uniqueness of the SVM Solution, Christopher J. C. Burges and David J. Crisp . . . 223

Model Selection for Support Vector Machines,
Olivier Chapelle and Vladimir N. Vapnik 230

*Dynamics of Supervised Learning with Restricted Training Sets and Noisy
Teachers,* A. C. C. Coolen and C. W. H. Mace 237

A Geometric Interpretation of ν-SVM Classifiers,
David J. Crisp and Christopher J. C. Burges 244

Efficient Approaches to Gaussian Process Classification,
Lehel Csató, Ernest Fokoué, Manfred Opper, Bernhard Schottky and Ole Winther . . 251

Potential Boosters?, Nigel Duffy and David Helmbold 258

Bayesian Averaging is Well-Temperated, Lars Kai Hansen 265

Regular and Irregular Gallager-type Error-Correcting Codes,
Yoshiyuki Kabashima, Tatsuto Murayama, David Saad and Renato Vicente 272

Mixture Density Estimation, Jonathan Q. Li and Andrew R. Barron 279

Statistical Dynamics of Batch Learning, Song Li and K. Y. Michael Wong 286

Neural Computation with Winner-Take-All as the Only Nonlinear Operation,
Wolfgang Maass 293

Boosting with Multi-Way Branching in Decision Trees,
Yishay Mansour and David McAllester 300

Inference for the Generalization Error, Claude Nadeau and Yoshua Bengio 307

Resonance in a Stochastic Neuron Model with Delayed Interaction,
Toru Ohira, Yuzuru Sato and Jack D. Cowan 314

*Understanding Stepwise Generalization of Support Vector Machines: a Toy
Model,* Sebastian Risau-Gusman and Mirta B. Gordon 321

*Lower Bounds on the Complexity of Approximating Continuous Functions by
Sigmoidal Neural Networks,* Michael Schmitt 328

Noisy Neural Networks and Generalizations,
Hava T. Siegelmann, Alexander Roitershtein and Asa Ben-Hur 335

The Entropy Regularization Information Criterion, Alexander J. Smola,
John Shawe-Taylor, Bernhard Schölkopf and Robert C. Williamson 342

Probabilistic Methods for Support Vector Machines, Peter Sollich 349

Algebraic Analysis for Non-regular Learning Machines, Sumio Watanabe 356

*Semiparametric Approach to Multichannel Blind Deconvolution of Nonminimum
Phase Systems,* L.-Q. Zhang, Shun-ichi Amari and A. Cichocki 363

*Some Theoretical Results Concerning the Convergence of Compositions of
Regularized Linear Functions,* Tong Zhang 370

Part IV Algorithms and Architecture

Robust Full Bayesian Methods for Neural Networks,
Christophe Andrieu, João F. G. de Freitas and Arnaud Doucet 379

Independent Factor Analysis with Temporally Structured Sources, Hagai Attias . . 386

Gaussian Fields for Approximate Inference in Layered Sigmoid Belief Networks,
David Barber and Peter Sollich 393

Modeling High-Dimensional Discrete Data with Multi-Layer Neural Networks,
Yoshua Bengio and Samy Bengio 400

Robust Neural Network Regression for Offline and Online Learning,
Thomas Briegel and Volker Tresp 407

Reconstruction of Sequential Data with Probabilistic Models and Continuity Constraints, Miguel Á. Carreira-Perpiñán 414

Transductive Inference for Estimating Values of Functions,
Olivier Chapelle, Vladimir N. Vapnik and Jason Weston 421

The Nonnegative Boltzmann Machine,
Oliver B. Downs, David J.C. MacKay and Daniel D. Lee 428

Differentiating Functions of the Jacobian with Respect to the Weights,
Gary William Flake and Barak A. Pearlmutter 435

Local Probability Propagation for Factor Analysis, Brendan J. Frey 442

Variational Inference for Bayesian Mixtures of Factor Analysers,
Zoubin Ghahramani and Matthew J. Beal 449

Bayesian Transduction, Thore Graepel, Ralf Herbrich and Klaus Obermayer 456

Learning to Parse Images,
Geoffrey E. Hinton, Zoubin Ghahramani and Yee Whye Teh 463

Maximum Entropy Discrimination, Tommi Jaakkola, Marina Meila and Tony Jebara 470

Topographic Transformation as a Discrete Latent Variable,
Nebojsa Jojic and Brendan J. Frey 477

An Improved Decomposition Algorithm for Regression Support Vector Machines,
Pavel Laskov 484

Algorithms for Independent Components Analysis and Higher Order Statistics,
Daniel D. Lee, Uri Rokni and Haim Sompolinsky 491

The Relaxed Online Maximum Margin Algorithm, Yi Li and Philip M. Long 498

Bayesian Network Induction via Local Neighborhoods,
Dimitris Margaritis and Sebastian Thrun 505

Boosting Algorithms as Gradient Descent,
Llew Mason, Jonathan Baxter, Peter Bartlett and Marcus Frean 512

A Multi-class Linear Learning Algorithm Related to Winnow, Chris Mesterharm . . 519

Invariant Feature Extraction and Classification in Kernel Spaces,
Sebastian Mika, Gunnar Rätsch, Jason Weston, Bernhard Schölkopf,
Alexander J. Smola and Klaus–Robert Müller 526

Approximate Inference Algorithms for Two-Layer Bayesian Networks,
Andrew Y. Ng and Michael I. Jordan 533

Optimal Kernel Shapes for Local Linear Regression,
Dirk Ormoneit and Trevor Hastie 540

Large Margin DAGs for Multiclass Classification,
John C. Platt, Nello Cristianini and John Shawe-Taylor 547

The Infinite Gaussian Mixture Model, Carl Edward Rasmussen 554

ν-Arc: Ensemble Learning in the Presence of Outliers, Gunnar Rätsch,
Bernhard Schölkopf, Alexander J. Smola, Klaus–Robert Müller, Takashi Onoda
and Sebastian Mika 561

Nonlinear Discriminant Analysis Using Kernel Functions,
Volker Roth and Volker Steinhage 568

An Analysis of Turbo Decoding with Gaussian Densities,
Paat Rusmevichientong and Benjamin Van Roy 575

Support Vector Method for Novelty Detection, Bernhard Schölkopf,
Robert C. Williamson, Alexander J. Smola, John Shawe-Taylor and John C. Platt . 582

*Better Generative Models for Sequential Data Problems: Bidirectional Recurrent
Mixture Density Networks,* Mike Schuster 589

Greedy Importance Sampling, Dale Schuurmans 596

*Bayesian Model Selection for Support Vector Machines, Gaussian Processes and
Other Kernel Classifiers,* Matthias Seeger 603

Leveraged Vector Machines, Yoram Singer 610

Agglomerative Information Bottleneck, Noam Slonim and Naftali Tishby 617

*Training Data Selection for Optimal Generalization in Trigonometric Polynomial
Networks,* Masashi Sugiyama and Hidemitsu Ogawa 624

Predictive Approaches for Choosing Hyperparameters in Gaussian Processes,
S. Sundararajan and S. Sathiya Keerthi 631

On Input Selection with Reversible Jump Markov Chain Monte Carlo Sampling,
Peter Sykacek 638

Building Predictive Models from Fractal Representations of Symbolic Sequences,
Peter Tiňo and Georg Dorffner 645

The Relevance Vector Machine, Michael E. Tipping 652

Support Vector Method for Multivariate Density Estimation,
Vladimir N. Vapnik and Sayan Mukherjee 659

Dual Estimation and the Unscented Transformation,
Eric A. Wan, Rudolph van der Merwe and Alex T. Nelson 666

*Correctness of Belief Propagation in Gaussian Graphical Models of Arbitrary
Topology,* Yair Weiss and William T. Freeman 673

A MCMC Approach to Hierarchical Mixture Modelling, Christopher K. I. Williams 680

*Data Visualization and Feature Selection: New Algorithms for Nongaussian
Data,* Howard Hua Yang and John Moody 687

Manifold Stochastic Dynamics for Bayesian Learning,
Mark Zlochin and Yoram Baram 694

Part V Implementation

The Parallel Problems Server: an Interactive Tool for Large Scale Machine Learning, Charles Lee Isbell, Jr. and Parry Husbands 703

An Oculo-Motor System with Multi-Chip Neuromorphic Analog VLSI Control, Oliver Landolt and Stève Gyger 710

A Winner-Take-All Circuit with Controllable Soft Max Property, Shih-Chii Liu . . . 717

A Neuromorphic VLSI System for Modeling the Neural Control of Axial Locomotion, Girish N. Patel, Edgar A. Brown and Stephen P. DeWeerth 724

Bifurcation Analysis of a Silicon Neuron, Girish N. Patel, Gennady S. Cymbalyuk, Ronald L. Calabrese and Stephen P. DeWeerth 731

An Analog VLSI Model of Periodicity Extraction, André van Schaik 738

Part VI Speech, Handwriting and Signal Processing

An Oscillatory Correlation Framework for Computational Auditory Scene Analysis, Guy J. Brown and DeLiang L. Wang 747

Bayesian Modelling of fMRI Time Series, Pedro A. d. F. R. Højen-Sørensen, Lars Kai Hansen and Carl Edward Rasmussen . 754

Neural System Model of Human Sound Localization, Craig T. Jin and Simon Carlile 761

Spectral Cues in Human Sound Localization, Craig T. Jin, Anna Corderoy, Simon Carlile and André van Schaik 768

Broadband Direction-Of-Arrival Estimation Based on Second Order Statistics, Justinian Rosca, Joseph Ó Ruanaidh, Alexander Jourjine and Scott Rickard 775

Constrained Hidden Markov Models, Sam Roweis 782

Online Independent Component Analysis with Local Learning Rate Adaptation, Nicol N. Schraudolph and Xavier Giannakopoulos 789

Speech Modelling Using Subspace and EM Techniques, Gavin Smith, João F. G. de Freitas, Tony Robinson and Mahesan Niranjan 796

Search for Information Bearing Components in Speech, Howard Hua Yang and Hynek Hermansky 803

Part VII Visual Processing

Audio Vision: Using Audio-Visual Synchrony to Locate Sounds, John Hershey and Javier R. Movellan 813

Bayesian Reconstruction of 3D Human Motion from Single-Camera Video, Nicholas R. Howe, Michael E. Leventon and William T. Freeman 820

Emergence of Topography and Complex Cell Properties from Natural Images using Extensions of ICA, Aapo Hyvärinen and Patrik Hoyer 827

An Information-Theoretic Framework for Understanding Saccadic Eye Movements, Tai Sing Lee and Stella X. Yu 834

Learning Sparse Codes with a Mixture-of-Gaussians Prior, Bruno A. Olshausen and K. Jarrod Millman 841

Hierarchical Image Probability (HIP) Models, Clay D. Spence and Lucas Parra . . 848

Scale Mixtures of Gaussians and the Statistics of Natural Images, Martin J. Wainwright and Eero P. Simoncelli 855

A SNoW-Based Face Detector, Ming-Hsuan Yang, Dan Roth and Narendra Ahuja . 862

Managing Uncertainty in Cue Combination, Zhiyong Yang and Richard S. Zemel . 869

Part VIII   Applications

Robust Learning of Chaotic Attractors, Rembrandt Bakker, Jaap C. Schouten, Marc-Olivier Coppens, Floris Takens, C. Lee Giles and Cor M. van den Bleek . . . 879

Image Representations for Facial Expression Coding, Marian Stewart Bartlett, Gianluca Donato, Javier R. Movellan, Joseph C. Hager, Paul Ekman and Terrence J. Sejnowski 886

Low Power Wireless Communication via Reinforcement Learning, Timothy X. Brown 893

Learning Informative Statistics: A Nonparametric Approach, John W. Fisher III, Alexander T. Ihler and Paul A. Viola 900

Kirchoff Law Markov Fields for Analog Circuit Design, Richard M. Golden 907

Learning the Similarity of Documents: An Information-Geometric Approach to Document Retrieval and Categorization, Thomas Hofmann 914

Constructing Heterogeneous Committees Using Input Feature Grouping: Application to Economic Forecasting, Yuansong Liao and John Moody 921

From Coexpression to Coregulation: An Approach to Inferring Transcriptional Regulation among Gene Classes from Large-Scale Expression Data, Eric Mjolsness, Tobias Mann, Rebecca Castaño and Barbara Wold 928

Churn Reduction in the Wireless Industry, Michael C. Mozer, Richard Wolniewicz, David B. Grimes, Eric Johnson and Howard Kaushansky . . . 935

Unmixing Hyperspectral Data, Lucas Parra, Clay D. Spence, Paul Sajda, Andreas Ziehe and Klaus–Robert Müller   942

Application of Blind Separation of Sources to Optical Recording of Brain Activity, Holger Schöner, Martin Stetter, Ingo Schießl, John E.W. Mayhew, Jennifer Lund, Niall McLoughlin and Klaus Obermayer 949

Reinforcement Learning for Spoken Dialogue Systems, Satinder Singh, Michael Kearns, Diane Litman and Marilyn Walker 956

Image Recognition in Context: Application to Microscopic Urinalysis, Xubo B. Song, Joseph Sill, Yaser Abu-Mostafa and Harvey Kasdan 963

Generalized Model Selection for Unsupervised Learning in High Dimensions,
Shivakumar Vaithyanathan and Byron Dom 970

Learning from User Feedback in Image Retrieval Systems,
Nuno Vasconcelos and Andrew Lippman 977

Part IX Control, Navigation and Planning

An Environment Model for Nonstationary Reinforcement Learning,
Samuel P. M. Choi, Dit-Yan Yeung and Nevin L. Zhang 987

State Abstraction in MAXQ Hierarchical Reinforcement Learning,
Thomas G. Dietterich 994

Approximate Planning in Large POMDPs via Reusable Trajectories,
Michael Kearns, Yishay Mansour and Andrew Y. Ng 1001

Actor-Critic Algorithms, Vijay R. Konda and John N. Tsitsiklis 1008

Bayesian Map Learning in Dynamic Environments, Kevin P. Murphy 1015

Policy Search via Density Estimation,
Andrew Y. Ng, Ronald Parr and Daphne Koller 1022

Neural Network Based Model Predictive Control, Stephen Piché, Jim Keeler,
Greg Martin, Gene Boe, Doug Johnson and Mark Gerules 1029

Reinforcement Learning Using Approximate Belief States,
Andrés Rodríguez, Ronald Parr and Daphne Koller 1036

Coastal Navigation with Mobile Robots, Nicholas Roy and Sebastian Thrun 1043

*Learning Factored Representations for Partially Observable Markov Decision
Processes,* Brian Sallans 1050

*Policy Gradient Methods for Reinforcement Learning with Function
Approximation,*
Richard S. Sutton, David McAllester, Satinder Singh and Yishay Mansour 1057

Monte Carlo POMDPs, Sebastian Thrun 1064

Index of Authors 1071

Keyword Index 1075

Preface

This volume contains the papers presented at the the thirteenth annual Neural Information Processing Systems (NIPS) conference, held in Colorado from November 29 through December 4, 1999. The conference spans a wide topical range, with contributions in Cognitive Science, Neuroscience, Learning Theory, Algorithms and Architectures, Implementations (both hardware and software), Speech and Signal Processing, Visual Processing, Applications, and Control and Navigation (which includes reinforcement learning). This topical breath is supported by contributors with intellectual roots in a variety of fields: neuroscience, cognitive science, statistics, mathematics, engineering, computer science, psychology, finance, and physics.

The challenge of maintaining high quality across such topical diversity is addressed through a rigorous evaluation process. The 150 papers presented here were chosen among 467 submissions; the selection was based on the recommendations of three to five reviewers for each full paper, and on a subsequent two-day plenary session of the program committee. This volume continues a series that enjoys a unique distinction among conference proceedings: it is widely considered to stand on par with archival journals, to the pleasure and pride of contributing authors.

As befits an active and mature field, the papers in this volume present extensions and applications of previous ideas, as well as truly novel developments. Work on Independent Component Analysis (ICA) ranges from fundamental and algorithmic considerations (Attias, D. Lee et al. for example) to the modeling of V1 complex cells (Hyvärinen and Hoyer). Progress in Support Vector Machines includes algorithms for density estimation (Vapnik and Mukherjee) and developments based on Bayesian methods. The Bayesian framework also finds a novel application in concept learning (Tenenbaum). In reinforcement learning, we find developments in policy optimization based on gradient methods (Konda and Tsitsiklis, Sutton et al.), and on the estimation of the density induced on states (Ng et al.). Note the algorithmic results for inference in graphical models (Rusmevichientong and Van Roy, Weiss and Freeman), and the theory and algorithm papers (Duffy and Helmbold, Mason et al.) that construct boosting algorithms as gradient descent. Neuroscience contributions capture a renewed focus on computational principles implicit in dynamical and statistical properties (Schneidman et al., Xie and Seung), as well as continued systems modeling. Finally, comprehensive results on density estimation by mixture models (Li and Barron) fill a gap in our understanding of generalization. (If this intentionally sparse list seduces the reader into browsing the volume and thus stumbling upon its many more treasures, then it will have served its purpose).

The program of contributed papers was complemented by lively invited talks, representing areas around the topical boundaries of the conference. Edward H. Adelson (MIT) delivered the banquet keynote address on "Lightness Perceptions and Lightness Illusions". Additional invited speakers were: Donald K. Eddington (Harvard Medical School and Cochlear Implant Research Lab) on "Sound Processing for Cochlear Implants: Rationale, Implementation and Patient Performance", Bard Ermentrout (University of Pittsburgh) on "Global Spatial Patterning Through Distance and Delay", Jessica K. Hodgins (Georgia Institute of Technology) on "Animation of Human Motion", Andrew W. Lo (MIT) on "How Anomalous are Anomalies in Financial Time Series?", and J. Anthony Movshon (Howard Hughes Medical Institute and New York University) on "Deconstructing Synchrony".

As is traditional, the conference was preceded by a day of tutorials and followed by two days of workshops. The tutorials, on topics of emerging interest to the NIPS community, were organized this year by Joachim Buhmann. The highly successful workshop program - an array of casual, involving, parallel topic sessions - was brilliantly organized this year by Sue Becker and Rich Caruana.

This year for the first time we used a web based process for paper submission and reviewing. Almost all of the submitting authors and fully all of our 215 reviewers used the new system, a tribute to their patience in the face of new procedures. That all bits and pieces of the new system functioned properly, from the submission of 467 papers through the delivery of 1428 reviews, speaks of the competence of our software developers: Doug Baker at Carnegie Mellon University, and Phil Galbiati at Oregon Graduate Institute.

Through the organization of this conference, we were continually impressed by the enthusiastic commitment of the many individuals who contribute their efforts to its success. We extend thanks to the organizing committee, and to the thirteen program co-chairs whose dedication and expertise are evident in the scientific quality of this meeting. The superb papers offered in this book rests upon the efforts of authors and reviewers; we thank them for their dedication. Thanks to the workshops co-chairs Sue Becker and Rich Caruana, the tutorials chair Joachim Buhmann, the publicity chair Lee Giles, the NIPS treasurer Bartlett Mel, and the local arrangements chair Arun Jagota. Doug Baker, the NIPS webmaster, deserves special thanks for his role in developing, testing, and overseeing our new web-based submission and manuscript distribution system. Sheri Dhuyvetter, Pat Dickerson, and Susannah Gardner tended to details too numerous to list, in their significant assistance to the program chair. It's a pleasure to extend warm thanks to Rosemary Miller and Leslie Anne Chaden for their efforts in handling conference logistics and administration, registration, dinner menus, and new poster arrangements; thanks also to the student volunteers who helped them on these tasks. Steven Lemm, Sebastian Mika, Andreas Ziehe, Gunnar Rätsch and Jens Kohlmorgen ably assisted the publication chair in editing and proofreading this volume. A special thanks to Thomas Petsche, who in his role of Publication Chair for NIPS*96 developed an excellent and comprehensive set of formatting tools for the production of both the Conference Program and the NIPS Proceedings.

Finally we thank the NIPS Foundation Board, whose work over the years has contributed to the development of a richly interdisciplinary community with high standards of excellence and dedication.

Sara A. Solla, Northwestern University
Todd K. Leen, Oregon Graduate Institute of Science & Technology
Klaus-Robert Müller, GMD First

January 2000

NIPS Committees

Organizing Committee

General Chair	*Sara A. Solla*, Northwestern University
Program Chair	*Todd K. Leen*, Oregon Graduate Institute
Workshops Co-Chairs	*Sue Becker*, McMaster University
	Rich Caruana, Carnegie Mellon University
Tutorials Chair	*Joachim Buhmann*, University of Bonn
Publicity Chair	*Lee Giles*, NEC Research Institute
Publications Chair	*Klaus–Robert Müller*, GMD First
Treasurer	*Bartlett Mel*, University of Southern California
Local Arrangements Chair	*Arun Jagota*, University of California Santa Cruz
Government Liaison	*Gary Blasdel*, Harvard Medical School
Contracts	*Steve Hanson*, Rutgers University
	Gerry Tesauro, IBM Watson Labs
Web Master	*Doug Baker*, Carnegie Mellon University

Program Committee

Program Chair	*Todd K. Leen*, Oregon Graduate Institute
Program Co-Chairs	*Leon Bottou*, AT&T Labs - Research
	Gary Cottrell, University of California San Diego
	Zoubin Ghahramani, University College London
	Tommi Jaakkola, MIT
	John Lazzaro, University of California Berkeley
	Barak Pearlmutter, University of New Mexico
	Alexandre Pouget, University of Rochester
	David Saad, Aston University
	Lawrence Saul, AT&T Labs - Research
	Xubo Song, Oregon Graduate Institute
	Sebastian Thrun, Carnegie Mellon University
	Benjamin Van Roy, Stanford University
	Paul Viola, MIT

NIPS Foundation Board Members

President	*Terrence Sejnowski*, The Salk Institute
Vice President for Development	*Gary Blasdel*, Harvard Medical School
Treasurer	*Eric Mjolsness*, Jet Propulsion Laboratory
Secretary	*Gerald Tesauro*, IBM Watson Labs
Members	*Leo Breiman*, University of California Berkeley
	Jack Cowan, University of Chicago
	Stephen J. Hanson, Rutgers University
	Michael I. Jordan, University of California Berkeley
	Michael S. Kearns, AT&T Labs – Research
	Scott Kirkpatrick, IBM Watson Labs
	Richard Lippmann, MIT Lincoln Laboratory
	John Moody, Oregon Graduate Institute
	Michael Mozer, University of Colorado Boulder
	Dave Touretzky, Carnegie Mellon University
Emeritus	*Terrence Fine*, Cornell University
	Eve Marder, Brandeis University
NIPS*99 General Chair	*Sara A. Solla*, Northwestern University

Reviewers

Shun-ichi Amari
Martin Anthony
Cynthia Archer
Amir Atiya
Chris Atkeson
Hagai Attias
Wyeth Bair
Pierre Baldi
Shumeet Baluja
David Barber
Peter Bartlett
Andrew Barto
Jonathan Baxter
Tony Bell
Yoshua Bengio
Samy Bengio
Michael Berry
Michael Biehl
Chris Bishop
Avrim Blum
Herve Bourlard
Justin A. Boyan
Matthew Brand
Chris Bregler
Leo Breiman
Nicolas Brunel
Joachim Buhmann
Christopher Burges
Neil Burgess
Matteo Carandini
Jean-François Cardoso
Rich Caruana
Nestor Caticha
Gert Cauwenberghs
Nicolo Cesa-Bianchi
Ton Coolen
Corinna Cortes
Gary Cottrell
Mark Craven
Bob Crites
Matt Dailey
Trevor Darrell
Peter Dayan

Jeremy De Bonet
Gustavo Deco
Joachim Diederich
Jeff Elman
Ralph Etienne-Cummings
Theodoros Evgeniou
Claude-Nicolas Fiechter
Gary Flake
Paolo Frasconi
Brendan Frey
Bernd Fritzke
Davi Geiger
Zoubin Ghahramani
C. Lee Giles
Mark Girolami
Moises Goldszmidt
Geoff Goodhill
Mirta B. Gordon
Dan Hammerstrom
Mary Hare
John G. Harris
Paul Hasler
David Heckerman
Ralf Herbrich
Tom Heskes
Thomas Hofmann
Reimar Hofmann
Tim Horiuchi
David Horn
Don Hush
Shiro Ikeda
Nathan Intrator
Malik Ismail
Tommi Jaakkola
Marwan Jabri
Robert Jacobs
Nathalie Japkowicz
Thorsten Joachims
Mike Jones
Michael I. Jordan
Carrie Joyce
Yoshiyuki Kabashima
Nandakishore Kambhatla

Hilbert J. Kappen
Daniel Kersten
Daphne Koller
Anders Krogh
Peter Latham
Yann LeCun
Te-Won Lee
Daniel D. Lee
Todd Leen
Michael Lewicki
Song Liao
Michael L. Littman
Bradley C. Love
Gabor Lugosi
Wolfgang Maass
David J.C. MacKay
Sridhar Mahadevan
Zach Mainen
Peter Marbach
Chris Meek
Marina Meila
Ron Meir
Bartlett W. Mel
Risto Miikkulainen
Ken Miller
Bradley A. Minch
Javier R. Movellan
Mike Mozer
Remi Munos
Noboru Murata
Kevin Murphy
Jean-Pierre Nadal
Radford Neal
Alex Nelson
Mahesan Niranjan
Alice J. O'Toole
Klaus Obermayer
Erkki Oja
Bruno A. Olshausen
Manfred Opper
Vassillis Papavassiliou
Ronald Parr
Lucas Parra

Steve D. Patek
Helene Paugam-Moisy
Misha Pavel
Barak Pearlmutter
John Pearson
Mark Pendrith
Michael P. Perrone
Fernando J. Pineda
John Platt
Massimiliano Pontil
Alex Pouget
Mazin Rahim
Anand Rangarajan
Rajesh Rao
Carl E. Rasmussen
Adam Reeves
Steve Rehfuss
Thomas Richardson
Denni Rognvaldsson
Sam Roweis
Henry Rowley
Paat Rusmevichientong
Flip Sabes
Matt Saffell
Maneesh Sahani
Emilio Salinas

Robert Schapire
Jeff Schneider
Bernhard Schölkopf
Paul Schrater
Dale Schuurmans
Sebastian Seung
John Sharpe
Jude Shavlik
John Shawe-Taylor
Barbara Shinn-Cunningham
Joe Sill
Patrice Simard
Eero Simoncelli
Satinder Singh
Malcolm Slaney
Padhraic Smyth
Peter Sollich
Xubo Song
Rich Sutton
Csaba Szepesvari
Joshua Tenenbaum
Sebastian Thrun
Rob Tibshirani
Mike Tipping
Naftali Tishby

Mike Titterington
Kari Torkkola
Dave Touretzky
Volker Tresp
Todd Troyer
Naonori Ueda
Robert Urbanczik
Joachim Utans
Chris van den Broeck
Benjamin Van Roy
Paul Viola
Eric Wan
Manfred Warmuth
Chris Watkins
Daphna Weinshall
Janet Wiles
Ronald J. Williams
Chris Williams
Laurenz Wiskott
Lizhong Wu
Howard Yang
Alan Yuille
Rich Zemel
Kechen Zhang
Geoff Zweig

Part I
Cognitive Science

Recognizing Evoked Potentials in a Virtual Environment *

Jessica D. Bayliss and Dana H. Ballard
Department of Computer Science
University of Rochester
Rochester, NY 14627
{bayliss,dana}@cs.rochester.edu

Abstract

Virtual reality (VR) provides immersive and controllable experimental environments. It expands the bounds of possible evoked potential (EP) experiments by providing complex, dynamic environments in order to study cognition without sacrificing environmental control. VR also serves as a safe dynamic testbed for brain-computer interface (BCI) research. However, there has been some concern about detecting EP signals in a complex VR environment. This paper shows that EPs exist at red, green, and yellow stop lights in a virtual driving environment. Experimental results show the existence of the P3 EP at "go" and "stop" lights and the contingent negative variation (CNV) EP at "slow down" lights. In order to test the feasibility of on-line recognition in VR, we looked at recognizing the P3 EP at red stop lights and the absence of this signal at yellow slow down lights. Recognition results show that the P3 may successfully be used to control the brakes of a VR car at stop lights.

1 Introduction

The controllability of VR makes it an excellent candidate for use in studying cognition. It expands the bounds of possible evoked potential (EP) experiments by providing complex, dynamic environments in order to study decision making in cognition without sacrificing environmental control. We have created a flexible system for real-time EEG collection and analysis from within virtual environments.

The ability of our system to give quick feedback enables it to be used in brain-computer interface (BCI) research, which is aimed at helping individuals with severe motor deficits to become more independent. Recent BCI work has shown the feasibility of on-line averaging and biofeedback methods in order to choose characters or move a cursor on a computer screen with up to 95% accuracy while sitting still and concentrating on the screen [McFarland *et al.*, 1993; Pfurtscheller *et al.*, 1996; Vaughn *et al.*, 1996; Farwell and Donchin, 1988]. Our focus is to dramatically extend the BCI by allowing evoked potentials to propel the user through alternate virtual environments. For example, a

---

*This research was supported by NIH/PHS grant1-P41-RR09283. It was also facilitated in part by a National Physical Science Consortium Fellowship and by stipend support from NASA Goddard Space Flight Center.

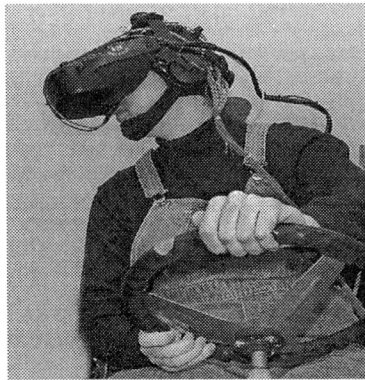 

Figure 1: (Left) An individual demonstrates driving in the modified go cart. (Right) A typical stoplight scene in the virtual environment.

user could choose a virtual living room from a menu of rooms, navigate to the living room automatically in the head-mounted display, and then choose to turn on the stereo.

As shown in [Farwell and Donchin, 1988], the P3 EP may be used for a brain-computer interface that picks characters on a computer monitor. Discovered by [Chapman and Bragdon, 1964; Sutton *et al.*, 1965] and extensively studied (see [Polich, 1998] for a literature review), the P3 is a positive waveform occurring approximately 300-500 ms after an infrequent task-relevant stimulus. We show that requiring subjects to stop or go at virtual traffic lights elicits this EP. The contingent negative variation (CNV), an EP that happens preceding an expected stimulus, occurs at slow down lights.

In order to test the feasibility of on-line recognition in the noisy VR environment, we recognized the P3 EP at red stop lights and the lack of this signal at yellow slow down lights. Results using a robust Kalman filter for off-line recognition indicate that the car may be stopped reliably with an average accuracy of 84.5% while the on-line average for car halting is 83%.

2 The Stoplight Experiments

The first experiment we performed in the virtual driving environment shows that a P3 EP is obtained when subjects stop or go at a virtual light and that a CNV occurs when subjects see a slow down light. Since all subjects received the same light colors for the slow down, go, and stop conditions we then performed a second experiment with different light colors in order to disambiguate light color from the occurrence of the P3 and CNV.

Previous P3 research has concentrated primarily on static environments such as the continuous performance task [Rosvold *et al.*, 1956]. In the visual continuous performance task (VCPT), static images are flashed on a screen and the subject is told to press a button when a rare stimulus occurs or to count the number of occurrences of a rare stimulus. This makes the stimulus both rare and task relevant in order to evoke a P3. As an example, given red and yellow stoplight pictures, a P3 should occur if the red picture is less frequent than the yellow and subjects are told to press a mouse button only during the red light. We assumed a similar response would occur in a VR driving world if certain lights were infrequent and subjects were told to stop or go at them. This differs from the VCPT in two important ways:

1. In the VCPT subjects sit passively and respond to stimuli. In the driving task,

subjects control when the stimuli appear by where they drive in the virtual world.

2. Since subjects are actively involved and fully immersed in the virtual world, they make more eye and head movements. The movement amount can be reduced by a particular experimental paradigm, but it can not be eliminated.

The first difference makes the VR environment a more natural experimental environment. The second difference means that subjects create more data artifacts with extra movement. We handled these artifacts by first manipulating the experimental environment to reduce movements where important stimulus events occurred. This meant that all stoplights were placed at the end of straight stretches of road in order to avoid the artifacts caused by turning a corner. For our on-line recognition, we then used the eye movement reduction technique described in [Semlitsch et al., 1986] in order to subtract a combination of the remaining eye and head movement artifact.

2.1 Experimental Setup

All subjects used a modified go cart in order to control the virtual car (see Figure 1). The virtual reality interface is rendered on a Silicon Graphics Onyx machine with 4 processors and an Infinite Reality Graphics Engine. The environment is presented to the subject through a head-mounted display (HMD). Since scalp EEG recordings are measured in microvolts, electrical signals may easily interfere during an experiment. We tested the effects of wearing a VR4 HMD containing an ISCAN eye tracker and discovered that the noise levels inside of the VR helmet were comparable to noise levels while watching a laptop screen [Bayliss and Ballard, 1998].

A trigger pulse containing information about the color of the light was sent to the EEG acquisition system whenever a light changed. While an epoch size from -100 ms to 1 sec was specified, the data was recorded continuously. Information about head position as well as gas, braking, and steering position were saved to an external file. Eight electrodes sites (FZ, CZ, CPZ, PZ, P3, P4, as well as 2 vertical EOG channels) were arranged on the heads of seven subjects with a linked mastoid reference. Electrode impedances were between 2 and 5 kohms for all subjects. Subjects ranged in age from 19 to 52 and most had no previous experiences in a virtual environment. The EEG signal was amplified using Grass amplifiers with an analog bandwidth from 0.1 to 100 Hz. Signals were then digitized at a rate of 500 Hz and stored to a computer.

2.2 Ordinary Traffic Light Color Experiment

Five subjects were instructed to slow down on yellow lights, stop for red lights, and go for green lights. These are normal traffic light colors. Subjects were allowed to drive in the environment before the experiment to get used to driving in VR.

In order to make slow down lights more frequent, all stoplights turned to the slow down color when subjects were further than 30 meters away from them. When the subject drove closer than 30 meters the light then turned to either the go or stop color with equal probability. The rest of the light sequence followed normal stoplights with the stop light turning to the go light after 3 seconds and the go light not changing.

We calculated the grand averages over red, green, and yellow light trials (see Figure 2a). Epochs affected by artifact were ignored in the averages in order to make sure that any existing movements were not causing a P3-like signal. Results show that a P3 EP occurs for both red and green lights. Back averaging from the green/red lights to the yellow light shows the existence of a CNV starting at approximately 2 seconds before the light changes to red or green.

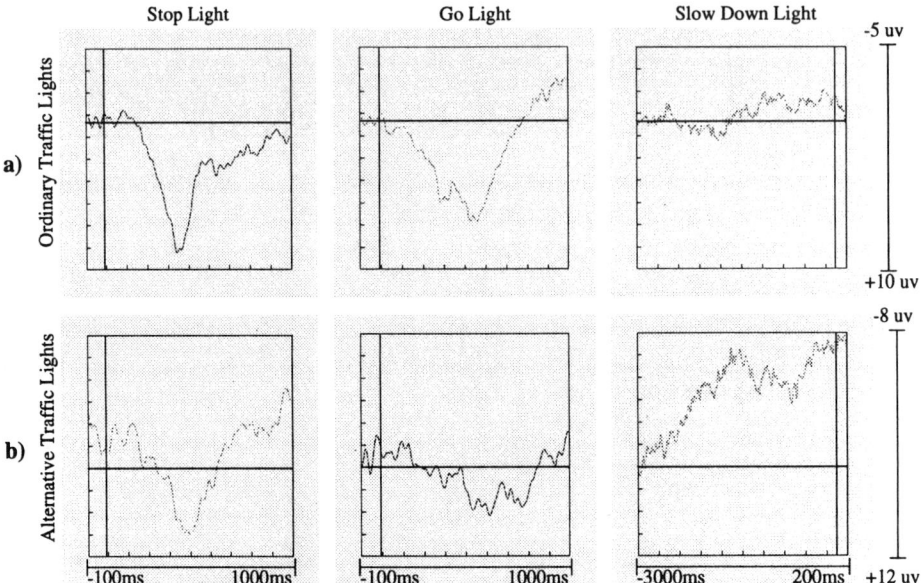

Figure 2: a) Grand averages for the red stop, green go, and yellow slow down lights. b) Grand averages for the yellow stop, red go, and green slow down lights. All slow down lights have been back-averaged from the occurrence of the go/stop light in order to show the existence of a CNV.

2.3 Alternative Traffic Light Colors

The P3 is related to task relevance and should not be related to color, but color needed to be disambiguated as the source of the P3 in the experiment. We had two subjects slow down at green lights, stop at yellow lights, and go at red lights. In order to get used to this combination of colors, subjects were allowed to drive in the town before the experiment.

The grand averages for each light color were calculated in the same manner as the averages above and are shown in Figure 2b. As expected, a P3 signal existed for the stop condition and a CNV for the slow down condition. The go condition P3 was much noisier for these two subjects, although a slight P3-like signal is still visible.

3 Single Trial Recognition Results

While averages show the existence of the P3 EP at red stop lights and the absence of such at yellow slow down lights, we needed to discover if the signal was clean enough for single trial recognition as the quick feedback needed by a BCI depends on quick recognition. While there were three light conditions to recognize, there were only two distinct kinds of evoked potentials. We chose to recognize the difference between the P3 and the CNV since their averages are very different. Recognizing the difference between two kinds of EPs gives us the ability to use a BCI in any task that can be performed using a series of binary decisions. We tried three methods for classification of the P3 EP: correlation, independent component analysis (ICA), and a robust Kalman filter.

Approximately, 90 slow down yellow light and 45 stop red light trials from each subject were classified. The reason we allowed a yellow light bias to enter recognition is because the yellow light currently represents an unimportant event in the environment. In a real BCI unimportant events are likely to occur more than user-directed actions, making this bias justifiable.

Table 1: Recognition Results ($p < 0.01$)

	Correlation %Correct			ICA %Correct			Robust Kalman Filter %Correct		
Subjects	Red	Yel	Total	Red	Yel	Total	Red	Yel	Total
S1	81	51	64	76	77	77	55	86	77
S2	95	63	73	86	88	87	82	94	90
S3	89	56	66	72	87	82	74	85	81
S4	81	60	67	73	69	71	65	91	82
S5	63	66	65	65	79	74	78	92	87

Table 2: Recognition Results for Return Subjects

	Robust K-Filter % Correct		
Subjects	Red	Yel	Total
S4	73	90	85
S5	67	87	80

As expected, the data obtained while driving contained artifacts, but in an on-line BCI these artifacts must be reduced in order to make sure that what the recognition algorithm is recognizing is not an artifact such as eye movement. In order to reduce these artifacts, we performed the on-line linear regression technique described in [Semlitsch et al., 1986] in order to subtract a combination of eye and head movement artifact.

In order to create a baseline from which to compare the performance of other algorithms, we calculated the correlation of all sample trials with the red and yellow light averages from each subject's maximal P3 electrode site using the following formula:

$$\text{correlation} = (\textbf{sample} * \textbf{ave}^T)/(\| \textbf{sample} \| * \| \textbf{ave} \|) \qquad (1)$$

where **sample** and **ave** are both 1×500 vectors representing the trial epochs and light averages (respectively). We used the whole trial epoch for recognition because it yielded better recognition than just the time area around the P3. If the highest correlation of a trial epoch with the red and yellow averages was greater than 0.0, then the signal was classified as that type of signal. If both averages correlated negatively with the single trial, then the trial was counted as a yellow light signal. As can be seen in Table 1, the correct signal identification of red lights was extremely high while the yellow light identification pulled the results down. This may be explained by the greater variance of the yellow light epochs. Correlations in general were poor with typical correlations around 0.25.

ICA has successfully been used in order to minimize artifacts in EEG data [Jung et al., 1997; Vigario, 1997] and has also proven useful in separating P3 component data from an averaged waveform [Makeig et al., 1997]. The next experiment used ICA in order to try to separate the background EEG signal from the P3 signal. Independent component analysis (ICA) assumes that n EEG data channels **x** are a linear combination of n statistically *independent* signals **s**:

$$\textbf{x} = A\textbf{s} \qquad (2)$$

where **x** and **s** are $n \times 1$ vectors. We used the matlab package mentioned in [Makeig et al., 1997] with default learning values, which finds a matrix W by stochastic gradient descent.

This matrix W performs component separation. All data was sphered in order to speed convergence time.

After training the W matrix, the source channel showing the closest P3-like signal (using correlation with the average) for the red light average data was chosen as the signal with which to correlate individual epochs. The trained W matrix was also used to find the sources of the yellow light average. The red and yellow light responses were then correlated with individual epoch sources in the manner of the first experiment.

The third experiment used the robust Kalman filter framework formulated by Rao [Rao, 1998]. The Kalman filter assumes a linear model similar to the one of ICA in equation 2, but assumes the EEG output $\mathbf{x}$ is the observable output of a generative or measurement matrix A and an internal state vector $\mathbf{s}$ of *Gaussian* sources. The output may also have an additional noise component $\mathbf{n}$, a Gaussian stochastic noise process with mean zero and a covariance matrix given by $\Sigma = E[\mathbf{n}\mathbf{n}^T]$, leading to the model expression: $\mathbf{x} = A\mathbf{s} + \mathbf{n}$. In order to find the most optimal value of $\mathbf{s}$, a weighted least-squares criterion is formulated:

$$J = (\mathbf{x} - A\mathbf{s})^T \Sigma^{-1} (\mathbf{x} - A\mathbf{s}) + (\mathbf{s} - \bar{\mathbf{s}})^T M^{-1} (\mathbf{s} - \bar{\mathbf{s}}) \qquad (3)$$

where s follows a Gaussian distribution with mean $\bar{\mathbf{s}}$ and covariance M. Minimizing this criterion by setting $\frac{\partial J}{\partial \mathbf{s}} = 0$ and using the substitution $N = (A^T \Sigma^{-1} U + M^{-1})^{-1}$ yields the Kalman filter equation, which is basically equal to the old estimate plus the Kalman gain times the residual error.

$$\mathbf{s} = \bar{\mathbf{s}} + N A^T \Sigma^{-1} (\mathbf{x} - A\bar{\mathbf{s}}) \qquad (4)$$

In an analogous manner, the measurement matrix A may be estimated (learned) if one assumes the physical relationships encoded by the measurement matrix are relatively stable. The learning rule for the measurement matrix may be derived in a manner similar to the rule for the internal state vector. In addition, a decay term is often needed in order to avoid overfitting the data set. See [Rao, 1998] for details.

In our experiments both the internal state matrix $\mathbf{s}$ and the measurement matrix A were learned by training them on the average red light signal and the average yellow light signal. The signal is measured from the start of the trial which is known since it is triggered by the light change. We used a Kalman gain of 0.6 and a decay of 0.3. After training, the signal estimate for each epoch is correlated with the red and yellow light signal estimates in the manner of experiment 1. We made the Kalman filter statistically robust by ignoring parts of the EEG signal that fell outside a standard deviation of 1.0 from the training signals.

The overall recognition results in Table 1 suggest that both the robust Kalman filter and ICA have a statistically significant advantage over correlation ($p < 0.01$). The robust Kalman filter has a very small advantage over ICA (not statistically significant).

In order to look at the reliability of the best algorithm and its ability to be used on-line two of the Subjects (S4 and S5) returned for another VR driving session. In these sessions the brakes of the driving simulator were controlled by the robust Kalman filter recognition algorithm for red stop and yellow slow down lights. Green lights were ignored. The results of this session using the Robust Kalman Filter trained on the first session are shown in Table 2. The recognition numbers for red and yellow lights between the two sessions were compared using correlation. Red light scores between the sessions correlated fairly highly - 0.82 for S4 and 0.69 for S5. The yellow light scores between sessions correlated poorly with both S4 and S5 at approximately -0.1. This indicates that the yellow light epochs tend to correlate poorly with each other due to the lack of a large component such as the P3 to tie them together.

4 Future Work

This paper showed the viability of recognizing the P3 EP in a VR environment. We plan to allow the P3 EP to propel the user through alternate virtual rooms through the use of various binary decisions. In order to improve recognition for the BCI we need to experiment with a wider and more complex variety of recognition algorithms. Our most recent work has shown a dependence between the human computer interface used in the BCI and recognition. We would like to explore this dependence in order to improve recognition as much as possible.

References

[Bayliss and Ballard, 1998] J.D. Bayliss and D.H. Ballard, "The Effects of Eye Tracking in a VR Helmet on EEG Recording," *TR 685, University of Rochester National Resource Laboratory for the Study of Brain and Behavior*, May 1998.

[Chapman and Bragdon, 1964] R.M. Chapman and H.R. Bragdon, "Evoked responses to numerical and non-numerical visual stimuli while problem solving.," *Nature*, 203:1155–1157, 1964.

[Farwell and Donchin, 1988] L.A. Farwell and E. Donchin, "Talking off the top of your head: toward a mental prosthesis utilizing event-related brain potentials," *Electroenceph. Clin. Neurophysiol.*, pages 510–523, 1988.

[Jung et al., 1997] T.P. Jung, C. Humphries, T. Lee, S. Makeig, M.J. McKeown, V. Iragui, and T.J. Sejnowski, "Extended ICA Removes Artifacts from Electroencephalographic Recordings," *to Appear in Advances in Neural Information Processing Systems*, 10, 1997.

[Makeig et al., 1997] S. Makeig, T. Jung, A.J. Bell, D. Ghahremani, and T.J. Sejnowski, "Blind Separation of Auditory Event-related Brain Responses into Independent Components," *Proc. Nat'l Acad. Sci. USA*, 94:10979–10984, 1997.

[McFarland et al., 1993] D.J. McFarland, G.W. Neat, R.F. Read, and J.R. Wolpaw, "An EEG-based method for graded cursor control," *Psychobiology*, 21(1):77–81, 1993.

[Pfurtscheller et al., 1996] G. Pfurtscheller, D. Flotzinger, M. Pregenzer, J. Wolpaw, and D. McFarland, "EEG-based Brain Computer Interface (BCI)," *Medical Progress through Technology*, 21:111–121, 1996.

[Polich, 1998] J. Polich, "P300 Clinical Utility and Control of Variability," *J. of Clinical Neurophysiology*, 15(1):14–33, 1998.

[Rao, 1998] R. P.N. Rao, "Visual Attention during Recognition," *Advances in Neural Information Processing Systems*, 10, 1998.

[Rosvold et al., 1956] H.E. Rosvold, A.F. Mirsky, I. Sarason, E.D. Bransome Jr., and L.H. Beck, "A Continuous Performance Test of Brain Damage," *J. Consult. Psychol.*, 20, 1956.

[Semlitsch et al., 1986] H.V. Semlitsch, P. Anderer, P Schuster, and O. Presslich, "A solution for reliable and valid reduction of ocular artifacts applied to the P300 ERP," *Psychophys.*, 23:695–703, 1986.

[Sutton et al., 1965] S. Sutton, M. Braren, J. Zublin, and E. John, "Evoked potential correlates of stimulus uncertainty," *Science*, 150:1187–1188, 1965.

[Vaughn et al., 1996] T.M. Vaughn, J.R. Wolpaw, and E. Donchin, "EEG-Based Communication: Prospects and Problems," *IEEE Trans. on Rehabilitation Engineering*, 4(4):425–430, 1996.

[Vigario, 1997] R. Vigario, "Extraction of ocular artifacts from eeg using independent component analysis," *Electroenceph. Clin. Neurophysiol.*, 103:395–404, 1997.

A Neurodynamical Approach to Visual Attention

Gustavo Deco
Siemens AG
Corporate Technology
Neural Computation, ZT IK 4
Otto-Hahn-Ring 6
81739 Munich, Germany
Gustavo.Deco@mchp.siemens.de

Josef Zihl
Institute of Psychology
Neuropsychology
Ludwig-Maximilians-University Munich
Leopoldstr. 13
80802 Munich, Germany

Abstract

The psychophysical evidence for "selective attention" originates mainly from visual search experiments. In this work, we formulate a hierarchical system of interconnected modules consisting in populations of neurons for modeling the underlying mechanisms involved in selective visual attention. We demonstrate that our neural system for visual search works across the visual field in parallel but due to the different intrinsic dynamics can show the two experimentally observed modes of visual attention, namely: the serial and the parallel search mode. In other words, neither explicit model of a focus of attention nor saliencies maps are used. The focus of attention appears as an emergent property of the dynamic behavior of the system. The neural population dynamics are handled in the framework of the mean-field approximation. Consequently, the whole process can be expressed as a system of coupled differential equations.

1 Introduction

Traditional theories of human vision considers two functionally distinct stages of visual processing [1]. The first stage, termed *the preattentive stage*, implies an unlimited-capacity system capable of processing the information contained in the entire visual field in parallel. The second stage is termed *the attentive or focal stage,* and is characterized by the serial processing of visual information corresponding to local spatial regions. This stage of processing is typically associated with a limited-capacity system which allocates its resources to a single particular location in visual space. The designed psychophysical experiments for testing this hypothesis consist of visual search tasks. In a visual search test the subject have to look at the display containing a frame filled with randomly positioned items in order to seek for an a priori defined target item. All other items in a frame which are not the target are called distractors. The number of items in a frame is called the frame size. The relevant variable to be measured is the reaction time as a function of the frame size. In this context, the *Feature Integration Theory,* assumes that the two stage processes operate sequentially [1]. The first early preattentive stage runs in parallel over the complete visual field extracting single *primitive features* without integrating them. The second attentive stage has been likened to a spotlight. This metaphor alludes that attention is focally allocated to a local region of the visual field where stimuli are processed in more detail and passed to higher level of processing, while, in the other regions not illuminated by the attentional spotlight, no further processing occurs. Computational models formulated in the framework of feature integration theory require the existence of a *saliency or priority map* for registering the potentially interesting areas of the retinal input, and a *gating* mechanism for reducing the amount of incoming visual information, so that limited computational resources in the system are not overloaded. The priority map serves to represent topographically the relevance of different parts of the visual field, in order to have a mechanism for guiding the attentional focus on salient regions of the retinal input. The focused area will be gated, such that only the information within will be passed further to yet higher levels, concerned with object recognition and action. The disparity between these two stages of attentional visual processing originated a vivid experimental disputation. Duncan and Humphreys [2] have postulated a hypothesis that integrates both attentional modes (parallel and serial) as an instantiates of a common principle. This principle sustains in both schemes that a selection is made. In the serial focal scheme, the selection acts on in the space dimension, while in the parallel spread scheme the selection concentrates in feature dimensions, e.g. color. On the other hand, Duncan's attentional theory [3] proposed that after a first parallel search a competition is initiated, which ends up by accepting only one object namely the target. Recently, several electrophysiological experiments have been performed which seems to support this hypothesis [4]. Chelazzi et al. [4] measured IT (inferotemporal) neurons in monkeys observing a display containing a target object (that the monkey has seen previously) and a distractor. They report a short period during which the neuron's response is enhanced. After this period the activity level of the neuron remains high if the target is the neuron's effective stimulus, and decay otherwise. The challenging question is therefore: is really the linear increasing reaction time observed in some visual search tests due to a serial mechanism? or is there only parallel processing followed by a dynamical time consuming latency? In other words, are really priority maps and spotlight paradigm required? or can a neurodynamical approach explain the observed psychophysical experiments?. Furthermore, it should be clarified if the feature dimension search is achieved independently in each feature dimension or is done after integrating the involved feature dimensions. We study in this paper these questions from a computational perspective. We formulate a neurodynamical model consisting in interconnected populations of biological neurons specially designed for visual search tasks. We demonstrate that it is plausible to build a neural system for visual search, which works across the visual field in parallel but due to the different intrinsic dynamics can show the two experimentally observed modes of visual attention, namely: the serial focal and the parallel spread over the space mode. In other words, neither explicit serial focal search nor saliency maps should be assumed. The focus of attention is not included in the system but just results after convergence of the dynamical behavior of the neural networks. The dynamics of the system can be interpreted as an intrinsic dynamical routing for binding features if top-down information is available. Our neurodynamical computational model requires independent competition mechanism along each feature dimension for explaining the experimental data, implying the necessity of the independent character of the search in separated and not integrated feature dimensions. The neural population dynamics are handled in the framework of the mean-field approximation yielding a system of coupled differential equations.

2 Neurodynamical model

We extend with the present model the approach of Usher and Niebur [5], which is based on the experimental data of Chelazzi et al. [4], for explaining the results of visual search experiments. The hierarchical architecture of our system is shown in Figure 1. The input retina is given as a matrix of visual items. The location of each item at the retina is specified by two indices ij meaning the position at the row i and the column j. The dimension of this matrix is SxS, i.e. the frame size is also SxS. The information is processed at each spatial location in parallel. Different feature maps extract for the item at each position the local values of the features. In the present work we hypothesize that selective attention is guided by an independent mechanism which corresponds to the independent search of each feature. Let us assume that each visual item can be defined by K features. Each feature k can adopt $L(k)$ values, for example the feature color can have the values red or green (in this case $L(color)=2$). For each feature map k exist $L(k)$ layers of neurons for characterizing the presence of each feature value.

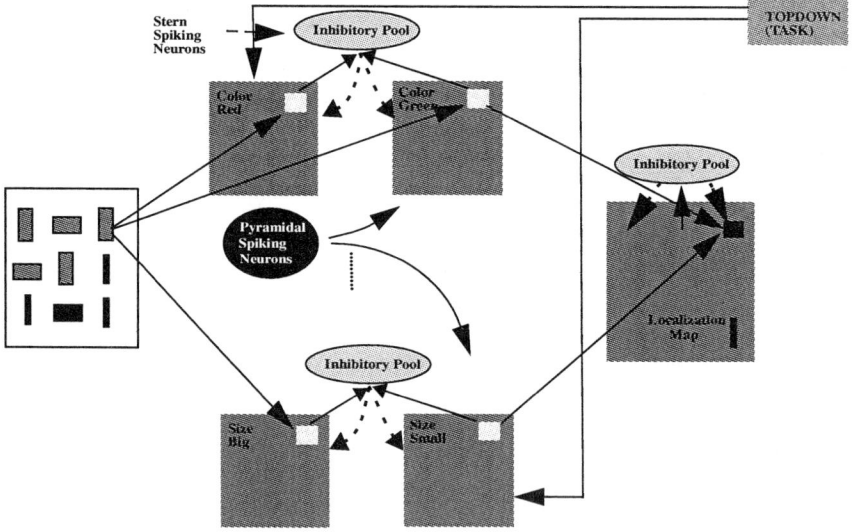

Figure 1: Hierarchical architecture of spiking neural modules for visual selective attention. Solid arrows denote excitatory connections and dotted arrows denote inhibitory connections

A cell assembly consisting in a population of full connected excitatory integrate-and-fire spiking neurons (pyramidal cells) is allocated in each layer and for each item location for encoding the presence of a specific feature value (e.g. color red) at the corresponding position. This corresponds to a sparse distributed representation. The feature maps are topographically ordered, i.e. the receptive fields of the neurons belonging to the cell assembly ij at one of these maps are sensible to the location ij at the retinal input. We further assume that the cell assemblies in layers corresponding to a feature dimension are mutually inhibitory. Inhibition is modeled, according to the constraint imposed by Dale's principle, by a different pool of inhibitory neurons. Each feature dimension has therefore an independent pool of inhibitory neurons. This accounts for the neurophysiological fact that the response of V4 neurons sensible to a specific feature value is enhanced and the activity of the other neurons sensible to other feature values are suppressed. A high level map consisting also in a topographically ordered excitatory cell assemblies is introduced for integration of the different feature dimension at each item location, i.e. for binding the features of each item. These cell assemblies are also mutually inhibited through a common pool of inhibitory neurons. This layer corresponds to the modeling of IT neurons, which show location specific enhancement of activity by suppression of the responses of the cell assemblies associated to other locations. This fact would yield a dynamical formation of a focus of attention without explicitly assuming any spotlight. Top-down information consisting in the feature values at each feature dimension of the target item is feed in the system by including an extra excitatory input to the corresponding feature layers. The whole system analyzes the information at all locations in parallel. Larger reaction times correspond to slower dynamical convergence at all levels, i.e. feature map and integration map levels.

Instead of solving the explicit set of integrate-and-fire neural equations, the Hebbian cell assemblies adopted representation impels to adopt a dynamic theory whose dependent variables are the activation levels of the cell populations. Assuming an ergodic behavior [5] it is possible to derive the dynamic equations for the cell assembly activities level by utilizing the mean-field approximation [5]. The essential idea consists in characterizing each cell assembly by means of each activity x, and an input current that is characteristic for all cells in the population, denoted by I, which satisfies:

$$x = F(I) = \frac{1}{T_r - \tau \log\left(1 - \frac{1}{\tau I}\right)} \quad (1)$$

which is the response function that transforms current into discharge rates for an integrate-and-fire spiking neuron with deterministic input, time membrane constant τ and absolute refractory time T_r. The system of differential equations describing the dynamics of the feature maps are:

$$\tau \frac{\partial}{\partial t} I_{ijkl}(t) = -I_{ijkl}(t) + aF(I_{ijkl}(t))$$
$$- bF(I^P_k(t)) + I_0 + I^F_{ijkl} + I^A_{kl} + \nu$$

$$\tau_P \frac{\partial}{\partial t} I^P_k(t) = -I^P_k(t) + c \sum_{i=1}^{S} \sum_{j=1}^{S} \sum_{k=1}^{L(k)} F(I_{ijkl}(t))$$
$$- dF(I^P_k(t))$$

where $I_{ijkl}(t)$ is the input current for the population with receptive field at location ij of the feature map k that analysis the value feature l, $I^P_k(t)$ is the current in the inhibitory pool bounded to the feature map layers of the feature dimension k. The frame size is S. The additive Gaussian noise ν considered has standard deviation 0.002. The synaptic time constants were $\tau = 5$ msec for the excitatory populations and $\tau_P = 20$ for the inhibitory pools. The synaptic weights chosen were: $a = 0.95, b = 0.8, c = 2.$ and $d = 0.1$. $I_0 = 0.025$ is a diffuse spontaneous background input, I^F_{ijkl} is the sensory input to the cells in feature map k sensible to the value l and with receptive fields at the location ij at the retina. This input characterizes the presence of the respective feature value at the corresponding position. A value of 0.05 corresponds to the presence of the respective feature value and a value of 0 to the absence of it. The top-down target information I^A_{kl} was equal 0.005 for the layers which code the target properties and 0 otherwise.

The higher level integrating assemblies are described by following differential equation system:

$$\tau_H \frac{\partial}{\partial t} I^H_{ij}(t) = -I_{ij}(t) + \widehat{a} F(I_{ij}(t)) - \widehat{b} F(I^{PH}(t))$$

$$I_0 + \widehat{w} \sum_{k=1}^{K} \sum_{l=1}^{L(k)} F(I_{ijkl}(t)) + \nu$$

$$\tau_{PH} \frac{\partial}{\partial t} I^{PH}(t) = -I^{PH}(t) + \widehat{c} \sum_{i=1}^{S} \sum_{j=1}^{S} F(I^H_{ij}(t))$$

$$- \widehat{d} F(I^{PH}(t))$$

where $I^H_{ij}(t)$ is the input current for the population with receptive field at location ij of the high level integrating map, $I^{PH}(t)$ is the associated current in the inhibitory pool. The synaptic time constants were $\tau_H = 5$ msec for the excitatory populations and $\tau_{PH} = 20$ for the inhibitory pools. The synaptic weights chosen were: $\widehat{a} = 0.95$, $\widehat{b} = 0.8$, $\widehat{w} = 1$, $\widehat{c} = 1$. and $\widehat{d} = 0.1$.

These systems of differential equations were integrated numerically until a convergence criterion were reached. This criterion were that the neurons in the high level map are polarized, i.e.

$$F(I^H_{i_{max} j_{max}}(t)) - \frac{\sum_{i \neq i_{max}} \sum_{j \neq j_{max}} F(I^H_{ij}(t))}{(S^2 - 1)} > \theta$$

where the index $i_{max} j_{max}$ denotes the cell assembly in the high level map with maximal activity and the threshold θ was chosen equal to 0.1. The second in the l.h.s measure the mean distractor activity. At each feature dimension the fixed point of the dynamic is given by the activity of cell assemblies at the layers with a common value with the target and corresponding to items having this value. For example, if the target is red, at the color map, the activity at the green layer will be suppressed and the cell assemblies corresponding to red items will be enhanced. At the high-level map, the populations corresponding to location which are maximally in all feature dimensions activated will be enhanced by suppressing the others. In other words, the location that shows all feature dimension equivalent at what top-down is stimulated and required, will be enhanced when the target is at this location.

3 Simulations of visual search tasks

In this section we present results simulating the visual search experiments involving *feature* and *conjunction search* [1]. Let us define the different kinds of search tasks by given a pair of numbers m and n, where m is the number of feature dimensions by which the distractors differ from the target and n is the number of feature dimensions by which the distractor groups simultaneously differ from the target. In other words, the feature search corresponds to a 1,1-search; a standard conjunction search corresponds to a 2,1-search; a triple conjunction search can be a 3,1 or a 3,2-search if the target differs from all distractor groups in one or in two features respectively. We assume that the items are defined by three feature dimensions ($K = 3$, e.g. color, size and position), each one having two values ($L(k) = 2$ for $k = 1, 2, 3$). At each size we repeat the experiment 100 times, each time with different randomly generated distractors and target.

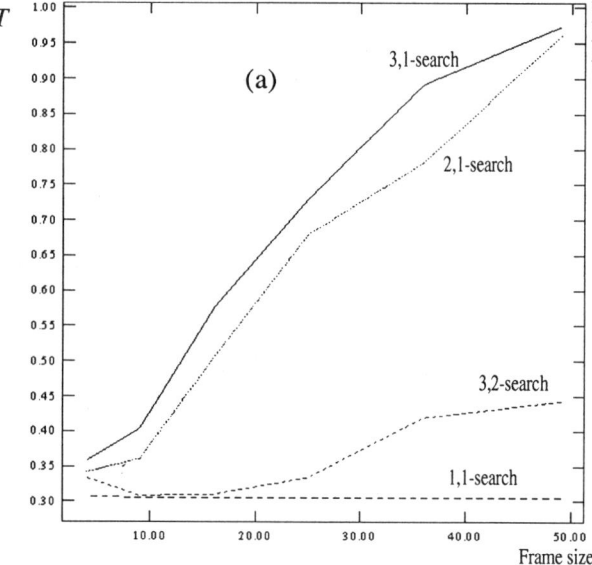

Figure 2: Search times for feature and conjunction searches obtained utilizing the presented model.

We plot as result the mean value T of the 100 simulated reaction times (in msec) as a function of the frame size. In Figure 2, the results obtained for 1,1; 2,1; 3,1 and 3,2-searches are shown. The slopes of the reaction time vs. frame size curves for all simulations are absolutely consistent with the existing experimental results[1]. The experimental work reports that in feature search (1,1) the target is detected in parallel across the visual field. Furthermore, the slopes corresponding to standard conjunction search and triple conjunction search are a linear function of the frame size, where by the slope of the triple conjunction search is steeper or very flat than in the case of standard search (2,1) if the target differs from the distractors in one (3,1) or two features (3,2) respectively. In order to analyze more carefully the dynamical evolution of the system, we plot in Figure 3 the temporal evolution of the rate activity corresponding to the target and to the distractors at the high-level integrating map and also separately for each feature dimension level for a parallel (1,1-search) and a serial (3,1-search) visual tasks. The frame size used is 25. It is interesting to note that in the case of 1,1-search the convergence time in all levels are very small and therefore this kind of search appears as a parallel search. In the case of 3,1-search the latency of the dynamic takes more time and therefore this kind of search appears as a serial one, in spite that the underlying mechanisms are parallel. In this case (see Figure 3-c) the large competition present in each feature dimension delays the convergence of the dynamics at each feature dimension and therefore also at the high-level map. Note in Figure 3-c the slow suppression of the distractor activity that reflects the underlying competition.

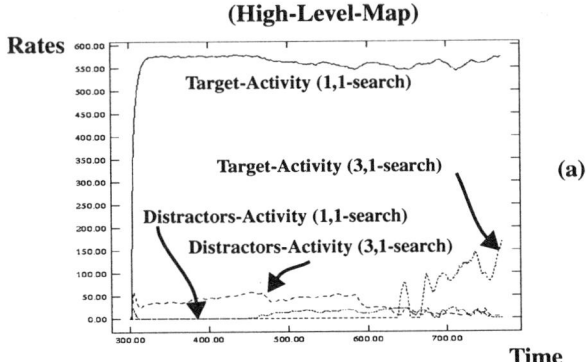
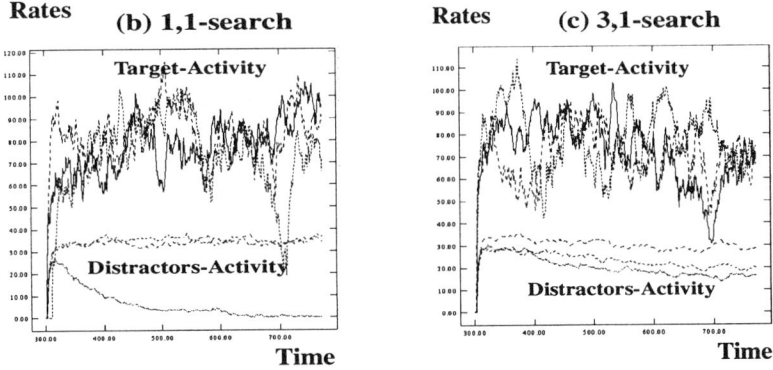

Figure 3: Activity levels during visual search experiments. (a) High-level-map rates for target $F(I^H_{i_{max}j_{max}}(t))$ and mean distractors-activity. (b) Feature-level map rates for target and one distractor activity for 1,1-search. There is one curve for each feature dimension (i.e. 3 for target and 3 for distractor. (c) the same as (b) but for 3,1-search.

References

[1] Treisman, A. (1988) Features and objects: The fourteenth Barlett memorial lecture. *The Quarterly Journal of Experimental Psychology*, **40A**, 201-237.

[2] Duncan, J. and Humphreys, G. (1989) Visual search and stimulus similarity. *Psychological Review*, **96**, 433-458.

[3] Duncan, J. (1980) The locus of interference in the perception of simultaneous stimuli. *Psychological Review*, **87**, 272-300.

[4] Chelazzi, L., Miller, E., Duncan, J. and Desimone, R. (1993) A neural basis for visual search in inferior temporal cortex. *Nature (London)*, **363**, 345-347.

[5] Usher, M. and Niebur, E. (1996) Modeling the temporal dynamics of IT neurons in visual search: A mechanism for top-down selective attention. *Journal of Cognitive Neuroscience*, **8**, 311-327.

Effects of Spatial and Temporal Contiguity on the Acquisition of Spatial Information

Thea B. Ghiselli-Crippa and Paul W. Munro
Department of Information Science and Telecommunications
University of Pittsburgh
Pittsburgh, PA 15260
tbgst@sis.pitt.edu, munro@sis.pitt.edu

Abstract

Spatial information comes in two forms: direct spatial information (for example, retinal position) and indirect temporal contiguity information, since objects encountered sequentially are in general spatially close. The acquisition of spatial information by a neural network is investigated here. Given a spatial layout of several objects, networks are trained on a prediction task. Networks using temporal sequences with no direct spatial information are found to develop internal representations that show distances correlated with distances in the external layout. The influence of spatial information is analyzed by providing direct spatial information to the system during training that is either consistent with the layout or inconsistent with it. This approach allows examination of the relative contributions of spatial and temporal contiguity.

1 Introduction

Spatial information is acquired by a process of exploration that is fundamentally temporal, whether it be on a small scale, such as scanning a picture, or on a larger one, such as physically navigating through a building, a neighborhood, or a city. Continuous scanning of an environment causes locations that are spatially close to have a tendency to occur in temporal proximity to one another. Thus, a temporal associative mechanism (such as a Hebb rule) can be used in conjunction with continuous exploration to capture the spatial structure of the environment [1]. However, the actual process of building a cognitive map need not rely solely on temporal associations, since some spatial information is encoded in the sensory array (position on the retina and proprioceptive feedback). Laboratory studies show different types of interaction between the relative contributions of temporal and spatial contiguities to the formation of an internal representation of space. While Clayton and Habibi's [2] series of recognition priming experiments indicates that priming is controlled only by temporal associations, in the work of McNamara et al. [3] priming in recognition is observed only when space and time are both contiguous. In addition, Curiel and Radvansky's [4] work shows that the effects of spatial and temporal contiguity depend on whether location or identity information is emphasized during learning. Moreover, other experiments ([3]) also show how the effects clearly depend on the task and can be quite different if an explicitly spatial task is used (e.g., additive effects in location judgments).

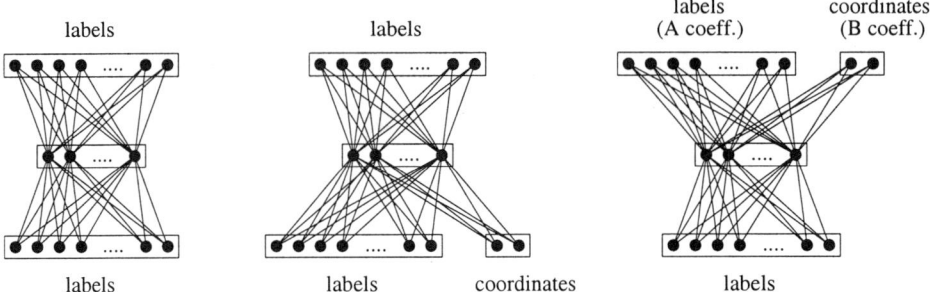

Figure 1: Network architectures: temporal-only network (left); spatio-temporal network with spatial units part of the input representation (center); spatio-temporal network with spatial units part of the output representation (right).

2 Network architectures

The goal of the work presented in this paper is to study the structure of the internal representations that emerge from the integration of temporal and spatial associations. An encoder-like network architecture is used (see Figure 1), with a set of N input units and a set of N output units representing N nodes on a 2-dimensional graph. A set of H units is used for the hidden layer. To include space in the learning process, additional spatial units are included in the network architecture. These units provide a representation of the spatial information directly available during the learning/scanning process. In the simulations described in this paper, two units are used and are chosen to represent the (x, y) coordinates of the nodes in the graph. The spatial units can be included as part of the input representation or as part of the output representation (see Figure 1, center and right panels): both choices are used in the experiments, to investigate whether the spatial information could better benefit training as an input or as an output [5]. In the second case, the relative contribution of the spatial information can be directly manipulated by introducing weighting factors in the cost function being minimized. A two-term cost function is used, with a cross-entropy term for the N label units and a squared error term for the 2 coordinate units,

$$E = A\left[-\sum_{i=1}^{N} t_i log_2(r_i) + (1-t_i)log_2(1-r_i)\right] + B\left[\frac{1}{2}\sum_{i=1}^{2}(t_i - r_i)^2\right] \quad (1)$$

r_i indicates the actual output of unit i and t_i its desired output. The relative influence of the spatial information is controlled by the coefficients A and B.

3 Learning tasks

The left panel of Figure 2 shows an example of the type of layout used; the effective layout used in the study consists of $N = 28$ nodes. For each node, a set of neighboring nodes is defined, chosen on the basis of how an observer might scan the layout to learn the node labels and their (spatial) relationships; in Figure 2, the neighborhood relationships are represented by lines connecting neighboring nodes. From any node in the layout, the only allowed transitions are those to a neighbor, thus defining the set of node pairs used to train the network (66 pairs out of $C(28, 2) = 378$ possible pairs). In addition, the probability of occurrence of a particular transition is computed as a function of the distance to the corresponding neighbor. It is then possible to generate a sequence of visits to the network nodes, aimed at replicating the scanning process of a human observer studying the layout.

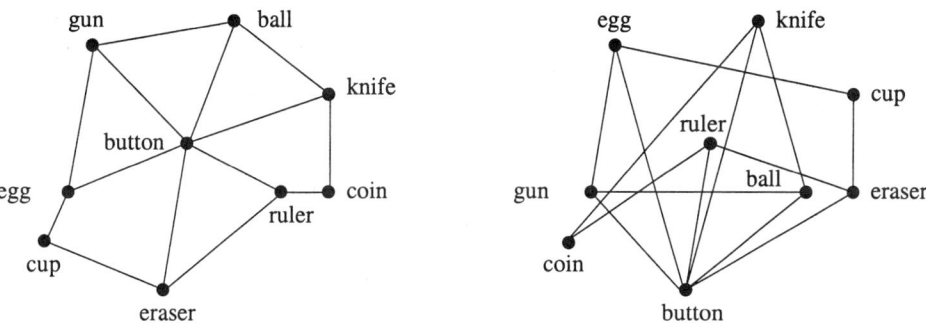

Figure 2: Example of a layout (left) and its permuted version (right). Links represent allowed transitions. A larger layout of 28 units was used in the simulations.

The basic learning task is similar to the grammar learning task of Servan-Schreiber et al. [6] and to the neighborhood mapping task described in [1] and is used to associate each of the N nodes on the graph and its (x, y) coordinates with the probability distribution of the transitions to its neighboring nodes. The mapping can be learned directly, by associating each node with the probability distribution of the transitions to all its neighbors: in this case, batch learning is used as the method of choice for learning the mapping. On the other hand, the mapping can be learned indirectly, by associating each node with itself and one of its neighbors, with online learning being the method of choice in this case; the neighbor chosen at each iteration is defined by the sequence of visits generated on the basis of the transition probabilities. Batch learning was chosen because it generally converges more smoothly and more quickly than online learning and gives qualitatively similar results. While the task and network architecture described in [1] allowed only for temporal association learning, in this study both temporal and spatial associations are learned simultaneously, thanks to the presence of the spatial units. However, the temporal-only (T-only) case, which has no spatial units, is included in the simulations performed for this study, to provide a benchmark for the evaluation of the results obtained with the spatio-temporal (S-T) networks.

The task described above allows the network to learn neighborhood relationships for which spatial and temporal associations provide consistent information, that is, nodes experienced contiguously in time (as defined by the sequence) are also contiguous in space (being spatial neighbors). To tease apart the relative contributions of space and time, the task is kept the same, but the data employed for training the network is modified: the same layout is used to generate the temporal sequence, but the x, y coordinates of the nodes are randomly permuted (see right panel of Figure 2). If the permuted layout is then scanned following the same sequence of node visits used in the original version, the net effect is that the temporal associations remain the same, but the spatial associations change so that temporally neighboring nodes can now be spatially close or distant: the spatial associations are no longer consistent with the temporal associations. As Figure 4 illustrates, the training pairs (filled circles) all correspond to short distances in the original layout, but can have a distance anywhere in the allowable range in the permuted layout. Since the temporal and spatial distances were consistent in the original layout, the original spatial distance can be used as an indicator of temporal distance and Figure 4 can be interpreted as a plot of temporal distance vs. spatial distance for the permuted layout.

The simulations described in the following include three experimental conditions: temporal only (no direct spatial information available); space and time consistent (the spatial coordinates and the temporal sequence are from the same layout); space and time inconsistent (the spatial coordinates and the temporal sequence are from different layouts).

Hidden unit representations are compared using Euclidean distance (cosine and inner product measures give consistent results); the internal representation distances are also used to compute their correlation with Euclidean distances between nodes in the layout (original and permuted). The correlations increase with the number of hidden units for values of H between 5 and 10 and then gradually taper off for values greater than 10. The results presented in the remainder of the paper all pertain to networks trained with $H = 20$ and with hidden units using a $tanh$ transfer function; all the results pertaining to S-T networks refer to networks with 2 spatial output units and cost function coefficients $A = 0.625$ and $B = 6.25$.

4 Results

Figure 3 provides a combined view of the results from all three experiments. The left panel illustrates the evolution of the correlation between internal representation distances and layout (original and permuted) distances. The right panel shows the distributions of the correlations at the end of training (1000 epochs). The first general result is that, when spatial information is available and consistent with the temporal information (original layout), the correlation between hidden unit distances and layout distances is consistently better than the correlation obtained in the case of temporal associations alone. The second general result is that, when spatial information is available but not consistent with the temporal information (permuted layout), the correlation between hidden unit distances and original layout distances (which represent temporal distances) is similar to that obtained in the case of temporal associations alone, except for the initial transient. When the correlation is computed with respect to the permuted layout distances, its value peaks early during training and then decreases rapidly, to reach an asymptotic value well below the other three cases. This behavior is illustrated in the boxplots in the right panel of Figure 3, which report the distribution of correlation values at the end of training.

4.1 Temporal-only vs. spatio-temporal

As a first step in this study, the effects of adding spatial information to the basic temporal associations used to train the network can be examined. Since the learning task is the same for both the T-only and the S-T networks except for the absence or presence of spatial information during training, the differences observed can be attributed to the additional spatial information available to the S-T networks. The higher correlation between internal representation distances and original layout distances obtained when spatial information is

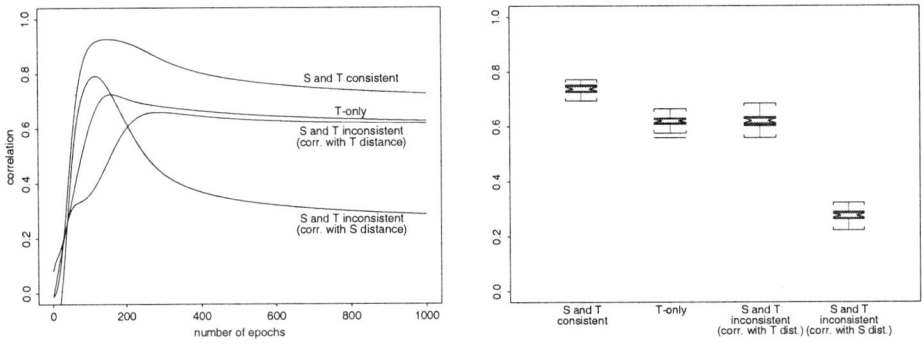

Figure 3: Evolution of correlation during training (0 - 1000 epochs) (left). Distributions of correlations at the end of training (1000 epochs) (right).

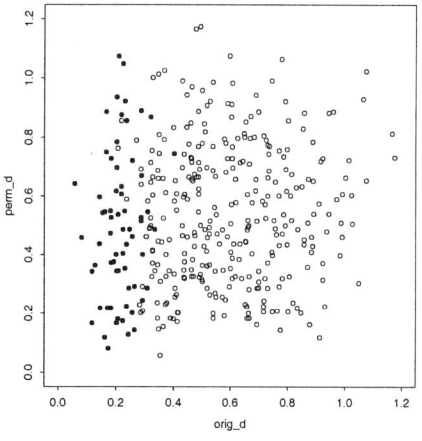 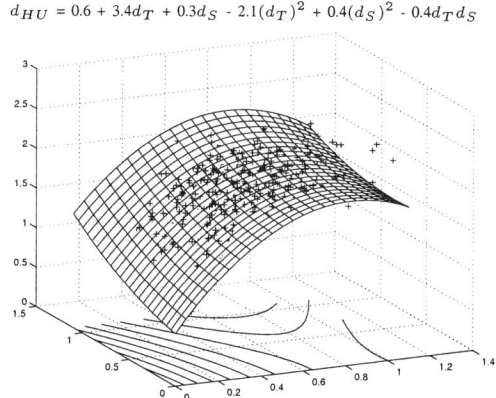

Figure 4: Distances in the original layout (x) vs. distances in the permuted layout (y). The 66 training pairs are identified by filled circles.

Figure 5: Similarities (Euclidean distances) between internal representations developed by a S-T network (after 300 epochs). Figure 4 projects the data points onto the x, y plane.

available (see Figure 3) is apparent also when the evolution of the internal representations is examined. As Figure 6 illustrates, the presence of spatial information results in better generalization for the pattern pairs outside the training set. While the distances between training pairs are mapped to similar distances in hidden unit space for both the T-only and the S-T networks, the T-only network tends to cluster the non-training pairs into a narrow band of distances in hidden unit space. In the case of the S-T network instead, the hidden unit distances between non-training pairs are spread out over a wider range and tend to reflect the original layout distances.

4.2 Permuted layout

As described above, with the permuted layout it is possible to decouple the spatial and temporal contributions and therefore study the effects of each. A comprehensive view of the results at a particular point during training (300 epochs) is presented in Figure 5, where the x, y plane represents temporal distance vs. spatial distance (see also Figure 4) and the z axis represents the similarity between hidden unit representations. The figure also includes a quadratic regression surface fitted to the data points. The coefficients in the equation of the surface provide a quantitative measure of the relative contributions of spatial (d_S) and temporal distances (d_T) to the similarity between hidden unit representations (d_{HU}):

$$d_{HU} = k_0 + k_1 d_T + k_2 d_S + k_3 (d_T)^2 + k_4 (d_S)^2 + k_5 d_T d_S \qquad (2)$$

In general, after the transient observed in early training (see Figure 3), the largest and most significant coefficients are found for d_T and $(d_T)^2$, indicating a stronger dependence of d_{HU} on temporal distance than on spatial distance.

The results illustrated in Figure 5 represent the situation at a particular point during training (300 epochs). Similar plots can be generated for different points during training, to study the evolution of the internal representations. A different view of the evolution process is provided by Figure 7, in which the data points are projected onto the x,z plane (top panel) and the y,z plane (bottom panel) at four different times during training. In the top panel,

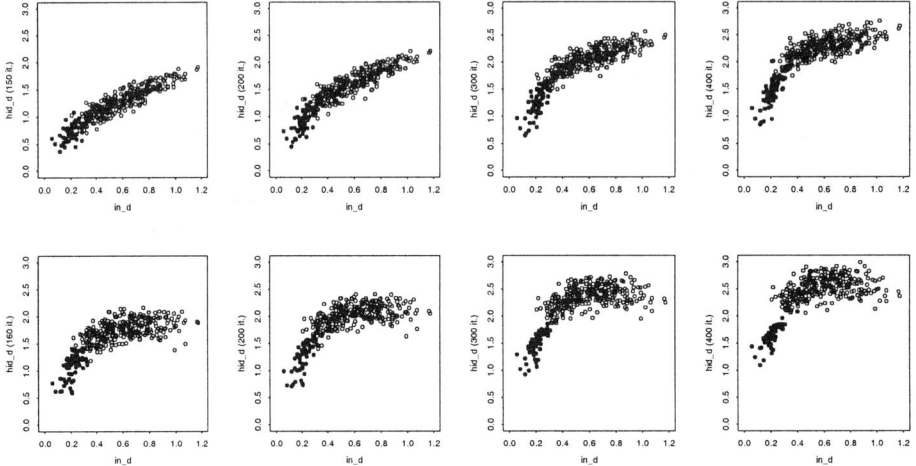

Figure 6: Internal representation distances vs. original layout distances: S-T network (top) vs. T-only network (bottom). The training pairs are identified by filled circles. The presence of spatial information results in better generalization for the pairs outside the training set.

the internal representation distances are plotted as a function of temporal distance (i.e., the spatial distance from the original layout), while in the bottom panel they are plotted as a function of spatial distance (from the permuted layout). The higher asymptotic correlation between internal representation distances and temporal distances, as opposed to spatial distances (see Figure 3), is apparent also from the examination of the evolutionary plots, which show an asymptotic behavior with respect to temporal distances (see Figure 7, top panel) very similar to the T-only case (see Figure 6, bottom panel).

5 Discussion

The first general conclusion that can be drawn from the examination of the results described in the previous section is that, when the spatial information is available and consistent with the temporal information (original layout), the similarity structure of the hidden unit representations is closer to the structure of the original layout than that obtained by using temporal associations alone. The second general conclusion is that, when the spatial information is available but not consistent with the temporal information (permuted layout), the similarity structure of the hidden unit representations seems to correspond to temporal more than spatial proximity. Figures 5 and 7 both indicate that temporal associations take precedence over spatial associations. This result is in agreement with the results described in [1], showing how temporal associations (plus some high-level constraints) significantly contribute to the internal representation of global spatial information. However, spatial information certainly is very beneficial to the (temporal) acquisition of a layout, as proven by the results obtained with the S-T network vs. the T-only network.

In terms of the model presented in this paper, the results illustrated in Figures 5 and 7 can be compared with the experimental data reported for recognition priming ([2], [3], [4]), with distance between internal representations corresponding to reaction time. The results of our model indicate that distances in both the spatially far and spatially close condition appear to be consistently shorter for the training pairs (temporally close) than for the non-training pairs (temporally distant), highlighting a strong temporal effect consistent with the data reported in [2] and [4] (for spatially far pairs) and in [3] (only for the spatially close

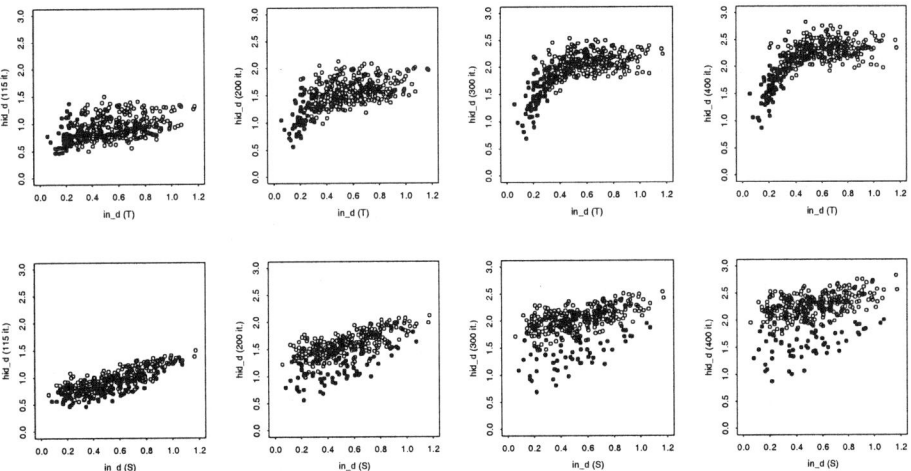

Figure 7: Internal representation distances vs. temporal distances (top) and vs. spatial distances (bottom) for a S-T network (permuted layout). The training pairs are identified by filled circles. The asymptotic behavior with respect to temporal distances (top panel) is similar to the T-only condition. The bottom panel indicates a weak dependence on spatial distances.

case). For the training pairs (temporally close), slightly shorter distances are obtained for spatially close pairs vs. spatially far pairs; this result does not provide support for the experimental data reported in either [3] (strong spatial effect) or [2] (no spatial effect). For the non-training pairs (temporally distant), long distances are found throughout, with no strong dependence on spatial distance; this effect is consistent with all the reported experimental data. Further simulations and statistical analyses are necessary for a more conclusive comparison with the experimental data.

References

[1] Ghiselli-Crippa, T.B. & Munro, P.W. (1994). Emergence of global structure from local associations. In J.D. Cowan, G. Tesauro, & J. Alspector (Eds.), *Advances in Neural Information Processing Systems 6*, pp. 1101-1108. San Francisco, CA: Morgan Kaufmann.

[2] Clayton, K.N. & Habibi, A. (1991). The contribution of temporal contiguity to the spatial priming effect. *Journal of Experimental Psychology: Learning, Memory, and Cognition* **17**:263-271.

[3] McNamara, T.P., Halpin, J.A. & Hardy, J.K. (1992). Spatial and temporal contributions to the structure of spatial memory. *Journal of Experimental Psychology: Learning, Memory, and Cognition* **18**:555-564.

[4] Curiel, J.M. & Radvansky, G.A. (1998). Mental organization of maps. *Journal of Experimental Psychology: Learning, Memory, and Cognition* **24**:202-214.

[5] Caruana, R. & de Sa, V.R. (1997). Promoting poor features to supervisors: Some inputs work better as outputs. In M.C. Mozer, M.I. Jordan, & T. Petsche (Eds.), *Advances in Neural Information Processing Systems 9*, pp. 389-395. Cambridge, MA: MIT Press.

[6] Servan-Schreiber, D., Cleeremans, A. & McClelland, J.L. (1989). Learning sequential structure in simple recurrent networks. In D.S. Touretzky (Ed.), *Advances in Neural Information Processing Systems 1*, pp. 643-652. San Mateo, CA: Morgan Kaufmann.

Acquisition in Autoshaping

Sham Kakade   **Peter Dayan**
Gatsby Computational Neuroscience Unit
17 Queen Square, London, England, WC1N 3AR.
sham@gatsby.ucl.ac.uk   dayan@gatsby.ucl.ac.uk

Abstract

Quantitative data on the speed with which animals acquire behavioral responses during classical conditioning experiments should provide strong constraints on models of learning. However, most models have simply ignored these data; the few that have attempted to address them have failed by at least an order of magnitude. We discuss key data on the speed of acquisition, and show how to account for them using a statistically sound model of learning, in which differential *reliabilities* of stimuli play a crucial role.

1 Introduction

Conditioning experiments probe the ways that animals make predictions about rewards and punishments and how those predictions are used to their advantage. Substantial quantitative data are available as to how pigeons and rats *acquire* conditioned responses during *autoshaping*, which is one of the simplest paradigms of classical conditioning.[4] These data are revealing about the statistical, and ultimately also the neural, substrate underlying the ways that animals learn about the causal texture of their environments.

In autoshaping experiments on pigeons, the birds acquire a peck response to a lighted key associated (irrespective of their actions) with the delivery of food. One attractive feature of autoshaping is that there is no need for separate 'probe trials' to assess the degree of association formed between the light and the food by the animal — rather, the rate of key pecking during the light (and before the food) can be used as a direct measure of this association. In particular, acquisition speeds are often measured by the number of trials until a certain behavioral criterion is met, such as pecking during the light on three out of four successive trials.[4,8,10]

As stressed persuasively by Gallistel & Gibbon[4] (GG; forthcoming), the critical feature of autoshaping is that there is substantial experimental evidence on how acquisition speed depends on the three critical variables shown in figure 1A. The first is I, the inter-trial interval; the second is T, the time during the trial for which the light is presented; the third is the training schedule, $1/S$, which is the fractional number of deliveries per light — some birds were only partially reinforced.

Figure 1 makes three key points. First, figure 1B shows that the median number of trials to the acquisition criterion depends on the *ratio* of I/T, and not on I and T separately – experiments reported for the same I/T are actually performed with I and T differing by more than an order of magnitude.[4,8] Second, figure 1B shows convincingly that the number of reinforcements is approximately inversely proportional to I/T — the relatively shorter presentation of light, the faster the learn-

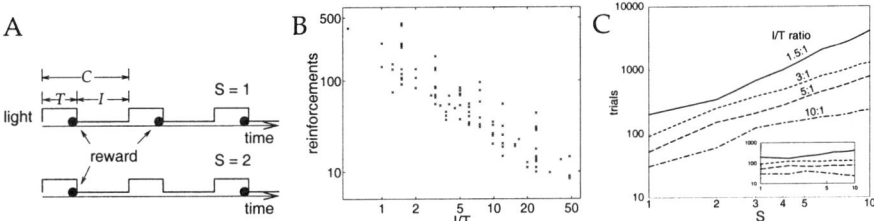

Figure 1: Autoshaping. A) Experimental paradigm. Top: the light is presented for T seconds every C seconds and is always followed by the delivery of food (filled circle). Bottom: the food is delivered with probability $1/S = 1/2$ per trial. In some cases I is stochastic, with the appropriate mean. B) Log-log plot[4] of the number of reinforcements to a given acquisition criterion versus the I/T ratio for $S = 1$. The data are median acquisition times from 12 different laboratories. C) Log-log acquisition curves for various I/T ratios and S values. The main graph shows *trials versus S*; the inset shows *reinforcements versus S*. (1999).

ing. Third, figure 1C shows that partial reinforcement has almost no effect when measured as a function of the number of reinforcements (rather than the number of trials),[4,10] since although it takes S times as many *trials* to acquire, there are *reinforcements* on only $1/S$ trials. Changing S does not change the effective I/T when measured as a function of reinforcements, so this result might actually be expected on the basis of figure 1B, and we only consider $S = 1$ in this paper. Altogether, the data show that:

$$n \approx 300 * T/I \qquad (1)$$

where n is the number of rewards to the acquisition criterion. Remarkably, these effects seem to hold for over an order of magnitude in both I/T and S.

These quantitative data should be a most seductive target for statistically sound models of learning. However, few models have even attempted to capture the strong constraints they provide, and those that have attempted, all fail in critical aspects. The best of them, rate estimation theory[4] (RET), is closely related to the Rescorla-Wagner[13] (RW) model, and actually captures the proportionality in equation 1. However, as shown below, RET grossly overestimates the observed speed of acquisition (underestimating the proportionality constant). Further, RET is designed to account for the time at which a particular, standard, acquisition criterion is met. Figure 2A shows that this is revealing only about the very early stages of learning — RET is silent about the remainder of the learning curve.

We look at additional quantitative data on learning, which collectively suggest that stimuli *compete* to predict the delivery of reward. Dayan & Long[3] (DL) discussed various statistically inspired competitive models of classical conditioning, concluding with one in which stimuli are differently *reliable* as predictors of reward. However, DL ignored the data shown in figures 1 and 2, basing their analysis on conditioning paradigms in which I/T was not a factor. Figures 1 and 2 demand a more sophisticated statistical model — building such a model is the focus of this paper.

2 Rate Estimation Theory

Gallistel & Gibbon[4] (GG; forthcoming) are amongst the strongest proponents of the quantitative relationships in figure 1. To account for them, GG suggest that animals are estimating the rates of rewards — one, λ_l, for the rate associated with the light and another, λ_b, for the rate associated with the *background context*. The context is the ever-present environment which can itself gain associative value. The overall

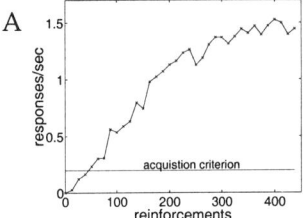 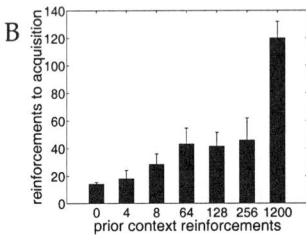

Figure 2: Additional Autoshaping Data. A) Acquisition of keypecking. The figure shows response rate *versus* reinforcements.[6] The acquisition criterion is satisfied at a relatively *early* time when the response curve crosses the acquisition criterion line. B) The effects of prior context reinforcements on subsequent acquisition speed. The data are taken from two experiments,[1,2] with $I/T = 6$.

predicted reward rate while the light is on is $\lambda_l + \lambda_b$, and the rate without the light is just λ_b.

The additive form of the model makes it similar to Rescorla-Wagner's[13] (RW) standard delta-rule model, for which the net prediction of the expected reward in a trial is the sum of the associative values of each active predictor (in this case, the context and light). If the rewards are modeled as being just present or absent, the expected value for a reward is just its *probability* of occurrence. Instead, RET uses *rates*, which are just probabilities per unit time.

GG[4] formulated their model from a frequentist viewpoint. However, it is easier to discuss a closely related Bayesian model which suffers from the same underlying problem. Instead of using RW's delta-rule for learning the rates, GG assume that reinforcements come from a constant rate Poisson process, and make sound statistical inferences about the rates given the data on the rewards. Using an improper flat prior over the rates, we can write the joint distribution as:

$$\mathcal{P}(\lambda_l \lambda_b \mid \text{data}) \propto \mathcal{P}(n \mid \lambda_l \lambda_b t_l t_b) \propto (\lambda_l + \lambda_b)^n e^{-(\lambda_l + \lambda_b) t_l} e^{-\lambda_b t_b} \qquad (2)$$

since all n rewards occur with the light, at rate $\lambda_l + \lambda_b$. Here, $t_l = nT$ is the total time the light is on, and $t_b = nI$ is the total time the light is off.

GG take the further important step of relating the inferred rates λ_l and λ_b to the decision of the animals to start responding (*ie* to satisfy the acquisition criterion). GG suggest that acquisition should occur when the animals have strong evidence that the fractional increase in the reward rate, whilst the light is on, is greater than some threshold. More formally, acquisition should occur when:

$$\mathcal{P}((\lambda_l + \lambda_b)/\lambda_b > \beta \mid n) = 1 - \alpha \qquad (3)$$

where α is the uncertainty threshold and β is slightly greater than one, reflecting the fractional increase. The n that first satisfies equation 3 can be found by integrating the joint probability in equation 2. It turns out that $n \propto t_l/t_b$, which has the approximate, linear dependence on the ratio I/T (as in figure 1B), since $t_l/t_b = nT/nI = T/I$. It also has no dependence on partial reinforcement, as observed in figure 1C.

However, even with a very low uncertainty, $\alpha = 0.001$, and a reasonable fractional increase, $\beta = 1.5$, this model predicts that learning should be more than ten times as fast as observed, since we get $n \approx 20 * T/I$ as opposed to the $300 * T/I$ observed. Equation 1 can only be satisfied by setting α between 10^{-20} and 10^{-50} (depending on the precise values of I/T and β)! This spells problems for GG as a normative, ideal detector model of learning — it cannot, for instance, be repaired with any reasonable prior for the rates, as α drops drastically with n. In other circumstances, though, Gallistel, Mark & King[5] (forthcoming) have shown that animals can be ideal detectors of changes in rates.

One hint of the flaw with GG is that simple manipulations to the context before starting autoshaping (in particular *extinction*) can produce very *rapid* learning.[2] More generally, the data show that acquisition speed is strongly controlled by prior rewards being given only in the context (without the light present).[2] Figure 2B shows a parametric study of subsequent acquisition speeds during autoshaping as a function of the *number* of rewards given only with the context. This effect cannot simply be modeled by assuming a different prior distribution for the rates (which does not fix the problem of the speed of acquisition in any case), since the *rate* at which these prior context rewards were given has little effect on subsequent acquisition speed for a given *number* of prior reinforcements.[9] Note that the data in figure 2B (*ie* equation 1) suggest that there were about thirty prior rewards in the context — this is consistent with the experimental procedures used,[8–10] although prior experience was not a carefully controlled factor.

3 The Competitive Model

Five sets of constraints govern our new model. First, since animals can be ideal detectors of rates in some circumstances,[5] we only consider accounts under which their acquisition of responding has a rational statistical basis. Second, the number of reinforcements to acquisition must be $n \approx 300 * T/I$, as in equation 1. This requires that the constant of proportionality should come from rational, not absurd, uncertainties. Third, pecking rates after the acquisition criterion is satisfied should also follow the form of figure 2A (in the end, we are preventing from a normative account of this by a dearth of data). Fourth, the overall learning speed should be strongly affected by the *number* of prior context rewards (figure 2B), but not by the *rate* at which they were presented. That is, the context, as an established predictor, regardless of the rate it predicts, should be able to substantially *block* learning to a less established predictor. Finally, the asymptotic accuracy of rate estimates should satisfy the substantial experimental data on the intrinsic uncertainty in the predictions in the form of a quantitative account called scalar expectancy theory[7] (SET).

In our model, as in DL, an *independent* prediction of the rate of reward delivery is made on the basis of each stimulus that is present (ω_c, for the context; ω_l for the light). These separate predictions are combined based on estimated *reliabilities* of the predictions. Here, we present a heuristic version of a more rigorously specified model.[12]

3.1 Rate Predictions

SET[7] was originally developed to capture the nature of uncertainty in the way that animals estimate time intervals. Its most important result is that the standard deviation of an estimate is consistently proportional to the mean, even after an asymptotic number of presentations of the interval. Since the estimated time to a reward is just the inverse rate, asymptotic rate estimates might also be expected to have constant coefficients of variation. Therefore, we constrain the standard deviations of rate estimates not to drop below a multiple of their means. Evidence suggests that this multiple is about 0.2.[7] RET clearly does not satisfy this constraint as the joint distribution (equation 2) becomes arbitrarily accurate over time.

Inspired by Sutton,[14] we consider Kalman filter models for *independent* log-predictions, $\log \omega_c(m)$ and $\log \omega_l(m)$, on trial m. The output models for the filters specify the relationship between the predicted and observed rates. We use a simple log-normal, $\mathcal{LN}$, approximation (to an underlying truly Poisson model):

$$\mathcal{P}(o_c(m) \mid \omega_c(m)) \sim \mathcal{LN}(\omega_c(m), v_c^2) \quad \mathcal{P}(o_l(m) \mid \omega_l(m)) \sim \mathcal{LN}(\omega_l(m), v_l^2) \quad (4)$$

where $o_*(m)$ is the observed average reward whilst predictor $*$ is present, so if a reward occurs with the light in trial m, then $o_l(m) = 1/T$ and $o_c(m) = 1/C$ (where $C = T + I$). The values of v_*^2 can be determined, from the Poisson model, to be $v_c^2 = v_l^2 = 1$.

The other part of the Kalman filter is a model of change in the world for the ω's:

$$\log \omega_c(m) = \log \omega_c(m-1) + \epsilon_c(m) \qquad \epsilon_c(m) \sim \mathcal{N}(0, (\eta(\eta+1))^{-1}) \quad (5)$$
$$\log \omega_l(m) = \log \omega_l(m-1) + \epsilon_l(m) \qquad \epsilon_l(m) \sim \mathcal{N}(0, (\eta(\eta+1))^{-1}) \quad (6)$$

We use log(rates) so that there is no inherent scale to change in the world. Here, η is a constant chosen to satisfy the SET constraint, imposed as $\sigma_* = \hat{\omega}_*/\sqrt{\eta}$ at asymptote. Notice that η acts as the effective number of rewards remembered, which will be less than 30, to get the observed coefficient of variation above 0.2.

After observing the data from m trials, the posterior distributions for the predictions will become approximately:

$$\mathcal{P}(\omega_c(m) \mid \text{data}) \sim \mathcal{N}(1/C, \sigma_c^2(m)) \quad \mathcal{P}(\omega_l(m) \mid \text{data}) \sim \mathcal{N}(1/T, \sigma_l^2(m)) \quad (7)$$

and, in about $m = \eta$ trials, $\sigma_c(m) \to (1/C)/\sqrt{\eta}$ and $\sigma_l(m) \to (1/T)/\sqrt{\eta}$. This captures the fastest acquisition in figure 2, and also extinction.

3.2 Cooperative Mixture of Experts

The two predictions (equation 7) are combined using the factorial experts model of Jacobs et al[11] that was also used by DL. For this, *during* the presentation of the light (and the context, of course), we consider that, independently, the relationships between the actual reward rate $r(m)$ and the outputs $\omega_l(m)$ and $\omega_c(m)$ of 'experts' associated with each stimulus are:

$$\mathcal{P}(\omega_l(m)|r(m)) \sim \mathcal{N}(r(m), \tfrac{1}{\rho_l(m)}) \quad , \quad \mathcal{P}(\omega_c(m)|r(m)) \sim \mathcal{N}(r(m), \tfrac{1}{\rho_c(m)}) \quad (8)$$

where $\rho_l(m)^{-1}$ and $\rho_c(m)^{-1}$ are inverse variances, or *reliabilities* for the stimuli. These reliabilities reflect the belief as to how close $\omega_l(m)$ and $\omega_c(m)$ are to $r(m)$. The estimates are combined, giving

$$\mathcal{P}(r(m) \mid \omega_l(m), \omega_c(m)) \sim \mathcal{N}(\hat{r}(m), (\rho_l(m) + \rho_c(m))^{-1})$$
$$\hat{r}(m) = \pi_l(m)\omega_l(m) + (1 - \pi_l(m))\omega_c(m) \quad \pi_l(m) = \rho_l(m)/(\rho_l(m) + \rho_c(m))$$

The prediction of the reward rate without the light $r_c(m)$ is determined just by the context value $\omega_c(m)$.

In this formulation, the context can block the light's prediction if it is more *reliable* ($\rho_c \gg \rho_l$), since $\pi_l \approx 0$, making the mean $\hat{r}(m) \approx \omega_c(m)$, and this blocking occurs regardless of the context's *rate*, $\omega_c(m)$. If ρ_l slowly increases, then $\hat{r}(m) \to \omega_l$ slowly as $\pi_l(m) \to 1$. We expect this to model the post-acquisition part of the learning shown in figure 2A.

A fully normative model of acquisition would come from a statistically correct account of how the reliabilities should change over time, which, in turn, would come from a statistical model of the expectations the animal has of how predictabilities change in the world. Unfortunately, the slow phase of learning in figure 2A, which should provide the most useful data on these expectations, is almost ubiquitously

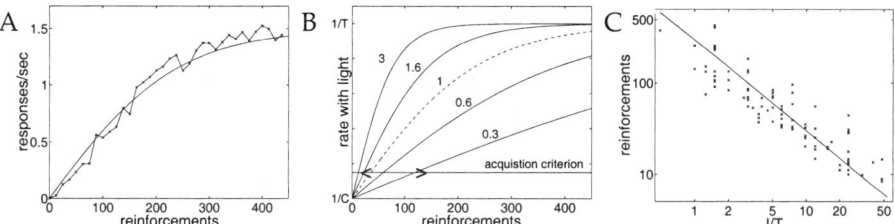

Figure 3: Satisfaction of the Constraints. A) The fit to the behavioral response curve (figure 2B), using equation 9 and $\pi_0 = 0.004$. B) Possible acquisition curves showing $\hat{r}(m)$ versus m. The $\longleftrightarrow$ on the criterion line denotes the range of 15 to 120 reinforcements that are indicated by figure 2B. The $--$ curve is the same as in Fig 3A. The parameters displayed are values for π_0 in multiples of π_0 for the center curve. C) A theoretical fit to the data using equation 11. Here, $\alpha = 5\%$ and $\pi_0 \sqrt{\rho_0} = 0.004$.

ignored in experiments. We therefore make two assumptions about this, which are chosen to fit the acquisition data, but whose normative underpinnings are unclear. The first assumption, chosen to obtain the slow learning curve, is that:

$$\pi_l(m) = \tanh \pi_0 m \qquad (9)$$

Assuming that the strength of the behavioral response is approximately proportional to $r(m) - r_c(m)$, which we will estimate by $\pi_l(m)(\hat{\omega}_l(m) - \hat{\omega}_c(m))$, figure 3A compares the rate of key pecking in the model with the data from figure 2A. Figure 3B shows the effect on the behavioral response of varying π_0. Within just a half an order magnitude of variation of π_0, the acquisition speeds (judged at the criterion line shown) due to between 1200 and 0 prior context rewards (figure 2B) can be obtained. Note the slightly counter-intuitive explanation — the actual reward rate associated with the light is established very quickly — slow learning comes from slow changes in the importance paid to these rates.

We make a second assumption that the coefficient of variation of the context's prediction, from equation 8, does not change significantly for the early trials before the acquisition criterion is met (it could change thereafter). This gives:

$$\rho_c(m) \approx \rho_0/\hat{\omega}_c(m)^2 \quad \text{for early } m \qquad (10)$$

It is plausible that the context is not becoming a relatively worse 'expert' for early m, since no other predictor has yet proven more reliable.

Following GG's suggestion, we model acquisition as occurring on trial m if $\mathcal{P}(r(m) > r_c(m)|\text{data}) \geq 1 - \alpha$, ie if the animal has sound reasons to expect a higher reward rate with the light. Integrating over the Kalman filter distributions in equation 7 gives the distribution of $r(m) - r_c(m)$ for early m as

$$\mathcal{P}(r(m) - r_c(m) \mid \text{data}) \sim \mathcal{N}((\tanh \pi_0 m)(1/T - 1/C), (\rho_0 C^2)^{-1})$$

where $\sigma_*(m)$ has dropped out due to $\pi_l(m)$ being small at early m. Finding the number of rewards, n, that satisfies the acquisition criterion gives:

$$n \approx \frac{\alpha}{\pi_0 \sqrt{\rho_0}} \frac{T}{I} \qquad (11)$$

where the factor of α depends on the uncertainty, α, used. Figure 3C shows the theoretical fit to the data.

4 Discussion

Although a noble attempt, RET fails to satisfy the strong body of constraints under which any acquisition model must labor. Under RET, the acquisition of responding cannot have a rational statistical basis, as the animal's modeled uncertainty in the association between light and reward at the time of acquisition is below 10^{-20}. Further, RET ignores constraints set forth by the data establishing SET and also data on prior context manipulations. These latter data show that the context, regardless of the rate it predicts, will substantially block learning to a less established predictor. Additive models, such as RET, are unable to capture this effect.

We have suggested a model in which each stimulus is like an 'expert' that learns independently about the world. Expert predictions can adapt quickly to changes in contingencies, as they are based on a Kalman filter model, with variances chosen to satisfy the constraint suggested by SET, and they can be combined based on their *reliabilities*. We have demonstrated the model's close fit to substantial experimental data. In particular, the new model captures the I/T dependence of the number of rewards to acquisition, with a constant of proportionality that reflects rational statistical beliefs. The slow learning that occurs in some circumstances, is due to a slow change in the reliabilities of predictors, not due to the rates being unable to adapt quickly. Although we have not shown it here, the model is also able to account for quantitative data as to the speed of extinction of the association between the light and the reward.

The model leaves many directions for future study. In particular, we have not specified a sound statistical basis for the changes in reliabilities given in equations 9 and 10. Such a basis is key to understanding the slow phase of learning. Second, we have not addressed data from more sophisticated conditioning paradigms. For instance, overshadowing, in which multiple conditioned stimuli are similarly predictive of the reward, should be able to be incorporated into the model in a natural way.

Acknowledgements

We are most grateful to Randy Gallistel and John Gibbon for freely sharing, prior to publication, their many ideas about timing and conditioning. We thank Sam Roweis for comments on an earlier version of the manuscript. Funding is from a NSF Graduate Research Fellowship (SK) and the Gatsby Charitable Foundation.

References

[1] Balsam, PD, & Gibbon, J (1988). *Journal of Experimental Psychology: Animal Behavior Processes*, **14**: 401-412.

[2] Balsam, PD, & Schwartz, AL (1981). *Journal of Experimental Psychology: Animal Behavior Processes*, **7**: 382-393.

[3] Dayan, P, & Long, T, (1997) *Neural Information Processing Systems*, **10**:117-124.

[4] Gallistel, CR, & Gibbon, J (1999). *Time, Rate, and Conditioning*. Forthcoming.

[5] Gallistel, CR, Mark, TS & King, A (1999). *Is the Rat an Ideal Detector of Changes in Rates of Reward?*. Forthcoming.

[6] Gamzu, ER, & Williams, DR (1973). *Journal of the Experimental Analysis of Behavior*, **19**:225-232.

[7] Gibbon, J (1977). *Psychological Review* **84**:279-325.

[8] Gibbon, J, Baldock, MD, Locurto, C, Gold, L & Terrace, HS (1977). *Journal of Experimental Psychology: Animal Behavior Processes*, **3**: 264-284.

[9] Gibbon, J & Balsam, P (1981). In CM Locurto, HS Terrace, & J Gibbon, editors, *Autoshaping and Conditioning Theory*. 219-253. New York, NY: Academic Press.

[10] Gibbon, J, Farrell, L, Locurto, CM, Duncan, JH & Terrace, HS (1980). *Animal Learning and Behavior*, **8**:45-59.

[11] Jacobs, RA, Jordan, MI, & Barto, AG (1991). *Cognitive Science* **15**:219-250.

[12] Kakade, S & Dayan, P (2000). In preparation.

[13] Rescorla, RA & Wagner, AR (1972). In AH Black & WF Prokasy, editors, *Classical Conditioning II: Current Research and Theory*, 64-69. New York, NY: Appleton-Century-Crofts.

[14] Sutton, R (1992). In *Proceedings of the 7th Yale Workshop on Adaptive and Learning Systems*.

Robust Recognition of Noisy and Superimposed Patterns via Selective Attention

Soo-Young Lee
Brain Science Research Center
Korea Advanced Institute of Science & Technology
Yusong-gu, Taejon 305-701 Korea
sylee@ee.kaist.ac.kr

Michael C. Mozer
Department of Computer Science
University of Colorado at Boulder
Boulder, CO 80309 USA
mozer@cs.colorado.edu

Abstract

In many classification tasks, recognition accuracy is low because input patterns are corrupted by noise or are spatially or temporally overlapping. We propose an approach to overcoming these limitations based on a model of human selective attention. The model, an early selection filter guided by top-down attentional control, entertains each candidate output class in sequence and adjusts attentional gain coefficients in order to produce a strong response for that class. The chosen class is then the one that obtains the strongest response with the least modulation of attention. We present simulation results on classification of corrupted and superimposed handwritten digit patterns, showing a significant improvement in recognition rates. The algorithm has also been applied in the domain of speech recognition, with comparable results.

1 Introduction

In many classification tasks, recognition accuracy is low because input patterns are corrupted by noise or are spatially or temporally overlapping. Approaches have been proposed to make classifiers more robust to such perturbations, e.g., by requiring classifiers to have low input-to-output mapping sensitivity [1]. We propose an approach that is based on human selective attention. People use selective attention to focus on critical features of a stimulus and to suppress irrelevant features. It seems natural to incorporate a selective-attention mechanism into pattern recognition systems for noisy real world applications.

Psychologists have for many years studied the mechanisms of selective attention (e.g., [2]-[4]). However, controversy still exists among competing theories, and only a few models are sufficiently well defined to apply to engineering pattern recognition problems.

Fukushima [5] has incorporated selective attention and attention-switching algorithms into his Neocognitron model, and has demonstrated good recognition performance on superimposed digits. However, the Neocognitron model has many unknown parameters which must be determined heuristically, and its performance is sensitive to the parameter values. Also, its computational requirements are prohibitively expensive for many real-time applications. Rao [6] has also recently introduced a selective attention model based on Kalman filters and demonstrated classifications of superimposed patterns. However, his model is based on linear systems, and a nonlinear extension is not straightforward. There being no definitive approach to incorporating selective attention into pattern recognition, we propose a novel approach and show it can improve recognition accuracy.

2 Psychological Views of Selective Attention

The modern study of selective attention began with Broadbent [7]. Broadbent presented two auditory channels to subjects, one to each ear, and asked subjects to shadow one channel. He observed that although subjects could not recall most of what took place in the unshadowed channel, they could often recall the last few seconds of input on that channel. Therefore, he suggested that the brain briefly stores incoming stimuli but the stimulus information fades and is neither admitted to the conscious mind nor is encoded in a way that would permit later recollection, unless attention is directed toward it. This view is known as an *early filtering* or *early selection* model. Treisman [8] proposed a modification to this view in which the filter merely attenuates the input rather than absolutely preventing further analysis. Although *late-selection* and hybrid views of attention have been proposed, it is clear that early selection plays a significant role in human information processing [3].

The question about where attention acts in the stream of processing is independent of another important issue: what factors drive attention to select one ear or one location instead of another. Attention may be directed based on low-level stimulus features, such as the amplitude of a sound or the color of a visual stimulus. This type of attentional control is often called *bottom up*. Attention may also be directed based on expectations and object knowledge, e.g., to a location where critical task-relevant information is expected. This type of attentional control is often called *top down*.

3 A Multilayer Perceptron Architecture for Selective Attention

We borrow the notion of an early selection filter with top-down control and integrate it into a multilayer perceptron (MLP) classifier, as depicted in Figure 1. The dotted box is a standard MLP classifier, and an attention layer with one-to-one connectivity is added in front of the input layer. Although we have depicted an MLP with a single hidden layer, our approach is applicable to general MLP architectures. The kth element of the input vector, denoted x_k, is gated to the kth input of the MLP by an attention gain or filtering coefficient a_k. Previously, the first author has shown a benefit of treating the a_k's like ordinary adaptive parameters during training [9]-[12].

In the present work, we fix the attention gains at 1 during training, causing the architecture to behave as an ordinary MLP. However, we allow the gains to be adjusted during classification of test patterns. Our basic conjecture is that recognition accuracy may be improved if attention can suppress noise along irrelevant dimensions and enhance a weak signal along relevant dimensions. "Relevant" and "irrelevant" are determined by top-down control of attention. Essentially, we use knowledge in the trained MLP to determine which input dimensions are critical for classifying a test pattern. To be concrete, consider an MLP trained to classify handwritten digits. When a test pattern is presented, we can adjust the attentional gains via gradient descent so as to make the input as good an example of the class "0" as possible. We do this for each of the different output classes, "0" through "9", and choose the class for which the strongest response is obtained with the smallest attentional modulation (the exact quantitative rule is presented below). The conjecture is that if the net can achieve a strong response for a class by making a small attentional modulation, that class is more likely to be correct than whichever class would have been selected without applying selective attention.

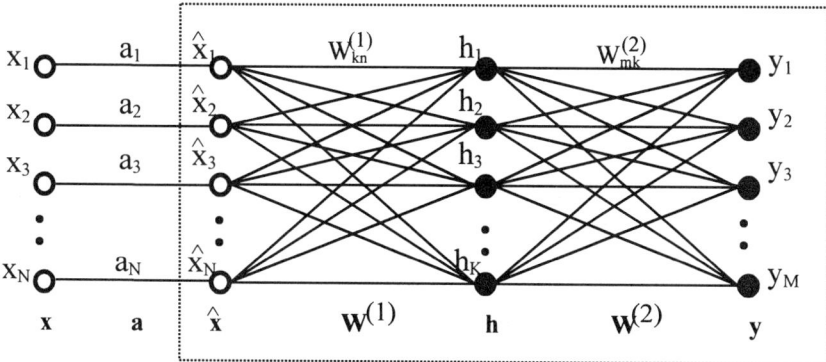

Figure 1: MLP architecture for selective attention

The process of adjusting the attentional gains to achieve a strong response from a particular class—call it the *attention class*—proceeds as follows. First, a target output vector $\mathbf{t}^s = [t_1^s \, t_2^s \cdots t_M^s]^T$ is defined. For bipolar binary output representations, $t_i^s = 1$ is for the attention class and -1 for the others. Second, the attention gain a_k's are set to 1. Third, the attention gain a_k's are adapted to minimize error $E^s \equiv \frac{1}{2} \sum_i (t_i^s - y_i)^2$ with the given input $\mathbf{x} = [x_1 \, x_2 \cdots x_N]^T$ and pre-trained and frozen synaptic weights W. The update rule is based on a gradient-descent algorithm with error back-propagation. At the $(n+1)$'th iterative epoch, the attention gain a_k is updated as

$$a_k[n+1] = a_k[n] - \eta (\partial E / \partial a_k)[n] = a_k[n] + \eta \, x_k \delta_k^{(0)}[n] \quad (1a)$$

$$\delta_k^{(0)} = \sum_j W_{jk}^{(1)} \delta_j^{(1)} \quad (1b)$$

where E denotes the attention output error, $\delta_j^{(1)}$ the j'th attribute of the back-propagated error at the first hidden-layer, and $W_{jk}^{(1)}$ the synaptic weight between the input $\hat{x}_k$ and the j'th neuron at the first hidden layer. Finally, η is a step size. The attention gains are thresholded to lie in [0, 1]. The application of selective attention to a test example is summarized as follows:

Step 1: Apply a test input pattern to the trained MLP and compute output values.
Step 2: For each of the classes with top m activation values,
    (1) Initialize all attention gain a_k's to 1 and set the target vector $\mathbf{t}^s$.
    (2) Apply the test pattern and attention gains to network and compute output.
    (3) Apply the selective attention algorithm in Eqs.(1) to adapt the attention gains.
    (4) Repeat steps (2) and (3) until the attention process converges.
    (5) Compute an attention measure M on the asymptotic network state.

Step 3: Select the class with a minimum attention measure M as the recognized class.

The attention measure is defined as

$$M \equiv D_I E_O, \tag{2a}$$

$$\begin{aligned} D_I &\equiv \sum_k (x_k - \hat{x}_k)^2 / 2N \\ &= \sum_k x_k^2 (1 - a_k)^2 / 2N \end{aligned} \tag{2b}$$

$$E_O \equiv \sum_i [t_i - y_i(\hat{\mathbf{x}})]^2 / 2M, \tag{2c}$$

where D_I is the square of Euclidean distance between two input patterns before and after the application of selective attention and E_O is the output error after the application of selective attention. Here, D_I and E_O are normalized with the number of input pixels and number of output classes, respectively. The superscript s for attention classes is omitted for simplicity. To make the measure M a dimensionless quantity, one may normalize the D_I and E_O with the input energy ($\sum_k x_k^2$) and the training output error, respectively. However, it does not affect the selection process in Step 3.

One can think of the attended input $\hat{\mathbf{x}}$ as the minimal deformation of the test input needed to trigger the attended class, and therefore the Euclidean distance between $\mathbf{x}$ and $\hat{\mathbf{x}}$ is a good measure for the classification confidence. In fact, D_I is basically the same quantity minimized by Rao [6]. However, the MLP classifier in our model is capable of nonlinear mapping between the input and output patterns. A nearest-neighbor classifier, with the training data as examples, could also be used to find the minimum-distance class. Our model with the MLP classifier computes a similar function without the large memory and computational requirements.

The proposed selective attention algorithm was tested on recognition of noisy numeral patterns. The numeral database consists of samples of the handwritten digits (0 through 9) collected from 48 people, for a total of 480 samples. Each digit is encoded as a 16x16 binary pixel array. Roughly 16% of the pixels are black and coded as 1; white pixels are coded as 0. Four experiments were conducted with different training sets of 280 training patterns each. A one hidden-layer MLP was trained by back propagation. The numbers of input, hidden, and output neurons were 256, 30, and 10, respectively. Three noisy test patterns were generated from each training pattern by randomly flipping each pixel value with a probability P_f, and the 840 test patterns were presented to the network for classification.

In Figure 2, the false recognition rate is plotted as a function of the number of candidates considered for the attentional manipulation, m. (Note that the run time of the algorithm is proportional to m, but that increasing m does not imply a more lax classification criterion, or additional external knowledge playing into the classification.) Results are shown for three different pixel inversion probabilities, P_f =0.05, 0.1, and 0.15. Considering the average 16% of black pixels in the data, the noisy input patterns with P_f = 0.15 correspond to a SNR of approximately 0 dB. For each condition in the figure, the false recognition rates for the four different training sets are marked with an 'o', and the means are connected by the solid curve.

A standard MLP classifier corresponds to $m = 1$ (i.e., only the most active output of the MLP is considered as a candidate response). The false recognition rate is clearly lower when the attentional manipulation is used to select a response from the MLP ($m > 1$). It appears that performance does not improve further by considering more than the top three candidates.

4 Attention Switching for Superimposed Patterns

Suppose that we superimpose the binary input patterns for two different handwritten digits using the logical OR operator (the pixels corresponding to the black ink have logical value 1). Can we use attention to recognize the two patterns in sequence? This is an extreme case of a situation that is common in visual pattern recognition—where two patterns are spatially overlapping.

We explore the following algorithm. First, one pattern is recognized with the selective attention process used in Section 3. Second, attention is *switched* from the recognized pattern to the remaining pixels in the image. Switching is accomplished by removing attention from the pixels of the recognized pattern: the attentional gain of an input is clamped to 0 following switching if and only if its value after the first-stage selective attention process was 1 (i.e., that input was attended during the recognition of the first pattern); all other gains are set to 1. Third, the recognition process with selective attention is performed again to recognize the second pattern.

The proposed selective attention and attention switching algorithm was tested for recognition of 2 superimposed numeral data. Again, four experiments were conducted with

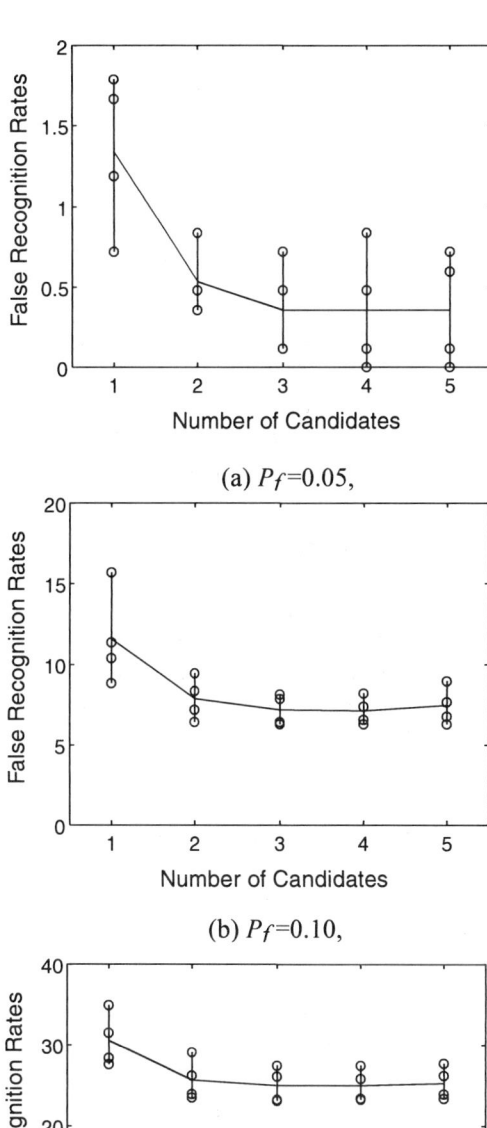

(a) P_f=0.05,

(b) P_f=0.10,

(c) P_f=0.15,

Figure 2: False recognition rates for noisy patterns as a function of the number of top candidates. Each binary pixel of training patterns is randomly inverted with a probability P_f.

different training sets. For each experiment, 40 patterns were selected from 280 training patterns, and 720 test patterns were generated by superimposing pairs of patterns from different output classes. The test patterns were still binary.

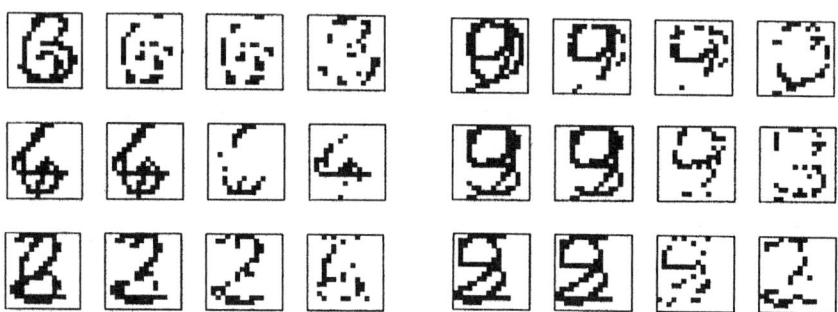

Figure 3: Examples of Selective Attention and Attention Switching

Figure 3 shows six examples of the selective attention and attention switching algorithm in action, each consisting of four panels in a horizontal sequence. The six examples were formed by superimposing instances of the following digit pairs: (6,3), (9,0), (6,4), (9,3), (2,6), and (5,2). The first panel for each example shows the superimposed pattern. The second panel shows the attended input $\hat{x}$ for the first round classification; because this input has continuous values, we have thresholded the values at 0.5 to facilitate viewing in the figure. The third panel shows the masking pattern for attention switching, generated by thresholding the input pattern at 1.0. The fourth panel shows the residual input pattern for the second round classification. The attended input $\hat{x}$ has analog values, but thresholded by 0.5 to be shown in the second rectangles. Figure 3 shows that attention switching is done effectively, and the remaining input patterns to the second classifier are quite visible.

We compared performance for three different methods. First, we simply selected the two MLP outputs with highest activity; this method utilizes neither selective attention. Second, we performed attention switching but did not apply selective attention (i.e., $m=1$). Third, we performed both attention switching and selective attention (with $m=3$). Table 1 summarizes the recognition rates for the first and the second patterns read out of the MLP for the three methods. As hypothesized, attention switching increases the recognition rate for the second pattern, and selective attention increases the recognition rate for both the first and the second pattern.

Table 1: Recognition Rates (%) of Two Superimposed Numeral Patterns

	First Pattern	Second Pattern
No selective attention or switching	91.3	62.7
Switching only	91.3	75.4
Switching & selective attention	95.9	77.4

5 Conclusion

In this paper, we demonstrated a selective-attention algorithm for noisy and superimposed patterns that obtains improved recognition rates. We also proposed a simple attention switching algorithm that utilizes the selective-attention framework to further improve performance on superimposed patterns. The algorithms are simple and easily implemented in feedforward MLPs. Although our experiments are preliminary, they suggest that attention-based algorithms will be useful for extracting and recognizing multiple patterns in a complex background. We have conducted further simulation studies supporting this conjecture in the domain of speech recognition, which we will integrate into this presentation if it is accepted at NIPS.

Acknowledgements

S.Y. Lee acknowledges supports from the Korean Ministry of Science and Technology. We thank Dr. Y. Le Cun for providing the handwritten digit database.

References

[1] Jeong D.G., and Lee, S.Y. (1996). Merging backpropagation and Hebbian learning rules for robust classification, *Neural Networks*, 9:1213-1222.
[2] Cowan, N. (1997). *Attention and Memory: An Integrated Framework*, Oxford Univ. Press.
[3] Pashler, H.E. (1998). *The Psychology of Attention*, MIT Press.
[4] Parasuraman, R. (ed.) (1998). *The Attentive Brain*, MIT Press.
[5] Fukushima, K. (1987). Neural network model for selective attention in visual pattern recognition and associative recall, *Applied Optics*, 26:4985-4992.
[6] Rao, R.P.N. (1998). Correlates of attention in a model of dynamic visual recognition. In *Neural Information Processing Systems 10*, MIT Press.
[7] Broadbent, D.E. (1958). *Perception and Communication*. Pergamon Press.
[8] Treisman, A. (1960). Contextual cues in selective listening, *Quarterly Journal of Experimental Psychology*, 12:242-248.
[9] Lee, H.J., Lee, S.Y. Lee, Shin, S.Y., and Koh, B.Y. (1991). TAG: A neural network model for large-scale optical implementation, *Neural Computation*, 3:135-143.
[10] Lee, S.Y., Jang, J.S., Shin, S.Y., & Shim, C.S. (1988). Optical Implementation of Associative Memory with Controlled Bit Significance, *Applied Optics*, 27:1921-1923.
[11] Kruschke, J.K. (1992). ALCOVE: An Examplar-Based Connectionist Model of Category Learning, *Psychological Review*, 99:22-44.
[12] Lee, S.Y., Kim, D.S., Ahn, K.H., Jeong, J.H., Kim, H., Park, S.Y., Kim, L.Y., Lee, J.S., & Lee, H.Y. (1997). Voice Command II: a DSP implementation of robust speech recognition in real-world noisy environments, *International Conference on Neural Information Processing*, pp. 1051-1054, Dunedin, New Zealand.

Perceptual Organization Based on Temporal Dynamics

Xiuwen Liu and DeLiang L. Wang
Department of Computer and Information Science
Center for Cognitive Science
The Ohio State University, Columbus, OH 43210-1277
Email: {liux, dwang}@cis.ohio-state.edu

Abstract

A figure-ground segregation network is proposed based on a novel boundary pair representation. Nodes in the network are boundary segments obtained through local grouping. Each node is excitatorily coupled with the neighboring nodes that belong to the same region, and inhibitorily coupled with the corresponding paired node. Gestalt grouping rules are incorporated by modulating connections. The status of a node represents its probability being figural and is updated according to a differential equation. The system solves the figure-ground segregation problem through temporal evolution. Different perceptual phenomena, such as modal and amodal completion, virtual contours, grouping and shape decomposition are then explained through local diffusion. The system eliminates combinatorial optimization and accounts for many psychophysical results with a fixed set of parameters.

1 Introduction

Perceptual organization refers to the ability of grouping similar features in sensory data. This, at a minimum, includes the operations of grouping and figure-ground segregation, which refers to the process of determining relative depths of adjacent regions in input data and thus proper occlusion hierarchy. Perceptual organization has been studied extensively and many of the existing approaches [5] [4] [8] [10] [3] start from detecting discontinuities, i.e. edges in the input; one or several configurations are then selected according to certain criteria, for example, non-accidentalness [5]. Those approaches have several disadvantages for perceptual organization. Edges should be localized between regions and an additional ambiguity, the ownership of a boundary segment, is introduced, which is equivalent to figure-ground segregation [7]. Due to that, regional attributions cannot be associated with boundary segments. Furthermore, because each boundary segment can belong to different regions, the potential search space is combinatorial.

To overcome some of the problems, we propose a laterally-coupled network based on a boundary-pair representation to resolve figure-ground segregation. An occluding boundary is represented by a pair of boundaries of the two associated regions, and

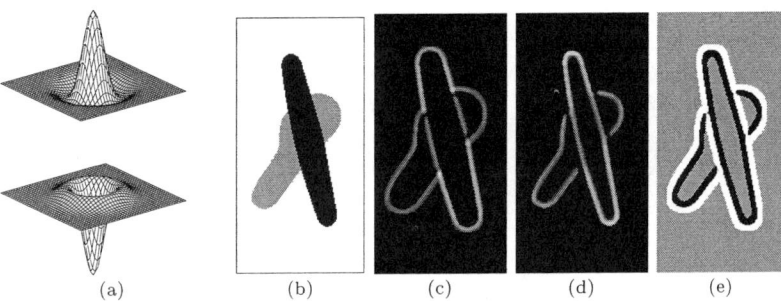

(a) (b) (c) (d) (e)

Figure 1: On- and off-center cell responses. (a) On- and off-center cells. (b) Input image. (c) On-center cell responses. (d) Off-center cell responses (e) Binarized on- and off-center cell responses, where white regions represent on-center response regions and black off-center regions.

initiates a competition between the regions. Each node in the network represents a boundary segment. Regions compete to be figural through boundary-pair competition and figure-ground segregation is resolved through temporal evolution. Gestalt grouping rules are incorporated by modulating coupling strengths between different nodes within a region, which influences the temporal dynamics and determines the percept of the system. Shape decomposition and grouping are then implemented through local diffusion using the results from figure-ground segregation.

2 Figure-Ground Segregation Network

The central problem in perceptual organization is to determine relative depths among regions. As figure reversal occurs in certain circumstances, figure-ground segregation cannot be resolved only based on local attributes.

2.1 The Network Architecture

The boundary-pair representation is motivated by on- and off-center cells, shown in Fig. 1(a). Fig. 1(b) shows an input image and Fig. 1(c) and (d) show the on- and off-center responses. Without zero-crossing, we naturally obtain double responses for each occluding boundary, as shown in Fig. 1(e). In our boundary-pair representation, each boundary is uniquely associated with a region.

In this paper, we obtain closed region boundaries from segmentation and form boundary segments using corners and junctions, which are detected through local corner and junction detectors. A node i in the figure-ground segregation network represents a boundary segment, and P_i represents its probability being figural, which is set to 0.5 initially. Each node is laterally coupled with neighboring nodes on the closed boundary. The connection weight from node i to j, w_{ij}, is 1 and can be modified by T-junctions and local shape information. Each occluding boundary is represented by a pair of boundary segments of the involved regions. For example, in Fig. 2(a), nodes 1 and 5 form a boundary pair, where node 1 belongs to the white region and node 5 belongs to the black region. Node i updates its status by:

$$\tau \frac{dP_i}{dt} = \mu_L \sum_{k \in N(i)} w_{ki}(P_k - P_i) + \mu_J (1 - P_i) \sum_{l \in J(i)} H(Q_{li}) + \mu_B (1 - P_i) \exp(-\frac{B_i}{K_B}) \quad (1)$$

Here $N(i)$ is the set of neighboring nodes of i, and μ_L, μ_J, and μ_B are parameters to determine the influences from lateral connections, junctions, and bias. $J(i)$ is

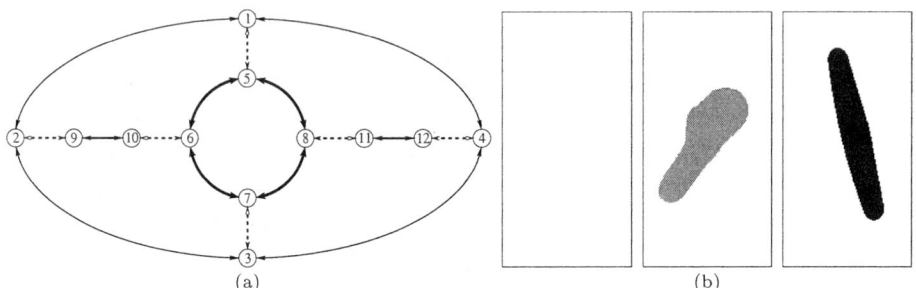

Figure 2: (a) The figure-ground segregation network for Fig. 1(b). Nodes 1, 2, 3 and 4 belong to the white region; nodes 5, 6, 7, and 8 belong to the black region; and nodes 9 and 10, and nodes 11 and 12 belong to the left and right gray regions respectively. Solid lines represent excitatory coupling while dashed lines represent inhibitory connections. (b) Result after surface completion. Left and right gray regions are grouped together.

the set of junctions that are associated with i and Q_{li} is the junction strength of node i of junction l. $H(x)$ is given by $H(x) = tanh(\beta(x - \theta_J))$, where β controls the steepness and θ_J is a threshold.

In (1), the first term on the right reflects the lateral influences. When nodes are strongly coupled, they are more likely to be in the same status, either figure or background. The second term incorporates junction information. In other words, at a T-junction, segments that vary more smoothly are more likely to be figural. The third term is a bias, where B_i is the bias introduced to simulate human perception. The competition between paired nodes i and j is through normalization based on the assumption that only one of the paired nodes should be figural at a given time: $P_i^{(t+1)} = P_i^t/(P_i^t + P_j^t)$ and $P_j^{(t+1)} = P_j^t/(P_i^t + P_j^t)$.

2.2 Incorporation of Gestalt Rules

To generate behavior that is consistent with human perception, we incorporate grouping cues and some Gestalt grouping principles. As the network provides a generic model, additional grouping rules can also be incorporated.

T-junctions T-junctions provide important cues for determining relative depths [7] [10]. In Williams and Hanson's model [10], T-junctions are imposed as topological constraints. Given a T-junction l, the initial strength for node i that is associated with l is:

$$Q_{li} = \frac{\exp(-\alpha_{(i,c(i))}/K_T)}{1/2 \sum_{k \in N_J(l)} \exp(-\alpha_{(k,c(k))}/K_T)},$$

where K_T is a parameter, $N_J(l)$ is a set of all the nodes associated with junction l, $c(i)$ is the other node in $N_J(l)$ that belongs to the same region as node i, and $\alpha_{(ij)}$ is the angle between segments i and j.

Non-accidentalness Non-accidentalness tries to capture the intrinsic relationships among segments [5]. In our system, an additional connection is introduced to node i if it is aligned well with a node j from the same region and $j \notin N(i)$ initially. The connection weight w_{ij} is a function of distance and angle between the involved ending points. This can be viewed as virtual junctions, resulting in virtual contours and conversion of a corner into a T-junction if involved nodes become figural. This corresponds to an organization criterion proposed by Geiger et al [3].

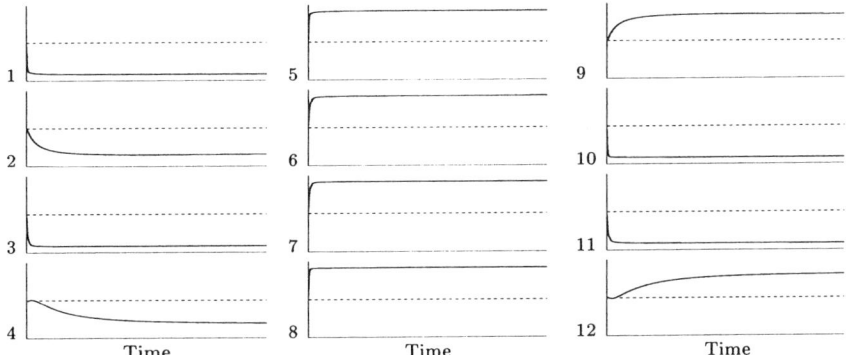

Figure 3: Temporal behavior of each node in the network shown in Fig. 2(a). Each plot shows the status of the corresponding node with respect to time. The dashed line is 0.5.

Shape information Shape information plays a central role in Gestalt principles and is incorporated through enhancing lateral connections. In this paper, we consider local symmetry. Let j and k be two neighboring nodes of i:

$$w_{ij} = 1 + C \exp(-|\alpha_{ij} - \alpha_{ki}|/K_\alpha) * \exp(-(L_j/L_k + L_k/L_j - 2)/K_L)),$$

where C, K_α, and K_L are parameters and L_j is the length of segment j. Essentially the lateral connections are strengthened when two neighboring segments of i are symmetric.

Preferences Human perceptual systems often prefer some organizations over others. Here we incorporated a well-known figure-ground segregation principle, called closeness. In other words, the system prefers filled regions over holes. In current implementation, we set $B_i = 1.0$ if node i is part of a hole and otherwise $B_i = 0$.

2.3 Temporal Properties of the Network

After we construct the figure-ground segregation network, each node is updated according to (1). Fig. 3 shows the temporal behavior of the network shown in Fig. 2(a). The system approaches to a stable solution. For figure-ground segregation, we can binarize the status of each node using threshold 0.5. Thus the system generates the desired percept in a few iterations. The black region occludes other regions while gray regions occlude the white region. For example, P_5 is close to 1 and thus segment 5 is figural, and P_1 is close to 0 and thus segment 1 is in the background.

2.4 Surface Completion

After figure-ground segregation is resolved, surface completion and shape decomposition are implemented through diffusion [3]. Each boundary segment is associated with regional attributes such as the average intensity value because its ownership is known. Boundary segments are then grouped into diffusion groups based on similarities of their regional attributes and if they are occluded by common regions. In Fig. 1(b), three diffusion groups are formed, namely, the black region, two gray regions, and the white region. Segments in one diffusion group are diffused simultaneously. For a figural segment, a buffer with a given radius is generated. Within the buffer, the values are fixed to 1 for pixels belonging to the region and 0 otherwise. Now the problem becomes a well-defined mathematical problem. We need to solve

Figure 4: Images with virtual contours. In each column, the top shows the input image and the bottom the surface completion result, where completed surfaces are shown according to their relative depths and the bottom one is the projection of all the completed surfaces. (a) Alternate pacman. (b) Reverse-contrast pacman. (c) Kanizsa triangle. (d) Woven square. (e) Double pacman.

the heat equation with given boundary conditions. Currently, the heat equation is solved through local diffusion. The results from diffusion are then binarized using threshold 0.5. Fig. 2(b) shows the results for Fig. 1(b) after surface completion. Here the two gray regions are grouped together through surface completion because occluded boundaries allow diffusion. The white region becomes the background, which is the entire image.

3 Experimental Results

Given an image, the system automatically constructs the network and establishes the connections based on the rules discussed in Section 2.2. For all the experiments shown here, a fixed set of parameters is used.

3.1 Modal and Amodal Completion

We first demonstrate that the system can simulate virtual contours and modal completion. Fig. 4 shows the input images and surface completion results. The system correctly solves figure-ground segregation problem and generates the most probable percept. Fig. 4 (a) and (b) show two variations of pacman images [9] [4]. Even though the edges have opposite contrast, the virtual rectangle is vivid. Through boundary-pair representation, our system can handle both cases using the same network. Fig. 4(c) shows a typical virtual image [6] and the system correctly simulates the percept. In Fig. 4(d) [6], the rectangular-like frame is tilted, making the order between the frame and virtual square not well-defined. Our system handles that in the temporal domain. At any given time, the system outputs one of the

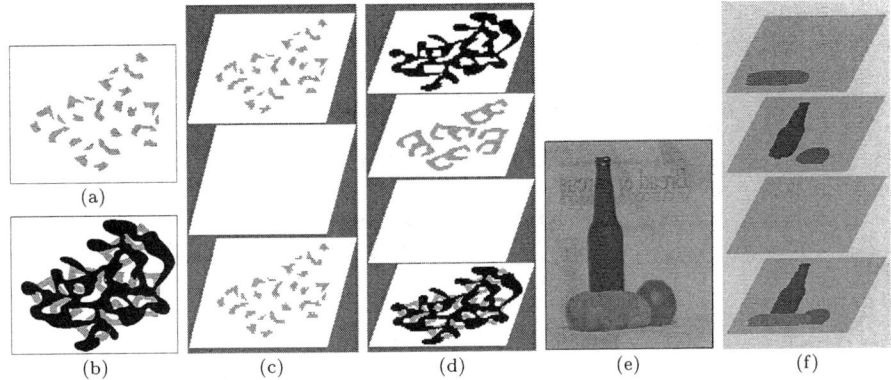

Figure 5: Surface completion results. (a) and (b) Bregman figures [1]. (c) and (d) Surface completion results for (a) and (b). (e) and (f) An image of some groceries and surface completion result.

completed surfaces. Due to this, the system can also handle the case in Fig. 4(e) [2], where the percept is bistable, as the order between the two virtual squares is not well defined.

Fig. 5(a) and (b) show the well-known Bregman figures [1]. In Fig. 5(a), there is no perceptual grouping and parts of B's remain fragmented. However, when occlusion is introduced as in Fig. 5(b), perceptual grouping is evident and fragments of B's are grouped together. Our results, shown in Fig. 5 (c) and (d), are consistent with the percepts. Fig. 5(e) shows an image of groceries, which is used extensively in [8]. Even though the T-junction at the bottom is locally confusing, our system gives the most plausible result through lateral influences of the other two strong T-junctions. Without search and parameter tuning, our system gives the optimal solution shown in Fig. 5(f).

3.2 Comparison with Existing Approaches

As mentioned earlier, at the minimum, figure-groud segregation and grouping need to be addresssed for perceptual organization. Edge-based approaches [4] [10] attempt to solve both problems simultaneously by preferring some configurations over combinatorially many ones according to certain creteria. There are several difficulties common to those approaches. First it cannot account for different human percepts of cases where edge elements are similar. Fig. 5 (a) and (b) are well-known examples in this regard. Another example is that the edge-only version of Fig. 4(c) does not give rise to a vivid virtual contour as in Fig. 4(c) [6]. To reduce the potential search space, often contrast signs of edges are used as additional contraints [10]. However, both Fig. 4 (a) and (b) give rise to virtual contours despite the opposite edge contrast signs. Essentially based on Fig. 4(b), Grossberg and Mingolla [4] claimed that illusory contours can join edges with different directions of contrast, which does not hold in general. As demonstrated through experiments, our approach does offer a common principle underlying these examples.

Our approach shares some similarities with the one by Geiger et al [3]. In both approaches, perceptual organization is solved in two steps. In [3], figure-ground segregation is encoded implicitly in hypotheses which are defined at junction points. Because potential hypotheses are combinatorial, only a few manually chosen ones are tested in their experiments, which is not sufficient for a general computational model. In our approach, by resolving figure-ground segregation, there is no need to define hypotheses explicitly. In both methods, grouping is implemented through diffusion. In [3], "heat" sources for diffusion are given manually for each hypothesis whereas our approach generates "heat" sources automatically using the figure-ground segregation results. Finally, in our approach, local ambiguities can be resolved through lateral connections using temporal dynamics, resulting in robust behavior. To obtain good results for Fig. 5(e), Nitzberg et al [8] need to tune parameters and increase their search space substantially due to the misleading T-junction at the bottom of Fig. 5(e).

4 Conclusion

In this paper we have proposed a network for perceptual organization using temporal dynamics. The pair-wise boundary representation resolves the ownership ambiguity inherent in an edge-based representation and is equivalent to a surface representation through diffusion, providing a unified edge- and surface-based representation. Through temporal dynamics, our model allows for interactions among different modules and top-down influences can be incorporated.

Acknowledgments

Authors would like to thank S. C. Zhu and M. Wu for their valuable discussions. This research is partially supported by an NSF grant (IRI-9423312) and an ONR Young Investigator Award (N00014-96-1-0676) to DLW.

References

[1] A. S. Bregman, "Asking the 'What for' question in auditory perception," In *Perceptual Organization*, M. Kubovy and J R. Pomerantz, eds., Lawrence Erlbaum Associates, Publishers, Hillsdale, New Jersey, pp. 99-118, 1981.

[2] M. Fahle and G. Palm, "Perceptual rivalry between illusory and real contours," *Biological Cybernetics*, vol. 66, pp. 1-8, 1991.

[3] D. Geiger, H. Pao, and N. Rubin, "Salient and multiple illusory surfaces," In *Proceedings of IEEE Computer Society Conference on Computer Vision and Pattern Recognition*, pp. 118-124, 1998.

[4] S. Grossberg and E. Mingolla, "Neural dynamics of perceptual grouping: textures, boundaries, and emergent segmentations," *Perception & Psychophysics*, vol. 38, pp. 141-170, 1985.

[5] D. G. Lowe, *Perceptual Organization and Visual Recognition*, Kluwer Academic Publishers, Boston, 1985.

[6] G. Kanizsa, *Organization in Vision*, Praeger, New York, 1979.

[7] K. Nakayama, Z. J. He, and S. Shimojo, "Visual surface representation: a critical link between lower-level and higher-level vision," In *Visual Cognition*, S. M. Kosslyn and D. N. Osherson, eds., The MIT Press, Cambridge, Massachusetts, vol. 2, pp. 1-70, 1995.

[8] M. Nitzberg, D. Mumford, and T. Shiota, *Filtering, Segmentation and Depth*, Springer-Verlag, New York, 1993.

[9] R. Shapley and J. Gordon, "The existence of interpolated illusory contours depends on contrast and spatial separation," In *The Perception of Illusory Contours*, S. Petry and G. E. Meyer, eds., Springer-Verlag, New York, pp. 109-115, 1987.

[10] L. R. Williams and A. R. Hanson, "Perceptual Completion of Occluded Surfaces," *Computer Vision and Image Understanding*, vol. 64, pp. 1-20, 1996.

Information Factorization in Connectionist Models of Perception

Javier R. Movellan
Department of Cognitive Science
Institute for Neural Computation
University of California San Diego

James L. McClelland
Center for the Neural Bases of Cognition
Department of Psychology
Carnegie Mellon University

Abstract

We examine a psychophysical law that describes the influence of stimulus and context on perception. According to this law choice probability ratios factorize into components independently controlled by stimulus and context. It has been argued that this pattern of results is incompatible with feedback models of perception. In this paper we examine this claim using neural network models defined via stochastic differential equations. We show that the law is related to a condition named channel separability and has little to do with the existence of feedback connections. In essence, channels are separable if they converge into the response units without direct lateral connections to other channels and if their sensors are not directly contaminated by external inputs to the other channels. Implications of the analysis for cognitive and computational neurosicence are discussed.

1 Introduction

We examine a psychophysical law, named the Morton-Massaro law, and its implications to connectionist models of perception and neural information processing. For an example of the type of experiments covered by the Morton-Massaro law consider an experiment by Massaro and Cohen (1983) in which subjects had to identify synthetic consonant sounds presented in the context of other phonemes. There were two response alternatives, seven stimulus conditions, and four context conditions. The response alternatives were /l/ and /r/, the stimuli were synthetic sounds generated by varying the onset frequency of the third formant, followed by the vowel /i/. Each of the 7 stimuli was placed after each of four different context consonants, /v/, /s/, /p/, and /t/. Morton (1969) and Massaro independently showed that in a remarkable range of experiments of this type, the influence of stimulus and context on response probabilities can be accounted for with a factorized version of Luce's strength model (Luce, 1959)

$$P(R = k \mid S = i, C = j) = \frac{\eta_S(i,k)\,\eta_C(j,k)}{\sum_l \eta_S(i,l)\,\eta_C(j,l)}, \text{ for } (i,j,k) \in \mathcal{S} \times \mathcal{C} \times \mathcal{R}. \quad (1)$$

Here S, C and R are random variables representing the stimulus, context and the subject's response, $\mathcal{S}$, $\mathcal{C}$ and $\mathcal{R}$ are the set of stimulus, context and response alternatives, $\eta_S(i,k) > 0$ represents the support of stimulus i for response k, and $\eta_C(j,k) > 0$ the support of context j for response k. Assuming no strength parameter is exactly zero, (1) is equivalent to

$$\frac{P(R=k \mid S=i, C=j)}{P(R=l \mid S=i, C=j)} = \left(\frac{\eta_S(i,k)}{\eta_S(i,l)}\right)\left(\frac{\eta_C(j,k)}{\eta_C(j,l)}\right), \text{ for all } (i,j,k) \in \mathcal{S} \times \mathcal{C} \times \mathcal{R}. \tag{2}$$

This says that response probability ratios factorize into two components, one which is affected by the stimulus but unaffected by the context and one affected by the context but unaffected by the stimulus.

2 Diffusion Models of Perception

Massaro (1989) conjectured that the Morton-Massaro law may be incompatible with feedback models of perception. This conjecture was based on the idea that in networks with feedback connections the stimulus can have an effect on the context units and the context can have an effect on the stimulus units making it impossible to factorize the influence of information sources. In this paper we analyze such a conjecture and show that, surprisingly, the Morton-Massaro law has little to do with the existence of feedback and lateral connections. We ground our analysis on continuous stochastic versions of recurrent neural networks [1]. We call these models diffusion (neural) networks for they are stochastic diffusion processes defined by adding Brownian motion to the standard recurrent neural network dynamics. Diffusion networks are defined by the following stochastic differential equation

$$dY_i(t) = \mu_i(Y(t), X)\, dt + \sigma\, dB_i(t) \quad \text{for } i \in \{1, \cdots, n\}, \tag{3}$$

where $Y_i(t)$ is a random variable representing the *internal potential* at time t of the ith unit, $Y(t) = (Y_1(t), \cdots, Y_n(t))'$, X represents the external input, which consists of stimulus and context, and B_i is Brownian motion, which acts as a stochastic driving term. The constant $\sigma > 0$, known as the *dispersion*, controls the amount of noise injected onto each unit. The function μ_i, known as the *drift*, determines the average instantaneous change of activation and is borrowed from the standard recurrent neural network literature: this change is modulated by a matrix w of connections between units, and a matrix v that controls the influence of the external inputs onto each unit.

$$\mu_i(Y_i(t), X) = \frac{1}{\kappa_i(Y_i(t))}(\bar{Y}_i(t) - Y_i(t)), \quad \text{for all } i \in \{1, \cdots, n\}, \tag{4}$$

where $1/\kappa_i$ is a positive function, named the capacitance, controlling the speed of processing and

$$\bar{Y}_i(t) = \sum_j w_{i,j}\, Z_j(t) + \sum_k v_{i,k} X_k, \quad \text{for all } i \in \{1, \cdots, n\}, \tag{5}$$

$$Z_j(t) = \varphi_i(Y_j(t)) = \varphi(\alpha_i Y_j(t)) = 1/(1 + e^{-\alpha_i Y_i(t)}). \tag{6}$$

Here $w_{i,j}$, an element of the connection matrix w, is the weight from unit j to unit i, $v_{i,k}$ is an element of the matrix v, φ is the logistic activation function and the $\alpha_i > 0$ terms are *gain* parameters, that control the sharpness of the activation functions. For large values of α_i the activation function of unit i converges to a step function. The variable $Z_j(t)$ represents a short-time mean firing rate (the activation) of unit

---
[1] For an analysis grounded on discrete time networks with binary states see McClelland (1991).

j scaled in the $(0,1)$ range. Intuition for equation (4) can be achieved by thinking of it as a the limit of a discrete time difference equation, in such case

$$Y(t + \Delta t) = Y_i(t) + \mu_i(Y_i(t), X)\Delta t + \sigma\sqrt{\Delta t} N_i(t), \quad (7)$$

where the $N_i(t)$ are independent standard Gaussian random variables. For a fixed state at time t there are two forces controlling the change in activation: the drift, which is deterministic, and the dispersion which is stochastic. This results in a distribution of states at time $t + \Delta t$. As Δt goes to zero, the solution to the difference equation (7) converges to the diffusion process defined in (4). In this paper we focus on the behavior of diffusion networks at stochastic equilibrium, i.e., we assume the network is given enough time to approximate stochastic equilibrium before its response is sampled.

3 Channel Separability

In this section we show that the Morton-Massaro is related to an architectural constraint named channel separability, which has nothing to do with the existence of feedback connections. In order to define channel separability it is useful to characterize the function of different units using the following categories: 1) *Response specification units*: A unit is a response specification unit, if, when the state of all the other units in the network is fixed, changing the state of this unit affects the probability distribution of overt responses. 2) *Stimulus units*: A unit belongs to the stimulus channel if : a) it is not a response unit, and b) when the state of the response units is fixed, the probability distribution of the activations of this unit is affected by the stimulus. 3) *Context units*: A unit belongs to the context channel if: a) it is not a response unit, and b) when the states of the response units are fixed, the probability distribution of the activations of this unit can be affected by the context. Given the above definitions, we say that a network has *separable stimulus and context channels* if the stimulus and context units are disjoint: no unit simultaneously belongs to the stimulus and context channels. In essence, channels are structurally separable if they converge into the response units without direct lateral connections to other channels and if their sensors are not directly contaminated by external inputs to the other channels (see Figure 1).

In the rest of the paper we show that if a diffusion network is structurally separable the Morton-Massaro law can be approximated with arbitrary precision regardless of the existence of feedback connections. For simplicity we examine the case in which the weight matrix is symmetric. In such case, each state has an associated goodness function that greatly simplifies the analysis. In a later section we discuss how the results generalize to the non-symmetric case.

Let $y \in \mathbb{R}^n$ represent the internal potential of a diffusion network. Let $z_i = \varphi(\alpha_i y_i)$ for $i = 1, \cdots, n$ represent the firing rates corresponding to y. Let z^s, z^c and z^r represent the components of z for the units in the stimulus channel, context channel and response specification module. Let x be a vector representing an input and let x^s, x^c be the components of x for the external stimulus and context. Let $\alpha = (\alpha_1, \cdots, \alpha_n)$ be a fixed gain vector and $Z^\alpha(t)$ a random vector representing the firing rates at time t of a network with gain vector α. Let $Z^\alpha = \lim_{t \to \infty} Z^\alpha(t)$, represent the firing rates at stochastic equilibrium. In Movellan (1998) it is shown that if the weights are symmetric i.e., $w = w'$ and $1/\kappa_i(x) = d\varphi_i(x)/dx$ then the equilibrium probability density of Z^α is as follows

$$p_{Z^\alpha | X}(z^s, z^c, z^r \mid x^s, x^c) = \frac{1}{K_\alpha(x_s, x_c)} \exp((2/\sigma^2)\, G_\alpha(z^s, z^r \mid x_s, x_c)), \quad (8)$$

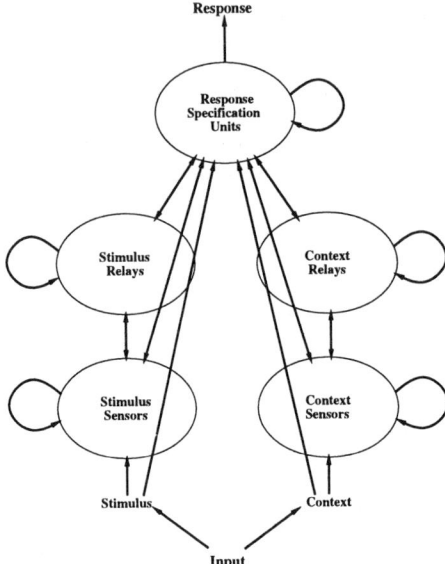

Figure 1: A network with separable context and stimulus processing channels. The stimulus sensor and stimulus relay units make up the stimulus channel units, and the context sensor and context channel units make up the context channel units. Note that any of the modules can be empty except the response module.

where

$$K_\alpha(x_s, x_c) = \int \exp((2/\sigma^2)\, G_\alpha(z \mid x_s, x_c))\, dz, \tag{9}$$

$$G_\alpha(z \mid x) = H(z \mid x) - \sum_{i=1}^{n} S_{\alpha_i}(z_i), \tag{10}$$

$$H(z \mid x) = z'\, w\, z/2 + z'\, v\, x, \tag{11}$$

$$S_{\alpha_i}(z_i) = \alpha_i \Big(\log(z_i) + \log(1 - z_i)\Big) + \frac{1}{\alpha_i}\Big(z_i \log(z_i) + (1 - z_i)\log(1 - z_i)\Big). \tag{12}$$

Without loss of generality hereafter we set $\sigma^2 = 2$. When there are no direct connections between the stimulus and context units there are no terms in the goodness function in which x^s or z^s occur jointly with x^c or z^c. Because of this, the goodness can be separated into three additive terms, that depend on x^s, x^c and a third term which depends on the response units:

$$G_\alpha(z^s, z^c, z^r \mid x^s, x^c) = G_\alpha^s(z^s, z^r \mid x^s) + G_\alpha^c(z^r, z^c \mid x^c) + G_\alpha^r(z^r), \tag{13}$$

where

$$G_\alpha^s(z^s, z^r \mid x^s) = (z^s)' w_{s,s} z^s/2 + (z^s)' w_{s,r} z^r + (z^s)' v_{s,s} x^s + (z^r)' v_{r,s} x^s - \sum_i S(z_i^s), \tag{14}$$

$$G_\alpha^c(z^c, z^r \mid x^s) = (z^c)' w_{c,c} z^c/2 + (z^c)' w_{c,r} z^r + (z^c)' v_{c,c} x^c + (z^r)' v_{r,c} x^c - \sum_i S(z_i^c), \tag{15}$$

$$G_\alpha^r(z^r) = (z_i^r)' w_{r,r} z^r/2 - \sum_i S(z_i^r). \tag{16}$$

where $w_{s,r}$ is a submatrix of w connecting the stimulus and response units. Similar notation is used for the other submatrices of w and v. It follows that we can write the ratio of the joint probability density' of two states z and $\tilde{z}$ as follows:

$$\frac{p_{Z_\alpha|X}(z^s, z^c, z^r \mid x^s, x^c)}{p_{Z_\alpha|X}(\tilde{z}^s, \tilde{z}^c, \tilde{z}^r \mid x^s, x^c)} = \frac{\exp(G_\alpha^s(z^s, z^r \mid x_s) + G_\alpha^c(z^c, z^r \mid x^c) + G_\alpha^r(z^r))}{\exp(G_\alpha^s(\tilde{z}^s, \tilde{z}^r \mid x_s) + G_\alpha^c(\tilde{z}^c, \tilde{z}^r \mid x^c) + G_\alpha^r(\tilde{z}^r))}, \quad (17)$$

which factorizes as desired. To get probability densities for the response units, we integrate over the states of all the other units

$$p_{Z_\alpha^r|X}(z^r \mid x^s, x^c) = \int \int p_{Z_\alpha|X}(z^s, z^c, z^r \mid x^s, x^c) \, dz^s \, dz^c, \quad (18)$$

and after rearranging terms

$$p_{Z_\alpha^r|X}(z^r \mid x^s, x^c) = \frac{1}{K_\alpha(x^s, x^c)} \left(\int \exp(G_x(z^s, z^r \mid x^s) + G_r(z^r)) \, dz^s \right) \left(\int \exp(G_c(z^c, z^r \mid x^c)) \, dz^c \right), \quad (19)$$

which also factorizes. All is left is mapping continuous states of the response units to discrete external responses. To do so we partition the space of the response specification units into discrete regions. The probability of a response becomes the integral of the probability density over the region corresponding to that response. The problem is that the integral of probability densities does not necessarily factorize even though the densities factorize at every point.

Fortunately there are two important cases for which the law holds, at least as a good approximation. The first case is when the response regions are small and thus we can approximate the integral over that region by the density at a point times the volume of the region. In such a case the ratio of the integrals can be approximated by the ratio of the probability densities of those individual states. The second case applies to models, like McClelland and Rumelhart's (1981) interactive activation model, in which each response is associated with a distinct response unit. These models typically have negative connections amongst the response units so that at equilibrium one unit tends to be active while the others are inactive. In such a case a common response policy picks the response corresponding to the active unit. We now show that such a policy can approximate the Morton-Massaro law to an arbitrary level of precision as the gain parameter of the response units is increased. Let z represent the joint state of a network and let the first r components of z be the states of the response specification units. Let $z^{(1)} = (1, 0, 0, \cdots, 0)'$, $z^{(2)} = (0, 1, 0, \cdots, 0)'$ be two r-dimensional vectors representing states of the response specification units. For $i \in \{1, 2\}$ and $\Delta \in (0, 1)$ let

$$z_\Delta^{(i)} = (1 - z^{(i)})\Delta + (z^{(i)})(1 - \Delta), \quad (20)$$

$$R_\Delta^{(i)} = \{x \in \mathbb{R}^r : x_j \in ((1-\Delta)z_j^{(i)}, \Delta + (1-\Delta)z_j^{(i)}), \text{ for } j = 1, \cdots, r\}. \quad (21)$$

The sets $R_\Delta^{(1)}$ and $R_\Delta^{(2)}$ are regions of the $[0, 1]^r$ space mapping into two distinct external responses. We now investigate the convergence of the probability ratio of these two responses as we let $\Delta \to 0$, i.e., as the response regions collapse into corners of $[0, 1]^r$.

$$\lim_{\Delta \to 0} \frac{P(Z_\alpha^r \in R_\Delta^{(2)} \mid X = x)}{P(Z_\alpha^r \in R_\Delta^{(1)} \mid X = x)} = \lim_{\Delta \to 0} \frac{\int_{R_\Delta^{(2)}} p_{Z_\alpha^r|X}(u \mid x) du}{\int_{R_\Delta^{(1)}} p_{Z_\alpha^r|X}(u \mid x) du} = \quad (22)$$

$$\lim_{\Delta \to 0} \frac{\Delta^r p_{Z_\alpha^r|X}(z_\Delta^{(2)} \mid x)}{\Delta^r p_{Z_\alpha^r|X}(z_\Delta^{(1)} \mid x)} = \lim_{\Delta \to 0} \frac{\int \int e^{G_\alpha^r(z_\Delta^{(2)}, z^s, z^c \mid x)} dz^s \, dz^c}{\int \int e^{G_\alpha(z_\Delta^{(1)}, z^s, z^c \mid x)} dz^s \, dz^c}. \quad (23)$$

Table 1: Predictions by the Morton-Massaro law (left side) versus diffusion network (square brackets) for subject 7 of Massaro and Cohen (1983) Experiment 2. Each prediction of the diffusion network is based on 100 random samples.

Stimulus	Context							
	V		S		P		T	
0	0.0017	[0.01]	0.0000	[0.00]	0.0152	[0.03]	0.9000	[0.91]
1	0.0126	[0.00]	0.0000	[0.00]	0.1008	[0.10]	0.9849	[0.97]
2	0.1105	[0.19]	0.0008	[0.00]	0.5208	[0.45]	0.9984	[1.00]
3	0.5463	[0.54]	0.0079	[0.00]	0.9133	[0.91]	0.9998	[1.00]
4	0.9827	[1.00]	0.2756	[0.30]	0.9980	[1.00]	0.9999	[1.00]
5	0.9999	[1.00]	0.9924	[0.99]	0.9999	[1.00]	1.0000	[1.00]
6	0.9999	[1.00]	0.9924	[1.00]	0.9999	[1.00]	1.0000	[1.00]

Now note that

$$G_\alpha(z_\Delta^{(1)}, z^s, z^c \mid x) = H(z_\Delta^{(1)}, z^s, z^c \mid x) - \sum_{i=1}^{r} S_{\alpha_i}(z_{\Delta,i}^{(1)}) - \sum_i S_{\alpha_i}(z_i^s) - \sum_j S_{\alpha_j}(z_j^c),$$
(24)

and since $\sum_{i=1}^{r} S_{\alpha_i}(z_{\Delta,i}^{(1)}) = \sum_{i=1}^{r} S_{\alpha_i}(z_{\Delta,i}^{(2)})$, it follows that

$$\lim_{\Delta \to 0} \frac{P(Z_\alpha^r \in R_\Delta^{(2)} \mid X = x)}{P(Z_\alpha^r \in R_\Delta^{(1)} \mid X = x)} = \frac{\int\int e^{H(z_\Delta^{(2)}, z^s, z^c \mid x) - \sum_i S_{\alpha_i}(z_i^s) - \sum_j S_{\alpha_j}(z_j^c)} dz^s \, dz^c}{\int\int e^{H(z_\Delta^{(1)}, z^s, z^c \mid x) - \sum_i S_{\alpha_i}(z_i^s) - \sum_j S_{\alpha_j}(z_j^c)} dz^s \, dz^c}.$$
(25)

It is easy to show that this ratio factorizes. Moreover, for all $\Delta > 0$ if we let $\alpha_1 = \cdots = \alpha_r = \alpha$, where $\alpha > 0$ then

$$\lim_{\alpha \to \infty} P(Z_\alpha^r \in [\Delta, 1-\Delta]^r) = 0,$$
(26)

since as the gain of the response units increases S_{α_i} decreases very fast at the corners of $(0,1)^r$. Thus as $\alpha \to \infty$ the random variable Z_α^r converges in distribution to a discrete random variable with mass at the corner of the $[0,1]^r$ hypercube and with factorized probability ratios as expressed on (25). Since the indexing of the response units is arbitrary the argument applies to all the responses.

□

4 Discussion

Our analysis establishes that in diffusion networks the Morton-Massaro law is not incompatible with the presence of feedback and lateral connections. Surprisingly, even though in diffusion networks with feedback connections stimulus and context units are interdependent, it is still possible to factorize the effect of stimulus and context on response probabilities.

The analysis shows that the Morton-Massaro can be arbitrarily approximated as the sharpness of the response units is increased. In practice we have found very good approximations with relatively small values of the sharpness parameter (see Table 1 for an example). The analysis assumed that the weights were symmetric. Mathematical analysis of the general case with non-symmetric weights is difficult.

However useful approximations exist (Movellan & McClelland, 1995) showing that if the noise parameter σ is relatively small or if the activation function φ is approximately linear, symmetric weights are not needed to exhibit the Morton-Massaro law.

The analysis presented here has potential applications to investigate models of perception and the functional architecture of the brain. For example the interactive activation model of word perception has a separable architecture and thus, diffusion versions of it adhere to the Morton Massaro law. The analysis also points to potential applications in computational neuroscience. It would be of interest to study whether the Morton-Massaro holds at the level of neural responses. For example, we may excite a neuron with two different sources of information and observe its short term average response to combination of stimuli. If the observed distribution of responses exhibits the Morton-Massaro law, this would be consistent with the existence of separable channels converging into that neuron. Otherwise, it would indicate that the channels from the two input areas to the response may not be structurally separable.

References

Luce, R. D. (1959). *Individual choice behavior*. New York: Wiley.

Massaro, D. W. (1989). Testing between the TRACE Model and the fuzzy logical model of speech perception. *Cognitive Psychology, 21*, 398–421.

Massaro, D. W. (1998). *Perceiving Talking Faces*. Cambridge, Massachusetts: MIT Press.

Massaro, D. W. & Cohen, M. M. (1983a). Phonological constraints in speech perception. *Perception and Psychophysics, 34*, 338–348.

McClelland, J. L. (1991). Stochastic interactive activation and the effect of context on perception. *Cognitive Psychology, 23*, 1–44.

Morton, J. (1969). The interaction of information in word recognition. *Psychological Review, 76*, 165–178.

Movellan, J. R. (1998). A Learning Theorem for Networks at Detailed Stochastic Equilibrium. *Neural Computation, 10*(5), 1157–1178.

Movellan, J. R. & McClelland, J. L. (1995). Stochastic interactive processing, channel separability and optimal perceptual inference: an examination of Morton's law. Technical Report PDP.CNS.95.4, Available at http://cnbc.cmu.edu, Carnegie Mellon University.

Graded grammaticality in Prediction Fractal Machines

Shan Parfitt, Peter Tiňo and Georg Dorffner
Austrian Research Institute for Artificial Intelligence,
Schottengasse 3, A-1010 Vienna, Austria.
{shan,petert,georg}@ai.univie.ac.at

Abstract

We introduce a novel method of constructing language models, which avoids some of the problems associated with recurrent neural networks. The method of creating a Prediction Fractal Machine (PFM) [1] is briefly described and some experiments are presented which demonstrate the suitability of PFMs for language modeling. PFMs distinguish reliably between minimal pairs, and their behavior is consistent with the hypothesis [4] that wellformedness is 'graded' not absolute. A discussion of their potential to offer fresh insights into language acquisition and processing follows.

1 Introduction

Cognitive linguistics has seen the development in recent years of two important, related trends. Firstly, a widespread renewal of interest in the statistical, 'graded' nature of language (e.g. [2]-[4]) is showing that the traditional all-or-nothing notion of well-formedness may not present an accurate picture of how the congruity of utterances is represented internally. Secondly, the analysis of state space trajectories in artificial neural networks (ANNs) has provided new insights into the types of processes which may account for the ability of learning devices to acquire and represent language, without appealing to traditional linguistic concepts [5]-[7]. Despite the remarkable advances which have come out of connectionist research (e.g. [8]), and the now common use of recurrent networks, and Simple Recurrent Networks (SRNs) [9] especially, in the study of language (e.g. [10]), recurrent neural networks suffer from particular problems which make them imperfectly suited to language tasks. The vast majority of work in this field employs small networks and datasets (usually artificial), and although many interesting linguistic issues may be thus tackled, real progress in evaluating the potentials of state trajectories and graded 'grammaticality' to uncover the underlying processes responsible for overt linguistic phenomena must inevitably be limited whilst the experimental tasks remain so small. Nevertheless, there are certain obstacles to the scaling-up of networks trained by back-propagation (BP). Such networks tend towards ever longer training times as the sizes of the input set and of the network increase, and although Real-Time Recurrent Learning (RTRL) and Back-propagation Through Time are potentially better at modeling temporal dependencies, training times are longer still [11]. Scaling-up is also difficult due to the potential for catastrophic interference and lack of adaptivity and stability [12]-[14]. Other problems include the rapid loss of information about past events as the distance from the present increases [15] and the dependence of learned state trajectories not only on the training data, but also upon such vagaries as initial weight vectors, making their analysis difficult [16]. Other types of learning device also suffer problems. Standard Markov models require the allocation of memory for every n-gram, such that large values of n are impractical; variable-length Markov models are more memory-efficient, but become unmanageable when trained on large data sets [17]. Two important, related concerns in cognitive linguistics are thus (a) to find a method which allows language models to be scaled up, which is similar in spirit to recurrent neural networks, but which does not encounter the same problems of scale, and (b) to use such a method to evince new insights into graded grammaticality from the state trajectories which arise given genuinely large, naturally-occurring data sets.

Accordingly, we present a new method of generating state trajectories which avoids most of these problems. Previously studied in a financial prediction task, the method creates a fractal map of the training data, from which state machines are built. The resulting models are known as Prediction Fractal Machines (PFMs) [18] and have some useful properties. The state trajectories in the fractal representation are fast and computationally efficient to generate, and are accurate and well-understood; it may be inferred that, even for very large vocabularies and training sets, catastrophic interference and lack of adaptivity and stability will not be a problem, given the way in which representations are built (demonstrating this is a topic for future work); training times are significantly less than for recurrent networks (in the experiments described below, the smallest models took a few minutes to build, while the largest ones took only around three hours; in comparison, all of the ANNs took longer - up to a day - to train); and there is little or no loss of information over the course of an input sequence (allowing for the finite precision of the computer). The scalability of the PFM was taken advantage of by training on a large corpus of naturally-occurring text. This enabled an assessment of what potential new insights might arise from the use of this method in truly large-scale language tasks.

2 Prediction Fractal Machines (PFMs)

A brief description of the method of creating a PFM will now be given. Interested readers should consult [1], since space constraints preclude a detailed examination here. The key idea behind our predictive model is a transformation F of symbol sequences from an alphabet (here, tagset) $\{1, 2, ..., N\}$ into points in a hypercube $H = [0, 1]^D$. The dimensionality D of the hypercube H should be large enough for each symbol $1, 2, ..., N$ to be identified with a *unique* vertex of H. The particular assignment of symbols to vertices is arbitrary. The transformation F has the crucial property that symbol sequences sharing the same suffix (context) are mapped close to each other. Specifically, the longer the common suffix shared by two sequences, the smaller the (Euclidean) distance between their point representations. The transformation F used in this study corresponds to an Iterative Function System [19] consisting of N affine maps $i : H \to H$, $i = 1, 2, ..., N$,

$$i(x) = \frac{1}{2}(x + t_i), \quad t_i \in \{0, 1\}^D, \quad t_i \neq t_j \text{ for } i \neq j. \tag{1}$$

Given a sequence $s_1 s_2 ... s_L$ of L symbols from the alphabet $1, 2, ..., N$, we construct its point representation as

$$s_L(s_{L-1}(...(s_2(s_1(x^*)))...)) = (s_L \circ s_{L-1} \circ ... \circ s_2 \circ s_1)(x^*), \tag{2}$$

where x^* is the center $\{\frac{1}{2}\}^D$ of the hypercube H. (Note that as is common in the Iterative Function Systems literature, i refers either to a symbol or to a map, depending upon the context.) PFMs are constructed on point representations of subsequences appearing in the training sequence. First, we slide the window of length $L > 1$ over the training sequence. At each position we transform the sequence of length L appearing in the window into a point. The set of points obtained by sliding through the whole training sequence is then partitioned into several classes by k-means vector quantization (in the Euclidean space), each class represented by a particular codebook vector. The number of codebook vectors required is chosen experimentally. Since quantization classes group points lying close together, sequences having point representations in the same class (potentially) share long suffixes. The quantization classes may then be treated as prediction contexts, and the corresponding predictive symbol probabilities computed by sliding the window over the training sequence again and counting, for each quantization class, how often a sequence mapped to that class was followed by a particular symbol. In test mode, upon seeing a new sequence of L symbols, the transformation F is again performed, the closest quantization center found, and the corresponding predictive probabilities used to predict the next symbol.

3 An experimental comparison of PFMs and recurrent networks

The performance of the PFM was compared against that of a RTRL-trained recurrent network on a next-tag prediction task. Sixteen grammatical tags and a 'sentence start' character were used. The models were trained on a concatenated sequence (22781 tags) of the top three-quarters of each of the 14 sub-corpora of the University of Pennsylvania 'Brown' corpus[1]. The remainder was used to create test data, as follows. Because in a large training corpus of naturally-occurring data, contexts in most cases have more than one possible correct continuation, simply counting correctly predicted symbols is insufficient to assess performance, since this fails to count correct responses which are not targets. The extent to which the models distinguished between grammatical and ungrammatical utterances was therefore additionally measured by generating minimal pairs and comparing their negative log likelihoods (NLLs) per symbol with respect to the model. Likelihood is computed by sliding through the test sequence and for each window position, determining the probability of the symbol that appears immediately beyond it. As processing progresses, these probabilities are multiplied. The negative of the natural logarithm is then taken and divided by the number of symbols. Significant differences in NLLs

---

[1] http://www.ldc.upenn.edu/

are much harder to achieve between members of minimal pairs than between grammatical and random sequences, and are therefore a good measure of model validity. Minimal pairs generated by theoretically-motivated manipulations tend to be no longer ungrammatical given a small tagset, because the removal of grammatical sub-classes necessarily also removes a large amount of information. Manipulations were therefore performed by switching the positions of two symbols in each sentence in the test sets. Symbols switched could be any distance apart within the sentence, as long as the resulting sentence was ungrammatical under all surface instantiations. By changing as little as possible to make the sentence ungrammatical, the goal was retained that the task of distinguishing between grammatical and ungrammatical sequences be as difficult as possible. The test data then consisted of 28 paired grammatical/ungrammatical test sets (around 570 tags each), plus an ungrammatical, 'meaningless' test set containing all 17 codes listed several times over, used to measure baseline performance. Ten 1st-order randomly-initialised networks were trained for 100 epochs using RTRL. The networks consisted of 1 input and 1 output layer, each with 17 units corresponding to the 17 tags, 2 hidden layers, each with 10 units, and 1 context layer of 10 units connected to the first hidden layer. The second hidden layer was used to increase the flexibility of the maps between the hidden representations in the recurrent portion and the tag activations at the output layer. A logistic sigmoid activation function was used, the learning rate and momentum were set to 0.05, and the training sequence was presented at the rate of one tag per clock tick. The PFMs were derived by clustering the fractal representation of the training data ten times for various numbers of codebook vectors between 5 and 200. More experiments were performed using PFMs than neural networks because in the former case, experience in choosing appropriate numbers of codebook vectors was initially lacking for this type of data.

The results which follow are given as averages, either over all neural networks, or else over all PFMs derived from a given number of codebook vectors. The networks correctly predicted 36.789% and 32.667% of next tags in the grammatical and ungrammatical test sets, respectively. The PFMs matched this performance at around 30 codebook vectors (37.134% and 32.814% respectively), and exceeded it for higher numbers of vectors (39.515% and 34.388% respectively at 200 vectors). The networks generated mean NLLs per symbol of 1.966 and 2.182 for the grammatical and ungrammatical test sets, respectively (a difference of 0.216) and 4.157 for the 'meaningless' test set (the difference between NLLs for grammatical and 'meaningless' data = 2.191). The PFMs matched this difference in NLLs at 40 codebook vectors (NLL grammatical = 1.999, NLL ungrammatical = 2.217; difference = 0.218). The NLL for the 'meaningless' data at 40 codebook vectors was 6.075 (difference between NLLs for grammatical and 'meaningless' data = 4.076). The difference between NLLs for grammatical and ungrammatical, and for grammatical and 'meaningless' data sets, became even larger with increased numbers of codebook vectors. The difference in performance between grammatical and ungrammatical test sets was thus highly significant in all cases ($p < .0005$): all the models distinguished what was grammatical from what was not. This conclusion is supported by the fact that the mean NLLs for the 'meaningless' test set were always noticeably higher than those for the minimal pair sets.

4 Discussion

The PFMs exceeded the performance of the networks for larger numbers of codebook vectors, but it is possible that networks with more hidden nodes would also do better. In terms of ease of use, however, as well as in their scaling-up potential, PFMs are certainly superior. Their other great advantage is that the representations created are dependable (see section 1), making hypothesis creation and testing not just more rapid, but also more straightforward: the speed with which PFMs may be trained made it possible to make statistically significant observations for a large number of clustering runs. In the introduction, 'graded' wellformedness was spoken of as being productive of new hypotheses about the nature of language. Our use of minimal pairs, designed to make a clear-cut distinction between grammatical and ungrammatical utterances, appears to leave this issue to one side. But in reality, our results were rather pertinent to it, as the use of the likelihood measure might indeed imply. The Brown corpus consists of subcorpora representative of 14 different discourse types, from fiction to government documents. Whereas traditional notions of grammaticality would lead us to treat all of the 'ungrammatical' sentences in the minimal pair test sets as equally ungrammatical, the NLLs in our experiments tell a different story. The grammatical versions consistently had a lower associated NLL (higher probability) than the ungrammatical versions, but the difference between these was much smaller than that between the 'meaningless' data and either the grammatical or the ungrammatical data. This supports the concept of 'graded grammaticality', and NLLs for 'meaningless' data such as ours might be seen as a sort of benchmark by which to measure all lesser degrees of ungrammaticality. (Note incidentally that the PFMs appear to associate with the 'meaningless' data a significantly higher NLL than did the networks, even though the difference between the NLLs of the grammatical and ungrammatical data was the same. This is suggestive of PFMs having greater powers of discrimination between grades of wellformedness than the recurrent networks used, but further research will be needed to ascertain the validity of this.) Moreover, the NLL varied not just between grammatical and ungrammatical test sets, but also from sentence to sentence, from word to word and from discourse style to discourse style. While it increased, often dramatically, when the manipulated portion of an ungrammatical sentence was encountered, some words in grammatical sentences exhibited a similar effect: thus, if a subsequence in a well-formed utterance occurs only rarely - or never - in a training set, it will have a high associated NLL in the same way as an ungrammatical one does. This is likely to happen even for very large corpora, since some grammatical structures are very rare. This is consistent with recent findings that, during human sentence processing, well-formedness is linked to conformity with expectation [20] as measured by CLOZE scores. Interesting also was the remarkable variation in NLL between discourse styles. Although the mean NLL across all discourse styles (test sets) is lower for the grammatical than for the ungrammatical versions, it cannot be guaranteed that the grammatical version of one test set will have a lower NLL than the *un*grammatical version of another. Indeed, the grammatical and ungrammatical NLLs interleave, as may be observed in figure 1, which shows the NLLs for the three discourse styles which lie at the bottom, middle and top of the range. Even more interestingly, if the NLLs for the grammatical versions of all discourse styles are ordered according to where they lie within this range, it becomes clear that NLL is a predictor of discourse style. Styles which linguists class as 'formal', e.g. those of

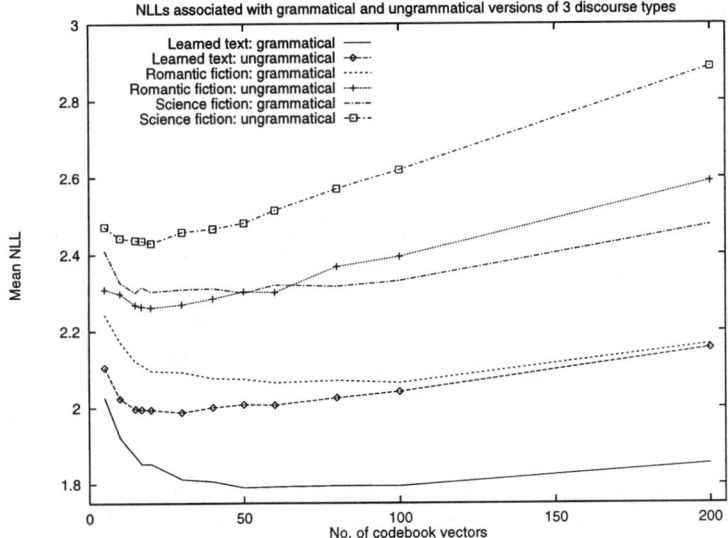

Figure 1: NLLs of minimal pair test sets containing different discourse styles suggest grades of wellformedness based upon prototypicality.

the Learned and Government Document test sets, have the lowest NLLs, with the three Press test sets clustering just above, and the Fiction test sets, exemplifying creative language use, clustering at the high end. Similarly, that the Learned and Government test sets have the lowest NLLs conforms with the intuition that their usage lies closest to what is grammatically 'prototypical' - even though in the training set, 6 out of the 14 test sets are fiction and thus might be expected to contribute more to the prototype. That they do not, suggests that usage varies significantly across fiction test sets.

5 Conclusion

Work on the use of PFMs in language modeling is at an early stage, but as results to date show, they have a lot to offer. A much larger project is planned, which will examine further Allen and Seidenberg's hypothesis that 'graded grammaticality' (or wellformedness) applies not only to syntax, but also to other language subdomains such as semantics, an integral part of this being the use of larger corpora and tagsets, and the identification of vertices with semantic/syntactic features rather than atomic symbols. Identifying the possibilities of combining PFMs with ANNs, for example as a means of bypassing the normal method of creating state-space trajectories, is the subject of current study.

Acknowledgments

This work was supported by the Austrian Science Fund (FWF) within the research project "Adaptive Information Systems and Modeling in Economics and Management Science" (SFB 010). The Austrian Research Institute for Artificial Intelligence is supported by the Austrian Federal Ministry of Science and Transport.

References

[1] P. Tiňo & G. Dorffner (1998). Constructing finite-context sources from fractal representations of symbolic sequences. Technical Report TR-98-18, Austrian Research Institute for AI, Vienna.

[2] J. R. Taylor (1995). *Linguistic categorisation: Prototypes in linguistic theory*. Clarendon, Oxford.

[3] J. R. Saffran, R. N. Aslin & E. L. Newport (1996). Statistical cues in language acquisition: Word segmentation by infants. In *Proc. of the Cognitive Science Society Conference*, 376–380, La Jolla, CA.

[4] J. Allen & M. S. Seidenberg (in press). The emergence of grammaticality in connectionist networks. In B. Macwhinney (ed.), *Emergentist approaches to language: Proc. of the 28th Carnegie Symposium on cognition*. Erlbaum.

[5] S. Parfitt (1997). *Aspects of anaphora resolution in artificial neural networks: Implications for nativism*. PhD thesis, Imperial College, London.

[6] D. Servan-Schreiber et al (1989). Graded state machines: The representation of temporal contingencies in Simple Recurrent Networks. In *Advances in Neural Information Processing Systems*, 643–652.

[7] W. Tabor & M. Tanenhaus (to appear). Dynamical models of sentence processing. Cognitive Science.

[8] J. L. Elman et al (1996). *Rethinking innateness: A connectionist perspective on development*. Bradford.

[9] J. L. Elman (1990). Finding structure in time. In: Cognitive Science, 14: 179-211.

[10] S. Lawrence, C. Lee Giles & S. Fong (in press). Natural language grammatical inference with recurrent neural networks. *IEEE Trans. on knowledge and data engineering*.

[11] J. Hertz, A. Krogh & R. G. Palmer (1991). *Introduction to the theory of neural computation*. Addison Wesley.

[12] M. McCloskey & N. J. Cohen (1989). Catastrophic interference in connectionist networks: The sequential learning problem. In G. Bower (ed.), *The psychology of learning and motivation, vol 24*. Academic, NY.

[13] J. K. Kruschke (1991). ALCOVE: A connectionist model of human category learning. In R. P. Lippman et al (eds.), *Advances in Neural Information Processing 3*, 649–655. Kaufmann, San Mateo, CA.

[14] S. Grossberg (ed.) (1988). *Neural networks and natural intelligence*. Bradford, MIT, Cambs, MA.

[15] Y. Bengio, P. Simard & P. Frasconi (1994). Learning long-term dependencies with gradient descent is difficult. *IEEE Trans. on neural networks*, 5(2).

[16] M. P. Casey (1996). The dynamics of discrete-time computation, with application to recurrent neural networks and finite-state machine extraction. *Neural Computation*, 8(6):1135–1178.

[17] D. Ron, Y. Singer & N. Tishby (1996). The power of amnesia. *Machine Learning*, 25.

[18] P. Tiňo, B. G. Horne, C. Lee Giles & P. C. Collingwood (1998). Finite state machines and recurrent neural networks - automata and dynamical systems approaches. In J. E. Dayhoff & O. Omidvar (eds.), *Neural Networks and Pattern Recognition*, 171–220. Academic.

[19] M. F. Barnsley (1988). *Fractals everywhere*. Academic, NY.

[20] S. Coulson, J. W. King & M. Kutas (1998). Expect the unexpected: Responses to morphosyntactic violations. *Language and Cognitive Processes*, 13(1).

Rules and Similarity in Concept Learning

Joshua B. Tenenbaum
Department of Psychology
Stanford University, Stanford, CA 94305
jbt@psych.stanford.edu

Abstract

This paper argues that two apparently distinct modes of generalizing concepts – abstracting rules and computing similarity to exemplars – should both be seen as special cases of a more general Bayesian learning framework. Bayes explains the specific workings of these two modes – which rules are abstracted, how similarity is measured – as well as why generalization should appear rule- or similarity-based in different situations. This analysis also suggests why the rules/similarity distinction, even if not computationally fundamental, may still be useful at the algorithmic level as part of a principled approximation to fully Bayesian learning.

1 Introduction

In domains ranging from reasoning to language acquisition, a broad view is emerging of cognition as a hybrid of two distinct modes of computation, one based on applying abstract rules and the other based on assessing similarity to stored exemplars [7]. Much support for this view comes from the study of concepts and categorization. In generalizing concepts, people's judgments often seem to reflect both rule-based and similarity-based computations [9], and different brain systems are thought to be involved in each case [8]. Recent psychological models of classification typically incorporate some combination of rule-based and similarity-based modules [1,4]. In contrast to this currently popular modularity position, I will argue here that rules and similarity are best seen as two ends of a continuum of possible concept representations. In [11,12], I introduced a general theoretical framework to account for how people can learn concepts from just a few positive examples based on the principles of Bayesian inference. Here I explore how this framework provides a unifying explanation for these two apparently distinct modes of generalization. The Bayesian framework not only includes both rules and similarity as special cases but also addresses several questions that conventional modular accounts do not. People employ particular algorithms for selecting rules and measuring similarity. Why these algorithms as opposed to any others? People's generalizations appear to shift from similarity-like patterns to rule-like patterns in systematic ways, e.g., as the number of examples observed increases. Why these shifts?

This short paper focuses on a simple learning game involving number concepts, in which both rule-like and similarity-like generalizations clearly emerge in the judgments of human subjects. Imagine that I have written some short computer programs which take as input a natural number and return as output either "yes" or "no" according to whether that number satisfies some simple concept. Some possible concepts might be "x is odd", "x is between 30 and 45", "x is a power of 3", or "x is less than 10". For simplicity, we assume that only numbers under 100 are under consideration. The learner is shown a few randomly chosen *positive* examples – numbers that the program says "yes" to – and must then identify the other numbers that the program would accept. This task, admittedly artificial, nonetheless draws on people's rich knowledge of number while remaining amenable to theoretical analysis. Its structure is meant to parallel more natural tasks, such as word learning, that often require meaningful generalizations from only a few positive examples of a concept.

Section 2 presents representative experimental data for this task. Section 3 describes a Bayesian model and contrasts its predictions with those of models based purely on rules or similarity. Section 4 summarizes and discusses the model's applicability to other domains.

2 The number concept game

Eight subjects participated in an experimental study of number concept learning, under essentially the same instructions as those given above [11]. On each trial, subjects were shown one or more random positive examples of a concept and asked to rate the probability that each of 30 test numbers would belong to the same concept as the examples observed. X denotes the set of examples observed on a particular trial, and n the number of examples.

Trials were designed to fall into one of three classes. Figure 1a presents data for two representative trials of each class. Bar heights represent the average judged probabilities that particular test numbers fall under the concept given one or more positive examples X, marked by "*"s. Bars are shown only for those test numbers rated by subjects; missing bars do *not* denote zero probability of generalization, merely missing data.

On class I trials, subjects saw only one example of each concept: e.g., $X = \{16\}$ and $X = \{60\}$. To minimize bias, these trials preceded all others on which multiple examples were given. Given only one example, people gave most test numbers fairly similar probabilities of acceptance. Numbers that were intuitively more similar to the example received slightly higher ratings: e.g., for $X = \{16\}$, 8 was more acceptable than 9 or 6, and 17 more than 87; for $X = \{60\}$, 50 was more acceptable than 51, and 63 more than 43.

The remaining trials each presented four examples and occured in pseudorandom order. On class II trials, the examples were consistent with a simple mathematical rule: $X = \{16, 8, 2, 64\}$ or $X = \{60, 80, 10, 30\}$. Note that the obvious rules, "powers of two" and "multiples of ten", are in no way logically implied by the data. "Multiples of five" is a possibility in the second case, and "even numbers" or "all numbers under 80" are possibilities in both, not to mention other logically possible but psychologically implausible candidates, such as "all powers of two, except 32 or 4". Nonetheless, subjects overwhelmingly followed an all-or-none pattern of generalization, with all test numbers rated near 0 or 1 according to whether they satisified the single intuitively "correct" rule. These preferred rules can be loosely characterized as the *most specific* rules (i.e., with smallest extension) that include all the examples and that also meet some criterion of psychological simplicity.

On class III trials, the examples satisified no simple mathematical rule but did have similar magnitudes: $X = \{16, 23, 19, 20\}$ and $X = \{60, 52, 57, 55\}$. Generalization now followed a similarity gradient along the dimension of magnitude. Probability ratings fell below 0.5 for numbers more than a characteristic distance ξ beyond the largest or smallest observed examples – roughly the typical distance between neighboring examples ($\sim$ 2 or 3). Logically, there is no reason why participants could not have generalized according to various complex rules that happened to pick out the given examples, or according to very different values of ξ, yet all subjects displayed more or less the same similarity gradients.

To summarize these data, generalization from a single example followed a weak similarity gradient based on both mathematical and magnitude properties of numbers. When several more examples were observed, generalization evolved into either an all-or-none pattern determined by the most specific simple rule, or, when no simple rule applied, a more articulated magnitude-based similarity gradient falling off with characteristic distance ξ roughly equal to the typical separation between neighboring examples. Similar patterns were observed on several trials not shown (including one with a different value of ξ) and on two other experiments in quite different domains (described briefly in Section 4).

3 The Bayesian model

In [12], I introduced a Bayesian framework for concept learning in the context of learning axis-parallel rectangles in a multidimensional feature space. Here I show that the same framework can be adapted to the more complex situation of learning number concepts and can explain all of the phenomena of rules and similarity documented above. Formally, we observe n positive examples $X = \{x^{(1)}, \ldots, x^{(n)}\}$ of concept C and want to compute $p(y \in C|X)$, the probability that some new object y belongs to C given the observations X. Inductive leverage is provided by a hypothesis space $\mathcal{H}$ of possible concepts and a probabilistic model relating hypotheses h to data X.

The hypothesis space. Elements of $\mathcal{H}$ correspond to subsets of the universe of objects that are psychologically plausible candidates for the extensions of concepts. Here the universe consists of numbers between 1 and 100, and the hypotheses correspond to subsets such as the even numbers, the numbers between 1 and 10, etc. The hypotheses can be thought of in terms of either rules or similarity, i.e., as potential rules to be abstracted or as features entering into a similarity computation, but Bayes does not distinguish these interpretations.

Because we can capture only a fraction of the hypotheses people might bring to this task, we would like an objective way to focus on the most relevant parts of people's hypothesis space. One such method is *additive clustering (ADCLUS)* [6,10], which extracts a set of features that best accounts for subjects' similarity judgments on a given set of objects. These features simply correspond to subsets of objects and are thus naturally identified with hypotheses for concept learning. Applications of ADCLUS to similarity judgments for the numbers 0-9 reveal two kinds of subsets [6,10]: numbers sharing a common mathematical property, such as $\{2, 4, 8\}$ and $\{3, 6, 9\}$, and consecutive numbers of similar magnitude, such as $\{1, 2, 3, 4\}$ and $\{2, 3, 4, 5, 6\}$. Applying ADCLUS to the full set of numbers from 1 to 100 is impractical, but we can construct an analogous hypothesis space for this domain based on the two kinds of hypotheses found in the ADCLUS solution for 0-9. One group of hypotheses captures salient mathematical properties: odd, even, square, cube, and prime numbers, multiples and powers of small numbers (≤ 12), and sets of numbers ending in the same digit. A second group of hypotheses, representing the dimension of numerical magnitude, includes all intervals of consecutive numbers with endpoints between 1 and 100.

Priors and likelihoods. The probabilistic model consists of a prior $p(h)$ over $\mathcal{H}$ and a likelihood $p(X|h)$ for each hypothesis $h \in H$. Rather than assigning prior probabilities to each of the 5083 hypotheses individually, I adopted a hierarchical approach based on the intuitive division of $\mathcal{H}$ into mathematical properties and magnitude intervals. A fraction λ of the total probability was allocated to the mathematical hypotheses as a group, leaving $(1 - \lambda)$ for the magnitude hypotheses. The λ probability was distributed uniformly across the mathematical hypotheses. The $(1-\lambda)$ probability was distributed across the magnitude intervals as a function of interval size according to an Erlang distribution, $p(h) \propto (|h|/\sigma^2)e^{-|h|/\sigma}$, to capture the intuition that intervals of some intermediate size are more likely than those of very large or small size. λ and σ are treated as free parameters of the model.

The likelihood is determined by the assumption of randomly sampled positive examples. In the simplest case, each example in X is assumed to be independently sampled from a uniform density over the concept C. For n examples we then have:

$$p(X|h) = 1/|h|^n \text{ if } \forall j, x^{(j)} \in h \qquad (1)$$
$$= 0 \text{ otherwise,}$$

where $|h|$ denotes the size of the subset h. For example, if h denotes the even numbers, then $|h| = 50$, because there are 50 even numbers between 1 and 100. Equation 1 embodies the *size principle* for scoring hypotheses: smaller hypotheses assign greater likelihood than do larger hypotheses to the same data, and they assign exponentially greater likelihood as the number of consistent examples increases. The size principle plays a key role in learning concepts from only positive examples [12], and, as we will see below, in determining the appearance of rule-like or similarity-like modes of generalization.

Given these priors and likelihoods, the posterior $p(h|X)$ follows directly from Bayes' rule. Finally, we compute the probability of generalization to a new object y by averaging the predictions of all hypotheses weighted by their posterior probabilities $p(h|X)$:

$$p(y \in C|X) = \sum_{h \in \mathcal{H}} p(y \in C|h) p(h|X). \qquad (2)$$

Equation 2 follows from the conditional independence of X and the membership of $y \in C$, given h. To evaluate Equation 2, note that $p(y \in C|h)$ is simply 1 if $y \in h$, and 0 otherwise.

Model results. Figure 1b shows the predictions of this Bayesian model (with $\lambda = 1/2$, $\sigma = 10$). The model captures the main features of the data, including convergence to the most specific rule on Class II trials and to appropriately shaped similarity gradients on Class III trials. We can understand the transitions between graded, similarity-like and all-or-none, rule-like regimes of generalization as arising from the interaction of the *size principle* (Equation 1) with *hypothesis averaging* (Equation 2). Because each hypothesis h contributes to the average in Equation 2 in proportion to its posterior probability $p(h|X)$, the degree of uncertainty in $p(h|X)$ determines whether generalization will be sharp or graded. When $p(h|X)$ is very spread out, many distinct hypotheses contribute significantly, resulting in a broad gradient of generalization. When $p(h|X)$ is concentrated on a single hypothesis h^*, only h^* contributes significantly and generalization appears all-or-none. The degree of uncertainty in $p(h|X)$ is in turn a consequence of the size principle. Given a few examples consistent with one hypothesis that is significantly smaller than the next-best competitor – such as $X = \{16, 8, 2, 64\}$, where "powers of two" is significantly smaller than "even numbers" – then the smallest hypothesis becomes exponentially more likely than any other and generalization appears to follow this most specific rule. However, given only one example (such as $X = \{16\}$), or given several examples consistent with many similarly sized hypotheses – such as $X = \{16, 23, 19, 20\}$, where the top candidates are all very similar intervals: "numbers between 16 and 23", "numbers between 15 and 24", etc. – the size-based likelihood favors the smaller hypotheses only slightly, $p(h|X)$ is spread out over many overlapping hypotheses and generalization appears to follow a gradient of similarity. That the Bayesian model predicts the right shape for the magnitude-based similarity gradients on Class III trials is no accident. The characteristic distance ξ of the Bayesian generalization gradient varies with the uncertainty in $p(h|X)$, which (for interval hypotheses) can be shown to covary with the intuitively relevant factor of average separation between neighboring examples.

Bayes vs. rules or similarity alone. It is instructive to consider two special cases of the Bayesian model that are equivalent to conventional similarity-based and rule-based algorithms from the concept learning literature. What I call the SIM algorithm was pioneered by [5] and also described in [2,3] as a Bayesian approach to learning concepts from both positive and negative evidence. SIM replaces the size-based likelihood with a binary likelihood that measures only whether a hypothesis is consistent with the examples: $p(X|h) = 1$ if $\forall j, x^{(j)} \in h$, and 0 otherwise. Generalization under SIM is just a count of the features shared by y and all the examples in X, independent of the frequency of those features or the number of examples seen. As Figure 1c shows, SIM successfully models generalization from a single example (Class I) but fails to capture how generalization sharpens up after multiple examples, to either the most specific rule (Class II) or a magnitude-based similarity gradient with appropriate characteristic distance ξ (Class III). What I call the MIN algorithm preserves the size principle but replaces the step of hypothesis averaging with maximization: $p(y \in C|X) = 1$ if $y \in \arg\max_h p(X|h)$, and 0 otherwise. MIN is perhaps the oldest algorithm for concept learning [3] and, as a maximum likelihood algorithm, is asymptotically equivalent to Bayes. Its success for finite amounts of data depends on how peaked $p(h|X)$ is (Figure 1d). MIN always selects the most specific consistent rule, which is reasonable when that hypothesis is much more probable than any other (Class II), but too conservative in other cases (Classes I and III). In quantitative terms, the predictions of Bayes correlate much more highly with the observed data ($R^2 = 0.91$) than do the predictions of either SIM ($R^2 = 0.74$) or MIN ($R^2 = 0.47$). In sum, only the full Bayesian framework can explain the full range of rule-like and similarity-like generalization patterns observed on this task.

4 Discussion

Experiments in two other domains provide further support for Bayes as a unifying framework for concept learning. In the context of multidimensional continuous feature spaces, similarity gradients are the default mode of generalization [5]. Bayes successfully models how the shape of those gradients depends on the distribution and number of examples; SIM and MIN do not [12]. Bayes also successfully predicts how fast these similarity gradients converge to the most specific consistent rule. Convergence is quite slow in this domain ($n \sim 50$) because the hypothesis space consists of densely overlapping subsets – axis-parallel rectangles – much like the interval hypotheses in the Class III number tasks.

Another experiment engaged a word-learning task, using photographs of real objects as stimuli and a cover story of learning a new language [11]. On each trial, subjects saw either one example of a novel word (e.g., a toy animal labeled with "Here is a blicket."), or three examples at one of three different levels of specificity: subordinate (e.g., 3 dalmatians labeled with "Here are three blickets."), basic (e.g., 3 dogs), or superordinate (e.g., 3 animals). They then were asked to pick the other instances of that concept from a set of 24 test objects, containing matches to the example(s) at all levels (e.g., other dalmatians, dogs, animals) as well as many non-matching objects. Figure 2 shows data and predictions for all three models. Similarity-like generalization given one example rapidly converged to the most specific rule after only three examples were observed, just as in the number task (Classes I and II) but in contrast to the axis-parallel rectangle task or the Class III number tasks, where similarity-like responding was still the norm after three or four examples. For modeling purposes, a hypothesis space was constructed from a hierarchical clustering of subjects' similarity judgments (augmented by an a priori preference for basic-level concepts) [11]. The Bayesian model successfully predicts rapid convergence from a similarity gradient to the minimal rule, because the smallest hypothesis consistent with each example set is significantly smaller than the next-best competitor (e.g., "dogs" is significantly smaller than "dogs and cats", just as with "multiples of ten" vs. "multiples of five"). Bayes fits the full data extremely well ($R^2 = 0.98$); by comparison, SIM ($R^2 = 0.83$) successfully accounts for only the $n = 1$ trials and MIN ($R^2 = 0.76$), the $n = 3$ trials.

In conclusion, a Bayesian framework is able to account for both rule- and similarity-like modes of generalization, as well as the dynamics of transitions between these modes, across several quite different domains of concept learning. The key features of the Bayesian model are *hypothesis averaging* and the *size principle*. The former allows either rule-like or similarity-like behavior depending on the uncertainty in the posterior probability. The latter determines this uncertainty as a function of the number and distribution of examples and the structure of the learner's hypothesis space. With *sparsely overlapping* hypotheses – i.e., the most specific hypothesis consistent with the examples is much smaller than its nearest competitors – convergence to a single rule occurs rapidly, after just a few examples. With *densely overlapping* hypotheses – i.e., many consistent hypotheses of comparable size – convergence to a single rule occurs much more slowly, and a gradient of similarity is the norm after just a few examples. Importantly, the Bayesian framework does not so much obviate the distinction between rules and similarity as explain why it might be useful in understanding the brain. As Figures 1 and 2 show, special cases of Bayes corresponding to the SIM and MIN algorithms consistently account for distinct and complementary regimes of generalization. SIM, without the size principle, works best given only one example or densely overlapping hypotheses, when Equation 1 does not generate large differences in likelihood. MIN, without hypothesis averaging, works best given many examples or sparsely overlapping hypotheses, when the most specific hypothesis dominates the sum over $\mathcal{H}$ in Equation 2. In light of recent brain-imaging studies dissociating rule- and exemplar-based processing [8], the Bayesian theory may best be thought of as a computational-level account of concept learning, with multiple subprocesses – perhaps subserving SIM and MIN – implemented in distinct neural circuits. I hope to explore this possibility in future work.

References

[1] M. Erickson & J. Kruschke (1998). Rules and exemplars in category learning. *JEP: General* **127**, 107-140.
[2] D. Haussler, M. Kearns, & R. Schapire (1994). Bounds on the sample complexity of Bayesian learning using information theory and the VC-dimension. *Machine Learning* **14**, 83-113.
[3] T. Mitchell (1997). *Machine Learning*. McGraw-Hill.
[4] R. Nosofsky & T. Palmeri (1998). A rule-plus-exception model for classifying objects in continuous-dimension spaces. *Psychonomic Bull. & Rev.* **5**, 345-369.
[5] R. Shepard (1987). Towards a universal law of generalization for psychological science. *Science* **237**, 1317-1323.
[6] R. Shepard & P. Arabie (1979). Additive clustering: Representation of similarities as combinations of discrete overlapping properties. *Psych. Rev.* **86**, 87-123.
[7] S. Sloman & L. Rips (1998). *Similarity and Symbols in Human Thinking*. MIT Press.
[8] E. Smith, A. Patalano & J. Jonides (1998). Alternative strategies of categorization. In [6].
[9] E. Smith & S. Sloman (1994). Similarity- vs. rule-based categorization. *Mem. & Cog.* **22**, 377.
[10] J. Tenenbaum (1996). Learning the structure of similarity. *NIPS 8*.
[11] J. Tenenbaum (1999). *A Bayesian Framework for Concept Learning*. Ph. D. Thesis, MIT.
[12] J. Tenenbaum (1999). Bayesian modeling of human concept learning. *NIPS 11*.

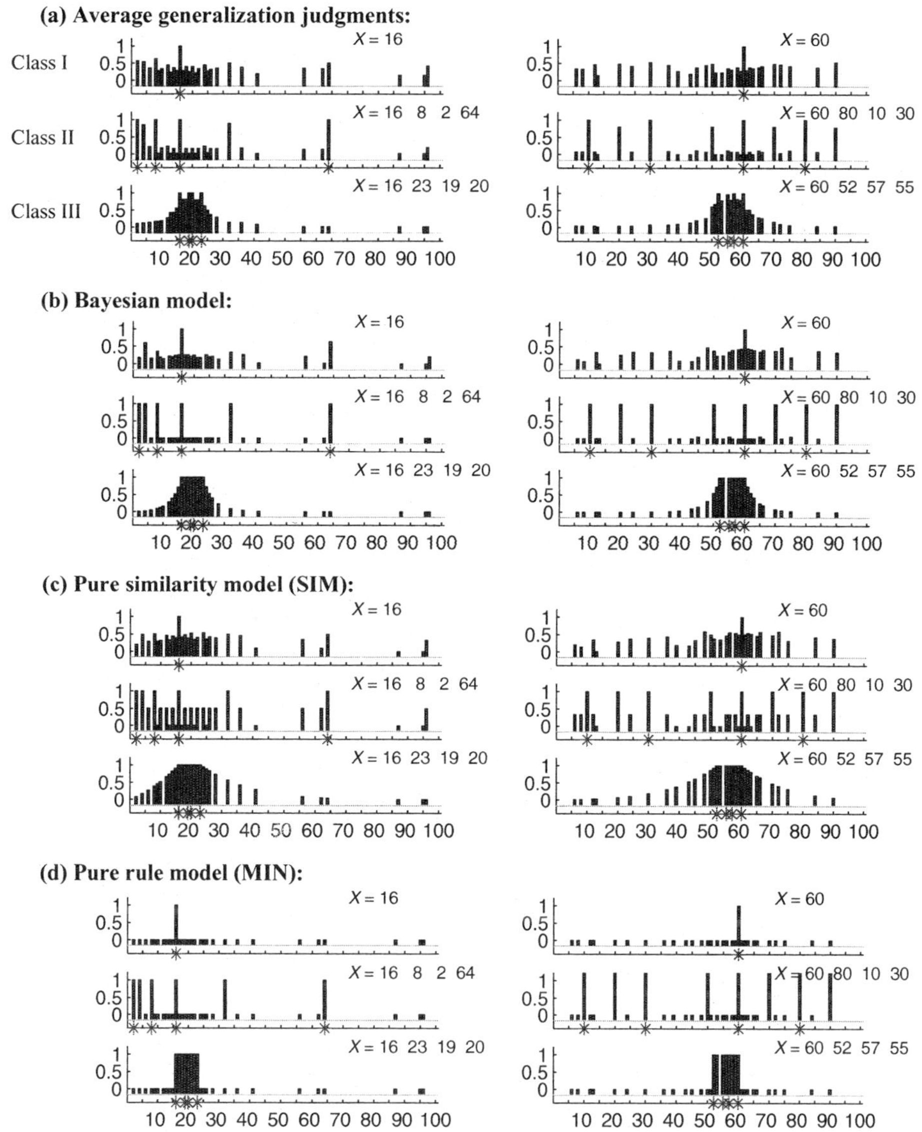

Rules and Similarity in Concept Learning

Figure 1: Data and model predictions for the number concept task.

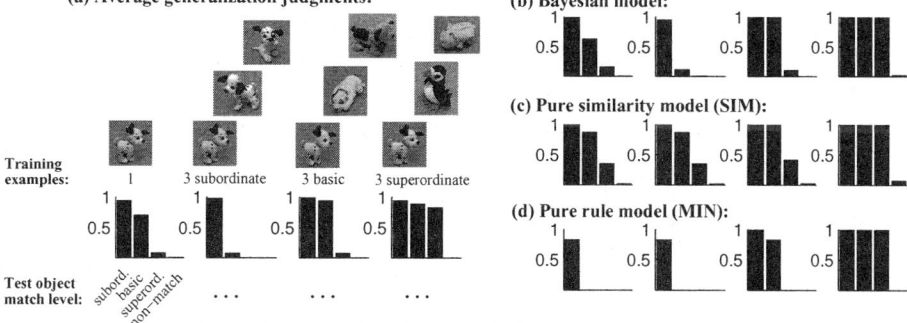

Figure 2: Data and model predictions for the word learning task.

Evolving Learnable Languages

Bradley Tonkes
Dept of Comp. Sci. and Elec. Engineering
University of Queensland
Queensland, 4072
Australia
btonkes@csee.uq.edu.au

Alan Blair
Department of Computer Science
University of Melbourne
Parkville, Victoria, 3052
Australia
blair@cs.mu.oz.au

Janet Wiles
Dept of Comp. Sci. and Elec. Engineering
School of Psychology
University of Queensland
Queensland, 4072
Australia
janetw@csee.uq.edu.au

Abstract

Recent theories suggest that language acquisition is assisted by the evolution of languages towards forms that are easily learnable. In this paper, we evolve combinatorial languages which can be learned by a recurrent neural network quickly and from relatively few examples. Additionally, we evolve languages for generalization in different "worlds", and for generalization from specific examples. We find that languages can be evolved to facilitate different forms of impressive generalization for a minimally biased, general purpose learner. The results provide empirical support for the theory that the language itself, as well as the language environment of a learner, plays a substantial role in learning: that there is far more to language acquisition than the language acquisition device.

1 Introduction: Factors in language learnability

In exploring issues of language learnability, the special abilities of humans to learn complex languages have been much emphasized, with one dominant theory based on innate, domain-specific learning mechanisms specifically tuned to learning human languages. It has been argued that without strong constraints on the learning mechanism, the complex syntax of language could not be learned from the sparse data that a child observes [1]. More recent theories challenge this claim and emphasize the interaction between learner and environment [2]. In addition to these two theories is the proposal that rather than "language-savvy infants", languages themselves adapt to human learners, and the ones that survive are "infant-friendly languages" [3–5]. To date, relatively few empirical studies have explored how such adaptation of language facilitates learning. Hare and Elman [6] demonstrated that classes of past tense forms could evolve over simulated generations in response to changes in the frequency of verbs, using neural networks. Kirby [7] showed, using a symbolic system, how compositional languages are more likely to emerge when learning is constrained to a limited set of examples. Batali [8] has evolved recurrent networks that communicate simple structured concepts.

Our argument is not that humans are general purpose learners. Rather, current research questions require exploring the nature and extent of biases that learners bring to language learning, and the ways in which languages exploit those biases [2]. Previous theories suggesting that many aspects of language were unlearnable without strong biases are gradually breaking down as new aspects of language are shown to be learnable with much weaker biases. Studies include the investigation of how languages may exploit biases as subtle as attention and memory limitations in children [9]. A complementary study has shown that general purpose learners can evolve biases in the form of initial starting weights that facilitate the learning of a family of recursive languages [10].

In this paper we present an empirical paradigm for continuing the exploration of factors that contribute to language learnability. The paradigm we propose necessitates the evolution of languages comprising recursive sentences over symbolic strings — languages whose sentences cannot be conveyed without combinatorial composition of symbols drawn from a finite alphabet. The paradigm is not based on any specific natural language, but rather, it is the simplest task we could find to illustrate the point that languages with compositional structure can be evolved to be learnable from few sentences. The simplicity of the communication task allows us to analyze the language and its generalizability, and highlight the nature of the generalization properties.

We start with the evolution of a recursive language that can be learned easily from five sentences by a minimally biased learner. We then address issues of robust learning of evolved languages, showing that different languages support generalization in different ways. We also address a factor to which scant regard has been paid, namely that languages may evolve not just to their learners, but also to be easily generalizable from a specific set of concepts. It seems almost axiomatic that learning paradigms should sample randomly from the training domain. It may be that human languages are not learnable from random sentences, but are easily generalizable from just those examples that a child is likely to be exposed to in its environment. In the third series of simulations, we test whether a language can adapt to be learnable from a core set of concepts.

2 A paradigm for exploring language learnability

We consider a simple language task in which two recurrent neural networks try to communicate a "concept" represented by a point in the unit interval, $[0,1]$ over a symbolic channel. An *encoder* network sends a sequence of symbols (thresholded outputs) for each concept, which a *decoder* network receives and processes back into a concept (the framework is described in greater detail in [11]). For communication to be successful, the decoder's output should approximate the encoder's input for all concepts.

The architecture for the encoder is a recurrent network with one input unit and five output units, and with recurrent connections from both the output and hidden units back to the hidden units. The encoder produces a sequence of up to five symbols (states of the output units) taken from $\Sigma = \{A, ..., J\}$, followed by the $ symbol, for each concept taken from $[0, 1]$. To encode a value $x \in [0, 1]$, the network

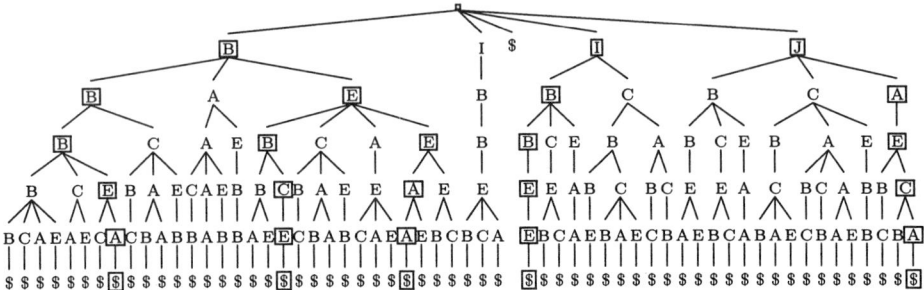

Figure 1: Hierarchical decomposition of the language produced by an encoder, with the first symbols produced appearing near the root of the tree. The ordering of leaves in the tree represent the input space, smaller inputs being encoded by those sentences on the left. The examples used to train the best decoder found during evolution are highlighted. The decoder must generalize to all other branches. In order to learn the task, the decoder must generalize systematically to novel states in the tree, including generalizing to symbols in different positions in the sequence. (Figure 2 shows the sequence of states of a successful decoder.)

is presented with a sequence of inputs $(x, 0, 0, ..)$. At each step, the output units of the network assume one of eleven states: all zero if no output is greater than 0.5 (denoted by \$); or the saturation of the two highest activations at 1.0 and the remainder at 0.0 (denoted by $A = [1, 1, 0, 0, 0]$ through $J = [0, 0, 0, 1, 1]$). If the zero output is produced, propagation is halted. Otherwise propagation continues for up to five steps, after which the output units assume the zero (\$) state.

The decoder is a recurrent network with 5 input units and a single output, and a recurrent hidden layer. Former work [11] has shown that due to conflicting constraints of the encoder and decoder, it is easier for the decoder to process strings which are in the *reverse order* to those produced by the encoder. Consequently, the input to the decoder is taken to be the reverse of the output from the decoder, except for \$, which remains the last symbol. (For clarity, strings are written in the order produced by the encoder.) Each input pattern presented to the decoder matches the output of the encoder — either two units are active, or none are. The network is trained with backpropagation through time to produce the desired value, x, on presentation of the final symbol in the sequence (\$).

A simple hill-climbing evolutionary strategy with a two-stage evaluation function is used to evolve an initially random encoder into one which produces a language which a random decoder can learn easily from few examples. The evaluation of an encoder, mutated from the current "champion" by the addition of Gaussian noise to the weights, is performed against two criteria. (1) The mutated network must produce a greater variety of sequences over the range of inputs; and (2) a decoder with initially small random weights, trained on the mutated encoder's output, must yield lower sum-squared error across the entire range of inputs than the champion.

Each mutant encoder is paired with a single decoder with initially random weights. If the mutant encoder-decoder pair is more successful than the champion, the mutant becomes champion and the process is repeated. Since the encoder's input space is continuous and impossible to examine in its entirety, the input range is approximated with 100 uniformly distributed examples from 0.00 to 0.99. The final output from the hill-climber is the language generated by the best encoder found.

2.1 Evolving an easily learnable language

Humans learn from sparse data. In the first series of simulations we test whether a compositional language can be evolved that learners can reliably and effectively learn from only five examples. From just five training examples, it seems unreasonable to expect that any decoder would learn the task. The task is intentionally hard in that a language is restricted to sequences of discrete symbols with which it must describe a continuous space. Note that simple linear interpolation is not possible due to the symbolic alphabet of the languages. Recursive solutions are possible but are unable to be learned by an *unbiased* learner. The decoder is a *minimally-biased* learner and as the simulations showed, performed much better than arguments based on learnability theory would predict.

Ten languages were evolved with the hill-climbing algorithm (outlined above) for 10000 generations.[1] For each language, 100 new random decoders were trained under the same conditions as during evolution (five examples, 400 epochs). All ten runs used encoders and decoders with five hidden units.

All of the evolved languages were learnable by some decoders (minimum 20, maximum 72, mean 48). A learner is said to have effectively learned the language if its sum-squared-error across the 100 points in the space is less than 1.0.[2] Encoders employed on average 36 sentences (minimum 21, maximum 60) to communicate the 100 points. The 5 training examples for each decoder were sampled randomly from $[0, 1]$ and hence some decoders faced very difficult generalization tasks. The difficulty of the task is demonstrated by the language analyzed in Figures 1 and 2. The evolved languages all contained similar compositional structure to that of the language described in Figures 1 and 2. The inherent biases of the decoder, although minimal, are clearly sufficient for learning the compositional structure.

3 Evolving languages for particular generalization

The first series of simulations demonstrate that we can find languages for which a minimally biased learner can generalize from few examples. In the next simulations we consider whether languages can be evolved to facilitate specific forms of generalization in their users. Section 2.1 considered the case where the decoder's required output was the same as the encoder's input. This setup yields the approximation to the line $y = x$ in Figure 2. The compositional structure of the evolved languages allows the decoder to generalize to unseen regions of the space. In the following series of simulations we consider the relationship between the structure of a language and the way in which the decoder is required to generalize. This association is studied by altering the desired relationship between the encoder's input (x) and the decoder's output (y).

Two sets of ten languages were evolved, one set requiring $y = x$ (*identity*, as in section 2.1), the other using a function resembling a series of five steps at random heights: $y = r(\lfloor 5x \rfloor); r = (0.3746, 0.5753, 0.8102, 0.7272, 0.4527)$ (*random step*)[3]. All conditions were as for section 2, with the exception that 10 training examples were used and the hill-climber ran for 1000 generations. On completion of evolution, 100 decoders were trained on the 20 final languages under both conditions above as

---

[1] One generation represents the creation of a more variable, mutated encoder and the subsequent training of a decoder.

[2] A language is said to be reliably learnable when at least 50% of random decoders are able to effectively learn it within 400 epochs.

[3] $\lfloor 5x \rfloor$ provides an index into the array r, based on the magnitude of x.

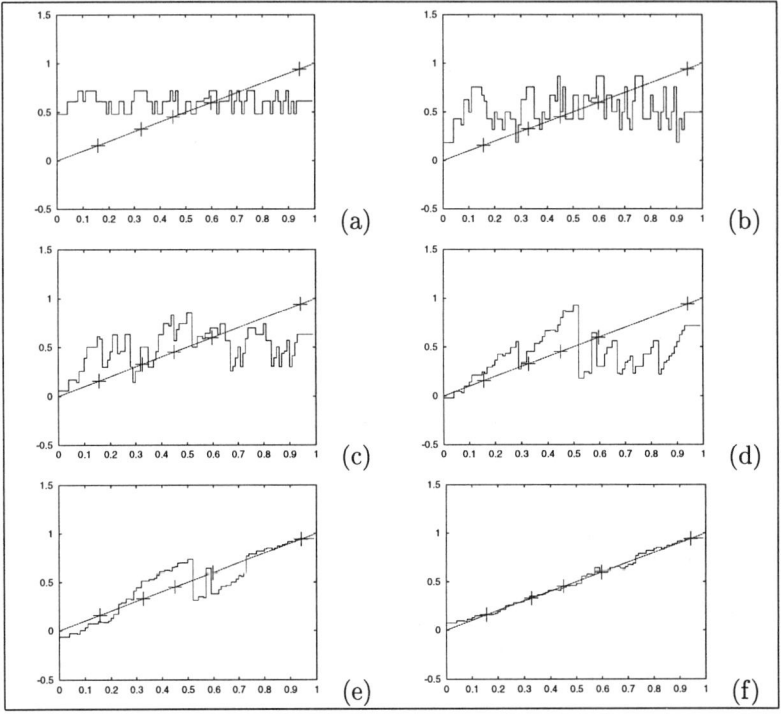

Figure 2: Decoder output after seeing the first n symbols in the message, for $n = 1$ (a) to $n = 6$ (f) (from the language in Figure 1). The X-axis is the encoder's input, the Y-axis is the decoder's output at that point in the sequence. The five points that the decoder was trained on are shown as crosses in each graph. After the first symbol (A, B, C, E or $), the decoder outputs one of five values (a); after the second symbol, more outputs are possible (b). Subsequent symbols in each string specify finer gradations in the output. Note that the output is not constructed monotonically, with each symbol providing a closer approximation to the target function, but rather recursively, only approximating the linear target at the final position in each sequence. Structure inherent in the sequences allows the system to generalize to parts of the space it has never seen. Note that the generalization is not based on interpolation between symbol values, but rather on their compositional structure.

well as two others, a *sine* function and a *cubic* function.

The results show that languages can be evolved to enhance generalization preferentially for one "world" over another. On average, the languages performed far better when tested in the world in which they were evolved than in other worlds. Languages evolved for the identity mapping were on average learned by 64% of decoders trained on the identity task compared with just 5% in the random step case. Languages evolved for the random step task were learned by 60% of decoders trained on the random step task but only 24% when trained on the identity task. Decoders generally performed poorly on the cubic function, and no decoder learned the sine task from either set of evolved languages. The second series of simulations show that the manner in which the decoder generalizes is not restricted to the task of section 2.1. Rather, the languages evolve to facilitate generalization by the decoder in different ways, aided by its minimal biases.

4 Generalization from core concepts

In the former simulations, randomly selected concepts were used to train decoders. In some cases a pathological distribution of points made learning extremely difficult. In contrast, it seems likely that human children learn language based on a common set of semantically-constrained core concepts ("Mom", "I want milk", "no", etc). For the third series of simulations, we tested whether selecting a fortuitous set of training concepts could have a positive affect on the success of an evolved language. The simulations with alternative generalization functions (section 3) indicated that decoders had difficulty generalizing to the sine function. Even when encoders were evolved specifically on the sine task, in the best of 10 systems only 13 of 100 random decoders successfully learned.

We evolved a new language on a specifically chosen set of 10 points for generalization to the sine function. One hundred decoders were then trained on the resulting language using either the same set of 10 points, or a random set. Of the networks trained on the fixed set, 92 learned the tasked, compared with 5 networks trained on the random sets. That a language evolves to communicate a restricted set of concepts is not particularly unusual. But what this simulation shows is the more surprising result that a language can evolve to generalize from specific core concepts to a whole recursive language in a particular way (in this case, a sine function).

5 Discussion

The first series of simulations show that a compositional language can be learned from five strings by an recurrent network. Generalization performance included correct decoding of novel branches and symbols in novel positions (Figure 1). The second series of simulations highlight how a language can be evolved to facilitate different forms of generalization in the decoder. The final simulation demonstrates that languages can also be tailored to generalize from a specific set of examples.

The three series of simulations modify the language environment of the decoder in three different ways: (1) the relationship between utterances and meaning; (2) the type of generalization required from the decoder; and (3) the particular utterances and meanings to which a learner is exposed. In each case, the language environment of the learner was sculpted to exploit the minimal biases present in the learner. While taking an approach similar to [10] of giving the learner an additional bias in the form of initial weights was also likely to have been effective, the purpose of the simulations was to investigate how strongly external factors could assist in simplifying learning.

6 Conclusions

> "The key to understanding language learnability does not lie in the richly social context of language training, nor in the incredibly prescient guesses of young language learners; rather, it lies in a process that seems otherwise far remote from the microcosm of toddlers and caretakers — language change. Although the rate of social evolutionary change in learning structure appears unchanging compared to the time it takes a child to develop language abilities, this process is crucial to understanding how the child can learn a language that on the surface appears impossibly complex and poorly taught." [3, p115].

In this paper we studied ways in which languages can adapt to their learners. By running simulations of a language evolution process, we contribute additional components to the list of aspects of language that can be learned by minimally-biased, general-purpose learners, namely that recursive structure can be learned from few examples, that languages can evolve to facilitate generalization in a particular way, and that they can evolve to be easily learnable from common sentences. In all the simulations in this paper, enhancement of language learnability is achieved through changes to the learner's environment without resorting to adding biases in the language acquisition device.

Acknowledgements

This work was supported by an APA to Bradley Tonkes, a UQ Postdoctoral Fellowship to Alan Blair and an ARC grant to Janet Wiles.

References

[1] N. Chomsky. *Language and Mind*. Harcourt, Brace, New York, 1968.

[2] J. L. Elman, E. A. Bates, M. H. Johnson, A. Karmiloff-Smith, D. Parisi, and K. Plunkett. *Rethinking Innateness: A Connectionist Perspective on Development*. MIT Press, Boston, 1996.

[3] T. W. Deacon. *The Symbolic Species: The Co-Evolution of Language and the Brain*. W. W. Norton and Company, New York, 1997.

[4] S. Kirby. Fitness and the selective adaptation of language. In J. Hurford, C. Knight, and M. Studdert-Kennedy, editors, *Approaches to the Evolution of Language*. Cambridge University Press, Cambridge, 1998.

[5] M. H. Christiansen. Language as an organism — implications for the evolution and acquisition of language. Unpublished manuscript, February 1995.

[6] M. Hare and J. L. Elman. Learning and morphological change. *Cognition*, 56:61–98, 1995.

[7] S. Kirby. Syntax without natural selection: How compositionality emerges from vocabulary in a population of learners. In C. Knight, J. Hurford, and M. Studdert-Kennedy, editors, *The Evolutionary Emergence of Language: Social function and the origins of linguistic form*. Cambridge University Press, Cambridge, 1999.

[8] J. Batali. Computational simulations of the emergence of grammar. In J. Hurford, C. Knight, and M. Studdert-Kennedy, editors, *Approaches to the Evolution of Language*, pages 405–426. Cambridge University Press, Cambridge, 1998.

[9] J. L. Elman. Learning and development in neural networks: The importance of starting small. *Cognition*, 48:71–99, 1993.

[10] J. Batali. Innate biases and critical periods: Combining evolution and learning in the acquisition of syntax. In R. Brooks and P. Maes, editors, *Proceedings of the Fourth Artificial Life Workshop*, pages 160–171. MIT Press, 1994.

[11] B. Tonkes, A. Blair, and J. Wiles. A paradox of neural encoders and decoders, or, why don't we talk backwards? In B. McKay, X. Yao, C. S. Newton, J. -H. Kim, and T. Furuhashi, editors, *Simulated Evolution and Learning*, volume 1585 of *Lecture Notes in Artificial Intelligence*. Springer, 1999.

Learning Statistically Neutral Tasks without Expert Guidance

Ton Weijters
Information Technology,
Eindhoven University,
The Netherlands

Antal van den Bosch
ILK,
Tilburg University,
The Netherlands

Eric Postma
Computer Science,
Universiteit Maastricht,
The Netherlands

Abstract

In this paper, we question the necessity of levels of expert-guided abstraction in learning hard, statistically neutral classification tasks. We focus on two tasks, date calculation and parity-12, that are claimed to require intermediate levels of abstraction that must be defined by a human expert. We challenge this claim by demonstrating empirically that a single hidden-layer BP-SOM network can learn both tasks without guidance. Moreover, we analyze the network's solution for the parity-12 task and show that its solution makes use of an elegant intermediary checksum computation.

1 Introduction

Breaking up a complex task into many smaller and simpler subtasks facilitates its solution. Such task decomposition has proved to be a successful technique in developing algorithms and in building theories of cognition. In their study and modeling of the human problem-solving process, Newell and Simon [1] employed protocol analysis to determine the subtasks human subjects employ in solving a complex task. Even nowadays, many cognitive scientists take task decomposition, i.e., the necessity of explicit levels of abstraction, as a fundamental property of human problem solving. Dennis Norris' [2] modeling study on the problem-solving capacity of autistic savants is a case in point. In the study, Norris focuses on the date-calculation task (i.e., to calculate the day of the week a given date fell on), which some autistic savants have been reported to perform flawlessly [3]. In an attempt to train a multi-layer neural network on the task, Norris failed to get a satisfactory level of generalization performance. Only by decomposing the task into three sub-tasks, and training the separate networks on each of the sub-tasks, the date-calculation task could be learned. Norris concluded that the date-calculation task is solvable (learnable) only when it is decomposed into intermediary steps using human assistance [2].

The date-calculation task is a very hard task for inductive learning algorithms, because it is a *statistically neutral* task: all conditional output probabilities on any input feature have chance values. Solving the task implies decomposing it, if possible, into subtasks that are not statistically neutral. The only suggested decomposition of the date-calculation task known to date involves explicit assistance

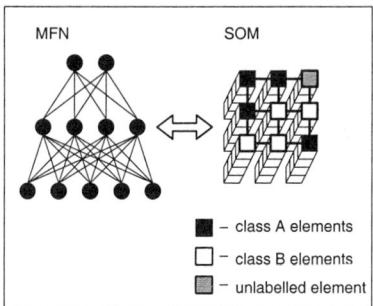

Figure 1: An example BP-SOM network.

from a human supervisor [2]. This paper challenges the decomposition assumption by showing that the date-calculation task can be learned in a single step with a appropriately constrained single hidden-layer neural network. In addition, another statistically neutral task, called the parity-n task (given an n-length bit string of 1's and 0's, calculate whether the number of 1's is even or odd) is investigated. In an experimental study by Dehaene, Bossini, and Giraux [4], it is claimed that humans decompose the parity-n task by first counting over the input string, and then perform the even/odd decision. In our study, parity-12 is shown to be learnable by a network with a single hidden layer.

2 BP-SOM

Below we give a brief characterization of the functioning of BP-SOM. For details we refer to [5]. The aim of the BP-SOM learning algorithm is to establish a cooperation between BP learning and SOM learning in order to find adequately constrained hidden-layer representations for learning classification tasks. To achieve this aim, the traditional MFN architecture [6] is combined with SOMs [7]: each hidden layer of the MFN is associated with one SOM (See Figure 1). During training of the weights in the MFN, the corresponding SOM is trained on the hidden-unit activation patterns.

After a number of training cycles of BP-SOM learning, each SOM develops a two-dimensional representation, that is translated into classification information, i.e., each SOM element is provided with a class label (one of the output classes of the task). For example, let the BP-SOM network displayed in Figure 1 be trained on a classification task which maps instances to either output class A or B. Three types of elements can be distinguished in the SOM: elements labelled with class A, elements labelled with class B, and unlabelled elements (no winning class could be found). The two-dimensional representation of the SOM is used as an addition to the standard BP learning rule [6]. Classification and reliability information from the SOMs is included when updating the connection weights of the MFN. The error of a hidden-layer vector is an accumulation of the error computed by the BP learning rule, and a SOM-error. The SOM-error is the difference between the hidden-unit activation vector and the vector of its best-matching element associated with the same class on the SOM.

An important effect of including SOM information in the error signals is that clusters of hidden-unit activation vectors of instances associated with the same class tend to become *increasingly similar* to each other. On top of this effect, individual hidden-unit activations tend to become more streamlined, and often end up having activations near one of a limited number of discrete values.

3 The date-calculation task

The first statistically neutral calculation task we consider is the date-calculation task: determining the day of the week on which a given date fell. (For instance, *October 24, 1997* fell on a Friday.) Solving the task requires an algorithmic approach that is typically hard for human calculators and requires one or more intermediate steps. It is generally assumed that the identity of these intermediate steps follows from the algorithmic solution, although variations exist in the steps as reportedly used by human experts [2]. We will show that such explicit abstraction is not needed, after reviewing the case for the necessity of "human assistance" in learning the task.

3.1 Date calculation with expert-based abstraction

Norris [2] attempted to model autistic savant date calculators using a multi-layer feedforward network (MFN) and the back-propagation learning rule [6]. He intended to build a model mimicking the behavior of the autistic savant without the need either to develop arithmetical skills or to encode explicit knowledge about regularities in the structure of dates. A standard multilayer network trained with backpropagation [6] was not able to solve the date-calculation task. Although the network was able to learn the examples used for training, it did not manage to generalize to novel date-day combinations. In a second attempt Norris split up the date-calculation task in three simpler subtasks and networks.

Using the three-stage learning strategy Norris obtained a nearly perfect performance on the training material and a performance of over 90% on the test material (errors are almost exclusively made on dates falling in January or February in leap years). He concludes with the observation that "The only reason that the network was able to learn so well was because it had some human assistance." [2, p.285]. In addition, Norris claims that "even if the [backpropagation] net did have the right number of layers there would be no way for the net to distribute its learning throughout the net such that each layer learned the appropriate step in computation." [2, p. 290].

3.2 Date calculation without expert-based abstraction

We demonstrate that with the BP-SOM learning rule, a single hidden-layer feedforward network can become a successful date calculator. Our experiment compares three types of learning: standard backpropagation learning (BP, [6]), backpropagation learning with weight decay (BPWD, [8]), and BP-SOM learning. Norris used BP learning in his experiment which leads to overfitting [2] (a considerably lower generalization accuracy on new material as compared to reproduction accuracy on training material); BPWD learning was included to avoid overfitting.

The parameter values for BP (including the number of hidden units for each task) were optimized by performing pilot experiments with BP. The optimal learning-rate and momentum values were 0.15 and 0.4, respectively. BP, BPWD, and BP-SOM were trained for a fixed number of cycles $m = 2000$. *Early stopping*, a common method to prevent overfitting, was used in all experiments with BP, BPWD, and BP-SOM [9].

In our experiments with BP-SOM, we used the same interval of dates as used by Norris, i.e., training and test dates ranged from *January 1, 1950* to *December 31, 1999*. We generated two training sets, each consisting of 3,653 randomly selected instances, i.e., one-fifth of all dates. We also generated two corresponding test sets and two validation sets (with 1,000 instances each) of new dates within the same 50-year period. In all our experiments, the training set, test set, and validation set

Table 1: Average generalization performances (plus standard deviation, after '±'; averaged over ten experiments) in terms of incorrectly-processed training and test instances, of BP, BPWD, and BP-SOM, trained on the date-calculation task and the parity-12 task.

Task	BP: % incorrect Train	BP: % incorrect Test	BPWD: % incorrect Train	BPWD: % incorrect Test	BP-SOM: % incorrect Train	BP-SOM: % incorrect Test
date calc.	20.8 ±5.4	28.8 ±7.8	1.5 ± 0.3	8.8 ±1.4	2.9 ±2.0	3.3 ±1.9
parity-12	14.1 ±18.8	27.4 ±16.4	21.6 ±24.2	22.4 ±18.3	5.9 ±10.2	6.2 ±10.7

had empty intersections. We partitioned the input into three fields, representing the day of the month (31 units), the month (12 units) and the year (50 units). The output is represented by 7 units, one for each day of the week. The MFN contained one hidden layer with 12 hidden units for BP, and 25 hidden units for BPWD and BP-SOM. The SOM of the BP-SOM network contained 12 × 12 elements. Each of the three learning types was tested on two different data sets. Five runs with different random weight initializations were performed on each set, yielding ten runs per learning type. The averaged classification errors on the test material are reported in Table 1.

From Table 1 it follows that the average classification error of BP is high: on test instances BP yields a classification error of 28.8%, while the classification error of BP on training instances is 20.8%. Compared to the classification error of BP, the classification errors on both training and test material of BPWD and BP-SOM are much lower. However, BPWD's generalization performance on the test material is considerably worse than its performance on the training material: a clear indication of overfitting. We note in passing that the results of BPWD contrast with Norris' [2] claim that BP is *unable* to learn the date-calculation task when it is not decomposed into subtasks. The inclusion of weight decay in BP is sufficient for a good approximation of the performance results of Norris' decomposed network.

The results in Table 1 also show that the performance of BP-SOM on test material is significantly better than that of BPWD ($t(19)=7.39$, $p<0.001$); BP-SOM has learned the date-calculation task at a level well beyond the average of human date calculators as reported by Norris [2]. In contrast with Norris' pre-structured network, BP-SOM does not rely on expert-based levels of abstraction for learning the date-calculation task.

4 The parity-12 task

The parity-n problem, starting from the XOR problem (parity-2), continues to be a relevant topic on the agenda of many neural network and machine learning researchers. Its definition is simple (determine whether there is an odd or even number of 1's in an n-length bit string of 1's and 0's), but established state-of-the-art algorithms such as C4.5 [10] and backpropagation [6] cannot learn it even with small n, i.e., backpropagation fails with $n \geq 4$ [11]. That is, these algorithms are unable to generalize from learning instances of a parity-n task to unseen new instances of the same task. As with date calculation, this is due to the statistical neutrality of the task. The solution of the problem must lie in having some comprehensive overview over *all* input values at an intermediary step before the odd/even decision is made. Indeed, humans appear to follow this strategy [4].

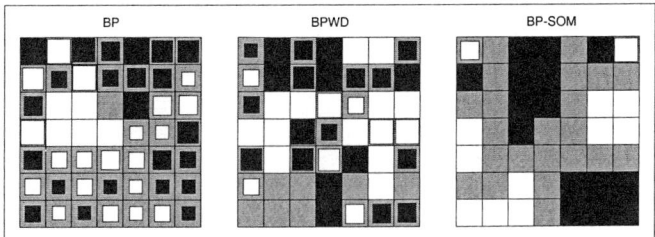

Figure 2: Graphic representation of a 7 × 7 SOM associated with a BP-trained MFN (left) and a BPWD-trained MFN (middle), and a 7 × 7 SOM associated with a BP-SOM network (right), all trained on the parity-12 task.

Analogous to our study of the date-calculation task presented in Section 3, we apply BP, BPWD, and BP-SOM to the parity-n task. We have selected n to be 12. The training set contained 1,000 different instances selected at random out of the set of 4,096 possible bit strings. The test set and the validation set contained 100 new instances each. The hidden layer of the MFN in all three algorithms contained 20 hidden units, and the SOM in BP-SOM contained 7 × 7 elements. The algorithms were run with 10 different random weight initializations. Table 1 displays the classification errors on training instances and test instances.

Analysis of the results shows that BP-SOM performs significantly better than BP and BPWD on test material (t(19)=3.42, p<0.01 and t(19)=2.42, p<0.05, respectively). (The average error of 6.2% made by BP-SOM stems from a single experiment out of the ten performing at chance level, and the remaining nine yielding about 1% error). BP-SOM is able to learn the parity-12 task quite accurately; BP and BPWD fail relatively, which is consistent with other findings [11].

As an additional analysis, we have investigated the differences in hidden unit activations after training with the three learning algorithms. To visualize the differences between the representations developed at the hidden layers of the MFNs trained with BP, BPWD, and BP-SOM, we also trained SOMs with the hidden layer activities of the trained BP and BPWD networks. The left part of Figure 2 visualizes the class labelling of the SOM attached to the BP-trained MFN after training; the middle part visualizes the SOM of the BPWD-trained MFN, and the right part displays the SOM of the BP-SOM network after training on the same material. The SOM of the BP-SOM network is much more organized and clustered than that of the SOMs corresponding with the BP-trained and BPWD-trained MFNs. The reliability values of the elements of all three SOMs are represented by the width of the black and white squares. It can be seen that the overall reliability and the degree of clusteredness of the SOM of the BP-SOM network is considerably higher than that of the SOM of the BP-trained and BPWD-trained MFNs.

5 How parity-12 is learned

Given the hardness of the task and the supposed necessity of expert guidance, and given BP-SOM's success in learning parity-12 in contrast, it is relevant to analyze what solution was found in the BP-SOM learning process. In this subsection we provide such an analysis, and show that the trained network performs an elegant checksum calculation at the hidden layer as the intermediary step.

All elements of SOMs of BP-SOM networks trained on the parity-12 task are either the prototype for training instances that are all labeled with the same class, or

Table 2: List of some training instances of the parity-12 task associated with SOM elements (1,1), (2,4), and (3,3) of a trained BP-SOM network.

SOM (1,1), class=even, reliability 1.0												
in1	in2	in3	in4	in5	in6	in7	in8	in9	in10	in11	in12	checksum
1	1	0	0	0	0	0	0	0	0	0	0	-2
0	0	1	0	0	0	1	0	1	1	0	0	-2
1	1	0	1	0	0	0	1	0	0	0	0	-2
. . .												
SOM (2,4), class=odd, reliability 1.0												
in1	in2	in3	in4	in5	in6	in7	in8	in9	in10	in11	in12	checksum
0	1	1	1	1	0	1	1	0	1	0	0	-1
1	1	1	0	1	1	1	0	1	1	0	1	-1
1	0	1	1	0	1	0	1	1	0	1	0	-1
. . .												
SOM (3,3), class=even, reliability 1.0												
in1	in2	in3	in4	in5	in6	in7	in8	in9	in10	in11	in12	checksum
0	0	1	1	0	0	1	1	0	1	0	1	0
1	1	1	1	1	0	1	0	0	0	1	1	0
1	0	1	1	1	1	0	1	1	0	0	1	0
. . .												
-	-	-	+	+	+	-	-	-	+	+	+	

prototype of no instances at all. Non-empty elements (the black and white squares in the right part of Figure 2) can thus be seen as containers of homogeneously-labeled subsets of the training set (i.e., fully reliable elements). The first step of our analysis consists of collecting, after training, for each non-empty SOM element all training instances clustered at that SOM element. As an illustration, Table 2 lists some training instances clustered at the SOM elements at coordinates (1,1), (2,4), and (3,3). At first sight the only common property of instances associated with the same SOM element is the class to which they belong; e.g., all instances of SOM element (1,1) are even, all instances of SOM element (2,4) are odd, and all instances of SOM element (3,3) are again even.

The second step of our analysis focuses on the sign of the weights of the connections between input and hidden units. Surprisingly, we find that the connections of each individual input unit to all hidden units have the same sign; each input unit can therefore be labeled with a sign marker (as displayed at the bottom of Table 2). This allows the clustering on the SOM to become interpretable. All weights from input unit 1, 2, 3, 7, 8, and 9 to all units of the hidden layer are negative, all weights from input unit 4, 5, 6, 10, 11, and 12 to all units of the hidden layer are positive. At the hidden layer, this information is gathered as if a *checksum* is computed; each SOM element contains instances that add up to an identical checksum. This can already be seen using only the sign information rather than the specific weights. For instance, all instances clustered at SOM element (1,1) lead to a checksum of -2 when a sum is taken of the product of all input values with all weight signs. Analogously, all instances of cluster (2,4) count up to -1 and the instances of cluster (3,3) to zero. The same regularity is present in the instances of the other SOM elements.

In sum, the BP-SOM solution to the parity-12 task can be interpreted as to transform it at the hidden layer into the mapping of different, approximately discrete, checksums to either class 'even' or 'odd'.

6 Conclusions

We have performed two learning experiments in which the BP-SOM learning algorithm was trained on the date-calculation task and on the parity-12 task. Both tasks are hard to learn because they are statistically neutral, but can be learned adequately and without expert guidance by the BP-SOM learning algorithm. The effect of the SOM part in BP-SOM (adequately constrained hidden-layer vectors, reliable clustering of vectors on the SOM, and streamlined hidden-unit activations) clearly contributes to this success.

From the results of the experiments on the date-calculation task, we conclude that Norris' claim that, without human assistance, a backpropagation net would never learn the date-calculation task is inaccurate. While BP with weight decay performs at Norris' target level of accuracy, BP-SOM performs even better. Apparently BP-SOM is able to distribute its learning throughout the net such that the two parts of the network (from input layer to hidden layer, and from hidden layer to output layer) perform the mapping with an appropriate intermediary step.

The parity-12 experiment exemplified that such a discovered intermediary step can be quite elegant; it consists of the computation of a checksum via the connection weights between the input and hidden layers. Unfortunately, a similar elegant simplicity was not found in the connection weights and SOM clustering of the date calculation task; future research will be aimed at developing more generic analyses for trained BP-SOM networks, so that automatically-discovered intermediary steps may be made understandably explicit.

References

[1] Newell, A. and Simon, H.A. (1972) *Human problem solving.* Engelwood Cliffs, NJ: Prentice-Hall.

[2] Norris, D. (1989). How to build a connectionist idiot (savant). *Cognition*, **35**, 277–291.

[3] Hill, A. L. (1975). An investigation of calendar calculating by an idiot savant. *American Journal of Psychiatry*, **132**, 557–560.

[4] Dehaene, P., Bossini, S., and Giraux, P. (1993). The mental representation of parity and numerical magnitude. *Journal of Experimental Psychology: General*, **122**, 371–396.

[5] Weijters, A., Van den Bosch, A., Van den Herik, H. J. (1997). Behavioural Aspects of Combining Backpropagation Learning and Self-organizing Maps. *Connection Science*, **9**, 235–252.

[6] Rumelhart, D. E., Hinton, G. E., and Williams, R. J. (1986). Learning internal representations by error propagation. In D. E. Rumelhart and J. L. McClelland (Eds.), *Parallel Distributed Processing: Explorations in the Microstructure of Cognition*, volume 1: Foundations (pp. 318–362). Cambridge, MA: The MIT Press.

[7] Kohonen, T. (1989). *Self-organisation and Associative Memory.* Berlin: Springer Verlag.

[8] Hinton, G. E. (1986). Learning distributed representations of concepts. In *Proceedings of the Eighth Annual Conference of the Cognitive Science Society*, 1–12. Hillsdale, NJ: Erlbaum.

[9] Prechelt, L. (1994). *Proben1: A set of neural network benchmark problems and benchmarking rules.* Technical Report 24/94, Fakultät für Informatik, Universität Karlsruhe, Germany.

[10] Quinlan, J. R. (1993). *C4.5: Programs for Machine Learning.* San Mateo, CA: Morgan Kaufmann.

[11] Thornton, C. (1996). Parity: the problem that won't go away. In G. McCalla (Ed.), *Proceeding of AI-96*, Toronto, Canada (pp. 362-374). Berlin: Springer Verlag.

A generative model for attractor dynamics

Richard S. Zemel
Department of Psychology
University of Arizona
Tucson, AZ 85721
zemel@u.arizona.edu

Michael C. Mozer
Department of Computer Science
University of Colorado
Boulder, CO 80309-0430
mozer@colorado.edu

Abstract

Attractor networks, which map an input space to a discrete output space, are useful for pattern completion. However, designing a net to have a given set of attractors is notoriously tricky; training procedures are CPU intensive and often produce spurious attractors and ill-conditioned attractor basins. These difficulties occur because each connection in the network participates in the encoding of multiple attractors. We describe an alternative formulation of attractor networks in which the encoding of knowledge is local, not distributed. Although localist attractor networks have similar dynamics to their distributed counterparts, they are much easier to work with and interpret. We propose a statistical formulation of localist attractor net dynamics, which yields a convergence proof and a mathematical interpretation of model parameters.

Attractor networks map an input space, usually continuous, to a sparse output space composed of a discrete set of alternatives. Attractor networks have a long history in neural network research.

Attractor networks are often used for *pattern completion*, which involves filling in missing, noisy, or incorrect features in an input pattern. The initial state of the attractor net is typically determined by the input pattern. Over time, the state is drawn to one of a predefined set of states—the *attractors*. Attractor net dynamics can be described by a state trajectory (Figure 1a). An attractor net is generally implemented by a set of visible units whose activity represents the instantaneous state, and optionally, a set of hidden units that assist in the computation. Attractor dynamics arise from interactions among the units. In most formulations of attractor nets,[2,3] the dynamics can be characterized by gradient descent in an energy landscape, allowing one to partition the output space into *attractor basins*. Instead of homogeneous attractor basins, it is often desirable to sculpt basins that depend on the recent history of the network and the arrangement of attractors in the space. In psychological models of human cognition, for example, *priming* is fundamental: after the model visits an attractor, it should be faster to fall into the same attractor in the near future, i.e., the attractor basin should be broadened.[1,6]

Another property of attractor nets is key to explaining behavioral data in psychological and neurobiological models: the *gang effect*, in which the strength of an attractor is influenced by other attractors in its neighborhood. Figure 1b illustrates the gang effect: the proximity of the two rightmost attractors creates a deeper attractor basin, so that if the input starts at the origin it will get pulled to the right.

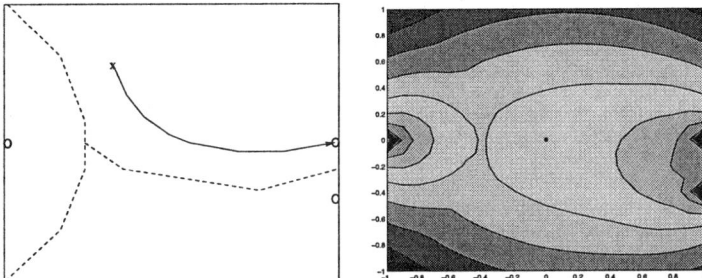

Figure 1: (a) A two-dimensional space can be carved into three regions (dashed lines) by an attractor net. The dynamics of the net cause an input pattern (the X) to be mapped to one of the attractors (the O's). The solid line shows the temporal trajectory of the network state. (b) the actual energy landscape for a localist attractor net as a function of $\hat{\mathbf{y}}$, when the input is fixed at the origin and there are three attractors, $\mathbf{w} = ((-1,0),(1,0),(1,-.4))$, with a uniform prior. The shapes of attractor basins are influenced by the proximity of attractors to one another (the *gang effect*). The origin of the space (depicted by a point) is equidistant from the attractor on the left and the attractor on the upper right, yet the origin clearly lies in the basin of the right attractors.

This effect is an emergent property of the distribution of attractors, and is the basis for interesting dynamics; it produces the mutually reinforcing or inhibitory influence of similar items in domains such as semantics,[9] memory,[10,12] and olfaction.[4]

Training an attractor net is notoriously tricky. Training procedures are CPU intensive and often produce spurious attractors and ill-conditioned attractor basins.[5,11] Indeed, we are aware of no existing procedure that can robustly translate an arbitrary specification of an attractor landscape into a set of weights. These difficulties are due to the fact that each connection participates in the specification of multiple attractors; thus, knowledge in the net is *distributed* over connections.

We describe an alternative attractor network model in which knowledge is *localized*, hence the name *localist attractor network*. The model has many virtues, including: a trivial procedure for wiring up the architecture given an attractor landscape; eliminating spurious attractors; achieving gang effects; providing a clear mathematical interpretation of the model parameters, which clarifies how the parameters control the qualitative behavior of the model (e.g., the magnitude of gang effects); and proofs of convergence and stability.

A localist attractor net consists of a set of n *state units* and m *attractor units*. Parameters associated with an attractor unit i encode the location of the attractor, denoted $\mathbf{w}_i$, and its "pull" or strength, denoted π_i, which influence the shape of the attractor basin. Its activity at time t, $q_i(t)$, reflects the normalized distance from the attractor center to the current state, $\mathbf{y}(t)$, weighted by the attractor strength:

$$q_i(t) = \frac{\pi_i g(\mathbf{y}(t), \mathbf{w}_i, \sigma(t))}{\sum_j \pi_j g(\mathbf{y}(t), \mathbf{w}_j, \sigma(t))} \quad (1)$$

$$g(\mathbf{y}, \mathbf{w}, \sigma) = \exp(-|\mathbf{y}-\mathbf{w}|^2/2\sigma^2) \quad (2)$$

Thus, the attractors form a layer of normalized radial-basis-function units.

The input to the net, $\mathcal{E}$, serves as the initial value of the state, and thereafter the state is pulled toward attractors in proportion to their activity. A straightforward expression of this behavior is:

$$\mathbf{y}(t+1) = \alpha(t)\mathcal{E} + (1-\alpha(t))\sum_i q_i(t)\mathbf{w}_i. \qquad (3)$$

where $\alpha(1) = 1$ on the first update and $\alpha(t) = 0$ for $t > 1$. More generally, however, one might want to gradually reduce α over time, allowing for a persistent effect of the external input on the asymptotic state. The variables $\sigma(t)$ and $\alpha(t)$ are not free parameters of the model, but can be derived from the formalism we present below.

The localist attractor net is motivated by a generative model of the input based on the attractor distribution, and the network dynamics corresponds to a search for a maximum likelihood interpretation of the observation. In the following section, we derive this result, and then present simulation studies of the architecture.

1 A MAXIMUM LIKELIHOOD FORMULATION

The starting point for the statistical formulation of a localist attractor network is a mixture of Gaussians model. A standard mixture of Gaussians consists of m Gaussian density functions in n dimensions. Each Gaussian is parameterized by a mean, a covariance matrix, and a mixture coefficient. The mixture model is *generative*, i.e., it is considered to have produced a set of observations. Each observation is generated by selecting a Gaussian based on the mixture coefficients and then stochastically selecting a point from the corresponding density function. The model parameters are adjusted to maximize the likelihood of a set of observations. The Expectation-Maximization (EM) algorithm provides an efficient procedure for estimating the parameters. The Expectation step calculates the posterior probability q_i of each Gaussian for each observation, and the Maximization step calculates the new parameters based on the previous values and the set of q_i.

The mixture of Gaussians model can provide an interpretation for a localist attractor network, in an unorthodox way. Each Gaussian corresponds to an attractor, and an observation corresponds to the state. Now, however, instead of fixing the observation and adjusting the Gaussians, we fix the Gaussians and adjust the observation. If there is a single observation, and $\alpha = 0$ and all Gaussians have uniform spread σ, then Equation 1 corresponds to the Expectation step, and Equation 3 to the Maximization step in this unusual mixture model.

Unfortunately, this simple characterization of the localist attractor network does not produce the desired behavior. Many situations produce partial solutions, in which the observation does not end up at an attractor. For example, if two unidimensional Gaussians overlap significantly, the most likely value for the observation is midway between them rather than at the mean of either Gaussian.

We therefore extend this mixture-of-Gaussians formulation to better characterize the localist attractor network. As in the simple model, each of the m attractors is a Gaussian generator, the mean of which is a location in the n-dimensional state space. The input to the net, $\mathcal{E}$, is considered to have been generated by a stochastic selection of one of the attractors, followed by the addition of zero-mean Gaussian noise with variance specified by the attractor. Given a particular observation $\mathcal{E}$, the an attractor's posterior probability is the normalized Gaussian probability of $\mathcal{E}$, weighted by its mixing proportion. This posterior distribution for the attractors corresponds to a distribution in state space that is a weighted sum of Gaussians.

We then consider the attractor network as encoding this distribution over states implied by the attractor posterior probabilities. At any one time, however, the attractor network can only represent a single position in state space, rather than the entire distribution over states. This restriction is appropriate when the state is an n-dimensional point represented by the pattern of activity over n state units. To accommodate this restriction, we change the standard mixture of Gaussians generative model by interjecting an intermediate level between the attractors and the observation. The first generative level consists of the discrete attractors, the second is the state space, and the third is the observation. Each observation is considered to have been generated by moving down this hierarchy:

1. select an attractor $\mathbf{x} = i$ from the set of attractors
2. select a state (i.e., a pattern of activity across the state units) based on the preferred location of that attractor: $\mathbf{y} = \mathbf{w}_i + \mathcal{N}_y$
3. select an observation $\mathbf{z} = \mathbf{y}\mathbf{G} + \mathcal{N}_z$

The observation $\mathbf{z}$ produced by a particular state $\mathbf{y}$ depends on the generative weight matrix $\mathbf{G}$. In the networks we consider here, the observation and state spaces are identical, so $\mathbf{G}$ is the identity matrix, but the formulation allows for $\mathbf{z}$ to lie in some other space. $\mathcal{N}_y$ and $\mathcal{N}_z$ describe the zero-mean, spherical Gaussian noise introduced at the two levels, with deviations σ_y and σ_z, respectively.

In comparison with the 2-level Gaussian mixture model described above, this 3-level model is more complicated but more standard: the observation $\mathcal{E}$ is preserved as stable data, and rather than the model manipulating the data here it can be viewed as iteratively manipulating an internal representation that fits the observation and attractor structure. The attractor dynamics correspond to an iterative search through state space to find the most likely single state that: (a) was generated by the mixture of Gaussian attractors, and (b) in turn generated the observation.

Under this model, one could fit an observation $\mathcal{E}$ by finding the posterior distribution over the hidden states (X and $\mathbf{Y}$) given the observation:

$$p(X = i, \mathbf{Y} = \mathbf{y} | \mathbf{Z} = \mathcal{E}) = \frac{p(\mathcal{E}|\mathbf{y}, i) p(\mathbf{y}, i)}{p(\mathcal{E})} = \frac{p(\mathcal{E}|\mathbf{y}) \pi_i p(\mathbf{y}|i)}{\int_\mathbf{y} p(\mathcal{E}|\mathbf{y}) \sum_i \pi_i p(\mathbf{y}|i) d\mathbf{y}} \quad (4)$$

where the conditional distributions are Gaussian: $p(\mathbf{Y} = \mathbf{y} | X = i) = \mathcal{G}(\mathbf{y} | \mathbf{w}_i, \sigma_y)$ and $p(\mathcal{E}|\mathbf{Y} = \mathbf{y}) = \mathcal{G}(\mathcal{E}|\mathbf{y}, \sigma_z)$. Evaluating the distribution in Equation 4 is tractable, because the partition function is a sum of a set of Gaussian integrals. Due to the restriction that the network cannot represent the entire distribution, we do not directly evaluate this distribution but instead adopt a mean-field approach, in which we approximate the posterior by another distribution $Q(X, \mathbf{Y}|\mathcal{E})$. Based on this approximation, the network dynamics can be seen as minimizing an objective function that describes an upper bound on the negative log probability of the observation given the model and mean-field parameters.

In this approach, one can choose any form of Q to estimate the posterior distribution, but a better estimate allows the network to approach a maximum likelihood solution.[13] We select a simple posterior: $Q(X, \mathbf{Y}) = q_i \delta(\mathbf{Y} = \hat{\mathbf{y}})$, where $q_i = Q(X = i)$ is the responsibility assigned to attractor i, and $\hat{\mathbf{y}}$ is the estimate of the state that accounts for the observation. The delta function over $\mathbf{Y}$ is motivated by the restriction that the explanation of an input consists of a single state.

Given this posterior distribution, the objective for the network is to minimize the free energy F, described here for a particular input example $\mathcal{E}$:

$$\begin{aligned} F(\mathbf{q}, \hat{\mathbf{y}} | \mathcal{E}) &= \sum_i \int Q(X = i, \mathbf{Y} = \mathbf{y}) \ln \frac{Q(X = i, \mathbf{Y} = \mathbf{y})}{P(\mathcal{E}, X = i, \mathbf{Y} = \mathbf{y})} d\mathbf{y} \\ &= \sum_i q_i \ln \frac{q_i}{\pi_i} - \ln p(\mathcal{E}|\hat{\mathbf{y}}) - \sum_i q_i \ln p(\hat{\mathbf{y}}|i) \end{aligned}$$

where π_i is the prior probability (mixture coefficient) associated with attractor i. These priors are parameters of the generative model, as are σ_y, σ_z, and **w**.

$$F(\mathbf{q},\hat{\mathbf{y}}|\mathcal{E}) = \sum_i q_i \ln \frac{q_i}{\pi_i} + \frac{1}{2\sigma_z^2}|\mathcal{E} - \hat{\mathbf{y}}|^2 + \frac{1}{2\sigma_y^2}\sum_i q_i|\hat{\mathbf{y}} - \mathbf{w}_i|^2 + n\ln(\sigma_y \sigma_z) \quad (5)$$

Given an observation, a good set of mean-field parameters can be determined by alternating between updating the generative parameters and the mean-field parameters. The update procedure is guaranteed to converge to a minimum of F, as long as the updates are done asynchronously and each update minimizes F with respect to a parameter.[8] The update equations for the mean-field parameters are:

$$\hat{\mathbf{y}} = \frac{\sigma_y^2 \mathcal{E} + \sigma_z^2 \sum_i q_i \mathbf{w}_i}{\sigma_y^2 + \sigma_z^2} \quad (6)$$

$$q_i = \frac{\pi_i p(\hat{\mathbf{y}}|i)}{\sum_j \pi_j p(\hat{\mathbf{y}}|j)} \quad (7)$$

In our simulations, we hold most of the parameters of the generative model constant, such as the priors π, the weights **w**, and the generative noise in the observation, σ_z. The only aspect that changes is the generative noise in the state, σ_y, which is a single parameter shared by all attractors:

$$\sigma_y^2 = \frac{1}{d}\sum_i q_i|\hat{\mathbf{y}} - \mathbf{w}_i|^2 \quad (8)$$

The updates of Equations 6-8 can be in any order. We typically initialize the state $\hat{\mathbf{y}}$ to $\mathcal{E}$ at time 0, and then cyclically update the q_i, σ_y, then $\hat{\mathbf{y}}$.

This generative model avoids the problem of spurious attractors described above for the standard Gaussian mixture model. Intuition into how the model avoids spurious attractors can be gained by inspecting the update equations. These equations effectively tie together two processes: moving $\hat{\mathbf{y}}$ closer to some $\mathbf{w}_i$ than the others, and increasing the corresponding responsibility q_i. As these two processes evolve together, they act to descrease the noise σ_y, which accentuates the pull of the attractor. Thus stable points that do not correspond to the attractors are rare.

2 SIMULATION STUDIES

To create an attractor net, we specify the parameters $(\pi_i, \mathbf{w}_i)$ associated with the attractors based on the desired structure of the energy landscape (e.g., Figure 1b). The only remaining free parameter, σ_z, plays an important role in determining how responsive the system is to the external input.

We have conducted several simulation studies to explore properties of localist attractor networks. Systematic investigations with a 200-dimensional state space and 200 attractors, randomly placed at corners of the 200-D hypercube, have demonstrated that spurious responses are exceedingly rare unless more than 85% of an input's features are distorted (Figure 2), and that manipulating parameters such as noise and prior probabilities has the predicted effects. We have also conducted studies of localist attractor networks in the domain of visual images of faces. These simulations have shown that gang effects arise when there is structure among the attractors. For example, when the attractor set consists of a single view of several different faces, and multiple views of one face, then an input that is a morphed face—a linear combination of one of the single-view faces and one view of the gang face—will end up in the gang attractor even when the initial weighting assigned to the gang face was less than 40%.

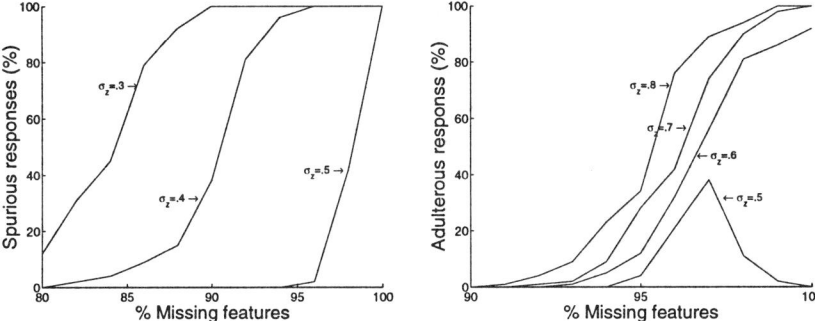

Figure 2: The input must be severely corrupted before the net makes *spurious* (final state not at an attractor) or *adulterous* (final state at a neighbor of the generating attractor) responses. (a) The percentage of spurious responses increases as σ_z is increased. (b) The percentage of adulterous responses increases as σ_z is decreased.

To test the architecture on a larger, structured problem, we modeled the domain of three-letter English words. The idea is to use the attractor network as a content addressable memory which might, for example, be queried to retrieve a word with P in the third position and any letter but A in the second position, a word such as HIP. The attractors consist of the 423 three-letter English words, from ACE to ZOO. The state space of the attractor network has one dimension for each of the 26 letters of the English alphabet in each of the 3 positions, for a total of 78 dimensions. We can refer to a given dimension by the letter and position it encodes, e.g., P_3 denotes the dimension corresponding to the letter P in the third position of the word. The attractors are at the corners of a $[-1, +1]^{78}$ hypercube. The attractor for a word such as HIP is located at the state having value -1 on all dimensions except for H_1, I_2, and P_3 which have value $+1$. The external input specifies a state that constrains the solution. For example, one might specify "P in the third position" by setting the external input to $+1$ on dimension P_3 and to -1 on dimensions α_3, for all letters α other than P. One might specify the absence of a constraint in a particular letter position, ρ, by setting the external input to 0 on dimensions α_ρ, for all letters α.

The network's task is to settle on a state corresponding to one of the words, given soft constraints on the letters. The interactive-activation model of word perception[7] performs a similar computation, and our implementation exhibits the key qualitative properties of their model. If the external input specifies a word, of course the attractor net will select that word. Interesting queries are those in which the external input underconstrains or overconstrains the solution. We illustrate with one example of the network's behavior, in which the external input specifies D_1, E_2, and G_3. Because DEG is a nonword, no attractor exists for that state. The closest attractors share two letters with DEG, e.g., PEG, BEG, DEN, and DOG. Figure 3 shows the effect of gangs on the selection of a response, BEG.

3 CONCLUSION

Localist attractor networks offer an attractive alternative to standard attractor networks, in that their dynamics are easy to control and adapt. We described a statistical formulation of a type of localist attractor, and showed that it provides a Lyapunov function for the system as well as a mathematical interpretation for the network parameters. The dynamics of this system are derived not from intuitive arguments but from this formal mathematical model. Simulation studies show that the architecture achieves gang effects, and spurious attractors are rare. This approach is inefficient if the attractors have compositional structure, but for many applications of pattern recognition or associative memory, the number of items

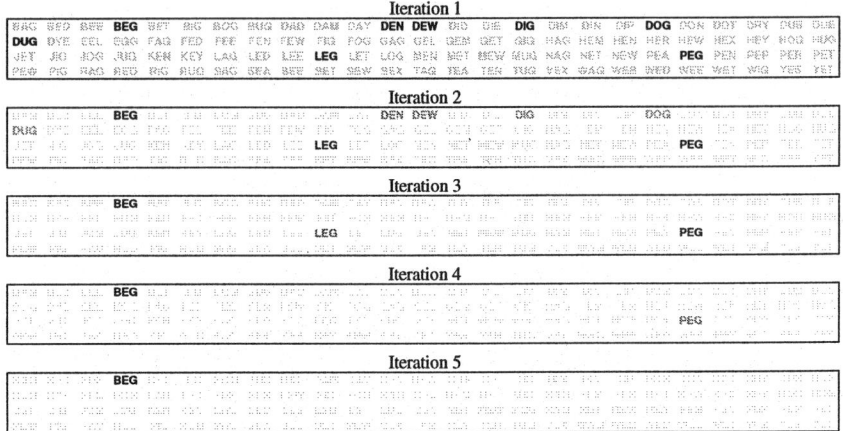

Figure 3: Simulation of the 3-letter word attractor network, queried with DEG. Each frame shows the relative activity of attractor units at various points in processing. Activity in each frame is normalized such that the most active unit is printed in black ink; the lighter the ink color, the less active the unit. Only attractor units sharing at least one letter with DEG are shown. The selection, BEG, is a product of a gang effect. The gangs in this example are formed by words sharing two letters. The most common word beginnings are PE– (7 instances) and DI– (6); the most common word endings are –AG (10) and –ET (10); the most common first-last pairings are B–G (5) and D–G (3). One of these gangs supports B_1, two support E_2, and three support G_3, hence BEG is selected.

being stored is small. The approach is especially useful in cases where attractor locations are known, and the key focus of the network is the mutual influence of the attractors, as in many cognitive modelling studies.

References

[1] Becker, S., Moscovitch, M., Behrmann, M., & Joordens, S. (1997). Long-term semantic priming: A computational account and empirical evidence. *Journal of Experimental Psychology: Learning, Memory, & Cognition, 23(5)*, 1059-1082.

[2] Golden, R. (1988). Probabilistic characterization of neural model computations. In D. Z. Anderson (Ed.), *Neural Information Processing Systems* (pp. 310-316). American Institute of Physics.

[3] Hopfield, J. J. (1982). Neural networks and physical systems with emergent collective computational abilities. *Proceedings of the National Academy of Sciences, 79*, 2554-2558.

[4] Kay, L.M., Lancaster, L.R., & Freeman W.J. (1996). Reafference and attractors in the olfactory system during odor recognition. *Int J Neural Systems, 7(4)*, 489-95.

[5] Mathis, D. (1997). *A computational theory of consciousness in cognition*. Unpublished Doctoral Dissertation. Boulder, CO: Department of Computer Science, University of Colorado.

[6] Mathis, D., & Mozer, M. C. (1996). Conscious and unconscious perception: A computational theory. In G. Cottrell (Ed.), *Proceedings of the Eighteenth Annual Conference of the Cognitive Science Society* (pp. 324-328). Erlbaum.

[7] McClelland, J. L. & Rumelhart, D. E. (1981). An interactive activation model of context effects in letter perception: Part I. An account of basic findings. *Psychological Review, 88*, 375-407.

[8] Neal, R. M. & Hinton, G. E. (1998). A view of the EM algorithm that justifies incremental, sparse, and other variants. In M. I. Jordan (Ed.), *Learning in Graphical Models*. Kluwer Academic Press.

[9] McRae, K., de Sa, V. R., & Seidenberg, M. S. (1997) On the nature and scope of featural representations of word meaning. *Journal of Experimental Psychology: General, 126(2)*, 99-130.

[10] Redish, A. D. & Touretzky, D. S. (1998). The role of the hippocampus in solving the Morris water maze. *Neural Computation, 10(1)*, 73-111.

[11] Rodrigues, N. C., & Fontanari, J. F. (1997). Multivalley structure of attractor neural networks. *Journal of Physics A (Mathematical and General), 30*, 7945-7951.

[12] Samsonovich, A. & McNaughton, B. L. (1997) Path integration and cognitive mapping in a continuous attractor neural network model. *Journal of Neuroscience, 17(15)*, 5900-5920.

[13] Saul, L.K., Jaakkola, T., & Jordan, M.I. (1996). Mean field theory for sigmoid belief networks. *Journal of AI Research, 4*, 61-76.

Part II
Neuroscience

Recurrent cortical competition: Strengthen or weaken?

Péter Adorján*, Lars Schwabe,
Christian Piepenbrock*, and Klaus Obermayer
Dept. of Comp. Sci., FR2-1, Technical University Berlin
Franklinstrasse 28/29 10587 Berlin, Germany
adorjan@epigenomics.com, {schwabe, oby}@cs.tu-berlin.de,
piepenbrock@epigenomics.com
http://www.ni.cs.tu-berlin.de

Abstract

We investigate the short term dynamics of the recurrent competition and neural activity in the primary visual cortex in terms of information processing and in the context of orientation selectivity. We propose that after stimulus onset, the strength of the recurrent excitation decreases due to fast synaptic depression. As a consequence, the network shifts from an initially highly nonlinear to a more linear operating regime. Sharp orientation tuning is established in the first highly competitive phase. In the second and less competitive phase, precise signaling of multiple orientations and long range modulation, e.g., by intra- and inter-areal connections becomes possible (surround effects). Thus the network first extracts the salient features from the stimulus, and then starts to process the details. We show that this signal processing strategy is optimal if the neurons have limited bandwidth and their objective is to transmit the maximum amount of information in any time interval beginning with the stimulus onset.

1 Introduction

In the last four decades there has been a vivid and highly polarized discussion about the role of recurrent competition in the primary visual cortex (V1) (see [12] for review). The main question is whether the recurrent excitation sharpens a weakly orientation tuned feed-forward input, or the feed-forward input is already sharply tuned, hence the massive recurrent circuitry has a different function. Strong cortical recurrency implements a highly nonlinear mapping of the feed-forward input, and obtains robust and sharply tuned cortical response even if only a weak or no feed-forward orientation bias is present [6, 11, 2]. However, such a competitive network in most cases fails to process multiple orientations within the classical receptive field and may signal spurious orientations [7]. This motivates the concept that the primary visual cortex maps an already sharply orientation tuned feed-forward input in a less competitive (more linear) fashion [9, 13].

Although these models for orientation selectivity in V1 vary on a wide scale, they have one common feature: each of them assumes that the synaptic strength is constant on the short time scale on which the network operates. Given the phenomenon of fast synaptic

---

*Current address: Epigenomics GmbH, Kastanienallee 24, D-10435 Berlin, Germany

dynamics this, however, does not need to be the case. Short term synaptic dynamics, e.g., of the recurrent excitatory synapses would allow a cortical network to operate in both—competitive and linear—regimes. We will show below (Section 2) that such a *dynamic cortical amplifier* network can establish sharp contrast invariant orientation tuning from a broadly tuned feed-forward input, while it is still able to respond correctly to multiple orientations.

We then show (Section 3) that decreasing the recurrent competition with time naturally follows from functional considerations, i.e. from the requirement that the mutual information between stimuli and representations is maximal for any time interval beginning with stimulus onset. We consider a free-viewing scenario, where the cortical layer represents a series of static images that are flashed onto the retina for a fixation period ($\Delta T = 200 - 300$ ms) between saccades. We also assume that the spike count in increasing time windows after stimulus onset carries the information. The key observations are that the signal-to-noise ratio of the cortical representation increases with time (because more spikes are available) and that the optimal strength of the recurrent connections (w.r.t. information transfer) decreases with the decreasing output noise. Consequently the model predicts that the information content per spike (or the SNR for a *fixed sliding* time window) decreases with time for a flashed static stimulus in accordance with recent experimental studies. The neural system thus adapts to its own internal changes by modifying its coding strategy, a phenomenon which one may refer to as *"dynamic coding"*.

2 Cortical amplifier with fast synaptic plasticity

To investigate our first hypothesis, we set up a model for an orientation-hypercolumn in the primary visual cortex with similar structure and parameters as in [7]. The important novel feature of our model is that fast synaptic depression is present at the recurrent excitatory connections. Neurons in the cortical layer receive orientation-tuned feed-forward input from the LGN and they are connected via a Mexican-hat shaped recurrent kernel in orientation space. In addition, the recurrent and feed-forward excitatory synapses exhibit fast depression due to the activity dependent depletion of the synaptic transmitter [1, 14]. We compare the response of the cortical amplifier models with and without fast synaptic plasticity at the recurrent excitatory connections to single and multiple bars within the classical receptive field.

The membrane potential $V(\theta, t)$ of a cortical cell tuned to an orientation θ decreases due to the leakage and the recurrent inhibition, and increases due to the recurrent excitation

$$\tau \frac{\partial}{\partial t} V(\theta, t) + V(\theta, t) = I^{\text{LGN}}(\theta, t) + I^{\text{exc}}(\theta, t) - I^{\text{inh}}(\theta, t), \tag{1}$$

where $\tau = 15$ ms is the membrane time constant and $I^{\text{LGN}}(\theta, t)$ is the input received from the LGN. The recurrent excitatory and inhibitory cortical inputs are given by

$$I^{\alpha}(\theta, t) = \int_{-\frac{\pi}{2}}^{+\frac{\pi}{2}} J^{\alpha}(\theta, \theta', t) \exp\left(-\frac{\Delta(\theta', \theta)^2}{2\sigma_\alpha^2}\right) f(\theta', t) \, d\theta' \tag{2}$$

where $\Delta(\theta', \theta)$ is a π periodic circular difference between the preferred orientations, $J^{\alpha}(\theta, \theta', t)$ are the excitatory and inhibitory connection strengths (with $\alpha \in \{\text{exc}, \text{inh}\}$, $J^{\text{exc}}_{\text{max}} = 0.2$ mV/Hz and $J^{\text{inh}}_{\text{max}} = 0.8$ mV/Hz), and f is the presynaptic firing rate. The excitatory synaptic efficacy J^{exc} is time dependent due to the fast synaptic depression, while the efficacy of inhibitory synapses J^{inh} is assumed to be constant. The recurrent excitation is sharply tuned $\sigma_{\text{exc}} = 7.5°$, while the inhibition has broad tuning $\sigma_{\text{inh}} = 90°$. The mapping from the membrane potential to firing rate is approximated by a linear function with a threshold at 0 ($f(\theta) = \beta \max(0, V(\theta))$, $\beta = 15$Hz/mV). Gaussian-noise with variances

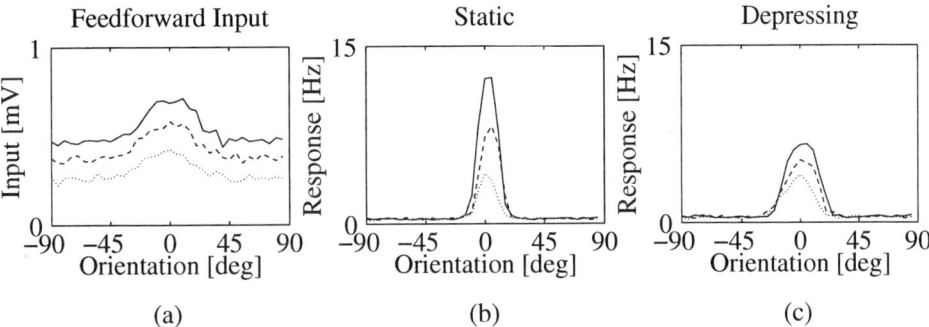

Figure 1: The feed-forward input (a), and the response of the cortical amplifier model with static recurrent synaptic strength (b), and a network with fast synaptic depression (c) if the stimulus is single bar with different stimulus contrasts (40%dotted; 60%dashed; 80%solid line). The cortical response is averaged over the first 100 ms after stimulus onset.

of 6 Hz and 1.6 Hz is added to the input intensities and to the output of cortical neurons. The orientation tuning curves of the feed-forward input I^{LGN} are Gaussians ($\sigma_{\mathrm{LGN}} = 18°$) resting on a strong additive orientation independent component which would correspond to a geniculo-cortical connectivity pattern with an approximate aspect ratio of 1:2. Both, the orientation dependent and independent components increase with contrast. Considering a free-viewing scenario where the environment is scanned by saccading around and fixating for short periods of $200-300$ ms we model stationary stimuli present for 300 ms. The stimuli are one or more bars with different orientations.

Feed-forward and recurrent excitatory synapses exhibit fast depression. Fast synaptic depression is modeled by the dynamics of the expected synaptic transmitter or "resource" $\bar{R}(t)$ for each synapse. The amount of the available transmitter decreases proportionally to the release probability p and to the presynaptic firing rate f, and it recovers exponentially ($\tau_{\mathrm{rec}}^{\mathrm{LGN}} = 120$ ms, $\tau_{\mathrm{rec}}^{\mathrm{Ctx}} = 850$ ms, $p^{\mathrm{LGN}} = 0.35$ and $p^{\mathrm{Ctx}} = 0.55$),

$$\frac{d}{dt}\bar{R}(t) = \frac{1 - \bar{R}(t)}{\tau_{\mathrm{rec}}} - f(t)p(t)\bar{R}(t) = -\frac{\bar{R}(t)}{\tau_{\mathrm{eff}}(f(t), p(t))} + \frac{1}{\tau_{\mathrm{rec}}}. \quad (3)$$

The change of the membrane potential on the postsynaptic cell at time t is proportional to the released transmitter $pR(t)$. The excitatory connectivity strength between neurons tuned to orientations θ and θ' is expressed as $J^{\mathrm{exc}}(\theta, \theta', t) = J_{\mathrm{max}}^{\mathrm{exc}} p R_{\theta\theta'}(t)$. Similarly this applies to the feed-forward synapses. Fast synaptic plasticity at the feed-forward synapses has been investigated in more detail in previous studies [3, 4].

In the following, we compare the predictions of the cortical amplifier model with and without fast synaptic depression at the recurrent excitatory connections. In both cases fast synaptic depression is present at the feed-forward connections limiting the duration of the effective feed-forward input to $200-400$ ms. Figure 1 shows the orientation tuning curves at different stimulus contrasts. The feed-forward input is noisy and broadly tuned (Fig. 1a). Both models exhibit contrast invariant tuning (Fig. 1b, c). If fast synaptic depression is present at the recurrent excitation, the cortical network sharpens the broadly tuned feed-forward input in the initial response phase. Once sharply tuned input is established, the tuning width does not change, only the response amplitude decreases in time.

The predictions of the two models differ substantially if multiple orientations are present (Fig. 2). At first, we test the cortical response to two bars separated by $60°$ with different intensities (Figs. 2a, b). If the recurrent synaptic weights are static and strong enough (Fig. 2a), then only one orientation is signaled. The cortical network selects the orientation

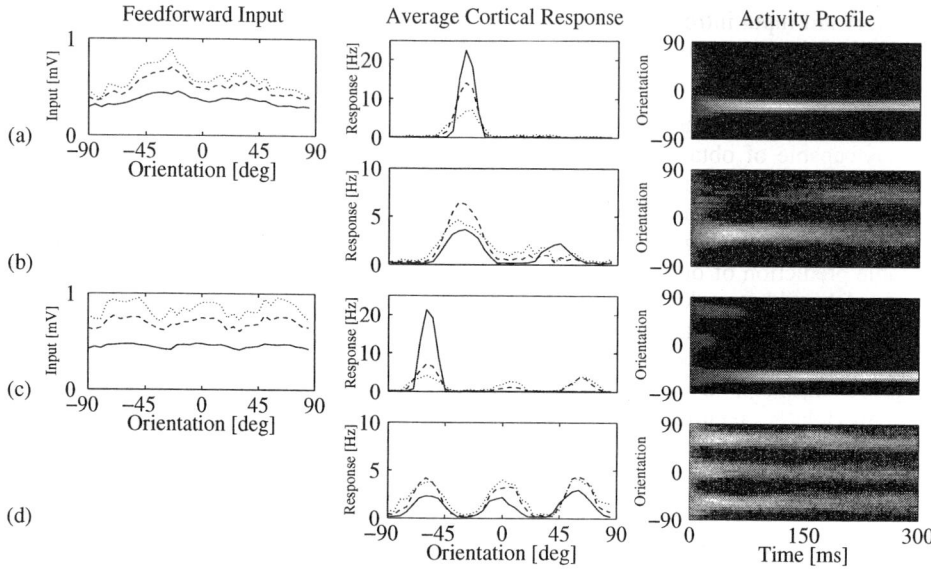

Figure 2: The response of the cortical amplifier model with static (a,c) and fast depressing recurrent synapses (b, d). In both models the feed-forward synapses are fast depressing. In the left column the feed-forward input is shown, that is same for both models. Two types of stimuli were applied. The first stimulus consists of a stronger ($\alpha = -30°$) and a weaker bar ($\alpha = +30°$) (a, b); the second stimulus consists of three equal intensity bars with orientations that are separated by $60°$ (c, d). In the middle column the cortical response is shown averaged for different time windows ([0..30] dotted; [0..80] dashed; [200..300] solid line). In the right column the cortical activity profile is plotted as a function of time. Gray values indicate the activity with bright denoting high activities.

with the highest amplitude in a winner-take-all fashion. In contrast, if synaptic depression is present at the recurrent excitatory synapses, both bars are signaled in parallel (at low release probability, Fig. 2b) or after each other (high release probability, data not shown). First, those cells fire which are tuned to the orientation of the bar with the stronger intensity, and a sharply tuned response emerges at a single orientation—the network operates in a winner-take-all regime. The synapses of these highly active cells then become strongly depressed and cortical competition decreases. As the network is shifted to a more linear operation regime, the second orientation is signaled too. Note that this phenomenon—together with the observed contrast invariant tuning—cannot be reproduced by simply decreasing the static synaptic weights in the cortical amplifier model. The recurrent synaptic efficacy changes inhomogeneously in the network depending on the activity. Only the synapses of the highly active cells depress strongly, and therefore a sharply tuned response can be evoked by a bar with weak intensity. Fast synaptic depression thus behaves as a local self-regulation that modulates competition with a certain delay. This delay, and therefore the delay of the rise of the response to the second bar depends on the effective time constant $\tau_{\text{eff}}(f(t), p) = \tau_{\text{rec}}/(1 + pf(t)\tau_{\text{rec}})$ of the synaptic depression at the recurrent connections. If the depression becomes faster due to an increase in the release probability p, then the delay decreases. The delay also scales with the difference between the bar intensities. The closer to each other they are, the shorter the delay will be.

In Figs. 2c, d the cortical response to three bars with equal intensities is presented. Cells tuned to the presented three orientations respond in parallel if fast synaptic depression at the recurrent excitation is present (Figs. 2d). The cortical network with strong *static* recurrent synapses again fails to signal faithfully its feed-forward input. Additive noise on the feed-forward input introduces a slight symmetry breaking and the network with static recurrent weights responds strongly at the orientation of only one of the presented bars (Fig. 2c).

In summary, our simulations revealed that a recurrent network with fast synaptic depression is capable of obtaining robust sharpening of its feed-forward input and it also responds correctly to multiple orientations. Note that other local activity dependent adaptation mechanisms, such as slow potassium current, would have similar effects as the synaptic depression on the highly orientation specific excitatory connections. An experimentally testable prediction of our model is that the response to a flashed bar with lower contrast can be delayed by masking it with a second bar with higher contrast (Fig. 2b, right). We also suggest that long range integration from outside of the classical receptive field could emerge with a similar delay. In the initial phase of the cortical response, strong local features are amplified. In the longer, second phase, recurrent competition decreases and then weak modulatory recurrent or feed-forward input has a stronger relative effect. In the following, we investigate whether this strategy is favorable from the point of view of cortical encoding.

3 Dynamic coding

In the previous section we have proposed that during cortical processing a highly nonlinear phase is followed by a more linear mode if we consider a short stimulus presentation or a fixation period. The simulations demonstrated that unless the recurrent competition is modulated in time, the network fails to account for more than one feature in its input. From a strictly functional point of view the question arises, why not to use weak recurrent competition during the whole processing period. We investigate this problem in an abstract signal-encoder framework

$$\vec{y} = g(\vec{x}) + \eta , \qquad (4)$$

where $\vec{x}$ is the input to the "cortical network", $g(\vec{x})$ is a nonlinear mapping and—for the sake of simplicity—η is additive Gaussian noise. Naturally, in a real recurrent network output noise becomes input noise because of the feedback. Here we use the simplifying assumption that only output noise is present on the transformed input signal (input noise would lead to different predictions that should be further investigated). Output noise can be interpreted as a noisy channel that projects out from, e.g., the primary visual cortex. The nonlinear transformation $g(\vec{x})$ here is considered as a functional description of a cortical amplifier network without analyzing how actually it is "implemented". Considering orientation selectivity, the signal $\vec{x}$ can be interpreted as a vector of intensities (or contrasts) of edges with different orientations. Edges which are not present have zero intensity. The coding capacity of a realistic neural network is limited. Among several other noise sources, this limitation could arise from imprecision in spike timing and a constraint on the maximal or average firing rate.

The input-output mapping $g(\vec{x})$ of a cortical amplifier network is approximated with the soft-max function

$$g_i(\vec{x}) = \frac{\exp(\beta x_i)}{\sum_i \exp(\beta x_i)} . \qquad (5)$$

The β parameter can be interpreted as the level of recurrent competition. As $\beta \to 0$ the network operates in a more linear mode, while $\beta \to \infty$ puts it into a highly nonlinear winner-take-all mode. In all cases the average activity in the network is constrained which has been suggested to minimize metabolic costs [5]. Let us consider a factorizing input distribution,

$$p(\vec{x}) = \frac{1}{Z} \Pi_i \exp\left(\frac{-x_i^\alpha}{\xi}\right) \quad \text{for } x \geq 0 , \qquad (6)$$

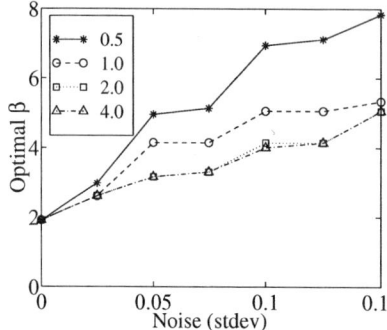

Figure 3: The optimal competition parameter β as a function of the standard deviation of the Gaussian output noise η. The optimal β is calculated for highly super-Gaussian, Gaussian, and sub-Gaussian stimulus densities. The sparsity parameter α is indicated in the legend.

where the exponent α determines the sparsity of the probability density function, Z is a normalizing constant, and ξ determines the variance. If $\alpha = 2$, the input density is the positive half of a multivariate Gaussian distribution. With $\alpha > 2$ the signal distribution becomes sub-Gaussian, and with $\alpha < 2$ it becomes super-Gaussian.

For optimal processing in *time* one needs to gain the maximal information about the signal for any increasing time window. Let us assume that the stimulus is static and it is presented for a limited time. As time goes ahead after stimulus onset, the time window for the encoding and the read-out mechanism increases. During a longer period more samples of the noisy network output are available, and thus the output noise level decreases with time. We suggest that the optimal competition parameter β^{opt}—at which the mutual information between input $\vec{x}$ and output $\vec{y}$ (Eq. 4) is maximized—depends on the noise level. As the noise decreases with time, β or the recurrent cortical competition should also change during cortical processing. To demonstrate this idea, the mutual information is calculated numerically for a three-dimensional state space.

One might expect that at higher noise levels the highest information transfer can be obtained if the typical and salient features are strongly amplified. Note that this is only true if the standard deviation of the noise scales sub-linearly with activity, which is true for an additive noise process as well as Poisson firing. As noise decreases (e.g., with increasing the time window for estimation), the level of competition should decrease distributing the available resources (e.g., spikes) among more units and letting the network respond to finer details at the input. Investigating the level of optimal competition β as a function of the standard deviation of the output noise (Fig. 3) this intuition is indeed justified. The optimal β scales with the standard deviation of the additive noise process. Comparing signal distributions with the same variance but with different sparsity exponents α, we find that the sparser the signal distribution is, the higher the optimal competition becomes, because multiple features are unlikely to be present at the same time if the input distribution is sparse. By enforcing competition, the optimal encoding strategy also generates an activity distribution where only few units fire for a presented stimulus. Since edges with different orientations form a sparse distributed representation of natural scenes [8], our work suggests that a strongly competitive visual cortical network could achieve a better performance on our visual environment than a simple linear network would do.

We can now interpret our simulation results presented in the Section 2 from a functional point of view and give a prediction for the dynamics of the recurrent cortical competition. Noting that the output noise is decreasing with increasing time-window for encoding, the cortical competition should also decrease following a similar trajectory as presented in Fig. 3. If competition is low and static, then the cumulative mutual information between input and output would converge only slowly towards the overall information that is available in the stimulus. If the competition is high during the whole observation period, then after a fast rise the cumulative mutual information would saturate well below the possible maximum. If the level of competition is dynamic, and it decreases from an initially highly competitive state, then the network obtains maximal information transfer in time.

One may argue that the *valuable* information about the signals mainly depends on the interest of the observer. Considering an encoding system for one variable it has been suggested that in a highly attentive state the recurrent competition increases [10]. In the view of our results we would refine this statement by suggesting that competition increases or decreases depending on the level of visual detail the observer pays attention to. Whenever representation of small details is also required, reducing competition is the optimal strategy given enough bandwidth.

In summary, using a detailed model for an orientation hypercolumn in V1 we have demonstrated that sharp contrast invariant tuning and faithful representation of multiple features can be achieved by a recurrent network if the recurrent competition decreases in time after stimulus onset. The model predicts that the cortical response to weak details in the stimulus emerges with a delay if a second stronger feature is also present. The modulation from, e.g., outside of the classical receptive field also has a delayed effect on cortical activity. Our study within an abstract framework revealed that weakening the recurrent cortical competition on a fast time scale is functionally advantageous, because a maximal amount of information can be transmitted in any time window after stimulus onset.

Acknowledgments Supported by the Boehringer Ingelheim Fonds (C. P.), by the German Science Foundation (DFG grant GK 120-2) and by Wellcome Trust 050080/Z/97.

References

[1] L. F. Abbott, J. A. Varela, K. Sen, and S. B. Nelson. Synaptic depression and cortical gain control. *Science*, 275:220–224, 1997.

[2] P. Adorján, J.B. Levitt, J.S. Lund, and K. Obermayer. A model for the intracortical origin of orientation preference and tuning in macaque striate cortex. *Vis. Neurosci.*, 16:303–318, 1999.

[3] P. Adorján, C. Piepenbrock, and K. Obermayer. Contrast adaptation and infomax in visual cortical neurons. *Rev. Neurosci.*, 10:181–200, 1999. ftp://ftp.cs.tu-berlin.de/pub/local/ni/papers/adp99-contrast.ps.gz.

[4] Ö. B. Artun, H. Z. Shouval, and L. N. Cooper. The effect of dynamic synapses on spatiotemporal receptive fields in visual cortex. *Proc. Natl. Acad. Sci.*, 95:11999–12003, 1998.

[5] R. Baddeley. An efficient code in V1? *Nature*, 381:560–561, 1996.

[6] R. Ben-Yishai, R. Lev Bar-Or, and H. Sompolinsky. Theory of orientation tuning in visual cortex. *Proc. Natl. Acad. Sci.*, 92:3844–3848, 1995.

[7] M. Carandini and D. L. Ringach. Predictions of a recurrent model of orientation selectivity. *Vision Res.*, 37:3061–3071, 1997.

[8] D. J. Field. What is the goal of sensory coding. *Neural Comput.*, 6:559–601, 1994.

[9] D. H. Hubel and T. N. Wiesel. Receptive fields, binocular interaction and functional architecture in cat's visual cortex. *J. Physiol.*, 165:559–568, 1962.

[10] D. K. Lee, L. Itti, C. Kock, and J. Braun. Attention activates winner-take-all competition among visual filters. *Nat. Neurosci.*, 2:375–381, 1999.

[11] D. C. Somers, S. B. Nelson, and M. Sur. An emergent model of orientation selectivity in cat visual cortical simple cells. *J. Neurosci.*, 15:5448–65, 1995.

[12] H. Sompolinsky and R. Shapley. New perspectives on the mechanisms for orientation selectivity. *Curr. Op. in Neurobiol.*, 7:514–522, 1997.

[13] T. W. Troyer, A. E. Krukowski, N. J. Priebe, and K. D. Miller. Contrast-invariant orientation tuning in visual cortex: Feedforward tuning and correlation-based intracortical connectivity. *J. Neurosci.*, 18:5908–5927, 1998.

[14] M. V. Tsodyks and H. Markram. The neural code between neocortical pyramidal neurons depends on neurotransmitter release probability. *Proc. Natl. Acad. Sci.*, 94:719–723, 1997.

Effective Learning Requires Neuronal Remodeling of Hebbian Synapses

Gal Chechik   Isaac Meilijson   Eytan Ruppin
School of Mathematical Sciences
Tel-Aviv University Tel Aviv, Israel
ggal@math.tau.ac.il   isaco@math.tau.ac.il   ruppin@math.tau.ac.il

Abstract

This paper revisits the classical neuroscience paradigm of Hebbian learning. We find that a necessary requirement for effective associative memory learning is that the efficacies of the incoming synapses should be uncorrelated. This requirement is difficult to achieve in a robust manner by Hebbian synaptic learning, since it depends on network level information. Effective learning can yet be obtained by a neuronal process that maintains a zero sum of the incoming synaptic efficacies. This normalization drastically improves the memory capacity of associative networks, from an essentially bounded capacity to one that linearly scales with the network's size. It also enables the effective storage of patterns with heterogeneous coding levels in a single network. Such neuronal normalization can be successfully carried out by activity-dependent homeostasis of the neuron's synaptic efficacies, which was recently observed in cortical tissue. Thus, our findings strongly suggest that effective associative learning with Hebbian synapses alone is biologically implausible and that Hebbian synapses must be continuously remodeled by neuronally-driven regulatory processes in the brain.

1 Introduction

Synapse-specific changes in synaptic efficacies, carried out by long-term potentiation (LTP) and depression (LTD) are thought to underlie cortical self-organization and learning in the brain. In accordance with the Hebbian paradigm, LTP and LTD modify synaptic efficacies as a function of the firing of pre and post synaptic neurons. This paper revisits the Hebbian paradigm showing that **synaptic learning alone cannot provide effective associative learning in a biologically plausible manner, and must be complemented with neuronally-driven synaptic remodeling.**

The importance of neuronally driven normalization processes has already been demonstrated in the context of self-organization of cortical maps [1, 2] and in continuous unsupervised learning as in principal-component-analysis networks [3]. In these scenarios normalization is necessary to prevent the excessive growth of synaptic efficacies that occurs when learning and neuronal activity are strongly coupled. In contradistinction, this paper focuses on associative memory learning where this excessive synaptic runaway growth is mild [4], and shows that even in this simple learning paradigm, normalization processes are essential. Moreover, while numerous normalization procedures can prevent synaptic runaway, our analysis shows that only a specific neuronally-driven correction procedure that preserves the total sum of synaptic efficacies leads to effective associative memory storage.

2 Effective Synaptic Learning rules

We study the computational aspects of associative learning in a model of a low-activity associative memory network with binary firing $\{0,1\}$ neurons. M uncorrelated memory patterns $\{\xi^\mu\}_{\mu=1}^M$ with coding level p (fraction of firing neurons) are stored in an N neurons network. The ith neuron updates its state X_i^t at time t by

$$X_i^{t+1} = \theta(f_i^t), \quad f_i^t = \frac{1}{N}\sum_{j=1}^{N} W_{ij} X_j^t - T, \quad \theta(f) = \frac{1 + sign(f)}{2}, \quad (1)$$

where f_i is its input field (postsynaptic potential) and T is its firing threshold. The synaptic weight W_{ij} between the jth (presynaptic) and ith (postsynaptic) neurons is determined by a general additive synaptic learning rule depending on the neurons' activity in each of the M stored memory patterns ξ^η

$$W_{ij} = \sum_{\eta=1}^{M} A(\xi_i^\eta, \xi_j^\eta), \quad A(\xi_i, \xi_j) = \text{postsynaptic}(\xi_i) \begin{array}{c} \text{presynaptic } (\xi_j) \\ \begin{array}{|c||c|c|} \hline & 1 & 0 \\ \hline\hline 1 & \alpha & \beta \\ \hline 0 & \gamma & \delta \\ \hline \end{array} \end{array}, \quad (2)$$

where the synaptic learning matrix $A(\xi_i^\eta, \xi_j^\eta)$ governs the incremental modifications to a synapse as a function of the firing of the presynaptic (column) and postsynaptic (row) neurons. In conventional biological terms, α denotes an increment following a long-term potentiation (LTP) event, β denotes heterosynaptic long-term depression (LTD), and γ a homosynaptic LTD event.

The parameters $\alpha, \beta, \gamma, \delta$ define a four dimensional space in which all linear additive Hebbian learning rules reside. However, in order to visualize this space, one may represent these Hebbian learning rules in a reduced, two-dimensional space utilizing a scaling invariance constraint and the requirement that the synaptic matrix should have a zero mean (otherwise the synaptic values diverge, the noise overshadows the signal term and no retrieval is possible [5]).

Figure 1A plots the memory capacity of the network as a function of the two free parameters α and β. It reveals that considerable memory storage may be obtained only along an essentially one dimensional curve, naturally raising the possibility of identifying an additional constraint on the relations between $(\alpha, \beta, \gamma, \delta)$. Such a constraint is revealed by a signal-to-noise analysis of the neuronal input field f_i during retrieval

$$\frac{Signal}{Noise} = \frac{E(f_i|\xi_i = 1) - E(f_i|\xi_i = 0)}{\sqrt{Var(f_i)}} \propto \frac{\sqrt{N}}{\sqrt{Var[W_{ij}] + NpCOV[W_{ij}, W_{ik}]}} \quad (3)$$

$$= \frac{\sqrt{N/M}}{\sqrt{Var[A(\xi_i, \xi_j)] + NpCOV[A(\xi_i, \xi_j), A(\xi_i, \xi_k)]}},$$

where averages are taken over the ensemble of stored memory patterns.

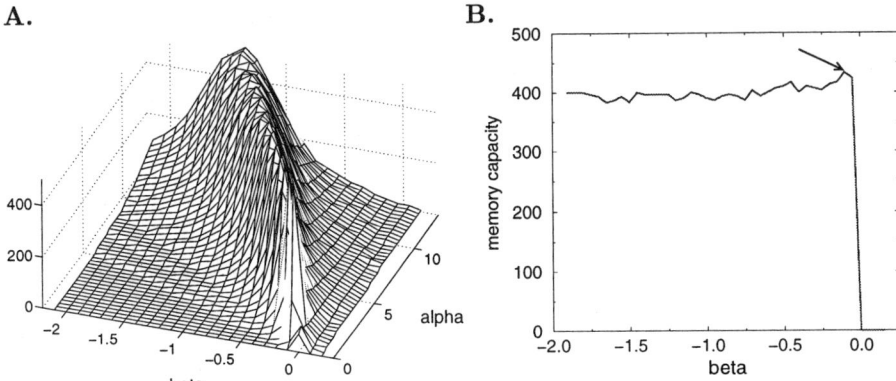

Figure 1: **A.** Memory capacity of a 1000-neurons network with $p = 0.05$ for different values of α and β as obtained in computer simulations. Capacity is defined as the maximal number of memories that can be retrieved with overlap bigger than 0.95 when presented with a degraded input cue with overlap 0.8. The overlap serves to measure retrieval acuity and is defined as $m^\eta = \frac{1}{p(1-p)N} \sum_{j=1}^{N} (\xi_j^\eta - p) X_j$. **B.** Memory capacity of the effective learning rules: The peak values on the ridge of Figure A, are displayed by tracing their projection on the β coordinate. The optimal learning rule $A(\xi_i, \xi_j) = (\xi_i - p)(\xi_j - p)$ [5], marked with an arrow, performs only slightly better than other effective learning rules.

As evident from equation (3) and already pointed out by [6], when the *postsynaptic covariance* $COV[A(\xi_i, \xi_j), A(\xi_i, \xi_k)]$ (determining the covariance between the incoming synapses of the postsynaptic neuron) is positive, the network's memory capacity is bounded, i.e., it does not scale with the network size. As the postsynaptic covariance is non negative, effective learning rules that obtain linear scaling of memory capacity as a function of the network's size require a vanishing postsynaptic covariance. Intuitively, when the synaptic weights are correlated, adding any new synapse contributes only little new information, thus limiting the number of beneficial synapses that help the neuron estimate whether it should fire or not. Figure 1B depicts the memory capacity of the effective synaptic learning rules which lie on the essentially one-dimensional ridge observed in Figure 1A. It shows that all these effective rules are only slightly inferior to the optimal synaptic learning rule calculated previously by [5, 6], which maximizes memory capacity.

The vanishing covariance constraint on effective learning rules implies a new requirement concerning the balance between synaptic depression and facilitation: $\beta = \frac{-p}{1-p} \alpha$. Thus, effective memory storage requires a delicate balance between LTP (x_P) and heterosynaptic depression (β), and is strongly dependent on the coding level p which is a global property of the network. It is thus difficult to see how effective rules can be implemented at the synaptic level. Moreover, as shown in Figure 1A, Hebbian learning rules lack robustness as small perturbations from the effective rules may result in large decrease in memory capacity.

Furthermore, these problems cannot be circumvented by introducing a nonlinear Hebbian learning rule of the form $W_{ij} = g\left(\sum_\eta A(\xi_i^\eta, \xi_j^\eta)\right)$ as even for a nonlinear function g the covariance $Cov\left[g(\sum_\eta A(\xi_i^\eta, \xi_j^\eta)), g(\sum_\eta A(\xi_i^\eta, \xi_k^\eta))\right]$ remains positive if $Cov(A(\xi_i, \xi_j), A(\xi_i, \xi_k))$ is positive. **These observations show that effective associative learning with Hebbian rules alone is implausible from a biological standpoint requiring locality of information.**

3 Effective Learning via Neuronal Weight Correction

The above results show that in order to obtain effective memory storage, the post-synaptic covariance must be kept negligible. **How then may effective storage take place in the brain with Hebbian learning?** We now proceed to show that a neuronally-driven procedure (essentially similar to that assumed by [2, 1] to occur during self-organization) can maintain a vanishing covariance and turn ineffective Hebbian synapses into effective ones. This enables the brain to utilize inefficient learning rules which use local information only, but still attain effective learning capabilities.

The solution emerges when rewriting the signal-to-noise equation (Eq. 3) as

$$\frac{Signal}{Noise} \propto \frac{N}{\sqrt{NVar[W_{ij}](1-p) + pVar(\sum_{j=1}^N W_{ij})}}. \qquad (4)$$

showing that the post synaptic covariance can be greatly diminished when the variance of the sum of incoming synapses is vanishing. We thus propose the following **neuronal weight correction** procedure: During learning, whenever a synapse is modified, its postsynaptic neuron additively modifies all its synapses to maintain the sum of their efficacies at a baseline zero level.

$$W_{ij} \Longrightarrow W_{ij} - \frac{1}{N}\sum_{j=1}^N W_{ij} \quad ; \quad \forall j = 1..N \qquad (5)$$

As this neuronal weight correction is additive, it can be performed either after several memories have been stored (as done in prescriptive learning), or during the storge of each memory pattern (as in developmental learning models).

Interestingly, the joint operation of weight correction over a linear Hebbian learning rule is equivalent to the storage of the same set of memory patterns with another Hebbian learning rule. We prove that this new rule has a zero-covariance learning matrix

	1	0
1	α	β
0	γ	δ

$\Longrightarrow$

	1	0
1	$(\alpha-\beta)(1-p)$	$(\alpha-\beta)(0-p)$
0	$(\gamma-\delta)(1-p)$	$(\gamma-\delta)(0-p)$

.

It should be reemphasized that the matrix on the right is not applied at the synaptic level but is the emergent result of the operation of the neuronal mechanism on the matrix on the left, and is used here as a mathematical tool to analyze network's performance. Thus, using a neuronal mechanism that maintains the sum of incoming synapses fixed enables the same level of effective performance as would have been achieved by using a zero-covariance Hebbian learning rule, but without the need to know the memories' coding level.

To demonstrate the beneficiary effects of neuronal weight correction we have first applied it to a common realization of the Hebb rule with inhibition added to obtain a zero-mean input field (otherwise the capacity vanishes) yielding $A(\xi_i, \xi_j) = \xi_i \xi_j - p^2$ [7]. Even though this learning rule has a zero mean synaptic matrix, its postsynaptic covariance is non-zero and is thus still an ineffective rule. Applying neuronal weight correction after learning with the above rule, results in a synaptic matrix which is identical to the one generated by the rule $A(\xi_i, \xi_j) = \xi_i(\xi_j - p)$ without neuronal weight correction, which has both zero mean and zero postsynaptic covariance. Figure 2A plots the memory capacity obtained with the zero mean Hebb rule, before and after neuronal weight correction, as a function of the network's size. After applying neuronal weight correction the originally bounded capacity turns to scale linearly with the network's size.

A. Ineffective learning rule **B. Variable coding level**

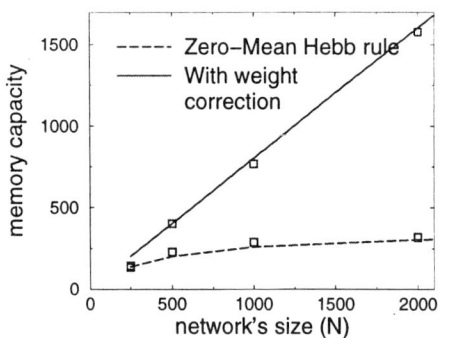
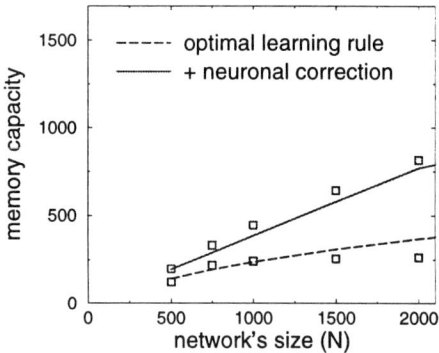

Figure 2: Network memory capacity as a function of network's size. **A.** While the original zero-mean learning rule has bounded memory capacity, the capacity becomes linear in the network's size when the same learning rule is coupled with neuronal-weight-correction. The lines plot analytical results and the squares designate simulation results ($p = 0.05$). **B.** Even the optimal learning rule becomes ineffective when the stored patterns have variable coding levels (coding levels are normally distributed $N(0.1, 0.02^2)$, but neuronal-weight-correction provides successful memory storage of such patterns. Results were obtained in a computer simulations.

As the effectiveness of the learning rule depends on the coding level of the stored patterns, all learning rules turn ineffective when the coding levels of the stored patterns are heterogeneous. Figure 2B compares the memory capacity of a network that uses the optimal learning rule ($A(\xi_i, \xi_j) = (\xi_i - p)(\xi_j - p)$) for a coding level of $p = 0.1$ but actually stores memory patterns with coding levels that are normally distributed around 0.1. Only the application of neuronal weight correction provides effective storage of such patterns while the optimal learning rule does not.

4 Neuronal Regulation Implements Weight Correction

Like previous normalization procedures, the proposed neuronal algorithm relies on the availability of explicit information about the total sum of synaptic efficacies at the neuronal level. However, as explicit information on the synaptic sum may not be available, several mechanisms for conservation of the total synaptic strength have been proposed (see [8] for a review). Here we focus on one such mechanism, Neuronal Regulation (NR), where the **total synaptic sum is regulated indirectly by estimating the neuron's average postsynaptic potential**. NR is a slow process, continuously modifying synaptic efficacies to maintain the homeostasis of neuronal activity. Such activity-dependent scaling of excitatory synapses, which acts to maintain the homeostasis of neuronal firing, has already been observed in cortical tissues by [9].

We have studied the operation of NR-driven correction compared with additive neuronal weight correction in an excitatory-inhibitory network. Figure 3 plots the memory capacity of networks storing memories according to the Hebb rule, showing how NR approximates the additive neuronal weight correction and succeeds in obtaining a linear growth of memory capacity.

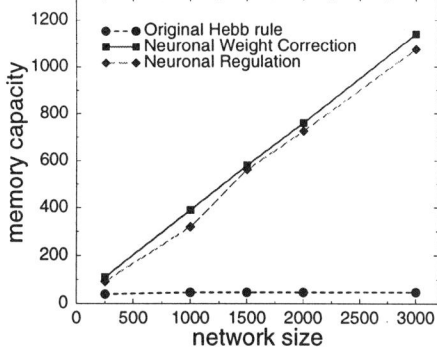

Figure 3. Applying NR achieves a linear scaling of memory capacity with a slightly inferior capacity compared with that obtained with neuronal weight correction. Memory patterns were stored according to the Hebb rule $W_{ij} = \sum_{\eta=1}^{M} \xi_i^\eta \xi_j^\eta$.

5 Summary

In this paper we have analyzed Hebbian learning rules in associative memory network models, and identified an essential requirement for effective memory storage: a vanishing postsynaptic covariance. We show that this constraint depends on the coding level of the stored memory patterns, thus requiring the use of network level information at the synaptic level. Moreover, when the stored memory patterns are heterogeneous, there is no single learning rule that can effectively store all patterns. We further show that applying a neuronally driven mechanism that preserves the total synaptic sum zeroes the catastrophic covariance and provides effective learning even for ineffective synaptic learning rules. **The resulting improvement in memory capacity is drastic: learning rules yielding bounded capacity are transformed into learning rules yielding linear memory capacity as a function of the network's size.** Finally, the normalization mechanism can be carried out by neuronal regulation (NR), a mechanism recently identified in mammalian cortical cultures.

The characterization of effective synaptic learning rules reopens the discussion of the computational role of heterosynaptic and homosynaptic depression. Previous studies have shown that long-term synaptic depression is necessary to prevent saturation of synaptic values [10], and to maintain zero mean synaptic efficacies [11]. Our study shows that effective learning requires proper heterosynaptic depression, but can be obtained regardless of the homosynaptic depression magnitude. The terms potentiation/depression used in the above context should be cautiously interpreted, as the apparent changes in synaptic efficacies measured in LTD/LTP experiments may involve two kinds of processes: Synaptic-driven processes, changing synapses according to the covariance between pre and post synaptic neurons, and neuronally-driven processes, operating to zero the covariance between incoming synapses of the neuron. These processes may be experimentally segregated as they operate on different time scales ([12, 9]), and their relative weights can be experimentally tested.

While several forms of synaptic constraints were suggested to improve the stability of Hebbian learning [2, 3], our analysis shows that effective memory storage requires that the sum of synaptic strengths which must be preserved, thus predicting that it is this specific form of normalization that occurs in the brain. The utilization of the simple McCullough-Pitts model studied here has enabled us to gain analytical insight to the phenomena in hand. Recent findings of neuronal weight normalization in spiking models [13], lead us to believe that these results will also extent to spiking neurons' networks.

Neuronal weight correction qualitatively improves the ability of a neuron to correctly discriminate between a large number of input patterns. It thus enhances the computational power of the single neuron and is likely to play a fundamental computational role in a variety of brain functions such as perceptual processing and associative learning.

References

[1] K.D. Miller and D.J.C MacKay. The role of constraints in Hebbian learning. *Neural Computation*, 6(1):100–126, 1994.

[2] C. von der Malsburg. Self organization of orientation sensitive cells in the striate cortex. *Kybernetik*, 14:85–100, 1973.

[3] Erkki Oja. A simplified neuron model as a principal component analyzer. *Journal of Mathematical Biology*, 15:267–273, 1982.

[4] A. Grinstein Massica and E. Ruppin. Synaptic runaway in associative networks and the pathogenesis of schizophrenia. *Neural Computation*, 10:451–465, 1998.

[5] P. Dayan and D.J. Willshaw. Optimizing synaptic learning rules in linear associative memories. *Biol. Cyber.*, 65:253, 1991.

[6] G. Palm and F. Sommer. Associative data storage and retrielval in neural networks. In E. Domani, J.L. vanHemmen, and eds. K. Schulten, editors, *Models of Neural Networks III. Association, Generalization and Represantation*, pages 79–118. Springer, 1996.

[7] M.V. Tsodyks. Associative memory in neural networks with Hebbian learning rule. *Modern Physics letters*, 3(7):555–560, 1989.

[8] K.D. Miller. Synaptic economics: Competition and cooperation in synaptic plasticity. *Neuron*, 17:371–374, 1996.

[9] G.G. Turrigano, K. Leslie, N. Desai, and S.B. Nelson. Activity dependent scaling of quantal amplitude in neocoritcal pyramidal neurons. *Nature*, 391(6670):892–896, 1998.

[10] T.J. Sejnowski. Statistical constraints on synaptic plasticity. *J. Theo. Biol.*, 69:385–389, 1977.

[11] D.J. Willshaw and P. Dayan. Optimal plasticity from matrix memories: What goes up must come down. *Neural Computation*, 2(1):85–93, 1990.

[12] M.F. Bear and W.C. Abraham. Long term depression in hippocampus. *Annu. Rev. Neurosci.*, 19:437–462, 1996.

[13] R. Kempter, W. Gerstner, and J.L. van Hemmen. Hebbian learning and spiking neurons. *Phys. Rev. E.*, 59(4), 1999.

Wiring optimization in the brain

Dmitri B. Chklovskii
Sloan Center for
Theoretical Neurobiology
The Salk Institute
La Jolla, CA 92037
mitya@salk.edu

Charles F. Stevens
Howard Hughes Medical Institute
and Molecular Neurobiology Lab
The Salk Institute
La Jolla, CA 92037
stevens@salk.edu

Abstract

The complexity of cortical circuits may be characterized by the number of synapses per neuron. We study the dependence of complexity on the fraction of the cortical volume that is made up of "wire" (that is, of axons and dendrites), and find that complexity is maximized when wire takes up about 60% of the cortical volume. This prediction is in good agreement with experimental observations. A consequence of our arguments is that any rearrangement of neurons that takes more wire would sacrifice computational power.

Wiring a brain presents formidable problems because of the extremely large number of connections: a microliter of cortex contains approximately 10^5 neurons, 10^9 synapses, and 4 km of axons, with 60% of the cortical volume being taken up with "wire", half of this by axons and the other half by dendrites.[1] Each cortical neighborhood must have exactly the right balance of components; if too many cell bodies were present in a particular mm cube, for example, insufficient space would remain for the axons, dendrites and synapses. Here we ask "What fraction of the cortical volume should be wires (axons + dendrites)?" We argue that physiological properties of axons and dendrites dictate an optimal wire fraction of 0.6, just what is actually observed.

To calculate the optimal wire fraction, we start with a real cortical region containing a fixed number of neurons, a mm cube, for example, and imagine perturbing it by adding or subtracting synapses and the axons and dendrites needed to support them. The rules for perturbing the cortical cube require that the existing circuit connections and function remain intact (except for what may have been removed in the perturbation), that no holes are created, and that all added (or subtracted) synapses are typical of those present; as wire volume is added, the volume of the cube of course increases. The ratio of the number of synapses per neuron in the perturbed cortex to that in the real cortex is denoted by θ, a parameter we call the *relative complexity*. We require that the volume of non-wire components (cell bodies, blood vessels, glia, etc) is unchanged by our perturbation and use ϕ to denote the volume fraction of the perturbed cortical region that is made up of wires (axons + dendrites; ϕ can vary between zero and one), with the fraction for the real brain being ϕ_0. The relation between relative complexity θ and wire volume fraction ϕ is given by the equation (derived in Methods)

$$\theta = \frac{1}{\lambda^5} \left(\frac{1-\phi}{1-\phi_0}\right)^{2/3} \frac{\phi}{\phi_0}. \tag{1}$$

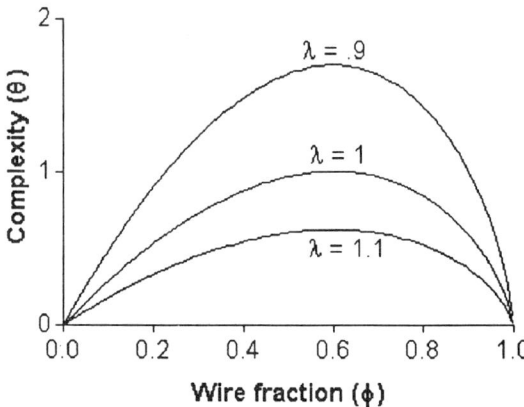

Figure 1: Relative complexity (θ) as a function of volume wire fraction (ϕ). The graphs are calculated from equation (1) for three values of the parameter λ as indicated; this parameter determines the average length of wire associated with a synapse (relative to this length for the real cortex, for which ($\lambda = 1$). Note that as the average length of wire per synapse increases, the maximum possible complexity decreases.

For the following discussion assume that $\lambda = 1$; we return to the meaning of this parameter later. To derive this equation two assumptions are made. First, we suppose that each added synapse requires extra wire equal to the average wire length and volume per synapse in the unperturbed cortex. Second, because adding wire for new synapses increases the brain volume and therefore increases the distance axons and dendrites must travel to maintain the connections they make in the real cortex, all of the dendrite and unmyelinated axon diameters are increased in proportion to the square of their length changes in order to maintain the intersynaptic conduction times[2] and dendrite cable lengths[3] as they are in the actual cortex. If the unmyelinated axon diameters were not increased as the axons become longer, for example, the time for a nerve impulse to propagate from one synapse to the next would be increased and we would violate our rule that the existing circuit and its function be unchanged. We note that the vast majority of cortical axons are unmyelinated.[1] The plot of θ as a function of ϕ is parabolic-like (see Figure 1) with a maximum value at $\phi = 0.6$, a point at which $d\theta/d\phi = 0$. This same maximum value is found for any possible value of ϕ_0, the real cortical wire fraction.

Why does complexity reach a maximum value at a particular wire fraction? When wire and synapses are added, a series of consequences can lead to a runaway situation we call the *wiring catastrophe*. If we start with a wire fraction less than 0.6, adding wire increases the cortical volume, increased volume makes longer paths for axons to reach their targets which requires larger diameter wires (to keep conduction delays or cable attenuation constant from one point to another), the larger wire diameters increase cortex volume which means wires must be longer, etc. While the wire fraction ϕ is less than 0.6, increasing complexity is accompanied by finite increases in ϕ. At $\phi = 0.6$ the rate at which wire fraction increases with complexity becomes infinite $d\phi/d\theta \to \infty$); we have reached the wiring catastrophe. At this point, adding wire becomes impossible without decreasing complexity or making other changes – like decreasing axon diameters – that alter cortical function. The physical cause of the catastrophe is a slow growth of conduction velocity and dendritic cable length with diameter combined with the requirement that the conduction times between synapses (and dendrite cable lengths) be unchanged in the perturbed cortex.

We assumed above that each synapse requires a certain amount of wire, but what if we could add new synapses using the wire already present? We do not know what factors determine the wire volume needed to support a synapse, but if the average amount of wire per synapse could be less (or more) than that in the actual cortex, the maximum wire fraction would still be 0.6. Each curve in Figure 1 corresponds to a different assumed average wire length required for a synapse (determined by λ), and the maximum always occurs at 0.6 independent of λ. In the following we consider only situations in which λ is fixed.

For a given λ, what complexity should we expect for the actual cortex? Three arguments favor the maximum possible complexity. The greatest complexity gives the largest number of synapses per neuron and this permits more bits of information to be represented per neuron. Also, more synapses per neuron decreases the relative effect caused by the loss or malfunction of a single synapse. Finally, errors in the local wire fraction would minimally affect the local complexity because $d\theta/d\phi = 0$ at $\phi = 0.6$. Thus one can understand why the actual cortex has the wire fraction we identify as optimal.[1]

This conclusion that the wire fraction is a maximum in the real cortex has an interesting consequence: components of an actual cortical circuit cannot be rearranged in a way that needs more wire without eliminating synapses or reducing wire diameters. For example, if intermixing the cell bodies of left and right eye cells in primate primary visual cortex (rather than separating them in ocular dominance columns) increased the average length of the wire[4] the existing circuit could not be maintained just by a finite increase in volume. This happens because a greater wire length demanded by the rearrangement of the same circuit would require longer wire per synapse, that is, an increased λ. As can be seen from Figure 1, brains with $\lambda > 1$ can never achieve the complexity reached at the maximum of the $\lambda = 1$ curve that corresponds to the actual cortex.

Our observations support the notion that brains are arranged to minimize wire length. This idea, dating back to Cajal[5], has recently been used to explain why retinotopic maps exist[6],[7], why cortical regions are separated, why ocular dominance columns are present in primary visual cortex[4],[8],[9] and why the cortical areas and flat worm ganglia are placed as they are.[10-13] We anticipate that maximal complexity/minimal wire length arguments will find further application in relating functional and anatomical properties of brain.

Methods

The volume of the cube of cortex we perturb is V, the volume of the non-wire portion is W (assumed to be constant), the fraction of V consisting of wires is ϕ, the total number of synapses is N, the average length of axonal wire associated with each synapse is s, and the average axonal wire volume per unit length is h; the corresponding values for dendrites are indicated by primes (s' and h'). The unperturbed value for each variable has a 0 subscript; thus the volume of the cortical cube before it is perturbed is

$$V_0 = W_0 + N_0(s_0 h_0 + s'_0 h'_0). \tag{2}$$

We now define a "virtual" perturbation that we use to explore the extent to which the actual cortical region contains an optimal fraction of wire. If we increase the number of synapses by a factor θ and the length of wire associated with each synapse by a factor λ, then the perturbed cortical cube's volume becomes

$$V_0 = W_0 + \lambda\theta \left(N_0 s_0 h_0 \frac{h}{h_0} + N_0 s'_0 h'_0 \frac{h'}{h'_0} \right) (V/V_0)^{1/3}. \tag{3}$$

This equation allows for the possibility that the average wire diameter has been perturbed and increases the length of all wire segments by the "mean field" quantity $(V/V_0)^{1/3}$ to take account of the expansion of the cube by the added wire; we require our perturbation disperses the added wire as uniformly as possible throughout the cortical cube.

To simplify this relation we must eliminate h/h_0 and h'/h'_0; we consider these terms in turn. When we perturb the brain we require that the average conduction time (s/u, where u is the conduction velocity) from one synapse to the next be unchanged so that $s/u = s_0/u_0$, or

$$\frac{u}{u_0} = \frac{s}{s_0} = \frac{\lambda s_0 (V/V_0)^{1/3}}{s_0} = \lambda (V/V_0)^{1/3}. \tag{4}$$

Because axon diameter is proportional to the square of conduction velocity u and the axon volume per unit length h is proportional to diameter squared, h is proportional to u^4 and the ratio h/h_0 can be written as

$$\frac{h}{h_0} = \left(\frac{u}{u_0}\right)^4 = \frac{s}{s_0} = \lambda^4 (V/V_0)^{4/3}. \tag{5}$$

For dendrites, we require that their length from one synapse to the next in units of the cable length constant be unchanged by the perturbation. The dendritic length constant is proportional to the square root of the dendritic diameter d, so $s/\sqrt{d} = s_0/\sqrt{d_0}$ or

$$\frac{d}{d_0} = \left(\frac{s'}{s'_0}\right)^2 = \left(\lambda(V/V_0)^{1/3}\right)^2 = \lambda^2 (V/V_0)^{2/3}. \tag{6}$$

Because dendritic volumes per unit length (h and h') vary as the square of the diameters, we have that

$$\frac{h'}{h'_0} = \left(\frac{d}{d_0}\right)^2 = \lambda^4 (V/V_0)^{4/3}. \tag{7}$$

The equation (2) can thus be rewritten as

$$V = W_0 + N_0(s_0 h_0 + s'_0 h'_0)\theta \lambda^5 (V/V_0)^{5/3}. \tag{8}$$

Divide this equation by V_0, define $\nu = V/V_0$, and recognize that $W_0/V_0 = (1 - \phi_0)$ and that $\phi_0 = N_0(s_0 h_0 + s'_0 h'_0)/V_0$; the result is

$$\nu = (1 - \phi_0) + \theta \lambda^5 \phi_0 \nu^{5/3}. \tag{9}$$

Because the non-wire volume is required not to change with the perturbation, we know that $W_0 = (1 - \phi_0)V_0 = (1 - \phi)V$ which means that $\nu = (1 - \phi_0)/(1 - \phi)$; substitute this in equation (9) and rearrange to give

$$\theta = \frac{1}{\lambda^5} \left(\frac{1 - \phi}{1 - \phi_0}\right)^{2/3} \frac{\phi}{\phi_0}. \tag{1}$$

the equation used in the main text.

We have assumed that conduction velocity and the dendritic cable length constant vary exactly with the square root of diameter[2],[14] but if the actual power were to deviate slightly from 1/2 the wire fraction that gives the maximum complexity would also differ slightly from 0.6.

Acknowledgments

This work was supported by the Howard Hughes Medical Institute and a grant from NIH to C.F.S. D.C. was supported by a Sloan Fellowship in Theoretical Neurobiology.

References

[1] Braitenberg, V. & Schuz, A. *Cortex: Statistics and Geometry of Neuronal Connectivity* (Springer, 1998).

[2] Rushton, W.A.H. A Theory of the Effects of Fibre Size in Medullated Nerve. J. Physiol. 115, 101-122 (1951).

[3] Bekkers, J.M. & Stevens, C.F. Two different ways evolution makes neurons larger. Prog Brain Res 83, 37-45 (1990).

[4] Mitchison, G. Neuronal branching patterns and the economy of cortical wiring. Proc R Soc Lond B Biol Sci 245, 151-158 (1991).

[5] Cajal, S.R.Y. *Histology of the Nervous System* 1-805 (Oxford University Press, 1995).

[6] Cowey, A. Cortical maps and visual perception: the Grindley Memorial Lecture. Q J Exp Phycol 31, 1-17 (1979).

[7] Allman J.M. & Kaas J.H. The organization of the second visual area (V II) in the owl monkey: a second order transformation of the visual hemifield. Brain Res 76: 247-65 (1974).

[8] Durbin, R. & Mitchison, G. A dimension reduction framework for understanding cortical maps. Nature 343, 644-647 (1990).

[9] Mitchison, G. Axonal trees and cortical architecture. Trends Neurosci 15, 122-126 (1992).

[10] Young, M.P. Objective analysis of the topological organization of the primate cortical visual system. Nature 358, 152-154 (1992).

[11] Cherniak, C. Local optimization of neuron arbors. Biol Cybern 66, 503-510 (1992).

[12] Cherniak, C. Component placement optimization in the brain. J Neurosci 14, 2418-2427 (1994).

[13] Cherniak, C. Neural component placement. Trends Neurosci 18, 522-527 (1995).

[14] Rall, W. in *Handbook of Physiology, The Nervous Systems, Cellular Biology of Neurons* (ed. Brookhart, J.M.M., V.B.) 39-97 (Am. Physiol. Soc., Bethesda, MD, 1977).

Optimal sizes of dendritic and axonal arbors

Dmitri B. Chklovskii
Sloan Center for Theoretical Neurobiology
The Salk Institute, La Jolla, CA 92037
mitya@salk.edu

Abstract

I consider a topographic projection between two neuronal layers with different densities of neurons. Given the number of output neurons connected to each input neuron (divergence or fan-out) and the number of input neurons synapsing on each output neuron (convergence or fan-in) I determine the widths of axonal and dendritic arbors which minimize the total volume of axons and dendrites. My analytical results can be summarized qualitatively in the following rule: neurons of the sparser layer should have arbors wider than those of the denser layer. This agrees with the anatomical data from retinal and cerebellar neurons whose morphology and connectivity are known. The rule may be used to infer connectivity of neurons from their morphology.

1 Introduction

Understanding brain function requires knowing connections between neurons. However, experimental studies of inter-neuronal connectivity are difficult and the connectivity data is scarce. At the same time neuroanatomists possess much data on cellular morphology and have powerful techniques to image neuronal shapes. This suggests using morphological data to infer inter-neuronal connections. Such inference must rely on rules which relate shapes of neurons to their connectivity.

The purpose of this paper is to derive such rule for a frequently encountered feature in the brain organization: a topographic projection. Two layers of neurons are said to form a topographic projection if adjacent neurons of the input layer connect to adjacent neurons of the output layer, Figure 1. As a result, output neurons form an orderly map of the input layer.

I characterize inter-neuronal connectivity for a topographic projection by divergence and convergence factors defined as follows, Figure 1. *Divergence*, D, of the projection is the number of output neurons which receive connections from an input neuron. *Convergence*, C, of the projection is the number of input neurons which connect with an output neuron. I assume that these numbers are the same for each neuron in a given layer. Furthermore, each neuron makes the required connections with the nearest neurons of the other layer. In most cases, this completely specifies the wiring diagram.

A typical topographic wiring diagram shown in Figure 1 misses an important biological detail. In real brains, connections between cell bodies are implemented by neuronal processes: axons which carry nerve pulses away from the cell bodies and dendrites which carry signals

Optimal Sizes of Dendritic and Axonal Arbors

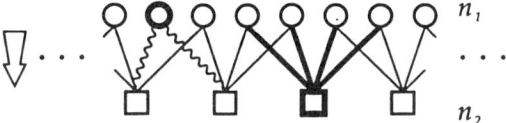

Figure 1: Wiring diagram of a topographic projection between input (circles) and output (squares) layers of neurons. Divergence, D, is the number of outgoing connections (here, $D = 2$) from an input neuron (wavey lines). Convergence, C, is the number of connections incoming (here, $C = 4$) to an output neuron (bold lines). Arrow shows the direction of signal propagation.

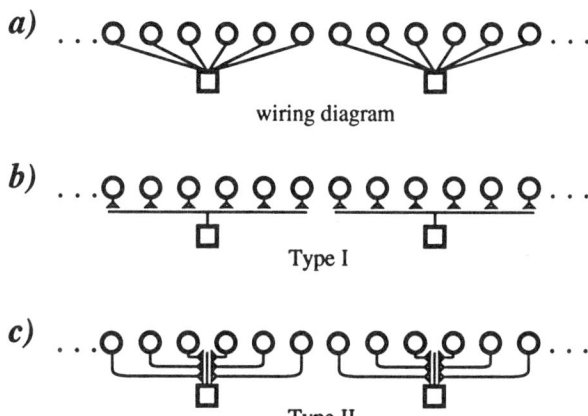

Figure 2: Two different arrangements implement the same wiring diagram. (a) Topographic wiring diagram with $C = 6$ and $D = 1$. (b) Arrangement with wide dendritic arbors and no axonal arbors (Type I) (c) Arrangement with wide axonal arbors and no dendritic arbors (Type II). Because convergence exceeds divergence type I has shorter wiring than type II.

towards cell bodies.[1] Therefore each connection is interrupted by a synapse which separates an axon of one neuron from a dendrite of another. Both axons and dendrites branch away from cell bodies forming arbors.

In general, a topographic projection with given divergence and convergence may be implemented by axonal and dendritic arbors of different sizes, which depend on the locations of synapses. For example, consider a wiring diagram with $D = 1$ and $C = 6$, Figure 2a. Narrow axonal arbors may synapse onto wide dendritic arbors, Figure 2b or wide axonal arbors may synapse onto narrow dendritic arbors, Figure 2c. I call these arrangements type I and type II, correspondingly. The question is: which arbor sizes are preferred?

I propose a rule which specifies the sizes of axonal arbors of input neurons and dendritic arbors of output neurons in a topographic projection: *High divergence/convergence ratio favors wide axonal and narrow dendritic arbors while low divergence/convergence ratio favors narrow axonal arbors and wide dendritic arbors.* Alternatively, this rule may be formulated in terms of neuronal densities in the two layers: *Sparser layer has wider arbors.* In the above example, divergence/convergence (and neuronal density) ratio is 1/6 and, according to the rule, type I arrangement, Figure 2b, is preferred.

In this paper I derive a quantitative version of this rule from the principle of wiring economy which can be summarized as follows. [2, 3, 4, 5, 6] Space constraints require keeping the brain volume to a minimum. Because wiring (axons and dendrites) takes up a significant fraction of the volume, evolution has probably designed axonal and dendritic arbors in a way that minimizes their total volume. Therefore we may understand the existing arbor sizes as a result of wiring optimization.

To obtain the rule I formulate and solve a wiring optimization problem. The goal is to find the sizes of axons and dendrites which minimize the total volume of wiring in a topographic wiring diagram for fixed locations of neurons. I specify the wiring diagram with divergence and convergence factors. Throughout most of the paper I assume that the cross-sectional area of dendrites and axons are constant and equal. Therefore, the problem reduces to the wire *length* minimization. Extension to unequal fiber diameters is given below.

2 Topographic projection in two dimensions

Consider two parallel layers of neurons with densities n_1 and n_2. The topographic wiring diagram has divergence and convergence factors, D and C, requiring each input neuron to connect with D nearest output neurons and each output neuron with C nearest input neurons. Again, the problem is to find the arrangement of arbors which minimizes the total length of axons and dendrites. For different arrangements I compare the wirelength per unit area, L. I assume that the two layers are close to each other and include only those parts of the wiring which are parallel to the layers.

I start with a special case where each input neuron connects with only one output neuron ($D = 1$). Consider an example with $C = 16$ and neurons arranged on a square grid in each layer, Figure 3a. Two extreme arrangements satisfy the wiring diagram: type I has wide dendritic arbors and no axonal arbors, Figure 3b; type II has wide axonal arbors and no dendritic arbors, Figure 3c. I take the branching angles equal to 120^0, an optimal value for constant crossectional area.[4] Assuming "point" neurons the ratio of wirelength for type I and type II arrangements:

$$\frac{L_I}{L_{II}} \approx 0.57. \quad (1)$$

Thus, the type I arrangement with wide dendritic arbors has shorter wire length. This conclusion holds for other convergence values much greater than one, provided $D = 1$. However, there are other arrangements with non-zero axonal arbors that give the same wire length. One of them is shown in Figure 3d. Degenerate arrangements have axonal arbor width $0 < s_a < 1/\sqrt{n_1}$ where the upper bound is given by the approximate inter-neuronal distance. This means that the optimal arbor size ratio for $D = 1$

$$\frac{s_d}{s_a} > \sqrt{\frac{n_1}{n_2}} \quad (2)$$

By using the symmetry in respect to the direction of signal propagation I adapt this result for the $C = 1$ case. For $D > 1$, arrangements with wide axonal arbors and narrow dendritic arbors ($0 < s_d < 1/\sqrt{n_2}$) have minimal wirelength. The arbor size ratio is

$$\frac{s_d}{s_a} < \sqrt{\frac{n_1}{n_2}}. \quad (3)$$

Next, I consider the case when both divergence and convergence are greater than one. Due to complexity of the problem I study the limit of large divergence and convergence ($D, C \gg 1$). I find analytically the optimal layout which minimizes the total length of axons and dendrites.

Notice that two neurons may form a synapse only if the axonal arbor of the input neuron overlaps with the dendritic arbor of the output neuron in a two-dimensional projection, Figure 4. Thus the goal is to design optimal dendritic and axonal arbors so that each dendritic arbor intersects C axonal arbors and each axonal arbor intersects D dendritic arbors.

To be specific, I consider a wiring diagram with convergence exceeding divergence, $C > D$ (the argument can be readily adapted for the opposite case). I make an assumption, to be

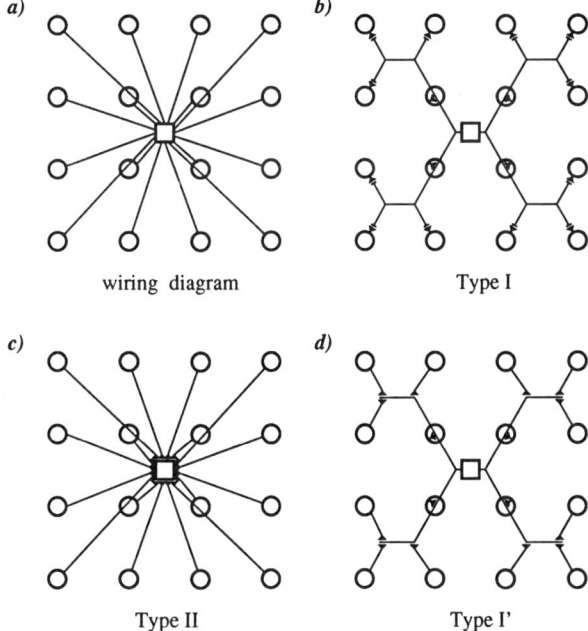

Figure 3: Different arrangements implement the same wiring diagram in two dimensions. (a) Topographic wiring diagram with $D = 1$ and $C = 16$. (b) Arrangement with wide dendritic arbors and no axonal arbors, Type I. (c) Arrangement with wide axonal arbors and no dendritic arbors, Type II. Because convergence exceeds divergence type I has shorter wiring than type II. (d) Intermediate arrangement which has the same wire length as type I.

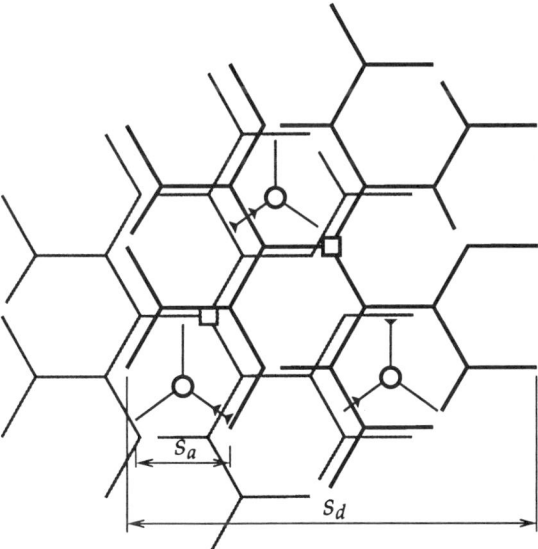

Figure 4: Topographic projection between the layers of input (circles) and output (squares) neurons. For clarity, out of the many input and output neurons with overlapping arbors only few are shown. The number of input neurons is greater than the number of output neurons ($C/D > 1$). Input neurons have narrow axonal arbors of width s_a connected to the wide but sparse dendritic arbors of width s_d. Sparseness of the dendritic arbor is given by s_a because all the input neurons spanned by the dendritic arbor have to be connected.

verified later, that dendritic arbor diameter s_d is greater than axonal one, s_a. In this regime each output neuron's dendritic arbor forms a sparse mesh covering the area from which signals are collected, Figure 4. Each axonal arbor in that area must intersect the dendritic arbor mesh to satisfy the wiring diagram. This requires setting mesh size equal to the axonal arbor diameter.

By using this requirement I express the total length of axonal and dendritic arbors as a function of only the axonal arbor size, s_a. Then I find the axonal arbor size which minimizes the total wirelength. Details of the calculation will be published elsewhere. Here, I give an intuitive argument for why in the optimal layout both axonal and dendritic size are non-zero. Consider two extreme layouts. In the first one, dendritic arbors have zero width, type II. In this arrangement axons have to reach out to every output neuron. For large convergence, $C \gg 1$, this is a redundant arrangement because of the many parallel axonal wires whose signals are eventually merged. In the second layout, axonal arbors are absent and dendrites have to reach out to every input neuron. Again, because each input neuron connects to many output neurons (large divergence, $D \gg 1$) many dendrites run in parallel inefficiently carrying the same signal. A non-zero axonal arbor rectifies this inefficiency by carrying signals to several dendrites along one wire.

I find that the optimal ratio of dendritic and axonal arbor diameters equals to the square root of the convergence/divergence ratio, or, alternatively, to the square root of the neuronal density ratio:

$$\frac{s_d}{s_a} = \sqrt{\frac{C}{D}} = \sqrt{\frac{n_1}{n_2}} \qquad (4)$$

Since I considered the case with $C > D$ this result also justifies the assumption about axonal arbors being smaller than dendritic ones.

For arbitrary axonal and dendritic cross-sectional areas, h_a and h_d, expressions of this Section are modified. The wiring economy principle requires minimizing the total volume occupied by axons and dendrites resulting in the following relation for the optimal arrangement:

$$\frac{s_d}{s_a} = \sqrt{\frac{C h_a}{D h_d}} = \sqrt{\frac{n_1 h_a}{n_2 h_d}} \qquad (5)$$

Notice that in the optimal arrangement the total axonal volume of input neurons is equal to the total dendritic volume of the output neurons.

3 Discussion

3.1 Comparison of the theory with anatomical data

This theory predicts a relationship between the con-/divergence ratio and the sizes of axonal and dendritic arbors. I test these predictions on several cases of topographic projection in two dimensions. The predictions depend on whether divergence and convergence are both greater than one or not. Therefore, I consider the two regimes separately.

First, I focus on topographic projections of retinal neurons whose divergence factor is equal or close to one. Because retinal neurons use mostly graded potentials the difference between axons and dendrites is small and I assume that their cross-sectional areas are equal. The theory predicts that the ratio of dendritic and axonal arbor sizes must be greater than the square root of the input/output neuronal density ratio, $s_d/s_a > (n_1/n_2)^{1/2}$ (Eq.2).

I represent the data on the plot of the relative arbor diameter, s_d/s_a, vs. the square root of the relative densities, $(n_1/n_2)^{1/2}$, (Figure 5). Because neurons located in the same layer may belong to different classes, each having different arbor size and connectivity, I plot data

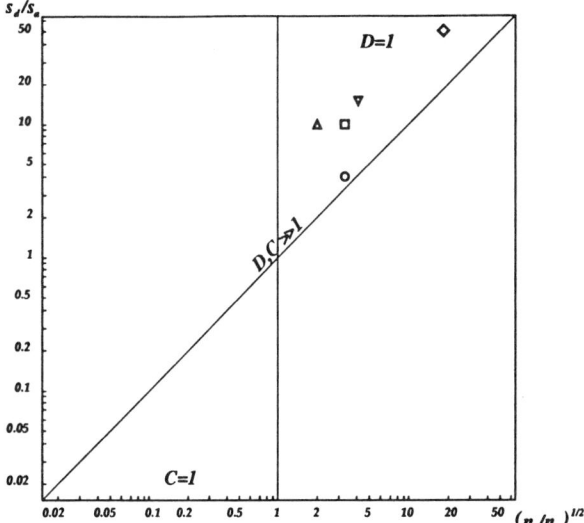

Figure 5: Anatomical data for several pairs of retinal cell classes which form topographic projections with $D = 1$. All the data points fall in the triangle above the $s_d/s_a = (n_1/n_2)^{1/2}$ line in agreement with the theoretical prediction, Eq.2. The following data has been used: ○ - midget bipolar → midget ganglion,[7, 8, 11]; ⊔ - diffuse bipolar → parasol ganglion,[7, 9]; ▽ - rods → rod bipolar,[10]; △ - cones → HI horizontals,[12]; ◇ - rods → telodendritic arbors of HI horizontals,[13].

from different classes separately. All the data points lie above the $s_d/s_a = (n_1/n_2)^{1/2}$ line in agreement with the prediction.

Second, I apply the theory to cerebellar neurons whose divergence and convergence are both greater than one. I consider a projection from granule cell axons (parallel fibers) onto Purkinje cells. Ratio of granule cells to Purkinje cells is 3300,[14], indicating a high convergence/divergence ratio. This predicts a ratio of dendritic and axonal arbor sizes of 58. This is qualitatively in agreement with wide dendritic arbors of Purkinje cells and no axonal arbors on parallel fibers.

Quantitative comparison is complicated because the projection is not strictly two-dimensional: Purkinje dendrites stacked next to each other add up to a significant third dimension. Naively, given that the dendritic arbor size is about $400\mu m$ Eq.4 predicts axonal arbor of about $7\mu m$. This is close to the distance between two adjacent Purkinje cell arbors of about $9\mu m$. Because the length of parallel fibers is greater than $7\mu m$ absence of axonal arbors comes as no surprise.

3.2 Other factors affecting arbor sizes

One may argue that dendrites and axons have functions other than linking cell bodies to synapses and, therefore, the size of the arbors may be dictated by other considerations. Although I can not rule out this possibility, the *primary* function of axons and dendrites is to connect cell bodies to synapses in order to conduct nerve pulses between them. Indeed, if neurons were not connected more sophisticated effects such as non-linear interactions between different dendritic inputs could not take place. Hence the most basic parameters of axonal and dendritic arbors such as their size should follow from considerations of connectivity.

Another possibility is that the size of dendritic arbors is dictated by the surface area needed to arrange all the synapses. This argument does not specify the arbor size, however: a compact dendrite of elaborate shape can have the same surface area as a wide dendritic arbor.

Finally, agreement of the predictions with the existing anatomical data suggests that the rule is based on correct principles. Further extensive testing of the rule is desirable. Violation of the rule in some system would suggest the presence of other overriding considerations in the design of that system, which is also interesting.

Acknowledgements

I benefited from helpful discussions with E.M. Callaway, E.J. Chichilnisky, H.J. Karten, C.F. Stevens and T.J. Sejnowski and especially with A.A. Koulakov. I thank G.D. Brown for suggesting that the size of axonal and dendritic arbors may be related to con-/divergence.

References

[1] Cajal, S.R.y. (1995a). Histology of the nervous system p.95 (Oxford University Press, New-York).
[2] Cajal, S.R.y. *ibid.* p.116.
[3] Mitchison, G. (1991). Neuronal branching patterns and the economy of cortical wiring. Proc R Soc Lond B Biol Sci 245, 151-8.
[4] Cherniak, C. (1992). Local optimization of neuron arbors, Biol Cybern 66, 503-510.
[5] Young, M.P. (1992). Objective analysis of the topological organization of the primate cortical visual system Nature 358, 152-5.
[6] Chklovskii, D.B. & Stevens, C.F. (1999). Wiring the brain optimally, submitted Nature Neuroscience.
[7] Watanabe, M. & Rodieck, R.W. (1989). Parasol and midget ganglion cells of the primate retina. J Comp Neurol 289, 434-54.
[8] Milam, A.H., Dacey, D.M. & Dizhoor, A.M. (1993). Recoverin immunoreactivity in mammalian cone bipolar cells. Vis Neurosci 10, 1-12.
[9] Grunert, U., Martin, P.R. & Wassle H. (1994). Immunocytochemical analysis of bipolar cells in the macaque monkey retina. J Comp Neurol 348, 607-27.
[10] Grunert, U. & Martin, P.R. (1991). Rod bipolar cells in the macaque monkey retina: immunoreactivity and connectivity. J Neurosci 11, 2742-58.
[11] Dacey, D.M. (1993). The mosaic of midget ganglion cells in the human retina. J Neurosci 13, 5334-55.
[12] Wassle, H., Boycott, B.B. & Rohrenbeck, J. (1989). Horizontal cells in the monkey retina: cone connections and dendritic network. Eur J Neurosci 1, 421-435.
[13] Rodieck, R.W. (1989) *The First Steps in Seeing* (Sinauer Associates, Sunderland, MA).
[14] Andersen, B.B., Korbo, L. & Pakkenberg, B. (1992). A quantitative study of the human cerebellum with unbiased stereological techniques. J Comp Neurol 326, 549-60.
[15] Peters A., Payne B.R. & Budd, J. (1994). A numerical analysis of the geniculocortical input to striate cortex in the monkey. Cereb Cortex 4, 215-229.
[16] Blasdel, G.G. & Lund, J.S. (1983) Termination of afferent axons in macaque striate cortex. J Neurosci 3, 1389-1413.
[17] Wiser, A.K. & Callaway, E.M. (1996). Contributions of individual layer 6 pyramidal neurons to local circuitry in macaque primary visual cortex. J Neurosci 16, 2724-2739.

Neural Representation of Multi-Dimensional Stimuli

Christian W. Eurich, Stefan D. Wilke and Helmut Schwegler
Institut für Theoretische Physik
Universität Bremen, Germany
(eurich,swilke,schwegler)@physik.uni-bremen.de

Abstract

The encoding accuracy of a population of stochastically spiking neurons is studied for different distributions of their tuning widths. The situation of identical radially symmetric receptive fields for all neurons, which is usually considered in the literature, turns out to be disadvantageous from an information-theoretic point of view. Both a variability of tuning widths and a fragmentation of the neural population into specialized subpopulations improve the encoding accuracy.

1 Introduction

The topic of neuronal tuning properties and their functional significance has focused much attention in the last decades. However, neither empirical findings nor theoretical considerations have yielded a unified picture of optimal neural encoding strategies given a sensory or motor task. More specifically, the question as to whether narrow tuning or broad tuning is advantageous for the representation of a set of stimulus features is still being discussed. Empirically, both situations are encountered: small receptive fields whose diameter is less than one degree can, for example, be found in the human retina [7], and large receptive fields up to $180°$ in diameter occur in the visual system of tongue-projecting salamanders [10]. On the theoretical side, arguments have been put forward for small [8] as well as for large [5, 1, 9, 3, 13] receptive fields.

In the last years, several approaches have been made to calculate the encoding accuracy of a neural population as a function of receptive field size [5, 1, 9, 3, 13]. It has turned out that for a firing rate coding, large receptive fields are advantageous provided that $D \geq 3$ stimulus features are encoded [9, 13]. For binary neurons, large receptive fields are advantageous also for $D = 2$ [5, 3].

However, so far only radially symmetric tuning curves have been considered. For neural populations which lack this symmetry, the situation may be very different. Here we study the encoding accuracy of a population of stochastically spiking neurons. A Fisher information analysis performed on different distributions of tunings widths will indeed reveal a much more detailed picture of neural encoding strategies.

2 Model

Consider a D-dimensional stimulus space, X. A stimulus is characterized by a position $\mathbf{x} = (x_1, \ldots, x_D) \in X$, where the value of feature i, x_i ($i = 1, \ldots, D$), is measured relative to the total range of values in the i-th dimension such that it is dimensionless. Information about the stimulus is encoded by a population of N stochastically spiking neurons. They are assumed to have independent spike generation mechanisms such that the joint probability distribution for observing $\mathbf{n} = (n^{(1)}, \ldots, n^{(k)}, \ldots, n^{(N)})$ spikes within a time interval τ, $P_s(\mathbf{n}; \mathbf{x})$, can be written in the form

$$P_s(\mathbf{n}; \mathbf{x}) = \prod_{k=1}^{N} P_s^{(k)}(n^{(k)}; \mathbf{x}), \tag{1}$$

where $P_s^{(k)}(n^{(k)}; \mathbf{x})$ is the single-neuron probability distribution of the number of observed spikes given the stimulus at position $\mathbf{x}$. Note that (1) does not exclude a correlation of the neural firing rates, i.e., the neurons may have common input or even share the same tuning function.

The firing rates depend on the stimulus via the local values of the tuning functions, such that $P_s^{(k)}(n^{(k)}; \mathbf{x})$ can be written in the form $P_s^{(k)}(n^{(k)}; \mathbf{x}) = S\left(n^{(k)}, f^{(k)}(\mathbf{x}), \tau\right)$, where the tuning function of neuron k, $f^{(k)}(\mathbf{x})$, gives its mean firing rate in response to the stimulus at position $\mathbf{x}$. We assume here a form of the tuning function that is not necessarily radially symmetric,

$$f^{(k)}(\mathbf{x}) = F\phi\left(\sum_{i=1}^{D} \frac{(x_i - c_i^{(k)})^2}{\sigma_i^{(k)2}}\right) =: F\phi\left(\xi^{(k)2}\right), \tag{2}$$

where $\mathbf{c}^{(k)} = (c_1^{(k)}, \ldots, c_D^{(k)})$ is the center of the tuning curve of neuron k, $\sigma_i^{(k)}$ is its tuning width in the i-th dimension, $\xi_i^{(k)2} := (x_i - c_i^{(k)})^2 / \sigma_i^{(k)2}$ for $i = 1, \ldots, D$, and $\xi^{(k)2} := \xi_1^{(k)2} + \ldots + \xi_D^{(k)2}$. $F > 0$ denotes the maximal firing rate of the neurons, which requires that $\max_{z \geq 0} \phi(z) = 1$.

We assume that the tuning widths $\sigma_1^{(k)}, \ldots, \sigma_D^{(k)}$ of each neuron k are drawn from a distribution $P_\sigma(\sigma_1, \ldots, \sigma_D)$. For a population of tuning functions with centers $\mathbf{c}^{(1)}, \ldots, \mathbf{c}^{(N)}$, a density $\eta(\mathbf{x})$ is introduced according to $\eta(\mathbf{x}) := \sum_{k=1}^{N} \delta(\mathbf{x} - \mathbf{c}^{(k)})$.

The encoding accuracy can be quantified by the Fisher information matrix, $\mathbf{J}$, which is defined as

$$J_{ij}(\mathbf{x}) := E\left[\left(\frac{\partial}{\partial x_i} \ln P(\mathbf{n}; \mathbf{x})\right)\left(\frac{\partial}{\partial x_j} \ln P(\mathbf{n}; \mathbf{x})\right)\right], \tag{3}$$

where $E[\ldots]$ denotes the expectation value over the probability distribution $P(\mathbf{n}; \mathbf{x})$ [2]. The Fisher information yields a lower bound on the expected error of an unbiased estimator that retrieves the stimulus $\mathbf{x}$ from the noisy neural activity (Cramér-Rao inequality) [2]. The minimal estimation error for the i-th feature x_i, $\epsilon_{i,\min}$, is given by $\epsilon_{i,\min}^2 = (\mathbf{J}^{-1})_{ii}$ which reduces to $\epsilon_{i,\min}^2 = 1/J_{ii}(\mathbf{x})$ if $\mathbf{J}$ is diagonal.

We shall now derive a general expression for the population Fisher information. In the next chapter, several cases and their consequences for neural encoding strategies will be discussed.

For model neuron (k), the Fisher information (3) reduces to

$$J_{ij}^{(k)}(\mathbf{x}; \sigma_1^{(k)}, \ldots, \sigma_D^{(k)}) = \frac{1}{\sigma_i^{(k)} \sigma_j^{(k)}} A_\phi\left(\xi^{(k)2}, F, \tau\right) \xi_i^{(k)} \xi_j^{(k)}, \tag{4}$$

where the dependence on the tuning widths is indicated by the list of arguments. The function A_ϕ depends on the shape of the tuning function and is given in [13]. The independence assumption (1) implies that the population Fisher information is the sum of the contributions of the individual neurons, $\sum_{k=1}^{N} J_{ij}^{(k)}(\mathbf{x}; \sigma_1^{(k)}, \ldots, \sigma_D^{(k)})$. We now define a population Fisher information which is averaged over the distribution of tuning widths $P_\sigma(\sigma_1, \ldots, \sigma_D)$:

$$\langle J_{ij}(\mathbf{x})\rangle_\sigma = \sum_{k=1}^{N} \int d\sigma_1 \ldots d\sigma_D \, P_\sigma(\sigma_1, \ldots, \sigma_D) \, J_{ij}^{(k)}(\mathbf{x}; \sigma_1, \ldots, \sigma_D). \quad (5)$$

Introducing the density of tuning curves, $\eta(\mathbf{x})$, into (5) and assuming a constant distribution, $\eta(\mathbf{x}) \equiv \eta \equiv \text{const.}$, one obtains the result that the population Fisher information becomes independent of $\mathbf{x}$ and that the off-diagonal elements of $\mathbf{J}$ vanish [13]. The average population Fisher information then becomes

$$\langle J_{ij}\rangle_\sigma = \eta D K_\phi(F, \tau, D) \left\langle \frac{\prod_{l=1}^{D} \sigma_l}{\sigma_i^2} \right\rangle_\sigma \delta_{ij}, \quad (6)$$

where K_ϕ depends on the geometry of the tuning curves and is defined in [13].

3 Results

In this section, we consider different distributions of tuning widths in (6) and discuss advantageous and disadvantageous strategies for obtaining a high representational accuracy in the neural population.

Radially symmetric tuning curves. For radially symmetric tuning curves of width $\bar{\sigma}$, the tuning-width distribution reads

$$P_\sigma(\sigma_1, \ldots, \sigma_D) = \prod_{i=1}^{D} \delta(\sigma_i - \bar{\sigma});$$

see Fig. 1a for a schematic visualization of the arrangement of the tuning widths for the case $D = 2$. The average population Fisher information (6) for $i = j$ becomes

$$\langle J_{ii}\rangle_\sigma = \eta D K_\phi(F, \tau, D) \bar{\sigma}^{D-2}, \quad (7)$$

a result already obtained by Zhang and Sejnowski [13]. Equation (7) basically shows that the minimal estimation error increases with $\bar{\sigma}$ for $D = 1$, that it does not depend on $\bar{\sigma}$ for $D = 2$, and that it decreases as $\bar{\sigma}$ increases for $D \geq 3$. We shall discuss the relevance of this case below.

Identical tuning curves without radial symmetry. Next we discuss tuning curves which are identical but not radially symmetric; the tuning-width distribution for this case is

$$P_\sigma(\sigma_1, \ldots, \sigma_D) = \prod_{i=1}^{D} \delta(\sigma_i - \bar{\sigma}_i),$$

where $\bar{\sigma}_i$ denotes the fixed width in dimension i. For $i = j$, the average population Fisher information (6) reduces to [11, 4]

$$\langle J_{ii}\rangle_\sigma = \eta D K_\phi(F, \tau, D) \frac{\prod_{l=1}^{D} \bar{\sigma}_l}{\bar{\sigma}_i^2}. \quad (8)$$

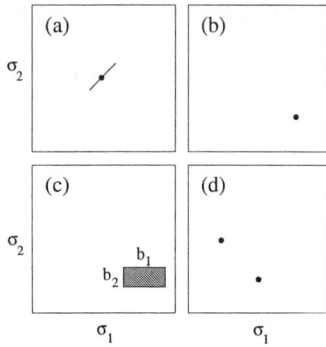

Figure 1: Visualization of different distributions of tuning widths for $D = 2$. (a) Radially symmetric tuning curves. The dot indicates a fixed $\overline{\sigma}$, while the diagonal line symbolizes a variation in $\overline{\sigma}$ discussed in [13]. (b) Identical tuning curves which are not radially symmetric. (c) Tuning widths uniformly distributed within a small rectangle. (d) Two subpopulations each of which is narrowly tuned in one dimension and broadly tuned in the other direction.

Equation (8) contains (7) as a special case. From (8) it becomes immediately clear that the expected minimal square encoding error for the i-th stimulus feature, $\epsilon_{i,\min}^2 = 1/\langle J_{ii}(\mathbf{x})\rangle_\sigma$, depends on i, i.e., *the population specializes in certain features*. The error obtained in dimension i thereby depends on the tuning widths in all dimensions.

Which encoding strategy is optimal for a population whose task it is to encode a single feature, say feature i, with high accuracy while not caring about the other dimensions? In order to answer this question, we re-write (8) in terms of receptive field overlap.

For the tuning functions $f^{(k)}(\mathbf{x})$ encountered empirically, large values of the single-neuron Fisher information (4) are typically restricted to a region around the center of the tuning function, $\mathbf{c}^{(k)}$. The fraction $p(\beta)$ of the Fisher information that falls into a region $E_D : \sqrt{\xi^{(k)2}} \leq \beta$ around $\mathbf{c}^{(k)}$ is given by

$$p(\beta) := \frac{\int_{E_D} d^D x \sum_{i=1}^D J_{ii}^{(k)}(\mathbf{x})}{\int_X d^D x \sum_{i=1}^D J_{ii}^{(k)}(\mathbf{x})} = \frac{\int_0^\beta d\xi\, \xi^{D+1} A_\phi(\xi^2, F, \tau)}{\int_0^\infty d\xi\, \xi^{D+1} A_\phi(\xi^2, F, \tau)}, \qquad (9)$$

where the index (k) was dropped because the tuning curves are assumed to have identical shapes. Equation (9) allows the definition of an effective receptive field, $\mathrm{RF}_{\mathrm{eff}}^{(k)}$, inside of which neuron k conveys a major fraction p_0 of Fisher information, $\mathrm{RF}_{\mathrm{eff}}^{(k)} := \left\{\mathbf{x}\,\middle|\,\sqrt{\xi^{(k)2}} \leq \beta_0\right\}$, where β_0 is chosen such that $p(\beta_0) = p_0$. The Fisher information a neuron k carries is small unless $\mathbf{x} \in \mathrm{RF}_{\mathrm{eff}}^{(k)}$. This has the consequence that a fixed stimulus $\mathbf{x}$ is actually encoded only by a subpopulation of neurons. The point $\mathbf{x}$ in stimulus space is covered by

$$N_{\mathrm{code}} := \eta\, \frac{2\pi^{D/2}(\beta_0)^D}{D\Gamma(D/2)} \prod_{j=1}^D \overline{\sigma}_j \qquad (10)$$

receptive fields. With the help of (10), the average population Fisher information (8) can be re-written as

$$\langle J_{ii}\rangle_\sigma = \frac{D^2 \Gamma(D/2)}{2\pi^{D/2}(\beta_0)^D} K_\phi(F, \tau, D) \frac{N_{\mathrm{code}}}{\overline{\sigma}_i^2}. \qquad (11)$$

Equation (11) can be interpreted as follows: We assume that the population of neurons encodes stimulus dimension i accurately, while all other dimensions are of secondary importance. The average population Fisher information for dimension i, $\langle J_{ii}\rangle_\sigma$, is determined by the tuning width in dimension i, $\overline{\sigma}_i$, and by the size of the active subpopulation, N_{code}. There is a tradeoff between these quantities. On the one hand, the encoding error can be decreased by decreasing $\overline{\sigma}_i$, which enhances the Fisher information carried by each single neuron. Decreasing $\bar{\sigma}_i$, on the other hand, will also shrink the active subpopulation via (10). This impairs the encoding accuracy, because the stimulus position is evaluated from the activity of fewer neurons. If (11) is valid due to a sufficient receptive field overlap, N_{code} can be increased by increasing the tuning widths, $\bar{\sigma}_j$, in all other dimensions $j \neq i$. This effect is illustrated in Fig. 2 for $D = 2$.

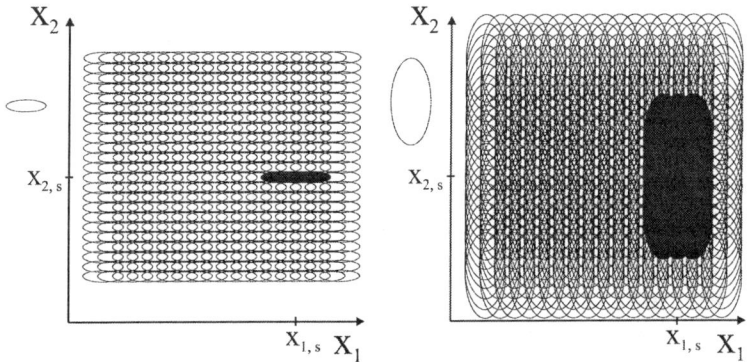

Figure 2: Encoding strategy for a stimulus characterized by parameters $x_{1,s}$ and $x_{2,s}$. Feature x_1 is to be encoded accurately. Effective receptive field shapes are indicated for both populations. If neurons are narrowly tuned in x_2 (left), the active population (solid) is small (here: $N_{\text{code}} = 3$). Broadly tuned receptive fields for x_2 (right) yield a much larger population (here: $N_{\text{code}} = 27$) thus increasing the encoding accuracy.

It shall be noted that although a narrow tuning width $\bar{\sigma}_i$ is advantageous, the limit $\bar{\sigma}_i \longrightarrow 0$ yields a bad representation. For narrowly tuned cells, gaps appear between the receptive fields: The condition $\eta(\mathbf{x}) \equiv \text{const.}$ breaks down, and (6) is no longer valid. A more detailed calculation shows that the encoding error diverges as $\bar{\sigma}_i \longrightarrow 0$ [4]. The fact that the encoding error decreases for both narrow tuning and broad tuning – due to (11) – proves the existence of an *optimal tuning width*. An example is given in Fig. 3a.

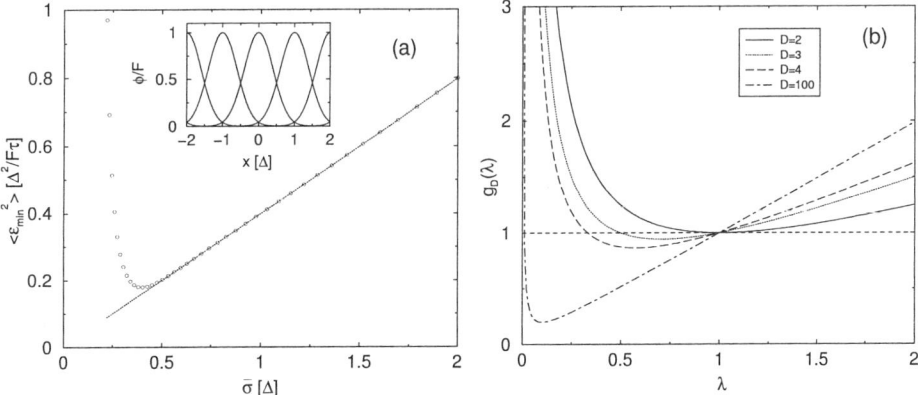

Figure 3: (a) Example for the encoding behavior with narrow tuning curves arranged on a regular lattice of dimension $D = 1$ (grid spacing Δ). Tuning curves are Gaussian, and neural firing is modeled as a Poisson process. Dots indicate the minimal square encoding error averaged over a uniform distribution of stimuli, $\langle \epsilon_{\min}^2 \rangle$, as a function of $\bar{\sigma}$. The minimum is clearly visible. The dotted line shows the corresponding approximation according to (8). The inset shows Gaussian tuning curves of optimal width, $\bar{\sigma}^{\text{opt}} \approx 0.4\Delta$. (b) $g_D(\lambda)$ as a function of λ for different values of D.

Narrow distribution of tuning curves. In order to study the effects of encoding the stimulus with distributed tuning widths instead of identical tuning widths as in the previous cases, we now consider the distribution

$$P_\sigma(\sigma_1,\ldots,\sigma_D) = \prod_{i=1}^{D} \frac{1}{b_i} \Theta\left[\sigma_i - (\overline{\sigma}_i - \frac{b_i}{2})\right] \Theta\left[(\overline{\sigma}_i + \frac{b_i}{2}) - \sigma_i\right], \qquad (12)$$

where Θ denotes the Heaviside step function. Equation (12) describes a uniform distribution in a D-dimensional cuboid of size $b_1,\ldots,b_D$ around $(\overline{\sigma}_1,\ldots\overline{\sigma}_D)$; cf. Fig. 1c. A straightforward calculation shows that in this case, the average population Fisher information (6) for $i = j$ becomes

$$\langle J_{ii}\rangle_\sigma = \eta D K_\phi(F,\tau,D) \frac{\prod_{l=1}^{D} \overline{\sigma}_l}{\overline{\sigma}_i^2} \left\{1 + \frac{1}{12}\left(\frac{b_i}{\overline{\sigma}_i}\right)^2 + \mathcal{O}\left[\left(\frac{b_i}{\overline{\sigma}_i}\right)^4\right]\right\}. \qquad (13)$$

A comparison with (8) yields the astonishing result that an increase in b_i results in an increase in the i-th diagonal element of the average population Fisher information matrix and thus in an improvement in the encoding of the i-th stimulus feature, while the encoding in dimensions $j \neq i$ is not affected. Correspondingly, the total encoding error can be decreased by increasing an arbitrary number of edge lengths of the cube. *The encoding by a population with a variability in the tuning curve geometries as described is more precise than that by a uniform population. This is true for arbitrary D.* Zhang and Sejnowski [13] consider the more artificial situation of a correlated variability of the tuning widths: tuning curves are always assumed to be radially symmetric. This is indicated by the diagonal line in Fig. 1a. A distribution of tuning widths restricted to this subset yields an average population Fisher information $\propto \langle\overline{\sigma}^{D-2}\rangle$ and does not improve the encoding for $D = 2$ or $D = 3$.

Fragmentation into D subpopulations. Finally, we study a family of distributions of tuning widths which also yields a lower minimal encoding error than the uniform population. Let the density of tuning curves be given by

$$P_\sigma(\sigma_1,\ldots,\sigma_D) = \frac{1}{D}\sum_{i=1}^{D} \delta(\sigma_i - \lambda\overline{\sigma}) \prod_{j\neq i} \delta(\sigma_j - \overline{\sigma}), \qquad (14)$$

where $\lambda > 0$. For $\lambda = 1$, the population is uniform as in (7). For $\lambda \neq 1$, the population is split up into D subpopulations; in subpopulation i, σ_i is modified while $\sigma_j \equiv \overline{\sigma}$ for $j \neq i$. See Fig. 1d for an example. The diagonal elements of the average population Fisher information are

$$\langle J_{ii}\rangle_\sigma = \eta D K_\phi(F,\tau,D) \overline{\sigma}^{D-2} \left\{\frac{1 + (D-1)\lambda^2}{D\lambda}\right\}, \qquad (15)$$

where the term in brackets will be abbreviated as $g_D(\lambda)$. $\langle J_{ii}\rangle_\sigma$ does not depend on i in this case because of the symmetry in the subpopulations. Equation (15) and the uniform case (7) differ by $g_D(\lambda)$ which will now be discussed. Figure 3b shows $g_D(\lambda)$ for different values of D. For $\lambda = 1$, $g_D(\lambda) = 1$ and (7) is recovered as expected. $g_D(\lambda) = 1$ also holds for $\lambda = 1/(D-1) < 1$: narrowing one tuning width in each subpopulation will at first decrease the resolution provided $D \geq 3$; this is due to the fact that N_{code} is decreased. For $\lambda < 1/(D-1)$, however, $g_D(\lambda) > 1$, and the resolution exceeds $\langle J_{ii}\rangle_\sigma$ in (7) because each neuron in the i-th subpopulation carries a high Fisher information in the i-th dimension. $D = 2$ is a special case where no impairment of encoding occurs because the effect of a decrease of N_{code} is less pronounced. Interestingly, an increase in λ also yields an improvement in the encoding accuracy. This is a combined effect resulting from an increase in N_{code} on the one hand and the existence of D subpopulations, $D - 1$ of which maintain their tuning widths in each dimension on the other hand. The discussion of $g_D(\lambda)$ leads to the following encoding strategy. For small λ, $\langle J_{ii} \rangle_\sigma$ increases rapidly, which suggests a fragmentation of the population into D subpopulations each of which encodes one feature with high accuracy, i.e., one tuning width in each subpopulation is small whereas the remaining tuning widths are broad. Like in the case discussed above, the theoretical limit of this method is a breakdown of the approximation of $\eta \equiv$ const. and the validity of (6) due to insufficient receptive field overlap.

4 Discussion and Outlook

We have discussed the effects of a variation of the tuning widths on the encoding accuracy obtained by a population of stochastically spiking neurons. The question of an optimal tuning strategy has turned out to be more complicated than previously assumed. More specifically, the case which focused most attention in the literature – radially symmetric receptive fields [5, 1, 9, 3, 13] – yields a worse encoding accuracy than most other cases we have studied: uniform populations with tuning curves which are not radially symmetric; distributions of tuning curves around some symmetric or non-symmetric tuning curve; and the fragmentation of the population into D subpopulations each of which is specialized in one stimulus feature.

In a next step, the theoretical results will be compared to empirical data on encoding properties of neural populations. One aspect is the existence of sensory maps which consist of neural subpopulations with characteristic tuning properties for the features which are represented. For example, receptive fields of auditory neurons in the midbrain of the barn owl have elongated shapes [6]. A second aspect concerns the short-term dynamics of receptive fields. Using single-unit recordings in anaesthetized cats, Wörgötter et al. [12] observed changes in receptive field size taking place in 50–100 ms. Our findings suggest that these dynamics alter the resolution obtained for the corresponding stimulus features. The observed effect may therefore realize a mechanism of an adaptable selective signal processing.

References

[1] Baldi, P. & Heiligenberg, W. (1988) *Biol. Cybern.* **59**:313–318.

[2] Deco, G. & Obradovic, D. (1997) *An Information-Theoretic Approach to Neural Computing.* New York: Springer.

[3] Eurich, C. W. & Schwegler, H. (1997) *Biol. Cybern.* **76**: 357–363.

[4] Eurich, C. W. & Wilke, S. D. (2000) *Neural Comp.* (in press).

[5] Hinton, G. E., McClelland, J. L. & Rumelhart, D. E (1986) In Rumelhart, D. E. & McClelland, J. L. (eds.), *Parallel Distributed Processing, Vol. 1*, pp. 77–109. Cambridge MA: MIT Press.

[6] Knudsen, E. I. & Konishi, M. (1978) *Science* **200**:795–797.

[7] Kuffler, S. W. (1953) *J. Neurophysiol.* **16**:37–68.

[8] Lettvin, J. Y., Maturana, H. R., McCulloch, W. S. & Pitts, W. H. (1959) *Proc. Inst. Radio Eng. NY* **47**:1940–1951.

[9] Snippe, H. P. & Koenderink, J. J. (1992) *Biol. Cybern.* **66**:543–551.

[10] Wiggers, W., Roth, G., Eurich, C. W. & Straub, A. (1995) *J. Comp. Physiol. A* **176**:365–377.

[11] Wilke, S. D. & Eurich, C. W. (1999) In Verleysen, M. (ed.), *ESANN 99, European Symposium on Artificial Neural Networks*, pp. 435–440. Brussels: D-Facto.

[12] Wörgötter, F., Suder, K., Zhao, Y., Kerscher, N., Eysel, U. T. & Funke, K. (1998) *Nature* **396**:165–168.

[13] Zhang, K. & Sejnowski, T. J. (1999) *Neural Comp.* **11**:75–84.

Spiking Boltzmann Machines

Geoffrey E. Hinton
Gatsby Computational Neuroscience Unit
University College London
London WC1N 3AR, UK
hinton@gatsby.ucl.ac.uk

Andrew D. Brown
Department of Computer Science
University of Toronto
Toronto, Canada
andy@cs.utoronto.ca

Abstract

We first show how to represent sharp posterior probability distributions using real valued coefficients on broadly-tuned basis functions. Then we show how the precise times of spikes can be used to convey the real-valued coefficients on the basis functions quickly and accurately. Finally we describe a simple simulation in which spiking neurons learn to model an image sequence by fitting a dynamic generative model.

1 Population codes and energy landscapes

A perceived object is represented in the brain by the activities of many neurons, but there is no general consensus on how the activities of individual neurons combine to represent the multiple properties of an object. We start by focussing on the case of a single object that has multiple instantiation parameters such as position, velocity, size and orientation. We assume that each neuron has an ideal stimulus in the space of instantiation parameters and that its activation rate or probability of activation falls off monotonically in all directions as the actual stimulus departs from this ideal. The semantic problem is to define exactly what instantiation parameters are being represented when the activities of many such neurons are specified.

Hinton, Rumelhart and McClelland (1986) consider binary neurons with receptive fields that are convex in instantiation space. They assume that when an object is present it activates all of the neurons in whose receptive fields its instantiation parameters lie. Consequently, if it is known that only one object is present, the parameter values of the object must lie within the feasible region formed by the *intersection* of the receptive fields of the active neurons. This will be called a *conjunctive* distributed representation. Assuming that each receptive field occupies only a small fraction of the whole space, an interesting property of this type of "coarse coding" is that the bigger the receptive fields, the more accurate the representation. However, large receptive fields lead to a loss of resolution when several objects are present simultaneously.

When the sensory input is noisy, it is impossible to infer the exact parameters of objects so it makes sense for a perceptual system to represent the probability distribution across parameters rather than just a single best estimate or a feasible region. The full probability distribution is essential for correctly combining infor-

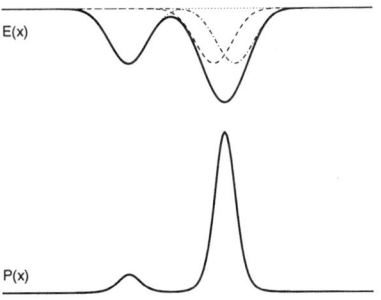

Figure 1: a) Energy landscape over a one-dimensional space. Each neuron adds a dimple (dotted line) to the energy landscape (solid line). b) The corresponding probability density. Where dimples overlap the corresponding probability density becomes sharper. Since the dimples decay to zero, the location of a sharp probability peak is not affected by distant dimples and multimodal distributions can be represented.

mation from different times or different sources. One obvious way to represent this distribution (Anderson and van Essen, 1994) is to allow each neuron to represent a fairly compact probability distribution over the space of instantiation parameters and to treat the activity levels of neurons as (unnormalized) mixing proportions. The semantics of this *disjunctive* distributed representation is precise, but the percepts it allows are not because it is impossible to represent distributions that are sharper than the individual receptive fields and, in high-dimensional spaces, the individual fields must be broad in order to cover the space. Disjunctive representations are used in Kohonen's self-organizing map which is why it is restricted to very low dimensional latent spaces.

The disjunctive model can be viewed as an attempt to approximate arbitrary smooth probability distributions by adding together probability distributions contributed by each active neuron. Coarse coding suggests a multiplicative approach in which the addition is done in the domain of energies (negative log probabilities). Each active neuron contributes an energy landscape over the whole space of instantiation parameters. The activity level of the neuron multiplies its energy landscape and the landscapes for all neurons in the population are added (Figure 1). If, for example, each neuron has a full covariance Gaussian tuning function, its energy landscape is a parabolic bowl whose curvature matrix is the inverse of the covariance matrix. The activity level of the neuron scales the inverse covariance matrix. If there are k instantiation parameters then only $k + k(k+1)/2$ real numbers are required to span the space of means and inverse covariance matrices. So the real-valued activities of $O(k^2)$ neurons are sufficient to represent arbitrary full covariance Gaussian distributions over the space of instantiation parameters.

Treating neural activities as multiplicative coefficients on additive contributions to energy landscapes has a number of advantages. Unlike disjunctive codes, vague distributions are represented by low activities so significant biochemical energy is only required when distributions are quite sharp. A central operation in Bayesian inference is to combine a prior term with a likelihood term or to combine two conditionally independent likelihood terms. This is trivially achieved by adding two energy landscapes[1].

---

[1] We thank Zoubin Ghahramani for pointing out that another important operation, convolving a probability distribution with Gaussian noise, is a difficult non-linear operation on the energy landscape.

2 Representing the coefficients on the basis functions

To perform perception at video rates, the probability distributions over instantiation parameters need to be represented at about 30 frames per second. This seems difficult using relatively slow spiking neurons because it requires the real-valued multiplicative coefficients on the basis functions to be communicated accurately and quickly using all-or-none spikes. The trick is to realise that when a spike arrives at another neuron it produces a postsynaptic potential that is a smooth function of time. So from the perspective of the postsynaptic neuron, the spike has been convolved with a smooth temporal function. By adding a number of these smooth functions together, with appropriate temporal offsets, it is possible to represent any smoothly varying sequence of coefficient values on a basis function, and this makes it possible to represent the temporal evolution of probability distributions as shown in Figure 2. The ability to vary the location of a spike in the single dimension of time thus allows real-valued control of the representation of probability distributions over multiple spatial dimensions.

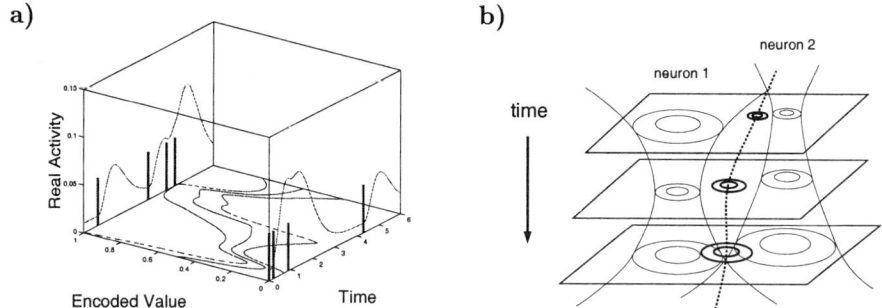

Figure 2: a)Two spiking neurons centered at 0 and 1 can represent the time-varying mean and standard deviation on a single spatial dimension. The spikes are first convolved with a temporal kernel and the resulting activity values are treated as exponents on Gaussian distributions centered at 0 and 1. The ratio of the activity values determines the mean and the sum of the activity values determines the inverse variance. b) The same method can be used for two (or more) spatial dimensions. Time flows from top to bottom. Each spike makes a contribution to the energy landscape that resembles an hourglass (thin lines). The waist of the hourglass corresponds to the time at which the spike has its strongest effect on some post-synaptic population. By moving the hourglasses in time, it is possible to get whatever temporal cross-sections are desired (thick lines) provided the temporal sampling rate is comparable to the time course of the effect of a spike.

Our proposed use of spike timing to convey real values quickly and accurately does not require precise coincidence detection, sub-threshold oscillations, modifiable time delays, or any of the other paraphernalia that has been invoked to explain how the brain could make effective use of the single, real-valued degree of freedom in the timing of a spike (Hopfield, 1995).

The coding scheme we have proposed would be far more convincing if we could show how it was learned and could demonstrate that it was effective in a simulation. There are two ways to design a learning algorithm for such spiking neurons. We could work in the relatively low-dimensional space of the instantiation parameters and design the learning to produce the right representations and interactions between representations in this space. Or we could treat this space as an implicit emergent property of the network and design the learning algorithm to optimize some objective function in the much higher-dimensional space of neural activities in the hope that this will create representations that can be understood using the implicit space of instantiation parameters. We chose the latter approach.

3 A learning algorithm for restricted Boltzmann machines

Hinton (1999) describes a learning algorithm for probabilistic generative models that are composed of a number of experts. Each expert specifies a probability distribution over the visible variables and the experts are combined by multiplying these distributions together and renormalizing.

$$p(\mathbf{d}|\theta_1...\theta_n) = \frac{\Pi_m p_m(\mathbf{d}|\theta_m)}{\sum_i \Pi_m p_m(\mathbf{c}_i|\theta_m)} \quad (1)$$

where $\mathbf{d}$ is a data vector in a discrete space, θ_m is all the parameters of individual model m, $p_m(\mathbf{d}|\theta_m)$ is the probability of $\mathbf{d}$ under model m, and i is an index over all possible vectors in the data space.

The coding scheme we have described is just a product of experts in which each spike is an expert. We first summarize the Product of Experts learning rule for a restricted Boltzmann machine (RBM) which consists of a layer of stochastic binary visible units connected to a layer of stochastic binary hidden units with no intralayer connections. We then extend RBM's to deal with temporal data.

In an RBM, each hidden unit is an expert. When it is off it specifies a uniform distribution over the states of the visible units. When it is on, its weight to each visible unit specifies the log odds that the visible unit is on. Multiplying together the distributions specified by different hidden units is achieved by adding the log odds. Inference in an RBM is much easier than in a causal belief net because there is no explaining away. The hidden states, s_j, are conditionally independent given the visible states, s_i, and the distribution of s_j is given by the standard logistic function σ: $p(s_j = 1) = \sigma(\sum_i w_{ij} s_i)$. Conversely, the hidden states of an RBM are *marginally* dependent so it is easy for an RBM to learn population codes in which units may be highly correlated. It is hard to do this in causal belief nets with one hidden layer because the generative model of a causal belief net assumes marginal independence.

An RBM can be trained by following the gradient of the log likelihood of the data:

$$\Delta w_{ij} = \epsilon \left(<s_i s_j>^0 - <s_i s_j>^\infty \right) \quad (2)$$

where $<s_i s_j>^0$ is the expected value of $s_i s_j$ when data is clamped on the visible units and the hidden states are sampled from their conditional distribution given the data, and $<s_i s_j>^\infty$ is the expected value of $s_i s_j$ after prolonged Gibbs sampling that alternates between sampling from the conditional distribution of the hidden states given the visible states and vice versa.

This learning rule not work well because the sampling noise in the estimate of $<s_i s_j>^\infty$ swamps the gradient. It is far more effective to maximize the *difference* between the log likelihood of the data and the log likelihood of the one-step reconstructions of the data that are produced by first picking binary hidden states from their conditional distribution given the data and then picking binary visible states from their conditional distribution given the hidden states. The gradient of the log likelihood of the one-step reconstructions is complicated because changing a weight changes the probability distribution of the reconstructions:

$$\frac{\partial L^1}{\partial w_{ij}} = <s_i s_j>^1 - <s_i s_j>^\infty + \frac{\partial Q^1}{\partial w_{ij}} \times \frac{\partial L^1}{\partial Q^1} \tag{3}$$

where Q^1 is the distribution of the one-step reconstructions of the training data and Q^∞ is the equilibrium distribution (*i.e.* the stationary distribution of prolonged Gibbs sampling). Fortunately, the cumbersome third term is sufficiently small that ignoring it does not prevent the vector of weight changes from having a positive cosine with the true gradient of the difference of the log likelihoods so the following very simple learning rule works much better than Eq. 2.

$$\Delta w_{ij} = \epsilon \left(<s_i s_j>^0 - <s_i s_j>^1 \right) \tag{4}$$

4 Restricted Boltzmann machines through time

Using a restricted Boltzmann machine we can represent time by *spatializing* it, *i.e.* taking each visible unit, i, and hidden unit, j, and replicating them through time with the constraint that the weight $w_{ij\tau}$ between replica t of i and replica $t + \tau$ of j does not depend on t. To implement the desired temporal smoothing, we also force the weights to be a smooth function of τ that has the shape of the temporal kernel, shown in Figure 3. The only remaining degree of freedom in the weights between replicas of i and replicas of j is the scale of the temporal kernel and it is this scale that is learned. The replicas of the visible and hidden units still form a bipartite graph and the probability distribution over the hidden replicas can be inferred exactly without considering data that lies further into the future than the width of the temporal kernel.

One problem with the restricted Boltzmann machine when we spatialize time is that hidden units at one time step have no memory of their states at previous time steps; they only see the data. If we were to add undirected connections between hidden units at different time steps, then the architecture would return to a fully connected Boltzmann machine in which the hidden units are no longer conditionally independent given the data. A useful trick borrowed from Elman nets is to allow the hidden units to see their previous states, but to treat these observations like data that cannot be modified by future hidden states. Thus, the hidden states may still be inferred independently without resorting to Gibbs sampling. The connections between hidden layer weights also follow the time course of the temporal kernel. These connections act as a predictive prior over the hidden units. It is important to note that these forward connections are not required for the network to model a sequence, but only for the purposes of extrapolating into the future.

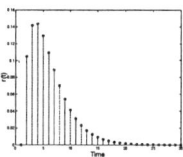

Figure 3: The form of the temporal kernel.

Now the probability that $s_j(t) = 1$ given the states of the visible units is,

$$P(s_j(t) = 1) = \sigma \left(\sum_i w_{ij} h_i(t) + \sum_k w_{kj} h_k(t) \right).$$

where $h_i(t)$ is the convolution of the history of visible unit i with the temporal kernel,

$$h_i(t) = \sum_{\tau=0}^{\infty} s_i(t-\tau) r(\tau),$$

and $h_k(t)$, the convolution of the hidden unit history, is computed similarly. [2] Learning the weights follows immediately from this formula for doing inference. In the positive phase the visible units are clamped at each time step and the posterior of the hidden units conditioned on the data is computed (we assume zero boundary conditions for time before $t = 0$). Then in the negative phase we sample from the posterior of the hidden units, and compute the distribution over the visible units at each time step given these hidden unit states. In each phase the correlations between the hidden and visible units are computed and the learning rule is,

$$\Delta w_{ij} = \sum_{t=0}^{\infty} \sum_{\tau=0}^{\infty} r(\tau) \left(\langle s_j(t) s_i(t-\tau) \rangle^0 - \langle s_j(t) s_i(t-\tau) \rangle^1 \right).$$

5 Results

We trained this network on a sequence of 8x8 synthetic images of a Gaussian blob moving in a circular path. In the following diagrams we display the time sequence of images as a matrix. Each row of the matrix represents a single image with its pixels stretched out into a vector in scanline order, and each column is the time course of a single pixel. The intensity f the pixel is represented by the area of the white patch. We used 20 hidden units. Figure 5a shows a segment (200 time steps) of the time series which was used in training. In this sequence the period of the blob is 80 time steps.

Figure 5b shows how the trained model reconstructs the data after we sample from the hidden layer units. Once we have trained the model it is possible to do forecasting by clamping visible layer units for a segment of a sequence and then doing iterative Gibbs sampling to generate future points in the sequence. Figure 5c shows that given 50 time steps from the series, the model can predict reasonably far into the future, before the pattern dies out. One problem with these simulations is that we are treating the real valued intensities in the images as probabilities. While this works for the blob images, where the values can be viewed as the probabilities of pixels in a binary image being on, this is not true for more natural images.

6 Discussion

In our initial simulations we used a causal sigmoid belief network (SBN) rather than a restricted Boltzmann machine. Inference in an SBN is *much* more difficult than in an RBM. It requires Gibbs sampling or severe approximations, and even if a temporal kernel is used to ensure that a replica of a hidden unit at one time

---

[2] Computing the conditional probability distribution over the visible units given the hidden states is done in a similar fashion, with the caveat that the weights in each direction must be symmetric. Thus, the convolution is done using the reverse kernel.

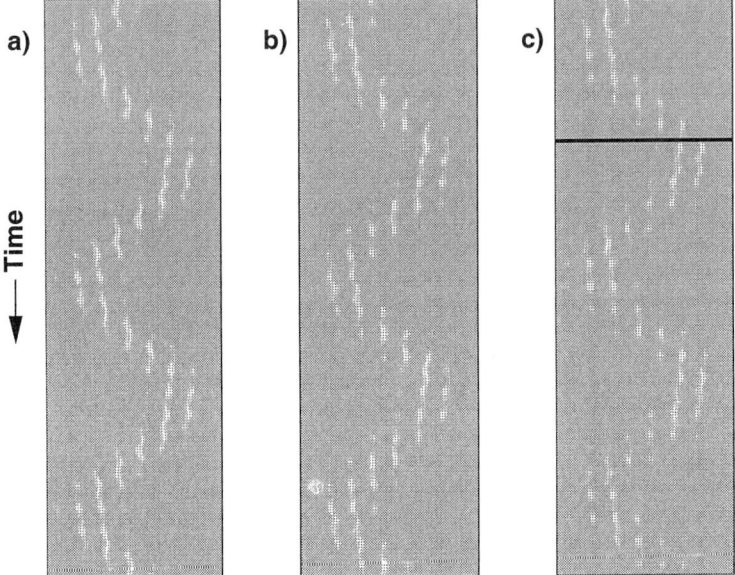

Figure 4: a) The original data, b) reconstruction of the data, and c) prediction of the data given 50 time steps of the sequence. The black line indicates where the prediction begins.

has no connections to replicas of visible units at very different times, the posterior distribution of the hidden units still depends on data far in the future. The Gibbs sampling made our SBN simulations very slow and the sampling noise made the learning far less effective than in the RBM. Although the RBM simulations seem closer to biological plausibility, they too suffer from a major problem. To apply the learning procedure it is necessary to reconstruct the data from the hidden states and we do not know how to do this without interfering with the incoming datastream. In our simulations we simply ignored this problem by allowing a visible unit to have both an observed value and a reconstructed value at the same time.

Acknowledgements

We thank Zoubin Ghahramani, Peter Dayan, Rich Zemel, Terry Sejnowski and Radford Neal for helpful discussions. This research was funded by grants from the Gatsby Foundation and NSERC.

References

Anderson, C.H. & van Essen, D.C (1994). Neurobiological computational systems. In J.M Zureda, R.J. Marks, & C.J. Robinson (Eds.), *Computational Intelligence Imitating Life* 213-222. New York: IEEE Press.

Hinton, G. E. (1999) Products of Experts. *ICANN 99: Ninth international conference on Artificial Neural Networks*, Edinburgh, 1-6.

Hinton, G. E., McClelland, J. L., & Rumelhart, D. E. (1986) Distributed representations. In Rumelhart, D. E. and McClelland, J. L., editors, *Parallel Distributed Processing: Explorations in the Microstructure of Cognition. Volume 1: Foundations*, MIT Press, Cambridge, MA.

Hopfield, J. (1995). Pattern recognition computation using action potential timing for stimulus representation. *Nature*, **376**, 33-36.

Distributed Synchrony of Spiking Neurons in a Hebbian Cell Assembly

David Horn   Nir Levy
School of Physics and Astronomy,
Raymond and Beverly Sackler Faculty of Exact Sciences,
Tel Aviv University, Tel Aviv 69978, Israel
horn@neuron.tau.ac.il   nirlevy@post.tau.ac.il

Isaac Meilijson   Eytan Ruppin
School of Mathematical Sciences,
Raymond and Beverly Sackler Faculty of Exact Sciences,
Tel Aviv University, Tel Aviv 69978, Israel
isaco@math.tau.ac.il   ruppin@math.tau.ac.il

Abstract

We investigate the behavior of a Hebbian cell assembly of spiking neurons formed via a temporal synaptic learning curve. This learning function is based on recent experimental findings. It includes potentiation for short time delays between pre- and post-synaptic neuronal spiking, and depression for spiking events occuring in the reverse order. The coupling between the dynamics of the synaptic learning and of the neuronal activation leads to interesting results. We find that the cell assembly can fire asynchronously, but may also function in complete synchrony, or in distributed synchrony. The latter implies spontaneous division of the Hebbian cell assembly into groups of cells that fire in a cyclic manner. We invetigate the behavior of distributed synchrony both by simulations and by analytic calculations of the resulting synaptic distributions.

1 Introduction

The Hebbian paradigm that serves as the basis for models of associative memory is often conceived as the statement that a group of excitatory neurons (the Hebbian cell assembly) that are coupled synaptically to one another fire together when a subset of the group is being excited by an external input. Yet the details of the temporal spiking patterns of neurons in such an assembly are still ill understood. Theoretically it seems quite obvious that there are two general types of behavior: synchronous neuronal firing, and asynchrony where no temporal order exists in the assembly and the different neurons fire randomly but with the same overall rate. Further subclassifications were recently suggested by [Brunel, 1999]. Experimentally this question is far from being settled because evidence for the associative memory paradigm is quite scarce. On one hand, one possible realization of associative memories in the brain was demonstrated by [Miyashita, 1988] in the inferotemporal cortex. This area was recently reinvestigated by [Yakovlev et al., 1998] who compared their experimental results with a model of asynchronized spiking neurons. On the other hand there exists experimental evidence [Abeles, 1982] for temporal activity patterns in the frontal cortex that Abeles called synfire-chains. Could they correspond to an alternative type of synchronous realization of a memory attractor?

To answer these questions and study the possible realizations of attractors in cortical-like networks we investigate the temporal structure of an attractor assuming the existence of a synaptic learning curve that is continuously applied to the memory system. This learning curve is motivated by the experimental observations of [Markram et al., 1997, Zhang et al., 1998] that synaptic potentiation or depression occurs within a critical time window in which both pre- and post-synaptic neurons have to fire. If the pre-synaptic neuron fires first within 30ms or so, potentiation will take place. Depression is the rule for the reverse order.

The regulatory effects of such a synaptic learning curve on the synapses of a *single neuron* that is subjected to external inputs were investigated by [Abbott and Song, 1999] and by [Kempter et al., 1999]. We investigate here the effect of such a rule within an *assembly of neurons* that are all excited by the same external input throughout a training period, and are allowed to influence one another through their resulting sustained activity.

2 The Model

We study a network composed of N_E excitatory and N_I inhibitory integrate-and-fire neurons. Each neuron in the network is described by its subthreshold membrane potential $V_i(t)$ obeying

$$\dot{V}_i(t) = -\frac{1}{\tau_n} V_i(t) + RI_i(t) \qquad (1)$$

where τ_n is the neuronal integration time constant. A spike is generated when $V_i(t)$ reaches the threshold $V_{rest} + \theta$, upon which a refractory period of τ_{RP} is set on and the membrane potential is reset to V_{reset} where $V_{rest} < V_{reset} < V_{rest} + \theta$. $I_i(t)$ is the sum of recurrent and external synaptic current inputs. The net synaptic input charging the membrane of excitatory neuron i at time t is

$$RI_i(t) = \sum_j J_{ij}^{EE}(t) \sum_l \delta\left(t - t_j^l - \tau_d\right) - \sum_j J_{ij}^{EI} \sum_m \delta\left(t - t_j^m - \tau_d\right) + I^{ext} \qquad (2)$$

summing over the different synapses of $j = 1, \ldots, N_E$ excitatory neurons and of $j = 1, \ldots, N_I$ inhibitory neurons, with postsynaptic efficacies $J_{ij}^{EE}(t)$ and J_{ij}^{EI} respectively. The sum over l (m) represents a sum on different spikes arriving at synapse j, at times $t = t_j^l + \tau_d$ ($t = t_j^m + \tau_d$), where t_j^l (t_j^m) is the emission time of the l-th (m-th) spike from the excitatory (inhibitory) neuron j and τ_d is the synaptic delay. I^{ext}, the external current, is assumed to be random and independent at each neuron and each time step, drawn from a Poisson distribution with mean λ^{ext}. Analogously, the synaptic input to the inhibitory neuron i at time t is

$$RI_i(t) = \sum_j J_{ij}^{IE} \sum_l \delta\left(t - t_j^l - \tau_d\right) - \sum_j J_{ij}^{II} \sum_m \delta\left(t - t_j^m - \tau_d\right) + I^{ext}. \qquad (3)$$

We assume full connectivity among the excitatory neurons, but only partial connectivity between all other three types of possible connnections, with connection probabilities denoted by C^{EI}, C^{IE} and C^{II}. In the following we will report simulation results in which the synaptic delays τ_d were assigned to each synapse, or pair of neurons, randomly, chosen from some finite set of values. Our analytic calculation will be done for one fixed value of this delay parameter.

The synaptic efficacies between excitatory neurons are assumed to be potentiated or depressed according to the firing patterns of the pre- and post-synaptic neurons. In addition we allow for a uniform synaptic decay. Thus each excitatory synapse obeys

$$\dot{J}_{ij}^{EE}(t) = -\frac{1}{\tau_s} J_{ij}^{EE}(t) + F_{ij}(t) \tag{4}$$

where the synaptic decay constant τ_s is assumed to be very large compared to the membrane time constant τ_n. $J_{ij}^{EE}(t)$ are constrained to vary in the range $[0, J_{max}]$. The change in synaptic efficacy is defined by $F_{ij}(t)$, as

$$F_{ij}(t) = \sum_{k,l} \left[\delta(t - t_i^k) K_P(t_j^l - t_i^k) + \delta(t - t_j^l) K_D(t_j^l - t_i^k) \right] \tag{5}$$

where K_P and K_D are the potentiation and depression branches of the kernel function

$$K(\delta) = -c\delta \exp\left[-(a\delta + b)^2 \right] \tag{6}$$

plotted in Figure 1. Following [Zhang et al., 1998] we distinguish between the situation where the postsynaptic spike, at t_i^k, appears after or before the presynaptic spike, at t_j^l, using the asymmetric kernel that captures the essence of their experimental observations.

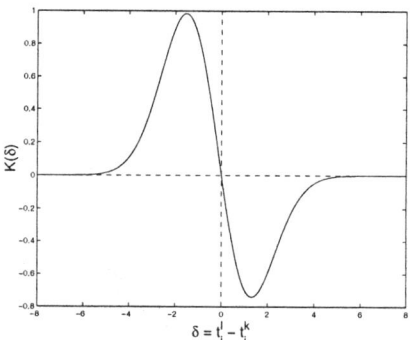

Figure 1: The kernel function whose left part, K_P, leads to potentiation of the synapse, and whose right branch, K_D, causes synaptic depression.

3 Distributed Synchrony of a Hebbian Assembly

We have run our system with synaptic delays chosen randomly to be either 1, 2, or $3ms$, and temporal parameters τ_n chosen as $40ms$ for excitatory neurons and $20ms$ for inhibitory ones. Turning external input currents off after a while we obtained sustained firing activities in the range of 100-150 Hz. We have found, in addition to synchronous and asynchronous realizations of this attractor, a mode of *distributed synchrony*. A characteristic example of a long cycle is shown in Figure 2: The 100 excitatory neurons split into groups such that each group fires at the same frequency and at a fixed phase difference from any other group. The J_{ij}^{EE} synaptic efficacies

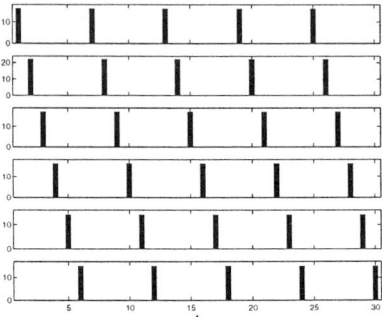

Figure 2: Distributed synchronized firing mode. The firing patterns of six cell assemblies of excitatory neurons are displayed *vs* time (in ms). These six groups of neurons formed in a self-organized manner for a kernel function with equal potentiation and depression. The delays were chosen randomly from three values, 1 2 or 3ms, and the system is monitored every 0.5ms.

are initiated as small random values. The learning process leads to the self-organized synaptic matrix displayed in Figure 3(a). The block form of this matrix represents the ordered couplings that are responsible for the fact that each coherent group of neurons feeds the activity of groups that follow it. The self-organized groups form spontaneously. When the synapses are affected by some external noise, as can come about from Hebbian learning in which these neurons are being coupled with other pools of neurons, the groups will change and regroup, as seen in Figure 3(b) and 3(c).

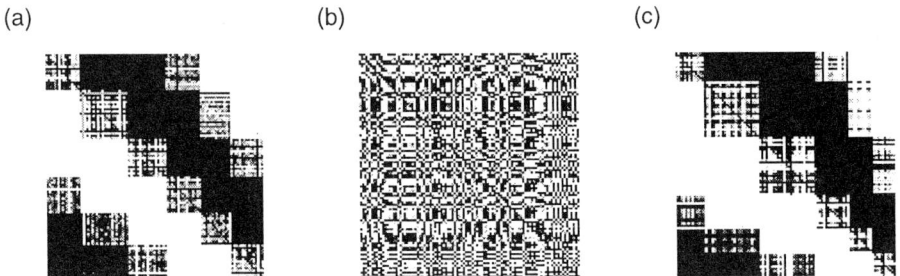

Figure 3: A synaptic matrix for $n = 6$ distributed synchrony. The synaptic matrix between the 100 excitatory neurons of our system is displayed in a grey-level code with black meaning zero efficacy and white standing for the synaptic upper-bound. (a) The matrix that exists during the distributed synchronous mode of Figure 2. Its basis is ordered such that neurons that fire together are grouped together. (b) Using the same basis as in (a) a new synaptic matrix is shown, one that is formed after stopping the sustained activity of Figure 2, introducing noise in the synaptic matrix, and reinstituting the original memory training. (c) The same matrix as (b) is shown in a new basis that exhibits connections that lead to a new and different realization of distributed synchrony.

A stable distributed synchrony cycle can be simply understood for the case of a single synaptic delay setting the basic step, or phase difference, of the cycle. When several delay parameters exist, a situation that probably more accurately represents the α-function character of synaptic transmission in cortical networks, distributed synchrony may still be obtained, as is evident from Figure 2. After some time the cycle may destabilize and regrouping may occur by itself, without external interference. The likelihood of this scenario is increased because different synaptic connections that have different delays can interfere with one another. Nonetheless, over time scales of the type shown in Figure 2, grouping is stable.

4 Analysis of a Cycle

In this section we analyze the dynamics of the network when it is in a stable state of distributed synchrony. We assume that n groups of neurons are formed and calculate the stationary distribution of $J_{ij}^{EE}(t)$. In this state the firing pattern of every two neurons in the network can be characterized by their frequency $\nu(t)$ and by their relative phase δ. We assume that δ is a random normal variable with mean μ_δ and standard deviation σ_δ. Thus, Eq. 4 can be rewritten as the following stochastic differential equation

$$dJ_{ij}^{EE}(t) = \left[\mu_{F_{ij}}(t) - \frac{1}{\tau_s}J_{ij}^{EE}(t)\right]dt + \sigma_{F_{ij}}(t)dW(t) \qquad (7)$$

where $F_{ij}(t)$ (Eq. 5) is represented here by a drift term $\mu_{F_{ij}}(t)$ and a diffusion term $\sigma_{F_{ij}}(t)$ which are its mean and standard deviation. $W(t)$ describes a Wiener process. Note that both $\mu_{F_{ij}}(t)$ and $\sigma_{F_{ij}}(t)$ are calculated for a specific distribution of δ and are functions of μ_δ and σ_δ.

The stochastic process that satisfies Eq. 7 will satisfy the Fokker-Plank equation for the probability distribution f of J_{ij}^{EE},

$$\frac{\partial f(J_{ij}^{EE},t)}{\partial t} = -\frac{\partial}{\partial J_{ij}^{EE}}\left[\left(\mu_{F_{ij}}(t) - \frac{1}{\tau_s}J_{ij}^{EE}\right)f(J_{ij}^{EE},t)\right] + \frac{\sigma_{F_{ij}}^2(t)}{2}\frac{\partial^2 f(J_{ij}^{EE},t)}{\partial J_{ij}^{EE2}} \qquad (8)$$

with reflecting boundary conditions imposed by the synaptic bounds, 0 and J_{max}. Since we are interested in the stable state of the process we solve the stationary equation. The resulting density function is

$$f(J_{ij}^{EE},\mu_\delta,\sigma_\delta) = \frac{\mathcal{N}}{\sigma_{F_{ij}}^2(t)}\exp\left[\frac{1}{\sigma_{F_{ij}}^2(t)}\left(2\mu_{F_{ij}}J_{ij}^{EE} - \frac{1}{\tau_s}J_{ij}^{EE2}\right)\right] \qquad (9)$$

where

$$\mathcal{N} = \left[\int_0^{J_{max}} f(J_{ij}^{EE},\mu_\delta,\sigma_\delta)dJ_{ij}^{EE}\right]^{-1} \qquad (10)$$

Eq. 9 enables us to calculate the stationary distribution of the synaptic efficacies between the presynaptic neuron i and the post-synaptic neuron j given their frequency ν and the parameters μ_δ and σ_δ. An example of a solution for a 3-cycle is shown in Figure 4. In this case all neurons fire with frequency $\nu = (3\tau_d)^{-1}$ and μ_δ takes one of the values $-\tau_d, 0, \tau_d$.

Simulation results of a 3-cycle in a network of excitatory and inhibitory integrate-and-fire neurons described in Section 2 are given in Figure 5. As can be seen the results obtained from the analysis match those observed in the simulation.

5 Discussion

The interesting experimental observations of synaptic learning curves [Markram et al., 1997, Zhang et al., 1998] have led us to study their implications for the firing patterns of a Hebbian cell assembly. We find that, in addition

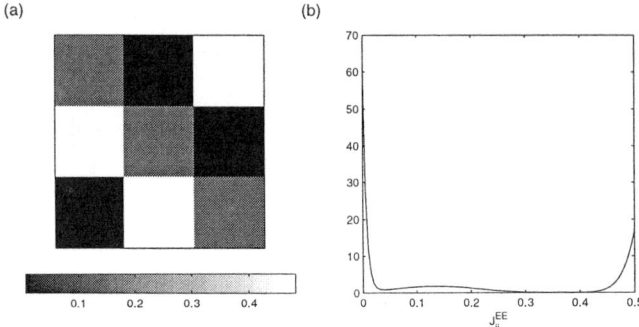

Figure 4: Results of the analysis for $n = 3$, $\sigma_\delta = 2ms$ and $\tau_d = 2.5ms$. (a) The synaptic matrix. Each of the nine blocks symbolizes a group of connections between neurons that have a common phase-lag μ_δ. The mean of J_{ij}^{EE} was calculated for each cell by Eq. 9 and its value is given by the gray scale tone. (b) The distribution of synaptic values between all excitatory neurons.

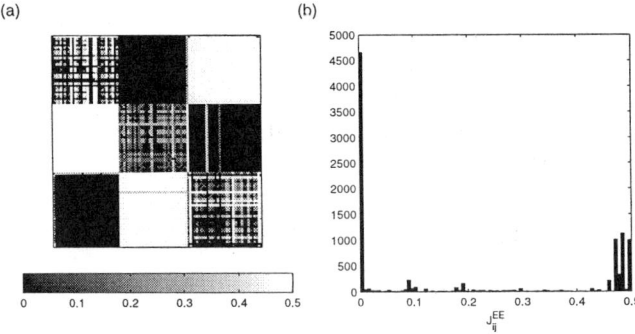

Figure 5: Simulation results for a network of $N_E = 100$ and $N_I = 50$ integrate-and-fire neurons, when the network is in a stable $n = 3$ state. $\tau_n = 10ms$ for both excitatory and inhibitory neurons. The average frequency of the neurons is 130 Hz. (a) The excitatory synaptic matrix. (b) Histogram of the synaptic efficacies.

to the expected synchronous and asynchronous modes, an interesting behavior of distributed synchrony can emerge. This is the phenomenon that we have investigated both by simulations and by analytic evaluation.

Distributed synchrony is a mode in which the Hebbian cell assembly breaks into an n-cycle. This cycle is formed by instantaneous symmetry breaking, hence specific classification of neurons into one of the n groups depends on initial conditions, noise, etc. Thus the different groups of a single cycle do not have a semantic invariant meaning of their own. It seems perhaps premature to try and identify these cycles with synfire chains [Abeles, 1982] that show recurrence of firing patterns of groups of neurons with periods of hundreds of ms. Note however, that if we make such an identification, it is a different explanation from the model of [Herrmann et al., 1995], which realizes the synfire chain by combining sets of preexisting patterns into a cycle.

The simulations in Figures 2 and 3 were carried out with a learning curve that possessed equal potentiation and depression branches, i.e. was completely antisymmetric in its argument. In that case no synaptic decay was allowed. Figure 5, on the other hand, had stronger potentiation than depression, and a finite synaptic decay time was assumed. Other conditions in these nets were different too, yet both had a window of parameters where distributed synchrony showed up. Using the analytic approach of section 4 we can derive the probability distribution of synaptic values once a definite cyclic pattern of distributed synchrony is formed. An analytic solution of the combined dynamics of both the synapses and the spiking neurons is still an open challenge. Hence we have to rely on the simulations to prove that distributed synchrony is a natural spatiotemporal behavior that follows from combined neuronal dynamics and synaptic learning as outlined in section 2. To the extent that both types of dynamics reflect correctly the dynamics of cortical neural networks, we may expect distributed synchrony to be a mode in which neuronal attractors are being realized.

The mode of distrbuted synchrony is of special significance to the field of neural computation since it forms a bridge between the feedback and feed-forward paradigms. Note that whereas the attractor that is formed by the Hebbian cell assembly is of global feedback nature, i.e. one may regard all neurons of the assembly as being connected to other neurons within the same assembly, the emerging structure of distributed synchrony shows that it breaks down into groups. These groups are connected to one another in a self-organized feed-forward manner, thus forming the cyclic behavior we have observed.

References

[Abbott and Song, 1999] L. F. Abbott and S. Song. Temporally asymmetric hebbian learning, spike timing and neuronal response variability. In M. S. Kearns, S. A. Solla, and D. A. Cohn, editors, *Advances in Neural Information Processing Systems 11: Proceedings of the 1998 Conference*, pages 69 – 75. MIT Press, 1999.

[Abeles, 1982] M. Abeles. *Local Cortical Circuits*. Springer, Berlin, 1982.

[Brunel, 1999] N. Brunel. Dynamics of sparsely connected networks of excitatory and inhibitory spiking neurons. *Journal of Computational Neuroscience*, 1999.

[Herrmann et al., 1995] M. Herrmann, J. Hertz, and A. Prügel-Bennet. Analysis of synfire chains. *Network: Comp. in Neural Systems*, 6:403 – 414, 1995.

[Kempter et al., 1999] R. Kempter, W. Gerstner, and J. Leo van Hemmen. Spike-based compared to rate-based hebbian learning. In M. S. Kearns, S. A. Solla, and D. A. Cohn, editors, *Advances in Neural Information Processing Systems 11: Proceedings of the 1998 Conference*, pages 125 – 131. MIT Press, 1999.

[Markram et al., 1997] H. Markram, J. Lübke, M. Frotscher, and B. Sakmann. Regulation of synaptic efficacy by coincidence of postsynaptic aps and epsps. *Science*, 275(5297):213 – 215, 1997.

[Miyashita, 1988] Y. Miyashita. Neuronal correlate of visual associative long-term memory in the primate temporal cortex. *Nature*, 335:817 – 820, 1988.

[Yakovlev et al., 1998] V. Yakovlev, S. Fusi, E. Berman, and E. Zohary. Inter-trial neuronal activity in inferior temporal cortex: a putative vehicle to generate long-term visual associations. *Nature Neurosc.*, 1(4):310 – 317, 1998.

[Zhang et al., 1998] L. I. Zhang, H. W. Tao, C. E. Holt, W. A. Harris, and M. Poo. A critical window for cooperation and competition among developing retinotectal synapses. *Nature*, 395:37 – 44, 1998.

Can V1 mechanisms account for figure-ground and medial axis effects?

Zhaoping Li
Gatsby Computational Neuroscience Unit
University College London
zhaoping@gatsby.ucl.ac.uk

Abstract

When a visual image consists of a figure against a background, V1 cells are physiologically observed to give higher responses to image regions corresponding to the figure relative to their responses to the background. The medial axis of the figure also induces relatively higher responses compared to responses to other locations in the figure (except for the boundary between the figure and the background). Since the receptive fields of V1 cells are very small compared with the global scale of the figure-ground and medial axis effects, it has been suggested that these effects may be caused by feedback from higher visual areas. I show how these effects can be accounted for by V1 mechanisms when the size of the figure is small or is of a certain scale. They are a manifestation of the processes of pre-attentive segmentation which detect and highlight the boundaries between homogeneous image regions.

1 Introduction

Segmenting figure from ground is one of the most important visual tasks. We neither know how to execute it on a computer in general, nor do we know how the brain executes it. Further, the medial axis of a figure has been suggested as providing a convenient skeleton representation of its shape (Blum 1973). It is therefore exciting to find that responses of cells in V1, which is usually considered a low level visual area, differentiate between figure and ground (Lamme 1995, Lamme, Zipser, and Spekreijse 1997, Zipser, Lamme, Schiller 1996) and highlight the medial axis (Lee, Mumford, Romero, and Lamme 1998). This happens even though the receptive fields in V1 are much smaller than the scale of these global and perceptually significant phenomena. A common assumption is that feedback from higher visual areas is mainly responsible for these effects. This is supported by the finding that the figure-ground effects in V1 can be strongly reduced or abolished by anaesthesia or lesions in higher visual areas (Lamme et al 1997).

However, in a related experiment (Gallant, van Essen, and Nothdurft 1995), V1 cells were found to give higher responses to global boundaries between two texture regions. Further, this border effect was significant only 10-15 milliseconds after the initial responses of the cells and was present even under anaesthesia. It is thus plausible that V1 mechanisms is mainly responsible for the border effect.

In this paper, I propose that the figure-ground and medial axis effects are manifestations of the border effect, at least for apropriately sized figures. The border effect is significant within a limited and finite distance from the figure border. Let us call the image region within this finite distance from the border the *effective border region*. When the size of the figure is small enough, all parts of the figure belong to the effective border region and can induce higher responses. This suggests that the figure-ground effect will be reduced or diminished as the size of the figure becomes larger, and the V1 responses to regions of the figure far away from the border will not be significantly higher than responses to background. This suggestion is supported by experimental findings (Lamme et al 1997). Furthermore, the border effect can create secondary ripples as the effect decays with distance from the border. Let us call the distance from the border to the ripple the *ripple wavelength*. When the size of a figure is roughly twice the ripple wavelength, the ripples from the two opposite borders of the figure can reinforce each other at the center of the figure to create the medial axis effect, which, indeed, is observed to occur only for figures of appropriate sizes (Lee et al 1998).

I validate this proposal using a biologically based model of V1 with intra-cortical interactions between cells with nearby but not necessarily overlapping receptive fields. Intra-cortical interactions cause the responses of a cell be modulated by nearby stimuli outside its classical receptive fields — the contextual influences that are observed physiologically (Knierim and van Essen 1992, Kapadia et al 1995). Contextual influences make V1 cells sensitive to global image features, despite their local receptive fields, as manifested in the border and other effects.

2 The V1 model

We have previously constructed a V1 model and shown it to be able to highlight smooth contours against a noisy background (Li 1998, 1999, 1999b) and also the boundaries between texture regions in images — the border effect. Its behavior agrees with physiological observations (Knierim and van Essen 1992, Kapadia et al 1995) that the neural response to a bar is suppressed strongly by contextual bars of similar orientatons — iso-orientation suppression; that the response is less suppressed by orthogonally or randomly oriented contextual bars; and that it is enhanced by contextual bars that are aligned to form a smooth contour in which the bar is within the receptive field — contour enhancement. Without loss of generality, the model ignores color, motion, and stereo dimensions, includes mainly layer 2-3 orientation selective cells, and ignores the intra-hypercolumnar mechanism by which their receptive fields are formed. Inputs to the model are images filtered by the edge- or bar-like local receptive fields (RFs) of V1 cells.[1] Cells influence each other contextually via horizontal intra-cortical connections (Rockland and Lund 1983, Gilbert, 1992), transforming patterns of inputs to patterns of cell responses. Fig. 1 shows the elements of the model and their interactions. At each location i there is a model V1 hypercolumn composed of K neuron pairs. Each pair (i, θ) has RF center i and preferred orientation $\theta = k\pi/K$ for $k = 1, 2, ...K$, and is called (the neural representation of) an edge segment. Based on experimental data (White, 1989), each edge segment consists of an excitatory and an inhibitory neuron that are interconnected, and each model cell represents a collection of local cells of similar types. The excitatory cell receives the visual input; its output is used as a measure of the response or salience of the edge segment and projects to higher visual areas. The inhibitory cells are treated as interneurons. Based on observations

---

[1]The terms 'edge' and 'bar' will be used interchangeably.

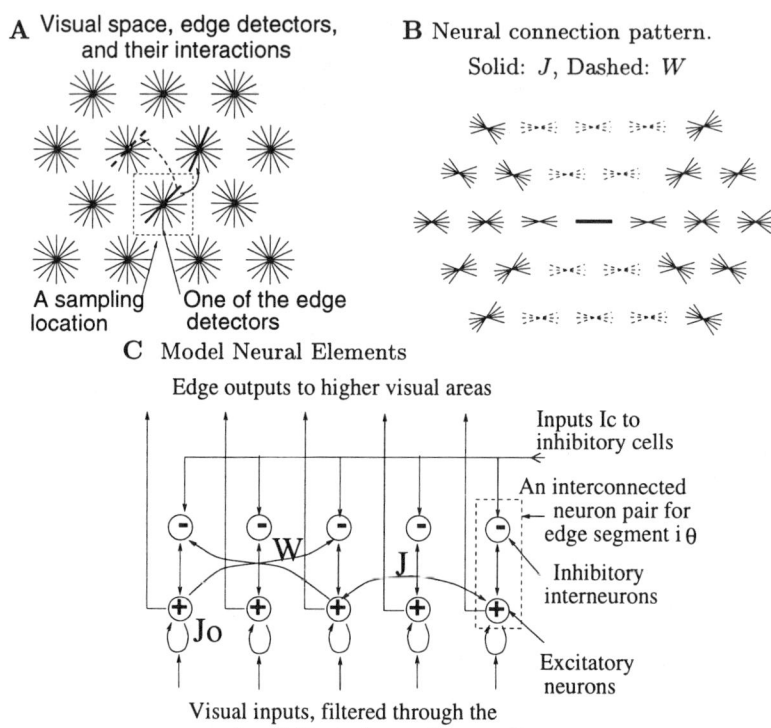

Figure 1: **A**: Visual inputs are sampled in a discrete grid of edge/bar detectors. Each grid point i has K neuron pairs (see **C**), one per bar segment, tuned to different orientations θ spanning 180°. Two segments at different grid points can interact with each other via monosynaptic excitation J (the solid arrow from one thick bar to anothe r) or disynaptic inhibition W (the dashed arrow to a thick dashed bar). See also **C**. **B**: A schematic of the neural connection pattern from the center (thick solid) bar to neighboring bars within a few sampling unit distances. J's contacts are shown by thin solid bars. W's are shown by thin dashed bars. The connection pattern is translation and rotation invariant. **C**: An input bar segment is directly processed by an interconnected pair of excitatory and inhibitory cells, each cell models abstractly a local group of cells of the same type. The excitatory cell receives visual input and sends output $g_x(x_{i\theta})$ to higher centers. The inhibitory cell is an interneuron. Visual space is taken as having periodic boundary conditions.

by Gilbert, Lund and their colleagues (Rockland and Lund, 1983, Gilbert 1992) horizontal connections $J_{i\theta,j\theta'}$ (respectively $W_{i\theta,j\theta'}$) mediate contextual influences via monosynaptic excitation (respectively disynaptic inhibition) from $j\theta'$ to $i\theta$ which have nearby but different RF centers, $i \neq j$, and similar orientation preferences, $\theta \sim \theta'$. The membrane potentials follow the equations:

$$\dot{x}_{i\theta} = -\alpha_x x_{i\theta} - \sum_{\Delta\theta} \psi(\Delta\theta) g_y(y_{i,\theta+\Delta\theta}) + J_o g_x(x_{i\theta}) + \sum_{j\neq i, \theta'} J_{i\theta,j\theta'} g_x(x_{j\theta'}) + I_{i\theta} + I_o$$

$$\dot{y}_{i\theta} = -\alpha_y y_{i\theta} + g_x(x_{i\theta}) + \sum_{j\neq i, \theta'} W_{i\theta,j\theta'} g_x(x_{j\theta'}) + I_c$$

where $\alpha_x x_{i\theta}$ and $\alpha_y y_{i\theta}$ model the decay to resting potential, $g_x(x)$ and $g_y(y)$ are sigmoid-like functions modeling cells' firing rates in response to membrane potentials x and y, respectively, $\psi(\Delta\theta)$ is the spread of inhibition within a hypercolumn, $J_o g_x(x_{i\theta})$ is self excitation, I_c and I_o are background inputs, including noise and inputs modeling the general and local normalization of activities (see Li (1998) for more details). Visual input $I_{i\theta}$ persists after onset, and initializes the activity levels $g_x(x_{i\theta})$. The activities are then modified by the contextual influences. Depending on the visual input, the system often settles into an oscillatory state (Gray and Singer, 1989, see the details in Li 1998). Temporal averages of $g_x(x_{i\theta})$ over several oscillation cycles are used as the model's output. The nature of the computation performed by the model is determined largely by the horizontal connections J and W, which are local (spanning only a few hypercolumns), and translation and rotation invariant (Fig. 1B).

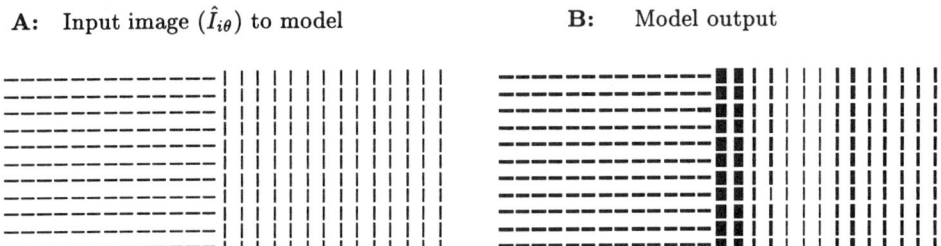

Figure 2: An example of the performance of the model. **A**: Input $\hat{I}_{i\theta}$ consists of two regions; each visible bar has the same input strength. **B**: Model output for **A**, showing non-uniform output strengths (temporal averages of $g_x(x_{i\theta})$) for the edges. The input and output strengths are proportional to the bar widths. Because of the noise in the system, the saliencies of the bars in the same column are not exactly the same, this is also the case in other figures.

The model was applied to some texture border and figure-ground stimuli, as shown in examples in the figures. The input values $\hat{I}_{i\theta}$ are the same for all visible bars in each example. The differences in the outputs are caused by intracortical interactions. They become significant about one membrane time constant after the initial neural response (Li, 1998). The widths of the bars in the figures are proportional to input and output strengths. The plotted region in each picture is often a small region of an extended image. The same model parameters (*e.g.* the dependence of the synaptic weights on distances and orientations, the thresholds and gains in the functions $g_x()$ and $g_y()$, and the level of input noise in I_o) are used for all the simulation examples.

Fig. 2 demonstrates that the model indeed gives higher responses to the boundaries between texture regions. This border effect is highly significant within a distance of about 2 texture element spacings from the border. Thus the effective border region is about 2 in texture element spacings in this example. Furthermore, at about 9 texture element spacings to the right of the texture border there is a much smaller but significant (visible on the figure) secondary peak in the response amplitude. Thus the ripple wavelength is about 9 texture element spacings here. The border effect is mainly caused by the fact that the texture elements at the border experience less iso-orientation suppression (which reduces the response levels to other texture bars in the middle of a homogeneous (texture) region) — the texture elements at the border have fewer neighboring texture bars of a similar orientation than the texture elements in the centers of the regions. The stronger responses to the effective border region cause extra iso-orientation suppression to texture bars near but right outside the effective border region. Let us call this region of stronger

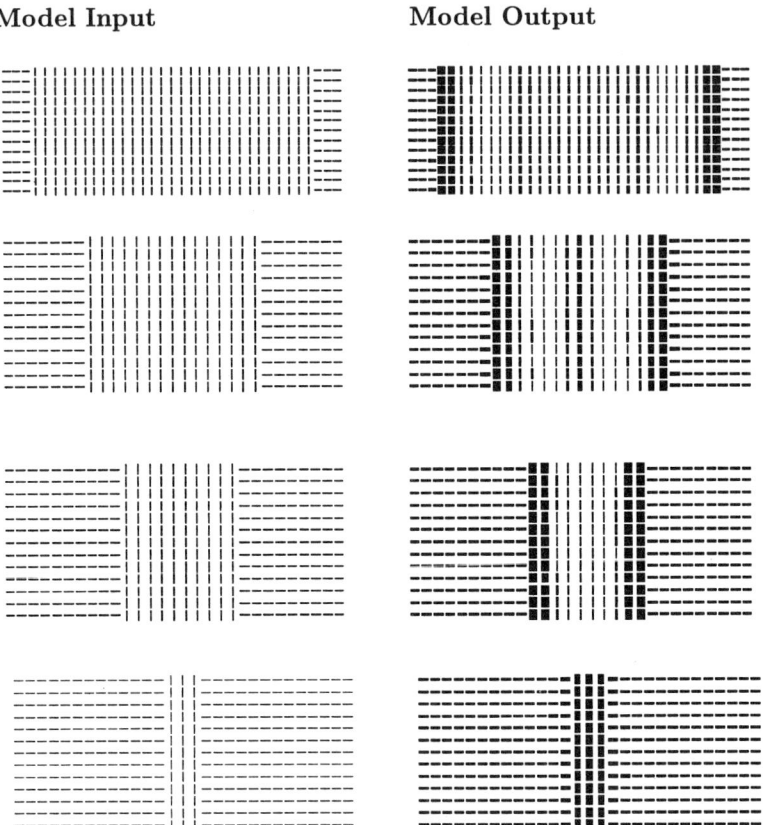

Figure 3: Dependence on the size of the figure. The figure-ground effect is most evident only for small figures, and the medial axis effect is most evident only for figures of finite and appropriate sizes.

suppression from the border the *border suppression region*, which is significant and visible in Fig. (2B). This region can reach no further than the longest length of the horizontal connenctions (mediating the suppresion) from the effective border region. Consequently, texture bars right outside the border suppression region not only escape the stronger suppression from the border, but also experience weaker iso-orientation suppression from the weakened texture bars in the nearby border suppression region. As a result, a second saliency peak appears — the ripple effect, and we can hence conclude that the ripple wavelength is of the same order of magnitude as the longest connection length of the cortical lateral connections mediating intra-cortical interactions.

Fig. 3 shows that for very small figures, the whole figure belongs to the effective border region and is highlighted in the V1 responses. As the figure size increases, the responses in the inside of the figure become smaller than the responses in the border region. However, when the size of the figure is appropriate, namely about twice the ripple wavelength, the center of the figure induces a secondary response highlight. In this case, the ripples or the secondary saliency peaks from both borders superpose onto each other at the same spatial location at the center of the figure. This reinforces the saliency peak at this medial axis since it has two border suppression regions (from two opposite borders), one on each side of it, as its contextual stimuli. For even larger figures, the medial axis effect diminishes because the ripples from

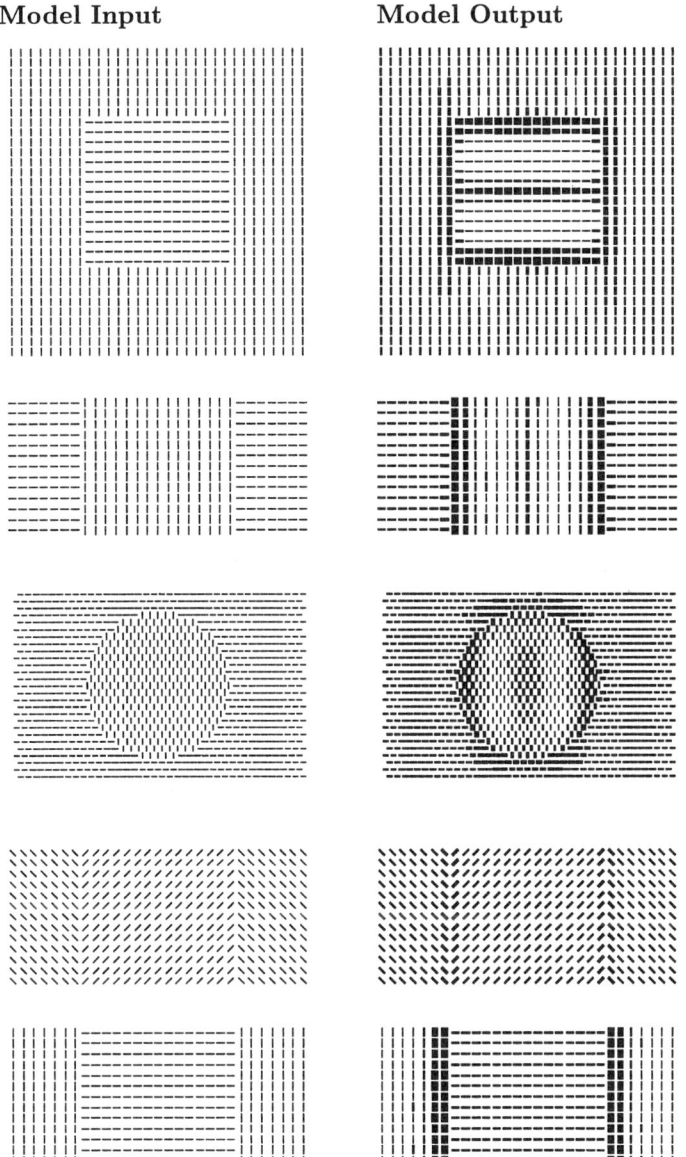

Figure 4: Dependence on the shape and texture feature of the figures.

the two opposite borders of the figure no longer reinforce each other.

Fig. 4 demonstrates that the border effect and its consequences for the medial axis also depend on the shape of the figures and the nature of the texture they contain (eg the orientations of the elements). Bars in the texture parallel to the border induce stronger highlights, and as a consequence, cause stronger ripple effects and medial axis highlights. This comes from the stronger co-linear, contour enhancing, inputs these bars receive than bars not parallel to the border.

3 Summary and Discussion

The model of V1 was originally proposed to account for pre-attentive contour enhancement and visual segmentation (Li 1998, 1999, 1999b). The contextual influences mediated by intracortical interactions enable each V1 neuron to process inputs from a local image area substantially larger than its classical receptive field. This enables cortical neurons to detect image locations where translation invariance in the input image breaks down, and highlight these image locations with higher neural activities, making them conspicuous. These highlights mark candidate locations for image region (or object surface) boundaries, smooth contours and small figures against backgrounds, serving the purpose of pre-attentive segmentation.

This paper has shown that the figure-ground and medial axis effects observed in the recent experiments can be accounted for using a purely V1 mechanism for border highlighting, provided that the sizes of the figures are small enough or of finite and appropriate scale. This has been the case in the existing experiments. We therefore suggest that feedbacks from higher visual areas are not necessary to explain the experimental observations, although we cannot, of course, exclude the possibilities that they also contribute.

References

[1] Lamme V.A. (1995) *Journal of Neuroscience* **15**(2), 1605-15.

[2] Lee T.S, Mumford D, Romero R. and Lamme V. A.F. (1998) *Vis. Res.* 38: 2429-2454.

[3] Zipser K., Lamme V. A., and Schiller P. H. (1996) *J. Neurosci.* **16** (22), 7376-89.

[4] Lamme V. A. F., Zipser K. and Spekreijse H. *Soc. Neuroscience Abstract* 603.1, 1997.

[5] Blum H. (1973) Biological shape and visual science *J. Theor. Biol.* 38: 205-87.

[6] Gallant J.L., van Essen D.C., and Nothdurft H.C. (1995) In *Early vision and beyond* eds. T. Papathomas, Chubb C, Gorea A., and Kowler E. (MIT press), pp 89-98.

[7] C. D. Gilbert (1992) *Neuron.* **9**(1), 1-13.

[8] C. M. Gray and W. Singer (1989) *Proc. Natl. Acad. Sci. USA* **86**, 1698-1702.

[9] M. K. Kapadia, M. Ito, C. D. Gilbert, and G. Westheimer (1995) *Neuron.* **15**(4), 843-56.

[10] J. J. Knierim and D. C. van Essen (1992) *J. Neurophysiol.* **67**, 961-980.

[11] Z. Li (1998) *Neural Computation* 10(4) p 903-940.

[12] Z. Li (1999) *Network: computations in neural systems* 10(2). p. 187-212.

[13] Z. Li (1999b) *Spatial Vision* 13(1) p. 25-50.

[14] K.S. Rockland and J. S. Lund (1983) *J. Comp. Neurol.* **216**, 303-318

[15] E. L. White (1989) *Cortical circuits* (Birkhauser).

Channel Noise in Excitable Neuronal Membranes

Amit Manwani,* Peter N. Steinmetz and Christof Koch
Computation and Neural Systems Program, M-S 139-74
California Institute of Technology Pasadena, CA 91125
{quixote,peter,koch}@klab.caltech.edu

Abstract

Stochastic fluctuations of voltage-gated ion channels generate current and voltage noise in neuronal membranes. This noise may be a critical determinant of the efficacy of information processing within neural systems. Using Monte-Carlo simulations, we carry out a systematic investigation of the relationship between channel kinetics and the resulting membrane voltage noise using a stochastic Markov version of the Mainen-Sejnowski model of dendritic excitability in cortical neurons. Our simulations show that kinetic parameters which lead to an increase in membrane excitability (increasing channel densities, decreasing temperature) also lead to an increase in the magnitude of the sub-threshold voltage noise. Noise also increases as the membrane is depolarized from rest towards threshold. This suggests that channel fluctuations may interfere with a neuron's ability to function as an integrator of its synaptic inputs and may limit the reliability and precision of neural information processing.

1 Introduction

Voltage-gated ion channels undergo random transitions between different conformational states due to thermal agitation. Generally, these states differ in their ionic permeabilities and the stochastic transitions between them give rise to conductance fluctuations which are a source of membrane noise [1]. In excitable cells, voltage-gated channel noise can contribute to the generation of spontaneous action potentials [2, 3], and the variability of spike timing [4]. Channel fluctuations can also give rise to bursting and chaotic spiking dynamics in neurons [5, 6].

Our interest in studying membrane noise is based on the thesis that noise ultimately limits the ability of neurons to transmit and process information. To study this problem, we combine methods from information theory, membrane biophysics and compartmental neuronal modeling to evaluate ability of different biophysical components of a neuron, such as the synapse, the dendritic tree, the soma and so on, to transmit information [7, 8, 9]. These neuronal components differ in the type, density, and kinetic properties of their constituent ion channels. Thus, measuring the impact of these differences on membrane noise rep-

---

*http://www.klab.caltech.edu/~quixote

resents a fundamental step in our overall program of evaluating information transmission within and between neurons.

Although information in the nervous system is mostly communicated in the form of action potentials, we first direct our attention to the study of sub-threshold voltage fluctuations for three reasons. Firstly, voltage fluctuations near threshold can cause variability in spike timing and thus directly influence the reliability and precision of neuronal activity. Secondly, many computations putatively performed in the dendritic tree (coincidence detection, multiplication, synaptic integration and so on) occur in the sub-threshold regime and thus are likely to be influenced by sub-threshold voltage noise. Lastly, several sensory neurons in vertebrates and invertebrates are non-spiking and an analysis of voltage fluctuations can be used to study information processing in these systems as well.

Extensive investigations of channel noise were carried out prior to the advent of the patch-clamp technique in order to provide indirect evidence for the existence of single ion channels (see [1] for an excellent review). More recently, theoretical studies have focused on the effect of random channel fluctuations on spike timing and reliability of individual neurons [4], as well as their effect on the dynamics of interconnected networks of neurons [5, 6]. In this paper, we determine the effect of varying the kinetic parameters, such as channel density and the rate of channel transitions, on the magnitude of sub-threshold voltage noise in an iso-potential membrane patches containing stochastic voltage-gated ion channels using Monte-Carlo simulations. The simulations are based on the Mainen-Sejnowski (MS) kinetic model of active channels in the dendrites of cortical pyramidal neurons [10]. By varying two model parameters (channel densities and temperature), we investigate the relationship between excitability and noise in neuronal membranes. By linearizing the channel kinetics, we derive analytical expressions which provide closed-form estimates of noise magnitudes; we contrast the results of the simulations with the linearized expressions to determine the parameter range over which they can be used.

2 Monte-Carlo Simulations

Consider an iso-potential membrane patch containing voltage-gated K$^+$ and Na$^+$ channels and leak channels,

$$-C \frac{dV_m}{dt} = g_K (V_m - E_K) + g_{Na} (V_m - E_{Na}) + g_L (V_m - E_L) + I_{inj} \quad (1)$$

where C is the membrane capacitance and g_K (g_{Na}, g_L) and E_K (E_{Na}, E_L) denote the K$^+$(Na$^+$, leak) conductance and the K$^+$(Na$^+$, leak) reversal potential respectively. Current injected into the patch is denoted by I_{inj}, with the convention that inward current is negative. The channels which give rise to potassium and sodium conductances switch randomly between different conformational states with voltage-dependent transition rates. Thus, g_K and g_{Na} are voltage-dependent random processes and eq. 1 is a non-linear stochastic differential equation. Generally, ion channel transitions are assumed to be Markovian [11] and the stochastic dynamics of eq. 1 can be studied using Monte-Carlo simulations of finite-state Markov models of channel kinetics.

Earlier studies have carried out simulations of stochastic versions of the classical Hodgkin-Huxley kinetic model [12] to study the effect of conductance fluctuations on neuronal spiking [13, 2, 4]. Since we are interested in sub-threshold voltage noise, we consider a stochastic Markov version of a less excitable kinetic model used to describe dendrites of cortical neurons [10]. We shall refer to it as the Mainen-Sejnowski (MS) kinetic scheme. The K$^+$ conductance is modeled by a single activation sub-unit (denoted by n) whereas the Na$^+$ conductance is comprised of three identical activation sub-units (denoted by m) and one inactivation sub-unit (denoted by h). Thus, the stochastic discrete-state Markov models of the K$^+$ and Na$^+$ channel have 2 and 8 states respectively (shown in Fig. 1). The single channel conductances and the densities of the ion channels (K^+, Na^+) are denoted by (γ_K, γ_{Na}) and (η_K, η_{Na}) respectively. Thus, g_K and g_{Na}) are given by the products of the respective single channel conductances and the corresponding numbers of channels in the conducting states.

A

$[n_0] \underset{\beta_n}{\overset{\alpha_n}{\rightleftarrows}} [n_1]$

$g_K(v,t) = \gamma_K [n_1]$

B

$[m_0h_1] \underset{\beta_m}{\overset{3\alpha_m}{\rightleftarrows}} [m_1h_1] \underset{2\beta_m}{\overset{2\alpha_m}{\rightleftarrows}} [m_2h_1] \underset{3\beta_m}{\overset{\alpha_m}{\rightleftarrows}} [m_3h_1]$

$\alpha_h \updownarrow \beta_h \quad \alpha_h \updownarrow \beta_h \quad \alpha_h \updownarrow \beta_h \quad \alpha_h \updownarrow \beta_h$

$[m_0h_0] \underset{\beta_m}{\overset{3\alpha_m}{\rightleftarrows}} [m_1h_0] \underset{2\beta_m}{\overset{2\alpha_m}{\rightleftarrows}} [m_2h_0] \underset{3\beta_m}{\overset{\alpha_m}{\rightleftarrows}} [m_3h_0]$

$g_{Na}(v,t) = \gamma_{Na} [m_3h_1]$

Figure 1: Kinetic scheme for the voltage-gated Mainen-Sejnowski K^+ (**A**) and Na^+ (**B**) channels. n_0 and n_1 represent the closed and open states of K^+ channel. $m_{0-2}h_1$ represent the 3 closed states, $m_{0-3}h_0$ the four inactivated states and m_3h_1 the open state of the Na^+ channel.

We performed Monte-Carlo simulations of the MS kinetic scheme using a fixed time step of $\Delta t = 10$ μsec. During each step, the number of sub-units undergoing transitions between states i and j was determined by drawing a pseudo-random binomial deviate (bnldev subroutine [14] driven by the ran2 subroutine of the 2nd edition) with N equal to the number of sub-units in state i and p given by the conditional probability of the transition between i and j. After updating the number of channels in each state, eq. 1 was integrated using fourth order Runge-Kutta integration with adaptive step size control [14]. During each step, the channel conductances were held at the fixed value corresponding to the new numbers of open channels. (See [4] for details of this procedure).

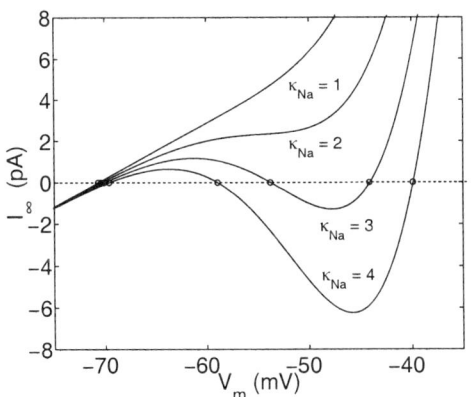

Figure 2: Steady-state I-V curves for different multiples (κ_{Na}) of the nominal MS Na^+ channel density. Circles indicate locations of fixed-points in the absence of current injection.

Due to random channel transitions, the membrane voltage fluctuates around the steady-state resting membrane voltage V_{rest}. By varying the magnitude of the constant injected current I_{inj}, the steady-state voltage can be varied over a broad range, which depends on the channel densities. The current required to maintain the membrane at a holding voltage V_{hold} can be determined from the steady-state I-V curve of the system, as shown in Fig. 2. Voltages for which the slope of the I-V curve is negative cannot be maintained as steady-states. By injecting an external current to offset the total membrane current, a fixed point in the negative slope region can be obtained but since the fixed point is unstable, any perturbation, such as a stochastic ion channel opening or closing, causes the system to be driven to the closest stable fixed point. We measured sub-threshold voltage noise only for stable steady-state holding voltages. A typical voltage trace from our simulations is shown in Fig. 3. To estimate the standard deviation of the voltage noise accurately, simulations were performed for a total of 492 seconds, divided into 60 blocks of 8.2 seconds each, for each steady-state value.

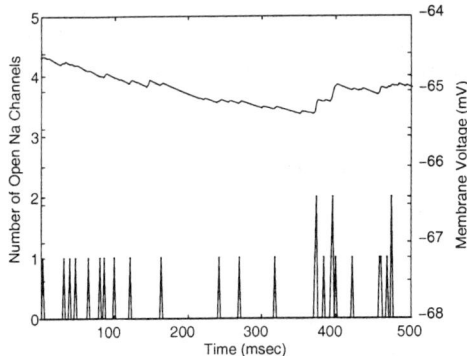

Figure 3: Monte-Carlo simulations of a 1000 μm^2 membrane patch with stochastic Na$^+$ and deterministic K$^+$ channels with MS kinetics. Bottom record shows the number of open Na$^+$ channels as a function of time. Top trace shows the corresponding fluctuations of the membrane voltage. Summary of nominal MS parameters: C_m = 0.75 $\mu F/cm^2$, η_K = 1.5 channels/μm^2, η_{Na} = 2 channels/μm^2, E_K = -90 mV, E_{Na} = 60 mV, E_L = -70 mV, g_L = 0.25 pS/μm^2, $\gamma_K = \gamma_{Na}$ = 20 pS.

3 Linearized Analysis

The non-linear stochastic differential equation (eq. 1) cannot be solved analytically. However, one can linearize it by expressing the ionic conductances and the membrane voltage as small perturbations (δ) around their steady-state values:

$$-C \frac{d\delta V_m}{dt} = (g_K^o + g_{Na}^o + g_L)\delta V_m + (V_m^o - E_K)\delta g_K + (V_m^o - E_{Na})\delta g_{Na} \quad (2)$$

where g_K^o and g_{Na}^o denote the values of the ionic conductances at the steady-state voltage V^o. $G = g_K^o + g_{Na}^o + g_L$ is the total steady-state patch conductance. Since the leak channel conductance is constant, $\delta g_L = 0$. On the other hand, δg_K and δg_{Na} depend on δV and t. It is known that, to first order, the voltage- and time-dependence of active ion channels can be modeled as phenomenological impedances [15, 16]. Fig. 4 shows the linearized equivalent circuit of a membrane patch, given by the parallel combination of the capacitance C, the conductance G and three series RL branches representing phenomenological models of K$^+$ activation, Na$^+$ activation and Na$^+$ inactivation.

$$I_n = \tilde{g}_K(E_K - V_m^o) + \tilde{g}_{Na}(E_{Na} - V_m^o) \quad (3)$$

represents the current noise due to fluctuations in the channel conductances (denoted by $\tilde{g}_K$ and $\tilde{g}_{Na}$) at the membrane voltage V_m^o (also referred to as holding voltage V_{hold}). The details of the linearization are provided [16]. The complex admittance (inverse of the impedance) of Fig. 4 is given by,

$$Y(f) = G + j2\pi fC + \frac{1}{r_n + j2\pi fl_n} + \frac{1}{r_m + j2\pi fl_m} + \frac{1}{r_h + j2\pi fl_h} \quad (4)$$

The variance of the voltage fluctuations σ_V^2 can be computed as,

$$\sigma_V^2 = \int_{-\infty}^{\infty} df \frac{S_{I_n}(f)}{|Y(f)|^2} \quad (5)$$

where the power spectral density of I_n is given by the sum of the individual channel current noise spectra, $S_{I_n}(f) = S_{I_K}(f) + S_{I_{Na}}(f)$.

For the MS scheme, the autocovariance of the K$^+$ current noise for patch of area A, clamped at a voltage V_m^o, can be derived using [1, 11],

$$C_{I_K}(t) = A\eta_K \gamma_K^2 (V_m^o - E_K)^2 n_\infty (1 - n_\infty) e^{-|t|/\tau_n} \quad (6)$$

where n_∞ and τ_n respectively denote the steady-state probability and time constant of the K$^+$ activation sub-unit at V_m^o. The power spectral density of the K$^+$ current noise $S_{I_K}(f)$ can be obtained from the Fourier transform of $C_{I_K}(t)$,

$$S_{I_K}(f) = \frac{2A\eta_K \gamma_K^2 (V_m^o - E_K)^2 n_\infty \tau_n}{1 + (2\pi f \tau_n)^2} \quad (7)$$

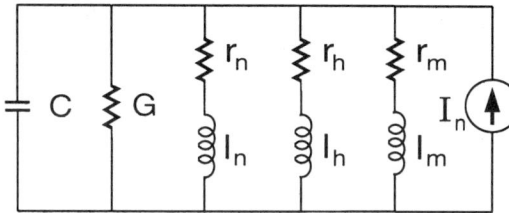

Figure 4: Linearized circuit of the membrane patch containing stochastic voltage-gated ion channels. C denotes the membrane capacitance, G is the sum of the steady-state conductances of the channels and the leak. r_i's and l_i's denote the phenomenological resistances and inductances due to the voltage- and time-dependent ionic conductances.

Thus, $S_{IK}(f)$ is a single Lorentzian spectrum with cut-off frequency determined by τ_n. Similarly, the auto-covariance of the MS Na$^+$current noise can be written as [1],

$$C_{INa}(t) = A\,\eta_{Na}\,\gamma_{Na}^2\,(V_m^o - E_{Na})^2\,m_\infty^3\,h_\infty\left[m^3(t)\,h(t) - m_\infty^3\,h_\infty\right] \qquad (8)$$

where

$$m(t) = m_\infty + (1 - m_\infty)\,e^{-t/\tau_m}, \quad h(t) = h_\infty + (1 - h_\infty)\,e^{-t/\tau_h} \qquad (9)$$

As before, m_∞ (h_∞) and τ_m (τ_h) are the open probability and the time constant of Na$^+$activation (inactivation) sub-unit. The Na$^+$current noise spectrum $S_{INa}(f)$ can be expressed as a sum of Lorentzian spectra with cut-off frequencies corresponding to the seven time constants τ_m, τ_h, $2\tau_m$, $3\tau_m$, $\tau_m + \tau_h$, $2\tau_m + \tau_h$ and $3\tau_m + \tau_h$. The details of the derivations can be found in [8].

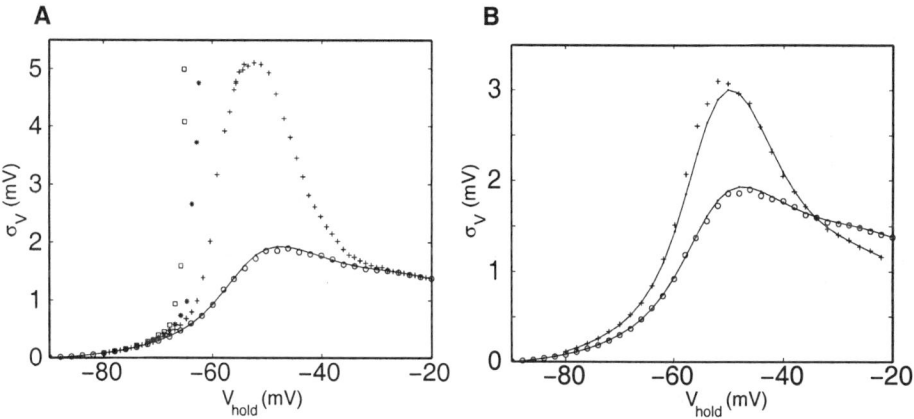

Figure 5: Standard deviation of the voltage noise σ_V in a 1000 μm^2 patch as a function of the holding voltage V_{hold}. Circles denote results of the Monte-Carlo simulations for the nominal MS parameter values (see Fig. 3). The solid curve corresponds to the theoretical expression obtained by linearizing the channel kinetics. (A) Effect of increasing the sodium channel density by a factor (compared to the nominal value) of 2 (pluses), 3 (asterisks) and 4 (squares) on the magnitude of voltage noise. (B) Effect of increasing both the sodium and potassium channel densities by a factor of two (pluses).

4 Effect of Varying Channel Densities

Fig. 5 shows the voltage noise for a 1000 μm^2 patch as a function of the holding voltage for different values of the channel densities. Noise increases as the membrane is depolarized from rest towards -50 mV and the rate of increase is higher for higher Na$^+$densities. The range of V_{hold} for sub-threshold behavior extends up to -20 mV for nominal densities, but does not exceed -60 mV for higher Na$^+$ densities. For moderate levels of depolarization, an increase in the magnitude of the ionic current noise with voltage is the dominant factor which leads to an increase in voltage noise; for higher voltages phenomenological impedances are large and shunt away the current noise. Increasing Na$^+$ density increases voltage noise, whereas, increasing K$^+$ density causes a decrease in noise magnitude (compare Fig. 5A and 5B). We linearized closed-form expressions provide accurate estimates of the noise magnitudes when the noise is small (of the order 3 mV).

5 Effect of Varying Temperature

Fig. 6 shows that voltage noise decreases with temperature. To model the effect of temperature, transition rates were scaled by a factor $Q_{10}^{\Delta T/10}$ ($Q_{10} = 2.3$ for K$^+$, $Q_{10} = 3$ for Na$^+$). Temperature increases the rates of channel transitions and thus the bandwidth of the ionic current noise fluctuations. The magnitude of the current noise, on the other hand, is independent of temperature. Since the membrane acts as a low-pass RC filter (at moderately depolarized voltages, the phenomenological inductances are small), increasing the bandwidth of the noise results in lower voltage noise as the high frequency components are filtered out.

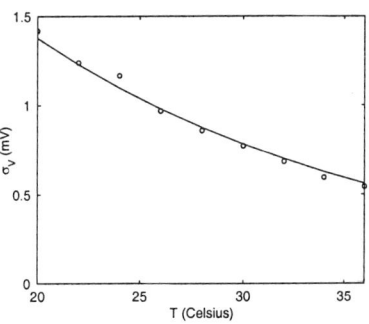

Figure 6: σ_V as a function of temperature for a 1000 μm^2 patch with MS kinetics ($V_{hold} = -60$ mV). Circles denote Monte-Carlo simulations, solid curve denotes linearized approximation.

6 Conclusions

We studied sub-threshold voltage noise due to stochastic ion channel fluctuations in an isopotential membrane patch with Mainen-Sejnowski kinetics. For the MS kinetic scheme, noise increases as the membrane is depolarized from rest, up to the point where the phenomenological impedances due to the voltage- and time-dependence of the ion channels become large and shunt away the noise. Increasing Na$^+$ channel density increases both the magnitude of the noise and its rate of increase with membrane voltage. On the other hand, increasing the rates of channel transitions by increasing temperature, leads to a decrease in noise. It has previously been shown that neural excitability increases with Na$^+$ channel density [17] and decreases with temperature [15]. Thus, our findings suggest that an increase in membrane excitability is inevitably accompanied by an increase in the magnitude of sub-threshold voltage noise fluctuations. The magnitude and the rapid increase of voltage noise with depolarization suggests that channel fluctuations can contribute significantly to the variability in spike timing [4] and the stochastic nature of ion channels may have a significant impact on information processing within individual neurons. It also potentially argues against the conventional role of a neuron as integrator of synaptic inputs [18], as the the slow depolarization associated with integration of small synaptic inputs would be accompanied by noise, making the membrane voltage a very unreliable indicator of the integrated inputs. We are actively investigating this issue more carefully.

When the magnitudes of the noise and the phenomenological impedances are small, the non-linear kinetic schemes are well-modeled by their linearized approximations. We have found this to be valid for other kinetic schemes as well [19]. These analytical approximations can be used to study noise in more sophisticated neuronal models incorporating realistic dendritic geometries, where Monte-Carlo simulations may be too computationally intensive to use.

Acknowledgments

This work was funded by NSF, NIMH and the Sloan Center for Theoretical Neuroscience. We thank our collaborators Michael London, Idan Segev and Yosef Yarom for their invaluable suggestions.

References

[1] DeFelice L.J. (1981). *Introduction to Membrane Noise*. Plenum Press: New York, New York.

[2] Strassberg A.F. & DeFelice L.J. (1993). Limitations of the Hodgkin-Huxley formalism: effect of single channel kinetics on transmembrane voltage dynamics. *Neural Computation*, 5:843–855.

[3] Chow C. & White J. (1996). Spontaneous action potentials due to channel fluctuations. *Biophy. J.*, 71:3013–3021.

[4] Schneidman E., Freedman B. & Segev I. (1998). Ion-channel stochasticity may be critical in determining the reliability and precision of spike timing. *Neural Computation*, 10:1679–1703.

[5] DeFelice L.J. & Isaac A. (1992). Chaotic states in a random world. *J. Stat. Phys.*, 70:339–352.

[6] White J.A., Budde T. & Kay A.R. (1995). A bifurcation analysis of neuronal subthreshold oscillations. *Biophy. J.*, 69:1203–1217.

[7] Manwani A. & Koch C. (1998). Synaptic transmission: An information-theoretic perspective. In: Jordan M., Kearns M.S. & Solla S.A., eds., *Advances in Neural Information Processing Systems 10*. pp 201-207. MIT Press: Cambridge, Massachusetts.

[8] Manwani A. & Koch C. (1999). Detecting and estimating signals in noisy cable structures: I. Neuronal noise sources. *Neural Computation*. In press.

[9] Manwani A. & Koch C. (1999). Detecting and estimating signals in noisy cable structures: II. Information-theoretic analysis. *Neural Computation*. In press.

[10] Mainen Z.F. & Sejnowski T.J. (1995). Reliability of spike timing in neocortical neurons. *Science*, 268:1503–1506.

[11] Johnston D. & Wu S.M. (1995). *Foundations of Cellular Neurophysiology*. MIT Press: Cambridge, Massachusetts.

[12] Hodgkin A.L. & Huxley A.F. (1952). A quantitative description of membrane current and its application to conduction and excitation in nerve. *J. Physiol. (London)*, 117:500–544.

[13] Skaugen E. & Walløe L. (1979). Firing behavior in a stochastic nerve membrane model based upon the Hodgkin-Huxley equations. *Acta Physiol. Scand.*, 107:343–363.

[14] Press W.H., Teukolsky S.A., Vetterling W.T. & Flannery B.P. (1992). *Numerical Recipes in C: The Art of Scientific Computing*. Cambridge University Press, second edn.

[15] Mauro A., Conti F., Dodge F. & Schor R. (1970). Subthreshold behavior and phenomenological impedance of the squid giant axon. *J. Gen. Physiol.*, 55:497–523.

[16] Koch C. (1984). Cable theory in neurons with active, linearized membranes. *Biol. Cybern.*, 50:15–33.

[17] Sabah N.H. & Leibovic K.N. (1972). The effect of membrane parameters on the properties of the nerve impulse. *Biophys. J.*, 12:1132–44.

[18] Shadlen M.N. & Newsome W.T. (1998). The variable discharge of cortical neurons: implications for connectivity, computation, and information coding. *J. Neurosci.*, 18:3870–3896.

[19] P. N. Steinmetz A. Manwani M.L. & Koch C. (1999). Sub-threshold voltage noise due to channel fluctuations in active neuronal membranes. In preparation.

LTD Facilitates Learning In a Noisy Environment

Paul Munro
School of Information Sciences
University of Pittsburgh
Pittsburgh PA 15260
pwm+@pitt.edu

Gerardina Hernandez
Intelligent Systems Program
University of Pittsburgh
Pittsburgh PA 15260
gehst5+@pitt.edu

Abstract

Long-term potentiation (LTP) has long been held as a biological substrate for associative learning. Recently, evidence has emerged that long-term depression (LTD) results when the presynaptic cell fires after the postsynaptic cell. The computational utility of LTD is explored here. Synaptic modification kernels for both LTP and LTD have been proposed by other laboratories based studies of one postsynaptic unit. Here, the interaction between time-dependent LTP and LTD is studied in small networks.

1 Introduction

Long term potentiation (LTP) is a neurophysiological phenomenon observed under laboratory conditions in which two neurons or neural populations are stimulated at a high frequency with a resulting measurable increase in synaptic efficacy between them that lasts for several hours or days [1]-[2] LTP thus provides direct evidence supporting the neurophysiological hypothesis articulated by Hebb [3].

This increase in synaptic strength must be countered by a mechanism for weakening the synapse [4]. The biological correlate, long-term depression (LTD) has also been observed in the laboratory; that is, synapses are observed to weaken when low presynaptic activity coincides with high postsynaptic activity [5]-[6].

Mathematical formulations of Hebbian learning produce weights, w_{ij}, (where i is the presynaptic unit and j is the postsynaptic unit), that capture the covariance [Eq. 1] between the instantaneous activities of pairs of units, a_i and a_j [7].

$$\dot{w}_{ij}(t) = (a_i(t) - \overline{a}_i)(a_j(t) - \overline{a}_j) \qquad [1]$$

This idea has been generalized to capture covariance between activities that are shifted in time [8]-[9], resulting in a framework that can model systems with temporal delays and dependencies [Eq. 2].

$$\dot{w}_{ij}(t) = \iint K(t'' - t') a_i(t'') a_j(t') dt'' dt' \qquad [2]$$

As will be shown in the following sections, depending on the choice of the function $K(\Delta t)$, this formulation encompasses a broad range of learning rules [10]-[12] and can support a comparably broad range of biological evidence.

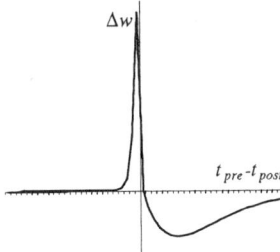

Figure 1. Synaptic change as a function of the time difference between spikes from the presynaptic neuron and the postsynaptic neuron. Note that for $t_{pre} < t_{post}$, LTP results ($\Delta w > 0$), and for $t_{pre} > t_{post}$, the result is LTD.

Recent biological data from [13]-[15], indicates an increase in synaptic strength (LTP) when presynaptic activity precedes postsynaptic activity, and LTD in the reverse case (postsynaptic precedes presynaptic). These ideas have started to appear in some theoretical models of neural computation [10]-[12], [16]-[18]. Thus, Figure 1 shows the form of the dependence of synaptic change, Δw on the difference in spike arrival times.

2 A General Framework

Given specific assumptions, the integral in Eq. 2 can be separated into two integrals, one representing LTP and one representing LTD [Eq. 3].

$$\dot{w}_{ij}(t) = \underbrace{\int_{t'=-\infty}^{t} K_P(t-t')a_i(t')a_j(.)dt'}_{LTP} + \underbrace{\int_{t'=-\infty}^{t} K_D(t-t')a_i(t)a_j(t')dt'}_{LTD} \quad [3]$$

The activities that do not depend on t' can be factored out of the integrals, giving two Hebb-like products, between the instantaneous activity in one cell and a weighted time average of the activity in the other [Eq. 4]:

$$\dot{w}_{ij}(t) = \left\langle a_i(t) \right\rangle_P a_j(t) - a_i(t)\left\langle a_j(t) \right\rangle_D \quad [4]$$

where $\left\langle f(t) \right\rangle_X \equiv | \int_{t'=-\infty}^{t} K_X(t-t')f(t')dt' |$ for $X \in \{P,D\}$

The kernel functions K_P and K_D can be chosen to select precise times out of the convoluted function $f(t)$, or to average across the functions for an arbitrary range. The alpha function is useful here [Eq. 5]. A high value of α selects an immediate time, while a small value approximates a longer time-average.

$$K_X(\tau) = \beta_X \tau e^{-\alpha_X \tau} \text{ for } X \in \{P,D\} \quad [5]$$
with $\alpha_P > 0, \alpha_D > 0, \beta_P > 0, \beta_D < 0$

For high values of α_P and α_D, only pre- and post- synaptic activities that are very close temporally will interact to modify the synapse. In a simulation with discrete step sizes, this can be reasonably approximated by only considering just a single time step [Eq. 6].

$$\Delta w_{ij}(t) = a_i(t-1)a_j(t) - a_i(t)a_j(t-1) \tag{6}$$

Summing $\Delta w_{ij}(t)$ and $\Delta w_{ij}(t+1)$ gives a net change in the weights $\Delta^{(2)} w_{ij} = w_{ij}(t+1) - w_{ij}(t-1)$ over the two time steps:

$$\Delta^{(2)} w_{ij}(t) = a_i(t)\Delta^{(2)} a_j(t) - a_j(t)\Delta^{(2)} a_i(t) \tag{7}$$

The first term is predictive in that it has the form of the delta rule where $a_j(t+1)$ acts as a training signal for $a_j(t-1)$, as in a temporal Hopfield network [9].

3 Temporal Contrast Enhancement

The computational role of the LTP term in Eq. 3 is well established, but how does the second term contribute? A possibility is that the term is analogous to lateral inhibition in the temporal domain; that is, that by suppressing associations in the "wrong" temporal direction, the system may be more robust against noise in the input. The resulting system may be able to detect the onset and offset of a signal more reliably than a system not using an anti-Hebbian LTD term.

The extent to which the LTD term is able to enhance temporal contrast is likely to depend idiosyncratically on the statistical qualities of a particular system. If so, the parameters of the system might only be valid for signals with specific statistical properties, or the parameters might be adaptive. Either of these possibilities lies beyond the scope of analysis for this paper.

4 Simulations

Two preliminary simulation studies illustrate the use of the learning rule for predictive behavior and for temporal contrast enhancement. For every simulation, kernel functions were specified by the parameters α and β, and the number of time steps, n_P and n_D, that were sampled for the approximation of each integral.

4.1 Task 1. A Sequential Shifter

The first task is a simple shifter over a set of 7 to 20 units. The system is trained on these stimuli and then tested to see if it can reconstruct the sequence given the initial input. The task is given with no noise and with temporal noise (see Figure 2). Task 1 is designed to examine the utility of LTD as an approach to learning a sequence with temporal noise. The ability of the network to reconstruct the noise-free sequence after training on the noisy sequence was tested for different LTD kernel functions.

Note that the same patterns are presented (for each time slice, just one of the n units is active), but the shifts either skip or repeat *in time*. Experiments were run with $k = 1, 2$, or 3 of the units active.

4.2 Task 2. Time series reconstruction.

In this task, a set of units was trained on external sinusoidal signals that varied according to frequency and phase. The purpose of this task is to examine the role of LTD in providing temporal context. The network was then tested under a condition in which the external signals were provided to all but one of the units. The activity of the deprived unit was then compared with its training signal

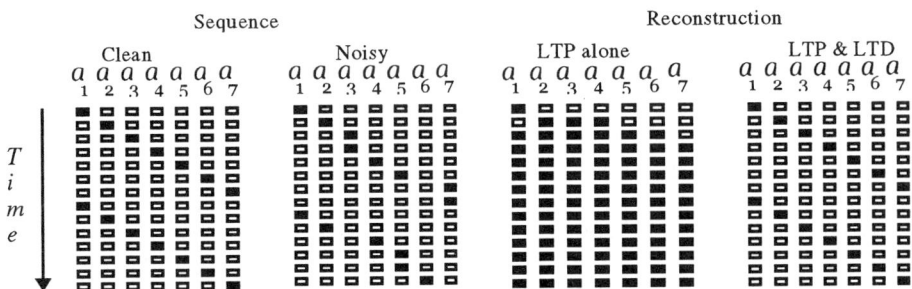

Figure 2. Reconstruction of clean shifter sequence using as input the noisy stimulus shifter sequence. For each time slice, just one of the 7 units is active. In the clean sequence, activity shifts cyclically around the 7 units. The noisy sequence has a random jitter of ±1.

5 ResultsSequential Shifter Results

All networks trained on the clean sequence can learn the task with LTP alone, but no networks could learn the shifter task based on a noisy training sequence unless there was also an LTD term. Without an LTD term, most units would saturate to maximum values. For a range of LTD parameters, the network would converge without saturating. Reconstruction performance was found to be sensitive to the LTD parameters. The parameters α and β shown in Table.1 needed to be chosen very specifically to get perfect reconstruction (this was done by trial and error). For a narrow range of parameters near the optimal values, the reconstructed sequence was close to the noise-free target. However, the parameters α and β shown in Table 2 are estimated from the experimental result of Zhang,et al [15].

Table 1. Results of the sequential shifter task.

k	n	n_r	α_P	β_P	n_P	α_D	β_D	n_D	Time
1	7	1	1	2.72	1	0.1	-0.4	5	208
2	7	1	1	2.72	1	0.1	-0.4	4	40
		2	0.5	0.4	3	0.2	-0.1	7	192
3	7	1	0.5	0.4	1	0.2	-0.1	6	168
1	10	1	1	2.72	1	0.1	-0.4	8	682
2	10	1	1	2.72	1	0.1	-0.4	7	99
1	15	1	1	2.72	1	0.1	-0.4	13	1136
1	20	1	1	2.72	1	0.1	-0.4	18	4000

The task was to shift a pattern 1 unit with each time step. A block of k of n units was active. The parameters of the kernel functions (α and β), the number of values sampled from the kernel (the number of time slices used to estimate the integral), n_P and n_D, and the number of steps used to begin the reconstruction, n_r (usually $n_r = 1$) are given in the table. The last column of the table (*Time*) reports the number of iterations required for perfect reconstruction.

Table 2. Results of the sequential shifter task using as parameters: $n_r = 1$; $n_P = 1$;
$\alpha_D = 0.125$; $\alpha_P = 0.5$; $\beta_D = -\alpha_D * e * 0.35$; $\beta_P = \alpha_P * e * 0.8$.

k	n	n_D	Time
1	7	6	288
2	7	5	96
3	7	4	64

For the above results, the k active units were always adjacent with respect to the shifting direction. For cases with noncontiguous active units, reconstruction was never exact. Networks trained with LTP alone would saturate, but would converge to a sequence "close" to the target (Fig. 3) if an LTD term was added.

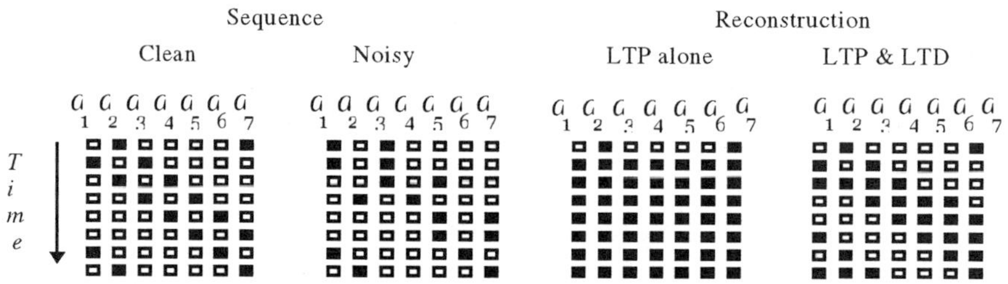

Figure 3. This base pattern ($k=2$, $n=7$) with noncontiguous active units was presented as a shifted sequence with noise. The target sequence is partially reconstructed only when LTP and LTD are used together.

5.1 Time Series Reconstruction Results

A network of just four units was trained for hundreds of iterations, the units were each externally driven by a sinusoidally varying input. Networks trained with LTP alone fail to reconstruct the time series on units deprived of external input during testing. In these simulations, there is no noise in the patterns, but LTD is shown to be necessary for reconstruction of the patterns (Fig. 4).

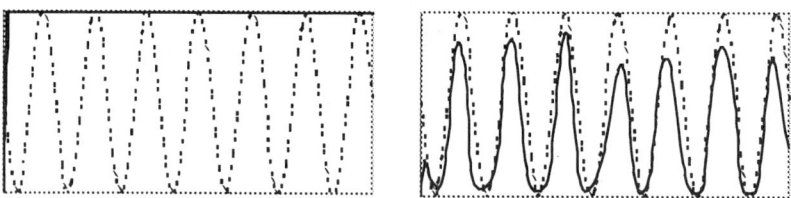

Figure 4. Reconstruction of sinusoids. Target signals from training (dashed) plotted with reconstructed signals (solid). Left: The best reconstruction using LTP alone. Right: A typical result with LTP and LTD together.

For high values of α_P and α_D, the reconstruction of sinusoids is very sensitive to the values of β_D and β_P. Figure 5 shows the results when $|\beta_D|$ and β_P values are close. In the first case (top), when $|\beta_D|$ is slightly smaller than β_P, the first two neurons (from left to right) saturate. And, in the contrary case (bottom) the first two neurons show almost null activation. However, the third and fourth neurons (from left to right) in both cases (top and bottom) show predictive behavior.

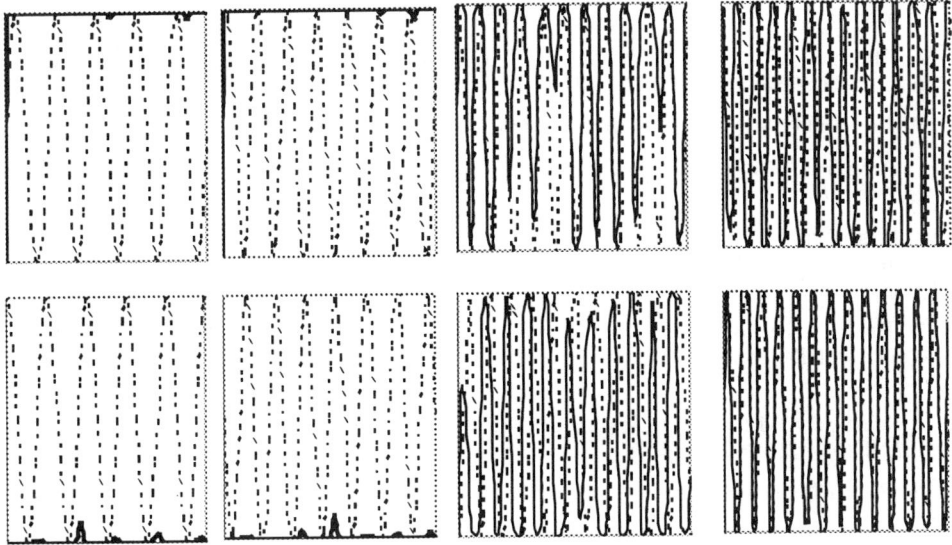

Figure 5. Reconstruction of sinusoids. Examples of target signals from training (dashed) plotted with reconstructed signals (solid). Top: When $|\beta_D|<\beta_P$. Bottom: When $|\beta_D|>\beta_P$.

6 Discussion

In the half century that has elapsed since Hebb articulated his neurophysiological postulate, the neuroscience community has come to recognize its fundamental role in plasticity. Hebb's hypothesis clearly transcends its original motivation to give a neurophysiologically based account of associative memory.

The phenomenon of LTP provides direct biological support for Hebb's postulate, and hence has clear cognitive implications. Initially after its discovery in the laboratory, the computational role of LTD was thought to be the flip side of LTP. This interpretation would have synapses strengthen when activities are correlated and have them weaken when they are anti-correlated. Such a theory is appealing for its elegance, and has formed the basis many network models [19]-[20]. However, the dependence of synaptic change on the relative timing of pre- and post- synaptic activity that has recently been shown in the laboratory is inconsistent with this story and calls for a computational interpretation. A network trained with such a learning rule cannot converge to a state where the weights are symmetric, for example, since $\Delta w_{ij} \neq \Delta w_{ji}$.

While the simulations reported here are simple and preliminary, they illustrate two tasks that benefit from the inclusion of time-dependent LTD. In the case of the sequential shifter, an examination of more complex predictive tasks is planned in the near future. It is expected that this will require architectures with unclamped (hidden) units. The role of LTD here is to temporally enhance contrast, in a way analogous to the role of lateral inhibition for computing spatial contrast enhancement in the retina. The time-series example illustrates the possible role of LTD for providing temporal context.

7 References

[1] Bliss TVP & Lømo T (1973) Long-lasting potentiation of synaptic in the dentate area of the unanaesthetized rabbit following stimulation of the perforant path. *J Physiol* **232**:331-356

[2] Malenka RC (1995) LTP and LTD: dynamic and interactive processes of synaptic plasticity. *The Neuroscientist* **1**:35-42.

[3] Hebb DO (1949) *The Organization of Behavior*. Wiley: NY.

[4] Stent G (1973) A physiological, mechanism for Hebb's postulate of learning. *Proc. Natl. Acad. Sci. USA* **70**: 997-1001

[5] Barrionuevo G, Schottler F & Lynch G (1980) The effects of repetitive low frequency stimulation on control and "pontentiated" synaptic responses in the hippocampus. *Life Sci* **27**:2385-2391.

[6] Thiels E, Xie X, Yeckel MF, Barrionuevo G & Berger TW (1996) NMDA Receptor-dependent LTD in different subfields of hippocampus in vivo and in vitro. *Hippocampus* **6**:43-51.

[7] Sejnowski T J (1977) Storing covariance with nonlinearly interacting neurons. *J. Math. Biol.* **4**:303-321.

[8] Sutton RS (1988) Learning to predict by the methods of temporal difference. *Machine Learning*. **3**:9-44

[9] Sompolinsky H and Kanter I (1986) Temporal association in asymmetric neural networks. *Phys.Rev.Letter.* **57**:2861-2864.

[10] Gerstner W, Kempter R, van Hemmen JL & Wagner H (1996) A neuronal learning rule for sub-millisecond temporal coding. *Nature* **383**:76-78.

[11] Kempter R, Gerstner W & van Hemmen JL (1999) Spike-based compared to rate-based hebbian learning. Kearns, Ms., Solla, S.A and Cohn, D.A. Eds. *Advances in Neural Information Processing Systems 11*. MIT Press, Cambridge MA.

[12] Kempter R, Gerstner W, van Hemmen JL & Wagner H (1996) Temporal coding in the sub-millisecond range: Model of barn owl auditory pathway. Touretzky, D.S, Mozer, M.C, Hasselmo, M.E, Eds. *Advances in Neural Information Processing Systems 8*. MIT Press, Cambridge MA pp.124-130.

[13] Markram H, Lubke J, Frotscher M & Sakmann B (1997) Regulation of synaptic efficacy by coincidence of postsynaptic Aps and EPPSPs. *Science* **275**:213-215.

[14] Markram H & Tsodyks MV (1996) Redistribution of synaptic efficacy between neocortical pyramidal neurons. *Nature* **382**:807-810.

[15] Zhang L, Tao HW, Holt CE & Poo M (1998) A critical window for cooperation and competition among developing retinotectal synapses. *Nature* **35**:37-44

[16] Abbott LF, & Blum KI (1996) Functional significance of long-term potentiation for sequence learning and prediction. *Cerebral Cortex* **6**: 406-416.

[17] Abbott LF, & Song S (1999) Temporally asymmetric hebbian learning, spike timing and neuronal response variability. Kearns, Ms., Solla, S.A and Cohn, D.A. Eds. *Advances in Neural Information Processing Systems 11*. MIT Press, Cambridge MA.

[18] Goldman MS, Nelson SB & Abbott LF (1998) Decorrelation of spike trains by synaptic depression. *Neurocomputing* (in press).

[19] Hopfield J (1982) Neural networks and physical systems with emergent collective computational properties. *Proc. Natl. Acad. Sci. USA*. **79**:2554-2558.

[20] Ackley DH, Hinton GE, Sejnowski TJ (1985) A learning algorithm for Boltzmann machines. *Cognitive Science* **9**:147-169.

Memory Capacity of Linear vs. Nonlinear Models of Dendritic Integration

Panayiota Poirazi[*]
Biomedical Engineering Department
University of Southern California
Los Angeles, CA 90089
poirazi@scf.usc.edu

Bartlett W. Mel[*]
Biomedical Engineering Department
University of Southern California
Los Angeles, CA 90089
mel@lnc.usc.edu

Abstract

Previous biophysical modeling work showed that nonlinear interactions among nearby synapses located on active dendritic trees can provide a large boost in the memory capacity of a cell (Mel, 1992a, 1992b). The aim of our present work is to quantify this boost by estimating the capacity of (1) a neuron model with passive dendritic integration where inputs are combined linearly across the entire cell followed by a single global threshold, and (2) an active dendrite model in which a threshold is applied separately to the output of each branch, and the branch subtotals are combined linearly. We focus here on the limiting case of binary-valued synaptic weights, and derive expressions which measure model capacity by estimating the number of distinct input-output functions available to both neuron types. We show that (1) the application of a fixed nonlinearity to each dendritic compartment substantially increases the model's flexibility, (2) for a neuron of realistic size, the capacity of the nonlinear cell can exceed that of the same-sized linear cell by more than an order of magnitude, and (3) the largest capacity boost occurs for cells with a relatively large number of dendritic subunits of relatively small size. We validated the analysis by empirically measuring memory capacity with randomized two-class classification problems, where a stochastic delta rule was used to train both linear and nonlinear models. We found that large capacity boosts predicted for the nonlinear dendritic model were readily achieved in practice.

[*]http://lnc.usc.edu

1 Introduction

Both physiological evidence and connectionist theory support the notion that in the brain, memories are stored in the pattern of learned synaptic weight values. Experiments in a variety of neuronal preparations however, indicate that the efficacy of synaptic transmission can undergo substantial fluctuations up or down, or both, during brief trains of synaptic stimuli. Large fluctuations in synaptic efficacy on short time scales seem inconsistent with the conventional connectionist assumption of stable, high-resolution synaptic weight values. Furthermore, a recent experimental study suggests that excitatory synapses in the hippocampus—a region implicated in certain forms of explicit memory—may exist in only a few long-term stable states, where the continuous grading of synaptic strength seen in standard measures of long-term potentiation (LTP) may exist only in the average over a large population of two-state synapses with randomly staggered thresholds for learning (Petersen, Malenka, Nicoll, & Hopfield, 1998). According to conventional connectionist notions, the possibility that individual synapses hold only one or two bits of long-term state information would seem to have serious implications for the storage capacity of neural tissue. Exploration of this question is one of the main themes of this paper.

In a related vein, we have found in previous biophysical modeling studies that nonlinear interactions between synapses co-activated on the same branch of an active dendritic tree could provide an alternative form of long-term storage capacity. This capacity, which is largely orthogonal to that tied up in conventional synaptic weights, is contained instead in the spatial permutation of synaptic connections onto the dendritic tree—which could in principle be modified in the course of learning or development (Mel, 1992a, 1992b). In a more abstract setting, we recently showed that a large repository of model flexibility lies in the *choice* as to which of a large number of possible interaction terms available in high dimension is actually included in a learning machine's discriminant function, and that the excess capacity contained in this "choice flexibility" can be quantified using straightforward counting arguments (Poirazi & Mel, 1999).

2 Two Alternative Models of Dendritic Integration

In this paper, we use a similar function-counting approach to address the more biologically relevant case of a neuron with multiple quasi-independent dendritic compartments (fig. 1). Our primary objective has been to compare the memory capacity of a cell assuming two different modes of dendritic integration. According to the linear model, the neuron's activation level $a_L(\mathbf{x})$ prior to thresholding is given by a weighted sum of of its inputs over the cell as a whole. According to the nonlinear model, the k synaptic inputs to each branch are first combined linearly, a static (e.g. sigmoidal) nonlinearity is applied to each of the m branch subtotals, and the resulting branch outputs are summed to produce the cell's overall activity $a_N(\mathbf{x})$:

$$a_L(\mathbf{x}) = \sum_{i=1}^{m}(\sum_{j=1}^{k} x_j^{(i)}) \qquad a_N(\mathbf{x}) = \sum_{i=1}^{m} g(\sum_{j=1}^{k} x_j^{(i)}) \qquad (1)$$

The expressions for a_L and a_N were written in similar form to emphasize that the models have an identical number of synaptic weights, differing only in the presence or absence of a fixed nonlinear function g applied to the branch subtotals. Though individual synaptic weights in both models are constrained to have a value of 1, any of the d input lines may form multiple connections on the same or different

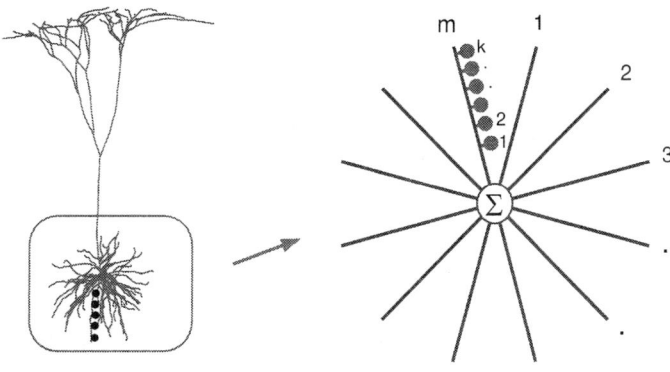

Figure 1: A cell is modeled as a set of m identical branches connected to a soma, where each branch contains k synaptic contacts driven by one of d distinct input lines.

branches as a means of representing graded synaptic strengths. Similarly, an input line which forms no connection has an implicit weight of 0. In light of this restriction to positive (or zero) weight values, both the linear and nonlinear models are split into two opponent channels a^+ and a^- dedicated to positive vs. negative coefficients, respectively. This leads to a final output for each model:

$$y_L(\mathbf{x}) = sgn\ [a_L^+(\mathbf{x}) - a_L^-(\mathbf{x})] \qquad y_N(\mathbf{x}) = sgn\ [a_N^+(\mathbf{x}) - a_N^-(\mathbf{x})] \qquad (2)$$

where the *sgn* operator maps the total activation level into a class label of {-1, 1}.

In the following, we derive expressions for the number of distinct parameter states available to the linear vs. nonlinear models, a measure which we have found to be a reliable predictor of storage capacity under certain restrictions (Poirazi & Mel, 1999). Based on these expressions, we compute the capacity boost provided by the branch nonlinearity as a function of the number of branches m, synaptic sites per branch k, and input space dimensionality d. Finally, we test the predictions of the analytical model by training both linear and nonlinear models on randomized classification problems using a stochastic delta rule, and empirically measure and compare the storage capacities of the two models.

3 Results

3.1 Counting Parameter States: Linear vs. Nonlinear Model

We derived expressions for B_L and B_N, which estimate the total number of parameter bits available to the linear vs. nonlinear models, respectively:

$$B_N = 2\log_2 \left(\binom{\binom{k+d-1}{k} + m - 1}{m} \right) \qquad B_L = 2\log_2 \binom{s+d-1}{s} \qquad (3)$$

These expressions estimate the number of non-redundant states in each neuron type, i.e., those assignments of input lines to dendritic sites which yield distinct input-output functions y_L or y_N.

These formulae are plotted in figure 2A with $d = 100$, where each curve represents a cell with a fixed number of branches (indicated by m). In each case, the capacity increases steadily as the number of synapses per branch, k, is increased. The logarithmic growth in the capacity of the linear model (evident in an asymptotic analysis of the expression for B_L) is shown at the bottom of the graph (circles), from which it may be seen that the boost in capacity provided by the dendritic branch nonlinearity increases steadily with the number of synaptic sites. For a cell with 100 branches containing 100 synaptic sites each, the capacity boost relative to the linear model exceeds a factor of 20.

Figure 2B shows that for a given total number of synaptic sites, in this case $s = m \cdot k = 10,000$, the capacity of the nonlinear cell is maximized for a specific choice of m and k. The peak of each of the three curves (computed for different values of d) occurs for a cell containing 1,250 branches with 8 synapses each. However, the capacity is only moderately sensitive to the branch count: the capacity of a cell with 100 branches of 100 synapses each, for example, lies within a factor of two of the optimal configuration. The linear cell capacities can be found at the far right edge of the plot ($m = 10,000$), since a nonlinear model with one synapse per branch has a number of trainable states identical to that of a linear model.

3.2 Validating the Analytical Model

To test the predictions of the analytical model, we trained both linear and nonlinear cells on randomized two-class classification problems. Training samples were drawn from a 40-dimensional spherical Gaussian distribution and were randomly assigned positive or negative labels—in some runs, training patterns were evenly divided between positive and negative labels, with similar results. Each of the 40 original input dimensions was recoded using a set of 10 1-dimensional binary, non-overlapping receptive fields with centers spaced along each dimension such that all receptive fields would be activated equally often. This manipulation mapped the original 40-dimensional learning problem into 400 dimensions, thereby increasing the discriminability of the training samples. The relative memory capacity of linear vs. nonlinear cells was then determined empirically by comparing the number of training patterns learnable at a fixed error rate of 2%.

The learning rule used for both cell types was similar to the "clusteron" learning rule described in (Mel, 1992a), and involved two mechanisms known to contribute to neural development: (1) random activity-independent synapse formation, and (2) activity-dependent synapse stabilization. In each iteration, a set of 25 synapses was chosen at random, and the "worst" synapse was identified based on the correlation over the training set of (i) the input's pre-synaptic activity, (ii) the post-synaptic activity (i.e. the local nonlinear branch response for the nonlinear energy model or a constant of 1 for the linear model), and (iii) a global "delta" signal with a value of 0 if the cell responded correctly to the input pattern, or ± 1 if the cell responded incorrectly. The poorest-performing synapse on the branch was then targeted for replacement with a new synapse drawn at random from the d input lines. The probability that the replacement actually occurred was given by a Boltzmann equation based on the difference in the training set error rates before and after the replacement. A "temperature" variable was gradually lowered over the course of the simulation, which was terminated when no further improvement in error rates was seen.

Results of the learning runs are shown in fig. 3 where the analytical capacity (measured in bits) was scaled to the numerical capacity (measured in training patterns

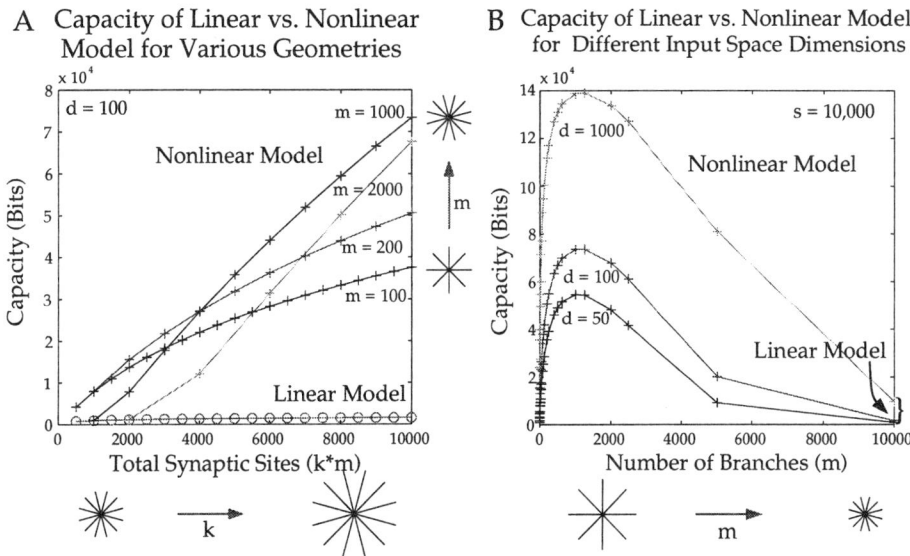

Figure 2: Comparison of linear vs. nonlinear model capacity as a function of branch geometry. A. Capacity in *bits* for linear and several nonlinear cells with different branch counts (for $d = 100$). For each curve indexed by branch count m, sites per branch k increases from left to right as indicated iconically beneath the x-axis. For all cells, capacity increases with an increasing number of sites, though the capacity of the linear model grows logarithmically, leading to an increasingly large capacity boost for the size-matched nonlinear cells. B. Capacity of a nonlinear model with 10,000 sites for different values of input space dimension d. Branch count m grows along the x-axis. Cells at right edge of plot contain only one synapse per branch, and thus have a number of modifiable parameters (and hence capacity) equivalent to that of the linear model. All three curves show that there exist an optimal geometry which maximizes the capacity of the nonlinear model (in this case 1,250 branches with 8 synapses each).

learned at 2% error). Two key features of the theoretical curves (dashed lines) are echoed in the empirical performance curves (solid lines), including the much larger storage capacity of the nonlinear cell model, and the specific cell geometry which maximizes the capacity boost.

4 Discussion

We found using both analytical and numerical methods that in the limit of low-resolution synaptic weights, application of a fixed output nonlinearity to each compartment of a dendritic tree leads to a significant boost in capacity relative to a cell whose post-synaptic integration is linear. For example, given a cell with 10,000 synaptic contacts originating from 400 distinct input lines, the analysis predicts a 23-fold increase in capacity for the nonlinear cell, while numerical simulations using a stochastic delta rule actually achieve a 15-fold boost.

Given that a linear and a nonlinear model have an identical number of synaptic contacts with uniform synaptic weight values, what accounts for the capacity boost? The principal insight gained in this work is that the attachment of a fixed nonlinearity to each branch in a neuron substantially increases its underlying "model

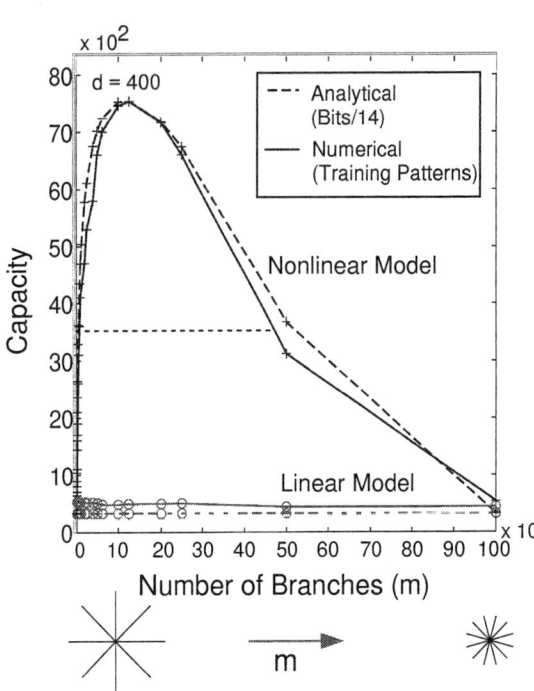

Figure 3: Comparison of capacity boost predicted by analysis vs. that observed empirically when linear and nonlinear models were trained using the same stochastic delta rule. Dashed lines: analytical curves for linear vs. nonlinear model for a cell with 10,000 sites show capacity for varying cell geometries. Solid lines: empirical performance for same two cells at 2% error criterion, using a subunit nonlinearity $g(x) = x^{10}$ (similar results were seen using a sigmoidal nonlinearity, though the parameters of the optimal sigmoid depended on the cell geometry). For both analytical and numerical curves, peak capacity is seen for cell with 1,000 branches (10 synapses per branch). Capacity exceeds that of same-sized linear model by a factor of 15 at the peak, and by more than a factor of 7 for cells ranging from about 3 to 60 synapses per branch (horizontal dotted line).

flexibility", i.e. confers upon the cell a much larger choice of distinct input-output relations from which to select during learning. This may be illustrated as follows. For the linear model, branching structure is irrelevant so that y_L depends only on the *number* of input connections formed from each of the d input lines. All spatial permutations of a set of input connections are thus interchangeable and produce identical cell responses. This massive redundancy confines the capacity of the linear model to grow only logarithmically with an increasing number of synaptic sites (fig. 1A), an unfortunate limitation for a brain in which the formation of large numbers of synaptic contacts between neurons is routine. In contrast, the model with nonlinear subunits contains many fewer redundancies: most spatial permutations of the same set of input connections lead to *non*-identical values of y_N, since an input x swapped from branch b_1 to branch b_2 leads to the elimination of the $k-1$ interaction terms involving x on branch b_1 and the creation of $k-1$ new interaction terms on branch b_2.

Interestingly, the particular form of the branch nonlinearity has virtually no effect on the capacity of the cell as far as the counting arguments are concerned (though it can have a profound effect on the cell's "representational bias"—see below), since the principal effect of the nonlinearity in our capacity calculations is to break the symmetry among the different branches.

The issue of representational bias is a critical one, however, and must be considered when attempting to predict absolute or relative performance rates for particular classifiers confronted with specific learning problems. Thus, intrinsic differences in the geometry of linear vs. nonlinear discriminant functions mean that the parameters available to the two models may be better or worse suited to solve a given learning problem, even if the two models were equated for total parameter flexibility. While such biases are not taken into account in our analysis, they could nonetheless have a substantial effect on measured error rates—and could thus throw a performance advantage to one machine or the other. One danger is that performance differences measured empirically could be misinterpreted as arising from differences in underlying model capacity, when in fact they arise from differential suitability of the two classifiers for the learning problem at hand. To avoid this difficulty, the random classification problems we used to empirically assess memory capacity were chosen to level the playing field for the linear vs. nonlinear cells, since in a previous study we found that the coefficients on linear vs. nonlinear (quadratic) terms were about equally efficient as features for this task. In this way, differences in measured performance on these tasks were primarily attributable to underlying capacity differences, rather than differences in representational bias. This experimental control permitted more meaningful comparisons between our analytical and empirical tests (fig. 3).

The problem of representational bias crops up in a second guise, wherein the analytical expressions for capacity in eq. 1 can significantly overestimate the actual performance of the cell. This occurs when a particular ensemble of learning problems fails to utilize all of the entropy available in the cell's parameter space—for example, by requiring the cell to visit only a small subset of its parameter states relatively often. This invalidates the maximum parameter entropy assumption made in the derivation of eq. 1, so that measured performance will tend to fall below predicted values. The actual performance of either model when confronted with an ensemble of learning problems will thus be determined by (1) the number of trainable parameters available to the neuron (as measured by eq. 1), (2) the suitability of the neuron's parameters for solving the assigned learning problems, and (3) the utilization of parameters, which relates to the entropy in the joint probability of the parameter values averaged over the ensemble of learning problems. In our comparisons here of linear and nonlinear cells, we we have calculated (1), and have attempted to control for (2) and (3).

In conclusion, our results build upon the results of earlier biophysical simulations, and indicate that in the limit of a large number of low-resolution synaptic weights, nonlinear dendritic processing could nonetheless have a major impact on the storage capacity of neural tissue.

References

Mel, B. W. (1992a). The clusteron: Toward a simple abstraction for a complex neuron. In Moody, J., Hanson, S., & Lippmann, R. (Eds.), *Advances in Neural Information Processing Systems, vol. 4*, pp. 35-42. Morgan Kaufmann, San Mateo, CA.

Mel, B. W. (1992b). NMDA-based pattern discrimination in a modeled cortical neuron. *Neural Comp., 4*, 502-516.

Petersen, C. C. H., Malenka, R. C., Nicoll, R. A., & Hopfield, J. J. (1998). All-or-none potentiation and CA3-CA1 synapses. *Proc. Natl. Acad. Sci. USA, 95*, 4732-4737.

Poirazi, P., & Mel, B. W. (1999). Choice and value flexibility jointly contribute to the capacity of a subsampled quadratic classifier. *Neural Comp., in press.*

Predictive Sequence Learning in Recurrent Neocortical Circuits[*]

R. P. N. Rao
Computational Neurobiology Lab and
Sloan Center for Theoretical Neurobiology
The Salk Institute, La Jolla, CA 92037
rao@salk.edu

T. J. Sejnowski
Computational Neurobiology Lab and
Howard Hughes Medical Institute
The Salk Institute, La Jolla, CA 92037
terry@salk.edu

Abstract

Neocortical circuits are dominated by massive excitatory feedback: more than eighty percent of the synapses made by excitatory cortical neurons are onto other excitatory cortical neurons. Why is there such massive recurrent excitation in the neocortex and what is its role in cortical computation? Recent neurophysiological experiments have shown that the plasticity of recurrent neocortical synapses is governed by a temporally asymmetric Hebbian learning rule. We describe how such a rule may allow the cortex to modify recurrent synapses for prediction of input sequences. The goal is to predict the next cortical input from the recent past based on previous experience of similar input sequences. We show that a temporal difference learning rule for prediction used in conjunction with dendritic back-propagating action potentials reproduces the temporally asymmetric Hebbian plasticity observed physiologically. Biophysical simulations demonstrate that a network of cortical neurons can learn to predict moving stimuli and develop direction selective responses as a consequence of learning. The space-time response properties of model neurons are shown to be similar to those of direction selective cells in alert monkey V1.

1 INTRODUCTION

The neocortex is characterized by an extensive system of recurrent excitatory connections between neurons in a given area. The precise computational function of this massive recurrent excitation remains unknown. Previous modeling studies have suggested a role for excitatory feedback in amplifying feedforward inputs [1]. Recently, however, it has been shown that recurrent excitatory connections between cortical neurons are modified according to a temporally asymmetric Hebbian learning rule: synapses that are activated slightly before the cell fires are strengthened whereas those that are activated slightly after are weakened [2, 3]. Information regarding the postsynaptic activity of the cell is conveyed back to the dendritic locations of synapses by back-propagating action potentials from the soma.

In this paper, we explore the hypothesis that recurrent excitation subserves the function of prediction and generation of temporal sequences in neocortical circuits [4, 5, 6]. We show

---

[*]This research was supported by the Sloan Foundation and Howard Hughes Medical Institute.

that a temporal difference based learning rule for prediction applied to backpropagating action potentials reproduces the experimentally observed phenomenon of asymmetric Hebbian plasticity. We then show that such a learning mechanism can be used to learn temporal sequences and the property of direction selectivity emerges as a consequence of learning to predict moving stimuli. Space-time response plots of model neurons are shown to be similar to those of direction selective cells in alert macaque V1.

2 TEMPORALLY ASYMMETRIC HEBBIAN PLASTICITY AND TEMPORAL DIFFERENCE LEARNING

To accurately predict input sequences, the recurrent excitatory connections in a network need to be adjusted such that the appropriate set of neurons are activated at each time step. This can be achieved by using a "temporal-difference" (TD) learning rule [5, 7]. In this paradigm of synaptic plasticity, an activated synapse is strengthened or weakened based on whether the difference between two temporally-separated predictions is positive or negative. This minimizes the errors in prediction by ensuring that the prediction generated by the neuron after synaptic modification is closer to the desired value than before (see [7] for more details).

In order to ascertain whether temporally-asymmetric Hebbian learning in cortical neurons can be interpreted as a form of temporal-difference learning, we used a two-compartment model of a cortical neuron consisting of a dendrite and a soma-axon compartment. The compartmental model was based on a previous study that demonstrated the ability of such a model to reproduce a range of cortical response properties [8]. The presence of voltage-activated sodium channels in the dendrite allowed back-propagation of action potentials from the soma into the dendrite. To study plasticity, excitatory postsynaptic potentials (EPSPs) were elicited at different time delays with respect to postsynaptic spiking by presynaptic activation of a single excitatory synapse located on the dendrite. Synaptic currents were calculated using a kinetic model of synaptic transmission with model parameters fitted to whole-cell recorded AMPA currents (see [9] for more details). Synaptic plasticity was simulated by incrementing or decrementing the value for maximal synaptic conductance by an amount proportional to the temporal-difference in the postsynaptic membrane potential at time instants $t + \Delta t$ and $t - \Delta t$ for presynaptic activation at time t. The delay parameter Δt was set to 5 ms to yield results consistent with previous physiological experiments [2]. Presynaptic input to the model neuron was paired with postsynaptic spiking by injecting a depolarizing current pulse (10 ms, 200 pA) into the soma. Changes in synaptic efficacy were monitored by applying a test stimulus before and after pairing, and recording the EPSP evoked by the test stimulus.

Figure 1A shows the results of pairings in which the postsynaptic spike was triggered 5 ms after and 5 ms before the onset of the EPSP respectively. While the peak EPSP amplitude was increased 58.5% in the former case, it was decreased 49.4% in the latter case, qualitatively similar to experimental observations [2]. The critical window for synaptic modifications in the model depends on the parameter Δt as well as the shape of the back-propagating action potential. This window of plasticity was examined by varying the time interval between presynaptic stimulation and postsynaptic spiking (with $\Delta t = 5$ ms). As shown in Figure 1B, changes in synaptic efficacy exhibited a highly asymmetric dependence on spike timing similar to physiological data [2]. Potentiation was observed for EPSPs that occurred between 1 and 12 ms before the postsynaptic spike, with maximal potentiation at 6 ms. Maximal depression was observed for EPSPs occurring 6 ms after the peak of the postsynaptic spike and this depression gradually decreased, approaching zero for delays greater than 10 ms. As in rat neocortical neurons, *Xenopus* tectal neurons, and cultured hippocampal neurons (see [2]), a narrow transition zone (roughly 3 ms in the model) separated the potentiation and depression windows.

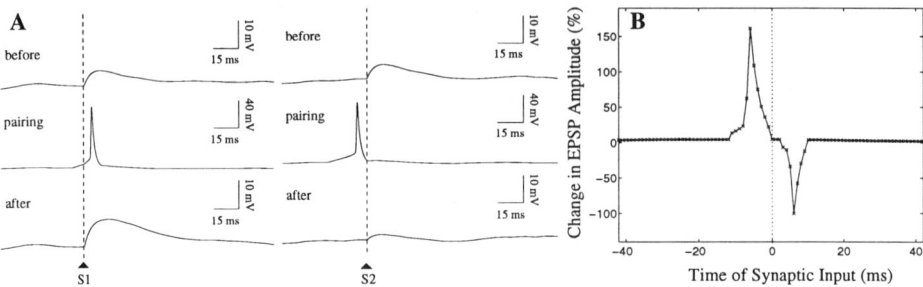

Figure 1: **Synaptic Plasticity in a Model Neocortical Neuron**. (**A**) (Left Panel) EPSP in the model neuron evoked by a presynaptic spike (S1) at an excitatory synapse ("before"). Pairing this presynaptic spike with postsynaptic spiking after a 5 ms delay ("pairing") induces long-term potentiation ("after"). (Right Panel) If presynaptic stimulation (S2) occurs 5 ms after postsynaptic firing, the synapse is weakened resulting in a corresponding decrease in peak EPSP amplitude. (**B**) Critical window for synaptic plasticity obtained by varying the delay between pre- and postsynaptic spiking (negative delays refer to presynaptic before postsynaptic spiking).

3 RESULTS

3.1 Learning Sequences using Temporally Asymmetric Hebbian Plasticity

To see how a network of model neurons can learn sequences using the learning mechanism described above, consider the simplest case of two excitatory neurons N1 and N2 connected to each other, receiving inputs from two separate input neurons I1 and I2 (Figure 2A). Suppose input neuron I1 fires before input neuron I2, causing neuron N1 to fire (Figure 2B). The spike from N1 results in a sub-threshold EPSP in N2 due to the synapse S2. If input arrives from I2 any time between 1 and 12 ms after this EPSP and the temporal summation of these two EPSPs causes N2 to fire, the synapse S2 will be strengthened. The synapse S1, on the other hand, will be weakened because the EPSP due to N2 arrives a few milliseconds after N1 has fired. Thus, on a subsequent trial, when input I1 causes neuron N1 to fire, N1 in turn causes N2 to fire several milliseconds *before* input I2 occurs due to the potentiation of the recurrent synapse S2 in previous trial(s) (Figure 2C). Input neuron I2 can thus be inhibited by the predictive feedback from N2 just before the occurrence of imminent input activity (marked by an asterisk in Figure 2C). This inhibition prevents input I2 from further exciting N2. Similarly, a positive feedback loop between neurons N1 and N2 is avoided because the synapse S1 was weakened in previous trial(s) (see arrows in Figures 2B and 2C). Figure 2D depicts the process of potentiation and depression of the two synapses as a function of the number of exposures to the I1-I2 input sequence. The decrease in latency of the predictive spike elicited in N2 with respect to the timing of input I2 is shown in Figure 2E. Notice that before learning, the spike occurs 3.2 ms after the occurrence of the input whereas after learning, it occurs 7.7 ms before the input.

3.2 Emergence of Direction Selectivity

In a second set of simulations, we used a network of recurrently connected excitatory neurons as shown in Figure 3A receiving retinotopic sensory input consisting of moving pulses of excitation (8 ms pulse of excitation at each neuron) in the rightward and leftward directions. The task of the network was to predict the sensory input by learning appropriate recurrent connections such that a given neuron in the network starts firing several milliseconds before the arrival of its input pulse of excitation. The network was comprised of two parallel chains of neurons with mutual inhibition (dark arrows) between corresponding pairs of neurons along the two chains. The network was initialized such that within a chain, a given

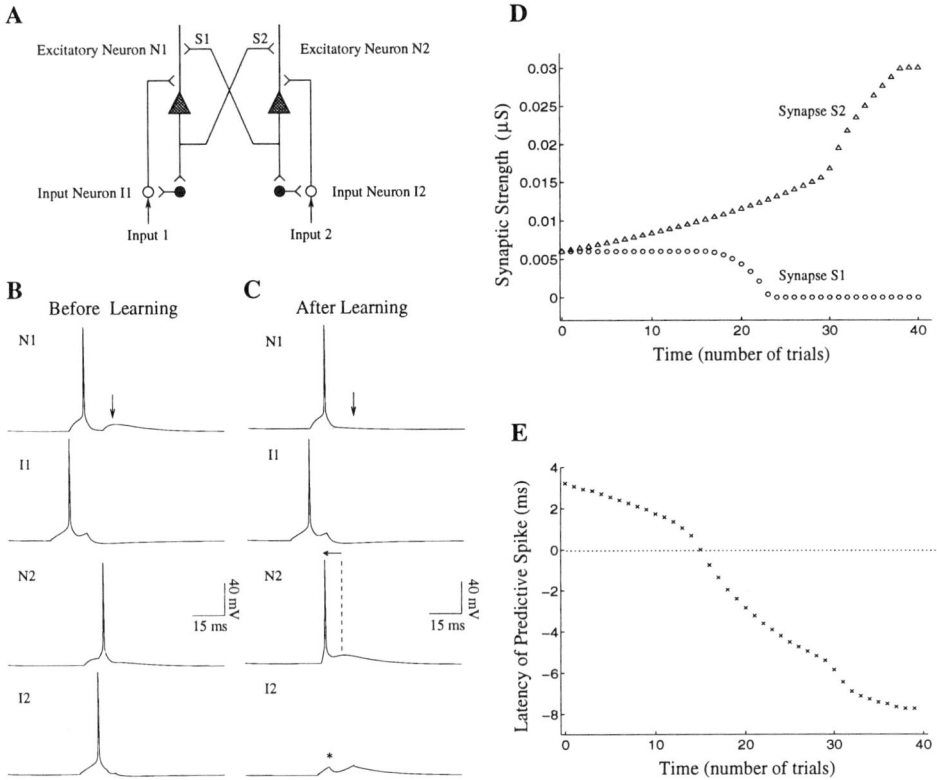

Figure 2: **Learning to Predict using Temporally Asymmetric Hebbian Learning**. (A) Network of two model neurons N1 and N2 recurrently connected via excitatory synapses S1 and S2, with input neurons I1 and I2. N1 and N2 inhibit the input neurons via inhibitory interneurons (darkened circles). (B) Network activity elicited by the sequence I1 followed by I2. (C) Network activity for the same sequence after 40 trials of learning. Due to strengthening of recurrent synapse S2, recurrent excitation from N1 now causes N2 to fire several ms before the expected arrival of input I2 (dashed line), allowing it to inhibit I2 (asterisk). Synapse S1 has been weakened, preventing re-excitation of N1 (downward arrows show decrease in EPSP). (D) Potentiation and depression of synapses S1 and S2 respectively during the course of learning. Synaptic strength was defined as maximal synaptic conductance in the kinetic model of synaptic transmission [9]. (E) Latency of predictive spike in N2 during the course of learning measured with respect to the time of input spike in I2 (dotted line).

excitatory neuron received both excitation and inhibition from its predecessors and successors (Figure 3B). Excitatory and inhibitory synaptic currents were calculated using kinetic models of synaptic transmission based on properties of AMPA and $GABA_A$ receptors as determined from whole-cell recordings [9]. Maximum conductances for all synapses were initialized to small positive values (dotted lines in Figure 3C) with a slight asymmetry in the recurrent excitatory connections for breaking symmetry between the two chains.

The network was exposed alternately to leftward and rightward moving stimuli for a total of 100 trials. The excitatory connections (labeled 'EXC' in Figure 3B) were modified according to the asymmetric Hebbian learning rule in Figure 1B while the excitatory connections onto the inhibitory interneuron (labeled 'INH') were modified according to an asymmetric anti-Hebbian learning rule that reversed the polarity of the rule in Figure 1B. The synaptic conductances learned by two neurons (marked N1 and N2 in Figure 3A) located at corresponding positions in the two chains after 100 trials of exposure to the moving stimuli are shown in Figure 3C (solid line). Initially, for rightward motion, the slight asymmetry in

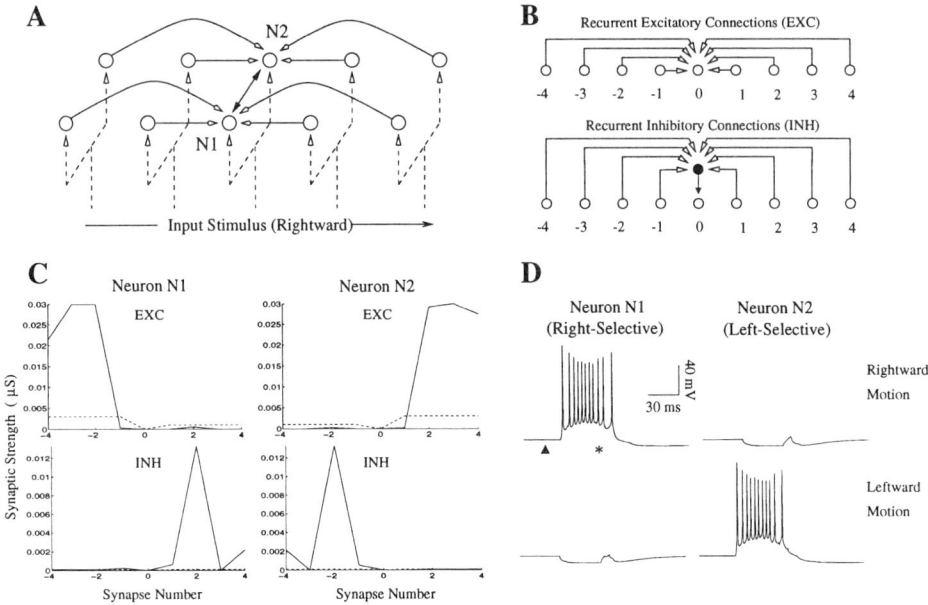

Figure 3: **Direction Selectivity in the Model.** (A) A model network consisting of two chains of recurrently connected neurons receiving retinotopic inputs. A given neuron receives recurrent excitation and recurrent inhibition (white-headed arrows) as well as inhibition (dark-headed arrows) from its counterpart in the other chain. (B) Recurrent connections to a given neuron (labeled '0') arise from 4 preceding and 4 succeeding neurons in its chain. Inhibition at a given neuron is mediated via a GABAergic interneuron (darkened circle). (C) Synaptic strength of recurrent excitatory (EXC) and inhibitory (INH) connections to neurons N1 and N2 before (dotted lines) and after learning (solid lines). Synapses were adapted during 100 trials of exposure to alternating leftward and rightward moving stimuli. (D) Responses of neurons N1 and N2 to rightward and leftward moving stimuli. As a result of learning, neuron N1 has become selective for rightward motion (as have other neurons in the same chain) while neuron N2 has become selective for leftward motion. In the preferred direction, each neuron starts firing several milliseconds before the actual input arrives at its soma (marked by an asterisk) due to recurrent excitation from preceding neurons. The dark triangle represents the start of input stimulation in the network.

the initial excitatory connections of neuron N1 allows it to fire slightly earlier than neuron N2 thereby inhibiting neuron N2. Additionally, since the EPSPs from neurons lying on the left of N1 occur before N1 fires, the excitatory synapses from these neurons are strengthened while the excitatory synapses from these same neurons to the inhibitory interneuron are weakened according to the two learning rules mentioned above. On the other hand, the excitatory synapses from neurons lying on the right side of N1 are weakened while inhibitory connections are strengthened since the EPSPs due to these connections occur after N1 has fired. The synapses on neuron N2 and its associated interneuron remain unaltered since there is no postsynaptic firing (due to inhibition by N1) and hence no back-propagating action potentials in the dendrite. As shown in Figure 3C, after 100 trials, the excitatory and inhibitory connections to neuron N1 exhibit a marked asymmetry, with excitation originating from neurons on the left and inhibition from neurons on the right. Neuron N2 exhibits the opposite pattern of connectivity. As expected, neuron N1 was found to be selective for rightward motion while neuron N2 was selective for leftward motion (Figure 3D). Moreover, when stimulus motion is in the preferred direction, each neuron starts firing several milliseconds before the time of arrival of the input stimulus at its soma (marked by an asterisk) due to recurrent excitation from preceding neurons. Conversely, motion in the non-preferred direction triggers recurrent inhibition from preceding neurons as well as inhibition

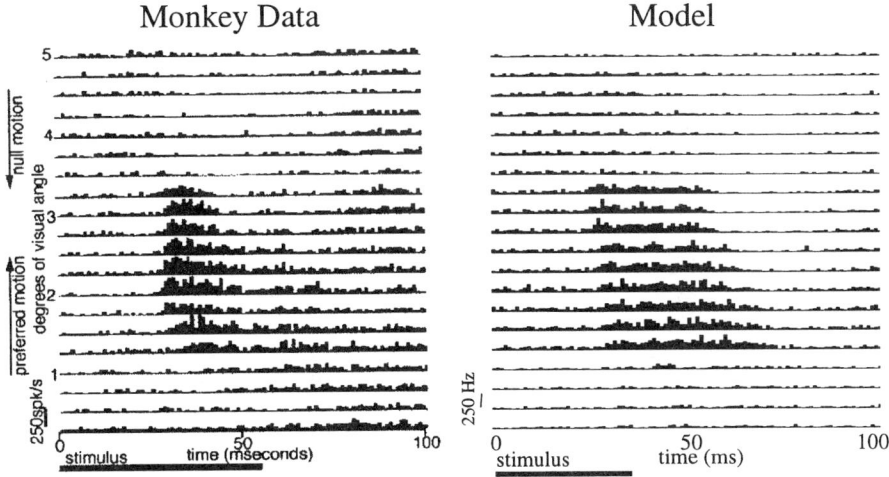

Figure 4: **Comparison of Monkey and Model Space-Time Response Plots.** (Left) Sequence of PSTHs obtained by flashing optimally oriented bars at 20 positions across the 5°-wide receptive field (RF) of a complex cell in alert monkey V1 (from [11]). The cell's preferred direction is from the part of the RF represented at the bottom towards the top. Flash duration = 56 ms; inter-stimulus delay = 100 ms; 75 stimulus presentations. (Right) PSTHs obtained from a model neuron after stimulating the chain of neurons at 20 positions to the left and right side of the given neuron. Lower PSTHs represent stimulations on the preferred side while upper PSTHs represent stimulations on the null side.

from the active neuron in the corresponding position in the other chain. Thus, the learned pattern of connectivity allows the direction selective neurons comprising the two chains in the network to conjointly code for and predict the moving input stimulus in each direction. The average firing rate of neurons in the network for the preferred direction was 75.7 Hz, which is in the range of cortical firing rates for moving bar stimuli. Assuming a 200 μm separation between excitatory model neurons in each chain and utilizing known values for the cortical magnification factor in monkey striate cortex, one can estimate the preferred stimulus velocity of model neurons to be 3.1°/s in the fovea and 27.9°/s in the periphery (at an eccentricity of 8°). Both of these values fall within the range of monkey striate cortical velocity preferences [11].

The model predicts that the neuroanatomical connections for a direction selective neuron should exhibit a pattern of asymmetrical excitation and inhibition similar to Figure 3C. A recent study of direction selective cells in awake monkey V1 found excitation on the preferred side of the receptive field and inhibition on the null side consistent with the pattern of connections learned by the model [11]. For comparison with this experimental data, spontaneous background activity in the model was generated by incorporating Poisson-distributed random excitatory and inhibitory alpha synapses on the dendrite of each model neuron. Post stimulus time histograms (PSTHs) and space-time response plots were obtained by flashing optimally oriented bar stimuli at random positions in the cell's activating region. As shown in Figure 4, there is good qualitative agreement between the response plot for a complex cell and that for the model. Both space-time plots show a progressive shortening of response onset time and an increase in response transiency going in the preferred direction: in the model, this is due to recurrent excitation from progressively closer cells on the preferred side. Firing is reduced to below background rates 40-60 ms after stimulus onset in the upper part of the plots: in the model, this is due to recurrent inhibition from cells on the null side. The response transiency and shortening of response time course appears as a slant in the space-time maps, which can be related to the neuron's velocity sensitivity [11].

4 CONCLUSIONS

Our results show that a network of recurrently connected neurons endowed with a temporal-difference based asymmetric Hebbian learning mechanism can learn a predictive model of its spatiotemporal inputs. When exposed to moving stimuli, neurons in a simulated network learned to fire several milliseconds before the expected arrival of an input stimulus and developed direction selectivity as a consequence of learning. The model predicts that a direction selective neuron should start responding several milliseconds before the preferred stimulus enters its retinal input dendritic field (such predictive neural activity has recently been reported in retinal ganglion cells [10]). Temporally asymmetric Hebbian learning has previously been suggested as a possible mechanism for sequence learning in the hippocampus [4] and as an explanation for the asymmetric expansion of hippocampal place fields during route learning [12]. Some of these theories require relatively long temporal windows of synaptic plasticity (on the order of several hundreds of milliseconds) [4] while others have utilized temporal windows in the millisecond range for coincidence detection [3]. Sequence learning in our model is based on a window of plasticity in the 10 to 15 ms range which is roughly consistent with recent physiological observations [2] (see also [13]). The idea that prediction and sequence learning may constitute an important goal of the neocortex has previously been suggested in the context of statistical and information theoretic models of cortical processing [4, 5, 6]. Our biophysical simulations suggest a possible implementation of such models in cortical circuitry. Given the universality of the problem of encoding and generating temporal sequences in both sensory and motor domains, the hypothesis of predictive sequence learning in recurrent neocortical circuits may help provide a unifying principle for studying cortical structure and function.

References

[1] R. J. Douglas et al., *Science* **269**, 981 (1995); H. Suarez et al., *J. Neurosci.* **15**, 6700 (1995); R. Maex and G. A. Orban, *J. Neurophysiol.* **75**, 1515 (1996); P. Mineiro and D. Zipser, *Neural Comput.* **10**, 353 (1998); F. S. Chance et al., *Nature Neuroscience* **2**, 277 (1999).

[2] H. Markram et al., *Science* **275**, 213 (1997); W. B. Levy and O. Steward, *Neuroscience* **8**, 791 (1983); D. Debanne et al., *Proc. Natl. Acad. Sci. U.S.A.* **91**, 1148 (1994); L. I. Zhang et al., *Nature* **395**, 37 (1998); G. Q. Bi and M. M. Poo, *J. Neurosci.* **18**, 10464 (1998).

[3] W. Gerstner et al., *Nature* **383**, 76 (1996); R. Kempter et al., in *Advances in Neural Info. Proc. Systems 11*, M. S. Kearns, S. A. Solla and D. A. Cohn, Eds. (MIT Press, Cambridge, MA, 1999), pp. 125–131.

[4] L. F. Abbott and K. I. Blum, *Cereb. Cortex* **6**, 406 (1996); W. Gerstner and L. F. Abbott, *J. Comput. Neurosci.* **4**, 79 (1997); A. A. Minai and W. B. Levy, in *Proceedings of the 1993 World Congress on Neural Networks* II, 505 (1993).

[5] P. R. Montague and T. J. Sejnowski, *Learning and Memory* **1**, 1 (1994); P. R. Montague et al., *Nature* **377**, 725 (1995); W. Schultz et al., *Science* **275**, 1593 (1997).

[6] R. P. N. Rao and D. H. Ballard, *Neural Computation* **9**, 721 (1997); R. P. N. Rao and D. H. Ballard, *Nature Neuroscience* **2**, 79 (1999); H. Barlow, *Perception* **27**, 885 (1998).

[7] R. S. Sutton, *Machine Learning* **3**, 9 (1988); R. S. Sutton and A. G. Barto, in *Learning and Computational Neuroscience: Foundations of Adaptive Networks*, M. Gabriel and J. W. Moore, editors (MIT Press, Cambridge, MA, 1990).

[8] Z. F. Mainen and T. J. Sejnowski, *Nature* **382**, 363 (1996).

[9] A. Destexhe et al., in *Methods in Neuronal Modeling*, C. Koch and I. Segev, editors, (MIT Press, Cambridge, MA, 1998).

[10] M. J. Berry et al., *Nature* **398**, 334 (1999).

[11] M. S. Livingstone, *Neuron* **20**, 509 (1998).

[12] M. R. Mehta et al., *Proc. Natl. Acad. Sci. U.S.A.* **94**, 8918 (1997).

[13] L. F. Abbott and S. Song, in *Advances in Neural Info. Proc. Systems 11*, M. S. Kearns, S. A. Solla and D. A. Cohn, Eds. (MIT Press, Cambridge, MA, 1999), pp. 69–75.

A recurrent model of the interaction between Prefrontal and Inferotemporal cortex in delay tasks

ALFONSO RENART, NÉSTOR PARGA
Departamento de Física Teórica
Universidad Autónoma de Madrid
Canto Blanco, 28049 Madrid, Spain
http://www.ft.uam.es/neurociencia/GRUPO/grupo_english.html
and
EDMUND T. ROLLS
Oxford University
Department of Experimental Psychology
South Parks Road, Oxford OX1 3UD, England

Abstract

A very simple model of two reciprocally connected attractor neural networks is studied analytically in situations similar to those encountered in delay match-to-sample tasks with intervening stimuli and in tasks of memory guided attention. The model qualitatively reproduces many of the experimental data on these types of tasks and provides a framework for the understanding of the experimental observations in the context of the attractor neural network scenario.

1 Introduction

Working memory is usually defined as the capability to actively hold information in memory for short periods of time. In primates, visual working memory is usually studied in experiments in which, after the presentation of a given visual stimulus, the monkey has to withhold its response during a certain delay period in which no specific visual stimulus is shown. After the delay, another stimulus is presented and the monkey has to make a response which depends on the interaction between the two stimuli. In order to bridge the temporal gap between the stimuli, the first one has to be held in memory during the delay. Electrophysiological recordings in primates during the performance of this type of tasks has revealed that some populations of neurons in different brain areas such as prefrontal (PF), inferotemporal (IT) or posterior parietal (PP) cortex, maintain approximately constant firing rates during the delay periods (for a review see [1]) and this delay activity states have been postulated as the internal representations of the stimuli provoking them [2]. Although up to now most of the modeling effort regarding the operation of networks able to support stable delay activity states has been put in the study of uni-modular (homogeneous) networks, there is evidence that in order for the monkey to solve the tasks satisfactorily, the interaction of several different neural structures is needed. A number of studies of delay match-to-sample tasks with intervening stimuli in primates performed by Desimone and colleagues has revealed that although IT cortex supports delay activity states and shows memory related effects (differential responses to the same, fixed stimulus depending on its status on the trial, e.g. whether it matches or not the sample), it cannot, by itself, provide the information necessary to solve the task, as the delay activity states elicited by each of the stimuli in a sequence are disrupted by the input information associated with each new stimulus presented [3, 4, 5]. Another structure is therefore needed to store the information for the whole duration of the trial. PF cortex is a candidate, since it shows selective delay activity maintained through entire trials even with intervening stimuli [6]. A series of parallel experiments by the same group on memory guided attention [7, 8] have also shown differential firing of IT neurons in response to the *same* visual stimulus shown after a delay (an array of figures), depending on previous information shown before the delay (one of the figures in the array working as a target stimulus). This evidence suggests a distributed memory system as the proper scenario to study working memory tasks as those described above. Taking into account that both IT and PF cortex are known to be able to support delay activity states, and that they are bi-directionally connected, in this paper we propose a simple model consisting of two reciprocally connected attractor neural networks to be identified with IT and PF cortex. Despite its simplicity, the model is able to qualitatively reproduce the behavior of IT and PF cortex during delay match-to-sample tasks with intervening stimuli, the behavior of IT cells during memory guided attention tasks, and to provide an unified picture of these experimental data in the context of associative memory and attractor neural networks.

2 Model and dynamics

The model network consists of a large number of (excitatory) neurons arranged in two modules. Following [9, 10], each neuron is assumed to be a dynamical element which transforms an incoming afferent current into an output spike rate according to a given transduction function. A given afferent current I_{ai} to neuron i ($i = 1, \ldots, N$) in module a ($a = \mathbf{IT}, \mathbf{PF}$) decays with a characteristic time constant $\mathcal{T}$ but increases proportionally to the spike rates ν_{bj} of the rest of the neurons in the network (both from inside and outside its module) connected to it, the contribution of each presynaptic neuron, e.g. neuron j from module b, being proportional to the synaptic efficacy J_{ij}^{ab} between the two. This can be expressed through the following equation

$$\frac{dI_{ai}(t)}{dt} = -\frac{I_{ai}(t)}{\mathcal{T}} + \sum_{bj} J_{ij}^{(a,b)} \nu_{bj} + h_{ai}^{(ext)} \; . \tag{1}$$

An external current $h_{ai}^{(ext)}$ from outside the network, representing the stimuli, can also be imposed on every neuron. Selective stimuli are modeled as proportional to the stored patterns, i.e. $h_{ai}^{\mu(ext)} = h_a \eta_{ai}^\mu$, where h_a is the intensity of the external current to module a.

The transduction function of the neurons transforming currents into rates has been chosen as a threshold hyperbolic tangent of gain G and threshold θ.

The synaptic efficacies between the neurons of each module and between the neurons in different modules are respectively [11, 12]

$$J_{ij}^{(a,a)} = \frac{J_0}{f(1-f)N_t} \sum_{\mu=1}^{P} (\eta_{ai}^\mu - f)(\eta_{aj}^\mu - f) \quad i \neq j \; ; \; a = \mathbf{IT}, \mathbf{PF} \tag{2}$$

$$J_{ij}^{(a,b)} = \frac{g}{f(1-f)N_t} \sum_{\mu=1}^{P} (\eta_{ai}^\mu - f)(\eta_{bj}^\mu - f) \quad \forall \; i,j \; ; \; a \neq b \; . \tag{3}$$

The intra-modular connections express the learning of P binary patterns $\{\eta_{ai}^\mu = 0, 1,\ \mu = 1,\ldots,P\}$ by each module, each of them signaling which neurons are active in each of the sustained activity configurations. Each variable η_{ai}^μ is supposed to take the values 1 and 0 with probabilities f and $(1-f)$ respectively, independently across neurons and across patterns. The inter-modular connections reflect the temporal associations between the sustained activity states of each module. In this way, every stored pattern μ in the IT module has an associated pattern in the PF module which is labelled by the same index. The normalization constant $N_t = N(J_0 + g)$ has been chosen so that the sum of the magnitudes of the inter- and the intra-modular connections remains constant and equal to 1 while their relative values are varied. When this constraint is imposed the strength of the connections can be expressed in terms of a single independent parameter g measuring the relative intensity of the inter- vs. the intra-modular connections (J_0 can be set equal to 1 everywhere). We will limit our study to the case where the number of stored patterns per module P does not increase proportionally to the size of the modules N since a large number of stored patterns does not seem necessary to describe the phenomenology of the delay match-to-sample experiments.

Since the number of neurons in a typical network one may be interested in is very large, e.g. $\sim 10^5 - 10^6$, the analytical treatment of the set of coupled differential equations (1) becomes intractable. On the other hand, when the number of neurons is large, a reliable description of the asymptotic solutions of these equations can be found using the techniques of statistical mechanics [13, 9]. In this framework, instead of characterizing the states of the system by the state of every neuron, this characterization is performed in terms of *macroscopic* quantities called *order parameters* which measure and quantify some global properties of the network as a whole. The relevant order parameters appearing in the description of our system are the overlaps of the state of each module with each of the stored patterns m_a^μ, defined as:

$$m_a^\mu = \frac{1}{\chi N} \ll \sum_i (\eta_{ai}^\mu - f)\nu_{ai} \gg_\eta , \qquad (4)$$

where the symbol $\ll \ldots \gg_\eta$ stands for an average over the stored patterns.

Using the free energy per neuron of the system at zero temperature $\mathcal{F}$ (which we do not write explicitly to reduce the technicalities to a minimum) we have modeled the experiments by giving the order parameters the following dynamics:

$$\mathcal{T} \frac{\partial m_a^\mu}{\partial t} = -\frac{\partial \mathcal{F}}{\partial m_a^\mu} . \qquad (5)$$

This dynamics ensures that the stationary solutions, corresponding to the values of the order parameters at the attractors, correspond also to minima of the free energy, and that, as the system evolves, the free energy is always minimized through its gradient. The time constant of the macroscopic dynamics is a free parameter which has been chosen equal to the time constant of the individual neurons, reflecting the assumption that neurons operate in parallel. Its value has been set to $\mathcal{T} = 10\ ms$. Equations (5) have been solved by a simple discretizing procedure (first order Runge-Kutta method).

Since not all neurons in the network receive the same inputs, not all of them behave in the same way, i.e. have the same firing rates. In fact, the neurons in each of the module can be split into different sub-populations according to their state of activity in each of the stored patterns. The mean firing rate of the neurons in each sub-population depends on the particular state realized by the network (characterized by the values of the order parameters). Associated to each pattern there are two larger sub-populations, to be denoted as foreground (all active neurons) and background (all inactive neurons) of that pattern.

The overlap with a given pattern can be expressed as the difference between the mean firing rate of the neurons in its foreground and its background. The average is performed over all other sub-populations to which each neuron in the foreground (background) may belong to, where the probability of a given sub-population is equal to the fraction of neurons in the module belonging to it (determined by the probability distribution of the stored patterns as given above). This partition of the neurons into sub-populations is appealing since, in experiments, cells are usually classified in terms of their response properties to a set of fixed stimuli, i.e. whether each stimulus is effective or ineffective in driving their response.

The modeling of the different experiments proceeded according to the macroscopic dynamics (5), where each stimulus was implemented as an extra current for a desired period of time.

3 Sequence with intervening stimuli

In order to study delay match-to-sample tasks with intervening stimuli [5, 6], the module to be identified with IT was sequentially stimulated with external currents proportional to some of the stored patterns with a delay between them. To take into account the large fraction of PF neurons with non-selective responses to the visual stimuli (which may be involved in other aspects of the task different from the identification of the stimuli), and since the neurons in our modules are, by definition, stimulus selective (although they are probably connected to the non-selective neurons) a constant, non-selective current of the same intensity as the selective input to the IT module was applied (during the same time) equally to all sub-populations of the PF module. The external current to the IT module was stimulus selective because the fraction of IT neurons with non-selective responses to the visual stimuli is very small [6]. The results can be seen in Figure 1 where the sequence **ABA** with **A** as the sample stimulus and **B** as a non-matching stimulus has been studied. The values of the model parameters are listed in the caption. In Figure 1a, the mean firing rates of the foreground populations of patterns A_{IT} and B_{IT} of the IT module have been plotted as a function of time. The main result is that, as observed in the experiments, the delay activity in the IT module is determined by the last stimulus presented. The delay activity provoked by a given stimulus is disrupted by the next, unless it corresponds to the same stimulus, in which case the effect of the stimulus is to increase the firing rate of the neurons in its foreground. We have checked that no noticeable effects occur if more non-matching stimuli are presented (they are all equivalent with respect to the sample) or if a non-match stimulus is repeated.

If the coupling g between the modules is weak enough [12] the behavior in the PF module is different. This can be seen in Figure 1b, where the time evolution of the mean firing rates of the foreground of the two associated patterns A_{PF} and B_{PF} stored in the PF module are shown. In agreement with the findings of Desimone and colleagues, the neurons in the PF module remain correlated with the sample for the whole trial, despite the non-selective signal received by *all* PF neurons (not only those in the foreground of the sample) and the fact that the selective current from the IT module tends to activate the pattern associated with the *current* stimulus.

Desimone and colleagues [5, 6] report that the response of some neurons (not necessarily those with sample selective delay activity or with stimulus selective responses) in both IT and PF cortex to some stimuli, is larger if those stimuli are matches in their trials than if the same stimuli are non-matches. This has been denoted as *match enhancement*. In the present scenario the explanation is straightforward: when a stimulus is a non-match, IT and PF are in different states and therefore send inconsistent signals to each other. The firing rate of the neurons of each module is maintained in that case solely by the contribution to the total current coming from the recurrent collaterals. On the other hand, when the stimulus is the match, both modules find themselves in states associated in the synapses

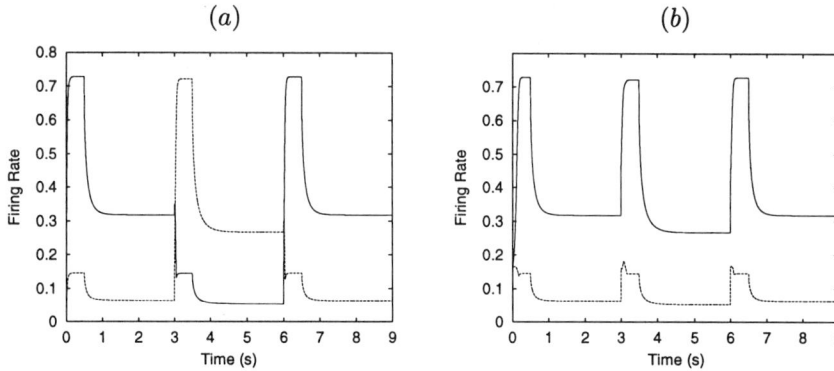

Figure 1: (a) Mean rates in the foreground of patterns $\mathbf{A}_{IT}$ (solid line) and $\mathbf{B}_{IT}$ (dashed line) in the IT module as a function of time. (b) Same but for patterns $\mathbf{A}_{PF}$ and $\mathbf{B}_{PF}$ of the PF module. Model parameters are $G = 1.3$, $\theta = 10^{-3}$, $f = 0.2$, $g = 10^{-2}$, $h = 0.13$. Stimuli are presented during $500\ ms$ at seconds 0, 3, and 6 following the sequence **ABA**.

between the neurons connecting them, PF because it has remained that way the whole trial, and IT because it is driven by the current stimulus. When this happens, the contribution to the total current from the recurrent collaterals and from the long range afferents add up consistently, and the firing rate increases. In order for this explanation to hold there should be a correlation between the top-down input from PF and the sensory bottom-up signal to IT. Indeed, experimental evidence for such a correlation has very recently been found [14]. This is an important experimental finding which supports our theory.

Looking at Figure 1, one sees that the effect is not evident in the model during the time of stimulus presentation, which is the period where it has been reported. The effect is, in fact, present, although its magnitude is too small to be noticeable in the figure. We would argue, however, that this quantitative difference is an artifact of the model. This is because the enhancement effect is very noticeable on the *delay* periods, where essentially the same neurons are active as during the stimulus presentations (i.e., where the same correlations between the top-down and bottom-up signals exist) but with lower firing rates. During stimulus presentations the firing rates are closer to the saturation regime, and therefore the dynamical response range of the neurons is largely reduced.

4 Memory guided attention

To test the differential response of cells as a function of the contents of memory, we have followed [7, 8] and studied a sub-population of IT cells which are simultaneously in the foreground of one of the patterns ($\mathbf{A}_{IT}$) and in the background of another ($\mathbf{B}_{IT}$) in the *same* conditions as the previous section (*same* model parameters). In Figure 2a the response of this sub-population as a function of time has been plotted in two different situations. In the first one, the effective stimulus $\mathbf{A}_{IT}$ was shown first (throughout this section non selective stimulation of PF proceeded as in the last section) and after a delay, a stimulus array equal to the sum of $\mathbf{A}_{IT}$ and $\mathbf{B}_{IT}$ was presented. The second situation is exactly equal, except for the fact that the cue stimulus shown first was the ineffective stimulus $\mathbf{B}_{IT}$. The response of the *same* sub-population to the *same* stimulus array is totally different and determined by the cue stimulus: If the sub-population is in the background of the cue, its response is null during the trial except for the initial period of the presentation of the array. In accordance with the experimental observations [7, 8], its response grows initially (as one would expect, since during the array presentation time, stimulation is symmetric with respect of **A** and **B**) but is later suppressed by the top-down signal being sent by the PF module. This suppression provides a clear example of a situation in which the contents of memory (in the form of an active PF activity state) are explicitly gating the access of sensory information to IT, implementing a non-spatial attentional mechanism.

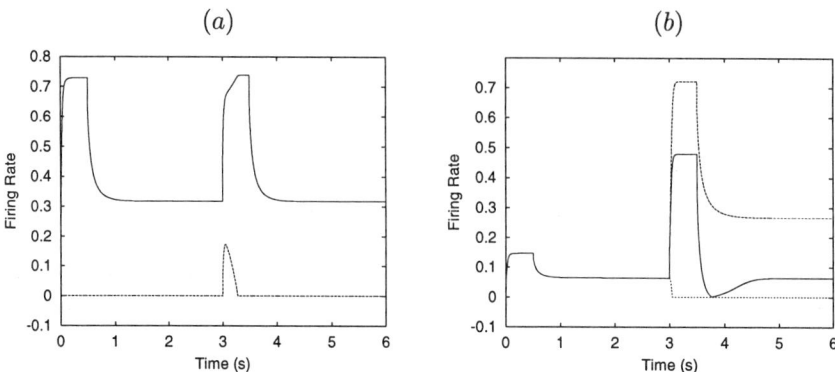

Figure 2: (*a*) Mean rates as a function of time in IT neurons which are both in the foreground $\mathbf{A}_{IT}$ and in the background of $\mathbf{B}_{IT}$ when the cue stimulus is $\mathbf{A}_{IT}$ (solid line) or $\mathbf{B}_{IT}$ (dashed line). (*b*) Mean rates of the same neurons when $\mathbf{C}_{IT}$ is the cue stimulus and the array is $\mathbf{A}_{IT}$ alone (long dashed line), $\mathbf{B}_{IT}$ alone (short dashed line) or the sum of $\mathbf{A}_{IT}$ and $\mathbf{B}_{IT}$ (solid line). Cue present until 500 ms. Array present from 3000 ms to 3500 ms. Model parameters as in Figure 1

In the model, the PF module remains in a state correlated with the cue during the whole trial (to our knowledge there are no measurements of PF activity during memory guided attention tasks) and therefore provides a persistent signal 'in the direction' of the cue which *biases* the competition between $\mathbf{A}_{IT}$ and $\mathbf{B}_{IT}$ established at the onset of the array. This is how the gating mechanism is implemented. The competitive interactions between the stimuli in the array are studied in Figure 2b, which is an emulation of the *target-absent* trials of [8]. In this figure, the same sub-population is studied under situations in which the cue stimulus is not present in the array (another one of the stored patterns, i.e. $\mathbf{C}_{IT}$) The three curves correspond to different arrays: The effective stimulus alone, the ineffective stimulus alone, and a sum of the two as in the previous experiment. In all three, the PF module remains in a sustained activity state correlated with $\mathbf{C}_{IT}$ the whole trial and therefore, since the patterns are independent, the signal it sends to IT is symmetric with respect of **A** and **B**. Thus, the response of the sub-population during the array is in this case unbiased, and the effect of the competitive interactions can be isolated. The result is that, as observed experimentally, the response to the complex array is intermediate between the one to the effective stimulus alone and the one to the ineffective stimulus alone. The nature of the competition in an attractor network like the one under study here is based on the fact that complex stimulus combinations are not stored in the recurrent collaterals of each module. These connections tend to stabilize the individual patterns which, being independent, tend to cancel each other when presented together. After the array is presented, the state of the IT module, which is correlated with $\mathbf{C}_{IT}$ in the initial delay, becomes correlated with $\mathbf{A}_{IT}$ or $\mathbf{B}_{IT}$ if they are presented alone. When the array contains both of them in a symmetric fashion, since the sum of the patterns is not a stored pattern itself, the IT module remains correlated with pattern $\mathbf{C}_{IT}$ due to the signal from the PF module.

5 Discussion

We have proposed a toy model consisting of two reciprocally connected attractor modules which reproduces nicely experimental observations regarding intra-trial data in delay match-to-sample and memory guided attention experiments in which the interaction between IT and PF cortex is relevant. Several important issues are taken into account in the model: a complex interaction between the PF and IT modules resultant from the association of frequent patterns of activity in both modules, delay activity states in each module which exert mutually modulatory influences on each other, and a common substrate (we emphasize that the results on Sections 3 and 4 where obtained with exactly the same model parameters, just by changing the type of task) for the explanation of apparently diverse phenomena. Perception is clearly an active process which results from the complex interactions between past experience and incoming sensory information. The main goal of this model was to show that a very simple associational (Hebbian) pattern of connectivity between a perceptual module and a 'working memory' module can provide the basic ingredients needed to explain coherently different experimentally found neural mechanisms related to this process. The model has clear limitations in terms of 'biological realism' which will have to be improved in order to use it to make quantitative predictions and comparisons, and does not provide a complete an exhaustive account of the very complex and diverse phenomena in which temporo-frontal interactions are relevant (there is, for example, the issue of how to reset PF activity in between trials [15]). However, it is precisely the simplicity of the mechanism it provides and the fact that it captures the essential features of the experiments, *despite* being so simple, what makes it likely that it will remain relevant after being refined.

Acknowledgements

This work was funded by a Spanish grant PB96-0047. We acknowledge the Max Planck Institute for Physics of Complex Systems in Dresden, Germany, for the hospitality received by A.R. and N.P. during the meeting held there from March 1 to 26, 1999.

References

[1] J. M. Fuster. *Memory in the cerebral cortex.* Cambridge, MA: MIT Press (1995)

[2] D. J. Amit. *Behavioral and Brain Sciences* **18**, 617-657 (1995)

[3] G. C. Baylis & E. T. Rolls. *Exp. Brain Res.* **65**, 614-622 (1987)

[4] E. K. Miller, L. Li & R. Desimone. *J. Neurosci.* **13**, 1460-1478 (1993)

[5] E. K. Miller & R. Desimone. *Science* **263**, 520-522 (1994)

[6] E. K. Miller, C. A. Erickson & R. Desimone. *J. Neurosci.* **16**, 5154-5167 (1996)

[7] L. Chelazzi, E. K. Miller, J. Duncan & R. Desimone. *Nature* **363**, 345-347 (1993)

[8] L. Chelazzi, J. Duncan, E. K. Miller & R. Desimone. *J. Neurophysiol. 80*, 2918-2940 (1998)

[9] R. Kuhn. In *Statistical Mechanics of Neural Networks.* (ed. L. Garrido), 19-32. Berlin: Springer-Verlag (1990)

[10] D. J. Amit & M. V. Tsodyks. *Network* **2**, 259-273 (1991)

[11] A. Renart, N. Parga & E. T. Rolls. *Neural Computation* **11**, 1349-1388 (1999).

[12] A. Renart, N. Parga & E. T. Rolls. *Network* **10**, 237-255 (1999).

[13] M. Mezard, G. Parisi & M. Virasoro. *Spin glass theory and beyond.* Singapore: World Scientific (1987)

[14] H. Tomita, M Ohbayashi, K. Nakahara, I. Hasegawa & Y. Miyashita. *Nature* **401**, 699-703 (1999)

[15] D. Durstewitz, M. Kelc & O. Güntürkün. *J. Neurosci.* **19**, 2807-2822 (1999)

Information Capacity and Robustness of Stochastic Neuron Models

Elad Schneidman   Idan Segev   Naftali Tishby
Institute of Computer Science,
Department of Neurobiology and
Center for Neural Computation,
Hebrew University
Jerusalem 91904, Israel
{elads,tishby}@cs.huji.ac.il, idan@lobster.ls.huji.ac.il

Abstract

The reliability and accuracy of spike trains have been shown to depend on the nature of the stimulus that the neuron encodes. Adding ion channel stochasticity to neuronal models results in a macroscopic behavior that replicates the input-dependent reliability and precision of real neurons. We calculate the amount of information that an ion channel based stochastic Hodgkin-Huxley (HH) neuron model can encode about a wide set of stimuli. We show that both the information rate and the information per spike of the stochastic model are similar to the values reported experimentally. Moreover, the amount of information that the neuron encodes is correlated with the amplitude of fluctuations in the input, and less so with the average firing rate of the neuron. We also show that for the HH ion channel density, the information capacity is robust to changes in the density of ion channels in the membrane, whereas changing the ratio between the Na^+ and K^+ ion channels has a considerable effect on the information that the neuron can encode. Finally, we suggest that neurons may maximize their information capacity by appropriately balancing the density of the different ion channels that underlie neuronal excitability.

1 Introduction

The capacity of neurons to encode information is directly connected to the nature of spike trains as a code. Namely, whether the fine temporal structure of the spike train carries information or whether the fine structure of the train is mainly noise (see e.g. [1, 2]). Experimental studies show that neurons *in vitro* [3, 4] and *in vivo* [5, 6, 7], respond to fluctuating inputs with repeatable and accurate spike trains, whereas slowly varying inputs result in lower repeatability and 'jitter' in the spike timing. Hence, it seems that the nature of the code utilized by the neuron depends on the input that it encodes [3, 6].

Recently, we suggested that the biophysical origin of this behavior is the stochasticity of single ion channels. Replacing the average conductance dynamics in the Hodgkin-Huxley (HH) model [8], with a stochastic channel population dynamics [9, 10, 11], yields a stochastic neuron model which replicates rather well the spike trains' reliability and precision of real neurons [12]. The stochastic model also shows subthreshold oscillations, spontaneous and missing spikes, all observed experimentally. Direct measurement of membranal noise has also been replicated successfully by such stochastic models [13]. Neurons use many tens of thousands of ion channels to encode the synaptic current that reaches the soma into trains of spikes [14]. The number of ion channels that underlies the spike generation mechanism, and their types, depend on the activity of the neuron [15, 16]. It is yet unclear how such changes may affect the amount and nature of the information that neurons encode.

Here we ask what is the information encoding capacity of the stochastic HH model neuron and how does this capacity depend on the densities of different of ion channel types in the membrane. We show that both the information rate and the information per spike of the stochastic HH model are similar to the values reported experimentally and that neurons encode more information about highly fluctuating inputs. The information encoding capacity is rather robust to changes in the channel densities of the HH model. Interestingly, we show that there is an optimal channel population size, around the natural channel density of the HH model. The encoding capacity is rather sensitive to changes in the distribution of channel types, suggesting that changes in the population ratios and adaptation through channel inactivation may change the information content of neurons.

2 The Stochastic HH Model

The stochastic HH (SHH) model expands the classic HH model [8], by incorporating the stochastic nature of single ion channels [9, 17]. Specifically, the membrane voltage dynamics is given by the HH description, namely,

$$c_m \frac{dV}{dt} = -g_L(V - V_L) - g_K(V,t)(V - V_K) - g_{Na}(V,t)(V - V_{Na}) + I \quad (1)$$

where V is the membrane potential, V_L, V_K and V_{Na} are the reversal potentials of the leakage, potassium and sodium currents, respectively, g_L, $g_K(V,t)$ and $g_{Na}(V,t)$ are the corresponding ion conductances, c_m is the membrane capacitance and I is the injected current. The ion channel stochasticity is introduced by replacing the equations describing the ion channel conductances with explicit voltage-dependent Markovian kinetic models for single ion channels [9, 10]. Based on the activation and inactivation variables of the deterministic HH model, each K^+ channel can be in one of five different states, and the rates for transition between these states are given in the following diagram,

$$[\mathbf{n_0}] \underset{\beta_n}{\overset{4\alpha_n}{\rightleftharpoons}} [\mathbf{n_1}] \underset{2\beta_n}{\overset{3\alpha_n}{\rightleftharpoons}} [\mathbf{n_2}] \underset{3\beta_n}{\overset{2\alpha_n}{\rightleftharpoons}} [\mathbf{n_3}] \underset{4\beta_n}{\overset{\alpha_n}{\rightleftharpoons}} [\mathbf{n_4}] \quad (2)$$

where $[\mathbf{n_j}]$ refers to the number of channels which are currently in the state n_j. Here $[n_4]$ labels the single open state of a potassium channel, and α_n, β_n, are the voltage-dependent rate-functions in the HH formalism. A similar model is used for the Na^+ channel (The Na^+ kinetic model has 8 states, with only one open state, see [12] for details).

The potassium and sodium membrane conductances are given by,

$$g_K(V,t) = \gamma_K [\mathbf{n_4}] \qquad g_{Na}(V,t) = \gamma_{Na} [\mathbf{m_3 h_1}] \quad (3)$$

where γ_K and γ_{Na} are the conductances of an ion channel for the K^+ and Na^+ respectively. We take the conductance of a single channel to be $20\,pS$ [14] for both the

K^+ and Na^+ channel types [1]. Each of the ion channels will thus respond stochastically by closing or opening its 'gates' according to the kinetic model, fluctuating around the average expected behavior. Figure 1 demonstrates the effect of the ion

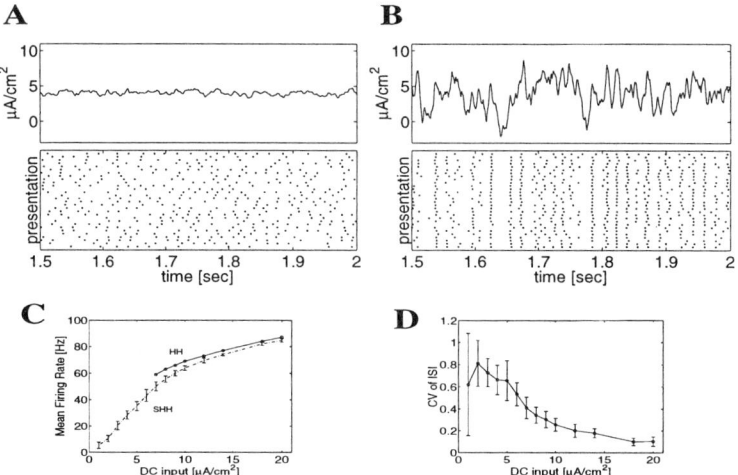

Figure 1: Reliability of firing patterns in a model of an isopotential Hodgkin-Huxley membrane patch in response to different current inputs. (A) Injecting a slowly changing current input (low-pass Gaussian white noise with a mean $\eta = 8\,\mu A/cm^2$, and standard deviation $\sigma = 1\,\mu A/cm^2$ which was convolved with an 'alpha-function' with a time constant $\tau_\alpha = 3\,msec$, top frame), results in high 'jitter' in the timing of the spikes (raster plots of spike responses, bottom frame). (B) The same patch was again stimulated repeatedly, with a highly fluctuating stimulus ($\eta = 8\,\mu A/cm^2$, $\sigma = 7\,\mu A/cm^2$ and $\tau_\alpha = 3\,msec$, top frame) The 'jitter' in spike timing is significantly smaller in B than in A (i.e. increased reliability for the fluctuating current input). Patch area used was $200\,\mu m^2$, with $3,600\,K^+$ channels and $12,000\,Na^+$ channels. (Compare to Fig.1 in see [3]). (C) Average firing rate in response to DC current input of both the HH and the stochastic HH model. (D) Coefficient of variation of the inter spike interval of the SHH model in response to DC inputs, giving values which are comparable to those observed in real neurons

channel stochasticity, showing the response of a $200\,\mu m^2$ SHH isopotential membrane patch (with the 'standard' SHH channel densities) to repeated presentation of suprathreshold current input. When the same slowly varying input is repeatedly presented (Fig. 1A), the spike trains are very different from each other, i.e., spike firing time is unreliable. On the other hand, when the input is highly fluctuating (Fig. 1B), the reliability of the spike timing is relatively high. The stochastic model thus replicates the input-dependent reliability and precision of spike trains observed in pyramidal cortical neurons [3]. As for cortical neurons, the *Repeatability* and *Precision* of the spike trains of the stochastic model (defined in [3]) are strongly correlated with the fluctuations in the current input and may get to sub-millisecond precision [12]. The f-I curve of the stochastic model (Fig. 1C) and the coefficient of variation (CV) of the inter-spike intervals (ISI) distribution for DC inputs (Fig. 1D) are both similar to the behavior of cortical neurons *in vivo* [18], in clear contrast to the deterministic model [2]

---

[1] The number of channels is thus the ratio between the total conductance of a single type of ion channels and the single channel conductance, and so the 'standard' SHH densities will be 60 Na^+ and 18 Na^+ channels per μm^2.

[2] Although the total number of channels in the model is very large, the microscopic level ion channel noise has a macroscopic effect on the spike train reliability, since the number

3 The Information Capacity of the SHH Neuron

Expanding the *Repeatability* and *Precision* measures [3], we turn to quantify how much information the neuron model encodes about the stimuli it receives. We thus present the model with a set of 'representative' input current traces, and the amount of information that the respective spike trains encode is calculated.

Following Mainen and Sejnowski [3], we use a set of input current traces which imitate the synaptic current that reaches the soma from the dendritic tree. We convolve a Gaussian white noise trace (with a mean current η and standard deviation σ) with an alpha function (with a $\tau_\alpha = 3\ msec$). Six different mean current values are used ($\eta = 0, 2, 4, 6, 8, 10\ \mu A/cm^2$), and five different std values ($\sigma = 1, 3, 5, 7, 9\ \mu A/cm^2$), yielding a set of 30 input current traces (each is 10 seconds long). This set of inputs is representative of the wide variety of current traces that neurons might encounter under *in vivo* conditions in the sense that the average firing rates for this set of inputs which range between $2 - 70\ Hz$ (not shown).

We present these input traces to the model, and calculate the amount of information that the resulting spike trains convey about each input, following [6, 19]. Each input is presented repeatedly and the resulting spike trains are discretized in $\Delta\tau$ bins, using a sliding 'window' of size T along the discretized sequence. Each train of spikes is thus transformed into a sequence of K-letter 'words' ($K = T/\Delta\tau$), consisting of 0's (no spike) and 1's (spike). We estimate $P(W)$, the probability of the word W to appear in the spike trains, and then compute the entropy rate of its total word distribution,

$$H_{total} = -\sum_W P(W) \log_2 P(W) \quad bits/word \quad (4)$$

which measures the capacity of information that the neuron spike trains hold [20, 6, 19]. We then examine the set of words that the neuron model used at a particular time t over all the repeated presentations of the stimulus, and estimate $P(W|t)$, the time-dependent word probability distribution. At each time t we calculate the time-dependent entropy rate, and then take the average of these entropies

$$H_{noise} = \langle -\sum_W P(W|t) \log_2 P(W|t) \rangle_t \quad bits/word \quad (5)$$

where $\langle ... \rangle_t$ denotes the average over all times t. H_{noise} is the noise entropy rate, which measures how much of the fine structure of the spike trains of the neuron is just noise. After performing the calculation for each of the inputs, using different word sizes [3], we estimate the limit of the total entropy and noise entropy rates at $T \to \infty$, where the entropies converge to their real values (see [19] for details).

Figure 2A shows the total entropy rate of the responses to the set of stimuli, ranging from 10 to 170 $bits/sec$. The total entropy rate is correlated with the firing rates of the neuron (not shown). The noise entropy rate however, depends in a different way on the input parameters: Figure 2B shows the noise entropy rate of the responses to the set of stimuli, which may get up to 100 $bits/sec$. Specifically, for inputs with high mean current values and low fluctuation amplitude, many of the spikes are

---

of ion channels which are open near the spike firing threshold is rather small [12]. The fluctuations in this small number of open channels near firing threshold give rise to the input-dependent reliability of the spike timing.

[3] the bin size $\tau = 2\ msec$ has been set to be small enough to keep the fine temporal structure of the spike train within the word sizes used, yet large enough to avoid undersampling problems

just noise, even if the mean firing rate is high. The difference between the neuron's entropy rate (the total capacity of information of the neuron's spike train) and the noise entropy rate, is exactly the average rate of information that the neuron's spike trains encode about the input, $I(stimulus, spike\ train) = H_{total} - H_{noise}$ [20, 6], this is shown in Figure 2C. The information rate is more sensitive to the size of

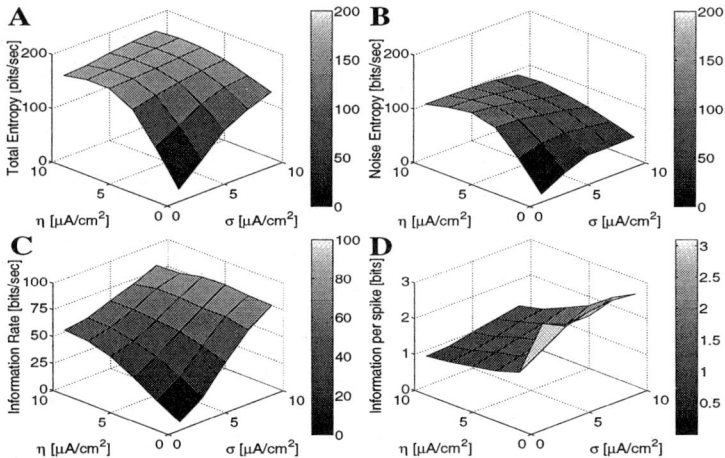

Figure 2: Information capacity of the SHH model. (A) The total spike train entropy rate of the SHH model as a function of η, the current input mean, and σ, the standard deviation (see text for details). Error bar values of this surface as well as for the other frames range between $1-6\%$ (not shown). (B) Noise entropy rate as a function of the current input parameters. (C) The information rate about the stimulus in the spike trains, as a function of the input parameters, calculated by subtracting noise entropy from the total entropy (note the change in grayscale in C and D). (D) Information per spike as a function of the input parameters, which is calculated by normalizing the results shown in C by the average firing rate of the responses to each of the inputs.

fluctuations in the input than to the mean value of the current trace (as expected, from the reliability and precision of spike timing observed *in vitro* [3] and *in vivo* [6] as well as in simulations [12]). The dependence of the neural code on the input parameters is better reflected when calculating the average amount of information per spike that the model gives for each of the inputs (Fig. 2D) (see for comparison the values for the Fly's H1 neuron [6]).

4 The effect of Changing the Neuron Parameters on the Information Capacity

Increasing the density of ion channels in the membrane compared to the 'standard' SHH densities, while keeping the ratio between the K^+ and Na^+ channels fixed, only diminishes the amount of information that the neuron encodes about any of the inputs in the set. However, the change is rather small: Doubling the channel density decreases the amount of information by $5-25\%$ (Fig. 3A), depending on the specific input. Decreasing the channel densities of both types, results in encoding more information about certain stimuli and less about others. Figure 3B shows that having half the channel densities would result with in 10% changes in the information in both directions. Thus, the information rates conveyed by the stochastic model are robust to changes in the ion channel density. Similar robustness (not shown) has been observed for changes in the membrane area (keeping channel density fixed) and in the temperature (which effects the channel kinetics). However,

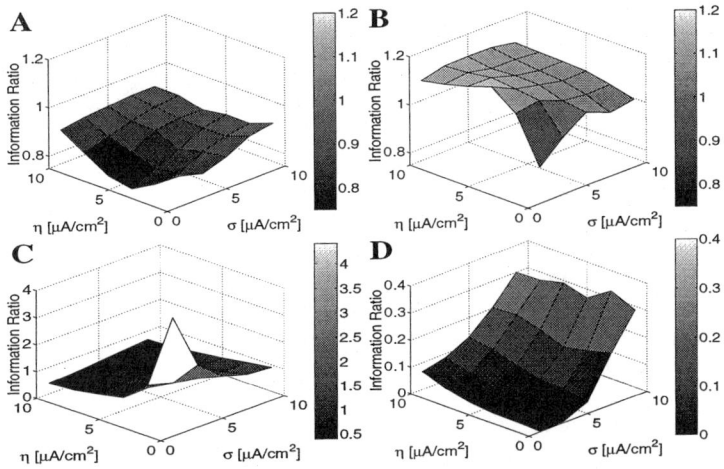

Figure 3: The effect of changing the ion channel densities on the information capacity. (A) The ratio of the information rate of the SHH model with twice the density of the 'standard' SHH densities divided by the information rate of the mode with 'standard' SHH densities. (B) As in A, only for the SHH model with half the 'standard' densities. (C) The ratio of the info rate of the SHH model with twice as many Na^+ channels, divided by the info rate of the standard SHH Na^+ channel density, where the K^+ channel density remains untouched (note the change in graycale in C and D). (D) As in C, only for the SHH model with the number of Na^+ channels reduced by half.

changing the density of the Na^+ channels alone has a larger impact on the amount of information that the neuron conveys about the stimuli. Increasing Na^+ channel density by a factor of two results in less information about most of the stimuli, and a gain in a few others (Fig. 3C). However, reducing the number of Na^+ channels by half results in drastic loss of information for all of the inputs (Fig. 3D).

5 Discussion

We have shown that the amount of information that the stochastic HH model encodes about its current input is highly correlated with the amplitude of fluctuations in the input and less so with the mean value of the input. The stochastic HH model, which incorporates ion channel noise, closely replicates the input-dependent reliability and precision of spike trains observed in cortical neurons. The information rates and information per spike are also similar to those of real neurons. As in other biological systems (e.g., [21]), we demonstrate robustness of macroscopic performance to changes in the cellular properties – the information coding rates of the SHH model are robust to changes in the ion channels densities as well as in the area of the excitable membrane patch and in the temperature (kinetics) of the channel dynamics. However, the information coding rates are rather sensitive to changes in the ratio between the densities of different ion channel types, suggests that the ratio between the density of the K^+ channels and the Na^+ channels in the 'standard' SHH model may be optimal in terms of the information capacity. This may have important implications on the nature of the neural code under adaptation and learning. We suggest that these notions of optimality and robustness may be a key biophysical principle of the operation of real neurons. Further investigations should take into account the activity-dependent nature of the channels and the neuron [15, 16] and the notion of local learning rules which could modify neuronal and suggest local learning rules as in [22].

Acknowledgements

This research was supported by a grant from the Ministry of Science, Israel.

References

[1] Rieke F., Warland D., de Ruyter van Steveninck R., and Bialek W. *Spike: Exploring the Neural Code*. MIT Press, 1997.

[2] Shadlen M. and Newsome W. Noise, neural codes and cortical organization. *Curr. Opin. Neurobiol.*, 4:569–579, 1994.

[3] Mainen Z. and Sejnowski T. Reliability of spike timing in neocortical neurons. *Science*, 268:1503–1508, 1995.

[4] Nowak L., Sanches-Vives M., and McCormick D. Influence of low and high frequency inputs on spike timing in visual cortical neurons. *Cerebral Cortex*, 7:487–501, 1997.

[5] Bair W. and Koch C. Temporal precision of spike trains in extrastriate cortex of the behaving macaque monkey. *Neural Comp.*, 8:1185–1202, 1996.

[6] de Ruyter van Steveninck R., Lewen G., Strong S., Koberle R., and Bialek W. Reproducibility and variability in neural spike trains. *Science*, 275:1805–1808, 1997.

[7] Reich D., Victor J., Knight B., Ozaki T., and Kaplan E. Response variability and timing precision of neuronal spike trains in vivo. *J. Neurophysiol.*, 77:2836:2841, 1997.

[8] Hodgkin A. and Huxley A. A quantitative description of membrane current and its application to conduction and excitation in nerve. *J. Physiol.*, 117:500–544, 1952.

[9] Fitzhugh R. A kinetic model of the conductance changes in nerve membrane. *J. Cell. Comp. Physiol.*, 66:111–118, 1965.

[10] DeFelice L. *Introduction to Membrane Noise*. Perseus Books, 1981.

[11] Skaugen E. and Walløe L. Firing behavior in a stochastic nerve membrane model based upon the Hodgkin-Huxley equations. *Acta Physiol. Scand.*, 107:343–363, 1979.

[12] Schneidman E., Freedman B., and Segev I. Ion channel stochasticity may be critical in determining the reliability and precision of spike timing. *Neural Comp.*, 10:1679–1704, 1998.

[13] White J., Klink R., Alonso A., and Kay A. Noise from voltage-gated channels may influence neuronal dynamics in the entorhinal cortex. *J Neurophysiol*, 80:262–9, 1998.

[14] Hille B. *Ionic Channels of Excitable Membrane*. Sinauer Associates, 2nd ed., 1992.

[15] Marder E., Abbott L., Turrigiano G., Liu Z., and Golowasch J. Memory from the dynamics of intrinsic membrane currents. *Proc. Natl. Acad. Sci.*, 93:13481–6, 1996.

[16] Toib A., Lyakhov V., and Marom S. Interaction between duration of activity and rate of recovery from slow inactivation in mammalian brain Na^+ channels. *J Neurosci.*, 18:1893–1903, 1998.

[17] Strassberg A. and DeFelice L. Limits of the HH formalism: Effects of single channel kinetics on transmembrane voltage dynamics. *Neural Comp.*, 5:843–856, 1993.

[18] Softky W. and Koch C. The highly irregular firing of cortical cells is inconsistent with temporal integration of random EPSPs. *J. Neurosci.*, 13:334–350, 1993.

[19] Strong S., Koberle R., de Ruyter van Steveninck R., and Bialek W. Entropy and information in neural spike trains. *Phys. Rev. Lett.*, 80:197–200, 1998.

[20] Cover T.M. and Thomas J.A. *Elements of Information Theory*. Wiley, 1991.

[21] Barkai N. and Leibler S. Robustness in simple biochemical networks. *Nature*, 387:913–917, 1997.

[22] Stemmler M. and Koch C. How voltage-dependent conductances can adapt to maximize the information encoded by neuronal firing rate. *Nat. Neurosci.*, 2:521–7, 1999.

An MEG Study of Response Latency and Variability in the Human Visual System During a Visual-Motor Integration Task

Akaysha C. Tang
Dept. of Psychology
University of New Mexico
Albuquerque, NM 87131
akaysha@unm.edu

Barak A. Pearlmutter
Dept. of Computer Science
University of New Mexico
Albuquerque, NM 87131
bap@cs.unm.edu

Tim A. Hely
Santa Fe Institute
1399 Hyde Park Road
Santa Fe, NM 87501
timhely@santafe.edu

Michael Zibulevsky
Dept. of Computer Science
University of New Mexico
Albuquerque, NM 87131
michael@cs.unm.edu

Michael P. Weisend
VA Medical Center
1501 San Pedro SE
Albuquerque, NM 87108
mweisend@unm.edu

Abstract

Human reaction times during sensory-motor tasks vary considerably. To begin to understand how this variability arises, we examined neuronal populational response time variability at early versus late visual processing stages. The conventional view is that precise temporal information is gradually lost as information is passed through a layered network of mean-rate "units." We tested in humans whether neuronal populations at different processing stages behave like mean-rate "units". A blind source separation algorithm was applied to MEG signals from sensory-motor integration tasks. Response time latency and variability for multiple visual sources were estimated by detecting single-trial stimulus-locked events for each source. In two subjects tested on four visual reaction time tasks, we reliably identified sources belonging to early and late visual processing stages. The standard deviation of response latency was smaller for early rather than late processing stages. This supports the hypothesis that human populational response time variability increases from early to late visual processing stages.

1 Introduction

In many situations, precise timing of a motor output is essential for successful task completion. Somehow the reliability in the output timing is related to the reliability of the underlying neural systems associated with different stages of processing. Recent literature from animal studies suggests that individual neurons from different brain regions and different species can be surprising reliable [1, 2, 5, 7–9, 14, 17, 18], on the order of a few milliseconds. Due to the low spatial resolution of electroencephalography (EEG) and the requirement of signal averaging due to noisiness of magnetoencephalography (MEG), *in vivo* measurement of human *populational* response time variability from different processing stages has not been available.

In four visual reaction time (RT) tasks, we estimated neuronal response time variability at different visual processing stages using MEG. One major obstacle that has prevented the analysis of response timing variability using MEG before is the relative weakness of the brain's magnetic signals (100fT) compared to noise in a shielded environment (magnetized lung contaminants: 10^6fT; abdominal currents 10^5fT; cardiogram and oculogram: 10^4fT; epileptic and spontaneous activity: 10^3fT) and in the sensors (10fT) [13]. Consequently, neuronal responses evoked during cognitive tasks often require signal averaging across many trials, making analysis of single-trial response times unfeasible.

Recently, Bell-Sejnowski Infomax [1995] and Fast ICA [10] algorithms have been used successfully to isolate and remove major artifacts from EEG and MEG data [11, 15, 20]. These methods greatly increase the effective signal-to-noise ratio and make single-trial analysis of EEG data feasible [12]. Here, we applied a Second-Order Blind Identification algorithm (SOBI) [4] (another blind source separation, or *BSS*, algorithm) to MEG data to find out whether *populational* response variability changes from early to late visual processing stages.

2 Methods

2.1 Experimental Design

Two volunteer normal subjects (females, right handed) with normal or corrected-to-normal visual acuity and binocular vision participated in four different visual RT tasks. Subjects gave informed consent prior to the experimental procedure. During each task we recorded continuous MEG signals at a 300Hz sampling rate with a band-pass filter of 1–100Hz using a 122 channel Neuromag-122.

In all four tasks, the subject was presented with a pair of abstract color patterns, one in the left and the other in the right visual field. One of the two patterns was a target pattern. The subject pressed either a left or right mouse button to indicate on which side the target pattern was presented. When a correct response was given, a low or high frequency tone was presented binaurally following respectively a correct or wrong response. The definition of the target pattern varied in the four tasks and was used to control task difficulty which ranged from easy (task 1) to more difficult (task 4) with increasing RTs. (The specific differences among the four tasks are not important for the analysis which follows and are not discussed further.)

In this study we focus on the one element that all tasks have in common, i.e. activation of multiple visual areas along the visual pathways. Our goal is to identify visual neuronal sources activated in all four visual RT tasks and to measure and compare response time variability between neuronal sources associated with early and later visual processing stages. Specifically, we test the hypothesis that populational neuronal response times increase from early to later visual processing stages.

2.2 Source Separation Using SOBI

In MEG, magnetic activity from different neuronal populations is observed by many sensors arranged around the subject's head. Each sensor responds to a mixture of the signals emitted by multiple sources. We used the Second-Order Blind Identification algorithm (SOBI) [4] (a BSS algorithm) to simultaneously separate neuromagnetic responses from different neuronal populations associated with different stages of visual processing. Responses from different neuronal populations will be referred to as *source responses* and the neuronal populations that give rise to these responses will be referred to as *neuronal sources* or simply *sources*. These neuronal sources often, but not always, consist of a spatially contiguous population of neurons. BSS separates the measured sensor signals into maximally independent components, each having its own spatial map. Previously we have shown that some of these BSS separated components correspond to noise sources, and many others correspond to neuronal sources [19].

To establish the identity of the components, we analyzed both temporal and spatial properties of the BSS separated components. Their temporal properties are displayed using *MEG images*, similar to the ERP images described by [12] but without smoothing across trials. These MEG images show stimulus or response locked responses across many trials in a map, from which response latencies across all displayed trials can be observed with a glance. The spatial properties of the separated components are displayed using a *field map* that shows the sensor projection of a given component. The intensity at each point on the field map indicates how strongly this component influences the sensor at this location.

The correspondence between the separated components and neuronal populational responses at different visual processing stages were established by considering both spatial and temporal properties of the separated components [19]. For example, a component was identified as an early visual neuronal source if and only if (1) the field pattern, or the sensor projection, of the separated component showed a focal response over the occipital lobe, and (2) the ERP image showed visual stimulus locked responses with latencies shorter than all other visual components and falling within the range of early visual responses reported in studies using other methods. *Only* those components consistent both spatially and temporally with known neurophysiology and neuroanatomy were identified as neuronal sources.

2.3 Single Event Detection and Response Latency Estimation

For all established visual components we calculated the single-trial response latency as follows. First, a detection window was defined using the stimulus-triggered average (STA). The beginning of the detection window was defined by the time at which the STA first exceeded the range of baseline fluctuation. Baseline fluctuation was estimated from the time of stimulus onset for approximately 50ms (the visual response occurred no earlier than 60ms after stimulus onset.) The detection window ended when the STA first returned to the same level as when the detection window began. The detection threshold was determined using a control window with the same width as the detection window, but immediately preceding the detection window. The threshold was adjusted until no more than five false detections occurred within the control window for each ninety trials. We estimated RTs using the leading edge of the response, rather than the time of the peak as this is more robust against noise.

3 Results

In both subjects across all four visual RT tasks, SOBI generated components that corresponded to neuronal populational responses associated with early and late stages of visual processing. In both subjects, we identified a single component with a sensor projection at the occipital lobe whose latency was the shortest among all

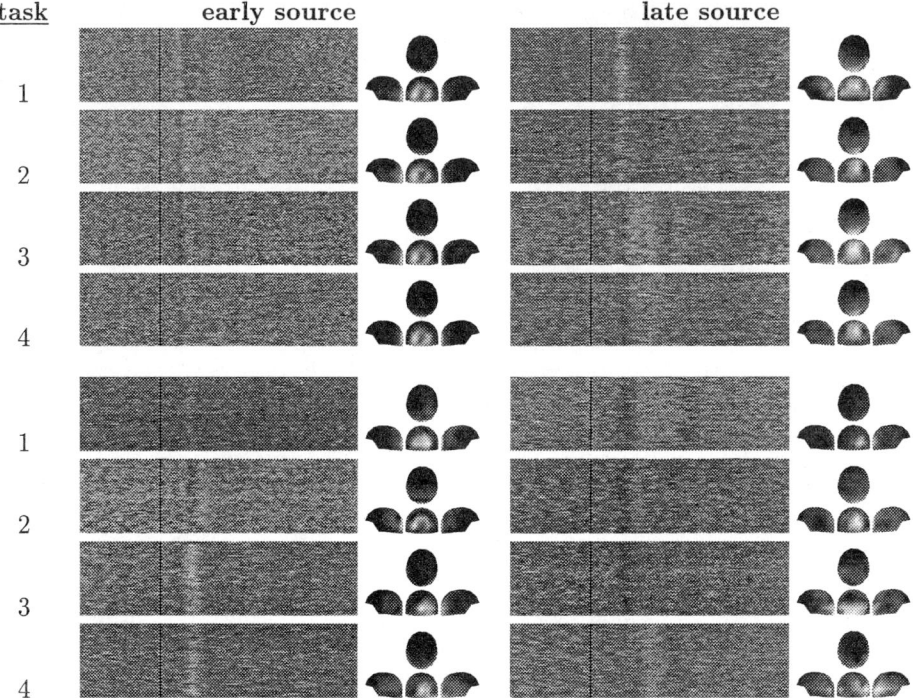

Figure 1: MEG images and field maps for an early and a late source from each task, for subject 1 (top) and subject 2 (bottom). MEG image pixels are brightness-coded source strength. Each row of a bitmap is one trial, running 1170ms from left to right. Vertical bars mark stimulus onset, and 333ms of pre-stimulus activity is shown. Each panel contains 90 trials. Field map brightness indicates the strength with which a source activates each of the 61 sensor pairs.

visual stimulus locked components within task and subject (Fig. 1 left). We identified multiple components that had sensor projections either at occipital-parietal, occipital-temporal, or temporal lobes, and whose response latencies are longer than early-stage components within task and subject (Fig. 1 right).

Fig. 2a shows examples of detected single-trial responses for one early and one late visual component (left: early; right: late) from one task. To minimize false positives, the detection threshold was set high (allowing 5 false detections out of 90 trials) at the expense of a low detection rate (15%–67%.) When Gaussian filters were applied to the raw separated data, the detection rates were increased to 22–91% (similar results hold but not shown). Fig. 2b shows such detected response time histograms superimposed on the stimulus triggered average using raw separated data. One early (top row) and two late visual components (middle and bottom rows) are plotted for each of the four experiments in subject one. The histogram width is smallest for early visual components (short mean response latency) and larger for late visual components (longer latency.)

We computed the standard deviation of component response times as a measure of response variability. Fig. 2c shows the response variability as a function of mean response latency for subject one. Early components (solid boxes, shorter mean latency) have smaller variability (height of the boxes) while late components (dashed boxes, longer mean latency) have larger variability (height of the boxes). Multiple

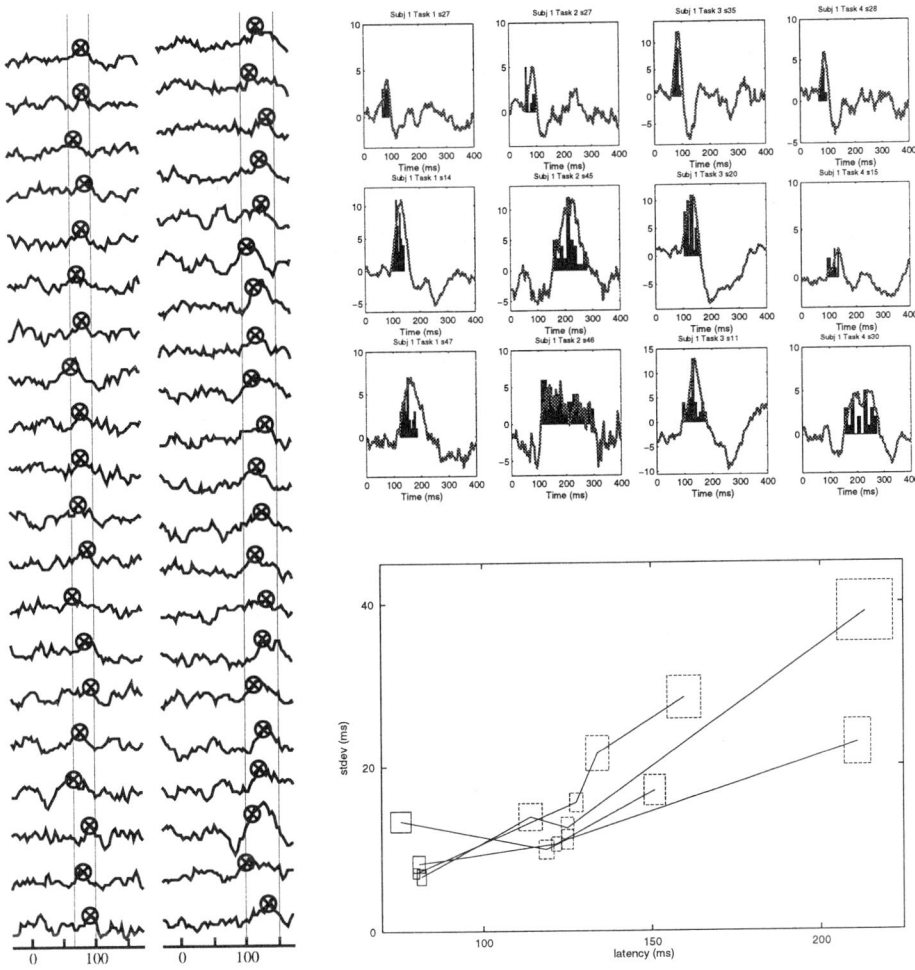

Figure 2: (**a**, left) Response onset was estimated for each trial via threshold crossing within a window of eligibility. (**b**, top right) The stimulus-locked averages for a number of sources overlaid on histograms of response onset times. (**c**, bottom right) Scatter plot of visual components from all experiments on subject 1 showing the standard deviation of the latency (y axis) versus the mean latency (x axis), with the error bars in each direction indicating one standard error in the respective measurement. Lines connect sources from each task.

visual components from each task are connected by a line. Four tasks were shown here. There is a general trend of increasing standard deviation of response times as a function of early-to-late processing stages (increasing mean latency from left to right). For the early visual components the standard deviation ranges from 6.6±0.63ms to 13.4±1.23ms, and for the late visual components, from 9.9±0.86ms to 38.8±3.73ms ($t = 3.565$, $p = 0.005$.)

4 Discussion

By applying SOBI to MEG data from four visual RT tasks, we separated components corresponding to neuronal populational responses associated with early and later stage visual processing in both subjects across all tasks. We performed single-trial RT detection on these early- and late-stage components and estimated both the mean and stdev of their response latency. We found that variability of the populational response latency increased from early to late processing stages.

These results contrast with single neuron recordings obtained previously. In early and late visual processing stages, the rise time of mean firing rate in single units remained constant, suggesting an invariance in RT variability [16]. Characterizing the precise relationship between single neuron and populational response reliability is difficult without careful simulations or simultaneous single unit and MEG recording. However, some major differences exist between the two types of studies. While MEG is more likely to sample a larger neuronal population, single unit studies are more likely to be selective to those neurons that are already highly reliable in their responses to stimulus presentation. It is possible that the most reliable neurons at both the early and late processing stages are equally reliable while large differences exist between the early and late stages for the low reliability neurons.

Previously, ICA algorithms have been used successfully to separate out various noise and neuronal sources in MEG data [19, 20]. Here we show that SOBI can also be used to separate different neuronal sources, particularly those associated with different processing stages. The SOBI algorithm assumes that the components are independent across multiple time scales and attempts to minimize the temporal correlation at these time scales. Although neuronal sources at different stages of processing are not completely independent as assumed in SOBI's derivation, BSS algorithms of this sort are quite robust even when the underlying assumptions are not fully met [6], *i.e.* the goodness of the separation is not significantly affected. The ultimate reality check should come from satisfying physiological and anatomical constraints derived from prior knowledge of the neural system under study. This was carried out for our analysis. Firstly, the average response latencies of the separated components fell within the range of latencies reported in MEG studies using conventional source modeling methods. Secondly, the spatial patterns of sensor responses to these separated components are consistent with the known functional anatomy of the visual system.

We have attempted to rule out many confounding factors. Our observed results cannot be accounted for by a higher signal to noise ratio in the early visual responses. The increase in measured onset response time variability from early to late visual processing stages was actually accompanied by an slightly *lower* signal-to-noise ratio among the early components. The number of events detected for the later components were also slightly greater than the earlier components. The higher signal-to-noise ratio at later components should *reduce* noise-induced variability in the later components, which would bias against the hypothesis that later visual responses have greater response time variability. We also found that response duration and detection window size cannot account for the observed differential variabilities. Later visual responses also had gentler onset slopes (as measured by the stimulus-triggered average). Sensor noise unavoidably introduces noise into the response onset detection process. We cannot rule out the possibility that the interaction of the noise with the response onset profiles might give rise to the observed differential variabilities. Similarly, we cannot rule out the possibility that even greater control of the experimental situation, such as better fixation and more effective head restraints, would differentially reduce the observed variabilities. In general, all measured variabilities can only be upper bounds, subject to downward revision as improved instrumentation and experiments become available. It is with this caution in mind that we conclude that response time variability of neuronal populations increases from early to late processing stages in the human visual system.

Acknowledgments

This research was supported by NSF CAREER award 97-02-311, and by the National Foundation for Functional Brain Imaging.

References

[1] M. Abeles, H. Bergman, E. Margalit, and E Vaadia. Spatiotemporal firing patterns in the frontal cortex of behaving monkeys. *J. Neurophys.*, 70:1629–1638, 1993.

[2] W. Bair and C. Koch. Temporal precision of spike trains in extrastriate cortex of the behaving macaque monkey. *Neural Computation*, 8(6):1184–1202, 1996.

[3] A. J. Bell and T. J. Sejnowski. An information-maximization approach to blind separation and blind deconvolution. *Neural Computation*, 7(6):1129–1159, 1995.

[4] A. Belouchrani, K. A. Meraim, J.-F. Cardoso, and E. Moulines. Second-order blind separation of correlated sources. In *Proc. Int. Conf. on Digital Sig. Proc.*, pages 346–351, Cyprus, 1993.

[5] M. J. Berry, W. K. Warland, and M. Meister. The structure and precision of retinal spike trains. *Proc. Natl. Acad. Sci. USA*, 94:5411–5416, 1997.

[6] J.-F. Cardoso. Blind signal separation: statistical principles. *Proceedings of the IEEE*, 9(10):2009–2025, October 1998.

[7] R. R. de Ruyter van Steveninck, G. D. Lewen, S. P. Strong, R. Koberle, and W. Bialek. Reproducibility and variability in neural spike trains. *Science*, 275:1805–1808, 1997.

[8] R. C. deCharms and M. M. Merzenich. Primary cortical representation of sounds by the coordination of action-potential timing. *Nature*, 381:610–3, 1996.

[9] M. Gur, A. Beylin, and D. M. Snodderly. Response variability of neurons in primary visual cortex (V1) of alert monkeys. *J. Neurosci.*, 17(8):2914–2920, 1997.

[10] A. Hyvarinen and E. Oja. A fast fixed-point algorithm for independent component analysis. *Neural Computation*, 9(7), October 1997.

[11] T.-P. Jung, C. Humphries, T.-W. Lee, M. J. McKeown, V. Iragui, S. Makeig, and T. J. Sejnowski. Removing electroencephalographic artifacts by blind source separation. *Psychophysiology*, 1999. In Press.

[12] T.-P. Jung, S. Makeig, M. Westerfield, J. Townsend, E. Courchesne, and T. J. Sejnowski. Analyzing and visualizing single-trial event-related potentials. In *Advances in Neural Information Processing Systems 11*, pages 118–124. MIT Press, 1999.

[13] J. D. Lewine and W. W. Orrison, II. Magnetoencephalography and magnetic source imaging. In *Functional Brain Imaging*, pages 369–417. Mosby, St. Louis, 1995.

[14] Z. F. Mainen and T. J. Sejnowski. Reliability of spike timing in neocortical neurons. *Science*, 268:1503–1506, 1995.

[15] S. Makeig, T.-P. Jung, A. J. Bell, D. Ghahremani, and T. J. Sejnowski. Blind separation of auditory event-related brain responses into independent components. *Proc. Nat. Acad. Sci.*, 94:10979–84, 1997.

[16] P. Marsalek, C. Koch, and J. Maunsell. On the relationship between synaptic input and spike output jitter in individual neurons. *Proc. Natl. Acad. Sci.*, 94:735–40, 1997.

[17] D. S. Reich, J. D. Victor, B. W. Knight, and T. Ozaki. Response variability and timing precision of neuronal spike trains *in vivo*. *J. Neurophys.*, 77:2836–2841, 1997.

[18] A. C. Tang, A. M. Bartels, and T. J. Sejnowksi. Effects of cholinergic modulation on responses of neocortical neurons to fluctuating inputs. *Cereb. Cortex*, 7:502–9, 1997.

[19] A. C. Tang, B. A. Pearlmutter, M. Zibulevsky, and R. Loring. Response time variability in the human sensory and motor systems. In *Computational Neuroscience*, 1999. To appear as a special issue of *Neurocomputing*.

[20] R. Vigário, V. Jousmäki, M. Hämäläinen, R. Hari, and E. Oja. Independent component analysis for identification of artifacts in magnetoencephalographic recordings. In *Advances in Neural Information Processing Systems 10*. MIT Press, 1998.

Population Decoding Based on an Unfaithful Model

S. Wu, H. Nakahara, N. Murata and S. Amari
RIKEN Brain Science Institute
Hirosawa 2-1, Wako-shi, Saitama, Japan
{phwusi, hiro, mura, amari}@brain.riken.go.jp

Abstract

We study a population decoding paradigm in which the maximum likelihood inference is based on an unfaithful decoding model (UMLI). This is usually the case for neural population decoding because the encoding process of the brain is not exactly known, or because a simplified decoding model is preferred for saving computational cost. We consider an unfaithful decoding model which neglects the pair-wise correlation between neuronal activities, and prove that UMLI is asymptotically efficient when the neuronal correlation is uniform or of limited-range. The performance of UMLI is compared with that of the maximum likelihood inference based on a faithful model and that of the center of mass decoding method. It turns out that UMLI has advantages of decreasing the computational complexity remarkably and maintaining a high-level decoding accuracy at the same time. The effect of correlation on the decoding accuracy is also discussed.

1 Introduction

Population coding is a method to encode and decode stimuli in a distributed way by using the joint activities of a number of neurons (e.g. Georgopoulos et al., 1986; Paradiso, 1988; Seung and Sompolinsky, 1993). Recently, there has been an expanded interest in understanding the population decoding methods, which particularly include the maximum likelihood inference (MLI), the center of mass (COM), the complex estimator (CE) and the optimal linear estimator (OLE) [see (Pouget et al., 1998; Salinas and Abbott, 1994) and the references therein]. Among them, MLI has an advantage of having small decoding error (asymptotic efficiency), but may suffers from the expense of computational complexity.

Let us consider a population of N neurons coding a variable x. The encoding process of the population code is described by a conditional probability $q(\mathbf{r}|x)$ (Anderson, 1994; Zemel et al., 1998), where the components of the vector $\mathbf{r} = \{r_i\}$ for $i = 1, \cdots, N$ are the firing rates of neurons. We study the following MLI estimator given by the value of x that maximizes the log likelihood $\ln p(\mathbf{r}|x)$, where $p(\mathbf{r}|x)$ is the decoding model which might be different from the encoding model $q(\mathbf{r}|x)$. So far, when people study MLI in a population code, it normally (*or implicitly*) assumes that $p(\mathbf{r}|x)$ is equal to the encoding model $q(\mathbf{r}|x)$. This requires that the estimator has full knowledge of the encoding process. Taking account of the complexity of the information process in the brain, it is more natural to assume $p(\mathbf{r}|x) \neq q(\mathbf{r}|x)$. Another reason for choosing this is for saving computational cost. Therefore, a decoding paradigm in which the assumed decoding model is different from the encoding one needs to be studied. In the context of statistical theory, this is called estimation based on an unfaithful or a misspecified model. Hereafter, we call the decoding paradigm of using MLI based on an unfaithful model, UMLI, to distinguish from that of MLI based on the faithful model, which is called FMLI. The unfaithful model studied in this paper is the one which neglects the pair-wise correlation between neural activities. It turns out that UMLI has attracting properties of decreasing the computational cost of FMLI remarkablely and at the same time maintaining a high-level decoding accuracy.

2 The Population Decoding Paradigm of UMLI

2.1 An Unfaithful Decoding Model of Neglecting the Neuronal Correlation

Let us consider a pair-wise correlated neural response model in which the neuron activities are assumed to be multivariate Gaussian

$$q(\mathbf{r}|x) = \frac{1}{\sqrt{(2\pi\sigma^2)^N \det(\mathbf{A})}} \exp[-\frac{1}{2\sigma^2} \sum_{i,j} A_{ij}^{-1}(r_i - f_i(x))(r_j - f_j(x))], \quad (1)$$

where $f_i(x)$ is the tuning function. In the present study, we will only consider the radial symmetry tuning function.

Two different correlation structures are considered. One is the uniform correlation model (Johnson, 1980; Abbott and Dayan, 1999), with the covariance matrix

$$A_{ij} = \delta_{ij} + c(1 - \delta_{ij}), \quad (2)$$

where the parameter c (with $-1 < c < 1$) determines the strength of correlation.

The other correlation structure is of limited-range (Johnson, 1980; Snippe and Koenderink, 1992; Abbott and Dayan, 1999), with the covariance matrix

$$A_{ij} = b^{|i-j|}, \quad (3)$$

where the parameter b (with $0 < b < 1$) determines the range of correlation. This structure has translational invariance in the sense that $A_{ij} = A_{kl}$, if $|i - j| = |k - l|$.

The unfaithful decoding model, treated in the present study, is the one which neglects the correlation in the encoding process but keeps the tuning functions unchanged, that is,

$$p(\mathbf{r}|x) = \frac{1}{\sqrt{(2\pi\sigma^2)^N}} \exp[-\frac{1}{2\sigma^2} \sum_i (r_i - f_i(x))^2]. \quad (4)$$

2.2 The decoding error of UMLI and FMLI

The decoding error of UMLI has been studied in the statistical theory (Akahira and Takeuchi, 1981; Murata et al., 1994). Here we generalize it to the population coding. For convenience, some notations are introduced. $\nabla f(\mathbf{r}, x)$ denotes $df(\mathbf{r}, x)/dx$. $E_q[f(\mathbf{r}, x)]$ and $V_q[f(\mathbf{r}, x)]$ denote, respectively, the mean value and the variance of $f(\mathbf{r}, x)$ with respect to the distribution $q(\mathbf{r}|x)$. Given an observation of the population activity $\mathbf{r}^\star$, the UMLI estimate $\hat{x}$ is the value of x that maximizes the log likelihood $L_p(\mathbf{r}^\star, x) = \ln p(\mathbf{r}^\star|x)$.

Denote by x_{opt} the value of x satisfying $E_q[\nabla L_p(\mathbf{r}, x_{\text{opt}})] = 0$. For the faithful model where $p = q$, $x_{\text{opt}} = x$. Hence, $(x_{\text{opt}} - x)$ is the error due to the unfaithful setting, whereas $(\hat{x} - x_{\text{opt}})$ is the error due to sampling fluctuations. For the unfaithful model (4), since $E_q[\nabla L_p(\mathbf{r}, x_{\text{opt}})] = 0$, $\sum_i [f_i(x) - f_i(x_{\text{opt}})] f_i'(x_{\text{opt}}) = 0$. Hence, $x_{\text{opt}} = x$ and UMLI gives an unbiased estimator in the present cases.

Let us consider the expansion of $\nabla L_p(\mathbf{r}^\star, \hat{x})$ at x,

$$\nabla L_p(\mathbf{r}^\star, \hat{x}) \simeq \nabla L_p(\mathbf{r}^\star, x) + \nabla \nabla L_p(\mathbf{r}^\star, x)(\hat{x} - x). \tag{5}$$

Since $\nabla L_p(\mathbf{r}^\star, \hat{x}) = 0$,

$$\frac{1}{N} \nabla \nabla L_p(\mathbf{r}^\star, x)(\hat{x} - x) \simeq -\frac{1}{N} \nabla L_p(\mathbf{r}^\star, x), \tag{6}$$

where N is the number of neurons. Only the large N limit is considered in the present study.

Let us analyze the properties of the two random variables $\frac{1}{N} \nabla \nabla L_p(\mathbf{r}^\star, x)$ and $\frac{1}{N} \nabla L_p(\mathbf{r}^\star, x)$. We consider first the uniform correlation model.

For the uniform correlation structure, we can write

$$r_i^\star = f_i(x) + \sigma(\epsilon_i + \eta), \tag{7}$$

where η and $\{\epsilon_i\}$, for $i = 1, \cdots, N$, are independent random variables having zero mean and variance c and $1 - c$, respectively. η is the common noise for all neurons, representing the uniform character of the correlation.

By using the expression (7), we get

$$\frac{1}{N} \nabla L_p(\mathbf{r}^\star, x) = \frac{1}{N\sigma} \sum_i \epsilon_i f_i'(x) + \frac{\eta}{N\sigma} \sum_i f_i'(x), \tag{8}$$

$$\frac{1}{N} \nabla \nabla L_p(\mathbf{r}^\star, x) = \frac{1}{N\sigma} \sum_i \epsilon_i f_i''(x) - \frac{1}{N\sigma^2} \sum_i f_i'(x)^2$$
$$+ \frac{\eta}{N\sigma} \sum_i f_i''(x). \tag{9}$$

Without loss of generality, we assume that the distribution of the preferred stimuli is uniform. For the radial symmetry tuning functions, $\frac{1}{N} \sum_i f_i'(x)$ and $\frac{1}{N} \sum_i f_i''(x)$ approaches zero when N is large. Therefore, the correlation contributions (the terms of η) in the above two equations can be neglected. UMLI performs in this case as if the neuronal signals are uncorrelated.

Thus, by the weak law of large numbers,

$$\frac{1}{N} \nabla \nabla L_p(\mathbf{r}^\star, x) \simeq -\frac{1}{N\sigma^2} \sum_i f_i'(x)^2$$
$$= \frac{Q_p}{N}, \tag{10}$$

where $Q_p \equiv E_q[\nabla \nabla L_p(\mathbf{r}, x)]$.

According to the central limit theorem, $\nabla L_p(\mathbf{r}^\star, x)/N$ converges to a Gaussian distribution

$$\frac{1}{N} \nabla L_p(\mathbf{r}^\star, x) \sim N(0, \frac{1-c}{N^2 \sigma^2} \sum_i f_i'(x)^2)$$
$$= N(0, \frac{G_p}{N^2}), \tag{11}$$

where $N(0, t^2)$ denoting the Gaussian distribution having zero mean and variance t, and $G_p \equiv V_q[\nabla L_p(\mathbf{r}, x)]$.

Combining the results of eqs.(6), (10) and (11), we obtain the decoding error of UMLI,

$$(\hat{x} - x)_{\text{UMLI}} \sim N(0, Q_p^{-2} G_p),$$
$$= N(0, \frac{(1-c)\sigma^2}{\sum_i f_i'(x)^2}). \quad (12)$$

In the similar way, the decoding error of FMLI is obtained,

$$(\hat{x} - x)_{\text{FMLI}} \sim N(0, Q_q^{-2} G_q),$$
$$= N(0, \frac{(1-c)\sigma^2}{\sum_i f_i'(x)^2}), \quad (13)$$

which has the same form as that of UMLI except that Q_q and G_q are now defined with respect to the faithful decoding model, i.e., $p(\mathbf{r}|x) = q(\mathbf{r}|x)$. To get eq.(13), the condition $\sum_i f_i'(x) = 0$ is used. Interestingly, UMLI and FMLI have the same decoding error. This is because the uniform correlation effect is actually neglected in both UMLI and FMLI.

Note that in FMLI, $Q_q = G_q = V_q[\nabla L_q(\mathbf{r}|x)]$ is the Fisher information. $Q_q^{-2} G_q$ is the Cramér-Rao bound, which is the optimal accuracy for an unbiased estimator to achieve. Eq.(13) shows that FMLI is asymptotically efficient. For an unfaithful decoding model, Q_p and G_p are usually different from the Fisher information. We call $Q_p^{-2} G_p$ the generalized Cramér-Rao bound, and UMLI quasi-asymptotically efficient if its decoding error approaches $Q_p^{-2} G_p$ asymptotically. Eq.(12) shows that UMLI is quasi-asymptotic efficient.

In the above, we have proved the asymptotic efficiency of FMLI and UMLI when the neuronal correlation is uniform. The result relies on the radial symmetry of the tuning function and the uniform character of the correlation, which make it possible to cancel the correlation contributions from different neurons. For general tuning functions and correlation structures, the asymptotic efficiency of UMLI and FMLI may not hold. This is because the law of large numbers (eq.(10)) and the central limit theorem (eq.(11)) are not in general applicable.

We note that for the limited-range correlation model, since the correlation is translational invariant and its strength decreases quickly with the dissimilarity in the neurons' preferred stimuli, the correlation effect in the decoding of FMLI and UMLI becomes negligible when N is large. This ensures that the law of large numbers and the central limit theorem hold in the large N limit. Therefore, UMLI and FMLI are asymptotically efficient. This is confirmed in the simulation in Sec.3.

When UMLI and FMLI are asymptotic efficient, their decoding errors in the large N limit can be calculated according to the Cramér-Rao bound and the generalized Cramér-Rao bound, respectively, which are

$$\langle (\hat{x} - x)^2 \rangle_{\text{UMLI}} \sim \frac{\sigma^2 \sum_{ij} A_{ij} f_i'(x) f_j'(x)}{[\sum_i (f_i'(x))^2]^2}, \quad (14)$$

$$\langle (\hat{x} - x)^2 \rangle_{\text{FMLI}} \sim \frac{\sigma^2}{\sum_{ij} A_{ij}^{-1} f_i'(x) f_j'(x)}. \quad (15)$$

3 Performance Comparison

The performance of UMLI is compared with that of FMLI and of the center of mass decoding method (COM). The neural population model we consider is a regular array of N neurons (Baldi and Heiligenberg, 1988; Snippe, 1996) with the preferred stimuli uniformly distributed in the range $[-D, D]$, that is, $c_i = -D + 2iD/(N+1)$, for $i = 1, \cdots, N$. The comparison is done at the stimulus $x = 0$.

COM is a simple decoding method without using any information of the encoding process, whose estimate is the averaged value of the neurons' preferred stimuli weighted by the responses (Georgopoulos et al., 1982; Snippe, 1996), i.e.,

$$\hat{x} = \frac{\sum_i r_i c_i}{\sum_i r_i}. \qquad (16)$$

The shortcoming of COM is a large decoding error.

For the population model we consider, the decoding error of COM is calculated to be

$$\langle (\hat{x} - x)^2 \rangle_{\text{COM}} \sim \frac{\sigma^2 \sum_{ij} A_{ij} c_i c_j}{[\sum_i f_i(x)]^2}, \qquad (17)$$

where the condition $\sum_i f_i(x) c_i = 0$ is used, due to the regularity of the distribution of the preferred stimuli.

The tuning function is Gaussian, which has the form

$$f_i(x) = \exp[-\frac{(x - c_i)^2}{2a^2}], \qquad (18)$$

where the parameter a is the tuning width.

We note that the Gaussian response model does not give zero probability for negative firing rates. To make it more reliable, we set $r_i = 0$ when $f_i(x) < 0.11$ ($|x - c_i| > 3a$), which means that only those neurons which are active enough contribute to the decoding. It is easy to see that this cut-off does not effect much the results of UMLI and FMLI, due to their nature of decoding by using the derivative of the tuning functions. Whereas, the decoding error of COM will be greatly enlarged without cut-off.

For the tuning width a, there are $N = \text{Int}[6a/d - 1]$ neurons involved in the decoding process, where d is the difference in the preferred stimuli between two consecutive neurons and the function $\text{Int}[\cdot]$ denotes the integer part of the argument.

In all experiment settings, the parameters are chosen as $a = 1$ and $\sigma = 0.1$. The decoding errors of the three methods are compared for different values of N when the correlation strength is fixed ($c = 0.5$ for the uniform correlation case and $b = 0.5$ for the limited-range correlation case), or different values of the correlation strength when N is fixed to be 50.

Fig.1 compares the decoding errors of the three methods for the uniform correlation model. It shows that UMLI has the same decoding error as that of FMLI, and a lower error than that of COM. The uniform correlation improves the decoding accuracies of the three methods (Fig.1b).

In Fig.2, the simulation results for the decoding errors of FMLI and UMLI in the limited-range correlation model are compared with those obtained by using the Cramér-Rao bound and the generalized Cramér-Rao bound, respectively. It shows that the two results agree very well when the number of neurons, N, is large, which means that FMLI and UMLI are asymptotic efficient as we analyzed. In the simulation, the standard gradient descent method is used to maximize the log likelihood, and the initial guess for the stimulus is chosen as the preferred stimulus of the most active neuron. The CPU time of UMLI is around $1/5$ of that of FMLI. UMLI reduces the computational cost of FMLI significantly.

Fig.3 compares the decoding errors of the three methods for the limited-range correlation model. It shows that UMLI has a lower decoding error than that of COM. Interestingly, UMLI has a comparable performance with that of FMLI for the whole range of correlation. The limited-range correlation degrades the decoding accuracies of the three methods when the strength is small and improves the accuracies when the strength is large (Fig.3b).

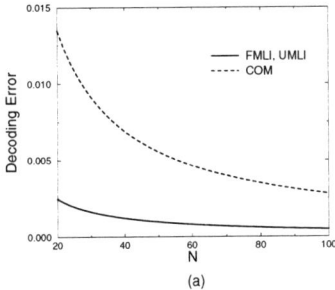 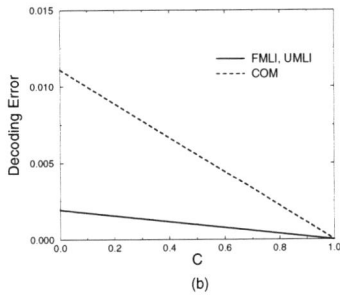

Figure 1: Comparing the decoding errors of UMLI, FMLI and COM for the uniform correlation model.

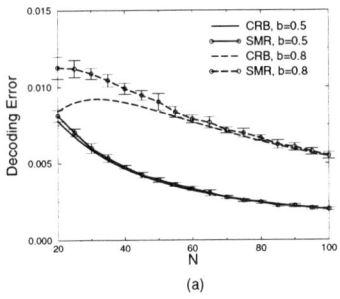 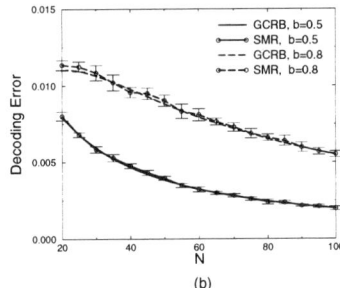

Figure 2: Comparing the simulation results of the decoding errors of UMLI and FMLI in the limited-range correlation model with those obtained by using the Cramér-Rao bound and the generalized Cramér-Rao bound, respectively. CRB denotes the Cramér-Rao bound, GCRB the generalized Cramér-Rao bound, and SMR the simulation result. In the simulation, 10 sets of data is generated, each of which is averaged over 1000 trials. (a) FMLI; (b) UMLI.

4 Discussions and Conclusions

We have studied a population decoding paradigm in which MLI is based on an unfaithful model. This is motivated by the facts that the encoding process of the brain is not exactly known by the estimator. As an example, we consider an unfaithful decoding model which neglects the pair-wise correlation between neuronal activities. Two different correlation structures are considered, namely, the uniform and the limited-range correlations. The performance of UMLI is compared with that of FMLI and COM. It turns out that UMLI has a lower decoding error than that of COM. Compared with FMLI, UMLI has comparable performance whereas with much less computational cost. It is our future work to understand the biological implication of UMLI.

As a by-product of the calculation, we also illustrate the effect of correlation on the decoding accuracies. It turns out that the correlation, depending on its form, can either improve or degrade the decoding accuracy. This observation agrees with the analysis of Abbott and Dayan (Abbott and Dayan, 1999), which is done with respect to the optimal decoding accuracy, i.e., the Cramér-Rao bound.

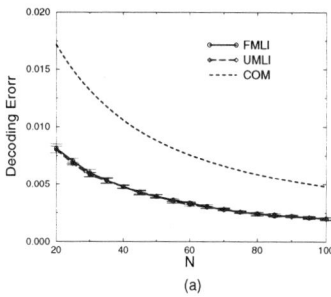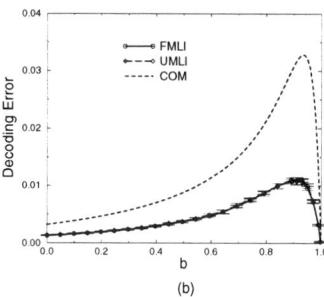

Figure 3: Comparing the decoding errors of UMLI, FMLI and COM for the limited-range correlation model.

Acknowledgment

We thank the three anonymous reviewers for their valuable comments and insight suggestion. S. Wu acknowledges helpful discussions with Danmei Chen.

References

L. F. Abbott and P. Dayan. 1999. The effect of correlated variability on the accuracy of a population code. *Neural Computation*, 11:91–101.

M. Akahira and K. Takeuchi. 1981. Asymptotic efficiency of statistical estimators: concepts and high order asymptotic efficiency. In *Lecture Notes in Statistics 7*.

C. H. Anderson. 1994. Basic elements of biological computational systems. *International Journal of Modern Physics C*, 5:135–137.

P. Baldi and W. Heiligenberg. 1988. How sensory maps could enhance resolution through ordered arrangements of broadly tuned receivers. *Biol. Cybern.*, 59:313–318.

A. P. Georgopoulos, J. F. Kalaska, R. Caminiti, and J. T. Massey. 1982. On the relations between the direction of two-dimensional arm movements and cell discharge in primate motor cortex. *J. Neurosci.*, 2:1527–1537.

K. O. Johnson. 1980. Sensory discrimination: neural processes preceding discrimination decision. *J. Neurophy.*, 43:1793–1815.

M. Murata, S. Yoshizawa, and S. Amari. 1994. Network information criterion-determining the number of hidden units for an artificial neural network model. *IEEE. Trans. Neural Networks*, 5:865–872.

A. Pouget, K. Zhang, S. Deneve, and P. E. Latham. 1998. Statistically efficient estimation using population coding. *Neural Computation*, 10:373–401.

E. Salinas and L. F. Abbott. 1994. Vector reconstruction from firing rates. *Journal of Computational Neuroscience*, 1:89–107.

H. P. Snippe and J. J. Koenderink. 1992. Information in channel-coded systems: correlated receivers. *Biological Cybernetics*, 67:183–190.

H. P. Snippe. 1996. Parameter extraction from population codes: a critical assessment. *Neural Computation*, 8:511–529.

R. S. Zemel, P. Dayan, and A. Pouget. 1998. Population interpolation of population codes. *Neural Computation*, 10:403–430.

Spike-based learning rules and stabilization of persistent neural activity

Xiaohui Xie and H. Sebastian Seung
Dept. of Brain & Cog. Sci., MIT, Cambridge, MA 02139
{xhxie, seung}@mit.edu

Abstract

We analyze the conditions under which synaptic learning rules based on action potential timing can be approximated by learning rules based on firing rates. In particular, we consider a form of plasticity in which synapses depress when a presynaptic spike is followed by a postsynaptic spike, and potentiate with the opposite temporal ordering. Such *differential anti-Hebbian plasticity* can be approximated under certain conditions by a learning rule that depends on the time derivative of the postsynaptic firing rate. Such a learning rule acts to stabilize persistent neural activity patterns in recurrent neural networks.

1 INTRODUCTION

Recent experiments have demonstrated types of synaptic plasticity that depend on the temporal ordering of presynaptic and postsynaptic spiking. At cortical[1] and hippocampal[2] synapses, long-term potentiation is induced by repeated pairing of a presynaptic spike and a succeeding postsynaptic spike, while long-term depression results when the order is reversed. The dependence of the change in synaptic strength on the difference $\Delta t = t_{post} - t_{pre}$ between postsynaptic and presynaptic spike times has been measured quantitatively. This *pairing function*, sketched in Figure 1A, has positive and negative

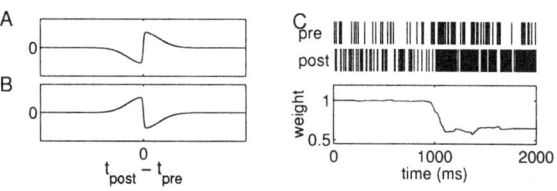

Figure 1: (A) Pairing function for differential Hebbian learning. The change in synaptic strength is plotted versus the time difference between postsynaptic and presynaptic spikes. (B) Pairing function for differential anti-Hebbian learning. (C) Differential anti-Hebbian learning is driven by changes in firing rates. The synaptic learning rule of Eq. (1) is applied to two Poisson spike trains. The synaptic strength remains roughly constant in time, except when the postsynaptic rate changes.

lobes correspond to potentiation and depression, and a width of tens of milliseconds. We will refer to synaptic plasticity associated with this pairing function as differential Hebbian plasticity—*Hebbian* because the conditions for potentiation are as predicted by Hebb[3], and *differential* because it is driven by the difference between the opposing processes of potentiation and depression.

The pairing function of Figure 1A is not characteristic of all synapses. For example, an opposite temporal dependence has been observed at electrosensory lobe synapses of electric fish[4]. As shown in Figure 1B, these synapses depress when a presynaptic spike is followed by a postsynaptic one, and potentiate when the order is reversed. We will refer to this as differential anti-Hebbian plasticity.

According to these experiments, the maximum ranges of the differential Hebbian and anti-Hebbian pairing functions are roughly 20 and 40 ms, respectively. This is fairly short, and seems more compatible with descriptions of neural activity based on spike timing rather than instantaneous firing rates[5, 6]. In fact, we will show that there are some conditions under which spike-based learning rules can be approximated by rate-based learning rules. Other people have also studied the relationship between spike-based and rate-based learning rules[7, 8].

The pairing functions of Figures 1A and 1B lead to rate-based learning rules like those traditionally used in neural networks, except that they depend on temporal derivatives of firing rates as well as firing rates themselves. We will argue that the differential anti-Hebbian learning rule of Figure 1B could be a general mechanism for tuning the strength of positive feedback in networks that maintain a short-term memory of an analog variable in persistent neural activity. A number of recurrent network models have been proposed to explain memory-related neural activity in motor [9] and prefrontal[10] cortical areas, as well as the head direction system [11] and oculomotor integrator[12, 13, 14]. All of these models require precise tuning of synaptic strengths in order to maintain continuously variable levels of persistent activity. As a simple illustration of tuning by differential anti-Hebbian learning, a model of persistent activity maintained by an integrate-and-fire neuron with an excitatory autapse is studied.

2 SPIKE-BASED LEARNING RULE

Pairing functions like those of Figure 1 have been measured using repeated pairing of a single presynaptic spike with a single postsynaptic spike. Quantitative measurements of synaptic changes due to more complex patterns of spiking activity have not yet been done. We will assume a simple model in which the synaptic change due to arbitrary spike trains is the sum of contributions from all possible pairings of presynaptic with postsynaptic spikes. The model is unlikely to be an exact description of real synapses, but could turn out to be approximately valid.

We will write the spike train of the ith neuron as a series of Dirac delta functions, $s_i(t) = \sum_n \delta(t - T_i^n)$, where T_i^n is the nth spike time of the ith neuron. The synaptic weight from neuron j to i at time t is denoted by $W_{ij}(t)$. Then the change in synaptic weight induced by presynaptic spikes occurring in the time interval $[0, T]$ is modeled as

$$W_{ij}(T + \lambda) - W_{ij}(\lambda) = \int_0^T dt_j \int_{-\infty}^{\infty} dt_i \, f(t_i - t_j) s_i(t_i) \, s_j(t_j) \quad (1)$$

Each presynaptic spike is paired with all postsynaptic spikes produced before and after. For each pairing, the synaptic weight is changed by an amount depending on the pairing function f. The pairing function is assumed to be nonzero inside the interval $[-\tau, \tau]$, and zero outside. We will refer to τ as the *pairing range*.

According to our model, each presynaptic spike results in induction of plasticity only after a latency λ. Accordingly, the arguments $T + \lambda$ and λ of W_{ij} on the left hand side of the equation are shifted relative to the limits T and 0 of the integral on the right hand side. We will assume that the latency λ is greater than the pairing range τ, so that W_{ij} at any time is only influenced by presynaptic and postsynaptic spikes that happened before that time, and therefore the learning rule is causal.

3 RELATION TO RATE-BASED LEARNING RULES

The learning rule of Eq. (1) is driven by correlations between presynaptic and postsynaptic activities. This dependence can be made explicit by making the change of variables $u = t_i - t_j$ in Eq. (1), which yields

$$W_{ij}(T + \lambda) - W_{ij}(\lambda) = \int_{-\tau}^{\tau} du\, f(u) C_{ij}(u) \tag{2}$$

where we have defined the cross-correlation

$$C_{ij}(u) = \int_0^T dt\, s_i(t + u)\, s_j(t)\ . \tag{3}$$

and made use of the fact that f vanishes outside the interval $[-\tau, \tau]$. Our immediate goal is to relate Eq. (2) to learning rules that are based on the cross-correlation between firing rates,

$$C_{ij}^{rate}(u) = \int_0^T dt\, \nu_i(t + u)\, \nu_j(t) \tag{4}$$

There are a number of ways of defining instantaneous firing rates. Sometimes they are computed by averaging over repeated presentations of a stimulus. In other situations, they are defined by temporal filtering of spike trains. The following discussion is general, and should apply to these and other definitions of firing rates.

The "rate correlation" is commonly subtracted from the total correlation to obtain the "spike correlation" $C_{ij}^{spike} = C_{ij} - C_{ij}^{rate}$. To derive a rate-based approximation to the learning rule (2), we rewrite it as

$$W_{ij}(T + \lambda) - W_{ij}(\lambda) = \int_{-\tau}^{\tau} du\, f(u) C_{ij}^{rate}(u) + \int_{-\tau}^{\tau} du\, f(u) C_{ij}^{spike}(u) \tag{5}$$

and simply neglect the second term. Shortly we will discuss the conditions under which this is a good approximation. But first we derive another form for the first term by applying the approximation $\nu_i(t + u) \approx \nu_i(t) + u\dot{\nu}_i(t)$ to obtain

$$\int_{-\tau}^{\tau} du\, f(u) C_{ij}^{rate}(u) \approx \int_0^T dt [\beta_0 \nu_i(t) + \beta_1 \dot{\nu}_i(t)] \nu_j(t) \tag{6}$$

where we define

$$\beta_0 = \int_{-\tau}^{\tau} du\, f(u) \qquad \beta_1 = \int_{-\tau}^{\tau} du\, u f(u) \tag{7}$$

This approximation is good when firing rates vary slowly compared to the pairing range τ. The learning rule depends on the postsynaptic rate through $\beta_0 \nu_i + \beta_1 \dot{\nu}_i$. When the first term dominates the second, then the learning rule is the conventional one based on correlations between firing rates, and the sign of β_0 determines whether the rule is Hebbian or anti-Hebbian.

In the remainder of the paper, we will discuss the more novel case where $\beta_0 = 0$. This holds for the pairing functions shown in Figures 1A and 1B, which have positive and negative lobes with areas that exactly cancel in the definition of β_0. Then the dependence on postsynaptic activity is purely on the time derivative of the firing rate. Differential Hebbian learning corresponds to $\beta_1 > 0$ (Figure 1A), while differential anti-Hebbian learning leads to $\beta_1 < 0$ (Figure 1B). To summarize the $\beta_0 = 0$ case, the synaptic changes due to rate correlations are approximated by

$$\dot{W}_{ij} \propto \dot{\nu}_i \nu_j \quad \text{(diff. Hebbian)} \qquad \dot{W}_{ij} \propto -\dot{\nu}_i \nu_j \quad \text{(diff. anti-Hebbian)} \qquad (8)$$

for slowly varying rates. These formulas imply that a constant postsynaptic firing rate causes no net change in synaptic strength. Instead, changes in rate are required to induce synaptic plasticity.

To illustrate this point, Figure 1C shows the result of applying differential anti-Hebbian learning to two spike trains. The presynaptic spike train was generated by a 50 Hz Poisson process, while the postsynaptic spike train was generated by an inhomogeneous Poisson process with rate that shifted from 50 Hz to 200 Hz at 1 sec. Before and after the shift, the synaptic strength fluctuates but remains roughly constant. But the upward shift in firing rate causes a downward shift in synaptic strength, in accord with the sign of the differential anti-Hebbian rule in Eq. (8).

The rate-based approximation works well for this example, because the second term of Eq. (5) is not so important. Let us return to the issue of the general conditions under which this term can be neglected. With Poisson spike trains, the spike correlations $C_{ij}^{spike}(u)$ are zero in the limit $T \to \infty$, but for finite T they fluctuate about zero. The integral over u in the second term of (5) dampens these fluctuations. The amount of dampening depends on the pairing range τ, which sets the limits of integration. In Figure 1C we used a relatively long pairing range of 100 ms, which made the fluctuations small even for small T. On the other hand, if τ were short, the fluctuations would be small only for large T. Averaging over large T is relevant when the amplitude of f is small, so that the rate of learning is slow. In this case, it takes a long time for significant synaptic changes to accumulate, so that plasticity is effectively driven by integrating over long time periods T in Eq. (1).

In the brain, nonvanishing spike correlations are sometimes observed even in the $T \to \infty$ limit, unlike with Poisson spike trains. These correlations are often roughly symmetric about zero, in which case they should produce little plasticity if the pairing functions are antisymmetric as in Figures 1A and 1B. On the other hand, if the spike correlations are asymmetric, they could lead to substantial effects[6].

4 EFFECTS ON RECURRENT NETWORK DYNAMICS

The learning rules of Eq. (8) depend on both presynaptic and postsynaptic rates, like learning rules conventionally used in neural networks. They have the special feature that they depend on time derivatives, which has computational consequences for recurrent neural networks of the form

$$\dot{x}_i + x_i = \sum_j W_{ij} \sigma(x_j) + b_i \qquad (9)$$

Such classical neural network equations can be derived from more biophysically realistic models using the method of averaging[15] or a mean field approximation[16]. The firing rate of neuron j is conventionally identified with $\nu_j = \sigma(x_j)$.

The cost function $E(\{x_i\}; \{W_{ij}\}) = \frac{1}{2} \sum_i \dot{\nu}_i^2$ quantifies the amount of drift in firing rate at the point $x_1, \ldots, x_N$ in the state space of the network. If we consider $\dot{\nu}_i$ to be a function of x_i and W_{ij} defined by (9), then the gradient of the cost function with respect to W_{ij} is given by $\partial E / \partial W_{ij} = \sigma'(x_i) \dot{\nu}_i \nu_j$. Assuming that σ is a monotonically increasing function so that $\sigma'(x_i) > 0$, it follows that the differential Hebbian update of (8) increases the cost function, and hence increases the magnitude of the drift velocity. In contrast, the differential anti-Hebbian update decreases the drift velocity. This suggests that the differential anti-Hebbian update could be useful for creating fixed points of the network dynamics (9).

5 PERSISTENT ACTIVITY IN A SPIKING AUTAPSE MODEL

The preceding arguments about drift velocity were based on approximate rate-based descriptions of learning and network dynamics. It is important to implement spike-based learning in a spiking network dynamics, to check that our approximations are valid. Therefore we have numerically simulated the simple recurrent circuit of integrate-and-fire neurons shown in Figure 2. The core of the circuit is the "memory neuron," which makes an excitatory autapse onto itself. It also receives synaptic input from three input neurons: a tonic neuron, an excitatory burst neuron, and an inhibitory burst neuron. It is known that this circuit can store a short-term memory of an analog variable in persistent activity, if the strengths of the autapse and tonic synapse are precisely tuned[17]. Here we show that this tuning can be accomplished by the spike-based learning rule of Eq. (1), with a differential anti-Hebbian pairing function like that of Figure 1B.

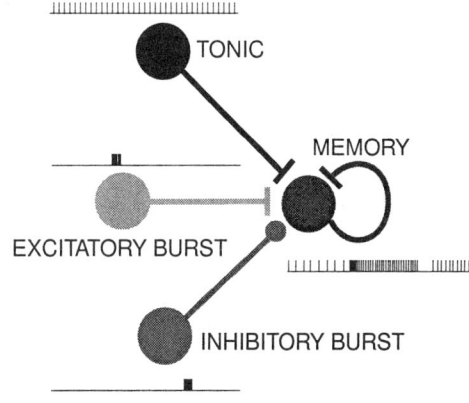

Figure 2: Circuit diagram for autapse model

The memory neuron is described by the equations

$$C_m \frac{dV}{dt} = -g_L(V - V_L) - g_E(V - V_E) - g_I(V - V_I) \qquad (10)$$

$$\tau_{syn} \frac{dr}{dt} + r = \alpha_r \sum_n \delta(t - T_n) \qquad (11)$$

where V is the membrane potential. When V reaches V_{thres}, a spike is considered to have occurred, and V is reset to V_{reset}. Each spike at time T_n causes a jump in the synaptic activation r of size α_r/τ_{syn}, after which r decays exponentially with time constant τ_{syn} until the next spike.

The synaptic conductances of the memory neuron are given by

$$g_E = Wr + W_0 r_0 + W_+ r_+ \qquad g_I = W_- r_- \qquad (12)$$

The term Wr is recurrent excitation from the autapse, where W is the strength of the autapse. The synaptic activations r_0, r_+, and r_- of the tonic, excitatory burst, and inhibitory burst neurons are governed by equations like (10) and (11), with a few differences. These neurons have no synaptic input; their firing patterns are instead determined by applied currents $I_{app,0}$, $I_{app,+}$ and $I_{app,-}$. The tonic neuron has a constant applied current, which makes it fire repetitively at roughly 20 Hz (Figure 3). For the excitatory and inhibitory burst neurons the applied current is normally zero, except for brief 100 ms current pulses that cause bursts of action potentials.

As shown in Figure 3, if the synaptic strengths W and W_0 are arbitrarily set before learning, the burst neurons cause only transient changes in the firing rate of the memory neuron. After applying the spike-based learning rule (1) to tune both W and W_0, the memory

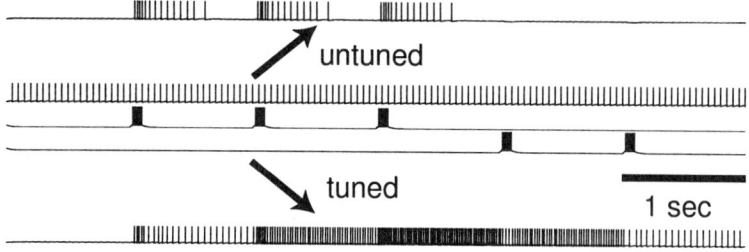

Figure 3: Untuned and tuned autapse activity. The middle three traces are the membrane potentials of the three input neurons in Figure 2 (spikes are drawn at the reset times of the integrate-and-fire neurons). Before learning, the activity of the memory neuron is not persistent, as shown in the top trace. After the spike-based learning rule (1) is applied to the synaptic weights W and W_0, then the burst inputs cause persistent changes in activity. $C_m = 1$ nF, $g_L = 0.025$ μS, $V_L = -70$ mV, $V_E = 0$ mV, $V_I = -70$ mV, $V_{thres} = -52$ mV, $V_{reset} = -59$ mV, $\alpha_s = 1$, $\tau_{syn} = 100$ ms, $I_{app,0} = 0.5203$ nA, $I_{app,\pm} = 0$ or 0.95 nA, $\tau_{syn,0} = 100$ ms, $\tau_{syn,+} = \tau_{syn,-} = 5$ ms, $W_+ = 0.1$, $W_- = 0.05$.

neuron is able to maintain persistent activity. During the interburst intervals (from λ after one burst until λ before the next), we made synaptic changes using the differential anti-Hebbian pairing function $f(t) = -A\sin(\pi t/\tau)$ for spike time differences in the range $[-\tau, \tau]$ with $A = 1.5 \times 10^{-4}$ and $\tau=\lambda=120$ ms. The resulting increase in persistence time can be seen in Figure 4A, along with the values of the synaptic weights versus time.

To quantify the performance of the system at maintaining persistent activity, we determined the relationship between $d\nu/dt$ and ν using a long sequence of interburst intervals, where ν was defined as the reciprocal of the interspike interval. If W and W_0 are fixed at optimally tuned values, there is still a residual drift, as shown in Figure 4B. But if these parameters are allowed to adapt continuously, even after good tuning has been achieved, then the residual drift is even smaller in magnitude. This is because the learning rule tweaks the synaptic weights during each interburst interval, reducing the drift for that particular firing rate.

Autapse learning is driven by the autocorrelation of the spike train, rather than a cross-correlation. The peak in the autocorrelogram at zero lag has no effect, since the pairing function is zero at the origin. Since the autocorrelation is zero for small time lags, we used a fairly large pairing range in our simulations. In a recurrent network of many neurons, a shorter pairing range would suffice, as the cross-correlation does not vanish near zero.

6 DISCUSSION

We have shown that differential anti-Hebbian learning can tune a recurrent circuit to maintain persistent neural activity. This behavior can be understood by reducing the spike-based learning rule (1) to the rate-based learning rules of Eqs. (6) and (8). The rate-based approximations are good if two conditions are satisfied. First, the pairing range must be large, or the rate of learning must be slow. Second, spike synchrony must be weak, or have little effect on learning due to the shape of the pairing function.

The differential anti-Hebbian pairing function results in a learning rule that uses $-\dot{\nu}_i$ as a negative feedback signal to reduce the amount of drift in firing rate, as illustrated by our simulations of an integrate-and-fire neuron with an excitatory autapse. More generally, the learning rule could be relevant for tuning the strength of positive feedback in networks that maintain a short-term memory of an analog variable in persistent neural activity.

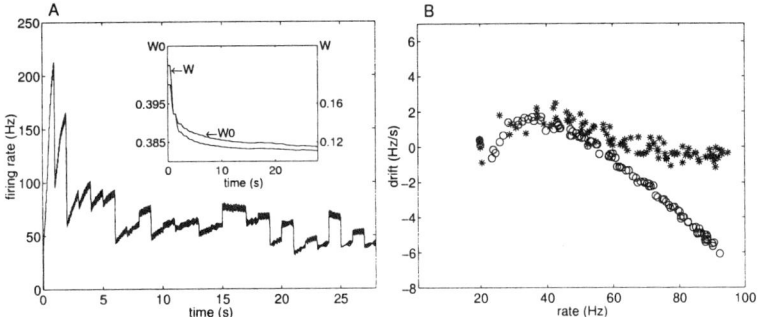

Figure 4: Tuning the autapse. (A) The persistence time of activity increases as the weights W and W_0 are tuned. Each transition is driven by pseudorandom bursts of input (B) Systematic relationship between drift $d\nu/dt$ in firing rate and ν, as measured from a long sequence of interburst intervals. If the weights are continuously fine-tuned ('*') the drift is less than with fixed well-tuned weights ('o').

For example, the learning rule could be used to improve the robustness of the oculomotor integrator[12, 13, 14] and head direction system[11] to mistuning of parameters. In deriving the differential forms of the learning rules in (8), we assumed that the areas under the positive and negative lobes of the pairing function are equal, so that the integral defining β_0 vanishes. In reality, this cancellation might not be exact. Then the ratio of β_1 and β_0 would limit the persistence time that can be achieved by the learning rule.

Both the oculomotor integrator and the head direction system are also able to integrate vestibular inputs to produce changes in activity patterns. The problem of finding generalizations of the present learning rules that train networks to integrate is still open.

References

[1] H. Markram, J. Lubke, M. Frotscher, and B. Sakmann. *Science*, 275(5297):213–5, 1997.

[2] G. Q. Bi and M. M. Poo. *J Neurosci*, 18(24):10464–72, 1998.

[3] D. O. Hebb. *Organization of behavior*. Wiley, New York, 1949.

[4] C. C. Bell, V. Z. Han, Y. Sugawara, and K. Grant. *Nature*, 387(6630):278–81, 1997.

[5] W. Gerstner, R. Kempter, J. L. van Hemmen, and H. Wagner. *Nature*, 383(6595):76–81, 1996.

[6] L. F. Abbott and S. Song. *Adv. Neural Info. Proc. Syst.*, 11, 1999.

[7] P. D. Roberts. *J. Comput. Neurosci.*, 7:235-246, 1999.

[8] R. Kempter, W. Gerstner, and J. L. van Hemmen. *Phys. Rev. E*, 59(4):4498-4514, 1999.

[9] A. P. Georgopoulos, M. Taira, and A. Lukashin. *Science*, 260:47–52, 1993.

[10] M. Camperi and X. J. Wang. *J Comput Neurosci*, 5(4):383–405, 1998.

[11] K. Zhang. *J. Neurosci.*, 16:2112–2126, 1996.

[12] S. C. Cannon, D. A. Robinson, and S. Shamma. *Biol. Cybern.*, 49:127–136, 1983.

[13] H. S. Seung. *Proc. Natl. Acad. Sci. USA*, 93:13339–13344, 1996.

[14] H. S. Seung, D. D. Lee, B. Y. Reis, and D. W. Tank. *Neuron*, 2000.

[15] B. Ermentrout. *Neural Comput.*, 6:679–695, 1994.

[16] O. Shriki, D. Hansel, and H. Sompolinsky. *Soc. Neurosci. Abstr.*, 24:143, 1998.

[17] H. S. Seung, D. D. Lee, B. Y. Reis, and D. W. Tank. *J. Comput. Neurosci.*, 2000.

Part III
Theory

A Variational Bayesian Framework for Graphical Models

Hagai Attias
hagai@gatsby.ucl.ac.uk
Gatsby Unit, University College London
17 Queen Square
London WC1N 3AR, U.K.

Abstract

This paper presents a novel practical framework for Bayesian model averaging and model selection in probabilistic graphical models. Our approach approximates full posterior distributions over model parameters and structures, as well as latent variables, in an analytical manner. These posteriors fall out of a free-form optimization procedure, which naturally incorporates conjugate priors. Unlike in large sample approximations, the posteriors are generally non-Gaussian and no Hessian needs to be computed. Predictive quantities are obtained analytically. The resulting algorithm generalizes the standard Expectation Maximization algorithm, and its convergence is guaranteed. We demonstrate that this approach can be applied to a large class of models in several domains, including mixture models and source separation.

1 Introduction

A standard method to learn a graphical model [1] from data is maximum likelihood (ML). Given a training dataset, ML estimates a single optimal value for the model parameters within a fixed graph structure. However, ML is well known for its tendency to overfit the data. Overfitting becomes more severe for complex models involving high-dimensional real-world data such as images, speech, and text. Another problem is that ML prefers complex models, since they have more parameters and fit the data better. Hence, ML cannot optimize model structure.

The Bayesian framework provides, in principle, a solution to these problems. Rather than focusing on a single model, a Bayesian considers a whole (finite or infinite) class of models. For each model, its posterior probability given the dataset is computed. Predictions for test data are made by averaging the predictions of all the individual models, weighted by their posteriors. Thus, the Bayesian framework avoids overfitting by integrating out the parameters. In addition, complex models are automatically penalized by being assigned a lower posterior probability, therefore optimal structures can be identified.

Unfortunately, computations in the Bayesian framework are intractable even for

---
[1] We use the term 'model' to refer collectively to parameters and structure.

very simple cases (e.g. factor analysis; see [2]). Most existing approximation methods fall into two classes [3]: Markov chain Monte Carlo methods and large sample methods (e.g., Laplace approximation). MCMC methods attempt to achieve exact results but typically require vast computational resources, and become impractical for complex models in high data dimensions. Large sample methods are tractable, but typically make a drastic approximation by modeling the posteriors over all parameters as Normal, even for parameters that are not positive definite (e.g., covariance matrices). In addition, they require the computation of the Hessian, which may become quite intensive.

In this paper I present *Variational Bayes* (VB), a practical framework for Bayesian computations in graphical models. VB draws together variational ideas from intractable latent variables models [8] and from Bayesian inference [4,5,9], which, in turn, draw on the work of [6]. This framework facilitates analytical calculations of posterior distributions over the hidden variables, parameters and structures. The posteriors fall out of a free-form optimization procedure which naturally incorporates conjugate priors, and emerge in standard forms, only one of which is Normal. They are computed via an iterative algorithm that is closely related to Expectation Maximization (EM) and whose convergence is guaranteed. No Hessian needs to be computed. In addition, averaging over models to compute predictive quantities can be performed analytically. Model selection is done using the posterior over structure; in particular, the BIC/MDL criteria emerge as a limiting case.

2 General Framework

We restrict our attention in this paper to directed acyclic graphs (DAGs, a.k.a. Bayesian networks). Let $Y = \{\mathbf{y}_1, ..., \mathbf{y}_N\}$ denote the visible (data) nodes, where $n = 1, ..., N$ runs over the data instances, and let $X = \{\mathbf{x}_1, ..., \mathbf{x}_N\}$ denote the hidden nodes. Let Θ denote the parameters, which are simply additional hidden nodes with their own distributions. A model with a fixed structure m is fully defined by the joint distribution $p(Y, X, \Theta \mid m)$. In a DAG, this joint factorizes over the nodes, i.e. $p(Y, X \mid \Theta, m) = \prod_i p(u_i \mid \mathbf{pa}_i, \theta_i, m)$, where $u_i \in Y \cup X$, $\mathbf{pa}_i$ is the set of parents of u_i, and $\theta_i \in \Theta$ parametrize the edges directed toward u_i. In addition, we usually assume independent instances, $p(Y, X \mid \Theta, m) = \prod_n p(\mathbf{y}_n, \mathbf{x}_n \mid \Theta, m)$.

We shall also consider a set of structures $m \in M$, where m controls the number of hidden nodes and the functional forms of the dependencies $p(u_i \mid \mathbf{pa}_i, \theta_i, m)$, including the range of values assumed by each node (e.g., the number of components in a mixture model). Associated with the set of structures is a structure prior $p(m)$.

Marginal likelihood and posterior over parameters. For a fixed structure m, we are interested in two quantities. The first is the *parameter posterior distribution* $p(\Theta \mid Y, m)$. The second is the *marginal likelihood* $p(Y \mid m)$, also known as the *evidence* assigned to structure m by the data. In the following, the reference to m is usually omitted but is always implied. Both quantities are obtained from the joint $p(Y, X, \Theta \mid m)$. For models with no hidden nodes the required computations can often be performed analytically. However, in the presence of hidden nodes, these quantities become computationally intractable. We shall approximate them using a variational approach as follows.

Consider the joint posterior $p(X, \Theta \mid Y)$ over hidden nodes and parameters. Since it is intractable, consider a *variational posterior* $q(X, \Theta \mid Y)$, which is restricted to the factorized form

$$q(X, \Theta \mid Y) = q(X \mid Y) q(\Theta \mid Y), \tag{1}$$

where given the data, the parameters and hidden nodes are independent. This restriction is the key: It makes q approximate but tractable. Notice that we do not require complete factorization, as the parameters and hidden nodes may still be correlated amongst themselves.

We compute q by optimizing a cost function $\mathcal{F}_m[q]$ defined by

$$\mathcal{F}_m[q] = \int d\Theta\, q(X)q(\Theta) \log \frac{p(Y, X, \Theta)}{q(X)q(\Theta)} \leq \log p(Y \mid m) , \quad (2)$$

where the inequality holds for an arbitrary q and follows from Jensen's inequality (see [6]); it becomes an equality when q is the true posterior. Note that q is always understood to include conditioning on Y as in (1). Since $\mathcal{F}_m$ is bounded from above by the marginal likelihood, we can obtain the optimal posteriors by maximizing it w.r.t. q. This can be shown to be equivalent to minimizing the KL distance between q and the true posterior. Thus, *optimizing $\mathcal{F}_m$ produces the best approximation to the true posterior within the space of distributions satisfying (1), as well as the tightest lower bound on the true marginal likelihood.*

Penalizing complex models. To see that the VB objective function $\mathcal{F}_m$ penalizes complexity, it is useful to rewrite it as

$$\mathcal{F}_m = \langle \log \frac{p(Y, X \mid \Theta)}{q(X)} \rangle_{X,\Theta} - KL[q(\Theta) \parallel p(\Theta)] , \quad (3)$$

where the average in the first term on the r.h.s. is taken w.r.t. $q(X, \Theta)$. The first term corresponds to the (averaged) likelihood. The second term is the KL distance between the prior and posterior over the parameters. As the number of parameters increases, the KL distance follows and consequently reduces $\mathcal{F}_m$.

This penalized likelihood interpretation becomes transparent in the large sample limit $N \to \infty$, where the parameter posterior is sharply peaked about the most probable value $\Theta = \Theta_0$. It can then be shown that the KL penalty reduces to $(\mid \Theta_0 \mid /2) \log N$, which is linear in the number of parameters $\mid \Theta_0 \mid$ of structure m. $\mathcal{F}_m$ then corresponds precisely the Bayesian information criterion (BIC) and the minimum description length criterion (MDL) (see [3]). Thus, these popular model selection criteria follow as a limiting case of the VB framework.

Free-form optimization and an EM-like algorithm. Rather than assuming a specific parametric form for the posteriors, we let them fall out of free-form optimization of the VB objective function. This results in an iterative algorithm directly analogous to ordinary EM. In the E-step, we compute the posterior over the hidden nodes by solving $\delta \mathcal{F}_m / \delta q(X) = 0$ to get

$$q(X) \propto e^{\langle \log p(Y, X \mid \Theta) \rangle_\Theta} , \quad (4)$$

where the average is taken w.r.t. $q(\Theta)$.

In the M-step, rather than the 'optimal' parameters, we compute the *posterior distribution over the parameters* by solving $\delta \mathcal{F}_m / \delta q(\Theta) = 0$ to get

$$q(\Theta) \propto e^{\langle \log p(Y, X \mid \Theta) \rangle_X} p(\Theta) , \quad (5)$$

where the average is taken w.r.t. $q(X)$.

This is where the concept of conjugate priors becomes useful. Denoting the exponential term on the r.h.s. of (5) by $f(\Theta)$, we choose the prior $p(\Theta)$ from a family of distributions such that $q(\Theta) \propto f(\Theta)p(\Theta)$ belongs to that same family. $p(\Theta)$ is then said to be *conjugate* to $f(\Theta)$. This procedure allows us to select a prior from a fairly large family of distributions (which includes non-informative ones as limiting cases) and thus not compromise generality, while facilitating mathematical simplicity and elegance. In particular, *learning in the VB framework simply amounts to updating the hyperparameters*, i.e., transforming the prior parameters to the posterior parameters. We point out that, while the use of conjugate priors is widespread in statistics, so far they could only be applied to models where all nodes were visible.

Structure posterior. To compute $q(m)$ we exploit Jensen's inequality once again to define a more general objective function, $\mathcal{F}[q] = \sum_{m \in M} q(m) \left[\mathcal{F}_m + \log p(m)/q(m) \right] \leq \log p(Y)$, where now $q = q(X \mid m, Y) q(\Theta \mid m, Y) q(m \mid Y)$. After computing $\mathcal{F}_m$ for each $m \in M$, the structure posterior is obtained by free-form optimization of $\mathcal{F}$:

$$q(m) \propto e^{\mathcal{F}_m} p(m) . \tag{6}$$

Hence, prior assumptions about the likelihood of different structures, encoded by the prior $p(m)$, affect the selection of optimal model structures performed according to $q(m)$, as they should.

Predictive quantities. The ultimate goal of Bayesian inference is to estimate predictive quantities, such as a density or regression function. Generally, these quantities are computed by averaging over all models, weighting each model by its posterior. In the VB framework, exact model averaging is approximated by replacing the true posterior $p(\Theta \mid Y)$ by the variational $q(\Theta \mid Y)$. In density estimation, for example, the density assigned to a new data point $\mathbf{y}$ is given by $p(\mathbf{y} \mid Y) = \int d\Theta \, p(\mathbf{y} \mid \Theta) \, q(\Theta \mid Y)$.

In some situations (e.g. source separation), an estimate of hidden node values $\mathbf{x}$ from new data $\mathbf{y}$ may be required. The relevant quantity here is the conditional $p(\mathbf{x} \mid \mathbf{y}, Y)$, from which the most likely value of hidden nodes is extracted. VB approximates it by $p(\mathbf{x} \mid \mathbf{y}, Y) \propto \int d\Theta \, p(\mathbf{y}, \mathbf{x} \mid \Theta) \, q(\Theta \mid Y)$.

3 Variational Bayes Mixture Models

Mixture models have been investigated and analyzed extensively over many years. However, the well known problems of regularizing against likelihood divergences and of determining the required number of mixture components are still open. Whereas in theory the Bayesian approach provides a solution, no satisfactory practical algorithm has emerged from the application of involved sampling techniques (e.g., [7]) and approximation methods [3] to this problem. We now present the solution provided by VB.

We consider models of the form

$$p(\mathbf{y}_n \mid \Theta, m) = \sum_{s=1}^{m} p(\mathbf{y}_n \mid s_n = s, \Theta) \, p(s_n = s \mid \Theta) , \tag{7}$$

where $\mathbf{y}_n$ denotes the nth observed data vector, and s_n denotes the hidden component that generated it. The components are labeled by $s = 1, ..., m$, with the structure parameter m denoting the number of components. Whereas our approach can be applied to arbitrary models, for simplicity we consider here Normal component distributions, $p(\mathbf{y}_n \mid s_n = s, \Theta) = \mathcal{N}(\boldsymbol{\mu}_s, \boldsymbol{\Gamma}_s)$, where $\boldsymbol{\mu}_s$ is the mean and $\boldsymbol{\Gamma}_s$ the precision (inverse covariance) matrix. The mixing proportions are $p(s_n = s \mid \Theta) = \pi_s$.

In hindsight, we use conjugate priors on the parameters $\Theta = \{\pi_s, \boldsymbol{\mu}_s, \boldsymbol{\Gamma}_s\}$. The mixing proportions are jointly Dirichlet, $p(\{\pi_s\}) = \mathcal{D}(\lambda^0)$, the means (conditioned on the precisions) are Normal, $p(\boldsymbol{\mu}_s \mid \boldsymbol{\Gamma}_s) = \mathcal{N}(\rho^0, \beta^0 \boldsymbol{\Gamma}_s)$, and the precisions are Wishart, $p(\boldsymbol{\Gamma}_s) = \mathcal{W}(\nu^0, \boldsymbol{\Phi}^0)$. We find that the parameter posterior for a fixed m

factorizes into $q(\Theta) = q(\{\pi_s\}) \prod_s q(\boldsymbol{\mu}_s, \boldsymbol{\Gamma}_s)$. The posteriors are obtained by the following iterative algorithm, termed VB-MOG.

E-step. Compute the responsibilities for instance n using (4):

$$\gamma_s^n \equiv q(s_n = s \mid \mathbf{y}_n) \propto \tilde{\pi}_s \, \tilde{\Gamma}_s^{1/2} \, e^{-(\mathbf{y}_n - \boldsymbol{\rho}_s)^T \bar{\boldsymbol{\Gamma}}_s (\mathbf{y}_n - \boldsymbol{\rho}_s)/2} \, e^{-d/2\beta_s} , \qquad (8)$$

noting that here $X = S$ and $q(S) = \prod_n q(s_n)$. This expression resembles the responsibilities in ordinary ML; the differences stem from integrating out the parameters. The special quantities in (8) are $\log \tilde{\pi}_s \equiv \langle \log \pi_s \rangle = \psi(\lambda_s) - \psi(\sum_{s'} \lambda_{s'})$, $\log \tilde{\Gamma}_s \equiv \langle \log |\boldsymbol{\Gamma}_s| \rangle = \sum_{i=1}^d \psi((\nu_s + 1 - i)/2) - \log |\boldsymbol{\Phi}_s| + d \log 2$, and $\bar{\boldsymbol{\Gamma}}_s \equiv \langle \boldsymbol{\Gamma}_s \rangle = \nu_s \boldsymbol{\Phi}_s^{-1}$, where $\psi(x) = d \log \Gamma(x)/dx$ is the digamma function, and the averages $\langle \cdot \rangle$ are taken w.r.t. $q(\Theta)$. The other parameters are described below.

M-step. Compute the parameter posterior in two stages. First, compute the quantities

$$\bar{\pi}_s = \frac{1}{N} \sum_{n=1}^N \gamma_s^n , \quad \bar{\boldsymbol{\mu}}_s = \frac{1}{\bar{N}_s} \sum_{n=1}^N \gamma_s^n \mathbf{y}_n , \quad \bar{\boldsymbol{\Sigma}}_s = \frac{1}{\bar{N}_s} \sum_{n=1}^N \gamma_s^n \mathbf{C}_s^n , \qquad (9)$$

where $\mathbf{C}_s^n = (\mathbf{y}_n - \bar{\boldsymbol{\mu}}_s)(\mathbf{y}_n - \bar{\boldsymbol{\mu}}_s)^T$ and $\bar{N}_s = N \bar{\pi}_s$. This stage is identical to the M-step in ordinary EM where it produces the new parameters. In VB, however, the quantities in (9) only help characterize the new parameter posteriors. These posteriors are functionally identical to the priors but have different parameter values. The mixing proportions are jointly Dirichlet, $q(\{\pi_s\}) = \mathcal{D}(\{\lambda_s\})$, the means are Normal, $q(\boldsymbol{\mu}_s \mid \boldsymbol{\Gamma}_s) = \mathcal{N}(\boldsymbol{\rho}_s, \beta_s \boldsymbol{\Gamma}_s)$, and the precisions are Wishart, $p(\boldsymbol{\Gamma}_s) = \mathcal{W}(\nu_s, \boldsymbol{\Phi}_s)$. The posterior parameters are updated in the second stage, using the simple rules

$$\begin{aligned}\lambda_s &= \bar{N}_s + \lambda^0 , & \boldsymbol{\rho}_s &= (\bar{N}_s \bar{\boldsymbol{\mu}}_s + \beta^0 \boldsymbol{\rho}^0)/(\bar{N}_s + \beta^0) , & \beta_s &= \bar{N}_s + \beta^0 , \\ \nu_s &= \bar{N}_s + \nu^0 , & \boldsymbol{\Phi}_s &= \bar{N}_s \bar{\boldsymbol{\Sigma}}_s + \bar{N}_s \beta^0 (\bar{\boldsymbol{\mu}}_s - \boldsymbol{\rho}^0)(\bar{\boldsymbol{\mu}}_s - \boldsymbol{\rho}^0)^T / (\bar{N}_s + \beta^0) + \boldsymbol{\Phi}^0 .\end{aligned} \qquad (10)$$

The final values of the posterior parameters form the output of the VB-MOG. We remark that (a) Whereas no specific assumptions have been made about them, the parameter posteriors emerge in suitable, non-trivial (and generally non-Normal) functional forms. (b) The computational overhead of the VB-MOG compared to EM is minimal. (c) The covariance of the parameter posterior is $\mathcal{O}(1/N)$, and VB-MOG reduces to EM (regularized by the priors) as $N \to \infty$. (d) VB-MOG has no divergence problems. (e) Stability is guaranteed by the existence of an objective function. (f) Finally, the approximate marginal likelihood $\mathcal{F}_m$, required to optimize the number of components via (6), can also be obtained in closed form (omitted).

Predictive Density. Using our posteriors, we can integrate out the parameters and show that the density assigned by the model to a new data vector $\mathbf{y}$ is a mixture of Student-t distributions,

$$p(\mathbf{y} \mid Y) = \sum_{s=1}^m \bar{\pi}_s \, t_{\omega_s}(\mathbf{y} \mid \boldsymbol{\rho}_s, \boldsymbol{\Lambda}_s) , \qquad (11)$$

where component s has $\omega_s = \nu_s + 1 - d$ d.o.f., mean $\boldsymbol{\rho}_s$, covariance $\boldsymbol{\Lambda}_s = ((\beta_s + 1)/\beta_s \omega_s) \boldsymbol{\Phi}_s$, and proportion $\bar{\pi}_s = \lambda_s / \sum_{s'} \lambda_{s'}$. (11) reduces to a MOG as $N \to \infty$.

Nonlinear Regression. We may divide each data vector into input and output parts, $\mathbf{y} = (\mathbf{y}^i, \mathbf{y}^o)$, and use the model to estimate the regression function $\hat{\mathbf{y}}^o = f(\mathbf{y}^i)$ and error spheres. These may be extracted from the conditional $p(\mathbf{y}^o \mid \mathbf{y}^i, Y) = \sum_{s=1}^m w_s \, t_{\omega_s'}(\mathbf{y}^o \mid \boldsymbol{\rho}_s', \boldsymbol{\Lambda}_s')$, which also turns out to be a mixture of Student-t distributions, with means $\boldsymbol{\rho}_s'$ being linear, and covariances $\boldsymbol{\Lambda}_s'$ and mixing proportions w_s nonlinear, in $\mathbf{y}^i$, and given in terms of the posterior parameters.

 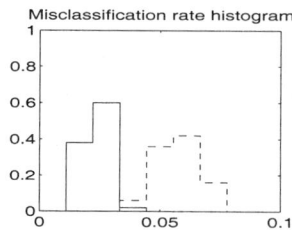

Figure 1: VB-MOG applied to handwritten digit recognition.

VB-MOG was applied to the Boston housing dataset (UCI machine learning repository), where 13 inputs are used to predict the single output, a house's price. 100 random divisions of the $N = 506$ dataset into 481 training and 25 test points were used, resulting in an average MSE of 11.9. Whereas ours is not a discriminative method, it was nevertheless competitive with Breiman's (1994) bagging technique using regression trees (MSE=11.7). For comparison, EM achieved MSE=14.6.

Classification. Here, a separate parameter posterior is computed for each class c from a training dataset Y^c. Test data vector y is then classified according to the conditional $p(c \mid y, \{Y^c\})$, which has a form identical to (11) (with c-dependent parameters) multiplied by the relative size of Y^c.

VB-MOG was applied to the Buffalo post office dataset, which contains 1100 examples for each digit $0 - 9$. Each digit is a gray-level 8×8 pixel array (see examples in Fig. 1 (left)). We used 10 random 500-digit batches for training, and a separate batch of 200 for testing. An average misclassification rate of .018 was obtained using $m = 30$ components; EM achieved .025. The misclassification histograms (VB=solid, EM=dashed) are shown in Fig. 1 (right).

4 VB and Intractable Models: a Blind Separation Example

The discussion so far assumed that a free-form optimization of the VB objective function is feasible. Unfortunately, for many interesting models, in particular models where ordinary ML is intractable, this is not the case. For such models, we modify the VB procedure as follows: (a) Specify a *parametric functional form* for the posterior over the hidden nodes $q(X)$, and optimize w.r.t. its parameters, in the spirit of [8]. (b) Let the parameter posterior $q(\Theta)$ fall out of free-form optimization, as before.

We illustrate this approach in the context of the blind source separation (BSS) problem (see, e.g., [1]). This problem is described by $y_n = Hx_n + u_n$, where x_n is an unobserved m-dim source vector at instance n, H is an unknown mixing matrix, and the noise u_n is Normally distributed with an unknown precision λI. The task is to construct a source estimate $\hat{x}_n$ from the observed d-dim data y. The sources are independent and non-Normally distributed. Here we assume the high-kurtosis distribution $p(x_i^n) \propto \cosh^{-2}(x_i^n/2)$, which is appropriate for modeling speech sources. One important but heretofore unresolved problem in BSS is determining the number m of sources from data. Another is to avoid overfitting the mixing matrix. Both problems, typical to ML algorithms, can be remedied using VB.

It is the non-Normal nature of the sources that renders the source posterior $p(X \mid Y)$ intractable even before a Bayesian treatment. We use a Normal variational posterior $q(X) = \prod_n \mathcal{N}(x_n \mid \rho_n, \Gamma_n)$ with instance-dependent mean and precision. The mixing matrix posterior $q(H)$ then emerges as Normal. For simplicity, λ is optimized rather than integrated out. The resulting VB-BSS algorithm runs as follows:

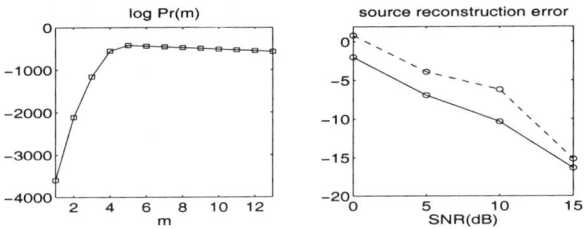

Figure 2: Application of VB to blind source separation algorithm (see text).

E-step. Optimize the variational mean ρ_n by iterating to convergence, for each n, the fixed-point equation $\lambda \bar{\mathbf{H}}^T(\mathbf{y}_n - \bar{\mathbf{H}}\rho_n) - \tanh \rho_n/2 = \mathbf{C}^{-1}\rho_n$, where $\mathbf{C}$ is the source covariance conditioned on the data. The variational precision matrix turns out to be n-independent: $\Gamma_n = \bar{\mathbf{A}}^T \Lambda \bar{\mathbf{A}} + \mathbf{I}/2 + \mathbf{C}^{-1}$.
M-step. Update the mean and precision of the posterior $q(\mathbf{H})$ (rules omitted).

This algorithm was applied to 11-dim data generated by linearly mixing 5 100msec-long speech and music signals obtained from commercial CDs. Gaussian noise were added at different SNR levels. A uniform structure prior $p(m) = 1/K$ for $m \leq K$ was used. The resulting posterior over the number of sources (Fig. 2 (left)) is peaked at the correct value $m = 5$. The sources were then reconstructed from test data via $p(\mathbf{x} \mid \mathbf{y}, Y)$. The log reconstruction error is plotted vs. SNR in Fig. 2 (right, solid). The ML error (which includes no model averaging) is also shown (dashed) and is larger, reflecting overfitting.

5 Conclusion

The VB framework is applicable to a large class of graphical models. In fact, it may be integrated with the junction tree algorithm to produce general inference engines with minimal overhead compared to ML ones. Dirichlet, Normal and Wishart posteriors are not special to models treated here but emerge as a general feature. Current research efforts include applications to multinomial models and to learning the structure of complex dynamic probabilistic networks.

Acknowledgements

I thank Matt Beal, Peter Dayan, David Mackay, Carl Rasmussen, and especially Zoubin Ghahramani, for important discussions.

References

[1] Attias, H. (1999). Independent Factor Analysis. *Neural Computation* **11**, 803-851.
[2] Bishop, C.M. (1999). Variational Principal Component Analysis. *Proc. 9th ICANN*.
[3] Chickering, D.M. & Heckerman, D. (1997). Efficient approximations for the marginal likelihood of Bayesian networks with hidden variables. *Machine Learning* **29**, 181-212.
[4] Hinton, G.E. & Van Camp, D. (1993). Keeping neural networks simple by minimizing the description length of the weights. *Proc. 6th COLT*, 5-13.
[5] Jaakkola, T. & Jordan, M.I. (1997). Bayesian logistic regression: A variational approach. *Statistics and Artificial Intelligence* **6** (Smyth, P. & Madigan, D., Eds).
[6] Neal, R.M. & Hinton, G.E. (1998). A view of the EM algorithm that justifies incremental, sparse, and other variants. *Learning in Graphical Models*, 355-368 (Jordan, M.I., Ed). Kluwer Academic Press, Norwell, MA.
[7] Richardson, S. & Green, P.J. (1997). On Bayesian analysis of mixtures with an unknown number of components. *Journal of the Royal Statistical Society B*, **59**, 731-792.
[8] Saul, L.K., Jaakkola, T., & Jordan, M.I. (1996). Mean field theory of sigmoid belief networks. *Journal of Artificial Intelligence Research* **4**, 61-76.
[9] Waterhouse, S., Mackay, D., & Robinson, T. (1996). Bayesian methods for mixture of experts. *NIPS-8* (Touretzky, D.S. et al, Eds). MIT Press.

Model selection in clustering by uniform convergence bounds*

Joachim M. Buhmann and Marcus Held
Institut für Informatik III,
Römerstraße 164, D-53117 Bonn, Germany
{jb,held}@cs.uni-bonn.de

Abstract

Unsupervised learning algorithms are designed to extract structure from data samples. Reliable and robust inference requires a guarantee that extracted structures are typical for the data source, i.e., similar structures have to be inferred from a second sample set of the same data source. The overfitting phenomenon in maximum entropy based annealing algorithms is exemplarily studied for a class of histogram clustering models. Bernstein's inequality for large deviations is used to determine the maximally achievable approximation quality parameterized by a minimal temperature. Monte Carlo simulations support the proposed model selection criterion by finite temperature annealing.

1 Introduction

Learning algorithms are designed to extract structure from data. Two classes of algorithms have been widely discussed in the literature – *supervised* and *unsupervised learning*. The distinction between the two classes depends on supervision or teacher information which is either available to the learning algorithm or missing. This paper applies statistical learning theory to the problem of unsupervised learning. In particular, error bounds as a protection against overfitting are derived for the recently developed **A**symmetric **C**lustering **M**odel (ACM) for co-occurrence data [6]. These theoretical results show that the continuation method "*deterministic annealing*" yields robustness of the learning results in the sense of statistical learning theory. The computational temperature of annealing algorithms plays the role of a control parameter which regulates the complexity of the learning machine. Let us assume that a hypothesis class $\mathcal{H}$ of loss functions $\mathbf{h}(\mathbf{x}; \alpha)$ is given. These loss functions measure the quality of structures in data. The complexity of $\mathcal{H}$ is controlled by coarsening, i.e., we define a γ–cover of $\mathcal{H}$. Informally, the inference principle advocated by us performs learning by two inference steps: (i) determine the optimal approximation level γ for consistent learning (in terms of large risk deviations); (ii) given the optimal approximation level γ, average over all hypotheses in an appropriate neighborhood of the empirical minimizer. The result of the inference

---
*This work has been supported by the German Israel Foundation for Science and Research Development (GIF) under grant #1-0403-001.06/95.

procedure is not a single hypothesis but a set of hypotheses. This set is represented either by an average of loss functions or, alternatively, by a typical member of this set. This induction approach is named *Empirical Risk Approximation* (ERA) [2].
The reader should note that the learning algorithm has to return an average structure which is *typical* in a γ-cover sense but it is not supposed to return the hypothesis with *minimal empirical risk* as in Vapnik's "Empirical Risk Minimization" (ERM) induction principle for classification and regression [9]. The loss function with minimal empirical risk is usually a structure with maximal complexity, e.g., in clustering the ERM principle will necessarily yield a solution with the maximal number of clusters. The ERM principle, therefore, is not suitable as a model selection principle to determine the number of clusters which are stable under sample fluctuations. The ERA principle with its approximation accuracy γ solves this problem by controlling the effective complexity of the hypothesis class.
In spirit, this approach is similar to the Gibbs–algorithm presented for example in [3]. The Gibbs–algorithm samples a random hypothesis from the version space to predict the label of the $l+1$th data point x_{l+1}. The version space is defined as the set of hypotheses which are consistent with the first l given data points. In our approach we use an alternative definition of consistency, where all hypothesis in an appropriate neighborhood of the empirical minimizer define the version space (see also [4]). Averaging over this neighborhood yields a structure with risk equivalent to the expected risk obtained by random sampling from this set of hypotheses. There exists also a tight methodological relationship to [7] and [4] where learning curves for the learning of two class classifiers are derived using techniques from statistical mechanics.

2 The Empirical Risk Approximation Principle

The data samples $\mathcal{Z} = \{\mathbf{z}_r \in \Omega, 1 \leq r \leq l\}$ which have to be analyzed by the unsupervised learning algorithm are elements of a suitable object (resp. feature) space Ω. The samples are distributed according to a measure μ which is not assumed to be known for the analysis.[1]
A mathematically precise statement of the ERA principle requires several definitions which formalize the notion of searching for structure in the data. The quality of structures extracted from the data set $\mathcal{Z}$ is evaluated by the *empirical risk* $\hat{\mathcal{R}}(\alpha; \mathcal{Z}) := \frac{1}{l} \sum_{r=1}^{l} \mathbf{h}(\mathbf{z}_r; \alpha)$ of a structure α given the training set $\mathcal{Z}$. The function $\mathbf{h}(\mathbf{z}; \alpha)$ is known as *loss function* in statistics. It measures the costs for processing a generic datum $\mathbf{z}$ with model α. Each value $\alpha \in \Lambda$ parameterizes an individual loss function with Λ denoting the set of possible parameters. The loss function which minimizes the empirical risk is denoted by $\hat{\alpha}^{\perp} := \arg\min_{\alpha \in \Lambda} \hat{\mathcal{R}}(\alpha; \mathcal{Z})$.
The relevant quality measure for learning is the *expected risk* $\mathcal{R}(\alpha) := \int_{\Omega} \mathbf{h}(\mathbf{z}; \alpha) \, d\mu(\mathbf{z})$. The optimal structure to be inferred from the data is $\alpha^{\perp} := \arg\min_{\alpha \in \Lambda} \mathcal{R}(\alpha)$. The distribution μ is assumed to decay sufficiently fast with bounded rth moments $\mathbf{E}_{\mu}\{|\mathbf{h}(\mathbf{z}; \alpha) - \mathcal{R}(\alpha)|^r\} \leq r! \tau^{r-2} \mathbf{V}_{\mu}\{\mathbf{h}(\mathbf{z}; \alpha)\}, \forall \alpha \in \Lambda$ ($r > 2$). $\mathbf{E}_{\mu}\{.\}$ and $\mathbf{V}_{\mu}\{.\}$ denote expectation and variance of a random variable, respectively. τ is a distribution dependent constant.
ERA requires the learning algorithm to determine a set hypotheses on the basis of the finest consistently learnable cover of the hypothesis class. Given a learning accuracy γ a subset of parameters $\Lambda_\gamma = \{\alpha_1, \ldots, \alpha_{|\Lambda_\gamma|-1}\} \cup \{\hat{\alpha}^{\perp}\}$ can be defined such that the hypothesis class $\mathcal{H}$ is covered by the function balls with index sets $\mathcal{B}_\gamma(\alpha) := \{\alpha' : \int_{\Omega} |\mathbf{h}(\mathbf{z}; \alpha') - \mathbf{h}(\mathbf{z}; \alpha)| \, d\mu(\mathbf{z}) \leq \gamma\}$, i. e. $\Lambda \subset \bigcup_{\alpha \in \Lambda_\gamma} \mathcal{B}_\gamma(\alpha)$. The em-

---

[1] Knowledge of covering numbers is required in the following analysis which is a weaker type of information than complete knowledge of the probability measure μ (see also [5]).

pirical minimizer $\hat{\alpha}^\perp$ has been added to the cover to simplify bounding arguments. Large deviation theory is used to determine the approximation accuracy γ for learning a hypothesis from the hypothesis class $\mathcal{H}$. The expected risk of the empirical minimizer exceeds the global minimum of the expected risk $\mathcal{R}(\alpha^\perp)$ by $\epsilon\sigma^\top$ with a probability bounded by Bernstein's inequality [8]

$$\mathbf{P}\left\{\mathcal{R}(\hat{\alpha}^\perp) - \mathcal{R}(\alpha^\perp) > \epsilon\sigma^\top\right\} \leq \mathbf{P}\left\{\sup_{\alpha \in \Lambda_\gamma} |\hat{\mathcal{R}}(\alpha) - \mathcal{R}(\alpha)| \geq \frac{1}{2}\left(\epsilon\sigma^\top - \gamma\right)\right\}$$
$$\leq 2|\Lambda_\gamma| \exp\left(-\frac{l\left(\epsilon - \gamma/\sigma^\top\right)^2}{8 + 4\tau\left(\epsilon - \gamma/\sigma^\top\right)}\right) \equiv \delta. \quad (1)$$

The complexity $|\Lambda_\gamma|$ of the coarsened hypothesis class has to be small enough to guarantee with high confidence small ϵ–deviations.[2] This large deviation inequality weighs two competing effects in the learning problem, i. e. the probability of a large deviation exponentially decreases with growing sample size l, whereas a large deviation becomes increasingly likely with growing cardinality of the γ–cover of the hypothesis class. According to (1) the sample complexity $l_0\left(\gamma, \epsilon, \delta\right)$ is defined by

$$\log |\Lambda_\gamma| - \frac{l_0\left(\epsilon - \gamma/\sigma^\top\right)^2}{8 + 4\tau\left(\epsilon - \gamma/\sigma^\top\right)} + \log \frac{2}{\delta} = 0. \quad (2)$$

With probability $1 - \delta$ the deviation of the empirical risk from the expected risk is bounded by $\frac{1}{2}\left(\epsilon^{\text{opt}}\sigma^\top - \gamma\right) =: \gamma^{\text{app}}$. Averaging over a set of functions which exceed the empirical minimizer by no more than $2\gamma^{\text{app}}$ in empirical risk yields an average hypothesis corresponding to the statistically significant structure in the data, i.e., $\hat{\mathcal{R}}(\alpha^\perp) - \hat{\mathcal{R}}(\hat{\alpha}^\perp) \leq \mathcal{R}(\alpha^\perp) + \gamma^{\text{app}} - (\mathcal{R}(\hat{\alpha}^\perp) - \gamma^{\text{app}}) \leq 2\gamma^{\text{app}}$ since $\mathcal{R}(\alpha^\perp) \leq \mathcal{R}(\hat{\alpha}^\perp)$ by definition. The key task in the following remains to calculate the minimal precision $\epsilon(\gamma)$ as a function of the approximation γ and to bound from above the cardinality $|\Lambda_\gamma|$ of the γ–cover for specific learning problems.

3 Asymmetric clustering model

The asymmetric clustering model was developed for the analysis resp. grouping of objects characterized by co–occurrence of objects and certain feature values [6]. Application domains for this explorative data analysis approach are for example texture segmentation, statistical language modeling or document retrieval.
Denote by $\Omega = \mathcal{X} \times \mathcal{Y}$ the product space of objects $\mathbf{x}_i \in \mathcal{X}, 1 \leq i \leq n$ and features $\mathbf{y}_j \in \mathcal{Y}, 1 \leq j \leq f$. The $\mathbf{x}_i \in \mathcal{X}$ are characterized by observations $\mathcal{Z} = \{\mathbf{z}_r\} = \{(\mathbf{x}_{i(r)}, \mathbf{y}_{j(r)}), r = 1, \ldots, l\}$. The sufficient statistics of how often the object–feature pair $(\mathbf{x}_i, \mathbf{y}_j)$ occurs in the data set $\mathcal{Z}$ is measured by the set of frequencies $\{\eta_{ij} : \text{number of observations}(\mathbf{x}_i, \mathbf{y}_j) / \text{total number of observations}\}$. Derived measurements are the frequency of observing object $\mathbf{x}_i$, i. e. $\eta_i = \sum_{j=1}^{f} \eta_{ij}$ and the frequency of observing feature $\mathbf{y}_j$ given object $\mathbf{x}_i$, i. e. $\eta_{j|i} = \eta_{ij}/\eta_i$. The asymmetric clustering model defines a generative model of a finite mixture of component probability distributions in feature space with cluster–conditional distributions $\mathbf{q} = (q_{j|\nu}), 1 \leq j \leq f, 1 \leq \nu \leq k$ (see [6]). We introduce indicator variables $\mathbf{M}_{i\nu} \in \{0, 1\}$ for the membership of object $\mathbf{x}_i$ in cluster $\nu \in \{1, \ldots, k\}$. $\sum_{\nu=1}^{k} \mathbf{M}_{i\nu} = 1 \; \forall i : 1 \leq i \leq n$ enforces the uniqueness constraint for assignments.

---
[2]The maximal standard deviation $\sigma^\top := \sup_{\alpha \in \Lambda_\gamma} \sqrt{\mathbf{V}\{\mathbf{h}(\mathbf{z};\alpha)\}}$ defines the scale to measure deviations of the empirical risk from the expected risk (see [2]).

Using these variables the observed data $\mathcal{Z}$ are distributed according to the generative model over $\mathcal{X} \times \mathcal{Y}$:

$$\mathbf{P}\{\mathbf{x}_i, \mathbf{y}_j | \mathbf{M}, \mathbf{q}\} = \frac{1}{n} \sum_{\nu=1}^{k} \mathbf{M}_{i\nu} q_{j|\nu}. \qquad (3)$$

For the analysis of the unknown data source — characterized (at least approximatively) by the empirical data $\mathcal{Z}$ — a structure $\alpha = (\mathbf{M}, \mathbf{q})$ with $\mathbf{M} \in \{0,1\}^{n \times k}$ has to be inferred. The aim of an ACM analysis is to group the objects $\mathbf{x}_i$ as coded by the unknown indicator variables $\mathbf{M}_{i\nu}$ and to estimate for each cluster ν a prototypical feature distribution $q_{j|\nu}$.

Using the *loss function* $\mathbf{h}(\mathbf{x}_i, \mathbf{y}_j; \alpha) = \log n - \sum_{\nu=1}^{k} \mathbf{M}_{i\nu} \log q_{j|\nu}$ the maximization of the likelihood can be formulated as minimization of the *empirical risk*: $\hat{\mathcal{R}}(\alpha; \mathcal{Z}) = \sum_{i=1}^{n} \sum_{j=1}^{f} \eta_{ij} \mathbf{h}(\mathbf{x}_i, \mathbf{y}_j; \alpha)$, where the essential quantity to be minimized is the *expected risk*: $\mathcal{R}(\alpha) = \sum_{i=1}^{n} \sum_{j=1}^{f} \mathbf{P}^{\text{true}}\{\mathbf{x}_i, \mathbf{y}_j\} \mathbf{h}(\mathbf{x}_i, \mathbf{y}_j; \alpha)$. Using the maximum entropy principle the following annealing equations are derived [6]:

$$\hat{q}_{j|\nu} = \frac{\sum_{i=1}^{n} \langle \mathbf{M}_{i\nu} \rangle \eta_{ij}}{\sum_{i=1}^{n} \langle \mathbf{M}_{i\nu} \rangle} = \sum_{i=1}^{n} \frac{\langle \mathbf{M}_{i\nu} \rangle \eta_i}{\sum_{h=1}^{n} \langle \mathbf{M}_{h\nu} \rangle} \eta_{j|i}, \qquad (4)$$

$$\langle \mathbf{M}_{i\nu} \rangle = \frac{\exp\left[\beta \sum_{j=1}^{f} \eta_{j|i} \log q_{j|\nu}\right]}{\sum_{\mu=1}^{k} \exp\left[\beta \sum_{j=1}^{f} \eta_{j|i} \log q_{j|\mu}\right]}. \qquad (5)$$

The critical temperature: Due to the limited precision of the observed data it is natural to study histogram clustering as a learning problem with the hypothesis class $\mathcal{H} = \{-\sum_\nu \mathbf{M}_{i\nu} \log q_{j|\nu} : \mathbf{M}_{i\nu} \in \{0,1\} \wedge \sum_\nu \mathbf{M}_{i\nu} = 1 \wedge q_{j|\nu} \in \{\frac{1}{l}, \frac{2}{l}, \cdots, 1\} \wedge \sum_j q_{j|\nu} = 1\}$. The limited number of observations results in a limited precision of the frequencies $\eta_{j|i}$. The value $q_{j|\nu} = 0$ has been excluded since it causes infinite expected risk for $\mathbf{P}^{\text{true}}\{\mathbf{y}_j|\mathbf{x}_i\} > 0$. The size of the regularized hypothesis class Λ_γ can be upper bounded by the cardinality of the complete hypothesis class divided by the minimal cardinality of a γ-function ball centered at a function of the γ-cover Λ_γ, i.e. $|\Lambda_\gamma| \leq |\mathcal{H}| / \min_{\tilde{\alpha} \in \Lambda_\gamma} |\mathcal{B}_\gamma(\tilde{\alpha})|$.

The cardinality of a function ball with radius γ can be approximated by adopting techniques from asymptotic analysis [1] ($\Theta(x) = \{\begin{smallmatrix}1\\0\end{smallmatrix}$ for $x \gtrless 0$):

$$|\mathcal{B}_\gamma(\tilde{\alpha})| = \sum_{\mathcal{M}} \sum_{\{q_{j|\alpha}\}} \Theta\left(\gamma - \sum_{i,j} \frac{1}{n} \mathbf{P}^{\text{true}}\{\mathbf{y}_j|\mathbf{x}_i\} \left|\log \frac{q_{j|m(i)}}{\tilde{q}_{j|\tilde{m}(i)}}\right|\right) \qquad (6)$$

$$= \frac{k^n l^{kf}}{(2\pi i)^k} \int_0^1 \cdots \int_0^1 \prod_{j=1}^{f} \prod_{\nu=1}^{k} dq_{j|\nu} \int_{-i\infty}^{+i\infty} \cdots \int_{-i\infty}^{+i\infty} dQ_\nu \int_{-i\infty}^{+i\infty} \frac{d\hat{x}}{2\pi i \hat{x}} \exp\left(n\mathcal{S}(\mathbf{q}, \mathbf{Q}, \hat{x})\right),$$

and the entropy $\mathcal{S}$ is given by

$$\mathcal{S}(\mathbf{q}, \mathbf{Q}, \hat{x}) = \gamma \hat{x} - \sum_\nu Q_\nu \left(\sum_j q_{j|\nu} - 1\right) +$$

$$\frac{1}{n} \sum_i \log \sum_\rho \exp\left(-\hat{x} \sum_j \mathbf{P}^{\text{true}}\{\mathbf{y}_j|\mathbf{x}_i\} \left|\log \frac{q_{j|\rho}}{\tilde{q}_{j|\tilde{m}(i)}}\right|\right). \qquad (7)$$

The auxiliary variables $\mathbf{Q} = \{Q_\nu\}_{\nu=1}^{k}$ are Lagrange parameters to enforce the normalizations $\sum_j q_{j|\nu} = 1$. Choosing $q_{j|\alpha} = \tilde{q}_{j|\tilde{m}(i)} \forall \tilde{m}(i) = \alpha$, we obtain an approximation of the integral. The reader should note that a saddlepoint approximation in the usual sense is only applicable for the parameter $\hat{x}$ but will fail for the $\mathbf{q}, \mathbf{Q}$ parameters since the integrand is maximal at the non–differentiability point of the absolute value function. We, therefore, expand $\mathcal{S}(\mathbf{q}, \mathbf{Q}, \hat{x})$ up to linear terms $\mathcal{O}(\mathbf{q} - \tilde{\mathbf{q}})$ and integrate piece–wise.

Using the abbreviation $\kappa_{i\nu} := \sum_j \mathbf{P}^{\text{true}}\{\mathbf{y}_j | \mathbf{x}_i\} \left| \log \frac{\tilde{q}_{j|\nu}}{\tilde{q}_{j|\tilde{m}(i)}} \right|$ the following saddle point approximation for the integral over $\hat{x}$ is obtained:

$$\gamma = \frac{1}{n} \sum_{i=1}^{n} \sum_{\mu=1}^{k} \mathbf{P}_{i\mu} \kappa_{j|\mu} \quad \text{with} \quad \mathbf{P}_{i\alpha} = \frac{\exp(-\hat{x}\kappa_{i\alpha})}{\sum_{\mu} \exp(-\hat{x}\kappa_{i\mu})}. \tag{8}$$

The entropy $\mathcal{S}$ evaluated at $\mathbf{q} = \tilde{\mathbf{q}}$ yields in combination with the Laplace approximation [1] an estimate for the cardinality of the γ–cover

$$\log |\Lambda_\gamma| = n(\log k - \mathcal{S}) + \frac{1}{2} \sum_{i,\rho} \kappa_{i\rho} \mathbf{P}_{i\rho} \left(\sum_\nu \mathbf{P}_{i\nu} \kappa_{i\nu} - \kappa_{i\rho} \right) \hat{x}^2 \tag{9}$$

where the second term results from the second order term of the Taylor expansion around the saddle point. Inserting this complexity in equation (2) yields an equation which determines the required number of samples l_0 for a fixed precision ϵ and confidence δ. This equation defines a functional relationship between the precision ϵ and the approximation quality γ for fixed sample size l_0 and confidence δ. Under this assumption the precision ϵ depends on γ in a non–monotone fashion, i. e.

$$\epsilon = \frac{\gamma}{\sigma^\tau} + \frac{2}{l_0} \left[\sqrt{2 l_0 C + \tau^2 C^2} + \tau C \right], \tag{10}$$

using the abbreviation $C = \log|\Lambda_\gamma| + \log \frac{2}{\delta}$. The minimum of the function $\epsilon(\gamma)$ defines a compromise between uncertainty originating from empirical fluctuations and the loss of precision due to the approximation by a γ–cover. Differentiating with respect to γ and setting the result to zero $(d\epsilon(\gamma)/d\gamma = 0)$ yields as upper bound for the inverse temperature:

$$\hat{x} \leq \frac{1}{\sigma^\tau} \frac{l_0}{2n} \left(\tau + \frac{l_0 + C\tau^2}{\sqrt{2 l_0 C + \tau^2 C^2}} \right)^{-1}. \tag{11}$$

Analogous to estimates of k–means, phase–transitions occur in ACM while lowering the temperature. The mixture model for the data at hand can be partitioned into more and more components, revealing finer and finer details of the generation process. The critical $\hat{x}^{\text{opt}}$ defines the resolution limit below which details can not be resolved in a reliable fashion on the basis of the sample size l_0.

Given the inverse temperature $\hat{x}$ the effective cardinality of the hypothesis class can be upper bounded via the solution of the fix point equation (8). On the other hand this cardinality defines with (11) and the sample size l_0 an upper bound on $\hat{x}$. Iterating these two steps we finally obtain an upper bound for the critical inverse temperature given a sample size l_0.

Empirical Results:
For the evaluation of the derived theoretical result a series of Monte–Carlo experiments on artificial data has been performed for the asymmetric clustering model. Given the number of objects $n = 30$, the number of groups $k = 5$ and the size of the histograms $f = 15$ the generative model for this experiments was created randomly and is summarized in fig. 1. From this generative model sample sets of arbitrary size can be generated and the true distributions $\mathbf{P}^{\text{true}}\{\mathbf{y}_j|\mathbf{x}_i\}$ can be calculated.
In figure 2a,b the predicted temperatures are compared to the empirically observed critical temperatures, which have been estimated on the basis of 2000 different samples of randomly generated co–occurrence data for each l_0. The expected risk (solid)

ν	$q_{j|\nu}$
1	{0.11, 0.01, 0.11, 0.07, 0.08, 0.04, 0.06, 0, 0.13, 0.07, 0.08, 0.1, 0, 0.11, 0.03}
2	{0.18, 0.1, 0.09, 0.02, 0.05, 0.09, 0.08, 0.03, 0.06, 0.07, 0.03, 0.02, 0.07, 0.06, 0.05}
3	{0.17, 0.05, 0.05, 0.06, 0.06, 0.05, 0.03, 0.11, 0.09, 0, 0.02, 0.1, 0.03, 0.07, 0.11}
4	{0.15, 0.07, 0.1, 0.03, 0.09, 0.03, 0.04, 0.05, 0.06, 0.05, 0.08, 0.04, 0.08, 0.09, 0.04}
5	{0.09, 0.09, 0.07, 0.1, 0.07, 0.06, 0.06, 0.11, 0.07, 0.07, 0.1, 0.02, 0.07, 0.02, 0}

$m(i) = (5, 3, 2, 5, 2, 2, 5, 4, 2, 2, 2, 4, 1, 5, 3, 5, 3, 4, 1, 2, 2, 3, 1, 1, 2, 5, 5, 2, 2, 1)$

Figure 1: Generative ACM model for the Monte–Carlo experiments.

and empirical risk (dashed) of these 2000 inferred models are averaged. Overfitting sets in when the expected risk rises as a function of the inverse temperature $\hat{x}$.
Figure 2c indicates that on average the minimal expected risk is assumed when the effective number is smaller than or equal 5, i. e. the number of clusters of the true generative model. Predicting the right computational temperature, therefore, also enables the data analyst to solve the cluster validation problem for the asymmetric clustering model. Especially for $l_0 = 800$ the sample fluctuations do not permit the estimate of five clusters and the minimal computational temperature prevents such an inference result. On the other hand for $l_0 = 1600$ and $l_0 = 2000$ the minimal temperature prevents the algorithm to infer too many clusters, which would be an instance of overfitting.
As an interesting point one should note that for an infinite number of observations the critical inverse temperature reaches a finite positive value and not more than the five effective clusters are extracted. At this point we conclude, that for the case of histogram clustering the *Empirical Risk Approximation* solves for realizable rules the problem of model validation, i. e. choosing the right number of clusters.
Figure 2d summarizes predictions of the critical temperature on the basis of the empirical distribution η_{ij} rather than the true distribution $\mathbf{P}^{\text{true}}\{\mathbf{x}_i, \mathbf{y}_j\}$. The empirical distribution has been generated by a training sample set with $\hat{x}$ of eq. (11) being used as a plug–in estimator. The histogram depicts the predicted inverse temperature for $l_0 = 1200$. The average of these plug–in estimators is equal to the predicted temperature for the true distribution. The estimates of $\hat{x}$ are biased towards too small inverse temperatures due to correlations between the parameter estimates and the stopping criterion. It is still an open question and focus of ongoing work to rigorously bound the variance of this plug–in estimator.
Empirically we observe a reduction of the variance of the expected risk occurring at the predicted temperature for higher sample sizes l_0.

4 Conclusions

The two conditions that the empirical risk has to uniformly converge towards the expected risk and that all loss functions within an $2\gamma^{\text{app}}$-range of the global empirical risk minimum have to be considered in the inference process limits the complexity of the underlying hypothesis class for a given number of samples. The maximum entropy method which has been widely employed in deterministic annealing procedures for optimization problems is substantiated by our analysis. Solutions with too many clusters clearly overfit the data and do not generalize. The condition that the hypothesis class should only be divided in function balls of size γ forces us to stop the stochastic search at the lower bound of the computational temperature.
Another important result of this investigation is the fact that choosing the right stopping temperature for the annealing process not only avoids overfitting but also solves the cluster validation problem in the realizable case of ACM. A possible inference of too many clusters using the empirical risk functional is suppressed.

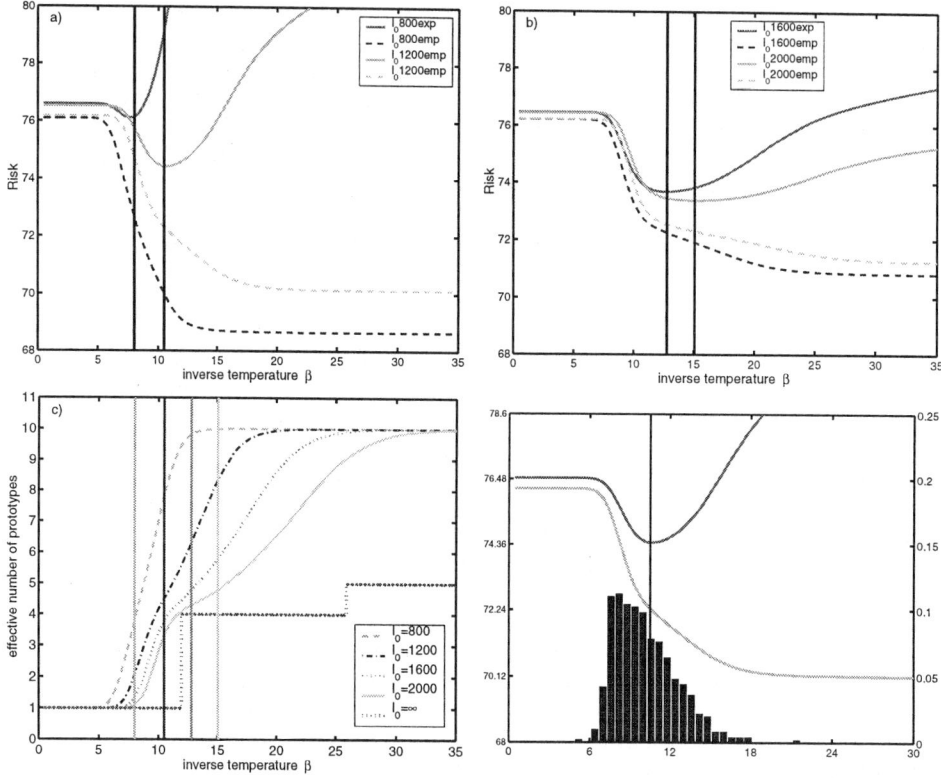

Figure 2: Comparison between the theoretically derived upper bound on $\hat{x}$ and the observed critical temperatures (minimum of the expected risk vs. $\hat{x}$ curve). Depicted are the plots for $l_0 = 800, 1200, 1600, 2000$. Vertical lines indicate the predicted critical temperatures. The average effective number of clusters is drawn in part c. In part d the distribution of the plug–in estimates is shown for $l_0 = 1200$.

References

[1] N. G. De Bruijn. *Asymptotic Methods in Analysis*. North-Holland Publishing Co., (repr. Dover), Amsterdam, 1958, (1981).

[2] J. M. Buhmann. Empirical risk approximation. Technical Report IAI-TR 98-3, Institut für Informatik III, Universität Bonn, 1998.

[3] D. Haussler, M. Kearns, and R. Schapire. Bounds on the sample complexity of Bayesian learning using information theory and the VC dimension. *Machine Learning*, 14(1):83–113, 1994.

[4] D. Haussler, M. Kearns, H.S. Seung, and N. Tishby. Rigorous learning curve bounds from statistical mechanics. *Machine Learning*, 25:195–236, 1997.

[5] D. Haussler and M. Opper. Mutual information, metric entropy and cumulative relative entropy risk. *Annals of Statistics*, December 1996.

[6] T. Hofmann, J. Puzicha, and M.I. Jordan. Learning from dyadic data. In M. S. Kearns, S. A. Solla, and D. A. Cohn, editors, *Advances in Neural Information Processing Systems 11*. MIT Press, 1999. to appear.

[7] H. S. Seung, H. Sompolinsky, and N. Tishby. Statistical mechanics of learning from examples. *Physical Review A*, 45(8):6056–6091, April 1992.

[8] A. W. van der Vaart and J. A. Wellner. *Weak Convergence and Empirical Processes*. Springer-Verlag, New York, Berlin, Heidelberg, 1996.

[9] V. N. Vapnik. *Statistical Learning Theory*. Wiley–Interscience, New York, 1998.

Uniqueness of the SVM Solution

Christopher J.C. Burges
Advanced Technologies,
Bell Laboratories,
Lucent Technologies
Holmdel, New Jersey
burges@lucent.com

David J. Crisp
Centre for Sensor Signal and
Information Processing,
Deptartment of Electrical Engineering,
University of Adelaide, South Australia
dcrisp@eleceng.adelaide.edu.au

Abstract

We give necessary and sufficient conditions for uniqueness of the support vector solution for the problems of pattern recognition and regression estimation, for a general class of cost functions. We show that if the solution is not unique, all support vectors are necessarily at bound, and we give some simple examples of non-unique solutions. We note that uniqueness of the primal (dual) solution does not necessarily imply uniqueness of the dual (primal) solution. We show how to compute the threshold b when the solution is unique, but when all support vectors are at bound, in which case the usual method for determining b does not work.

1 Introduction

Support vector machines (SVMs) have attracted wide interest as a means to implement structural risk minimization for the problems of classification and regression estimation. The fact that training an SVM amounts to solving a convex quadratic programming problem means that the solution found is global, and that if it is not unique, then the set of global solutions is itself convex; furthermore, if the objective function is strictly convex, the solution is guaranteed to be unique [1][1]. For quadratic programming problems, convexity of the objective function is equivalent to positive semi-definiteness of the Hessian, and strict convexity, to positive definiteness [1]. For reference, we summarize the basic uniqueness result in the following theorem, the proof of which can be found in [1]:

Theorem 1: The solution to a convex programming problem, for which the objective function is strictly convex, is unique. Positive definiteness of the Hessian implies strict convexity of the objective function.

Note that in general strict convexity of the objective function does not neccesarily imply positive definiteness of the Hessian. Furthermore, the solution can still be unique, even if the objective function is loosely convex (we will use the term "loosely convex" to mean convex but not strictly convex). Thus the question of uniqueness

---

[1]This is in contrast with the case of neural nets, where local minima of the objective function can occur.

for a convex programming problem for which the objective function is loosely convex is one that must be examined on a case by case basis. In this paper we will give necessary and sufficient conditions for the support vector solution to be unique, even when the objective function is loosely convex, for both the clasification and regression cases, and for a general class of cost function.

One of the central features of the support vector method is the implicit mapping Φ of the data $z \in \Re^n$ to some feature space $\mathcal{F}$, which is accomplished by replacing dot products between data points z_i, z_j, wherever they occur in the train and test algorithms, with a symmetric function $K(z_i, z_j)$, which is itself an inner product in $\mathcal{F}$ [2]: $K(z_i, z_j) = \langle \Phi(z_i), \Phi(z_j) \rangle = \langle x_i, x_j \rangle$, where we denote the mapped points in $\mathcal{F}$ by $x = \Phi(z)$. In order for this to hold the kernel function K must satisfy Mercer's positivity condition [3]. The algorithms then amount to constructing an optimal separating hyperplane in $\mathcal{F}$, in the pattern recognition case, or fitting the data to a linear regression tube (with a suitable choice of loss function [4]) in the regression estimation case. Below, without loss of generality, we will work in the space $\mathcal{F}$, whose dimension we denote by d_F. The conditions we will find for non-uniqueness of the solution will not depend explicitly on $\mathcal{F}$ or Φ.

Most approaches to solving the support vector training problem employ the Wolfe dual, which we describe below. By uniqueness of the primal (dual) solution, we mean uniqueness of the set of primal (dual) variables at the solution. Notice that strict convexity of the primal objective function does not imply strict convexity of the dual objective function. For example, for the optimal hyperplane problem (the problem of finding the maximal separating hyperplane in input space, for the case of separable data), the primal objective function is strictly convex, but the dual objective function will be loosely convex whenever the number of training points exceeds the dimension of the data in input space. In that case, the dual Hessian H will necessarily be positive semidefinite, since H (or a submatrix of H, for the cases in which the cost function also contributes to the (block-diagonal) Hessian) is a Gram matrix of the training data, and some rows of the matrix will then necessarily be linearly dependent [5][2]. In the cases of support vector pattern recognition and regression estimation studied below, one of four cases can occur: (1) both primal and dual solutions are unique; (2) the primal solution is unique while the dual solution is not; (3) the dual is unique but the primal is not; (4) both solutions are not unique. Case (2) occurs when the unique primal solution has more than one expansion in terms of the dual variables. We will give an example of case (3) below. It is easy to construct trivial examples where case (1) holds, and based on the discussion below, it will be clear how to construct examples of (4). However, since the geometrical motivation and interpretation of SVMs rests on the primal variables, the theorems given below address uniqueness of the primal solution[3].

2 The Case of Pattern Recognition

We consider a slightly generalized form of the problem given in [6], namely to minimize the objective function

$$F = (1/2) \|w\|^2 + \sum_i C_i \xi_i^p \quad (1)$$

---

[2]Recall that a Gram matrix is a matrix whose ij'th element has the form $\langle x_i, x_j \rangle$ for some inner product $\langle , \rangle$, where x_i is an element of a vector space, and that the rank of a Gram matrix is the maximum number of linearly independent vectors x_i that appear in it [6].

[3]Due to space constraints some proofs and other details will be omitted. Complete details will be given elsewhere.

with constants $p \in [1, \infty)$, $C_i > 0$, subject to constraints:

$$y_i(w \cdot x_i + b) \geq 1 - \xi_i, \quad i = 1, \cdots, l \tag{2}$$
$$\xi_i \geq 0, \quad i = 1, \cdots, l \tag{3}$$

where w is the vector of weights, b a scalar threshold, ξ_i are positive slack variables which are introduced to handle the case of nonseparable data, the y_i are the polarities of the training samples ($y_i \in \{\pm 1\}$), x_i are the images of training samples in the space $\mathcal{F}$ by the mapping Φ, the C_i determine how much errors are penalized (here we have allowed each pattern to have its own penalty), and the index i labels the l training patterns. The goal is then to find the values of the primal variables $\{w, b, \xi_i\}$ that solve this problem. Most workers choose $p = 1$, since this results in a particularly simple dual formulation, but the problem is convex for any $p \geq 1$. We will not go into further details on support vector classification algorithms themselves here, but refer the interested reader to [3], [7]. Note that, at the solution, b is determined from w and ξ_i by the Karush Kuhn Tucker (KKT) conditions (see below), but we include it in the definition of a solution for convenience.

Note that Theorem 1 gives an immediate proof that the solution to the optimal hyperplane problem is unique, since there the objective function is just $(1/2)\|w\|^2$, which is strictly convex, and the constraints (Eq. (2) with the ξ variables removed) are linear inequality constraints which therefore define a convex set[4].

For the discussion below we will need the dual formulation of this problem, for the case $p = 1$. It takes the following form: minimize $\frac{1}{2}\sum_{ij} \alpha_i \alpha_j y_i y_j \langle x_i, x_j \rangle - \sum_i \alpha_i$ subject to constraints:

$$\eta_i \geq 0, \quad \alpha_i \geq 0 \tag{4}$$
$$C_i = \alpha_i + \eta_i \tag{5}$$
$$\sum_i \alpha_i y_i = 0 \tag{6}$$

and where the solution takes the form $w = \sum_i \alpha_i y_i x_i$, and the KKT conditions, which are satisfied at the solution, are $\eta_i \xi_i = 0$, $\alpha_i(y_i(w \cdot x_i + b) - 1 + \xi_i) = 0$, where η_i are Lagrange multipliers to enforce positivity of the ξ_i, and α_i are Lagrange multipliers to enforce the constraint (2). The η_i can be implicitly encapsulated in the condition $0 \leq \alpha_i \leq C_i$, but we retain them to emphasize that the above equations imply that whenever $\xi_i \neq 0$, we must have $\alpha_i = C_i$. Note that, for a given solution, a support vector is defined to be any point x_i for which $\alpha_i > 0$. Now suppose we have some solution to the problem (1), (2), (3). Let $\mathcal{N}_1$ denote the set $\{i : y_i = 1, w \cdot x_i + b < 1\}$, $\mathcal{N}_2$ the set $\{i : y_i = -1, w \cdot x_i + b > -1\}$, $\mathcal{N}_3$ the set $\{i : y_i = 1, w \cdot x_i + b = 1\}$, $\mathcal{N}_4$ the set $\{i : y_i = -1, w \cdot x_i + b = -1\}$, $\mathcal{N}_5$ the set $\{i : y_i = 1, w \cdot x_i + b > 1\}$, and $\mathcal{N}_6$ the set $\{i : y_i = -1, w \cdot x_i + b < -1\}$. Then we have the following theorem:

Theorem 2: The solution to the soft-margin problem, (1), (2) and (3), is unique for $p > 1$. For $p = 1$, the solution is not unique if and only if at least one of the following two conditions holds:

$$\sum_{i \in \mathcal{N}_2 \cup \mathcal{N}_4} C_i = \sum_{i \in \mathcal{N}_1} C_i \tag{7}$$

$$\sum_{i \in \mathcal{N}_1 \cup \mathcal{N}_3} C_i = \sum_{i \in \mathcal{N}_2} C_i \tag{8}$$

Furthermore, whenever the solution is not unique, all solutions share the same w, and any support vector x_i has Lagrange multiplier satisfying $\alpha_i = C_i$, and when (7)

---
[4]This is of course not a new result: see for example [3].

holds, then $\mathcal{N}_3$ contains no support vectors, and when (8) holds, then $\mathcal{N}_4$ contains no support vectors.

Proof: For the case $p > 1$, the objective function F is strictly convex, since a sum of strictly convex functions is a strictly convex function, and since the function $g(v) = v^p$, $v \in \Re_+$ is strictly convex for $p > 1$. Furthermore the constraints define a convex set, since any set of simultaneous linear inequality constraints defines a convex set. Hence by Theorem 1 the solution is unique.

For the case $p = 1$, define z to be that $d_F + l$-component vector with $z_i = w_i$, $i = 1, \cdots, d_F$, and $z_i = \xi_i$, $i = d_F + 1, \cdots, d_F + l$. In terms of the variables z, the problem is still a convex programming problem, and hence has the property that any solution is a global solution. Suppose that we have two solutions, z_1 and z_2. Then we can form the family of solutions z_t, where $z_t \equiv (1-t)z_1 + tz_2$, and since the solutions are global, we have $F(z_1) = F(z_2) = F(z_t)$. By expanding $F(z_t) - F(z_1) = 0$ in terms of z_1 and z_2 and differentiating twice with respect to t we find that $w_1 = w_2$. Now given w and b, the ξ_i are completely determined by the KKT conditions. Thus the solution is not unique if and only if b is not unique.

Define $\delta \equiv \min\{\min_{i \in \mathcal{N}_1} \xi_i, \min_{i \in \mathcal{N}_6}(-1 - w \cdot x_i - b)\}$, and suppose that condition (7) holds. Then a different solution $\{w', b', \xi'\}$ is given by $w' = w$, $b' = b + \delta$, and $\xi'_i = \xi_i - \delta$, $\forall i \in \mathcal{N}_1$, $\xi'_i = \xi_i + \delta$, $\forall i \in \mathcal{N}_2 \cup \mathcal{N}_4$, all other $\xi_i = 0$, since by construction F then remains the same, and the constraints (2), (3) are satisfied by the primed variables. Similarly, suppose that condition (8) holds. Define $\delta \equiv \min\{\min_{i \in \mathcal{N}_2} \xi_i, \min_{i \in \mathcal{N}_5}(w \cdot x_i + b - 1)\}$. Then a different solution $\{w', b', \xi'\}$ is given by $w' = w$, $b' = b - \delta$, and $\xi'_i = \xi_i - \delta$, $\forall i \in \mathcal{N}_2$, $\xi'_i = \xi_i + \delta$, $\forall i \in \mathcal{N}_1 \cup \mathcal{N}_3$, all other $\xi_i = 0$, since again by construction F is unchanged and the constraints are still met. Thus the given conditions are sufficient for the solution to be non-unique. To show necessity, assume that the solution is not unique: then by the above argument, the solutions must differ by their values of b. Given a particular solution b, suppose that $b + \delta$, $\delta > 0$ is also a solution. Since the set of solutions is itself convex, then $b + \delta'$ will also correspond to a solution for all $\delta' : 0 \le \delta' \le \delta$. Given some $b' = b + \delta'$, we can use the KKT conditions to compute all the ξ_i, and we can choose δ' sufficiently small so that no ξ_i, $i \in \mathcal{N}_6$ that was previously zero becomes nonzero. Then we find that in order that F remain the same, condition (7) must hold. If $b - \delta$, $\delta > 0$ is a solution, similar reasoning shows that condition (8) must hold. To show the final statement of the theorem, we use the equality constraint (6), together with the fact that, from the KKT conditions, all support vectors x_i with indices in $\mathcal{N}_1 \cup \mathcal{N}_2$ satisfy $\alpha_i = C_i$. Substituting (6) in (7) then gives $\sum_{\mathcal{N}_3} \alpha_i + \sum_{\mathcal{N}_4}(C_i - \alpha_i) = 0$ which implies the result, since all α_i are non-negative. Similarly, substituting (6) in (8) gives $\sum_{\mathcal{N}_3}(C_i - \alpha_i) + \sum_{\mathcal{N}_4} \alpha_i = 0$ which again implies the result. □

Corollary: For any solution which is not unique, letting $\mathcal{S}$ denote the set of indices of the corresponding set of support vectors, then we must have $\sum_{i \in \mathcal{S}} C_i y_i = 0$. Furthermore, if the number of data points is finite, then for at least one of the family of solutions, all support vectors have corresponding $\xi_i \ne 0$.

Note that it follows from the corollary that if the C_i are chosen such that there exists no subset $\mathcal{T}$ of the train data such that $\sum_{i \in \mathcal{T}} C_i y_i = 0$, then the solution is guaranteed to be unique, even if $p = 1$. Furthermore this can be done by choosing all the C_i very close to some central value C, although the resulting solution can depend sensitively on the values chosen (see the example immediately below). Finally, note that if all C_i are equal, the theorem shows that a necessary condition for the solution to be non-unique is that the negative and positive polarity support vectors be equal in number.

A simple example of a non-unique solution, for the case $p = 1$, is given by a train set in one dimension with just two examples, $\{x_1 = 1, y_1 = 1\}$ and $\{x_2 = -1, y_2 = -1\}$, with $C_1 = C_2 \equiv C$. It is straightforward to show analytically that for $C \geq \frac{1}{2}$, the solution is unique, with $w = 1$, $\xi_1 = \xi_2 = b = 0$, and margin[5] equal to 2, while for $C < \frac{1}{2}$ there is a family of solutions, with $-1 + 2C \leq b \leq 1 - 2C$ and $\xi_1 = 1 - b - 2C$, $\xi_2 = 1 + b - 2C$, and margin $1/C$. The case $C < \frac{1}{2}$ corresponds to Case (3) in Section (1) (dual unique but primal not), since the dual variables are uniquely specified by $\alpha = C$. Note also that this family of solutions also satisfies the condition that any solution is smoothly deformable into another solution [7]. If $C_1 > C_2$, the solution becomes unique, and is quite different from the unique solution found when $C_2 > C_1$. When the C's are not equal, one can interpret what happens in terms of the mechanical analogy [8], with the central separating hyperplane sliding away from the point that exerts the higher force, until that point lies on the edge of the margin region.

Note that if the solution is not unique, the possible values of b fall on an interval of the real line: in this case a suitable choice would be one that minimizes an estimate of the Bayes error, where the SVM output densities are modeled using a validation set[6]. Alternatively, requiring continuity with the cases $p > 1$, so that one would choose that value of b that would result by considering the family of solutions generated by different choices of p, and taking the limit from above of $p \to 1$, would again result in a unique solution.

3 The Case of Regression Estimation[7]

Here one has a set of l pairs $\{x_1, y_1\}, \{x_2, y_2\}, \cdots, \{x_l, y_l\}$, $\{x_i \in \mathcal{F}, y_i \in \Re\}$, and the goal is to estimate the unknown functional dependence $\hat{f}$ of the y on the x, where the function $\hat{f}$ is assumed to be related to the measurements $\{x_i, y_i\}$ by $y_i = \hat{f}(x_i) + n_i$, and where n_i represents noise. For details we refer the reader to [3], [9]. Again we generalize the original formulation [10], as follows: for some choice of positive error penalties C_i, and for positive ϵ_i, minimize

$$F = \frac{1}{2}\|w\|^2 + \sum_{i=1}^{l}(C_i \xi_i^p + C_i^* (\xi_i^*)^p) \tag{9}$$

with constant $p \in [1, \infty)$, subject to constraints

$$y_i - w \cdot x_i - b \leq \epsilon_i + \xi_i \tag{10}$$
$$w \cdot x_i + b - y_i \leq \epsilon_i + \xi_i^* \tag{11}$$
$$\xi_i^{(*)} \geq 0 \tag{12}$$

where we have adopted the notation $\xi_i^{(*)} \equiv \{\xi_i, \xi_i^*\}$ [9]. This formulation results in an "ϵ insensitive" loss function, that is, there is no penalty ($\xi_i^{(*)} = 0$) associated with point x_i if $|y_i - w \cdot x_i - b| \leq \epsilon_i$. Now let β, β^* be the Lagrange multipliers introduced to enforce the constraints (10), (11). The dual then gives

$$\sum_i \beta_i = \sum_i \beta_i^*, \quad 0 \leq \beta_i \leq C_i, \quad 0 \leq \beta_i^* \leq C_i^*, \tag{13}$$

---

[5] The margin is defined to be the distance between the two hyperplanes corresponding to equality in Eq. (2), namely $2/\|w\|$, and the margin region is defined to be the set of points between the two hyperplanes.

[6] This method was used to estimate b under similar circumstances in [8].

[7] The notation in this section only coincides with that used in section 2 where convenient.

which we will need below. For this formulation, we have the following

Theorem 3: For a given solution, define $f(x_i, y_i) \equiv y_i - w \cdot x_i - b$, and define $\mathcal{N}_1$ to be the set of indices $\{i : f(x_i, y_i) > \epsilon_i\}$, $\mathcal{N}_2$ the set $\{i : f(x_i, y_i) = \epsilon_i\}$, $\mathcal{N}_3$ the set $\{i : f(x_i, y_i) = -\epsilon_i\}$, and $\mathcal{N}_4$ the set $\{i : f(x_i, y_i) < -\epsilon_i\}$. Then the solution to (9) - (12) is unique for $p > 1$, and for $p = 1$ it is not unique if and only if at least one of the following two conditions holds:

$$\sum_{i \in \mathcal{N}_1 \cup \mathcal{N}_2} C_i = \sum_{i \in \mathcal{N}_4} C_i^* \tag{14}$$

$$\sum_{i \in \mathcal{N}_3 \cup \mathcal{N}_4} C_i^* = \sum_{i \in \mathcal{N}_1} C_i \tag{15}$$

Furthermore, whenever the solution is not unique, all solutions share the same w, and all support vectors are at bound (that is[8], either $\beta_i = C_i$ or $\beta_i^* = C_i^*$), and when (14) holds, then $\mathcal{N}_3$ contains no support vectors, and when (15) holds, then $\mathcal{N}_2$ contains no support vectors.

The theorem shows that in the non-unique case one will only be able to move the tube (and get another solution) if one does not change its normal w. A trivial example of a non-unique solution is when all the data fits inside the ϵ-tube with room to spare, in which case for all the solutions, the normal to the ϵ-tubes always lies along the y direction. Another example is when all C_i are equal, all data falls outside the tube, and there are the same number of points above the tube as below it.

4 Computing b when all SVs are at Bound

The threshold b in Eqs. (2), (10) and (11) is usually determined from that subset of the constraint equations which become equalities at the solution and for which the corresponding Lagrange multipliers are not at bound. However, it may be that at the solution, this subset is empty. In this section we consider the situation where the solution is unique, where we have solved the optimization problem and therefore know the values of all Lagrange multipliers, and hence know also w, and where we wish to find the unique value of b for this solution. Since the $\xi_i^{(*)}$ are known once b is fixed, we can find b by finding that value which both minimizes the cost term in the primal Lagrangian, and which satisfies all the constraint equations. Let us consider the pattern recognition case first. Let S_+ (S_-) denote the set of indices of positive (negative) polarity support vectors. Also let V_+ (V_-) denote the set of indices of positive (negative) vectors which are not support vectors. It is straightforward to show that if $\sum_{i \in S_-} C_i > \sum_{i \in S_+} C_i$, then $b = \max \{\max_{i \in S_-}(-1 - w \cdot x_i), \max_{i \in V_+}(1 - w \cdot x_i)\}$, while if $\sum_{i \in S_-} C_i < \sum_{i \in S_+} C_i$, then $b = \min \{\min_{i \in S_+}(1 - w \cdot x_i), \min_{i \in V_-}(-1 - w \cdot x_i)\}$. Furthermore, if $\sum_{i \in S_-} C_i = \sum_{i \in S_+} C_i$, and if the solution is unique, then these two values coincide.

In the regression case, let us denote by S the set of indices of all support vectors, $\bar{S}$ its complement, S_1 the set of indices for which $\beta_i = C_i$, and S_2 the set of indices for which $\beta_i^* = C_i^*$, so that $S = S_1 \cup S_2$ (note $S_1 \cap S_2 = \emptyset$). Then if $\sum_{i \in S_2} C_i^* > \sum_{i \in S_1} C_i$, the desired value of b is $b = \max \{\max_{i \in S}(y_i - w \cdot x_i + \epsilon_i), \max_{i \in \bar{S}}(y_i - w \cdot x_i - \epsilon_i)\}$ while if $\sum_{i \in S_2} C_i^* < \sum_{i \in S_1} C_i$, then $b = \min \{\min_{i \in S}(y_i - w \cdot x_i - \epsilon_i), \min_{i \in \bar{S}}(y_i - w \cdot x_i + \epsilon_i)\}$.

---
[8]Recall that if $\epsilon_i > 0$, then $\beta_i \beta_i^* = 0$.

Again, if the solution is unique, and if also $\sum_{i \in S_2} C_i^* = \sum_{i \in S_1} C_i$, then these two values coincide.

5 Discussion

We have shown that non-uniqueness of the SVM solution will be the exception rather than the rule: it will occur only when one can rigidly parallel transport the margin region without changing the total cost. If non-unique solutions are encountered, other techniques for finding the threshold, such as minimizing the Bayes error arising from a model of the SVM posteriors [8], will be needed. The method of proof in the above theorems is straightforward, and should be extendable to similar algorithms, for example Mangasarian's Generalized SVM [11]. In fact one can extend this result to any problem whose objective function consists of a sum of strictly convex and loosely convex functions: for example, it follows immediately that for the case of the ν-SVM pattern recognition and regression estimation algorithms [12], with arbitrary convex costs, the value of the normal w will always be unique.

Acknowledgments

C. Burges wishes to thank W. Keasler, V. Lawrence and C. Nohl of Lucent Technologies for their support.

References

[1] R. Fletcher. *Practical Methods of Optimization.* John Wiley and Sons, Inc., 2nd edition, 1987.

[2] B. E. Boser, I. M. Guyon, and V .Vapnik. A training algorithm for optimal margin classifiers. In *Fifth Annual Workshop on Computational Learning Theory*, Pittsburgh, 1992. ACM.

[3] V. Vapnik. *Statistical Learning Theory.* John Wiley and Sons, Inc., New York, 1998.

[4] A.J. Smola and B. Schölkopf. On a kernel-based method for pattern recognition, regression, approximation and operator inversion. *Algorithmica*, 22:211 – 231, 1998.

[5] Roger A. Horn and Charles R. Johnson. *Matrix Analysis.* Cambridge University Press, 1985.

[6] C. Cortes and V. Vapnik. Support vector networks. *Machine Learning*, 20:273–297, 1995.

[7] C.J.C. Burges. A tutorial on support vector machines for pattern recognition. *Data Mining and Knowledge Discovery*, 2(2):121–167, 1998.

[8] C. J. C. Burges and B. Schölkopf. Improving the accuracy and speed of support vector learning machines. In M. Mozer, M. Jordan, and T. Petsche, editors, *Advances in Neural Information Processing Systems 9*, pages 375–381, Cambridge, MA, 1997. MIT Press.

[9] A. Smola and B. Schölkopf. A tutorial on support vector regression. *Statistics and Computing*, 1998. In press: also, COLT Technical Report TR-1998-030.

[10] V. Vapnik, S. Golowich, and A. Smola. Support vector method for function approximation, regression estimation, and signal processing. *Advances in Neural Information Processing Systems*, 9:281–287, 1996.

[11] O.L. Mangarasian. Generalized support vector machines, mathematical programming technical report 98-14. Technical report, University of Wisconsin, October 1998.

[12] B. Schölkopf, A. Smola, R. Williamson and P. Bartlett, New Support Vector Algorithms, NeuroCOLT2 NC2-TR-1998-031, 1998.

Model Selection for Support Vector Machines

Olivier Chapelle*,†, Vladimir Vapnik*
* AT&T Research Labs, Red Bank, NJ
† LIP6, Paris, France
{chapelle,vlad}@research.att.com

Abstract

New functionals for parameter (model) selection of Support Vector Machines are introduced based on the concepts of the *span* of support vectors and rescaling of the feature space. It is shown that using these functionals, one can both predict the best choice of parameters of the model and the relative quality of performance for any value of parameter.

1 Introduction

Support Vector Machines (SVMs) implement the following idea : they map input vectors into a high dimensional feature space, where a maximal margin hyperplane is constructed [6]. It was shown that when training data are separable, the error rate for SVMs can be characterized by

$$h = R^2/M^2, \qquad (1)$$

where R is the radius of the smallest sphere containing the training data and M is the margin (the distance between the hyperplane and the closest training vector in feature space). This functional estimates the VC dimension of hyperplanes separating data with a given margin M.

To perform the mapping and to calculate R and M in the SVM technique, one uses a positive definite kernel $K(\mathbf{x}, \mathbf{x}')$ which specifies an inner product in feature space. An example of such a kernel is the Radial Basis Function (RBF),

$$K(\mathbf{x}, \mathbf{x}') = e^{-||\mathbf{x}-\mathbf{x}'||^2/2\sigma^2}.$$

This kernel has a free parameter σ and more generally, most kernels require some parameters to be set. When treating noisy data with SVMs, another parameter, penalizing the training errors, also needs to be set. The problem of choosing the values of these parameters which minimize the expectation of test error is called the model selection problem.

It was shown that the parameter of the kernel that minimizes functional (1) provides a good choice for the model : the minimum for this functional coincides with the minimum of the test error [1]. However, the shapes of these curves can be different.

In this article we introduce refined functionals that not only specify the best choice of parameters (both the parameter of the kernel and the parameter penalizing training error), but also produce curves which better reflect the actual error rate.

Model Selection for Support Vector Machines

The paper is organized as follows. Section 2 describes the basics of SVMs, section 3 introduces a new functional based on the concept of the span of support vectors, section 4 considers the idea of rescaling data in feature space and section 5 discusses experiments of model selection with these functionals.

2 Support Vector Learning

We introduce some standard notation for SVMs; for a complete description, see [6]. Let $(\mathbf{x}_i, y_i)_{1 \leq i \leq \ell}$ be a set of training examples, $\mathbf{x}_i \in \mathbb{R}^n$ which belong to a class labeled by $y_i \in \{-1, 1\}$. The decision function given by a SVM is :

$$f(\mathbf{x}) = sgn \left(\sum_{i=1}^{\ell} \alpha_i^0 y_i K(\mathbf{x}_i, \mathbf{x}) + b \right), \tag{2}$$

where the coefficients α_i^0 are obtained by maximizing the following functional :

$$W(\alpha) = \sum_{i=1}^{\ell} \alpha_i - \frac{1}{2} \sum_{i,j=1}^{\ell} \alpha_i \alpha_j y_i y_j K(\mathbf{x}_i, \mathbf{x}_j) \tag{3}$$

under constraints

$$\sum_{i=1}^{\ell} \alpha_i y_i = 0 \text{ and } 0 \leq \alpha_i \leq C \ \ i = 1, ..., \ell.$$

C is a constant which controls the tradeoff between the complexity of the decision function and the number of training examples misclassified. SVM are linear maximal margin classifiers in a high-dimensional feature space where the data are mapped through a non-linear function $\Phi(\mathbf{x})$ such that $\Phi(\mathbf{x}_i) \cdot \Phi(\mathbf{x}_j) = K(\mathbf{x}_i, \mathbf{x}_j)$.

The points $\mathbf{x}_i$ with $\alpha_i > 0$ are called support vectors. We distinguish between those with $0 < \alpha_i < C$ and those with $\alpha_i = C$. We call them respectively support vectors of the first and second category.

3 Prediction using the span of support vectors

The results introduced in this section are based on the leave-one-out cross-validation estimate. This procedure is usually used to estimate the probability of test error of a learning algorithm.

3.1 The leave-one-out procedure

The *leave-one-out* procedure consists of removing from the training data one element, constructing the decision rule on the basis of the remaining training data and then testing the removed element. In this fashion one tests all ℓ elements of the training data (using ℓ different decision rules). Let us denote the number of errors in the leave-one-out procedure by $\mathcal{L}(\mathbf{x}_1, y_1, ..., \mathbf{x}_\ell, y_\ell)$. It is known [6] that the the leave-one-out procedure gives an almost unbiased estimate of the probability of test error : the expectation of test error for the machine trained on $\ell - 1$ examples is equal to the expectation of $\frac{1}{\ell}\mathcal{L}(\mathbf{x}_1, y_1, ..., \mathbf{x}_\ell, y_\ell)$.

We now provide an analysis of the number of errors made by the leave-one-out procedure. For this purpose, we introduce a new concept, called the *span* of support vectors [7].

3.2 Span of support vectors

Since the results presented in this section do not depend on the feature space, we will consider without any loss of generality, linear SVMs, i.e. $K(\mathbf{x}_i, \mathbf{x}_j) = \mathbf{x}_i \cdot \mathbf{x}_j$.

Suppose that $\boldsymbol{\alpha}^0 = (\alpha_1^0, ..., \alpha_n^0)$ is the solution of the optimization problem (3).

For any fixed support vector $\mathbf{x}_p$ we define the set Λ_p as constrained linear combinations of the support vectors of the first category $(\mathbf{x}_i)_{i \neq p}$:

$$\Lambda_p = \left\{ \sum_{\{i \neq p/\ 0 < \alpha_i^0 < C\}}^{\ell} \lambda_i \mathbf{x}_i, \quad \sum_{i=1,\ i \neq p}^{\ell} \lambda_i = 1,\ 0 \leq \alpha_i^0 + y_i y_p \alpha_p^0 \lambda_i \leq C \right\}. \quad (4)$$

Note that λ_i can be less than 0.

We also define the quantity S_p, which we call the *span* of the support vector $\mathbf{x}_p$ as the minimum distance between $\mathbf{x}_p$ and this set (see figure 1)

$$S_p^2 = d^2(\mathbf{x}_p, \Lambda_p) = \min_{\mathbf{x} \in \Lambda_p} (\mathbf{x}_p - \mathbf{x})^2. \quad (5)$$

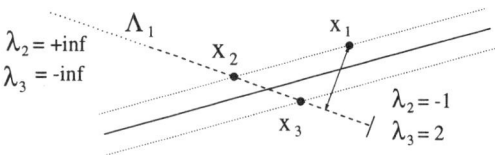

Figure 1: *Three support vectors with $\alpha_1 = \alpha_2 = \alpha_3/2$. The set Λ_1 is the semi-opened dashed line.*

It was shown in [7] that the set Λ_p is not empty and that $S_p = d(\mathbf{x}_p, \Lambda_p) \leq D_{SV}$, where D_{SV} is the diameter of the smallest sphere containing the support vectors.

Intuitively, the smaller $S_p = d(\mathbf{x}_p, \Lambda_p)$ is, the less likely the leave-one-out procedure is to make an error on the vector $\mathbf{x}_p$. Formally, the following theorem holds :

Theorem 1 *[7] If in the leave-one-out procedure a support vector $\mathbf{x}_p$ corresponding to $0 < \alpha_p < C$ is recognized incorrectly, then the following inequality holds*

$$\alpha_p^0 \geq \frac{1}{S_p \max(D, 1/\sqrt{C})}.$$

This theorem implies that in the separable case ($C = \infty$), the number of errors made by the leave-one-out procedure is bounded as follows : $\mathcal{L}(\mathbf{x}_1, y_1, ..., \mathbf{x}_\ell, y_\ell) \leq \sum_p \alpha_p^0 \max_p S_p D = \max_p S_p D/M^2$, because $\sum \alpha_p^0 = 1/M^2$ [6]. This is already an improvement compared to functional (1), since $S_p \leq D_{SV}$. But depending on the geometry of the support vectors the value of the span S_p can be much less than the diameter D_{SV} of the support vectors and can even be equal to zero.

We can go further under the assumption that the set of support vectors does not change during the leave-one-out procedure, which leads us to the following theorem :

Theorem 2 *If the sets of support vectors of first and second categories remain the same during the leave-one-out procedure, then for any support vector $\mathbf{x}_p$, the following equality holds :*

$$y_p[f^0(\mathbf{x}_p) - f^p(\mathbf{x}_p)] = \alpha_p^0 S_p^2$$

where f^0 and f^p are the decision function (2) given by the SVM trained respectively on the whole training set and after the point $\mathbf{x}_p$ has been removed.

The proof of the theorem follows the one of Theorem 1 in [7].

The assumption that the set of support vectors does not change during the leave-one-out procedure is obviously not satisfied in most cases. Nevertheless, the proportion of points which violate this assumption is usually small compared to the number of support vectors. In this case, Theorem 2 provides a good approximation of the result of the leave-one procedure, as pointed out by the experiments (see Section 5.1, figure 2).

As already noticed in [1], the larger α_p is, the more "important" in the decision function the support vector $\mathbf{x}_p$ is. Thus, it is not surprising that removing a point $\mathbf{x}_p$ causes a change in the decision function proportional to its Lagrange multiplier α_p. The same kind of result as Theorem 2 has also been derived in [2], where for SVMs without threshold, the following inequality has been derived : $y_p(f^0(\mathbf{x}_p) - f^p(\mathbf{x}_p)) \leq \alpha_p^0 K(\mathbf{x}_p, \mathbf{x}_p)$. The span S_p takes into account the geometry of the support vectors in order to get a precise notion of how "important" is a given point.

The previous theorem enables us to compute the number of errors made by the leave-one-out procedure :

Corollary 1 *Under the assumption of Theorem 2, the test error prediction given by the leave-one-out procedure is*

$$t_\ell = \frac{1}{\ell}\mathcal{L}(\mathbf{x}_1, y_1, ..., \mathbf{x}_\ell, y_\ell) = \frac{1}{\ell} Card\{p/\ \alpha_p^0 S_p^2 \geq y_p f^0(\mathbf{x}_p)\} \qquad (6)$$

Note that points which are not support vectors are correctly classified by the leave-one-out procedure. Therefore t_ℓ defines the number of errors of the leave-one-out procedure on the entire training set.

Under the assumption in Theorem 2, the box constraints in the definition of Λ_p (4) can be removed. Moreover, if we consider only hyperplanes passing through the origin, the constraint $\sum \lambda_i = 1$ can also be removed. Therefore, under those assumptions, the computation of the span S_p is an unconstrained minimization of a quadratic form and can be done analytically. For support vectors of the first category, this leads to the closed form $S_p^2 = 1/(K_{SV}^{-1})_{pp}$, where K_{SV} is the matrix of dot products between support vectors of the first category. A similar result has also been obtained in [3].

In Section 5, we use the span-rule (6) for model selection in both separable and non-separable cases.

4 Rescaling

As we already mentioned, functional (1) bounds the VC dimension of a linear margin classifier. This bound is tight when the data almost "fills" the surface of the sphere enclosing the training data, but when the data lie on a flat ellipsoid, this bound is poor since the radius of the sphere takes into account only the components with the largest deviations. The idea we present here is to make a rescaling of our data in feature space such that the radius of the sphere stays constant but the margin increases, and then apply this bound to our rescaled data and hyperplane.

Let us first consider linear SVMs, i.e. without any mapping in a high dimensional space. The rescaling can be achieved by computing the covariance matrix of our data and rescaling according to its eigenvalues. Suppose our data are centered and let $(\varphi_1, \ldots, \varphi_n)$ be the normalized eigenvectors of the covariance matrix of our data. We can then compute the smallest enclosing box containing our data, centered at the origin and whose edges are parallels to $(\varphi_1, \ldots, \varphi_n)$. This box is an approximation of the smallest enclosing ellipsoid. The length of the edge in the direction φ_k is $\mu_k = \max_i |\mathbf{x}_i \cdot \varphi_k|$. The rescaling consists of the following diagonal transformation :

$$D : \mathbf{x} \longrightarrow D\mathbf{x} = \sum_k \mu_k (\mathbf{x} \cdot \varphi_k) \, \varphi_k.$$

Let us consider $\tilde{\mathbf{x}}_i = D^{-1} \mathbf{x}_i$ and $\tilde{\mathbf{w}} = D\mathbf{w}$. The decision function is not changed under this transformation since $\tilde{\mathbf{w}} \cdot \tilde{\mathbf{x}}_i = \mathbf{w} \cdot \mathbf{x}_i$ and the data $\tilde{\mathbf{x}}_i$ fill a box of side length 1. Thus, in functional (1), we replace R^2 by 1 and $1/M^2$ by $\tilde{\mathbf{w}}^2$. Since we rescaled our data in a box, we actually estimated the radius of the enclosing ball using the ℓ_∞-norm instead of the classical ℓ_2-norm. Further theoretical works needs to be done to justify this change of norm.

In the non-linear case, note that even if we map our data in a high dimensional feature space, they lie in the linear subspace spanned by these data. Thus, if the number of training data ℓ is not too large, we can work in this subspace of dimension at most ℓ. For this purpose, one can use the tools of kernel PCA [5] : if A is the matrix of normalized eigenvectors of the Gram matrix $K_{ij} = K(\mathbf{x}_i, \mathbf{x}_j)$ and (λ_i) the eigenvalues, the dot product $\mathbf{x}_i \cdot \varphi_k$ is replaced by $\sqrt{\lambda_k} A_{ik}$ and $\mathbf{w} \cdot \varphi_k$ becomes $\sqrt{\lambda_k} \sum_i A_{ik} y_i \alpha_i$. Thus, we can still achieve the diagonal transformation A and finally functional (1) becomes

$$\sum_k \lambda_k^2 \max_i A_{ik}^2 (\sum_i A_{ik} y_i \alpha_i)^2.$$

5 Experiments

To check these new methods, we performed two series of experiments. One concerns the choice of σ, the width of the RBF kernel, on a linearly separable database, the postal database. This dataset consists of 7291 handwritten digit of size 16x16 with a test set of 2007 examples. Following [4], we split the training set in 23 subsets of 317 training examples. Our task consists of separating digit 0 to 4 from 5 to 9. Error bars in figures 2a and 3 are standard deviations over the 23 trials. In another experiment, we try to choose the optimal value of C in a noisy database, the breast-cancer database[1]. The dataset has been split randomly 100 times into a training set containing 200 examples and a test set containing 77 examples.

Section 5.1 describes experiments of model selection using the span-rule (6), both in the separable case and in the non-separable one, while Section 5.2 shows VC bounds for model selection in the separable case both with and without rescaling.

5.1 Model selection using the span-rule

In this section, we use the prediction of test error derived from the span-rule (6) for model selection. Figure 2a shows the test error and the prediction given by the span for different values of the width σ of the RBF kernel on the postal database. Figure 2b plots the same functions for different values of C on the breast-cancer database. We can see that the method predicts the correct value of the minimum. Moreover, the prediction is very accurate and the curves are almost identical.

---

[1]Available from http://horn.first.gmd.de/~raetsch/data/breast-cancer

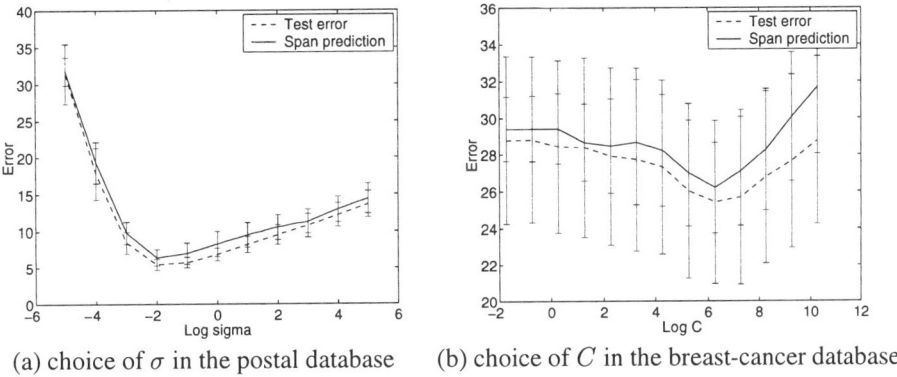

(a) choice of σ in the postal database   (b) choice of C in the breast-cancer database

Figure 2: *Test error and its prediction using the span-rule (6).*

The computation of the span-rule (6) involves computing the span S_p (5) for every support vector. Note, however, that we are interested in the inequality $S_p^2 \leq y_p f(\mathbf{x}_p)/\alpha_p^0$, rather than the exact value of the span S_p. Thus, while minimizing $S_p = d(\mathbf{x}_p, \Lambda_p)$, if we find a point $\mathbf{x}^* \in \Lambda_p$ such that $d(\mathbf{x}_p, \mathbf{x}^*)^2 \leq y_p f(\mathbf{x}_p)/\alpha_p^0$, we can stop the minimization because this point will be correctly classified by the leave-one-out procedure.

It turned out in the experiments that the time required to compute the span was not prohibitive, since it is was about the same than the training time.

There is a noteworthy extension in the application of the span concept. If we denote by θ one hyperparameter of the kernel and if the derivative $\frac{\partial K(\mathbf{x}_i, \mathbf{x}_j)}{\partial \theta}$ is computable, then it is possible to compute analytically $\frac{\partial \sum \alpha_i S_i^2 - y_i f^0(\mathbf{x}_i)}{\partial \theta}$, which is the derivative of an upper bound of the number of errors made by the leave-one-out procedure (see Theorem 2). This provides us a more powerful technique in model selection. Indeed, our initial approach was to choose the value of the width σ of the RBF kernel according to the minimum of the span-rule. In our case, there was only hyperparamter so it was possible to try different values of σ. But, if we have several hyperparameters, for example one σ per component, $K(\mathbf{x}, \mathbf{x}') = e^{-\sum_k \frac{(\mathbf{x}_k - \mathbf{x}'_k)^2}{2\sigma_k^2}}$, it is not possible to do an exhaustive search on all the possible values of of the hyperparameters. Nevertheless, the previous remark enables us to find their optimal value by a classical gradient descent approach.

Preliminary results seem to show that using this approach with the previously mentioned kernel improve the test error significantely.

5.2 VC dimension with rescaling

In this section, we perform model selection on the postal database using functional (1) and its rescaled version. Figure 3a shows the values of the classical bound R^2/M^2 for different values of σ. This bound predicts the correct value for the minimum, but does not reflect the actual test error. This is easily understandable since for large values of σ, the data in input space tend to be mapped in a very flat ellipsoid in feature space, a fact which is not taken into account [4]. Figure 3b shows that by performing a rescaling of our data, we manage to have a much tighter bound and this curve reflects the actual test error, given in figure 2a.

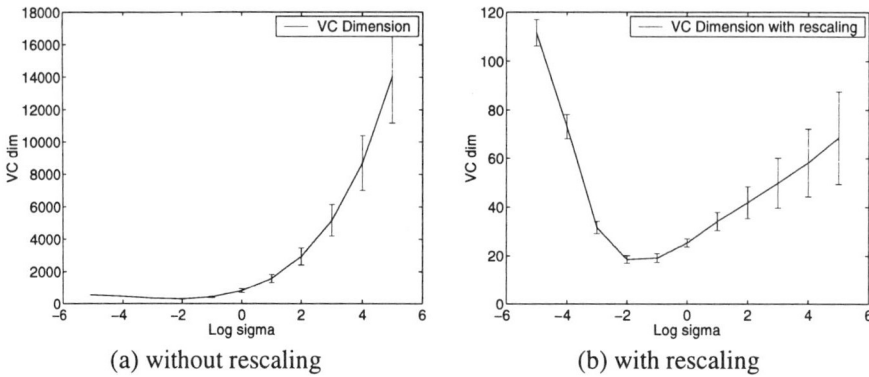

(a) without rescaling   (b) with rescaling

Figure 3: *Bound on the VC dimension for different values of σ on the postal database. The shape of the curve with rescaling is very similar to the test error on figure 2.*

6 Conclusion

In this paper, we introduced two new techniques of model selection for SVMs. One is based on the span, the other is based on rescaling of the data in feature space. We demonstrated that using these techniques, one can both predict optimal values for the parameters of the model and evaluate relative performances for different values of the parameters. These functionals can also lead to new learning techniques as they establish that generalization ability is not only due to margin.

Acknowledgments

The authors would like to thank Jason Weston and Patrick Haffner for helpfull discussions and comments.

References

[1] C. J. C. Burges. A tutorial on support vector machines for pattern recognition. *Data Mining and Knowledge Discovery*, 2(2):121–167, 1998.

[2] T. S. Jaakkola and D. Haussler. Probabilistic kernel regression models. In *Proceedings of the 1999 Conference on AI and Statistics*, 1999.

[3] M. Opper and O. Winther. Gaussian process classification and SVM: Mean field results and leave-one-out estimator. In *Advances in Large Margin Classifiers*. MIT Press, 1999. to appear.

[4] B. Schölkopf, J. Shawe-Taylor, A. J. Smola, and R. C. Williamson. Kernel-dependent Support Vector error bounds. In *Ninth International Conference on Artificial Neural Networks*, pp. 304 - 309

[5] B. Schölkopf, A. Smola, and K.-R. Müller. Kernel principal component analysis. In *Artificial Neural Networks — ICANN'97*, pages 583 – 588, Berlin, 1997. Springer Lecture Notes in Computer Science, Vol. 1327.

[6] V. Vapnik. *Statistical Learning Theory*. Wiley, New York, 1998.

[7] V. Vapnik and O. Chapelle. Bounds on error expectation for SVM. *Neural Computation*, 1999. Submitted.

Dynamics of Supervised Learning with Restricted Training Sets and Noisy Teachers

A.C.C. Coolen
Dept of Mathematics
King's College London
The Strand, London WC2R 2LS, UK
tcoolen@mth.kcl.ac.uk

C.W.H. Mace
Dept of Mathematics
King's College London
The Strand, London WC2R 2LS, UK
cmace@mth.kcl.ac.uk

Abstract

We generalize a recent formalism to describe the dynamics of supervised learning in layered neural networks, in the regime where data recycling is inevitable, to the case of noisy teachers. Our theory generates reliable predictions for the evolution in time of training- and generalization errors, and extends the class of mathematically solvable learning processes in large neural networks to those situations where overfitting can occur.

1 Introduction

Tools from statistical mechanics have been used successfully over the last decade to study the dynamics of learning in layered neural networks (for reviews see e.g. [1] or [2]). The simplest theories result upon assuming the data set to be much larger than the number of weight updates made, which rules out recycling and ensures that any distribution of relevance will be Gaussian. Unfortunately, both in terms of applications and in terms of mathematical interest, this regime is not the most relevant one. Most complications and peculiarities in the dynamics of learning arise precisely due to data recycling, which creates for the system the possibility to improve performance by memorizing answers rather than by learning an underlying rule. The dynamics of learning with restricted training sets was first studied analytically in [3] (linear learning rules) and [4] (systems with binary weights). The latter studies were ahead of their time, and did not get the attention they deserved just because at that stage even the simpler learning dynamics without data recycling had not yet been studied. More recently attention has moved back to the dynamics of learning in the recycling regime. Some studies aimed at developing a general theory [5, 6, 7], some at finding exact solutions for special cases [8]. All general theories published so far have in common that they as yet considered realizable scenario's: the rule to be learned was implementable by the student, and overfitting could not yet occur. The next hurdle is that where restricted training sets are combined with unrealizable rules. Again some have turned to non-typical but solvable cases, involving Hebbian rules and noisy [9] or 'reverse wedge' teachers [10]. More recently the cavity method has been used to build a general theory [11] (as yet for batch learning only). In this paper we generalize the general theory launched in [6, 5, 7], which applies to arbitrary learning rules, to the case of noisy teachers. We will mirror closely the presentation in [6] (dealing with the simpler case of noise-free teachers), and we refer to [5, 7] for background reading on the ideas behind the formalism.

2 Definitions

As in [6, 5] we restrict ourselves for simplicity to perceptrons. A student perceptron operates a linear separation, parametrised by a weight vector $J \in \Re^N$:

$$S : \{-1, 1\}^N \to \{-1, 1\} \qquad S(\xi) = \mathrm{sgn}\,[J \cdot \xi]$$

It aims to emulate a teacher operating a similar rule, which, however, is characterized by a variable weight vector $B \in \Re^N$, drawn at random from a distribution $P(B)$ such as

$$\text{output noise}: \qquad P(B) = \lambda \delta[B + B^\star] + (1 - \lambda)\delta[B - B^\star] \qquad (1)$$

$$\text{Gaussian weight noise}: \qquad P(B) = [\Sigma\sqrt{2\pi}/N]^{-N}\, e^{-\frac{1}{2}N(B - B^\star)^2/\Sigma^2} \qquad (2)$$

The parameters λ and Σ control the amount of teacher noise, with the noise-free teacher $B = B^\star$ recovered in the limits $\lambda \to 0$ and $\Sigma \to 0$. The student modifies J iteratively, using examples of input vectors ξ which are drawn at random from a fixed (randomly composed) training set containing $p = \alpha N$ vectors $\xi^\mu \in \{-1, 1\}^N$ with $\alpha > 0$, and the corresponding values of the teacher outputs. We choose the teacher noise to be consistent, i.e. the answer given by the teacher to a question ξ^μ will remain the same when that particular question re-appears during the learning process. Thus $T(\xi^\mu) = \mathrm{sgn}[B^\mu \cdot \xi^\mu]$, with p teacher weight vectors B^μ, drawn randomly and independently from $P(B)$, and we generalize the training set accordingly to $\tilde{D} = \{(\xi^1, B^1), \ldots, (\xi^p, B^p)\}$. Consistency of teacher noise is natural in terms of applications, and a prerequisite for overfitting phenomena. Averages over the training set will be denoted as $\langle \ldots \rangle_{\tilde{D}}$; averages over all possible input vectors $\xi \in \{-1, 1\}^N$ as $\langle \ldots \rangle_\xi$. We analyze two classes of learning rules, of the form $J(\ell+1) = J(\ell) + \Delta J(\ell)$:

$$\begin{aligned}\text{on-line}: \quad & \Delta J(\ell) = \tfrac{\eta}{N}\{\xi(\ell)\,\mathcal{G}\,[J(\ell)\cdot\xi(\ell), B(\ell)\cdot\xi(\ell)] - \gamma J(\ell)\} \\ \text{batch}: \quad & \Delta J(\ell) = \tfrac{\eta}{N}\{\langle \xi\,\mathcal{G}\,[J(\ell)\cdot\xi, B\cdot\xi]\rangle_{\tilde{D}} - \gamma J(m)\}\end{aligned} \qquad (3)$$

In on-line learning one draws at each step ℓ a question/answer pair $(\xi(\ell), B(\ell))$ at random from the training set. In batch learning one iterates a deterministic map which is an average over all data in the training set. Our performance measures are the training- and generalization errors, defined as follows (with the step function $\theta[x > 0] = 1$, $\theta[x < 0] = 0$):

$$E_\mathrm{t}(J) = \langle \theta[-(J\cdot\xi)(B\cdot\xi)]\rangle_{\tilde{D}} \qquad E_\mathrm{g}(J) = \langle \theta[-(J\cdot\xi)(B^\star\cdot\xi)]\rangle_\xi \qquad (4)$$

We introduce macroscopic observables, taylored to the present problem, generalizing [5, 6]:

$$Q[J] = J^2, \qquad R[J] = J\cdot B^\star, \qquad P[x, y, z; J] = \langle \delta[x - J\cdot\xi]\delta[y - B^\star\cdot\xi]\delta[z - B\cdot\xi]\rangle_{\tilde{D}} \qquad (5)$$

As in [5, 6] we eliminate technical subtleties by assuming the number of arguments (x, y, z) for which $P[x, y, z; J]$ is evaluated to go to infinity after the limit $N \to \infty$ has been taken.

3 Derivation of Macroscopic Laws

Upon generalizing the calculations in [6, 5], one finds for on-line learning:

$$\frac{d}{dt}Q = 2\eta\int dxdydz\, P[x, y, z]\, x\mathcal{G}[x, z] - 2\eta\gamma Q + \eta^2\int dxdydz\, P[x, y, z]\,\mathcal{G}^2[x, z] \qquad (6)$$

$$\frac{d}{dt}R = \eta\int dxdydz\, P[x, y, z]\, y\mathcal{G}[x, z] - \eta\gamma R \qquad (7)$$

$$\frac{\partial}{\partial t}P[x, y, z] = \frac{1}{\alpha}\int dx'\, P[x', y, z]\,\{\delta[x - x' - \eta G[x', z]] - \delta[x - x']\}$$

$$-\eta\frac{\partial}{\partial x}\int dx'dy'dz'\int dx'dy'dz'\,\mathcal{G}[x', z]\mathcal{A}[x, y, z; x', y', z'] + \eta\gamma\frac{\partial}{\partial x}\{xP[x, y, z]\}$$

$$+\frac{1}{2}\eta^2\int dx'dy'dz'\, P[x', y', z']\mathcal{G}^2[x', z']\frac{\partial^2}{\partial x^2}P[x, y, z] \qquad (8)$$

The complexity of the problem is concentrated in a Green's function:
$$\mathcal{A}[x,y,z;x',y',z'] = \lim_{N\to\infty}$$
$$\langle\langle\langle[1-\delta_{\xi\xi'}]\delta[x-\boldsymbol{J}\cdot\boldsymbol{\xi}]\delta[y-\boldsymbol{B}^\star\cdot\boldsymbol{\xi}]\delta[z-\boldsymbol{B}\cdot\boldsymbol{\xi}](\boldsymbol{\xi}\cdot\boldsymbol{\xi}')\delta[x'-\boldsymbol{J}\cdot\boldsymbol{\xi}']\delta[y'-\boldsymbol{B}^\star\cdot\boldsymbol{\xi}']\delta[y'-\boldsymbol{B}\cdot\boldsymbol{\xi}']\rangle_{\tilde{D}}\rangle_{\tilde{D}}\rangle_{\text{QRP};t}$$

It involves a conditional average of the form $\langle K[\boldsymbol{J}]\rangle_{\text{QRP};t} = \int d\boldsymbol{J}\, p_t(\boldsymbol{J}|Q,R,P) K[\boldsymbol{J}]$, with

$$p_t(\boldsymbol{J}|Q,R,P) = \frac{p_t(\boldsymbol{J})\, \delta[Q-Q[\boldsymbol{J}]]\delta[R-R[\boldsymbol{J}]]\prod_{xyz}\delta[P[x,y,z]-P[x,y,z;\boldsymbol{J}]]}{\int d\boldsymbol{J}\, p_t(\boldsymbol{J})\, \delta[Q-Q[\boldsymbol{J}]]\delta[R-R[\boldsymbol{J}]]\prod_{xyz}\delta[P[x,y,z]-P[x,y,z;\boldsymbol{J}]]}$$

in which $p_t(\boldsymbol{J})$ is the weight probability density at time t. The solution of (6,7,8) can be used to generate the $N\to\infty$ performance measures (4) at any time:

$$E_t = \int dx\,dy\,dz\, P[x,y,z]\theta[-xz] \qquad E_g = \pi^{-1}\arccos[R/\sqrt{Q}] \qquad (9)$$

Expansion of these equations in powers of η, and retaining only the terms linear in η, gives the corresponding equations describing batch learning. So far this analysis is exact.

4 Closure of Macroscopic Laws

As in [6, 5] we close our macroscopic laws (6,7,8) by making the two key assumptions underlying dynamical replica theory:

(i) For $N\to\infty$ our macroscopic observables obey *closed* dynamic equations.

(ii) These equations are self-averaging with respect to the specific realization of $\tilde{D}$.

(i) implies that probability variations within $\{Q,R,P\}$ subshells are either absent or irrelevant to the macroscopic laws. We may thus make the simplest choice for $p_t(\boldsymbol{J}|Q,R,P)$:

$$p_t(\boldsymbol{J}|Q,R,P) \to \delta[Q-Q[\boldsymbol{J}]]\,\delta[R-R[\boldsymbol{J}]]\prod_{xyz}\delta[P[x,y,z]-P[x,y,z;\boldsymbol{J}]] \qquad (10)$$

The procedure (10) leads to exact laws if our observables $\{Q,R,P\}$ indeed obey closed equations for $N\to\infty$. It is a maximum entropy approximation if not. (ii) allows us to average the macroscopic laws over all training sets; it is observed in simulations, and proven using the formalism of [4]. Our assumptions (10) result in the closure of (6,7,8), since now the Green's function can be written in terms of $\{Q,R,P\}$. The final ingredient of dynamical replica theory is doing the average of fractions with the replica identity

$$\left\langle \frac{\int d\boldsymbol{J}\, W[\boldsymbol{J}|\tilde{D}]G[\boldsymbol{J}|\tilde{D}]}{\int d\boldsymbol{J}\, W[\boldsymbol{J}|\tilde{D}]}\right\rangle_{\text{sets}} = \lim_{n\to 0}\int d\boldsymbol{J}^1\cdots d\boldsymbol{J}^n\, \langle G[\boldsymbol{J}^1|\tilde{D}]\prod_{\alpha=1}^n W[\boldsymbol{J}^\alpha|\tilde{D}]\rangle_{\text{sets}}$$

Our problem has been reduced to calculating (non-trivial) integrals and averages. One finds that $P[x,y,z] = P[x,z|y]P[y]$ with $P[y] = (2\pi)^{-\frac{1}{2}}\exp[-\frac{1}{2}y^2]$. With the short-hands $Dy = P[y]dy$ and $\langle f(x,y,z)\rangle = \int Dy\,dx\,dz\, P[x,z|y]f(x,y,z)$ we can write the resulting macroscopic laws, for the case of output noise (1), in the following compact way:

$$\frac{d}{dt}Q = 2\eta(V-\gamma Q) + \eta^2 Z \qquad \frac{d}{dt}R = \eta(W-\gamma R) \qquad (11)$$

$$\frac{\partial}{\partial t}P[x,z|y] = \frac{1}{\alpha}\int dx'\, P[x',z|y]\left\{\delta[x-x'-\eta G[x',z]]-\delta[x-x']\right\} + \frac{1}{2}\eta^2 Z\frac{\partial^2}{\partial x^2}P[x,z|y]$$

$$-\eta\frac{\partial}{\partial x}\left\{P[x,z|y]\left[U(x-Ry)+Wy-\gamma x+[V-RW-(Q-R^2)U]\Phi[x,y,z]\right]\right\} \qquad (12)$$

with
$$U = \langle\Phi[x,y,z]\mathcal{G}[x,z]\rangle, \quad V = \langle x\mathcal{G}[x,z]\rangle, \quad W = \langle y\mathcal{G}[x,z]\rangle, \quad Z = \langle\mathcal{G}^2[x,z]\rangle$$

The solution of (12) is at any time of the following form:

$$P[x,z|y] = (1-\lambda)\delta[y-z]P^+[x|y] + \lambda\delta[y+z]P^-[x|y] \qquad (13)$$

Finding the function $\Phi[x,y,z]$ (in replica symmetric ansatz) requires solving a saddle-point problem for a scalar observable q and two functions $M^\pm[x|y]$. Upon introducing

$$B = \frac{\sqrt{qQ-R^2}}{Q(1-q)} \qquad \langle f[x,y]\rangle_\star^\pm = \frac{\int dx\, M^\pm[x|y]e^{Bxs}f[x,y]}{\int dx\, M^\pm[x|y]e^{Bxs}}$$

(with $\int dx\, M^\pm[x|y] = 1$ for all y) the saddle-point equations acquire the form

$$\text{for all } X, y: \qquad P^\pm[X|y] = \int Ds\, \langle\delta[X-x]\rangle_\star^\pm \tag{14}$$

$$\langle(x-Ry)^2\rangle + (qQ-R^2)[1-\frac{1}{\alpha}] = \frac{qQ+Q-2R^2}{\sqrt{qQ-R^2}}\int Dy Ds\, s[(1-\lambda)\langle x\rangle_\star^+ + \lambda\langle x\rangle_\star^-] \tag{15}$$

The equations (14) which determine $M^\pm[x|y]$ have the same structure as the corresponding (single) equation in [5, 6], so the proofs in [5, 6] again apply, and the solutions $M^\pm[x|y]$, given a q in the physical range $q \in [R^2/Q, 1]$, are unique. The function $\Phi[x,y,z]$ is then given by

$$\Phi[X,y,z] = \int \frac{Ds\, s}{\sqrt{qQ-R^2}P[X,z|y]}\left\{(1-\lambda)\delta[z-y]\langle\delta[X-x]\rangle_\star^+ + \lambda\delta[z+y]\langle\delta[X-x]\rangle_\star^-\right\} \tag{16}$$

Working out predictions from these equations is generally CPU-intensive, mainly due to the functional saddle-point equation (14) to be solved at each time step. However, as in [7] one can construct useful approximations of the theory, with increasing complexity:

(i) Large α approximation (giving the simplest theory, without saddle-point equations)
(ii) Conditionally Gaussian approximation for $M[x|y]$ (with y-dependent moments)
(iii) Annealed approximation of the functional saddle-point equation

5 Benchmark Tests: The Limits $\alpha \to \infty$ and $\lambda \to 0$

We first show that in the limit $\alpha \to \infty$ our theory reduces to the simple (Q,R) formalism of infinite training sets, as worked out for noisy teachers in [12]. Upon making the ansatz

$$P^\pm[x|y] = P[x|y] = [2\pi(Q-R^2)]^{-\frac{1}{2}}e^{-\frac{1}{2}[x-Ry]^2/(Q-R^2)} \tag{17}$$

one finds

$$M^\pm[x|y] = P[x|y], \qquad q = R^2/Q, \qquad \Phi[x,y,z] = (x-Ry)/(Q-R^2)$$

Insertion of our ansatz into (12), followed by rearranging of terms and usage of the above expression for $\Phi[x,y,z]$, shows that (12) is satisfied. The remaining equations (11) involve only averages over the Gaussian distribution (17), and indeed reduce to those of [12]:

$$\frac{1}{\eta}\frac{d}{dt}Q = (1-\lambda)\left\{2\langle x\mathcal{G}[x,y]\rangle + \eta\langle\mathcal{G}^2[x,y]\rangle\right\} + \lambda\left\{2\langle x\mathcal{G}[x,-y]\rangle + \eta\langle\mathcal{G}^2[x,-y]\rangle\right\} - 2\gamma Q$$

$$\frac{1}{\eta}\frac{d}{dt}R = (1-\lambda)\langle y\mathcal{G}[x,y]\rangle + \lambda\langle y\mathcal{G}[x,-y]\rangle - \gamma R$$

Next we turn to the limit $\lambda \to 0$ (restricted training sets & noise-free teachers) and show that here our theory reproduces the formalism of [6, 5]. Now we make the following ansatz:

$$P^+[x|y] = P[x|y], \qquad P[x,z|y] = \delta[z-y]P[x|y] \tag{18}$$

Insertion shows that for $\lambda = 0$ solutions of this form indeed solve our equations, giving $\Phi[x,y,z] \to \Phi[x,y]$ and $M^+[x|y] = M[x|y]$, and leaving us exactly with the formalism of [6, 5] describing the case of noise-free teachers and restricted training sets (apart from some new terms due to the presence of weight decay, which was absent in [6, 5]).

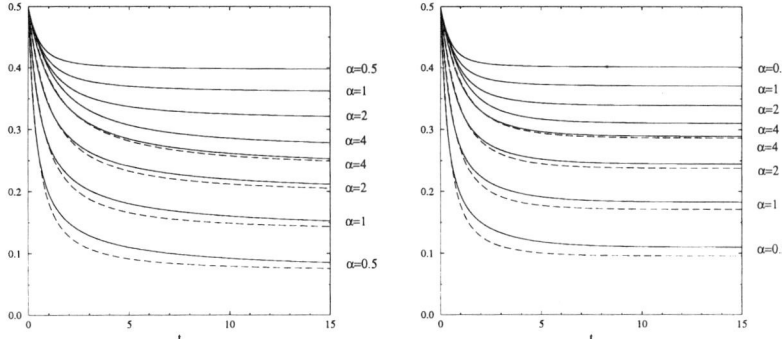

Figure 1: On-line Hebbian learning: conditionally Gaussian approximation versus exact solution in [9] ($\eta = 1$, $\lambda = 0.2$). Left: $\gamma = 0.1$, right: $\gamma = 0.5$. Solid lines: approximated theory, dashed lines: exact result. Upper curves: E_g as functions of time (here the two theories agree), lower curves: E_t as functions of time.

6 Benchmark Tests: Hebbian Learning

The special case of Hebbian learning, i.e. $\mathcal{G}[x, z] = \text{sgn}(z)$, can be solved exactly at any time, for arbitrary $\{\alpha, \lambda, \gamma\}$ [9], providing yet another excellent benchmark for our theory. For batch execution of Hebbian learning the macroscopic laws are obtained upon expanding (11,12) and retaining only those terms which are linear in η. All integrations can now be done and all equations solved explicitly, resulting in $U = 0$, $Z = 1$, $W = (1-2\lambda)\sqrt{2/\pi}$, and

$$Q = Q_0 \, e^{-2\eta\gamma t} + \frac{2R_0(1-2\lambda)}{\gamma} e^{-\eta\gamma t}[1-e^{-\eta\gamma t}]\sqrt{\frac{2}{\pi}} + \left[\frac{2}{\pi}(1-2\lambda)^2 + \frac{1}{\alpha}\right]\frac{[1-e^{-\eta\gamma t}]^2}{\gamma^2}$$

$$R = R_0 \, e^{-\eta\gamma t} + (1-2\lambda)\sqrt{2/\pi}[1-e^{-\eta\gamma t}]/\gamma \qquad q = [\alpha R^2 + (1-e^{-\eta\gamma t})^2/\gamma^2]/\alpha Q$$

$$P^{\pm}[x|y] = [2\pi(Q-R^2)]^{-\frac{1}{2}} e^{-\frac{1}{2}[x-Ry\mp \text{sgn}(y)[1-e^{-\eta\gamma t}]/\alpha\gamma]^2/(Q-R^2)} \qquad (19)$$

From these results, in turn, follow the performance measures $E_g = \pi^{-1}\arccos[R/\sqrt{Q}]$ and

$$E_t = \frac{1}{2} - \frac{1}{2}(1-\lambda)\int Dy \, \text{erf}[\frac{|y|R+[1-e^{-\eta\gamma t}]/\alpha\gamma}{\sqrt{2(Q-R^2)}}] + \frac{1}{2}\lambda\int Dy \, \text{erf}[\frac{|y|R-[1-e^{-\eta\gamma t}]/\alpha\gamma}{\sqrt{2(Q-R^2)}}]$$

Comparison with the exact solution, calculated along the lines of [9] or, equivalently, obtained upon putting $t \ll \eta^{-2}$ in [9], shows that the above expressions are all exact.

For on-line execution we cannot (yet) solve the functional saddle-point equation in general. However, some analytical predictions can still be extracted from (11,12,13):

$$Q = Q_0 \, e^{-2\eta\gamma t} + \frac{2R_0(1-2\lambda)}{\gamma} e^{-\eta\gamma t}[1-e^{-\eta\gamma t}]\sqrt{\frac{2}{\pi}} + \left[\frac{2}{\pi}(1-2\lambda)^2 + \frac{1}{\alpha}\right]\frac{[1-e^{-\eta\gamma t}]^2}{\gamma^2}$$

$$R = R_0 \, e^{-\eta\gamma t} + (1-2\lambda)\sqrt{2/\pi}[1-e^{-\eta\gamma t}]/\gamma \qquad\qquad + \frac{\eta}{2\gamma}[1-e^{-2\eta\gamma t}]$$

$$\int dx \, xP^{\pm}[x|y] = Ry \pm \text{sgn}(y)[1-e^{-\eta\gamma t}]/\alpha\gamma$$

with $U = 0$, $W = (1-2\lambda)\sqrt{2/\pi}$, $V = WR + [1-e^{-\eta\gamma t}]/\alpha\gamma$, and $Z = 1$. Comparison with the results in [9] shows that the above expressions, and thus also that of E_g, are all fully exact, at any time. Observables involving $P[x, y, z]$ (including the training error) are not as easily solved from our equations. Instead we used the conditionally Gaussian approximation (found to be adequate for the noiseless Hebbian case [5, 6, 7]). The result is shown in figure 1. The agreement is reasonable, but significantly less than that in [6]; apparently teacher noise adds to the deformation of the field distribution away from a Gaussian shape.

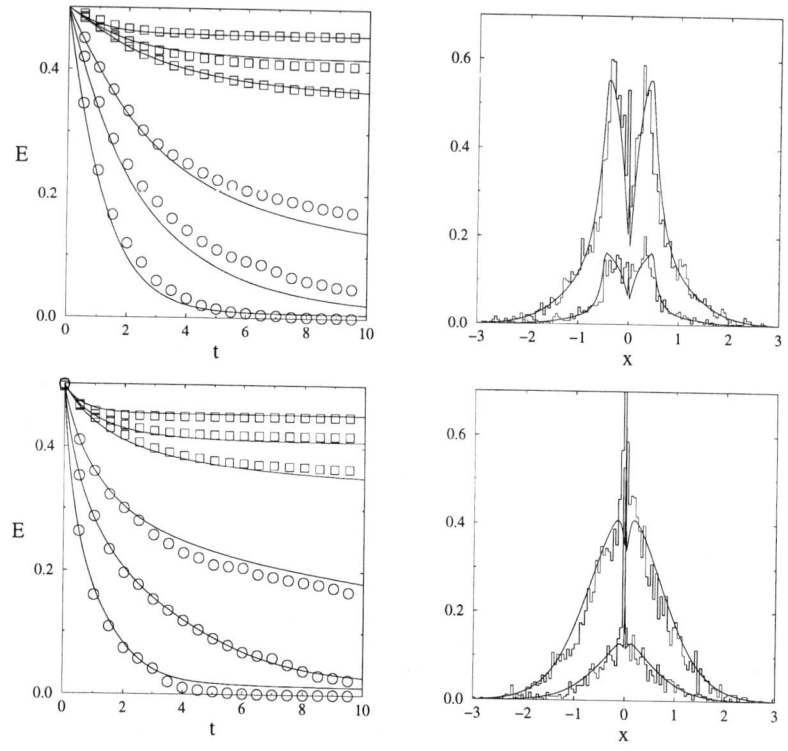

Figure 2: Large α approximation versus numerical simulations (with $N = 10{,}000$), for $\gamma = 0$ and $\lambda = 0.2$. Top row: Perceptron rule, with $\eta = \frac{1}{2}$. Bottom row: Adatron rule, with $\eta = \frac{3}{2}$. Left: training errors E_t and generalisation errors E_g as functions of time, for $\alpha \in \{\frac{1}{2}, 1, 2\}$. Lines: approximated theory, markers: simulations (circles: E_t, squares: E_g). Right: joint distributions for student field and teacher noise $P^\pm[x] = \int dy\, P[x,y,z=\pm y]$ (upper: $P^+[x]$, lower: $P^-[x]$). Histograms: simulations, lines: approximated theory.

7 Non-Linear Learning Rules: Theory versus Simulations

In the case of non-linear learning rules no exact solution is known against which to test our formalism, leaving numerical simulations as the yardstick. We have evaluated numerically the large α approximation of our theory for Perceptron learning, $\mathcal{G}[x,z] = \text{sgn}(z)\theta[-xz]$, and for Adatron learning, $\mathcal{G}[x,z] = \text{sgn}(z)|z|\theta[-xz]$. This approximation leads to the following fully explicit equation for the field distributions:

$$\frac{d}{dt}P^\pm[x|y] = \frac{1}{\alpha}\int dx'\, P^\pm[x'|y]\left\{\delta[x-x'-\eta\mathcal{F}[x',\pm y]] - \delta[x-x']\right\} + \frac{1}{2}\eta^2 Z \frac{\partial^2}{\partial x^2}P^\pm[x|y]$$

with

$$-\eta\frac{\partial}{\partial x}\left\{P[x|y]\left[Wy - \gamma x + \frac{U[\overline{x}^\pm(y) - Ry] + (V-RW)[x-\overline{x}^\pm(y)]}{Q-R^2}\right]\right\}$$

$$U = \int Dy\, dx\, \{(1-\lambda)P^+[x|y][x-\overline{x}^+(y)]\mathcal{G}[x,y] + \lambda P^-[x|y][x-\overline{x}^-(y)]\mathcal{G}[x,-y]\}$$

$$V = \int Dy\, dx\, x\, \{(1-\lambda)P^+[x|y]\mathcal{G}[x,y] + \lambda P^-[x|y]\mathcal{G}[x,-y]\}$$

$$W = \int Dy\, dx\, y\, \{(1-\lambda)P^+[x|y]\mathcal{G}[x,y] + \lambda P^-[x|y]\mathcal{G}[x,-y]\}$$

$$Z = \int Dy\, dx\, \{(1-\lambda)P^+[x|y]\mathcal{G}^2[x,y] + \lambda P^-[x|y]\mathcal{G}^2[x,-y]\}$$

and with the short-hands $\overline{x}^{\pm}(y) = \int dx\, xP^{\pm}[x|y]$. The result of our comparison is shown in figure 2. Note: E_t increases monotonically with α, and E_g decreases monotonically with α, at any t. As in the noise-free formalism [7], the large α approximation appears to capture the dominant terms both for $\alpha \to \infty$ and for $\alpha \to 0$. The predicting power of our theory is mainly limited by numerical constraints. For instance, the Adatron learning rule generates singularities at $x = 0$ in the distributions $P^{\pm}[x|y]$ (especially for small η) which, although predicted by our theory, are almost impossible to capture in numerical solutions.

8 Discussion

We have shown how a recent theory to describe the dynamics of supervised learning with restricted training sets (designed to apply in the data recycling regime, and for arbitrary on-line and batch learning rules) [5, 6, 7] in large layered neural networks can be generalized successfully in order to deal also with noisy teachers. In our generalized approach the joint distribution $P[x, y, z]$ for the fields of student, 'clean' teacher, and noisy teacher is taken to be a dynamical order parameter, in addition to the conventional observables Q and R. From the order parameter set $\{Q, R, P\}$ we derive the generalization error E_g and the training error E_t. Following the prescriptions of dynamical replica theory one finds a diffusion equation for $P[x, y, z]$, which we have evaluated by making the replica-symmetric ansatz. We have carried out several orthogonal benchmark tests of our theory: (i) for $\alpha \to \infty$ (no data recycling) our theory is exact, (ii) for $\lambda \to 0$ (no teacher noise) our theory reduces to that of [5, 6, 7], and (iii) for batch Hebbian learning our theory is exact. For on-line Hebbian learning our theory is exact with regard to the predictions for Q, R, E_g and the y-dependent conditional averages $\int dx\, xP^{\pm}[x|y]$, at any time, and a crude approximation of our equations already gives reasonable agreement with the exact results [9] for E_t. For non-linear learning rules (Perceptron and Adatron) we have compared numerical solution of a simple large α aproximation of our equations to numerical simulations, and found satisfactory agreement. This paper is a preliminary presentation of results obtained in the second stage of a research programme aimed at extending our theoretical tools in the arena of learning dynamics, building on [5, 6, 7]. Ongoing work is aimed at systematic application of our theory and its approximations to various types of non-linear learning rules, and at generalization of the theory to multi-layer networks.

References

[1] Mace C.W.H. and Coolen A.C.C (1998), *Statistics and Computing* **8**, 55

[2] Saad D. (ed.) (1998), *On-Line Learning in Neural Networks* (Cambridge: CUP)

[3] Hertz J.A., Krogh A. and Thorgersson G.I. (1989), *J. Phys. A* **22**, 2133

[4] Horner H. (1992a), *Z. Phys. B* **86**, 291 *and* Horner H. (1992b), *Z. Phys. B* **87**, 371

[5] Coolen A.C.C. and Saad D. (1998), in *On-Line Learning in Neural Networks*, Saad D. (ed.), (Cambridge: CUP)

[6] Coolen A.C.C. and Saad D. (1999), in Advances in Neural Information Processing Systems 11, Kearns D., Solla S.A., Cohn D.A. (eds.), (MIT press)

[7] Coolen A.C.C. and Saad D. (1999), *preprints KCL-MTH-99-32 & KCL-MTH-99-33*

[8] Rae H.C., Sollich P. and Coolen A.C.C. (1999), in Advances in Neural Information Processing Systems 11, Kearns D., Solla S.A., Cohn D.A. (eds.), (MIT press)

[9] Rae H.C., Sollich P. and Coolen A.C.C. (1999), *J. Phys. A* **32**, 3321

[10] Inoue J.I. (1999) *private communication*

[11] Wong K.Y.M., Li S. and Tong Y.W. (1999), *preprint cond-mat/9909004*

[12] Biehl M., Riegler P. and Stechert M. (1995), *Phys. Rev. E* **52**, 4624

A Geometric Interpretation of ν−SVM Classifiers

David J. Crisp
Centre for Sensor Signal and
Information Processing,
Deptartment of Electrical Engineering,
University of Adelaide, South Australia
dcrisp@eleceng.adelaide.edu.au

Christopher J.C. Burges
Advanced Technologies,
Bell Laboratories,
Lucent Technologies
Holmdel, New Jersey
burges@lucent.com

Abstract

We show that the recently proposed variant of the Support Vector machine (SVM) algorithm, known as ν-SVM, can be interpreted as a maximal separation between subsets of the convex hulls of the data, which we call soft convex hulls. The soft convex hulls are controlled by choice of the parameter ν. If the intersection of the convex hulls is empty, the hyperplane is positioned halfway between them such that the distance between convex hulls, measured along the normal, is maximized; and if it is not, the hyperplane's normal is similarly determined by the soft convex hulls, but its position (perpendicular distance from the origin) is adjusted to minimize the error sum. The proposed geometric interpretation of ν-SVM also leads to necessary and sufficient conditions for the existence of a choice of ν for which the ν-SVM solution is nontrivial.

1 Introduction

Recently, Schölkopf et al. [1] introduced a new class of SVM algorithms, called ν-SVM, for both regression estimation and pattern recognition. The basic idea is to remove the user-chosen error penalty factor C that appears in SVM algorithms by introducing a new variable ρ which, in the pattern recognition case, adds another degree of freedom to the margin. For a given normal to the separating hyperplane, the size of the margin increases linearly with ρ. It turns out that by adding ρ to the primal objective function with coefficient $-\nu$, $\nu \geq 0$, the variable C can be absorbed, and the behaviour of the resulting SVM - the number of margin errors and number of support vectors - can to some extent be controlled by setting ν. Moreover, the decision function produced by ν-SVM can also be produced by the original SVM algorithm with a suitable choice of C.

In this paper we show that ν-SVM, for the pattern recognition case, has a clear geometric interpretation, which also leads to necessary and sufficient conditions for the existence of a nontrivial solution to the ν-SVM problem. All our considerations apply to feature space, after the mapping of the data induced by some kernel. We adopt the usual notation: w is the normal to the separating hyperplane, the mapped

A Geometric Interpretation of ν-SVM Classifiers

data is denoted by $x_i \in \Re^N$, $i = 1, \cdots, l$, with corresponding labels $y_i \in \{\pm 1\}$, b, ρ are scalars, and ξ_i, $i = 1, \cdots, l$ are positive scalar slack variables.

2 ν-SVM Classifiers

The ν-SVM formulation, as given in [1], is as follows: minimize

$$F' = \frac{1}{2}\|w'\|^2 - \nu\rho' + \frac{1}{l}\sum_i \xi_i' \quad (1)$$

with respect to w', b', ρ', ξ_i', subject to:

$$y_i(w' \cdot x_i + b') \geq \rho' - \xi_i', \quad \xi_i' \geq 0, \quad \rho' \geq 0. \quad (2)$$

Here ν is a user-chosen parameter between 0 and 1. The decision function (whose sign determines the label given to a test point x) is then:

$$f'(x) = w' \cdot x + b'. \quad (3)$$

The Wolfe dual of this problem is: maximize $F_D' = -\frac{1}{2}\sum_{ij} \alpha_i \alpha_j y_i y_j x_i \cdot x_j$ subject to

$$0 \leq \alpha_i \leq \frac{1}{l}, \quad \sum_i \alpha_i y_i = 0, \quad \sum_i \alpha_i \geq \nu \quad (4)$$

with w' given by $w' = \sum_i \alpha_i y_i x_i$. Schölkopf et al. [1] show that ν is an upper bound on the fraction of margin errors[1], a lower bound on the fraction of support vectors, and that both of these quantities approach ν asymptotically.

Note that the point $w' = b' = \rho = \xi_i' = 0$ is feasible, and that at this point, $F' = 0$. Thus any solution of interest must have $F' \leq 0$. Furthermore, if $\nu\rho' = 0$, the optimal solution is at $w' = b' = \rho = \xi_i' = 0$[2]. Thus we can assume that $\nu\rho' > 0$ (and therefore $\nu > 0$) always. Given this, the constraint $\rho' \geq 0$ is in fact redundant: a negative value of ρ' cannot appear in a solution (to the problem with this constraint removed) since the above (feasible) solution (with $\rho' = 0$) gives a lower value for F'. Thus below we replace the constraints (2) by

$$y_i(w' \cdot x_i + b') \geq \rho' - \xi_i', \quad \xi_i' \geq 0. \quad (5)$$

2.1 A Reparameterization of ν−SVM

We reparameterize the primal problem by dividing the objective function F' by $\nu^2/2$, the constraints (5) by ν, and by making the following substitutions:

$$\mu = \frac{2}{\nu l}, \quad w = \frac{w'}{\nu}, \quad b = \frac{b'}{\nu}, \quad \rho = \frac{\rho'}{\nu}, \quad \xi_i = \frac{\xi_i'}{\nu}. \quad (6)$$

---
[1] A margin error x_i is defined to be any point for which $\xi_i > 0$ (see [1]).
[2] In fact we can prove that, even if the optimal solution is not unique, the global solutions still all have $w = 0$: see Burges and Crisp, "Uniqueness of the SVM Solution" in this volume.

This gives the equivalent formulation: minimize

$$F = \|w\|^2 - 2\rho + \mu \sum_i \xi_i \qquad (7)$$

with respect to w, b, ρ, ξ_i, subject to:

$$y_i(w \cdot x_i + b) \geq \rho - \xi_i, \quad \xi_i \geq 0. \qquad (8)$$

If we use as decision function $f(x) \equiv f'(x)/\nu$, the formulation is exactly equivalent, although both primal and dual appear different. The dual problem is now: minimize

$$F_D = \frac{1}{4} \sum_{i,j} \alpha_i \alpha_j y_i y_j x_i \cdot x_j \qquad (9)$$

with respect to the α_i, subject to:

$$\sum_i \alpha_i y_i = 0, \quad \sum_i \alpha_i = 2, \quad 0 \leq \alpha_i \leq \mu \qquad (10)$$

with w given by $w = \frac{1}{2}\sum_i \alpha_i y_i x_i$. In the following, we will refer to the reparameterized version of ν-SVM given above as μ-SVM, although we emphasize that it describes the same problem.

3 A Geometric Interpretation of ν–SVM

In the separable case, it is clear that the optimal separating hyperplane is just that hyperplane which bisects the shortest vector joining the convex hulls of the positive and negative polarity points[3]. We now show that this geometric interpretation can be extended to the case of ν–SVM for both separable and nonseparable cases.

3.1 The Separable Case

We start by giving the analysis for the separable case. The convex hulls of the two classes are

$$H_+ = \left\{ \sum_{i:y_i=+1} \alpha_i x_i \,\bigg|\, \sum_{i:y_i=+1} \alpha_i = 1, \; \alpha_i \geq 0 \right\} \qquad (11)$$

and

$$H_- = \left\{ \sum_{i:y_i=-1} \alpha_i x_i \,\bigg|\, \sum_{i:y_i=-1} \alpha_i = 1, \; \alpha_i \geq 0 \right\}. \qquad (12)$$

Finding the two closest points can be written as the following optimization problem:

$$\min_\alpha \left\| \sum_{i:y_i=+1} \alpha_i x_i - \sum_{i:y_i=-1} \alpha_i x_i \right\|^2 \qquad (13)$$

---

[3]See, for example, K. Bennett, 1997, in http://www.rpi.edu/b̃ennek/svmtalk.ps (also, to appear).

subject to:
$$\sum_{i:y_i=+1} \alpha_i = 1, \quad \sum_{i:y_i=-1} \alpha_i = 1, \quad \alpha_i \geq 0 \quad (14)$$

Taking the decision boundary $\tilde{f}(x) = w \cdot x + \tilde{b} = 0$ to be the perpendicular bisector of the line segment joining the two closest points means that at the solution,

$$w = \frac{1}{2}(\sum_{i:y_i=+1} \alpha_i x_i - \sum_{i:y_i=-1} \alpha_i x_i) \quad (15)$$

and $\tilde{b} = -w \cdot p$, where

$$p = \frac{1}{2}(\sum_{i:y_i=+1} \alpha_i x_i + \sum_{i:y_i=-1} \alpha_i x_i). \quad (16)$$

Thus w lies along the line segment (and is half its size) and p is the midpoint of the line segment. By rescaling the objective function and using the class labels $y_i = \pm 1$ we can rewrite this as[4]:

$$\min_{\alpha} \quad \|w\|^2 = \frac{1}{4}\sum_{ij} \alpha_i \alpha_j y_i y_j x_i \cdot x_j \quad (17)$$

subject to
$$\sum_i \alpha_i y_i = 0, \quad \sum_i \alpha_i = 2, \quad \alpha_i \geq 0. \quad (18)$$

The associated decision function is $\tilde{f}(x) = w \cdot x + \tilde{b}$ where $w = \frac{1}{2}\sum_i \alpha_i y_i x_i$, $p = \frac{1}{2}\sum_i \alpha_i x_i$ and $\tilde{b} = -w.p = -\frac{1}{4}\sum_{ij} \alpha_i y_i \alpha_j x_i \cdot x_j$.

3.2 The Connection with ν–SVM

Consider now the two sets of points defined by:

$$H_{+\mu} = \left\{ \sum_{i:y_i=+1} \alpha_i x_i \,\bigg|\, \sum_{i:y_i=+1} \alpha_i = 1, \quad 0 \leq \alpha_i \leq \mu \right\} \quad (19)$$

and

$$H_{-\mu} = \left\{ \sum_{i:y_i=-1} \alpha_i x_i \,\bigg|\, \sum_{i:y_i=-1} \alpha_i = 1, \quad 0 \leq \alpha_i \leq \mu \right\}. \quad (20)$$

We have the following simple proposition:

Proposition 1: $H_{+\mu} \subset H_+$ and $H_{-\mu} \subset H_-$, and $H_{+\mu}$ and $H_{-\mu}$ are both convex sets. Furthermore, the positions of the points $H_{+\mu}$ and $H_{-\mu}$ with respect to the x_i do not depend on the choice of origin.

Proof: Clearly, since the α_i defined in $H_{+\mu}$ is a subset of the α_i defined in H_+, $H_{+\mu} \subset H_+$, similarly for H_-. Now consider two points in $H_{+\mu}$ defined by α_1, α_2. Then all points on the line joining these two points can be written as $\sum_{i:y_i=+1}((1-\lambda)\alpha_{1i} + \lambda\alpha_{2i})x_i$, $0 \leq \lambda \leq 1$. Since α_{1i} and α_{2i} both satisfy $0 \leq \alpha_i \leq \mu$, so does $(1-\lambda)\alpha_{1i}+\lambda\alpha_{2i}$, and since also $\sum_{i:y_i=+1}(1-\lambda)\alpha_{1i}+\lambda\alpha_{2i} = 1$, the set $H_{+\mu}$ is convex.

---

[4]That one can rescale the objective function without changing the constraints follows from uniqueness of the solution. See also Burges and Crisp, "Uniqueness of the SVM Solution" in this volume.

The argument for $H_{-\mu}$ is similar. Finally, suppose that every x_i is translated by x_0, i.e. $x_i \to x_i + x_0$ $\forall i$. Then since $\sum_{i:y_i=+1} \alpha_i = 1$, every point in $H_{+\mu}$ is also translated by the same amount, similarly for $H_{-\mu}$. □

The problem of finding the optimal separating hyperplane between the convex sets $H_{+\mu}$ and $H_{-\mu}$ then becomes:

$$\min_\alpha \quad \|w\|^2 = \frac{1}{4} \sum_{ij} \alpha_i \alpha_j y_i y_j x_i \cdot x_j \tag{21}$$

subject to

$$\sum_i \alpha_i y_i = 0, \quad \sum_i \alpha_i = 2, \quad 0 \leq \alpha_i \leq \mu. \tag{22}$$

Since Eqs. (21) and (22) are identical to (9) and (10), we see that the ν-SVM algorithm is in fact finding the optimal separating hyperplane between the convex sets $H_{+\mu}$ and $H_{-\mu}$. We note that the convex sets $H_{+\mu}$ and $H_{-\mu}$ are not simply uniformly scaled versions of H_+ and H_-. An example is shown in Figure 1.

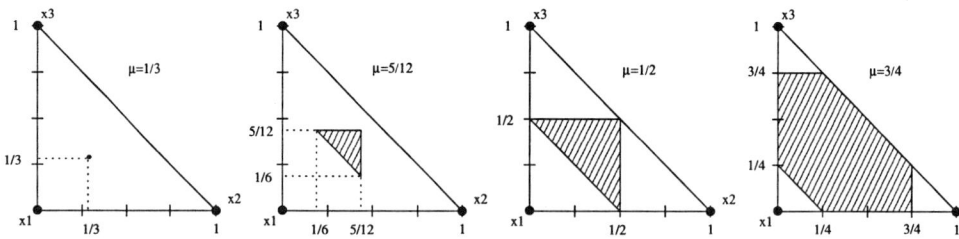

Figure 1: The soft convex hull for the vertices of a right isosceles triangle, for various μ. Note how the shape changes as the set grows and is constrained by the boundaries of the encapsulating convex hull. For $\mu < \frac{1}{3}$, the set is empty.

Below, we will refer to the formulation given in this section as the soft convex hull formulation, and the sets of points defined in Eqs. (19) and (20) as soft convex hulls.

3.3 Comparing the Offsets and Margin Widths

The natural value of the offset $\tilde{b}$ in the soft convex hull approach, $\tilde{b} = -w \cdot p$, arose by asking that the separating hyperplane lie halfway between the closest extremities of the two soft convex hulls. Different choices of b just amount to hyperplanes with the same normal but at different perpendicular distances from the origin. This value of b will not in general be the same as that for which the cost term in Eq. (7) is minimized. We can compare the two values as follows. The KKT conditions for the μ-SVM formulation are

$$(\mu - \alpha_i)\xi_i = 0 \tag{23}$$
$$\alpha_i(y_i(w \cdot x_i + b) - \rho + \xi_i) = 0 \tag{24}$$

Multiplying (24) by y_i, summing over i and using (23) gives

… A Geometric Interpretation of ν-SVM Classifiers … 249

$$b = \tilde{b} - \frac{\mu}{2}\sum_i y_i \xi_i. \tag{25}$$

Thus the separating hyperplane found in the μ-SVM algorithm sits a perpendicular distance $|\frac{\mu}{2\|w\|}\sum_i y_i \xi_i|$ away from that found in the soft convex hull formulation. For the given w, this choice of b results in the lowest value of the cost, $\mu\sum_i \xi_i$.

The soft convex hull approach suggests taking $\tilde{\rho} = w \cdot w$, since this is the value $|\tilde{f}|$ takes at the points $\sum_{y_i=+1} \alpha_i x_i$ and $\sum_{y_i=-1} \alpha_i x_i$. Again, we can use the KKT conditions to compare this with ρ. Summing (24) over i and using (23) gives

$$\rho = \tilde{\rho} + \frac{\mu}{2}\sum_i \xi_i. \tag{26}$$

Since $\tilde{\rho} = w \cdot w$, this again shows that if $\rho = 0$ then $w = \xi_i = 0$, and, by (25), $b = 0$.

3.4 The Primal for the Soft Convex Hull Formulation

By substituting (25) and (26) into the μ-SVM primal formulation (7) and (8) we obtain the primal formulation for the soft convex hull problem: minimize

$$\tilde{F} = \|w\|^2 - 2\tilde{\rho} \tag{27}$$

with respect to $w, \tilde{b}, \tilde{\rho}, \xi_i$, subject to:

$$y_i(w \cdot x_i + \tilde{b}) \geq \tilde{\rho} - \xi_i + \mu \sum_j \frac{1 + y_i y_j}{2}\xi_j, \qquad \xi_i \geq 0. \tag{28}$$

It is straightforward to check that the dual is exactly (9) and (10). Moreover, by summing the relevant KKT conditions, as above, we see that $\tilde{b} = -w \cdot p$ and $\tilde{\rho} = w \cdot w$. Note that in this formulation the variables ξ_i retain their meaning according to (8).

4 Choosing ν

In this section we establish some results on the choices for ν, using the μ-SVM formulation. First, note that $\sum_i \alpha_i y_i = 0$ and $\sum_i \alpha_i = 2$ implies $\sum_{i:y_i=+1} \alpha_i = \sum_{i:y_i=-1} \alpha_i = 1$. Then $\alpha_i \geq 0$ gives $\alpha_i \leq 1$, $\forall i$. Thus choosing $\mu > 1$, which corresponds to choosing $\nu < 2/l$, results in the same solution *of the dual* (and hence the same normal w) as choosing $\mu = 1$. (Note that different values of $\mu > 1$ can still result in different values of the other primal variables, e.g. b).

The equalities $\sum_{i:y_i=+1} \alpha_i = \sum_{i:y_i=-1} \alpha_i = 1$ also show that if $\mu < 2/l$ then the feasible region for the dual is empty and hence the problem is insoluble. This corresponds to the requirement $\nu < 1$. However, we can improve upon this. Let l_+ (l_-) be the number of positive (negative) polarity points, so that $l_+ + l_- = l$. Let $l_{min} \equiv \min\{l_+, l_-\}$. Then the minimal value of μ which still results in a nonempty feasible region is $\mu_{min} = 1/l_{min}$. This gives the condition $\nu \leq 2l_{min}/l$.

We define a "nontrivial" solution of the problem to be any solution with $w \neq 0$. The following proposition gives conditions for the existence of nontrivial solutions.

Proposition 2: A value of ν exists which will result in a nontrivial solution to the ν–SVM classification problem if and only if $\{H_{+\mu} : \mu = \mu_{min}\} \cap \{H_{-\mu} : \mu = \mu_{min}\} = \emptyset$.

Proof: Suppose that $\{H_{+\mu} : \mu = \mu_{min}\} \cap \{H_{-\mu} : \mu = \mu_{min}\} \neq \emptyset$. Then for all allowable values of μ (and hence ν), the two convex hulls will intersect, since $\{H_{+\mu} : \mu = \mu_{min}\} \subset \{H_{+\mu} : \mu \geq \mu_{min}\}$ and $\{H_{-\mu} : \mu = \mu_{min}\} \subset \{H_{-\mu} : \mu \geq \mu_{min}\}$. If the two convex hulls intersect, then the solution is trivial, since by definition there then exist feasible points z such that $z = \sum_{i:y_i=+1} \alpha_i x_i$ and $z = \sum_{i:y_i=-1} \alpha_i x_i$, and hence $2w = \sum_i \alpha_i y_i x_i = \sum_{i:y_i=+1} \alpha_i x_i - \sum_{i:y_i=-1} \alpha_i x_i = 0$ (cf. (21), (22)). Now suppose that $\{H_{+\mu} : \mu = \mu_{min}\} \cap \{H_{-\mu} : \mu = \mu_{min}\} = \emptyset$. Then clearly a nontrivial solution exists, since the shortest distance between the two convex sets $\{H_{+\mu} : \mu = \mu_{min}\}$ and $\{H_{-\mu} : \mu = \mu_{min}\}$ is not zero, hence the corresponding $w \neq 0$. □

Note that when $l_+ = l_-$, the condition amounts to the requirement that the centroid of the positive examples does not coincide with that of the negative examples. Note also that this shows that, given a data set, one can find a lower bound on ν, by finding the largest μ that satisfies $H_{-\mu} \cap H_{+\mu} = \emptyset$.

5 Discussion

The soft convex hull interpretation suggests that an appropriate way to penalize positive polarity errors differently from negative is to replace the sum $\mu \sum_i \xi_i$ in (7) with $\mu_+ \sum_{i:y_i=+1} \xi_i + \mu_- \sum_{i:y_i=-1} \xi_i$. In fact one can go further and introduce a μ for every train point. The μ-SVM formulation makes this possibility explicit, which it is not in original ν-SVM formulation.

Note also that the fact that ν-SVM leads to values of b which differ from that which would place the optimal hyperplane halfway between the soft convex hulls suggests that there may be principled methods for choosing the best b for a given problem, other than that dictated by minimizing the sum of the ξ_i's. Indeed, originally, the sum of ξ_i's term arose in an attempt to approximate the *number* of errors on the train set [2]. The above reasoning in a sense separates the justification for w from that for b. For example, given w, a simple line search could be used to find that value of b which actually does minimize the number of errors on the train set. Other methods (for example, minimizing the estimated Bayes error [3]) may also prove useful.

Acknowledgments

C. Burges wishes to thank W. Keasler, V. Lawrence and C. Nohl of Lucent Technologies for their support.

References

[1] B. Schölkopf and A. Smola and R. Williamson and P. Bartlett. New support vector algorithms, neurocolt2 nc2-tr-1998-031. Technical report, GMD First and Australian National University, 1998.

[2] C. Cortes and V. Vapnik. Support vector networks. *Machine Learning*, 20:273–297, 1995.

[3] C. J. C. Burges and B. Schölkopf. Improving the accuracy and speed of support vector learning machines. In M. Mozer, M. Jordan, and T. Petsche, editors, *Advances in Neural Information Processing Systems 9*, pages 375–381, Cambridge, MA, 1997. MIT Press.

Efficient Approaches to Gaussian Process Classification

Lehel Csató, Ernest Fokoué, Manfred Opper, Bernhard Schottky
Neural Computing Research Group
School of Engineering and Applied Sciences
Aston University Birmingham B4 7ET, UK.
{opperm,csatol}@aston.ac.uk

Ole Winther
Theoretical Physics II, Lund University, Sölvegatan 14 A,
S-223 62 Lund, Sweden
winther@thep.lu.se

Abstract

We present three simple approximations for the calculation of the posterior mean in Gaussian Process classification. The first two methods are related to mean field ideas known in Statistical Physics. The third approach is based on Bayesian online approach which was motivated by recent results in the Statistical Mechanics of Neural Networks. We present simulation results showing: 1. that the mean field Bayesian evidence may be used for hyperparameter tuning and 2. that the online approach may achieve a low training error fast.

1 Introduction

Gaussian processes provide promising non-parametric Bayesian approaches to regression and classification [2, 1]. In these statistical models, it is assumed that the likelihood of an output or target variable y for a given input $\mathbf{x} \in R^N$ can be written as $P(y|a(\mathbf{x}))$ where $a : R^N \to R$ are functions which have a Gaussian prior distribution, i.e. a is (a priori) assumed to be a Gaussian random field. This means that any finite set of field variables $a(\mathbf{x}_i)$, $i = 1, \ldots, l$ are jointly Gaussian distributed with a given covariance $\mathbf{E}[a(\mathbf{x}_i)a(\mathbf{x}_j)] = K(\mathbf{x}_i, \mathbf{x}_j)$ (we will also assume a zero mean throughout the paper).

Predictions on $a(\mathbf{x})$ for novel inputs $\mathbf{x}$, when a set D of m training examples $(\mathbf{x}_i, y_i)$ $i = 1, \ldots, m$, is given, can be computed from the posterior distribution of the $m+1$ variables $a(\mathbf{x})$ and $a(\mathbf{x}_1), \ldots, a(\mathbf{x}_m)$. A major technical problem of the Gaussian process models is the difficulty of computing posterior averages as high dimensional integrals, when the likelihood is not Gaussian. This happens for example in classification problems. So far, a variety of approximation techniques have been discussed: Monte Carlo sampling [2], the MAP approach [4], bounds on the likelihood [3] and a TAP mean field approach [5]. In this paper, we will introduce three different novel methods for approximating the posterior mean of the random field $a(\mathbf{x})$, which we think are simple enough to be used in practical applications. Two of the techniques are based on mean field ideas from Statistical Mechanics, which in contrast to the previously developed TAP approach are easier to implement. They also yield simple approximations to the total likelihood of the data (the evidence) which can be used to tune the hyperparameters in the covariance kernel K (The Bayesian evidence (or MLII) framework aims at maximizing the likelihood of the data).

We specialize to the case of a binary classification problem, where for simplicity, the class label $y = \pm 1$ is assumed to be noise free and the likelihood is chosen as

$$P(y|a) = \Theta(ya) ,\qquad(1)$$

where $\Theta(x)$ is the unit step function, which equals 1 for $x > 0$ and zero else. We are interested in computing efficient approximations to the posterior mean $\langle a(\mathbf{x})\rangle$, which we will use for a prediction of the labels via $y = \text{sign}\langle a(\mathbf{x})\rangle$, where $\langle\ldots\rangle$ denotes the posterior expectation. If the posterior distribution of $a(\mathbf{x})$ is symmetric around its mean, this will give the Bayes optimal prediction.

Before starting, let us add two comments on the likelihood (1). First, the MAP approach (i.e. predicting with the fields a that maximize the posterior) would not be applicable, because it gives the trivial result $a(\mathbf{x}) = 0$. Second, noise can be easily introduced within a *probit* model [2], all subsequent calculations will only be slightly altered. Moreover, the Gaussian average involved in the definition of the probit likelihood can always be shifted from the likelihood into the Gaussian process prior, by a redefinition of the fields a (which does not change the prediction), leaving us with the simple likelihood (1) and a modified process covariance [5].

2 Exact Results

At first glance, it may seem that in order to calculate $\langle a(\mathbf{x})\rangle$ we have to deal with the joint posterior of the fields $a_i = a(\mathbf{x}_i)$, $i = 1,\ldots,m$ together with the field at the test point $a(\mathbf{x})$. This would imply that for any test point, a different new $m+1$ dimensional average has to be performed. Actually, we will show that this is not the case. As above let $\mathbf{E}$ denote the expectation over the Gaussian prior. The posterior expectation at any point, say $\mathbf{x}$

$$\langle a(\mathbf{x})\rangle = \frac{\mathbf{E}\left[a(\mathbf{x})\prod_{j=1}^{m} P(y_j|a_j)\right]}{\mathbf{E}\left[\prod_{j=1}^{m} P(y_j|a_j)\right]} \qquad(2)$$

can by integration by parts–for any likelihood–be written as

$$\langle a(\mathbf{x})\rangle = \sum_j K(\mathbf{x},\mathbf{x}_j)\alpha_j y_j \quad\text{and}\quad \alpha_j \doteq y_j \left\langle\frac{\partial \ln P(y_j|a_j)}{\partial a_j}\right\rangle \qquad(3)$$

showing that α_j is not dependent on the test point $\mathbf{x}$. It is therefore not necessary to compute a $m+1$ dimensional average for every prediction.

We have chosen the specific definition (3) in order to stress the similarity to predictions with Support Vector Machines (for the likelihood (1), the α_j will come out nonnegative). In the next sections we will develop three approaches for an approximate computation of the α_j.

3 Mean Field Method I: Ensemble Learning

Our first goal is to approximate the true posterior distribution

$$p(\mathbf{a}|D_m) = \frac{1}{Z}\frac{1}{\sqrt{(2\pi)^m \det \mathbf{K}}}e^{-\frac{1}{2}\mathbf{a}^T \mathbf{K}^{-1}\mathbf{a}}\prod_{j=1}^{m} P(y_j|a_j) \qquad(4)$$

of $\mathbf{a} \doteq (a_1, \ldots, a_m)$ by a simpler, tractable distribution q. Here, $\mathbf{K}$ denotes the covariance matrix with elements $K_{ij} = K(\mathbf{x}_i, \mathbf{x}_j)$. In the variational mean field approach–known as *ensemble learning* in the Neural Computation Community,– the relative entropy distance $KL(q,p) = \int d\mathbf{a}\, q(\mathbf{a}) \ln \frac{q(\mathbf{a})}{p(\mathbf{a})}$ is minimized in the family of *product distributions* $q(\mathbf{a}) = \prod_{j=1}^{m} q_j(a_j)$. This is in contrast to [3], where a variational bound on the likelihood is computed. We get

$$KL(q,p) = \sum_i \int da_i q_i(a_i) \ln \frac{q_i(a_i)}{P(y_i|a_i)} + \frac{1}{2} \sum_{i,j,i\neq j} [\mathbf{K}^{-1}]_{ij} \langle a_i \rangle_0 \langle a_j \rangle_0 + \frac{1}{2} \sum_i [\mathbf{K}^{-1}]_{ii} \langle a_i^2 \rangle_0$$

where $\langle \ldots \rangle_0$ denotes expectation w.r.t. q. By setting the functional derivative of $KL(q,p)$ with respect to $q_i(a)$ equal to zero, we find that the best product distribution is a Gaussian prior times the original Likelihood:

$$q_i(a) \propto P(y_i|a) \frac{1}{\sqrt{2\pi \lambda_i}} e^{-\frac{(a-m_i)^2}{2\lambda_i}}, \tag{5}$$

where $m_i = -\lambda_i \sum_{j,j\neq i} (\mathbf{K}^{-1})_{ij} \langle \mathbf{a_j} \rangle_0$ and $\lambda_i = [\mathbf{K}^{-1}]_{ii}^{-1}$. Using this specific form for the approximated posterior $q(a)$, replacing the average over the true posterior in (3) by the approximation (5), we get (using the likelihood (1)) a set of m nonlinear equations in the unknowns α_j:

$$\alpha_j = y_j \left\langle \frac{\partial \ln P(y_j|a_j)}{\partial a_j} \right\rangle_0 = \frac{1}{\sqrt{\lambda_j}} \frac{D(\frac{m_j}{\sqrt{\lambda_j}})}{\Phi(y_j \frac{m_j}{\sqrt{\lambda_j}})} \quad \text{and} \quad m_j = \sum_i K_{ji} y_i \alpha_i - \lambda_j y_j \alpha_j, \tag{6}$$

where $D(z) = e^{-z^2/2}/\sqrt{2\pi}$ and $\Phi(z) = \int_{-\infty}^{z} dt\, D(t)$. As a useful byproduct of the variational approximation, an upper bound on the Bayesian evidence $P(D) = \int d\mathbf{a}\, \pi(\mathbf{a}) P(D|\mathbf{a})$ can be derived. (π denotes the Gaussian process prior and $P(D|\mathbf{a}) = \prod_{j=1}^{m} P(y_j|a_j)$). The bound can be written in terms of the mean field 'free energy' as

$$\begin{aligned}
-\ln P(D) &\leq \mathbf{E}_q \ln q(\mathbf{a}) - \mathbf{E}_q \ln[\pi(\mathbf{a}) P(D|\mathbf{a})] \\
&= -\sum_i \ln \Phi\left(y_i \frac{m_j}{\sqrt{\lambda_i}}\right) + \frac{1}{2} \sum_{ij} y_i \alpha_i (K_{ij} - \delta_{ij} \lambda_i) y_j \alpha_j \\
&\quad + \frac{1}{2} \ln \det \mathbf{K} - \frac{1}{2} \sum_i \ln \lambda_i
\end{aligned} \tag{7}$$

which can be used as a yardstick for selecting appropriate hyperparameters in the covariance kernel.

The ensemble learning approach has the little drawback, that it requires inversion of the covariance matrix $\mathbf{K}$ and, for the free energy (7) one must compute a determinant. A second, simpler approximation avoids these computations.

4 Mean Field Theory II: A 'Naive' Approach

The second mean field theory aims at working directly with the variables α_j. As a starting point, we consider the partition function (evidence),

$$Z = P(D) = \int d\mathbf{z}\, e^{-\frac{1}{2}\mathbf{z}^T \mathbf{K} \mathbf{z}} \prod_{j=1}^{m} \hat{P}(y_j|z_j), \tag{8}$$

which follows from (4) by a standard Gaussian integration, introducing the Fourier transform of the Likelihood $\hat{P}(y|z) = \int \frac{da}{2\pi} e^{iaz} P(y|a)$ with i being the imaginary unit. It is tempting to view (8) as a normalizing partition function for a Gaussian process z_i having covariance matrix $\mathbf{K}^{-1}$ and likelihood $\hat{P}$. Unfortunately, $\hat{P}$ is not a real number and precludes a proper probabilistic interpretation. Nevertheless, dealing formally with the complex measure defined by (8), integration by parts shows that one has $y_j \alpha_j = -i \langle z_j \rangle_*$, where the brackets $\langle \ldots \rangle_*$ denote a average over the complex measure. This suggests a simple approximation for calculating the α_j. One may think of trying a saddle-point (or steepest descent) approximation to (8) and replace $\langle z_j \rangle_*$ by the value of z_j (in the complex z plane) which makes the integrand stationary thereby neglecting the fluctuations of the z_j. Hence, this approximation would treat expectations of products as $\langle z_i z_j \rangle_*$ as $\langle z_i \rangle_* \langle z_j \rangle_*$, which may be reasonable for $i \neq j$, but definitely not for the self-correlation $i = j$. According to the general formalism of mean field theories (outlined e.g. in [6]), one can improve on that idea, by treating the 'self-interactions' z_i^2 separately. This can be done by replacing all z_i (except in the form z_i^2) by a new variable μ_i by inserting a Dirac δ function representation $\delta(z - \mu) = \int \frac{dm}{2\pi} e^{-im(z-\mu)}$ into (8) and integrate over the z and a variables exactly (the integral factorizes), and finally perform a saddle-point integration over the m and μ variables. The details of this calculation will be given elsewhere. Within the saddle-point approximation, we get the system of nonlinear equations

$$\alpha_j = -iy_j \mu_j = \frac{1}{\sqrt{K_{jj}}} \frac{D(\frac{m_j}{\sqrt{K_{jj}}})}{\Phi(y_j \frac{m_j}{\sqrt{K_{jj}}})} \quad \text{and} \quad m_j = \sum_{i, i \neq j} K_{ji}(-i\mu_i) = \sum_{i, i \neq j} K_{ji} y_i \alpha_i \quad (9)$$

which is of the same form as (6) with λ_j replaced by the simpler K_{jj}. These equations have also been derived by us in [5] using a Callen identity, but our present derivation allows also for an approximation to the evidence. By plugging the saddle-point values back into the partition function, we get

$$-\ln P(D) \approx -\sum_i \ln \Phi\left(y_i \frac{m_i}{\sqrt{K_{ii}}}\right) + \frac{1}{2} \sum_{ij} y_i \alpha_i (K_{ij} - \delta_{ij} K_{ii}) y_j \alpha_j$$

which is also simpler to compute than (7) but does not give a bound on the true evidence.

5 A sequential Approach

Both previous algorithms do not give an explicit expression for the posterior mean, but require the solution of a set of nonlinear equations. These must be obtained by an iterative procedure. We now present a different approach for an approximate computation of the posterior mean, which is based on a single sequential sweep through the whole dataset giving an explicit update of the posterior.

The algorithm is based on a recently proposed Bayesian approach to online learning (see [8] and the articles of Opper and Winther & Solla in [9]). Its basic idea applied to the Gaussian process scenario, is as follows: Suppose, that q_t is a Gaussian approximation to the posterior after having seen t examples. This means that we approximate the posterior process by a Gaussian process with mean $\langle a(\mathbf{x}) \rangle_t$ and covariance $K_t(\mathbf{x}, \mathbf{y})$, starting with $\langle a(\mathbf{x}) \rangle_0 = 0$ and $K_0(\mathbf{x}, \mathbf{y}) = K(\mathbf{x}, \mathbf{y})$. After a new data point y_{t+1} is observed, the posterior is updated according to Bayes rule. The new non-Gaussian posterior $\hat{q}_t$ is projected back into the family of Gaussians by choosing the closest Gaussian q_{t+1} minimizing the relative entropy $KL(\hat{q}_t, q_{t+1})$

in order to keep the loss of information small. This projection is equivalent to a matching of the first two moments of $\hat{q}_t$ and q_{t+1}. E.g., for the first moment we get

$$\langle a(\mathbf{x})\rangle_{t+1} = \frac{\langle a(\mathbf{x}) \ P(y_{t+1}|a(\mathbf{x}_{t+1}))\rangle_t}{\langle P(y_{t+1}|a(\mathbf{x}_{t+1}))\rangle_t} = \langle a(\mathbf{x})\rangle_t + \kappa_1(t) K_t(\mathbf{x}, \mathbf{x}_{t+1})$$

where the second line follows again from an integration by parts and $\kappa_1(t) = \frac{y_{t+1}}{\sigma} \frac{\phi'(z_t)}{\phi(z_t)}$ with $z_t = \frac{y_{t+1}\langle a(\mathbf{x}_{t+1})\rangle_t}{\sigma(t)}$ and $\sigma^2(t) = K_t(\mathbf{x}_{t+1}, \mathbf{x}_{t+1})$. This recursion and the corresponding one for K_t can be solved by the ansatz

$$\langle a(\mathbf{x})\rangle_t = \sum_{j=1}^{t} K(\mathbf{x}, \mathbf{x}_j) y_j \alpha_j(t) \qquad (10)$$

$$K_t(\mathbf{x}, \mathbf{y}) = \sum_{i,j} K(\mathbf{x}, \mathbf{x}_i) C_{ij}(t) K(\mathbf{x}, \mathbf{x}_j) + K(\mathbf{x}, \mathbf{y}) \qquad (11)$$

where the vector $\alpha(t) = (a_1, \ldots, a_t, 0, 0, \ldots)$ and the matrix $C(t)$ (which has also only $t \times t$ nonzero elements) are updated as

$$\alpha(t+1) = \alpha(t) + \kappa_1(t) \left(\mathbf{C}(t)\mathbf{k_{t+1}} + \mathbf{e_{t+1}}\right) \otimes \mathbf{y}$$
$$\mathbf{C}(t+1) = \mathbf{C}(t) + \kappa_2(t) \left(\mathbf{C}(t)\mathbf{k_{t+1}} + \mathbf{e_{t+1}}\right) \left(\mathbf{C}(t)\mathbf{k_{t+1}} + \mathbf{e_{t+1}}\right)^T \qquad (12)$$

where $\kappa_2(t) = \frac{1}{\sigma^2}\left\{\frac{\Phi''(z_t)}{\Phi(z_t)} - \left(\frac{\Phi'(z_t)}{\Phi(z_t)}\right)^2\right\}$, $\mathbf{k_t}$ is the vector with elements K_{tj}, $j = 1 \ldots, t$ and $\otimes$ denotes the element-wise product between vectors. The sequential algorithm defined by (10)-(12) has the advantage of not requiring any matrix inversions. There is also no need to solve a numerical optimization problem at each time as in the approach of [11] where a different update of a Gaussian posterior approximation was proposed. Since we do not require a linearization of the likelihood, the method is not equivalent to the extended Kalman Filter approach.

Since it is possible to compute the evidence of the new datapoint $P(y_{t+1}) = \langle P(y_{t+1}|a_{t+1})\rangle_t$ based on the old posterior, we can compute a further approximation to the log evidence for m data via $\ln P(D_m) = \sum_{t=1}^{m-1} \ln \langle P(y_{t+1}|a_{t+1})\rangle_t$.

6 Simulations

We present two sets of simulations for the mean field approaches. In the first, we test the Bayesian evidence framework for tuning the hyperparameters of the covariance function (kernel). In the second, we test the ability of the sequential approach to achieve low training error and a stable test error for fixed hyperparameters.

For the evidence framework, we give simulation results for both mean field free energies (7) and (10) on a single data set, 'Pima Indian Diabetes (with 200/332 training/test-examples and input dimensionality $d = 7$) [7]. The results should therefore not be taken as a conclusive evidence for the merits of these approaches, but simply as an indication that they may give reasonable results. We use the radial basis function covariance function $K(\mathbf{x}, \mathbf{x}') = \exp\left(-\frac{1}{2}\sum_l^d w_l(x_l - x'_l)^2\right)$. A diagonal term v is added to the covariance matrix corresponding to a Gaussian noise added to the fields with variance v [5]. The free energy, $-\ln P(D)$ is minimized by gradient descent with respect to v and the lengthscale parameters $w_1, \ldots, w_d$ and the mean field equations for α_j are solved by iteration before each update of the hyperparameters (further details will be given elsewhere). Figure 1 shows the evolution of the naive mean free energy and the test error starting from uniform ws. It typically requires of the order of 10 iteration steps of the α_j-equations between each hyperparameter update. We also used hybrid approaches, where the free energy was minimized by one mean field algorithm and the hyperparameters used in the other. As it may be seen from table 1, the naive mean field theory can overestimate the free energy (since the ensemble free energy is an upper bound to the free energy). The overestimation is not nearly as severe at the minimum of the naive mean field free energy. Another interesting observation is that as long as the same hyperparameters are used the actual performance (as measured by the test error) is not very sensitive to the algorithm used. This also seems to be the case for the TAP mean field approach and Support Vector Machines [5].

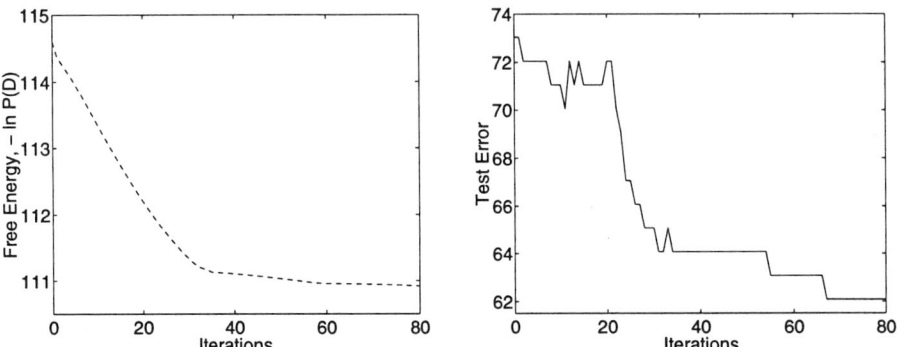

Figure 1: Hyperparameter optimization for the Pima Indians data set using the naive mean field free energy. Left figure: The free energy as a function of the number of hyperparameter updates. Right figure: The test error count (out of 332) as a function of the number of hyperparameter updates.

Table 1: Pima Indians dataset. Hyperparameters found by free energy minimization. Left column gives the free energy $-\ln P(D)$ used in hyperparameter optimization. Test error counts in range 63- 75 have previously been reported [5]

	Ensemble MF		Naive MF	
Free Energy minimization	Error	$-\ln P(D)$	Error	$-\ln P(D)$
Ensemble Mean Field, eq. (7)	72	100.6	70	183.2
Naive Mean Field, eq. (10)	62	107.0	62	110.9

For the sequential algorithm, we have studied the *sonar* [10] and *crab* [7] datasets. Since we have not computed an approximation to the evidence so far, a simple fixed polynomial kernel was used. Although a probabilistic justification of the algorithm is only valid, when a *single* sweep through the data is used (the independence of the data is assumed), it is tempting to reuse the same data and iterate the procedure as a heuristic. The two plots show that in this way, only a small improvement is obtained, and it seems that the method is rather efficient in extracting the information from the data in a single presentation. For the sonar dataset, a single sweep is enough to achieve zero training error.

Acknowledgements: BS would like to thank the Leverhulme Trust for their support (F/250/K). The work was also supported by EPSRC Grant GR/L52093.

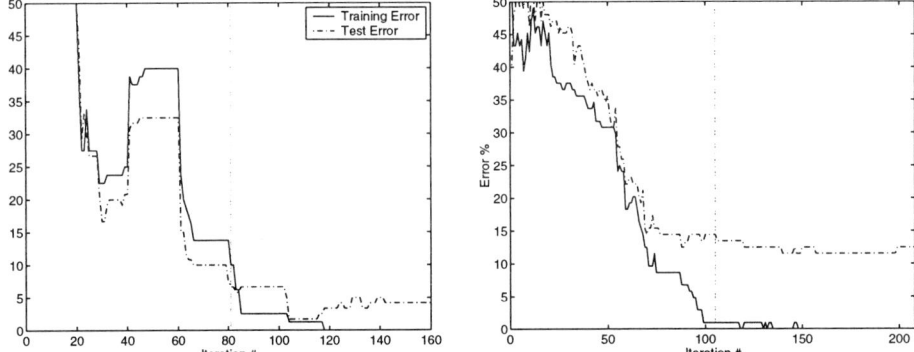

Figure 2: Training and test errors during learning for the sonar (left) and crab dataset (right). The vertical dash-dotted line marks the end of the training set and the starting point of reusing of it. The kernel function used is $K(\mathbf{x}, \mathbf{x}') = (1 + \mathbf{x} \cdot \mathbf{x}'/m)^k$ with order $k = 2$ (m is the dimension of inputs).

References

[1] Williams C.K.I. and Rasmussen C.E., Gaussian Processes for Regression, in *Neural Information Processing Systems 8*, Touretzky D.S, Mozer M.C. and Hasselmo M.E. (eds.), 514-520, MIT Press (1996).

[2] Neal R.M, *Monte Carlo Implementation of Gaussian Process Models for Bayesian Regression and Classification*, Technical Report 9702, Department of Statistics, University of Toronto (1997).

[3] Gibbs M.N. and Mackay D.J.C., *Variational Gaussian Process Classifiers*, Preprint Cambridge University (1997).

[4] Williams C.K.I. and Barber D, *Bayesian Classification with Gaussian Processes*, IEEE Trans Pattern Analysis and Machine Intelligence, **20** 1342-1351 (1998).

[5] Opper M. and Winther O. *Gaussian Processes for Classification: Mean Field Algorithms*, Submitted to Neural Computation, http://www.thep.lu.se /tf2/staff/winther/ (1999).

[6] Zinn-Justin J, *Quantum Field Theory and Critical Phenomena*, Clarendon Press Oxford (1990).

[7] Ripley B.D, *Pattern Recognition and Neural Networks*, Cambridge University Press (1996).

[8] Opper M., Online versus Offline Learning from Random Examples: General Results, Phys. Rev. Lett. 77, 4671 (1996).

[9] *Online Learning in Neural Networks*, Cambridge University Press, D. Saad (ed.) (1998).

[10] Gorman R.P and Sejnowski T.J, *Analysis of hidden units in a layered network trained to classify sonar targets*, Neural Networks 1, (1988).

[11] Jaakkola T. and Haussler D. *Probabilistic kernel regression*, In Online Proceedings of 7-th Int. Workshop on AI and Statistics (1999), http://uncertainty99.microsoft.com/proceedings.htm.

Potential Boosters ?

Nigel Duffy
Department of Computer Science
University of California
Santa Cruz, CA 95064
nigeduff@cse.ucsc.edu

David Helmbold
Department of Computer Science
University of California
Santa Cruz, CA 95064
dph@cse.ucsc.edu

Abstract

Recent interpretations of the Adaboost algorithm view it as performing a gradient descent on a potential function. Simply changing the potential function allows one to create new algorithms related to AdaBoost. However, these new algorithms are generally not known to have the formal boosting property. This paper examines the question of which potential functions lead to new algorithms that are boosters. The two main results are general sets of conditions on the potential; one set implies that the resulting algorithm is a booster, while the other implies that the algorithm is not. These conditions are applied to previously studied potential functions, such as those used by LogitBoost and Doom II.

1 Introduction

The first boosting algorithm appeared in Rob Schapire's thesis [1]. This algorithm was able to boost the performance of a weak PAC learner [2] so that the resulting algorithm satisfies the strong PAC learning [3] criteria. We will call any method that builds a strong PAC learning algorithm from a weak PAC learning algorithm a *PAC boosting algorithm*. Freund and Schapire later found an improved PAC boosting algorithm called AdaBoost [4], which also tends to improve the hypotheses generated by practical learning algorithms [5].

The AdaBoost algorithm takes a labeled training set and produces a *master hypothesis* by repeatedly calling a given learning method. The given learning method is used with different distributions on the training set to produce different *base hypotheses*. The master hypothesis returned by AdaBoost is a weighted vote of these base hypotheses. AdaBoost works iteratively, determining which examples are poorly classified by the current weighted vote and selecting a distribution on the training set to emphasize those examples.

Recently, several researchers [6, 7, 8, 9, 10] have noticed that Adaboost is performing a constrained gradient descent on an exponential potential function of the margins of the examples. The margin of an example is $yF(x)$ where y is the ± 1 valued label of the example x and $F(x) \in \Re$ is the net weighted vote of master hypothesis F. Once Adaboost is seen this way it is clear that further algorithms may be derived by changing the potential function [6, 7, 9, 10].

The exponential potential used by AdaBoost has the property that the influence of a data point increases exponentially if it is repeatedly misclassified by the base hypotheses. This concentration on the "hard" examples allows AdaBoost to rapidly obtain a consistent hypothesis (assuming that the base hypotheses have certain properties). However, it also means that an incorrectly labeled or noisy example can quickly attract much of the distribution. It appears that this lack of noise-tolerance is one of AdaBoost's few drawbacks [11]. Several researchers [7, 8, 9, 10] have proposed potential functions which do not concentrate as much on these "hard" examples. However, they generally do not show that the derived algorithms have the PAC boosting property.

In this paper we return to the original motivation behind boosting algorithms and ask: "for which potential functions does gradient descent lead to PAC boosting algorithms" (i.e. boosters that create strong PAC learning algorithms from arbitrary weak PAC learners). We give necessary conditions that are met by some of the proposed potential functions (most notably the LogitBoost potential introduced by Friedman et al. [7]). Furthermore, we show that simple gradient descent on other proposed potential functions (such as the sigmoidal potential used by Mason et al. [10]) cannot convert arbitrary weak PAC learning algorithms into strong PAC learners. The aim of this work is to identify properties of potential functions required for PAC boosting, in order to guide the search for more effective potentials.

Some potential functions have an additional tunable parameter [10] or change over time [12]. Our results do not yet apply to such dynamic potentials.

2 PAC Boosting

Here we define the notions of PAC learning[1] and boosting, and define the notation used throughout the paper.

A *concept* C is a subset of the learning domain $\mathcal{X}$. A *random example* of C is a pair ($x \in \mathcal{X}, y \in \{-1, +1\}$) where x is drawn from some distribution on $\mathcal{X}$ and $y = 1$ if $x \in C$ and -1 otherwise. A *concept class* is a set of concepts.

Definition 1 *A (strong) PAC learner for concept class $\mathcal{C}$ has the property that for every distribution D on $\mathcal{X}$, all concepts $C \in \mathcal{C}$, and all $0 < \epsilon, \delta < 1/2$: with probability at least $1 - \delta$ the algorithm outputs a hypothesis h where $\mathbf{P}_D[h(x) \neq C(x)] \leq \epsilon$. The learning algorithm is given $\mathcal{C}$, ϵ, δ, and the ability to draw random examples of C (w.r.t. distribution D), and must run in time bounded by $\mathrm{poly}(1/\epsilon, 1/\delta)$.*

Definition 2 *A weak PAC learner is similar to a strong PAC learner, except that it need only satisfy the conditions for a particular $0 < \epsilon_0, \delta_0 < 1/2$ pair, rather than for all ϵ, δ pairs.*

Definition 3 *A PAC boosting algorithm is a generic algorithm which can leverage any weak PAC learner to meet the strong PAC learning criteria.*

In the remainder of the paper we emphasize boosting the accuracy ϵ as it is much easier to boost the confidence δ, see Haussler et al. [13] and Freund [14] for details. Furthermore, we emphasize boosting by re-sampling, where the strong PAC learner draws a large sample, and each iteration the weak learning algorithm is called with some distribution over this sample.

---
[1]To simplify the presentation we omit the instance space dimension and target representation length parameters.

Throughout the paper we use the following notation.

- m is the cardinality of the fixed sample $\{(x_1, y_1), \ldots, (x_m, y_m)\}$.
- $h_t(x)$ is the ± 1 valued weak hypothesis created at iteration t.
- α_t is the weight or vote of h_t in the master hypothesis, the α's may or may not be normalized so that $\sum_{t'=1}^{t} \alpha_{t'} = 1$.
- $F_t(x) = \sum_{t'=1}^{t}(\alpha_{t'} h_{t'}(x)/\sum_{\tau=1}^{t}\alpha_\tau) \in \Re$, is the master hypothesis[2] at iteration t.
- $u_{i,t} = y_i \sum_{t'=1}^{t} \alpha_{t'} h_{t'}(x)$ is the margin of x_i after iteration t; the t subscript is often omitted. Note that the margin is positive when the master hypothesis is correct, and the *normalized margin* is $u_{i,t}/\sum_{t'=1}^{t}\alpha_{t'}$.
- $p(u)$ is the *potential* of an instance with margin u, and the total potential is $\sum_{i=1}^{m} p(u_i)$.
- $\mathbf{P}_D[\ ], \mathbf{P}_S[\ ]$, and $\mathbf{E}_S[\ ]$ are the probability with respect to the unknown distribution over the domain, and the probability and expectations with respect to the uniform distribution over the sample, respectively.

Our results apply to total potential functions of the form $\sum_{i=1}^{m} p(u_i)$ where p is positive and strictly decreasing.

3 Leveraging Learners by Gradient Descent

AdaBoost [4] has recently been interpreted as gradient descent independently by several groups [6, 7, 8, 9, 10]. Under this interpretation AdaBoost is seen as minimizing the total potential $\sum_{i=1}^{m} p(u_i) = \sum_{i=1}^{m} \exp(-u_i)$ via feasible direction gradient descent. On each iteration $t+1$, AdaBoost chooses the direction of steepest descent as the distribution on the sample, and calls the weak learner to obtain a new base hypothesis h_{t+1}. The weight α_{t+1} of this new weak hypothesis is calculated to minimize[3] the resulting potential $\sum_{i=1}^{m} p(u_{i,t+1}) = \sum_{i=1}^{m} \exp(-(u_{i,t}+\alpha_{t+1} y_i h_{t+1}(x_i)))$.

This gradient descent idea has been generalized to other potential functions [6, 7, 10]. Duffy *et al.* [9] prove bounds for a similar gradient descent technique using a non-componentwise, non-monotonic potential function.

Note that if the weak learner returns a good hypothesis h_t (with training error at most $\epsilon < 1/2$), then $\sum_{i=1}^{m} D_t(x_i) y_i h_t(x_i) > 1 - 2\epsilon > 0$. We set $r = 1 - 2\epsilon$, and assume that each base hypothesis produced satisfies $\sum_{i=1}^{m} D_t(x_i) y_i h_t(x_i) \geq r$.

In this paper we consider this general gradient descent approach applied to various potentials $\sum_{i=1}^{m} p(u_i)$. Note that each potential function p has two corresponding gradient descent algorithms (see [6]). The *un-normalized* algorithms (like AdaBoost) continually add in new weak hypotheses while preserving the old α's. The *normalized* algorithms re-scale the α's so that they always sum to 1. In general, we call such algorithms "leveraging algorithms", reserving the term "boosting" for those that actually have the PAC boosting property.

4 Potentials that Don't Boost

In this section we describe sufficient conditions on potential functions so that the corresponding leveraging algorithm does not have the PAC boosting property. We

---

[2] The prediction of the master hypothesis on instance x is the sign of $F_t(x)$.

[3] Our current proofs require that the actual α_t's be no greater than a constant (say 1). Therefore, this minimizing α may need to be reduced.

apply these conditions to show that two potentials from the literature do not lead to boosting algorithms.

Theorem 1 *Let $p(u)$ be a potential function for which:*
1) the derivative, $p'(u)$, is increasing ($-p'(u)$ decreasing) in $\Re_+$, and
2) $\exists \beta > 0$ such that for all $u > 0$, $-\beta p'(u) \geq -p'(-2u)$.
Then neither the normalized nor the un-normalized leveraging algorithms corresponding to potential p have the PAC boosting property.

This theorem is proven by an adversary argument. Whenever the concept class is sufficiently rich[4], the adversary can keep a constant fraction of the sample from being correctly labeled by the master hypothesis. Thus as the error tolerance ϵ goes to zero, the master hypotheses will not be sufficiently accurate.

We now apply this theorem to two potential functions from the literature.

Friedman et al. [7] describe a potential they call "Squared Error(p)" where the potential at x_i is $\left(\frac{y_i+1}{2} - \frac{e^{F(x_i)}}{e^{F(x_i)} + e^{-F(x_i)}}\right)^2$. This potential can be re-written as $p_{SE}(u_i) = \frac{1}{4}\left(1 + 2\frac{e^{-u_i} - e^{u_i}}{e^{u_i} + e^{-u_i}} + \left(\frac{e^{-u_i} - e^{u_i}}{e^{u_i} + e^{-u_i}}\right)^2\right)$.

Corollary 1 *Potential "Squared Error(p)" does not lead to a boosting algorithm.*

Proof: This potential satisfies the conditions of Theorem 1. It is strictly decreasing, and the second condition holds for $\beta = 2$.

Mason et al. [10] examine a normalized algorithm using the potential $p_D(u) = 1 - \tanh(\lambda u)$. Their algorithm optimizes over choices of λ via cross-validation, and uses weak learners with slightly different properties. However, we can plug this potential directly into the gradient descent framework and examine the resulting algorithms.

Corollary 2 *The DOOMII potential p_D does not lead to a boosting algorithm for any fixed λ.*

Proof: The potential is strictly decreasing, and the second condition of Theorem 1 holds for $\beta = 1$.

Our techniques show that potentials that are sigmoidal in nature do not lead to algorithms with the PAC boosting property. Since sigmoidal potentials are generally better over-estimates of the $0, 1$ loss than the potential used by AdaBoost, our results imply that boosting algorithms must use a potential with more subtle properties than simply upper bounding the $0, 1$ loss.

5 Potential Functions That Boost

In this section we give sufficient conditions on a potential function for it's corresponding un-normalized algorithm to have the PAC boosting property. This result implies that AdaBoost [4] and LogitBoost [7] have the PAC boosting property (Although this was previously known for AdaBoost [4], we believe this is a new result for LogitBoost).

---

[4]The VC-dimension 4 concept class consisting of pairs of intervals on the real line is sufficient for our adversary.

One set of conditions on the potential imply that it decreases roughly exponentially when the (un-normalized) margins are large. Once the margins are in this exponential region, ideas similar to those used in AdaBoost's analysis show that the minimum *normalized* margin quickly becomes bounded away from zero. This allows us to bound the generalization error using a theorem from Bartlett et al. [15].

A second set of conditions governs the behavior of the potential function before the un-normalized margins are large enough. These conditions imply that the total potential decreases by a constant factor each iteration. Therefore, too much time will not be spent before all the margins enter the exponential region.

The margin value bounding the exponential region is U, and once $\sum_{i=1}^{t} p(u_i) \leq p(U)$, all margins $p(u_i)$ will remain in the exponential region. The following theorem gives conditions on p ensuring that $\sum_{i=1}^{t} p(u_i)$ quickly becomes less than $p(U)$.

Theorem 2 *If the following conditions hold for $p(u)$ and U:*

1. *$-p'(u)$ is strictly decreasing and $0 < p''(u) \leq B$, and*
2. *$\exists q > 0$ such that $p(u) \leq -qp'(u) \ \forall u > U$,*

then $\sum_{i=1}^{m} p(u_i) \leq p(U)$ after $T_1 \geq \dfrac{4Bq^2 m^2 p(0) \ln\left(\frac{mp(0)}{p(U)}\right)}{p(U)^2 r^2}$ iterations.

The proof of this theorem approximates the new total potential by the old potential minus α times a linear term, plus an error. By bounding the error as a function of α and minimizing we demonstrate that some values of α give a sufficient decrease in the total potential.

Theorem 3 *If the following conditions hold for $p(u)$, U, q, and iteration T_1:*

1. *$\exists \beta \geq \sqrt{3}$ such that $-p'(u+v) \leq p(u+v) \leq -p'(u)\beta^{-v}q$ whenever $-1 \leq v \leq 1$ and $u > U$,*
2. *$\sum_{i=1}^{m} p(u_{i,T_1}) \leq p(U)$,*
3. *$-p'(u)$ is strictly decreasing, and*
4. *$\exists C > 0, \gamma > 1$ such that $Cp(u) \geq \gamma^{-u} \ \forall u > U$*

then $\mathbf{P}_S[yF_T(x) \leq \theta] \leq \dfrac{qC}{m} \gamma^{\theta T_1} p(U) \left(\gamma^\theta q \sqrt{1-r^2}\right)^{(T-T_1)}$ which decreases exponentially in $T - T_1$ if $\theta < \dfrac{-\ln(q\sqrt{1-r^2})}{\ln(\gamma)}$.

The proof of this theorem is a generalization of the AdaBoost proof.

Combining these two theorems, and the generalization bound from Theorem 2 of Bartlett et al. [15] gives the following result, where d is the VC dimension of the weak hypothesis class.

Theorem 4 *If for all edges $0 < r < 1/2$ there exists $T_{1,r} \leq \text{poly}(m, 1/r)$, U_r, and q_r satisfying the conditions of Theorem 3 such that $p(U_r) \geq \text{poly}(r)$ and $q_r \sqrt{1-r^2} = l(r) < 1 - \text{poly}(r)$, then in time $\text{poly}(m, 1/r)$ all examples have nor-*

malized margin at least $\theta = \ln\left(\frac{l(r)+1}{2l(r)}\right)/\ln(\gamma)$ and

$$\mathbf{P}_D[yF_T(x) \leq 0] \in O\left(\frac{1}{\sqrt{m}}\left(\frac{\ln^2(\gamma)d\log^2(m/d)}{(\ln(l(r)+1)-\ln(2l(r)))^2} + \log(1/\delta)\right)^{\frac{1}{2}}\right).$$

Choosing m appropriately makes the error rate sufficiently small so that the algorithm corresponding to p has the PAC boosting property.

We now apply Theorem 4 to show that the AdaBoost and LogitBoost potentials lead to boosting algorithms.

6 Some Boosting Potentials

In this section we show as a direct consequence of our Theorem 4 that the potential functions for AdaBoost and LogitBoost lead to boosting algorithms. Note that the LogitBoost algorithm we analyze is not exactly the same as that described by Friedman et al. [7], their "weak learner" optimizes a square loss which appears to better fit the potential. First we re-derive the boosting property for AdaBoost.

Corollary 3 *AdaBoost's [16] potential boosts.*

Proof: To prove this we simply need to show that the potential $p(u) = \exp(-u)$ satisfies the conditions of Theorem 4. This is done by setting $U_r = -\ln(m)$, $q_r = 1$, $\gamma = \beta = e$, $C = 1$, and $T_1 = 0$.

Corollary 4 *The log-likelihood potential (as used in LogitBoost [7]) boosts.*

Proof: In this case $p(u) = \ln(1+e^{-u})$ and $-p'(u) = \frac{e^{-u}}{1+e^{-u}}$. We set $\gamma = \beta = e$, $C = 2$, $U_r = -\ln\left(\frac{\sqrt{1-\epsilon^2/2}}{\sqrt{1-\epsilon^2}} - 1\right)$ and $q_r = 1 + \exp(-U_r) = \frac{\sqrt{1-\epsilon^2/2}}{\sqrt{1-\epsilon^2}}$. Now Theorem 2 shows that after $T_1 \leq \text{poly}(m, 1/r)$ iterations the conditions of Theorem 4 are satisfied.

7 Conclusions

In this paper we have examined leveraging weak learners using a gradient descent approach [9]. This approach is a direct generalization of the Adaboost [4, 16] algorithm, where Adaboost's exponential potential function is replaced by alternative potentials. We demonstrated properties of potentials that are sufficient to show that the resulting algorithms are PAC boosters, and other properties that imply that the resulting algorithms are not PAC boosters. We applied these results to several potential functions from the literature [7, 10, 16].

New insight can be gained from examining our criteria carefully. The conditions that show boosting leave tremendous freedom in the choice of potential function for values less than some U, perhaps this freedom can be used to choose potential functions which do not overly concentrate on noisy examples.

There is still a significant gap between these two sets of properties, we are still a long way from classifying arbitrary potential functions as to their boosting properties.

There are other classes of leveraging algorithms. One class looks at the distances between successive distributions [17, 18]. Another class changes their potential over time [6, 8, 12, 14]. The criteria for boosting may change significantly with these different approaches. For example, Freund recently presented a boosting algorithm [12] that uses a time-varying sigmoidal potential. It would be interesting to adapt our techniques to such dynamic potentials.

References

[1] Robert E. Schapire. *The Design and Analysis of Efficient Learning Algorithms*. MIT Press, 1992.

[2] Michael Kearns and Leslie Valiant. Cryptographic limitations on learning Boolean formulae and finite automata. *Journal of the ACM*, 41(1):67–95, January 1994.

[3] L. G. Valiant. A theory of the learnable. *Commun. ACM*, 27(11):1134–1142, November 1984.

[4] Yoav Freund and Robert E. Schapire. A decision-theoretic generalization of on-line learning and an application to boosting. *Journal of Computer and System Sciences*, 55(1):119–139, August 1997.

[5] Eric Bauer and Ron Kohavi. An empirical comparison of voting classification algorithms: Bagging, boosting and variants. *Machine Learning*, 36(1–2):105–39, 1999.

[6] Leo Breiman. Arcing the edge. Technical Report 486, Department of Statistics, University of California, Berkeley., 1997. available at www.stat.berkeley.edu.

[7] Jerome Friedman, Trevor Hastie, and Robert Tibshirani. Additive logistic regression: a statistical view of boosting. Technical report, Stanford University, 1998.

[8] G. Rätsch, T. Onoda, and K.-R. Müller. Soft margins for AdaBoost. *Machine Learning*, 2000. To appear.

[9] Nigel Duffy and David P. Helmbold. A geometric approach to leveraging weak learners. In Paul Fischer and Hans Ulrich Simon, editors, *Computational Learning Theory: 4th European Conference (EuroCOLT '99)*, pages 18–33. Springer-Verlag, March 1999.

[10] Llew Mason, Jonathan Baxter, Peter Bartlett, and Marcus Frean. Boosting algorithms as gradient descent. To appear in NIPS 2000.

[11] Thomas G. Dietterich. An experimental comparison of three methods for constructing ensembles of decision trees: Bagging, Boosting, and Randomization. *Machine Learning*. To appear.

[12] Yoav Freund. An adaptive version of the boost-by-majority algorithm. In *Proc. 12th Annu. Conf. on Comput. Learning Theory*, pages 102–113. ACM, 1999.

[13] David Haussler, Michael Kearns, Nick Littlestone, and Manfred K. Warmuth. Equivalence of models for polynomial learnability. *Information and Computation*, 95(2):129–161, December 1991.

[14] Y. Freund. Boosting a weak learning algorithm by majority. *Information and Computation*, 121(2):256–285, September 1995.

[15] Robert E. Schapire, Yoav Freund, Peter Bartlett, and Wee Sun Lee. Boosting the margin: A new explanation for the effectiveness of voting methods. *The Annals of Statistics*, 26(5):1651–1686, 1998.

[16] Robert E. Schapire and Yoram Singer. Improved boosting algorithms using confidence-rated predictions. *Machine Learning*, 37(3):297–336, December 1999.

[17] Jyrki Kivinen and Manfred K. Warmuth. Boosting as entropy projection. In *Proc. 12th Annu. Conf. on Comput. Learning Theory*, pages 134–144. ACM, 1999.

[18] John Lafferty. Additive models, boosting, and inference for generalized divergences. In *Proc. 12th Annu. Conf. on Comput. Learning Theory*, pages 125–133. ACM.

Bayesian averaging is well-temperated

Lars Kai Hansen
Department of Mathematical Modelling
Technical University of Denmark B321
DK-2800 Lyngby, Denmark
lkhansen@imm.dtu.dk

Abstract

Bayesian predictions are stochastic just like predictions of any other inference scheme that generalize from a finite sample. While a simple variational argument shows that Bayes averaging is generalization optimal given that the prior matches the teacher parameter distribution the situation is less clear if the teacher distribution is unknown. I define a class of averaging procedures, the temperated likelihoods, including both Bayes averaging with a uniform prior and maximum likelihood estimation as special cases. I show that Bayes is generalization optimal in this family for any teacher distribution for two learning problems that are analytically tractable: learning the mean of a Gaussian and asymptotics of smooth learners.

1 Introduction

Learning is the stochastic process of generalizing from a random finite sample of data. Often a learning problem has natural quantitative measure of generalization. If a loss function is defined the natural measure is the *generalization error*, i.e., the *expected loss* on a random sample independent of the training set. Generalizability is a key topic of learning theory and much progress has been reported. Analytic results for a broad class of machines can be found in the litterature [8, 12, 9, 10] describing the asymptotic generalization ability of supervised algorithms that are continuously parameterized. Asymptotic bounds on generalization for general machines have been advocated by Vapnik [11]. Generalization results valid for finite training sets can only be obtained for specific learning machines, see e.g. [5]. A very rich framework for analysis of generalization for Bayesian averaging and other schemes is defined in [6].

Averaging has become popular as a tool for improving generalizability of learning machines. In the context of (time series) forecasting averaging has been investigated intensely for decades [3]. Neural network ensembles were shown to improve generalization by simple voting in [4] and later work has generalized these results to other types of averaging. Boosting, Bagging, Stacking, and Arcing are recent examples of averaging procedures based on data resampling that have shown useful see [2] for a recent review with references. However, Bayesian averaging in particular is attaining a kind of cult status. Bayesian averaging is indeed provably optimal in a number various ways (admissibility, the likelihood principle etc) [1]. While it follows by construction that Bayes is generalization optimal if given the correct prior information, i.e., the teacher parameter distribution, the situation is less clear if the teacher distribution is unknown. Hence, the pragmatic Bayesians downplay the role of the prior. Instead the averaging aspect is emphasized and "vague" priors are invoked. It is important to note that whatever prior is used Bayesian predictions are stochastic just like predictions of any other inference scheme that generalize from a finite sample.

In this contribution I analyse two scenarios where averaging can improve generalizability and I show that the vague Bayes average is in fact optimal among the averaging schemes investigated. Averaging is shown to reduce variance at the cost of introducing bias, and Bayes happens to implement the optimal bias-variance trade-off.

2 Bayes and generalization

Consider a model that is smoothly parametrized and whose predictions can be described in terms of a density function[1]. Predictions in the model are based on a given training set: a finite sample $D = \{x_\alpha\}_{\alpha=1}^N$ of the stochastic vector x whose density – the teacher – is denoted $p(x|\theta_0)$. In other words the true density is assumed to be defined by a fixed, but unknown, teacher parameter vector θ_0. The model, denoted H, involves the parameter vector θ and the predictive density is given by

$$p(x|D, H) = \int p(x|\theta, H) p(\theta|D, H) d\theta \qquad (1)$$

$p(\theta|D, H)$ is the parameter distribution produced in training process. In a maximum likelihood scenario this distribution is a delta function centered on the most likely parameters under the model for the given data set. In ensemble averaging approaches, like boosting bagging or stacking, the distribution is obtained by training on resampled traning sets. In a Bayesian scenario, the parameter distribution is the posterior distribution,

$$p(\theta|D, H) = \frac{p(D|\theta, H) p(\theta|H)}{\int p(D|\theta', H) p(\theta'|H) d\theta'} \qquad (2)$$

where $p(\theta|H)$ is the prior distribution (probability density of parameters if D is empty). In the sequel we will only consider one model hence we suppress the model conditioning label H.

The generalization error is the average negative log density (also known as simply the "log loss" – in some applied statistics works known as the "deviance")

$$\Gamma(D|\theta_0) = \int -\log p(x|D) p(x|\theta_0) dx, \qquad (3)$$

The expected value of the generalization error for training sets produced by the given teacher is given by

$$\Gamma(\theta_0) = \int \int -\log p(x|D) p(x|\theta_0) dx p(D|\theta_0) dD. \qquad (4)$$

---

[1]This does not limit us to conventional density estimation; pattern recognition and many functional approximations problems can be formulated as density estimation problems as well.

Playing the game of "guessing a probability distribution" [6] we not only face a random training set, we also face a teacher drawn from the teacher distribution $p(\theta_0)$. The teacher averaged generalization must then be defined as

$$\Gamma = \int \Gamma(\theta_0) p(\theta_0) d\theta_0. \qquad (5)$$

This is the typical generalization error for a random training set from the randomly chosen teacher – produced by the model H. The generalization error is minimized by Bayes averaging if the teacher distribution is used as prior. To see this, form the Lagrangian functional

$$\mathcal{L}[q(x|D)] = \int \int \int -\log q(x|D) p(x|\theta_0) dx p(D|\theta_0) dD p(\theta_0) d\theta_0 + \lambda \int q(x|D) dx \qquad (6)$$

defined on positive functions $q(x|D)$. The second term is used to ensure that $q(x|D)$ is a normalized density in x. Now compute the variational derivative to obtain

$$\frac{\delta \mathcal{L}}{\delta q(x|D)} = -\frac{1}{q(x|D)} \int p(x|\theta_0) p(D|\theta_0) p(\theta_0) d\theta_0 + \lambda. \qquad (7)$$

Equating this derivative to zero we recover the predictive distribution of Bayesian averaging,

$$q(x|D) = \int p(x|\theta) \frac{p(D|\theta) p(\theta)}{\int p(D|\theta') p(\theta') d\theta'} d\theta, \qquad (8)$$

where we used that $\lambda = \int p(D|\theta) p(\theta) d\theta$ is the appropriate normalization constant. It is easily verified that this is indeed the global minimum of the averaged generalization error. We also note that if the Bayes average is performed with another prior than the teacher distribution $p(\theta_0)$, we can expect a higher generalization error. The important question from a Bayesian point of view is then: Are there cases where averaging with generic priors (e.g. vague or uniform priors) can be shown to be optimal?

3 Tempered likelihoods

To come closer to a quantitative statement about when and why vague Bayes is the better procedure we will analyse two problems for which some analytical progress is possible. We will consider a one-parameter family of learning procedures including both a Bayes and the maximum likelihood procedure,

$$p(\theta|\beta, D, H) = \frac{p^\beta(D|\theta)}{\int p^\beta(D|\theta') d\theta'}, \qquad (9)$$

where β is a positive parameter (plying the role of an inverse temperature). The family of procedures are all averaging procedures, and β controls the width of the average. Vague Bayes (here used synonymously with Bayes with a uniform prior) is recoved for $\beta = 1$, while the maximum posterior procedure is obtained by cooling to zero width $\beta \to \infty$.

In this context the generalization design question can be frased as follows: *is there an optimal temperature in the family of the temperated likelihoods?*

3.1 Example: 1D normal variates

Let the teacher distribution be given by

$$p(x|\theta_0) = \frac{1}{\sqrt{2\pi\sigma^2}} \exp\left(-\frac{1}{2\sigma^2}(x - \theta_0)^2\right) \qquad (10)$$

The model density is of the same form with θ unknown and σ^2 assumed to be known. For N examples the posterior (with a uniform prior) is,

$$p(\theta|D) = \sqrt{\frac{N}{2\pi\sigma^2}} \exp\left(-\frac{N}{2\sigma^2}(\overline{x}-\theta)^2\right), \quad (11)$$

with $\overline{x} = 1/N \sum_\alpha x_\alpha$. The temperated likelihood is obtained by raising to the β'th power and normalizing,

$$p(\theta|D,\beta) = \sqrt{\frac{\beta N}{2\pi\sigma^2}} \exp\left(-\frac{\beta N}{2\sigma^2}(\overline{x}-\theta)^2\right). \quad (12)$$

The predictive distribution is found by integrating w.r.t. θ,

$$p(x|D,\beta) = \int p(x|\theta)p(\theta|D,\beta)d\theta = \frac{1}{\sqrt{2\pi\sigma_\beta^2}} \exp\left(-\frac{1}{2\sigma_\beta^2}(\overline{x}-x)^2\right), \quad (13)$$

with $\sigma_\beta^2 = \sigma^2(1+1/\beta N)$. We note that this distribution is wider for all the averaging procedures than it is for maximum likelihood ($\beta \to \infty$), i.e., less variant. For very small β the predictive distribution is almost independent of the data set, hence highly biased.

It is straightforward to compute the generalization error of the predictive distribution for general β. First we compute the generalization error for the specific training set D,

$$\Gamma(D,\beta,\theta_0) = \int -\log p(x|D,\beta)p(x|\theta_0)dx = \log\sqrt{2\pi\sigma_\beta^2} + \frac{1}{2\sigma_\beta^2}\left((\overline{x}-\theta_0)^2 + \sigma^2\right), \quad (14)$$

The average generalization error is then found by averaging w.r.t the sampling distribution using $\overline{x} \sim \mathcal{N}(\theta_0, \sigma^2/N)$.,

$$\Gamma(\beta) = \int \Gamma(D,\beta)dDp(D|\theta_0) = \log\sqrt{2\pi\sigma_\beta^2} + \frac{\sigma^2}{2\sigma_\beta^2}\left(\frac{1}{N}+1\right), \quad (15)$$

We first note that the generalization error is independent of the teacher θ_0 parameter, this happened because θ is a "location" parameter. The β-dependency of the averaged generalization error is depicted in Figure 1. Solving $\partial\Gamma(\beta)/\partial\beta = 0$ we find that the optimal β solves

$$\sigma_\beta^2 \equiv \sigma^2\left(\frac{1}{\beta N}+1\right) = \sigma^2\left(\frac{1}{N}+1\right) \Rightarrow \beta = 1 \quad (16)$$

Note that this result holds for any N and is independent of the teacher parameter. The Bayes averaging at unit temperature is optimal for any given value of θ_0, hence, for any teacher distribution. We may say that the vague Bayes scheme is robust to the teacher distribution in this case. Clearly this is a much stronger optimality than the more general result proven above.

3.2 Bias-variance tradeoff

It is interesting to decompose the generalization error in Eq. 15 in bias and variance components. We follow Heskes [7] and define the bias error as the generalization error of the geometric average distribution,

$$B(\beta) \equiv \int -\log\overline{p}(x)p(x|\theta_0)dx, \quad (17)$$

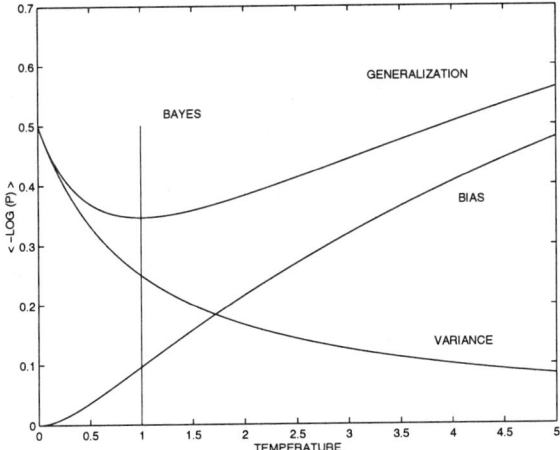

Figure 1: Bias-variance trade-off as function of the width of the temperated likelihood ensemble (temperature $= 1/\beta$) for $N = 1$. The bias is computed as the generalization error of the predictive distribution obtained from the geometric average distribution w.r.t. training set fluctuations as proposed by Heskes. The predictive distribution produced by Bayesian averaging corresponds to unit temperature (vertical line) and it achieves the minimal generalization error. Maximum-likelihood estimation for reference is recovered as the zero width/temperature limit.

with

$$\overline{p}(x) = Z^{-1} \exp\left(\int \log[p(x|D)] p(D|\theta_0) dD\right). \tag{18}$$

Inserting from Eq. (13), we find

$$\overline{p}(x) = \frac{1}{\sqrt{2\pi\sigma_\beta^2}} \exp\left(-\frac{1}{2\sigma_\beta^2}(x - \theta_0)^2\right). \tag{19}$$

Integrating over the teacher distribution we find,

$$B(\beta) = \frac{1}{2}\log 2\pi\sigma_\beta^2 + \frac{\sigma^2}{2\sigma_\beta^2} \tag{20}$$

The variance error is given by $V(\beta) = \Gamma(\beta) - B(\beta)$,

$$V(\beta) = \frac{\sigma^2}{2N\sigma_\beta^2} \tag{21}$$

We can now quantify the statements above. By averaging a bias is introduced –the predictive distribution becomes wider– which decrease the variance contribution initially so that the generalization error being the sum of the two decreases. At still higher temperatures the bias becomes too strong and the generalization error start to increase. The Bayes average at unit temperature is the optimal trade-off within the given family of procedures.

3.3 Asymptotics for smoothly parameterized models

We now go on to show that a similar result also holds for general learning problems in limit of large data sets. We consider a system parameterized by a finite dimensional parameter vector θ. For a given large training set and for a smooth likelihood function, the tempered likelihood is approximately Gaussian centered at the maximum posterior parameters[13], hence the normalized temperated posterior reads

$$P(\theta|\beta D, H) = \sqrt{\left|\frac{\beta N A(D, \theta_{ML})}{2\pi}\right|} \exp\left(-\frac{\beta N}{2} \delta\theta' A(D, \theta_{ML}) \delta\theta\right) \quad (22)$$

where $\delta\theta = \theta - \theta_{ML}$, with $\theta_{ML} = \theta_{ML}(D)$ denoting the maximum likelihood solution for the given training sample. The second derivative or *Hessian* matrix is given by

$$A(D, \theta) = \frac{1}{N}\sum_{\alpha=1}^{N} A(x_\alpha, \theta) \quad (23)$$

$$A(x, \theta) = \frac{\partial^2}{\partial\theta\partial\theta'} - \log p(x|\theta) \quad (24)$$

The predictive distribution is given by

$$p(x|\beta, D) = \int p(x|\theta)p(\theta|\beta, D)d\theta \quad (25)$$

we write $p(x|\theta) = \exp(-\epsilon(x|\theta))$ and expand $\epsilon(x|\theta)$ around θ_{ML} to second order, we find

$$p(x|\theta) \approx p(x|\theta_{ML}) \exp\left(-a(x|\theta_{ML})'\delta\theta - \tfrac{1}{2}\delta\theta' A(x|\theta_{ML})\delta\theta\right). \quad (26)$$

We are then in position to perform the integration over the posterior to find the normalized predictive distribution,

$$p(x|\beta, D) = p(x|\theta_{ML})\sqrt{\frac{|\beta N A(D)|}{|\beta N A(D) + A(x)|}} \exp\left(\tfrac{1}{2}a(x|\theta_{ML})' A(x|\theta_{ML})a(x|\theta_{ML})\right). \quad (27)$$

Proceeding as above, we compute the generalization error

$$\Gamma(\beta, \theta_0) = \int\int -\log p(x|\beta, D) p(x|\theta_0) dx p(D|\theta_0) dD \quad (28)$$

For sufficiently smooth likelihoods, fluctuations in the maximum likelihood parameters will be asymptotic normal, see e.g. [8], and furthermore fluctuations in $A(D)$ can be neglected, this means that we can approximate,

$$A(x) + A(D) \approx (\frac{1}{N} + 1)A_0, \quad A_0 = \int A(x|\theta_0) p(x|\theta_0) dx \quad (29)$$

where A_0 is the averaged Fisher information matrix. With these approximations (valid as $N \to \infty$) the generalization error can be found,

$$\Gamma(\beta, \theta_0) \approx \Gamma(\infty) + \frac{d}{2}\log\left(1 + \frac{1}{\beta N}\right) - \frac{d}{2}\frac{1 + \frac{1}{N}}{1 + \beta N}. \quad (30)$$

with $d = \dim(\theta)$ denoting the dimension of the parameter vector. Like in the 1D example (Eq. (15)) we find the generalization error is asymptotically independent of the teacher parameters. It is minimized for $\beta = 1$ and we conclude that Bayes is well-tempered in the asymptotics and that this holds for any teacher distribution. In the Bayes literature this is refered to as the prior is overwhelmed by data [1]. Decomposing the errors in bias and variance contributions we find similar results as for in 1D example, Bayes introduces the optimal bias by averaging at unit temperature.

4 Discussion

We have seen two examples of Bayes averaging being optimal, in particular improving on maximum likelihood estimation. We found that averaging introduces a bias and reduces variance so that the generalization error (being the sum of bias and variance) initially decrease. Bayesian averaging at unit temperature is the optimal width of the averaging distribution. For larger temperatures (widths) the bias is too strong and the generalization error increases. Both examples were special in the sense that they lead to generalization errors that are independent of the random teacher parameter. This is not generic, of course, rather the generic case is that a mis-specified prior can lead to arbitrary large learning catastrophes.

Acknowledgments

I thank the organizers of the 1999 Max Planck Institute Workshop on Statistical Physics of Neural Networks Michael Biehl, Wolfgang Kinzel and Ido Kanter, where this work was initiated. I thank Carl Edward Rasmussen, Jan Larsen, and Manfred Opper for stimulating discussions on Bayesian averaging. This work was funded by the Danish Research Councils through the Computational Neural Network Center CONNECT and the THOR Center for Neuroinformatics.

References

[1] C.P. Robert: *The Bayesian Choice - A Decision-Theoretic Motivation.* Springer Texts in Statistics, Springer Verlag, New York (1994). A. Ohagan: *Bayesian Inference.* Kendall's Advanced Theory of Statistics. Vol 2B. The University Press, Cambridge (1994).

[2] L. Breiman: *Using adaptive bagging to debias regressions.* Technical Report 547, Statistics Dept. U.C. Berkeley, (1999).

[3] R.T. Clemen *Combining forecast: A review and annotated bibliography.* Journal of Forecasting **5**, 559 (1989).

[4] L.K. Hansen and P. Salamon: *Neural Network Ensembles.* IEEE Transactions on Pattern Analysis and Machine Intelligence, **12**, 993-1001 (1990).

[5] L.K. Hansen: *Stochastic Linear Learning: Exact Test and Training Error Averages.* Neural Networks **6**, 393-396, (1993)

[6] D. Haussler and M. Opper: *Mutual Information, Metric Entropy, and Cumulative Relative Entropy Risk* Annals of Statistics **25** 2451-2492 (1997)

[7] T. Heskes: *Bias/Variance Decomposition for Likelihood-Based Estimators.* Neural Computation **10**, pp 1425-1433, (1998).

[8] L. Ljung: *System Identification: Theory for the User.* Englewood Cliffs, New Jersey: Prentice-Hall, (1987).

[9] J. Moody: "Note on Generalization, Regularization, and Architecture Selection in Nonlinear Learning Systems," in B.H. Juang, S.Y. Kung & C.A. Kamm (eds.) *Proceedings of the first IEEE Workshop on Neural Networks for Signal Processing*, Piscataway, New Jersey: IEEE, 1–10, (1991).

[10] N. Murata, S. Yoshizawa & S. Amari: *Network Information Criterion — Determining the Number of Hidden Units for an Artificial Neural Network Model.* IEEE Transactions on Neural Networks, vol. 5, no. 6, pp. 865–872, 1994.

[11] V. Vapnik: *Estimation of Dependences Based on Empirical Data.* Springer-Verlag New York (1982).

[12] H. White, "Consequences and Detection of Misspecified Nonlinear Regression Models," *Journal of the American Statistical Association*, **76**(374), 419–433, (1981).

[13] D.J.C MacKay: *Bayesian Interpolation,* Neural Computation **4**, 415-447, (1992).

Regular and Irregular Gallager-type Error-Correcting Codes

Y. Kabashima and T. Murayama
Dept. of Compt. Intl. & Syst. Sci.
Tokyo Institute of Technology
Yokohama 2268502, Japan

D. Saad and R. Vicente
Neural Computing Research Group
Aston University
Birmingham B4 7ET, UK

Abstract

The performance of regular and irregular Gallager-type error-correcting code is investigated via methods of statistical physics. The transmitted codeword comprises products of the original message bits selected by two randomly-constructed sparse matrices; the number of non-zero row/column elements in these matrices constitutes a family of codes. We show that Shannon's channel capacity may be saturated in equilibrium for many of the regular codes while slightly lower performance is obtained for others which may be of higher practical relevance. Decoding aspects are considered by employing the TAP approach which is identical to the commonly used belief-propagation-based decoding. We show that irregular codes may saturate Shannon's capacity but with improved dynamical properties.

1 Introduction

The ever increasing information transmission in the modern world is based on reliably communicating messages through noisy transmission channels; these can be telephone lines, deep space, magnetic storing media etc. Error-correcting codes play a significant role in correcting errors incurred during transmission; this is carried out by encoding the message prior to transmission and decoding the corrupted received code-word for retrieving the original message.

In his ground breaking papers, Shannon[1] analyzed the capacity of communication channels, setting an upper bound to the achievable noise-correction capability of codes, given their code (or symbol) rate, constituted by the ratio between the number of bits in the original message and the transmitted code-word. Shannon's bound is non-constructive and does not provide a recipe for devising optimal codes. The quest for more efficient codes, in the hope of saturating the bound set by Shannon, has been going on ever since, providing many useful but sub-optimal codes.

One family of codes, presented originally by Gallager[2], attracted significant interest recently as it has been shown to outperform most currently used techniques[3]. Gallager-type codes are characterized by several parameters, the choice of which defines a particular member of this family of codes. Current theoretical results[3] offer only bounds on the error probability of various architectures, proving the existence of very good codes under some restrictions; decoding issues are examined via numerical simulations.

In this paper we analyze the typical performance of Gallager-type codes for several parameter choices via methods of statistical mechanics. We then validate the analytical solution by comparing the results to those obtained by the TAP approach and via numerical methods.

2 The general framework

In a general scenario, a message represented by an N dimensional Boolean vector $\boldsymbol{\xi}$ is encoded to the M dimensional vector $\boldsymbol{J^0}$ which is transmitted through a noisy channel with some flipping probability p per bit (other noise types may also be studied). The received message $\boldsymbol{J}$ is then decoded to retrieve the original message.

In this paper we analyze a slightly different version of Gallager-type codes termed the MN code[3] that is based on choosing two randomly-selected sparse matrices A and B of dimensionality $M \times N$ and $M \times M$ respectively; these are characterized by K and L non-zero unit elements per row and C and L per column respectively. The finite numbers K, C and L define a particular code; both matrices are known to both sender and receiver. Encoding is carried out by constructing the modulo 2 inverse of B and the matrix $B^{-1}A$ (mod 2); the vector $\boldsymbol{J^0} = B^{-1}A\,\boldsymbol{\xi}$ (mod 2, $\boldsymbol{\xi}$ Boolean vector) constitutes the codeword. Decoding is carried out by taking the product of the matrix B and the received message $\boldsymbol{J} = \boldsymbol{J^0} + \boldsymbol{\zeta}$ (mod 2), corrupted by the Boolean noise vector $\boldsymbol{\zeta}$, resulting in $A\boldsymbol{\xi}+B\boldsymbol{\zeta}$. The equation

$$A\boldsymbol{\xi} + B\boldsymbol{\zeta} = A\boldsymbol{S} + B\boldsymbol{\tau} \pmod{2} \tag{1}$$

is solved via the iterative methods of Belief Propagation (BP)[3] to obtain the most probable Boolean vectors $\boldsymbol{S}$ and $\boldsymbol{\tau}$; BP methods in the context of error-correcting codes have recently been shown to be identical to a TAP[4] based solution of a similar physical system[5].

The similarity between error-correcting codes of this type and Ising spin systems was first pointed out by Sourlas[6], who formulated the mapping of a simpler code, somewhat similar to the one presented here, onto an Ising spin system Hamiltonian. We recently extended the work of Sourlas, that focused on extensively connected systems, to the finite connectivity case[5] as well as to the case of MN codes [7].

To facilitate the current investigation we first map the problem to that of an Ising model with finite connectivity. We employ the binary representation (± 1) of the dynamical variables $\boldsymbol{S}$ and $\boldsymbol{\tau}$ and of the vectors $\boldsymbol{J}$ and $\boldsymbol{J^0}$ rather than the Boolean $(0,1)$ one; the vector $\boldsymbol{J^0}$ is generated by taking products of the relevant binary message bits $J_\mu^0 = \prod_{i \in \mu} \xi_i$, where the indices $\mu = \langle i_1, \ldots i_K \rangle$ correspond to the non-zero elements of $B^{-1}A$, producing a binary version of $\boldsymbol{J^0}$. As we use statistical mechanics techniques, we consider the message and codeword dimensionality (N and M respectively) to be infinite, keeping the ratio between them $R = N/M$, which constitutes the code rate, finite. Using the thermodynamic limit is quite natural as Gallager-type codes are usually used for transmitting long (10^4-10^5) messages, where finite size corrections are likely to be negligible. To explore the system's capabilities we examine the Hamiltonian

$$\mathcal{H} = \sum_{\mu,\sigma} \mathcal{D}_{\mu\sigma}\, \delta\!\left[-1\,;\, \mathcal{J}_{\mu\sigma} \prod_{i \in \mu} S_i \prod_{j \in \sigma} \tau_j \right] - \frac{F_s}{\beta} \sum_{i=1}^{N} S_i - \frac{F_\tau}{\beta} \sum_{j=1}^{M} \tau_j\ .$$

The tensor product $\mathcal{D}_{\mu\sigma}\mathcal{J}_{\mu\sigma}$, where $\mathcal{J}_{\mu\sigma} = \prod_{i\in\mu} \xi_i \prod_{j\in\sigma} \zeta_j$ and $\sigma = \langle j_1,\ldots j_L \rangle$, is the binary equivalent of $A\boldsymbol{\xi}+B\boldsymbol{\zeta}$, treating both signal ($\boldsymbol{S}$ and index i) and noise ($\boldsymbol{\tau}$ and index j) simultaneously. Elements of the sparse connectivity tensor $\mathcal{D}_{\mu\sigma}$ take the value 1 if the corresponding indices of both signal and noise are chosen (i.e., if all corresponding indices of the matrices A and B are 1) and 0 otherwise; it has C unit elements per i-index and L per j-index representing the system's degree of connectivity. The δ function provides 1 if the selected sites' product $\prod_{i\in\mu} S_i \prod_{j\in\sigma} \tau_j$ is in disagreement with the corresponding element $\mathcal{J}_{\mu\sigma}$, recording an error, and 0 otherwise. Notice that this term is not frustrated, as there are $M+N$ degrees of freedom and only M constraints from Eq.(1), and can therefore vanish at sufficiently low temperatures. The last two terms on the right represent our prior knowledge in the case of sparse or biased messages F_s and of the noise level F_τ and require assigning certain values to these additive fields. The choice of $\beta \to \infty$ imposes the restriction of Eq.(1), limiting the solutions to those for which the first term of Eq.(2) vanishes, while the last two terms, scaled with β, survive. Note that the noise dynamical variables $\boldsymbol{\tau}$ are irrelevant to measuring the retrieval success $m = \frac{1}{N} \left\langle \sum_{i=1}^{N} \xi_i \, \text{sign} \, \langle S_i \rangle_\beta \right\rangle_\xi$. The latter monitors the normalized mean overlap between the Bayes-optimal retrieved message, shown to correspond to the alignment of $\langle S_i \rangle_\beta$ to the nearest binary value[6], and the original message; the subscript β denotes thermal averaging.

Since the first part of Eq.(2) is invariant under the map $S_i \to S_i \xi_i$, $\tau_j \to \tau_j \zeta_j$ and $\mathcal{J}_{\mu\sigma} \to \mathcal{J}_{\mu\sigma} \prod_{i\in\mu} \xi_i \prod_{j\in\sigma} \zeta_j = 1$, it is useful to decouple the correlation between the vectors $\boldsymbol{S}, \boldsymbol{\tau}$ and $\boldsymbol{\xi}, \boldsymbol{\zeta}$. Rewriting Eq.(2) one obtains a similar expression apart from the last terms on the right which become $F_s/\beta \sum_k S_k \, \xi_k$ and $F_\tau/\beta \sum_k \tau_k \, \zeta_k$.

The random selection of elements in $\mathcal{D}$ introduces disorder to the system which is treated via methods of statistical physics. More specifically, we calculate the partition function $\mathcal{Z}(\mathcal{D}, \boldsymbol{J}) = \text{Tr}_{\{\boldsymbol{S},\boldsymbol{\tau}\}} \exp[-\beta\mathcal{H}]$ averaged over the disorder and the statistical properties of the message and noise, using the replica method[5, 8, 9]. Taking $\beta \to \infty$ gives rise to a set of order parameters

$$q_{\alpha,\beta,\ldots,\gamma} = \left\langle \frac{1}{N} \sum_{i=1}^{N} Z_i \, S_i^\alpha \, S_i^\beta, \ldots, S_i^\gamma \right\rangle_{\beta\to\infty} \qquad r_{\alpha,\beta,\ldots,\gamma} = \left\langle \frac{1}{M} \sum_{i=1}^{M} Y_j \, \tau_j^\alpha \, \tau_j^\beta, \ldots, \tau_j^\gamma \right\rangle_{\beta\to\infty} \tag{2}$$

where $\alpha, \beta, \ldots$ represent replica indices, and the variables Z_i and Y_j come from enforcing the restriction of C and L connections per index respectively[5]:

$$\delta\left(\sum_{\langle i_2,\ldots,i_K \rangle} \mathcal{D}_{<i,i_2,\ldots,j_L>} - C \right) = \oint_0^{2\pi} \frac{dZ}{2\pi} Z^{\sum_{\langle i_2,\ldots,i_K \rangle} \mathcal{D}_{<i,i_2,\ldots,j_L>} - (C+1)}, \tag{3}$$

and similarly for the restriction on the j indices.

To proceed with the calculation one has to make an assumption about the order parameters symmetry. The assumption made here, and validated later on, is that of replica symmetry in the following representation of the order parameters and the related conjugate variables

$$q_{\alpha,\beta\ldots\gamma} = a_q \int dx \, \pi(x) \, x^l \, , \quad \widehat{q}_{\alpha,\beta\ldots\gamma} = a_{\widehat{q}} \int d\hat{x} \, \widehat{\pi}(\hat{x}) \, \hat{x}^l \tag{4}$$

$$r_{\alpha,\beta\ldots\gamma} = a_r \int dy \, \rho(y) \, y^l \, , \quad \widehat{r}_{\alpha,\beta\ldots\gamma} = a_{\widehat{r}} \int d\hat{y} \, \widehat{\rho}(\hat{y}) \, \hat{y}^l \, ,$$

where l is the number of replica indices, a_* are normalization coefficients, and $\pi(x), \widehat{\pi}(\hat{x}), \rho(y)$ and $\widehat{\rho}(\hat{y})$ represent probability distributions. Unspecified integrals are over the range $[-1, +1]$. One then obtains an expression for the free energy per spin expressed in terms of these probability distributions $1/N \langle \ln \mathcal{Z} \rangle_{\xi,\varsigma,\mathcal{D}}$. The free energy can then be calculated via the saddle point method. Solving the equations obtained by varying the free energy w.r.t the probability distributions $\pi(x), \widehat{\pi}(\widehat{x}), \rho(y)$ and $\widehat{\rho}(\widehat{y})$, is difficult as they generally comprise both delta peaks and regular[9] solutions for the ferromagnetic and paramagnetic phases (there is no spin-glass solution here as the system is not frustrated). The solutions obtained in the case of unbiased messages (the most interesting case as most messages are compressed prior to transmission) are for the ferromagnetic phase:

$$\pi(x) = \delta(x-1) \; , \; \widehat{\pi}(\widehat{x}) = \delta(\widehat{x}-1) \; , \; \rho(y) = \delta(y-1) \; , \; \widehat{\rho}(\widehat{y}) = \delta(\widehat{y}-1) \; , \quad (5)$$

and for the paramagnetic phase:

$$\begin{aligned}\pi(x) &= \delta(x) \; , \; \widehat{\pi}(\widehat{x}) = \delta(\widehat{x}) \; , \; \widehat{\rho}(\widehat{y}) = \delta(\widehat{y}) \\ \rho(y) &= \frac{1+\tanh F_\tau}{2} \delta(y - \tanh F_\tau) + \frac{1-\tanh F_\tau}{2} \delta(y + \tanh F_\tau) \; .\end{aligned} \quad (6)$$

These solutions obey the saddle point equations. However, it is unclear whether the contribution of other delta peaks or of an additional continuous solution will be significant and whether the solutions (5) and (6) are stable or not. In addition, it is also necessary to validate the replica symmetric ansatz itself. To address these questions we obtained solutions to the system described by the Hamiltonian (2) via TAP methods of finitely connected systems[5]; we solved the saddle point equations derived from the free energy numerically, representing all probability distributions by up to 10^4 bin models and by carrying out the integrations via Monte-Carlo methods; finally, to show the consistency between theory and practice we carried out large scale simulations for several cases, which will be presented elsewhere.

3 Structure of the solutions

The various methods indicate that the solutions may be divided to two different categories: $K=L=2$ and either $K \geq 3$ or $L \geq 3$. We therefore treat them separately.

For unbiased messages and either $K \geq 3$ or $L \geq 3$ we obtain the solutions (5) and (6) both by applying the TAP approach and by solving the saddle point equations numerically. The former was carried out at the value of F_τ which corresponds to the true noise and input bias levels (for unbiased messages $F_s = 0$) and thus to Nishimori's condition[10], where no replica symmetry breaking effects are expected. This is equivalent to having the correct prior within the Bayesian framework[6] and enables one to obtain analytic expressions for some observables as long as some gauge requirements are obeyed[10]. Numerical solutions show the emergence of stable dominant delta peaks, consistent with those of (5) and (6). The question of longitudinal mode stability (corresponding to the replica symmetric solution) was addressed by setting initial conditions for the numerical solutions close to the solutions (5) and (6), showing that they converge back to these solutions which are therefore stable.

The most interesting quantity to examine is the maximal code rate, for a given corruption process, for which messages can be perfectly retrieved. This is defined in the case of $K, L \geq 3$ by the value of $R = K/C = N/M$ for which the free energy of the ferromagnetic solution becomes smaller than that of the paramagnetic solution, constituting a first order phase transition. A schematic description of the solutions obtained is shown in the inset of Fig.1a. The paramagnetic solution $(m=0)$ has a lower free energy than the ferromagnetic one (low/high free energies are denoted by the thick and thin lines respectively, there are no axis lines at $m = 0, 1$) for noise levels $p > p_c$ and vice versa for $p \leq p_c$; both solutions are stable. The critical code rate is derived by equating the ferromagnetic and paramagnetic free energies to obtain $R_c = 1 - H_2(p) = 1 + (p \log_2 p + (1-p) \log_2(1-p))$. This coincides with *Shannon's capacity*. To validate these results we obtained TAP solutions for the unbiased message case ($K = L = 3$, $C = 6$) as shown in Fig.1a (as +) in comparison to Shannon's capacity (solid line).

Analytical solutions for the saddle point equations cannot be obtained for biased patterns and we therefore resort to numerical methods and the TAP approach. The maximal information rate (i.e., code-rate $\times H_2(f_s = (1 + \tanh F_s)/2)$ - the source redundancy) obtained by the TAP method ($\diamond$) and numerical solutions of the saddle point equations ($\square$), for each noise level, are shown in Fig.1a. Numerical results have been obtained using $10^3 - 10^4$ bin models for each probability distribution and had been run for 10^5 steps per noise level point. The various results are highly consistent and practically saturate Shannon's bound for the same noise level.

The MN code for $K, L \geq 3$ seems to offer optimal performance. However, the main drawback is rooted in the co-existence of the stable $m = 1$ and $m = 0$ solutions, shown in Fig.1a (inset), which implies that from some initial conditions the system will converge to the undesired paramagnetic solution. Moreover, studying the ferromagnetic solution numerically shows a highly limited basin of attraction, which becomes smaller as K and L increase, while the paramagnetic solution at $m = 0$ *always* enjoys a wide basin of attraction. Computer simulations (see also [3]) show that as initial conditions for the decoding process are typically of close-to-zero magnetization (almost no prior information about the original message is assumed) it is likely that the decoding process will converge to the paramagnetic solution.

While all codes with $K, L \geq 3$ saturate Shannon's bound in their equilibrium properties and are characterized by a first order, paramagnetic to ferromagnetic, phase transition, codes with $K = L = 2$ show lower performance and different physical characteristics. The analytical solutions (5) and (6) are unstable at some flip rate levels and one resorts to solving the saddle point equations numerically and to TAP based solutions. The picture that emerges is sketched in the inset of Fig.1b: The paramagnetic solution dominates the high flip rate regime up to the point p_1 (denoted as 1 in the inset) in which a stable, ferromagnetic solution, of higher free energy, appears (thin lines at $m = \pm 1$). At a lower flip rate value p_2 the paramagnetic solution becomes unstable (dashed line) and is replaced by two stable sub-optimal ferromagnetic (broken symmetry) solutions which appear as a couple of peaks in the various probability distributions; typically, these have a lower free energy than the ferromagnetic solution until p_3, after which the ferromagnetic solution becomes dominant. Still, only once the sub-optimal ferromagnetic solutions disappear, at the spinodal point p_s, a unique ferromagnetic solution emerges as a single delta peak in the numerical results (plus a mirror solution). The point in which the sub-optimal ferromagnetic solutions disappear constitutes the maximal practical flip rate for the current code-rate and was defined numerically ($\diamond$) and via TAP solutions (+) as shown in Fig.1b.

Notice that initial conditions for TAP and the numerical solutions were chosen almost randomly, with a slight bias of $\mathcal{O}(10^{-12})$, in the initial magnetization. The TAP dynamical equations are identical to those used for practical BP decoding[5], and therefore provide equivalent results to computer simulations with the same parameterization, supporting the analytical results. The excellent convergence results obtained point out the existence of a unique pair of global solutions to which the system converges (below p_s) *from practically all initial conditions*. This observation and the practical implications of using $K = L = 2$ code have not been obtained by information theory methods (e.g.[3]); these prove the existence of very good codes for $C=L\geq 3$, and examine decoding properties only via numerical simulations.

4 Irregular Constructions

Irregular codes with non-uniform number of non-zero elements per column and uniform number of elements per row were recently introduced [11, 12] and were found to outperform regular codes. It is relatively straightforward to adapt our methods to study these particular constructions. The restriction of the number of connections per index can be replaced by a set of N restrictions of the form (1), enforcing C_j non-zero elements in the j-th column of the matrix A, and other M restrictions enforcing L_l non-zero elements in the l-th column of the matrix B. By construction these restrictions must obey the relations $\sum_{j=1}^{N} C_j = MK$ and $\sum_{l=1}^{M} L_l = ML$. One can assume that a particular set of restrictions is generated independently by the probability distributions $\mathcal{P}(C)$ and $\mathcal{P}(L)$. With that we can compute average properties of irregularly constructed codes generated by arbitrary distributions.

Proceeding along the same lines to those of the regular case one can find a very similar expression for the free energy which can be interpreted as a mixture of regular codes with column weights sampled with probabilities $\mathcal{P}(C)$ and $\mathcal{P}(L)$. As long as we choose probability distributions which vanish for $C, L = 0$ (avoiding trivial non-invertible matrices) and $C, L = 1$ (avoiding single checked bits), the solutions to the saddle point equations are the same as those obtained in the regular case (Eqs.5, 6) leading to exactly the same predictions for the maximum performance. The differences between regular and irregular codes show up in their dynamical behavior. In the irregular case with $K > 2$ and for biased messages the basin of attraction is larger for higher noise levels [13].

5 Conclusion

In this paper we examined the typical performance of Gallager-type codes. We discovered that for a certain choice of parameters, either $K \geq 3$ or $L \geq 3$, one potentially obtains optimal performance, saturating Shannon's bound. This comes at the expense of a decreasing basin of attraction making the decoding process increasingly impractical. Another code, $K = L = 2$, shows close to optimal performance with a very large basin of attraction, making it highly attractive for practical purposes. The decoding performance of both code types was examined by employing the TAP approach, an iterative method identical to the commonly used BP. Both numerical and TAP solutions agree with the theoretical results. The equilibrium properties of regular and irregular constructions is shown to be the same. The improved performance of irregular codes reported in the literature can be explained as consequence of dynamical properties. This study examines the typical performance of these increasingly important error-correcting codes, from which optimal parameter choices can be derived, complementing the bounds and empirical results provided in the information theory literature . Important aspects that are yet to be investigated include other noise types, finite size effects and the decoding dynamics itself.

Acknowledgement Support by the JSPS RFTF program (YK), The Royal Society and EPSRC grant GR/N00562 (DS) is acknowledged.

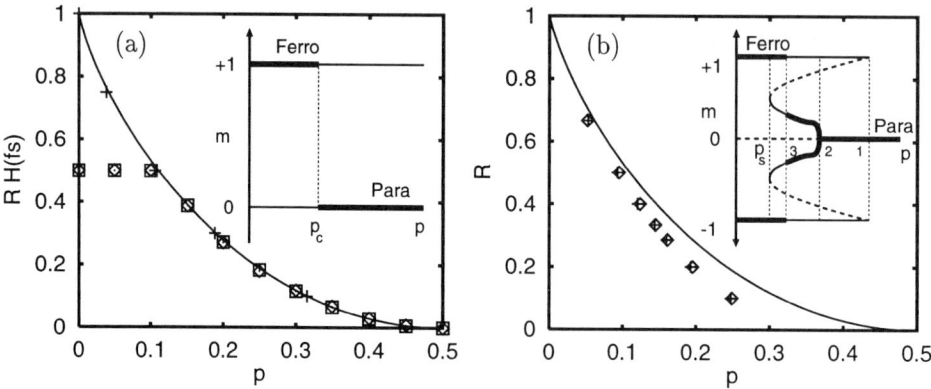

Figure 1: Critical code rate as a function of the flip rate p, obtained from numerical solutions and the TAP approach ($N = 10^4$), and averaged over 10 different initial conditions with error bars much smaller than the symbols size. (a) Numerical solutions for $K=L=3$, $C=6$ and varying input bias f_s ($\square$) and TAP solutions for both unbiased (+) and biased ($\diamond$) messages; initial conditions were chosen close to the analytical ones. The critical rate is multiplied by the source information content to obtain the maximal information transmission rate, which clearly does not go beyond $R=3/6$ in the case of biased messages; for unbiased patterns $H_2(f_s) = 1$. Inset: The ferromagnetic and paramagnetic solutions as functions of p; thick and thin lines denote stable solutions of lower and higher free energies respectively. (b) For the unbiased case of $K = L = 2$; initial conditions for the TAP (+) and the numerical solutions ($\diamond$) are of almost zero magnetization. Inset: The ferromagnetic (optimal/sub-optimal) and paramagnetic solutions as functions of p; thick and thin lines are as in (a), dashed lines correspond to unstable solutions.

References

[1] C.E. Shannon, *Bell Sys.Tech.J.*, **27**, 379 (1948); **27**, 623 (1948).

[2] R.G. Gallager, *IRE Trans.Info.Theory*, **IT-8**, 21 (1962).

[3] D.J.C. MacKay, *IEEE Trans.IT*, **45**, 399 (1999).

[4] D. Thouless, P.W. Anderson and R.G. Palmer, *Phil. Mag.*, **35**, 593 (1977).

[5] Y. Kabashima and D. Saad, *Europhys.Lett.*, **44** 668 (1998) and **45** 97 (1999).

[6] N. Sourlas, *Nature*, **339**, 693 (1989) and *Euro.Phys.Lett.*, **25**, 159 (1994).

[7] Y. Kabashima, T. Murayama and D. Saad, *Phys.Rev.Lett.*, (1999) in press.

[8] K.Y.M. Wong and D. Sherrington, *J.Phys.A*, **20**, L793 (1987).

[9] C. De Dominicis and P.Mottishaw, *J.Phys.A*, **20**, L1267 (1987).

[10] H. Nishimori, *Prog.Theo.Phys.*, **66**, 1169 (1981).

[11] M. Luby et. al, *IEEE proceedings of ISIT98* (1998) and Analysis of Low Density Codes and Improved Designs Using Irregular Graphs, preprint.

[12] D.J.C. MacKay et. al, *IEEE Trans.Comm.*, **47**, 1449 (1999).

[13] R. Vicente et. al, http://xxx.lanl.gov/abs/cond-mat/9908358 (1999).

Mixture Density Estimation

Jonathan Q. Li
Department of Statistics
Yale University
P.O. Box 208290
New Haven, CT 06520
Qiang.Li@aya.yale.edu

Andrew R. Barron
Department of Statistics
Yale University
P.O. Box 208290
New Haven, CT 06520
Andrew.Barron@yale.edu

Abstract

Gaussian mixtures (or so-called radial basis function networks) for density estimation provide a natural counterpart to sigmoidal neural networks for function fitting and approximation. In both cases, it is possible to give simple expressions for the iterative improvement of performance as components of the network are introduced one at a time. In particular, for mixture density estimation we show that a k-component mixture estimated by maximum likelihood (or by an iterative likelihood improvement that we introduce) achieves log-likelihood within order $1/k$ of the log-likelihood achievable by any convex combination. Consequences for approximation and estimation using Kullback-Leibler risk are also given. A Minimum Description Length principle selects the optimal number of components k that minimizes the risk bound.

1 Introduction

In density estimation, Gaussian mixtures provide flexible-basis representations for densities that can be used to model heterogeneous data in high dimensions. We introduce an index of regularity c_f of density functions f with respect to mixtures of densities from a given family. Mixture models with k components are shown to achieve Kullback-Leibler approximation error bounded by c_f^2/k for every k. Thus in a manner analogous to the treatment of sinusoidal and sigmoidal networks in Barron [1],[2], we find classes of density functions f such that reasonable size networks (not exponentially large as function of the input dimension) achieve suitable approximation and estimation error.

Consider a parametric family $G = \{\phi_\theta(x), x \in \mathcal{X} \subset R^{d'} : \theta \in \Theta \subset R^d\}$ of probability density functions parameterized by $\theta \in \Theta$. Then consider the class $\mathcal{C} = CONV(G)$ of density functions for which there is a mixture representation of the form

$$f_P(x) = \int_\Theta \phi_\theta(x) P(d\theta) \qquad (1)$$

where $\phi_\theta(x)$ are density functions from G and P is a probability measure on Θ.

The main theme of the paper is to give approximation and estimation bounds of arbitrary densities by finite mixture densities. We focus our attention on densities inside $\mathcal{C}$ first and give an approximation error bound by finite mixtures for arbitrary $f \in \mathcal{C}$. The approximation error is measured by Kullback-Leibler divergence between two densities, defined as

$$D(f\|g) = \int f(x)\log[f(x)/g(x)]dx. \tag{2}$$

In density estimation, D is more natural to use than the L^2 distance often seen in the function fitting literature. Indeed, D is invariant under scale transformations (and other 1-1 transformation of the variables) and it has an intrinsic connection with Maximum Likelihood, one of the most useful methods in the mixture density estimation. The following result quantifies the approximation error.

THEOREM 1 Let $G = \{\phi_\theta(x) : \theta \in \Theta\}$ and $\mathcal{C} = CONV(G)$. Let $f(x) = \int \phi_\theta(x) P(d\theta) \in \mathcal{C}$. There exists f_k, a k-component mixture of ϕ_θ, such that

$$D(f\|f_k) \leq \frac{c_f^2 \gamma}{k}. \tag{3}$$

In the bound, we have

$$c_f^2 = \int \frac{\int \phi_\theta^2(x) P(d\theta)}{\int \phi_\theta(x) P(d\theta)} dx, \tag{4}$$

and $\gamma = 4[\log(3\sqrt{e}) + a]$, where

$$a = \sup_{\theta_1,\theta_2,x} \log \frac{\phi_{\theta_1}(x)}{\phi_{\theta_2}(x)}. \tag{5}$$

Here, a characterizes an upper bound of the log ratio of the densities in G, when the parameters are restricted to Θ and the variable to $\mathcal{X}$.

Note that the rate of convergence, $1/k$, is not related to the dimensions of Θ or $\mathcal{X}$. The behavior of the constants, though, depends on the choices of G and the target f.

For example we may take G to be the Gaussian location family, which we restrict to a set $\mathcal{X}$ which is a cube of side-length A. Likewise we restrict the parameters to be in the same cube. Then,

$$a \leq \frac{dA^2}{\sigma^2}. \tag{6}$$

In this case, a is linear in dimension.

The value of c_f^2 depends on the target density f. Suppose f is a finite mixture with M components, then

$$c_f^2 \leq M, \tag{7}$$

with equality if and only if those M components are disjoint. Indeed, suppose $f(x) = \sum_{i=1}^M p_i \phi_{\theta_i}(x)$, then $p_i \phi_{\theta_i}(x) / \sum_{i=1}^M p_i \phi_{\theta_i}(x) \leq 1$ and hence

$$c_f^2 = \int \frac{\sum_{i=1}^M (p_i \phi_{\theta_i}(x))\phi_{\theta_i}(x)}{\sum_{i=1}^M p_i \phi_{\theta_i}(x)} dx \leq \int \sum_{i=1}^M (1)\phi_{\theta_i}(x) dx = M. \tag{8}$$

Genovese and Wasserman [3] deal with a similar setting. A Kullback-Leibler approximation bound of order $1/\sqrt{k}$ for one-dimensional mixtures of Gaussians is given by them.

In the more general case that f is not necessarily in $\mathcal{C}$, we have a competitive optimality result. Our density approximation is nearly at least as good as any g_P in $\mathcal{C}$.

THEOREM 2 *For every* $g_P(x) = \int \phi_\theta(x) P(d\theta)$,

$$D(f\|f_k) \leq D(f\|g_P) + \frac{c_{f,P}^2}{k}\gamma. \tag{9}$$

Here,

$$c_{f,P}^2 = \int \frac{\int \phi_\theta^2(x) P(d\theta)}{(\int \phi_\theta(x) P(d\theta))^2} f(x) dx. \tag{10}$$

In particular, we can take infimum over all $g_P \in \mathcal{C}$, and still obtain a bound.

Let $D(f\|\mathcal{C}) = \inf_{g \in \mathcal{C}} D(f\|g)$. A theory of information projection shows that if there exists a sequence of f_k such that $D(f\|f_k) \to D(f\|\mathcal{C})$, then f_k converges to a function f^*, which achieves $D(f\|\mathcal{C})$. Note that f^* is not necessarily an element in $\mathcal{C}$. This is developed in Li[4] building on the work of Bell and Cover[5]. As a consequence of Theorem 2 we have

$$D(f\|f_k) \leq D(f\|f^*) + \frac{c_{f,*}^2}{k}\gamma \tag{11}$$

where $c_{f,*}^2$ is the smallest limit of $c_{f,P}^2$ for sequences of P achieving $D(f\|g_P)$ that approaches the infimum $D(f\|\mathcal{C})$.

We prove Theorem 1 by induction in the following section. An appealing feature of such an approach is that it provides an iterative estimation procedure which allows us to estimate one component at a time. This greedy procedure is shown to perform almost as well as the full-mixture procedures, while the computational task of estimating one component is considerably easier than estimating the full mixtures.

Section 2 gives the iterative construction of a suitable approximation, while Section 3 shows how such mixtures may be estimated from data. Risk bounds are stated in Section 4.

2 An iterative construction of the approximation

We provide an iterative construction of f_k's in the following fashion. Suppose during our discussion of approximation that f is given. We seek a k-component mixture f_k close to f. Initialize f_1 by choosing a single component from G to minimize $D(f\|f_1) = D(f\|\phi_\theta)$. Now suppose we have $f_{k-1}(x)$. Then let $f_k(x) = (1-\alpha)f_{k-1}(x) + \alpha\phi_\theta(x)$ where α and θ are chosen to minimize $D(f\|f_k)$. More generally let f_k be any sequence of k-component mixtures, for $k = 1, 2, \ldots$ such that $D(f\|f_k) \leq \min_{\alpha,\theta} D(f\|(1-\alpha)f_{k-1} + \alpha\phi_\theta)$. We prove that such sequences f_k achieve the error bounds in Theorem 1 and Theorem 2.

Those familiar with the iterative Hilbert space approximation results of Jones[6], Barron[1], and Lee, Bartlett and Williamson[7], will see that we follow a similar strategy. The use of L_2 distance measures for density approximation involves L_2 norms of component densities that are exponentially large with dimension. Naive Taylor expansion of the Kullback-Leibler divergence leads to an L_2 norm approximation (weighted by the reciprocal of the density) for which the difficulty remains (Zeevi & Meir[8], Li[9]). The challenge for us was to adapt iterative approximation to the use of Kullback-Leibler divergence in a manner that permits the constant a in the bound to involve the *logarithm* of the density ratio (rather than the ratio itself) to allow more manageable constants.

The proof establishes the inductive relationship

$$D_k \leq (1-\alpha)D_{k-1} + \alpha^2 B, \tag{12}$$

where B is bounded and $D_k = D(f\|f_k)$. By choosing $\alpha_1 = 1, \alpha_2 = 1/2$ and thereafter $\alpha_k = 2/k$, it's easy to see by induction that $D_k \leq 4B/k$.

To get (12), we establish a quadratic upper bound for $-\log \frac{f_k}{f} = -\log \frac{((1-\alpha)f_{k-1} + \alpha\phi_\theta)}{f}$. Three key analytic inequalities regarding to the logarithm will be handy for us,

$$-\log(r) \leq -(r-1) + \left[\frac{-\log(r_0) + r_0 - 1}{(r_0 - 1)^2}\right](r-1)^2 \tag{13}$$

for $r \geq r_0 > 0$,

$$2\left[\frac{-\log(r) + r - 1}{r-1}\right] \leq \log r, \tag{14}$$

and

$$\frac{-\log(r) + r - 1}{(r-1)^2} \leq 1/2 + \log^-(r) \tag{15}$$

where $\log^-(\cdot)$ is the negative part of the logarithm. The proof of of inequality (13) is done by verifying that $\frac{-\log(r)+r-1}{(r-1)^2}$ is monotone decreasing in r. Inequalities (14) and (15) are shown by separately considering the cases that $r < 1$ and $r > 1$ (as well as the limit as $r \to 1$). To get the inequalities one multiplies through by $(r-1)$ or $(r-1)^2$, respectively, and then takes derivatives to obtain suitable monotonicity in r as one moves away from $r = 1$.

Now apply the inequality (13) with $r = \frac{(1-\alpha)f_{k-1} + \alpha\phi_\theta}{g}$ and $r_0 = \frac{(1-\alpha)f_{k-1}}{g}$, where g is an arbitrary density in $\mathcal{C}$ with $g = \int \phi_\theta P(d\theta)$. Note that $r \geq r_0$ in this case because $\frac{\alpha\phi_\theta}{g} \geq 0$. Plug in $r = r_0 + \alpha\frac{\phi_\theta}{g}$ at the right side of (13) and expand the square. Then we get

$$\begin{aligned}
-\log(r) &\leq -(r_0 + \frac{\alpha\phi}{g} - 1) + \left[\frac{-\log(r_0) + r_0 - 1}{(r_0 - 1)^2}\right][(r_0 - 1) + (\frac{\alpha\phi}{g})]^2 \\
&= -\frac{\alpha\phi}{g} - \log(r_0) + \alpha^2 \frac{\phi^2}{g^2}\left[\frac{-\log(r_0) + r_0 - 1}{(r_0 - 1)^2}\right] + 2\alpha\frac{\phi}{g}\left[\frac{-\log(r_0) + r_0 - 1}{r_0 - 1}\right].
\end{aligned}$$

Now apply (14) and (15) respectively. We get

$$-\log(r) \leq -\log(r_0) - \frac{\alpha\phi}{g} + \alpha^2 \frac{\phi^2}{g^2}(1/2 + \log^-(r_0)) + \alpha\frac{\phi}{g}\log(r_0). \tag{16}$$

Note that in our application, r_0 is a ratio of densities in $\mathcal{C}$. Thus we obtain an upper bound for $\log^-(r_0)$ involving a. Indeed we find that $(1/2 + \log^-(r_0)) \leq \gamma/4$ where γ is as defined in the theorem.

In the case that f is in $\mathcal{C}$, we take $g = f$. Then taking the expectation with respect to f of both sides of (16), we acquire a quadratic upper bound for D_k, noting that $r = \frac{f_k}{f}$. Also note that D_k is a function of θ. The greedy algorithm chooses θ to minimize $D_k(\theta)$. Therefore

$$D_k \leq \min_\theta D_k(\theta) \leq \int D_k(\theta) P(d\theta). \tag{17}$$

Plugging the upper bound (16) for $D_k(\theta)$ into (17), we have

$$D_k \leq \int_\theta \int_x [-\log(r_0) - \frac{\alpha\phi}{g} + \alpha^2 \frac{\phi^2}{g^2}(\gamma/4) + \alpha\frac{\phi}{g}\log(r_0)] f(x) dx P(d\theta). \tag{18}$$

where $r_0 = (1-\alpha)f_{k-1}(x)/g(x)$ and P is chosen to satisfy $\int_\theta \phi_\theta(x)P(d\theta) = g(x)$. Thus

$$D_k \leq (1-\alpha)D_{k-1} + \alpha^2 \int \frac{\phi_\theta^2(x)P(d\theta)}{(g(x))^2} f(x)dx(\gamma/4) + \alpha\log(1-\alpha) - \alpha - \log(1-\alpha). \tag{19}$$

It can be shown that $\alpha\log(1-\alpha) - \alpha - \log(1-\alpha) \leq 0$. Thus we have the desired inductive relationship,

$$D_k \leq (1-\alpha)D_{k-1} + \alpha^2 c_{f,P}^2 \gamma/4. \tag{20}$$

Therefore, $D_k \leq \frac{\gamma c_{f,P}^2}{k}$.

In the case that f does not have a mixture representation of the form $\int \phi_\theta P(d\theta)$, i.e. f is outside the convex hull $\mathcal{C}$, we take D_k to be $\int f(x) \log \frac{g_P(x)}{f_k(x)} dx$ for any given $g_P(x) = \int \phi_\theta(x) P(d\theta)$. The above analysis then yields $D_k = D(f\|f_k) - D(f\|g_P) \leq \frac{\gamma c_{f,P}^2}{k}$ as desired. That completes the proof of Theorems 1 and 2.

3 A greedy estimation procedure

The connection between the K-L divergence and the MLE helps to motivate the following estimation procedure for f_k if we have data $X_1, ..., X_n$ sampled from f. The iterative construction of f_k can be turned into a sequential maximum likelihood estimation by changing $\min D(f\|f_k)$ to $\max \sum_{i=1}^n \log f_k(X_i)$ at each step. A surprising result is that the resulting estimator $\hat{f}_k$ has a log likelihood almost at least as high as log likelihood achieved by any density g_P in $\mathcal{C}$ with a difference of order $1/k$. We formally state it as

$$\frac{1}{n}\sum_{i=1}^n \log \hat{f}_k(X_i) \geq \frac{1}{n}\sum_{i=1}^n \log g_P(X_i) - \gamma \frac{c_{F_n,P}^2}{k} \tag{21}$$

for all $g_P \in \mathcal{C}$. Here F_n is the empirical distribution, for which $c_{F_n,P}^2 = (1/n)\sum_{i=1}^n c_{X_i,P}^2$ where

$$c_{x,P}^2 = \frac{\int \phi_\theta^2(x) P(d\theta)}{(\int \phi_\theta(x) P(d\theta))^2}. \tag{22}$$

The proof of this result (21) follows as in the proof in the last section, except that now we take $D_k = E_{F_n} \log g_P(X)/f_k(X)$ to be the expectation with respect to F_n instead of with respect to the density f.

Let's look at the computation at each step to see the benefits this new greedy procedure can bring for us. We have $\hat{f}_k(x) = (1-\alpha)\hat{f}_{k-1}(x) + \alpha\phi_\theta(x)$ with θ and α chosen to maximize

$$\sum_{i=1}^n \log[(1-\alpha)\hat{f}_{k-1}(X_i) + \alpha\phi_\theta(X_i)] \tag{23}$$

which is a simple two component mixture problem, with one of the two components, $\hat{f}_{k-1}(x)$, fixed. To achieve the bound in (21), α can either be chosen by this iterative maximum likelihood or it can be held fixed at each step to equal α_k (which as before is $\alpha_k = 2/k$ for $k > 2$). Thus one may replace the MLE-computation of a k-component mixture by successive MLE-computations of two-component mixtures. The resulting estimate is guaranteed to have almost at least as high a likelihood as is achieved by any mixture density.

A disadvantage of the greedy procedure is that it may take a number of steps to adequately downweight poor initial choices. Thus it is advisable at each step to retune the weights of convex combinations of previous components (and even perhaps to adjust the locations of these components), in which case, the result from the previous iterations (with $k-1$ components) provide natural initialization for the search at step k. The good news is that as long as for each k, given $\hat{f}_{k-1}$, the $\hat{f}_k$ is chosen among k component mixtures to achieve likelihood at least as large as the choice achieving $\max_\theta \sum_{i=1}^n \log[(1-\alpha_k)\hat{f}_{k-1}(X_i) + \alpha_k \phi_\theta(X_i)]$, that is, we require that

$$\sum_{i=1}^n \log \hat{f}_k(X_i) \geq \max_\theta \sum_{i=1}^n \log[(1-\alpha_k)\hat{f}_{k-1}(X_i) + \alpha_k \phi_\theta(X_i)], \quad (24)$$

then the conclusion (21) will follow.

In particular, our likelihood results and risk bound results apply both to the case that $\hat{f}_k$ is taken to be global maximizer of the likelihood over k-component mixtures as well as to the case that $\hat{f}_k$ is the result of the greedy procedure.

4 Risk bounds for the MLE and the iterative MLE

The metric entropy of the family G is controlled to obtain the risk bound and to determine the precisions with which the coordinates of the parameter space are allowed to be represented. Specifically, the following Lipschitz condition is assumed: for $\theta \in \Theta \subset R^d$ and $x \in \mathcal{X} \subset R^d$,

$$\sup_{x \in \mathcal{X}} |\log \phi_\theta(x) - \log \phi_{\theta'}(x)| \leq B \sum_{j=1}^d |\theta_j - \theta'_j| \quad (25)$$

where θ_j is the j-th coordinate of the parameter vector. Note that such a condition is satisfied by a Gaussian family with x restricted to a cube with sidelength A and has a location parameter θ that is also prescribed to be in the same cube. In particular, if we let the variance be σ^2, we may set $B = 2A/\sigma^2$.

Now we can state the bound on the K-L risk of $\hat{f}_k$.

THEOREM 3 *Assume the condition (25). Also assume Θ to be a cube with sidelength A. Let $\hat{f}_k(x)$ be either the maximizer of the likelihood over k-component mixtures or more generally any sequence of density estimates $\hat{f}_k$ satisfying (24). We have*

$$E(D(f\|\hat{f}_k)) - D(f\|\mathcal{C}) \leq \gamma^2 \frac{c_{f,*}^2}{k} + \gamma \frac{2kd}{n} \log(nABe). \quad (26)$$

From the bound on risk, a best choice of k would be of order roughly $\sqrt{n}$ leading to a bound on $ED(f\|\hat{f}_k) - D(f\|\mathcal{C})$ of order $1/\sqrt{n}$ to within logarithmic factors. However the best such bound occurs with $k = \gamma c_{f,*}\sqrt{n}/\sqrt{2d\log(nABe)}$ which is not available when the value of $c_{f,*}$ is unknown. More importantly, k should not be chosen merely to optimize an upper bound on risk, but rather to balance whatever approximation and estimation sources of error actually occur. Toward this end we optimize a penalized likelihood criterion related to the minimum description length principle, following Barron and Cover [10].

Let $l(k)$ be a function of k that satisfies $\sum_{k=1}^\infty e^{-l(k)} \leq 1$, such as $l(k) = 2\log(k+1)$.

A penalized MLE (or MDL) procedure picks k by minimizing

$$\frac{1}{n}\sum_{i=1}^{n} \log \frac{1}{\hat{f}_k(X_i)} + 2kd\frac{\log(nABe)}{n} + 2l(k)/n. \qquad (27)$$

Then we have

$$E(D(f\|\hat{f}_k)) - D(f\|\mathcal{C}) \leq \min_k \{\gamma^2 \frac{c_{f,*}^2}{k} + \gamma \frac{2kd}{n}\log(nABe) + 2l(k)/n\}. \qquad (28)$$

A proof of these risk bounds is given in Li[4]. It builds on general results for maximum likelihood and penalized maximum likelihood procedures.

Recently, Dasgupta [11] has established a randomized algorithm for estimating mixtures of Gaussians, in the case that data are drawn from a finite mixture of sufficiently separated Gaussian components with common covariance, that runs in time linear in the dimension and quadratic in the sample size. However, present forms of his algorithm require impractically large sample sizes to get reasonably accurate estimates of the density. It is not yet known how his techniques will work for more general mixtures. Here we see that iterative likelihood maximization provides a better relationship between accuracy, sample size and number of components.

References

[1] Barron, Andrew (1993) Universal Approximation Bounds for Superpositions of a Sigmoidal Function. *IEEE Transactions on Information Theory* **39**, No. 3: 930-945

[2] Barron, Andrew (1994) Approximation and Estimation Bounds for Artificial Neural Networks. *Machine Learning* **14**: 115-133.

[3] Genovese, Chris and Wasserman, Larry (1998) Rates of Convergence for the Gaussian Mixture Seive. Manuscript.

[4] Li, Jonathan Q. (1999) Estimation of Mixture Models. Ph.D Dissertation. The Department of Statistics. Yale University.

[5] Bell, Robert and Cover, Thomas (1988) Game-theoretic optimal portfolios. *Management Science* **34**: 724-733.

[6] Jones, Lee (1992) A simple lemma on greedy approximation in Hilbert space and convergence rates for projection pursuit regression and neural network training. *Annals of Statistics* **20**: 608-613.

[7] Lee, W.S., Bartlett, P.L. and Williamson R.C. (1996) Efficient Agnostic Learning of Neural Networks with Bounded Fan-in. *IEEE Transactions on Information Theory* **42**, No. 6: 2118-2132.

[8] Zeevi, Assaf and Meir Ronny (1997) Density Estimation Through Convex Combinations of Densities: Approximation and Estimation Bounds. *Neural Networks* **10**, No.1: 99-109.

[9] Li, Jonathan Q. (1997) Iterative Estimation of Mixture Models. Ph.D. Prospectus. The Department of Statistics. Yale University.

[10] Barron, Andrew and Cover, Thomas (1991) Minimum Complexity Density Estimation. *IEEE Transactions on Information Theory* **37**: 1034-1054.

[11] Dasgupta, Sanjoy (1999) Learning Mixtures of Gaussians. *Proc. IEEE Conf. on Foundations of Computer Science*, 634-644.

Statistical Dynamics of Batch Learning

S. Li and K. Y. Michael Wong
Department of Physics, Hong Kong University of Science and Technology
Clear Water Bay, Kowloon, Hong Kong
{phlisong, phkywong}@ust.hk

Abstract

An important issue in neural computing concerns the description of learning dynamics with macroscopic dynamical variables. Recent progress on *on-line* learning only addresses the often unrealistic case of an infinite training set. We introduce a new framework to model batch learning of restricted sets of examples, widely applicable to *any* learning cost function, and fully taking into account the temporal correlations introduced by the recycling of the examples. For illustration we analyze the effects of weight decay and early stopping during the learning of teacher-generated examples.

1 Introduction

The dynamics of learning in neural computing is a complex multi-variate process. The interest on the macroscopic level is thus to describe the process with macroscopic dynamical variables. Recently, much progress has been made on modeling the dynamics of *on-line* learning, in which an independent example is generated for each learning step [1, 2]. Since statistical correlations among the examples can be ignored, the dynamics can be simply described by instantaneous dynamical variables.

However, most studies on on-line learning focus on the ideal case in which the network has access to an almost infinite training set, whereas in many applications, the collection of training examples may be costly. A restricted set of examples introduces extra temporal correlations during learning, and the dynamics is much more complicated. Early studies briefly considered the dynamics of Adaline learning [3, 4, 5], and has recently been extended to *linear* perceptrons learning nonlinear rules [6, 7]. Recent attempts, using the *dynamical replica theory*, have been made to study the learning of restricted sets of examples, but so far exact results are published for simple learning rules such as Hebbian learning, beyond which appropriate approximations are needed [8].

In this paper, we introduce a new framework to model batch learning of restricted sets of examples, widely applicable to any learning rule which minimizes an *arbitrary* cost function by gradient descent. It fully takes into account the temporal correlations during learning, and is therefore exact for large networks.

2 Formulation

Consider the single layer perceptron with $N \gg 1$ input nodes $\{\xi_j\}$ connecting to a single output node by the weights $\{J_j\}$. For convenience we assume that the inputs ξ_j are Gaussian variables with mean 0 and variance 1, and the output state S is a function $f(x)$ of the *activation* x at the output node, i.e.

$$S = f(x); \quad x = \vec{J} \cdot \vec{\xi}. \tag{1}$$

The network is assigned to "learn" $p \equiv \alpha N$ examples which map inputs $\{\xi_j^\mu\}$ to the outputs $\{S_\mu\}$ ($\mu = 1, \ldots, p$). S_μ are the outputs generated by a teacher perceptron $\{B_j\}$, namely

$$S_\mu = f(y_\mu); \quad y_\mu = \vec{B} \cdot \vec{\xi}^\mu. \tag{2}$$

Batch learning by gradient descent is achieved by adjusting the weights $\{J_j\}$ iteratively so that a certain cost function in terms of the student and teacher activations $\{x_\mu\}$ and $\{y_\mu\}$ is minimized. Hence we consider a general cost function

$$E = -\sum_\mu g(x_\mu, y_\mu). \tag{3}$$

The precise functional form of $g(x, y)$ depends on the adopted learning algorithm. For the case of binary outputs, $f(x) = \text{sgn} x$. Early studies on the learning dynamics considered Adaline learning [3, 4, 5], where $g(x, y) = -(S - x)^2/2$ with $S = \text{sgn} y$. For recent studies on Hebbian learning [8], $g(x, y) = xS$.

To ensure that the perceptron is regularized after learning, it is customary to introduce a weight decay term. Furthermore, to avoid the system being trapped in local minima, noise is often added in the dynamics. Hence the gradient descent dynamics is given by

$$\frac{dJ_j(t)}{dt} = \frac{1}{N} \sum_\mu g'(x_\mu(t), y_\mu) \xi_j^\mu - \lambda J_j(t) + \eta_j(t), \tag{4}$$

where, here and below, $g'(x, y)$ and $g''(x, y)$ respectively represent the first and second partial derivatives of $g(x, y)$ with respect to x. λ is the weight decay strength, and $\eta_j(t)$ is the noise term at temperature T with

$$\langle \eta_j(t) \rangle = 0 \quad \text{and} \quad \langle \eta_j(t)\eta_k(s) \rangle = \frac{2T}{N} \delta_{jk} \delta(t - s). \tag{5}$$

3 The Cavity Method

Our theory is the dynamical version of the cavity method [9, 10, 11]. It uses a self-consistency argument to consider what happens when a new example is added to a training set. The central quantity in this method is the *cavity activation*, which is the activation of a new example for a perceptron trained without that example. Since the original network has no information about the new example, the cavity activation is stochastic. Specifically, denoting the new example by the label 0, its cavity activation at time t is

$$h_0(t) = \vec{J}(t) \cdot \vec{\xi}^0. \tag{6}$$

For large N and independently generated examples, $h_0(t)$ is a Gaussian variable. Its covariance is given by the correlation function $C(t, s)$ of the weights at times t and s, that is,

$$\langle h_0(t) h_0(s) \rangle = \vec{J}(t) \cdot \vec{J}(s) \equiv C(t, s), \tag{7}$$

where ξ_j^0 and ξ_k^0 are assumed to be independent for $j \neq k$. The distribution is further specified by the teacher-student correlation $R(t)$, given by

$$\langle h_0(t) y_0 \rangle = \vec{J}(t) \cdot \vec{B} \equiv R(t). \tag{8}$$

Now suppose the perceptron incorporates the new example at the batch-mode learning step at time s. Then the activation of this new example at a subsequent time $t > s$ will no longer be a random variable. Furthermore, the activations of the original p examples at time t will also be adjusted from $\{x_\mu(t)\}$ to $\{x_\mu^0(t)\}$ because of the newcomer, which will in turn affect the evolution of the activation of example 0, giving rise to the so-called Onsager reaction effects. This makes the dynamics complex, but fortunately for large $p \sim N$, we can assume that the adjustment from $x_\mu(t)$ to $x_\mu^0(t)$ is small, and perturbative analysis can be applied.

Suppose the weights of the original and new perceptron at time t are $\{J_j(t)\}$ and $\{J_j^0(t)\}$ respectively. Then a perturbation of (4) yields

$$\left(\frac{d}{dt} + \lambda\right)(J_j^0(t) - J_j(t)) = \frac{1}{N} g'(x_0(t), y_0) \xi_j^0$$
$$+ \frac{1}{N} \sum_{\mu k} \xi_j^\mu g''(x_\mu(t), y_\mu) \xi_k^\mu (J_k^0(t) - J_k(t)). \tag{9}$$

The first term on the right hand side describes the primary effects of adding example 0 to the training set, and is the driving term for the difference between the two perceptrons. The second term describes the secondary effects due to the changes to the original examples caused by the added example, and is referred to as the Onsager reaction term. One should note the difference between the cavity and generic activations of the added example. The former is denoted by $h_0(t)$ and corresponds to the activation in the perceptron $\{J_j(t)\}$, whereas the latter, denoted by $x_0(t)$ and corresponding to the activation in the perceptron $\{J_j^0(t)\}$, is the one used in calculating the gradient in the driving term of (9). Since their notations are sufficiently distinct, we have omitted the superscript 0 in $x_0(t)$, which appears in the background examples $x_\mu^0(t)$.

The equation can be solved by the Green's function technique, yielding

$$J_j^0(t) - J_j(t) = \sum_k \int ds\, G_{jk}(t,s) \left(\frac{1}{N} g_0'(s) \xi_k^0\right), \tag{10}$$

where $g_0'(s) = g'(x_0(s), y_0)$ and $G_{jk}(t,s)$ is the *weight Green's function* satisfying

$$G_{jk}(t,s) = G^{(0)}(t-s)\delta_{jk} + \frac{1}{N} \sum_{\mu i} \int dt'\, G^{(0)}(t-t') \xi_j^\mu g_\mu''(t') \xi_i^\mu G_{ik}(t'-s), \tag{11}$$

$G^{(0)}(t-s) \equiv \Theta(t-s) \exp(-\lambda(t-s))$ is the bare Green's function, and Θ is the step function. The weight Green's function describes how the effects of example 0 propagates from weight J_k at learning time s to weight J_j at a subsequent time t, including both primary and secondary effects. Hence all the temporal correlations have been taken into account.

For large N, the equation can be solved by a diagrammatic approach similar to [5]. The weight Green's function is self-averaging over the distribution of examples and is diagonal, i.e. $\lim_{N \to \infty} G_{jk}(t,s) = G(t,s) \delta_{jk}$, where

$$G(t,s) = G^{(0)}(t-s) + \alpha \int dt_1 \int dt_2\, G^{(0)}(t-t_1) \langle g_\mu''(t_1) D_\mu(t_1, t_2) \rangle G(t_2, s). \tag{12}$$

$D_\mu(t,s)$ is the *example Green's function* given by

$$D_\mu(t,s) = \delta(t-s) + \int dt' G(t,t') g''_\mu(t') D_\mu(t',s). \tag{13}$$

This allows us to express the generic activations of the examples in terms of their cavity counterparts. Multiplying both sides of (10) and summing over j, we get

$$x_0(t) - h_0(t) = \int ds G(t,s) g'_0(s). \tag{14}$$

This equation is interpreted as follows. At time t, the generic activation $x_0(t)$ deviates from its cavity counterpart because its gradient term $g'_0(s)$ was present in the batch learning step at previous times s. This gradient term propagates its influence from time s to t via the Green's function $G(t,s)$. Statistically, this equation enables us to express the activation distribution in terms of the cavity activation distribution, thereby getting a macroscopic description of the dynamics.

To solve for the Green's functions and the activation distributions, we further need the fluctuation-response relation derived by linear response theory,

$$C(t,s) = \alpha \int dt' G^{(0)}(t-t') \langle g'_\mu(t') x_\mu(s) \rangle + 2T \int dt' G^{(0)}(t-t') G(s,t'). \tag{15}$$

Finally, the teacher-student correlation is given by

$$R(t) = \alpha \int dt' G^{(0)}(t-t') \langle g'_\mu(t') y_\mu \rangle. \tag{16}$$

4 A Solvable Case

The cavity method can be applied to the dynamics of learning with an arbitrary cost function. When it is applied to the Hebb rule, it yields results identical to the exact results in [8]. Here we present the results for the Adaline rule to illustrate features of learning dynamics derivable from the study. This is a common learning rule and bears resemblance with the more common back-propagation rule. Theoretically, its dynamics is particularly convenient for analysis since $g''(x) = -1$, rendering the weight Green's function time translation invariant, i.e. $G(t,s) = G(t-s)$. In this case, the dynamics can be solved by Laplace transform.

To monitor the progress of learning, we are interested in three performance measures: (a) *Training error* ϵ_t, which is the probability of error for the training examples. It is given by $\epsilon_t = \langle \Theta(-x \operatorname{sgn} y) \rangle_{xy}$, where the average is taken over the joint distribution $p(x,y)$ of the training set. (b) *Test error* ϵ_{test}, which is the probability of error when the inputs ξ_j^μ of the training examples are corrupted by an additive Gaussian noise of variance Δ^2. This is a relevant performance measure when the perceptron is applied to process data which are the corrupted versions of the training data. It is given by $\epsilon_{test} = \langle H(x \operatorname{sgn} y / \Delta \sqrt{C(t,t)}) \rangle_{xy}$. When $\Delta^2 = 0$, the test error reduces to the training error. (c) *Generalization error* ϵ_g, which is the probability of error for an arbitrary input ξ_j when the teacher and student outputs are compared. It is given by $\epsilon_g = \arccos[R(t)/\sqrt{C(t,t)}]/\pi$.

Figure 1(a) shows the evolution of the generalization error at $T = 0$. When the weight decay strength varies, the steady-state generalization error is minimized at the optimum

$$\lambda_{opt} = \frac{\pi}{2} - 1, \tag{17}$$

which is independent of α. It is interesting to note that in the cases of the linear perceptron, the optimal weight decay strength is also independent of α and only determined by the output noise and unlearnability of the examples [5, 7]. Similarly, here the student is only provided the coarse-grained version of the teacher's activation in the form of binary bits.

For $\lambda < \lambda_{opt}$, the generalization error is a non-monotonic function in learning time. Hence the dynamics is plagued by *overtraining*, and it is desirable to introduce *early stopping* to improve the perceptron performance. Similar behavior is observed in linear perceptrons [5, 6, 7].

To verify the theoretical predictions, simulations were done with $N = 500$ and using 50 samples for averaging. As shown in Fig. 1(a), the agreement is excellent.

Figure 1(b) compares the generalization errors at the steady-state and the early stopping point. It shows that early stopping improves the performance for $\lambda < \lambda_{opt}$, which becomes near-optimal when compared with the best result at $\lambda = \lambda_{opt}$. Hence early stopping can speed up the learning process without significant sacrifice in the generalization ability. However, it cannot outperform the optimal result at steady-state. This agrees with a recent empirical observation that a careful control of the weight decay may be better than early stopping in optimizing generalization [12].

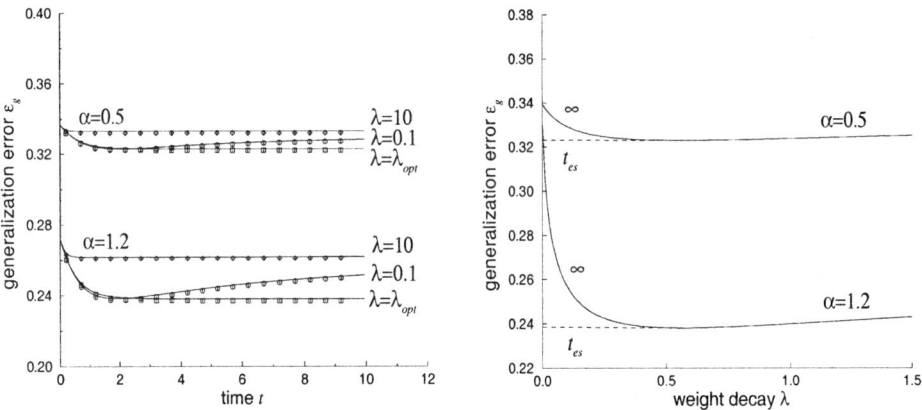

Figure 1: (a) The evolution of the generalization error at $T = 0$ for $\alpha = 0.5, 1.2$ and different weight decay strengths λ. Theory: solid line, simulation: symbols. (b) Comparing the generalization error at the steady state (∞) and at the early stopping point (t_{es}) for $\alpha = 0.5, 1.2$ and $T = 0$.

In the search for optimal learning algorithms, an important consideration is the environment in which the performance is tested. Besides the generalization performance, there are applications in which the test examples have inputs correlated with the training examples. Hence we are interested in the evolution of the test error for a given additive Gaussian noise Δ in the inputs. Figure 2(a) shows, again, that there is an optimal weight decay parameter λ_{opt} which minimizes the test error. Furthermore, when the weight decay is weak, early stopping is desirable.

Figure 2(b) shows the value of the optimal weight decay as a function of the input noise variance Δ^2. To the lowest order approximation, $\lambda_{opt} \propto \Delta^2$ for sufficiently large Δ^2. The dependence of λ_{opt} on input noise is rather general since it also holds in the case of random examples [13]. In the limit of small Δ^2, λ_{opt} vanishes as Δ^2 for $\alpha < 1$, whereas λ_{opt} approaches a nonzero constant for $\alpha > 1$. Hence for

$\alpha < 1$, weight decay is not necessary when the training error is optimized, but when the perceptron is applied to process increasingly noisy data, weight decay becomes more and more important in performance enhancement.

Figure 2(b) also shows the phase line $\lambda_{ot}(\Delta^2)$ below which overtraining occurs. Again, to the lowest order approximation, $\lambda_{ot} \propto \Delta^2$ for sufficiently large Δ^2. However, unlike the case of generalization error, the line for the onset of overtraining does not coincide exactly with the line of optimal weight decay. In particular, for an intermediate range of input noise, the optimal line lies in the region of overtraining, so that the optimal performance can only be attained by tuning *both* the weight decay strength and learning time. However, at least in the present case, computational results show that the improvement is marginal.

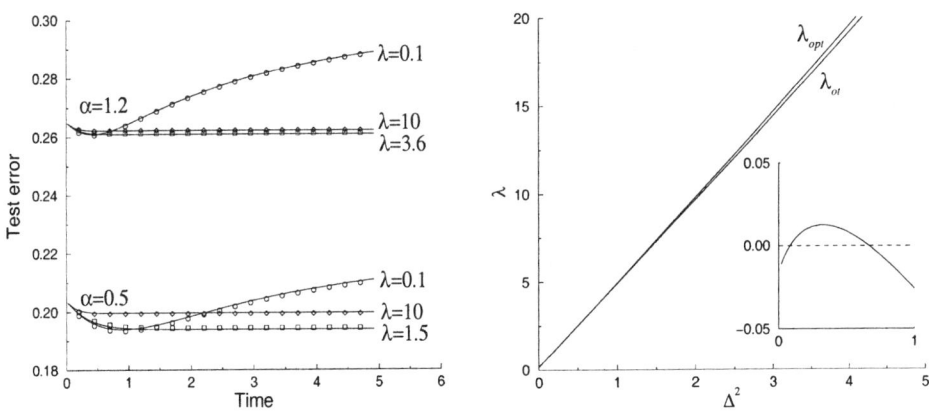

Figure 2: (a) The evolution of the test error for $\Delta^2 = 3$, $T = 0$ and different weight decay strengths λ ($\lambda_{opt} \approx 1.5, 3.6$ for $\alpha = 0.5, 1.2$ respectively). (b) The lines of the optimal weight decay and the onset of overtraining for $\alpha = 5$. Inset: The same data with $\lambda_{ot} - \lambda_{opt}$ (magnified) versus Δ^2.

5 Conclusion

Based on the cavity method, we have introduced a new framework for modeling the dynamics of learning, which is applicable to *any* learning cost function, making it a versatile theory. It takes into full account the temporal correlations generated by the use of a restricted set of examples, which is more realistic in many situations than theories of on-line learning with an infinite training set.

While the Adaline rule is solvable by the cavity method, it is still a relatively simple model approachable by more direct methods. Hence the justification of the method as a general framework for learning dynamics hinges on its applicability to less trivial cases. In general, $g''_\mu(t')$ in (13) is not a constant and $D_\mu(t,s)$ has to be expanded as a series. The dynamical equations can then be considered as the starting point of a perturbation theory, and results in various limits can be derived, e.g. the limits of small α, large α, large λ, or the asymptotic limit. Another area for the useful application of the cavity method is the case of batch learning with very large learning steps. Since it has been shown recently that such learning converges in a few steps [6], the dynamical equations remain simple enough for a meaningful study. Preliminary results along this direction are promising and will be reported elsewhere.

An alternative general theory for learning dynamics, the dynamical replica theory, has recently been developed [8]. It yields exact results for Hebbian learning, and approximate results for more non-trivial cases. Based on certain self-averaging assumptions, the theory is able to approximate the dynamics by the evolution of single-time functions, at the expense of having to solve a set of saddle point equations in the replica formalism at every learning instant. On the other hand, our theory retains the functions $G(t,s)$ and $C(t,s)$ with double arguments, but develops naturally from the stochastic nature of the cavity activations. Contrary to a suggestion [14], the cavity method can also be applied to the on-line learning with restricted sets of examples. It is hoped that by adhering to an exact formalism, the cavity method can provide more fundamental insights when the studies are extended to more sophisticated multilayer networks of practical importance.

The method enables us to study the effects of weight decay and early stopping. It shows that the optimal strength of weight decay is determined by the imprecision in the examples, or the level of input noise in anticipated applications. For weaker weight decay, the generalization performance can be made near-optimal by early stopping. Furthermore, depending on the performance measure, optimality may only be attained by a combination of weight decay and early stopping. Though the performance improvement is marginal in the present case, the question remains open in the more general context.

We consider the present work as the beginning of an in-depth study of learning dynamics. Many interesting and challenging issues remain to be explored.

Acknowledgments

We thank A. C. C. Coolen and D. Saad for fruitful discussions during NIPS. This work was supported by the grant HKUST6130/97P from the Research Grant Council of Hong Kong.

References

[1] D. Saad and S. Solla, *Phys. Rev. Lett.* **74**, 4337 (1995).

[2] D. Saad and M. Rattray, *Phys. Rev. Lett.* **79**, 2578 (1997).

[3] J. Hertz, A. Krogh and G. I. Thorbergssen, *J. Phys. A* **22**, 2133 (1989).

[4] M. Opper, *Europhys. Lett.* **8**, 389 (1989).

[5] A. Krogh and J. A. Hertz, *J. Phys. A* **25**, 1135 (1992).

[6] S. Bös and M. Opper, *J. Phys. A* **31**, 4835 (1998).

[7] S. Bös, *Phys. Rev. E* **58**, 833 (1998).

[8] A. C. C. Coolen and D. Saad, in *On-line Learning in Neural Networks*, ed. D. Saad (Cambridge University Press, Cambridge, 1998).

[9] M. Mézard, G. Parisi and M. Virasoro, *Spin Glass Theory and Beyond* (World Scientific, Singapore) (1987).

[10] K. Y. M. Wong, *Europhys. Lett.* **30**, 245 (1995).

[11] K. Y. M. Wong, *Advances in Neural Information Processing Systems* **9**, 302 (1997).

[12] L. K. Hansen, J. Larsen and T. Fog, *IEEE Int. Conf. on Acoustics, Speech, and Signal Processing* **4**, 3205 (1997).

[13] Y. W. Tong, K. Y. M. Wong and S. Li, to appear in *Proc. of IJCNN'99* (1999).

[14] A. C. C. Coolen and D. Saad, Preprint KCL-MTH-99-33 (1999).

Neural Computation with Winner-Take-All as the only Nonlinear Operation

Wolfgang Maass
Institute for Theoretical Computer Science
Technische Universität Graz
A-8010 Graz, Austria
email: maass@igi.tu-graz.ac.at
http://www.cis.tu-graz.ac.at/igi/maass

Abstract

Everybody "knows" that neural networks need *more than a single layer of nonlinear units* to compute interesting functions. We show that *this is false* if one employs *winner-take-all* as nonlinear unit:

- Any boolean function can be computed by a *single k-winner-take-all* unit applied to weighted sums of the input variables.

- Any continuous function can be approximated arbitrarily well by a *single* soft winner-take-all unit applied to weighted sums of the input variables.

- Only positive weights are needed in these (linear) weighted sums. This may be of interest from the point of view of *neurophysiology*, since only 15% of the synapses in the cortex are inhibitory. In addition it is widely believed that there are special microcircuits in the cortex that compute winner-take-all.

- Our results support the view that winner-take-all is a very useful basic computational unit in *Neural VLSI*:
    - it is wellknown that winner-take-all of n input variables can be computed very efficiently with $2n$ transistors (and a total wire length and area that is linear in n) in analog VLSI [Lazzaro et al., 1989]
    - we show that winner-take-all is not just useful for special purpose computations, but may serve as the only nonlinear unit for neural circuits with universal computational power
    - we show that any multi-layer perceptron needs quadratically in n many gates to compute winner-take-all for n input variables, hence winner-take-all provides a substantially more powerful computational unit than a perceptron (at about the same cost of implementation in analog VLSI).

Complete proofs and further details to these results can be found in [Maass, 2000].

1 Introduction

Computational models that involve competitive stages have so far been neglected in computational complexity theory, although they are widely used in computational brain models, artificial neural networks, and analog VLSI. The circuit of [Lazzaro et al., 1989] computes an approximate version of winner-take-all on n inputs with just $2n$ transistors and wires of length $O(n)$, with lateral inhibition implemented by adding currents on a single wire of length $O(n)$. Numerous other efficient implementations of winner-take-all in analog VLSI have subsequently been produced. Among them are circuits based on silicon spiking neurons ([Meador and Hylander, 1994], [Indiveri, 1999]) and circuits that emulate attention in artificial sensory processing ([Horiuchi et al., 1997], [Indiveri,1999]). Preceding analytical results on winner-take-all circuits can be found in [Grossberg, 1973] and [Brown, 1991].

We will analyze in section 4 the computational power of the most basic competitive computational operation: winner-take-all (= 1-WTA$_n$). In section 2 we will discuss the somewhat more complex operation k-winner-take-all (k-WTA$_n$), which has also been implemented in analog VLSI [Urahama and Nagao, 1995]. Section 3 is devoted to soft winner-take-all, which has been implemented by [Indiveri, 1999] in analog VLSI via temporal coding of the output.

Our results shows that winner-take-all is a surprisingly powerful computational module in comparison with threshold gates (= McCulloch-Pitts neurons) and sigmoidal gates. Our theoretical analysis also provides answers to two basic questions that have been raised by neurophysiologists in view of the well-known asymmetry between excitatory and inhibitory connections in cortical circuits: how much computational power of neural networks is lost if only positive weights are employed in weighted linear sums, and how much learning capability is lost if only the positive weights are subject to plasticity.

2 Restructuring Neural Circuits with Digital Output

We investigate in this section the computational power of a k-winner-take-all gate computing the function $\quad k - WTA_n \ : \ \mathbb{R}^n \to \{0,1\}^n$

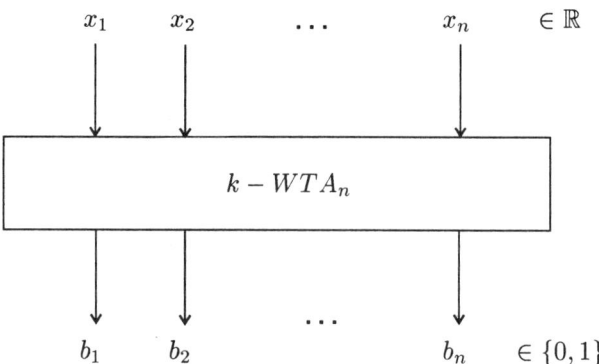

with

$b_i = 1 \leftrightarrow x_i$ is among the k largest of the inputs $x_1, \ldots, x_n$.

[precisely: $b_i = 1 \leftrightarrow x_j > x_i$ holds for at most $k-1$ indices j]

Theorem 1. *Any two-layer feedforward circuit C (with m analog or binary input variables and one binary output variable) consisting of threshold gates (=perceptrons) can be simulated by a circuit W consisting of a single k-winner-take-all gate k-WTA_n[1] applied to weighted sums of the input variables with positive weights. This holds for all digital inputs, and for analog inputs except for some set $S \subseteq \mathbb{R}^m$ of inputs that has measure 0.*

In particular, any boolean function

$$f : \{0, 1\}^m \to \{0, 1\}$$

can be computed by a single k-winner-take-all gate applied to positive weighted sums of the input bits.

Remarks

1. If C has polynomial size and integer weights, whose size is bounded by a polynomial in m, then the number of linear gates S in W can be bounded by a polynomial in m, and all weights in the simulating circuit W are natural numbers whose size is bounded by a polynomial in m.

2. The exception set of measure 0 in this result is a union of finitely many hyperplanes in $\mathbb{R}^m$. One can easily show that this exception set S of measure 0 in Theorem 1 is *necessary*.

3. Any circuit that has the structure of W can be converted back into a 2-layer threshold circuit, with a number of gates that is quadratic in the number of weighted sums (=linear gates) in W. This relies on the construction in section 4.

Proof of Theorem 1: Since the outputs of the gates on the hidden layer of C are from $\{0, 1\}$, we can assume without loss of generality that the weights $\alpha_1, \ldots, \alpha_n$ of the output gate G of C are from $\{-1, 1\}$ (see for example [Siu et al., 1995] for details; one first observes that it suffices to use integer weights for threshold gates with binary inputs, one can then normalize these weights to values in $\{-1, 1\}$ by duplicating gates on the hidden layer of C). Thus for any circuit input $\underline{z} \in \mathbb{R}^m$ we have $C(\underline{z}) = 1 \Leftrightarrow \sum_{j=1}^{n} \alpha_j G_j(\underline{z}) \geq \Theta$, where $G_1, \ldots, G_n$ are the threshold gates on the hidden layer of C, $\alpha_1, \ldots, \alpha_n$ are from $\{-1, 1\}$, and Θ is the threshold of the output gate G. In order to eliminate the negative weights in G we replace each gate G_j for which $\alpha_j = -1$ by another threshold gate $\hat{G}_j$ so that $\hat{G}_j(\underline{z}) = 1 - G_j(\underline{z})$ for all $\underline{z} \in \mathbb{R}^m$ except on some hyperplane.[2] We set $\hat{G}_j := G_j$ for all $j \in \{1, \ldots, n\}$ with $\alpha_j = 1$. Then we have for all $\underline{z} \in \mathbb{R}^m$, except for $\underline{z}$ from some exception set S consisting of up to n hyperplanes,

$$\sum_{j=1}^{n} \alpha_j G_j(\underline{z}) = \sum_{j=1}^{n} \hat{G}_j(\underline{z}) - |\{j \in \{1, \ldots, n\} : \alpha_j = -1\}|.$$

Hence $C(\underline{z}) = 1 \Leftrightarrow \sum_{j=1}^{n} \hat{G}_j(\underline{z}) \geq \hat{k}$ for all $\underline{z} \in \mathbb{R}^m - S$, for some suitable $\hat{k} \in \mathbb{N}$.

Let $w_1^j, \ldots, w_m^j \in \mathbb{R}$ be the weights and $\Theta^j \in \mathbb{R}$ be the threshold of gate $\hat{G}_j$, $j = 1, \ldots, n$.

---

[1] of which we only use its last output bit

[2] We exploit here that $\neg \sum_{i=1}^{m} w_i z_i \geq \Theta \Leftrightarrow \sum_{i=1}^{m} (-w_i) z_i > -\Theta$ for arbitrary $w_i, z_i, \Theta \in \mathbb{R}$.

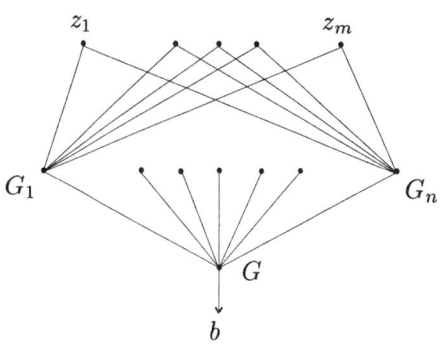

$G_1, \ldots, G_n$ are arbitrary threshold gates, G is a threshold gate with weights from $\{-1,1\}$

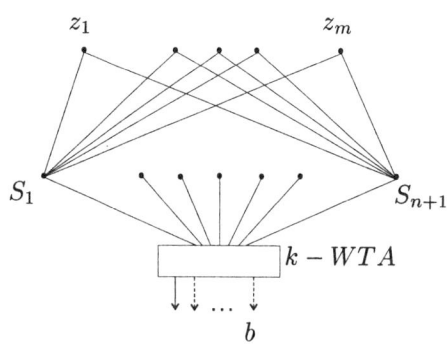

$S_1, \ldots, S_{n+1}$ are linear gates (with positive weights only, which are sums of absolute values of weights from the gates $G_1, \ldots, G_n$)

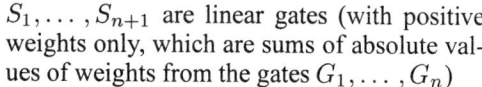

Thus $\hat{G}_j(\underline{z}) = 1 \Leftrightarrow \sum_{i:w_i^j>0} |w_i^j|z_i - \sum_{i:w_i^j<0} |w_i^j|z_i \geq \Theta^j$. Hence with

$$S_j := \sum_{i:w_i^j<0} |w_i^j|z_i + \Theta^j + \sum_{\ell \neq j} \sum_{i:w_i^\ell>0} |w_i^\ell|z_i \quad \text{for } j = 1, \ldots, n$$

and

$$S_{n+1} := \sum_{j=1}^{n} \sum_{i:w_i^j>0} |w_i^j|z_i$$

we have for every $j \in \{1, \ldots, n\}$ and every $\underline{z} \in \mathbb{R}^m$:

$$S_{n+1} \geq S_j \Leftrightarrow \sum_{i:w_i^j>0} |w_i^j|z_i - \sum_{i:w_i^j<0} |w_i^j|z_i \geq \Theta^j \Leftrightarrow \hat{G}_j(\underline{z}) = 1.$$

This implies that the $(n+1)$st output b_{n+1} of the k-winner-take-all gate k-WTA$_{n+1}$ for

$k := n - \hat{k} + 1$ applied to $S_1, \ldots, S_{n+1}$ satisfies

$$\begin{aligned}
b_{n+1} = 1 \quad &\Leftrightarrow |\{j \in \{1, \ldots, n+1\} : S_j > S_{n+1}\}| \leq n - \hat{k} \\
&\Leftrightarrow |\{j \in \{1, \ldots, n+1\} : S_{n+1} \geq S_j\}| \geq \hat{k} + 1 \\
&\Leftrightarrow |\{j \in \{1, \ldots, n\} : S_{n+1} \geq S_j\}| \geq \hat{k} \\
&\Leftrightarrow \sum_{j=1}^{n} \hat{G}_j(\underline{z}) \geq \hat{k} \\
&\Leftrightarrow C(\underline{z}) = 1 \; .
\end{aligned}$$

Note that all the coefficients in the sums $S_1, \ldots, S_{n+1}$ are positive. ∎

3 Restructuring Neural Circuits with Analog Output

In order to approximate arbitrary continuous functions with values in $[0, 1]$ by circuits that have a similar structure as those in the preceding section, we consider here a variation of a winner-take-all gate that outputs analog numbers between 0 and 1, whose values depend on the rank of the corresponding input in the linear order of all the n input numbers. One may argue that such gate is no longer a "winner-take-all" gate, but in agreement with common terminology we refer to it as a *soft winner-take-all* gate. Such gate computes a function from $\mathbb{R}^n$ into $[0, 1]^n$

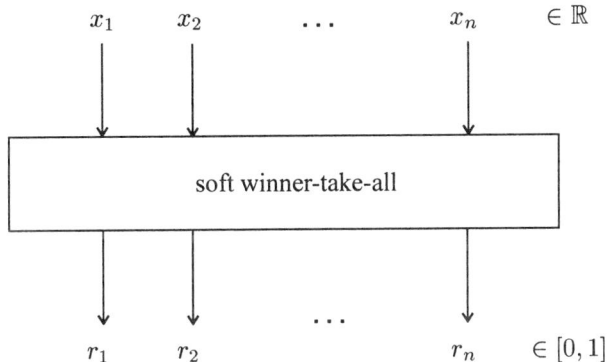

whose ith output $r_i \in [0, 1]$ is roughly proportional to the rank of x_i among the numbers $x_1, \ldots, x_n$. More precisely: for some parameter $T \in \mathbb{N}$ we set

$$r_i = \frac{|\{j \in \{1, \ldots, n\} : x_i \geq x_j\}| - \frac{n}{2}}{T},$$

rounded to 0 or 1 if this value is outside $[0, 1]$. Hence this gate focuses on those inputs x_i whose rank among the n input numbers $x_1, \ldots, x_n$ belongs to the set $\{\frac{n}{2}, \frac{n}{2} + 1, \ldots, \min\{n, T + \frac{n}{2}\}\}$. These ranks are linearly scaled into $[0, 1]$.[3]

Theorem 2. *Circuits consisting of a single soft winner-take-all gate (of which we only use its first output r_1) applied to positive weighted sums of the input variables are universal approximators for arbitrary continuous functions from $\mathbb{R}^m$ into $[0, 1]$.* ∎

---

[3] It is shown in [Maass, 2000] that actually any continuous monotone scaling into $[0, 1]$ can be used instead.

A circuit of the type considered in Theorem 2 (with a soft winner-take-all gate applied to n positive weighted sums $S_1, \ldots, S_n$) has a very simple geometrical interpretation: Over each point $\underline{z}$ of the input "plane" $\mathbb{R}^m$ we consider the relative heights of the n hyperplanes $H_1, \ldots, H_n$ defined by the n positive weighted sums $S_1, \ldots, S_n$. The circuit output depends only on how many of the other hyperplanes $H_2, \ldots, H_n$ are above H_1 at this point $\underline{z}$.

4 A Lower Bound Result for Winner-Take-All

One can easily see that any k-WTA gate with n inputs can be computed by a 2-layer threshold circuit consisting of $\binom{n}{2} + n$ threshold gates:

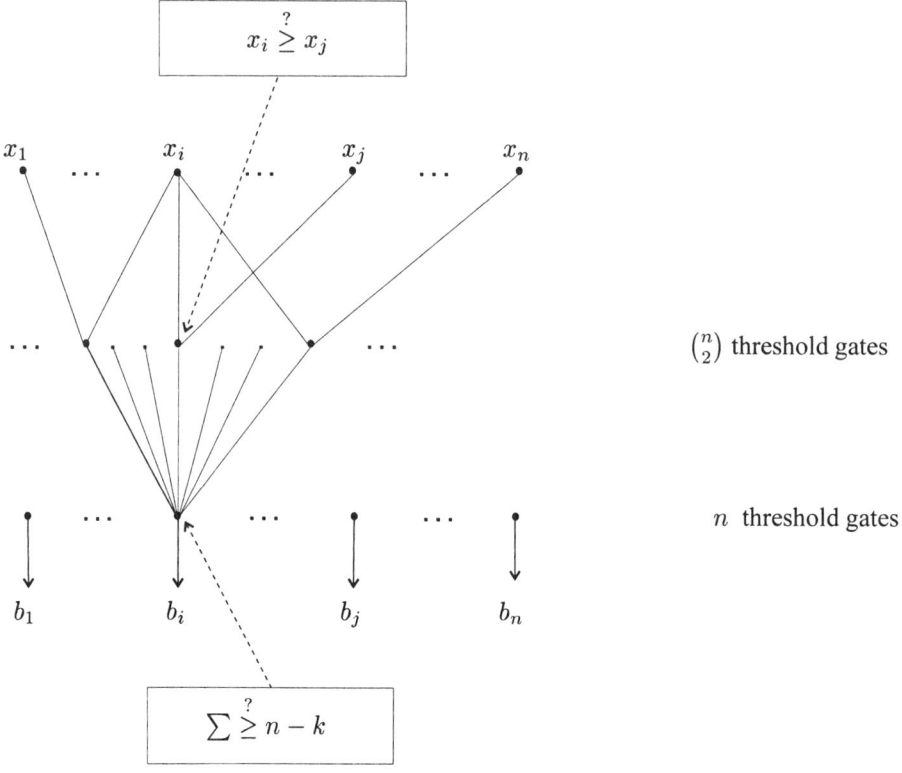

Hence the following result provides an *optimal* lower bound.

Theorem 3. Any *feedforward threshold circuit (=multi-layer perceptron) that computes 1-WTA for n inputs needs to have at least $\binom{n}{2} + n$ gates.* ∎

5 Conclusions

The lower bound result of Theorem 3 shows that the computational power of winner-take-all is quite large, even if compared with the arguably most powerful gate commonly studied in circuit complexity theory: the threshold gate (also referred to a McCulloch-Pitts neuron or perceptron).

It is well known ([Minsky and Papert, 1969]) that a single threshold gate is not able to compute certain important functions, whereas circuits of moderate (i.e., polynomial) size consisting of two layers of threshold gates with polynomial size integer weights have remarkable computational power (see [Siu et al., 1995]). We have shown in Theorem 1 that any such 2-layer (i.e., 1 hidden layer) circuit can be simulated by a single k-winner-take-all gate, applied to polynomially many weighted sums with positive integer weights of polynomial size.

We have also analyzed the computational power of soft winner-take-all gates in the context of *analog* computation. It is shown in Theorem 2 that a single soft winner-take-all gate may serve as the only nonlinearity in a class of circuits that have universal computational power in the sense that they can approximate any continuous functions.

Furthermore our novel universal approximators require only *positive* linear operations besides soft winner-take-all, thereby showing that in principle no computational power is lost if in a biological neural system inhibition is used exclusively for unspecific lateral inhibition, and no adaptive flexibility is lost if synaptic plasticity (i.e., "learning") is restricted to excitatory synapses.

Our somewhat surprising results regarding the computational power and universality of winner-take-all point to further opportunities for low-power analog VLSI chips, since winner-take-all can be implemented very efficiently in this technology.

References

[Brown, 1991] Brown, T. X. (1991). *Neural Network Design for Switching Network Control.*. Ph.-D.-Thesis, CALTECH.

[Grossberg, 1973] Grossberg, S. (1973). Contour enhancement, short term memory, and constancies in reverberating neural networks. *Studies in Applied Mathematics*, vol. 52, 217–257.

[Horiuchi et al., 1997] Horiuchi, T. K., Morris, T. G., Koch, C., DeWeerth, S. P. (1997). Analog VLSI circuits for attention-based visual tracking. *Advances in Neural Information Processing Systems*, vol. 9, 706–712.

[Indiveri, 1999] Indiveri, G. (1999). Modeling selective attention using a neuromorphic analog VLSI device, submitted for publication.

[Lazzaro et al., 1989] Lazzaro, J., Ryckebusch, S., Mahowald, M. A., Mead, C. A. (1989). Winner-take-all networks of $O(n)$ complexity. *Advances in Neural Information Processing Systems*, vol. 1, Morgan Kaufmann (San Mateo), 703-711.

[Maass, 2000] Maass, W. (2000). On the computational power of winner-take-all, *Neural Computation*, in press.

[Meador and Hylander, 1994] Meador, J. L., and Hylander, P. D. (1994). Pulse coded winner-take-all networks. In: *Silicon Implementation of Pulse Coded Neural Networks*, Zaghloul, M. E., Meador, J., and Newcomb, R. W., eds., Kluwer Academic Publishers (Boston), 79–99.

[Minsky and Papert, 1969] Minsky, M. C., Papert, S. A. (1969). *Perceptrons*, MIT Press (Cambridge).

[Siu et al., 1995] Siu, K.-Y., Roychowdhury, V., Kailath, T. (1995). *Discrete Neural Computation: A Theoretical Foundation*. Prentice Hall (Englewood Cliffs, NJ, USA).

[Urahama and Nagao, 1995] Urahama, K., and Nagao, T. (1995). k-winner-take-all circuit with $O(N)$ complexity. *IEEE Trans. on Neural Networks*, vol.6, 776–778.

Boosting with Multi-Way Branching in Decision Trees

Yishay Mansour   David McAllester

AT&T Labs-Research
180 Park Ave
Florham Park NJ 07932
{mansour, dmac}@research.att.com

Abstract

It is known that decision tree learning can be viewed as a form of boosting. However, existing boosting theorems for decision tree learning allow only binary-branching trees and the generalization to multi-branching trees is not immediate. Practical decision tree algorithms, such as CART and C4.5, implement a trade-off between the number of branches and the improvement in tree quality as measured by an index function. Here we give a boosting justification for a particular quantitative trade-off curve. Our main theorem states, in essence, that if we require an improvement proportional to the log of the number of branches then top-down greedy construction of decision trees remains an effective boosting algorithm.

1 Introduction

Decision trees have been proved to be a very popular tool in experimental machine learning. Their popularity stems from two basic features — they can be constructed quickly and they seem to achieve low error rates in practice. In some cases the time required for tree growth scales linearly with the sample size. Efficient tree construction allows for very large data sets. On the other hand, although there are known theoretical handicaps of the decision tree representations, it seem that in practice they achieve accuracy which is comparable to other learning paradigms such as neural networks.

While decision tree learning algorithms are popular in practice it seems hard to quantify their success in a theoretical model. It is fairly easy to see that even if the target function can be described using a small decision tree, tree learning algorithms may fail to find a good approximation. Kearns and Mansour [6] used the weak learning hypothesis to show that standard tree learning algorithms perform boosting. This provides a theoretical justification for decision tree learning similar to justifications that have been given for various other boosting algorithms, such as AdaBoost [4].

Most decision tree learning algorithms use a top-down growth process. Given a current tree the algorithm selects some leaf node and extends it to an internal node by assigning to it some "branching function" and adding a leaf to each possible output value of this branching function. The set of branching functions may differ from one algorithm to another, but most algorithms used in practice try to keep the set of branching functions fairly simple. For example, in C4.5 [7], each branching function depends on a single attribute. For categorical attributes, the branching is according to the attribute's value, while for continuous attributes it performs a comparison of the attribute with some constant.

Of course such top-down tree growth can over-fit the data — it is easy to construct a (large) tree whose error rate on the training data is zero. However, if the class of splitting functions has finite VC dimension then it is possible to prove that, with high confidence of the choice of the training data, for all trees T the true error rate of T is bounded by $\hat{\epsilon}(T) + O\left(\sqrt{|T|/m}\right)$ where $\hat{\epsilon}(T)$ is the error rate of T on the training sample, $|T|$ is the number of leaves of T, and m is the size of the training sample. Over-fitting can be avoided by requiring that top-down tree growth produce a small tree. In practice this is usually done by constructing a large tree and then pruning away some of its nodes. Here we take a slightly different approach. We assume a given target tree size s and consider the problem of constructing a tree T with $|T| = s$ and $\hat{\epsilon}(T)$ as small as possible. We can avoid over-fitting by selecting a small target value for the tree size.

A fundamental question in top-down tree growth is how to select the branching function when growing a given leaf. We can think of the target size as a "budget". A four-way branch spends more of the tree size budget than does a two-way branch — a four-way branch increases the tree size by roughly the same amount as two two-way branches. A sufficiently large branch would spend the entire tree size budget in a single step. Branches that spend more of the tree size budget should be required to achieve more progress than branches spending less of the budget. Naively, one would expect that the improvement should be required to be roughly linear in the number of new leaves introduced — one should get a return proportional to the expense. However, a weak learning assumption and a target tree size define a nontrivial game between the learner and an adversary. The learner makes moves by selecting branching functions and the adversary makes moves by presenting options consistent with the weak learning hypothesis. We prove here that the learner achieve a better value in this game by selecting branches that get a return considerably smaller than the naive linear return. Our main theorem states, in essence, that the return need only be proportional to the log of the number of branches.

2 Preliminaries

We assume a set $\mathcal{X}$ of instances and an unknown target function f mapping $\mathcal{X}$ to $\{0,1\}$. We assume a given "training set" S which is a set of pairs of the form $\langle x, f(x) \rangle$. We let $\mathcal{H}$ be a set of potential branching functions where each $h \in \mathcal{H}$ is a function from $\mathcal{X}$ to a finite set R_h — we allow different functions in $\mathcal{H}$ to have different ranges. We require that for any $h \in \mathcal{H}$ we have $|R_h| \geq 2$. An $\mathcal{H}$-tree is a tree where each internal node is labeled with an branching function $h \in \mathcal{H}$ and has children corresponding to the elements of the set R_h. We define $|T|$ to be the number of leaf nodes of T. We let $L(T)$ be the set of leaf nodes of T. For a given tree T, leaf node ℓ of T and sample S we write S_ℓ to denote the subset of the sample S reaching leaf ℓ. For $\ell \in T$ we define $\hat{p}_\ell$ to be the fraction of the sample reaching leaf ℓ, i.e., $|S_\ell|/|S|$. We define $\hat{q}_\ell$ to be the fraction of the pairs $\langle x, f(x) \rangle$ in S_ℓ for which $f(x) = 1$. The training error of T, denoted $\hat{\epsilon}(T)$, is $\sum_{\ell \in L(T)} \hat{p}_\ell \min(\hat{q}_\ell, 1 - \hat{q}_\ell)$.

3 The Weak Learning Hypothesis and Boosting

Here, as in [6], we view top-down decision tree learning as a form of Boosting [8, 3]. Boosting describes a general class of iterative algorithms based on a weak learning hypothesis. The classical weak learning hypothesis applies to classes of Boolean functions. Let $\mathcal{H}_2$ be the subset of branching functions $h \in \mathcal{H}$ with $|R_h| = 2$. For $\delta > 0$ the classical δ-weak learning hypothesis for $\mathcal{H}_2$ states that for any distribution on $\mathcal{X}$ there exists an $h \in \mathcal{H}_2$ with $Pr_D(h(x) \neq f(x)) \leq 1/2 - \delta$. Algorithms designed to exploit this particular hypothesis for classes of Boolean functions have proved to be quite useful in practice [5].

Kearns and Mansour show [6] that the key to using the weak learning hypothesis for decision tree learning is the use of an index function $I : [0, 1] \to [0, 1]$ where $I(q) \leq 1$, $I(q) \geq \min(q, (1-q))$ and where $I(T)$ is defined to be $\sum_{\ell \in L(T)} \hat{p}_\ell I(\hat{q}_\ell)$. Note that these conditions imply that $\hat{\epsilon}(T) \leq I(T)$. For any sample W let q_W be the fraction of pairs $\langle x, f(x) \rangle \in W$ such that $f(x) = 1$. For any $h \in \mathcal{H}$ let T_h be the decision tree consisting of a single internal node with branching function h plus a leaf for each member of $|R_h|$. Let $I_W(T_h)$ denote the value of $I(T_h)$ as measured with respect to the sample W. Let $\Delta(W, h)$ denote $I(q_W) - I_W(T_h)$. The quantity $\Delta(W, h)$ is the reduction in the index for sample W achieved by introducing a single branch. Also note that $\hat{p}_\ell \Delta(S_\ell, h)$ is the reduction in $I(T)$ when the leaf ℓ is replaced by the branch h. Kearns and Mansour [6] prove the following lemma.

Lemma 3.1 (Kearns & Mansour) *Assuming the δ-weak learning hypothesis for $\mathcal{H}_2$, and taking $I(q)$ to be $2\sqrt{q(1-q)}$, we have that for any sample W there exists an $h \in \mathcal{H}_2$ such that $\Delta(W, h) \geq \frac{\delta^2}{16} I(q_W)$.*

This lemma motivates the following definition.

Definition 1 *We say that $\mathcal{H}_2$ and I satisfies the γ-weak tree-growth hypothesis if for any sample W from $\mathcal{X}$ there exists an $h \in \mathcal{H}_2$ such that $\Delta(W, h) \geq \gamma I(q_W)$.*

Lemma 3.1 states, in essence, that the classical weak learning hypothesis implies the weak tree growth hypothesis for the index function $I(q) = 2\sqrt{q(1-q)}$. Empirically, however, the weak tree growth hypothesis seems to hold for a variety of index functions that were already used for tree growth prior to the work of Kearns and Mansour. The Ginni index $I(q) = 4q(1-q)$ is used in CART [1] and the entropy $I(q) = -q \log q - (1-q) \log(1-q)$ is used in C4.5 [7]. It has long been empirically observed that it is possible to make steady progress in reducing $I(T)$ for these choices of I while it is difficult to make steady progress in reducing $\hat{\epsilon}(T)$.

We now define a simple binary branching procedure. For a given training set S and target tree size s this algorithm grows a tree with $|T| = s$. In the algorithm

$\emptyset$ denotes the trivial tree whose root is a leaf node and $T_{\ell,h}$ denotes the result of replacing the leaf ℓ with the branching function h and a new leaf for each element of R_h.

$T = \emptyset$
WHILE ($|T| < s$) **DO**
$\qquad \ell \leftarrow \text{argmax}_\ell \ \hat{p}_\ell I(\hat{q}_\ell)$
$\qquad h \leftarrow \text{argmax}_{h \in \mathcal{H}_2} \Delta(S_\ell, h)$
$\qquad T \leftarrow T_{\ell,h};$
END-WHILE

We now define $e(n)$ to be the quantity $\prod_{i=1}^{n-1}(1 - \frac{\gamma}{n})$. Note that $e(n) \leq \prod_{i=1}^{n-1} e^{-\frac{\gamma}{i}} = e^{-\gamma \sum_{i=1}^{n-1} 1/i} \leq e^{-\gamma \ln n} = n^{-\gamma}$.

Theorem 3.2 (Kearns & Mansour) *If $\mathcal{H}_2$ and I satisfy the γ-weak tree growth hypothesis then the binary branching procedure produces a tree T with $\hat{\epsilon}(T) \leq I(T) \leq e(|T|) \leq |T|^{-\gamma}$.*

Proof: The proof is by induction on the number of iterations of the procedure. We have that $I(\emptyset) \leq 1 = e(1)$ so the initial tree immediately satisfies the condition. We now assume that the condition is satisfied by T at the begining of an iteration and prove that it remains satisfied by $T_{\ell,h}$ at the end of the iteration. Since $I(T) = \sum_{\ell \in T} \hat{p}_\ell I(\hat{q}_\ell)$ we have that the leaf ℓ selected by the procedure is such that $\hat{p}_\ell I(\hat{q}_\ell) \geq \frac{I(T)}{|T|}$. By the γ-weak tree growth assumption the function h selected by the procedure has the property that $\Delta(S_\ell, h) \geq \gamma I(\hat{q}_\ell)$. We now have that $I(T) - I(T_{\ell,h}) = \hat{p}_\ell \Delta(S_\ell, h) \geq \hat{p}_\ell \gamma I(\hat{q}_\ell) \geq \gamma \frac{I(T)}{|T|}$. This implies that $I(T_{\ell,h}) \leq I(T) - \frac{\gamma}{|T|} I(T) = (1 - \frac{\gamma}{|T|}) I(T) \leq (1 - \frac{\gamma}{|T|}) e(|T|) = e(|T|+1) = e(|T_{\ell,h}|)$. $\square$

4 Statement of the Main Theorem

We now construct a tree-growth algorithm that selects multi-way branching functions. As with many weak learning hypotheses, the γ-weak tree-growth hypothesis can be viewed as defining a game between the learner and an adversary. Given a tree T the adversary selects a set of branching functions allowed at each leaf of the tree subject to the constraint that at each leaf ℓ the adversary must provide a binary branching function h with $\Delta(S_\ell, h) \geq \gamma I(\hat{q}_\ell)$. The learner then selects a leaf ℓ and a branching function h and replaces T by $T_{\ell,h}$. The adversary then again selects a new set of options for each leaf subject to the γ-weak tree growth hypothesis. The proof of theorem 3.2 implies that even when the adversary can reassign all options at every move there exists a learner strategy, the binary branching procedure, guaranteed to achieves a final error rate of $|T|^{-\gamma}$.

Of course the optimal play for the adversary in this game is to only provide a single binary option at each leaf. However, in practice the "adversary" will make mistakes and provide options to the learner which can be exploited to achieve even lower error rates. Our objective now is to construct a strategy for the learner which can exploit multi-way branches provided by the adversary.

We first say that a branching function h is *acceptable* for tree T and target size

s if either $|R_h| = 2$ or $|T| < e(|R_h|)s\gamma/(2|R_h|)$. We also define $g(k)$ to be the quantity $(1 - e(k))/\gamma$. It should be noted that $g(2) = 1$. It should also be noted that $e(k) \sim e^{-\gamma \ln k}$ and hence for $\gamma \ln k$ small we have $e(k) \sim 1 - \gamma \ln k$ and hence $g(k) \sim \ln k$. We now define the following multi-branch tree growth procedure.

$T = \emptyset$
WHILE $(|T| < s)$ **DO**
    $\ell \leftarrow \text{argmax}_\ell \; \hat{p}_\ell I(\hat{q}_\ell)$
    $h \leftarrow \text{argmax}_{h \in \mathcal{H}, \; h \text{ acceptable for } T \text{ and } s} \; \Delta(S_\ell, h)/g(|R_h|)$
    $T \leftarrow T_{\ell, h};$
END-WHILE

A run of the multi-branch tree growth procedure will be called γ-boosting if at each iteration the branching function h selected has the property that $\Delta(S_\ell, h)/g(|R_h|) \geq \gamma I(\hat{q}_\ell)$. The γ-weak tree growth hypothesis implies that $\Delta(S_\ell, h)/g(|R_h|) \geq \gamma I(\hat{q}_\ell)/g(2) = \gamma I(\hat{q}_\ell)$. Therefore, the γ-weak tree growth hypothesis implies that every run of the multi-branch growth procedure is γ-boosting. But a run can be γ-boosting by exploiting mutli-way branches even when the γ-weak tree growth hypothesis fails. The following is the main theorem of this paper.

Theorem 4.1 *If T is produced by a γ-boosting run of the multi-branch tree-growth procedure then $I(T) \leq e(|T|) \leq |T|^{-\gamma}$.*

5 Proof of Theorem 4.1

To prove the main theorem we need the concept of a visited weighted tree, or VW-tree for short. A VW-tree is a tree in which each node m is assigned both a rational weight $w_m \in [0, 1]$ and an integer visitation count $v_m \geq 1$. We now define the following VW tree growth procedure. In the procedure T_w is the tree consisting of a single root node with weight w and visitation count 1. The tree $T_{\ell, w_1, \ldots, w_k}$ is the result of inserting k new leaves below the leaf ℓ where the ith new leaf has weight w_i and new leaves have visitation count 1.

$w \leftarrow$ any rational number in $[0, 1]$
$T \leftarrow T_w$
FOR ANY NUMBER OF STEPS REPEAT THE FOLLOWING
    $\ell \leftarrow \text{argmax}_\ell \; \frac{e(v_\ell) w_\ell}{v_\ell}$
    $v_\ell \leftarrow v_\ell + 1$
    OPTIONALLY $T \leftarrow T_{\ell, w_1, \ldots, w_{v_\ell}}$ **WITH** $w_1 + \ldots w_{v_\ell} \leq e(v_\ell) w_\ell$

We first prove an analog of theorem 3.2 for the above procedure. For a VW-tree T we define $|T|$ to be $\sum_{\ell \in L(T)} v_\ell$ and we define $I(T)$ to be $\sum_{\ell \in L(T)} e(v_\ell) w_\ell$.

Lemma 5.1 *The VW procedure maintains the invariant that $I(T) \leq e(|T|)$.*

Proof: The proof is by induction on the number of iterations of the algorithm. The result is immediate for the initial tree since $e(1) = 1$. We now assume that $I(T) \leq e(|T|)$ at the start of an iteration and show that this remains true at the end of the iteration.

We can associate each leaf ℓ with v_ℓ "subleaves" each of weight $e(v_\ell)w_\ell/v_\ell$. We have that $|T|$ is the total number of these subleaves and $I(T)$ is the total weight of these subleaves. Therefore there must exist a subleaf whose weight is at least $I(T)/|T|$. Hence there must exist a leaf ℓ satisfying $e(v_\ell)w_\ell/v_\ell \geq I(T)/|T|$. Therefore this relation must hold of the leaf ℓ selected by the procedure.

Let T' be the tree resulting from incrementing v_ℓ. We now have $I(T) - I(T') = e(v_\ell)w_\ell - e(v_\ell+1)w_\ell = e(v_\ell)w_\ell - (1-\frac{\gamma}{v_\ell})e(v_\ell)w_\ell = \frac{\gamma}{v_\ell}e(v_\ell)w_\ell \geq \gamma\frac{I(T)}{|T|}$. So we have $I(T') \leq (1-\frac{\gamma}{|T|})I(T) \leq (1-\frac{\gamma}{|T|})e(|T|) = e(|T'|)$.

Finally, if the procedure grows new leaves we have that the $I(T)$ does not increase and that $|T|$ remains the same and hence the invariant is maintained. □

For any internal node m in a tree T let $C(m)$ denote the set of nodes which are children of m. A VW-tree will be called *locally-well-formed* if for every internal node m we have that $v_m = |C(m)|$, that $\sum_{n \in C(m)} w_n \leq e(|C(m)|)w_m$. A VW-tree will be called *globally-safe* if $\max_{\ell \in L(T)} e(v_\ell)w_\ell/v_\ell \leq \min_{m \in N(T)} e(v_\ell-1)w_\ell/(v_\ell-1)$ where $N(T)$ denotes the set of internal nodes of T.

Lemma 5.2 *If T is a locally well-formed and globally safe VW-tree, then T is a possible output of the VW growth procedure and therefore $I(T) \leq e(|T|)$.*

Proof: Since T is locally well formed we can use T as a "template" for making nondeterministic choices in the VW growth procedure. This process is guaranteed to produce T provided that the growth procedure is never forced to visit a node corresponding to a leaf of T. But the global safety condition guarantees that any unfinished internal node of T has a weight as least as large as any leaf node of T. □

We now give a way of mapping $\mathcal{H}$-trees into VW-trees. More specifically, for any $\mathcal{H}$-tree T we define $VW(T)$ to be the result of assigning each node m in T the weight $\hat{p}_m I(\hat{q}_m)$, each internal node a visitation count equal to its number of children, and each leaf node a visitation count equal to 1. We now have the following lemmas.

Lemma 5.3 *If T is grown by a γ-boosting run of the multi-branch procedure then $VW(T)$ is locally well-formed.*

Proof: Note that the children of an internal node m are derived by selecting a branching function h for the node m. Since the run is γ-boosting we have $\Delta(S_\ell, h)/g(|R_h|) \geq \gamma I(\hat{q}_\ell)$. Therefore $\Delta(S_\ell, h) = (I(\hat{q}_\ell) - I_{S_\ell}(T_h)) \geq I(\hat{q}_\ell)(1 - e(|R_h|))$. This implies that $I_{S_\ell}(T_h) \leq e(|R_h|)I(\hat{q}_\ell)$. Multiplying by $\hat{p}_\ell$ and transforming the result into weights in the tree $VW(T)$ gives the desired result. □

The following lemma now suffices for theorem 4.1.

Lemma 5.4 *If T is grown by a γ-boosting run of the multi-branch procedure then $VW(T)$ is globally safe.*

Proof: First note that the following is an invariant of a γ-boosting run of the multi-branch procedure.

$$\max_{\ell \in L(VW(T))} w_\ell \leq \min_{m \in N(VW(T))} w_\ell$$

The proof is a simple induction on γ-boosting tree growth using the fact that the procedure always expands a leaf node of maximal weight.

We must now show that for every internal node m and every leaf ℓ we have that $w_\ell \leq e(k-1)w_m/(k-1)$ where k is the number of children of m. Note that if $k=2$ then this reduces to $w_\ell \leq w_m$ which follows from the above invariant. So we can assume without loss of generality that $k > 2$. Also, since $e(k)/k < e(k-1)/(k-1)$, it suffices to show that $w_\ell \leq e(k)w_m/k$.

Let m be an internal node with $k > 2$ children and let T' be the tree at the time m was selected for expansion. Let w_ℓ be the maximum weight of a leaf in the final tree T. By the definition of the acceptability condition, in the last $s/2$ iterations we are performing only binary branching. Each binary expansion reduces the index by at least γ times the weight of the selected node. Since the sequence of nodes selected in the multi-branch procedure has non-increasing weights, we have that in any iteration the weight of the selected node is at least w_ℓ. Since there are at least $s/2$ binary expansions after the expansion of m, each of which reduces I by at least γw_ℓ, we have that $s\gamma w_\ell/2 \leq I(T')$ so $w_\ell \leq 2I(T')/(\gamma s)$. The acceptability condition can be written as $2/(\gamma s) \leq e(k)/(k|T'|)$ which now yields $w_l \leq I(T')e(k)/(k|T'|)$. But we have that $I(T')/|T'| \leq w_m$ which now yields $w_l \leq e(k)w_m/k$ as desired. □

References

[1] Leo Breiman, Jerome H. Friedman, Richard A. Olshen, and Charles J. Stone. *Classification and Regression Trees.* Wadsworth International Group, 1984.

[2] Tom Dietterich, Michael Kearns and Yishay Mansour. Applying the Weak Learning Framework to understand and improve C4.5. In Proc. of *Machine Learning*, 96-104, 1996.

[3] Yoav Freund. Boosting a weak learning algorithm by majority. *Information and Computation*, 121(2):256–285, 1995.

[4] Yoav Freund and Robert E. Schapire. A decision-theoretic generalization of on-line learning and an application to boosting. In *Computational Learning Theory: Second European Conference, EuroCOLT '95*, pages 23–37. Springer-Verlag, 1995.

[5] Yoav Freund and Robert E. Schapire. Experiments with a new boosting algorithm. In *Machine Learning: Proceedings of the Thirteenth International Conference*, pages 148–156, 1996.

[6] Michael Kearns and Yishay Mansour. On the boosting ability of top-down decision tree learning. In *Proceedings of the Twenty-Eighth ACM Symposium on the Theory of Computing*, pages 459–468, 1996.

[7] J. Ross Quinlan. *C4.5: Programs for Machine Learning.* Morgan Kaufmann, 1993.

[8] Robert E. Schapire. The strength of weak learnability. *Machine Learning*, 5(2):197–227, 1990.

Inference for the Generalization Error

Claude Nadeau
CIRANO
2020, University,
Montreal, Qc, Canada, H3A 2A5
jcnadeau@altavista.net

Yoshua Bengio
CIRANO and *Dept. IRO*
Université de Montréal
Montreal, Qc, Canada, H3C 3J7
bengioy@iro.umontreal.ca

Abstract

In order to to compare learning algorithms, experimental results reported in the machine learning litterature often use statistical tests of significance. Unfortunately, most of these tests do not take into account the variability due to the choice of training set. We perform a theoretical investigation of the variance of the cross-validation estimate of the generalization error that takes into account the variability due to the choice of training sets. This allows us to propose two new ways to estimate this variance. We show, via simulations, that these new statistics perform well relative to the statistics considered by Dietterich (Dietterich, 1998).

1 Introduction

When applying a learning algorithm (or comparing several algorithms), one is typically interested in estimating its generalization error. Its point estimation is rather trivial through cross-validation. Providing a variance estimate of that estimation, so that hypothesis testing and/or confidence intervals are possible, is more difficult, especially, as pointed out in (Hinton et al., 1995), if one wants to take into account the variability due to the choice of the training sets (Breiman, 1996). A notable effort in that direction is Dietterich's work (Dietterich, 1998). Careful investigation of the variance to be estimated allows us to provide new variance estimates, which turn out to perform well.

Let us first lay out the framework in which we shall work. We assume that data are available in the form $Z_1^n = \{Z_1, \ldots, Z_n\}$. For example, in the case of supervised learning, $Z_i = (X_i, Y_i) \in \mathcal{Z} \subseteq \mathbb{R}^{p+q}$, where p and q denote the dimensions of the X_i's (inputs) and the Y_i's (outputs). We also assume that the Z_i's are independent with $Z_i \sim P(Z)$. Let $\mathcal{L}(D; Z)$, where D represents a subset of size $n_1 \leq n$ taken from Z_1^n, be a function $\mathcal{Z}^{n_1} \times \mathcal{Z} \to \mathbb{R}$. For instance, this function could be the loss incurred by the decision that a learning algorithm trained on D makes on a new example Z. We are interested in estimating $_n\mu \equiv E[\mathcal{L}(Z_1^n; Z_{n+1})]$ where $Z_{n+1} \sim P(Z)$ is independent of Z_1^n. Subscript n stands for the size of the training set (Z_1^n here). The above expectation is taken over Z_1^n and Z_{n+1}, meaning that we are interested in the performance of an algorithm rather than the performance of the specific decision function it yields on the data at hand. According to Dietterich's taxonomy (Dietterich, 1998), we deal with problems of type 5 through 8, (evaluating learning algorithms) rather then type 1 through 4 (evaluating decision functions). We call $_n\mu$ the generalization error even though it can also represent an error difference:

- **Generalization error**
We may take

$$\mathcal{L}(D; Z) = \mathcal{L}(D; (X, Y)) = Q(F(D)(X), Y), \tag{1}$$

where $F(D)$ ($F(D) : \mathbb{R}^p \to \mathbb{R}^q$) is the decision function obtained when training an algorithm on D, and Q is a loss function measuring the inaccuracy of a decision. For instance, we could have $Q(\hat{y}, y) = I[\hat{y} \neq y]$, where $I[\ ]$ is the indicator function, for classification problems and $Q(\hat{y}, y) = \| \hat{y} - y \|^2$, where is $\| \cdot \|$ is the Euclidean norm, for "regression" problems. In that case $_n\mu$ is what most people call the generalization error.

- **Comparison of generalization errors**

Sometimes, we are not interested in the performance of algorithms *per se*, but instead in how two algorithms compare with each other. In that case we may want to consider

$$\mathcal{L}(D; Z) = \mathcal{L}(D; (X, Y)) = Q(F_A(D)(X), Y) - Q(F_B(D)(X), Y), \qquad (2)$$

where $F_A(D)$ and $F_B(D)$ are decision functions obtained when training two algorithms (A and B) on D, and Q is a loss function. In this case $_n\mu$ would be a difference of generalization errors as outlined in the previous example.

The generalization error is often estimated via some form of cross-validation. Since there are various versions of the latter, we lay out the specific form we use in this paper.

- Let S_j be a random set of n_1 distinct integers from $\{1, \ldots, n\}$ ($n_1 < n$). Here n_1 represents the size of the training set and we shall let $n_2 = n - n_1$ be the size of the test set.

- Let $S_1, \ldots S_J$ be independent such random sets, and let $S_j^c = \{1, \ldots, n\} \setminus S_j$ denote the complement of S_j.

- Let $Z_{S_j} = \{Z_i | i \in S_j\}$ be the training set obtained by subsampling Z_1^n according to the random index set S_j. The corresponding test set is $Z_{S_j^c} = \{Z_i | i \in S_j^c\}$.

- Let $L(j, i) = \mathcal{L}(Z_{S_j}; Z_i)$. According to (1), this could be the error an algorithm trained on the training set Z_{S_j} makes on example Z_i. According to (2), this could be the difference of such errors for two different algorithms.

- Let $\hat{\mu}_j = \frac{1}{K} \sum_{k=1}^{K} L(j, i_k^j)$ where $i_1^j, \ldots, i_K^j$ are randomly and independently drawn from S_j^c. Here we draw K examples from the test set $Z_{S_j^c}$ with replacement and compute the average error committed. The notation does not convey the fact that $\hat{\mu}_j$ depends on K, n_1 and n_2.

- Let $\hat{\mu}_j^\infty = \lim_{K \to \infty} \hat{\mu}_j = \frac{1}{n_2} \sum_{i \in S_j^c} L(j, i)$ denote what $\hat{\mu}_j$ becomes as K increases without bounds. Indeed, when sampling infinitely often from $Z_{S_j^c}$, each Z_i ($i \in S_j^c$) is chosen with relative frequency $\frac{1}{n_2}$, yielding the usual "average test error". The use of K is just a mathematical device to make the test examples sampled independently from S_j^c.

Then the cross-validation estimate of the generalization error considered in this paper is

$$_{n_1}^{n_2}\hat{\mu}_J^K = \frac{1}{J} \sum_{j=1}^{J} \hat{\mu}_j.$$

We note that this an unbiased estimator of $_{n_1}\mu = E[\mathcal{L}(Z_1^{n_1}, Z_{n+1})]$ (not the same as $_n\mu$).

This paper is about the estimation of the variance of $_{n_1}^{n_2}\hat{\mu}_J^\infty$. We first study theoretically this variance in section 2, leading to two new variance estimators developed in section 3. Section 4 shows part of a simulation study we performed to see how the proposed statistics behave compared to statistics already in use.

2 Analysis of $Var[\,_{n_1}^{n_2}\hat{\mu}_J^K]$

Here we study $Var[\,_{n_1}^{n_2}\hat{\mu}_J^\infty]$. This is important to understand why some inference procedures about $_{n_1}\mu$ presently in use are inadequate, as we shall underline in section 4. This investigation also enables us to develop estimators of $Var[\,_{n_1}^{n_2}\hat{\mu}_J^\infty]$ in section 3. Before we proceed, we state the following useful lemma, proved in (Nadeau and Bengio, 1999).

Lemma 1 *Let $U_1, \ldots, U_k$ be random variables with common mean β, common variance δ and $Cov[U_i, U_j] = \gamma$, $\forall i \neq j$. Let $\pi = \frac{\gamma}{\delta}$ be the correlation between U_i and U_j ($i \neq j$). Let $\bar{U} = k^{-1} \sum_{i=1}^{k} U_i$ and $S_U^2 = \frac{1}{k-1} \sum_{i=1}^{k} (U_i - \bar{U})^2$ be the sample mean and sample variance respectively. Then $E[S_U^2] = \delta - \gamma$ and $Var[\bar{U}] = \gamma + \frac{(\delta - \gamma)}{k} = \delta \left(\pi + \frac{1-\pi}{k} \right)$.*

To study $Var[\,^{n_2}_{n_1}\hat{\mu}_J^K]$ we need to define the following covariances.

- Let $\sigma_0 = \sigma_0(n_1) = Var[L(j, i)]$ when i is randomly drawn from S_j^c.
- Let $\sigma_1 = \sigma_1(n_1, n_2) = Cov[L(j, i), L(j, i')]$ for i and i' randomly and independently drawn from S_j^c.
- Let $\sigma_2 = \sigma_2(n_1, n_2) = Cov[L(j, i), L(j', i')]$, with $j \neq j'$, i and i' randomly and independently drawn from S_j^c and $S_{j'}^c$ respectively.
- Let $\sigma_3 = \sigma_3(n_1) = Cov[L(j, i), L(j, i')]$ for $i, i' \in S_j^c$ and $i \neq i'$. This is not the same as σ_1. In fact, it may be shown that

$$\sigma_1 = Cov[L(j, i), L(j, i')] = \frac{\sigma_0}{n_2} + \frac{(n_2 - 1)\sigma_3}{n_2} = \sigma_3 + \frac{\sigma_0 - \sigma_3}{n_2}. \quad (3)$$

Let us look at the mean and variance of $\hat{\mu}_j$ and $\,^{n_2}_{n_1}\hat{\mu}_J^K$. Concerning expectations, we obviously have $E[\hat{\mu}_j] = {}_{n_1}\mu$ and thus $E[\,^{n_2}_{n_1}\hat{\mu}_J^K] = {}_{n_1}\mu$. From Lemma 1, we have $Var[\hat{\mu}_j] = \sigma_1 + \frac{\sigma_0 - \sigma_1}{K}$ which implies

$$Var[\hat{\mu}_j^\infty] = Var[\lim_{K \to \infty} \hat{\mu}_j] = \lim_{K \to \infty} Var[\hat{\mu}_j] = \sigma_1.$$

It can also be shown that $Cov[\hat{\mu}_j, \hat{\mu}_{j'}] = \sigma_2$, $j \neq j'$, and therefore (using Lemma 1)

$$Var[\,^{n_2}_{n_1}\hat{\mu}_J^K] = \sigma_2 + \frac{Var[\hat{\mu}_j] - \sigma_2}{J} = \sigma_2 + \frac{\sigma_1 + \frac{\sigma_0 - \sigma_1}{K} - \sigma_2}{J}. \quad (4)$$

We shall often encounter $\sigma_0, \sigma_1, \sigma_2, \sigma_3$ in the future, so some knowledge about those quantities is valuable. Here's what we can say about them.

Proposition 1 *For given n_1 and n_2, we have $0 \leq \sigma_2 \leq \sigma_1 \leq \sigma_0$ and $0 \leq \sigma_3 \leq \sigma_1$.*
Proof *See (Nadeau and Bengio, 1999).*

A natural question about the estimator $\,^{n_2}_{n_1}\hat{\mu}_J^K$ is how n_1, n_2, K and J affect its variance.

Proposition 2 *The variance of $\,^{n_2}_{n_1}\hat{\mu}_J^K$ is non-increasing in J, K and n_2.*
Proof *See (Nadeau and Bengio, 1999).*

Clearly, increasing K leads to smaller variance because the noise introduced by sampling with replacement from the test set disappears when this is done over and over again. Also, averaging over many train/test (increasing J) improves the estimation of $\,_{n_1}\mu$. Finally, all things equal elsewhere (n_1 fixed among other things), the larger the size of the test sets, the better the estimation of $\,_{n_1}\mu$.

The behavior of $Var[\,^{n_2}_{n_1}\hat{\mu}_J^K]$ with respect to n_1 is unclear, but we conjecture that **in most situations it should decrease in n_1**. Our argument goes like this. The variability in $\,^{n_2}_{n_1}\hat{\mu}_J^K$ comes from two sources: sampling decision rules (training process) and sampling testing examples. Holding n_2, J and K fixed freezes the second source of variation as it solely depends on those three quantities, not n_1. The problem to solve becomes: how does n_1 affect the first source of variation? It is not unreasonable to say that the decision function yielded by a learning algorithm is less variable when the training set is large. We conclude that the first source of variation, and thus the total variation (that is $Var[\,^{n_2}_{n_1}\hat{\mu}_J^K]$) is decreasing in n_1. We advocate the use of the estimator

$$\,^{n_2}_{n_1}\hat{\mu}_J^\infty = \frac{1}{J} \sum_{j=1}^{J} \hat{\mu}_j^\infty \quad (5)$$

as it is easier to compute and has smaller variance than ${}^{n_2}_{n_1}\hat{\mu}^K_J$ (J, n_1, n_2 held constant).

$$Var[{}^{n_2}_{n_1}\hat{\mu}^\infty_J] = \lim_{K \to \infty} Var[{}^{n_2}_{n_1}\hat{\mu}^K_J] = \sigma_2 + \frac{\sigma_1 - \sigma_2}{J} = \sigma_1 \left(\rho + \frac{1-\rho}{J}\right). \quad (6)$$

where $\rho = \frac{\sigma_2}{\sigma_1} = Corr[\hat{\mu}^\infty_j, \hat{\mu}^\infty_{j'}]$.

3   Estimation of $Var[{}^{n_2}_{n_1}\hat{\mu}^\infty_J]$

We are interested in estimating ${}^{n_2}_{n_1}\sigma^2_J \equiv Var[{}^{n_2}_{n_1}\hat{\mu}^\infty_J]$ where ${}^{n_2}_{n_1}\hat{\mu}^\infty_J$ is as defined in (5). We provide two different estimators of $Var[{}^{n_2}_{n_1}\hat{\mu}^\infty_J]$. The first is simple but may have a positive or negative bias for the actual variance. The second is meant to be conservative, that is, if our conjecture of the previous section is correct, its expected value exceeds the actual variance.

1st Method: Corrected Resampled t-Test. Let us recall that ${}^{n_2}_{n_1}\hat{\mu}^\infty_J = \frac{1}{J}\sum_{j=1}^J \hat{\mu}^\infty_j$. Let $\tilde{\sigma}^2$ be the sample variance of the $\hat{\mu}^\infty_j$'s. According to Lemma 1,

$$E[\tilde{\sigma}^2] = \sigma_1(1-\rho) = \frac{1-\rho}{\rho + \frac{1-\rho}{J}}\sigma_1\left(\rho + \frac{1-\rho}{J}\right) = \frac{\sigma_1\left(\rho + \frac{1-\rho}{J}\right)}{\frac{1}{J} + \frac{\rho}{1-\rho}} = \frac{Var[{}^{n_2}_{n_1}\hat{\mu}^\infty_J]}{\frac{1}{J} + \frac{\rho}{1-\rho}}, \quad (7)$$

so that $\left(\frac{1}{J} + \frac{\rho}{1-\rho}\right)\tilde{\sigma}^2$ is an unbiased estimator of $Var[{}^{n_2}_{n_1}\hat{\mu}^\infty_J]$. The only problem is that $\rho = \rho(n_1, n_2) = \frac{\sigma_2(n_1,n_2)}{\sigma_1(n_1,n_2)}$, the correlation between the $\hat{\mu}^\infty_j$'s, is unknown and difficult to estimate. We use a naive surrogate for ρ as follows. Let us recall that $\hat{\mu}^\infty_j = \frac{1}{n_2}\sum_{i \in S^c_j} \mathcal{L}(Z_{S_j}; Z_i)$. For the purpose of building our estimator, let us make the approximation that $\mathcal{L}(Z_{S_j}; Z_i)$ depends only on Z_i and n_1. Then it is not hard to show (see (Nadeau and Bengio, 1999)) that the correlation between the $\hat{\mu}^\infty_j$'s becomes $\frac{n_2}{n_1+n_2}$. Therefore our first estimator of $Var[{}^{n_2}_{n_1}\hat{\mu}^\infty_J]$ is $\left(\frac{1}{J} + \frac{\rho_o}{1-\rho_o}\right)\tilde{\sigma}^2$ where $\rho_o = \rho_o(n_1, n_2) = \frac{n_2}{n_1+n_2}$, that is $\left(\frac{1}{J} + \frac{n_2}{n_1}\right)\tilde{\sigma}^2$. This will tend to overestimate or underestimate $Var[{}^{n_2}_{n_1}\hat{\mu}^\infty_J]$ according to whether $\rho_o > \rho$ or $\rho_o < \rho$. Note that this first method basically does not require any more computations than that already performed to estimate generalization error by cross-validation.

2nd Method: Conservative Z. Our second method aims at overestimating $Var[{}^{n_2}_{n_1}\hat{\mu}^\infty_J]$ which will lead to conservative inference, that is tests of hypothesis with actual size less than the nominal size. This is important because techniques currently in use have the opposite defect, that is they tend to be liberal (tests with actual size exceeding the nominal size), which is typically regarded as less desirable than conservative tests.

Estimating ${}^{n_2}_{n_1}\sigma^2_J$ unbiasedly is not trivial as hinted above. However we may estimate unbiasedly ${}^{n_2}_{n'_1}\sigma^2_J = Var[{}^{n_2}_{n'_1}\hat{\mu}^\infty_J]$ where $n'_1 = \lfloor \frac{n}{2} \rfloor - n_2 < n_1$. Let ${}^{n_2}_{n'_1}\hat{\sigma}^2_J$ be the unbiased estimator, developed below, of the above variance. We argued in the previous section that $Var[{}^{n_2}_{n'_1}\hat{\mu}^\infty_J] \geq Var[{}^{n_2}_{n_1}\hat{\mu}^\infty_J]$. Therefore ${}^{n_2}_{n'_1}\hat{\sigma}^2_J$ will tend to overestimate ${}^{n_2}_{n_1}\sigma^2_J$, that is $E[{}^{n_2}_{n'_1}\hat{\sigma}^2_J] = {}^{n_2}_{n'_1}\sigma^2_J \geq {}^{n_2}_{n_1}\sigma^2_J$.

Here's how we may estimate ${}^{n_2}_{n'_1}\sigma^2_J$ without bias. For simplicity, assume that n is even. We have to randomly split our data Z^n_1 into two distinct data sets, D_1 and D^c_1, of size $\frac{n}{2}$ each. Let $\hat{\mu}_{(1)}$ be the statistic of interest (${}^{n_2}_{n'_1}\hat{\mu}^\infty_J$) computed on D_1. This involves, among other things, drawing J train/test subsets from D_1. Let $\hat{\mu}^c_{(1)}$ be the statistic computed on D^c_1. Then $\hat{\mu}_{(1)}$ and $\hat{\mu}^c_{(1)}$ are independent since D_1 and D^c_1 are independent data sets, so that $(\hat{\mu}_{(1)} - \frac{\hat{\mu}_{(1)}+\hat{\mu}^c_{(1)}}{2})^2 + (\hat{\mu}^c_{(1)} - \frac{\hat{\mu}_{(1)}+\hat{\mu}^c_{(1)}}{2})^2 = \frac{1}{2}(\hat{\mu}_{(1)} - \hat{\mu}^c_{(1)})^2$ is an unbiased estimate of ${}^{n_2}_{n'_1}\sigma^2_J$. This splitting process may be repeated M times. This yields D_m and D^c_m, with

$D_m \cup D_m^c = Z_1^n$, $D_m \cap D_m^c = \emptyset$ for $m = 1, \ldots, M$. Each split yields a pair $(\hat{\mu}_{(m)}, \hat{\mu}_{(m)}^c)$ that is such that $\frac{1}{2}(\hat{\mu}_{(m)} - \hat{\mu}_{(m)}^c)^2$ is unbiased for $\frac{n_2}{n_1'}\sigma_J^2$. This allows us to use the following unbiased estimator of $\frac{n_2}{n_1'}\sigma_J^2$:

$$\frac{n_2}{n_1'}\hat{\sigma}_J^2 = \frac{1}{2M} \sum_{m=1}^{M} (\hat{\mu}_{(m)} - \hat{\mu}_{(m)}^c)^2. \tag{8}$$

Note that, according to Lemma 1, $Var[\frac{n_2}{n_1'}\hat{\sigma}_J^2] = \frac{1}{4} Var[(\hat{\mu}_{(m)} - \hat{\mu}_{(m)}^c)^2] \left(r + \frac{1-r}{M}\right)$ with $r = Corr[(\hat{\mu}_{(i)} - \hat{\mu}_{(i)}^c)^2, (\hat{\mu}_{(j)} - \hat{\mu}_{(j)}^c)^2]$ for $i \neq j$. Simulations suggest that r is usually close to 0, so that the above variance decreases roughly like $\frac{1}{M}$ for M up to 20, say. The second method is therefore a bit more computation intensive, since requires to perform cross-validation M times, but it is expected to be conservative.

4 Simulation study

We consider five different test statistics for the hypothesis $H_0 : {}_{n_1}\mu = \mu_0$. The first three are methods already in use in the machine learning community, the last two are the new methods we put forward. They all have the following form

$$\text{reject } H_0 \text{ if } \left|\frac{\hat{\mu} - \mu_0}{\hat{\sigma}}\right| > c. \tag{9}$$

Table 1 describes what they are [1]. We performed a simulation study to investigate the size (probability of rejecting the null hypothesis when it is true) and the power (probability of rejecting the null hypothesis when it is false) of the five test statistics shown in Table 1. We consider the problem of estimating generalization errors in the Letter Recognition classification problem (available from www.ics.uci.edu/pub/machine-learning-databases). The learning algorithms are

1. **Classification tree**
   We used the function **tree** in Splus version 4.5 for Windows. The default arguments were used and no pruning was performed. The function **predict** with option **type="class"** was used to retrieve the decision function of the tree: $F_A(Z_S)(X)$. Here the classification loss function $L_A(j, i) = I[F_A(Z_{S_j})(X_i) \neq Y_i]$ is equal to 1 whenever this algorithm misclassifies example i when the training set is S_j; otherwise it is 0.

2. **First nearest neighbor**
   We apply the first nearest neighbor rule with a distorted distance metric to pull down the performance of this algorithm to the level of the classification tree (as in (Dietterich, 1998)). We have $L_B(j, i)$ equal to 1 whenever this algorithm misclassifies example i when the training set is S_j; otherwise it is 0.

In addition to inference about the generalization errors ${}_{n_1}\mu_A$ and ${}_{n_1}\mu_B$ associated with those two algorithms, we also consider inference about ${}_{n_1}\mu_{A-B} = {}_{n_1}\mu_A - {}_{n_1}\mu_B = E[L_{A-B}(j,i)]$ where $L_{A-B}(j,i) = L_A(j,i) - L_B(j,i)$.

We sample, without replacement, 300 examples from the 20000 examples available in the Letter Recognition data base. Repeating this 500 times, we obtain 500 sets of data of the form $\{Z_1, \ldots, Z_{300}\}$. Once a data set $Z_1^{300} = \{Z_1, \ldots Z_{300}\}$ has been generated, we may

---

[1] When comparing two classifiers, (Nadeau and Bengio, 1999) show that the t-test is closely related to McNemar's test described in (Dietterich, 1998). The 5 × 2 cv procedure was developed in (Dietterich, 1998) with solely the comparison of classifiers in mind but may trivially be extended to other problems as shown in (Nadeau and Bengio, 1999).

Name	$\hat{\mu}$	$\hat{\sigma}^2$	c	$\frac{Var[\hat{\mu}]}{E[\hat{\sigma}^2]}$
t-test (McNemar)	$_{n_1}^{n_2}\hat{\mu}_1^\infty$	$\frac{1}{n_2}SV(L(1,i))$	$t_{n_2-1, 1-\alpha/2}$	$\frac{n_2\sigma_3+(\sigma_0-\sigma_3)}{\sigma_0-\sigma_3} > 1$
resampled t	$_{n_1}^{n_2}\hat{\mu}_J^\infty$	$\frac{1}{J}\tilde{\sigma}^2$	$t_{J-1, 1-\alpha/2}$	$1 + J\frac{\rho}{1-\rho} > 1$
Dietterich's 5 × 2 cv	$_{n/2}^{n/2}\hat{\mu}_1^\infty$	see (Dietterich, 1998)	$t_{5, 1-\alpha/2}$	?
1: conservative Z	$_{n_1}^{n_2}\hat{\mu}_J^\infty$	$_{n_1'}^{n_2}\hat{\sigma}_J^2$	$Z_{1-\alpha/2}$	$\frac{\frac{n_2}{n_1}\sigma_J^2}{\frac{n_2}{n_1'}\sigma_J^2} < 1$
2: corr. resampled t	$_{n_1}^{n_2}\hat{\mu}_J^\infty$	$\left(\frac{1}{J}+\frac{n_2}{n_1}\right)\tilde{\sigma}^2$	$t_{J-1, 1-\alpha/2}$	$\frac{1+J\frac{\rho}{1-\rho}}{1+J\frac{n_2}{n_1}}$

Table 1: Description of five test statistics in relation to the rejection criteria shown in (9). Z_p and $t_{k,p}$ refer to the quantile p of the $N(0,1)$ and Student t_k distribution respectively. $\tilde{\sigma}^2$ is as defined above (7) and $SV(L(1,i))$ is the sample variance of the $L(1,i)$'s involved in $_{n_1}^{n_2}\hat{\mu}_1^\infty$. The $\frac{Var[\hat{\mu}]}{E[\hat{\sigma}^2]}$ ratio (which comes from proper application of Lemma 1, except for Dietterich's 5 × 2 cv and the Conservative Z) indicates if a test will tend to be conservative (ratio less than 1) or liberal (ratio greater than 1).

perform hypothesis testing based on the statistics shown in Table 1. A difficulty arises however. For a given n ($n = 300$ here), those methods don't aim at inference for the same generalization error. For instance, Dietterich's 5 × 2 cv test aims at $_{n/2}\mu$, while the others aim at $_{n_1}\mu$ where n_1 would usually be different for different methods (e.g. $n_1 = \frac{2n}{3}$ for the t test statistic, and $n_1 = \frac{9n}{10}$ for the resampled t test statistic, for instance). In order to compare the different techniques, for a given n, we shall always aim at $_{n/2}\mu$, i.e. use $n_1 = \frac{n}{2}$. However, for statistics involving $_{n_1}^{n_2}\hat{\mu}_J^\infty$ with $J > 1$, normal usage would call for n_1 to be 5 or 10 times larger than n_2, not $n_1 = n_2 = \frac{n}{2}$. Therefore, for those statistics, we also use $n_1 = \frac{n}{2}$ and $n_2 = \frac{n}{10}$ so that $\frac{n_1}{n_2} = 5$. To obtain $_{n/2}^{n/10}\hat{\mu}_J^\infty$ we simply throw out 40% of the data. For the conservative Z, we do the variance calculation as we would normally do ($n_2 = \frac{n}{10}$ for instance) to obtain $_{n/2-n_2}^{n_2}\hat{\sigma}_J^2 = _{2n/5}^{n/10}\hat{\sigma}_J^2$. However, in the numerator we compute both $_{n/2}^{n/2}\hat{\mu}_J^\infty$ and $_{n/2}^{n_2}\hat{\mu}_J^\infty = _{n/2}^{n/10}\hat{\mu}_J^\infty$ instead of $_{n-n_2}^{n_2}\hat{\mu}_J^\infty$, as explained above. Note that the rationale that led to the conservative Z statistics is maintained, that is $_{2n/5}^{n/10}\hat{\sigma}_J^2$ overestimates both $Var[_{n/2}^{n/10}\hat{\mu}_J^\infty]$ and $Var[_{n/2}^{n/2}\hat{\mu}_J^\infty]$: $E\left[_{2n/5}^{n/10}\hat{\sigma}_J^2\right] \geq Var[_{n/2}^{n/10}\hat{\mu}_J^\infty] \geq Var[_{n/2}^{n/2}\hat{\mu}_J^\infty]$.

Figure 1 shows the estimated power of different statistics when we are interested in μ_A and μ_{A-B}. We estimate powers by computing the proportion of rejections of H_0. We see that tests based on the t-test or resampled t-test are liberal, they reject the null hypothesis with probability greater than the prescribed $\alpha = 0.1$, when the null hypothesis is true. The other tests appear to have sizes that are either not significantly larger the 10% or barely so. Note that Dietterich's 5 × 2cv is not very powerful (note that its curve has the lowest power on the extreme values of mu_0). To make a fair comparison of power between two curves, one should mentally align the size (bottom of the curve) of these two curves. Indeed, even the resampled t-test and the conservative Z that throw out 40% of the data are more powerful. That is of course due to the fact that the 5 × 2 cv method uses $J = 1$ instead of $J = 15$.

This is just a glimpse of a much larger simulation study. When studying the corrected resampled t-test and the conservative Z in their natural habitat ($n_1 = \frac{9n}{10}$ and $n_2 = \frac{n}{10}$), we see that they are usually either right on the money in term of size, or slightly conservative. Their powers appear equivalent. The simulations were performed with J up to 25 and M up to 20. We found that taking J greater than 15 did not improve much the power of the

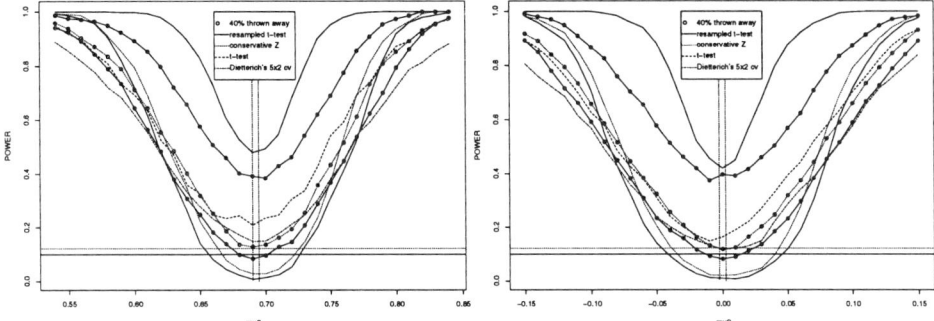

Figure 1: Powers of the tests about $H_0 : \mu_A = \mu_0$ (left panel) and $H_0 : \mu_{A-B} = \mu_0$ (right panel) at level $\alpha = 0.1$ for varying μ_0. The dotted vertical lines correspond to the 95% confidence interval for the actual μ_A or μ_{A-B}, therefore that is where the actual size of the tests may be read. The solid horizontal line displays the nominal size of the tests, i.e. 10%. Estimated probabilities of rejection laying above the dotted horizontal line are significatively greater than 10% (at significance level 5%). Solid curves either correspond to the resampled t-test or the corrected resampled t-test. The resampled t-test is the one that has ridiculously high size. Curves with circled points are the versions of the ordinary and corrected resampled t-test and conservative Z with 40% of the data thrown away. Where it matters $J = 15$, $M = 10$ were used.

statistics. Taking $M = 20$ instead of $M = 10$ does not lead to any noticeable difference in the distribution of the conservative Z. Taking $M = 5$ makes the statistic slightly less conservative. See (Nadeau and Bengio, 1999) for further details.

5 Conclusion

This paper addresses a very important practical issue in the empirical validation of new machine learning algorithms: how to decide whether one algorithm is significantly better than another one. We argue that it is important to take into account the variability due to the choice of training set. (Dietterich, 1998) had already proposed a statistic for this purpose. We have constructed two new variance estimates of the cross-validation estimator of the generalization error. These enable one to construct tests of hypothesis and confidence intervals that are seldom liberal. Furthermore, tests based on these have powers that are unmatched by any known techniques with comparable size. One of them (corrected resampled t-test) can be computed without any additional cost to the usual K-fold cross-validation estimates. The other one (conservative Z) requires M times more computation, where we found sufficiently good values of M to be between 5 and 10.

References

Breiman, L. (1996). Heuristics of instability and stabilization in model selection. *Annals of Statistics*, 24 (6):2350–2383.

Dietterich, T. (1998). Approximate statistical tests for comparing supervised classification learning algorithms. *Neural Computation*, 10 (7):1895–1924.

Hinton, G., Neal, R., Tibshirani, R., and DELVE team members (1995). Assessing learning procedures using DELVE. Technical report, University of Toronto, Department of Computer Science.

Nadeau, C. and Bengio, Y. (1999). Inference for the generalisation error. Technical Report in preparation, CIRANO.

Resonance in a Stochastic Neuron Model with Delayed Interaction

Toru Ohira*
Sony Computer Science Laboratory
3-14-13 Higashi-gotanda
Shinagawa, Tokyo 141, Japan
ohira@csl.sony.co.jp

Yuzuru Sato
Institute of Physics,
Graduate School of Arts and Science, University of Tokyo
3-8-1 Komaba, Meguro, Tokyo 153 Japan
ysato@sacral.c.u-tokyo.ac.jp

Jack D. Cowan
Department of Mathematics
University of Chicago
5734 S. University, Chicago, IL 60637, U.S.A
cowan@math.uchicago.edu

Abstract

We study here a simple stochastic single neuron model with delayed self–feedback capable of generating spike trains. Simulations show that its spike trains exhibit resonant behavior between "noise" and "delay". In order to gain insight into this resonance, we simplify the model and study a stochastic binary element whose transition probability depends on its state at a fixed interval in the past. With this simplified model we can analytically compute interspike interval histograms, and show how the resonance between noise and delay arises. The resonance is also observed when such elements are coupled through delayed interaction.

1 Introduction

"Noise" and "delay" are two elements which are associated with many natural and artificial systems and have been studied in diverse fields. Neural networks provide representative examples of information processing systems with noise and delay. Though much research has gone into the investigation of these two factors in the community, they have mostly been separately studied (see e.g. [1]). Neural

---
*Affiliated also with the Laboratory for Information Synthesis, RIKEN Brain Science Institute, Wako, Saitama, Japan

models incorporating both noise and delay are more realistic [2], but their complex characteristics have yet to be explored both theoretically and numerically.

The main theme of this paper is the study of a simple stochastic neural model with delayed interaction which can generate spike trains. The most striking feature of this model is that it can show a regular spike pattern with suitably "tuned" noise and delay [3]. Stochastic resonance in neural information processing has been investigated by others (see e.g. [4]). This model, however, introduces a different type of such resonance, via delay rather than through an external oscillatory signal. It can be classified with models of stochastic resonance without an external signal [5].

The novelty of this model is the use of delay as the source of its oscillatory dynamics. To gain insight into the resonance, we simplify the model and study a stochastic binary element whose transition probability depends on its state at a fixed interval in the past. With this model, we can analytically compute interspike interval histograms, and show how the resonance between noise and delay arises. We further show that the resonance also occurs when such stochastic binary elements are coupled through delayed interaction.

2 Single Delayed-feedback Stochastic Neuron Model

Our model is described by the following equations:

$$\mu \frac{d}{dt} V(t) = -V(t) + W\phi(V(t-\tau)) + \xi_L(t)$$
$$\phi(V(t)) = \frac{2}{1+e^{-\eta(V(t)-\theta)}} - 1 \quad (1)$$

where η and θ are constants, and V is the membrane potential of the neuron. The noise term ξ_L has the following probability distribution.

$$P(\xi = u) = \frac{1}{2L} \quad (-L \leq u \leq L)$$
$$= 0 \quad (u < -L, u > L), \quad (2)$$

i.e., ξ_L is a time uncorrelated uniformly distributed noise in the range $(-L, L)$. It can be interpreted as a fluctuation that is much faster than the membrane relaxation time μ. The model can be interpreted as a stochastic neuron model with delayed self–feedback of weight W, which is an extension of a model with no delay previously studied using the Fokker–Planck equation [6].

We numerically study the following discretized version:

$$V(t+1) = \frac{2}{1+e^{-\eta(V(t-\tau)-\theta)}} - 1 + \xi_L \quad (3)$$

We fix η and θ so that this map has two basins of attractors of differing size with no delay, as shown in Figure 1(A). We have simulated the map (3) with various noise widths and delays and find regular spiking behavior as shown in Fig 1(C) for tuned noise width and delay. In case the noise width is too large or too small given self-feedback delay, this rhythmic behavior does not emerge, as shown in Fig1(B) and (D).

We argue that the delay changes the effective shape of the basin of attractors into an oscillatory one, just like that due to an external oscillating force which, as is well-known, leads to stochastic resonance with a tuned noise width. The analysis of the dynamics given by (1) or (3), however, is a non–trivial task, particularly with respect to the spike trains. A previous analysis using the Fokker–Planck equation cannot capture this emergence of regular spiking behavior. This difficulty motivates us to further simplify our model, as described in the next section.

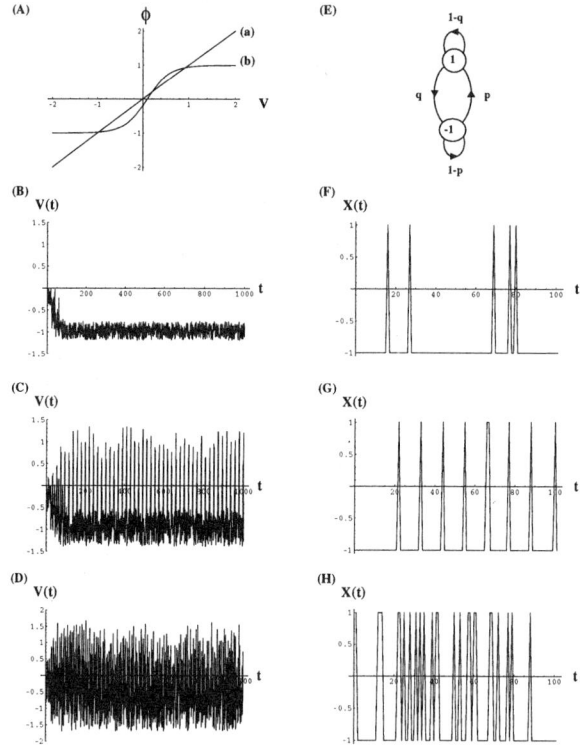

Figure 1: (A) The shape of the sigmoid function ϕ (b) for $\eta = 4$ and $\theta = 0.1$. The straight line (a) is $\phi = V$ and the crossings of the two lines indicate the stationary point of the dynamics. Also, the typical dynamics of $V(t)$ from the map model are shown as we change noise width L. The values of L are (B) $L = 0.2$, (C) $L = 0.4$, (D) $L = 0.7$. The data is taken with $\tau = 20$, $\eta = 4.0$, $\theta = 0.1$ and the initial condition $V(t) = 0.0$ for $t \in [-\tau, 0]$. The plots are shown between $t = 0$ to 1000. (E) Schematic view of the single binary model. Some typical dynamics from the binary model are also shown. The values of parameters are $\tau = 10$, $q = 0.5$, and (F) $p = 0.005$, (G) $p = 0.05$, and (H) $p = 0.2$.

3 Delayed Stochastic Binary Neuron Model

The model we now discuss is an approximation of the dynamics that retains the asymmetric stochastic transition and delay. The state $X(t)$ of the system at time step t is either -1 or 1. With the same noise ξ_L, the model is described as follows:

$$\begin{aligned} X(t+1) &= \theta[f(X(t-\tau)) + \xi_L], \\ f(n) &= \frac{1}{2}((a+b) + n(a-b)), \\ \theta[n] &= 1 \;\; (0 \leq n), \quad -1 \;\; (0 > n), \end{aligned} \quad (4)$$

where a and b are parameters such that $|a| \leq L$ and $|b| \leq L$, and τ is the delay. This model is an approximate discretization of the space of map (3) into two states with a and b controlling the bias of transition depending on the state of X τ steps earlier. When $a \neq b$, the transition between the two states is asymmetric, reflecting the two differing sized basins of attractors.

We can describe this model more concisely in probability space (Figure 1(E)). The formal definition is given as follows:

$$\begin{aligned} P(1, t+1) &= p, & X(t-\tau) &= -1, \\ &= 1-q, & X(t-\tau) &= 1, \\ P(-1, t+1) &= q, & X(t-\tau) &= 1, \\ &= 1-p, & X(t-\tau) &= -1, \\ p &= \frac{1}{2}(1 + \frac{b}{L}), \\ q &= \frac{1}{2}(1 - \frac{a}{L}), \end{aligned} \quad (5)$$

where $P(s, t)$ is the probability that $X(t) = s$. Hence, the transition probability of the model depends on its state τ steps in the past, and is a special case of a delayed random walk [7].

We randomly generate $X(t)$ for the interval $t = (-\tau, 0)$. Simulations are performed in which parameters are varied and $X(t)$ is recorded for up to 10^6 steps. They appear to be qualitatively similar to those generated by the map dynamics (Figure 1(F),(G),(H)). ¿From the trajectory $X(t)$, we construct a residence time histogram $h(u)$ for the system to be in the state -1 for u consecutive steps. Some examples of the histograms are shown in Figure 2 ($q = 1 - q = 0.5$, $\tau = 10$). We note that with $p \ll 0.5$, as in Figure 2(A), the model has a tendency to switch or spike to the $X = 1$ state after the time step interval of τ. But the spike trains do not last long and result in a small peak in the histogram. For the case of Figure 2(C) where p is closer to 0.5, we observe less regular transitions and the peak height is again small. With appropriate p as in Figure 2(B), spikes tend to appear at the interval τ more frequently, resulting in higher peaks in the histogram. This is what we mean by stochastic resonance (Figure 2(D)). Choosing an appropriate p is equivalent to "tuning" the noise width L, with other parameters appropriately fixed. In this sense, our model exhibits stochastic resonance.

This model can be treated analytically. The first observation to make with the model is that given τ, it consists of statistically independent $\tau + 1$ Markov chains. Each Markov chain has its state appearing at every $\tau+1$ interval. With this property of the model, we label time step t by the two integers s and k as follows

$$t = s(\tau + 1) + k, \quad (0 \leq s, 0 \leq k \leq \tau) \quad (6)$$

Let $P_{\pm}(t) \equiv P_{\pm}(s, k)$ be the probability for the state to be in the ± 1 state at time t or (s, k). Then, it can be shown that

$$\begin{aligned} P_+(s, k) &= \alpha(1 - \gamma^s) + \gamma^s P_+(s=0, k), \\ P_-(s, k) &= \beta(1 - \gamma^s) + \gamma^s P_-(s=0, k), \\ \alpha &= \frac{p}{p+q}, \\ \beta &= \frac{q}{p+q}, \\ \gamma &= 1 - (p+q). \end{aligned} \quad (7)$$

In the steady state, $P_+(s \to \infty, k) \equiv P_+ = \alpha$ and $P_-(s \to \infty, k) \equiv P_- = \beta$. The steady state residence time histogram can be obtained by computing the following quantity, $h(u) \equiv P(+;-,u;+)$, which is the probability that the system takes consecutive -1 states u times between two $+1$ states. With the definition of the model and statistical independence between Markov chains in the sequence, the following expression can be derived:

$$P(+;-,u;+) = P_+(P_-)^u P_+ = (\beta)^u (\alpha)^2 \quad (1 \leq u < \tau) \tag{8}$$
$$= P_+(P_-)^\tau (1-q) = (\beta)^\tau (\alpha)(1-q) \quad (u = \tau) \tag{9}$$
$$= P_+(P_-)^\tau (q)(1-p)^{u-\tau}(p) = (\beta)^u (p)^2 \quad (u > \tau) \tag{10}$$

With appropriate normalization, this expression reflects the shape of the histogram obtained by numerical simulations, as shown in Figure 2. Also, by differentiating equation (9) with respect to p, we derive the resonant condition for the peak to reach maximum height as

$$q = p\tau \tag{11}$$

or, equivalently,

$$L - a = (L+b)\tau. \tag{12}$$

In Figure 2(D), we see that maximum peak amplitude is reached by choosing parameters according to equation (11). We note that this analysis for the histogram is exact in the stationary limit, which makes this model unique among those showing stochastic resonance.

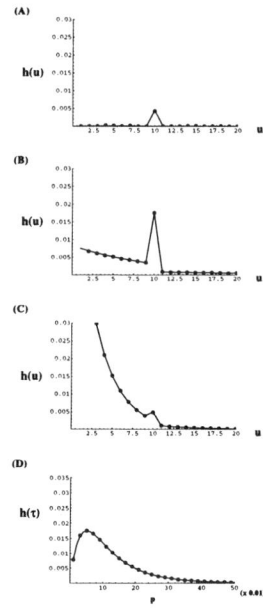

Figure 2: Residence time histogram and dynamics of $X(t)$ as we change p. The values of p are (A) $p = 0.005$, (B) $p = 0.05$, (C) $p = 0.2$. The solid line in the histogram is from the analytical expression given in equations (8-10). Also, in (D) we show a plot of peak height by varying p. The solid line is from equation (9). The parameters are $\tau = 10$, $q = 0.5$.

4 Delay Coupled Two Neuron Case

We now consider a circuit comprising two such stochastic binary neurons coupled with delayed interaction. We observe again that resonance between noise and delay takes place. The coupled two neuron model is a simple extension of the model in the previous section. The transition probability of each neuron is dependent on the other neuron's state at a fixed interval in the past. Formally, it can be described in probability space as follows.

$$
\begin{aligned}
P_1(1, t+1) &= p_1, & X_2(t-\tau_2) &= -1, \\
&= 1-q_1, & X_2(t-\tau_2) &= 1, \\
P_1(-1, t+1) &= q_1, & X_2(t-\tau_2) &= 1, \\
&= 1-p_1, & X_2(t-\tau_2) &= -1, \\
P_2(1, t+1) &= p_2, & X_1(t-\tau_1) &= -1, \\
&= 1-q_2, & X_1(t-\tau_1) &= 1, \\
P_2(-1, t+1) &= q_2, & X_1(t-\tau_1) &= 1, \\
&= 1-p_2, & X_1(t-\tau_1) &= -1
\end{aligned}
\quad (13)
$$

$P_i(s,t)$ is the probability that the state of the neuron i is $X_i(t) = s$. We have performed simulation experiments on the model and have again found resonance between noise and delay. Though more intricate than the single neuron model, we can perform a similar theoretical analysis of the histograms and have obtained approximate results for some cases. For example, we obtain the following approximate analytical results for the peak height of the interspike histogram of X_1 for the case $\tau_1 = \tau_2 \equiv \tau$. (The peak occurs at $\tau_1 + \tau_2 + 1$.)

$$
\begin{aligned}
H(p_1, p_2, q_1, q_2) &= \{\mu_3(p_1, p_2, q_1, q_2)q_1 + \mu_4(p_1, p_2, q_1, q_2)(1-p_1)\}^\tau \quad (14) \\
&\quad \{\mu_1(p_1, p_2, q_1, q_2)(q_1 q_2 p_1 + q_1(1-q_2)(1-q_1)) \\
&\quad + \mu_2(p_1, p_2, q_1, q_2)((1-p_1)q_2 p_1 + (1-p_1)(1-q_2)(1-q_1))\} \\
\mu_1(p_1, p_2, q_1, q_2) &= \frac{f_1(p_1, p_2, q_1, q_2) f_2(p_1, p_2, q_1, q_2)}{s(p_1, p_2, q_1, q_2)} \quad (15) \\
\mu_2(p_1, p_2, q_1, q_2) &= \frac{f_1(p_1, p_2, q_1, q_2)}{s(p_1, p_2, q_1, q_2)} \quad (16) \\
\mu_3(p_1, p_2, q_1, q_2) &= \frac{f_2(p_1, p_2, q_1, q_2)}{s(p_1, p_2, q_1, q_2)} \quad (17) \\
\mu_4(p_1, p_2, q_1, q_2) &= \frac{1}{s(p_1, p_2, q_1, q_2)} \quad (18) \\
f_1(p_1, p_2, q_1, q_2) &= \frac{p_1(1-p_2) + p_2(1-q_1)}{q_1(1-q_2) + q_2(1-q_1)} \quad (19) \\
f_2(p_1, p_2, q_1, q_2) &= \frac{p_2 + p_1(1-p_2-q_2)}{q_2 + q_1(1-p_2-q_2)} \quad (20) \\
s(p_1, p_2, q_1, q_2) &= f_1(p_1, p_2, q_1, q_2) f_2(p_1, p_2, q_1, q_2) \\
&\quad + f_1(p_1, p_2, q_1, q_2) + f_2(p_1, p_2, q_1, q_2) + 1 \quad (21)
\end{aligned}
$$

These analytical results are compared with the simulation experiments, examples of which are shown in Figure 3. A detailed analysis, particularly for the case of $\tau_1 \neq \tau_2$, is quite intricate and is left for the future.

5 Discussion

There are two points to be noted. Firstly, although there are examples which may indicate that stochastic resonance is utilized in biological information processing, it is yet to be explored if the resonance between noise and delay has some role in

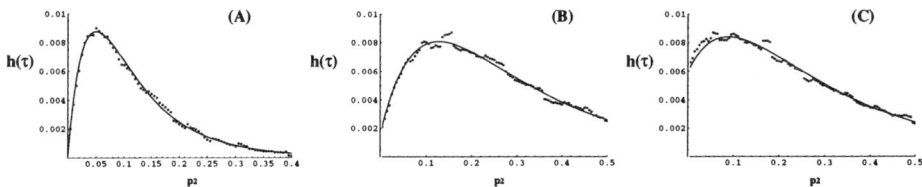

Figure 3: A plot of peak height by varying p_2. The solid line is from equation (14-20). The parameters are $\tau_1 = \tau_2 = 10$, $q_1 = q_2 = 0.5$, (A)$p_1 = p_2$, (B) $p_1 = 0.005$, (C) $p_1 = 0.025$.

neural information processing. Secondly, there are many investigations of spiking neural models and their applications (see e.g., [8]). Our model can be considered as a new mechanism for generating controlled stochastic spike trains. One can predict its application to weak signal transmission analogous to recent research using stochastic resonance with a larger number of units in series [9]. Investigations of the network model with delayed interactions are currently underway.

References

[1] Hertz, J. A., Krogh, A., & Palmer, R. G. (1991). *Introduction to the Theory of Neural Computation*. Redwood City: Addison-Wesley.

[2] Foss, J., Longtin, A., Mensour, B., & Milton, J. G. (1996). Multistability and Delayed Recurrent Loops. *Physical Review Letters, 76*, 708–711; Pham, J., Pakdaman, K., Vibert, J.-F. (1998). Noise–induced coherent oscillations in randomly connected neural networks. *Physical Review E, 58*, 3610–3622; Kim, S., Park, S. H., Pyo, H.-B. (1999). Stochastic Resonance in Coupled Oscillator Systems with Time Delay. *Physical Review Letters, 82*, 1620–1623; Bressloff, P. C. (1999). Synaptically Generated Wave Propagation in Excitable Neural Media. *Physical Review Letters, 82*, 2979–2982.

[3] Ohira, T. & Sato, Y. (1999). Resonance with Noise and Delay. *Physical Review Letters, 82*, 2811–2815.

[4] Gammaitoni, L., Hänggi, P., Jung, P., & Marchesoni, F.(1998). Stochastic Resonance. *Review of Modern Physics, 70*, 223–287.

[5] Gang, H., Ditzinger, T., Ning, C. Z., & Haken, H.(1993) Stochastic Resonance without External Periodic Force. *Physical Review Letters, 71*, 807–810; Rappel, W-J. & Strogatz, S. H. (1994). Stochastic resonance in an autonomous system with a nonuniform limit cycle. *Physical Review E, 50*, 3249–3250; Longtin, A. (1997). Autonomous stochastic resonance in bursting neurons. *Physical Review E, 55*, 868–876.

[6] Ohira, T. & Cowan J. D. (1995). Stochastic Single Neurons, *Neural Communication, 7* 518–528.

[7] Ohira, T. & Milton, J. G. (1995). Delayed Random Walks. *Physical Review E, 52*, 3277–3280; Ohira, T. (1997). Oscillatory Correlation of Delayed Random Walks, *Physical Review E, 55*, R1255–1258.

[8] Maas, W. (1997). Fast Sigmoidal Network via Spiking Neurons. *Neural Computation, 9*(2), 279–304; Maas, W. (1996). Lower Bounds for the Computational Power of Networks of Spiking Neurons. *Neural Computation, 8*(1), 1–40.

[9] Löcher, M., Cigna, D., and Hunt, E. R. (1998). Noise Sustained Propagation of a Signal in Coupled Bistable Electric Elements *Physical Review Letters, 80*, 5212–5215.

Understanding stepwise generalization of Support Vector Machines: a toy model

Sebastian Risau-Gusman and Mirta B. Gordon
DRFMC/SPSMS CEA Grenoble, 17 av. des Martyrs
38054 Grenoble cedex 09, France

Abstract

In this article we study the effects of introducing structure in the input distribution of the data to be learnt by a simple perceptron. We determine the learning curves within the framework of Statistical Mechanics. Stepwise generalization occurs as a function of the number of examples when the distribution of patterns is highly anisotropic. Although extremely simple, the model seems to capture the relevant features of a class of Support Vector Machines which was recently shown to present this behavior.

1 Introduction

A new approach to learning has recently been proposed as an alternative to feedforward neural networks: the Support Vector Machines (SVM) [1]. Instead of trying to learn a non linear mapping between the input patterns and internal representations, like in multilayered perceptrons, the SVMs choose *a priori* a non-linear kernel that transforms the input space into a high dimensional feature space. In binary classification tasks like those considered in the present paper, the SVMs look for linear separation with optimal margin in feature space. The main advantage of SVMs is that learning becomes a convex optimization problem. The difficulties of having many local minima that hinder the process of training multilayered neural networks is thus avoided. One of the questions raised by this approach is why SVMs do not overfit the data in spite of the extremely large dimensions of the feature spaces considered.

Two recent theoretical papers [2, 3] studied a family of SVMs with the tools of Statistical Mechanics, predicting typical properties in the limit of large dimensional spaces. Both papers considered mappings generated by polynomial kernels, and more specifically quadratic ones. In these, the input vectors $\mathbf{x} \in \mathbf{R}^N$ are transformed to $N(N+1)/2$-dimensional feature vectors $\Phi(\mathbf{x})$. More precisely, the mapping $\Phi_1(\mathbf{x}) = (\mathbf{x}, x_1\mathbf{x}, x_2\mathbf{x}, \cdots, x_k\mathbf{x})$ has been studied in [3] as a function of k, the number of quadratic features, and $\Phi_2(\mathbf{x}) = (\mathbf{x}, x_1\mathbf{x}/N, x_2\mathbf{x}/N, \cdots, x_N\mathbf{x}/N)$ has been considered in [2], leading to different results. These mappings are particular cases of quadratic kernels. In particular, in the case of learning quadratically separable tasks with mapping Φ_2, the generalization error decreases up to a lower bound for a number of examples proportional to N, followed by a further decrease if the number of examples increases proportionally to the dimension of the feature space, *i.e.* to N^2. In fact, this behavior is not specific of the SVMs. It also arises in the typical case of Gibbs learning (defined below) in quadratic feature spaces [4]: on increasing the training set size, the quadratic components of the discriminating surface are learnt after the linear ones. In the case of learning linearly separable tasks in quadratic feature spaces, the effect of overfitting is harmless, as it only slows down the decrease of the generalization error with the training set size. In the case of mapping Φ_1, overfitting is dramatic, as the generalization error at any given training set size increases with the number k of features.

The aim of the present paper is to understand the influence of the mapping scaling-factor on the generalization performance of the SVMs. To this end, it is worth to remark that features Φ_2 may be obtained by compressing the quadratic subspace of Φ_1 by a fixed factor. In order to mimic this contraction, we consider a linearly separable task in which the input patterns have a highly anisotropic distribution, so that the variance in one subspace is much smaller than in the orthogonal directions. We show that in this simple toy model, the generalization error as a function of the training set size exhibits a cross-over between two different behaviors: a rapid decrease corresponding to learning the components in the uncompressed space, followed by a slow improvement in which mainly the components in the compressed space are learnt. The latter would correspond, in this highly stylized model, to learning the scaled quadratic features in the SVM with mapping Φ_2.

The paper is organized as follows: after a short presentation of the model, we describe the main steps of the Statistical Mechanics calculation. The order parameters caracterizing the properties of the learning process are defined, and their evolution as a function of the training set size is analyzed. The two regimes of the generalization error are described, and we determine the training set size per input dimension at the crossover, as a function of the pertinent parameters. Finally we discuss our results, and their relevance to the understanding of the generalization properties of SVMs.

2 The model

We consider the problem of learning a binary classification task from examples. The training data set $\mathcal{D}_\alpha$ contains $P = \alpha N$ N-dimensional patterns $(\boldsymbol{\xi}^\mu, \tau^\mu)$ $(\mu = 1, \cdots, P)$ where $\tau^\mu = \text{sign}(\boldsymbol{\xi}^\mu \cdot \mathbf{w}^*)$ is given by a teacher of weights $\mathbf{w}^* = (w_1, w_2, ..., w_n)$. Without any loss of generality we consider normalized teachers: $\mathbf{w}^* \cdot \mathbf{w}^* = N$. We assume that the components ξ_i, $(i = 1, \cdots, N)$ of the input patterns $\boldsymbol{\xi}$ are independent, identically distributed random variables drawn from a zero-mean gaussian distribution, with variance σ along N_c directions and unit variance in the N_u remaining ones $(N_c + N_u = N)$:

$$P(\boldsymbol{\xi}) = \prod_{i \in N_c} \frac{1}{\sqrt{2\pi\sigma^2}} \exp\left(-\frac{\xi_i^2}{2\sigma^2}\right) \prod_{i \in N_u} \frac{1}{\sqrt{2\pi}} \exp\left(-\frac{\xi_i^2}{2}\right). \qquad (1)$$

We take $\sigma < 1$ without any loss of generality, as the case $\sigma > 1$ may be deduced from the former through a straightforward rescaling of N_c and N_u. Hereafter, the subspace of dimension N_c and variance σ will be called *compressed* subspace. The corresponding orthogonal subspace, of dimension $N_u = N - N_c$, will be called *uncompressed* subspace.

We study the typical generalization error of a student perceptron learning the classification task, using the tools of Statistical Mechanics. The pertinent cost function is the number of misclassified patterns:

$$E(\mathbf{w}; \mathcal{D}_\alpha) = \sum_{\mu=1}^{P} \Theta(-\tau^\mu \boldsymbol{\xi}^\mu \cdot \mathbf{w}), \qquad (2)$$

The weight vectors in version space correspond to a vanishing cost (2). Choosing a $\mathbf{w}$ at random from the *a posteriori* distribution

$$P(\mathbf{w}|\mathcal{D}_\alpha) = Z^{-1} P_0(\mathbf{w}) \exp\left(-\beta E(\mathbf{w}; \mathcal{D}_\alpha)\right), \qquad (3)$$

in the limit of $\beta \to \infty$ is called Gibbs' learning. In eq. (3), β is equivalent to an inverse temperature in the Statistical Mechanics formulation, the cost (2) being the energy function. We assume that P_0, the *a priori* distribution of the weights, is uniform on the hypersphere of radius $\sqrt{N}$:

$$P_0(\mathbf{w}) = (2\pi e)^{-N/2} \delta(\mathbf{w} \cdot \mathbf{w} - N). \qquad (4)$$

The normalization constant $(2\pi e)^{N/2}$ is the leading order term of the hypersphere's surface in N-dimensional space. Z is the partition function ensuring the correct normalization of $P(\mathbf{w}|\mathcal{D}_\alpha)$:

$$Z(\beta; \mathcal{D}_\alpha) = \int d\mathbf{w} \, P_0(\mathbf{w}) \exp\left(-\beta E(\mathbf{w}; \mathcal{D}_\alpha)\right). \qquad (5)$$

In general, the properties of the student are related to those of the free energy $F(\beta; \mathcal{D}_\alpha) = -\ln Z(\beta; \mathcal{D}_\alpha)/\beta$. In the limit $N \to \infty$ with the training set size per input dimension $\alpha \equiv P/N$ constant, the properties of the student weights become independant of the particular training set $\mathcal{D}_\alpha$. They are deduced from the averaged free energy per degree of freedom, calculated using the replica trick:

$$f(\beta) = -\frac{1}{N\beta} \overline{\ln Z(\beta; \mathcal{D}_\alpha)} = -\frac{1}{N\beta} \lim_{n \to 0} \frac{\ln \overline{Z^n(\beta; \mathcal{D}_\alpha)}}{n} \qquad (6)$$

where the overline represents the average over $\mathcal{D}_\alpha$, composed of patterns selected according to (1). In the case of Gibbs learning, the typical behavior of any intensive quantity is obtained in the zero temperature limit $\beta \to \infty$. In this limit, only error-free solutions, with vanishing cost, have non-vanishing posterior probability (3). Thus, Gibbs learning corresponds to picking at random a student in version space, *i.e.* a vector $\mathbf{w}$ that classifies correctly the training set $\mathcal{D}_\alpha$, with a probability proportional to $P_0(\mathbf{w})$.

In the case of an isotropic pattern distribution, which corresponds to $\sigma = 1$ in (1), the properties of cost function (2) have been extensively studied [5]. The case of patterns drawn from two gaussian clusters in which the symmetry axis of the clusters is the same [6] and different [7] from the teacher's axis, have recently been addressed. Here we consider the problem where, instead of having a single direction along which the patterns' distribution is contracted (or expanded), there is a *finite* fraction of compressed dimensions. In this case, all the properties of the student's perceptron may be expressed in terms of the following order parameters, that have to satisfy corresponding extremum conditions of the free energy:

$$\tilde{q}_c^{ab} = \langle \frac{1}{N} \sum_{i \in N_c} w_{ia} w_{ib} \rangle \qquad (7)$$

$$\tilde{q}_u^{ab} = \langle \frac{1}{N} \sum_{i \in N_u} w_{ia} w_{ib} \rangle \qquad (8)$$

$$\tilde{R}_c^a = \langle \frac{1}{N} \sum_{i \in N_c} w_{ia} w_i^* \rangle \qquad (9)$$

$$\tilde{R}_u^a = \langle \frac{1}{N} \sum_{i \in N_u} w_{ia} w_i^* \rangle \qquad (10)$$

$$Q^a = \langle \frac{1}{N} \sum_{i \in N_c} (w_{ia})^2 \rangle \qquad (11)$$

where $\langle \cdots \rangle$ indicates the average over the posterior (3); a, b are replica indices, and the subcripts c and u stand for compressed and uncompressed respectively. Notice that we do not impose that Q^a, the typical squared norm of the student's components in the compressed subspace, be equal to the corresponding teacher's norm $Q^* = \sum_{i \in N_c} (w_i^*)^2 / N$.

3 Order parameters and learning curves

Assuming that the order parameters are invariant under permutation of replicas, we can drop the replica indices in equations (7) to (11). We expect that this hypothesis of replica symmetry is consistent, like it is in other cases of perceptrons learning realizable tasks. The problem is thus reduced to the determination of five order parameters. Their meaning becomes clearer if we consider the following combinations:

$$q_c = \frac{\tilde{q}_c}{Q}, \qquad (12)$$

$$q_u = \frac{\tilde{q}_u}{1-Q}, \qquad (13)$$

$$R_c = \frac{\tilde{R}_c}{\sqrt{Q}\sqrt{Q^*}}, \qquad (14)$$

$$R_u = \frac{\tilde{R}_u}{\sqrt{1-Q}\sqrt{1-Q^*}}, \qquad (15)$$

$$Q = \langle \frac{1}{N} \sum_{i \in N_c} (w_i)^2 \rangle. \qquad (16)$$

q_c and q_u are the typical overlaps between the components of two student vectors in the compressed and the uncompressed subspaces respectively. Similarly, R_c and R_u are the corresponding overlaps between a typical student and the teacher. In terms of this set of parameters, the typical generalization error is $\epsilon_g = (1/\pi) \arccos R$ with

$$R = \frac{\sigma^2 R_c \sqrt{QQ^*} + R_u \sqrt{(1-Q)(1-Q^*)}}{\sqrt{\sigma^2 Q + (1-Q)}\sqrt{\sigma^2 Q^* + (1-Q^*)}}. \qquad (17)$$

Given α, the general solution to the extremum conditions depends on the three parameters of the problem, namely σ, Q^* and $n_c \equiv N_c/N$. An interesting case is the one where the teacher's anisotropy is consistent with that of the pattern's distribution, i.e. $Q^* = n_c$. In this case, it easy to show that $Q = Q^*$, $q_c = R_c$ and $q_u = R_u$. Thus,

$$R = \frac{n_u R_u + \sigma^2 n_c R_c}{n_u + \sigma^2 n_c}, \qquad (18)$$

where $n_u \equiv N_u/N$, R_u and R_c are given by the following equations:

$$\frac{R_c}{1-R_c} = \frac{\sigma^2}{\sigma^2 n_c + n_u} \frac{\alpha}{\pi \sqrt{1-R}} \int \mathcal{D}t \frac{\exp(-Rt^2/2)}{H(t\sqrt{R})}, \qquad (19)$$

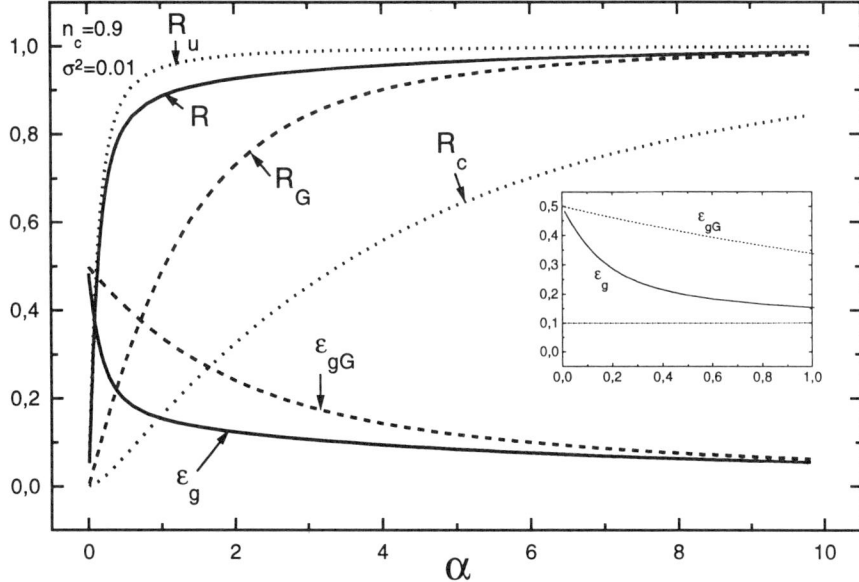

Figure 1: Order parameters and generalization error for the case $Q^* = n_c = 0.9$, $\sigma^2 = 10^{-2}$. The curves for the case of spherically distributed patterns is shown for comparison. The inset shows the first step of learning and its *plateau* (see text).

$$\frac{R_c}{1 - R_c} = \sigma^2 \frac{R_u}{1 - R_u}. \qquad (20)$$

where $\mathcal{D}t = dt\, e^{-t^2/2}/\sqrt{2\pi}$ and $H(x) = \int_x^\infty \mathcal{D}t$. If $\sigma^2 = 1$, we recover the equations corresponding to Gibbs learning of isotropic pattern distributions [5].

The order parameters are represented as a function of α on figure 1, for a particular choice of n_c and σ. R_u grows much faster than R_c, meaning that it is easier to learn the components of the uncompressed space. As a result, R (and therefore the generalization error ϵ_g) presents a cross-over between two behaviors. At small α, both $R_u \ll 1$ and $R_c \ll 1$, so that $R(\alpha, \sigma^2) = R_G(\alpha(n_u + \sigma^4 n_c)/(n_u + \sigma^2 n_c)^2)$ where R_G is the overlap for Gibbs learning with an isotropic ($\sigma^2 = 1$) distribution [5]. Learning the anisotropic distribution is faster (in α) than learning the isotropic one. If $\sigma \ll 1$ the anisotropy is very large and R increases like R_G but with an effective training set size per input dimension $\sim \alpha/n_u > \alpha$. On increasing α, there is an intermediate regime in which R_u increases but $R_c \ll 1$, so that $R \simeq R_u n_u/(n_u + \sigma^2 n_c)$. The corresponding generalization error seems to reach a *plateau* corresponding to $R_u = 1$ and $R_c = 0$. At $\alpha \gg 1$, $R(\alpha, \sigma^2) \simeq R_G(\alpha)$, the asymptotic behavior is independent of the details of the distribution, like in [7]. The crossover between these two regimes, when $\sigma^2 \ll 1$, occurs at $\alpha_0 \approx \sqrt{2(n_u + \sigma^2 n_c)/(\sigma^2 n_c)}$.

The cases $Q^* = 1$ and $Q^* = 0$ are also of interest. $Q^* = 1$ corresponds to a teacher having all the weights components in the compressed subspace, whereas $Q^* = 0$

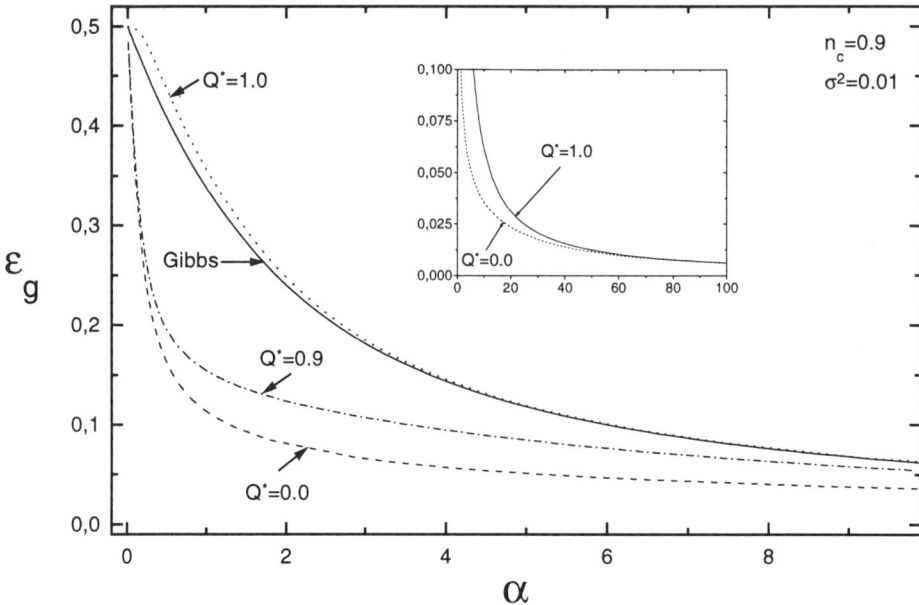

Figure 2: Generalization errors as a function of α for different teachers ($Q^* = 1$, $Q^* = 0.9$ and $Q^* = 1$), for the case $n_c = 0.9$ and $\sigma^2 = 10^{-2}$. The curve for spherically distributed patterns [5] is included for comparison. The inset shows the large alpha behaviors.

corresponds to a teacher orthogonal to the compressed subspace, *i.e.* with all the components in the uncompressed subspace. They correspond respectively to tasks where either the uncompressed or the compressed components are irrelevant for the patterns' classification. In Figure 2 we show all the generalization error curves, including the generalization error ϵ_{gG} for a uniform distribution [5] for comparison. The behaviour of $\epsilon_g(\alpha)$ is very sensitive to the value of Q^*. If $Q^* = 1$, the teacher is in the compressed subspace where learning is difficult. Consequently, $\epsilon_g(\alpha) > \epsilon_{gG}(\alpha)$ as expected. On the contrary, for $Q^* = 0$, only the components in the uncompressed space are relevant for the classification task. In this subspace learning is easy and $\epsilon_g(\alpha) < \epsilon_{gG}(\alpha)$. At $Q^* \neq 0, 1$ there is a crossover between these regimes, as already discussed. All the curves merge in the asymptotic regime $\alpha \to \infty$, as may be seen in the inset of Figure 2.

4 Discussion

We analyzed the typical learning behavior of a toy perceptron model that allows to clarify some aspects of generalization in high dimensional feature spaces. In particular, it captures an element essential to obtain stepwise learning, which is shown to stem from the compression of high order features. The components in the compressed space are more difficult to learn than those not compressed. Thus, if the training set is not large enough, mainly the latter are learnt.

Our results allow to understand the importance of the scaling of high order features in the SVMs kernels. In fact, with SVMs one has to choose *a priori* the kernel that maps the input space to the feature space. If high order features are conveniently compressed, hierarchical learning occurs. That is, low order features are learnt first; higher order features are only learnt if the training set is large enough. In the cases where the higher order features are irrelevant, it is likely that they will not hinder the learning process. This interesting behavior allows to avoid overfitting. Computer simulations currently in progress, of SVMs generated by quadratic kernels with and without the $1/N$ scaling, show a behavior consistent with the theoretical predictions [2, 3]. These may be understood with the present toy model.

References

[1] V. Vapnik (1995) The nature of statistical learning theory. Springer Verlag, New York.

[2] R. Dietrich, M. Opper, and H. Sompolinsky (1999) Statistical Mechanics of Support Vector Networks. Phys. Rev. Lett. 82, 2975-2978.

[3] A. Buhot and M. B. Gordon (1999) Statistical mechanics of support vector machines. *ESANN'99-European Symposium on Artificial Neural Networks* Proceedings, Michel Verleysen ed. 201-206; A. Buhot and M. B. Gordon (1998) Learning properties of support vector machines. Cond-Mat/9802179.

[4] H. Yoon and J.-H. Oh (1998) Learning of higher order perceptrons with tunable complexities J. Phys. A: Math. Gen. 31, 7771-7784.

[5] G. Györgyi and N. Tishby (1990) Statistical Theory of Learning a Rule. In Neural Networks and Spin Glasses (W. K. Theumann and R. Köberle, Worls Scientific), 3-36.

[6] R. Meir (1995) Empirical risk minimizaton. A case study. Neural Comp. 7, 144-157.

[7] C. Marangi, M. Biehl, S. A. Solla (1995) Supervised Learning from Clustered Examples Europhys. Lett. 30 (2), 117-122.

Lower Bounds on the Complexity of Approximating Continuous Functions by Sigmoidal Neural Networks

Michael Schmitt
Lehrstuhl Mathematik und Informatik
Fakultät für Mathematik
Ruhr-Universität Bochum
D–44780 Bochum, Germany
mschmitt@lmi.ruhr-uni-bochum.de

Abstract

We calculate lower bounds on the size of sigmoidal neural networks that approximate continuous functions. In particular, we show that for the approximation of polynomials the network size has to grow as $\Omega((\log k)^{1/4})$ where k is the degree of the polynomials. This bound is valid for any input dimension, i.e. independently of the number of variables. The result is obtained by introducing a new method employing upper bounds on the Vapnik-Chervonenkis dimension for proving lower bounds on the size of networks that approximate continuous functions.

1 Introduction

Sigmoidal neural networks are known to be universal approximators. This is one of the theoretical results most frequently cited to justify the use of sigmoidal neural networks in applications. By this statement one refers to the fact that sigmoidal neural networks have been shown to be able to approximate any continuous function arbitrarily well. Numerous results in the literature have established variants of this universal approximation property by considering distinct function classes to be approximated by network architectures using different types of neural activation functions with respect to various approximation criteria, see for instance [1, 2, 3, 5, 6, 11, 12, 14, 15]. (See in particular Scarselli and Tsoi [15] for a recent survey and further references.)

All these results and many others not referenced here, some of them being constructive, some being merely existence proofs, provide upper bounds for the network size asserting that good approximation is possible if there are sufficiently many network nodes available. This, however, is only a partial answer to the question that mainly arises in practical applications: "Given some function, how many network nodes are needed to approximate it?" Not much attention has been focused on establishing lower bounds on the network size and, in particular, for the approximation of functions over the reals. As far as the computation of binary-valued functions by sigmoidal networks is concerned (where the output value of a network is thresholded to yield 0 or 1) there are a few results in this direction. For a specific Boolean function Koiran [9] showed that networks using the standard sigmoid $\sigma(y) = 1/(1 + e^{-y})$ as activation function must have size $\Omega(n^{1/4})$ where n is the number of inputs. (When measuring network size we do not count the input nodes here and in what follows.) Maass [13] established a larger lower bound by constructing a binary-valued function over $\mathbb{R}^n$ and showing that standard sigmoidal networks require $\Omega(n)$ many network nodes for computing this function. The first work on the complexity of sigmoidal networks for approximating continuous functions is due to DasGupta and Schnitger [4]. They showed that the standard sigmoid in network nodes can be replaced by other types of activation functions without increasing the size of the network by more than a polynomial. This yields indirect lower bounds for the size of sigmoidal networks in terms of other network types. DasGupta and Schnitger [4] also claimed the size bound $A^{\Omega(1/d)}$ for sigmoidal networks with d layers approximating the function $\sin(Ax)$.

In this paper we consider the problem of using the standard sigmoid $\sigma(y) = 1/(1 + e^{-y})$ in neural networks for the approximation of polynomials. We show that at least $\Omega((\log k)^{1/4})$ network nodes are required to approximate polynomials of degree k with small error in the l_∞ norm. This bound is valid for arbitrary input dimension, i.e., it does not depend on the number of variables. (Lower bounds can also be obtained from the results on binary-valued functions mentioned above by interpolating the corresponding functions by polynomials. This, however, requires growing input dimension and does not yield a lower bound in terms of the degree.) Further, the bound established here holds for networks of any number of layers. As far as we know this is the first lower bound result for the approximation of polynomials. From the computational point of view this is a very simple class of functions; they can be computed using the basic operations addition and multiplication only. Polynomials also play an important role in approximation theory since they are dense in the class of continuous functions and some approximation results for neural networks rely on the approximability of polynomials by sigmoidal networks (see, e.g., [2, 15]).

We obtain the result by introducing a new method that employs upper bounds on the Vapnik-Chervonenkis dimension of neural networks to establish lower bounds on the network size. The first use of the Vapnik-Chervonenkis dimension to obtain a lower bound is due to Koiran [9] who calculated the above-mentioned bound on the size of sigmoidal networks for a Boolean function. Koiran's method was further developed and extended by Maass [13] using a similar argument but another combinatorial dimension. Both papers derived lower bounds for the computation of binary-valued functions (Koiran [9] for inputs from $\{0,1\}^n$, Maass [13] for inputs from $\mathbb{R}^n$). Here, we present a new technique to show that and how lower bounds can be obtained for networks that approximate continuous functions. It rests on two fundamental results about the Vapnik-Chervonenkis dimension of neural networks. On the one hand, we use constructions provided by Koiran and Sontag [10] to build networks that have large Vapnik-Chervonenkis dimension and consist of gates that compute certain arithmetic functions. On the other hand, we follow the lines of reasoning of Karpinski and Macintyre [7] to derive an upper bound for the Vapnik-Chervonenkis dimension of these networks from the estimates of Khovanskiĭ [8] and a result due to Warren [16].

In the following section we give the definitions of sigmoidal networks and the Vapnik-Chervonenkis dimension. Then we present the lower bound result for function approximation. Finally, we conclude with some discussion and open questions.

2 Sigmoidal Neural Networks and VC Dimension

We briefly recall the definitions of a sigmoidal neural network and the Vapnik-Chervonenkis dimension (see, e.g., [7, 10]). We consider *feedforward neural networks* which have a certain number of input nodes and one output node. The nodes which are not input nodes are called *computation nodes* and associated with each of them is a real number t, the *threshold*. Further, each edge is labelled with a real number w called *weight*. Computation in the network takes place as follows: The input values are assigned to the input nodes. Each computation node applies the standard sigmoid $\sigma(y) = 1/(1 + e^{-y})$ to the sum $w_1 x_1 + \cdots + w_r x_r - t$ where $x_1, \ldots, x_r$ are the values computed by the node's predecessors, $w_1, \ldots, w_r$ are the weights of the corresponding edges, and t is the threshold. The output value of the network is defined to be the value computed by the output node. As it is common for approximation results by means of neural networks, we assume that the output node is a linear gate, i.e., it just outputs the sum $w_1 x_1 + \cdots + w_r x_r - t$. (Clearly, for computing functions on finite sets with output range $[0, 1]$ the output node may apply the standard sigmoid as well.) Since σ is the only sigmoidal function that we consider here we will refer to such networks as *sigmoidal neural networks*. (Sigmoidal functions in general need to satisfy much weaker assumptions than σ does.) The definition naturally generalizes to networks employing other types of gates that we will make use of (e.g. linear, multiplication, and division gates).

The Vapnik-Chervonenkis dimension is a combinatorial dimension of a function class and is defined as follows: A *dichotomy* of a set $S \subseteq \mathbb{R}^n$ is a partition of S into two disjoint subsets (S_0, S_1) such that $S_0 \cup S_1 = S$. Given a set $\mathcal{F}$ of functions mapping $\mathbb{R}^n$ to $\{0, 1\}$ and a dichotomy (S_0, S_1) of S, we say that $\mathcal{F}$ *induces* the dichotomy (S_0, S_1) on S if there is some $f \in \mathcal{F}$ such that $f(S_0) \subseteq \{0\}$ and $f(S_1) \subseteq \{1\}$. We say further that $\mathcal{F}$ *shatters* S if $\mathcal{F}$ induces all dichotomies on S. The *Vapnik-Chervonenkis (VC) dimension* of $\mathcal{F}$, denoted VCdim($\mathcal{F}$), is defined as the largest number m such that there is a set of m elements that is shattered by $\mathcal{F}$. We refer to the VC dimension of a neural network, which is given in terms of a "feedforward architecture", i.e. a directed acyclic graph, as the VC dimension of the class of functions obtained by assigning real numbers to all its programmable parameters, which are in general the weights and thresholds of the network or a subset thereof. Further, we assume that the output value of the network is thresholded at $1/2$ to obtain binary values.

3 Lower Bounds on Network Size

Before we present the lower bound on the size of sigmoidal networks required for the approximation of polynomials we first give a brief outline of the proof idea. We will define a sequence of univariate polynomials $(p_n)_{n \geq 1}$ by means of which we show how to construct neural architectures $\mathcal{N}_n$ consisting of various types of gates such as linear, multiplication, and division gates, and, in particular, gates that compute some of the polynomials. Further, this architecture has a single weight as programmable parameter (all other weights and thresholds are fixed). We then demonstrate that, assuming the gates computing the polynomials can be approximated by sigmoidal neural networks sufficiently well, the architecture $\mathcal{N}_n$ can shatter a certain set by assigning suitable values to its programmable weight. The final step is to reason along the lines of Karpinski and Macintyre [7] to obtain via Khovanskiĭ's estimates [8] and Warren's result [16] an upper bound on the VC dimension of $\mathcal{N}_n$ in terms of the number of its computation nodes. (Note that we cannot directly apply Theorem 7 of [7] since it does not deal with division gates.) Comparing this bound with the cardinality of the shattered set we will then be able

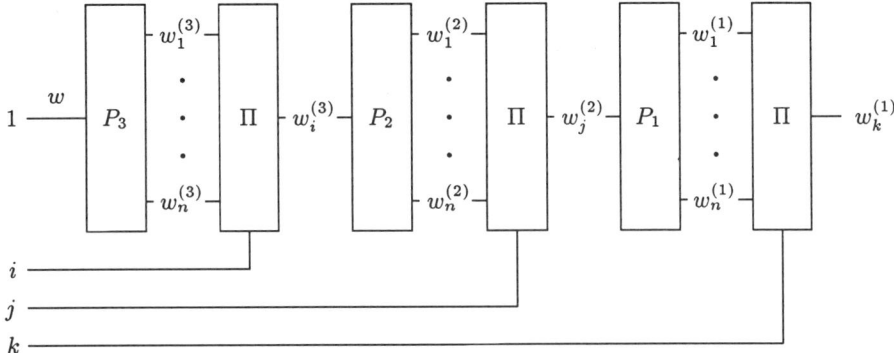

Figure 1: The network $\mathcal{N}_n$ with values $k,j,i,1$ assigned to the input nodes x_1, x_2, x_3, x_4 respectively. The weight w is the only programmable parameter of the network.

to conclude with a lower bound on the number of computation nodes in $\mathcal{N}_n$ and thus in the networks that approximate the polynomials.

Let the sequence $(p_n)_{n\geq 1}$ of polynomials over $\mathbb{R}$ be inductively defined by

$$p_n(x) = \begin{cases} 4x(1-x) & n=1, \\ p(p_{n-1}(x)) & n \geq 2. \end{cases}$$

Clearly, this uniquely defines p_n for every $n \geq 1$ and it can readily be seen that p_n has degree 2^n. The main lower bound result is made precise in the following statement.

Theorem 1 *Sigmoidal neural networks that approximate the polynomials $(p_n)_{n\geq 1}$ on the interval $[0,1]$ with error at most $O(2^{-n})$ in the l_∞ norm must have at least $\Omega(n^{1/4})$ computation nodes.*

Proof. For each n a neural architecture $\mathcal{N}_n$ can be constructed as follows: The network has four input nodes x_1, x_2, x_3, x_4. Figure 1 shows the network with input values assigned to the input nodes in the order $x_4 = 1, x_3 = i, x_2 = j, x_1 = k$. There is one weight which we consider as the (only) programmable parameter of $\mathcal{N}_n$. It is associated with the edge outgoing from input node x_4 and is denoted by w. The computation nodes are partitioned into six levels as indicated by the boxes in Figure 1. Each level is itself a network. Let us first assume, for the sake of simplicity, that all computations over real numbers are exact. There are three levels labeled with Π, having $n+1$ input nodes and one output node each, that compute so-called projections $\pi : \mathbb{R}^{n+1} \to \mathbb{R}$ where $\pi(y_1, \ldots, y_n, a) = y_a$ for $a \in \{1, \ldots, n\}$.

The levels labeled P_3, P_2, P_1 have one input node and n output nodes each. Level P_3 receives the constant 1 as input and thus the value w which is the parameter of the network. We define the output values of level P_λ for $\lambda = 3, 2, 1$ by

$$w_b^{(\lambda)} = p_{b \cdot n^{\lambda-1}}(v), \quad b = 1, \ldots, n$$

where v denotes the input value to level P_λ. This value is equal to w for $\lambda = 3$ and $\pi(w_1^{(\lambda+1)}, \ldots, w_n^{(\lambda+1)}, x_{\lambda+1})$ otherwise. We observe that $w_{b+1}^{(\lambda)}$ can be calculated from

$w_b^{(\lambda)}$ as $p_{n^{\lambda-1}}(w_b^{(\lambda)})$. Therefore, the computations of level P_λ can be implemented using n gates each of them computing the function $p_{n^{\lambda-1}}$.

We show now that $\mathcal{N}_n$ can shatter a set of cardinality n^3. Let $S = \{1, \ldots, n\}^3$. It has been shown in Lemma 2 of [10] that for each $(\beta_1, \ldots, \beta_r) \in \{0,1\}^r$ there exists some $w \in [0,1]$ such that for $q = 1, \ldots, r$

$$p_q(w) \in [0, 1/2) \text{ if } \beta_q = 0, \text{ and } p_q(w) \in (1/2, 1] \text{ if } \beta_q = 1.$$

This implies that, for each dichotomy (S_0, S_1) of S there is some $w \in [0,1]$ such that for every $(i, j, k) \in S$

$$p_k(p_{j \cdot n}(p_{i \cdot n^2}(w))) < 1/2 \quad \text{if} \quad (i, j, k) \in S_0,$$
$$p_k(p_{j \cdot n}(p_{i \cdot n^2}(w))) > 1/2 \quad \text{if} \quad (i, j, k) \in S_1.$$

Note that $p_k(p_{j \cdot n}(p_{i \cdot n^2}(w)))$ is the value computed by $\mathcal{N}_n$ given input values $k, j, i, 1$. Therefore, choosing a suitable value for w, which is the parameter of $\mathcal{N}_n$, the network can induce any dichotomy on S. In other words, S is shattered by $\mathcal{N}_n$.

It has been shown in Lemma 1 of [10] that there is an architecture $\mathcal{A}_n$ such that for each $\varepsilon > 0$ weights can be chosen for $\mathcal{A}_n$ such that the function $f_{n,\varepsilon}$ computed by this network satisfies $\lim_{\varepsilon \to 0} f_{n,\varepsilon}(y_1, \ldots, y_n, a) = y_a$. Moreover, this architecture consists of $O(n)$ computation nodes, which are linear, multiplication, and division gates. (Note that the size of $\mathcal{A}_n$ does not depend on ε.) Therefore, choosing ε sufficiently small, we can implement the projections π in $\mathcal{N}_n$ by networks of $O(n)$ computation nodes such that the resulting network $\mathcal{N}_n'$ still shatters S. Now in $\mathcal{N}_n'$ we have $O(n)$ computation nodes for implementing the three levels labeled Π and we have in each level P_λ a number of $O(n)$ computation nodes for computing $p_{n^{\lambda-1}}$, respectively. Assume now that the computation nodes for $p_{n^{\lambda-1}}$ can be replaced by sigmoidal networks such that on inputs from S and with the parameter values defined above the resulting network $\mathcal{N}_n''$ computes the same functions as $\mathcal{N}_n'$. (Note that the computation nodes for $p_{n^{\lambda-1}}$ have no programmable parameters.)

We estimate the size of $\mathcal{N}_n''$. According to Theorem 7 of Karpinski and Macintyre [7] a sigmoidal neural network with l programmable parameters and m computation nodes has VC dimension $O((ml)^2)$. We have to generalize this result slightly before being able to apply it. It can readily be seen from the proof of Theorem 7 in [7] that the result also holds if the network additionally contains linear and multiplication gates. For division gates we can derive the same bound taking into account that for a gate computing division, say x/y, we can introduce a defining equality $x = z \cdot y$ where z is a new variable. (See [7] for how to proceed.) Thus, we have that a network with l programmable parameters and m computation nodes, which are linear, multiplication, division, and sigmoidal gates, has VC dimension $O((ml)^2)$. In particular, if m is the number of computation nodes of $\mathcal{N}_n''$, the VC dimension is $O(m^2)$. On the other hand, as we have shown above, $\mathcal{N}_n''$ can shatter a set of cardinality n^3. Since there are $O(n)$ sigmoidal networks in $\mathcal{N}_n''$ computing the functions $p_{n^{\lambda-1}}$, and since the number of linear, multiplication, and division gates is bounded by $O(n)$, for some value of λ a single network computing $p_{n^{\lambda-1}}$ must have size at least $\Omega(\sqrt{n})$. This yields a lower bound of $\Omega(n^{1/4})$ for the size of a sigmoidal network computing p_n.

Thus far, we have assumed that the polynomials p_n are computed exactly. Since polynomials are continuous functions and since we require them to be calculated only on a finite set of input values (those resulting from S and from the parameter values chosen for w to shatter S) an approximation of these polynomials is sufficient. A straightforward analysis, based on the fact that the output value of the network has a "tolerance" close to $1/2$, shows that if p_n is approximated with error $O(2^{-n})$

in the l_∞ norm, the resulting network still shatters the set S. This completes the proof of the theorem. □

The statement of the previous theorem is restricted to the approximation of polynomials on the input domain $[0, 1]$. However, the result immediately generalizes to any arbitrary interval in $\mathbb{R}$. Moreover, it remains valid for multivariate polynomials of arbitrary input dimension.

Corollary 2 *The approximation of polynomials of degree k by sigmoidal neural networks with approximation error $O(1/k)$ in the l_∞ norm requires networks of size $\Omega((\log k)^{1/4})$. This holds for polynomials over any number of variables.*

4 Conclusions and Open Questions

We have established lower bounds on the size of sigmoidal networks for the approximation of continuous functions. In particular, for a concrete class of polynomials we have calculated a lower bound in terms of the degree of the polynomials. The main result already holds for the approximation of univariate polynomials. Intuitively, approximation of multivariate polynomials seems to become harder when the dimension increases. Therefore, it would be interesting to have lower bounds both in terms of the degree and the input dimension.

Further, in our result the approximation error and the degree are coupled. Naturally, one would expect that the number of nodes has to grow for each fixed function when the error decreases. At present we do not know of any such lower bound.

We have not aimed at calculating the constants in the bounds. For practical applications such values are indispensable. Refining our method and using tighter results it should be straightforward to obtain such numbers. Further, we expect that better lower bounds can be obtained by considering networks of restricted depth.

To establish the result we have introduced a new method for deriving lower bounds on network sizes. One of the main arguments is to use the functions to be approximated to construct networks with large VC dimension. The method seems suitable to obtain bounds also for the approximation of other types of functions as long as they are computationally powerful enough.

Moreover, the method could be adapted to obtain lower bounds also for networks using other activation functions (e.g. more general sigmoidal functions, ridge functions, radial basis functions). This may lead to new separation results for the approximation capabilities of different types of neural networks. In order for this to be accomplished, however, an essential requirement is that small upper bounds can be calculated for the VC dimension of such networks.

Acknowledgments

I thank Hans U. Simon for helpful discussions. This work was supported in part by the ESPRIT Working Group in Neural and Computational Learning II, Neuro-COLT2, No. 27150.

References

[1] A. Barron. Universal approximation bounds for superposition of a sigmoidal function. *IEEE Transactions on Information Theory*, 39:930–945, 1993.

[2] C. K. Chui and X. Li. Approximation by ridge functions and neural networks with one hidden layer. *Journal of Approximation Theory*, 70:131–141, 1992.

[3] G. Cybenko. Approximation by superpositions of a sigmoidal function. *Mathematics of Control, Signals, and Systems*, 2:303–314, 1989.

[4] B. DasGupta and G. Schnitger. The power of approximating: A comparison of activation functions. In C. L. Giles, S. J. Hanson, and J. D. Cowan, editors, *Advances in Neural Information Processing Systems 5*, pages 615–622, Morgan Kaufmann, San Mateo, CA, 1993.

[5] K. Hornik. Approximation capabilities of multilayer feedforward networks. *Neural Networks*, 4:251–257, 1991.

[6] K. Hornik, M. Stinchcombe, and H. White. Multilayer feedforward networks are universal approximators. *Neural Networks*, 2:359–366, 1989.

[7] M. Karpinski and A. Macintyre. Polynomial bounds for VC dimension of sigmoidal and general Pfaffian neural networks. *Journal of Computer and System Sciences*, 54:169–176, 1997.

[8] A. G. Khovanskiĭ. *Fewnomials*, volume 88 of *Translations of Mathematical Monographs*. American Mathematical Society, Providence, RI, 1991.

[9] P. Koiran. VC dimension in circuit complexity. In *Proceedings of the 11th Annual IEEE Conference on Computational Complexity CCC'96*, pages 81–85, IEEE Computer Society Press, Los Alamitos, CA, 1996.

[10] P. Koiran and E. D. Sontag. Neural networks with quadratic VC dimension. *Journal of Computer and System Sciences*, 54:190–198, 1997.

[11] V. Y. Kreinovich. Arbitrary nonlinearity is sufficient to represent all functions by neural networks: A theorem. *Neural Networks*, 4:381–383, 1991.

[12] M. Leshno, V. Y. Lin, A. Pinkus, and S. Schocken. Multilayer feedforward networks with a nonpolynomial activation function can approximate any function. *Neural Networks*, 6:861–867, 1993.

[13] W. Maass. Noisy spiking neurons with temporal coding have more computational power than sigmoidal neurons. In M. Mozer, M. I. Jordan, and T. Petsche, editors, *Advances in Neural Information Processing Systems 9*, pages 211–217. MIT Press, Cambridge, MA, 1997.

[14] H. Mhaskar. Neural networks for optimal approximation of smooth and analytic functions. *Neural Computation*, 8:164–177, 1996.

[15] F. Scarselli and A. C. Tsoi. Universal approximation using feedforward neural networks: A survey of some existing methods and some new results. *Neural Networks*, 11:15–37, 1998.

[16] H. E. Warren. Lower bounds for approximation by nonlinear manifolds. *Transactions of the American Mathematical Society*, 133:167–178, 1968.

Noisy Neural Networks and Generalizations

Hava T. Siegelmann
Industrial Eng. and Management, Mathematics
Technion - IIT
Haifa 32000, Israel
iehava@ie.technion.ac.il

Alexander Roitershtein
Mathematics
Technion - IIT
Haifa 32000, Israel
roiterst@math.technion.ac.il

Asa Ben-Hur
Industrial Eng. and Management
Technion - IIT
Haifa 32000, Israel
asa@tx.technion.ac.il

Abstract

In this paper we define a probabilistic computational model which generalizes many noisy neural network models, including the recent work of Maass and Sontag [5]. We identify weak ergodicity as the mechanism responsible for restriction of the computational power of probabilistic models to *definite languages*, independent of the characteristics of the noise: whether it is discrete or analog, or if it depends on the input or not, and independent of whether the variables are discrete or continuous. We give examples of weakly ergodic models including noisy computational systems with noise depending on the current state and inputs, aggregate models, and computational systems which update in continuous time.

1 Introduction

Noisy neural networks were recently examined, e.g. in. [1, 4, 5]. It was shown in [5] that Gaussian-like noise reduces the power of analog recurrent neural networks to the class of definite languages, which are a strict subset of regular languages. Let Σ be an arbitrary alphabet. $L \subseteq \Sigma^*$ is called a *definite language* if for some integer r any two words coinciding on the last r symbols are either both in L or neither in L. The ability of a computational system to recognize only definite languages can be interpreted as saying that the system forgets all its input signals, except for the most recent ones. This property is reminiscent of human short term memory.

"Definite probabilistic computational models" have their roots in Rabin's pioneering work on probabilistic automata [9]. He identified a condition on probabilistic automata with a finite state space which restricts them to definite languages. Paz [8] generalized Rabin's condition, applying it to automata with a countable state space, and calling it *weak ergodicity* [7, 8]. In their ground-breaking paper [5],

Maass and Sontag extended the principle leading to definite languages to a finite interconnection of *continuous-valued* neurons. They proved that in the presence of "analog noise" (e.g. Gaussian), recurrent neural networks are limited in their computational power to definite languages. Under a different noise model, Maass and Orponen [4] and Casey [1] showed that such neural networks are reduced in their power to regular languages.

In this paper we generalize the condition of weak ergodicity, making it applicable to numerous probabilistic computational machines. In our general probabilistic model, the state space can be *arbitrary*: it is not constrained to be a finite or infinite set, to be a discrete or non-discrete subset of some Euclidean space, or even to be a metric or topological space. The input alphabet is arbitrary as well (e.g., bits, rationals, reals, etc.). The stochasticity is not necessarily defined via a transition probability function (TPF) as in all the aforementioned probabilistic and noisy models, but through the more general *Markov operators acting on measures*. Our *Markov Computational Systems* (MCS's) include as special cases Rabin's actual probabilistic automata with cut-point [9], the quasi-definite automata by Paz [8], and the noisy analog neural network by Maass and Sontag [5]. Interestingly, our model also includes: analog dynamical systems and neural models, which have no underlying deterministic rule but rather update probabilistically by using finite memory; neural networks with an unbounded number of components; networks of variable dimension (e.g., "recruiting networks"); hybrid systems that combine discrete and continuous variables; stochastic cellular automata; and stochastic coupled map lattices.

We prove that all weakly ergodic Markov systems are stable, i.e. are robust with respect to architectural imprecisions and environmental noise. This property is desirable for both biological and artificial neural networks. This robustness was known up to now only for the classical discrete probabilistic automata [8, 9]. To enable practicality and ease in deciding weak ergodicity for given systems, we provide two conditions on the transition probability functions under which the associated computational system becomes weakly ergodic. One condition is based on a version of Doeblin's condition [5] while the second is motivated by the theory of scrambling matrices [7, 8]. In addition we construct various examples of weakly ergodic systems which include synchronous or asynchronous computational systems, and hybrid continuous and discrete time systems.

2 Markov Computational System (MCS)

Instead of describing various types of noisy neural network models or stochastic dynamical systems we define a general abstract probabilistic model. When dealing with systems containing inherent elements of uncertainty (e.g., noise) we abandon the study of individual trajectories in favor of an examination of the flow of state distributions. The noise models we consider are homogeneous in time, in that they may depend on the input, but do not depend on time. The dynamics we consider is defined by operators acting in the space of measures, and are called *Markov operators* [6]. In the following we define the concepts which are required for such an approach.

Let Σ be an arbitrary alphabet and Ω be an abstract state space. We assume that a σ-algebra $\mathcal{B}$ (not necessarily Borel sets) of subsets of Ω is given, thus $(\Omega, \mathcal{B})$ is a measurable space. Let us denote by $\mathcal{P}$ the set of probability measures on $(\Omega, \mathcal{B})$. This set is called a *distribution space*.

Let $\mathcal{E}$ be a space of finite measures on $(\Omega, \mathcal{B})$ with the total variation norm defined

by
$$\|\mu\|_1 = |\mu|(\Omega) = \sup_{A \in \mathcal{B}} \mu(A) - \inf_{A \in \mathcal{B}} \mu(A). \tag{1}$$

Denote by $\mathcal{L}$ the set of all bounded linear operators acting from $\mathcal{E}$ to itself. The $\|\cdot\|_1$- norm on $\mathcal{E}$ induces a norm $\|P\|_1 = \sup_{\mu \in \mathcal{P}} \|P\mu\|_1$ in $\mathcal{L}$. An operator $P \in \mathcal{L}$ is said to be a *Markov operator* if for any probability measure $\mu \in \mathcal{P}$, the image $P\mu$ is again a probability measure. For a Markov operator, $\|P\|_1 = 1$.

Definition 2.1 A *Markov system* is a set of Markov operators $T = \{P_u : u \in \Sigma\}$.

With any Markov system T, one can associate a probabilistic computational system. If the probability distribution on the initial states is given by the probability measure μ_0, then the distribution of states after n computational steps on inputs $w = w_0, w_1, ..., w_n$, is defined as in [5, 8]
$$P_w \mu_0(A) = P_{w_n} \cdot \ldots \cdot P_{w_1} P_{w_0} \mu_0. \tag{2}$$

Let $\mathcal{A}$ and $\mathcal{R}$ be two subset of $\mathcal{P}$ with the property of having a ρ-gap
$$dist(\mathcal{A}, \mathcal{R}) = \inf_{\mu \in \mathcal{A}, \nu \in \mathcal{R}} \|\mu - \nu\|_1 = \rho > 0 \tag{3}$$

The first set is called a set of *accepting distributions* and the second is called a set of *rejecting distributions*. A language $L \in \Sigma^*$ is said to be *recognized* by Markov computational system $\mathcal{M} = \langle \mathcal{E}, \mathcal{A}, \mathcal{R}, \Sigma, \mu_0, T \rangle$ if

$$w \in L \Leftrightarrow P_w \mu_0 \in \mathcal{A}$$
$$w \notin L, \Leftrightarrow P_w \mu_0 \in \mathcal{R}.$$

This model of language recognition with a gap between accepting and rejecting spaces agrees with Rabin's model of probabilistic automata with isolated cut-point [9] and the model of analog probabilistic computation [4, 5].

An example of a Markov system is a system of operators defined by TPF on $(\Omega, \mathcal{B})$. Let $P_u(x, A)$ be the probability of moving from a state x to the set of states A upon receiving the input signal $u \in \Sigma$. The function $P_u(x, \cdot)$ is a probability measure for all $x \in \Omega$ and $P_u(\cdot, A)$ is a measurable function of x for any $A \in \mathcal{B}$. In this case, $P_u\mu(A)$ are defined by
$$P_u\mu(A) = \int_\Omega P_u(x, A)\mu(dx). \tag{4}$$

3 Weakly Ergodic MCS

Let $P \in \mathcal{L}$ be a Markov operator. The real number $\gamma(P) = 1 - \frac{1}{2}\sup_{\mu,\nu \in \mathcal{P}} \|P\mu - P\nu\|_1$ is called *the ergodicity coefficient of the Markov operator*. We denote $\delta(P) = 1 - \gamma(P)$. It can be proven that for any two Markov operators P_1, P_2, $\delta(P_1 P_2) \leq \delta(P_1)\delta(P_2)$. The ergodicity coefficient was introduced by Dobrushin [2] for the particular case of Markov operators induced by TPF $P(x, A)$. In this special case $\gamma(P) = 1 - \sup_{x,y} \sup_A |P(x, A) - P(y, A)|$.

Weakly ergodic systems were introduced and studied by Paz in the particular case of a denumerable state space Ω, where Markov operators are represented by infinite dimensional matrices. The following definition makes no assumption on the associated measurable space.

Definition 3.1 A Markov system $\{P_u, u \in \Sigma\}$ is called *weakly ergodic* if for any $\alpha > 0$, there is an integer $r = r(\alpha)$ such that for any $w \in \Sigma^{\geq r}$ and any $\mu, \nu \in \mathcal{P}$,
$$\delta(P_w) = \frac{1}{2}\|P_w\mu - P_w\nu\|_1 \leq \alpha. \tag{5}$$

An MCS $\mathcal{M}$ is called *weakly ergodic* if its associated Markov system $\{P_u, u \in \Sigma\}$ is weakly ergodic. ∎

An MCS $\mathcal{M}$ is weakly ergodic if and only if there is an integer r and real number $\alpha < 1$, such that $\|P_w\mu - P_w\nu\|_1 \leq \alpha$ for any word w of length r. Our most general characterization of weak ergodicity is as follows: [11]:

Theorem 1 *An abstract MCS $\mathcal{M}$ is weakly ergodic if and only if there exists a multiplicative operator's norm $\|\cdot\|_{**}$ on $\mathcal{L}$ equivalent to the norm $\|\cdot\|_{\mathcal{B}} := \sup_{\{\lambda:\lambda\Omega=0\}} \frac{\|P\lambda\|_1}{\|\lambda\|_1}$, and such that $\sup_{u\in\Sigma}\|P_u\|_{**} \leq \varepsilon$ for some number $\varepsilon < 1$.* ∎

The next theorem connects the computational power of weakly ergodic MCS's with the class of definite languages, generalizing the results by Rabin [9], Paz [8, p. 175], and Maass and Sontag [5].

Theorem 2 *Let $\mathcal{M}$ be a weakly ergodic MCS. If a language L can be recognized by $\mathcal{M}$, then it is definite.* ∎

4 The Stability Theorem of Weakly Ergodic MCS

An important issue for any computational system is whether the machine is robust with respect to small perturbations of the system's parameters or under some external noise. The stability of language recognition by weakly ergodic MCS's under perturbations of their Markov operators was previously considered by Rabin [9] and Paz [7, 8]. We next state a general version of the stability theorem that is applicable to our wide notion of weakly ergodic systems.

We first define two MCS's $\mathcal{M}$ and $\widetilde{\mathcal{M}}$ to be *similar* if they share the same measurable space $(\Omega, \mathcal{B})$, alphabet Σ, and sets $\mathcal{A}$ and $\mathcal{R}$, and if they differ only by their associated Markov operators.

Theorem 3 *Let $\mathcal{M}$ and $\widetilde{\mathcal{M}}$ be two similar MCS's such that the first is weakly ergodic. Then there is $\alpha > 0$, such that if $\|P_u - \tilde{P}_u\|_1 \leq \alpha$ for all $u \in \Sigma$, then the second is also weakly ergodic. Moreover, these two MCS's recognize exactly the same class of languages.* ∎

Corollary 3.1 *Let $\mathcal{M}$ and $\widetilde{\mathcal{M}}$ be two similar MCS's. Suppose that the first is weakly ergodic. Then there exists $\beta > 0$, such that if $\sup_{A\in\mathcal{B}} |P_u(x, A) - \tilde{P}_u(x, A)| \leq \beta$ for all $u \in \Sigma, x \in \Omega$, the second is also weakly ergodic. Moreover, these two MCS's recognize exactly the same class of languages.* ∎

A mathematically deeper result which implies Theorem 3 was proven in [11]:

Theorem 4 *Let $\mathcal{M}$ and $\widetilde{\mathcal{M}}$ be two similar MCS's, such that the first is weakly ergodic and the second is arbitrary. Then, for any $\alpha > 0$ there exists $\varepsilon > 0$ such that $\|P_u - \tilde{P}_u\|_1 \leq \varepsilon$ for all $u \in \Sigma$ implies $\|P_w - \tilde{P}_w\|_1 \leq \alpha$ for all words $w \in \Sigma^*$.* ∎

Theorem 3 follows from Theorem 4. To see this, one can chose any $\alpha < \rho$ in Theorem 4 and observe that $\|P_w - \tilde{P}_w\|_1 \leq \alpha < \rho$ implies that the word w is accepted or rejected by $\widetilde{\mathcal{M}}$ in accordance to whether it is accepted or rejected by $\mathcal{M}$.

5 Conditions on the Transition Probabilities

This section discusses practical conditions for weakly ergodic MCS's in which the Markov operators P_u are induced by transition probability functions as in (4). Clearly, a simple sufficient condition for an MCS to be weakly ergodic is given by $\sup_{u \in \Sigma} \delta(P_u) \leq 1 - c$, for some $c > 0$.

Maass and Sontag used Doeblin's condition to prove the computational power of noisy neural networks [5]. Although the networks in [5] constitute a very particular case of weakly ergodic MCS's, Doeblin's condition is applicable also to our general model. The following version of Doeblin's condition was given by Doob [3]:

Definition 5.1 [3] Let $P(x, A)$ be a TPF on $(\Omega, \mathcal{B})$. We say that it satisfies Doeblin condition, D_0^n, if there exists a constant c and a probability measure μ on $(\Omega, \mathcal{B})$ such that $P^n(x, A) \geq c\mu(A)$ for any set $A \in \mathcal{B}$. ∎

If an MCS $\mathcal{M}$ is weakly ergodic, then all its associated TPF $P_w(x, A), w \in \Sigma$ must satisfy D_0^n for some $n = n(w)$. Doob has proved [3, p. 197] that if $P(x, A)$ satisfies Doeblin's condition D_0^1 with constant c, then for any $\mu, \nu \in \mathcal{P}$, $\|P\mu - P\nu\|_1 \leq (1-c)\|\mu - \nu\|_1$, i.e., $\delta(P) \leq 1 - c$. This leads us to the following definition.

Definition 5.2 Let $\mathcal{M}$ be an MCS. We say that the space Ω is *small* with respect to $\mathcal{M}$ if there exists an $m > 0$ such that all associated TPF $P_w(x, A)$, $w \in \Sigma^m$ satisfy Doeblin's condition D_0^1 uniformly with the same constant c, i.e., $P_w(x, A) \geq c\mu_w(A)$, $w \in \Sigma^m$. ∎

The following theorem strengthens the result by Maass and Sontag [5].

Theorem 5 *Let $\mathcal{M}$ be an MCS. If the space Ω is small with respect to $\mathcal{M}$, then $\mathcal{M}$ is weakly ergodic, and it can recognize only definite languages.* ∎

This theorem provides a convenient method for checking weak ergodicity in a given TPF. The theorem implies that it is sufficient to execute the following simple check: choose any integer n, and then verify that for every state x and all input strings $w \in \Sigma^n$, the "absolutely continuous" part of all TPF $P_w, w \in \Sigma^n$ is uniformly bounded from below:

$$\psi_w\left(\{y : p_w(x, y) \geq c_1 \quad \text{for all } w \in \Sigma^n\}\right) \geq c_2, \tag{6}$$

where $p_w(x, y)$ is the density of the absolutely continuous component of $P_w(x, \cdot)$ with respect to ψ_w, and c_1, c_2 are positive numbers.

Most practical systems can be defined by null preserving TPF (including for example the systems in [5]). For these systems we provide (Theorem 6) a sufficient and necessary condition in terms of density kernels. A TPF $P_u(x, A)$, $u \in \Sigma$ is called *null preserving* with respect to a probability measure $\mu \in \mathcal{P}$ if it has a density with respect to μ i.e., $P(x, A) = \int_A p_u(x, z)\mu(dz)$. It is not hard to see, that the property of null preserving per letter $u \in \Sigma$ implies that all TPF $P_w(x, A)$ of words $w \in \Sigma^*$ are null preserving as well. In this case $\delta(P_u) = 1 - \inf_{x,y} \int_\Omega \min\{p_u(x, z), p_u(y, z)\}\mu_u(dz)$ and we have:

Theorem 6 *Let $\mathcal{M}$ be an MCS defined by null preserving transition probability functions $P_u, u \in \Sigma$. Then, $\mathcal{M}$ is weakly ergodic if and only if there exists n such that $\inf_{w \in \Sigma^n} \inf_{x,y} \int_\Omega \min\{p_u(x, z), p_u(y, z)\}\mu_u(dz) > 0$.* ∎

A similar result was previously established by Paz [7, 8] for the case of a denumerable state space Ω. This theorem allows to treat examples which are not covered by

Theorem 5. For example, suppose that the space Ω is not small with respect to an MCS $\mathcal{M}$, but for some n and any $w \in \Sigma^n$ there exists a measure ψ_w on $(\Omega, \mathcal{B})$ with the property that for any couple of states $x, y \in \Omega$

$$\psi_w \left(\{ z : \min\{p_w(x,z), p_w(y,z)\} \geq c_1 \} \right) \geq c_2, \tag{7}$$

where $p_w(x,y)$ is the density of $P_w(x, \cdot)$ with respect to ψ_w, and c_1, c_2 are positive numbers. This condition may occur even if there is no y such that $p_u(x,y) \leq c_1$ for all $x \in \Omega$.

6 Examples of Weakly Ergodic Systems

1. The Synchronous Parallel Model

Let $(\Omega_i, \mathcal{B}_i), i = 1, 2, ..., N$ be a collection of measurable sets. Define $\Omega^{\mathbf{i}} = \prod_{j \neq i} \Omega_j$ and $\mathcal{B}^{\mathbf{i}} = \prod_{j \neq i} \mathcal{B}_j$. Then $(\Omega^{\mathbf{i}}, \mathcal{B}^{\mathbf{i}})$ are measurable spaces. Define also $\Sigma_i = \Sigma \times \Omega^{\mathbf{i}}$, and $T_i = \{P_{\mathbf{x^i}, u}(x_i, A_i) : (\mathbf{x^i}, u) \in \Sigma_i\}$ be given stochastic kernels. Each set T_i defines an MCS $\mathcal{M}_i$. We can define an *aggregate* MCS by setting $\Omega = \prod_i \Omega_i$, $\mathcal{B} = \prod_i \mathcal{B}_i$, $S = \prod_i S_i$, $R = \prod_i R_i$, and

$$P_u(x, A) = \prod_i P_{\mathbf{x^i}, u}(x_i, A_i). \tag{8}$$

This describes a model of N noisy computational systems that update in synchronous parallelism. The state of the whole aggregate is a vector of states of the individual components, and each receives the states of all other components as part of its input.

Theorem 7 *[12] Let $\mathcal{M}$ be an MCS defined by equation (8). It is weakly ergodic if at least one set of operators T^i is such that $\delta(P^i_{u, \mathbf{x^i}}) \leq 1 - c$ for any $u \in \Sigma$, $\mathbf{x^i} \in \Omega^{\mathbf{i}}$ and some positive number c.* ∎

2. The Asynchronous Parallel Model

In this model, at every step only one component is activated. Suppose that a collection of N *similar* MCS's $\mathcal{M}_i, i = 1, \ldots, N$ is given. Consider a probability measure $\varepsilon = \{\varepsilon_1, \ldots, \varepsilon_N\}$ on the set $K = \{1, \ldots, N\}$. Assume that in each computational step only one MCS is activated. The current state of the whole aggregate is represented by the state of its active component. Assume also that the probability of a computational system $\mathcal{M}_i$ to be activated, is time-independent and is given by $Prob(\mathcal{M}_i) = \varepsilon_i$. The aggregate system is then described by stochastic kernels

$$P_u(x, A) = \sum_{i=1}^{N} \varepsilon_i P^i_u(x, A). \tag{9}$$

Theorem 8 *[12] Let $\mathcal{M}$ be an MCS defined by formula (9). It is weakly ergodic if at least one set of operators $\{P^1_u\}, \ldots, \{P^N_u\}$ is weakly ergodic.* ∎

3. Hybrid Weakly Ergodic Systems

We now present a hybrid weakly ergodic computational system consisting of both continuous and discrete elements. The evolution of the system is governed by a differential equation, while its input arrives at discrete times. Let $\Omega = \mathbb{R}^n$, and consider a collection of differential equations

$$\dot{x}_u(s) = \psi_u(x_u(s)), \ u \in \Sigma, \ s \in [0, \infty). \tag{10}$$

Suppose that $\psi_u(x)$ is sufficiently smooth to ensure the existence and uniqueness of solutions of Equation (10) for $s \in [0, 1]$ and for any initial condition.

Consider a computational system which receives an input $u(t)$ at discrete times $t_0, t_1, t_2 \ldots$. In the interval $t \in [t_i, t_{i+1}]$ the behavior of the system is described by Equation (10), where $s = t - t_i$. A random initial condition for the time t_n is defined by

$$Prob[x_{u(t_n)}(0) \in A] = P_u(x_{u(t_{n-1})}(1), A), \tag{11}$$

where $x_{u(t_{n-1})}(1)$ is the state of the system after previously completed computations, and $P_u(x, A), u \in \Sigma$ is a family of stochastic kernels on $\Omega \times \mathcal{B}$. This describes a system which receives inputs in discrete instants of time; the input letters $u \in \Sigma$ cause random perturbations of the state $x_{u(t-1)}(1)$ governed by the transition probability functions $P_{u(t)}(x_{u(t-1)}, A)$. In all other times the system is a noise-free continuous computational system which evolves according to equation (10).

Let $\Omega = \mathbb{R}^n$, $x_0 \in \Omega$ be a distinguished initial state, and let S and R be two subsets of Ω with the property of having a ρ-gap: $dist(S, R) = \inf_{x \in S, y \in R} \|x - y\| = \rho > 0$. The first set is called a set of *accepting final states* and the second is called a set of *rejecting final states*. We say that the *hybrid computational system* $\mathcal{M} = \langle \Omega, \Sigma, x_0, \psi_u, S, R \rangle$ recognizes $L \subseteq \Sigma^*$ if for all $w = w_0 \ldots w_n \in \Sigma^*$ and the end letter $\$ \notin \Sigma$ the following holds: $w \in L \Leftrightarrow Prob(x_{w_n\$}(1) \in S) > \frac{1}{2} + \varepsilon$, and $w \notin L \Leftrightarrow Prob(x_{w_n\$}(1) \in R) > \frac{1}{2} + \varepsilon$.

Theorem 9 *[12] Let $\mathcal{M}$ be a hybrid computational system. It is weakly ergodic if its set of evolution operators $T = \{P_u : u \in \Sigma\}$ is weakly ergodic.* ∎

References

[1] Casey, M., The Dynamics of Discrete-Time Computation, With Application to Recurrent Neural Networks and Finite State Machine Extraction, Neural Computation 8, 1135-1178, 1996.

[2] Dobrushin, R. L., Central limit theorem for nonstationary Markov chains I, II. *Theor. Probability Appl.* vol. 1, 1956, pp 65–80, 298–383.

[3] Doob J. L., *Stochastic Processes*. John Wiley and Sons, Inc., 1953.

[4] W. Maass and Orponen, P., On the effect of analog noise in discrete time computation, *Neural Computation*, 10(5), 1998, pp. 1071–1095.

[5] W. Maass and Sontag, E., Analog neural nets with Gaussian or other common noise distribution cannot recognize arbitrary regular languages, *Neural Computation*, 11, 1999, pp. 771–782.

[6] Neveu J., *Mathematical Foundations of the Calculus of Probability*. Holden Day, San Francisco, 1964.

[7] Paz A., Ergodic theorems for infinite probabilistic tables. *Ann. Math. Statist.* vol. 41, 1970, pp. 539–550.

[8] Paz A., *Introduction to Probabilistic Automata*. Academic Press, Inc., London, 1971.

[9] Rabin, M., Probabilistic automata, *Information and Control*, vol 6, 1963, pp. 230-245.

[10] Siegelmann H. T., *Neural Networks and Analog Computation: Beyond the Turing Limit*. Birkhauser, Boston, 1999.

[11] Siegelmann H. T. and Roitershtein A., On weakly ergodic computational systems, 1999, *submitted*.

[12] Siegelmann H. T., Roitershtein A., and Ben-Hur, A., On noisy computational systems, 1999, *Discrete Applied Mathematics*, accepted.

The Entropy Regularization Information Criterion

Alex J. Smola
Dept. of Engineering and RSISE
Australian National University
Canberra ACT 0200, Australia
Alex.Smola@anu.edu.au

John Shawe-Taylor
Royal Holloway College
University of London
Egham, Surrey TW20 0EX, UK
john@dcs.rhbnc.ac.uk

Bernhard Schölkopf
Microsoft Research Limited
St. George House, 1 Guildhall Street
Cambridge CB2 3NH
bsc@microsoft.com

Robert C. Williamson
Dept. of Engineering
Australian National University
Canberra ACT 0200, Australia
Bob.Williamson@anu.edu.au

Abstract

Effective methods of capacity control via uniform convergence bounds for function expansions have been largely limited to Support Vector machines, where good bounds are obtainable by the entropy number approach. We extend these methods to systems with expansions in terms of arbitrary (parametrized) basis functions and a wide range of regularization methods covering the whole range of general linear additive models. This is achieved by a data dependent analysis of the eigenvalues of the corresponding design matrix.

1 INTRODUCTION

Model selection criteria based on the Vapnik-Chervonenkis (VC) dimension are known to be difficult to obtain, worst case, and often not very tight. Yet they have the theoretical appeal of providing bounds, with few or no assumptions made.

Recently new methods [8, 7, 6] have been developed which are able to provide a better characterization of the complexity of function classes than the VC dimension, and moreover, are easily obtainable and take advantage of the data at hand (i.e. they employ the concept of luckiness). These techniques, however, have been limited to linear functions or expansions of functions in terms of kernels as happens to be the case in Support Vector (SV) machines.

In this paper we show that the previously mentioned techniques can be extended to expansions in terms of arbitrary basis functions, covering a large range of practical algorithms such as general linear models, weight decay, sparsity regularization [3], and regularization networks [4].

2 SUPPORT VECTOR MACHINES

Support Vector machines carry out an effective means of capacity control by minimizing a weighted sum of the training error

$$R_{\text{emp}}[f] := \frac{1}{m} \sum_{i=1}^{m} c(x_i, y_i, f(x_i)) \tag{1}$$

and a regularization term $Q[f] = \frac{1}{2}\|w\|^2$; i.e. they minimize the regularized risk functional

$$R_{\text{reg}}[f] := R_{\text{emp}}[f] + \lambda Q[f] = \frac{1}{m} \sum_{i=1}^{m} c(x_i, y_i, f(x_i)) + \frac{\lambda}{2}\|w\|^2. \tag{2}$$

Here $X := \{x_1, \ldots x_m\} \subset \mathcal{X}$ denotes the training set, $Y := \{y_1, \ldots y_m\} \subset \mathcal{Y}$ the corresponding labels (target values), $\mathcal{X}, \mathcal{Y}$ the corresponding domains, $\lambda > 0$ a regularization constant, $c : \mathcal{X} \times \mathcal{Y} \times \mathcal{Y} \to \mathbb{R}_0^+$ a cost function, and $f : \mathcal{X} \to \mathcal{Y}$ is given by

$$f(x) := \langle x, w \rangle, \text{ or in the nonlinear case } f(x) := \langle \Phi(x), w \rangle. \tag{3}$$

Here $\Phi : \mathcal{X} \to \mathcal{F}$ is a map into a feature space $\mathcal{F}$. Finally, dot products in feature space can be written as $\langle \Phi(x), \Phi(x') \rangle = k(x, x')$ where k is a so-called Mercer kernel.

For $n \in \mathbb{N}$, $\mathbb{R}^n$ denotes the n-dimensional space of vectors $x = (x_1, \ldots, x_n)$. We define spaces ℓ_p^n as follows: as vector spaces, they are identical to $\mathbb{R}^n$, in addition, they are endowed with p-norms:

$$\|x\|_{\ell_p^n} := \|x\|_p = \left(\sum_{j=1}^{n} |x_j|^p\right)^{1/p} \quad \text{for } 0 < p < \infty$$

$$\|x\|_{\ell_\infty^n} := \max_{j=1,\ldots,n} |x_j| \quad \text{for } p = \infty$$

We write $\ell_p = \ell_p^\infty$. Furthermore let $U_{\ell_p^n} := \{x : \|x\|_{\ell_p^n} \leq 1\}$ be the unit ℓ_p^n-ball.

For model selection purposes one wants to obtain bounds on the richness of the map S_X

$$S_X : w \mapsto (f(x_1), \ldots, f(x_m)) = (\langle \Phi(x_1), w \rangle, \ldots, \langle \Phi(x_m), w \rangle). \tag{4}$$

where w is restricted to an ℓ_2 unit ball of some radius Λ (this is equivalent to choosing an appropriate value of λ — an increase in λ decreases Λ and vice versa). By the "richness" of S_X specifically we mean the ℓ_∞^m ϵ-covering numbers $\mathcal{N}(\epsilon, S_X(\Lambda U_{\ell_p^m}), \ell_\infty^m)$ of the set $S_X(\Lambda U_{\ell_p^m})$. In the standard COLT notation, we mean

$$\mathcal{N}(\epsilon, S_X(\Lambda U_{\ell_p^m}), \ell_\infty^m) := \min \left\{ n \;\middle|\; \begin{array}{l} \text{There exists a set } \{z_1, \ldots z_n\} \subset F \text{ such that for all} \\ z \in S_X(\Lambda U_{\ell_p^m}) \text{ we have } \min_{1 \leq i \leq n} \|z - z_i\|_{\ell_\infty^m} \leq \epsilon \end{array} \right\}$$

See [8] for further details.

When carrying out model selection in this case, advanced methods [6] exploit the *distribution* of X mapped into feature space $\mathcal{F}$, and thus of the spectral properties of the operator S_X by analyzing the spectrum of the Gram matrix $G = [g_{ij}]_{ij}$, where $g_{ij} := k(x_i, x_j)$.

All this is possible since $k(x_i, x_j)$ can be seen as a dot product of x_i, x_j mapped into some feature space $\mathcal{F}$, i.e. $k(x_i, x_j) = \langle \Phi(x_i), \Phi(x_j) \rangle$. This property, whilst true for SV machines with Mercer kernels, does not hold in general case where f is expanded in terms of more or less arbitrary basis functions.

3 THE BASIC PROBLEMS

One basic problem is that when expanding f into

$$f(x) = \sum_{i=1}^{n} \alpha_i f_i(x) \text{ where } \alpha_i \in \mathbb{R} \tag{5}$$

with $f_i(x)$ being arbitrary functions, it is not immediately obvious how to regard f as a dot product in some feature space. One can show that the VC dimension of a set of n linearly independent functions is n. Hence one would intuitively try to restrict the class of admissible models by controlling the number of basis functions n in terms of which f can be expanded.

Now consider an extreme case. In addition to the n basis functions f_i defined previously, we are given n further basis functions f'_i, linearly independent of the previous ones, which differ from f_i only on a small domain $\mathcal{X}'$, i.e. $f_i|_{\mathcal{X}\setminus\mathcal{X}'} = f'_i|_{\mathcal{X}\setminus\mathcal{X}'}$. Since this new set of functions is linearly independent, the VC dimension of the joint set is given by $2n$. On the other hand, if hardly any data occurs on the domain $\mathcal{X}'$, one would not notice the difference between f_i and f'_i. In other words, the joint system of functions would behave as if we only had the initial system of n basis functions.

An analogous situation occurs if $f'_i = f_i + \epsilon g_i$ where ϵ is a small constant and g_i was bounded, say, within $[0, 1]$. Again, in this case, the additional effect of the set of functions f'_i would be hardly noticeable, but still, the joint set of functions would count as one with VC dimension $2n$. This already indicates, that simply counting the number of basis functions may not be a good idea after all.

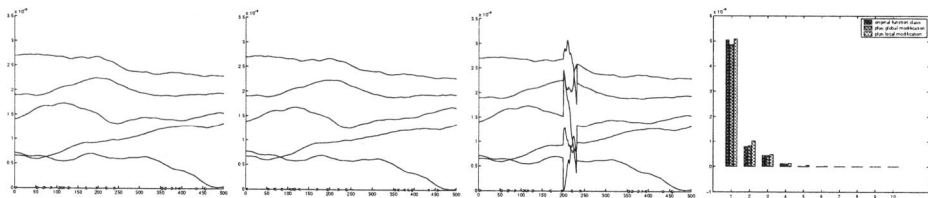

Figure 1: From left to right: (a) initial set of functions $f_1, \ldots, f_5$ (dots on the x-axis indicate sampling points); (b) additional set of functions $f'_1, \ldots, f'_5$ which differ globally, but only by a small amount; (c) additional set of functions $f'_1, \ldots, f'_5$ which differ locally, however by a large amount; (d) spectrum of the corresponding design matrices - the bars denote the cases (a)-(c) in the corresponding order. Note that the difference is quite small.

On the other hand, the spectra of the corresponding design matrices (see Figure 1) are very similar. This suggests the use of the latter for a model selection criterion.

Finally we have the practical problem that capacity control, which in SV machines was carried out by minimizing the length of the "weight vector" w in feature space, cannot be done in an analogous way either. There are several ways to do this. Below we consider three that have appeared in the literature and for which there exist effective algorithms.

Example 1 (Weight Decay) *Define $Q[f] := \frac{1}{2} \sum_i \alpha_i^2$; i.e. the coefficients α_i of the function expansion are constrained to an ℓ_2 ball. In this case we can consider the following operator $S_X^{(1)} : \ell_2^n \to \ell_\infty^m$, where*

$$S_X^{(1)} : \alpha \mapsto (f(x_1), \ldots, f(x_m)) = (\langle f(x_1), \alpha \rangle, \ldots, \langle f(x_m), \alpha \rangle) = F\alpha \tag{6}$$

Here $f(x) := (f_1(x), \ldots f_n(x))$, $F_{ij} := f_i(x_j)$, $\alpha := (\alpha_1, \ldots, \alpha_n)$ and $\alpha \in \Lambda U_{\ell_2^n}$ for some $\Lambda > 0$.

Example 2 (Sparsity Regularization) *In this case $Q[f] := \sum_i |\alpha_i|$, i.e. the coefficients α_i of the function expansion are constrained to an ℓ_1 ball to enforce sparseness [3]. Thus $S_X^{(2)}: \ell_1^n \to \ell_\infty^m$ with $S_X^{(2)}$ mapping α as in (6) except $\alpha \in \Lambda U_{\ell_1^n}$. This is similar to expansions encountered in boosting or in linear programming machines.*

Example 3 (Regularization Networks) *Finally one could set $Q[f] := \frac{1}{2}\alpha^\top Q\alpha$ for some positive definite matrix Q. For instance, Q_{ij} could be obtained from $\langle Pf_i, Pf_j \rangle$ where P is a regularization operator penalizing non-smooth functions [4]. In this case α lives inside some n–dimensional ellipsoid. By substituting $\alpha' := Q^{\frac{1}{2}}\alpha$ one can reduce this setting to the case of example 1 with a different set of basis functions ($f'(x) = Q^{-\frac{1}{2}}f(x)$) and consider an evaluation operator $S_X^{(3)}: \ell_2^n \to \ell_\infty^m$ given by*

$$S_X^{(3)}: \alpha' \mapsto (f(x_1), \ldots, f(x_m)) = (\langle Q^{-\frac{1}{2}}f(x_1), \alpha' \rangle, \ldots, \langle Q^{-\frac{1}{2}}f(x_m), \alpha' \rangle) = Q^{-\frac{1}{2}}F\alpha' \tag{7}$$

where $\alpha' \in \Lambda U_{\ell_2^n}$ for some $\Lambda > 0$ and $F_{ij} = f_i(x_j)$ as in example 1.

Example 4 (Support Vector Machines) *An important special case of example 3 are Support Vector Machines where we have $Q_{ij} = k(x_i, x_j)$ and $f_i(x) = k(x_i, x)$, hence $Q = F$. Hence the possible values generated by a Support Vector Machine can be written as*

$$S_X^{(4)}: \alpha' \mapsto (f(x_1), \ldots, f(x_m)) = (\langle Q^{-\frac{1}{2}}f(x_1), \alpha' \rangle, \ldots, \langle Q^{-\frac{1}{2}}f(x_m), \alpha' \rangle) = F^{\frac{1}{2}}\alpha' \tag{8}$$

where $\alpha' \in \Lambda U_{\ell_2^n}$ for some $\Lambda > 0$.

4 ENTROPY NUMBERS

Covering numbers characterize the difficulty of learning elements of a function class. Entropy numbers of operators can be used to compute covering numbers more easily and more tightly than the traditional techniques based on VC-like dimensions such as the fat shattering dimension [1]. Knowing $e_l(S_X) = \epsilon$ (see below for the definition) tells one that $\log \mathcal{N}(\epsilon, F, \ell_\infty^m) \leq l$, where F is the effective class of functions used by the regularised learning machines under consideration. In this section we summarize a few basic definitions and results as presented in [8] and [2].

The lth entropy number $\epsilon_l(F)$ of a set F with a corresponding metric d is the precision up to which F can be approximated by l elements of F; i.e. for all $f \in F$ there exists some $\bar{f}_i \in \{\bar{f}_1, \ldots, \bar{f}_l\}$ such that $d(f, \bar{f}_i) \leq \epsilon_l$. Hence $\epsilon_l(F)$ is the functional inverse of the covering number of F.

The entropy number of an bounded linear operator $T: A \to B$ between normed linear spaces A and B is defined as $\epsilon_l(T) := \epsilon_l(T(U_A))$ with the metric d being induced by $\|\cdot\|_B$. The *dyadic entropy numbers* e_l are defined by $e_l := \epsilon_{2^l+1}$ (the latter quantity is often more convenient to deal with since it corresponds to the log of the covering number).

We make use of the following three results on entropy numbers of the identity mapping from $\ell_{p_1}^n$ into $\ell_{p_2}^n$, diagonal operators, and products of operators. Let

$$\mathrm{id}_{p_1, p_2}^n : \ell_{p_1}^n \to \ell_{p_2}^n \quad ; \quad \mathrm{id}_{p_1, p_2}^n : x \mapsto x$$

The following result is due to Schütt; the constants 9.94 and 1.86 were obtained in [9].

Proposition 1 (Entropy numbers for identity operators) *Be $m \in \mathbb{N}$. Then*

$$e_l(\mathrm{id}_{1,2}^n) \leq 9.94 \left(\frac{1}{l} \log\left(1 + \frac{n}{l}\right)\right)^{\frac{1}{2}} \quad \& \quad e_l(\mathrm{id}_{2,\infty}^n) \leq 1.86 \left(\frac{1}{l} \log\left(1 + \frac{n}{l}\right)\right)^{\frac{1}{2}} \tag{9}$$

Proposition 2 (Carl and Stephani [2, p. 11]) *Let E, F, G be Banach spaces, $R : F \to G$, and $S : E \to F$. Then, for $n, t \in \mathbb{N}$,*

$$e_{n+t-1}(RS) \leq e_n(R)e_t(S), \ e_n(RS) \leq e_n(R)\|S\| \text{ and } e_n(RS) \leq e_n(S)\|R\|. \quad (10)$$

Note that the latter two inequalities follow directly from the fact that $\epsilon_1(R) = \|R\|$ for all $R : F \to G$ by definition of the operator norm $\|R\|$.

Proposition 3 *Let $\sigma_1 \geq \sigma_2 \geq \cdots \geq \sigma_j \geq \cdots \geq 0$, $1 \leq p \leq \infty$ and*

$$Dx = (\sigma_1 x_1, \sigma_2 x_2, \ldots, \sigma_j x_j, \ldots) \quad (11)$$

for $x = (x_1, x_2, \ldots, x_j, \ldots) \in \ell_p$ be the diagonal operator from ℓ_p into itself, generated by the sequence $(\sigma_j)_j$. Then for all $n \in \mathbb{N}$,

$$\sup_{j \in \mathbb{N}} 2^{-\frac{n-1}{j}} (\sigma_1 \sigma_2 \cdots \sigma_j)^{\frac{1}{j}} \leq e_n(D) \leq 6 \sup_{j \in \mathbb{N}} 2^{-\frac{n-1}{j}} (\sigma_1 \sigma_2 \cdots \sigma_j)^{\frac{1}{j}}. \quad (12)$$

5 THE MAIN RESULT

We can now state the main theorem which gives bounds on the entropy numbers of $S_X^{(i)}$ for the first three examples of model selection described above (since Support Vector Machines are a special case of example 3 we will not deal with it separately).

Proposition 4 *Let f be expanded in a linear combination of basis functions as $f := \sum_{i=1}^{n} \alpha_i f_i$ and the coefficients α restricted to one of the convex sets as described in the examples 1 to 3. Moreover denote by $F_{ij} := f_j(x_i)$ the design matrix on a particular sample X, and by Q the regularization matrix in the case of example 3. Then the following bound on S_X holds.*

1. *In the case of weight decay (ex. 1) (with $l_1 + l_2 \geq l + 1$)*

$$e_l(S_X^{(1)}) \leq 1.96 \left(l_1^{-1} \log(1 + m/l_1)\right)^{\frac{1}{2}} e_{l_2}(\Sigma). \quad (13)$$

2. *In the case of weight sparsity regularization (ex. 2) (with $l_1 + l_2 + l_3 \geq l + 2$)*

$$e_l(S_X^{(2)}) \leq 18.48 \left(l_1^{-1} \log(1 + m/l_1)\right)^{\frac{1}{2}} e_{l_2}(\Sigma) \left(l_3^{-1} \log(1 + m/l_3)\right)^{\frac{1}{2}}. \quad (14)$$

3. *Finally, in the case of regularization networks (ex. 3) (with $l_1 + l_2 \geq l + 1$)*

$$e_l(S_X^{(3)}) \leq 1.96 \left(l_1^{-1} \log(1 + m/l_1)\right)^{\frac{1}{2}} e_{l_2}(\Sigma). \quad (15)$$

Here Σ is a diagonal scaling operator (matrix) with (i, i) entries $\sqrt{\sigma_i}$ and $(\sqrt{\sigma_i})_i$ are the eigenvalues (sorted in decreasing order) of the matrix $FF^\top$ in the case of examples 1 and 2, and $FQ^{-1}F^\top$ in the case of example 3.

The entropy number of Σ is readily bounded in terms of $(\sigma_i)_i$ by using (3). One can see that the first setting (weight decay) is a special case of the third one, namely when $Q = 1$, i.e. when Q is just the identity matrix.

Proof The proof relies on a factorization of $S_X^{(i)}$ ($i = 1, 2, 3$) in the following way. First we consider the equivalent operator $\hat{S}_X$ mapping from ℓ_2^n to ℓ_2^m and perform a singular value decomposition [5] of the latter into $\hat{S}_X = V \Sigma W$ where V, W are operators of norm 1, and Σ contains the singular values of $S_X^{(i)}$, i.e. the singular values of F and $FQ^{-\frac{1}{2}}$

respectively. The latter, however, are identical to the square root of the eigenvalues of $FF^\top$ or $FQ^{-1}F^\top$. Consequently we can factorize $S_X^{(i)}$ as in the diagram

$$\begin{array}{ccccc}
& & S_X^{(2)} & & \\
& \overbrace{} & & & \\
\ell_1^n & \xrightarrow{\mathrm{id}} & \ell_2^n & \xrightarrow{\{S_X^{(1)}, S_X^{(3)}\}} & \ell_\infty^m \\
& & \downarrow W & & \uparrow \mathrm{id} \\
& & \ell_2^m \xrightarrow{\Sigma} \ell_2^m \xrightarrow{V} \ell_2^m &
\end{array} \qquad (16)$$

Finally, in order to compute the entropy number of the overall operator one only has to use the factorization of S_X into $S_X^{(i)} = \mathrm{id}_{2,\infty}^m V\Sigma W$ for $i \in \{1,3\}$ and into $S_X^{(2)} = \mathrm{id}_{2,\infty}^m V\Sigma W \mathrm{id}_{1,2}^n$ for example 2, and apply Proposition 2 several times. We also exploit the fact that for singular value decompositions $\|V\|, \|W\| \leq 1$. ∎

The present theorem allows us to compute the entropy numbers (and thus the complexity) of a class of functions on the current sample X. Going back to the examples of section 3, which led to large bounds on the VC dimension one can see that the new result is much less susceptible to such modifications: the addition of $f_1', \ldots f_n'$ to $f_1, \ldots f_n$ does not change the eigenspectrum Σ of the design matrix significantly (possibly only doubling the nominal value of the singular values), if the functions f_i' differ from f_i only slightly. Consequently also the bounds will not change significantly even though the number of basis functions just doubled.

Also note that the current error bounds reduce to the results of [6] in the SV case: here $Q_{ij} = F_{ij} = k(x_i, x_j)$ (both the design matrix F and the regularization matrix Q are determined by kernels) and therefore $FQ^{-1}F = Q$. Thus the analysis of the singular values of $FQ^{-1}F$ leads to an analysis of the eigenvalues of the kernel matrix, which is exactly what is done when dealing with SV machines.

6 ERROR BOUNDS

To use the above result we need a bound on the expected error of a hypothesis f in terms of the empirical error (training error) and the observed entropy numbers $\epsilon_n(\mathcal{F})$. We use [6, Theorem 4.1] with a small modification.

Theorem 1 *Let $\mathcal{F}$ be a set of linear functions as described in the previous examples with $e_n(S_X)$ as the corresponding bound on the observed entropy numbers of $\mathcal{F}$ on the dataset X. Moreover suppose that for a fixed threshold $b \in \mathbb{R}$ for some $f \in \mathcal{F}$, $\mathrm{sgn}(f - b)$ correctly classifies the set X with a margin $\gamma := \min_{1 \leq i \leq m} |f(x_i) - b|$.*

Finally let $U := \min\{n \in \mathbb{N}$ with $e_n(S_X) \leq \gamma/8.001\}$ and $\alpha(U, \delta) := 3.08(1 + \frac{1}{U} \ln \frac{1}{\delta})$. Then with confidence $1 - \delta$ over X (drawn randomly from P^m where P is some probability distribution) the expected error of $\mathrm{sgn}(f - b)$ is bounded from above by

$$\epsilon(m, U, \delta) = \frac{2}{m} \left(U \left(1 + \alpha \left(U, \frac{\delta}{2}\right) \log\left(\frac{5em}{U}\right) \log(17m)\right) + \log\left(\frac{16m}{\delta}\right) \right). \qquad (17)$$

The proof is essentially identical to that of [6, Theorem 4.1] and is omitted. [6] also shows how to compute $e_n(S_X)$ efficiently including an explicit formula for evaluating $e_l(\Sigma)$.

7 DISCUSSION

We showed how improved bounds could be obtained on the entropy numbers of a wide class of popular statistical estimators ranging from weight decay to sparsity regularization (with SV machines being a special case thereof). The results are given in a way that is directly useable for practicioners without any tedious calculations of the VC dimension or similar combinatorial quantities. In particular, our method ignores (nearly) linear dependent basis functions automatically. Finally, it takes advantage of favourable distributions of data by using the *observed* entropy numbers as a base for stating bounds on the true entropy numbers with respect to the function class under consideration.

Whilst this leads to significantly improved bounds (we achieved an improvement of approximately two orders of magnitude over previous VC-type bounds involving only the radius of the data R and the weight vector $\|w\|$ in the experiments) on the expected risk, the bounds are still not good enough to become predictive. This indicates that possibly rather than using the standard uniform convergence bounds (as used in the previous section) one might want to use other techniques such as a PAC-Bayesian treatment (as recently suggested by Herbrich and Graepel) in combination with the bounds on eigenvalues of the design matrix.

Acknowledgements: This work was supported by the Australian Research Council and a grant of the Deutsche Forschungsgemeinschaft SM 62/1-1.

References

[1] N. Alon, S. Ben-David, N. Cesa-Bianchi, and D. Haussler. Scale–sensitive Dimensions, Uniform Convergence, and Learnability. *J. of the ACM*, 44(4):615–631, 1997.

[2] B. Carl and I. Stephani. *Entropy, compactness, and the approximation of operators.* Cambridge University Press, Cambridge, UK, 1990.

[3] S. Chen, D. Donoho, and M. Saunders. Atomic decomposition by basis pursuit. Technical Report 479, Department of Statistics, Stanford University, 1995.

[4] F. Girosi, M. Jones, and T. Poggio. Regularization theory and neural networks architectures. *Neural Computation*, 7:219–269, 1995.

[5] R. A. Horn and C. R. Johnson. *Matrix Analysis*. Cambridge University Press, Cambridge, 1992.

[6] B. Schölkopf, J. Shawe-Taylor, A. J. Smola, and R. C. Williamson. Generalization bounds via eigenvalues of the gram matrix. Technical Report NC-TR-99-035, NeuroColt2, University of London, UK, 1999.

[7] J. Shawe-Taylor and R. C. Williamson. Generalization performance of classifiers in terms of observed covering numbers. In *Proc. EUROCOLT'99*, 1999.

[8] R. C. Williamson, A. J. Smola, and B. Schölkopf. Generalization performance of regularization networks and support vector machines via entropy numbers of compact operators. NeuroCOLT NC-TR-98-019, Royal Holloway College, 1998.

[9] R. C. Williamson, A. J. Smola, and B. Schölkopf. A Maximum Margin Miscellany. Typescript, 1999.

Probabilistic methods for Support Vector Machines

Peter Sollich
Department of Mathematics, King's College London
Strand, London WC2R 2LS, U.K. Email: peter.sollich@kcl.ac.uk

Abstract

I describe a framework for interpreting Support Vector Machines (SVMs) as maximum a posteriori (MAP) solutions to inference problems with Gaussian Process priors. This can provide intuitive guidelines for choosing a 'good' SVM kernel. It can also assign (by evidence maximization) optimal values to parameters such as the noise level C which cannot be determined unambiguously from properties of the MAP solution alone (such as cross-validation error). I illustrate this using a simple approximate expression for the SVM evidence. Once C has been determined, error bars on SVM predictions can also be obtained.

1 Support Vector Machines: A probabilistic framework

Support Vector Machines (SVMs) have recently been the subject of intense research activity within the neural networks community; for tutorial introductions and overviews of recent developments see [1, 2, 3]. One of the open questions that remains is how to set the 'tunable' parameters of an SVM algorithm: While methods for choosing the width of the kernel function and the noise parameter C (which controls how closely the training data are fitted) have been proposed [4, 5] (see also, very recently, [6]), the effect of the overall shape of the kernel function remains imperfectly understood [1]. Error bars (class probabilities) for SVM predictions — important for safety-critical applications, for example — are also difficult to obtain. In this paper I suggest that a probabilistic interpretation of SVMs could be used to tackle these problems. It shows that the SVM kernel defines a prior over functions on the input space, avoiding the need to think in terms of high-dimensional feature spaces. It also allows one to define quantities such as the evidence (likelihood) for a set of hyperparameters (C, kernel amplitude K_0 etc). I give a simple approximation to the evidence which can then be maximized to set such hyperparameters. The evidence is sensitive to the values of C and K_0 individually, in contrast to properties (such as cross-validation error) of the deterministic solution, which only depends on the product CK_0. It can therefore be used to assign an unambiguous value to C, from which error bars can be derived.

I focus on two-class classification problems. Suppose we are given a set D of n training examples (x_i, y_i) with binary outputs $y_i = \pm 1$ corresponding to the two classes. The basic SVM idea is to map the inputs x onto vectors $\phi(x)$ in some high-dimensional feature space; ideally, in this feature space, the problem should be linearly separable. Suppose first that this is true. Among all decision hyperplanes $\mathbf{w}\cdot\phi(x) + b = 0$ which separate the training examples (i.e. which obey $y_i(\mathbf{w}\cdot\phi(x_i) + b) > 0$ for all $x_i \in D_X$, D_X being the set of training inputs), the SVM solution is chosen as the one with the largest *margin*, i.e. the largest minimal distance from any of the training examples. Equivalently, one specifies the margin to be one and minimizes the squared length of the weight vector $||\mathbf{w}||^2$ [1], subject to the constraint that $y_i(\mathbf{w}\cdot\phi(x_i) + b) \geq 1$ for all i. If the problem is not linearly separable, 'slack variables' $\xi_i \geq 0$ are introduced which measure how much the margin constraints are violated; one writes $y_i(\mathbf{w}\cdot\phi(x_i) + b) \geq 1 - \xi_i$. To control the amount of slack allowed, a penalty term $C\sum_i \xi_i$ is then added to the objective function $\frac{1}{2}||\mathbf{w}||^2$, with a penalty coefficient C. Training examples with $y_i(\mathbf{w}\cdot\phi(x_i) + b) \geq 1$ (and hence $\xi_i = 0$) incur no penalty; all others contribute $C[1 - y_i(\mathbf{w}\cdot\phi(x_i) + b)]$ each. This gives the SVM optimization problem: Find $\mathbf{w}$ and b to minimize

$$\tfrac{1}{2}||\mathbf{w}||^2 + C\sum_i l(y_i[\mathbf{w}\cdot\phi(x_i) + b]) \qquad (1)$$

where $l(z)$ is the (shifted) 'hinge loss', $l(z) = (1-z)\Theta(1-z)$.

To interpret SVMs probabilistically, one can regard (1) as defining a (negative) log-posterior probability for the parameters $\mathbf{w}$ and b of the SVM, given a training set D. The first term gives the prior $Q(\mathbf{w}, b) \sim \exp(-\frac{1}{2}||\mathbf{w}||^2 - \frac{1}{2}b^2 B^{-2})$. This is a Gaussian prior on $\mathbf{w}$; the components of $\mathbf{w}$ are uncorrelated with each other and have unit variance. I have chosen a Gaussian prior on b with variance B^2; the flat prior implied by (1) can be recovered[1] by letting $B \to \infty$. Because only the 'latent variable' values $\theta(x) = \mathbf{w}\cdot\phi(x) + b$ — rather than $\mathbf{w}$ and b individually — appear in the second, data dependent term of (1), it makes sense to express the prior directly as a distribution over these. The $\theta(x)$ have a joint Gaussian distribution because the components of $\mathbf{w}$ do, with covariances given by $\langle\theta(x)\theta(x')\rangle = \langle(\phi(x)\cdot\mathbf{w})(\mathbf{w}\cdot\phi(x'))\rangle + B^2 = \phi(x)\cdot\phi(x') + B^2$. The SVM prior is therefore simply a *Gaussian process* (GP) over the functions θ, with covariance function $K(x, x') = \phi(x)\cdot\phi(x') + B^2$ (and zero mean). This correspondence between SVMs and GPs has been noted by a number of authors, *e.g.* [6, 7, 8, 9, 10].

The second term in (1) becomes a (negative) log-likelihood if we define the probability of obtaining output y for a given x (and θ) as

$$Q(y=\pm 1|x, \boldsymbol{\theta}) = \kappa(C)\exp[-Cl(y\theta(x))] \qquad (2)$$

We set $\kappa(C) = 1/[1 + \exp(-2C)]$ to ensure that the probabilities for $y = \pm 1$ never add up to a value larger than one. The likelihood for the complete data set is then $Q(D|\boldsymbol{\theta}) = \prod_i Q(y_i|x_i, \boldsymbol{\theta})Q(x_i)$, with some input distribution $Q(x)$ which remains essentially arbitrary at this point. However, this likelihood function is not normalized, because

$$\nu(\theta(x)) = Q(1|x, \boldsymbol{\theta}) + Q(-1|x, \boldsymbol{\theta}) = \kappa(C)\{\exp[-Cl(\theta(x))] + \exp[-Cl(-\theta(x))]\} < 1$$

---
[1]In the probabilistic setting, it actually makes more sense to keep B finite (and small); for $B \to \infty$, only training sets with all y_i equal have nonzero probability.

except when $|\theta(x)| = 1$. To remedy this, I write the actual probability model as

$$P(D, \boldsymbol{\theta}) = Q(D|\boldsymbol{\theta})Q(\boldsymbol{\theta})/\mathcal{N}(D). \tag{3}$$

Its posterior probability $P(\boldsymbol{\theta}|D) \sim Q(D|\boldsymbol{\theta})Q(\boldsymbol{\theta})$ is independent of the normalization factor $\mathcal{N}(D)$; by construction, the MAP value of $\boldsymbol{\theta}$ is therefore the SVM solution. The simplest choice of $\mathcal{N}(D)$ which normalizes $P(D, \boldsymbol{\theta})$ is D-independent:

$$\mathcal{N} = \overline{N^n} = \int d\boldsymbol{\theta}\, Q(\boldsymbol{\theta})N^n(\boldsymbol{\theta}), \quad N(\boldsymbol{\theta}) = \int dx\, Q(x)\, \nu(\theta(x)). \tag{4}$$

Conceptually, this corresponds to the following procedure of sampling from $P(D, \boldsymbol{\theta})$: First, sample $\boldsymbol{\theta}$ from the GP prior $Q(\boldsymbol{\theta})$. Then, for each data point, sample x from $Q(x)$. Assign outputs $y = \pm 1$ with probability $Q(y|x, \boldsymbol{\theta})$, respectively; with the *remaining* probability $1 - \nu(\theta(x))$ (the 'don't know' class probability in [11]), restart the whole process by sampling a new $\boldsymbol{\theta}$. Because $\nu(\theta(x))$ is smallest[2] inside the 'gap' $|\theta(x)| < 1$, functions $\boldsymbol{\theta}$ with many values in this gap are less likely to 'survive' until a dataset of the required size n is built up. This is reflected in an n-dependent factor in the (effective) prior, which follows from (3,4) as $P(\boldsymbol{\theta}) \sim Q(\boldsymbol{\theta})N^n(\boldsymbol{\theta})$. Correspondingly, in the likelihood

$$P(y|x, \boldsymbol{\theta}) = Q(y|x, \boldsymbol{\theta})/\nu(\theta(x)), \quad P(x|\boldsymbol{\theta}) \sim Q(x)\,\nu(\theta(x)) \tag{5}$$

(which now is normalized over $y = \pm 1$), the input density is influenced by the function $\boldsymbol{\theta}$ itself; it is reduced in the 'uncertainty gaps' $|\theta(x)| < 1$.

To summarize, eqs. (2-5) define a probabilistic data generation model whose MAP solution $\boldsymbol{\theta}^* = \arg\max P(\boldsymbol{\theta}|D)$ for a given data set D is identical to a standard SVM. The effective prior $P(\boldsymbol{\theta})$ is a GP prior modified by a data set size-dependent factor; the likelihood (5) defines not just a conditional output distribution, but also an input distribution (relative to some arbitrary $Q(x)$). All relevant properties of the feature space are encoded in the underlying GP prior $Q(\boldsymbol{\theta})$, with covariance matrix equal to the kernel $K(x, x')$. The log-posterior of the model

$$\ln P(\boldsymbol{\theta}|D) = -\tfrac{1}{2} \int dx\, dx'\, \theta(x) K^{-1}(x, x') \theta(x') - C \sum_i l(y_i \theta(x_i)) + \text{const} \tag{6}$$

is just a transformation of (1) from $\mathbf{w}$ and b to $\boldsymbol{\theta}$. By differentiating w.r.t. the $\theta(x)$ for non-training inputs, one sees that its maximum is of the standard form $\theta^*(x) = \sum_i \alpha_i y_i K(x, x_i)$; for $y_i \theta^*(x_i) > 1$, < 1, and $= 1$ one has $\alpha_i = 0$, $\alpha_i = C$ and $\alpha_i \in [0, C]$ respectively. I will call the training inputs x_i in the last group marginal; they form a subset of all support vectors (the x_i with $\alpha_i > 0$). The sparseness of the SVM solution (often the number of support vectors is $\ll n$) comes from the fact that the hinge loss $l(z)$ is constant for $z > 1$. This contrasts with other uses of GP models for classification (see *e.g.* [12]), where instead of the likelihood (2) a sigmoidal (often logistic) 'transfer function' with nonzero gradient everywhere is used. Moreover, in the noise free limit, the sigmoidal transfer function becomes a step function, and the MAP values $\boldsymbol{\theta}^*$ will tend to the trivial solution $\theta^*(x) = 0$. This illuminates from an alternative point of view why the margin (the 'shift' in the hinge loss) is important for SVMs.

Within the probabilistic framework, the main effect of the kernel in SVM classification is to change the properties of the underlying GP prior $Q(\boldsymbol{\theta})$ in $P(\boldsymbol{\theta}) \sim$

---

[2] This is true for $C > \ln 2$. For smaller C, $\nu(\theta(x))$ is actually higher in the gap, and the model makes less intuitive sense.

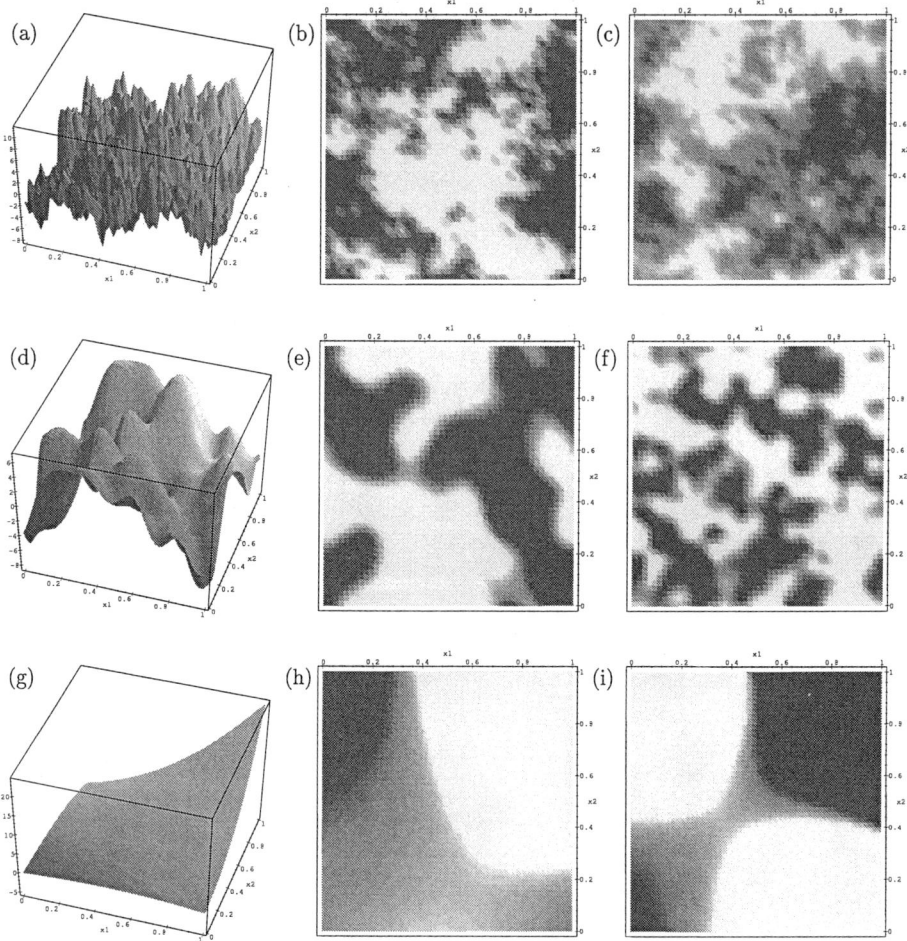

Figure 1: Samples from SVM priors; the input space is the unit square $[0,1]^2$. 3d plots are samples $\theta(x)$ from the underlying Gaussian process prior $Q(\boldsymbol{\theta})$. 2d greyscale plots represent the output distributions obtained when $\theta(x)$ is used in the likelihood model (5) with $C = 2$; the greyscale indicates the probability of $y = 1$ (black: 0, white: 1). (a,b) Exponential (Ornstein-Uhlenbeck) kernel/covariance function $K_0 \exp(-|x - x'|/l)$, giving rough $\theta(x)$ and decision boundaries. Length scale $l = 0.1$, $K_0 = 10$. (c) Same with $K_0 = 1$, i.e. with a reduced amplitude of $\theta(x)$; note how, in a sample from the prior corresponding to this new kernel, the grey 'uncertainty gaps' (given roughly by $|\theta(x)| < 1$) between regions of definite outputs (black/white) have widened. (d,e) As first row, but with squared exponential (RBF) kernel $K_0 \exp[-(x - x')^2/(2l^2)]$, yielding smooth $\theta(x)$ and decision boundaries. (f) Changing l to 0.05 (while holding K_0 fixed at 10) and taking a new sample shows how this parameter sets the typical length scale for decision regions. (g,h) Polynomial kernel $(1 + x \cdot x')^p$, with $p = 5$; (i) $p = 10$. The absence of a clear length scale and the widely differing magnitudes of $\theta(x)$ in the bottom left ($x = [0,0]$) and top right ($x = [1,1]$) corners of the square make this kernel less plausible from a probabilistic point of view.

$Q(\boldsymbol{\theta})N^n(\boldsymbol{\theta})$. Fig. 1 illustrates this with samples from $Q(\boldsymbol{\theta})$ for three different types of kernels. The effect of the kernel on smoothness of decision boundaries, and typical sizes of decision regions and 'uncertainty gaps' between them, can clearly be seen. When prior knowledge about these properties of the target is available, the probabilistic framework can therefore provide intuition for a suitable choice of kernel. Note that the samples in Fig. 1 are from $Q(\boldsymbol{\theta})$, rather than from the effective prior $P(\boldsymbol{\theta})$. One finds, however, that the n-dependent factor $N^n(\boldsymbol{\theta})$ does not change the properties of the prior qualitatively[3].

2 Evidence and error bars

Beyond providing intuition about SVM kernels, the probabilistic framework discussed above also makes it possible to apply Bayesian methods to SVMs. For example, one can define the evidence, i.e. the likelihood of the data D, given the model as specified by the hyperparameters C and (some parameters defining) $K(x,x')$. It follows from (3) as

$$P(D) = Q(D)/\overline{N^n}, \qquad Q(D) = \int d\boldsymbol{\theta}\, Q(D|\boldsymbol{\theta})Q(\boldsymbol{\theta}). \tag{7}$$

The factor $Q(D)$ is the 'naive' evidence derived from the unnormalized likelihood model; the correction factor $\overline{N^n}$ ensures that $P(D)$ is normalized over all data sets. This is crucial in order to guarantee that optimization of the (log) evidence gives optimal hyperparameter values at least on average (M Opper, private communication). Clearly, $P(D)$ will in general depend on C and $K(x,x')$ separately. The actual SVM solution, on the other hand, i.e. the MAP values $\boldsymbol{\theta}^*$, can be seen from (6) to depend on the product $CK(x,x')$ only. Properties of the deterministically trained SVM alone (such as test or cross-validation error) cannot therefore be used to determine C and the resulting class probabilities (5) unambiguously.

I now outline how a simple approximation to the naive evidence can be derived. $Q(D)$ is given by an integral over all $\theta(x)$, with the log integrand being (6) up to an additive constant. After integrating out the Gaussian distributed $\theta(x)$ with $x \notin D_X$, an intractable integral over the $\theta(x_i)$ remains. However, progress can be made by expanding the log integrand around its maximum $\theta^*(x_i)$. For all non-marginal training inputs this is equivalent to Laplace's approximation: the first terms in the expansion are quadratic in the deviations from the maximum and give simple Gaussian integrals. For the remaining $\theta(x_i)$, the leading terms in the log integrand vary *linearly* near the maximum. Couplings between these $\theta(x_i)$ only appear at the next (quadratic) order; discarding these terms as subleading, the integral factorizes over the $\theta(x_i)$ and can be evaluated. The end result of this calculation is:

$$\ln Q(D) \approx -\tfrac{1}{2}\sum_i y_i\alpha_i\theta^*(x_i) - C\sum_i l(y_i\theta^*(x_i)) - n\ln(1+e^{-2C}) - \tfrac{1}{2}\ln\det(\mathbf{L}_m\mathbf{K}_m) \tag{8}$$

The first three terms represent the maximum of the log integrand, $\ln Q(D|\boldsymbol{\theta}^*)$; the last one comes from the integration over the fluctuations of the $\theta(x)$. Note that it only contains information about the *marginal* training inputs: $\mathbf{K}_m$ is the corresponding submatrix of $K(x,x')$, and $\mathbf{L}_m$ is a diagonal matrix with entries

---

[3]Quantitative changes arise because function values with $|\theta(x)| < 1$ are 'discouraged' for large n; this tends to increase the size of the decision regions and narrow the uncertainty gaps. I have verified this by comparing samples from $Q(\boldsymbol{\theta})$ and $P(\boldsymbol{\theta})$.

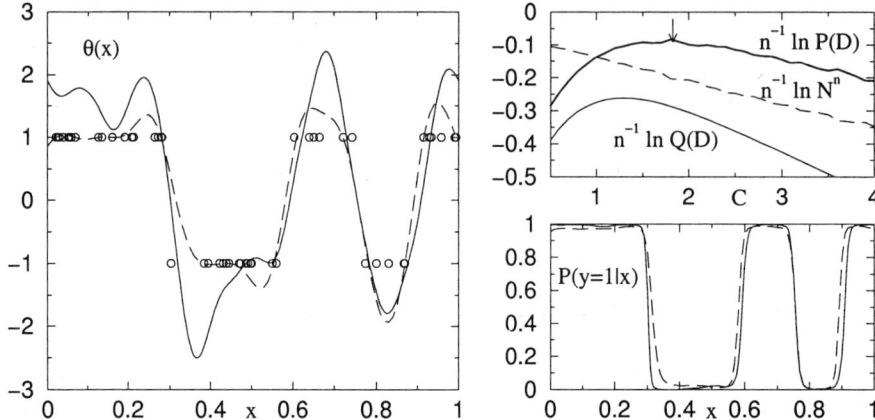

Figure 2: Toy example of evidence maximization. Left: Target 'latent' function $\theta(x)$ (solid line). A SVM with RBF kernel $K(x,x') = K_0 \exp[-(x-x')^2/(2l^2)]$, $l = 0.05$, $CK_0 = 2.5$ was trained (dashed line) on $n = 50$ training examples (circles). Keeping CK_0 constant, the evidence $P(D)$ (top right) was then evaluated as a function of C using (7,8). Note how the normalization factor $\overline{N^n}$ shifts the maximum of $P(D)$ towards larger values of C than in the naive evidence $Q(D)$. Bottom right: Class probability $P(y=1|x)$ for the target (solid), and prediction at the evidence maximum $C \approx 1.8$ (dashed). The target was generated from (3) with $C=2$.

$2\pi[\alpha_i(C-\alpha_i)/C]^2$. Given the sparseness of the SVM solution, these matrices should be reasonably small, making their determinants amenable to numerical computation or estimation [12]. Eq. (8) diverges when $\alpha_i \to 0$ or $\to C$ for one of the marginal training inputs; the approximation of retaining only linear terms in the log integrand then breaks down. I therefore adopt the simple heuristic of replacing $\det(\mathbf{L}_m\mathbf{K}_m)$ by $\det(\mathbf{I} + \mathbf{L}_m\mathbf{K}_m)$, which prevents these spurious singularities ($\mathbf{I}$ is the identity matrix). This choice also keeps the evidence continuous when training inputs move in or out of the set of marginal inputs as hyperparameters are varied.

Fig. 2 shows a simple application of the evidence estimate (8). For a given data set, the evidence $P(D)$ was evaluated[4] as a function of C. The kernel amplitude K_0 was varied simultaneously such that CK_0 and hence the SVM solution itself remained unchanged. Because the data set was generated artificially from the probability model (3), the 'true' value of $C = 2$ was known; in spite of the rather crude approximation for $Q(D)$, the maximum of the full evidence $P(D)$ identifies $C \approx 1.8$ quite close to the truth. The approximate class probability prediction $P(y=1|x,D)$ for this value of C is also plotted in Fig. 2; it overestimates the noise in the target somewhat. Note that $P(y|x,D)$ was obtained simply by inserting the MAP values $\theta^*(x)$ into (5). In a proper Bayesian treatment, an average over the posterior distribution $P(\theta|D)$ should of course be taken; I leave this for future work.

---

[4]The normalization factor $\overline{N^n}$ was estimated, for the assumed uniform input density $Q(x)$ of the example, by sampling from the GP prior $Q(\theta)$. If $Q(x)$ is unknown, the empirical training input distribution can be used as a proxy, and one samples instead from a multivariate Gaussian for the $\theta(x_i)$ with covariance matrix $K(x_i,x_j)$. This gave very similar values of $\ln \overline{N^n}$ in the example, even when only a subset of 30 training inputs was used.

In summary, I have described a probabilistic framework for SVM classification. It gives an intuitive understanding of the effect of the kernel, which determines a Gaussian process prior. More importantly, it also allows a properly normalized evidence to be defined; from this, optimal values of hyperparameters such as the noise parameter C, and corresponding error bars, can be derived. Future work will have to include more comprehensive experimental tests of the simple Laplace-type estimate of the (naive) evidence $Q(D)$ that I have given, and comparison with other approaches. These include variational methods; very recent experiments with a Gaussian approximation for the posterior $P(\theta|D)$, for example, seem promising [6]. Further improvement should be possible by dropping the restriction to a 'factor-analysed' covariance form [6]. (One easily shows that the optimal Gaussian covariance matrix is $(\mathbf{D} + \mathbf{K}^{-1})^{-1}$, parameterized only by a diagonal matrix $\mathbf{D}$.) It will also be interesting to compare the Laplace and Gaussian variational results for the evidence with those from the 'cavity field' approach of [10].

Acknowledgements

It is a pleasure to thank Tommi Jaakkola, Manfred Opper, Matthias Seeger, Chris Williams and Ole Winther for interesting comments and discussions, and the Royal Society for financial support through a Dorothy Hodgkin Research Fellowship.

References

[1] C J C Burges. A tutorial on support vector machines for pattern recognition. *Data Mining and Knowledge Discovery*, 2:121–167, 1998.

[2] A J Smola and B Schölkopf. A tutorial on support vector regression. 1998. Neuro COLT Technical Report TR-1998-030; available from http://svm.first.gmd.de/.

[3] B Schölkopf, C Burges, and A J Smola. *Advances in Kernel Methods: Support Vector Machines*. MIT Press, Cambridge, MA, 1998.

[4] B Schölkopf, P Bartlett, A Smola, and R Williamson. Shrinking the tube: a new support vector regression algorithm. In *NIPS 11*.

[5] N Cristianini, C Campbell, and J Shawe-Taylor. Dynamically adapting kernels in support vector machines. In *NIPS 11*.

[6] M Seeger. Bayesian model selection for Support Vector machines, Gaussian processes and other kernel classifiers. Submitted to *NIPS 12*.

[7] G Wahba. Support vector machines, reproducing kernel Hilbert spaces and the randomized GACV. Technical Report 984, University of Wisconsin, 1997.

[8] T S Jaakkola and D Haussler. Probabilistic kernel regression models. In *Proceedings of The 7th International Workshop on Artificial Intelligence and Statistics*. To appear.

[9] A J Smola, B Schölkopf, and K R Müller. The connection between regularization operators and support vector kernels. *Neural Networks*, 11:637–649, 1998.

[10] M Opper and O Winther. Gaussian process classification and SVM: Mean field results and leave-one-out estimator. In *Advances in Large Margin Classifiers*. MIT Press. To appear.

[11] P Sollich. Probabilistic interpretation and Bayesian methods for Support Vector Machines. Submitted to ICANN 99.

[12] C K I Williams. Prediction with Gaussian processes: From linear regression to linear prediction and beyond. In M I Jordan, editor, *Learning and Inference in Graphical Models*, pages 599–621. Kluwer Academic, 1998.

Algebraic Analysis for Non-Regular Learning Machines

Sumio Watanabe
Precision and Intelligence Laboratory
Tokyo Institute of Technology
4259 Nagatsuta, Midori-ku, Yokohama 223 Japan
swatanab@pi.titech.ac.jp

Abstract

Hierarchical learning machines are non-regular and non-identifiable statistical models, whose true parameter sets are analytic sets with singularities. Using algebraic analysis, we rigorously prove that the stochastic complexity of a non-identifiable learning machine is asymptotically equal to $\lambda_1 \log n - (m_1 - 1) \log \log n + $ const., where n is the number of training samples. Moreover we show that the rational number λ_1 and the integer m_1 can be algorithmically calculated using resolution of singularities in algebraic geometry. Also we obtain inequalities $0 < \lambda_1 \leq d/2$ and $1 \leq m_1 \leq d$, where d is the number of parameters.

1 Introduction

Hierarchical learning machines such as multi-layer perceptrons, radial basis functions, and normal mixtures are non-regular and non-identifiable learning machines. If the true distribution is almost contained in a learning model, then the set of true parameters is not one point but an analytic variety [4][9][3][10]. This paper establishes the mathematical foundation to analyze such learning machines based on algebraic analysis and algebraic geometry.

Let us consider a learning machine represented by a conditional probability density $p(x|w)$ where x is an M dimensional vector and w is a d dimensional parameter. We assume that n training samples $X^n = \{X_i; i = 1, 2, ..., n\}$ are independently taken from the true probability distribution $q(x)$, and that the set of true parameters

$$W_0 = \{w \in W \; ; \; p(x|w) = q(x) \quad (\text{a.s. } q(x)) \;\}$$

is not empty. In Bayes statistics, the estimated distribution $p(x|X^n)$ is defined by

$$p(x|X^n) = \int p(x|w) \, \rho_n(w) dw, \quad \rho_n(w) = \frac{1}{Z_n} \prod_{i=1}^{n} p(X_i|w) \, \varphi(w),$$

where $\varphi(w)$ is an *a priori* probability density on R^d, and Z_n is a normalizing constant. The *generalization error* is defined by

$$K(n) = E_{X^n} \{ \int q(x) \, \log \frac{q(x)}{p(x|X^n)} \, dx \}$$

where $E_{X^n}\{\cdot\}$ shows the expectation value over all training samples X^n. One of the main purposes in learning theory is to clarify how fast $K(n)$ converges to zero as n tends to infinity. Using the log-loss function $h(x,w) = \log q(x) - \log p(x,w)$, we define the Kullback distance and the empirical one,

$$H(w) = \int h(x,w)q(x)dx, \quad H(w, X^n) = \frac{1}{n}\sum_{i=1}^{n} h(X_i, w).$$

Note that the set of true parameters is equal to the set of zeros of $H(w)$, $W_0 = \{w \in W \; ; \; H(w) = 0\}$. If the true parameter set W_0 consists of only one point, the learning machine $p(x|w)$ is called *identifiable*, if otherwise *non-identifiable*. It should be emphasized that, in non-identifiable learning machines, W_0 is not a manifold but an *analytic set* with singular points, in general. Let us define the *stochastic complexity* by

$$F(n) = -E_{X^n}\{\log \int \exp(-nH(w, X^n))\varphi(w)dw\}. \tag{1}$$

Then we have an important relation between the stochastic complexity $F(n)$ and the generalization error $K(n)$

$$K(n) = F(n+1) - F(n),$$

which represents that $K(n)$ is equal to the increase of $F(n)$ [1]. In this paper, we show the rigorous asymptotic form of the stochastic complexity $F(n)$ for general non-identifiable learning machines.

2 Main Results

We need three assumptions upon which the main results are proven.

(A.1) The probability density $\varphi(w)$ is infinite times continuously differentiable and its support, $W \equiv \mathrm{supp}\,\varphi$, is compact. In other words, $\varphi \in C_0^\infty$.

(A.2) The log loss function, $h(x,w) = \log q(x) - \log p(x,w)$, is continuous for x in the support $Q \equiv \mathrm{supp}\, q$, and is analytic for w in an open set $W' \supset W$.

(A.3) Let $\{r_j(x, w^*); j = 1, 2, ..., d\}$ be the associated convergence radii of $h(x,w)$ at w^*, in other words, Taylor expansion of $h(x,w)$ at $w^* = (w_1^*, ..., w_d^*)$,

$$h(x,w) = \sum_{k_1,...,k_d=0}^{\infty} a_{k_1 k_2 ... k_d}(x)(w_1 - w_1^*)^{k_1}(w_2 - w_2^*)^{k_2} \cdots (w_d - w_d^*)^{k_d},$$

absolutely converges in $|w_j - w_j^*| < r_j(x, w^*)$. Assume $\inf_{x \in Q} \inf_{w^* \in W} r_j(x, w^*) > 0$ for $j = 1, 2, ..., d$.

Theorem 1 *Assume (A.1),(A.2), and (A.3). Then, there exist a rational number $\lambda_1 > 0$, a natural number m_1, and a constant C, such that*

$$|F(n) - \lambda_1 \log n + (m_1 - 1) \log \log n| < C$$

holds for an arbitrary natural number n.

Remarks. (1) If $q(x)$ is compact supported, then the assumption (A.3) is automatically satisfied. (2) Without assumptions (A.1) and (A.3), we can prove the upper bound, $F(n) \leq \lambda_1 \log n - (m_1 - 1) \log \log n + const$.

From Theorem 1, if the generalization error $K(n)$ has the asymptotic expansion, then it should be
$$K(n) = \frac{\lambda_1}{n} - \frac{m_1 - 1}{n \log n} + o(\frac{1}{n \log n}).$$
As is well known, if the model is identifiable and has the positive definite Fisher information matrix, then $\lambda_1 = d/2$ (d is the dimension of the parameter space) and $m_1 = 1$. However, hierarchical learning models such as multi-layer perceptrons, radial basis functions, and normal mixtures have smaller λ_1 and larger m_1, in other words, hierarchical models are better learning machines than regular ones if Bayes estimation is applied. Constants λ_1 and m_1 are characterized by the following theorem.

Theorem 2 *Assume the same conditions as theorem 1. Let $\epsilon > 0$ be a sufficiently small constant. The holomorphic function in $Re(z) > 0$,*
$$J(z) = \int_{H(w) < \epsilon} H(w)^z \varphi(w) dw,$$
can be analytically continued to the entire complex plane as a meromorphic function whose poles are on the negative part of the real axis, and the constants $-\lambda_1$ and m_1 in theorem 1 are equal to the largest pole of $J(z)$ and its multiplicity, respectively.

The proofs of above theorems are explained in the following section. Let $w = g(u)$ is an arbitrary analytic function from a set $U \subset R^d$ to W. Then $J(z)$ is invariant under the mapping,
$$\{H(w), \varphi(w)\} \rightarrow \{H(g(u)), \varphi(g(u))|g'(u)|\},$$
where $|g'(u)| = |\det(\partial w_i / \partial u_j)|$ is Jacobian. This fact shows that λ_1 and m_1 are invariant under a bi-rational mapping. In section 4, we show an algorithm to calculate λ_1 and m_1 by using this invariance and resolution of singularities.

3 Mathematical Structure

In this section, we present an outline of the proof and its mathematical structure.

3.1 Upper bound and b-function

For a sufficiently small constant $\epsilon > 0$, we define $F^*(n)$ by
$$F^*(n) = -\log \int_{H(w) < \epsilon} \exp(-nH(w)) \, \varphi(w) \, dw.$$
Then by using the *Jensen's inequality*, we obtain $F(n) \leq F^*(n)$. To evaluate $F^*(n)$, we need the b-function in algebraic analysis [6][7]. Sato, Bernstein, Björk, and Kashiwara proved that, for an arbitrary analytic function $H(w)$, there exist a differential operator $D(w, \partial_w, z)$ which is a polynomial for z, and a polynomial $b(z)$ whose zeros are rational numbers on the negative part of the real axis, such that
$$D(w, \partial_w, z) H(w)^{z+1} = b(z) H(w)^z \qquad (2)$$
for any $z \in C$ and any $w \in W_\epsilon = \{w \in W; H(w) < \epsilon\}$. By using the relation eq.(2), the holomorphic function $J(z)$ in $Re(z) > 0$,
$$J(z) \equiv \int_{H(w) < \epsilon} H(w)^z \varphi(w) dw = \frac{1}{b(z)} \int_{H(w) < \epsilon} H(w)^{z+1} D_w^* \varphi(w) dw,$$

can be analytically continued to the entire complex plane as a meromorphic function whose poles are on the negative part of the real axis. The poles, which are rational numbers and ordered from the origin to the minus infinity, are referred to as $-\lambda_1, -\lambda_2, -\lambda_3, ...$, and their multiplicities are also referred to as $m_1, m_2, m_3, ...$ Let c_{km} be the coefficient of the m-th order of Laurent expansion of $J(z)$ at $-\lambda_k$. Then,

$$J_K(z) \equiv J(z) - \sum_{k=1}^{K} \sum_{m=1}^{m_k} \frac{c_{km}}{(z+\lambda_k)^{-m}} \quad (3)$$

is holomorphic in $\operatorname{Re}(z) > -\lambda_{K+1}$, and $|J_K(z)| \to 0$ ($|z| \to \infty$, $\operatorname{Re}(z) > -\lambda_{K+1}$). Let us define a function

$$I(t) = \int \delta(t - H(w))\varphi(w)dw$$

for $0 < t < \epsilon$ and $I(t) = 0$ for $\epsilon \leq t \leq 1$. Then $I(t)$ connects the function $F^*(n)$ with $J(z)$ by the relations,

$$J(z) = \int_0^1 t^z I(t) \, dt,$$

$$F^*(n) = -\log \int_0^1 \exp(-nt) I(t) \, dt.$$

The inverse Laplace transform gives the asymptotic expansion of $I(t)$ as $t \to 0$,

$$I(t) = \sum_{k=1}^{\infty} \sum_{m=1}^{m_k} \frac{c_{km}}{(m-1)!} t^{\lambda_k - 1} (-\log t)^{m-1},$$

resulting in the asymptotic expansion of $F^*(n)$,

$$F^*(n) = -\log \int_0^n \exp(-t) I(\frac{t}{n}) \frac{dt}{n}$$
$$= \lambda_1 \log n - (m_1 - 1) \log \log n + O(1),$$

which is the upper bound of $F(n)$.

3.2 Lower Bound

We define a random variable

$$A(X^n) = \sup_{w \in W} | n^{1/2}(H(w, X^n) - H(w)) / H(w)^{1/2} |. \quad (4)$$

Then, we prove in Appendix that there exists a constant c_0 which is independent of n such that

$$E_{X^n}\{A(X^n)^2\} < c_0. \quad (5)$$

By using an inequality $ab \leq (a^2 + b^2)/2$,

$$nH(w, X^n) \geq nH(w) - A(X^n)(nH(w))^{1/2} \geq \frac{1}{2}\{nH(w) - A(X^n)^2\},$$

which derives a lower bound,

$$F(n) \geq -E_{X^n}\{\log \int \exp(-\frac{1}{2}\{nH(w) - A(X^n)^2\})\varphi(w)dw\}$$
$$= -\frac{1}{2}E_{X^n}\{A(X^n)^2\} - \log \int \exp(-\frac{nH(w)}{2})\varphi(w)dw \quad (6)$$

The first term in eq.(6) is bounded. Let the second term be $F_*(n)$, then

$$F_*(n) = -\log(Z_1 + Z_2)$$
$$Z_1 = \int_{H(w)<\epsilon} \exp(-\frac{nH(w)}{2}) \varphi(w)dw \cong const. \, n^{-\lambda_1} (\log n)^{m_1-1}$$
$$Z_2 = \int_{H(w)\geq\epsilon} \exp(-\frac{nH(w)}{2}) \varphi(w)dw \leq \exp(-\frac{n\epsilon}{2}),$$

which proves the lower bound of $F(n)$,

$$F(n) \geq \lambda_1 \log n - (m_1 - 1) \log\log n + const.$$

4 Resolution of Singularities

In this section, we construct a method to calculate λ_1 and m_1. First of all, we cover the compact set W_0 with a finite union of open sets W^α. In other words, $W_0 \subset \cup_\alpha W^\alpha$. Hironaka's resolution of singularities [5][2] ensures that, for an arbitrary analytic function $H(w)$, we can algorithmically find an open set $U^\alpha \subset R^d$ (U^α contains the origin) and an analytic function $g_\alpha : U^\alpha \to W^\alpha$ such that

$$H(g_\alpha(u)) = a(u) \, u_1^{k_1} u_2^{k_2} \cdots u_d^{k_d} \quad (u \in U^\alpha) \tag{7}$$

where $a(u) > 0$ is a positive function and $k_i \geq 0$ ($1 \leq i \leq d$) are even integers ($a(u)$ and k_i depend on U^α). Note that Jacobian $|g'_\alpha(u)| = 0$ if and only if $u \in g_\alpha^{-1}(W_0)$.

$$\varphi(g_\alpha(u))|g'_\alpha(u)| = \sum_{(p_1,p_2,\ldots,p_d)}^{\text{finite}} c_{p_1,p_2,\ldots,p_d} \, u_1^{p_1} u_2^{p_2} \cdots u_d^{p_d} + R(u), \tag{8}$$

By combining eq.(7) with eq.(8), we obtain

$$J_\alpha(z) \equiv \int_{W^\alpha} H(w)^z \varphi(w)$$
$$= \int_{U^\alpha} a(u) \, \{u_1^{k_1} u_2^{k_2} \cdots u_d^{k_d}\}^z \, u_1^{p_1} u_2^{p_2} \cdots u_d^{p_d} \, du_1 \, du_2 \cdots du_d.$$

For real z, $\max_\alpha J_\alpha(z) \leq J(z) \leq \sum_\alpha J_\alpha(z)$,

$$\lambda_1 = \min_\alpha \, \min_{(p_1,\ldots,p_d)} \, \min_{1\leq q\leq d} \frac{p_q + 1}{k_q}$$

and m_1 is equal to the number of q which attains the minimum, $\min_{1\leq q\leq d}$.

Remark. In a neighborhood of $w_0 \in W_0$, the analytic function $H(w)$ is equivalent to a polynomial $H_{w_0}(w)$, in other words, there exists constants $c_1, c_2 > 0$ such that $c_1 H_{w_0}(w) \leq H(w) \leq c_2 H_{w_0}(w)$. Hironaka's theorem constructs the resolution map g_α for any polynomial $H_{w_0}(w)$ algorithmically in the finite procedures (blowing-ups for nonsingular manifolds in singularities are recursively applied [5]). From the above discussion, we obtain an inequality, $1 \leq m \leq d$. Moreover there exists $\gamma > 0$ such that $H(w) \leq \gamma |w - w_0|^2$ in the neighborhood of $w_0 \in W_0$, we obtain $\lambda_1 \leq d/2$.

Example. Let us consider a model $(x, y) \in R^2$ and $w = (a, b, c, d) \in R^4$,

$$p(x, y|w) = p_0(x) \frac{1}{(2\pi)^{1/2}} \exp(-\frac{1}{2}(y - \psi(x, w))^2),$$
$$\psi(x, a, b, c, d) = a\tanh(bx) + c\tanh(dx),$$

where $p_0(x)$ is a compact support probability density (not estimated). We also assume that the true regression function is $y = \psi(x, 0, 0, 0, 0)$. The set of true parameters is

$$W_0 = \{E_X \psi(X, a, b, c, d)^2 = 0\} = \{ab + cd = 0 \text{ and } ab^3 + cd^3 = 0\}.$$

Assumptions (A.1),(A.2), and (A.3) are satisfied. The singularity in W_0 which gives the smallest λ_1 is the origin and the average loss function in the neighborhood W^o of the origin is equivalent to the polynomial $H_0(a, b, c, d) = (ab+cd)^2 + (ab^3+cd^3)^2$, (see[9]). Using blowing-ups, we find a map $g : (x, y, z, w) \mapsto (a, b, c, d)$,

$$a = x, \quad b = y^3 w - yzw, \quad c = zwx, \quad d = y,$$

by which the singularity at the origin is resolved.

$$\begin{aligned} J(z) &= \int_{W^o} H_0(a, b, c, d)^z \varphi(a, b, c, d) da\, db\, dc\, dd \\ &= \int \{ x^2 y^6 w^2 [1 + (z + w^2(y^2 - z)^3)^2] \}^z |xy^3 w| \varphi(g(x, y, z, w))\, dxdydzdw, \end{aligned}$$

which shows that $\lambda_1 = 2/3$ and $m_1 = 1$, resulting that $F(n) = (2/3) \log n + Const$. If the generalization error can be asymptotically expanded, then $K(n) \cong (2/3n)$.

5 Conclusion

Mathematical foundation for non-identifiable learning machines is constructed based on algebraic analysis and algebraic geometry. We obtained both the rigorous asymptotic form of the stochastic complexity and an algorithm to calculate it.

Appendix

In the appendix, we show the inequality eq.(5).

Lemma 1 *Assume conditions (A.1), (A.2) and (A.3). Then*

$$E_{X^n} \{ \sup_{w \in W} | \frac{1}{\sqrt{n}} \sum_{i=1}^n [\, h(X_i, w) - E_X h(X, w)\,]\, |^2 \} < \infty.$$

This lemma is proven by using just the same method as [10]. In order to prove (5), we divide '$\sup_{w \in W}$' in eq.(4) into '$\sup_{H(w) \geq \epsilon}$' and '$\sup_{H(w) < \epsilon}$'. Finiteness of the first half is directly proven by Lemma 1. Let us prove the second half is also finite. We can assume without loss of generality that w is in the neighborhood of $w_0 \in W_0$, because W can be covered by a finite union of neighborhoods. In each neighborhood, by using Taylor expansion of an analytic function, we can find functions $\{f_j(x, w)\}$ and $\{g_j(w) = \prod_i (w_i - w_{0i})^{a_i}\}$ such that

$$h(x, w) = \sum_{j=1}^J g_j(w) f_j(x, w), \qquad (9)$$

where $\{f_j(x, w_0)\}$ are linearly independent functions of x and $g_j(w_0) = 0$. Since $g_j(w) f_j(x, w)$ is a part of Taylor expansion among w_0, $f_j(x, w)$ satisfies

$$E_{X^n} \{ \sup_{w \in W_\epsilon} | \frac{1}{\sqrt{n}} \sum_{i=1}^n (f_j(X_i, w) - E_X f_j(X, w))|^2 \} < \infty. \qquad (10)$$

By using a definition $\hat{H}(w) \equiv |H(w, X^n) - H(w)|$,

$$\hat{H}(w)^2 = |\frac{1}{n}\sum_{i=1}^{n}\{\sum_{j=1}^{J} g_j(w)(f_j(X_i, w) - E_X f_j(X, w))\}|^2$$

$$\leq \sum_{j=1}^{J} g_j(w)^2 \sum_{j=1}^{J}\{\frac{1}{n}\sum_{i=1}^{n}(f_j(X_i, w) - E_X f_j(X, w))\}^2$$

where we used Cauchy-Schwarz's inequality. On the other hand, the inequality $\log x \geq (1/2)(\log x)^2 - x + 1$ $(x > 0)$ shows that

$$H(w) = \int q(x) \log \frac{q(x)}{p(x,w)} dx \geq \frac{1}{2}\int q(x)(\log \frac{q(x)}{p(x,w)})^2 dx \geq \frac{a_0}{2}\sum_{j=1}^{J} g_j(w)^2$$

where $a_0 > 0$ is the smallest eigen value of the positive definite symmetric matrix $E_X\{f_j(X,w_0)f_k(X,w_0)\}$. Lastly, combining

$$A(X^n) = \sup_{w \in W_\epsilon} \frac{n\hat{H}(w)^2}{H(w)} \leq \frac{a_0}{2} \sup_{w \in W_\epsilon} \sum_{j=1}^{J}\{\frac{1}{\sqrt{n}}\sum_{i=1}^{n}(f_j(X_i,w) - E_X f_j(X,w))\}^2$$

with eq.(10), we obtain eq.(5).

Acknowledgments

This research was partially supported by the Ministry of Education, Science, Sports and Culture in Japan, Grant-in-Aid for Scientific Research 09680362.

References

[1] Amari,S., Murata, N.(1993) Statistical theory of learning curves under entropic loss. *Neural Computation*, **5** (4) pp.140-153.

[2] Atiyah, M.F. (1970) Resolution of singularities and division of distributions. *Comm. Pure and Appl. Math.*, **13** pp.145-150.

[3] Fukumizu,K. (1999) Generalization error of linear neural networks in unidentifiable cases.*Lecture Notes in Computer Science*, **1720** Springer, pp.51-62.

[4] Hagiwara,K., Toda,N., Usui,S. (1993) On the problem of applying AIC to determine the structure of a layered feed-forward neural network. *Proc. of IJCNN*, **3** pp.2263-2266.

[5] Hironaka, H. (1964) Resolution of singularities of an algebraic variety over a field of characteristic zero, I,II. *Annals of Math.*, **79** pp.109-326.

[6] Kashiwara, M. (1976) B-functions and holonomic systems, *Invent. Math.*, **38** pp.33-53.

[7] Oaku, T. (1997) An algorithm of computing b-funcitions. *Duke Math. J.*, **87** pp.115-132.

[8] Sato, M., Shintani,T. (1974) On zeta functions associated with prehomogeneous vector space.*Annals of Math.*, **100**, pp.131-170.

[9] Watanabe, S.(1998) On the generalization error by a layered statistical model with Bayesian estimation. *IEICE Trans.*, **J81-A** pp.1442-1452. English version: *Elect. Comm. in Japan.*, to appear.

[10] Watanabe, S. (1999) Algebraic analysis for singular statistical estimation. *Lecture Notes in Computer Science*, **1720** Springer, pp.39-50.

Semiparametric Approach to Multichannel Blind Deconvolution of Nonminimum Phase Systems

L.-Q. Zhang, S. Amari and A. Cichocki
Brain-style Information Systems Research Group, BSI
The Institute of Physical and Chemical Research
Wako shi, Saitama 351-0198, JAPAN
zha@open.brain.riken.go.jp
{amari,cia}@brain.riken.go.jp

Abstract

In this paper we discuss the semiparametric statistical model for blind deconvolution. First we introduce a Lie Group to the manifold of noncausal FIR filters. Then blind deconvolution problem is formulated in the framework of a semiparametric model, and a family of estimating functions is derived for blind deconvolution. A natural gradient learning algorithm is developed for training noncausal filters. Stability of the natural gradient algorithm is also analyzed in this framework.

1 Introduction

Recently blind separation/deconvolution has been recognized as an increasing important research area due to its rapidly growing applications in various fields, such as telecommunication systems, image enhancement and biomedical signal processing. Refer to review papers [7] and [13] for details. A semiparametric statistical model treats a family of probability distributions specified by a finite-dimensional parameter of interest and an infinite-dimensional nuisance parameter [12]. Amari and Kumon [10] have proposed an approach to semiparametric statistical models in terms of estimating functions and elucidated their geometric structures and efficiencies by information geometry [1]. Blind source separation can be formulated in the framework of semiparametric statistical models. Amari and Cardoso [5] applied information geometry of estimating functions to blind source separation and derived an admissible class of estimating functions which includes efficient estimators. They showed that the manifold of mixtures is $m-$curvature free, so that we can design algorithms of blind separation without taking much care of misspecification of source probability functions.

The theory of estimating functions has also been applied to the case of instantaneous mixtures, where independent source signals have unknown temporal correlations [3]. It is also applied to derive efficiency and superefficiency of demixing learning algorithms [4].

Most of these theories treat only blind source separation of instantaneous mixtures. It is only recently that the natural gradient approach has been proposed for multichannel blind deconvolution [8], [18]. The present paper extends the geometrical theory of estimating functions to the semiparametric model of multichannel blind deconvolution. For the limited space, the detailed derivations and proofs are left to a full paper.

2 Blind Deconvolution Problem

In this paper, as a convolutive mixing model, we consider a multichannel linear time-invariant (LTI) systems, with no poles on the unit circle, of the form

$$\mathbf{x}(k) = \sum_{p=-\infty}^{\infty} \mathbf{H}_p \mathbf{s}(k-p), \quad (1)$$

where $\mathbf{s}(k)$ is an n-dimensional vector of source signals which are spatially mutually independent and temporarily identically independently distributed, and $\mathbf{x}(k)$ is an n-dimensional sensor vector at time k, $k = 1, 2, \cdots$. We denote the unknown mixing filter by $\mathbf{H}(z) = \sum_{p=-\infty}^{\infty} \mathbf{H}_p z^{-p}$. The goal of multichannel blind deconvolution is to retrieve source signals $\mathbf{s}(k)$ only using sensor signals $\mathbf{x}(k), k = 1, 2, \cdots$, and certain knowledge of the source signal distributions and statistics. We carry out blind deconvolution by using another multichannel LTI system of the form

$$\mathbf{y}(k) = \mathbf{W}(z)\mathbf{x}(k), \quad (2)$$

where $\mathbf{W}(z) = \sum_{p=-N}^{N} \mathbf{W}_p z^{-p}$, N is the length of FIR filter $\mathbf{W}(z)$, $\mathbf{y}(k) = [y_1(k), \cdots, y_n(k)]^T$ is an n-dimensional vector of the outputs, which is used to estimate the source signals.

When we apply $\mathbf{W}(z)$ to the sensor signal $\mathbf{x}(k)$, the global transfer function from $\mathbf{s}(k)$ to $\mathbf{y}(k)$ is defined by $\mathbf{G}(z) = \mathbf{W}(z)\mathbf{H}(z)$. The goal of the blind deconvolution task is to find $\mathbf{W}(z)$ such that $\mathbf{G}(z) = \mathbf{P}\mathbf{\Lambda}\mathbf{D}(z)$, where $\mathbf{P} \in \mathbf{R}^{n \times n}$ is a permutation matrix, $\mathbf{D}(z) = \mathrm{diag}\{z^{-d_1}, \cdots, z^{-d_n}\}$, and $\mathbf{\Lambda} \in \mathbf{R}^{n \times n}$ is a nonsingular diagonal scaling matrix.

3 Lie Group on $\mathcal{M}(N, N)$

In this section, we introduce a Lie group to the manifold of noncausal FIR filters. The Lie group operations play a crucial role in the following discussion. The set of all the noncausal FIR filters $\mathbf{W}(z)$ of length N, having the constraint that $\mathcal{W}$ is nonsingular, is denoted by

$$\mathcal{M}(N, N) = \left\{ \mathbf{W}(z) \mid \mathbf{W}(z) = \sum_{p=-N}^{N} \mathbf{W}_p z^{-p},\ det(\mathcal{W}) \neq 0 \right\}, \quad (3)$$

where $\mathcal{W}$ is an $N \times N$ block matrix,

$$\mathcal{W} = \begin{bmatrix} \mathbf{W}_0 & \mathbf{W}_{-1} & \cdots & \mathbf{W}_{-N+1} \\ \mathbf{W}_1 & \mathbf{W}_0 & \cdots & \mathbf{W}_{-N+2} \\ \vdots & \vdots & \ddots & \vdots \\ \mathbf{W}_{N-1} & \mathbf{W}_{N-2} & \cdots & \mathbf{W}_0 \end{bmatrix} \quad (4)$$

$\mathcal{M}(N, N)$ is a manifold of dimension $n^2(2N+1)$. In general, multiplication of two filters in $\mathcal{M}(N, N)$ will enlarge the filter length and the result does belong to $\mathcal{M}(N, N)$ anymore. This makes it difficult to introduce the Riemannian structure to the manifold of noncausal FIR filters. In order to explore possible geometrical structures of $\mathcal{M}(N, N)$ which will lead to effective learning algorithms for $\mathbf{W}(z)$, we define algebraic operations of filters in the Lie group framework. First, we introduce a novel filter decomposition of noncausal filters in $\mathcal{M}(N, N)$ into a product of two one-sided FIR filters [19], which is illustrated in Fig. 1.

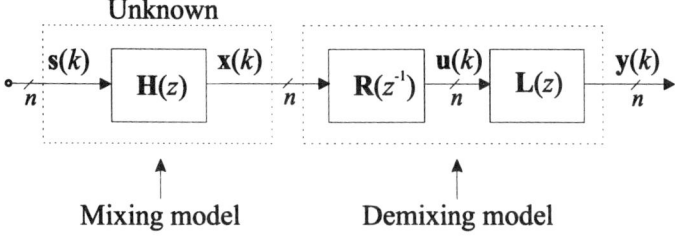

Figure 1: Illustration of decomposition of noncausal filters in $\mathcal{M}(N,N)$

Lemma 1 *[19] If the matrix $\mathcal{W}$ is nonsingular, any noncausal filter $\mathbf{W}(z)$ in $\mathcal{M}(N,N)$ has the decomposition $\mathbf{W}(z) = \mathbf{R}(z)\mathbf{L}(z^{-1})$, where $\mathbf{R}(z) = \sum_{p=0}^{N} \mathbf{R}_p z^{-p}$, $\mathbf{L}(z^{-1}) = \sum_{p=0}^{N} \mathbf{L}_p z^p$ are one-sided FIR filters.*

In the manifold $\mathcal{M}(N,N)$, Lie operations, *multiplication* $*$ and *inverse* $\dagger$, are defined as follows: For $\mathbf{B}(z), \mathbf{C}(z) \in \mathcal{M}(N,N)$,

$$\mathbf{B}(z) * \mathbf{C}(z) = [\mathbf{B}(z)\mathbf{C}(z)]_N, \quad \mathbf{B}^\dagger(z) = \mathbf{L}^\dagger(z^{-1})\mathbf{R}^\dagger(z), \tag{5}$$

where $[\mathbf{B}(z)]_N$ is the truncating operator that any terms with orders higher than N in the polynomial $\mathbf{B}(z)$ are truncated, and the inverse of one-side FIR filters is recurrently defined by $\mathbf{R}_0^\dagger = \mathbf{R}_0^{-1}$, $\mathbf{R}_p^\dagger = -\sum_{q=1}^{p} \mathbf{R}_{p-q}^\dagger \mathbf{R}_q \mathbf{R}_0^{-1}$, $p = 1, \cdots, N$. Refer to [18] for the detailed derivation. With these operations, both $\mathbf{B}(z) * \mathbf{C}(z)$ and $\mathbf{B}^\dagger(z)$ still remain in the manifold $\mathcal{M}(N,N)$. It is easy to verify that the manifold $\mathcal{M}(N,N)$ with the above operations forms a Lie Group. The identity element is $\mathbf{E}(z) = \mathbf{I}$.

4 Semiparametric Approach to Blind Deconvolution

We first introduce the basic theory of semiparametric models, and formulate blind deconvolution problem in the framework of the semiparametric models.

4.1 Semiparametric model

Consider a general statistical model $\{p(\mathbf{x}; \boldsymbol{\theta}, \boldsymbol{\xi})\}$, where $\mathbf{x}$ is a random variable whose probability density function is specified by two parameters, $\boldsymbol{\theta}$ and $\boldsymbol{\xi}$, $\boldsymbol{\theta}$ being the parameter of interest, and $\boldsymbol{\xi}$ being the nuisance parameter. When the nuisance parameter is of infinite dimensions or of functional degrees of freedom, the statistical model is called a semiparametric model [12]. The gradient vectors of the log likelihood $\mathbf{u}(x; \boldsymbol{\theta}, \boldsymbol{\xi}) = \frac{\partial \log p(\boldsymbol{x};\boldsymbol{\theta},\boldsymbol{\xi})}{\partial \boldsymbol{\theta}}$, $\mathbf{v}(x; \boldsymbol{\theta}, \boldsymbol{\xi}) = \frac{\partial \log p(\boldsymbol{x};\boldsymbol{\theta},\boldsymbol{\xi})}{\partial \boldsymbol{\xi}}$, are called the score functions of the parameter of interest or shortly $\boldsymbol{\theta}$−score and the nuisance score or shortly $\boldsymbol{\xi}$−score, respectively.

In the semiparametric model, it is difficult to estimate both the parameters of interest and nuisance parameters at the same time, since the nuisance parameter $\boldsymbol{\xi}$ is of infinite degrees of freedom. The semiparametric approach suggests to use an estimating function to estimate the parameters of interest, regardless of the nuisance parameters. The estimating function is a vector function $\mathbf{z}(\mathbf{x}, \boldsymbol{\theta})$, independent of nuisance parameters $\boldsymbol{\xi}$, satisfying the following conditions

1) $E_{\boldsymbol{\theta},\boldsymbol{\xi}}[\mathbf{z}(\mathbf{x},\boldsymbol{\theta})] = 0,$ \hfill (6)

2) $det(\mathcal{K}) \neq 0$, where $\mathcal{K} = E_{\boldsymbol{\theta},\boldsymbol{\xi}}[\frac{\partial \mathbf{z}(\mathbf{x},\boldsymbol{\theta})}{\partial \boldsymbol{\theta}}].$ \hfill (7)

$$3) \quad E_{\theta,\xi}[\mathbf{z}(\mathbf{x},\boldsymbol{\theta})\mathbf{z}^T(\mathbf{x},\boldsymbol{\theta})] < \infty, \tag{8}$$

for all $\boldsymbol{\theta}$ and $\boldsymbol{\xi}$. Generally speaking, it is difficult to find an estimating function. Amari and Kawanabe [9] studied the information geometry of estimating functions and provided a novel approach to find all the estimating functions. In this paper, we follow the approach to find a family of estimating functions for bind deconvolution.

4.2 Semiparametric Formulation for Blind Deconvolution

Now we turn to formulate the blind deconvolution problem in the framework of semiparametric models. From the statistical point of view, the blind deconvolution problem is to estimate $\mathbf{H}(z)$ or $\mathbf{H}^{-1}(z)$ from the observed data $\mathcal{D}_L = \{\mathbf{x}(k), k = 1, 2, \cdots\}$. The estimate includes two unknowns: One is the mixing filter $\mathbf{H}(z)$ which is the parameter of interest, and the other is the probability density function $p(\mathbf{s})$ of sources, which is the nuisance parameter in the present case. For blind deconvolution problem, we usually assume that source signals are zero-mean, $E[s_i] = 0$, for $i = 1, \cdots, n$. In addition, we generally impose constraints on the recovered signals to remove the indeterminacy,

$$E[k_i(s_i)] = 0, \text{ for } i = 1, \cdots, n. \tag{9}$$

A typical example of the constraint is $k_i(s_i) = s_i^4 - 1$. Since the source signals are spatially mutually independent and temporally iid, the pdf $r(\mathbf{s})$ can be factorized into a product form $r(\mathbf{s}) = \prod_{i=1}^{n} r(s_i)$. The purpose of this paper is to find a family of estimating functions for blind deconvolution. Remarkable progress has been made recently in the theory of the semiparametric approach [9],[12]. It has been shown that the efficient score itself is an estimating function for blind separation.

5 Estimating Functions

In this section, we give an explicit form of the score function matrix of interest and the nuisance tangent space, by using a local nonholonomic reparameterization. We then derive a family of estimating functions from it.

5.1 Score function matrix and its representation

Since the mixing model is a matrix filter, we write an estimating function in the same matrix filter format

$$\mathbf{F}(\mathbf{x}; \mathbf{H}(z)) = \sum_{p=-N}^{N} \mathbf{F}_p(\mathbf{x}; \mathbf{H}(z)) z^{-p}, \tag{10}$$

where $\mathbf{F}_p(\mathbf{x}; \mathbf{H}(z))$ are $n \times n$-matrices. In order to derive the explicit form of the H-score, we reparameterize the filter in a small neighborhood of $\mathbf{H}(z)$ by using a new variable matrix filter as $\mathbf{H}(z) * (\mathbf{I} - \mathbf{X}(z))$, where $\mathbf{I}$ is the identity element of the manifold $\mathcal{M}(N,N)$. The variation $\mathbf{X}(z)$ represents a local coordinate system at the neighborhood $\mathcal{N}_\mathbf{H}$ of $\mathbf{H}(z)$ on the manifold $\mathcal{M}(N,N)$. The variation $d\mathbf{H}(z)$ of $\mathbf{H}(z)$ is represented as $d\mathbf{H}(z) = -\mathbf{H}(z) * d\mathbf{X}(z)$. Letting $\mathbf{W}(z) = \mathbf{H}^{\dagger}(z)$, we have

$$d\mathbf{X}(z) = d\mathbf{W}(z) * \mathbf{W}^{\dagger}(z), \tag{11}$$

which is a nonholonomic differential variable [6] since (11) is not integrable. With this representation of the parameters, we can obtain learning algorithms having the equivariant property [14] since the deviation $d\mathbf{X}(z)$ is independent of a specific $\mathbf{H}(z)$. The relative or the natural gradient of a cost function on the manifold can be automatically derived from this representation [2], [14], [18].

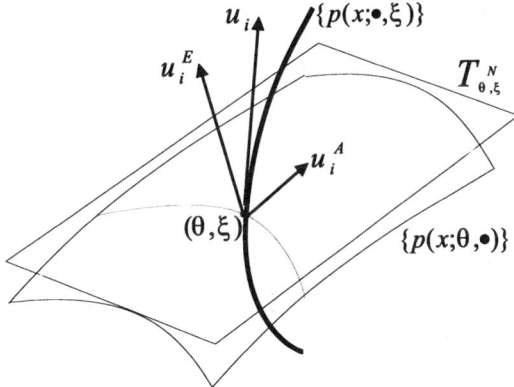

Figure 2: Illustration of orthogonal decomposition of score functions

The derivative of any cost function $l(\mathbf{H}(z))$ with respect to a noncausal filter $\mathbf{X}(z) = \sum_{p=-N}^{N} \mathbf{X}_p z^{-p}$ is defined by

$$\frac{\partial l(\mathbf{H}(z))}{\partial \mathbf{X}(z)} = \sum_{p=-N}^{N} \frac{\partial l(\mathbf{H}(z))}{\partial \mathbf{X}_p} z^{-p} \qquad (12)$$

Now we can easily calculate the score function matrix of noncausal filter $\mathbf{X}(z)$,

$$\frac{\partial \log p(\mathbf{x}; \mathbf{H}(z), r)}{\partial \mathbf{X}(z)} = \sum_{p=-N}^{N} \varphi(\mathbf{y}) \mathbf{y}^T (k-p) z^{-p}, \qquad (13)$$

where $\varphi(\mathbf{y}) = (\varphi_i(y_i), \cdots, \varphi_n(y_n))^T$, $\varphi_i(y_i) = \frac{d \log r_i(y_i)}{dy_i}$. and $\mathbf{y} = \mathbf{H}^\dagger(z)\mathbf{x}$.

5.2 Efficient scores

The efficient scores, denoted by $\mathbf{U}^E(\mathbf{s}; \mathbf{H}(z), r)$, can be obtained by projecting the score function to the space orthogonal to the nuisance tangent space $\mathcal{T}_{\mathbf{H}(z),r}^N$, which is illustrated in figure 2. In this section, we give an explicit form of the efficient scores for blind deconvolution.

Lemma 2 [5] *The tangent nuisance space $\mathcal{T}_{\mathbf{H}(z),r}^N$ is a linear space spanned by the nuisance score functions, denoted by $\mathcal{T}_{\mathbf{H}(z),r}^N = \{\sum_{i=1}^{n} c_i \alpha_i(s_i)\}$, where c_i are coefficients, and $\alpha_i(s_i)$ are arbitrary functions, satisfying the following conditions*

$$E[\alpha_i(s_i)^2] < \infty, \ E[s\alpha_i(s_i)] = 0, \ E[k(s_i)\alpha_i(s_i)] = 0. \qquad (14)$$

We rewrite the score function (13) into the form $\mathbf{U}(\mathbf{s}; \mathbf{H}(z), r) = \sum_{p=-N}^{N} \mathbf{U}_p z^{-p}$, where $U_p = (\varphi(s_i(k))s_j(k-p))_{n \times n}$.

Lemma 3 *The off-diagonal elements $u_{0,ij}(\mathbf{s}; \mathbf{H}(z), r)$, $i \neq j$, and the delay elements $u_{p,ij}(\mathbf{s}; \mathbf{H}(z), r)$, $p \neq 0$, of the score functions are orthogonal to the nuisance tangent space $\mathcal{T}_{\mathbf{H}(z),r}^N$.*

Lemma 4 *The projection of $u_{0,ii}$ to the space orthogonal to the nuisance tangent space $\mathcal{T}_{\mathbf{H}(z),r}^N$ is of the form $w(s_i) = c_0 + c_1 s_i + c_2 k(s_i)$, where c_i are any constants.*

In summary we have the following theorem

Theorem 1 *The efficient score, $\mathbf{U}^E(\mathbf{s}; \mathbf{H}(z), r) = \sum_{p=-N}^{N} \mathbf{U}_p^E z^{-p}$, is given by*

$$\mathbf{U}_p^E = \varphi(\mathbf{s})\mathbf{s}^T(k-p), \text{ for } p \neq 0; \tag{15}$$

$$\mathbf{U}_0^E = \begin{cases} \varphi(\mathbf{s})\mathbf{s}^T, & \text{for off diagonal elements,} \\ c_0 + c_1 s + c_2 k(s), & \text{for diagonal elements.} \end{cases} \tag{16}$$

For the instantaneous mixture case, it has been proven [9] that the semiparametric model for blind separation is information m-curvature free. This is also true in the multichannel blind deconvolution case. As a result, the efficient score function is an estimating function for blind deconvolution. Using this result, we easily derive a family of estimating functions for blind deconvolution

$$\mathbf{F}(\mathbf{x}(k); \mathbf{W}(z)) = \sum_{p=-N}^{N} \varphi(\mathbf{y}(k))\mathbf{y}(k-p)^T z^{-p} - \mathbf{I}, \tag{17}$$

where $\mathbf{y}(k) = \mathbf{W}(z)\mathbf{x}(k)$, and φ is a given function vector. The estimating function is the efficient score function, when $c_0 = c_1 = 0$, $c_2 = 1$ and $k_i(s_i) = \varphi_i(s_i)s_i - 1$.

6 Natural Gradient Learning and its Stability

Ordinary stochastic gradient methods for parameterized systems suffer from slow convergence due to the statistical correlations of the processes signals. While quasi-Newton and related methods can be used to improve convergence, they also suffer from the mass computation and numerical instability, as well as local convergence.

The natural gradient approach was developed to overcome the drawback of the ordinary gradient algorithm in the Riemannian spaces [2, 8, 15]. It has been proven that the natural gradient algorithm is an efficient algorithm in blind separation and blind deconvolution [2].

The efficient score function (the estimating function) gives an efficient search direction for updating filter $\mathbf{X}(z)$. Therefore, the updating rule for $\mathbf{X}(z)$ is described by

$$\mathbf{X}_{k+1}(z) = \mathbf{X}_k(z) - \eta \mathbf{F}(\mathbf{x}(k), \mathbf{W}_k(z)), \tag{18}$$

where η is a learning rate. Since the new parameterization $\mathbf{X}(z)$ is defined by a nonholonomic transformation $d\mathbf{X}(z) = d\mathbf{W}(z) * \mathbf{W}^\dagger(z)$, the deviation of $\mathbf{W}(z)$ is given by

$$\Delta \mathbf{W}(z) = \Delta \mathbf{X}(z) * \mathbf{W}(z). \tag{19}$$

Hence, the natural gradient learning algorithm for $\mathbf{W}(z)$ is described as

$$\mathbf{W}_{k+1}(z) = \mathbf{W}_k(z) - \eta \mathbf{F}(\mathbf{x}(k), \mathbf{W}_k(z)) * \mathbf{W}_k(z), \tag{20}$$

where $\mathbf{F}(\mathbf{x}, \mathbf{W}(z))$ is an estimating function in the form (17). The stability of the algorithm (20) is equivalent to the one of algorithm (18). Consider the averaged version of algorithm (18)

$$\Delta \mathbf{X}(z) = -\eta E[\mathbf{F}(\mathbf{x}(k), \mathbf{W}_k(z))]. \tag{21}$$

Analyzing the variational equation of the above equation and using the mutual independence and i.i.d. properties of source signals, we derive the stability conditions of learning algorithm (21) at vicinity of the true solution

$$m_i + 1 > 0, \quad \kappa_i > 0, \quad \kappa_i \kappa_j \sigma_i^2 \sigma_j^2 > 1, \tag{22}$$

for $i, j = 1, \cdots, n$, where $m_i = E(\varphi'(y_i(k))y_i^2(k))$, $\kappa_i = E[\varphi_i'(y_i)]$, $\sigma_i^2 = E[|y_i|^2]$.

Therefore, we have the following theorem:

Theorem 2 *If the conditions (22) are satisfied, then the natural gradient learning algorithm (20) is locally stable.*

References

[1] S. Amari. *Differential–geometrical methods in statistics, Lecture Notes in Statistics*, volume 28. Springer, Berlin, 1985.

[2] S. Amari. Natural gradient works efficiently in learning. *Neural Computation*, 10:251–276, 1998.

[3] S. Amari. ICA of temporally correlated signals – Learning algorithm. In *Proceeding of 1st Inter. Workshop on Independent Component Analysis and Signal Separation*, pages 37–42, Aussois, France, January, 11-15 1999.

[4] S. Amari. Superefficiency in blind source separation. *IEEE Trans. on Signal Processing*, 47(4):936–944, April 1999.

[5] S. Amari and J.-F. Cardoso. Blind source separation– semiparametric statistical approach. *IEEE Trans. Signal Processing*, 45:2692–2700, Nov. 1997.

[6] S. Amari, T. Chen, and A. Cichocki. Nonholonomic orthogonal constraints in blind source separation. *Neural Comput.*, to be published.

[7] S. Amari and A. Cichocki. Adaptive blind signal processing– neural network approaches. *Proceedings of the IEEE*, 86(10):2026–2048, 1998.

[8] S. Amari, S. Douglas, A. Cichocki, and H. Yang. Multichannel blind deconvolution and equalization using the natural gradient. In *Proc. IEEE Workshop on Signal Processing Adv. in Wireless Communications*, pages 101–104, Paris, France, April 1997.

[9] S. Amari and M. Kawanabe. Estimating functions in semiparametric statistical models. In I. V. Basawa, V.P. Godambe, and R.L. Taylor, editors, *Estimating Functions*, volume 32 of *Monograph Series*, pages 65–81. IMS, 1998.

[10] S. Amari and M. Kumon. Estimation in the presence of infinitely many nuisance parameters in semiparametric statistical models. *Ann. Statistics*, 16:1044–1068, 1988.

[11] A.J. Bell and T.J. Sejnowski. An information maximization approach to blind separation and blind deconvolution. *Neural Computation*, 7:1129–1159, 1995.

[12] P. Bickel, C. Klaassen, Y. Ritov, and J. Wellner. *Efficient and Adaptive Estimation for Semiparametric Models*. The Johns Hopkins Univ. Press, Baltimore and London, 1993.

[13] J.-F Cardoso. Blind signal separation: Statistical principles. *Proceedings of the IEEE*, 86(10):2009–2025, 1998.

[14] J.-F. Cardoso and B. Laheld. Equivariant adaptive source separation. *IEEE Trans. Signal Processing*, SP-43:3017–3029, Dec 1996.

[15] A. Cichocki and R. Unbehauen. Robust neural networks with on-line learning for blind identification and blind separation of sources. *IEEE Trans Circuits and Systems I : Fundamentals Theory and Applications*, 43(11):894–906, 1996.

[16] L. Tong, R.W. Liu, V.C. Soon, and Y.F. Huang. Indeterminacy and identifiability of blind identification. *IEEE Trans. Circuits, Syst.*, 38(5):499–509, May 1991.

[17] H. Yang and S. Amari. Adaptive on-line learning algorithms for blind separation: Maximum entropy and minimal mutual information. *Neural Comput.*, 9:1457–1482, 1997.

[18] L. Zhang, A. Cichocki, and S. Amari. Geometrical structures of FIR manifold and their application to multichannel blind deconvolution. In *Proceeding of NNSP'99*, pages 303–312, Madison, Wisconsin, August 23-25 1999.

[19] L. Zhang, A. Cichocki, and S. Amari. Multichannel blind deconvolution of nonminimum phase systems using information backpropagation. In *Proceedings of the Fifth International Conference on Neural Information Processing(ICONIP'99)*, page 210-216, Perth, Australia, Nov. 16-20 1999.

Some Theoretical Results Concerning the Convergence of Compositions of Regularized Linear Functions

Tong Zhang
Mathematical Sciences Department
IBM T.J. Watson Research Center
Yorktown Heights, NY 10598
tzhang@watson.ibm.com

Abstract

Recently, sample complexity bounds have been derived for problems involving linear functions such as neural networks and support vector machines. In this paper, we extend some theoretical results in this area by deriving dimensional independent covering number bounds for regularized linear functions under certain regularization conditions. We show that such bounds lead to a class of new methods for training linear classifiers with similar theoretical advantages of the support vector machine. Furthermore, we also present a theoretical analysis for these new methods from the asymptotic statistical point of view. This technique provides better description for large sample behaviors of these algorithms.

1 Introduction

In this paper, we are interested in the generalization performance of linear classifiers obtained from certain algorithms. From computational learning theory point of view, such performance measurements, or sample complexity bounds, can be described by a quantity called covering number [11, 15, 17], which measures the size of a parametric function family. For two-class classification problem, the covering number can be bounded by a combinatorial quantity called VC-dimension [12, 17]. Following this work, researchers have found other combinatorial quantities (dimensions) useful for bounding the covering numbers. Consequently, the concept of VC-dimension has been generalized to deal with more general problems, for example in [15, 11].

Recently, Vapnik introduced the concept of support vector machine [16] which has been successful applied to many real problems. This method achieves good generalization by restricting the 2-norm of the weights of a separating hyperplane. A similar technique has been investigated by Bartlett [3], where the author studied the performance of neural networks when the 1-norm of the weights is bounded. The same idea has also been applied in [13] to explain the effectiveness of the boosting algorithm. In this paper, we will extend their results and emphasize the importance of dimension independence. Specifically, we consider the following form of regularization method (with an emphasis on classification problems) which has been widely studied for regression problems both in statistics and in

numerical mathematics:
$$\inf_w E_{x,y} L(w, x, y) = \inf_w E_{x,y} f(w^T xy) + \lambda g(w), \quad (1)$$
where $E_{x,y}$ is the expectation over a distribution of (x, y), and $y \in \{-1, 1\}$ is the binary label of data vector x. To apply this formulation for the purpose of training linear classifiers, we can choose f as a decreasing function, such that $f(\cdot) \geq 0$, and choose $g(w) \geq 0$ as a function that penalizes large w ($\lim_{w \to \infty} g(w) \to \infty$). λ is an appropriately chosen positive parameter to balance the two terms.

The paper is organized as follows. In Section 2, we briefly review the concept of covering numbers as well as the main results related to analyzing the performance of learning algorithms. In Section 3, we introduce the regularization idea. Our main goal is to construct regularization conditions so that dimension independent bounds on covering numbers can be obtained. Section 4 extends results from the previous section to nonlinear compositions of linear functions. In Section 5, we give an asymptotic formula for the generalization performance of a learning algorithm, which will then be used to analyze an instance of SVM. Due to the space limitation, we will only present the main results and discuss their implications. The detailed derivations can be found in [18].

2 Covering numbers

We formulate the learning problem as to find a parameter from random observations to minimize risk: given a loss function $L(\alpha, x)$ and n observations $X_1^n = \{x_1, \ldots, x_n\}$ independently drawn from a fixed but unknown distribution D, we want to find α that minimizes the expected loss over x (*risk*):
$$R(\alpha) = E_x L(\alpha, x) = \int L(\alpha, x) \, dP(x). \quad (2)$$
The most natural method for solving (2) using a limited number of observations is by the *empirical risk minimization* (ERM) method (*cf.* [15, 16]). We simply choose a parameter α that minimizes the observed risk:
$$R(\alpha, X_1^n) = \frac{1}{n} \sum_{i=1}^n L(\alpha, x_i). \quad (3)$$
We denote the parameter obtained in this way as $\alpha_{\text{erm}}(X_1^n)$. The convergence behavior of this method can be analyzed by using the VC theoretical point of view, which relies on the uniform convergence of the empirical risk (the uniform law of large numbers): $\sup_\alpha |R(\alpha, X_1^n) - R(\alpha)|$. Such a bound can be obtained from quantities that measure the size of a Glivenko-Cantelli class. For finite number of indices, the family size can be measured simply by its cardinality. For general function families, a well known quantity to measure the degree of uniform convergence is the *covering number* which can be be dated back to Kolmogrov [8, 9]. The idea is to discretize (which can depend on the data X_1^n) the parameter space into N values $\alpha_1, \ldots, \alpha_N$ so that each $L(\alpha, \cdot)$ can be approximated by $L(\alpha_i, \cdot)$ for some i. We shall only describe a simplified version relevant for our purposes.

Definition 2.1 *Let B be a metric space with metric ρ. Given a norm p, observations $X_1^n = [x_1, \ldots, x_n]$, and vectors $f(\alpha, X_1^n) = [f(\alpha, x_1), \ldots, f(\alpha, x_n)] \in B^n$ parameterized by α, the covering number in p-norm, denoted as $\mathcal{N}_p(f, \epsilon, X_1^n)$, is the minimum number of a collection of vectors $v_1, \ldots, v_m \in B^n$ such that $\forall \alpha, \exists v_i : \|\rho(f(\alpha, X_1^n), v_i)\|_p \leq n^{1/p} \epsilon$. We also denote $\mathcal{N}_p(f, \epsilon, n) = \max_{X_1^n} \mathcal{N}_p(f, \epsilon, X_1^n)$.*

Note that from the definition and the Jensen's inequality, we have $\mathcal{N}_p \leq \mathcal{N}_q$ for $p \leq q$. We will always assume the metric on R to be $|x_1 - x_2|$ if not explicitly specified otherwise. The following theorem is due to Pollard [11]:

Theorem 2.1 ([11]) $\forall n, \epsilon > 0$ and distribution D.

$$P[\sup_\alpha |R(\alpha, X_1^n) - R(\alpha)| > \epsilon] \leq 8E[\mathcal{N}_1(L, \epsilon/8, X_1^n)] \exp(\frac{-n\epsilon^2}{128M^2}),$$

where $M = \sup_{\alpha,x} L(\alpha, x) - \inf_{\alpha,x} L(\alpha, x)$, and $X_1^n = \{x_1, \ldots, x_n\}$ are independently drawn from D.

The constants in the above theorem can be improved for certain problems; see [4, 6, 15, 16] for related results. However, they yield very similar bounds. The result most relevant for this paper is a lemma in [3] where the 1-norm covering number is replaced by the ∞-norm covering number. The latter can be bounded by a scale-sensitive combinatorial dimension [1], which can be bounded from the 1-norm covering number if this covering number does not depend on n. These results can replace Theorem 2.1 to yield better estimates under certain circumstances.

Since Bartlett's lemma in [3] is only for binary loss functions, we shall give a generalization so that it is comparable to Theorem 2.1:

Theorem 2.2 Let f_1 and f_2 be two functions: $R^n \to [0, 1]$ such that $|y_1 - y_2| \leq \gamma$ implies $f_1(y_1) \leq f_3(y_2) \leq f_2(y_1)$ where $f_3 : R^n \to [0, 1]$ is a reference separating function, then

$$P[\sup_\alpha [E_x f_1(L(\alpha, x)) - E_{X_1^n} f_2(L(\alpha, x))] > \epsilon] \leq 4E[\mathcal{N}_\infty(L, \gamma, X_1^n)] \exp(\frac{-n\epsilon^2}{32}).$$

Note that in the extreme case that some choice of α achieves perfect generalization: $E_x f_2(L(\alpha, x)) = 0$, and assume that our choices of $\alpha(X_1^n)$ always satisfy the condition $E_{X_1^n} f_2(L(\alpha, x)) = 0$, then better bounds can be obtained by using a refined version of the Chernoff bound.

3 Covering number bounds for linear systems

In this section, we present a few new bounds on covering numbers for the following form of real valued loss functions:

$$L(w, x) = x^T w = \sum_{i=1}^{d} x_i w_i. \tag{4}$$

As we shall see later, these bounds are relevant to the convergence properties of (1). Note that in order to apply Theorem 2.1, since $\mathcal{N}_1 \leq \mathcal{N}_2$, therefore it is sufficient to estimate $\mathcal{N}_2(L, \epsilon, n)$ for $\epsilon > 0$. It is clear that $\mathcal{N}_2(L, \epsilon, n)$ is not finite if no restrictions on x and w are imposed. Therefore in the following, we will assume that each $\|x_i\|_p$ is bounded, and study conditions of $\|w\|_q$ so that $\log \mathcal{N}(f, \epsilon, n)$ is independent or weakly dependent of d.

Our first result generalizes a theorem of Bartlett [3]. The original results is with $p = \infty$ and $q = 1$, and the related technique has also appeared in [10, 13]. The proof uses a lemma that is attributed to Maurey (cf. [2, 7]).

Theorem 3.1 If $\|x_i\|_p \leq b$ and $\|w\|_q \leq a$, where $1/p + 1/q = 1$ and $2 \leq p \leq \infty$, then

$$\log_2 \mathcal{N}_2(L, \epsilon, n) \leq \lceil \frac{a^2 b^2}{\epsilon^2} \rceil \log_2(2d + 1).$$

The above bound on the covering number depends logarithmically on d, which is already quite weak (as compared to linear dependency on d in the standard situation). However, the bound in Theorem 3.1 is not tight for $p < \infty$. For example, the following theorem improves the above bound for $p = 2$. Our technique of proof relies on the SVD decomposition [5] for matrices, which improves a similar result in [14] by a logarithmic factor.

Theorem 3.2 If $\|x_i\|_2 \leq b$ and $\|w\|_2 \leq a$, then
$$\log_2 \mathcal{N}_2(L, \epsilon, n) \leq \lceil \frac{2a^2 b^2}{\epsilon^2} \rceil \log_2(4a^2 b^2/\epsilon^2 + 1).$$

The next theorem shows that if $1/p + 1/q > 1$, then the 2-norm covering number is also independent of dimension.

Theorem 3.3 Let $L(w, x) = x^T w$. If $\|x_i\|_p \leq b$ and $\|w\|_q \leq a$, where $1 \leq q \leq 2$ and $\delta = 1/p + 1/q - 1 > 0$, then
$$\log_2 \mathcal{N}_2(L, \epsilon, n) \leq \lceil \frac{4a^2 b^2}{\epsilon^2} \rceil \log_2(2(2ab/\epsilon)^{1/\delta} + 1).$$

One consequence of this theorem is a potentially refined explanation for the boosting algorithm. In [13], the boosting algorithm has been analyzed by using a technique related to results in [3] which essentially rely on Theorem 3.1 with $p = \infty$. Unfortunately, the bound contains a logarithmic dependency on d (in the most general case) which does not seem to fully explain the fact that in many cases the performance of the boosting algorithm keeps improving as d increases. However, this seemingly mysterious behavior might be better understood from Theorem 3.3 under the assumption that the data is more restricted than simply being ∞-norm bounded. For example, when the contribution of the wrong predictions is bounded by a constant (or grow very slowly as d increases), then we can regard its p-th norm bounded for some $p < \infty$. In this case, Theorem 3.3 implies dimensional independent generalization.

If we want to apply Theorem 2.2, then it is necessary to obtain bounds for infinity-norm covering numbers. The following theorem gives such bounds by using a result from online learning.

Theorem 3.4 If $\|x_i\|_p \leq b$ and $\|w\|_q \leq a$, where $2 \leq p < \infty$ and $1/p + 1/q = 1$, then $\forall \epsilon > 0$,
$$\log_2 \mathcal{N}_\infty(L, \epsilon, n) \leq 36(p-1)\frac{a^2 b^2}{\epsilon^2} \log_2[2\lceil 4ab/\epsilon + 2\rceil n + 1].$$

In the case of $p = \infty$, an entropy condition can be used to obtain dimensional independent covering number bounds.

Definition 3.1 Let $\mu = [\mu_i]$ be a vector with positive entries such that $\|\mu\|_1 = 1$ (in this case, we call μ a distribution vector). Let $x = [x_i] \neq 0$ be a vector of the same length, then we define the weighted relative entropy of x with respect to μ as:
$$\text{entro}_\mu(x) = \sum_i |x_i| \ln \frac{|x_i|}{\mu_i \|x\|_1}.$$

Theorem 3.5 Given a distribution vector μ, If $\|x_i\|_\infty \leq b$ and $\|w\|_1 \leq a$ and $\text{entro}_\mu(w) \leq c$, where we assume that w has non-negative entries, then $\forall \epsilon > 0$,
$$\log_2 \mathcal{N}_\infty(L, \epsilon, n) \leq \frac{36 b^2(a^2 + ac)}{\epsilon^2} \log_2[2\lceil 4ab/\epsilon + 2\rceil n + 1].$$

Theorems in this section can be combined with Theorem 4.1 to form more complex covering number bounds for nonlinear compositions of linear functions.

4 Nonlinear extensions

Consider the following system:
$$L([\alpha, w], x) = f(g(\alpha, x) + w^T h(\alpha, x)), \quad (5)$$
where x is the observation, and $[\alpha, w]$ is the parameter. We assume that f is a nonlinear function with bounded total variation.

Definition 4.1 *A function $f : R \to R$ is said to satisfy the Lipschitz condition with parameter γ if $\forall x, y$: $|f(x) - f(y)| \leq \gamma |x - y|$.*

Definition 4.2 *The total variation of a function $f : R \to R$ is defined as*
$$\mathrm{TV}(f, x) = \sup_{x_0 < x_1 \cdots < x_\ell \leq x} \sum_{i=1}^{\ell} |f(x_i) - f(x_{i-1})|.$$
We also denote $\mathrm{TV}(f, \infty)$ as $\mathrm{TV}(f)$.

Theorem 4.1 *If $L([\alpha, w], x) = f(g(\alpha, x) + w^T h(\alpha, x))$, where $\mathrm{TV}(f) < \infty$ and f is Lipschitz with parameter γ. Assume also that w is a d-dimensional vector and $\|w\|_q \leq c$, then $\forall \epsilon_1, \epsilon_2 > 0$, and $n > 2(d+1)$:*
$$\log_2 \mathcal{N}_r(L, \epsilon_1 + \epsilon_2, n) \leq (d+1) \log_2 [\frac{en}{d+1} \max(\lfloor \frac{\mathrm{TV}(f)}{2\epsilon_1} \rfloor, 1)] + \log_2 \mathcal{N}_r([g, h], \epsilon_2/\gamma, n),$$
where the metric of $[g, h]$ is defined as $|g_1 - g_2| + c\|h_1 - h_2\|_p$ $(1/p + 1/q = 1)$.

Example 4.1 Consider classification by hyperplane: $L(w, x) = I(w^T x < 0)$ where I is the set indicator function. Let $L'(w, x) = f_0(w^T x)$ be another loss function where
$$f_0(z) = \begin{cases} 1 & z < 0 \\ 1 - z & z \in [0, 1] \\ 0 & z > 1 \end{cases}.$$

Instead of using ERM for estimating parameter that minimizes the risk of L, consider the scheme of minimize empirical risk associated with L', under the assumption that $\|x\|_2 \leq b$ and constraint that $\|w\|_2 \leq a$. Denote the estimated parameter by w_n. It follows from the covering number bounds and Theorem 2.1 that with probability of at least $1 - \eta$:
$$E_x I(w_n^T x \leq 0) \leq \inf_{\|w\|_2 \leq a} E_x f_0(w^T x) + O(\sqrt{\frac{n^{1/2} ab \ln(nab + 2) + \ln \frac{1}{\eta}}{n}}).$$
If we apply a slight generalization of Theorem 2.2 and the covering number bound of Theorem 3.4, then with probability of at least $1 - \eta$:
$$E_x I(w_n^T x \leq 0) \leq E_{X_1^n} I(w_n^T x \leq 2\gamma) + O(\sqrt{\frac{1}{n}(\frac{a^2 b^2}{\gamma^2} \ln(ab/\gamma + 2) + \ln n + \ln \frac{1}{\eta})})$$
for all $\gamma \in (0, 1]$. □

Bounds given in this paper can be applied to show that under appropriate regularization conditions and assumptions on the data, methods based on (1) lead to generalization performances of the form $\tilde{O}(1/\sqrt{n})$, where $\tilde{O}$ symbol (which is independent of d) is used to indicate that the hidden constant may include a polynomial dependency on $\log(n)$. It is also important to note that in certain cases, λ will not appear (or it has a small influence on the convergence) in the constant of $\tilde{O}$, as being demonstrated by the example in the next section.

5 Asymptotic analysis

The convergence results in the previous sections are in the form of VC style convergence in probability, which has a combinatorial flavor. However, for problems with differentiable function families involving vector parameters, it is often convenient to derive precise asymptotic results using the differential structure.

Assume that the parameter $\alpha \in R^m$ in (2) is a vector and L is a smooth function. Let α^* denote the optimal parameter; ∇_α denote the derivative with respect to α; and $\Psi(\alpha, x)$ denote $\nabla_\alpha L(\alpha, x)$. Assume that

$$V = \int \nabla_\alpha \Psi(\alpha^*, x) \, dP(x)$$

$$U = \int \Psi(\alpha^*, x) \Psi(\alpha^*, x)^T \, dP(x).$$

Then under certain regularity conditions, the asymptotic expected generalization error is given by

$$E\, R(\alpha_{\mathrm{erm}}) = R(\alpha^*) + \frac{1}{2n}\mathrm{tr}(V^{-1}U). \tag{6}$$

More generally, for any evaluation function $h(\alpha)$ such that $\nabla h(\alpha^*) = 0$:

$$E\, h(\alpha_{\mathrm{erm}}) \approx h(\alpha^*) + \frac{1}{2n}\mathrm{tr}(V^{-1}\nabla^2 h \cdot V^{-1}U), \tag{7}$$

where $\nabla^2 h$ is the Hessian matrix of h at α^*. Note that this approach assumes that the optimal solution is unique. These results are exact asymptotically and provide better bounds than those from the standard PAC analysis.

Example 5.1 We would like to study a form of the support vector machine: Consider $L(\alpha, x) = f(\alpha^T x) + \frac{1}{2}\lambda \alpha^2$,

$$f(z) = \begin{cases} 1 - z & z \leq 1 \\ 0 & z > 1 \end{cases}.$$

Because of the discontinuity in the derivative of f, the asymptotic formula may not hold. However, if we make an assumption on the smoothness of the distribution x, then the expectation of the derivative over x can still be smooth. In this case, the smoothness of f itself is not crucial. Furthermore, in a separate report, we shall illustrate that similar small sample bounds without any assumption on the smoothness of the distribution can be obtained by using techniques related to asymptotic analysis.

Consider the optimal parameter α^* and let $S = \{x : \alpha^{*T} x \leq 1\}$. Note that $\lambda \alpha^* = E_{x \in S} x$, and $U = E_{x \in S}(x - E_{x \in S} x)(x - E_{x \in S} x)^T$. Assume that $\exists \gamma > 0$ s.t. $P(\alpha^{*T} x \leq \gamma) = 0$, then $V = \lambda I + B$ where B is a positive semi-definite matrix. It follows that

$$\mathrm{tr}(V^{-1}U) \leq \mathrm{tr}(U)/\lambda \leq \frac{E_{x \in S} x^2}{E_{x \in S} \alpha^{*T} x}\|\alpha^*\|_2^2 \leq \sup \|x\|_2^2 \|\alpha^*\|_2^2 / \gamma.$$

Now, consider α_n obtained from observations $X_1^n = [x_1, \ldots, x_n]$ by minimizing empirical risk associated with loss function $L(\alpha, x)$, then

$$E_x L(\alpha_{\mathrm{emp}}, x) \leq \inf_\alpha E_x L(\alpha, x) + \frac{1}{2\gamma n} \sup \|x\|_2^2 \|\alpha^*\|_2^2$$

asymptotically. Let $\lambda \to 0$, this scheme becomes the optimal separating hyperplane [16]. This asymptotic bound is better than typical PAC bounds with fixed λ. □

Note that although the bound obtained in the above example is very similar to the mistake bound for the perceptron online update algorithm, we may in practice obtain much better estimates from (6) by plugging in the empirical data.

References

[1] N. Alon, S. Ben-David, N. Cesa-Bianchi, and D. Haussler. Scale-sensitive dimensions, uniform convergence, and learnability. *Journal of the ACM*, 44(4):615–631, 1997.

[2] A.R. Barron. Universal approximation bounds for superpositions of a sigmoidal function. *IEEE Transactions on Information Theory*, 39(3):930–945, 1993.

[3] P.L. Bartlett. The sample complexity of pattern classification with neural networks: the size of the weights is more important than the size of the network. *IEEE Transactions on Information Theory*, 44(2):525–536, 1998.

[4] R.M. Dudley. *A course on empirical processes*, volume 1097 of *Lecture Notes in Mathematics*. 1984.

[5] G.H. Golub and C.F. Van Loan. *Matrix computations*. Johns Hopkins University Press, Baltimore, MD, third edition, 1996.

[6] D. Haussler. Generalizing the PAC model: sample size bounds from metric dimension-based uniform convergence results. In *Proc. 30th IEEE Symposium on Foundations of Computer Science*, pages 40–45, 1989.

[7] Lee K. Jones. A simple lemma on greedy approximation in Hilbert space and convergence rates for projection pursuit regression and neural network training. *Ann. Statist.*, 20(1):608–613, 1992.

[8] A.N. Kolmogorov. Asymptotic characteristics of some completely bounded metric spaces. *Dokl. Akad. Nauk. SSSR*, 108:585–589, 1956.

[9] A.N. Kolmogorov and V.M. Tihomirov. ϵ-entropy and ϵ-capacity of sets in functional spaces. *Amer. Math. Soc. Transl.*, 17(2):277–364, 1961.

[10] Wee Sun Lee, P.L. Bartlett, and R.C. Williamson. Efficient agnostic learning of neural networks with bounded fan-in. *IEEE Transactions on Information Theory*, 42(6):2118–2132, 1996.

[11] D. Pollard. *Convergence of stochastic processes*. Springer-Verlag, New York, 1984.

[12] N. Sauer. On the density of families of sets. *Journal of Combinatorial Theory (Series A)*, 13:145–147, 1972.

[13] Robert E. Schapire, Yoav Freund, Peter Bartlett, and Wee Sun Lee. Boosting the margin: a new explanation for the effectiveness of voting methods. *Ann. Statist.*, 26(5):1651–1686, 1998.

[14] J. Shawe-Taylor, P.L. Bartlett, R.C. Williamson, and M. Anthony. Structural risk minimization over data-dependent hierarchies. *IEEE Trans. Inf. Theory*, 44(5):1926–1940, 1998.

[15] V.N. Vapnik. *Estimation of dependences based on empirical data*. Springer-Verlag, New York, 1982. Translated from the Russian by Samuel Kotz.

[16] V.N. Vapnik. *The nature of statistical learning theory*. Springer-Verlag, New York, 1995.

[17] V.N. Vapnik and A.J. Chervonenkis. On the uniform convergence of relative frequencies of events to their probabilities. *Theory of Probability and Applications*, 16:264–280, 1971.

[18] Tong Zhang. Analysis of regularized linear functions for classification problems. Technical Report RC-21572, IBM, 1999.

PART IV
ALGORITHMS AND ARCHITECTURE

Robust Full Bayesian Methods for Neural Networks

Christophe Andrieu[*]
Cambridge University
Engineering Department
Cambridge CB2 1PZ
England
ca226@eng.cam.ac.uk

João FG de Freitas
UC Berkeley
Computer Science
387 Soda Hall, Berkeley
CA 94720-1776 USA
jfgf@cs.berkeley.edu

Arnaud Doucet
Cambridge University
Engineering Department
Cambridge CB2 1PZ
England
ad2@eng.cam.ac.uk

Abstract

In this paper, we propose a full Bayesian model for neural networks. This model treats the model dimension (number of neurons), model parameters, regularisation parameters and noise parameters as random variables that need to be estimated. We then propose a reversible jump Markov chain Monte Carlo (MCMC) method to perform the necessary computations. We find that the results are not only better than the previously reported ones, but also appear to be robust with respect to the prior specification. Moreover, we present a geometric convergence theorem for the algorithm.

1 Introduction

In the early nineties, Buntine and Weigend (1991) and Mackay (1992) showed that a principled Bayesian learning approach to neural networks can lead to many improvements [1,2]. In particular, Mackay showed that by approximating the distributions of the weights with Gaussians and adopting smoothing priors, it is possible to obtain estimates of the weights and output variances and to automatically set the regularisation coefficients. Neal (1996) cast the net much further by introducing advanced Bayesian simulation methods, specifically the hybrid Monte Carlo method, into the analysis of neural networks [3]. Bayesian sequential Monte Carlo methods have also been shown to provide good training results, especially in time-varying scenarios [4]. More recently, Rios Insua and Müller (1998) and Holmes and Mallick (1998) have addressed the issue of selecting the number of hidden neurons with growing and pruning algorithms from a Bayesian perspective [5,6]. In particular, they apply the reversible jump Markov Chain Monte Carlo (MCMC) algorithm of Green [7] to feed-forward sigmoidal networks and radial basis function (RBF) networks to obtain joint estimates of the number of neurons and weights.

We also apply the reversible jump MCMC simulation algorithm to RBF networks so as to compute the joint posterior distribution of the radial basis parameters and the number of basis functions. However, we advance this area of research in two important directions. Firstly, we propose a full hierarchical prior for RBF networks. That

---
[*]Authorship based on alphabetical order.

is, we adopt a full Bayesian model, which accounts for model order uncertainty and regularisation, and show that the results appear to be robust with respect to the prior specification. Secondly, we present a geometric convergence theorem for the algorithm. The complexity of the problem does not allow for a comprehensive discussion in this short paper. We have, therefore, focused on describing our objectives, the Bayesian model, convergence theorem and results. Readers are encouraged to consult our technical report for further results and implementation details [8][1].

2 Problem statement

Many physical processes may be described by the following nonlinear, multivariate input-output mapping:

$$\mathbf{y}_t = \mathbf{f}(\mathbf{x}_t) + \mathbf{n}_t \quad (1)$$

where $\mathbf{x}_t \in \mathbb{R}^d$ corresponds to a group of input variables, $\mathbf{y}_t \in \mathbb{R}^c$ to the target variables, $\mathbf{n}_t \in \mathbb{R}^c$ to an unknown noise process and $t = \{1, 2, \cdots\}$ is an index variable over the data. In this context, the learning problem involves computing an approximation to the function $\mathbf{f}$ and estimating the characteristics of the noise process given a set of N input-output observations: $\mathcal{O} = \{\mathbf{x}_1, \mathbf{x}_2, \cdots, \mathbf{x}_N, \mathbf{y}_1, \mathbf{y}_2, \cdots, \mathbf{y}_N\}$ Typical examples include regression, where $\mathbf{y}_{1:N,1:c}$[2] is continuous; classification, where $\mathbf{y}$ corresponds to a group of classes and nonlinear dynamical system identification, where the inputs and targets correspond to several delayed versions of the signals under consideration.

We adopt the approximation scheme of Holmes and Mallick (1998), consisting of a mixture of k RBFs and a linear regression term. Yet, the work can be easily extended to other regression models. More precisely, our model $\mathcal{M}$ is:

$$\begin{aligned} \mathcal{M}_0 : &\quad \mathbf{y}_t = b + \beta' \mathbf{x}_t + \mathbf{n}_t &\quad k = 0 \\ \mathcal{M}_k : &\quad \mathbf{y}_t = \sum_{j=1}^{k} \mathbf{a}_j \phi(\|\mathbf{x}_t - \boldsymbol{\mu}_j\|) + b + \beta' \mathbf{x}_t + \mathbf{n}_t &\quad k \geq 1 \end{aligned} \quad (2)$$

where $\|\cdot\|$ denotes a distance metric (usually Euclidean or Mahalanobis), $\boldsymbol{\mu}_j \in \mathbb{R}^d$ denotes the j-th RBF centre for a model with k RBFs, $\mathbf{a}_j \in \mathbb{R}^c$ the j-th RBF amplitude and $b \in \mathbb{R}^c$ and $\beta \in \mathbb{R}^d \times \mathbb{R}^c$ the linear regression parameters. The noise sequence $\mathbf{n}_t \in \mathbb{R}^c$ is assumed to be zero-mean white Gaussian. It is important to mention that although we have not explicitly indicated the dependency of b, β and $\mathbf{n}_t$ on k, these parameters are indeed affected by the value of k. For convenience, we express our approximation model in vector-matrix form:

$$\begin{bmatrix} y_{1,1} \cdots y_{1,c} \\ y_{2,1} \cdots y_{2,c} \\ \vdots \\ y_{N,1} \cdots y_{N,c} \end{bmatrix} = \begin{bmatrix} 1 & \mathbf{x}_{1,1} \cdots \mathbf{x}_{1,d} & \phi(\mathbf{x}_1, \boldsymbol{\mu}_1) \cdots \phi(\mathbf{x}_1, \boldsymbol{\mu}_k) \\ 1 & \mathbf{x}_{2,1} \cdots \mathbf{x}_{2,d} & \phi(\mathbf{x}_2, \boldsymbol{\mu}_1) \cdots \phi(\mathbf{x}_2, \boldsymbol{\mu}_k) \\ \vdots & \vdots & \vdots \\ 1 & \mathbf{x}_{N,1} \cdots \mathbf{x}_{N,d} & \phi(\mathbf{x}_N, \boldsymbol{\mu}_1) \cdots \phi(\mathbf{x}_N, \boldsymbol{\mu}_k) \end{bmatrix} \begin{bmatrix} b_1 \cdots b_c \\ \beta_{1,1} \cdots \beta_{1,c} \\ \vdots \\ \beta_{d,1} \cdots \beta_{d,c} \\ \mathbf{a}_{1,1} \cdots \mathbf{a}_{1,c} \\ \vdots \\ \mathbf{a}_{k,1} \cdots \mathbf{a}_{k,c} \end{bmatrix} + \mathbf{n}_{1:N}$$

---

[1] The software is available at http://www.cs.berkeley.edu/~jfgf.

[2] $\mathbf{y}_{1:N,1:c}$ is an N by c matrix, where N is the number of data and c the number of outputs. We adopt the notation $\mathbf{y}_{1:N,j} \triangleq (y_{1,j}, y_{2,j}, \ldots, y_{N,j})'$ to denote all the observations corresponding to the j-th output (j-th column of $\mathbf{y}$). To simplify the notation, $\mathbf{y}_t$ is equivalent to $\mathbf{y}_{t,1:c}$. That is, if one index does not appear, it is implied that we are referring to all of its possible values. Similarly, $\mathbf{y}$ is equivalent to $\mathbf{y}_{1:N,1:c}$. We will favour the shorter notation and only adopt the longer notation to avoid ambiguities and emphasise certain dependencies.

where the noise process is assumed to be normally distributed $\mathbf{n}_t \sim \mathcal{N}(0, \sigma_i^2)$ for $i = 1, \ldots, c$. In shorter notation, we have:

$$\mathbf{y} = \mathbf{D}(\boldsymbol{\mu}_{1:k,1:d}, \mathbf{x}_{1:N,1:d})\boldsymbol{\alpha}_{1:1+d+k,1:c} + \mathbf{n}_t \quad (3)$$

We assume here that the number k of RBFs and their parameters $\boldsymbol{\theta} \triangleq \{\boldsymbol{\alpha}_{1:m,1:c}, \boldsymbol{\mu}_{1:k,1:d}, \sigma_{1:c}^2\}$, with $m = 1 + d + k$, are unknown. Given the data set $\{\mathbf{x}, \mathbf{y}\}$, our objective is to estimate k and $\boldsymbol{\theta} \in \Theta_k$.

3 Bayesian model and aims

We follow a Bayesian approach where the unknowns k and $\boldsymbol{\theta}$ are regarded as being drawn from appropriate prior distributions. These priors reflect our degree of belief on the relevant values of these quantities [9]. Furthermore, we adopt a hierarchical prior structure that enables us to treat the priors' parameters (hyper-parameters) as random variables drawn from suitable distributions (hyper-priors). That is, instead of fixing the hyper-parameters arbitrarily, we acknowledge that there is an inherent uncertainty in what we think their values should be. By devising probabilistic models that deal with this uncertainty, we are able to implement estimation techniques that are robust to the specification of the hyper-priors.

The overall parameter space $\Theta \times \Psi$ can be written as a finite union of subspaces $\Theta \times \Psi = (\cup_{k=0}^{k_{\max}} \{k\} \times \Theta_k) \times \Psi$ where $\Theta_0 \triangleq (\mathbb{R}^{d+1})^c \times (\mathbb{R}^+)^c$ and $\Theta_k \triangleq (\mathbb{R}^{d+1+k})^c \times (\mathbb{R}^+)^c \times \Omega_k$ for $k \in \{1, \ldots, k_{\max}\}$. That is, $\boldsymbol{\alpha} \in (\mathbb{R}^{d+1+k})^c$, $\boldsymbol{\sigma} \in (\mathbb{R}^+)^c$ and $\boldsymbol{\mu} \in \Omega_k$. The hyper-parameter space $\Psi \triangleq (\mathbb{R}^+)^{c+1}$, with elements $\psi \triangleq \{\Lambda, \delta^2\}$, will be discussed at the end of this section. The space of the radial basis centres Ω_k is defined as a compact set including the input data: $\Omega_k \triangleq \{\boldsymbol{\mu}; \boldsymbol{\mu}_{1:k,i} \in [\min(\mathbf{x}_{1:N,i}) - \iota\Xi_i, \max(\mathbf{x}_{1:N,i}) + \iota\Xi_i]^k$ for $i = 1, \ldots, d$ with $\mu_{j,i} \neq \mu_{l,i}$ for $j \neq l\}$. $\Xi_i = \|\max(\mathbf{x}_{1:N,i}) - \min(\mathbf{x}_{1:N,i})\|$ denotes the Euclidean distance for the i-th dimension of the input and ι is a user specified parameter that we only need to consider if we wish to place basis functions outside the region where the input data lie. That is, we allow Ω_k to include the space of the input data and extend it by a factor which is proportional to the spread of the input data. The hyper-volume of this space is: $\Im^k \triangleq \left(\prod_{i=1}^d (1 + 2\iota)\Xi_i\right)^k$.

The maximum number of basis functions is defined as $k_{\max} \triangleq (N - (d+1))$ We also define $\Omega \triangleq \cup_{k=0}^{k_{\max}} \{k\} \times \Omega_k$ with $\Omega_0 \triangleq \emptyset$. Under the assumption of independent outputs given $(k, \boldsymbol{\theta})$, the likelihood $p(\mathbf{y}|k, \boldsymbol{\theta}, \psi, \mathbf{x})$ for the approximation model described in the previous section is:

$$\prod_{i=1}^{c} (2\pi\sigma_i^2)^{-N/2} \exp\left(-\frac{1}{2\sigma_i^2}(\mathbf{y}_{1:N,i} - \mathbf{D}(\boldsymbol{\mu}_{1:k}, \mathbf{x})\boldsymbol{\alpha}_{1:m,i})'(\mathbf{y}_{1:N,i} - \mathbf{D}(\boldsymbol{\mu}_{1:k}, \mathbf{x})\boldsymbol{\alpha}_{1:m,i})\right)$$

We assume the following structure for the prior distribution:

$$p(k, \boldsymbol{\theta}, \psi) = p(\boldsymbol{\alpha}_{1:m}|k, \sigma^2, \delta^2) p(\boldsymbol{\mu}_{1:k}|k) p(k|\Lambda) p(\sigma^2) p(\Lambda) p(\delta^2)$$

where the scale parameters σ_i^2, are assumed to be independent of the hyper-parameters (i.e. $p(\sigma^2|\Lambda, \delta^2) = p(\sigma^2)$), independent of each other ($p(\sigma^2) = \prod_{i=1}^{c} p(\sigma_i^2)$) and distributed according to conjugate inverse-Gamma prior distributions: $\sigma_i^2 \sim \mathcal{IG}\left(\frac{v_0}{2}, \frac{\gamma_0}{2}\right)$. When $v_0 = 0$ and $\gamma_0 = 0$, we obtain Jeffreys' uninformative prior [9]. For a given σ^2, the prior distribution $p(k, \boldsymbol{\alpha}_{1:m}, \boldsymbol{\mu}_{1:k}|\sigma^2, \Lambda, \delta^2)$ is:

$$\left[\prod_{i=1}^{c} |2\pi\sigma_i^2\delta_i^2\mathbf{I}_m|^{-1/2} \exp\left(-\frac{1}{2\sigma_i^2\delta_i^2}\boldsymbol{\alpha}'_{1:m,i}\boldsymbol{\alpha}_{1:m,i}\right)\right]\left[\frac{\mathbb{I}_\Omega(k, \boldsymbol{\mu}_{1:k})}{\Im^k}\right]\left[\frac{\Lambda^k/k!}{\sum_{j=0}^{k_{\max}} \Lambda^j/j!}\right]$$

where $\mathbf{I}_m$ denotes the identity matrix of size $m \times m$ and $\mathbb{I}_\Omega(k, \boldsymbol{\mu}_{1:k})$ is the indicator function of the set Ω (1 if $(k, \boldsymbol{\mu}_{1:k}) \in \Omega$, 0 otherwise).

The prior model order distribution $p(k|\Lambda)$ is a truncated Poisson distribution. Conditional upon k, the RBF centres are uniformly distributed. Finally, conditional upon $(k, \boldsymbol{\mu}_{1:k})$, the coefficients $\boldsymbol{\alpha}_{1:m,i}$ are assumed to be zero-mean Gaussian with variance $\delta_i^2 \sigma_i^2$. The hyper-parameters $\boldsymbol{\delta}^2 \in (\mathbb{R}^+)^c$ and $\Lambda \in \mathbb{R}^+$ can be respectively interpreted as the expected signal to noise ratios and the expected number of radial basis. We assume that they are independent of each other, i.e. $p(\Lambda, \boldsymbol{\delta}^2) = p(\Lambda)p(\boldsymbol{\delta}^2)$. Moreover, $p(\boldsymbol{\delta}^2) = \prod_{i=1}^c p(\delta_i^2)$. As $\boldsymbol{\delta}^2$ is a scale parameter, we ascribe a vague conjugate prior density to it: $\delta_i^2 \sim \mathcal{IG}(\alpha_{\delta^2}, \beta_{\delta^2})$ for $i = 1, \ldots, c$, with $\alpha_{\delta^2} = 2$ and $\beta_{\delta^2} > 0$. The variance of this hyper-prior with $\alpha_{\delta^2} = 2$ is infinite. We apply the same method to Λ by setting an uninformative conjugate prior [9]: $\Lambda \sim \mathcal{Ga}(1/2 + \varepsilon_1, \varepsilon_2)$ $(\varepsilon_i \ll 1\; i = 1, 2)$.

3.1 Estimation and inference aims

The Bayesian inference of k, $\boldsymbol{\theta}$ and $\boldsymbol{\psi}$ is based on the joint posterior distribution $p(k, \boldsymbol{\theta}, \boldsymbol{\psi}|\mathbf{x}, \mathbf{y})$ obtained from Bayes' theorem. Our aim is to estimate this joint distribution from which, by standard probability marginalisation and transformation techniques, one can "theoretically" obtain all posterior features of interest. We propose here to use the reversible jump MCMC method to perform the necessary computations, see [8] for details. MCMC techniques were introduced in the mid 1950's in statistical physics and started appearing in the fields of applied statistics, signal processing and neural networks in the 1980's and 1990's [3,5,6,10,11]. The key idea is to build an ergodic Markov chain $(k^{(i)}, \boldsymbol{\theta}^{(i)}, \boldsymbol{\psi}^{(i)})_{i \in \mathbb{N}}$ whose equilibrium distribution is the desired posterior distribution. Under weak additional assumptions, the $P \gg 1$ samples generated by the Markov chain are asymptotically distributed according to the posterior distribution and thus allow easy evaluation of all posterior features of interest. For example:

$$\widehat{p}(k = j|\mathbf{x}, \mathbf{y}) = \frac{1}{P}\sum_{i=1}^{P} \mathbb{I}_{\{j\}}(k^{(i)}) \text{ and } \widehat{\mathbb{E}}(\boldsymbol{\theta}|k = j, \mathbf{x}, \mathbf{y}) = \frac{\sum_{i=1}^{P} \boldsymbol{\theta}^{(i)} \mathbb{I}_{\{j\}}(k^{(i)})}{\sum_{i=1}^{P} \mathbb{I}_{\{j\}}(k^{(i)})} \quad (4)$$

In addition, we can obtain predictions, such as:

$$\widehat{\mathbb{E}}(\mathbf{y}_{N+1}|\mathbf{x}_{1:N+1}, \mathbf{y}_{1:N}) = \frac{1}{P}\sum_{i=1}^{P} \mathbf{D}(\boldsymbol{\mu}_{1:k}^{(i)}, \mathbf{x}_{N+1})\boldsymbol{\alpha}_{1:m}^{(i)} \quad (5)$$

3.2 Integration of the nuisance parameters

According to Bayes theorem, we can obtain the posterior distribution as follows:

$$p(k, \boldsymbol{\theta}, \boldsymbol{\psi}|\mathbf{x}, \mathbf{y}) \propto p(\mathbf{y}|k, \boldsymbol{\theta}, \boldsymbol{\psi}, \mathbf{x})p(k, \boldsymbol{\theta}, \boldsymbol{\psi})$$

In our case, we can integrate with respect to $\boldsymbol{\alpha}_{1:m}$ (Gaussian distribution) and with respect to σ_i^2 (inverse Gamma distribution) to obtain the following expression for the posterior:

$$p(k, \boldsymbol{\mu}_{1:k}, \Lambda, \boldsymbol{\delta}^2|\mathbf{x}, \mathbf{y}) \propto \left[\prod_{i=1}^{c} (\delta_i^2)^{-m/2}|\mathbf{M}_{i,k}|^{1/2} \left(\frac{\gamma_0 + \mathbf{y}'_{1:N,i}\mathbf{P}_{i,k}\mathbf{y}_{1:N,i}}{2}\right)^{(-\frac{N+v_0}{2})}\right] \times$$

$$\left[\frac{\mathbb{I}_\Omega(k, \boldsymbol{\mu}_k)}{\mathfrak{S}^k}\right]\left[\frac{\Lambda^k/k!}{\sum_{j=0}^{k_{max}} \Lambda^j/j!}\right]\left[\prod_{i=1}^{c}(\delta_i^2)^{-(\alpha_{\delta^2}+1)} \exp\left(-\frac{\beta_{\delta^2}}{\delta_i^2}\right)\right]\left[(\Lambda)^{(\varepsilon_1 - 1/2)} \exp\left(-\varepsilon_2 \Lambda\right)\right]$$

$$(6)$$

It is worth noticing that the posterior distribution is highly non-linear in the RBF centres $\boldsymbol{\mu}_k$ and that an expression of $p(k|\mathbf{x},\mathbf{y})$ cannot be obtained in closed-form.

4 Geometric convergence theorem

It is easy to prove that the reversible jump MCMC algorithm applied to our model converges, that is, that the Markov chain $\left(k^{(i)}, \boldsymbol{\mu}_{1:k}^{(i)}, \Lambda^{(i)}, \delta^{2(i)}\right)_{i \in \mathbb{N}}$ is ergodic. We present here a stronger result, namely that $\left(k^{(i)}, \boldsymbol{\mu}_{1:k}^{(i)}, \Lambda^{(i)}, \delta^{2(i)}\right)_{i \in \mathbb{N}}$ converges to the required posterior distribution at a geometric rate:

Theorem 1 Let $\left(k^{(i)}, \boldsymbol{\mu}_{1:k}^{(i)}, \Lambda^{(i)}, \delta^{2(i)}\right)_{i \in \mathbb{N}}$ be the Markov chain whose transition kernel has been described in Section 3. This Markov chain converges to the probability distribution $p\left(k, \boldsymbol{\mu}_{1:k}, \Lambda, \delta^2 | \mathbf{x}, \mathbf{y}\right)$. Furthermore this convergence occurs at a geometric rate, that is, for almost every initial point $\left(k^{(0)}, \boldsymbol{\mu}_{1:k}^{(0)}, \Lambda^{(0)}, \delta^{2(0)}\right) \in \Omega \times \Psi$ there exists a function of the initial states $C_0 > 0$ and a constant and $\rho \in [0,1)$ such that

$$\left\| p^{(i)}\left(k, \boldsymbol{\mu}_{1:k}, \Lambda, \delta^2\right) - p\left(k, \boldsymbol{\mu}_{1:k}, \Lambda, \delta^2 | \mathbf{x}, \mathbf{y}\right) \right\|_{TV} \leq C_0 \rho^{\lfloor i/k_{\max} \rfloor} \quad (7)$$

where $p^{(i)}\left(k, \boldsymbol{\mu}_{1:k}, \Lambda, \delta^2\right)$ is the distribution of $\left(k^{(i)}, \boldsymbol{\mu}_{1:k}^{(i)}, \Lambda^{(i)}, \delta^{2(i)}\right)$ and $\|\cdot\|_{TV}$ is the total variation norm [11]. **Proof.** See [8] ∎

Corollary 1 If for each iteration i one samples the nuisance parameters $(\boldsymbol{\alpha}_{1:m}, \sigma_k^2)$ then the distribution of the series $(k^{(i)}, \boldsymbol{\alpha}_{1:m}^{(i)}, \boldsymbol{\mu}_{1:k}^{(i)}, \sigma_k^{2(i)}, \Lambda^{(i)}, \delta^{2(i)})_{i \in \mathbb{N}}$ converges geometrically towards $p(k, \boldsymbol{\alpha}_{1:m}, \boldsymbol{\mu}_{1:k}, \sigma_k^2, \Lambda, \delta^2 | \mathbf{x}, \mathbf{y})$ at the same rate ρ.

5 Demonstration: robot arm data

This data is often used as a benchmark to compare learning algorithms[3]. It involves implementing a model to map the joint angle of a robot arm (x_1, x_2) to the position of the end of the arm (y_1, y_2). The data were generated from the following model:

$$\begin{aligned} y_1 &= 2.0 \cos(x_1) + 1.3 \cos(x_1 + x_2) + \epsilon_1 \\ y_2 &= 2.0 \sin(x_1) + 1.3 \sin(x_1 + x_2) + \epsilon_2 \end{aligned}$$

where $\epsilon_i \sim \mathcal{N}(0, \sigma^2)$; $\sigma = 0.05$. We use the first 200 observations of the data set to train our models and the last 200 observations to test them. In the simulations, we chose to use cubic basis functions. Figure 1 shows the 3D plots of the training data and the contours of the training and test data. The contour plots also include the typical approximations that were obtained using the algorithm. We chose uninformative priors for all the parameters and hyper-parameters (Table 1). To demonstrate the robustness of our algorithm, we chose different values for β_{δ^2} (the only critical hyper-parameter as it quantifies the mean of the spread $\boldsymbol{\delta}$ of $\boldsymbol{\alpha}_k$). The obtained mean square errors and probabilities for δ_1, δ_2, $\sigma_{1,k}^2$, $\sigma_{2,k}^2$ and k, shown in Figure 2, clearly indicate that our algorithm is robust with respect to prior specification. Our mean square errors are of the same magnitude as the ones reported by other researchers [2,3,5,6]; slightly better (Not by more than 10%). Moreover, our algorithm leads to more parsimonious models than the ones previously reported.

---
[3]The robot arm data set can be found in David Mackay's home page: http://wol.ra.phy.cam.ac.uk/mackay/

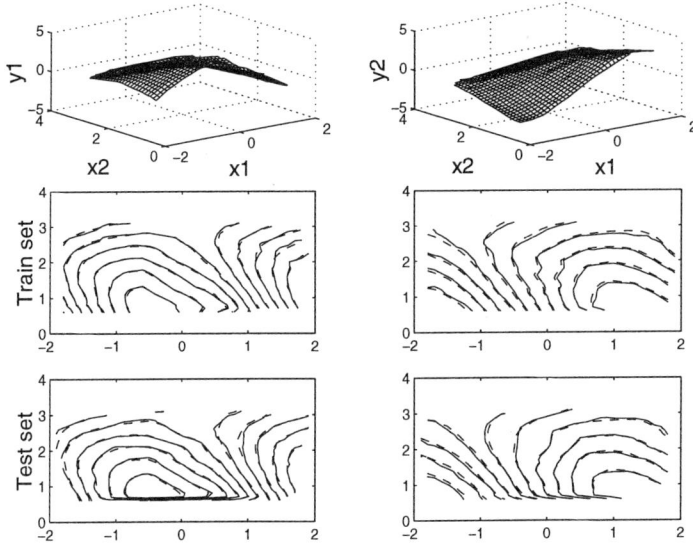

Figure 1: The top plots show the training data surfaces corresponding to each coordinate of the robot arm's position. The middle and bottom plots show the training and validation data [- -] and the respective RBF network mappings [—].

Table 1: Simulation parameters and mean square test errors.

α_{δ^2}	β_{δ^2}	v_0	γ_0	ε_1	ε_2	**MS ERROR**
2	0.1	0	0	0.0001	0.0001	0.00505
2	10	0	0	0.0001	0.0001	0.00503
2	100	0	0	0.0001	0.0001	0.00502

6 Conclusions

We presented a general methodology for estimating, jointly, the noise variance, parameters and number of parameters of an RBF model. In adopting a Bayesian model and the reversible jump MCMC algorithm to perform the necessary integrations, we demonstrated that the method is very accurate. Contrary to previous reported results, our experiments indicate that our model is robust with respect to the specification of the prior. In addition, we obtained more parsimonious RBF networks and better approximation errors than the ones previously reported in the literature. There are many avenues for further research. These include estimating the type of basis functions, performing input variable selection, considering other noise models and extending the framework to sequential scenarios. A possible solution to the first problem can be formulated using the reversible jump MCMC framework. Variable selection schemes can also be implemented via the reversible jump MCMC algorithm. We are presently working on a sequential version of the algorithm that allows us to perform model selection in non-stationary environments.

References

[1] Buntine, W.L. & Weigend, A.S. (1991) Bayesian back-propagation. *Complex Systems* **5**:603-643.

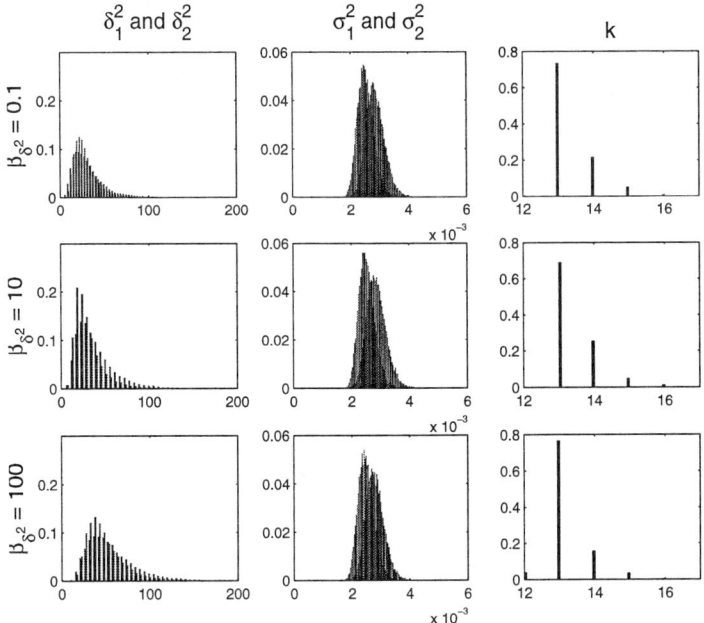

Figure 2: Histograms of smoothness constraints (δ_1 and δ_2), noise variances ($\sigma_{1,k}^2$ and $\sigma_{2,k}^2$) and model order (k) for the robot arm data using 3 different values for β_{δ^2}. The plots confirm that the algorithm is robust to the setting of β_{δ^2}.

[2] Mackay, D.J.C. (1992) A practical Bayesian framework for backpropagation networks. *Neural Computation* **4**:448-472.

[3] Neal, R.M. (1996) *Bayesian Learning for Neural Networks*. New York: Lecture Notes in Statistics No. 118, Springer-Verlag.

[4] de Freitas, J.F.G., Niranjan, M., Gee, A.H. & Doucet, A. (1999) Sequential Monte Carlo methods to train neural network models. To appear in *Neural Computation*.

[5] Rios Insua, D. & Müller, P. (1998) Feedforward neural networks for nonparametric regression. *Technical report* 98-02. Institute of Statistics and Decision Sciences, Duke University, http://www.stat.duke.edu.

[6] Holmes, C.C. & Mallick, B.K. (1998) Bayesian radial basis functions of variable dimension. *Neural Computation* **10**:1217-1233.

[7] Green, P.J. (1995) Reversible jump Markov chain Monte Carlo computation and Bayesian model determination. *Biometrika* **82**:711-732.

[8] Andrieu, C., de Freitas, J.F.G. & Doucet, A. (1999) Robust full Bayesian learning for neural networks. *Technical report* CUED/F-INFENG/TR 343. Cambridge University, http://svr-www.eng.cam.ac.uk/.

[9] Bernardo, J.M. & Smith, A.F.M. (1994) *Bayesian Theory*. Chichester: Wiley Series in Applied Probability and Statistics.

[10] Besag, J., Green, P.J., Hidgon, D. & Mengersen, K. (1995) Bayesian computation and stochastic systems. *Statistical Science* **10**:3-66.

[11] Tierney, L. (1994) Markov chains for exploring posterior distributions. *The Annals of Statistics.* **22**(4):1701-1762.

Independent Factor Analysis with Temporally Structured Sources

Hagai Attias
hagai@gatsby.ucl.ac.uk
Gatsby Unit, University College London
17 Queen Square
London WC1N 3AR, U.K.

Abstract

We present a new technique for time series analysis based on dynamic probabilistic networks. In this approach, the observed data are modeled in terms of unobserved, mutually independent factors, as in the recently introduced technique of Independent Factor Analysis (IFA). However, unlike in IFA, the factors are not i.i.d.; each factor has its own temporal statistical characteristics. We derive a family of EM algorithms that learn the structure of the underlying factors and their relation to the data. These algorithms perform source separation and noise reduction in an integrated manner, and demonstrate superior performance compared to IFA.

1 Introduction

The technique of independent factor analysis (IFA) introduced in [1] provides a tool for modeling L'-dim data in terms of L unobserved factors. These factors are mutually independent and combine linearly with added noise to produce the observed data. Mathematically, the model is defined by

$$\mathbf{y}_t = \mathbf{H}\mathbf{x}_t + \mathbf{u}_t , \qquad (1)$$

where $\mathbf{x}_t$ is the vector of factor activities at time t, $\mathbf{y}_t$ is the data vector, $\mathbf{H}$ is the $L' \times L$ mixing matrix, and $\mathbf{u}_t$ is the noise.

The origins of IFA lie in applied statistics on the one hand and in signal processing on the other hand. Its statistics ancestor is ordinary factor analysis (FA), which assumes Gaussian factors. In contrast, IFA allows each factor to have its own arbitrary distribution, modeled semi-parametrically by a 1-dim mixture of Gaussians (MOG). The MOG parameters, as well as the mixing matrix and noise covariance matrix, are learned from the observed data by an expectation-maximization (EM) algorithm derived in [1]. The signal processing ancestor of IFA is the independent component analysis (ICA) method for blind source separation [2]-[6]. In ICA, the factors are termed *sources*, and the task of blind source separation is to recover them from the observed data with no knowledge of the mixing process. The sources in ICA have non-Gaussian distributions, but unlike in IFA these distributions are usually fixed by prior knowledge or have quite limited adaptability. More significant restrictions are that their number is set to the data dimensionality, i.e. $L = L'$ ('square mixing'), the mixing matrix is assumed invertible, and the data are assumed noise-free ($\mathbf{u}_t = 0$). In contrast, IFA allows any L, L' (including more sources than sensors, $L > L'$), as well as non-zero noise with unknown covariance. In addition, its use of the flexible MOG model often proves crucial for achieving successful separation [1].

Therefore, IFA generalizes and unifies FA and ICA. Once the model has been learned, it can be used for classification (fitting an IFA model for each class), completing missing data, and so on. In the context of blind separation, an optimal reconstruction of the sources $\mathbf{x}_t$ from data is obtained [1] using a MAP estimator.

However, IFA and its ancestors suffer from the following shortcoming: They are oblivious to temporal information since they do not attempt to model the temporal statistics of the data (but see [4] for square, noise-free mixing). In other words, the model learned would not be affected by permuting the time indices of $\{\mathbf{y}_t\}$. This is unfortunate since modeling the data as a time series would facilitate filtering and forecasting, as well as more accurate classification. Moreover, for source separation applications, learning temporal statistics would provide additional information on the sources, leading to cleaner source reconstructions.

To see this, one may think of the problem of blind separation of noisy data in terms of two components: source separation and noise reduction. A possible approach might be the following two-stage procedure. First, perform noise reduction using, e.g., Wiener filtering. Second, perform source separation on the cleaned data using, e.g., an ICA algorithm. Notice that this procedure directly exploits temporal (second-order) statistics of the data in the first stage to achieve stronger noise reduction. An alternative approach would be to exploit the temporal structure of the data indirectly, by using a temporal source model. In the resulting single-stage algorithm, *the operations of source separation and noise reduction are coupled.* This is the approach taken in the present paper.

In the following, we present a new approach to the independent factor problem based on dynamic probabilistic networks. In order to capture temporal statistical properties of the observed data, we describe each source by a hidden Markov model (HMM). The resulting dynamic model describes a multivariate time series in terms of several independent sources, each having its own temporal characteristics. Section 2 presents an EM learning algorithm for the zero-noise case, and section 3 presents an algorithm for the case of isotropic noise. The case of non-isotropic noise turns out to be computationally intractable; section 4 provides an approximate EM algorithm based on a variational approach.

Notation: The multivariable Gaussian density is denoted by $\mathcal{G}(\mathbf{z}, \mathbf{\Sigma}) = | 2\pi\mathbf{\Sigma} |^{-1/2} \exp(-\mathbf{z}^T \mathbf{\Sigma}^{-1} \mathbf{z}/2)$. We work with T-point time blocks denoted $\mathbf{x}_{1:T} = \{\mathbf{x}_t\}_{t=1}^T$. The ith coordinate of $\mathbf{x}_t$ is x_t^i. For a function f, $\langle f(\mathbf{x}_{1:T}) \rangle$ denotes averaging over an ensemble of $\mathbf{x}_{1:T}$ blocks.

2 Zero Noise

The MOG source model employed in IFA [1] has the advantages that (i) it is capable of approximating arbitrary densities, and (ii) it can be learned efficiently from data by EM. The Gaussians correspond to the hidden states of the sources, labeled by s. Assume that at time t, source i is in state $s_t^i = s$. Its signal x_t^i is then generated by sampling from a Gaussian distribution with mean μ_s^i and variance ν_s^i. In order to capture temporal statistics of the data, we endow the sources with temporal structure by introducing a transition matrix $a_{s's}^i$ between the states. Focusing on a time block $t = 1, ..., T$, the resulting probabilistic model is defined by

$$p(s_t^i = s \mid s_{t-1}^i = s') = a_{s's}^i, \qquad p(s_0^i = s) = \pi_s^i,$$
$$p(x_t^i \mid s_t^i = s) = \mathcal{G}(x_t^i - \mu_s^i, \nu_s^i), \qquad p(\mathbf{y}_{1:T}) = |\det \mathbf{G}|^T p(\mathbf{x}_{1:T}), \qquad (2)$$

where $p(\mathbf{x}_{1:T})$ is the joint density of all sources $x_t^i, i = 1, ..., L$ at all time points, and the last equation follows from $\mathbf{x}_t = \mathbf{G}\mathbf{y}_t$ with $\mathbf{G} = \mathbf{H}^{-1}$ being the unmixing matrix. As usual in the noise-free scenario (see [2]; section 7 of [1]), we are assuming that the mixing matrix is square and invertible.

The graphical model for the observed density $p(\mathbf{y}_{1:T} \mid W)$ defined by (2) is parametrized by $W = \{G_{ij}, \mu_s^i, \nu_s^i, \pi_s^i, a_{s's}^i\}$. This model describes each source as a first-order HMM; it reduces to a time-independent model if $a_{s's}^i = \pi_s^i$. Whereas temporal structure can be described by other means, e.g. a moving-average [4] or autoregressive [6] model, the HMM is advantageous since it models high-order temporal statistics and facilitates EM learning. Omitting the derivation, maximization with respect to G_{ij} results in the incremental update rule

$$\delta \mathbf{G} = \epsilon \mathbf{G} - \epsilon \frac{1}{T} \sum_{t=1}^T \phi(\mathbf{x}_t) \mathbf{x}_t^T \mathbf{G}, \qquad (3)$$

where $\phi(x_t^i) = \sum_s \gamma_t^i(s)(x_t^i - \mu_s^i)/\nu_s^i$, and the natural gradient [3] was used; ϵ is an appropriately chosen learning rate. For the source parameters we obtain the update rules

$$\mu_s^i = \frac{\sum_t \gamma_t^i(s) x_t^i}{\sum_t \gamma_t^i(s)}, \qquad \nu_s^i = \frac{\sum_t \gamma_t^i(s)(x_t^i - \mu_s^i)^2}{\sum_t \gamma_t^i(s)}, \qquad a_{s's}^i = \frac{\sum_t \xi_t^i(s', s)}{\sum_t \gamma_{t-1}^i(s')}, \qquad (4)$$

with the initial probabilities updated via $\pi_s^i = \gamma_0^i(s)$. We used the standard HMM notation $\gamma_t^i(s) = p(s_t^i = s \mid x_{1:T}^i)$, $\xi_t^i(s', s) = p(s_{t-1}^i = s', s_t^i = s \mid x_{1:T}^i)$. These posterior densities are computed in the E-step for each source, which is given in terms of the data via $x_t^i = \sum_j G_{ij} y_t^j$, using the forward-backward procedure [7].

The algorithm (3–4) may be used in several possible generalized EM schemes. An efficient one is given by the following two-phase procedure: (i) freeze the source parameters and learn the separating matrix $\mathbf{G}$ using (3); (ii) freeze $\mathbf{G}$ and learn the source parameters using (4), then go back to (i) and repeat. Notice that the rule (3) is similar to a natural gradient version of Bell and Sejnowski's ICA rule [2]; in fact, the two coincide for time-independent sources where $\phi(x_i) = -\partial \log p(x_i)/\partial x_i$. We also recognize (4) as the Baum-Welch method. Hence, in phase (i) our algorithm separates the sources using a generalized ICA rule, whereas in phase (ii) it learns an HMM for each source.

Remark. Often one would like to model a given L'-variable time series in terms of a smaller number $L \leq L'$ of factors. In the framework of our noise-free model $\mathbf{y}_t = \mathbf{H}\mathbf{x}_t$, this can be achieved by applying the above algorithm to the L largest principal components of the data; notice that if the data were indeed generated by L factors, the remaining $L' - L$ principal components would vanish. Equivalently, one may apply the algorithm to the data directly, using a non-square $L \times L'$ unmixing matrix $\mathbf{G}$.

Results. Figure 1 demonstrates the performance of the above method on a 4×4 mixture of speech signals, which were passed through a non-linear function to modify their distributions. This mixture is inseparable to ICA because the source model used by the latter does not fit the actual source densities (see discussion in [1]). We also applied our dynamic network to a mixture of speech signals whose distributions

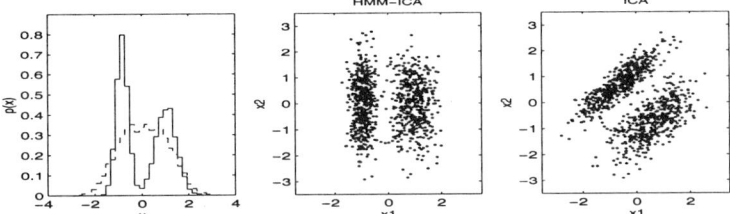

Figure 1: Left: Two of the four source distributions. Middle: Outputs of the EM algorithm (3–4) are nearly independent. Right: the outputs of ICA [2] are correlated.

were made Gaussian by an appropriate non-linear transformation. Since temporal information is crucial for separation in this case (see [4],[6]), this mixture is inseparable to ICA and IFA; however, the algorithm (3–4) accomplished separation successfully.

3 Isotropic Noise

We now turn to the case of non-zero noise $\mathbf{u}_t \neq 0$. We assume that the noise is white and has a zero-mean Gaussian distribution with covariance matrix $\mathbf{\Lambda}$. In general, this case is computationally intractable (see section 4). The reason is that the E-step requires computing the posterior distribution $p(\mathbf{s}_{0:T}, \mathbf{x}_{1:T} \mid \mathbf{y}_{1:T})$ not only over the source states (as in the zero-noise case) but also over the source signals, and this posterior has a quite complicated structure. We now show that if we assume isotropic noise, i.e. $\Lambda_{ij} = \lambda \delta_{ij}$, as well as square invertible mixing as above, this posterior simplifies considerably, making learning and inference tractable. This is done by adapting an idea suggested in [8] to our dynamic probabilistic network.

We start by pre-processing the data using a linear transformation that makes their covariance matrix unity, i.e., $\langle \mathbf{y}_t \mathbf{y}_t^T \rangle = \mathbf{I}$ ('sphering'). Here $\langle \cdot \rangle$ denotes averaging over T-point time blocks. From (1) it follows that $\mathbf{HSH}^T = \lambda'\mathbf{I}$, where $\mathbf{S} = \langle \mathbf{x}_t \mathbf{x}_t^T \rangle$ is the diagonal covariance matrix of the sources, and $\lambda' = 1 - \lambda$. This, for a square invertible $\mathbf{H}$, implies that $\mathbf{H}^T\mathbf{H}$ is diagonal. In fact, since the unobserved sources can be determined only to within a scaling factor, we can set the variance of each source to unity and obtain the *orthogonality property* $\mathbf{H}^T\mathbf{H} = \lambda'\mathbf{I}$. It can be shown that the source posterior now factorizes into a product over the individual sources, $p(\mathbf{s}_{0:T}, \mathbf{x}_{1:T} \mid \mathbf{y}_{1:T}) = \prod_i p(s_{0:T}^i, x_{1:T}^i \mid \mathbf{y}_{1:T})$, where

$$p(s_{0:T}^i, x_{1:T}^i \mid \mathbf{y}_{1:T}) \propto \left[\prod_{t=1}^{T} \mathcal{G}(x_t^i - \eta_t^i, \sigma_t^i) \cdot v_t^i p(s_t^i \mid s_{t-1}^i) \right] v_0^i p(s_0^i) . \quad (5)$$

The means and variances at time t in (5), as well as the quantities v_t^i, depend on both the data $\mathbf{y}_t$ and the states s_t^i; in particular, $\eta_t^i = (\sum_j H_{ji} y_t^j + \lambda \mu_s^i)/(\lambda' \nu_s + \lambda)$ and $\sigma_t^i = \lambda \nu_s^i / (\lambda' \nu_s + \lambda)$, using $s = s_t^i$; the expression for the v_t^i are omitted. The transition probabilities are the same as in (2). Hence, the posterior distribution (5) effectively defines a new HMM for each source, with $\mathbf{y}_t$-dependent emission and transition probabilities.

To derive the learning rule for $\mathbf{H}$, we should first compute the conditional mean $\bar{\mathbf{x}}_t$ of the source signals at time t given the data. This can be done recursively using (5) as in the forward-backward procedure. We then obtain

$$\mathbf{H} = \sqrt{\lambda'}\mathbf{C}(\mathbf{C}^T\mathbf{C})^{-1/2}, \quad \mathbf{C} = \frac{1}{T}\sum_{t=1}^{T} \mathbf{y}_t \bar{\mathbf{x}}_t^T . \quad (6)$$

This fractional form results from imposing the orthogonality constraint $\mathbf{H}^T\mathbf{H} = \lambda'\mathbf{I}$ using Lagrange multipliers and can be computed via a diagonalization procedure. The source parameters are computed using a learning rule (omitted) similar to the noise-free rule (4). It is easy to derive a learning rule for the noise level λ as well; in fact, the ordinary FA rule would suffice. We point out that, while this algorithm has been derived for the case $L = L'$, it is perfectly well defined (though sub-optimal: see below) for $L \leq L'$.

4 Non-Isotropic Noise

The general case of non-isotropic noise and non-square mixing is computationally intractable. This is because the exact E-step requires summing over all possible source configurations $(s_{t_1}^1, ..., s_{t_L}^L)$ at all times $t_1, ..., t_L = 1, ..., T$. The intractability problem stems from the fact that, while the sources are independent, the sources *conditioned on a data vector* $\mathbf{y}_{1:T}$ are correlated, resulting in a large number of hidden configurations. This problem does not arise in the noise-free case, and can be avoided in the case of isotropic noise and square mixing using the orthogonality property; in both cases, the exact posterior over the sources factorizes.

The EM algorithm derived below is based on a variational approach. This approach was introduced in [9] in the context of sigmoid belief networks, but constitutes a general framework for ML learning in intractable probabilistic networks; it was used in a HMM context in [10]. The idea is to use an approximate but tractable posterior to place a lower bound on the likelihood, and optimize the parameters by maximizing this bound.

A starting point for deriving a bound on the likelihood $\mathcal{L}$ is Neal and Hinton's [11] formulation of the EM algorithm:

$$\mathcal{L} = \log p(\mathbf{y}_{1:T}) \geq \sum_{t=1}^{T} E_q \log p(\mathbf{y}_t \mid \mathbf{x}_t) + \sum_{i=1}^{L} E_q \log p(s_{0:T}^i, x_{1:T}^i) - E_q \log q , \quad (7)$$

where E_q denotes averaging with respect to an arbitrary posterior density over the hidden variables given the observed data, $q = q(\mathbf{s}_{0:T}, \mathbf{x}_{1:T} \mid \mathbf{y}_{1:T})$. Exact EM, as shown in [11], is obtained by maximizing the bound (7) with respect to both the posterior q (corresponding to the E-step) and the model parameters W (M-step). However, the resulting q is the true but intractable posterior. In contrast, in variational EM we choose a q that differs from the true posterior, but facilitates a tractable E-step.

E-Step. We use $q(\mathbf{s}_{0:T}, \mathbf{x}_{1:T} \mid \mathbf{y}_{1:T}) = \prod_i q(s_{0:T}^i \mid \mathbf{y}_{1:T}) \prod_t q(\mathbf{x}_t \mid \mathbf{y}_{1:T})$, parametrized as

$$q(s_t^i = s \mid s_{t-1}^i = s', \mathbf{y}_{1:T}) \propto \lambda_{s,t}^i a_{s's}^i , \quad q(s_0^i = s \mid \mathbf{y}_{1:T}) \propto \lambda_{s,t}^i \pi_s^i ,$$
$$q(\mathbf{x}_t \mid \mathbf{y}_{1:T}) = \mathcal{G}(\mathbf{x}_t - \boldsymbol{\rho}_t, \boldsymbol{\Sigma}_t) . \quad (8)$$

Thus, the variational transition probabilities in (8) are described by multiplying the original ones $a_{s's}^i$ by the parameters $\lambda_{s,t}^i$, subject to the normalization constraints. The source signals $\mathbf{x}_t$ at time t are jointly Gaussian with mean $\boldsymbol{\rho}_t$ and covariance $\boldsymbol{\Sigma}_t$. The means, covariances and transition probabilities are all time- and data-dependent, i.e., $\boldsymbol{\rho}_t = f(\mathbf{y}_{1:T}, t)$ etc. This parametrization scheme is motivated by the form of the posterior in (5); notice that the quantities $\eta_t^i, \sigma_t^i, v_{s,t}^i$ there become the *variational parameters* $\rho_t^i, \Sigma_t^{ij}, \lambda_{s,t}^i$ of (8). A related scheme was used in [10] in a different context. Since these parameters will be adapted independently of the model parameters, the non-isotropic algorithm is expected to give superior results compared to the isotropic one.

Dynamic Independent Factor Analysis

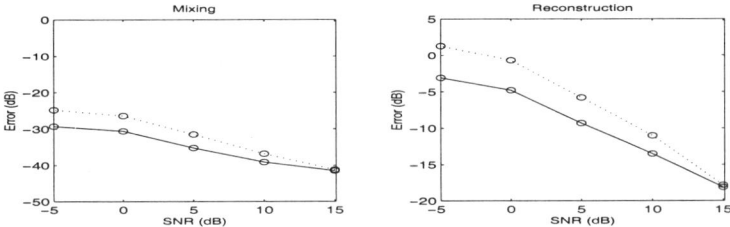

Figure 2: Left: quality of the model parameter estimates. Right: quality of the source reconstructions. (See text).

Of course, in the *true* posterior the $\mathbf{x}_t$ are correlated, both temporally among themselves and with $\mathbf{s}_t$, and the latter do not factorize. To best approximate it, the variational parameters $V = \{\rho_t^i, \Sigma_t^{ij}, \lambda_{s,t}^i\}$ are optimized to maximize the bound on $\mathcal{L}$, or equivalently to minimize the KL distance between q and the true posterior. This requirement leads to the fixed point equations

$$\rho_t = (\mathbf{H}^T \Lambda^{-1} \mathbf{H} + \mathbf{B}_t)^{-1} (\mathbf{H}^T \Lambda^{-1} \mathbf{y}_t + \mathbf{b}_t), \quad \Sigma_t = (\mathbf{H}^T \Lambda^{-1} \mathbf{H} + \mathbf{B}_t)^{-1},$$

$$\lambda_{s,t}^i = \frac{1}{z_t^i} \exp\left[-\frac{1}{2} \log \nu_s^i - \frac{(\rho_t^i - \mu_s^i)^2 + \Sigma_t^{ii}}{2\nu_s^i}\right], \quad (9)$$

where $B_t^{ij} = \sum_s [\gamma_t^i(s)/\nu_s^i]\delta_{ij}$, $b_t^i = \sum_s \gamma_t^i(s)\mu_s^i/\nu_s^i$, and the factors z_t^i ensure normalization. The HMM quantities $\gamma_t^i(s)$ are computed by the forward-backward procedure using the *variational* transition probabilities (8). The variational parameters are determined by solving eqs. (9) iteratively for each block $\mathbf{y}_{1:T}$; in practice, we found that less then 20 iterations are usually required for convergence.

M-Step. The update rules for W are given for the mixing parameters by

$$\mathbf{H} = \left[\sum_t \mathbf{y}_t \rho_t^T\right]\left[\sum_t (\rho_t \rho_t^T + \Sigma_t)\right]^{-1}, \quad \Lambda = \frac{1}{T}\sum_t (\mathbf{y}_t \mathbf{y}_t^T - \mathbf{y}_t \rho_t^T \mathbf{H}^T), \quad (10)$$

and for the source parameters by

$$\mu_s^i = \frac{\sum_t \gamma_t^i(s)\rho_t^i}{\sum_t \gamma_t^i(s)}, \quad \nu_s^i = \frac{\sum_t \gamma_t^i(s)((\rho_t^i - \mu_s^i)^2 + \Sigma_t^{ii})}{\sum_t \gamma_t^i(s)},$$

$$a_{s's}^i = \frac{\sum_t \xi_t^i(s',s)}{\sum_t \gamma_{t-1}^i(s')}, \quad \pi_s^i = \gamma_0^i(s), \quad (11)$$

where the $\xi_t^i(s',s)$ are computed using the variational transition probabilities (8). Notice that the learning rules for the source parameters have the Baum-Welch form, in spite of the correlations between the conditioned sources. In our variational approach, these correlations are hidden in V, as manifested by the fact that the fixed point equations (9) couple the parameters V across time points (since $\gamma_t^i(s)$ depends on $\lambda_{s,t=1:T}^i$) and sources.

Source Reconstruction. From $q(\mathbf{x}_t \mid \mathbf{y}_{1:T})$ (8), we observe that the MAP source estimate is given by $\hat{\mathbf{x}}_t = \rho_t(\mathbf{y}_{1:T})$, and depends on both W and V.

Results. The above algorithm is demonstrated on a source separation task in Figure 2. We used 6 speech signals, transformed by non-linearities to have arbitrary one-point densities, and mixed by a random 8×6 matrix $\mathbf{H}_0$. Different signal-to-noise (SNR) levels were used. The error in the estimated $\mathbf{H}$ (left, solid line) is quantified by the size of the non-diagonal elements of $(\mathbf{H}^T\mathbf{H})^{-1}\mathbf{H}^T\mathbf{H}_0$ relative to the diagonal; the results obtained by IFA [1], which does not use temporal information, are plotted for reference (dotted line). The mean squared error of the reconstructed sources (right, solid line) and the corresponding IFA result (right, dashed line) are also shown. The estimate and reconstruction errors of this algorithm are consistently smaller than those of IFA, reflecting the advantage of exploiting the temporal structure of the data. Additional experiments with different numbers of sources and sensors gave similar results. Notice that this algorithm, unlike the previous two, allows both $L \leq L'$ and $L > L'$. We also considered situations where the number of sensors was smaller than the number of sources; the separation quality was good, although, as expected, less so than in the opposite case.

5 Conclusion

An important issue that has not been addressed here is model selection. When applying our algorithms to an arbitrary dataset, the number of factors and of HMM states for each factor should be determined. Whereas this could be done, in principle, using cross-validation, the required computational effort would be fairly large. However, in a recent paper [12] we develop a new framework for Bayesian model selection, as well as model averaging, in probabilistic networks. This framework, termed *Variational Bayes*, proposes an EM-like algorithm which approximates full posterior distributions over not only hidden variables but also parameters and model structure, as well as predictive quantities, in an analytical manner. It is currently being applied to the algorithms presented here with good preliminary results.

One field in which our approach may find important applications is speech technology, where it suggests building more economical signal models based on combining independent low-dimensional HMMs, rather than fitting a single complex HMM. It may also contribute toward improving recognition performance in noisy, multi-speaker, reverberant conditions which characterize real-world auditory scenes.

References

[1] Attias, H. (1999). Independent factor analysis. *Neur. Comp.* **11**, 803-851.
[2] Bell, A.J. & Sejnowski, T.J. (1995). An information-maximization approach to blind separation and blind deconvolution. *Neur. Comp.* **7**, 1129-1159.
[3] Amari, S., Cichocki, A. & Yang, H.H. (1996). A new learning algorithm for blind signal separation. *Adv. Neur. Info. Proc. Sys.* **8**, 757-763 (Ed. by Touretzky, D.S. et al). MIT Press, Cambridge, MA.
[4] Pearlmutter, B.A. & Parra, L.C. (1997). Maximum likelihood blind source separation: A context-sensitive generalization of ICA. *Adv. Neur. Info. Proc. Sys.* **9**, 613-619 (Ed. by Mozer, M.C. et al). MIT Press, Cambridge, MA.
[5] Hyvärinen, A. & Oja, E. (1997). A fast fixed-point algorithm for independent component analysis. *Neur. Comp.* **9**, 1483-1492.
[6] Attias, H. & Schreiner, C.E. (1998). Blind source separation and deconvolution: the dynamic component analysis algorithm. *Neur. Comp.* **10**, 1373-1424.
[7] Rabiner, L. & Juang, B.-H. (1993). *Fundamentals of Speech Recognition*. Prentice Hall, Englewood Cliffs, NJ.
[8] Lee, D.D. & Sompolinsky, H. (1999), unpublished; D.D. Lee, personal communication.
[9] Saul, L.K., Jaakkola, T., and Jordan, M.I. (1996). Mean field theory of sigmoid belief networks. *J. Art. Int. Res.* **4**, 61-76.
[10] Ghahramani, Z. & Jordan, M.I. (1997). Factorial hidden Markov models. *Mach. Learn.* **29**, 245-273.
[11] Neal, R.M. & Hinton, G.E. (1998). A view of the EM algorithm that justifies incremental, sparse, and other variants. *Learning in Graphical Models*, 355-368 (Ed. by Jordan, M.I.). Kluwer Academic Press.
[12] Attias, H. (2000). A variational Bayesian framework for graphical models. *Adv. Neur. Info. Proc. Sys.* **12** (Ed. by Leen, T. et al). MIT Press, Cambridge, MA.

Gaussian Fields for Approximate Inference in Layered Sigmoid Belief Networks

David Barber*
Stichting Neurale Netwerken
Medical Physics and Biophysics
Nijmegen University, The Netherlands
barberd@aston.ac.uk

Peter Sollich
Department of Mathematics
King's College, University of London
London WC2R 2LS, U.K.
peter.sollich@kcl.ac.uk

Abstract

Layered Sigmoid Belief Networks are directed graphical models in which the local conditional probabilities are parameterised by weighted sums of parental states. Learning and inference in such networks are generally intractable, and approximations need to be considered. Progress in *learning* these networks has been made by using variational procedures. We demonstrate, however, that variational procedures can be inappropriate for the equally important issue of *inference* - that is, calculating marginals of the network. We introduce an alternative procedure, based on assuming that the weighted input to a node is approximately Gaussian distributed. Our approach goes beyond previous Gaussian field assumptions in that we take into account correlations between parents of nodes. This procedure is specialized for calculating marginals and is significantly faster and simpler than the variational procedure.

1 Introduction

Layered Sigmoid Belief Networks [1] are directed graphical models [2] in which the local conditional probabilities are parameterised by weighted sums of parental states, see fig(1). This is a graphical representation of a distribution over a set of binary variables $s_i \in \{0, 1\}$. Typically, one supposes that the states of the nodes at the bottom of the network are *generated* by states in previous layers. Whilst, in principle, there is no restriction on the number of nodes in any layer, typically, one considers structures similar to the "fan out" in fig(1) in which higher level layers provide an "explanation" for patterns generated in lower layers. Such graphical models are attractive since they correspond to layers of information processors, of potentially increasing complexity. Unfortunately, learning and inference in such networks is generally intractable, and approximations need to be considered. Progress in learning has been made by using variational procedures [3, 4, 5]. However, another crucial aspect remains inference [2]. That is, given some evidence (or none), calculate the marginal of a variable, conditional on this evidence. This assumes that we have found a suitable network from some learning procedure, and now wish

---
*Present Address: NCRG, Aston University, Birmingham B4 7ET, U.K.

to query this network. Whilst the variational procedure is attractive for learning, since it generally provides a bound on the likelihood of the visible units, we demonstrate that it may not always be equally appropriate for the inference problem.

A directed graphical model defines a distribution over a set of variables $\mathbf{s} = (s_1 \ldots s_n)$ that factorises into the local conditional distributions,

$$p(s_1 \ldots s_n) = \prod_{i=1}^{n} p(s_i | \pi_i) \quad (1)$$

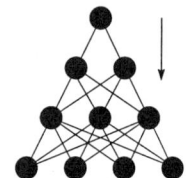

Figure 1: A Layered Sigmoid Belief Network

where π_i denotes the parent nodes of node i. In a layered network, these are the nodes in the proceeding layer that feed into node i. In a sigmoid belief network the local probabilities are defined as

$$p(s_i = 1 | \pi_i) = \sigma \left(\sum_j w_{ij} s_j + \theta_i \right) = \sigma(h_i) \quad (2)$$

where the "field" at node i is defined as $h_i = \sum_j w_{ij} s_j + \theta_i$ and $\sigma(h) = 1/(1 + e^{-h})$. w_{ij} is the strength of the connection between node i and its parent node j; if j is not a parent of i we set $w_{ij} = 0$. θ_i is a bias term that gives a parent-independent bias to the state of node i.

We are interested in inference - in particular, calculating marginals of the network for cases with and without evidential nodes. In section (2) we describe how to approximate the quantities $p(s_i = 1)$ and discuss in section (2.1) why our method can improve on the standard variational mean field theory. Conditional marginals, such as $p(s_i = 1 | s_j = 1, s_k = 0)$ are considered in section (3).

2 Gaussian Field Distributions

Under the 0/1 coding for the variables s_i, the mean of a variable, m_i is given by the probability that it is in state 1. Using the fact from (2) that the local conditional distribution of node i is dependent on its parents *only* through its field h_i, we have

$$m_i = p(s_i = 1) = \int p(s_i = 1 | h_i) p(h_i) dh_i \equiv \langle \sigma(h_i) \rangle_{p(h_i)} \quad (3)$$

where we use the notation $\langle (\cdot) \rangle_p$ to denote an average with respect to the distribution p. If there are many parents of node i, a reasonable assumption is that the distribution of the field h_i will be Gaussian, $p(h_i) \approx N(\mu_i, \sigma_i^2)$. Under this Gaussian Field (GF) assumption, we need to work out the mean and variance, which are given by

$$\mu_i = \langle h_i \rangle = \sum_j w_{ij} \langle s_j \rangle + \theta_i = \sum_j w_{ij} m_j + \theta_i \quad (4)$$

$$\sigma_i^2 = \left\langle (\Delta h_i)^2 \right\rangle = \sum_{j,k} w_{ij} w_{ik} R_{jk} \quad (5)$$

where $R_{jk} = \langle \Delta s_j \Delta s_k \rangle$. We use the notation $\Delta(\cdot) \equiv (\cdot) - \langle (\cdot) \rangle$.

The diagonal terms of the node covariance matrix are $R_{ii} = m_i(1 - m_i)$. In contrast to previous studies, we include off diagonal terms in the calculation of R [4]. From

(5) we only need to find correlations between parents i and j of a node. These are easy to calculate in the layered networks that we are considering, because neither i nor j is a descendant of the other:

$$R_{ij} = p(s_i = 1, s_j = 1) - m_i m_j \qquad (6)$$

$$= \int p(s_i = 1|h_i) p(s_j = 1|h_j) p(h_i, h_j) dh - m_i m_j \qquad (7)$$

$$= \langle \sigma(h_i) \sigma(h_j) \rangle_{p(h_i, h_j)} - m_i m_j \qquad (8)$$

Assuming that the joint distribution $p(h_i, h_j)$ is Gaussian, we again need its mean and covariance, given by

$$\mu^T = (\langle h_i \rangle, \langle h_j \rangle) = \left(\sum_k w_{ik} m_k + \theta_i, \sum_l w_{jl} m_l + \theta_j \right) \qquad (9)$$

$$\Sigma_{ij} = \langle \Delta h_i \Delta h_j \rangle = \sum_{kl} w_{ik} w_{jl} \langle \Delta s_k \Delta s_l \rangle = \sum_{kl} w_{ik} w_{jl} R_{kl} \qquad (10)$$

Under this scheme, we have a closed set of equations, (4,5,8,10) for the means m_i and covariance matrix R_{ij} which can be solved by forward propagation of the equations. That is, we start from nodes without parents, and then consider the next layer of nodes, repeating the procedure until a full sweep through the network has been completed. The one and two dimensional field averages, equations (3) and (8), are computed using Gaussian Quadrature. This results in an extremely fast procedure for approximating the marginals m_i, requiring only a single sweep through the network.

Our approach is related to that of [6] by the common motivating assumption that each node has a large number of parents. This is used in [6] to obtain actual bounds on quantities of interest such as joint marginals. Our approach does not give bounds. Its advantage, however, is that it allows fluctuations in the fields h_i, which are effectively excluded in [6] by the assumed scaling of the weights w_{ij} with the number of parents per node.

2.1 Relation to Variational Mean Field Theory

In the variational approach, one fits a tractable approximating distribution Q to the SBN. Taking Q factorised, $Q(\mathbf{s}) = \prod_i m_i^{s_i} (1 - m_i)^{1-s_i}$ we have the bound

$$\ln p(s_1 \ldots s_n) \geq \sum_i \{-m_i \ln m_i - (1 - m_i) \ln (1 - m_i)\}$$

$$+ \sum_i \left\{ \sum_j m_i w_{ij} m_j + \theta_i m_i - \langle \ln (1 + e^{h_i}) \rangle_Q \right\} \qquad (11)$$

The final term in (11) causes some difficulty even in the case in which Q is a factorised model. Formally, this is because this term does not have the same graphical structure as the tractable model Q. One way around around this difficulty is to employ a further bound, with associated variational parameters [7]. Another approach is to make the Gaussian assumption for the field h_i as in section (2). Because Q is factorised, corresponding to a diagonal correlation matrix R, this gives [4]

$$\langle \ln (1 + e^{h_i}) \rangle_Q \approx \langle \ln (1 + e^{h_i}) \rangle_{N(\mu_i, \sigma_i^2)} \qquad (12)$$

where $\mu_i = \sum_j w_{ij} m_j + \theta_i$ and $\sigma_i^2 = \sum_j w_{ij}^2 m_j (1 - m_j)$. Note that this is a one dimensional integral of a smooth function. In contrast to [4] we therefore evaluate this quantity using Gaussian Quadrature. This has the advantage that no extra variational parameters need to be introduced. Technically, the assumption of a Gaussian field distribution means that (11) is no longer a bound. Nevertheless, in practice it is found that this has little effect on the quality of the resulting solution. In our implementation of the variational approach, we find the optimal parameters m_i by maximising the above equation for each component m_i separately, cycling through the nodes until the parameters m_i do not change by more than 10^{-10}. This is repeated 5 times, and the solution with the highest bound score is chosen. Note that these equations cannot be solved by forward propagation alone since the final term contains contributions from all the nodes in the network. This is in contrast to the GF approach of section (2). Finding appropriate parameters m_i by the variational approach is therefore rather slower than using the GF method.

In arriving at the above equations, we have made two assumptions. The first is that the intractable distribution is well approximated by a factorised model. The second is that the field distribution is Gaussian. The first step is necessary in order to obtain a bound on the likelihood of the model (although this is slightly compromised by the Gaussian field assumption). In the GF approach we dispense with this assumption of an effectively factorised network (partially because if we are only interested in inference, a bound on the model likelihood is less relevant). The GF method may therefore prove useful for a broader class of networks than the variational approach.

2.2 Results for unconditional marginals

We compared three procedures for estimating the conditional values $p(s_i = 1)$ for all the nodes in the network, namely the variational theory, as described in section (2.1), the diagonal Gaussian field theory, and the non-diagonal Gaussian field theory which includes correlation effects between parents. Results for small weight values w_{ij} are shown in fig(2). In this case, all three methods perform reasonably well, although there is a significant improvement in using the GF methods over the variational procedure; parental correlations are not important (compare figs(2b) and (2c)). In fig(3) the weights and biases are chosen such that the exact mean variables m_i are roughly 0.5 with non-trivial correlation effects between parents. Note that the variational mean field theory now provides a poor solution, whereas the GF methods are relatively accurate. The effect of using the non-diagonal R terms is beneficial, although not dramatically so.

3 Calculating Conditional Marginals

We consider now how to calculate conditional marginals, given some evidential nodes. (In contrast to [6], any set of nodes in the network, not just output nodes, can be considered evidential.) We write the evidence in the following manner

$$E = \{s_{c_1} = S_{c_1}, \ldots s_{c_n} = S_{c_n}\} = \{E_{c_1} \ldots E_{c_n}\}$$

The quantities that we are interested in are conditional marginals which, from Bayes rule are related to the joint distribution by

$$p(s_i = 1 | E) = \frac{p(s_i = 1, E)}{p(s_i = 0, E) + p(s_i = 1, E)} \tag{13}$$

That is, provided that we have a procedure for estimating joint marginals, we can obtain conditional marginals too. Without loss of generality, we therefore consider

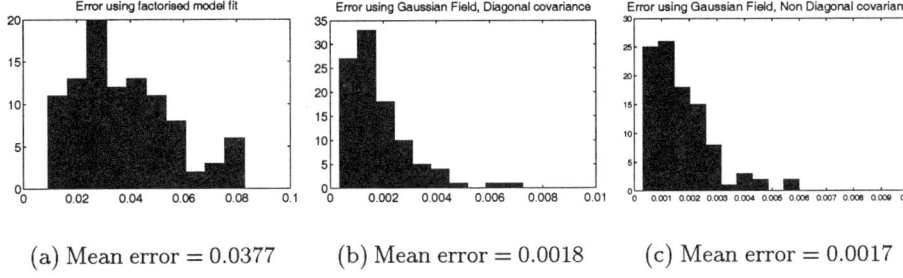

(a) Mean error = 0.0377   (b) Mean error = 0.0018   (c) Mean error = 0.0017

Figure 2: Error in approximating $p(s_i = 1)$ for the network in fig(1), averaged over all the nodes in the network. In each of 100 trials, weights were drawn from a zero mean, unit variance Gaussian; biases were set to 0. Note the different scale in (b) and (c). In (a) we use the variational procedure with a factorised Q, as in section (2.1). In (b) we use the Gaussian field equations, assuming a diagonal covariance matrix R. This procedure was repeated in (c) including correlations between parents.

$E^+ = E \cup \{s_i = 1\}$, which then contains $n+1$ "evidential" variables. That is, the desired marginal variable is absorbed into the evidence set. For convenience, we then split the nodes into two sets, those containing the evidential or "clamped" nodes, C, and the remaining "free" nodes F. The joint evidence is then given by

$$p(E^+) = \sum_{s_F} p\left(E_{c_1}, \ldots E_{c_{n+1}}, s_{f_1}, \ldots s_{f_m}\right) \tag{14}$$

$$= \sum_{s_F} p\left(E_{c_1}|\pi^*_{c_1}\right) \ldots p\left(E_{n+1}|\pi^*_{c_{n+1}}\right) p\left(s_{f_1}|\pi^*_{f_1}\right) \ldots p\left(s_{f_m}|\pi^*_{f_m}\right) \tag{15}$$

where π^*_i are the parents of node i, with any evidential parental nodes set to their values as specified in E^+. In the sigmoid belief network

$$p(E_k|\pi^*_k) = \sigma\left((2S_k - 1)\left(\sum_i w_{ki} s^*_i + \theta_k\right)\right), \quad s^*_i = \begin{cases} S_i, & \text{if } i \text{ is an evidential node} \\ s_i, & \text{otherwise} \end{cases} \tag{16}$$

$p(E_k|\pi^*_k)$ is therefore determined by the distribution of the field $h^*_k = \sum_i w_{ki} s^*_i + \theta_k$. Examining (15), we see that the product over the "free" nodes defines a SBN in which the local probability distributions are given by those of the original network, but with any evidential parental nodes clamped to their evidence values. Therefore,

$$p\left(E^+\right) = \left\langle \prod_{i=1}^{n+1} \sigma\left((2S_{c_i} - 1)h^*_{c_i}\right) \right\rangle_{p\left(h^*_{c_1} \ldots h^*_{c_{n+1}}\right)} \tag{17}$$

Consistent with our previous assumptions, we assume that the distribution of the fields $\mathbf{h}^* = \left(h^*_{c_1} \ldots h^*_{c_{n+1}}\right)$ is jointly Gaussian. We can then find the mean and covariance matrix for the distribution of $\mathbf{h}^*$ by repeating the calculation of section (2) in which evidential nodes have been clamped to their evidence values. Once this Gaussian has been determined, it can be used in (17) to determine $p(E^+)$. Gaussian averages of products of sigmoids are calculated by drawing 1000 samples from the Gaussian over which we wish to integrate[1]. Note that if there are evidential nodes

---

[1] In one and two dimensions ($n = 0, 1$), or $n = 1$, we use Gaussian Quadrature.

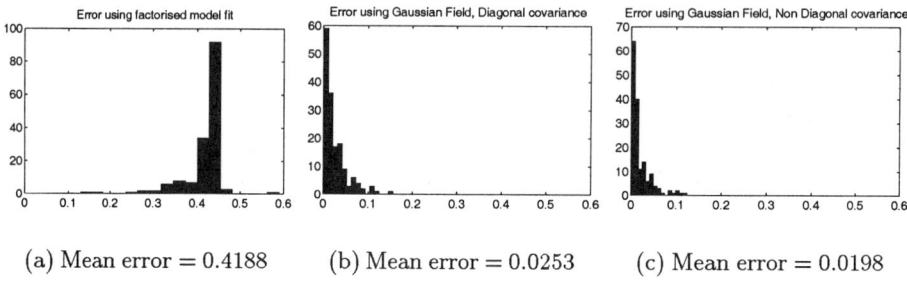

(a) Mean error = 0.4188   (b) Mean error = 0.0253   (c) Mean error = 0.0198

Figure 3: All weights are set to uniformly from 0 to 50. Biases are set to -0.5 of the summed parental weights plus a uniform random number from -2.5 to 2.5. The root node is set to be 1 with probability 0.5. This has the effect of making all the nodes in the exact network roughly 0.5 in mean, with non-negligible correlations between parental nodes. 160 simulations were made.

in different layers, we require the correlations between their fields h to evaluate (17). Such 'inter-layer' correlations were not required in section (2), and to be able to use the same calculational scheme we simply neglect them. (We leave a study of the effects of this assumption for future work.) The average in (17) then factors into groups, where each group contains evidential terms in a particular layer.

The conditional marginal for node i is obtained from repeating the above procedure in which the desired marginal node is clamped to its opposite value, and then using these results in (13). The above procedure is repeated for each conditional marginal that we are interested in. Although this may seem computationally expensive, the marginal for each node is computed quickly, since the equations are solved by one forward propagation sweep only.

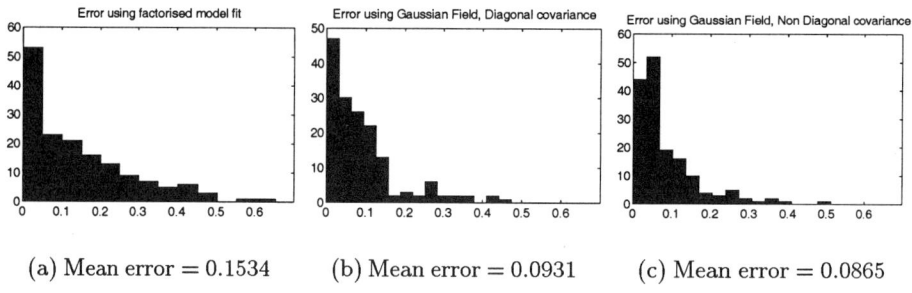

(a) Mean error = 0.1534   (b) Mean error = 0.0931   (c) Mean error = 0.0865

Figure 4: Estimating the conditional marginal of the top node being in state 1, given that the four bottom nodes are in state 1. Weights were drawn from a zero mean Gaussian with variance 5, with biases set to -0.5 the summed parental weights plus a uniform random number from -2.5 to 2.5. Results of 160 simulations.

3.1 Results for conditional marginals

We used the same structure as in the previous experiments, as shown in fig(1). We are interested here in calculating the probability that the top node is in state 1, given that the four bottom nodes are in state 1. Weights were chosen from a zero mean Gaussian with variance 5. Biases were set to negative half of the summed parent weights, plus a uniform random value from -2.5 to 2.5. Correlation effects in these networks are not as strong as in the experiments in section (2.2), although the improvement of the GF theory over the variational theory seen in fig(4) remains clear. The improvement from the off diagonal terms in R is minimal.

4 Conclusion

Despite their appropriateness for learning, variational methods may not be equally suited to inference, making more tailored methods attractive. We have considered an approximation procedure that is based on assuming that the distribution of the weighted input to a node is approximately Gaussian. Correlation effects between parents of a node were taken into account to improve the Gaussian theory, although in our examples this gave only relatively modest improvements.

The variational mean field theory performs poorly in networks with strong correlation effects between nodes. On the other hand, one may conjecture that the Gaussian Field approach will not generally perform catastrophically worse than the factorised variational mean field theory. One advantage of the variational theory is the presence of an objective function against which competing solutions can be compared. However, finding an optimum solution for the mean parameters m_i from this function is numerically complex. Since the Gaussian Field theory is extremely fast to solve, an interesting compromise might be to prime the variational solution with the results from the Gaussian Field theory.

Acknowledgments

DB would like to thank Bert Kappen and Wim Wiegerinck for stimulating and helpful discussions. PS thanks the Royal Society for financial support.

[1] R. Neal. Connectionist learning of Belief Networks. *Artificial Intelligence*, 56:71–113, 1992.

[2] E. Castillo, J. M. Gutierrez, and A. S. Hadi. *Expert Systems and Probabilistic Network Models*. Springer, 1997.

[3] M. I. Jordan, Z. Gharamani, T. S. Jaakola, and L. K. Saul. An Introduction to Variational Methods for Graphical Models. In M. I. Jordan, editor, *Learning in Graphical Models*, pages 105–161. Kluwer, 1998.

[4] L. Saul and M. I. Jordan. A mean field learning algorithm for unsupervised neural networks. In M. I. Jordan, editor, *Learning in Graphical Models*, 1998.

[5] D. Barber and W Wiegerinck. Tractable variational structures for approximating graphical models. In M.S. Kearns, S.A. Solla, and D.A. Cohn, editors, *Advances in Neural Information Processing Systems NIPS 11*. MIT Press, 1999.

[6] M. Kearns and L. Saul. Inference in Multilayer Networks via Large Deviation Bounds. In *Advances in Neural Information Processing Systems NIPS 11*, 1999.

[7] L. K. Saul, T. Jaakkola, and M. I. Jordan. Mean Field Theory for Sigmoid Belief Networks. *Journal of Artificial Intelligence Research*, 4:61–76, 1996.

Modeling High-Dimensional Discrete Data with Multi-Layer Neural Networks

Yoshua Bengio
Dept. IRO
Université de Montréal
Montreal, Qc, Canada, H3C 3J7
bengioy@iro.umontreal.ca

Samy Bengio[*]
IDIAP
CP 592, rue du Simplon 4,
1920 Martigny, Switzerland
bengio@idiap.ch

Abstract

The curse of dimensionality is severe when modeling high-dimensional discrete data: the number of possible combinations of the variables explodes exponentially. In this paper we propose a new architecture for modeling high-dimensional data that requires resources (parameters and computations) that grow only at most as the square of the number of variables, using a multi-layer neural network to represent the joint distribution of the variables as the product of conditional distributions. The neural network can be interpreted as a graphical model without hidden random variables, but in which the conditional distributions are tied through the hidden units. The connectivity of the neural network can be pruned by using dependency tests between the variables. Experiments on modeling the distribution of several discrete data sets show statistically significant improvements over other methods such as naive Bayes and comparable Bayesian networks, and show that significant improvements can be obtained by pruning the network.

1 Introduction

The curse of dimensionality hits particularly hard on models of high-dimensional discrete data because there are many more possible combinations of the values of the variables than can possibly be observed in any data set, even the large data sets now common in data-mining applications. In this paper we are dealing in particular with multivariate discrete data, where one tries to build a model of the distribution of the data. This can be used for example to detect anomalous cases in data-mining applications, or it can be used to model the class-conditional distribution of some observed variables in order to build a classifier. A simple multinomial maximum likelihood model would give zero probability to all of the combinations not encountered in the training set, i.e., it would most likely give zero probability to most out-of-sample test cases. Smoothing the model by assigning the same non-zero probability for all the unobserved cases would not be satisfactory either because it would not provide much generalization from the training set. This could be obtained by using a multivariate multinomial model whose parameters θ are estimated by the maximum a-posteriori (MAP) principle, i.e., those that have the greatest probability, given the training data D, and using a diffuse prior $P(\theta)$ (e.g. Dirichlet) on the parameters.

A graphical model or Bayesian network [6, 5] represents the joint distribution of random variables $Z_1 \ldots Z_n$ with

$$P(Z_1 \ldots Z_n) = \prod_{i=1}^{n} P(Z_i | \text{Parents}_i)$$

---
[0]Part of this work was done while S.B. was at CIRANO, Montreal, Qc. Canada.

where Parents$_i$ is the set of random variables which are called the **parents** of variable i in the graphical model because they directly condition Z_i, and an arrow is drawn, in the graphical model, to Z_i, from each of its parents. A fully connected "left-to-right" graphical model is illustrated in Figure 1 (left), which corresponds to the model

$$P(Z_1 \ldots Z_n) = \prod_{i=1}^{n} P(Z_i | Z_1 \ldots Z_{i-1}). \tag{1}$$

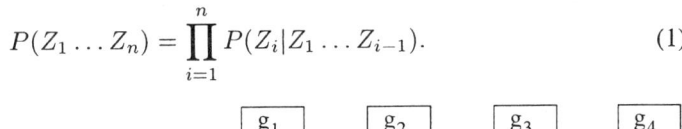
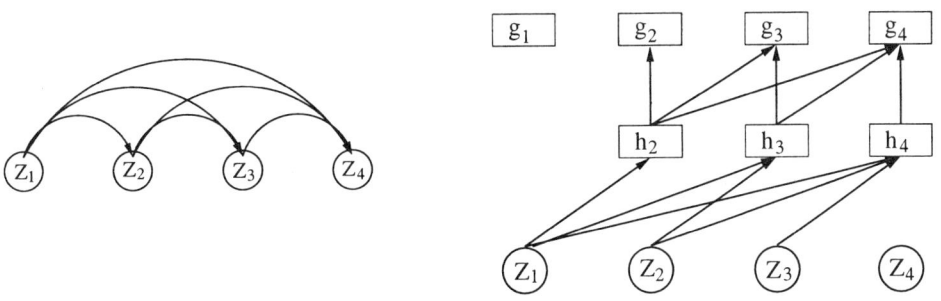

Figure 1: Left: a fully connected "left-to-right" graphical model.
Right: the architecture of a neural network that simulates a fully connected "left-to-right" graphical model. The observed values $Z_i = z_i$ are encoded in the corresponding input unit group. h_i is a group of hidden units. g_i is a group of output units, which depend on $z_1 \ldots z_{i-1}$, representing the parameters of a distribution over Z_i. These conditional probabilities $P(Z_i | Z_1 \ldots Z_{i-1})$ are multiplied to obtain the joint distribution.

Note that this representation depends on the ordering of the variables (in that all previous variables in this order are taken as parents). We call each combination of the values of Parents$_i$ a *context*. In the "exact" model (with the full table of all possible contexts) all the orders are equivalent, but if approximations are used, different predictions could be made by different models assuming different orders.

In graphical models, the curse of dimensionality shows up in the representation of conditional distributions $P(Z_i|\text{Parents}_i)$ where Z_i has many parents. If $Z_j \in$ Parents$_i$ can take n_j values, there are $\prod_j n_j$ different contexts which can occur in which one would like to estimate the distribution of Z_i. This serious problem has been addressed in the past by two types of approaches, which are sometimes combined:

1. *Not modeling all the dependencies between all the variables*: this is the approach mainly taken with most graphical models or Bayes networks [6, 5]. The set of independencies can be assumed using a-priori or human expert knowledge or can be learned from data. See also [2] in which the set *Parents$_i$* is restricted to at most one element, which is chosen to maximize the correlation with Z_i.

2. *Approximating the mathematical form of the joint distribution* with a form that takes only into account dependencies of lower order, or only takes into account some of the possible dependencies, e.g., with the Rademacher-Walsh expansion or multi-binomial [1, 3], which is a low-order polynomial approximation of a full joint binomial distribution (and is used in the experiments reported in this paper).

The approach we are putting forward in this paper is mostly of the second category, although we are using simple non-parametric statistics of the dependency between pairs of variables to further reduce the number of required parameters.

In the multi-binomial model [3], the joint distribution of a set of binary variables is approximated by a polynomial. Whereas the "exact" representation of $P(Z_1 = z_1, \ldots Z_n = z_n)$ as a function of $z_1 \ldots z_n$ is a polynomial of degree n, it can be approximated with a lower degree polynomial, and this approximation can be easily computed using the Rademacher-Walsh expansion [1] (or other similar expansions, such as the Bahadur-Lazarsfeld expansion [1]). Therefore, instead of having 2^n parameters, the approximated model for $P(Z_1, \ldots Z_n)$ only requires $O(n^k)$ parameters. Typically, order $k = 2$ is used. The model proposed here also requires $O(n^2)$ parameters, but it allows to model dependencies between tuples of variables, with more than 2 variables at a time.

In previous related work by Frey [4], a fully-connected graphical model is used (see Figure 1, left) but each of the conditional distributions is represented by a logistic, which take into account only first-order dependency between the variables:

$$P(Z_i = 1 | Z_1 \ldots Z_{i-1}) = \frac{1}{1 + \exp(-w_0 - \sum_{j<i} w_j Z_j)}.$$

In this paper, we basically extend Frey's idea to using a neural network with a hidden layer, with a particular architecture, allowing multinomial or continuous variables, and we propose to prune down the network weights. Frey has named his model a *Logistic Autoregressive Bayesian Network* or LARC. He argues that the prior variances on the logistic weights (which correspond to inverse weight decays) should be chosen inversely proportional to the number of conditioning variables (i.e. the number of inputs to the particular output neuron). The model was tested on a task of learning to classify digits from 8x8 binary pixel images. Models with different orderings of the variables were compared and did not yield significant differences in performance. When averaging the predictive probabilities from 10 different models obtained by considering 10 different random orderings, Frey obtained small improvements in likelihood but not in classification. The model performed better or equivalently to other models tested: CART, naive Bayes, K-nearest neighbors, and various Bayesian models with hidden variables (Helmholtz machines). These results are impressive, taking into account the simplicity of the LARC model.

2 Proposed Architecture

The proposed architecture is a "neural network" implementation of a graphical model where all the variables are observed in the training set, with the hidden units playing a significant role to share parameters across different conditional distributions. Figure 1 (right) illustrates the model in the simpler case of a fully connected (left-to-right) graphical model (Figure 1, left). The neural network represents the parametrized function

$$f_\theta(z_1, \ldots, z_n) = log(\hat{P}_\theta(Z_1 = z_1, \ldots, Z_n = z_n)) \qquad (2)$$

approximating the joint distribution of the variables, with parameters θ being the weights of the neural network. The architecture has three layers, with each layer organized in **groups** associated to each of the variables. The above log-probability is computed as the sum of conditional log-probabilities

$$f_\theta(z_1, \ldots, z_n) = \sum_{i=1}^{n} log(P(Z_i = z_i | g_i(z_1, \ldots, z_{i-1})))$$

where $g_i(z_1, \ldots, z_{i-1})$ is the vector-valued output of the i-th group of output units, and it gives the value of the parameters of the distribution of Z_i when $Z_1 = z_1, Z_2 = z_2, \ldots, Z_{i-1} = z_{i-1}$. For example, in the ordinary discrete case, g_i may be the vector of probabilities associated with each of the possible values of the multinomial random variable Z_i. In this case, we have

$$P(Z_i = i' | g_i) = g_{i,i'}$$

In this example, a *softmax* output for the i-th group may be used to force these parameters to be positive and sum to 1, i.e.,

$$g_{i,i'} = \frac{e^{g'_{i,i'}}}{\sum_{i'} e^{g'_{i,i'}}}$$

where $g'_{i,i'}$ are linear combinations of the hidden units outputs, with i' ranging over the number of elements of the parameter vector associated with the distribution of Z_i (for a fixed value of $Z_1 \ldots Z_{i-1}$). To guarantee that the functions $g_i(z_1, \ldots, z_{i-1})$ only depend on $z_1 \ldots z_{i-1}$ and not on any of $z_i \ldots z_n$, the connectivity struture of the hidden units must be constrained as follows:

$$g'_{i,i'} = b_{i,i'} + \sum_{j \leq i} \sum_{j'=1}^{m_j} w_{i,i',j,j'} h_{j,j'}$$

where the b's are biases and the w's are weights of the output layer, and the $h_{j,j'}$ is the output of the j'-th unit (out of m_j such units) in the j-th group of hidden layer nodes. It may be computed as follows:

$$h_{j,j'} = \tanh(c_{j,j'} + \sum_{k<j} \sum_{k'=1}^{n_k} v_{j,j',k,k'} z_{k,k'})$$

where the c's are biases and the v's are the weights of the hidden layer, and $z_{k,k'}$ is k'-th element of the vectorial input representation of the value $Z_k = z_k$. For example, in the binary case ($z_i = 0$ or 1) we have used only one input node, i.e.,

$$Z_i \text{ binomial} \rightarrow z_{i,0} = z_i$$

and in the multinomial case we use the one-hot encoding,

$$Z_i \in \{0, 1, \ldots n_i - 1\} \rightarrow z_{i,i'} = \delta_{z_i, i'}$$

where $\delta_{i,i'} = 1$ if $i = i'$ and 0 otherwise. The input layer has $n - 1$ groups because the value $Z_n = z_n$ is not used as an input. The hidden layer also has $n - 1$ groups corresponding to the variables $j = 2$ to n (since $P(Z_1)$ is represented unconditionally in the first output group, its corresponding group does not need any hidden units or inputs, but just has biases).

2.1 Discussion

The number of free parameters of the model is $O(n^2 H)$ where $H = \max_i m_j$ is the maximum number of hidden units per hidden group (i.e., associated with one of the variables). This is basically quadratic in the number of variables, like the multi-binomial approximation that uses a polynomial expansion of the joint distribution. However, as H is increased, representation theorems for neural networks suggest that we should be able to approximate with arbitrary precision the true joint distribution. Of course the true limiting factor is the amount of data, and H should be tuned according to the amount of data. In our experiments we have used cross-validation to choose a value of $m_j = H$ for all the hidden groups. In this sense, this neural network representation of $P(Z_1 \ldots Z_n)$ is to the polynomial expansions (such as the multi-binomial) what ordinary multilayer neural networks for function approximation are to polynomial function approximators. It allows to capture high-order dependencies, but not all of them. It is the number of hidden units that controls "how many" such dependencies will be captured, and it is the data that "chooses" which of the actual dependencies are most useful in maximizing the likelihood.

Unlike Bayesian networks with hidden random variables, learning with the proposed architecture is very simple, even when there are no conditional independencies. To optimize the parameters we have simply used gradient-based optimization methods, either using conjugate or stochastic (on-line) gradient, to maximize the total log-likelihood which is the sum of values of f (eq. 2) for the training examples. A prior on the parameters can be incorporated in the cost function and the MAP estimator can be obtained as easily, by maximizing the total log-likelihood plus the log-prior on the parameters. In our experiments we have used a "weight decay" penalty inspired by the analysis of Frey [4], with a penalty proportional to the number of weights incoming into a neuron.

However, it is not so clear how the distribution could be generally marginalized, except by summing over possibly many combinations of the values of variables to be integrated. Another related question is whether one could deal with missing values: if the total number of values that the missing variables can take is reasonably small, then one can sum over these values in order to obtain a marginal probability and maximize this probability. If some variables have more systematically missing values, they can be put at the end of the variable ordering, and in this case it is very easy to compute the marginal distribution (by taking only the product of the output probabilities up to the missing variables). Similarly, one can easily compute the predictive distribution of the last variable given the first $n - 1$ variables.

The framework can be easily extended to hybrid models involving both continuous and discrete variables. In the case of continuous variables, one has to choose a parametric form for the distribution of the continuous variable when all its parents (i.e., the conditioning context) are fixed. For example one could use a normal, log-normal, or mixture of normals. Instead of having softmax outputs, the i-th output group would compute the parameters of this continuous distribution (e.g., mean and log-variance). Another type of extension allows to build a conditional distribution, e.g., to model $P(Z_1 \ldots Z_n | X_1 \ldots X_m)$. One just adds extra input units to represent the values of the conditioning variables $X_1 \ldots X_m$. Finally, an architectural extension that we have implemented is to allow direct input-to-output connections (still following the rules of ordering which allow g_i to depend only on $z_1 \ldots z_{i-1}$). Therefore in the case where the number of hidden units is 0 ($H = 0$) we obtain the LARC model proposed by Frey [4].

2.2 Choice of topology

Another type of extension of this model which we have found very useful in our experiments is to allow the user to choose a topology that is not fully connected (left-to-right). In our experiments we have used non-parametric tests to heuristically eliminate some of the connections in the network, but one could also use expert or prior knowledge, just as with regular graphical models, in order to cut down on the number of free parameters.

In our experiments we have used for a pairwise test of statistical dependency the Kolmogorov-Smirnov statistic (which works both for continuous and discrete variables). The statistic for variables X and Y is

$$s = \sqrt{l} \sup_i |\hat{P}(X \leq x_i, Y \leq y_i) - \hat{P}(X \leq x_i)\hat{P}(Y \leq y_i)|$$

where l is the number of examples and $\hat{P}$ is the empirical distribution (obtained by counting over the training data). We have ranked the pairs according to their value of the statistic s, and we have chosen those pairs for which the value of statistic is above a threshold value s^*, which was chosen by cross-validation. When the pairs $\{(Z_i, Z_j)\}$ are chosen to be part of the model, and assuming without loss of generality that $i < j$ for those pairs, then the only connections that are kept in the network (in addition to those from the k-th hidden group to the k-th output group) are those from hidden group i to output group j, and from input group i to hidden group j, for every such (Z_i, Z_j) pair.

3 Experiments

In the experiments we have compared the following models:

- Naive Bayes: the likelihood is obtained as a product of multinomials (one per variable). Each multinomial is smoothed with a Dirichlet prior.
- Multi-Binomial (using Rademacher-Walsh expansion of order 2) [3]. Since this only handles the case of binary data, it was only applied to the DNA data set.
- A simple graphical model with the same pairs of variables and variable ordering as selected for the neural network, but in which each of the conditional distribution is modeled

by a separate multinomial for each of the conditioning context. This works only if the number of conditioning variables is small so in the Mushroom, Audiology, and Soybean experiments we had to reduce the number of conditioning variables (following the order given by the above tests). The multinomials are also smoothed with a Dirichlet prior.
- Neural network: the architecture described above, with or without hidden units (i.e., LARC), with or without pruning.

5-fold cross-validation was used to select the number of hidden units per hidden group and the weight decay for the neural network and LARC. Cross-validation was also used to choose the amount of pruning in the neural network and LARC, and the amount of smoothing in the Dirichlet priors for the multinomials of the naive Bayes model and the simple graphical model.

3.1 Results

All four data sets were obtained on the web from the UCI Machine Learning and STATLOG databases. Most of these are meant to be for classification tasks but we have instead ignored the classification and used the data to learn a probabilistic model of all the input features.

- DNA (from STATLOG): there are 180 binary features. 2000 cases were used for training and cross-validation, and 1186 for testing.
- Mushroom (from UCI): there are 22 discrete features (taking each between 2 and 12 values). 4062 cases were used for training and cross-validation, and 4062 for testing.
- Audiology (from UCI): there are 69 discrete features (taking each between 2 and 7 values). 113 cases are used for training and 113 for testing (the original train-test partition was 200 + 26 and we concatenated and re-split the data to obtain more significant test figures).
- Soybean (from UCI): there are 35 discrete features (taking each between 2 and 8 values). 307 cases are used for training and 376 for testing.

Table 1 clearly shows that the proposed model yields promising results since the pruned neural network was superior to all the other models in all 4 cases, and the pairwise differences with the other models are statistically significant in all 4 cases (except Audiology, where the difference with the network without hidden units, LARC, is not significant).

4 Conclusion

In this paper we have proposed a new application of multi-layer neural networks to the modelization of high-dimensional distributions, in particular for discrete data (but the model could also be applied to continuous or mixed discrete / continuous data). Like the polynomial expansions [3] that have been previously proposed for handling such high-dimensional distributions, the model approximates the joint distribution with a reasonable ($O(n^2)$) number of free parameters but unlike these it allows to capture high-order dependencies even when the number of parameters is small. The model can also be seen as an extension of the previously proposed auto-regressive logistic Bayesian network [4], using hidden units to capture some high-order dependencies.

Experimental results on four data sets with many discrete variables are very encouraging. The comparisons were made with a naive Bayes model, with a multi-binomial expansion, with the LARC model and with a simple graphical model, showing that a neural network did significantly better in terms of out-of-sample log-likelihood in all cases.

The approach to pruning the neural network used in the experiments, based on pairwise statistical dependency tests, is highly heuristic and better results might be obtained using approaches that take into account the higher order dependencies when selecting the conditioning variables. Methods based on pruning the fully connected network (e.g., with a "weight elimination" penalty) should also be tried. Also, we have not tried to optimize

	DNA		Mushroom	
	mean (stdev)	p-value	mean (stdev)	p-value
naive Bayes	100.4 (.18)	<1e-9	47.00 (.29)	<1e-9
multi-Binomial order 2	117.8 (.01)	<1e-9		
ordinary graph. model	108.1 (.06)	<1e-9	44.68 (.26)	<1e-9
LARC	83.2 (.24)	7e-5	42.51 (.16)	<1e-9
pruned LARC	91.2 (.15)	<1e-9	43.87 (.13)	<1e-9
full-conn. neural net.	120.0 (.02)	<1e-9	33.58 (.01)	<1e-9
pruned neural network	82.9 (.21)		31.25 (.04)	
	Audiology		Soybean	
	mean (stdev)	p-value	mean (stdev)	p-value
naive Bayes	36.40 (2.9)	<1e-9	34.74 (1.0)	<1e-9
multi-Binomial order 2				
ordinary graph. model	16.56 (.48)	6.8e-4	43.65 (.07)	<1e-9
LARC	17.69 (.65)	<1e-9	16.95 (.35)	5.5e-4
pruned LARC	16.69 (.41)	0.20	19.06 (.43)	<1e-9
full-conn. neural net.	17.39 (.58)	<1e-9	21.65 (.43)	<1e-9
pruned neural network	16.37 (.45)		16.55 (.27)	

Table 1: *Average out-of-sample negative log-likelihood obtained with the various models on four data sets (standard deviations of the average in parenthesis and p-value to test the null hypotheses that a model has same true generalization error as the pruned neural network). The pruned neural network was better than all the other models in in all cases, and the pair-wise difference is always statistically significant (except with respect to the pruned LARC on Audiology).*

the order of the variables, or combine different networks obtained with different orders, like [4].

References

[1] R.R. Bahadur. A representation of the joint distribution of responses to n dichotomous items. In ed. H. Solomon, editor, *Studies in Item Analysis and Predictdion*, pages 158–168. Stanford University Press, California, 1961.

[2] C.K. Chow. A recognition method using neighbor dependence. *IRE Trans. Elec. Comp.*, EC-11:683–690, October 1962.

[3] R.O. Duda and P.E. Hart. *Pattern Classification and Scene Analysis*. Wiley, New York, 1973.

[4] B. Frey. *Graphical models for machine learning and digital communication*. MIT Press, 1998.

[5] Steffen L. Lauritzen. The EM algorithm for graphical association models with missing data. *Computational Statistics and Data Analysis*, 19:191–201, 1995.

[6] Judea Pearl. *Probabilistic Reasoning in Intelligent Systems : Networks of Plausible Inference*. Morgan Kaufmann, 1988.

Robust Neural Network Regression for Offline and Online Learning

Thomas Briegel*
Siemens AG, Corporate Technology
D-81730 Munich, Germany
thomas.briegel@mchp.siemens.de

Volker Tresp
Siemens AG, Corporate Technology
D-81730 Munich, Germany
volker.tresp@mchp.siemens.de

Abstract

We replace the commonly used Gaussian noise model in nonlinear regression by a more flexible noise model based on the Student-t-distribution. The degrees of freedom of the t-distribution can be chosen such that as special cases either the Gaussian distribution or the Cauchy distribution are realized. The latter is commonly used in robust regression. Since the t-distribution can be interpreted as being an infinite mixture of Gaussians, parameters and hyperparameters such as the degrees of freedom of the t-distribution can be learned from the data based on an EM-learning algorithm. We show that modeling using the t-distribution leads to improved predictors on real world data sets. In particular, if outliers are present, the t-distribution is superior to the Gaussian noise model. In effect, by adapting the degrees of freedom, the system can "learn" to distinguish between outliers and non-outliers. Especially for online learning tasks, one is interested in avoiding inappropriate weight changes due to measurement outliers to maintain stable online learning capability. We show experimentally that using the t-distribution as a noise model leads to stable online learning algorithms and outperforms state-of-the art online learning methods like the extended Kalman filter algorithm.

1 INTRODUCTION

A commonly used assumption in nonlinear regression is that targets are disturbed by independent additive Gaussian noise. Although one can derive the Gaussian noise assumption based on a maximum entropy approach, the main reason for this assumption is practicability: under the Gaussian noise assumption the maximum likelihood parameter estimate can simply be found by minimization of the squared error. Despite its common use it is far from clear that the Gaussian noise assumption is a good choice for many practical problems. A reasonable approach therefore would be a noise distribution which contains the Gaussian as a special case but which has a tunable parameter that allows for more flexible distributions. In this paper we use the Student-t-distribution as a noise model which contains two free parameters – the degrees of freedom ν and a width parameter σ^2. A nice feature of the t-distribution is that if the degrees of freedom ν approach infinity, we recover the Gaussian noise model. If $\nu < \infty$ we obtain distributions which are more heavy-tailed than the Gaussian distribution including the Cauchy noise model with $\nu = 1$. The latter

---

*Now with McKinsey & Company, Inc.

is commonly used for robust regression. The first goal of this paper is to investigate if the additional free parameters, e.g. ν, lead to better generalization performance for real world data sets if compared to the Gaussian noise assumption with $\nu = \infty$. The most common reason why researchers depart from the Gaussian noise assumption is the presence of outliers. Outliers are errors which occur with low probability and which are not generated by the data-generation process that is subject to identification. The general problem is that a few (maybe even one) outliers of high leverage are sufficient to throw the standard Gaussian error estimators completely off-track (Rousseeuw & Leroy, 1987). In the second set of experiments we therefore compare how the generalization performance is affected by outliers, both for the Gaussian noise assumption and for the t-distribution assumption. Dealing with outliers is often of critical importance for online learning tasks. Online learning is of great interest in many applications exhibiting non-stationary behavior like tracking, signal and image processing, or navigation and fault detection (see, for instance the NIPS*98 Sequential Learning Workshop). Here one is interested in avoiding inappropriate weight chances due to measurement outliers to maintain stable online learning capability. Outliers might result in highly fluctuating weights and possible even instability when estimating the neural network weight vector online using a Gaussian error assumption. State-of-the art online algorithms like the extended Kalman filter, for instance, are known to be nonrobust against such outliers (Meinhold & Singpurwalla, 1989) since they are based on a Gaussian output error assumption.

The paper is organized as follows. In Section 2 we adopt a probabilistic view to outlier detection by taking as a heavy-tailed observation error density the Student-t-distribution which can be derived from an infinite mixture of Gaussians approach. In our work we use the multi-layer perceptron (MLP) as nonlinear model. In Section 3 we derive an EM algorithm for estimating the MLP weight vector and the hyperparameters offline. Employing a state-space representation to model the MLP's weight evolution in time we extend the batch algorithm of Section 3 to the online learning case (Section 4). The application of the computationally efficient Fisher scoring algorithm leads to posterior mode weight updates and an online EM-type algorithm for approximate maximum likelihood (ML) estimation of the hyperparameters. In in the last two sections (Section 5 and Section 6) we present experiments and conclusions, respectively.

2 THE t-DENSITY AS A ROBUST ERROR DENSITY

We assume a nonlinear regression model where for the t-th data point the noisy target $y_t \in \mathbf{R}$ is generated as

$$y_t = g(x_t; w_t) + v_t \tag{1}$$

and $x_t \in \mathbf{R}^k$ is a k-dimensional known input vector. $g(.; w_t)$ denotes a neural network model characterized by weight vector $w_t \in \mathbf{R}^n$, in our case a multi-layer perceptron (MLP). In the offline case the weight vector w_t is assumed to be a fixed unknown constant vector, i.e. $w_t \equiv w$. Furthermore, we assume that v_t is uncorrelated noise with density $p_{v_t}(.)$. In the offline case, we assume $p_{v_t}(.)$ to be independent of t, i.e. $p_{v_t}(.) \equiv p_v(.)$. In the following we assume that $p_v(.)$ is a Student-t-density with ν degrees of freedom with

$$p_v(z) = \mathcal{T}(z|\sigma^2, \nu) = \frac{\Gamma\left(\frac{\nu+1}{2}\right)}{\sigma\sqrt{\pi\nu}\,\Gamma(\frac{\nu}{2})} \left(1 + \frac{z^2}{\sigma^2 \nu}\right)^{-\frac{\nu+1}{2}}, \quad \nu, \sigma > 0. \tag{2}$$

It is immediately apparent that for $\nu = 1$ we recover the heavy-tailed Cauchy density. What is not so obvious is that for $\nu \to \infty$ we obtain a Gaussian density. For the derivation of the EM-learning rules in the next section it is important to note that the t-denstiy can be thought of as being an infinite mixture of Gaussians of the form

$$\mathcal{T}(z|\sigma^2, \nu) = \int \mathcal{N}(z|0, \sigma^2/u)\, p(u)\, du \tag{3}$$

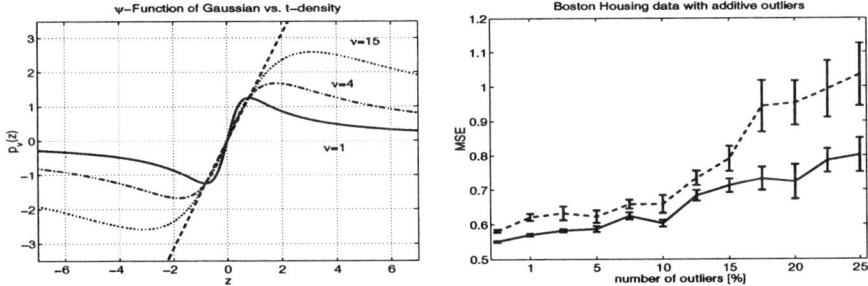

Figure 1: **Left**: $\psi(.)$-functions for the Gaussian density (dashed) and t-densities with $\nu = 1, 4, 15$ degrees of freedom. **Right**: MSE on Boston Housing data test set for additive outliers. The dashed line shows results using a Gaussian error measure and the continuous line shows the results using the Student-t-distribution as error measure.

where $\mathcal{T}(z|\sigma^2, \nu)$ is the Student-t-density with ν degrees of freedom and width parameter σ^2, $\mathcal{N}(z|0, \sigma^2/u)$ is a Gaussian density with center 0 and variance σ^2/u and $u \sim \chi_\nu^2/\nu$ where χ_ν^2 is a Chi-square distribution with ν degrees of freedom evaluated at $u > 0$.

To compare different noise models it is useful to evaluate the "ψ-function" defined as (Huber, 1964)

$$\psi(z) = -\partial \log p_v(z)/\partial z \qquad (4)$$

i.e. the negative score-function of the noise density. In the case of i.i.d. samples the ψ-function reflects the influence of a single measurement on the resulting estimator. Assuming Gaussian measurement errors $p_v(z) = \mathcal{N}(z|0, \sigma^2)$ we derive $\psi(z) = z/\sigma^2$ which means that for $|z| \to \infty$ a single outlier z can have an infinite leverage on the estimator. In contrast, for constructing robust estimators West (1981) states that large outliers should not have *any* influence on the estimator, i.e. $\psi(z) \to 0$ for $|z| \to \infty$. Figure 1 (left) shows $\psi(z)$ for different ν for the Student-t-distribution. It can be seen that the degrees of freedom ν determine how much weight outliers obtain in influencing the regression. In particular, for finite ν, the influence of outliers with $|z| \to \infty$ approaches zero.

3 ROBUST OFFLINE REGRESSION

As stated in Equation (3), the t-density can be thought of as being generated as an infinite mixture of Gaussians. Maximum likelihood adaptation of parameters and hyperparameters can therefore be performed using an EM algorithm (Lange *et al.*, 1989). For the t-th sample, a complete data point would consist of the triple (x_t, y_t, u_t) of which only the first two are known and u_t is missing.

In the *E-step* we estimate for every data point indexed by t

$$\alpha_t = (\nu^{\text{old}} + 1)/(\nu^{\text{old}} + \delta_t) \qquad (5)$$

where $\alpha_t = E[u_t|y_t, x_t]$ is the expected value of the unknown u_t given the available data (x_t, y_t) and where $\delta_t = \left(y_t - g(x_t; w^{\text{old}})\right)^2/\sigma^{2,\text{old}}$.

In the *M-step* the weights w and the hyperparameters σ^2 and ν are optimized using

$$w^{\text{new}} = \arg\min_w \left\{ \sum_{t=1}^{T} \alpha_t \left(y_t - g(x_t; w)\right)^2 \right\} \qquad (6)$$

$$\sigma^{2,\text{new}} = \frac{1}{T}\sum_{t=1}^{T}\alpha_t\left[\left(y_t - g(x_t;w^{\text{new}})\right)^2\right] \quad (7)$$

$$\nu^{\text{new}} = \arg\max_{\nu}\Big\{\frac{T\nu}{2}\log\frac{\nu}{2} - T\log\{\Gamma(\frac{\nu}{2})\}$$

$$+(\frac{\nu}{2}-1)\sum_{t=1}^{T}\beta_t - \frac{\nu}{2}\sum_{t=1}^{T}\alpha_t\Big\} \quad (8)$$

where

$$\beta_t = \text{DG}\left(\frac{\nu^{\text{old}}+1}{2}\right) - \log\left(\frac{1}{2}(\nu^{\text{old}}+\delta_t)\right) \quad (9)$$

with the Digamma function $\text{DG}(z) = \partial\Gamma(z)/\partial z$. Note that the M-step for ν is a one-dimensional nonlinear optimization problem. Also note that the M-steps for the weights in the MLP reduce to a weighted least squares regression problem in which outliers tend to be weighted down. The exception of course is the Gaussian case with $\nu \to \infty$ in which all terms obtain equal weight.

4 ROBUST ONLINE REGRESSION

For robust online regression, we assume that the model Equation (1) is still valid but that w can change over time, i.e. $w \equiv w_t$. In particular we assume that w_t follows a first order random walk with normally distributed increments, i.e.

$$w_t|w_{t-1} \sim \mathcal{N}(w_{t-1}, Q_t) \quad (10)$$

and where w_0 is normally distributed with center a_0 and covariance Q_0. Clearly, due to the nonlinear nature of g and due to the fact that the noise process is non-Gaussian, a fully Bayesian online algorithm — which for the linear case with Gaussian noise can be realized using the Kalman filter — is clearly infeasible.

On the other hand, if we consider data $\mathcal{D} = \{x_t, y_t\}_{t=1}^{T}$, the negative log-posterior $-\log p(W_T|\mathcal{D})$ of the parameter sequence $W_T = (w_0^\top, \ldots, w_T^\top)^\top$ is up to a normalizing constant

$$-\log p(W_T|\mathcal{D}) \propto -\sum_{t=1}^{T}\log p_\nu\big(y_t - g(x_t;w_t)\big) + \frac{1}{2}(w_0 - a_0)^\top Q_0^{-1}(w_0 - a_0)$$

$$+ \frac{1}{2}\sum_{t=1}^{T}(w_t - w_{t-1})^\top Q_t^{-1}(w_t - w_{t-1}) \quad (11)$$

and can be used as the appropriate cost function to derive the *posterior mode estimate* W_T^{MAP} for the weight sequence. The two differences to the presentation in the last section are that first, w_t is allowed to change over time and that second, penalty terms, stemming from the prior and the transition density, are included. The penalty terms are penalizing roughness of the weight sequence leading to smooth weight estimates.

A suitable way to determine a stationary point of $-\log p(W_T|\mathcal{D})$, the posterior mode estimate of W_T, is to apply *Fisher scoring*. With the current estimate W_T^{old} we get a better estimate $W_T^{\text{new}} = W_T^{\text{old}} + \eta\gamma$ for the unknown weight sequence W_T where γ is the solution of

$$\mathcal{S}(W_T^{\text{old}})\gamma = s(W_T^{\text{old}}) \quad (12)$$

with the negative score function $s(W_T) = -\partial\log p(W_T|\mathcal{D})/\partial W_T$ and the expected information matrix $\mathcal{S}(W_T) = \mathrm{E}[\partial^2 \log p(W_T|\mathcal{D})/\partial W_T \partial W_T^\top]$. By applying the ideas given in Fahrmeir & Kaufmann (1991) to robust neural network regression it turns out that solving (12), i.e. to compute the inverse of the expected information matrix, can be performed by

Cholesky decomposition in one forward and backward pass through the set of data $\mathcal{D}$. Note that the expected information matrix is a positive definite block-tridiagonal matrix. The forward-backward steps have to be iterated to obtain the posterior mode estimate W_T^{MAP} for W_T.

For *online posterior mode smoothing*, it is of interest to smooth backwards after each filter step t. If Fisher scoring steps are applied sequentially for $t = 1, 2, \ldots$, then the posterior mode smoother at time-step $t-1$, $W_{t-1}^{\mathrm{MAP}} = (w_{0|t-1}^\top, \ldots, w_{t-1|t-1}^\top)^\top$ together with the step-one predictor $w_{t|t-1} = w_{t-1|t-1}$ is a reasonable starting value for obtaining the posterior mode smoother W_t^{MAP} at time t. One can reduce the computational load by limiting the backward pass to a sliding time window, e.g. the last τ_t time steps, which is reasonable in non-stationary environments for online purposes. Furthermore, if we use the underlying assumption that in most cases a new measurement y_t should not change estimates too drastically then a *single* Fisher scoring step often suffices to obtain the new posterior mode estimate at time t. The resulting single Fisher scoring step algorithm with lookback parameter τ_t has in fact just one additional line of code involving simple matrix manipulations compared to online Kalman smoothing and is given here in pseudo-code. Details about the algorithm and a full description can be found in Briegel & Tresp (1999).

Online single Fisher scoring step algorithm (pseudo-code)

for $t = 1, 2, \ldots$ repeat the following four steps:

- Evaluate the step-one predictor $w_{t|t-1}$.
- Perform the forward recursions for $s = t - \tau_t, \ldots, t$.
- New data point (x_t, y_t) arrives: evaluate the corrector step $w_{t|t}$.
- Perform the backward smoothing recursions $w_{s-1|t}$ for $s = t, \ldots, t - \tau_t$.

For the adaptation of the parameters in the t-distribution, we apply results from Fahrmeir & Künstler (1999) to our nonlinear assumptions and use an online EM-type algorithm for approximate maximum likelihood estimation of the hyperparameters ν_t and σ_t^2. We assume the scale factors σ_t^2 and the degrees of freedom ν_t being fixed quantities in a certain time window of length $\tilde{\tau}_t$, e.g. $\sigma_t^2 = \sigma^2, \nu_t = \nu, t \in \{t - \tilde{\tau}_t, t\}$. For deriving online EM update equations we treat the weight sequence w_t together with the mixing variables u_t as missing. By linear Taylor series expansion of $g(.; w_s)$ about the Fisher scoring solutions $w_{s|t}$ and by approximating posterior expectations $\mathrm{E}[w_s|\mathcal{D}]$ with posterior modes $w_{s|t}, s \in \{t - \tilde{\tau}_t, t\}$ and posterior covariances $\mathrm{cov}[w_s|\mathcal{D}]$ with curvatures $\Sigma_{s|t} = \mathrm{E}[(w_s - w_{s|t})(w_s - w_{s|t})^\top | \mathcal{D}]$ in the E-step, a somewhat lengthy derivation results in approximate maximum likelihood update rules for σ^2 and ν similar to those given in Section 3. Details about the online EM-type algorithm can be found in Briegel & Tresp (1999).

5 EXPERIMENTS

1. Experiment: Real World Data Sets. In the first experiment we tested if the Student-t-distribution is a useful error measure for real-world data sets. In training, the Student-t-distribution was used and both, the degrees of freedom ν and the width parameter σ^2 were adapted using the EM update rules from Section 3. Each experiment was repeated 50 times with different divisions into training and test data. As a comparison we trained the neural networks to minimize the squared error cost function (including an optimized weight decay term). On the test data set we evaluated the performance using a squared error cost function. Table 1 provides some experimental parameters and gives the test set performance based on the 50 repetitions of the experiments. The additional explained variance is defined as [in percent] $100 \times (1 - \mathrm{MSPE}_\mathcal{T}/\mathrm{MSPE}_\mathcal{N})$ where $\mathrm{MSPE}_\mathcal{T}$ is the mean squared prediction error using the t-distribution and $\mathrm{MSPE}_\mathcal{N}$ is the mean squared prediction error using the Gaussian error measure. Furthermore we supply the standard

Table 1: Experimental parameters and test set performance on real world data sets.

Data Set	# Inputs/Hidden	Training	Test	Add.Exp.Var. [%]	Std. [%]
Boston Housing	(13/6)	400	106	4.2	0.93
Sunspot	(12/7)	221	47	5.3	0.67
Fraser River	(12/7)	600	334	5.4	0.75

error based on the 50 experiments. In all three experiments the networks optimized with the t-distribution as noise model were 4-5% better than the networks optimized using the Gaussian as noise model and in all experiments the improvements were significant based on the paired t-test with a significance level of 1%. The results show clearly that the additional free parameter in the Student-t-distribution does not lead to overfitting but is used in a sensible way by the system to value down the influence of extreme target values. Figure 2 shows the normal probability plots. Clearly visible is the derivation from the Gaussian distribution for extreme target values. We also like to remark that we did not apply any preselection process in choosing the particular data sets which indicates that non-Gaussian noise seems to be the rule rather than the exception for real world data sets.

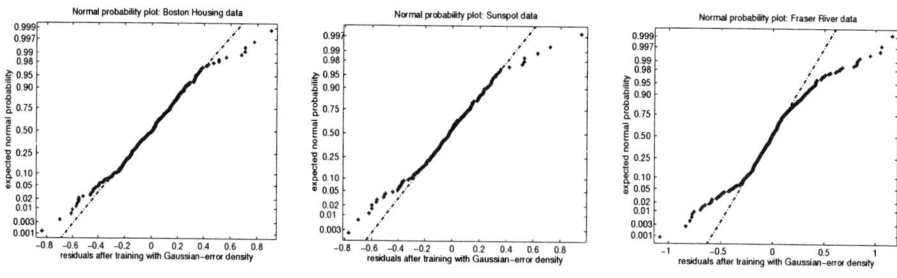

Figure 2: Normal probability plots of the three training data sets after learning with the Gaussian error measure. The dashed line show the expected normal probabilities. The plots show clearly that the residuals follow a more heavy-tailed distribution than the normal distribution.

2. Experiment: Outliers. In the second experiment we wanted to test how our approach deals with outliers which are artificially added to the data set. We started with the Boston housing data set and divided it into training and test data. We then randomly selected a subset of the training data set (between 0.5% and 25%) and added to the targets a uniformly generated real number in the interval $[-5, 5]$. Figure 1 (right) shows the mean squared error on the test set for different percentages of added outliers. The error bars are derived from 20 repetitions of the experiment with different divisions into training and test set. It is apparent that the approach using the t-distribution is consistently better than the network which was trained based on a Gaussian noise assumption.

3. Experiment: Online Learning. In the third experiment we examined the use of the t-distribution in online learning. Data were generated from a nonlinear map $y = 0.6x^2 + b\sin(6x) - 1$ where $b = -0.75, -0.4, -0.1, 0.25$ for the first, second, third and fourth set of 150 data points, respectively. Gaussian noise with variance 0.2 was added and for training, a MLP with 4 hidden units was used. In the first experiment we compare the performance of the EKF algorithm with our single Fisher scoring step algorithm. Figure 3 (left) shows that our algorithm converges faster to the correct map and also handles the transition in the model (parameter b) much better than the EKF. In the second experiment with a probability of 10% outliers uniformly drawn from the interval $[-5, 5]$ were added to the targets. Figure 3 (middle) shows that the single Fisher scoring step algorithm using the

t-distribution is consistently better than the same algorithm using a Gaussian noise model and the EKF. The two plots on the right in Figure 3 compare the nonlinear maps learned after 150 and 600 time steps, respectively.

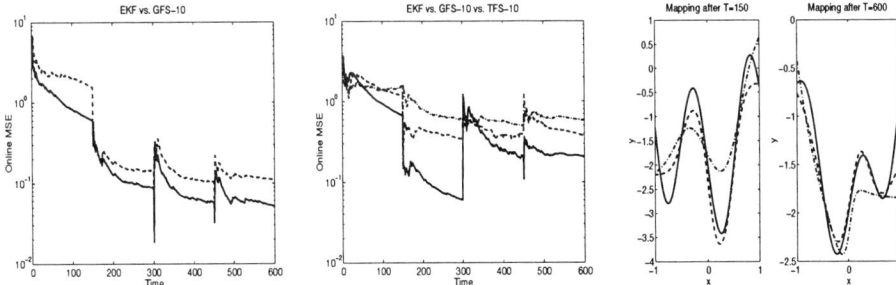

Figure 3: **Left & Middle**: Online MSE over each of the 4 sets of training data. On the left we compare extended Kalman filtering (EKF) (dashed) with the single Fisher scoring step algorithm with $\tau_t = 10$ (GFS-10) (continuous) for additive Gaussian noise. The second figure shows EKF (dashed-dotted), Fisher scoring with Gaussian error noise (GFS-10) (dashed) and t-distributed error noise (TFS-10) (continuous), respectively for data with additive outliers. **Right**: True map (continuous), EKF learned map (dashed-dotted) and TFS-10 map (dashed) after $T = 150$ and $T = 600$ (data sets with additive outliers).

6 CONCLUSIONS

We have introduced the Student-t-distribution to replace the standard Gaussian noise assumption in nonlinear regression. Learning is based on an EM algorithm which estimates both the scaling parameters and the degrees of freedom of the t-distribution. Our results show that using the Student-t-distribution as noise model leads to 4-5% better test errors than using the Gaussian noise assumption on real world data set. This result seems to indicate that non-Gaussian noise is the rule rather than the exception and that extreme target values should in general be weighted down. Dealing with outliers is particularly important for online tasks in which outliers can lead to instability in the adaptation process. We introduced a new online learning algorithm using the t-distribution which leads to better and more stable results if compared to the extended Kalman filter.

References

Briegel, T. and Tresp, V. (1999) *Dynamic Neural Regression Models*, Discussion Paper, Seminar für Statistik, Ludwig Maximilians Universität München.

de Freitas, N., Doucet, A. and Niranjan, M. (1998) *Sequential Inference and Learning*, NIPS*98 Workshop, Breckenridge, CO.

Fahrmeir, L. and Kaufmann, H. (1991) *On Kalman Filtering, Posterior Mode Estimation and Fisher Scoring in Dynamic Exponential Family Regression*, Metrika 38, pp. 37-60.

Fahrmeir, L. and Künstler, R. (1999) *Penalized likelihood smoothing in robust state space models*, Metrika 49, pp. 173-191.

Huber, P.J. (1964) *Robust Estimation of Location Parameter*, Annals of Mathematical Statistics 35, pp. 73-101.

Lange, K., Little, L., Taylor, J. (1989) *Robust Statistical Modeling Using the t-Distribution*, JASA 84, pp. 881-896.

Meinhold, R. and Singpurwalla, N. (1989) *Robustification of Kalman Filter Models*, JASA 84, pp. 470-496.

Rousseeuw, P. and Leroy, A. (1987) *Robust Regression and Outlier Detection*, John Wiley & Sons.

West, M. (1981) *Robust Sequential Approximate Bayesian Estimation*, JRSS B 43, pp. 157-166.

Reconstruction of Sequential Data with Probabilistic Models and Continuity Constraints

Miguel Á. Carreira-Perpiñán
Dept. of Computer Science, University of Sheffield, UK
miguel@dcs.shef.ac.uk

Abstract

We consider the problem of reconstructing a temporal discrete sequence of multidimensional real vectors when part of the data is missing, under the assumption that the sequence was generated by a continuous process. A particular case of this problem is multivariate regression, which is very difficult when the underlying mapping is one-to-many. We propose an algorithm based on a joint probability model of the variables of interest, implemented using a nonlinear latent variable model. Each point in the sequence is potentially reconstructed as any of the modes of the conditional distribution of the missing variables given the present variables (computed using an exhaustive mode search in a Gaussian mixture). Mode selection is determined by a dynamic programming search that minimises a geometric measure of the reconstructed sequence, derived from continuity constraints. We illustrate the algorithm with a toy example and apply it to a real-world inverse problem, the acoustic-to-articulatory mapping. The results show that the algorithm outperforms conditional mean imputation and multilayer perceptrons.

1 Definition of the problem

Consider a mobile point following a continuous trajectory in a subset of $\mathbb{R}^D$. Imagine that it is possible to obtain a finite number of measurements of the position of the point. Suppose that these measurements are corrupted by noise and that sometimes part of, or all, the variables are missing. The problem considered here is to reconstruct the sequence from the part of it which is observed. In the particular case where the present variables and the missing ones are the same for every point, the problem is one of multivariate regression. If the pattern of missing variables is more general, the problem is one of missing data reconstruction.

Consider the problem of regression. If the present variables uniquely identify the missing ones at every point of the data set, the problem can be adequately solved by a universal function approximator, such as a multilayer perceptron. In a probabilistic framework, the conditional mean of the missing variables given the present ones will minimise the average squared reconstruction error [3]. However, if the underlying mapping is one-to-many, there will be regions in the space for which the present variables do not identify uniquely the missing ones. In this case, the conditional mean mapping will fail, since it will give a compromise value—an average of the correct ones. *Inverse problems*, where the inverse of a mapping is one-to-many, are of this type. They include the acoustic-to-articulatory mapping in speech [15], where different vocal tract shapes may produce the same acoustic signal, or the robot arm problem [2], where different configurations of the joint angles may place the hand in the same position.

In some situations, data reconstruction is a means to some other objective, such as classification or inference. Here, we deal solely with data reconstruction of temporally continuous sequences according to the squared error. Our algorithm does not apply for data sets that either lack continuity (e.g. discrete variables) or have lost it (e.g. due to undersampling or shuffling).

We follow a statistical learning approach: we attempt to reconstruct the sequence by learning the mapping from a training set drawn from the probability distribution of the data, rather than by solving a physical model of the system. Our algorithm can be described briefly as follows. First, a joint density model of the data is learned in an unsupervised way from a sample of the data[1]. Then, pointwise reconstruction is achieved by computing all the modes of the conditional distribution of the missing variables given the present ones at the current point. In principle, any of these modes is potentially a plausible reconstruction. When reconstructing a sequence, we repeat this mode search for every point in the sequence, and then find the combination of modes that minimises a geometric sequence measure, using dynamic programming. The sequence measure is derived from local continuity constraints, e.g. the curve length.

The algorithm is detailed in §2 to §4. We illustrate it with a 2D toy problem in §5 and apply it to an acoustic-to-articulatory-like problem in §6. §7 discusses the results and compares the approach with previous work.

Our notation is as follows. We represent the observed variables in vector form as $\mathbf{t} = (t_1, \ldots, t_D) \in \mathbb{R}^D$. A data set (possibly a temporal sequence) is represented as $\{\mathbf{t}_n\}_{n=1}^N$. Groups of variables are represented by sets of indices $\mathcal{I}, \mathcal{J} \in \{1, \ldots, D\}$, so that if $\mathcal{I} = \{1, 7, 3\}$, then $\mathbf{t}_\mathcal{I} = (t_1 t_7 t_3)$.

2 Joint generative modelling using latent variables

Our starting point is a joint probability model of the observed variables $p(\mathbf{t})$. From it, we can compute conditional distributions of the form $p(\mathbf{t}_\mathcal{J}|\mathbf{t}_\mathcal{I})$ and, by picking representative points, derive a (multivalued) mapping $\mathbf{t}_\mathcal{I} \to \mathbf{t}_\mathcal{J}$. Thus, contrarily to other approaches, e.g. [6], we adopt *multiple pointwise imputation*. In §4 we show how to obtain a single reconstructed sequence of points.

Although density estimation requires more parameters than mapping approximation, it has a fundamental advantage [6]: the density model represents the relation between any variables, which allows to choose any missing/present variable combination. A mapping approximator treats asymmetrically some variables as inputs (present) and the rest as outputs (missing) and can't easily deal with other relations.

The existence of functional relationships (even one-to-many) between the observed variables indicates that the data must span a low-dimensional manifold in the data space. This suggests the use of latent variable models for modelling the joint density. However, it is possible to use other kinds of density models.

In latent variable modelling the assumption is that the observed high-dimensional data $\mathbf{t}$ is generated from an underlying low-dimensional process defined by a small number L of *latent variables* $\mathbf{x} = (x_1, \ldots, x_L)$ [1]. The latent variables are mapped by a fixed

---

[1]In our examples we only use complete training data (i.e., with no missing data), but it is perfectly possible to estimate a probability model with incomplete training data by using an EM algorithm [6].

transformation into a D-dimensional data space and noise is added there. A particular model is specified by three parametric elements: a prior distribution in latent space $p(\mathbf{x})$, a smooth mapping $\mathbf{f}$ from latent space to data space and a noise model in data space $p(\mathbf{t}|\mathbf{x})$. Marginalising the joint probability density function $p(\mathbf{t},\mathbf{x})$ over the latent space gives the distribution in data space, $p(\mathbf{t})$. Given an observed sample in data space $\{\mathbf{t}_n\}_{n=1}^N$, a parameter estimate can be found by maximising the log-likelihood, typically using an EM algorithm. We consider the following latent variable models, both of which allow easy computation of conditional distributions of the form $p(\mathbf{t}_\mathcal{J}|\mathbf{t}_\mathcal{I})$:

Factor analysis [1], in which the mapping is linear, the prior in latent space is unit Gaussian and the noise model is diagonal Gaussian. The density in data space is then Gaussian with a constrained covariance matrix. We use it as a baseline for comparison with more sophisticated models.

The generative topographic mapping (GTM) [4] is a nonlinear latent variable model, where the mapping is a generalised linear model, the prior in latent space is discrete uniform and the noise model is isotropic Gaussian. The density in data space is then a constrained mixture of isotropic Gaussians.

In latent variable models that sample the latent space prior distribution (like GTM), the mixture centroids in data space (associated to the latent space samples) are not trainable parameters. We can then improve the density model at a higher computational cost with no generalisation loss by increasing the number of mixture components. Note that the number of components required will depend exponentially on the intrinsic dimensionality of the data (ideally coincident with that of the latent space, L) and not on the observed one, D.

3 Exhaustive mode finding

Given a conditional distribution $p(\mathbf{t}_\mathcal{J}|\mathbf{t}_\mathcal{I})$, we consider all its modes as plausible predictions for $\mathbf{t}_\mathcal{J}$. This requires an exhaustive mode search in the space of $\mathbf{t}_\mathcal{J}$. For Gaussian mixtures, we do this by using a maximisation algorithm starting from each centroid[2], such as a fixed-point iteration or gradient ascent combined with quadratic optimisation [5]. In the particular case where all variables are missing, rather than performing a mode search, we return as predictions all the component centroids. It is also possible to obtain error bars at each mode by locally approximating the density function by a normal distribution. However, if the dimensionality of $\mathbf{t}_\mathcal{J}$ is high, the error bars become very wide due to the curse of the dimensionality.

An advantage of multiple pointwise imputation is the easy incorporation of extra constraints on the missing variables. Such constraints might include keeping only those modes that lie in an interval dependent on the present variables [8] or discarding low-probability (spurious) modes—which speeds up the reconstruction algorithm and may make it more robust.

A faster way to generate representative points of $p(\mathbf{t}_\mathcal{J}|\mathbf{t}_\mathcal{I})$ is simply to draw a fixed number of samples from it—which may also give robustness to poor density models. However, in practice this resulted in a higher reconstruction error.

4 Continuity constraints and dynamic programming (DP) search

Application of the exhaustive mode search to the conditional distribution at every point of the sequence produces one or more candidate reconstructions per point. To select a

---

[2]Actually, given a value of $\mathbf{t}_\mathcal{I}$, most centroids have negligible posterior probability and can be removed from the mixture with practically no loss of accuracy. Thus, a large number of mixture components may be used without deteriorating excessively the computational efficiency.

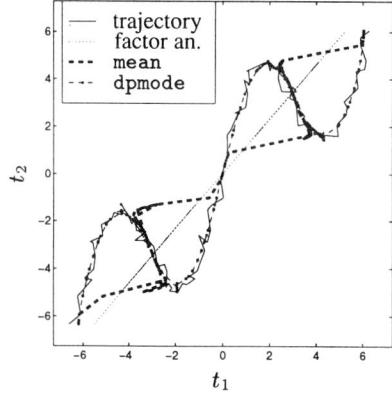

Average squared reconstruction error

Missing pattern	Factor analysis	MLP[a]	GTM		
			mean	dpmode	cmode
t_2	3.8902	0.2046	0.2044	0.2168	0.2168
t_1	4.3226	2.5126	2.4224	0.0522	0.0522
t_1 or t_2	4.2020	—	1.2963	0.1305	0.1305
10%	1.0983	—	0.3970	0.0253	0.0251
50%	6.2914	—	4.6530	0.1176	0.0771
90%	21.4942	—	20.7877	2.2261	0.0643

[a]The MLP cannot be applied to varying patterns of missing data.

Table 1: Trajectory reconstruction for a 2D problem. The table gives the average squared reconstruction error when t_2 is missing (row 1), t_1 is missing (row 2), exactly one variable per point is missing at random (row 3) or a percentage of the values are missing at random (rows 4–6). The graph shows the reconstructed trajectory when t_1 is missing: factor analysis (straight, dotted line), mean (thick, dashed), dpmode (superimposed on the trajectory).

single reconstructed sequence, we define a *local continuity constraint*: consecutive points in time should also lie nearby in data space. That is, if δ is some suitable distance in $\mathbb{R}^D$, $\delta(\mathbf{t}_n, \mathbf{t}_{n+1})$ should be small. Then we define a *global geometric measure* $\mathscr{C}$ for a sequence $\{\mathbf{t}_n\}_{n=1}^N$ as $\mathscr{C}\left(\{\mathbf{t}_n\}_{n=1}^N\right) \stackrel{\text{def}}{=} \sum_{n=1}^{N-1} \delta(\mathbf{t}_n, \mathbf{t}_{n+1})$. We take δ as the Euclidean distance, so $\mathscr{C}$ becomes simply the length of the sequence (considered as a polygonal line). Finding the sequence of modes with minimal $\mathscr{C}$ is efficiently achieved by dynamic programming.

5 Results with a toy problem

To illustrate the algorithm, we generated a 2D data set from the curve $(t_1, t_2) = (x, x + 3\sin(x))$ for $x \in [-2\pi, 2\pi]$, with normal isotropic noise (standard deviation 0.2) added. Thus, the mapping $t_1 \to t_2$ is one-to-one but the inverse one, $t_2 \to t_1$, is multivalued. One-dimensional factor analysis (6 parameters) and GTM models (21 parameters) were estimated from a 1000-point sample, as well as two 48-hidden-unit multilayer perceptrons (98 parameters), one for each mapping. For GTM we tried several strategies to select points from the conditional distribution: mean (the conditional mean), dpmode (the mode selected by dynamic programming) and cmode (the closest mode to the actual value of the missing variable). The cmode, unknown in practice, is used here to compute a lower bound on the performance of any mode-based strategy. Other strategies, such as picking the global mode, a random mode or using a local (greedy) search instead of dynamic programming, gave worse results than the dpmode.

Table 1 shows the results for reconstructing a 100-point trajectory. The nonlinear nature of the problem causes factor analysis to break down in all cases. For the one-to-one mapping case (t_2 missing) all the other methods perform well and recover the original trajectory, with mean attaining the lowest error, as predicted by the theory[3]. For the one-to-many case (t_1 missing, see fig.), both the MLP and the mean are unable to track more than one branch of the mapping, but the dpmode still recovers the original mapping. For random missing

---

[3]A combined strategy could retain the optimality of the mean in the one-to-one case and the advantage of the modes in the one-to-many case, by choosing the conditional mean (rather than the mode) when the conditional distribution is unimodal, and all the modes otherwise.

Missing pattern	Factor analysis	GTM		
		mean	dpmode	cmode
PLP	0.9165	0.6217	0.6250	0.4587
EPG	3.7177	2.3729	2.0613	1.0538
10%	0.2046	0.0947	0.0903	0.0841
50%	1.1285	0.7540	0.6527	0.6023
blocks	0.1950	0.1669	0.1005	0.0925

Table 2: Average squared reconstruction error for an utterance. The last row corresponds to a missing pattern of square blocks totalling 10% of the utterance.

patterns[4], the dpmode is able to cope well with high amounts of missing data.

The consistently low error of the cmode shows that the modes contain important information about the possible options to predict the missing values. The performance of the dpmode, close to that of the cmode even for large amounts of missing data, shows that application of the continuity constraint allows to recover that information.

6 Results with real speech data

We report a preliminary experiment using acoustic and electropalatographic (EPG) data[5] for the utterance "Put your hat on the hatrack and your coat in the cupboard" (speaker FG) from the ACCOR database [10]. 12th-order perceptual linear prediction coefficients [7] plus the log-energy were computed at 200 Hz from its acoustic waveform. The EPG data consisted of 62-bit frames sampled at 200 Hz, which we consider as 62-dimensional vectors of real numbers. No further preprocessing of the data was carried out. Thus, the resulting sequence consisted of over 600 75-dimensional real vectors. We constructed a training set by picking, in random order, 80% of these vectors. The whole utterance was used for the reconstruction test.

We trained two density models: a 9-dimensional factor analysis (825 parameters) and a two-dimensional[6] GTM (3676 parameters) with a 20×20 grid (resulting in a mixture of 400 isotropic Gaussians in the 75-dimensional data space). Table 2 confirms again that the linear method (factor analysis) fares worst (despite its use of a latent space of dimension $L = 9$). The dpmode attains almost always a lower error than the conditional mean, with up to a 40% improvement (the larger the higher the amount of missing data). When a shuffled version of the utterance (thus having lost its continuity) was reconstructed, the error of the dpmode was consistently higher than that of the mean, indicating that the application of the continuity constraint was responsible for the error decrease.

7 Discussion

Using a joint probability model allows flexible construction of predictive distributions for the missing data: varying patterns of missing data and multiple pointwise imputations are possible, as opposed to standard function approximators. We have shown that the modes of the conditional distribution of the missing variables given the present ones are potentially

---

[4]Note that the nature of the missing pattern (missing at random, missing completely at random, etc. [9]) does not matter for reconstruction—although it does for estimation.

[5]An EPG datum is the (binary) contact pattern between the tongue and the palate at selected locations in the latter. Note that it is an incomplete articulatory representation of speech.

[6]A latent space of 2 dimensions is clearly too low for this data, but the computational complexity of GTM prevents the use of a higher one. Still, its nonlinear character compensates partly for this.

plausible reconstructions of the missing values, and that the application of local continuity constraints—when they hold—can help to recover the actually plausible ones.

Previous work The key aspects of our approach are the use of a joint density model (learnt in an unsupervised way), the exhaustive mode search, the definition of a geometric trajectory measure derived from continuity constraints and its implementation by dynamic programming. Several of these ideas have been applied earlier in the literature, which we review briefly.

The use of the joint density model for prediction is the basis of the statistical technique of *multiple imputation* [9]. Here, several versions of the complete data set are generated from the appropriate conditional distributions, analysed by standard complete-data methods and the results combined to produce inferences that incorporate missing-data uncertainty. Ghahramani and Jordan [6] also proposed the use of the joint density model to generate a single estimate of the missing variables and applied it to a classification problem.

Conditional distributions have been approximated by MLPs rather than by density estimation [16], but this lacks flexibility to varying patterns of missing data and requires an extra model of the input variables distribution (unless assumed uniform).

Rohwer and van der Rest [12] introduce a cost function with a description length interpretation whose minimum is approximated by the densest mode of a distribution. A neural network trained with this cost function can learn one branch of a multivariate mapping, but is unable to select other branches which may be correct at a given time.

Continuity constraints implemented via dynamic programming have been used for the acoustic-to-articulatory mapping problem [15]. Reasonable results (better than using an MLP to approximate the mapping) can be obtained using a large codebook of acoustic and articulatory vectors. Rahim et al. [11] achieve similar quality with much less computational requirements using an assembly of MLPs, each one trained in a different area of the acoustic-articulatory space, to locally approximate the mapping. However, clustering the space is heuristic (with no guarantee that the mapping is one-to-one in each region) and training the assembly is difficult. It also lacks flexibility to varying missingness patterns.

A number of trajectory measures have been used in the robot arm problem literature [2] and minimised by dynamic programming, such as the energy, torque, acceleration, jerk, etc.

Temporal modelling It is important to remark that our approach does not attempt to model the temporal evolution of the system. The joint probability model is estimated statically. The temporal aspect of the data appears indirectly and a posteriori through the application of the continuity constraints to select a trajectory[7]. In this respect, our approach differs from that of dynamical systems or from models based in Markovian assumptions, such as hidden Markov models or other trajectory models [13, 14]. However, the fact that the duration or speed of the trajectory plays no role in the algorithm may make it invariant to time warping (e.g. robust to fast/slow speech styles).

Choice of density model The fact that the modes are a key aspect of our approach make it sensitive to the density model. With finite mixtures, spurious modes can appear as ripple superimposed on the density function in regions where the mixture components are sparsely distributed and have little interaction. Such modes can lead the DP search to a wrong trajectory. Possible solutions are to improve the density model (perhaps by increasing the number of components, see §2, or by regularisation), to smooth the conditional distribution or to look for *bumps* (regions of high probability mass) instead of modes.

---

[7]However, the method may be derived by assuming a distribution over the whole sequence with a normal, Markovian dependence between adjacent frames.

Computational cost The DP search has complexity $\mathcal{O}(NM^2)$, where M is an average of the number of modes per sequence point and N the number of points in the sequence. In our experiments M is usually small and the DP search is fast even for long sequences. The bottleneck of the reconstruction part of the algorithm is obtaining the modes of the conditional distribution for every point in the sequence when there are many missing variables.

Further work We envisage more thorough experiments using data from the Wisconsin X-ray microbeam database and comparing with recurrent MLPs or an MLP committee, which may be more suitable for multivalued mappings. Extensions of our algorithm include different geometric measures (e.g. curvature-based rather than length-based), different strategies for multiple pointwise imputation (e.g. bump searching) or multidimensional constraints (e.g. temporal and spatial). Other practical applications include audiovisual mappings for speech, hippocampal place cell reconstruction and wind vector retrieval from scatterometer data.

Acknowledgments

We thank Steve Renals for useful conversations and for comments about this paper.

References

[1] D. J. Bartholomew. *Latent Variable Models and Factor Analysis*. Charles Griffin & Company Ltd., London, 1987.

[2] N. Bernstein. *The Coordination and Regulation of Movements*. Pergamon, Oxford, 1967.

[3] C. M. Bishop. *Neural Networks for Pattern Recognition*. Oxford University Press, 1995.

[4] C. M. Bishop, M. Svensén, and C. K. I. Williams. GTM: The generative topographic mapping. *Neural Computation*, 10(1):215–234, Jan. 1998.

[5] M. Á. Carreira-Perpiñán. Mode-finding in Gaussian mixtures. Technical Report CS–99–03, Dept. of Computer Science, University of Sheffield, UK, Mar. 1999. Available online at http://www.dcs.shef.ac.uk/~miguel/papers/cs-99-03.html.

[6] Z. Ghahramani and M. I. Jordan. Supervised learning from incomplete data via an EM approach. In *NIPS 6*, pages 120–127, 1994.

[7] H. Hermansky. Perceptual linear predictive (PLP) analysis of speech. *J. Acoustic Soc. Amer.*, 87(4):1738–1752, Apr. 1990.

[8] L. Josifovski, M. Cooke, P. Green, and A. Vizinho. State based imputation of missing data for robust speech recognition and speech enhancement. In *Proc. Eurospeech 99*, pages 2837–2840, 1999.

[9] R. J. A. Little and D. B. Rubin. *Statistical Analysis with Missing Data*. John Wiley & Sons, New York, London, Sydney, 1987.

[10] A. Marchal and W. J. Hardcastle. ACCOR: Instrumentation and database for the cross-language study of coarticulation. *Language and Speech*, 36(2, 3):137–153, 1993.

[11] M. G. Rahim, C. C. Goodyear, W. B. Kleijn, J. Schroeter, and M. M. Sondhi. On the use of neural networks in articulatory speech synthesis. *J. Acoustic Soc. Amer.*, 93(2):1109–1121, Feb. 1993.

[12] R. Rohwer and J. C. van der Rest. Minimum description length, regularization, and multimodal data. *Neural Computation*, 8(3):595–609, Apr. 1996.

[13] S. Roweis. Constrained hidden Markov models. In *NIPS 12 (this volume)*, 2000.

[14] L. K. Saul and M. G. Rahim. Markov processes on curves for automatic speech recognition. In *NIPS 11*, pages 751–757, 1999.

[15] J. Schroeter and M. M. Sondhi. Techniques for estimating vocal-tract shapes from the speech signal. *IEEE Trans. Speech and Audio Process.*, 2(1):133–150, Jan. 1994.

[16] V. Tresp, R. Neuneier, and S. Ahmad. Efficient methods for dealing with missing data in supervised learning. In *NIPS 7*, pages 689–696, 1995.

Transductive Inference for Estimating Values of Functions

Olivier Chapelle*, Vladimir Vapnik*,†, Jason Weston††,†,*
* AT&T Research Laboratories, Red Bank, USA.
† Royal Holloway, University of London, Egham, Surrey, UK.
†† Barnhill BioInformatics.com, Savannah, Georgia, USA.
{chapelle,vlad,weston}@research.att.com

Abstract

We introduce an algorithm for estimating the values of a function at a set of test points $x_{\ell+1}, \ldots, x_{\ell+m}$ given a set of training points $(x_1, y_1), \ldots, (x_\ell, y_\ell)$ without estimating (as an intermediate step) the regression function. We demonstrate that this direct (transductive) way for estimating values of the regression (or classification in pattern recognition) can be more accurate than the traditional one based on two steps, first estimating the function and then calculating the values of this function at the points of interest.

1 Introduction

Following [6] we consider a general scheme of transductive inference. Suppose there exists a function $y^* = f_0(x)$ from which we observe the measurements corrupted with noise

$$((x_1, y_1), \ldots (x_\ell, y_\ell)), \quad y_i = y_i^* + \xi_i. \tag{1}$$

Find an algorithm A that using both the given set of training data (1) and the given set of test data

$$(x_{\ell+1}, \ldots, x_{\ell+m}) \tag{2}$$

selects from a set of functions $\{x \mapsto f(x)\}$ a function

$$y = f(x) = f_A(x|x_1, y_1, \ldots, x_\ell, y_\ell, x_{\ell+1}, \ldots, x_{\ell+m}) \tag{3}$$

and minimizes at the points of interest the functional

$$R(A) = E\left(\sum_{i=\ell+1}^{\ell+m}(y_i^* - f_A(x_i|x_1, y_1, \ldots, x_\ell, y_\ell, x_{\ell+1}, \ldots, x_{\ell+m}))^2\right) \tag{4}$$

where expectation is taken over x and ξ. For the training data we are given the vector x and the value y, for the test data we are only given x.

Usually, the problem of estimating values of a function at points of interest is solved in two steps: first in a given set of functions $f(x, \alpha)$, $\alpha \in \Lambda$ one estimates the regression, i.e the function which minimizes the functional

$$R(\alpha) = \int((y - f(x, \alpha))^2 dF(x, y), \tag{5}$$

(the inductive step) and then using the estimated function $y = f(x, \alpha_\ell)$ we calculate the values at points of interest

$$y_i^* = f(x_i^*, \alpha_\ell) \tag{6}$$

(the deductive step).

Note, however, that the estimation of a function is equivalent to estimating its values in the continuum points of the domain of the function. Therefore, by solving the regression problem using a restricted amount of information, we are looking for a more general solution than is required. In [6] it is shown that using a direct estimation method one can obtain better bounds than through the two step procedure.

In this article we develop the idea introduced in [5] for estimating the values of a function only at the given points.

The material is organized as follows. In Section 1 we consider the classical (inductive) Ridge Regression procedure, and the leave–one–out technique which is used to measure the quality of its solutions. Section 2 introduces the transductive method of inference for estimation of the values of a function based on this leave–one–out technique. In Section 3 experiments which demonstrate the improvement given by transductive inference compared to inductive inference (in both regression and pattern recognition) are presented. Finally, Section 4 summarizes the results.

2   Ridge Regression and the Leave–One–Out procedure

In order to describe our transductive method, let us first discuss the classical two-step (inductive plus deductive) procedure of Ridge Regression. Consider the set of functions linear in their parameters

$$f(x, \alpha) = \sum_{i=1}^{n} \alpha_i \phi_i(x). \tag{7}$$

To minimize the expected loss (5), where $F(x, y)$ is unknown, we minimize the following empirical functional (the so–called Ridge Regression functional [1])

$$R_{emp}(\alpha) = \frac{1}{\ell} \sum_{i=1}^{\ell} (y_i - f(x_i, \alpha))^2 + \gamma ||\alpha||^2 \tag{8}$$

where γ is a fixed positive constant, called the regularization parameter. The minimum is given by the vector of coefficients

$$\alpha_\ell = \alpha(x_1, y_1, \ldots, x_\ell, y_\ell) = (K^T K + \gamma I)^{-1} K^T Y \tag{9}$$

where

$$Y = (y_1, \ldots, y_\ell)^T, \tag{10}$$

and K is a matrix with elements:

$$K_{ij} = \phi_j(x_i), \quad i = 1, \ldots, \ell, \quad j = 1, \ldots, n. \tag{11}$$

The problem is to choose the value γ which provides small expected loss for training on a sample $S_\ell = \{(x_1, y_1), \ldots, (x_\ell, y_\ell)\}$.

For this purpose, we would like to choose γ such that f_γ minimizing (8) also minimizes

$$R = \int (y^* - f_\gamma(x^*|S_\ell))^2 dF(x^*, y^*) dF(S_\ell). \tag{12}$$

Since $F(x,y)$ is unknown one cannot estimate this minimum directly. To solve this problem we instead use the leave–one–out procedure, which is an almost unbiased estimator of (12). The leave–one–out error of an algorithm on the training sample S_ℓ is

$$T_{loo}(\gamma) = \frac{1}{\ell} \sum_{i=1}^{\ell} (y_i - f_\gamma(x_i|S_\ell \setminus (x_i, y_i)))^2 . \qquad (13)$$

The leave–one–out procedure consists of removing from the training data one element (say (x_i, y_i)), constructing the regression function only on the basis of the remaining training data and then testing the removed element. In this fashion one tests all ℓ elements of the training data using ℓ different decision rules. The minimum over γ of (13) we consider as the minimum over γ of (12) since the expectation of (13) coincides with (12) [2].

For Ridge Regression, one can derive a closed form expression for the leave–one–out error. Denoting

$$A_\gamma^{-1} = (K^T K + \gamma I)^{-1} \qquad (14)$$

the error incurred by the leave–one–out procedure is [6]

$$T_{loo}(\gamma) = \frac{1}{\ell} \sum_{i=1}^{\ell} \left(\frac{y_i - k_i^T A_\gamma^{-1} K^T Y}{1 - k_i^T A_\gamma^{-1} k_i} \right)^2 \qquad (15)$$

where

$$k_t = (\phi_1(x_t) \ldots, \phi_n(x_t))^T . \qquad (16)$$

Let $\gamma = \gamma^0$ be the minimum of (15). Then the vector

$$Y^0 = K^*(K^T K + \gamma^0 I)^{-1} K^T Y \qquad (17)$$

where

$$K^* = \begin{pmatrix} \phi(x_{\ell+1}) & \cdots & \phi_n(x_{\ell+1}) \\ \vdots & & \vdots \\ \phi_1(x_{\ell+m}) & \cdots & \phi_n(x_{\ell+m}) \end{pmatrix} \qquad (18)$$

is the Ridge Regression estimate of the unknown values $(y_{\ell+1}^*, \ldots, y_{\ell+m}^*)$.

3 Leave–One–Out Error for Transductive Inference

In transductive inference, our goal is to find an algorithm A which minimizes the functional (4) using both the training data (1) and the test data (2). We suggest the following method: predict $(y_{\ell+1}^*, \ldots, y_{\ell+m}^*)$ by finding those values which minimize the leave–one–out error of Ridge Regression training on the joint set

$$(x_1, y_1), \ldots, (x_\ell, y_\ell), (x_{\ell+1}, y_{\ell+1}^*), \ldots, (x_{\ell+m}, y_{\ell+m}^*). \qquad (19)$$

This is achieved in the following way. Suppose we treat the unknown values $(y_{\ell+1}^*, \ldots, y_{\ell+m}^*)$ as variables and for some fixed value of these variables we minimize the following empirical functional

$$R_{emp}(\alpha|y_1^*, \ldots, y_m^*) = \frac{1}{\ell+m} \left(\sum_{i=1}^{\ell} (y_i - f(x_i, \alpha))^2 + \sum_{i=\ell+1}^{\ell+m} (y_i^* - f(x_i, \alpha))^2 \right) + \gamma \|\alpha\|^2. \qquad (20)$$

This functional differs only in the second term from the functional (8) and corresponds to performing Ridge Regression with the extra pairs

$$(x_{\ell+1}, y_{\ell+1}^*), \ldots, (x_{\ell+m}, y_{\ell+m}^*). \qquad (21)$$

Suppose that vector $Y^* = (y_1^*, \ldots, y_m^*)$ is taken from some set $Y^* \in \mathcal{Y}$ such that the pairs (21) can be considered as a sample drawn from the same distribution as the pairs $(x_1, y_1^*), \ldots, (x_\ell, y_\ell^*)$. In this case the leave–one–out error of minimizing (20) over the set (19) approximates the functional (4). We can measure this leave–one–out error using the same technique as in Ridge Regression. Using the closed form (15) one obtains

$$T_{loo}(\gamma|y_1^*, \ldots, y_m^*) = \frac{1}{\ell+m} \sum_{i=1}^{\ell+m} \left(\frac{\hat{Y}_i - \hat{k}_i^T \hat{A}_\gamma^{-1} \hat{K}^T \hat{Y}}{1 - \hat{k}_i^T \hat{A}_\gamma^{-1} \hat{k}_i} \right)^2. \tag{22}$$

where we denote $\hat{x} = (x_1, \ldots, x_{\ell+m})$, $\hat{Y} = (y_1, \ldots, y_\ell, y_{\ell+1}^*, \ldots, y_{\ell+m}^*)^T$, and

$$\hat{A}_\gamma^{-1} = (\hat{K}^T \hat{K} + \gamma I)^{-1} \tag{23}$$

$$\hat{K}_{ij} = \phi_j(\hat{x}_i), \quad i = 1, \ldots, \ell+m, \quad j = 1, \ldots, n. \tag{24}$$

$$\hat{k}_t = (\phi_1(\hat{x}_t) \ldots, \phi_n(\hat{x}_t))^T. \tag{25}$$

Now let us rewrite the expression (22) in an equivalent form to separate the terms with $\hat{Y}$ from the terms with x. Introducing

$$C = I - \hat{K} A_\gamma^{-1} \hat{K}^T, \tag{26}$$

and the matrix M with elements

$$M_{ij} = \sum_{k=1}^{\ell+m} \frac{C_{ik} C_{kj}}{C_{kk}^2} \tag{27}$$

we obtain the equivalent expression of (22)

$$T_{loo}(\gamma|y_1^*, \ldots, y_m^*) = \frac{1}{\ell+m} (\hat{Y}^T M \hat{Y}). \tag{28}$$

In order for the Y^* which minimize the leave–one–out procedure to be valid it is required that the pairs (21) are drawn from the same distribution as the pairs $(x_1, y_1^*), \ldots, (x_\ell, y_\ell^*)$. To satisfy this constraint we choose vectors Y^* from the set

$$\mathcal{Y} = \{Y^* : ||Y^* - Y^0|| \leq R\} \tag{29}$$

where the vector Y^0 is the solution obtained from classical Ridge Regression.

To minimize (28) under constraint (29) we use the functional

$$T_{loo}^{\gamma^*}(\gamma) = \hat{Y}^T M \hat{Y} + \gamma^* ||Y^* - Y^0||^2 \tag{30}$$

where γ^* is a constant depending on R.

Now, to find the values at the given points of interest (2) all that remains is to find the minimum of (30) in Y^*. Note that the matrix M is obtained using only the vectors $\hat{x}$. Therefore, to find the minimum of this functional we rewrite Equation (30) as

$$T_{loo}^{\gamma^*}(\gamma) = Y^T M_0 Y + 2Y^{*T} M_1 Y + Y^{*T} M_2 Y^* + \gamma^* ||Y^* - Y^0||^2 \tag{31}$$

where

$$M = \begin{vmatrix} M_0 & M_1 \\ M_1^T & M_2 \end{vmatrix} \tag{32}$$

and M_0 is a $\ell \times \ell$ matrix, M_1 is a $\ell \times m$ matrix and M_2 is a $m \times m$ matrix. Taking the derivative of (31) in Y^* we obtain the condition for the solution

$$2M_1Y + 2M_2Y^* - 2\gamma^* Y^0 + 2\gamma^* Y^* = 0 \qquad (33)$$

which gives the predictions

$$Y^* = (\gamma^* I + M_2)^{-1}(-M_1 Y + \gamma^* Y^0). \qquad (34)$$

In this algorithm (which we will call Transductive Regression) we have two parameters to control: γ and γ^*. The choice of γ can be found using the leave-one-out estimator (15) for Ridge Regression. This leaves γ^* as the only free parameter.

4 Experiments

To compare our one–step transductive approach with the classical two–step approach we performed a series of experiments on regression problems. We also describe experiments applying our technique to the problem of pattern recognition.

4.1 Regression

We conducted computer simulations for the regression problem using two datasets from the DELVE repository: **boston** and **kin-32fh**.

The **boston** dataset is a well-known problem where one is required to estimate house prices according to various statistics based on 13 locational, economic and structural features from data collected by the U.S Census Service in the Boston Massachusetts area.

The **kin-32fh** dataset is a realistic simulation of the forward dynamics of an 8 link all-revolute robot arm. The task is to predict the distance of the end-effector from a target, given 32 inputs which contain information on the joint positions, twist angles and so forth.

Both problems are nonlinear and contain noisy data. Our objective is to compare our transductive inference method directly with the inductive method of Ridge Regression. To do this we chose the set of basis functions $\phi_i(x) = \exp\left(-\|x - x_i\|^2/2\sigma^2\right)$, $i = 1, \ldots, \ell$, and found the values of γ and σ for Ridge Regression which minimized the leave–one–out bound (15). We then used the same values of these parameters in our transductive approach, and using the basis functions $\phi_i(x) = \exp\left(-\|x - \hat{x}_i\|^2/2\sigma^2\right)$, $i = 1, \ldots, \ell + m$, we then chose a fixed value of γ^*.

For the **boston** dataset we followed the same experimental setup as in [4], that is, we partitioned the training set of 506 observations randomly 100 times into a training set of 481 observations and a testing set of 25 observations. We chose the values of γ and σ by taking the minimum average leave–one–out error over five more random splits of the data stepping over the parameter space. The minimum was found at $\gamma = 0.005$ and $\log \sigma = 0.7$. For our transductive method, we also chose the parameter $\gamma^* = 10$. In Figure 1a we plot mean squared error (MSE) on the test set averaged over the 100 runs against $\log \sigma$ for Ridge Regression and Transductive Regression. Transductive Regression outperforms Ridge Regression, especially at the minimum.

To observe the influence of the number of test points m on the generalization ability of our transductive method, we ran further experiments, setting $\gamma^* = \ell/2m$ for

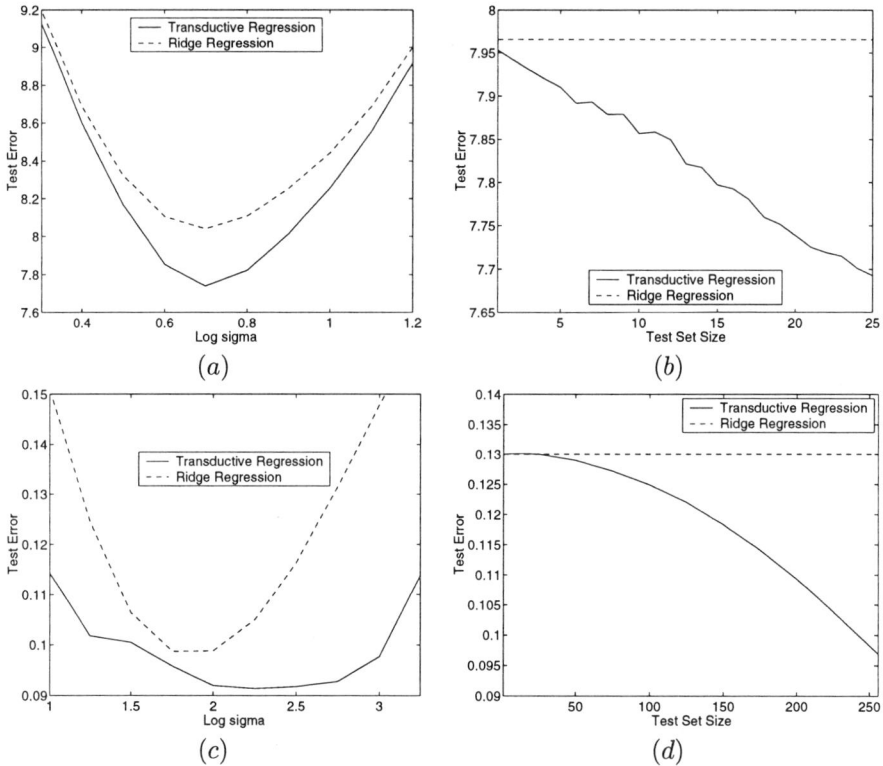

Figure 1: *A comparison of Transductive Regression to Ridge Regression on the* **boston** *dataset: (a) error rates for varying σ, (b) varying the test set size, m, and on the* **kin-32fh** *dataset: (c) error rates for varying σ, (d) varying the test set size.*

different values of m. In Figure 1b we plot m against MSE on the testing set, at $\log \sigma = 0.7$. The results indicate that increasing the test set size gives improved performance in Transductive Regression. For Ridge Regression, of course, the size of the testing set has no influence on the generalization ability.

We then performed similar experiments on the **kin-32fh** dataset. This time, as we were interested in large testing sets giving improved performance for Transductive Regression we chose 100 splits where we took a subset of only 64 observations for training and 256 for testing. Again the leave–one–out estimator was used to find the values $\gamma = 0.1$ and $\log \sigma = 2$ for Ridge Regression, and for Transductive Regression we also chose the parameter $\gamma^* = 0.1$. We plotted MSE on the testing set against $\log \sigma$ (Figure 1c) and the size of the test set m for $\log \sigma = 2.75$ (also, $\gamma^* = 50/m$) (Figure 1d) for the two algorithms. For large test set sizes our method outperforms Ridge Regression.

4.2 Pattern Recognition

This technique can also be applied for pattern recognition problems by solving them based on minimizing functional (8) with $y = \pm 1$. Such a technique is known as a Linear Discriminant (LD) technique.

	AB	AB$_R$	SVM	TLD
Postal	–	–	5.5	4.7
Banana	12.3	10.9	11.5	11.4
Diabetes	26.5	23.8	23.5	23.3
Titanic	22.6	22.6	22.4	22.4
Breast Cancer	30.4	26.5	26.0	25.7
Heart	20.3	16.6	16.0	15.7
Thyroid	4.4	4.6	4.8	4.0

Table 1: *Comparison of percentage test error of AdaBoost (AB), Regularized AdaBoost (AB$_R$), Support Vector Machines (SVM) and Transductive Linear Discrimination (TLD) on seven datasets.*

Table 1 describes results of experiments on classification in the following problems: 2 class digit recognition (0 − 4 versus 5 − 9) splitting the training set into 23 runs of 317 observations and considering a testing set of 2000 observations, and six problems from the UCI database. We followed the same experimental setup as in [3]: the performance of a classifier is measured by its average error over one hundred partitions of the datasets into training and testing sets. Free parameter(s) are chosen via validation on the first five training datasets. The performance of the transductive LD technique was compared to Support Vector Machines, AdaBoost and Regularized AdaBoost [3].

It is interesting to note that in spite of the fact that LD technique is one of the simplest pattern recognition techniques, transductive inference based upon this method performs well compared to state of the art methods of pattern recognition.

5 Summary

In this article we performed transductive inference in the problem of estimating values of functions at the points of interest. We demonstrate that estimating the unknown values via a one–step (transductive) procedure can be more accurate than the traditional two–step (inductive plus deductive) one.

References

[1] A. Hoerl and R. W. Kennard. Ridge regression: Biased estimation for nonorthogonal problems. *Technometrics*, 12(1):55–67, 1970.

[2] A. Luntz and V. Brailovsky. On the estimation of characters obtained in statistical procedure of recognition,. *Technicheskaya Kibernetica*, 1969. [In Russian].

[3] G. Rätsch, T. Onoda, and K.-R. Müller. Soft margins for adaboost. Technical report, Royal Holloway, University of London, 1998. TR–98–21.

[4] C. Saunders, A. Gammermann, and V. Vovk. Ridge regression learning algorithm in dual variables. In *Proccedings of the 15th International Conference on Machine Learning*, pages 515–521. Morgan Kaufmann, 1998.

[5] V. Vapnik. Estimating of values of regression at the point of interest. In *Method of Pattern Recognition*. Sovetskoe Radio, 1977. [In Russian].

[6] V. Vapnik. *Estimation of Dependences Based on Empirical Data.* Springer-Verlag, New York, 1982.

The Nonnegative Boltzmann Machine

Oliver B. Downs
Hopfield Group
Schultz Building
Princeton University
Princeton, NJ 08544
obdowns@princeton.edu

David J.C. MacKay
Cavendish Laboratory
Madingley Road
Cambridge, CB3 0HE
United Kingdom
mackay@mrao.cam.ac.uk

Daniel D. Lee
Bell Laboratories
Lucent Technologies
700 Mountain Ave.
Murray Hill, NJ 07974
ddlee@bell-labs.com

Abstract

The nonnegative Boltzmann machine (NNBM) is a recurrent neural network model that can describe multimodal nonnegative data. Application of maximum likelihood estimation to this model gives a learning rule that is analogous to the binary Boltzmann machine. We examine the utility of the mean field approximation for the NNBM, and describe how Monte Carlo sampling techniques can be used to learn its parameters. Reflective slice sampling is particularly well-suited for this distribution, and can efficiently be implemented to sample the distribution. We illustrate learning of the NNBM on a translationally invariant distribution, as well as on a generative model for images of human faces.

Introduction

The multivariate Gaussian is the most elementary distribution used to model generic data. It represents the *maximum entropy* distribution under the constraint that the mean and covariance matrix of the distribution match that of the data. For the case of binary data, the maximum entropy distribution that matches the first and second order statistics of the data is given by the Boltzmann machine [1]. The probability of a particular state in the Boltzmann machine is given by the exponential form:

$$P(\{s_i = \pm 1\}) = \frac{1}{Z} \exp\left(-\frac{1}{2} \sum_{ij} s_i A_{ij} s_j + \sum_i b_i s_i\right). \tag{1}$$

Interpreting Eq. 1 as a neural network, the parameters A_{ij} represent symmetric, recurrent weights between the different units in the network, and b_i represent local biases. Unfortunately, these parameters are not simply related to the observed mean and covariance of the

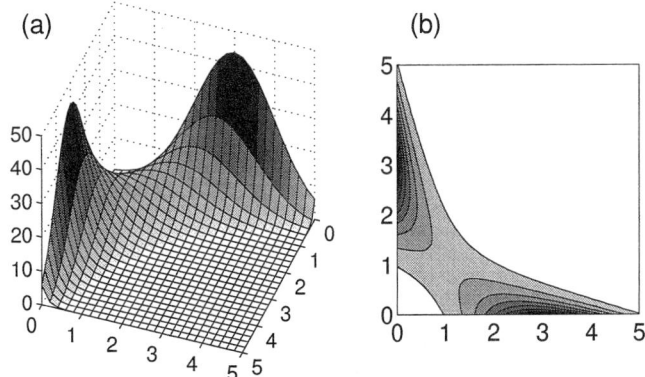

Figure 1: a) Probability density and b) shaded contour plot of a two dimensional competitive NNBM distribution. The energy function $E(x)$ for this distribution contains a saddle point and two local minima, which generates the observed multimodal distribution.

data as they are for the normal Gaussian. Instead, they need to be adapted using an iterative learning rule that involves difficult sampling from the binary distribution [2].

The Boltzmann machine can also be generalized to continuous and nonnegative variables. In this case, the maximum entropy distribution for nonnegative data with known first and second order statistics is described by a distribution previously called the "rectified Gaussian" distribution [3]:

$$P(x) = \begin{cases} \frac{1}{Z} \exp[-E(x)] & \text{if } x_i \geq 0 \, \forall i, \\ 0 & \text{if any } x_i < 0, \end{cases} \quad (2)$$

where the energy function $E(x)$ and normalization constant Z are:

$$E(x) = \frac{1}{2} x^T A x - b^T x, \quad (3)$$

$$Z = \int_{x \geq 0} dx \, \exp[-E(x)]. \quad (4)$$

The properties of this nonnegative Boltzmann machine (NNBM) distribution differ quite substantially from that of the normal Gaussian. In particular, the presence of the nonnegativity constraints allows the distribution to have multiple modes. For example, Fig. 1 shows a two-dimensional NNBM distribution with two separate maxima located against the rectifying axes. Such a multimodal distribution would be poorly modelled by a single normal Gaussian.

In this submission, we discuss how a multimodal NNBM distribution can be learned from nonnegative data. We show the limitations of mean field approximations for this distribution, and illustrate how recent developments in efficient sampling techniques for continuous belief networks can be used to tune the weights of the network [4]. Specific examples of learning are demonstrated on a translationally invariant distribution, as well as on a generative model for face images.

Maximum Likelihood

The learning rule for the NNBM can be derived by maximizing the log likelihood of the observed data under Eq. 2. Given a set of nonnegative vectors $\{\vec{x}^\mu\}$, where $\mu = 1..M$

indexes the different examples, the log likelihood is:

$$L = \frac{1}{M}\sum_{\mu=1}^{M}\log P(\vec{x}^{\mu}) = -\frac{1}{M}\sum_{\mu=1}^{M}E(\vec{x}^{\mu}) - \log Z. \qquad (5)$$

Taking the derivatives of Eq. 5 with respect to the parameters A and b gives:

$$\frac{\partial L}{\partial A_{ij}} = \langle x_i x_j \rangle_{\text{f}} - \langle x_i x_j \rangle_{\text{c}} \qquad (6)$$

$$\frac{\partial L}{\partial b_i} = \langle x_i \rangle_{\text{c}} - \langle x_i \rangle_{\text{f}}, \qquad (7)$$

where the subscript "c" denotes a "clamped" average over the data, and the subscript "f" denotes a "free" average over the NNBM distribution:

$$\langle f(x) \rangle_{\text{c}} = \frac{1}{M}\sum_{\mu=1}^{M} f(\vec{x}^{\mu}) \qquad (8)$$

$$\langle f(x) \rangle_{\text{f}} = \int_{x \geq 0} dx\, P(x) f(x). \qquad (9)$$

These derivatives are used to define a gradient ascent learning rule for the NNBM that is similar to that of the binary Boltzmann machine. The contrast between the clamped and free covariance matrix is used to update the iteractions A, while the difference between the clamped and free means is used to update the local biases b.

Mean field approximation

The major difficulty with this learning algorithm lies in evaluating the averages $\langle x_i x_j \rangle_{\text{f}}$ and $\langle x_i \rangle_{\text{f}}$. Because it is analytically intractable to calculate these free averages exactly, approximations are necessary for learning. Mean field approximations have previously been proposed as a deterministic alternative for learning in the binary Boltzmann machine, although there have been contrasting views on their validity [5, 6]. Here, we investigate the utility of mean field theory for approximating the NNBM distribution.

The mean field equations are derived by approximating the NNBM distribution in Eq. 2 with the factorized form:

$$Q(x) = \prod_i Q_{\tau_i}(x_i) = \prod_i \frac{1}{\gamma!}\frac{1}{\tau_i}\left(\frac{x_i}{\tau_i}\right)^{\gamma} e^{-\frac{x_i}{\tau_i}}, \qquad (10)$$

where the different marginal densities $Q(x_i)$ are characterized by the means τ_i with a fixed constant γ. The product of γ-distributions is the natural factorizable distribution for non-negative random variables.

The optimal mean field parameters τ_i are determined by minimizing the Kullback-Leibler divergence between the NNBM distribution and the factorized distribution:

$$D_{KL}(Q\|P) = \int dx\, Q(x) \log\left[\frac{Q(x)}{P(x)}\right] = \langle E(x) \rangle_{Q(x)} + \log Z - H(Q). \qquad (11)$$

Finding the minimum of Eq. 11 by setting its derivatives with respect to the mean field parameters τ_i to zero gives the simple mean field equations:

$$A_{ii}\tau_i = (\gamma + 1)\left[b_i - \sum_j A_{ij}\tau_j + \frac{1}{\tau_i}\right] \qquad (12)$$

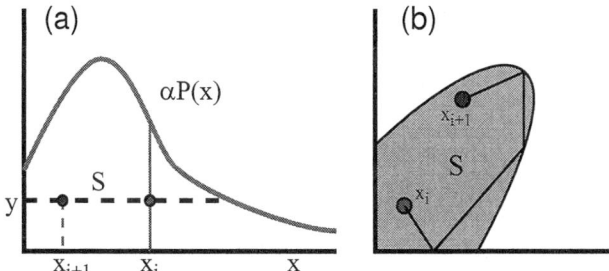

Figure 2: a) Slice sampling in one dimension. Given the current sample point, x_i, a height $y \in [0, \alpha P(x)]$ is randomly chosen. This defines a slice $(x \in S | \alpha P(x) \geq y)$ in which a new x_{i+1} is chosen. b) For a multidimensional slice S, the new point x_{i+1} is chosen using ballistic dynamics with specular reflections off the interior boundaries of the slice.

These equations can then be solved self-consistently for τ_i. The "free" statistics of the NNBM are then replaced by their statistics under the factorized distribution $Q(x)$:

$$\langle x_i \rangle_f \approx \tau_i, \quad \langle x_i x_j \rangle_f \approx [(\gamma+1)^2 + (\gamma+1)\delta_{ij}]\tau_i \tau_j. \tag{13}$$

The fidelity of this approximation is determined by how well the factorized distribution $Q(x)$ models the NNBM distribution. Unfortunately, for distributions such as the one shown in Fig. 3, the mean field approximation is quite different from that of the true multimodal NNBM distribution. This suggests that the naive mean field approximation is inadequate for learning in the NNBM, and in fact attempts to use this approximation fail to learn the examples given in following sections. However, the mean field approximation can still be used to initialize the parameters to reasonable values before using the sampling techniques that are described below.

Monte-Carlo sampling

A more direct approach to calculating the "free" averages in Eq. 6–7 is to numerically approximate them. This can be accomplished by using Monte Carlo sampling to generate a representative set of points that sufficiently approximate the statistics of the continuous distribution. In particular, Markov chain Monte-Carlo methods employ an iterative stochastic dynamics whose equilibrium distribution converges to that of the desired distribution [4]. For the binary Boltzmann machine, such sampling dynamics involves random "spin flips" which change the value of a single binary component. Unfortunately, these single component dynamics are easily caught in local energy minima, and can converge very slowly for large systems. This makes sampling the binary distribution very difficult, and more specialized computational techniques such as simulated annealing, cluster updates, etc., have been developed to try to circumvent this problem.

For the NNBM, the use of continuous variables makes it possible to investigate different stochastic dynamics in order to more efficiently sample the distribution. We first experimented with Gibbs sampling with ordered overrelaxation [7], but found that the required inversion of the error function was too computationally expensive. Instead, the recently developed method of slice sampling [8] seems particularly well-suited for implementation in the NNBM.

The basic idea of the slice sampling algorithm is shown in Fig. 2. Given a sample point x_i, a random $y \in [0, \alpha P(x_i)]$ is first uniformly chosen. Then a slice S is defined as the connected set of points $(x \in S \mid \alpha P(x) \geq y)$, and the new point $x_{i+1} \in S$ is chosen

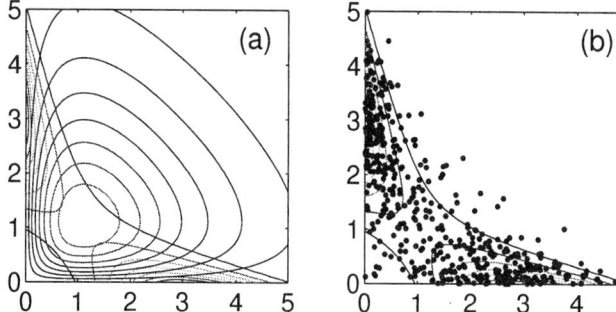

Figure 3: Contours of the two-dimensional competitive NNBM distribution overlaid by a) $\gamma = 1$ mean field approximation and b) 500 reflected slice samples.

randomly from this slice. The distribution of x_n for large n can be shown to converge to the desired density $P(x)$. Now, for the NNBM, solving the boundary points along a particular direction in a given slice is quite simple, since it only involves solving the roots of a quadratic equation. In order to efficiently choose a new point within a particular slice, reflective "billiard ball" dynamics are used. A random initial velocity is chosen, and the new point is evolved by travelling a certain distance from the current point while specularly reflecting from the boundaries of the slice. Intuitively, the reversibility of these reflections allows the dynamics to satisfy detailed balance.

In Fig. 3, the mean field approximation and reflective slice sampling are used to model the two-dimensional competitive NNBM distribution. The poor fit of the mean field approximation is apparent from the unimodality of the factorized density, while the sample points from the reflective slice sampling algorithm are more representative of the underlying NNBM distribution. For higher dimensional data, the mean field approximation becomes progressively worse. It is therefore necessary to implement the numerical slice sampling algorithm in order to accurately approximate the NNBM distribution.

Translationally invariant model

Ben-Yishai et al. have proposed a model for orientation tuning in primary visual cortex that can be interpreted as a cooperative NNBM distribution [9]. In the absence of visual input, the firing rates of N cortical neurons are described as minimizing the energy function $E(x)$ with parameters:

$$\frac{A_{ij}}{\beta} = \delta_{ij} + \frac{1}{N} - \frac{\epsilon}{N}\cos(\frac{2\pi}{N}|i-j|) \qquad (14)$$
$$\frac{b_i}{\beta} = 1$$

This distribution was used to test the NNBM learning algorithm. First, a large set of $N = 25$ dimensional nonnegative training vectors were generated by sampling the distribution with $\beta = 50$ and $\epsilon = 4$. Using these samples as training data, the A and b parameters were learned from a unimodal initialization by evolving the training vectors using reflective slice sampling, and these evolved vectors were used to calculate the "free" averages in Eq. 6–7. The A and b estimates were then updated, and this procedure was iterated until the evolved averages matched that of the training data. The learned A and b parameters were then found to almost exactly match the original form in Eq. 14. Some representative samples from the learned NNBM distribution are shown in Fig. 4.

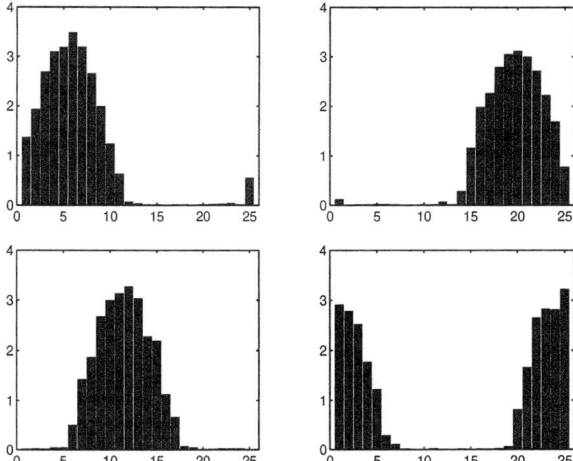

Figure 4: Representative samples taken from a NNBM after training to learn a translationally invariant cooperative distribution with $\beta = 50$ and $\epsilon = 4$.

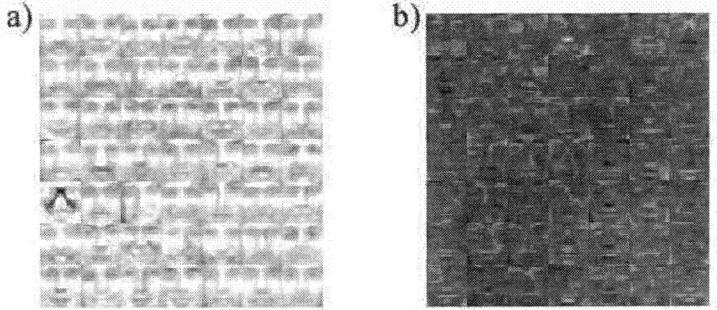

Figure 5: a) Morphing of a face image by successive sampling from the learned NNBM distribution. b) Samples generated from a normal Gaussian.

Generative model for faces

We have also used the NNBM to learn a generative model for images of human faces. The NNBM is used to model the correlations in the coefficients of the nonnegative matrix factorization (NMF) of the face images [10]. NMF reduces the dimensionality of nonnegative data by decomposing the face images into parts correponding to eyes, noses, ears, etc. Since the different parts are coactivated in reconstructing a face, the activations of these parts contain significant correlations that need to be captured by a generative model. Here we briefly demonstrate how the NNBM is able to learn these correlations.

Sampling from the NNBM stochastically generates coefficients which can graphically be displayed as face images. Fig. 5 shows some representative face images as the reflective slice sampling dynamics evolves the coefficients. Also displayed in the figure are the analogous images generated if a normal Gaussian is used to model the correlations instead. It is clear that the nonnegativity constraints and multimodal nature of the NNBM results in samples which are cleaner and more distinct as faces.

Discussion

Here we have introduced the NNBM as a recurrent neural network model that is able to describe multimodal nonnegative data. Its application is made practical by the efficiency of the slice sampling Monte Carlo method. The learning algorithm incorporates numerical sampling from the NNBM distribution and is able to learn from observations of nonnegative data. We have demonstrated the application of NNBM learning to a cooperative, translationally invariant distribution, as well as to real data from images of human faces.

Extensions to the present work include incorporating hidden units into the recurrent network. The addition of hidden units implies modelling certain higher order statistics in the data, and requires calculating averages over these hidden units. We anticipate the marginal distribution over these units to be most commonly unimodal, and hence mean field theory should be valid for approximating these averages.

Another possible extension involves generalizing the NNBM to model continuous data confined within a certain range, i.e. $0 \leq x_i \leq 1$. In this situation, slice sampling techniques would also be used to efficiently generate representative samples. In any case, we hope that this work stimulates more research into using these types of recurrent neural networks to model complex, multimodal data.

Acknowledgements

The authors acknowledge useful discussion with John Hopfield, Sebastian Seung, Nicholas Socci, and Gayle Wittenberg, and are indebted to Haim Sompolinsky for pointing out the maximum entropy interpretation of the Boltzmann machine. This work was funded by Bell Laboratories, Lucent Technologies.

O.B. Downs is grateful for the moral support, and open ears and minds of Beth Brittle, Gunther Lenz, and Sandra Scheitz.

References

[1] Hinton, GE & Sejnowski, TJ (1983). Optimal perceptual learning. *IEEE Conference on Computer Vision and Pattern Recognition*, Washington, DC, 448–453.

[2] Ackley, DH, Hinton, GE, & Sejnowski, TJ (1985). A learning algorithm for Boltzmann machines. *Cognitive Science* **9**, 147–169.

[3] Socci, ND, Lee, DD, and Seung, HS (1998). The rectified Gaussian distribution. *Advances in Neural Information Processing Systems* **10**, 350–356.

[4] MacKay, DJC (1998). Introduction to Monte Carlo Methods. *Learning in Graphical Models*. Kluwer Academic Press, NATO Science Series, 175–204.

[5] Galland, CC (1993). The limitations of deterministic Boltzmann machine learning. *Network* **4**, 355–380.

[6] Kappen, HJ & Rodriguez, FB (1997). Mean field approach to learning in Boltzmann machines. *Pattern Recognition in Practice V)*, Amsterdam.

[7] Neal, RM (1995). Suppressing random walks in Markov chain Monte Carlo using ordered overrelaxation. Technical Report 9508, Dept. of Statistics, University of Toronto.

[8] Neal, RM (1997). Markov chain Monte Carlo methods based on "slicing" the density function. Technical Report 9722, Dept. of Statistics, University of Toronto.

[9] Ben-Yishai, R, Bar-Or, RL, & Sompolinsky, H (1995). Theory of orientation tuning in visual cortex. *Proc. Nat. Acad. Sci. USA* **92**, 3844–3848.

[10] Lee, DD, and Seung, HS (1999) Learning the parts of objects by non-negative matrix factorization. *Nature* **401**, 788-791.

Differentiating Functions of the Jacobian with Respect to the Weights

Gary William Flake
NEC Research Institute
4 Independence Way
Princeton, NJ 08540
flake@research.nj.nec.com

Barak A. Pearlmutter
Dept of Computer Science, FEC 313
University of New Mexico
Albuquerque, NM 87131
bap@cs.unm.edu

Abstract

For many problems, the correct behavior of a model depends not only on its input-output mapping but also on properties of its Jacobian matrix, the matrix of partial derivatives of the model's outputs with respect to its inputs. We introduce the *J-prop* algorithm, an efficient general method for computing the exact partial derivatives of a variety of simple functions of the Jacobian of a model with respect to its free parameters. The algorithm applies to any parametrized feedforward model, including nonlinear regression, multilayer perceptrons, and radial basis function networks.

1 Introduction

Let $f(x, w)$ be an n input, m output, twice differentiable feedforward model parameterized by an input vector, x, and a weight vector w. Its Jacobian matrix is defined as

$$J = \begin{bmatrix} \frac{\partial f_1}{\partial x_1} & \cdots & \frac{\partial f_1}{\partial x_n} \\ \vdots & \ddots & \vdots \\ \frac{\partial f_m}{\partial x_1} & \cdots & \frac{\partial f_m}{\partial x_n} \end{bmatrix} = \frac{df(x, w)}{dx}.$$

The algorithm we introduce can be used to optimize functions of the form

$$E_u(w) = \frac{1}{2} \left\| J^T u - a \right\|^2 \qquad (1)$$

or

$$E_v(w) = \frac{1}{2} \left\| J v - b \right\|^2 \qquad (2)$$

where u, v, a, and b are user-defined constants. Our algorithm, which we call *J-prop*, can be used to calculate the exact value of both $\partial E_u / \partial w$ or $\partial E_v / \partial w$ in $O(1)$ times the time required to calculate the normal gradient. Thus, J-prop is suitable for training models to have specific first derivatives, or for implementing several other well-known algorithms such as Double Backpropagation [1] and Tangent Prop [2].

Clearly, being able to optimize Equations 1 and 2 is useful; however, we suspect that the formalism which we use to derive our algorithm is actually more interesting because it allows us to modify J-prop to easily be applicable to a wide-variety of model types and objective functions. As such, we spend a fair portion of this paper describing the mathematical framework from which we later build J-prop.

This paper is divided into four more sections. Section 2 contains background information and motivation for why optimizing the properties of the Jacobian is an important problem. Section 3 introduces our formalism and contains the derivation of the J-prop algorithm. Section 4 contains a brief numerical example of J-prop. And, finally, Section 5 describes further work and gives our conclusions.

2 Background and motivation

Previous work concerning the modeling of an unknown function and its derivatives can be divided into works that are descriptive or prescriptive. Perhaps the best known descriptive result is due to White *et al.* [3, 4], who show that given noise-free data, a multilayer perceptron (MLP) can approximate the higher derivatives of an unknown function in the limit as the number of training points goes to infinity. The difficulty with applying this result is the strong requirements on the amount and integrity of the training data; requirements which are rarely met in practice. This problem was specifically demonstrated by Principe, Rathie and Kuo [5] and Deco and Schürmann [6], who showed that using noisy training data from chaotic systems can lead to models that are accurate in the input-output sense, but inaccurate in their estimates of quantities related to the Jacobian of the unknown system, such as the largest Lyapunov exponent and the correlation dimension.

MLPs are particularly problematic because large weights can lead to saturation at a particular sigmoidal neuron which, in turn, results in extremely large first derivatives at the neuron when evaluated near the center of the sigmoid transition. Several methods to combat this type of over-fitting have been proposed. One of the earliest methods, weight decay [7], uses a penalty term on the magnitude of the weights. Weight decay is arguably optimal for models in which the output is linear in the weights because minimizing the magnitude of the weights is equivalent to minimizing the magnitude of the model's first derivatives. However, in the nonlinear case, weight decay can have suboptimal performance [1] because large (or small) weights do not always correspond to having large (or small) first derivatives.

The Double Backpropagation algorithm [1] adds an additional penalty term to the error function equal to $||\partial E/\partial x||^2$. Training on this function results in a form of regularization that is in many ways an elegant combination of weight decay and training with noise: it is strictly analytic (unlike training with noise) but it explicitly penalizes large first derivatives of the model (unlike weight decay). Double Backpropagation can be seen as a special case of J-prop, the algorithm derived in this paper.

As to the general problem of coercing the first derivatives of a model to specific values, Simard, *et al.*, [2] introduced the Tangent Prop algorithm, which was used to train MLPs for optical character recognition to be insensitive to small affine transformations in the character space. Tangent Prop can also be considered a special case of J-prop.

3 Derivation

We now define a formalism under which J-prop can be easily derived. The method is very similar to a technique introduced by Pearlmutter [8] for calculating the product of the Hessian of an MLP and an arbitrary vector. However, where Pearlmutter used differential operators applied to a model's weight space, we use differential operators defined with respect to a model's input space.

Our entire derivation is presented in five steps. First, we will define an auxiliary error function that has a few useful mathematical properties that simplify the derivation. Next, we will define a special differential operator that can be applied to both the auxiliary error function, and its gradient with respect to the weights. We will then see that the result of applying the differential operator to the gradient of the auxiliary error function is equivalent to analytically calculating the derivatives required to optimize Equations 1 and 2. We then show an example of the technique applied to an MLP. Finally, in the last step, the complete algorithm is presented.

To avoid confusion, when referring to generic data-driven models, the model will always be expressed as a vector function $y = f(x, w)$, where x refers to the model input and w refers to a vector of all of the tunable parameters of the model. In this way, we can talk about models while ignoring the mechanics of how the models work internally. Complementary to the generic vector notation, the notation for an MLP uses only scalar symbols; however, these symbols must refer to internal variable of the model (e.g., neuron thresholds, net inputs, weights, etc.), which can lead to some ambiguity. To be clear, when using vector notation, the input and output of an MLP will always be denoted by x and y, respectively, and the collection of all of the weights (including biases) map to the vector w. However, when using scalar arithmetic, the scalar notation for MLPs will apply.

3.1 Auxiliary error function

Our auxiliary error function, $\tilde{E}$, is defined as

$$\tilde{E}(x, w) = u^T f(x, w). \tag{3}$$

Note that we never actually optimize with respect $\tilde{E}$; we define it only because it has the property that $\partial \tilde{E}/\partial x = u^T J$, which will be useful to the derivation shortly. Note that $\partial \tilde{E}/\partial x$ appears in the Taylor expansion of $\tilde{E}$ about a point in input space:

$$\tilde{E}(x + \Delta x, w) = \tilde{E}(x, w) + \frac{\partial \tilde{E}}{\partial x}^T \Delta x + O\left(||\Delta x||^2\right). \tag{4}$$

Thus, while holding the weights, w, fixed and letting Δx be a perturbation of the input, x, Equation 4 characterizes how small changes in the input of the model change the value of the auxiliary error function.

Be setting $\Delta x = rv$, with v being an arbitrary vector and r being a small value, we can rearrange Equation 4 into the form:

$$\begin{aligned}\frac{\partial \tilde{E}}{\partial x}^T v &= \frac{1}{r}\left[\tilde{E}(x+rv, w) - \tilde{E}(x, w)\right] + O(r) \\ &\vdots = \lim_{r \to 0} \frac{1}{r}\left[\tilde{E}(x+rv, w) - \tilde{E}(x, w)\right] \\ u^T J v &= \left.\frac{\partial}{\partial r}\tilde{E}(x+rv, w)\right|_{r=0}.\end{aligned} \tag{5}$$

This final expression will allow us to define the differential operator in the next subsection.

3.2 Differential operator

Let $h(x, w)$ be an arbitrary twice differentiable function. We define the differentiable operator

$$R_v\{h(x, w)\} \equiv \left.\frac{\partial}{\partial r}h(x+rv, w)\right|_{r=0}, \tag{6}$$

which has the property that $R_{\mathbf{v}}\{\tilde{E}(x, w)\} = u^T J v$. Being a differential operator, $R_{\mathbf{v}}\{\cdot\}$ obeys all of the standard rules for differentiation:

$$\begin{aligned}
R_{\mathbf{v}}\{c\} &= 0 \\
R_{\mathbf{v}}\{c \cdot h(x, w)\} &= c \cdot R_{\mathbf{v}}\{h(x, w)\} \\
R_{\mathbf{v}}\{h(x, w) + g(x, w)\} &= R_{\mathbf{v}}\{h(x, w)\} + R_{\mathbf{v}}\{g(x, w)\} \\
R_{\mathbf{v}}\{h(x, w) \cdot g(x, w)\} &= R_{\mathbf{v}}\{h(x, w)\} \cdot g(x, w) + h(x, w) \cdot R_{\mathbf{v}}\{g(x, w)\} \\
R_{\mathbf{v}}\{h(g(x, w), w)\} &= h'(g(x, w)) \cdot R_{\mathbf{v}}\{g(x, w)\} \\
R_{\mathbf{v}}\left\{\frac{d}{dt} h(x, w)\right\} &= \frac{d}{dt} R_{\mathbf{v}}\{h(x, w)\}
\end{aligned}$$

The operator also yields the identity $R_{\mathbf{v}}\{\mathbf{x}\} = \mathbf{v}$.

3.3 Equivalence

We will now see that the result of calculating $R_{\mathbf{v}}\{\partial \tilde{E}/\partial w\}$ can be used to calculate both $\partial E_u/\partial w$ and $\partial E_v/\partial w$. Note that Equations 3–5 all assume that both u and v are independent of x and w. To calculate $\partial E_u/\partial w$ and $\partial E_v/\partial w$, we will actually set u or v to a value that depends on both x and w; however, the derivation still works because our choices are explicitly made in such a way that the chain rule of differentiation is *not* supposed to be applied to these terms. Hence, the correct analytical solution is obtained despite the dependence.

To optimize with respect to Equation 1, we use:

$$\frac{\partial}{\partial w} \frac{1}{2} \left\| J^T u - a \right\|^2 = \left(\frac{\partial u^T J}{\partial w}\right)^T (J^T u - a) = R_{\mathbf{v}}\left\{\frac{\partial \tilde{E}}{\partial w}\right\}, \tag{7}$$

with $v = (J^T u - a)$. To optimize with respect to Equation 2, we use:

$$\frac{\partial}{\partial w} \frac{1}{2} \|J v - b\|^2 = (J v - b)^T \left(\frac{\partial J v}{\partial w}\right) = R_{\mathbf{v}}\left\{\frac{\partial \tilde{E}}{\partial w}\right\}, \tag{8}$$

with $u = (J v - b)$.

3.4 Method applied to MLPs

We are now ready to see how this technique can be applied to a specific type of model. Consider an MLP with $L + 1$ layers of nodes defined by the equations:

$$y_i^l = g(x_i^l) \tag{9}$$

$$x_i^l = \sum_j^{N_l} y_j^{l-1} w_{ij}^l - \theta_i^l. \tag{10}$$

In these equations, superscripts denote the layer number (starting at 0), subscripts index over terms in a particular layer, and N_l is the number of input nodes in layer l. Thus, y_i^l is the output of neuron i at node layer l, and x_i^l is the net input coming into the same neuron. Moreover, y_i^L is an output of the entire MLP while y_i^0 is an input going into the MLP.

The feedback equations calculated with respect to $\tilde{E}$ are:

$$\frac{\partial \tilde{E}}{\partial y_i^L} = u_i \tag{11}$$

$$\frac{\partial \tilde{E}}{\partial y_i^l} = \sum_j^{N_{l+1}} w_{ij}^{l+1} \frac{\partial \tilde{E}}{\partial x_j^{l+1}} \quad \text{(for } l < L\text{)} \tag{12}$$

$$\frac{\partial \tilde{E}}{\partial x_i^l} = \frac{\partial \tilde{E}}{\partial y_i^l} g'(x_i^l) \tag{13}$$

$$\frac{\partial \tilde{E}}{\partial w_{ij}^l} = \frac{\partial \tilde{E}}{\partial x_i^l} y_j^{l-1} \tag{14}$$

$$\frac{\partial \tilde{E}}{\partial \theta_j^l} = \frac{\partial \tilde{E}}{\partial x_i^l}, \tag{15}$$

where the u_i term is a component in the vector u from Equation 1. Applying the $R_\mathbf{v}\{\cdot\}$ operator to the feedforward equations yields:

$$R_\mathbf{v}\{y_i^0\} = v_i \tag{16}$$

$$R_\mathbf{v}\{y_i^l\} = g'(x_i^l) R_\mathbf{v}\{x_i^l\} \quad \text{(for } l > 0\text{)} \tag{17}$$

$$R_\mathbf{v}\{x_i^l\} = \sum_j^{N_l} R_\mathbf{v}\{y_j^{l-1}\} w_{ij}^l, \tag{18}$$

where the v_i term is a component in the vector v from Equation 2. As the final step, we apply the $R_\mathbf{v}\{\cdot\}$ operator to the feedback equations, which yields:

$$R_\mathbf{v}\left\{\frac{\partial \tilde{E}}{\partial y_i^L}\right\} = 0 \tag{19}$$

$$R_\mathbf{v}\left\{\frac{\partial \tilde{E}}{\partial y_i^l}\right\} = \sum_j^{N_{l+1}} w_{ij}^{l+1} R_\mathbf{v}\left\{\frac{\partial \tilde{E}}{\partial x_j^{l+1}}\right\} \quad \text{(for } l < L\text{)} \tag{20}$$

$$R_\mathbf{v}\left\{\frac{\partial \tilde{E}}{\partial x_i^l}\right\} = R_\mathbf{v}\left\{\frac{\partial \tilde{E}}{\partial y_i^l}\right\} g'(x_i^l) + \frac{\partial \tilde{E}}{\partial y_i^l} g''(x_i^l) R_\mathbf{v}\{x_i^l\} \tag{21}$$

$$R_\mathbf{v}\left\{\frac{\partial \tilde{E}}{\partial w_{ij}^l}\right\} = R_\mathbf{v}\left\{\frac{\partial \tilde{E}}{\partial x_i^l}\right\} y_j^{l-1} + \frac{\partial \tilde{E}}{\partial x_i^l} R_\mathbf{v}\{y_j^{l-1}\} \tag{22}$$

$$R_\mathbf{v}\left\{\frac{\partial \tilde{E}}{\partial \theta_j^l}\right\} = R_\mathbf{v}\left\{\frac{\partial \tilde{E}}{\partial x_i^l}\right\}. \tag{23}$$

3.5 Complete algorithm

Implementing this algorithm is nearly as simple as implementing normal gradient descent. For each type of variable that is used in an MLP (net input, neuron output, weights, thresholds, partial derivatives, etc.), we require that an extra variable be allocated to hold the result of applying the $R_\mathbf{v}\{\cdot\}$ operator to the original variable. With this change in place, the complete algorithm to compute $\partial E_u / \partial w$ is as follows:

- Set u and a to the user specified vectors from Equation 1.
- Set the MLP inputs to the value of x that J is to be evaluated at.
- Perform a normal feedforward pass using Equations 9 and 10.
- Set $\partial \tilde{E}/\partial y_i^L$ to u_i.

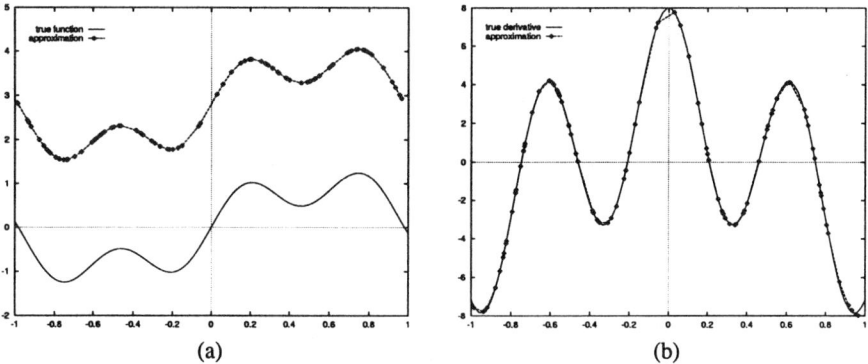

Figure 1: Learning only the derivative: showing (a) poor approximation of the function with (b) excellent approximation of the derivative.

- Perform the feedback pass with Equations 11–15. Note that values in the $\partial \tilde{E}/\partial y_i^0$ terms are now equal to $J^T u$.

- Set v to $(J^T u - a)$

- Perform a $R_v\{\cdot\}$ forward pass with Equations 16–18.

- Set the $R_v\{\partial \tilde{E}/\partial y_i^L\}$ terms to 0.

- Perform a $R_v\{\cdot\}$ backward pass with Equations 19–23.

After the last step, the values in the $R_v\{\partial \tilde{E}/\partial w_{ij}^l\}$ and $R_v\{\partial \tilde{E}/\partial \theta_j^l\}$ terms contain the required result. It is important to note that the time complexity of the "J-forward" and "J-backward" calculations are nearly identical to the typical output and gradient evaluations (i.e., the "forward" and "backward" passes) of the models used.

A similar technique can be used for calculating $\partial E_v/\partial w$. The main difference is that the $R_v\{\cdot\}$ forward pass is performed between the normal forward and backward passes because u can only be determined after the $R_v\{f(x,w)\}$ has been calculated.

4 Experimental results

To demonstrate the effectiveness and generality of the J-prop algorithm, we have implemented it on top of an existing neural network library [9] in such a way that the algorithm can be used on a large number of architectures, including MLPs, radial basis function networks, and higher order networks.

We trained an MLP with ten hidden tanh nodes on 100 points with conjugate gradient. The training exemplars consisted of inputs in $[-1, 1]$ and a target derivative from $3\cos(3x) + 5\cos(10x)$. Our unknown function (which the MLP never sees data from) is $\sin(3x) + \frac{1}{2}\sin(10x)$. The model quickly converges to a solution in approximately 100 iterations.

Figure 1 shows the performance of the MLP. Having never seen data from the unknown function, the MLP yields a poor approximation of the function, but a very accurate approximation of the function's derivative. We could have trained on both outputs and derivatives, but our goal was to illustrate that J-prop can target derivatives alone.

5 Conclusions

We have introduced a general method for calculating the weight gradient of functions of the Jacobian matrix of feedforward nonlinear systems. The method can be easily applied to most nonlinear models in common use today. The resulting algorithm, J-prop, can be easily modified to minimize functionals from several application domains [10]. Some possible uses include: targeting known first derivatives, implementing Tangent Prop and Double Backpropagation, enforcing identical I/O sensitivities in auto-encoders, deflating the largest eigenvalue and minimizing all eigenvalue bounds, optimizing the determinant for blind source separation, and building nonlinear controllers.

While some special cases of the J-prop algorithm have already been studied, a great deal is unknown about how optimization of the Jacobian changes the overall optimization problem. Some anecdotal evidence seems to imply that optimization of the Jacobian can lead to better generalization and faster training. It remains to be seen if J-prop used on a nonlinear extension of linear methods will lead to superior solutions.

Acknowledgements

We thank Frans Coetzee, Yannis Kevrekidis, Joe O'Ruanaidh, Lucas Parra, Scott Rickard, Justinian Rosca, and Patrice Simard for helpful discussions. GWF would also like to thank Eric Baum and the NEC Research Institute for funding the time to write up these results.

References

[1] H. Drucker and Y. Le Cun. Improving generalization performance using double backpropagation. *IEEE Transactions on Neural Networks*, 3(6), November 1992.

[2] P. Simard, B. Victorri, Y. Le Cun, and J. Denker. Tangent prop—A formalism for specifying selected invariances in an adaptive network. In John E. Moody, Steve J. Hanson, and Richard P. Lippmann, editors, *Advances in Neural Information Processing Systems*, volume 4, pages 895–903. Morgan Kaufmann Publishers, Inc., 1992.

[3] H. White and A. R. Gallant. On learning the derivatives of an unknown mapping with multilayer feedforward networks. In Halbert White, editor, *Artificial Neural Networks*, chapter 12, pages 206–223. Blackwell, Cambridge, Mass., 1992.

[4] H. White, K. Hornik, and M. Stinchcombe. Universal approximation of an unknown mapping and its derivative. In Halbert White, editor, *Artificial Neural Networks*, chapter 6, pages 55–77. Blackwell, Cambridge, Mass., 1992.

[5] J. Principe, A. Rathie, and J. Kuo. Prediction of chaotic time series with neural networks and the issues of dynamic modeling. *Bifurcations and Chaos*, 2(4), 1992.

[6] G. Deco and B. Schürmann. Dynamic modeling of chaotic time series. In Russell Greiner, Thomas Petsche, and Stephen José Hanson, editors, *Computational Learning Theory and Natural Learning Systems*, volume IV of *Making Learning Systems Practical*, chapter 9, pages 137–153. The MIT Press, Cambridge, Mass., 1997.

[7] G. E. Hinton. Learning distributed representations of concepts. In *Proc. Eigth Annual Conf. Cognitive Science Society*, pages 1–12, Hillsdale, NJ, 1986. Erlbaum.

[8] Barak A. Pearlmutter. Fast exact multiplication by the Hessian. *Neural Computation*, 6(1):147–160, 1994.

[9] G. W. Flake. Industrial strength modeling tools. Submitted to NIPS 99, 1999.

[10] G. W. Flake and B. A. Pearlmutter. Optimizing properties of the Jacobian of nonlinear feedforward systems. In preperation, 1999.

Local probability propagation for factor analysis

Brendan J. Frey
Computer Science, University of Waterloo, Waterloo, Ontario, Canada

Abstract

Ever since Pearl's probability propagation algorithm in graphs with cycles was shown to produce excellent results for error-correcting decoding a few years ago, we have been curious about whether local probability propagation could be used successfully for machine learning. One of the simplest adaptive models is the factor analyzer, which is a two-layer network that models bottom layer sensory inputs as a linear combination of top layer factors plus independent Gaussian sensor noise. We show that local probability propagation in the factor analyzer network usually takes just a few iterations to perform accurate inference, even in networks with 320 sensors and 80 factors. We derive an expression for the algorithm's fixed point and show that this fixed point matches the exact solution in a variety of networks, even when the fixed point is unstable. We also show that this method can be used successfully to perform inference for approximate EM and we give results on an online face recognition task.

1 Factor analysis

A simple way to encode input patterns is to suppose that each input can be well-approximated by a linear combination of component vectors, where the amplitudes of the vectors are modulated to match the input. For a given training set, the most appropriate set of component vectors will depend on how we expect the modulation levels to behave and how we measure the distance between the input and its approximation. These effects can be captured by a generative probability model that specifies a distribution $p(\mathbf{z})$ over modulation levels $\mathbf{z} = (z_1, \ldots, z_K)^{\mathrm{T}}$ and a distribution $p(\mathbf{x}|\mathbf{z})$ over sensors $\mathbf{x} = (x_1, \ldots, x_N)^{\mathrm{T}}$ given the modulation levels. Principal component analysis, independent component analysis and factor analysis can be viewed as maximum likelihood learning in a model of this type, where we assume that over the training set, the appropriate modulation levels are independent and the overall distortion is given by the sum of the individual sensor distortions.

In factor analysis, the modulation levels are called *factors* and the distributions have the following form:

$$p(z_k) = \mathcal{N}(z_k; 0, 1), \quad p(\mathbf{z}) = \prod_{k=1}^{K} p(z_k) = \mathcal{N}(\mathbf{z}; \mathbf{0}, \mathbf{I}),$$

$$p(x_n|\mathbf{z}) = \mathcal{N}(x_n; \sum_{k=1}^{K} \lambda_{nk} z_k, \psi_n), \quad p(\mathbf{x}|\mathbf{z}) = \prod_{n=1}^{N} p(x_n|\mathbf{z}) = \mathcal{N}(\mathbf{x}; \mathbf{\Lambda}\mathbf{z}, \mathbf{\Psi}). \quad (1)$$

The parameters of this model are the factor loading matrix $\mathbf{\Lambda}$, with elements λ_{nk}, and the diagonal sensor noise covariance matrix $\mathbf{\Psi}$, with diagonal elements ψ_n. A belief network for the factor analyzer is shown in Fig. 1a. The likelihood is

$$p(\mathbf{x}) = \int_{\mathbf{z}} \mathcal{N}(\mathbf{z}; \mathbf{0}, \mathbf{I}) \mathcal{N}(\mathbf{x}; \mathbf{\Lambda}\mathbf{z}, \mathbf{\Psi}) d\mathbf{z} = \mathcal{N}(\mathbf{x}; \mathbf{0}, \mathbf{\Lambda}\mathbf{\Lambda}^{\mathrm{T}} + \mathbf{\Psi}), \quad (2)$$

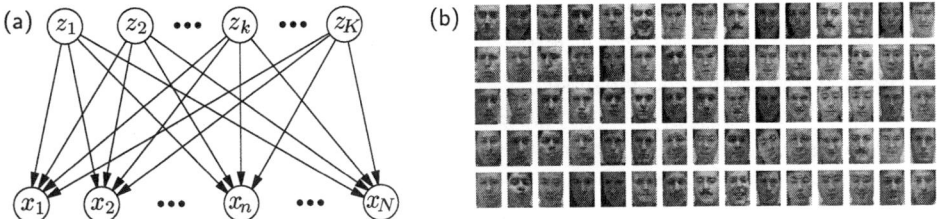

Figure 1: (a) A belief network for factor analysis. (b) High-dimensional data ($N = 560$).

and online factor analysis consists of adapting $\boldsymbol{\Lambda}$ and $\boldsymbol{\Psi}$ to increase the likelihood of the current input, such as a vector of pixels from an image in Fig. 1b.

Probabilistic inference – computing or estimating $p(\mathbf{z}|\mathbf{x})$ – is needed to do dimensionality reduction and to fill in the unobserved factors for online EM-type learning. In this paper, we focus on methods that infer *independent* factors. $p(\mathbf{z}|\mathbf{x})$ is Gaussian and it turns out that the posterior means and variances of the factors are

$$\mathrm{E}[\mathbf{z}|\mathbf{x}] = (\boldsymbol{\Lambda}^{\mathrm{T}}\boldsymbol{\Psi}^{-1}\boldsymbol{\Lambda} + \mathbf{I})^{-1}\boldsymbol{\Lambda}^{\mathrm{T}}\boldsymbol{\Psi}^{-1}\mathbf{x},$$
$$\mathrm{diag}(\mathrm{COV}(\mathbf{z}|\mathbf{x})) = \mathrm{diag}((\boldsymbol{\Lambda}^{\mathrm{T}}\boldsymbol{\Psi}^{-1}\boldsymbol{\Lambda} + \mathbf{I})^{-1}). \qquad (3)$$

Given $\boldsymbol{\Lambda}$ and $\boldsymbol{\Psi}$, computing these values exactly takes $\mathcal{O}(K^2N)$ computations, mainly because of the time needed to compute $\boldsymbol{\Lambda}^{\mathrm{T}}\boldsymbol{\Psi}^{-1}\boldsymbol{\Lambda}$. Since there are only KN connections in the network, exact inference takes at least $\mathcal{O}(K)$ bottom-up/top down iterations.

Of course, if the *same* network is going to be applied more than K times for inference (*e.g.*, for batch EM), then the matrices in (3) can be computed once and reused. However, this is not directly applicable in online learning and in biological models. One way to circumvent computing the matrices is to keep a separate recognition network, which approximates $\mathrm{E}[\mathbf{z}|\mathbf{x}]$ with $\mathbf{R}\mathbf{x}$ (Dayan *et al.*, 1995). The optimal recognition network, $\mathbf{R} = (\boldsymbol{\Lambda}^{\mathrm{T}}\boldsymbol{\Psi}^{-1}\boldsymbol{\Lambda}+\mathbf{I})^{-1}\boldsymbol{\Lambda}^{\mathrm{T}}\boldsymbol{\Psi}^{-1}$, can be approximated by jointly estimating the generative network and the recognition network using online wake-sleep learning (Hinton *et al.*, 1995).

2 Probability propagation in the factor analyzer network

Recent results on error-correcting coding show that in some cases Pearl's probability propagation algorithm, which does exact probabilistic inference in graphs that are trees, gives excellent performance *even if the network contains so many cycles that its minimal cut set is exponential* (Frey and MacKay, 1998; Frey, 1998; MacKay, 1999). In fact, the probability propagation algorithm for decoding low-density parity-check codes (MacKay, 1999) and turbocodes (Berrou and Glavieux, 1996) is widely considered to be a major breakthrough in the information theory community.

When the network contains cycles, the local computations give rise to an iterative algorithm, which hopefully converges to a good answer. Little is known about the convergence properties of the algorithm. Networks containing a single cycle have been successfully analyzed by Weiss (1999) and Smyth *et al.* (1997), but results for networks containing many cycles are much less revealing.

The probability messages produced by probability propagation in the factor analyzer network of Fig. 1a are Gaussians. Each iteration of propagation consists of passing a mean and a variance along each edge in a bottom-up pass, followed by passing a mean and a variance along each edge in a top-down pass. At any instant, the bottom-up means and variances can be combined to form estimates of the means and variances of the modulation levels given the input.

Initially, the variance and mean sent from the kth top layer unit to the nth sensor is set to $\nu_{kn}^{(0)} = 1$ and $\eta_{kn}^{(0)} = 0$. The bottom-up pass begins by computing a noise level and an error signal at each sensor using the top-down variances and means from the previous iteration:

$$s_n^{(i)} = \psi_n + \sum_{k=1}^{K} \lambda_{nk}^2 \nu_{kn}^{(i-1)}, \quad e_n^{(i)} = x_n - \sum_{k=1}^{K} \lambda_{nk} \eta_{kn}^{(i-1)}. \tag{4}$$

These are used to compute bottom-up variances and means as follows:

$$\phi_{nk}^{(i)} = s_n^{(i)}/\lambda_{nk}^2 - \nu_{kn}^{(i-1)}, \quad \mu_{nk}^{(i)} = e_n^{(i)}/\lambda_{nk} + \eta_{kn}^{(i-1)}. \tag{5}$$

The bottom-up variances and means are then combined to form the current estimates of the modulation variances and means:

$$v_k^{(i)} = 1/(1 + \sum_{n=1}^{N} 1/\phi_{nk}^{(i)}), \quad \hat{z}_k^{(i)} = v_k^{(i)} \sum_{n=1}^{N} \mu_{nk}^{(i)}/\phi_{nk}^{(i)}. \tag{6}$$

The top-down pass proceeds by computing top-down variances and means as follows:

$$\nu_{kn}^{(i)} = 1/(1/v_k^{(i)} - 1/\phi_{nk}^{(i)}), \quad \eta_{kn}^{(i)} = \nu_{kn}^{(i)}(\hat{z}_k^{(i)}/v_k^{(i)} - \mu_{nk}^{(i)}/\phi_{nk}^{(i)}). \tag{7}$$

Notice that the variance updates are independent of the mean updates, whereas the mean updates depend on the variance updates.

2.1 Performance of local probability propagation.

We created a total of 200,000 factor analysis networks with 20 different sizes ranging from $K = 5, N = 10$ to $K = 80, N = 320$ and for each size of network we measured the inference error as a function of the number of iterations of propagation. Each of the 10,000 networks of a given size was produced by drawing the λ_{nk}s from standard normal distributions and then drawing each sensor variance ψ_n from an exponential distribution with mean $\sum_{k=1}^{K} \lambda_{nk}^2$. (A similar procedure was used by Neal and Dayan (1997).)

For each random network, a pattern was simulated from the network and probability propagation was applied using the simulated pattern as input. We measured the error between the estimate $\hat{\mathbf{z}}^{(i)}$ and the correct value $\mathrm{E}[\mathbf{z}|\mathbf{x}]$ by computing the difference between their coding costs under the exact posterior distribution and then normalizing by K to get an average number of nats per top layer unit.

Fig. 2a shows the inference error on a logarithmic scale versus the number of iterations (maximum of 20) in the 20 different network sizes. In all cases, the median error is reduced below .01 nats within 6 iterations. The rate of convergence of the error improves for larger N, as indicated by a general trend for the error curves to drop when N is increased. In contrast, the rate of convergence of the error appears to worsen for larger K, as shown by a general slight trend for the error curves to rise when K is increased.

For $K \geq N/8$, 0.1% of the networks actually diverge. To better understand the divergent cases, we studied the means and variances for all of the divergent networks. In all cases, the variances converge within a few iterations whereas the means oscillate and diverge. For $K = 5, N = 10$, 54 of the 10,000 networks diverged and 5 of these are shown in Fig. 2b. This observation suggests that in general the dynamics are determined by the dynamics of the mean updates.

2.2 Fixed points and a condition for global convergence.

When the variance updates converge, the dynamics of probability propagation in factor analysis networks become linear. This allows us to derive the fixed point of propagation in closed form and write an eigenvalue condition for global convergence.

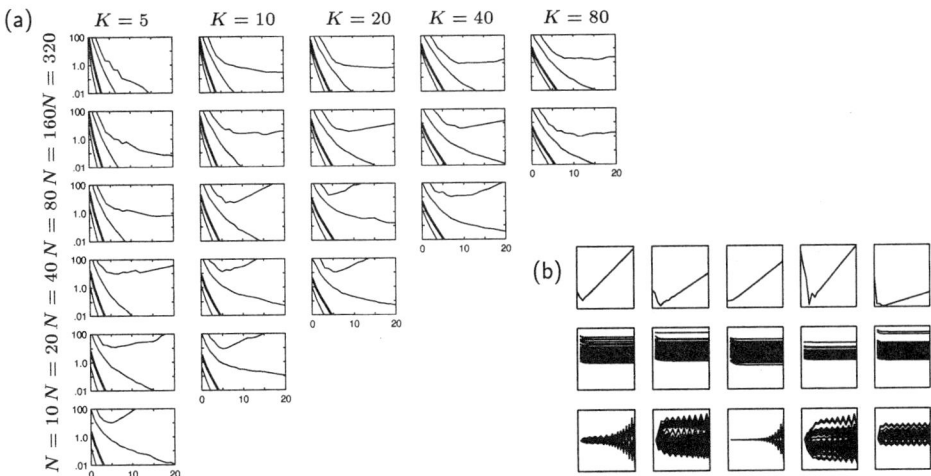

Figure 2: (a) Performance of probability propagation. Median inference error (bold curve) on a logarithmic scale as a function of the number of iterations for different sizes of network parameterized by K and N. The two curves adjacent to the bold curve show the range within which 98% of the errors lie. 99.9% of the errors were below the fourth, topmost curve. (b) The error, bottom-up variances and top-down means as a function of the number of iterations (maximum of 20) for 5 divergent networks of size $K = 5$, $N = 10$.

To analyze the system of mean updates, we define the following length KN vectors of means and the input: $\tilde{\eta}^{(i)} = (\eta_{11}^{(i)}, \eta_{21}^{(i)}, \ldots, \eta_{K1}^{(i)}, \eta_{12}^{(i)}, \ldots, \eta_{KN}^{(i)})^{\mathrm{T}}$, $\tilde{\mu}^{(i)} = (\mu_{11}^{(i)}, \mu_{12}^{(i)}, \ldots, \mu_{1K}^{(i)}, \mu_{21}^{(i)}, \ldots, \mu_{NK}^{(i)})^{\mathrm{T}}$, $\tilde{\mathbf{x}} = (x_1, x_1, \ldots, x_1, x_2, \ldots, x_2, x_N, \ldots, x_N)^{\mathrm{T}}$, where each x_n is repeated K times in the last vector. The network parameters are represented using $KN \times KN$ diagonal matrices, $\tilde{\mathbf{\Lambda}}$ and $\tilde{\mathbf{\Psi}}$. The diagonal of $\tilde{\mathbf{\Lambda}}$ is $\lambda_{11}, \ldots, \lambda_{1K}, \lambda_{21}, \ldots, \lambda_{NK}$, and the diagonal of $\tilde{\mathbf{\Psi}}$ is $\psi_1 \mathbf{I}, \psi_2 \mathbf{I}, \ldots, \psi_N \mathbf{I}$, where $\mathbf{I}$ is the $K \times K$ identity matrix. The converged bottom-up variances are represented using a diagonal matrix $\tilde{\mathbf{\Phi}}$ with diagonal $\phi_{11}, \ldots, \phi_{1K}, \phi_{21}, \ldots, \phi_{NK}$.

The summation operations in the propagation formulas are represented by a $KN \times KN$ matrix $\tilde{\mathbf{\Sigma}}_z$ that sums over means sent down from the top layer and a $KN \times KN$ matrix $\tilde{\mathbf{\Sigma}}_x$ that sums over means sent up from the sensory input:

$$\tilde{\mathbf{\Sigma}}_z = \begin{pmatrix} \mathbf{1} & & & \\ & \mathbf{1} & & \\ & & \ldots & \\ & & & \mathbf{1} \end{pmatrix}, \quad \tilde{\mathbf{\Sigma}}_x = \begin{pmatrix} \mathbf{I} & \mathbf{I} & \ldots & \mathbf{I} \\ \mathbf{I} & \mathbf{I} & \ldots & \mathbf{I} \\ \ldots & \ldots & \ldots & \ldots \\ \mathbf{I} & \mathbf{I} & \ldots & \mathbf{I} \end{pmatrix}. \tag{8}$$

These are $N \times N$ matrices of $K \times K$ blocks, where $\mathbf{1}$ is the $K \times K$ block of ones and $\mathbf{I}$ is the $K \times K$ identity matrix.

Using the above representations, the bottom-up pass is given by

$$\tilde{\mu}^{(i)} = \tilde{\mathbf{\Lambda}}^{-1}\tilde{\mathbf{x}} - \tilde{\mathbf{\Lambda}}^{-1}(\tilde{\mathbf{\Sigma}}_z - \mathbf{I})\tilde{\mathbf{\Lambda}}\tilde{\eta}^{(i-1)}, \tag{9}$$

and the top-down pass is given by

$$\tilde{\eta}^{(i)} = \left(\mathbf{I} + \mathrm{diag}(\tilde{\mathbf{\Sigma}}_x \tilde{\mathbf{\Phi}}^{-1} \tilde{\mathbf{\Sigma}}_x) - \tilde{\mathbf{\Phi}}^{-1}\right)^{-1}(\tilde{\mathbf{\Sigma}}_x - \mathbf{I})\tilde{\mathbf{\Phi}}^{-1}\tilde{\mu}^{(i)}. \tag{10}$$

Substituting (10) into (9), we get the linear update for $\tilde{\mu}$:

$$\tilde{\mu}^{(i)} = \tilde{\mathbf{\Lambda}}^{-1}\tilde{\mathbf{x}} - \tilde{\mathbf{\Lambda}}^{-1}(\tilde{\mathbf{\Sigma}}_z - \mathbf{I})\tilde{\mathbf{\Lambda}}\left(\mathbf{I} + \mathrm{diag}(\tilde{\mathbf{\Sigma}}_x \tilde{\mathbf{\Phi}}^{-1} \tilde{\mathbf{\Sigma}}_x) - \tilde{\mathbf{\Phi}}^{-1}\right)^{-1}(\tilde{\mathbf{\Sigma}}_x - \mathbf{I})\tilde{\mathbf{\Phi}}^{-1}\tilde{\mu}^{(i-1)}. \tag{11}$$

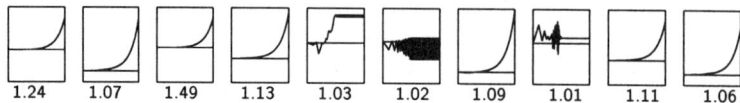

Figure 3: The error (log scale) versus number of iterations (log scale, max. of 1000) in 10 of the divergent networks with $K = 5$, $N = 10$. The means were *initialized* to the fixed point solutions and machine round-off errors cause divergence from the fixed points, whose errors are shown by horizontal lines.

The fixed point of this dynamic system, when it exists, is

$$\tilde{\boldsymbol{\mu}}^* = \tilde{\boldsymbol{\Phi}}\Big(\tilde{\boldsymbol{\Lambda}}\tilde{\boldsymbol{\Phi}} + (\tilde{\boldsymbol{\Sigma}}_z - \mathbf{I})\tilde{\boldsymbol{\Lambda}}\big(\mathbf{I} + \mathrm{diag}(\tilde{\boldsymbol{\Sigma}}_x\tilde{\boldsymbol{\Phi}}^{-1}\tilde{\boldsymbol{\Sigma}}_x) - \tilde{\boldsymbol{\Phi}}^{-1}\big)^{-1}(\tilde{\boldsymbol{\Sigma}}_x - \mathbf{I})\Big)^{-1}\tilde{\mathbf{x}}. \quad (12)$$

A fixed point exists if the determinant of the expression in large braces in (12) is nonzero. We have found a simplified expression for this determinant in terms of the determinants of smaller, $K \times K$ matrices.

Reinterpreting the dynamics in (11) as dynamics for $\tilde{\boldsymbol{\Lambda}}\tilde{\boldsymbol{\mu}}^{(i)}$, the stability of a fixed point is determined by the largest eigenvalue of the update matrix, $(\tilde{\boldsymbol{\Sigma}}_z - \mathbf{I})\tilde{\boldsymbol{\Lambda}}\big(\mathbf{I} + \mathrm{diag}(\tilde{\boldsymbol{\Sigma}}_x\tilde{\boldsymbol{\Phi}}^{-1}\tilde{\boldsymbol{\Sigma}}_x) - \tilde{\boldsymbol{\Phi}}^{-1}\big)^{-1}(\tilde{\boldsymbol{\Sigma}}_x - \mathbf{I})\tilde{\boldsymbol{\Phi}}^{-1}\tilde{\boldsymbol{\Lambda}}^{-1}$. If the modulus of the largest eigenvalue is less than 1, the fixed point is stable. Since the system is linear, if a stable fixed point exists, the system will be globally convergent to this point.

Of the 200,000 networks we explored, about 99.9% of the networks converged. For 10 of the divergent networks with $K = 5$, $N = 10$, we used 1000 iterations of probability propagation to compute the steady state variances. Then, we computed the modulus of the largest eigenvalue of the system and we computed the fixed point. After initializing the bottom-up means to the fixed point values, we performed 1000 iterations to see if numerical errors due to machine precision would cause divergence from the fixed point. Fig. 3 shows the error versus number of iterations (on logarithmic scales) for each network, the error of the fixed point, and the modulus of the largest eigenvalue. In some cases, the network diverges from the fixed point and reaches a dynamic equilibrium that has a lower average error than the fixed point.

3 Online factor analysis

To perform maximum likelihood factor analysis in an online fashion, each parameter should be modified to slightly increase the log-probability of the current sensory input, $\log p(\mathbf{x})$. However, since the factors are hidden, they must be probabilistically "filled in" using inference before an incremental learning step is performed.

If the estimated mean and variance of the kth factor are $\hat{z}_k$ and v_k, then it turns out (*e.g.*, Neal and Dayan, 1997) the parameters can be updated as follows:

$$\lambda_{nk} \leftarrow \lambda_{nk} + \eta[\hat{z}_k(x_n - \sum_{j=1}^K \lambda_{nj}\hat{z}_j) - v_k\lambda_{nk}]/\psi_n,$$
$$\psi_n \leftarrow (1-\eta)\psi_n + \eta[(x_n - \sum_{j=1}^K \lambda_{nj}\hat{z}_j)^2 + \sum_{j=1}^K v_k\lambda_{nj}^2], \quad (13)$$

where η is a learning rate.

Online learning consists of performing some number of iterations of probability propagation for the current input (*e.g.*, 4 iterations) and then modifying the parameters before processing the next input.

3.1 Results on simulated data. We produced 95 training sets of 200 cases each, with input sizes ranging from 20 sensors to 320 sensors. For each of 19 sizes of factor analyzer, we randomly selected 5 sets of parameters as described above and generated a training set. The factor analyzer sizes were $K \in \{5, 10, 20, 40, 80\}$,

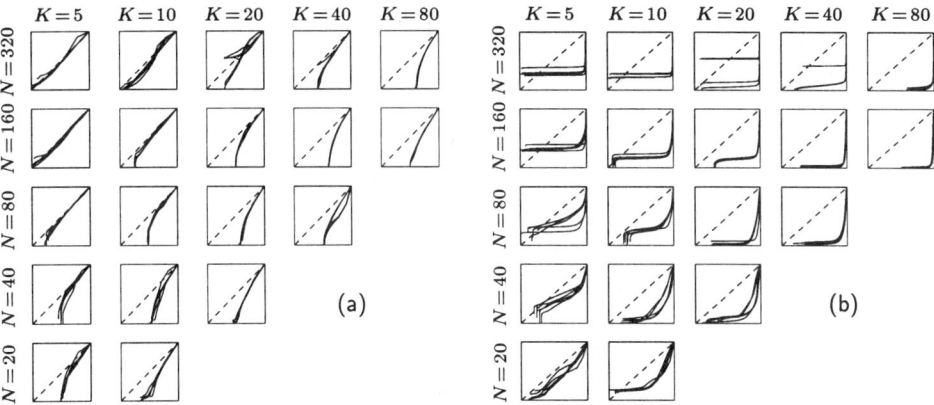

Figure 4: (a) Achievable errors after the same number of epochs of learning using 4 iterations versus 1 iteration. The horizontal axis gives the log-probability error (log scale) for learning with 1 iteration and the vertical axis gives the error after the same number of epochs for learning with 4 iterations. (b) The achievable errors for learning using 4 iterations of propagation versus wake-sleep learning using 4 iterations.

$N \in \{20, 40, 80, 160, 320\}$, $N > K$. For each factor analyzer and simulated data set, we estimated the optimal log-probability of the data using 100 iterations of EM.

For learning, the size of the model to be trained was set equal to the size of the model that was used to generate the data. To avoid the issue of how to schedule learning rates, we searched for *achievable* learning curves, regardless of whether or not a simple schedule for the learning rate exists. So, for a given method and randomly initialized parameters, we performed one separate epoch of learning using each of the learning rates, $1, 0.5, \ldots, 0.5^{20}$ and picked the learning rate that most improved the log-probability. Each successive learning rate was determined by comparing the performance using the old learning rate and one 0.75 times smaller.

We are mainly interested in comparing the achievable curves for different methods and how the differences scale with K and N. For two methods with the same K and N trained on the same data, we plot the log-probability error (optimal log-probability minus log-probability under the learned model) of one method against the log-probability error of the other method.

Fig. 4a shows the achievable errors using 4 iterations versus using 1 iteration. Usually, using 4 iterations produces networks with lower errors than those learned using 1 iteration. The difference is most significant for networks with large K, where in Sec. 2.1 we found that the convergence of the inference error was slower.

Fig. 4b shows the achievable errors for learning using 4 iterations of probability propagation versus wake-sleep learning using 4 iterations. Generally, probability propagation achieves much smaller errors than wake-sleep learning, although for small K wake-sleep performs better very close to the optimum log-probability. The most significant difference between the methods occurs for large K, where aside from local optima probability propagation achieves nearly optimal log-probabilities while the log-probabilities for wake-sleep learning are still close to their values at the start of learning.

4 Online face recognition

Fig. 1b shows examples from a set of 30,000 20×28 greyscale face images of 18 different people. In contrast to other data sets used to test face recognition methods, these faces include wide variation in expression and pose. To make classification more difficult, we normalized the images for each person so that each pixel has the same mean and variance. We used probability propagation and a recognition network in a factor analyzer to reduce the dimensionality of the data online from 560 dimensions to 40 dimensions. For probability propagation, we rather arbitrarily chose a learning rate of 0.0001, but for wake-sleep learning we tried learning rates ranging from 0.1 down to 0.0001. A multilayer perceptron with one hidden layer of 160 tanh units and one output layer of 18 softmax units was simultaneously being trained using gradient descent to predict face identity from the mean factors. The learning rate for the multilayer perceptron was set to 0.05 and this value was used for both methods.

For each image, a prediction was made before the parameters were modified. Fig. 5 shows online error curves obtained by filtering the losses. The curve for probability propagation is generally below the curves for wake-sleep learning.

The figure also shows the error curves for two forms of online nearest neighbors, where only the most recent W cases are used to make a prediction. The form of nearest neighbors that performs the worst has W set so that the storage requirements are the same as for the factor analysis / multilayer perceptron method. The better form of nearest neighbors has W set so that the number of computations is the same as for the factor analysis / multilayer perceptron method.

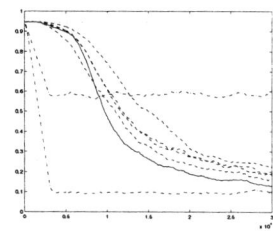

Number of pattern presentations

Figure 5: Online error curves for probability propagation (solid), wake-sleep learning (dashed), nearest neighbors (dot-dashed) and guessing (dotted).

5 Summary

It turns out that iterative probability propagation can be fruitful when used for learning in a graphical model with cycles, even when the model is *densely* connected. Although we are more interested in extending this work to more complex models where exact inference takes exponential time, studying iterative probability propagation in the factor analyzer allowed us to compare our results with exact inference and allowed us to derive the fixed point of the algorithm. We are currently applying iterative propagation in multiple cause networks for vision problems.

References

C. Berrou and A. Glavieux 1996. Near optimum error correcting coding and decoding: Turbo-codes. *IEEE Trans. on Communications*, **44**, 1261–1271.

P. Dayan, G. F. Hinton, R. M. Neal and R. S. Zemel 1995. The Helmholtz machine. *Neural Computation* **7**, 889–904.

B. J. Frey and D. J. C. MacKay 1998. A revolution: Belief propagation in graphs with cycles. In M. Jordan, M. Kearns and S. Solla (eds), *Advances in Neural Information Processing Systems 10*, Denver, 1997.

B. J. Frey 1998. *Graphical Models for Machine Learning and Digital Communication.* MIT Press, Cambridge MA. See http://www.cs.utoronto.ca/~frey.

G. E. Hinton, P. Dayan, B. J. Frey and R. M. Neal 1995. The wake-sleep algorithm for unsupervised neural networks. *Science* **268**, 1158–1161.

D. J. C. MacKay 1999. *Information Theory, Inference and Learning Algorithms.* Book in preparation, currently available at http://wol.ra.phy.cam.ac.uk/mackay.

R. M. Neal and P. Dayan 1997. Factor analysis using delta-rule wake-sleep learning. *Neural Computation* **9**, 1781–1804.

P. Smyth, R. J. McEliece, M. Xu, S. Aji and G. Horn 1997. Probability propagation in graphs with cycles. Presented at the workshop on *Inference and Learning in Graphical Models*, Vail, Colorado.

Y. Weiss 1998. Correctness of local probability propagation in graphical models. To appear in *Neural Computation.*

Variational Inference for Bayesian Mixtures of Factor Analysers

Zoubin Ghahramani and Matthew J. Beal
Gatsby Computational Neuroscience Unit
University College London
17 Queen Square, London WC1N 3AR, England
{zoubin,m.beal}@gatsby.ucl.ac.uk

Abstract

We present an algorithm that infers the model structure of a mixture of factor analysers using an efficient and deterministic variational approximation to full Bayesian integration over model parameters. This procedure can automatically determine the optimal number of components and the local dimensionality of each component (i.e. the number of factors in each factor analyser). Alternatively it can be used to infer posterior distributions over number of components and dimensionalities. Since all parameters are integrated out the method is not prone to overfitting. Using a stochastic procedure for adding components it is possible to perform the variational optimisation incrementally and to avoid local maxima. Results show that the method works very well in practice and correctly infers the number and dimensionality of nontrivial synthetic examples.

By importance sampling from the variational approximation we show how to obtain unbiased estimates of the true evidence, the exact predictive density, and the KL divergence between the variational posterior and the true posterior, not only in this model but for variational approximations in general.

1 Introduction

Factor analysis (FA) is a method for modelling correlations in multidimensional data. The model assumes that each p-dimensional data vector $\mathbf{y}$ was generated by first linearly transforming a $k < p$ dimensional vector of unobserved independent zero-mean unit-variance Gaussian sources, $\mathbf{x}$, and then adding a p-dimensional zero-mean Gaussian noise vector, $\mathbf{n}$, with diagonal covariance matrix Ψ: i.e. $\mathbf{y} = \Lambda \mathbf{x} + \mathbf{n}$. Integrating out $\mathbf{x}$ and $\mathbf{n}$, the marginal density of $\mathbf{y}$ is Gaussian with zero mean and covariance $\Lambda \Lambda^T + \Psi$. The matrix Λ is known as the factor loading matrix. Given data with a sample covariance matrix Σ, factor analysis finds the Λ and Ψ that optimally fit Σ in the maximum likelihood sense. Since $k < p$, a single factor analyser can be seen as a reduced parametrisation of a full-covariance Gaussian.[1]

---

[1] Factor analysis and its relationship to principal components analysis (PCA) and mixture models is reviewed in [10].

A *mixture* of factor analysers (MFA) models the density for **y** as a weighted average of factor analyser densities

$$P(\mathbf{y}|\Lambda, \Psi, \pi) = \sum_{s=1}^{S} P(s|\pi) P(\mathbf{y}|s, \Lambda^s, \Psi), \qquad (1)$$

where π is the vector of mixing proportions, s is a discrete indicator variable, and Λ^s is the factor loading matrix for factor analyser s which includes a mean vector for **y**.

By exploiting the factor analysis parameterisation of covariance matrices, a mixture of factor analysers can be used to fit a mixture of Gaussians to correlated high dimensional data without requiring $O(p^2)$ parameters or undesirable compromises such as axis-aligned covariance matrices. In an MFA each Gaussian cluster has intrinsic dimensionality k (or k_s if the dimensions are allowed to vary across clusters). Consequently, the mixture of factor analysers simultaneously addresses the problems of clustering and local dimensionality reduction. When Ψ is a multiple of the identity the model becomes a mixture of probabilistic PCAs. Tractable maximum likelihood procedure for fitting MFA and MPCA models can be derived from the Expectation Maximisation algorithm [4, 11].

The maximum likelihood (ML) approach to MFA can easily get caught in local maxima.[2] Ueda et al. [12] provide an effective deterministic procedure for avoiding local maxima by considering splitting a factor analyser in one part of space and merging two in a another part. But splits and merges have to be considered simultaneously because the number of factor analysers has to stay the same since adding a factor analyser is always expected to increase the training likelihood.

A fundamental problem with maximum likelihood approaches is that they fail to take into account model complexity (i.e. the cost of coding the model parameters). So more complex models are not penalised, which leads to overfitting and the inability to determine the best model size and structure (or distributions thereof) without resorting to costly cross-validation procedures. Bayesian approaches overcome these problems by treating the parameters θ as unknown random variables and averaging over the ensemble of models they define:

$$P(Y) = \int d\theta \, P(Y|\theta) P(\theta). \qquad (2)$$

$P(Y)$ is the *evidence* for a data set $Y = \{\mathbf{y}^1, \ldots, \mathbf{y}^N\}$. Integrating out parameters penalises models with more degrees of freedom since these models can *a priori* model a larger range of data sets. All information inferred from the data about the parameters is captured by the posterior distribution $P(\theta|Y)$ rather than the ML point estimate $\hat{\theta}$.[3]

While Bayesian theory deals with the problems of overfitting and model selection/averaging, in practice it is often computationally and analytically intractable to perform the required integrals. For Gaussian mixture models *Markov chain Monte Carlo* (MCMC) methods have been developed to approximate these integrals by sampling [8, 7]. The main criticism of MCMC methods is that they are slow and

---

[2]Technically, the log likelihood is not bounded above if no constraints are put on the determinant of the component covariances. So the real ML objective for MFA is to find the highest finite local maximum of the likelihood.

[3]We sometimes use θ to refer to the parameters and sometimes to all the unknown quantities (parameters and hidden variables). Formally the only difference between the two is that the number of hidden variables grows with N, whereas the number of parameters usually does not.

it is usually difficult to assess convergence. Furthermore, the posterior density over parameters is stored as a set of samples, which can be inefficient.

Another approach to Bayesian integration for Gaussian mixtures [9] is the *Laplace approximation* which makes a local Gaussian approximation around a maximum *a posteriori* parameter estimate. These approximations are based on large data limits and can be poor, particularly for small data sets (for which, in principle, the advantages of Bayesian integration over ML are largest). Local Gaussian approximations are also poorly suited to bounded or positive parameters such as the mixing proportions of the mixture model. Finally, it is difficult to see how this approach can be applied to online incremental changes to model structure.

In this paper we employ a third approach to Bayesian inference: *variational approximation*. We form a lower bound on the log evidence using Jensen's inequality:

$$\mathcal{L} \equiv \ln P(Y) = \ln \int d\theta\, P(Y,\theta) \geq \int d\theta\, Q(\theta) \ln \frac{P(Y,\theta)}{Q(\theta)} \equiv \mathcal{F}, \qquad (3)$$

which we seek to maximise. Maximising $\mathcal{F}$ is equivalent to minimising the KL-divergence between $Q(\theta)$ and $P(\theta|Y)$, so a tractable Q can be used as an approximation to the intractable posterior. This approach draws its roots from one way of deriving mean field approximations in physics, and has been used recently for Bayesian inference [13, 5, 1].

The variational method has several advantages over MCMC and Laplace approximations. Unlike MCMC, convergence can be assessed easily by monitoring $\mathcal{F}$. The approximate posterior is encoded efficiently in $Q(\theta)$. Unlike Laplace approximations, the form of Q can be tailored to each parameter (in fact the optimal form of Q for each parameter falls out of the optimisation), the approximation is global, and Q optimises an objective function. Variational methods are generally fast, $\mathcal{F}$ is guaranteed to increase monotonically and transparently incorporates model complexity. To our knowledge, no one has done a full Bayesian analysis of mixtures of factor analysers.

Of course, vis-a-vis MCMC, the main disadvantage of variational approximations is that they are not guaranteed to find the exact posterior in the limit. However, with a straightforward application of sampling, it is possible to take the result of the variational optimisation and use it to sample from the exact posterior and exact predictive density. This is described in section 5.

In the remainder of this paper we first describe the mixture of factor analysers in more detail (section 2). We then derive the variational approximation (section 3). We show empirically that the model can infer both the number of components and their intrinsic dimensionalities, and is not prone to overfitting (section 6). Finally, we conclude in section 7.

2 The Model

Starting from (1), the evidence for the Bayesian MFA is obtained by averaging the likelihood under priors for the parameters (which have their own hyperparameters):

$$\begin{aligned} P(Y) = & \int d\pi P(\pi|\alpha) \int d\nu P(\nu|a,b) \int d\Lambda\, P(\Lambda|\nu) \cdot \\ & \prod_{n=1}^{N} \left[\sum_{s^n=1}^{S} P(s^n|\pi) \int d\mathbf{x}^n P(\mathbf{x}^n) P(\mathbf{y}^n|\mathbf{x}^n, s^n, \Lambda^s, \Psi) \right]. \end{aligned} \qquad (4)$$

Here $\{\alpha, a, b, \Psi\}$ are hyperparameters[4], ν are precision parameters (i.e. inverse variances) for the columns of Λ. The conditional independence relations between the variables in this model are shown graphically in the usual belief network representation in Figure 1.

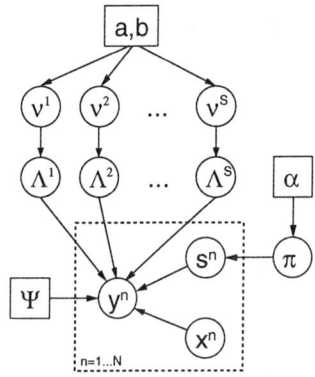

Figure 1: Generative model for variational Bayesian mixture of factor analysers. Circles denote random variables, solid rectangles denote hyperparameters, and the dashed rectangle shows the plate (i.e. repetitions) over the data.

While arbitrary choices could be made for the priors on the first line of (4), choosing priors that are conjugate to the likelihood terms on the second line of (4) greatly simplifies inference and interpretability.[5] So we choose $P(\pi|\alpha)$ to be symmetric Dirichlet, which is conjugate to the multinomial $P(s|\pi)$.

The prior for the factor loading matrix plays a key role in this model. Each component of the mixture has a Gaussian prior $P(\Lambda^s|\nu^s)$, where each element of the vector ν^s is the precision of a *column* of Λ. If one of these precisions $\nu_l^s \to \infty$, then the outgoing weights for factor $\mathbf{x}_l$ will go to zero, which allows the model to reduce the intrinsic dimensionality of $\mathbf{x}$ if the data does not warrant this added dimension. This method of intrinsic dimensionality reduction has been used by Bishop [2] for Bayesian PCA, and is closely related to MacKay and Neal's method for automatic relevance determination (ARD) for inputs to a neural network [6].

To avoid overfitting it is important to integrate out all parameters whose cardinality scales with model complexity (i.e. number of components and their dimensionalities). We therefore also integrate out the precisions using Gamma priors, $P(\nu|a,b)$.

3 The Variational Approximation

Applying Jensen's inequality repeatedly to the log evidence (4) we lower bound it using the following factorisation of the distribution of parameters and hidden variables: $Q(\Lambda)Q(\pi,\nu)Q(s,\mathbf{x})$. Given this factorisation several additional factorisations fall out of the conditional independencies in the model resulting in the variational objective function:

$$\mathcal{F} = \int d\pi \, Q(\pi) \ln \frac{P(\pi|\alpha)}{Q(\pi)} + \sum_{s=1}^{S} \int d\nu^s Q(\nu^s) \left[\ln \frac{P(\nu^s|a,b)}{Q(\nu^s)} + \int d\Lambda^s Q(\Lambda^s) \ln \frac{P(\Lambda^s|\nu^s)}{Q(\Lambda^s)} \right]$$

$$+ \sum_{n=1}^{N} \sum_{s^n=1}^{S} Q(s^n) \left[\int d\pi \, Q(\pi) \ln \frac{P(s^n|\pi)}{Q(s^n)} + \int d\mathbf{x}^n Q(\mathbf{x}^n|s^n) \ln \frac{P(\mathbf{x}^n)}{Q(\mathbf{x}^n|s^n)} \right.$$

$$\left. + \int d\Lambda^s Q(\Lambda^s) \int d\mathbf{x}^n Q(\mathbf{x}^n|s^n) \ln P(\mathbf{y}^n|\mathbf{x}^n, s^n, \Lambda^s, \Psi) \right] \quad (5)$$

The variational posteriors $Q(\cdot)$, as given in the Appendix, are derived by performing a free-form extremisation of $\mathcal{F}$ w.r.t. Q. It is not difficult to show that these extrema are indeed maxima of $\mathcal{F}$. The optimal posteriors Q are of the same conjugate forms as the priors. The model hyperparameters which govern the priors can be estimated in the same fashion (see the Appendix).

---

[4]We currently do not integrate out Ψ, although this can also be done.
[5]Conjugate priors have the same effect as pseudo-observations.

4 Birth and Death

When optimising $\mathcal{F}$, occasionally one finds that for some s: $\sum_n Q(s^n) = 0$. These zero responsibility components are the result of there being insufficient support from the local data to overcome the dimensional complexity prior on the factor loading matrices. So components of the mixture die of natural causes when they are no longer needed. Removing these redundant components increases $\mathcal{F}$.

Component birth does not happen spontaneously, so we introduce a heuristic. Whenever $\mathcal{F}$ has stabilised we pick a parent-component stochastically with probability proportional to $e^{-\beta \mathcal{F}_s}$ and attempt to split it into two; $\mathcal{F}_s$ is the s-specific contribution to $\mathcal{F}$ with the last bracketed term in (5) normalised by $\sum_n Q(s^n)$. This works better than both cycling through components and picking them at random as it concentrates attempted births on components that are faring poorly. The parameter distributions of the two Gaussians created from the split are initialised by partitioning the responsibilities for the data, $Q(s^n)$, along a direction sampled from the parent's distribution. This usually causes $\mathcal{F}$ to decrease, so by monitoring the future progress of $\mathcal{F}$ we can reject this attempted birth if $\mathcal{F}$ does not recover.

Although it is perfectly possible to start the model with many components and let them die, it is computationally more efficient to start with one component and allow it to spawn more when necessary.

5 Exact Predictive Density, True Evidence, and KL

By importance sampling from the variational approximation we can obtain unbiased estimates of three important quantities: the exact predictive density, the true log evidence $\mathcal{L}$, and the KL divergence between the variational posterior and the true posterior. Letting $\theta = \{\Lambda, \pi\}$, we sample $\theta_i \sim Q(\theta)$. Each such sample is an instance of a mixture of factor analysers with predictive density given by (1). We weight these predictive densities by the importance weights $w_i = P(\theta_i, Y)/Q(\theta_i)$, which are easy to evaluate. This results in a *mixture* of mixtures of factor analysers, and will converge to the exact predictive density, $P(\mathbf{y}|Y)$, as long as $Q(\theta) > 0$ wherever $P(\theta|Y) > 0$. The true log evidence can be similarly estimated by $\mathcal{L} = \ln \langle w \rangle$, where $\langle \cdot \rangle$ denotes averaging over the importance samples. Finally, the KL divergence is given by: $\mathrm{KL}(Q(\theta)\|P(\theta|Y)) = \ln \langle w \rangle - \langle \ln w \rangle$.

This procedure has three significant properties. First, the same importance weights can be used to estimate all three quantities. Second, while importance sampling can work very poorly in high dimensions for ad hoc proposal distributions, here the variational optimisation is used in a principled manner to pick Q to be a good approximation to P and therefore hopefully a good proposal distribution. Third, this procedure can be applied to any variational approximation. A detailed exposition can be found in [3].

6 Results

Experiment 1: Discovering the number of components. We tested the model on synthetic data generated from a mixture of 18 Gaussians with 50 points per cluster (Figure 2, top left). The variational algorithm has little difficulty finding the correct number of components and the birth heuristics are successful at avoiding local maxima. After finding the 18 Gaussians repeated splits are attempted and rejected. Finding a distribution over number of components using $\mathcal{F}$ is also simple.

Experiment 2: The shrinking spiral. We used the dataset of 800 data points from a shrinking spiral from [12] as another test of how well the algorithm could

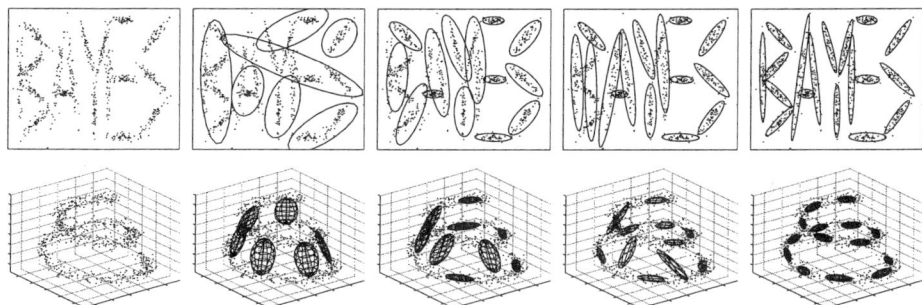

Figure 2: **(top)** Exp 1: The frames from left to right are the data, and the 2 S.D. Gaussian ellipses after 7, 14, 16 and 22 accepted births. **(bottom)** Exp 2: Shrinking spiral data and 1 S.D. Gaussian ellipses after 6, 9, 12, and 17 accepted births. Note that the number of Gaussians increases from left to right.

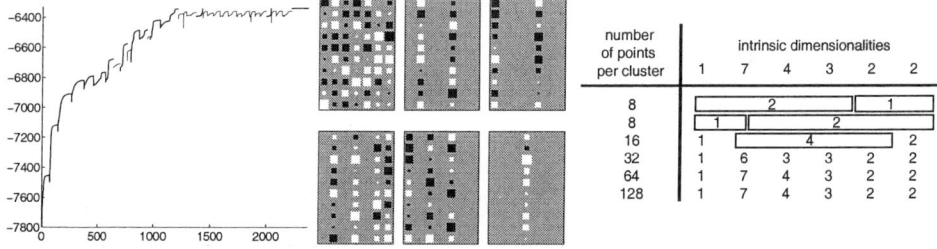

Figure 3: **(left)** Exp 2: $\mathcal{F}$ as function of iteration for the spiral problem on a typical run. Drops in $\mathcal{F}$ constitute component births. Thick lines are accepted attempts, thin lines are rejected attempts. **(middle)** Exp 3: Means of the factor loading matrices. These results are analogous to those given by Bishop [2] for Bayesian PCA. **(right)** Exp 3: Table with learned number of Gaussians and dimensionalities as training set size increases. Boxes represent model components that capture several of the clusters.

escape local maxima and how robust it was to initial conditions (Figure 2, bottom). Again local maxima did not pose a problem and the algorithm always found between 12-14 Gaussians regardless of whether it was initialised with 0 or 200. These runs took about 3-4 minutes on a 500MHz Alpha EV6 processor. A plot of $\mathcal{F}$ shows that most of the compute time is spent on accepted moves (Figure 3, left).

Experiment 3: Discovering the local dimensionalities. We generated a synthetic data set of 300 data points in each of 6 Gaussians with intrinsic dimensionalities (7 4 3 2 2 1) embedded in 10 dimensions. The variational Bayesian approach correctly inferred both the number of Gaussians and their intrinsic dimensionalities (Figure 3, middle). We varied the number of data points and found that as expected with fewer points the data could not provide evidence for as many components and intrinsic dimensions (Figure 3, right).

7 Discussion

Search over model structures for MFAs is computationally intractable if each factor analyser is allowed to have different intrinsic dimensionalities. In this paper we have shown that the variational Bayesian approach can be used to efficiently infer this model structure while avoiding overfitting and other deficiencies of ML approaches. One attraction of our variational method, which can be exploited in other models, is that once a factorisation of Q is assumed all inference is automatic and exact. We can also use $\mathcal{F}$ to get a distribution over structures if desired. Finally we derive a generally applicable importance sampler that gives us unbiased estimates of the true evidence, the exact predictive density, and the KL divergence between the variational posterior and the true posterior.

Encouraged by the results on synthetic data, we have applied the Bayesian mixture of factor analysers to a real-world unsupervised digit classification problem. We will report the results of these experiments in a separate article.

Appendix: Optimal Q Distributions and Hyperparameters

$$Q(\mathbf{x}^n|s^n) \sim \mathcal{N}(\overline{\mathbf{x}}^{n,s}, \Sigma^s) \quad Q(\Lambda_q^s) \sim \mathcal{N}(\overline{\Lambda}_q^s, \Sigma^{q,s}) \quad Q(\boldsymbol{\nu}_l^s) \sim \mathcal{G}(a_l^s, b_l^s) \quad Q(\boldsymbol{\pi}) \sim \mathcal{D}(\omega \mathbf{u})$$

$$\ln Q(s^n) = [\psi(\omega u_s) - \psi(\omega)] + \frac{1}{2}\ln|\Sigma^s| + \langle \ln P(\mathbf{y}^n|\mathbf{x}^n, s^n, \Lambda^s, \Psi)\rangle + c$$

$$\overline{\mathbf{x}}^{n,s} = \Sigma^s \overline{\Lambda}^{s\top} \Psi^{-1} \mathbf{y}^n, \quad \overline{\Lambda}_q^s = \left[\Psi^{-1}\sum_{n=1}^N Q(s^n) \mathbf{y}^n \overline{\mathbf{x}}^{n,s\top} \Sigma^{q,s}\right]_q, \quad a_l^s = a + \frac{p}{2}, \quad b_l^s = b + \frac{1}{2}\sum_{q=1}^p \langle \Lambda_{ql}^{s\,2}\rangle$$

$$\Sigma^{s\,-1} = \langle \Lambda^{s\top}\Psi^{-1}\Lambda^s\rangle + I, \quad \Sigma^{q,s\,-1} = \Psi_{qq}^{-1}\sum_{n=1}^N Q(s^n)\langle \mathbf{x}^n \mathbf{x}^{n\top}\rangle + \mathrm{diag}\langle \boldsymbol{\nu}^s\rangle, \quad \omega u_s = \frac{\alpha}{S} + \sum_{n=1}^N Q(s^n)$$

where $\{\mathcal{N}, \mathcal{G}, \mathcal{D}\}$ denote Normal, Gamma and Dirichlet distributions respectively, $\langle \cdot \rangle$ denotes expectation under the variational posterior, and $\psi(x)$ is the *digamma* function $\psi(x) \equiv \frac{\partial}{\partial x}\ln\Gamma(x)$. Note that the optimal distributions $Q(\Lambda^s)$ have block diagonal covariance structure; even though each Λ^s is a $p \times q$ matrix, its covariance only has $O(pq^2)$ parameters. Differentiating $\mathcal{F}$ with respect to the parameters, a and b, of the precision prior we get fixed point equations $\psi(a) = \langle \ln \boldsymbol{\nu}\rangle + \ln b$ and $b = a/\langle \boldsymbol{\nu}\rangle$. Similarly the fixed point for the parameters of the Dirichlet prior is $\psi(\alpha) - \psi(\alpha/S) + \sum [\psi(\omega u_s) - \psi(\omega)]/S = 0$.

References

[1] H. Attias. Inferring parameters and structure of latent variable models by variational Bayes. In *Proc. 15th Conf. on Uncertainty in Artificial Intelligence*, 1999.

[2] C.M. Bishop. Variational PCA. In *Proc. Ninth Int. Conf. on Artificial Neural Networks. ICANN*, 1999.

[3] Z. Ghahramani, H. Attias, and M.J. Beal. Learning model structure. Technical Report GCNU-TR-1999-006, (in prep.) Gatsby Unit, Univ. College London, 1999.

[4] Z. Ghahramani and G.E. Hinton. The EM algorithm for mixtures of factor analyzers. Technical Report CRG-TR-96-1 [http://www.gatsby.ucl.ac.uk/~zoubin/papers/tr-96-1.ps.gz], Dept. of Comp. Sci., Univ. of Toronto, 1996.

[5] D.J.C. MacKay. Ensemble learning for hidden Markov models. Technical report, Cavendish Laboratory, University of Cambridge, 1997.

[6] R.M. Neal. Assessing relevance determination methods using DELVE. In C.M. Bishop, editor, *Neural Networks and Machine Learning*, 97–129. Springer-Verlag, 1998.

[7] C.E. Rasmussen. The infinite gaussian mixture model. In *Adv. Neur. Inf. Proc. Sys. 12*. MIT Press, 2000.

[8] S. Richardson and P.J. Green. On Bayesian analysis of mixtures with an unknown number of components. *J. Roy. Stat. Soc.-Ser. B*, 59(4):731–758, 1997.

[9] S.J. Roberts, D. Husmeier, I. Rezek, and W. Penny. Bayesian approaches to Gaussian mixture modeling. *IEEE PAMI*, 20(11):1133–1142, 1998.

[10] S. T. Roweis and Z. Ghahramani. A unifying review of linear Gaussian models. *Neural Computation*, 11(2):305–345, 1999.

[11] M.E. Tipping and C.M. Bishop. Mixtures of probabilistic principal component analyzers. *Neural Computation*, 11(2):443–482, 1999.

[12] N. Ueda, R. Nakano, Z. Ghahramani, and G.E. Hinton. SMEM algorithm for mixture models. In *Adv. Neur. Inf. Proc. Sys. 11*. MIT Press, 1999.

[13] S. Waterhouse, D.J.C. Mackay, and T. Robinson. Bayesian methods for mixtures of experts. In *Adv. Neur. Inf. Proc. Sys. 7*. MIT Press, 1995.

Bayesian Transduction

Thore Graepel, Ralf Herbrich and Klaus Obermayer
Department of Computer Science
Technical University of Berlin
Franklinstr. 28/29, 10587 Berlin, Germany
{*graepel2, ralfh, oby*}@*cs.tu-berlin.de*

Abstract

Transduction is an inference principle that takes a training sample and aims at estimating the values of a function at given points contained in the so-called working sample as opposed to the whole of input space for induction. Transduction provides a confidence measure on single predictions rather than classifiers — a feature particularly important for risk-sensitive applications. The possibly infinite number of functions is reduced to a finite number of equivalence classes on the working sample. A rigorous Bayesian analysis reveals that for standard classification loss we cannot benefit from considering more than one test point at a time. The probability of the label of a given test point is determined as the posterior measure of the corresponding subset of hypothesis space. We consider the PAC setting of binary classification by linear discriminant functions (perceptrons) in kernel space such that the probability of labels is determined by the volume ratio in version space. We suggest to sample this region by an ergodic billiard. Experimental results on real world data indicate that Bayesian Transduction compares favourably to the well-known Support Vector Machine, in particular if the posterior probability of labellings is used as a confidence measure to exclude test points of low confidence.

1 Introduction

According to Vapnik [9], *when solving a given problem one should avoid solving a more general problem as an intermediate step.* The reasoning behind this principle is that in order to solve the more general task resources may be wasted or compromises may have to be made which would not have been necessary for the solution of the problem at hand. A direct application of this common-sense principle reduces the more general problem of inferring a functional dependency on the whole of input space to the problem of estimating the values of a function at given points (working sample), a paradigm referred to as *transductive inference*. More formally, given a probability measure $\mathbf{P}_{\mathsf{XY}}$ on the space of data $\mathcal{X} \times \mathcal{Y} = \mathcal{X} \times \{-1, +1\}$, a *training sample* $S = \{(\mathbf{x}_1, y_1), \ldots, (\mathbf{x}_\ell, y_\ell)\}$ is generated i.i.d. according to $\mathbf{P}_{\mathsf{XY}}$. Additional m data points $W = \{\mathbf{x}_{\ell+1}, \ldots, \mathbf{x}_{\ell+m}\}$ are drawn: the *working sample*. The goal is to label the objects of the working sample W using a fixed set $\mathcal{H}$ of functions

$f: \mathcal{X} \mapsto \{-1, +1\}$ so as to minimise a predefined loss. In contrast, *inductive inference*, aims at choosing a *single* function $f_\ell \in \mathcal{H}$ best suited to capture the dependency expressed by the unknown $\mathbf{P_{XY}}$. Obviously, if we have a transductive algorithm $\mathcal{A}(W, S, \mathcal{H})$ that assigns to each working sample W a set of labels given the training sample S and the set $\mathcal{H}$ of functions, we can define a function $f_S : \mathcal{X} \mapsto \{-1, +1\}$ by $f_S(\mathbf{x}) = \mathcal{A}(\{\mathbf{x}\}, S, \mathcal{H})$ as a result of the transduction algorithm. There are two crucial differences to induction, however: i) $\mathcal{A}(\{\mathbf{x}\}, S, \mathcal{H})$ is not restricted to select a single decision function $f \in \mathcal{H}$ for each $\mathbf{x}$, ii) a transduction algorithm can give performance guarantees on particular labellings instead of functions. In practical applications this difference may be of great importance.

After all, in risk sensitive applications (medical diagnosis, financial and critical control applications) it often matters to know how *confident* we are about a given prediction. In this case a general confidence measure of the classifier w.r.t. the whole input distribution would not provide the desired warranty at all. Note that for linear classifiers some guarantee can be obtained by the margin [7] which in Section 4 we will demonstrate to be too coarse a confidence measure. The idea of transduction was put forward in [8], where also first algorithmic ideas can be found. Later [1] suggested an algorithm for transduction based on linear programming and [3] highlighted the need for confidence measures in transduction.

The paper is structured as follows: A Bayesian approach to transduction is formulated in Section 2. In Section 3 the function class of kernel perceptrons is introduced to which the Bayesian transduction scheme is applied. For the estimation of volumes in parameter space we present a kernel billiard as an efficient sampling technique. Finally, we demonstrate experimentally in Section 4 how the confidence measure for labellings helps Bayesian Transduction to achieve low generalisation error at a low rejection rate of test points and thus to outperform Support Vector Machines (SVMs).

2 Bayesian Transductive Classification

Suppose we are given a training sample $S = \{(\mathbf{x}_1, y_1), \ldots, (\mathbf{x}_\ell, y_\ell)\}$ drawn i.i.d. from $\mathbf{P_{XY}}$ and a working sample $W = \{\mathbf{x}_{\ell+1}, \ldots, \mathbf{x}_{\ell+m}\}$ drawn i.i.d. from $\mathbf{P_X}$. Given a *prior* $\mathbf{P_H}$ over the set $\mathcal{H}$ of functions and a likelihood $\mathbf{P}_{(XY)^\ell | H=f}$ we obtain a posterior probability $\mathbf{P}_{H|(XY)^\ell = S} \stackrel{\text{def}}{=} \mathbf{P}_{H|S}$ by Bayes' rule. This posterior measure induces a probability measure on labellings $\mathbf{b} \in \{-1, +1\}^m$ of the working sample by[1]

$$\mathbf{P}_{Y^m|S,W}(\mathbf{b}) \stackrel{\text{def}}{=} \mathbf{P}_{H|S}(\{f : \forall \mathbf{x}_{\ell+i} \in W \quad f(\mathbf{x}_{\ell+i}) = b_i\}) . \quad (1)$$

For the sake of simplicity let us assume a PAC style setting, i.e. there exists a function f^* in the space $\mathcal{H}$ such that $\mathbf{P}_{Y|X=\mathbf{x}}(y) = \delta(y - f^*(\mathbf{x}))$. In this case one can define the so-called *version-space* as the set of functions that is consistent with the training sample

$$V(S) = \{f : \forall (\mathbf{x}_i, y_i) \in S \quad f(\mathbf{x}_i) = y_i\} , \quad (2)$$

outside which the posterior $\mathbf{P}_{H|S}$ vanishes. Then $\mathbf{P}_{Y^m|S,W}(\mathbf{b})$ represents the prior measure of functions consistent with the training sample S *and* the labelling $\mathbf{b}$ on the working sample W normalised by the prior measure of functions consistent with S alone. The measure $\mathbf{P_H}$ can be used to incorporate prior knowledge into

---

[1] Note that the number of different labellings $\mathbf{b}$ implementable by $\mathcal{H}$ is bounded above by the value of the growth function $\Pi_\mathcal{H}(|W|)$ [8, p. 321].

the inference process. If no such knowledge is available, considerations of symmetry may lead to "uninformative" priors.

Given the measure $\mathbf{P}_{\mathsf{Y}^m|\mathsf{S},\mathsf{W}}$ over labellings, in order to arrive at a risk minimal decision w.r.t. the labelling we need to define a loss function $l : \mathcal{Y}^m \times \mathcal{Y}^m \mapsto \mathbb{R}^+$ between labellings and minimise its expectation,

$$R(\mathbf{b}, S, W) = \mathbf{E}_{\mathsf{Y}^m|\mathsf{S},\mathsf{W}}\left[l(\mathbf{b}, \mathsf{Y}^m)\right] = \sum_{\{\mathbf{b}'\}} l(\mathbf{b}, \mathbf{b}') \mathbf{P}_{\mathsf{Y}^m|\mathsf{S},\mathsf{W}}(\mathbf{b}'), \qquad (3)$$

where the summation runs over all the 2^m possible labellings $\mathbf{b}'$ of the working sample. Let us consider two scenarios:

1. A 0–1–loss on the exact labelling $\mathbf{b}$, i.e. for two labellings $\mathbf{b}$ and $\mathbf{b}'$

$$l_c(\mathbf{b}, \mathbf{b}') = 1 - \prod_{i=1}^{m} \delta(b_i - b_i') \quad \Leftrightarrow \quad R_c(\mathbf{b}, S, W) = 1 - \mathbf{P}_{\mathsf{Y}^m|\mathsf{S},\mathsf{W}}(\mathbf{b}). \qquad (4)$$

In this case choosing the labelling $\mathbf{b}_c = \mathrm{argmin}_\mathbf{b}\, R_c(\mathbf{b}, S, W)$ of the highest joint probability $\mathbf{P}_{\mathsf{Y}^m|\mathsf{S},\mathsf{W}}(\mathbf{b})$ minimises the risk. This non-labelwise loss is appropriate if the goal is to *exactly* identify a combination of labels, e.g. the combination of handwritten digits defining a postal zip code. Note that classical SVM transduction (see, e.g. [8, 1]) by maximising the margin on the combined training and working sample approximates this strategy and hence does not minimise the standard classification risk on single instances as intended.

2. A 0–1–loss on the single labels b_i, i.e. for two labellings $\mathbf{b}$ and $\mathbf{b}'$

$$\begin{aligned} l_s(\mathbf{b}, \mathbf{b}') &= \frac{1}{m} \sum_{i=1}^{m} (1 - \delta(b_i - b_i')), & (5) \\ R_s(\mathbf{b}, S, W) &= \frac{1}{m} \sum_{i=1}^{m} \sum_{\{\mathbf{b}'\}} (1 - \delta(b_i - b_i')) \mathbf{P}_{\mathsf{Y}^m|\mathsf{S},\mathsf{W}}(\mathbf{b}') \\ &= \frac{1}{m} \sum_{i=1}^{m} (1 - \mathbf{P}_{\mathsf{H}|\mathsf{S}}(\{f : f(\mathbf{x}_{\ell+i}) = b_i\})). \end{aligned}$$

Due to the independent treatment of the loss at working sample points the risk $R_s(\mathbf{b}, S, W)$ is minimised by the labelling of highest marginal probability of the labels, i.e.

$$b_i = \mathrm{argmax}_{y \in \mathcal{Y}}\, \mathbf{P}_{\mathsf{H}|\mathsf{S}}(\{f : f(\mathbf{x}_{\ell+i}) = y\}).$$

Thus in the case of the labelwise loss (5) a working sample of $m > 1$ point does not offer any advantages over larger working samples w.r.t. the Bayes-optimal decision. Since this corresponds to the standard classification setting, we will restrict ourselves to working samples of size $m = 1$, i.e. to one working point $\mathbf{x}_{\ell+1}$.

3 Bayesian Transduction by Volume

3.1 The Kernel Perceptron

We consider transductive inference for the class of kernel perceptrons. The decision functions are given by

$$f(\mathbf{x}) = \mathrm{sign}(\langle \mathbf{w}, \phi(\mathbf{x}) \rangle_{\mathcal{F}}) = \mathrm{sign}\left(\sum_{i=1}^{\ell} \alpha_i k(\mathbf{x}_i, \mathbf{x})\right) \qquad \mathbf{w} = \sum_{i=1}^{\ell} \alpha_i \phi(\mathbf{x}_i) \in \mathcal{F},$$

Bayesian Transduction

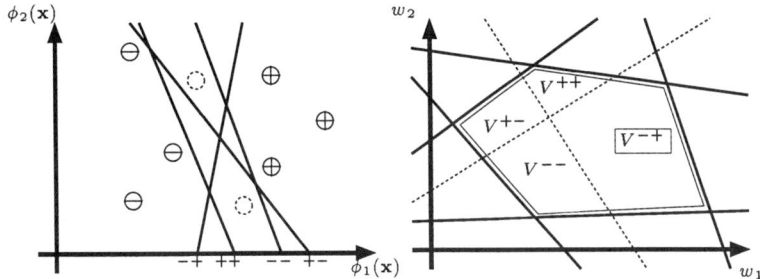

Figure 1: Schematic view of data space (left) and parameter space (right) for a classification toy example. Using the duality given by $\langle \mathbf{w}, \phi(\mathbf{x}) \rangle_{\mathcal{F}} = 0$ data points on the left correspond to hyperplanes on the right, while hyperplanes on the left can be thought of as points on the right.

where the mapping $\phi : \mathcal{X} \mapsto \mathcal{F}$ maps from input space $\mathcal{X}$ to a *feature space* $\mathcal{F}$ completely determined by the inner product function (*kernel*) $k : \mathcal{X} \times \mathcal{X} \mapsto \mathbb{R}$ (see [9, 10]). Given a training sample $S = \{(\mathbf{x}_i, y_i)\}_{i=1}^{\ell}$ we can define the version space — the set of all perceptrons compatible with the training data — as in (2) having the additional constraint $\|\mathbf{w}\|_{\mathcal{F}} = 1$ ensuring uniqueness. In order to obtain a prediction on the label b_1 of the working point $\mathbf{x}_{\ell+1}$ we note that $\mathbf{x}_{\ell+1}$ may bisects the volume V of version space into two sub-volumes V^+ and V^-, where the perceptrons in V^+ would classify $\mathbf{x}_{\ell+1}$ as $b_1 = +1$ and those in V^- as $b_1 = -1$. The ratio $p^+ = V^+/V$ is the probability of the labelling $b_1 = +1$ given a uniform prior $\mathbf{P}_H$ over $\mathbf{w}$ and the class of kernel perceptrons, accordingly for $b_1 = -1$ (see Figure 1). Already Vapnik in [8, p. 323] noticed that it is troublesome to estimate sub-volumes of version space. As the solution to this problem we suggest to use a billiard algorithm.

3.2 Kernel Billiard for Volume Estimation

The method of playing billiard in version space was first introduced by Rujan [6] for the purpose of estimating its centre of mass and consequently refined and extended to kernel spaces by [4]. For Bayesian Transduction the idea is to bounce the billiard ball in version space and to record how much time it spends in each of the sub-volumes of interest. Under the assumption of ergodicity [2] w.r.t. the uniform measure in the limit the accumulated flight times for each sub-volume are proportional to the sub-volume itself.

Since the trajectory is located in $\mathcal{F}$ each position $\mathbf{w}$ and direction $\mathbf{v}$ of the ball can be expressed as linear combinations of the $\phi(\mathbf{x}_i)$, i.e.

$$\mathbf{w} = \sum_{i=1}^{\ell} \alpha_i \phi(\mathbf{x}_i) \quad \mathbf{v} = \sum_{i=1}^{\ell} \beta_i \phi(\mathbf{x}_i) \quad \langle \mathbf{w}, \mathbf{v} \rangle_{\mathcal{F}} = \sum_{i,j=1}^{\ell} \alpha_i \beta_j k(\mathbf{x}_i, \mathbf{x}_j)$$

where $\boldsymbol{\alpha}, \boldsymbol{\beta}$ are real vectors with ℓ components and fully determine the state of the billiard. The algorithm for the determination of the label b_1 of $\mathbf{x}_{\ell+1}$ proceeds as follows:

1. Initialise the starting position $\mathbf{w}_0$ in $V(S)$ using any kernel perceptron algorithm that achieves zero training error (e.g. SVM [9]). Set $V^+ = V^- = 0$.

2. Find the closest boundary of $V(S)$ starting from current $\mathbf{w}$ into direction $\mathbf{v}$, where the flight times τ_j for all points including $\mathbf{x}_{\ell+1}$ are determined using

$$\tau_j = -\frac{\langle \mathbf{w}, \phi(\mathbf{x}_j)\rangle_{\mathcal{F}}}{\langle \mathbf{v}, \phi(\mathbf{x}_j)\rangle_{\mathcal{F}}}.$$

The smallest positive flight time $\tau_c = \min_{j:\tau_j>0} \tau_j$ in kernel space corresponds to the closest data point boundary $\phi(\mathbf{x}_c)$ on the hypersphere. Note, that if $\tau_c \to \infty$ we randomly generate a direction $\mathbf{v}$ pointing *towards* version space, i.e. $y\langle \mathbf{v}, \phi(\mathbf{x})\rangle_{\mathcal{F}} > 0$ assuming the last bounce was at $\phi(\mathbf{x})$.

3. Calculate the ball's new position $\mathbf{w}'$ according to

$$\mathbf{w}' = \frac{\mathbf{w} + \tau_c \mathbf{v}}{\|\mathbf{w} + \tau_c \mathbf{v}\|_{\mathcal{F}}}.$$

Calculate the distance $t_i^y = \|\mathbf{w} - \mathbf{w}'\|_{\text{sphere}} = \arccos\left(1 - \|\mathbf{w} - \mathbf{w}'\|_{\mathcal{F}}^2/2\right)$ on the hypersphere and add it to the volume estimate V^y corresponding to the current label $y = \text{sign}(\langle \mathbf{w} + \mathbf{w}', \phi(\mathbf{x}_{\ell+1})\rangle_{\mathcal{F}})$. If the test point $\phi(\mathbf{x}_{\ell+1})$ was hit, i.e. $c = \ell + 1$, keep the old direction vector $\mathbf{v}$. Otherwise update to the reflection direction $\mathbf{v}'$,

$$\mathbf{v}' = \mathbf{v} - 2\langle \mathbf{v}, \phi(\mathbf{x}_c)\rangle_{\mathcal{F}} \phi(\mathbf{x}_c).$$

Go back to step 2 unless the stopping criterion (8) is met.

Note that in practice one trajectory can be calculated in advance and can be used for all test points. The estimators of the probability of the labellings are then given by $\widehat{p}^+ = V^+/(V^+ + V^-)$ and $\widehat{p}^- = V^-/(V^+ + V^-)$. Thus, the algorithm outputs $\widehat{b}_1$ with confidence $\widehat{c}_{\text{trans}}$ according to

$$\widehat{b}_1 \stackrel{\text{def}}{=} \text{argmax}_{y \in \mathcal{Y}} \widehat{p}^y, \tag{6}$$

$$\widehat{c}_{\text{trans}} \stackrel{\text{def}}{=} (2 \cdot \max(\widehat{p}^+, \widehat{p}^-) - 1) \in [0, 1]. \tag{7}$$

Note that the Bayes Point Machine (BPM) [4] aims at an optimal approximation of the transductive classification (6) by a single function $f \in \mathcal{H}$ and that the well known SVM can be viewed as an approximation of the BPM by the centre of the largest ball in version space. Thus, treating the real valued output $|f(\mathbf{x}_{\ell+1})| \stackrel{\text{def}}{=} \widehat{c}_{\text{ind}}$ of SVM classifiers as a confidence measure can be considered an approximation of (7). The consequences will be demonstrated experimentally in the following section.

Disregarding the issue of mixing time [2] and the dependence of trajectories we assume for the stopping criterion that the fraction p_i^+ of time t_i^+ spent in volume V^+ on trajectory i of length $(t_i^+ + t_i^-)$ is a random variable having expectation p^+. Hoeffding's inequality [5] bounds the probability of deviation from the expectation p^+ by more than ϵ,

$$\mathbf{P}\left(\frac{1}{n}\sum_{i=1}^n p_i^+ - p^+ \geq \epsilon\right) \leq \exp(-2n\epsilon^2) \stackrel{\text{def}}{=} \eta. \tag{8}$$

Thus if we want the deviation ϵ from the true label probability to be less than $\epsilon < 0.05$ with probability at least $1 - \eta = 0.99$ we need approximately $n \approx 1000$ bounces. The computational effort of the above algorithm for a working set of size m is of order $\mathcal{O}(n\ell(m + \ell))$.

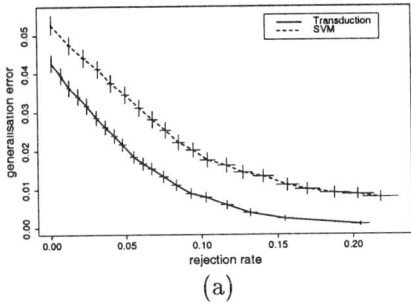 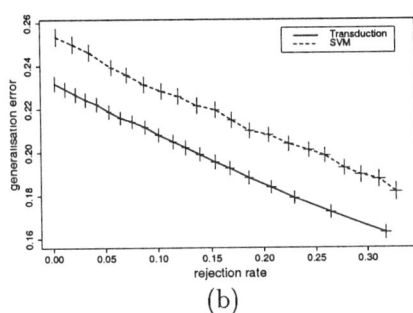

Figure 2: Generalisation error vs. rejection rate for Bayesian Transduction and SVMs for the thyroid data set ($\sigma = 3$) (a) and the heart data set ($\sigma = 10$). The error bars in both directions indicate one standard deviation of the estimated means. The upper curve depicts the result for the SVM algorithm; the lower curve is the result obtained by Bayesian Transduction.

4 Experimental Results

We focused on the confidence $\widehat{c}_{\text{trans}}$ Bayesian Transduction provides together with the prediction $\widehat{b}_1$ of the label. If the confidence $\widehat{c}_{\text{trans}}$ reflects reliability of a label estimate at a given test point then rejecting those test points whose predictions carry low confidence should lead to a reduction in generalisation error on the remaining test points. In the experiments we varied a rejection threshold θ between $[0, 1]$ thus obtaining for each θ a rejeection rate together with an estimate of the generalisation error at non-rejected points. Both these curves were linked by their common θ-axis resulting in a generalisation error versus rejection rate plot.

We used the UCI[2] data sets thyroid and heart because they are medical applications for which the confidence of single predictions is particularly important. Also a high rejection rate due to too conservative a confidence measure may incur considerable costs. We trained a Support Vector Machine using RBF kernels $k(\mathbf{x}, \mathbf{x}') = \exp\left(-\|\mathbf{x} - \mathbf{x}'\|^2 / 2\sigma^2\right)$ with σ chosen such as to insure the existence of a version space. We used 100 different training samples obtained by random 60%:40% splits of the whole data set. The margin $\widehat{c}_{\text{ind}}$ of each test point was calculated as a confidence measure of SVM classifications. For comparison we determined the labels $\widehat{b}_1$ and resulting confidences $\widehat{c}_{\text{trans}}$ using the Bayesian Transduction algorithm (see Section 3) with the same value of the kernel parameter. Since the rejection for the Bayesian Transduction was in both cases higher than for SVMs at the same level θ we determined $\theta_{\max}$ which achieves the same rejection rate for the SVM confidence measures as Bayesian Transduction achieves at $\theta = 1$ (thyroid: $\theta_{\max} = 2.15$, heart: $\theta_{\max} = 1.54$). The results for the two data sets are depicted in Figure 2.

In the thyroid example Figure 2 (a) one can see that $\widehat{c}_{\text{trans}}$ is indeed an appropriate indicator of confidence: at a rejection rate of approximately 20% the generalisation error approaches zero at minimal variance. For any desired generalisation error Bayesian Transduction needs to reject significantly less examples of the test set as compared to SVM classifiers, e.g. 4% less at 2.3% generalisation error. The results of the heart data set show even more pronounced characteristics w.r.t. to the rejection

---

[2]UCI University of California at Irvine: Machine Learning Repository

rate. Note that those confidence measures considered cannot capture the effects of noise in the data which leads to a generalisation error of 16.4% even at maximal rejection $\theta = 1$ corresponding to the Bayes error under the given function class.

5 Conclusions and Future Work

In this paper we a presented a Bayesian analysis of transduction. The required volume estimates for kernel perceptrons in version space are performed by an ergodic billiard in kernel space. Most importantly, transduction not only determines the label of a given point but also returns a confidence measure of the classification in the form of the probability of the label under the model. Using this confidence measure to reject test examples then lead to improved generalisation error over SVMs. The billiard algorithm can be extended to the case of non-zero training error by allowing the ball to penetrate walls, a property that is captured by adding a constant λ to the diagonal of the kernel matrix [4]. Further research will aim at the discovery of PAC-Bayesian bounds on the generalisation error of transduction.

Acknowledgements

We are greatly indebted to U. Kockelkorn for many interesting suggestions and discussions. This project was partially funded by Technical University of Berlin via FIP 13/41.

References

[1] K. Bennett. *Advances in Kernel Methods — Support Vector Learning*, chapter 19, Combining Support Vector and Mathematical Programming Methods for Classification, pages 307–326. MIT Press, 1998.

[2] I. Cornfeld, S. Fomin, and Y. Sinai. *Ergodic Theory*. Springer Verlag, 1982.

[3] A. Gammerman, V. Vovk, and V. Vapnik. Learning by transduction. In *Proceedings of Uncertainty in AI*, pages 148–155, Madison, Wisconsin, 1998.

[4] R. Herbrich, T. Graepel, and C. Campbell. Bayesian learning in reproducing kernel Hilbert spaces. Technical report, Technical University Berlin, 1999. TR 99-11.

[5] W. Hoeffding. Probability inequalities for sums of bounded random variables. *Journal of the American Statistical Association*, 58:13–30, 1963.

[6] P. Ruján. Playing billiard in version space. *Neural Computation*, 9:99–122, 1997.

[7] J. Shawe-Taylor. Confidence estimates of classification accuracy on new examples. Technical report, Royal Holloway, University of London, 1996. NC2–TR–1996-054.

[8] V. Vapnik. *Estimation of Dependences Based on Empirical Data*. Springer, 1982.

[9] V. Vapnik. *The Nature of Statistical Learning Theory*. Springer, 1995.

[10] G. Wahba. *Spline Models for Observational Data*. Society for Industrial and Applied Mathematics, Philadelphia, 1990.

Learning to Parse Images

Geoffrey E. Hinton and Zoubin Ghahramani
Gatsby Computational Neuroscience Unit
University College London
London, United Kingdom WC1N 3AR
{*hinton,zoubin*}@*gatsby.ucl.ac.uk*

Yee Whye Teh
Department of Computer Science
University of Toronto
Toronto, Ontario, Canada M5S 3G4
ywteh@cs.utoronto.ca

Abstract

We describe a class of probabilistic models that we call credibility networks. Using parse trees as internal representations of images, credibility networks are able to perform segmentation and recognition simultaneously, removing the need for *ad hoc* segmentation heuristics. Promising results in the problem of segmenting handwritten digits were obtained.

1 Introduction

The task of recognition has been the main focus of attention of statistical pattern recognition for the past 40 years. The paradigm problem is to classify an object from a vector of features extracted from the image. With the advent of backpropagation [1], the choice of features and the choice of weights to put on these features became part of a single, overall optimization and impressive performance was obtained for restricted but important tasks such as handwritten character identification [2].

A significant weakness of many current recognition systems is their reliance on a separate preprocessing stage that segments one object out of a scene and approximately normalizes it. Systems in which segmentation precedes recognition suffer from the fact that the segmenter does not know the shape of the object it is segmenting so it cannot use shape information to help it. Also, by segmenting an image, we remove the object to be recognized from the context in which it arises. Although this helps in removing the clutter present in the rest of the image, it might also reduce the ability to recognize an object correctly because the context in which an object arises gives a great deal of information about the nature of the object. Finally, each object can be described in terms of its parts, which can also be viewed as objects in their own right. This raises the question of how fine-grained the segmentations should be. In the words of David Marr : "Is a nose an object? Is a head one? ... What about a man on a horseback?" [3].

The successes of structural linguistics inspired an alternative approach to pattern recognition in which the paradigm problem was to parse an image using a hierarchical grammar of scenes and objects. Within linguistics, the structural approach was seen as an advance over earlier statistical approaches and for many years linguists eschewed probabilities, even though it had been known since the 1970's that a version of the EM algorithm could be used to fit stochastic context free grammars. Structural pattern recognition inherited the linguists aversion to probabilities and as a result it never worked very well for real data. With the advent of graphical models it has become clear that structure and probabilities can coexist. Moreover, the "explaining away" phenomenon that is central to inference in directed acyclic graphical models is exactly what is needed for performing inferences about possible segmentations of an image.

In this paper we describe an image interpretation system which combines segmentation and recognition into the same inference process. The central idea is the use of parse trees of images. Graphical models called credibility networks which describe the joint distribution over the latent variables and over the possible parse trees are used. In section 2 we describe some current statistical models of image interpretation. In section 3 we develop credibility networks and in section 4 we derive useful learning and inference rules for binary credibility networks. In section 5 we demonstrate that binary credibility networks are useful in solving the problem of classifying and segmenting binary handwritten digits. Finally in section 6 we end with a discussion and directions for future research.

2 Related work

Neal [4] introduced generative models composed of multiple layers of stochastic logistic units connected in a directed acyclic graph. In general, as each unit has multiple parents, it is intractable to compute the posterior distribution over hidden variables when certain variables are observed. However, Neal showed that Gibbs sampling can be used effectively for inference [4]. Efficient methods of approximating the posterior distribution were introduced later [5, 6, 7] and these approaches were shown to yield good density models for binary images of handwritten digits [8]. The problem with these models which make them inappropriate for modeling images is that they fail to respect the 'single-parent' constraint : in the correct interpretation of an image of opaque objects each object-part belongs to at most one object – images need parse trees, not parse DAGs.

Multiscale models [9] are interesting generative models for images that use a fixed tree structure. Nodes high up in the tree control large blocks of the image while bottom level leaves correspond to individual pixels. Because a tree structure is used, it is easy to compute the exact posterior distribution over the latent (non-terminal) nodes given an image. As a result, the approach has worked much better than Markov random fields which generally involve an intractable partition function. A disadvantage is that there are serious block boundary artifacts, though overlapping trees can be used to smooth the transition from one block to another [10]. A more serious disadvantage is that the tree cannot possibly correspond to a parse tree because it is the same for every image.

Zemel, Mozer and Hinton [11] proposed a neural network model in which the activities of neurons are used to represent the instantiation parameters of objects or their parts, i.e. the viewpoint-dependent coordinate transformation between an object's intrinsic coordinate system and the image coordinate system. The weights on connections are then used to represent the viewpoint-invariant relationship between the instantiation parameters of a whole, rigid object and the instantiation parameters of its parts. This model captures viewpoint invariance nicely and corresponds to the way viewpoint effects are handled in computer graphics, but there was no good inference procedure for hierarchical models and no systematic way of sharing modules that recognize parts of objects among multiple competing object models.

Simard et al [12] noted that small changes in object instantiation parameters result in approximately linear changes in (real-valued) pixel intensities. These can be captured successfully by linear models. To model larger changes, many locally linear models can be pieced together. Hinton, Dayan and Revow [13] proposed a mixture of factor analyzers for this. Tipping and Bishop have recently shown how to make this approach much more computationally efficient [14]. To make the approach really efficient, however, it is necessary to have multiple levels of factor analyzers and to allow an analyzer at one level to be shared by several competing analyzers at the next level up. Deciding which subset of the analyzers at one level should be controlled by one analyzer at the level above is equivalent to image segmentation or the construction of part of a parse tree and the literature on linear models contains no proposals on how to achieve this.

3 A new approach to image interpretation

We developed a class of graphical models called credibility networks in which the possible interpretations of an image are parse trees, with nodes representing object-parts and containing latent variables. Given a DAG, the possible parse trees of an image are constrained to be individual or collections of trees where each unit satisfies the single-parent constraint, with the leaves being the pixels of an image. Credibility networks describe a joint distribution over the latent variables and possible tree structures. The EM algorithm [15] can be used to fit credibility networks to data.

Let $i \in I$ be a node in the graph. There are three random variables associated with i. The first is a multinomial variate $\lambda_i = \{\lambda_{ij}\}_{j \in pa(i)}$ which describes the parent of i from among the potential parents $pa(i)$:

$$\lambda_{ij} = \begin{cases} 1 & \text{if parent of } i \text{ is } j, \\ 0 & \text{if parent of } i \text{ is not } j. \end{cases} \quad (1)$$

The second is a binary variate s_i which determines whether the object i^1 is present ($s_i = 1$) or not ($s_i = 0$). The third is the latent variables x_i that describe the pose and deformation of the object. Let $\Lambda = \{\lambda_i : i \in I\}, S = \{s_i : i \in I\}$ and $X = \{x_i : i \in I\}$.

Each connection $j \to i$ has three parameters also. The first, c_{ij} is an unnormalized prior probability that j is i's parent given that object j is present. The actual prior probability is

$$\pi_{ij} = \frac{c_{ij} s_j}{\sum_{k \in pa(i)} c_{ik} s_k} \quad (2)$$

We assume there is always a unit $1 \in pa(i)$ such that $s_1 = 1$. This acts as a default parent when no other potential parent is present and makes sure the denominator in (2) is never 0. The second parameter, p_{ij}, is the conditional probability that object i is present given that j is i's parent ($\lambda_{ij} = 1$). The third parameter t_{ij} characterizes the distribution of x_i given $\lambda_{ij} = 1$ and x_j. Let $\theta = \{c_{ij}, p_{ij}, t_{ij} : i \in I, j \in pa(i)\}$.

Using Bayes' rule the joint distribution over Λ, S and X given θ is $p(\Lambda, S, X|\theta) = p(\Lambda, S|\theta)p(X|\Lambda, S, \theta)$. Note that Λ and S together define a parse tree for the image. Given the parse tree the distribution over latent variables $p(X|\Lambda, S, \theta)$ can be

---

[1]Technically this should be the object represented by node i.

efficiently inferred from the image. The actual form of $p(X|\Lambda, S, \theta)$ is unimportant. The joint distribution over Λ and S is

$$P(\Lambda, S|\theta) = \prod_{i \in I} \prod_{j \in pa(i)} \left(\pi_{ij} p_{ij}^{s_i}(1-p_{ij})^{1-s_i}\right)^{\lambda_{ij}} \quad (3)$$

4 Binary credibility networks

The simulation results in section 5 are based on a simplified version of credibility networks in which the latent variables X are ignored. Notice that we can sum out Λ from the joint distribution (3), so that

$$P(S|\theta) = \prod_{i \in I} \sum_{j \in pa(i)} \pi_{ij} p_{ij}^{s_i}(1-p_{ij})^{1-s_i} \quad (4)$$

Using Bayes' rule and dividing (3) by (4), we have

$$P(\Lambda|S, \theta) = \prod_{i \in I} \prod_{j \in pa(i)} \left(\frac{c_{ij} s_j p_{ij}^{s_i}(1-p_{ij})^{1-s_i}}{\sum_{k \in pa(i)} c_{ik} s_k p_{ik}^{s_i}(1-p_{ik})^{1-s_i}} \right)^{\lambda_{ij}} \quad (5)$$

Let $r_{ij} = c_{ij} p_{ij}^{s_i}(1-p_{ij})^{1-s_i}$. We can view r_{ij} as the unnormalized posterior probability that j is i's parent given that object j is present. The actual posterior is the fraction in (5) :

$$\omega_{ij} = \frac{r_{ij} s_j}{\sum_{k \in pa(i)} r_{ik} s_k} \quad (6)$$

Given some observations $\mathcal{O} \subset S$, let $\mathcal{H} = S \setminus \mathcal{O}$ be the hidden variables. We approximate the posterior distribution for $\mathcal{H}$ using a factored distribution

$$Q(\mathcal{H}) = \prod_{i \in I} \sigma_i^{s_i}(1-\sigma_i)^{1-s_i} \quad (7)$$

The variational free energy, $\mathcal{F}(Q, \theta) = E_Q[-\log P(S|\theta) + \log Q(S)]$ is

$$\mathcal{F}(Q, \theta) = \sum_{i \in I} \left(E_Q\left[\log \sum_{j \in pa(i)} c_{ij} s_j - \log \sum_{j \in pa(i)} c_{ij} s_j p_{ij}^{s_i}(1-p_{ij})^{1-s_i}\right] \right) +$$
$$\sum_{i \in I} \left(\sigma_i \log \sigma_i + (1-\sigma_i) \log(1-\sigma_i) \right) \quad (8)$$

The negative of the free energy $-\mathcal{F}$ is a lower bound on the log likelihood of generating the observations $\mathcal{O}$. The variational EM algorithm improves this bound by iteratively improving $-\mathcal{F}$ with respect to Q (E-step) and to θ (M-step). Let $ch(i)$ be the possible children of i. The inference rules can be derived from (8) :

$$\sigma_i = sigmoid \left(\begin{array}{c} E_Q\left[\log \sum_{j \in pa(i)} c_{ij} s_j p_{ij} - \log \sum_{j \in pa(i)} c_{ij} s_j (1-p_{ij})\right] \\ + \sum_{l \in ch(i)} E_Q\left[\log \sum_{j \in pa(l)} r_{lj} s_j - \log \sum_{j \in pa(l)} c_{lj} s_j\right]_{\sigma_i=0}^{\sigma_i=1} \end{array} \right) \quad (9)$$

Let D be the training set and Q_d be the mean field approximation to the posterior distribution over $\mathcal{H}$ given the training data (observation) $d \in D$. Then the learning

Learning to Parse Images

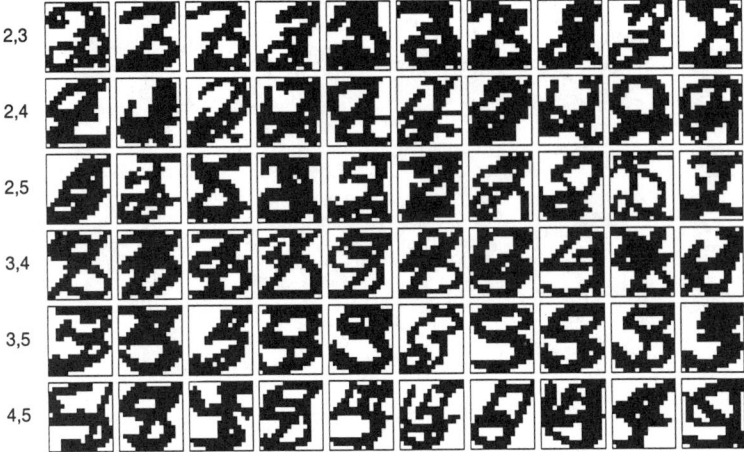

Figure 1: Sample images from the test set. The classes of the two digits in each image in a row are given to the left.

rules are

$$\frac{\partial - \sum_d \mathcal{F}(Q_d, \theta)}{\partial \log c_{ij}} = \sum_{d \in D} E_{Q_d}[\omega_{ij} - \pi_{ij}] \quad (10)$$

$$p_{ij}^{new} = \frac{\sum_{d \in D} E_{Q_d}[\omega_{ij} s_i]}{\sum_{d \in D} E_{Q_d}[\omega_{ij}]} \quad (11)$$

For an efficient implementation of credibility networks using mean field approximations, we still need to evaluate terms of the form $E[\log x]$ and $E[1/x]$ where x is a weighted sum of binary random variates. In our implementation we used the simplest approximations : $E[\log x] \approx \log E[x]$ and $E[1/x] \approx 1/E[x]$. Although biased the implementation works well enough in general.

5 Segmenting handwritten digits

Hinton and Revow [16] used a mixture of factor analyzers model to segment and estimate the pose of digit strings. When the digits do not overlap, the model was able to identify the digits present and segment the image easily. The hard cases are those in which two or more digits overlap significantly. To assess the ability of credibility networks at segmenting handwritten digits, we used superpositions of digits at exactly the same location. This problem is much harder than segmenting digit strings in which digits partially overlap.

The data used is a set of 4400 images of single digits from the classes 2, 3, 4 and 5 derived from the CEDAR CDROM 1 database [17]. Each image has size 16x16. The size of the credibility network is 256-64-4. The 64 middle layer units are meant to encode low level features, while each of the 4 top level units are meant to encode a digit class. We used 700 images of single digits from each class to train the network. So it was not trained to segment images. During training we clamped at 1 the activation of the top layer unit corresponding to the class of the digit in the current image while fixing the rest at 0.

After training, the network was first tested on the 1600 images of single digits not in the training set. The predicted class of each image was taken to be the

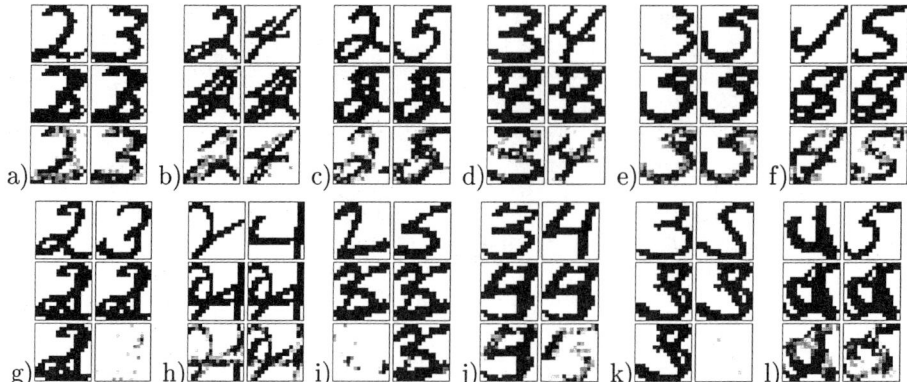

Figure 2: Segmentations of pairs of digits. (To make comparisons easier we show the overlapping image in both columns of a)-l).)

class corresponding to the top layer unit with the highest activation. The error rate was 5.5%. We then showed the network 120 images of two overlapping digits from distinct classes. There were 20 images per combination of two classes. Some examples are given in Figure 1. The predicted classes of the two digits are chosen to be the corresponding classes of the 2 top layer units with the highest activations. A human subject (namely the third author) was tested on the same test set. The network achieved an error rate of 21.7% while the author erred on 19.2% of the images.

We can in fact produce a segmentation of each image into an image for each class present. Recall that given the values of S the posterior probability of unit j being pixel i's parent is ω_{ij}. Then the posterior probability of pixel i belonging to digit class k is $\sum_j E_Q[\omega_{ij}\omega_{jk}]$.

This gives a simple way to segment the image. Figure 2 shows a number of segmentations. Note that for each pixel, the sum of the probabilities of the pixel belonging to each digit class is 1. To make the picture clearer, a white pixel means a probability of $\leq .1$ of belonging to a class, while black means $\geq .6$ probability, and the intensity of a gray pixel describes the size of the probability if it is between .1 and .6. Figures 2a) to 2f) shows successful segmentations, while Figure 2g) to 2l) shows unsuccessful segmentations.

6 Discussion

Using parse trees as the internal representations of images, credibility networks avoid the usual problems associated with a bottom-up approach to image interpretation. Segmentation can be carried out in a statistically sound manner, removing the need for hand crafted *ad hoc* segmentation heuristics. The granularity problem for segmentation is also resolved since credibility networks use parse trees as internal representations of images. The parse trees describe the segmentations of the image at every level of granularity, from individual pixels to the whole image.

We plan to develop and implement credibility networks in which each latent variable x_i is a multivariate Gaussian, so that a node can represent the position, orientation and scale of a 2 or 3D object, and the conditional probability models on the links can represent the relationship between a moderately deformable object and its parts.

Acknowledgments

We thank Chris Williams, Stuart Russell and Phil Dawid for helpful discussions and NSERC and ITRC for funding.

References

[1] D. E. Rumelhart, G. E. Hinton, and R. J. Williams. Learning internal representations by error propagation. In D. E. Rumelhart, J. L. McClelland, and the PDP Research Group, editors, *Parallel Distributed Processing : Explorations in The Microstructure of Cognition. Volume 1 : Foundations.* The MIT Press, 1986.

[2] Y. Le Cun, B. Boser, J. S. Denker, S. Solla, R. E. Howard, and L. D. Jackel. Back-propagation applied to handwritten zip code recognition. *Neural Computation*, 1(4):541–551, 1989.

[3] D. Marr. *Vision : A Computational Investigation into the Human Representation and Processing of Visual Information.* W. H. Freeman and company, San Francisco, 1980.

[4] R. M. Neal. Connectionist learning of belief networks. *Artificial Intelligence*, 56:71–113, 1992.

[5] P. Dayan, G. E. Hinton, R. M. Neal, and R. S. Zemel. Helmholtz machines. *Neural Computation*, 7:1022–1037, 1995.

[6] G. E. Hinton, P. Dayan, B. J. Frey, and R. M. Neal. The wake-sleep algorithm for self-organizing neural networks. *Science*, 268:1158–1161, 1995.

[7] L. K. Saul and M. I. Jordan. Attractor dynamics in feedforward neural networks. Submitted for publication.

[8] B. J. Frey, G. E. Hinton, and P. Dayan. Does the wake-sleep algorithm produce good density estimators? In D. Touretzky, M. Mozer, and M. Hasselmo, editors, *Advances in Neural Information Processing Systems*, volume 8. The MIT Press, 1995.

[9] M. R. Luettgen and A. S. Willsky. Likelihood calculation for a class of multiscale stochastic models, with application to texture discrimination. *IEEE Transactions on Image Processing*, 4(2):194–207, 1995.

[10] W. W. Irving, P. W. Fieguth, and A. S. Willsky. An overlapping tree approach to multiscale stochastic modeling and estimation. *IEEE Transactions on Image Processing*, 1995.

[11] R. S. Zemel, M. C. Mozer, and G. E. Hinton. TRAFFIC: Recognizing objects using hierarchical reference frame transformations. In *Advances in Neural Information Processing Systems*, volume 2. Morgan Kaufmann Publishers, San Mateo CA, 1990.

[12] P. Simard, Y. Le Cun, and J. Denker. Efficient pattern recognition using a new transformation distance. In S. Hanson, J. Cowan, and L. Giles, editors, *Advances in Neural Information Processing Systems*, volume 5. Morgan Kaufmann Publishers, San Mateo CA, 1992.

[13] G. E. Hinton, P. Dayan, and M. Revow. Modeling the manifolds of images of handwritten digits. *IEEE Transactions on Neural Networks*, 8:65–74, 1997.

[14] M. E. Tipping and C. M. Bishop. Mixtures of probabilistic principal component analysis. Technical Report NCRG/97/003, Aston University, Department of Computer Science and Applied Mathematics, 1997.

[15] A.P. Dempster, N.M. Laird, and D.B. Rubin. Maximum likelihood from incomplete data via the EM algorithm. *Journal of the Royal Statistical Society B*, 39:1–38, 1977.

[16] G. E. Hinton and M. Revow. Using mixtures of factor analyzers for segmentation and pose estimation, 1997.

[17] J. J. Hull. A database for handwritten text recognition research. *IEEE Transactions on Pattern Analysis and Machine Intelligence*, 16(5):550–554, 1994.

Maximum entropy discrimination

Tommi Jaakkola
MIT AI Lab
545 Technology Sq.
Cambridge, MA 02139
tommi@ai.mit.edu

Marina Meila
MIT AI Lab
545 Technology Sq.
Cambridge, MA 02139
mmp@ai.mit.edu

Tony Jebara
MIT Media Lab
20 Ames St.
Cambridge, MA 02139
jebara@media.mit.edu

Abstract

We present a general framework for discriminative estimation based on the maximum entropy principle and its extensions. All calculations involve distributions over structures and/or parameters rather than specific settings and reduce to relative entropy projections. This holds even when the data is not separable within the chosen parametric class, in the context of anomaly detection rather than classification, or when the labels in the training set are uncertain or incomplete. Support vector machines are naturally subsumed under this class and we provide several extensions. We are also able to estimate exactly and efficiently discriminative distributions over tree structures of class-conditional models within this framework. Preliminary experimental results are indicative of the potential in these techniques.

1 Introduction

Effective discrimination is essential in many application areas. Employing generative probability models such as mixture models in this context is attractive but the criterion (e.g., maximum likelihood) used for parameter/structure estimation is suboptimal. Support vector machines (SVMs) are, for example, more robust techniques as they are specifically designed for discrimination [9].

Our approach towards general discriminative training is based on the well known maximum entropy principle (e.g., [3]). This enables an appropriate training of both ordinary and structural parameters of the model (cf. [5, 7]). The approach is not limited to probability models and extends, e.g., SVMs.

2 Maximum entropy classification

Consider a two-class classification problem[1] where labels $y \in \{-1, 1\}$ are assigned

---
[1]The extension to a multi-class is straightforward[4]. The formulation also admits an easy extension to regression problems, analogously to SVMs.

to examples $X \in \mathcal{X}$. Given two generative probability distributions $P(X|\theta_y)$ with parameters θ_y, one for each class, the corresponding decision rule follows the sign of the *discriminant function*:

$$\mathcal{L}(X|\Theta) = \log \frac{P(X|\theta_1)}{P(X|\theta_{-1})} + b \qquad (1)$$

where $\Theta = \{\theta_1, \theta_{-1}, b\}$ and b is a bias term, usually expressed as a log-ratio $b = \log p/(1-p)$. The class-conditional distributions may come from different families of distributions or the parametric discriminant function could be specified directly without any reference to models. The parameters θ_y may also include the model structure (see later sections).

The parameters $\Theta = \{\theta_1, \theta_{-1}, b\}$ should be chosen to maximize classification accuracy. We consider here the more general problem of finding a distribution $P(\Theta)$ over parameters and using a convex combination of discriminant functions, i.e., $\int P(\Theta) \mathcal{L}(X|\Theta) d\Theta$ in the decision rule. The search for the optimal $P(\Theta)$ can be formalized as a *maximum entropy* (ME) estimation problem. Given a set of training examples $\{X_1, \ldots, X_T\}$ and corresponding labels $\{y_1, \ldots, y_T\}$ we find a distribution $P(\Theta)$ that maximizes the entropy $H(P)$ subject to the classification constraints $\int P(\Theta) [y_t \mathcal{L}(X_t|\Theta)] d\Theta \geq \gamma$ for all t. Here $\gamma > 0$ specifies a desired classification margin. The solution is unique (if it exists) since $H(P)$ is concave and the linear constraints specify a convex region. Note that the preference towards high entropy distributions (fewer assumptions) applies only within the admissible set of distributions $\mathcal{P}_\gamma$ consistent with the constraints. See [2] for related work.

We will extend this basic idea in a number of ways. The ME formulation assumes, for example, that the training examples can be separated with the specified margin. We may also have a reason to prefer some parameter values over others and would therefore like to incorporate a prior distribution $P_0(\Theta)$. Other extensions and generalizations will be discussed later in the paper.

A more complete formulation is based on the following *minimum relative entropy* principle:

Definition 1 *Let $\{X_t, y_t\}$ be the training examples and labels, $\mathcal{L}(X|\Theta)$ a parametric discriminant function, and $\gamma = [\gamma_1, \ldots, \gamma_t]$ a set of margin variables. Assuming a prior distribution $P_0(\Theta, \gamma)$, we find the discriminative minimum relative entropy (MRE) distribution $P(\Theta, \gamma)$ by minimizing $D(P\|P_0)$ subject to*

$$\int P(\Theta, \gamma) [y_t \mathcal{L}(X_t|\Theta) - \gamma_t] d\Theta d\gamma \geq 0 \qquad (2)$$

for all t. Here $\hat{y} = \text{sign} \left(\int P(\Theta) \mathcal{L}(X|\Theta) d\Theta \right)$ specifies the decision rule for any new example X.

The margin constraints and the preference towards large margin solutions are encoded in the prior $P_0(\gamma)$. Allowing negative margin values with non-zero probabilities also guarantees that the admissible set $\mathcal{P}$ consisting of distributions $P(\Theta, \gamma)$ consistent with the constraints, is never empty. Even when the examples cannot be separated by any discriminant function in the parametric class (e.g., linear), we get a valid solution. The miss-classification penalties follow from $P_0(\gamma)$ as well.

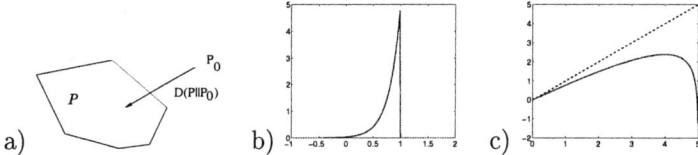

Figure 1: a) Minimum relative entropy (MRE) projection from the prior distribution to the admissible set. b) The margin prior $P_0(\gamma_t)$. c) The potential terms in the MRE formulation (solid line) and in SVMs (dashed line). $c = 5$ in this case.

Suppose $P_0(\Theta, \gamma) = P_0(\Theta) P_0(\gamma)$ and $P_0(\gamma) = \prod_t P_0(\gamma_t)$, where

$$P_0(\gamma_t) = c\, e^{-c(1-\gamma_t)} \quad \text{for } \gamma_t \leq 1, \tag{3}$$

This is shown in Figure 1b. The penalty for margins smaller than $1 - 1/c$ (the prior mean of γ_t) is given by the relative entropy distance between $P(\gamma)$ and $P_0(\gamma)$. This is similar but not identical to the use of slack variables in support vector machines. Other choices of the prior are discussed in [4].

The MRE solution can be viewed as a relative entropy projection from the prior distribution $P_0(\Theta, \gamma)$ to the admissible set $\mathcal{P}$. Figure 1a illustrates this view. From the point of view of regularization theory, the prior probability P_0 specifies the entropic regularization used in this approach.

Theorem 1 *The solution to the MRE problem has the following general form [1]*

$$P(\Theta, \gamma) = \frac{1}{Z(\lambda)} P_0(\Theta, \gamma)\, e^{\sum_t \lambda_t [y_t \mathcal{L}(X_t|\Theta) - \gamma_t]} \tag{4}$$

where $Z(\lambda)$ is the normalization constant (partition function) and $\lambda = \{\lambda_1, \ldots, \lambda_T\}$ defines a set of non-negative Lagrange multipliers, one for each classification constraint. λ are set by finding the unique maximum of the following jointly concave objective function: $J(\lambda) = -\log Z(\lambda)$

The solution is *sparse*, i.e., only a few Lagrange multipliers will be non-zero. This arises because many of the classification constraints become irrelevant once the constraints are enforced for a small subset of examples. Sparsity leads to immediate but weak generalization guarantees expressed in terms of the number of non-zero Lagrange multipliers [4]. Practical leave-one-out cross-validation estimates can be also derived.

2.1 Practical realization of the MRE solution

We now turn to finding the MRE solution. To begin with, we note that any disjoint factorization of the prior $P_0(\Theta, \gamma)$, where the corresponding parameters appear in distinct additive components in $y_t \mathcal{L}(X_t, \Theta) - \gamma_t$, leads to a disjoint factorization of the MRE solution $P(\Theta, \gamma)$. For example, $\{\Theta \setminus b, b, \gamma\}$ provides such a factorization. As a result of this factorization, the bias term could be eliminated by imposing additional constraints on the Lagrange multipliers [4]. This is analogous to the handling of the bias term in support vector machines [9].

We consider now a few specific realizations such as support vector machines and a class of graphical models.

2.1.1 Support vector machines

It is well known that the log-likelihood ratio of two Gaussian distributions with equal covariance matrices yields a linear decision rule. With a few additional assumptions, the MRE formulation gives support vector machines:

Theorem 2 *Assuming $\mathcal{L}(X, \Theta) = \theta^T X - b$ and $P_0(\Theta, \gamma) = P_0(\theta) P_0(b) P_0(\gamma)$ where $P_0(\theta)$ is $N(0, I)$, $P_0(b)$ approaches a non-informative prior, and $P_0(\gamma)$ is given by eq. (3) then the Lagrange multipliers λ are obtained by maximizing $J(\lambda)$ subject to $0 \leq \lambda_t \leq c$ and $\sum_t \lambda_t y_t = 0$, where*

$$J(\lambda) = \sum_t [\lambda_t + \log(1 - \lambda_t/c)] - \frac{1}{2} \sum_{t,t'} \lambda_t \lambda_{t'} y_t y_{t'} (X_t^T X_{t'}) \tag{5}$$

The only difference between our $J(\lambda)$ and the (dual) optimization problem for SVMs is the additional potential term $\log(1 - \lambda_t/c)$. This highlights the effect of the different miss-classification penalties, which in our case come from the MRE projection. Figure 1b shows, however, that the additional potential term does not always carry a huge effect (for $c = 5$). Moreover, in the separable case, letting $c \to \infty$, the two methods coincide. The decision rules are formally identical.

We now consider the case where the discriminant function $\mathcal{L}(X, \Theta)$ corresponds to the log-likelihood ratio of two Gaussians with different (and adjustable) covariance matrices. The parameters Θ in this case are both the means and the covariances. The prior $P_0(\Theta)$ must be the conjugate Normal-Wishart to obtain closed form integrals[2] for the partition function, Z. Here, $P(\Theta_1, \Theta_{-1})$ is $P(m_1, V_1) P(m_{-1}, V_{-1})$, a density over means and covariances.

The prior distribution has the form $P_0(\Theta_1) = \mathcal{N}(m_1; m_0, V_1/k) \mathcal{IW}(V_1; kV_0, k)$ with parameters (k, m_0, V_0) that can be specified manually or one may let $k \to 0$ to get a non-informative prior. Integrating over the parameters and the margin, we get $Z = Z_\gamma \times Z_1 \times Z_{-1}$, where

$$Z_1 \propto N_1^{-d/2} |\pi S_1|^{-N_1/2} \Pi_{j=1}^d \Gamma((N_1 + 1 - j)/2) \tag{6}$$

$N_1 \triangleq \sum_t w_t$, $\bar{X}_1 \triangleq \sum_t \frac{w_t}{N_1} X_t$, $S_1 \triangleq \sum_t w_t X_t X_t^T - N_1 \bar{X}_1 \bar{X}_1^T$. Here, w_t is a scalar weight given by $w_t = u(y_t) + y_t \lambda_t$. For Z_{-1}, the weights are set to $w_t = u(-y_t) - y_t \lambda_t$; $u(\cdot)$ is the step function. Given Z, updating λ is done by maximizing $J(\lambda)$. The resulting marginal MRE distribution over the parameters (normalized by $Z_1 \times Z_{-1}$) is a Normal-Wishart distribution itself, $P(\Theta_1) = \mathcal{N}(m_1; \bar{X}_1, V_1/N_1) \mathcal{IW}(V_1; S_1, N_1)$ with the final λ values. Predicting the label for a new example X involves taking expectations of the discriminant function under a Normal-Wishart. This is

$$E_{P(\Theta_1)}[\log P(X|\Theta_1)] = \text{constant} - \frac{N_1}{2}(X - \bar{X}_1)^T S_1^{-1}(X - \bar{X}_1) \tag{7}$$

We thus obtain discriminative *quadratic* decision boundaries. These extend the linear boundaries without (explicitly) resorting to *kernels*. More generally, the covariance estimation in this framework adaptively modifies the kernel.

---

[2] This can be done more generally for conjugate priors in the exponential family.

2.1.2 Graphical models

We consider here graphical models with no hidden variables. The ME (or MRE) distribution is in this case a distribution over both structures and parameters. Finding the distribution over parameters can be done in closed form for conjugate priors when the observations are complete. The distribution over structures is, in general, intractable. A notable exception is a tree model that we discuss in the forthcoming.

A tree graphical model is a graphical model for which the structure is a *tree*. This model has the property that its log-likelihood can be expressed as a sum of local terms [8]

$$\log P(X, E|\theta) = \sum_u h_u(X, \theta) + \sum_{uv \in E} w_{uv}(X, \theta) \qquad (8)$$

The discriminant function consisting of the log-likelihood ratio of a pair of tree models (depending on the edge sets E_1, E_{-1}, and parameters θ_1, θ_{-1}) can be also expressed in this form.

We consider here the ME distribution over tree structures for fixed parameters[3]. The treatment of the general case (i.e. including the parameters) is a direct extension of this result. The ME distribution over the edge sets E_1 and E_{-1} factorizes with components

$$P(E_{\pm 1}) = \frac{1}{Z_{\pm 1}} e^{\pm \sum_t \lambda_t y_t [\sum_{uv \in E_{\pm 1}} w_{uv}^{\pm 1}(X_t, \theta_{\pm 1}) + \sum_u h_u(X_t, \theta_{\pm 1})]} = \frac{h^{\pm 1}}{Z_{\pm 1}} \prod_{uv \in E_{\pm 1}} W_{uv}^{\pm 1} \qquad (9)$$

where $Z_{\pm 1}, h^{\pm 1}, W^{\pm 1}$ are functions of the same Lagrange multipliers λ. To completely define the distribution we need to find λ that optimize $J(\lambda)$ in Theorem 1; for classification we also need to compute averages with respect to $P(E_{\pm 1})$. For these, it suffices to obtain an expression of the partition function(s) $Z_{\pm 1}$.

P is a discrete distribution over all possible tree structures for n variables (there are n^{n-2} trees). However, a remarkable graph theory result, called the *Matrix Tree Theorem* [10], enables us to perform all necessary summations in closed form in polynomial time. On the basis of this result, we find

Theorem 3 *The normalization constant Z of a distribution of the form (9) is*

$$Z = h \cdot \sum_E \prod_{uv \in E} W_{uv} = h \cdot |Q(W)|, \quad \text{where} \qquad (10)$$

$$Q_{uv}(W) = \begin{cases} -W_{uv} & u \neq v \\ \sum_{v'=1}^n W_{v'v} & u = v \end{cases} \qquad (11)$$

This shows that summing over the distribution of all trees, when this distribution factors according to the trees' edges, can be done in closed form by computing the value of a determinant in time $\mathcal{O}(n^3)$. Since we obtain a closed form expression, optimization of the Lagrange multipliers and evaluating the resulting classification rule are also tractable.

Figure 2a provides a comparison of the discriminative tree approach and a maximum likelihood tree estimation method on a DNA splice junction problem.

---

[3]Each tree relies on a different set of $n-1$ pairwise node marginals. In our experiments the class-conditional pairwise marginals were obtained directly from data.

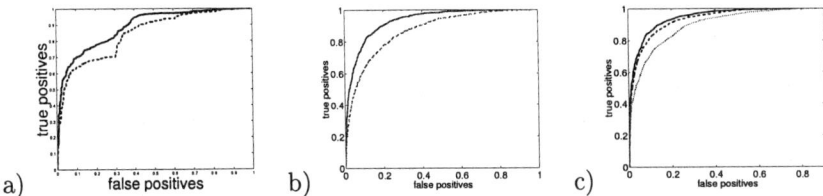

Figure 2: ROC curves based on independent test sets. a) Tree estimation: discriminative (solid) and ML (dashed) trees. b) Anomaly detection: MRE (solid) and Bayes (dashed). c) Partially labeled case: 100% labeled (solid), 10% labeled + 90% unlabeled (dashed), and 10% labeled + 0% unlabeled training examples (dotted).

3 Extensions

Anomaly detection: In anomaly detection we are given a set of training examples representing only one class, the "typical" examples. We attempt to capture regularities among the examples to be able to recognize unlikely members of this class. Estimating a probability distribution $P(X|\theta)$ on the basis of the training set $\{X_1, \ldots, X_T\}$ via the ML (or analogous) criterion is not appropriate; there is no reason to further increase the probability of those examples that are already well captured by the model. A more relevant measure involves the level sets $\mathcal{X}_\gamma = \{ X \in \mathcal{X} : \log P(X|\theta) \geq \gamma \}$ which are used in deciding the class membership in any case. We estimate the parameters θ to optimize an appropriate level set.

Definition 2 *Given a probability model $P(X|\theta)$, $\theta \in \Theta$, a set of training examples $\{X_1, \ldots, X_T\}$, a set of margin variables $\gamma = [\gamma_1, \ldots, \gamma_T]$, and a prior distribution $P_0(\theta, \gamma)$ we find the MRE distribution $P(\theta, \gamma)$ such that minimizes $D(P\|P_0)$ subject to the constraints $\int P(\theta, \gamma) [\log P(X_t|\theta) - \gamma_t] d\theta d\gamma \geq 0$ for all $t = 1, \ldots, T$.*

Note that this again a MRE projection whose solution can be obtained as before. The choice of $P_0(\gamma)$ in $P_0(\theta, \gamma) = P_0(\theta) P_0(\gamma)$ is not as straightforward as before since each margin γ_t needs to be close to achievable log-probabilities. We can nevertheless find a reasonable choice by relating the prior mean of γ_t to some α-percentile of the training set log-probabilities generated through ML or other estimation criterion. Denote the resulting value by l_α and define the prior $P_0(\gamma_t)$ as $P_0(\gamma_t) = c e^{-c(l_\alpha - \gamma_t)}$ for $\gamma_t \leq l_\alpha$. In this case the prior mean of γ_t is $l_\alpha - 1/c$.

Figure 2b shows in the context of a simple product distribution that this choice of prior together with the MRE framework leads to a real improvement over standard (Bayesian) approach. We believe, however, that the effect will be more striking for sophisticated models such as HMMs that may otherwise easily capture spurious regularities in the data. An extension of this formalism to latent variable models is provided in [4].

Uncertain or incompletely labeled examples: Examples with uncertain labels are hard to deal with in any (probabilistic or not) discriminative classification method. Uncertain labels can be, however, handled within the maximum entropy formalism: let $y = \{y_1, \ldots, y_T\}$ be a set of binary variables corresponding to the labels for the training examples. We can define a prior uncertainty over the labels by specifying $P_0(y)$; for simplicity, we can take this to be a product distribution

$P_0(y) = \prod_t P_{t,0}(y_t)$ where a different level of uncertainty can be assigned to each example. Consequently, we find the minimum relative entropy projection from the prior distribution $P_0(\Theta, \gamma, y) = P_0(\Theta) P_0(\gamma) P_0(y)$ to the admissible set of distributions (no longer a function of the labels) that are consistent with the constraints: $\sum_y \int_{\Theta, \gamma} P(\Theta, \gamma, y) \left[y_t \mathcal{L}(X_t, \Theta) - \gamma_t \right] d\Theta \, d\gamma \geq 0$ for all $t = 1, \ldots, T$. The MRE principle differs from *transduction* [9], provides a soft rather than hard assignment of unlabeled examples, and is fundamentally driven by large margin classification. The MRE solution is not, however, often feasible to obtain in practice. We can nevertheless formulate an efficient mean field approach in this context [4]. Figure 2c demonstrates that even the approximate method is able to reap most of the benefit from unlabeled examples (compare, e.g., [6]). The results are for a DNA splice junction classification problem. For more details see [4].

4 Discussion

We have presented a general approach to discriminative training of model parameters, structures, or parametric discriminant functions. The formalism is based on the minimum relative entropy principle reducing all calculations to relative entropy projections. The idea naturally extends beyond standard classification and covers anomaly detection, classification with partially labeled examples, and feature selection.

References

[1] Cover and Thomas (1991). *Elements of information theory*. John Wiley & Sons.

[2] Kivinen J. and Warmuth M. (1999). Boosting as Entropy Projection. *Proceedings of the 12th Annual Conference on Computational Learning Theory*.

[3] Levin and Tribus (eds.) (1978). *The maximum entropy formalism*. Proceedings of the Maximum entropy formalism conference, MIT.

[4] Jaakkola T., Meilă M. and Jebara T. (1999). Maximum entropy discrimination. MIT AITR-1668, http://www.ai.mit.edu/~tommi/papers.html.

[5] Jaakkola T. and Haussler D. (1998). Exploiting generative models in discriminative classifiers. NIPS 11.

[6] Joachims, T. (1999). Transductive inference for text classification using support vector machines. *International conference on Machine Learning*.

[7] Jebara T. and Pentland A. (1998). Maximum conditional likelihood via bound maximization and the CEM algorithm. NIPS 11.

[8] Meilă M. and Jordan M. (1998). Estimating dependency structure as a hidden variable. NIPS 11.

[9] Vapnik V. (1998). *Statistical learning theory*. John Wiley & Sons.

[10] West D. (1996). *Introduction to graph theory*. Prentice Hall.

Topographic Transformation as a Discrete Latent Variable

Nebojsa Jojic
Beckman Institute
University of Illinois at Urbana
www.ifp.uiuc.edu/~jojic

Brendan J. Frey
Computer Science
University of Waterloo
www.cs.uwaterloo.ca/~frey

Abstract

Invariance to topographic transformations such as translation and shearing in an image has been successfully incorporated into feedforward mechanisms, *e.g.*, "convolutional neural networks", "tangent propagation". We describe a way to add transformation invariance to a generative density model by approximating the nonlinear transformation manifold by a discrete set of transformations. An EM algorithm for the original model can be extended to the new model by computing expectations over the set of transformations. We show how to add a discrete transformation variable to Gaussian mixture modeling, factor analysis and mixtures of factor analysis. We give results on filtering microscopy images, face and facial pose clustering, and handwritten digit modeling and recognition.

1 Introduction

Imagine what happens to the point in the N-dimensional space corresponding to an N-pixel image of an object, while the object is deformed by shearing. A very small amount of shearing will move the point only slightly, so deforming the object by shearing will trace a continuous curve in the space of pixel intensities. As illustrated in Fig. 1a, extensive levels of shearing will produce a highly nonlinear curve (consider shearing a thin vertical line), although the curve can be approximated by a straight line locally.

Linear approximations of the transformation manifold have been used to significantly improve the performance of feedforward discriminative classifiers such as nearest neighbors (Simard *et al.*, 1993) and multilayer perceptrons (Simard *et al.*, 1992). Linear generative models (factor analysis, mixtures of factor analysis) have also been modified using linear approximations of the transformation manifold to build in some degree of transformation invariance (Hinton *et al.*, 1997).

In general, the linear approximation is accurate for transformations that couple neighboring pixels, but is inaccurate for transformations that couple nonneighboring pixels. In some applications (*e.g.*, handwritten digit recognition), the input can be blurred so that the linear approximation becomes more robust.

For significant levels of transformation, the nonlinear manifold can be better modeled using a discrete approximation. For example, the curve in Fig. 1a can be

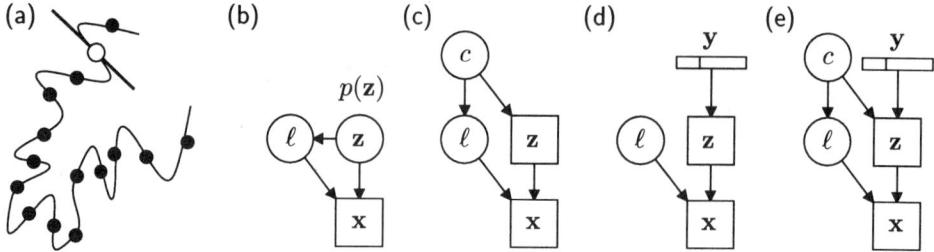

Figure 1: (a) An N-pixel greyscale image is represented by a point (unfilled disc) in an N-dimensional space. When the object being imaged is deformed by shearing, the point moves along a continuous curve. Locally, the curve is linear, but high levels of shearing produce a highly nonlinear curve, which we approximate by discrete points (filled discs) indexed by ℓ. (b) A graphical model showing how a discrete transformation variable ℓ can be added to a density model $p(\mathbf{z})$ for a *latent image* $\mathbf{z}$ to model the observed image $\mathbf{x}$. The Gaussian pdf $p(\mathbf{x}|\ell, \mathbf{z})$ captures the ℓth transformation plus a small amount of pixel noise. (We use a box to represent variables that have Gaussian conditional pdfs.) We have explored (c) transformed mixtures of Gaussians, where c is a discrete cluster index; (d) transformed component analysis (TCA), where $\mathbf{y}$ is a vector of Gaussian factors, some of which may model locally linear transformation perturbations; and (e) mixtures of transformed component analyzers, or transformed mixtures of factor analyzers.

represented by a set of points (filled discs). In this approach, a discrete set of possible transformations is specified beforehand and parameters are learned so that the model is invariant to the set of transformations. This approach has been used to design "convolutional neural networks" that are invariant to translation (Le Cun et al., 1998) and to develop a general purpose learning algorithm for generative topographic maps (Bishop et al., 1998).

We describe how invariance to a discrete set of *known* transformations (like translation) can be built into a generative density model and we show how an EM algorithm for the original density model can be extended to the new model by computing expectations over the set of transformations. We give results for 5 different types of experiment involving translation and shearing.

2 Transformation as a Discrete Latent Variable

We represent transformation ℓ by a sparse transformation generating matrix $\mathbf{G}_\ell$ that operates on a vector of pixel intensities. For example, integer-pixel translations of an image can be represented by permutation matrices. Although other types of transformation matrix may not be accurately represented by permutation matrices, many useful types of transformation can be represented by sparse transformation matrices. For example, rotation and blurring can be represented by matrices that have a small number of nonzero elements per row (e.g., at most 6 for rotations).

The observed image $\mathbf{x}$ is linked to the nontransformed *latent image* $\mathbf{z}$ and the transformation index $\ell \in \{1, \ldots, L\}$ as follows:

$$p(\mathbf{x}|\ell, \mathbf{z}) = \mathcal{N}(\mathbf{x}; \mathbf{G}_\ell \mathbf{z}, \mathbf{\Psi}), \qquad (1)$$

where $\mathbf{\Psi}$ is a diagonal matrix of pixel noise variances. Since the probability of a transformation may depend on the latent image, the joint distribution over the latent image $\mathbf{z}$, the transformation index ℓ and the observed image $\mathbf{x}$ is

$$p(\mathbf{x}, \ell, \mathbf{z}) = \mathcal{N}(\mathbf{x}; \mathbf{G}_\ell \mathbf{z}, \mathbf{\Psi}) P(\ell|\mathbf{z}) p(\mathbf{z}). \qquad (2)$$

The corresponding graphical model is shown in Fig. 1b. For example, to model noisy transformed images of just one shape, we choose $p(\mathbf{z})$ to be a Gaussian distribution.

2.1 Transformed mixtures of Gaussians (TMG).

Fig. 1c shows the graphical model for a TMG, where different clusters may have different transformation probabilities. Cluster c has mixing proportion π_c, mean $\boldsymbol{\mu}_c$ and diagonal covariance matrix $\boldsymbol{\Phi}_c$. The joint distribution is

$$p(\mathbf{x}, \ell, \mathbf{z}, c) = \mathcal{N}(\mathbf{x}; \mathbf{G}_\ell \mathbf{z}, \boldsymbol{\Psi}) \mathcal{N}(\mathbf{z}; \boldsymbol{\mu}_c, \boldsymbol{\Phi}_c) \rho_{\ell c} \pi_c, \qquad (3)$$

where the probability of transformation ℓ for cluster c is $\rho_{\ell c}$. Marginalizing over the latent image gives the cluster/transformation conditional likelihood,

$$p(\mathbf{x}|\ell, c) = \mathcal{N}(\mathbf{x}; \mathbf{G}_\ell \boldsymbol{\mu}_c, \mathbf{G}_\ell \boldsymbol{\Phi}_c \mathbf{G}_\ell^T + \boldsymbol{\Psi}), \qquad (4)$$

which can be used to compute $p(\mathbf{x})$ and the cluster/transformation responsibility $P(\ell, c|\mathbf{x})$. This likelihood looks like the likelihood for a mixture of factor analyzers (Ghahramani and Hinton, 1997). However, whereas the likelihood computation for N latent pixels takes order N^3 time in a mixture of factor analyzers, it takes *linear* time, order N, in a TMG, because $\mathbf{G}_\ell \boldsymbol{\Phi}_c \mathbf{G}_\ell^T + \boldsymbol{\Psi}$ is sparse.

2.2 Transformed component analysis (TCA).

Fig. 1d shows the graphical model for TCA (or "transformed factor analysis"). The latent image is modeled using linearly combined Gaussian factors, $\mathbf{y}$. The joint distribution is

$$p(\mathbf{x}, \ell, \mathbf{z}, \mathbf{y}) = \mathcal{N}(\mathbf{x}; \mathbf{G}_\ell \mathbf{z}, \boldsymbol{\Psi}) \mathcal{N}(\mathbf{z}; \boldsymbol{\mu} + \boldsymbol{\Lambda} \mathbf{y}, \boldsymbol{\Phi}) \mathcal{N}(\mathbf{y}; \mathbf{0}, \mathbf{I}) \rho_\ell, \qquad (5)$$

where $\boldsymbol{\mu}$ is the mean of the latent image, $\boldsymbol{\Lambda}$ is a matrix of latent image components (the factor loading matrix) and $\boldsymbol{\Phi}$ is a diagonal noise covariance matrix for the latent image. Marginalizing over the factors and the latent image gives the transformation conditional likelihood,

$$p(\mathbf{x}|\ell) = \mathcal{N}(\mathbf{x}; \mathbf{G}_\ell \boldsymbol{\mu}, \mathbf{G}_\ell (\boldsymbol{\Lambda} \boldsymbol{\Lambda}^T + \boldsymbol{\Phi}) \mathbf{G}_\ell^T + \boldsymbol{\Psi}), \qquad (6)$$

which can be used to compute $p(\mathbf{x})$ and the transformation responsibility $p(\ell|\mathbf{x})$. $\mathbf{G}_\ell (\boldsymbol{\Lambda} \boldsymbol{\Lambda}^T + \boldsymbol{\Phi}) \mathbf{G}_\ell^T$ is not sparse, so computing this likelihood exactly takes N^3 time. However, the likelihood *can* be computed in linear time if we assume $|\mathbf{G}_\ell (\boldsymbol{\Lambda} \boldsymbol{\Lambda}^T + \boldsymbol{\Phi}) \mathbf{G}_\ell^T + \boldsymbol{\Psi}| \approx |\mathbf{G}_\ell (\boldsymbol{\Lambda} \boldsymbol{\Lambda}^T + \boldsymbol{\Phi}) \mathbf{G}_\ell^T|$, which corresponds to assuming that the observed noise is smaller than the variation due to the latent image, or that the observed noise is accounted for by the latent noise model, $\boldsymbol{\Phi}$. In our experiments, this approximation did not lead to degenerate behavior and produced useful models.

By setting columns of $\boldsymbol{\Lambda}$ equal to the derivatives of $\boldsymbol{\mu}$ with respect to continuous transformation parameters, a TCA can accommodate *both* a local linear approximation and a discrete approximation to the transformation manifold.

2.3 Mixtures of transformed component analyzers (MTCA).

A combination of a TMG and a TCA can be used to jointly model clusters, linear components and transformations. Alternatively, a mixture of Gaussians that is invariant to a discrete set of transformations *and* locally linear transformations can be obtained by combining a TMG with a TCA whose components are all set equal to transformation derivatives.

The joint distribution for the combined model in Fig. 1e is

$$p(\mathbf{x}, \ell, \mathbf{z}, c, \mathbf{y}) = \mathcal{N}(\mathbf{x}; \mathbf{G}_\ell \mathbf{z}, \boldsymbol{\Psi}) \mathcal{N}(\mathbf{z}; \boldsymbol{\mu}_c + \boldsymbol{\Lambda}_c \mathbf{y}, \boldsymbol{\Phi}_c) \mathcal{N}(\mathbf{y}; \mathbf{0}, \mathbf{I}) \rho_{\ell c} \pi_c. \qquad (7)$$

The cluster/transformation likelihood is $p(\mathbf{x}|\ell, c) = \mathcal{N}(\mathbf{x}; \mathbf{G}_\ell \boldsymbol{\mu}_c, \mathbf{G}_\ell (\boldsymbol{\Lambda}_c \boldsymbol{\Lambda}_c^T + \boldsymbol{\Phi}_c) \mathbf{G}_\ell^T + \boldsymbol{\Psi})$, which can be approximated in linear time as for TCA.

3 Mixed Transformed Component Analysis (MTCA)

We present an EM algorithm for MTCA; EM algorithms for TMG or TCA emerge by setting the number of factors to 0 or setting the number of clusters to 1.

Let θ represent a parameter in the generative model. For i.i.d. data, the derivative of the log-likelihood of a training set $\mathbf{x}_1, \ldots, \mathbf{x}_T$ with respect to θ can be written

$$\frac{\partial \log p(\mathbf{x}_1, \ldots, \mathbf{x}_T)}{\partial \theta} = \sum_{t=1}^{T} \mathrm{E}\Big[\frac{\partial}{\partial \theta} \log p(\mathbf{x}_t, c, \ell, \mathbf{z}, \mathbf{y}) \Big| \mathbf{x}_t \Big], \tag{8}$$

where the expectation is taken over $p(c, \ell, \mathbf{z}, \mathbf{y}|\mathbf{x}_t)$. The EM algorithm iteratively solves for a new set of parameters using the old parameters to compute the expectations. This procedure consistently increases the likelihood of the training data.

By setting (8) to 0 and solving for the new parameter values, we obtain update equations based on the expectations given in the Appendix. Notation: $\langle \cdot \rangle = \frac{1}{T}\sum_{t=1}^{T}(\cdot)$ is a sufficient statistic computed by averaging over the training set; diag($\mathbf{A}$) gives a vector containing the diagonal elements of matrix $\mathbf{A}$; diag($\mathbf{a}$) gives a diagonal matrix whose diagonal contains the elements of vector $\mathbf{a}$; and $\mathbf{a} \circ \mathbf{b}$ gives the element-wise product of vectors $\mathbf{a}$ and $\mathbf{b}$. Denoting the updated parameters by " $\tilde{}$ ", we have

$$\tilde{\pi}_c = \langle P(c|\mathbf{x}_t) \rangle, \qquad \tilde{\rho}_{\ell c} = \langle P(\ell|\mathbf{x}_t, c) \rangle, \tag{9}$$

$$\tilde{\boldsymbol{\mu}}_c = \frac{\langle P(c|\mathbf{x}_t)\mathrm{E}[\mathbf{z} - \boldsymbol{\Lambda}_c \mathbf{y}|\mathbf{x}_t, c]\rangle}{\langle P(c|\mathbf{x}_t)\rangle}, \tag{10}$$

$$\tilde{\boldsymbol{\Phi}}_c = \frac{\mathrm{diag}(\langle P(c|\mathbf{x}_t)\mathrm{E}[(\mathbf{z}-\boldsymbol{\mu}_c-\boldsymbol{\Lambda}_c\mathbf{y})\circ(\mathbf{z}-\boldsymbol{\mu}_c-\boldsymbol{\Lambda}_c\mathbf{y})|\mathbf{x}_t, c]\rangle)}{\langle P(c|\mathbf{x}_t)\rangle}, \tag{11}$$

$$\tilde{\boldsymbol{\Psi}} = \mathrm{diag}(\langle \mathrm{E}[(\mathbf{x}_t - \mathbf{G}_\ell \mathbf{z}) \circ (\mathbf{x}_t - \mathbf{G}_\ell \mathbf{z})|\mathbf{x}_t] \rangle), \tag{12}$$

$$\tilde{\boldsymbol{\Lambda}}_c = \langle P(c|\mathbf{x}_t)\mathrm{E}[(\mathbf{z}-\boldsymbol{\mu}_c)\mathbf{y}^T|\mathbf{x}_t]\rangle \langle P(c|\mathbf{x}_t)\mathrm{E}[\mathbf{y}\mathbf{y}^T|\mathbf{x}_t]\rangle^{-1}. \tag{13}$$

To reduce the number of parameters, we will sometimes assume $\rho_{\ell c}$ does not depend on c or even that $\rho_{\ell c}$ is held constant at a uniform distribution.

4 Experiments

4.1 Filtering Images from a Scanning Electron Microscope (SEM).

SEM images (*e.g.*, Fig. 2a) can have a very low signal to noise ratio due to a high variance in electron emission rate and modulation of this variance by the imaged material (Golem and Cohen, 1998). To reduce noise, multiple images are usually averaged and the pixel variances can be used to estimate certainty in rendered structures. Fig. 2b shows the estimated means and variances of the pixels from 230 140 × 56 SEM images like the ones in Fig. 2a. In fact, averaging images does not take into account spatial uncertainties and filtering in the imaging process introduced by the electron detectors and the high-speed electrical circuits.

We trained a single-cluster TMG with 5 horizontal shifts and 5 vertical shifts on the 230 SEM images using 30 iterations of EM. To keep the number of parameters almost equal to the number of parameters estimated using simple averaging, the transformation probabilities were not learned and the pixel variances in the observed image were set equal after each M step. So, TMG had 1 more parameter. Fig. 2c shows the mean and variance learned by the TMG. Compared to simple averaging, the TMG finds sharper, more detailed structure. The variances are significantly lower, indicating that the TMG produces a more confident estimate of the image.

Topographic Transformation as a Discrete Latent Variable 481

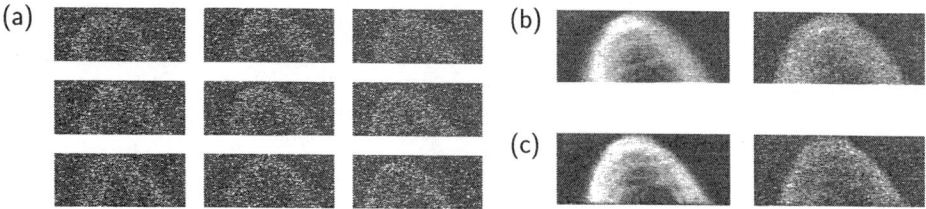

Figure 2: (a) 140 × 56 pixel SEM images. (b) The mean and variance of the image pixels. (c) The mean and variance found by a TMG reveal more structure and less uncertainty.

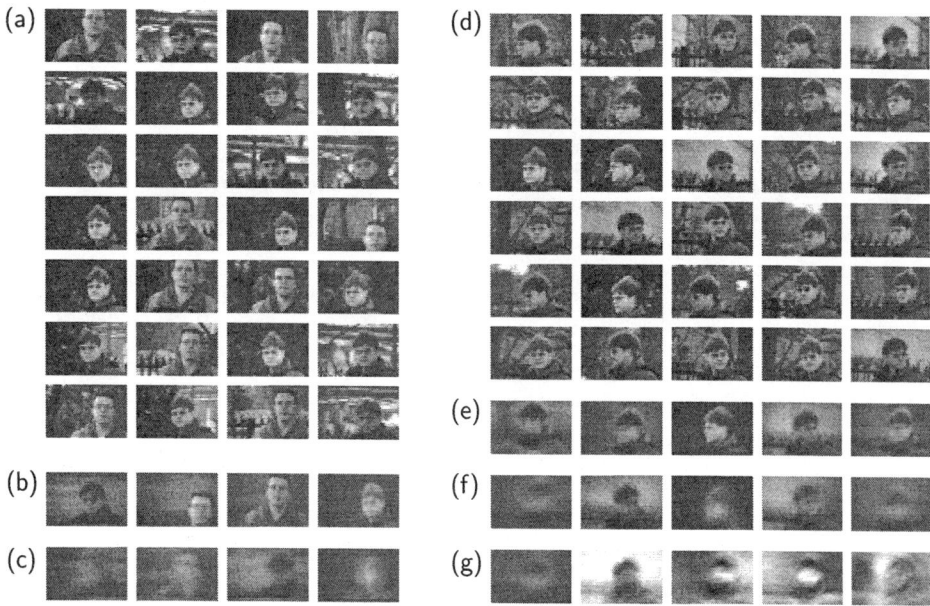

Figure 3: (a) Frontal face images of two people. (b) Cluster means learned by a TMG and (c) a mixture of Gaussians. (d) Images of one person with different poses. (e) Cluster means learned by a TMG. (f) Less detailed cluster means learned by a mixture of Gaussians. (g) Mean and first 4 principal components of the data, which mostly model lighting and translation.

4.2 Clustering Faces and Poses. Fig. 3a shows examples from a training set of 400 jerky images of two people walking across a cluttered background. We trained a TMG with 4 clusters, 11 horizontal shifts and 11 vertical shifts using 15 iterations of EM after initializing the weights to small, random values. The loop-rich MATLAB script executed in 40 minutes on a 500MHz Pentium processor. Fig. 3b shows the cluster means, which include two sharp representations of each person's face, with the background clutter suppressed. Fig. 3c shows the much blurrier means for a mixture of Gaussians trained using 15 iterations of EM.

Fig. 3d shows examples from a training set of 400 jerky images of one person with different poses. We trained a TMG with 5 clusters, 11 horizontal shifts and 11 vertical shifts using 40 iterations of EM. Fig. 3e shows the cluster means, which capture 4 poses and mostly suppress the background clutter. The mean for cluster 4 includes part of the background, but this cluster also has a low mixing proportion of 0.1. A traditional mixture of Gaussians trained using 40 iterations of EM finds blurrier means, as shown in Fig. 3f. The first 4 principal components mostly try to account for lighting and translation, as shown in Fig. 3g.

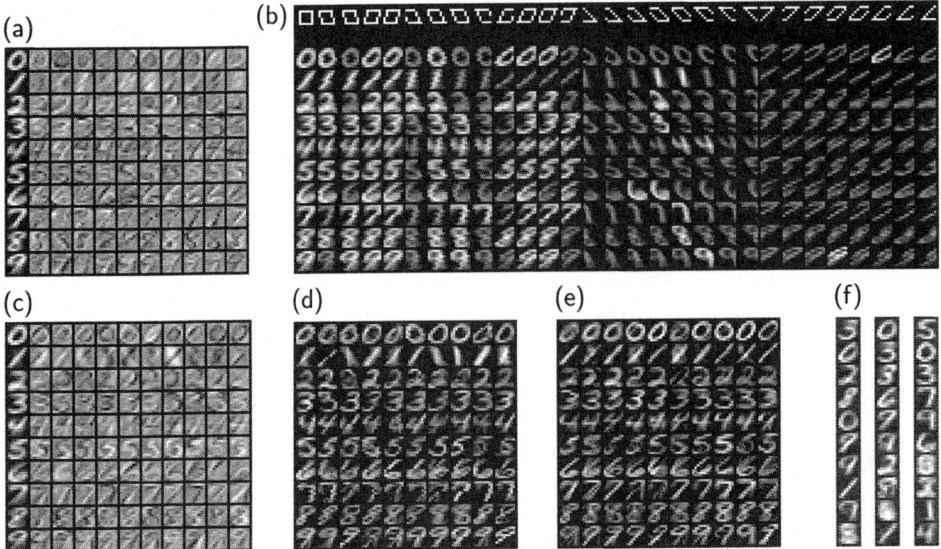

Figure 4: Modeling handwritten digits. (a) Means and components and (b) the sheared + translated means (dimmed transformations have low probability) for each of 10 TCA models trained on 200 examples of each digit. (c) Means and components of 10 FA models trained on the same data. (d) Digits generated from the 10 TCA models and (e) the 10 FA models. (f) The means for a mixture of 10 Gaussians, a mixture of 10 factor analyzers and a 10-cluster TMG trained on all 2000 digits. In each case, the best of 10 experiments was selected.

4.3 Modeling Handwritten Digits. We performed both supervised and unsupervised learning experiments on 8 × 8 greyscale versions of 2000 digits from the CEDAR CDROM (Hull, 1994). Although the preprocessed images fit snugly in the 8 × 8 window, there is wide variation in "writing angle" (*e.g.*, the vertical stroke of the 7 is at different angles). So, we produced a set of 29 shearing+translation transformations (see the top row of Fig. 4b) to use in transformed density models.

In our supervised learning experiments, we trained one 10-component TCA on each class of digit using 30 iterations of EM. Fig. 4a shows the mean and 10 components for each of the 10 models. The lower 10 rows of images in Fig. 4b show the sheared and translated means. In cases where the transformation probability is below 1%, the image is dimmed. We also trained one 10-component factor analyzer on each class of digit using 30 iterations of EM. The means and components are shown in Fig. 4c. The means found by TCA are sharper and whereas the components found by factor analysis often account for writing angle (*e.g.*, see the components for 7) the components found by TCA tend to account for line thickness and arc size. Fig. 4d and e show digits that were randomly generated from the TCAs and the factor analyzers. Since different components in the factor analyzers account for different stroke angles, the simulated digits often have an extra stroke, whereas digits simulated from the TCAs contain fewer spurious strokes.

To test recognition performance, we trained 10-component factor analyzers and TCAs on 200 examples of each digit using 50 iterations of EM. Each set of models used Bayes rule to classify 1000 test patterns and while factor analysis gave an error rate of 3.2%, TCA gave an error rate of only 2.7%.

In our unsupervised learning experiments, we fit 10-cluster mixture models to the entire set of 2000 digits to see which models could identify all 10 digits. We tried a mixture of 10 Gaussians, a mixture of 10 factor analyzers and a 10-cluster TMG. In each case, 10 models were trained using 100 iterations of EM and the model with the highest likelihood was selected and is shown in Fig. 4f. Compared to the TMG, the first two methods found blurred and repeated classes. After identifying each cluster with its most prevalent class of digit, we found that the first two methods had error rates of 53% and 49%, but the TMG had a much lower error rate of 26%.

5 Summary

In many learning applications, we know beforehand that the data includes transformations of an easily specified nature (*e.g.*, shearing of digit images). If a generative density model is learned from the data, the model must extract a model of both the transformations and the more interesting and potentially useful structure. We described a way to add transformation invariance to a generative density model by approximating the transformation manifold with a discrete set of points. This releases the generative model from needing to model the transformations. 5 different types of experiment show that the method is effective and quite efficient.

Although the time needed by this method scales exponentially with the dimensionality of the transformation manifold, we believe that it will be useful in many practical applications and that it illustrates what is possible with a generative model that incorporates a latent transformation variable. We are exploring the performance of a faster variational learning method and extending the model to time series.

Acknowledgements. We used CITO, NSERC, NSF and Beckman Foundation grants.

References

C. M. Bishop, M. Svensen and C. K. I. Williams 1998. GTM: The generative topographic mapping. *Neural Computation* **10:1**, 215–235.

G. E. Hinton, P. Dayan and M. Revow 1997. Modeling the manifolds of images of handwritten digits. *IEEE Trans. on Neural Networks* **8**, 65–74.

Z. Ghahramani and G. E. Hinton 1997. The EM algorithm for mixtures of factor analyzers. University of Toronto Technical Report CRG-TR-96-1. Available at www.gatsby.ucl.ac.uk/~zoubin.

R. Golem and I. Cohen 1998. Scanning electron microscope image enhancement. School of Computer and Electrical Engineering project report, Ben-Gurion University.

J. J. Hull 1994. A database for handwritten text recognition research. *IEEE Trans. on Pattern Analysis and Machine Intelligence* **16:5**, 550–554.

Y. Le Cun, L. Bottou, Y. Bengio and P. Haffner 1998. Gradient-based learning applied to document recognition. *Proceedings of the IEEE* **86:11**, November, 2278–2324.

P. Y. Simard, B. Victorri, Y. Le Cun and J. Denker 1992. Tangent Prop – A formalism for specifying selected invariances in an adaptive network. In *Advances in Neural Information Processing Systems 4*, Morgan Kaufmann, San Mateo, CA.

P. Y. Simard, Y. Le Cun and J. Denker 1993. Efficient pattern recognition using a new transformation distance. In S. J. Hanson, J. D. Cowan and C. L. Giles, *Advances in Neural Information Processing Systems 5*, Morgan Kaufmann, San Mateo, CA.

Appendix: The Sufficient Statistics Found in the E-Step

The sufficient statistics for the M-Step are computed in the E-Step using sparse linear algebra during a single pass through the training set. Before making this pass, the following matrices are computed: $\Omega_{\ell,c} = \text{COV}(\mathbf{z}|\mathbf{x},\mathbf{y},\ell,c) = (\Phi_c^{-1} + \mathbf{G}_\ell' \Psi^{-1} \mathbf{G}_\ell)^{-1}$, $\beta_{\ell,c} = \text{COV}(\mathbf{y}|\mathbf{x},\ell,c) = (\mathbf{I} + \Lambda_c' \Phi_c^{-1} \Lambda_c - \Lambda_c' \Phi_c^{-1} \Omega_{\ell,c} \Phi_c^{-1} \Lambda_c)^{-1}$. For each case in the training set, $P(c,\ell|\mathbf{x}_t)$ is first computed for each combination of c,ℓ, before computing $\text{E}[\mathbf{y}|\mathbf{x}_t,\ell,c] = \beta_{\ell,c} \Lambda_c' \Phi_c^{-1} [\Omega_{\ell,c} \mathbf{G}_\ell' \Psi^{-1} \mathbf{x}_t - (\mathbf{I} - \Omega_{\ell,c} \Phi_c^{-1}) \boldsymbol{\mu}_c]$, $\text{E}[\mathbf{z}|\mathbf{x}_t,\ell,c] = \boldsymbol{\mu}_c + \Omega_{\ell,c} \mathbf{G}_\ell' \Psi^{-1} (\mathbf{x}_t - \mathbf{G}_\ell \boldsymbol{\mu}_c) + \Omega_\ell \Phi^{-1} \Lambda_c \beta_{\ell,c} \Lambda_c' \Phi_c^{-1} \Omega_{\ell,c} \mathbf{G}_\ell' \Psi^{-1} (\mathbf{x}_t - \mathbf{G}_\ell \boldsymbol{\mu}_c)$, $\text{E}[(\mathbf{z}-\boldsymbol{\mu}_c)(\mathbf{z}-\boldsymbol{\mu}_c)'|\mathbf{x}_t,\ell,c] = (\text{E}[\mathbf{z}|\mathbf{x}_t,\ell,c]-\boldsymbol{\mu}_c)(\text{E}[\mathbf{z}|\mathbf{x}_t,\ell,c]-\boldsymbol{\mu}_c)' + \text{diag}(\Omega_{\ell,c}) + \text{diag}(\Omega_{\ell,c} \Phi_c^{-1} \Lambda_c \beta_{\ell,c} \Lambda_c' \Phi_c^{-1} \Omega_{\ell,c})$, $\text{E}[(\mathbf{z}-\boldsymbol{\mu}_c)\mathbf{y}'|\mathbf{x}_t,\ell,c] = (\text{E}[\mathbf{z}|\mathbf{x}_t,\ell,c] - \boldsymbol{\mu}_c) \text{E}[\mathbf{y}|\mathbf{x}_t,\ell,c]' + \Omega_{\ell,c} \Phi_c^{-1} \Lambda_c \beta_{\ell,c}$. The expectations needed in (10)-(13) are then computed from $P(c|\mathbf{x}_t) \text{E}[\mathbf{z} - \Lambda_c \mathbf{y}|\mathbf{x}_t,c] = \sum_\ell P(c,\ell|\mathbf{x}_t)(\text{E}[\mathbf{z}|\mathbf{x}_t,\ell,c] - \Lambda_c \text{E}[\mathbf{y}|\mathbf{x}_t,\ell,c])$, $P(c|\mathbf{x}_t) \text{E}[(\mathbf{z}-\boldsymbol{\mu}_c-\Lambda_c \mathbf{y}) \circ (\mathbf{z}-\boldsymbol{\mu}_c-\Lambda_c \mathbf{y})|\mathbf{x}_t,c] = \sum_\ell P(c,\ell|\mathbf{x}_t) \{\text{E}[(\mathbf{z}-\boldsymbol{\mu}_c) \circ (\mathbf{z}-\boldsymbol{\mu}_c)|\mathbf{x}_t,\ell,c] + \text{diag}(\Lambda_c \beta_{\ell,c} \Lambda_c') - 2\text{diag}(\Lambda_c \text{E}[(\mathbf{z}-\boldsymbol{\mu}_c) \mathbf{y}'|\mathbf{x}_t,\ell,c]') + (\Lambda_c \text{E}[\mathbf{y}|\mathbf{x}_t,\ell,c]) \circ (\Lambda_c \text{E}[\mathbf{y}|\mathbf{x}_t,\ell,c])\}$, $\text{E}[(\mathbf{x}_t - \mathbf{G}_\ell \mathbf{z})\circ(\mathbf{x}_t - \mathbf{G}_\ell \mathbf{z})|\mathbf{x}_t] = \sum_{c,\ell} P(c,\ell|\mathbf{x}_t) \{(\mathbf{x}_t - \mathbf{G}_\ell \text{E}[\mathbf{z}|\mathbf{x}_t,\ell,c]) \circ (\mathbf{x}_t - \mathbf{G}_\ell \text{E}[\mathbf{z}|\mathbf{x}_t,\ell,c]) + \text{diag}(\mathbf{G}_\ell \Omega_{\ell,c} \mathbf{G}_\ell') + \text{diag}(\mathbf{G}_\ell \Omega_{\ell,c} \Phi_c^{-1} \Lambda_c \beta_{\ell,c} \Lambda_c' \Phi_c^{-1} \Omega_{\ell,c} \mathbf{G}_\ell')\}$, $P(c|\mathbf{x}_t) \text{E}[(\mathbf{z}-\boldsymbol{\mu})\mathbf{y}'|\mathbf{x}_t,c] = \sum_\ell P(c,\ell|\mathbf{x}_t) \text{E}[(\mathbf{z}-\boldsymbol{\mu})\mathbf{y}'|\mathbf{x}_t,\ell,c]$, $P(c|\mathbf{x}_t) \text{E}[\mathbf{y}\mathbf{y}'|\mathbf{x}_t,c] = \sum_\ell P(c,\ell|\mathbf{x}_t) \beta_{\ell,c} + \sum_\ell P(c,\ell|\mathbf{x}_t) \text{E}[\mathbf{y}|\mathbf{x}_t,\ell,c] \text{E}[\mathbf{y}|\mathbf{x}_t,\ell,c]'$.

An Improved Decomposition Algorithm for Regression Support Vector Machines

Pavel Laskov
Department of Computer and Information Sciences
University of Delaware
Newark, DE 19718
laskov@asel.udel.edu

Abstract

A new decomposition algorithm for training regression Support Vector Machines (SVM) is presented. The algorithm builds on the basic principles of decomposition proposed by Osuna et. al., and addresses the issue of optimal working set selection. The new criteria for testing optimality of a working set are derived. Based on these criteria, the principle of "maximal inconsistency" is proposed to form (approximately) optimal working sets. Experimental results show superior performance of the new algorithm in comparison with traditional training of regression SVM without decomposition. Similar results have been previously reported on decomposition algorithms for pattern recognition SVM. The new algorithm is also applicable to advanced SVM formulations based on regression, such as density estimation and integral equation SVM.

1 Introduction

The increasing interest in applications of Support Vector Machines (SVM) to large-scale problems ushers in new requirements for computational complexity of their training algorithms. Requests have been recently made for algorithms capable of handling problems containing 10^5 - 10^6 examples [1]. Training an SVM constitutes a quadratic programming problem, and a typical SVM package uses an off-the-shelf optimization software to obtain a solution to it. The number of variables in the optimization problem is equal to the number of training data points (for the pattern recognition SVM) or twice that number (for the regression SVM). The speed of general-purpose optimization methods is insufficient for problems containing more than a few thousand examples. This has motivated a quest for special-purpose training algorithms to take advantage of the particular structure of SVM training problems.

The main avenue of research in SVM training algorithms is decomposition. The key idea of decomposition, due to Osuna et. al. [2], is to freeze all but a small number of optimization variables, and to solve a sequence of small fixed-size problems. The set of variables whose values are optimized at a current iteration is called the *working set*. Complexity of re-optimizing the working set is assumed to be constant-time.

In order for a decomposition algorithm to be successful, the working set must be selected in a smart way. The fastest known decomposition algorithm is due to Joachims [3]. It is based on Zoutendijk's method of feasible directions proposed in the optimization community in the early 1960's. However Joachims' algorithm is limited to pattern recognition SVM because it makes use of labels being ± 1. The current article presents a similar algorithm for the regression SVM.

The new algorithm utilizes a slightly different background from optimization theory. The Karush-Kuhn-Tucker Theorem is used to derive conditions for determining whether or not a given working set is optimal. These conditions become the algorithm's termination criteria, as an alternative to Osuna's criteria (also used by Joachims without modification) which used conditions for individual points. The advantage of the new conditions is that knowledge of the hyperplane's constant factor b, which in some cases is difficult to compute, is not required. Further investigation of the new termination conditions allows to form the strategy for selecting an optimal working set. The new algorithm is applicable to the pattern recognition SVM, and is provably equivalent to Joachims' algorithm. One can also interpret the new algorithm in the sense of the method of feasible directions. Experimental results presented in the last section demonstrate superior performance of the new method in comparison with traditional training of regression SVM.

2 General Principles of Regression SVM Decomposition

The original decomposition algorithm proposed for the pattern recognition SVM in [2] has been extended to the regression SVM in [4]. For the sake of completeness I will repeat the main steps of this extension with the aim of providing terse and streamlined notation to lay the ground for working set selection.

Given the training data of size l, training of the regression SVM amounts to solving the following quadratic programming problem in $2l$ variables:

$$
\begin{aligned}
\text{Maximize} \quad & W(\tilde{\alpha}) = \tilde{y}^T \tilde{\alpha} - \frac{1}{2} \tilde{\alpha}^T D \tilde{\alpha} \\
\text{subject to:} \quad & c^T \tilde{\alpha} = 0 \\
& \tilde{\alpha} - C\mathbf{1} \leq 0 \\
& \tilde{\alpha} \geq 0
\end{aligned}
\quad (1)
$$

where

$$
\tilde{\alpha} = \begin{bmatrix} \alpha \\ \alpha^* \end{bmatrix}, \quad \tilde{y} = \begin{bmatrix} y - \epsilon \mathbf{1} \\ -y - \epsilon \mathbf{1} \end{bmatrix}, \quad D = \begin{bmatrix} K & -K \\ -K & K \end{bmatrix}, \quad c = \begin{bmatrix} 1 \\ -1 \end{bmatrix}
$$

The basic idea of decomposition is to split the variable vector $\tilde{\alpha}$ into the working set $\tilde{\alpha}_B$ of fixed size q and the non-working set $\tilde{\alpha}_N$ containing the rest of the variables. The corresponding parts of vectors c and $\tilde{y}$ will also bear subscripts N and B. The matrix D is partitioned into D_{BB}, $D_{BN} = D_{NB}^T$ and D_{NN}. A further requirement is that, for the i-th element of the training data, both α_i and α_i^* are either included in or omitted from the working set.[1] The values of the variables in the non-working set are frozen for the iteration, and optimization is only performed with respect to the variables in the working set.

Optimization of the working set is also a quadratic program. This can be seen by re-arranging the terms of the objective function and the equality constraint in

---

[1]This rule facilitates formulation of sub-problems to be solved at each iteration.

(1) and dropping the terms independent of $\tilde{\alpha}_B$ from the objective. The resulting quadratic program (sub-problem) is formulated as follows:

$$\begin{aligned}
\text{Maximize} \quad W_B(\tilde{\alpha}_B) &= (\tilde{\mathbf{y}}_B^T - \tilde{\alpha}_N^T D_{NB})\tilde{\alpha}_B - \frac{1}{2}\tilde{\alpha}_B^T D_{BB}\tilde{\alpha}_B \\
\text{subject to:} \quad \mathbf{c}_B^T \tilde{\alpha}_B + \mathbf{c}_N^T \tilde{\alpha}_N &= 0 \\
\tilde{\alpha}_B - C\mathbf{1} &\leq 0 \\
\tilde{\alpha}_B &\geq 0
\end{aligned} \quad (2)$$

The basic decomposition algorithm chooses the first working set at random, and proceeds iteratively by selecting sub-optimal working sets and re-optimizing them, by solving quadratic program (2), until all subsets of size q are optimal. The precise formulation of termination conditions will be developed in the following section.

3 Optimality of a Working Set

In order to maintain strict improvement of the objective function, the working set must be sub-optimal before re-optimization. The classical Karush-Kuhn-Tucker (KKT) conditions are necessary and sufficient for optimality of a quadratic program. I will use these conditions applied to the standard form of a quadratic program, as described in [5], p. 36.

The standard form of a quadratic program requires that all constraints are of equality type except for non-negativity constraints. To cast the regression SVM quadratic program (1) into the standard form, the slack variables $\mathbf{s}^T = (s_1, \ldots, s_{2l})$ corresponding to the box constraints, and the following matrices are introduced:

$$E = \begin{bmatrix} 1 & I & 0 \\ -1 & 0 & I \end{bmatrix}, \quad \tilde{E} = \begin{bmatrix} E \\ I \end{bmatrix}, \quad \mathbf{z} = \begin{bmatrix} \tilde{\alpha} \\ 0 \\ \mathbf{s} \end{bmatrix}, \quad \mathbf{f} = \begin{bmatrix} 0 \\ \mathbf{C} \end{bmatrix} \quad (3)$$

where $\mathbf{1}$ is a vector of length l, $\mathbf{C}$ is a vector of length $2l$. The zero element in vector $\mathbf{z}$ reflects the fact that a slack variable for the equality constraint must be zero. In the matrix notation all constraints of problem (1) can be compactly expressed as:

$$\begin{aligned} \tilde{E}^T \mathbf{z} &= \mathbf{f} \\ \mathbf{z} &\geq 0 \end{aligned} \quad (4)$$

In this notation the Karush-Kuhn-Tucker Theorem can be stated as follows:

Theorem 1 (Karush-Kuhn-Tucker Theorem) *The primal vector $\mathbf{z}$ solves the quadratic problem (1) if and only if it satisfies (4) and there exists a dual vector $\mathbf{u}^T = (\mathbf{\Pi}^T \ \mathbf{w}^T) = (\mathbf{\Pi}^T \ (\mu \ \Upsilon^T))$ such that:*

$$\begin{aligned} \mathbf{\Pi} &= D\tilde{\alpha} + E\mathbf{w} - \tilde{\mathbf{y}} \geq 0 & (5) \\ \Upsilon &\geq 0 & (6) \\ \mathbf{u}^T \mathbf{z} &= 0 & (7) \end{aligned}$$

It follows from the Karush-Kuhn-Tucker Theorem that if for all $\mathbf{u}$ satisfying conditions (6) – (7) the system of inequalities (5) is inconsistent then the solution of problem (1) is *not* optimal. Since the objective function of sub-problem (2) was obtained by merely re-arranging terms in the objective function of the initial problem (1), the same conditions guarantee that the sub-problem (2) is not optimal. Thus, the main strategy for identifying sub-optimal working sets will be to enforce inconsistency of the system (5) while satisfying conditions (6) – (7).

Let us further analyze inequalities in (5). Each inequality has one of the following forms:

$$\pi_i = -\phi_i + \epsilon + v_i + \mu \geq 0 \tag{8}$$
$$\pi_i^* = \phi_i + \epsilon - v_i^* - \mu \geq 0 \tag{9}$$

where

$$\phi_i = y_i - \sum_{j=1}^{l}(\alpha_j - \alpha_j^*)K_{ij}$$

Consider the values α_i can possible take:

1. $\alpha_i = 0$. In this case $s_i = C$, and, by complementarity condition (7), $v_i = 0$. Then inequality (8) becomes:
$$\pi_i = -\phi_i + \epsilon + \mu \geq 0 \quad \Rightarrow \quad \mu \geq \phi_i - \epsilon$$

2. $\alpha_i = C$. By complementarity condition (7), $\pi_i = 0$. Then inequality (8) becomes:
$$-\phi_i + \epsilon + \mu + v_i = 0 \quad \Rightarrow \quad \mu \leq \phi_i - \epsilon$$

3. $0 < \alpha_i < C$. By complementarity condition (7), $v_i = 0$, $\pi_i = 0$. Then inequality (8) becomes:
$$-\phi_i + \epsilon + \mu = 0 \quad \Rightarrow \quad \mu = \phi_i - \epsilon$$

Similar reasoning for α_i^* and inequality (9) yields the following results:

1. $\alpha_i^* = 0$. Then
$$\mu \leq \phi_i + \epsilon$$

2. $\alpha_i^* = C$. Then
$$\mu \geq \phi_i + \epsilon$$

3. $0 < \alpha_i^* < C$. Then
$$\mu = \phi_i + \epsilon$$

As one can see, the only free variable in system (5) is μ. Each inequality restricts μ to a certain interval on a real line. Such intervals will be denoted as μ-*sets* in the rest of the exposition. Any subset of inequalities in (5) is inconsistent if the intersection of the corresponding μ-sets is empty. This provides a lucid rule for determining optimality of any working set: it is sub-optimal if the intersection of μ-sets of all its points is empty. A sub-optimal working set will also be denoted as "inconsistent". The following summarizes the rules for calculation of μ-sets, taking into account that for regression SVM $\alpha_i \alpha_i^* = 0$:

$$\mathcal{M}_i = \begin{cases} [\phi_i - \epsilon, \phi_i + \epsilon], & \text{if } \alpha_i = 0,\ \alpha_i^* = 0 \\ [\phi_i - \epsilon, \phi_i - \epsilon], & \text{if } 0 < \alpha_i < C,\ \alpha_i^* = 0 \\ (-\infty, \phi_i - \epsilon], & \text{if } \alpha_i = C,\ \alpha_i^* = 0 \\ [\phi_i + \epsilon, \phi_i + \epsilon], & \text{if } \alpha_i = 0,\ 0 < \alpha_i^* < C \\ [\phi_i + \epsilon, +\infty), & \text{if } \alpha_i = 0,\ \alpha_i^* = C \end{cases} \tag{10}$$

4 Maximal Inconsistency Algorithm

While inconsistency of the working set at each iteration guarantees convergence of decomposition, the rate of convergence is quite slow if arbitrary inconsistent working sets are chosen. A natural heuristic is to select "maximally inconsistent" working sets, in a hope that such choice would provide the greatest improvement of the objective function. The notion of "maximal inconsistency" is easy to define: let it be the gap between the smallest right boundary and the largest left boundary of μ-sets of elements in the training set:

$$G = L - R$$
$$L = \max_{0<i<l} \mu_i^l, \quad R = \min_{0<i<l} \mu_i^r$$

where μ_i^l, μ_i^r are the left and the right boundaries respectively (possibly minus or plus infinity) of the μ-set $\mathcal{M}_i$. It is convenient to require that the largest possible inconsistency gap be maintained between all pairs of points comprising the working set. The obvious implementation of such strategy is to select $q/2$ elements with the largest values of μ^l and $q/2$ elements with the smallest values of μ^r. The maximal inconsistency strategy is summarized in Algorithm 1.

Algorithm 1 Maximal inconsistency SVM decomposition algorithm.

Let S be the list of all samples.
while $(L > R)$

- compute $\mathcal{M}_i$ according to the rules (10) for all elements in S
- select $q/2$ elements with the largest values of μ^l ("left pass")
- select $q/2$ elements with the smallest values of μ^r ("right pass")
- re-optimize the working set

Although the motivation provided for the maximal inconsistency algorithm is purely heuristic, the algorithm can be rigorously derived, in a similar fashion as Joachims' algorithm, from Zoutendijk's feasible direction problem. Details of such derivation cannot be presented here due to space constraints. Because of this relationship I will further refer to both algorithms as "feasible direction" algorithms.

5 Experimental Results

Experimental evaluation of the new algorithm was performed on the modified KDD Cup 1998 data set. The original data set is available under *http://www.ics.uci.edu/~kdd/databases/kddcup98/kddcup98.html*. The following modifications were made to obtain a pure regression problem:

- All 75 character fields were eliminated.
- Numeric fields CONTROLN, ODATEDW, TCODE and DOB were elimitated.

The remaining 400 features and the labels were scaled between 0 and 1. Initial subsets of the training database of different sizes were selected for evaluation of the scaling properties of the new algorithm. The training times of the algorithms, with and without decomposition, the numbers of support vectors, including bounded support vectors, and the experimental scaling factors, are displayed in Table 1.

Table 1: Training time (sec) and number of SVs for the KDD Cup problem

Examples	no dcmp	dcmp	total SV	BSV
500	39	10	274	0
1000	226	41	518	3
2000	1490	158	970	5
3000	5744	397	1429	7
5000	27052	1252	2349	15
scaling factor:	2.84	2.08		
SV-scaling factor:	3.06	2.24		

Table 2: Training time (sec) and number of SVs for the KDD Cup problem, reduced feature space.

Examples	no dcmp	dcmp	total SV	BSV
500	56	18	170	30
1000	346	44	374	62
2000	1768	198	510	144
3000	4789	366	729	222
5000	22115	863	1139	354
scaling factor:	2.55	1.72		
SV-scaling factor:	3.55	2.35		

The experimental scaling factors are obtained by fitting lines to log-log plots of the running times against sample sizes, in the number of examples and the number of unbounded support vectors respectively. Experiments were run on SGI Octane with 195MHz clock and 256M RAM. RBF kernel with $\gamma = 10$, $C = 1$, termination accuracy 0.001, working set size of 20, and cache size of 5000 samples were used.

A similar experiment was performed on a reduced feature set consisting of the first 50 features selected from the full-size data set. This experiment illustrates the behavior of the algorithms when the large number of support vectors are bounded. The results are presented in Table 2.

6 Discussion

It comes at no surprise that the decomposition algorithm outperforms the conventional training algorithm by an order of magnitude. Similar results have been well established for pattern recognition SVM. Remarkable is the co-incidence of scaling factors of the maximal inconsistency algorithm and Joachims' algorithm: his scaling factors range from 1.7 to 2.1 [3]. I believe however, that a more important performance measure is SV-scaling factor, and the results above suggest that this factor is consistent even for problems with significantly different compositions of support vectors. Further experiments should investigate properties of this measure.

Finally, I would like to mention other methods proposed in order to speed-up training of SVM, although no experimental results have been reported for these methods with regard to training of the regression SVM. Chunking [6], p. 366, iterates through the training data accumulating support vectors and adding a "chunk" of new data until no more changes to a solution occur. The main problem with this method is that when the percentage of support vectors is high it essentially solves the problem of almost the same size more than once. Sequential Minimal Optimization (SMO), proposed by Platt [7] and easily extendable to the regression SVM [1], employs an idea similar to decomposition but always uses the working set of size 2. For such a working set, a solution can be calculated "by hand" without numerical optimization. A number of heuristics is applied in order to choose a good working set. It is difficult to draw a comparison between the working set selection mechanisms of SMO and the feasible direction algorithms but experimental results of Joachims [3] suggest that SMO is slower. Another advantage of feasible direction algorithms is that the size of the working set is not limited to 2, as in SMO. Practical experience shows that the optimal size of the working set is between 10 and 100. Lastly, traditional optimization methods, such as Newton's or conjugate gradient methods, can be modified to yield the complexity of $O(s^3)$, where s is the number of detected support vectors [8]. This can be a considerable improvement over the methods that have complexity of $O(l^3)$, where l is the total number of training samples.

The real challenge lies in attaining sub-$O(s^3)$ complexity. While the experimental results suggest that feasible direction algorithms might attain such complexity, their complexity is not fully understood from the theoretical point of view. More specifically, the convergence rate, and its dependence on the number of support vectors, needs to be analyzed. This will be the main direction of the future research in feasible direction SVM training algorithms.

References

[1] Smola, A., Schölkopf, B. (1998) A Tutorial on Support Vector Regression. *NeuroCOLT2 Technical Report NC2-TR-1998-030.*

[2] Osuna, E., Freund, R., Girosi, F. (1997) An Improved Training Algorithm for Support Vector Machines. *Proceedings of IEEE NNSP'97.* Amelia Island FL.

[3] Joachims, T. (1998) Making Large-Scale SVM Learning Practical. *Advances in Kernel Methods – Support Vector Learning.* B. Schölkopf, C. Burges, A. Smola, (eds.) MIT-Press.

[4] Osuna, E. (1998) Support Vector Machines: Training and Applications. Ph. D. Dissertation. Operations Research Center, MIT.

[5] Boot, J. (1964) *Quadratic Programming. Algorithms – Anomalies – Applications.* North Holland Publishing Company, Amsterdam.

[6] Vapnik, V. (1982) *Estimation of Dependencies Based on Empirical Data.* Springer-Verlag.

[7] Platt, J. (1998) Fast Training of Support Vector Machines Using Sequential Minimal Optimization. *Advances in Kernel Methods – Support Vector Learning.* B. Schölkopf, C. Burges, A. Smola, (eds.) MIT-Press.

[8] Kaufman, L. (1998) Solving the Quadratic Programming Problem Arising in SupportVector Classification. *Advances in Kernel Methods – Support Vector Learning.* B. Schölkopf, C. Burges, A. Smola, (eds.) MIT-Press.

Algorithms for Independent Components Analysis and Higher Order Statistics

Daniel D. Lee
Bell Laboratories
Lucent Technologies
Murray Hill, NJ 07974

Uri Rokni and Haim Sompolinsky
Racah Institute of Physics and
Center for Neural Computation
Hebrew University
Jerusalem, 91904, Israel

Abstract

A latent variable generative model with finite noise is used to describe several different algorithms for Independent Components Analysis (ICA). In particular, the Fixed Point ICA algorithm is shown to be equivalent to the Expectation-Maximization algorithm for maximum likelihood under certain constraints, allowing the conditions for global convergence to be elucidated. The algorithms can also be explained by their generic behavior near a singular point where the size of the optimal generative bases vanishes. An expansion of the likelihood about this singular point indicates the role of higher order correlations in determining the features discovered by ICA. The application and convergence of these algorithms are demonstrated on a simple illustrative example.

Introduction

Independent Components Analysis (ICA) has generated much recent theoretical and practical interest because of its successes on a number of different signal processing problems. ICA attempts to decompose the observed data into components that are as statistically independent from each other as possible, and can be viewed as a nonlinear generalization of Principal Components Analysis (PCA). Some applications of ICA include blind separation of audio signals, beamforming of radio sources, and discovery of features in biomedical traces [1].

There have also been a number of approaches to deriving algorithms for ICA [2, 3, 4]. Fundamentally, they all consider the problem of recovering independent source signals $\{\vec{s}\}$ from observations $\{\vec{x}\}$ such that:

$$x_i = \sum_{j=1}^{M} W_{ij} s_j, \ i = 1..N \quad (1)$$

Here, W_{ij} is a $N \times M$ mixing matrix where the number of sources M is not greater than the dimensionality N of the observations. Thus, the columns of W represent the different independent features present in the observed data.

Bell and Sejnowski formulated their Infomax algorithm for ICA as maximizing the mutual information between the data and a nonlinearly transformed version of the data [5]. The covariant version of this algorithm uses the natural gradient of the mutual information to iteratively update the estimate for the demixing matrix W^{-1} in terms of the estimated components $s = W^{-1}x$ [6]:

$$\Delta W^{-1} \propto \left[I - \langle g(s)s^T \rangle\right] W^{-1}, \qquad (2)$$

The nonlinearity $g(s)$ differentiates the features learned by the Infomax ICA algorithm from those found by conventional PCA. Fortunately, the exact form of the nonlinearity used in Eq. 2 is not crucial for the success of the algorithm, as long as it preserves the sub-Gaussian or super-Gaussian nature of the sources [7].

Another approach to ICA due to Hyvarinen and Oja was derived from maximizing objective functions motivated by projection pursuit [8]. Their Fixed Point ICA algorithm attempts to self-consistently solve for the extremum of a nonlinear objective function. The simplest formulation considers a single source $M = 1$ so that the mixing matrix is a single vector w, constrained to be unit length $|w| = 1$. Assuming the data is first preprocessed and whitened, the Fixed Point ICA algorithm iteratively updates the estimate of w as follows:

$$\begin{aligned} w &\leftarrow \langle x g(w^T x) \rangle - \lambda_G w \\ w &\leftarrow \frac{w}{|w|}, \end{aligned} \qquad (3)$$

where $g(w^T x)$ is a nonlinear function and λ_G is a constant given by the integral over the Gaussian:

$$\lambda_G = \frac{1}{\sqrt{2\pi}} \int_{-\infty}^{\infty} d\eta \, e^{-\eta^2/2} \, g'(\eta). \qquad (4)$$

The Fixed Point algorithm can be extended to an arbitrary number $M \leq N$ of sources by using Eq. 3 in a serial deflation scheme. Alternatively, the M columns of the mixing matrix W can be updated simultaneously by orthogonalizing the $N \times M$ matrix:

$$W \leftarrow \langle x g(W^T x)^T \rangle - \lambda_G W. \qquad (5)$$

Under the assumption that the observed data match the underlying ICA model, $x = Ws$, it has been shown that the Fixed Point algorithm converges locally to the correct solution with at least quadratic convergence. However, the global convergence of the generic Fixed Point ICA algorithm is uncertain. This is in contrast to the gradient-based Infomax algorithm whose convergence is guaranteed as long as a sufficiently small step size is chosen.

In this paper, we first review the latent variable generative model framework for Independent Components Analysis. We then consider the generative model in the presence of finite noise, and show how the Fixed Point ICA algorithm can be related to an Expectation-Maximization algorithm for maximum likelihood. This allows us to elucidate the conditions under which the Fixed Point algorithm is guaranteed to globally converge. Assuming that the data are indeed generated from independent components, we derive the optimal parameters for convergence. We also investigate how the optimal size of the ICA mixing matrix varies as a function of the added noise, and demonstrate the presence of a singular point. By expanding the likelihood about this singular point, the behavior of the ICA algorithms can be related to the higher order statistics present in the data. Finally, we illustrate the application and convergence of these ICA algorithms on some artificial data.

Generative model

A convenient method for interpreting the different ICA algorithms is in terms of the hidden, or latent, variable generative model shown in Fig. 1 [9, 10]. The hidden variables $\{s_j\}$

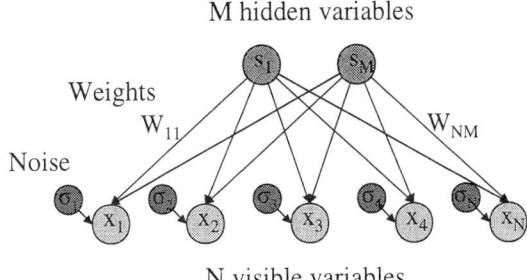

Figure 1: Generative model for ICA algorithms. s are the hidden variables, σ are additive Gaussian noise terms, and $x = Ws + \sigma$ are the visible variables.

correspond to the different independent components and are assumed to have the factorized non-Gaussian prior probability distribution:

$$P(s) = \prod_{j=1}^{M} e^{-F(s_j)}. \qquad (6)$$

Once the hidden variables are instantiated, the visible variables $\{x_i\}$ are generated via a linear mapping through the generative weights W:

$$P(x|s) = \prod_{i=1}^{N} \frac{1}{\sqrt{2\pi\sigma^2}} \exp\left[-\frac{1}{2\sigma^2}(x_i - \sum_j W_{ij} s_j)^2\right], \qquad (7)$$

where σ^2 is the variance of the Gaussian noise added to the visible variables.

The probability of the data given this model is then calculated by integrating over all possible values of the hidden variables:

$$P(x) = \int ds\, P(s) P(x|s) = \frac{1}{(2\pi\sigma^2)^{N/2}} \int ds\, \exp\left[-F(s) - \frac{1}{2\sigma^2}(x - Ws)^2\right] \qquad (8)$$

In the limit that the added noise vanishes, $\sigma^2 \to 0$, it has previously been shown that maximizing the likelihood of Eq. 8 is equivalent to the Infomax algorithm in Eq. 2 [11]. In the following analysis, we will consider the situation when the variance of the noise is nonzero, $\sigma^2 \neq 0$.

Expectation-Maximization

We assume that the data has initially been preprocessed and spherized: $\langle x_i x_j \rangle = \delta_{ij}$. Unfortunately, for finite noise σ^2 and an arbitrary prior $F(s_j)$, deriving a learning rule for W in closed form is analytically intractable. However, it becomes possible to derive a simple Expectation–Maximization (EM) learning rule under the constraint:

$$W = \xi W_0, \quad W_0^T W_0 = I, \qquad (9)$$

which implies that W is orthogonal, and ξ is the length of the individual columns of W. Indeed, for data that obeys the ICA model, $x = Ws$, it can be shown that the optimal W must satisfy this orthogonality condition. By assuming the constraint in Eq. 9 for arbitrary data, the posterior distribution $P(s|x)$ becomes conveniently factorized:

$$P(s|x) \propto \prod_{j=1}^{M} \exp\left[-F(s_j) + \frac{1}{\sigma^2}[(W^T x)_j s_j - \frac{1}{2}\xi^2 s_j^2\right]. \qquad (10)$$

For the E-step, this factorized form allows the expectation function $\int ds\, P(s|x)s = g(W^T x)$ to be analytically evaluated. This expectation is then used in the M-step to find the new estimate W':

$$\langle xg(W^T x)^T \rangle - \Lambda_S W' = 0, \qquad (11)$$

where Λ_S is a symmetric matrix of Lagrange multipliers that constrain the new W' to be orthogonal. Eq. 11 is easily solved by taking the reduced singular value decomposition of the rectangular matrix:

$$UDV^T = \langle xg(W^T x)^T \rangle, \qquad (12)$$

where $U^T U = V V^T = I$ and D is a diagonal $M \times M$ matrix. Then the solution for the EM estimate of the mixing matrix is given by:

$$W' = \xi UV^T \qquad (13)$$
$$\Lambda_S = \frac{1}{\xi} UDU^T. \qquad (14)$$

As a specific example, consider the following prior for binary hidden variables: $P(s) = \frac{1}{2}[\delta(s-1) + \delta(s+1)]$. In this case, the expectation $\int ds\, P(s|x)s = \tanh(W^T x/\sigma^2)$ and so the EM update rule is given by orthogonalizing the matrix:

$$W \leftarrow \left\langle x \tanh(\frac{1}{\sigma^2} W^T x) \right\rangle. \qquad (15)$$

Fixed Point ICA

Besides the presence of the linear term $\lambda_G W$ in Eq. 5, the EM update rule looks very much like that of the Fixed Point ICA algorithm. It turns out that without this linear term, the convergence of the naive EM algorithm is much slower than that of Eq. 5. Here we show that it is possible to interpret the role of this linear term in the Fixed Point ICA algorithm within the framework of this generative model.

Suppose that the distribution of the observed data $P_D(x)$ is actually a mixture between an isotropic distribution $P_0(x)$ and a non-isotropic distribution $P_1(x)$:

$$P_D(x) = \alpha P_0(x) + (1-\alpha) P_1(x). \qquad (16)$$

Because the isotropic part does not break rotational symmetry, it does not affect the choice of the directions of the learned basis W. Thus, it is more efficient to apply the learning algorithm to only the non-isotropic portion of the distribution, $P_1(x) \propto P_D(x) - \alpha P_0(x)$, rather than to the whole observed distribution $P_D(x)$. Applying EM to $P_1(x)$ results in a correction term arising from the subtracted isotropic distribution. With this correction, the EM update becomes:

$$W \leftarrow \langle xg(W^T x) \rangle - \alpha \lambda_G W \qquad (17)$$

which is equivalent to the Fixed Point ICA algorithm when $\alpha = 1$.

Unfortunately, it is not clear how to compute an appropriate value for α to use in fitting data. Taking a very small value, $\alpha \ll 1$, will result in a learning rule that is very similar to the naive EM update rule. This implies that the algorithm will be guaranteed to monotonically converge, albeit very slowly, to a local maximum of the likelihood. On the other hand, choosing a large value, $\alpha \gg 1$, will result in a subtracted probability density $P_1(x)$ that is negative everywhere. In this case, the algorithm will converge slowly to a local minimum of the likelihood. For the Fixed Point algorithm which operates in the intermediate regime, $\alpha \approx 1$, the algorithm is likely to converge most rapidly. However, it is also in this situation that the subtracted density $P_1(x)$ could have both positive and negative regions, and the algorithm is no longer guaranteed to converge.

ICA Algorithms and Higher Order Statistics

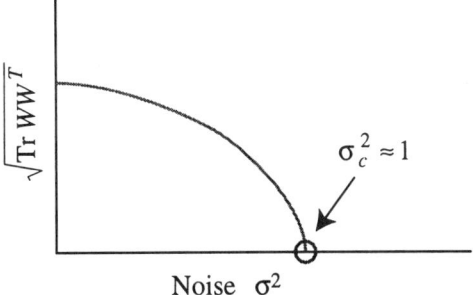

Figure 2: Size of the optimal generative bases as a function of the added noise σ^2, showing the singular point behavior around $\sigma_c^2 \approx 1$.

Optimal value of α

In order to determine the optimal value of α, we make the assumption that the observed data obeys the ICA model, $x = As$. Note that the statistics of the sources in the data need not match the assumed prior distribution of the sources in the generative model Eq. 6. With this assumption, which is not related to the mixture assumption in Eq. 16, it is easy to show that $W = A$ is a fixed point of the algorithm. By analyzing the behavior of the algorithm in the vicinity of this fixed point, a simple expression emerges for the change in deviations from this fixed point, δW, after a single iteration of Eq. 17:

$$\delta W_{ij} \leftarrow \frac{\langle g'(s) \rangle - \alpha \lambda_G}{\langle sg(s) \rangle - \alpha \lambda_G} \delta W_{ij} + O(\delta W^3) \tag{18}$$

where the averaging here is over the true source distribution, assumed for simplicity to be identical for all sources. Thus, the algorithm converges most rapidly if one chooses:

$$\alpha_{opt} = \frac{\langle g'(s) \rangle}{\lambda_G}, \tag{19}$$

so that the local convergence is cubic. From Eq. 18 one can show that the condition for the stability of the fixed point is given by $\alpha < \alpha_c$, where:

$$\alpha_c = \frac{\langle sg(s) + g'(s) \rangle}{2\lambda_G}. \tag{20}$$

Thus, for $\alpha = 0$, the stability criterion in Eq. 18 is equivalent to $\langle sg(s) \rangle > \langle g'(s) \rangle$. For the cubic nonlinearity $g(s) = s^3$, this implies that the algorithm will find the true independent features only if the source distribution has positive kurtosis.

Singular point expansion

Let us now consider how the optimal size ξ of the weights W varies as a function of the noise parameter σ^2. For very small $\sigma^2 \ll 1$, the weights W are approximately described by the Infomax algorithm of Eq. 2, and the lengths of the columns should be unity in order to match the covariance of the data. For large $\sigma^2 \gg 1$, however, the optimal size of the weights should be very small because the covariance of the noise is already larger than that of the data. In fact, for Factor Analysis which is a special case of the generative model with $F(s) = \frac{1}{2}s^2$ in Eq. 6, it can be shown that the weights are exactly zero, $W = 0$, for $\sigma^2 > 1$.

Thus, the size of the optimal generative weights W varies with σ^2 as shown qualitatively in Fig. 2. Above a certain critical noise value $\sigma_c^2 \approx 1$, the weights are exactly equal to

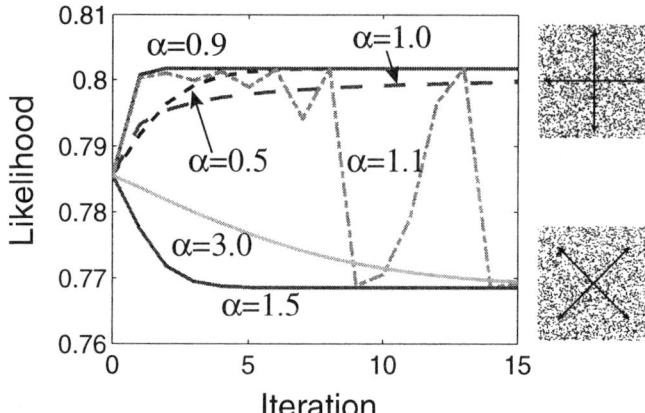

Figure 3: Convergence of the modified EM algorithm as a function of α. With $g(s) = \tanh(s)$ as the nonlinearity, the likelihood $\langle \ln \cosh(W^T x) \rangle$ is plotted as a function of the iteration number. The optimal basis W are plotted on the two-dimensional data distribution when the likelihood is maximized (top) and minimized (bottom).

zero, $W = 0$. Only below this critical value do the weights become nonzero. We expand the likelihood of the generative model in the vicinity of this singular point. This expansion is well-behaved because the size of the generative weights W acts as a small perturbative parameter in this expansion. The log likelihood of the model around this singular value is then given by:

$$L = -\frac{1}{4}\text{Tr}\left[WW^T - (1-\sigma^2)I\right]^2 \tag{21}$$
$$+\frac{1}{4!}\sum_{ijklm} \text{kurt}(s_m) \langle x_i x_j x_k x_l \rangle_c W_{im} W_{jm} W_{km} W_{lm}$$
$$+O(1-\sigma^2)^3,$$

where $\text{kurt}(s_m)$ represents the kurtosis of the prior distribution over the hidden variables. Note that this expansion is valid for any symmetric prior, and differs from other expansions that assume small deviations from a Gaussian prior [12, 13]. Eq. 21 shows the importance of the fourth-order cumulant of the observed data in breaking the rotational degeneracy of the weights W. The generic behavior of ICA is manifest in optimizing the cumulant term in Eq.21, and again depends crucially on the sign of the kurtosis that is used for the prior.

Example with artificial data

As an illustration of the convergence of the algorithm in Eq. 17, we consider the simple two-dimensional uniform distribution:

$$P(x_1, x_2) = \begin{cases} 1/12, & -\sqrt{3} \leq x_1, x_2 \leq \sqrt{3} \\ 0, & \text{otherwise} \end{cases} \tag{22}$$

With $g(s) = \tanh(s)$ as the nonlinearity, Fig. 3 shows how the overall likelihood converges for different values of the parameter α as the algorithm is iterated. For $\alpha \leq 1.0$, the algorithm converges to a maximum of the likelihood, with the fastest convergence at $\alpha_{opt} = 0.9$. However, for $\alpha > 1.2$, the algorithm converges to a minimum of the likelihood. At an intermediate value, $\alpha = 1.1$, the likelihood does not converge at all, fluctuating wildly between the maximum and minimum likelihood solutions. The maximum likelihood solution shows the basis vectors in W aligned with the sides of the square distribution, whereas the minimum likelihood solution has the basis aligned with the diagonals. These solutions can also be understood as maximizing and minimizing the kurtosis terms in Eq. 21.

Discussion

The utility of the latent variable generative model is demonstrated on deriving algorithms for ICA. By constraining the generative weights to be orthogonal, an EM algorithm is analytically obtained. By interpreting the data to be fitted as a mixture of isotropic and non-isotropic parts, a simple correction to the EM algorithm is derived. Under certain conditions, this modified algorithm is equivalent to the Fixed Point ICA algorithm, and converges much more rapidly than the naive EM algorithm. The optimal parameter for convergence is derived assuming the data is consistent with the ICA generative model. There also exists a critical value for the noise parameter in the generative model, about which a controlled expansion of the likelihood is possible. This expansion makes clear the role of higher order statistics in determining the generic behavior of different ICA algorithms.

We acknowledge the support of Bell Laboratories, Lucent Technologies, the US-Israel Binational Science Foundation, and the Israel Science Foundation. We also thank Hagai Attias, Simon Haykin, Juha Karhunen, Te-Won Lee, Erkki Oja, Sebastian Seung, Boris Shraiman, and Oren Shriki for helpful discussions.

References

[1] Haykin, S (1999). *Neural networks: a comprehensive foundation.* 2nd ed., Prentice-Hall, Upper Saddle River, NJ.

[2] Jutten, C & Herault, J (1991). Blind separation of sources, part I: An adaptive algorithm based on neuromimetic architecture. *Signal Processing* **24**, 1–10.

[3] Comon, P (1994). Independent component analysis: a new concept? *Signal Processing* **36**, 287–314.

[4] Roth, Z & Baram, Y (1996). Multidimensional density shaping by sigmoids. *IEEE Trans. Neural Networks* **7**, 1291–1298.

[5] Bell, AJ & Sejnowski, TJ (1995). An information maximization approach to blind separation and blind deconvolution. *Neural Computation* **7**, 1129–1159.

[6] Amari, S, Cichocki, A & Yang, H (1996). A new learning algorithm for blind signal separation. *Advances in Neural Information Processing Systems* **8**, 757–763.

[7] Lee, TW, Girolami, M, & Sejnowski, TJ (1999). Independent component analysis using an extended infomax algorithm for mixed sub-gaussian and super-gaussian sources. *Neural Computation* **11**, 609–633.

[8] Hyvarinen, A & Oja, E (1997). A fast fixed-point algorithm for independent component analysis. *Neural Computation* **9**, 1483–1492.

[9] Hinton, G & Ghahramani, Z (1997). Generative models for discovering sparse distributed representations. *Philosophical Transactions Royal Society B* **352**, 1177–1190.

[10] Attias, H (1998). Independent factor analysis. *Neural Computation* **11**, 803–851.

[11] Pearlmutter, B & Parra, L (1996). A context-sensitive generalization of ICA. In ICONIP '96, 151–157.

[12] Nadal, JP & Parga, N (1997). Redundancy reduction and independent component analysis: conditions on cumulants and adaptive approaches. *Neural Computation* **9**, 1421–1456.

[13] Cardoso, JF (1999). High-order contrasts for independent component analysis. *Neural Computation* **11**, 157–192.

The Relaxed Online Maximum Margin Algorithm

Yi Li and Philip M. Long
Department of Computer Science
National University of Singapore
Singapore 119260, Republic of Singapore
{*liyi,plong*}@*comp.nus.edu.sg*

Abstract

We describe a new incremental algorithm for training linear threshold functions: the Relaxed Online Maximum Margin Algorithm, or ROMMA. ROMMA can be viewed as an approximation to the algorithm that repeatedly chooses the hyperplane that classifies previously seen examples correctly with the maximum margin. It is known that such a maximum-margin hypothesis can be computed by minimizing the length of the weight vector subject to a number of linear constraints. ROMMA works by maintaining a relatively simple relaxation of these constraints that can be efficiently updated. We prove a mistake bound for ROMMA that is the same as that proved for the perceptron algorithm. Our analysis implies that the more computationally intensive maximum-margin algorithm also satisfies this mistake bound; this is the first worst-case performance guarantee for this algorithm. We describe some experiments using ROMMA and a variant that updates its hypothesis more aggressively as batch algorithms to recognize handwritten digits. The computational complexity and simplicity of these algorithms is similar to that of perceptron algorithm, but their generalization is much better. We describe a sense in which the performance of ROMMA converges to that of SVM in the limit if bias isn't considered.

1 Introduction

The perceptron algorithm [10, 11] is well-known for its simplicity and effectiveness in the case of linearly separable data. Vapnik's support vector machines (SVM) [13] use quadratic programming to find the weight vector that classifies all the training data correctly and maximizes the margin, i.e. the minimal distance between the separating hyperplane and the instances. This algorithm is slower than the perceptron algorithm, but generalizes better. On the other hand, as an incremental algorithm, the perceptron algorithm is better suited for online learning, where the algorithm repeatedly must classify patterns one at a time, then finds out the correct classification, and then updates its hypothesis before making the next prediction.

In this paper, we design and analyze a new simple online algorithm called ROMMA (the **R**elaxed **O**nline **M**aximum **M**argin **A**lgorithm) for classification using a linear threshold function. ROMMA has similar time complexity to the perceptron algorithm, but its generalization performance in our experiments is much better on average. Moreover, ROMMA can be applied with kernel functions.

We conducted experiments similar to those performed by Cortes and Vapnik [2] and Freund and Schapire [3] on the problem of handwritten digit recognition. We tested the standard perceptron algorithm, the voted perceptron algorithm (for details, see [3]) and our new algorithm, using the polynomial kernel function with $d = 4$ (the choice that was best in [3]). We found that our new algorithm performed better than the standard perceptron algorithm, had slightly better performance than the voted perceptron.

For some other research with aims similar to ours, we refer the reader to [9, 4, 5, 6].

The paper is organized as follows. In Section 2, we describe ROMMA in enough detail to determine its predictions, and prove a mistake bound for it. In Section 3, we describe ROMMA in more detail. In Section 4, we compare the experimental results of ROMMA and an aggressive variant of ROMMA with the perceptron and the voted perceptron algorithms.

2 A mistake-bound analysis

2.1 The online algorithms

For concreteness, our analysis will concern the case in which instances (also called patterns) and weight vectors are in $\mathbf{R}^n$. Fix $n \in \mathbf{N}$. In the standard online learning model [7], learning proceeds in *trials*. In the tth trial, the algorithm is first presented with an instance $\vec{x}_t \in \mathbf{R}^n$. Next, the algorithm outputs a prediction $\hat{y}_t$ of the classification of $\vec{x}_t$. Finally, the algorithm finds out the correct classification $y_t \in \{-1, 1\}$. If $\hat{y}_t \neq y_t$, then we say that the algorithm makes a mistake. It is worth emphasizing that in this model, when making its prediction for the tth trial, the algorithm only has access to instance-classification pairs for previous trials.

All of the online algorithms that we will consider work by maintaining a weight vector $\vec{w}_t$ which is updated between trials, and predicting $\hat{y}_t = \text{sign}(\vec{w}_t \cdot \vec{x}_t)$, where $\text{sign}(z)$ is 1 if z is positive, -1 if z is negative, and 0 otherwise.[1]

The perceptron algorithm. The perceptron algorithm, due to Rosenblatt [10, 11], starts off with $\vec{w}_1 = 0$. When its prediction differs from the label y_t, it updates its weight vector by $\vec{w}_{t+1} = \vec{w}_t + y_t \vec{x}_t$. If the prediction is correct then the weight vector is not changed.

The next three algorithms that we will consider assume that all of the data seen by the online algorithm is collectively linearly separable, i.e. that there is a weight vector $\vec{u}$ such that for all each trial t, $y_t = \text{sign}(\vec{u} \cdot \vec{x}_t)$. When kernel functions are used, this is often the case in practice.

The ideal online maximum margin algorithm. On each trial t, this algorithm chooses a weight vector $\vec{w}_t$ for which for all previous trials $s \leq t$, $\text{sign}(\vec{w}_t \cdot \vec{x}_s) = y_s$, and which maximizes the minimum distance of any $\vec{x}_s$ to the separating hyperplane. It is known [1, 14] that this can be implemented by choosing $\vec{w}_t$ to minimize $\|\vec{w}_t\|$ subject to the constraints that $y_s(\vec{w}_t \cdot \vec{x}_s) \geq 1$ for all $s \leq t$. These constraints define a convex polyhedron in weight space which we will refer to as P_t.

The relaxed online maximum margin algorithm. This is our new algorithm. The first difference is that trials in which mistakes are not made are ignored. The second difference

---

[1]The prediction of 0, which ensures a mistake, is to make the proofs simpler. The usual mistake bound proof for the perceptron algorithm goes through with this change.

is in how the algorithm responds to mistakes. The relaxed algorithm starts off like the ideal algorithm. Before the second trial, it sets $\vec{w}_2$ to be the shortest weight vector such that $y_1(\vec{w}_2 \cdot \vec{x}_1) \geq 1$. If there is a mistake on the second trial, it chooses $\vec{w}_3$ as would the ideal algorithm, to be the smallest element of

$$\{\vec{w} : y_1(\vec{w} \cdot \vec{x}_1) \geq 1\} \cap \{\vec{w} : y_2(\vec{w} \cdot \vec{x}_2) \geq 1\}. \tag{1}$$

However, if the third trial is a mistake, then it behaves differently. Instead of choosing $\vec{w}_4$ to be the smallest element of

$$\{\vec{w} : y_1(\vec{w} \cdot \vec{x}_1) \geq 1\} \cap \{\vec{w} : y_2(\vec{w} \cdot \vec{x}_2) \geq 1\} \cap \{\vec{w} : y_3(\vec{w} \cdot \vec{x}_3) \geq 1\},$$

it lets $\vec{w}_4$ be the smallest element of

$$\{\vec{w} : \vec{w}_3 \cdot \vec{w} \geq ||\vec{w}_3||^2\} \cap \{\vec{w} : y_3(\vec{w} \cdot \vec{x}_3) \geq 1\}.$$

This can be thought of as, before the third trial, replacing the polyhedron defined by (1) with the halfspace $\{\vec{w} : \vec{w}_3 \cdot \vec{w} \geq ||\vec{w}_3||^2\}$ (see Figure 1).

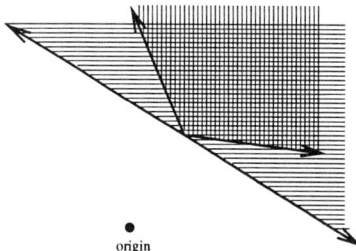

Figure 1: In ROMMA, a convex polyhedron in weight space is replaced with the halfspace with the same smallest element.

Note that this halfspace contains the polyhedron of (1); in fact, it contains any convex set whose smallest element is $\vec{w}_3$. Thus, it can be thought of as the least restrictive convex constraint for which the smallest satisfying weight vector is $\vec{w}_3$. Let us call this halfspace H_3. The algorithm continues in this manner. If the tth trial is a mistake, then $\vec{w}_{t+1}$ is chosen to be the smallest element of $H_t \cap \{\vec{w} : y_t(\vec{w} \cdot \vec{x}_t) \geq 1\}$, and H_{t+1} is set to be $\{\vec{w} : \vec{w}_{t+1} \cdot \vec{w} \geq ||\vec{w}_{t+1}||^2\}$. If the tth trial is not a mistake, then $\vec{w}_{t+1} = \vec{w}_t$ and $H_{t+1} = H_t$. We will call H_t the old constraint, and $\{\vec{w} : y_t(\vec{w} \cdot \vec{x}_t) \geq 1\}$ the new constraint.

Note that after each mistake, this algorithm needs only to solve a quadratic programming problem with two linear constraints. In fact, there is a simple closed-form expression for $\vec{w}_{t+1}$ as a function of $\vec{w}_t$, $\vec{x}_t$ and y_t that enables it to be computed incrementally using time similar to that of the perceptron algorithm. This is described in Section 3.

The relaxed online maximum margin algorithm with aggressive updating. The algorithm is the same as the previous algorithm, except that an update is made after any trial in which $y_t(\vec{w}_t \cdot \vec{x}_t) < 1$, not just after mistakes.

2.2 Upper bound on the number of mistakes made

Now we prove a bound on the number of mistakes made by ROMMA. As in previous mistake bound proofs (e.g. [8]), we will show that mistakes result in an increase in a "measure of progress", and then appeal to a bound on the total possible progress. Our proof will use the squared length of $\vec{w}_t$ as its measure of progress.

First we will need the following lemmas.

Lemma 1 *On any run of ROMMA on linearly separable data, if trial t was a mistake, then the new constraint is binding at the new weight vector, i.e. $y_t(\vec{w}_{t+1} \cdot \vec{x}_t) = 1$.*

Proof: For the purpose of contradiction suppose the new constraint is not binding at the new weight vector $\vec{w}_{t+1}$. Since $\vec{w}_t$ fails to satisfy this constraint, the line connecting $\vec{w}_{t+1}$ and $\vec{w}_t$ intersects with the border hyperplane of the new constraint, and we denote the intersecting point $\vec{w}_q$. Then $\vec{w}_q$ can be represented as $\vec{w}_q = \alpha \vec{w}_t + (1-\alpha)\vec{w}_{t+1}, 0 < \alpha < 1$.

Since the square of Euclidean length $\|\cdot\|^2$ is a convex function, the following holds:

$$\|\vec{w}_q\|^2 \leq \alpha \|\vec{w}_t\|^2 + (1-\alpha)\|\vec{w}_{t+1}\|^2$$

Since $\vec{w}_t$ is the unique smallest member of H_t and $\vec{w}_{t+1} \neq \vec{w}_t$, we have $\|\vec{w}_t\|^2 < \|\vec{w}_{t+1}\|^2$, which implies

$$\|\vec{w}_q\|^2 < \|\vec{w}_{t+1}\|^2 \tag{2}$$

Since $\vec{w}_t$ and $\vec{w}_{t+1}$ are both in H_t, $\vec{w}_q$ is too, and hence (2) contradicts the definition of $\vec{w}_{t+1}$. □

Lemma 2 *On any run of ROMMA on linearly separable data, if trial t was a mistake, and not the first one, then the old constraint is binding at the new weight vector, i.e.* $\vec{w}_{t+1} \cdot \vec{w}_t = \|\vec{w}_t\|^2$.

Proof: Let A_t be the plane of weight vectors that make the new constraint tight, i.e. $A_t = \{\vec{w} : y_t(\vec{w} \cdot \vec{x}_t) = 1\}$. By Lemma 1, $\vec{w}_{t+1} \in A_t$. Let $\vec{a}_t = y_t \vec{x}_t / \|\vec{x}_t\|^2$ be the element of A_t that is perpendicular to it. Then each $\vec{w} \in A_t$ satisfies $\|\vec{w}\|^2 = \|\vec{a}_t\|^2 + \|\vec{w} - \vec{a}_t\|^2$, and therefore the length of a vector $\vec{w}$ in A_t is minimized when $\vec{w} = \vec{a}_t$ and is monotone in the distance from $\vec{w}$ to $\vec{a}_t$. Thus, if the old constraint is not binding, then $\vec{w}_{t+1} = \vec{a}_t$, since otherwise the solution could be improved by moving $\vec{w}_{t+1}$ a little bit toward $\vec{a}_t$. But the old constraint requires that $(\vec{w}_t \cdot \vec{w}_{t+1}) \geq \|\vec{w}_t\|^2$, and if $\vec{w}_{t+1} = \vec{a}_t = y_t \vec{x}_t / \|\vec{x}_t\|^2$, this means that $\vec{w}_t \cdot (y_t \vec{x}_t / \|\vec{x}_t\|^2) \geq \|\vec{w}_t\|^2$. Rearranging, we get $y_t(\vec{w}_t \cdot \vec{x}_t) \geq \|\vec{x}_t\|^2 \|\vec{w}_t\|^2 > 0$ ($\|x_t\| > 0$ follows from the fact that the data is linearly separable, and $\|w_t\| > 0$ follows from the fact that there was at least one previous mistake). But since trial t was a mistake, $y_t(\vec{w}_t \cdot \vec{x}_t) \leq 0$, a contradiction. □

Now we're ready to prove the mistake bound.

Theorem 3 *Choose* $m \in \mathbf{N}$, *and a sequence* $(\vec{x}_1, y_1), \cdots, (\vec{x}_m, y_m)$ *of pattern-classification pairs in* $\mathbf{R}^n \times \{-1, +1\}$. *Let* $R = \max_t \|\vec{x}_t\|$. *If there is a weight vector* $\vec{u}$ *such that* $y_t(\vec{u} \cdot \vec{x}_t) \geq 1$ *for all* $1 \leq t \leq m$, *then the number of mistakes made by ROMMA on* $(\vec{x}_1, y_1), \cdots, (\vec{x}_m, y_m)$ *is at most* $R^2 \|\vec{u}\|^2$.

Proof: First, we claim that for all t, $\vec{u} \in H_t$. This is easily seen since $\vec{u}$ satisfies all the constraints that are ever imposed on a weight vector, and therefore all relaxations of such constraints. Since $\vec{w}_t$ is the smallest element of H_t, we have $\|\vec{w}_t\| \leq \|\vec{u}\|$.

We have $\vec{w}_2 = y_1 \vec{x}_1 / \|\vec{x}_1\|^2$, and therefore $\|\vec{w}_2\| = 1/\|\vec{x}_1\| \geq 1/R$ which implies $\|\vec{w}_2\|^2 \geq 1/R^2$. We claim that if any trial $t > 1$ is a mistake, then $\|\vec{w}_{t+1}\|^2 \geq \|\vec{w}_t\|^2 + 1/R^2$. This will imply by induction that after M mistakes, the squared length of the algorithm's weight vector is at least M/R^2, which, since all of the algorithm's weight vectors are no longer than $\vec{u}$, will complete the proof.

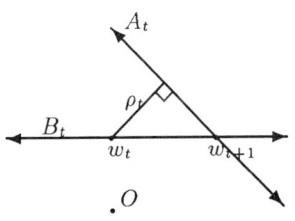

Figure 2: A_t, B_t, and ρ_t

Choose an index $t > 1$ of a trial in which a mistake is made. Let $A_t = \{\vec{w} : y_t(\vec{w} \cdot \vec{x}_t) = 1\}$ and $B_t = \{\vec{w} : (\vec{w} \cdot \vec{w}_t) = \|\vec{w}_t\|^2\}$. By Lemmas 1 and 2, $\vec{w}_{t+1} \in A_t \cap B_t$.

The distance from $\vec{w}_t$ to A_t (call it ρ_t) satisfies

$$\rho_t = \frac{|y_t(\vec{x}_t \cdot \vec{w}_t) - 1|}{\|\vec{x}_t\|} \geq \frac{1}{\|\vec{x}_t\|} \geq \frac{1}{R}, \tag{3}$$

since the fact that there was a mistake in trial t implies $y_t(\vec{x}_t \cdot \vec{w}_t) \leq 0$. Also, since $\vec{w}_{t+1} \in A_t$,

$$\|w_{t+1} - w_t\| \geq \rho_t. \tag{4}$$

Because $\vec{w}_t$ is the normal vector of B_t and $\vec{w}_{t+1} \in B_t$, we have

$$\|\vec{w}_{t+1}\|^2 = \|\vec{w}_t\|^2 + \|\vec{w}_{t+1} - \vec{w}_t\|^2.$$

Thus, applying (3) and (4), we have $\|\vec{w}_{t+1}\|^2 - \|\vec{w}_t\|^2 = \|\vec{w}_{t+1} - \vec{w}_t\|^2 \geq \rho_t^2 \geq 1/R^2$, which, as discussed above, completes the proof. $\square$

Using the fact, easily proved using induction, that for all t, $P_t \subseteq H_t$, we can easily prove the following, which complements analyses of the maximum margin algorithm using independence assumptions [1, 14, 12]. Details are omitted due to space constraints.

Theorem 4 *Choose* $m \in \mathbf{N}$, *and a sequence* $(\vec{x}_1, y_1), \cdots, (\vec{x}_m, y_m)$ *of pattern-classification pairs in* $\mathbf{R}^n \times \{-1, +1\}$. *Let* $R = \max_t \|\vec{x}_t\|$. *If there is a weight vector* $\vec{u}$ *such that* $y_t(\vec{u} \cdot \vec{x}_t) \geq 1$ *for all* $1 \leq t \leq m$, *then the number of mistakes made by the ideal online maximum margin algorithm on* $(\vec{x}_1, y_1), \cdots, (\vec{x}_m, y_m)$ *is at most* $R^2 \|\vec{u}\|^2$.

In the proof of Theorem 3, if an update is made and $y_t(\vec{w}_t \cdot \vec{x}_t) < 1 - \delta$ instead of $y_t(\vec{w}_t \cdot \vec{x}_t) \leq 0$, then the progress made can be seen to be at least δ^2/R^2. This can be applied to prove the following.

Theorem 5 *Choose* $\delta > 0$, $m \in \mathbf{N}$, *and a sequence* $(\vec{x}_1, y_1), \cdots, (\vec{x}_m, y_m)$ *of pattern-classification pairs in* $\mathbf{R}^n \times \{-1, +1\}$. *Let* $R = \max_t \|\vec{x}_t\|$. *If there is a weight vector* $\vec{u}$ *such that* $y_t(\vec{u} \cdot \vec{x}_t) \geq 1$ *for all* $1 \leq t \leq m$, *then if* $(\vec{x}_1, y_1), \cdots, (\vec{x}_m, y_m)$ *are presented on line the number of trials in which aggressive ROMMA has* $y_t(\vec{w}_t \cdot \vec{x}_t) < 1 - \delta$ *is at most* $R^2 \|\vec{u}\|^2/\delta^2$.

Theorem 5 implies that, in a sense, repeatedly cycling through a dataset using aggressive ROMMA will eventually converge to SVM; note however that bias is not considered.

3 An efficient implementation

When the prediction of ROMMA differs from the expected label, the algorithm chooses $\vec{w}_{t+1}$ to minimize $\|\vec{w}_{t+1}\|$ subject to $A\vec{w}_{t+1} = b$, where $A = \begin{pmatrix} \vec{w}_t^T \\ \vec{x}_t^T \end{pmatrix}$ and $b = \begin{pmatrix} \|\vec{w}_t\|^2 \\ y_t \end{pmatrix}$. Simple calculation shows that

$$\vec{w}_{t+1} = A^T(AA^T)^{-1}b$$
$$= \left(\frac{\|\vec{x}_t\|^2 \|\vec{w}_t\|^2 - y_t(\vec{w}_t \cdot \vec{x}_t)}{\|\vec{x}_t\|^2 \|\vec{w}_t\|^2 - (\vec{w}_t \cdot \vec{x}_t)^2}\right) \vec{w}_t + \left(\frac{\|\vec{w}_t\|^2 (y_t - (\vec{w}_t \cdot \vec{x}_t))}{\|\vec{x}_t\|^2 \|\vec{w}_t\|^2 - (\vec{w}_t \cdot \vec{x}_t)^2}\right) \vec{x}_t. \quad (5)$$

If on trials t in which a mistake is made, $c_t = \frac{\|\vec{x}_t\|^2 \|\vec{w}_t\|^2 - y_t(\vec{w}_t \cdot \vec{x}_t)}{\|\vec{x}_t\|^2 \|\vec{w}_t\|^2 - (\vec{w}_t \cdot \vec{x}_t)^2}$ and $d_t = \frac{\|\vec{w}_t\|^2 (y_t - (\vec{w}_t \cdot \vec{x}_t))}{\|\vec{x}_t\|^2 \|\vec{w}_t\|^2 - (\vec{w}_t \cdot \vec{x}_t)^2}$, and on other trials $c_t = 1$ and $d_t = 0$, then always $\vec{w}_{t+1} = c_t \vec{w}_t + d_t \vec{x}_t$. Note that based on Lemmas 1 and 2, the denominators in (5) will never be equal to zero.

Since the computations required by ROMMA involve inner products together with a few operations on scalars, we can apply the kernel method to our algorithm, efficiently solving the original problem in a very high dimensional space. Computationally, we only need to modify the algorithm by replacing each inner product computation $(\vec{x}_i \cdot \vec{x}_j)$ with a kernel function computation $\mathcal{K}(\vec{x}_i, \vec{x}_j)$.

To make a prediction for the tth trial, the algorithm must compute the inner product between $\vec{x}_t$ and prediction vector $\vec{w}_t$. In order to apply the kernel function, as in [1, 3], we store each prediction vector $\vec{w}_t$ in an implicit manner, as the weighted sum of examples on which mistakes occur during the training. In particular, each $\vec{w}_t$ is represented as

$$\vec{w}_t = \left(\prod_{j=1}^{t-1} c_j\right) \vec{w}_1 + \sum_{j=1}^{t-1} \left(\prod_{n=j+1}^{t-1} c_n\right) d_j \vec{x}_j$$

The above formula may seem daunting; however, making use of the recurrence $(\vec{w}_{t+1} \cdot \vec{x}) = c_t(\vec{w}_t \cdot \vec{x}) + d_t(\vec{x}_t \cdot \vec{x})$, it is obvious that the complexity of our new algorithm is similar to that of perceptron algorithm. This was born out by our experiments.

The implementation for aggressive ROMMA is similar to the above.

4 Experiments

We did some experiments using the ROMMA and aggressive ROMMA as batch algorithms on the MNIST OCR database.[2] We obtained a batch algorithm from our online algorithm in the usual way, making a number of passes over the dataset and using the final weight vector to classify the test data.

Every example in this database has two parts, the first is a 28×28 matrix which represents the image of the corresponding digit. Each entry in the matrix takes value from $\{0, \cdots, 255\}$. The second part is a label taking a value from $\{0, \cdots, 9\}$. The dataset consists of $60,000$ training examples and $10,000$ test examples. We adopt the following polynomial kernel: $\mathcal{K}(\vec{x}_i, \vec{x}_j) = (1 + (\vec{x}_i \cdot \vec{x}_j))^d$. This corresponds to using an expanded collection of features including all products of at most d components of the original feature vector (see [14]). Let us refer to the mapping from the original feature vector to the expanded feature vector as Φ. Note that one component of $\Phi(\vec{x})$ is always 1, and therefore the component of the weight vector corresponding to that component can be viewed as a bias. In our experiments, we set $\vec{w}_1 = \Phi(\vec{0})$ rather than $\vec{0}$ to speed up the learning of the coefficient corresponding to the bias. We chose $d = 4$ since in experiments on the same problem conducted in [3, 2], the best results occur with this value.

To cope with multiclass data, we trained ROMMA and aggressive ROMMA once for each of the 10 labels. Classification of an unknown pattern is done according to the maximum output of these ten classifiers.

As every entry in the image matrix takes value from $\{0, \cdots, 255\}$, the order of magnitude of $\mathcal{K}(\vec{x}, \vec{x})$ is at least 10^{26}, which might cause round-off error in the computation of c_i and d_i. We scale the data by dividing each entry with 1100 when training with ROMMA.

Table 1: Experimental results on MNIST data

	$T=1$		$T=2$		$T=3$		$T=4$	
	Err	MisNo	Err	MisNo	Err	MisNo	Err	MisNo
percep	2.84	7970	2.27	10539	1.99	11945	1.85	12800
voted-percep	2.26	7970	1.88	10539	1.76	11945	1.69	12800
ROMMA	2.48	7963	1.96	9995	1.79	10971	1.77	11547
agg-ROMMA	2.14	6077	1.82	7391	1.71	7901	1.67	8139
agg-ROMMA(NC)	2.05	5909	1.76	6979	1.67	7339	1.63	7484

Since the performance of online learning is affected by the order of sample sequence, all the results shown in Table 1 average over 10 random permutations. The columns marked

---

[2]National Institute for Standards and Technology, special database 3. See http://www.research.att.com/~yann/ocr for information on obtaining this dataset.

"MisNo" in Table 1 show the total number of mistakes made during the training for the 10 labels. Although online learning would involve only one epoch, we present results for a batch setting until four epochs (T in Table 1 represents the number of epochs).

To deal with data which are linearly inseparable in the feature space, and also to improve generalization, Friess et al [4] suggested the use of quadratic penalty in the cost function, which can be implemented using a slightly different kernel function [4, 5]: $\tilde{\mathcal{K}}(x_k, x_j) = \mathcal{K}(x_k, x_j) + \delta_{kj}\lambda$, where δ_{kj} is the Kronecker delta function. The last row in Table 1 is the result of aggressive ROMMA using this method to control noise ($\lambda = 30$ for 10 classifiers).

We conducted three groups of experiments, one for the perceptron algorithm (denoted "percep"), the second for the voted perceptron (denoted "voted-percep") whose description is in [3], the third for ROMMA, aggressive ROMMA (denoted "agg-ROMMA"), and aggressive ROMMA with noise control (denoted "agg-ROMMA(NC)"). Data in the third group are scaled. All three groups set $\vec{w}_1 = \Phi(\vec{0})$.

The results in Table 1 demonstrate that ROMMA has better performance than the standard perceptron, aggressive ROMMA has slightly better performance than the voted perceptron. Aggressive ROMMA with noise control should not be compared with perceptrons without noise control. Its presentation is used to show what performance our new online algorithm could achieve (of course it's not the best, since all 10 classifiers use the same λ). A remarkable phenomenon is that our new algorithm behaves very well at the first two epochs.

References

[1] B. E. Boser, I. M. Guyon, and V. N. Vapnik. A training algorithm for optimal margin classifiers. *Proceedings of the 1992 Workshop on Computational Learning Theory*, pages 144–152, 1992.

[2] C. Cortes and V. Vapnik. Support-vector networks. *Machine Learning*, 20(3):273–297, 1995.

[3] Y. Freund and R. E. Schapire. Large margin classification using the perceptron algorithm. *Proceedings of the 1998 Conference on Computational Learning Theory*, 1998.

[4] T. T. Friess, N. Cristianini, and C. Campbell. The kernel adatron algorithm: a fast and simple learning procedure for support vector machines. In *Proc. 15th Int. Conf. on Machine Learning*. Morgan Kaufman Publishers, 1998.

[5] S. S. Keerthi, S. K. Shevade, C. Bhattacharyya, and K. R. K. Murthy. A fast iterative nearest point algorithm for support vector machine classiifer design. Technical report, Indian Institute of Science, 99. TR-ISL-99-03.

[6] Adam Kowalczyk. Maximal margin perceptron. In Smola, Bartlett, Scholkopf, and Schuurmans, editors, *Advances in Large Margin Classifiers*, 1999. MIT-Press.

[7] N. Littlestone. Learning quickly when irrelevant attributes abound: a new linear-threshold algorithm. *Machine Learning*, 2:285–318, 1988.

[8] N. Littlestone. *Mistake Bounds and Logarithmic Linear-threshold Learning Algorithms*. PhD thesis, UC Santa Cruz, 1989.

[9] John C. Platt. Fast training of support vector machines using sequential minimal optimization. In B. Scholkopf, C. Burges, A. Smola, editors, *Advances in Kernel Methods: Support Vector Machines*, 1998. MIT Press.

[10] F. Rosenblatt. The perceptron: A probabilistic model for information storage and organization in the brain. *Psychological Review*, 65:386–407, 1958.

[11] F. Rosenblatt. *Principles of Neurodynamics: Perceptrons and the Theory of Brain Mechanisms*. Spartan Books, Washington, D. C., 1962.

[12] J. Shawe-Taylor, P. Bartlett, R. Williamson, and M. Anthony. A framework for structural risk minimization. In *Proc. of the 1996 Conference on Computational Learning Theory*, 1996.

[13] V. N. Vapnik. *Estimation of Dependencies based on Empirical Data*. Springer Verlag, 1982.

[14] V. N. Vapnik. *The Nature of Statistical Learning Theory*. Springer, 1995.

Bayesian Network Induction via Local Neighborhoods

Dimitris Margaritis
Department of Computer Science
Carnegie Mellon University
Pittsburgh, PA 15213
D.Margaritis@cs.cmu.edu

Sebastian Thrun
Department of Computer Science
Carnegie Mellon University
Pittsburgh, PA 15213
S.Thrun@cs.cmu.edu

Abstract

In recent years, Bayesian networks have become highly successful tool for diagnosis, analysis, and decision making in real-world domains. We present an efficient algorithm for learning Bayes networks from data. Our approach constructs Bayesian networks by first identifying each node's Markov blankets, then connecting nodes in a maximally consistent way. In contrast to the majority of work, which typically uses hill-climbing approaches that may produce dense and causally incorrect nets, our approach yields much more compact causal networks by heeding independencies in the data. Compact causal networks facilitate fast inference and are also easier to understand. We prove that under mild assumptions, our approach requires time polynomial in the size of the data and the number of nodes. A randomized variant, also presented here, yields comparable results at much higher speeds.

1 Introduction

A great number of scientific fields today benefit from being able to automatically estimate the probability of certain quantities of interest that may be difficult or expensive to observe directly. For example, a doctor may be interested in estimating the probability of heart disease from indications of high blood pressure and other directly measurable quantities. A computer vision system may benefit from a probability distribution of buildings based on indicators of horizontal and vertical straight lines. Probability densities proliferate the sciences today and advances in its estimation are likely to have a wide impact on many different fields.

Bayesian networks are a succinct and efficient way to represent a joint probability distribution among a set of variables. As such, they have been applied to fields such as those mentioned [Herskovits90][Agosta88]. Besides their ability for density estimation, their semantics lend them to what is sometimes loosely referred to as *causal discovery*, namely directional relationships among quantities involved. It has been widely accepted that the most parsimonious representation for a Bayesian net is one that closely represents the causal independence relationships that may exist. For these reasons, there has been great interest in automatically inducing the structure of Bayesian nets automatically from data, preferably also preserving the independence relationships in the process.

Two research approaches have emerged. The first employs independence properties of the underlying network that produced the data in order to discover parts of its structure. This approach is mainly exemplified by the SGS and PC algorithms in [Spirtes93], as well

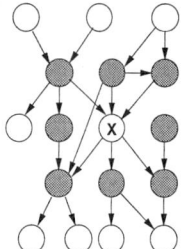 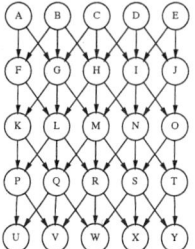 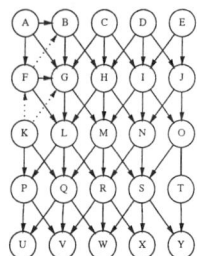

Figure 1: On the left, an example of a Markov blanket of variable X is shown. The members of the blanket are shown shaded. On the right, an example reconstruction of a 5×5 rectangular net of branching factor 3 by the algorithm presented in this paper using 20000 samples. Indicated by dotted lines are 3 directionality errors.

as for restricted classes such as trees [Chow68] and polytrees [Rebane87]. The second approach is concerned more with data prediction, disregarding independencies in the data. It is typically identified with a greedy hill-climbing or best-first beam search in the space of legal structures, employing as a scoring function a form of data likelihood, sometimes penalized for network complexity. The result is a local maximum score network structure for representing the data, and is one of the more popular techniques used today.

This paper presents an approach that belongs in the first category. It addresses the two main shortcomings of the prior work which, we believe, are preventing its use from becoming more widespread. These two disadvantages are: exponential execution times, and proneness to errors in dependence tests used. The former problem is addressed in this paper in two ways. One is by identifying the local neighborhood of each variable in the Bayesian net as a preprocessing step, in order to facilitate the recovery of the local structure around each variable in polynomial time under the assumption of bounded neighborhood size. The second, randomized version goes one step further, employing a user-specified number of randomized tests (constant or logarithmic) in order to ascertain the same result with high probability. The second disadvantage of this research approach, namely proneness to errors, is also addressed by the randomized version, by using multiple data sets (if available) and Bayesian accumulation of evidence.

2   The Grow-Shrink Markov Blanket Algorithm

The concept of the *Markov blanket* of a variable or a set of variables is central to this paper. The concept itself is not new. For example, see [Pearl88]. It is surprising, however, how little attention it has attracted for all its being a fundamental property of a Bayesian net. What is new in this paper is the introduction of the explicit use of this idea to effectively limit unnecessary computation, as well as a simple algorithm to compute it. The definition of a Markov blanket is as follows: denoting $\mathbf{V}$ as the set of variables and $X \leftrightarrow_\mathbf{S} Y$ as the conditional dependence of X and Y given the set $\mathbf{S}$, the Markov blanket $\mathbf{BL}(X) \subseteq \mathbf{V}$ of $X \in \mathbf{V}$ is any set of variables such that for any $Y \in \mathbf{V} - \mathbf{BL}(X) - \{X\}$, $X \not\leftrightarrow_{\mathbf{BL}(X)} Y$. In other words, $\mathbf{BL}(X)$ completely shields variable X from any other variable in $\mathbf{V}$. The notion of a *minimal Markov blanket*, called a *Markov boundary*, is also introduced in [Pearl88] and its uniqueness shown under certain conditions. The Markov boundary is not unique in certain pathological situations, such as the equality of two variables. In our following discussion we will assume that the conditions necessary for its existence and uniqueness are satisfied and we will identify the Markov blanket with the Markov boundary, using the notation $\mathbf{B}(X)$ for the blanket of variable X from now on. It is also illuminating to mention that, in the Bayesian net framework, the Markov blanket of a node X is easily identifiable from the graph: it consists of all parents, children and parents of children of X. An example Markov blanket is shown in Fig. 1. Note that any of these nodes, say Y, is dependent with X given $\mathbf{B}(X) - \{Y\}$.

1. $\mathbf{S} \leftarrow \emptyset$.

2. While $\exists Y \in \mathbf{V} - \{X\}$ such that $Y \leftrightarrow_{\mathbf{S}} X$, do $\mathbf{S} \leftarrow \mathbf{S} \cup \{Y\}$. [Growing phase]

3. While $\exists Y \in \mathbf{S}$ such that $Y \not\leftrightarrow_{\mathbf{S}-\{Y\}} X$, do $\mathbf{S} \leftarrow \mathbf{S} - \{Y\}$. [Shrinking phase]

4. $\mathbf{B}(X) \leftarrow \mathbf{S}$.

Figure 2: The basic Markov blanket algorithm.

The algorithm for the recovery of the Markov blanket of X is shown in Fig. 2. The idea behind step 2 is simple: as long as the Markov blanket property of X is violated (*ie.* there exists a variable in $\mathbf{V}$ that is dependent on X), we add it to the current set $\mathbf{S}$ until there are no more such variables. In this process however, there may be some variables that were added to $\mathbf{S}$ that were really outside the blanket. Such variables would have been rendered independent from X at a later point when "intervening" nodes of the underlying Bayesian net were added to $\mathbf{S}$. This observation necessitates step 3, which identifies and removes those variables. The algorithm is efficient, requiring only $O(n)$ conditional tests, making its running time $O(n|\mathbf{D}|)$, where $n = |\mathbf{V}|$ and $\mathbf{D}$ is the set of examples. For a detailed derivation of this bound as well as a formal proof of correctness, see [Margaritis99]. In practice one may try to minimize the number of tests in step 3 by heuristically ordering the variables in the loop of step 2, for example by ascending mutual information or probability of dependence between X and Y (as computed using the χ^2 test, see section 5).

3 Grow-Shrink (GS) Algorithm for Bayesian Net Induction

The recovery of the local structure around each node is greatly facilitated by the knowledge of the nodes' Markov blankets. What would normally be a daunting task of employing dependence tests conditioned on an exponential number of subsets of large sets of variables—even though most of their members may be irrelevant—can now be focused on the Markov blankets of the nodes involved, making structure discovery much faster and more reliable. We present below the plain version of the GS algorithm that utilizes blanket information for inducing the structure of a Bayesian net. At a later point of this paper, we will present a robust, randomized version that has the potential of being faster and more reliable, as well as being able to operate in an "anytime" manner.

In the following $\mathbf{N}(X)$ represents the direct neighbors of X.

[**Compute Markov Blankets**]
  For all $X \in \mathbf{V}$, compute the Markov blanket $\mathbf{B}(X)$.

[**Compute Graph Structure**]
  For all $X \in \mathbf{V}$ and $Y \in \mathbf{B}(X)$, determine Y to be a direct neighbor of X if X and Y are dependent given $\mathbf{S}$ for all $\mathbf{S} \subseteq \mathbf{T}$, where $\mathbf{T}$ is the smaller of $\mathbf{B}(X) - \{Y\}$ and $\mathbf{B}(Y) - \{X\}$.

[**Orient Edges**]
  For all $X \in \mathbf{V}$ and $Y \in \mathbf{N}(X)$, orient $Y \to X$ if there exists a variable $Z \in \mathbf{N}(X) - \mathbf{N}(Y) - \{Y\}$ such that Y and Z are dependent given $\mathbf{S} \cup \{X\}$ for all $\mathbf{S} \subseteq \mathbf{U}$, where $\mathbf{U}$ is the smaller of $\mathbf{B}(Y) - \{Z\}$ and $\mathbf{B}(Z) - \{Y\}$.

[**Remove Cycles**]
  Do the following while there exist cycles in the graph:

  1. Compute the set of edges $\mathbf{C} = \{X \to Y \text{ such that } X \to Y \text{ is part of a cycle}\}$.

  2. Remove the edge in $\mathbf{C}$ that is part of the greatest number of cycles, and put it in $\mathbf{R}$.

[Reverse Edges]
Insert each edge from **R** in the graph, reversed.
[Propagate Directions]
For all $X \in \mathbf{V}$ and $Y \in \mathbf{N}(X)$ such that neither $Y \to X$ nor $X \to Y$, execute the following rule until it no longer applies: If there exists a directed path from X to Y, orient $X \to Y$.

In the algorithm description above, step 2 determines which of the members of the blanket of each node are actually direct neighbors (parents and children). Assuming, without loss of generality, that $\mathbf{B}(X) - \{Y\}$ is the smaller set, if any of the tests are successful in separating (making independent) X from Y, the algorithm determines that there is no direct connection between them. That would happen when the conditioning set **S** includes all parents of X and no common children of X and Y. It is interesting to note that the motivation behind selecting the smaller set to condition on stems not only from computational efficiency but from reliability as well: a conditioning set **S** causes the data set to be split into $2^{|\mathbf{S}|}$ partitions; smaller conditioning sets cause the data set to be split into larger partitions and make dependence tests more reliable.

Step 3 exploits the fact that two variables that have a common descendant become dependent when conditioning on a set that includes any such descendant. Since the direct neighbors of X and Y are known from step 2, we can determine whether a direct neighbor Y is a parent of X if there exists another node Z (which, coincidentally, is also a parent) such that any attempt to separate Y and Z by conditioning on a subset of the blanket of Y that includes X, fails (assuming that $\mathbf{B}(Y)$ is smaller than $\mathbf{B}(Z)$). If the directionality is indeed $Y \to X \leftarrow Z$, there should be no such subset since, by conditioning on X, a permanent dependency path between Y and Z is created. This would not be the case if Y were a child of X.

It is straightforward to show that the algorithm requires $O(n^2 + nb^2 2^b)$ conditional independence tests, where $b = \max_X(|\mathbf{B}(X)|)$. Under the assumption that b is bounded by a constant, this algorithm is $O(n^2)$ in the number of conditional independence tests. It is worthwhile to note that the time to compute a conditional independence test by a pass over the data set **D** is $O(n |\mathbf{D}|)$ and *not* $O(2^{|\mathbf{V}|})$. An analysis and a formal proof of correctness of the algorithm is presented in [Margaritis99].

Discussion

The main advantage of the algorithm comes through the use of Markov blankets to restrict the size of the conditioning sets. The Markov blankets may be usually wrong in the side of including too many nodes because they are represented by a disjunction of tests for all values of the conditioning set, on the same data. This emphasizes the importance of the "direct neighbors" step which removes nodes that were incorrectly added during the Markov blanket computation step by admitting variables whose dependence was shown high confidence in a large number of different tests.

It is also possible that an edge direction is wrongly determined during step 3 due to non-representative or noisy data. This may lead to directed cycles in the resulting graph. It is therefore necessary to remove those cycles by identifying the minimum set of edges than need to be reversed for all cycles to disappear. This problem is closely related [Margaritis99] to the *Minimum Feedback Arc Set* problem, which is concerned with identifying a minimum set of edges that need to be removed from a graph that possibly contains directed cycles, in order for all such cycles to disappear. Unfortunately, this problem is NP-complete in its generality [Jünger85]. We introduce here a reasonable heuristic for its solution that is based on the number of cycles that an edge that is part of a cycle is involved in.

Not all edge directions can be determined during the last two steps. For example, nodes with a single parent or multi-parent nodes (called *colliders*) whose parents are directly connected do not apply to step 3, and steps 4 and 5 are only concerned with already directed edges. Step 6 attempts to ameliorate that, through orienting edges in a way that does not introduce a cycle, if the reverse direction necessarily does. It is not obvious that, for example, if the direction $X \to Y$ produces a cycle in an otherwise acyclic graph, the opposite direction $Y \to X$ will not also. However, this is the case. For the proof of this, see [Margaritis99].

The algorithm is similar to the SGS algorithm presented in [Spirtes93], but differs in a number of ways. Its main difference lies in the use of Markov blankets to dramatically improve performance (in many cases where the bounded blanket size assumptions hold). Its structure is similar to SGS, and the stability (frequently referred to as robustness in the following discussion) arguments presented in [Spirtes93] apply. Increased reliability stems from the use of smaller conditioning sets, leading to greater number of examples per test. The PC algorithm, also in [Spirtes93], differs from the GS algorithm in that it involves linear probing for a separator set, which makes it unnecessarily inefficient.

4 Randomized Version of the GS Algorithm

The GS algorithm, as presented above, is appropriate for situations where the maximum Markov blanket of each of a set of variables is small. While it is reasonable to assume that in many real-life problems where high-level variables are involved this may be the case, other problems such as Bayesian image retrieval in computer vision, may employ finer representations. In these cases the variables used may depend in a direct manner on many others. For example, we may choose to use variables to characterize local texture in different parts of an image. If the resolution of the mapping from textures to variables is increasingly fine, direct dependencies among those variables may be plentiful and therefore the maximum Markov blanket size may be significant.

Another problem that has plagued independence-test based algorithms for Bayesian net structure induction in general is that their decisions are based on a single or a few tests ("hard" decisions), making them prone to errors due to noise in the data. This also applies to the the GS algorithm. It would therefore be advantageous to employ multiple tests before deciding on a direct neighbor or the direction of an edge.

The randomized version of the GS algorithm addresses these two problems. Both of them are tackled through randomized testing and Bayesian evidence accumulation. The problem of exponential running times in the maximum blanket size of steps 2 and 3 of the plain algorithm is overcome by replacing them by a series of tests, whose number may be specified by the user, with the members of the conditioning set chosen randomly from the smallest blanket of the two variables. Each such test provides evidence for or against the direct connection between the two variables, appropriately weighted by the probability that circumstances causing that event occur or not, and due to the fact that connectedness is the conjunction of more elementary events.

This version of the algorithm is not shown here in detail due to space restrictions. Its operation follows closely the one of the plain GS version. The main difference lies in the usage of Bayesian updating of the posterior probability of a direct link (or a dependence through a collider) between a pair of variables X and Y using conditional dependence tests that take into account independent evidence. The posterior probability p_i of a link between X and Y after executing i dependence tests $d_j, j = 1, \ldots, i$ is

$$p_i = \frac{p_{i-1} d_i}{p_{i-1} d_i + (1 - p_{i-1})(G + 1 - d_i)}$$

where $G \equiv G(X, Y) = 1 - (\frac{1}{2})^{|\mathbf{T}|}$ is a factor that takes values in the interval $[0, 1)$ and can be interpreted as the "(un)importance" of the truth of each test d_i, while $\mathbf{T}$ is the smaller of $\mathbf{B}(X) - \{Y\}$ and $\mathbf{B}(Y) - \{X\}$. We can use this accumulated evidence to guide our decisions to the hypothesis that we feel most confident about. Besides being able to do that in a timely manner due to the user-specified number of tests, we also note how this approach also addresses the robustness problem mentioned above through the use of multiple weighted tests, and leaving for the end the "hard" decisions that involve a threshold (ie. comparing the posterior probability with a threshold, which in our case is $\frac{1}{2}$).

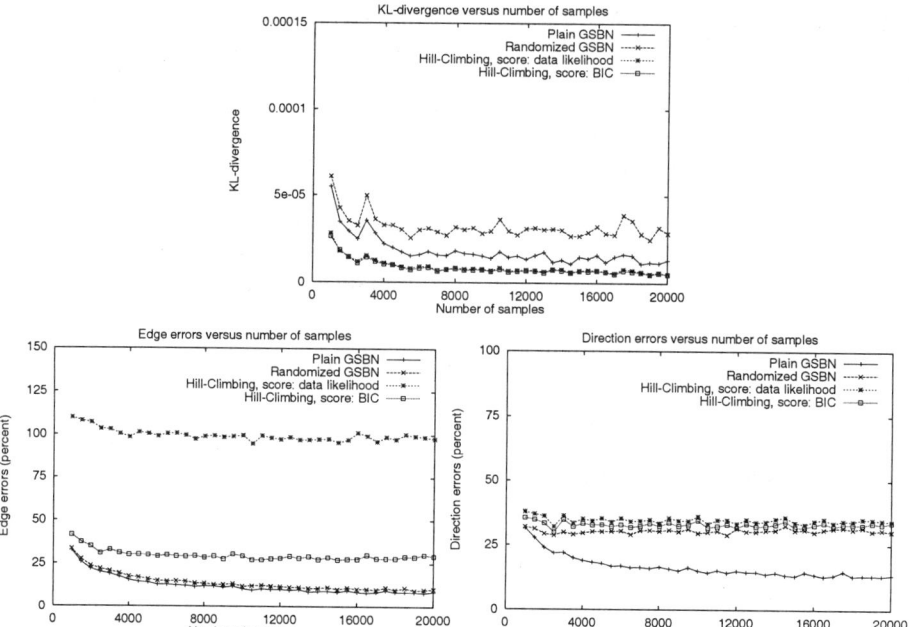

Figure 3: Results for a 5 × 5 rectangular net with branching factor 2 (in both directions, blanket size 8) as a function of the number of samples. On the top, KL-divergence is depicted for the plain GS, randomized GS, and hill-climbing algorithms. On the bottom, the percentage of edge and direction errors are shown. Note that certain edge error rates for the hill-climbing algorithm exceed 100%.

5 Results

Throughout the algorithms presented in this paper we employ standard chi-square (χ^2) conditional dependence tests (as is done also in [Spirtes93]) in order to compare the histograms $\widehat{P}(X)$ and $\widehat{P}(X \mid Y)$. The χ^2 test gives us a probability of the error of assuming that the two variables are dependent when in fact they are not (type II error of a dependence test), from which we can easily derive the probability that X and Y are dependent. There is an implicit confidence threshold τ involved in each dependence test, indicating how certain we wish to be about the correctness of the test without unduly rejecting dependent pairs, something that is always possible in reality due to the presence of noise. In all experiments we used $\tau = 0.95$, which corresponds to a 95% confidence test.

We test the effectiveness of the algorithms through the following procedure: we generate a random rectangular net of specified dimensions and up/down branching factor. A number of examples are drawn from that net using logic sampling and they are used as input to the algorithm under test. The resulting nets can be compared with the original ones along dimensions of KL-divergence and difference in edges and edge directionality. The KL-divergence was estimated using a Monte Carlo procedure. An example reconstruction was shown in the beginning of the paper, Fig. 1.

Fig. 3 shows how the KL-divergence between the original and the reconstructed net as well as edge omissions/false additions/reversals as a function of number of samples used. It demonstrates two facts. First, that typical KL-divergence for both GS and hill-climbing algorithms is low (with hill-climbing slightly lower), which shows good performance for applications where prediction is of prime concern. Second, the number of incorrect edges and the errors in the directionality of the edges present is much higher for the hill-climbing algorithm, making it unsuitable for accurate Bayesian net reconstruction.

Fig. 4 shows the effects of increasing the Markov blanket through an increasing branching factor. As expected, we see a dramatic (exponential) increase in execution time of the plain

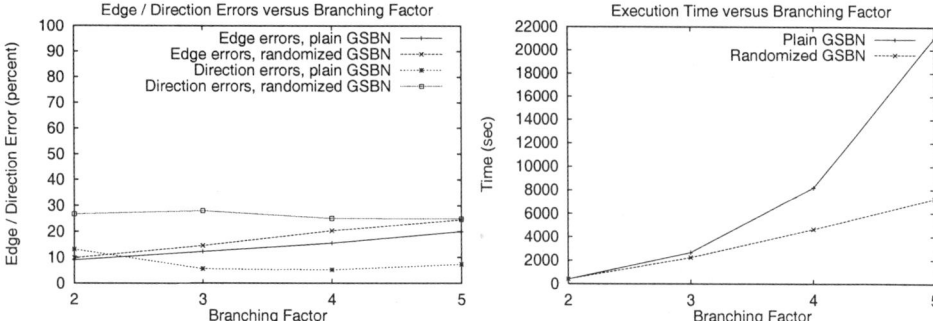

Figure 4: Results for a 5 × 5 rectangular net from which 10000 samples were generated and used for reconstruction, versus increasing branching factor. On the left, errors are slowly increasing as expected, but comparable for the plain and randomized versions of the GS algorithm. On the right, corresponding execution times are shown.

GS algorithm, though only a mild increase of the randomized version. The latter uses 200 (constant) conditional tests per decision, and its execution time increase can be attributed to the (quadratic) increase in the number of decisions. Note that the error percentages between the plain and the randomized version remain relatively close. The number of direction errors for the GS algorithm actually decreases due to the larger number of parents for each node (more "V" structures), which allows a greater number of opportunities to recover the directionality of an edge (using an increased number of tests).

6 Discussion

In this paper we presented an efficient algorithm for computing the Markov blanket of a node and then used it in the two versions of the GS algorithm (plain and randomized) by exploiting the properties of the Markov blanket to facilitate fast reconstruction of the local neighborhood around each node, under assumptions of bounded neighborhood size. We also presented a randomized variant that has the advantages of faster execution speeds and added reconstruction robustness due to multiple tests and Bayesian accumulation of evidence. Simulation results demonstrate the reconstruction accuracy advantages of the algorithms presented here over hill-climbing methods. Additional results also show that the randomized version has a dramatical execution speed benefit over the plain one in cases where the assumption of bounded neighborhood does not hold, without significantly affecting the reconstruction error rate.

References

[Chow68]   C.K. Chow and C.N. Liu. Approximating discrete probability distributions with dependence trees. *IEEE Transactions on Information Theory*, 14, 1968.

[Herskovits90]   E.H. Herskovits and G.F. Cooper. Kutató: An entropy-driven system for construction of probabilistic expert systems from databases. UAI-90.

[Spirtes93]   P. Spirtes, C. Glymour, and R. Scheines. *Causation, Prediction, and Search*, Springer, 1993.

[Pearl88]   J. Pearl. *Probabilistic Reasoning in Intelligent Systems*, Morgan Kaufmann, 1988.

[Rebane87]   G. Rebane and J. Pearl. The recovery of causal poly-trees from statistical data. UAI-87.

[Verma90]   T.S. Verma, and J. Pearl. Equivalence and Synthesis of Causal Models. UAI-90.

[Agosta88]   J.M. Agosta. The structure of Bayes networks for visual recognition. UAI-88.

[Cheng97]   J. Cheng, D.A. Bell, W. Liu, An algorithm for Bayesian network construction from data. AI and Statistics, 1997.

[Margaritis99]   D. Margaritis, S. Thrun, Bayesian Network Induction via Local Neighborhoods. TR CMU-CS-99-134, forthcoming.

[Jünger85]   M. Jünger, *Polyhedral combinatorics and the acyclic subdigraph problem*, Heldermann, 1985.

Boosting Algorithms as Gradient Descent

Llew Mason
Research School of Information
Sciences and Engineering
Australian National University
Canberra, ACT, 0200, Australia
lmason@syseng.anu.edu.au

Jonathan Baxter
Research School of Information
Sciences and Engineering
Australian National University
Canberra, ACT, 0200, Australia
Jonathan.Baxter@anu.edu.au

Peter Bartlett
Research School of Information
Sciences and Engineering
Australian National University
Canberra, ACT, 0200, Australia
Peter.Bartlett@anu.edu.au

Marcus Frean
Department of Computer Science
and Electrical Engineering
The University of Queensland
Brisbane, QLD, 4072, Australia
marcusf@elec.uq.edu.au

Abstract

We provide an abstract characterization of boosting algorithms as gradient decsent on cost-functionals in an inner-product function space. We prove convergence of these functional-gradient-descent algorithms under quite weak conditions. Following previous theoretical results bounding the generalization performance of convex combinations of classifiers in terms of general cost functions of the margin, we present a new algorithm (DOOM II) for performing a gradient descent optimization of such cost functions. Experiments on several data sets from the UC Irvine repository demonstrate that DOOM II generally outperforms AdaBoost, especially in high noise situations, and that the overfitting behaviour of AdaBoost is predicted by our cost functions.

1 Introduction

There has been considerable interest recently in *voting methods* for pattern classification, which predict the label of a particular example using a weighted vote over a set of base classifiers [10, 2, 6, 9, 16, 5, 3, 19, 12, 17, 7, 11, 8]. Recent theoretical results suggest that the effectiveness of these algorithms is due to their tendency to produce *large margin classifiers* [1, 18]. Loosely speaking, if a combination of classifiers correctly classifies most of the training data with a large margin, then its error probability is small.

In [14] we gave improved upper bounds on the misclassification probability of a combined classifier in terms of the average over the training data of a certain *cost function* of the margins. That paper also described DOOM, an algorithm for directly minimizing the margin cost function by adjusting the weights associated with each base classifier (the base classifiers are suppiled to DOOM). DOOM exhibits performance improvements over AdaBoost, even when using the same base hypotheses, which provides additional empirical evidence that these margin cost functions are appropriate quantities to optimize.

In this paper, we present a general class of algorithms (called AnyBoost) which are gradient descent algorithms for choosing linear combinations of elements of an inner product function space so as to minimize some cost functional. The normal operation of a weak learner is shown to be equivalent to maximizing a certain inner product. We prove convergence of AnyBoost under weak conditions. In Section 3, we show that this general class of algorithms includes as special cases nearly all existing voting methods. In Section 5, we present experimental results for a special case of AnyBoost that minimizes a theoretically-motivated margin cost functional. The experiments show that the new algorithm typically outperforms AdaBoost, and that this is especially true with label noise. In addition, the theoretically-motivated cost functions provide good estimates of the error of AdaBoost, in the sense that they can be used to predict its overfitting behaviour.

2 AnyBoost

Let (x, y) denote *examples* from $X \times Y$, where X is the space of measurements (typically $X \subseteq \mathbb{R}^N$) and Y is the space of labels (Y is usually a discrete set or some subset of $\mathbb{R}$). Let $\mathcal{F}$ denote some class of functions (the base hypotheses) mapping $X \to Y$, and $\text{lin}(\mathcal{F})$ denote the set of all linear combinations of functions in $\mathcal{F}$. Let $\langle,\rangle$ be an *inner product* on $\text{lin}(\mathcal{F})$, and

$$C: \text{lin}(\mathcal{F}) \to \Re$$

a cost *functional* on $\text{lin}(\mathcal{F})$.

Our aim is to find a function $F \in \text{lin}(\mathcal{F})$ minimizing $C(F)$. We will proceed iteratively via a gradient descent procedure.

Suppose we have some $F \in \text{lin}(\mathcal{F})$ and we wish to find a new $f \in \mathcal{F}$ to add to F so that the cost $C(F + \epsilon f)$ decreases, for some small value of ϵ. Viewed in function space terms, we are asking for the "direction" f such that $C(F + \epsilon f)$ most rapidly decreases. The desired direction is simply the negative of the functional derivative of C at F, $-\nabla C(F)$, where:

$$\nabla C(F)(x) := \left. \frac{\partial C(F + \alpha 1_x)}{\partial \alpha} \right|_{\alpha=0}, \quad (1)$$

where 1_x is the indicator function of x. Since we are restricted to choosing our new function f from $\mathcal{F}$, in general it will not be possible to choose $f = -\nabla C(F)$, so instead we search for an f with greatest inner product with $-\nabla C(F)$. That is, we should choose f to maximize $-\langle \nabla C(F), f \rangle$. This can be motivated by observing that, to first order in ϵ, $C(F + \epsilon f) = C(F) + \epsilon \langle \nabla C(F), f \rangle$ and hence the greatest reduction in cost will occur for the f maximizing $-\langle \nabla C(F), f \rangle$.

For reasons that will become obvious later, an algorithm that chooses f attempting to maximize $-\langle \nabla C(F), f \rangle$ will be described as a *weak learner*.

The preceding discussion motivates Algorithm 1 (AnyBoost), an iterative algorithm for finding linear combinations F of base hypotheses in $\mathcal{F}$ that minimize the cost functional $C(F)$. Note that we have allowed the base hypotheses to take values in an arbitrary set Y, we have not restricted the form of the cost or the inner product, and we have not specified what the step-sizes should be. Appropriate choices for these things will be made when we apply the algorithm to more concrete situations. Note also that the algorithm terminates when $-\langle \nabla C(F_t), f_{t+1} \rangle \leq 0$, i.e when the weak learner $\mathcal{L}$ returns a base hypothesis f_{t+1} which *no longer points in the downhill direction* of the cost function $C(F)$. Thus, the algorithm terminates when, to first order, a step in function space in the direction of the base hypothesis returned by $\mathcal{L}$ would increase the cost.

Algorithm 1 : AnyBoost

Require :
- An inner product space $(\mathcal{X}, \langle, \rangle)$ containing functions mapping from X to some set Y.
- A class of base classifiers $\mathcal{F} \subseteq \mathcal{X}$.
- A differentiable cost functional $C \colon \mathrm{lin}(\mathcal{F}) \to \mathbb{R}$.
- A weak learner $\mathcal{L}(F)$ that accepts $F \in \mathrm{lin}(\mathcal{F})$ and returns $f \in \mathcal{F}$ with a large value of $-\langle \nabla C(F), f \rangle$.

Let $F_0(x) := 0$.
for $t := 0$ to T **do**
  Let $f_{t+1} := \mathcal{L}(F_t)$.
  if $-\langle \nabla C(F_t), f_{t+1} \rangle \leq 0$ **then**
    return F_t.
  end if
  Choose w_{t+1}.
  Let $F_{t+1} := F_t + w_{t+1} f_{t+1}$.
end for
return F_{T+1}.

---

3 A gradient descent view of voting methods

We now restrict our attention to base hypotheses $f \in \mathcal{F}$ mapping to $Y = \{\pm 1\}$, and the inner product

$$\langle F, G \rangle := \frac{1}{m} \sum_{i=1}^{m} F(x_i) G(x_i) \qquad (2)$$

for all $F, G \in \mathrm{lin}(\mathcal{F})$, where $S = \{(x_1, y_1), \ldots, (x_n, y_n)\}$ is a set of training examples generated according to some unknown distribution $\mathcal{D}$ on $X \times Y$. Our aim now is to find $F \in \mathrm{lin}(\mathcal{F})$ such that $\Pr_{(x,y) \sim \mathcal{D}} \mathrm{sgn}(F(x)) \neq y$ is minimal, where $\mathrm{sgn}(F(x)) = -1$ if $F(x) < 0$ and $\mathrm{sgn}(F(x)) = 1$ otherwise. In other words, $\mathrm{sgn}\, F$ should minimize the misclassification probability.

The *margin* of $F \colon X \to \Re$ on example (x, y) is defined as $yF(x)$. Consider *margin cost-functionals* defined by

$$C(F) := \frac{1}{m} \sum_{i=1}^{m} c(y_i F(x_i))$$

where $c \colon \Re \to \Re$ is any differentiable real-valued function of the margin. With these definitions, a quick calculation shows:

$$-\langle \nabla C(F), f \rangle = -\frac{1}{m^2} \sum_{i=1}^{m} y_i f(x_i) c'(y_i F(x_i)).$$

Since positive margins correspond to examples correctly labelled by $\mathrm{sgn}\, F$ and negative margins to incorrectly labelled examples, any sensible cost function of the

Table 1: Existing voting methods viewed as AnyBoost on margin cost functions.

Algorithm	Cost function	Step size
AdaBoost [9]	$e^{-yF(x)}$	Line search
ARC-X4 [2]	$(1 - yF(x))^5$	$1/t$
ConfidenceBoost [19]	$e^{-yF(x)}$	Line search
LogitBoost [12]	$\ln(1 + e^{-yF(x)})$	Newton-Raphson

margin will be monotonically decreasing. Hence $-c'(y_i F(x_i))$ will always be positive. Dividing through by $-\sum_{i=1}^{m} c'(y_i F(x_i))$, we see that finding an f maximizing $-\langle \nabla C(F), f \rangle$ is equivalent to finding an f minimizing the weighted error

$$\sum_{i:\, f(x_i) \neq y_i} D(i) \quad \text{where} \quad D(i) := \frac{c'(y_i F(x_i))}{\sum_{i=1}^{m} c'(y_i F(x_i))} \quad \text{for } i = 1, \ldots, m.$$

Many of the most successful voting methods are, for the appropriate choice of margin cost function c and step-size, specific cases of the AnyBoost algorithm (see Table 3). A more detailed analysis can be found in the full version of this paper [15].

4 Convergence of AnyBoost

In this section we provide convergence results for the AnyBoost algorithm, under quite weak conditions on the cost functional C. The prescriptions given for the step-sizes w_t in these results are for convergence guarantees only: in practice they will almost always be smaller than necessary, hence fixed small steps or some form of line search should be used.

The following theorem (proof omitted, see [15]) supplies a specific step-size for AnyBoost and characterizes the limiting behaviour with this step-size.

Theorem 1. *Let $C \colon \mathrm{lin}(\mathcal{F}) \to \mathbb{R}$ be any lower bounded, Lipschitz differentiable cost functional (that is, there exists $L > 0$ such that $\|\nabla C(F) - \nabla C(F')\| \leq L\|F - F'\|$ for all $F, F' \in \mathrm{lin}(\mathcal{F})$). Let $F_0, F_1, \ldots$ be the sequence of combined hypotheses generated by the AnyBoost algorithm, using step-sizes*

$$w_{t+1} := -\frac{\langle \nabla C(F_t), f_{t+1} \rangle}{L\|f_{t+1}\|^2}. \tag{3}$$

Then AnyBoost either halts on round T with $-\langle \nabla C(F_T), f_{T+1} \rangle \leq 0$, or $C(F_t)$ converges to some finite value C^*, in which case $\lim_{t \to \infty} \langle \nabla C(F_t), f_{t+1} \rangle = 0$.

The next theorem (proof omitted, see [15]) shows that if the weak learner can always find the best weak hypothesis $f_t \in \mathcal{F}$ on each round of AnyBoost, and if the cost functional C is convex, then any accumulation point F of the sequence (F_t) generated by AnyBoost with the step sizes (3) is a global minimum of the cost. For ease of exposition, we have assumed that rather than terminating when $-\langle \nabla C(F_T), f_{T+1} \rangle \leq 0$, AnyBoost simply continues to return F_T for all subsequent time steps t.

Theorem 2. *Let $C \colon \mathrm{lin}(\mathcal{F}) \to \mathbb{R}$ be a convex cost functional with the properties in Theorem 1, and let (F_t) be the sequence of combined hypotheses generated by the AnyBoost algorithm with step sizes given by (3). Assume that the weak hypothesis class $\mathcal{F}$ is negation closed ($f \in \mathcal{F} \implies -f \in \mathcal{F}$) and that on each round* the AnyBoost algorithm finds a function f_{t+1} maximizing $-\langle \nabla C(F_t), f_{t+1}\rangle$. Then any accumulation point F of the sequence (F_t) satisfies $\sup_{f\in\mathcal{F}} -\langle \nabla C(F), f\rangle = 0$, and $C(F) = \inf_{G\in\text{lin}(\mathcal{F})} C(G)$.

5 Experiments

AdaBoost had been perceived to be resistant to overfitting despite the fact that it can produce combinations involving very large numbers of classifiers. However, recent studies have shown that this is not the case, even for base classifiers as simple as decision stumps [13, 5, 17]. This overfitting can be attributed to the use of exponential margin cost functions (recall Table 3).

The results in in [14] showed that overfitting may be avoided by using margin cost functionals of a form qualitatively similar to

$$C(F) = \frac{1}{m}\sum_{i=1}^{m} 1 - \tanh(\lambda y_i F(x_i)), \tag{4}$$

where λ is an adjustable parameter controlling the steepness of the margin cost function $c(z) = 1 - \tanh(\lambda z)$. For the theoretical analysis of [14] to apply, F must be a *convex* combination of base hypotheses, rather than a general linear combination. Henceforth (4) will be referred to as the *normalized sigmoid cost functional*. AnyBoost with (4) as the cost functional and (2) as the inner product will be referred to as **DOOM II**. In our implementation of DOOM II we use a fixed small step-size ϵ (for all of the experiments $\epsilon = 0.05$). For all details of the algorithm the reader is referred to the full version of this paper [15].

We compared the performance of DOOM II and AdaBoost on a selection of nine data sets taken from the UCI machine learning repository [4] to which various levels of label noise had been applied. To simplify matters, only binary classification problems were considered. For all of the experiments axis orthogonal hyperplanes (also known as decision stumps) were used as the weak learner. Full details of the experimental setup may be found in [15]. A summary of the experimental results is shown in Figure 1. The improvement in test error exhibited by DOOM II over AdaBoost is shown for each data set and noise level. DOOM II generally outperforms AdaBoost and the improvement is more pronounced in the presence of label noise.

The effect of using the normalized sigmoid cost function rather than the exponential cost function is best illustrated by comparing the cumulative margin distributions generated by AdaBoost and DOOM II. Figure 2 shows comparisons for two data sets with 0% and 15% label noise applied. For a given margin, the value on the curve corresponds to the proportion of training examples with margin less than or equal to this value. These curves show that in trying to increase the margins of negative examples AdaBoost is willing to sacrifice the margin of positive examples significantly. In contrast, DOOM II 'gives up' on examples with large negative margin in order to reduce the value of the cost function.

Given that AdaBoost does suffer from overfitting and is guaranteed to minimize an exponential cost function of the margins, this cost function certainly does not relate to test error. How does the value of our proposed cost function correlate against AdaBoost's test error? Figure 3 shows the variation in the normalized sigmoid cost function, the exponential cost function and the test error for AdaBoost for two UCI data sets over 10000 rounds. There is a strong correlation between the normalized sigmoid cost and AdaBoost's test error. In both data sets the minimum

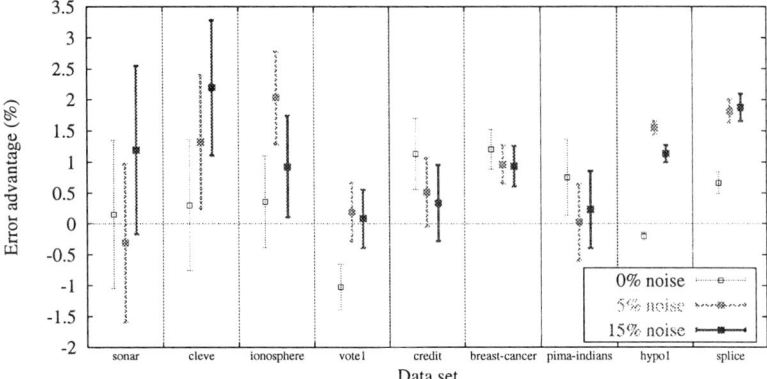

Figure 1: Summary of test error advantage (with standard error bars) of DOOM II over AdaBoost with varying levels of noise on nine UCI data sets.

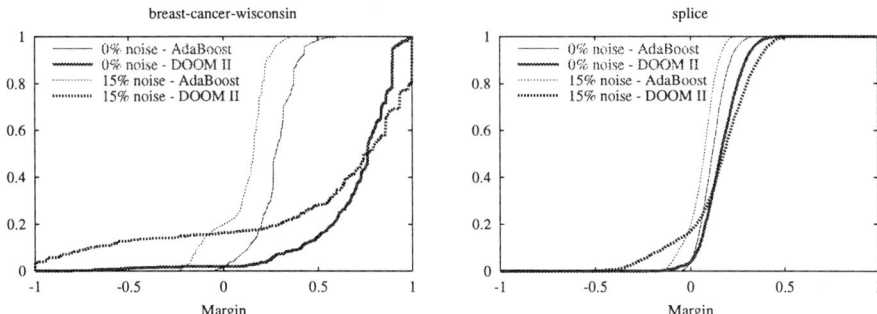

Figure 2: Margin distributions for AdaBoost and DOOM II with 0% and 15% label noise for the `breast-cancer` and `splice` data sets.

of AdaBoost's test error and the minimum of the normalized sigmoid cost very nearly coincide, showing that the sigmoid cost function predicts when AdaBoost will start to overfit.

References

[1] P. L. Bartlett. The sample complexity of pattern classification with neural networks: the size of the weights is more important than the size of the network. *IEEE Transactions on Information Theory*, 44(2):525–536, March 1998.

[2] L. Breiman. Bagging predictors. *Machine Learning*, 24(2):123–140, 1996.

[3] L. Breiman. Prediction games and arcing algorithms. Technical Report 504, Department of Statistics, University of California, Berkeley, 1998.

[4] E. Keogh C. Blake and C. J. Merz. UCI repository of machine learning databases, 1998. http://www.ics.uci.edu/~mlearn/MLRepository.html.

[5] T.G. Dietterich. An experimental comparison of three methods for constructing ensembles of decision trees: Bagging, boosting, and randomization. Technical report, Computer Science Department, Oregon State University, 1998.

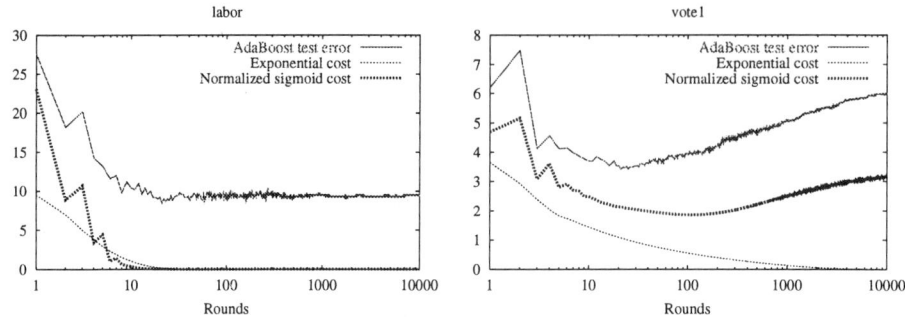

Figure 3: AdaBoost test error, exponential cost and normalized sigmoid cost over 10000 rounds of AdaBoost for the `labor` and `vote1` data sets. Both costs have been scaled in each case for easier comparison with test error.

[6] H. Drucker and C. Cortes. Boosting decision trees. In *Advances in Neural Information Processing Systems 8*, pages 479–485, 1996.

[7] N. Duffy and D. Helmbold. A geometric approach to leveraging weak learners. In *Computational Learning Theory: 4th European Conference*, 1999. (to appear).

[8] Y. Freund. An adaptive version of the boost by majority algorithm. In *Proceedings of the Twelfth Annual Conference on Computational Learning Theory*, 1999. (to appear).

[9] Y. Freund and R. E. Schapire. Experiments with a new boosting algorithm. In *Machine Learning: Proceedings of the Thirteenth International Conference*, pages 148–156, 1996.

[10] Y. Freund and R. E. Schapire. A decision-theoretic generalization of on-line learning and an application to boosting. *Journal of Computer and System Sciences*, 55(1):119–139, August 1997.

[11] J. Friedman. Greedy function approximation : A gradient boosting machine. Technical report, Stanford University, 1999.

[12] J. Friedman, T. Hastie, and R. Tibshirani. Additive logistic regression : A statistical view of boosting. Technical report, Stanford University, 1998.

[13] A. Grove and D. Schuurmans. Boosting in the limit: Maximizing the margin of learned ensembles. In *Proceedings of the Fifteenth National Conference on Artificial Intelligence*, pages 692–699, 1998.

[14] L. Mason, P. L. Bartlett, and J. Baxter. Improved generalization through explicit optimization of margins. *Machine Learning*, 1999. (to appear).

[15] Llew Mason, Jonathan Baxter, Peter Bartlett, and Marcus Frean. Functional Gradient Techniques for Combining Hypotheses. In Alex Smola, Peter Bartlett, Bernard Schölkopf, and Dale Schuurmanns, editors, *Large Margin Classifiers*. MIT Press, 1999. To appear.

[16] J. R. Quinlan. Bagging, boosting, and C4.5. In *Proceedings of the Thirteenth National Conference on Artificial Intelligence*, pages 725–730, 1996.

[17] G. Rätsch, T. Onoda, and K.-R. Müller. Soft margins for AdaBoost. Technical Report NC-TR-1998-021, Department of Computer Science, Royal Holloway, University of London, Egham, UK, 1998.

[18] R. E. Schapire, Y. Freund, P. L. Bartlett, and W. S. Lee. Boosting the margin : A new explanation for the effectiveness of voting methods. *Annals of Statistics*, 26(5):1651–1686, October 1998.

[19] R. E. Schapire and Y. Singer. Improved boosting algorithms using confidence-rated predictions. In *Proceedings of the Eleventh Annual Conference on Computational Learning Theory*, pages 80–91, 1998.

A Multi-class Linear Learning Algorithm Related to Winnow

Chris Mesterharm*
Rutgers Computer Science Department
110 Frelinghuysen Road
Piscataway, NJ 08854
mesterha@paul.rutgers.edu

Abstract

In this paper, we present Committee, a new multi-class learning algorithm related to the Winnow family of algorithms. Committee is an algorithm for combining the predictions of a set of sub-experts in the on-line mistake-bounded model of learning. A sub-expert is a special type of attribute that predicts with a distribution over a finite number of classes. Committee learns a linear function of sub-experts and uses this function to make class predictions. We provide bounds for Committee that show it performs well when the target can be represented by a few relevant sub-experts. We also show how Committee can be used to solve more traditional problems composed of attributes. This leads to a natural extension that learns on multi-class problems that contain both traditional attributes and sub-experts.

1 Introduction

In this paper, we present a new multi-class learning algorithm called Committee. Committee learns a k class target function by combining information from a large set of sub-experts. A sub-expert is a special type of attribute that predicts with a distribution over the target classes. The target space of functions are linear-max functions. We define these as functions that take a linear combination of sub-expert predictions and return the class with maximum value. It may be useful to think of the sub-experts as individual classifying functions that are attempting to predict the target function. Even though the individual sub-experts may not be perfect, Committee attempts to learn a linear-max function that represents the target function. In truth, this picture is not quite accurate. The reason we call them sub-experts and not experts is because even though a individual sub-expert might be poor at prediction, it may be useful when used in a linear-max function. For example, some sub-experts might be used to add constant weights to the linear-max function.

The algorithm is analyzed for the on-line mistake-bounded model of learning [Lit89]. This is a useful model for a type of incremental learning where an algorithm can use feedback about its current hypothesis to improve its performance. In this model, the algorithm goes through a series of learning trials. A trial is composed of three steps. First, the algorithm

---
*Part of this work was supported by NEC Research Institute, Princeton, NJ.

receives an instance, in this case, the predictions of the sub-experts. Second, the algorithm predicts a label for the instance; this is the global prediction of Committee. And last, the algorithm receives the true label of the instance; Committee uses this information to update its estimate of the target. The goal of the algorithm is to minimize the total number of prediction mistakes the algorithm makes while learning the target.

The analysis and performance of Committee is similar to another learning algorithm, Winnow [Lit89]. Winnow is an algorithm for learning a linear-threshold function that maps attributes in $[0, 1]$ to a binary target. It is an algorithm that is effective when the concept can be represented with a few relevant attributes, irrespective of the behavior of the other attributes. Committee is similar but deals with learning a target that contains only a few relevant sub-experts. While learning with sub-experts is interesting in it's own right, it turns out the distinction between the two tasks is not significant. We will show in section 5 how to transform attributes from $[0, 1]$ into sub-experts. Using particular transformations, Committee is identical to the Winnow algorithms, Balanced and WMA [Lit89]. Furthermore, we can generalize these transformations to handle attribute problems with multi-class targets. These transformations naturally lead to a hybrid algorithm that allows a combination of sub-experts and attributes for multi-class learning problems. This opens up a range of new practical problems that did not easily fit into the previous framework of $[0, 1]$ attributes and binary classification.

2 Previous work

Many people have successfully tried the Winnow algorithms on real-world tasks. In the course of their work, they have made modifications to the algorithms to fit certain aspects of their problem. These modifications include multi-class extensions.

For example, [DKR97] use Winnow algorithms on text classification problems. This multi-class problem has a special form; a document can belong to more than one class. Because of this property, it makes sense to learn a different binary classifier for each class. The linear functions are allowed, even desired, to overlap. However, this paper is concerned with cases where this is not possible. For example, in [GR96] the correct spelling of a word must be selected from a set of many possibilities. In this setting, it is more desirable to have the algorithm select a single word.

The work in [GR96] presents many interesting ideas and modifications of the Winnow algorithms. At a minimum, these modification are useful for improving the performance of Winnow on those particular problems. Part of that work also extends the Winnow algorithm to general multi-class problems. While the results are favorable, the contribution of this paper is to give a different algorithm that has a stronger theoretical foundation for customizing a particular multi-class problem.

Blum also works with multi-class Winnow algorithms on the calendar scheduling problem of [MCF+94]. In [Blu95], a modified Winnow is given with theoretical arguments for good performance on certain types of multi-class disjunctions. In this paper, these results are extended, with the new algorithm Committee, to cover a wider range of multi-class linear functions.

Other related theoretical work on multi-class problems includes the regression algorithm $EG^{\pm}$. In [KW97], Kivinen and Warmuth introduce $EG^{\pm}$, an algorithm related to Winnow but used on regression problems. In general, while regression is a useful framework for many multi-class problems, it is not straightforward how to extend regression to the concepts learned by Committee. A particular problem is the inability of current regression techniques to handle 0-1 loss.

3 Algorithm

This section of the paper describes the details of Committee. Near the end of the section, we will give a formal statement of the algorithm.

3.1 Prediction scheme

Assume there are n sub-experts. Each sub-expert has a positive weight that is used to vote for k different classes; let w_i be the weight of sub-expert i. A sub-expert can vote for several classes by spreading its weight with a prediction distribution. For example, if $k = 3$, a sub-expert may give 3/5 of its weight to class 1, 1/5 of its weight to class 2, and 1/5 of its weight to class 3. Let x_i represent this prediction distribution, where x_i^j is the fraction of the weight sub-expert i gives to class j. The vote for class j is $\sum_{i=1}^{n} w_i x_i^j$. Committee predicts the class that has the highest vote. (On ties, the algorithm picks one of the classes involved in the tie.) We call the function computed by this prediction scheme a linear-max function, since it is the maximum class value taken from a linear combination of the sub-expert predictions.

3.2 Target function

The goal of Committee is to minimize the number of mistakes by quickly learning sub-expert weights that correctly classify the target function. Assume there exists μ, a vector of nonnegative weights that correctly classifies the target. Notice that μ can be multiplied by any constant without changing the target. To remove this confusion, we will normalize the weights to sum to 1, i.e., $\sum_{i=1}^{n} \mu_i = 1$. Let $\zeta(j)$ be the target's vote for class j.

$$\zeta(j) = \sum_{i=1}^{n} \mu_i x_i^j$$

Part of the difficulty of the learning problem is hidden in the target weights. Intuitively, a target function will be more difficult to learn if there is a small difference between the ζ votes of the correct and incorrect classes. We measure this difficulty by looking at the minimum difference, over all trials, of the vote of the correct label and the vote of the other labels. Assume for trial t that ρ_t is the correct label.

$$\delta = \min_{t \in Trials} \left(\min_{j \neq \rho_t} (\zeta(\rho_t) - \zeta(j)) \right)$$

Because these are the weights of the target, and the target always makes the correct prediction, $\delta > 0$.

One problem with the above assumptions is that they do not allow noise (cases where $\delta \leq 0$). However, there are variations of the analysis that allow for limited amounts of noise [Lit89, Lit91]. Also experimental work [Lit95, LM] shows the family of Winnow algorithms to be much more robust to noise than the theory would predict. Based on the similarity of the algorithm and analysis, and some preliminary experiments, Committee should be able to tolerate some noise.

3.3 Updates

Committee only updates on mistakes using multiplicative updates. The algorithm starts by initializing all weights to $1/n$. During the trials, let ρ be the correct label and λ be the predicted label of Committee. When $\lambda \neq \rho$ the weight of each sub-expert i is multiplied by $\alpha^{x_i^\rho - x_i^\lambda}$. This corresponds to increasing the weights of the sub-experts who predicted the correct label instead of the label Committee predicted. The value of α is initialized at the start of the algorithm. The optimal value of α for the bounds depends on δ. Often δ is not known in advance, but experiments on Winnow algorithms suggest that these algorithms are more flexible, often performing well with a wider range of α values [LM]. Last, the weights are renormalize to sum to 1. While this is not strictly necessary, normalizing has several advantages including reducing the likelyhood of underflow/overflow errors.

3.4 Committee code

Initialization

$\forall i \in \{1,\ldots,n\}\ w_i := 1/n$.
Set $\alpha > 1$.

Trials

Instance sub-experts $(x_1, \ldots, x_n)$.
Prediction λ is the first class c such that for all other classes j,
$\sum_{i=1}^{n} w_i x_i^c \geq \sum_{i=1}^{n} w_i x_i^j$.
Update Let ρ be the correct label. If mistake ($\lambda \neq \rho$)
for i:=1 to n
$w_i := \alpha^{x_i^\rho - x_i^\lambda} w_i$.
Normalize weights, $\sum_{i=1}^{n} w_i = 1$

3.5 Mistake bound

We do not have the space to give the proof for the mistake bound of Committee, but the technique is similar to the proof of the Winnow algorithm, Balanced, given in [Lit89]. For the complete proof, the reader can refer to [Mes99].

Theorem 1 *Committee makes at most $2\ln(n)/\delta^2$ mistakes when the target conditions in section 3.2 are satisfied and α is set to $(1-\delta)^{-1/2}$.*

Surprisingly, this bound does not refer to the number of classes. The effects of larger values of k show up indirectly in the δ value.

While it is not obvious, this bound shows that Committee performs well when the target can be represented by a small fraction of the sub-experts. Call the sub-experts in the target the relevant sub-experts. Since δ is a function of the target, δ only depends on the relevant sub-experts. On the other hand, the remaining sub-experts have a small effect on the bound since they are only represented in the $\ln(n)$ factor. This means that the mistake bound of Committee is fairly stable even when adding a large number of additional sub-experts. In truth, this doesn't mean that the algorithm will have a good bound when there are few relevant sub-experts. In some cases, a small number of sub-experts can give an arbitrarily small δ value. (This is a general problem with all the Winnow algorithms.) What it does mean is that, given any problem, increasing the number of irrelevant sub-experts will only have a logarithmic effect on the mistake bound.

4 Attributes to sub-experts

Often there are no obvious sub-experts to use in solving a learning problem. Many times the only information available is a set of attributes. For attributes in $[0, 1]$, we will show how to use Committee to learn a natural kind of k class target function, a linear machine. To learn this target, we will transform each attribute into k separate sub-experts. We will use some of the same notion as Committee to help understand the transformation.

4.1 Attribute target (linear machine)

A linear machine [DH73] is a prediction function that divides the feature space into disjoint convex regions where each class corresponds to one region. The predictions are made by a comparing the value of k different linear functions where each function corresponds to a class.

More formally, assume there are $m - 1$ attributes and k classes. Let $z_i \in [0, 1]$ be attribute i. Assume the target function is represented using k linear functions of the attributes. Let $\zeta(j) = \sum_{i=1}^{m} \mu_i^j z_i$ be the linear function for class j where μ_i^j is the weight of attribute i in class j. Notice that we have added one extra attribute. This attribute is set to 1 and is needed for the constant portion of the linear functions. The target function labels an instance with the class of the largest ζ function. (Ties are not defined.) Therefore, $\zeta(j)$ is similar to the voting function for class j used in Committee.

4.2 Transforming the target

One difficulty with these linear functions is that they may have negative weights. Since Committee only allows targets with nonnegative weights, we need transform to an equivalent problem that has nonnegative weights. This is not difficult. Since we are only concerned with the relative difference between the ζ functions, we are allowed to add any function to the ζ functions as long as we add it to all ζ functions. This gives us a simple procedure to remove negative weights. For example, if $\zeta(1) = 3z_1 - 2z_2 + 1z_3 - 4$, we can add $2z_2 + 4$ to every ζ function to remove the negative weights from $\zeta(1)$. It is straightforward to extend this and remove all negative weights.

We also need to normalize the weights. Again, since only the relative difference between the ζ functions matter, we can divide all the ζ functions by any constant. We normalize the weights to sum to 1, i.e., $\sum_{j=1}^{k}\sum_{i=1}^{n} \mu_i^j = 1$. At this point, without loss of generality, assume that the original ζ functions are nonnegative and normalized.

The last step is to identify a δ value. We use the same definition of δ as Committee substituting the corresponding ζ functions of the linear machine. Assume for trial t that ρ_t is the correct label.

$$\delta = \min_{t \in Trials} \left(\min_{j \neq \rho_t}(\zeta(\rho_t) - \zeta(j)) \right)$$

4.3 Transforming the attributes

The transformation works as follows: convert attribute z_i into k sub-experts. Each sub-expert will always vote for one of the k classes with value z_i. The target weight for each of these sub-experts is the corresponding target weight of the attribute, label pair in the ζ functions. Do this for every attribute.

$$z_i \Longrightarrow \mu_i^1 \begin{pmatrix} z_i \\ 0 \\ \vdots \\ 0 \end{pmatrix} + \mu_i^2 \begin{pmatrix} 0 \\ z_i \\ 0 \\ \vdots \end{pmatrix} + \cdots + \mu_i^k \begin{pmatrix} 0 \\ \vdots \\ 0 \\ z_i \end{pmatrix}$$

Notice that we are not using distributions for the sub-expert predictions. A sub-expert's prediction can be converted to a distribution by adding a constant amount to each class prediction. For example, a sub-expert that predicts $z_1 = .7$, $z_2 = 0$, $z_3 = 0$ can be changed to $z_1 = .8$, $z_2 = .1$, $z_3 = .1$ by adding .1 to each class. This conversion does not affect the predicting or updating of Committee.

Theorem 2 *Committee makes at most $2\ln(mk)/\delta^2$ mistakes on a linear machine, as defined in this section, when α is set to $(1-\delta)^{-1/2}$.*

Proof: The above target transformation creates mk normalized target sub-experts that vote with the same ζ functions as the linear machine. Therefore, this set of sub-experts has the same δ value. Plugging these values into the bound for Committee gives the result.

This transformation provides a simple procedure for solving linear machine problems. While the details of the transformation may look cumbersome, the actual implementation of the algorithm is relatively simple. There is no need to explicitly keep track of the sub-experts. Instead, the algorithm can use a linear machine type representation. Each class keeps a vector of weights, one weight for each attribute. During an update, only the correct class weights and the predicted class weights are changed. The correct class weights are multiplied by α^{z_i}; the predicted class weights are multiplied by α^{-z_i}.

The above procedure is very similar to the Balanced algorithm from [Lit89], in fact, for $k = 2$, it is identical. A similar transformation duplicates the behavior of the linear-threshold learning version of WMA as given in [Lit89].

$$z_i \implies \begin{pmatrix} z_i \\ 1 - z_i \end{pmatrix}$$

While this transformation shows some advantages for $k = 2$, more research is needed to determine the proper way to generalize to the multi-class case. For both of these transformations, the bounds given in this paper are equivalent (except for a superficial adjustment in the δ notation of WMA) to the original bounds given in [Lit89].

4.4 Combining attributes and sub-experts

These transformations suggest the proper way to do a hybrid algorithm that combines sub-experts and attributes: use the transformations to create new sub-experts from the attributes and combine them with the original sub-experts when running Committee. It may even be desirable to break original sub-experts into attributes and use both in the algorithm because some sub-experts may perform better on certain classes. For example, if it is felt that a sub-expert is particularly good at class 1, we can perform the following transformation.

$$\begin{pmatrix} x_1 \\ x_2 \\ x_3 \end{pmatrix} \implies \begin{pmatrix} x_1 \\ x_2 \\ x_3 \end{pmatrix} \begin{pmatrix} x_1 \\ 0 \\ 0 \end{pmatrix} \begin{pmatrix} 0 \\ x_1 \\ 0 \end{pmatrix} \begin{pmatrix} 0 \\ 0 \\ x_1 \end{pmatrix}$$

Now, instead of using one weight for the whole sub-expert, Committee can also learn based on the sub-expert's performance for the first class. Even if a good target is representable only with the original sub-experts, these additional sub-experts will not have a large effect because of the logarithmic bound. In the same vein, it may be useful to add constant attributes to a set of sub-experts. These add only k extra sub-experts, but allow the algorithm to represent a larger set of target functions.

5 Conclusion

In this paper, we have introduced Committee, a multi-class learning algorithm. We feel that this algorithm will be important in practice, extending the range of problems that can be handled by the Winnow family of algorithms. With a solid theoretical foundation, researchers can customize Winnow algorithms to handle various multi-class problems.

Part of this customization includes feature transformations. We show how Committee can handle general linear machine problems by transforming attributes into sub-experts. This suggests a way to do a hybrid learning algorithm that allows a combination of sub-experts and attributes. This same techniques can also be used to add to the representational power on a standard sub-expert problem.

In the future, we plan to empirically test Committee and the feature transformations on real world problems. Part of this testing will include modifying the algorithm to use extra information, that is related to the proof technique [Mes99], in an attempt to lower the number of mistakes. We speculate that adjusting the multiplier to increase the change in progress per trial will be useful for certain types of multi-class problems.

Acknowledgments

We thank Nick Littlestone for stimulating this work by suggesting techniques for converting the Balanced algorithm to multi-class targets. Also we thank Haym Hirsh, Nick Littlestone and Warren Smith for providing valuable comments and corrections.

References

[Blu95] Avrim Blum. Empirical support for winnow and weighted-majority algorithms: results on a calendar scheduling domain. In *ML-95*, pages 64–72, 1995.

[DH73] R. O. Duda and P. Hart. *Pattern Classification and Scene Analysis*. Wiley, New York, 1973.

[DKR97] I. Dagan, Y. Karov, and D. Roth. Mistake-driven learning in text categorization. In *EMNLP-97*, pages 55–63, 1997.

[GR96] A. R. Golding and D. Roth. Applying winnow to context-sensitive spelling correction. In *ML-96*, 1996.

[KW97] Jyrki Kivinen and Manfred K. Warmuth. Additive versus exponentiated gradient updates for linear prediction. *Information and Computation*, 132(1):1–64, 1997.

[Lit89] Nick Littlestone. *Mistake bounds and linear-threshold learning algorithms*. PhD thesis, University of California, Santa Cruz, 1989. Technical Report UCSC-CRL-89-11.

[Lit91] Nick Littlestone. Redundant noisy attributes, attribute errors, and linear-threshold learning using winnow. In *COLT-91*, pages 147–156, 1991.

[Lit95] Nick Littlestone. Comparing several linear-threshold learning algorithms on tasks involving superfluous attributes. In *ML-95*, pages 353–361, 1995.

[LM] Nick Littlestone and Chris Mesterharm. A simulation study of winnow and related algorithms. Work in progress.

[MCF+94] T. Mitchell, R. Caruana, D. Freitag, J. McDermott, and D. Zabowski. Experience with a personal learning assistant. *CACM*, 37(7):81–91, 1994.

[Mes99] Chris Mesterharm. A multi-class linear learning algorithm related to winnow with proof. Technical report, Rutgers University, 1999.

Invariant Feature Extraction and Classification in Kernel Spaces

Sebastian Mika[1], Gunnar Rätsch[1], Jason Weston[2],
Bernhard Schölkopf[3], Alex Smola[4], and Klaus-Robert Müller[1]

1 GMD FIRST, Kekulèstr. 7, 12489 Berlin, Germany
2 Barnhill BioInformatics, 6709 Waters Av., Savannah, GR 31406, USA
3 Microsoft Research Ltd., 1 Guildhall Street, Cambridge CB2 3NH, UK
4 Australian National University, Canberra, 0200 ACT, Australia

{mika, raetsch, klaus}@first.gmd.de, jasonw@dcs.rhbnc.ac.uk
bsc@microsoft.com, Alex.Smola.anu.edu.au

Abstract

We incorporate prior knowledge to construct nonlinear algorithms for invariant feature extraction and discrimination. Employing a unified framework in terms of a nonlinear variant of the Rayleigh coefficient, we propose non-linear generalizations of Fisher's discriminant and oriented PCA using Support Vector kernel functions. Extensive simulations show the utility of our approach.

1 Introduction

It is common practice to preprocess data by extracting linear or nonlinear features. The most well-known feature extraction technique is principal component analysis PCA (e.g. [3]). It aims to find an orthonormal, ordered basis such that the i-th direction describes as much variance as possible while maintaining orthogonality to all other directions. However, since PCA is a linear technique, it is too limited to capture interesting nonlinear structure in a data set and nonlinear generalizations have been proposed, among them Kernel PCA [14], which computes the principal components of the data set mapped nonlinearly into some high dimensional feature space $\mathcal{F}$.

Often one has prior information, for instance, we might know that the sample is corrupted by noise or that there are invariances under which a classification should not change. For feature extraction, the concepts of known noise or transformation invariance are to a certain degree equivalent, i.e. they can both be interpreted as causing a change in the feature which ought to be minimized. Clearly, invariance alone is not a sufficient condition for a good feature, as we could simply take the constant function. What one would like to obtain is a feature which is as invariant as possible while still covering as much of the information necessary for describing the particular data. Considering only one (linear) feature vector w and restricting to first and second order statistics of the data one arrives at a maximization of the so called *Rayleigh* coefficient

$$J(w) = \frac{w^\top S_I w}{w^\top S_N w}, \tag{1}$$

where w is the feature vector and S_I, S_N are matrices describing the desired and undesired properties of the feature, respectively (e.g. information and noise). If S_I is the data covariance and S_N the noise covariance, we obtain *oriented PCA* [3]. If we leave the field of data description to perform supervised classification, it is common to choose S_I as the separability of class centers (between class variance) and S_N to be the within class variance. In that case, we recover the well known Fisher Discriminant [7]. The ratio in (1) is maximized when we cover much of the information coded by S_I while avoiding the one coded by S_N. The problem is known to be solved, in analogy to PCA, by a generalized symmetric eigenproblem $S_I w = \lambda S_N w$ [3], where $\lambda \in \mathbb{R}$ is the corresponding (biggest) eigenvalue.

In this paper we generalize this setting to a nonlinear one. In analogy to [8, 14] we first map the data via some nonlinear mapping Φ to some high-dimensional feature space $\mathcal{F}$ and then optimize (1) in $\mathcal{F}$. To avoid working with the mapped data explicitly (which might be impossible if $\mathcal{F}$ is infinite dimensional) we introduce support vector kernel functions [11], the well-known kernel trick. These kernel functions $k(x, y)$ compute a dot product in some feature space $\mathcal{F}$, i.e. $k(x,y) = (\Phi(x) \cdot \Phi(y))$. Formulating the algorithms in $\mathcal{F}$ using Φ only in dot products, we can replace any occurrence of a dot product by the kernel function k. Possible choices for k which have proven useful e.g. in Support Vector Machines [2] or Kernel PCA [14] are Gaussian RBF, $k(x, y) = \exp(-\|x - y\|^2/c)$, or polynomial kernels, $k(x,y) = (x \cdot y)^d$, for some positive constants $c \in \mathbb{R}$ and $d \in \mathbb{N}$, respectively.

The remainder of this paper is organized as follows: The next section shows how to formulate the optimization problem induced by (1) in feature space. Section 3 considers various ways to find Fisher's Discriminant in $\mathcal{F}$; we conclude with extensive experiments in section 4 and a discussion of our findings.

2 Kernelizing the Rayleigh Coefficient

To optimize (1) in some kernel feature space $\mathcal{F}$ we need to find a formulation which uses only dot products of Φ-images. As numerator and denominator are both scalars this can be done independently. Furthermore, the matrices S_I and S_N are basically covariances and thus the sum over outer products of Φ-images. Therefore, and due to the linear nature of (1) every solution $w \in \mathcal{F}$ can be written as an expansion in terms of mapped training data[1], i.e.

$$w = \sum_{i=1}^{\ell} \alpha_i \Phi(x_i). \qquad (2)$$

To define some common choices in $\mathcal{F}$ let $\mathcal{X} = \{x_1, \ldots, x_\ell\}$ be our training sample and, where appropriate, $\mathcal{X}_1 \cup \mathcal{X}_2 = \mathcal{X}, \mathcal{X}_1 \cap \mathcal{X}_2 = \emptyset$, two subclasses (with $|\mathcal{X}_i| = \ell_i$). We get the full covariance of $\mathcal{X}$ by

$$C = \frac{1}{\ell} \sum_{x \in \mathcal{X}} (\Phi(x) - m)(\Phi(x) - m)^\top \text{ with } m = \frac{1}{\ell} \sum_{x \in \mathcal{X}} \Phi(x), \qquad (3)$$

---

[1] S_B and S_W are operators on a (finite-dimensional) subspace spanned by the $\Phi(x_i)$ (in a possibly infinite space). Let $w = v_1 + v_2$, where $v_1 \in \text{Span}(\Phi(x_i) : i = 1, \ldots, \ell)$ and $v_2 \perp \text{Span}(\Phi(x_i) : i = 1, \ldots, \ell)$. Then for $S = S_W$ or $S = S_B$ (which are both symmetric)

$$\begin{aligned}
\langle w, Sw \rangle &= \langle (v_1 + v_2), S(v_1 + v_2) \rangle \\
&= \langle (v_1 + v_2)S, v_1 \rangle \\
&= \langle v_1, Sv_1 \rangle
\end{aligned}$$

As v_1 lies in the span of the $\Phi(x_i)$ and S only operates on this subspace there exist an expansion of w which maximizes $J(w)$.

which could be used as S_I in oriented Kernel PCA. For S_N we could use an estimate of the noise covariance, analogous to the definition of C but over mapped patterns sampled from the assumed noise distribution. The standard formulation of the Fisher discriminant in $\mathcal{F}$, yielding the *Kernel Fisher Discriminant* (KFD) [8] is given by

$$S_W = \sum_{i=1,2} \sum_{x \in \mathcal{X}_i} (\Phi(x) - m_i)(\Phi(x) - m_i)^\top \quad \text{and} \quad S_B = (m_2 - m_1)(m_2 - m_1)^\top,$$

the within-class scatter S_W (as S_N), and the between class scatter S_B (as S_I). Here m_i is the sample mean for patterns from class i.

To incorporate a known invariance e.g. in oriented Kernel PCA, one could use the tangent covariance matrix [12],

$$T = \frac{1}{\ell t^2} \sum_{x \in \mathcal{X}} (\Phi(x) - \Phi(\mathcal{L}_t x))(\Phi(x) - \Phi(\mathcal{L}_t x))^\top \text{ for some small } t > 0. \qquad (4)$$

Here $\mathcal{L}_t$ is a local 1-parameter transformation. T is a finite difference approximation t of the covariance of the tangent of $\mathcal{L}_t$ at point $\Phi(x)$ (details e.g. in [12]). Using $S_I = C$ and $S_N = T$ in oriented Kernel PCA, we impose invariance under the local transformation $\mathcal{L}_t$. Crucially, this matrix is not only constructed from the training patterns $\mathcal{X}$. Therefore, the argument used to find the expansion (2) is slightly incorrect. Nevertheless, we can assume that (2) is a reasonable approximation for describing the variance induced by T.

Multiplying either of these matrices from the left and right with the expansion (2), we can find a formulation which uses only dot products. For the sake of brevity, we only give the explicit formulation of (1) in $\mathcal{F}$ for KFD (cf. [8] for details). Defining $(\boldsymbol{\mu}_i)_j = \frac{1}{\ell_i} \sum_{x \in \mathcal{X}_i} \mathrm{k}(x_j, x)$ we can write (1) for KFD as

$$J(\boldsymbol{\alpha}) = \frac{(\boldsymbol{\alpha}^\top \boldsymbol{\mu})^2}{\boldsymbol{\alpha}^\top N \boldsymbol{\alpha}} = \frac{\boldsymbol{\alpha}^\top M \boldsymbol{\alpha}}{\boldsymbol{\alpha}^\top N \boldsymbol{\alpha}}, \qquad (5)$$

where $N = KK^\top - \sum_{i=1,2} \ell_i \boldsymbol{\mu}_i \boldsymbol{\mu}_i^\top$, $\boldsymbol{\mu} = \boldsymbol{\mu}_2 - \boldsymbol{\mu}_1$, $M = \boldsymbol{\mu}\boldsymbol{\mu}^\top$, and $K_{ij} = \mathrm{k}(x_i, x_j)$. The results for other choices of S_I and S_N in $\mathcal{F}$ as for the cases of oriented kernel PCA or transformation invariance can be obtained along the same lines. Note that we still have to maximize a Rayleigh coefficient. However, now it is a quotient in terms of expansion coefficients $\boldsymbol{\alpha}$, and not in terms of $w \in \mathcal{F}$ which is a potentially infinite-dimensional space. Furthermore, it is well known that the solution for this special eigenproblem is in the direction of $N^{-1}(\boldsymbol{\mu}_2 - \boldsymbol{\mu}_1)$ [7], which can be solved using e.g. a Cholesky factorization of N. The projection of a new pattern x onto w in $\mathcal{F}$ can then be computed by

$$(w \cdot \Phi(x)) = \sum_{i=1}^{\ell} \alpha_i \mathrm{k}(x_i, x). \qquad (6)$$

3 Algorithms

Estimating a covariance matrix with rank up to ℓ from ℓ samples is ill-posed. Furthermore, by performing an explicit centering in $\mathcal{F}$ each covariance matrix loses one more dimension, i.e. it has only rank $\ell - 1$ (even worse, for KFD the matrix N has rank $\ell - 2$). Thus the ratio in (1) is not well defined anymore, as the denominator might become zero. In the following we will propose several ways to deal with this problem in KFD. Furthermore we will tackle the question how to solve the optimization problem of KFD more efficiently. So far, we have an eigenproblem of size $\ell \times \ell$. If ℓ becomes large this is numerically demanding. Reformulations of the original problem allow to overcome some of these limitations. Finally, we describe the connection between KFD and RBF networks.

3.1 Regularization and Solution on a Subspace

As noted before, the matrix N has only rank $\ell - 2$. Besides numerical problems which can cause the matrix N to be not even positive, we could think of imposing some regularization to control capacity in $\mathcal{F}$. To this end, we simply add a multiple of the identity matrix to N, i.e. replace N by N_μ where

$$N_\mu := N + \mu I. \tag{7}$$

This can be viewed in different ways: (i) for $\mu > 0$ it makes the problem feasible and numerically more stable as N_μ becomes positive; (ii) it can be seen as decreasing the bias in sample based estimation of eigenvalues (cf. [6]); (iii) it imposes a regularization on $\|\alpha\|^2$, favoring solutions with small expansion coefficients. Furthermore, one could use other regularization type additives to N, e.g. penalizing $\|w\|^2$ in analogy to SVM (by adding the kernel matrix $K_{ij} = \mathrm{k}(x_i, x_j)$).

To optimize (5) we need to solve an $\ell \times \ell$ eigenproblem, which might be intractable for large ℓ. As the solutions are not sparse one can not directly use efficient algorithms like chunking for Support Vector Machines (cf. [13]). To this end, we might restrict the solution to lie in a subspace, i.e. instead of expanding w by (2) we write

$$w = \sum_{i=1}^{m} \alpha_i \Phi(z_i), \tag{8}$$

with $m < l$. The patterns z_i could either be a subset of the training patterns $\mathcal{X}$ or e.g. be estimated by some clustering algorithm. The derivation of (5) does not change, only K is now $m \times \ell$ and we end up with $m \times m$ matrices N and M. Another advantage is, that it increases the rank of N (relative to its size) although there still might be some need for regularization.

3.2 Quadratic optimization and Sparsification

Even if N has full rank, maximizing (5) is underdetermined: if α is optimal, then so is any multiple thereof. Since $\alpha^\top M \alpha = (\alpha^\top \mu)^2$, M has rank one. Thus we can seek for a vector α, such that $\alpha^\top N \alpha$ is minimal for fixed $\alpha^\top \mu$ (e.g. to 1). The solution is unique and we can find the optimal α by solving the quadratic optimization problem:

$$\min \ \alpha^\top N \alpha \quad \text{subject to} \quad \alpha^\top \mu = 1. \tag{9}$$

Although the quadratic optimization problem is not easier to solve than the eigenproblem, it has an appealing interpretation. The constraint $\alpha^\top \mu = 1$ ensures, that the average class distance, projected onto the direction of discrimination, is constant, while the intra class variance is minimized, i.e. we maximize the *average* margin. Contrarily, the SVM approach [2] optimizes for a large *minimal* margin. Considering (9) we are able to overcome another shortcoming of KFD. The solutions α are *not* sparse and thus evaluating (6) is expensive. To solve this we can add an l_1-regularizer $\lambda \|\alpha\|_1$ to the objective function, where λ is a regularization parameter allowing us to adjust the degree of sparseness.

3.3 Connection to RBF Networks

Interestingly, there exists a close connection between RBF networks (e.g. [9, 1]) and KFD. If we add no regularization and expand in all training patterns, we find that an optimal α is given by $\alpha = K^{-1} y$, where K is the symmetric, positive matrix of all kernel elements $\mathrm{k}(x_i, x_j)$ and y the ± 1 label vector[2]. A RBF-network with the

---

[2] To see this, note that N can be written as $N = KDK$ where $D = I - y_1 y_1^\top - y_2 y_2^\top$ has rank $\ell - 2$, while y_i is the vector of $1/\sqrt{\ell_i}$'s for patterns from class i and zero otherwise.

	RBF	AB	AB$_R$	SVM	KFD
Banana	**10.8±0.06**	12.3±0.07	*10.9±0.04*	11.5±0.07	**10.8±0.05**
B.Cancer	27.6±0.47	30.4±0.47	26.5±0.45	*26.0±0.47*	**25.8±0.46**
Diabetes	24.3±0.19	26.5±0.23	23.8±0.18	*23.5±0.17*	**23.2±0.16**
German	24.7±0.24	27.5±0.25	24.3±0.21	**23.6±0.21**	*23.7±0.22*
Heart	17.6±0.33	20.3±0.34	16.5±0.35	**16.0±0.33**	*16.1±0.34*
Image	3.3±0.06	**2.7±0.07**	**2.7±0.06**	*3.0±0.06*	4.8±0.06
Ringnorm	1.7±0.02	1.9±0.03	*1.6±0.01*	1.7±0.01	**1.5±0.01**
F.Sonar	34.4±0.20	35.7±0.18	34.2±0.22	**32.4±0.18**	*33.2±0.17*
Splice	*10.0±0.10*	10.1±0.05	**9.5±0.07**	10.9±0.07	10.5±0.06
Thyroid	4.5±0.21	*4.4±0.22*	4.6±0.22	4.8±0.22	**4.2±0.21**
Titanic	23.3±0.13	*22.6±0.12*	*22.6±0.12*	**22.4±0.10**	23.2±0.20
Twonorm	2.9±0.03	3.0±0.03	*2.7±0.02*	3.0±0.02	**2.6±0.02**
Waveform	10.7±0.11	10.8±0.06	**9.8±0.08**	*9.9±0.04*	*9.9±0.04*

Table 1: Comparison between KFD, single RBF classifier, AdaBoost (AB), regul. AdaBoost (AB$_R$) and SVMs (see text). Best result in bold face, second best in italics.

same kernel at each sample and fixed kernel width gives the same solution, if the mean squared error between labels and output is minimized. Also for the case of restricted expansions (8) there exists a connection to RBF networks with a smaller number of centers (cf. [4]).

4 Experiments

Kernel Fisher Discriminant Figure 1 shows an illustrative comparison of the features found by KFD, and Kernel PCA. The KFD feature discriminates the two classes, the first Kernel PCA feature picks up the important nonlinear structure.
To evaluate the performance of the KFD on real data sets we performed an extensive comparison to other state-of-the-art classifiers, whose details are reported in [8].[3]
We compared the Kernel Fisher Discriminant and Support Vector Machines, both with Gaussian kernel, to AdaBoost [5], and regularized AdaBoost [10] (cf. table 1). For KFD we used the regularized within-class scatter (7) and computed projections onto the optimal direction $w \in \mathcal{F}$ by means of (6). To use w for classification we have to estimate a threshold. This can be done by e.g. trying all thresholds between two outputs on the training set and selecting the median of those with the smallest empirical error, or (as we did here) by computing the threshold which maximizes the margin on the outputs in analogy to a Support Vector Machine, where we deal with errors on the trainig set by using the SVM soft margin approach. A disadvantage of this is, however, that we have to control the regularization constant for the slack variables. The results in table 1 show the average test error and the standard

---

If K has full rank, the null space of D, which is spanned by y_1 and y_2, is the null space of N. For $\bar{\alpha} = K^{-1}y$ we get $\bar{\alpha}^T N \bar{\alpha} = 0$ and $\bar{\alpha}^T \mu \neq 0$. As we are free to fix the constraint $\alpha^T \mu$ to any positive constant (not just 1), $\bar{\alpha}$ is also feasible.

[3]The breast cancer domain was obtained from the University Medical Center, Inst. of Oncology, Ljubljana, Yugoslavia. Thanks to M. Zwitter and M. Soklic for the data. All data sets used in the experiments can be obtained via http://www.first.gmd.de/~raetsch/.

Figure 1: Comparison of feature found by KFD (left) and first Kernel PCA feature (right). Depicted are two classes (information only used by KFD) as dots and crosses and levels of same feature value. Both with polynomial kernel of degree two, KFD with the regularized within class scatter (7) ($\mu = 10^{-3}$).

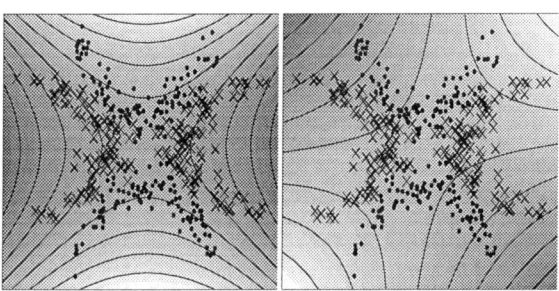

deviation of the averages' estimation, over 100 runs with different realizations of the datasets. To estimate the necessary parameters, we ran 5-fold cross validation on the first five realizations of the training sets and took the model parameters to be the median over the five estimates (see [10] for details of the experimental setup).

Using prior knowledge. A toy example (figure 2) shows a comparison of Kernel PCA and oriented Kernel PCA, which used S_I as the full covariance (3) and as noise matrix S_N the tangent covariance (4) of (i) rotated patterns and (ii) along the x-axis translated patterns. The toy example shows how imposing the desired invariance yields meaningful invariant features.

In another experiment we incorporated prior knowledge in KFD. We used the USPS database of handwritten digits, which consists of 7291 training and 2007 test patterns, each 256 dimensional gray scale images of the digits $0\ldots9$. We used the regularized within-class scatter (7) ($\mu = 10^{-3}$) as S_N and added to it an multiple λ of the tangent covariance (4), i.e. $S_N = N_\mu + \lambda T$. As invariance transformations we have chosen horizontal and vertical translation, rotation, and thickening (cf. [12]), where we simply averaged the matrices corresponding to each transformation. The feature was extracted by using the restricted expansion (8), where the patterns z_i were the first 3000 training samples. As kernel we have chosen a Gaussian of width $0.3 \cdot 256$, which is optimal for SVMs [12]. For each class we trained one KFD which classified this class against the rest and computed the 10-class error by the winner-takes-all scheme. The threshold was estimated by minimizing the empirical risk on the normalized outputs of KFD.

Without invariances, i.e. $\lambda = 0$, we achieved a test error of 3.7%, slightly better than a plain SVM with the same kernel (4.2%) [12]. For $\lambda = 10^{-3}$, using the tangent covariance matrix led to a very slight improvement to 3.6%. That the result was not significantly better than the corresponding one for KFD (3.7%) can be attributed to the fact that we used the same expansion coefficients in both cases. The tangent covariance matrix, however, lives in a slightly different subspace. And indeed, a subsequent experiment where we used vectors which were obtained by clustering a larger dataset, including virtual examples generated by the appropriate invariance transformation, led to 3.1%, comparable to an SVM using prior knowledge (e.g. [12]; best SVM result 2.9% with local kernel and virtual support vectors).

5 Conclusion

In the task of learning from data it is equivalent to have prior knowledge about e.g. invariances or about specific sources of noise. In the case of feature extraction, we seek features which are sufficiently (noise-) invariant while still describing interesting structure. Oriented PCA and, closely related, Fisher's Discriminant, use particularly simple features, since they only consider first and second order statistics for maximizing the Rayleigh coefficient (1). Since linear methods can be too restricted in many real-world applications, we used Support Vector Kernel functions to obtain nonlinear versions of these algorithms, namely oriented Kernel PCA and Kernel Fisher Discriminant analysis.

Our experiments show that the Kernel Fisher Discriminant is competitive or in

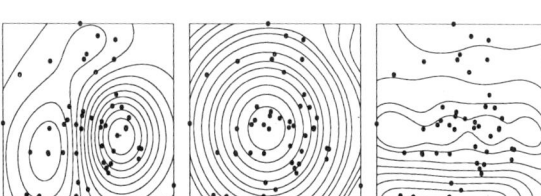

Figure 2: Comparison of first features found by Kernel PCA and oriented Kernel PCA (see text); from left to right: KPCA, OKPCA with rotation and translation invariance; all with Gaussian kernel.

some cases even superior to the other state-of-the-art algorithms tested. Interestingly, both SVM and KFD construct a hyperplane in $\mathcal{F}$ which is in some sense optimal. In many cases, the one given by the solution w of KFD is superior to the one of SVMs. Encouraged by the preliminary results for digit recognition, we believe that the reported results can be improved, by incorporating different invariances and using e.g. local kernels [12].

Future research will focus on further improvements on the algorithmic complexity of our new algorithms, which is so far larger than the one of the SVM algorithm, and on the connection between KFD and Support Vector Machines (cf. [16, 15]).

Acknowledgments This work was partially supported by grants of the DFG (JA 379/5-2,7-1,9-1) and the EC STORM project number 25387 and carried out while BS and AS were with GMD First.

References

[1] C.M. Bishop. *Neural Networks for Pattern Recognition.* Oxford Univ. Press, 1995.

[2] B. Boser, I. Guyon, and V.N. Vapnik. A training algorithm for optimal margin classifiers. In D. Haussler, editor, *Proc. COLT*, pages 144–152. ACM Press, 1992.

[3] K.I. Diamantaras and S.Y. Kung. *Principal Component Neural Networks.* Wiley, New York, 1996.

[4] B.Q. Fang and A.P. Dawid. Comparison of full bayes and bayes-least squares criteria for normal discrimination. *Chinese Journal of Applied Probability and Statistics*, 12:401–410, 1996.

[5] Y. Freund and R.E. Schapire. A decision-theoretic generalization of on-line learning and an application to boosting. In *EuroCOLT 94*. LNCS, 1994.

[6] J.H. Friedman. Regularized discriminant analysis. *Journal of the American Statistical Association*, 84(405):165–175, 1989.

[7] K. Fukunaga. *Introduction to Statistical Pattern Recognition.* Academic Press, San Diego, 2nd edition, 1990.

[8] S. Mika, G. Rätsch, J. Weston, B. Schölkopf, and K.-R. Müller. Fisher discriminant analysis with kernels. In Y.-H. Hu, J. Larsen, E. Wilson, and S. Douglas, editors, *Neural Networks for Signal Processing IX*, pages 41–48. IEEE, 1999.

[9] J. Moody and C. Darken. Fast learning in networks of locally-tuned processing units. *Neural Computation*, 1(2):281–294, 1989.

[10] G. Rätsch, T. Onoda, and K.-R. Müller. Soft margins for adaboost. Technical Report NC-TR-1998-021, Royal Holloway College, University of London, UK, 1998.

[11] S. Saitoh. *Theory of Reproducing Kernels and its Applications.* Longman Scientific & Technical, Harlow, England, 1988.

[12] B. Schölkopf. *Support vector learning.* Oldenbourg Verlag, 1997.

[13] B. Schölkopf, C.J.C. Burges, and A.J. Smola, editors. *Advances in Kernel Methods – Support Vector Learning.* MIT Press, 1999.

[14] B. Schölkopf, A.J. Smola, and K.-R. Müller. Nonlinear component analysis as a kernel eigenvalue problem. *Neural Computation*, 10:1299–1319, 1998.

[15] A. Shashua. On the relationship between the support vector machine for classification and sparsified fisher's linear discriminant. *Neural Processing Letters*, 9(2):129–139, April 1999.

[16] S. Tong and D. Koller. Bayes optimal hyperplanes $\rightarrow$ maximal margin hyperplanes. Submitted to IJCAI'99 Workshop on Support Vector Machines (robotics.stanford.edu/~koller/), 1999.

Approximate inference algorithms for two-layer Bayesian networks

Andrew Y. Ng
Computer Science Division
UC Berkeley
Berkeley, CA 94720
ang@cs.berkeley.edu

Michael I. Jordan
Computer Science Division and
Department of Statistics
UC Berkeley
Berkeley, CA 94720
jordan@cs.berkeley.edu

Abstract

We present a class of approximate inference algorithms for graphical models of the QMR-DT type. We give convergence rates for these algorithms and for the Jaakkola and Jordan (1999) algorithm, and verify these theoretical predictions empirically. We also present empirical results on the difficult QMR-DT network problem, obtaining performance of the new algorithms roughly comparable to the Jaakkola and Jordan algorithm.

1 Introduction

The graphical models formalism provides an appealing framework for the design and analysis of network-based learning and inference systems. The formalism endows graphs with a joint probability distribution and interprets most queries of interest as marginal or conditional probabilities under this joint. For a fixed model one is generally interested in the conditional probability of an output given an input (for prediction), or an input conditional on the output (for diagnosis or control). During learning the focus is usually on the likelihood (a marginal probability), on the conditional probability of unobserved nodes given observed nodes (e.g., for an EM or gradient-based algorithm), or on the conditional probability of the parameters given the observed data (in a Bayesian setting).

In all of these cases the key computational operation is that of marginalization. There are several methods available for computing marginal probabilities in graphical models, most of which involve some form of message-passing on the graph. Exact methods, while viable in many interesting cases (involving sparse graphs), are infeasible in the dense graphs that we consider in the current paper. A number of approximation methods have evolved to treat such cases; these include search-based methods, loopy propagation, stochastic sampling, and variational methods.

Variational methods, the focus of the current paper, have been applied successfully to a number of large-scale inference problems. In particular, Jaakkola and Jordan (1999) developed a variational inference method for the QMR-DT network, a benchmark network involving over 4,000 nodes (see below). The variational method provided accurate approximation to posterior probabilities within a second of computer time. For this difficult inference problem exact methods are entirely infeasible (see below), loopy propagation does not converge to correct posteriors (Murphy, Weiss, & Jordan, 1999), and stochastic sampling methods are slow and unreliable (Jaakkola & Jordan, 1999).

A significant step forward in the understanding of variational inference was made by Kearns and Saul (1998), who used large deviation techniques to analyze the convergence rate of a simplified variational inference algorithm. Imposing conditions on the magnitude of the weights in the network, they established a $O(\sqrt{\log N/N})$ rate of convergence for the error of their algorithm, where N is the fan-in.

In the current paper we utilize techniques similar to those of Kearns and Saul to derive a new set of variational inference algorithms with rates that are faster than $O(\sqrt{\log N/N})$. Our techniques also allow us to analyze the convergence rate of the Jaakkola and Jordan (1999) algorithm. We test these algorithms on an idealized problem and verify that our analysis correctly predicts their rates of convergence. We then apply these algorithms to the difficult the QMR-DT network problem.

2 Background

2.1 The QMR-DT network

The QMR-DT (Quick Medical Reference, Decision-Theoretic) network is a bipartite graph with approximately 600 top-level nodes d_i representing diseases and approximately 4000 lower-level nodes f_j representing findings (observed symptoms). All nodes are binary-valued. Each disease is given a prior probability $P(d_i = 1)$, obtained from archival data, and each finding is parameterized as a "noisy-OR" model:

$$P(f_i = 1|d) = 1 - e^{-\theta_{i0} - \sum_{j \in \pi_i} \theta_{ij} d_j},$$

where π_i is the set of parent diseases for finding f_i, and where the parameters θ_{ij} are obtained from assessments by medical experts (see Shwe, et al., 1991).

Letting $z_i = \theta_{i0} + \sum_{j \in \pi_i} \theta_{ij} d_j$, we have the following expression for the likelihood[1]:

$$P(f) = \sum_{\{d\}} \left[\prod_{i=1}^{K} (1 - e^{-z_i})^{f_i} \prod_{i=1}^{K} (e^{-z_i})^{1-f_i} \prod_{j=1}^{N} P(d_j) \right], \quad (1)$$

where the sum is a sum across the approximately 2^{600} configurations of the diseases. Note that the second product, a product over the negative findings, factorizes across the diseases d_j; these factors can be absorbed into the priors $P(d_j)$ and have no significant effect on the complexity of inference. It is the positive findings which couple the diseases and prevent the sum from being distributed across the product.

Generic exact algorithms such as the junction tree algorithm scale exponentially in the size of the maximal clique in a moralized, triangulated graph. Jaakkola and Jordan (1999) found cliques of more than 150 nodes in QMR-DT; this rules out the junction tree algorithm. Heckerman (1989) discovered a factorization specific to QMR-DT that reduces the complexity substantially; however the resulting algorithm still scales exponentially in the number of positive findings and is only feasible for a small subset of the benchmark cases.

---

[1] In this expression, the factors $P(d_j)$ are the probabilities associated with the (parent-less) disease nodes, the factors $(1 - e^{-z_i})$ are the probabilities of the (child) finding nodes that are observed to be in their positive state, and the factors e^{-z_i} are the probabilities of the negative findings. The resulting product is the joint probability $P(f, d)$, which is marginalized to obtain the likelihood $P(f)$.

2.2 The Jaakkola and Jordan (JJ) algorithm

Jaakkola and Jordan (1999) proposed a variational algorithm for approximate inference in the QMR-DT setting. Briefly, their approach is to make use of the following variational inequality:

$$1 - e^{-z_i} \leq e^{\lambda_i z_i - c_i},$$

where c_i is a deterministic function of λ_i. This inequality holds for arbitrary values of the free "variational parameter" λ_i. Substituting these variational upper bounds for the probabilities of positive findings in Eq. (1), one obtains a factorizable upper bound on the likelihood. Because of the factorizability, the sum across diseases can be distributed across the joint probability, yielding a product of sums rather than a sum of products. One then minimizes the resulting expression with respect to the variational parameters to obtain the tightest possible variational bound.

2.3 The Kearns and Saul (KS) algorithm

A simplified variational algorithm was proposed by Kearns and Saul (1998), whose main goal was the theoretical analysis of the rates of convergence for variational algorithms. In their approach, the local conditional probability for the finding f_i is approximated by its value at a point a small distance ε_i above or below (depending on whether upper or lower bounds are desired) the mean input $E[z_i]$. This yields a variational algorithm in which the values ε_i are the variational parameters to be optimized. Under the assumption that the weights θ_{ij} are bounded in magnitude by τ/N, where τ is a constant and N is the number of parent ("disease") nodes, Kearns and Saul showed that the error in likelihood for their algorithm converges at a rate of $O(\sqrt{\log N/N})$.

3 Algorithms based on local expansions

Inspired by Kearns and Saul (1998), we describe the design of approximation algorithms for QMR-DT obtained by expansions around the mean input to the finding nodes. Rather than using point approximations as in the Kearns-Saul (KS) algorithm, we make use of Taylor expansions. (See also Plefka (1982), and Barber and van de Laar (1999) for other perturbational techniques.)

Consider a generalized QMR-DT architecture in which the noisy-OR model is replaced by a general function $\psi(z) : \mathbb{R} \to [0, 1]$ having uniformly bounded derivatives, i.e., $|\psi^{(i)}(z)| \leq B_i$. Define $F(z_1, \ldots, z_K) = \prod_{i=1}^{K} (\psi(z_i))^{f_i} \prod_{i=1}^{K} (1 - \psi(z_i))^{1-f_i}$ so that the likelihood can be written as

$$P(f) = \mathrm{E}_{\{z_i\}}[F(z_1, \ldots, z_K)]. \qquad (2)$$

Also define $\mu_i = \mathrm{E}[z_i] = \theta_{i0} + \sum_{j=1}^{N} \theta_{ij} P(d_j = 1)$.

A simple mean-field-like approximation can be obtained by evaluating F at the mean values μ_i:

$$P(f) \approx F(\mu_1, \ldots, \mu_K). \qquad (3)$$

We refer to this approximation as "MF(0)."

Expanding the function F to second order, and defining $\epsilon_i = z_i - \mu_i$, we have:

$$\begin{aligned}
P(f) &= \mathrm{E}_{\{\epsilon_i\}} \Bigg[F(\vec{\mu}) + \sum_{i_1=1}^{K} F_{i_1}(\vec{\mu}) \epsilon_{i_1} + \frac{1}{2!} \sum_{i_1=1}^{K} \sum_{i_2=1}^{K} F_{i_1 i_2}(\vec{\mu}) \epsilon_{i_1} \epsilon_{i_2} + \\
&\quad \frac{1}{3!} \sum_{i_1=1}^{K} \sum_{i_2=1}^{K} \sum_{i_3=1}^{K} F_{i_1 i_2 i_3}(\vec{\xi}_\epsilon) \epsilon_{i_1} \epsilon_{i_2} \epsilon_{i_3} \Bigg]
\end{aligned} \qquad (4)$$

where the subscripts on F represent derivatives. Dropping the remainder term and bringing the expectation inside, we have the "MF(2)" approximation:

$$P(f) \approx F(\vec{\mu}) + \frac{1}{2} \sum_{i_1=1}^{K} \sum_{i_2=1}^{K} F_{i_1 i_2}(\vec{\mu}) \mathrm{E}[\epsilon_{i_1} \epsilon_{i_2}]$$

More generally, we obtain a "MF(i)" approximation by carrying out a Taylor expansion to i-th order.

3.1 Analysis

In this section, we give two theorems establishing convergence rates for the MF(i) family of algorithms and for the Jaakkola and Jordan algorithm. As in Kearns and Saul (1998), our results are obtained under the assumption that the weights are of magnitude at most $O(1/N)$ (recall that N is the number of disease nodes). For large N, this assumption of "weak interactions" implies that each z_i will be close to its mean value with high probability (by the law of large numbers), and thereby gives justification to the use of local expansions for the probabilities of the findings.

Due to space constraints, the detailed proofs of the theorems given in this section are deferred to the long version of this paper, and we will instead only sketch the intuitions for the proofs here.

Theorem 1 *Let K (the number of findings) be fixed, and suppose $|\theta_{ij}| \leq \frac{\tau}{N}$ for all i, j for some fixed constant τ. Then the absolute error of the MF(k) approximation is $O\left(\frac{1}{N^{(k+1)/2}}\right)$ for k odd and $O\left(\frac{1}{N^{(k/2+1)}}\right)$ for k even.*

Proof intuition. First consider the case of odd k. Since $|\theta_{ij}| \leq \frac{\tau}{N}$, the quantity $\epsilon_i = z_i - \mu_i = \sum_j \theta_{ij}(d_j - \mathrm{E}[d_j])$ is like an average of N random variables, and hence has standard deviation on the order $1/\sqrt{N}$. Since MF(k) matches F up to the k-th order derivatives, we find that when we take a Taylor expansion of MF(k)'s error, the leading non-zero term is the $k+1$-st order term, which contains quantities such as ϵ_i^{k+1}. Now because ϵ_i has standard deviation on the order $1/\sqrt{N}$, it is unsurprising that $\mathrm{E}[\epsilon_i^{k+1}]$ is on the order $1/N^{(k+1)/2}$, which gives the error of MF(k) for odd k.

For k even, the leading non-zero term in the Taylor expansion of the error is a $k+1$-st order term with quantities such as ϵ_i^{k+1}. But if we think of ϵ_i as converging (via a central limit theorem effect) to a symmetric distribution, then since symmetric distributions have small odd central moments, $\mathrm{E}[\epsilon_i^{k+1}]$ would be small. This means that for k even, we may look to the order $k+2$ term for the error, which leads to MF(k) having the the same big-O error as MF($k+1$). Note this is also consistent with how MF(0) and MF(1) always give the same estimates and hence have the same absolute error. $\square$

A theorem may also be proved for the convergence rate of the Jaakkola and Jordan (JJ) algorithm. For simplicity, we state it here only for noisy-OR networks.[2] A closely related result also holds for sigmoid networks with suitably modified assumptions; see the full paper.

Theorem 2 *Let K be fixed, and suppose $\psi(z) = 1-e^{-z}$ is the noisy-OR function. Suppose further that $0 \leq \theta_{ij} \leq \frac{\tau}{N}$ for all i, j for some fixed constant τ, and that $\mu_i \geq \mu_{\min}$ for all i, for some fixed $\mu_{\min} > 0$. Then the absolute error of the JJ approximation is $O\left(\frac{1}{N}\right)$.*

---

[2] Note in any case that JJ can be applied only when ψ is log-concave, such as in noisy-OR networks (where incidentally all weights are non-negative).

The condition of some $\mu_{\min}$ lowerbounding the μ_i's ensures that the findings are not too unlikely; for it to hold, it is sufficient that there be bias ("leak") nodes in the network with weights bounded away from zero.

Proof intuition. Neglecting negative findings, (which as discussed do not need to be handled variationally,) this result is proved for a "simplified" version of the JJ algorithm, that always chooses the variational parameters so that for each i, the exponential upperbound on $\psi(z_i)$ is tangent to ψ at $z_i = \mu_i$. (The "normal" version of JJ can have error no worse than this simplified one.) Taking a Taylor expansion again of the approximation's error, we find that since the upperbound has matched zeroth and first derivatives with F, the error is a second order term with quantities such as ϵ_i^2. As discussed in the MF(k) proof outline, this quantity has expectation on the order $1/N$, and hence JJ's error is $O(1/N)$. □

To summarize our results in the most useful cases, we find that MF(0) has a convergence rate of $O(1/N)$, both MF(2) and MF(3) have rates of $O(1/N^2)$, and JJ has a convergence rate of $O(1/N)$.

4 Simulation results

4.1 Artificial networks

We carried out a set of simulations that were intended to verify the theoretical results presented in the previous section. We used bipartite noisy-OR networks, with full connectivity between layers and with the weights θ_{ij} chosen uniformly in $(0, 2/N)$. The number N of top-level ("disease") nodes ranged from 10 to 1000. Priors on the disease nodes were chosen uniformly in $(0, 1)$.

The results are shown in Figure 1 for one and five positive findings (similar results where obtained for additional positive findings).

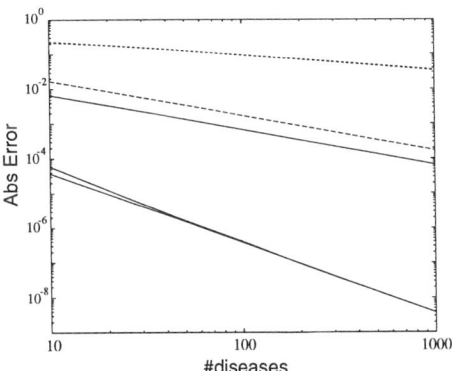
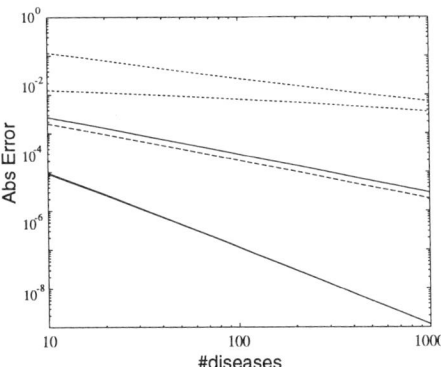

Figure 1: Absolute error in likelihood (averaged over many randomly generated networks) as a function of the number of disease nodes for various algorithms. The short-dashed lines are the KS upper and lower bounds (these curves overlap in the left panel), the long-dashed line is the JJ algorithm and the solid lines are MF(0), MF(2) and MF(3) (the latter two curves overlap in the right panel).

The results are entirely consistent with the theoretical analysis, showing nearly exactly the expected slopes of -1/2, -1 and -2 on a loglog plot.[3] Moreover, the asymptotic results are

---

[3] The anomalous behavior of the KS lower bound in the second panel is due to the fact that the algorithm generally finds a vacuous lower bound of 0 in this case, which yields an error which is essentially constant as a function of the number of diseases.

also predictive of overall performance: the MF(2) and MF(3) algorithms perform best in all cases, MF(0) and JJ are roughly equivalent, and KS is the least accurate.

4.2 QMR-DT network

We now present results for the QMR-DT network, in particular for the four benchmark CPC cases studied by Jaakkola and Jordan (1999). These cases all have fewer than 20 positive findings; thus it is possible to run the Heckerman (1989) "Quickscore" algorithm to obtain the true likelihood.

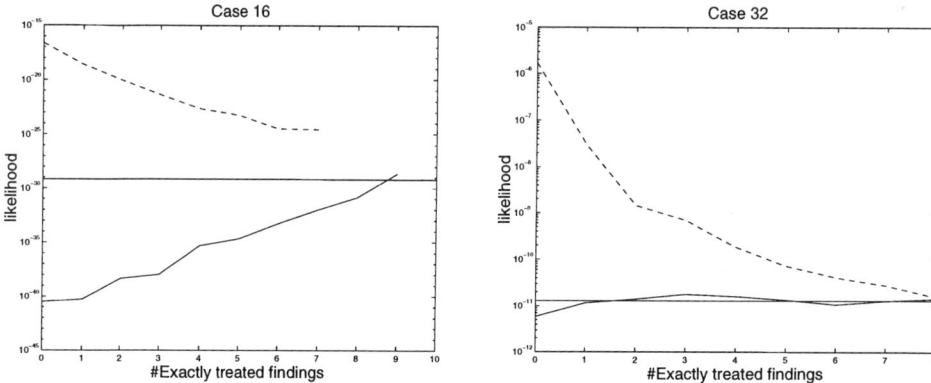

Figure 2: Results for CPC cases 16 and 32, for different numbers of exactly treated findings. The horizontal line is the true likelihood, the dashed line is JJ's estimate, and the lower solid line is MF(3)'s estimate.

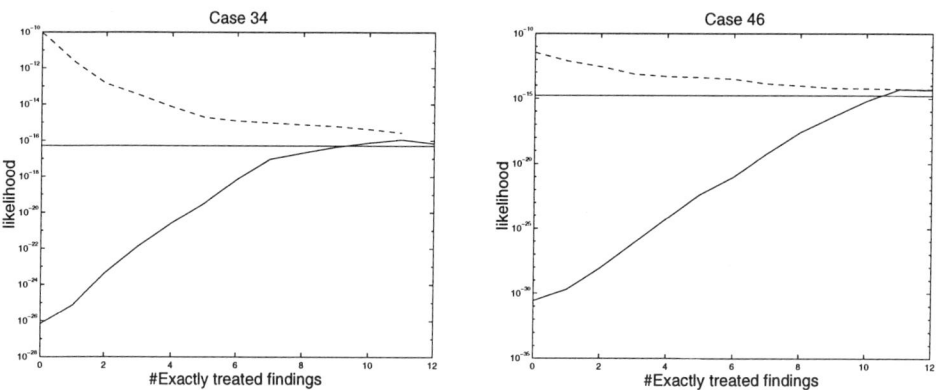

Figure 3: Results for CPC cases 34 and 46. Same legend as above.

In Jaakkola and Jordan (1999), a hybrid methodology was proposed in which only a portion of the findings were treated approximately; exact methods were used to treat the remaining findings. Using this hybrid methodology, Figures 2 and 3 show the results of running JJ and MF(3) on these four cases.[4]

---

[4]These experiments were run using a version of the JJ algorithm that optimizes the variational parameters just once without any findings treated exactly, and then uses these fixed values of the parameters thereafter. The order in which findings are chosen to be treated exactly is based on JJ's estimates, as described in Jaakkola and Jordan (1999). Missing points in the graphs for cases 16 and

The results show the MF algorithm yielding results that are comparable with the JJ algorithm.

5 Conclusions and extension to multilayer networks

This paper has presented a class of approximate inference algorithms for graphical models of the QMR-DT type, supplied a theoretical analysis of convergence rates, verified the rates empirically, and presented promising empirical results for the difficult QMR-DT problem.

Although the focus of this paper has been two-layer networks, the MF(k) family of algorithms can also be extended to multilayer networks. For example, consider a 3-layer network with nodes b_i being parents of nodes d_i being parents of nodes f_i. To approximate $\Pr[f]$ using (say) MF(2), we first write $\Pr[f]$ as an expectation of a function (F) of the z_i's, and approximate this function via a second-order Taylor expansion. To calculate the expectation of the Taylor approximation, we need to calculate terms in the expansion such as $E[d_i]$, $E[d_i d_j]$ and $E[d_i^2]$. When d_i had no parents, these quantities were easily derived in terms of the disease prior probabilities. Now, they instead depend on the joint distribution of d_i and d_j, which we use our two-layer version of MF(k), applied to the first two (b_i and d_i) layers of the network, to approximate. It is important future work to carefully study the performance of this algorithm in the multilayer setting.

Acknowledgments

We wish to acknowledge the helpful advice of Tommi Jaakkola, Michael Kearns, Kevin Murphy, and Larry Saul.

References

[1] Barber, D., & van de Laar, P. (1999) Variational cumulant expansions for intractable distributions. *Journal of Artificial Intelligence Research, 10*, 435–455.

[2] Heckerman, D. (1989). A tractable inference algorithm for diagnosing multiple diseases. In *Proceedings of the Fifth Conference on Uncertainty in Artificial Intelligence*.

[3] Jaakkola, T. S., & Jordan, M. I. (1999). Variational probabilistic inference and the QMR-DT network. *Journal of Artificial Intelligence Research, 10*, 291–322.

[4] Jordan, M. I., Ghahramani, Z., Jaakkola, T. S., & Saul, L. K. (1998). An introduction to variational methods for graphical models. In *Learning in Graphical Models*. Cambridge: MIT Press.

[5] Kearns, M. J., & Saul, L. K. (1998). Large deviation methods for approximate probabilistic inference, with rates of convergence. In G. F. Cooper & S. Moral (Eds.), *Proceedings of the Fourteenth Conference on Uncertainty in Artificial Intelligence*. San Mateo, CA: Morgan Kaufmann.

[6] Murphy, K. P., Weiss, Y., & Jordan, M. I. (1999). Loopy belief propagation for approximate inference: An empirical study. In *Proceedings of the Fifteenth Conference on Uncertainty in Artificial Intelligence*.

[7] Plefka, T. (1982). Convergence condition of the TAP equation for the infinite-ranged Ising spin glass model. In *J. Phys. A: Math. Gen., 15*(6).

[8] Shwe, M., Middleton, B., Heckerman, D., Henrion, M., Horvitz, E., Lehmann, H., & Cooper, G. (1991). Probabilistic diagnosis using a reformulation of the INTERNIST-1/QMR knowledge base I. The probabilistic model and inference algorithms. *Methods of Information in Medicine, 30*, 241–255.

---

34 correspond to runs where our implementation of the Quickscore algorithm encountered numerical problems.

Optimal Kernel Shapes for Local Linear Regression

Dirk Ormoneit   Trevor Hastie
Department of Statistics
Stanford University
Stanford, CA 94305-4065
ormoneit@stat.stanford.edu

Abstract

Local linear regression performs very well in many low-dimensional forecasting problems. In high-dimensional spaces, its performance typically decays due to the well-known "curse-of-dimensionality". A possible way to approach this problem is by varying the "shape" of the weighting kernel. In this work we suggest a new, data-driven method to estimating the optimal kernel shape. Experiments using an artificially generated data set and data from the UC Irvine repository show the benefits of kernel shaping.

1 Introduction

Local linear regression has attracted considerable attention in both statistical and machine learning literature as a flexible tool for nonparametric regression analysis [Cle79, FG96, AMS97]. Like most statistical smoothing approaches, local modeling suffers from the so-called "curse-of-dimensionality", the well-known fact that the proportion of the training data that lie in a fixed-radius neighborhood of a point decreases to zero at an exponential rate with increasing dimension of the input space. Due to this problem, the bandwidth of a weighting kernel must be chosen very big so as to contain a reasonable sample fraction. As a result, the estimates produced are typically highly biased. One possible way to reduce the bias of local linear estimates is to vary the "shape" of the weighting kernel. In this work, we suggest a method for estimating the optimal kernel shape using the training data. For this purpose, we parameterize the kernel in terms of a suitable "shape matrix", L, and minimize the mean squared forecasting error with respect to L. For such an approach to be meaningful, the "size" of the weighting kernel must be constrained during the minimization to avoid overfitting. We propose a new, entropy-based measure of the kernel size as a constraint. By analogy to the nearest neighbor approach to bandwidth selection [FG96], the suggested measure is adaptive with regard to the local data density. In addition, it leads to an efficient gradient descent algorithm for the computation of the optimal kernel shape. Experiments using an artificially generated data set and data from the UC Irvine repository show that kernel shaping can improve the performance of local linear estimates substantially.

The remainder of this work is organized as follows. In Section 2 we briefly review local linear models and introduce our notation. In Section 3 we formulate an objective function for kernel shaping, and in Section 4 we discuss entropic neighborhoods. Section 5 describes our experimental results and Section 6 presents conclusions.

2 Local Linear Models

Consider a nonlinear regression problem where a continuous response $y \in \mathbb{R}$ is to be predicted based on a d-dimensional predictor $x \in \mathbb{R}^d$. Let $D \equiv \{(x_t, y_t), t = 1, \ldots, T\}$ denote a set of training data. To estimate the conditional expectation $f(x_0) \equiv E[y|x_0]$, we consider the local linear expansion $f(x) \approx \alpha_0 + (x - x_0)'\beta_0$ in the neighborhood of x_0. In detail, we minimize the weighted least squares criterion

$$\mathcal{C}(\alpha, \beta; x_0) \equiv \sum_{t=1}^{T}(y_t - \alpha - (x_t - x_0)'\beta)^2 k(x_t, x_0) \qquad (1)$$

to determine estimates of the parameters α_0 and β_0. Here $k(x_t, x_0)$ is a non-negative *weighting kernel* that assigns more weight to residuals in the neighborhood of x_0 than to residuals distant from x_0. In multivariate problems, a standard way of defining $k(x_t, x_0)$ is by applying a univariate, non-negative "mother kernel" $\phi(z)$ to the distance measure $||x_t - x_0||_\Omega \equiv \sqrt{(x_t - x_0)'\Omega(x_t - x_0)}$:

$$k(x_t, x_0) \equiv \frac{\phi(||x_t - x_0||_\Omega)}{\sum_{s=1}^{T} \phi(||x_s - x_0||_\Omega)}. \qquad (2)$$

Here Ω is a positive definite $d \times d$ matrix determining the relative importance assigned to different directions of the input space. For example, if $\phi(z)$ is a standard normal density, $k(x_t, x_0)$ is a normalized multivariate Gaussian with mean x_0 and covariance matrix Ω^{-1}. Note that $k(x_t, x_0)$ is normalized so as to satisfy $\sum_{t=1}^{T} k(x_t, x_0) = 1$. Even though this restriction is not relevant directly with regard to the estimation of α_0 and β_0, it will be needed in our discussion of entropic neighborhoods in Section 4.

Using the shorthand notation $\hat{\gamma}(x_0, \Omega) \equiv (\hat{\alpha}_0, \hat{\beta}_0')'$, the solution of the minimization problem (1) may be written conveniently as

$$\hat{\gamma}(x_0, \Omega) = (X'WX)^{-1}X'WY, \qquad (3)$$

where X is the $T \times (d+1)$ design matrix with rows $(1, x_t' - x_0')'$, Y is the vector of response values, and W is a $T \times T$ diagonal matrix with entries $W_{t,t} = k(x_t, x_0)$. The resulting local linear fit at x_0 using the inverse covariance matrix Ω is simply $\hat{f}(x_0; \Omega) \equiv \hat{\alpha}_0$. Obviously, $\hat{f}(x_0; \Omega)$ depends on Ω through the definition of the weighting kernel (2). In the discussion below, our focus is on choices of Ω that lead to favorable estimates of the unknown function value $f(x_0)$.

3 Kernel Shaping

The local linear estimates resulting from different choices of Ω vary considerably in practice. A common strategy is to choose Ω proportional to the inverse sample covariance matrix. The remaining problem of finding the optimal scaling factor is equivalent to the problem of bandwidth selection in univariate smoothing [FG96, BBB99]. For example, the bandwidth is frequently chosen as a function of the distance between x_0 and its kth nearest neighbor in practical applications [FG96]. In this paper, we take a different viewpoint and argue that optimizing the "shape" of the weighting kernel is at least as important as optimizing the bandwidth. More specifically, for a fixed "volume" of the weighting kernel, the bias of the estimate can be reduced drastically by shrinking the kernel in directions of large nonlinear variation of $f(x)$, and stretching it in directions of small nonlinear variation. This idea is illustrated using the example shown in Figure 1. The plotted function is sigmoidal along an index vector κ and constant in directions orthogonal to κ. Therefore, a "shaped" weighting kernel is shrunk in the direction κ and stretched orthogonally to κ, minimizing the exposure of the kernel to the nonlinear variation.

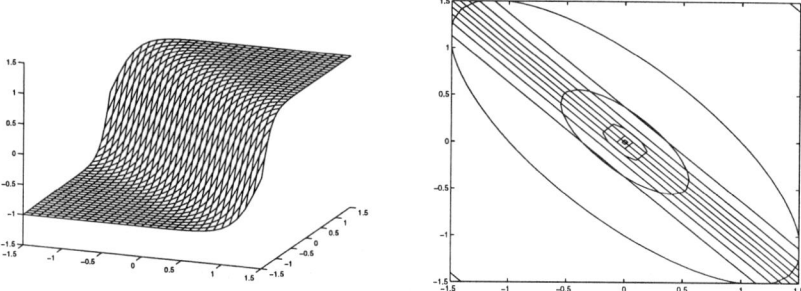

Figure 1: *Left:* Example of a single index model of the form $y = g(x'\kappa)$ with $\kappa = (1, 1)$ and $g(z) = \tanh(3z)$. *Right:* The contours of $g(z)$ are straight lines orthogonal to κ.

To distinguish formally the metric and the bandwidth of the weighting kernel, we rewrite Ω as follows:

$$\Omega \equiv \lambda \cdot (LL' + I). \qquad (4)$$

Here λ corresponds to the inverse bandwidth, and L may be interpreted as a metric- or shape-matrix. Below we suggest an algorithm which is designed to minimize the bias with respect to the kernel metric. Clearly, for such an approach to be meaningful, we need to restrict the "volume" of the weighting kernel; otherwise, the bias of the estimate could be minimized trivially by choosing a zero bandwidth. For example, we might define λ contingent on L so as to satisfy $|\Omega| = c$ for some constant c. A serious disadvantage of this idea is that, by contrast to the nearest neighbor approach, $|\Omega|$ is independent of the design. As a more appropriate alternative, we define λ in terms of a measure of the number of neighboring observations. In detail, we fix the volume of $k(x_t, x_0)$ in terms of the "entropy" of the weighting kernel. Then, we choose λ so as to satisfy the resulting entropy constraint. Given this definition of the bandwidth, we determine the metric of $k(x_t, x_0)$ by minimizing the mean squared prediction error:

$$\mathcal{C}(L; D) \equiv \sum_{t=1}^{T} (y_t - f(x_t; \Omega))^2 \qquad (5)$$

with respect to L. In this way, we obtain an approximation of the optimal kernel shape because the expectation of $\mathcal{C}(L; D)$ differs from the bias only by a variance term which is independent of L. Details of the entropic neighborhood criterion and of the numerical minimization procedure are described next.

4 Entropic Neighborhoods

We mentioned previously that, for a given shape matrix L, we choose the bandwidth parameter λ in (4) so as to fulfill a volume constraint on the weighting kernel. For this purpose, we interpret the kernel weights $k(x_t, x_0)$ as probabilities. In particular, as $k(x_t, x_0) > 0$ and $\sum_t k(x_t, x_0) = 1$ by definition (2), we can formulate the local *entropy* of $k(x_t, x_0)$:

$$H(\Omega) \equiv -\sum_{t=1}^{T} k(x_t, x_0) \log k(x_t, x_0). \qquad (6)$$

The entropy of a probability distribution is typically thought of as a measure of uncertainty. In the context of the weighting kernel $k(x_t, x_0)$, $H(\Omega)$ can be used as a smooth measure of the "size" of the neighborhood that is used for averaging. To see this, note that in the extreme case where equal weights are placed on all observations in D, the entropy is maximized. At the other extreme, if the single nearest neighbor of x_0 is assigned the entire weight of one, the entropy attains its minimum value zero. Thus, fixing the entropy at a constant value c is similar to fixing the number k in the nearest neighbor approach. Besides justifying (6), the correspondence between k and c can also be used to derive a more intuitive volume parameter than the entropy level c. We specify c in terms of a hypothetical weighting kernel that places equal weight on the k nearest neighbors of x_0 and zero weight on the remaining observations. Note that the entropy of this hypothetical kernel is $\log k$. Thus, it is natural to characterize the size of an entropic neighborhood in terms of k, and then to determine λ by numerically solving the nonlinear equation system (for details, see [OH99])

$$H(\Omega) = \log k. \qquad (7)$$

More precisely, we report the number of neighbors in terms of the *equivalent sample fraction* $\rho \equiv k/T$ to further intuition. This idea is illustrated in Figure 2 using a one- and a two-dimensional example. The equivalent sample fractions are $\rho = 30\%$ and $\rho = 50\%$, respectively. Note that in both cases the weighting kernel is wider in regions with few observations, and narrower in regions with many observations. As a consequence, the number of observations within contours of equal weighting remains approximately constant across the input space.

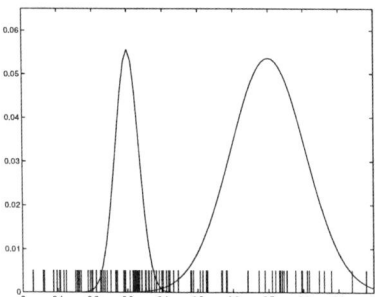
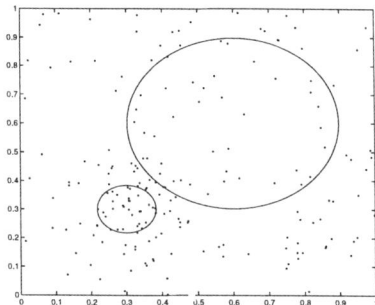

Figure 2: *Left:* Univariate weighting kernel $k(\cdot, x_0)$ evaluated at $x_0 = 0.3$ and $x_0 = 0.7$ based on a sample data set of 100 observations (indicated by the bars at the bottom). *Right:* Multivariate weighting kernel $k(\cdot, x_0)$ based on a sample data set of 200 observations. The two ellipsoids correspond to 95% contours of a weighting kernel evaluated at $(0.3, 0.3)'$ and $(0.6, 0.6)'$.

To summarize, we define the value of λ by fixing the equivalent sample fraction parameter ρ, and subsequently minimize the prediction error on the training set with respect to the shape matrix L. Note that we allow for the possibility that L may be of reduced rank $l \leq d$ as a means of controlling the number of free parameters. As a minimization procedure, we use a variant of gradient descent that accounts for the entropy constraint. In particular, our algorithm relies on the fact that (7) is differentiable with respect to L. Due to space limitations, the interested reader is referred to [OH99] for a formal derivation of the involved gradients and for a detailed description of the optimization procedure.

5 Experiments

In this section we compare kernel shaping to standard local linear regression using a fixed spherical kernel in two examples. First, we evaluate the performance using a simple toy problem which allows us to estimate confidence intervals for the prediction accuracy using Monte Carlo simulation. Second, we investigate a data set from the machine learning data base at UC Irvine [BKM98].

5.1 Mexican Hat Function

In our first example, we employ Monte Carlo simulation to evaluate the performance of kernel shaping in a five-dimensional regression problem. For this purpose, 20 sets of 500 data points each are generated independently according to the model

$$y = \cos(5\sqrt{x_1^2 + x_2^2}) \cdot \exp(-(x_1^2 + x_2^2)). \tag{8}$$

Here the predictor variables $x_1, \ldots, x_5$ are drawn according to a five-dimensional standard normal distribution. Note that, even though the regression is carried out in a five-dimensional predictor space, y is really only a function of the variables x_1 and x_2. In particular, as dimensions two through five do not contribute any information with regard to the value of y, kernel shaping should effectively discard these variables. Note also that there is no noise in this example.

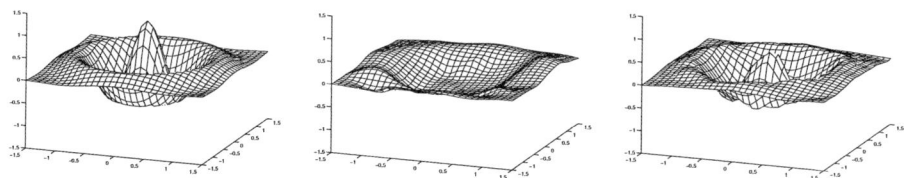

Figure 3: *Left:* "True" Mexican hat function. *Middle:* Local linear estimate using a spherical kernel ($\rho = 2\%$). *Right:* Local linear estimate using kernel shaping ($\rho = 2\%$). Both estimates are based on a training set consisting of 500 data points.

Figure 3 shows a plot of the true function, the spherical estimate, and the estimate using kernel shaping as functions of x_1 and x_2. The true function has the familiar "Mexican hat" shape, which is recovered by the estimates to different degrees. We evaluate the local linear estimates for values of the equivalent neighborhood fraction parameter ρ in the range from 1% to 15%. Note that, to warrant a fair comparison, we used the entropic neighborhood also to determine the bandwith of the spherical estimate. For each value of ρ, 20 models are estimated using the 20 artificially generated training sets, and subsequently their performance is evaluated on the training set and on the test set of 31×31 grid points shown in Figure 3. The shape matrix L has maximal rank $l = 5$ in this experiment. Our results for local linear regression using the spherical kernel and kernel shaping are summarized in Table 1. Performance is measured in terms of the mean R^2-value of the 20 models, and standard deviations are reported in parenthesis.

Algorithm		Training R^2	Test R^2
spherical kernel	$\rho = 1\%$	0.961 (0.005)	0.215 (0.126)
spherical kernel	$\rho = 2\%$	0.871 (0.014)	<u>0.293</u> (0.082)
spherical kernel	$\rho = 5\%$	0.680 (0.029)	0.265 (0.043)
spherical kernel	$\rho = 10\%$	0.507 (0.038)	0.213 (0.030)
spherical kernel	$\rho = 20\%$	0.341 (0.039)	0.164 (0.021)
kernel shaping	$\rho = 1\%$	0.995 (0.001)	0.882 (0.024)
kernel shaping	$\rho = 2\%$	0.984 (0.002)	<u>0.909</u> (0.017)
kernel shaping	$\rho = 5\%$	0.923 (0.009)	0.836 (0.023)
kernel shaping	$\rho = 15\%$	0.628 (0.035)	0.517 (0.035)

Table 1: Performances in the toy problem. The results for kernel shaping were obtained using 200 gradient descent steps with step size $\alpha = 0.2$.

The results in Table 1 indicate that the optimal performance on the test set is obtained using the parameter values $\rho = 2\%$ both for kernel shaping ($R^2 = 0.909$) and for the spherical kernel ($R^2 = 0.293$). Given the large difference between the R^2 values, we conclude that kernel shaping clearly outperforms the spherical kernel on this data set.

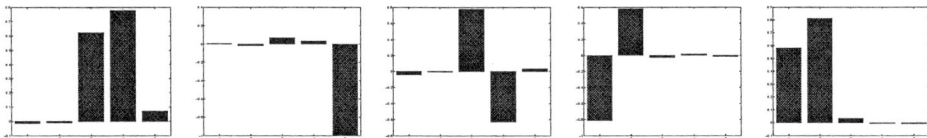

Figure 4: The eigenvectors of the estimate of Ω obtained on the first of 20 training sets. The graphs are ordered from left to right by increasing eigenvalues (decreasing extension of the kernel in that direction): 0.76, 0.76, 0.76, 33.24, 34.88.

Finally, Figure 4 shows the eigenvectors of the optimized Ω on the first of the 20 training sets. The eigenvectors are arranged according to the size of the corresponding eigenvalues. Note that the two rightmost eigenvectors, which correspond to the directions of minimum kernel extension, span exactly the x_1-x_2-space where the true function lives. The kernel is stretched in the remaining directions, effectively discarding nonlinear contributions from x_3, x_4, and x_5.

5.2 Abalone Database

The task in our second example is to predict the age of abalone based on several measurements. More specifically, the response variable is obtained by counting the number of rings in the shell in a time-consuming procedure. Preferably, the age of the abalone could be predicted from alternative measurements that may be obtained more easily. In the data set, eight candidate measurements including sex, dimensions, and various weights are reported along with the number of rings of the abalone as predictor variables. We normalize these variables to zero mean and unit variance prior to estimation. Overall, the data set consists of 4177 observations. To prevent possible artifacts resulting from the order of the data records, we randomly draw 2784 observations as a training set and use the remaining 1393 observations as a test set. Our results are summarized in Table 2 using various settings for the rank l, the equivalent fraction parameter ρ, and the gradient descent step size α. The optimal choice for ρ is 20% both for kernel shaping ($R^2 = 0.582$) and for the spherical kernel ($R^2 = 0.572$). Note that the performance improvement due to kernel shaping is negligible in this experiment.

Kernel		Training R^2	Test R^2
spherical kernel	$\rho = 0.05$	0.752	0.543
spherical kernel	$\rho = 0.10$	0.686	0.564
spherical kernel	$\rho = 0.20$	0.639	0.572
spherical kernel	$\rho = 0.50$	0.595	0.565
spherical kernel	$\rho = 0.70$	0.581	0.552
spherical kernel	$\rho = 0.90$	0.568	0.533
kernel shaping	$l = 5, \rho = 0.20, \alpha = 0.5$	0.705	0.575
kernel shaping	$l = 5, \rho = 0.20, \alpha = 0.2$	0.698	0.577
kernel shaping	$l = 2, \rho = 0.10, \alpha = 0.2$	0.729	0.574
kernel shaping	$l = 2, \rho = 0.20, \alpha = 0.2$	0.663	0.582
kernel shaping	$l = 2, \rho = 0.50, \alpha = 0.2$	0.603	0.571
kernel shaping	$l = 2, \rho = 0.20, \alpha = 0.5$	0.669	0.582

Table 2: Results using the Abalone database after 200 gradient descent steps.

6 Conclusions

We introduced a data-driven method to improve the performance of local linear estimates in high dimensions by optimizing the shape of the weighting kernel. In our experiments we found that kernel shaping clearly outperformed local linear regression using a spherical kernel in a five-dimensional toy example, and led to a small performance improvement in a second, real-world example. To explain the results of the second experiment, we note that kernel shaping aims at exploiting global structure in the data. Thus, the absence of a larger performance improvement may suggest simply that no corresponding structure prevails in that data set. That is, even though optimal kernel shapes exist *locally*, they may vary accross the predictor space so that they cannot be approximated by any particular *global* shape. Preliminary experiments using a localized variant of kernel shaping did not lead to significant performance improvements in our experiments.

Acknowledgments

The work of Dirk Ormoneit was supported by a grant of the Deutsche Forschungsgemeinschaft (DFG) as part of its post-doctoral program. Trevor Hastie was partially supported by NSF grant DMS-9803645 and NIH grant ROI-CA-72028-01. Carrie Grimes pointed us to misleading formulations in earlier drafts of this work.

References

[AMS97] C. G. Atkeson, A. W. Moore, and S. Schaal. Locally weighted learning. *Artificial Intelligence Review*, 11:11–73, 1997.

[BBB99] M. Birattari, G. Bontempi, and H. Bersini. Lazy learning meets the recursive least squares algorithm. In M. J. Kearns, S. A. Solla, and D. A. Cohn, editors, *Advances in Neural Information Processing Systems 11*. The MIT Press, 1999.

[BKM98] C. Blake, E. Koegh, and C. J. Merz. UCI Repository of machine learning databases. http://www.ics.uci.edu/~mlearn/MLRepository.html.

[Cle79] W. S. Cleveland. Robust locally weighted regression and smoothing scatterplots. *Journal of the American Statistical Association*, 74:829–836, 1979.

[FG96] J. Fan and I. Gijbels. *Local Polynomial Modelling and Its Applications*. Chapman & Hall, 1996.

[OH99] D. Ormoneit and T. Hastie. Optimal kernel shapes for local linear regression. Tech. report 1999-11, Department of Statistics, Stanford University, 1999.

Large Margin DAGs for Multiclass Classification

John C. Platt
Microsoft Research
1 Microsoft Way
Redmond, WA 98052
jplatt@microsoft.com

Nello Cristianini
Dept. of Engineering Mathematics
University of Bristol
Bristol, BS8 1TR - UK
nello.cristianini@bristol.ac.uk

John Shawe-Taylor
Department of Computer Science
Royal Holloway College - University of London
EGHAM, Surrey, TW20 0EX - UK
j.shawe-taylor@dcs.rhbnc.ac.uk

Abstract

We present a new learning architecture: the Decision Directed Acyclic Graph (DDAG), which is used to combine many two-class classifiers into a multiclass classifier. For an N-class problem, the DDAG contains $N(N-1)/2$ classifiers, one for each pair of classes. We present a VC analysis of the case when the node classifiers are hyperplanes; the resulting bound on the test error depends on N and on the margin achieved at the nodes, but not on the dimension of the space. This motivates an algorithm, DAGSVM, which operates in a kernel-induced feature space and uses two-class maximal margin hyperplanes at each decision-node of the DDAG. The DAGSVM is substantially faster to train and evaluate than either the standard algorithm or Max Wins, while maintaining comparable accuracy to both of these algorithms.

1 Introduction

The problem of multiclass classification, especially for systems like SVMs, doesn't present an easy solution. It is generally simpler to construct classifier theory and algorithms for two mutually-exclusive classes than for N mutually-exclusive classes. We believe constructing N-class SVMs is still an unsolved research problem.

The standard method for N-class SVMs [10] is to construct N SVMs. The ith SVM will be trained with all of the examples in the ith class with positive labels, and all other examples with negative labels. We refer to SVMs trained in this way as *1-v-r* SVMs (short for one-versus-rest). The final output of the N 1-v-r SVMs is the class that corresponds to the SVM with the highest output value. Unfortunately, there is no bound on the generalization error for the 1-v-r SVM, and the training time of the standard method scales linearly with N.

Another method for constructing N-class classifiers from SVMs is derived from previous research into combining two-class classifiers. Knerr [5] suggested constructing all possible two-class classifiers from a training set of N classes, each classifier being trained on only two out of N classes. There would thus be $K = N(N-1)/2$ classifiers. When applied to SVMs, we refer to this as *1-v-1* SVMs (short for one-versus-one).

Knerr suggested combining these two-class classifiers with an "AND" gate [5]. Friedman [4] suggested a Max Wins algorithm: each 1-v-1 classifier casts one vote for its preferred class, and the final result is the class with the most votes. Friedman shows circumstances in which this algorithm is Bayes optimal. Kreßel [6] applies the Max Wins algorithm to Support Vector Machines with excellent results.

A significant disadvantage of the 1-v-1 approach, however, is that, unless the individual classifiers are carefully regularized (as in SVMs), the overall N-class classifier system will tend to overfit. The "AND" combination method and the Max Wins combination method do not have bounds on the generalization error. Finally, the size of the 1-v-1 classifier may grow superlinearly with N, and hence, may be slow to evaluate on large problems.

In Section 2, we introduce a new multiclass learning architecture, called the Decision Directed Acyclic Graph (DDAG). The DDAG contains $N(N-1)/2$ nodes, each with an associated 1-v-1 classifier. In Section 3, we present a VC analysis of DDAGs whose classifiers are hyperplanes, showing that the margins achieved at the decision nodes and the size of the graph both affect their performance, while the dimensionality of the input space does not. The VC analysis indicates that building large margin DAGs in high-dimensional feature spaces can yield good generalization performance. Using such bound as a guide, in Section 4, we introduce a novel algorithm for multiclass classification based on placing 1-v-1 SVMs into nodes of a DDAG. This algorithm, called DAGSVM, is efficient to train and evaluate. Empirical evidence of this efficiency is shown in Section 5.

2 Decision DAGs

A Directed Acyclic Graph (DAG) is a graph whose edges have an orientation and no cycles. A Rooted DAG has a unique node such that it is the only node which has no arcs pointing into it. A Rooted Binary DAG has nodes which have either 0 or 2 arcs leaving them. We will use Rooted Binary DAGs in order to define a class of functions to be used in classification tasks. The class of functions computed by Rooted Binary DAGs is formally defined as follows.

Definition 1 Decision DAGs (DDAGs). *Given a space X and a set of boolean functions $\mathcal{F} = \{f : X \to \{0, 1\}\}$, the class $\text{DDAG}(\mathcal{F})$ of Decision DAGs on N classes over $\mathcal{F}$ are functions which can be implemented using a rooted binary DAG with N leaves labeled by the classes where each of the $K = N(N-1)/2$ internal nodes is labeled with an element of $\mathcal{F}$. The nodes are arranged in a triangle with the single root node at the top, two nodes in the second layer and so on until the final layer of N leaves. The i-th node in layer $j < N$ is connected to the i-th and $(i+1)$-st node in the $(j+1)$-st layer.*

To evaluate a particular DDAG G on input $x \in X$, starting at the root node, the binary function at a node is evaluated. The node is then exited via the left edge, if the binary function is zero; or the right edge, if the binary function is one. The next node's binary function is then evaluated. The value of the decision function $D(x)$ is the value associated with the final leaf node (see Figure 1(a)). The path taken through the DDAG is known as the *evaluation path*. The input x reaches a node of the graph, if that node is on the evaluation path for x. We refer to the decision node distinguishing classes i and j as the ij-node. Assuming that the number of a leaf is its class, this node is the i-th node in the $(N - j + i)$-th layer provided $i < j$. Similarly the j-nodes are those nodes involving class j, that is, the internal nodes on the two diagonals containing the leaf labeled by j.

The DDAG is equivalent to operating on a list, where each node eliminates one class from the list. The list is initialized with a list of all classes. A test point is evaluated against the decision node that corresponds to the first and last elements of the list. If the node prefers

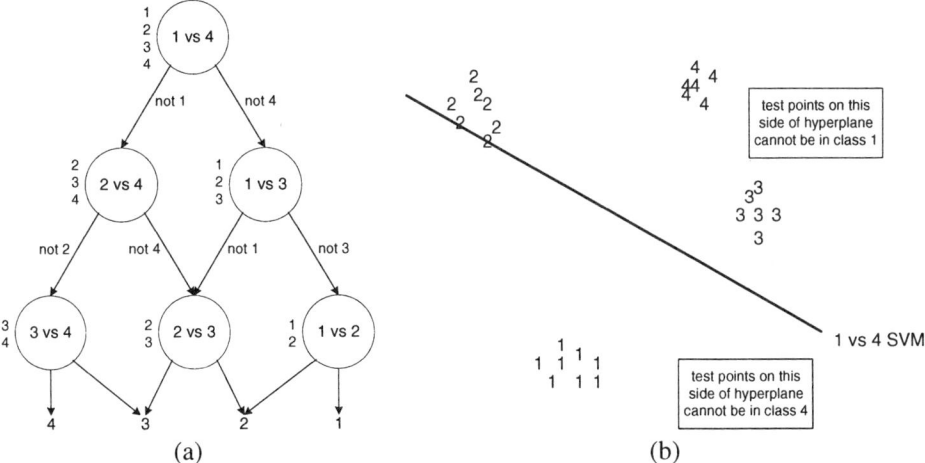

Figure 1: (a) The decision DAG for finding the best class out of four classes. The equivalent list state for each node is shown next to that node. (b) A diagram of the input space of a four-class problem. A 1-v-1 SVM can only exclude one class from consideration.

one of the two classes, the other class is eliminated from the list, and the DDAG proceeds to test the first and last elements of the new list. The DDAG terminates when only one class remains in the list. Thus, for a problem with N classes, $N-1$ decision nodes will be evaluated in order to derive an answer.

The current state of the list is the total state of the system. Therefore, since a list state is reachable in more than one possible path through the system, the decision graph the algorithm traverses is a DAG, not simply a tree.

Decision DAGs naturally generalize the class of Decision Trees, allowing for a more efficient representation of redundancies and repetitions that can occur in different branches of the tree, by allowing the merging of different decision paths. The class of functions implemented is the same as that of Generalized Decision Trees [1], but this particular representation presents both computational and learning-theoretical advantages.

3 Analysis of Generalization

In this paper we study DDAGs where the node-classifiers are hyperplanes. We define a *Perceptron DDAG* to be a DDAG with a perceptron at every node. Let w be the (unit) weight vector correctly splitting the i and j classes at the ij-node with threshold θ. We define the margin of the ij-node to be $\gamma = \min_{c(x)=i,j} \{|\langle w, x \rangle - \theta|\}$, where $c(x)$ is the class associated to training example x. Note that, in this definition, we only take into account examples with class labels equal to i or j.

Theorem 1 *Suppose we are able to classify a random m sample of labeled examples using a Perceptron DDAG on N classes containing K decision nodes with margins γ_i at node i, then we can bound the generalization error with probability greater than $1 - \delta$ to be less than*

$$\frac{130R^2}{m}\left(D' \log(4em)\log(4m) + \log\frac{2(2m)^K}{\delta}\right),$$

where $D' = \sum_{i=1}^{K} \frac{1}{\gamma_i^2}$, and R is the radius of a ball containing the distribution's support.

Proof: see Appendix □

Theorem 1 implies that we can control the capacity of DDAGs by enlarging their margin. Note that, in some situations, this bound may be pessimistic: the DDAG partitions the input space into polytopic regions, each of which is mapped to a leaf node and assigned to a specific class. Intuitively, the only margins that should matter are the ones relative to the boundaries of the cell where a given training point is assigned, whereas the bound in Theorem 1 depends on all the margins in the graph.

By the above observations, we would expect that a DDAG whose j-node margins are large would be accurate at identifying class j, even when other nodes do not have large margins. Theorem 2 substantiates this by showing that the appropriate bound depends only on the j-node margins, but first we introduce the notation, $\epsilon_j(G) = P\{x : (x \text{ in class } j \text{ and } x \text{ is misclassified by } G) \text{ or } x \text{ is misclassified as class } j \text{ by } G\}$.

Theorem 2 *Suppose we are able to correctly distinguish class j from the other classes in a random m-sample with a DDAG G over N classes containing K decision nodes with margins γ_i at node i, then with probability $1 - \delta$,*

$$\epsilon_j(G) \leq \frac{130R^2}{m}\left(D'\log(4em)\log(4m) + \log\frac{2(2m)^{N-1}}{\delta}\right),$$

where $D' = \sum_{i \in j\text{-nodes}} \frac{1}{\gamma_i^2}$, and R is the radius of a ball containing the support of the distribution.

Proof: follows exactly Lemma 4 and Theorem 1, but is omitted. □

4 The DAGSVM algorithm

Based on the previous analysis, we propose a new algorithm, called the Directed Acyclic Graph SVM (DAGSVM) algorithm, which combines the results of 1-v-1 SVMs. We will show that this combination method is efficient to train and evaluate.

The analysis of Section 3 indicates that maximizing the margin of all of the nodes in a DDAG will minimize a bound on the generalization error. This bound is also independent of input dimensionality. Therefore, we will create a DDAG whose nodes are maximum margin classifiers over a kernel-induced feature space. Such a DDAG is obtained by training each ij-node only on the subset of training points labeled by i or j. The final class decision is derived by using the DDAG architecture, described in Section 2.

The DAGSVM separates the individual classes with large margin. It is safe to discard the losing class at each 1-v-1 decision because, for the hard margin case, all of the examples of the losing class are far away from the decision surface (see Figure 1(b)).

For the DAGSVM, the choice of the class order in the list (or DDAG) is arbitrary. The experiments in Section 5 simply use a list of classes in the natural numerical (or alphabetical) order. Limited experimentation with re-ordering the list did not yield significant changes in accuracy performance.

The DAGSVM algorithm is superior to other multiclass SVM algorithms in both training and evaluation time. Empirically, SVM training is observed to scale super-linearly with the training set size m [7], according to a power law: $T = cm^\gamma$, where $\gamma \approx 2$ for algorithms based on the decomposition method, with some proportionality constant c. For the standard 1-v-r multiclass SVM training algorithm, the entire training set is used to create all N classifiers. Hence the training time for 1-v-r is

$$T_{1-\text{v-r}} = cNm^\gamma. \tag{1}$$

Assuming that the classes have the same number of examples, training each 1-v-1 SVM only requires $2m/N$ training examples. Thus, training K 1-v-1 SVMs would require

$$T_{1-\text{v-1}} = c\frac{N(N-1)}{2}\left(\frac{2m}{N}\right)^\gamma \approx 2^{\gamma-1}cN^{2-\gamma}m^\gamma. \tag{2}$$

For a typical case, where $\gamma = 2$, the amount of time required to train all of the 1-v-1 SVMs is independent of N, and is only twice that of training a single 1-v-r SVM. Using 1-v-1 SVMs with a combination algorithm is thus preferred for training time.

5 Empirical Comparisons and Conclusions

The DAGSVM algorithm was evaluated on three different test sets: the USPS handwritten digit data set [10], the UCI Letter data set [2], and the UCI Covertype data set [2]. The USPS digit data consists of 10 classes (0-9), whose inputs are pixels of a scaled input image. There are 7291 training examples and 2007 test examples. The UCI Letter data consists of 26 classes (A-Z), whose inputs are measured statistics of printed font glyphs. We used the first 16000 examples for training, and the last 4000 for testing. All inputs of the UCI Letter data set were scaled to lie in $[-1, 1]$. The UCI Covertype data consists of 7 classes of trees, where the inputs are terrain features. There are 11340 training examples and 565893 test examples. All of the continuous inputs for Covertype were scaled to have zero mean and unit variance. Discrete inputs were represented as a 1-of-n code.

On each data set, we trained N 1-v-r SVMs and K 1-v-1 SVMs, using SMO [7], with soft margins. We combined the 1-v-1 SVMs both with the Max Wins algorithm and with DAGSVM. The choice of kernel and of the regularizing parameter C was determined via performance on a validation set. The validation performance was measured by training on 70% of the training set and testing the combination algorithm on 30% of the training set (except for Covertype, where the UCI validation set was used). The best kernel was selected from a set of polynomial kernels (from degree 1 through 6), both homogeneous and inhomogeneous; and Gaussian kernels, with various σ. The Gaussian kernel was always found to be best.

	σ	C	Error Rate (%)	Kernel Evaluations	Training CPU Time (sec)	Classifier Size (Kparameters)
USPS						
1-v-r	3.58	100	4.7	2936	3532	760
Max Wins	5.06	100	4.5	1877	307	487
DAGSVM	5.06	100	4.4	819	307	487
Neural Net [10]			5.9			
UCI Letter						
1-v-r	0.447	100	2.2	8183	1764	148
Max Wins	0.632	100	2.4	7357	441	160
DAGSVM	0.447	10	2.2	3834	792	223
Neural Net			4.3			
UCI Covertype						
1-v-r	1	10	30.2	7366	4210	105
Max Wins	1	10	**29.0**	7238	1305	107
DAGSVM	1	10	29.2	4390	1305	107
Neural Net [2]			30			

Table 1: Experimental Results

Table 1 shows the results of the experiments. The optimal parameters for all three multiclass SVM algorithms are very similar for both data sets. Also, the error rates are similar for all three algorithms for both data sets. Neither 1-v-r nor Max Wins is statistically significantly better than DAGSVM using McNemar's test [3] at a 0.05 significance level for USPS or UCI Letter. For UCI Covertype, Max Wins is slightly better than either of the other SVM-based algorithms. The results for a neural network trained on the same data sets are shown for a baseline accuracy comparison.

The three algorithms distinguish themselves in training time, evaluation time, and classifier size. The number of kernel evaluations is a good indication of evaluation time. For 1-v-r and Max Wins, the number of kernel evaluations is the total number of unique support vectors for all SVMs. For the DAGSVM, the number of kernel evaluations is the number of unique support vectors averaged over the evaluation paths through the DDAG taken by the test set. As can be seen in Table 1, Max Wins is faster than 1-v-r SVMs, due to shared support vectors between the 1-v-1 classifiers. The DAGSVM has the fastest evaluation. The DAGSVM is between a factor of 1.6 and 2.3 times faster to evaluate than Max Wins.

The DAGSVM algorithm is also substantially faster to train than the standard 1-v-r SVM algorithm: a factor of 2.2 and 11.5 times faster for these two data sets. The Max Wins algorithm shares a similar training speed advantage.

Because the SVM basis functions are drawn from a limited set, they can be shared across classifiers for a great savings in classifier size. The number of parameters for DAGSVM (and Max Wins) is comparable to the number of parameters for 1-v-r SVM, even though there are $N(N-1)/2$ classifiers, rather than N.

In summary, we have created a Decision DAG architecture, which is amenable to a VC-style bound of generalization error. Using this bound, we created the DAGSVM algorithm, which places a two-class SVM at every node of the DDAG. The DAGSVM algorithm was tested versus the standard 1-v-r multiclass SVM algorithm, and Friedman's Max Wins combination algorithm. The DAGSVM algorithm yields comparable accuracy and memory usage to the other two algorithms, but yields substantial improvements in both training and evaluation time.

6 Appendix: Proof of Main Theorem

Definition 2 *Let $\mathcal{F}$ be a set of real valued functions. We say that a set of points X is γ-shattered by $\mathcal{F}$ relative to $r = (r_x)_{x \in X}$, if there are real numbers r_x, indexed by $x \in X$, such that for all binary vectors b indexed by X, there is a function $f_b \in \mathcal{F}$ satisfying $(2b_x - 1)f_b(x) \geq (2b_x - 1)r_x + \gamma$. The fat shattering dimension, fat_F, of the set $\mathcal{F}$ is a function from the positive real numbers to the integers which maps a value γ to the size of the largest γ-shattered set, if the set is finite, or maps to infinity otherwise.*

As a relevant example, consider the class $\mathcal{F}_{\text{lin}} = \{x \to \langle w, x \rangle - \theta : \|w\| = 1\}$. We quote the following result from [1].

Theorem 3 *Let $\mathcal{F}_{\text{lin}}$ be restricted to points in a ball of n dimensions of radius R about the origin. Then*

$$\mathrm{fat}_{\mathcal{F}_{\text{lin}}}(\gamma) \leq \min\{R^2/\gamma^2, n+1\}.$$

We will bound generalization with a technique that closely resembles the technique used in [1] to study Perceptron Decision Trees. We will now give a lemma and a theorem: the lemma bounds the probability over a double sample that the first half has zero error and the second error greater than an appropriate ϵ. We assume that the DDAG on N classes has $K = N(N-1)/2$ nodes and we denote $\mathrm{fat}_{\mathcal{F}_{\text{lin}}}(\gamma)$ by $\mathrm{fat}(\gamma)$.

Lemma 4 *Let G be a DDAG on N classes with $K = N(N-1)/2$ decision nodes with margins $\gamma^1, \gamma^2, \ldots, \gamma^K$ at the decision nodes satisfying $k_i = \mathrm{fat}(\gamma_i/8)$, where fat is continuous from the right. Then the following bound holds, $P^{2m}\{\mathbf{xy}: \exists \text{ a graph } G : G \text{ which separates classes } i \text{ and } j \text{ at the } ij\text{-node for all } x \text{ in } \mathbf{x}, \text{ a fraction of points misclassified in } y > \epsilon(m, K, \delta).\} < \delta$ where $\epsilon(m, K, \delta) = \frac{1}{m}(D \log(8m) + \log \frac{2^K}{\delta})$ and $D = \sum_{i=1}^{K} k_i \log(4em/k_i)$.*

Proof The proof of Lemma 4 is omitted for space reasons, but is formally analogous to the proof of Lemma 4.4 in [8], and can easily be reconstructed from it. □

Lemma 4 applies to a particular DDAG with a specified margin γ_i at each node. In practice, we observe these quantities after generating the DDAG. Hence, to obtain a bound that can be applied in practice, we must bound the probabilities uniformly over all of the possible margins that can arise. We can now give the proof for Theorem 1.

Proof of Main Theorem: We must bound the probabilities over different margins. We first use a standard result due to Vapnik [9, page 168] to bound the probability of error in terms of the probability of the discrepancy between the performance on two halves of a double sample. Then we combine this result with Lemma 4. We must consider all possible patterns of k_i's over the decision nodes. The largest allowed value of k_i is m, and so, for fixed K, we can bound the number of possibilities by m^K. Hence, there are m^K of applications of Lemma 4 for a fixed N. Since $K = N(N-1)/2$, we can let $\delta_k = \delta/m^K$, so that the sum $\sum_{k=1}^{m} \delta_k = \delta$. Choosing

$$\epsilon\left(m, K, \frac{\delta_k}{2}\right) = \frac{65R^2}{m}\left(D'\log(4em)\log(4m) + \log\frac{2(2m)^K}{\delta}\right) \qquad (3)$$

in the applications of Lemma 4 ensures that the probability of any of the statements failing to hold is less than $\delta/2$. Note that we have replaced the constant $8^2 = 64$ by 65 in order to ensure the continuity from the right required for the application of Lemma 4 and have upper bounded $\log(4em/k_i)$ by $\log(4em)$. Applying Vapnik's Lemma [9, page 168] in each case, the probability that the statement of the theorem fails to hold is less than δ. □

More details on this style of proof, omitted in this paper for space constraints, can be found in [1].

References

[1] K. Bennett, N. Cristianini, J. Shawe-Taylor, and D. Wu. Enlarging the margin in perceptron decision trees. *Machine Learning (submitted)*. http://lara.enm.bris.ac.uk/cig/pubs/ML-PDT.ps.

[2] C. Blake, E. Keogh, and C. Merz. UCI repository of machine learning databases. Dept. of information and computer sciences, University of California, Irvine, 1998. http://www.ics.uci.edu/~mlearn/MLRepository.html.

[3] T. G. Dietterich. Approximate statistical tests for comparing supervised classification learning algorithms. *Neural Computation*, 10:1895–1924, 1998.

[4] J. H. Friedman. Another approach to polychotomous classification. Technical report, Stanford Department of Statistics, 1996. http://www-stat.stanford.edu/reports/friedman/poly.ps.Z.

[5] S. Knerr, L. Personnaz, and G. Dreyfus. Single-layer learning revisited: A stepwise procedure for building and training a neural network. In Fogelman-Soulie and Herault, editors, *Neurocomputing: Algorithms, Architectures and Applications*, NATO ASI. Springer, 1990.

[6] U. Kreßel. Pairwise classification and support vector machines. In B. Schölkopf, C. J. C. Burges, and A. J. Smola, editors, *Advances in Kernel Methods: Support Vector Learning*, pages 255–268. MIT Press, Cambridge, MA, 1999.

[7] J. Platt. Fast training of support vector machines using sequential minimal optimization. In B. Schölkopf, C. J. C. Burges, and A. J. Smola, editors, *Advances in Kernel Methods — Support Vector Learning*, pages 185–208. MIT Press, Cambridge, MA, 1999.

[8] J. Shawe-Taylor and N. Cristianini. Data dependent structural risk minimization for perceptron decision trees. In M. Jordan, M. Kearns, and S. Solla, editors, *Advances in Neural Information Processing Systems*, volume 10, pages 336–342. MIT Press, 1999.

[9] V. Vapnik. *Estimation of Dependences Based on Empirical Data [in Russian]*. Nauka, Moscow, 1979. (English translation: Springer Verlag, New York, 1982).

[10] V. Vapnik. *Statistical Learning Theory*. Wiley, New York, 1998.

The Infinite Gaussian Mixture Model

Carl Edward Rasmussen
Department of Mathematical Modelling
Technical University of Denmark
Building 321, DK-2800 Kongens Lyngby, Denmark
carl@imm.dtu.dk http://bayes.imm.dtu.dk

Abstract

In a Bayesian mixture model it is not necessary a priori to limit the number of components to be finite. In this paper an infinite Gaussian mixture model is presented which neatly sidesteps the difficult problem of finding the "right" number of mixture components. Inference in the model is done using an efficient parameter-free Markov Chain that relies entirely on Gibbs sampling.

1 Introduction

One of the major advantages in the Bayesian methodology is that "overfitting" is avoided; thus the difficult task of adjusting model complexity vanishes. For neural networks, this was demonstrated by Neal [1996] whose work on infinite networks led to the reinvention and popularisation of Gaussian Process models [Williams & Rasmussen, 1996]. In this paper a Markov Chain Monte Carlo (MCMC) implementation of a hierarchical infinite Gaussian mixture model is presented. Perhaps surprisingly, inference in such models is possible using finite amounts of computation.

Similar models are known in statistics as Dirichlet Process mixture models and go back to Ferguson [1973] and Antoniak [1974]. Usually, expositions start from the Dirichlet process itself [West et al, 1994]; here we derive the model as the limiting case of the well-known finite mixtures. Bayesian methods for mixtures with an unknown (finite) number of components have been explored by Richardson & Green [1997], whose methods are not easily extended to multivariate observations.

2 Finite hierarchical mixture

The finite Gaussian mixture model with k components may be written as:

$$p(y|\mu_1, \ldots, \mu_k, s_1, \ldots, s_k, \pi_1, \ldots, \pi_k) = \sum_{j=1}^{k} \pi_j \mathcal{N}(\mu_j, s_j^{-1}), \qquad (1)$$

where μ_j are the means, s_j the *precisions* (inverse variances), π_j the mixing proportions (which must be positive and sum to one) and $\mathcal{N}$ is a (normalised) Gaussian with specified mean and variance. For simplicity, the exposition will initially assume scalar observations, n of which comprise the training data $\mathbf{y} = \{y_1, \ldots, y_n\}$. First we will consider these models for a fixed value of k, and later explore the properties in the limit where $k \to \infty$.

Gibbs sampling is a well known technique for generating samples from complicated multivariate distributions that is often used in Monte Carlo procedures. In its simplest form, Gibbs sampling is used to update each variable in turn from its conditional distribution given all other variables in the system. It can be shown that Gibbs sampling generates samples from the joint distribution, and that the entire distribution is explored as the number of Gibbs sweeps grows large.

We introduce stochastic *indicator* variables, c_i, one for each observation, whose role is to encode which class has generated the observation; the indicators take on values $1\ldots k$. Indicators are often referred to as "missing data" in a mixture model context.

In the following sections the priors on component parameters and hyperparameters will be specified, and the conditional distributions for these, which will be needed for Gibbs sampling, will be derived. In general the form of the priors are chosen to have (hopefully) reasonable modelling properties, with an eye to mathematical convenience (through the use of conjugate priors).

2.1 Component parameters

The component means, μ_j, are given Gaussian priors:

$$p(\mu_j|\lambda,r) \sim \mathcal{N}(\lambda, r^{-1}), \qquad (2)$$

whose mean, λ, and precision, r, are hyperparameters common to all components. The hyperparameters themselves are given vague Normal and Gamma priors:

$$p(\lambda) \sim \mathcal{N}(\mu_y, \sigma_y^2), \qquad p(r) \sim \mathcal{G}(1, \sigma_y^{-2}) \propto r^{-1/2}\exp(-r\sigma_y^2/2), \qquad (3)$$

where μ_y and σ_y^2 are the mean and variance of the observations[1]. The shape parameter of the Gamma prior is set to unity, corresponding to a very broad (vague) distribution.

The conditional posterior distributions for the means are obtained by multiplying the likelihood from eq. (1) conditioned on the indicators, by the prior, eq. (2):

$$p(\mu_j|\mathbf{c}, \mathbf{y}, s_j, \lambda, r) \sim \mathcal{N}\Big(\frac{\bar{y}_j n_j s_j + \lambda r}{n_j s_j + r}, \frac{1}{n_j s_j + r}\Big), \qquad \bar{y}_j = \frac{1}{n_j}\sum_{i:c_i=j} y_i, \qquad (4)$$

where the *occupation number*, n_j, is the number of observations belonging to class j, and $\bar{y}_j$ is the mean of these observations. For the hyperparameters, eq. (2) plays the role of the likelihood which together with the priors from eq. (4) give conditional posteriors of standard form:

$$p(\lambda|\mu_1,\ldots,\mu_k,r) \sim \mathcal{N}\Big(\frac{\mu_y\sigma_y^{-2} + r\sum_{j=1}^k \mu_j}{\sigma_y^{-2} + kr}, \frac{1}{\sigma_y^{-2} + kr}\Big),$$

$$p(r|\mu_1,\ldots,\mu_k,\lambda) \sim \mathcal{G}\Big(k+1, \big[\frac{1}{k+1}(\sigma_y^2 + \sum_{j=1}^k(\mu_j - \lambda)^2)\big]^{-1}\Big). \qquad (5)$$

The component precisions, s_j, are given Gamma priors:

$$p(s_j|\beta, w) \sim \mathcal{G}(\beta, w^{-1}), \qquad (6)$$

whose shape, β, and mean, w^{-1}, are hyperparameters common to all components, with priors of inverse Gamma and Gamma form:

$$p(\beta^{-1}) \sim \mathcal{G}(1,1) \Longrightarrow p(\beta) \propto \beta^{-3/2}\exp\big(-1/(2\beta)\big), \qquad p(w) \sim \mathcal{G}(1, \sigma_y^2). \qquad (7)$$

---

[1] Strictly speaking, the priors ought not to depend on the observations. The current procedure is equivalent to normalising the observations and using unit priors. A wide variety of reasonable priors will lead to similar results.

The conditional posterior precisions are obtained by multiplying the likelihood from eq. (1) conditioned on the indicators, by the prior, eq. (6):

$$p(s_j|\mathbf{c}, \mathbf{y}, \mu_j, \beta, w) \sim \mathcal{G}\Big(\beta + n_j, \big[\frac{1}{\beta + n_j}(w\beta + \sum_{i:c_i=j}(y_i - \mu_j)^2)\big]^{-1}\Big). \tag{8}$$

For the hyperparameters, eq. (6) plays the role of likelihood which together with the priors from eq. (7) give:

$$p(w|s_1, \ldots, s_k, \beta) \sim \mathcal{G}\Big(k\beta + 1, \big[\frac{1}{k\beta + 1}(\sigma_y^{-2} + \beta \sum_{j=1}^{k} s_j)\big]^{-1}\Big), \tag{9}$$

$$p(\beta|s_1, \ldots, s_k, w) \propto \Gamma\big(\frac{\beta}{2}\big)^{-k} \exp\big(\frac{-1}{2\beta}\big)\big(\frac{\beta}{2}\big)^{(k\beta-3)/2} \prod_{j=1}^{k}(s_j w)^{\beta/2} \exp\big(-\frac{\beta s_j w}{2}\big).$$

The latter density is not of standard form, but it can be shown that $p(\log(\beta)|s_1, \ldots, s_k, w)$ is log-concave, so we may generate independent samples from the distribution for $\log(\beta)$ using the Adaptive Rejection Sampling (ARS) technique [Gilks & Wild, 1992], and transform these to get values for β.

The mixing proportions, π_j, are given a symmetric Dirichlet (also known as multivariate beta) prior with concentration parameter α/k:

$$p(\pi_1, \ldots, \pi_k|\alpha) \sim \text{Dirichlet}(\alpha/k, \ldots, \alpha/k) = \frac{\Gamma(\alpha)}{\Gamma(\alpha/k)^k} \prod_{j=1}^{k} \pi_j^{\alpha/k-1}, \tag{10}$$

where the mixing proportions must be positive and sum to one. Given the mixing proportions, the prior for the occupation numbers, n_j, is multinomial and the joint distribution of the indicators becomes:

$$p(c_1, \ldots, c_k|\pi_1, \ldots, \pi_k) = \prod_{j=1}^{k} \pi_j^{n_j}, \quad n_j = \sum_{i=1}^{n} \delta_{\text{Kronecker}}(c_i, j). \tag{11}$$

Using the standard Dirichlet integral, we may integrate out the mixing proportions and write the prior directly in terms of the indicators:

$$p(c_1, \ldots, c_k|\alpha) = \int p(c_1, \ldots, c_k|\pi_1, \ldots, \pi_k) p(\pi_1, \ldots, \pi_k) d\pi_1 \cdots d\pi_k \tag{12}$$

$$= \frac{\Gamma(\alpha)}{\Gamma(\alpha/k)^k} \int \prod_{j=1}^{k} \pi_j^{n_j + \alpha/k - 1} d\pi_j = \frac{\Gamma(\alpha)}{\Gamma(n+\alpha)} \prod_{j=1}^{k} \frac{\Gamma(n_j + \alpha/k)}{\Gamma(\alpha/k)}.$$

In order to be able to use Gibbs sampling for the (discrete) indicators, c_i, we need the conditional prior for a single indicator given all the others; this is easily obtained from eq. (12) by keeping all but a single indicator fixed:

$$p(c_i = j|\mathbf{c}_{-i}, \alpha) = \frac{n_{-i,j} + \alpha/k}{n - 1 + \alpha}, \tag{13}$$

where the subscript $-i$ indicates all indexes except i and $n_{-i,j}$ is the number of observations, excluding y_i, that are associated with component j. The posteriors for the indicators are derived in the next section.

Lastly, a vague prior of inverse Gamma shape is put on the concentration parameter α:

$$p(\alpha^{-1}) \sim \mathcal{G}(1,1) \Longrightarrow p(\alpha) \propto \alpha^{-3/2} \exp\big(-1/(2\alpha)\big). \tag{14}$$

The likelihood for α may be derived from eq. (12), which together with the prior from eq. (14) gives:

$$p(n_1,\ldots,n_k|\alpha) = \frac{\alpha^k \Gamma(\alpha)}{\Gamma(n+\alpha)}, \qquad p(\alpha|k,n) \propto \frac{\alpha^{k-3/2}\exp\bigl(-1/(2\alpha)\bigr)\Gamma(\alpha)}{\Gamma(n+\alpha)}. \tag{15}$$

Notice, that the conditional posterior for α depends only on number of observations, n, and the number of components, k, and not on how the observations are distributed among the components. The distribution $p(\log(\alpha)|k,n)$ is log-concave, so we may efficiently generate independent samples from this distribution using ARS.

3 The infinite limit

So far, we have considered k to be a fixed finite quantity. In this section we will explore the limit $k \to \infty$ and make the final derivations regarding the conditional posteriors for the indicators. For all the model variables except the indicators, the conditional posteriors for the infinite limit is obtained by substituting for k the number of classes that have data associated with them, k_{rep}, in the equations previously derived for the finite model. For the indicators, letting $k \to \infty$ in eq. (13), the conditional prior reaches the following limits:

$$\begin{aligned}
\text{components where } n_{-i,j} > 0: &\quad p(c_i = j|\mathbf{c}_{-i},\alpha) &=& \frac{n_{-i,j}}{n-1+\alpha}, \\
\text{all other components combined:} &\quad p(c_i \neq c_{i'} \text{ for all } i' \neq i|\mathbf{c}_{-i},\alpha) &=& \frac{\alpha}{n-1+\alpha}.
\end{aligned} \tag{16}$$

This shows that the conditional class prior for components that are associated with other observations is proportional to the number of such observations; the combined prior for all other classes depends only on α and n. Notice how the analytical tractability of the integral in eq. (12) is essential, since it allows us to work directly with the (finite number of) indicator variables, rather than the (infinite number of) mixing proportions. We may now combine the likelihood from eq. (1) conditioned on the indicators with the prior from eq. (16) to obtain the conditional posteriors for the indicators:

$$\text{components for which } n_{-i,j} > 0: \quad p(c_i = j|\mathbf{c}_{-i},\mu_j,s_j,\alpha) \propto \tag{17}$$

$$p(c_i = j|\mathbf{c}_{-i},\alpha)p(y_i|\mu_j,s_j,\mathbf{c}_{-i}) \propto \frac{n_{-i,j}}{n-1+\alpha} s_j^{1/2} \exp\bigl(-s_j(y_i-\mu_j)^2/2\bigr),$$

all other components combined: $p(c_i \neq c_{i'} \text{ for all } i \neq i'|\mathbf{c}_{-i},\lambda,r,\beta,w,\alpha) \propto$

$$p(c_i \neq c_{i'} \text{ for all } i \neq i'|\mathbf{c}_{-i},\alpha) \int p(y_i|\mu_j,s_j)p(\mu_j,s_j|\lambda,r,\beta,w)d\mu_j ds_j.$$

The likelihood for components with observations other than y_i currently associated with them is Gaussian with component parameters μ_j and s_j. The likelihood pertaining to the currently unrepresented classes (which have no parameters associated with them) is obtained through integration over the prior distribution for these. Note, that we need not differentiate between the infinitely many unrepresented classes, since their parameter distributions are all identical. Unfortunately, this integral is not analytically tractable; I follow Neal [1998], who suggests to sample from the priors (which are Gaussian and Gamma shaped) in order to generate a Monte Carlo estimate of the probability of "generating a new class". Notice, that this approach effectively generates parameters (by sampling from the prior) for the classes that are unrepresented. Since this Monte Carlo estimate is unbiased, the resulting chain will sample from *exactly* the desired distribution, no matter how many samples are used to approximate the integral; I have found that using a single sample works fairly well in many applications.

In detail, there are three possibilities when computing conditional posterior class probabilities, depending on the number of observations associated with the class:

if $n_{-i,j} > 0$: there are other observations associated with class j, and the posterior class probability is as given by the top line of eq. (17).

if $n_{-i,j} = 0$ and $c_i = j$: observation y_i is currently the only observation associated with class j; this is an peculiar situation, since there are no other observations associated with the class, but the class still has parameters. It turns out that this situation should be handled as an unrepresented class, but rather than sampling for the parameters, one simply uses the class parameters; consult [Neal 1998] for a detailed derivation.

unrepresented classes: values for the mixture parameters are picked at random from the prior for these parameters, which is Gaussian for μ_j and Gamma shaped for s_j.

Now that all classes have parameters associated with them, we can easily evaluate their likelihoods (which are Gaussian) and the priors, which take the form $n_{-i,j}/(n-1+\alpha)$ for components with observations other than y_i associated with them, and $\alpha/(n-1+\alpha)$ for the remaining class. When hitherto unrepresented classes are chosen, a new class is introduced in the model; classes are removed when they become empty.

4 Inference; the "spirals" example

To illustrate the model, we use the 3 dimensional "spirals" dataset from [Ueda et al, 1998], containing 800 data point, plotted in figure 1. Five data points are generated from each of 160 isotropic Gaussians, whose means follow a spiral pattern.

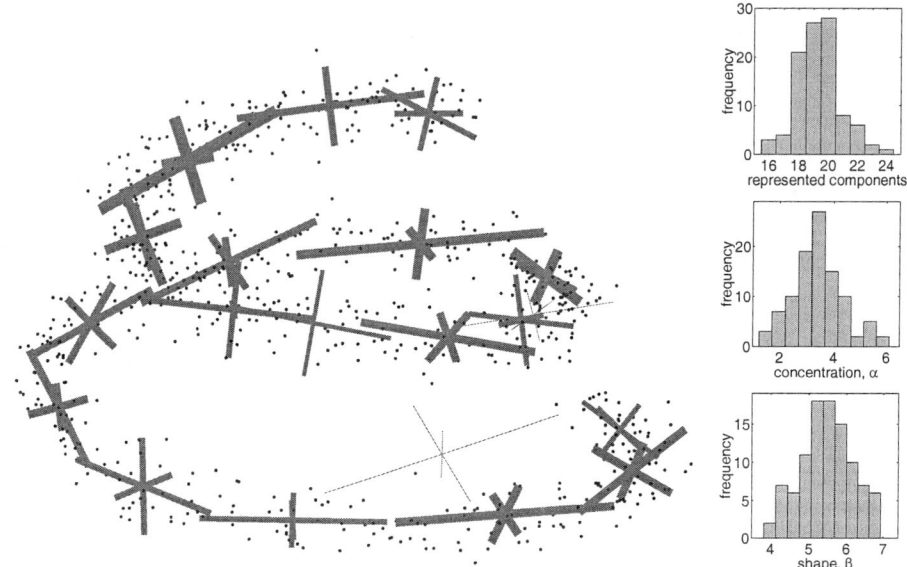

Figure 1: The 800 cases from the three dimensional spirals data. The crosses represent a single (random) sample from the posterior for the mixture model. The $k_{\text{rep}} = 20$ represented classes account for $n/(n+\alpha) \simeq 99.6\%$ of the mass. The lines indicate 2 std. dev. in the Gaussian mixture components; the thickness of the lines represent the mass of the class. To the right histograms for 100 samples from the posterior for k_{rep}, α and β are shown.

4.1 Multivariate generalisation

The generalisation to multivariate observations is straightforward. The means, μ_j, and precisions, s_j, become vectors and matrices respectively, and their prior (and posterior)

The Infinite Gaussian Mixture Model

distributions become multivariate Gaussian and Wishart. Similarly, the hyperparameter λ becomes a vector (multivariate Gaussian prior) and r and w become matrices with Wishart priors. The β parameter stays scalar, with the prior on $(\beta - D + 1)^{-1}$ being Gamma with mean $1/D$, where D is the dimension of the dataset. All other specifications stay the same. Setting $D = 1$ recovers the scalar case discussed in detail.

4.2 Inference

The mixture model is started with a single component, and a large number of Gibbs sweeps are performed, updating all parameters and hyperparameters in turn by sampling from the conditional distributions derived in the previous sections. In figure 2 the auto-covariance for several quantities is plotted, which reveals a maximum correlation-length of about 270. Then 30000 iterations are performed for modelling purposes (taking 18 minutes of CPU time on a Pentium PC): 3000 steps initially for "burn-in", followed by 27000 to generate 100 roughly independent samples from the posterior (spaced evenly 270 apart). In figure 1, the represented components of one sample from the posterior is visualised with the data. To the right of figure 1 we see that the posterior number of represented classes is very concentrated around $18 - 20$, and the concentration parameter takes values around $\alpha \simeq 3.5$ corresponding to only $\alpha/(n+\alpha) \simeq 0.4\%$ of the mass of the predictive distribution belonging to unrepresented classes. The shape parameter β takes values around $5-6$, which gives the "effective number of points" contributed from the prior to the covariance matrices of the mixture components.

4.3 The predictive distribution

Given a particular state in the Markov Chain, the predictive distribution has two parts: the represented classes (which are Gaussian) and the unrepresented classes. As when updating the indicators, we may chose to approximate the unrepresented classes by a finite mixture of Gaussians, whose parameters are drawn from the prior. The final predictive distribution is an average over the (eg. 100) samples from the posterior. For the spirals data this density has roughly 1900 components for the represented classes plus however many are used to represent the remaining mass. I have not attempted to show this distribution. However, one can imagine a smoothed version of the single sample shown in figure 1, from averaging over models with slightly varying numbers of classes and parameters. The (small) mass from the unrepresented classes spreads diffusely over the entire observation range.

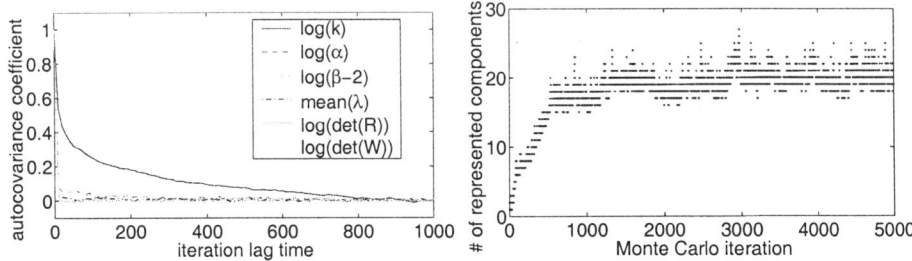

Figure 2: The left plot shows the auto-covariance length for various parameters in the Markov Chain, based on 10^5 iterations. Only the number of represented classes, k_{rep}, has a significant correlation; the effective correlation length is approximately 270, computed as the sum of covariance coefficients between lag -1000 and 1000. The right hand plot shows the number of represented classes growing during the initial phase of sampling. The initial 3000 iterations are discarded.

5 Conclusions

The infinite hierarchical Bayesian mixture model has been reviewed and extended into a practical method. It has been shown that good performance (without overfitting) can be achieved on multidimensional data. An efficient and practical MCMC algorithm with no free parameters has been derived and demonstrated on an example. The model is fully automatic, without needing specification of parameters of the (vague) prior. This corroborates the falsity of the common misconception that "the only difference between Bayesian and non-Bayesian methods is the prior, which is arbitrary anyway ... ".

Further tests on a variety of problems reveals that the infinite mixture model produces densities whose generalisation is highly competitive with other commonly used methods. Current work is undertaken to explore performance on high dimensional problems, in terms of computational efficiency and generalisation.

The infinite mixture model has several advantages over its finite counterpart: 1) in many applications, it may be more appropriate not to limit the number of classes, 2) the number of represented classes is automatically determined, 3) the use of MCMC effectively avoids local minima which plague mixtures trained by optimisation based methods, eg. EM [Ueda et al, 1998] and 4) it is much simpler to handle the infinite limit than to work with finite models with unknown sizes, as in [Richardson & Green, 1997] or traditional approaches based on extensive crossvalidation. The Bayesian infinite mixture model solves simultaneously several long-standing problems with mixture models for density estimation.

Acknowledgments

Thanks to Radford Neal for helpful comments, and to Naonori Ueda for making the spirals data available. This work is funded by the Danish Research Councils through the Computational Neural Network Center (CONNECT) and the THOR Center for Neuroinformatics.

References

Antoniak, C. E. (1974). Mixtures of Dirichlet processes with applications to Bayesian nonparametric problems. *Annals of Statistics 2*, 1152–1174.

Ferguson, T. S. (1973). A Bayesian analysis of some nonparametric problems. *Annals of Statistics 1*, 209–230.

Gilks, W. R. and P. Wild (1992). Adaptive rejection sampling for Gibbs sampling. *Applied Statistics 41*, 337–348.

Neal, R. M. (1996). Bayesian Learning for Neural Networks, Lecture Notes in Statistics No. 118, New York: Springer-Verlag.

Neal, R. M. (1998). Markov chain sampling methods for Dirichlet process mixture models. Technical Report 4915, Department of Statistics, University of Toronto.
http://www.cs.toronto.edu/~radford/mixmc.abstract.html.

Richardson, S. and P. Green (1997). On Bayesian analysis of mixtures with an unknown number of components. *Journal of the Royal Statistical Society, B 59*, 731–792.

Ueda, N., R. Nakano, Z. Ghahramani and G. E. Hinton (1998). SMEM Algorithm for Mixture Models, NIPS 11, MIT Press.

West, M., P. Müller and M. D. Escobar (1994). Hierarchical priors and mixture models with applications in regression and density estimation. In P. R. Freeman and A. F. M. Smith (editors), *Aspects of Uncertainty*, pp. 363–386. John Wiley.

Williams, C. K. I. and C. E. Rasmussen (1996). Gaussian Processes for Regression, in D. S. Touretzky, M. C. Mozer and M. E. Hasselmo (editors), NIPS 8, MIT Press.

ν-Arc: Ensemble Learning in the Presence of Outliers

G. Rätsch[†], B. Schölkopf[‡], A. Smola[*],
K.-R. Müller[†], T. Onoda[††], and S. Mika[†]

† GMD FIRST, Rudower Chaussee 5, 12489 Berlin, Germany
‡ Microsoft Research, 1 Guildhall Street, Cambridge CB2 3NH, UK
* Dep. of Engineering, ANU, Canberra ACT 0200, Australia
†† CRIEPI, 2-11-1, Iwado Kita, Komae-shi, Tokyo, Japan
{raetsch, klaus, mika}@first.gmd.de, bsc@microsoft.com,
Alex.Smola@anu.edu.au, onoda@criepi.denken.or.jp

Abstract

AdaBoost and other ensemble methods have successfully been applied to a number of classification tasks, seemingly defying problems of overfitting. AdaBoost performs gradient descent in an error function with respect to the margin, asymptotically concentrating on the patterns which are hardest to learn. For very noisy problems, however, this can be disadvantageous. Indeed, theoretical analysis has shown that the margin *distribution*, as opposed to just the minimal margin, plays a crucial role in understanding this phenomenon. Loosely speaking, some outliers should be tolerated if this has the benefit of substantially increasing the margin on the remaining points. We propose a new boosting algorithm which allows for the possibility of a pre-specified fraction of points to lie in the margin area or even on the wrong side of the decision boundary.

1 Introduction

Boosting and related Ensemble learning methods have been recently used with great success in applications such as Optical Character Recognition (e.g. [8, 16]).
The idea of a large minimum margin [17] explains the good generalization performance of AdaBoost in the low noise regime. However, AdaBoost performs worse on noisy tasks [10, 11], such as the *iris* and the *breast cancer* benchmark data sets [1]. On the latter tasks, a large margin on *all* training points cannot be achieved without adverse effects on the generalization error. This experimental observation was supported by the study of [13] where the generalization error of ensemble methods was bounded by the sum of the fraction of training points which have a margin smaller than some value ρ, say, plus a complexity term depending on the base hypotheses and ρ. While this bound can only capture part of what is going on in practice, it nevertheless already conveys the message that in some cases it pays to allow for some points which have a small margin, or are misclassified, if this leads to a larger overall margin on the remaining points.
To cope with this problem, it was mandatory to construct *regularized* variants of AdaBoost, which traded off the number of margin errors and the size of the margin

[9, 11]. This goal, however, had so far been achieved in a heuristic way by introducing regularization parameters which have no immediate interpretation and which cannot be adjusted easily.

The present paper addresses this problem in two ways. Primarily, it makes an *algorithmic* contribution to the problem of constructing regularized boosting algorithms. However, compared to the previous efforts, it parameterizes the above trade-off in a much more intuitive way: its only free parameter directly determines the fraction of margin errors. This, in turn, is also appealing from a *theoretical* point of view, since it involves a parameter which controls a quantity that plays a crucial role in the generalization error bounds (cf. also [9, 13]). Furthermore, it allows the user to roughly specify this parameter once a reasonable estimate of the expected error (possibly from other studies) can be obtained, thus reducing the training time.

2 Boosting and the Linear Programming Solution

Before deriving a new algorithm, we briefly discuss the properties of the solution generated by standard AdaBoost and, closely related, Arc-GV [2], and show the relation to a linear programming (LP) solution over the class of base hypotheses G. Let $\{g_t(\mathbf{x}) : t = 1, \ldots, T\}$ be a sequence of hypotheses and $\boldsymbol{\alpha} = [\alpha_1 \ldots \alpha_T]$ their weights satisfying $\alpha_t \geq 0$. The hypotheses g_t are elements of a hypotheses class $G = \{g : \mathbf{x} \mapsto [-1, 1]\}$, which is defined by a base learning algorithm.

The ensemble generates the label which is the weighted majority of the votes by

$$\text{sign}(f(\mathbf{x})) \quad \text{where} \quad f(\mathbf{x}) = \sum_t \frac{\alpha_t}{\|\boldsymbol{\alpha}\|_1} g_t(\mathbf{x}). \tag{1}$$

In order to express that f and therefore also the margin ρ depend on $\boldsymbol{\alpha}$ and for ease of notation we define

$$\rho(\mathbf{z}, \boldsymbol{\alpha}) := y f(\mathbf{x}) \text{ where } \mathbf{z} := (\mathbf{x}, y) \text{ and } f \text{ is defined as in (1)}. \tag{2}$$

Likewise we use the *normalized* margin:

$$\rho(\boldsymbol{\alpha}) := \min_{1 \leq i \leq m} \rho(\mathbf{z}_i, \boldsymbol{\alpha}) , \tag{3}$$

Ensemble learning methods have to find both, the hypotheses $g_t \in G$ used for the combination and their weights $\boldsymbol{\alpha}$. In the following we will consider only AdaBoost algorithms (including Arcing). For more details see e.g. [4, 2]. The main idea of AdaBoost is to introduce weights $w_t(\mathbf{z}_i)$ on the training patterns. They are used to control the importance of each single pattern in learning a new hypothesis (i.e. while repeatedly running the base algorithm). Training patterns that are difficult to learn (which are misclassified repeatedly) become more important.

The minimization objective of AdaBoost can be expressed in terms of margins as

$$\mathcal{G}(\boldsymbol{\alpha}) := \sum_{i=1}^{m} \exp(-\|\boldsymbol{\alpha}\|_1 \rho(\mathbf{z}_i, \boldsymbol{\alpha})) . \tag{4}$$

In every iteration, AdaBoost tries to minimize this error by a stepwise maximization of the margin. It is widely believed that AdaBoost tries to maximize the *smallest margin* on the training set [2, 5, 3, 13, 11]. Strictly speaking, however, a general proof is missing. It would imply that AdaBoost asymptotically approximates (up to scaling) the solution of the following linear programming problem over the complete hypothesis set G (cf. [7], assuming a *finite* number of basis hypotheses):

$$\begin{aligned} \text{maximize} \quad & \rho \\ \text{subject to} \quad & \rho(\mathbf{z}_i, \boldsymbol{\alpha}) \geq \rho \quad \text{for all } 1 \leq i \leq m \\ & \alpha_t, \rho \geq 0 \quad \text{for all } 1 \leq t \leq |G| \\ & \|\boldsymbol{\alpha}\|_1 = 1 \end{aligned} \tag{5}$$

Since such a linear program cannot be solved exactly for a infinite hypothesis set in general, it is interesting to analyze approximation algorithms for this kind of problems.

Breiman [2] proposed a modification of AdaBoost – Arc-GV – making it possible to show the asymptotic convergence of $\rho(\boldsymbol{\alpha}^t)$ to the global solution ρ^{lp}:

Theorem 1 (Breiman [2]). *Choose α_t in each iteration as*

$$\alpha_t := \operatorname*{argmin}_{\alpha \in [0,1]} \sum_i \exp\left[-\|\boldsymbol{\alpha}^t\|_1 \left(\rho(\mathbf{z}_i, \boldsymbol{\alpha}^t) - \rho(\boldsymbol{\alpha}^{t-1})\right)\right], \tag{6}$$

and assume that the base learner always finds the hypothesis $g \in G$ which minimizes the weighted training error with respect to the weights. Then

$$\lim_{t \to \infty} \rho(\boldsymbol{\alpha}^t) = \rho^{\text{lp}}.$$

Note that the algorithm above can be derived from the modified error function

$$\mathcal{G}_{\text{gv}}(\boldsymbol{\alpha}^t) := \sum_i \exp\left[-\|\boldsymbol{\alpha}^t\|_1 \left(\rho(\mathbf{z}_i, \boldsymbol{\alpha}^t) - \rho(\boldsymbol{\alpha}^{t-1})\right)\right]. \tag{7}$$

The question one might ask now is whether to use AdaBoost or rather Arc-GV in practice. Does Arc-GV converge fast enough to benefit from its asymptotic properties? In [12] we conducted experiments to investigate this question. We empirically found that (a) AdaBoost has problems finding the optimal combination if $\rho^{\text{lp}} < 0$, (b) Arc-GV's convergence does not depend on ρ^{lp}, and (c) for $\rho^{\text{lp}} > 0$, AdaBoost usually converges to the maximum margin solution slightly faster than Arc-GV. Observation (a) becomes clear from (4): $\mathcal{G}(\boldsymbol{\alpha})$ will not converge to 0 and $\|\boldsymbol{\alpha}\|_1$ can be bounded by some value. Thus the asymptotic case cannot be reached, whereas for Arc-GV the optimum is always found.

Moreover, the number of iterations necessary to converge to a *good* solution seems to be reasonable, but for a near *optimal* solution the number of iterations is rather high. This implies that for real world hypothesis sets, the number of iterations needed to find an almost optimal solution can become prohibitive, but we conjecture that in practice a reasonably good approximation to the optimum is provided by both AdaBoost and Arc-GV.

3 ν-Algorithms

For the LP-AdaBoost [7] approach it has been shown for noisy problems that the generalization performance is usually not as good as the one of AdaBoost [7, 2, 11]. From Theorem 5 in [13] (cf. Theorem 3 on page 5) this fact becomes clear, as the minimum of the right hand side of inequality (cf. (13)) need not necessarily be achieved with a maximum margin. We now propose an algorithm to directly control the number of margin errors and therefore also the contribution of both terms in the inequality separately (cf. Theorem 3). We first consider a small hypothesis class and end up with a linear program – ν-LP-AdaBoost. In subsection 3.2 we then combine this algorithm with the ideas from section 2 and get a new algorithm – ν-Arc – which approximates the ν-LP solution.

3.1 ν-LP-AdaBoost

Let us consider the case where we are given a (finite) set $G = \{g : \mathbf{x} \mapsto [-1, 1]\}$ of T hypotheses. To find the coefficients $\boldsymbol{\alpha}$ for the combined hypothesis $f(\mathbf{x})$ we extend the LP-AdaBoost algorithm [7, 11] by incorporating the parameter ν [15] and solve the following linear optimization problem:

$$\begin{array}{ll}
\text{maximize} & \rho - \frac{1}{\nu m} \sum_{i=1}^m \xi_i \\
\text{subject to} & \rho(\mathbf{z}_i, \boldsymbol{\alpha}) \geq \rho - \xi_i \quad \text{for all } 1 \leq i \leq m \\
& \xi_i, \alpha_t, \rho \geq 0 \quad \text{for all } 1 \leq t \leq T \text{ and } 1 \leq i \leq m \\
& \|\boldsymbol{\alpha}\|_1 = 1
\end{array} \tag{8}$$

This algorithm does not force all margins to be beyond zero and we get a *soft margin* classification (cf. SVMs) with a regularization constant $\frac{1}{\nu m}$. The following proposition shows that ν has an immediate interpretation:

Proposition 2 (Rätsch et al. [12]). *Suppose we run the algorithm given in (8) on some data with the resulting optimal $\rho > 0$. Then*

1. *ν upper bounds the fraction of margin errors.*

2. *$1 - \nu$ upper bounds the fraction of patterns with margin larger than ρ.*

Since the slack variables ξ_i only enter the cost function linearly, their absolute size is not important. Loosely speaking, this is due to the fact that for the optimum of the primal objective function, only *derivatives* wrt. the primal variables matter, and the derivative of a linear function is constant.

In the case of SVMs [14], where the hypotheses can be thought of as vectors in some feature space, this statement can be translated into a precise rule for distorting training patterns without changing the solution: we can move them locally orthogonal to a separating hyperplane. This yields a desirable *robustness* property. Note that the algorithm essentially depends on the *number* of outliers, not on the size of the error [15].

3.2 The ν-Arc Algorithm

Suppose we have a very large (but finite) base hypothesis class G. Then it is difficult to solve (8) as (5) directly. To this end, we propose a new algorithm – ν-Arc – that approximates the solution of (8).

The optimal ρ for fixed margins $\rho(\mathbf{z}_i, \boldsymbol{\alpha})$ in (8) can be written as

$$\rho_\nu(\boldsymbol{\alpha}) := \underset{\rho \in [0,1]}{\operatorname{argmax}} \left(\rho - \frac{1}{\nu m} \sum_{i=1}^m (\rho - \rho(\mathbf{z}_i, \boldsymbol{\alpha}))_+ \right). \quad (9)$$

where $(\xi)_+ := \max(\xi, 0)$. Setting $\xi_i := (\rho_\nu(\boldsymbol{\alpha}) - \rho(\mathbf{z}_i, \boldsymbol{\alpha}))_+$ and subtracting $\frac{1}{\nu m} \sum_{i=1}^m \xi_i$ from the resulting inequality on both sides yields (for all $1 \leq i \leq m$)

$$\rho(\mathbf{z}_i, \boldsymbol{\alpha}) + \xi_i - \frac{1}{\nu m} \sum_{i=1}^m \xi_i \geq \rho_\nu(\boldsymbol{\alpha}) - \frac{1}{\nu m} \sum_{i=1}^m \xi_i. \quad (10)$$

Two more substitutions are needed to transform the problem into one which can be solved by the AdaBoost algorithm. In particular we have to get rid of the slack variables ξ_i again by absorbing them into quantities similar to $\rho(\mathbf{z}_i, \boldsymbol{\alpha})$ and $\rho(\boldsymbol{\alpha})$. This works as follows: on the right hand side of (10) we have the objective function (cf. (8)) and on the left hand side a term that depends nonlinearly on $\boldsymbol{\alpha}$. Defining

$$\tilde{\rho}_\nu(\boldsymbol{\alpha}) := \rho_\nu(\boldsymbol{\alpha}) - \frac{1}{\nu m} \sum_{i=1}^m \xi_i \quad \text{and} \quad \tilde{\rho}_\nu(\mathbf{z}_i, \boldsymbol{\alpha}) := \rho(\mathbf{z}_i, \boldsymbol{\alpha}) + \xi_i - \frac{1}{\nu m} \sum_{i=1}^m \xi_i, \quad (11)$$

which we substitute for $\rho(\boldsymbol{\alpha})$ and $\rho(\mathbf{z}, \boldsymbol{\alpha})$ in (5), respectively, we obtain a new optimization problem. Note that $\tilde{\rho}_\nu(\boldsymbol{\alpha})$ and $\tilde{\rho}_\nu(\mathbf{z}_i, \boldsymbol{\alpha})$ play the role of a *corrected* or *virtual* margin. We obtain a nonlinear min-max problem

$$\begin{aligned}
\text{maximize} \quad & \tilde{\rho}(\boldsymbol{\alpha}) \\
\text{subject to} \quad & \tilde{\rho}(\mathbf{z}_i, \boldsymbol{\alpha}) \geq \tilde{\rho}(\boldsymbol{\alpha}) \quad \text{for all } 1 \leq i \leq m \\
& \alpha_t \geq 0 \quad \text{for all } 1 \leq t \leq T \\
& \|\boldsymbol{\alpha}\|_1 = 1
\end{aligned} \quad (12)$$

which Arc-GV can solve approximately (cf. section 2). Hence, by replacing the margin $\rho(\mathbf{z}, \boldsymbol{\alpha})$ by $\tilde{\rho}(\mathbf{z}, \boldsymbol{\alpha})$ in equation (4) and the other formulas for Arc-GV (cf. [2]), we obtain a new algorithm which we refer to as ν-Arc.

We can now state interesting properties for ν-Arc by using Theorem 5 of [13] that bounds the generalization error $R(f)$ for ensemble methods. In our case $R_\rho(f) \leq \nu$ by construction (i.e. the number of patterns with a margin smaller than ρ, cf. Proposition 2), thus we get the following simple reformulation of this bound:

Theorem 3. *Let $p(\mathbf{x}, y)$ be a distribution over $\mathcal{X} \times [-1, 1]$, and let X be a sample of m examples chosen iid according to p. Suppose the base-hypothesis space G has VC dimension h, and let $\delta > 0$. Then with probability at least $1 - \delta$ over the random choice of the training set X, Y, every function f generated by ν-Arc, where $\nu \in (0, 1)$ and $\rho_\nu > 0$, satisfies the following bound:*

$$R(f) \leq \nu + \sqrt{\frac{c}{m}\left(\frac{h\log^2(m/h)}{\rho_\nu^2} + \log\left(\frac{1}{\delta}\right)\right)}. \tag{13}$$

So, for minimizing the right hand side we can tradeoff between the first and the second term by controlling an easily interpretable regularization parameter ν.

4 Experiments

We show a set of toy experiments to illustrate the general behavior of ν-Arc. As base hypothesis class G we use the RBF networks of [11], and as data a two-class problem generated from several 2D Gauss blobs (cf. **Banana shape** dataset from http://www.first.gmd.de/~data/banana.html.). We obtain the following results:

- ν-Arc leads to approximately νm patterns that are effectively used in the training of the base learner: Figure 1 (left) shows the fraction of patterns that have high average weights during the learning process (i.e. $\sum_{t=1}^T w_t(\mathbf{z}_i) > 1/2m$). We find that the number of the latter increases (almost) linearly with ν. This follows from (11) as the (soft) margin of patterns with $\rho(\mathbf{z}, \boldsymbol{\alpha}) < \rho_\nu$ is set to ρ_ν and the weight of those patterns will be the same.

- The (estimated) test error, averaged over 10 training sets, exhibits a rather flat minimum in ν (Figure 1 (lower)). This indicates that just as for ν-SVMs, where corresponding results have been obtained, ν is a well-behaved parameter in the sense that a slight misadjustment it is not harmful.

- ν-Arc leads to the fraction ν of margin errors (cf. dashed line in Figure 1) exactly as predicted in Proposition 2.

- Finally, a good value of ν can already be inferred from prior knowledge of the expected error. Setting it to a value similar to the latter provides a good starting point for further optimization (cf. Theorem 3).

Note that for $\nu = 1$, we recover the Bagging algorithm (if we used bootstrap samples), as the weights of all patterns will be the same ($w_t(\mathbf{z}_i) = 1/m$ for all $i = 1, \ldots, m$) and also the hypothesis weights will be constant ($\alpha_t \sim 1/T$ for all $t = 1, \ldots, T$).

Finally, we present a small comparison on ten benchmark data sets obtained from the UCI [1] benchmark repository (cf. http://ida.first.gmd.de/~raetsch/data/benchmarks.html). We analyze the performance of single RBF networks, AdaBoost, ν-Arc and RBF-SVMs. For AdaBoost and ν-Arc we use RBF networks [11] as base hypothesis. The model parameters of RBF (number of centers etc.), ν-Arc (ν) and SVMs (σ, C) are optimized using 5-fold cross-validation. More details on the experimental setup can

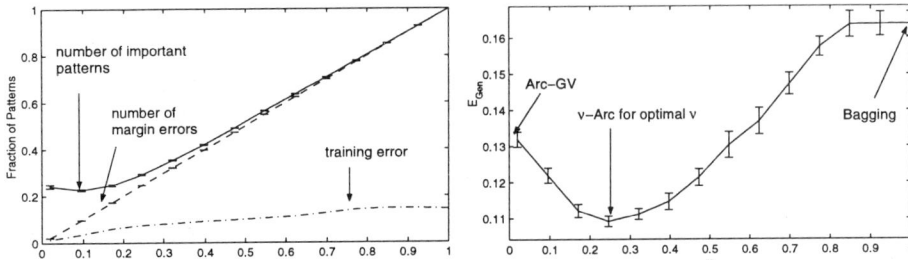

Figure 1: Toy experiment ($\sigma = 0$): the left graph shows the average fraction of *important* patterns, the av. fraction of margin errors and the av. training error for different values of the regularization constant ν for ν-Arc. The right graph shows the corresponding generalization error. In both cases, the parameter ν allows us to reduce the test errors to values much lower than for the hard margin algorithm (for $\nu = 0$ we recover Arc-GV/AdaBoost, and for $\nu = 1$ we get Bagging.)

be found in [11]. Fig. 1 shows the generalization error estimates (after averaging over 100 realizations of the data sets) and the confidence interval. The results of the best classifier and the classifiers that are not significantly worse are set in bold face. To test the significance, we used a t-test ($p = 80\%$). On eight out of the ten data sets, ν-Arc performs significantly better than AdaBoost. This clearly shows the superior performance of ν-Arc for noisy data sets and supports this soft margin approach for AdaBoost. Furthermore, we find comparable performances for ν-Arc and SVMs. In three cases the SVM performs better and in two cases ν-Arc performs best. Summarizing, AdaBoost is useful for low noise cases, where the classes are separable. ν-Arc extends the applicability of boosting to problems that are difficult to separate and should be applied if the data are noisy.

5 Conclusion

We analyzed the AdaBoost algorithm and found that Arc-GV and AdaBoost are efficient for approximating the solution of non-linear min-max problems over huge hypothesis classes. We re-parameterized the LP$_{Reg}$-AdaBoost algorithm (cf. [7, 11]) and introduced a new regularization constant ν that controls the fraction of patterns inside the margin area. The new parameter is highly intuitive and has to be optimized only on a fixed interval $[0, 1]$.

Using the fact that Arc-GV can approximately solve min-max problems, we found a formulation of Arc-GV – ν-Arc – that implements the ν-idea for Boosting by defining an appropriate *soft margin*. The present paper extends previous work on regularizing boosting (DOOM [9], AdaBoost$_{Reg}$ [11]) and shows the utility and flexibility of the soft margin approach for AdaBoost.

	RBF	AB	ν-Arc	SVM
Banana	10.8 ± 0.06	12.3 ± 0.07	**10.6 ± 0.05**	11.5 ± 0.07
B.Cancer	27.6 ± 0.47	30.4 ± 0.47	**25.8 ± 0.46**	**26.0 ± 0.47**
Diabetes	24.3 ± 0.19	26.5 ± 0.23	**23.7 ± 0.20**	**23.5 ± 0.17**
German	24.7 ± 0.24	27.5 ± 0.25	24.4 ± 0.22	**23.6 ± 0.21**
Heart	17.6 ± 0.33	20.3 ± 0.34	**16.5 ± 0.36**	**16.0 ± 0.33**
Ringnorm	**1.7 ± 0.02**	1.9 ± 0.03	**1.7 ± 0.02**	**1.7 ± 0.01**
F.Sonar	34.4 ± 0.20	35.7 ± 0.18	34.4 ± 0.19	**32.4 ± 0.18**
Thyroid	**4.5 ± 0.21**	4.4 ± 0.22	4.4 ± 0.22	4.8 ± 0.22
Titanic	23.3 ± 0.13	**22.6 ± 0.12**	23.0 ± 0.14	**22.4 ± 0.10**
Waveform	10.7 ± 0.11	10.8 ± 0.06	**10.0 ± 0.07**	9.9 ± 0.04

Table 1: Generalization error estimates and confidence intervals. The best classifiers for a particular data set are marked in bold face (see text).

We found empirically that the generalization performance in ν-Arc depends only slightly on the choice of the regularization constant. This makes model selection (e.g. via cross-validation) easier and faster.

Future work will study the detailed regularization properties of the regularized versions of AdaBoost, in particular in comparison to ν-LP Support Vector Machines.

Acknowledgments: Partial funding from DFG grant (Ja 379/52) is gratefully acknowledged. This work was done while AS and BS were at GMD FIRST.

References

[1] C. Blake, E. Keogh, and C. J. Merz. UCI repository of machine learning databases, 1998. http://www.ics.uci.edu/~mlearn/MLRepository.html.

[2] L. Breiman. Prediction games and arcing algorithms. Technical Report 504, Statistics Department, University of California, December 1997.

[3] M. Frean and T. Downs. A simple cost function for boosting. Technical report, Dept. of Computer Science and Electrical Eng., University of Queensland, 1998.

[4] Y. Freund and R. E. Schapire. A decision-theoretic generalization of on-line learning and an application to boosting. In *Computational Learning Theory: Eurocolt '95*, pages 23–37. Springer-Verlag, 1995.

[5] Y. Freund and R. E. Schapire. A decision-theoretic generalization of on-line learning and an application to boosting. *J. of Comp. & Syst. Sc.*, 55(1):119–139, 1997.

[6] J. Friedman, T. Hastie, and R. Tibshirani. Additive logistic regression: a statistical view of boosting. Technical report, Stanford University, 1998.

[7] A. Grove and D. Schuurmans. Boosting in the limit: Maximizing the margin of learned ensembles. In *Proc. of the 15th Nat. Conf. on AI*, pages 692–699, 1998.

[8] Y. LeCun, L. D. Jackel, L. Bottou, C. Cortes, J. S. Denker, H. Drucker, I. Guyon, U. A. Müller, E. Säckinger, P. Simard, and V. Vapnik. Learning algorithms for classification: A comparison on handwritten digit recognition. *Neural Networks*, pages 261–276, 1995.

[9] L. Mason, P. L. Bartlett, and J. Baxter. Improved generalization through explicit optimization of margins. *Machine Learning*, 1999. to appear.

[10] J. R. Quinlan. Boosting first-order learning (invited lecture). *Lecture Notes in Computer Science*, 1160:143, 1996.

[11] G. Rätsch, T. Onoda, and K.-R. Müller. Soft margins for AdaBoost. Technical Report NC-TR-1998-021, Department of Computer Science, Royal Holloway, University of London, Egham, UK, 1998. To appear in Machine Learning.

[12] G. Rätsch, B. Schökopf, A. Smola, S. Mika, T. Onoda, and K.-R. Müller. Robust ensemble learning. In A.J. Smola, P.L. Bartlett, B. Schölkopf, and D. Schuurmans, editors, *Advances in LMC*, pages 207–219. MIT Press, Cambridge, MA, 1999.

[13] R. Schapire, Y. Freund, P. L. Bartlett, and W. Sun Lee. Boosting the margin: A new explanation for the effectiveness of voting methods. *Annals of Statistics*, 1998. (Earlier appeared in: D. H. Fisher, Jr. (ed.), Proc. ICML97, M. Kaufmann).

[14] B. Schölkopf, C. J. C. Burges, and A. J. Smola. *Advances in Kernel Methods — Support Vector Learning*. MIT Press, Cambridge, MA, 1999.

[15] B. Schölkopf, A. Smola, R. C. Williamson, and P. L. Bartlett. New support vector algorithms. *Neural Computation*, 12:1083 – 1121, 2000.

[16] H. Schwenk and Y. Bengio. Training methods for adaptive boosting of neural networks. In Michael I. Jordan, Michael J. Kearns, and Sara A. Solla, editors, *Advances in Neural Inf. Processing Systems*, volume 10. The MIT Press, 1998.

[17] V. Vapnik. *The Nature of Statistical Learning Theory*. Springer Verlag, New York, 1995.

Nonlinear Discriminant Analysis using Kernel Functions

Volker Roth & Volker Steinhage
University of Bonn, Institut of Computer Science III
Römerstrasse 164, D-53117 Bonn, Germany
{*roth, steinhag*}@*cs.uni-bonn.de*

Abstract

Fishers linear discriminant analysis (LDA) is a classical multivariate technique both for dimension reduction and classification. The data vectors are transformed into a low dimensional subspace such that the class centroids are spread out as much as possible. In this subspace LDA works as a simple prototype classifier with linear decision boundaries. However, in many applications the linear boundaries do not adequately separate the classes. We present a nonlinear generalization of discriminant analysis that uses the *kernel trick* of representing dot products by kernel functions. The presented algorithm allows a simple formulation of the EM-algorithm in terms of kernel functions which leads to a unique concept for unsupervised mixture analysis, supervised discriminant analysis and semi-supervised discriminant analysis with partially unlabelled observations in feature spaces.

1 Introduction

Classical linear discriminant analysis (LDA) projects N data vectors that belong to c different classes into a $(c-1)$–dimensional space in such way that the ratio of *between group scatter* S_B and *within group scatter* S_W is maximized [1]. LDA formally consists of an eigenvalue decomposition of $S_W^{-1} S_B$ leading to the so called *canonical variates* which contain the whole class specific information in a $(c-1)$-dimensional subspace. The canonical variates can be ordered by decreasing eigenvalue size indicating that the first variates contain the major part of the information. As a consequence, this procedure allows low dimensional representations and therefore a *visualization* of the data. Besides from interpreting LDA only as a technique for dimensionality reduction, it can also be seen as a multi-class classification method: the set of linear discriminant functions define a partition of the projected space into regions that are identified with class membership. A new observation x is assigned to the class with centroid closest to x in the projected space.

To overcome the limitation of only linear decision functions some attempts have been made to incorporate nonlinearity into the classical algorithm. HASTIE *et al.* [2] introduced the so called model of *Flexible Discriminant Analysis*: LDA is reformulated in the framework of linear regression estimation and a generalization of this method is given by using nonlinear regression techniques. The proposed regression techniques implement the idea of using nonlinear mappings to transform the input data into a new space in which again a linear regression is performed. In real world applications this approach has to deal with numerical problems due to the dimensional explosion resulting from nonlinear mappings. In the recent years approaches that avoid such *explicit* mappings by using *kernel functions* have become popular. The main idea is to construct algorithms that only afford dot products of pattern vectors which can be computed efficiently in high-dimensional spaces. Examples of this type of algorithms are the *Support Vector Machine* [3] and *Kernel Principal Component Analysis* [4].

In this paper we show that it is possible to formulate classical linear regression and therefore also linear discriminant analysis exclusively in terms of dot products. Therefore, kernel methods can be used to construct a nonlinear variant of discriminant analysis. We call this technique *Kernel Discriminant Analysis* (KDA). Contrary to a similar approach that has been published recently [5], our algorithm is a real multi-class classifier and inherits from classical LDA the convenient property of data *visualization*.

2 Review of Linear Discriminant Analysis

Under the assumption of the data being centered (i.e. $\sum_i x_i = 0$) the *scatter matrices* S_B and S_W are defined by

$$S_B = \sum_{j=1}^{c} \frac{1}{n_j} \sum_{l,m=1}^{n_j} \left(x_l^{(j)}\right) \left(x_m^{(j)}\right)^T \tag{1}$$

$$S_W = \sum_{j=1}^{c} \sum_{l=1}^{n_j} \left(x_l^{(j)} - \frac{1}{n_j} \sum_{l=1}^{n_j} x_l^{(j)}\right) \left(x_l^{(j)} - \frac{1}{n_j} \sum_{m=1}^{n_j} x_m^{(j)}\right)^T, \tag{2}$$

where n_j is the number of patterns $x_l^{(j)}$ that belong to class j.

LDA chooses a transformation matrix V that maximizes the objective function

$$J(V) = \frac{|V^T S_B V|}{|V^T S_W V|}. \tag{3}$$

The columns of an optimal V are the generalized eigenvectors that correspond to the nonzero eigenvalues in $S_B v_i = \lambda_i S_W v_i$.

In [6] and [7] we have shown, that the standard LDA algorithm can be restated exclusively in terms of dot products of input vectors. The final equation is an eigenvalue equation in terms of dot product matrices which are of size $N \times N$. Since the solution of high-dimensional generalized eigenvalue equations may cause numerical problems (N may be large in real world applications), we present an improved algorithm that reformulates discriminant analysis as a regression problem. Moreover, this version allows a simple implementation of the EM-algorithm in feature spaces.

3 Linear regression analysis

In this section we give a brief review of linear regression analysis which we use as "building block" for LDA. The task of linear regression analysis is to approximate the regression function by a linear function

$$r(x) = E(\mathcal{Y}|\mathcal{X} = x) \approx c + x^T \beta. \tag{4}$$

on the basis of a sample $(y_1, x_1), \cdots, (y_N, x_N)$. Let now y denote the vector $(y_1, \ldots, y_N)^T$ and X denote the data matrix which rows are the input vectors. Using a quadratic loss function, the optimal parameters c and β are chosen to minimize the average squared residual

$$ASR = N^{-1} \|y - c\mathbf{1}_N + X\beta\|^2 + \beta^T \Omega \beta. \tag{5}$$

$\mathbf{1}_N$ denotes a N-vector of ones, Ω denotes a ridge-type penalty matrix $\Omega = \epsilon I$ which penalizes the coefficients of β. Assuming the data being centered, i.e $\sum_{i=1}^{N} x_i = 0$, the parameters of the regression function are given by:

$$c = N^{-1} \sum_{i=1}^{N} y_i =: \mu_y, \qquad \beta = (X^T X + \epsilon I)^{-1} X^T y. \tag{6}$$

4 LDA by optimal scoring

In this section the LDA problem is linked to linear regression using the framework of *penalized optimal scoring*. We give an overview over the detailed derivation in [2] and [8]. Considering again the problem with c classes and N data vectors, the class-memberships are represented by a categorical response variable $\mathcal{G}$ with c levels. It is useful to code the n responses in terms of the indicator matrix Z: $Z_{i,j} = 1$, if the i-th data vector belongs to class j, and 0 otherwise. The point of optimal scoring is to turn categorical variables into quantitative ones by assigning scores to classes: the score vector $\boldsymbol{\theta}$ assigns the real number $\boldsymbol{\theta}_j$ to the j-th level of $\mathcal{G}$. The vector $Z\boldsymbol{\theta}$ then represents a vector of scored training data and is regressed onto the data matrix X. The simultaneous estimation of scores and regression coefficients constitutes the optimal scoring problem: minimize the criterion

$$ASR(\boldsymbol{\theta}, \boldsymbol{\beta}) = N^{-1}[\|Z\boldsymbol{\theta} - X\boldsymbol{\beta}\|^2 + \boldsymbol{\beta}^T \Omega \boldsymbol{\beta}] \quad (7)$$

under the constraint $\frac{1}{N}\|Z\boldsymbol{\theta}\|^2 = 1$. According to (6), for a given score $\boldsymbol{\theta}$ the minimizing $\boldsymbol{\beta}$ is given by

$$\boldsymbol{\beta}_{OS} = (X^T X + \Omega)^{-1} X^T Z \boldsymbol{\theta}, \quad (8)$$

and the partially minimized criterion becomes:

$$\min_{\boldsymbol{\beta}} ASR(\boldsymbol{\theta}, \boldsymbol{\beta}) = 1 - N^{-1} \boldsymbol{\theta}^T Z^T M(\Omega) Z \boldsymbol{\theta}, \quad (9)$$

where $M(\Omega) = X(X^T X + \Omega)^{-1} X^T$ denotes the regularized *hat* or *smoother* matrix. Minimizing of (9) under the constraint $\frac{1}{N}\|Z\boldsymbol{\theta}\|^2 = 1$ can be performed by the following procedure:

1. Choose an initial matrix Θ_0 satisfying the constraint $N^{-1} \Theta_0^T Z^T Z \Theta_0 = I$ and set $\Theta_0^* = Z\Theta_0$
2. Run a multi-response regression of Θ_0^* onto X: $\hat{\Theta}_0^* = M(\Omega)\Theta_0^* = XB$, where B is the matrix of regression coefficients.
3. Eigenanalyze $\Theta_0^{*T} \hat{\Theta}_0^*$ to obtain the optimal scores, and update the matrix of regression coefficients: $B^* = BW$, with W being the matrix of eigenvectors.

It can be shown, that the final matrix B^* is, up to a diagonal scale matrix, equivalent to the matrix of LDA-vectors, see [8].

5 Ridge regression using only dot products

The penalty matrix Ω in (5) assures that the penalized $d \times d$ covariance matrix $\tilde{\Sigma} = X^T X + \epsilon I$ is a symmetric nonsingular matrix. Therefore, it has d eigenvectors e_i with accomplished positive eigenvalues γ_i such that the following equations hold:

$$\tilde{\Sigma} e_i = \sum_{j=1}^{N} x_j x_j^T e_i + \epsilon e_i = \gamma_i e_i, \quad \tilde{\Sigma}^{-1} = \sum_{i=1}^{d} \frac{1}{\gamma_i} e_i e_i^T \quad (10)$$

The first equation implies that the first l leading eigenvectors e_i with eigenvalues $\gamma_i > \epsilon$ have an expansion in terms of the input vectors. Note that l is the number of nonzero eigenvalues of the unpenalized covariance matrix $X^T X$. Together with (6), it follows for the general case, when the dimensionality d may extend l, that β can be written as the sum of two terms: an expansion in terms of the vectors x_i with coefficients α_i and a similar expansion in terms of the remaining eigenvectors:

$$\beta = \sum_{i=1}^{N} \alpha_i x_i + \sum_{j=l+1}^{d} \xi_j e_j = X^T \boldsymbol{\alpha} + \sum_{j=l+1}^{d} \xi_j e_j, \quad (11)$$

with $\boldsymbol{\alpha} = (\alpha_1 \cdots \alpha_n)^T$. However, the last term can be dropped, since every eigenvector e_j, $j = l+1, \ldots, d$ is orthogonal to *every* vector x_i and does not influence the value of the regression function (4).

The problem of penalized linear regression can therefore be stated as minimizing

$$ASR(\alpha) = N^{-1}\big[\,\|y - XX^T\alpha\|^2 + \alpha^T X\Omega X^T\alpha\,\big]. \tag{12}$$

A stationary vector α is determined by
$$\alpha = (XX^T + \Omega)^{-1}y. \tag{13}$$

Let now the *dot product matrix* K be defined by $K_{ij} = x_i^T x_j$ and let for a given test point (x_l) the dot product vector k_l be defined by $k_l = Xx_l$. With this notation the regression function of a test point (x_l) reads
$$r(x_l) = \mu_y + k_l^T(K + \epsilon I)^{-1}y. \tag{14}$$

This equation requires only dot products and we can apply the *kernel trick*. The final equation (14), up to the constant term μ_y, has also been found by SAUNDERS et al., [9]. They restated ridge regression in dual variables and optimized the resulting criterion function with a lagrange multiplier technique. Note that our derivation, which is a direct generalization of the standard linear regression formalism, leads in a natural way to a class of more general regression functions including the constant term.

6 LDA using only dot products

Setting $\beta = X^T\alpha$ as in (11) and using the notation of section 5, for a given score θ the optimal vector α is given by:
$$\alpha_{OS} = (XX^T + \Omega)^{-1}Z\theta. \tag{15}$$

Analogous to (9), the partially minimized criterion becomes:
$$\min_{\alpha} ASR(\theta, \alpha) = 1 - N^{-1}\theta^T Z^T \tilde{M}(\Omega) Z\theta, \tag{16}$$

with
$$\tilde{M}(\Omega) = XX^T(XX^T + \Omega)^{-1} = K(K + \epsilon I)^{-1}.$$

To minimize (16) under the constraint $\frac{1}{N}\|Z\theta\|^2 = 1$ the procedure described in section 4 can be used when $M(\Omega)$ is substituted by $\tilde{M}(\Omega)$. The matrix Y which rows are the input vectors projected onto the column vectors of B^* is given by:
$$Y = XB^* = K(K + \epsilon I)^{-1}Z\Theta_0 W. \tag{17}$$

Note that again the dot product matrix K is all that is needed to calculate Y.

7 The kernel trick

The main idea of constructing nonlinear algorithms is to apply the linear methods not in the space of observations but in a *feature space* F that is related to the former by a nonlinear mapping $\phi : \mathbf{R}^N \to F$, $x \to \phi(x)$.
Assuming that the mapped data are centered in F, i.e. $\sum_{i=1}^{n} \phi(x_i) = 0$, the presented algorithms remain formally unchanged if the dot product matrix K is computed in F: $K_{ij} = (\phi(x_i) \cdot \phi(x_j))$. As shown in [4], this assumption can be dropped by writing $\tilde{\phi}$ instead of the mapping ϕ: $\quad \tilde{\phi}(x_i) := \phi(x_i) - \frac{1}{n}\sum_{i=1}^{n}\phi(x_i)$.
Computation of dot products in feature spaces can be done efficiently by using *kernel functions* $k(x_i, x_j)$ [3]: For some choices of k there exists a mapping ϕ into some feature space F such that k acts as a dot product in F. Among possible kernel functions there are e.g. Radial Basis Function (RBF) kernels of the form $k(x, y) = \exp(-\|x - y\|^2/c)$.

8 The EM-algorithm in feature spaces

LDA can be derived as the maximum likelihood method for normal populations with different means and common covariance matrix Σ (see [11]). Coding the class membership of the observations in the matrix Z as in section 4, LDA maximizes the (complete data) log-likelihood function

$$l(\mu_k, \Sigma, \pi_k) \propto - \sum_{k=1}^{c} \sum_{Z_{ik}=1} \log\left((x_i - \mu_k)^T \Sigma^{-1} (x_i - \mu_k)\right) - N \log |\Sigma|. \quad (18)$$

This concept can be generalized for the case that only the group membership of $N_C < N$ observations is known ([14], p.679): the EM-algorithm provides a convenient method for maximizing the likelihood function with missing data:
E-step: set $p_{ki} = \text{Prob}(x_i \in \text{class } k)$

$$p_{ki} = \begin{cases} Z_{ik}, & \text{if the class membership of } x_i \text{ has been observed} \\ \frac{\pi_k \phi_k(x_i)}{\sum_{k=1}^{c} \pi_k \phi_k(x_i)}, & \text{otherwise}, \quad \phi_k(x_i) \propto \exp[-1/2(x_i - \mu_k)^T \Sigma^{-1}(x_i - \mu_k)] \end{cases}$$

M-step: set

$$\pi_k = \frac{1}{N} \sum_{i=1}^{N} p_{ki}, \quad \mu_k = \frac{1}{N \pi_k} \sum_{i=1}^{N} p_{ki} x_i, \quad \Sigma = \frac{1}{N} \sum_{k=1}^{c} \sum_{i=1}^{N} p_{ki} (x_i - \mu_k)(x_i - \mu_k)^T$$

The idea behind this approach is that even an unclassified observation can be used for estimation if it is given a proper weight according to its posterior probability for class membership. The M-step can be seen as weighted mean and covariance maximum likelihood estimates in a weighted and augmented problem: we augment the data by replicating the N observations c times, with the l-th such replication having observation weights p_{li}. The maximization of the likelihood function can be achieved via a weighted and augmented LDA. It turns out that it is *not* necessary to explicitly replicate the observations and run a standard LDA: the optimal scoring version of LDA described in section 4 allows an implicit solution of the augmented problem that still uses only N observations. Instead of using a response indicator matrix Z, one uses a *blurred* response Matrix $\tilde{Z}$, whose rows consist of the current class probabilities for each observation. At each M-step this $\tilde{Z}$ is used in a multiple linear regression followed by an eigen-decomposition. A detailed derivation is given in [11]. Since we have shown that the optimal scoring problem can be solved in feature spaces using kernel functions this is also the case for the whole EM-algorithm: the E-step requires only *differences* in Mahalonobis distances which are supplied by KDA.

After iterated application of the E- and M-step an observation is classified to the class k with highest probability p_k. This leads to a unique framework for pure mixture analysis ($N_C = 0$), pure discriminant analysis ($N_C = N$) and the semi-supervised models of discriminant analysis with partially unclassified observations ($0 < N_C < N$) in feature spaces.

9 Experiments

Waveform data: We illustrate KDA on a popular simulated example, taken from [10], p.49-55 and used in [2, 11]. It is a three class problem with 21 variables. The learning set consisted of 100 observations per class. The test set was of size 1000. The results are given in table 1.

Table 1: Results for waveform data. The values are averages over 10 simulations. The 4 entries above the line are taken from [11]. QDA: quadratic discriminant analysis, FDA: flexible discriminant analysis, MDA: mixture discriminant analysis.

Technique	Training Error [%]	Test Error [%]
LDA	12.1(0.6)	19.1(0.6)
QDA	3.9(0.4)	20.5(0.6)
FDA (best model parameters)	10.0(0.6)	19.1(0.6)
MDA (best model parameters)	13.9(0.5)	15.5(0.5)
KDA (RBF kernel, $\sigma = 2, \epsilon = 1.5$)	10.7(0.6)	14.1(0.7)

The Bayes risk for the problem is about 14% [10]. KDA outperforms the other nonlinear versions of discriminant analysis and reaches the Bayes rate within the error bounds, indicating that one cannot expect significant further improvement using other classifiers. Figure 1 demonstrates the *data visualization* property of KDA. Since for a 3 class problem the dimensionality of the projected space equals 2, the data can be visualized without any loss of information. In the left plot one can see the projected learn data and the class centroids, the right plot shows the test data and again the class centroids of the learning set.

Figure 1: Data visualization with KDA. Left: learn set, right: test set

To demonstrate the effect of using unlabeled data for classification we repeated the experiment with waveform data using only 20 labeled observations per class. We compared the the classification results on a test set of size 300 using only the labeled data (error rate E_1) with the results of the EM-model which considers the test data as incomplete measurements during an iterative maximization of the likelihood function (error rate E_2). Using a RBF kernel ($\sigma = 250$), we obtained the following mean error rates over 20 simulations: $E_1 = 30.5(3.6)\%$, $E_2 = 17.1(2.7)\%$. The classification performance could be drastically improved when including the unlabelled data into the learning process.

Object recognition: We tested KDA on the *MPI Chair Database*[1]. It consists of 89 regular spaced views form the upper viewing hemisphere of 25 different classes of chairs as a training set and 100 random views of each class as a test set. The available images are downscaled to 16 × 16 pixels. We did not use the additional 4 edge detection patterns for each view. Classification results for several classifiers are given in table 2.

Table 2: Test error rates (%). **S**upport **V**ector **M**achine , **M**ulti **L**ayer **P**erceptron, **O**riented **F**ilter, taken from [12].

SVM	MLP	OF	KDA, RBF kernel	KDA poly. kernel
2.0	7.2	21.0	1.9	2.1

For a comparison of the computational performance we also trained the *SVM-light* implementation (V 2.0) on the data, [13]. In this experiment with 25 classes the KDA algorithm showed to be significantly faster than the SVM: using the RBF-kernel, KDA was 3 times faster, with the polynomial kernel KDA was 20 times faster than *SVM-light*.

10 Discussion

In this paper we present a nonlinear version of classical linear discriminant analysis. The main idea is to map the input vectors into a high- or even infinite dimensional feature space and to apply LDA in this enlarged space. Restating LDA in a way that only dot products of input vectors are needed makes it possible to use *kernel representations* of dot products. This overcomes numerical problems in high-dimensional

---

[1]The database is available via ftp://ftp.mpik-tueb.mpg.de/pub/chair_dataset/

feature spaces. We studied the classification performance of the KDA classifier on simulated waveform data and on the MPI chair database that has been widely used for benchmarking in the literature. For medium size problems, especially if the number of classes is high, the KDA algorithm showed to be significantly faster than a SVM while leading to the same classification performance. From classical LDA the presented algorithm inherits the convenient property of *data visualization*, since it allows low dimensional views of the data vectors. This makes an intuitive interpretation possible, which is helpful in many practical applications. The presented KDA algorithm can be used as the maximization step in an EM algorithm in feature spaces. This allows to include unlabeled observation into the learning process which can improve classification results. Studying the performance of KDA for other classification problems as well as a theoretical comparison of the optimization criteria used in the KDA- and SVM-algorithm will be subject of future work.

Acknowledgements
This work was supported by Deutsche Forschungsgemeinschaft, DFG. We heavily profitted from discussions with Armin B. Cremers, John Held and Lothar Hermes.

References

[1] R. Duda and P. Hart, *Pattern Classification and Scene Analysis*. Wiley & Sons, 1973.

[2] T. Hastie, R. Tibshirani, and A. Buja, "Flexible discriminant analysis by optimal scoring," *JASA*, vol. 89, pp. 1255–1270, 1994.

[3] V. N. Vapnik, *Statistical learning theory*. Wiley & Sons, 1998.

[4] B. Schölkopf, A. Smola, and K.-R. Muller, "Nonlinear component analysis as a kernel eigenvalue problem," *Neural Computation*, vol. 10, no. 5, pp. 1299–1319, 1998.

[5] S. Mika, G. Rätsch, J. Weston, B. Schölkopf, and K.-R. Müller, "Fisher discriminant analysis with kernels," in *Neural Networks for Signal Processing IX* (Y.-H. Hu, J. Larsen, E. Wilson, and S. Douglas, eds.), pp. 41–48, IEEE, 1999.

[6] V. Roth and V. Steinhage, "Nonlinear discriminant analysis using kernel functions," Tech. Rep. IAI-TR-99-7, Department of Computer Science III, Bonn University, 1999.

[7] V. Roth, A. Pogoda, V. Steinhage, and S. Schröder, "Pattern recognition combining feature- and pixel-based classification within a real world application," in *Mustererkennung 1999* (W. Förstner, J. Buhmann, A. Faber, and P. Faber, eds.), Informatik aktuell, pp. 120–129, 21. DAGM Symposium, Bonn, Springer, 1999.

[8] T. Hastie, A. Buja, and R. Tibshirani, "Penalized discriminant analysis," *AnnStat*, vol. 23, pp. 73–102, 1995.

[9] S. Saunders, A. Gammermann, and V. Vovk, "Ridge regression learning algorithm in dual variables," tech. rep., Royal Holloway, University of London, 1998.

[10] L. Breiman, J. H. Friedman, R. A. Olshen, and C. J. Stone, *Classification and Regression Trees*. Monterey, CA: Wadsworth and Brooks/Cole, 1984.

[11] T. Hastie and R. Tibshirani, "Discriminant analysis by gaussian mixtures," *JRSSB*, vol. 58, pp. 158–176, 1996.

[12] B. Schölkopf, *Support Vector Learning*. PhD thesis, 1997. R. Oldenbourg Verlag, Munich.

[13] T. Joachims, "Making large-scale svm learning practical," in *Advances in Kernel Methods – Support Vector Learning* (B. Schölkopf, C. Burges, and A. Smola, eds.), MIT Press, 1999.

[14] B. Flury, *A First Course in Multivariate Statistics*. Springer, 1997.

An Analysis of Turbo Decoding with Gaussian Densities

Paat Rusmevichientong and Benjamin Van Roy
Stanford University
Stanford, CA 94305
{paatrus,bvr}@stanford.edu

Abstract

We provide an analysis of the turbo decoding algorithm (TDA) in a setting involving Gaussian densities. In this context, we are able to show that the algorithm converges and that – somewhat surprisingly – though the density generated by the TDA may differ significantly from the desired posterior density, the means of these two densities coincide.

1 Introduction

In many applications, the state of a system must be inferred from noisy observations. Examples include digital communications, speech recognition, and control with incomplete information. Unfortunately, problems of inference are often intractable, and one must resort to approximation methods. One approximate inference method that has recently generated spectacular success in certain coding applications is the turbo decoding algorithm [1, 2], which bears a close resemblance to message–passing algorithms developed in the coding community a few decades ago [4]. It has been shown that the TDA is also related to well–understood exact inference algorithms [5, 6], but its performance on the intractable problems to which it is applied has not been explained through this connection.

Several other papers have further developed an understanding of the turbo decoding algorithm. The exact inference algorithms to which turbo decoding has been related are variants of belief propagation [7]. However, this algorithm is designed for inference problems for which graphical models describing conditional independencies form trees, whereas graphical models associated with turbo decoding possess many loops. To understand the behavior of belief propagation in the presence of loops, Weiss has analyzed the algorithm for cases where only a single loop is present [11]. Other analyses that have shed significant light on the performance of the TDA in its original coding context include [8, 9, 10].

In this paper, we develop a new line of analysis for a restrictive setting in which underlying distributions are Gaussian. In this context, inference problems are tractable and the use of approximation algorithms such as the TDA are unnecessary. However, studying the TDA in this context enables a streamlined analysis that generates new insights into its behavior. In particular, we will show that the algorithm converges and that the mean of the resulting distribution coincides with that of the desired posterior distribution.

While preparing this paper, we became aware of two related initiatives, both involving analysis of belief propagation when priors are Gaussian and graphs possess cycles. Weiss and Freeman [12] were studying the case of graphs possessing only cliques of size two. Here, they were able to show that, if belief propagation converges, the mean of the resulting approximation coincides with that of the true posterior distribution. At the same time, Frey [3] studied a case involving graphical structures that generalize those employed in turbo decoding. He also conducted an empirical study.

The paper is organized as follows. In Section 2, we provide our working definition of the TDA. In Section 3, we analyze the case of Gaussian densities. Finally, a discussion of experimental results and open issues is presented in Section 4.

2 A Definition of Turbo Decoding

Consider a random variable x taking on values in $\Re^n$ distributed according to a density p_0. Let y_1 and y_2 be two random variables that are conditionally independent given x. For example, y_1 and y_2 might represent outcomes of two independent transmissions of the signal x over a noisy communication channel. If y_1 and y_2 are observed, then one might want to infer a posterior density f for x conditioned on y_1 and y_2. This can be obtained by first computing densities p_1^* and p_2^*, where the first is conditioned on y_1 and the second is conditioned on y_2. Then,

$$f = \alpha \left(\frac{p_1^* p_2^*}{p_0} \right),$$

where α is a "normalizing operator" defined by

$$\alpha g \equiv \frac{g}{\int g(\bar{x}) d\bar{x}},$$

and multiplication/division are carried out pointwise.

Unfortunately, the problem of computing f is generally intractable. The computational burden associated with storing and manipulating high–dimensional densities appears to be the primary obstacle. This motivates the idea of limiting attention to densities that factor. In this context, it is convenient to define an operator π that generates a density that factors while possessing the same marginals as another density. In particular, this operator is defined by

$$(\pi g)(a) \equiv \prod_{i=1}^{n} \int_{\{\bar{x} \in \Re^n | \bar{x}_i = a_i\}} g(\bar{x}) d\bar{x} \wedge d\bar{x}_i$$

for all densities g and all $a \in \Re^n$, where $d\bar{x} \wedge d\bar{x}_i = d\bar{x}_1 \cdots d\bar{x}_{i-1} d\bar{x}_{i+1} \cdots d\bar{x}_n$. One may then aim at computing πf as a proxy for f. Unfortunately, even this problem is generally intractable. The TDA can be viewed as an iterative algorithm for approximating πf.

Let operators F_1 and F_2 be defined by

$$F_1 g = \alpha \left(\left(\pi \frac{p_1^* g}{p_0} \right) \frac{p_0}{g} \right),$$

and

$$F_2 g = \alpha \left(\left(\pi \frac{g p_2^*}{p_0} \right) \frac{p_0}{g} \right),$$

for any density g. The TDA is applicable in cases where computation of these two operations is tractable. The algorithm generates sequences $q_1^{(k)}$ and $q_2^{(k)}$ according to
$$q_1^{(k+1)} = F_1 q_2^{(k)} \quad \text{and} \quad q_2^{(k+1)} = F_2 q_1^{(k)}.$$
initialized with densities $q_1^{(0)}$ and $q_2^{(0)}$ that factor. The hope is that $\alpha(q_1^{(k)} q_2^{(k)}/p_0)$ converges to an approximation of πf.

3 The Gaussian Case

We will consider a setting in which joint density of x, y_1, and y_2, is Gaussian. In this context, application of the TDA is not warranted – there are tractable algorithms for computing conditional densities when priors are Gaussian. Our objective, however, is to provide a setting in which the TDA can be analyzed and new insights can be generated.

Before proceeding, let us define some notation that will facilitate our exposition. We will write $g \sim N(\mu_g, \Sigma_g)$ to denote a Gaussian density g whose mean vector and covariance matrix are μ_g and Σ_g, respectively. For any matrix A, $\delta(A)$ will denote a diagonal matrix whose entries are given by the diagonal elements of A. For any diagonal matrices X and Y, we write $X \leq Y$ if $X_{ii} \leq Y_{ii}$ for all i. For any pair of nonsingular covariance matrices Σ_u and Σ_v such that $\Sigma_u^{-1} + \Sigma_v^{-1} - I$ is nonsingular, let a matrix A_{Σ_u, Σ_v} be defined by

$$A_{\Sigma_u, \Sigma_v} \equiv (\Sigma_u^{-1} + \Sigma_v^{-1} - I)^{-1}.$$

To reduce notation, we will sometimes denote this matrix by A_{uv}.

When the random variables x, y_1, and y_2 are jointly Gaussian, the densities p_1^*, p_2^*, f, and p_0 are also Gaussian. We let

$$p_1^* \sim N(\mu_1, \Sigma_1), \quad p_2^* \sim N(\mu_2, \Sigma_2), \quad f \sim N(\mu, \Sigma),$$

and assume that both Σ_1 and Σ_2 are symmetric positive definite matrices. We will also assume that $p_0 \sim N(0, I)$ where I is the identity matrix. It is easy to show that A_{Σ_1, Σ_2} is well–defined.

The following lemma provides formulas for the means and covariances that arise from multiplying and rescaling Gaussian densities. The result follows from simple algebra, and we state it without proof.

Lemma 1 *Let $u \sim N(\mu_u, \Sigma_u)$ and $v \sim N(\mu_v, \Sigma_v)$, where Σ_u and Σ_v are positive definite. If $\Sigma_u^{-1} + \Sigma_v^{-1} - I$ is positive definite then*

$$\alpha\left(\frac{uv}{p_0}\right) \sim N\left(A_{uv}\left(\Sigma_u^{-1}\mu_u + \Sigma_v^{-1}\mu_v\right), A_{uv}\right).$$

One immediate consequence of this lemma is an expression for the mean of f:

$$\mu = A_{\Sigma_1, \Sigma_2}\left(\Sigma_1^{-1}\mu_1 + \Sigma_2^{-1}\mu_2\right).$$

Let $\mathcal{S}$ denote the set of covariance matrices that are diagonal and positive definite. Let $\mathcal{G}$ denote the set of Gaussian densities with covariance matrices in $\mathcal{S}$. We then have the following result, which we state without proof.

Lemma 2 *The set $\mathcal{G}$ is closed under F_1 and F_2.*

If the TDA is initialized with $q_1^{(0)}, q_2^{(0)} \in \mathcal{G}$, this lemma allows us to represent all iterates using appropriate mean vectors and covariance matrices.

3.1 Convergence Analysis

Under suitable technical conditions, it can be shown that the sequence of mean vectors and covariance matrices generates by the TDA converges. Due to space limitations, we will only present results pertinent to the convergence of covariance matrices. Furthermore, we will only present certain central components of the analyses. For more complete results and detailed analyses, we refer the reader to our upcoming full–length paper.

Recall that the TDA generates sequences $q_1^{(k)}$ and $q_2^{(k)}$ according to

$$q_1^{(k+1)} = F_1 q_2^{(k)} \quad \text{and} \quad q_2^{(k+1)} = F_2 q_1^{(k)}.$$

As discussed earlier, if the algorithm is initialized with elements of $\mathcal{G}$, by Lemma 2,

$$q_1^{(k)} \sim N\left(m_1^{(k)}, \Sigma_1^{(k)}\right) \quad \text{and} \quad q_2^{(k)} \sim N\left(m_2^{(k)}, \Sigma_2^{(k)}\right),$$

for appropriate sequences of mean vectors and covariance matrices. It turns out that there are mappings $\mathcal{T}_1 : \mathcal{S} \mapsto \mathcal{S}$ and $\mathcal{T}_2 : \mathcal{S} \mapsto \mathcal{S}$ such that

$$\Sigma_1^{(k+1)} = \mathcal{T}_1\left(\Sigma_2^{(k)}\right) \quad \text{and} \quad \Sigma_2^{(k+1)} = \mathcal{T}_2\left(\Sigma_1^{(k)}\right),$$

for all k. Let $\mathcal{T} \equiv \mathcal{T}_1 \circ \mathcal{T}_2$. To establish convergence of $\Sigma_1^{(k)}$ and $\Sigma_2^{(k)}$, it suffices to show that $\mathcal{T}^n(\Sigma_2^{(0)})$ converges. The following theorem establishes this and further points out that the limit does not depend on the initial iterates.

Theorem 1 *There exists a matrix $V^* \in \mathcal{S}$ such that*

$$\lim_{n \to \infty} \mathcal{T}^n(V) = V^*,$$

for all $V \in \mathcal{S}$.

3.1.1 Preliminary Lemmas

Our proof of Theorem 1 relies on a few lemmas that we will present in this section. We begin with a lemma that captures important abstract properties of the function $\mathcal{T}$. Due to space constraints, we omit the proof, even though it is nontrivial.

Lemma 3
(a) There exists a matrix $\overline{D} \in \mathcal{S}$ such that for all $D \in \mathcal{S}$, $\overline{D} \leq \mathcal{T}(D) \leq I$.
(b) For all $X, Y \in \mathcal{S}$, if $X \leq Y$ then $\mathcal{T}(X) \leq \mathcal{T}(Y)$.
(c) The function $\mathcal{T}$ is continuous on $\mathcal{S}$.
(d) For all $\beta \in (0,1)$ and $D \in \mathcal{S}$, $(\beta + \alpha)\mathcal{T}(D) \leq \mathcal{T}(\beta D)$ for some $\alpha > 0$.

The following lemma establishes convergence when the sequence of covariance matrices is initialized with the identity matrix.

Lemma 4 *The sequence $\mathcal{T}^n(I)$ converges in $\mathcal{S}$ to a fixed point of $\mathcal{T}$.*

Proof: By Lemma 3(a), $\mathcal{T}(I) \leq I$, and it follows from monotonicity of $\mathcal{T}$ (Lemma 3(b)) that $\mathcal{T}^{n+1}(I) \leq \mathcal{T}^n(I)$ for all n. Since $\mathcal{T}^n(I)$ is bounded below by a matrix $\overline{D} \in \mathcal{S}$, the sequence converges in $\mathcal{S}$. The fact that the limit is a fixed point of $\mathcal{T}$ follows from the continuity of $\mathcal{T}$ (Lemma 3(c)). ∎

Let $V^* = \lim_{n \to \infty} \mathcal{T}^n(I)$. This matrix plays the following special role.

Lemma 5 *The matrix V^* is the unique fixed point in $\mathcal{S}$ of $\mathcal{T}$.*

Proof: Because $T^n(I)$ converges to V^* and T is monotonic, no matrix $V \in S$ with $V \neq V^*$ and $V^* \leq V \leq I$ can be a fixed point. Furthermore, by Lemma 3(a), no matrix $V \in S$ with $V \geq I$ and $V \neq I$ can be a fixed point. For any $V \in S$ with $V \leq V^*$, let

$$\beta_V = \sup\left\{\beta \in (0,1] \big| \beta V^* \leq V\right\}.$$

For any $V \in S$ with $V \neq V^*$ and $V \leq V^*$, we have $\beta_V < 1$. For such a V, by Lemma 3(d), there is an $\alpha > 0$ such that $T(\beta_V V^*) \geq (\beta_V + \alpha)V^*$, and therefore $T(V) \neq V$. The result follows. ∎

3.1.2 Proof of Theorem 1

Proof: For $V \in S$ with $V^* \leq V \leq I$ convergence to V^* follows from Lemma 4 and monotonicity (Lemma 3(b)). For $V \in S$ with $V \geq I$, convergence follows from the fact that $V^* \leq T(V) \leq I$, which is a consequence of the two previously invoked lemmas together with Lemma 3(a).

Let us now address the case of $V \in S$ with $V \leq V^*$. Let β_V be defined as in the proof of Lemma 5. Then, $\beta_V V^* \leq T(\beta_V V^*)$. By monotonicity, $T^n(\beta_V V^*) \leq T^{n+1}(\beta_V V^*) \leq V^*$ for all n. It follows that $T^n(\beta_V V^*)$ converges, and since T is continuous, the limit must be the unique fixed point V^*. We have established convergence for elements V of S satisfying $V \leq V^*$ or $V \geq V^*$. For other elements of S, convergence follows from the monotonicity of T. ∎

3.2 Analysis of the Fixed Point

As discussed in the previous section, under suitable conditions, $F_1 \circ F_2$ and $F_2 \circ F_1$ each possess a unique fixed point, and the TDA converges on these fixed points. Let $q_1^* \sim N(\mu_{q_1^*}, \Sigma_{q_1^*})$ and $q_2^* \sim N(\mu_{q_2^*}, \Sigma_{q_2^*})$ denote the fixed points of $F_1 \circ F_2$ and $F_2 \circ F_1$, respectively. Based on Theorem 1, $\Sigma_{q_1^*}$ and $\Sigma_{q_2^*}$ are in S.

The following lemma provides an equation relating means associated with the fixed points. It is not hard to show that $A_{q_1^* q_2^*}$, $A_{\Sigma_1, \Sigma_{q_2^*}}$, and $A_{\Sigma_{q_1^*}, \Sigma_2}$, which are used in the statement, are well-defined.

Lemma 6

$$A_{q_1^* q_2^*}\left(\Sigma_{q_1^*}^{-1}\mu_{q_1^*} + \Sigma_{q_2^*}^{-1}\mu_{q_2^*}\right) = A_{\Sigma_1, \Sigma_{q_2^*}}\left(\Sigma_1^{-1}\mu_1 + \Sigma_{q_2^*}^{-1}\mu_{q_2^*}\right) = A_{\Sigma_{q_1^*}, \Sigma_2}\left(\Sigma_{q_1^*}^{-1}\mu_{q_1^*} + \Sigma_2^{-1}\mu_2\right)$$

Proof: It follows from the definitions of F_1 and F_2 that, if $q_1^* = F_1 q_2^*$ and $q_2^* = F_2 q_1^*$,

$$\alpha \frac{q_1^* q_2^*}{p_0} = \alpha\pi \frac{p_1^* q_2^*}{p_0} = \alpha\pi \frac{q_1^* p_2^*}{p_0}.$$

The result then follows from Lemma 1 and the fact that π does not alter the mean of a distribution. ∎

We now prove a central result of this paper: the mean of the density generated by the TDA coincides with the mean μ of the desired posterior density f.

Theorem 2 $\alpha(q_1^* q_2^*/p_0) \sim N(\mu, A_{q_1^* q_2^*})$

Proof: By Lemma 1, $\mu = A_{\Sigma_1, \Sigma_2}\left(\Sigma_1^{-1}\mu_1 + \Sigma_2^{-1}\mu_2\right)$, while the mean of $\alpha(q_1^* q_2^*/p_0)$ is $A_{q_1^* q_2^*}\left(\Sigma_{q_1^*}^{-1}\mu_{q_1^*} + \Sigma_{q_2^*}^{-1}\mu_{q_2^*}\right)$. We will show that these two expressions are equal.

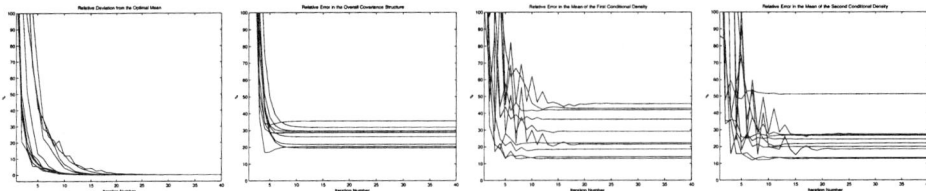

Figure 1: Evolution of errors.

Multiplying the equations from Lemma 6 by appropriate matrices, we obtain

$$A_{q_1^* q_2^*} A_{\Sigma_1, \Sigma_{q_2^*}}^{-1} A_{q_1^* q_2^*} \left(\Sigma_{q_1^*}^{-1} \mu_{q_1^*} + \Sigma_{q_2^*}^{-1} \mu_{q_2^*} \right) = A_{q_1^* q_2^*} \left(\Sigma_1^{-1} \mu_1 + \Sigma_{q_2^*}^{-1} \mu_{q_2^*} \right),$$

and

$$A_{q_1^* q_2^*} A_{\Sigma_{q_1^*}, \Sigma_2}^{-1} A_{q_1^* q_2^*} \left(\Sigma_{q_1^*}^{-1} \mu_{q_1^*} + \Sigma_{q_2^*}^{-1} \mu_{q_2^*} \right) = A_{q_1^* q_2^*} \left(\Sigma_{q_1^*}^{-1} \mu_{q_1^*} + \Sigma_2^{-1} \mu_2 \right).$$

It follows that

$$\left(A_{q_1^* q_2^*} (A_{\Sigma_1, \Sigma_{q_2^*}}^{-1} + A_{\Sigma_{q_1^*}, \Sigma_2}^{-1}) - I \right) A_{q_1^* q_2^*} \left(\Sigma_{q_1^*}^{-1} \mu_{q_1^*} + \Sigma_{q_2^*}^{-1} \mu_{q_2^*} \right) = A_{q_1^* q_2^*} \left(\Sigma_1^{-1} \mu_1 + \Sigma_2^{-1} \mu_2 \right),$$

and therefore

$$\left(A_{\Sigma_1, \Sigma_{q_2^*}}^{-1} + A_{\Sigma_{q_1^*}, \Sigma_2}^{-1} - A_{q_1^* q_2^*}^{-1} \right) A_{q_1^* q_2^*} \left(\Sigma_{q_1^*}^{-1} \mu_{q_1^*} + \Sigma_{q_2^*}^{-1} \mu_{q_2^*} \right) = \Sigma_1^{-1} \mu_1 + \Sigma_2^{-1} \mu_2.$$

Note that $A_{\Sigma_1, \Sigma_{q_2^*}}^{-1} + A_{\Sigma_{q_1^*}, \Sigma_2}^{-1} - A_{q_1^* q_2^*}^{-1} = A_{\Sigma_1, \Sigma_2}^{-1}$. It follows that

$$A_{q_1^* q_2^*} \left(\Sigma_{q_1^*}^{-1} \mu_{q_1^*} + \Sigma_{q_2^*}^{-1} \mu_{q_2^*} \right) = A_{\Sigma_1, \Sigma_2} (\Sigma_1^{-1} \mu_1 + \Sigma_2^{-1} \mu_2) = \mu.$$

■

4 Discussion and Experimental Results

The limits of convergence q_1^* and q_2^* of the TDA provide an approximation $\alpha(q_1^* q_2^*/p_0)$ to πf. We have established that the mean of this approximation coincides with that of the desired density. One might further expect that the covariance matrix of $\alpha(q_1^* q_2^*/p_0)$ approximates that of πf, and even more so, that q_1^* and q_2^* bear some relation to p_1^* and p_2^*. Unfortunately, as will be illustrated by experimental results in this section, such expectations appear to be inaccurate.

We performed experiments involving 20 and 50 dimensional Gaussian densities (i.e., x was either 20 or 50 dimensional in each instance). Problem instances were sampled randomly from a fixed distribution. Due to space limitations, we will not describe the tedious details of the sampling mechanism.

Figure 1 illustrates the evolution of certain "errors" during representative runs of the TDA on 20–dimensional problems. The first graph plots relative errors in means of densities $\alpha(q_1^{(n)} q_2^{(n)}/p_0)$ generated by iterates of the TDA. As indicated by our analysis, these errors converge to zero. The second chart plots a measure of relative error for the covariance of $\alpha(q_1^{(n)} q_2^{(n)}/p_0)$ versus that of πf for representative runs. Though these covariances converge, the ultimate errors are far from zero. The two

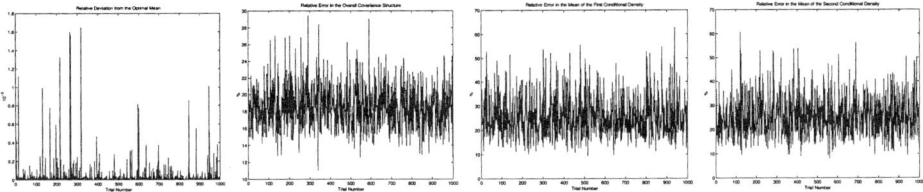

Figure 2: Errors after 50 iterations.

final graphs plot errors between the means of $q_1^{(n)}$ and $q_2^{(n)}$ and those of p_1^* and p_2^*, respectively. Again, though these means converge, the ultimate errors can be large.

Figure 2 provides plots of the same sorts of errors measured on 1000 different instances of 50–dimensional problems after the 50th iteration of the TDA. The horizontal axes are labeled with indices of the problem instances. Note that the errors in the first graph are all close to zero (the units on the vertical axis must be multiplied by 10^{-5} and errors are measured in relative terms). On the other hand, errors in the other graphs vary dramatically.

It is intriguing that – at least in the context of Gaussian densities – the TDA can effectively compute conditional means without accurately approximating conditional densities. It is also interesting to note that, in the context of communications, the objective is to choose a code word $\bar{x}$ that is comes close to the transmitted code x. One natural way to do this involves assigning to $\bar{x}$ the code word that maximizes the conditional density f, i.e., the one that has the highest chance of being correct. In the Gaussian case that we have studied, this corresponds to the mean of f – a quantity that is computed correctly by the TDA! It will be interesting to explore generalizations of the line of analysis presented in this paper to other classes of densities.

References

[1] S. Benedetto and G. Montorsi, "Unveiling turbo codes: Some results on parallel concatenated coding schemes," in *IEEE Trans. Inform. Theory*, vol. 42, pp. 409-428, Mar. 1996.

[2] G. Berrou, A. Glavieux, and P. Thitimajshima, "Near Shannon limit error-correcting coding: Turbo codes," in *Proc. 1993 Int. Conf. Commun.*, Geneva, Switzerland, May 1993, pp. 1064-1070.

[3] B. Frey, "Turbo Factor Analysis." To appear in *Advances in Neural Information Processing Systems 12*.

[4] R. G. Gallager, *Low–Density Parity–Check Codes*. Cambridge, MA: MIT Press, 1963.

[5] F. R. Kschischang and B. J. Frey, "Iterative Decoding of Compound Codes by Probability Propagation in Graphical Models," in *IEEE Journal on Selected Areas in Commun.*, vol. 16, 2, pp. 219-230, Feb. 1998.

[6] R. J. McEliece, D. J. C. MacKay, and J-F. Cheng, "Turbo Decoding as an Instance of Pearl's "Belief Propagation" Algorithm," in *IEEE Journal on Selected Areas in Commun.*, vol. 16, 2, pp. 140-152, Feb. 1998.

[7] J. Pearl, *Probabilistic Reasoning in Intelligent Systems: Networks of Plausible Inference*. San Mateo, CA: Morgan Kaufmann, 1988.

[8] T. Richardson, "The Geometry of Turbo-Decoding Dynamics," Dec. 1998. To appear in *IEEE Trans. Inform. Theory*.

[9] T. Richardson and R. Urbanke, "The Capacity of Low-Density Parity Check Codes under Message-Passing Decoding", submitted to the *IEEE Trans. on Information Theory*.

[10] T. Richardson, A. Shokrollahi, and R. Urbanke, "Design of Provably Good Low-Density Parity Check Codes," submitted to the *IEEE Trans. on Information Theory*.

[11] Y. Weiss, "Belief Propagation and Revision in Networks with Loops," November 1997. Available by ftp to publications.ai.mit.edu.

[12] Y. Weiss and W. T. Freeman, "Correctness of belief propagation in Gaussian graphical models of arbitrary topology." To appear in *Advances in Neural Information Processing Systems 12*.

Support Vector Method for Novelty Detection

Bernhard Schölkopf*, **Robert Williamson**[§],
Alex Smola[§], **John Shawe-Taylor**[†], **John Platt***

* Microsoft Research Ltd., 1 Guildhall Street, Cambridge, UK
[§] Department of Engineering, Australian National University, Canberra 0200
[†] Royal Holloway, University of London, Egham, UK
* Microsoft, 1 Microsoft Way, Redmond, WA, USA
bsc/jplatt@microsoft.com, Bob.Williamson/Alex.Smola@anu.edu.au, john@dcs.rhbnc.ac.uk

Abstract

Suppose you are given some dataset drawn from an underlying probability distribution P and you want to estimate a "simple" subset S of input space such that the probability that a test point drawn from P lies outside of S equals some a priori specified ν between 0 and 1.

We propose a method to approach this problem by trying to estimate a function f which is positive on S and negative on the complement. The functional form of f is given by a kernel expansion in terms of a potentially small subset of the training data; it is regularized by controlling the length of the weight vector in an associated feature space. We provide a theoretical analysis of the statistical performance of our algorithm.

The algorithm is a natural extension of the support vector algorithm to the case of unlabelled data.

1 INTRODUCTION

During recent years, a new set of kernel techniques for supervised learning has been developed [8]. Specifically, support vector (SV) algorithms for pattern recognition, regression estimation and solution of inverse problems have received considerable attention. There have been a few attempts to transfer the idea of using kernels to compute inner products in feature spaces to the domain of *unsupervised* learning. The problems in that domain are, however, less precisely specified. Generally, they can be characterized as estimating *functions* of the data which tell you something interesting about the underlying distributions. For instance, kernel PCA can be characterized as computing functions which on the training data produce unit variance outputs while having minimum norm in feature space [4]. Another kernel-based unsupervised learning technique, regularized principal manifolds [6], computes functions which give a mapping onto a lower-dimensional manifold minimizing a regularized quantization error. Clustering algorithms are further examples of unsupervised learning techniques which can be kernelized [4].

An extreme point of view is that unsupervised learning is about estimating densities. Clearly, knowledge of the density of P would then allow us to solve whatever problem can be solved on the basis of the data. The present work addresses an easier problem: it proposes an algorithm which computes a binary function which is supposed to capture regions in input space where the probability density lives (its support), i.e. a function such that most of the data will live in the region where the function is nonzero [5]. In doing so, it is in line with Vapnik's principle never to solve a problem which is more general than the one we actually need to solve. Moreover, it is applicable also in cases where the density of the data's distribution is not even well-defined, e.g. if there are singular components. Part of the motivation for the present work was the paper [1]. It turns out that there is a considerable amount of prior work in the statistical literature; for a discussion, cf. the full version of the present paper [3].

2 ALGORITHMS

We first introduce terminology and notation conventions. We consider training data $\mathbf{x}_1, \ldots, \mathbf{x}_\ell \in \mathcal{X}$, where $\ell \in \mathbb{N}$ is the number of observations, and $\mathcal{X}$ is some set. For simplicity, we think of it as a compact subset of $\mathbb{R}^N$. Let Φ be a feature map $\mathcal{X} \to F$, i.e. a map into a dot product space F such that the dot product in the image of Φ can be computed by evaluating some simple kernel [8]

$$k(\mathbf{x}, \mathbf{y}) = (\Phi(\mathbf{x}) \cdot \Phi(\mathbf{y})), \tag{1}$$

such as the Gaussian kernel

$$k(\mathbf{x}, \mathbf{y}) = e^{-\|\mathbf{x}-\mathbf{y}\|^2/c}. \tag{2}$$

Indices i and j are understood to range over $1, \ldots, \ell$ (in compact notation: $i, j \in [\ell]$). Bold face greek letters denote ℓ-dimensional vectors whose components are labelled using normal face typeset.

In the remainder of this section, we shall develop an algorithm which returns a function f that takes the value $+1$ in a "small" region capturing most of the data points, and -1 elsewhere. Our strategy is to map the data into the feature space corresponding to the kernel, and to separate them from the origin with maximum margin. For a new point $\mathbf{x}$, the value $f(\mathbf{x})$ is determined by evaluating which side of the hyperplane it falls on, in feature space. Via the freedom to utilize different types of kernel functions, this simple geometric picture corresponds to a variety of nonlinear estimators in input space.

To separate the data set from the origin, we solve the following quadratic program:

$$\min_{w \in F, \boldsymbol{\xi} \in \mathbb{R}^\ell, \rho \in \mathbb{R}} \quad \tfrac{1}{2}\|w\|^2 + \tfrac{1}{\nu\ell}\sum_i \xi_i - \rho \tag{3}$$

$$\text{subject to} \quad (w \cdot \Phi(\mathbf{x}_i)) \geq \rho - \xi_i, \; \xi_i \geq 0. \tag{4}$$

Here, $\nu \in (0, 1)$ is a parameter whose meaning will become clear later. Since nonzero slack variables ξ_i are penalized in the objective function, we can expect that if w and ρ solve this problem, then the decision function $f(\mathbf{x}) = \text{sgn}((w \cdot \Phi(\mathbf{x})) - \rho)$ will be positive for most examples $\mathbf{x}_i$ contained in the training set, while the SV type regularization term $\|w\|$ will still be small. The actual trade-off between these two goals is controlled by ν. Deriving the dual problem, and using (1), the solution can be shown to have an SV expansion

$$f(\mathbf{x}) = \text{sgn}\left(\sum_i \alpha_i k(\mathbf{x}_i, \mathbf{x}) - \rho\right) \tag{5}$$

(patterns $\mathbf{x}_i$ with nonzero α_i are called SVs), where the coefficients are found as the solution of the dual problem:

$$\min_{\boldsymbol{\alpha}} \frac{1}{2}\sum_{ij}\alpha_i\alpha_j k(\mathbf{x}_i, \mathbf{x}_j) \quad \text{subject to} \quad 0 \leq \alpha_i \leq \frac{1}{\nu\ell}, \quad \sum_i \alpha_i = 1. \tag{6}$$

This problem can be solved with standard QP routines. It does, however, possess features that sets it apart from generic QPs, most notably the simplicity of the constraints. This can be exploited by applying a variant of SMO developed for this purpose [3].

The offset ρ can be recovered by exploiting that for any α_i which is not at the upper or lower bound, the corresponding pattern $\mathbf{x}_i$ satisfies $\rho = (w \cdot \Phi(\mathbf{x}_i)) = \sum_j \alpha_j k(\mathbf{x}_j, \mathbf{x}_i)$.

Note that if ν approaches 0, the upper boundaries on the Lagrange multipliers tend to infinity, i.e. the second inequality constraint in (6) becomes void. The problem then resembles the corresponding *hard margin* algorithm, since the penalization of errors becomes infinite, as can be seen from the primal objective function (3). It can be shown that if the data set is separable from the origin, then this algorithm will find the unique supporting hyperplane with the properties that it separates all data from the origin, and its distance to the origin is maximal among all such hyperplanes [3]. If, on the other hand, ν approaches 1, then the constraints alone only allow one solution, that where all α_i are at the upper bound $1/(\nu \ell)$. In this case, for kernels with integral 1, such as normalized versions of (2), the decision function corresponds to a thresholded Parzen windows estimator.

To conclude this section, we note that one can also use *balls* to describe the data in feature space, close in spirit to the algorithms of [2], with hard boundaries, and [7], with "soft margins." For certain classes of kernels, such as Gaussian RBF ones, the corresponding algorithm can be shown to be equivalent to the above one [3].

3 THEORY

In this section, we show that the parameter ν characterizes the fractions of SVs and outliers (Proposition 1). Following that, we state a robustness result for the soft margin (Proposition 2) and error bounds (Theorem 5). Further results and proofs are reported in the full version of the present paper [3]. We will use italic letters to denote the feature space images of the corresponding patterns in input space, i.e. $x_i := \Phi(\mathbf{x}_i)$.

Proposition 1 *Assume the solution of (4) satisfies $\rho \neq 0$. The following statements hold:*
(i) ν is an upper bound on the fraction of outliers.
(ii) ν is a lower bound on the fraction of SVs.
(iii) Suppose the data were generated independently from a distribution $P(\mathbf{x})$ which does not contain discrete components. Suppose, moreover, that the kernel is analytic and nonconstant. With probability 1, asymptotically, ν equals both the fraction of SVs and the fraction of outliers.

The proof is based on the constraints of the dual problem, using the fact that outliers must have Lagrange multipliers at the upper bound.

Proposition 2 *Local movements of outliers parallel to w do not change the hyperplane.*

We now move on to the subject of generalization. Our goal is to bound the probability that a novel point drawn from the same underlying distribution lies outside of the estimated region by a certain margin. We start by introducing a common tool for measuring the capacity of a class $\mathcal{F}$ of functions that map $\mathcal{X}$ to $\mathbb{R}$.

Definition 3 *Let (X, d) be a pseudo-metric space,[1] let A be a subset of X and $\epsilon > 0$. A set $B \subseteq X$ is an ϵ-cover for A if, for every $a \in A$, there exists $b \in B$ such that $d(a, b) \leq \epsilon$. The ϵ-covering number of A, $\mathcal{N}_d(\epsilon, A)$, is the minimal cardinality of an ϵ-cover for A (if there is no such finite cover then it is defined to be ∞).*

---
[1] i.e. with a distance function that differs from a metric in that it is only semidefinite

The idea is that B should be finite but approximate all of A with respect to the pseudometric d. We will use the l_∞ distance over a finite sample $X = (x_1, \ldots, x_\ell)$ for the pseudometric in the space of functions, $d_X(f, g) = \max_{i \in [\ell]} |f(x_i) - g(x_i)|$. Let $\mathcal{N}(\epsilon, \mathcal{F}, \ell) = \sup_{X \in \mathcal{X}^\ell} \mathcal{N}_{d_X}(\epsilon, \mathcal{F})$. Below, logarithms are to base 2.

Theorem 4 *Consider any distribution P on $\mathcal{X}$ and any $\theta \in \mathbb{R}$. Suppose $x_1, \ldots, x_\ell$ are generated i.i.d. from P. Then with probability $1 - \delta$ over such an ℓ-sample, if we find $f \in \mathcal{F}$ such that $f(x_i) \geq \theta + \gamma$ for all $i \in [\ell]$,*

$$P\{x : f(x) < \theta - \gamma\} \leq \tfrac{2}{\ell}(k + \log \tfrac{2\ell}{\delta}),$$

where $k = \lceil \log \mathcal{N}(\gamma, \mathcal{F}, 2\ell) \rceil$.

We now consider the possibility that for a small number of points $f(x_i)$ fails to exceed $\theta + \gamma$. This corresponds to having a non-zero slack variable ξ_i in the algorithm, where we take $\theta + \gamma = \rho / \|w\|$ and use the class of linear functions in feature space in the application of the theorem. There are well-known bounds for the log covering numbers of this class.

Let f be a real valued function on a space $\mathcal{X}$. Fix $\theta \in \mathbb{R}$. For $x \in \mathcal{X}$, define

$$d(x, f, \gamma) = \max\{0, \theta + \gamma - f(x)\}.$$

Similarly for a training sequence X, we define $\mathcal{D}(X, f, \gamma) = \sum_{x \in X} d(x, f, \gamma)$.

Theorem 5 *Fix $\theta \in \mathbb{R}$. Consider a fixed but unknown probability distribution P on the input space $\mathcal{X}$ and a class of real valued functions $\mathcal{F}$ with range $[a, b]$. Then with probability $1 - \delta$ over randomly drawn training sequences x of size ℓ, for all $\gamma > 0$ and any $f \in \mathcal{F}$,*

$$P\{x : f(x) < \theta - \gamma \text{ and } x \notin X\} \leq \tfrac{2}{\ell}(k + \log \tfrac{4\ell}{\delta}),$$

where $k = \left\lceil \log \mathcal{N}(\gamma/2, \mathcal{F}, 2\ell) + \frac{64(b-a)\mathcal{D}(X,f,\gamma)}{\gamma^2} \log\left(\frac{e\ell\gamma}{8\mathcal{D}(X,f,\gamma)}\right) \log\left(\frac{32\ell(b-a)^2}{\gamma^2}\right) \right\rceil$.

The theorem bounds the probability of a new point falling in the region for which $f(x)$ has value less than $\theta - \gamma$, this being the complement of the estimate for the support of the distribution. The choice of γ gives a trade-off between the size of the region over which the bound holds (increasing γ increases the size of the region) and the size of the probability with which it holds (increasing γ decreases the size of the log covering numbers).

The result shows that we can bound the probability of points falling outside the region of estimated support by a quantity involving the ratio of the log covering numbers (which can be bounded by the fat shattering dimension at scale proportional to γ) and the number of training examples, plus a factor involving the 1-norm of the slack variables. It is stronger than related results given by [1], since their bound involves the square root of the ratio of the Pollard dimension (the fat shattering dimension when γ tends to 0) and the number of training examples.

The output of the algorithm described in Sec. 2 is a function $f(x) = \sum_i \alpha_i k(x_i, x)$ which is greater than or equal to $\rho - \xi_i$ on example x_i. Though non-linear in the input space, this function is in fact linear in the feature space defined by the kernel k. At the same time the 2-norm of the weight vector is given by $B = \sqrt{\alpha^T K \alpha}$, and so we can apply the theorem with the function class $\mathcal{F}$ being those linear functions in the feature space with 2-norm bounded by B. If we assume that θ is fixed, then $\gamma = \rho - \theta$, hence the support of the distribution is the set $\{x : f(x) \geq \theta - \gamma = 2\theta - \rho\}$, and the bound gives the probability of a randomly generated point falling outside this set, in terms of the log covering numbers of the function class $\mathcal{F}$ and the sum of the slack variables ξ_i. Since the log covering numbers at scale $\gamma/2$ of the class $\mathcal{F}$ can be bounded by $O(\frac{R^2 B^2}{\gamma^2} \log^2 \ell)$ this gives a bound in terms of the 2-norm of the weight vector.

Ideally, one would like to allow θ to be chosen after the value of ρ has been determined, perhaps as a fixed fraction of that value. This could be obtained by another level of structural risk minimisation over the possible values of ρ or at least a mesh of some possible values. This result is beyond the scope of the current preliminary paper, but the form of the result would be similar to Theorem 5, with larger constants and log factors.

Whilst it is premature to give specific theoretical recommendations for practical use yet, one thing is clear from the above bound. To generalize to novel data, the decision function to be used should employ a threshold $\eta \cdot \rho$, where $\eta < 1$ (this corresponds to a nonzero γ).

4 EXPERIMENTS

We apply the method to artificial and real-world data. Figure 1 displays 2-D toy examples, and shows how the parameter settings influence the solution.

Next, we describe an experiment on the USPS dataset of handwritten digits. The database contains 9298 digit images of size $16 \times 16 = 256$; the last 2007 constitute the test set. We trained the algorithm, using a Gaussian kernel (2) of width $c = 0.5 \cdot 256$ (a common value for SVM classifiers on that data set, cf. [2]), on the test set and used it to identify outliers — it is folklore in the community that the USPS test set contains a number of patterns which are hard or impossible to classify, due to segmentation errors or mislabelling. In the experiment, we augmented the input patterns by ten extra dimensions corresponding to the class labels of the digits. The rationale for this is that if we disregarded the labels, there would be no hope to identify *mislabelled* patterns as outliers. Fig. 2 shows the 20 worst outliers for the USPS test set. Note that the algorithm indeed extracts patterns which are very hard to assign to their respective classes. In the experiment, which took 36 seconds on a Pentium II running at 450 MHz, we used a ν value of 5%.

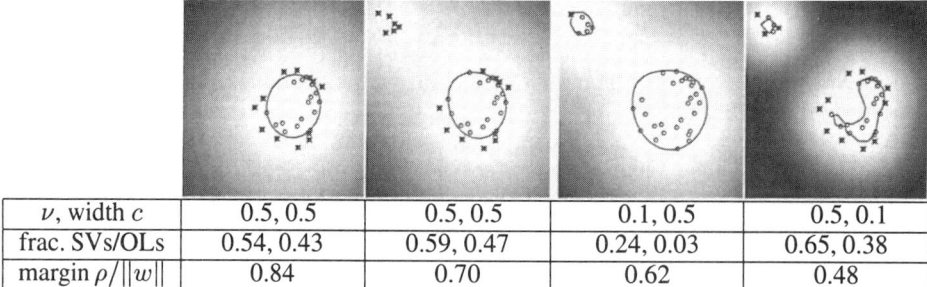

ν, width c	0.5, 0.5	0.5, 0.5	0.1, 0.5	0.5, 0.1
frac. SVs/OLs	0.54, 0.43	0.59, 0.47	0.24, 0.03	0.65, 0.38
margin $\rho/\|w\|$	0.84	0.70	0.62	0.48

Figure 1: *First two pictures:* A single-class SVM applied to two toy problems; $\nu = c = 0.5$, domain: $[-1, 1]^2$. Note how in both cases, at least a fraction of ν of all examples is in the estimated region (cf. table). The large value of ν causes the additional data points in the upper left corner to have almost no influence on the decision function. For smaller values of ν, such as 0.1 *(third picture)*, the points cannot be ignored anymore. Alternatively, one can force the algorithm to take these 'outliers' into account by changing the kernel width (2): in the *fourth picture*, using $c = 0.1, \nu = 0.5$, the data is effectively analyzed on a different length scale which leads the algorithm to consider the outliers as meaningful points.

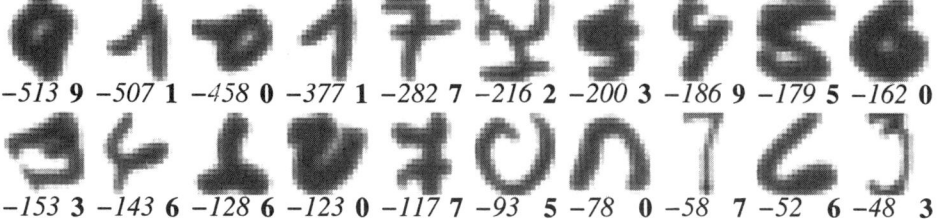

Figure 2: Outliers identified by the proposed algorithm, ranked by the negative output of the SVM (the argument of the sgn in the decision function). The outputs (for convenience in units of 10^{-5}) are written underneath each image in italics, the (alleged) class labels are given in bold face. Note that most of the examples are "difficult" in that they are either atypical or even mislabelled.

5 DISCUSSION

One could view the present work as an attempt to provide an algorithm which is in line with Vapnik's principle never to solve a problem which is more general than the one that one is actually interested in. E.g., in situations where one is only interested in detecting *novelty*, it is not always necessary to estimate a full density model of the data. Indeed, density estimation is more difficult than what we are doing, in several respects.

Mathematically speaking, a density will only exist if the underlying probability measure possesses an absolutely continuous distribution function. The general problem of estimating the measure for a large class of sets, say the sets measureable in Borel's sense, is not solvable (for a discussion, see e.g. [8]). Therefore we need to restrict ourselves to making a statement about the measure of *some* sets. Given a small class of sets, the simplest estimator accomplishing this task is the empirical measure, which simply looks at how many training points fall into the region of interest. Our algorithm does the opposite. It starts with the number of training points that are supposed to fall into the region, and then estimates a region with the desired property. Often, there will be many such regions — the solution becomes unique only by applying a regularizer, which in our case enforces that the region be small in a feature space associated to the kernel. This, of course, implies, that the measure of smallness in this sense depends on the kernel used, in a way that is no different to any other method that regularizes in a feature space. A similar problem, however, appears in density estimation already when done in input space. Let p denote a density on $\mathcal{X}$. If we perform a (nonlinear) coordinate transformation in the input domain $\mathcal{X}$, then the density values will *change*; loosely speaking, what remains constant is $p(x) \cdot dx$, while dx is transformed, too. When directly estimating the probability *measure* of regions, we are not faced with this problem, as the regions automatically change accordingly.

An attractive property of the measure of smallness that we chose to use is that it can also be placed in the context of regularization theory, leading to an interpretation of the solution as maximally smooth in a sense which depends on the specific kernel used [3].

The main inspiration for our approach stems from the earliest work of Vapnik and collaborators. They proposed an algorithm for characterizing a set of unlabelled data points by separating it from the origin using a hyperplane [9]. However, they quickly moved on to two-class classification problems, both in terms of algorithms and in the theoretical development of statistical learning theory which originated in those days. From an algorithmic point of view, we can identify two shortcomings of the original approach which may have caused research in this direction to stop for more than three decades. Firstly, the original algorithm in was limited to linear decision rules in input space, secondly, there was no way of dealing with outliers. In conjunction, these restrictions are indeed severe — a generic dataset need not be separable from the origin by a hyperplane in input space. The two modifications that we have incorporated dispose of these shortcomings. Firstly, the kernel trick allows for a much larger class of functions by nonlinearly mapping into a high-dimensional feature space, and thereby increases the chances of separability from the origin. In particular, using a Gaussian kernel (2), such a separation exists for any data set $x_1, \ldots, x_\ell$: to see this, note that $k(x_i, x_j) > 0$ for all i, j, thus all dot products are positive, implying that all mapped patterns lie inside the same orthant. Moreover, since $k(x_i, x_i) = 1$ for all i, they have unit length. Hence they are separable from the origin. The second modification allows for the possibility of outliers. We have incorporated this 'softness' of the decision rule using the ν-trick and thus obtained a direct handle on the fraction of outliers.

We believe that our approach, proposing a concrete algorithm with well-behaved computational complexity (convex quadratic programming) for a problem that so far has mainly been studied from a theoretical point of view has abundant practical applications. To turn the algorithm into an easy-to-use black-box method for practicioners, questions like the selection of kernel parameters (such as the width of a Gaussian kernel) have to be tackled. It is our expectation that the theoretical results which we have briefly outlined in this paper will provide a foundation for this formidable task.

Acknowledgement. Part of this work was supported by the ARC and the DFG (# Ja 379/9-1), and done while BS was at the Australian National University and GMD FIRST. AS is supported by a grant of the Deutsche Forschungsgemeinschaft (Sm 62/1-1). Thanks to S. Ben-David, C. Bishop, C. Schnörr, and M. Tipping for helpful discussions.

References

[1] S. Ben-David and M. Lindenbaum. Learning distributions by their density levels: A paradigm for learning without a teacher. *Journal of Computer and System Sciences*, 55:171–182, 1997.

[2] B. Schölkopf, C. Burges, and V. Vapnik. Extracting support data for a given task. In U. M. Fayyad and R. Uthurusamy, editors, *Proceedings, First International Conference on Knowledge Discovery & Data Mining*. AAAI Press, Menlo Park, CA, 1995.

[3] B. Schölkopf, J. Platt, J. Shawe-Taylor, A.J. Smola, and R.C. Williamson. Estimating the support of a high-dimensional distribution. TR MSR 99 - 87, Microsoft Research, Redmond, WA, 1999.

[4] B. Schölkopf, A. Smola, and K.-R. Müller. Kernel principal component analysis. In B. Schölkopf, C. Burges, and A. Smola, editors, *Advances in Kernel Methods — Support Vector Learning*. MIT Press, Cambridge, MA, 1999. 327 – 352.

[5] B. Schölkopf, R. Williamson, A. Smola, and J. Shawe-Taylor. Single-class support vector machines. In J. Buhmann, W. Maass, H. Ritter, and N. Tishby, editors, *Unsupervised Learning*, Dagstuhl-Seminar-Report 235, pages 19 – 20, 1999.

[6] A. Smola, R. C. Williamson, S. Mika, and B. Schölkopf. Regularized principal manifolds. In *Computational Learning Theory: 4th European Conference*, volume 1572 of *Lecture Notes in Artificial Intelligence*, pages 214 – 229. Springer, 1999.

[7] D.M.J. Tax and R.P.W. Duin. Data domain description by support vectors. In M. Verleysen, editor, *Proceedings ESANN*, pages 251 – 256, Brussels, 1999. D Facto.

[8] V. Vapnik. *Statistical Learning Theory*. Wiley, New York, 1998.

[9] V. Vapnik and A. Lerner. Pattern recognition using generalized portraits. *Avtomatika i Telemekhanika*, 24:774 – 780, 1963.

Better Generative Models for Sequential Data Problems: Bidirectional Recurrent Mixture Density Networks

Mike Schuster
ATR Interpreting Telecommunications Research Laboratories
2-2 Hikaridai, Seika-cho, Soraku-gun, Kyoto 619-02, JAPAN
gustl@itl.atr.co.jp

Abstract

This paper describes bidirectional recurrent mixture density networks, which can model multi-modal distributions of the type $P(\mathbf{x}_t|\mathbf{y}_1^T)$ and $P(\mathbf{x}_t|\mathbf{x}_1, \mathbf{x}_2, \ldots, \mathbf{x}_{t-1}, \mathbf{y}_1^T)$ without any explicit assumptions about the use of context. These expressions occur frequently in pattern recognition problems with sequential data, for example in speech recognition. Experiments show that the proposed generative models give a higher likelihood on test data compared to a traditional modeling approach, indicating that they can summarize the statistical properties of the data better.

1 Introduction

Many problems of engineering interest can be formulated as sequential data problems in an abstract sense as *supervised learning from sequential data*, where an input vector (dimensionality D) sequence $\mathbf{X} = \mathbf{x}_1^T = \{\mathbf{x}_1, \mathbf{x}_2, \ldots, \mathbf{x}_{T-1}, \mathbf{x}_T\}$ living in space $\mathcal{X}$ has to be mapped to an output vector (dimensionality K) target sequence $\mathbf{T} = \mathbf{t}_1^T = \{\mathbf{t}_1, \mathbf{t}_2, \ldots, \mathbf{t}_{T-1}, \mathbf{t}_T\}$ in space[1] $\mathcal{Y}$, that often embodies correlations between neighboring vectors $\mathbf{x}_t, \mathbf{x}_{t+1}$ and $\mathbf{t}_t, \mathbf{t}_{t+1}$. In general there are a number of training data sequence pairs (input and target), which are used to estimate the parameters of a given model structure, whose performance can then be evaluated on another set of test data pairs. For many applications the problem becomes to *predict* the *best* sequence $\mathbf{Y}^\star$ given an arbitrary input sequence $\mathbf{X}$, with *'best'* meaning the sequence that minimizes an error using a suitable metric that is yet to be defined. Making use of the theory of pattern recognition [2] this problem is often simplified by treating any sequence as one pattern. This makes it possible to express the objective of sequence prediction with the well known expression $\mathbf{Y}^\star = \arg\max_\mathcal{Y} P(\mathbf{Y}|\mathbf{X})$, with $\mathbf{X}$ being the input sequence, $\mathbf{Y}$ being any valid output sequence and $\mathbf{Y}^\star$ being the predicted sequence with the highest probability[2]

---

[1] a sample sequence of the *training target data* is denoted as $\mathbf{T}$, while an output sequence in general is denoted as $\mathbf{Y}$, both live in the output space $\mathcal{Y}$.

[2] to simplify notation, random variables and their values, are *not* denoted as different symbols. This means, $P(\mathbf{x}) = P(X = \mathbf{x})$.

among all possible sequences.

Training of a sequence prediction system corresponds to estimating the distribution [3] $P(\mathbf{Y}|\mathbf{X})$ from a number of samples which includes (a) defining an appropriate model representing this distribution and (b) estimating its parameters such that $P(\mathbf{Y}|\mathbf{X})$ for the training data is maximized. In practice the model consists of several modules with each of them being responsible for a different part of $P(\mathbf{Y}|\mathbf{X})$.

Testing (usage) of the trained system or *recognition* for a given input sequence $\mathbf{X}$ corresponds principally to the evaluation of $P(\mathbf{Y}|\mathbf{X})$ for all possible output sequences to find the best one $\mathbf{Y}^\star$. This procedure is called the *search* and its efficient implementation is important for many applications.

In order to build a model to predict sequences it is necessary to decompose the sequences such that modules responsible for smaller parts can be build. An often used approach is the decomposition into a generative and prior model part, using $P(B|A) = P(A|B)P(B)/P(A)$ and $P(A,B) = P(A)P(B|A)$, as:

$$\begin{aligned}\mathbf{Y}^\star &= \arg\max_y P(\mathbf{Y}|\mathbf{X}) = \arg\max_y P(\mathbf{X}|\mathbf{Y})P(\mathbf{Y}) \\ &= \arg\max_y \underbrace{\Big[\prod_{t=1}^T P(\mathbf{x}_t|\mathbf{x}_1,\mathbf{x}_2,\ldots,\mathbf{x}_{t-1},\mathbf{y}_1^T)\Big]}_{\text{generative part}} \underbrace{\Big[\prod_{t=1}^T P(\mathbf{y}_t|\mathbf{y}_1,\mathbf{y}_2,\ldots,\mathbf{y}_{t-1})\Big]}_{\text{prior part}} \quad (1)\end{aligned}$$

For many applications (1) is approximated by simpler expressions, for example as a first order Markov Model

$$\mathbf{Y}^\star \approx \arg\max_y \Big[\prod_{t=1}^T P(\mathbf{x}_t|\mathbf{y}_t)\Big]\Big[\prod_{t=1}^T P(\mathbf{y}_t|\mathbf{y}_{t-1})\Big] \quad (2)$$

making some simplifying approximations. These are for this example:

- Every output $\mathbf{y}_t$ depends only on the previous output $\mathbf{y}_{t-1}$ and not on all previous outputs:
$$P(\mathbf{y}_t|\mathbf{y}_1,\mathbf{y}_2,\ldots,\mathbf{y}_{t-1}) \Rightarrow P(\mathbf{y}_t|\mathbf{y}_{t-1}) \quad (3)$$
- The inputs are assumed to be statistically independent in time:
$$P(\mathbf{x}_t|\mathbf{x}_1,\mathbf{x}_2,\ldots,\mathbf{x}_{t-1},\mathbf{y}_1^T) \Rightarrow P(\mathbf{x}_t|\mathbf{y}_1^T) \quad (4)$$
- The likelihood of an input vector x_t given the complete output sequence $\mathbf{y}_1^T$ is assumed to depend only on the output found at t and not on any other ones:
$$P(\mathbf{x}_t|\mathbf{y}_1^T) \Rightarrow P(\mathbf{x}_t|\mathbf{y}_t) \quad (5)$$

Assuming that the output sequences are categorical sequences (consisting of symbols), approximation (2) and derived expressions are the basis for many applications. For example, using Gaussian mixture distributions to model $P(\mathbf{x}_t|\mathbf{y}_t) = P_k(\mathbf{x}) \; \forall \; K$ occuring symbols, approach (2) is used in a more sophisticated form in most state-of-the-art speech recognition systems.

Focus of this paper is to present some models for the generative part of (1) which need less assumptions. Ideally this means to be able to model directly expressions of the form $P(\mathbf{x}_t|\mathbf{x}_1,\mathbf{x}_2,\ldots,\mathbf{x}_{t-1},\mathbf{y}_1^T)$, the possibly (multi-modal) distribution of a vector conditioned on previous $\mathbf{x}$ vectors $\mathbf{x}_t,\mathbf{x}_{t-1},\ldots,\mathbf{x}_1$ and a complete sequence $\mathbf{y}_1^T$, as shown in the next section.

---

[3] there is no distinction made between probability mass and density, usually denoted as P and p, respectively. If the quantity to model is categorical, a probability mass is assumed, if it is continuous, a probability density is assumed.

2 Mixture density recurrent neural networks

Assume we want to model a continuous vector sequence, conditioned on a sequence of categorical variables as shown in Figure 1. One approach is to assume that the vector sequence can be modeled by a uni-modal Gaussian distribution with a constant variance, making it a uni-modal regression problem. There are many practical examples where this assumption doesn't hold, requiring a more complex output distribution to model multi-modal data. One example is the attempt to model the sounds of phonemes based on data from multiple speakers. A certain phoneme will sound completely different depending on its phonetic environment or on the speaker, and using a single Gaussian with a constant variance would lead to a crude averaging of all examples.

The traditional approach is to build generative models for each symbol separately, as suggested by (2). If conventional Gaussian mixtures are used to model the observed input vectors, then the parameters of the distribution (means, covariances, mixture weights) in general do not change with the temporal position of the vector to model within a given state segment of that symbol. This can be a bad representation for the data in some areas (shown are here the means of a very bi-modal looking distribution), as indicated by the two shown variances for the state 'E'. When used to model speech, a procedure often used to cope with this problem is to increase the number of symbols by grouping often appearing symbol sub-strings into a new symbol and by subdividing each original symbol into a number of states.

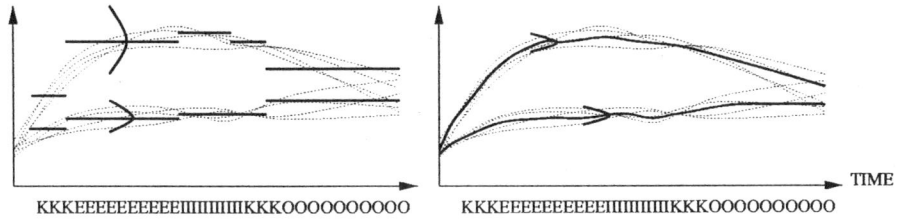

Figure 1: Conventional Gaussian mixtures (left) and mixture density BRNNs (right) for multi-modal regression

Another alternative is explored here, where all parameters of a Gaussian mixture distribution modeling the continuous targets are predicted by one bidirectional recurrent neural network, extended to model mixture densities conditioned on a complete vector sequence, as shown on the right side of Figure 1. Another extension (section 2.1) to the architecture allows the estimation of time varying mixture densities conditioned on a hypothesized output sequence *and* a continuous vector sequence to model exactly the generative term in (1) without *any* explicit approximations about the use of context.

Basics of non-recurrent mixture density networks (MLP type) can be found in [1][2]. The extension from uni-modal to multi-modal regression is somewhat involved but straightforward for the two interesting cases of having a radial covariance matrix or a diagonal covariance matrix per mixture component. They are trained with gradient-descent procedures as regular uni-modal regression NNs. Suitable equations to calculate the error that is back-propagated can be found in [6] for the two cases mentioned, a derivation for the simple case in [1][2].

Conventional recurrent neural networks (RNNs) can model expressions of the form $P(\mathbf{x}_t|\mathbf{y}_1, \mathbf{y}_2, \ldots, \mathbf{y}_t)$, the distribution of a vector given an input vector plus its past input vectors. *Bidirectional* recurrent neural networks (BRNNs) [5][6] are a simple extension of conventional RNNs. The extension allows one to model expressions of the form $P(\mathbf{x}_t|\mathbf{y}_1^T)$, the distribution of a vector given an input vector plus its past *and following* input vectors.

2.1 Mixture density extension for BRNNs

Here two types of extensions of BRNNs to mixture density networks are considered:

I) An extension to model expressions of the type $P(\mathbf{x}_t|\mathbf{y}_1^T)$, a multi-modal distribution of a continuous vector conditioned on a vector sequence $\mathbf{y}_1^T$, here labeled as mixture density BRNN of *Type I*.

II) An extension to model expressions of the type $P(\mathbf{x}_t|\mathbf{x}_1, \mathbf{x}_2, \ldots, \mathbf{x}_{t-1}, \mathbf{y}_1^T)$, a probability distribution of a continuous vector conditioned on a vector sequence $\mathbf{y}_1^T$ *and* on its previous context in time $\mathbf{x}_1, \mathbf{x}_2, \ldots, \mathbf{x}_{t-1}$. This architecture is labeled as mixture density BRNN of *Type II*.

The first extension of conventional uni-modal regression BRNNs to mixture density networks is not particularly difficult compared to the non-recurrent implementation, because the changes to model multi-modal distributions are completely independent of the structural changes that have to be made to form a BRNN.

The second extension involves a structural change to the basic BRNN structure to incorporate the $\mathbf{x}_1, \mathbf{x}_2, \ldots, \mathbf{x}_{t-1}$ as additional inputs, as shown in Figure 2. For any t the neighboring $\mathbf{x}_{t-1}, \mathbf{x}_{t-2}, \ldots$ are incorporated by adding an additional set of weights to feed the hidden forward states with the extended inputs (the targets for the outputs) from the time step before. This includes $\mathbf{x}_{t-1}$ directly and $\mathbf{x}_{t-2}, \mathbf{x}_{t-3}, \ldots \mathbf{x}_1$ indirectly through the hidden forward neurons. This architecture allows one to estimate the generative term in (1) without making the explicit assumptions (4) and (5), since all the information $\mathbf{x}_t$ is conditioned on, is theoretically available.

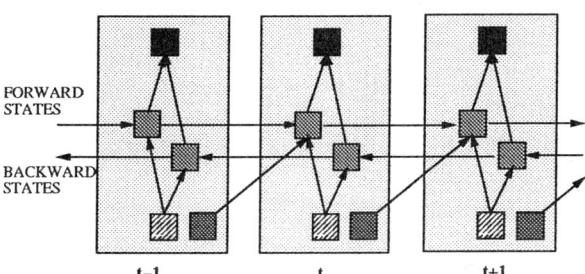

Figure 2: BRNN mixture density extension (Type II) (inputs: striped, outputs: black, hidden neurons: grey, additional inputs: dark grey). Note that without the backward states and the additional inputs this structure is a conventional RNN, unfolded in time.

Different from non-recurrent mixture density networks, the extended BRNNs can predict the parameters of a Gaussian mixture distribution conditioned on a vector *sequence* rather than a single vector, that is, at each (time) position t one parameter set (means, variances (actually standard variations), mixture weights) conditioned on $\mathbf{y}_1^T$ for the BRNN of type I and on $\mathbf{x}_1, \mathbf{x}_2, \ldots, \mathbf{x}_{t-1}, \mathbf{y}_1^T$ for the BRNN of type II.

3 Experiments and Results

The goal of the experiments is to show that the proposed models are more suitable to model speech data than traditional approaches, because they rely on fewer assumptions. The speech data used here has observation vector sequences representing the original waveform in a compressed form, where each vector is mapped to exactly one out of K phonemes. Here three approaches are compared, which allow the estimation of the likelihood $P(\mathbf{X}|\mathbf{Y})$ with various degrees of approximations:

Conventional Gaussian mixture model, $P(\mathbf{X}|\mathbf{Y}) \approx \prod_{t=1}^{T} P(\mathbf{x}_t|\mathbf{y}_t)$:
According to (2) the likelihood of a phoneme class vector is approximated by a conventional Gaussian mixture distribution, that is, a separate mixture model is built to estimate $P(\mathbf{x}|\mathbf{y}) = P_k(\mathbf{x})$ for each of the possible K categorical states in $\mathcal{Y}$. In this case the two assumptions (4) and (5) are necessary. For the variance a radial covariance matrix (diagonal single variance for all vector components) is chosen to match it to the conditions for the BRNN cases below. The number of parameters for the complete model is $KM(D+2)$ for $M > 1$. Several models of different complexity were trained (Table 1).

Mixture density BRNN I, $P(\mathbf{X}|\mathbf{Y}) \approx \prod_{t=1}^{T} P(\mathbf{x}_t|\mathbf{y}_1^T)$: One mixture density BRNN of type I, with the same number of mixture components and a radial covariance matrix for its output distribution as in the approach above, is trained by presenting complete sample sequences to it. Note that for type I all possible context-dependencies (assumption (5)) are automatically taken care of, because the probability is conditioned on complete sequences $\mathbf{y}_1^T$. The sequence $\mathbf{y}_1^T$ contains for any t not only the information about neighboring phonemes, but also the position of a frame within a phoneme. In conventional systems this can only be modeled crudely by introducing a certain number of states per phoneme. The number of outputs for the network depends on the number of mixture components and is $M(D+2)$. The total number of parameters can be adjusted by changing the number of hidden forward and backward state neurons, and was set here to 64 each.

Mixture density BRNN II, $P(\mathbf{X}|\mathbf{Y}) = \prod_{t=1}^{T} P(\mathbf{x}_t|\mathbf{x}_1, \mathbf{x}_2, \ldots, \mathbf{x}_{t-1}, \mathbf{y}_1^T)$:
One mixture density BRNN of type II, again with the same number of mixture components and a radial covariance matrix, is trained under the same conditions as above. Note that in this case both assumptions (4) and (5) are taken care of, because exactly expressions of the required form can be modeled by a mixture density BRNN of type II.

3.1 Experiments

The recommended training and test data of the TIMIT speech database [3] was used for the experiments. The TIMIT database comes with hand-aligned phonetic transcriptions for all utterances, which were transformed to sequences of categorical class numbers (training = 702438, test = 256617 vec.). The number of possible categorical classes is the number of phonemes, $K = 61$. The categorical data (input data for the BRNNs) is represented as K-dimensional vectors with the kth component being one and all others zero. The feature extraction for the waveforms, which resulted in the vector sequences $\mathbf{x}_1^T$ to model, was done as in most speech recognition systems [7]. The variances were normalized with respect to all training data, such that a radial variance for each mixture component in the model is a reasonable choice.

All three model types were trained with $M = 1, 2, 3, 4$, the conventional Gaussian mixture model also with $M = 8, 16$ mixture components. The number of resulting parameters, used as a rough complexity measure for the models, is shown in Table 1. The states of the triphone models were not clustered.

Table 1: Number of parameters for different types of models

mixture components	mono61 1-state	mono61 3-state	tri571 3-state	BRNN I	BRNN II
1	1952	5856	54816	20256	22176
2	3904	11712	109632	24384	26304
3	5856	17568	164448	28512	30432
4	7808	23424	219264	32640	34560
8	15616	46848	438528	–	–
16	31232	93696	877056	–	–

Training for the conventional approach using M mixtures of Gaussians was done using the EM algorithm. For some classes with only a few samples M had to be reduced to reach a stationary point of the likelihood. Training of the BRNNs of both types must be done using a gradient descent algorithm. Here a modified version of RPROP [4] was used, which is in more detail described in [6].

The measure used in comparing the tested approaches is the log-likelihood of training and test data given the models built on the training data. In absence of a search algorithm to perform recognition this is a valid measure to evaluate the models since maximizing log-likelihood on the training data is the objective for all model types. Note that the given alignment of vectors to phoneme classes for the test data is used in calculating the log-likelihood on the test data – there is no search for the best alignment.

3.2 Results

Figure 3 shows the average log-likelihoods depending on the number of mixture components for all tested approaches on training (upper line) and test data (lower line). The baseline 1-state monophones give the lowest likelihood. The 3-state monophones are slightly better, but have a larger gap between training and test data likelihood. For comparison on the training data a system with 571 distinct triphones with 3 states each was trained also. Note that this system has a lot more parameters than the BRNN systems (see Table 1) it was compared to. The results for the traditional Gaussian mixture systems show how the models become better by building more detailed models for different (phonetic) context, i.e., by using more states and more context classes.

The mixture density BRNN of type I gives a higher likelihood than the traditional Gaussian mixture models. This was expected because the BRNN type I models are, in contrast to the traditional Gaussian mixture models, able to include all possible phonetic context effects by removing assumption (5) – i.e. a frame of a certain phoneme surrounded by frames of any other phonemes with theoretically no restriction about the range of the contextual influence.

The mixture density BRNN of type II, which in addition removes the independence assumption (4), gives a significant higher likelihood than all other models. Note that the difference in likelihood on training and test data for this model is very small, indicating a useful model for the underlying distribution of the data.

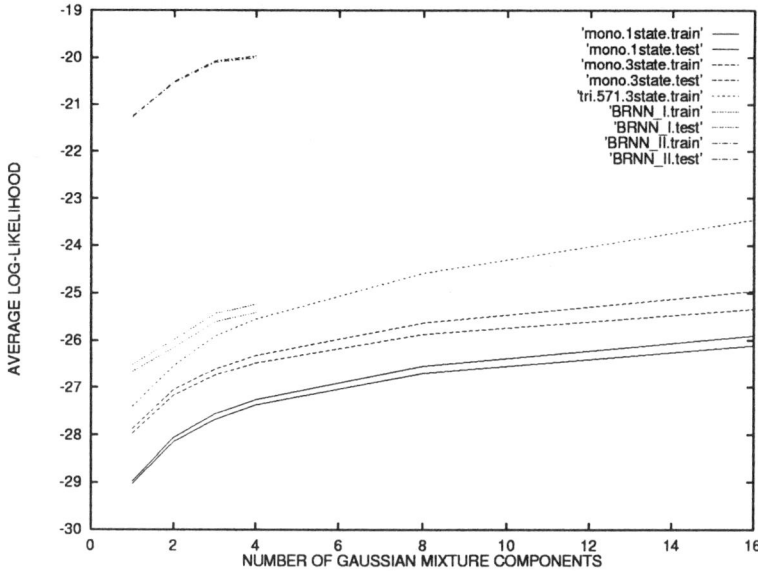

Figure 3: Mixture density BRNNs for multi-modal regression: Results

4 Conclusions

The mixture density BRNNs allow one to model probabilistic expressions frequently occurring in sequence processing problems, with less assumptions than traditionally necessary. Here it was shown that they can model the statistical properties of speech data better than the traditional approach using Gaussian mixture models, making mixture density BRNNs and approximations to them potential candidates for improved speech recognition, coding and synthesis.

Many issues couldn't be covered in this paper because of space limitations. A more detailed description of these models can be found in [6].

References

[1] C. M. Bishop. Mixture density networks. Technical Report NCRG/94/004, Neural Computing Research Group, Aston University, Birmingham, England, 1994.

[2] C. M. Bishop. *Neural Networks for Pattern Recognition*. Clarendon Press, Oxford, England, 1995.

[3] Linguistic Data Consortium. TIMIT Acoustic-Phonetic Continuous Speech Corpus, 1993. (http://morph.ldc.upenn.edu/Catalog/LDC93S1.html).

[4] M. Riedmiller and H. Braun. A direct adaptive method for faster back-propagation learning: The RPROP algorithm. In *Proceedings of the IEEE International Conference on Neural Networks*, pages 586–591, 1993.

[5] M. Schuster and K. K. Paliwal. Bidirectional recurrent neural networks. *IEEE Transactions on Neural Networks*, 45(11):2673–2681, 1997.

[6] M. Schuster. *On supervised learning from sequential data with applications for speech recognition*. PhD thesis, Nara Institute of Science and Technology, Nara, JAPAN, 1999. (http://isw3.aist-nara.ac.jp/IS/Shikano-lab/database/library/paper/DT9661205.ps.gz).

[7] S. Young. A review of large vocabulary speech recognition. *IEEE Signal Processing Magazine*, 15(5):45–57, 1996.

Greedy importance sampling

Dale Schuurmans
Department of Computer Science
University of Waterloo
dale@cs.uwaterloo.ca

Abstract

I present a simple variation of importance sampling that explicitly searches for important regions in the target distribution. I prove that the technique yields unbiased estimates, and show empirically it can reduce the variance of standard Monte Carlo estimators. This is achieved by concentrating samples in more significant regions of the sample space.

1 Introduction

It is well known that general inference and learning with graphical models is computationally hard [1] and it is therefore necessary to consider restricted architectures [13], or approximate algorithms to perform these tasks [3, 7]. Among the most convenient and successful techniques are stochastic methods which are guaranteed to converge to a correct solution in the limit of large samples [10, 11, 12, 15]. These methods can be easily applied to complex inference problems that overwhelm deterministic approaches.

The family of stochastic inference methods can be grouped into the *independent* Monte Carlo methods (importance sampling and rejection sampling [4, 10, 14]) and the *dependent* Markov Chain Monte Carlo (MCMC) methods (Gibbs sampling, Metropolis sampling, and "hybrid" Monte Carlo) [5, 10, 11, 15]. The goal of all these methods is to simulate drawing a random sample from a target distribution $P(x)$ (generally defined by a Bayesian network or graphical model) that is difficult to sample from directly.

This paper investigates a simple modification of importance sampling that demonstrates some advantages over independent and dependent-Markov-chain methods. The idea is to explicitly search for important regions in a target distribution P when sampling from a simpler proposal distribution Q. Some MCMC methods, such as Metropolis and "hybrid" Monte Carlo, attempt to do something like this by biasing a local random search towards higher probability regions, while preserving the asymptotic "fair sampling" properties of the exploration [11, 12]. Here I investigate a simple direct approach where one draws points from a proposal distribution Q but then explicitly searches in P to find points from significant regions. The main challenge is to maintain correctness (*i.e.*, unbiasedness) of the resulting procedure, which we achieve by independently sampling search subsequences and then weighting the sample points so that their expected weight under the proposal distribution Q matches their true probability under the target P.

Importance sampling
- Draw $x_1, ..., x_n$ independently from Q.
- Weight each point x_i by $w(x_i) = \frac{P(x_i)}{Q(x_i)}$.
- For a random variable, f, estimate $\mathrm{E}_{P(x)} f(x)$ by $\hat{f} = \frac{1}{n} \sum_{i=1}^{n} f(x_i) w(x_i)$.

"Indirect" importance sampling
- Draw $x_1, ..., x_n$ independently from Q.
- Weight each point x_i by $u(x_i) = \frac{\beta P(x_i)}{Q(x_i)}$.
- For a random variable, f, estimate $\mathrm{E}_{P(x)} f(x)$ by $\hat{f} = \sum_{i=1}^{n} f(x_i) u(x_i) / \sum_{i=1}^{n} u(x_i)$.

Figure 1: Regular and "indirect" importance sampling procedures

2 Generalized importance sampling

Many inference problems in graphical models can be cast as determining the expected value of a random variable of interest, f, given observations drawn according to a target distribution P. That is, we are interested in computing the expectation $\mathrm{E}_{P(x)} f(x)$. Usually the random variable f is simple, like the indicator of some event, but the distribution P is generally not in a form that we can sample from efficiently. *Importance sampling* is a useful technique for estimating $\mathrm{E}_{P(x)} f(x)$ in these cases. The idea is to draw independent points $x_1, ..., x_n$ from a simpler "proposal" distribution Q, but then weight these points by $w(x) = P(x)/Q(x)$ to obtain a "fair" representation of P. Assuming that we can efficiently evaluate $P(x)$ at each point, the weighted sample can be used to estimate desired expectations (Figure 1). The correctness (*i.e.*, unbiasedness) of this procedure is easy to establish, since the expected weighted value of f under Q is just $\mathrm{E}_{Q(x)} f(x) w(x) = \sum_{x \in X} [f(x) w(x)] Q(x) = \sum_{x \in X} \left[f(x) \frac{P(x)}{Q(x)} \right] Q(x) = \sum_{x \in X} f(x) P(x) = \mathrm{E}_{P(x)} f(x)$.

This technique can be implemented using "indirect" weights $u(x) = \beta P(x)/Q(x)$ and an alternative estimator (Figure 1) that only requires us to compute a fixed multiple of $P(x)$. This preserves asymptotic correctness because $\frac{1}{n} \sum_{i=1}^{n} f(x_i) u(x_i)$ and $\frac{1}{n} \sum_{i=1}^{n} u(x_i)$ converge to $\beta \mathrm{E}_{P(x)} f(x)$ and β respectively, which yields $\hat{f} \to \mathrm{E}_{P(x)} f(x)$ (generally [4]). It will always be possible to apply this extended approach below, but we drop it for now.

Importance sampling is an effective estimation technique when Q approximates P over most of the domain, but it fails when Q misses high probability regions of P and systematically yields samples with small weights. In this case, the resulting estimator will have high variance because the sample will almost always contain unrepresentative points but is sometimes dominated by a few high weight points. To overcome this problem it is critical to obtain data points from the important regions of P. Our goal is to avoid generating systematically under-weight samples by *explicitly* searching for significant regions in the target distribution P. To do this, and maintain the unbiasedness of the resulting procedure, we develop a series of extensions to importance sampling that are each provably correct.

The first extension is to consider sampling *blocks* of points instead of just individual points. Let $\mathcal{B}$ be a partition of X into finite blocks B, where $\bigcup_{B \in \mathcal{B}} B = X$, $B \cap B' = \emptyset$, and each B is finite. (Note that $\mathcal{B}$ can be infinite.) The "block" sampling procedure (Figure 2) draws independent blocks of points to construct the final sample, but then weights points by their target probability $P(x)$ divided by the total block probability $Q(B(x))$. For discrete spaces it is easy to verify that this procedure yields unbiased estimates, since $\mathrm{E}_{Q(x)} \left[\sum_{x_j \in B(x)} f(x_j) w(x_j) \right] = \sum_{x \in X} \left[\sum_{x_j \in B(x)} f(x_j) w(x_j) \right] Q(x) = \sum_{B \in \mathcal{B}} \sum_{x_i \in B} \left[\sum_{x_j \in B} f(x_j) w(x_j) \right] Q(x_i) = \sum_{B \in \mathcal{B}} \left[\sum_{x_j \in B} f(x_j) w(x_j) \right] Q(B) = \sum_{B \in \mathcal{B}} \left[\sum_{x_j \in B} f(x_j) \frac{P(x_j)}{Q(B)} \right] Q(B) = \sum_{B \in \mathcal{B}} \left[\sum_{x_j \in B} f(x_j) P(x_j) \right] = \sum_{x \in X} f(x) P(x)$.

"Block" importance sampling
- Draw $x_1, ..., x_n$ independently from Q.
- For x_i, recover block $B_i = \{x_{i,1}, ..., x_{i,b_i}\}$.
- Create a large sample out of the blocks
  $x_{1,1}, ..., x_{1,b_1}, x_{2,1}, ..., x_{2,b_2}, ..., x_{n,1}, ..., x_{n,b_n}$.
- Weight each $x_{i,j}$ by $w(x_{i,j}) = \frac{P(x_{i,j})}{\sum_{j=1}^{b_i} Q(x_{i,j})}$.
- For a random variable, f, estimate $\mathrm{E}_{P(x)} f(x)$
  by $\hat{f} = \frac{1}{n} \sum_{i=1}^{n} \sum_{j=1}^{b_i} f(x_{i,j}) w(x_{i,j})$.

"Sliding window" importance sampling
- Draw $x_1, ..., x_n$ independently from Q.
- For x_i, recover block B_i, and let $x_{i,1} = x_i$:
  - Get $x_{i,1}$'s successors $x_{i,1}, x_{i,2}, ..., x_{i,m}$
    by climbing up $m - 1$ steps from $x_{i,1}$.
  - Get predecessors $x_{i,-m+1}, , ..., x_{i,-1}, x_{i,0}$
    by climbing down $m - 1$ steps from $x_{i,1}$.
  - Weight $w(x_{i,j}) = P(x_{i,j}) / \sum_{k=j-m+1}^{j} Q(x_{i,k})$
- Create final sample from *successor* points
  $x_{1,1}, ..., x_{1,m}, x_{2,1}, ..., x_{2,m}, ..., x_{n,1}, ..., x_{n,m}$.
- For a random variable, f, estimate $\mathrm{E}_{P(x)} f(x)$
  by $\hat{f} = \frac{1}{n} \sum_{i=1}^{n} \sum_{j=1}^{m} f(x_{i,j}) w(x_{i,j})$.

Figure 2: "Block" and "sliding window" importance sampling procedures

Crucially, this argument does not depend on *how* the partition of X is chosen. In fact, we could fix any partition, even one that depended on the target distribution P, and still obtain an unbiased procedure (so long as the partition remains fixed). Intuitively, this works because blocks are drawn independently from Q and the weighting scheme still produces a "fair" representation of P. (Note that the results presented in this paper can all be extended to continuous spaces under mild technical restrictions. However, for the purposes of clarity we will restrict the technical presentation in this paper to the discrete case.)

The second extension is to allow countably infinite blocks that each have a discrete total order $\cdots < x_{i-1} < x_i < x_{i+1} < \cdots$ defined on their elements. This order could reflect the relative probability of x_i and x_j under P, but for now we just consider it to be an arbitrary discrete order. To cope with blocks of unbounded length, we employ a "sliding window" sampling procedure that selects a contiguous sub-block of size m from within a larger selected block (Figure 2). This procedure builds each independent subsample by choosing a random point x_1 from the proposal distribution Q, determining its containing block $B(x_1)$, and then climbing up $m - 1$ steps to obtain the successors $x_1, x_2, ..., x_m$, and climbing down $m - 1$ steps to obtain the predecessors $x_{-m+1}, ..., x_{-1}, x_0$. The successor points (including x_1) appear in the final sample, but the predecessors are only used to determine the weights of the sample points. Weights are determined by the target probability $P(x)$ divided by the probability that the point x appears in a random reconstruction under Q. This too yields an unbiased estimator since $\mathrm{E}_{Q(x)}\left[\sum_{j=1}^{m} f(x_j) w(x_j)\right] = \sum_{x_\ell \in X} \left[\sum_{j=\ell}^{\ell+m-1} f(x_j) \frac{P(x_j)}{\sum_{k=j-m+1}^{j} Q(x_k)}\right] Q(x_\ell) =$
$\sum_{B \in \mathcal{B}} \sum_{x_\ell \in B} \sum_{j=\ell}^{\ell+m-1} \frac{f(x_j) P(x_j) Q(x_\ell)}{\sum_{k=j-m+1}^{j} Q(x_k)} = \sum_{B \in \mathcal{B}} \sum_{x_j \in B} \sum_{\ell=j-m+1}^{j} \frac{f(x_j) P(x_j) Q(x_\ell)}{\sum_{k=j-m+1}^{j} Q(x_k)} =$
$\sum_{B \in \mathcal{B}} \sum_{x_j \in B} f(x_j) P(x_j) \frac{\sum_{\ell=j-m+1}^{j} Q(x_\ell)}{\sum_{k=j-m+1}^{j} Q(x_k)} = \sum_{B \in \mathcal{B}} \sum_{x_j \in B} f(x_j) P(x_j) = \sum_{x \in X} f(x) P(x)$.
(The middle line breaks the sum into disjoint blocks and then reorders the sum so that instead of first choosing the start point x_ℓ and then x_ℓ's successors $x_\ell, ..., x_{\ell+m-1}$, we first choose the successor point x_j and then the start points $x_{j-m+1}, ..., x_j$ that could have led to x_j). Note that this derivation does not depend on the particular block partition nor on the particular discrete orderings, so long as they remain fixed. This means that, again, we can use partitions and orderings that explicitly depend on P and still obtain a correct procedure.

"Greedy" importance sampling (1-D)
- Draw $x_1, ..., x_n$ independently from Q.
- For each x_i, let $x_{i,1} = x_i$:
  - Compute successors $x_{i,1}, x_{i,2}, ..., x_{i,m}$ by taking $m-1$ size ϵ steps in the direction of increase.
  - Compute predecessors $x_{i,-m+1}, ..., x_{i,-1}, x_{i,0}$ by taking $m-1$ size ϵ steps in the direction of decrease.
  - If an improper ascent or descent occurs, truncate paths as shown on the upper right.
  - Weight $w(x_{i,j}) = P(x_{i,j}) / \sum_{k=j-m+1}^{j} Q(x_{i,k})$.
- Create the final sample from successor points $x_{1,1}, ..., x_{1,m}, x_{2,1}, ..., x_{2,m}, ..., x_{n,1}, ..., x_{n,m}$.
- For a random variable, f, estimate $\mathrm{E}_{P(x)} f(x)$ by $\hat{f} = \frac{1}{n} \sum_{i=1}^{n} \sum_{j=1}^{m} f(x_{i,j}) w(x_{i,j})$.

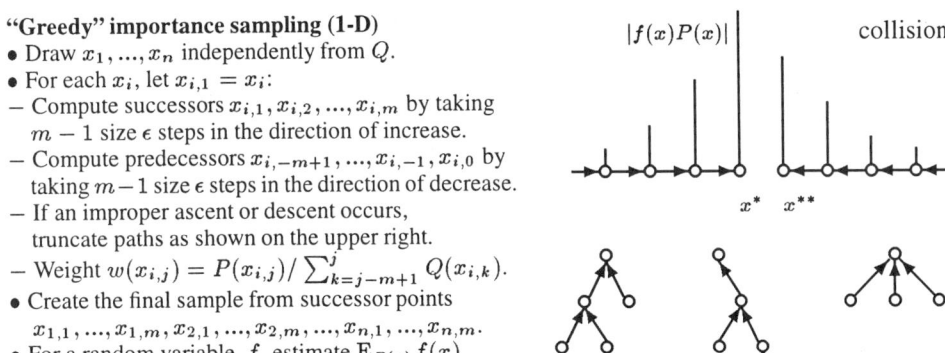

Figure 3: "Greedy" importance sampling procedure; "colliding" and "merging" paths.

3 Greedy importance sampling: 1-dimensional case

Finally, we apply the sliding window procedure to conduct an explicit search for important regions in X. It is well known that the optimal proposal distribution for importance sampling is just $Q^*(x) = |f(x)P(x)| / \sum_{x \in X} |f(x)P(x)|$ (which minimizes variance [2]). Here we apply the sliding window procedure using an order structure that is determined by the objective $|f(x)P(x)|$. The hope is to obtain reduced variance by sampling independent blocks of points where each block (by virtue of being constructed via an explicit search) is likely to contain at least one or two high weight points. That is, by capturing a moderate size sample of independent high weight points we intuitively expect to outperform standard methods that are unlikely to observe such points by chance. Our experiments below verify this intuition (Figure 4).

The main technical issue is maintaining unbiasedness, which is easy to establish in the 1-dimensional case. In the simple 1-d setting, the "greedy" importance sampling procedure (Figure 3) first draws an initial point x_1 from Q and then follows the direction of increasing $|f(x)P(x)|$, taking fixed size ϵ steps, until either $m-1$ steps have been taken or we encounter a critical point. A single "block" in our final sample is comprised of a complete sequence captured in one ascending search. To weight the sample points we account for all possible ways each point could appear in a subsample, which, as before, entails climbing down $m-1$ steps in the descent direction (to calculate the denominators). The unbiasedness of the procedure then follows directly from the previous section, since greedy importance sampling is equivalent to sliding window importance sampling in this setting.

The only nontrivial issue is to maintain disjoint search paths. Note that a search path must terminate whenever it steps from a point x^* to a point x^{**} with lower value; this indicates that a collision has occurred because some other path must reach x^* from the "other side" of the critical point (Figure 3). At a collision, the largest ascent point x^* must be allocated to a single path. A reasonable policy is to allocate x^* to the path that has the lowest weight penultimate point (but the only critical issue is ensuring that it gets assigned to a single block). By ensuring that the critical point is included in only one of the two distinct search paths, a practical estimator can be obtained that exhibits no bias (Figure 4).

To test the effectiveness of the greedy approach I conducted several 1-dimensional experiments which varied the relationship between P, Q and the random variable f (Figure 4). In these experiments greedy importance sampling strongly outperformed standard methods, including regular importance sampling and directly sampling from the target distribution P (rejection sampling and Metropolis sampling were not competitive). The results not only verify the unbiasedness of the greedy procedure, but also show that it obtains significantly smaller variances across a wide range of conditions. Note that the greedy procedure actually uses m out of $2m - 1$ points sampled for each block and therefore effectively uses a double sample. However, Figure 4 shows that the greedy approach often obtains variance reductions that are far greater than 2 (which corresponds to a standard deviation reduction of $\sqrt{2}$).

4 Multi-dimensional case

Of course, this technique is worthwhile only if it can be applied to multi-dimensional problems. In principle, it is straightforward to apply the greedy procedure of Section 3 to multi-dimensional sample spaces. The only new issue is that discrete search paths can now possibly "merge" as well as "collide"; see Figure 3. (Recall that paths could not merge in the previous case.) Therefore, instead of decomposing the domain into a collection of disjoint search paths, the objective $|f(x)P(x)|$ now decomposes the domain into a forest of disjoint search *trees*. However, the same principle could be used to devise an unbiased estimator in this case: one could assign a weight to a sample point x that is just its target probability $P(x)$ divided by the total Q-probability of the subtree of points that lead to x in fewer than m steps. This weighting scheme can be shown to yield an unbiased estimator as before. However, the resulting procedure is impractical because in an N-dimensional sample space a search tree will typically have a branching factor of $\Omega(N)$; yielding exponentially large trees. Avoiding the need to exhaustively examine such trees is the critical issue in applying the greedy approach to multi-dimensional spaces.

The simplest conceivable strategy is just to ignore merge events. Surprisingly, this turns out to work reasonably well in many circumstances. Note that merges will be a measure zero event in many continuous domains. In such cases one could hope to ignore merges and trust that the probability of "double counting" such points would remain near zero. I conducted simple experiments with a version of greedy importance sampling procedure that ignored merges. This procedure searched in the gradient ascent direction of the objective $|f(x)p(x)|$ and heuristically inverted search steps by climbing in the gradient *descent* direction. Figures 5 and 6 show that, despite the heuristic nature of this procedure, it nevertheless demonstrates credible performance on simple tasks.

The first experiment is a simple demonstration from [12, 10] where the task is to sample from a bivariate Gaussian distribution P of two highly correlated random variables using a "weak" proposal distribution Q that is standard normal (depicted by the elliptical and circular one standard deviation contours in Figure 5 respectively). Greedy importance sampling once again performs very well (Figure 5); achieving unbiased estimates with lower variance than standard Monte Carlo estimators, including common MCMC methods.

To conduct a more significant study, I applied the heuristic greedy method to an inference problem in graphical models: recovering the hidden state sequence from a dynamic probabilistic model, given a sequence of observations. Here I considered a simple Kalman filter model which had one state variable and one observation variable per time-step, and used the conditional distributions $X_t|X_{t-1} \sim N(x_{t-1}, \sigma_s^2)$, $Z_t|X_t \sim N(x_t, \sigma_o^2)$ and initial distribution $X_1 \sim N(0, \sigma_s^2)$. The problem was to infer the value of the final state variable x_t given the observations $z_1, z_2, ..., z_t$. Figure 6 again demonstrates that the greedy approach has a strong advantage over standard importance sampling. (In fact, the greedy approach can be applied to "condensation" [6, 8] to obtain further improvements on this task, but space bounds preclude a detailed discussion.)

Overall, these preliminary results show that despite the heuristic choices made in this section, the greedy strategy still performs well relative to common Monte Carlo estimators, both in terms of bias and variance (at least on some low and moderate dimension problems). However, the heuristic nature of this procedure makes it extremely unsatisfying. In fact, merge points can easily make up a significant fraction of *finite* domains. It turns out that a rigorously unbiased and feasible procedure can be obtained as follows. First, take greedy fixed size steps in axis parallel directions (which ensures the steps can be inverted). Then, rather than exhaustively explore an entire predecessor tree to calculate the weights of a sample point, use the well known technique of Knuth [9] to sample a *single* path from the root and obtain an unbiased estimate of the total Q-probability of the tree. This procedure allows one to formulate an asymptotically unbiased estimator that is nevertheless feasible to implement. It remains important future work to investigate this approach and compare it to other Monte Carlo estimation methods on large dimensional problems—in particular hybrid Monte Carlo [11, 12]. The current results already suggest that the method could have benefits.

References

[1] P. Dagum and M. Luby. Approximating probabilistic inference in Bayesian belief networks is NP-hard. *Artif Intell*, 60:141–153, 1993.

[2] M. Evans. Chaining via annealing. *Ann Statist*, 19:382–393, 1991.

[3] B. Frey. *Graphical Models for Machine Learning and Digital Communication*. MIT Press, Cambridge, MA, 1998.

[4] J. Geweke. Baysian inference in econometric models using Monte Carlo integration. *Econometrica*, 57:1317–1339, 1989.

[5] W. Gilks, S. Richardson, and D. Spiegelhalter. *Markov chain Monte Carlo in practice*. Chapman and Hall, 1996.

[6] M. Isard and A. Blake. Coutour tracking by stochastic propagation of conditional density. In *ECCV*, 1996.

[7] M. Jordan, Z. Ghahramani, T. Jaakkola, and L. Saul. An introduction to variational methods for graphical models. In *Learning in Graphical Models*. Kluwer, 1998.

[8] K. Kanazawa, D. Koller, and S. Russell. Stochastic simulation algorithms for dynamic probabilistic networks. In *UAI*, 1995.

[9] D. Knuth. Estimating the efficiency of backtracking algorithms. *Math. Comput.*, 29(129):121–136, 1975.

[10] D. MacKay. Intro to Monte Carlo methods. In *Learning in Graphical Models*. Kluwer, 1998.

[11] R. Neal. Probabilistic inference using Markov chain Monte Carlo methods. 1993.

[12] R. Neal. *Bayesian Learning for Neural Networks*. Springer, New York, 1996.

[13] J. Pearl. *Probabilistic Reasoning in Intelligence Systems*. Morgan Kaufmann, 1988.

[14] R. Shacter and M. Peot. Simulation approaches to general probabilistic inference in belief networks. In *Uncertainty in Artificial Intelligence 5*. Elsevier, 1990.

[15] M. Tanner. *Tools for statistical inference: Methods for exploration of posterior distributions and likelihood functions*. Springer, New York, 1993.

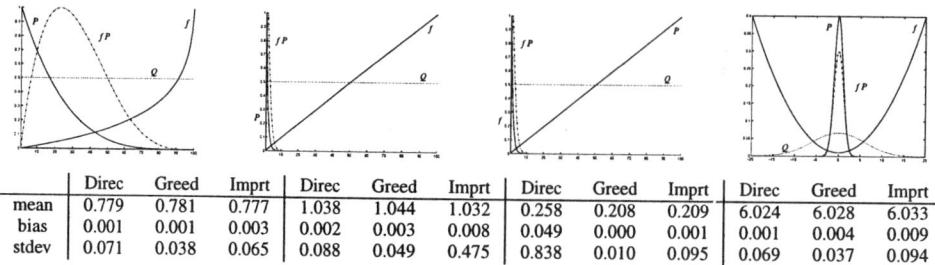

Figure 4: 1-dimensional experiments: 1000 repetitions on estimation samples of size 100. Problems with varying relationships between P, Q, f and $|fP|$.

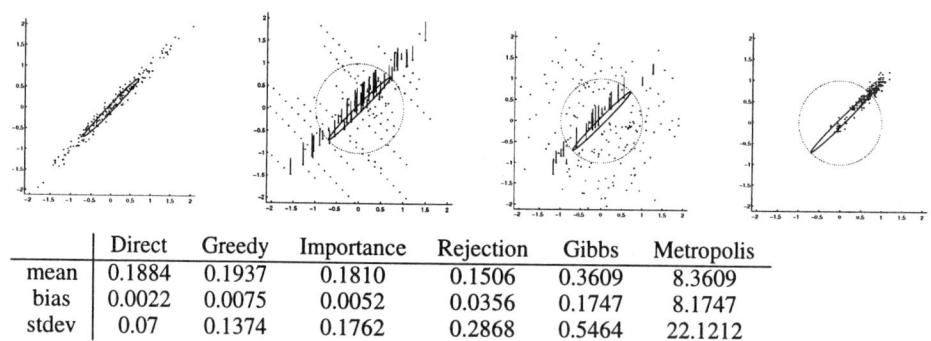

Figure 5: 2-dimensional experiments: 500 repetitions on estimation samples of size 200. Pictures depict: direct, greedy importance, regular importance, and Gibbs sampling, showing 1 standard deviation countours (dots are sample points, vertical lines are weights).

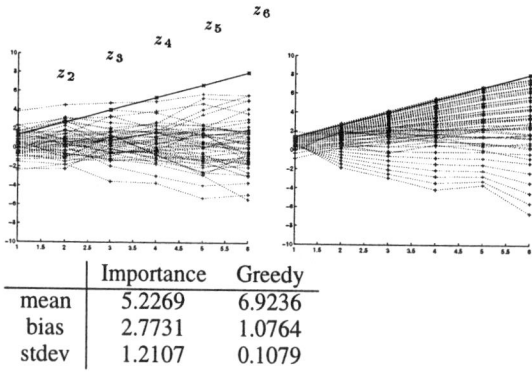

Figure 6: A 6-dimensional experiment: 500 repetitions on estimation samples of size 200. Estimating the value of x_t given the observations $z_1, ..., z_t$. Pictures depict paths sampled by regular versus greedy importance sampling.

Bayesian model selection for Support Vector machines, Gaussian processes and other kernel classifiers

Matthias Seeger
Institute for Adaptive and Neural Computation
University of Edinburgh
5 Forrest Hill, Edinburgh EH1 2QL
seeger@dai.ed.ac.uk

Abstract

We present a variational Bayesian method for model selection over families of kernels classifiers like Support Vector machines or Gaussian processes. The algorithm needs no user interaction and is able to adapt a large number of kernel parameters to given data without having to sacrifice training cases for validation. This opens the possibility to use sophisticated families of kernels in situations where the small "standard kernel" classes are clearly inappropriate. We relate the method to other work done on Gaussian processes and clarify the relation between Support Vector machines and certain Gaussian process models.

1 Introduction

Bayesian techniques have been widely and successfully used in the neural networks and statistics community and are appealing because of their conceptual simplicity, generality and consistency with which they solve learning problems. In this paper we present a new method for applying the Bayesian methodology to Support Vector machines. We will briefly review Gaussian Process and Support Vector classification in this section and clarify their relationship by pointing out the common roots. Although we focus on classification here, it is straightforward to apply the methods to regression problems as well. In section 2 we introduce our algorithm and show relations to existing methods. Finally, we present experimental results in section 3 and close with a discussion in section 4.

Let X be a measure space (e.g. $X = \mathbb{R}^d$) and $D = (\mathcal{X}, t) = \{(x_1, t_1), \ldots, (x_n, t_n)\}$, $x_i \in X$, $t_i \in \{-1, +1\}$ a noisy i.i.d. sample from a *latent function* $y : X \to \mathbb{R}$, where $P(t|y)$ denotes the noise distribution. Given further points x_* we wish to predict t_* so as to minimize the error probability $P(t|x_*, D)$, or (more difficult) to estimate this probability. *Generative Bayesian* methods attack this problem by placing a stochastic process prior $P(y(\cdot))$ over the space of latent functions and then compute *posterior* and *predictive distributions* $P(\boldsymbol{y}|D)$, $P(y_*|\boldsymbol{x}_*,D)$ as

$$P(\boldsymbol{y}|D) = \frac{P(D|\boldsymbol{y})P(\boldsymbol{y})}{P(D)},$$
$$P(y_*|D,\boldsymbol{x}_*) = \int P(y_*|\boldsymbol{y})P(\boldsymbol{y}|D)\,d\boldsymbol{y} \qquad (1)$$

where $\boldsymbol{y} = (y(\boldsymbol{x}_i))_i$, $y_* = y(\boldsymbol{x}_*)$, the likelihood $P(D|\boldsymbol{y}) = \prod_i P(t_i|y_i)$ and $P(D)$ is a normalization constant. $P(t|\boldsymbol{x}_*,D)$ can then be obtained by averaging $P(t|y_*)$ over $P(y_*|\boldsymbol{x}_*,D)$. *Gaussian process (GP)* or *spline smoothing* models use a Gaussian process prior on $y(\cdot)$ which can be seen as function of X into a set of random variables such that for each finite $X_1 \subset X$ the corresponding variables are jointly Gaussian (see [15] for an introduction). A GP is determined by a mean function[1] $\boldsymbol{x} \mapsto \mathrm{E}[\,y(\boldsymbol{x})\,]$ and a positive definite *covariance kernel* $K(\boldsymbol{x},\tilde{\boldsymbol{x}})$. *Gaussian process classification (GPC)* amounts to specifying available prior knowledge by choosing a class of kernels $K(\boldsymbol{x},\boldsymbol{x}|\boldsymbol{\theta})$, $\boldsymbol{\theta} \in \Theta$, where $\boldsymbol{\theta}$ is a vector of *hyperparameters*, and a *hyperprior* $P(\boldsymbol{\theta})$. Usually, these choices are guided by simple attributes of $y(\cdot)$ such as smoothness, trends, differentiability, but more general approaches to kernel design have also been considered [5]. For 2-class classification the most common noise distribution is the *binomial* one where $P(t|y) = \sigma(ty)$, $\sigma(u) = (1+\exp(-u))^{-1}$ the *logistic* function, and y is the *logit* $\log(P(+1|\boldsymbol{x})/P(-1|\boldsymbol{x}))$ of the target distribution. For this noise model the integral in (1) is not analytically tractable, but a range of approximative techniques based on *Laplace approximations* [16], *Markov chain Monte Carlo* [7], variational methods [2] or mean field algorithms [8] are known.

We follow [16]. The Laplace approach to GPC is to approximate the posterior $P(\boldsymbol{y}|D,\boldsymbol{\theta})$ by the Gaussian distribution $N(\hat{\boldsymbol{y}},\mathcal{H}^{-1})$ where $\hat{\boldsymbol{y}} = \mathrm{argmax}\,P(\boldsymbol{y}|D,\boldsymbol{\theta})$ is the posterior mode and $\mathcal{H} = \nabla'_\mathbf{y}\nabla_\mathbf{y}(-\log P(\boldsymbol{y}|D,\boldsymbol{\theta}))$, evaluated at $\hat{\boldsymbol{y}}$. Then it is easy to show that the predictive distribution is Gaussian with mean $\boldsymbol{k}(\boldsymbol{x}_*)'\mathcal{K}^{-1}\hat{\boldsymbol{y}}$ and variance $k_* - \boldsymbol{k}(\boldsymbol{x}_*)'\mathcal{K}^{-1}\boldsymbol{k}(\boldsymbol{x}_*)$ where $\mathcal{K}$ is the covariance matrix $(K(\boldsymbol{x}_i,\boldsymbol{x}_j))_{ij}$, $\boldsymbol{k}(\cdot) = (K(\boldsymbol{x}_i,\cdot))_i$, $k_* = K(\boldsymbol{x}_*,\boldsymbol{x}_*)$ and the prime denotes transposition. The final discriminant is therefore a linear combination of the $K(\boldsymbol{x}_i,\cdot)$.

The *discriminative* approach to the prediction problem is to choose a *loss function* $g(t,y)$, being an approximation to the *misclassification loss*[2] $I_{\{ty \le 0\}}$ and then to search for a discriminant $y(\cdot)$ which minimizes $\mathrm{E}[\,g(t,y(\boldsymbol{x}_*))\,]$ for the points $\boldsymbol{x}_*$ of interest (see [14]). *Support Vector classification (SVC)* uses the ε-insensitive loss (SVC loss) $g(t,y) = [1-ty]_+$, $[u]_+ = uI_{\{u \ge 0\}}$ which is an upper bound on the misclassification loss, and a *reproducing kernel Hilbert space (RKHS)* with kernel $K(\boldsymbol{x},\tilde{\boldsymbol{x}}|\boldsymbol{\theta})$ as hypothesis space for $y(\cdot)$. Indeed, Support Vector models and the Laplace method for Gaussian processes are special cases of *spline smoothing* models in RKHS where the aim is to minimize the functional

$$\sum_{i=1}^n g(t_i,y_i) + \lambda\|y(\cdot)\|_K^2 \qquad (2)$$

where $\|\cdot\|_K$ denotes the norm of the RKHS. It can be shown that the minimizer of (2) can be written as $\boldsymbol{k}(\cdot)'\mathcal{K}^{-1}\hat{\boldsymbol{y}}$ where $\hat{\boldsymbol{y}}$ maximizes

$$-\sum_{i=1}^n g(t_i,y_i) - \lambda \boldsymbol{y}'\mathcal{K}^{-1}\boldsymbol{y}. \qquad (3)$$

All these facts can be found in [13]. Now (3) is, up to terms not depending on $\boldsymbol{y}$, the log posterior in the above GP framework if we choose $g(t,y) = -\log P(t|y)$ and

---
[1] W.l.o.g. we only consider GPs with mean function 0 in what follows.
[2] I_A denotes the indicator function of the set $A \subset \mathbb{R}$.

absorb λ into $\boldsymbol{\theta}$. For the SVC loss, (3) can be transformed into a dual problem via $\boldsymbol{y} = \mathcal{K}\boldsymbol{\alpha}$, where $\boldsymbol{\alpha}$ is a vector of dual variables, which can be efficiently solved using quadratic programming techniques. [12] is an excellent reference.

Note that the SVC loss cannot be written as the negative log of a noise distribution, so we cannot reduce SVC to a special case of a Gaussian process classification model. Although a generative model for SVC is given in [11], it is easier and less problematic to regard SVC as efficient approximation to a proper Gaussian process model. Various such models have been proposed (see [8],[4]). In this work, we simply normalize the SVC loss pointwise, i.e. use a Gaussian process model with the *normalized SVC loss* $g(t, y) = [1 - ty]_+ + \log Z(y)$, $Z(y) = \exp(-[1 - y]_+) + \exp(-[1 + y]_+)$. Note that $g(t, y)$ is a close approximation of the (unnormalized) SVC loss. The reader might miss the SVM *bias parameter* which we dropped here for clarity, but it is straightforward to apply this *semiparametric* extension to GP models too[3].

2 A variational method for kernel classification

The real Bayesian way to deal with the hyperparameters $\boldsymbol{\theta}$ is to average $P(y_*|\boldsymbol{x}_*, D, \boldsymbol{\theta})$ over the posterior $P(\boldsymbol{\theta}|D)$ in order to obtain the predictive distribution $P(y_*|\boldsymbol{x}_*, D)$. This can be approximated by Markov chain Monte Carlo methods [7], [16] or simply by $P(y_*|\boldsymbol{x}_*, D, \hat{\boldsymbol{\theta}})$, $\hat{\boldsymbol{\theta}} = \arg\max P(\boldsymbol{\theta}|D)$. The latter approach, called *maximum a-posteriori (MAP)*, can be justified in the limit of large n and often works well in practice. The basic challenge of MAP is to calculate the *evidence*

$$P(D|\boldsymbol{\theta}) = \int P(D, \boldsymbol{y}|\boldsymbol{\theta})\, d\boldsymbol{y} = \int \exp\left(-\sum_{i=1}^n g(t_i, y_i)\right) N(\boldsymbol{y}|\mathbf{0}, \mathcal{K}(\boldsymbol{\theta}))\, d\boldsymbol{y}. \quad (4)$$

Our plan is to attack (4) by a *variational* approach. Let $\tilde{P}$ be a density from a model class Γ chosen to approximate the posterior $P(\boldsymbol{y}|D, \boldsymbol{\theta})$. Then:

$$\begin{aligned}-\log P(D|\boldsymbol{\theta}) &= -\int \tilde{P}(\boldsymbol{y}) \log\left(\frac{P(D, \boldsymbol{y}|\boldsymbol{\theta})\tilde{P}(\boldsymbol{y})}{P(\boldsymbol{y}|D, \boldsymbol{\theta})\tilde{P}(\boldsymbol{y})}\right) d\boldsymbol{y} \\ &= F(\tilde{P}, \boldsymbol{\theta}) - \int \tilde{P}(\boldsymbol{y}) \log\left(\frac{\tilde{P}(\boldsymbol{y})}{P(\boldsymbol{y}|D, \boldsymbol{\theta})}\right) d\boldsymbol{y}\end{aligned} \quad (5)$$

where we call $F(\tilde{P}, \boldsymbol{\theta}) = \mathrm{E}_{\tilde{P}}[-\log P(D, \boldsymbol{y}|\boldsymbol{\theta})] + \mathrm{E}_{\tilde{P}}[\log \tilde{P}(\boldsymbol{y})]$ the *variational free energy*. The second term in (5) is the well-known *Kullback-Leibler divergence* between $\tilde{P}$ and the posterior which is nonnegative and equals zero iff $\tilde{P}(\boldsymbol{y}) = P(\boldsymbol{y}|D, \boldsymbol{\theta})$ almost everywhere with respect to the distribution $\tilde{P}$. Thus, F is an upper bound on $-\log P(D|\boldsymbol{\theta})$, and changing $(\tilde{P}, \boldsymbol{\theta})$ to decrease F enlarges the evidence or decreases the divergence between the posterior and its approximation, both being favourable. This idea has been introduced in [3] as *ensemble learning*[4] and has been successfully applied to MLPs [1]. The latter work also introduced the model class Γ we use here, namely the class of Gaussians with mean $\boldsymbol{\mu}$ and *factor-analyzed* covariance $\Sigma = \mathcal{D} + \sum_{j=1}^M \boldsymbol{c}_j \boldsymbol{c}_j'$, $\mathcal{D}$ diagonal with positive elements[5]. Hinton and

---
[3]This is the "random effects model with improper prior" of [13], p.19, and works by placing a flat improper prior on the bias parameter.
[4]We average different discriminants (given by $\boldsymbol{y}$) over the ensemble $\tilde{P}$.
[5]Although there is no danger of overfitting, the use of full covariances would render the optimization more difficult, time and memory consuming.

van Camp [3] used diagonal covariances which would be $M = 0$ in our setting. By choosing a small M, we are able to track the most important correlations between the components in the posterior using $O(Mn)$ parameters to represent $\tilde{P}$.

Having agreed on Γ, the criterion F and its gradients with respect to θ and the parameters of $\tilde{P}$ can easily and efficiently be computed except for the generic term

$$\mathrm{E}_{\tilde{P}}\left[\sum_{i=1}^{n} g(t_i, y_i)\right], \qquad (6)$$

a sum of one-dimensional Gaussian expectations which are, depending on the actual g, either analytically tractable or can be approximated using a quadrature algorithm. For example, the expectation for the normalized SVC loss can be decomposed into expectations over the (unnormalized) SVC loss and over $\log Z(y)$ (see end of section 1). While the former can be computed analytically, the latter expectation can be handled by replacing $\log Z(y)$ by a piecewise defined tight bound such that the integral can be solved analytically. For the GPC loss (6) cannot be solved analytically and was in our experiments approximated by Gaussian quadrature.

We can optimize F using a nested loop algorithm as follows. In the inner loop we run an optimizer to minimize F w.r.t. $\tilde{P}$ for fixed θ. We used a *conjugate gradients* optimizer since the number of parameters of $\tilde{P}$ is rather large. The outer loop is an optimizer minimizing F w.r.t. θ, and we chose a *Quasi-Newton* method here since the dimension of Θ is usually rather small and gradients w.r.t. θ are costly to evaluate.

We can use the resulting minimizer $(\tilde{P}, \hat{\theta})$ of F in two different ways. The most natural is to discard $\tilde{P}$, plug $\hat{\theta}$ into the original architecture and predict using the mode of $P(y|D, \hat{\theta})$ as an approximation to the true posterior mode, benefitting from a kernel now adapted to the given data. This is particularly interesting for Support Vector machines due to the sparseness of the final kernel expansion (typically only a small fraction of the components in the weight vector $\mathcal{K}^{-1}\hat{y}$ is non-zero, the corresponding datapoints are termed *Support Vectors*) which allows very efficient predictions for a large number of test points. However, we can also retain $\tilde{P}$ and use it as a Gaussian approximation of the posterior $P(y|D, \hat{\theta})$. Doing so, we can use the variance of the approximative predictive distribution $P(y_*|x_*, D)$ to derive *error bars* for our predictions, although the interpretation of these figures is somewhat complicated in the case of kernel discriminants like SVM whose loss function does not correspond to a noise distribution.

2.1 Relations to other methods

Let us have a look at alternative ways to maximize (4). If the loss $g(t, y)$ is twice differentiable everywhere, progress can be made by replacing g by its second order Taylor expansion around the mode of the integrand. This is known as *Laplace approximation* and is used in [16] to maximize (4) approximately. However, this technique cannot be used for nondifferentiable losses of the ε-insensitive type[6].

Nevertheless, for the SVC loss the evidence (4) can be approximated in a Laplace-like fashion [11], and it will be interesting to compare the results of this work with ours. This approximation can be evaluated very efficiently, but is not continuous[7]

---

[6]The nondifferentiabilities cannot be ignored since with probability one a nonzero number of the $\hat{y}_i$ sit exactly at these margin locations.

[7]Although continuity can be accomplished by a further modification, see [11].

w.r.t. $\boldsymbol{\theta}$ and difficult to optimize if the dimension of Θ is not small. Opper and Winther [8] use mean field ideas to derive an approximate leave-one-out test error estimator which can be quickly evaluated, but suffers from the typical noisiness of cross-validation scores. Kwok [6] applies the evidence framework to Support Vector machines, but the technique seems to be restricted to kernels with a finite eigenfunction expansion (see [13] for details).

It is interesting to compare our variational method to the Laplace method of [16] and the variational technique of [2]. Let $g(t,y)$ be differentiable and suppose that for given $\boldsymbol{\theta}$ we restrict ourselves to approximate (6) by replacing $g(t_i, y_i)$ by the expansion

$$g(t_i, \mu_i) + \frac{\partial g}{\partial y}(t_i, \mu_i)(y_i - \mu_i) + \frac{1}{2}\frac{\partial^2 g}{\partial y^2}(t_i, \hat{y}_i)(y_i - \mu_i)^2, \qquad (7)$$

where $\hat{y}$ is the posterior mean. This will change the criterion F to F_{approx}, say. Then it is easy to show that the Gaussian approximation to the posterior employed by the Laplace method, namely $N(\hat{y}, (\mathcal{K}^{-1}+\mathcal{W})^{-1})$, $\mathcal{W} = \text{diag}(\sigma(\hat{y}_i)(1-\sigma(\hat{y}_i)))$, minimizes F_{approx} w.r.t. $\tilde{P}$ if full covariances Σ are used, and plugging this minimizer into F_{approx} we end up with the evidence approximation which is maximized by the Laplace method. The latter is not a variational technique since the approximation (7) to the loss function is not an upper bound, and works only for differentiable loss functions. If we upper bound the loss function $g(t,y)$ by a quadratic polynomial and add the variational parameters of this bound to the parameters of $\tilde{P}$, our method becomes broadly similar to the lower bound algorithm of [2]. Indeed, since for fixed variational parameters of the polynomials we can easily solve for the mean and covariance of $\tilde{P}$, the former parameters are the only essential ones. However, the quadratic upper bound is poor for functions like the SVC loss, and in these cases our bound is expected to be tighter.

3 Experiments

We tested our variational algorithm on a number of datasets from the *UCI machine learning repository* and the *DELVE archive* of the University of Toronto[8]: *Leptograpsus crabs*, *Pima Indian diabetes*, *Wisconsin Breast Cancer*, *Ringnorm*, *Twonorm* and *Waveform* (class 1 against 2). Descriptions may be found on the web. In each case we normalized the whole set to zero mean, unit variance in all input columns, picked a training set at random and used the rest for testing. We chose (for $X = \mathbb{R}^d$) the well-known *squared-exponential kernel* (see [15]):

$$K(\boldsymbol{x}, \tilde{\boldsymbol{x}}|\boldsymbol{\theta}) = C\left(\exp\left(-\frac{1}{2d}\sum_{i=1}^{d} w_i(x_i - \tilde{x}_i)^2\right) + v\right), \quad \boldsymbol{\theta} = ((w_i)_i', C, v)'. \qquad (8)$$

All parameters are constrained to be positive, so we chose the representation $\theta_i = \nu_i^2$. We did not use a prior on $\boldsymbol{\theta}$ (see comment at end of this section). For comparison we trained a Gaussian Process classifier with the Laplace method (also without hyperprior) and a Support Vector machine using 10-fold cross-validation to select the free parameters. In the latter case we constrained the scale parameters w_i to be equal (it is infeasible to adapt $d+2$ hyperparameters to the data using cross-validation) and dropped the v parameter while allowing for a bias parameter. As mentioned above, within the variational method we can use the posterior mode $\hat{y}$

---

[8]See http://www.cs.utoronto.ca/~delve and http://www.ics.uci.edu/~mlearn/MLRepository.html.

Name	train size	test size	Var. GP $\hat{y}$	μ	GP Lapl.	Var. SVM $\hat{y}$	μ	SVM 10-CV	Lin. discr.
crabs	80	120	3	4	4	4	4	4	3
pima	200	332	66	66	68	64	66	67	67
wdbc	300	269	11	11	8	10	10	9	19
twonorm	300	7100	233	224	297	260	223	163	207
ringnorm	400	7000	119	124	184	129	126	160	1763
waveform	800	2504	206	204	221	211	206	197	220

Table 1: Number of test errors for various methods.

as well as the mean μ of $\tilde{P}$ for prediction, and we tested both methods. Error bars were not computed. The baseline method was a linear discriminant trained to minimize the squared error. Table 1 shows the test errors the different methods attained.

These results show that the new algorithm performs equally well as the other methods we considered. They have of course to be regarded in combination with how much effort was necessary to produce them. It took us almost a whole day and a lot of user interactions to do the cross-validation model selection. The rule-of-thumb that a lot of Support Vectors at the upper bound indicate too large a parameter C in (8) failed for at least two of these sets, so we had to start with very coarse grids and sweep through several stages of refinement.

An effect known as *automatic relevance determination (ARD)* (see [7]) can be nicely observed on some of the datasets, by monitoring the length scale parameters w_i in (8). Indeed, our variational SVC algorithm almost completely ignored (by driving their length scales to very small values) 3 of the 5 dimensions in "crabs", 2 of 7 in "pima" and 3 of 21 in "waveform". On "wdbc", it detected dimension 24 as particularly important with regard to separation, all this in harmony with the GP Laplace method. Thus, a sensible parameterized kernel family together with a method of the Bayesian kind allows us to gain additional important information from a dataset which might be used to improve the experimental design.

Results of experiments with the methods tested above and hyperpriors as well as a more detailed analysis of the experiments can be found in [9].

4 Discussion

We have shown how to perform model selection for Support Vector machines using approximative Bayesian variational techniques. Our method is applicable to a wide range of loss functions and is able to adapt a large number of hyperparameters to given data. This allows for the use of sophisticated kernels and Bayesian techniques like *automatic relevance determination* (see [7]) which is not possible using other common model selection criteria like *cross-validation*. Since our method is fully automatic, it is easy for non-experts to use[9], and as the evidence is computed on the training set, no training data has to be sacrificed for validation. We refer to [9] where the topics of this paper are investigated in much greater detail.

A pressing issue is the unfortunate scaling of the method with the training set

---

[9]As an aside, this opens the possibility of comparing SVMs against other fully-automatic methods within the *DELVE* project (see section 3).

size n which is currently $O(n^3)$[10]. We are currently exploring the applicability of the powerful approximations of [10] which might bring us very much closer to the desired $O(n^2)$ scaling (see also [2]). Another interesting issue would be to connect our method with the work of [5] who use generative models to derive kernels in situations where the "standard kernels" are not applicable or not reasonable.

Acknowledgments

We thank Chris Williams, Amos Storkey, Peter Sollich and Carl Rasmussen for helpful and inspiring discussions. This work was partially funded by a scholarship of the *Dr. Erich Müller foundation*. We are grateful to the Division of Informatics for supporting our visit in Edinburgh, and to Chris Williams for making it possible.

References

[1] David Barber and Christopher Bishop. Ensemble learning for multi-layer networks. In *Advances in NIPS*, number 10, pages 395–401. MIT Press, 1997.

[2] Mark N. Gibbs. *Bayesian Gaussian Processes for Regression and Classification*. PhD thesis, University of Cambridge, 1997.

[3] Geoffrey E. Hinton and D. Van Camp. Keeping neural networks simple by minimizing the description length of the weights. In *Proceedings of the 6th annual conference on computational learning theory*, pages 5–13, 1993.

[4] Tommi Jaakkola, Marina Meila, and Tony Jebara. Maximum entropy discrimination. In *Advances in NIPS*, number 13. MIT Press, 1999.

[5] Tommi S. Jaakkola and David Haussler. Exploiting generative models in discriminative classifiers. In *Advances in NIPS*, number 11, 1998.

[6] James Tin-Tau Kwok. Integrating the evidence framework and the Support Vector machine. Submitted to ESANN 99, 1999.

[7] Radford M. Neal. Monte Carlo implementation of Gaussian process models for Bayesian classification and regression. Technical Report 9702, Department of Statistics, University of Toronto, January 1997.

[8] Manfred Opper and Ole Winther. GP classification and SVM: Mean field results and leave-one-out estimator. In *Advances in Large Margin Classifiers*. MIT Press, 1999.

[9] Matthias Seeger. Bayesian methods for Support Vector machines and Gaussian processes. Master's thesis, University of Karlsruhe, Germany, 1999. Available at http://www.dai.ed.ac.uk/~seeger.

[10] John Skilling. *Maximum entropy and Bayesian methods*. Cambridge University Press, 1988.

[11] Peter Sollich. Probabilistic methods for Support Vector machines. In *Advances in NIPS*, number 13. MIT Press, 1999.

[12] Vladimir N. Vapnik. *Statistical Learning Theory*. Wiley, 1998.

[13] Grace Wahba. *Spline Models for Observational Data*. CBMS-NSF Regional Conference Series. SIAM, 1990.

[14] Grace Wahba. Support Vector machines, reproducing kernel Hilbert spaces and the randomized GACV. Technical Report 984, University of Wisconsin, 1997.

[15] Christopher K. I. Williams. Prediction with Gaussian processes: From linear regression to linear prediction and beyond. In M. I. Jordan, editor, *Learning in Graphical Models*. Kluwer, 1997.

[16] Christopher K.I. Williams and David Barber. Bayesian classification with Gaussian processes. *IEEE Trans. PAMI*, 20(12):1342–1351, 1998.

---

[10] The running time is essentially the same as that of the Laplace method, thus being comparable to the fastest known Bayesian GP algorithm.

Leveraged Vector Machines

Yoram Singer
Hebrew University
singer@cs.huji.ac.il

Abstract

We describe an iterative algorithm for building vector machines used in classification tasks. The algorithm builds on ideas from support vector machines, boosting, and generalized additive models. The algorithm can be used with various continuously differential functions that bound the discrete (0-1) classification loss and is very simple to implement. We test the proposed algorithm with two different loss functions on synthetic and natural data. We also describe a norm-penalized version of the algorithm for the exponential loss function used in AdaBoost. The performance of the algorithm on natural data is comparable to support vector machines while typically its running time is shorter than of SVM.

1 Introduction

Support vector machines (SVM) [1, 13] and boosting [10, 3, 4, 11] are highly popular and effective methods for constructing linear classifiers. The theoretical basis for SVMs stems from Vapnik's seminal on learning and generalization [12] and has proved to be of great practical usage. The first boosting algorithms [10, 3], on the other hand, were developed to answer certain fundamental questions about PAC-learnability [6]. While mathematically beautiful, these algorithms were rather impractical. Later, Freund and Schapire [4] developed the AdaBoost algorithm, which proved to be a practically useful meta-learning algorithm. AdaBoost works by making repeated calls to a *weak learner*. On each call the weak learner generates a single *weak hypothesis*, and these weak hypotheses are combined into an ensemble called *strong hypothesis*. Recently, Schapire and Singer [11] studied a simple generalization of AdaBoost in which a weak-hypothesis can assign a real-valued *confidence* to each prediction. Even more recently, Friedman, Hastie, and Tibshirani [5] presented an alternative view of boosting from a statistical point of view and also described a new family of algorithms for constructing generalized additive models of base learners in a similar fashion to AdaBoost. The work of Friedman, Hastie, and Tibshirani generated lots of attention and motivated research in classification algorithms that employ various loss functions [8, 7].

In this work we combine ideas from the research mentioned above and devise an alternative approach to construct vector machines for classification. As in SVM, the base predictors that we use are Mercer kernels. The value of a kernel evaluated at an input pattern, i.e., the dot-product between two instances embedded in a high-dimensional space, is viewed as a real-valued prediction. We describe a simple extension to additive models in which the prediction of a base-learner is a linear transformation of a given kernel. We then describe an iterative algorithm that greedily adds kernels. We derive our algorithm using the exponential loss function used in AdaBoost and the loss function used by Friedman, Hastie, and Tibshirani [5] in "LogitBoost". For brevity we call the resulting classifiers boosted vector machines (BVM) and logistic vector machines (LVM). We would like to note in passing that the resulting algorithms are *not* boosting algorithms in the PAC sense. For instance, the weak-learnability assumption that the weak-learner can always find a weak-hypothesis is violated. We therefore adopt the terminology used in [2] and call the resulting classifiers *leveraged vector machines*.

The leveraging procedure we give adopts the chunking technique from SVM. After presenting the basic leveraging algorithms we compare their performance with SVM on synthetic data. The experimental results show that the leveraged vector machines achieve similar performance to SVM and often the resulting vector machines are smaller than the ones obtained by SVM. The experiments also demonstrate that BVM is especially sensitive to (malicious) label noise while LVM seems to be more insensitve. We also describe a simple norm-penalized extension of BVM that provides a partial solution to overfitting in the p-resence of noise. Finally, we give results of experiments performed with natural data from the UCI repository and conclude.

2 Preliminaries

Let $S = \langle (x_1, y_1), \ldots, (x_m, y_m) \rangle$ be a sequence of training examples where each *instance* x_i belongs to a *domain* or *instance space* $\mathcal{X}$, and each *label* y_i is in $\{-1, +1\}$. (The methods described in this paper to build vector machines and SVMs can be extended to solve multiclass problems using, for instance, error correcting output coding. Such methods are beyond the scope of this paper and will be discussed elsewhere). For convenience, we will use $\tilde{y}_i$ to denote $(y_i + 1)/2 \in \{0, 1\}$.

As is boosting, we assume access to a *weak* or *base* learning algorithm which accepts as input a *weighted* sequence of training examples S. Given such input, the weak learner computes a weak (or base) *hypothesis* h. In general, h has the form $h : \mathcal{X} \to \mathbb{R}$. We interpret the sign of $h(x)$ as the predicted label (-1 or $+1$) to be assigned to instance x, and the magnitude $|h(x)|$ as the "confidence" in this prediction.

To build vector machines we use the notion of confidence-rated predictions, take for base hypotheses sample-based Mercer kernels [13], and define the confidence (i.e., the magnitude of prediction) of a base learner to be the value of its dot-product with another instance. The sign of the prediction is set to be the label of the corresponding instance. Formally, for each base hypothesis h there exist $(x_j, y_j) \in S$ such that $h(x) = y_j K(x_j, x)$ and $K(u, v)$ defines an inner product in a feature space: $K(u, v) = \sum_{k=1}^{\infty} a_k \psi_k(u) \psi_k(v)$. We denote the function induced by an instance label pair (x_j, y_j) with a kernel K by $\phi_j(x) = y_j K(x_j, x)$. Our goal is to find a classifier $f(x)$, called a strong hypothesis in the context of boosting algorithms, of the form $f(x) = \sum_{t=1}^{T} \alpha_t h_t(x) + \beta$, such that the signs of the predictions of the classifier should agree, as much as possible, with the labels of the training instances.

The leverage algorithm we describe maintains a distribution D over $\{1, \ldots, m\}$, i.e., over the indices of S. This distribution is simply a vector of non-negative weights, one weight per example and is an exponential function of the classifier f which is built incrementally,

$$D(i) = \frac{1}{Z} \exp(-y_i f(x_i)) \text{ where } Z = \sum_{i=1}^{m} \exp(-y_i f(x_i)). \quad (1)$$

For a random function g of the input instances and the labels, we denote the *sample* expectation of g according to D by $\bar{E}_D(g) = \sum_{i=1}^{m} D(i) g(x_i, y_i)$. We also use this notation to denote the expectation of matrices of random functions. We will convert a confidence-rated classifier f into a randomized predictor by using the soft-max function and denote it by $P(x_i)$ where

$$P(x_i) = \frac{\exp(f(x_i))}{\exp(f(x_i)) + \exp(-f(x_i))} = \frac{1}{1 + \exp(-2f(x_i))}. \quad (2)$$

3 The leveraging algorithm

The basic procedure to construct leveraged vector machines builds on ideas from [11, 5] by extending the prediction to be a linear function of the base classifiers. The algorithm works in rounds, constructing a new classifier f_t from the previous one f_{t-1} by adding a new base hypothesis h_t to the current classifier, f_t. Denoting by D_t and P_{t+1} the distribution and probability given by Eqn. (1) and Eqn. (2) using f_t and f_{t+1}, the algorithm attempts to minimize either the exponential function that arise in AdaBoost:

$$\begin{aligned} Z &= \sum_{i=1}^{m} \exp\left(-y_i f_t(x_i)\right) = \sum_{i=1}^{m} \exp\left(-y_i(f_{t-1}(x_i) + \alpha_t h_t(x_i) + \beta_t)\right) \\ &\sim \sum_{i=1}^{m} D_t(i) \exp\left(-y_i(\alpha_t h_t(x_i) + \beta_t)\right), \end{aligned} \quad (3)$$

or the logistic loss function:

$$\begin{aligned} L &= \sum_{i=1}^{m} \log\left(1 + \exp\left(-2y_i f_t(x_i)\right)\right) \quad (4) \\ &= \sum_{i=1}^{m} \log\left(1 + \exp\left(-2y_i(f_{t-1}(x_i) + \alpha_t h_t(x_i) + \beta_t)\right)\right) \\ &= -\sum_{i=1}^{m} \left(\tilde{y}_i \log(P_{t+1}(x_i)) + (1 - \tilde{y}_i) \log(1 - P_{t+1}(x_i))\right). \quad (5) \end{aligned}$$

We initialize $f_0(x)$ to be zero everywhere and run the procedure for a predefined number of rounds T. The final classifier is therefore $f_T(x) = \sum_{t=1}^{T}(\alpha_t h_t(x) + \beta_t) = \beta + \sum_{t=1}^{T} \alpha_t h_t(x)$ where $\beta = \sum_t \beta_t$. We would like to note parenthetically that it is possible to use other loss functions that bound the 0-1 (classification) loss (see for instance [8]). Here we focus on the above loss functions, L and Z. Fixing f_{t-1} and h_t, these functions are convex in α_t and β_t which guarantees, under mild conditions (details omitted due to lack of space), the uniqueness of α_t and β_t.

On each round we look for the current base hypothesis h_t that will reduce the loss function (Z or L) the most. As discussed before, each input instance x_j defines a function $\phi_j(x)$ and is a candidate for $h_t(x)$. In general, there is no close form solution for Eqn. (3) and (5) and finding α and β for each possible input instance is time consuming. We therefore use a quadratic approximation for the loss functions. Using the quadratic approximation, for each ϕ_j we can find α and β analytically and calculate the reduction in the loss function. Let $\nabla Z = (\frac{\partial Z}{\partial \alpha}, \frac{\partial Z}{\partial \beta})^T$ and $\nabla L = (\frac{\partial L}{\partial \alpha}, \frac{\partial L}{\partial \beta})^T$ be the column vectors of the partial derivatives of Z and L w.r.t α and β (fixing f_{t-1} and h_t). Similarly, let $\nabla^2 Z$ and $\nabla^2 L$ be the 2×2 matrices of second order derivatives of Z and L with respect to α and β. Then, quadratic approximation yields that $(\alpha, \beta)^T = (\nabla^2 Z)^{-1} \nabla Z$ and $(\alpha, \beta)^T = (\nabla^2 L)^{-1} \nabla L$. On each round t we maintain a distribution D_t which is defined from f_t as given by Eqn. (1) and conditional class probability estimates $P_t(x_i)$ as given by Eqn. (2). Solving the linear equation above for α and β for each possible instance is done by setting $h_t(x) = \phi_j(x)$, we get for Z

$$\begin{pmatrix} \alpha_j \\ \beta_j \end{pmatrix} = \left[E_{D_t} \begin{pmatrix} \phi_j^2 & \phi_j \\ \phi_j & 1 \end{pmatrix} \right]^{-1} E_{D_t}\left[y \begin{pmatrix} \phi_j \\ 1 \end{pmatrix} \right], \quad (6)$$

and for L

$$\begin{pmatrix} \alpha_j \\ \beta_j \end{pmatrix} = \frac{1}{2} \left[E_{D_t}\left[P(1-P) \begin{pmatrix} \phi_j^2 & \phi_j \\ \phi_j & 1 \end{pmatrix} \right] \right]^{-1} E_{D_t}\left[(\tilde{y} - P) \begin{pmatrix} \phi_j \\ 1 \end{pmatrix} \right]. \quad (7)$$

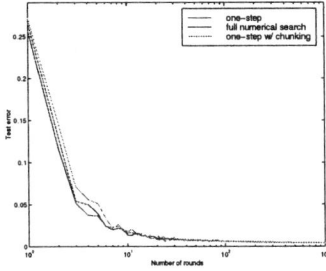

Figure 1: Comparison of the test error as a function of number of leveraging rounds when using full numerical search for α and β, a "one-step" numerical search based on a quadratic approximation of the loss function, and a one-step search with chunking of the instances.

Note that the equations above share much in common and require, after pre-computing $P(x_i)$, the same amount of computation time.

After calculating the value of α and β for each instance (x_j, y_j), we simply evaluate the corresponding value of the loss function, choose the instance (x_{j^*}, y_{j^*}) that attains the minimal loss, and set $h_t = \phi_{j^*}$. We then numerically search for the optimal value of α and β by iterating Eqn. (6) or Eqn. (7) and summing the values into α_t and β_t. We would like to note that typically two or three iterations suffice and we can save time by using the value of α and β found using the quadratic approximation without a full numerical search for the optimal value of α and β. (See also Fig. 1.) We repeat this process for T rounds or until no instance can serve as a base hypothesis. We note that the same instance can be chosen more than once, although not in consecutive iterations, and typically only a small fraction of the instances is actually used in building f. Roughly speaking, these instances are the "support patterns" of the leveraged machines although they are not necessarily the geometric support patterns.

As in SVMs, in order to make the search for a base hypothesis efficient we pre-compute and store $K(x, x')$ for all pairs $x \neq x'$ from S. Storing these values require $|S|^2$ space, which might be prohibited in large problems. To save space, we employ the idea of chunking used in SVM. We partition S into r blocks $S_1, S_2, \ldots, S_r$ of about the same size. We divide the iterations into sub-groups such that all iterations belonging to the ith sub-group use and evaluate kernels based on instances from the ith block only. When switching to a new block k we need to compute the values $K(x, x')$ for $x \in S$ and $x' \in S_k$. This division into blocks might be more expensive since we typically use each block of instances more than once. However, the storage of the kernel values can be done in place and we thus save a factor of r in memory requirements. In practice we found that chunking does not hurt the performance. In Fig. 1 we show the test error as a function of number of rounds when using (a) full numerical search to determine α and β on each round, (b) using the quadratic approximation ("one-step") to find α and β, and (c) using quadratic approximation with chunking. The number of instances in the experiment is 1000, each block for chunking is of size 100, and we switch to a different block every 100 iterations. (Further description of the data is given in the next section.) In this example, after 10 iterations, there is virtually no difference in the performance of the different schemes.

4 Experiments with synthetic data

In this section we describe experiments with synthetic data comparing different aspects of leveraged vector machines to SVMs. The original instance space is two dimensional where the positive class includes all points inside a circle of radius R, i.e., an instance $(u_1, u_2) \in \mathbb{R}^2$ is labeled $+1$ iff $u_1^2 + u_2^2 \leq R$. The instances were picked at random according to a zero mean unit variance normal distribution and R was set such exactly half of the instances belong to the positive class. In all the experiments described in this section we generated 10 groups of training and test sets each of which includes 1000 train and test examples. Overall, there are $10,000$ training examples and $10,000$ test examples. The

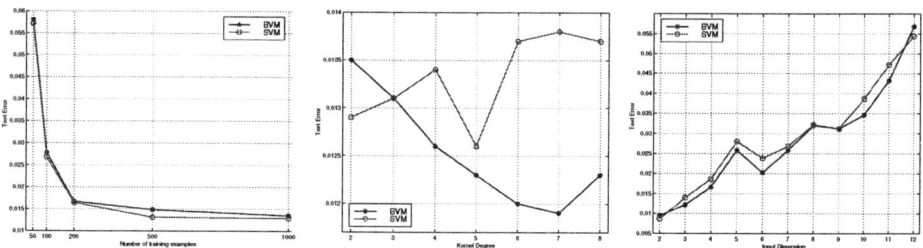

Figure 2: Performance comparison of SVM and BVM as a function of the training data size (left), the dimension of the kernels (middle), and the number of redundant features.

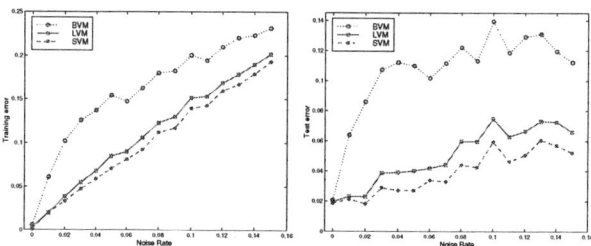

Figure 3: Train and test errors for SVM, LVM, and BVM as a function of the label noise.

average variance of the estimates of the empirical errors across experiments is about 0.2%. For SVM we set the regularization parameter, C, to 100 and used 500 iterations to build leveraged machines. In all the experiments without noise the results for BVM and LVM were practically the same. We therefore only compare BVM to SVM in Fig. 2. Unless said otherwise we used polynomials of degree two as kernels: $K(x,'x) = (x \cdot x' + 1)^2$. Hence, the data is separable in the absence of noise.

In the first experiment we tested the sensitivity to the number of training examples by omitting examples from the training data (without any modification to the test sets). On the left part of Fig. 2 we plot the test error as a function of the number of training examples. The test error of BVM is almost indistinguishable from the error of SVM and performance of both methods improves very fast as a function of training examples. Next, we compared the performance as a function of the dimension of polynomial constituting the kernel. We ran the algorithms with kernels of the form $K(x,'x) = (x \cdot x' + 1)^d$ for $d = 2, \ldots, 8$. The results are depicted in the middle plots of Fig. 2. Again, the performance of BVM and SVM is very close (note the small scale of the y axis for the test error in this experiment). To conclude the experiments with clean, realizable, data we checked the sensitivity to irrelevant features of the input. Each input instance (u_1, u_2) was augmented with random elements $u_3, \ldots, u_l$ to form an input vector of dimension l. The right hand side graphs of Fig. 2 shows the test error as a function of l for $l = 2, \ldots, 12$. Once more we see that the performance of both algorithms is very similar.

We next compared the performance of the algorithms in the presence of noise. We used kernels of dimension two and instances without redundant features. The label of each instance was flipped with probability ϵ. We ran 15 sets of experiments, for $\epsilon = 0.01, \ldots, 0.15$. As before, each set included 10 runs each of which used 1000 training examples and 1000 test examples. In Fig. 3 we show the average training error (left), and the average test error (right), for each of the algorithms. It is apparent from the graphs that BVMs built based on the exponential loss are much more sensitive to noise than SVMs and LVMs, and their generalization error degrades significantly, even for low noise rates. The generalization error of LVMs is, on the other hand, only slightly worse than the that of SVMs, although the

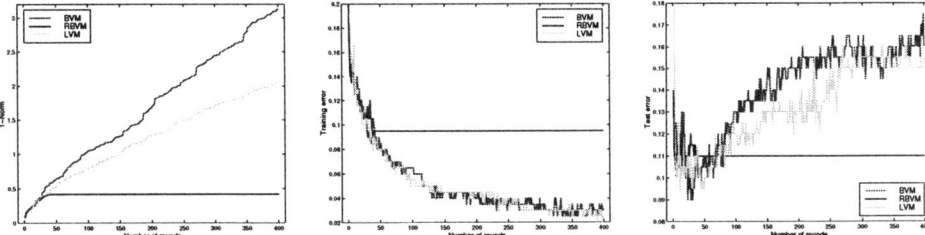

Figure 4: The training error, test error, and the cumulative L_1 norm ($\sum_{t'=1}^{t} |\alpha'_t|$) as a function of the number of leveraging iterations for LVM, BVM, and PBVM.

only algorithmic difference in constructing BVMs and LVMs is in the loss function. The fact that LVMs exhibit performance similar to SVM can be partially attributed to the fact that the asymptotic behavior of their loss functions is the same.

5 A norm-penalized version

One of the problems with boosting and the corresponding leveraging algorithm with the exponential loss described here, is that it might increase the confidence on a few instances while misclassifying many other instances, albeit with a small confidence. This often happens on late rounds, during which the distribution $D_t(i)$ is concentrated on a few examples, and the leveraging algorithm typically assigns a large weight to a weak hypothesis that does not effect most of the instances. It is therefore desired to control the complexity of the leveraged classifiers by limiting the magnitude of base hypotheses' weights. Several methods have been proposed to limit the confidence of AdaBoost, using, for instance, regularization (e.g., [9]) or "smoothing" the predictions [11]. Here we propose a norm-penalized method for BVM that is very simple to implement and maintains the convexity properties of the objective function. Following the idea Cortes and Vapnik's of SVMs in the non-separable case [1] we add the following penalization term: $\gamma_0 \exp \left(\sum_{t=1}^{T} |\alpha_t|^p \right)$. Simple algebraic manipulation implies that the objective function at the tth round for BVMs with the penalization term above is,

$$\tilde{Z}_t = \sum_{i=1}^{m} D_t(i) \exp\left(-y_i(\alpha_t h_t(x_i) + \beta_t)\right) + \gamma_t \exp(|\alpha_t|^p) . \qquad (8)$$

It is also easy to show that the penalty parameter should be updated after each round is: $\gamma_t = \gamma_{t-1} \exp(|\alpha_{t-1}|^p)/Z_{t-1}$. Since $Z_t < 1$, unless there is no kernel function better than random, γ_t typically increases as a function of t, forcing more and more the new weights to be small. Note that Eqn. (8) implies that the search for a base predictor h_t and weights α_t, β_t on each round can still be done independently of previous rounds by maintaining the distribution D_t and a single regularization value γ_t. The penalty term for $p = 1$ and $p = 2$ simply adds a diagonal term to the matrix of second order derivatives (Eqn. (6)) and the algorithm follows the same line (details omitted). For brevity we call the norm-penalized leveraging procedure PBVM. In Fig. 4 we plot the test error (right), training error (middle), and $\sum_t |\alpha_t|$ as functions of number of rounds for LVM, BVM, and PBVM with $p = 1$ $\gamma_0 = 0.01$. The training set in this example was made small on purpose (200 examples) and was contaminated with 5% label noise. In this very small example both LVM and BVM overfit while PBVM stops increasing the weights and finds a reasonably good classifier. The plots demonstrate that the norm-penalized version can safeguard against overfitting by preventing the weights from growing arbitrarily large, and that the effect of the penalized version is very similar to early stopping. We would like

| | #Example | SVM | LVM | BVM | RBVM | SVM | LVM | BVM | PBVM |
| Data Set | & | Size | Size | Size | Size | Error | Error | Error | Error |
(Source)	#Feature								
labor (uci)	57 : 16	12.5	13.7	16.1	13.6	**6.0**	14.0	14.0	12.0
echocard. (uci)	74 : 12	7.8	13.0	12.6	12.4	8.6	**5.7**	10.0	10.0
bridges (uci)	102 : 7	27.2	20.2	18.5	17.9	15.0	15.0	23.0	**14.0**
hepatitis (uci)	155 : 19	41.2	13.5	17.4	14.0	21.3	22.0	22.7	22.0
horse-colic (uci)	300 : 23	122.0	13.0	13.0	13.0	14.7	14.7	14.7	**13.2**
liver (uci)	345 : 6	228.6	11.3	12.8	10.7	33.8	35.6	**33.5**	35.6
ionosphere (uci)	351 : 34	63.4	58.9	67.9	59.1	13.7	**13.1**	16.9	13.7
vote (uci)	435 : 16	37.0	37.0	41.0	37.0	**4.4**	5.2	5.9	5.2
ticket1 (att)	556 : 78	48.1	84.6	89.3	82.3	8.4	**3.3**	11.5	5.1
ticket2 (att)	556 : 53	52.6	77.1	75.4	74.0	6.6	**6.4**	8.0	**6.4**
ticket3 (att)	556 : 61	46.1	76.2	77.8	73.3	6.9	**4.9**	7.6	6.7
bands (uci)	690 : 39	265.5	78.2	76.4	75.6	**32.8**	33.2	34.3	33.3
breast-wisc (uci)	699 : 9	49.3	26.5	24.4	24.0	**3.5**	3.6	4.1	4.1
pima (uci)	768 : 8	360.7	47.7	30.3	22.8	23.0	22.6	23.2	**22.1**
german (uci)	1000 : 10	485.2	89.8	96.5	87.0	**23.5**	24.0	23.8	24.1
weather (uci)	1000 : 35	562.0	52.0	52.0	52.0	25.9	**25.4**	**25.4**	**25.4**
network (att)	2600 : 35	1031.0	42.0	43.0	42.0	24.8	**21.2**	23.5	**21.2**
splice (uci)	3190 : 60	318.0	153.0	156.0	153.0	**8.0**	8.4	8.4	8.4
boa (att)	5000 : 68	637.0	183.0	178.0	160.0	41.5	**40.8**	**40.8**	41.0

Table 1: Summary of results for a collection of binary classification problems.

to note that we found experimentally that the norm-penalized version does compensate for incorrect estimates of α and β due to malicious label noise. The experimental results given in the next section show, however, that it does indeed help in preventing overfitting when the training set is small.

6 Experiments with natural data

We compared the practical performance of leveraged vector machines with SVMs on a collection of nineteen dataset from the UCI machine learning repository and AT&T networking and marketing data. For SVM we set $C = 100$. We built each of the leveraged vector machines using 500 rounds. For PBVM we used again $p = 1$ and $\gamma_0 = 0.01$. We used chunking in building the leveraged vector machines, dividing each training set into 10 blocks. For all the datasets, with the exception of "boa", we used 10-fold cross validation to calculate the test error. (The dataset "boa" has 5000 training examples and 6000 test examples.) The performance of SVM, LVM, and PBVM seem comparable. In fact, with the exception of a very few datasets the differences in error rates are *not* statistically significant. Of the three methods (SVM, PBVM, and LVM), LVM is the simplest to implement the time required to build an LVM is typically much shorter than that of an SVM. It is also worth noting that the size of leveraged machines is often smaller than the size of the corresponding SVM. Finally, it apparent that PBVMs frequently yield better results than BVMs, especially for small and medium size datasets.

References

[1] Corinna Cortes and Vladimir Vapnik. Support-vector networks. *Machine Learning*, 20(3):273–297, September 1995.
[2] N. Duffy and D. Helmbold. A geometric approach to leveraging weak learners. EuroCOLT '99.
[3] Yoav Freund. Boosting a weak learning algorithm by majority. *Information and Computation*, 121(2):256–285, 1995.
[4] Yoav Freund and Robert E. Schapire. A decision-theoretic generalization of on-line learning and an application to boosting. *Journal of Computer and System Sciences*, 55(1):119–139, August 1997.
[5] J. Friedman, T. Hastie, and R. Tibshirani. Additive logistic regression: a statistical view of boosting. Tech. Report, 1998.
[6] Michael Kearns and Leslie G. Valiant. Cryptographic limitations on learning Boolean formulae and finite automata. *Journal of the Association for Computing Machinery*, 41(1):67–95, January 1994.
[7] John D. Lafferty. Additive models, boosting and inference for generalized divergences. In *Proceedings of the Twelfth Annual Conference on Computational Learning Theory*, 1999.
[8] L. Mason, J. Baxter, P. Bartlett, and M. Frean. Doom II. Technical report, Depa. of Sys. Eng. ANU 1999.
[9] G. Rätsch, T.Onoda, and K.-R. Müller. Regularizing adaboost. In *Advances in Neural Info. Processing Systems 12*, 1998.
[10] Robert E. Schapire. The strength of weak learnability. *Machine Learning*, 5(2):197–227, 1990.
[11] Robert E. Schapire and Yoram Singer. Improved boosting algorithms using confidence-rated predictions. COLT'98.
[12] V. N. Vapnik. *Estimation of Dependences Based on Empirical Data*. Springer-Verlag, 1982.
[13] Vladimir N. Vapnik. *The Nature of Statistical Learning Theory*. Springer, 1995.

Agglomerative Information Bottleneck

Noam Slonim   Naftali Tishby*
Institute of Computer Science and
Center for Neural Computation
The Hebrew University
Jerusalem, 91904 Israel
email: {noamm,tishby}@cs.huji.ac.il

Abstract

We introduce a novel distributional clustering algorithm that maximizes the mutual information per cluster between data and given categories. This algorithm can be considered as a bottom up hard version of the recently introduced "Information Bottleneck Method". The algorithm is compared with the top-down soft version of the information bottleneck method and a relationship between the hard and soft results is established. We demonstrate the algorithm on the *20 Newsgroups* data set. For a subset of two newsgroups we achieve compression by 3 orders of magnitudes loosing only 10% of the original mutual information.

1 Introduction

The problem of self-organization of the members of a set X based on the similarity of the conditional distributions of the members of another set, Y, $\{p(y|x)\}$, was first introduced in [8] and was termed "distributional clustering".

This question was recently shown in [9] to be a special case of a much more fundamental problem: *What are the features of the variable X that are relevant for the prediction of another, relevance, variable Y?* This general problem was shown to have a natural information theoretic formulation: *Find a compressed representation of the variable X, denoted $\tilde{X}$, such that the mutual information between $\tilde{X}$ and Y, $I(\tilde{X};Y)$, is as high as possible, under a constraint on the mutual information between X and $\tilde{X}$, $I(X;\tilde{X})$*. Surprisingly, this variational problem yields an exact self-consistent equations for the conditional distributions $p(y|\tilde{x})$, $p(x|\tilde{x})$, and $p(\tilde{x})$. This constrained information optimization problem was called in [9] *The Information Bottleneck Method*.

The original approach to the solution of the resulting equations, used already in [8], was based on an analogy with the "deterministic annealing" approach to clustering (see [7]). This is a top-down hierarchical algorithm that starts from a single cluster and undergoes a cascade of cluster splits which are determined stochastically (as phase transitions) into a "soft" (fuzzy) tree of clusters.

In this paper we propose an alternative approach to the information bottleneck problem, based on a greedy bottom-up merging. It has several advantages over the top-down method. It is fully deterministic, yielding (initially) "hard clusters", for any desired number of clusters. It gives higher mutual information per-cluster than the deterministic annealing algorithm and it can be considered as the hard (zero temperature) limit of deterministic annealing, for any prescribed number of clusters. Furthermore, using the bottleneck self-consistent equations one can "soften" the resulting hard clusters and recover the deterministic annealing solutions without the need to identify the cluster splits, which is rather tricky. The main disadvantage of this method is computational, since it starts from the limit of a cluster per each member of the set X.

1.1 The information bottleneck method

The mutual information between the random variables X and Y is the symmetric functional of their joint distribution,

$$I(X;Y) = \sum_{x \in X, y \in Y} p(x,y) \log \left(\frac{p(x,y)}{p(x)p(y)} \right) = \sum_{x \in X, y \in Y} p(x)p(y|x) \log \left(\frac{p(y|x)}{p(y)} \right) . \quad (1)$$

The objective of the information bottleneck method is to extract a compact representation of the variable X, denoted here by $\tilde{X}$, with minimal loss of mutual information to another, *relevance*, variable Y. More specifically, we want to find a (possibly stochastic) map, $p(\tilde{x}|x)$, that minimizes the (lossy) coding length of X via $\tilde{X}$, $I(X;\tilde{X})$, under a constraint on the mutual information to the relevance variable $I(\tilde{X};Y)$. In other words, we want to find an efficient representation of the variable X, $\tilde{X}$, such that the predictions of Y from X through $\tilde{X}$ will be as close as possible to the direct prediction of Y from X.

As shown in [9], by introducing a positive Lagrange multiplier β to enforce the mutual information constraint, the problem amounts to minimization of the Lagrangian:

$$\mathcal{L}[p(\tilde{x}|x)] = I(X;\tilde{X}) - \beta I(\tilde{X};Y) , \quad (2)$$

with respect to $p(\tilde{x}|x)$, subject to the Markov condition $\tilde{X} \to X \to Y$ and normalization.

This minimization yields directly the following self-consistent equations for the map $p(\tilde{x}|x)$, as well as for $p(y|\tilde{x})$ and $p(\tilde{x})$:

$$\begin{cases} p(\tilde{x}|x) = \frac{p(\tilde{x})}{Z(\beta,x)} \exp\left(-\beta D_{KL}[p(y|x)\|p(y|\tilde{x})]\right) \\ p(y|\tilde{x}) = \sum_x p(y|x) p(\tilde{x}|x) \frac{p(x)}{p(\tilde{x})} \\ p(\tilde{x}) = \sum_x p(\tilde{x}|x) p(x) \end{cases} \quad (3)$$

where $Z(\beta,x)$ is a normalization function. The functional $D_{KL}[p\|q] \equiv \sum_y p(y) \log \frac{p(y)}{q(y)}$ is the Kulback-Liebler divergence [3], which *emerges* here from the variational principle. These equations can be solved by iterations that are proved to converge for any finite value of β (see [9]). The Lagrange multiplier β has the natural interpretation of inverse temperature, which suggests deterministic annealing [7] to explore the hierarchy of solutions in $\tilde{X}$, an approach taken already in [8].

The variational principle, Eq.(2), determines also the shape of the annealing process, since by changing β the mutual informations $I_X \equiv I(X;\tilde{X})$ and $I_Y \equiv I(Y;\tilde{X})$ vary such that

$$\frac{\delta I_Y}{\delta I_X} = \beta^{-1} . \quad (4)$$

Thus the optimal curve, which is analogous to the rate distortion function in information theory [3], follows a strictly concave curve in the (I_X, I_Y) plane, called the *information plane*. Deterministic annealing, at fixed number of clusters, follows such a concave curve as well, but this curve is suboptimal beyond a certain critical value of β.

Another interpretation of the bottleneck principle comes from the relation between the mutual information and Bayes classification error. This error is bounded above and below (see [6]) by an important information theoretic measure of the class conditional distributions $p(x|y_i)$, called the *Jensen-Shannon divergence*. This measure plays an important role in our context.

The Jensen-Shannon divergence of M class distributions, $p_i(x)$, each with a prior π_i, $1 \leq i \leq M$, is defined as, [6, 4].

$$JS_\pi[p_1, p_2, ..., p_M] \equiv H[\sum_{i=1}^{M} \pi_i p_i(x)] - \sum_{i=1}^{M} \pi_i H[p_i(x)] \ , \tag{5}$$

where $H[p(x)]$ is Shannon's entropy, $H[p(x)] = -\sum_x p(x) \log p(x)$. The convexity of the entropy and Jensen inequality guarantees the non-negativity of the JS-divergence.

1.2 The hard clustering limit

For any finite cardinality of the representation $|\tilde{X}| \equiv m$ the limit $\beta \to \infty$ of the Eqs.(3) induces a hard partition of X into m disjoint subsets. In this limit each member $x \in X$ belongs only to the subset $\tilde{x} \in \tilde{X}$ for which $p(y|\tilde{x})$ has the smallest $D_{KL}[p(y|x)\|p(y|\tilde{x})]$ and the probabilistic map $p(\tilde{x}|x)$ obtains the limit values 0 and 1 only.

In this paper we focus on a bottom up agglomerative algorithm for generating "good" hard partitions of X. We denote an m-partition of X, i.e. $\tilde{X}$ with cardinality m, also by $Z_m = \{z_1, z_2, ..., z_m\}$, in which case $p(\tilde{x}) = p(z_i)$. We say that Z_m is an *optimal m-partition* (not necessarily unique) of X if for every other m-partition of X, Z'_m, $I(Z_m; Y) \geq I(Z'_m; Y)$. Starting from the trivial N-partition, with $N = |X|$, we seek a sequence of merges into coarser and coarser partitions that are as close as possible to optimal.

It is easy to verify that in the $\beta \to \infty$ limit Eqs.(3) for the *m-partition distributions* are simplified as follows. Let $\tilde{x} \equiv z = \{x_1, x_2, ..., x_{|z|}\}$, $x_i \in X$ denote a specific component (i.e. cluster) of the partition Z_m, then

$$\begin{cases} p(z|x) = \begin{cases} 1 & \text{if } x \in z \\ 0 & \text{otherwise} \end{cases} \forall x \in X \\ p(y|z) = \frac{1}{p(z)} \sum_{i=1}^{|z|} p(x_i, y) \ \forall y \in Y \\ p(z) = \sum_{i=1}^{|z|} p(x_i) \end{cases} \tag{6}$$

Using these distributions one can easily evaluate the mutual information between Z_m and Y, $I(Z_m; Y)$, and between Z_m and X, $I(Z_m; X)$, using Eq.(1).

Once any hard partition, or hard clustering, is obtained one can apply "reverse annealing" and "soften" the clusters by *decreasing* β in the self-consistent equations, Eqs.(3). Using this procedure we in fact recover the stochastic map, $p(\tilde{x}|x)$, from the hard partition without the need to identify the cluster splits. We demonstrate this reverse deterministic annealing procedure in the last section.

1.3 Relation to other work

A similar agglomerative procedure, without the information theoretic framework and analysis, was recently used in [1] for text categorization on the 20 newsgroup corpus. Another approach that stems from the distributional clustering algorithm was given in [5] for clustering dyadic data. An earlier application of mutual information for semantic clustering of words was used in [2].

2 The agglomerative information bottleneck algorithm

The algorithm starts with the trivial partition into $N = |X|$ clusters or components, with each component contains exactly one element of X. At each step we *merge* several components of the current partition into a single new component in a way that locally minimizes the loss of mutual information $I(\tilde{X}; Y) = I(Z_m; Y)$.

Let Z_m be the current *m-partition* of X and $Z_{\bar{m}}$ denote the new $\bar{m}$-*partition* of X after the merge of several components of Z_m. Obviously, $\bar{m} < m$. Let $\{z_1, z_2, ..., z_k\} \subseteq Z_m$ denote the set of components to be merged, and $\bar{z}_k \in Z_{\bar{m}}$ the new component that is generated by the merge, so $\bar{m} = m - k + 1$.

To evaluate the reduction in the mutual information $I(Z_m; Y)$ due to this merge one needs the distributions that define the new $\bar{m}$-*partition*, which are determined as follows. For every $z \in Z_{\bar{m}}, z \neq \bar{z}_k$, its probability distributions $(p(z), p(y|z), p(z|x))$ remains equal to its distributions in Z_m. For the new component, $\bar{z}_k \in Z_{\bar{m}}$, we define,

$$\begin{cases} p(\bar{z}_k) = \sum_{i=1}^{k} p(z_i) \\ p(y|\bar{z}_k) = \frac{1}{p(\bar{z}_k)} \sum_{i=1}^{k} p(z_i, y) \quad \forall y \in Y \\ p(\bar{z}|x) = \begin{cases} 1 & \text{if } x \in z_i \text{ for some } 1 \leq i \leq k \\ 0 & \text{otherwise} \end{cases} \quad \forall x \in X \end{cases} \quad (7)$$

It is easy to verify that $Z_{\bar{m}}$ is indeed a valid $\bar{m}$-*partition* with proper probability distributions.

Using the same notations, for every *merge* we define the additional quantities:

- The **merge prior distribution**: defined by $\Pi_k \equiv (\pi_1, \pi_2, ..., \pi_k)$, where π_i is the prior probability of z_i in the merged subset, i.e. $\pi_i \equiv \frac{p(z_i)}{p(\bar{z}_k)}$.
- The **Y-information decrease**: the decrease in the mutual information $I(\tilde{X}; Y)$ due to a single merge, $\delta I_y(z_1, ..., z_k) \equiv I(Z_m; Y) - I(Z_{\bar{m}}; Y)$
- The **X-information decrease**: the decrease in the mutual information $I(\tilde{X}, X)$ due to a single merge, $\delta I_x(z_1, z_2, ..., z_k) \equiv I(Z_m; X) - I(Z_{\bar{m}}; X)$

Our algorithm is a *greedy* procedure, where in each step we perform "the best possible merge", i.e. merge the components $\{z_1, ..., z_k\}$ of the current *m-partition* which minimize $\delta I_y(z_1, ..., z_k)$. Since $\delta I_y(z_1, ..., z_k)$ can only increase with k (corollary 2), for a *greedy* procedure it is enough to check only the possible merging of pairs of components of the current *m-partition*. Another advantage of merging only pairs is that in this way we go through all the possible cardinalities of $Z = \tilde{X}$, from N to 1.

For a given *m-partition* $Z_m = \{z_1, z_2, ..., z_m\}$ there are $\frac{m(m-1)}{2}$ possible pairs to merge. To find "the best possible merge" one must evaluate the reduction of information $\delta I_y(z_i, z_j) = I(Z_m; Y) - I(Z_{m-1}; Y)$ for every pair in Z_m, which is $O(m \cdot |Y|)$ operations for every pair. However, using *proposition 1* we know that $\delta I_y(z_i, z_j) = (p(z_i) + p(z_j)) \cdot JS_{\Pi_2}(p(Y|z_i), p(Y|z_j))$, so the reduction in the mutual information due to the merge of z_i and z_j can be evaluated directly (looking only at this pair) in $O(|Y|)$ operations, a reduction of a factor of m in time complexity (for every merge).

Input: Empirical probability matrix $p(x,y)$, $N = |X|$, $M = |Y|$

Output: Z_m : m-partition of X into m clusters, for every $1 \leq m \leq N$

Initialization:
- Construct $Z \equiv X$
  - For $i = 1...N$
    * $z_i = \{x_i\}$
    * $p(z_i) = p(x_i)$
    * $p(y|z_i) = p(y|x_i)$ for every $y \in Y$
    * $p(z|x_j) = 1$ if $j = i$ and 0 otherwise
  - $Z = \{z_1, ..., z_N\}$
- for every $i, j = 1...N$, $i < j$, calculate
  $d_{i,j} = (p(z_i) + p(z_j)) \cdot JS_{\Pi_2}[p(y|z_i), p(y|z_j)]$
  (every $d_{i,j}$ points to the corresponding couple in Z)

Loop:
- For $t = 1...(N-1)$
  - Find $\{\alpha, \beta\} = argmin_{i,j}\{d_{i,j}\}$
    (if there are several minima choose arbitrarily between them)
  - Merge $\{z_\alpha, z_\beta\} \Rightarrow \bar{z}$:
    * $p(\bar{z}) = p(z_\alpha) + p(z_\beta)$
    * $p(y|\bar{z}) = \frac{1}{p(\bar{z})}(p(z_\alpha, y) + p(z_\beta, y))$ for every $y \in Y$
    * $p(\bar{z}|x) = 1$ if $x \in z_\alpha \cup z_\beta$ and 0 otherwise, for every $x \in X$
  - Update $Z = \{Z - \{z_\alpha, z_\beta\}\} \bigcup \{\bar{z}\}$
    (Z is now a new $(N-t)$-partition of X with $N-t$ clusters)
  - Update $d_{i,j}$ costs and pointers w.r.t. $\bar{z}$
    (only for couples contained z_α or z_β).
- **End For**

Figure 1: Pseudo-code of the algorithm.

3 Discussion

The algorithm is non-parametric, it is a simple *greedy* procedure, that depends only on the input empirical joint distribution of X and Y. The output of the algorithm is the hierarchy of all m-partitions Z_m of X for $m = N, (N-1), ..., 2, 1$. Moreover, unlike most other clustering heuristics, it has a built in measure of efficiency even for sub-optimal solutions, namely, the mutual information $I(Z_m; Y)$ which bounds the Bayes classification error. The quality measure of the obtained Z_m partition is the fraction of the mutual information between X and Y that Z_m captures. This is given by the curve $\frac{I(Z_m;Y)}{I(X;Y)}$ vs. $m = |Z_m|$. We found that empirically this curve was *concave*. If this is always true the decrease in the mutual information at every step, given by $\delta(m) \equiv \frac{I(Z_m;Y) - I(Z_{m-1};Y)}{I(X;Y)}$ can only *increase* with decreasing m. Therefore, if at some point $\delta(m)$ becomes relatively high it is an indication that we have reached a value of m with "meaningful" partition or clusters. Further merging results in substantial loss of information and thus significant reduction in the performance of the clusters as features. However, since the computational cost of the final (low m) part of the procedure is very low we can just as well complete the merging to a single cluster.

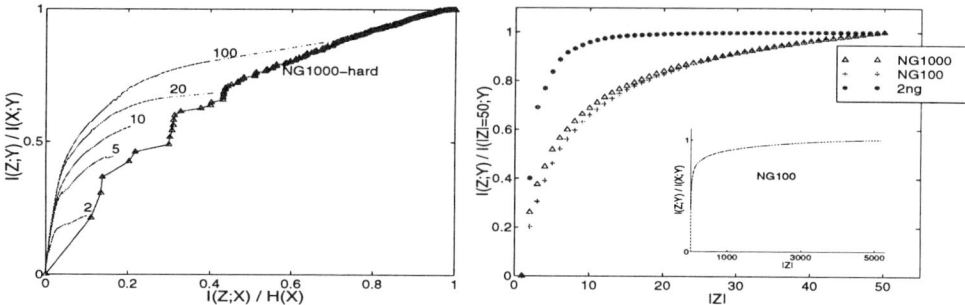

Figure 2: On the left figure the results of the agglomerative algorithm are shown in the "information plane", normalized $I(Z;Y)$ vs. normalized $I(Z;X)$ for the NG1000 dataset. It is compared to the soft version of the information bottleneck via "reverse annealing" for $|Z| = 2, 5, 10, 20, 100$ (the smooth curves on the left). For $|Z| = 20, 100$ the annealing curve is connected to the starting point by a dotted line. In this plane the hard algorithm is clearly inferior to the soft one.

On the right-hand side: $I(Z_m, Y)$ of the agglomerative algorithm is plotted vs. the cardinality of the partition m for three subsets of the newsgroup dataset. To compare the performance over the different data cardinalities we normalize $I(Z_m; Y)$ by the value of $I(Z_{50}; Y)$, thus forcing all three curves to start (and end) at the same points. The predictive information on the newsgroup for NG1000 and NG100 is very similar, while for the dichotomy dataset, 2ng, a much better prediction is possible at the same $|Z|$, as can be expected for dichotomies. The inset presents the full curve of the normalized $I(Z;Y)$ vs. $|Z|$ for NG100 data for comparison. In this plane the hard partitions are superior to the soft ones.

4 Application

To evaluate the ideas and the algorithm we apply it to several subsets of the *20Newsgroups* dataset, collected by Ken Lang using 20,000 articles evenly distributed among 20 UseNet discussion groups (see [1]). We replaced every digit by a single character and by another to mark non-alphanumeric characters. Following this pre-processing, the first dataset contained the 530 strings that appeared more then 1000 times in the data. This dataset is referred as *NG*1000. Similarly, all the strings that appeared more then 100 times constitutes the *NG*100 dataset and it contains 5148 different strings. To evaluate also a dichotomy data we used a corpus consisting of only two discussion groups out of the *20Newsgroups* with similar topics: *alt.atheism* and *talk.religion.misc*. Using the same pre-processing, and removing strings that occur less then 10 times, the resulting "lexicon" contained 5765 different strings. We refer to this dataset as *2ng*.

We plot the results of our algorithm on these three data sets in two different planes. First, the normalized information $\frac{I(Z;Y)}{I(X;Y)}$ vs. the size of partition of X (number of clusters), $|Z|$. The greedy procedure directly tries to maximize $I(Z;Y)$ for a given $|Z|$, as can be seen by the strong concavity of these curves (figure 2, right). Indeed the procedure is able to maintain a high percentage of the relevant mutual information of the original data, while reducing the dimensionality of the "features",

$|Z|$, by several orders of magnitude.

On the right hand-side of figure 2 we present a comparison between the efficiency of the procedure for the three datasets. The two-class data, consisting of 5765 different strings, is compressed by two orders of magnitude, into 50 clusters, almost without loosing any of the mutual information about the news groups (the decrease in $I(\tilde{X};Y)$ is about 0.1%). Compression by three orders of magnitude, into 6 clusters, maintains about 90% of the original mutual information.

Similar results, even though less striking, are obtained when Y contain all 20 newsgroups. The *NG100* dataset was compressed from 5148 strings to 515 clusters, keeping 86% of the mutual information, and into 50 clusters keeping about 70% of the information. About the same compression efficiency was obtained for the *NG1000* dataset.

The relationship between the soft and hard clustering is demonstrated in the *Information plane*, i.e., the normalized mutual information values, $\frac{I(Z;Y)}{I(X;Y)}$ vs. $\frac{I(Z;X)}{H(X)}$. In this plane, the soft procedure is optimal since it is a direct maximization of $I(Z;Y)$ while constraining $I(Z;X)$. While the hard partition is suboptimal in this plane, as confirmed empirically, it provides an excellent starting point for reverse annealing. In figure 2 we present the results of the agglomerative procedure for *NG1000* in the information plane, together with the reverse annealing for different values of $|Z|$. As predicted by the theory, the annealing curves merge at various critical values of β into the globally optimal curve, which correspond to the "rate distortion function" for the information bottleneck problem. With the reverse annealing ("heating") procedure there is no need to identify the cluster splits as required in the original annealing ("cooling") procedure. As can be seen, the "phase diagram" is much better recovered by this procedure, suggesting a combination of agglomerative clustering and reverse annealing as the ultimate algorithm for this problem.

References

[1] L. D. Baker and A. K. McCallum. Distributional Clustering of Words for Text Classification In *ACM SIGIR 98*, 1998.

[2] P. F. Brown, P.V. deSouza, R.L. Mercer, V.J. DellaPietra, and J.C. Lai. Class-based n-gram models of natural language. In *Computational Linguistics*, 18(4):467-479, 1992.

[3] T. M. Cover and J. A. Thomas. *Elements of Information Theory*. John Wiley & Sons, New York, 1991.

[4] R. El-Yaniv, S. Fine, and N. Tishby. Agnostic classification of Markovian sequences. In *Advances in Neural Information Processing (NIPS'97)* , 1998.

[5] T. Hofmann, J. Puzicha, and M. Jordan. Learning from dyadic data. In *Advances in Neural Information Processing (NIPS'98)*, 1999.

[6] J. Lin. Divergence Measures Based on the Shannon Entropy. *IEEE Transactions on Information theory*, 37(1):145-151, 1991.

[7] K. Rose. Deterministic Annealing for Clustering, Compression, Classification, Regression, and Related Optimization Problems. *Proceedings of the IEEE*, 86(11):2210-2239, 1998.

[8] F.C. Pereira, N. Tishby, and L. Lee. Distributional clustering of English words. In *30th Annual Meeting of the Association for Computational Linguistics, Columbus, Ohio*, pages 183-190, 1993.

[9] N. Tishby, W. Bialek, and F. C. Pereira. The information bottleneck method: Extracting relevant information from concurrent data. Yet unpublished manuscript, NEC Research Institute TR, 1998.

Training Data Selection for Optimal Generalization in Trigonometric Polynomial Networks

Masashi Sugiyama*and Hidemitsu Ogawa
Department of Computer Science, Tokyo Institute of Technology,
2-12-1, O-okayama, Meguro-ku, Tokyo, 152-8552, Japan.
sugi@cs.titech.ac.jp

Abstract

In this paper, we consider the problem of active learning in trigonometric polynomial networks and give a necessary and sufficient condition of sample points to provide the optimal generalization capability. By analyzing the condition from the functional analytic point of view, we clarify the mechanism of achieving the optimal generalization capability. We also show that a set of training examples satisfying the condition does not only provide the optimal generalization but also reduces the computational complexity and memory required for the calculation of learning results. Finally, examples of sample points satisfying the condition are given and computer simulations are performed to demonstrate the effectiveness of the proposed active learning method.

1 Introduction

Supervised learning is obtaining an underlying rule from training examples, and can be formulated as a function approximation problem. If sample points are actively designed, then learning can be performed more efficiently. In this paper, we discuss the problem of designing sample points, referred to as *active learning*, for optimal generalization.

Active learning is classified into two categories depending on the optimality. One is *global optimal*, where a set of all training examples is optimal (e.g. Fedorov [3]). The other is *greedy optimal*, where the next training example to sample is optimal in each step (e.g. MacKay [5], Cohn [2], Fukumizu [4], and Sugiyama and Ogawa [10]). In this paper, we focus on the global optimal case and give a new active learning method in trigonometric polynomial networks. The proposed method does not employ any approximations in its derivation, so that it provides exactly the optimal generalization capability. Moreover, the proposed method reduces the computational complexity and memory required for the calculation of learning results. Finally, the effectiveness of the proposed method is demonstrated through computer simulations.

---

*http://ogawa-www.cs.titech.ac.jp/~sugi.

2 Formulation of supervised learning

In this section, the supervised learning problem is formulated from the functional analytic point of view (see Ogawa [7]). Then, our learning criterion and model are described.

2.1 Supervised learning as an inverse problem

Let us consider the problem of obtaining the optimal approximation to a target function $f(x)$ of L variables from a set of M training examples. The training examples are made up of sample points $x_m \in \mathcal{D}$, where $\mathcal{D}$ is a subset of the L-dimensional Euclidean space $\mathbf{R}^L$, and corresponding sample values $y_m \in \mathbf{C}$:

$$\{(x_m, y_m) \mid y_m = f(x_m) + n_m\}_{m=1}^{M}, \quad (1)$$

where y_m is degraded by zero-mean additive noise n_m. Let n and y be M-dimensional vectors whose m-th elements are n_m and y_m, respectively. y is called a *sample value vector*. In this paper, the target function $f(x)$ is assumed to belong to a *reproducing kernel Hilbert space* H (Aronszajn [1]). If H is unknown, then it can be estimated by model selection methods (e.g. Sugiyama and Ogawa [9]). Let $K(\cdot, \cdot)$ be the reproducing kernel of H. If a function $\psi_m(x)$ is defined as $\psi_m(x) = K(x, x_m)$, then the value of f at a sample point x_m is expressed as $f(x_m) = \langle f, \psi_m \rangle$, where $\langle \cdot, \cdot \rangle$ stands for the inner product. For this reason, ψ_m is called a *sampling function*. Let A be an operator defined as

$$A = \sum_{m=1}^{M} \left(e_m \otimes \overline{\psi_m} \right), \quad (2)$$

where e_m is the m-th vector of the so-called standard basis in $\mathbf{C}^M$ and $(\cdot \otimes \overline{\cdot})$ stands for the *Neumann-Schatten product*[1]. A is called a *sampling operator*. Then, the relationship between f and y can be expressed as

$$y = Af + n. \quad (3)$$

Let us denote a mapping from y to a learning result f_0 by X:

$$f_0 = Xy, \quad (4)$$

where X is called a *learning operator*. Then, the supervised learning problem is reformulated as an inverse problem of obtaining X providing the best approximation f_0 to f under a certain learning criterion.

2.2 Learning criterion and model

As mentioned above, function approximation is performed on the basis of a learning criterion. Our purpose of learning is to minimize the *generalization error* of the learning result f_0 measured by

$$J_G = E_n \|f_0 - f\|^2, \quad (5)$$

where E_n denotes the ensemble average over noise. In this paper, we adopt *projection learning* as our learning criterion. Let A^*, $\mathcal{R}(A^*)$, and $P_{\mathcal{R}(A^*)}$ be the adjoint operator of A, the range of A^*, and the orthogonal projection operator onto $\mathcal{R}(A^*)$, respectively. Then, projection learning is defined as follows.

---
[1] For any fixed g in a Hilbert space H_1 and any fixed f in a Hilbert space H_2, the Neumann-Schatten product $(f \otimes \overline{g})$ is an operator from H_1 to H_2 defined by using any $h \in H_1$ as $(f \otimes \overline{g})h = \langle h, g \rangle f$.

Definition 1 (Projection learning) *(Ogawa [6]) An operator X is called the projection learning operator if X minimizes the functional $J_P[X] = E_n \|Xn\|^2$ under the constraint $XA = P_{\mathcal{R}(A^*)}$.*

It is well-known that Eq.(5) can be decomposed into the *bias* and *variance*:

$$J_G = \|P_{\mathcal{R}(A^*)}f - f\|^2 + E_n\|Xn\|^2. \tag{6}$$

Eq.(6) implies that the projection learning criterion reduces the bias to a certain level and minimizes the variance.

Let us consider the following function space.

Definition 2 (Trigonometric polynomial space) *Let $x = (\xi^{(1)}, \xi^{(2)}, \cdots, \xi^{(L)})^\top$. For $1 \leq l \leq L$, let N_l be a positive integer and $\mathcal{D}_l = [-\pi, \pi]$. Then, a function space H is called a trigonometric polynomial space of order $(N_1, N_2, \cdots, N_L)$ if H is spanned by*

$$\left\{ \prod_{l=1}^{L} \exp(in_l \xi^{(l)}) \right\}_{n_1=-N_1, n_2=-N_2, \cdots, n_L=-N_L}^{N_1, N_2, \cdots, N_L} \tag{7}$$

defined on $\mathcal{D}_1 \times \mathcal{D}_2 \times \cdots \times \mathcal{D}_L$, and the inner product in H is defined as

$$\langle f, g \rangle = \frac{1}{(2\pi)^L} \int_{-\pi}^{\pi} \int_{-\pi}^{\pi} \cdots \int_{-\pi}^{\pi} f(x)\overline{g(x)} d\xi^{(1)} d\xi^{(2)} \cdots d\xi^{(L)}. \tag{8}$$

The dimension μ of a trigonometric polynomial space of order $(N_1, N_2, \cdots, N_L)$ is $\mu = \prod_{l=1}^{L}(2N_l + 1)$, and the reproducing kernel of this space is expressed as

$$K(x, x') = \prod_{l=1}^{L} K_l(\xi^{(l)}, \xi^{(l)\prime}), \tag{9}$$

where

$$K_l(\xi^{(l)}, \xi^{(l)\prime}) = \begin{cases} \sin \frac{(2N_l+1)(\xi^{(l)} - \xi^{(l)\prime})}{2} \Big/ \sin \frac{\xi^{(l)} - \xi^{(l)\prime}}{2} & \text{if } \xi^{(l)} \neq \xi^{(l)\prime}, \\ 2N_l + 1 & \text{if } \xi^{(l)} = \xi^{(l)\prime}. \end{cases} \tag{10}$$

3 Active learning in trigonometric polynomial space

The problem of active learning is to find a set $\{x_m\}_{m=1}^{M}$ of sample points providing the optimal generalization capability. In this section, we give the optimal solution to the active learning problem in the trigonometric polynomial space.

Let $A^\dagger$ be the *Moore-Penrose generalized inverse*[2] of A. Then, the following proposition holds.

Proposition 1 *If the noise covariance matrix Q is given as $Q = \sigma^2 I$ with $\sigma^2 > 0$, then the projection learning operator X is expressed as $X = A^\dagger$.*

Note that the sampling operator A is uniquely determined by $\{x_m\}_{m=1}^{M}$ (see Eq.(2)).

From Eq.(6), the bias of a learning result f_0 becomes zero for all f in H if and only if $\mathcal{N}(A) = \{0\}$, where $\mathcal{N}(\cdot)$ stands for the null space of an operator. For this reason,

---

[2] An operator X is called the Moore-Penrose generalized inverse of an operator A if X satisfies $AXA = A$, $XAX = X$, $(AX)^* = AX$, and $(XA)^* = XA$.

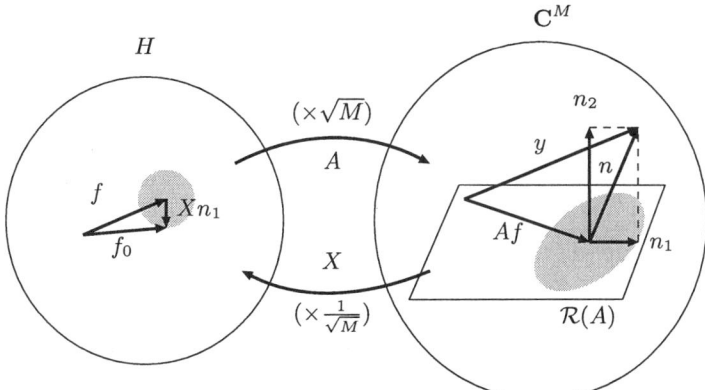

Figure 1: Mechanism of noise suppression by Theorem 1. If a set $\{x_m\}_{m=1}^M$ of sample points satisfies $A^*A = MI$, then $XAf = f$, $\|Xn_1\| = \frac{1}{\sqrt{M}}\|n_1\|$, and $Xn_2 = 0$.

we consider the case where a set $\{x_m\}_{m=1}^M$ of sample points satisfies $\mathcal{N}(A) = \{0\}$. In this case, Eq.(6) is reduced to

$$J_G = E_n \|A^\dagger n\|^2, \tag{11}$$

which is equivalent to the noise variance in H. Consequently, the problem of active learning becomes the problem of finding a set $\{x_m\}_{m=1}^M$ of sample points minimizing Eq.(11) under the constraint $\mathcal{N}(A) = \{0\}$.

First, we derive a condition for optimal generalization in terms of the sampling operator A.

Theorem 1 *Assume that the noise covariance matrix Q is given as $Q = \sigma^2 I$ with $\sigma^2 > 0$. Then, J_G in Eq.(11) is minimized under the constraint $\mathcal{N}(A) = \{0\}$ if and only if*

$$A^*A = MI, \tag{12}$$

where I denotes the identity operator on H. In this case, the minimum value of J_G is $\sigma^2 \mu/M$, where μ is the dimension of H.

Eq.(12) implies that $\{\frac{1}{\sqrt{M}}\psi_m\}_{m=1}^M$ forms a *pseudo orthonormal basis* (Ogawa [8]) in H, which is an extension of orthonormal bases. The following lemma gives interpretation of Theorem 1.

Lemma 1 *When a set $\{x_m\}_{m=1}^M$ of sample points satisfies Eq.(12), it holds that*

$$XAf = f \quad \text{for all } f \in H, \tag{13}$$

$$\|Af\| = \sqrt{M}\|f\| \quad \text{for all } f \in H, \tag{14}$$

$$\|Xu\| = \begin{cases} \frac{1}{\sqrt{M}}\|u\| & \text{for } u \in \mathcal{R}(A), \\ 0 & \text{for } u \in \mathcal{R}(A)^\perp. \end{cases} \tag{15}$$

Eqs.(14) and (15) imply that $\frac{1}{\sqrt{M}}A$ becomes an *isometry* and $\sqrt{M}X$ becomes a *partial isometry* with the initial space $\mathcal{R}(A)$, respectively. Let us decompose the noise n as $n = n_1 + n_2$, where $n_1 \in \mathcal{R}(A)$ and $n_2 \in \mathcal{R}(A)^\perp$. Then, the sample value vector y is rewritten as $y = Af + n_1 + n_2$. It follows from Eq.(13) that the signal component Af is transformed into the original function f by X. From Eq.(15), X suppresses the magnitude of noise n_1 in $\mathcal{R}(A)$ by $\frac{1}{\sqrt{M}}$ and completely removes the

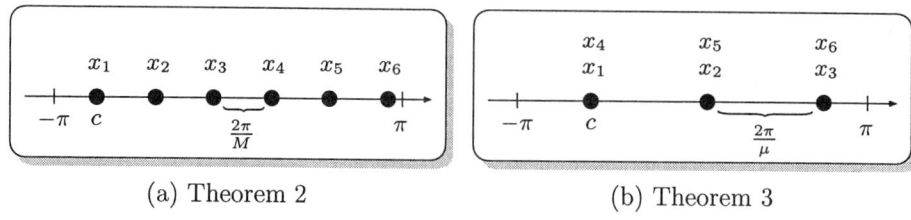

(a) Theorem 2 (b) Theorem 3

Figure 2: Two examples of sample points such that Condition (12) holds ($\mu = 3$ and $M = 6$).

noise n_2 in $\mathcal{R}(A)^\perp$. This analysis is summarized in Fig.1. Note that Theorem 1 and its interpretation are valid for all Hilbert spaces such that $K(x,x)$ is a constant for any x.

In Theorem 1, we have given a necessary and sufficient condition to minimize J_G in terms of the sampling operator A. Now we give two examples of sample points $\{x_m\}_{m=1}^M$ such that Condition (12) holds. From here on, we focus on the case when the dimension L of the input x is 1 for simplicity. However, the following results can be easily scaled to the case when $L > 1$.

Theorem 2 *Let $M \geq \mu$, where μ is the dimension of H. Let c be an arbitrary constant such that $-\pi \leq c \leq -\pi + \frac{2\pi}{M}$. If a set $\{x_m\}_{m=1}^M$ of sample points is determined as*

$$x_m = c + \frac{2\pi}{M}(m-1), \tag{16}$$

then Eq.(12) holds.

Theorem 3 *Let $M = k\mu$ where k is a positive integer. Let c be an arbitrary constant such that $-\pi \leq c \leq -\pi + \frac{2\pi}{\mu}$. If a set $\{x_m\}_{m=1}^M$ of sample points is determined as*

$$x_m = c + \frac{2\pi}{\mu}r, \quad \text{where} \quad r = m - 1 \;(mod\; \mu), \tag{17}$$

then Eq.(12) holds.

Theorem 2 means that M sample points are fixed to $2\pi/M$ intervals in the domain $[-\pi, \pi]$ and sample values are gathered once at each point (see Fig.2 (a)). In contrast, Theorem 3 means that μ sample points are fixed to $2\pi/\mu$ intervals in the domain and sample values are gathered k times at each point (see Fig.2 (b)).

Now, we discuss calculation methods of the projection learning result $f_0(x)$. Let h_m be the m-th column vector of the M-dimensional matrix $(AA^*)^\dagger$. Then, for general sample points, the projection learning result $f_0(x)$ can be calculated as

$$f_0(x) = \sum_{m=1}^M \langle y, h_m \rangle \psi_m(x). \tag{18}$$

When we use the optimal sample points satisfying Condition (12), the following theorems hold.

Theorem 4 *When Eq.(12) holds, the projection learning result $f_0(x)$ can be calculated as*

$$f_0(x) = \frac{1}{M}\sum_{m=1}^M y_m \psi_m(x). \tag{19}$$

Theorem 5 *When sample points are determined following Theorem 3, the projection learning result $f_0(x)$ can be calculated as*

$$f_0(x) = \frac{1}{\mu} \sum_{p=1}^{\mu} \overline{y_p} \psi_p(x), \quad \text{where} \quad \overline{y_p} = \frac{1}{k} \sum_{q=1}^{k} y_{p+\mu(q-1)}. \tag{20}$$

In Eq.(18), the coefficient of $\psi_m(x)$ is obtained by the inner product $\langle y, h_m \rangle$. In contrast, it is replaced with y_m/M in Eq.(19), which implies that the Moore-Penrose generalized inverse of AA^* is not required for calculating $f_0(x)$. This property is quite useful when the number M of training examples is very large since the calculation of the Moore-Penrose generalized inverse of high dimensional matrices is sometimes unstable. In Eq.(20), the number of basis functions is reduced to μ and the coefficient of $\psi_p(x)$ is obtained by $\overline{y_p}/\mu$, where $\overline{y_p}$ is the mean sample values at x_p.

For general sample points, the computational complexity and memory required for calculating $f_0(x)$ by Eq.(18) are both $O(M^2)$. In contrast, Theorem 4 states that if a set of sample points satisfies Eq.(12), then both the computational complexity and memory are reduced to $O(M)$. Hence, Theorem 1 and Theorem 4 do not only provide the optimal generalization but also reduce the computational complexity and memory. Moreover, if we determine sample points following Theorem 3 and calculate the learning result $f_0(x)$ by Theorem 5, then the computational complexity and memory are reduced to $O(\mu)$. This is extremely efficient since μ does not depend on the number M of training examples. The above results are shown in Tab.1.

4 Simulations

In this section, the effectiveness of the proposed active learning method is demonstrated through computer simulations.

Let H be a trigonometric polynomial space of order 100, and the noise covariance matrix Q be $Q = I$. Let us consider the following three sampling schemes.

(A) Optimal sampling: Training examples are gathered following Theorem 3.

(B) Experimental design: Eq.(2) in Cohn [2] is adopted as the active learning criterion. The value of this criterion is evaluated by 30 reference points. The sampling location is determined by multi-point-search with 3 candidates.

(C) Passive learning: Training examples are given unilaterally.

Fig.3 shows the relation between the number of training examples and the generalization error. The horizontal and vertical axes display the number of training examples and the generalization error J_G measured by Eq.(5), respectively. The solid line shows the sampling scheme (A). The dashed and dotted lines denote the averages of 10 trials of the sampling schemes (B) and (C), respectively. When the number of training examples is 201, the generalization error of the sampling scheme (A) is 1 while the generalization errors of the sampling schemes (B) and (C) are 3.18×10^4 and 8.75×10^4, respectively. This graph illustrates that the proposed sampling scheme gives much better generalization capability than the sampling schemes (B) and (C) especially when the number of training examples is not so large.

5 Conclusion

We proposed a new active learning method in the trigonometric polynomial space. The proposed method provides exactly the optimal generalization capability and

Table 1: Computational complexity and memory required for projection learning.

Calculation methods	Computational Complexity and Memory
Eq.(18)	$O(M^2)$
Theorem 4	$O(M)$
Theorem 5[§]	$O(\mu)$

[§] $M = k\mu$ where μ is the dimension of H and k is a positive integer.

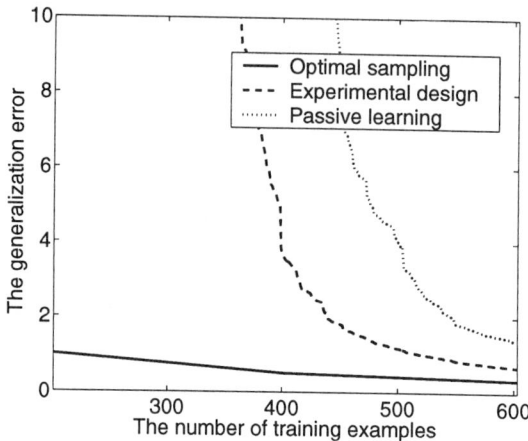

Figure 3: Relation between the number of training examples and the generalization error.

at the same time, it reduces the computational complexity and memory required for the calculation of learning results. The mechanism of achieving the optimal generalization was clarified from the functional analytic point of view.

References

[1] N. Aronszajn. Theory of reproducing kernels. *Transactions on American Mathematical Society*, 68:337–404, 1950.

[2] D. Cohn. Neural network exploration using optimal experiment design. In J. Cowan et al. (Eds.), *Advances in Neural Information Processing Systems 6*, pp. 679–686. Morgan-Kaufmann Publishers Inc., San Mateo, CA, 1994.

[3] V. V. Fedorov. *Theory of Optimal Experiments*. Academic Press, New York, 1972.

[4] K. Fukumizu. Active learning in multilayer perceptrons. In D. Touretzky et al. (Eds.), *Advances in Neural Information Processing Systems 8*, pp. 295–301. The MIT Press, Cambridge, 1996.

[5] D. MacKay. Information-based objective functions for active data selection. *Neural Computation*, 4(4):590–604, 1992.

[6] H. Ogawa. Projection filter regularization of ill-conditioned problem. In *Proceedings of SPIE, 808, Inverse Problems in Optics*, pp. 189–196, 1987.

[7] H. Ogawa. Neural network learning, generalization and over-learning. In *Proceedings of the ICIIPS'92, International Conference on Intelligent Information Processing & System*, vol. 2, pp. 1–6, Beijing, China, 1992.

[8] H. Ogawa. Theory of pseudo biorthogonal bases and its application. In *Research Institute for Mathematical Science, RIMS Kokyuroku, 1067, Reproducing Kernels and their Applications*, pp. 24–38, 1998.

[9] M. Sugiyama and H. Ogawa. Functional analytic approach to model selection—Subspace information criterion. In *Proceedings of 1999 Workshop on Information-Based Induction Sciences (IBIS'99)*, pp. 93–98, Syuzenji, Shizuoka, Japan, 1999 (Its complete version is available at ftp://ftp.cs.titech.ac.jp/pub/TR/99/TR99-0009.ps.gz).

[10] M. Sugiyama and H. Ogawa. Incremental active learning in consideration of bias, *Technical Report of IEICE*, NC99-56, pp. 15–22, 1999 (Its complete version is available at ftp://ftp.cs.titech.ac.jp/pub/TR/99/TR99-0010.ps.gz).

Predictive Approaches For Choosing Hyperparameters in Gaussian Processes

S. Sundararajan
Computer Science and Automation
Indian Institute of Science
Bangalore 560 012, India
sundar@csa.iisc.ernet.in

S. Sathiya Keerthi
Mechanical and Production Engg.
National University of Singapore
10 Kentridge Crescent, Singapore 119260
mpessk@guppy.mpe.nus.edu.sg

Abstract

Gaussian Processes are powerful regression models specified by parametrized mean and covariance functions. Standard approaches to estimate these parameters (known by the name Hyperparameters) are Maximum Likelihood (ML) and Maximum APosterior (MAP) approaches. In this paper, we propose and investigate predictive approaches, namely, maximization of Geisser's Surrogate Predictive Probability (GPP) and minimization of mean square error with respect to GPP (referred to as Geisser's Predictive mean square Error (GPE)) to estimate the hyperparameters. We also derive results for the standard Cross-Validation (CV) error and make a comparison. These approaches are tested on a number of problems and experimental results show that these approaches are strongly competitive to existing approaches.

1 Introduction

Gaussian Processes (GPs) are powerful regression models that have gained popularity recently, though they have appeared in different forms in the literature for years. They can be used for classification also; see MacKay (1997), Rasmussen (1996) and Williams and Rasmussen (1996). Here, we restrict ourselves to regression problems. Neal (1996) showed that a large class of neural network models converge to a Gaussian Process prior over functions in the limit of an infinite number of hidden units. Although GPs can be created using infinite networks, often GPs are specified directly using parametric forms for the mean and covariance functions (Williams and Rasmussen (1996)). We assume that the process is zero mean. Let $\mathbf{Z}_N = \{\mathbf{X}_N, \mathbf{y}_N\}$ where $\mathbf{X}_N = \{\mathbf{x}(i) : i = 1, \ldots, N\}$ and $\mathbf{y}_N = \{y(i) : i = 1, \ldots, N\}$. Here, $\mathbf{y}(i)$ represents the output corresponding to the input vector $\mathbf{x}(i)$. Then, the Gaussian prior over the functions is given by

$$p(\mathbf{y}_N | \mathbf{X}_N, \bar{\boldsymbol{\theta}}) = \frac{exp(-\mathbf{y}_N^T \bar{\mathbf{C}}_N^{-1} \mathbf{y}_N)}{(2\pi)^{\frac{N}{2}} |\bar{\mathbf{C}}_N|^{\frac{1}{2}}} \tag{1}$$

where $\bar{\mathbf{C}}_N$ is the covariance matrix with $(i,j)^{th}$ element $[\bar{\mathbf{C}}_N]_{i,j} = \bar{C}(\mathbf{x}(i), \mathbf{x}(j); \bar{\boldsymbol{\theta}})$ and $\bar{C}(.; \bar{\boldsymbol{\theta}})$ denotes the parametrized covariance function. Now, assuming that the observed output $\mathbf{t}_N$ is modeled as $\mathbf{t}_N = \mathbf{y}_N + \boldsymbol{\epsilon}_N$ and $\boldsymbol{\epsilon}_N$ is zero mean multivariate Gaussian with covariance matrix $\sigma^2 \mathbf{I}_N$ and is independent of $\mathbf{y}_N$, we get

$$p(\mathbf{t}_N|\mathbf{X}_N, \boldsymbol{\theta}) = \frac{exp(-\mathbf{t}_N^T \mathbf{C}_N^{-1} \mathbf{t}_N)}{(2\pi)^{\frac{N}{2}} |\mathbf{C}_N|^{\frac{1}{2}}} \quad (2)$$

where $\mathbf{C}_N = \bar{\mathbf{C}}_N + \sigma^2 \mathbf{I}_N$. Therefore, $[\mathbf{C}_N]_{i,j} = [\bar{\mathbf{C}}_N]_{i,j} + \sigma^2 \delta_{i,j}$, where $\delta_{i,j} = 1$ when $i = j$ and zero otherwise. Note that $\boldsymbol{\theta} = (\bar{\boldsymbol{\theta}}, \sigma^2)$ is the new set of hyperparameters. Then, the predictive distribution of the output $y(N+1)$ for a test case $\mathbf{x}(N+1)$ is also Gaussian with mean and variance

$$\hat{y}(N+1) = \mathbf{k}_{N+1}^T \mathbf{C}_N^{-1} \mathbf{t}_N \quad (3)$$

and

$$\sigma_{y(N+1)}^2 = b_{N+1} - \mathbf{k}_{N+1}^T \mathbf{C}_N^{-1} \mathbf{k}_{N+1} \quad (4)$$

where $b_{N+1} = C(\mathbf{x}(N+1), \mathbf{x}(N+1); \boldsymbol{\theta})$ and $\mathbf{k}_{N+1}$ is an $N \times 1$ vector with i^{th} element given by $C(\mathbf{x}(N+1), \mathbf{x}(i); \boldsymbol{\theta})$. Now, we need to specify the covariance function $C(.; \boldsymbol{\theta})$. Williams and Rasmussen (1996) found the following covariance function to work well in practice.

$$\bar{C}(\mathbf{x}(i), \mathbf{x}(j); \bar{\boldsymbol{\theta}}) = a_0 + a_1 \sum_{p=1}^{M} x_p(i) x_p(j) + v_0 exp\left(-\frac{1}{2} \sum_{p=1}^{M} w_p (x_p(i) - x_p(j))^2\right) \quad (5)$$

where $x_p(i)$ is the pth component of ith input vector $\mathbf{x}(i)$. The w_p are the Automatic Relevance Determination (ARD) parameters. Note that $C(\mathbf{x}(i), \mathbf{x}(j); \boldsymbol{\theta}) = \bar{C}(\mathbf{x}(i), \mathbf{x}(j); \bar{\boldsymbol{\theta}}) + \sigma^2 \delta_{i,j}$. Also, all the parameters are positive and it is convenient to use logarithmic scale. Hence, $\boldsymbol{\theta}$ is given by $log(a_0, a_1, v_0, w_1, \ldots, w_M, \sigma^2)$. Then, the question is: how do we handle $\boldsymbol{\theta}$? More sophisticated techniques like Hybrid Monte Carlo (HMC) methods (Rasmussen (1996) and Neal (1997)) are available which can numerically integrate over the hyperparameters to make predictions. Alternately, we can estimate $\boldsymbol{\theta}$ from the training data. We restrict to the latter approach here. In the classical approach, $\boldsymbol{\theta}$ is assumed to be deterministic but unknown and the estimate is found by maximizing the likelihood (2). That is, $\boldsymbol{\theta}_{ML} = \underset{\boldsymbol{\theta}}{argmax}\, p(\mathbf{t}_N|\mathbf{X}_N, \boldsymbol{\theta})$. In the Bayesian approach, $\boldsymbol{\theta}$ is assumed to be random and a prior $p(\boldsymbol{\theta})$ is specified. Then, the MAP estimate $\boldsymbol{\theta}_{MP}$ is obtained as $\boldsymbol{\theta}_{MP} = \underset{\boldsymbol{\theta}}{argmax}\, p(\mathbf{t}_N|\mathbf{X}_N, \boldsymbol{\theta}) p(\boldsymbol{\theta})$ with the motivation that the the predictive distribution $p(y(N+1)|\mathbf{x}(N+1), \mathbf{Z}_N)$ can be approximated as $p(y(N+1)|\mathbf{x}(N+1), \mathbf{Z}_N, \boldsymbol{\theta}_{MP})$. With this background, in this paper we propose and investigate different predictive approaches to estimate the hyperparameters from the training data.

2 Predictive approaches for choosing hyperparameters

Geisser (1975) proposed Predictive Sample Reuse (PSR) methodology that can be applied for both model selection and parameter estimation problems. The basic idea is to define a partition scheme $P(N, n, \Gamma)$ such that $P_{N-n}^{(i)} = (\mathbf{Z}_{N-n}^{ir}; \mathbf{Z}_n^{io})$ is i^{th} partition belonging to a set Γ of partitions with $\mathbf{Z}_{N-n}^{ir}$, $\mathbf{Z}_n^{io}$ representing the $N - n$ retained and n omitted data sets respectively. Then, the unknown $\boldsymbol{\theta}$ is estimated (or a model M_j is chosen among a set of models indexed by $j = 1, \ldots, J$) by means of optimizing a predictive measure that measures the predictive performance on the omitted observations $\mathbf{X}_n^{io}$ by using the retained observations $\mathbf{Z}_{N-n}^{ir}$ averaged over the partitions ($i \in \Gamma$). In the special case of $n = 1$, we have the leave one out strategy. Note that this approach was independently presented in the name of cross-validation (CV) by Stone (1974). The well known examples are the standard CV error and negative of average predictive likelihood. Geisser and Eddy (1979) proposed to maximize $\prod_{i=1}^{N} p(t(i)|\mathbf{x}(i), \mathbf{Z}_N^{(i)}, M_j)$ (known as Geisser's surrogate Predictive Probability (GPP)) by synthesizing Bayesian and PSR methodology in the context of (parametrized) model selection. Here, we propose to maximize $\prod_{i=1}^{N} p(t(i)|\mathbf{x}(i), \mathbf{Z}_N^{(i)}, \boldsymbol{\theta})$ to estimate $\boldsymbol{\theta}$, where $\mathbf{Z}_N^{(i)}$ is obtained from $\mathbf{Z}_N$ by removing the ith sample. Note that $p(t(i)|\mathbf{x}(i), \mathbf{Z}_N^{(i)}, \boldsymbol{\theta})$ is nothing but the predictive distribution $p(y(i)|\mathbf{x}(i), \mathbf{Z}_N^{(i)}, \boldsymbol{\theta})$ evaluated at $y(i) = t(i)$. Also, we introduce the notion of Geisser's Predictive mean square Error (GPE) defined as $\frac{1}{N} \sum_{i=1}^{N} E((y(i) - t(i))^2)$ (where the expectation operation is defined with respect to $p(y(i)|\mathbf{x}(i), \mathbf{Z}_N^{(i)}, \boldsymbol{\theta})$) and propose to estimate $\boldsymbol{\theta}$ by minimizing GPE.

2.1 Expressions for GPP and its gradient

The objective function corresponding to GPP is given by

$$G(\boldsymbol{\theta}) = -\frac{1}{N} \sum_{i=1}^{N} log(p(t(i)|\mathbf{x}(i), \mathbf{Z}_N^{(i)}, \boldsymbol{\theta})) \tag{6}$$

From (3) and (4) we get

$$G(\boldsymbol{\theta}) = \frac{1}{N} \sum_{i=1}^{N} \frac{(t(i) - \hat{y}(i))^2}{2\sigma_{y(i)}^2} + \frac{1}{2N} \sum_{i=1}^{N} log \, \sigma_{y(i)}^2 + \frac{1}{2} log \, 2\pi \tag{7}$$

where $\hat{y}(i) = [\mathbf{c}_i^{(i)}]^T [\mathbf{C}_N^{(i)}]^{-1} \mathbf{t}_N^{(i)}$ and $\sigma_{y(i)}^2 = c_{ii} - [\mathbf{c}_i^{(i)}]^T [\mathbf{C}_N^{(i)}]^{-1} \mathbf{c}_i^{(i)}$. Here, $\mathbf{C}_N^{(i)}$ is an $N-1 \times N-1$ matrix obtained from $\mathbf{C}_N$ by removing the ith column and i^{th} row. Similarly, $\mathbf{t}_N^{(i)}$ and $\mathbf{c}_i^{(i)}$ are obtained from $\mathbf{t}_N$ and $\mathbf{c}_i$ (i.e., i^{th} column of $\mathbf{C}_N$) respectively by removing the ith element. Then, $G(\boldsymbol{\theta})$ and its gradient can be computed efficiently using the following result.

Theorem 1 *The objective function $G(\boldsymbol{\theta})$ under the Gaussian Process model is given by*

$$G(\boldsymbol{\theta}) = \frac{1}{2N} \sum_{i=1}^{N} \frac{q_N^2(i)}{\bar{c}_{ii}} - \frac{1}{2N} \sum_{i=1}^{N} log \bar{c}_{ii} + \frac{1}{2} log 2\pi \tag{8}$$

where $\bar{c}_{ii}$ denotes the ith diagonal entry of $\mathbf{C}_N^{-1}$ and $q_N(i)$ denotes the ith element of $\mathbf{q}_N = \mathbf{C}_N^{-1} \mathbf{t}_N$. Its gradient is given by

$$\frac{\partial G(\boldsymbol{\theta})}{\partial \theta_j} = \frac{1}{2N} \sum_{i=1}^{N} \left(1 + \frac{q_N^2(i)}{\bar{c}_{ii}}\right) \left(\frac{s_{j,i}}{\bar{c}_{ii}}\right) + \frac{1}{N} \sum_{i=1}^{N} q_N(i) \left(\frac{r_j(i)}{\bar{c}_{ii}}\right) \tag{9}$$

where $s_{j,i} = \bar{\mathbf{c}}_i^T \frac{\partial \mathbf{C}_N}{\partial \theta_j} \bar{\mathbf{c}}_i$, $\mathbf{r}_j = -\mathbf{C}_N^{-1} \frac{\partial \mathbf{C}_N}{\partial \theta_j} \mathbf{C}_N^{-1} \mathbf{t}_N$ and $\mathbf{q}_N = \mathbf{C}_N^{-1} \mathbf{t}_N$. Here, $\bar{\mathbf{c}}_i$ denotes the ith column of the matrix $\mathbf{C}_N^{-1}$.

Thus, using (8) and (9) we can compute the GPP and its gradient. We will give meaningful interpretation to the different terms shortly.

2.2 Expressions for CV function and its gradient

We define the CV function as

$$H(\boldsymbol{\theta}) = \frac{1}{N} \sum_{i=1}^{N} (t(i) - \hat{y}(i))^2 \tag{10}$$

where $\hat{y}(i)$ is the mean of the conditional predictive distribution as given above. Now, using the following result we can compute $H(\boldsymbol{\theta})$ efficiently.

Theorem 2 *The CV function $H(\boldsymbol{\theta})$ under the Gaussian model is given by*

$$H(\boldsymbol{\theta}) = \frac{1}{N} \sum_{i=1}^{N} \left(\frac{q_N(i)}{\bar{c}_{ii}}\right)^2 \tag{11}$$

and its gradient is given by

$$\frac{\partial H(\boldsymbol{\theta})}{\partial \theta_j} = \frac{1}{N} \sum_{i=1}^{N} \left(\frac{2}{\bar{c}_{ii}}\right) \left(\frac{q_N(i) r_j(i)}{\bar{c}_{ii}} + \left(\frac{q_N^2(i)}{\bar{c}_{ii}}\right)\left(\frac{s_{j,i}}{\bar{c}_{ii}}\right)\right) \tag{12}$$

where $s_{j,i}, r_j, q_N(i)$ and $\bar{c}_{ii}$ are as defined in theorem 1.

2.3 Expressions for GPE and its gradient

The GPE function is defined as

$$G_E(\boldsymbol{\theta}) = \frac{1}{N} \sum_{i=1}^{N} \int (t(i) - y(i))^2 \, p(y(i)|\mathbf{x}(i), \mathbf{Z}_N^{(i)}, \boldsymbol{\theta}) \, dy(i) \tag{13}$$

which can be readily simplified to

$$G_E(\boldsymbol{\theta}) = \frac{1}{N} \sum_{i=1}^{N} (t(i) - \hat{y}(i))^2 + \frac{1}{N} \sum_{i=1}^{N} \sigma_{y(i)}^2 \tag{14}$$

On comparing (14) with (10), we see that while CV error minimizes the deviation from the predictive mean, GPE takes predictive variance also into account. Now, the gradient can be written as

$$\frac{\partial G_E(\boldsymbol{\theta})}{\partial \theta_j} = \frac{\partial H(\boldsymbol{\theta})}{\partial \theta_j} + \frac{1}{N} \sum_{i=1}^{N} \left(\frac{1}{\bar{c}_{ii}}\right)^2 \bar{\mathbf{c}}_i^T \frac{\partial \mathbf{C}_N}{\partial \theta_j} \bar{\mathbf{c}}_i \tag{15}$$

where we have used the results $\sigma_{y(i)}^2 = \frac{1}{\bar{c}_{ii}}$, $\frac{\partial \bar{c}_{ii}}{\partial \theta_j} = \mathbf{e}_i^T \frac{\partial \mathbf{C}_N^{-1}}{\partial \theta_j} \mathbf{e}_i$ and $\frac{\partial \mathbf{C}_N^{-1}}{\partial \theta_j} = -\mathbf{C}_N^{-1} \frac{\partial \mathbf{C}_N}{\partial \theta_j} \mathbf{C}_N^{-1}$. Here $\mathbf{e}_i$ denotes the ith column vector of the identity matrix $\mathbf{I}_N$.

2.4 Interpretations

More insight can be obtained from reparametrizing the covariance function as follows.

$$C(\mathbf{x}(i), \mathbf{x}(j); \boldsymbol{\theta}) = \sigma^2 \left(\bar{a}_0 + \bar{a}_1 \sum_{p=1}^{M} x_p(i) x_p(j) + \bar{v}_0 exp(-\frac{1}{2} \sum_{p=1}^{M} w_p (x_p(i) - x_p(j))^2) + \delta_{i,j}\right) \tag{16}$$

where $a_0 = \sigma^2 \bar{a}_0$, $a_1 = \sigma^2 \bar{a}_1$, $v_0 = \sigma^2 \bar{v}_0$. Let us define $P(\mathbf{x}(i), \mathbf{x}(j); \boldsymbol{\theta}) = \frac{1}{\sigma^2} C(\mathbf{x}(i), \mathbf{x}(j); \boldsymbol{\theta})$. Then $\mathbf{P}_N^{-1} = \sigma^2 \mathbf{C}_N^{-1}$. Therefore, $\bar{c}_{i,j} = \frac{\bar{p}_{i,j}}{\sigma^2}$ where $\bar{c}_{i,j}, \bar{p}_{i,j}$ denote the $(i,j)^{th}$ element of the matrices $\mathbf{C}_N^{-1}$ and $\mathbf{P}_N^{-1}$ respectively. From theorem 2 (see (10) and (11)) we have $t(i) - \hat{y}(i) = \frac{q_N(i)}{\bar{c}_{ii}} = \frac{\bar{\mathbf{c}}_i^T \mathbf{t}_N}{\bar{c}_{ii}}$. Then, we can rewrite (8) as

$$G(\boldsymbol{\theta}) = \frac{1}{2N\sigma^2} \sum_{i=1}^{N} \frac{\bar{q}_N^2(i)}{\bar{p}_{ii}} - \frac{1}{2N} \sum_{i=1}^{N} log \bar{p}_{ii} + \frac{1}{2} log 2\pi\sigma^2 \tag{17}$$

Here, $\bar{q}_N = \mathbf{P}_N^{-1}\mathbf{t}_N$ and, $\bar{\mathbf{p}}_i, \bar{p}_{ii}$ denote, respectively, the ith column and i^{th} diagonal entry of the matrix $\mathbf{P}_N^{-1}$. Now, by setting the derivative of (17) with respect to σ^2 to zero, we can infer the noise level as

$$\hat{\sigma}^2 = \frac{1}{N} \sum_{i=1}^{N} \frac{\bar{q}_N^2(i)}{\bar{p}_{ii}} \qquad (18)$$

Similarly, the CV error (10) can be rewritten as

$$H(\boldsymbol{\theta}) = \frac{1}{N} \sum_{i=1}^{N} \frac{\bar{q}_N^2(i)}{\bar{p}_{ii}^2} \qquad (19)$$

Note that $H(\boldsymbol{\theta})$ is dependent only on the ratio of the hyperparameters (i.e., on $\bar{a}_0, \bar{a}_1, \bar{v}_0$) apart from the ARD parameters. Therefore, we cannot infer the noise level uniquely. However, we can estimate the ARD parameters and the ratios $\bar{a}_0, \bar{a}_1, \bar{v}_0$. Once we have estimated these parameters, then we can use (18) to estimate the noise level. Next, we note that the noise level preferred by the GPE criterion is zero. To see this, first let us rewrite (14) under reparametrization as

$$G_E(\boldsymbol{\theta}) = \frac{1}{N} \sum_{i=1}^{N} \frac{\bar{q}_N^2(i)}{\bar{p}_{ii}^2} + \frac{\sigma^2}{N} \sum_{i=1}^{N} \frac{1}{\bar{p}_{ii}} \qquad (20)$$

Since $\bar{q}_N(i)$ and $\bar{p}_{ii}$ are independent of σ^2, it follows that the GPE prefers zero as the noise level, which is not true. Therefore, this approach can be applied when, either the noise level is known or a good estimate of it is available.

3 Simulation results

We carried out simulation on four data sets. We considered MacKay's robot arm problem and its modified version introduced by Neal (1996). We used the same data set as MacKay (2-inputs and 2-outputs), with 200 examples in the training set and 200 in the test set. This data set is referred to as 'data set 1' in Table 1. Next, to evaluate the ability of the predictive approaches in estimating the ARD parameters, we carried out simulation on the robot arm data with 6 inputs (Neal's version), denoted as 'data set 2' in Table 1. This data set was generated by adding four further inputs, two of which were copies of the two inputs corrupted by additive zero mean Gaussian noise of standard deviation 0.02 and two further irrelevant Gaussian noise inputs with zero mean and unit variance (Williams and Rasmussen (1996)). The performance measures chosen were average of Test Set Error (normalized by true noise level of 0.0025) and average of negative logarithm of predictive probability (NLPP) (computed from Gaussian density function with (3) and (4)). Friedman's [1] data sets 1 and 2 were based on the problem of predicting impedance and phase respectively from four parameters of an electrical circuit. Training sets of three different sizes (50, 100, 200) and with a signal-to-noise ratio of about 3:1 were replicated 100 times and for each training set (at each sample size N), scaled integral squared error ($ISE = \frac{\int_D (y(\mathbf{x}) - \hat{y}(\mathbf{x}))^2 d\mathbf{x}}{var_D\, y(\mathbf{x})}$) and NLPP were computed using 5000 data points randomly generated from a uniform distribution over D (Friedman (1991)). In the case of GPE (denoted as G_E in the tables), we used the noise level estimate generated from Gaussian distribution with mean NL_T (true noise level) and standard deviation 0.03 NL_T. In the case of CV, we estimated the hyperparameters in the reparametrized form and estimated the noise level using (18). In the case of MAP (denoted as MP in the tables), we used the same prior

Table 1: Results on robot arm data sets. Average of normalized test set error (TSE) and negative logarithm of predictive probability (NLPP) for various methods.

	Data Set : 1		Data Set : 2	
	TSE	NLPP	TSE	NLPP
ML	1.126	-1.512	1.131	-1.512
MP	1.131	-1.511	1.181	-1.489
G_P	1.115	-1.524	1.116	-1.516
CV	1.112	-1.518	1.146	-1.514
G_E	1.111	-1.524	1.112	-1.524

Table 2: Results on Friedman's data sets. Average of scaled integral squared error and negative logarithm of predictive probability (given in brackets) for different training sample sizes and various methods.

	Data Set : 1			Data Set : 2		
	N = 50	N = 100	N = 200	N = 50	N = 100	N = 200
ML	0.43(7.24)	0.19(6.71)	0.10(6.49)	0.26(1.05)	0.16(0.82)	0.11(0.68)
MP	0.42(7.18)	0.22(6.78)	0.12(6.56)	0.25(1.01)	0.16(0.82)	0.11(0.69)
G_P	0.47(7.29)	0.20(6.65)	0.10(6.44)	0.33(1.25)	0.20(0.86)	0.12(0.70)
CV	0.55(7.27)	0.22(6.67)	0.10(6.44)	0.42(1.36)	0.21(0.91)	0.13(0.70)
G_E	0.35(7.10)	0.15(6.60)	0.08(6.37)	0.28(1.20)	0.18(0.85)	0.12(0.63)

given in Rasmussen (1996). The GPP approach is denoted as G_P in the tables. For all these methods, conjugate gradient (CG) algorithm (Rasmussen (1996)) was used to optimize the hyperparameters. The termination criterion (relative function error) with a tolerance of 10^{-7} was used, but with a constraint on the maximum number of CG iterations set to 100. In the case of robot arm data sets, the algorithm was run with ten different initial conditions and the best solution (chosen from respective best objective function value) is reported. The optimization was carried out separately for the two outputs and the results reported are the average TSE, NLPP. In the case of Friedman's data sets, the optimization algorithm was run with three different initial conditions and the best solution was picked up. When $N = 200$, the optimization algorithm was run with only one initial condition. For all the data sets, both the inputs and outputs were normalized to zero mean and unit variance.

From Table 1, we see that the performances (both TSE and NLPP) of the predictive approaches are better than ML and MAP approaches for both the data sets. In the case of data set 2, we observed that like ML and MAP methods, all the predictive approaches rightly identified the irrelevant inputs. The performance of GPE approach is the best on the robot arm data and demonstrates the usefulness of this approach when a good noise level estimate is available. In the case of Friedman's data set 1 (see Table 2), the important observation is that the performances (both ISE and NLPP) of GPP, CV approaches are relatively poor at low sample size ($N = 50$) and improve very well as N increases. Note that the performances of the predictive approaches are better compared to the ML and MAP methods starting from $N = 100$ onwards (see NLPP). Again, GPE gives the best performance and the performance at low sample size ($N = 50$) is also quite good. In the case of Friedman's data set 2, the ML and MAP approaches perform better compared to the predictive approaches except GPE. The performances of GPP and CV improve as N increases and are very close to the ML and MAP methods when $N = 200$. Next, it is clear that the MAP method gives the best performance at low sample size. This behavior, we believe, is because the prior plays an important role and hence is very useful. Also, note that unlike data set 1, the performance of GPE is inferior to ML and MAP approaches at low sample sizes and improves over these approaches (see NLPP) as N increases. This suggests that the knowledge of the noise level alone is not the only issue. The basic issue we think is that the predictive approaches estimate the predictive performance of a given model from the training samples. Clearly, the quality of the estimate will become better as N increases. Also, knowing the noise level improves the quality of the estimate.

4 Discussion

Simulation results indicate that the size N required to get good estimates of predictive performance will be dependent on the problem. When N is sufficiently large, we find that the predictive approaches perform better than ML and MAP approaches. The *sufficient* number of samples can be as low as 100 as evident from our results on Friedman's data set 1. Also, MAP approach is the best, when N is very low. As one would expect, the performances of ML and MAP approaches are nearly same as N increases. The comparison with the existing approaches indicate that the predictive approaches developed here are strongly competitive. The overall cost for computing the function and the gradient (for all three predictive approaches) is $O(MN^3)$. The cost for making prediction is same as the one required for ML and MAP methods. The proofs of the results and detailed simulation results will be presented in another paper (Sundararajan and Keerthi, 1999).

References

Friedman, J.H., (1991) Multivariate Adaptive Regression Splines, *Ann. of Stat.*, **19**, 1-141.

Geisser, S., (1975) The Predictive Sample Reuse Method with Applications, *Journal of the American Statistical Association*, **70**, 320-328.

Geisser, S., and Eddy, W.F., (1979) A Predictive Approach to Model Selection, *Journal of the American Statistical Association*, **74**, 153-160.

MacKay, D.J.C. (1997) Gaussian Processes - *A replacement for neural networks ?*, Available in Postscript via URL http://www.wol.ra.phy.cam.ac.uk/mackay/.

Neal, R.M. (1996) *Bayesian Learning for Neural Networks*, New York: Springer-Verlag.

Neal, R.M. (1997) Monte Carlo Implementation of Gaussian Process Models for Bayesian Regression and Classification. Tech. Rep. No. 9702, Dept. of Statistics, University of Toronto.

Rasmussen, C. (1996) *Evaluation of Gaussian Processes and other Methods for Non-Linear Regression*, Ph.D. Thesis, Dept. of Computer Science, University of Toronto.

Stone, M. (1974) Cross-Validatory Choice and Assessment of Statistical Predictions (with discussion), *Journal of Royal Statistical Society, ser.B*, **36**, 111-147.

Sundararajan, S., and Keerthi, S.S. (1999) Predictive Approaches for Choosing Hyperparameters in Gaussian Processes, submitted to *Neural Computation*, available at: http://guppy.mpe.nus.edu.sg/~mpessk/gp/gp.html.

Williams, C.K.I., and Rasmussen, C.E. (1996) Gaussian Processes for Regression. In *Advances in Neural Information Processing Systems 8*, ed. by D.S.Touretzky, M.C.Mozer, and M.E.Hasselmo. MIT Press.

On input selection with reversible jump Markov chain Monte Carlo sampling

Peter Sykacek
Austrian Research Institute for Artificial Intelligence (ÖFAI)
Schottengasse 3, A-1010 Vienna, Austria
peter@ai.univie.ac.at

Abstract

In this paper we will treat input selection for a radial basis function (RBF) like classifier within a Bayesian framework. We approximate the a-posteriori distribution over both model coefficients and input subsets by samples drawn with Gibbs updates and reversible jump moves. Using some public datasets, we compare the classification accuracy of the method with a conventional ARD scheme. These datasets are also used to infer the a-posteriori probabilities of different input subsets.

1 Introduction

Methods that aim to determine relevance of inputs have always interested researchers in various communities. Classical feature subset selection techniques, as reviewed in [1], use search algorithms and evaluation criteria to determine *one* optimal subset. Although these approaches can improve classification accuracy, they do not explore different equally probable subsets. Automatic relevance determination (ARD) is another approach which determines relevance of inputs. ARD is due to [6] who uses Bayesian techniques, where hierarchical priors penalize irrelevant inputs.

Our approach is also "Bayesian": Relevance of inputs is measured by a probability distribution over all possible feature subsets. This probability measure is determined by the Bayesian evidence of the corresponding models. The general idea was already used in [7] for variable selection in linear regression models. Though our interest is different as we select inputs for a nonlinear classification model. We want an approximation of the true distribution over *all* different subsets. As the number of subsets grows exponentially with the total number of inputs, we can not calculate Bayesian model evidence directly. We need a method that samples efficiently across different dimensional parameter spaces. The most general method that can do this is the reversible jump Markov chain Monte Carlo sampler (reversible jump MC) recently proposed in [4]. The approach was successfully applied by [8] to determine a probability distribution in a mixture density model with variable number of kernels and in [5] to sample from the posterior of RBF regression networks with variable number of kernels. A Markov chain that switches between different input subsets is useful for two tasks: Counting how often a particular subset was visited gives us a relevance measure of the corresponding inputs; For classification, we approximate the integral over input sets and coefficients by summation over samples from the Markov chain.

The next sections will show how to implement such a reversible jump MC and apply the proposed algorithm to classification and input evaluation using some public datasets. Though the approach could not improve the MLP-ARD scheme from [6] in terms of classification accuracy, we still think that it is interesting: We can assess the importance of different *feature subsets* which is different than importance of *single features* as estimated by ARD.

2 Methods

The classifier used in this paper is a RBF like model. Inference is performed within a Bayesian framework. When conditioning on *one* set of inputs, the posterior over model parameters is already multimodal. Therefore we resort to Markov chain Monte Carlo (MCMC) sampling techniques to approximate the desired posterior over both model coefficients and feature subsets. In the next subsections we will propose an appropriate architecture for the classifier and a *hybrid sampler* for model inference. This hybrid sampler consists of two parts: We use Gibbs updates ([2]) to sample when conditioning on a particular set of inputs and reversible jump moves that carry out dimension switching updates.

2.1 The classifier

In order to allow input relevance determination by Bayesian model selection, the classifier needs at least one coefficient that is associated with each input: Roughly speaking, the probability of each model is proportional to the likelihood of the most probable coefficients, weighted by their posterior width divided by their prior width. The first factor always increases when using more coefficients (or input features). The second will decrease the more inputs we use and together this gives a peak for the most probable model. A classifier that satisfies these constraints is the so called *classification in the sampling paradigm*. We model class conditional densities and together with class priors express posterior probabilities for classes. In neural network literature this approach was first proposed in [10]. We use a model that allows for overlapping class conditional densities:

$$p(\underline{x}|k) = \sum_{d=1}^{D} w_{kd} p(\underline{x}|\Phi_d) \ , \ p(\underline{x}) = \sum_{k=1}^{K} P_k p(\underline{x}|k) \tag{1}$$

Using P_k for the K class priors and $p(\underline{x}|k)$ for the class conditional densities, (1) expresses posterior probabilities for classes as $P(k|\underline{x}) = P_k p(\underline{x}|k)/p(\underline{x})$. We choose the component densities, $p(\underline{x}|\Phi_d)$, to be Gaussian with restricted parametrisation: Each kernel is a multivariate normal distribution with a mean and a diagonal covariance matrix. For all Gaussian kernels together, we get $2*D*I$ parameters, with I denoting the current input dimension and D denoting the number of kernels. Apart from kernel coefficients, Φ_d, (1) has D coefficients per class, w_{kd}, indicating the prior kernel allocation probabilities and K class priors. Model (1) allows to treat labels of patterns as *missing data* and use labeled as well as unlabeled data for model inference. In this case training is carried out using the likelihood of observing inputs *and* targets:

$$p(\mathcal{T}, \mathcal{X}|\underline{\Theta}) = \Pi_{k=1}^{K} \Pi_{n_k=1}^{N_k} P_k p_k(\underline{x}_{n_k}|\underline{\Theta}_k) \Pi_{m=1}^{M} p(\underline{x}_m|\underline{\Theta}), \tag{2}$$

where $\mathcal{T}$ denotes labeled and $\mathcal{X}$ unlabeled training data. In (2) $\underline{\Theta}_k$ are all coefficients the k-th class conditional density depends on. We further use $\underline{\Theta}$ for all model coefficients together, n_k as number of samples belonging to class k and m as index for unlabeled samples. To make Gibbs updates possible, we further introduce two latent allocation variables. The first one, d, indicates the kernel number each sample was generated from, the second one is the unobserved class label c, introduced for unlabeled data. Typical approaches for training models like (1), e.g. [3] and [9], use the EM algorithm, which is closely related to the Gibbs sampler introduce in the next subsection.

2.2 Fixed dimension sampling

In this subsection we will formulate Gibbs updates for sampling from the posterior when conditioning on a fixed set of inputs. In order to allow sampling from the full conditional, we have to choose priors over coefficients from their *conjugate family*:

- Each component mean, $\underline{m}_d$, is given a Gaussian prior: $\underline{m}_d \sim \mathcal{N}_d(\underline{\xi}, \underline{\kappa})$.

- The inverse variance of input i and kernel d gets a Gamma prior: $\sigma_{id}^{-2} \sim \Gamma(\alpha, \beta_i)$.

- All d variances of input i have a common hyperparameter, β_i, that has itself a Gamma hyperprior: $\beta_i \sim \Gamma(g, h_i)$.

- The mixing coefficients, $\underline{w}_k$, get a Dirichlet prior: $\underline{w}_k \sim \mathcal{D}(\delta_w, ..., \delta_w)$.

- Class priors, $\underline{P}$, also get a Dirichlet prior: $\underline{P} \sim \mathcal{D}(\delta_P, ..., \delta_P)$.

The quantitative settings are similar to those used in [8]: Values for α are between 1 and 2, g is usually between 0.2 and 1 and h_i is typically between $1/R_i^2$ and $10/R_i^2$, with R_i denoting the i'th input range. The mean gets a Gaussian prior centered at the midpoint, $\underline{\xi}$, with diagonal inverse covariance matrix $\underline{\kappa}$, with $\kappa_{ii} = 1/R_i^2$. The prior counts δ_w and δ_P are set to 1 to give the corresponding probabilities non-informative proper Dirichlet priors.

The Gibbs sampler uses updates from the full conditional distributions in (3). For notational convenience we use $\underline{\Theta}_k$ for the parameters that determine class conditional densities. We use m as index over unlabeled data and c_m as latent class label. The index for all data is n, d_n are the latent kernel allocations and n_d the number of samples allocated by the d-th component. One distribution does not occur in the prior specification. That is $\mathcal{M}n(1, ...)$ which is a multinomial-one distribution. Finally we need some counters: $m_1 ... m_K$ are the counts per class and $m_{1k} .. m_{Dk}$ count kernel allocations of class-k-patterns. The full conditional of the d-th kernel variances and the hyper parameter β_i contain i as index of the input dimension. There we express each $\sigma_{i,d}^{-2}$ separately. In the expression of the d-th kernel mean,

$\underline{m}_d$, we use $\underline{V}_d$ to denote the entire covariance matrix.

$$p(c_m|...) = \mathcal{M}n\left(1, \left\{\frac{P_k p(\underline{x}_m|\Theta_k)}{\sum_k P_k p(\underline{x}_m|\Theta_k)}, k=1..K\right\}\right) \quad (3)$$

$$p(d_n|...) = \mathcal{M}n\left(1, \left\{\frac{w_{t_n d} p(\underline{x}_n|\Phi_d)}{\sum_l w_{t_n d} p(\underline{x}_n|\Phi_d)}, d=1..D\right\}\right)$$

$$p(\underline{\beta}_i|...) = \Gamma\left(g + D\alpha, h_i + \sum_d \sigma_{d,i}^{-2}\right)$$

$$p(\underline{w}_k|...) = \mathcal{D}(\delta_w + m_{1k},..., \delta_w + m_{Dk})$$

$$p(\underline{P}|...) = \mathcal{D}(\delta_P + m_1,..., \delta_P + m_K)$$

$$p(\underline{m}_d|...) = \mathcal{N}\left((n_d \underline{V}_d^{-1} + \underline{\kappa})^{-1}(n_d \underline{V}_d^{-1} \underline{\bar{x}}_d + \underline{\kappa}\underline{\xi}), (n_d \underline{V}_d^{-1} + \underline{\kappa})^{-1}\right)$$

$$p(\sigma_{i,d}^{-2}|...) = \Gamma\left(\alpha + \frac{n_d}{2}, \beta_i + \frac{1}{2}\sum_{\underline{x}_n \forall n|d_n=d}(\underline{x}_{n,i} - \underline{m}_{d,i})^2\right)$$

2.3 Moving between different input subsets

The core part of this sampler are reversible jump updates, where we move between different feature subsets. The probability of a feature subset will be determined by the corresponding Bayesian model evidence and by an additional prior over number of inputs. In accordance with [7], we use the truncated Poisson prior:

$$p(I) = 1/\binom{I_{max}}{I} c\frac{\lambda^I}{I!}, \text{ where } c \text{ is a constant and } I_{max} \text{ the total nr. of inputs.}$$

Reversible jump updates are generalizations of conventional Metropolis-Hastings updates, where moves are bijections $(x, u) \leftrightarrow (x', u')$. For a thorough treatment we refer to [4]. In order to switch subsets efficiently, we will use two different types of moves. The first consist of a step where we add one input chosen at random and a matching step that removes one randomly chosen input. A second move exchanges two inputs which allows "tunneling" through low likelihood areas.

Adding an input, we have to increase the dimension of all kernel means and diagonal covariances. These coefficients are drawn from their priors. In addition the move proposes new allocation probabilities in a semi deterministic way. Assuming the ordering, $w_{k,d} \leq w_{k,d+1}$:

$$\delta_p = \text{Beta}(b_a, b_b + I)$$

$$\forall d \leq D/2 \quad \begin{cases} w'_{k,D+1-d} = w_{k,D+1-d} + w_{k,d}\delta_p \\ w'_{k,d} = w_{k,d}(1 - \delta_p) \end{cases} \quad (4)$$

The matching step proposes removing a randomly chosen input. Removing corresponding kernel coefficients is again combined with a semi deterministic proposal of new allocation probabilities, which is exactly symmetric to the proposal in (4).

Table 1: Summary of experiments

Data	avg(#)	max(#)	RBF (%,n_a)	MLP (%,n_b)
Ionosphere	4.3	9	(91.5,11)	(95.5,4)
Pima	4	7	(78.9,11)	(79.8,8)
Wine	4.4	8	(100, 0)	(96.8,2)

We accept births with probability:

$$\alpha_b = \min(1, \text{lh. rt.} \times \frac{p(I+1)}{p(I)} \left(\frac{1}{R'}\sqrt{2\pi}\right)^D \prod_D \exp\left(-0.5\frac{1}{R'^2}(\mu'_d - \xi'_d)^2\right)$$

$$\times \left(\frac{\beta'^\alpha}{\Gamma(\alpha)}\right)^D \prod_D (\sigma'^{-2}_d)^{\alpha-1} \exp(-\beta'\sigma'^{-2}_d)$$

$$\times \frac{d_m/(I+1)}{b_m/(I_{max}-I)} \times \frac{1}{\left(\frac{1}{R'}\sqrt{2\pi}\right)^D \prod_D \exp\left(-0.5\frac{1}{R'^2}(\mu'_d - \xi'_d)^2\right)}$$

$$\times \frac{1}{\left(\frac{\beta'^\alpha}{\Gamma(\alpha)}\right)^D \prod_D (\sigma'^{-2}_d)^{\alpha-1} \exp(-\beta'\sigma'^{-2}_d)}). \quad (5)$$

The first line in (5) are the likelihood and prior ratio. The prior ratio results from the difference in input dimension, which affects the kernel means and the prior over number of inputs. The first term of the proposal ratio is from proposing to add or remove one input. The second term is the proposal density of the additional kernel components which cancels with the corresponding term in the prior ratio. Due to symmetry of the proposal (4) and its reverse in a death move, there is no contribution from changing allocation probabilities. Death moves are accepted with probability $\alpha_d = 1/\alpha_b$.

The second type of move is an exchange move. We select a new input and one from the model inputs and propose new mean coefficients. This gives the following acceptance probability:

$$\alpha_c = min(1, \text{lh. ratio} \times \frac{\left(\frac{1}{R'}\sqrt{2\pi}\right)^D \prod_D \exp\left(-0.5\frac{1}{R'^2}(\mu'_d - \xi'_d)^2\right)}{\left(\frac{1}{R'}\sqrt{2\pi}\right)^D \prod_D \exp\left(-0.5\frac{1}{R'^2}(\mu_d - \xi_d)^2\right)} \quad (6)$$

$$\times \frac{c_m/I}{c_m/(I_{max}-I)} \times \frac{\prod_D \mathcal{N}(\mu_d|...)}{\prod_D \mathcal{N}(\mu'_d|...)}).$$

The first line of (6) are again likelihood and prior ratio. For exchange moves, the prior ratio is just the ratio from different values in the kernel means. The first term in the proposal ratio is from proposing to exchange an input. The second term is the proposal density of new kernel mean components. The last part is from proposing new allocation probabilities.

3 Experiments

Although the method can be used with labeled and unlabeled data, the following experiments were performed using only labeled data. For all experiments we set $\alpha = 2$ and $g = 0.2$. The first two data sets are from the UCI repository[1]. We use

---
[1] Available at http://www.ics.uci.edu/ mlearn/MLRepository.html.

the Ionosphere data which has 33 inputs, 175 training and 176 test samples. For this experiment we use 6 kernels and set $h = 0.5$. The second data is the wine recognition data which provides 13 inputs, 62 training and 63 test samples. For this data, we use 3 kernels and set $h = 0.28$. The third experiment is performed with the Pima data provided by B. D. Ripley[2]. For this one we use 3 kernels and set $h = 0.16$.

For all experiments we draw 15000 samples from the posterior over coefficients and input subsets. We discard the first 5000 samples as burn in and use the rest for predictions. Classification accuracy, is compared with an MLP classifier using R. Neals hybrid Monte Carlo sampling with ARD priors on inputs. These experiments use 25 hidden units. Table 1 contains further details: avg(#) is the average and max(#) the maximal number of inputs used by the hybrid sampler; RBF (%, n_a) is the classification accuracy of the hybrid sampler and the number of errors it made that were not made by the ARD-MLP; MLP(%, n_b) is the same for the ARD-MLP. We compare classifiers by testing (n_a, n_b) against the null hypothesis that this is an observation from a Binomial $\mathcal{B}n(n_a + n_b, 0.5)$ distribution. This reveals that neither difference is significant. Although we could not improve classification accuracy on these data, this does not really matter because ARD methods usually lead to high generalization accuracy and we can compete.

The real benefit from using the hybrid sampler is that we can infer probabilities telling us how much different subsets contribute to an explanation of the target variables. Figure 3 shows the occurrence probabilities of feature subsets and features. Note that table 1 has also details about how many features were used in these problems. Especially the results from Ionosphere data are interesting as on average we use only 4.3 out of 33 input features. For ionosphere and wine data the Markov chain visits about 500 different input subsets within 10000 samples. For the Pima data the number is about 60 and an order of magnitude smaller.

4 Discussion

In this paper we have discussed a hybrid sampler that uses Gibbs updates and reversible jump moves to approximate the a-posteriori distribution over parameters and input subsets in nonlinear classification problems. The classification accuracy of the method could compete with R. Neals MLP-ARD implementation. However the real advantage of the method is that it provides us with a relevance measure of feature subsets. This allows to infer the optimal number of inputs and how many different explanations the data provides.

Acknowledgements

I want to thank several people for having used resources they provide: I have used R.Neals hybrid Markov chain sampler for the MLP experiments; The data used for the experiments were obtained form the University at Irvine repository and from B. D. Ripley. Furthermore I want to express gratitude to the anonymous reviewers for their comments and to J.F.G. de Freitas for useful discussions during the conference. This work was done in the framework of the research project GZ 607.519/2-V/B/9/98 "Verbesserung der Biosignalverarbeitung durch Beruecksichtigung von Unsicherheit und Konfidenz", funded by the Austrian federal ministry of science and transport (BMWV).

---

[2] Available at http://www.stats.ox.ac.uk

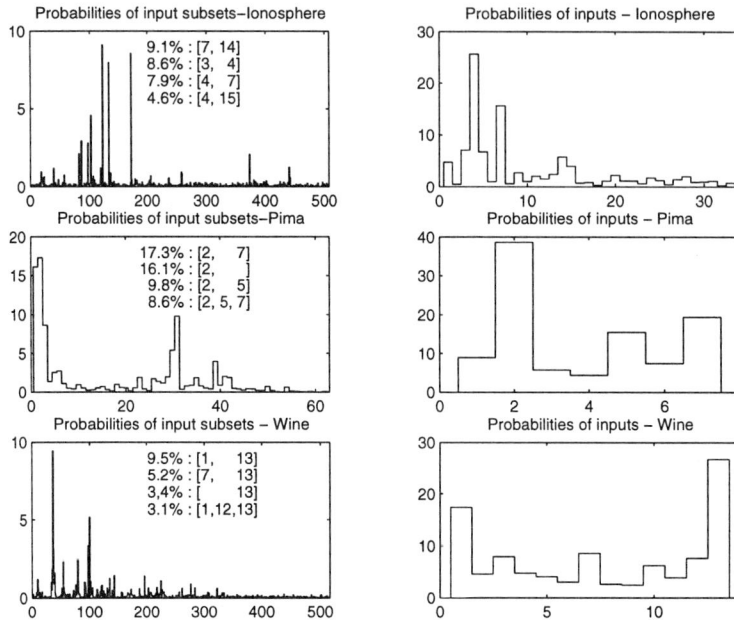

Figure 1: Probabilities of inputs and input subsets measuring their relevance.

References

[1] P. A. Devijver and J. V. Kittler. *Pattern Recognition. A Statistical Approach.* Prentice-Hall, Englewood Cliffs, NJ, 1982.

[2] S. Geman and D. Geman. Stochastic relaxation, gibbs distributions and the bayesian restoration of images. *IEEE Trans. Pattn. Anal. Mach. Intel.*, 6:721–741, 1984.

[3] Z. Ghahramani, M.I. Jordan Supervised Learning from Incomplete Data via an EM Approach In Cowan J.D., et al.(eds.), Advances in Neural Information Processing Systems 6, Morgan Kaufmann, Los Altos/Palo Alto/San Francisco, pp.120-127, 1994.

[4] P. J. Green. Reversible jump markov chain monte carlo computation and bayesian model determination. *Biometrika*, 82:711–732, 1995.

[5] C. C. Holmes and B. K. Mallick. Bayesian radial basis functions of variable dimension. *Neural Computation*, 10:1217–1234, 1998.

[6] R. M. Neal. Bayesian Learning for Neural Networks. Springer, New York, 1986.

[7] D. B. Phillips and A. F. M. Smith. Bayesian model comparison via jump diffusioons. In W.R. Gilks, S. Richardson, and D.J. Spiegelhalter, editors, *Markov Chain Monte Carlo in Practice*, pages 215–239, London, 1996. Chapman & Hall.

[8] S. Richardson and P.J. Green On Bayesian Analysis of Mixtures with an unknown number of components *Journal Royal Stat. Soc. B*, 59:731–792, 1997.

[9] M. Stensmo, T.J. Sejnowski A Mixture Model System for Medical and Machine Diagnosis In Tesauro G., et al.(eds.), Advances in Neural Information Processing System 7, MIT Press, Cambridge/Boston/London, pp.1077-1084, 1995.

[10] H. G. C. Tråvén A neural network approach to statistical pattern classification by "semiparametric" estimation of probability density functions IEEE Trans. Neur. Net., 2:366–377, 1991.

Building Predictive Models from Fractal Representations of Symbolic Sequences

Peter Tiño   Georg Dorffner
Austrian Research Institute for Artificial Intelligence
Schottengasse 3, A-1010 Vienna, Austria
{*petert,georg*}@*ai.univie.ac.at*

Abstract

We propose a novel approach for building finite memory predictive models similar in spirit to variable memory length Markov models (VLMMs). The models are constructed by first transforming the n-block structure of the training sequence into a spatial structure of points in a unit hypercube, such that the longer is the common suffix shared by any two n-blocks, the closer lie their point representations. Such a transformation embodies a Markov assumption – n-blocks with long common suffixes are likely to produce similar continuations. Finding a set of prediction contexts is formulated as a resource allocation problem solved by vector quantizing the spatial n-block representation. We compare our model with both the classical and variable memory length Markov models on three data sets with different memory and stochastic components. Our models have a superior performance, yet, their construction is fully automatic, which is shown to be problematic in the case of VLMMs.

1 Introduction

Statistical modeling of complex sequences is a prominent theme in machine learning due to its wide variety of applications (see e.g. [5]). Classical Markov models (MMs) of finite order are simple, yet widely used models for sequences generated by stationary sources. However, MMs can become hard to estimate due to the familiar explosive increase in the number of free parameters when increasing the model order. Consequently, only low order MMs can be considered in practical applications. Some time ago, Ron, Singer and Tishby [4] introduced at this conference a Markovian model that could (at least partially) overcome the curse of dimensionality in classical MMs. The basic idea behind their model was simple: instead of fixed-order MMs consider variable memory length Markov models (VLMMs) with a "deep" memory just where it is really needed (see also e.g. [5][7]).

The size of VLMMs is usually controlled by one or two construction parameters. Unfortunately, constructing a series of increasingly complex VLMMs (for example to enter a model selection phase on a validation set) by varying the construction parameters can be a troublesome task [1]. Construction often does not work "smoothly" with varying the parameters. There are large intervals of parameter values yielding unchanged VLMMs interleaved with tiny parameter regions corresponding to a large spectrum of VLMM sizes. In such cases it is difficult to fully automize the VLMM construction.

To overcome this drawback, we suggest an alternative predictive model similar in spirit to VLMMs. Searching for the relevant prediction contexts is reformulated as a resource allocation problem in Euclidean space solved by vector quantization. A potentially prohibitively large set of all length-L blocks is assigned to a much smaller set of prediction contexts on a suffix basis. To that end, we first transform the set of L-blocks appearing in the training sequence into a set of points in Euclidean space, such that points corresponding to blocks sharing a long common suffix are mapped close to each other. Vector quantization on such a set partitions the set of L-blocks into several classes dominated by common suffixes. Quantization centers play the role of predictive contexts. A great advantage of our model is that vector quantization can be performed on a completely self-organized basis.

We compare our model with both classical MMs and VLMMs on three data sets representing a wide range of grammatical and statistical structure. First, we train the models on the Feigenbaum binary sequence with a very strict topological and metric organization of allowed subsequences. Highly specialized, deep prediction contexts are needed to model this sequence. Classical Markov models cannot succeed and the full power of admitting a limited number of variable length contexts can be exploited. The second data set consists of quantized daily volatility changes of the Dow Jones Industrial Average (DJIA). Predictive models are used to predict the direction of volatility move for the next day. Financial time series are known to be highly stochastic with a relatively shallow memory structure. In this case, it is difficult to beat low-order classical MMs. One can perform better than MMs only by developing a few deeper specialized contexts, but that, on the other hand, can lead to overfitting. Finally, we test our model on the experiments of Ron, Singer and Tishby with language data from the Bible [5]. They trained classical MMs and a VLMM on the books of the Bible except for the book of Genesis. Then the models were evaluated on the bases of negative log-likelihood on an unseen text from Genesis. We compare likelihood results of our model with those of MMs and VLMMs.

2 Predictive models

We consider sequences $S = s_1 s_2 ...$ over a finite alphabet $\mathcal{A} = \{1, 2, ..., A\}$ generated by stationary sources. The set of all sequences over $\mathcal{A}$ with exactly n symbols is denoted by $\mathcal{A}^n$.

An information source over $\mathcal{A} = \{1, 2, ..., A\}$ is defined by a family of consistent probability measures P_n on $\mathcal{A}^n$, $n = 0, 1, 2, ..., \sum_{s \in \mathcal{A}} P_{n+1}(ws) = P_n(w)$, for all $w \in \mathcal{A}^n$ ($\mathcal{A}^0 = \{\Lambda\}$ and $P_0(\Lambda) = 1$, Λ denotes the empty string).

In applications it is useful to consider probability functions P_n that are easy to handle. This can be achieved, for example, by assuming a finite source memory of length at most L, and formulating the conditional measures $P(s|w) = P_{L+1}(ws)/P_L(w)$, $w \in \mathcal{A}^L$, using a function $c : \mathcal{A}^L \to \mathcal{C}$, from L-blocks over $\mathcal{A}$ to a (presumably small) finite set $\mathcal{C}$ of prediction contexts:

$$P(s|w) = P(s|c(w)). \tag{1}$$

In *Markov models* (MMs) of order $n \leq L$, for all L-blocks $w \in \mathcal{A}^L$, $c(w)$ is the length-n

suffix of w, i.e. $c(uv) = v$, $v \in \mathcal{A}^n$, $u \in \mathcal{A}^{L-n}$.

In *variable memory length Markov models* (VLMMs), the suffices $c(w)$ of L-blocks $w \in \mathcal{A}^L$ can have different lengths, depending on the particular L-block w. For strategies of selecting and representing the prediction contexts through prediction suffix trees and/or probabilistic suffix automata see, for example, [4][5]. VLMM construction is controlled by one, or several parameters regulating selection of candidate contexts and growing/pruning decisions.

Prediction context function $c : \mathcal{A}^L \to \mathcal{C}$ in Markov models of order $n \leq L$, can be interpreted as a natural homomorphism $c : \mathcal{A}^L \to \mathcal{A}^L|_{\mathcal{E}}$ corresponding to the equivalence relation $\mathcal{E} \subseteq \mathcal{A}^L \times \mathcal{A}^L$ on L-blocks over $\mathcal{A}$: two L-blocks u, v are in the same class, i.e. $(u, v) \in \mathcal{E}$, if they share the same suffix of length n. The factor set $\mathcal{A}^L|_{\mathcal{E}} = \mathcal{C} = \mathcal{A}^n$ consists of all n-blocks over $\mathcal{A}$. Classical MMs define the equivalence $\mathcal{E}$ on the suffix bases, but *regardless of the suffix structure present in the training data*. Our idea is to keep the Markov-motivated suffix strategy for constructing $\mathcal{E}$, but at the same time *take into an account the data suffix structure*.

Vector quantization on a set of B points in a Euclidean space positions $N << B$ codebook vectors (CVs), each CV representing a subset of points that are closer to it than to any other CV, so that the overall error of substituting CVs for points they represent is minimal. In other words, CVs tend to represent points lying close to each other (in a Euclidean metric). In order to use vector quantization for determining relevant predictive contexts we need to do two things:

1. Define a suitable metric in the sequence space that would correspond to Markov assumptions:

    (a) two sequences are "close" if they share a common suffix
    (b) the longer is the common suffix the closer are the sequences

2. Define a uniformly continuous map from the sequence metric space to the Euclidean space, i.e. sequences that are close in the sequence space (i.e. share a long common suffix) are mapped close to each other in the Euclidean space.

In [6] we rigorously study a class of such spatial representations of symbolic structures. Specifically, a family of distances between two L-blocks $u = u_1 u_2 ... u_{L-1} u_L$ and $v = v_1 v_2 ... v_{L-1} v_L$ over $\mathcal{A} = \{1, 2, ..., A\}$, expressed as

$$d_k(u, v) = \sum_{i=1}^{L} k^{L-i+1} \delta(u_i, v_i), \quad k \leq \frac{1}{2}, \qquad (2)$$

with $\delta(i, j) = 1$ if $i = j$, and $\delta(i, j) = 0$ otherwise, correspond to Markov assumption. The parameter k influences the rate of "forgetting the past". We construct a map from the sequence metric space to the Euclidean space as follows: Associate with each symbol $i \in \mathcal{A}$ a map

$$i(x) = kx + (1-k)t_i, \quad t_i \in \{0, 1\}^D, \quad x \in [0, 1]^D \qquad (3)$$

operating on a unit D-dimensional hypercube $[0, 1]^D$. Dimension of the hypercube should be large enough so that each symbol i is associated with a unique vertex, i.e. $D = \lceil \log_2 A \rceil$ and $t_i \neq t_j$ whenever $i \neq j$. The map $\sigma : \mathcal{A}^L \to [0, 1]^D$, from L-blocks $v_1 v_2 ... v_L$ over $\mathcal{A}$ to the unit hypercube,

$$\sigma(v_1 v_2 ... v_L) = v_L(v_{L-1}(...(v_2(v_1(x^*)))...)) = (v_L \circ v_{L-1} \circ ... \circ v_2 \circ v_1)(x^*), \qquad (4)$$

where $x^* = \{\frac{1}{2}\}^D$ is the center of the hypercube, is "uniformly continuous". Indeed, whenever two sequences u, v share a common suffix of length Q, the Euclidean distance between their point representations $\sigma(u)$ and $\sigma(v)$ is less than $\sqrt{2}k^Q$. Strictly speaking, for a mathematically correct treatment of uniform continuity, we would need to consider infinite sequences. Finite blocks of symbols would then correspond to cylinder sets (see [6]). For sake of simplicity we only deal with finite sequences.

As with classical Markov models, we define the prediction context function $c : \mathcal{A}^L \to \mathcal{C}$ via an equivalence $\mathcal{E}$ on L-blocks over $\mathcal{A}$: two L-blocks u, v are in the same class if their images under the map σ are represented by the same codebook vector. In this case, the set of prediction contexts $\mathcal{C}$ can be identified with the set of codebook vectors $\{b_1, b_2, ..., b_N\}$, $b_i \in \Re^D$, $i = 1, 2, ..., N$. We refer to predictive models with such a context function as *prediction fractal machines* (PFMs). The prediction probabilities (1) are determined by

$$P(s|b_i) = \frac{N(i,s)}{\sum_{a \in \mathcal{A}} N(i,a)}, \quad s \in \mathcal{A}, \tag{5}$$

where $N(i, a)$ is the number of $(L+1)$-blocks $ua, a \in \mathcal{A}^L, a \in \mathcal{A}$, in the training sequence, such that the point $\sigma(u)$ is allocated to the codebook vector b_i.

3 Experiments

In all experiments we constructed PFMs using a contraction coefficient $k = \frac{1}{2}$ (see eq. (3)) and K-means as a vector quantization tool.

The first data set is the Feigenbaum sequence over the binary alphabet $\mathcal{A} = \{1, 2\}$. This sequence is well-studied in symbolic dynamics and has a number of interesting properties. First, the topological structure of the sequence can only be described using a context sensitive tool – a restricted indexed context-free grammar. Second, for each block length $n = 1, 2, ...$, the distribution of n-blocks is either uniform, or has just two probability levels. Third, the n-block distributions are organized in a self-similar fashion (see [2]). The sequence can be specified by the subsequence composition rule

$$a_0 = 2, \quad a_1 = 21, \quad a_{n+1} = a_n a_{n-1} a_{n-1}. \tag{6}$$

We chose to work with the Feigenbaum sequence, because increasingly accurate modeling of the sequence with finite memory models requires a selective mechanism for deep prediction contexts.

We created a large portion of the Feigenbaum sequence and trained a series of classical MMs, variable memory length MMs (VLMMs), and prediction fractal machines (PFMs) on the first 260,000 symbols. The following 200,000 symbols formed a test set. Maximum memory length L for VLMMs and PFMs was set to 30.

As mentioned in the introduction, constructing a series of increasingly complex VLMMs by varying the construction parameters appeared to be a troublesome task. We spent a fair amount of time finding "critical" parameter values at which the model size changed. In contrast, a fully automatic construction of PFMs involved sliding a window of length $L = 30$ through the training set; for each window position, mapping the L-block u appearing in the window to the point $\sigma(u)$ (eq. (4)), vector-quantizing the resulting set of points (up to 30 codebook vectors). After the quantization step we computed predictive probabilities according to eq. (5).

Table 1: Normalized negative log-likelihoods (NNL) on the Feigenbaum test set.

model	# contexts	NNL	captured block distribution
PFM	2–4	0.6666	1–3
	5–7	0.3333	1–6
	8–22	0.1666	1–12
	23–	0.0833	1–24
VLMM	2–4	0.6666	1–3
	5	0.3333	1–6
	11	0.1666	1–12
	23	0.0833	1–24
MM	2,4,8,16,32	0.6666	1–3

Negative log-likelihoods per symbol (the base of logarithm is always taken to be the number of symbols in the alphabet) of the test set computed using the fitted models exhibited a step-like increasing tendency shown in Table 1. We also investigated the ability of the models to reproduce the n-block distribution found in the training and test sets. This was done by letting the models generate sequences of length equal to the length of the training sequence and for each block length $n = 1, 2, ..., 30$, computing the L_1 distance between the n-block distribution of the training and model-generated sequences. The n-block distributions on the test and training sets were virtually the same for $n = 1, 2, ...30$. In Table 1 we show block lengths for which the L_1 distance does not exceed a small threshold Δ. We set $\Delta = 0.005$, since in this experiment, either the L_1 distance was less 0.005, or exceeded 0.005 by a large amount.

An explanation of the step-like behavior in the log-likelihood and n-block modeling behavior of VLMMs and PFMs is out of the scope of this paper. We briefly mention, however, that by combining the knowledge about the topological and metric structures of the Feigenbaum sequence (e.g. [2]) with a careful analysis of the models, one can show why and when an inclusion of a prediction context leads to an abrupt improvement in the modeling performance. In fact, we can show that VLMMs and PFMs constitute increasingly better approximations to the infinite self-similar Feigenbaum machine known in symbolic dynamics [2].

The classical MM totally fails in this experiment, since the context length 5 is far too small to enable the MM to mimic the complicated subsequence structure in the Feigenbaum sequence. PFMs and VLMMs quickly learn to explore a limited number of deep prediction contexts and perform comparatively well.

In the second experiment, a time series $\{x_t\}$ of the daily values of the Dow Jones Industrial Average (DJIA) from Feb. 1 1918 until April 1 1997 was transformed into a time series of returns $r_t = \log x_{t+1} - \log x_t$, and divided into 12 partially overlapping epochs, each containing about 2300 values (spanning approximately 9 years). We consider the squared return r_t^2 a volatility estimate for day t. Volatility change forecasts (volatility is going to increase or decrease) based on historical returns can be interpreted as a buying or selling signal for a straddle (see e.g. [3]). If the volatility decreases we go short (straddle is sold), if it increases we take a long position (straddle is bought). In this respect, the quality of a volatility model can be measured by the percentage of correctly predicted directions of daily volatility differences.

Table 2: Prediction performance on the DJIA volatility series.

model	Percent correct on test set					
	1	2	3	4	5	6
PFM	71.08	70.39	69.70	70.05	72.12	72.46
VLMM	68.67	68.18	68.79	69.25	69.41	68.29
MM	68.56	69.11	69.78	68.28	69.50	73.13
	7	8	9	10	11	12
PFM	74.01	71.77	73.84	73.84	71,77	74.19
VLMM	69.83	67.00	67.96	70.76	69.80	70.25
MM	74.16	71.96	69.95	69.16	71.74	71.07

The series $\{r_{t+1}^2 - r_t^2\}$ of differences between the successive squared returns is transformed into a sequence $\{D_t\}$ over 4 symbols by quantizing the series $\{r_{t+1}^2 - r_t^2\}$ as follows:

$$D_t = \begin{cases} 1 \text{ (extreme down)}, & \text{if } r_{t+1}^2 - r_t^2 < \theta_1 < 0 \\ 2 \text{ (normal down)}, & \text{if } \theta_1 \leq r_{t+1}^2 - r_t^2 < 0 \\ 3 \text{ (normal up)}, & \text{if } 0 \leq r_{t+1}^2 - r_t^2 < \theta_2 \\ 4 \text{ (extreme up)}, & \text{if } \theta_2 \leq r_{t+1}^2 - r_t^2, \end{cases} \quad (7)$$

where the parameters θ_1 and θ_2 correspond to Q percent and $(100 - Q)$ percent sample quantiles, respectively. So, the upper (lower) $Q\%$ of all daily volatility increases (decreases) in the sample are considered extremal, and the lower (upper) $(50 - Q)\%$ of daily volatility increases (decreases) are viewed as normal.

Each epoch is partitioned into training, validation and test parts containing 110, 600 and 600 symbols, respectively. Maximum memory length L for VLMMs and PFMs was set to 10 (two weeks). We trained classical MMs, VLMMs and PFMs with various numbers of prediction contexts (up to 256) and extremal event quantiles $Q \in \{5, 10, 15, ..., 45\}$. For each model class, the model size and the quantile Q to be used on the test set were selected according to the validation set performance. Performance of the models was quantified as the percentage of correct guesses of the volatility change direction for the next day. If the next symbol is 1 or 2 (3 or 4) and the sum of conditional next symbol probabilities for 1 and 2 (3 and 4) given by a model is greater than 0.5, the model guess is considered correct. Results are shown in Table 2. Paired t-test reveals that PFMs significantly ($p < 0.005$) outperform both VLMMs and classical MMs.

Of course, fixed-order MMs are just special cases of VLMMs, so theoretically, VLMMs cannot perform worse than MMs. We present separate results for MMs and VLMMs to illustrate *practical* problems in fitting VLMMs. Besides familiar problems with setting the construction parameter values, one-parameter-schemes (like that presented in [4] and used here) operate only on small subsets of potential VLMMs. On data sets with a rather shallow memory structure, this can have a negative effect.

The third experiment extends the work of Ron, Singer and Tishby [5]. They tested classical MMs and VLMMs on the Bible. The alphabet is English letters and the blank character (27 symbols). The training set consisted of the Bible except for the book of Genesis. The test set was a portion of 236 characters from the book of Genesis. They set the maximal memory depth to $L = 30$ and constructed a VLMM with about 3000 contexts. Summarizing the results in [5], classical MMs of order 0, 1, 2 and 3 achieved negative log-likelihoods per character (NNL) of 0.853, 0.681, 0.560 and 0.555, respectively. The authors point out a huge difference between the number of states in MMs of order 2 and 3: $27^3 - 27^2 = 18954$. **VLMM** performed much better and achieved an NNL of **0.456**. In our experiments, we set the maximal memory length to $L = 30$ (the same maximal memory length was used for VLMM construction in [5]). PFMs were constructed by vector quantizing a 5-dimensional (alphabet has 27 symbols) spatial representation of 30-blocks appearing in the training set. On the test set, **PFMs** with 100, 500, 1000 and 3000 predictive contexts achieved an NNL of 0.622, 0.518, 0.510 and **0.435**.

4 Conclusion

We presented a novel approach for building finite memory predictive models similar in spirit to variable memory length Markov models (VLMMs). Constructing a series of VLMMs is often a troublesome and highly time-consuming task requiring a lot of interactive steps. Our predictive models, prediction fractal machines (PFMs), can be constructed in a completely automatic and intuitive way - the number of codebook vectors in the vector quantization PFM construction step corresponds to the number of predictive contexts.

We tested our model on three data sets with different memory and stochastic components. VLMMs excel over the classical MMs on the Feigenbaum sequence requiring deep prediction contexts. On this sequence, PFMs achieved the same performance as their rivals - VLMMs. On financial time series, PFMs significantly outperform the purely symbolic Markov models - MMs and VLMMs. On natural language Bible data, our PFM outperforms a VLMM of comparable size.

Acknowledgments

This work was supported by the Austrian Science Fund (FWF) within the research project "Adaptive Information Systems and Modeling in Economics and Management Science" (SFB 010) and the Slovak Academy of Sciences grant SAV 2/6018/99. The Austrian Research Institute for Artificial Intelligence is supported by the Austrian Federal Ministry of Science and Transport.

References

[1] P. Bühlmann. Model selection for variable length Markov chains and tuning the context algorithm. *Annals of the Institute of Statistical Mathematics*, (in press), 1999.

[2] J. Freund, W. Ebeling, and K. Rateitschak. Self-similar sequences and universal scaling of dynamical entropies. *Physical Review E*, 54(5), pp. 5561–5566, 1996.

[3] J. Noh, R.F. Engle, and A. Kane. Forecasting volatility and option prices of the s&p 500 index. *Journal of Derivatives*, pp. 17–30, 1994.

[4] D. Ron, Y. Singer, and N. Tishby. The power of amnesia. In *Advances in Neural Information Processing Systems 6*, pp. 176–183. Morgan Kaufmann, 1994.

[5] D. Ron, Y. Singer, and N. Tishby. The power of amnesia. *Machine Learning*, 25, 1996.

[6] P. Tiňo. Spatial representation of symbolic sequences through iterative function system. *IEEE Transactions on Systems, Man, and Cybernetics Part A: Systems and Humans*, 29(4), pp. 386–392, 1999.

[7] M.J. Weinberger, J.J. Rissanen, and M. Feder. A universal finite memory source. *IEEE Transactions on Information Theory*, 41(3), pp. 643–652, 1995.

The Relevance Vector Machine

Michael E. Tipping
Microsoft Research
St George House, 1 Guildhall Street
Cambridge CB2 3NH, U.K.
mtipping@microsoft.com

Abstract

The support vector machine (SVM) is a state-of-the-art technique for regression and classification, combining excellent generalisation properties with a sparse kernel representation. However, it does suffer from a number of disadvantages, notably the absence of probabilistic outputs, the requirement to estimate a trade-off parameter and the need to utilise 'Mercer' kernel functions. In this paper we introduce the *Relevance Vector Machine* (RVM), a Bayesian treatment of a generalised linear model of identical functional form to the SVM. The RVM suffers from none of the above disadvantages, and examples demonstrate that for comparable generalisation performance, the RVM requires dramatically fewer kernel functions.

1 Introduction

In *supervised learning* we are given a set of examples of input vectors $\{\mathbf{x}_n\}_{n=1}^N$ along with corresponding targets $\{t_n\}_{n=1}^N$, the latter of which might be real values (in *regression*) or class labels (*classification*). From this 'training' set we wish to learn a model of the dependency of the targets on the inputs with the objective of making accurate predictions of t for previously unseen values of $\mathbf{x}$. In real-world data, the presence of noise (in regression) and class overlap (in classification) implies that the principal modelling challenge is to avoid 'over-fitting' of the training set.

A very successful approach to supervised learning is the *support vector machine* (SVM) [8]. It makes predictions based on a function of the form

$$y(\mathbf{x}) = \sum_{n=1}^{N} w_n K(\mathbf{x}, \mathbf{x}_n) + w_0, \qquad (1)$$

where $\{w_n\}$ are the model 'weights' and $K(\cdot,\cdot)$ is a *kernel* function. The key feature of the SVM is that, in the classification case, its target function attempts to minimise the number of errors made on the training set while simultaneously maximising the 'margin' between the two classes (in the feature space implicitly defined by the kernel). This is an effective 'prior' for avoiding over-fitting, which leads to good generalisation, and which furthermore results in a *sparse* model dependent only on a subset of kernel functions: those associated with training examples $\mathbf{x}_n$ that lie either on the margin or on the 'wrong' side of it. State-of-the-art results have been reported on many tasks where SVMs have been applied.

However, the support vector methodology does exhibit significant disadvantages:

- Predictions are not *probabilistic*. In regression the SVM outputs a point estimate, and in classification, a 'hard' binary decision. Ideally, we desire to estimate the conditional distribution $p(t|\mathbf{x})$ in order to capture uncertainty in our prediction. In regression this may take the form of 'error-bars', but it is particularly crucial in classification where posterior probabilities of class membership are necessary to adapt to varying class priors and asymmetric misclassification costs.
- Although relatively sparse, SVMs make liberal use of kernel functions, the requisite number of which grows steeply with the size of the training set.
- It is necessary to estimate the error/margin trade-off parameter 'C' (and in regression, the insensitivity parameter 'ϵ' too). This generally entails a cross-validation procedure, which is wasteful both of data and computation.
- The kernel function $K(\cdot, \cdot)$ must satisfy Mercer's condition.

In this paper, we introduce the 'relevance vector machine' (RVM), a probabilistic sparse kernel model identical in functional form to the SVM. Here we adopt a Bayesian approach to learning, where we introduce a prior over the weights governed by a set of hyperparameters, one associated with each weight, whose most probable values are iteratively estimated from the data. Sparsity is achieved because in practice we find that the posterior distributions of many of the weights are sharply peaked around zero. Furthermore, unlike the support vector classifier, the non-zero weights in the RVM are *not* associated with examples close to the decision boundary, but rather appear to represent 'prototypical' examples of classes. We term these examples 'relevance' vectors, in deference to the principle of *automatic relevance determination* (ARD) which motivates the presented approach [4, 6].

The most compelling feature of the RVM is that, while capable of generalisation performance comparable to an equivalent SVM, it typically utilises dramatically fewer kernel functions. Furthermore, the RVM suffers from none of the other limitations of the SVM outlined above.

In the next section, we introduce the Bayesian model, initially for regression, and define the procedure for obtaining hyperparameter values, and thus weights. In Section 3, we give brief examples of application of the RVM in the regression case, before developing the theory for the classification case in Section 4. Examples of RVM classification are then given in Section 5, concluding with a discussion.

2 Relevance Vector Regression

Given a dataset of input-target pairs $\{\mathbf{x}_n, t_n\}_{n=1}^{N}$, we follow the standard formulation and assume $p(t|\mathbf{x})$ is Gaussian $\mathcal{N}(t|y(\mathbf{x}), \sigma^2)$. The mean of this distribution for a given $\mathbf{x}$ is modelled by $y(\mathbf{x})$ as defined in (1) for the SVM. The likelihood of the dataset can then be written as

$$p(\mathbf{t}|\mathbf{w}, \sigma^2) = (2\pi\sigma^2)^{-N/2} \exp\left\{-\frac{1}{2\sigma^2}\|\mathbf{t} - \mathbf{\Phi}\mathbf{w}\|^2\right\}, \qquad (2)$$

where $\mathbf{t} = (t_1 \ldots t_N)$, $\mathbf{w} = (w_0 \ldots w_N)$ and $\mathbf{\Phi}$ is the $N \times (N+1)$ 'design' matrix with $\mathbf{\Phi}_{nm} = K(\mathbf{x}_n, \mathbf{x}_{m-1})$ and $\mathbf{\Phi}_{n1} = 1$. Maximum-likelihood estimation of $\mathbf{w}$ and σ^2 from (2) will generally lead to severe overfitting, so we encode a preference for smoother functions by defining an ARD Gaussian prior [4, 6] over the weights:

$$p(\mathbf{w}|\boldsymbol{\alpha}) = \prod_{i=0}^{N} \mathcal{N}(w_i|0, \alpha_i^{-1}), \qquad (3)$$

with $\boldsymbol{\alpha}$ a vector of $N+1$ hyperparameters. This introduction of an individual hyperparameter for every weight is the key feature of the model, and is ultimately responsible for its sparsity properties. The posterior over the weights is then obtained from Bayes' rule:

$$p(\mathbf{w}|\mathbf{t},\boldsymbol{\alpha},\sigma^2) = (2\pi)^{-(N+1)/2}|\boldsymbol{\Sigma}|^{-1/2}\exp\left\{-\frac{1}{2}(\mathbf{w}-\boldsymbol{\mu})^{\mathrm{T}}\boldsymbol{\Sigma}^{-1}(\mathbf{w}-\boldsymbol{\mu})\right\}, \quad (4)$$

with

$$\boldsymbol{\Sigma} = (\boldsymbol{\Phi}^{\mathrm{T}}\mathbf{B}\boldsymbol{\Phi} + \mathbf{A})^{-1}, \quad (5)$$

$$\boldsymbol{\mu} = \boldsymbol{\Sigma}\boldsymbol{\Phi}^{\mathrm{T}}\mathbf{B}\mathbf{t}, \quad (6)$$

where we have defined $\mathbf{A} = \mathrm{diag}(\alpha_0, \alpha_1, \ldots, \alpha_N)$ and $\mathbf{B} = \sigma^{-2}\mathbf{I}_N$. Note that σ^2 is also treated as a hyperparameter, which may be estimated from the data.

By integrating out the weights, we obtain the *marginal likelihood*, or *evidence* [2], for the hyperparameters:

$$p(\mathbf{t}|\boldsymbol{\alpha},\sigma^2) = (2\pi)^{-N/2}|\mathbf{B}^{-1} + \boldsymbol{\Phi}\mathbf{A}^{-1}\boldsymbol{\Phi}^{\mathrm{T}}|^{-1/2}\exp\left\{-\frac{1}{2}\mathbf{t}^{\mathrm{T}}(\mathbf{B}^{-1} + \boldsymbol{\Phi}\mathbf{A}^{-1}\boldsymbol{\Phi}^{\mathrm{T}})^{-1}\mathbf{t}\right\}. \quad (7)$$

For ideal Bayesian inference, we should define hyperpriors over $\boldsymbol{\alpha}$ and σ^2, and integrate out the hyperparameters too. However, such marginalisation cannot be performed in closed-form here, so we adopt a pragmatic procedure, based on that of MacKay [2], and *optimise* the marginal likelihood (7) with respect to $\boldsymbol{\alpha}$ and σ^2, which is essentially the *type II maximum likelihood* method [1]. This is equivalent to finding the maximum of $p(\boldsymbol{\alpha}, \sigma^2|\mathbf{t})$, assuming a uniform (and thus improper) hyperprior. We then make predictions, based on (4), using these maximising values.

2.1 Optimising the hyperparameters

Values of $\boldsymbol{\alpha}$ and σ^2 which maximise (7) cannot be obtained in closed form, and we consider two alternative formulae for iterative re-estimation of $\boldsymbol{\alpha}$. First, by considering the weights as 'hidden' variables, an EM approach gives:

$$\alpha_i^{\mathrm{new}} = \frac{1}{\langle w_i^2 \rangle_{p(\mathbf{w}|\mathbf{t},\boldsymbol{\alpha},\sigma^2)}} = \frac{1}{\Sigma_{ii} + \mu_i^2}. \quad (8)$$

Second, direct differentiation of (7) and rearranging gives:

$$\alpha_i^{\mathrm{new}} = \frac{\gamma_i}{\mu_i^2}, \quad (9)$$

where we have defined the quantities $\gamma_i = 1 - \alpha_i \Sigma_{ii}$, which can be interpreted as a measure of how 'well-determined' each parameter w_i is by the data [2]. Generally, this latter update was observed to exhibit faster convergence.

For the noise variance, both methods lead to the same re-estimate:

$$(\sigma^2)^{\mathrm{new}} = \|\mathbf{t} - \boldsymbol{\Phi}\boldsymbol{\mu}\|^2 / (N - \sum_i \gamma_i). \quad (10)$$

In practice, during re-estimation, we find that many of the α_i approach infinity, and from (4), $p(w_i|\mathbf{t},\boldsymbol{\alpha},\sigma^2)$ becomes infinitely peaked at zero — implying that the corresponding kernel functions can be 'pruned'. While space here precludes a detailed explanation, this occurs because there is an 'Occam' penalty to be paid for smaller values of α_i, due to their appearance in the determinant in the marginal likelihood (7). For some α_i, a lesser penalty can be paid by explaining the data with increased noise σ^2, in which case those $\alpha_i \to \infty$.

3 Examples of Relevance Vector Regression

3.1 Synthetic example: the 'sinc' function

The function $\text{sinc}(x) = |x|^{-1}\sin|x|$ is commonly used to illustrate support vector regression [8], where in place of the classification margin, the ϵ-*insensitive region* is introduced, a 'tube' of $\pm\epsilon$ around the function within which errors are not penalised. In this case, the support vectors lie on the edge of, or outside, this region. For example, using linear spline kernels and with $\epsilon = 0.01$, the approximation of $\text{sinc}(x)$ based on 100 uniformly-spaced noise-free samples in $[-10, 10]$ utilises 39 support vectors [8].

By comparison, we approximate the same function with a relevance vector model utilising the same kernel. In this case the noise variance is fixed at 0.01^2 and $\boldsymbol{\alpha}$ alone re-estimated. The approximating function is plotted in Figure 1 (left), and requires only 9 relevance vectors. The largest error is 0.0087, compared to 0.01 in the SV case. Figure 1 (right) illustrates the case where Gaussian noise of standard deviation 0.2 is added to the targets. The approximation uses 6 relevance vectors, and the noise is automatically estimated, using (10), as $\sigma = 0.189$.

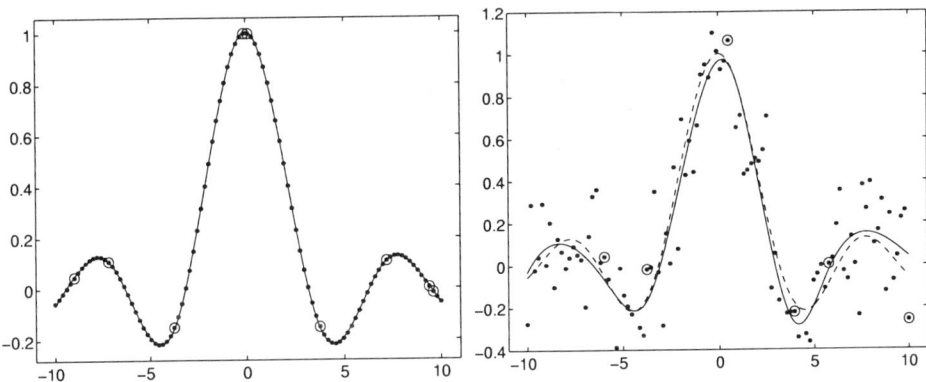

Figure 1: Relevance vector approximation to $\text{sinc}(x)$: noise-free data (left), and with added Gaussian noise of $\sigma = 0.2$ (right). The estimated functions are drawn as solid lines with relevance vectors shown circled, and in the added-noise case (right) the true function is shown dashed.

3.2 Some benchmarks

The table below illustrates regression performance on some popular benchmark datasets — Friedman's three synthetic functions (results averaged over 100 randomly generated training sets of size 240 with a 1000-example test set) and the 'Boston housing' dataset (averaged over 100 randomised 481/25 train/test splits). The prediction error obtained and the number of kernel functions required for both support vector regression (SVR) and relevance vector regression (RVR) are given.

	errors		kernels	
Dataset	SVR	RVR	SVR	RVR
Friedman #1	2.92	2.80	116.6	59.4
Friedman #2	4140	3505	110.3	6.9
Friedman #3	0.0202	0.0164	106.5	11.5
Boston Housing	8.04	7.46	142.8	39.0

4 Relevance Vector Classification

We now extend the relevance vector approach to the case of classification — i.e. where it is desired to predict the posterior probability of class membership given the input **x**. We generalise the linear model by applying the logistic sigmoid function $\sigma(y) = 1/(1+e^{-y})$ to $y(\mathbf{x})$ and writing the likelihood as

$$P(\mathbf{t}|\mathbf{w}) = \prod_{n=1}^{N} \sigma\{y(\mathbf{x}_n)\}^{t_n} [1 - \sigma\{y(\mathbf{x}_n)\}]^{1-t_n}. \qquad (11)$$

However, we cannot integrate out the weights to obtain the marginal likelihood analytically, and so utilise an iterative procedure based on that of MacKay [3]:

1. For the current, fixed, values of $\boldsymbol{\alpha}$ we find the most probable weights $\mathbf{w}_{\text{MP}}$ (the location of the posterior mode). This is equivalent to a standard optimisation of a regularised logistic model, and we use the efficient iteratively-reweighted least-squares algorithm [5] to find the maximum.

2. We compute the Hessian at $\mathbf{w}_{\text{MP}}$:

$$\nabla\nabla \log p(\mathbf{t}, \mathbf{w}|\boldsymbol{\alpha})\big|_{\mathbf{w}_{\text{MP}}} = -(\boldsymbol{\Phi}^{\text{T}} \mathbf{B} \boldsymbol{\Phi} + \mathbf{A}), \qquad (12)$$

where $\mathbf{B}_{nn} = \sigma\{y(\mathbf{x}_n)\}[1 - \sigma\{y(\mathbf{x}_n)\}]$, and this is negated and inverted to give the covariance $\boldsymbol{\Sigma}$ for a Gaussian approximation to the posterior over weights, and from that the hyperparameters $\boldsymbol{\alpha}$ are updated using (9). Note that there is no 'noise' variance σ^2 here.

This procedure is repeated until some suitable convergence criteria are satisfied. Note that in the Bayesian treatment of multilayer neural networks, the Gaussian approximation is considered a weakness of the method if the posterior mode is unrepresentative of the overall probability mass. However, for the RVM, we note that $p(\mathbf{t}, \mathbf{w}|\boldsymbol{\alpha})$ is log-concave (i.e. the Hessian is negative-definite everywhere), which gives us considerably more confidence in the Gaussian approximation.

5 Examples of RVM Classification

5.1 Synthetic example: Gaussian mixture data

We first utilise artificially generated data in two dimensions in order to illustrate graphically the selection of relevance vectors. Class 1 (denoted by '×') was sampled from a single Gaussian, and overlaps to a small degree class 2 ('•'), sampled from a mixture of two Gaussians.

A relevance vector classifier was compared to its support vector counterpart, using the same Gaussian kernel. A value of C for the SVM was selected using 5-fold cross-validation on the training set. The results for a typical dataset of 200 examples are given in Figure 2. The test errors for the RVM (9.32%) and SVM (9.48%) are comparable, but the remarkable feature of contrast is the complexity of the classifiers. The support vector machine utilises 44 kernel functions compared to just 3 for the relevance vector method.

It is also notable that the relevance vectors are some distance from the decision boundary (in **x**-space). Given further analysis, this observation can be seen to be consistent with the hyperparameter update equations. A more qualitative explanation is that the output of a basis function lying on or near the decision boundary is a poor indicator of class membership, and such basis functions are naturally 'penalised' under the Bayesian framework.

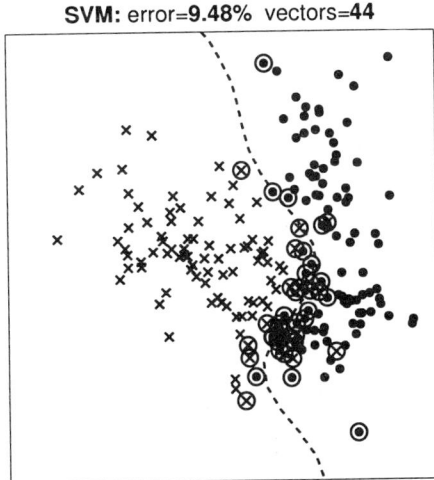 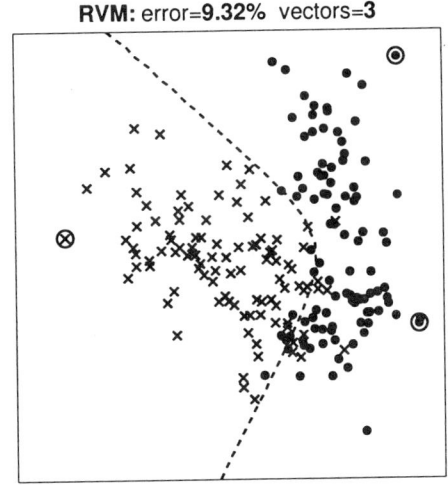

Figure 2: Results of training functionally identical SVM (left) and RVM (right) classifiers on a typical synthetic dataset. The decision boundary is shown dashed, and relevance/support vectors are shown circled to emphasise the dramatic reduction in complexity of the RVM model.

5.2 Real examples

In the table below we give error and complexity results for the 'Pima Indian diabetes' and the 'U.S.P.S. handwritten digit' datasets. The former task has been recently used to illustrate Bayesian classification with the related *Gaussian Process* (GP) technique [9], and we utilised those authors' split of the data into 200 training and 332 test examples and quote their result for the GP case. The latter dataset is a popular support vector benchmark, comprising 7291 training examples along with a 2007-example test set, and the SVM result is quoted from [7].

Dataset	errors			kernels		
	SVM	GP	RVM	SVM	GP	RVM
Pima Indians	67	68	65	109	200	4
U.S.P.S.	4.4%	–	5.1%	2540	–	316

In terms of prediction accuracy, the RVM is marginally superior on the Pima set, but outperformed by the SVM on the digit data. However, consistent with other examples in this paper, the RVM classifiers utilise many fewer kernel functions. Most strikingly, the RVM achieves state-of-the-art performance on the diabetes dataset with only 4 kernels. It should be noted that *reduced set* methods exist for subsequently pruning support vector models to reduce the required number of kernels at the expense of some increase in error (*e.g.* see [7] for some example results on the U.S.P.S. data).

6 Discussion

Examples in this paper have effectively demonstrated that the relevance vector machine can attain a comparable (and for regression, apparently superior) level of generalisation accuracy as the well-established support vector approach, while at the same time utilising dramatically fewer kernel functions — implying a considerable saving in memory and computation in a practical implementation. Importantly, we also benefit from the absence of any additional nuisance parameters to set, apart from the need to choose the type of kernel and any associated parameters.

In fact, for the case of kernel parameters, we have obtained improved (both in terms of accuracy and sparsity) results for all the benchmarks given in Section 3.2 when optimising the marginal likelihood with respect to multiple input scale parameters in Gaussian kernels (q.v. [9]). Furthermore, we may also exploit the Bayesian formalism to guide the choice of kernel itself [2], and it should be noted that the presented methodology is applicable to arbitrary basis functions, so we are not limited, for example, to the use of 'Mercer' kernels as in the SVM.

A further advantage of the RVM classifier is its standard formulation as a probabilistic generalised linear model. This implies that it can be extended to the multiple-class case in a straightforward and principled manner, without the need to train and heuristically combine multiple dichotomous classifiers as is standard practice for the SVM. Furthermore, the estimation of posterior probabilities of class membership is a major benefit, as these convey a principled measure of uncertainty of prediction, and are essential if we wish to allow adaptation for varying class priors, along with incorporation of asymmetric misclassification costs.

However, it must be noted that the principal disadvantage of relevance vector methods is in the complexity of the training phase, as it is necessary to repeatedly compute and invert the Hessian matrix, requiring $O(N^2)$ storage and $O(N^3)$ computation. For large datasets, this makes training considerably slower than for the SVM. Currently, memory constraints limit us to training on no more than 5,000 examples, but we have developed approximation methods for handling larger datasets which were employed on the U.S.P.S. handwritten digit database. We note that while the case for Bayesian methods is generally strongest when data is scarce, the sparseness of the resulting classifier induced by the Bayesian framework presented here is a compelling motivation to apply relevance vector techniques to larger datasets.

Acknowledgements

The author wishes to thank Chris Bishop, John Platt and Bernhard Schölkopf for helpful discussions, and JP again for his Sequential Minimal Optimisation code.

References

[1] J. O. Berger. *Statistical decision theory and Bayesian analysis*. Springer, New York, second edition, 1985.

[2] D. J. C. Mackay. Bayesian interpolation. *Neural Computation*, 4(3):415–447, 1992.

[3] D. J. C. Mackay. The evidence framework applied to classification networks. *Neural Computation*, 4(5):720–736, 1992.

[4] D. J. C. Mackay. Bayesian non-linear modelling for the prediction competition. In *ASHRAE Transactions*, vol. 100, pages 1053–1062. ASHRAE, Atlanta, Georgia, 1994.

[5] I. T. Nabney. Efficient training of RBF networks for classification. In *Proceedings of ICANN99*, pages 210–215, London, 1999. IEE.

[6] R. M. Neal. *Bayesian Learning for Neural Networks*. Springer, New York, 1996.

[7] B. Schölkopf, S. Mika, C. J. C. Burges, P. Knirsch, K.-R. Müller, G. Rätsch, and A. J. Smola. Input space versus feature space in kernel-based methods. *IEEE Transactions on Neural Networks*, 10(5):1000–1017, 1999.

[8] V. N. Vapnik. *Statistical Learning Theory*. Wiley, New York, 1998.

[9] C. K. I. Williams and D. Barber. Bayesian classification with Gaussian processes. *IEEE Trans. Pattern Analysis and Machine Intelligence*, 20(12):1342–1351, 1998.

Support Vector Method for Multivariate Density Estimation

Vladimir N. Vapnik
Royal Halloway College and
AT&T Labs, 100 Schultz Dr.
Red Bank, NJ 07701
vlad@research.att.com

Sayan Mukherjee
CBCL, MIT E25-201
Cambridge, MA 02142
sayan@ai.mit.edu

Abstract

A new method for multivariate density estimation is developed based on the Support Vector Method (SVM) solution of inverse ill-posed problems. The solution has the form of a mixture of densities. This method with Gaussian kernels compared favorably to both Parzen's method and the Gaussian Mixture Model method. For synthetic data we achieve more accurate estimates for densities of 2, 6, 12, and 40 dimensions.

1 Introduction

The problem of multivariate density estimation is important for many applications, in particular, for speech recognition [1] [7]. When the unknown density belongs to a parametric set satisfying certain conditions one can estimate it using the maximum likelihood (ML) method. Often these conditions are too restrictive. Therefore, non-parametric methods were proposed.

The most popular of these, Parzen's method [5], uses the following estimate given data $x_1, ..., x_\ell$:

$$P(t, \gamma_\ell) = \frac{1}{\ell} \sum_{i=1}^{\ell} K_{\gamma_\ell}(t - x_i), \qquad (1)$$

where $K_{\gamma_\ell}(t - x_i)$ is a smooth function such that $\int K_{\gamma_\ell}(t - x_i) dt = 1$. Under some conditions on γ_ℓ and $K_{\gamma_\ell}(t - x_i)$, Parzen's method converges with a fast asymptotic rate. An example of such a function is a Gaussian with one free parameter γ_ℓ^2 (the width)

$$K_{\gamma_\ell}(\mathbf{t} - \mathbf{x}_i) = \frac{1}{(2\pi)^{n/2} \gamma_\ell^n} \exp\left\{-(\mathbf{t} - \mathbf{x}_i)^T \left(\gamma_\ell^2 I\right)^{-1} (\mathbf{t} - \mathbf{x}_i)\right\}. \qquad (2)$$

The structure of the Parzen estimator is too complex: the number of terms in (1) is equal to the number of observations (which can be hundreds of thousands).

Researchers believe that for practical problems densities can be approximated by a mixture with few elements (Gaussians for Gaussian Mixture Models (GMM)). Therefore, the following parametric density model was introduced

$$P(\mathbf{x}, \mathbf{a}, \Sigma) = \sum_{i=1}^{m} \alpha_i P(\mathbf{x}, \mathbf{a}_i, \Sigma_i), \quad \alpha \geq 0, \quad \sum_{i=1}^{m} \alpha_i = 1, \qquad (3)$$

where $P(\mathbf{x}, \mathbf{a}_i, \Sigma_i)$ are Gaussians with different vectors $\mathbf{a}_i$ and different diagonal covariance matrices Σ_i; α_i is the proportion of the i-th Gaussian in the mixture.

It is known [9] that for general forms of Gaussian mixtures the ML estimate does not exist. To use the ML method two values are specified: a lower bound on diagonal elements of the covariance matrix and an upper bound on the number of mixture elements. Under these constraints one can estimate the mixture parameters using the EM algorithm. This solution, however, is based on predefined parameters.

In this article we use an SVM approach to obtain an estimate in the form of a mixture of densities. The approach has no free parameters. In our experiments it performs better than the GMM method.

2 Density estimation is an ill-posed problem

A density $p(t)$ is defined as the solution of the equation

$$\int_{-\infty}^{x} p(t)\, dt = F(x), \qquad (4)$$

where $F(x)$ is the probability distribution function. Estimating a density from data involves solving equation (4) on a given set of densities when the distribution function $F(x)$ is unknown but a random i.i.d. sample $x_1, ..., x_\ell$ is given. The empirical distribution function $F_\ell(x)$ is a good approximation of the actual distribution,

$$F_\ell(x) = \frac{1}{\ell} \sum_{i=1}^{\ell} \theta(x - x_i),$$

where $\theta(u)$ is the step-function. In the univariate case, for sufficiently large ℓ the distribution of the supremum error between $F(x)$ and $F_\ell(x)$ is given by the Kolmogorov-Smirnov distribution

$$P\{\sup_x |F(x) - F_\ell(x)| < \varepsilon/\sqrt{\ell}\} = 1 - 2 \sum_{k=1}^{\infty} (-1)^{k-1} \exp\{-2\varepsilon^2 k^2\}. \qquad (5)$$

Hence, the problem of density estimation can be restated as solving equation (4) but replacing the distribution function $F(x)$ with the empirical distribution function $F_\ell(x)$ which converges to the true one with the (fast) rate $O(\frac{1}{\sqrt{\ell}})$, for univariate and multivariate cases.

The problem of solving the linear operator equation $Ap = F$ with approximation $F_\ell(x)$ is ill-posed.

In the 1960's methods were proposed for solving ill-posed problems using approximations F_ℓ converging to F as ℓ increases. The idea of these methods was to introduce a regularizing functional $\Omega(p)$ (a semi-continuous, positive functional for which $\Omega(p) \leq c$, $c > 0$ is a compactum) and define the solution p_ℓ which is a trade-off between $\Omega(p)$ and $||Ap - F_\ell||$.

The following two methods which are asymptotically equivalent [11] were proposed by Tikhonov [8] and Phillips [6]

$$\min_p \left[||Ap - F_\ell||^2 + \gamma_\ell \Omega(p)\right], \quad \gamma_\ell > 0, \quad \gamma_\ell \to 0, \tag{6}$$

$$\min_p \Omega(p) \quad s.t. \quad ||Ap - F_\ell|| < \varepsilon_\ell, \quad \varepsilon_\ell > 0, \quad \varepsilon_\ell \to 0. \tag{7}$$

For the stochastic case it can be shown for both methods that if $F_\ell(x)$ converges in probability to $F(x)$ and $\gamma_\ell \to 0$ then for sufficiently large ℓ and arbitrary ν and μ the following inequality holds [10] [9] [3]

$$P(\rho_{E_1}(p, p_\ell) > \nu) \leq P(\rho_{E_2}(F, F_\ell) > \sqrt{\gamma_\ell \mu}) \tag{8}$$

where $\ell > \ell_0(\nu, \mu)$ and $\rho_{E_1}(p, p_\ell)$, $\rho_{E_2}(F, F_\ell)$ are metrics in the spaces p and F. Since $F_\ell(x) \to F(x)$ in probability with the rate $O(\frac{1}{\sqrt{\ell}})$, from equation (8) it follows that if $\gamma_\ell > O(\frac{1}{\sqrt{\ell}})$ the solutions of equation (4) are consistent.

3 Choice of regularization parameters

For the deterministic case the residual method [2] can be used to set the regularization parameters (γ_ℓ in (6) and ε_ℓ in (7)) by setting the parameter (γ_ℓ or ε_ℓ) such that p_ℓ satisfies the following

$$||Ap_\ell - F_\ell|| = ||F(x) - F_\ell(x)|| = \sigma_\ell, \tag{9}$$

where σ_ℓ is the known accuracy of approximation of $F(x)$ by $F_\ell(x)$. We use this idea for the stochastic case. The Kolmogorov-Smirnov distribution is used to set σ_ℓ, $\sigma_\ell = c/\sqrt{\ell}$, where c corresponds to an appropriate quantile. For the multivariate case one can either evaluate the appropriate quantile analytically [4] or by simulations.

The density estimation problem can be solved using either regularization method (6) or (7). Using method (6) with a L_2 norm in image space F and regularization functional $\Omega(p) = (\mathcal{T}p, \mathcal{T}p)$ where $\mathcal{T}$ is a convolution operator, one obtains Parzen's method [10] [9] with kernels defined by operator $\mathcal{T}$.

4 SVM for density estimation

We apply the SVM technique to equation (7) for density estimation. We use the C norm in (7) and solve equation (4) in a set of functions belonging to a Reproducing Kernel Hilbert Space (RKHS). We use the regularization functional

$$\Omega(p) = ||p||_{\mathcal{H}}^2 = (p, p)_{\mathcal{H}}. \tag{10}$$

A RKHS can be defined by a positive definite kernel $K(x, y)$ and an inner product $(f, g)_{\mathcal{H}}$ in Hilbert space $\mathcal{H}$ such that

$$(f(x), K(x, y))_{\mathcal{H}} = f(y) \quad \forall f \in \mathcal{H}. \tag{11}$$

Note that any positive definite function $K(x,y)$ has an expansion

$$K(x,y) = \sum_{i=1}^{\infty} \lambda_i \phi_i(x) \phi_i(y) \tag{12}$$

where λ_i and $\phi_i(x)$ are eigenvalues and eigenfunctions of $K(x,y)$. Consider the set of functions

$$f(x,c) = \sum_{i=1}^{\infty} c_i \phi_i(x) \tag{13}$$

and the inner product

$$(f(x,c^*), f(x,c^{**})) = \sum_{i=1}^{\infty} \frac{c_i^* c_i^{**}}{\lambda_i}. \tag{14}$$

Kernel (12), inner product (14), and set (13) define a RKHS and

$$(f(x), K(x,y))_{\mathcal{H}} = \left(\sum_{i=1}^{\infty} c_i \phi_i(x), K(x,y) \right)_{\mathcal{H}} =$$

$$\left(\sum_{i=1}^{\infty} c_i \phi_i(x), \sum_{i=1}^{\infty} \lambda_i \phi_i(x) \phi_i(y) \right)_{\mathcal{H}} = \sum_{i=1}^{\infty} \frac{c_i \lambda_i \phi_i(y)}{\lambda_i} = f(y).$$

For functions from a RKHS the functional (10) has the form

$$\Omega(p) = \sum_{i=1}^{\infty} \frac{c_i^2}{\lambda_i}, \tag{15}$$

where λ_i is the i-th eigenvalue of the kernel $K(x,y)$. The choice of the kernel defines smoothness properties on the solution.

To use method (7) to solve for the density in equation (4) in a RKHS with a solution satisfying condition (9) we minimize

$$\Omega(p) = (p,p)_{\mathcal{H}}$$

subject to the constraint

$$\max_i \left| F_\ell(x) - \int_{-\infty}^{x} p(t) dt \right|_{x=x_i} = \sigma_\ell.$$

We look for a solution of equation (4) with the form

$$p(t) = \sum_{i=1}^{\ell} \beta_i K_{\gamma_\ell}(x_i, t). \tag{16}$$

Accounting for (16) and (11) minimizing (10) is equivalent to minimizing

$$\Omega(p,p) = (p,p)_{\mathcal{H}} = \sum_{i,j=1}^{\ell} \beta_i \beta_j K_{\gamma_\ell}(x_i, x_j) \tag{17}$$

subject to constraints

$$\max_i \left| F_\ell(x) - \sum_{j=1}^{\ell} \beta_j \int_{-\infty}^{x} K_{\gamma_\ell}(x_j, t) dt \right|_{x=x_i} = \sigma_\ell, \tag{18}$$

$$\beta_i \geq 0, \quad \sum_{i=1}^{\ell} \beta_i = 1. \tag{19}$$

This optimization problem is closely related to the SV regression problem with an σ_ℓ-insensitive zone [9]. It can be solved using the standard SVM technique.

Generally, only a few of the β_i will be nonzero, the x_i corresponding to these β_i are called support vectors.

Note that kernel (2) has width parameter γ_ℓ. We call the value of this parameter admissible if it satisfies constraint (18) (the solution satisfies condition (9)). The admissible set $\gamma_{min} \leq \gamma_\ell \leq \gamma_{max}$ is not empty since for Parzen's method (which also has form (16)) such a value does exist. Among the γ_ℓ in this admissible set we select the one for which $\Omega(p)$ is smallest or the number of support vectors is minimum.

Choosing other kernels (for example Laplacians) one can estimate densities using non-Gaussian mixture models which for some problems are more appropriate [1].

5 Experiments

Several trials of estimates constructed from sampling distributions were examined. Boxplots were made of the $L_1(p)$ norm over the trials. The horizontal lines of the boxplot indicate the 5%, 25%, 50%, 75%, and 95% quantiles of the error distribution.

For the SVM method we set $\sigma_\ell = c/\sqrt{\ell}$, where $c = .36, .41, .936$, and 1.75 for two, six, twelve and forty dimensions. For Parzen's method γ_ℓ was selected using a leave-one out procedure. The GMM method uses the EM algorithm and sets all parameters except n, the upper bound on the number of terms in the mixture [7].

Figure (1) shows plots of the SVM estimate using a Gaussian kernel and the GMM estimate when 60 points were drawn form a mixture of a Gaussian and Laplacian in two dimensions.

Figure (2a) shows four boxplots of estimating a density defined by a mixture of two Laplacians in a two dimensional space using 200 observations. Each boxplot shows outcomes of 100 trials: for the SVM method, Parzen's method, and the GMM method with parameters $n = 2$, and $n = 4$. Figure (2c) shows the distribution of the number of terms for the SVM method.

Figure (2b) shows boxplots of estimating a density defined by the mixture of four Gaussians in a six dimensional space using 600 observations. Each boxplot shows outcomes of 50 trials: for the SVM method, Parzen's method, and the GMM method with parameters $n = 4$, and $n = 8$. Figure (2c) shows the distribution of the number of terms for the SVM method.

Figure (3a) shows boxplots of outcomes of estimating a density defined by the mixture of four Gaussians and four Laplacians in a twelve dimensional space using

400 observations. Each boxplot shows outcomes of 50 trials: for the SVM method, Parzen's method, and the GMM method with parameter $n = 8$. Figure (3c) shows the distribution of the number of terms for the SVM method.

Figure (3b) shows boxplots of outcomes of estimating a density defined by the mixture of four Gaussians and four Laplacians in a forty dimensional space using 480 observations. Each box-plot shows outcomes of 50 trials: for the SVM method, Parzen's method, and the GMM method with parameter $n = 8$. Figure (3c) shows the distribution of the number of terms for the SVM method.

6 Summary

A method for multivariate density estimation based on the SVM technique for solving ill-posed problems is introduced. This method has a form of a mixture of densities. The estimate in general has only a few terms. In experiments on synthetic data this method is more accurate than the GMM method.

References

[1] S. Basu and C.A. Micchelli. Parametric density estimation for the classification of acoustic feature vectors in speech recognition. In *Nonlinear Modeling, Advanced Black-Box Techniques*. Kluwer Publishers, 1998.

[2] V.A. Morozov. *Methods for solving incorrectly posed problems*. Springer-Verlag, Berlin, 1984.

[3] S. Mukherjee and V. Vapnik. Multivariate density estimation: An svm approach. AI Memo 1653, Massachusetts Institute of Technology, 1999.

[4] S. Paramasamy. On multivariate kolmogorov-smirnov distribution. *Statistics & Probability Letters*, 15:140–155, 1992.

[5] E. Parzen. On estimation of a probability density function and mode. *Ann. Math. Statis.*, 33:1065–1076, 1962.

[6] D.L. Phillips. A technique for the numerical solution of integral equations of the first kind. *J.Assoc. Comput. Machinery*, 9:84–97, 1962.

[7] D. Reynolds and R. Rose. Robust text-independent speaker identification using gaussian mixture speaker models. *IEEE Trans on Speech and Audio Processing*, 3(1):1–27, 1995.

[8] A. N. Tikhonov. Solution of incorrectly formulated problems and the regularization method. *Soviet Math. Dokl.*, 4:1035–1038, 1963.

[9] V. N. Vapnik. *Statistical learning theory*. J. Wiley, 1998.

[10] V.N. Vapnik and A.R. Stefanyuk. Nonparametric methods for restoring probability densities. *Avtomatika i Telemekhanika*, (8):38–52, 1978.

[11] V.V. Vasin. Relationship of several variational methods for the approximate solution of ill-posed problems. *Math Notes*, 7:161–166, 1970.

Support Vector Method for Multivariate Density Estimation

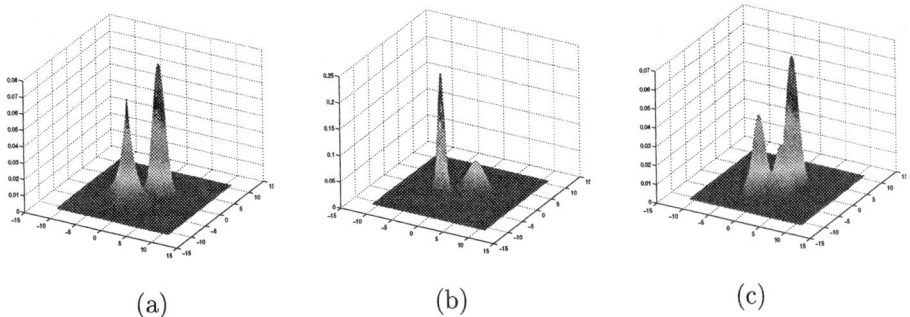

(a) (b) (c)

Figure 1: (a) The true distribution (b) the GMM case with 4 mixtures (c) the Parzen case (d) the SVM case for 60 points.

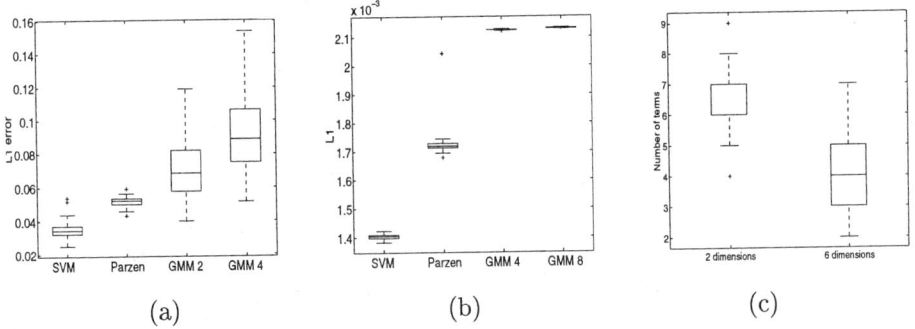

(a) (b) (c)

Figure 2: (a) Boxplots of the $L_1(p)$ error for the mixture of two Laplacians in two dimensions for the SVM method, Parzen's method, and the GMM method with 2 and 4 Gaussians. (b) Boxplots of the $L_1(p)$ error for mixture of four Gaussians in six dimensions with the SVM method, Parzen's method, and the GMM method with 4 mixtures. (c) Boxplots of distribution of the number of terms for the SVM method for the two and six dimensional cases.

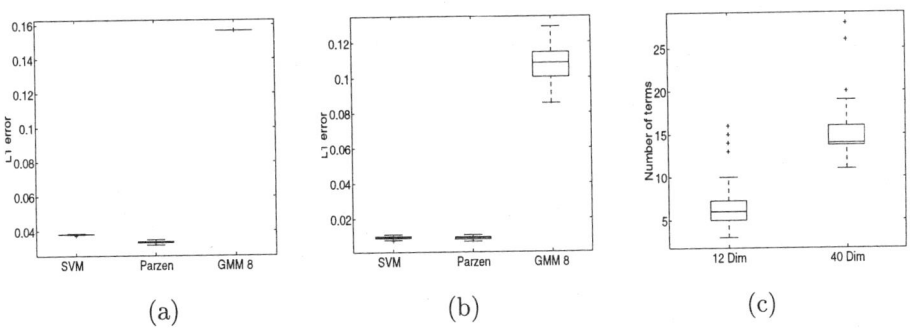

(a) (b) (c)

Figure 3: (a) Boxplots of the $L_1(p)$ error for the mixture of four Laplacians and four Gaussians in twelve dimensions for the SVM method, Parzen's method, and the GMM method with 8 Gaussians. (b) Boxplots of the $L_1(p)$ error for the mixture of four Laplacians and four Gaussians in forty dimensions for the SVM method, Parzen's method, and the GMM method with 8 Gaussians. (c) Boxplots of distribution of the number of terms for the SVM method for the twelve and forty dimensional cases.

Dual Estimation and the Unscented Transformation

Eric A. Wan
ericwan@ece.ogi.edu

Rudolph van der Merwe
rudmerwe@ece.ogi.edu

Alex T. Nelson
atnelson@ece.ogi.edu

Oregon Graduate Institute of Science & Technology
Department of Electrical and Computer Engineering
20000 N.W. Walker Rd., Beaverton, Oregon 97006

Abstract

Dual estimation refers to the problem of simultaneously estimating the state of a dynamic system and the model which gives rise to the dynamics. Algorithms include expectation-maximization (EM), dual Kalman filtering, and joint Kalman methods. These methods have recently been explored in the context of *nonlinear* modeling, where a neural network is used as the functional form of the unknown model. Typically, an extended Kalman filter (EKF) or smoother is used for the part of the algorithm that estimates the clean state given the current estimated model. An EKF may also be used to estimate the weights of the network. This paper points out the flaws in using the EKF, and proposes an improvement based on a new approach called the *unscented transformation* (UT) [3]. A substantial performance gain is achieved with the same order of computational complexity as that of the standard EKF. The approach is illustrated on several dual estimation methods.

1 Introduction

We consider the problem of learning both the hidden states $\mathbf{x}_k$ and parameters $\mathbf{w}$ of a discrete-time nonlinear dynamic system,

$$\mathbf{x}_{k+1} = F(\mathbf{x}_k, \mathbf{v}_k, \mathbf{w}) \qquad (1)$$
$$\mathbf{y}_k = H(\mathbf{x}_k, \mathbf{n}_k, \mathbf{w}), \qquad (2)$$

where $\mathbf{y}_k$ is the only observed signal. The *process* noise $\mathbf{v}_k$ drives the dynamic system, and the *observation* noise is given by $\mathbf{n}_k$. Note that we are not assuming additivity of the noise sources.

A number of approaches have been proposed for this problem. The *dual EKF* algorithm uses two separate EKFs: one for signal estimation, and one for model estimation. The states are estimated given the current weights and the weights are estimated given the current states. In the *joint EKF*, the state and model parameters are concatenated within a combined state vector, and a single EKF is used to estimate both quantities simultaneously. The *EM* algorithm uses an extended Kalman smoother for the E-step, in which forward and backward passes are made through the data to estimate the signal. The model is updated during a separate M-step.

For a more thorough treatment and a theoretical basis on how these algorithms relate, see Nelson [6]. Rather than provide a comprehensive comparison between the different algorithms, the goal of this paper is to point out the assumptions and flaws in the EKF (Section 2), and offer a improvement based on the unscented transformation/filter (Section 3). The *unscented filter* has recently been proposed as a substitute for the EKF in nonlinear control problems (known dynamic model) [3]. This paper presents new research on the use of the UF within the dual estimation framework for both state and weight estimation. In the case of weight estimation, the UF represents a new efficient "second-order" method for training neural networks in general.

2 Flaws in the EKF

Assume for now that we know the model (weight parameters) for the dynamic system in Equations 1 and 2. Given the noisy observation $\mathbf{y}_k$, a recursive estimation for $\hat{\mathbf{x}}_k$ can be expressed in the form,

$$\hat{\mathbf{x}}_k = (\text{optimal prediction of } \mathbf{x}_k) + G_k \times [\mathbf{y}_k - (\text{optimal prediction of } \mathbf{y}_k)] \qquad (3)$$

This recursion provides the optimal MMSE estimate for $\mathbf{x}_k$ assuming the prior estimate $\hat{\mathbf{x}}_k$ and current observation $\mathbf{y}_k$ are Gaussian. We need not assume linearity of the model. The optimal terms in this recursion are given by

$$\hat{\mathbf{x}}_k^- = E[F(\hat{\mathbf{x}}_{k-1}, \mathbf{v}_{k-1})] \qquad G_k = \mathbf{P}_{\mathbf{x}_k \mathbf{y}_k} \mathbf{P}_{\tilde{\mathbf{y}}_k \tilde{\mathbf{y}}_k}^{-1} \qquad \hat{\mathbf{y}}_k^- = E[H(\hat{\mathbf{x}}_k^-, \mathbf{n}_k)], \qquad (4)$$

where the optimal prediction $\hat{\mathbf{x}}_k^-$ is the expectation of a nonlinear function of the random variables $\hat{\mathbf{x}}_{k-1}$ and $\mathbf{v}_{k-1}$ (similar interpretation for the optimal prediction of $\mathbf{y}_k$). The optimal gain term is expressed as a function of posterior covariance matrices (with $\tilde{\mathbf{y}}_k = \mathbf{y}_k - \hat{\mathbf{y}}_k^-$). Note these terms also require taking expectations of a nonlinear function of the prior state estimates.

The Kalman filter calculates these quantities exactly in the linear case. For nonlinear models, however, the extended KF approximates these as:

$$\hat{\mathbf{x}}_k^- \approx F(\hat{\mathbf{x}}_{k-1}, \bar{\mathbf{v}}) \qquad G_k \approx \hat{\mathbf{P}}_{\mathbf{x}_k \mathbf{y}_k} \hat{\mathbf{P}}_{\tilde{\mathbf{y}}_k \tilde{\mathbf{y}}_k}^{-1} \qquad \hat{\mathbf{y}}_k^- = H(\hat{\mathbf{x}}_k^-, \bar{\mathbf{n}}), \qquad (5)$$

where predictions are approximated as simply the function of the prior *mean* value for estimates (no expectation taken). The covariance are determined by linearizing the dynamic equations ($\mathbf{x}_{k+1} \approx A\mathbf{x}_k + B\mathbf{v}_k$, $\mathbf{y}_k \approx C\mathbf{x}_k + D\mathbf{n}_k$), and then determining the posterior covariance matrices analytically for the linear system. As such, the EKF can be viewed as providing "first-order" approximations to the optimal terms (in the sense that expressions are approximated using a first-order Taylor series expansion of the nonlinear terms around the mean values). While "second-order" versions of the EKF exist, their increased implementation and computational complexity tend to prohibit their use.

3 The Unscented Transformation/Filter

The unscented transformation (UT) is a method for calculating the statistics of a random variable which undergoes a nonlinear transformation [3]. Consider propagating a random variable α (dimension L) through a nonlinear function, $\beta = g(\alpha)$. Assume α has mean $\bar{\alpha}$ and covariance $\mathbf{P}_\alpha$. To calculate the statistics of β, we form a matrix $\mathcal{X}$ of $2L+1$ *sigma* vectors $\mathcal{X}_i$, where the first vector ($\mathcal{X}_0$) corresponds to $\bar{\alpha}$, and the rest are computed from the mean (+)plus and (-)minus each column of the matrix square-root of $\mathbf{P}_\alpha$. These sigma vectors are propagated through the nonlinear function, and the mean and covariance for β are approximated using a weighted sample mean and covariance,

$$\bar{\beta} \approx \frac{1}{L+\kappa} \left\{ \kappa g(\mathcal{X}_0) + \frac{1}{2} \sum_{i=1}^{2L} g(\mathcal{X}_i) \right\}, \quad (6)$$

$$\mathbf{P}_\beta \approx \frac{1}{L+\kappa} \left\{ \kappa [g(\mathcal{X}_0) - \bar{\beta}][g(\mathcal{X}_0) - \bar{\beta}]^T + \frac{1}{2} \sum_{i=1}^{2L} [g(\mathcal{X}_i) - \bar{\beta}][g(\mathcal{X}_i) - \bar{\beta}]^T \right\} \quad (7)$$

where κ is a scaling factor. Note that this method differs substantially from general "sampling" methods (e.g., Monte-Carlo methods and particle filters [1]) which require orders of magnitude more sample points in an attempt to propagate an accurate (possibly non-Gaussian) distribution of the state. The UT approximations are accurate to the third order for Gaussian inputs for all nonlinearities. For non-Gaussian inputs, approximations are accurate to at least the second-order, with the accuracy determined by the choice of κ [3]. A simple example is shown in Figure 1 for a 2-dimensional system: the left plots shows the true mean and covariance propagation using Monte-Carlo sampling; the center plots show the performance of the UT (note only 5 sigma points are required); the right plots show the results using a linearization approach as would be done in the EKF. The superior performance of the UT is clear.

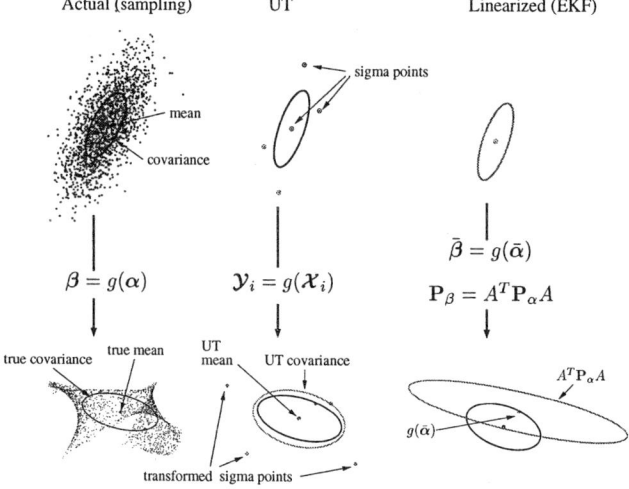

Figure 1: Example of the UT for mean and covariance propagation. a) actual, b) UT, c) first-order linear (EKF).

The *unscented filter* (UF) [3] is a straightforward extension of the UT to the recursive estimation in Equation 3, where we set $\alpha = \hat{\mathbf{x}}_k$, and denote the corresponding sigma matrix as $\mathcal{X}(k|k)$. The UF equations are given on the next page. It is interesting to note that no explicit calculation of Jacobians or Hessians are necessary to implement this algorithm. The total number of computations is only order L^2 as compared to L^3 for the EKF.[1]

4 Application to Dual Estimation

This section shows the use of the UF within several dual estimation approaches. As an application domain for comparison, we consider modeling a noisy time-series as a nonlinear

---
[1]Note that a matrix square-root using the Cholesky factorization is of order $L^3/6$. However, the covariance matrices are expressed recursively, and thus the square-root can be computed in only order L^2 by performing a recursive update to the Cholesky factorization.

$$
\boxed{\begin{array}{l}
\text{UF Equations} \\
W_0 = \kappa/(L+\kappa) \quad , \quad W_1 \ldots W_{2L} = 1/2(L+\kappa) \\
\mathcal{X}(k|k-1) = \mathbf{F}[\mathcal{X}(k-1|k-1), \mathbf{P}_{\mathbf{vv}}^{1/2}] \\
\hat{\mathbf{x}}_k^- = \sum_{i=0}^{2L} W_i \mathcal{X}_i(k|k-1) \\
\mathbf{P}_k^- = \sum_{i=0}^{2L} W_i [\mathcal{X}_i(k|k-1) - \hat{\mathbf{x}}_k^-][\mathcal{X}_i(k|k-1) - \hat{\mathbf{x}}_k^-]^T \\
\mathcal{Y}(k|k-1) = \mathbf{H}[\mathcal{X}(k|k-1), \mathbf{P}_{\mathbf{nn}}^{1/2}] \\
\hat{\mathbf{y}}_k^- = \sum_{i=0}^{2L} W_i \mathcal{Y}_i(k|k-1) \\
\mathbf{P}_{\tilde{\mathbf{y}}_k \tilde{\mathbf{y}}_k} = \sum_{i=0}^{2L} W_i [\mathcal{Y}_i(k|k-1) - \hat{\mathbf{y}}_k^-][\mathcal{Y}_i(k|k-1) - \hat{\mathbf{y}}_k^-]^T \\
\mathbf{P}_{\mathbf{x}_k \mathbf{y}_k} = \sum_{i=0}^{2L} W_i [\mathcal{X}_i(k|k-1) - \hat{\mathbf{x}}_k^-][\mathcal{Y}_i(k|k-1) - \hat{\mathbf{y}}_k^-]^T \\
\hat{\mathbf{x}}_k = \hat{\mathbf{x}}_k^- + \mathbf{P}_{\mathbf{x}_k \mathbf{y}_k} \mathbf{P}_{\tilde{\mathbf{y}}_k \tilde{\mathbf{y}}_k}^{-1} (\mathbf{y}_k - \hat{\mathbf{y}}_k^-) \\
\mathbf{P}_k = \mathbf{P}_k^- - \mathbf{P}_{\mathbf{x}_k \mathbf{y}_k} (\mathbf{P}_{\tilde{\mathbf{y}}_k \tilde{\mathbf{y}}_k}^{-1})^T \mathbf{P}_{\mathbf{x}_k \mathbf{y}_k}^T
\end{array}}
$$

autoregression:

$$x_k = f(x_{k-1}, \ldots x_{k-M}, \mathbf{w}) + v_k \tag{8}$$
$$y_k = x_k + n_k, \qquad \forall k \in \{1 \ldots N\}$$

The underlying clean signal x_k is a nonlinear function of its past M values, driven by white Gaussian process noise v_k with variance σ_v^2. The observed data point y_k includes the additive noise n_k, which is assumed to be Gaussian with variance σ_n^2. The corresponding state-space representation for the signal x_k is given by:

$$\mathbf{x}_k = F(\mathbf{x}_{k-1}, \mathbf{w}) + B \cdot v_{k-1} \tag{9}$$

$$\begin{bmatrix} x_k \\ x_{k-1} \\ \vdots \\ x_{k-M+1} \end{bmatrix} = \begin{bmatrix} f(x_{k-1}, \ldots, x_{k-M}, \mathbf{w}) \\ \begin{bmatrix} 1 & 0 & 0 & 0 \\ 0 & \ddots & 0 & \vdots \\ 0 & 0 & 1 & 0 \end{bmatrix} \begin{bmatrix} x_{k-1} \\ \vdots \\ x_{k-M} \end{bmatrix} \end{bmatrix} + \begin{bmatrix} 1 \\ 0 \\ \vdots \\ 0 \end{bmatrix} \cdot v_{k-1}$$

$$y_k = [1 \ 0 \ \cdots \ 0] \cdot \mathbf{x}_k + n_k \tag{10}$$

In this context, the dual estimation problem consists of simultaneously estimating the clean signal x_k and the model parameters $\mathbf{w}$ from the noisy data y_k.

4.1 Dual EKF / Dual UF

One dual estimation approach is the *dual extended Kalman filter* developed in [8, 6]. The dual EKF requires separate state-space representation for the signal and the weights. A state-space representation for the weights is generated by considering them to be a stationary process with an identity state transition matrix, driven by process noise $\mathbf{u}_k$:

$$\mathbf{w}_k = \mathbf{w}_{k-1} + \mathbf{u}_k \tag{11}$$
$$y_k = f(\mathbf{x}_{k-1}, \mathbf{w}_k) + v_k + n_k. \tag{12}$$

The noisy measurement y_k has been rewritten as an observation on $\mathbf{w}$. This allows the use of an EKF for weight estimation (representing a "second-order" optimization procedure) [7]. Two EKFs can now be run simultaneously for signal and weight estimation. At every time-step, the current estimate of the weights is used in the signal-filter, and the current estimate of the signal-state is used in the weight-filter.

The *dual UF/EKF* algorithm is formed by simply replacing the EKF for state-estimation with the UF while still using an EKF for weight-estimation. In the *dual UF* algorithm both state- and weight-estimation are done with the UF. Note that the state-transition is linear in the weight filter, so the nonlinearity is restricted to the measurement equation. Here, the UF gives a more exact measurement-update phase of estimation. The use of the UF for weight estimation in general is discussed in further detail in Section 5.

4.2 Joint EKF / Joint UF

An alternative approach to dual estimation is provided by the *joint extended Kalman filter* [4, 5]. In this framework the signal-state and weight vector are concatenated into a single, *joint* state vector: $\mathbf{z}_k = [\mathbf{x}_k^T \; \mathbf{w}_k^T]^T$. The estimation of $\mathbf{z}_k$ can be done recursively by writing the state-space equations for the joint state as:

$$\mathbf{z}_k = \begin{bmatrix} F(\mathbf{x}_{k-1}, \mathbf{w}_{k-1}) \\ \mathbf{I} \cdot \mathbf{w}_{k-1} \end{bmatrix} + \begin{bmatrix} B \cdot v_k \\ \mathbf{u}_k \end{bmatrix} \quad \text{and} \quad y_k = [1 \; 0 \; \cdots \; 0]\mathbf{z}_k + n_k, \qquad (13)$$

and running an EKF on the joint state-space to produce simultaneous estimates of the states $\mathbf{x}_k$ and $\mathbf{w}$. As discussed in [6], the joint EKF provides approximate MAP estimates by maximizing the joint density of the signal and weights given the noisy data. Again, our approach in this paper is to use the UF instead of the EKF to provide more accurate estimation of the state, resulting in the *joint UF* algorithm.

4.3 EM - Unscented Smoothing

A somewhat different iterative approach to dual estimation is given by the expectation-maximization (EM) algorithm applied to nonlinear dynamic systems [2]. In each iteration, the conditional expectation of the signal is computed, given the data and the current estimate of the model (E-step). Then the model is found that maximizes a function of this conditional mean (M-step). For linear models, the M-step can be solved in closed form. The E-step is computed with a Kalman smoother, which combines the forward-time estimated mean and covariance ($\hat{\mathbf{x}}_k^f, \mathbf{P}_k^f$) of the signal given *past* data, with the backward-time predicted mean and covariance ($\hat{\mathbf{x}}_k^b, \mathbf{P}_k^b$) given the *future* data, producing the following smoothed statistics given *all* the data:

$$(\mathbf{P}_k^s)^{-1} = (\mathbf{P}_k^f)^{-1} + (\mathbf{P}_k^b)^{-1} \qquad (14)$$

$$\hat{\mathbf{x}}_k^s = \mathbf{P}_k^s[(\mathbf{P}_k^b)^{-1}\hat{\mathbf{x}}_k^b - (\mathbf{P}_k^f)^{-1}\hat{\mathbf{x}}_k^f]. \qquad (15)$$

When a MLP neural network model is used, the M-step can no longer be computed in closed-form, and a gradient-based approach is used instead. The resulting algorithm is usually referred to as generalized EM (GEM) [2]. The E-step is typically approximated by an extended Kalman smoother, wherein a linearization of the model is used for backward propagation of the state estimates.

We propose improving the E-step of the EM algorithm for nonlinear models by using a UF instead of an EKF to compute both the forward and backward passes in the Kalman smoother. Rather than linearize the model for the backward pass, as in [2], a neural network is trained on the backward dynamics (as well as the forward dynamics). This allows for a more exact backward estimation phase using the UF, and enables the development of an *unscented smoother* (US).

---

[2] An exact M-step is possible using RBF networks [2].

4.4 Experiments

We present results on two simple time-series to provide a clear illustration of the use of the UF over the EKF. The first series is the Mackey-Glass chaotic series with additive WGN (SNR $\approx 3dB$). The second time series (also chaotic) comes from an autoregressive neural network with random weights driven by Gaussian process noise and also corrupted by additive WGN (SNR $\approx 3dB$). A standard 5-3-1 MLP with $tanh$ hidden activation functions and a linear output layer was used in all the filters. The process and measurement noise variances were assumed to be known.

Results on training and testing data, as well as training curves for the different dual estimation methods are shown below. The quoted numbers are normalized (clean signal variance) mean-square estimation and prediction errors. The superior performance of the UT based algorithms (especially the *dual UF*) are clear. Note also the more stable learning curves using the UF approaches. These improvements have been found to be consistent and statistically significant on a number of additional experiments.

Mackey-Glass	Train		Test	
Algorithm	Est.	Pred.	Est.	Pred.
Dual EKF	0.20	0.50	0.21	0.54
Dual UF/EKF	0.19	0.50	0.19	0.53
Dual UF	0.15	0.45	0.14	0.48
Joint EKF	0.22	0.53	0.22	0.56
Joint UF	0.19	0.50	0.18	0.53

Chaotic AR-NN	Train		Test	
Algorithm	Est.	Pred.	Est.	Pred.
Dual EKF	0.32	0.62	0.36	0.69
Dual UF/EKF	0.26	0.58	0.28	0.69
Dual UF	0.23	0.55	0.27	0.63
Joint EKF	0.29	0.58	0.34	0.72
Joint UF	0.25	0.55	0.30	0.67

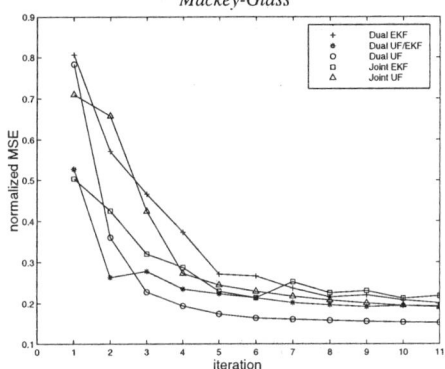

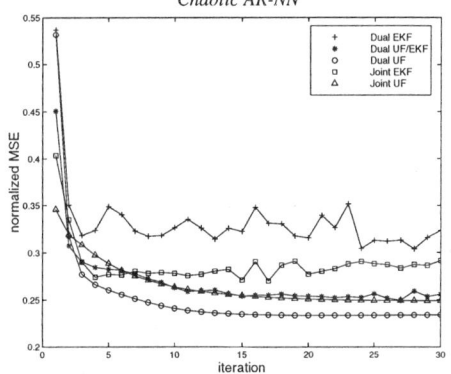

The final table below compares *smoother* performance used for the E-step in the EM algorithm. In this case, the network models are trained on the clean time-series, and then tested on the noisy data using either the standard Kalman smoother with linearized backward model (EKS1), a Kalman smoother with a second nonlinear backward model (EKS2), and the unscented smoother (US). The forward (F), backward (B), and smoothed (S) estimation errors are reported. Again the performance benefits of the unscented approach is clear.

Mackey-Glass	Norm. MSE		
Algorithm	F	B	S
EKS1	0.20	0.70	0.27
EKS2	0.20	0.31	0.19
US	0.10	0.24	0.08

Chaotic AR-NN	Norm. MSE		
Algorithm	F	B	S
EKS1	0.35	0.32	0.28
EKS2	0.35	0.22	0.23
US	0.23	0.21	0.16

5 UF Neural Network Training

As part of the dual UF algorithm, we introduced the use of the UF for weight estimation. The approach can also be seen as a new method for the general problem of training neural networks (*i.e.*, for regression or classification problems where the input **x** is observed and no state-estimation is required). The advantage of the UF over the EKF in this case is not as obvious, as the state-transition function is linear (See Equation 11). However, as pointed out earlier, the observation is nonlinear. Effectively, the EKF builds up an approximation to the expected Hessian by taking outer products of the gradient. The UF, however, may provide a more accurate estimate through direct approximation of the expectation of the Hessian. We have performed a number of preliminary experiments on standard benchmark data. The figure below shows the mean and std. of learning curves (computed over 100 experiments with different initial weights) for the Mackay Robot Arm Mapping dataset. Note the faster convergence, lower variance, and lower final MSE performance of the UF weight training. While these results are encouraging, further study is still necessary to fully contrast differences between UF and EKF weight training.

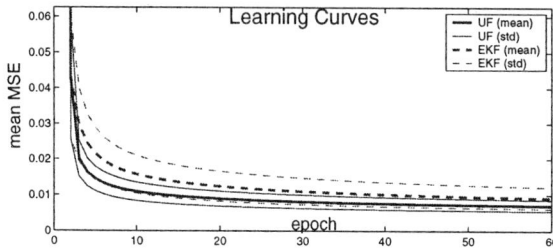

6 Conclusions

The EKF has been widely accepted as a standard tool in the machine learning community. In this paper we have presented an alternative to the EKF using the unscented filter. The UF consistently achieves a better level of accuracy than the EKF at a comparable level of complexity. We demonstrated this performance gain on a number of dual estimation methods as well as standard regression modeling.

Acknowledgements

This work was sponsored in part by the NSF under grant IRI-9712346.

References

[1] J. F. G. de Freitas, M. Niranjan, A. H. Gee, and A. Doucet. Sequential Monte Carlo methods for optimisation of neural network models. Technical Report TR-328, Cambridge University Engineering Department, Cambridge, England, November 1998.

[2] Z. Ghahramani and S. T. Roweis. Learning nonlinear dynamical systems using an EM algorithm. In M. J. Kearns, S. A. Solla, and D. A. Cohn, editors, *Advances in Neural Information Processing Systems 11: Proceedings of the 1998 Conference.* MIT Press, 1999.

[3] S. J. Julier and J. K. Uhlmann. A New Extension of the Kalman Filter to Nonlinear Systems. In *Proc. of AeroSense: The 11th International Symposium on Aerospace/Defence Sensing, Simulation and Controls, Orlando, Florida.*, 1997.

[4] R. E. Kopp and R. J. Orford. Linear regression applied to system identification for adaptive control systems. *AIAA J.*, 1:2300–06, October 1963.

[5] M. B. Matthews and G. S. Moschytz. Neural-network nonlinear adaptive filtering using the extended Kalman filter algorithm. In *INNC*, pages 115–8, 1990.

[6] A. T. Nelson. *Nonlinear Estimation and Modeling of Noisy Time-Series by Dual Kalman Filtering Methods.* PhD thesis, Oregon Graduate Institute, 1999. In preparation.

[7] S. Singhal and L. Wu. Training multilayer perceptrons with the extended Kalman filter. In *Advances in Neural Information Processing Systems 1*, pages 133–140, San Mateo, CA, 1989. Morgan Kauffman.

[8] E. A. Wan and A. T. Nelson. Dual Kalman filtering methods for nonlinear prediction, estimation, and smoothing. In *Advances in Neural Information Processing Systems 9*, 1997.

Correctness of belief propagation in Gaussian graphical models of arbitrary topology

Yair Weiss
Computer Science Division
UC Berkeley, 485 Soda Hall
Berkeley, CA 94720-1776
Phone: 510-642-5029
yweiss@cs.berkeley.edu

William T. Freeman
Mitsubishi Electric Research Lab
201 Broadway
Cambridge, MA 02139
Phone: 617-621-7527
freeman@merl.com

Abstract

Local "belief propagation" rules of the sort proposed by Pearl [15] are guaranteed to converge to the correct posterior probabilities in singly connected graphical models. Recently, a number of researchers have empirically demonstrated good performance of "loopy belief propagation"– using these same rules on graphs with loops. Perhaps the most dramatic instance is the near Shannon-limit performance of "Turbo codes", whose decoding algorithm is equivalent to loopy belief propagation.

Except for the case of graphs with a single loop, there has been little theoretical understanding of the performance of loopy propagation. Here we analyze belief propagation in networks with arbitrary topologies when the nodes in the graph describe jointly Gaussian random variables. We give an analytical formula relating the true posterior probabilities with those calculated using loopy propagation. We give sufficient conditions for convergence and show that when belief propagation converges it gives the correct posterior means *for all graph topologies*, not just networks with a single loop.

The related "max-product" belief propagation algorithm finds the maximum posterior probability estimate for singly connected networks. We show that, even for non-Gaussian probability distributions, the convergence points of the max-product algorithm in loopy networks are maxima over a particular large local neighborhood of the posterior probability. These results help clarify the empirical performance results and motivate using the powerful belief propagation algorithm in a broader class of networks.

Problems involving probabilistic belief propagation arise in a wide variety of applications, including error correcting codes, speech recognition and medical diagnosis. If the graph is singly connected, there exist local message-passing schemes to calculate the posterior probability of an unobserved variable given the observed variables. Pearl [15] derived such a scheme for singly connected Bayesian networks and showed that this "belief propagation" algorithm is guaranteed to converge to the correct posterior probabilities (or "beliefs").

Several groups have recently reported excellent experimental results by running algorithms equivalent to Pearl's algorithm on networks with loops [8, 13, 6]. Perhaps the most dramatic instance of this performance is for "Turbo code" [2] error correcting codes. These codes have been described as "the most exciting and potentially important development in coding theory in many years" [12] and have recently been shown [10, 11] to utilize an algorithm equivalent to belief propagation in a network with loops.

Progress in the analysis of loopy belief propagation has been made for the case of networks with a single loop [17, 18, 4, 1]. For these networks, it can be shown that (1) unless all the compatabilities are deterministic, loopy belief propagation will converge. (2) The difference between the loopy beliefs and the true beliefs is related to the convergence rate of the messages — the faster the convergence the more exact the approximation and (3) If the hidden nodes are binary, then the loopy beliefs and the true beliefs are both maximized by the same assignments, although the confidence in that assignment is wrong for the loopy beliefs.

In this paper we analyze belief propagation in graphs of *arbitrary topology*, for nodes describing jointly Gaussian random variables. We give an exact formula relating the correct marginal posterior probabilities with the ones calculated using loopy belief propagation. We show that if belief propagation converges, then it will give the correct posterior means *for all graph topologies*, not just networks with a single loop. We show that the covariance estimates will generally be incorrect but present a relationship between the error in the covariance estimates and the convergence speed. For Gaussian *or* non-Gaussian variables, we show that the "max-product" algorithm, which calculates the MAP estimate in singly connected networks, only converges to points that are maxima over a particular large neighborhood of the posterior probability of loopy networks.

1 Analysis

To simplify the notation, we assume the graphical model has been preprocessed into an undirected graphical model with pairwise potentials. Any graphical model can be converted into this form, and running belief propagation on the pairwise graph is equivalent to running belief propagation on the original graph [18]. We assume each node x_i has a local observation y_i. In each iteration of belief propagation, each node x_i sends a message to each neighboring x_j that is based on the messages it received from the other neighbors, its local observation y_i and the pairwise potentials $\Psi_{ij}(x_i, x_j)$ and $\Psi_{ii}(x_i, y_i)$. We assume the message-passing occurs in parallel.

The idea behind the analysis is to build an unwrapped tree. The unwrapped tree is the graphical model which belief propagation is solving exactly when one applies the belief propagation rules in a loopy network [9, 20, 18]. It is constructed by maintaining the same local neighborhood structure as the loopy network but nodes are replicated so there are no loops. The potentials and the observations are replicated from the loopy graph. Figure 1 (a) shows an unwrapped tree for the diamond shaped graph in (b). By construction, the belief at the root node $\tilde{x}_1$ is identical to that at node x_1 in the loopy graph after four iterations of belief propagation. Each node has a shaded observed node attached to it, omitted here for clarity.

Because the original network represents jointly Gaussian variables, so will the unwrapped tree. Since it is a tree, belief propagation is guaranteed to give the correct answer for the unwrapped graph. We can thus use Gaussian marginalization formulae to calculate the true mean and variances in both the original and the unwrapped networks. In this way, we calculate the accuracy of belief propagation for Gaussian networks of arbitrary topology.

We assume that the joint mean is zero (the means can be added-in later). The joint distri-

Correctness of Belief Propagation

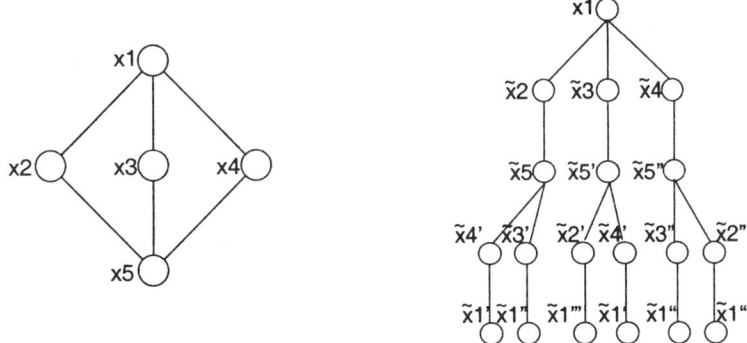

Figure 1: **Left:** A Markov network with multiple loops. **Right:** The unwrapped network corresponding to this structure.

bution of $z = \begin{pmatrix} x \\ y \end{pmatrix}$ is given by $P(z) = \alpha e^{-\frac{1}{2} z^T V z}$, where $V = \begin{pmatrix} V_{xx} & V_{xy} \\ V_{yx} & V_{yy} \end{pmatrix}$. It is straightforward to construct the inverse covariance matrix V of the joint Gaussian that describes a given Gaussian graphical model [3].

Writing out the exponent of the joint and completing the square shows that the mean μ of x, given the observations y, is given by:

$$V_{xx}\mu = -V_{xy}y, \tag{1}$$

and the covariance matrix $C_{x|y}$ of x given y is: $C_{x|y} = V_{xx}^{-1}$. We will denote by $C_{x_i|y}$ the ith row of $C_{x|y}$ so the marginal posterior variance of x_i given the data is $\sigma^2(i) = C_{x_i|y}(i)$.

We will use ˜ for unwrapped quantities. We scan the tree in *breadth first* order and denote by $\tilde{x}$ the vector of values in the hidden nodes of the tree when so scanned. Similarly, we denote by $\tilde{y}$ the observed nodes scanned in the same order and $\tilde{V}_{xx}, \tilde{V}_{xy}$ the inverse covariance matrices. Since we are scanning in breadth first order the last nodes are the leaf nodes and we denote by L the number of leaf nodes. By the nature of unwrapping, $\tilde{\mu}(1)$ is the mean of the belief at node x_1 after t iterations of belief propagation, where t is the number of unwrappings. Similarly $\tilde{\sigma}^2(1) = \tilde{C}_{x_1|y}(1)$ is the variance of the belief at node x_1 after t iterations.

Because the data is replicated we can write $\tilde{y} = Oy$ where $O(i,j) = 1$ if $\tilde{y}_i$ is a replica of y_j and 0 otherwise. Since the potentials $\Psi(x_i, y_i)$ are replicated, we can write $\tilde{V}_{xy}O = OV_{xy}$. Since the $\Psi(x_i, x_j)$ are also replicated and all non-leaf $\tilde{x}_i$ have the same connectivity as the corresponding x_i, we can write $\tilde{V}_{xx}O = OV_{xx} + E$ where E is zero in all but the last L rows. When these relationships between the loopy and unwrapped inverse covariance matrices are substituted into the loopy and unwrapped versions of equation 1, one obtains the following expression, true for any iteration [19]:

$$\tilde{\mu}(1) = \mu(1) + \tilde{C}_{x_1|y}e \tag{2}$$

where e is a vector that is zero everywhere but the last L components (corresponding to the leaf nodes). Our choice of the node for the root of the tree is arbitrary, so this applies to all nodes of the loopy network. This formula relates, for any node of a network with loops, the means calculated at each iteration by belief propagation with the true posterior means.

Similarly when the relationship between the loopy and unwrapped inverse covariance matrices is substituted into the loopy and unwrapped definitions of $C_{x|y}$ we can relate the

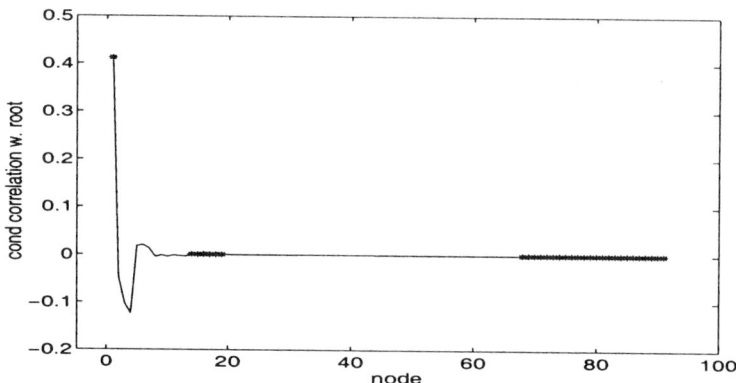

Figure 2: The conditional correlation between the root node and all other nodes in the unwrapped tree of Fig. 1 after eight iterations. Potentials were chosen randomly. Nodes are presented in breadth first order so the last elements are the correlations between the root node and the leaf nodes. We show that if this correlation goes to zero, belief propagation converges and the loopy means are exact. Symbols plotted with a star denote correlations with nodes that correspond to the node x_1 in the loopy graph. The sum of these correlations gives the correct variance of node x_1 while loopy propagation uses only the first correlation.

marginalized covariances calculated by belief propagation to the true ones [19]:

$$\tilde{\sigma}^2(1) = \sigma^2(1) + \tilde{C}_{x_1|y} e_1 - \tilde{C}_{x_1|y} e_2 \qquad (3)$$

where e_1 is a vector that is zero everywhere but the last L components while e_2 is equal to 1 for all nodes in the unwrapped tree that are replicas of x_1 except for $\tilde{x}_1$. All other components of e_2 are zero,

Figure 2 shows $\tilde{C}_{x_1|y}$ for the diamond network in Fig. 1. We generated random potential functions and observations and calculated the conditional correlations in the unwrapped tree. Note that the conditional correlation decreases with distance in the tree — we are scanning in breadth first order so the last L components correspond to the leaf nodes. As the number of iterations of loopy propagation is increased the size of the unwrapped tree increases and the conditional correlation between the leaf nodes and the root node decreases.

From equations 2–3 it is clear that if the conditional correlation between the leaf nodes and the root nodes are zero for all sufficiently large unwrappings then (1) belief propagation converges (2) the means are exact and (3) the variances may be incorrect. In practice the conditional correlations will not actually be equal to zero for any finite unwrapping. In [19] we give a more precise statement: if the conditional correlation of the root node and the leaf nodes decreases rapidly enough then (1) belief propagation converges (2) the means are exact and (3) the variances may be incorrect. We also show sufficient conditions on the potentials $\Psi(x_i, x_j)$ for the correlation to decrease rapidly enough: the rate at which the correlation decreases is determined by the ratio of off-diagonal and diagonal components in the quadratic form defining the potentials [19].

How wrong will the variances be? The term $\tilde{C}_{x_1|y} e_2$ in equation 3 is simply the sum of many components of $\tilde{C}_{x_1|y}$. Figure 2 shows these components. The correct variance is the sum of all the components while the belief propagation variance approximates this sum with the first (and dominant) term. Whenever there is a positive correlation between the root node and other replicas of x_1 the loopy variance is strictly less than the true variance — the loopy estimate is overconfident.

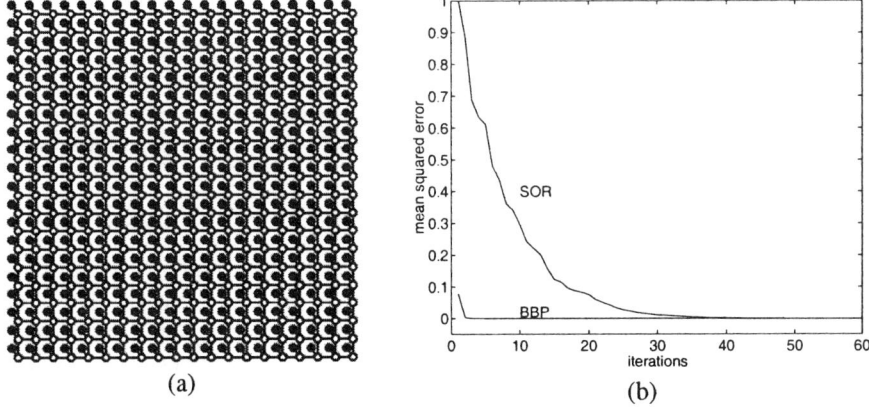

Figure 3: (a) 25×25 graphical model for simulation. The unobserved nodes (unfilled) were connected to their four nearest neighbors and to an observation node (filled). (b) The error of the estimates of loopy propagation and successive over-relaxation (SOR) as a function of iteration. Note that belief propagation converges much faster than SOR.

Note that when the conditional correlation decreases rapidly to zero two things happen. First, the convergence is faster (because $\tilde{C}_{x_1|y}e_1$ approaches zero faster). Second, the approximation error of the variances is smaller (because $\tilde{C}_{x_1|y}e_2$ is smaller). Thus we have shown, as in the single loop case, quick convergence is correlated with good approximation.

2 Simulations

We ran belief propagation on the 25×25 2D grid of Fig. 3 a. The joint probability was:

$$P(x,y) = exp(-\sum_{ij} w_{ij}(x_i - x_j)^2 - \sum_i w_{ii}(x_i - y_i)^2) \qquad (4)$$

where $w_{ij} = 0$ if nodes x_i, x_j are not neighbors and 0.01 otherwise and w_{ii} was randomly selected to be 0 or 1 for all i with probability of 1 set to 0.2. The observations y_i were chosen randomly. This problem corresponds to an approximation problem from sparse data where only 20% of the points are visible.

We found the exact posterior by solving equation 1. We also ran belief propagation and found that when it converged, the calculated means were identical to the true means up to machine precision. Also, as predicted by the theory, the calculated variances were too small — the belief propagation estimate was overconfident.

In many applications, the solution of equation 1 by matrix inversion is intractable and iterative methods are used. Figure 3 compares the error in the means as a function of iterations for loopy propagation and successive-over-relaxation (SOR), considered one of the best relaxation methods [16]. Note that after essentially five iterations loopy propagation gives the right answer while SOR requires many more. As expected by the fast convergence, the approximation error in the variances was quite small. The median error was 0.018. For comparison the true variances ranged from 0.01 to 0.94 with a mean of 0.322. Also, the nodes for which the approximation error was worse were indeed the nodes that converged slower.

3 Discussion

Independently, two other groups have recently analyzed special cases of Gaussian graphical models. Frey [7] analyzed the graphical model corresponding to factor analysis and gave conditions for the existence of a stable fixed-point. Rusmevichientong and Van Roy [14] analyzed a graphical model with the topology of turbo decoding but a Gaussian joint density. For this specific graph they gave sufficient conditions for convergence and showed that the means are exact.

Our main interest in the Gaussian case is to understand the performance of belief propagation in general networks with multiple loops. We are struck by the similarity of our results for Gaussians in arbitrary networks and the results for single loops of arbitrary distributions [18]. First, in single loop networks with binary nodes, loopy belief at a node and the true belief at a node are maximized by the same assignment while the confidence in that assignment is incorrect. In Gaussian networks with multiple loops, the mean at each node is correct but the confidence around that mean may be incorrect. Second, for both single-loop and Gaussian networks, fast belief propagation convergence correlates with accurate beliefs. Third, in both Gaussians and discrete valued single loop networks, the statistical dependence between root and leaf nodes governs the convergence rate and accuracy.

The two models are quite different. Mean field approximations are exact for Gaussian MRFs while they work poorly in sparsely connected discrete networks with a single loop. The results for the Gaussian and single-loop cases lead us to believe that similar results may hold for a larger class of networks.

Can our analysis be extended to non-Gaussian distributions? The basic idea applies to arbitrary graphs and arbitrary potentials: belief propagation is performing exact inference on a tree that has the same local neighbor structure as the loopy graph. However, the linear algebra that we used to calculate exact expressions for the error in belief propagation at any iteration holds only for Gaussian variables.

We have used a similar approach to analyze the related "max-product" belief propagation algorithm on arbitrary graphs with arbitrary distributions [5] (both discrete and continuous valued nodes). We show that if the max-product algorithm converges, the max-product assignment has greater posterior probability then any assignment in a particular large region around that assignment. While this is a weaker condition than a global maximum, it is much stronger than a simple local maximum of the posterior probability.

The sum-product and max-product belief propagation algorithms are fast and parallelizable. Due to the well known hardness of probabilistic inference in graphical models, belief propagation will obviously not work for arbitrary networks and distributions. Nevertheless, a growing body of empirical evidence shows its success in many networks with loops. Our results justify applying belief propagation in certain networks with multiple loops. This may enable fast, approximate probabilistic inference in a range of new applications.

References

[1] S.M. Aji, G.B. Horn, and R.J. McEliece. On the convergence of iterative decoding on graphs with a single cycle. In *Proc. 1998 ISIT*, 1998.

[2] C. Berrou, A. Glavieux, and P. Thitimajshima. Near Shannon limit error-correcting coding and decoding: Turbo codes. In *Proc. IEEE International Communications Conference '93*, 1993.

[3] R. Cowell. Advanced inference in Bayesian networks. In M.I. Jordan, editor, *Learning in Graphical Models*. MIT Press, 1998.

[4] G.D. Forney, F.R. Kschischang, and B. Marcus. Iterative decoding of tail-biting trellisses. preprint presented at 1998 Information Theory Workshop in San Diego, 1998.

[5] W. T. Freeman and Y. Weiss. On the fixed points of the max-product algorithm. Technical Report 99–39, MERL, 201 Broadway, Cambridge, MA 02139, 1999.

[6] W.T. Freeman and E.C. Pasztor. Learning to estimate scenes from images. In M.S. Kearns, S.A. Solla, and D.A. Cohn, editors, *Adv. Neural Information Processing Systems 11*. MIT Press, 1999.

[7] B.J. Frey. Turbo factor analysis. In *Adv. Neural Information Processing Systems 12*. 2000. to appear.

[8] Brendan J. Frey. *Bayesian Networks for Pattern Classification, Data Compression and Channel Coding*. MIT Press, 1998.

[9] R.G. Gallager. *Low Density Parity Check Codes*. MIT Press, 1963.

[10] F. R. Kschischang and B. J. Frey. Iterative decoding of compound codes by probability propagation in graphical models. *IEEE Journal on Selected Areas in Communication*, 16(2):219–230, 1998.

[11] R.J. McEliece, D.J.C. MackKay, and J.F. Cheng. Turbo decoding as as an instance of Pearl's 'belief propagation' algorithm. *IEEE Journal on Selected Areas in Communication*, 16(2):140–152, 1998.

[12] R.J. McEliece, E. Rodemich, and J.F. Cheng. The Turbo decision algorithm. In *Proc. 33rd Allerton Conference on Communications, Control and Computing*, pages 366–379, Monticello, IL, 1995.

[13] K.P. Murphy, Y. Weiss, and M.I. Jordan. Loopy belief propagation for approximate inference: an empirical study. In *Proceedings of Uncertainty in AI*, 1999.

[14] Rusmevichientong P. and Van Roy B. An analysis of Turbo decoding with Gaussian densities. In *Adv. Neural Information Processing Systems 12*. 2000. to appear.

[15] Judea Pearl. *Probabilistic Reasoning in Intelligent Systems: Networks of Plausible Inference*. Morgan Kaufmann, 1988.

[16] Gilbert Strang. *Introduction to Applied Mathematics*. Wellesley-Cambridge, 1986.

[17] Y. Weiss. Belief propagation and revision in networks with loops. Technical Report 1616, MIT AI lab, 1997.

[18] Y. Weiss. Correctness of local probability propagation in graphical models with loops. *Neural Computation*, to appear, 2000.

[19] Y. Weiss and W. T. Freeman. Loopy propagation gives the correct posterior means for Gaussians. Technical Report UCB.CSD-99-1046, Berkeley Computer Science Dept., 1999. www.cs.berkeley.edu yweiss/.

[20] N. Wiberg. *Codes and decoding on general graphs*. PhD thesis, Department of Electrical Engineering, U. Linkoping, Sweden, 1996.

A MCMC approach to Hierarchical Mixture Modelling

Christopher K. I. Williams
Institute for Adaptive and Neural Computation
Division of Informatics, University of Edinburgh
5 Forrest Hill, Edinburgh EH1 2QL, Scotland, UK
ckiw@dai.ed.ac.uk   http://anc.ed.ac.uk

Abstract

There are many hierarchical clustering algorithms available, but these lack a firm statistical basis. Here we set up a hierarchical probabilistic mixture model, where data is generated in a hierarchical tree-structured manner. Markov chain Monte Carlo (MCMC) methods are demonstrated which can be used to sample from the posterior distribution over trees containing variable numbers of hidden units.

1 Introduction

Over the past decade or two mixture models have become a popular approach to clustering or competitive learning problems. They have the advantage of having a well-defined objective function and fit in with the general trend of viewing neural network problems in a statistical framework. However, one disadvantage is that they produce a "flat" cluster structure rather than the hierarchical tree structure that is returned by some clustering algorithms such as the agglomerative single-link method (see e.g. [12]). In this paper I formulate a hierarchical mixture model, which retains the advantages of the statistical framework, but also features a tree-structured hierarchy.

The basic idea is illustrated in Figure 1(a). At the root of the tree (level 1) we have a single centre (marked with a ×). This is the mean of a Gaussian with large variance (represented by the large circle). A random number of centres (in this case 3) are sampled from the level 1 Gaussian, to produce 3 new centres (marked with o's). The variance associated with the level 2 Gaussians is smaller. A number of level 3 units are produced and associated with the level 2 Gaussians. The centre of each level 3 unit (marked with a +) is sampled from its parent Gaussian. This hierarchical process could be continued indefinitely, but in this example we generate data from the level 3 Gaussians, as shown by the dots in Figure 1(a).

A three-level version of this model would be a standard mixture model with a Gaussian prior on where the centres are located. In the four-level model the third level centres are clumped together around the second level means, and it is this that distinguishes the model from a flat mixture model. Another view of the generative process is given in Figure 1(b), where the tree structure denotes which nodes are children of particular parents. Note also that this is a *directed* acyclic graph, with the arrows denoting dependence of the position of the child on that of the parent.

In section 2 we describe the theory of probabilistic hierarchical clustering and give a discussion of related work. Experimental results are described in section 3.

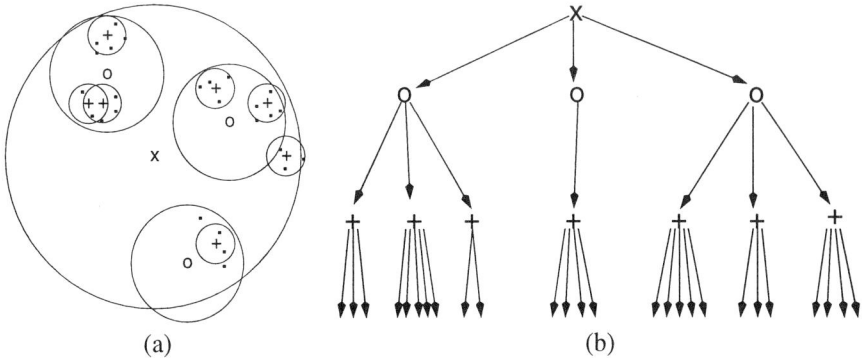

Figure 1: The basic idea of the hierarchical mixture model. (a) × denotes the root of the tree, the second level centres are denoted by o's and the third level centres by +'s. Data is generated from the third level centres by sampling random points from Gaussians whose means are the third level centres. (b) The corresponding tree structure.

2 Theory

We describe in turn (i) the prior over trees, (ii) the calculation of the likelihood given a data vector, (iii) Markov chain Monte Carlo (MCMC) methods for the inference of the tree structure given data and (iv) related work.

2.1 Prior over trees

We describe first the prior over the number of units in each layer, and then the prior on connections between layers. Consider a L layer hierarchical model. The root node is in level 1, there are n_2 nodes in level 2, and so on down to n_L nodes on level L. These n's are collected together in the vector $\mathbf{n}$. We use a Markovian model for $P(\mathbf{n})$, so that $P(\mathbf{n}) = P(n_1)P(n_2|n_1)\ldots P(n_L|n_{L-1})$ with $P(n_1) = \delta(n_1, 1)$. Currently these are taken to be Poisson distributions offset by 1, so that $P(n_{i+1}|n_i) \sim \text{Po}(\lambda_i n_i) + 1$, where λ_i is a parameter associated with level i. The offset is used so that there must always be at least one unit in any layer.

Given $\mathbf{n}$, we next consider how the tree is formed. The tree structure describes which node in the ith layer is the parent of each node in the $(i+1)$th layer, for $i = 1, \ldots, L-1$. Each unit has an indicator vector which stores the index of the parent to which it is attached. We collect all these indicator vectors together into a matrix, denoted $Z(\mathbf{n})$. The probability of a node in layer $(i+1)$ connecting to any node in layer i is taken to be $1/n_i$. Thus

$$P(\mathbf{n}, Z(\mathbf{n})) = P(\mathbf{n})P(Z(\mathbf{n})|\mathbf{n}) = P(\mathbf{n}) \prod_{i=1}^{L-1} (1/n_i)^{n_{i+1}}.$$

We now describe the generation of a random tree given $\mathbf{n}$ and $Z(\mathbf{n})$. For simplicity we describe the generation of points in 1-d below, although everything can be extended to arbitrary dimension very easily. The mean μ^1 of the level 1 Gaussian is at the origin[1]. The

---

[1]It is easy to relax this assumption so that μ^1 has a prior Gaussian distribution, or is located at some point other than the origin.

level 2 means μ_j^2, $j = 1, \ldots, n_2$ are generated from $\mathcal{N}(\mu^1, \sigma_1^2)$, where σ_1^2 is the variance associated with the level 1 node. Similarly, the position of each level 3 node is generated from its level 2 parent as a displacement from the position of the level 2 parent. This displacement is a Gaussian RV with zero mean and variance σ_2^2. This process continues on down to the visible variables. In order for this model to be useful, we require that $\sigma_1^2 > \sigma_2^2 > \ldots > \sigma_{L-1}^2$, i.e. that the variability introduced at successive levels declines monotonically (cf scaling of wavelet coefficients).

2.2 Calculation of the likelihood

The data that we observe are the positions of the points in the final layer; this is denoted $\mathbf{x}$. To calculate the likelihood of $\mathbf{x}$ under this model, we need to integrate out the locations of the means of the hidden variables in levels 2 through to $L - 1$. This can be done explicitly, however, we can shorten this calculation by realizing that given $Z(\mathbf{n})$, the generative distribution for the observables $\mathbf{x}$ is Gaussian $\mathcal{N}(0, C)$. The covariance matrix C can be calculated as follows. Consider two leaf nodes indexed by k and l. The Gaussian RVs that generated the position of these two leaves can be denoted

$$x_k = w_k^1 + w_k^2 + \ldots + w_k^{(L-1)}, \qquad x_l = w_l^1 + w_l^2 + \ldots + w_l^{(L-1)}.$$

To calculate the covariance between x_k and x_l, we simply calculate $\langle x_k x_l \rangle$. This depends crucially on how many of the w's are shared between nodes k and l (cf path analysis). For example, if $w_k^1 \neq w_l^1$, i.e. the nodes lie in different branches of the tree at level 1, their covariance is zero. If $k = l$, the variance is just the sum of the variances of each RV in the tree. In between, the covariance of x_k and x_l can be determined by finding at what level in the tree their common parent occurs.

Under these assumptions, the log likelihood L of $\mathbf{x}$ given $Z(\mathbf{n})$ is

$$L = -\frac{1}{2}\mathbf{x}^T C^{-1} \mathbf{x} - \frac{1}{2}\log|C| - \frac{n_L}{2}\log 2\pi. \tag{1}$$

In fact this calculation can be speeded up by taking account of the tree structure (see e.g. [8]). Note also that the posterior means (and variances) of the hidden variables can be calculated based on the covariances between the hidden and visible nodes. Again, this calculation can be carried out more efficiently; see Pearl [11] (section 7.2) for details.

2.3 Inference for n and $Z(\mathbf{n})$

Given $\mathbf{n}$ we have the problem of trying to infer the connectivity structure Z given the observations $\mathbf{x}$. Of course what we are interested in is the posterior distribution over Z, i.e. $P(Z|\mathbf{x}, \mathbf{n})$. One approach is to use a Markov chain Monte Carlo (MCMC) method to sample from this posterior distribution. A straightforward way to do this is to use the Metropolis algorithm, where we propose changes in the structure by changing the parent of a single node at a time. Note the similarities of this algorithm to the work of Williams and Adams [14] on Dynamic Trees (DTs); the main differences are (i) that disconnections are not allowed, i.e. we maintain a single tree (rather than a forest), and (ii) that the variables in the DT image models are discrete rather than Gaussian.

We also need to consider moves that change $\mathbf{n}$. This can be effected with a split/merge move. In the split direction, consider a node with a parent and several children. Split this node and randomly assign the children to the two split nodes. Each of the split nodes keeps the same parent. The probability of accepting this move under the Metropolis-Hastings scheme is

$$\alpha = \min\left(1, \frac{P(\mathbf{n}', Z(\mathbf{n}')|\mathbf{x})Q(\mathbf{n}', Z(\mathbf{n}'); \mathbf{n}, Z(\mathbf{n}))}{P(\mathbf{n}, Z(\mathbf{n})|\mathbf{x})Q(\mathbf{n}, Z(\mathbf{n}); \mathbf{n}', Z(\mathbf{n}'))}\right),$$

where $Q(\mathbf{n}', Z(\mathbf{n}'); \mathbf{n}, Z(\mathbf{n}))$ is the proposal probability of configuration $(\mathbf{n}', Z(\mathbf{n}'))$ given configuration $(\mathbf{n}, Z(\mathbf{n}))$. This scheme is based on the work on MCMC model composition (MC^3) by Madigan and York [9], and on Green's work on reversible jump MCMC [5].

Another move that changes $\mathbf{n}$ is to remove "dangling" nodes, i.e. nodes which have no children. This occurs when all the nodes in a given layer "decide" not to use one or more nodes in the layer above.

An alternative to sampling from the posterior is to use approximate inference, such as mean-field methods. These are currently being investigated for DT models [1].

2.4 Related work

There are a very large number of papers on hierarchical clustering; in this work we have focussed on expressing hierarchical clustering in terms of probabilistic models. For example Ambros-Ingerson et al [2] and Mozer [10] developed models where the idea is to cluster data at a coarse level, subtract out mean and cluster the residuals (recursively). This paper can be seen as a probabilistic interpretation of this idea.

The reconstruction of phylogenetic trees from biological sequence (DNA or protein) information gives rise to the problem of inferring a binary tree from the data. Durbin et al [3] (chapter 8) show how a probabilistic formulation of the problem can be developed, and the link to agglomerative hierarchical clustering algorithms as approximations to the full probabilistic method (see §8.6 in [3]). Much of the biological sequence work uses discrete variables, which diverges somewhat from the focus of the current work. However work by Edwards (1970) [4] concerns a branching Brownian-motion process, which has some similarities to the model described above. Important differences are that Edwards' model is in continuous time, and the the variances of the particles are derived from a Wiener process (and so have variance proportional to the lifetime of the particle). This is in contrast to the decreasing sequence of variances at a given number of levels assumed in the above model. One important difference between the model discussed in this paper and the phylogenetic tree model is that points in higher levels of the phylogenetic tree are taken to be individuals at an earlier time in evolutionary history, which is not the interpretation we require here.

An very different notion of hierarchy in mixture models can be found in the work on the AutoClass system [6]. They describe a model involving class hierarchy and inheritance, but their trees specify over which *dimensions* sharing of parameters occurs (e.g. means and covariance matrices for Gaussians). In contrast, the model in this paper creates a hierarchy over examples labelled $1, \ldots, n$ rather than dimensions.

Xu and Pearl [15] discuss the inference of a tree-structured belief network based on knowledge of the covariances of the leaf nodes. This algorithm cannot be applied directly in our case as the covariances are not known, although we note that if multiple runs from a given tree structure were available the covariances might be approximated using sample estimates.

Other ideas concerning hierarchical clustering are discussed in [13] and [7].

3 Experiments

We describe two sets of experiments to explore these ideas.

3.1 Searching over Z with n fixed

100 4-level random trees were generated from the prior, using values of $\lambda_1 = 1.5$, $\lambda_2 = 2$, $\lambda_3 = 3$, and $\sigma_1^2 = 10$, $\sigma_2^2 = 1$, $\sigma_3^2 = 0.01$. These trees had between 4 and 79 leaf

nodes, with an average of 30. For each tree **n** was kept the same as in the generative tree, and sampling was carried out over Z starting from a random initial configuration. A given node proposes changing its parent, and this proposal is accepted or rejected with the usual Metropolis probability. In one *sweep*, each node in levels 3 and 4 makes such a move. (Level 2 nodes only have one parent so there is no point in such a move there.) To obtain a representative sample of $P(Z(\mathbf{n})|\mathbf{n}, \mathbf{x})$, we should run the chain for as long as possible. However, we can also use the chain to find configurations with high posterior probability, and in this case running for longer only increases the chances of finding a better configuration. In our experiments the sampler was run for 100 sweeps. As $P(Z(\mathbf{n})|\mathbf{n})$ is uniform for fixed **n**, the posterior is simply proportional to the likelihood term. It would also be possible to run simulated annealing with the same move set to search explicitly for the *maximum a posteriori* (MAP) configuration.

The results are that for 76 of the 100 cases the tree with the highest posterior probability (HPP) configuration had higher posterior probability than the generative tree, for 20 cases the same tree was found and in 4 cases the HPP solution was inferior to the generative tree. The fact that in almost all cases the sampler found a configuration as good or better than the generative one in a relatively small number of sweeps is very encouraging.

In Figure 2 the generative (left column) and HPP trees for fixed **n** (middle column) are plotted for two examples. In panel (b) note the "dangling" node in level 2, which means that the level 3 nodes to the left end up in a inferior configuration to (a). By contrast, in panel (e) the sampler has found a better (less tangled) configuration than the generative model (d).

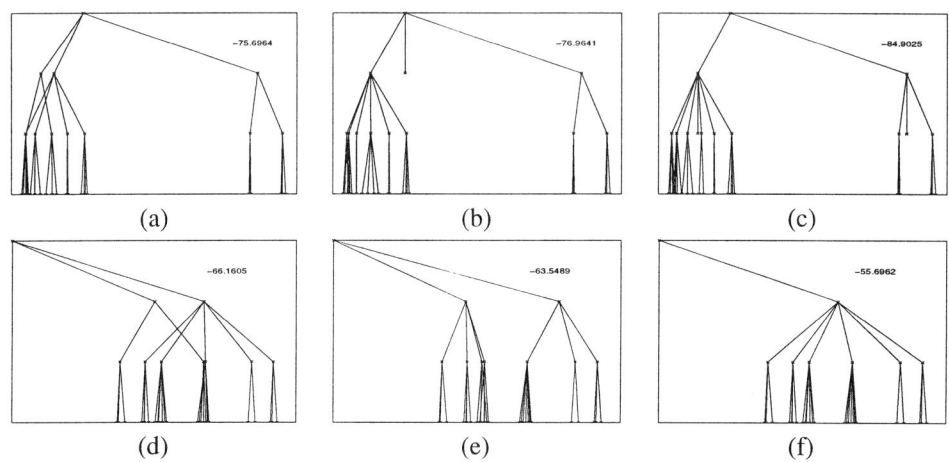

Figure 2: (a) and (d) show the generative trees for two examples. The corresponding HPP trees for fixed **n** are plotted in (b) and (e) and those for variable **n** in (c) and (f). The number in each panel is the log posterior probability of the configuration. The nodes in levels 2 and 3 are shown located at their posterior means. Apparent non-tree structures are caused by two nodes being plotted almost on top of each other.

3.2 Searching over both n and Z

Given some data **x** we will not usually know appropriate numbers of hidden units. This motivates searching over both Z and **n**, which can be achieved using the split/merge moves discussed in section 2.3.

In the experiments below the initial numbers of units in levels 2 and 3 (denoted $\hat{n}_2$ and

$\hat{n}_3$) were set using the simple-minded formulae $\hat{n}_3 = \lceil \dim(\mathbf{x})/\lambda_3 \rceil$ $\hat{n}_2 = \lceil \hat{n}_3/\lambda_2 \rceil$. A proper inferential calculation for n_2 and n_3 can be carried out, but it requires the solution of a non-linear optimization problem. Given $\hat{n}_2$ and $\hat{n}_3$, the initial connection configuration was chosen randomly.

The search method used was to propose a split/merge move (with probability 0.5:0.5) in level 2, then to sample the level 2 to level 3 connections, and then to propose a split-merge move in level 3, and then update the level 3 to level 4 connections. This comprised a single *sweep*, and as above 100 sweeps were used.

Experiments were conducted on the same trees used in section 3.1. In this case the results were that for 50 out of the 100 cases, the HPP configuration had higher posterior probability than the generative tree, for 11 cases the same tree was found and in 39 cases the HPP solution was inferior to the generative tree. Overall these results are less good than the ones in section 3.1, but it should be remembered that the search space is now much larger, and so it would be expected that one would need to search longer. Comparing the results from fixed **n** against those with variable **n** shows that in 42 out of 100 cases the variable **n** method gave a higher posterior probability, in 45 cases it was lower and in 13 cases the same trees were found.

The rightmost column of Figure 2 shows the HPP configurations when sampling with variable **n** on the two examples discussed above. In panel (c) the solution found is not very dissimilar to that in panel (b), although the overall probability is lower. In (f), the solution found uses just one level 2 centre rather than two, and obtains a higher posterior probability than the configurations in (e) and (d).

4 Discussion

The results above indicate that the proposed model behaves sensibly, and that reasonable solutions can be found with relatively short amounts of search. The method has been demonstrated on univariate data, but extending it to multivariate Gaussian data for which each dimension is independent given the tree structure is very easy as the likelihood calculation is independent on each dimension.

There are many other directions is which the model can be developed. Firstly, the model as presented has uniform mixing proportions, so that children are equally likely to connect to each potential parent. This can be generalized so that there is a non-uniform vector of connection probabilities in each layer. Also, given a tree structure and independent Dirichlet priors over these probability vectors, these parameters can be integrated out analytically. Secondly, the model can be made to generate iid data by regarding the penultimate layer as mixture centres; in this case the term $P(n_L|n_{L-1})$ would be ignored when computing the probability of the tree. Thirdly, it would be possible to add the variance variables to the MCMC scheme, e.g. using the Metropolis algorithm, after defining a suitable prior on the sequence of variances $\sigma_1^2, \ldots, \sigma_{L-1}^2$. The constraint that all variances in the same level are equal could also be relaxed by allowing them to depend on hyperparameters set at every level. Fourthly, there may be improved MCMC schemes that can be devised. For example, in the current implementation the posterior means of the candidate units are not taken into account when proposing merge moves (*cf* [5]). Fifthly, for the multivariate Gaussian version we can consider a tree-structured factor analysis model, so that higher levels in the tree need not have the same dimensionality as the data vectors.

One can also consider a version where each dimension is a multinomial rather than a continuous variable. In this case one might consider a model where a multinomial parameter vector $\boldsymbol{\theta}_l$ in the tree is generated from its parent by $\boldsymbol{\theta}_l = \gamma \boldsymbol{\theta}_{l-1} + (1-\gamma)\mathbf{r}$ where $\gamma \in [0,1]$ and **r** is a random vector of probabilities. An alternative model could be to build a tree structured prior on the α parameters of the Dirichlet prior for the multinomial distribution.

Acknowledgments

This work is partially supported through EPSRC grant GR/L78161 *Probabilistic Models for Sequences*. I thank the Gatsby Computational Neuroscience Unit (UCL) for organizing the "Mixtures Day" in March 1999 and supporting my attendance, and Peter Green, Phil Dawid and Peter Dayan for helpful discussions at the meeting. I also thank Amos Storkey for helpful discussions and Magnus Rattray for (accidentally!) pointing me towards the chapters on phylogenetic trees in [3].

References

[1] N. J. Adams, A. Storkey, Z. Ghahramani, and C. K. I. Williams. MFDTs: Mean Field Dynamic Trees. Submitted to ICPR 2000, 1999.

[2] J. Ambros-Ingerson, R. Granger, and G. Lynch. Simulation of Paleocortex Performs Hierarchical Clustering. *Science*, 247:1344–1348, 1990.

[3] R. Durbin, S. Eddy, A. Krogh, and G. Mitchison. *Biological Sequence Analysis*. Cambridge University Press, Cambridge, UK, 1998.

[4] A. W. F. Edwards. Estimation of the Branch Points of a Branching Diffusion Process. *Journal of the Royal Statistical Society B*, 32(2):155–174, 1970.

[5] P. J. Green. Reversible Jump Markov chain Monte Carlo computation and Bayesian model determination. *Biometrika*, 82(4):711–732, 1995.

[6] R. Hanson, J. Stutz, and P. Cheeseman. Bayesian Classification with Correlation and Inheritance. In *IJCAI-91: Proceedings of the Twelfth International Joint Conference on Artificial Intelligence*, 1991. Sydney, Australia.

[7] T. Hofmann and J. M. Buhmann. Hierarchical Pairwise Data Clustering by Mean-Field Annealing. In F. Fogelman-Soulie and P. Gallinari, editors, *Proc. ICANN 95*. EC2 et Cie, 1995.

[8] M. R. Luettgen and A. S. Willsky. Likelihood Calculation for a Class of Multiscale Stochastic Models, with Application to Texture Discrimination. *IEEE Trans. Image Processing*, 4(2):194–207, 1995.

[9] D. Madigan and J. York. Bayesian Graphical Models for Discrete Data. *International Statistical Review*, 63:215–232, 1995.

[10] M. C. Mozer. Discovering Discrete Distributed Representations with Iterated Competitive Learning. In R. P. Lippmann, J. E. Moody, and D. S. Touretzky, editors, *Advances in Neural Information Processing Systems 3*. Morgan Kaufmann, 1991.

[11] J. Pearl. *Probabilistic Reasoning in Intelligent Systems: Networks of Plausible Inference*. Morgan Kaufmann, San Mateo, CA, 1988.

[12] B. Ripley. *Pattern Recognition and Neural Networks*. Cambridge University Press, Cambridge, UK, 1996.

[13] N. Vasconcelos and A. Lippmann. Learning Mixture Hierarchies. In M. S. Kearns, S. A. Solla, and D. A. Cohn, editors, *Advances in Neural Information Processing Systems 11*, pages 606–612. MIT Press, 1999.

[14] C. K. I. Williams and N. J. Adams. DTs: Dynamic Trees. In M. J. Kearns, S. A. Solla, and D. A. Cohn, editors, *Advances in Neural Information Processing Systems 11*. MIT Press, 1999.

[15] L. Xu and J. Pearl. Structuring Causal Tree Models with Continuous Variables. In L. N. Kanal, T. S. Levitt, and J. F. Lemmer, editors, *Uncertainty in Artificial Intelligence 3*. Elsevier, 1989.

Data Visualization and Feature Selection: New Algorithms for Nongaussian Data

Howard Hua Yang and John Moody
Oregon Graduate Institute of Science and Technology
20000 NW, Walker Rd., Beaverton, OR97006, USA
hyang@ece.ogi.edu, moody@cse.ogi.edu, FAX:503 7481406

Abstract

Data visualization and feature selection methods are proposed based on the *joint mutual information* and ICA. The visualization methods can find many good 2-D projections for high dimensional data interpretation, which cannot be easily found by the other existing methods. The new variable selection method is found to be better in eliminating redundancy in the inputs than other methods based on simple mutual information. The efficacy of the methods is illustrated on a radar signal analysis problem to find 2-D viewing coordinates for data visualization and to select inputs for a neural network classifier.

Keywords: feature selection, joint mutual information, ICA, visualization, classification.

1 INTRODUCTION

Visualization of input data and feature selection are intimately related. A good feature selection algorithm can identify meaningful coordinate projections for low dimensional data visualization. Conversely, a good visualization technique can suggest meaningful features to include in a model.

Input variable selection is the most important step in the model selection process. Given a target variable, a set of input variables can be selected as explanatory variables by some prior knowledge. However, many irrelevant input variables cannot be ruled out by the prior knowledge. Too many input variables irrelevant to the target variable will not only severely complicate the model selection/estimation process but also damage the performance of the final model.

Selecting input variables after model specification is a model-dependent approach[6]. However, these methods can be very slow if the model space is large. To reduce the computational burden in the estimation and selection processes, we need model-independent approaches to select input variables before model specification. One such approach is δ-Test [7]. Other approaches are based on the *mutual information* (MI) [2, 3, 4] which is very effective in evaluating the relevance of each input variable, but it fails to eliminate redundant variables.

In this paper, we focus on the model-independent approach for input variable selection based on joint mutual information (JMI). The increment from MI to JMI is the conditional MI. Although the conditional MI was used in [4] to show the monotonic property of the MI, it was not used for input selection.

Data visualization is very important for human to understand the structural relations among variables in a system. It is also a critical step to eliminate some unrealistic models. We give two methods for data visualization. One is based on the JMI and another is based on Independent Component Analysis (ICA). Both methods perform better than some existing methods such as the methods based on PCA and canonical correlation analysis (CCA) for nongaussian data.

2 Joint mutual information for input/feature selection

Let Y be a target variable and X_i's are inputs. The relevance of a single input is measured by the MI
$$I(X_i; Y) = K(p(x_i, y) \| p(x_i) p(y))$$
where $K(p\|q)$ is the Kullback-Leibler divergence of two probability functions p and q defined by $K(p(x)\|q(x)) = \sum_x p(x) \log \frac{p(x)}{q(x)}$.

The relevance of a set of inputs is defined by the *joint mutual information*
$$I(X_i, \cdots, X_k; Y) = K(p(x_i, \cdots, x_k, y) \| p(x_i, \cdots, x_k) p(y)).$$

Given two selected inputs x_j and x_k, the conditional MI is defined by
$$I(X_i; Y | X_j, X_k) = \sum_{x_j, x_k} p(x_j, x_k) K(p(x_i, y | x_j, x_k) \| p(x_i | x_j, x_k) p(y | x_j, x_k)).$$

Similarly define $I(X_i; Y | X_j, \cdots, X_k)$ conditioned on more than two variables.

The conditional MI is always non-negative since it is a weighted average of the Kullback-Leibler divergence. It has the following property
$$I(X_1, \cdots, X_{n-1}, X_n; Y) - I(X_1, \cdots, X_{n-1}; Y) = I(X_n; Y | X_1, \cdots, X_{n-1}) \geq 0.$$

Therefore, $I(X_1, \cdots, X_{n-1}, X_n; Y) \geq I(X_1, \cdots, X_{n-1}; Y)$, i.e., adding the variable X_n will always increase the mutual information. The information gained by adding a variable is measured by the conditional MI.

When X_n and Y are conditionally independent given $X_1, \cdots, X_{n-1}$, the conditional MI between X_n and Y is
$$I(X_n; Y | X_1, \cdots, X_{n-1}) = 0, \qquad (1)$$
so X_n provides no extra information about Y when $X_1, \cdots, X_{n-1}$ are known. In particular, when X_n is a function of $X_1, \cdots, X_{n-1}$, the equality (1) holds. This is the reason why the joint MI can be used to eliminate redundant inputs.

The conditional MI is useful when the input variables cannot be distinguished by the mutual information $I(X_i; Y)$. For example, assume $I(X_1; Y) = I(X_2; Y) = I(X_3; Y)$, and the problem is to select $(x_1, x_2), (x_1, x_3)$ or (x_2, x_3). Since
$$I(X_1, X_2; Y) - I(X_1, X_3; Y) = I(X_2; Y | X_1) - I(X_3; Y | X_1),$$
we should choose (x_1, x_2) rather than (x_1, x_3) if $I(X_2; Y | X_1) > I(X_3; Y | X_1)$. Otherwise, we should choose (x_1, x_3). All possible comparisons are represented by a binary tree in Figure 1.

To estimate $I(X_1, \cdots, X_k; Y)$, we need to estimate the joint probability $p(x_1, \cdots, x_k, y)$. This suffers from the curse of dimensionality when k is large.

Sometimes, we may not be able to estimate high dimensional MI due to the sample shortage. Further work is needed to estimate high dimensional joint MI based on parametric and non-parametric density estimations, when the sample size is not large enough.

In some real world problems such as mining large data bases and radar pulse classification, the sample size is large. Since the parametric densities for the underlying distributions are unknown, it is better to use non-parametric methods such as histograms to estimate the joint probability and the joint MI to avoid the risk of specifying a wrong or too complicated model for the true density function.

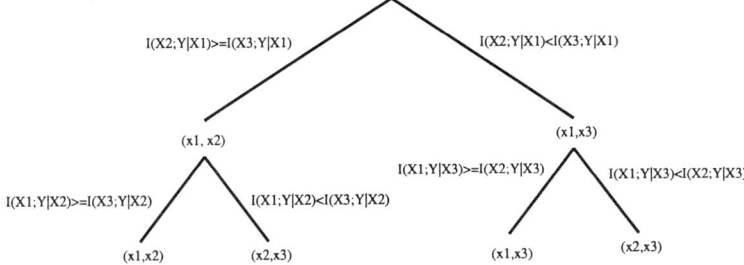

Figure 1: Input selection based on the conditional MI.

In this paper, we use the joint mutual information $I(X_i, X_j; Y)$ instead of the mutual information $I(X_i; Y)$ to select inputs for a neural network classifier. Another application is to select two inputs most relevant to the target variable for data visualization.

3 Data visualization methods

We present supervised data visualization methods based on joint MI and discuss unsupervised methods based on ICA.

The most natural way to visualize high-dimensional input patterns is to display them using two of the existing coordinates, where each coordinate corresponds to one input variable. Those inputs which are most relevant to the target variable corresponds the best coordinates for data visualization. Let $(i^*, j^*) = \arg\max_{(i,j)} I(X_i, X_j; Y)$. Then, the coordinate axes (x_{i^*}, x_{j^*}) should be used for visualizing the input patterns since the corresponding inputs achieve the maximum joint MI. To find the maximum $I(X_{i^*}, X_{j^*}|Y)$, we need to evaluate every joint MI $I(X_i, X_j; Y)$ for $i < j$. The number of evaluations is $O(n^2)$.

Noticing that $I(X_i, X_j; Y) = I(X_i; Y) + I(X_j; Y|X_i)$, we can first maximize the MI $I(X_i; Y)$, then maximize the conditional MI. This algorithm is suboptimal, but only requires $n-1$ evaluations of the joint MIs. Sometimes, this is equivalent to exhaustive search. One such example is given in next section.

Some existing methods to visualize high-dimensional patterns are based on dimensionality reduction methods such as PCA and CCA to find the new coordinates to display the data. The new coordinates found by PCA and CCA are orthogonal in Euclidean space and the space with Mahalanobis inner product, respectively. However, these two methods are not suitable for visualizing nongaussian data because the projections on the PCA or CCA coordinates are not statistically independent for nongaussian vectors. Since the JMI method is model-independent, it is better for analyzing nongaussian data.

Both CCA and maximum joint MI are supervised methods while the PCA method is unsupervised. An alternative to these methods is ICA for visualizing clusters [5]. The ICA is a technique to transform a set of variables into a new set of variables, so that statistical dependency among the transformed variables is minimized. The version of ICA that we use here is based on the algorithms in [1, 8]. It discovers a non-orthogonal basis that minimizes mutual information between projections on basis vectors. We shall compare these methods in a real world application.

4 Application to Signal Visualization and Classification

4.1 Joint mutual information and visualization of radar pulse patterns

Our goal is to design a classifier for radar pulse recognition. Each radar pulse pattern is a 15-dimensional vector. We first compute the joint MIs, then use them to select inputs for the visualization and classification of radar pulse patterns.

A set of radar pulse patterns is denoted by $D = \{(\boldsymbol{x}^i, y^i) : i = 1, \cdots, N\}$ which consists of patterns in three different classes. Here, each $\boldsymbol{x}^i \in R^{15}$ and each $y^i \in \{1, 2, 3\}$.

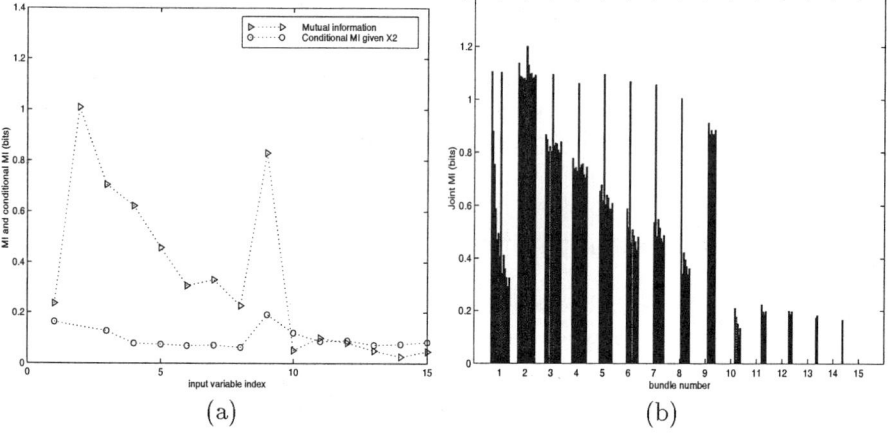

Figure 2: (a) MI vs conditional MI for the radar pulse data; maximizing the MI then the conditional MI with $O(n)$ evaluations gives $I(X_{i_1}, X_{j_1}; Y) = 1.201$ bits. (b) The joint MI for the radar pulse data; maximizing the joint MI gives $I(X_{i^*}, X_{j^*}; Y) = 1.201$ bits with $O(n^2)$ evaluations of the joint MI. $(i_1, j_1) = (i^*, j^*)$ in this case.

Let $i_1 = \arg\max_i I(X_i; Y)$ and $j_1 = \arg\max_{j \neq i_1} I(X_j; Y|X_{i_1})$. From Figure 2(a), we obtain $(i_1, j_1) = (2, 9)$ and $I(X_{i_1}, X_{j_1}; Y) = I(X_{i_1}; Y) + I(X_{j_1}; Y|X_{i_1}) = 1.201$ bits. If the number of total inputs is n, then the number of evaluations for computing the mutual information $I(X_i; Y)$ and the conditional mutual information $I(X_j; Y|X_{i_1})$ is $O(n)$.

To find the maximum $I(X_{i^*}, X_{j^*}; Y)$, we evaluate every $I(X_i, X_j; Y)$ for $i < j$. These MIs are shown by the bars in Figure 2(b), where the i-th bundle displays the MIs $I(X_i, X_j; Y)$ for $j = i+1, \cdots, 15$.

In order to compute the joint MIs, the MI and the conditional MI is evaluated $O(n)$ and $O(n^2)$ times respectively. The maximum joint MI is $I(X_{i^*}, X_{j^*}; Y) = 1.201$ bits. Generally, we only know $I(X_{i_1}, X_{j_1}; Y) \leq I(X_{i^*}, X_{j^*}; Y)$. But in this particular

Data Visualization and Feature Selection

application, the equality holds. This suggests that sometimes we can use an efficient algorithm with only linear complexity to find the optimal coordinate axis view (x_{i^*}, x_{j^*}). The joint MI also gives other good sets of coordinate axis views with high joint MI values.

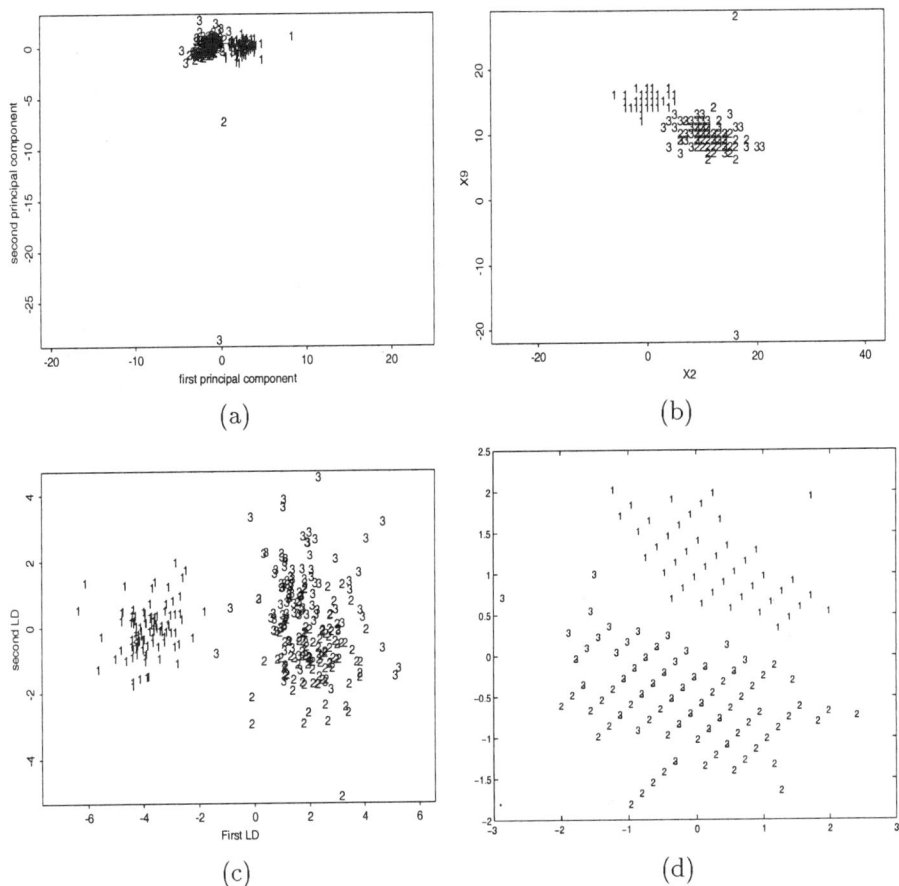

Figure 3: (a) Data visualization by two principal components; the spatial relation between patterns is not clear. (b) Use the optimal coordinate axis view (x_{i^*}, x_{j^*}) found via joint MI to project the radar pulse data; the patterns are well spread to give a better view on the spatial relation between patterns and the boundary between classes. (c) The CCA method. (d) The ICA method.

Each bar in Figure 2(b) is associated with a pair of inputs. Those pairs with high joint MI give good coordinate axis view for data visualization. Figure 3 shows that the data visualizations by the maximum JMI and the ICA is better than those by the PCA and the CCA because the data is nongaussian.

4.2 Radar pulse classification

Now we train a two layer feed-forward network to classify the radar pulse patterns. Figure 3 shows that it is very difficult to separate the patterns by using just two inputs. We shall use all inputs or four selected inputs. The data set D is divided into a training set D_1 and a test set D_2 consisting of 20 percent patterns in D. The network trained on the data set D_1 using all input variables is denoted by

$$Y = f(X_1, \cdots, X_n; \boldsymbol{W}_1, \boldsymbol{W}_2, \theta)$$

where $\boldsymbol{W}_1$ and $\boldsymbol{W}_2$ are weight matrices and θ is a vector of thresholds for the hidden layer.

From the data set D, we estimate the mutual information $I(X_i; Y)$ and select $i_1 = \arg\max_i I(X_i; Y)$. Given X_{i_1}, we estimate the conditional mutual information $I(X_j; Y | X_{i_1})$ for $j \neq i_1$. Choose three inputs X_{i_2}, X_{i_3} and X_{i_4} with the largest conditional MI. We found a quartet $(i_1, i_2, i_3, i_4) = (1, 2, 3, 9)$. The two-layer feed-forward network trained on D_1 with four selected inputs is denoted by

$$Y = g(X_1, X_2, X_3, X_9; \boldsymbol{W}'_1, \boldsymbol{W}'_2, \theta').$$

There are 1365 choices to select 4 input variables out of 15. To set a reference performance for network with four inputs for comparison. Choose 20 quartets from the set $Q = \{(j_1, j_2, j_3, j_4) : 1 \leq j_1 < j_2 < j_3 < j_4 \leq 15\}$. For each quartet (j_1, j_2, j_3, j_4), a two-layer feed-forward network is trained using inputs $(X_{j_1}, X_{j_2}, X_{j_3}, X_{j_4})$. These networks are denoted by

$$Y = h_i(X_{j_1}, X_{j_2}, X_{j_3}, X_{j_4}; \boldsymbol{W}''_1, \boldsymbol{W}''_2, \theta''), \quad i = 1, 2, \cdots, 20.$$

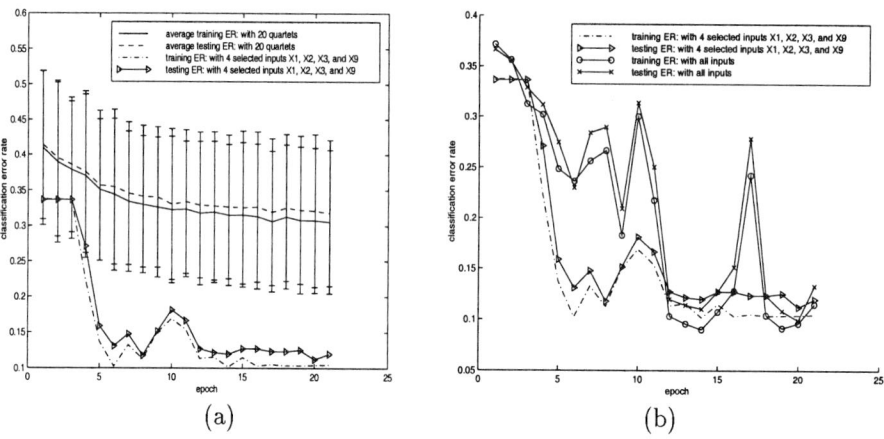

Figure 4: (a) The error rates of the network with four inputs (X_1, X_2, X_3, X_9) selected by the joint MI are well below the average error rates (with error bars attached) of the 20 networks with different input quartets randomly selected; this shows that the input quartet (X_1, X_2, X_3, X_9) is rare but informative. (b) The network with the inputs (X_1, X_2, X_3, X_9) converges faster than the network with all inputs. The former uses 65% fewer parameters (weights and thresholds) and 73% fewer inputs than the latter. The classifier with the four best inputs is less expensive to construct and use, in terms of data acquisition costs, training time, and computing costs for real-time application.

The mean and the variance of the error rates of the 20 networks are then computed. All networks have seven hidden units. The training and testing error rates of the networks at each epoch are shown in Figure 4, where we see that the network with four inputs selected by the joint MI performs better than the networks with randomly selected input quartets and converges faster than the network with all inputs. The network with fewer inputs is not only faster in computing but also less expensive in data collection.

5 CONCLUSIONS

We have proposed data visualization and feature selection methods based on the *joint mutual information* and ICA.

The maximum JMI method can find many good 2-D projections for visualizing high dimensional data which cannot be easily found by the other existing methods. Both the maximum JMI method and the ICA method are very effective for visualizing nongaussian data.

The variable selection method based on the JMI is found to be better in eliminating redundancy in the inputs than other methods based on simple mutual information. Input selection methods based on mutual information (MI) have been useful in many applications, but they have two disadvantages. First, they cannot distinguish inputs when all of them have the same MI. Second, they cannot eliminate the redundancy in the inputs when one input is a function of other inputs. In contrast, our new input selection method based on the *joint* MI offers significant advantages in these two aspects.

We have successfully applied these methods to visualize radar patterns and to select inputs for a neural network classifier to recognize radar pulses. We found a smaller yet more robust neural network for radar signal analysis using the JMI.

Acknowledgement: This research was supported by grant ONR N00014-96-1-0476.

References

[1] S. Amari, A. Cichocki, and H. H. Yang. A new learning algorithm for blind signal separation. In *Advances in Neural Information Processing Systems, 8*, eds. David S. Touretzky, Michael C. Mozer and Michael E. Hasselmo, MIT Press: Cambridge, MA., pages 757–763, 1996.

[2] G. Barrows and J. Sciortino. A mutual information measure for feature selection with application to pulse classification. In *IEEE Intern. Symposium on Time-Frequency and Time-Scale Analysis*, pages 249–253, 1996.

[3] R. Battiti. Using mutual information for selecting features in supervised neural net learning. *IEEE Trans. on Neural Networks*, 5(4):537–550, July 1994.

[4] B. Bonnlander. Nonparametric selection of input variables for connectionist learning. Technical report, PhD Thesis. University of Colorado, 1996.

[5] C. Jutten and J. Herault. Blind separation of sources, part i: An adaptive algorithm based on neuromimetic architecture. *Signal Processing*, 24:1–10, 1991.

[6] J. Moody. Prediction risk and architecture selection for neural network. In V. Cherkassky, J.H. Friedman, and H. Wechsler, editors, *From Statistics to Neural Networks: Theory and Pattern Recognition Applications*. NATO ASI Series F, Springer-Verlag, 1994.

[7] H. Pi and C. Peterson. Finding the embedding dimension and variable dependencies in time series. *Neural Computation*, 6:509–520, 1994.

[8] H. H. Yang and S. Amari. Adaptive on-line learning algorithms for blind separation: Maximum entropy and minimum mutual information. *Neural Computation*, 9(7):1457–1482, 1997.

Manifold Stochastic Dynamics for Bayesian Learning

Mark Zlochin
Department of Computer Science
Technion - Israel Institute of Technology
Technion City, Haifa 32000, Israel
zmark@cs.technion.ac.il

Yoram Baram
Department of Computer Science
Technion - Israel Institute of Technology
Technion City, Haifa 32000, Israel
baram@cs.technion.ac.il

Abstract

We propose a new Markov Chain Monte Carlo algorithm which is a generalization of the stochastic dynamics method. The algorithm performs exploration of the state space using its intrinsic geometric structure, facilitating efficient sampling of complex distributions. Applied to Bayesian learning in neural networks, our algorithm was found to perform at least as well as the best state-of-the-art method while consuming considerably less time.

1 Introduction

In the Bayesian framework predictions are made by integrating the function of interest over the *posterior* parameter distribution, the latter being the normalized product of the *prior* distribution and the *likelihood*. Since in most problems the integrals are too complex to be calculated analytically, approximations are needed.

Early works in Bayesian learning for nonlinear models [Buntine and Weigend 1991, MacKay 1992] used Gaussian approximations to the posterior parameter distribution. However, the Gaussian approximation may be poor, especially for complex models, because of the multi-modal character of the posterior distribution.

Hybrid Monte Carlo (HMC) [Duane et al. 1987] introduced to the neural network community by [Neal 1996], deals more successfully with multi-modal distributions but is very time consuming. One of the main causes of HMC inefficiency is the anisotropic character of the posterior distribution - the density changes rapidly in some directions while remaining almost constant in others.

We present a novel algorithm which overcomes the above problem by using the intrinsic geometrical structure of the model space.

2 Hybrid Monte Carlo

Markov Chain Monte Carlo (MCMC) [Gilks et al. 1996] approximates the value

$$E[a] = \int a(\theta) Q(\theta) d\theta$$

by the mean

$$\bar{a} = \frac{1}{N} \sum_{t=1}^{N} a(\theta^{(t)})$$

where $\theta^{(1)}, \ldots, \theta^{(N)}$ are successive states of the ergodic Markov chain with invariant distribution $Q(\theta)$.

In addition to ergodicity and invariance of $Q(\theta)$ another quality we would like the Markov chain to have is rapid exploration of the state space. While the first two qualities are rather easily attained, achieving rapid exploration of the state space is often nontrivial.

A state-of-the-art MCMC method, capable of sampling from complex distributions, is Hybrid Monte Carlo [Duane et al. 1987].

The algorithm is expressed in terms of sampling from *canonical* distribution for the state, q, of a "physical" system, defined in terms of the energy function $E(q)$ [1]:

$$P(q) \propto \exp(-E(q)) \qquad (1)$$

To allow the use of dynamical methods, a "momentum" variable, p, is introduced, with the same dimensionality as q. The canonical distribution over the "phase space" is defined to be:

$$P(q, p) \propto \exp(-H(q, p)) \qquad (2)$$

where $H(q, p) = E(q) + K(p)$ is the "Hamiltonian", which represents the total energy. $K(p)$ is the "kinetic energy" due to momentum, defined as

$$K(p) = \sum_{i=1}^{n} \frac{p_i^2}{2m_i} \qquad (3)$$

where $p_i, i = 1, \ldots, n$ are the momentum components and m_i is the "mass" associated with i'th component, so that different components can be given different weight.

Sampling from the canonical distribution can be done using *stochastic dynamics* method [Andersen 1980], in which the task is split into two subtasks - sampling uniformly from values of q and p with a fixed total energy, $H(q, p)$, and sampling states with different values of H. The first task is done by simulating the *Hamiltonian dynamics* of the system:

$$\frac{dq_i}{d\tau} = +\frac{\partial H}{\partial p_i} = \frac{p_i}{m_i}$$

$$\frac{dp_i}{d\tau} = -\frac{\partial H}{\partial q_i} = -\frac{\partial E}{\partial q_i}$$

Different energy levels are obtained by occasional stochastic Gibbs sampling [Geman and Geman 1984] of the momentum. Since q and p are independent, p may be updated without reference to q by drawing a value with probability density proportional to $\exp(-K(p))$, which, in the case of (3), can be easily done, since the p_i's have independent Gaussian distributions.

In practice, Hamiltonian dynamics cannot be simulated exactly, but can be approximated by some discretization using finite time steps. One common approximation is *leapfrog* discretization [Neal 1996].

In the hybrid Monte Carlo method stochastic dynamic transitions are used to generate candidate states for the Metropolis algorithm [Metropolis et al. 1953]. This eliminates certain

---

[1] Note that any probability density that is nowhere zero can be put in this form, by simply defining $E(q) = -\log P(q) - \log Z$, for any convenient Z).

drawbacks of the stochastic dynamics such as systematic errors due to leapfrog discretization, since Metropolis algorithm ensures that every transition keeps canonical distribution invariant. However, the empirical comparison between the uncorrected stochastic dynamics and the HMC in application to Bayesian learning in neural networks [Neal 1996] showed that with appropriate discretization stepsize there is no notable difference between the two methods.

A modification proposed in [Horowitz 1991] instead of Gibbs sampling of momentum, is to replace p each time by $p \cdot \cos(\theta) + \zeta \cdot \sin(\theta)$, where θ is a small angle and ζ is distributed according to $N(0, I)$. While keeping canonical distribution invariant, this scheme, called *momentum persistence*, improves the rate of exploration.

3 Riemannian geometry

A Riemannian manifold [Amari 1997] is a set $\Theta \subseteq R^n$ equipped with a *metric tensor* G which is a positive semidefinite matrix defining the inner product between infinitesimal increments as:

$$< d\theta_1, d\theta_2 > = d\theta_1^T \cdot G \cdot d\theta_2$$

Let us denote entries of G by $G_{i,j}$ and entries of G^{-1} by $G^{i,j}$. This inner product naturally gives us the norm

$$\| d\theta \|_G^2 = < d\theta, d\theta > = d\theta^T \cdot G \cdot d\theta.$$

The Jeffrey prior over Θ is defined by the density function:

$$\pi(\theta) \propto \sqrt{|G(\theta)|}$$

where $|\cdot|$ denotes determinant.

3.1 Hamiltonian dynamics over a manifold

For Riemannian manifold the dynamics take a more general form than the one described in section 2.

If the metric tensor is G and all masses are set to one then the Hamiltonian is given by:

$$H(q, p) = E(q) + \frac{1}{2} p^T \cdot G^{-1} \cdot p \qquad (4)$$

The dynamics are governed by the following set of differential equations [Chavel 1993]:

$$\frac{d^2 q_i}{d\tau^2} = -\sum_j G^{i,j} \frac{\partial E}{\partial q_j} - \sum_{j,k} \Gamma^i_{j,k} \dot{q}_i \dot{q}_j$$

where $\Gamma^i_{j,k}$ are the *Christoffel symbols* given by:

$$\Gamma^i_{j,k} = \frac{1}{2} \sum_m G^{i,m} \left(\frac{\partial G_{m,k}}{\partial q_j} + \frac{\partial G_{m,j}}{\partial q_k} - \frac{\partial G_{j,k}}{\partial q_m} \right)$$

and $\dot{q} = \frac{dq}{d\tau}$ is related to p by $\dot{q} = G^{-1} p$.

3.2 Riemannian geometry of functions

In regression the log-likelihood is proportional to the empirical error, which is simply the Euclidean distance between the target point, t, and candidate function evaluated over the sample. Therefore, the most natural distance measure between the models is the Euclidean seminorm:

$$d(\theta^1, \theta^2)^2 = \| f_{\theta^1} - f_{\theta^2} \|_l^2 = \sum_{i=1}^{l} (f(x_i, \theta^1) - f(x_i, \theta^2))^2 \tag{5}$$

The resulting metric tensor is:

$$G = \sum_{i=1}^{l} \{ \nabla_\theta f(x_i, \theta) \cdot \nabla_\theta f(x_i, \theta)^T \} = J^T \cdot J \tag{6}$$

where ∇_θ denotes gradient and $J = [\frac{\partial f(x_i)}{\partial \theta_j}]$ is the Jacobian matrix.

3.3 Bayesian geometry

A Bayesian approach would suggest the inclusion of prior assumptions about the parameters in the manifold geometry.

If, for example, *a priori* $\theta \sim N(0, I/\alpha)$, then the log-posterior can be written as:

$$\log p(\theta|x) = \beta \sum_{i=1}^{l} (f(x_i, \theta_1) - t)^2 + \alpha \sum_{k=1}^{n} (\theta_k - 0)^2$$

where β is inverse noise variance.

Therefore, the natural metric in the model space is

$$d(\theta^1, \theta^2)^2 = \beta \sum_{i=1}^{l} (f(x_i, \theta^1) - f(x_i, \theta^2))^2 + \alpha \sum_{k=1}^{n} (\theta_k^1 - \theta_k^2)^2$$

with the metric tensor:

$$G_B = \beta \cdot G + \alpha \cdot I = \hat{J}^T \cdot \hat{J} \tag{7}$$

where $\hat{J}$ is the "extended Jacobian":

$$\hat{J}_{i,j} = \begin{cases} \sqrt{\beta} \cdot \dfrac{\partial f(x_i)}{\partial \theta_j} & i \leq l \\ \sqrt{\alpha} \cdot \delta_{i-l,j} & i > l \end{cases} \tag{8}$$

where $\delta_{i,j}$ is the Kroneker's delta.

Note, that as $\alpha \to 0$, $G_B \to \beta G$, hence as the prior becomes vaguer we approach a non-Bayesian paradigm. If, on the other hand, $\alpha \to \infty$ or $\beta \cdot G \to 0$, the Bayesian geometry approaches the Euclidean geometry of the parameter space. These are the qualities that we would like the Bayesian geometry to have - if the prior is "strong" in comparison to the likelihood, the exact form of G should be of little importance.

The definitions above can be applied to any log-concave prior distribution with the inverse Hessian of the log-prior, $(\nabla\nabla \log p(\theta))^{-1}$, replacing αI in (7). The framework is not restricted to regression. For a general distribution class it is natural to use Fisher information matrix, $\mathcal{I}$, as a metric tensor [Amari 1997]. The Bayesian metric tensor then becomes:

$$G_B = \mathcal{I} + (\nabla\nabla \log p(\theta))^{-1} \tag{9}$$

4 Manifold Stochastic Dynamics

As mentioned before, the energy landscape in many regression problems is anisotropic. This degrades the performance of HMC in two aspects:

- The dynamics may not be optimal for efficient exploration of the posterior distribution as suggested by the studies of Gaussian diffusions [Hwang et al. 1993].
- The resulting differential equations are *stiff* [Gear 1971], leading to large discretization errors, which in turn necessitates small time steps, implying that the computational burden is high.

Both of these problems disappear if instead of the Euclidean Hamiltonian dynamics used in HMC we simulate dynamics over the manifold equipped with the metric tensor G_B proposed in the previous section.

In the context of regression from the definition $G_B = \hat{J}^T \cdot \hat{J}$, we obtain an alternative equation for $\dfrac{d^2 q}{d\tau^2}$, in a matrix form:

$$\frac{d^2 q}{d\tau^2} = -G_B^{-1}(\nabla E + \hat{J}^T \frac{\partial \hat{J}}{\partial \tau} \dot{q}) \tag{10}$$

In the canonical distribution $P(q,p) \propto \exp(-H(q,p))$ the conditional distribution of p given q is a zero-mean Gaussian with the covariance matrix $G_B(q)$ and the marginal distribution over q is proportional to $\exp(-E(q))\pi(q)$. This is equivalent to multiplying the prior by the Jeffrey prior[2].

The sampling from the canonical distribution is two-fold:

- Simulate the Hamiltonian dynamics (3.1) for one time-step using leapfrog discretisation.
- Replace p using momentum persistence. Unlike the HMC case, the momentum perturbation ζ is distributed according to $N(0, G_B)$.

The actual weights multiplying the matrices I and G in (7) may be chosen to be different from the specified α and β, so as to improve numerical stability.

5 Empirical comparison

5.1 Robot arm problem

We compared the performance of the Manifold Stochastic Dynamics (MSD) algorithm with the standard HMC. The comparison was carried using MacKay's robot arm problem which is a common benchmark for Bayesian methods in neural networks [MacKay 1992, Neal 1996].

The robot arm problem is concerned with the mapping:

$$y_1 = 2.0\cos x_1 + 1.3\cos(x_1 + x_2) + e_1, \quad y_2 = 2.0\sin x_1 + 1.3\sin(x_1 + x_2) + e_2$$

where e_1, e_2 are independent Gaussian noise variables of standard deviation 0.05. The dataset used by Neal and Mackay contained 200 examples in the training set and 400 in the test set.

---

[2]In fact, since the actual prior over the weights is unknown, a truly Bayesian approach would be to use a non-informative prior such as $\pi(q)$. In this paper we kept the modified prior which is the product of $\pi(q)$ and a zero-mean Gaussian.

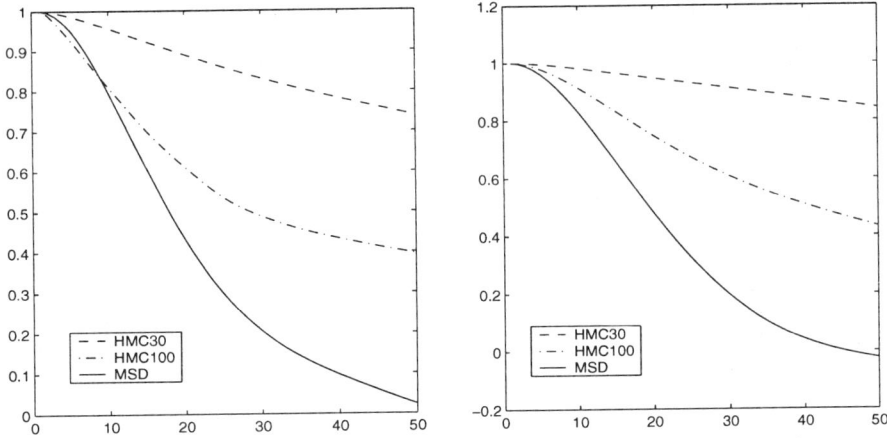

Figure 1: Average (over the 10 runs) autocorrelation of input-to-hidden (left) and hidden-to-output (right) weights for HMC with 100 and 30 leapfrog steps per iteration and MSD with single leapfrog step per iteration. The horizontal axis gives the lags, measured in number of iterations.

We used a neural network with two input units, one hidden layer containing 8 tanh units and two linear output units.

The hyperparameter β was set to its correct value of 400 and α was chosen to be 1.

5.2 Algorithms

We compared MSD with two versions of HMC - with 30 and with 100 leapfrog steps per iteration, henceforth referred to as HMC30 and HMC100. MSD was run with a single leapfrog step per iteration. In all three algorithms momentum was resampled using persistence with $\cos(\theta) = 0.95$.

A single iteration of HMC100 required about $4.8 \cdot 10^6$ floating point operations (flops), HMC30 required $1.4 \cdot 10^6$ flops and MSD required $0.5 \cdot 10^6$ flops. Hence the computational load of MSD was about one third of that of HMC30 and 10 times lower than that of HMC100.

The discretization stepsize for HMC was chosen so as to keep the rejection rate below 5%. An equivalent criterion of average error in the Hamiltonian around 0.05 was used for the MSD.

All three sampling algorithms were run 10 times, each time for 3000 iteration with the first 1000 samples discarded in order to allow the algorithms to reach the regions of high probability.

5.3 Results

One appropriate measure for the rate of state space exploration is weights autocorrelation [Neal 1996]. As shown in Figure 1, the behavior of MSD was clearly superior to that of HMC.

Another value of interest is the total squared error over the test set. The predictions for the test set were made as follows. A subsample of 100 parameter vectors was generated by taking every twentieth sample vector starting from 1001 and on. The predicted value was the average over the empirical function distribution of this subsample.

The total squared errors, normalized with respect to the variance on the test cases, have the following statistics (over the 10 runs):

	average	standard deviation
HMC30	1.314	0.074
HMC100	1.167	0.044
MSD	1.161	0.023

The average error of HMC30 is high, indicating that the algorithm failed to reach the region of high probability. The errors of HMC100 and MSD are comparable but the standard deviation for MSD is twice as low as that for HMC100, meaning that the estimate obtained using MSD is more reliable.

6 Conclusion

We have described a new algorithm for efficient sampling from complex distributions such as those appearing in Bayesian learning with non-linear models. The empirical comparison shows that our algorithm achieves results superior to the best achieved by existing algorithms in considerably smaller computation time.

References

[Amari 1997] Amari S., "Natural Gradient Works Efficiently in Learning", *Neural Computation*, vol. 10, pp.251-276.

[Andersen 1980] Andersen H.C., "Molecular dynamics simulations at constant pressure and/or temperature", *Journal of Chemical Physics*, vol. 3, pp. 589-603.

[Buntine and Weigend 1991] "Bayesian back-propagation", *Complex systems*, vol. 5, pp. 603-643.

[Chavel 1993] Chavel I., *Riemannian Geometry: A Modern Introduction*, University Press, Cambridge.

[Duane et al. 1987] "Hybrid Monte Carlo", *Physics Letters B*, vol. 195, pp. 216-222.

[Gear 1971] Gear C.W., *Numerical initial value problems in ordinary differential equations*, Prentice Hall.

[Geman and Geman 1984] Geman S., Geman D., "Stochastic relaxation, Gibbs distributions and the Bayesian restoration of images", *IEEE Trans., PAMI-6*, 721-741.

[Gilks et al. 1996] Gilks W.R., Richardson S. and Spiegelhalter D.J., *Markov Chain Monte Carlo in Practice*, Chapman&Hall.

[Hwang et al. 1993] Hwang, C.,-R, Hwang-Ma S.,-Y. and Shen. S.,-J., "Accelerating Gaussian diffusions", *Ann. Appl. Prob.*, vol. 3, 897-913.

[Horowitz 1991] Horowitz A.M., "A generalized guided Monte Carlo algorithm", *Physics Letters B*, vol. 268, pp. 247-252.

[MacKay 1992] MacKay D.J.C., *Bayesian Methods for Adaptive Models*, Ph.D. thesis, California Institute of Technology.

[Metropolis et al. 1953] Metropolis N., Rosenbluth A.W., Rosenbluth M.N., Teller A.H. and Teller E., "Equation of State Calculations by Fast Computing Machines", *Journal of Chemical Physics*, vol.21, pp. 1087-1092.

[Neal 1996] Neal, R.M., *Bayesian Learning for Neural Networks*, Springer 1996.

Part V
Implementation

The Parallel Problems Server: an Interactive Tool for Large Scale Machine Learning

Charles Lee Isbell, Jr.
isbell@research.att.com
AT&T Labs
180 Park Avenue Room A255
Florham Park, NJ 07932-0971

Parry Husbands
PJRHusbands@lbl.gov
Lawrence Berkeley National Laboratory/NERSC
1 Cyclotron Road, MS 50F
Berkeley, CA 94720

Abstract

Imagine that you wish to classify data consisting of tens of thousands of examples residing in a twenty thousand dimensional space. How can one apply standard machine learning algorithms? We describe the Parallel Problems Server (PPServer) and MATLAB*P. In tandem they allow users of networked computers to work transparently on large data sets from within Matlab. This work is motivated by the desire to bring the many benefits of scientific computing algorithms and computational power to machine learning researchers.

We demonstrate the usefulness of the system on a number of tasks. For example, we perform *independent components analysis* on very large text corpora consisting of tens of thousands of documents, making minimal changes to the original Bell and Sejnowski Matlab source (Bell and Sejnowski, 1995). Applying ML techniques to data previously beyond their reach leads to interesting analyses of both data and algorithms.

1 Introduction

Real-world data sets are extremely large by the standards of the machine learning community. In text retrieval, for example, we often wish to process collections consisting of tens or hundreds of thousands of documents and easily as many different words. Naturally, we would like to apply machine learning techniques to this problem; however, the sheer size of the data makes this difficult.

This paper describes the Parallel Problems Server (PPServer) and MATLAB*P. The PPServer is a "linear algebra server" that executes distributed memory algorithms on large data sets. Together with MATLAB*P, users can manipulate large data sets within Matlab transparently. This system brings the efficiency and power of highly-optimized parallel computation to researchers using networked machines but maintain the many benefits of interactive environments.

We demonstrate the usefulness of the PPServer on a number of tasks. For example, we perform *independent components analysis* on very large text corpora consisting of tens of thousands of documents with minimal changes to the original Bell and Sejnowski Matlab source (Bell and Sejnowski, 1995). Applying ML techniques to datasets previously beyond

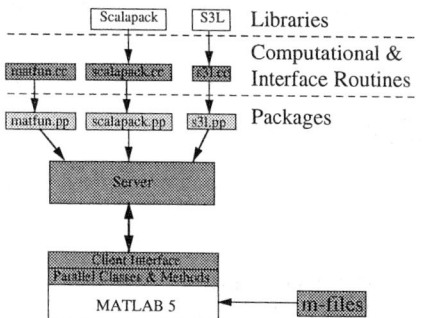 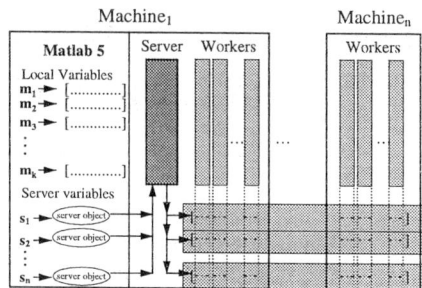

Figure 1: Use of the PPServer by Matlab is almost completely transparent. PPServer variables are tied to the PPServer itself while Matlab maintains *handles* to the data. Using Matlab's object system, functions using PPServer variables invoke PPServer commands implicitly.

their reach, we discover interesting analyses of both data and algorithms.

2 The Parallel Problems Server

The Parallel Problems Server (PPServer) is the foundation of this work. The PPServer is a realization of a novel client-server model for computation on very large matrices. It is compatible with any Unix-like platform supporting the Message Passing Interface (MPI) library (Gropp, Lusk and Skjellum, 1994). MPI is the standard for multi-processor communication and is the most portable way for writing parallel code.

The PPServer implements functions for creating and removing distributed matrices, loading and storing them from/to disk using a portable format, and performing elementary matrix operations. Matrices are two-dimensional single or double precision arrays created on the PPServer itself (functions are provided for transferring matrix sections to and from a client). The PPServer supports both dense and sparse matrices.

The PPServer communicates with clients using a simple request-response protocol. A client requests an action by issuing a command with the appropriate arguments, the server executes that command, and then notifies the client that the command is complete.

The PPServer is directly extensible via compiled libraries called *packages*. The PPServer implements a robust protocol for communicating with packages. Clients (and other packages) can load and remove packages on-the-fly, as well as execute commands within packages.

Package programmers have direct access to information about the PPServer and its matrices. Each package represents its own namespace, defining a set of visible function names. This supports data encapsulation and allows users to hide a subset of functions in one package by loading another that defines the same function names. Finally, packages support common parallel idioms (*eg* applying a function to every element of a matrix), making it easier to add common functionality.

All but a few PPServer commands are implemented in packages, including basic matrix operations. Many highly-optimized public libraries have been realized as packages using appropriate wrapper functions. These packages include ScaLAPACK (Blackford et al., 1997), S3L (Sun's optimized version of ScaLAPACK), PARPACK (Maschhoff and Sorensen, 1996), and PETSc (PETSc,).

```
1  function H=hilb(n)
2      J = 1:n;
3      J = J(ones(n,1),:);
4      I = J';
5      E = ones(n,n);
6      H = E./(I+J-1);
```

Figure 2: Matlab code for producing Hilbert matrices. When n is influenced by P, each of the constructors creates a PPServer object instead of a Matlab object.

3 MATLAB*P

By directly using the PPServer's client communication interface, it is possible for other applications to use the PPServer's functionality. We have implemented a client interface for Matlab, called MATLAB*P. MATLAB*P is a collection of Matlab 5 objects, Matlab m-files (Matlab's scripting language) and Matlab MEX programs (Matlab's external language API) that allows for the transparent integration of Matlab as a front end for the Parallel Problems Server.

The choice of Matlab was influenced by several factors. It is the *de facto* standard for scientific computing, enjoying wide use in industry and academia. In the machine learning community, for example, algorithms are often written as Matlab scripts and made freely available. In the scientific computing community, algorithms are often first prototyped in Matlab before being optimized for languages such as Fortran.

We endeavor to make interaction with the PPServer as transparent as possible for the user. In principle, a typical Matlab user should never have to make explicit calls to the PPServer. Further, current Matlab programs should not have to be rewritten to take advantage of the PPServer.

Space does not permit a complete discussion of MATLAB*P (we refer the reader to (Husbands and Isbell, 1999)); however, we will briefly discuss how to use prewritten Matlab scripts without modification. This is accomplished through the simple but innovative P notation.

We use Matlab 5's object oriented features to create PPServer objects automatically. P is a special object we introduce in Matlab that acts just like the integer 1. A user typing a=ones(1000*P,1000) or b=rand(1000,1000*P) obtains two 1000-by-1000 matrices distributed in parallel. The reader can guess the use of P here: it indicates that a is distributed by rows and b by columns.

To a user, a and b are matrices, but within Matlab, they are handles to special distributed types that exist on the PPServer. Any further references to these variables (e.g. via such commands as eig, svd, inv, *, +, -) are recognized as a call to the PPServer rather than as a traditional Matlab command.

Figure 2 shows the code for Matlab's built in function hilb. The call hilb(n) produces the $n \times n$ Hilbert matrix ($H_{ij} = \frac{1}{i+j-1}$). When n is influenced by P, a parallel array results:

- J=1:n in line 2 creates the PPServer vector $1, 2, \cdots, n$ and places a handle to it in J. Note that this behavior does not interfere with the semantics of for loops (for i=1:n) as Matlab assigns to i the value of each column of 1:n: the numbers $1, 2, \ldots, n$.
- ones(n,1) in line 3 produces a PPServer matrix.
- Emulation of Matlab's indexing functions results in the correct execution of line 3.

- Overloading of ' (the transpose operator) executes line 4 on the PPServer.
- In line 5, E is generated on the PPServer because of the overloading of ones.
- Overloading elementary matrix operations makes H a PPServer matrix (line 6).

The Parallel Problems Server and MATLAB*P have been tested extensively on a variety of platforms. They currently run on Cray supercomputers[1], clusters of symmetric multiprocessors from Sun Microsystems and DEC as well as on clusters of networked Intel PCs. The PPServer has also been tested with other clients, including Common LISP.

Although computational performance varies depending upon the platform, it is clear that the system provides distinct computational advantages. Communication overhead (in our experiments, roughly two milliseconds per PPServer command) is negligible compared to the computational and space advantage afforded by transparent access to highly-optimized linear algebra algorithms.

4 Applications in Text Retrieval

In this section we demonstrate the efficacy of the PPServer on real-world machine learning problems. In particular we explore the use of the PPServer and MATLAB*P in the text retrieval domain.

The task in text retrieval is to find the subset of a collection of documents relevant to a user's information request. Standard approaches are based on the Vector Space Model (VSM). A document is a vector where each dimension is a count of the occurrence of a different word. A collection of documents is a matrix, D, where each column is a document vector d_i. The similarity between two documents is their inner product, $d_i^T d_j$. Queries are just like documents, so the relevance of documents to a query, q, is $D^T q$.

Typical small collections contain a thousand vectors in a ten thousand dimensional space, while large collections may contain 500,000 vectors residing in hundreds of thousands of dimensions. Clearly, well-understood standard machine learning techniques may exhibit unpredictable behavior under such circumstances, or simply may not scale at all.

Classically, ML-like approaches try to construct a set of linear operators which extract the underlying "topic" structure of documents. Documents and queries are projected into that new (usually smaller) space before being compared using the inner product.

The large matrix support in MATLAB*P enables us to use matrix decomposition techniques for extracting linear operators easily. We have explored several different algorithms(Isbell and Viola, 1998). Below, we discuss two standard algorithms to demonstrate how the PPServer allows us to perform interesting analysis on large datasets.

4.1 Latent Semantic Indexing

Latent Semantic Indexing (LSI) (Deerwester et al., 1990) constructs a smaller document matrix by using the Singular Value Decomposition (SVD): $D = USV^T$. U contains the eigenvectors of the co-occurrence matrix while the diagonal elements of S (referred to as *singular values*) contain the square roots of their corresponding eigenvalues. The eigenvectors with the largest eigenvalues capture the axes of largest variation in the data.

LSI projects documents onto the k-dimensional subspace spanned by the first k columns of U (denoted U_k) so that the documents are now: $V_k^T = S_k^{-1} U_k$. Queries are similarly projected. Thus, the document-query scores for LSI can be obtained with simple Matlab code:

---

[1] Although there is no Matlab for the Cray, we are still able to use it to "execute" Matlab code in parallel.

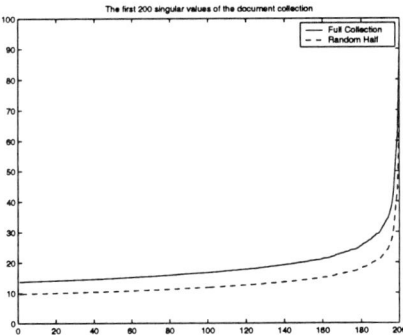

Figure 3: The first 200 singular values of a collection of about 500,000 documents and 200,000 terms, and singular values for half of that collection. Computation for on the full collection took only 62 minutes using 32 processors on a Cray T3E.

```
D=dsparse('term-doc');      %D SPARSE reads a sparse matrix
Q=dsparse('queries');
[U,S,V]=svds(D,k);          % compute the k-SVD of D
sc=getlsiscores(U,S,V,Q);   % computes v*(1/s)*u'*q
```

The scores that are returned can then be combined with relevance judgements to obtain precision/recall curves that are displayed in Matlab:

```
r=dsparse('judgements');
[pr,re]=precisionrecall(sc,r);
plot(re('@'),pr('@'));
```

In addition to evaluating the performance of various techniques, we can also explore characteristics of the data itself. For example, many implementations of LSI on large collections use only a subset of the documents for computational reasons. This leads one to question how the SVD is affected. Figure 3 shows the first singular values for one large collection as well as for a random half of that collection. It shows that the shape of the curves are remarkably similar (as they are for the *other* half). This suggests that we can derive a projection matrix from just half of the collection. An evaluation of this technique can easily be performed using our system. Premlinary experiments show nearly identical retrieval performance.

4.2 What are the Independent Components of Documents?

Independent components analysis (ICA)(Bell and Sejnowski, 1995) also recovers linear projections from data. Unlike LSI, which finds principal components, ICA finds axes that are statistically independent. ICA's biggest success is probably its application to the *blind source separation* or *cocktail party* problem. In this problem, one observes the output of a number of microphones. Each microphone is assumed to be recording a linear mixture of a number of unknown sources. The task is to recover the original sources.

There is a natural embedding of text retrieval within this framework. The words that are observed are like microphone signals, and underlying "topics" are the source signals that give rise to them.

Figure 4 shows a typical distribution of words projected along axes found by ICA.[2] Most words have a value close to zero. The histogram shows only the words large positive or

---

[2] These results are from a collection containing transcripts of White House press releases from 1993. There are 1585 documents and 18,675 distinct words.

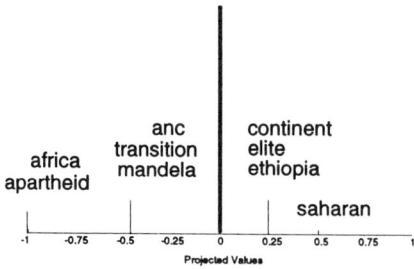

Figure 4: Distribution of words with large magnitude an ICA axis from White House text.

negative values. One group of words is made up of highly-related terms; namely, "africa," "apartheid," and "mandela." The other group of words are not directly related, but each co-occurs with different individual words in the first group. For example, "saharan" and "africa" occur together many times, but not in the context of apartheid and South Africa; rather, in documents concerning US policy toward Africa in general. As it so happens, "saharan" acts as a discriminating word for these subtopics.

As observed in (Isbell and Viola, 1998), it appears that ICA is finding a set of words, S, that selects for related documents, H, along with another set of words, T, whose elements do not select for H, but co-occur with elements of S. Intuitively, S selects for documents in a general subject area, and T removes a specific subset of those documents, leaving a small set of highly related documents. This suggests a straightforward algorithm to achieve the same goal directly. This local clustering approach is similar to an unsupervised version of Rocchio with Query Zoning (Singhal, 1997).

Further analysis of ICA on similar collections reveals other interesting behavior on large datasets. For example, it is known that ICA will attempt to find an unmixing matrix that is full rank. This is in conflict with the notion that these collections actually reside in a much smaller subspace. We have found in our experiments with ICA that some axes are highly *kurtotic* while others produce gaussian-like distributions. We conjecture that any axis that results in a gaussian-like distribution will be split arbitrarily among all "empty" axes. For all intents and purposes, these axes are uninformative. This provides an automatic noise-reduction technique for ICA when applied to large datasets.

For the purposes of comparison, Figure 5 illustrates the performance of several algorithms (including ICA and various clustering techniques) on articles from the Wall Street Journal.[3]

5 Discussion

We have shown that MATLAB*P enables portable, high-performance interactive supercomputing using the Parallel Problems Server, a powerful mechanism for writing and accessing optimized algorithms. Further, the client communication protocol makes it possible to implement transparent integration with sufficiently powerful clients, such as Matlab 5.

With such a tool, researchers can now use Matlab as something more than just a way for prototyping algorithms and working on small problems. MATLAB*P makes it possible to interactively operate on and visualize large data sets. We have demonstrated this last claim by using the PPServer system to apply ML techniques to large datasets, allowing for analyses of both data and algorithms. MATLAB*P has also been used to implement versions of Diverse Density(Maron, 1998), MIMIC(DeBonet, Isbell and Viola, 1996), and gradient descent.

---

[3]The WSJ collection contains 42,652 documents and 89,757 words

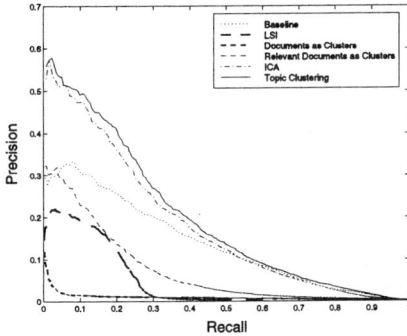

Figure 5: A comparison of different algorithms on the Wall Street Journal

References

Bell, A. and Sejnowski, T. (1995). An information-maximizaton approach to blind source separation and blind deconvolution. *Neural Computation*, 7:1129–1159.

Blackford, L. S., Choi, J., Cleary, A., D'Azevedo, E., Demmel, J., Dhilon, I., Dongarra, J., Hammarling, S., Henry, G., Petitet, A., Stanley, K., Walker, D., and Whaley, R. (1997). ScaLAPACK Users' Guide. http://www.netlib.org/scalapack/slug/scalapack_slug.html.

DeBonet, J., Isbell, C., and Viola, P. (1996). Mimic: Finding optima by estimating probability densities. In *Advances in Neural Information Processing Systems*.

Deerwester, S., Dumais, S. T., Landauer, T. K., Furnas, G. W., and Harshman, R. A. (1990). Indexing by latent semantic analysis. *Journal of the Society for Information Science*, 41(6):391–407.

Frakes, W. B. and Baeza-Yates, R., editors (1992). *Information Retrieval: Data Structures and Algorithms*. Prentice-Hall.

Gropp, W., Lusk, E., and Skjellum, A. (1994). *Using MPI: Portable Parallel Programming with the Message-Passing Interface*. The MIT Press.

Husbands, P. and Isbell, C. (1999). MITMatlab: A tool for interactive supercomputing. In *Proceedings of the Ninth SIAM Conference on Parallel Processing for Scientific Computing*.

Isbell, C. and Viola, P. (1998). Restructuring sparse high dimensional data for effective retrieval. In *Advances in Neural Information Processing Systems*.

Kwok, K. L. (1996). A new method of weighting query terms for ad-hoc retrieval. In *Proceedings of the 19th ACM/SIGIR Conference*, pages 187–195.

Maron, O. (1998). A framework for multiple-instance learning. In *Advances in Neural Information Processing Systems*.

Maschhoff, K. J. and Sorensen, D. C. (1996). A Portable Implementation of ARPACK for Distributed Memory Parallel Computers. In *Preliminary Proceedings of the Copper Mountain Conference on Iterative Methods*.

O'Brien, G. W. (1994). Information management tools for updating an svd-encoded indexing scheme. Technical Report UT-CS-94-259, University of Tennessee.

PETSc. The Portable, Extensible Toolkit for Scientific Computation. http://www.mcs.anl.gov/home/group/petsc.html.

PPServer. The Parallel Problems Server Web Page. http://www.ai.mit.edu/projects/ppserver.

Sahami, M., Hearst, M., and Saund, E. (1996). Applying the multiple cause mixture model to text categorization. In *Proceedings of the 13th International Machine Learning Conference*.

Singhal, A. (1997). Learning routing queries in a query zone. In *Proceedings of the 20th International Conference on Research and Development in Information Retrieval*.

An Oculo-Motor System with Multi-Chip Neuromorphic Analog VLSI Control

Oliver Landolt*
CSEM SA
2007 Neuchâtel / Switzerland
E-mail: landolt@caltech.edu

Stève Gyger
CSEM SA
2007 Neuchâtel / Switzerland
E-mail: steve.gyger@csem.ch

Abstract

A system emulating the functionality of a moving eye—hence the name *oculo-motor system*—has been built and successfully tested. It is made of an optical device for shifting the field of view of an image sensor by up to 45° in any direction, four neuromorphic analog VLSI circuits implementing an oculo-motor control loop, and some off-the-shelf electronics. The custom integrated circuits communicate with each other primarily by non-arbitrated address-event buses. The system implements the behaviors of saliency-based *saccadic exploration*, and *smooth pursuit* of light spots. The duration of saccades ranges from 45 ms to 100 ms, which is comparable to human eye performance. Smooth pursuit operates on light sources moving at up to 50°/s in the visual field.

1 INTRODUCTION

Inspiration from biology has been recognized as a seminal approach to address some engineering challenges, particularly in the computational domain [1]. Researchers have borrowed architectures, operating principles and even micro-circuits from various biological neural structures and turned them into analog VLSI circuits [2]. Neuromorphic approaches are often considered to be particularly suited for machine vision, because even simple animals are fitted with neural systems that can easily outperform most sequential digital computers in visual processing tasks. It has long been recognized that the level of visual processing capability needed for practical applications would require more circuit area than can be fitted on a single chip. This observation has triggered the development of inter-chip communication schemes suitable for neuromorphic analog VLSI circuits [3]-[4], enabling the combination of several chips into a system capable of addressing tasks of higher complexity. Despite the availability of these communication protocols, only few successful implementations of multi-chip neuromorphic systems have been reported so far (see [5] for a review). The present contribution reports the completion of a fully functional multi-chip system emulating the functionality of a moving eye, hence the denomination *oculo-motor system*. It is made of two 2D VLSI retina chips, two custom analog VLSI control chips, dedicated optical and mechanical devices and off-the-shelf electronic components. The four neuromorphic chips communicate mostly by pulse streams mediated by non-arbitrated address-event buses [4]. In its current version, the system can generate *saccades* (quick eye

---

* Now with Koch Lab, Division of Biology 139-74, Caltech, Pasadena, CA 91125, USA

movements) toward salient points of the visual scene, and track moving light spots. The purpose of the saccadic operating mode is to explore the visual scene efficiently by allocating processing time proportionally to significance. The purpose of tracking (also called *smooth pursuit*) is to slow down or suppress the retina image slip of moving objects in order to leave visual circuitry more time for processing. The two modes—saccadic exploration and smooth pursuit—operate concurrently and interact with each other. The development of this oculo-motor system was meant as a framework in which some general issues pertinent to neuromorphic engineering could be addressed. In this respect, it complements Horiuchi's pioneering work [6]-[7], which consisted of developing a 1D model of the primate oculo-motor system with a focus on automatic on-chip learning of the correct control function. The new system addresses different issues, notably 2D operation and the problem of strongly non-linear mapping between 2D visual and motor spaces.

2 SYSTEM DESCRIPTION

The oculo-motor system is made of three modules (Fig. 1). The moving eye module contains a 35 by 35 pixels electronic retina [8] fitted with a light deflection device driven by two motors. This device can shift the field of view of the retina by up to 45° in any direction. The optics are designed to cover only a narrow field of view of about 12°. Thereby, the retina serves as a high-resolution "spotlight" gathering details of interesting areas of the visual scene, similarly to the fovea of animals. Two position control loops implemented by off-the-shelf components keep the optical elements in the position specified by input signals applied to this module. The other modules control the moving eye in two types of behavior, namely *saccadic exploration* and *smooth pursuit*. They are implemented as physically distinct printed circuit boards which can be enabled or disabled independently.

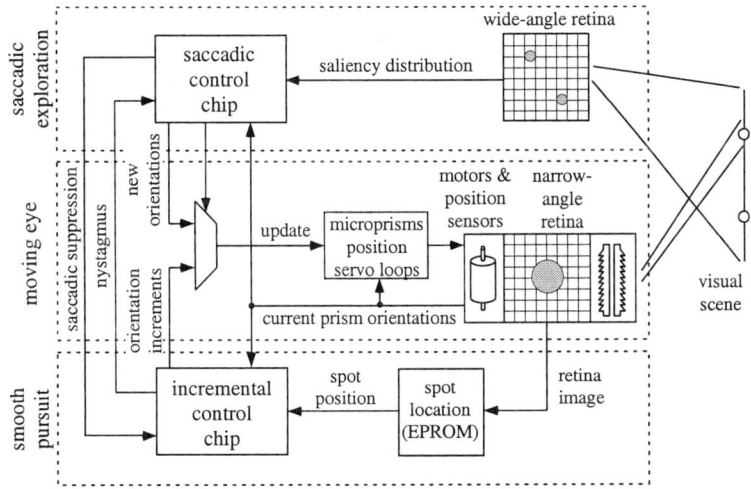

Figure 1: Oculo-motor system architecture

The light deflection device is made of two transparent and flat disks with a micro-prism grating on one side, mounted perpendicularly to the optical axis of a lens. Each disk can rotate without restriction around this axis, independently from the other. As a whole, each micro-prism grating acts on light essentially like a single large prism, except that it takes much less space (Fig. 2). Although a single fixed prism cannot have an adjustable deflection angle, with two mobile prisms, any magnitude and direction of deflection within some boundary can be selected, because the two contributions may combine either constructively or destructively depending on the relative prism orientations. The relationship between prism orientations and deflection angle has been derived in [9]. The advantage of this system over many other designs is that only two small passive optical elements have to move whereas most of the components are fixed, which enables fast movements and avoids electrical connections to moving parts. The drawback of this principle is that optical aberrations introduced by the prisms degrade image quality. However, when the device is used in conjunction with a typical electronic retina, this degradation is not limiting because these image sensors are characterized by a modest resolution due to focal-plane electronic processing.

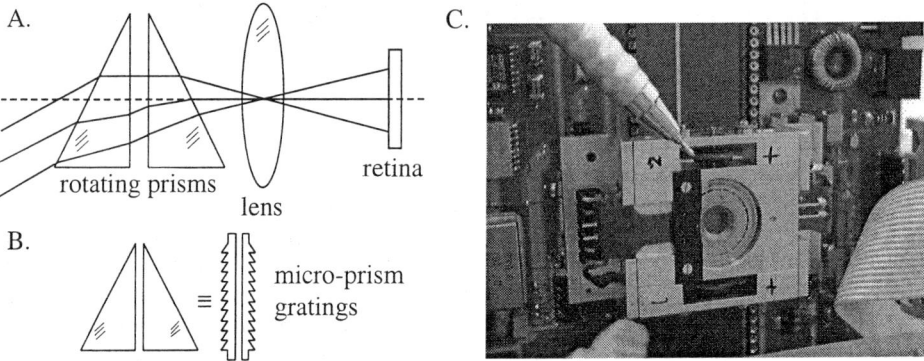

Figure 2: A. Light deflection device principle. B. Replacement of conventional prisms by micro-prism gratings. C. Photograph of the prototype with motors and orientation sensors.

The saccadic exploration module (Fig. 1) consists of an additional retina fitted with a fixed wide-angle lens, and a neuromorphic saccadic control chip. The retina gathers low-resolution information from the whole visual scene accessible to the moving eye, determines the degree of interest—or *saliency* [10]—of every region and transmits the resulting saliency distribution to the saccadic control chip. In the current version of the system, the distribution of saliency is just the raw output image of the retina, whereby saliency is determined by the brightness of visual scene locations. By inserting additional visual processing hardware between the retina and the saccadic control chip, it would be possible to generate interest for more sophisticated cues like edges, motion or specific shapes or patterns. The saccadic control chip (Fig. 3) determines the sequence and timing of an endless succession of quick jumps—or *saccades*—to be executed by the moving eye, in such a way that salient locations are attended longer and more frequently than less significant locations. The chip contains a 2D array of about 900 cells, which is called *visual map* because its organization matches the topology of the visual field accessible by the moving eye. The chip also contains two 1D arrays of 64 cells called *motor maps*, which encode micro-prism orientations in the light deflection device. Each cell of the visual map is externally stimulated by a stream of brief pulses, the frequency of which encodes saliency. The cells integrate incoming pulses over time on a capacitor, thereby building up an internal voltage at a rate proportional to pulse frequency. A global comparison circuit—called *winner-take-all*—selects the cell with the highest internal voltage. In the winning cell, a leakage mechanism slowly decrease the internal voltage over time, thereby eventually leading another cell to win. With this principle, any cell stimulated to some degree wins from time to time. The frequency of winning and the time ellapsed until another cell wins increases with saliency. The visual map and the two motor maps are interconnected by a so-called *network of links* [9], which embodies the mapping between visual and motor spaces. This network consists of a pair of wires running from each visual cell to one cell in each of the two motor maps. Thereby, the winning cell in the visual map stimulates exactly one cell in each motor map. The *location* of the active cell in a motor map encodes the orientation of a micro-prism grating, therefore this representation convention is called *place coding* [9]. The addresses of the active cells on the motor maps are transmitted to the moving eye, which triggers micro-prism displacements toward the specified orientations.

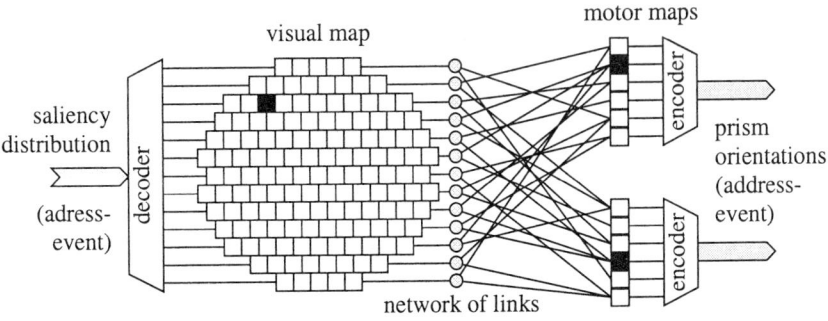

Figure 3: Schematic of the saccadic control chip

The smooth pursuit module consists of an EPROM chip and a neuromorphic incremental control chip (Fig. 1). The address-event stream delivered by the narrow-field retina is applied to the EPROM. The field of view of this retina has been divided up into eight angular sectors and a center region (Fig. 4A). The EPROM maps the addresses of pixels located in the same sector onto a common output address, thereby summing their spiking frequencies. The resulting address-event stream is applied to a topological map of eight cells constituting one of the inputs of the neuromorphic incremental control chip. If a single bright spot is focused on the retina away from the center, a large sum is produced in one or two neighboring cells of this map, whereas the other cells receive only background stimulation levels close to zero. Thereby, the angular position of the light spot is encoded by the location of the spot of activity on the map—in other words place coding. Other objects than light spots could be processed similarly after insertion of relevant detection hardware between the retina and the EPROM. The incremental control chip has two additional input maps representing the current orientations of the two prisms (Fig. 4B). These maps are connected to position sensors incorporated into the moving eye module (Fig. 1). These additional inputs are necessary because the control actions depends not only on the location of the target on the retina, but also on the current prism orientations [9]. The control actions are computed by three networks of links relating the primary inputs maps to the final output map via an intermediate layer. The purpose of this intermediate stage is to break down the control function of three variables into three functions of only two variables, which can be implemented by a lower number of links [11]. As in the saccadic control chip, the mapping between the input and output spaces has been calculated numerically prior to chip fabrication, then hardwired as electrical connections. The final outputs of the chip are pulse streams encoding the direction and rate at which each micro-prism grating must rotate in order to shift the target toward the center of the retina. These pulses incrementally update prism orientations settings at the input of the moving eye module (Fig. 1).

Since two different modules control the same moving eye, it is necessary to coordinate them in order to avoid conflicts. Saccadic module interventions occur whenever a saccade is generated, namely every 200–500 ms in typical operating conditions. At the instant a saccade is requested, the smooth pursuit module is shut off in order to prevent it from reacting against the saccade. A similar mechanism called *saccadic suppression* exists in biology. When the eye reaches the target location, control is left entirely to the smooth pursuit module until the next saccade is generated. Reciprocally, if an object tracked by

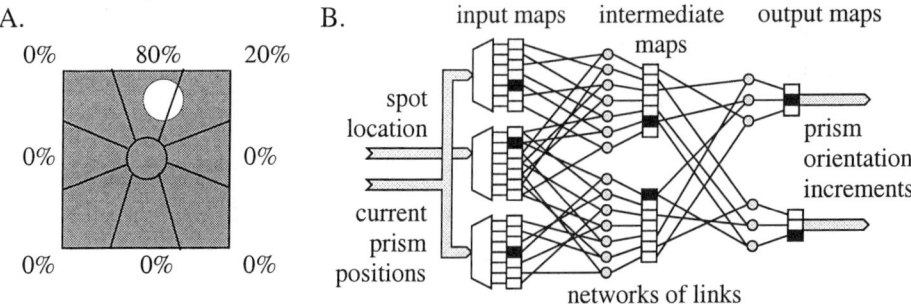

Figure 4: A. Place-coded spot location obtained by summing the outputs of pixels belonging to the same sector. B. Architecture of the incremental control chip

the smooth pursuit module reaches the boundary of the global visual field, the incremental control chip sends a signal triggering a saccade back toward the center of the visual field—which is called *nystagmus* in biology. The reason for splitting control into two modules is that visuo-motor coordinate mappings are very different for saccadic exploration and for smooth pursuit [9]. In the former case, visual input is related to the global field of view covered by the fixed wide-angle retina, and outputs are absolute micro-prism orientations. Saccade targets need not be initially visible to the moving eye. Since saccades are executed without permanent visual feedback, their accuracy is limited by the mapping hardwired in the control chip. Inversely, smooth pursuit is based on information extracted directly from the retina image of the moving eye. The output of the incremental control chip are small changes in micro-prism orientations instead of absolute positions. Thereby, the smooth pursuit module operates under closed-loop visual feedback, which confers it high accuracy. However, operation under visual feedback is slower than open-loop saccadic movements, and smooth pursuit inherently applies only to a single target. Thus, the two control modules are very complementary in purpose and performance.

3 EXPERIMENTAL RESULTS

The present section reports both qualitative observations and quantitative measurements made on the oculo-motor system, because the complexity of its behavior is difficult to convey by just a few numbers. The measurement setup consisted of a black board on which high efficiency white light emitting diodes were mounted, the intensity of which could be set individually. The visual scene was placed about 70 cm away from the moving eye. The axes of the two retinas were parallel at a distance of 6.5 cm. It was necessary to take this spacing into account for the visuo-motor coordinate mapping. The saliency distribution produced by the visual scene was measured by analyzing the output image of the wide-angle retina chip (Fig. 1).

When a single torchlight was waved in front of the moving eye, it was found that the smooth pursuit system indeed keeps the center of gravity of the light source image at the center of the narrow field of view. The maximum tracking velocity depends on the intensity ratio—contrast—between the light spot and the background. This behavior was expected because by construction, the incremental control chip generates correction pulses at a rate proportional to the magnitude of its input signals. At the highest contrast, we were able to achieve a maximum tracking speed of 50°/s. For comparison, smooth pursuit in humans can in principle reach up to 180°/s, but tracking is accurate only up to about 30°/s [7].

When shown two fixed light spots, the moving eye jumps from one to the other periodically.

The relative time spent on each light source depends on their intensity ratio. The duty cycle has been measured for ratios ranging from 0.1 to 10 (Fig. 5A). It is close to 50% for equal saliency, and tends toward a ratio of 10 to 1 in favor of the brightest spot at the extremities of the range. The delay between onset of a saccade and stabilization on the target ranges from 45 ms to 100 ms. The delay is not constant because it depends to some extent on saccade magnitude, and because of occasional mechanical slipping at the onset. In humans, the duration of saccades tends to be proportional to their amplitude, and ranges between 25 ms and 200 ms.

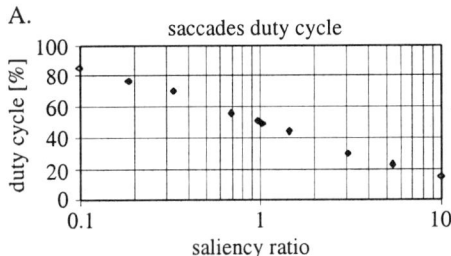
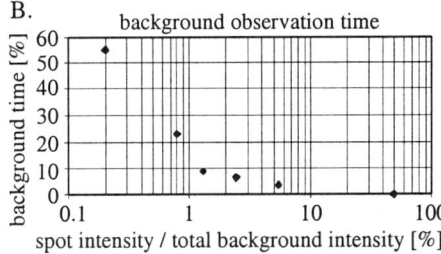

Figure 5: Measured data plots. A. Gaze time sharing between two salient spots versus saliency ratio. B. Gaze time on background versus spot-to-background intensity ratio.

When more than two spots are turned on, the saccadic exploration is not obviously periodic anymore, but the eye keeps spending most time on the light spots, with a noticeable preference for larger intensities. This behavior is consistent with measurements previously made on the saccadic control chip alone under electrical stimulation [9]. Saccades towards locations in the background are rare and brief if the intensity ratio between the light sources and the background is high enough. This phenomenon has been studied quantitatively by measuring the fraction of time spent on background locations for different light source intensities (Fig. 5B). The quantity on the horizontal axis of the plot is the ratio between the total intensity in light spots and the total background intensity. These two quantities are measured by summing the outputs of wide-angle retina pixels belonging to the light spot images and to the background respectively. It can be seen that if this ratio is above 1, less than 10% of the time is spent scanning the background.

Open-loop saccade accuracy has been evaluated by switching off the smooth pursuit module, and measuring the error vector between the center of gravity of the light spot and the center of the narrow-field retina after each saccade, for six different light spots spread over the field of view. The error vectors were found to be always less than 2° in magnitude, with different orientations in each case. Whenever the moving eye returned to a same light spot, the error vector was the same. This shows that the residual error is not due to random noise, but to the limited accuracy of visuo-motor mapping within the saccadic control chip. The magnitude of the error is always low enough that the target light spot is completely visible by the moving eye, thereby ensuring that the smooth pursuit module can indeed correct the error when enabled.

4 CONCLUSION

The oculo-motor system described herein performs as intended, thereby demonstrating the value of a neuromorphic engineering approach in the case of a relatively complex task involving mechanical and optical components. This system provides an experimental platform for studying *active vision*, whereby a visual system acts on itself in order to facilitate perception of its surroundings. Besides saccadic exploration and smooth pursuit, a moving eye can be exploited to improve vision in many other ways. For instance, resolution shortcomings in retinas incorporating only a modest number of pixels can be overcome by continuously sweeping the field of view back and forth, thereby providing continuous information in space—although not simultaneously in time. In binocular vision, 3D information perception by stereopsis is also made easier if the fields of view can be aligned by vergence control [12]. Besides active vision, the oculo-motor system also lends itself as a framework for testing and demonstrating other analog VLSI vision circuits. As already mentioned, due to its modular architecture, it is possible to insert additional visual processing chips either in the saccadic exploration module, or in the smooth pursuit module, in order to make the current light-source oriented system suitable for operation in natural visual environments.

Acknowledgments

The authors wish to express their gratitude to all their colleagues at CSEM who contributed to this work. Special thanks are due to Patrick Debergh for the micro-prism light deflection concept, to Friedrich Heitger for designing and building the mechanical device, and to Edoardo Franzi for designing and building the related electronic interface. Thanks are also due to Arnaud Tisserand, Friedrich Heitger, Eric Vittoz, Reid Harrison, Theron Stanford, and Edoardo Franzi for helpful comments on the manuscript. Mr. Roland Lagger, from Portescap, La Chaux-de-Fonds, Switzerland, provided friendly assistance in a critical mechanical assembly step.

References

[1] C. Mead. *Analog VLSI and Neural Systems*. Addison Wesley, 1989.

[2] T.S. Lande, editor. *Neuromorphic Systems Engineering*. Kluwer Academic Publishers, Dordrecht, 1998.

[3] K. Boahen. Retinomorphic vision systems II: Communication channel design. In *IEEE Int. Symp. Circuits and Systems (ISCAS'96)*, Atlanta, May 1996.

[4] A. Mortara, E. Vittoz, and P. Venier. A communication scheme for analog VLSI perceptive systems. *IEEE Journal of Solid-State Circuits*, 30, June 1995.

[5] C.M. Higgins. Multi-chip neuromorphic motion processing. In *Conference on Advanced Research in VLSI*, Atlanta, March 1999.

[6] T.K. Horiuchi, B. Bishofberger, and C. Koch. An analog VLSI saccadic eye movement system. In *Advances in Neural Processing Systems 6*, 1994.

[7] T.K. Horiuchi. *Analog VLSI-Based, Neuromorphic Sensorimotor Systems: Modeling the Primate Oculomotor System*. PhD thesis, Caltech, Pasadena, 1997.

[8] P. Venier. A constrast sensitive silicon retina based on conductance modulation in a diffusion network. In *6th Int. Conf. Microelectronics for Neural Networks and Fuzzy Systems (MicroNeuro'97)*, Dresden, Sept 1997.

[9] O. Landolt. *Place Coding in Analog VLSI - A Neuromorphic Approach to Computation*. Kluwer Academic Publishers, Dordrecht, 1998.

[10] T.G. Morris and S.P. DeWeerth. Analog VLSI excitatory feedback circuits for attentional shifts and tracking. *Analog Integrated Circuits and Signal Processing*, 13, May-June 1997.

[11] O. Landolt. Place coding in analog VLSI and its application to the control of a light deflection system. In *MicroNeuro'97*, Dresden, Sept 1997.

[12] M. Mahowald. *An Analog VLSI System for Stereoscopic Vision*. Kluwer Academic Publishers, Boston, 1994.

A Winner-Take-All Circuit with Controllable Soft Max Property

Shih-Chii Liu
Institute for Neuroinformatics, ETH/UNIZ
Winterthurstrasse 190, CH-8057 Zurich
Switzerland
shih@ini.phys.ethz.ch

Abstract

I describe a silicon network consisting of a group of excitatory neurons and a global inhibitory neuron. The output of the inhibitory neuron is normalized with respect to the input strengths. This output models the normalization property of the wide-field direction-selective cells in the fly visual system. This normalizing property is also useful in any system where we wish the output signal to code only the strength of the inputs, and not be dependent on the number of inputs. The circuitry in each neuron is equivalent to that in Lazzaro's winner-take-all (WTA) circuit with one additional transistor and a voltage reference. Just as in Lazzaro's circuit, the outputs of the excitatory neurons code the neuron with the largest input. The difference here is that multiple winners can be chosen. By varying the voltage reference of the neuron, the network can transition between a soft-max behavior and a hard WTA behavior. I show results from a fabricated chip of 20 neurons in a 1.2μm CMOS technology.

1 Introduction

Lazzaro and colleagues (Lazzaro, 1988) were the first to implement a hardware model of a winner-take-all (WTA) network. This network consists of N excitatory cells that are inhibited by a global signal. Improvements of this network with addition of positive feedback and lateral connections have been described (Morris, 1998; Indiveri, 1998). The dynamics and stability properties of networks of coupled excitatory and inhibitory neurons have been analyzed by many (Amari, 1982; Grossberg, 1988). Grossberg described conditions under which these networks will exhibit WTA behavior. Lazzaro's network computes a single winner as reflected by the outputs of the excitatory cells. Several winners can be chosen by using more localized inhibition.

In this work, I describe two variants of a similar architecture where the outputs of the excitatory neurons code the relative input strengths as in a soft-max computation. The relative values of the outputs depend on the number of inputs, their relative strengths and two parameter settings in the network. The global inhibitory

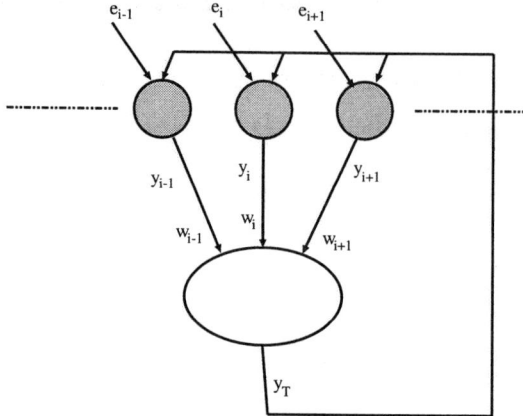

Figure 1: Network model of recurrent inhibitory network.

signal can also be used as an output. This output saturates with increasing number of active inputs, and the saturation level depends on the input strengths and parameter settings. This normalization property is similar to the normalization behavior of the wide-field direction-selective cells in the fly visual system. These cells code the temporal frequency of the visual inputs and are largely independent of the stimulation size. The circuitry in each neuron in the silicon network is equivalent to that in Lazzaro et. al.'s hard WTA network with an additional transistor and a voltage reference. By varying the voltage reference, the network can transition between a soft-max computation and a hard WTA computation. In the two variants, the outputs of the excitatory neurons either code the strength of the inputs or are normalized with respect to a constant bias current. Results from a fabricated network of 20 neurons in a 1.2μm AMI CMOS show the different regimes of operation.

2 Network with Global Inhibition

The generic architecture of a recurrent network with excitatory neurons and a single inhibitory neuron is shown in Figure 1. The excitatory neurons receive an external input, and they synapse onto a global inhibitory neuron. The inhibitory neuron, in turn, inhibits the excitatory neurons. The dynamics of the network is described as follows:

$$\frac{dy_i}{dt} = -y_i + e_i - g(\sum_{j=1}^{N} w_j y_j) \qquad (1)$$

where w_j is the weight of the synapse between the jth excitatory neuron and the inhibitory neuron, and y_j is the state of the jth neuron. Under steady-state conditions, $y_i = e_i - y_T$, where $y_T = g(\sum_{j=1}^{N} w_j y_j)$.

Assume a linear relationship between y_T and y_j, and letting $w_j = w$,

$$y_T = w \sum_{j=1}^{N} y_j = \frac{w \sum_{j=1}^{N} e_j}{1 + wN}$$

As N increases, $y_T = \frac{\sum_{j=1}^{N} e_j}{N}$. If all inputs have the same level, e, then $y_T = e$.

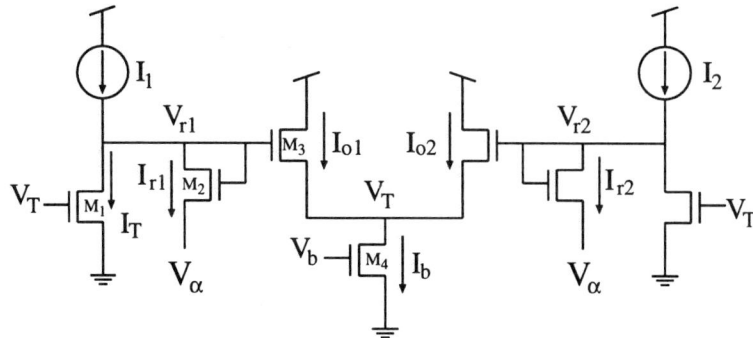

Figure 2: First variant of the architecture. Here we show the circuit for two excitatory neurons and the global inhibition neuron, M_4. The circuit in each excitatory neuron consists of an input current source, I_1, and transistors, M_1 to M_3. The inhibitory transistor is a fixed current source, I_b. The inputs to the inhibitory transistor, I_{o1} and I_{o2} are normalized with respect to I_b.

3 First Variant of Network with Fixed Current Source

In Sections 3 and 4, I describe two variants of the architecture shown in Figure 1. The two variants differ in the way that the inhibition signal is generated. The first network in Figure 2 shows the circuitry for two excitatory neurons and the inhibition neuron. Each excitatory neuron is a linear threshold unit and consists of an input current, I_1, and transistors, M_1, M_2, and M_3. The state of the neuron is represented by the current, I_{r1}. The diode-connected transistor, M_2, introduces a rectifying nonlinearity into the system since I_{r1} cannot be negative. The inhibition current, I_T, is sunk by M_1, and is determined by the gate voltage, V_T. The inhibition neuron consists of a current source, I_b, and V_T is determined by the corresponding current, I_{r1} and the corresponding transistor, M_3 in each neuron. Notice that I_T cannot be greater than the largest input to the network and the inputs to this network can only be excitatory. The input currents into the transistor, M_4, are defined as I_{o1} and I_{o2} and are normalized with respect to the current source, I_b. In the hard WTA condition, the output current of the winning neuron is equal to the bias current, I_b.

This network exhibits either a soft-maximum behavior or a hard WTA behavior depending on the value of an external bias, V_α. The inhibition current, I_T, is derived as:

$$I_T = \frac{I_\alpha N I_i}{I_b + I_\alpha N} = \frac{N I_i}{I_b/I_\alpha + N} \qquad (2)$$

where N is the number of "active" excitatory neurons (that is, neurons whose $I_i > I_T$), I_i is the same input current to each neuron, and $I_\alpha = I_0 e^{\kappa V_\alpha/U_T}$. In deriving the above equation, we assumed that $\kappa = 1$. The inhibition current, I_T, is a linear combination of the states of the neurons because $I_T = \sum_i^N I_{ri} \times I_\alpha/I_b$.

Figure 3(a) shows the response of the common-node voltage, V_T, as a function of the number of inputs for different input values measured from a fabricated silicon network of 20 neurons. The input current to each neuron is provided by a pFET transistor that is driven by the gate voltage, V_{in}. All input currents are equal in this figure. The saturation behavior of the network as a function of the number

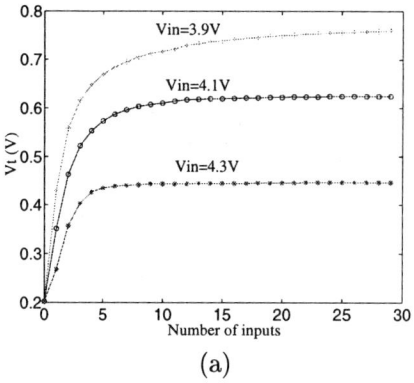 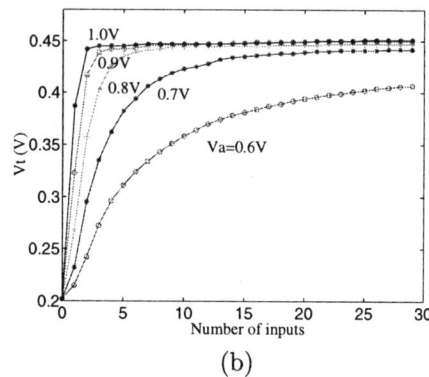

Figure 3: (a) Common-node voltage, V_T, as a function of the number of input stimuli. $V_\alpha = 0.8\text{V}$. (b) Common-node voltage, V_T, as a function of the number of inputs with an input voltage of 4.3V and $V_b = 0.7\text{V}$. The curves correspond to different values of V_α.

of inputs can be seen in the different traces and the saturation level increases as V_{in} decreases. As seen in Equation 2, the point at which the response saturates is dependent on the ratio, I_b/I_α. In Figure 3(b), I show how the curve saturates at different points for different values of V_α and a fixed I_b and V_{in}.

In Figure 4, I set all inputs to zero except for two inputs, V_{in1} and V_{in2} that are set to the same value. I measured I_{o1} and I_{o1} as a function of V_α as shown in Figure 4(a). The four curves correspond to four values of V_{in}. Initially both currents I_{o1} and I_{o2} are equal as is expected in the soft-max condition. As V_α increases, the network starts exhibiting a WTA behavior. One of the output currents finally goes to zero above a critical value of V_α. This critical value increases for higher input currents because of transistor backgate effects. In Figure 4(b), I show how the output currents respond as a function of the differential voltage between the two inputs as shown in Figure 4. Here, I fixed one input at 4.3V and swept the second input differentially around it. The different curves correspond to different values of V_α. For a low value of V_α, the linear differential input range is about 100mV. This linear range decreases as V_α is increased (corresponding to the WTA condition).

4 Second Variant with Diode-Connected Inhibition Transistor

In the second variant shown in Figure 5, the current source, M_4 is replaced by a diode-connected transistor and the output currents, I_{oi}, follow the magnitude of the input currents. The inhibition current, I_T, can be expressed as follows:

$$I_T = (I_{ri}/I_{oi}) \times I_\alpha \tag{3}$$

where I_α is defined in Section 3. We sum Equation 3 over all neurons and assuming equal inputs, we get $I_T = \sqrt{\sum I_{ri} \times I_\alpha}$. This equation shows that the feedback signal has a square root dependence on the neuron states. As we will see, this causes the feedback signal to saturate quickly with the number of inputs.

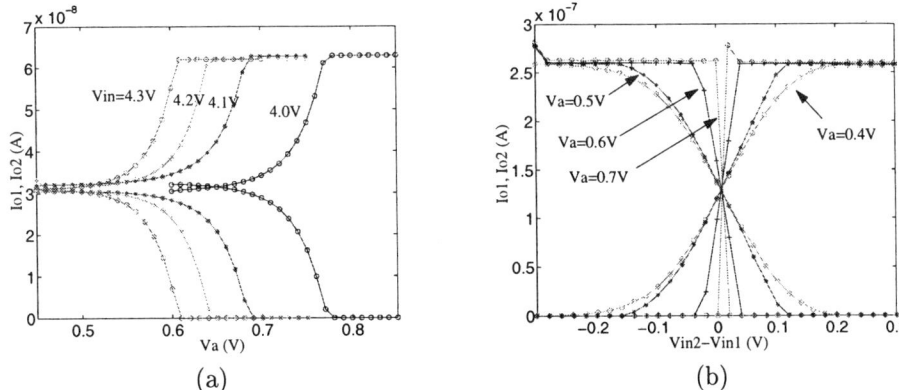

Figure 4: (a) Output currents, I_{o1} and I_{o2}, as a function of V_α for a subthreshold bias current and $V_{in} = 4.0\text{V}$ to 4.3V. (b) Outputs, I_{o1} and I_{o2}, as a function of the differential input voltage, ΔV_{in}, with $V_{in1} = 4.3\text{V}$.

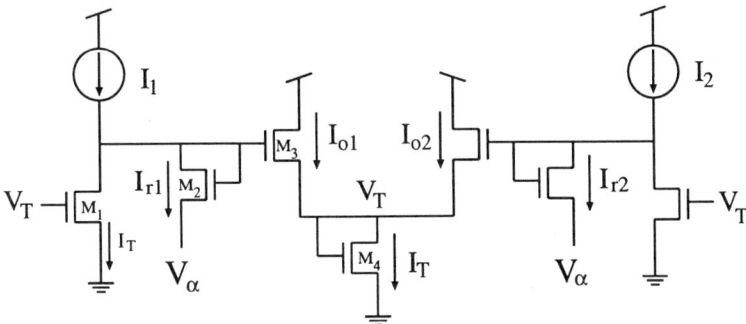

Figure 5: Second variant of network. The schematic shows two excitatory neurons with diode-connected inhibition transistor.

Substituting $I_{ri} = I_i - I_T$ in Equation 3, we solve for I_T,

$$I_T = -I_\alpha N + \sqrt{(I_\alpha N)^2 + 4I_\alpha \sum_i^N I_i} \qquad (4)$$

From measurements from a fabricated circuit with 20 neurons, I show the dependence of V_T (the natural logarithm of I_T) on the number of inputs in Figure 6(a). The output saturates quickly with the number of inputs and the level of saturation increases with increased input strengths. All the inputs have the same value.

The network can also act as a WTA by changing V_α. Again, all inputs are set to zero except for two inputs whose gate voltages are both set at 4.2V. As shown in Figure 6(b), the output currents, I_{o1} and I_{o2}, are initially equal, and as V_α increases above 0.6V, the output currents split apart and eventually, $I_{o2} = 0\text{A}$. The final value of I_{o1} depends on the maximum input current. This data shows that the network acts as a WTA circuit when $V_\alpha > 0.73\text{V}$. If I set $V_{in2} = 4.25\text{V}$ instead, the output currents split at a lower value of V_α.

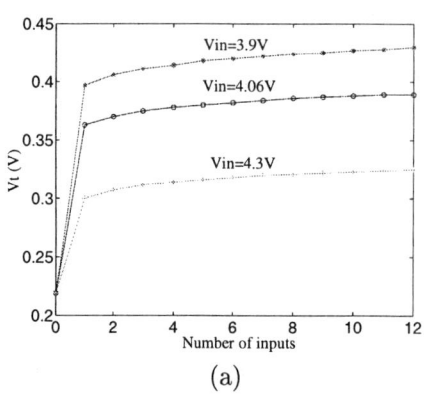 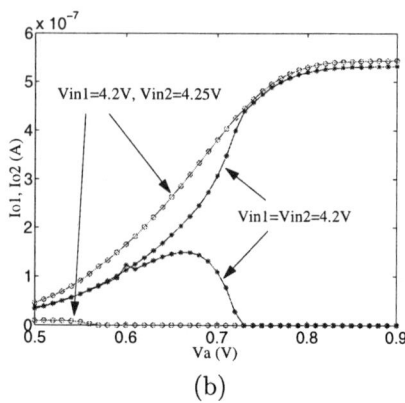

Figure 6: (a) Common-node voltage, V_T, as a function of the number of inputs for input voltages, 3.9V, 4.06V, and 4.3V for $V_\alpha = 0.4$V. (b) Outputs, I_{o1} and I_{o2}, as a function of V_α for $V_{in1} = 4.2$V, $V_{in2} = 4.25$V for the 2 curves with asterisks and for $V_{in1} = V_{in2} = 4.2$V for the 2 curves with circles.

5 Inhibition

The WTA property arises in both variants of this network if the gain parameter, V_α, is increased so that the diode-connected transistor, M_2, can be ignored. Both variants then reduce to Lazzaro's network. In the first variant, the feedback current (I_T) is a linear combination of the neuron states. However, when the gain parameter is increased so that M_2 can be ignored, the feedback current is now a nonlinear combination of the input states so the WTA behavior is exhibited by these reduced networks.

Under hard WTA conditions, if I_T is initially smaller than all the input currents, the capacitances C at the nodes V_{r1} and V_{r2} are charged up by the difference between the individual input current and I_T, i.e., $\frac{dV_{ri}}{dt} = \frac{I_i - I_T}{C}$. Since the inhibition current is a linear combination of I_{ri} and I_{ri} is exponential in V_{ri}, we can see that I_T is a sum of the exponentials of the input currents, I_i. Hence the feedback current is nonlinear in the input currents. Another way of viewing this condition in electronic terms is that in the soft WTA condition, the output node of each neuron is a soft-impedance node, or a low-gain node. In the hard WTA case, the output node is now a high-impedance node or a high-gain node. Any input differences are immediately amplified in the circuit.

6 Discussion

Hahnloser (Hahnloser, 1998) recently implemented a silicon network of linear threshold excitatory neurons that are coupled to a global inhibitory neuron. The inhibitory signal is a linear combination of the output states of the excitatory neurons. This network does not exhibit WTA behavior unless the excitatory neurons include a self-excitatory term. The inhibition current in his network is also generated via a diode-connected transistor. The circuitry in two variants described here is more compact than the circuitry in his network.

Recurrent networks with the architecture described in this paper have been proposed by Reichardt and colleagues (Reichardt, 1983) in modelling the aggregation property of the wide-field direction-selective cells in flies. The synaptic inputs are inhibited by a wide-field cell that pools all the synaptic inputs. Similar networks have also been used to model cortical processing, for example, orientation selectivity (Douglas, 1995).

The network implemented here can model the aggregation property of the direction-selective cells in the fly. By varying a voltage reference, the network implements either a soft-max computation or a hard WTA computation. This circuitry will be useful in hardware models of cortical processing or motion processing in invertebrates.

Acknowledgments

I thank Rodney Douglas for supporting this work, and the MOSIS foundation for fabricating this circuit. I also thank Tobias Delbrück for proofreading this document. This work was supported in part by the Swiss National Foundation Research SPP grant and the U.S. Office of Naval Research.

References

Amari, S., and Arbib, M. A., "Competition and cooperation in neural networks," New York, Springer-Verlag, 1982.

Grossberg, W., "Nonlinear neural networks: Principles, mechanisms, and architectures," *Neural Networks*, **1**, 17–61, 1988.

Hanhloser, R., "About the piecewise analysis of networks of linear threshold neurons," *Neural Networks*, **11**, 691–697, 1988.

Hahnloser, R., "Computation in recurrent networks of linear threshold neurons: Theory, simulation and hardware implementation," *Ph.D. Thesis*, Swiss Federal Institute of Technology, 1998.

Lazzaro, J., Ryckebusch, S. Mahowald, M.A., and Mead. C., "Winner-take-all networks of 0(n) complexity," In Tourestzky, D. (ed), Advances in Neural Information Processing Systems 1, San Mateo, CA: Morgan Kaufman Publishers, pp. 703–711, 1988.

Morris, T.G., Horiuchi, T. and Deweerth, S.P., "Object-based selection within an analog VLSI visual attention system," *IEEE Trans. on Circuits and Systems II*, **45:12**, 1564–1572, 1998.

Indiveri, G., "Winner-take-all networks with lateral excitation," *Neuromorphic Systems Engineering*, Editor, Lande, TS., 367–380, Kluwer Academic, Norwell, MA, 1998.

Reichardt, W., Poggio, T., and Hausen, K., "Figure-ground discrimination by relative movement in the visual system of the fly," *Biol. Cybern.*, **46**, 1–30, 1983.

Douglas, RJ., Koch, C., Mahowald, M., Martin, KAC., and Suarez, HH., "Recurrent excitation in neocortical circuits," *Science*, **269:5226**, 981–985, 1995.

A Neuromorphic VLSI System for Modeling the Neural Control of Axial Locomotion

Girish N. Patel
girish@ece.gatech.edu

Edgar A. Brown
ebrown@ece.gatech.edu

Stephen P. DeWeerth
steved@ece.gatech.edu

School of Electrical and Computer Engineering
Georgia Institute of Technology
Atlanta, Ga. 30332-0250

Abstract

We have developed and tested an analog/digital VLSI system that models the coordination of biological segmental oscillators underlying axial locomotion in animals such as leeches and lampreys. In its current form the system consists of a chain of twelve pattern generating circuits that are capable of arbitrary contralateral inhibitory synaptic coupling. Each pattern generating circuit is implemented with two independent silicon Morris–Lecar neurons with a total of 32 programmable (floating-gate based) inhibitory synapses, and an asynchronous address-event interconnection element that provides synaptic connectivity and implements axonal delay. We describe and analyze the data from a set of experiments exploring the system behavior in terms of synaptic coupling.

1 Introduction

In recent years, neuroscientists and modelers have made great strides towards illuminating structure and computational properties in biological motor systems. For example, much progress has been made toward understanding the neural networks that elicit rhythmic motor behaviors, including leech heartbeat, crustacean stomatogastric mill and lamprey swimming (a good review on these is in [1] and [2]). It is thought that these same mechanisms form the basis for more complex motor behaviors. The neural substrate for these control mechanisms are called central pattern generators (CPG). In the case of locomotion these circuits are distributed along the body (in the spinal cord of vertebrates or in the ganglia of invertebrates) and are richly interactive with sensory input and descending connections from the brain, giving rise to a highly distributed system as shown in Figure 1. In cases in which axial locomotion is involved, such as leech and lamprey swimming, synaptic interconnection patterns among autonomous segmental oscillators along the animal's axis produce coordinated motor patterns. These *intersegmental coordination* architectures have been well studied through both physiological experimentation and mathematical modeling. In addition, undulatory gaits in snakes have also been studied from a robotics perspective [3]. However, a thorough understanding of the computational principles in these systems is still lacking.

A Neuromorphic System for Modeling Axial Locomotion

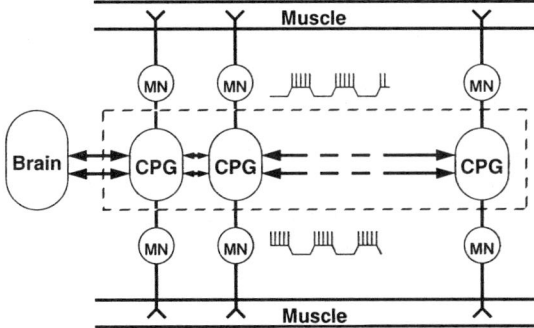

Figure 1: Neuroanatomy of segmented animals.

In order to better understand the computational paradigms that mediate intersegmental coordination and the resulting neural control of axial locomotion (and other motor patterns), we are using neuromorphic very large-scale integrated (VLSI) circuits to develop models of these biological systems. The goals in our research are (i) to study how the properties of individual neurons in a network affect the overall system behavior; (ii) to facilitate the validation of the principles underlying intersegmental coordination; and (iii) to develop a real-time, low power, motion control system. We want to exploit these principles and architectures both to improve our understanding of the biology and to design artificial systems that perform autonomously in various environments.

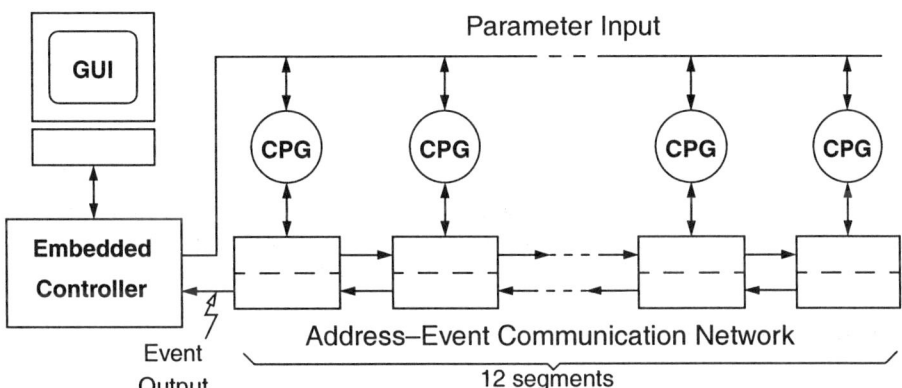

Figure 2: Block-level diagram of the implemented system. The intersegmental communications network facilitates communication among the intrasegmental units with pipelined stages.

In this paper, we present a VLSI model of intersegmental coordination as shown in Figure 2. Each segment in our system is implemented with a custom IC containing a CPG consisting of two silicon model neurons, each one with 16 inhibitory synapses whose values are stored on chip and are continuously variable; an asynchronous address event communications IC that implements the queuing and delaying of events providing synaptic connectivity and thus simulating axonal properties; and a microcontroller (with internal A/D converter and timer) that facilitates the modification of individual parameters through a serial bus. The entire system consists of twelve such segments linked to a computer on which a graphical user interface (GUI) is implemented. By using the GUI, we are able to control all of the synaptic connections in the system and to measure the resulting neural outputs. We present the system model, and we investigate the role of synaptic coupling in the establishment of phase lags along this chain of neural oscillators.

2 Pattern generating circuits

The smallest neural system capable of generating the basic alternating activity that characterizes the swimming CPGs is the *half-center* oscillator, essentially two bursting neurons with reciprocally inhibitory connections [1] as shown in Figure 3a. In biological systems, the associated neurons have both slow and fast time constants to facilitate the fast spiking (action potentials) and the slower bursting oscillations that control the elicited movements as shown in Figure 3b. To simplify the parameter space of our system, we use reduced two-state silicon neurons [4]. The output of each silicon neuron is an oscillation that represents the envelope of the bursting activity (i.e. the spiking activity and corresponding fast time constants are eliminated) as shown in Figure 3c. Each neuron also has 16 analog synapses that receive off-chip input. The synaptic parameters are stored in an array of floating-gate transistors [5] that provide nonvolatile analog memory.

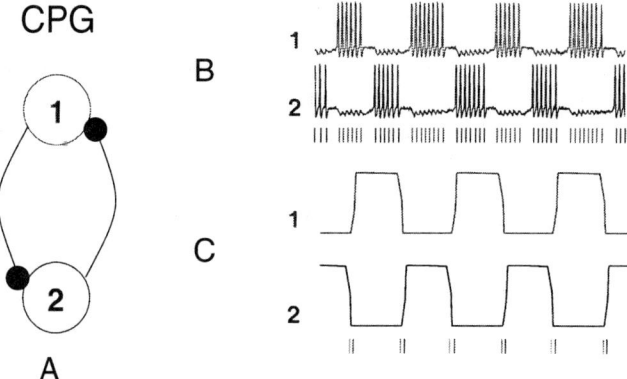

Figure 3: Half-center oscillator and the generation of events in spiking and nonspiking silicon neurons. Events are generated by detecting rapid rises in the membrane potential of spiking neurons or by detecting rapid rises and falls in nonspiking neurons.

3 Intersegmental communication

Our segmented system consists of an array of CPG circuits interconnected via an communication network that implements an asynchronous, address–event protocol [6][7]. Each CPG is connected to one node of this address–event intersegmental communication system as illustrated in Figure 2. This application-specific architecture uses a pipelined broadcast scheme that is based upon its biological counterpart. The principal advantage of using this custom scheme is that requisite addresses and delays are generated implicitly based upon the system architecture. In particular the system implements distance-dependent delays and relative addressing. The delays, which are thought to be integral to the network computation, replicate the axonal delays that result as action potentials propagate down an animal's body [2]. The relative addressing greatly simplifies the implementation of synaptic spread [8], the hypothesized translational invariance in the intersegmental connectivity in biological axial locomotion systems. Thus, we can set the synaptic parameters identically at every segment, greatly reducing system complexity.

In this architecture (which is described in more depth in [4]), each event is passed from segment to neighboring segment bidirectionally down the length of the one-dimensional communications network. By delaying each event at every segment, the pipeline architecture facilitates the creation of distance-dependent delays. The other primary advantage of this architecture is that it can easily generate a relative addressing scheme. Figure 4 illustrates the event-passing architecture with respect to the relative addressing and distance-dependent delays. Each event, generated at a particular node (the center node, in this example), is transmitted bidirectionally down the length of the network. It is delayed by time ΔT at each segment, not including the initiating segment.

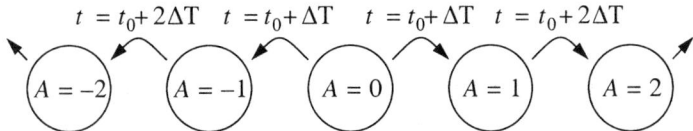

Figure 4: Relative addressing and distance-dependent delays.

The events are generated by the neurons in each segment. Because these are not spiking neurons, we could not use the typical scheme of generating one event per action potential. Instead, we generate one event at the beginning and end of each burst (as illustrated in Figure 3) and designate the individual events as rising or falling. In each segment the events are stored in a queue (Figure 5), which implements delay based upon uniform conduction velocities. As an event arrives at each new segment, it is time stamped, its relative address is incremented (or decremented), and then it is stored in the queue for the ΔT interval. As the event exits the queue, its data is decoded by the intrasegmental units, and synaptic inputs are applied to the appropriate intrasegmental neurons.

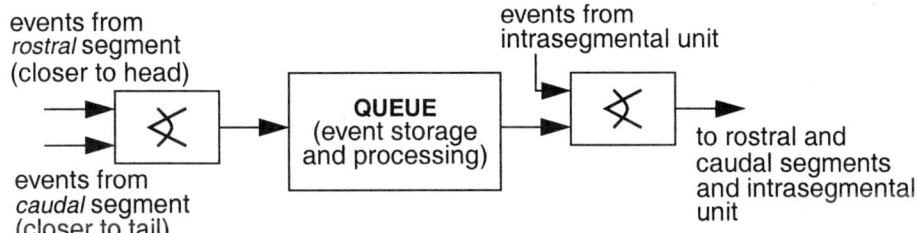

Figure 5: Block-level diagram of a communications node illustrating how events enter and exit each stage of the pipeline.

4 Experiments and Discussion

We have implemented the complete system shown in Figure 2, and have performed a number of experiments on the system. In Figure 6, we show the behaviors the system exhibits when it is configured with asymmetrical nearest-neighbor connections. The system displays traveling waves whose directions depend on the direction of the dominant coupling. Note that the intersegmental phase lags vary for different swim frequencies.

One important set of experiments focussed on the role of long-distance connections on the system behaviors. In these experiments, we configured the system with strong descending (towards the tail) connections such that robust rearward traveling waves (forward swimming) are observed. The long-distance connections are weak enough to avoid any *bifurcations* in behavior (different type of behavior). Thus, the traveling wave solution resulting from the nearest-neighbor connections persists as we progressively add long-distance connections. In Figure 7 we show the dependency of the swim frequency and the total phase lag (summation of the normalized intersegmental phase lags, where $1 \equiv 360°$) on the extent of the connections. The results show a clear difference in behav-

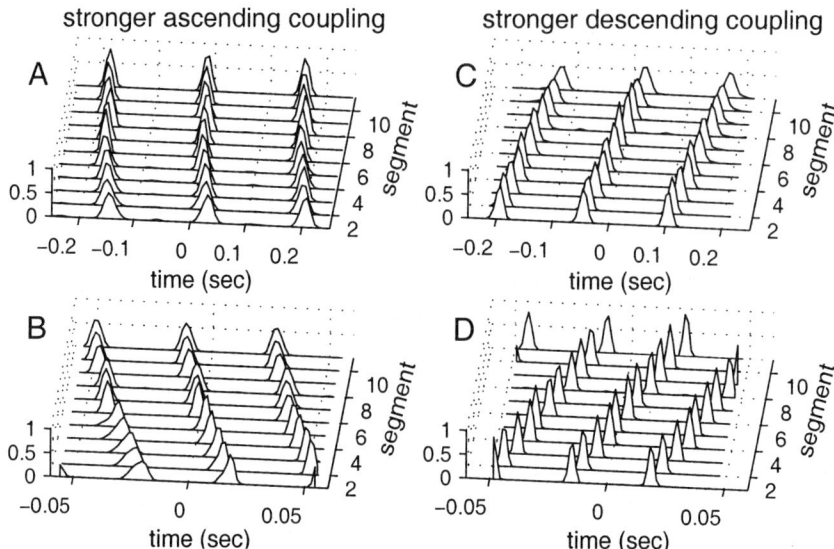

Figure 6: Traveling waves in the system with asymmetrical, nearest-neighbor connections. Plots are cross-correlations between rising edge events generated by a neuron in segment six and events generated by homolog neurons in each segment. Stronger ascending connections (A & B) produce forward traveling waves (backward swimming) and stronger descending connections (C & D) produce rearward traveling waves (forward swimming). An externally applied current (I_{ext}) controls the swim frequency. At small values of I_{ext} (6.7 nA) the periods of the swim cycles are approximately 0.180 ms and 0.150 ms for A & C, respectively; for large values of I_{ext} (32.8 nA), the periods of the swim cycles are approximately 36 ms and 33 ms for B & D, respectively.

iors between the lowest tonic drive (I_{ext} = 21.9 nA) and the two higher tonic drives. (By tonic drive, we mean a constant dc current is applied to all neurons.) In the former, the sensitivity of long-distance connections on frequency and intersegmental phase lags is considerably greater than in the latter. The demarcation in behavior may be attributed to different behaviors at different tonic drives. For lower tonic drive, the long-distance connections tend to synchronize the system (decrease the intersegmental phase lags). At the higher tonic drives, long-distance connections do not affect the system considerably. For I_{ext} = 32.8 nA, connections that span up to four segments aid in producing uniformity in the intersegmental phase lags. Although this does not hold for I_{ext} = 48.1 nA, long-distance connections play a more significant role in preserving the total phase difference. At I_{ext} = 32.8 nA and I_{ext} = 48.1 nA, the system with short-distance connections produces a total phase difference of 1.19 and 1.33, respectively. In contrast, for I_{ext} = 32.8 nA and I_{ext} = 48.1 nA, the system with long-distance connections that span up to seven segments produces a total phase difference of 1.20 and 1.25, respectively.

In the above experiments, we have demonstrated that, in a specific parameter regime, weak long-distance connections can affect the intersegmental phase lags. However, these weight profiles should not be construed as a possible explanation on what the weight profiles in a biological system might be. The parameter regime in which we observed this behavior is small; at moderate strengths of coupling, the traveling wave solutions disappear and move towards synchronous behavior. Recent experiments done on spinalized lampreys reveal that long-distance connections are moderately strong [10]. Thus, our current model is unable to replicate this aspect of intersegmental coordination. There are several explanations that may account for this discrepancy.

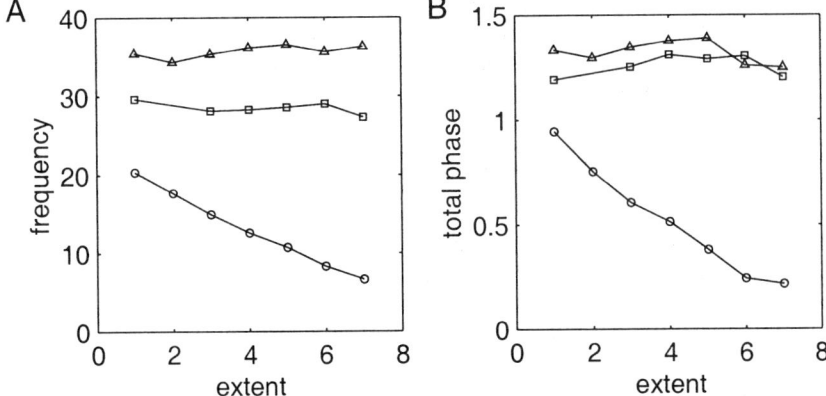

Figure 7: Effects of weak long-distance connections on swimming frequency (A), on the total phase difference (summation of the normalized intersegmental phase lags) (B), and on the standard deviation of the intersegmental phase lags (C). $\triangle$ $\square$ $\circ$ denote I_{ext} = 48.1 nA, 32.8 nA, and 21 nA, respectively.

In the segmental CPG network of the animal, there are many classes of neurons that send projections to many other classes of neurons. The phase a connection imposes is determined by which neuron class connects with which other neuron class. In our system, the segmental CPG network has only a single class of neurons upon which the long-distance connections can impose their phase. Depending on where in parameter space we operate our system, the long-distance connections have too little or too great an effect on the behavior of the system. At high tonic drives, the sensitivity of the weak long-distance connections on the intersegmental phase lags is small, whereas for small tonic drives, the long-distance connections have a great effect on the intersegmental phase lags.

It has been shown that if the waveform of the oscillators is sinusoidal (i.e., the time scales of the two state variables are not too different), traveling wave solutions exist and have a large basin of attraction [11]. However, as the disparity between the two time scales is made larger (i.e., the neurons are stiff and the waveform of the oscillations appears square-wave like), the system will move towards synchrony. In our implementation, to facilitate accurate communication of events, we bias the neurons with relatively large differences in the time scales. Thus, this restriction reduces the parameter regime in which we can observe stable traveling waves.

Another factor that determines the range of parameters in which stable traveling waves are observed is the slope of our synaptic coupling function. When the slope of the coupling function is steep, the total synaptic current over a cycle can increase significantly, causing weak connections to appear strong. This has an overall effect of synchronizing the network [11]. For coupling functions whose slopes are shallow, the total synaptic current over a cycle is reduced; therefore, the connections appear weak and larger intersegmental phase lags are possible. Thus, the sharp synaptic coupling function in our implementation, which is necessary for communication, is another factor that diminishes the parameter regime in which we can observe stable traveling waves.

The above factors limit the parameter range in which we observe traveling waves. However, all of these issues can be addressed by improving our CPG network. The first issue can be addressed by increasing the number of neuron classes or adding more segments. The second and third issues can be addressed by adding spiking neurons in our CPG network so that the form of the oscillations can be coded in the spike train and the synaptic coupling functions can be implemented on the receiving side of the CPG chip. The fourth issue can be addressed by designing self-adapting neurons that tune their internal parameters so that their waveforms and intrinsic frequencies are matched. Although weak coupling may not be biologically plausible, producing traveling waves based on phase oscillators would be an interesting research direction.

5 Conclusions and Future Work

In this paper, we described a functional, neuromorphic VLSI system that implements an array of neural oscillators interconnected by an address–event communication network. This system represents our most ambitious neuromorphic VLSI effort to date, combining 24 custom ICs, a special-purpose asynchronous communication architecture designed analogously to its biological counterpart, large-scale synaptic interconnectivity with parameters stored using floating-gate devices, and a computer interface for setting the parameters and for measuring the neural activity. The working system represents the culmination of a four-year effort, and now provides a testbed for exploring a variety of biological hypotheses and theoretical predictions.

Our future directions in the development of this system are threefold. First, we will continue to explore, in depth, the operation of the present system, comparing it to theoretical predictions and biological hypotheses. Second, we are implementing a segmented mechanical system that will provide a moving output and will facilitate the implementation of sensory feedback. Third, we are developing new CPG model centered around sensory feedback and motor learning. The modular design of the system, which puts all of the neural and synaptic specificity on the CPG IC, allows us to design a completely new CPG and to replace it in the system without changing the communication architecture.

References

[1] E. Marder & R.L. Calabrese. Principles of rhythmic motor pattern generation. *Physiological Reviews* 76 (3): 687–717, 1996.

[2] A.H. Cohen, G.B. Ermentrout, T. Kiemel, N. Kopell, K.A. Sigvardt, & T.L. Williams. Modeling of intersegmental coordination in the lamprey central pattern generator for locomotion. *TINS* 15:434–438, 1992.

[3] S. Hirose. *Biologically Inspired Robots: Snake-like Locomotors and Manipulators*. Oxford University Press, 1993.

[4] S. DeWeerth, G. Patel, D. Schimmel, M. Simoni, & R.L. Calabrese. A VLSI Architecture for Modeling Intersegmental Coordination. In *Proceedings of the Seventeenth Conference on Advanced Research in VLSI*, R.B. Brown and A.T. Ishii (eds), Los Alamitos, CA: IEEE Computer Society, 182–200, 1997.

[5] P. Hasler, B.A. Minch, and C. Diorio. Adaptive circuits using pFet floating-gate devices. In Scott Wills and Stephen DeWeerth editors, *20th Conference of Advanced Research in VLSI*, pages 215–230, Los Alamitos, California, CA: IEEE Computer Society, 1999.

[6] M.A. Mahowald. VLSI Analogs of Neuronal Visual Processing: A Synthesis of Form and Function. *Ph.D. Thesis, California Institute of Technology*, Pasadena, CA, 1992.

[7] K.A. Boahen. Communicating Neuronal Ensembles between Neuromorphic Chips. *Analog Integrated Circuits and Signal Processing*, 1997.

[8] T. Willams. Phase Coupling and Synaptic Spread in Chains of Coupled Neuronal Oscillators. *Science*, vol. 258, 1992.

[9] G. Patel. A Neuromorphic Architecture for Modeling Intersegmental Coordination. *Ph.D. Thesis, Georgia Institute of Technology*, Atlanta, GA, 1999.

[10] A. H. Cohen. Personal communication.

[11] D. Somers & N. Kopell. Waves and synchrony in networks of oscillators of relaxation and non-relaxation type. *Phyica D*, 89:169–183, 1995.

[12] N. Kopell & G.B. Ermentrout. Coupled oscillators and the design of central pattern generators. *Mathematical Biosciences*, 90:87–109, 1988.

Bifurcation Analysis of a Silicon Neuron

Girish N. Patel[1], Gennady S. Cymbalyuk[2,3],
Ronald L. Calabrese[2], and Stephen P. DeWeerth[1]

[1]School of Electrical and Computer Engineering
Georgia Institute of Technology
Atlanta, Ga. 30332-0250
{girish.patel, steve.deweerth}@ece.gatech.edu

[2]Department of Biology
Emory University
1510 Clifton Road, Atlanta, GA 30322
{gcym, rcalabre}@biology.emory.edu

[3]Institute of Mathematical Problems in Biology RAS
Pushchino, Moscow Region, Russia 142292 (on leave)

Abstract

We have developed a VLSI silicon neuron and a corresponding mathematical model that is a two state-variable system. We describe the circuit implementation and compare the behaviors observed in the silicon neuron and the mathematical model. We also perform bifurcation analysis of the mathematical model by varying the externally applied current and show that the behaviors exhibited by the silicon neuron under corresponding conditions are in good agreement to those predicted by the bifurcation analysis.

1 Introduction

The use of hardware models to understand dynamical behaviors in biological systems is an approach that has a long and fruitful history [1][2]. The implementation in silicon of oscillatory neural networks that model rhythmic motor-pattern generation in animals is one recent addition to these modeling efforts [3][4]. The oscillatory patterns generated by these systems result from intrinsic membrane properties of individual neurons and their synaptic interactions within the network [5]. As the complexity of these oscillatory silicon systems increases, effective mathematical analysis becomes increasingly more important to our understanding their behavior. However, the nonlinear dynamical behaviors of the model neurons and the large-scale interconnectivity among these neurons makes it very difficult to analyze theoretically the behavior of the resulting very large-scale integrated (VLSI) systems. Thus, it is important to first identify methods for modeling the model neurons that underlie these oscillatory systems.

Several simplified neuronal models have been used in the mathematical simulations of pattern generating networks [6][7][8]. In this paper, we describe the implementation of a two-state-variable silicon neuron that has been used effectively to develop oscillatory networks [9][10]. We then derive a mathematical model of this implementation and analyze the neuron and the model using nonlinear dynamical techniques including bifurcation analysis [11]. Finally, we compare the experimental data derived from the silicon neuron to that obtained from the mathematical model.

2 The silicon model neuron

The schematic for our silicon model neuron is shown in Figure 1. This silicon neuron is inspired by the two-state, Morris–Lecar neuron model [12][13]. Transistor M_1, analogous to the voltage-gated calcium channel in the Morris–Lecar model, provides an instantaneous inward current that raises the membrane potential towards V_{High} when the membrane is depolarized. Transistor M_2, analogous to the voltage-gated potassium channel in the Morris–Lecar model, provides a delayed outward current that lowers the membrane potential toward V_{Low} when the membrane is depolarized. V_H and V_L are analogous to the half-activation voltages for the inward and outward currents, respectively. The voltages across C_1 and C_2 are the state variables representing the membrane potential, V, and the slow "activation" variable of the outward current, W, respectively. The W-nullcline represents its steady-state activation curve. Unlike the Morris–Lecar model, our silicon neuron model does not possess a leak current.

Using current conservation at node V, the net current charging C_1 is given by

$$C_1 \dot{V} = I_{ext}\alpha_P + i_H \alpha_P - i_L \alpha_N \tag{1}$$

where i_H and i_L are the output currents of a differential pair circuit, and α_P and α_N describe the ohmic effects of transistors M_1 and M_2, respectively. The net current into C_2 is given by

$$C_2 \dot{W} = i_X \beta_P \beta_N \tag{2}$$

where i_X is the output current of the OTA, and β_P and β_N account for ohmic effects of the pull-up and the pull-down transistors inside the OTA.

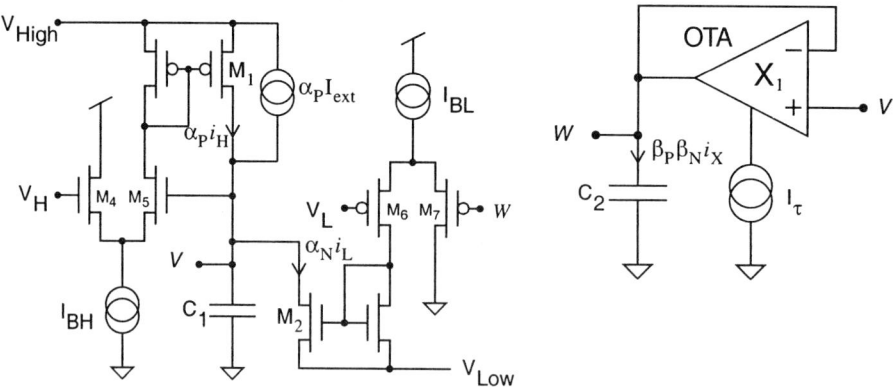

Figure 1: Circuit diagram of the silicon neuron. The circuit incorporates analog building blocks including two differential pair circuits composed of a bias current, IB_H, and transistors M_4–M_5, and a bias current, IB_L, and transistors M_6–M_7, and a single follower–integrator circuit composed of an operational transconductance amplifier (OTA), X_1 in the configuration shown and a load capacitor, C_2. The response of the follower–integrator circuit is similar to a first-order low-pass filter.

The output currents of the differential-pair and an OTA circuits, derived by using sub-threshold transistor equations [2], are a Fermi function and a hyperbolic-tangent function, respectively [2]. Substituting these functions for i_H, i_L, and i_X in (1) and (2) yields

$$C_1 \dot{V} = I_{ext}\alpha_P + I_{BH} \frac{e^{\kappa(V-V_H)/U_T}}{1+e^{\kappa(V-V_H)/U_T}} \alpha_P - I_{BL} \frac{e^{\kappa(W-V_L)/U_T}}{1+e^{\kappa(W-V_L)/U_T}} \alpha_N \qquad (3)$$

$$C_2 \dot{W} = I_\tau \tanh\left(\kappa \frac{V-W}{2U_T}\right) \beta_P \beta_N$$

where

$$\alpha_P = 1 - e^{V-V_{High}/U_T} \qquad \alpha_N = 1 - e^{V_{Low}-V/U_T} \qquad (4)$$

$$\beta_P = 1 - e^{W-V_{dd}/U_T} \qquad \beta_N = 1 - e^{-W/U_T}$$

U_T is the thermal voltage, V_{dd} is the supply voltage, and κ is a fabrication dependent parameter. The terms α_P and α_N limit the range of V to within V_{High} and V_{Low}, and the terms β_P and β_N limit the range of W to within the supply rails (V_{dd} and Gnd).

In order to compare the model to the experimental results, we needed to determine values for all of the model parameters. V_{High}, V_{Low}, V_H, V_L, and V_{dd} were directly measured in experiments. The parameters I_{BH} and I_{BL} were measured by voltage-clamp experiments performed on the silicon neuron. At room temperature, $U_T \approx 0.025$ volts. The value of $\kappa \approx 0.65$ was estimated by measuring the slope of the steady-state activation curve of inward current. Because W was implemented as an inaccessible node, I_τ could only be estimated. Based on the circuit design, we can assume that the bias currents I_τ and I_{BH} are of the same order of magnitude. We choose $I_\tau \approx 2.2$ nA to fit the bifurcation diagram (see Figure 3). C1 and C2, which are assumed to be identical according to the physical design, are time scaling parameters in the model. We choose their values (C1 = C2 = 28 pF) to fit frequency dependence on I_{ext} (see Figure 4).

3 Bifurcation analysis

The silicon neuron and the mathematical model[1] described by (3) demonstrate various dynamical behaviors under different parametric conditions. In particular, stable oscillations and steady-state equilibria are observed for different values of the externally applied current, I_{ext}. We focused our analysis on the influence of I_{ext} on the neuron behavior for two reasons: (i) it provides insight about effects of synaptic currents, and (ii) it allows comparison with neurophysiological experiments in which polarizing current is used as a primary control parameter. The main results of this work are presented as the comparison between the mathematical models and the experimental data represented as bifurcation diagrams and frequency dependencies.

The nullclines described by (3) and for $I_{ext} = 32$ nA are shown in Figure 2A. In the regime that we operate the circuit, the W-nullcline is an almost-linear curve and the V-nullcline is an N-shaped curve. From (3), it can be seen that when $IB_H + I_{ext} > IB_L$ the nullclines cross at $(V, W) \approx (V_{High}, V_{High})$ and the system has high voltage (about 5 volts) steady-state equilibrium. Similarly, for I_{ext} close to zero, the system has one stable equilibrium point close to $(V, W) \approx (V_{Low}, V_{Low})$.

---

[1]The parameters used throughout the analyses of the model are $V_{Low} = 0$ V, $V_{High} = 5$ V, $V_L = V_H = 2.5$ V, $I_{BH} = 6.5$ nA, $I_{BL} = 42$ nA, $I_\tau = 2.2$ nA, $V_{dd} = 5$ V, $U_t = 0.025$ mV, and $\kappa = 0.65$.

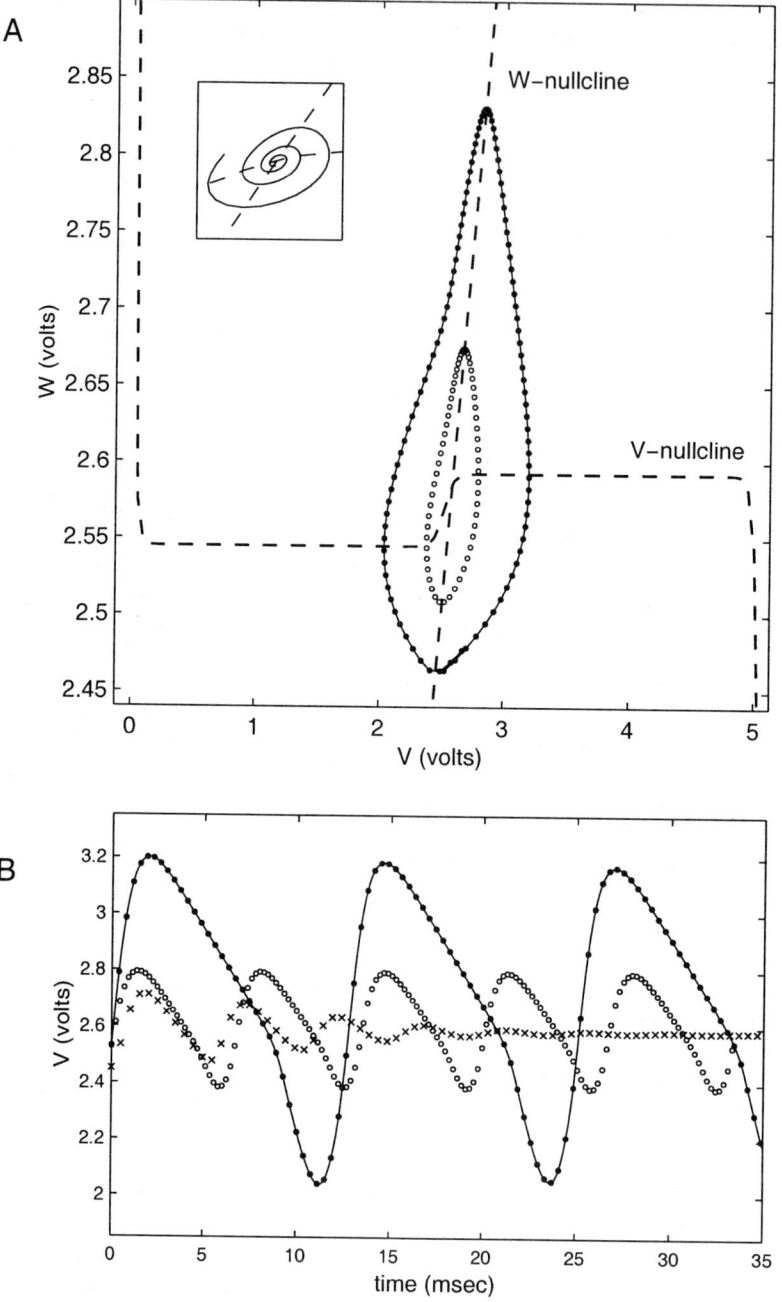

Figure 2: Nullclines and trajectories in the model of the silicon neuron for $I_{ext} = 32$ nA. The system exhibits a stable limit-cycle (filled circles), an unstable limit-cycle (unfilled circles), and stable equilibrium point. Unstable limit-cycle separates the basins of attraction of the stable limit-cycle and stable equilibrium point. Thus, trajectories initiated within the area bounded by the unstable limit-cycle approach the stable equilibrium point (solid line in A's inset, and "x's" in B). Trajectories initiated outside the unstable limit-cycle approach the stable limit-cycle. In A, the inset shows an expansion at the intersection of the V- and W-nullclines.

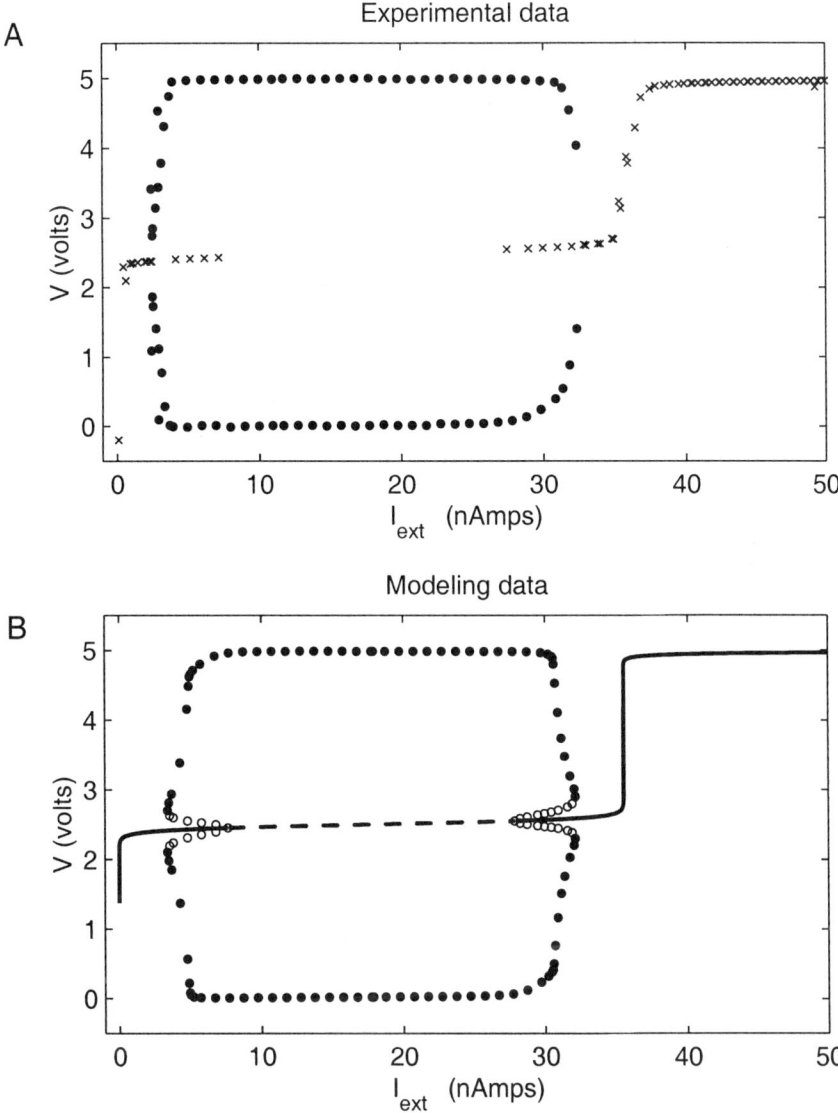

Figure 3: Bifurcation diagrams of the hardware implementation (A) and of the mathematical model (B) under variation of the externally applied current. In A, the steady-state equilibrium potential of V is denoted by "x"s. The maximum and minimum values of V during stable oscillations are denoted by the filled circles. In B, the stable and unstable equilibrium points are denoted by the solid and dashed curve, respectively, and the minimum and maximum values of the stable and unstable oscillations are denoted by the filled and unfilled circles, respectively. In B, limit-cycle oscillations appear and disappear via sub-critical Andronov–Hopf bifurcations. The bifurcation diagram (B) was computed with the LOCBIF program [14].

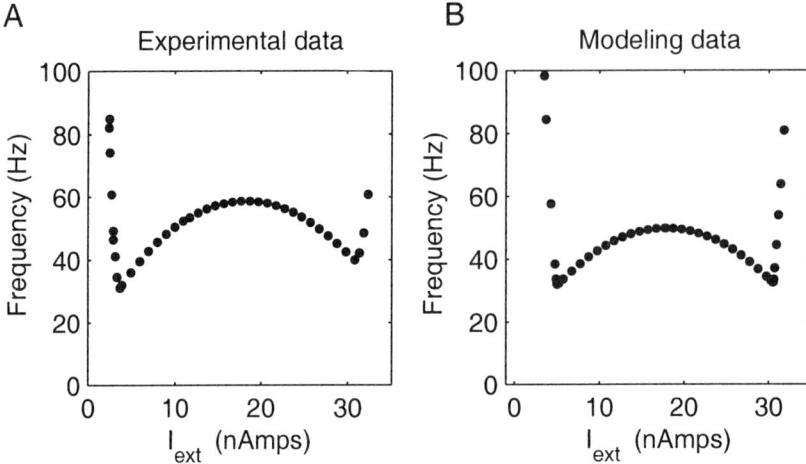

Figure 4: Frequency dependence of the silicon neuron (A) and the mathematical model (B) on the externally applied current.

For moderate values of I_{ext} ([1 nA, 34 nA]), the stable and unstable equilibrium points are close to $(V, W) \approx (V_H, V_L)$ (Figure 3). In experiments in which I_{ext} was varied, we observed a hard loss of the stability of the steady-state equilibrium and a transition into oscillations at $I_{ext} = 7.2$ nA ($I_{ext} = 27.5$ nA). In the mathematical model, at the critical value of $I_{ext} = 7.7$ nA ($I_{ext} = 27.8$ nA), an unstable limit cycle appears via a subcritical Andronov-Hopf bifurcation. This unstable limit cycle merges with the stable limit cycle at the fold bifurcation at $I_{ext} = 3.4$ nA ($I_{ext} = 32.1$ nA). Similarly, in the experiments, we observed hard loss of stability of oscillations at $I_{ext} = 2.0$ nA ($I_{ext} = 32.8$ nA). Thus, the system demonstrates hysteresis. For example, when $I_{ext} = 20$ nA the silicon neuron has only one stable regime, namely, stable oscillations. Then if external current is slowly increased to $I_{ext} = 32.8$ nA, the form of oscillations changes. At this critical value of the current, the oscillations suddenly lose stability, and only steady-state equilibrium is stable. Now, when the external current is reduced, the steady-state equilibrium is observed at the values of the current where oscillations were previously exhibited. Thus, within the ranges of externally applied currents (2.0, 7.2) and (27.5, 32.8), oscillations and a steady-state equilibrium are stable regimes as shown in Figure 2.

4 Discussion

We have developed a two-state silicon neuron and a mathematical model that describes the behavior of this neuron. We have shown experimentally and verified mathematically that this silicon neuron has three regions of operation under the variation of its external current (one of its parameters). We also perform bifurcation analysis of the mathematical model by varying the externally applied current and show that the behaviors exhibited by the silicon neuron under corresponding conditions are in good agreement to those predicted by the bifurcation analysis.

This analysis and comparison to experiment is an important step toward our understanding of a variety of oscillatory hardware networks that we and others are developing. The model facilitates an understanding of the neurons that the hardware alone does not provide. In particular for this neuron, the model allows us to determine the location of the unstable fixed points and the types of bifurcations that are exhibited. In higher-order systems, we expect that the model will provide us insight about observed behaviors and complex bifurcations in the phase space. The good matching between the model and the experimental data described in this paper gives us some confidence that future analysis efforts will prove fruitful.

Acknowledgments

S. DeWeerth and G. Patel are funded by NSF grant IBN-9511721, G.S. Cymbalyuk is supported by Russian Foundation of Fundamental Research grant 99-04-49112, R.L. Calabrese and G.S. Cymbalyuk are supported by NIH grants NS24072 and NS34975.

References

[1] Van Der Pol, B (1939) Biological rhythms considered as relaxation oscillations In H. Bremmer and C.J. Bouwkamp (eds) *Selected Scientific Papers*, Vol 2, North Holland Pub. Co., 1960.

[2] Mead, C.A. *Analog VLSI and Neural Systems*. Addison-Wesley, Reading, MA, 1989.

[3] Simoni, M.F., Patel, G.N., DeWeerth, S.P., & Calabrese, R.L. Analog VLSI model of the leech heartbeat elemental oscillator. Sixth Annual Computational Neuroscience Meeting, 1997. in Big Sky, Montana.

[4] DeWeerth, S., Patel, G., Schimmel, D., Simoni, M. and Calabrese, R. (1997). In *Proceedings of the Seventeenth Conference on Advanced Research in VLSI*, R.B. Brown and A.T. Ishii (eds), Los Alamitos, CA: IEEE Computer Society, 182–200.

[5] Marder, E. & Calabrese, R.L. (1996) Principles of rhythmic motor pattern generation. *Physiological Reviews* **76** (3): 687-717.

[6] Kopell, N. & Ermentrout, B. (1988) Coupled oscillators and the design of central pattern generators. *Mathematical biosciences* 90: 87-109.

[7] Skinner, F.K., Turrigiano, G.G., & Marder, E. (1993) Frequency and burst duration in oscillating neurons and two-cell networks. *Biological Cybernetics* **69**: 375-383.

[8] Skinner, F.K., Gramoll, S., Calabrese, R.L., Kopell, N. & Marder, E. (1994) Frequency control in biological half-center oscillators. In F.H. Eeckman (ed.), *Computation in neurons and neural systems,* pp. 223-228, Boston: Kluwer Academic Publishers.

[9] Patel, G. Holleman, J., DeWeerth, S. Analog VLSI model of intersegmental coordination with nearest-neighbor coupling. In , 1997.

[10] Patel, G. *A neuromorphic architecture for modelling intersegmental coordination.* Ph.D. dissertation, Georgia Institute of Technology, 1999.

[11] J. Guckenheimer and P. Holmes. *Nonlinear Oscillations, Dynamical Systems, and Bifurcation of Vector Fields*. Applied Mathematical Sciences, 42. Springer-Verlag, New York, New York, Heidelberg, Berlin, 1983.

[12] Morris, C. and Lecar, H. (1981) Voltage oscillations in the barnacle giant muscle fiber. *Biophys. J*, 35: 193–213.

[13] Rinzel, J. & Ermentrout, G.B. (1989) Analysis of Neural Excitability and Oscillations. In C. Koch and I. Segev (eds) *Methods in Neuronal Modeling from Synapses to Networks*. MIT press, Cambridge, MA.

[14] Khibnik, A.I., Kuznetsov, Yu.A., Levitin, V.V., Nikolaev, E.V. (1993) Continuation techniques and interactive software for bifurcation analysis of ODEs and iterated maps. *Physica D* **62** (1-4): 360-367.

An Analog VLSI Model of Periodicity Extraction

André van Schaik
Computer Engineering Laboratory
J03, University of Sydney, NSW 2006
Sydney, Australia
andre@ee.usyd.edu.au

Abstract

This paper presents an electronic system that extracts the periodicity of a sound. It uses three analogue VLSI building blocks: a silicon cochlea, two inner-hair-cell circuits and two spiking neuron chips. The silicon cochlea consists of a cascade of filters. Because of the delay between two outputs from the silicon cochlea, spike trains created at these outputs are synchronous only for a narrow range of periodicities. In contrast to traditional band-pass filters, where an increase in selectivity has to be traded off against a decrease in response time, the proposed system responds quickly, independent of selectivity.

1 Introduction

The human ear transduces airborne sounds into a neural signal using three stages in the inner ear's cochlea: (i) the mechanical filtering of the Basilar Membrane (BM), (ii) the transduction of membrane vibration into neurotransmitter release by the Inner Hair Cells (IHCs), and (iii) spike generation by the Spiral Ganglion Cells (SGCs), whose axons form the auditory nerve. The properties of the BM are such that close to the entrance of the cochlea (the base) the BM is most sensitive to high frequencies and at the apex the BM responds best to low frequencies. Along the BM the best-frequency decreases in an exponential manner with distance along the membrane. For frequencies below a given point's best-frequency the response drops off gradually, but for frequencies above the best-frequency the response drops off rapidly (see Fig. 1b for examples of such frequency-gain functions).

An Inner Hair Cell senses the local vibration of a section of the Basilar Membrane. The intracellular voltage of an IHC resembles a half-wave-rectified version of the local BM vibration, low-pass filtered at 1 kHz. The IHC voltage has therefore lost it's AC component almost completely for frequencies above about 4 kHz. Well below this frequency, however, the IHC voltage has a clear temporal structure, which will be reflected in the spike trains on the auditory nerve.

These spike trains are generated by the spiral ganglion cells. These SGCs spike with a probability roughly proportional to the instantaneous inner hair cell voltage. Therefore, for the lower sound frequencies, the spectrum of the input waveform is not only encoded in the form of an average spiking rate of different fibers along the cochlea (place coding), but also in the periodicity of spiking of the individual auditory nerve fibers. It has been shown that this periodicity information is a much more robust cue than the spatial distribution of average firing rates [1]. Some periodicity information can already be detected at intensities 20 dB below the intensity needed to obtain a change in average rate. Periodicity information is retained at intensities in the range of 60-90 dB SPL, for which the average rate of the majority of the auditory nerve fibers is saturated. Moreover, the positions of the fibers responding best to a given frequency move with changing sound intensity, whereas the periodicity information remains constant. Furthermore, the frequency selectivity of a given fiber's spiking rate is drastically reduced at medium and high sound intensities. The robustness of periodicity information makes it likely that the brain actually uses this information.

2 Modelling periodicity extraction

Several models have been proposed that extract periodicity information using the phase encoding of fibers connected to the same inner hair cell or that use the synchronicity of firing on auditory nerve fibers connected to different inner hair cells (see [2] for 4 examples of these models). The simplest of the phase encoding schemes correlate the output of the cochlea at a given position with a delayed version of itself. It is easy to see that for pure tones, the comparison $sin(2 \pi f t) = sin(2 \pi f (t - \Delta))$ is only true for frequencies that are a multiple of $1/\Delta$, i.e., for these frequencies the signals are in perfect synchrony and thus perfectly correlated. We can adapt the delay Δ to each cochlear output, so that $1/\Delta$ equals the best frequency of that cochlear output. In this case higher multiples of $1/\Delta$ will be suppressed due to the very steep cut-off of the cochlear filters for frequencies above the best frequency. Each synchronicity detector will then only be sensitive to the best frequency of the filter to which it is connected. If we code the direct signal and the delayed signal with two spike trains, with one spike per period at a fixed phase each, it becomes a very simple operation to detect the synchronicity. A simple digital AND operator will be enough to detect overlap between two spikes. These spikes will overlap perfectly when $f = 1/\Delta$, but some overlap will still be present for frequencies close to $1/\Delta$, since the spikes have a finite width. The bandwidth of the AND output can thus be controlled by the spike width.

It is possible to create a silicon implementation of this scheme using an artificial cochlea, an IHC circuit, and a spiking neuron circuit together with additional circuits to create the delays. A chip along these lines has been developed by John Lazzaro [3] and functioned correctly. A disadvantage of this scheme, however, is the fact that the delay associated with a cochlear output has to be matched to the inverse of the best frequency of that cochlear output. For a cochlea whose best frequency changes exponentially with filter number in the cascade from 4 kHz (the upper range of phase locking on the auditory nerve) to 100 Hz, we will have to create delays that range from 0.25 ms to 10 ms. In the brain, such a large variation in delays is unlikely to be provided by an axonal delay circuit because it would require an excessively large variation in axon length.

A possible solution comes from the observation that the phase of a pure tone of a given frequency on the basilar membrane increases from base to apex, and the phase changes rapidly around the best frequency. The silicon cochlea, which is implemented with a cascade of second-order low-pass filters (Fig. 1a), also functions as a delay line, and each filter adds a delay which corresponds to $\pi/2$ at the cut-off frequency of that filter. If we assume that filter i and filter i-4 have the same cut-off frequency (which is not the case), the delay between the output of both filters will correspond to a full period (2π) at the cut-off frequency.

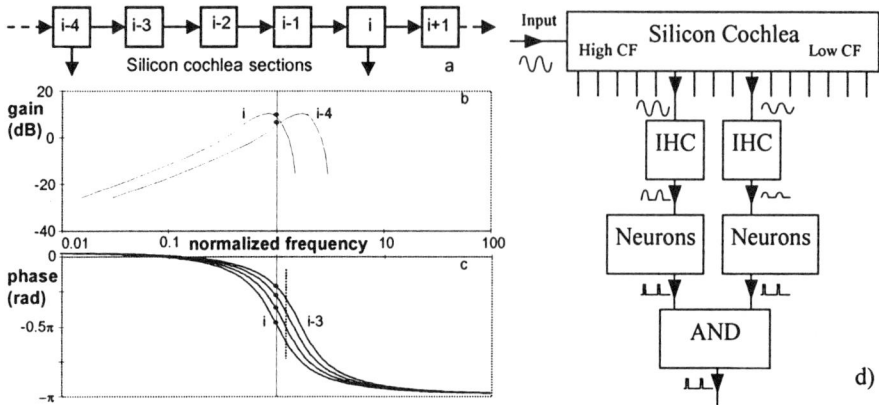

Figure 1: a) Part of a silicon cochlea. Each section contains a second-order low-pass filter and a derivator; b) accumulated gain at output i and i-4; c) phase curves of the individual stages between output i and output i-4; d) proposed implementation of the periodicity extraction model.

In reality, the filters along the cochlea will have different cut-off frequencies, as shown in Fig. 1. Here we show the *accumulated* gain at the outputs i and i-4 (Fig. 1b), and the delay added by each *individual* filter between these two outputs (Fig. 1c) as a function of frequency (normalized to the cut-off frequency of filter i). The solid vertical line represents this cut-off frequency, and we can see that only filter i adds a delay of $\pi/2$, and the other filters add less. However, if we move the vertical line to the right (indicated by the dotted vertical line), the delay added by each filter will increase relatively quickly, and at some frequency slightly higher than the cut-off frequency of filter i, the sum of the delays will become 2π (dashed line). At this frequency neither filter i nor filter i-4 has maximum gain, but if the cut-off frequency of both filters is not too different, the gain will still be high enough for both filters at the correlator frequency to yield output signals with reasonable amplitudes.

The improved model can be implemented using building blocks as shown in Fig. 1d. Each of these building blocks have previously been presented (refer to [4] for additional details). The silicon cochlea is used to filter and delay the signal, and has been adjusted so that the cut-off frequency decreases by one octave every twenty stages, so that the cut-off frequencies of neighboring filters are almost equal. The IHC circuit half-wave rectifies the signal in the implementation of Figure 1d. The low-pass filtering of the biological Inner Hair Cell can be ignored for frequencies below the approximately 1kHz cut-off frequency of the cell. Since we limited our measurements to this range, the low-pass filtering has not been modeled by the circuit. Two chips containing electronic leaky-integrate-and-fire neurons have been used to create the two spike trains. In the first series of measurements, each chip generates exactly one spike per period of the input signal. A final test will set the 32 neurons on each chip to behave more like biological spiral ganglion cells and the effect on periodicity extraction will be shown. A digital AND gate is used to compare the output spikes of the two chips, and the spike rate at the output of the AND gate is the measure of activity used.

3 Test results

The first experiment measures the number of spikes per second at the output of the AND gate as a function of input frequency, using different cochlear filter combinations. Twelve filter pairs have been measured, each combining a filter output with the output of a filter four sections earlier in the cascade. The best frequency of the filter with the lowest best frequency of the pairs ranged from 200 Hz to 880 Hz. The results are shown in Fig. 2a.

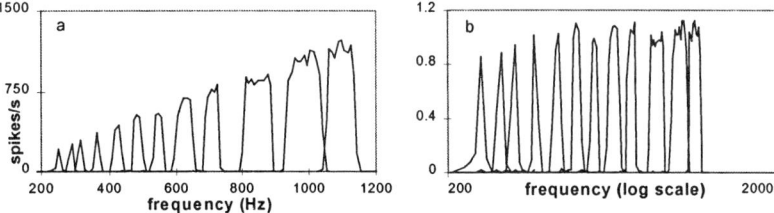

Figure 2: a) measured output rate at different cochlear positions, and b) spike rate normalized to best input frequency, plotted on a log frequency scale.

The maximum spike rate increases approximately linearly with frequency; this is to be expected, since we will have approximately one spike per signal period. Furthermore the best response frequencies of the filters sensitive to higher frequencies are further apart, due to the exponential scaling of the frequencies along the cochlea. Finally, a given time delay corresponds to a larger phase delay for the higher frequencies, so that the absolute bandwidth of the coincidence detectors, i.e., the range of input frequencies to which they respond, is larger. When we normalize the spike rate and plot the curves on a logarithmic frequency scale, as in Fig. 2b, we see that the best frequencies of the correlators follow the exponential scaling of the best frequencies of the cochlear filters, and that the relative bandwidth is fairly constant.

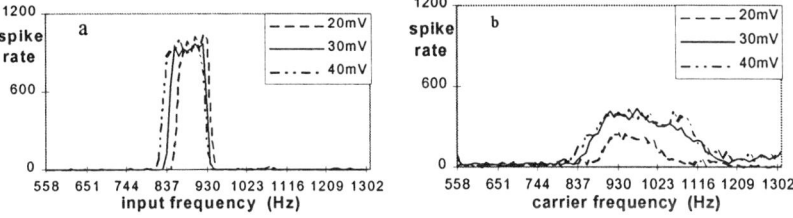

Figure 3: Frequency selectivity for different input intensities. a) pure tones b) AM signals.

Using the same settings as in the previous experiment, the output spike rate of the system for different input amplitudes has been measured, using the cochlear filter pair with best frequencies of 710 Hz and 810 Hz. In principle, the amplitude of the input signal should have no effect on the output of the system, since the system only uses phase information. However, this is only true if the spikes are always created at the same phase of the output signal of the cochlear filters, for instance at the peak, or the zero crossing. Fig. 3 shows however that the resulting filter selectivity shifts to lower frequencies for higher intensity input signals.

This is a result of the way the spikes are created on the neuron chip. The neurons have been adjusted to spike once per period, but the phase at which they spike with respect to the half-wave-rectified waveform depends on the integration time of the neuron, which is the time needed with a given input current to reach the spike threshold voltage from the zero resting voltage. This time depends on the amplitude of the input current, which in turn is proportional to the amplitude of the input signal. Since the amplitude gain of the two cochlear filters used is not the same, the amplitude of the current input to the two neuron chips is different. Therefore, they do not spike at the same phase with respect to their respective input waveforms. This causes the frequency selectivity of the system to shift to lower frequencies with increasing intensity. However, this is an artifact of the spike generation used to simplify the system. On the auditory nerve, spikes arrive with a probability roughly proportional to the half-wave rectified waveform. The most probable phase for a spike is therefore always at the maximum of the waveform, independent of intensity. In such a system, the frequency selectivity will therefore be independent of amplitude. A second advantage of coding (at least half of) the waveform in spike probability is that it does not assume that the input waveform is sinusoidal. Coding a waveform with just one spike per period can only code the frequency and phase of the waveform, but not its shape. A square wave and a sine wave would both yield the same spike train. We will discuss the "auditory-nerve-like" coding at the end of this section.

To test the model with a more complex waveform, a 930 Hz sine wave 100% amplitude-modulated at 200 Hz generated on a computer has been used. The carrier frequency was varied by playing the whole waveform a certain percentage slower or faster. Therefore the actual modulation frequency changes with the same factor as the carrier frequency. The results of this test are shown in Fig. 3b for three different input amplitudes. Compared to the measurements in Fig. 3a, we see that the filter is less selective and centered at a higher input frequency. The shift towards a higher frequency can be explained by the fact that the average amplitude of a half-wave rectified amplitude modulated signal is lower than in for a half-wave rectified pure tone with the same maximum amplitude. Furthermore, the amplitude of the positive half-cycle of the output of the IHC circuit changes from cycle to cycle because of the amplitude modulation. We have seen that the amplitude of the input signal changes the frequency for which the two spike trains are synchronous, which means that the frequency which yields the best response changes from cycle to cycle with a periodicity equal to the modulation frequency. This introduces a sort of "roaming" of the frequencies in the input signal, effectively reducing the selectivity of the filters. Finally, because of the 100% depth of the amplitude modulation, the amplitude of the input will be too low during some cycles to create a spike, which therefore reduces the total number of spikes which can coincide.

Fig. 3b shows that this model detects periodicity and not spectral content. The spectrum of a 930 Hz pure tone 100% amplitude modulated at 200 Hz contains, apart from a 930 Hz carrier component, components both at 730 Hz and 1130 Hz, with half the amplitude of the carrier component. When the speed of the waveform playback is varied so that the carrier frequency is either 765 Hz or 1185 Hz, one of these spectral side bands will be at 930 Hz, but the system does not respond at these carrier frequencies. This is explained by the fact that the periodicity of the zero crossings, and thus of the positive half cycles of the IHC output, is always equal to the carrier frequency.

Traditional band-pass filters with a very high quality factor (Q) can also yield a narrow pass-band, but their step response takes about 1.5Q cycles at the center frequency to reach steady state. The periodicity selectivity of the synchronicity detector shown in Fig. 3a corresponds to a quality factor of 14; a traditional band-pass filter would take about 21 cycles of the 930Hz input signal to reach 95% of it's final output value. Fig. 4 shows the temporal aspect of the synchronicity detection in our system. The top trace in this figure shows the output of the cochlear filter with the highest best frequency (index i-4 in Fig. 1) and the spikes generated based on this output. The second trace shows the same for the output of the cochlear filter with the lower best frequency (index i in Fig. 1). The third trace shows the output of the AND gate with the above inputs, which are slightly above its best periodicity. Coincidences are detected at the onset of the tone, even when it is not of the correct periodicity, but only for the first one or two cycles. The bottom trace shows the output of the AND gate for an input at best frequency. The system thus responds to the presence of a pure tone of the correct periodicity after only a few cycles, independent of the filters selectivity.

An Analog VLSI Model of Periodicity Extraction

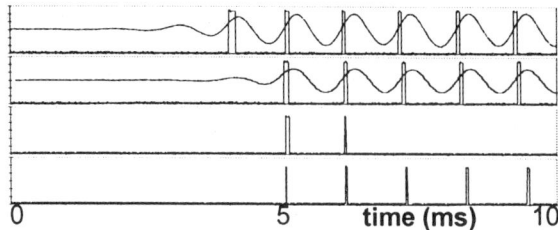

Figure 4: Oscilloscope traces of the temporal aspect of synchronicity detection. The vertical scale is 20mV per square for the cochlear outputs, the spikes are 5V in amplitude.

To show this more dramatically, we have reduced the spike width to 10 µs, to obtain a high periodicity selectivity as shown in Fig. 5a. The bandwidth of this filter is only 20 Hz at 930 Hz, equivalent to a quality factor of 46.5. A traditional filter with such a quality factor would only settle 70 cycles after the onset of the signal, whereas the periodicity detector still settles after the first few cycles, as shown in Fig. 5b. We can compare this result with the response of a classic RLC band-pass filter with a 930 Hz center frequency and a quality factor of 46.5 as shown in Fig. 6. After 18 cycles of the input signal, the output of the band-pass filter has only reached 65% of its final value. Thresholding the RLC output could signal the presence of a periodicity faster, but it would then still respond very slowly to the offset of the tone as the RLC filter will continue ringing after the offset.

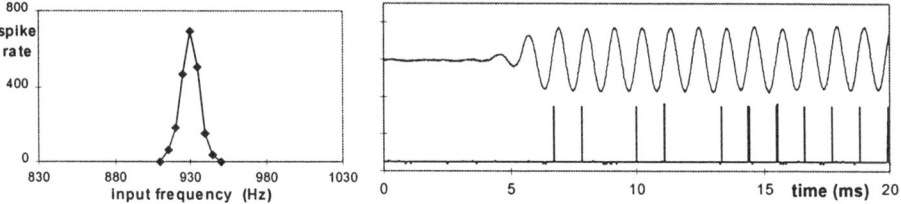

Figure 5: a) Frequency selectivity with a 10µs spike width. b) Cochlear output (top, 40 mV scale) and coincidences (bottom) for a signal at best frequency.

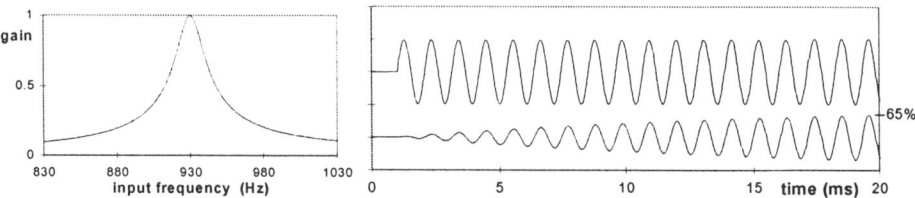

Figure 6: Simulated response of the RLC band-pass filter. a) frequency selectivity, b) transient response (scale units are 40 mV).

In the previous experiments we simplified the model to use one spike per period in order to understand the principle behind the periodicity detection. However, we have seen that this implementation leads to a shift in best periodicity with changing amplitude, because the phase at which the 'single neuron' spikes changes with intensity. Now, we will change the settings to be more realistic, so that each of the 32 neurons cannot spike at every period, and we will reduce the output gain of the IHC circuit so that the neurons receive less signal current, and thus have a lower input SNR. The resulting spike distribution is a better simulation of the spike distribution on the auditory nerve. This is shown in Fig. 7 for a group of 32 neurons stimulated by and IHC circuit connected to a single cochlear output. The bottom trace shows the sum of spikes over the 32 neurons on an arbitrary scale. When we use this spike distribution and repeat the pure-tone detection experiment of Fig. 3a at different input intensities, we obtain the curve of Fig. 7b. Indeed, in this case, the best periodicity does not change; the curves are remarkably independent of input intensity. However, the selectivity curve is about twice as wide at the base as the ones in Fig. 3a, but the slopes of the selectivity curve rise and fall much more gradually. This means that we can easily increase the selectivity of these curves by setting a higher threshold, e.g., discarding spike rates below 70 spikes per second. Because of the steep slopes in Fig. 3a such an operation would hardly increase the selectivity for that case.

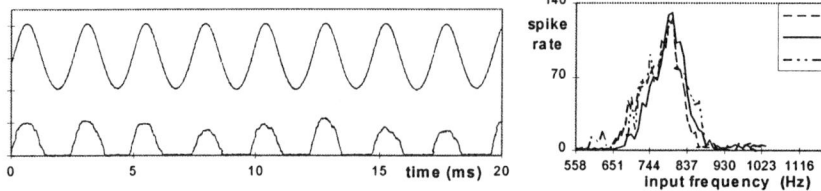

Figure 7: a) Cochlear output (top) and population average of the auditory nerve spikes (bottom); b) periodicity selectivity with auditory nerve like spike distribution.

4 Conclusions

In this paper we have presented a neural system for periodicity detection implemented with three analogue VLSI building blocks. The system uses the delay between the outputs at two points along the cochlea and synchronicity of the spike trains created from these cochlear outputs to detect the periodicity of the input signal. An especially useful property of the cochlea is that the delay between two points a fixed distance apart corresponds to a full period at a frequency that scales in the same way as the best frequency along the cochlea, i.e., decreases exponentially.

If we always create spikes at the same phase of the output signal at each filter, or simply have the highest spiking probability for the maximum instantaneous amplitude of the output signal, then both outputs will only have synchronous spikes for a certain periodicity, and we can easily detect this synchronicity with coincidence detectors. This system offers a way to obtain very selective filters using spikes. Even though they react to a very narrow range of periodicities, these filters are able to react after only a few periods. Furthermore, the range of periodicities it responds to can be made independent of input intensity, which is not the case with the cochlear output itself. This clearly demonstrates the advantages of using spikes in the detection of periodicity.

Acknowledgements

The author thanks Eric Fragnière, Eric Vittoz and the Swiss NSF for their support.

References

[1] Evans, "Functional anatomy of the auditory system," in Barlow and Mollon (editors), *The Senses*, Cambridge University Press, pp. 251-306, 1982.

[2] Seneff, Shamma, Deng, & Ghitza, *Journal of Phonetics*, Vol. 16, pp. 55-123, 1988.

[3] Lazzaro, "A silicon model of an auditory neural representation of spectral shape." *IEEE Journal of Solid-State Circuits*, Vol. 26, No. 5, pp. 772-777, 1991.

[4] van Schaik, "An Analogue VLSI Model of Periodicity Extraction in the Human Auditory System," to appear in *Analog Integrated Circuits and Signal Processing*, Kluwer, 2000.

PART VI
SPEECH, HANDWRITING AND SIGNAL PROCESSING

An Oscillatory Correlation Framework for Computational Auditory Scene Analysis

Guy J. Brown
Department of Computer Science
University of Sheffield
Regent Court, 211 Portobello Street,
Sheffield S1 4DP, UK
Email: g.brown@dcs.shef.ac.uk

DeLiang L. Wang
Department of Computer and Information
Science and Centre for Cognitive Science
The Ohio State University
Columbus, OH 43210-1277, USA
Email: dwang@cis.ohio-state.edu

Abstract

A neural model is described which uses oscillatory correlation to segregate speech from interfering sound sources. The core of the model is a two-layer neural oscillator network. A sound stream is represented by a synchronized population of oscillators, and different streams are represented by desynchronized oscillator populations. The model has been evaluated using a corpus of speech mixed with interfering sounds, and produces an improvement in signal-to-noise ratio for every mixture.

1 Introduction

Speech is seldom heard in isolation: usually, it is mixed with other environmental sounds. Hence, the auditory system must parse the acoustic mixture reaching the ears in order to retrieve a description of each sound source, a process termed *auditory scene analysis* (ASA) [2]. Conceptually, ASA may be regarded as a two-stage process. The first stage (which we term 'segmentation') decomposes the acoustic stimulus into a collection of sensory elements. In the second stage ('grouping'), elements that are likely to have arisen from the same environmental event are combined into a perceptual structure called a *stream*. Streams may be further interpreted by higher-level cognitive processes.

Recently, there has been a growing interest in the development of computational systems that mimic ASA [4], [1], [5]. Such computational auditory scene analysis (CASA) systems are inspired by auditory function but do not model it closely; rather, they employ symbolic search or high-level inference engines. Although the performance of these systems is encouraging, they are no match for the abilities of a human listener; also, they tend to be complex and computationally intensive. In short, CASA currently remains an unsolved problem for real-time applications such as automatic speech recognition.

Given that human listeners can segregate concurrent sounds with apparent ease, computational systems that are more closely modelled on the neurobiological mechanisms of hearing may offer a performance advantage over existing CASA systems. This observation – together with a desire to understand the neurobiological basis of ASA – has led some investigators to propose neural network models of ASA. Most recently, Brown and Wang [3] have given an account of concurrent vowel separation based on *oscillatory correlation*. In this framework, oscillators that represent a perceptual stream are synchronized (phase locked with zero phase lag), and are desynchronized from oscillators that represent different streams [8]. Evidence for the oscillatory correlation theory comes from neurobiological studies which report synchronised oscillations in the auditory, visual and olfactory cortices (see [10] for a review).

In this paper, we propose a neural network model that uses oscillatory correlation as the underlying neural mechanism for ASA; streams are formed by synchronizing oscillators in a two-dimensional time-frequency network. The model is evaluated on a task that involves the separation of two time-varying sounds. It therefore extends our previous study [3], which only considered the segregation of vowel sounds with static spectra.

2 Model description

The input to the model consists of a mixture of speech and an interfering sound source, sampled at a rate of 16 kHz with 16 bit resolution. This input signal is processed in four stages described below (see [10] for a detailed account).

2.1 Peripheral auditory processing

Peripheral auditory frequency selectivity is modelled using a bank of 128 gammatone filters with center frequencies equally distributed on the equivalent rectangular bandwidth (ERB) scale between 80 Hz and 5 kHz [1]. Subsequently, the output of each filter is processed by a model of inner hair cell function. The output of the hair cell model is a probabilistic representation of auditory nerve firing activity.

2.2 Mid-level auditory representations

Mechanisms similar to those underlying pitch perception can contribute to the perceptual separation of sounds that have different fundamental frequencies (F0s) [3]. Accordingly, the second stage of the model extracts periodicity information from the simulated auditory nerve firing patterns. This is achieved by computing a running autocorrelation of the auditory nerve activity in each channel, forming a representation known as a *correlogram* [1], [5]. At time step j, the autocorrelation $A(i,j,\tau)$ for channel i with time lag τ is given by:

$$A(i, j, \tau) = \sum_{k=0}^{K-1} r(i, j-k) r(i, j-k-\tau) w(k) \quad (1)$$

Here, r is the output of the hair cell model and w is a rectangular window of width K time steps. We use $K = 320$, corresponding to a window width of 20 ms. The autocorrelation lag τ is computed in L steps of the sampling period between 0 and L-1; we use $L = 201$, corresponding to a maximum delay of 12.5 ms. Equation (1) is computed for M time frames, taken at 10 ms intervals (i.e., at intervals of 160 steps of the time index j).

For periodic sounds, a characteristic 'spine' appears in the correlogram which is centered on the lag corresponding to the stimulus period (Figure 1A). This pitch-related structure can be emphasized by forming a 'pooled' correlogram $s(j,\tau)$, which exhibits a prominent peak at the delay corresponding to perceived pitch:

$$s(j, \tau) = \sum_{i=1}^{N} A(i, j, \tau) \quad (2)$$

It is also possible to extract harmonics and formants from the correlogram, since frequency channels that are excited by the same acoustic component share a similar pattern of periodicity. Bands of coherent periodicity can be identified by cross-correlating adjacent correlogram channels; regions of high correlation indicate a harmonic or formant [1]. The cross-correlation $C(i,j)$ between channels i and $i+1$ at time frame j is defined as:

$$C(i, j) = \frac{1}{L} \sum_{\tau=0}^{L-1} \hat{A}(i, j, \tau) \hat{A}(i+1, j, \tau) \quad (1 \leq i \leq N-1) \quad (3)$$

Here, $\hat{A}(i, j, \tau)$ is the autocorrelation function of (1) which has been normalized to have zero mean and unity variance. A typical cross-correlation function is shown in Figure 1A.

2.3 Neural oscillator network: overview

Segmentation and grouping take place within a two-layer oscillator network (Figure 1B). The basic unit of the network is a single oscillator, which is defined as a reciprocally connected excitatory variable x and inhibitory variable y [7]. Since each layer of the network takes the form of a time-frequency grid, we index each oscillator according to its frequency channel (i) and time frame (j):

$$\dot{x}_{ij} = 3x_{ij} - x_{ij}^3 + 2 - y_{ij} + I_{ij} + S_{ij} + \rho \qquad (4a)$$

$$\dot{y}_{ij} = \varepsilon(\gamma(1 + \tanh(x_{ij}/\beta)) - y_{ij}) \qquad (4b)$$

Here, I_{ij} represents external input to the oscillator, S_{ij} denotes the coupling from other oscillators in the network, ε, γ and β are parameters, and ρ is the amplitude of a Gaussian noise term. If coupling and noise are ignored and I_{ij} is held constant, (4) defines a relaxation oscillator with two time scales. The x-nullcline, i.e. $\dot{x}_{ij} = 0$, is a cubic function and the y-nullcline is a sigmoid function. If $I_{ij} > 0$, the two nullclines intersect only at a point along the middle branch of the cubic with β chosen small. In this case, the oscillator exhibits a stable limit cycle for small values of ε, and is referred to as *enabled*. The limit cycle alternates between *silent* and *active* phases of near steady-state behaviour. Compared to motion within each phase, the alternation between phases takes place rapidly, and is referred to as *jumping*. If $I_{ij} < 0$, the two nullclines intersect at a stable fixed point. In this case, no oscillation occurs. Hence, oscillations in (4) are stimulus-dependent.

2.4 Neural oscillator network: segment layer

In the first layer of the network, *segments* are formed – blocks of synchronised oscillators that trace the evolution of an acoustic component through time and frequency. The first layer is a two-dimensional time-frequency grid of oscillators with a global inhibitor (see Figure 1B). The coupling term S_{ij} in (4a) is defined as

$$S_{ij} = \sum_{kl \in N(i,j)} W_{ij,kl} H(x_{kl} - \theta_x) - W_z H(z - \theta_z) \qquad (5)$$

where H is the Heaviside function (i.e., $H(x) = 1$ for $x \geq 0$, and zero otherwise), $W_{ij,kl}$ is the connection weight from an oscillator (i,j) to an oscillator (k,l) and $N(i,j)$ is the four nearest neighbors of (i,j). The threshold θ_x is chosen so that an oscillator has no influence on its

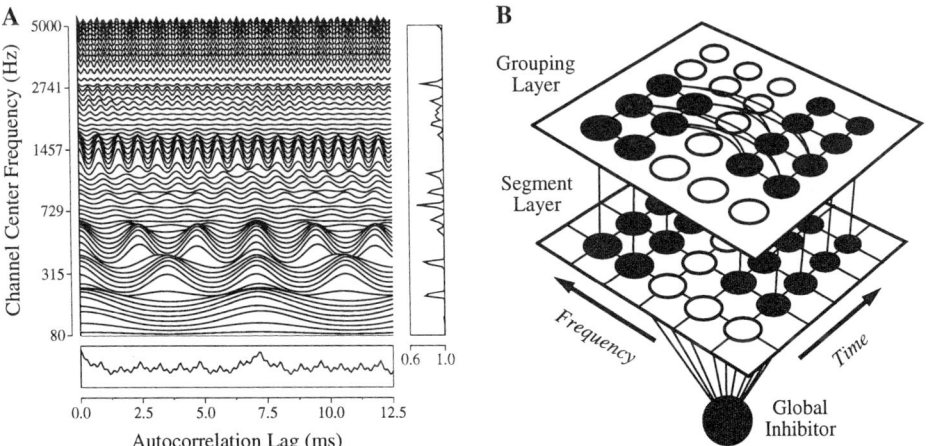

Figure 1: A. Correlogram of a mixture of speech and trill telephone, taken 450 ms after the start of the stimulus. The pooled correlogram is shown in the bottom panel, and the cross-correlation function is shown on the right. B. Structure of the two-layer oscillator network.

neighbors unless it is in the active phase. The weight of neighboring connections along the time axis is uniformly set to 1. The connection weight between an oscillator (i,j) and its vertical neighbor $(i+1,j)$ is set to 1 if $C(i,j)$ exceeds a threshold θ_c; otherwise it is set to 0. W_z is the weight of inhibition from the global inhibitor z, defined as

$$\dot{z} = \sigma_\infty - z \qquad (6)$$

where $\sigma_\infty = 1$ if $x_{ij} \geq \theta_z$ for at least one oscillator (i,j), and $\sigma_\infty = 0$ otherwise. Hence θ_z is a threshold. If $\sigma_\infty = 1$, $z \to 1$.

Small segments may form which do not correspond to perceptually significant acoustic components. In order to remove these noisy fragments, we introduce a lateral potential p_{ij} for oscillator (i,j), defined as [11]:

$$\dot{p}_{ij} = (1 - p_{ij}) H \left[\sum_{kl \in N_p(i,j)} H(x_{kl} - \theta_x) - \theta_p \right] - \varepsilon p_{ij} \qquad (7)$$

Here, θ_p is a threshold. $N_p(i,j)$ is called the potential neighborhood of (i,j), which is chosen to be $(i,j-1)$ and $(i,j+1)$. If both neighbors of (i,j) are active, p_{ij} approaches 1 on a fast time scale; otherwise, p_{ij} relaxes to 0 on a slow time scale determined by ε.

The lateral potential plays its role by gating the input to an oscillator. More specifically, we replace (4a) with

$$\dot{x}_{ij} = 3x_{ij} - x_{ij}^3 + 2 - y_{ij} + I_{ij} H(p_{ij} - \theta) + S_{ij} + \rho \qquad (4a')$$

With p_{ij} initialized to 1, it follows that p_{ij} will drop below the threshold θ unless the oscillator (i,j) receives excitation from its entire potential neighborhood. Given our choice of neighborhood in (5), this implies that a segment must extend for at least three consecutive time frames. Oscillators that are stimulated but cannot maintain a high potential are relegated to a discontiguous 'background' of noisy activity.

An oscillator (i,j) is stimulated if its corresponding input $I_{ij} > 0$. Oscillators are stimulated only if the energy in their corresponding correlogram channel exceeds a threshold θ_a. It is evident from (1) that the energy in a correlogram channel i at time j corresponds to $A(i,j,0)$; thus we set $I_{ij} = 0.2$ if $A(i,j,0) > \theta_a$, and $I_{ij} = -5$ otherwise.

Figure 2A shows the segmentation of a mixture of speech and trill telephone. The network was simulated by the LEGION algorithm [8], producing 94 segments (each represented by a distinct gray level) plus the background (shown in black). For convenience we show all segments together in Figure 2A, but each actually arises during a unique time interval.

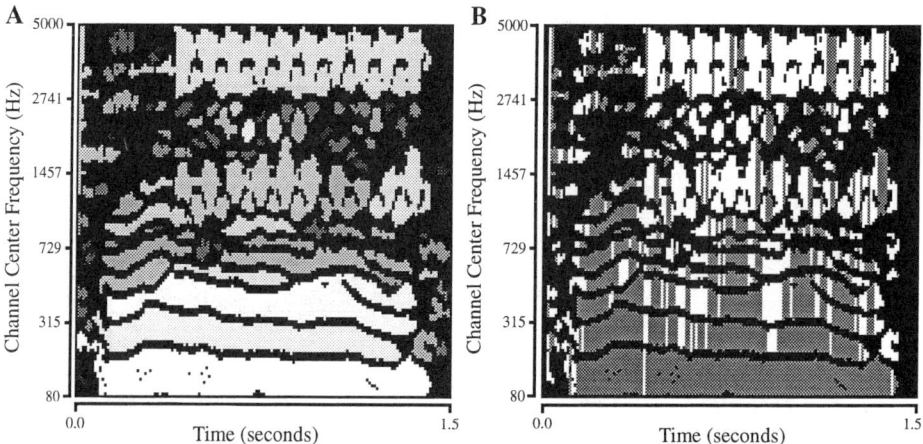

Figure 2: A. Segments formed by the first layer of the network for a mixture of speech and trill telephone. B. Categorization of segments according to F0. Gray pixels represent the set P, and white pixels represent regions that do not agree with the F0.

2.5 Neural oscillator network: grouping layer

The second layer is a two-dimensional network of laterally coupled oscillators without global inhibition. Oscillators in this layer are stimulated if the corresponding oscillator in the first layer is stimulated and does not form part of the background. Initially, all oscillators have the same phase, implying that all segments from the first layer are allocated to the same stream. This initialization is consistent with psychophysical evidence suggesting that perceptual fusion is the default state of auditory organisation [2]. In the second layer, an oscillator has the same form as in (4), except that x_{ij} is changed to:

$$\dot{x}_{ij} = 3x_{ij} - x_{ij}^3 + 2 - y_{ij} + I_{ij}[1 + \mu H(p_{ij} - \theta)] + S_{ij} + \rho \tag{4a''}$$

Here, μ is a small positive parameter; this implies that an oscillator with a high lateral potential gets a slightly higher external input. We choose $N_p(i,j)$ and θ_p so that oscillators which correspond to the longest segment from the first layer are the first to jump to the active phase. The longest segment is identified by using the mechanism described in [9].

The coupling term in (4a'') consists of two types of coupling:

$$S_{ij} = S_{ij}^e + S_{ij}^v \tag{8}$$

Here, S_{ij}^e represents mutual excitation between oscillators within each segment. We set $S_{ij}^e = 4$ if the active oscillators from the same segment occupy more than half of the length of the segment; otherwise $S_{ij}^e = 0.1$ if there is at least one active oscillator from the same segment.

The coupling term S_{ij}^v denotes vertical connections between oscillators corresponding to different frequency channels and different segments, but within the same time frame. At each time frame, an F0 is estimated from the pooled correlogram (2) and this is used to classify frequency channels into two categories: a set of channels, P, that are consistent with the F0, and a set of channels that are not (Figure 2B). Given the delay τ_m at which the largest peak occurs in the pooled correlogram, for each channel i at time frame j, $i \in P$ if

$$A(i, j, \tau_m) / A(i, j, 0) > \theta_d \tag{9}$$

Since $A(i,j,0)$ is the energy in correlogram channel i at time j, (9) amounts to classification on the basis of an energy threshold. We use $\theta_d = 0.95$. The delay τ_m can be found by using a winner-take-all network, although for simplicity we currently apply a maximum selector.

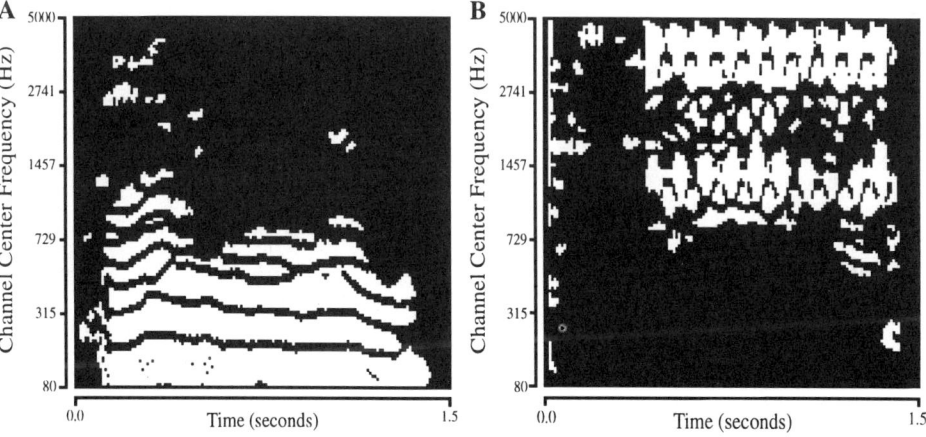

Figure 3: A. Snapshot showing the activity of the second layer shortly after the start of simulation. Active oscillators (white pixels) correspond to the speech stream. B. Another snapshot, taken shortly after A. Active oscillators correspond to the telephone stream.

The F0 classification process operates on channels, rather than segments. As a result, channels within the same segment at a particular time frame may be allocated to different F0 categories. Since segments cannot be decomposed, we enforce a rule that all channels of the same frame within each segment must belong to the same F0 category as that of the majority of channels. After this conformational step, vertical connections are formed such that, at each time frame, two oscillators of different segments have mutual excitatory links if the two corresponding channels belong to the same F0 category; otherwise they have mutual inhibitory links. S_{ij}^v is set to -0.5 if (i,j) receives an input from its inhibitory links; similarly, S_{ij}^v is set to 0.5 if (i,j) receives an input from its vertical excitatory links.

At present, our model has no mechanism for grouping segments that do not overlap in time. Accordingly, we limit operation of the second layer to the time span of the longest segment. After forming lateral connections and trimming by the longest segment, the network is numerically solved using the singular limit method [6].

Figure 3 shows the response of the second layer to the mixture of speech and trill telephone. The figure shows two snapshots of the second layer, where a white pixel indicates an active oscillator and a black pixel indicates a silent oscillator. The network quickly forms two synchronous blocks, which desynchronize from each other. Figure 3A shows a snapshot taken when the oscillator block (stream) corresponding to the segregated speech is in the active phase; Figure 3B shows a subsequent snapshot when the oscillator block corresponding to the trill telephone is in the active phase. Hence, the activity in this layer of the network embodies the result of ASA; the components of an acoustic mixture have been separated using F0 information and represented by oscillatory correlation.

2.6 Resynthesis

The last stage of the model is a resynthesis path. Phase-corrected output from the gammatone filterbank is divided into 20 ms sections, overlapping by 10 ms and windowed with a raised cosine. A weighting is then applied to each section, which is unity if the corresponding oscillator is in its active phase, and zero otherwise. The weighted filter outputs are summed across all channels to yield a resynthesized waveform.

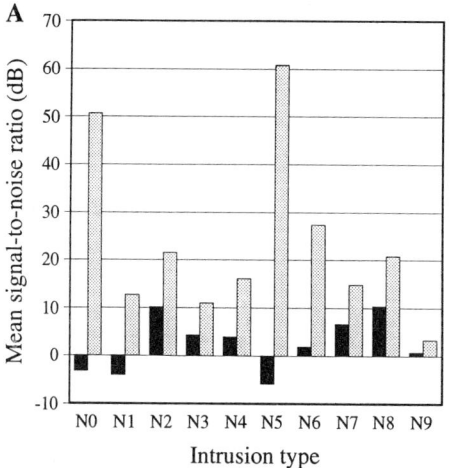
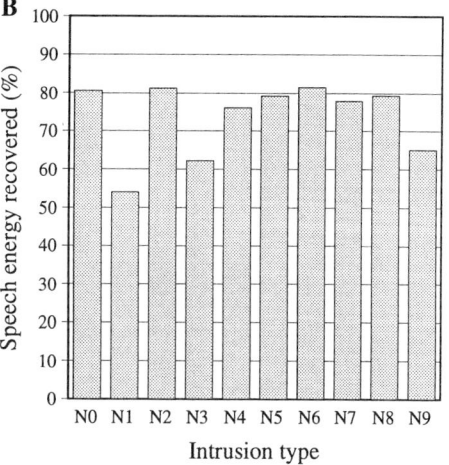

Figure 4: A. SNR before (black bar) and after (grey bar) separation by the model. Results are shown for voiced speech mixed with ten intrusions (N0 = 1 kHz tone; N1 = random noise; N2 = noise bursts; N3 = 'cocktail party' noise; N4 = rock music; N5 = siren; N6 = trill telephone; N7 = female speech; N8 = male speech; N9 = female speech). B. Percentage of speech energy recovered from each mixture after separation by the model.

3 Evaluation

The model has been evaluated using 100 mixtures of speech and noise [4]. The mixtures are obtained by adding the waveforms of ten voiced utterances to each of ten intrusive sounds. Since separate speech and noise waveforms are available, a signal-to-noise ratio (SNR) can be computed for each mixture. Also, the SNR can be estimated after processing by the model using separated speech and noise waveforms from the resynthesis path [10].

The SNR before and after separation by the model is shown in Figure 4A, averaged across the ten utterances for each noise condition. Dramatic improvements in SNR are obtained when the interfering noise is narrowband (1 kHz tone and siren); such intrusions tend to be represented as a single segment, which can be segregated very effectively from the speech source. Informal listening tests suggest that the intelligibility of the resynthesized speech is good. Also, we have quantified the percentage of speech energy that is recovered by the segregation process: typically, this is between 55% and 80% (Figure 4B).

4 Discussion

A significant feature of the model proposed here is that each stage has a neurobiological foundation. The peripheral auditory model is based upon the gammatone filter, which is derived from physiological measurement of auditory nerve impulse responses. Similarly, our mid-level auditory representations are consistent with the physiology of the higher auditory system [1]. Overall, the model is based on a framework – oscillatory correlation – which is supported by recent neurophysiological findings.

The neural oscillator network performs ASA in a distributed manner; each oscillator behaves autonomously and in parallel with the other oscillators. Although there are issues regarding real-time implementation of the model that must be resolved [10], there is a real possibility that the oscillator network can be implemented in analog VLSI. This feature is very attractive, since the high speed and compact size of analog VLSI will be needed if CASA is to provide an effective front-end for automatic speech recognition systems.

References

[1] Brown, G. J. & Cooke, M. (1994) Computational auditory scene analysis. *Computer Speech and Language*, **8**, pp. 297-336.
[2] Bregman, A. S. (1990) *Auditory scene analysis*. Cambridge MA: MIT Press.
[3] Brown, G. J. & Wang, D. L. (1997) Modelling the perceptual segregation of double vowels with a network of neural oscillators. *Neural Networks*, **10**, pp. 1547-1558.
[4] Cooke, M. (1993) *Modelling auditory processing and organization*. Cambridge U.K.: Cambridge University Press.
[5] Ellis, D. P. W. (1996) *Prediction-driven computational auditory scene analysis*. Ph.D. Dissertation, MIT Department of Electrical Engineering and Computer Science.
[6] Linsay, P. S. & Wang, D. L. (1998) Fast numerical integration of relaxation oscillator networks based on singular limit solutions. *IEEE Transactions on Neural Networks*, **9**, pp. 523-532.
[7] Terman, D. & Wang, D. L. (1995) Global competition and local cooperation in a network of neural oscillators, *Physica D*, **81**, pp. 148-176.
[8] Wang, D. L. (1996) Primitive auditory segregation based on oscillatory correlation, *Cognitive Science*, **20**, pp. 409-456.
[9] Wang, D. L. (1999) Object selection based on oscillatory correlation, *Neural Networks*, **12**, pp. 579-592.
[10] Wang, D. L. & Brown, G. J. (1999) Separation of speech from interfering sounds based on oscillatory correlation. *IEEE Transactions on Neural Networks*, **10**, pp. 684-697.
[11] Wang, D. L. & Terman, D. (1997) Image segmentation based on oscillatory correlation, *Neural Computation*, **9**, pp. 805-836 (for errata see *Neural Computation*, **9**, pp. 1623-1626, 1997).

Bayesian modelling of fMRI time series

Pedro A. d. F. R. Højen-Sørensen, Lars K. Hansen and **Carl Edward Rasmussen**
Department of Mathematical Modelling, Building 321
Technical University of Denmark
DK-2800 Lyngby, Denmark
`phs,lkhansen,carl@imm.dtu.dk`

Abstract

We present a Hidden Markov Model (HMM) for inferring the hidden psychological state (or neural activity) during single trial fMRI activation experiments with blocked task paradigms. Inference is based on Bayesian methodology, using a combination of analytical and a variety of Markov Chain Monte Carlo (MCMC) sampling techniques. The advantage of this method is that detection of short time learning effects between repeated trials is possible since inference is based only on single trial experiments.

1 Introduction

Functional magnetic resonance imaging (fMRI) is a non-invasive technique that enables indirect measures of neuronal activity in the working human brain. The most common fMRI technique is based on an image contrast induced by temporal shifts in the relative concentration of oxyhemoglobin and deoxyhemoglobin (BOLD contrast). Since neuronal activation leads to an increased blood flow, the so-called *hemodynamic response*, the measured fMRI signal reflects neuronal activity. Hence, when analyzing the BOLD signal there are two unknown factors to consider; the task dependent neuronal activation and the hemodynamic response. Bandettini et al. [1993] analyzed the correlation between a binary reference function (representing the stimulus/task sequence) and the BOLD signal. In the following we will also make reference to the binary representation of the task as the *paradigm*. Lange and Zeger [1997] discuss a parameterized hemodynamic response adapted by a least squares procedure. Multivariate strategies have been pursued in [Worsley et al. 1997, Hansen et al. 1999]. Several explorative strategies have been proposed for finding spatio-temporal activation patterns without explicit reference to the activation paradigm. McKeown et al. [1998] used independent component analysis and found several types of activations including components with "transient task related" response, i.e., responses that could not simply be accounted for by the paradigm. The model presented in this paper draws on the experimental observation that the basic coupling between the net neural activity and hemodynamic response is roughly linear while the relation between neuronal response and stimulus/task parameters is often nonlinear [Dale 1997]. We will represent the neuronal activity (integrated over the voxel and sampling time interval) by a binary signal while we will represent the hemodynamic response as a linear filter of unknown form and temporal extent.

2 A Bayesian model of fMRI time series

Let $s = \{s_t : t = 0, \ldots, T - 1\}$ be a hidden sequence of binary state variables $s_t \in \{0, 1\}$, representing the state of a single voxel over time; the time variable, t, indexes the sequence of fMRI scans. Hence, s_t is a binary representation of the neural state. The hidden sequence is governed by a symmetric first order Hidden Markov Model (HMM) with transition probability $\alpha = P(S_{t+1} = j | S_t = j)$. We expect the activation to mimic the blocked structure of the experimental paradigm so for this reason we restrict α to be larger than one half. The *predicted signal* (noiseless signal) is given by $y_t = h*s + \theta_0 + \theta_1 t$, where $*$ denotes the linear convolution and h is the impulse response of a linear system of order M_f. The dc off-set and linear trend which are typically seen in fMRI time series are given by θ_0 and θ_1, respectively. Finally, it is assumed that the observable is given by $z_t = y_t + \varepsilon_t$, where ε_t is iid. Gaussian noise with variance σ_n^2. The generative model considered is therefore given by:

$$
\begin{aligned}
p(s_t | s_{t-1}, \alpha) &= \alpha \delta_{s_t, s_{t-1}} + (1 - \alpha)(1 - \delta_{s_t, s_{t-1}}), \\
p(z | s, \sigma_n, \theta, M_f) &\sim \mathcal{N}(y, \sigma_n^2 I), \text{ where } y = \{y_t\} = H_s \theta, \text{ and } z = \{z_t\}.
\end{aligned}
\tag{$*$}
$$

Furthermore, $\delta_{s_t, s_{t-1}}$ is the usual Kronecker delta and $H_s = [\mathbf{1}, \xi, \gamma_0 s, \gamma_1 s, \ldots, \gamma_{M_f - 1} s]$, where $\mathbf{1} = (1, \ldots 1)'$, $\xi = (1, \ldots, T)'/T$ and γ_i is a i-step shift operator, that is $\gamma_i s = (\underbrace{0, \ldots, 0}_{i}, s_0, s_1, \ldots, s_{T-1-i})'$. The linear parameters are collected in $\theta = (\theta_0, \theta_1, h)'$.

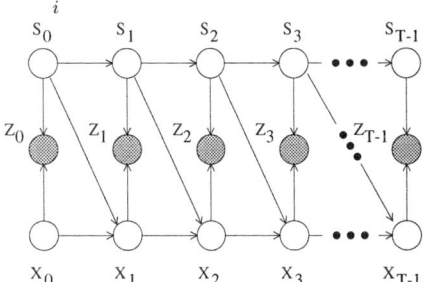

The graphical model. The hidden states $X_t = (S_{t-1}, S_{t-2}, \ldots, S_{t-(M_f-1)})$ have been introduced to make the model first order.

3 Analytic integration and Monte Carlo sampling

In this section we introduce priors over the model parameters and show how inference may be performed. The filter coefficients and noise parameters may be handled analytically, whereas the remaining parameters are treated using sampling procedures (a combination of Gibbs and Metropolis sampling). Like in the previous section explicit reference to the filter order M_f may be omitted to ease the notation.

The dc off-set θ_0 and the linear trend θ_1 are given (improper) uniform priors. The filter coefficients are given priors that are uniform on an interval of length β independently for each coefficient:

$$
p(h | M_f) = \begin{cases} \beta^{-M_f} & \text{for } |h_i| < \frac{\beta}{2}, \quad 0 \leq i \leq M_f - 1 \\ 0 & \text{otherwise} \end{cases}
$$

Assuming that all the values of θ for which the associated likelihood has non-vanishing contributions lie inside the box where the prior for θ has support, we may integrate out the filter coefficients via a Gaussian integral:

$$
p(z | \sigma_n, s, M_f) = \int p(z | \theta, \sigma_n, s, M_f) p(\theta | M_f) d\theta = \frac{(2\pi \sigma_n^2)^{\frac{M_f - T}{2} + 1}}{\beta^{M_f} \sqrt{|H_s' H_s|}} \exp\left(-\frac{z'z - \hat{y}_s' \hat{y}_s}{2\sigma_n^2}\right).
$$

We have here defined the *mean filter*, $\hat{\theta}_s = (H'_s H_s)^{-1} H_s z$ and *mean predicted signal*, $\hat{y}_s = H_s \hat{\theta}_s$, for given state and filter length. We set the interval-length, β to be 4 times the standard deviation of the observed signal z. This is done, since the response from the filter should be able to model the signal, for which it is thought to need an interval of plus/minus two standard deviations.

We now proceed to integrate over the noise parameter; using the (improper) non-informative Jeffreys prior, $p(\sigma_n) \propto \sigma_n^{-1}$, we get a Gamma integral:

$$p(z|s, M_f) = \int p(z|\sigma_n, s, M_f) p(\sigma_n) d\sigma_n = \frac{1}{2} \Gamma\left(\frac{T - M_f}{2} - 1\right) \frac{\left(\pi(z'z - \hat{y}'_s \hat{y}_s)\right)^{\frac{M_f - T}{2} + 1}}{\beta^{M_f} \sqrt{|H'_s H_s|}}.$$

The remaining variables cannot be handled analytically, and will be treated using various forms of sampling as described in the following sections.

3.1 Gibbs and Metropolis updates of the state sequence

We use a flat prior on the states, $p(s_t = 0) = p(s_t = 1)$, together with the first order Markov property for the hidden states and Bayes' rule to get the conditional posterior for the individual states:

$$p(s_t = j | s \backslash s_t, \alpha, M_f) \propto p(s_t = j | s_{t-1}, \alpha) p(s_{t+1} | s_t = j, \alpha) p(z | s, M_f).$$

These probabilities may (in normalized form) be used to implement Gibbs updates for the hidden state variables, updating one variable at a time and sweeping through all variables. However, it turns out that there are significant correlations between states which makes it difficult for the Markov Chain to move around in the hidden state-space using only Gibbs sampling (where a single state is updated at a time). To improve the situation we also perform global state updates, consisting of proposing to move the entire state sequence one step forward or backward (the direction being chosen at random) and accepting the proposed state using the Metropolis acceptance procedure. The proposed movements are made using periodic boundary conditions. The Gibbs sweep is computationally involved, since it requires computation of several matrix expressions for every state-variable.

3.2 Adaptive Rejection Sampling for the transition probability

The likelihood for the transition probability α is derived from the Hidden Markov Model:

$$p(s|\alpha) = p(s_0) \prod_{t=1}^{T-1} p(s_t | s_{t-1}, \alpha) = \frac{1}{2} \alpha^{E(s)} (1 - \alpha)^{T-1-E(s)},$$

where $E(s) = \sum_{t=1}^{T-1} \delta_{s_t, s_{t-1}}$ is the number of neighboring states in s with identical values. The prior on the transition probabilities is uniform, but restricted to be larger than one half, since we expect the activation to mimic the blocked structure of the experimental paradigm. It is readily seen that $p(\alpha|s) \propto p(s|\alpha)$, $\alpha \in [\frac{1}{2}, 1]$ is log-concave. Hence, we may use the Adaptive Rejection Sampling algorithm [Gilks and Wild, 1992] to sample from the distribution for the transition probability.

3.3 Metropolis updates for the filter length

In practical applications using real fMRI data, we do typically not know the necessary length of the filter. The problem of finding the "right" model order is difficult and has received a lot of attention. Here, we let the Markov Chain sample over different filter lengths, effectively integrating out the filter-length rather than trying to optimize it. Although the value of M_f determines the dimensionality of the parameter space, we do not need to use specialized sampling methodology (such as Reversible Jump MCMC [Green, 1995]), since those parameters are handled analytically in our model. We put a flat (improper) prior on M_f and propose new filter lengths using a Gaussian proposal centered on the current value, with a standard deviation of 3 (non-positive proposed orders are rejected). This choice of the standard deviation only effects the mixing rate of the Markov chain and does not have any influence on the stationary distribution. The proposed values are accepted using the Metropolis algorithm, using $p(M_f|s,y) \propto p(y|s,M_f)$.

3.4 The posterior mean and uncertainty of the predicted signal

Since θ has a flat prior the conditional probability for the filter coefficients is proportional to the likelihood $p(z|\theta,\cdot)$ and by $(*)$ we get:

$$p(\theta|z,s,\sigma_n,M_f) \sim \mathcal{N}(D_s z, \sigma_n^2 D_s D_s'), \quad D_s = (H_s' H_s)^{-1} H_s'\ .$$

The posterior mean of the predicted signal, $\hat{y}$, is then readily computed as:

$$\hat{y} = \left\langle y_{\theta,\sigma_n,s,M_f} \right\rangle_{\theta,\sigma_n,s,M_f} = \langle \hat{y}_s \rangle_{s,M_f} = \langle H_s \hat{\theta}_s \rangle_{s,M_f} = \langle F_s \rangle_{s,M_f} z\ ,$$

where $F_s = H_s D_s$. Here, the average over θ and σ_n is done analytically, and the average over the state and filter length is done using Monte Carlo. The uncertainty in the posterior, can also be estimated partly by analytical averaging, and partly Monte Carlo:

$$\Sigma_y = \left\langle (y_{\theta,\sigma_n,s,M_f} - \hat{y})(y_{\theta,\sigma_n,s,M_f} - \hat{y})' \right\rangle_{\theta,\sigma_n,s,M_f}$$
$$= \frac{1}{T - M_f - 2} \left\langle (z'z - \hat{y}_s' \hat{y}_s) F_s F_s' \right\rangle_{s,M_f} + \left\langle F_s z z' F_s' \right\rangle_{s,M_f} - \hat{y}\hat{y}'\ .$$

4 Example: synthetic data

In order to test the model, we first present some results on a synthetic data set. A signal z of length 100 is generated using a $M_f = 10$ order filter, and a hidden state sequence s consisting of two activation bursts (indicated by dotted bars in figure 1 top left). In this example, the hidden sequence is actually not generated from the generative model $(*)$; however, it still exhibits the kind of block structure that we wish to be able to recover. The model is run for 10000 iterations, which is sufficient to generate 500 approximately independent samples from the posterior; figure 2 (right) shows the auto-covariance for M_f as a function of the iteration lag. It is thought that changes in M_f are indicative of correlation time of the overall system.

The correlation plot for the hidden states (figure 2, left) shows that the state activation onset correlates strongly with the second onset and negatively with the end of the activation (and vice versa). This indicates that the Metropolis updates described in section 3.1 may indeed be effective. Notice also that the very strong correlation among state variables does not strongly carry over to the predicted signal (figure 1, bottom right).

To verify that the model can reasonably recover the parameters used to generate the data, posterior samples from some of the model variables are shown in figure 3. For all these parameters the posterior density is large around the correct values. Notice, that there in the original model $(*)$ is an indeterminacy in the simultaneous inference of the state sequence and the filter parameters (but no indeterminacy in the predicted signal); for example, the same signal is predicted by shifting the state sequence backward in time and introducing leading zero filter coefficients. However, the Bayesian methodology breaks this symmetry by penalizing complex models.

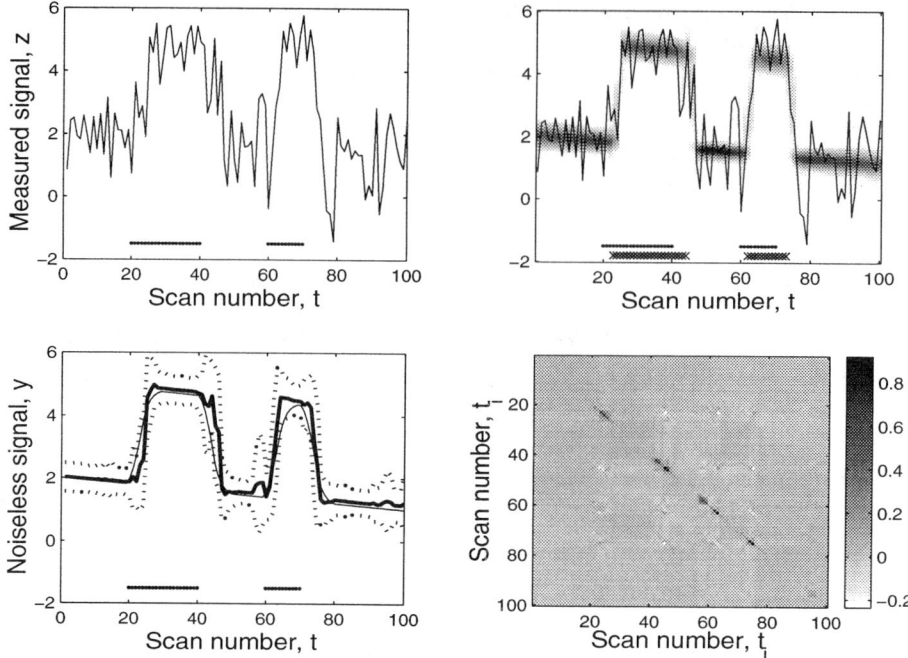

Figure 1: Experiments with synthetic data. Top left, the measured response from a voxel is plotted for 100 consecutive scans. In the bottom left, the underlying signal is seen in thin, together with the posterior mean, $\hat{y}$ (thick), and two std. dev. error-bars in dotted. Top right, the posterior probabilities are shown as a grey level, for each scan. The true activated instances are indicated by the dotted bars and the pseudo MAP estimate of the activation sequence is given by the crossed bars. Bottom right, shows the posterior uncertainty Σ_y.

The posterior mean and the two standard deviations are plotted in figure 1 bottom left. Notice, however, that the distribution of y is not Gaussian, but rather a mixture of Gaussians, and is not necessarily well characterized by mean and variance alone. In figure 1 (top left), the distribution of y_t is visualized using grey-scale to represent density.

5 Simulations on real fMRI data and discussion

In figure 4 the model has been applied to two measurements in the same voxel in visual cortex. The fMRI scans were acquired every 330 ms. The experimental paradigm consisted of 30 scans of rest followed by 30 scans of activation and 40 rest. Visual activation consisted of a flashing (8 Hz) annular checkerboard pattern. The model readily identifies the activation burst of somewhat longer duration than the visual stimulus and delayed around 2 seconds. The delay is in part caused by the delay in the hemodynamic response.

These results show that the integration procedure works in spite of the very limited data at hand. In figure 4 (top) the posterior model size suggests that (at least) two competing models can explain the signal from this trial. One of these models explains the measured signal as a simple square wave function which seems reasonable by considering the signal. Conversely, figure 4 (bottom), suggests that the signal from the second trial can not be explained by a simple model. This too, seems reasonable because of the long signal raise interval suggested in the signal.

Bayesian Modelling of fMRI Time Series

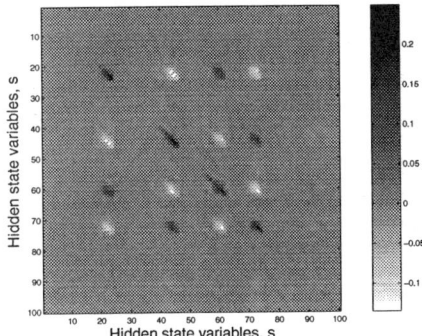 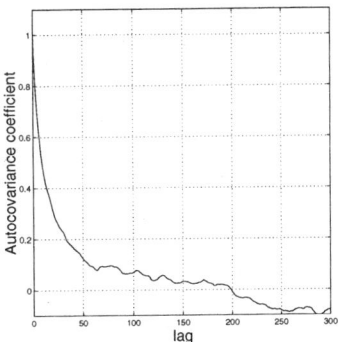

Figure 2: The covariance of the hidden states based on a long run of the model is shown to the left. Notice, that the states around the front (back) of the activity "bumps" are highly (anti-) correlated. Right: The auto-covariance for the filter length M_f as a function of the lag time in iterations. The correlation length is about 20, computed as the sum of auto-covariance coefficients from lag -400 to 400.

Since the posterior distribution of the filter length is very broad it is questionable whether an optimization based procedure such as maximum likelihood estimation would be able to make useful inference in this case were data is very limited. Also, it is not obvious how one may use cross-validation in this setting. One might expect such optimization based strategies to get trapped in suboptimal solutions. This, of course, remains to be investigated.

6 Conclusion

We have presented a model for voxel based explorative data analysis of single trial fMRI signals during blocked task activation studies. The model is founded on the experimental observation that the basic coupling between the net neural activity and hemodynamic response is roughly linear. The preliminary investigation reported here are encouraging in that the model reliably detects reasonable hidden states from the very noisy fMRI data.

One drawback of this method is that the Gibbs sampling step is computational expensive. To improve on this step one could make use of the large class of variational/mean field methods known from the graphical models literature. Finally, current work is in progress for generalizing the model to multiple voxels, including spatial correlation due to e.g. spill-over effects.

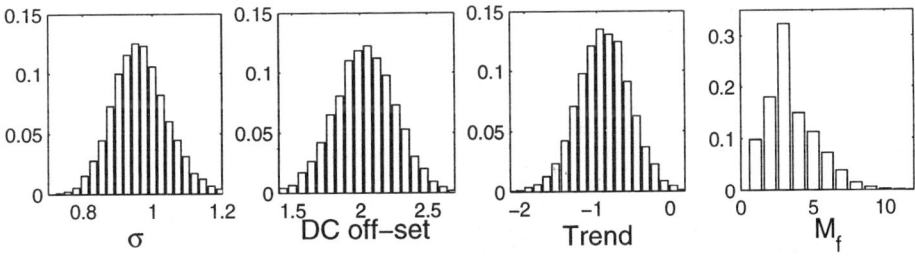

Figure 3: Posterior distributions of various model parameters. The parameters used to generate the data are: $\sigma = 1.0$, DC off-set $= 2$, trend $= -1$ and filter order $M_f = 10$.

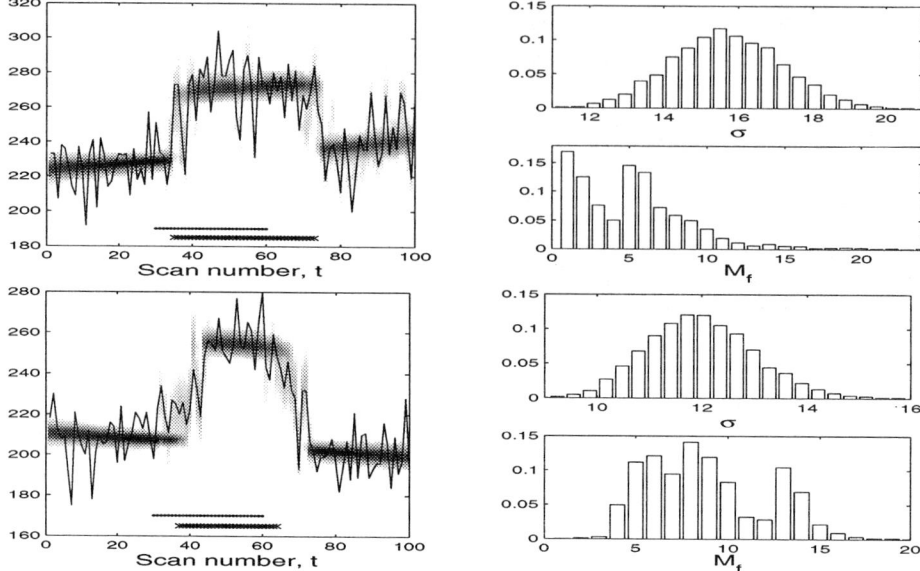

Figure 4: Analysis of two experimental trials of the same voxel in visual cortex. The left hand plot shows the posterior inferred signal distribution superimposed by the measured signal. The dotted bar indicates the experimental paradigm and the crossed bar indicates the pseudo MAP estimate of the neural activity. To the right the posterior noise level and inferred filter length are displayed.

Acknowledgments

Thanks to Egill Rostrup for providing the fMRI data. This work is funded by the Danish Research Councils through the Computational Neural Network Center (CONNECT) and the THOR Center for Neuroinformatics.

References

Bandettini, P. A. (1993). Processing strategies for time-course data sets in functional MRI of the human brain *Magnetic Resonance in Medicine 30*, 161–173.

Dale, A. M. and R. L. Buckner (1997). Selective Averaging of Individual Trials Using fMRI. *NeuroImage 5*, Abstract S47.

Green, P. J. (1995). Reversible jump Markov chain Monte Carlo computation and Bayesian model determination. *Biometrika 82*, 711–732.

Gilks, W. R. and P. Wild (1992). Adaptive rejection sampling for Gibbs sampling. *Applied Statistics 41*, 337–348.

Hansen, L. K. et al. (1999). Generalizable Patterns in Neuroimaging: How Many Principal Components? *NeuroImage*, to appear.

Lange, N. and S. L. Zeger (1997). Non-linear Fourier time series analysis for human brain mapping by functional magnetic resonance imaging. *Journal of the Royal Statistical Society - Series C Applied Statistics 46*, 1–30.

McKeown, M. J. et al. (1998). Spatially independent activity patterns in functional magnetic resonance imaging data during the stroop color-naming task. *Proc. Natl. Acad. Sci. USA. 95*, 803–810.

Worsley, K. J. et al. (1997). Characterizing the Response of PET and fMRI Data Using Multivariate Linear Models (MLM). *NeuroImage 6*, 305–319.

Neural System Model of Human Sound Localization

Craig T. Jin
Department of Physiology and
Department of Electrical Engineering,
Univ. of Sydney, NSW 2006, Australia

Simon Carlile
Department of Physiology
and Institute of Biomedical Research,
Univ. of Sydney, NSW 2006, Australia

Abstract

This paper examines the role of biological constraints in the human auditory localization process. A psychophysical and neural system modeling approach was undertaken in which performance comparisons between competing models and a human subject explore the relevant biologically plausible "realism constraints". The directional acoustical cues, upon which sound localization is based, were derived from the human subject's head-related transfer functions (HRTFs). Sound stimuli were generated by convolving bandpass noise with the HRTFs and were presented to both the subject and the model. The input stimuli to the model was processed using the Auditory Image Model of cochlear processing. The cochlear data was then analyzed by a time-delay neural network which integrated temporal and spectral information to determine the spatial location of the sound source. The combined cochlear model and neural network provided a system model of the sound localization process. Human-like localization performance was qualitatively achieved for broadband and bandpass stimuli when the model architecture incorporated frequency division (or tonotopicity), and was trained using variable bandwidth and center-frequency sounds.

1 Introduction

The ability to accurately estimate the location of a sound source has obvious evolutionary advantages in terms of avoiding predators and finding prey. Indeed, humans are very accurate in their ability to localize broadband sounds. There has been a considerable amount of psychoacoustical research into the auditory processes involved in human sound localization (recent review [1]). Furthermore, numerous models of the human and animal sound localization process have been proposed (recent reviews [2, 3]). However, there still remains a large gap between the psychophysical and the model explanations. Principal congruence between the two approaches exists for localization performance under restricted conditions, such as for narrowband sounds where spectral integration is not required, or for restricted regions of space. Unfortunately, there is no existing computational model that accounts well for human sound localization performance for a wide-range of sounds (e.g., varying in bandwidth and center-frequency). Furthermore, the biological constraints pertinent to sound localization have generally not been explored by these models. These include the spectral resolution of the auditory system in terms of the number and bandwidth of frequency channels and the role of tonotopic processing. In addition, the performance requirements of such a system are substantial and involve, for example, the accomodation of spectrally complex sounds, the robustness to irregularity in the sound source spectrum, and the channel based structure of spatial coding as evidenced by auditory spatial after-effects [4]. The crux of the matter is the notion that "biologically-likely realism", if built into a model, provides for a better understanding of the underlying processes.

This work attempts to bridge part of this gap between the modeling and psychophysics. It describes the development and use (for the first time, to the authors' knowledge) of a time-delay neural network model that integrates both spectral and temporal cues for auditory sound localization and compares the performance of such a model with the corresponding human psychophysical evidence.

2 Sound Localization

The sound localization performance of a normal hearing human subject was tested using stimuli consisting of three different band-passed sounds: (1) a low-passed sound (300 – 2000 Hz) (2) a high-passed sound (2000 – 14000 Hz) and (3) a broadband sound (300 – 14000 Hz). These frequency bands respectively cover conditions in which either temporal cues, spectral cues, or both dominate the localization process (see [1]). The subject performed five localization trials for each sound condition, each with 76 test locations evenly distributed about the subject's head. The detailed methods used in free-field sound localization can be found in [5]. A short summary is presented below.

2.1 Sound Localization Task

Human sound localization experiments were carried out in a darkened anechoic chamber. Free-field sound stimuli were presented from a loudspeaker carried on a semicircular robotic arm. These stimuli consisted of "fresh" white Gaussian noise appropriately band-passed for each trial. The robotic arm allowed for placement of the speaker at almost any location on the surface of an imaginary sphere, one meter in radius, centered on the subject's head. The subject indicated the location of the sound source by pointing his nose in the perceived direction of the sound. The subject's head orientation was monitored using an electromagnetic sensor system (Polhemus, Inc.).

2.2 Measurement and Validation of Outer Ear Acoustical Filtering

The cues for sound localization depend not only upon the spectral and temporal properties of the sound stimulus, but also on the acoustical properties of the individual's outer ears. It is generally accepted that the relevant acoustical cues (i.e., the interaural time difference, ITD; interaural level difference, ILD; and spectral cues) to a sound's location in the free-field are described by the head-related transfer function (HRTF) which is typically represented by a finite-length impulse response (FIR) filter [1]. Sounds filtered with the HRTF should be localizable when played over ear-phones which bypass the acoustical filtering of the outer ear. The illusion of free-field sounds using head-phones is known as virtual auditory space (VAS).

Thus in order to incorporate outer ear filtering into the modelling process, measurements of the subject's HRTFs were carried out in the anechoic chamber. The measurements were made for both ears simultaneously using a "blocked ear" technique [1]. 393 measurements were made at locations evenly distributed on the sphere. In order to establish that the HRTFs appropriately indicated the direction of a sound source the subject repeated the localization task as above with the stimulus presented in VAS.

2.3 Human Sound Localization Performance

The sound localization performance of the human subject in three different stimulus conditions (broadband, high-pass, low-pass) was examined in both the free-field and in virtual auditory space. Comparisons between the two (using correlational statistics, data not shown, but see [3]) across all sound conditions demonstrated their equivalence. Thus the measured HRTFs were highly effective.

Localization data across all three sound conditions (single trial VAS data shown in Fig. 1a) shows that the subject performed well in both the broadband and high-pass sound conditions and rather poorly in the low-pass condition, which is consistent with other studies [6]. The data is illustrated using spherical localization plots which well demonstrates the global distribution of localization responses. Given the large qualitative differences in the data sets presented below, this visual method of analysis was sufficient for evaluating the competing models. For each condition, the target and response locations are shown for both the left (L) and right (R) hemispheres of space. It is clear that in the low-pass condition, the subject demonstrated gross mislocalizations with the responses clustering toward the lower and frontal hemispheres. The gross mislocalizations correspond mainly to the traditional cone of confusion errors [6].

3 Localization Model

The sound localization model consisted of two basic system components: (1) a modified version of the physiological Auditory Image Model [7] which simulates the spectro-temporal characteristics of peripheral auditory processing, and (2) the computational architecture of a time-delay neural network. The sounds presented to the model were filtered using the subject's HRTFs in exactly the same manner as was used in producing VAS. Therefore, the modeling results can be compared with human localization performance on an individual basis.

The modeling process can be broken down into four stages. In the first stage a sound stimulus was generated with specific band-pass characteristics. The sound stimulus was then filtered with the subject's right and left ear HRTFs to render an auditory stimulus originating from a particular location in space. The auditory stimulus was then processed by the Auditory Image Model (AIM) to generate a neural activity profile that simulates the output of the inner hair cells in the organ of Corti and indicates the spiking probability of auditory nerve fibers. Finally, in the fourth and last stage, a time-delay neural network (TDNN) computed the spatial direction of the sound input based on the distribution of neural activity calculated by AIM.

A detailed presentation of the modeling process can be found in [3], although a brief summary is presented here. The distribution of cochlear filters across frequency in AIM was chosen such that the minimum center frequency was 300 Hz and the maximum center frequency was 14 kHz with 31 filters essentially equally spaced on a logarithmic scale. In order to fully describe a computational layer of the TDNN, four characteristic numbers must be specified: (1) the number of neurons; (2) the kernel length, a number which determines the size of the current layer's time-window in terms of the number of time-steps of the previous layer; (3) the kernel width, a number which specifies how many neurons in the previous layer with which there are actual connections; and (4) the undersampling factor, a number describing the multiplicative factor by which the current layer's time-step interval is increased from the previous layer's. Using this nomenclature, the architecture of the different layers of one TDNN is summarized in Table 1, with the smallest time-step being 0.15 ms. The exact connection arrangement of the network is described in the next section.

Table 1: The Architecture of the TDNN.

Layer	Neurons	Kernel Length	Kernel Width	Undersampling
Input	62	—	—	—
Hidden 1	50	15	6	2
Hidden 2	28	10	4, 5, 6	2
Output	393	4	28	1

The spatial location of a sound source was encoded by the network as a distributed response with the peak occurring at the output neuron representing the target location of the input sound. The output response would then decay away in the form of a two-dimensional Gaussian as one moves to neurons further away from the target location. This derives from the well-established paradigm that the nervous system uses overlapping receptive fields to encode properties of the physical world.

3.1 Networks with Frequency Division and Tonotopicity

The major auditory brainstem nuclei demonstrate substantial frequency division within their structure. The tonotopic organization of the primary auditory nerve fibers that innervate the cochlea carries forward to the brainstem's auditory nuclei. This arrangement is described as a tonotopic organization. Despite this fact and to our knowledge, no previous network model for sound localization incorporates such frequency division within its architecture. Typically (e.g., [8]) all of the neurons in the first computational layer are fully connected to *all* of the input cochlear frequency channels. In this work, different architectures were examined with varying amounts of frequency division imposed upon the network structure. The network with the architecture described above had its network connections constrained by frequency in a tonotopic like arrangement. The 31 input cochlear frequency channels for each ear were split into ten overlapping groups consisting generally of six contiguous frequency channels. There were five neurons in the first hidden layer for each group of input channels. The kernel widths of these neurons were set, not to the total number of frequency channels in the input layer, but only to the six contiguous frequency channels defining the group. Information across the different groups of frequency channels was progressively integrated in the higher layers of the network.

3.2 Network Training

Sounds with different center-frequency and bandwidth were used for training the networks. In one particular training paradigm, the center-frequency and bandwidth of the noise were chosen randomly. The center-frequency was chosen using a uniform probability distribution on a logarithmic scale that was similar to the physiological distribution of output frequency channels from AIM. In this manner, each frequency region was trained equally based on the density of neurons in that frequency region. During training, the error back-propagation algorithm was used with a summed squared error measure. It is a natural feature of the learning rule that a given neuron's weights are only updated when there is activity in its respective cochlear channels. So, for example, a training sound containing only low frequencies will not train the high-frequency neurons and vice versa. All modeling results correspond with a *single* tonotopically organized TDNN trained using random sounds (unless explicitly stated otherwise).

4 Localization Performance of a Tonotopic Network

Experimentation with the different network architectures clearly demonstrated that a network with frequency division vastly improved the localization performance of the TDNNs (Figure 1). In this case, frequency division was essential to producing a reasonable neural system model that would localize similarly to the human subject across *all* of the different band-pass conditions. For any single band-pass condition, it was found that the TDNN did not require frequency division within its architecture to produce quality solutions when trained *only* on these band-passed sounds.

As mentioned above it was observed that a tonotopic network, one that divides the input frequency channels into different groups and then progressively interconnects the neurons in the higher layers across frequency, was more robust in its localization performance across sounds with variable center-frequency and bandwidth than a simple fully connected network. There are two likely explanations for this observation. One line of reasoning argues that it was easier for the tonotopic network to prevent a narrow band of frequency channels from dominating the localization computation across the entire set of sound stimuli. Or expressed slightly differently, it may have been easier for it to incorporate the relevant information across the different frequency channels. A second line of reasoning argues that the tonotopic network structure (along with the training with variable sounds) encouraged the network to develop meaningful connections for all frequencies.

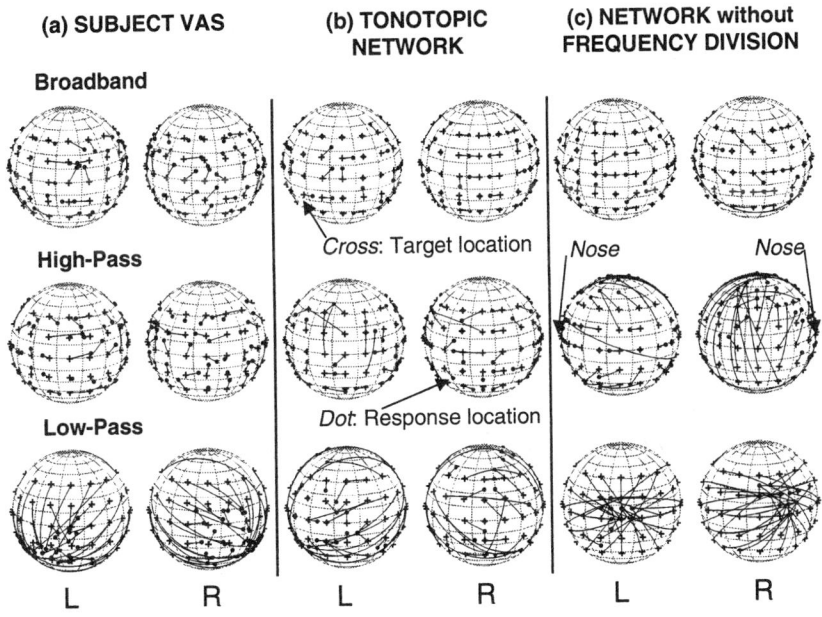

Figure 1: Comparison of the subject's VAS localization performance and the model's localization performance both with and without frequency division. The viewpoint is from an outside observer, with the target location shown by a cross and the response location shown by a black dot.

5 Matched Filtering and Sound Localization

A number of previous sound localization models have used a relatively straight-forward matched filter or template matching analysis [9]. In such cases, the ITD and spectrum of a given input sound is commonly cross-correlated with the ITD and spectrum of an entire database of sounds for which the location is known. The location with the highest correlation is then chosen as the optimal source location.

Matched filtering analysis is compared with the localization performance of both the human subject and the neural system model using a bandpass sound with restricted high-frequencies (Figure 2). The matched filtering localizes the sounds much better than the subject or the TDNN model. The matched filtering model used the same number of cochlear channels as the TDNNs and therefore contained the same inherent spectral resolution. This spectral resolution (31 cochlear channels) is certainly less than the spectral resolution of the human cochlea. This shows that although there was sufficient information to localize the sounds from the point of view of matched filtering, neither the human nor TDNN demonstrated such ability in their performance. In order for the TDNN to localize similarly to the matched filtering model, the network weights corresponding to a given location need to assume the form of the filter template for that location. As all of the training sounds were flat-spectrum, the TDNN received no ambiguity as far as the source spectrum was concerned. Thus it is likely that the difference in the distribution of localization responses in Figure 2b, as compared with that in Figure 2c, has been encouraged by using training sounds with random center-frequency and bandwidth, providing a partial explanation as to why the human localization performance is not optimal from a matched filtering standpoint.

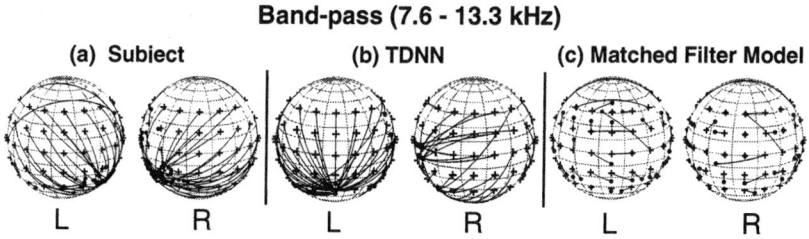

Figure 2: Comparison of the localization performances of the subject, the TDNN model, and a matched filtering model. Details as in Fig. 1.

6 Varying Sound Levels and the ILD Cue

The training of the TDNNs was performed in such a fashion, that for any particular location in space, the sound level (67 dB SPL) did not vary by more than 1 dB SPL during repeated presentations of the sound. The localization performance of the neural system model was then examined, using a broadband sound source, across a range of sound levels varying from 60 dB SPL to 80 dB SPL. The spherical correlation coefficient between the target and response locations ([10], values above 0.8 indicate "high" correlation) remained above 0.8 between 60 and 75 dB SPL demonstrating that there was a graceful degradation in localization performance over a range in sound level of 15 dB.

The network was also tested on broadband sounds, 10 dB louder in one ear than the other. The results of these tests are shown in Figure 3 and clearly illustrate that the localization responses were pulled toward the side with the louder sound. While the magnitude of this effect is certainly not human-like, such behaviour suggests that interaural level difference cues were a prominent and constant feature of the data that conferred a measure of robustness to sound level variations.

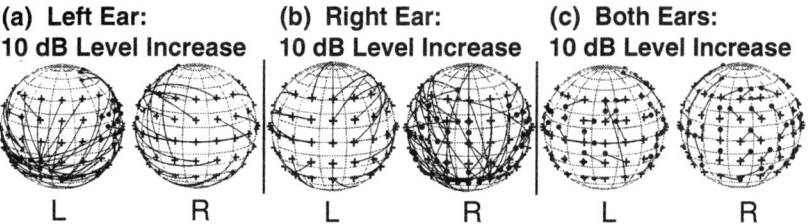

Figure 3: Model's localization performance with a 10 dB increase in sound level: (a,b) monaurally, (c) binaurally.

7 Conclusions

A neural system model was developed in which physiological constraints were imposed upon the modeling process: (1) a TDNN model was used to incorporate the important role of spectral-temporal processing in the auditory nervous system, (2) a tonotopic structure was added to the network, (3) the training sounds contained randomly varying center-frequencies and bandwidths. This biologically plausible model provided increased understanding of the role that these constraints play in determining localization performance.

Acknowledgments

The authors thank Markus Schenkel and André van Schaik for valuable comments. This research was supported by the NHMRC, ARC, and a Dora Lush Scholarship to CJ.

References

[1] S. Carlile, *Virtual auditory space: Generation and applications.* New York: Chapman and Hall, 1996.

[2] R. H. Gilkey and T. R. Anderson, *Binaural and Spatial Hearing in real and virtual environments.* Mahwah, New Jersey: Lawrence Erlbaum Associates, Publishers, 1997.

[3] C. Jin, M. Schenkel, and S. Carlile, "Neural system identification model of human sound localisation," *(Submitted to J. Acoust. Soc. Am.)*, 1999.

[4] S. Hyams and S. Carlile, "After-effects in auditory localization: evidence for channel based processing," *Submitted to the J. Acoust. Soc. Am.*, 2000.

[5] S. Carlile, P. Leong, and S. Hyams, "The nature and distribution of errors in the localization of sounds by humans," *Hearing Research*, vol. 114, pp. 179–196, 1997.

[6] S. Carlile, S. Delaney, and A. Corderoy, "The localization of spectrally restricted sounds by human listeners," *Hearing Research*, vol. 128, pp. 175–189, 1999.

[7] C. Giguère and P. C. Woodland, "A computational model of the auditory periphery for speech and hearing research. i. ascending path," *J. Acoust. Soc. Am.*, vol. 95, pp. 331–342, 1994.

[8] C. Neti, E. Young, and M. Schneider, "Neural network models of sound localization based on directional filtering by the pinna," *J. Acoust. Soc. Am.*, vol. 92, no. 6, pp. 3140–3156, 1992.

[9] J. Middlebrooks, "Narrow-band sound localization related to external ear acoustics," *J. Acoust. Soc. Am.*, vol. 92, no. 5, pp. 2607–2624, 1992.

[10] N. Fisher, I, T. Lewis, and B. J. J. Embleton, *Statistical analysis of spherical data.* Cambridge: Cambridge University Press, 1987.

Spectral Cues in Human Sound Localization

Craig T. Jin
Department of Physiology and
Department of Electrical Engineering,
Univ. of Sydney, NSW 2006, Australia

Anna Corderoy
Department of Physiology
Univ. of Sydney, NSW 2006, Australia

Simon Carlile
Department of Physiology
and Institute of Biomedical Research
Univ. of Sydney, NSW 2006, Australia

André van Schaik
Department of Electrical Engineering,
Univ. of Sydney, NSW 2006, Australia

Abstract

The differential contribution of the monaural and interaural spectral cues to human sound localization was examined using a combined psychophysical and analytical approach. The cues to a sound's location were correlated on an individual basis with the human localization responses to a variety of spectrally manipulated sounds. The spectral cues derive from the acoustical filtering of an individual's auditory periphery which is characterized by the measured head-related transfer functions (HRTFs). Auditory localization performance was determined in virtual auditory space (VAS). Psychoacoustical experiments were conducted in which the amplitude spectra of the sound stimulus was varied *independently* at each ear while preserving the normal timing cues, an impossibility in the free-field environment. Virtual auditory noise stimuli were generated over earphones for a specified target direction such that there was a "false" flat spectrum at the left eardrum. Using the subject's HRTFs, the sound spectrum at the right eardrum was then adjusted so that either the true right monaural spectral cue or the true interaural spectral cue was preserved. All subjects showed systematic mislocalizations in both the true right and true interaural spectral conditions which was absent in their control localization performance. The analysis of the different cues along with the subjects' localization responses suggests there are significant differences in the use of the monaural and interaural spectral cues and that the auditory system's reliance on the spectral cues varies with the sound condition.

1 Introduction

Humans are remarkably accurate in their ability to localize transient, broadband noise, an ability with obvious evolutionary advantages. The study of human auditory localization has a considerable and rich history (recent review [1]) which demonstrates that there are three general classes of acoustical cues involved in the localization process: (1) interaural time differences, ITDs; (2) interaural level differences, ILDs; and (3) the spectral cues resulting from the auditory periphery. It is generally accepted that for humans, the ITD and ILD cues only specify the location of the sound source to within a "cone of confusion" [1], i.e., a locus of points approximating the surface of a cone symmetric with respect to the interaural axis. It remains, therefore, for the localization system to extract a more precise sound source location from the spectral cues.

The utilization of the outer ear spectral cues during sound localization has been analyzed both as a statistical estimation problem, (e.g., [2]) and as optimization problem, often using neural networks, (e.g., [3]). Such computational models show that sufficient localization information is provided by the spectral cues to resolve the cone of confusion ambiguity which corroborates the psychoacoustical evidence. Furthermore, it is commonly argued that the interaural spectral cue, because of its natural robustness to level and spectral variations, has advantages over the monaural spectral cues alone. Despite these observations, there is still considerable contention as to the relative role or contribution of the monaural versus the interaural spectral cues.

In this study, each subject's spectral cues were characterized by measuring their head related transfer functions (HRTFs) for 393 evenly distributed positions in space. Measurements were carried out in an anechoic chamber and were made for both ears simultaneously using a "blocked ear" technique [1]. Sounds filtered with the HRTFs and played over earphones, which bypass the acoustical filtering of the outer ear, result in the illusion of free-field sounds which is known as virtual auditory space (VAS). The HRTFs were used to generate virtual sound sources in which the spectral cues were manipulated systematically. The recorded HRTFs along with the Glasberg and Moore cochlear model [4] were also used to generate neural excitation patterns (frequency representations of the sound stimulus within the auditory nerve) which were used to estimate the different cues available to the subject during the localization process. Using this analysis, the interaural spectral cue was characterized and the different localization cues have been correlated with each subjects' VAS localization responses.

2 VAS Sound Localization

The sound localization performance of four normal hearing subjects was examined in VAS using broadband white noise (300 – 14 000 Hz). The stimuli were filtered under three differing spectral conditions. (1) control: stimuli were filtered with spectrally correct left and right ear HRTFs for a given target location, (2) veridical interaural: stimuli at the left ear were made spectrally flat with an appropriate dB sound level for the given target location, while the stimuli at the right ear were spectrally shaped to preserve the correct interaural spectrum, (3) veridical right monaural: stimuli at the left ear were spectrally flat as in the second condition, while the stimuli at the right ear were filtered with the correct HRTF for the given target location, resulting in an inappropriate interaural spectral difference. For each condition, a minimum-phase filter spectral approximation was made and the interaural time difference was modeled as an all-pass delay [5]. Sounds were presented at approximately 70 dB SPL and with duration 150 ms (with 10 ms raised-cosine onset and offset ramps). Each subject performed five trials at each of 76 test positions for each stimulus condition. Detailed sound localization methods can be found in [1]. A short summary is presented below.

2.1 Sound Localization Task

The human localization experiments were carried out in a darkened anechoic chamber. Virtual auditory sound stimuli were presented using earphones (ER-2, Etymōtic Research, with a flat frequency response, within 3 dB, between 200–16 000 Hz). The perceived location of the virtual sound source was indicated by the subject pointing his/her nose in the direction of the perceived source. The subject's head orientation and position were monitored using an electromagnetic sensor system (Polhemus, Inc.).

2.2 Human Sound Localization Performance

The sound localization performance of two subjects in the three different stimulus conditions are shown in Figure 1. The pooled data across 76 locations and five trials is presented for both the left (L) and right (R) hemispheres of space from the viewpoint of an outside observer. The target location is shown by a cross and the centroid of the subjects responses for each location is shown by a black dot with the standard deviation indicated by an ellipse. Front-back confusions are plotted, although, they were removed for calculating the standard deviations. The subjects localized the control broadband sounds accurately (Figure 1a). In contrast, the subjects demonstrated systematic mislocalizations for both the veridical interaural and veridical monaural spectral conditions (Figures 1b,c). There is clear pulling of the localization responses to particular regions of space with evident intersubject variations.

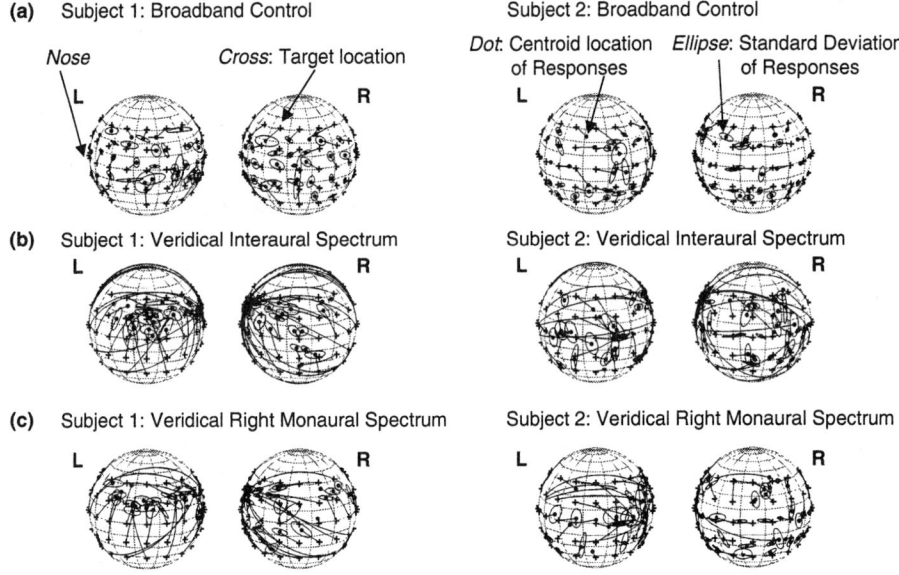

Figure 1: Localization performance for two subjects in the three sound conditions: (a) control broadband; (b) veridical interaural; (c) veridical monaural. See text for details.

3 Extraction of Acoustical Cues

With accurate measurements of each individual's outer ear filtering, the different acoustical cues can be compared with human localization performance on an individual basis. In order to extract the different acoustical cues in a biologically plausible manner, a model of peripheral auditory processing was used. A virtual source sound stimulus was prepared as described in Secion 2 for a particular target location. The stimulus was then filtered using a cochlear model based on the work of Glasberg and Moore [4]. This cochlear model consisted of a set of modified rounded-exponential auditory filters. The width and shape of the auditory filters change as a function of frequency (and sound level) in a manner consistent with the known physiological and psychophysical data. These filters were logarithmically spaced on the frequency axis with a total of 200 filters between 300 Hz and 14 kHz. The cochlea's compressive non-linearity was modelled mathematically using a logarithmic function. Thus the logarithm of the output energy of a given filter indicated the amount of neural activity in that particular cochlear channel.

The relative activity across the different cochlear channels was representative of the neural excitation pattern (EP) along the auditory nerve and it is from this excitation pattern that the different spectral cues were estimated. For a given location, the left and right EPs themselves represent the monaural spectral cues. The difference in the total energy (calculated as the area under the curve) between the left and right EPs was taken as a measure of the interaural level difference and the interaural spectral shape cue was calculated as the difference between the left and right EPs. The fourth cue, interaural time difference, is a measure of the time lag between the signal in one ear as compared to the other and depends principally upon the geometrical relationship between the sound source and the human subject. This time delay was calculated using the acoustical impulse response for both ears as measured during the HRTF recordings.

4 Correlation of Cues and Location

For each stimulus condition and location, the acoustical cues were calculated as described above for all 393 HRTF locations. Locations at which a given cue correlates well with the stimulus cue for a particular target location were taken as analytical predictions of the subject's response locations according to that cue. As the spectral content of the signal is varied, the cue(s) available may strongly match the cue(s) normally arising from locations other than the target location. Therefore the aim of this analysis is to establish for which locations and stimulus conditions a given response most correlated with a particular cue.

The following analyses (using a Matlab toolbox developed by the authors) hinge upon the calculation of "cue correlation values". To a large extent, these calculations follow the examples described by [6] and are briefly described here. For each stimulus condition and target location, the subject performed five localizations trials. For each of the subject's five response locations, each possible cue was estimated (Section 3) assuming a flat-spectrum broadband Gaussian white noise as the stimulus. A mathematical quantity was then calculated which would give a measure of the similarity of the response location cues with the corresponding stimulus cues. The method of calculation depended on the cue and several alternative methods were tried. Generally, for a given cue, these different methods demonstrated the same basic pattern and the term "cue correlation value" has been given to the mathematical quantity that was used to measure cue similarity. The methods are as follows.

For the ITD cue, the negative of the absolute value of the difference between possible response location ITDs and the stimulus ITD was used as the ITD cue correlation values (the more positive a value, the higher its correlation). The ILD cue correlation value was calculated in a similar fashion. The cue correlation values for the left and right monaural spectral cues (in this case, the shape of the neural excitation pattern) was calculated by taking the difference between the stimulus EP and the possible response location EPs and then summing across frequency the variation of this difference about its mean value. For the interaural spectral cue, the vector difference between the left and right EPs was calculated for both the stimulus and the possible response locations. The dot product between the stimulus and the possible response location vectors gave the ISD cue correlation values.

The cue correlation values were normalized in order to facilitate meaningful comparisons across the different acoustical cues. Following Middlebrooks [6], a "z-score normalized" cue value, for each response location corresponding to a given target location, was obtained by subtracting the mean correlation value (across all possible locations) and dividing by the standard deviation. For these new cue values, termed the cue z-score values, a score of 1.0 or greater indicates good correlation.

5 Relationship between the ISD and the Cone-of-Confusion

The distribution of a given cue's z-score values around the sphere of space surrounding the subject reveals the spatial directions for that cue that correlate best with the given stimulus and target location being examined. An examination of the interaural spectral cue indicated that, unlike the other cues, the range of its cue z-score variation was relatively restricted on the ipsilateral hemisphere of space relative to the sound stimulus (values on the ipsilateral side were approximately 1.0, those on the contralateral side, -1.0). This was the first indication of the more moderate variation of the ISD cue across space as compared with the monaural spectral cues.

Closer examination of the ISD cue revealed more detailed variational properties. In order to facilitate meaningful comparisons with the other cues, the ISD cue z-score values were adjusted such that all negative values (i.e., those values at locations generally contralateral to the stimulus) were set to 0.0 and the cue z-score values recalculated. The spatial distribution of the rescaled ISD cue z-score values, as compared with the cue z-score values for the other cues, is shown in Figure 2. The cone of confusion described by the ITD and ILD is clearly evident (Fig. 2a,b) and it can be seen that the ISD cue is closely aligned with these cues (Fig. 2c). Furthermore, the ISD cue demonstrates significant asymmetry along the front-back dimensions. These novel observations demonstrate that while previous work [3, 2] indicates that the ISD cue provides *sufficient* information to determine a sound's location exactly along the cone of confusion, the variation of the cue z-score values along the cone is substantially *less* than that for the monaural spectral cues (Fig. 2d), suggesting perhaps that this acts to make the monaural spectral cue a more salient cue.

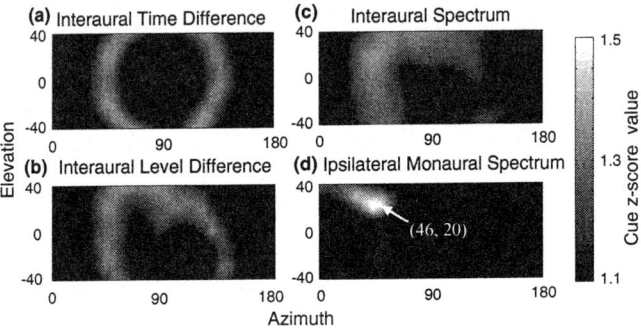

Figure 2: Spatial plot of the cue z-score values for a *single* target location (46° azimuth, 20° elevation) and broadband sound condition. Gray-scale color values indicate the cue's correlation in different spatial directions with the stimulus cue at the target location. (Z-score values for the ISD cue have been rescaled, see text.)

6 Analysis of Subjects Responses using Cue Z-score Values

A given cue's z-score values for the subject's responses across all 76 test locations and five trials were averaged. The mean and standard deviation are presented in a bar graph (Fig. 3). The subjects' response locations correlate highly with the ITD and ILD cue and the standard deviation of the correlation was low (Fig. 3a,b). In other words, subjects' responses stayed on the cone of confusion of the target location. A similar analysis of the more restricted, rescaled version of the interaural spectral cue shows that despite the spectral manipulations and systematic mislocalizations, subject's were responding to locations which were highly correlated with the interaural spectral cue (Fig. 3c). The bar graphs for the monaural spectral cues ipsilateral and contralateral to the target location show the average correlation of the subjects' responses with these cues varied considerably with the stimulus condition (Fig. 3d-g) and to a lesser extent across subjects.

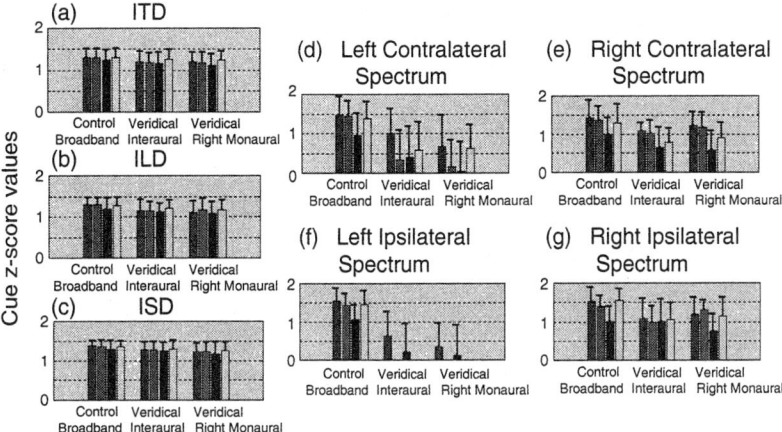

Figure 3: Correlation of the four subjects' (indicated by different gray bars) localization responses with the different acoustical cues for each stimulus condition. The bar heights indicates the mean cue z-score value, while the error bars indicate standard deviation.

7 Spatial Plots of Correlation Regions

As the localization responses tended to lie along the cone of confusion, the relative importance of the spectral cues along the cone of confusion was examined. The correlation values for the spectral cues associated with the subjects' responses were recalculated as a z-score value using *only* the distribution of values restricted to the cone of confusion. This demonstrates whether the spectral cues associated with the subjects' response locations were better correlated with the stimulus cues, than for any *random* location on the cone of confusion.

Spatial plots of the recalculated response cue z-score values for the spectral cues of one subject (similar trends across subjects), obtained for each stimulus location and across the three different sound conditions, is shown in Figure 4. Spatial regions of both high and low correlation are evident that vary with the stimulus spectrum. The z-score values for the ISD cue shows greater bilateral correlation across space in the veridical interaural condition (Fig. 4d) than for the veridical monaural condition (Fig. 4g), while the right monaural spectral cue demonstrates higher correlation in the right hemisphere of space for the veridical monaural condition (Fig. 4i) as opposed to the veridical interaural condition (Fig. 4f). This result (although not surprising) demonstrates that the auditory system is extracting cues to source location in a manner *dependent* on the input sound spectrum and in a manner *consistent* with the spectral information available in the sound spectrum. Figures 4e,h clearly demonstrate that the flat sound spectrum in the left ear was strongly correlated with and influenced the subject's localization judgements for specific regions of space.

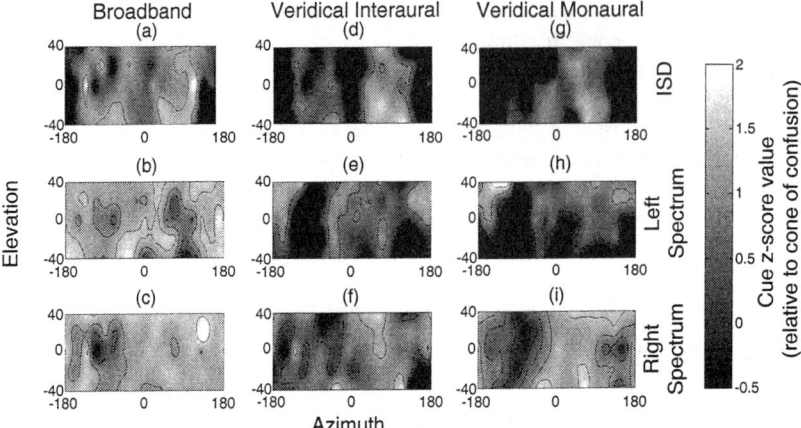

Figure 4: Spatial plot of the spectral cue z-score values for one subject's localization responses across the three different sound conditions.

8 Conclusions

The correlation of human sound localization responses with the available acoustical cues across three spectrally different sound conditions has provided insights into the human auditory system and its integration of cues to produce a coherent percept of spatial location. These data suggest an interrelationship between the interaural spectral cue and the cone of confusion. The ISD cue is front-back asymmetrical along the cone and its cue correlation values vary more moderately as a function of space than those of the monaural spectral cues. These data shed light on the relative role and importance of the interaural and monaural spectral cues.

Acknowledgments

This research was supported by the ARC, NHMRC, and Dora Lush Scholarship to CJ.

References

[1] S. Carlile, *Virtual auditory space: Generation and applications.* New York: Chapman and Hall, 1996.

[2] R. O. Duda, "Elevation dependence of the interaural transfer function," in *Binaural and spatial hearing in real and virtual environments* (R. H. Gilkey and T. R. Anderson, eds.), ch. 3, pp. 49–75, Mahwah, New Jersey: Lawrence Erlbaum Associates, 1997.

[3] J. A. Janko, T. R. Anderson, and R. H. Gilkey, "Using neural networks to evaluate the viability of monaural and interaural cues for sound localization," in *Binaural and Spatial Hearing in real and virtual environments* (R. H. Gilkey and T. R. Anderson, eds.), ch. 26, pp. 557–570, Mahwah, New Jersey: Lawrence Erlbaum Associates, 1997.

[4] B. Glasberg and B. Moore, "Derivation of auditory filter shapes from notched-noise data," *Hearing Research*, vol. 47, no. 1-2, pp. 103–138, 1990.

[5] F. Wightman and D. Kistler, "The dominant role of low-frequency interaural time differences in sound localization," *J. Acoust. Soc. Am.*, vol. 91, no. 3, pp. 1648–1661, 1992.

[6] J. Middlebrooks, "Narrow-band sound localization related to external ear acoustics," *J. Acoust. Soc. Am.*, vol. 92, no. 5, pp. 2607–2624, 1992.

Broadband Direction-Of-Arrival Estimation Based On Second Order Statistics

Justinian Rosca   Joseph Ó Ruanaidh   Alexander Jourjine   Scott Rickard

{rosca,oruanaidh,jourjine,rickard}@scr.siemens.com

Siemens Corporate Research, Inc.
755 College Rd E
Princeton, NJ 08540

Abstract

N wideband sources recorded using N closely spaced receivers can feasibly be separated based only on second order statistics when using a physical model of the mixing process. In this case we show that the parameter estimation problem can be essentially reduced to considering directions of arrival and attenuations of each signal. The paper presents two demixing methods operating in the time and frequency domain and experimentally shows that it is always possible to demix signals arriving at different angles. Moreover, one can use spatial cues to solve the channel selection problem and a post-processing Wiener filter to ameliorate the artifacts caused by demixing.

1 Introduction

Blind source separation (BSS) is capable of dramatic results when used to separate mixtures of independent signals. The method relies on simultaneous recordings of signals from two or more input sensors and separates the original sources purely on the basis of statistical independence between them. Unfortunately, BSS literature is primarily concerned with the idealistic instantaneous mixing model.

In this paper, we formulate a low dimensional and fast solution to the problem of separating two signals from a mixture recorded using two closely spaced receivers. Using a physical model of the mixing process reduces the complexity of the model and allows one to identify and to invert the mixing process using second order statistics only.

We describe the theoretical basis of the new approach, and then focus on two algorithms, which were implemented and successfully applied to extensive sets of real-world data. In essence, our separation architecture is a system of adaptive directional receivers designed using the principles of BSS. The method bears resemblance to methods in beamforming [8] in that it works by spatial filtering. Array processing techniques [2] reduce noise by separating signal space from noise space, which necessitates more receivers than emitters. The main differences are that standard beamforming and array processing techniques [8, 2] are generally strictly concerned with processing directional narrowband signals. The difference with BSS [7, 6] is that our approach is model-based and therefore the elements of the mixing matrix are highly constrained: a feature that aids in the robust and reliable identification of the mixing process.

The layout of the paper is as follows. Sections 2 and 3 describe the theoretical foundation of the separation method that was pursued. Section 4 presents algorithms that were developed and experimental results. Finally we summarize and conclude this work.

2 Theoretical foundation for the BSS solution

As a first approximation to the general multi-path model, we use the delay-mixing model. In this model, only direct path signal components are considered. Signal components from one source arrive with a fractional delay between the time of arrivals at two receivers. By fractional delays, we mean that delays between receivers are not generally integer multiples of the sampling period. The delay depends on the position of the source with respect to the receiver axis and the distance between receivers. Our BSS algorithms demix by compensating for the fractional delays. This, in effect, is a form of adaptive beamforming with directional notches being placed in the direction of sources of interference [8]. A more detailed account of the analytical structure of the solutions can be found in [1].

Below we address the case of two inputs and two outputs but there is no reason why the discussion cannot be generalized to multiple inputs and multiple outputs. Assume a linear mixture of two sources, where source amplitude drops off in proportion to distance:

$$x_i(t) = \frac{1}{R_{i1}} s_1(t - \frac{R_{i1}}{c}) + \frac{1}{R_{i2}} s_2(t - \frac{R_{i2}}{c}) \qquad (1)$$

$j = 1, 2$, where c is the speed of wave propagation, and R_{ij} indicates the distance from receiver i to source j. This describes signal propagation through a uniform non-dispersive medium. In the Fourier domain, Equation 1 results in a *mixing matrix* $A(\omega)$ given by:

$$A(\omega) = \begin{bmatrix} \frac{1}{R_{11}} e^{-j\omega \frac{R_{11}}{c}} & \frac{1}{R_{12}} e^{-j\omega \frac{R_{12}}{c}} \\ \frac{1}{R_{21}} e^{-j\omega \frac{R_{21}}{c}} & \frac{1}{R_{22}} e^{-j\omega \frac{R_{22}}{c}} \end{bmatrix} \qquad (2)$$

It is important to note that the columns can be scaled arbitrarily without affecting separation of sources because rescaling is absorbed into the sources. This implies that row scaling in the demixing matrix (the inverse of $A(\omega)$) is arbitrary.

Using the Cosine Rule, R_{ij} can be expressed in terms of the distance R_j of source j to the midpoint between two receivers, the direction of arrival of source j, and the distance between receivers, d, as follows:

$$R_{ij} = \left[R_j^2 + \left(\frac{d}{2}\right)^2 + 2(-1)^i \left(\frac{d}{2}\right) R_j \cos\theta_j \right]^{\frac{1}{2}} \qquad (3)$$

Expanding the right term above using the binomial expansion and preserving only zeroth and first order terms, we can express distance from the receivers to the sources as:

$$R_{ij} = \left(R_j + \frac{d^2}{8R_j} \right) + (-1)^i \left(\frac{d}{2}\right) \cos\theta_j \qquad (4)$$

This approximation is valid within a 5% relative error when $d \leq \frac{R_j}{2}$. With the substitution for R_{ij} and with the redefinition of source j to include the delay due to the term within brackets in Equation 4 divided by c, Equation 1 becomes:

$$x_i(t) = \sum_j \frac{1}{R_{ij}} . s_j \left(t + (-1)^i . \left(\frac{d}{2c}\right) . \cos\theta_j \right), i = 1, 2 \qquad (5)$$

In the Fourier domain, equation 5 results in the simplification to the mixing matrix $A(\omega)$:

$$A(\omega) = \begin{bmatrix} \frac{1}{R_{11}} . e^{-j\omega\delta_1} & \frac{1}{R_{12}} . e^{-j\omega\delta_2} \\ \frac{1}{R_{21}} . e^{j\omega\delta_1} & \frac{1}{R_{22}} . e^{j\omega\delta_2} \end{bmatrix} \qquad (6)$$

Here phases are functions of the directions of arrival θ_j (defined with respect to the midpoint between receivers), the distance between receivers d, and the speed of propagation c: $\delta_i = \frac{d}{2c} \cos \theta_i, i = 1, 2$. R_{ij} are unknown, but we can again redefine sources so diagonal elements are unity:

$$A(\omega) = \begin{bmatrix} e^{-j\omega\delta_1} & c_1 . e^{-j\omega\delta_2} \\ c_2 . e^{j\omega\delta_1} & e^{j\omega\delta_2} \end{bmatrix} \quad (7)$$

where c_1, c_2 are two positive real numbers. In wireless communications sources are typically distant compared to antenna distance. For distant sources and a well matched pair of receivers $c_1 \approx c_2 \approx 1$. Equation 7 describes the mixing matrix for the delay model in the frequency domain, in terms of four parameters, $\delta_1, \delta_2, c_1, c_2$.

The corresponding ideal demixing matrix $W(\omega)$, for each frequency ω, is given by:

$$W(\omega) = [A(\omega)]^{-1} = \frac{1}{\det A(\omega)} \begin{bmatrix} e^{j\omega\delta_2} & -c_1 . e^{-j\omega\delta_2} \\ -c_2 . e^{j\omega\delta_1} & e^{-j\omega\delta_1} \end{bmatrix} \quad (8)$$

The outputs, estimating the sources, are:

$$\begin{bmatrix} z_1(\omega) \\ z_2(\omega) \end{bmatrix} = W(\omega) \begin{bmatrix} x_1(\omega) \\ x_2(\omega) \end{bmatrix} = \frac{1}{\det A(\omega)} \begin{bmatrix} e^{j\omega\delta_2} & -c_1 e^{-j\omega\delta_2} \\ -c_2 e^{j\omega\delta_1} & e^{-j\omega\delta_1} \end{bmatrix} \begin{bmatrix} x_1(\omega) \\ x_2(\omega) \end{bmatrix} \quad (9)$$

Making the transition back to the time domain results in the following estimate of the outputs:

$$\begin{bmatrix} z_1(t) \\ z_2(t) \end{bmatrix} = h(t, \delta_1, \delta_2, c_1, c_2) \otimes \begin{bmatrix} x_1(t + \delta_2) - c_1 x_2(t - \delta_2) \\ -c_2 x_1(t + \delta_1) + x_2(t - \delta_1) \end{bmatrix} \quad (10)$$

where $\otimes$ is convolution, and

$$h(t, \delta_1, \delta_2, c_1, c_2) = \frac{1}{2\pi} \int e^{j\omega t} H(\omega, \delta_1, \delta_2, c_1, c_2) d\omega \quad (11)$$

$$H(\omega, \delta_1, \delta_2, c_1, c_2) = \frac{1}{\det A(\omega)} = \frac{1}{e^{j\omega(\delta_2 - \delta_1)} - c_1 c_2 e^{-j\omega(\delta_2 - \delta_1)}}$$

Formulae 9 and 10 form the basis for two algorithms to be described next, in the time domain and the frequency domains. The algorithms have the role of determining the four unknown parameters. Note that the filter corresponding to $H(\omega, \delta_1, \delta_2, c_1, c_2)$ should be applied to the output estimates in order to map back to the original inputs.

3 Delay and attenuation compensation algorithms

The estimation of the four unknown parameters $\delta_1, \delta_2, c_1, c_2$ can be carried out based on second order criteria that impose the constraint that outputs are decorrelated ([9, 4, 6, 5]).

3.1 Time and frequency domain approaches

The time domain algorithm is based on the idea of imposing the decorrelation constraint $\langle z_1(t), z_2(t) \rangle = 0$ between the estimates of the outputs, as a function of the delays D_1 and D_2 and scalar coefficients c_1 and c_2. This is equivalent to the following criterion:

$$\{\hat{D}_1, \hat{D}_2, \hat{c}_1, \hat{c}_2\} = \arg\min\{F(D_1, D_2, c_1, c_2)\} \quad (12)$$

where $F(.)$ measures the cross-correlations between the signals given below, representing filtered versions of the differences of fractionally delayed measurements:

$$z_1(t) = h(t, D_1, D_2, c_1, c_2) \otimes (x_1(t + D_2) - c_1 x_2(t)) \tag{13}$$
$$z_2(t) = h(t, D_1, D_2, c_1, c_2) \otimes (c_2 x_1(t + D_2) - x_2(t))$$
$$F(D_1, D_2, c_1, c_2) = \langle z_1(t), z_2(t) \rangle$$

In the frequency domain, the cross-correlation of the inputs is expressed as follows:

$$R^X(\omega) = A(\omega) R^S(\omega) A^H(\omega) \tag{14}$$

The mixing matrix in the frequency domain has the form given in Equation 7. Inverting this cross correlation equation yields four equations that are written in matrix form as:

$$R^S(\omega) = A^{-1}(\omega) R^X(\omega) A^{-H}(\omega) \tag{15}$$

Source orthogonality implies that the off-diagonal terms in the covariance matrix must be zero:

$$R^S_{12}(\omega) = 0 \tag{16}$$
$$R^S_{21}(\omega) = 0$$

For far field conditions (i.e. the distance between the receivers is much less than the distance from sources) one obtains the following equations:

$$R^S_{12}(\omega) = \bar{c}_1 \frac{a}{b} R^X_{11}(\omega) - c_2 \frac{b}{a} R^X_{22}(\omega) - \bar{c}_1 c_2 ab R^X_{21}(\omega) - \frac{1}{ab} R^X_{12}(\omega) = 0 \tag{17}$$
$$R^S_{21}(\omega) = c_1 \frac{b}{a} R^X_{11}(\omega) - \bar{c}_2 \frac{a}{b} R^X_{22}(\omega) - ab R^X_{21}(\omega) - \frac{c_1 \bar{c}_2}{ab} R^X_{12}(\omega) = 0$$

The terms $a = e^{-j\omega \delta_1}$ and $b = e^{-j\omega \delta_2}$ are functions of the time delays. Note that there is a pair of equations of this kind for each frequency. In practice, the unknowns should be estimated from data at all available frequencies to obtain a robust estimate.

3.2 Channel selection

Up to this point, there was no guarantee that estimated parameters would ensure source separation in some specific order. We could not decide a priori whether estimated parameters for the first output channel correspond to the first or second source. However, the dependence of the phase delays on the angles of arrival suggests a way to break the permutation symmetry in source estimation, that is to decide precisely which estimate to present on the first channel (and henceforth on the second channel as well).

The core idea is that directionality and spatial cues provide the information required to break the symmetry. The criterion we use is to sort sources in order of increasing delay. Note that the correspondence between delays and sources is unique when sources are not symmetrical with respect to the receiver axis. When sources are symmetric there is no way of distinguishing between their positions because the cosine of the angles of arrival, and hence the delay, is invariant to the sign of the angle.

4 Experimental results

A robust implementation of criterion 12 averages cross-correlations over a number of windows, of given size. More precisely F is defined as follows:

$$F(\delta_1, \delta_2) = \sum_{\text{Blocks}} |\langle z_1(t), z_2(t) \rangle|^q \tag{18}$$

Normally $q = 1$ to obtain a robust estimate. Ngo and Bhadkamkar [5] suggest a similar criterion using $q = 2$ without making use of the determinant of the mixing matrix.

After taking into account all terms from Equation 18, including the determinant of the mixing matrix A, we obtain the function to be used for parameter estimation in the frequency domain:

$$F(\delta_1, \delta_2) = \sum_\omega \frac{1}{\{\det A\}^2 + \eta} \cdot \left| \frac{a}{b} R_{11}^X(\omega) - \frac{b}{a} R_{22}^X(\omega) - ab R_{21}^X(\omega) - \frac{1}{ab} R_{12}^X(\omega) \right|^q \quad (19)$$

where η is a (Wiener Filter-like) constant that helps prevent singularities and q is normally set to one.

Computing the separated sources using only time differences leads to highpass filtered outputs. In order to implement exactly the theoretical demixing procedure presented one has to divide by the determinant of the mixing matrix. Obviously one could filter using the inverse of the determinant to obtain optimal results. This can be implemented in the form of a Wiener filter. The Wiener filter requires knowledge both of the signal and noise power spectral densities. This information is not available to us but a reasonable approximation is to assume that the (wideband) sources have a flat spectral density and the noise corrupting the mixtures is white. In this case, the Wiener Filter becomes:

$$H(\omega) = \left(\frac{\{\det A(\omega)\}^2}{\{\det A(\omega)\}^2 + \eta} \right) \frac{1}{\det A(\omega)} \quad (20)$$

where the parameter η has been empirically set to the variance of the mixture. Applying this choice of filter usually dramatically improves the quality of the separated outputs.

The technique of postprocessing using the determinant of the mixing matrix is perfectly general and applies equally well to demixtures computed using matrices of FIR filters. The quality of the result depends primarily on the care with which the inverse filter is implemented. It also depends on the accuracy of the estimate for the mixing parameters. One should avoid using the Wiener filter for near-degenerate mixtures.

The proof of concept for the theory outlined above was obtained using speech signals which if anything pose a greater challenge to separation algorithms because of the correlation structure of speech. Two kinds of data are considered in this paper: synthetic direct propagation delay data and synthetic multi-path data. Data can be characterized along two dimensions of difficulty: synthetic vs. real-world, and direct path vs. multi-path. Combinations along these dimensions represented the main type of data we used.

The value of distance between receivers dictates the order of delays that can appear due to direct path propagation, which is used by the demixing algorithms. Data was generated synthetically employing fractional delays corresponding to the various positions of the sources [3].

We modeled multi-path by taking into account the decay in signal amplitude due to propagation distance as well as the absorption of waves. Only the direct path and one additional path were considered.

The algorithms developed proved successful for separation of two voices from direct path mixtures, even where the sources had very similar spectral power characteristics, and for separation of one source for multi-path mixtures. Moreover, outputs were free from artifacts and were obtained with modest computational requirements.

Figure 1 presents mean separation results of the first and second channels, which correspond to the first and second sources, for various synthetic data sets. Separation depends on the angles of arrival. Plots show no separation in the degenerate case of equal or closeby angles of arrival, but more than 10dB mean separation in the anechoic case and 5dB in the multi-path case.

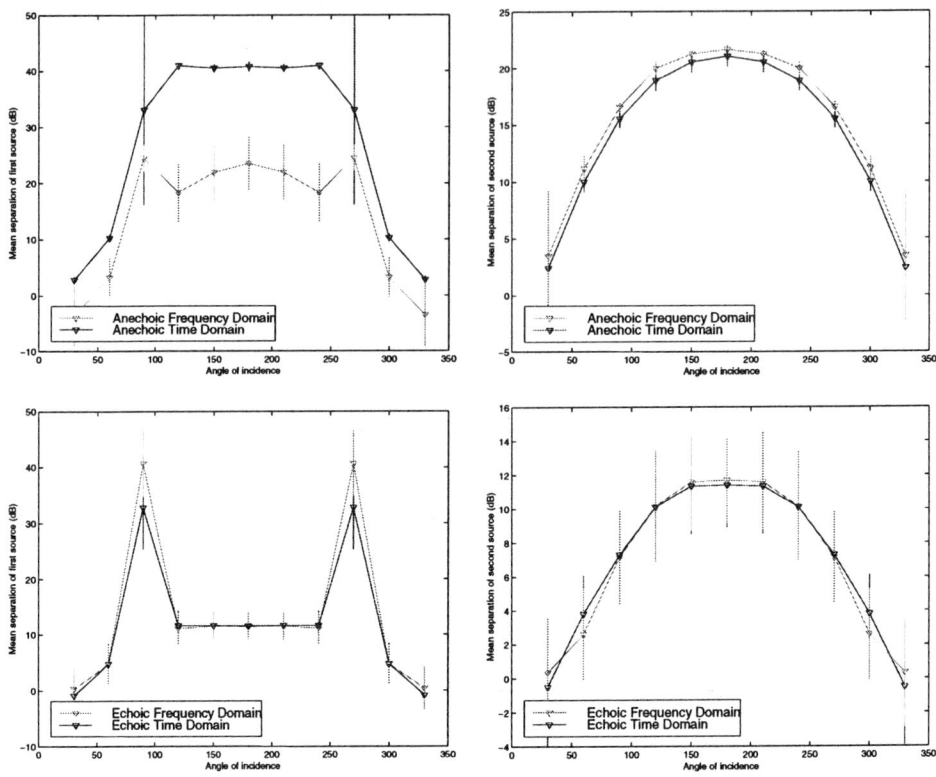

Figure 1: Two sources were positioned at a relatively large distance from a pair of closely spaced receivers. The first source was always placed at zero degrees whilst the second source was moved uniformly from 30 to 330 degrees in steps of 30 degrees. The above shows mean separation and standard deviation error bars of first and second sources for six synthetic delay mixtures or synthetic multi-path data mixtures using the time and frequency domain algorithms.

5 Conclusions

The present source separation approach is based on minimization of cross-correlations of the estimated sources, in the time or frequency domains, when using a delay model and explicitly employing dirrection of arrival. The great advantage of this approach is that it reduces source separation to a decorrelation problem, which is theoretically solved by a system of equations. Although the delay model used generates essentially anechoic time delay algorithms, the results of this work show systematic improvements even when the algorithms are applied to real multi-path data. In all cases separation improvement is robust with respect to the power ratios of sources.

Acknowledgments

We thank Radu Balan and Frans Coetzee for useful discussions and proofreading various versions of this document and our collaborators within Siemens for providing extensive data for testing.

References

[1] A. Jourjine, S. Rickard, J. Ó Ruanaidh, and J. Rosca. Demixing of anechoic time delay mixtures using second order statistics. Technical Report SCR-99-TR-657, Siemens Corporate Research, 755 College Road East, Princeton, New Jersey, 1999.

[2] Hamid Krim and Mats Viberg. Two decades of array signal processing research. *IEEE Signal Processing Magazine*, 13(4), 1996.

[3] Tim Laakso, Vesa Valimaki, Matti Karjalainen, and Unto Laine. Splitting the unit delay. *IEEE Signal Processing Magazine*, pages 30–60, 1996.

[4] L. Molgedey and H.G. Schuster. Separation of a mixture of independent signals using time delayed correlations. *Phys.Rev.Lett.*, 72(23):3634–3637, July 1994.

[5] T. J. Ngo and N.A. Bhadkamkar. Adaptive blind separation of audio sources by a physically compact device using second order statistics. In *First International Workshop on ICA and BSS*, pages 257–260, Aussois, France, January 1999.

[6] Lucas Parra, Clay Spence, and Bert De Vries. Convolutive blind source separation based on multiple decorrelation. In *NNSP98*, 1988.

[7] K. Torkolla. Blind separation for audio signals: Are we there yet? In *First International Workshop on Independent component analysis and blind source separation*, pages 239–244, Aussois, France, January 1999.

[8] V. Van Veen and Kevin M. Buckley. Beamforming: A versatile approach to spatial filtering. *IEEE ASSP Magazine*, 5(2), 1988.

[9] E. Weinstein, M. Feder, and A. Oppenheim. Multi-channel signal separation by decorrelation. *IEEE Trans. on Speech and Audio Processing*, 1(4):405–413, 1993.

Constrained Hidden Markov Models

Sam Roweis
roweis@gatsby.ucl.ac.uk
Gatsby Unit, University College London

Abstract

By thinking of each state in a hidden Markov model as corresponding to some spatial region of a fictitious *topology space* it is possible to naturally define neighbouring states as those which are connected in that space. The transition matrix can then be constrained to allow transitions only between neighbours; this means that all valid state sequences correspond to connected paths in the topology space. I show how such *constrained HMMs* can learn to discover underlying structure in complex sequences of high dimensional data, and apply them to the problem of recovering mouth movements from acoustics in continuous speech.

1 Latent variable models for structured sequence data

Structured time-series are generated by systems whose underlying state variables change in a continuous way but whose state to output mappings are highly nonlinear, many to one and not smooth. Probabilistic unsupervised learning for such sequences requires models with two essential features: latent (hidden) variables and *topology* in those variables. Hidden Markov models (HMMs) can be thought of as dynamic generalizations of discrete state static data models such as Gaussian mixtures, or as discrete state versions of linear dynamical systems (LDSs) (which are themselves dynamic generalizations of continuous latent variable models such as factor analysis). While both HMMs and LDS provide probabilistic latent variable models for time-series, both have important limitations. Traditional HMMs have a very powerful model of the relationship between the underlying state and the associated observations because each state stores a private distribution over the output variables. This means that any change in the hidden state can cause arbitrarily complex changes in the output distribution. However, it is extremely difficult to capture reasonable dynamics on the discrete latent variable because in principle any state is reachable from any other state at any time step and the next state depends only on the current state. LDSs, on the other hand, have an extremely impoverished representation of the outputs as a function of the latent variables since this transformation is restricted to be global and linear. But it is somewhat easier to capture state dynamics since the state is a multidimensional vector of continuous variables on which a matrix "flow" is acting; this enforces some continuity of the latent variables across time. *Constrained hidden Markov models* address the modeling of state dynamics by building some topology into the hidden state representation. The essential idea is to constrain the transition parameters of a conventional HMM so that the discrete-valued hidden state evolves in a structured way.[1] In particular, below I consider parameter restrictions which constrain the state to evolve as a discretized version of a continuous multivariate variable, i.e. so that it inscribes only connected paths in some space. This lends a physical interpretation to the discrete state trajectories in an HMM.

---

[1] A standard trick in traditional speech applications of HMMs is to use "left-to-right" transition matrices which are a special case of the type of constraints investigated in this paper. However, left-to-right (Bakis) HMMs force state trajectories that are inherently one-dimensional and uni-directional whereas here I also consider higher dimensional topology and free omni-directional motion.

2 An illustrative game

Consider playing the following game: divide a sheet of paper into several contiguous, non-overlapping regions which between them cover it entirely. In each region inscribe a symbol, allowing symbols to be *repeated* in different regions. Place a pencil on the sheet and move it around, reading out (in order) the symbols in the regions through which it passes. Add some *noise* to the observation process so that some fraction of the time incorrect symbols are reported in the list instead of the correct ones. The game is to reconstruct the configuration of regions on the sheet from only such an ordered list(s) of noisy symbols. Of course, the absolute scale, rotation and reflection of the sheet can never be recovered, but learning the essential *topology* may be possible.[2] Figure 1 illustrates this setup.

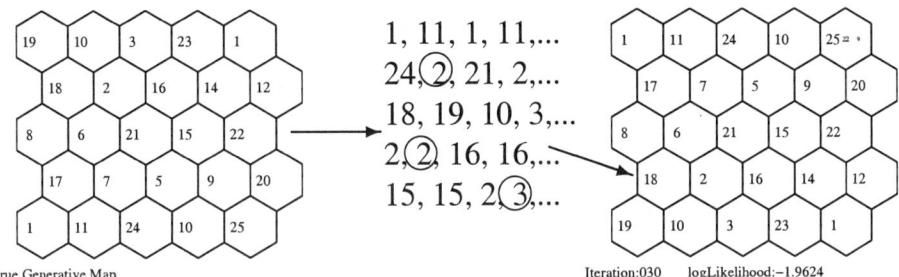

Figure 1: (**left**) True map which generates symbol sequences by random movement between connected cells. (**centre**) An example noisy output sequence with noisy symbols circled. (**right**) Learned map after training on 3 sequences (with 15% noise probability) each 200 symbols long. Each cell actually contains an entire distribution over all observed symbols, though in this case only the upper right cell has significant probability mass on more than one symbol (see figure 3 for display details).

Without noise or repeated symbols, the game is easy (non-probabilistic methods can solve it) but in their presence it is not. One way of mitigating the noise problem is to do statistical averaging. For example, one could attempt to use the average separation *in time* of each pair of symbols to define a dissimilarity between them. It then would be possible to use methods like multi-dimensional scaling or a sort of *Kohonen mapping though time*[3] to explicitly construct a configuration of points obeying those distance relations. However, such methods still cannot deal with many-to-one state to output mappings (repeated numbers in the sheet) because by their nature they assign a unique spatial location to each symbol.

Playing this game is analogous to doing unsupervised learning on structured sequences. (The game can also be played with continuous outputs, although often high-dimensional data can be effectively clustered around a manageable number of prototypes; thus a vector time-series can be converted into a sequence of symbols.) Constrained HMMs incorporate latent variables with topology yet retain powerful nonlinear output mappings and can deal with the difficulties of noise and many-to-one mappings mentioned above; so they can "win" our game (see figs. 1 & 3). The key insight is that the game generates sequences exactly according to a hidden Markov process whose transition matrix allows only transitions between neighbouring cells and whose output distributions have most of their probability on a single symbol with a small amount on all other symbols to account for noise.

---

[2]The observed symbol sequence must be "informative enough" to reveal the map structure (this can be quantified using the idea of *persistent excitation* from control theory).

[3]Consider a network of units which compete to explain input data points. Each unit has a position in the output space as well as a position in a lower dimensional topology space. The winning unit has its position in output space updated towards the data point; but also the recent (in time) winners have their positions in topology space updated towards the topology space location of the current winner. Such a rule works well, and yields topological maps in which *nearby units code for data that typically occur close together in time*. However it cannot learn many-to-one maps in which more than one unit at different topology locations have the same (or very similar) outputs.

3 Model definition: state topologies from cell packings

Defining a constrained HMM involves identifying each state of the underlying (hidden) Markov chain with a spatial cell in a fictitious *topology space*. This requires selecting a *dimensionality d* for the topology space and choosing a *packing* (such as hexagonal or cubic) which fills the space. The number of cells in the packing is equal to the number of states M in the original Markov model. Cells are taken to be all of equal size and (since the scale of the topology space is completely arbitrary) of unit volume. Thus, the packing covers a volume M in topology space with a side length ℓ of roughly $\ell = M^{1/d}$. The dimensionality and packing together define a vector-valued function $\mathbf{x}(m)$, $m = 1 \ldots M$ which gives the location of cell m in the packing. (For example, a cubic packing of d dimensional space defines $\mathbf{x}(m+1)$ to be $[m, m/\ell, m/\ell^2, \ldots, m/\ell^{d-1}]$ mod ℓ.) State m in the Markov model is assigned to cell m in the packing, thus giving it a location $\mathbf{x}(m)$ in the topology space. Finally, we must choose a *neighbourhood rule* in the topology space which defines the neighbours of cell m; for example, all "connected" cells, all face neighbours, or all those within a certain radius. (For cubic packings, there are 3^d-1 connected neighbours and $2d$ face neighbours in a d dimensional topology space.) The neighbourhood rule also defines the boundary conditions of the space – e.g. periodic boundary conditions would make cells on opposite extreme faces of the space neighbours with each other.

The transition matrix of the HMM is now *preprogrammed* to only allow transitions between neighbours. All other transition probabilities are set to zero, making the transition matrix very sparse. (I have set all permitted transitions to be equally likely.) Now, *all valid state sequences in the underlying Markov model represent connected ("city block") paths through the topology space*. Figure 2 illustrates this for a three-dimensional model.

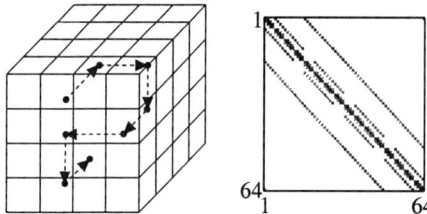

Figure 2: (left) Physical depiction of the topology space for a constrained HMM with $d=3, \ell=4$ and $M=64$ showing an example state trajectory. (right) Corresponding transition matrix structure for the 64-state HMM computed using face-centred cubic packing. The gaps in the inner bands are due to edge effects.

4 State inference and learning

The constrained HMM has exactly the same inference procedures as a regular HMM: the *forward-backward algorithm* for computing state occupation probabilities and the *Viterbi decoder* for finding the single best state sequence. Once these discrete state inferences have been performed, they can be transformed using the state position function $\mathbf{x}(m)$ to yield probability distributions over the topology space (in the case of forward-backward) or paths through the topology space (in the case of Viterbi decoding). This transformation makes the outputs of state decodings in constrained HMMs comparable to the outputs of inference procedures for continuous state dynamical systems such as Kalman smoothing.

The learning procedure for constrained HMMs is also almost identical to that for HMMs. In particular, the EM algorithm (Baum-Welch) is used to update model parameters. The crucial difference is that the transition probabilities which are precomputed by the topology and packing are never updated during learning. In fact, this makes learning much easier in some cases. Not only do the transition probabilities not have to be learned, but their structure constrains the hidden state sequences in such a way as to make the learning of the output parameters much more efficient when the underlying data really does come from a spatially structured generative model. Figure 3 shows an example of parameter learning for the game discussed above. Notice that in this case, each part of state space had only a single output (except for noise) so the final learned output distributions became essentially minimum entropy. But constrained HMMs can in principle model stochastic or multimodal output processes since each state stores an entire private distribution over outputs.

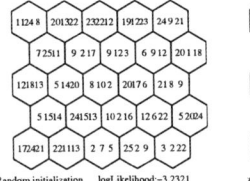 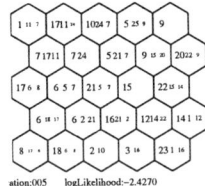 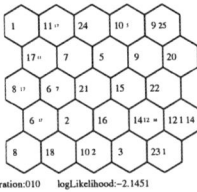 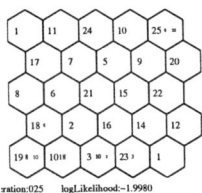

Figure 3: Snapshots of model parameters during constrained HMM learning for the game described in section 2. At every iteration each cell in the map has a complete distribution over all of the observed symbols. Only the top three symbols of each cell's histogram are show, with *font size proportional to the square root of probability* (to make ink roughly proportional). The map was trained on 3 noisy sequences each 200 symbols long generated from the map on the left of figure 1 using 15% noise probability. The final map after convergence (30 iterations) is shown on the right of figure 1.

5 Recovery of mouth movements from speech audio

I have applied the constrained HMM approach described above to the problem of recovering mouth movements from the acoustic waveform in human speech. Data containing simultaneous audio and articulator movement information was obtained from the University of Wisconsin X-ray microbeam database [9]. Eight separate points (four on the tongue, one on each lip and two on the jaw) located in the midsaggital plane of the speaker's head were tracked while subjects read various words, sentences, paragraphs and lists of numbers. The x and y coordinates (to within about ± 1mm) of each point were sampled at 146Hz by an X-ray system which located gold beads attached to the feature points on the mouth, producing a 16-dimensional vector every 6.9ms. The audio was sampled at 22kHz with roughly 14 bits of amplitude resolution but in the presence of machine noise.

These data are well suited to the constrained HMM architecture. They come from a system whose state variables are known, because of physical constraints, to move in connected paths in a low degree-of-freedom space. In other words the (normally hidden) articulators (movable structures of the mouth), whose positions represent the underlying state of the speech production system,[4] move slowly and smoothly. The observed speech signal—the system's output—can be characterized by a sequence of short-time spectral feature vectors, often known as a *spectrogram*. In the experiments reported here, I have characterized the audio signal using 12 line spectral frequencies (LSFs) measured every 6.9ms (to coincide with the articulatory sampling rate) over a 25ms window. These LSF vectors characterize only the *spectral shape* of the speech waveform over a short time but not its energy. Average energy (also over a 25ms window every 6.9ms) was measured as a separate one dimensional signal. Unlike the movements of the articulators, the audio spectrum/energy can exhibit quite abrupt changes, indicating that the mapping between articulator positions and spectral shape is not smooth. Furthermore, the mapping is many to one: *different* articulator configurations can produce very similar spectra (see below).

The unsupervised learning task, then, is to explain the complicated sequences of observed spectral features (LSFs) and energies as the outputs of a system with a low-dimensional state vector that changes slowly and smoothly. In other words, can we learn the parameters[5] of a constrained HMM such that connected paths through the topology space (state space) generate the acoustic training data with high likelihood? Once this unsupervised learning task has been performed, we can (as I show below) relate the learned trajectories in the topology space to the true (measured) articulator movements.

---

[4] Articulator positions do not provide complete state information. For example, the excitation signal (voiced or unvoiced) is not captured by the bead locations. They do, however, provide much important information; other state information is easily accessible directly from acoustics.

[5] Model structure (dimensionality and number of states) is currently set using cross validation.

While many models of the speech production process predict the many-to-one and non-smooth properties of the articulatory to acoustic mapping, it is useful to confirm these features by looking at real data. Figure 4 shows the experimentally observed distribution of articulator configurations used to produce similar sounds. It was computed as follows. All the acoustic and articulatory data for a single speaker are collected together. Starting with some sample called the *key sample*, I find the 1000 samples "nearest" to this key by two measures: articulatory distance, defined using the Mahalanobis norm between two position vectors under the global covariance of all positions for the appropriate speaker, and spectral shape distance, again defined using the Mahalanobis norm but now between two line spectral frequency vectors using the global LSF covariance of the speaker's audio data. In other words, I find the 1000 samples that "look most like" the key sample in mouth shape and that "sound most like" the key sample in spectral shape. I then plot the tongue bead positions of the key sample (as a thick cross), and the 1000 nearest samples by mouth shape (as a thick ellipse) and spectral shape (as dots). The points of primary interest are the dots; they show the distribution of tongue positions used to generate very similar sounds. (The thick ellipses are shown only as a control to ensure that many nearby points to the key sample *do* exist in the dataset.) Spread or multimodality in the dots indicates that many *different* articulatory configurations are used to generate the *same* sound.

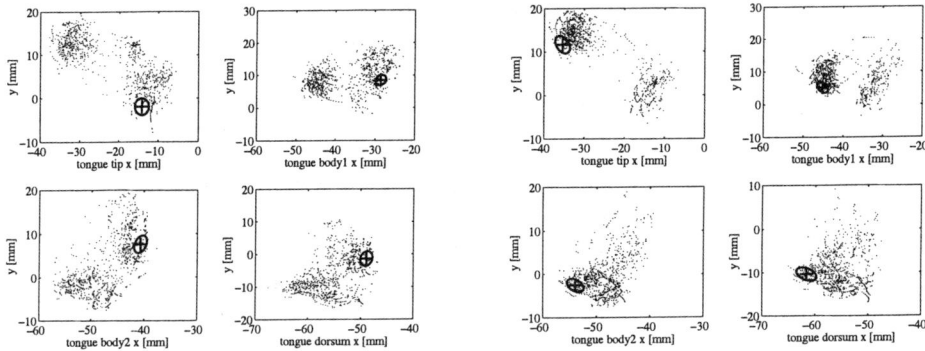

Figure 4: Inverse mapping from acoustics to articulation is ill-posed in real speech production data. Each group of four articulator-space plots shows the 1000 samples which are "nearest" to one key sample (thick cross). The dots are the 1000 nearest samples using an acoustic measure based on line spectral frequencies. Spread or multimodality in the dots indicates that many different articulatory configurations are used to generate very similar sounds. Only the positions of the four tongue beads have been plotted. Two examples (with different key samples) are shown, one in the left group of four panels and another in the right group. The thick ellipses (shown as a control) are the two-standard deviation contour of the 1000 nearest samples using an articulatory position distance metric.

Why not do direct supervised learning from short-time spectral features (LSFs) to the articulator positions? The ill-posed nature of the inverse problem as shown in figure 4 makes this impossible. To illustrate this difficulty, I have attempted to recover the articulator positions from the acoustic feature vectors using Kalman smoothing on a LDS. In this case, since we have access to both the hidden states (articulator positions) and the system outputs (LSFs) we can compute the optimal parameters of the model directly. (In particular, the state transition matrix is obtained by regression from articulator positions and velocities at time t onto positions at time $t+1$; the output matrix by regression from articulator positions and velocities onto LSF vectors; and the noise covariances from the residuals of these regressions.) Figure 5b shows the results of such smoothing; the recovery is quite poor.

Constrained HMMs can be applied to this recovery problem, as previously reported [6]. (My earlier results used a small subset of the same database that was not continuous speech and did not provide the hard experimental verification (fig. 4) of the many-to-one problem.)

Constrained Hidden Markov Models

Figure 5: (A) Recovered articulator movements using state inference on a constrained HMM. A four-dimensional model with 4096 states was trained on data (all beads) from a single speaker but not including the test utterance shown. Dots show the actual measured articulator movements for a single bead coordinate versus time; the thin lines are estimated movements from the corresponding acoustics. (B) Unsuccessful recovery of articulator movements using Kalman smoothing on a global LDS model. All the (speaker-dependent) parameters of the underlying linear dynamical system are known; they have been set to their optimal values using the true movement information from the training data. Furthermore, for this example, the test utterance shown was included in the training data used to estimate model parameters. (C) All 16 bead coordinates; all vertical axes are the same scale. Bead names are shown on the left. Horizontal movements are plotted in the left-hand column and vertical movements in the right-hand column. The separation between the two horizontal lines near the centre of the right panel indicates the machine measurement error.

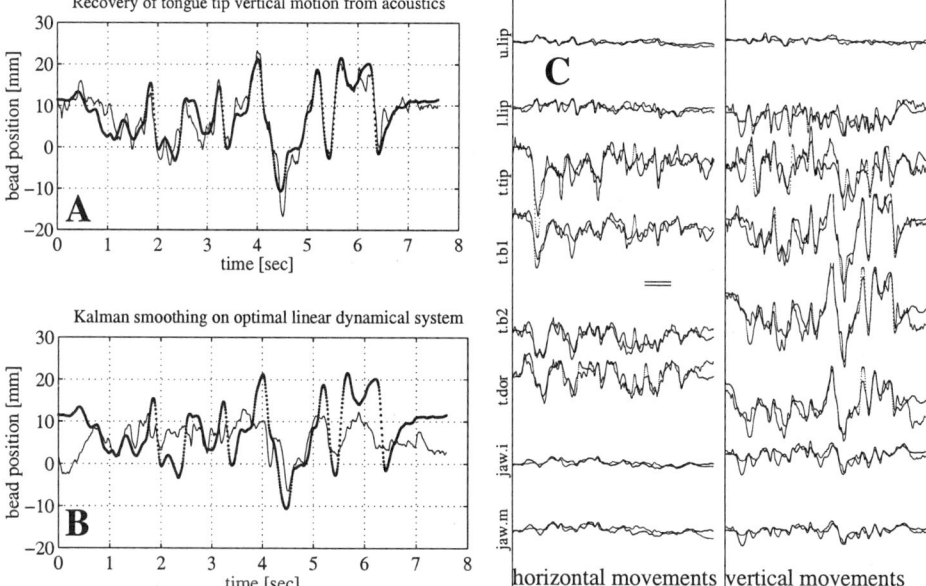

The basic idea is to train (unsupervised) on sequences of acoustic-spectral features and then map the topology space state trajectories onto the measured articulatory movements. Figure 5 shows movement recovery using state inference in a four-dimensional model with 4096 states ($d=4, \ell=8, M=4096$) trained on data (all beads) from a single speaker. (Naive unsupervised learning runs into severe local minima problems. To avoid these, in the simulations shown above, models were trained by slowly annealing two learning parameters[6]: a term ϵ^β was used in place of the zeros in the sparse transition matrix, and γ_t^β was used in place of $\gamma_t = p(m_t|observations)$ during inference of state occupation probabilities. Inverse temperature β was raised from 0 to 1.) To infer a continuous state trajectory from an utterance after learning, I first do Viterbi decoding on the acoustics to generate a discrete state sequence m_t and then interpolate smoothly between the positions $\mathbf{x}(m_t)$ of each state.

---

[6]An easier way (which I have used previously) to find good minima is to initialize the models using the articulatory data themselves. This does not provide as impressive "structure discovery" as annealing but still yields a system capable of inverting acoustics into articulatory movements on previously unseen test data. First, a constrained HMM is trained on just the articulatory movements; this works easily because of the natural geometric (physical) constraints. Next, I take the distribution of acoustic features (LSFs) over all times (in the training data) when Viterbi decoding places the model in a particular state and use those LSF distributions to initialize an equivalent acoustic constrained HMM. This new model is then retrained until convergence using Baum-Welch.

After unsupervised learning, a single linear fit is performed between these continuous state trajectories and actual articulator movements on the training data. (The model cannot discover the units system or axes used to represent the articulatory data.) To recover articulator movements from a previously unseen test utterance, I infer a continuous state trajectory as above and then apply the single linear mapping (learned only once from the training data).

6 Conclusions, extensions and other work

By enforcing a simple constraint on the transition parameters of a standard HMM, a link can be forged between discrete state dynamics and the motion of a real-valued state vector in a continuous space. For complex time-series generated by systems whose underlying latent variables do in fact change slowly and smoothly, such constrained HMMs provide a powerful unsupervised learning paradigm. They can model state to output mappings that are highly nonlinear, many to one and not smooth. Furthermore, they rely only on well understood learning and inference procedures that come with convergence guarantees.

Results on synthetic and real data show that these models can successfully capture the low-dimensional structure present in complex vector time-series. In particular, I have shown that a speaker dependent constrained HMM can accurately recover articulator movements from continuous speech to within the measurement error of the data. This acoustic to articulatory inversion problem has a long history in speech processing (see e.g. [7] and references therein). Many previous approaches have attempted to exploit the smoothness of articulatory movements for inversion or modeling: Hogden *et.al* (e.g. [4]) provided early inspiration for my ideas, but do not address the many-to-one problem; Simon Blackburn [1] has investigated a *forward* mapping from articulation to acoustics but does not explicitly attempt inversion; early work at Waterloo [5] suggested similar constraints for improving speech recognition systems but did look at real articulatory data, more recent work at Rutgers [2] developed a very similar system much further with good success. Perpiñán [3], considers a related problem in sequence learning using EPG speech data as an example.

While in this note I have described only "diffusion" type dynamics (transitions to all neighbours are equally likely) it is also possible to consider *directed flows* which give certain neighbours of a state lower (or zero) probability. The left-to-right HMMs mentioned earlier are an example of this for one-dimensional topologies. For higher dimensions, flows can be derived from discretization of matrix (linear) dynamics or from other physical/structural constraints. It is also possible to have many connected local flow regimes (either diffusive or directed) rather than one global regime as discussed above; this gives rise to *mixtures* of constrained HMMs which have block-structured rather than banded transition matrices. Smyth [8] has considered such models in the case of one-dimensional topologies and directed flows; I have applied these to learning character sequences from English text. Another application I have investigated is map learning from multiple sensor readings. An explorer (robot) navigates in an unknown environment and records at each time many local measurements such as altitude, pressure, temperature, humidity, etc. We wish to reconstruct from only these sequences of readings the topographic maps (in each sensor variable) of the area as well as the trajectory of the explorer. A final application is tracking (inferring movements) of articulated bodies using video measurements of feature positions.

References
[1] S. Blackburn & S. Young. *ICSLP 1996*, Philadephia, v.2 pp.969–972
[2] S. Chennoukh *et.al*, *Eurospeech 1997*, Rhodes, Greece, v.1 pp.429–432
[3] M. Carreira-Perpiñán. *NIPS'12*, 2000. (This volume.)
[4] D. Nix & J. Hogden. *NIPS'11*, 1999, pp.744–750
[5] G. Ramsay & L. Deng. *J. Acoustical Society of America*, 95(5), 1994, p.2873
[6] S. Roweis & A. Alwan. *Eurospeech 1997*, Rhodes, Greece, v.3 pp.1227–1230
[7] J. Schroeter & M. Sondhi. *IEEE Trans.Speech & Audio Processing*, 2(1p2), 1994, pp.133–150
[8] P. Smyth. *NIPS'9*, 1997, pp.648–654
[9] J. Westbury. X-ray microbeam speech production database user's handbook version 1.0. University of Wisconsin, Madison, June 1994.

Online Independent Component Analysis With Local Learning Rate Adaptation

Nicol N. Schraudolph
nic@idsia.ch

Xavier Giannakopoulos
xavier@idsia.ch

IDSIA, Corso Elvezia 36
6900 Lugano, Switzerland
http://www.idsia.ch/

Abstract

Stochastic meta-descent (SMD) is a new technique for online adaptation of local learning rates in arbitrary twice-differentiable systems. Like matrix momentum it uses full second-order information while retaining $O(n)$ computational complexity by exploiting the efficient computation of Hessian-vector products. Here we apply SMD to independent component analysis, and employ the resulting algorithm for the blind separation of time-varying mixtures. By matching individual learning rates to the rate of change in each source signal's mixture coefficients, our technique is capable of simultaneously tracking sources that move at very different, *a priori* unknown speeds.

1 Introduction

Independent component analysis (ICA) methods are typically run in batch mode in order to keep the stochasticity of the empirical gradient low. Often this is combined with a global learning rate annealing scheme that negotiates the tradeoff between fast convergence and good asymptotic performance. For time-varying mixtures, this must be replaced by a learning rate *adaptation* scheme. Adaptation of a single, global learning rate, however, facilitates the tracking only of sources whose mixing coefficients change at comparable rates [1], *resp.* switch all at the same time [2]. In cases where some sources move much faster than others, or switch at different times, individual weights in the unmixing matrix must adapt at different rates in order to achieve good performance.

We apply stochastic meta-descent (SMD), a new online adaptation method for local learning rates [3, 4], to an extended Bell-Sejnowski ICA algorithm [5] with natural gradient [6] and kurtosis estimation [7] modifications. The resulting algorithm is capable of separating and tracking a time-varying mixture of 10 sources whose unknown mixing coefficients change at different rates.

2 The SMD Algorithm

Given a sequence $\vec{x}_0, \vec{x}_1, \ldots$ of data points, we minimize the expected value of a twice-differentiable loss function $f_{\vec{w}}(\vec{x})$ with respect to its parameters $\vec{w}$ by stochastic gradient descent:

$$\vec{w}_{t+1} = \vec{w}_t + \vec{p}_t \cdot \vec{\delta}_t, \quad \text{where} \quad \vec{\delta}_t \equiv -\frac{\partial f_{\vec{w}_t}(\vec{x}_t)}{\partial \vec{w}} \tag{1}$$

and · denotes component-wise multiplication. The local learning rates $\vec{p}$ are best adapted by exponentiated gradient descent [8, 9], so that they can cover a wide dynamic range while staying strictly positive:

$$\ln \vec{p}_t = \ln \vec{p}_{t-1} - \mu \frac{\partial f_{\vec{w}_t}(\vec{x}_t)}{\partial \ln \vec{p}}$$

$$\vec{p}_t = \vec{p}_{t-1} \cdot \exp(\mu \vec{\delta}_t \cdot \vec{v}_t), \quad \text{where} \quad \vec{v}_t \equiv \frac{\partial \vec{w}_t}{\partial \ln \vec{p}} \tag{2}$$

and μ is a global meta-learning rate. This approach rests on the assumption that each element of $\vec{p}$ affects $f_{\vec{w}}(\vec{x})$ only through the corresponding element of $\vec{w}$. With considerable variation, (2) forms the basis of most local rate adaptation methods found in the literature.

In order to avoid an expensive exponentiation [10] for each weight update, we typically use the linearization $e^u \approx 1 + u$, valid for small $|u|$, giving

$$\vec{p}_t = \vec{p}_{t-1} \cdot \max(\varrho, 1 + \mu \vec{\delta}_t \cdot \vec{v}_t), \tag{3}$$

where we constrain the multiplier to be at least (typically) $\varrho = 0.1$ as a safeguard against unreasonably small — or negative — values. For the meta-level gradient descent to be stable, μ must in any case be chosen such that the multiplier for $\vec{p}$ does not stray far from unity; under these conditions we find the linear approximation (3) quite sufficient.

Definition of $\vec{v}$. The *gradient trace* $\vec{v}$ should accurately measure the effect that a change in local learning rate has on the corresponding weight. It is tempting to consider only the *immediate* effect of a change in $\vec{p}_t$ on $\vec{w}_{t+1}$: declaring $\vec{w}_t$ and $\vec{\delta}_t$ in (1) to be independent of $\vec{p}_t$, one then quickly arrives at

$$\vec{v}_{t+1} \equiv \frac{\partial \vec{w}_{t+1}}{\partial \ln \vec{p}_t} = \vec{p}_t \cdot \vec{\delta}_t \tag{4}$$

However, this common approach [11, 12, 13, 14, 15] fails to take into account the incremental nature of gradient descent: a change in $\vec{p}$ affects not only the current update of $\vec{w}$, but also future ones. Some authors account for this by setting $\vec{v}$ to an exponential average of past gradients [2, 11, 16]; we found empirically that the method of Almeida *et al.* [15] can indeed be improved by this approach [3]. While such averaging serves to reduce the stochasticity of the product $\vec{\delta}_t \cdot \vec{\delta}_{t-1}$ implied by (3) and (4), the average remains one of immediate, single-step effects.

By contrast, Sutton [17, 18] models the long-term effect of $\vec{p}$ on future weight updates in a linear system by carrying the relevant partials forward through time, as is done in real-time recurrent learning [19]. This results in an iterative update rule for $\vec{v}$, which we have extended to nonlinear systems [3, 4]. We define $\vec{v}$ as an exponential average of the effect of *all* past changes in $\vec{p}$ on the current weights:

$$\vec{v}_{t+1} \equiv (1-\lambda) \sum_{i=0}^{\infty} \lambda^i \frac{\partial \vec{w}_{t+1}}{\partial \ln \vec{p}_{t-i}} \quad (5)$$

The *forgetting factor* $0 \leq \lambda \leq 1$ is a free parameter of the algorithm. Inserting (1) into (5) gives

$$\begin{aligned}
\vec{v}_{t+1} &= \sum_{i=0}^{\infty} \frac{\lambda^i \partial \vec{w}_t}{\partial \ln \vec{p}_{t-i}} + \sum_{i=0}^{\infty} \lambda^i \frac{\partial(\vec{p}_t \cdot \vec{\delta}_t)}{\partial \ln \vec{p}_{t-i}} \\
&\approx \lambda \vec{v}_t + \vec{p}_t \cdot \vec{\delta}_t - \vec{p}_t \cdot \left[\frac{\partial^2 f_{\vec{w}_t}(\vec{x}_t)}{\partial \vec{w}_t \partial \vec{w}_t^T} \sum_{i=0}^{\infty} \frac{\lambda^i \partial \vec{w}_t}{\partial \ln \vec{p}_{t-i}} \right] \\
&= \lambda \vec{v}_t + \vec{p}_t \cdot (\vec{\delta}_t - \lambda H_t \vec{v}_t), \quad (6)
\end{aligned}$$

where H_t denotes the instantaneous Hessian of $f_{\vec{w}}(\vec{x})$ at time t. The approximation in (6) assumes that $(\forall i > 0)\, \partial \vec{p}_t / \partial \vec{p}_{t-i} = 0$; this signifies a certain dependence on an appropriate choice of meta-learning rate μ. Note that there is an efficient $O(n)$ algorithm to calculate $H_t \vec{v}_t$ without ever having to compute or store the matrix H_t itself [20]; we shall elaborate on this technique for the case of independent component analysis below.

Meta-level conditioning. The gradient descent in $\vec{p}$ at the meta-level (2) may of course suffer from ill-conditioning just like the descent in $\vec{w}$ at the main level (1); the meta-descent in fact *squares* the condition number when $\vec{v}$ is defined as the previous gradient, or an exponential average of past gradients. Special measures to improve conditioning are thus required to make meta-descent work in non-trivial systems.

Many researchers [11, 12, 13, 14] use the sign function to radically normalize the $\vec{p}$-update. Unfortunately such a nonlinearity does not preserve the zero-mean property that characterizes stochastic gradients in equilibrium — in particular, it will translate any skew in the equilibrium distribution into a non-zero mean change in $\vec{p}$. This causes convergence to non-optimal step sizes, and renders such methods unsuitable for online learning. Notably, Almeida *et al.* [15] avoid this pitfall by using a running estimate of the gradient's stochastic variance as their meta-normalizer.

In addition to modeling the long-term effect of a change in local learning rate, our iterative gradient trace serves as a highly effective conditioner for the meta-descent: the fixpoint of (6) is given by

$$\vec{v}_t = [\lambda H_t + (1-\lambda)\operatorname{diag}(1/\vec{p}_t)]^{-1} \vec{\delta}_t \quad (7)$$

— a modified Newton step, which for typical values of λ (*i.e.*, close to 1) scales with the inverse of the gradient. Consequently, we can expect the product $\vec{\delta}_t \cdot \vec{v}_t$ in (2) to be a very well-conditioned quantity. Experiments with feedforward multi-layer perceptrons [3, 4] have confirmed that SMD does not require explicit meta-level normalization, and converges faster than alternative methods.

3   Application to ICA

We now apply the SMD technique to independent component analysis, using the Bell-Sejnowski algorithm [5] as our base method. The goal is to find an *unmixing* matrix W_t which — up to scaling and permutation — provides a good linear estimate $\vec{y}_t \equiv W_t \vec{x}_t$ of the independent sources $\vec{s}_t$ present in a given mixture signal $\vec{x}_t$. The mixture is generated linearly according to $\vec{x}_t = A_t \vec{s}_t$, where A_t is an unknown (and unobservable) full rank matrix.

We include the well-known natural gradient [6] and kurtosis estimation [7] modifications to the basic algorithm, as well as a matrix P_t of local learning rates. The resulting online update for the weight matrix W_t is

$$W_{t+1} = W_t - P_t \cdot D_t, \qquad (8)$$

where the gradient D_t is given by

$$D_t \equiv \frac{\partial f_{W_t}(\vec{x}_t)}{\partial W_t} = ([\vec{y}_t \pm \tanh(\vec{y}_t)]\vec{y}_t^T - I)W_t, \qquad (9)$$

with the sign for each component of the $\tanh(\vec{y}_t)$ term depending on its current kurtosis estimate.

Following Pearlmutter [20], we now define the differentiation operator

$$\mathcal{R}_{V_t}(g(W_t)) \equiv \left. \frac{\partial g(W_t + rV_t)}{\partial r} \right|_{r=0} \qquad (10)$$

which describes the effect on g of a perturbation of the weights in the direction of V_t. We can use $\mathcal{R}_{V_t}$ to efficiently calculate the Hessian-vector product

$$H_t \star V_t \equiv \operatorname{vec}^{-1}[H_t \operatorname{vec}(V_t)] = \mathcal{R}_{V_t}(D_t) \qquad (11)$$

where "vec" is the operator that concatenates all columns of a matrix into a single column vector. Since $\mathcal{R}_{V_t}$ is a linear operator, we have

$$\mathcal{R}_{V_t}(W_t) = V_t, \qquad (12)$$
$$\mathcal{R}_{V_t}(\vec{y}_t) = \mathcal{R}_{V_t}(W_t \vec{x}_t) = V_t \vec{x}_t, \qquad (13)$$
$$\mathcal{R}_{V_t}(\tanh(\vec{y}_t)) = \operatorname{diag}(\tanh'(\vec{y}_t)) V_t \vec{x}_t, \qquad (14)$$

and so forth (cf. [20]). Starting from (9), we apply the $\mathcal{R}_{V_t}$ operator to obtain

$$\begin{aligned}
H_t \star V_t &= \mathcal{R}_{V_t}[([\vec{y}_t \pm \tanh(\vec{y}_t)]\vec{y}_t^T - I)W_t] \\
&= ([\vec{y}_t \pm \tanh(\vec{y}_t)]\vec{y}_t^T - I) V_t + \mathcal{R}_{V_t}([\vec{y}_t \pm \tanh(\vec{y}_t)]\vec{y}_t^T - I) W_t \\
&= ([\vec{y}_t \pm \tanh(\vec{y}_t)]\vec{y}_t^T - I) V_t + \\
&\quad [(I \pm \operatorname{diag}[\tanh'(\vec{y}_t)]) V_t \vec{x}_t \vec{y}_t^T + [\vec{y}_t \pm \tanh(\vec{y}_t)](V_t \vec{x}_t)^T] W_t
\end{aligned} \qquad (15)$$

In conjunction with the matrix versions of our learning rate update (3)

$$P_t = P_{t-1} \max(\varrho, \, 1 - \mu D_t \cdot V_t) \qquad (16)$$

and gradient trace (6)

$$V_{t+1} = \lambda V_t - P_t \cdot (D_t + \lambda H_t \star V_t) \qquad (17)$$

this constitutes our SMD-ICA algorithm.

4 Experiment

The algorithm was tested on an artificial problem where 10 sources follow elliptic trajectories according to

$$\vec{x}_t = (A_{base} + A_1 \sin(\vec{\omega}t) + A_2 \cos(\vec{\omega}t))\, \vec{s}_t \tag{18}$$

where A_{base} is a normally distributed mixing matrix, as well as A_1 and A_2, whose columns represent the axes of the ellipses on which the sources travel. The velocities $\vec{\omega}$ are normally distributed around a mean of one revolution for every 6 000 data samples. All sources are supergaussian.

The ICA-SMD algorithm was implemented with only online access to the data, including on-line whitening [21]. Whenever the condition number of the estimated whitening matrix exceeded a large threshold (set to 350 here), updates (16) and (17) were disabled to prevent the algorithm from diverging. Other parameters settings were $\mu = 0.1$, $\lambda = 0.999$, and $\rho = 0.2$.

Results that were not separating the 10 sources without ambiguity were discarded. Figure 1 shows the performance index from [6] (the lower the better, zero being the ideal case) along with the condition number of the mixing matrix, showing that the algorithm is robust to a temporary confusion in the separation. The ordinate represents 3 000 data samples, divided into mini-batches of 10 each for efficiency.

Figure 2 shows the match between an actual mixing column and its estimate, in the subspace spanned by the elliptic trajectory. The singularity occurring halfway through is not damaging performance. Globally the algorithm remains stable as long as degenerate inputs are handled correctly.

5 Conclusions

Once SMD-ICA has found a separating solution, we find it possible to simultaneously track ten sources that move independently at very different, *a priori* unknown

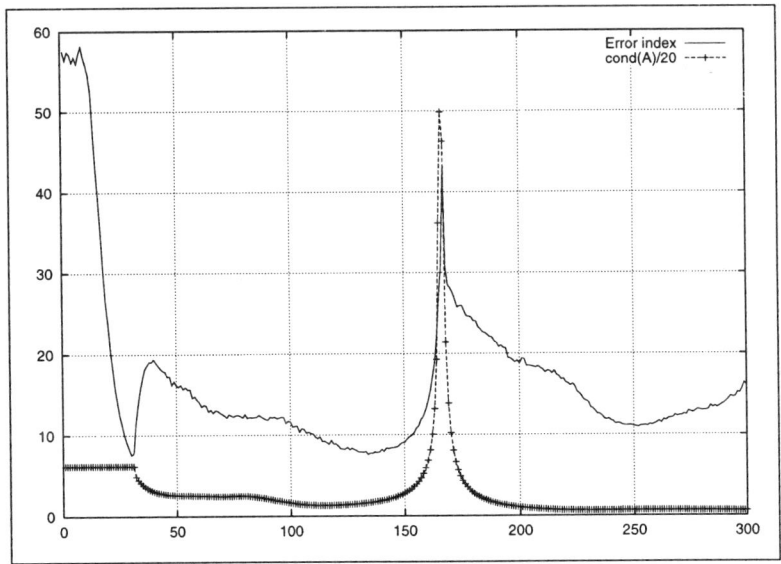

Figure 1: Global view of the quality of separation

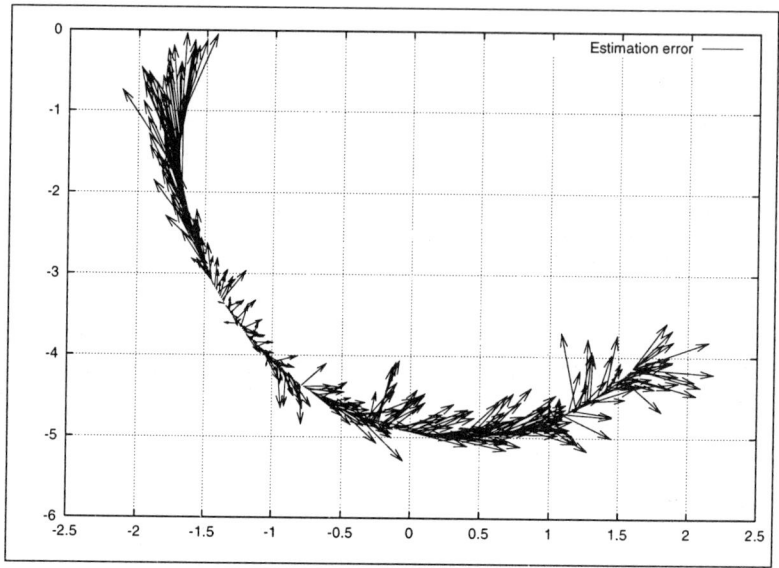

Figure 2: Projection of a column from the mixing matrix. Arrows link the exact point with its estimate; the trajectory proceeds from lower right to upper left.

speeds. To continue tracking over extended periods it is necessary to handle momentary singularities, through online estimation of the number of sources or some other heuristic solution. SMD's adaptation of local learning rates can then facilitate continuous, online use of ICA in rapidly changing environments.

Acknowledgments

This work was supported by the Swiss National Science Foundation under grants number 2000–052678.97/1 and 2100–054093.98.

References

[1] J. Karhunen and P. Pajunen, "Blind source separation and tracking using nonlinear PCA criterion: A least-squares approach", in *Proc. IEEE Int. Conf. on Neural Networks*, Houston, Texas, 1997, pp. 2147–2152.

[2] N. Murata, K.-R. Müller, A. Ziehe, and S.-i. Amari, "Adaptive on-line learning in changing environments", in *Advances in Neural Information Processing Systems*, M. C. Mozer, M. I. Jordan, and T. Petsche, Eds. 1997, vol. 9, pp. 599–605, The MIT Press, Cambridge, MA.

[3] N. N. Schraudolph, "Local gain adaptation in stochastic gradient descent", in *Proceedings of the 9th International Conference on Artificial Neural Networks*, Edinburgh, Scotland, 1999, pp. 569–574, IEE, London, ftp://ftp.idsia.ch/pub/nic/smd.ps.gz.

[4] N. N. Schraudolph, "Online learning with adaptive local step sizes", in *Neural Nets — WIRN Vietri-99: Proceedings of the 11th Italian Workshop on Neural Nets*, M. Marinaro and R. Tagliaferri, Eds., Vietri sul Mare, Salerno, Italy, 1999, Perspectives in Neural Computing, pp. 151–156, Springer Verlag, Berlin.

[5] A. J. Bell and T. J. Sejnowski, "An information-maximization approach to blind separation and blind deconvolution", *Neural Computation*, 7(6):1129–1159, 1995.

[6] S.-i. Amari, A. Cichocki, and H. H. Yang, "A new learning algorithm for blind signal separation", in *Advances in Neural Information Processing Systems*, D. S. Touretzky, M. C. Mozer, and M. E. Hasselmo, Eds. 1996, vol. 8, pp. 757–763, The MIT Press, Cambridge, MA.

[7] M. Girolami and C. Fyfe, "Generalised independent component analysis through unsupervised learning with emergent bussgang properties", in *Proc. IEEE Int. Conf. on Neural Networks*, Houston, Texas, 1997, pp. 1788–1791.

[8] J. Kivinen and M. K. Warmuth, "Exponentiated gradient versus gradient descent for linear predictors", Tech. Rep. UCSC-CRL-94-16, University of California, Santa Cruz, June 1994.

[9] J. Kivinen and M. K. Warmuth, "Additive versus exponentiated gradient updates for linear prediction", in *Proc. 27th Annual ACM Symposium on Theory of Computing*, New York, NY, May 1995, pp. 209–218, The Association for Computing Machinery.

[10] N. N. Schraudolph, "A fast, compact approximation of the exponential function", *Neural Computation*, 11(4):853–862, 1999.

[11] R. Jacobs, "Increased rates of convergence through learning rate adaptation", *Neural Networks*, 1:295–307, 1988.

[12] T. Tollenaere, "SuperSAB: fast adaptive back propagation with good scaling properties", *Neural Networks*, 3:561–573, 1990.

[13] F. M. Silva and L. B. Almeida, "Speeding up back-propagation", in *Advanced Neural Computers*, R. Eckmiller, Ed., Amsterdam, 1990, pp. 151–158, Elsevier.

[14] M. Riedmiller and H. Braun, "A direct adaptive method for faster backpropagation learning: The RPROP algorithm", in *Proc. International Conference on Neural Networks*, San Francisco, CA, 1993, pp. 586–591, IEEE, New York.

[15] L. B. Almeida, T. Langlois, J. D. Amaral, and A. Plakhov, "Parameter adaptation in stochastic optimization", in *On-Line Learning in Neural Networks*, D. Saad, Ed., Publications of the Newton Institute, chapter 6. Cambridge University Press, 1999, ftp://146.193.2.131/pub/lba/papers/adsteps.ps.gz.

[16] M. E. Harmon and L. C. Baird III, "Multi-player residual advantage learning with general function approximation", Tech. Rep. WL-TR-1065, Wright Laboratory, WL/AACF, 2241 Avionics Circle, Wright-Patterson Air Force Base, OH 45433-7308, 1996, http://www.leemon.com/papers/sim_tech/sim_tech.ps.gz.

[17] R. S. Sutton, "Adapting bias by gradient descent: an incremental version of delta-bar-delta", in *Proc. 10th National Conference on Artificial Intelligence*. 1992, pp. 171–176, The MIT Press, Cambridge, MA, ftp://ftp.cs.umass.edu/pub/anw/pub/sutton/sutton-92a.ps.gz.

[18] R. S. Sutton, "Gain adaptation beats least squares?", in *Proc. 7th Yale Workshop on Adaptive and Learning Systems*, 1992, pp. 161–166, ftp://ftp.cs.umass.edu/pub/anw/pub/sutton/sutton-92b.ps.gz.

[19] R. Williams and D. Zipser, "A learning algorithm for continually running fully recurrent neural networks", *Neural Computation*, 1:270–280, 1989.

[20] B. A. Pearlmutter, "Fast exact multiplication by the Hessian", *Neural Computation*, 6(1):147–160, 1994.

[21] J. Karhunen, E. Oja, L. Wang, R. Vigario, and J. Joutsensalo, "A class of neural networks for independent component analysis", *IEEE Trans. on Neural Networks*, 8(3):486–504, 1997.

Speech Modelling Using Subspace and EM Techniques

Gavin Smith
Cambridge University
Engineering Department
Cambridge CB2 1PZ
England
gas1003@eng.cam.ac.uk

João FG de Freitas
Computer Science Division
487 Soda Hall
UC Berkeley
CA 94720-1776, USA.
jfgf@cs.berkeley.edu [1]

Tony Robinson
Cambridge University
Engineering Department
Cambridge CB2 1PZ
England
ajr@eng.cam.ac.uk

Mahesan Niranjan
Computer Science
Sheffield University
Sheffield. S1 4DP
England
m.niranjan@dcs.shef.ac.uk

Abstract

The speech waveform can be modelled as a piecewise-stationary linear stochastic state space system, and its parameters can be estimated using an expectation-maximisation (EM) algorithm. One problem is the initialisation of the EM algorithm. Standard initialisation schemes can lead to poor formant trajectories. But these trajectories however are important for vowel intelligibility. The aim of this paper is to investigate the suitability of subspace identification methods to initialise EM.

The paper compares the subspace state space system identification (4SID) method with the EM algorithm. The 4SID and EM methods are similar in that they both estimate a state sequence (but using Kalman filters and Kalman smoothers respectively), and then estimate parameters (but using least-squares and maximum likelihood respectively). The similarity of 4SID and EM motivates the use of 4SID to initialise EM. Also, 4SID is non-iterative and requires no initialisation, whereas EM is iterative and requires initialisation. However 4SID is sub-optimal compared to EM in a probabilistic sense. During experiments on real speech, 4SID methods compare favourably with conventional initialisation techniques. They produce smoother formant trajectories, have greater frequency resolution, and produce higher likelihoods.

---

[1] Work done while in Cambridge Engineering Dept., UK.

1 Introduction

This paper models speech using a stochastic state space model, where model parameters are estimated using the expectation-maximisation (EM) technique. One problem is the initialisation of the EM algorithm. Standard initialisation schemes can lead to poor formant trajectories. These trajectories are however important for vowel intelligibility. This paper investigates the suitability of subspace state space system identification (4SID) techniques [10,11], which are popular in system identification, for EM initialisation.

Speech is split into fixed-length, overlapping frames. Overlap encourages temporally smoother parameter transitions between frames. Due to the slow non-stationary behaviour of speech, each frame of speech is assumed quasi-stationary and represented as a linear time-invariant stochastic state space (SS) model.

$$\mathbf{x}_{t+1} = \mathbf{A}\mathbf{x}_t + \mathbf{w}_t \tag{1}$$
$$y_t = \mathbf{c}\mathbf{x}_t + v_t \tag{2}$$

The system order is p. $\mathbf{x}_t \in \mathbb{R}^{p \times 1}$ is the state vector. $\mathbf{A} \in \mathbb{R}^{p \times p}$ and $\mathbf{c} \in \mathbb{R}^{1 \times p}$ are system parameters. The output $y_t \in \mathbb{R}$ is the speech signal at the microphone. Process and observation noises are modelled as white zero-mean Gaussian stationary noises $\mathbf{w}_t \in \mathbb{R}^{p \times 1} \sim N(\mathbf{0}, \mathbf{Q})$ and $v_t \in \mathbb{R} \sim N(0, R)$ respectively. The problem definition is to estimate parameters $\Theta = (\mathbf{A}, \mathbf{c}, \mathbf{Q}, R)$ from speech y_t only.

The structure of the paper is as follows. The theory section describes EM and 4SID applied to the parameter estimation of the above SS model. The similarity of 4SID and EM motivates the use of 4SID to initialise EM. Experiments on real speech then compare 4SID with more conventional initialisation methods. The discussion then compares 4SID with EM.

2 Theory

2.1 The Expectation-Maximisation (EM) Technique

Given a sequence of N observations $\mathbf{y}_{1:N}$ of a signal such as speech, the maximum likelihood estimate for the parameters is $\hat{\Theta}_{ML} = \arg\max_\Theta p(\mathbf{y}_{1:N}|\Theta)$. EM breaks the maximisation of this potentially difficult likelihood function down into an iterative maximisation of a simpler likelihood function, generating a new estimate Θ_k each iteration. Rewriting $p(\mathbf{y}_{1:N}|\Theta)$ in terms of a hidden state sequence $\mathbf{x}_{1:N}$, and taking expectations over $p(\mathbf{x}_{1:N}|\mathbf{y}_{1:N}, \Theta_k)$

$$\log p(\mathbf{y}_{1:N}|\Theta) = \log p(\mathbf{x}_{1:N}, \mathbf{y}_{1:N}|\Theta) - \log p(\mathbf{x}_{1:N}|\mathbf{y}_{1:N}, \Theta) \tag{3}$$
$$\log p(\mathbf{y}_{1:N}|\Theta) = E_k[\log p(\mathbf{x}_{1:N}, \mathbf{y}_{1:N}|\Theta)] - E_k[\log p(\mathbf{x}_{1:N}|\mathbf{y}_{1:N}, \Theta)] \tag{4}$$

Iterative maximisation of the first expectation in equation 4 guarantees an increase in $\log p(\mathbf{y}_{1:N}|\Theta)$.

$$\Theta_{k+1} = \arg\max_\Theta E_k[\log p(\mathbf{x}_{1:N}, \mathbf{y}_{1:N}|\Theta_k)] \tag{5}$$

This converges to a local or global maximum depending on the initial parameter estimate Θ_0. Refer to [8] for more details. EM can thus be applied to the stochastic state space model of equations 1 and 2 to determine optimal parameters Θ. An explanation is given in [3]. The EM algorithm applied to the SS system consists of two stages per iteration. Firstly, given current parameter estimates, states are estimated using a Kalman smoother. Secondly, given these states, new parameters are estimated by maximising the expected log likelihood function. We employ the Rauch-Tung-Striebel formulation of the Kalman smoother [2].

2.2 The State-Space Model

Equations 1 and 2 can be cast in block matrix form and are termed the state sequence and block output equations respectively [10]. Note that the use of blocking and fixed-length signals applies restrictions to the general model in section 1. $i > p$ is the block size.

$$\mathbf{X}_{i+1,i+j} = \mathbf{A}^i \mathbf{X}_{1,j} + \mathbf{\Delta}_i^w \mathbf{W}_{1|i} \quad (6)$$
$$\mathbf{Y}_{1|i} = \mathbf{\Gamma}_i \mathbf{X}_{1,j} + \mathbf{H}_i^w \mathbf{W}_{1|i} + \mathbf{V}_{1|i} \quad (7)$$

$\mathbf{X}_{i+1,i+j}$ is a state sequence matrix; its columns are the state vectors from time $(i+1)$ to $(i+j)$. $\mathbf{X}_{1,j}$ is similarly defined. $\mathbf{Y}_{1|i}$ is a Hankel matrix of outputs from time 1 to $(i+j-1)$. $\mathbf{W}$ and $\mathbf{V}$ are similarly defined. $\mathbf{\Delta}_i^w$ is a reversed extended controllability-type matrix, $\mathbf{\Gamma}_i$ is the extended observability matrix and $\mathbf{H}_i^w$ is a Toeplitz matrix. These are all defined below where $\mathbf{I}^{p \times p}$ is an identity matrix.

$$\mathbf{X}_{1,j} \stackrel{def}{=} [\mathbf{x}_1 \ \mathbf{x}_2 \ \mathbf{x}_3 \ \ldots \ \mathbf{x}_j] \qquad \mathbf{\Gamma}_i \stackrel{def}{=} \begin{bmatrix} \mathbf{c} \\ \mathbf{cA} \\ \vdots \\ \mathbf{cA}^{i-1} \end{bmatrix}$$

$$\mathbf{\Delta}_i^w \stackrel{def}{=} [\mathbf{A}^{i-1} \ \mathbf{A}^{i-2} \ \ldots \ \mathbf{I}]$$

$$\mathbf{Y}_{1|i} \stackrel{def}{=} \begin{bmatrix} y_1 & y_2 & \cdots & y_j \\ y_2 & y_3 & \cdots & y_{j+1} \\ \vdots & \vdots & & \vdots \\ y_i & y_{i+1} & \cdots & y_{i+j-1} \end{bmatrix} \qquad \mathbf{H}_i^w \stackrel{def}{=} \begin{bmatrix} 0 & & & 0 \\ \mathbf{c} & 0 & & \\ \vdots & & \ddots & \ddots \\ \mathbf{cA}^{i-2} & \cdots & \mathbf{c} & 0 \end{bmatrix}$$

A sequence of outputs can be separated into two block output equations containing *past* and *future* outputs denoted with subscripts p and f respectively. With $\mathbf{Y}_p \stackrel{def}{=} \mathbf{Y}_{1|i}$, $\mathbf{Y}_f \stackrel{def}{=} \mathbf{Y}_{i+1|2i}$ and similarly for $\mathbf{W}$ and $\mathbf{V}$, and $\mathbf{X}_p \stackrel{def}{=} \mathbf{X}_{1,j}$ and $\mathbf{X}_f \stackrel{def}{=} \mathbf{X}_{i+1,i+j}$, past and future are related by the equations

$$\mathbf{X}_f = \mathbf{A}^i \mathbf{X}_p + \mathbf{\Delta}_i^w \mathbf{W}_p \quad (8)$$
$$\mathbf{Y}_p = \mathbf{\Gamma}_i \mathbf{X}_p + \mathbf{H}_i^w \mathbf{W}_p + \mathbf{V}_p \quad (9)$$
$$\mathbf{Y}_f = \mathbf{\Gamma}_i \mathbf{X}_f + \mathbf{H}_i^w \mathbf{W}_f + \mathbf{V}_f \quad (10)$$

2.3 Subspace State Space System Identification (4SID) Techniques

Comments throughout this section on 4SID are largely taken from the work of Van Overschee and De Moor [10]. 4SID methods are related to instrumental variable (IV) methods [11]. 4SID algorithms are composed of two stages. Stage one involves the low-rank approximation and estimation of the extended observability matrix directly from the output data. For example, consider the future output block equation 10. $\mathbf{Y}_f$ undergoes an orthogonal projection onto the row space of $\mathbf{Y}_p$. This is denoted by $\mathbf{Y}_f/\mathcal{Y}_p = \mathbf{Y}_f \mathbf{Y}_p^T (\mathbf{Y}_p \mathbf{Y}_p^T)^\dagger \mathbf{Y}_p$, where $\dagger$ is the Moore-Penrose inverse.

$$\begin{aligned} \mathbf{Y}_f/\mathcal{Y}_p &= \Gamma_i \mathbf{X}_f/\mathcal{Y}_p + \mathbf{H}_i^w \mathbf{W}_f/\mathcal{Y}_p + \mathbf{V}_f/\mathcal{Y}_p \\ \mathbf{Y}_f/\mathcal{Y}_p &= \Gamma_i \mathbf{X}_f/\mathcal{Y}_p \end{aligned} \quad (11)$$

Stage two involves estimation of system parameters. The singular value decomposition of $\mathbf{Y}_f/\mathcal{Y}_p$ allows the observability and state sequence matrices to be estimated to within a similarity transform from the column and row spaces respectively. From these two matrices, system parameters $(\mathbf{A}, \mathbf{c}, \mathbf{Q}, R)$ can be determined by least-squares.

There are two interesting comments. Firstly, the orthogonal projection from stage one coincides with a minimum error between true data $\mathbf{Y}_f$ and its linear prediction from $\mathbf{Y}_p$ in the Frobenius norm. Greater flexibility is obtained by weighting the projection with matrices $\mathbf{W}_1$ and $\mathbf{W}_2$ and analysing this: $\mathbf{W}_1(\mathbf{Y}_f/\mathcal{Y}_p)\mathbf{W}_2$. 4SID and IV methods differ with respect to these weighting matrices. Weighting is similar to prefiltering the observations prior to analysis to preferentially weight some frequency domain, as is common in identification theory [6]. Secondly, the state estimates from stage two can be considered as outputs from a parallel bank of Kalman filters, each one estimating a state from the previous i observations, and initialised using zero conditions.

The particular subspace algorithm and software used in this paper is the *sto_pos* algorithm as detailed in [10]. Although this algorithm introduces a small bias into some of the parameter estimates, it guarantees positive realness of the covariance sequence, which in turn guarantees the definition of a forward innovations model.

3 Experiments

Experiments are conducted on the phrase *"in arithmetic"*, spoken by an adult male. The speech waveform is obtained from the Eurom 0 database [4] and sampled at 16 kHz. The speech waveform is divided into fixed-length, overlapping frames, the mean is subtracted and then a hamming window is applied. Frames are 15 ms in duration, shifted 7.5 ms each frame. Speech is modelled as detailed in section 1. All models are order 8. A frame is assumed silent and no analysis done when the mean energy per sample is less than an empirically defined threshold.

For the EM algorithm, a modified version of the software in [3] is used. The initial state vector and covariance matrix are set to zero and identity respectively, and 50 iterations are applied. $\mathbf{Q}$ is updated by taking its diagonal only in the M-step for numerical stability (see [3]).

In these experiments, three schemes are compared at initialising parameters for the EM algorithm, that is the estimation of Θ_0. These schemes are compared in terms of their formant trajectories relative to the spectrogram and their likelihoods. The three schemes are

- **4SID**. This is the subspace method in section 2.3 with block size 16.
- **ARMA**. This estimates Θ_0 using the customised Matlab *armax* function[1], which models the speech waveform as an autoregressive moving average (ARMA) process, with order 8 polynomials.

---

[1]*armax* minimises a robustified quadratic prediction error criterion using an iterative Gauss-Newton algorithm, initialised using a four-stage least-squares instrumental variables algorithm [7].

- **AR(1)**. This uses a simplistic method, and models the speech waveform as a first order autoregressive (AR) process with some randomness introduced into the estimation. It still initialises all parameters fully[2].

Results are shown in Figures 1 and 2. Figure 1 shows the speech waveform, spectrogram and formant trajectories for EM with all three initialisation schemes. Here formant frequencies are derived from the phase of the positive phase eigenvalues of **A** after 50 iterations of EM. Comparison with the spectrogram shows that for this order 8 model, 4SID-EM produces best formant trajectories. Figure 2 shows mean average plots of likelihood against EM iteration number for each initialisation scheme. 4SID-EM gives greater likelihoods than ARMA-EM and AR(1)-EM. The difference in formant trajectories between subspace-EM and ARMA-EM despite the high likelihoods, demonstrates the multi-modality of the likelihood function. For AR(1)-EM, a few frames were not estimated due to numerical instability.

4 Discussion

Both the 4SID and EM algorithms employ similar methodologies: states are first estimated using a Kalman device, and then these states are used to estimate system parameters according to similar criteria. However in EM, states are estimated using past, present and future observations with a Kalman smoother; system parameters are then estimated using maximum likelihood (ML). Whereas in 4SID, states are estimated using the previous i observations only with non-steady state Kalman filters. System parameters are then estimated using least-squares (LS) subject to a positive realness constraint for the covariance sequence. Refer also to [5] for a similar comparison.

4SID algorithms are sub-optimal for three reasons. Firstly, states are estimated using only partial observations sequences. Secondly, the LS criterion is only an approximation to the ML criterion. Thirdly, the positive realness constraint introduces bias. A positive realness constraint is necessary due to a finite amount of data and any lacking in the SS model. For this reason, 4SID methods are used to initialise rather than replace EM in these experiments.

4SID methods also have some advantages. Firstly, they are linear and non-iterative, and do not suffer from the disadvantages typical of iterative algorithms (including EM) such as sensitivity to initial conditions, convergence to local minima, and the definition of convergence criteria. Secondly, they require little prior parameterisation except the definition of the system order, which can be determined *in situ* from observation of the singular values of the orthogonal projection. Thirdly, the use of the SVD gives numerical robustness to the algorithms. Fourthly, they have higher frequency resolution than prediction error minimisation methods such as ARMA and AR [1].

5 Conclusions

4SID methods can be used to initialise EM giving better formant tracks, higher likelihoods and better frequency resolution than more conventional initialisation methods. In the future we hope to compare 4SID methods with EM in a principled probabilistic manner, investigate weighting matrices further, and apply these methods to speech enhancement. Further work is done by Smith et al. in [9], and similar work done by Grivel et al. in [5].

Acknowledgements
We are grateful for the use of 4SID software supplied with [10] and the EM software of

---

[2]Presented in the software in [3], this method is best used when the dimensions of the state space and observations are the same.

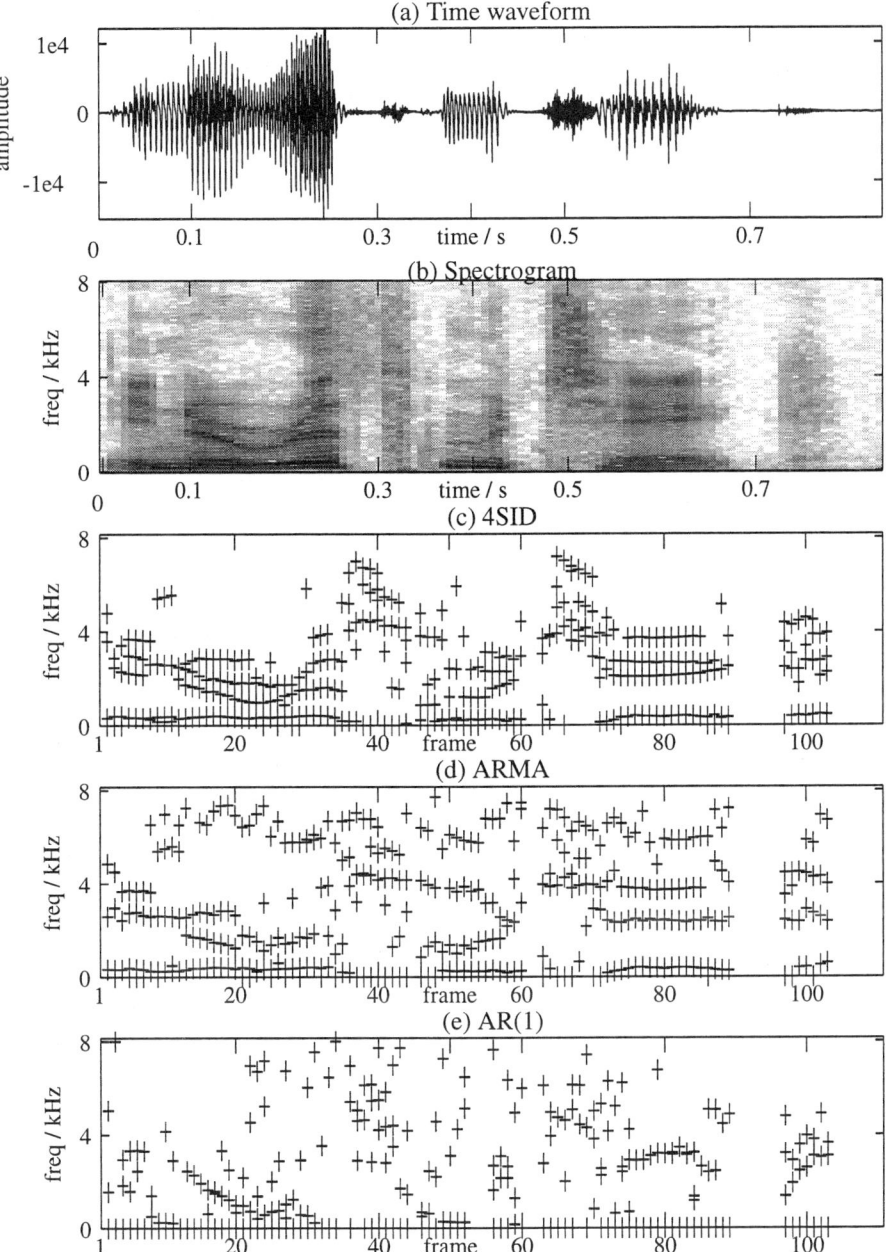

Figure 1: (a) Time waveform and (b) spectrogram for "*in arithmetic*". Formant trajectories are estimated using EM and a SS model initialised with three different schemes: (d) 4SID, (e) ARMA and (f) AR(1).

Zoubin Ghahramani [3]. Gavin Smith is supported by the Schiff Foundation, Cambridge University. At the time of writing, Nando de Freitas was supported by two University of the Witwatersrand Merit Scholarships, a Foundation for Research Development Scholarship (South Africa), an ORS award and a Trinity College External Research Studentship (Cambridge).

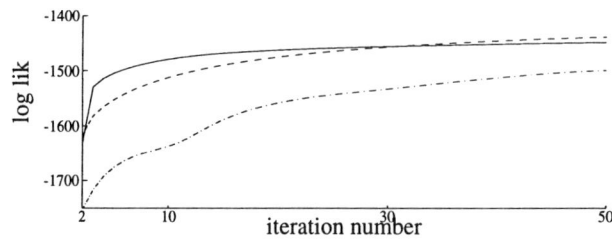

Figure 2: Likelihood convergence plots for EM and the SS model initialised with 4SID [- -], ARMA [–] and AR(1) [-.] for the experiments in Figure 1. Plots are the mean average over all frames where analysed.

6 References

[1] Arun, K.S. & Kung, S.Y. (1990) Balanced Approximation of Stochastic Systems. SIAM Journal on Matrix Analysis and Applications, vol. 11, no. 1, pp. 42–68.

[2] Gelb, A. ed., (1974) *Applied Optimal Estimation*. Cambridge, MA: MIT Press.

[3] Ghahramani, Z. & Hinton, G. (1996) Parameter Estimation for Linear Dynamical Systems, Tech. rep. CRG-TR-96-2, Dept. of Computer Science, Univ. of Toronto. Software at *www.gatsby.ucl.ac.uk/~zoubin/software.html*.

[4] Grice, M. & Barry, W. (1989) Multi-lingual Speech Input/Output: Assessment, Methodology and Standardization, Tech. rep., University College, London, ESPRIT Project 1541 (SAM), extension phase final report.

[5] Grivel, E., Gabrea, M. & Najim, M. (1999) Subspace State Space Model Identification For Speech Enhancement, Paper 1622, ICASSP'99.

[6] Ljung, L. (1987) *System Identification: Theory for the User*. Englewood Cliffs, NJ: Prentice-Hall, Inc.

[7] Ljung, L. (1991) *System Identification Toolbox For Use With MatLab*. 24 Prime Park Way, Natrick, MA, USA: The MathWorks, Inc.

[8] McLachlan, G.J. & Krishnan, T. (1997) *The EM Algorithm and Extensions*. John Wiley and Sons Inc.

[9] Smith, G.A. & Robinson, A.J. & Niranjan, M. (2000) A Comparison Between the EM and Subspace Algorithms for the Time-Invariant Linear Dynamical System. Tech. rep. CUED/F-INFENG/TR.366, Engineering Dept., Cambridge Univ., UK.

[10] Van Overschee, P. & De Moor, B. (1996) *Subspace Identification for Linear Systems: Theory, Implementation, Applications*. Dordrecht, Netherlands: Kluwer Academic Publishers.

[11] Viberg, M. & Wahlberg, B. & Ottersten, B. (1997) Analysis of State Space System Identification Methods Based on Instrumental Variables and Subspace Fitting. Automatica, vol. 33, no. 9, pp. 1603–1616.

Search for Information Bearing Components in Speech

Howard Hua Yang and Hynek Hermansky
Department of Electrical and Computer Engineering
Oregon Graduate Institute of Science and Technology
20000 NW, Walker Rd., Beaverton, OR97006, USA
{hyang,hynek}@ece.ogi.edu, FAX:503 7481406

Abstract

In this paper, we use mutual information to characterize the distributions of phonetic and speaker/channel information in a time-frequency space. The mutual information (MI) between the phonetic label and one feature, and the joint mutual information (JMI) between the phonetic label and two or three features are estimated. The Miller's bias formulas for entropy and mutual information estimates are extended to include higher order terms. The MI and the JMI for speaker/channel recognition are also estimated. The results are complementary to those for phonetic classification. Our results show how the phonetic information is locally spread and how the speaker/channel information is globally spread in time and frequency.

1 Introduction

Speech signals typically carry information about number of target sources such as linguistic message, speaker identity, and environment in which the speech was produced. In most realistic applications of speech technology, only one or a few information targets are important. For example, one may be interested in identifying the message in the signal regardless of the speaker or the environments in which the speech was produced, or the identification of the speaker is needed regardless of the words the targeted speaker is saying. Thus, not all components of the signal may be equally relevant for a decoding of the targeted information in the signal.

The speech research community has at its disposal rather large speech databases which are mainly used for training and testing automatic speech recognition (ASR) systems. There have been relatively few efforts to date to use such databases for deriving reusable knowledge about speech and speech communication processes which could be used for improvements of ASR technology. In this paper we apply information-theoretic approaches to study a large hand-labeled data set of fluent speech to learn about the information structure of the speech signal including the distribution of speech information in frequency and in time.

Based on the labeled data set, we analyze the relevancy of the features for phonetic classifications and speaker/channel variability. The features in this data set are labeled with respect to underlying phonetic classes and files from which the features come from. The phoneme labels relate to the linguistic message in the signal, and the file labels carry the information about speakers and communication channels (each file contains speech of a single speaker transmitted through one telephone channel). Thus, phoneme and file labels are two target variables for statistical inference. The phoneme labels take 19 different values corresponding to 19 broad phoneme categories in the OGI Stories database [2]. The file labels take different values representing different speakers in the OGI Stories database.

The relevancy of a set of features is measured by the joint mutual information (JMI) between the features and a target variable. The phoneme target variable represents in our case the linguistic message. The file target variable represents both different speakers and different telephone channels. The joint mutual information between a target variable and the features quantifies the relevancy of the features for that target variable.

Mutual information measure the statistical dependence between random variables. Morris et al (1993) used mutual information to find the critical points of information for classifying French Vowel-Plosive-Vowel utterances. Bilmes(1998) showed recently that the information appears to be spread over relatively long temporal spans. While Bilmes used mutual information between two variables on non-labeled data to reveal the mutual dependencies between the components of the spectral energies in time and frequency, we focused on joint mutual information between the phoneme labels or file labels and one, two or three feature variables in the time-frequency plane[7, 6] and used this concept to gain insight into how information about phonemes and speaker/channel variability is distributed in the time-frequency plane.

2 Data Set and Preprocessing

The data set used in this paper is 3-hour phonetically labeled telephone speech, a subset of the English portion (Stories) of the OGI multi-lingual database [2] containing approximately 50 seconds of extemporaneous speech from each of 210 different speakers. The speech data is labeled by a variable Y taking 19 values representing 19 most often occurring phoneme categories. The average phoneme duration is about 65 ms and the number of phoneme instances is 65421.

Acoustic features $X(f_k, t)$ for the experiments are derived from a short-time analysis of the speech signal with a 20 ms analysis window (Hamming) at the frame t advanced in 10 ms steps. The logarithmic energy at a frequency f_k is computed from the squared magnitude FFT using a critical-band spaced (log-like in the frequency variable) weighting function in a manner similar to that of the computation of Perceptual Linear Prediction coefficients [3]. In particular, the 5-th, 8-th and 12-th bands are centered around 0.5, 1 and 2 kHz respectively. Each feature $X(f_k, t)$ is labeled by a phoneme label $Y^p(t)$ and a file label $Y^f(t)$. We use mutual information to measure the relevancy of $X(f_k, t-d)$ across all frequencies f_k and in a context window $-D \leq d \leq +D$ for the phoneme classification and the speaker/channel identification.

3 Estimation of MI and Bias Correction

In this paper, we only consider the mutual information (MI) between discrete random variables. The phoneme label and the file label are discrete random variables.

However, the feature variables are bounded continuous variables. To obtain the quantized features, we divide the maximum range of the observed features into cells of equal volume so that we can use histogram to estimate mutual information defined by

$$I(X;Y) = \sum_{x,y} p(x,y) \log_2 \frac{p(x,y)}{p(x)p(y)}.$$

If X and Y are jointly Gaussian, then $I(X;Y) = -\frac{1}{2}\ln(1-\rho^2)$ where ρ is the correlation coefficient between X and Y. However, for speech data the feature variables are generally non-Gaussian and target variables are categorical type variables. Correlations involving a categorical variable are meaningless.

The MI can also be written as

$$\begin{aligned} I(X;Y) &= H(X) + H(Y) - H(X,Y) \\ &= H(Y) - H(Y|X) = H(X) - H(X|Y) \end{aligned} \quad (1)$$

where $H(Y|X)$ is a conditional entropy defined by

$$H(Y|X) = -\sum_x p(x) \sum_y p(y|x) \log_2 p(y|x).$$

The two equations in (1) mean that the MI is the uncertainty reduction about Y give X or the uncertainty reduction about X give Y.

Based on the histogram, $H(X)$ is estimated by

$$\hat{H}(X) = -\sum_i \frac{n_i}{n} \log_2 \frac{n_i}{n}$$

where n_i is the number of data points in the i-th cell and n is the data size. And $I(X;Y)$ is estimated by

$$\hat{I}(X;Y) = \hat{H}(X) + \hat{H}(Y) - \hat{H}(X,Y).$$

Miller(1954)[4] has shown that $\hat{H}(X)$ is an underestimate of $H(X)$ and $\hat{I}(X;Y)$ is an overestimate of $I(X;Y)$. The biases are

$$E[\hat{H}(X)] - H(X) = -\frac{r-1}{2\ln(2)n} + O(\frac{1}{n^2}) \quad (2)$$

$$E[\hat{I}(X;Y)] - I(X;Y) = \frac{(r-1)(c-1)}{2\ln(2)n} + O(\frac{1}{n^2}) \quad (3)$$

where r and c are the number of cells for X and Y respectively.

Interestingly, the first order terms in (2) and (3) do not depend on the probability distribution. After using these formulas to correct the estimates, the new estimates have the same variances as the old estimates but with reduced biases. However, these formulas break down when r and n are of the same order. Extending Miller's approach, we find a high order correction for the bias. Let $\{p_i\}$ be the probability distribution of X, then

$$\begin{aligned} E[\hat{H}(X)] - H(X) &= -\frac{r-1}{2\ln(2)n} + \frac{1}{6\ln(2)n^2}(S(\{p_i\}) - 3r + 2) \\ &\quad - \frac{1}{4n^3}(S(\{p_i\}) - 1) + O(\frac{1}{n^4}) \end{aligned} \quad (4)$$

where $S(\{p_i\}) = \sum_{i=1, p_i \neq 0}^{r} \frac{1}{p_i}$.

The last two terms in the bias (4) depend on the unknown probabilities $\{p_i\}$. In practice they are approximated by the relative frequency estimates.

Similarly, we can find the bias formulas of the high order terms $O(\frac{1}{n^2})$ and $O(\frac{1}{n^3})$ for the MI estimate.

When X is evenly distributed, $p_i = 1/r$, so $S(\{p_i\}) = r^2$ and

$$E[\hat{H}(X)] - H(X) = -\frac{r-1}{2\ln(2)n} + \frac{1}{6\ln(2)n^2}(r^2 - 3r + 2) - \frac{1}{4n^3}(r^2 - 1) + O(\frac{1}{n^4}).$$

Theoretically $S(\{p_i\})$ has no upper bound when one of the probabilities is close to zero. However, in practice it is hard to collect a sample to estimate a very small probability. For this reason, we assume that p_i is either zero or greater than ε/r where $\varepsilon > 0$ is a small constant does not depend on n or r. Under this assumption $S(\{p_i\}) \leq r^2/\varepsilon$ and the amplitude of the last term in (4) is less than $\frac{1}{4n^3}(r^2/\varepsilon - 1)$.

4 MI in Speech for Phonetic Classification

The three hour telephone speech in the OGI database gives us a sample size greater than 1 million, $n = 1050000$. To estimate the mutual information between three features and a target variable, we need to estimate the entropy $H(X_1, X_2, X_3, Y)$. Take $B = 20$ as the number of bins for each feature variable and $C = 19$ is the number of phoneme categories. Then the total number of cells is $r = B^3 * C$. After a constant adjustment, assuming $\varepsilon = 1$, the bias is

$$O(\frac{1}{n^2}) = \frac{1}{6\ln(2)n^2}(r^2 - 3r + 2) = 0.005 (\text{bits}).$$

It is shown in Fig. 1(a) that $X(f_4, t)$ and $X(f_5, t)$ are most relevant features for phonetic classification. From Fig. 1(b), at 5 Bark the MI spread around the current frame is 200 ms.

Given one feature X_1, the information gain due to the second feature is the difference

$$I(X_1, X_2; Y) - I(X_1; Y) = I(X_2; Y|X_1)$$

where $I(X_2; Y|X_1)$ is called the information gain of X_2 given X_1. It is a conditional mutual information defined by

$$I(X_2; Y|X_1) = \sum_{x_1} p(x_1) \sum_{x_2, y} p(x_2, y|x_1) \log_2 \frac{p(x_2, y|x_1)}{p(x_2|x_1)p(y|x_1)}$$

It is shown in Fig. 1(c)-(d) that given $X(f_5, t)$ across different bands the maximum information gain is achieved by $X(f_9, t)$, and within 5 Bark band the maximum information gain is achieved by $X(f_5, t - 5)$. The mutual informations $I(X(f_4, t), X(f_k, t + d); Y)$ for $k = 1, \cdots, 15, k \neq 4$, and $d = \pm 1, \cdots, \pm 10$, the information gain from the second feature in the vicinity of the first one, are shown in Fig. 2. The asymmetric distribution of the MI around the neighborhood $(f_5, d = 0)$ indicates that the phonetic information is spread asymmetrically through time but localized in about 200 ms around the current frame.

Based on our data set, we have $\hat{H}(Y) = 3.96$ (bits). The JMI for three frequency features and three temporal features are shown in Fig. 1(e)-(f). Based on these estimates, the three frequency features give 28% reduction in uncertainty about Y while the three temporal features give 19% reduction.

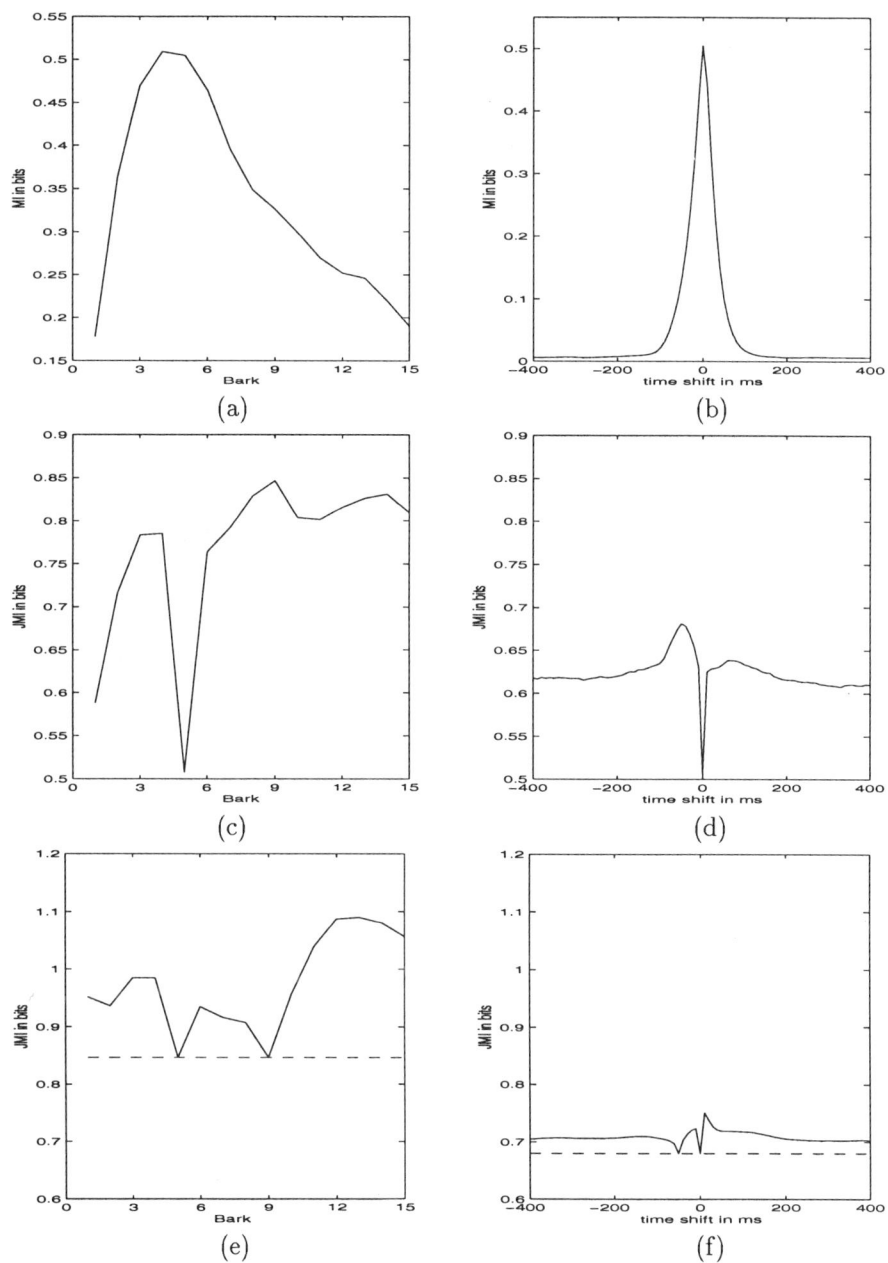

Figure 1: (a) MIs of individual features in different bands. (b) MIs of individual feature at 5 Bark with different 10ms-frame shifts. (c) JMIs of two features: at 5 Bark and in other bands. (d) JMIs of two features: current frame and shifted frames, both at 5 Bark. (e) JMIs of three features: at 5 Bark, 9 Bark and in other bands. The dashed line is the JMI level achieved by the two features $X(f_5,t)$ and $X(f_9,t)$. (f) JMIs of three features: current frame, 5th frame before current frame, and other shifted frames, all at 5 Bark. The dashed line is the JMI level achieved by $X(f_5,t)$ and $X(f_5,t-5)$.

The size of our data set is $n = 1050000$. Therefore, we can reliably estimate the joint

MI between three features and the phoneme label. However, to estimate the JMI for more than 3 features we have the problem of curse of dimensionality since for k features, $r = B^k * C$ is exponential increasing. For example, when $k = 4, B = 20$, and $C = 19$, the second order bias is $O(1/n^2) = 2.02$ (bits) which is too high to be ignored. To extend our approach beyond the current three-feature level, we need either to enlarge our data set or to find an alternative to the histogram based MI estimation.

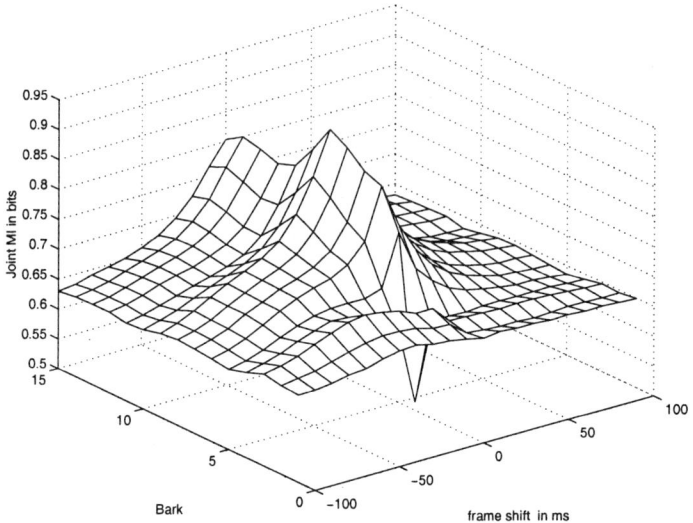

Figure 2: The 3-D plot of joint mutual information around $X(f_4, t)$. An asymmetric distribution is apparent especially around 4 Bark and 5 Bark.

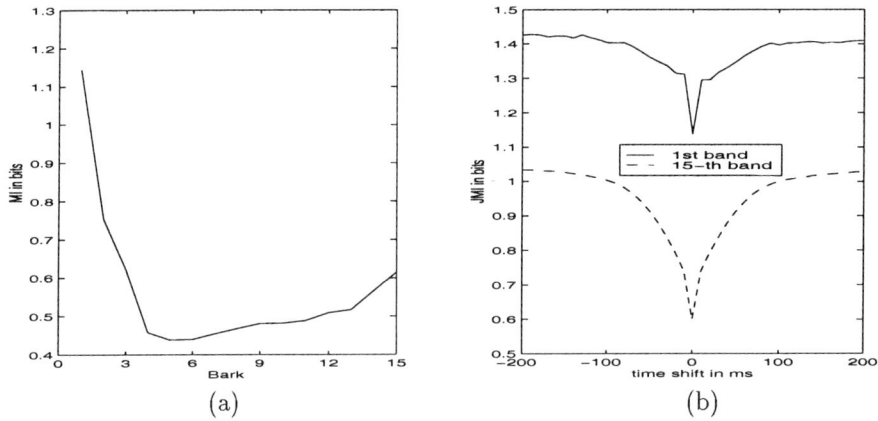

Figure 3: (a) The MI between one frequency feature and the file label. (b) The JMI between two features and the file identity labels.

5 MI in Speech for Speaker/Channel Recognition

The linguistic variability expressed by phoneme labels is not the only variability present in speech. We use the mutual information to evaluate relevance to other sources of variabilities such as speaker/channel variability. Taking the file label as a target variable, we estimated the mutual information for one and two features.

It is shown in Fig. 3(a) that the most relevant features are in the very low frequency channels, which in our case of telephone speech carry only very little speech information. Fig. 3(b) shows that the second most relevant feature for speaker/channel recognition is at least 150 ms apart from the first most relevant feature. These results suggest that the information about the speaker and the communication channel is not localized in time. These results are complementary to the results for phonetic classification shown in Fig. 1(a) and (d).

6 CONCLUSIONS

Our results have shown that the information theoretic analysis of labeled speech data is feasible and useful for obtaining reusable knowledge about speech/channel variabilities. The joint mutual information of two features for phonetic classification is asymmetric around the current frame. We also estimated the joint mutual information between the phoneme labels and three feature variables. The uncertainty about the phonetic classification is reduced by adding more features. The maximum uncertainty reductions due to three frequency features and three temporal features are 28% and 19% respectively.

The mutual informations of one and two features for speaker/channel recognition are estimated. The results show that the most relevant features are in the very low frequency bands. At 1 Bark and 5 Bark, the second most relevant temporal feature for speaker/channel recognition is at least 150 ms apart from the first most relevant feature. These results suggest that the information about the speaker and the communication channel is not localized in time. These results are complementary to the results for phonetic classification for which the mutual information is generally localized with some time spread.

References

[1] J. A. Bilmes. Maximum mutual information based reduction strategies for cross-correlation based joint distribution modeling. In *ICASSP98*, pages 469–472, April 1998.

[2] R. Cole, M. Fanty, M. Noel, and T. Lander. Telephone speech corpus development at CSLU. In *ICSLP*, pages 1815–1818, Yokohama, Sept. 1994.

[3] H. Hermansky. Perceptual linear predictive (PLP) analysis of speech. *J. Acoust. Soc. Am.*, 87(4):1738–1752, April 1990.

[4] G. A. Miller. Note on the bias of information estimates. In H. Quastler, editor, *Information Theory and Psychology*, pages 95–100. The Free Press, Illinois, 1954.

[5] Andrew Morris, Jean-Luc Schwartz, and Pierre Escudier. An information theoretical investigation into the distribution of phonetic information across the auditory spectogram. *Computer Speech & Language*, 7(2):121–136, April 1993.

[6] H. H. Yang, S. Van Vuuren, , S. Sharma, and H. Hermansky. Relevancy of time-frequency features for phonetic classification and speaker-channel recognition. *Accepted by Speech Communication*, 1999.

[7] H. H. Yang, S. Van Vuuren, and H. Hermansky. Relevancy of time-frequency features for phonetic classification measured by mutual information. In *ICASSP99*, pages I:225–228, Phoenix, March 1999.

Part VII
Visual Processing

Audio-Vision:
Using Audio-Visual Synchrony to Locate Sounds

John Hershey [*]
jhershey@cogsci.ucsd.edu
Department of Cognitive Science
University of California, San Diego
La Jolla, CA 92093-0515

Javier Movellan
movellan@cogsci.ucsd.edu
Department of Cognitive Science
University of California, San Diego
La Jolla, CA 92093-0515

Abstract

Psychophysical and physiological evidence shows that sound localization of acoustic signals is strongly influenced by their synchrony with visual signals. This effect, known as ventriloquism, is at work when sound coming from the side of a TV set feels as if it were coming from the mouth of the actors. The ventriloquism effect suggests that there is important information about sound location encoded in the synchrony between the audio and video signals. In spite of this evidence, audiovisual synchrony is rarely used as a source of information in computer vision tasks. In this paper we explore the use of audio visual synchrony to locate sound sources. We developed a system that searches for regions of the visual landscape that correlate highly with the acoustic signals and tags them as likely to contain an acoustic source. We discuss our experience implementing the system, present results on a speaker localization task and discuss potential applications of the approach.

Introduction

We present a method for locating sound sources by sampling regions of an image that correlate in time with the auditory signal. Our approach is inspired by psychophysical and physiological evidence suggesting that audio-visual contingencies play an important role in the localization of sound sources: sounds seem to emanate from visual stimuli that are synchronized with the sound. This effect becomes particularly noticeable when the perceived source of the sound is known to be false, as in the case of a ventriloquist's dummy, or a television screen. This phenomenon is known in the psychophysical community as the *ventriloquism effect*, defined as a mislocation of sounds toward their apparent visual source. The effect is robust in a wide variety of conditions, and has been found to be strongly dependent on the degree of "synchrony" between the auditory and visual signals (Driver, 1996; Bertelson, Vroomen, Wiegeraad & de Gelder, 1994).

---
[*] To whom correspondence should be addressed.

The ventriloquism effect is in fact less speech-specific than first thought. For example the effect is not disrupted by an upside-down lip signal (Bertelson, Vroomen, Wiegeraad & de Gelder, 1994) and is just as strong when the lip signals are replaced by light flashes that are synchronized with amplitude peaks in the audio signal (Radeau & Bertelson, 1977). The crucial aspect here is correlation between visual and auditory intensity over time. When the light flashes are not synchronized the effect disappears.

The ventriloquism effect is strong enough to produce an enduring localization bias, known as the *ventriloquism aftereffect*. Over time, experience with spatially offset auditory-visual stimuli causes a persistent shift in subsequent auditory localization. Exposure to audio-visual stimuli offset from each other by only 8 degrees of azimuth for 20-30 minutes is sufficient to shift auditory localization by the same amount. A corresponding shift in neural processing has been detected in macaque monkeys as early as primary auditory cortex(Recanzone, 1998). In barn owls a misalignment of visual and auditory stimuli during development causes the realignment of the auditory and visual maps in the optic tectum(Zheng & Knudsen, 1999; Stryker, 1999; Feldman & Knudsen, 1997).

The strength of the psychophysical and physiological evidence suggests that audio-visual contingency may be used as an important source of information that is currently underutilized in computer vision tasks. Visual and auditory sensor systems carry information about the same events in the world, and this information must be combined correctly in order for a useful interaction of the two modalities. Audiovisual contingency can be exploited to help determine which signals in different modalities share a common origin. The benefits are two-fold: the two signals can help localize each other, and once paired can help interpret each other. To this effect we developed a system to localize speakers using input from a camera and a single microphone. The approach is based on searching for regions of the image which are "synchronized" with the acoustic signal.

Measuring Synchrony

The concept of audio-visual *synchrony* is not well formalized in the psychophysical literature, so for a working definition we interpret synchrony as the degree of mutual information between audio and spatially localized video signals. Ultimately it is a *causal* relationship that we are often interested in, but causes can only be inferred from effects such as synchrony. Let $a(t) \in \mathbb{R}^n$ be a vector describing the acoustic signal at time t. The components of $a(t)$ could be cepstral coefficients, pitch measurements, or the outputs of a filter bank. Let $v(x, y, t) \in \mathbb{R}^m$ be a vector describing the visual signal at time t, pixel (x, y). The components of $v(x, y, t)$ could represent Gabor energy coefficients, RGB color values, etc.

Consider now a set of s audio and visual vectors $\mathcal{S} = (a(t_l), v(x, y, t_l))_{l=k-s-1,\cdots,k}$ sampled at times $t_{k-s-1}, \cdots, t_k$ and at spatial coordinates (x, y). Given this set of vectors our goal is to provide a number that describes the temporal contingency between audio and video at time t_k. The approach we take is to consider each vector in $\mathcal{S}$ as an independent sample from a joint multivariate Gaussian process $(A(t_k), V(x, y, t_k))$ and define audio-visual synchrony at time t_k as the estimate of the mutual information between the audio and visual components of the process.

Let $A(t_k) \sim \mathcal{N}_n(\mu_A(t_k), \Sigma_A(t_k))$, and $V(x, y, t_k) \sim \mathcal{N}_m(\mu_V(x, y, t), \Sigma_V(x, y, t_k))$, where μ represents means and Σ covariance matrices. Let $A(t_k)$ and $V(x, y, t_k)$ be jointly Gaussian, i.e., $(A(t_k), V(x, y, t_k)) \sim \mathcal{N}_{n+m}(\mu_{A,V}(x, y, t_k), \Sigma_{A,V}(x, y, t_k))$.

The mutual information between $A(x, y, t_k)$ and $V(t_k)$ can be shown to be as follows

$$\begin{aligned} I(A(t_k); V(x,y,t_k)) &= H(A(t_k)) + H(V(x,y,t_k)) - H(A(t_k), V(x,y,t_k)) \\ &= \frac{1}{2}\log(2\pi e)^n |\Sigma_A(t_k)| + \frac{1}{2}\log(2\pi e)^m |\Sigma_V(x,y,t_k)| \quad (1) \\ &\quad - \frac{1}{2}\log(2\pi e)^{n+m} |\Sigma_{A,V}(x,y,t_k)| \\ &\quad\quad\quad\quad\quad\quad\quad\quad\quad\quad\quad\quad\quad\quad\quad\quad\quad\quad (2) \\ &= \frac{1}{2} \log \frac{|\Sigma_A(t_k)||\Sigma_V(x,y,t_k)|}{|\Sigma_{A,V}(x,y,t_k)|}. \quad (3) \end{aligned}$$

In the special case that $n = m = 1$, then

$$I(A(t_k); V(x,y,t_k)) = -\frac{1}{2}\log(1 - \rho^2(x,y,t_k)), \quad (4)$$

where $\rho(x, y, t_k)$ is the Pearson correlation coefficient between $A(t_k)$ and $V(x, y, t_k)$.

For each triple (x, y, t_k) we estimate the mutual information between $A(t_k)$ and $V(x, y, t_k)$ by considering each element of S as an independent sample from the random vector $(A(t_k), V(x, y, t_k))$. This amounts to computing estimates of the joint covariance matrix $\Sigma_{A,V}(x, y, t_k)$. For example the estimate of the covariance between the ith audio component and the jth video component would be as follows

$$S_{A_i,V_j}(x,y,t_k) = \frac{1}{s-1} \sum_{l=0}^{s-1} (a_i(t_{k-l}) - \bar{a}_i(t_k))(v_j(x,y,t_{k-l}) - \bar{v}_j(x,y,t_k)), \quad (5)$$

where

$$\bar{a}_i(t_k) = \frac{1}{s} \sum_{l=0}^{s-1} a_i(t_{k-l}), \quad (6)$$

$$\bar{v}_j(t_k) = \frac{1}{s} \sum_{l=0}^{s-1} v_j(x,y,t_{k-l}). \quad (7)$$

$$\quad (8)$$

These simple covariance estimates can be computed recursively in constant time with respect to the number of timepoints. The independent treatment of pixels would lend well to a parallel implementation.

To measure performance, a secondary system produces a single estimate of the auditory location, for use with a database of labeled solitary audiovisual sources. Unfortunately there are many ways of producing such estimates so it becomes difficult to separate performance of the measure from the underlying system. The model used here is a centroid computation on the mutual information estimates, with some enhancements to aid tracking and reduce background noise.

Implementation Issues

A real time system was prototyped using a QuickCam on the Linux operating system and then ported to NT as a DirectShow filter. This platform provides input from real-time audio and video capture hardware as well as from static movie files. The video output could also be rendered live or compressed and saved in a movie file. The implementation was challenging in that it turns out to be rather difficult

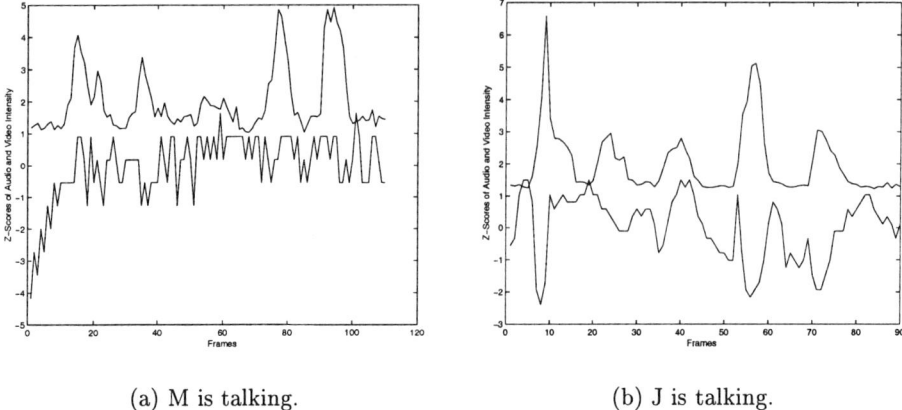

(a) M is talking. (b) J is talking.

Figure 1: Normalized audio and visual intensity across sequences of frames in which a sequence of four numbers is spoken. The top trace is the contour of the acoustic energy from one of two speakers, M or J, and the bottom trace is the contour of intensity values for a single pixel, (147,100), near the mouth of J.

to process precisely time-synchronized audio and video on a serial machine in real time. Multiple threads are required to read from the peripheral audio and visual devices. By the time the audio and visual streams reach the AV filter module, they are quite separate and asynchronous. The separately threaded auditory and visual packet streams must be synchronized, buffered, and finally matched and aligned by time-stamps before they can finally be processed. It is interesting that successful biologial audiovisual systems employ a parallel architecture and thus avoid this problem.

Results

To obtain a performance baseline we first tried the simplest possible approach: A single audio and visual feature per location: $n = m = 1$, $v(x, y, t) \in \mathbb{R}$ is the intensity of pixel (x, y) at time t, and $a(t) \in \mathbb{R}$ is the average acoustic energy over the interval $[t - \Delta t, t]$, where $\Delta t = 1/30\ msec$, the sampling period for the NTSC video signal. Figure 1 illustrates the time course of these signals for a non-synchronous and a synchronous pair of acoustic energy and pixel intensity. Notice in particular that in the synchonous pair, 1(b), where the sound and pixel values come from the same speaker, the relationship between the signals changes over time. There are regions of positive and negative covariance strung together in succession. Clearly the relationship over the entire sequence is far from linear. However over shorter time periods a linear relationship looks like a better approximation. Our window size of 16 samples (i.e., $s = 16$ in 5 coincides approximately with this time-scale. Perhaps by averaging over many small windows we can capture on a larger scale what would be lost to the same method applied with a larger window. Of course there is a trade-off in the time-scale between sensitivity to spurious transients, and the response time of the system.

We applied this mutual information measure to all the pixels in a movie, in the spirit of the perceptual maps of the brain. The result is a changing topographic map of audiovisual mutual information. Figure 2 illustrates two snapshots in which

(a) Frame 206: M (at left) is talking. (b) Frame 104: J (at right) is talking.

Figure 2: Estimated mutual information between pixel intensity and audio intensity (bright areas indicate greater mutual information) overlaid on stills from the video where one person is in mid-utterance.

different parts of the face are synchronous (possibly with different sign) with the sound they take part in producing. It is interesting that the synchrony is shared by some parts, such as the eyes, that do not directly contribute to the sound, but contribute to the communication nonetheless.

To estimate the position of the speaker we computed a centroid were each point was weighted by the estimated mutual information between the corresponding pixel and the audio signal. At each time step the mutual information was estimated using 16 past frames (i.e., $s = 16$) In order to reduce the intrusion of spurious correlations from competing targets, once a target has been found, we employ a Gaussian *influence function*. (Goodall, 1983) The influence function reduces the weight given to mutual information from locations far from the current centroid when computing the next centroid. To allow for the speedy disengagement from a dwindling source of mutual information we set a threshold on the mutual information. Measurements under the threshold are treated as zero. This threshold also reduces the effects of unwanted background noise, such as camera and microphone jitter.

$$\hat{S}_x(t) = \frac{\sum_x \sum_y x\, \theta(\log(1 - \hat{\rho}^2(x,y,t)))\psi(x, \hat{S}_x(t-1))}{\sum_x \sum_y \theta(\log(1 - \hat{\rho}^2(x,y,t)))\psi(x, \hat{S}_x(t-1))} \quad (9)$$

where $\hat{S}_x(t)$ represents the estimate of the x coordinate for the position of the speaker at time t. $\theta(.)$ is the thresholding function, and $\psi(x, \hat{S}_x(t-1))$ is the influence function, which depends upon the position x of the pixel being sampled and the prior estimate $\hat{S}_x(t-1)$. $\hat{\rho}^2(x,y,t)$ is the estimate of the correlation between the intensity in pixel (x,y) and the acoustic enery, when using the 16 past video frames. $-\frac{1}{2}\log(1 - \hat{\rho}^2(x,y,t))$ is the corresponding estimate of mutual information (the factor, $-\frac{1}{2}$ cancels out in the quotient after adjusting the threshold function accordingly.)

We tried the approach on a movie of two people (M and J) taking turns while saying random digits. Figure 3 shows the estimates of the actual positions of the speaker as a function of time. The estimates clearly provide information that could be used to localize the speaker, especially in combination with other approaches (e.g., flesh detection).

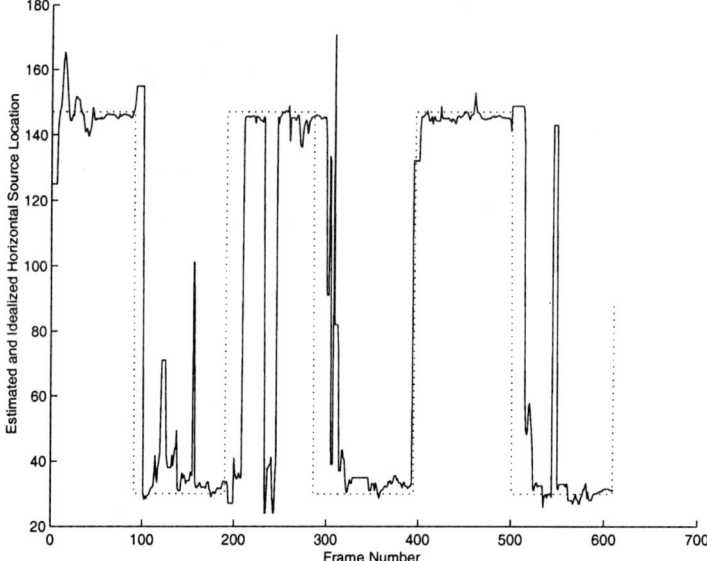

Figure 3: Estimated and actual position of speaker at each frame for six hundred frames. The sources, M and J, took turns uttering a series of four digits, for three turns each. The actual positions and alternation times were measured by hand from the video recording

Conclusions

We have presented exploratory work on a system for localizing sound sources on a video signal by tagging regions of the image that are correlated in time with the auditory signal. The approach was motivated by the wealth of evidence in the psychophysical and physiological literature showing that sound localization is strongly influenced by synchrony with the visual signal. We presented a measure of local synchrony based on modeling the audio-visual signal as a non-stationary Gaussian process. We developed a general software tool that accepts as inputs all major video and audio file formats as well as direct input from a video camera. We tested the tool on a speaker localization task with very encouraging results. The approach could have practical applications for localizing sound sources in situations where where acoustic stereo cues are inexistent or unreliable. For example the approach could be used to help localize the actor talking in a video scene and put closed-captioned text near the audio source. The approach could also be used to guide a camera in teleconferencing applications.

While the results reported here are very encouraging, more work needs to be done before practical applications are developed. For example we need to investigate more sophisticated methods for processing the audio and video signals. At this point we use average energy to represent the video and thus changes in the fundamental frequency that do not affect the average energy would not be captured by our model. Similarly local video decompositions, like spatio-temporal Gabor filtering, or approaches designed to enhance the lip regions may be helpful. The changing symmetry observed between audio and video signals might be addressed rectifying or squaring the normalized signals and derivatives. Finally, relaxing the Gaussian constraints in our measure of audio-visual contingency may help improve performance. While the work shown here is exploratory at this point, the approach is very promising: It emphasizes the idea of machine perception as a multimodal process it is backed by psychophysical evidence, and when combined with other approaches it may help improve robustness in tasks such as localization and separation of sound sources.

References

Bertelson, P., Vroomen, J., Wiegeraad, G., & de Gelder, B. (1994). Exploring the relation between McGurk interference and ventriloquism. In *Proceedings of the 1994 International Conference on Spoken Language Processing*, volume 2, pages 559–562.

Driver, J. (1996). Enhancement of selective listening by illusory mislocation of speech sounds due to lip-reading. *Nature*, *381*, 66–68.

Feldman, D. E. & Knudsen, E. I. (1997). An anatomical basis for visual calibration of the auditiory space map in the barn owl's midbrain. *The Journal of Neuroscience*, *17*(17), 6820–6837.

Goodall, C. (1983). M-Estimators of Location: an outline of the theory. Wiley series in probability and mathematical statistics. Applied probability and statistics.

Radeau, M. & Bertelson, P. (1977). Adaptation to auditory-visual discordance and ventriloquism in semi-realistic situations. *Perception and Psychophysics*, *22*, 137–146.

Recanzone, G. H. (1998). Rapidly induced auditory plasticity: The ventriloquism aftereffect. *Proceedings of the National Academy of Sciences, USA*, *95*, 869–875.

Stryker, M. P. (1999). Sensory Maps on the Move. *Science*, 925–926.

Zheng, W. & Knudsen, E. I. (1999). Functional Selection of Adaptive Auditory Space Map by GABAA-Mediated Inhibition, 962–965.

Bayesian Reconstruction of 3D Human Motion from Single-Camera Video

Nicholas R. Howe
Department of Computer Science
Cornell University
Ithaca, NY 14850
nihowe@cs.cornell.edu

Michael E. Leventon
Artificial Intelligence Lab
Massachusetts Institute of Technology
Cambridge, MA 02139
leventon@ai.mit.edu

William T. Freeman
MERL – a Mitsubishi Electric Research Lab
201 Broadway
Cambridge, MA 02139
freeman@merl.com

Abstract

The three-dimensional motion of humans is underdetermined when the observation is limited to a single camera, due to the inherent 3D ambiguity of 2D video. We present a system that reconstructs the 3D motion of human subjects from single-camera video, relying on prior knowledge about human motion, learned from training data, to resolve those ambiguities. After initialization in 2D, the tracking and 3D reconstruction is automatic; we show results for several video sequences. The results show the power of treating 3D body tracking as an inference problem.

1 Introduction

We seek to capture the 3D motions of humans from video sequences. The potential applications are broad, including industrial computer graphics, virtual reality, and improved human-computer interaction. Recent research attention has focused on unencumbered tracking techniques that don't require attaching markers to the subject's body [4, 5], see [12] for a survey. Typically, these methods require simultaneous views from multiple cameras.

Motion capture from a single camera is important for several reasons. First, though underdetermined, it is a problem people can solve easily, as anyone viewing a dancer in a movie can confirm. Single camera shots are the most convenient to obtain, and, of course, apply to the world's film and video archives. It is an appealing computer vision problem that emphasizes inference as much as measurement.

This problem has received less attention than motion capture from multiple cameras. Goncalves et.al. rely on perspective effects to track only a single arm, and thus need not deal with complicated models, shadows, or self-occlusion [7]. Bregler & Malik develop a body tracking system that may apply to a single camera, but performance in that domain is not clear; most of the examples use multiple cameras [4]. Wachter & Nagel use an iterated extended Kalman filter, although their body model is limited in degrees of freedom [12]. Brand [3] uses an learning-based approach, although with representational expressiveness restricted by the number of HMM states. An earlier version of the work reported here [10] required manual intervention for the 2D tracking.

This paper presents our system for single-camera motion capture, a learning-based approach, relying on prior information learned from a labeled training set. The system tracks joints and body parts as they move in the 2D video, then combines the tracking information with the prior model of human motion to form a best estimate of the body's motion in 3D. Our reconstruction method can work with incomplete information, because the prior model allows spurious and distracting information to be discarded. The 3D estimate provides feedback to influence the 2D tracking process to favor more likely poses.

The 2D tracking and 3D reconstruction modules are discussed in Sections 3 and 4, respectively. Section 4 describes the system operation and presents performance results. Finally, Section 5 concludes with possible improvements.

2 2D Tracking

The 2D tracker processes a video stream to determine the motion of body parts in the image plane over time. The tracking algorithm used is based on one presented by Ju et. al. [9], and performs a task similar to one described by Morris & Rehg [11]. Fourteen body parts are modeled as planar patches, whose positions are controlled by 34 parameters. Tracking consists of optimizing the parameter values in each frame so as to minimize the mismatch between the image data and a projection of the body part maps. The 2D parameter values for the first frame must be initialized by hand, by overlaying a model onto the 2D image of the first frame.

We extend Ju et. al.'s tracking algorithm in several ways. We track the entire body, and build a model of each body part that is a weighted average of several preceding frames, not just the most recent one. This helps eliminate tracking errors due to momentary glitches that last for a frame or two.

We account for self-occlusions through the use of support maps [4, 1]. It is essential to address this problem, as limbs and other body parts will often partly or wholly obscure one another. For the single-camera case, there are no alternate views to be relied upon when a body part cannot be seen.

The 2D tracker returns the coordinates of each limb in each successive frame. These in turn yield the positions of joints and other control points needed to perform 3D reconstruction.

3 3D Reconstruction

3D reconstruction from 2D tracking data is underdetermined. At each frame, the algorithm receives the positions in two dimensions of 20 tracked body points, and must to infer the correct depth of each point. We rely on a training set of 3D human motions to determine which reconstructions are plausible. Most candidate projections are unnatural motions, if not anatomically impossible, and can be eliminated on this basis. We adopt a Bayesian framework, and use the training data to compute prior probabilities of different 3D motions.

We model plausible motions as a mixture of Gaussian probabilities in a high-dimensional space. Motion capture data gathered in a professional studio provide the training data: frame-by-frame 3D coordinates for 20 tracked body points at 20-30 frames per second. We want to model the probabilities of human motions of some short duration, long enough be informative, but short enough to characterize probabilistically from our training data. We assembled the data into short motion elements we called *snippets* of 11 successive frames, about a third of a second. We represent each snippet from the training data as a large column vector of the 3D positions of each tracked body point in each frame of the snippet.

We then use those data to build a mixture-of-Gaussians probability density model [2]. For computational efficiency, we used a clustering approach to approximate the fitting of an EM algorithm. We use k-means clustering to divide the snippets into m groups, each of which will be modeled by a Gaussian probability cloud. For each cluster, the matrix M_j is formed, where the columns of M_j are the n_j individual motion snippets after subtracting the mean μ_j. The singular value decomposition (SVD) gives $M_j = U_j S_j V_j^T$, where S_j contains the singular values along the diagonal, and U_j contains the basis vectors. (We truncate the SVD to include only the 50 largest singular values.) The cluster can be modeled by a multidimensional Gaussian with covariance $\Lambda_j = \frac{1}{n_j} U_j S_j^2 U_j^T$. The prior probability of a snippet $\vec{x}$ over all the models is a sum of the Gaussian probabilities weighted by the probability of each model.

$$P(\vec{x}) = \sum_{j=1}^{m} k\pi_j e^{-\frac{1}{2}(\vec{x}-\mu_j)^T \Lambda^{-1}(\vec{x}-\mu_j)} \quad (1)$$

Here k is a normalization constant, and π_j is the *a priori* probability of model j, computed as the fraction of snippets in the knowledge base that were originally placed in cluster j. Given this approximately derived mixture-of-factors model [6], we can compute the prior probability of any snippet.

To estimate the data term (likelihood) in Bayes' law, we assume that the 2D observations include some Gaussian noise with variance σ. Combined with the prior, the expression for the probability of a given snippet $\vec{x}$ given an observation $\vec{y}$ becomes

$$P(\vec{x}, \theta, s, \vec{v} | \vec{y}) = k' \left(e^{-\|\vec{y} - R_{\theta,s,\vec{v}}(\vec{x})\|^2/(2\sigma^2)} \right) \left(\sum_{j=1}^{m} k\pi_j e^{-\frac{1}{2}(\vec{x}-\mu_j)^T \Lambda^{-1}(\vec{x}-\mu_j)} \right) \quad (2)$$

In this equation, $R_{\theta,s,\vec{v}}(\vec{x})$ is a rendering function which maps a 3D snippet $\vec{x}$ into the image coordinate system, performing scaling s, rotation about the vertical axis θ, and image-plane translation $\vec{v}$. We use the EM algorithm to find the probabilities of each Gaussian in the mixture and the corresponding snippet $\vec{x}$ that maximizes the probability given the observations [6]. This allows the conversion of eleven frames of 2D tracking measurements into the most probable corresponding 3D snippet. In cases where the 2D tracking is poor, the reconstruction may be improved by matching only the more reliable points in the likelihood term of Equation 2. This adds a second noise process to explain the outlier data points in the likelihood term.

To perform the full 3D reconstruction, the system first divides the 2D tracking data into snippets, which provides the $\vec{y}$ values of Eq. 2, then finds the best (MAP) 3D snippet for each of the 2D observations. The 3D snippets are stitched together, using a weighted interpolation for frames where two snippets overlap. The result is a Bayesian estimate of the subject's motion in three dimensions.

4 Performance

The system as a whole will track and successfully 3D reconstruct simple, short video clips with no human intervention, apart from 2D pose initialization. It is not currently reliable enough to track difficult footage for significant lengths of time. However, analysis of short clips demonstrates that the system can successfully reconstruct 3D motion from ambiguous

2D video. We evaluate the two stages of the algorithm independently at first, and then consider their operation as a system.

4.1 Performance of the 3D reconstruction

The 3D reconstruction stage is the heart of the system. To our knowledge, no similar 2D to 3D reconstruction technique relying on prior information has been published. ([3], developed simultaneously, also uses an inference-based approach). Our tests show that the module can restore deleted depth information that looks realistic and is close to the ground truth, at least when the knowledge base contains some examples of similar motions. This makes the 3D reconstruction stage itself an important result, which can easily be applied in conjunction with other tracking technologies.

To test the reconstruction with known ground truth, we held back some of the training data for testing. We artificially provided perfect 2D marker position data, $\vec{y}$ in Eq. 2, and tested the 3D reconstruction stage in isolation. After removing depth information from the test sequence, the sequence is reconstructed as if it had come from the 2D tracker. Sequences produced in this manner look very much like the original. They show some rigid motion error along the line of sight. An analysis of the uncertainty in the posterior probability predicts high uncertainty for the body motion mode of rigid motion parallel to the orthographic projection [10]. This slipping can be corrected by enforcing ground-contact constraints. Figure 1 shows a reconstructed running sequence corrected for rigid motion error and superimposed on the original. The missing depth information is reconstructed well, although it sometimes lags or anticipates the true motion slightly. Quantitatively, this error is a relatively small effect. After subtracting rigid motion error, the mean residual 3D errors in limb position are the same order of magnitude as the small frame-to frame changes in those positions.

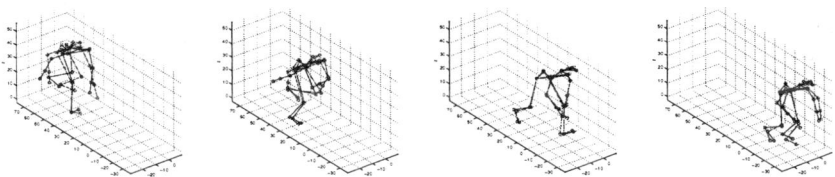

Figure 1: Original and reconstructed running sequences superimposed (frames 1, 7, 14, and 21).

4.2 Performance of the 2D tracker

The 2D tracker performs well under constant illumination, providing quite accurate results from frame to frame. The main problem it faces is the slow accumulation of error. On longer sequences, the errors can build up to the point where the module is no longer tracking the body parts it was intended to track. The problem is worsened by low contrast, occlusion and lighting changes. More careful body modeling [5], lighting models, and modeling of the background may address these issues. The sequences we used for testing were several seconds long and had fairly good contrast. Although adequate to demonstrate the operation of our system, the 2D tracker contains the most open research issues.

4.3 Overall system performance

Three example reconstructions are given, showing a range of different tracking situations. The first is a reconstruction of a stationary figure waving one arm, with most of the motion in the image plane. The second shows a figure bringing both arms together towards the camera, resulting in a significant amount of foreshortening. The third is a reconstruction of a figure walking sideways, and includes significant self-occlusion

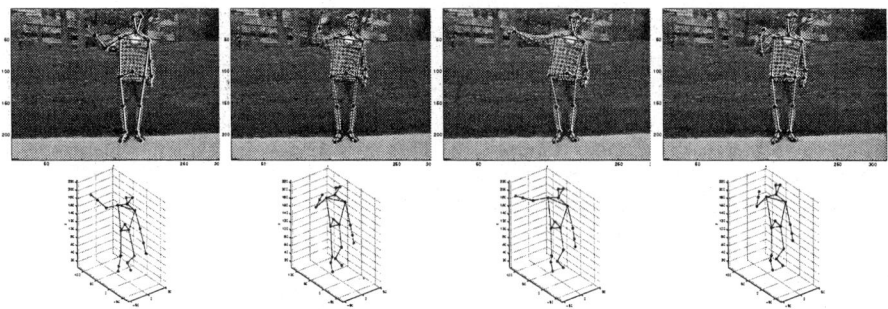

Figure 2: First clip and its reconstruction (frames 1, 25, 50, and 75).

The first video is the easiest to track because there is little or no occlusion and change in lighting. The reconstruction is good, capturing the stance and motion of the arm. There is some rigid motion error, which is corrected through ground friction constraints. The knees are slightly bent; this may be because the subject in the video has different body proportions than those represented in the training database.

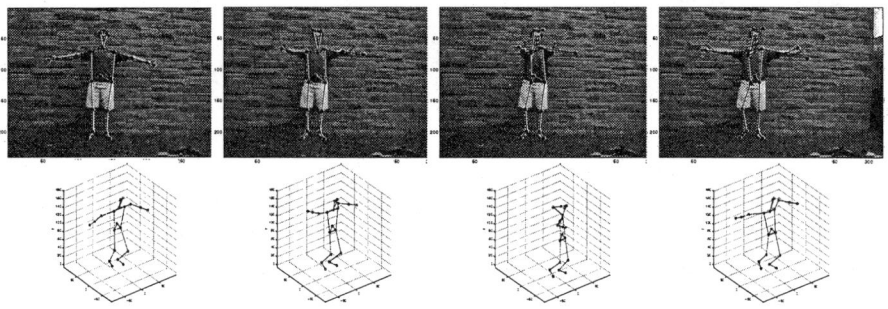

Figure 3: Second clip and its reconstruction (frames 1, 25, 50, and 75).

The second video shows a figure bringing its arms together towards the camera. The only indication of this is in the foreshortening of the limbs, yet the 3D reconstruction correctly captures this in the right arm. (Lighting changes and contrast problems cause the 2D tracker to lose the left arm partway through, confusing the reconstruction of that limb, but the right arm is tracked accurately throughout.)

The third video shows a figure walking to the right in the image plane. This clip is the hardest for the 2D tracker, due to repeated and prolonged occlusion of some body parts. The tracker loses the left arm after 15 frames due to severe occlusion, yet the remaining tracking information is still sufficient to perform an adequate reconstruction. At about frame 45, the left leg has crossed behind the right several times and is lost, at which point the reconstruction quality begins to degrade. The key to a more reliable reconstruction on this sequence is better tracking.

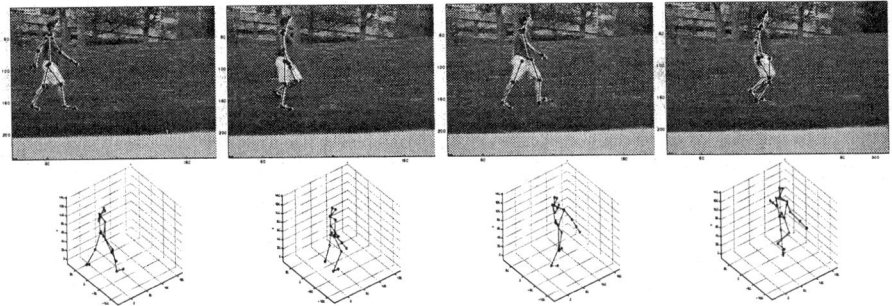

Figure 4: Third clip and its reconstruction (frames 6, 16, 26, and 36).

5 Conclusion

We have demonstrated a system that tracks human figures in short video sequences and reconstructs their motion in three dimensions. The tracking is unassisted, although 2D pose initialization is required. The system uses prior information learned from training data to resolve the inherent ambiguity in going from two to three dimensions, an essential step when working with a single-camera video source. To achieve this end, the system relies on prior knowledge, extracted from examples of human motion. Such a learning-based approach could be combined with more sophisticated measurement-based approaches to the tracking problem [12, 8, 4].

References

[1] J. R. Bergen, P. Anandan, K. J. Hanna, and R. Hingorani. Hierarchical model-based motion estimation. In *European Conference on Computer Vision*, pages 237–252, 1992.

[2] C. M. Bishop. *Neural networks for pattern recognition*. Oxford, 1995.

[3] M. Brand. Shadow puppetry. In *Proc. 7th Intl. Conf. on Computer Vision*, pages 1237–1244. IEEE, 1999.

[4] C. Bregler and J. Malik. Tracking people with twists and exponential maps. In *IEEE Computer Society Conference on Computer Vision and Pattern Recognition*, Santa Barbera, 1998.

[5] D. M. Gavrila and L. S. Davis. 3d model-based tracking of humans in action: A multi-view approach. In *IEEE Computer Society Conference on Computer Vision and Pattern Recognition*, San Francisco, 1996.

[6] Z. Ghahramani and G. E. Hinton. The EM algorithm for mixtures of factor analyzers. Technical report, Department of Computer Science, University of Toronto, May 21 1996. (revised Feb. 27, 1997).

[7] L. Goncalves, E. Di Bernardo, E. Ursella, and P. Perona. Monocular tracking of the human arm in 3D. In *Proceedings of the Third International Conference on Computer Vision*, 1995.

[8] M. Isard and A. Blake. Condensation – conditional density propagation for visual tracking. *International Journal of Computer Vision*, 29(1):5–28, 1998.

[9] S. X. Ju, M. J. Black, and Y. Yacoob. Cardboard people: A parameterized model of articulated image motion. In *2nd International Conference on Automatic Face and Gesture Recognition*, 1996.

[10] M. E. Leventon and W. T. Freeman. Bayesian estimation of 3-d human motion from an image sequence. Technical Report TR98-06, Mitsubishi Electric Research Lab, 1998.

[11] D. D. Morris and J. Rehg. Singularity analysis for articulated object tracking. In *IEEE Computer Society Conference on Computer Vision and Pattern Recognition*, Santa Barbera, 1998.

[12] S. Wachter and H.-H. Nagel. Tracking of persons in monocular image sequences. In *Nonrigid and Articulated Motion Workshop*, 1997.

Emergence of Topography and Complex Cell Properties from Natural Images using Extensions of ICA

Aapo Hyvärinen and Patrik Hoyer
Neural Networks Research Center
Helsinki University of Technology
P.O. Box 5400, FIN-02015 HUT, Finland
aapo.hyvarinen@hut.fi, patrik.hoyer@hut.fi
http://www.cis.hut.fi/projects/ica/

Abstract

Independent component analysis of natural images leads to emergence of simple cell properties, i.e. linear filters that resemble wavelets or Gabor functions. In this paper, we extend ICA to explain further properties of V1 cells. First, we decompose natural images into independent subspaces instead of scalar components. This model leads to emergence of phase and shift invariant features, similar to those in V1 complex cells. Second, we define a topography between the linear components obtained by ICA. The topographic distance between two components is defined by their higher-order correlations, so that two components are close to each other in the topography if they are strongly dependent on each other. This leads to simultaneous emergence of both topography and invariances similar to complex cell properties.

1 Introduction

A fundamental approach in signal processing is to design a statistical generative model of the observed signals. Such an approach is also useful for modeling the properties of neurons in primary sensory areas. The basic models that we consider here express a static monochrome image $I(x,y)$ as a linear superposition of some features or basis functions $b_i(x,y)$:

$$I(x,y) = \sum_{i=1}^{n} b_i(x,y)s_i \qquad (1)$$

where the s_i are stochastic coefficients, different for each image $I(x,y)$. Estimation of the model in Eq. (1) consists of determining the values of s_i and $b_i(x,y)$ for all i and (x,y), given a sufficient number of observations of images, or in practice, image patches $I(x,y)$. We restrict ourselves here to the basic case where the $b_i(x,y)$ form an invertible linear system. Then we can invert $s_i = <w_i, I>$ where the w_i denote the inverse filters, and $<w_i, I> = \sum_{x,y} w_i(x,y) I(x,y)$ denotes the dot-product.

The $w_i(x, y)$ can then be identified as the receptive fields of the model simple cells, and the s_i are their activities when presented with a given image patch $I(x, y)$.

In the basic case, we assume that the s_i are nongaussian, and mutually independent. This type of decomposition is called independent component analysis (ICA) [3, 9, 1, 8], or sparse coding [13]. Olshausen and Field [13] showed that when this model is estimated with input data consisting of patches of natural scenes, the obtained filters $w_i(x, y)$ have the three principal properties of simple cells in V1: they are localized, oriented, and bandpass (selective to scale/frequency). Van Hateren and van der Schaaf [15] compared quantitatively the obtained filters $w_i(x, y)$ with those measured by single-cell recordings of the macaque cortex, and found a good match for most of the parameters.

We show in this paper that simple extensions of the basic ICA model explain emergence of further properties of V1 cells: topography and the invariances of complex cells. Due to space limitations, we can only give the basic ideas in this paper. More details can be found in [6, 5, 7].

First, using the method of feature subspaces [11], we model the response of a complex cell as the norm of the projection of the input vector (image patch) onto a linear subspace, which is equivalent to the classical energy models. Then we maximize the independence between the norms of such projections, or energies. Thus we obtain features that are localized in space, oriented, and bandpass, like those given by simple cells, or Gabor analysis. In contrast to simple linear filters, however, the obtained feature subspaces also show emergence of phase invariance and (limited) shift or translation invariance. Maximizing the independence, or equivalently, the sparseness of the norms of the projections to feature subspaces thus allows for the emergence of exactly those invariances that are encountered in complex cells.

Second, we extend this model of independent subspaces so that we have overlapping subspaces, and every subspace corresponds to a neighborhood on a topographic grid. This is called topographic ICA, since it defines a topographic organization between components. Components that are far from each other on the grid are independent, like in ICA. In contrast, components that are near to each other are not independent: they have strong higher-order correlations. This model shows emergence of both complex cell properties and topography from image data.

2 Independent subspaces as complex cells

In addition to the simple cells that can be modelled by basic ICA, another important class of cells in V1 is complex cells. The two principal properties that distinguish complex cells from simple cells are phase invariance and (limited) shift invariance. The purpose of the first model in this paper is to explain the emergence of such phase and shift invariant features using a modification of the ICA model. The modification is based on combining the principle of invariant-feature subspaces [11] and the model of multidimensional independent component analysis [2].

Invariant feature subspaces. The principle of invariant-feature subspaces states that one may consider an invariant feature as a linear subspace in a feature space. The value of the invariant, higher-order feature is given by (the square of) the norm of the projection of the given data point on that subspace, which is typically spanned by lower-order features. A feature subspace, as any linear subspace, can always be represented by a set of orthogonal basis vectors, say $w_i(x, y), i = 1, ..., m$, where m is the dimension of the subspace. Then the value $F(I)$ of the feature F with input vector $I(x, y)$ is given by $F(I) = \sum_{i=1}^{m} <w_i, I>^2$, where a square root might be taken. In fact, this is equivalent to computing the distance between the input vector $I(x,y)$ and a general linear combination of the basis vectors (filters) $w_i(x,y)$ of the feature subspace [11]. In [11], it was shown that this principle, when combined with competitive learning techniques, can lead to emergence of invariant image features.

Multidimensional independent component analysis. In multidimensional independent component analysis [2] (see also [12]), a linear generative model as in Eq. (1) is assumed. In contrast to ordinary ICA, however, the components (responses) s_i are not assumed to be all mutually independent. Instead, it is assumed that the s_i can be divided into couples, triplets or in general m-tuples, such that the s_i inside a given m-tuple may be dependent on each other, but dependencies between different m-tuples are not allowed. Every m-tuple of s_i corresponds to m basis vectors $b_i(x,y)$. The m-dimensional probability densities inside the m-tuples of s_i is not specified in advance in the general definition of multidimensional ICA [2]. In the following, let us denote by J the number of independent feature subspaces, and by $S_j, j = 1,...,J$ the set of the indices of the s_i belonging to the subspace of index j.

Independent feature subspaces. Invariant-feature subspaces can be embedded in multidimensional independent component analysis by considering probability distributions for the m-tuples of s_i that are *spherically symmetric*, i.e. depend only on the norm. In other words, the probability density $p_j(.)$ of the m-tuple with index $j \in \{1,...,J\}$, can be expressed as a function of the sum of the squares of the $s_i, i \in S_j$ only. For simplicity, we assume further that the $p_j(.)$ are equal for all j, i.e. for all subspaces.

Assume that the data consists of K observed image patches $I_k(x,y), k = 1,...,K$. Then the logarithm of the likelihood L of the data given the model can be expressed as

$$\log L(w_i(x,y), i=1...n) = \sum_{k=1}^{K} \sum_{j=1}^{J} \log p(\sum_{i \in S_j} <w_i, I_k>^2) + K \log|\det \mathbf{W}| \quad (2)$$

where $p(\sum_{i \in S_j} s_i^2) = p_j(s_i, i \in S_j)$ gives the probability density inside the j-th m-tuple of s_i, and $\mathbf{W}$ is a matrix containing the filters $w_i(x,y)$ as its columns.

As in basic ICA, prewhitening of the data allows us to consider the $w_i(x,y)$ to be orthonormal, and this implies that $\log|\det \mathbf{W}|$ is zero [6]. Thus we see that the likelihood in Eq. (2) is a function of the norms of the projections of $I_k(x,y)$ on the subspaces indexed by j, which are spanned by the orthonormal basis sets given by $w_i(x,y), i \in S_j$. Since the norm of the projection of visual data on practically any subspace has a supergaussian distribution, we need to choose the probability density p in the model to be sparse [13], i.e. supergaussian [8]. For example, we could use the following probability distribution

$$\log p(\sum_{i \in S_j} s_i^2) = -\alpha [\sum_{i \in S_j} s_i^2]^{1/2} + \beta, \quad (3)$$

which could be considered a multi-dimensional version of the exponential distribution. Now we see that the estimation of the model consists of finding subspaces such that the *norms of the projections of the (whitened) data on those subspaces have maximally sparse distributions*.

The introduced "independent (feature) subspace analysis" is a natural generalization of ordinary ICA. In fact, if the projections on the subspaces are reduced to dot-products, i.e. projections on 1-D subspaces, the model reduces to ordinary ICA (provided that, in addition, the independent components are assumed to have non-skewed distributions). It is to be expected that the norms of the projections on the subspaces represent some higher-order, invariant features. The exact nature of the invariances has not been specified in the model but will emerge from the input data, using only the prior information on their independence.

When independent subspace analysis is applied to natural image data, we can identify the norms of the projections $(\sum_{i \in S_j} s_i^2)^{1/2}$ as the responses of the complex cells. If the individual filter vectors $w_i(x,y)$ are identified with the receptive fields of simple cells, this can be interpreted as a hierarchical model where the complex cell response is computed from simple cell responses s_i, in a manner similar to the classical energy models for complex cells. Experiments (see below and [6]) show that the model does lead to emergence of those invariances that are encountered in complex cells.

3 Topographic ICA

The independent subspace analysis model introduces a certain dependence structure for the components s_i. Let us assume that the distribution in the subspace is sparse, which means that the norm of the projection is most of the time very near to zero. This is the case, for example, if the densities inside the subspaces are specified as in (3). Then the model implies that two components s_i and s_j that belong to the same subspace tend to be nonzero simultaneously. In other words, s_i^2 and s_j^2 are positively correlated. This seems to be a preponderant structure of dependency in most natural data. For image data, this has also been noted by Simoncelli [14].

Now we generalize the model defined by (2) so that it models this kind of dependence not only inside the m-tuples, but among all "neighboring" components. A neighborhood relation defines a topographic order [10]. (A different generalization based on an explicit generative model is given in [5].) We define the model by the following likelihood:

$$\log L(w_i(x,y), i=1,...,n) = \sum_{k=1}^{K} \sum_{j=1}^{n} G(\sum_{i=1}^{n} h(i,j) <w_i, I_k>^2) + K \log |\det \mathbf{W}| \quad (4)$$

Here, $h(i,j)$ is a neighborhood function, which expresses the strength of the connection between the i-th and j-th units. The neighborhood function can be defined in the same way as with the self-organizing map [10]. Neighborhoods can thus be defined as one-dimensional or two-dimensional; 2-D neighborhoods can be square or hexagonal. A simple example is to define a 1-D neighborhood relation by

$$h(i,j) = \begin{cases} 1, & \text{if } |i-j| \leq m \\ 0, & \text{otherwise.} \end{cases} \quad (5)$$

The constant m defines here the width of the neighborhood.

The function G has a similar role as the log-density of the independent components in classic ICA. For image data, or other data with a sparse structure, G should be chosen as in independent subspace analysis, see Eq. (3).

Properties of the topographic ICA model. Here, we consider for simplicity only the case of sparse data. The first basic property is that all the components s_i are uncorrelated, as can be easily proven by symmetry arguments [5]. Moreover, their variances can be defined to be equal to unity, as in classic ICA. Second, components s_i and s_j that are near to each other, i.e. such that $h(i,j)$ is significantly non-zero, tend to be active (non-zero) at the same time. In other words, their energies s_i^2 and s_j^2 are positively correlated. Third, latent variables that are far from each other are practically independent. Higher-order correlation decreases as a function of distance, assuming that the neighborhood is defined in a way similar to that in (5). For details, see [5].

Let us note that our definition of *topography by higher-order correlations* is very different from the one used in practically all existing topographic mapping methods. Usually, the distance is defined by basic geometrical relations like Euclidean distance or correlation. Interestingly, our principle makes it possible to define a topography even among a set of orthogonal vectors whose Euclidean distances are all equal. Such orthogonal vectors are actually encountered in ICA, where the basis vectors and filters can be constrained to be orthogonal in the whitened space.

4 Experiments with natural image data

We applied our methods on natural image data. The data was obtained by taking 16×16 pixel image patches at random locations from monochrome photographs depicting wild-life scenes (animals, meadows, forests, etc.). Preprocessing consisted of removing the DC component and reducing the dimension of the data to 160 by PCA. For details on the experiments, see [6, 5].

Fig. 1 shows the basis vectors of the 40 feature subspaces (complex cells), when subspace dimension was chosen to be 4. It can be seen that the basis vectors associated with a single complex cell all have approximately the same orientation and frequency. Their locations are not identical, but close to each other. The phases differ considerably. Every feature subspace can thus be considered a generalization of a quadrature-phase filter pair as found in the classical energy models, enabling the cell to be selective to some given orientation and frequency, but invariant to phase and somewhat invariant to shifts. Using 4 dimensions instead of 2 greatly enhances the shift invariance of the feature subspace.

In topographic ICA, the neighborhood function was defined so that every neighborhood consisted of a 3×3 square of 9 units on a 2-D torus lattice [10]. The obtained basis vectors, are shown in Fig. 2. The basis vectors are similar to those obtained by ordinary ICA of image data [13, 1]. In addition, they have a clear topographic organization. In addition, the connection to independent subspace analysis is clear from Fig. 2. Two neighboring basis vectors in Fig. 2 tend to be of the same orientation and frequency. Their locations are near to each other as well. In contrast, their phases are very different. This means that a neighborhood of such basis vectors, i.e. simple cells, is similar to an independent subspace. Thus it functions as a complex cell. This was demonstrated in detail in [5].

5 Discussion

We introduced here two extensions of ICA that are especially useful for image modelling. The first model uses a subspace representation to model invariant features. It turns out that the independent subspaces of natural images are similar to complex cells. The second model is a further extension of the independent subspace model. This topographic ICA model is a generative model that combines topographic mapping with ICA. As in all topographic mappings, the distance in the representation space (on the topographic "grid") is related to some measure of distance between represented components. In topographic ICA, the distance between represented components is defined by higher-order correlations, which gives the natural distance measure in the context of ICA.

An approach closely related to ours is given by Kohonen's Adaptive Subspace Self-Organizing Map [11]. However, the emergence of shift invariance in [11] was conditional to restricting consecutive patches to come from nearby locations in the image, giving the input data a temporal structure like in a smoothly changing image sequence. Similar developments were given by Földiák [4]. In contrast to these two theories, we formulated an explicit image model. This independent subspace analysis model shows that emergence of complex cell properties is possible using patches at random, independently selected locations, which proves that there is enough information in static images to explain the properties of complex cells. Moreover, by extending this subspace model to model topography, we showed that *the emergence of both topography and complex cell properties can be explained by a single principle*: neighboring cells should have strong higher-order correlations.

References

[1] A.J. Bell and T.J. Sejnowski. The 'independent components' of natural scenes are edge filters. *Vision Research*, 37:3327–3338, 1997.

[2] J.-F. Cardoso. Multidimensional independent component analysis. In *Proc. IEEE Int. Conf. on Acoustics, Speech and Signal Processing (ICASSP'98)*, Seattle, WA, 1998.

[3] P. Comon. Independent component analysis – a new concept? *Signal Processing*, 36:287–314, 1994.

[4] P. Földiák. Learning invariance from transformation sequences. *Neural Computation*, 3:194–200, 1991.

[5] A. Hyvärinen and P. O. Hoyer. Topographic independent component analysis. 1999. Submitted, available at http://www.cis.hut.fi/~aapo/.

[6] A. Hyvärinen and P. O. Hoyer. Emergence of phase and shift invariant features by decomposition of natural images into independent feature subspaces. *Neural Computation*, 2000. (in press).

[7] A. Hyvärinen, P. O. Hoyer, and M. Inki. The independence assumption: Analyzing the independence of the components by topography. In M. Girolami, editor, *Advances in Independent Component Analysis*. Springer-Verlag, 2000. in press.

[8] A. Hyvärinen and E. Oja. A fast fixed-point algorithm for independent component analysis. *Neural Computation*, 9(7):1483–1492, 1997.

[9] C. Jutten and J. Herault. Blind separation of sources, part I: An adaptive algorithm based on neuromimetic architecture. *Signal Processing*, 24:1–10, 1991.

[10] T. Kohonen. *Self-Organizing Maps*. Springer-Verlag, Berlin, Heidelberg, New York, 1995.

[11] T. Kohonen. Emergence of invariant-feature detectors in the adaptive-subspace self-organizing map. *Biological Cybernetics*, 75:281–291, 1996.

[12] J. K. Lin. Factorizing multivariate function classes. In *Advances in Neural Information Processing Systems*, volume 10, pages 563–569. The MIT Press, 1998.

[13] B. A. Olshausen and D. J. Field. Emergence of simple-cell receptive field properties by learning a sparse code for natural images. *Nature*, 381:607–609, 1996.

[14] E. P. Simoncelli and O. Schwartz. Modeling surround suppression in V1 neurons with a statistically-derived normalization model. In *Advances in Neural Information Processing Systems 11*, pages 153–159. MIT Press, 1999.

[15] J. H. van Hateren and A. van der Schaaf. Independent component filters of natural images compared with simple cells in primary visual cortex. *Proc. Royal Society ser. B*, 265:359–366, 1998.

Emergence of V1 properties using Extensions of ICA

Figure 1: Independent subspaces of natural image data. The model gives Gabor-like basis vectors for image windows. Every group of four basis vectors corresponds to one independent feature subspace, or complex cell. Basis vectors in a subspace are similar in orientation, location and frequency. In contrast, their phases are very different.

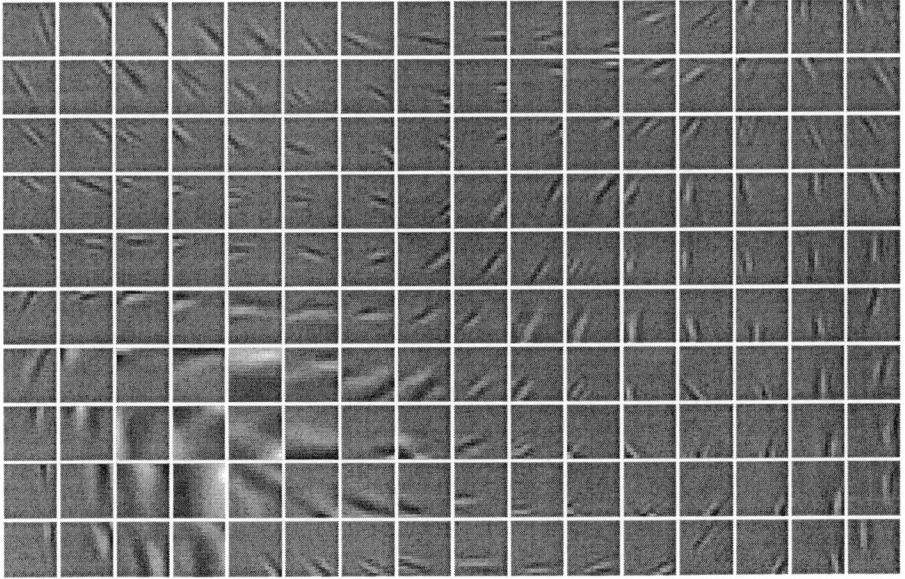

Figure 2: Topographic ICA of natural image data. This gives Gabor-like basis vectors as well. Basis vectors that are similar in orientation, location and/or frequency are close to each other. The phases of nearby basis vectors are very different, giving each neighborhood properties similar to a complex cell.

An Information-Theoretic Framework for Understanding Saccadic Eye Movements

Tai Sing Lee [*]
Department of Computer Science
Carnegie Mellon University
Pittsburgh, PA 15213
tai@cs.cmu.edu

Stella X. Yu
Robotics Institute
Carnegie Mellon University
Pittsburgh, PA 15213
stella@cnbc.cmu.edu

Abstract

In this paper, we propose that information maximization can provide a unified framework for understanding saccadic eye movements. In this framework, the mutual information among the cortical representations of the retinal image, the priors constructed from our long term visual experience, and a dynamic short-term internal representation constructed from recent saccades provides a map for guiding eye navigation. By directing the eyes to locations of maximum complexity in neuronal ensemble responses at each step, the automatic saccadic eye movement system greedily collects information about the external world, while modifying the neural representations in the process. This framework attempts to connect several psychological phenomena, such as pop-out and inhibition of return, to long term visual experience and short term working memory. It also provides an interesting perspective on contextual computation and formation of neural representation in the visual system.

1 Introduction

When we look at a painting or a visual scene, our eyes move around rapidly and constantly to look at different parts of the scene. Are there rules and principles that govern where the eyes are going to look next at each moment? In this paper, we sketch a theoretical framework based on information maximization to reason about the organization of saccadic eye movements.

---

[*]Both authors are members of the Center for the Neural Basis of Cognition – a joint center between University of Pittsburgh and Carnegie Mellon University. Address: Rm 115, Mellon Institute, Carnegie Mellon University, Pittsburgh, PA 15213.

Vision is fundamentally a Bayesian inference process. Given the measurement by the retinas, the brain's memory of eye positions and its prior knowledge of the world, our brain has to make an inference about what is where in the visual scene. The retina, unlike a camera, has a peculiar design. It has a small foveal region dedicated to high-resolution analysis and a large low-resolution peripheral region for monitoring the rest of the visual field. At about $2.5°$ visual angle away from the center of the fovea, visual acuity is already reduced by a half. When we 'look' (foveate) at a certain location in the visual scene, we direct our high-resolution fovea to analyze information in that location, taking a snap shot of the scene using our retina. Figure 1A-C illustrate what a retina would see at each fixation. It is immediately obvious that our retinal image is severely limited – it is clear only in the fovea and is very blurry in the surround, posing a severe constraint on the information available to our inference system. Yet, in our subjective experience, the world seems to be stable, coherent and complete in front of us. This is a paradox that have engaged philosophical and scientific debates for ages. To overcome the constraint of the retinal image, during perception, the brain actively moves the eyes around to (1) gather information to construct a mental image of the world, and (2) to make inference about the world based on this mental image. Understanding the forces that drive saccadic eye movements is important to elucidating the principles of active perception.

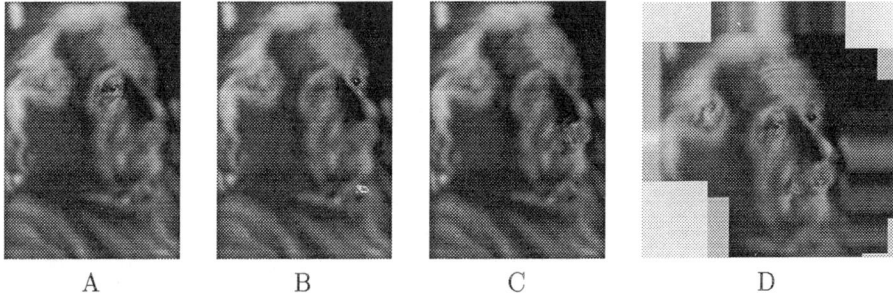

Figure 1. A-C: retinal images in three separate fixations. D: a mental mosaic created by integrating the retinal images from these three and other three fixations.

It is intuitive to think that eye movements are used to gather information. Eye movements have been suggested to provide a means for measuring the allocation of attention or the values of each kind of information in a particular context [16]. The basic assumption of our theory is that we move our eyes around to maximize our information intake from the world, for constructing the mental image and for making inference of the scene. Therefore, the system should always look for and attentively fixate at a location in the retinal image that is the most unusual or the most unexplained – and hence carries the maximum amount of information.

2 Perceptual Representation

How can the brain decide which part of the retinal image is more unusual? First of all, we know the responses of V1 simple cells, modeled well by the Gabor wavelet pyramid [3,7], can be used to reconstruct completely the retinal image. It is also well established that the receptive fields of these neurons developed in such a way as to provide a compact code for natural images [8,9,13,14]. The idea of compact code or sparse code, originally proposed by Barlow [2], is that early visual neurons capture the statistical correlations in natural scenes so that only a small number of cells out of a large set will be activated to represent a particular scene at each moment. Extending this logic, we suggest that the complexity or the entropy of the neuronal ensemble response of a hypercolumn in V1 is therefore closely related to the strangeness of the image features being analyzed by the machinery in that hypercolumn. A frequent event will have a more compact representation in the neuronal ensemble response. Entropy is an information measure that captures the complexity or the variability of signals. The entropy of a neuronal ensemble in a hypercolumn can therefore be used to quantify the strangeness of a particular event.

A hypercolumn in the visual cortex contains roughly 200,000 neurons, dedicated to analyzing different aspects of the image in its 'visual window'. These cells are tuned to different spatial positions, orientations, spatial frequency, color disparity and other cues. There might also be a certain degree of redundancy, i.e. a number of neurons are tuned to the same feature. Thus a hypercolumn forms the fundamental computational unit for image analysis within a particular window in visual space. Each hypercolumn contains cells with receptive fields of different sizes, many significantly smaller than the aggregated 'visual window' of the hypercolumn. The entropy of a hypercolumn's ensemble response at a certain time t is the sum of entropies of all the channels, given by,

$$H(u(R_{\vec{x}},t)) = -\sum_{\theta,\sigma}\sum_{v} p(u(R_{\vec{x}},v,\sigma,\theta,t)) \log_2 p(u(R_{\vec{x}},v,\sigma,\theta,t))$$

where $u(R_{\vec{x}},t)$ denotes the responses of all complex cell channels inside the visual window $R_{\vec{x}}$ of a hypercolumn at time t, computed within a 20 msec time window. $u(\vec{x},\sigma,\theta,t)$ is the response of a V1 complex cell channel of a particular scale σ and orientation σ at spatial location $\vec{x}$ at t. $p(u(R_{\vec{x}},v,\sigma,\theta,t))$ is the probability of cells in that channel within the visual window $R_{\vec{x}}$ of the hypercolumn firing v number of spikes. v can be computed as the power modulus of the corresponding simple cell channels, modeled by Gabor wavelets [see 7]. $\sum_v p(u(R_{\vec{x}},v,\sigma,\theta,t)) = 1$. The probability $p(u(R_{\vec{x}},v,\sigma,\theta,t))$ can be computed at each moment in time because of the variations in spatial position of the receptive fields of similar cell within the hypercolumn – hence the 'same' cells in the hypercolumn are analyzing different image patches, and also because of the redundancy of cells coding similar features.

The neurons' responses in a hypercolumn are subject to contextual modulation from other hypercolumns, partly in the form of lateral inhibition from cells with similar tunings. The net observed effect is that the later part of V1 neurons' response, starting at about 80 msec, exhibits differential suppression depending on the spatial extent and the nature of the surround stimulus. The more similar the surround stimulus is to the center stimuli, and the larger the spatial extent of the 'similar surround', the stronger is the suppressive effect [e.g. 6]. Simoncelli and Schwartz [15] have proposed that the steady state responses of the cells can be modeled by dividing the response of the cell (i.e. modeled by the wavelet coefficient or its power modulus) by a weighted combination of the responses of its spatial neighbors in order to remove the statistical dependencies between the responses of spatial neighbors. These weights are found by minimizing a predictive error between the center signal from the surround signals. In our context, this idea of predictive coding [see also 14] is captured by the concept of mutual information between the ensemble responses of the different hypercolumns as given below,

$$\begin{aligned}I(u(R_{\vec{x}},t);u(\Omega_{\vec{x}},t-\delta t_1)) &= H(u(R_{\vec{x}},t)) - H(u(R_{\vec{x}},t)|u(\Omega_{\vec{x}},t-\delta t_1)) \\ &= \sum_{\sigma,\theta}\sum_{v_R,v_\Omega}[p(u(R_{\vec{x}},v_R,\sigma,\theta,t),u(\Omega_{\vec{x}},v_\Omega,\sigma,\theta,t)) \\ &\quad \log_2 \frac{p(u(R_{\vec{x}},v_R,\sigma,\theta,t),u(\Omega_{\vec{x}},v_\Omega,\sigma,\theta,t))}{p(u(R_{\vec{x}},v_R,\sigma,\theta,t)),p(u(\Omega_{\vec{x}},v_\Omega,\sigma,\theta,t))}].\end{aligned}$$

where $u(R_{\vec{x}},t)$ is the ensemble response of the hypercolumn in question, and $u(\Omega_{\vec{x}},t)$ is the ensemble response of the surrounding hypercolumns. $p(u(R_{\vec{x}},v_R,\sigma,\theta,t))$ is the probability that cells of a channel in the center hypercolumn assumes the response value v_R and $p(u(\Omega_{\vec{x}},v_R,\sigma,\theta,t))$ the probability that cells of a similar channel in the surrounding hypercolumns assuming the response value v_Ω. t_1 is the delay by which the surround information exerts its effect on the center hypercolumn. The mutual information I can be computed from the joint probability of ensemble responses of the center and the surround.

The steady state responses of the V1 neurons, as a result of this contextual modulation, are said to be more correlated to perceptual pop-out than the neurons' initial responses [5,6]. The complexity of the steady state response in the early visual cortex is described by the following conditional entropy,

$$H(u(R_{\vec{x}},t)|u(\Omega_{\vec{x}},t-\delta t_1)) = H(u(R_{\vec{x}},t)) - I(u(R_{\vec{x}},t);u(\Omega_{\vec{x}},t-\delta t_1)).$$

However, the computation in V1 is not limited to the creation of compact representation through surround inhibition. In fact, we have suggested that V1 plays an active role in scene interpretation particularly when such inference involves high resolution details [6]. Visual tasks such as the inference of contour and surface likely involve V1 heavily. These computations could further modify the steady state responses of V1, and hence the control of saccadic eye movements.

3 Mental Mosaic Representation

The perceptual representation provides the basic force for the brain to steer the high resolution fovea to locations of maximum uncertainty or maximum signal complexity. Foveation captures the maximum amount of available information in a location. Once a location is examined by the fovea, its information uncertainty is greatly reduced. The eyes should move on and not to return to the same spot within a certain period of time. This is called the 'inhibition of return'.

How can we model this reduction of interest? We propose that the mind creates a mental mosaic of the scene in order to keep track of the information that have been gathered. By mosaic, we mean that the brain can assemble successive retinal images obtained from multiple fixations into a coherent mental picture of the scene. Figure 1D provides an example of a mental mosaic created by combining information from the retinal images from 6 fixations. Whether the brain actually keeps such a mental mosaic of the scene is currently under debate. McConkie and Rayner [10] had suggested the idea of an integrative visual buffer to integrate information across multiple saccades. However, numerous experiments demonstrated we actually remember relatively little across saccades [4]. This lead to the idea that brain may not need an explicit internal representation of the world. Since the world is always out there, the brain can access whatever information it needs at the appropriate details by moving the eyes to the appropriate place at the appropriate time. The subjective feeling of a coherent and a complete world in front of us is a mere illusion [e.g. 1].

The mental mosaic represented in Figure 1D might resemble McConkie and Rayner's theory superficially. But the existence of such a detailed high-resolution buffer with a large spatial support in the brain is rather biologically implausible. Rather, we think that the information corresponding to the mental mosaic is stored in an *interpreted* and *semantic* form in a mesh of Bayesian belief networks in the brain (e.g. involving PO, IT and area 46). This distributed semantic representation of the mental mosaic, however, is capable of generating detailed (sometimes false) imagery in early visual cortex using the massive recurrent convergent feedback from the higher areas to V1. However, because of the limited support provided by V1 machinery, the instantiation of mental imagery in V1 has to be done sequentially one 'retinal image' frame at a time, presumably in conjunction with eye movement, even when the eyes are closed. This might explain why vivid visual dream is always accompanied by rapid eye movement in REM sleep. The mental mosaic accumulates information from the retinal images up to the last fixation and can provide prediction on what the retina will see in the current fixation. For each $u(\vec{x},\sigma,\theta)$ cell, there is a corresponding effective prediction signal $m(\vec{x},\sigma,\theta)$ fed back from the mental mosaic.

This prediction signal can reduce the conditional entropy or complexity of the ensemble response in the perceptual representation by discounting the mutual information between the ensemble response to the retinal image and the mental mosaic prediction as follow,

$$H(u(R_{\vec{x}},t)|m(R_{\vec{x}},t-\delta t_2)) = H(u(R_{\vec{x}},t)) - I(u(R_{\vec{x}},t),m(R_{\vec{x}},t-\delta t_2))$$

where δt_2 is the transmission delay from the mental mosaic back to V1.

At places where the fovea has visited, the mental mosaic representation has high resolution information and $m(\vec{x},\sigma,\theta,t-\delta t_2)$ can explain $u(\vec{x},\sigma,\theta,t)$ fully. Hence, the mutual information is high at those hypercolumns and the conditional entropy $H(u(R_{\vec{x}},t)|m(R_{\vec{x}},t-\delta t_2))$ is low, with two consequences: (1) the system will not get the eyes stuck at a particular location; once the information at $\vec{x}$ is updated to the mental mosaic, the system will lose interest and move on; (2) the system will exhibit 'inhibition of return' as the information in the visited locations are fully predicted by the mental mosaic. Also, from this standpoint, the 'habituation dynamics' often observed in visual neurons when the same stimulus is presented multiple times might not be simply due to neuro-chemical fatigue, but might be understood in terms of mental mosaic being updated and then fed back to explain the perceptual representation in V1. The mental mosaic is in effect our short-term memory of the scene. It has a forgetting dynamics, and needs to be periodically updated. Otherwise, it will rapidly fade away.

4 Overall Reactive Saccadic Behaviors

Now, we can combine the influence of the two predictive processes to arrive at a discounted complexity measure of the hypercolumn's ensemble response:

$$\begin{aligned}H(u(R_{\vec{x}},t)|u(\Omega_{\vec{x}},t-\delta t_1),m(R_{\vec{x}},t-\delta t_2)) =\ & H(u(R_{\vec{x}},t)) \\ & -I(u(R_{\vec{x}},t);u(\Omega_{\vec{x}},t-\delta t_1)) \\ & -I(u(R_{\vec{x}},t);m(R_{\vec{x}},t-\delta t_2)) \\ & +I(u(\Omega_{\vec{x}},t-\delta t_1);m(R_{\vec{x}},t-\delta t_2))\end{aligned}$$

If we can assume the long range surround priors and the mental mosaic short term memory are independent processes, we can leave out the last term, $I(u(\Omega_{\vec{x}},t-\delta t_1);m(R_{\vec{x}},t-\delta t_2))$, of the equation.

The system, after each saccade, will evaluate the new retinal scene and select the location where the perceptual representation has the maximum conditional entropy. To maximize the information gain, the system must constantly search for and make a saccade to the locations of maximum uncertainty (or complexity) computed from the hypercolumn ensemble responses in V1 at each fixation. Unless the number of saccades is severely limited, this locally greedy algorithm, coupled the inhibition of return mechanism, will likely steer the system to a relatively optimal global sampling of the world – in the sense that the average information gain per saccade is maximized, and the mental mosaic's dissonance with the world is minimized.

5 Task-dependent schema Representation

However, human eye movements are not simply controlled by the generic information in a bottom-up fashion. Yarbus [16] has shown that, when staring at a face, subjects' eyes tend to go back to the same locations (eyes, mouth) over and over again. Further, he showed that when asked different questions, subjects exhibited different kinds of scan-paths when looking at the same picture. Norton and Stark [12] also showed that eye movements are not random, but often exhibit repetitive or even idiosyncratic path patterns.

To capture these ideas, we propose a third representation, called task schema, to provide the necessary *top-down* information to bias the eye movement control. It specifies the learned or habitual scan-paths for a particular task in a particular context or assigns weights to different types of information. Given that we arenot mostly unconscious of the scan-path patterns we are making, these task-sensitive or context-sensitive habitual scan-patterns might be encoded at the levels of motor programs, and be downloaded when needed without our conscious control. These motor programs for scan-paths can be trained from reinforcement learning. For example, since the eyes and the mouths convey most of the emotional content of a facial expression, a successful interpretation of another person's emotion could provide the reward signal to reinforce the motor programs just executed or the fixations to certain facial features. These unconscious scan-path motor programs could provide the additional modulation to automatic saccadic eye movement generation.

6 Discussion

In this paper, we propose that information maximization might provide a theoretical framework to understand the automatic saccadic eye movement behaviors in human. In this proposal, each hypercolumn in V1 is considered a fundamental computational unit. The relative complexity or entropy of the neuronal ensemble response in the V1 hypercolumns, discounted by the predictive effect of the surround, higher order representations and working memory, creates a force field to guide eye navigation.

The framework we sketched here bridge natural scene statistics to eye movement control via the more established ideas of sparse coding and predictive coding in neural representation. Information maximization has been suggested to be a possible explanation for shaping the receptive fields in the early visual cortex according to the statistics of natural images [8,9,13,14] to create a minimum-entropy code [2,3]. As a result, a frequent event is represented efficiently with the response of a few neurons in a large set, resulting in a lower hypercolumn ensemble entropy, while unusual events provoke ensemble responses of higher complexity. We suggest that higher complexity in ensemble responses will arouse attention and draw scrutiny by the eyes, forcing the neural representation to continue adapting to the statistics of the natural scenes. The formulation here also suggests that information maximization might provide an explanation for the formation of horizontal predictive network in V1 as well as higher order internal representations, consistent with the ideas of predictive coding [11, 14, 15]. Our theory hence predicts that the adaptation of the neural representations to the statistics of natural scenes will lead to the adaptation of saccadic eye movement behaviors.

Acknowledgements

The authors have been supported by a grant from the McDonnell Foundation and a NSF grant (LIS 9720350). Yu is also being supported in part by a grant to Takeo Kanade.

References

[1] Ballard, D. Hayhoe, M.M. Pook, P.K. & Rao, R.P.N. (1997). Deictic codes for the embodiment of cognition. *Behavioral and Brain Science*, **20:4**, December, 723-767.

[2] Barlow, H.B. (1989). Unsupervised learning. *Neural Computation*, 1, 295-311.

[3] Daugman, J.G. (1989). Entropy reduction and decorrelation in visual coding by oriented neural receptive fields. *IEEE Transactions on Biomedical Engineering 36:*, 107-114.

[4] Irwin, D. E, 1991. Information Integration across Saccadic Eye Movements. *Cognitive Psychology*, 23(3):420-56.

[5] Knierim, J. & Van Essen, D.C. Neural response to static texture patterns in area V1 of macaque monkey. *J. Neurophysiology*, **67:** 961-980.

[6] Lee, T.S., Mumford, D., Romero R. & Lamme, V.A.F. (1998). The role of primary visual cortex in higher level vision. *Vision Research* **38**, 2429-2454.

[7] Lee, T.S. (1996). Image representation using 2D Gabor wavelets. *IEEE Transaction of Pattern Analysis and Machine Intelligence.* **18:10**, 959-971.

[8] Lewicki, M. & Olshausen, B. (1998). Inferring sparse, overcomplete image codes using an efficient coding framework. In *Advances in Neural Information Processing System 10*, M. Jordan, M. Kearns and S. Solla (eds). MIT Press.

[9] Linsker, R. (1989). How to generate ordered maps by maximizing the mutual information between input and output signals. *Neural Computation*, **1:** 402-411.o

[10] McConkie, G.W. & Rayner, K. (1976). Identifying the span of effective stimulus in reading. Literature review and theories of reading. In H. Singer and R.B. Ruddell (Eds), *Theoretical models and processes of reading*, 137-162. Newark, D.E.: International Reading Association.

[11] Mumford, D. (1992). On the computational architecture of the neocortex II. *Biological cybernetics,* **66**, 241-251.

[12] Norton, D. and Stark, L. (1971) Eye movements and visual perception. *Scientific American*, **224**, 34-43.

[13] Olshausen, B.A., & Field, D.J. (1996), Emergence of simple cell receptive field properties by learning a sparse code for natural images. *Nature*, **381:** 607-609.

[14] Rao R., & Ballard, D.H. (1999). Predictive coding in the visual cortex: a functional interpretation of some extra-classical receptive field effects. *Nature Neuroscience*, **2:1** 79-87.

[15] Simoncelli, E.P. & Schwartz, O. (1999). Modeling surround suppression in V1 neurons with a statistically-derived normalization model. In *Advances in Neural Information Processing Systems 11*, . M.S. Kearns, S.A. Solla, and D.A. Cohn (eds). MIT Press.

[16] Yarbus, A.L. (1967). Eye movements and vision. Plenum Press.

Learning sparse codes with a mixture-of-Gaussians prior

Bruno A. Olshausen
Department of Psychology and
Center for Neuroscience, UC Davis
1544 Newton Ct.
Davis, CA 95616
baolshausen@ucdavis.edu

K. Jarrod Millman
Center for Neuroscience, UC Davis
1544 Newton Ct.
Davis, CA 95616
kjmillman@ucdavis.edu

Abstract

We describe a method for learning an overcomplete set of basis functions for the purpose of modeling sparse structure in images. The sparsity of the basis function coefficients is modeled with a mixture-of-Gaussians distribution. One Gaussian captures non-active coefficients with a small-variance distribution centered at zero, while one or more other Gaussians capture active coefficients with a large-variance distribution. We show that when the prior is in such a form, there exist efficient methods for learning the basis functions as well as the parameters of the prior. The performance of the algorithm is demonstrated on a number of test cases and also on natural images. The basis functions learned on natural images are similar to those obtained with other methods, but the sparse form of the coefficient distribution is much better described. Also, since the parameters of the prior are adapted to the data, no assumption about sparse structure in the images need be made *a priori*, rather it is learned from the data.

1 Introduction

The general problem we address here is that of learning a set of basis functions for representing natural images efficiently. Previous work using a variety of optimization schemes has established that the basis functions which best code natural images in terms of sparse, independent components resemble a Gabor-like wavelet basis in which the basis functions are spatially localized, oriented and bandpass in spatial-frequency [1, 2, 3, 4]. In order to tile the joint space of position, orientation, and spatial-frequency in a manner that yields useful image representations, it has also been advocated that the basis set be *overcomplete* [5], where the number of basis functions exceeds the dimensionality of the images being coded. A major challenge in learning overcomplete bases, though, comes from the fact that the posterior distribution over the coefficients must be sampled during learning. When the posterior is sharply peaked, as it is when a sparse prior is imposed, then conventional sampling methods become especially cumbersome.

One approach to dealing with the problems associated with overcomplete codes and sparse priors is suggested by the form of the resulting posterior distribution over the coefficients averaged over many images. Shown below is the posterior distribution of one of the coefficients in a 4×'s overcomplete representation. The sparse prior that was imposed in learning was a Cauchy distribution and is overlaid (dashed line). It would seem that the coefficients do not fit this imposed prior very well, and instead want to occupy one of two states: an *inactive* state in which the coefficient is set nearly to zero, and an *active* state in which the coefficient takes on some significant non-zero value along a continuum. This suggests that the appropriate choice of prior is one that is capable of capturing these two discrete states.

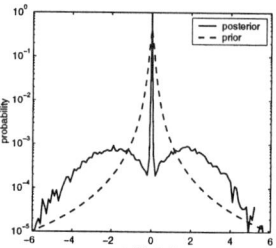

Figure 1: Posterior distribution of coefficients with Cauchy prior overlaid.

Our approach to modeling this form of sparse structure uses a *mixture-of-Gaussians* prior over the coefficients. A set of binary or ternary state variables determine whether the coefficient is in the active or inactive state, and then the coefficient distribution is Gaussian distributed with a variance and mean that depends on the state variable. An important advantage of this approach, with regard to the sampling problems mentioned above, is that the use of Gaussian distributions allows an analytical solution for integrating over the posterior distribution for a given setting of the state variables. The only sampling that needs to be done then is over the binary or ternary state variables. We show here that this problem is a tractable one. This approach differs from that taken previously by Attias [6] in that we do not use variational methods to approximate the posterior, but rather we rely on sampling to adequately characterize the posterior distribution over the coefficients.

2 Mixture-of-Gaussians model

An image, $I(x,y)$, is modeled as a linear superposition of basis functions, $\phi_i(x,y)$, with coefficients a_i, plus Gaussian noise $\nu(x,y)$:

$$I(x,y) = \sum_i a_i\, \phi_i(x,y) + \nu(x,y) \tag{1}$$

In what follows this will be expressed in vector-matrix notation as $\mathbf{I} = \boldsymbol{\Phi}\,\mathbf{a} + \nu$.

The prior probability distribution over the coefficients is factorial, with the distribution over each coefficient a_i modeled as a mixture-of-Gaussians distribution with either two or three Gaussians (fig. 2). A set of binary or ternary state variables s_i then determine which Gaussian is used to describe the coefficients.

The total prior over both sets of variables, $\mathbf{a}$ and $\mathbf{s}$, is of the form

$$P(\mathbf{a},\mathbf{s}) = \prod_i P(a_i|s_i)\, P(s_i) \tag{2}$$

Learning Sparse Codes with a Mixture-of-Gaussians Prior

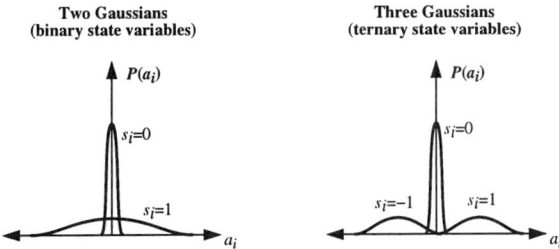

Figure 2: Mixture-of-Gaussians prior.

where $P(s_i)$ determines the probability of being in the active or inactive states, and $P(a_i|s_i)$ is a Gaussian distribution whose mean and variance is determined by the current state s_i.

The total image probability is then given by

$$P(\mathbf{I}|\theta) = \sum_{\mathbf{s}} P(\mathbf{s}|\theta) \int P(\mathbf{I}|\mathbf{a},\theta) P(\mathbf{a}|\mathbf{s},\theta) d\mathbf{a} \quad (3)$$

where

$$P(\mathbf{I}|\mathbf{a},\theta) = \frac{1}{Z_{\lambda_N}} e^{-\frac{\lambda_N}{2}|\mathbf{I}-\Phi\mathbf{a}|^2} \quad (4)$$

$$P(\mathbf{a}|\mathbf{s},\theta) = \frac{1}{Z_{\Lambda_\mathbf{a}(\mathbf{s})}} e^{-\frac{1}{2}(\mathbf{a}-\mu(\mathbf{s}))^t \Lambda_\mathbf{a}(\mathbf{s})(\mathbf{a}-\mu(\mathbf{s}))} \quad (5)$$

$$P(\mathbf{s}|\theta) = \frac{1}{Z_{\Lambda_\mathbf{s}}} e^{-\frac{1}{2}\mathbf{s}^t \Lambda_\mathbf{s} \mathbf{s}} \quad (6)$$

and the parameters θ include λ_N, Φ, $\Lambda_\mathbf{a}(\mathbf{s})$, $\mu(\mathbf{s})$, and $\Lambda_\mathbf{s}$. $\Lambda_\mathbf{a}(\mathbf{s})$ is a diagonal inverse covariance matrix with elements $\Lambda_\mathbf{a}(\mathbf{s})_{ii} = \lambda_{a_i}(s_i)$. (The notations $\Lambda_\mathbf{a}(\mathbf{s})$ and $\mu(\mathbf{s})$ are used here to explicitly reflect the dependence of the means and variances of the a_i on s_i.) $\Lambda_\mathbf{s}$ is also diagonal (for now) with elements $\Lambda_{\mathbf{s}ii} = \lambda_{s_i}$. The model is illustrated graphically in figure 3.

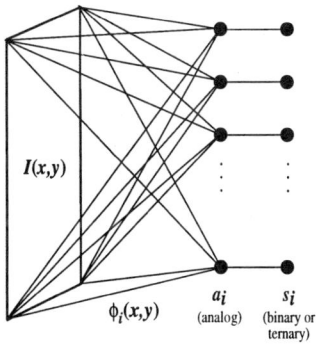

Figure 3: Image model.

3 Learning

The objective function for learning the parameters of the model is the average log-likelihood:
$$\mathcal{L} = \langle \log P(\mathbf{I}|\theta) \rangle \quad (7)$$
Maximizing this objective will minimize the lower bound on coding length.

Learning is accomplished via gradient ascent on the objective, $\mathcal{L}$. The learning rules for the parameters $\mathbf{\Lambda_s}$, $\mathbf{\Lambda_a(s)}$, $\mu(\mathbf{s})$ and $\mathbf{\Phi}$ are given by:

$$\Delta \lambda_{s_i} \propto \frac{\partial \mathcal{L}}{\partial \lambda_{s_i}}$$
$$= \frac{1}{2}\left[\langle s_i \rangle_{P(s_i|\theta)} - \langle s_i \rangle_{P(\mathbf{s}|\mathbf{I},\theta)}\right] \quad (8)$$

$$\Delta \lambda_{a_i}(u) \propto \frac{\partial \mathcal{L}}{\partial \lambda_{a_i}(u)}$$
$$= \frac{1}{2}\left[\frac{\langle \delta(s_i - u)\rangle_{P(\mathbf{s}|\mathbf{I},\theta)}}{\lambda_{a_i}(u)} - \right.$$
$$\left. \langle \delta(s_i - u)\left(K_{ii}(u) - 2\hat{a}_i(u)\mu_i(u) + \mu_i^2(u)\right)\rangle_{P(\mathbf{s}|\mathbf{I},\theta)}\right] \quad (9)$$

$$\Delta \mu_i(u) \propto \frac{\partial \mathcal{L}}{\partial \mu_i(u)}$$
$$= \lambda_{a_i}(u) \langle \delta(s_i - u)\left(\hat{a}_i(u) - \mu_i(u)\right)\rangle \quad (10)$$

$$\Delta \mathbf{\Phi} \propto \frac{\partial \mathcal{L}}{\partial \mathbf{\Phi}}$$
$$= \lambda_N \left[\mathbf{I} \langle \hat{\mathbf{a}}(\mathbf{s}) \rangle_{P(\mathbf{s}|\mathbf{I},\theta)} - \mathbf{\Phi} \langle \mathbf{K}(\mathbf{s}) \rangle_{P(\mathbf{s}|\mathbf{I},\theta)}\right] \quad (11)$$

where u takes on values 0,1 (binary) or -1,0,1 (ternary) and $\mathbf{K}(\mathbf{s}) = \mathbf{H}^{-1}(\mathbf{s}) + \hat{\mathbf{a}}(\mathbf{s})\hat{\mathbf{a}}(\mathbf{s})^T$. ($\hat{\mathbf{a}}$ and $\mathbf{H}$ are defined in eqs. 15 and 16 in the next section.) Note that in these expressions we have dropped the outer brackets averaging over images simply to reduce clutter.

Thus, for each image we must sample from the posterior $P(\mathbf{s}|\mathbf{I},\theta)$ in order to collect the appropriate statistics needed for learning. These statistics must be accumulated over many different images, and then the parameters are updated according to the rules above. Note that this approach differs from that of Attias [6] in that we do not attempt to sum over all states, $\mathbf{s}$, or to use the variational approximation to approximate the posterior. Instead, we are effectively summing only over those states that are most probable according to the posterior. We conjecture that this scheme will work in practice because the posterior has significant probability only for a small fraction of states $\mathbf{s}$, and so it can be well-characterized by a relatively small number of samples. Next we present an efficient method for Gibbs sampling from the posterior.

4 Sampling and inference

In order to sample from the posterior $P(\mathbf{s}|\mathbf{I},\theta)$, we first cast it in Boltzmann form:
$$P(\mathbf{s}|\mathbf{I},\theta) \propto e^{-E(\mathbf{s})} \quad (12)$$
where
$$E(\mathbf{s}) = -\log P(\mathbf{s},\mathbf{I}|\theta) = -\log P(\mathbf{s}|\theta) \int P(\mathbf{I}|\mathbf{a},\theta)P(\mathbf{a}|\mathbf{s},\theta)d\mathbf{a}$$

$$= \frac{1}{2}\mathbf{s}^T \mathbf{\Lambda_s} \mathbf{s} + \log Z_{\mathbf{\Lambda_a(s)}} + E_{\mathbf{a|s}}(\hat{\mathbf{a}},\mathbf{s}) + \frac{1}{2}\log\det \mathbf{H(s)} + \text{const.} \quad (13)$$

and

$$E_{\mathbf{a|s}}(\mathbf{a},\mathbf{s}) \equiv \frac{\lambda_N}{2}|\mathbf{I}-\mathbf{\Phi a}|^2 + \frac{1}{2}(\mathbf{a}-\mu(\mathbf{s}))^T \mathbf{\Lambda_a(s)}(\mathbf{a}-\mu(\mathbf{s})) \quad (14)$$

$$\hat{\mathbf{a}} = \arg\min_{\mathbf{a}} E_{\mathbf{a|s}}(\mathbf{a},\mathbf{s}) \quad (15)$$

$$\mathbf{H(s)} = \nabla\nabla_{\mathbf{a}} E_{\mathbf{a|s}}(\mathbf{a},\mathbf{s}) = \lambda_N \mathbf{\Phi}^T\mathbf{\Phi} + \mathbf{\Lambda_a(s)} \quad (16)$$

Gibbs-sampling on $P(\mathbf{s}|\mathbf{I},\theta)$ can be performed by flipping state variables s_i according to

$$P(s_i \leftarrow s^\alpha) = \frac{1}{1+e^{\Delta E(s_i \leftarrow s^\alpha)}} \quad \text{(binary)} \quad (17)$$

$$P(s_i \leftarrow s^\alpha) = \frac{1}{1+e^{\Delta E(s_i \leftarrow s^\alpha)}\left[1+e^{-\Delta E(s_i \leftarrow s^\beta)}\right]} \quad \text{(ternary)} \quad (18)$$

Where $s^\alpha = \overline{s_i}$ in the binary case, and s^α and s^β are the two alternative states in the ternary case. $\Delta E(s_i \leftarrow s^\alpha)$ denotes the change in $E(\mathbf{s})$ due to changing s_i to s^α and is given by:

$$\Delta E(s_i \leftarrow s^\alpha) = \frac{1}{2}\left[\log\frac{\lambda_{a_i}(s_i)}{\lambda_{a_i}(s^{(\alpha)})} + \Delta s_i \lambda_{s_i} + \log(1+\Delta\lambda_{a_i} J_{ii}) + \frac{\Delta\lambda_{a_i}\hat{a}_i^2 - 2\hat{a}_i\Delta v_i - J_{ii}\Delta v_i^2}{1+\Delta\lambda_{a_i} J_{ii}} + \Delta(\mu_i v_i)\right] \quad (19)$$

where $\Delta s_i = s^\alpha - s_i$, $\Delta\lambda_{a_i} = \lambda_{a_i}(s^\alpha) - \lambda_{a_i}(s_i)$, $\mathbf{J} = \mathbf{H}^{-1}$, and $v_i = \lambda_{a_i}(s_i)\mu_i(s_i)$. Note that all computations for considering a change of state are local and involve only terms with index i. Thus, deciding whether or not to change state can be computed quickly. However, if a change of state is accepted, then we must update $\mathbf{J}$. Using the Sherman-Morrison formula, this can be kept to an $O(N^2)$ computation:

$$\mathbf{J} \leftarrow \mathbf{J} - \left[\frac{\Delta\lambda_{a_k}}{1+\Delta\lambda_{a_k} J_{kk}}\right]\mathbf{J}_k \mathbf{J}_k^T \quad (20)$$

As long as accepted state changes are rare (which we have found to be the case for sparse distributions), then Gibbs sampling may be performed quickly and efficiently. In addition, $\mathbf{H}$ and $\mathbf{J}$ are generally very sparse matrices, so as the system is scaled up the number of elements of $\mathbf{a}$ that are affected by a flip of s_i will be relatively few.

In order to code images under this model, a single state of the coefficients must be chosen for a given image. We use for this purpose the MAP estimator:

$$\hat{\mathbf{a}} = \arg\max_{\mathbf{a}} P(\mathbf{a}|\mathbf{I},\hat{\mathbf{s}},\theta) \quad (21)$$

$$\hat{\mathbf{s}} = \arg\max_{\mathbf{s}} P(\mathbf{s}|\mathbf{I},\theta) \quad (22)$$

Maximizing the posterior distribution over $\mathbf{s}$ is accomplished by assigning a temperature,

$$P(\mathbf{s}|\mathbf{I},\theta) \propto e^{-E(\mathbf{s})/T} \quad (23)$$

and gradually lowering it until there are no more state changes.

5 Results

5.1 Test cases

We first trained the algorithm on a number of test cases containing known forms of both sparse and non-sparse (bi-modal) structure, using both critically sampled (complete) and 2×'s overcomplete basis sets. The training sets consisted of 6x6 pixel image patches that were created by a sparse superposition of basis functions (36 or 72) with $P(|s_i| = 1) = 0.2$, $\lambda_{a_i}(0) = 1000$, and $\lambda_{a_i}(1) = 10$. The results of these test cases confirm that the algorithm is capable of correctly extracting both sparse and non-sparse structure from data, and they are not shown here for lack of space.

5.2 Natural images

We trained the algorithm on 8x8 image patches extracted from pre-whitened natural images. In all cases, the basis functions were initialized to random functions (white noise) and the prior was initialized to be Gaussian (both Gaussians of roughly equal variance). Shown in figure 4a,b are the results for a set of 128 basis functions (2×'s overcomplete) in the two-Gausian case. In the three-Gaussian case, the prior was initialized to be platykurtic (all three Gaussians of equal variance but offset at three different positions). Thus, in this case the sparse form of the prior emerged completely from the data. The resulting priors for two of the coefficients are shown in figure 4c, with the posterior distribution averaged over many images overlaid. For some of the coefficients the posterior distribution matches the mixture-of-Gaussians prior well, but for others the tails appear more Laplacian in form. Also, it appears that the extra complexity offered by having three Gaussians is not utilized: Both Gaussians move to the center position and have about the same mean. When a non-sparse, bimodal prior is imposed, the basis function solution does not become localized, oriented, and bandpass as it does with sparse priors.

5.3 Coding efficiency

We evaluated the coding efficiency by quantizing the coefficients to different levels and calculating the total coefficient entropy as a function of the distortion introduced by quantization. This was done for basis sets containing 48, 64, 96, and 128 basis functions. At high SNR's the overcomplete basis sets yield better coding efficiency, despite the fact that there are more coefficients to code. However, the point at which this occurs appears to be well beyond the point where errors are no longer perceptually noticeable (around 14 dB).

6 Conclusions

We have shown here that both the prior and basis functions of our image model can be adapted to natural images. Without sparseness being imposed, the model both seeks distributions that are sparse and learns the appropriate basis functions for this distribution. Our conjecture that a small number of samples allows the posterior to be sufficiently characterized appears to hold. In all cases here, averages were collected over 40 Gibbs sweeps, with 10 sweeps for initialization. The algorithm proved capable of extracting the structure in challenging datasets in high dimensional spaces.

The overcomplete image codes have the lowest coding cost at high SNR levels, but at levels that appear higher than is practically useful. On the other hand, the

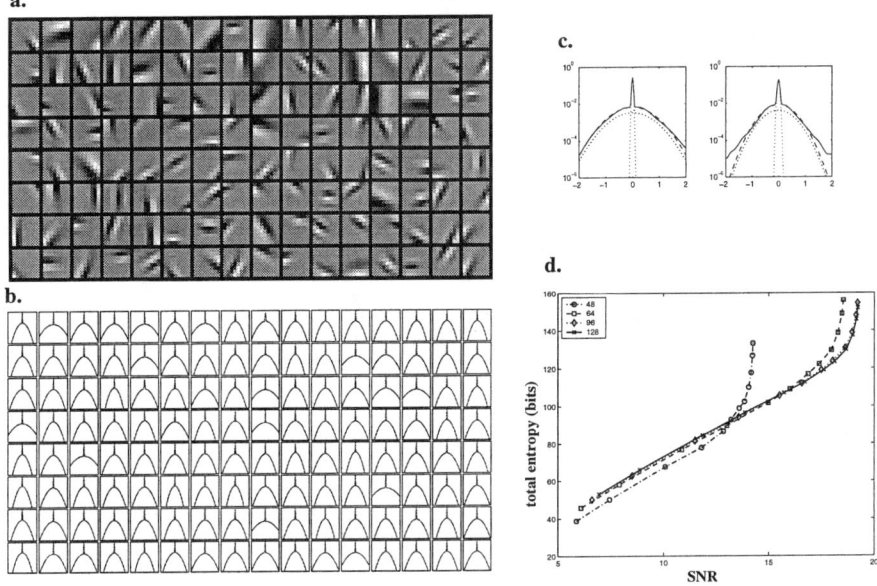

Figure 4: An overcomplete set of 128 basis functions (a) and priors (b, vertical axis is log-probability) learned from natural images. c, Two of the priors learned from a three-Gaussian mixture using 64 basis functions, with the posterior distribution averaged over many coefficients overlaid. d, Rate distortion curve comparing the coding efficiency of different learned basis sets.

sum of marginal entropies likely underestimates the true entropy of the coefficients considerably, as there are certainly statistical dependencies among the coefficients. So it may still be the case that the overcomplete bases will show a win at lower SNR's when these dependencies are included in the model (through the coupling term Λ_s).

Acknowledgments

This work was supported by NIH grant R29-MH057921.

References

[1] Olshausen BA, Field DJ (1997) "Sparse coding with an overcomplete basis set: A strategy employed by V1?" Vision Research, 37: 3311-3325.

[2] Bell AJ, Sejnowski TJ (1997) "The independent components of natural images are edge filters," Vision Research, 37: 3327-3338.

[3] van Hateren JH, van der Schaaff A (1997) "Independent component filters of natural images compared with simple cells in primary visual cortex," Proc. Royal Soc. Lond. B, 265: 359-366.

[4] Lewicki MS, Olshausen BA (1999) "A probabilistic framework for the adaptation and comparison of image codes," JOSA A, 16(7): 1587-1601.

[5] Simoncelli EP, Freeman WT, Adelson EH, Heeger DJ (1992) "Shiftable multiscale transforms," IEEE Transactions on Information Theory, 38(2): 587-607.

[6] Attias H (1999) "Independent factor analysis," Neural Computation, 11: 803-852.

Hierarchical Image Probability (HIP) Models

Clay D. Spence and Lucas Parra
Sarnoff Corporation
CN5300
Princeton, NJ 08543-5300
{cspence, lparra}@sarnoff.com

Abstract

We formulate a model for probability distributions on image spaces. We show that any distribution of images can be factored exactly into conditional distributions of feature vectors at one resolution (pyramid level) conditioned on the image information at lower resolutions. We would like to factor this over positions in the pyramid levels to make it tractable, but such factoring may miss long-range dependencies. To fix this, we introduce hidden class labels at each pixel in the pyramid. The result is a hierarchical mixture of conditional probabilities, similar to a hidden Markov model on a tree. The model parameters can be found with maximum likelihood estimation using the EM algorithm. We have obtained encouraging preliminary results on the problems of detecting various objects in SAR images and target recognition in optical aerial images.

1 Introduction

Many approaches to object recognition in images estimate $\Pr(\text{class} \mid \text{image})$. By contrast, a model of the probability distribution of images, $\Pr(\text{image})$, has many attractive features. We could use this for object recognition in the usual way by training a distribution for each object class and using Bayes' rule to get $\Pr(\text{class} \mid \text{image}) = \Pr(\text{image} \mid \text{class}) \Pr(\text{class}) / \Pr(\text{image})$. Clearly there are many other benefits of having a model of the distribution of images, since any kind of data analysis task can be approached using knowledge of the distribution of the data. For classification we could attempt to detect unusual examples and reject them, rather than trusting the classifier's output. We could also compress, interpolate, suppress noise, extend resolution, fuse multiple images, etc.

Many image analysis algorithms use probability concepts, but few treat the distribution of images. Zhu, Wu and Mumford [9] do this by computing the maximum entropy distribution given a set of statistics for some features. This seems to work well for textures but it is not clear how well it will model the appearance of more structured objects.

There are several algorithms for modeling the distributions of features extracted from the image, instead of the image itself. The Markov Random Field (*MRF*) models are an example of this line of development; see, e.g., [5, 4]. Unfortunately they tend to be very expensive computationally.

In De Bonet and Viola's flexible histogram approach [2, 1], features are extracted at multiple image scales, and the resulting feature vectors are treated as a set of independent

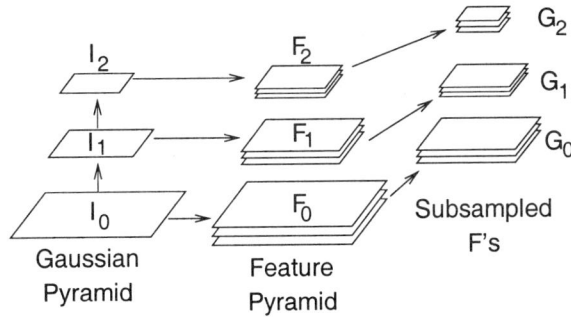

Figure 1: Pyramids and feature notation.

samples drawn from a distribution. They then model this distribution of feature vectors with Parzen windows. This has given good results, but the feature vectors from neighboring pixels are treated as independent when in fact they share exactly the same components from lower-resolutions. To fix this we might want to build a model in which the features at one pixel of one pyramid level condition the features at each of several child pixels at the next higher-resolution pyramid level. The multiscale stochastic process (*MSP*) methods do exactly that. Luettgen and Willsky [7], for example, applied a scale-space auto-regression (AR) model to texture discrimination. They use a quadtree or quadtree-like organization of the pixels in an image pyramid, and model the features in the pyramid as a stochastic process from coarse-to-fine levels along the tree. The variables in the process are hidden, and the observations are sums of these hidden variables plus noise. The Gaussian distributions are a limitation of MSP models. The result is also a model of the probability of the observations on the tree, not of the image.

All of these methods seem well-suited for modeling texture, but it is unclear how we might build the models to capture the appearance of more structured objects. We will argue below that the presence of objects in images can make local conditioning like that of the flexible histogram and MSP approaches inappropriate. In the following we present a model for probability distributions of images, in which we try to move beyond texture modeling. This hierarchical image probability (*HIP*) model is similar to a hidden Markov model on a tree, and can be learned with the EM algorithm. In preliminary tests of the model on classification tasks the performance was comparable to that of other algorithms.

2 Coarse-to-fine factoring of image distributions

Our goal will be to write the image distribution in a form similar to $\Pr(I) \sim \Pr(\mathbf{F}_0 \,|\, \mathbf{F}_1) \Pr(\mathbf{F}_1 \,|\, \mathbf{F}_2) \ldots$, where $\mathbf{F}_l$ is the set of feature images at pyramid level l. We expect that the short-range dependencies can be captured by the model's distribution of individual feature vectors, while the long-range dependencies can be captured somehow at low resolution. The large-scale structures affect finer scales by the conditioning.

In fact we can prove that a coarse-to-fine factoring like this is correct. From an image I we build a Gaussian pyramid (repeatedly blur-and-subsample, with a Gaussian filter). Call the l-th level I_l, e.g., the original image is I_0 (Figure 1). From each Gaussian level I_l we extract some set of feature images $\mathbf{F}_l$. Sub-sample these to get feature images $\mathbf{G}_l$. Note that the images in $\mathbf{G}_l$ have the same dimensions as I_{l+1}. We denote by $\tilde{\mathbf{G}}_l$ the set of images containing I_{l+1} and the images in $\mathbf{G}_l$. We further denote the mapping from I_l to $\tilde{\mathbf{G}}_l$ by $\tilde{\mathcal{G}}_l$.

Suppose now that $\tilde{\mathcal{G}}_0 : I_0 \mapsto \tilde{\mathbf{G}}_0$ is invertible. Then we can think of $\tilde{\mathcal{G}}_0$ as a change of variables. If we have a distribution on a space, its expressions in two different coordinate systems are related by multiplying by the Jacobian. In this case we get $\Pr(I_0) = |\tilde{\mathcal{G}}_0| \Pr(\tilde{\mathbf{G}}_0)$. Since $\tilde{\mathbf{G}}_0 = (\mathbf{G}_0, I_1)$, we can factor $\Pr(\tilde{\mathbf{G}}_0)$ to get $\Pr(I_0) = |\tilde{\mathcal{G}}_0| \Pr(\mathbf{G}_0 \mid I_1) \Pr(I_1)$. If $\tilde{\mathcal{G}}_l$ is invertible for all $l \in \{0, \ldots, L-1\}$ then we can simply repeat this change of variable and factoring procedure to get

$$\Pr(I) = \left[\prod_{l=0}^{L-1} |\tilde{\mathcal{G}}_l| \Pr(\mathbf{G}_l \mid I_{l+1}) \right] \Pr(I_L) \qquad (1)$$

This is a very general result, valid for all $\Pr(I)$, no doubt with some rather mild restrictions to make the change of variables valid. The restriction that $\tilde{\mathcal{G}}_l$ be invertible is strong, but many such feature sets are known to exist, e.g., most wavelet transforms on images. We know of a few ways that this condition can be relaxed, but further work is needed here.

3 The need for hidden variables

For the sake of tractability we want to factor $\Pr(\mathbf{G}_l \mid I_{l+1})$ over positions, something like $\Pr(I) \sim \prod_l \prod_{x \in I_{l+1}} \Pr(\mathbf{g}_l(x) \mid \mathbf{f}_{l+1}(x))$ where $\mathbf{g}_l(x)$ and $\mathbf{f}_{l+1}(x)$ are the feature vectors at position x. The dependence of $\mathbf{g}_l$ on $\mathbf{f}_{l+1}$ expresses the persistence of image structures across scale, e.g., an edge is usually detectable as such in several neighboring pyramid levels. The flexible histogram and MSP methods share this structure. While it may be plausible that $\mathbf{f}_{l+1}(x)$ has a strong influence on $\mathbf{g}_l(x)$, we argue now that this factorization and conditioning is not enough to capture some properties of real images.

Objects in the world cause correlations and non-local dependencies in images. For example, the presence of a particular object might cause a certain kind of texture to be visible at level l. Usually local features $\mathbf{f}_{l+1}$ by themselves will not contain enough information to infer the object's presence, but the entire image I_{l+1} at that layer might. Thus $\mathbf{g}_l(x)$ is influenced by more of I_{l+1} than the local feature vector.

Similarly, objects create long-range dependencies. For example, an object class might result in a kind of texture across a large area of the image. If an object of this class is always present, the distribution may factor, but if such objects aren't always present and can't be inferred from lower-resolution information, the presence of the texture at one location affects the probability of its presence elsewhere.

We introduce hidden variables to represent the non-local information that is not captured by local features. They should also constrain the variability of features at the next finer scale. Denoting them collectively by A, we assume that conditioning on A allows the distributions over feature vectors to factor. In general, the distribution over images becomes

$$\Pr(I) \propto \sum_A \left\{ \prod_{l=0}^{L-1} \prod_{x \in I_{l+1}} \Pr(\mathbf{g}_l(x) \mid \mathbf{f}_{l+1}(x), A) \Pr(A \mid I_L) \right\} \Pr(I_L). \qquad (2)$$

As written this is absolutely general, so we need to be more specific. In particular we would like to preserve the conditioning of higher-resolution information on coarser-resolution information, and the ability to factor over positions.

Hierarchical Image Probability (HIP) Models

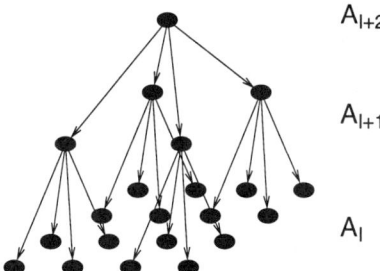

Figure 2: Tree structure of the conditional dependency between hidden variables in the HIP model. With subsampling by two, this is sometimes called a quadtree structure.

As a first model we have chosen the following structure for our HIP model:[1]

$$\Pr(I) \propto \sum_{A_0,\ldots,A_{L-1}} \prod_{l=0}^{L} \prod_{x \in I_{l+1}} \Big[\Pr\big(\mathbf{g}_l(x) \,|\, \mathbf{f}_{l+1}(x), a_l(x)\big) \Pr\big(a_l(x) \,|\, a_{l+1}(x)\big) \Big]. \quad (3)$$

To each position x at each level l we attach a hidden discrete index or label $a_l(x)$. The resulting label image A_l for level l has the same dimensions as the images in $\tilde{\mathbf{G}}_l$.

Since $a_l(x)$ codes non-local information we can think of the labels A_l as a segmentation or classification at the l-th pyramid level. By conditioning $a_l(x)$ on $a_{l+1}(x)$, we mean that $a_l(x)$ is conditioned on a_{l+1} at the *parent* pixel of x. This parent-child relationship follows from the sub-sampling operation. For example, if we sub-sample by two in each direction to get $\mathbf{G}_l$ from $\mathbf{F}_l$, we condition the variable a_l at (x,y) in level l on a_{l+1} at location $(\lfloor x/2 \rfloor, \lfloor y/2 \rfloor)$ in level $l+1$ (Figure 2). This gives the dependency graph of the hidden variables a tree structure. Such a probabilistic tree of discrete variables is sometimes referred to as a belief network. By conditioning child labels on their parents information propagates though the layers to other areas of the image while accumulating information along the way.

For the sake of simplicity we've chosen $\Pr(\mathbf{g}_l \,|\, \mathbf{f}_{l+1}, a_l)$ to be normal with mean $\bar{\mathbf{g}}_{l,a_l} + M_{a_l} \mathbf{f}_{l+1}$ and covariance Σ_{a_l}. We also constrain M_{a_l} and Σ_{a_l} to be diagonal.

4 EM algorithm

Thanks to the tree structure, the belief network for the hidden variables is relatively easy to train with an EM algorithm. The expectation step (summing over a_l's) can be performed directly. If we had chosen a more densely-connected structure with each child having several parents, we would need either an approximate algorithm or Monte Carlo techniques. The expectation is weighted by the probability of a label or a parent-child pair of labels given the image. This can be computed in a fine-to-coarse-to-fine procedure, i.e. working from leaves to the root and then back out to the leaves. The method is based on belief propagation [6]. With some care an efficient algorithm can be worked out, but we omit the details due to space constraints.

Once we can compute the expectations, the normal distribution makes the M-step tractable; we simply compute the updated $\bar{\mathbf{g}}_{a_l}, \Sigma_{a_l}, M_{a_l}$, and $\Pr(a_l \,|\, a_{l+1})$ as combinations of various expectation values.

---

[1] The proportionality factor includes $\Pr(A_L, I_L)$ which we model as $\prod_x \Pr(\mathbf{g}_L(X) \,|\, a_L(x)) \Pr(a_L(x))$. This is the $l = L$ factor of Equation 3, which should be read as having no quantities $\mathbf{f}_{L+1}$ or a_{L+1}.

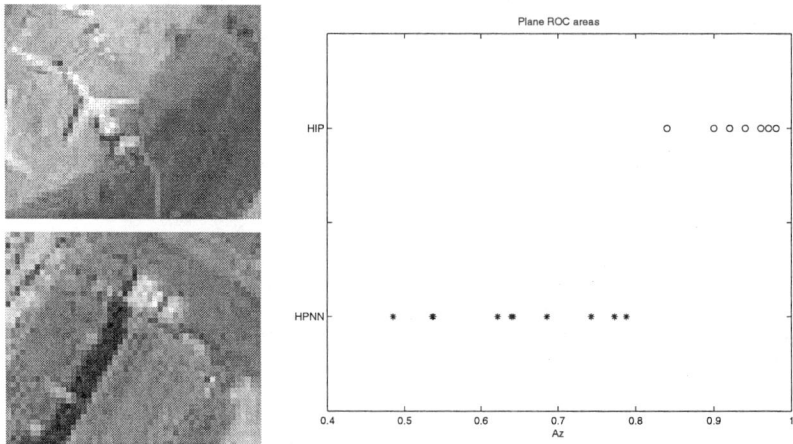

Figure 3: Examples of aircraft ROIs. On the right are A_z values from a jack-knife study of detection performance of HIP and HPNN models.

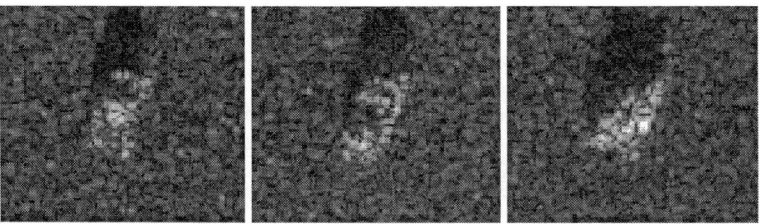

Figure 4: SAR images of three types of vehicles to be detected.

5 Experiments

We applied HIP to the problem of detecting aircraft in an aerial photograph of Logan airport. A simple template-matching algorithm was used to select forty candidate aircraft, twenty of which were false positives (Figure 3). Ten of the plane examples were used for training one HIP model and ten negative examples were used to train another. Because of thesmall number of examples, we performed a jack-knife study with ten random splits of the data. For features we used filter kernels that were polynomials of up to third order multiplying Gaussians. The HIP pyramid used subsampling by three in each direction. The test set ROC area for HIP had a mean of $A_z = 0.94$, while our HPNN algorithm [8] gave a mean A_z of 0.65. The individual values shown in Figure 3. (We compared with the HPNN because it had given $A_z = 0.86$ on a larger set of aircraft images including these with a different set of features and subsampling by two.)

We also performed an experiment with the three target classes in the MSTAR public targets data set, to compare with the results of the flexible histogram approach of De Bonet, et al [1]. We trained three HIP models, one for each of the target vehicles BMP-2, BTR-70 and T-72 (Figure 4). As in [1] we trained each model on ten images of its class, one image for each of ten aspect angles, spaced approximately $36°$ apart. We trained one model for all ten images of a target, whereas De Bonet et al trained one model per image.

We first tried discriminating between vehicles of one class and other objects by thresholding $\log \Pr(I \mid \text{class})$, i.e., no model of other objects is used. For the tests, the other objects were taken from the test data for the two other vehicle classes, plus seven other vehicle classes.

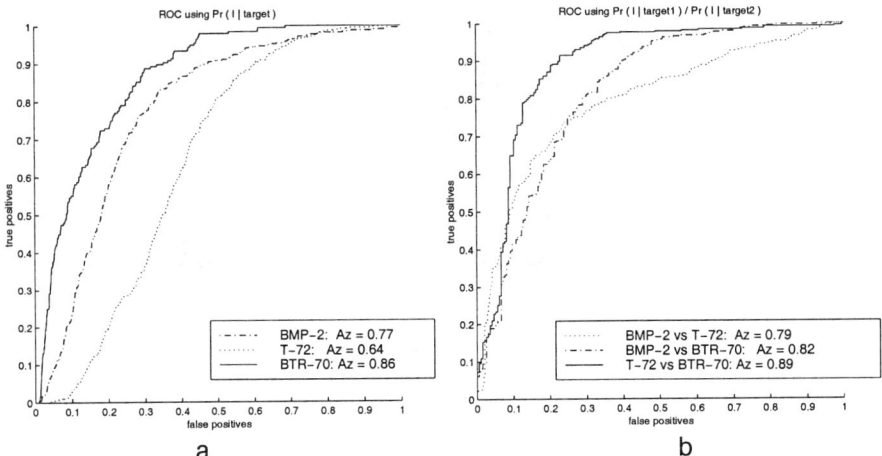

Figure 5: ROC curves for vehicle detection in SAR imagery. (a) ROC curves by thresholding HIP likelihood of desired class. (b) ROC curves for inter-class discrimination using ratios of likelihoods as given by HIP models.

There were 1,838 image from these seven other classes, 391 BMP2 test images, 196 BTR70 test images, and 386 T72 test images. The resulting ROC curves are shown in Figure 5a.

We then tried discriminating between pairs target classes using HIP model likelihood ratios, i.e., $\log \Pr(I \mid \text{class1}) - \log \Pr(I \mid \text{class2})$. Here we could not use the extra seven vehicle classes. The resulting ROC curves are shown in Figure 5b. The performance is comparable to that of the flexible histogram approach.

6 Conditional distributions of features

To further test the HIP model's fit to the image distribution, we computed several distributions of features $g_l(x)$ conditioned on the parent feature $f_{l+1}(x)$.[2] The empirical and computed distributions for a particular parent-child pair of features are shown in Figure 6. The conditional distributions we examined all had similar appearance, and all fit the empirical distributions well. Buccigrossi and Simoncelli [3] have reported such "bow-tie" shape conditional distributions for a variety of features. We want to point out that such conditional distributions are naturally obtained for any mixture of Gaussian distributions with varying scales and zero means. The present HIP model learns such conditionals, in effect describing the features as non-stationary Gaussian variables.

7 Conclusion

We have developed a class of image probability models we call hierarchical image probability or HIP models. To justify these, we showed that image distributions can be exactly represented as products over pyramid levels of distributions of sub-sampled feature images conditioned on coarser-scale image information. We argued that hidden variables are needed to capture long-range dependencies while allowing us to further factor the distributions over position. In our current model the hidden variables act as indices of mixture

---

[2]This is somewhat involved; $\Pr(g_l \mid f_{l+1})$ is not just $\Pr(g_l \mid f_{l+1}, a_l) \Pr(a_l)$ summed over a_l, but $\sum_{a_l} \Pr(g_l, a_l \mid f_{l+1}) = \sum_{a_l} \Pr(g_l \mid f_{l+1}, a_l) \Pr(a_l \mid f_{l+1})$.

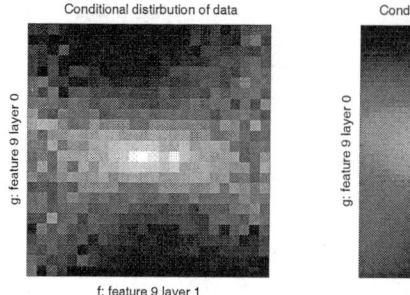
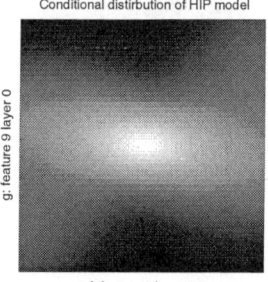

Figure 6: Empirical and HIP estimates of the distribution of a feature $g_l(x)$ conditioned on its parent feature $f_{l+1}(x)$.

components. The resulting model is somewhat like a hidden Markov model on a tree. Our early results on classification problems showed good performance.

Acknowledgements

We thank Jeremy De Bonet and John Fisher for kindly answering questions about their work and experiments. Supported by the United States Government.

References

[1] J. S. De Bonet, P. Viola, and J. W. Fisher III. Flexible histograms: A multiresolution target discrimination model. In E. G. Zelnio, editor, *Proceedings of SPIE*, volume 3370, 1998.

[2] Jeremy S. De Bonet and Paul Viola. Texture recognition using a non-parametric multi-scale statistical model. In *Conference on Computer Vision and Pattern Recognition*. IEEE, 1998.

[3] Robert W. Buccigrossi and Eero P. Simoncelli. Image compression via joint statistical characterization in the wavelet domain. Technical Report 414, U. Penn. GRASP Laboratory, 1998. Available at ftp://ftp.cis.upenn.edu/pub/eero/buccigrossi97.ps.gz.

[4] Rama Chellappa and S. Chatterjee. Classification of textures using Gaussian Markov random fields. *IEEE Trans. ASSP*, 33:959–963, 1985.

[5] Stuart Geman and Donald Geman. Stochastic relaxation, Gibbs distributions, and the Bayesian restoration of images. *IEEE Trans. PAMI*, PAMI-6(6):194–207, November 1984.

[6] Michael I. Jordan, editor. *Learning in Graphical Models*, volume 89 of *NATO Science Series D: Behavioral and Brain Sciences*. Kluwer Academic, 1998.

[7] Mark R. Luettgen and Alan S. Willsky. Likelihood calculation for a class of multiscale stochastic models, with application to texture discrimination. *IEEE Trans. Image Proc.*, 4(2):194–207, 1995.

[8] Clay D. Spence and Paul Sajda. Applications of multi-resolution neural networks to mammography. In Michael S. Kearns, Sara A. Solla, and David A. Cohn, editors, *NIPS 11*, pages 981–988, Cambridge, MA, 1998. MIT Press.

[9] Song Chun Zhu, Ying Nian Wu, and David Mumford. Minimax entropy principle and its application to texture modeling. *Neural Computation*, 9(8):1627–1660, 1997.

Scale Mixtures of Gaussians and the Statistics of Natural Images

Martin J. Wainwright
Stochastic Systems Group
Electrical Engineering & CS
MIT, Building 35-425
Cambridge, MA 02139
mjwain@mit.edu

Eero P. Simoncelli
Ctr. for Neural Science, and
Courant Inst. of Mathematical Sciences
New York University
New York, NY 10012
eero.simoncelli@nyu.edu

Abstract

The statistics of photographic images, when represented using multiscale (wavelet) bases, exhibit two striking types of non-Gaussian behavior. First, the marginal densities of the coefficients have extended heavy tails. Second, the joint densities exhibit variance dependencies not captured by second-order models. We examine properties of the class of Gaussian scale mixtures, and show that these densities can accurately characterize both the marginal and joint distributions of natural image wavelet coefficients. This class of model suggests a Markov structure, in which wavelet coefficients are linked by hidden scaling variables corresponding to local image structure. We derive an estimator for these hidden variables, and show that a nonlinear "normalization" procedure can be used to Gaussianize the coefficients.

Recent years have witnessed a surge of interest in modeling the statistics of natural images. Such models are important for applications in image processing and computer vision, where many techniques rely (either implicitly or explicitly) on a prior density. A number of empirical studies have demonstrated that the power spectra of natural images follow a $1/f^\gamma$ law in radial frequency, where the exponent γ is typically close to two [e.g., 1]. Such second-order characterization is inadequate, however, because images usually exhibit highly non-Gaussian behavior. For instance, the marginals of wavelet coefficients typically have much heavier tails than a Gaussian [2]. Furthermore, despite being approximately decorrelated (as suggested by theoretical analysis of $1/f$ processes [3]), orthonormal wavelet coefficients exhibit striking forms of statistical dependency [4, 5]. In particular, the standard deviation of a wavelet coefficient typically scales with the absolute values of its neighbors [5].

A number of researchers have modeled the marginal distributions of wavelet coefficients with generalized Laplacians, $p_Y(y) \propto \exp(-|y/\lambda|^p)$ [e.g. 6, 7, 8]. Special cases include the Gaussian ($p = 2$) and the Laplacian ($p = 1$), but appropriate ex-

---

Research supported by NSERC 1969 fellowship 160833 to MJW, and NSF CAREER grant MIP-9796040 to EPS.

Mixing density	GSM density	GSM char. function
$\sqrt{Z(\gamma)}$	symmetrized Gamma	$(1 + \frac{t^2}{2\lambda^2})^{-\gamma}, \quad \gamma > 0$
$1/\sqrt{Z(\beta - \frac{1}{2})}$	Student: $[1/(\lambda^2 + y^2)]^\beta, \quad \beta > \frac{1}{2}$	No explicit form
Positive, $\sqrt{\frac{\alpha}{2}}$ - stable	α-stable	$\exp(-|\lambda t|^\alpha), \quad \alpha \in (0, 2]$
No explicit form	generalized Laplacian: $\exp(-|y/\lambda|^p), \quad p \in (0, 2]$	No explicit form

Table 1. Example densities from the class of Gaussian scale mixtures. $Z(\gamma)$ denotes a positive gamma variable, with density $p(z) = [1/\Gamma(\gamma)] z^{\gamma-1} \exp(-z)$. The characteristic function of a random variable x is defined as $\phi_x(t) \triangleq \int_{-\infty}^{\infty} p(x) \exp(jxt) \, dx$.

ponents for natural images are typically less than one. Simoncelli [5, 9] has modeled the variance dependencies of pairs of wavelet coefficients. Romberg et al. [10] have modeled wavelet densities using two-component mixtures of Gaussians. Huang and Mumford [11] have modeled marginal densities and cross-sections of joint densities with multi-dimensional generalized Laplacians.

In the following sections, we explore the semi-parametric class of *Gaussian scale mixtures*. We show that members of this class satisfy the dual requirements of being heavy-tailed, and exhibiting multiplicative scaling between coefficients. We also show that a particular member of this class, in which the multiplier variables are distributed according to a gamma density, captures the range of joint statistical behaviors seen in wavelet coefficients of natural images. We derive an estimator for the multipliers, and show that a nonlinear "normalization" procedure can be used to Gaussianize the wavelet coefficients. Lastly, we form random cascades by linking the multipliers on a multiresolution tree.

1 Scale Mixtures of Gaussians

A random vector Y is a Gaussian scale mixture (GSM) if $Y \stackrel{d}{=} zU$, where $\stackrel{d}{=}$ denotes equality in distribution; $z \geq 0$ is a scalar random variable; $U \sim \mathcal{N}(0, Q)$ is a Gaussian random vector; and z and U are independent.

As a consequence, any GSM variable has a density given by an integral:

$$p_Y(Y) = \int_{-\infty}^{\infty} \frac{1}{[2\pi]^{\frac{N}{2}} |z^2 Q|^{1/2}} \exp\left(-\frac{Y^T Q^{-1} Y}{2z^2}\right) \phi_z(z) dz.$$

where ϕ_z is the probability density of the mixing variable z (henceforth the multiplier). A special case of a GSM is a finite mixture of Gaussians, where z is a discrete random variable. More generally, it is straightforward to provide conditions on either the density [12] or characteristic function of X that ensure it is a GSM, but these conditions do not necessarily provide an explicit form of ϕ_z. Nevertheless, a number of well-known distributions may be written as Gaussian scale mixtures. For the scalar case, a few of these densities, along with their associated characteristic functions, are listed in Table 1. Each variable is characterized by a scale parameter λ, and a tail parameter. All of the GSM models listed in Table 1 produce heavy-tailed marginal and variance-scaling joint densities.

Scale Mixtures of Gaussians and the Statistics of Natural Images

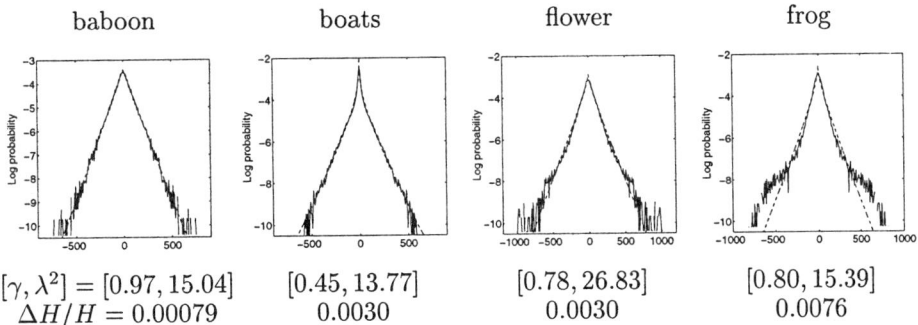

baboon	boats	flower	frog
$[\gamma, \lambda^2] = [0.97, 15.04]$	$[0.45, 13.77]$	$[0.78, 26.83]$	$[0.80, 15.39]$
$\Delta H/H = 0.00079$	0.0030	0.0030	0.0076

Figure 1. GSMs (dashed lines) fitted to empirical histograms (solid lines). Below each plot are the parameter values, and the relative entropy between the histogram (with 256 bins) and the model, as a fraction of the histogram entropy.

2 Modeling Natural Images

As mentioned in the introduction, natural images exhibit striking non-Gaussian behavior, both in their marginal and joint statistics. In this section, we show that this behavior is consistent with a GSM, using the first of the densities given in Table 1 for illustration.

2.1 Marginal distributions

We begin by examining the symmetrized Gamma class as a model for marginal distributions of wavelet coefficients. Figure 1 shows empirical histograms of a particular wavelet subband[1] for four different natural images, along with the best fitting instance of the symmetrized Gamma distribution. Fitting was performed by minimizing the relative entropy (i.e., the Kullback-Leibler divergence, denoted ΔH) between empirical and theoretical histograms. In general, the fits are quite good: the fourth plot shows one of the worst fits in our data set.

2.2 Normalized components

For a GSM random vector $Y \stackrel{d}{=} zU$, the normalized variable Y/z formed by component-wise division is Gaussian-distributed. In order to test this behavior empirically, we model a given wavelet coefficient y_0 and a collection of neighbors $\{y_1, \ldots, y_N\}$ as a GSM vector. For our examples, we use a neighborhood of $N = 11$ coefficients corresponding to basis functions at 4 adjacent positions, 5 orientations, and 2 scales. Although the multiplier z is unknown, we can estimate it by maximizing the log likelihood of the observed coefficients: $\hat{z} \stackrel{\Delta}{=} \arg\max_z \{\log p(Y|z)\}$. Under reasonable conditions, the normalized quantity $Y/\hat{z}$ should converge in distribution to a Gaussian as the number of neighbors increases. The estimate $\hat{z}$ is simple to derive:

$$\begin{aligned}
\hat{z} &= \arg\max_z \{\log p(Y|z)\} \\
&= \arg\min_z \{N \log(z) + Y^T Q^{-1} Y/2z^2\} \\
&= \sqrt{Y^T Q^{-1} Y/N},
\end{aligned}$$

---

[1] We use the steerable pyramid, an overcomplete multiscale representation described in [13]. The marginal and joint statistics of other multiscale oriented representations are similar.

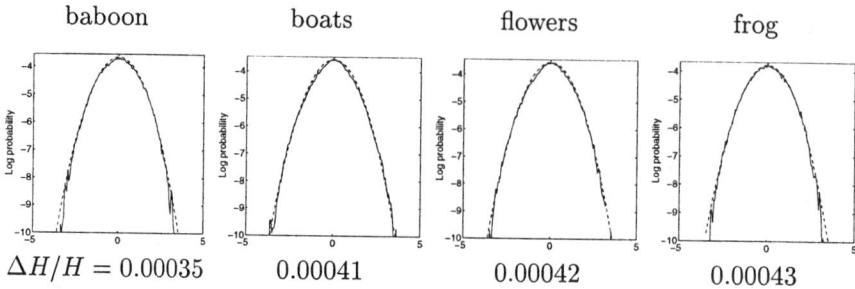

Figure 2. Marginal log histograms (solid lines) of the normalized coefficient ν for a single subband of four natural images. Each shape is close to an inverted parabola, in agreement with Gaussians (dashed lines) of equivalent empirical variance. Below each plot is the relative entropy between the histogram (with 256 bins) and a variance-matched Gaussian, as a fraction of the total histogram entropy.

where $Q \triangleq \mathbb{E}\left[UU^T\right]$ is the positive definite covariance matrix of the underlying Gaussian vector U.

Given the estimate $\widehat{z}$, we then compute the normalized coefficient $\nu \triangleq y_0/\widehat{z}$. This is a generalization of the variance normalization proposed by Ruderman and Bialek[1], and the weighted sum of squares normalization procedure used by Simoncelli [5, 14]. Figure 2 shows the marginal histograms (in the log domain) of this normalized coefficient for four natural images, along with Gaussians of equal empirical variance. In contrast to histograms of the raw coefficients (shown in Figure 1), the histograms of normalized coefficients are nearly Gaussian.

The GSM model makes a stronger prediction: that normalized quantities corresponding to nearby wavelet pairs should be *jointly* Gaussian. Specifically, a pair of normalized coefficients should be either correlated or uncorrelated Gaussians, depending on whether the underlying Gaussians $U = [u_1 \, u_2]^T$ are correlated or uncorrelated. We examine this prediction by collecting joint conditional histograms of normalized coefficients. The top row of Figure 3 shows joint conditional histograms for raw wavelet coefficients (taken from the same four natural images as Figure 2). The first two columns correspond to adjacent spatial scales; though decorrelated, they exhibit the familiar form of multiplicative scaling. The latter two columns correspond to adjacent orientations; in addition to being correlated, they also exhibit the multiplicative form of dependency.

The bottom row shows the same joint conditional histograms, after the coefficients have been normalized. Whereas Figure 2 demonstrates that normalized coefficients are close to *marginally* Gaussian, Figure 3 demonstrates that they are also approximately *jointly* Gaussian. These observations support the use of a Gaussian scale mixture for modeling natural images.

2.3 Joint distributions

The GSM model is a reasonable approximation for groups of nearby wavelet coefficients. However, the components of GSM vectors are highly dependent, whereas the dependency between wavelet coefficients decreases as (for example) their spatial separation increases. Consequently, the simple GSM model is inadequate for global modeling of coefficients. We are thus led to use a graphical model (such as tree) that specifies probabilistic relations between the multipliers. The wavelet coefficients themselves are considered observations, and are linked indirectly by their shared dependency on the (hidden) multipliers.

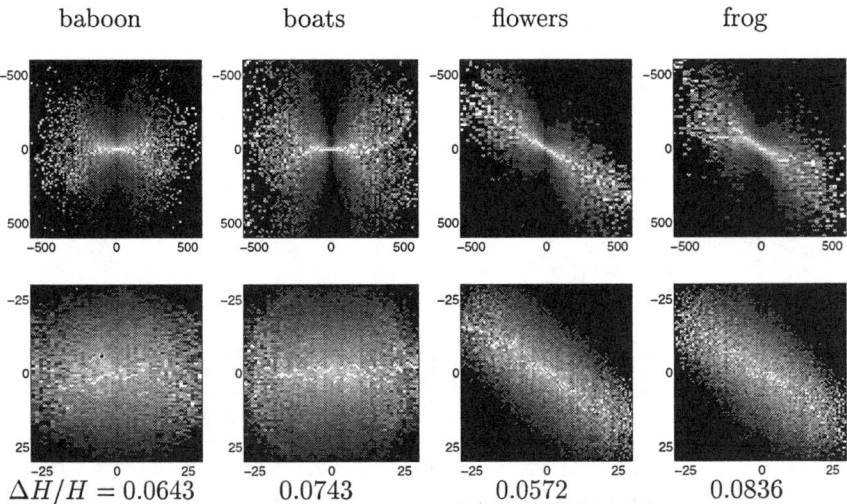

Figure 3. Top row: joint conditional histograms of raw wavelet coefficients for four natural images. Bottom row: joint conditional histograms of normalized pairs of coefficients. Below each plot is the relative entropy between the joint histogram (with 256 × 256 bins) and a covariance-matched Gaussian, as a fraction of the total histogram entropy.

For concreteness, we model the wavelet coefficient at node s as $y(s) \stackrel{d}{=} \|x(s)\| u(s)$, where $x(s)$ is Gaussian, so that $z \stackrel{\triangle}{=} \|x\|$ is the square root of a gamma variable of index 0.5. For illustration, we assume that the multipliers are linked by a multiscale autoregressive (MAR) process [15] on a tree:

$$x(s) = \mu\, x(p(s)) + \sqrt{1-\mu^2}\, w(s)$$

where $p(s)$ is the parent of node s. Two wavelet coefficients $y(s)$ and $y(t)$ are linked through the multiplier at their common ancestral node denoted $s \wedge t$. In particular, the joint distributions are given by

$$y(s) = \left\|\mu^{d(s,s\wedge t)} x(s \wedge t) + v_1(s)\right\| u(s)$$
$$y(t) = \left\|\mu^{d(t,s\wedge t)} x(s \wedge t) + v_2(t)\right\| u(t)$$

where v_1, v_2 are independent white noise processes; and $d(\,,\,)$ denotes the distance between a node and one of its ancestors on the tree (e.g., $d(s, p(s)) = 1$). For nodes s and t at the same scale and orientation but spatially separated by a distance of $\Delta(s,t)$, the distance between s and the common ancestor $s \wedge t$ grows as $d(s, s \wedge t) \sim [\log_2(\Delta(s,t)) + 1]$.

The first row of Figure 4 shows the range of behaviors seen in joint distributions taken from a wavelet subband of a particular natural image, compared to simulated GSM gamma distributions with $\mu = 0.92$. The first column corresponds to a pair of wavelet filters in quadrature phase (i.e., related by a Hilbert transform). Note that for this pair of coefficients, the contours are nearly circular, an observation that has been previously made by Zetzsche [4]. Nevertheless, these two coefficients are dependent, as shown by the multiplicative scaling in the conditional histogram of the third row. This type of scaling dependency has been extensively documented by Simoncelli [5, 9]. Analogous plots for the simulated Gamma model, with zero spatial separation are shown in rows 2 and 4. As in the image data, the contours of the joint density are very close to circular, and the conditional distribution shows a striking variance dependency.

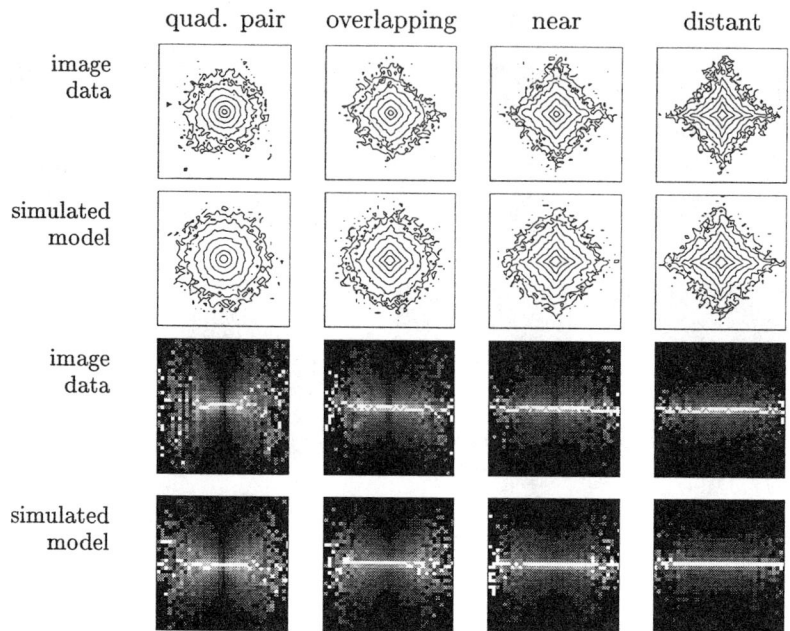

Figure 4. Examples of empirically observed distributions of wavelet coefficients, compared with simulated distributions from the GSM gamma model. First row: Empirical joint histograms for the "mountain" image, for four pairs of wavelet coefficients, corresponding to basis functions with spatial separations $\Delta = \{0, 4, 8, 128\}$. Second row: Simulated joint distributions for Gamma variables with $\mu = 0.92$ and the same spatial separations. Contour lines are drawn at equal intervals of log probability. Third row: Empirical conditional histograms for the "mountain" image. Fourth row: Simulated conditional histograms for Gamma variables. For these conditional distributions, intensity corresponds to probability, except that each column has been independently rescaled to fill the full range of intensities.

The remaining three columns of figure 4 show pairs of coefficients drawn from identical wavelet filters at spatial displacements $\Delta = \{4, 8, 128\}$, corresponding to a pair of overlapping filters, a pair of nearby filters, and a distant pair. Note the progression in the contour shapes from off-circular, to a diamond shape, to a concave "star" shape. The model distributions behave similarly, and show the same range of contours for simulated pairs of coefficients. Thus, consistent with empirical observations, a GSM model can produce a range of dependency between pairs of wavelet coefficients. Again, the marginal histograms retain the same form throughout this range.

3 Conclusions

We have proposed the class of Gaussian scale mixtures for modeling natural images. Models in this class typically exhibit heavy-tailed marginals, as well as multiplicative scaling between adjacent coefficients. We have demonstrated that a particular GSM (the symmetrized Gamma family) accounts well for both the marginal and joint distributions of wavelet coefficients from natural images. More importantly, this model suggests a hidden Markov structure for natural images, in which wavelet coefficients are linked by hidden multipliers. Romberg et al. [10] have made a related proposal using two-state discrete multipliers, corresponding to a finite mixture of Gaussians.

We have demonstrated that the hidden multipliers can be locally estimated from measurements of wavelet coefficients. Thus, by conditioning on fixed values of the multipliers, estimation problems may be reduced to the classical Gaussian case. Moreover, we described how to link the multipliers on a multiresolution tree, and showed that such a random cascade model accounts well for the drop-off in dependence of spatially separated coefficients. We are currently exploring EM-like algorithms for the problem of dual parameter and state estimation.

Acknowledgements

We thank Bill Freeman, David Mumford, Mike Schneider, Ilya Pollak, and Alan Willsky for helpful discussions.

References

[1] D. L. Ruderman and W. Bialek. Statistics of natural images: Scaling in the woods. *Phys. Rev. Letters*, 73(6):814–817, 1994.

[2] D. J. Field. Relations between the statistics of natural images and the response properties of cortical cells. *J. Opt. Soc. Am. A*, 4(12):2379–2394, 1987.

[3] A. H. Tewfik and M. Kim. Correlation structure of the discrete wavelet coefficients of fractional Brownian motion. *IEEE Trans. Info. Theory*, 38:904–909, Mar. 1992.

[4] C. Zetzsche, B. Wegmann, and E. Barth. Nonlinear aspects of primary vision: Entropy reduction beyond decorrelation. In *Int'l Symp. Soc. for Info. Display*, volume 24, pages 933–936, 1993.

[5] E. P. Simoncelli. Statistical models for images: Compression, restoration and synthesis. In *31st Asilomar Conf.*, pages 673–678, Nov. 1997.

[6] S. G. Mallat. A theory for multiresolution signal decomposition: the wavelet representation. *IEEE Pat. Anal. Mach. Intell.*, 11:674–693, July 1989.

[7] E. P. Simoncelli and E. H. Adelson. Noise removal via Bayesian wavelet coring. In *Proc. IEEE ICIP*, volume I, pages 379–382, September 1996.

[8] P. Moulin and J. Liu. Analysis of multiresolution image denoising schemes using a generalized Gaussian and complexity priors. *IEEE Trans. Info. Theory*, 45:909–919, Apr. 1999.

[9] R. W. Buccigrossi and E. P. Simoncelli. Image compression via joint statistical characterization in the wavelet domain. *IEEE Trans. Image. Proc.*, 8(12):1688–1701, Dec. 1999.

[10] J.K. Romberg, H. Choi, and R.G. Baraniuk. Bayesian wavelet domain image modeling using hidden Markov trees. In *Proc. IEEE ICIP*, Kobe, Japan, Oct. 1999.

[11] J. Huang and D. Mumford. Statistics of natural images and models. In *CVPR*, paper 216, 1999.

[12] D.F. Andrews and C.L. Mallows. Scale mixtures of normal distributions. *J. Royal Stat. Soc.*, 36:99–102, 1974.

[13] E. P. Simoncelli and W. T. Freeman. The steerable pyramid: A flexible architecture for multi-scale derivative computation. In *Proc. IEEE ICIP*, volume III, pages 444–447, Oct. 1995.

[14] E. P. Simoncelli and O. Schwartz. Image statistics and cortical normalization models. In M. S. Kearns, S. A. Solla, and D. A. Cohn, editors, *Adv. Neural Information Processing Systems*, volume 11, pages 153–159, Cambridge, MA, May 1999.

[15] K. Chou, A. Willsky, and R. Nikoukhah. Multiscale systems, Kalman filters, and Riccati equations. *IEEE Trans. Automatic Control*, 39(3):479–492, Mar. 1994.

A SNoW-Based Face Detector

Ming-Hsuan Yang   Dan Roth   Narendra Ahuja
Department of Computer Science and the Beckman Institute
University of Illinois at Urbana-Champaign
Urbana, IL 61801
mhyang@vision.ai.uiuc.edu   danr@cs.uiuc.edu   ahuja@vision.ai.uiuc.edu

Abstract

A novel learning approach for human face detection using a network of linear units is presented. The SNoW learning architecture is a sparse network of linear functions over a pre-defined or incrementally learned feature space and is specifically tailored for learning in the presence of a very large number of features. A wide range of face images in different poses, with different expressions and under different lighting conditions are used as a training set to capture the variations of human faces. Experimental results on commonly used benchmark data sets of a wide range of face images show that the SNoW-based approach outperforms methods that use neural networks, Bayesian methods, support vector machines and others. Furthermore, learning and evaluation using the SNoW-based method are significantly more efficient than with other methods.

1 Introduction

Growing interest in intelligent human computer interactions has motivated a recent surge in research on problems such as face tracking, pose estimation, face expression and gesture recognition. Most methods, however, assume human faces in their input images have been detected and localized.

Given a single image or a sequence of images, the goal of face detection is to identify and locate human faces regardless of their positions, scales, orientations, poses and illumination. To support automated solutions for the above applications, this has to be done efficiently and robustly. The challenge in building an efficient and robust system for this problem stems from the fact that human faces are highly non-rigid objects with a high degree of variability in size, shape, color and texture.

Numerous intensity-based methods have been proposed recently to detect human faces in a single image or a sequence of images. Sung and Poggio [24] report an example-based learning approach for locating vertical frontal views of human faces. They use a number of Gaussian clusters to model the distributions of face and non-face patterns. A small window is moved over an image to determine whether a face exists using the estimated distributions. In [16], a detection algorithm is proposed that combines template matching and feature-based detection method using hierarchical Markov random fields (MRF) and maximum *a posteriori* probability (MAP) estimation. Colmenarez and Huang [4] apply Kullback relative information for maximal discrimination between positive and negative examples of faces. They use a family of discrete Markov processes to model faces and background patterns and estimate the density functions. Detection of a face is based on the likelihood ratio computed during training. Moghaddam and Pentland [12] propose a probabilistic method that is based on density estimation in a high dimensional space using an eigenspace decomposition. In [20], Rowley et al. use an ensemble of neural networks to learn face and non-face patterns for face detection. Schneiderman et al. describe a probabilistic method based on local appearance and principal component analysis [23]. Their method gives some preliminary results on profile face detection. Finally, hidden Markov models [17], higher order statistics [17], and support vector machines (SVM) [14] have also been applied to face detection and demonstrated some success in detecting upright frontal faces under certain lighting conditions.

In this paper, we present a face detection method that uses the SNoW learning architecture [18, 3] to detect faces with different features and expressions, in different poses, and under different lighting conditions. SNoW (Sparse Network of Winnows) is a sparse network of linear functions that utilizes the Winnow update rule [10]. SNoW is specifically tailored for learning in domains in which the potential number of features taking part in decisions is very large, but may be unknown a priori. Some of the characteristics of this learning architecture are its sparsely connected units, the allocation of features and links in a data driven way, the decision mechanism and the utilization of an efficient update rule. SNoW has been used successfully on a variety of large scale learning tasks in the natural language domain [18, 13, 5, 19] and this is its first use in the visual processing domain.

In training the SNoW-based face detector, we use a set of 1,681 face images from Olivetti [22], UMIST [6], Harvard [7], Yale [1] and FERET [15] databases to capture the variations in face patterns. In order to compare our approach with other methods, our experiments involve two benchmark data sets [20, 24] that have been used in other works on face detection. The experimental results on these benchmark data sets (which consist of 225 images with 619 faces) show that our method outperforms all other methods evaluated on this problem, including those using neural networks [20], Kullback relative information [4], naive Bayes [23] and support vector machines [14], while being significantly more efficient computationally. Along with these experimental results we describe further experiments that provide insight into some of the theoretical and practical considerations of SNoW-based learning systems. In particular, we study the effect of learning with primitive as well as with multi-scale features, and discuss some of the sources of the success of the approach.

2 The SNoW System

The SNoW (Sparse Network of Winnows) learning architecture is a sparse network of linear units over a common pre-defined or incrementally learned feature space. Nodes in the input layer of the network represent simple relations over the input and are being used as the input features. Each linear unit is called a *target node* and represents relations which are of interest over the input examples; in the current application, only two target nodes are being used, one as a representation for a *face* pattern and the other for a *non-face* pattern. Given a set of relations (i.e., *types* of features) that may be of interest in the input image, each input image is mapped into a set of features which are *active* (present) in it; this representation is presented to the input layer of SNoW and propagates to the target nodes. (Features may take either binary value, just indicating the fact that the feature is active (present) or real values, reflecting its strength; in the current application, all features are binary. See Sec 3.1.) Target nodes are linked via weighted edges to (some of the) input features. Let $\mathcal{A}_t = \{i_1, \ldots, i_m\}$ be the set of features that are active in an example and are linked to the target node t. Then the linear unit is *active* if and only if $\sum_{i \in \mathcal{A}_t} w_i^t > \theta_t$, where w_i^t is the weight on the edge connecting the ith feature to the target node t, and θ_t is its threshold.

In the current application a single SNoW *unit* which includes two subnetworks, one for each of the targets, is used. A given example is treated autonomously by each target subnetwork; that is, an image labeled as a face is used as a positive example for the *face* target and as a negative example for the *non-face* target, and vice-versa.

The learning policy is on-line and mistake-driven; several update rules can be used within SNoW. The most successful update rule, and the only one used in this work is a variant of Littlestone's Winnow update rule, a multiplicative update rule tailored to the situation in which the set of input features is not known a priori, as in the infinite attribute model [2]. This mechanism is implemented via the sparse architecture of SNoW. That is, (1) input features are allocated in a data driven way – an input node for the feature i is allocated only if the feature i is active in the input image and (2) a link (i.e., a non-zero weight) exists between a target node t and a feature i if and only if i has been active in an image labeled t. Thus, the architecture also supports augmenting the feature types at later stages or from external sources in a flexible way, an option we do not use in the current work.

The Winnow update rule has, in addition to the threshold θ_t at the target t, two update parameters: a *promotion* parameter $\alpha > 1$ and a *demotion* parameter $0 < \beta < 1$. These are being used to update the current representation of the target t (the set of weights w_i^t) only when a mistake in prediction is made. Let $\mathcal{A}_t = \{i_1, \ldots, i_m\}$ be the set of active features that are linked to the target node t. If the algorithm predicts 0 (that is, $\sum_{i \in \mathcal{A}_t} w_i^t \leq \theta_t$) and the received label is 1, the active weights in the current example are *promoted* in a multiplicative fashion: $\forall i \in \mathcal{A}_t, w_i^t \leftarrow \alpha \cdot w_i^t$. If the algorithm predicts 1 ($\sum_{i \in \mathcal{A}_t} w_i^t > \theta_t$) and the received label is 0, the active weights in the current example are *demoted*: $\forall i \in \mathcal{A}_t, w_i^t \leftarrow \beta \cdot w_i^t$. All other weights are unchanged. The key property of the Winnow update rule is that the number of examples[1] it requires to learn a linear function grows linearly with the number of *relevant* features and only logarithmically with the total number of features. This property seems crucial in domains in which the number of potential features is vast, but a relatively small number of them is relevant (this does not mean that only a small number of them will be active, or have non-zero weights). Winnow is known to learn efficiently any linear threshold function and to be robust in the presence of various kinds of noise and in cases where no linear-threshold function can make perfect classification, and still maintain its abovementioned dependence on the number of total and relevant attributes [11, 9]. Once target subnetworks have been learned and the network is being evaluated, a winner-take-all mechanism selects the dominant active target node in the SNoW unit to produce a final prediction. In general, but not in this work, units' output may be cached and processed along with the output of other SNoW units to produce a coherent output.

3 Learning to detect faces

For training, we use a set of 1,681 face images (collected from Olivetti [22], UMIST [6], Harvard [7], Yale [1] and FERET [15] databases) which have wide variations in pose, facial expression and lighting condition. For negative examples we start with 8,422 non-face examples from 400 images of landscapes, trees, buildings, etc. Although it is extremely difficult to collect a representative set of non-face examples, the bootstrap method [24] is used to include more non-face examples during training. For positive examples, each face sample is manually cropped and normalized such that it is aligned vertically and its size is 20×20 pixels. To make the detection method less sensitive to scale and rotation variation, 10 face examples are generated from each original sample. The images are produced by randomly rotating the images by up to 15 degrees with scaling between 80% and 120%. This produces 16,810 face samples. Then, histogram equalization is performed that maps the

---

[1] In the on-line setting [10] this is usually phrased in terms of a mistake-bound but is known to imply convergence in the PAC sense [25, 8].

intensity values to expand the range of intensities. The same procedure is applied to input images in detection phase.

3.1 Primitive Features

The SNoW-based face detector makes use of Boolean features that encode the positions and intensity values of pixels. Let the pixel at (x, y) of an image with width w and height h have intensity value $I(x, y)$ ($0 \leq I(x, y) \leq 255$). This information is encoded as a feature whose index is $256(y * w + x) + I(x, y)$. This representation ensures that different points in the {position × intensity} space are mapped to different features. (That is, the feature indexed $256(y * w + x) + I(x, y)$ is *active* if and only if the intensity in position (x, y) is $I(x, y)$.) In our experiments, the values for w and h are 20 since each face sample has been normalized to an image of 20×20 pixels. Note that although the number of potential features in our representation is 102400 (400×256), only 400 of those are active (present) in each example, and it is plausible that many features will never be active. Since the algorithm's complexity depends on the number of active features in an example, rather than the total number of features, the sparseness also ensures efficiency.

3.2 Multi-scale Features

Many vision problems have utilized multi-scale features to capture the structures of an object. However, extracting detailed multi-scale features using edge or region information from segmentation is a computationally expensive task. Here we use the SNoW paradigm to extract Boolean features that represent multi-scale information. This is done in a similar way to the {position × intensity} used in Sec. 3.1, only that in this case we encode, in addition to position, the mean and variance of a multi-scale pixel. The hope is that the multi-scale feature will capture information that otherwise requires many pixel-based features to represent, and thus simplify the learning problem. Uninformative multi-scale features will be quickly assigned low weights by the learning algorithm and will not degrade performance. Since each face sample is normalized to be a rectangular image of the same size, it suffices to consider rectangular sub-images with varying size from face samples, and for each generate features in terms of the means and variances of their intensity values. Empirical results show that faces can be described effectively this way.

Instead of using the absolute values of the mean and variance when encoding the features, we discretize these values into a predefined number of classes. Since the distribution of the mean values as well as the variance values is normal, the discretization is finer near the means of these distributions. The total number of values was determined empirically to be 100, out of which 80 ended up near the mean. Given that, we use the same scheme as in Sec. 3.1 to map the {position × intensity mean × intensity variance} space into the Boolean feature space. This is done separately for four different sub-image scales, of 1×1, 2×2, 4×4 to 10×10 pixels. The multi-scale feature vector consists of active features corresponding to all these scales. The number of active features in each example is therefore $400 + 100 + 25 + 4$, although the total number of features is much larger.

In recent work we have used more sophisticated conjunctive features for this purpose yielding even better results. However, the emphasis here is that with the SNoW approach, even very simplistic features support excellent performance.

4 Empirical Results

We tested the SNoW-based approach with both sets of features on the two sets of images collected by Rowley [20], and Sung [24]. Each image is scanned with a rectangular window to determine whether a face exists in the window or not. To detect faces of different scales, each input image is repeatedly subsampled by a factor of 1.2 and scanned through for 10 iterations. Table 1 shows the reported experimental results of the SNoW-based face detectors and several face detection systems using the two benchmark data sets (available at http://www.cs.cmu.edu/ ~har/ faces.html). The first data set consists of 130 images with 507 frontal faces and the second data set consists of 23 images with 155 frontal faces. There are a few hand drawn faces and cartoon faces in both sets. Since some methods use intensity values as their features, systems 1-4 and 7 discard these such hand drawn and cartoon faces. Therefore, there are 125 images with 483 faces in test set 1 and 20 images with 136 faces in test set 2 respectively. The reported detection rate is computed as the ratio between the number of faces detected in the images by the system and the number of faces identified there by humans. The number of false detections is the number of non-faces detected as faces.

It is difficult to evaluate the performance of different methods even though they use the same benchmark data sets because different criteria (e.g. training time, number of training examples involved, execution time, number of scanned windows in detection) can be applied to favor one over another. Also, one can tune the parameters of one's method to increase the detection rates while increasing also the false detections. The methods using neural networks [20], distribution-based [24], Kullback relative information [4] and naive Bayes [23] report several experimental results based on different sets of parameters. Table 1 summarizes the best detection rates and corresponding false detections of these methods. Although the method in [4] has the highest detection rates in one benchmark test, this was done by significantly increasing the number of false detections. Other than that, it is evident that the SNoW-based face detectors outperforms others in terms of the overall performance. These results show the credibility of SNoW for these tasks, as well

Table 1: Experimental results on images from test set 1 (125 images with 483 faces) in [20] and test set 2 (20 images with 136 faces) in [24] (see text for details)

Method	Test Set 1		Test Set 2	
	Detect Rate	False Detects	Detect Rate	False Detects
SNoW w/ primitive features	**94.2%**	**84**	**93.6%**	**3**
SNoW w/ multi-scale features	**94.8%**	**78**	**94.1%**	**3**
Mixture of factor analyzers [26]	92.3%	82	89.4%	3
Fisher linear discriminant [27]	93.6%	74	91.5%	1
Distribution-based [24]	N/A	N/A	81.9%	13
Neural network [20]	92.5%	862	90.3%	42
Naive Bayes [23]	93.0%	88	91.2%	12
Kullback relative information [4]	98.0%	12758	N/A	N/A
Support vector machine [14]	N/A	N/A	74.2%	20

as exhibit the improvement achieved by increasing the expressiveness of the features. This may indicate that further elaboration of the features, which can be done in a very general and flexible way within SNoW, would yield further improvements.

In addition to comparing feature sets, we started to investigate some of the reasons for the success of SNoW in this domain, which we discuss briefly below. Two potential contributions are the Winnow update rule and the architecture. First, we studied the update rule in isolation, independent of the SNoW architecture. The results we got when using the Winnow simply as a discriminator were fairly poor (63.9%/65.3% for Test Set 1, primitive and multi-scale features, respectively, and similar results for the Test Set 2.). The results are not surprising, given that Winnow is used here only as a discriminator and is using only positive weights. Investigating the architecture in isolation reveals that weighting or discarding features based on their contribution to mistakes during training, as is done within SNoW, is crucial. Considering the active features uniformly (separately for faces and non-faces) yields poor results. Specifically, studying the resulting SNoW network shows that the total number of features that were active with non-faces is 102,208, out of 102,400 possible (primitive) features. The total number of active features in faces was only 82,608, most of which are active only a few times. In retrospect, this is clear given the diverse set of images used as negative examples, relative to the somewhat restricted (by nature) set of images that constitute faces. (Similar phenomenon occurs with the multi-scale features, where the numbers are 121572 and 90528, respectively, out of 135424.) Overall it exhibits that the architecture, the learning regime and the update rule all contribute significantly to the success of the approach.

Figure 1 shows some faces detected in our experiments. Note that profile faces and faces under heavy illumination are detected. Experimental results show that profile faces and faces under different illumination are detected very well by our method. Note that although there may exist several detected faces around each face, only one window is drawn to enclose each detected face for clear presentation.

Figure 1: Sample experimental results using our method on images from two benchmark data sets. Every detected face is shown with an enclosing window.

5 Discussion and Conclusion

Many theoretical and experimental issues are to be addressed before a learning system of this sort can be used to detect faces efficiently and robustly under general conditions. In terms of the face detection problem, the presented method is still not able to detect rotated faces. A recent method [21], addresses this problem by building upon a upright face detector [20] and rotating each test sample to upright position. However, it suffers from degraded detection rates and more false detections. Given our results, we believe that the SNoW approach, if adapted in similar ways, would generalize very well to detect faces under more general conditions.

In terms of the SNoW architecture, although the main ingredients of it are understood theoretically, more work is required to better understand its strengths. This is increasingly interesting given that the architecture has been found to perform very well in large-scale problem in the natural language domain as well

The contributions of this paper can be summarized as follows. We have introduced the SNoW learning architecture to the domain of visual processing and described an approach that detect faces regardless of their poses, facial features and illumination conditions. Experimental results show that this method outperforms other methods in terms of detection rates and false detectionss, while being more efficient both in learning and evaluation.

References

[1] P. Belhumeur, J. Hespanha, and D. Kriegman. Eigenfaces vs. fisherfaces: Recognition using class specific linear projection. *IEEE Transactions on Pattern Analysis and Machine Intelligence*, 19(7):711–720, 1997.

[2] A. Blum. Learning boolean functions in an infinite attribute space. *Machine Learning*, 9(4):373–386, 1992.

[3] A. Carleson, C. Cumby, J. Rosen, and D. Roth. The SNoW learning architecture. Technical Report UIUCDCS-R-99-2101, UIUC Computer Science Department, May 1999.

[4] A. J. Colmenarez and T. S. Huang. Face detection with information-based maximum discrimination. In *Proceedings of the IEEE Computer Society Conference on Computer Vision and Pattern Recognition*, pages 782–787, 1997.

[5] A. R. Golding and D. Roth. A winnow based approach to context-sensitive spelling correction. *Machine Learning*, 34:107–130, 1999. Special Issue on Machine Learning and Natural Language.

[6] D. B. Graham and N. M. Allinson. Characterizing virtual eigensignatures for general purpose face recognition. In H. Wechsler, P. J. Phillips, V. Bruce, F. Fogelman-Soulie, and T. S. Huang, editors, *Face Recognition: From Theory to Applications*, volume 163 of *NATO ASI Series F, Computer and Systems Sciences*, pages 446–456. Springer, 1998.

[7] P. Hallinan. *A Deformable Model for Face Recognition Under Arbitrary Lighting Conditions*. PhD thesis, Harvard University, 1995.

[8] D. Helmbold and M. K. Warmuth. On weak learning. *Journal of Computer and System Sciences*, 50(3):551–573, June 1995.

[9] J. Kivinen and M. K. Warmuth. Exponentiated gradient versus gradient descent for linear predictors. In *Proceedings of the Annual ACM Symposium on the Theory of Computing*, 1995.

[10] N. Littlestone. Learning quickly when irrelevant attributes abound: A new linear-threshold algorithm. *Machine Learning*, 2:285–318, 1988.

[11] N. Littlestone. Redundant noisy attributes, attribute errors, and linear threshold learning using winnow. In *Proceedings of the fourth Annual Workshop on Computational Learning Theory*, pages 147–156, 1991.

[12] B. Moghaddam and A. Pentland. Probabilistic visual learning for object recognition. *IEEE Transactions on Pattern Analysis and Machine Intelligence*, 19(7):696–710, 1997.

[13] M. Munoz, V. Punyakanok, D. Roth, and D. Zimak. A learning approach to shallow parsing. In *EMNLP-VLC'99, the Joint SIGDAT Conference on Empirical Methods in Natural Language Processing and Very Large Corpora*, June 1999.

[14] E. Osuna, R. Freund, and F. Girosi. Training support vector machines: an application to face detection. In *Proceedings of the IEEE Computer Society Conference on Computer Vision and Pattern Recognition*, pages 130–136, 1997.

[15] P. J. Phillips, H. Moon, S. Rizvi, and P. Rauss. The feret evaluation. In H. Wechsler, P. J. Phillips, V. Bruce, F. Fogelman-Soulie, and T. S. Huang, editors, *Face Recognition: From Theory to Applications*, volume 163 of *NATO ASI Series F, Computer and Systems Sciences*, pages 244–261. Springer, 1998.

[16] R. J. Qian and T. S. Huang. Object detection using hierarchical mrf and map estimation. In *Proceedings of the IEEE Computer Society Conference on Computer Vision and Pattern Recognition*, pages 186–192, 1997.

[17] A. N. Rajagopalan, K. S. Kumar, J. Karlekar, R. Manivasakan, and M. M. Patil. Finding faces in photographs. In *Proceedings of the Sixth International Conference on Computer Vision*, pages 640–645, 1998.

[18] D. Roth. Learning to resolve natural language ambiguities: A unified approach. In *Proceedings of the Fifteenth National Conference on Artificial Intelligence*, pages 806–813, 1998.

[19] D. Roth and D. Zelenko. Part of speech tagging using a network of linear separators. In *COLING-ACL 98, The 17th Int. Conference on Computational Linguistics*, pages 1136–1142, 1998.

[20] H. Rowley, S. Baluja, and T. Kanade. Neural network-based face detection. *IEEE Transactions on Pattern Analysis and Machine Intelligence*, 20(1):23–38, 1998.

[21] H. Rowley, S. Baluja, and T. Kanade. Rotation invariant neural network-based face detection. In *Proceedings of the IEEE Computer Society Conference on Computer Vision and Pattern Recognition*, pages 38–44, 1998.

[22] F. S. Samaria. *Face Recognition Using Hidden Markov Models*. PhD thesis, University of Cambridge, 1994.

[23] H. Schneiderman and T. Kanade. Probabilistic modeling of local appearance and spatial relationships for object recognition. In *Proceedings of the IEEE Computer Society Conference on Computer Vision and Pattern Recognition*, pages 45–51, 1998.

[24] K.-K. Sung and T. Poggio. Example-based learning for view-based human face detection. *IEEE Transactions on Pattern Analysis and Machine Intelligence*, 20(1):39–51, 1998.

[25] L. G. Valiant. A theory of the learnable. *Commun. ACM*, 27(11):1134–1142, Nov. 1984.

[26] M.-H. Yang, N. Ahuja, and D. Kriegman. Face detection using a mixture of factor analyzers. In *Proceedings of the IEEE International Conference on Image Processing*, 1999.

[27] M.-H. Yang, N. Ahuja, and D. Kriegman. Mixtures of linear subspaces for face detection. In *Proceedings of the Foruth IEEE International Conference on Automatic Face and Gesture Recognition*, 2000.

Managing Uncertainty in Cue Combination

Zhiyong Yang
Department of Neurobiology, Box 3209
Duke University Medical Center
Durham, NC 27710
zhyyang@duke.edu

Richard S. Zemel
Department of Psychology
University of Arizona
Tucson, AZ 85721
zemel@u.arizona.edu

Abstract

We develop a hierarchical generative model to study cue combination. The model maps a global shape parameter to local cue-specific parameters, which in turn generate an intensity image. Inferring shape from images is achieved by inverting this model. Inference produces a probability distribution at each level; using distributions rather than a single value of underlying variables at each stage preserves information about the validity of each local cue for the given image. This allows the model, unlike standard combination models, to adaptively weight each cue based on general cue reliability and specific image context. We describe the results of a cue combination psychophysics experiment we conducted that allows a direct comparison with the model. The model provides a good fit to our data and a natural account for some interesting aspects of cue combination.

Understanding cue combination is a fundamental step in developing computational models of visual perception, because many aspects of perception naturally involve multiple cues, such as binocular stereo, motion, texture, and shading. It is often formulated as a problem of inferring or estimating some relevant parameter, e.g., depth, shape, position, by combining estimates from individual cues.

An important finding of psychophysical studies of cue combination is that cues vary in the degree to which they are used in different visual environments. Weights assigned to estimates derived from a particular cue seem to reflect its estimated reliability in the current scene and viewing conditions. For example, motion and stereo are weighted approximately equally at near distances, but motion is weighted more at far distances, presumably due to distance limits on binocular disparity.[3] Experiments have also found these weightings sensitive to image manipulations; if a cue is weakened, such as by adding noise, then the uncontaminated cue is utilized more in making depth judgments.[9] A recent study[2] has shown that observers can adjust the weighting they assign to a cue based on its relative utility for a particular task. From these and other experiments, we can identify two types of information that determine relative cue weightings: (1) *cue reliability*: its relative utility in the context of the task and general viewing conditions; and (2) *region informativeness*: cue information available locally in a given image.

A central question in computational models of cue combination then concerns how these forms of uncertainty can be combined. We propose a hierarchical generative model. Generative models have a rich history in cue combination, as they underlie models of Bayesian perception that have been developed in this area.[10,5] The novelty in the generative model proposed here lies in its hierarchical nature and use of distributions throughout, which allows for both context-dependent and image-specific uncertainty to be combined in a principled manner.

Our aims in this paper are dual: to develop a combination model that incorporates cue reliability and region informativeness (estimated across and within images), and to use this model to account for data and provide predictions for psychophysical experiments. Another motivation for the approach here stems from our recent probabilistic framework,[11] which posits that every step of processing entails the representation of an entire probability distribution, rather than just a single value of the relevant underlying variable(s). Here we use separate local probability distributions for each cue estimated directly from an image. Combination then entails transforming representations and integrating distributions across both space and cues, taking across- and within-image uncertainty into account.

1 IMAGE GENERATION

In this paper we study the case of combining shading and texture. Standard shape-from-shading models exclude texture,[1,8] while standard shape-from-texture models exclude shading.[7] Experimental results and computational arguments have supported a strong interaction between these cues,[10] but no model accounting for this interaction has yet been worked out.

The shape used in our experiments is a simple surface:

$$Z = B(1 - x^2), |x| <= 1, |y| <= 1 \qquad (1)$$

where Z is the height from the xy plane. B is the only shape parameter.

Our image formation model is a hierarchical generative model (see Figure 1). The top layer contains the global parameter B. The second layer contains local shading and texture parameters $\mathbf{S}, \mathbf{T} = \{S_i, T_i\}$, where i indexes image regions. The generation of local cues from a global parameter is intended to allow local uncertainties to be introduced separately into the cues. This models specific conditions in realistic images, such as shading uncertainty due to shadows or specularities, and texture uncertainty when prior assumptions such as isotropicity are violated.[4] Here we introduce uncertainty by adding independent local noise to the underlying shape parameter; this manipulation is less realistic but easier to control.

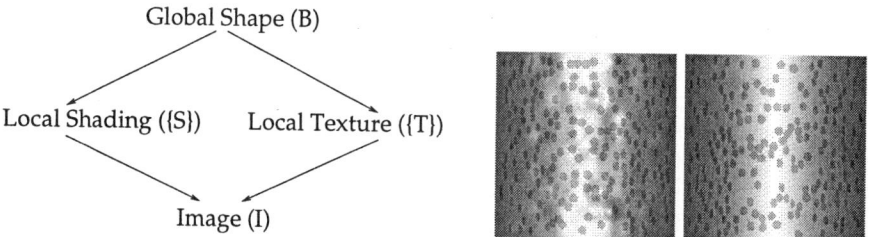

Figure 1: Left: The generative model of image formation. Right: Two sample images generated by the image formation procedure. $B = 1.4$ in both. Left: $\sigma_s = 0.05, \sigma_t = 0$. Right: $\sigma_s = 0, \sigma_t = 0.05$.

The local cues are sampled from Gaussian distributions: $p(S_i|B) = \mathcal{N}(f(B); \sigma_s)$; $p(T_i|B) = \mathcal{N}(g(B); \sigma_t)$. $f(B), g(B)$ describe how the local cue parameters depend on the shape parameter B, while σ_s and σ_t represent the degree of noise in each cue. In this paper, to simplify the generation process we set $f(B) = g(B) = B$. From $\{S_i\}$ and $\{T_i\}$, two surfaces are generated; these are essentially two separate noisy local versions of B. The intensity image combines these surfaces. A set of same-intensity texsels sampled from a uniform distribution are mapped onto the texture surface, and then projected onto the image plane under orthogonal projection. The intensity of surface pixels not contained within these texsels are determined generated from the shading surface using Lambertian shading. Each image is composed of 10×10 non-overlapping regions, and contains 400×400 pixels. Figure 1 shows two images generated by this procedure.

2 COMBINATION MODEL

We create a combination, or recognition model by inverting the generative model of Figure 1 to infer the shape parameter B from the image. An important aspect of the combination model is the use of distributions to represent parameter estimates at each stage. This preserves uncertainty information at each level, and allows it to play a role in subsequent inference.

The overall goal of combination is to infer an estimate of B given some image I. We derive our main inference equation using a Bayesian integration over distributions:

$$P(B|I) = \int P(B|\mathbf{S},\mathbf{T}) P(\mathbf{S},\mathbf{T}|I) d\mathbf{S} d\mathbf{T} \qquad (2)$$

$$P(\mathbf{S},\mathbf{T}|I) \sim \prod_i P(S_i|I) P(T_i|I) \qquad (3)$$

$$P(B|\mathbf{S},\mathbf{T}) = P(B) P(\mathbf{S},\mathbf{T}|B) / \int P(B) P(\mathbf{S},\mathbf{T}|B) db \sim \prod_i P(S_i|B) P(T_i|B) \qquad (4)$$

To simplify the two components we have assumed that the prior over B is uniform, and that the $\mathbf{S}, \mathbf{T}$ are conditionally independent given B, and given the image. This third assumption is dubious but is not essential in the model, as discussed below. We now consider these two components in turn.

2.1 Obtaining local cue-specific representations from an image

One component in the inference equation, $P(\mathbf{S},\mathbf{T}|I)$, describes local cue-dependent information in the particular image I. We first define intermediate representations S, T that are dependent on shading and texture cues, respectively. The shading representation is the curvature of a horizontal section: $S = f(B) = 2B(1 + 4x^2B^2)^{-3/2}$. The texture representation is the cosine of the surface slant: $T = g(B) = (1 + 4x^2B^2)^{-1/2}$. Note that these S, T variables do not match those used in the generative model; ideally we could have used these cue-dependent variables, but generating images from them proved difficult.

Some image pre-processing must take place in order to estimate values and uncertainties for these particular local variables. The approach we adopt involves a simple statistical matching procedure, similar to k-nearest neighbors, applied to local image patches. After applying Gaussian smoothing and band-pass filtering to the image, two representations of each patch are obtained using separate shading and texture filters. For shading, image patches are represented by forming a histogram of $\frac{\Delta I}{I}$; for texture, the patch is represented by the mean and standard deviation of the amplitude of Gabor filter responses at 4 scales and orientations. This representation of a shading patch is then compared to a database of similar patch representations. Entries in the shading database are formed by first selecting a particular value of B and σ_s, generating an image patch, and applying the appropriate filters. Thus $S = f(B)$ and the noise level σ_s are known for each entry, allowing an estimate of these variables for the new patch to be formed as a linear combination of the entries with similar representations. An analogous procedure, utilizing a separate database, allows T and an uncertainty estimate to be derived for texture. Both databases have 60 different b, σ pairs, and 10 samples of each pair.

Based on this procedure we obtain for each image patch mean values M_i^s, M_i^t and uncertainty values V_i^s, V_i^t for S_i, T_i. These determine $P(I|S), P(I|T)$, which are approximated as Gaussians. Taking into account the Gaussian priors for S_i, T_i,

$$P(S_i|I) = P(I|S_i)P(S_i) \sim \exp(-\frac{V_i^s}{2}(S-M_i^s)^2)\exp(-\frac{V_0^s}{2}(S-M_0^s)^2) \quad (5)$$

$$P(T_i|I) = P(I|T_i)P(T_i) \sim \exp(-\frac{V_i^t}{2}(T-M_i^t)^2)\exp(-\frac{V_0^t}{2}(T-M_0^t)^2) \quad (6)$$

Note that the independence assumption of Equation 3 is not necessary, as the matching procedure could use a single database indexed by both the shading and texture representations of a patch.

2.2 Transforming and combining cue-specific local representations

The other component of the inference equation describes the relationship between the intermediate, cue-specific representations S, T and the shape parameter B:

$$P(S|B) \sim \exp(-\frac{V_b^s}{2}(S-f(B))^2) \; ; \; P(T|B) \sim \exp(-\frac{V_b^t}{2}(T-g(B))^2) \quad (7)$$

The two parameters V_b^s, V_b^t in this equation describe the uncertainty in the relationship between the intermediate parameters S, T and B; they are invariant across space. These two, along with the parameters of the priors—$M_0^s, M_0^t, V_0^s, V_0^t$—are the free parameters of this model. Note that this combination model neatly accounts for both types of cue validity we identified: the variance in $P(S|B)$ describes the *general uncertainty* of a given cue, while the local variance in $P(S|I)$ describes the *image-specific uncertainty* of the cue.

Combining Equations 3-7, and completing the integral in Equation 2, we have:

$$P(B|I) \sim \exp\left[-\frac{1}{2}\sum_i a_1 f(B)^2 + a_2 g(B)^2 - 2a_3 f(B) - 2a_4 g(B)\right] \quad (8)$$

$a_1 = \frac{V_b^s(V_i^s+V_0^s)}{V_b^s+V_i^s+V_0^s}, a_2 = \frac{V_b^t(V_i^t+V_0^t)}{V_b^t+V_i^t+V_0^t}, a_3 = \frac{V_b^s(V_i^s M_i^s+V_0^s M_0^s)}{V_b^s+V_i^s+V_0^s}, a_4 = \frac{V_b^t(V_i^t M_i^t+V_0^t M_0^t)}{V_b^t+V_i^t+V_0^t}$. Approximating $P(B|I)$ as a Gaussian, we obtain the mean $\mathcal{U}$ and std. deviation Σ:

$$\frac{\partial \log(-P(B|I))}{\partial B}|_{\mathcal{U}} = 0 \; ; \; \Sigma = [\frac{\partial^2(-\log P(B|I))}{\partial^2 B}|_{\mathcal{U}}]^{-1/2} \quad (9)$$

Thus our model infers from any image a mean $\mathcal{U}$ and variance Σ^2 for B as nonlinear combinations of the cue estimates, taking into account the various forms of uncertainty.

3 A CUE COMBINATION PSYCHOPHYSICS EXPERIMENT

We have conducted psychophysical experiments using stimuli generated by the procedure described above. In each experimental trial, a stimulus image and four views of a mesh surface are displayed side-by-side on a computer screen. The subject's task is to manipulate the curvature of the mesh to match the stimulus. The final shape of the mesh surface describes the subject's estimate of the shape parameter B on that trial. The subject's variance is computed across repeated trials with an identical stimulus. In a given block of trials, the stimulus may contain only shading information (no texture elements), only texture information uniform shading), or both. The local cue noise (σ_s, σ_t) is zero in some blocks, non-zero in others. The primary experimental findings (see Figure 2) are:

- Shape from shading alone produces underestimates of B. Shape from texture alone also leads to underestimation, but to a lesser degree.

- Shape from both cues leads to almost perfect estimation, with smaller variance than shape from either cue alone. Thus *cue enhancement*—more accurate and robust judgements for stimuli containing multiple cues than just individual cues—applies to this paradigm.

- The variance of a subject's estimation increases with B.

- Noise in either shading or texture systematically biases the estimation from the true values: the greater the noise level, the greater the bias.

- Shape from both cues is more robust against noise than shape from either cue alone, providing evidence of another form of cue enhancement.

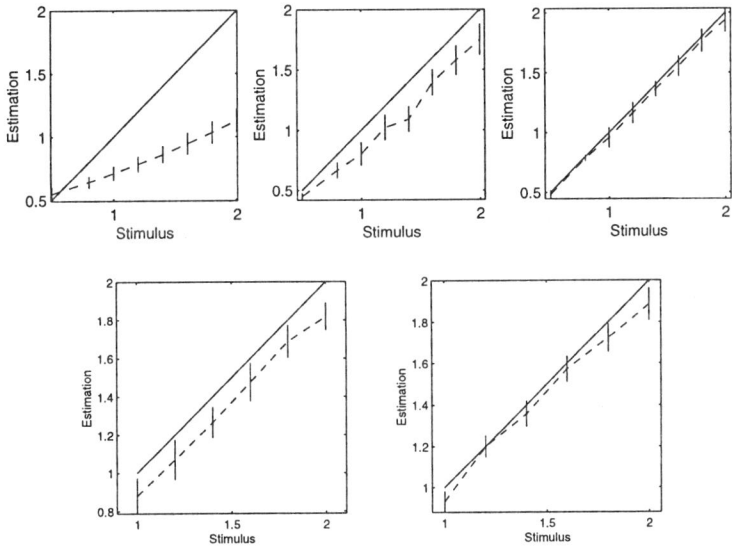

Figure 2: Means and standard errors are shown for the shape matching experiment, for different values of B, under different stimulus conditions. TOP: No noise in local shape parameters. Left: Shape from shading alone. Middle: Shape from texture alone. Right: Shape from shading and texture. BOTTOM: Shape from shading and texture. Left: $\sigma_s = 0.05$, $\sigma_t = 0$. Right: $\sigma_s = 0$, $\sigma_t = 0.05$.

4 MODELING RESULTS

The model was trained using a subset of data from these experiments. The error criteria was mean relative error (MRE) between the model outputs ($\mathcal{U}, \Sigma$) and

B	σ_s	σ_t	data ($\mathcal{U}/\Sigma$)	model ($\mathcal{U}/\Sigma$)
1.4	0.10	0	1.18/0.072	1.20/0.06
1.6	0.10	0	1.34/0.075	1.35/0.063
1.4	0.05	0	1.32/0.042	1.4/0.067
1.6	0.05	0	1.52/0.049	1.46/0.069
1.2	0	0.05	1.20/0.052	1.14/0.056
1.4	0	0.05	1.36/0.062	1.30/0.063

Table 1: Data versus model predictions on images outside the training class. The first column of means and variances are from the experimental data, the second column from the model.

experimental data (subject mean and variance on the same image). The six free parameters of the model were described as the sum of third order polynomials of local S, T and the noise levels. Gradient descent was used to train the model.

The model was trained and tested on three different subsets of the experimental data. When trained on data in which only B varied, the model output accurately predicts unseen experimental data of the same type. When the data varied in B and σ_s or σ_t, the model outputs agree very well with subject data ($MRE \sim 5-8\%$). When trained on data where all three variables vary, the model fits the data reasonably well ($MRE \sim 8-13\%$). For a model of the first type, Figure 3 compares model predictions to data from within the same set, while Table 1 shows model outputs and subject responses for test examples from outside the training class.

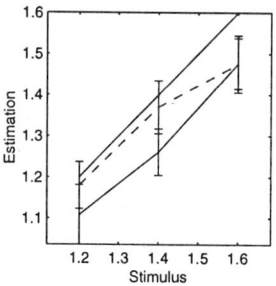

Figure 3: Model performance on data in which $\sigma_s = 0, \sigma_t = 0.10$. Upper line: perfect estimation. Lower line: experimental data. Dashed line: model prediction.

The model accounts for some important aspects of cue combination. Trained model parameters reveal that the texture prior is considerably weaker than the shading prior, and texture has a more reliable relationship with B. Consequently, at equal noise levels texture outweighs shading in the combination model. These factors account for the degree of underestimation found in each single-cue experiment, and the greater accuracy (i.e., enhancement) with combined-cues. Our studies also reveal a novel form of cue interaction: for some image patches, esp. at high curvature and noise levels, shading information becomes *harmful*, i.e., curvature estimation becomes less reliable when shading information is taken into account. Note that this differs from cue veto, in that texture does not veto shading.

Finally, the primary contribution of our model lies in its ability to predict the effect of continuous within-image variation in cue reliability on combination. Figure 4 shows how the estimation becomes more accurate and less variable with increasing certainty in shading information. Standard cue combination models cannot produce similar behavior, as they do not estimate within-image cue reliabilities.

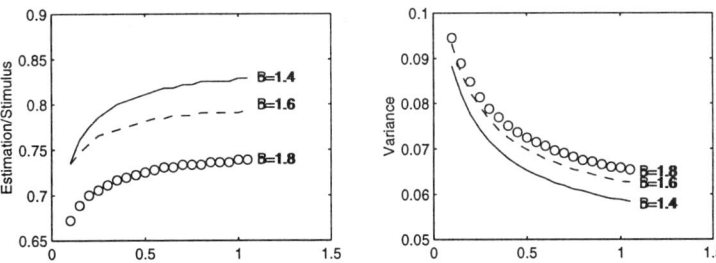

Figure 4: Mean (left) and variance (right) of model output as a function of V_i^s, for different values of B. Here $\sigma_s = 0.15, \sigma_t = 0$, all model parameters held constant.

5 CONCLUSION

We have proposed a hierarchical generative model to study cue combination. Inferring parameters from images is achieved by inverting this model. Inference produces probability distributions at each level: a set of local distributions, separately representing each cue, are combined to form a distribution over a relevant scene variable. The model naturally handles variations in cue reliability, which depend both on spatially local image context and general cue characteristics. This form of representation, incorporating image-specific cue utilities, makes this model more powerful than standard combination models. The model provides a good fit to our psychophysics results on shading and texture combination and an account for several aspects of cue combination; it also provides predictions for how varying noise levels, both within and across images, will effect combination.

We are extending this work in a number of directions. We are conducting experiments to obtain local shape estimates from subjects. We are considering better ways to extract local representations and distributions over them directly from an image, and methods of handling natural outliers such as shadows and occlusion.

References

[1] Horn, B. K. P. (1977). Understanding image intensities. *AI 8*, 201-231.
[2] Jacobs, R. A. & Fine I. (1999). Experience-dependent integration of texture and motion cues to depth. *Vis. Res.*, 39, 4062-4075.
[3] Johnston, E. B., Cumming, B. G., & Landy, M. S. (1994). Integration of depth modules: Stereopsis and texture. *Vis. Res. 34*, 2259-2275.
[4] Knill, D. C. (1998). Surface orientation from texture: ideal observers, generic observers and the information content of texture cues. *Vis. Res.* 38, 1655-1682.
[5] Knill, D. C., Kersten, D., & Mamassian P. (1996). Implications of a Bayesian formulation of visual information for processing for psychophysics. In *Perception as Bayesian Inference*, D. C. Knill and W. Richards (Eds.), 239-286, Cambridge Univ Press.
[6] Landy, M. S., Maloney, L. T., Johnston, E. B., & Young, M. J. (1995). Measurement and modeling of depth cue combination: In defense of weak fusion. *Vis. Res. 35*, 389-412.
[7] Malik, J. & Rosenholtz, R. (1997). Computing local surface orientation and shape from texture for curved surfaces. *IJCV 23*, 149-168.
[8] Pentland, A. (1984). Local shading analysis. *IEEE PAMI, 6*, 170-187.
[9] Young, M.J., Landy, M.S., & Maloney, L.T. (1993). A perturbation analysis of depth perception from combinations of texture and motion cues. *Vis. Res. 33*, 2685-2696.
[10] Yuille, A. & Bulthoff, H. H. (1996). Bayesian decision theory and psychophysics. In *Perception as Bayesian Inference*, D. C. Knill and W. Richards (Eds.), 123-161, Cambridge Univ Press.
[11] Zemel, R. S., Dayan, P., & Pouget, A. (1998). Probabilistic interpretation of population codes. *Neural Computation*, 403-430.

Part VIII
Applications

Robust Learning of Chaotic Attractors

Rembrandt Bakker*
Chemical Reactor Engineering
Delft Univ. of Technology
r.bakker@stm.tudelft.nl

Jaap C. Schouten
Chemical Reactor Engineering
Eindhoven Univ. of Technology
J.C.Schouten@tue.nl

Marc-Olivier Coppens
Chemical Reactor Engineering
Delft Univ. of Technology
coppens@stm.tudelft.nl

Floris Takens
Dept. Mathematics
University of Groningen
F.Takens@math.rug.nl

C. Lee Giles
NEC Research Institute
Princeton NJ
giles@research.nj.nec.com

Cor M. van den Bleek
Chemical Reactor Engineering
Delft Univ. of Technology
vdbleek@stm.tudelft.nl

Abstract

A fundamental problem with the modeling of chaotic time series data is that minimizing short-term prediction errors does *not guarantee* a match between the reconstructed attractors of model and experiments. We introduce a modeling paradigm that simultaneously learns to short-term predict and to locate the outlines of the attractor by a new way of nonlinear principal component analysis. Closed-loop predictions are constrained to stay within these outlines, to prevent divergence from the attractor. Learning is exceptionally fast: parameter estimation for the 1000 sample laser data from the 1991 Santa Fe time series competition took less than a minute on a 166 MHz Pentium PC.

1 Introduction

We focus on the following objective: given a set of experimental data and the assumption that it was produced by a deterministic chaotic system, find a set of model equations that will produce a time-series with identical chaotic characteristics, having the same chaotic attractor. The common approach consists of two steps: (1) identify a model that makes accurate short-term predictions; and (2) generate a long time-series with the model and compare the nonlinear-dynamic characteristics of this time-series with the original, measured time-series.

Principe *et al.* [1] found that in many cases the model can make good short-term predictions but does *not* learn the chaotic attractor. The method would be greatly improved if we could minimize directly the difference between the reconstructed attractors of the model-generated and measured data, instead of minimizing prediction errors. However, we cannot reconstruct the attractor without first having a prediction model. Until now research has focused on how to optimize both step 1 and step 2. For example, it is important to optimize the prediction horizon of the model [2] and to reduce complexity as much as possible. This way it was possible to learn the attractor of the benchmark laser time series data from the 1991 Santa Fe

---

*DelftChemTech, Chemical Reactor Engineering Lab, Julianalaan 136, 2628 BL, Delft, The Netherlands; http://www.cpt.stm.tudelft.nl/cpt/cre/research/bakker/.

time series competition. While training a neural network for this problem, we noticed [3] that the attractor of the model fluctuated from a good match to a complete mismatch from one iteration to another. We were able to circumvent this problem by selecting exactly that model that matches the attractor. However, after carrying out more simulations we found that what we neglected as an unfortunate phenomenon [3] is really a fundamental limitation of current approaches.

An important development is the work of Principe *et al.* [4] who use Kohonen Self Organizing Maps (SOMs) to create a discrete representation of the state space of the system. This creates a partitioning of the input space that becomes an infrastructure for local (linear) model construction. This partitioning enables to verify if the model input is near the original data (*i.e.*, detect if the model is not extrapolating) without keeping the training data set with the model. We propose a different partitioning of the input space that can be used to (i) learn the outlines of the chaotic attractor by means of a new way of nonlinear Principal Component Analysis (PCA), and (ii) *enforce* the model never to predict outside these outlines. The nonlinear PCA algorithm is inspired by the work of Kambhatla and Leen [5] on local PCA: they partition the input space and perform local PCA in each region. Unfortunately, this introduces discontinuities between neighboring regions. We resolve them by introducing a hierarchical partitioning algorithm that uses fuzzy boundaries between the regions. This partitioning closely resembles the hierarchical mixtures of experts of Jordan and Jacobs [6].

In Sec. 2 we put forward the fundamental problem that arises when trying to learn a chaotic attractor by creating a short-term prediction model. In Sec. 3 we describe the proposed partitioning algorithm. In Sec. 4 it is outlined how this partitioning can be used to learn the outline of the attractor by defining a potential that measures the distance to the attractor. In Sec. 5 we show modeling results on a toy example, the logistic map, and on a more serious problem, the laser data from the 1991 Santa Fe time series competition. Section 6 concludes.

2 The attractor learning dilemma

Imagine an experimental system with a chaotic attractor, and a time-series of noise-free measurements taken from this system. The data is used to fit the parameters of the model $\vec{z}_{t+1} = F_{\vec{w}}(\vec{z}_t, \vec{z}_{t-1}, \ldots, \vec{z}_{t-m})$ where F is a nonlinear function, $\vec{w}$ contains its adjustable parameters and m is a positive constant. What happens if we fit the parameters $\vec{w}$ by nonlinear least squares regression? Will the model be stable, *i.e.*, will the closed-loop long term prediction converge to the same attractor as the one represented by the measurements?

Figure 1 shows the result of a test by Diks *et al.* [7] that compares the difference between the model and measured attractor. The figure shows that while the neural network is trained to predict chaotic data, the model quickly converges to the measured attractor (S=0), but once in a while, from one iteration to another, the match between the attractors is lost.

To understand what causes this instability, imagine that we try to fit the parameters of a model $\vec{z}_{t+1} = \vec{a} + B\vec{z}_t$ while the real system has a point attractor, $\vec{z} = \vec{\alpha}$, where $\vec{z}$ is the state of the system and $\vec{\alpha}$ its attracting value. Clearly, measurements taken from this system contain no information to

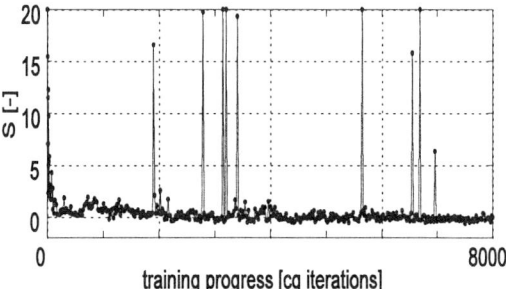

Figure 1: Diks test monitoring curve for a neural network model trained on data from an experimental chaotic pendulum [3].

estimate both $\vec{a}$ and B. If we fit the model parameters with non-robust linear least squares, B may be assigned any value and if its largest eigenvalue happens to be greater than zero, the model will be unstable!

For the linear model this problem has been solved a long time ago with the introduction of singular value decomposition. There still is a need for a nonlinear counterpart of this technique, in particular since we have to work with very flexible models that are designed to fit a wide variety of nonlinear shapes, see for example the early work of Lapedes and Farber [8]. It is already common practice to control the complexity of nonlinear models by pruning or regularization. Unfortunately, these methods do not always solve the attractor learning problem, since there is a good chance that a nonlinear term explains a lot of variance in one part of the state space, while it causes instability of the attractor (without affecting the one-step-ahead prediction accuracy) elsewhere. In Secs. 3 and 4 we will introduce a new method for nonlinear principal component analysis that will detect and prevent unstable behavior.

3. The split and fit algorithm

The nonlinear regression procedure of this section will form the basis of the nonlinear principal component algorithm in Sec. 4. It consists of (i) a partitioning of the input space, (ii) a local linear model for each region, and (iii) fuzzy boundaries between regions to ensure global smoothness. The partitioning scheme is outlined in Procedure 1:

Procedure 1: Partitioning the input space

1) Start with the entire set Z of input data

2) Determine the direction of largest variance of Z: perform a singular value decomposition of Z into the product $U\Sigma V^T$ and take the eigenvector (column of V) with the largest singular value (on the diagonal of Σ).

3) Split the data in two subsets (to be called: clusters) by creating a plane perpendicular to the direction of largest variance, through the center of gravity of Z.

4) Next, select the cluster with the largest sum squared error to be split next, and recursively apply 2-4 until a stopping criteria is met.

Figures 2 and 3 show examples of the partitioning. The disadvantage of dividing regression problems into localized subproblems was pointed out by Jordan and Jacobs [6]: the spread of the data in each region will be much smaller than the spread of the data as a whole, and this will increase the variance of the model parameters. Since we always split perpendicular to the direction of maximum variance, this problem is minimized.

The partitioning can be written as a binary tree, with each non-terminal node being a split and each terminal node a cluster. Procedure 2 creates fuzzy boundaries between the clusters.

Procedure 2. Creating fuzzy boundaries

1) An input $\vec{z}$ enters the tree at the top of the partitioning tree.

2) The Euclidean distance to the splitting hyperplane is divided by the bandwidth β of the split, and passed through a sigmoidal function with range [0,1]. This results in $\vec{z}$'s share σ in the subset on $\vec{z}$'s side of the splitting plane. The share in the other subset is $1-\sigma$.

3) The previous step is carried out for all non-terminal nodes of the tree.

4) The membership μ_c of $\vec{z}$ to subset (terminal node) c is computed by taking the product of all previously computed shares σ along the path from the terminal node to the top of the tree.

If we would make all parameters adjustable, that is (i) the orientation of the splitting hyperplanes, (ii) the bandwidths β, and (iii) the local linear model parameters, the above model structure would be identical to the *hierarchical mixtures of experts* of Jordan and Jacobs [6]. However, we already fixed the hyperplanes and use Procedure 3 to compute the bandwidths:

Procedure 3. Computing the Bandwidths

1) The bandwidths of the terminal nodes are taken to be a constant (we use 1.65, the 90% confidence limit of a normal distribution) times the variance of the subset *before it was last split*, in the direction of the eigenvector of that last split.

2) The other bandwidths do depend on the input $\vec{z}$. They are computed by climbing upward in the tree. The bandwidth of node n is computed as a weighted sum between the βs of its right and left child, by the implicit formula $\beta_n = \sigma_L \beta_L \; \sigma_R \beta_R$, in which σ_L and σ_R depend on β_n. Starting from initial guess $\beta_n = \beta_L$ if $\sigma_L > 0.5$, or else $\beta_n = \beta_R$, the formula is solved in a few iterations.

This procedure is designed to create large overlap between neighboring regions and almost no overlap between non-neighboring regions. What remains to be fitted is the set of the local linear models. The j-th output of the split&fit model for a given input $\vec{z}_p$ is computed:

$$\hat{y}_{j,p} = \sum_{c=1}^{C} \mu_p^c \{\vec{a}_j^c \vec{z}_p + b_j^c\}, \text{where } \vec{a}^c \text{ and } b^c \text{ contain the linear model parameters of subset } c,$$

and C is the number of clusters. We can determine the parameters of all local linear models in one global fit that is linear in the parameters. However, we prefer to locally optimize the parameters for two reasons: (i) it makes it possible to locally control the stability of the attractor and do the principal component analysis of Sec. 4; and (ii) the computing time for a linear regression problem with r regressors scales $\sim O(r^3)$. If we would adopt global fitting, r would scale linearly with C and, while growing the model, the regression problem would quickly become intractable. We use the following iterative local fitting procedure instead.

Procedure 4. Iterative Local Fitting

1) Initialize a J by N matrix of residuals R to zero, J being the number of outputs and N the number of data.

2) For cluster c, if an estimate for its linear model parameters already exists, for each input vector $\vec{z}_p$ add $\mu_p^c \hat{y}_{j,p}$ to the matrix of residuals, otherwise add $\mu_p^c y_{j,p}$ to R, $y_{j,p}$ being the j-th element of the desired output vector for sample p.

3) Least squares fit the linear model parameters of cluster c to predict the current residuals R, and subtract the (new) estimate, $\mu_p^c \hat{y}_{j,p}$, from R.

4) Do 2-4 for each cluster and repeat the fitting several times (default: 3).

From simulations we found that the above fast optimization method converges to the global minimum if it is repeated many times. Just as with neural network training, it is often better to use early stopping when the prediction error on an independent test set starts to increase.

4. Nonlinear Principal Component Analysis

To learn a chaotic attractor from a single experimental time-series we use the *method of delays*: the state $\vec{z}$ consists of m delays taken from the time series. The embedding dimension m must be chosen large enough to ensure that it contains sufficient information for faithful reconstruction of the chaotic attractor, see Takens [9]. Typically, this results in an m-dimensional state space with all the measurements covering only a much lower dimensional, but non-linearly shaped, subspace. This creates the danger pointed out in Sec. 2: the stability of the model in directions perpendicular to this low dimensional subspace cannot be guaranteed.

With the split & fit algorithm from Sec. 3 we can learn the non-linear shape of the low dimensional subspace, and, if the state of the system escapes from this subspace, we use the algorithm to redirect the state to the nearest point on the subspace. See Malthouse [10] for limitations of existing nonlinear PCA approaches. To obtain the low dimensional subspace, we proceed according to Procedure 5.

Procedure 5. Learning the Low-dimensional Subspace
1) Augment the output of the model with the m-dimensional state $\vec{z}$: the model will learn to predict its own input.
2) In each cluster c, perform a singular value decomposition to create a set of m principal directions, sorted in order of decreasing explained variance. The result of this decomposition is also used in step 3 of Procedure 4.
3) Allow the local linear model of each cluster to use no more than m_{red} of these principal directions.
4) Define a potential P to be the squared Euclidian distance between the state $\vec{z}$ and its prediction by the model.

The potential P implicitly defines the lower dimensional subspace: if a state $\vec{z}$ is on the subspace, P will be zero. P will increase with the distance of $\vec{z}$ from the subspace. The model has learned to predict its own input with small error, meaning that it has tried to reduce P as much as possible at exactly those points in state space where the training data was sampled. In other words, P will be low if the input $\vec{z}$ is close to one of the original points in the training data set. From the split&fit algorithm we can analytically compute the gradient $dP/d\vec{z}$. Since the evaluation of the split&fit model involves a backward (computing the bandwidths) and forward pass (computing memberships), the gradient algorithm involves a forward and backward pass through the tree. The gradient is used to project states that are off the nonlinear subspace onto the subspace

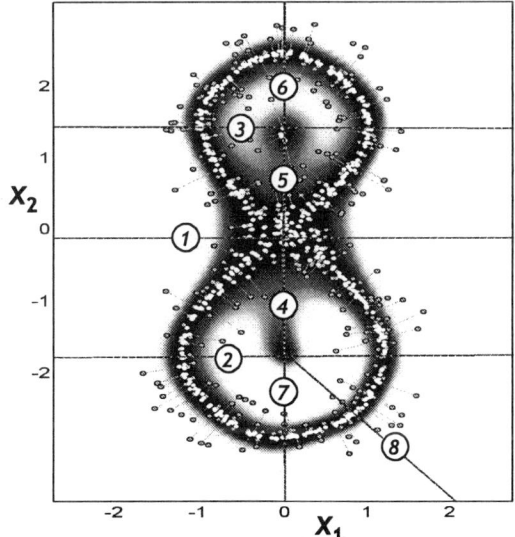

Figure 2. Projecting two-dimensional data on a one-dimensional self-intersecting subspace. The colorscale represents the potential P, white indicates $P>0.04$..

in one or a few Newton-Rhapson iterations. Figure 2 illustrates the algorithm for the problem of creating a one-dimensional representation of the number '8'. The training set consists of 136 clean samples, and Fig. 2 shows how a set of 272 noisy inputs is projected by a 48 subset split&fit model onto the one-dimensional subspace. Note that the center of the '8' cannot be well represented by a one-dimensional space. We leave development of an algorithm that automatically detects the optimum local subspace dimension for future research.

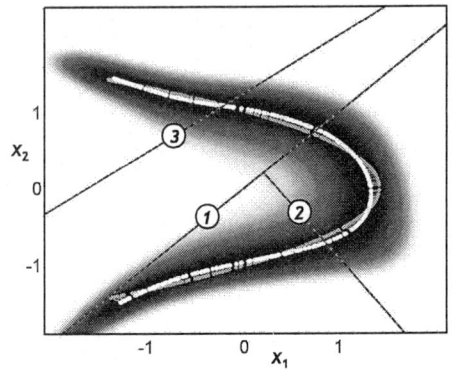

Figure 3. Learning the attractor of the two-input logistic map. The order of creation of the splits is indicated. The colorscale represents the potential P, white indicates $P>0.05$.

5. Application Examples

First we show the nonlinear principal component analysis result for a toy example, the logistic map $z_{t+1} = 4z_t(1-z_t)$. If we use a model $z_{t+1} = F_{\bar{w}}(z_t)$, where the prediction only depends on one previous output, there is no lower dimensional space to which the attractor is confined. However, if we allow the output to depend on more than a single delay, we create a possibility for unstable behavior. Figure 3 shows how well the split&fit algorithm learns the one-dimensional shape of the attractor after creating only five regions. The parabola is slightly deformed (seen from the white lines perpendicular to the attractor), but this may be solved by increasing the number of splits.

Next we look at the laser data. The complex behavior of chaotic systems is caused by an interplay of destabilizing and stabilizing forces: the destabilizing forces make nearby points in state space diverge, while the stabilizing forces keep the state of the system bounded. This process, known as 'stretching and folding', results in the attractor of the system: the set of points that the state of the system will visit after all transients have died out. In the case of the laser data this behavior is clear cut: destabilizing forces make the signal grow exponentially until the increasing amplitude triggers a collapse that reinitiates the sequence. We have seen in neural network based models [3] and in this study that it is very hard for the models to cope with the sudden collapses. Without the nonlinear subspace correction of Sec. 4, most of the

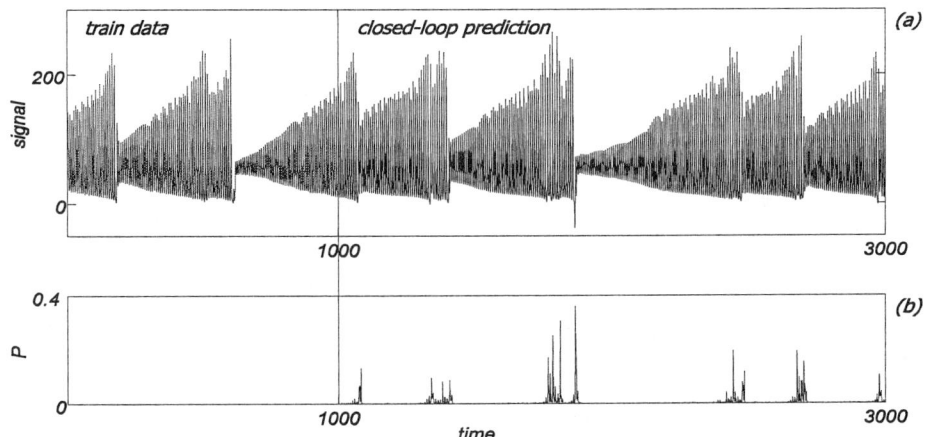

Figure 4. Laser data from the Santa Fe time series competition. The 1000 sample train data set is followed by iterated prediction of the model (a). After every prediction a correction is made to keep P (see Sec. 4) small. Plot (b) shows P before this correction.

models we tested grow without bounds after one or more rise and collapse sequences. That is not very surprising - the training data set contains only three examples of a collapse. Figure 4 shows how this is solved with the subspace correction: every time the model is about to grow to infinity, a high potential P is detected (depicted in Fig. 3b) and the state of the system is directed to the nearest point on the subspace as learned from the nonlinear principal component analysis. After some trial and error, we selected an embedding dimension m of 12 and a reduced dimension m_{red} of 4. The split&fit model starts with a single dataset, and was grown until 48 subsets. At that point, the error on the 1000 sample train set was still decreasing rapidly but the error on an independent 1000 sample test set increased. We compared the reconstructed attractors of the model and measurements, using 9000 samples of closed-loop generated and 9000 samples of measured data. No significant difference between the two could be detected by the Diks test [7].

6. Conclusions

We present an algorithm that robustly models chaotic attractors. It simultaneously learns (1) to make accurate short term predictions; and (2) the outlines of the attractor. In closed-loop prediction mode, the state of the system is corrected after every prediction, to stay within these outlines. The algorithm is very fast, since the main computation is to least squares fit a set of local linear models. In our implementation the largest matrix to be stored is N by C, N being the number of data and C the number of clusters. We see many applications other than attractor learning: the split&fit algorithm can be used as a fast learning alternative to neural networks and the new form of nonlinear PCA will be useful for data reduction and object recognition. We envisage to apply the technique to a wide range of applications, from the control and modeling of chaos in fluid dynamics to problems in finance and biology to fluid dynamics.

Acknowledgements

This work is supported by the Netherlands Foundation for Chemical Research (SON) with financial aid from the Netherlands Organization for Scientific Research (NWO).

References

[1] J.C. Principe, A. Rathie, and J.M. Kuo, "Prediction of Chaotic Time Series with Neural Networks and the Issue of Dynamic Modeling", *Int. J. Bifurcation and Chaos*, 2, 1992, p 989.

[2] J.M. Kuo, and J.C. Principe, "Reconstructed Dynamics and Chaotic Signal Modeling", In *Proc. IEEE Int'l Conf. Neural Networks*, 5, 1994, p 3131.

[3] R. Bakker, J.C. Schouten, C.L. Giles, F. Takens, C.M. van den Bleek, "Learning Chaotic Attractors by Neural Networks", submitted.

[4] J.C. Principe, L. Wang, M.A. Motter, "Local Dynamic Modeling with Self-Organizing Maps and Applications to Nonlinear System Identification and Control",*Proc. IEEE*, 86(11), 1998.

[5] N. Kambhatla, T.K. Leen, "Dimension Reduction by Local PCA", *Neural Computation*, 9, 1997, p. 1493

[6] M.I. Jordan, R.A. Jacobs, "Hierarchical Mixtures of Experts and the EM Algorithm", *Neural Compution*, 6, 1994, p. 181.

[7] C. Diks, W.R. van Zwet, F. Takens, and J. de Goede, "Detecting differences between delay vector distributions", *Physical Review E*, 53, 1996, p. 2169.

[8] A. Lapedes, R. Farber, "Nonlinear Signal Processing Using Neural Networks: Prediction and System Modelling", *Los Alamos Technical Report* LA-UR-87-2662.

[9] F. Takens, "Detecting strange attractors in turbulence", *Lecture notes in Mathematics*, **898**, 1981, p. 365.

[10] E.C. Malthouse, "Limitations of Nonlinear PCA as performed with Generic Neural Networks, *IEEE Trans. Neural Networks*, 9(1), 1998, p. 165.

Image representations for facial expression coding

Marian Stewart Bartlett[*]
U.C. San Diego
marni@salk.edu

Gianluca Donato
Digital Persona, Redwood City, CA
gianlucad@digitalpersona.com

Javier R. Movellan
U.C. San Diego
movellan@cogsci.ucsd.edu

Joseph C. Hager
Network Information Res., SLC, Utah
jchager@ibm.com

Paul Ekman
U.C. San Francisco
ekman@compuserve.com

Terrence J. Sejnowski
Howard Hughes Medical Institute
The Salk Institute; U.C. San Diego
terry@salk.edu

Abstract

The Facial Action Coding System (FACS) (9) is an objective method for quantifying facial movement in terms of component actions. This system is widely used in behavioral investigations of emotion, cognitive processes, and social interaction. The coding is presently performed by highly trained human experts. This paper explores and compares techniques for automatically recognizing facial actions in sequences of images. These methods include unsupervised learning techniques for finding basis images such as principal component analysis, independent component analysis and local feature analysis, and supervised learning techniques such as Fisher's linear discriminants. These data-driven bases are compared to Gabor wavelets, in which the basis images are predefined. Best performances were obtained using the Gabor wavelet representation and the independent component representation, both of which achieved 96% accuracy for classifying 12 facial actions. The ICA representation employs 2 orders of magnitude fewer basis images than the Gabor representation and takes 90% less CPU time to compute for new images. The results provide converging support for using local basis images, high spatial frequencies, and statistical independence for classifying facial actions.

1 Introduction

Facial expressions provide information not only about affective state, but also about cognitive activity, temperament and personality, truthfulness, and psychopathology. The Facial Action Coding System (FACS) (9) is the leading method for measuring facial movement in behavioral science. FACS is performed manually by highly trained human experts. A FACS coder decomposes a facial expression into component muscle movements (Figure 1). Ekman and Friesen described 46 distinct facial movements, and over 7000 distinct combinations of such movements have

---

[*] To whom correspondence should be addressed. (UCSD 0523, La Jolla, CA 92093.) This research was supported by NIH Grant No. 1F32 MH12417-01.

been observed in spontaneous behavior. An automated system would make facial expression measurement more widely accessible as a research tool for behavioral science and medicine. Such a system would also have application in human-computer interaction tools and low bandwidth facial animation coding.

A number of systems have appeared in the computer vision literature for classifying facial expressions into a few basic categories of emotion, such as happy, sad, or surprised. While such approaches are important, an objective and detailed measure of facial activity such as FACS is needed for basic research into facial behavior. In a system being developed concurrently for automatic facial action coding, Cohn and colleagues (7) employ feature point tracking of a select set of image points. Techniques employing 2-D image filters have proven to be more effective than feature-based representations for face image analysis [e.g. (6)]. Here we examine image analysis techniques that densely analyze graylevel information in the face image.

This work surveys and compares techniques for face image analysis as applied to automated FACS encoding.[1] The analysis focuses on methods for face image representation in which image graylevels are described as a linear superposition of basis images. The techniques were compared on a common image testbed using common similarity measures and classifiers.

We compared four representations in which the basis images were learned from the statistics of the face image ensemble. These include unsupervised learning techniques such as principal component analysis (PCA), and local feature analysis (LFA), which are learned from the second-order dependences among the image pixels, and independent component analysis (ICA) which is learned from the high-order dependencies as well. We also examined a representation obtained through supervised learning on the second-order image statistics, Fisher's linear discriminants (FLD). Classification performances with these data-driven basis images were compared to Gabor wavelets, in which the basis images were pre-defined. We examined properties of optimal basis images, where optimal was defined in terms of classification.

Generalization to novel faces was evaluated using leave-one-out cross-validation. Two basic classifiers were employed: nearest neighbor and template matching, where the templates were the mean feature vectors for each class. Two similarity measures were employed for each classifier: Euclidean distance and cosine of the angle between feature vectors.

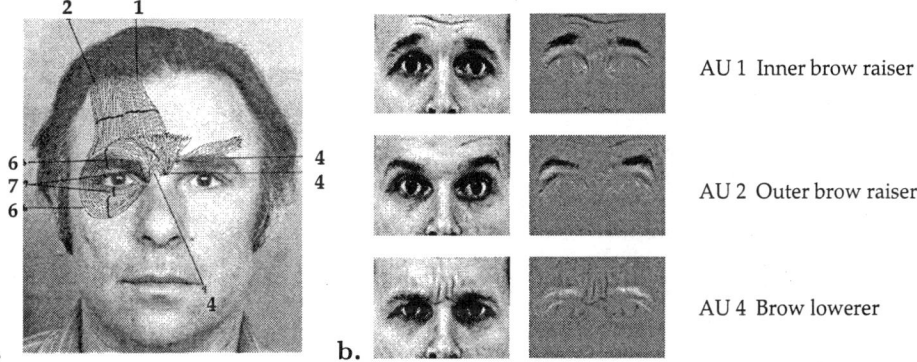

Figure 1: a. The facial muscles underlying six of the 46 facial actions. b. Cropped face images and δ-images for three facial actions (AU's).

---

[1] A detailed description of this work appears in (8).

2 Image Database

We collected a database of image sequences of subjects performing specified facial actions. The database consisted of image sequences of subjects performing specified facial actions. Each sequence began with a neutral expression and ended with a high magnitude muscle contraction. For this investigation, we used 111 sequences from 20 subjects and attempted to classify 12 actions: 6 upper face actions and 6 lower face actions. Upper and lower-face actions were analyzed separately since facial motions in the lower face do not effect the upper face, and vice versa (9).

The face was located in the first frame in each sequence using the centers of the eyes and mouth. These coordinates were obtained manually by a mouse click. The coordinates from Frame 1 were used to register the subsequent frames in the sequence. The aspect ratios of the faces were warped so that the eye and mouth centers coincided across all images. The three coordinates were then used to rotate the eyes to horizontal, scale, and finally crop a window of 60 × 90 pixels containing the upper or lower face. To control for variations in lighting, logistic thresholding and luminance scaling was performed (13). Difference images (δ-images) were obtained by subtracting the neutral expression in the first image of each sequence from the subsequent images in the sequence.

3 Unsupervised learning

3.1 Eigenfaces (PCA)

A number of approaches to face image analysis employ data-driven basis vectors learned from the statistics of the face image ensemble. Techniques such as eigenfaces (17) employ principal component analysis, which is an unsupervised learning method based on the second-order dependencies among the pixels (the pixelwise covariances). PCA has been applied successfully to recognizing facial identity (17), and full facial expressions (14).

Here we performed PCA on the dataset of δ-images, where each δ-image comprised a point in R^n given by the brightness of the n pixels. The PCA basis images were the eigenvectors of the covariance matrix (see Figure 2a), and the first p components comprised the representation. Multiple ranges of components were tested, from $p = 10$ to $p = 200$, and performance was also tested excluding the first 1-3 components. Best performance of 79.3% correct was obtained with the first 30 principal components, using the Euclidean distance similarity measure and template matching classifier.

Padgett and Cottrell (14) found that a local PCA representation outperformed global PCA for classifying full facial expressions of emotion. Following the methods in (14), a set of local basis images was derived from the principal components of 15×15 image patches from randomly sampled locations in the δ-images (see Figure 2d.) The first p principal components comprised a basis set for all image locations, and the representation was downsampled by a factor of 4. Best performance of 73.4% was obtained with components 2-30, using Euclidean distance and template matching. Unlike the findings in (14), local basis images obtained through PCA were not more effective than global PCA for facial action coding. A second local implementation of PCA, in which the principal components were calculated for *fixed* 15×15 image patches also failed to improve over global PCA.

3.2 Local Feature Analysis (LFA)

Penev and Atick (15) recently developed a local, topographic representation based on second-order image statistics called local feature analysis (LFA). The kernels are derived from the principal component axes, and consist of a "whitening" step to equalize the variance of the PCA coefficients, followed by a rotation to pixel space.

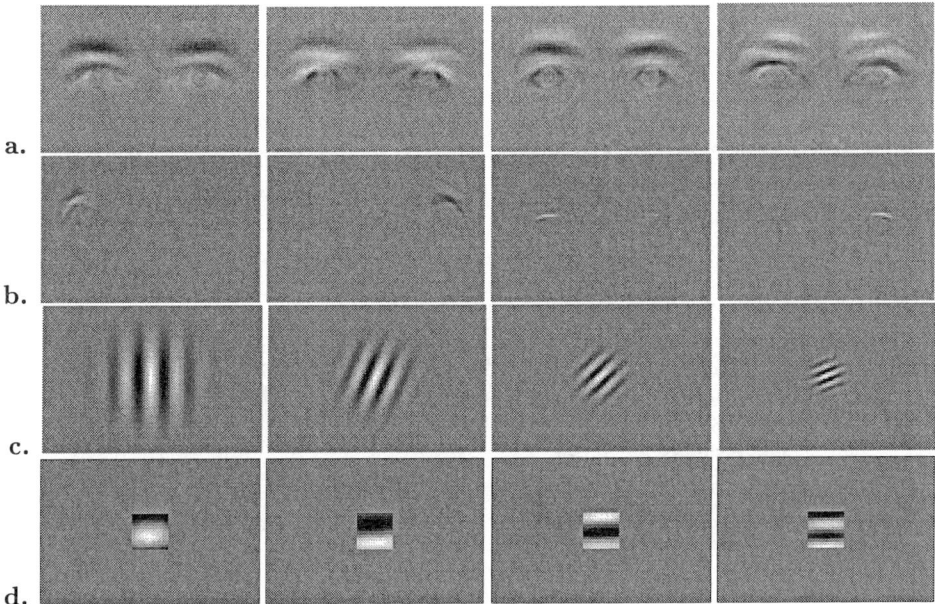

Figure 2: a. First 4 PCA basis images. b. Four ICA basis images. The ICA basis images are local, spatially opponent, and adaptive. c. Gabor kernels are local, spatially opponent, and predefined. d. First 4 local PCA basis images.

We begin with the matrix P containing the principal component eigenvectors in its columns, and λ_i are the corresponding eigenvalues. Each row of the matrix K serves as an element of the LFA image dictionary[2]

$$K = PVP^T \quad \text{where} \quad V = D^{-\frac{1}{2}} = \text{diag}(\frac{1}{\sqrt{\lambda_i}}) \quad i = 1,\ldots,p \qquad (1)$$

where λ_i are the eigenvalues. The rows of K were found to have spatially local properties, and are "topographic" in the sense that they are indexed by spatial location (15). The dimensionality of the LFA representation was reduced by employing an iterative sparsification algorithm based on multiple linear regression described in (15).

The LFA representation attained 81.1% correct classification performance. Best performance was obtained using the first 155 kernels, the cosine similarity measure, and nearest neighbor classifier. Classification performance using LFA was not significantly different from the performance using PCA. Although a face recognition algorithm based on the principles of LFA outperformed Eigenfaces in the March 1995 FERET competition, the exact algorithm has not been disclosed. Our results suggest that an aspect of the algorithm other than the LFA representation accounts for the difference in performance.

3.3 Independent Component Analysis (ICA)

Representations such as Eigenfaces, LFA, and FLD are based on the second-order dependencies among the pixels, but are insensitive to the high-order dependencies. High-order dependencies are relationships that cannot be described by a linear predictor. Independent component analysis (ICA) learns the high-order dependencies in addition to the second-order dependencies among the pixels.

---

[2] An image dictionary is a set of images that decomposes other images, e.g. through inner product. Here it finds the coefficients for the basis set K^{-1}

The ICA representation was obtained by performing Bell & Sejnowski's infomax algorithm (4) (5) on the ensemble of δ–images in the rows of the matrix X. The images in X were assumed to be a linear mixture of an unknown set of independent source images which were recovered through ICA. In contrast to PCA, the ICA source images were local in nature (see Figure 2b). These source images provided a basis set for the expression images. The coefficients of each image with respect to the new basis set were obtained from the estimated mixing matrix $A \triangleq W^{-1}$, where W is the ICA weight matrix [see (1), (2)].

Unlike PCA, there is no inherent ordering to the independent components of the dataset. We therefore selected as an ordering parameter the class discriminability of each component, defined as the ratio of between-class to within-class variance. Best performance of 95.5% was obtained with the first 75 components selected by class discriminability, using the cosine similarity measure, and nearest neighbor classifier. Independent component analysis gave the best performance among all of the data-driven image kernels. Class discriminability analysis of a PCA representation was previously found to have little effect on classification performance with PCA (2).

4 Supervised learning: Fisher's Linear Discriminants (FLD)

A class specific linear projection of a PCA representation of faces was recently shown to improve identity recognition performance (3). The method employs a classic pattern recognition technique, Fisher's linear discriminant (FLD), to project the images into a $c - 1$ dimensional subspace in which the c classes are maximally separated. Best performance was obtained by choosing $p = 30$ principal components to first reduce the dimensionality of the data. The data was then projected down to 5 dimensions via the FLD projection matrix, W_{fld}. The FLD image dictionary was thus $W_{pca} * W_{fld}$. Best performance of 75.7% correct was obtained with the Euclidean distance similarity measure and template matching classifier.

FLD provided a much more compact representation than PCA. However, unlike the results obtained by (3) for identity recognition, Fisher's Linear Discriminants did not improve over basic PCA (Eigenfaces) for facial action classification. The difference in performance may be due to the low dimensionality of the final representation here. Class discriminations that are approximately linear in high dimensions may not be linear when projected down to as few as 5 dimensions.

5 Predefined image kernels: Gabor wavelets

An alternative to the adaptive bases described above are wavelet decompositions based on predefined families of Gabor kernels. Gabor kernels are 2-D sine waves modulated by a Gaussian (Figure 2c). Representations employing families of Gabor filters at multiple spatial scales, orientations, and spatial locations have proven successful for recognizing facial identity in images (11). Here, the δ–images were convolved with a family of Gabor kernels ψ_i, defined as

$$\psi_i(\vec{x}) = \frac{\|\vec{k}_i\|^2}{\sigma^2} e^{-\frac{\|\vec{k}_i\|^2 \|\vec{x}\|^2}{2\sigma^2}} \left[e^{j\vec{k}_i \vec{x}} - e^{-\frac{\sigma^2}{2}} \right] \quad (2)$$

where $\vec{k}_i = \begin{pmatrix} f_\nu \cos\varphi_\mu \\ f_\nu \sin\varphi_\mu \end{pmatrix}$, $f_\nu = 2^{-\frac{\nu+2}{2}} \pi$, $\varphi_\mu = \mu \frac{\pi}{8}$.

Following (11), the representation consisted of the amplitudes at 5 frequencies ($\nu = 0 - 4$) and 8 orientations ($\mu = 1 - 8$). Each filter output was downsampled by a factor q and normalized to unit length. We tested the performance of the system using $q = 1, 4, 16$ and found that $q = 16$ yielded the best generalization rate. Best performance was obtained with the cosine similarity measure and nearest neighbor classifier. Classification performance with the Gabor representation was 95.5%. This performance was significantly higher than all of the data-driven approaches in the comparison except independent component analysis, with which it tied.

6 Results and Conclusions

PCA	Local PCA	LFA	ICA	FLD	Gabor
79.3 ±3.9	73.4 ±4.2	81.1 ±3.7	95.5 ±2.0	75.7 ±4.1	95.5 ±2.0

Table 1: Summary of classification performance for 12 facial actions.

We have compared a number of different image analysis methods on a difficult classification problem, the classification of facial actions. Best performances were obtained with the Gabor and ICA representations, which both achieved 95.5% correct classification (see Table 1). The performance of these two methods equaled the agreement level of expert human subjects on these images (94%). Image representations derived from the second-order statistics of the dataset (PCA and LFA) performed in the 80% accuracy range. An image representation derived from supervised learning on the second-order statistics (FLD) also did not significantly differ from PCA. We also obtained evidence that high spatial frequencies are important for classifying facial actions. Classification with the three highest frequencies of the Gabor representation ($\nu = 0, 1, 2$, cycles/face $= 15, 18, 21$ cycles/face) was 93% compared to 84% with the three lowest frequencies ($\nu = 2, 3, 4$, cycles/face $= 9, 12, 15$).

The two representations that significantly outperformed the others, Gabor and Independent Components, employed local basis images, which supports recent findings that local basis images are important for face image analysis (14) (10) (12). The local property alone, however, does not account for the good performance of these two representations, as LFA performed no better than PCA on this classification task, nor did local implementations of PCA.

In addition to spatial locality, the ICA representation and the Gabor filter representation share the property of redundancy reduction, and have relationships to representations in the visual cortex. The response properties of primary visual cortical cells are closely modeled by a bank of Gabor kernels. Relationships have been demonstrated between Gabor kernels and independent component analysis. Bell & Sejnowski (5) found using ICA that the kernels that produced independent outputs from natural scenes were spatially local, oriented edge kernels, similar to a bank of Gabor kernels. It has also been shown that Gabor filter outputs of natural images are at least pairwise independent (16).

The Gabor wavelets and ICA each provide a way to represent face images as a linear superposition of basis functions. Gabor wavelets employ a set of pre-defined basis images, whereas ICA learns basis images that are adapted to the data ensemble. The Gabor wavelets are not specialized to the particular data ensemble, but would be advantageous when the amount of data is small. The ICA representation has the advantage of employing two orders of magnitude fewer basis images. This can be an advantage for classifiers that involve parameter estimation. In addition, the ICA representation takes 90% less CPU time than the Gabor representation to compute once the ICA weights are learned, which need only be done once.

In summary, this comparison provided converging support for using local basis images, high spatial frequencies, and statistical independence for classifying facial actions. Best performances were obtained with Gabor wavelet decomposition and independent component analysis. These two representations employ graylevel basis functions that share properties of spatial locality, independence, and have relationships to the response properties of visual cortical neurons.

An outstanding issue is whether our findings depend on the simple recognition engines we employed. Would a smarter recognition engine alter the relative performances? Our preliminary investigations suggest that is not the case. Hidden Markov models (HMM's) were trained on the PCA, ICA and Gabor representations. The Gabor representation was reduced to 75 dimensions using PCA before training the HMM. The HMM improved classification performance with ICA to 96.3%, and it did not change the overall findings, as it gave similar percent improvements to the PCA and PCA-reduced Gabor representations over their nearest neighbor performances. The dimensionality reduction of the Gabor representation, however, caused its nearest neighbor performance to drop, and the performance with the HMM was 92.7%. The lower dimensionality of the ICA representation was an advantage when employing the HMM.

7 References

[1] M.S. Bartlett. *Face Image Analysis by Unsupervised Learning and Redundancy Reduction*. PhD thesis, University of California, San Diego, 1998.

[2] M.S. Bartlett, H.M. Lades, and T.J. Sejnowski. Independent component representations for face recognition. In T. Rogowitz, B. & Pappas, editor, *Proceedings of the SPIE Symposium on Electonic Imaging: Science and Technology; Human Vision and Electronic Imaging III*, volume 3299, pages 528–539, San Jose, CA, 1998. SPIE Press.

[3] P.N. Belhumeur, J.P. Hespanha, and D.J. Kriegman. Eigenfaces vs. fisherfaces: Recognition using class specific linear projection. *IEEE Transations on Pattern Analysis and Machine Intelligence*, 19(7):711–720, 1997.

[4] A.J. Bell and T.J. Sejnowski. An information-maximization approach to blind separation and blind deconvolution. *Neural Computation*, 7(6):1129–1159, 1995.

[5] A.J. Bell and T.J. Sejnowski. The independent components of natural scenes are edge filters. *Vision Research*, 37(23):3327–3338, 1997.

[6] R. Brunelli and T. Poggio. Face recognition: Features versus templates. *IEEE transactions on pattern analysis and machine intelligence*, 15(10):1042–1052, 1993.

[7] J.F. Cohn, A.J. Zlochower, J.J. Lien, Y-T Wu, and T. Kanade. Automated face coding: A computer-vision based method of facial expression analysis. *Psychophysiology*, 35(1):35–43, 1999.

[8] G. Donato, M. Bartlett, J. Hager, P. Ekman, and T. Sejnowski. Classifying facial actions. *IEEE Transactions on Pattern Analysis and Machine Intelligence*, 21(10):974–989, 1999.

[9] P. Ekman and W. Friesen. *Facial Action Coding System: A Technique for the Measurement of Facial Movement*. Consulting Psychologists Press, Palo Alto, CA, 1978.

[10] M.S. Gray, J. Movellan, and T.J. Sejnowski. A comparison of local versus global image decomposition for visual speechreading. In *Proceedings of the 4th Joint Symposium on Neural Computation*, pages 92–98. Institute for Neural Computation, La Jolla, CA, 92093-0523, 1997.

[11] M. Lades, J. Vorbrüggen, J. Buhmann, J. Lange, W. Konen, C. von der Malsburg, and R. Würtz. Distortion invariant object recognition in the dynamic link architecture. *IEEE Transactions on Computers*, 42(3):300–311, 1993.

[12] D.D. Lee and S. Seung. Learning the parts of objects by non-negative matrix factorization. *Nature*, 401:788–791, 1999.

[13] J.R. Movellan. Visual speech recognition with stochastic networks. In G. Tesauro, D.S. Touretzky, and T. Leen, editors, *Advances in Neural Information Processing Systems*, volume 7, pages 851–858. MIT Press, Cambridge, MA, 1995.

[14] C. Padgett and G. Cottrell. Representing face images for emotion classification. In M. Mozer, M. Jordan, and T. Petsche, editors, *Advances in Neural Information Processing Systems*, volume 9, Cambridge, MA, 1997. MIT Press.

[15] P.S. Penev and J.J. Atick. Local feature analysis: a general statistical theory for object representation. *Network: Computation in Neural Systems*, 7(3):477–500, 1996.

[16] E. P. Simoncelli. Statistical models for images: Compression, restoration and synthesis. In *31st Asilomar Conference on Signals, Systems and Computers*, Pacific Grove, CA, November 2-5 1997.

[17] M. Turk and A. Pentland. Eigenfaces for recognition. *Journal of Cognitive Neuroscience*, 3(1):71–86, 1991.

Low Power Wireless Communication via Reinforcement Learning

Timothy X Brown
Electrical and Computer Engineering
University of Colorado
Boulder, CO 80309-0530
timxb@colorado.edu

Abstract

This paper examines the application of reinforcement learning to a wireless communication problem. The problem requires that channel utility be maximized while simultaneously minimizing battery usage. We present a solution to this multi-criteria problem that is able to significantly reduce power consumption. The solution uses a variable discount factor to capture the effects of battery usage.

1 Introduction

Reinforcement learning (RL) has been applied to resource allocation problems in telecommunications, e.g., channel allocation in wireless systems, network routing, and admission control in telecommunication networks [1, 2, 8, 10]. These have demonstrated reinforcement learning can find good policies that significantly increase the application reward within the dynamics of the telecommunication problems. However, a key issue is how to treat the commonly occurring multiple reward and constraint criteria in a consistent way.

This paper will focus on power management for wireless packet communication channels. These channels are unlike wireline channels in that channel quality is poor and varies over time, and often one side of the wireless link is a battery operated device such as a laptop computer. In this environment, power management decides when to transmit and receive so as to simultaneously maximize channel utility and battery life.

A number of power management strategies have been developed for different aspects of battery operated computer systems such as the hard disk and CPU [4, 5]. Managing the channel is different in that some control actions such as shutting off the wireless transmitter make the state of the channel and the other side of the communication unobservable.

In this paper, we consider the problem of finding a power management policy that simultaneously maximizes the radio communication's earned revenue while minimizing battery usage. The problem is recast as a stochastic shortest path problem which in turn is mapped to a discounted infinite horizon with a variable discount factor. Results show significant reductions in power usage.

Figure 1: The five components of the radio communication system.

2 Problem Description

The problem is comprised of five components as shown in Figure 1: mobile application, mobile radio, wireless channel, base station radio, and base station application. The applications on each end generate packets that are sent via a radio across the channel to the radio and then application on the other side. The application also defines the utility of a given end-to-end performance. The radios implement a simple acknowledgment/retransmit protocol for reliable transmission. The base station is fixed and has a reliable power supply and therefore is not power constrained. The mobile power is limited by a battery and it can choose to turn its radio off for periods of time to reduce power usage. Note that even with the radio off, the mobile system continues to draw power for other uses. The channel adds errors to the packets. The rate of errors depends on many factors such as location of mobile and base station, intervening distance, and levels of interference. The problem requires models for each of these components. To be concrete, the specific models used in this paper are described in the following sections. It should be emphasized that in order to focus on the machine learning issues, simple models have been chosen. More sophisticated models can readily be included.

2.1 The Channel

The channel carries fixed-size packets in synchronous time slots. All packet rates are normalized by the channel rate so that the channel carries one packet per unit time in each direction. The forward and reverse channels are orthogonal and do not interfere.

Wireless data channels typically have low error rates. Occasionally, due to interference or signal fading, the channel introduces many errors. This variation is possible even when the mobile and base station are stationary. The channel is modeled by a two state Gilbert-Elliot model [3]. In this model, the channel is in either a "good" or a "bad" state with a packet error probabilities p_g and p_b where $p_g < p_b$. The channel is symmetric with the same loss rate in both directions. The channel stays in each state with a geometrically distributed holding time with mean holding times h_g and h_b time slots.

2.2 Mobile and Base Station Application

The traffic generated by the source is a bursty ON/OFF model that alternates between generating no packets and generating packets at rate r_{ON}. The holding times are geometrically distributed with mean holding times h_{ON} and h_{OFF}. The traffic in each direction is independent and identically distributed.

2.3 The Radios

The radios can transmit data from the application and send it on the channel and simultaneously receive data from the other radio and pass it on to its application. The radios implement a simple packet protocol to ensure reliability. Packets from the sources are queued in the radio and sent one by one. Packets consist of a header and data. The header carries acknowledgements (ACK's) with the most recent packet received without error. The header contains a checksum so that errors in the payload can be detected. Errored packets

Parameter Name	Symbol	Value
Channel Error Rate, Good	p_g	0.01
Channel Error Rate, Bad	p_b	0.20
Channel Holding Time, Good	h_g	100
Channel Holding Time, Bad	h_b	10
Source On Rate	r_{ON}	1.0
Source Holding Time, On	h_{ON}	1
Source Holding Time, Off	h_{OFF}	10
Power, Radio Off	P_{OFF}	7 W
Power, Radio On	P_{ON}	8.5 W
Power, Radio Transmitting	P_{TX}	10 W
Real Time Max Delay	d_{max}	3
Web Browsing Time Scale	d_0	3

Table 1: Application parameters.

cause the receiving radio to send a packet with a negative acknowledgment (NACK) to the other radio instructing it to retransmit the packet sequence starting from the errored packet. The NACK is sent immediately even if no data is waiting and the radio must send an empty packet. Only unerrored packets are sent on to the application. The header is assumed to always be received without error[1].

Since the mobile is constrained by power, the mobile is considered the master and the base station the slave. The base station is always on and ready to transmit or receive. The mobile can turn its radio off to conserve power. Every ON-OFF and OFF-ON transition generates a packet with a message in the header indicating the change of state to the base station. These message packets carry no data. The mobile expends power at three levels—P_{OFF}, P_{ON}, and P_{tx}—corresponding to the radio off, receiver on but no packet transmitted, and receiver on packet transmitted.

2.4 Reward Criteria

Reward is earned for packets passed in each direction. The amount depends on the application. In this paper we consider three types of applications, an e-mail application, a real-time application, and a web browsing application. In the e-mail application, a unit reward is given for every packet received by the application. In the real time application a unit reward is given for every packet received by the application with delay less than d_{max}. The reward is zero otherwise. In the web browsing application, time is important but not critical. The value of a packet with delay d is $(1 - 1/d_0)^d$, where d_0 is the desired time scale of the arrivals.

The specific parameters used in this experiment are given in Table 1. These were gathered as typical values from [7, 9]. It should be emphasized that this model is the simplest model that captures the essential characteristics of the problem. More realistic channels, protocols, applications, and rewards can readily be incorporated but for this paper are left out for clarity.

---

[1] A packet error rate of 20% implies a bit error rate of less than 1%. Error correcting codes in the header can easily reduce this error rate to a low value. The main intent is to simplify the protocol for this paper so that time-outs and other mechanisms do not need to be considered.

Component	States
Channel	{good,bad}
Application	{ON,OFF}
Mobile	{ON,OFF}
Mobile	{List of waiting and unacknowledged packets and their current delay}
Base Station	{List of waiting and unacknowledged packets and their current delay}

Table 2: Components to System State.

3 Markov Decision Processes

At any given time slot, t, the system is in a particular configuration, x, defined by the state of each of the components in Table 2. The system state is $s = (x, t)$ where we include the time in order to facilitate accounting for the battery. The mobile can choose to toggle its radio between the ON and OFF state and rewards are generated by successfully received packets. The task of the learner is to determine a radio ON/OFF policy that maximizes the total reward for packets received before batteries run out.

The battery life is not a fixed time. First, it depends on usage. Second, for a given drain, the capacity depends on how long the battery was charged, how long it has sat since being charged, the age of the battery, etc. In short, the battery runs out at a random time. The system can be modeled as a stochastic shortest path problem whereby there exists a terminal state, s_0, that corresponds to the battery empty in which no more reward is possible and the system remains permanently at no cost.

3.1 Multi-criteria Objective

Formally, the goal is to learn a policy for each possible system state so as to *maximize*

$$J^\pi(s) = E\left\{ \sum_{t=0}^{T} c(t) \Bigg| s, \pi \right\},$$

where $E\{\cdot|s,\pi\}$ is the expectation over possible trajectories starting from state s using policy π, $c(t)$ is the reward for packets received at time t, and T is the last time step before the batteries run out.

Typically, T is very large and this inhibits fast learning. So, in order to promote faster learning we convert this problem to a discounted problem that removes the variance caused by the random stopping times. At time t, given action $a(t)$, while in state $s(t)$ the terminal state is reached with probability $p_{s(t)}(a(t))$. Setting the value of the terminal state to 0, we can convert our new criterion to maximize:

$$J^\pi(s) = E\left\{ \sum_{t=0}^{\infty} c(t) \prod_{\tau=0}^{t-1} (1 - p_{s(\tau)}(a(\tau))) \Bigg| s, \pi \right\},$$

where the product is the probability of reaching time t. In words, future rewards are discounted by $1 - p_s(a)$, and the discounting is larger for actions that drain the batteries faster. Thus a more power efficient strategy will have a discount factor closer to one which correctly extends the effective horizon over which reward is captured.

3.2 Q-learning

RL methods solve MDP problems by learning good approximations to the optimal value function, J^*, given by the solution to the Bellman optimality equation which takes the following form:

$$J^*(s) = \max_{a \in A(s)} [E_{s'}\{c(s,a,s') + (1-p_s(a))J^*(s')\}] \quad (1)$$

where $A(s)$ is the set of actions available in the current state s, $c(s,a,s')$ is the effective immediate payoff, and $E_{s'}\{\cdot\}$ is the expectation over possible next states s'.

We learn an approximation to J^* using Watkin's Q-learning algorithm. Bellman's equation can be rewritten in Q-factor as

$$J^*(s) = \max_{a \in A(s)} Q^*(s,a) \quad (2)$$

In every time step the following decision is made. The Q-value of turning on in the next state is compared to the Q-value of turning off in the next state. If turning on has higher value the mobile turns on. Else, the mobile turns off.

Whatever our decision, we update our value function as follows: on a transition from state s to s' on action a,

$$Q(s,a) = (1-\gamma)Q(s,a) + \gamma\left(c(s,a,s') + (1-p_s(a))\max_{b \in A(s')} Q(s',b)\right) \quad (3)$$

where γ is the learning rate. In order for Q-learning to perform well, all potentially important state-action pairs (s,a) must be explored. At each state, with probability 0.1 we apply a random action instead of the action recommended by the Q-value. However, we still use (3) to update Q-values using the action b recommended by the Q-values.

3.3 Structural Limits to the State Space

For theoretical reasons it is desirable to use a table lookup representation. In practice, since the mobile radio decides using information available to it, this is impossible for the following reasons. The state of the channel is never known directly. The receiver only observes errored packets. It is possible to infer the state, but, only when packets are actually received and channel state changes introduce inference errors.

Traditional packet applications rarely communicate state information to the transport layer. This state information could also be inferred. But, given the quickly changing application dynamics, the application state is often ignored. For the particular parameters in Table 1, (i.e. $r_{ON} = 1.0$) the application is on if and only if it generates a packet so its state is completely specified by the packet arrivals and does not need to be inferred.

The most serious deficiency to a complete state space representation is that when the mobile radio turns OFF, it has no knowledge of state changes in the base station. Even when it is ON, the protocol does not have provisions for transferring directly the state information. Again, this implies that state information must be inferred.

One approach to these structural limits is to use a POMDP approach [6] which we leave to future work. In this paper, we simply learn deterministic policies on features that estimate the state.

3.4 Simplifying Assumptions

Beyond the structural problems of the previous section we must treat the usual problem that the state space is huge. For instance, assuming even moderate maximum queue sizes and maximum wait times yields 10^{20} states. If one considers e-mail like applications where

Component	Feature
Mobile Radio	is radio ON or OFF
Mobile Radio	number of packets waiting at the mobile
Mobile Radio	wait time of first packet waiting at the mobile
Channel	number of errors received in last 4 time slots
Base Radio	number of time slots since mobile was last ON

Table 3: Decision Features Measured by Mobile Radio

wait times of minutes (1000's of time slot wait times) with many packets waiting possible, the state space exceeds 10^{100} states. Thus we seek a representation to reduce the size and complexity of the state space. This reduction is taken in two parts. The first is a feature representation that is possible given the structural limits of the previous section, the second is a function approximation based on these feature vectors.

The feature vectors are listed in Table 3. These are chosen since they are measurable at the mobile radio. For function approximation, we use state aggregation since it provably converges.

4 Simulation Results

This section describes simulation-based experiments on the mobile radio control problem. For this initial study, we simplified the problem by setting $p_g = p_b = 0$ (i.e. no channel errors).

State aggregation was used with 4800 aggregate states. The battery termination probability, $p_s(a)$ was simply $P/1000$ where P is the power appropriate for the state and action chosen from Table 1. This was chosen to have an expected battery life much longer than the time scale of the traffic and channel processes.

Three policies were learned, one for each application reward criteria. The resulting policies are tested by simulating for 10^6 time slots.

In each test run, an upper and lower bound on the energy usage is computed. The upper bound is the case of the mobile radio always on[2]. The lower bound is a policy that ignores the reward criteria but still delivers all the packets. In this policy, the radio is off and packets are accumulated until the latter portion of the test run when they are sent in one large group. Policies are compared using the normalized power savings. This is a measure of how close the policy is to the lower bound with 0% and 100% being the upper and lower bound.

The results are given in Table 4. The table also lists the average reward per packet received by the application. For the e-mail application, which has no constraints on the packets, the average reward is identically one.

5 Conclusion

This paper showed that reinforcement learning was able to learn a policy that significantly reduced the power consumption of a mobile radio while maintaining a high application utility. It used a novel variable discount factor that captured the impact of different actions on battery life. This was able to gain 50% to 80% of the possible power savings.

---

[2]There exist policies that exceed this power, e.g. if they toggle ONand OFFoften and generate many notification packets. But, the always on policy is the baseline that we are trying to improve upon.

Application	Normalized Power Savings	Average Reward
E-mail	81%	1
Real Time	49%	1.00
Web Browsing	48%	0.46

Table 4: Simulation Results.

In the application the paper used a simple model of the radio, channel, battery, etc. It also used simple state aggregation and ignored the partially observable aspects of the problem. Future work will address more accurate models, function approximation, and POMDP approaches.

Acknowledgment

This work was supported by CAREER Award: NCR-9624791 and NSF Grant NCR-9725778.

References

[1] Boyan, J.A., Littman, M.L., "Packet routing in dynamically changing networks: a reinforcement learning approach," in Cowan, J.D., et al., ed. *Advances in NIPS 6*, Morgan Kauffman, SF, 1994. pp. 671–678.

[2] Brown, T.X, Tong, H., Singh, S., "Optimizing admission control while ensuring quality of service in multimedia networks via reinforcement learning," in *Advances in Neural Information Processing Systems 12*, ed. M. Kearns, et al., MIT Press, 1999, pp. 982–988.

[3] Goldsmith, A.J., Varaiya, P.P., "Capacity, mutual information, and coding for finite state Markov channels," *IEEE T. on Info. Thy.*, v. 42, pp. 868–886, May 1996.

[4] Govil, K., Chan, E., Wasserman, H., "Comparing algorithms for dynamic speed-setting of a low-power cpu," *Proceedings of the First ACM Int. Conf. on Mobile Computing and Networking (MOBICOM)*, 1995.

[5] Helmbold, D., Long, D.D.E., Sherrod, B., "A dynamic disk spin-down technique for mobile computing. *Proceedings of the Second ACM Int. Conf. on Mobile Computing and Networking (MOBICOM)*, 1996.

[6] Jaakola, T., Singh, S., Jordan, M.I., "Reinforcement Learning Algorithm for Partially Observable Markov Decision Problems," in *Advances in Neural Information Processing Systems 7*, ed. G. Tesauro, et al., MIT Press, 1995, pp. 345–352.

[7] Kravits, R., Krishnan, P., "Application-Driven Power Management for Mobile Communication," Wireless Networks, 1999.

[8] Marbach, P., Mihatsch, O., Schulte, M., Tsitsiklis, J.N., "Reinforcement learning for call admission control and routing in integrated service networks," in Jordan, M., et al., ed. *Advances in NIPS 10*, MIT Press, 1998.

[9] Rappaport, T.S., *Wireless Communications: Principles and Practice,* Prentice-Hall Pub., Englewood Cliffs, NJ, 1996.

[10] Singh, S.P., Bertsekas, D.P., "Reinforcement learning for dynamic channel allocation in cellular telephone systems," in *Advances in NIPS 9*, ed. Mozer, M., et al., MIT Press, 1997. pp. 974–980.

Learning Informative Statistics: A Nonparametric Approach

John W. Fisher III, Alexander T. Ihler, and Paul A. Viola
Massachusetts Institute of Technology
77 Massachusetts Ave., 35-421
Cambridge, MA 02139
{fisher,ihler,viola}@ai.mit.edu

Abstract

We discuss an information theoretic approach for categorizing and modeling dynamic processes. The approach can learn a compact and informative statistic which summarizes past states to predict future observations. Furthermore, the uncertainty of the prediction is characterized nonparametrically by a joint density over the learned statistic and present observation. We discuss the application of the technique to both noise driven dynamical systems and random processes sampled from a density which is conditioned on the past. In the first case we show results in which both the dynamics of random walk and the statistics of the driving noise are captured. In the second case we present results in which a summarizing statistic is learned on noisy random telegraph waves with differing dependencies on past states. In both cases the algorithm yields a principled approach for discriminating processes with differing dynamics and/or dependencies. The method is grounded in ideas from information theory and nonparametric statistics.

1 Introduction

Noisy dynamical processes abound in the world – human speech, the frequency of sun spots, and the stock market are common examples. These processes can be difficult to model and categorize because current observations are dependent on the past in complex ways. Classical models come in two sorts: those that assume that the dynamics are linear and the noise is Gaussian (e.g. Weiner etc.); and those that assume that the dynamics are discrete (e.g. HMM's). These approach are wildly popular because they are tractable and well understood. Unfortunately there are many processes where the underlying theoretical assumptions of these models are false. For example we may wish to analyze a system with linear dynamics and non-Gaussian noise or we may wish to model a system with an unknown number of discrete states.

We present an information-theoretic approach for analyzing stochastic dynamic processes which can model simple processes like those mentioned above, while retaining the flexibility to model a wider range of more complex processes. The key insight is that we can often learn a simplifying informative statistic of the past from samples using nonparametric estimates of both entropy and mutual information. Within this framework we can predict future states and, of equal importance, characterize the uncertainty accompanying those predictions. This non-parametric model is flexible enough to describe uncertainty which is more complex than second-order statistics. In contrast techniques which use squared prediction error to drive learning are focused on the mode of the distribution.

Taking an example from financial forecasting, while the *most likely* sequence of pricing events is of interest, one would also like to know the accompanying distribution of price values (i.e. even if the most likely outcome is appreciation in the price of an asset, knowledge of lower, but not insignificant, probability of depreciation is also valuable). Towards that end we describe an approach that allows us to simultaneously learn the dependencies of the process on the past as well as the uncertainty of future states. Our approach is novel in that we fold in concepts from information theory, nonparametric statistics, and learning.

In the two types of stochastic processes we will consider, the challenge is to summarize the past in an efficient way. In the absence of a known dynamical or probabilistic model, can we learn an informative statistic (ideally a sufficient statistic) of the past which minimizes our uncertainty about future states? In the classical linear state-space approach, uncertainty is characterized by mean squared error (MSE) which implicitly assume Gaussian statistics. There are, however, linear systems with interesting behavior due to non-Gaussian statistics which violate the assumption underlying MSE. There are also nonlinear systems and purely probabilistic processes which exhibit complex behavior and are poorly characterized by mean square error and/or the assumption of Gaussian noise.

Our approach is applicable to both types of processes. Because it is based on non-parametric statistics we characterize the uncertainty of predictions in a very general way: by a density of possible future states. Consequently the resulting system captures both the dynamics of the systems (through a parameterization) and the statistics of driving noise (through a nonparametric modeling). The model can then be used to classify new signals and make predictions about the future.

2 Learning from Stationary Processes

In this paper we will consider two related types of stochastic processes, depicted in figure 1. These processes differ in how current observations are related to the past. The first type of process, described by the following set of equations, is a discrete time dynamical (possibly nonlinear) system:

$$x_k = G(\{x_{k-1}\}_N; w_g) + \eta_k \quad ; \{x_k\}_N = \{x_k, \ldots, x_{k-(N-1)}\} \quad (1)$$

where, x_k, the state of the process at time k, is a function of the N previous states and the present value of η. In general the sequence $\{x_k\}$ is not stationary (in the strict sense); however, under fairly mild conditions on $\{\eta_k\}$, namely that $\{\eta_k\}$ is a sequence of i.i.d. random variables (which we will always assume to be true), the sequence:

$$\epsilon_k = x_k - G(\{x_{k-1}\}_N; w_g) \quad (2)$$

is stationary. Often termed an innovation sequence, for our purpose the stationarity of 2 will suffice. This leads to a prediction framework for estimating the dynamical parameters, w_g, of the system and to which we will adjoin a nonparametric characterization of uncertainty.

The second type of process we consider is described by a conditional probability density:

$$x_k \sim p(x_k \| \{x_{k-1}\}_N) \quad (3)$$

In this case it is only the conditional statistics of $\{x_k\}$ that we are concerned with and they are, by definition, constant.

3 Learning Informative Statistics with Nonparametric Estimators

We propose to determine the system parameters by minimizing the entropy of the error residuals for systems of type (a). Parametric entropy optimization approaches have been

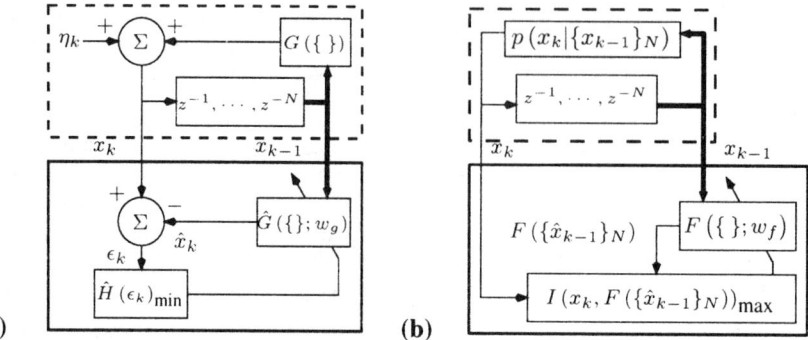

Figure 1: Two related systems: (a) dynamical system driven by stationary noise and (b) probabilistic system dependent on the finite past. Dotted box indicates source of stochastic process, while solid box indicates learning algorithm

proposed (e.g. [4]), the novelty of our approach; however, is that we estimate entropy nonparametrically. That is,

$$\hat{w}_g = \arg\min_{w_g} \hat{H}(\epsilon) \quad \hat{H}(\epsilon) \approx \int \hat{p}(\epsilon)\log\hat{p}(\epsilon)d\epsilon \quad \hat{p}(\epsilon) = -\frac{1}{M}\sum_{k=0}^{M-1}\kappa(\epsilon_k - \epsilon) \;, \quad (4)$$

where the differential entropy integral is approximated using a function of the Parzen kernel density estimator [5] (in all experiments we use the Gaussian kernel). It can be shown that minimizing the entropy of the error residuals is equivalent to maximizing their likelihood [1]. In this light, the proposed criterion is seeking the maximum likelihood estimate of the system parameters using a nonparametric description of the noise density. Consequently, we solve for the system parameters and the noise density jointly.

While there is no explicit dynamical system in the second system type we do assume that the conditional statistics of the observed sequence are constant (or at worst slowly changing for an on-line learning algorithm). In this case we desire to minimize the uncertainty of predictions from future samples by summarizing information from the past. The challenge is to do so efficiently via a function of recent samples. Ideally we would like to find a sufficient statistic of the past; however, without an explicit description of the density we opt instead for an *informative* statistic. By *informative* statistic we simply mean one which reduces the conditional entropy of future samples. If the statistic were *sufficient* then the mutual information has reached a maximum [1]. As in the previous case, we propose to find such a statistic by maximizing the *nonparametric* mutual information as defined by

$$w_f = \arg\min_{w_f} \hat{I}(x_k, F(\{x_{k-1}\}_N; w_f)) \quad (5)$$

$$= \arg\min_{w_f} \hat{H}(x_k) + \hat{H}(F(\{\ \}; w_f)) - \hat{H}(x_k, F(\{\ \}; w_f))) \quad (6)$$

$$= \arg\min_{w_f} \hat{H}(x_k) - \hat{H}(x_k|F(\{\ \}; w_f))) \quad (7)$$

By equation 6 this is equivalent to optimizing the joint and marginal entropies (which we do in practice) or, by equation 7, minimizing the conditional entropy.

We have previously presented two related methods for incorporating kernel based density estimators into an information theoretic learning framework [2, 3]. We chose the method of [3] because it provides an exact gradient of an *approximation* to entropy, but more importantly can be converted into an implicit error function thereby reducing computation cost.

4 Distinguishing Random Walks: An Example

In random walk the feedback function $G(\{x_{k-1}\}_1) = x_{k-1}$. The noise is assumed to be independent and identically distributed (i.i.d.). Although the sequence, x_k, is non-stationary the increments (x_k-x_{k-1}) are stationary. In this context, estimating the statistics of the residuals allows for discrimination between two random walk process with differing noise densities. Furthermore, as we will demonstrate empirically, even when one of the processes is driven by Gaussian noise (an implicit assumption of the MMSE criterion), such knowledge may not be sufficient to distinguish one process from another.

Figure 2 shows two random walk realizations and their associate noise densities (solid lines). One is driven by Gaussian noise ($\eta_k \sim N(0,1)$), while the other is driven by a bi-modal mixture of gaussians ($\eta_k \sim \frac{1}{2}N(0.95, 0.3) + \frac{1}{2}N(-0.95, 0.3)$) (note: both densities are zero-mean and unit variance). During learning, the process was modeled as fifth-order auto-regressive (AR$_5$). One hundred samples were drawn from a realization of each type and the AR parameters were estimated using the standard MMSE approach and the approach described above. With regards to parameter estimation, both methods (as expected) yield essentially the same parameters with the first coefficient being near unity and the remaining coefficients being near zero.

We are interested in the ability to distinguish one process from another. As mentioned, the current approach jointly estimates the parameters of the system as well as the density of the noise. The nonparametric estimates are shown in figure 2 (dotted lines). These estimates are then be used to compute the accumulated average log-likelihood ($L(\epsilon_k) = \frac{1}{k}\sum_{i=1}^{k} \log p(x_i)$) of the residual sequence ($\epsilon_k \approx \eta_k$) under the known and learned densities (figure 3). It is striking (but not surprising) that $L(\epsilon_k)$ of the bi-modal mixture under the Gaussian model (dashed lines, top) does not differ significantly from the Gaussian driven increments process (solid lines, top). The explanation follows from the fact that

$$\lim_{k \to \infty} L(\epsilon_k) = -(H(p_\epsilon(\epsilon)) + D(p(\epsilon)\|p_\epsilon(\epsilon))) \tag{8}$$

where $p_\epsilon(\epsilon)$ is the true density of ϵ (bi-modal), $p(\epsilon)$ is the assumed density of the likelihood test (unit-variance Gaussian), and $D(\|)$ is the Kullback-Leibler divergence [1]. In this case, $D(p(\epsilon)\|p_\epsilon(\epsilon))$ is relatively small (not true for $D(p_\epsilon(\epsilon)\|p(\epsilon))$ and $H(p_\epsilon(\epsilon))$ is less than the entropy of the unit-variance Gaussian (for fixed variance, the Gaussian density has maximum entropy). The consequence is that the likelihood test under the Gaussian assumption does not reliably distinguish the two processes. The likelihood test under the bi-modal density or its nonparametric estimate (figure 3, bottom) does distinguish the two.

The method described is not limited to linear dynamic models. It can certainly be used for nonlinear models, so long as the dynamic can be well approximated by differentiable functions. Examples for multi-layer perceptrons are described in [3].

5 Learning the Structure of a Noisy Random Telegraph Wave

A noisy random telegraph wave (RTW) can be described by figure 1(b). Our goal is not to demonstrate that we can analyze random telegraph waves, rather that we can robustly learn an informative statistic of the past for such a process. We define a noisy random telegraph wave as a sequence $x_k \sim N(\mu_k, \sigma)$ where μ_k is binomially distributed:

$$\mu_k \in \{\pm\mu\} \quad P\{\mu_k = -\mu_{k-1}\} = \alpha \frac{|\frac{1}{N}\sum_{i=1}^{N} x_{k-i}|}{\frac{1}{N}\sum_{i=1}^{N} |x_{k-i}|}, \tag{9}$$

$N(\mu_k, \sigma)$ is Gaussian and $\alpha < 1$. This process is interesting because the parameters are random functions of a nonlinear combination of the set $\{x_k\}_N$. Depending on the value of N, we observe different switching dynamics. Figure 4 shows examples of such signals for

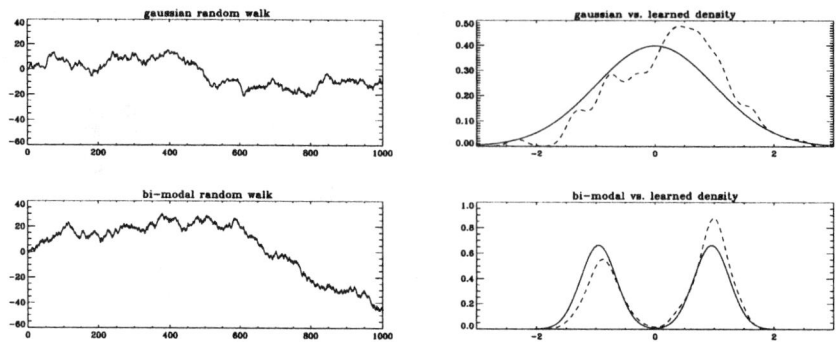

Figure 2: Random walk examples (left), comparison of known to learned densities (right).

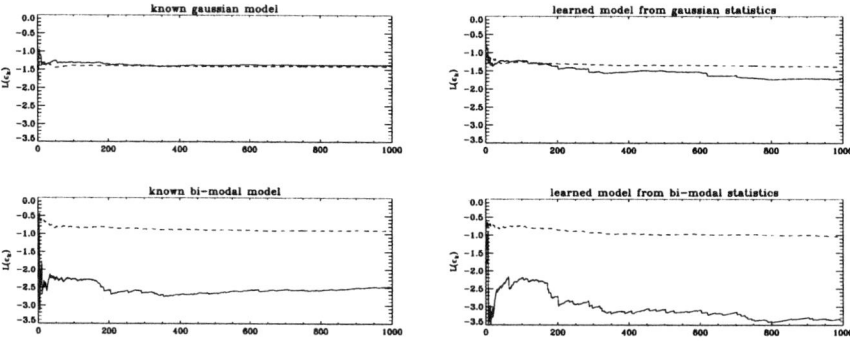

Figure 3: $L(\epsilon_k)$ under known models (left) as compared to learned models (right).

$N = 20$ (left) and $N = 4$ (right). Rapid switching dynamics are possible for both signals while $N = 20$ has periods with longer duration than $N = 4$.

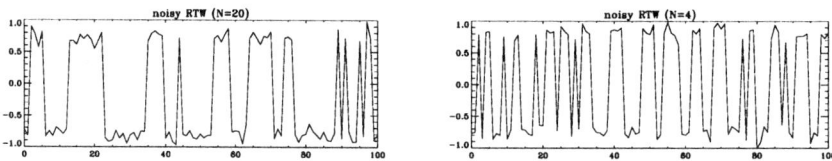

Figure 4: Noisy random telegraph wave: $N = 20$ (left), $N = 4$ (right)

In our experiments we learn a sufficient statistic which has the form

$$F(\{x_k\}_{\text{past}}) = \sigma\left(\sum_{i=1}^{M} w_{f_i} x_{k-i}\right), \quad (10)$$

where $\sigma(\ )$ is the hyperbolic tangent function (i.e. $F\{\ \}$ is a one layer perceptron). Note that a multi-layer perceptron could also be used [3].

In our experiments we train on 100 samples of noisy RTW$_{(N=20)}$ and RTW$_{(N=4)}$. We then learn statistics for each type of process using $M = \{4, 5, 15, 20, 25\}$. This tests for situations in which the depth is both under-specified and over-specified (as well as perfectly

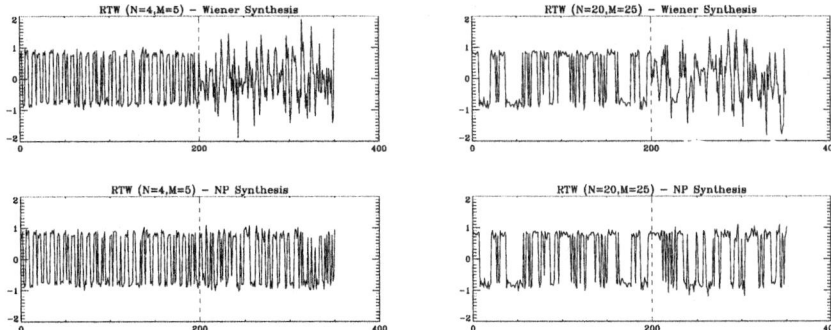

Figure 5: Comparison of Wiener filter (top) nonparametric approach (bottom) for synthesis.

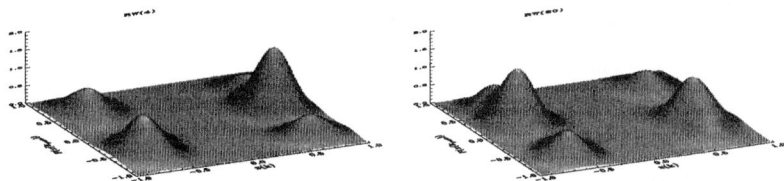

Figure 6: Informative Statistics for noisy random telegraph waves. $M = 25$ trained on N equal 4 (left) and 20 (right).

specified). We will denote $F_N(\{x_k\}_M)$ as the statistic which was trained on an RTW$_{(N)}$ process with a memory depth of M.

Since we implicitly learn a joint density over $(x_k, F_N(\{x_k\}_M))$ synthesis is possible by sampling from that density. Figure 5 compares synthesis using the described method (bottom) to a Wiener filter (top) estimated over the same data. The results using the information theoretic approach (bottom) preserve the structure of the RTW while the Wiener filter results do not. This was achieved by collapsing the information of past samples into a single statistic (avoiding high dimension density estimation). Figure 6 shows the joint density over $(x_k, F_N(\{x_k\}_M))$ for $N = \{4, 20\}$ and $M = 25$. We see that the estimated densities are not separable and by virtue of this fact the learned statistic conveys information about the future. Figure 7 shows results from 100 monte carlo trials. In this case the depth of the statistic is matched to the process. Each plot shows the accumulated conditional log likelihood ($L(\epsilon_k) = \frac{1}{k}\sum_{i=1}^{k} \log \hat{p}(x_i|F_N(\{x_{k-1}\}_M))$) under the learned statistic with error bars. Figure 8 shows similar results after varying the memory depth $M = \{4, 5, 15, 20, 25\}$ of the statistic. The figures illustrate robustness to choice of memory depth M. This is not to say that memory depth doesn't matter; that is, there must be some information to exploit, but the empirical results indicate that useful information was extracted.

6 Conclusions

We have described a nonparametric approach for finding *informative* statistics. The approach is novel in that learning is derived from nonparametric estimators of entropy and mutual information. This allows for a means by which to 1) efficiently summarize the past, 2) predict the future and 3) characterize the uncertainty of those predictions beyond second-order statistics. Futhermore, this was accomplished without the strong assumptions accompanying parametric approaches.

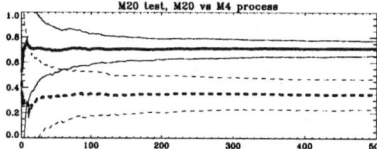
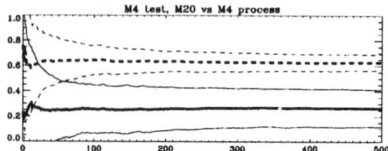

Figure 7: Conditional $L(\epsilon_k)$. Solid line indicates $\text{RTW}_{(N=20)}$ while dashed line indicates $\text{RTW}_{(N=4)}$. Thick lines indicate the average over all monte carlo runs while the thin lines indicate ± 1 standard deviation. The left plot uses a statistic trained on $\text{RTW}_{(N=20)}$ while the right plot uses a statistic trained on $\text{RTW}_{(N=4)}$.

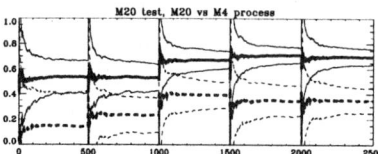
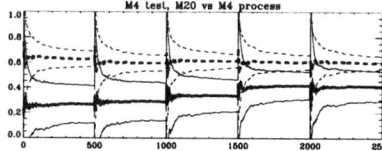

Figure 8: Repeat of figure 7 for cases with $M = \{4, 5, 15, 20, 25\}$. Obvious breaks indicate a new set of trials

We also presented empirical results which illustrated the utility of our approach. The example of random walk served as a simple illustration in learning a dynamic system in spite of the over-specification of the AR model. More importantly, we demonstrated the ability to learn both the dynamic and the statistics of the underlying noise process. This information was later used to distinguish realizations by their nonparametric densities, something not possible using MMSE error prediction.

An even more compelling result were the experiments with noisy random telegraph waves. We demonstrated the algorithms ability to learn a compact statistic which efficiently summarized the past for process identification. The method exhibited robustness to the number of parameters of the learned statistic. For example, despite overspecifying the dependence of the memory-4 in three of the cases, a useful statistic was still found. Conversely, despite the memory-20 statistic being underspecified in three of the experiments, useful information from the available past was extracted.

It is our opinion that this method provides an alternative to some of the traditional and connectionist approaches to time-series analysis. The use of nonparametric estimators adds flexibility to the class of densities which can be modeled and places less of a constraint on the exact form of the summarizing statistic.

References

[1] T. Cover and J. Thomas. *Elements of Information Theory*. John Wiley & Sons, New York, 1991.

[2] P. Viola et al. Empricial entropy manipulation for real world problems. In Mozer Touretsky and Hasselmo, editors, *Advances in Neural Information Processing Systems*, pages ?–?, 1996.

[3] J.W. Fisher and J.C. Principe. A methodology for information theoretic feature extraction. In A. Stuberud, editor, *Proc. of the IEEE Int Joint Conf on Neural Networks*, pages ?–?, 1998.

[4] J. Kapur and H. Kesavan. *Entropy Optimization Principles with Applications*. Academic Press, New York, 1992.

[5] E. Parzen. On estimation of a probability density function and mode. *Ann. of Math Stats.*, 33:1065–1076, 1962.

Kirchoff Law Markov Fields for Analog Circuit Design

Richard M. Golden [*]
RMG Consulting Inc.
2000 Fresno Road, Plano, Texas 75074
RMGCONSULT@AOL.COM,
www.neural-network.com

Abstract

Three contributions to developing an algorithm for assisting engineers in designing analog circuits are provided in this paper. First, a method for representing highly nonlinear and non-continuous analog circuits using Kirchoff current law potential functions within the context of a Markov field is described. Second, a relatively efficient algorithm for optimizing the Markov field objective function is briefly described and the convergence proof is briefly sketched. And third, empirical results illustrating the strengths and limitations of the approach are provided within the context of a JFET transistor design problem. The proposed algorithm generated a set of circuit components for the JFET circuit model that accurately generated the desired characteristic curves.

1 Analog circuit design using Markov random fields

1.1 Markov random field models

A Markov random field (MRF) is a generalization of the concept of a Markov chain. In a Markov field one begins with a set of random variables and a *neighborhood relation* which is represented by a graph. Each random variable will be assumed in this paper to be a discrete random variable which takes on one of a finite number of possible values. Each node of the graph indexes a specific random variable. A link from the jth node to the ith node indicates that the conditional probability distribution of the ith random variable in the field is functionally dependent upon the jth random variable. That is, random variable j is a *neighbor* of random variable i. The only restriction upon the definition of a Markov field (i.e., the *positivity condition*) is that the probability of every realization of the field is strictly positive. The essential idea behind Markov field design is that one specifies a potential (energy) function for every clique in the neighborhood graph such that the subset of random variables associated with that clique obtain their optimal values when that clique's potential function obtains its minimal value (for reviews see [1]-[2]).

---

[*] Associate Professor at University of Texas at Dallas (*www.utdallas.edu/~golden*)

Markov random field models provide a convenient mechanism for probabilistically representing and optimally combining combinations of local constraints.

1.2 Analog circuit design using SPICE

In some mixed signal ASIC (Application Specific Integrated Circuit) design problems, most of the circuit design specifications are well known but the introduction of a single constraint (e.g., an increase in substrate noise) could result in a major redesign of an entire circuit. The industry standard tool for aiding engineers in solving analog circuit design problems is SPICE which is a software environment for simulation of large scale electronic circuits. SPICE does have special optimization options for fitting circuit parameters to desired input-output characteristics but typically such constraints are too weak for SPICE to solve analog circuit design problems with large numbers of free parameters (see [3] for an introduction to SPICE). Another difficulty with using SPICE is that it does not provide a global confidence factor for indicating its confidence in a generated design or local confidence factors for determining the locations of "weak points" in the automatically generated circuit design solution.

1.3 Markov field approaches to analog circuit design

In this paper, an approach for solving real-world analog circuit design problems using an appropriately constructed Markov random is proposed which will be referred to as MRFSPICE. Not only are desired input-output characteristics directly incorporated into the construction of the potential functions for the Markov field but additional constraints based upon Kirchoff's current law are directly incorporated into the field. This approach thus differs from the classic SPICE methodology because Kirchoff current law constraints are explicitly incorporated into an objective function which is minimized by the "optimal design". This approach also differs from previous Markov field approaches (i.e., the "Harmony" neural network model [4] and the "Brain-State-in-a-Box" neural network model [5]) designed to qualitatively model human understanding of electronic circuit behavior since those approaches used pair-wise correlational (quadratic) potential functions as opposed to the highly nonlinear potential functions that will be used in the approach described in this paper.

1.4 Key contributions

This paper thus makes three important contributions to the application of Markov random fields to the analog circuit design problem. First, a method for representing highly nonlinear and non-continuous analog circuits using Kirchoff current law potential functions within the context of a Markov field is described. Second, a relatively efficient algorithm for optimizing the Markov field objective function is briefly described and the convergence proof is briefly sketched. And third, empirical results illustrating the strengths and limitations of the approach is provided within the context of a JFET transistor design problem.

2 Modeling assumptions and algorithms

2.1 Probabilistic modeling assumptions

A given circuit circuit design problem consists of a number of design decision variables. Denote those design decision variables by the discrete random variables

$\tilde{x}_1, \ldots, \tilde{x}_d$. Let the MRF be denoted by the set $\tilde{\mathbf{x}} = [\tilde{x}_1, \ldots, \tilde{x}_d]$ so that a realization of $\tilde{\mathbf{x}}$ is the d-dimensional real vector $\mathbf{x}$. A realization of $\tilde{\mathbf{x}}$ is referred to as a *circuit design solution*.

Let the joint (global) probability mass function for $\tilde{\mathbf{x}}$ be denoted by p_G. It is assumed that $p_G(\mathbf{x}) > p_G(\mathbf{y})$ if and only if the circuit design solution $\mathbf{x}$ is preferred to the circuit design solution $\mathbf{y}$. Thus, $p_G(\mathbf{x})$ specifies a type of probabilistic fuzzy measure [1].

For example, the random variable $\tilde{x}_i$ might refer to a design decision concerning the choice of a particular value for a capacitor C_{14}. From previous experience, it is expected that the value of C_{14} may be usually constrained without serious difficulties to one of ten possible values:

$$0.1\mu F, 0.2\mu F, 0.3\mu F, 0.4\mu F, 0.5\mu F, 0.6\mu F, 0.7\mu F, 0.8\mu F, 0.9\mu F, \text{ or } 1\mu F.$$

Thus, $k_i = 10$ in this example. By limiting the choice of C_{14} to a small number of finite values, this permits the *introduction of design expertise hints* directly into the problem formulation without making strong committments to the ultimate choice of the value of capacitor C_{14}. Other examples of design decision variable values include: resistor values, inductor values, transistor types, diode types, or even fundamentally different circuit topologies.

The problem that is now considered will be to assign design preference probabilities in a meaningful way to alternative design solutions. The strategy for doing this will be based upon constructing p_G with the property that if $p_G(\mathbf{x}) > p_G(\mathbf{y})$, then circuit design solution $\mathbf{x}$ exhibits the requisite operating characteristics with respect to a set of M "test circuits" more effectively than circuit design solution $\mathbf{y}$. An optimal analog circuit design solution $\mathbf{x}^*$ then may be defined as a global maximum of p_G. The specific details of this strategy for constructing p_G are now discussed by first carefully defining the concept of a "test circuit".

Let $\mathcal{V} = \{0, 1, 2, \ldots, m\}$ be a finite set of integers (i.e., the unique "terminals" in the test circuit) which index a set of m complex numbers, $v_0, v_1, v_2, \ldots, v_m$ which will be referred to as *voltages*. The magnitude of v_k indicates the voltage magnitude while the angle of v_k indicates the voltage phase shift. By convention the *ground voltage*, v_0, is always assigned the value of 0. Let $d \in \mathcal{V} \times \mathcal{V}$ (i.e., an ordered pair of elements in $\mathcal{V}$). A *circuit component current source* is defined with respect to $\mathcal{V}$ by a complex-valued function $i_{a,b}$ whose value is typically functionally dependent upon v_a and v_b but may also be functionally dependent upon other voltages and circuit component current sources associated with $\mathcal{V}$.

For example, a "resistor" circuit component current source would be modeled by choosing $i_{a,b} = (v_b - v_a)/R$ where R is the resistance in ohms of some resistor, v_b is the voltage observed on one terminal of the resistor, and v_a is the voltage observed on the other terminal of the resistor. The quantity $i_{a,b}$ is the current flowing through the resistor from terminal a to terminal b. Similarly, a "capacitor" circuit component current source would be modeled by choosing $i_{a,b} = (v_b - v_a)/[2\pi j f]$ where $j = \sqrt{-1}$ and f is the frequency in Hz of the test circuit. A "frequency specific voltage controlled current source" circuit component current source may be modeled by making $i_{a,b}$ functionally dependent upon some subset of voltages in the test circuit. See [6] for additional details regarding the use of complex arithmetic for analog circuit analysis and design.

An important design constraint is that Kirchoff's current law should be satisfied at every voltage node. Kirchoff's current law states that the sum of the currents entering a voltage node must be equal to zero [6]. We will now show how this physical law can be directly embodied as a system of nonlinear constraints on the behavior of the MRF.

We say that the kth voltage node in test circuit q is *clamped* if the voltage v_k is known. For example, node k in circuit q might be directly grounded, node k might be directly connected to a grounded voltage source, or the voltage at node k, v_k, might be a desired known target voltage.

If voltage node k in test circuit q is clamped, then Kirchoff's current law at voltage node k in circuit q is simply assumed to be satisfied which, in turn, implies that the *voltage potential function* $\Phi_{q,k} = 0$.

Now suppose that voltage node k in test circuit q is not clamped. This means that the voltage at node k must be estimated. If there are no controlled current sources in the test circuit (i.e., only passive devices), then the values of the voltages at the unclamped nodes in the circuit can be calculated by solving a system of linear equations where the current choice of circuit component values are treated as constants. In the more general case where controlled current sources exist in the test circuit, then an approximate iterative gradient descent algorithm (such as the algorithm used by SPICE) is used to obtain improved estimates of the voltages of the unclamped nodes. The iterative algorithm is always run for a fixed number of iterations.

Now the value of $\Phi_{q,k}$ must be computed. The current entering node k via arc j in test circuit q is denoted by the two-dimensional real vector $\mathbf{I}_{k,j}^q$ whose first component is the real part of the complex current and whose second component is the imaginary part.

The average current entering node k in test circuit q is given by the formula:

$$\bar{\mathbf{I}}_k^q = (1/n_k) \sum_{j=1}^{n_k} \mathbf{I}_{k,j}^q.$$

Design circuit components (e.g., resistors, capacitors, diodes, etc.) which minimize $\bar{\mathbf{I}}_k^q$ will satisfy Kirchoff's current law at node k in test circuit q. However, the measure $\bar{\mathbf{I}}_k^q$ is an not entirely adequate indicator of the degree to which Kirchoff's current law is satisfied since $\bar{\mathbf{I}}_k^q$ may be small in magnitude not necessarily because Kirchoff's current law is satisfied but simply because all currents entering node k are small in magnitude. To compensate for this problem, a normalized current signal magnitude to current signal variability ratio is minimized at node k in test circuit q. This ratio decreases in magnitude if $\bar{\mathbf{I}}_k^q$ has a magnitude which is small relative to the magnitude of individual currents entering node k in test circuit q.

The voltage potential function, $\Phi_{q,k}$, for voltage node k in test circuit q is now formally defined as follows. Let

$$\mathbf{Q}_{k,q} = (1/n_k) \sum_{j=1}^{n_k} (\mathbf{I}_{k,j}^q - \bar{\mathbf{I}}_k^q)(\mathbf{I}_{k,j}^q - \bar{\mathbf{I}}_k^q)^T.$$

Let $\lambda_1, \ldots, \lambda_u$ be those eigenvalues of $\mathbf{Q}_{k,q}$ whose values are strictly greater than some small positive number ϵ. Let $\mathbf{e}_i$ be the eigenvector associated with eigenvalue λ_i. Define

$$\mathbf{Q}_{k,q}^{-1} = \sum_{j=1}^{u} (1/\lambda_j) \mathbf{e}_j \mathbf{e}_j^T.$$

Thus, if $\mathbf{Q}_{k,q}$ has all positive eigenvalues, then $\mathbf{Q}_{k,q}$ is simply the matrix inverse of $\mathbf{Q}_{k,q}^{-1}$. Using this notation, the voltage potential function for the unclamped voltage

node k in test circuit q may be expressed by the formula:
$$\Phi_{q,k} = [\bar{\mathbf{I}}_k^q]^T \mathbf{Q}^{-1} \bar{\mathbf{I}}_k^q.$$

Now define the global probability or "global preference" of a particular design configuration by the formula:
$$p_G(\mathbf{x}) = (1/Z) exp(-U(\mathbf{x})) \qquad (1)$$
where $U = (1/N) \sum_q \sum_k \Phi_{q,k}$ and where N is the total number of voltage nodes across all test circuits. The most preferred (i.e., "most probable") design are the design circuit components that maximize p_G. Note that probabilities have been assigned such that circuit configurations which are less consistent with Kirchoff's current law are considered "less probable" (i.e., "less preferred").

Because the normalization constant Z in (1) is computationally intractable to compute, it is helpful to define the easily computable *circuit confidence factor*, CCF, given by the formula: $CCF(\mathbf{x}) = exp(-U(\mathbf{x})) = Zp_G(\mathbf{x})$. Note that the global probability p is directly proportional to the CCF. Since U is always non-negative and complete satisfaction of Kirchoff's current laws corresponds to the case where $U = 0$, it follows that $CCF(\mathbf{x})$ has a lower bound of 0 (indicating "no subjective confidence" in the design solution $\mathbf{x}$) and an upper bound of 1 (indicating "absolute subjective confidence" in the design solution $\mathbf{x}$).

In addition, local conditional probabilities of the form
$$p_i = p(\tilde{x}_i = x_i | x_1, \ldots, x_{i-1}, x_{i+1}, \ldots, x_d)$$
can be computed using the formula:
$$p_i = \frac{p_G(x_1, \ldots, x_{i-1}, x_i, x_{i+1}, \ldots, x_d)}{\sum_k p_G(x_1, \ldots, x_{i-1}, x_k, x_{i+1}, \ldots, x_d)}.$$

Such local conditional probabilities are helpful for explicitly computing the probability or "preference" for selecting one design circuit component value given a subset of other design component values have been accepted. Remember that probability (i.e., "preference") is essentially a measure of the degree to which the chosen design components and pre-specified operating characteristic voltage versus frequency curves of the circuit satisfy Kirchoff's current laws.

2.2 MRFSPICE algorithm

The MRFSPICE algorithm is a combination of the Metropolis and Besag's ICM (Iterated Conditional Modes) algorithms [1]-[2]. The stochastic Metropolis algorithm (with temperature parameter set equal to one) is used to sample from $p(\mathbf{x})$. As each design solution is generated, the CCF for that design solution is computed and the design solution with the best CCF is kept as an initial design solution guess $\mathbf{x}_0$. Next, the deterministic ICM algorithm is then initialized with $\mathbf{x}_0$ and the ICM algorithm is applied until an equilibrium point is reached.

A simulated annealing method involving decreasing the temperature parameter according to a logarithmic cooling schedule in Step 1 through Step 5 could easily be used to guarantee convergence in distribution to a uniform distribution over the global maxima of p_G (i.e., convergence to an optimal solution) [1]-[2]. However, for the test problems considered thus far, equally effective results have been obtained by using the above fast heuristic algorithm which is guaranteed to converge to a local maximum as opposed to a global maximum. It is proposed that in situations where the convergence rate is slow or the local maximum generated by MRFSPICE is a poor design solution with low CCF, that appropriate local conditional probabilites be computed and provided as feedback to a human design engineer. The human design engineer can then make direct alterations to the sample space of p_G (i.e., the domain of CCF) in order to appropriately simply the search space. Finally, the ICM algorithm can be easily viewed as an artificial neural network algorithm and in fact is a generalization of the classic Hopfield (1982) model as noted in [1].

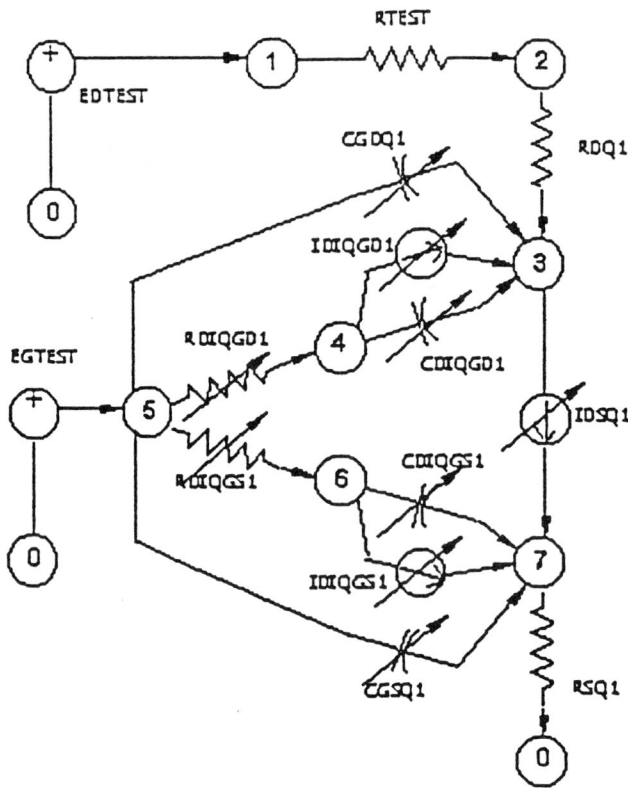

Figure 1: As external input voltage generator EGTEST and external supply voltage EDTEST are varied, current IRTEST flowing through external resistor RTEST is measured.

3 JFET design problem

In this design problem, specific combinations of free parameters for a macroequivalent JFET transistor model were selected on the basis of a given set of characteristic curves specifying how the drain to source current of the JFET varied as a function of the gate voltage and drain voltage at $0Hz$ and $1MHz$. Specifically, a JFET transistor model was simulated using the classic Shichman and Hodges (1968) large-signal n-channel JFET model as described by Vladimirescu [3] (pp. 96-100). The circuit diagram of this transistor model is shown in Figure 1. The only components in the circuit diagram which are not part of the JFET transistor model are the external voltage generators EDTEST and EGTEST, and external resistor RTEST. The specific functions which describe how IDIQGD1, CDIQGD1, RDIQGD1, IDIQGS1, CDIQGS1, RDIQGS1, CGDQ1, and CGSQ1 change as a function of EGTEST and the current IRTEST (which flows through RTEST) are too long and complex to be presented here (for more details see [3] pp. 96-100).

Five design decision variables were defined. The first design decision variable, XDIQGS1, specified a set of parameter values for the large signal gate to source diode model portion of the JFET model. There were 20 possible choices for the value of XDIQGS1. Similarly, the second design decision variable, XDIQGD1, had 20 possible values and specified a set of parameter values for the large signal gate to drain diode model portion of the JFET model. The third design decision variable was XQ1 which also had 20 possible values were each value specified a set of choices for JFET-type specific parameters. The fourth and fifth design decision variables were the resistors RSQ1 and RSD1 each of which could take on one of 15 possible values.

The results of the JFET design problem are shown in Table 1. The phase angle for IRTEST at $1MHz$ was specified to be approximately 10 degrees, while the observed phase angle for IRTEST ranged from 7 to 9 degrees. The computing time was approximately $2-4$ hours using unoptimized prototype MATLAB code on a 200 MHZ Pentium Processor. The close agreement between the desired and actual results suggests further research in this area would be highly rewarding.

Table 1: Evaluation of MRFSPICE-generated JFET design

EGTEST	EDTEST	IRTEST @ DC (ma) (desired/actual)	IRTEST @ 1MHZ (ma) (desired/actual)
0	1.5	1.47/1.50	1.19/1.21
0	2.0	1.96/1.99	1.60/1.62
0	3.0	2.94/2.99	2.43/2.43
-0.5	1.5	1.47/1.50	1.07/1.11
-0.5	2.0	1.96/2.00	1.49/1.52
-0.5	3.0	2.95/2.99	2.34/2.35
-1.0	1.5	1.48/1.50	0.96/1.02
-1.0	2.0	1.97/2.00	1.39/1.44
-1.0	3.0	2.96/3.00	2.27/2.29

Acknowledgments

This research was funded by Texas Instruments Inc. through the direct efforts of Kerry Hanson. Both Kerry Hanson and Ralph Golden provided numerous key insights and knowledge substantially improving this project's quality.

References

[1] Golden, R. M. (1996) *Mathematical methods for neural network analysis and design.* Cambridge: MIT Press.

[2] Winkler, G. (1995) *Image analysis, random fields, and dynamic Monte Carlo methods: A mathematical introduction.* New York: Springer-Verlag.

[3] Vladimirescu, A. (1994) *The SPICE book.* New York: Wiley.

[4] Smolensky, P. (1986). Information processing in dynamical systems: Foundations of Harmony theory. In D. E. Rumelhart and J. L. McClelland (eds.), *Parallel distributed processing. Volume 1: Foundations,* pp. 194-281. Cambridge: MIT Press.

[5] Anderson, J. A. (1995). *An introduction to neural networks.* Cambridge: MIT Press.

[6] Skilling, H. (1959) *Electrical engineering circuits.* New York: Wiley.

Learning the Similarity of Documents:
An Information-Geometric Approach to Document Retrieval and Categorization

Thomas Hofmann
Department of Computer Science
Brown University, Providence, RI
hofmann@cs.brown.edu, www.cs.brown.edu/people/th

Abstract

The project pursued in this paper is to develop from first information-geometric principles a general method for learning the similarity between text documents. Each individual document is modeled as a memoryless information source. Based on a latent class decomposition of the term-document matrix, a low-dimensional (curved) multinomial subfamily is learned. From this model a canonical similarity function – known as the Fisher kernel – is derived. Our approach can be applied for unsupervised and supervised learning problems alike. This in particular covers interesting cases where both, labeled and unlabeled data are available. Experiments in automated indexing and text categorization verify the advantages of the proposed method.

1 Introduction

The computer-based analysis and organization of large document repositories is one of today's great challenges in machine learning, a key problem being the quantitative assessment of *document similarities*. A reliable similarity measure would provide answers to questions like: How similar are two text documents and which documents match a given query best? In a time, where searching in huge on-line (hyper-)text collections like the World Wide Web becomes more and more popular, the relevance of these and related questions needs not to be further emphasized.

The focus of this work is on data-driven methods that *learn* a similarity function based on a training corpus of text documents without requiring domain-specific knowledge. Since we do not assume that labels for text categories, document classes, or topics, etc. are given at this stage, the former is by definition an *unsupervised* learning problem. In fact, the general problem of learning object similarities precedes many "classical" unsupervised learning methods like data clustering that already presuppose the availability of a metric or similarity function. In this paper, we develop a framework for learning similarities between text documents from first principles. In doing so, we try to span a bridge from the foundations of statistics in *information geometry* [13, 1] to real-world applications in *information retrieval* and text learning, namely *ad hoc* retrieval and text categorization. Although the developed general methodology is not limited to text documents, we will for sake of concreteness restrict our attention exclusively to this domain.

2 Latent Class Decomposition

Memoryless Information Sources Assume we have available a set of documents $\mathcal{D} = \{d_1, \ldots, d_N\}$ over some fixed vocabulary of words (or terms) $\mathcal{W} = \{w_1, \ldots, w_M\}$. In an information-theoretic perspective, each document d_i can be viewed as an information source, *i.e.* a probability distribution over word sequences. Following common practice in information retrieval, we will focus on the more restricted case where text documents are modeled on the level of single word occurrences. This means that we we adopt the bag–of–words view and treat documents as *memoryless* information sources.[1]

A. Modeling assumption: Each document is a memoryless information source.

This assumption implies that each document can be represented by a multinomial probability distribution $P(w_j|d_i)$, which denotes the (unigram) probability that a generic word occurrence in document d_i will be w_j. Correspondingly, the data can be reduced to some simple sufficient statistics which are counts $n(d_i, w_j)$ of how often a word w_j occurred in a document d_i. The rectangular $N \times M$ matrix with coefficients $n(d_i, w_j)$ is also called the *term-document matrix*.

Latent Class Analysis Latent class analysis is a decomposition technique for contingency tables (cf. [5, 3] and the references therein) that has been applied to language modeling [15] ("aggregate Markov model") and in information retrieval [7] ("probabilistic latent semantic analysis"). In latent class analysis, an unobserved class variable $z_k \in \mathcal{Z} = \{z_1, \ldots, z_K\}$ is associated with each observation, *i.e.* with each word occurrence (d_i, w_j). The joint probability distribution over $\mathcal{D} \times \mathcal{W}$ is a mixture model that can be parameterized in two equivalent ways

$$P(d_i, w_j) = \sum_{k=1}^{K} P(z_k) P(d_i|z_k) P(w_j|z_k) = P(d_i) \sum_{k=1}^{K} P(w_j|z_k) P(z_k|d_i). \quad (1)$$

The latent class model (1) introduces a conditional independence assumption, namely that d_i and w_j are independent conditioned on the state of the associated latent variable. Since the cardinality of z_k is typically smaller than the number of documents/words in the collection, z_k acts as a bottleneck variable in predicting words conditioned on the context of a particular document.

To give the reader a more intuitive understanding of the latent class decomposition, we have visualized a representative subset of 16 "factors" from a $K = 64$ latent class model fitted from the Reuters21578 collection (cf. Section 4) in Figure 1. Intuitively, the learned parameters seem to be very meaningful in that they represent identifiable topics and capture the corresponding vocabulary quite well.

By using the latent class decomposition to model a collection of memoryless sources, we implicitly assume that the overall collection will help in estimating parameters for individual sources, an assumption which has been validated in our experiments.

B. Modeling assumption: Parameters for a collection of memoryless information sources are estimated by latent class decomposition.

Parameter Estimation The latent class model has an important geometrical interpretation: the parameters $\phi_j^k \equiv P(w_j|z_k)$ define a low-dimensional subfamily of the multinomial family, $\mathcal{S}(\phi) \equiv \{\pi \in [0;1]^M : \pi_j = \sum_k \psi_k \phi_j^k \text{ for some } \psi \in [0;1]^K, \sum_k \psi_k = 1\}$, *i.e.* all multinomials π that can be obtained by convex combinations from the set of "basis" vectors $\{\phi^k : 1 \leq k \leq K\}$. For given ϕ–parameters,

---

[1] Extensions to the more general case are possible, but beyond the scope of this paper.

government	president	banks	pct	union	marks	gold	billion
tax	chairman	debt	january	air	currency	steel	dlrs
budget	executive	brazil	february	workers	dollar	plant	year
cut	chief	new	rise	strike	german	mining	surplus
spending	officer	loans	rose	airlines	bundesbank	copper	deficit
cuts	vice	dlrs	1986	aircraft	central	tons	foreign
deficit	company	bankers	december	port	mark	silver	current
taxes	named	bank	year	boeing	west	metal	trade
reform	board	payments	fell	employees	dollars	production	account
billion	director	billion	prices	airline	dealers	ounces	reserves
trading	american	trade	oil	vs	areas	food	house
exchange	general	japan	crude	cts	weather	drug	reagan
futures	motors	japanese	energy	net	area	study	president
stock	chrysler	ec	petroleum	loss	normal	aids	administration
options	gm	states	prices	mln	good	product	congress
index	car	united	bpd	shr	crop	treatment	white
contracts	ford	officials	barrels	qtr	damage	company	secretary
market	test	community	barrel	revs	caused	environmental	told
london	cars	european	exploration	profit	affected	products	volcker
exchanges	motor	imports	price	note	people	approval	reagans

Figure 1: 16 selected factors from a 64 factor decomposition of the Reuters21578 collection. The displayed terms are the 10 most probable words in the class-conditional distribution $P(w_j|z_k)$ for 16 selected states z_k after the exclusion of stop words.

each ψ^i, $\psi_k^i \equiv P(z_k|d_i)$, will define a unique multinomial distribution $\pi^i \in S(\phi)$. Since $S(\phi)$ defines a submanifold on the multinomial simplex, it corresponds to a *curved exponential subfamily*.[2] We would like to emphasis that we propose to learn both, the parameters within the family (the ψ's or mixing proportions $P(z_k|d_i)$) *and* the parameters that define the subfamily (the ϕ's or class-conditionals $P(w_j|z_k)$).

The standard procedure for maximum likelihood estimation in latent variable models is the Expectation Maximization (EM) algorithm. In the E–step one computes posterior probabilities for the latent class variables,

$$P(z_k|d_i,w_j) = \frac{P(z_k)P(d_i|z_k)P(w_j|z_k)}{\sum_l P(z_l)P(d_i|z_l)P(w_j|z_l)} = \frac{P(z_k)P(d_i|z_k)P(w_j|z_k)}{P(d_i,w_j)}. \quad (2)$$

The M-step formulae can be written compactly as

$$\left. \begin{array}{c} P(d_i|z_k) \\ P(w_j|z_k) \\ P(z_k) \end{array} \right\} \propto \sum_{n=1}^{N}\sum_{m=1}^{M} n(d_n,w_m)P(z_k|d_n,w_m) \times \left\{ \begin{array}{c} \delta_{in} \\ \delta_{jm} \\ 1 \end{array} \right., \quad (3)$$

where δ denotes the Kronecker delta.

Related Models As demonstrated in [7], the latent class model can be viewed as a probabilistic variant of Latent Semantic Analysis [2], a dimension reduction technique based on Singular Value Decomposition. It is also closely related to the non-negative matrix decomposition discussed in [12] which uses a Poisson sampling model and has been motivated by imposing non-negativity constraints on a decomposition by PCA. The relationship of the latent class model to clustering models like distributional clustering [14] has been investigated in [8]. [6] presents yet another approach to dimension reduction for multinomials which is based on spherical models, a different type of curved exponential subfamilies than the one presented here which is affine in the mean-value parameterization.

---

[2]Notice that graphical models with latent variable are in general stratified exponential families [4], yet in our case the geometry is simpler. The geometrical view also illustrates the well-known identifiability problem in latent class analysis. The interested reader is referred to [3]. As a practical remedy, we have used a Bayesian approach with conjugate (Dirichlet) prior distributions over all multinomials which for the sake of clarity is not described in this paper since it is very technical but nevertheless rather straightforward.

3 Fisher Kernel and Information Geometry

The Fisher Kernel We follow the work of [9] to derive kernel functions (and hence similarity functions) from generative data models. This approach yields a uniquely defined and intrinsic (*i.e.* coordinate invariant) kernel, called the *Fisher kernel*. One important implication is that yardsticks used for statistical models carry over to the selection of appropriate similarity functions. In spite of the purely unsupervised manner in which a Fisher kernel can be learned, the latter is also very useful in *supervised* learning, where it provides a way to take advantage of additional unlabeled data. This is important in text learning, where digital document databases and the World Wide Web offer a huge background text repository.

As a starting point, we partition the data log-likelihood into contributions from the various documents. The average log-probability of a document d_i, *i.e.* the probability of all the word occurrences in d_i normalized by document length is given by,

$$l(d_i) = \sum_{j=1}^{M} \hat{P}(w_j|d_i) \log \sum_{k=1}^{K} P(w_j|z_k) P(z_k|d_i), \quad \hat{P}(w_j|d_i) \equiv \frac{n(d_i, w_j)}{\sum_m n(d_i, w_m)} \quad (4)$$

which is up to constants the negative Kullback-Leibler divergence between the empirical distribution $\hat{P}(w_j|d_i)$ and the model distribution represented by (1).

In order to derive the Fisher kernel, we have to compute the Fisher scores $u(d_i; \theta)$, *i.e.* the gradient of $l(d_i)$ with respect to θ, as well as the Fisher information $I(\theta)$ in some parameterization θ [13]. The Fisher kernel at $\hat{\theta}$ is then given by [9]

$$\mathcal{K}(d_i, d_n) = \langle u(d_i; \hat{\theta}), I(\hat{\theta})^{-1} u(d_n; \hat{\theta}) \rangle. \quad (5)$$

Computational Considerations For computational reasons we propose to approximate the (inverse) information matrix by the identity matrix, thereby making additional assumptions about information orthogonality. More specifically, we use a variance stabilizing parameterization for multinomials – the square-root parameterization – which yields an isometric embedding of multinomial families on the positive part of a hypersphere [11]. In this parameterization, the above approximation will be exact for the multinomial family (disregarding the normalization constraint). We conjecture that it will also provide a reasonable approximation in the case of the subfamily defined by the latent class model.

C. Simplifying assumption: The Fisher information in the square-root parameterization can be approximated by the identity matrix.

Interpretation of Results Instead of going through the details of the derivation which is postponed to the end of this section, it is revealing to relate the results back to our main problem of defining a similarity function between text documents. We will have a closer look at the two contributions resulting from different sets of parameters. The contribution which stems from (square-root transformed) parameters $P(z_k)$ is (in a simplified version) given by

$$\tilde{\mathcal{K}}(d_i, d_n) = \sum_k P(z_k|d_i) P(z_k|d_n) / P(z_k). \quad (6)$$

$\tilde{\mathcal{K}}$ is a weighted inner product in the low-dimensional factor representation of the documents by mixing weights $P(z_k|d_i)$. This part of the kernel thus computes a "topical" overlap between documents and is thereby able to capture *synonyms*, i.e., words with an identical or similar meaning, as well as words referring to the same topic. Notice, that it is not required that d_i and d_n actually have (many) terms in common in order to get a high similarity score.

The contribution due to the parameters $P(w_j|z_k)$ is of a very different type. Again using the approximation of the Fisher matrix, we arrive at the inner product

$$\bar{K}(d_i, d_n) = \sum_j \hat{P}(w_j|d_i)\hat{P}(w_j|d_n) \sum_k \frac{P(z_k|d_i, w_j)P(z_k|d_n, w_j)}{P(w_j|z_k)}. \quad (7)$$

$\bar{K}$ has also a very appealing interpretation: It essentially computes an inner product between the empirical distributions of d_i and d_n, a scheme that is very popular in the context of information retrieval in the vector space model. However, common words only contribute, if they are explained by the same factor(s), i.e., if the respective posterior probabilities overlap. This allows to capture words with multiple meanings, so-called *polysems*. For example, in the factors displayed in Figure 1 the term "president" occurs twice (as the president of a company and as the president of the US). Depending on the document the word occurs in, the posterior probability will be high for either one of the factors, but typically not for both. Hence, the same term used in different context and different meanings will generally not increase the similarity between documents, a distinction that is absent in the naive inner product which corresponds to the degenerate case of $K = 1$.

Since the choice of K determines the coarseness of the identified "topics" and different resolution levels possibly contribute useful information, we have combined models by a simple additive combination of the derived inner products. This combination scheme has experimentally proven to be very effective and robust.

D. Modeling assumption: Similarities derived from latent class decompositions at different levels of resolution are additively combined.

In summary, the emergence of important language phenomena like synonymy and polysemy from information-geometric principles is very satisfying and proves in our opinion that interesting similarity functions can be rigorously derived, without specific domain knowledge and based on few, explicitly stated assumptions (A-D).

Technical Derivation Define $\rho_{jk} \equiv 2\sqrt{P(w_j|z_k)}$, then

$$\begin{aligned}
\frac{\partial l(d_i)}{\partial \rho_{jk}} &= \frac{\partial l(d_i)}{\partial P(w_j|z_k)}\frac{\partial P(w_j|z_k)}{\partial \rho_{jk}} = \sqrt{P(w_j|z_k)}\frac{\hat{P}(w_j|d_i)}{P(w_j|d_i)}P(z_k|d_i) \\
&= \frac{\hat{P}(w_j|d_i)P(z_k|d_i, w_j)}{\sqrt{P(w_j|z_k)}}.
\end{aligned}$$

Similarly we define $\rho_k = 2\sqrt{P(z_k)}$. Applying Bayes' rule to substitute $P(z_k|d_i)$ in $l(d_i)$ (i.e. $P(z_k|d_i) = P(z_k)P(d_i|z_k)/P(d_i)$) yields

$$\begin{aligned}
\frac{\partial l(d_i)}{\partial \rho_k} &= \frac{\partial l(d_i)}{\partial P(z_k)}\frac{\partial P(z_k)}{\partial \rho_k} = \sqrt{P(z_k)}\frac{P(d_i|z_k)}{P(d_i)}\sum_j \frac{\hat{P}(w_j|d_i)}{P(w_j|d_i)}P(w_j|z_k) \\
&= \frac{P(z_k|d_i)}{\sqrt{P(z_k)}}\sum_j \frac{\hat{P}(w_j|d_i)}{P(w_j|d_i)}P(w_j|z_k) \approx \frac{P(z_k|d_i)}{\sqrt{P(z_k)}}.
\end{aligned}$$

The last (optional) approximation step makes sense whenever $\hat{P}(w_j|d_i) \approx P(w_j|d_i)$. Notice that we have ignored the normalization constraints which would yield a (reactive) term that is constant for each multinomial. Experimentally, we have observed no deterioration in performance by making these additional simplifications.

	Medline	Cranfield	CACM	CISI
VSM	44.3	29.9	17.9	12.7
VSM++	67.2	37.9	27.5	20.3

Table 1: Average precision results for the vector space baseline method (VSM) and the Fisher kernel approach (VSM++) for 4 standard test collections, Medline, Cranfield, CACM, and CISI.

		earn	acq	money	grain	crude	average	improv.
20x sub	SVM	5.51	7.67	3.25	2.06	2.50	4.20	-
	SVM++	4.56	5.37	2.08	1.71	1.53	3.05	+27.4%
	kNN	5.91	9.64	3.24	2.54	2.42	4.75	-
	kNN++	5.05	7.80	3.11	2.35	1.95	4.05	+14.7%
10x sub	SVM	4.88	5.54	2.38	1.71	1.88	3.27	-
	SVM++	4.11	4.84	2.08	1.42	1.45	2.78	+15.0%
	kNN	5.51	9.23	2.64	2.55	2.42	4.47	-
	kNN++	4.94	7.47	2.42	2.28	1.88	3.79	+15.2%
5x sub	SVM	4.09	4.40	2.10	1.32	1.46	2.67	-
	SVM++	3.64	4.15	1.78	0.98	1.19	2.35	+12.1%
	kNN	5.13	8.70	2.27	2.40	2.23	4.14	-
	kNN++	4.74	6.99	2.22	2.18	1.74	3.57	+13.7%
all data 10x cv	SVM	2.92	3.21	1.20	0.77	0.92	1.81	-
	SVM++	2.98	3.15	1.21	0.76	0.86	1.79	+0.6%
	kNN	4.17	6.69	1.78	1.73	1.42	3.16	-
	kNN++	4.07	5.34	1.73	1.58	1.18	2.78	+12.0%

Table 2: Classification errors for k-nearest neighbors (kNN) SVMs (SVM) with the naive kernel and with the Fisher kernel(++) (derived from $K = 1$ and $K = 64$ models) on the 5 most frequent categories of the Reuters21578 corpus (earn, acq, monex-fx, grain, and crude) at different subsampling levels.

4 Experimental Results

We have applied the proposed method for *ad hoc* information retrieval, where the goal is to return a list of documents, ranked with respect to a given query. This obviously involves computing similarities between documents and queries. In a follow-up series of experiments to the ones reported in [7] – where kernels $\tilde{\mathcal{K}}(d_i, d_n) = \sum_k P(z_k|d_i)P(z_k|d_n)$ and $\bar{\mathcal{K}}(d_i, d_n) = \sum_j \hat{P}(w_j|d_i)\hat{P}(w_j|d_n)$ have been proposed in an *ad hoc* manner – we have been able to obtain a rigorous theoretical justification as well as some additional improvements. Average precision-recall values for four standard test collections reported in Table 1 show that substantial performance gains can be achieved with the help of a generative model (cf. [7] for details on the conducted experiments).

To demonstrate the utility of our method for supervised learning problems, we have applied it to text categorization, using a standard data set in the evaluation, the Reuters21578 collections of news stories. We have tried to boost the performance of two classifiers that are known to be highly competitive for text categorization: the k-nearest neighbor method and Support Vector Machines (SVMs) with a linear kernel [10]. Since we are particularly interested in a setting, where the generative model is trained on a larger corpus of unlabeled data, we have run experiments where the classifier was only trained on a subsample (at subsampling factors 20x,10x,5x). The results are summarized in Table 2. Free parameters of the base classifiers have been optimized in extensive simulations with held-out data. The results indicate that substantial performance gains can be achieved over the standard k-nearest neighbor method at all subsampling levels. For SVMs the gain is huge on the subsampled data collections, but insignificant for SVMs trained on all data. This seems to indicate that the generative model does not provide any extra information, if the SVM classifier is trained on the same data. However, notice that many interesting applications in text categorization operate in the small sample limit with lots of unlabeled data. Examples include the definition of personalized news categories by just a few example, the classification and/or filtering of email, on-line topic spotting and tracking, and many more.

5 Conclusion

We have presented an approach to learn the similarity of text documents from first principles. Based on a latent class model, we have been able to derive a similarity function, that is theoretically satisfying, intuitively appealing, and shows substantial performance gains in the conducted experiments. Finally, we have made a contribution to the relationship between unsupervised and supervised learning as initiated in [9] by showing that generative models can help to exploit unlabeled data for classification problems.

References

[1] Shun'ichi Amari. *Differential-geometrical methods in statistics.* Springer-Verlag, Berlin, New York, 1985.

[2] S. Deerwester, S. T. Dumais, G. W. Furnas, T. K. Landauer, and R. Harshman. Indexing by latent semantic analysis. *Journal of the American Society for Information Science*, 41:391–407, 1990.

[3] M. J. Evans, Z. Gilula, and I. Guttman. Latent class analysis of two-way contingency tables by Bayesian methods. *Biometrika*, 76(3):557–563, 1989.

[4] D. Geiger, D. Heckerman, H. King, and C. Meek. Stratified exponential families: Graphical models and model selection. Technical Report MSR-TR-98-31, Microsoft Research, 1998.

[5] Z. Gilula and S. J. Haberman. Canonical analysis of contingency tables by maximum likelihood. *Journal of the American Statistical Association*, 81(395):780–788, 1986.

[6] A. Gous. *Exponential and Spherical Subfamily Models.* PhD thesis, Stanford, Statistics Department, 1998.

[7] T. Hofmann. Probabilistic latent semantic indexing. In *Proceedings of the 22th International Conference on Research and Development in Information Retrieval (SIGIR)*, pages 50–57, 1999.

[8] T. Hofmann, J. Puzicha, and M. I. Jordan. Unsupervised learning from dyadic data. In *Advances in Neural Information Processing Systems 11*. MIT Press, 1999.

[9] T. Jaakkola and D. Haussler. Exploiting generative models in discriminative classifiers. In *Advances in Neural Information Processing Systems 11*. MIT Press, 1999.

[10] T. Joachims. Text categorization with support vector machines: Learning with many relevant features. In *International Conference on Machine Learning (ECML)*, 1998.

[11] R.E. Kass and P. W. Vos. *Geometrical foundations of asymptotic inference.* Wiley, New York, 1997.

[12] D. Lee and S. Seung. Learning the parts of objects by non-negative matrix factorization. *Nature*, 401:788–791, 1999.

[13] M. K. Murray and J. W. Rice. *Differential geometry and statistics.* Chapman & Hall, London, New York, 1993.

[14] F.C.N. Pereira, N.Z. Tishby, and L. Lee. Distributional clustering of English words. In *Proceedings of the ACL*, pages 183–190, 1993.

[15] L. Saul and F. Pereira. Aggregate and mixed-order Markov models for statistical language processing. In *Proceedings of the 2nd International Conference on Empirical Methods in Natural Language Processing*, 1997.

Constructing Heterogeneous Committees Using Input Feature Grouping: Application to Economic Forecasting

Yuansong Liao and John Moody

Department of Computer Science, Oregon Graduate Institute,
P.O.Box 91000, Portland, OR 97291-1000

Abstract

The committee approach has been proposed for reducing model uncertainty and improving generalization performance. The advantage of committees depends on (1) the performance of individual members and (2) the correlational structure of errors between members. This paper presents an input grouping technique for *designing* a *heterogeneous committee*. With this technique, all input variables are first grouped based on their mutual information. Statistically similar variables are assigned to the same group. Each member's input set is then formed by input variables extracted from different groups. Our *designed committees* have less error correlation between its members, since each member observes different input variable combinations. The individual member's feature sets contain less redundant information, because highly correlated variables will not be combined together. The member feature sets contain almost complete information, since each set contains a feature from each information group. An empirical study for a noisy and nonstationary economic forecasting problem shows that committees constructed by our proposed technique outperform committees formed using several existing techniques.

1 Introduction

The committee approach has been widely used to reduce model uncertainty and improve generalization performance. Developing methods for generating candidate committee members is a very important direction of committee research. Good candidate members of a committee should have (1) good (not necessarily excellent) individual performance and (2) small residual error correlations with other members.

Many techniques have been proposed to reduce residual correlations between members. These include resampling the training and validation data [3], adding randomness to data [7], and decorrelation training [8]. These approaches are only effective for certain models and problems. Genetic algorithms have also been used to generate good and diverse members [6].

Input feature selection is one of the most important stages of the model learning process. It has a crucial impact both on the learning complexity and the generalization performance. It is essential that a feature vector gives sufficient information for estimation. However, too many redundant input features not only burden the whole learning process, but also degrade the achievable generalization performance.

Input feature selection for individual estimators has received a lot of attention because of its importance. However, there has not been much research on feature selection for estimators in the context of committees. Previous research found that giving committee members different input features is very useful for improving committee performance [4], but is difficult to implement [9]. The feature selection problem for committee members is conceptually different than for single estimators. When using committees for estimation, as we stated previously, committee members not only need to have reasonable performance themselves, but should also make decisions independently.

When all committee members are trained to model the same underlying function, it is difficult for committee members to optimize both criteria at the same time. In order to generate members that provide a good balance between the two criteria, we propose a feature selection approach, called **input feature grouping**, for committee members. The idea is to give each member estimator of a committee a rich but distinct feature sets, in the hope that each member will generalize independently with reduced error correlations.

The proposed method first groups input features using a hierarchical clustering algorithm based on their mutual information, such that features in different groups are less related to each other and features within a group are statistically similar to each other. Then the feature set for each committee member is formed by selecting a feature from each group. Our empirical results demonstrate that forming a heterogeneous committee using input feature grouping is a promising approach.

2 Committee Performance Analysis

There are many ways to construct a committee. In this paper, we are mainly interested in heterogeneous committees whose members have different input feature sets. Committee members are given different subsets of the available feature set. They are trained independently, and the committee output is either a weighted or unweighted combination of individual members' outputs.

In the following, we analyze the relationship between committee errors and average member errors from the regression point of view and discuss how the residual correlations between members affect the committee error. We define the training data $\mathcal{D} = \{(X^\beta, Y^\beta); \beta = 1, 2, \ldots N\}$ and the test data $\mathcal{T} = \{(X^\mu, Y^\mu); \mu = 1, 2, \ldots \infty\}$, where both are assumed to be generated by the model: $Y = t(X) + \epsilon$, $\epsilon \sim \mathcal{N}(0, \sigma^2)$. The data $\mathcal{D}$ and $\mathcal{T}$ are independent, and inputs are drawn from an unknown distribution. Assume that a committee has K members. Denote the available input features as $X = [x_1, x_2, \ldots, x_m]$, the feature sets for the ith and j^{th} members as $X_i = [x_{i_1}, x_{i_2}, \ldots, x_{m_i}]$ and $X_j = [x_{j_1}, x_{j_2}, \ldots, x_{m_j}]$ respectively, where $X_i \in X$, $X_j \in X$ and $X_i \neq X_j$, and the mapping function of the ith and j^{th} member models trained on data from $\mathcal{D}$ as $f_i(X_i)$ and $f_j(X_j)$. Define the *model error* $e_i^\mu = t^\mu - f_i(X_i^\mu)$, for all $\mu = 1, 2, 3, \ldots, \infty$ and $i = 1, 2, \ldots, K$.

The MSE of a committee is

$$E_C = \mathcal{E}_\mu\left[\left(t^\mu - \frac{1}{K}\sum_{i=1}^K f_i(X_i^\mu)\right)^2\right] = \frac{1}{K^2}\sum_{i=1}^K \mathcal{E}_\mu[(e_i^\mu)^2] + \frac{1}{K^2}\sum_{i\neq j}^K \mathcal{E}_\mu[e_i^\mu e_j^\mu], \quad (1)$$

and the average MSE made by the committee members acting individually is

$$E_{\text{ave}} = \frac{1}{K}\sum_{i=1}^K \mathcal{E}_\mu[(e_i^\mu)^2], \quad (2)$$

where $\mathcal{E}[\cdot]$ denotes the expectation over all test data $\mathcal{T}$. Using Jensen's inequality, we get $E_C \leq E_{\text{ave}}$, which indicates that the performance of a committee is always equal to or better than the average performance of its members.

We define the *average model error correlation* as $C = \frac{1}{K(K-1)}\sum_{i\neq j}^K \mathcal{E}_\mu[e_i^\mu e_j^\mu]$, and then have

$$E_C = \frac{1}{K}E_{\text{ave}} + \frac{K-1}{K}C = (\frac{1}{K} + \frac{K-1}{K}q)E_{\text{ave}}, \quad (3)$$

where $q = \frac{C}{E_{\text{ave}}}$. We consider the following four cases of q:

- **Case 1:** $-\frac{1}{K-1} \leq q < 0$. In this case, the model errors between members are anti-correlated, which might be achieved through decorrelation training.

- **Case 2:** $q = 0$. In this case, the *model errors* between members are uncorrelated, and we have: $E_C = \frac{1}{K}E_{\text{ave}}$. That is to say, a committee can do much better than the average performance of its members.

- **Case 3:** $0 < q < 1$. If E_{ave} is bounded above, when the committee size $K \longrightarrow \infty$, we have $E_C = qE_{\text{ave}}$. This gives the asymptotic limit of a committee's performance. As the size of a committee goes to infinity, the committee error is equal to the average model error correlation C. The difference between E_C and E_{ave} is determined by the ratio q.

- **Case 4:** $q = 1$. In this case, E_C is equal to E_{ave}. This happens only when $e_i = e_j$, for all $i, j = 1, \ldots, K$. It is obvious that there is no advantage to combining a set of models that act identically.

It is clear from the analyses above that a committee shows its advantage when the ratio q is less than one. The smaller the ratio q is, the better the committee performs compared to the average performance of its members. For the committee to achieve substantial improvement over a single model, committee members not only should have small errors individually, but also should have small residual correlations between each other.

3 Input Feature Grouping

One way to construct a feature subset for a committee member is by randomly picking a certain number of features from the original feature set. The advantage of this method is that it is simple. However, we have no control on each member's performance or on the residual correlation between members by randomly selecting subsets.

Instead of randomly picking a subset of features for a member, we propose an input feature grouping method for forming committee member feature sets. The input grouping method first groups features based on a relevance measure in a way such that features between different groups are less related to one another and features within a group are more related to one another.

After grouping, there are two ways to form member feature sets. One method is to construct the feature set for each member by selecting a feature from each group. Forming a member's feature set in this way, each member will have enough information to make decision, and its feature set has less redundancy. This is the method we use in this paper.

Another way is to use each group as the feature set for a committee member. In this method each member will only have partial information. This is likely to hurt individual member's performance. However, because the input features for different members are less dependent, these members tend to make decisions more independently. There is always a trade-off between increasing members' independence and hurting individual members' performance. If there is no redundancy among input feature representations, removing several features may hurt individual members' performance badly, and the overall committee performance will be hurt even though members make decisions independently. This method is currently under investigation.

The mutual information $I(x_i; x_j)$ between two input variables x_i and x_j is used as the relevance measure to group inputs. The mutual information $I(x_i; x_j)$, which is defined in equation 4, measures the dependence between the two random variables.

$$I(x_i; x_j) = H(x_i) - H(x_i|x_j) = \sum_{x_i, x_j} p(x_i, y_i) \log \frac{p(x_i, x_j)}{p(x_i)p(x_j)} . \qquad (4)$$

If features x_i and x_j are highly dependent, $I(x_i; x_j)$ will be large. Because the mutual information measures arbitrary dependencies between random variables, it has been effectively used for feature selections in complex prediction tasks [1], where methods bases on linear relations like the correlation are likely to make mistakes. The fact that the mutual information is independent of the coordinates chosen permits a robust estimation.

4 Empirical Studies

We apply the input grouping method to predict the one-month rate of change of the Index of Industrial Production (IP), one of the key measures of economic activity. It is computed and published monthly. Figure 4 plots monthly IP data from 1967 to 1993.

Nine macroeconomic time series, whose names are given in Table 1, are used for forecasting IP. Macroeconomic forecasting is a difficult task because data are usually limited, and these series are intrinsically very noise and nonstationary. These series are preprocessed before they are applied to the forecasting models. The representation used for input series is the first difference on one month time scales of the logged series. For example, the notation IP.L.D1 represents IP.L.D1 $\equiv ln(\text{IP}(t)) - ln(\text{IP}(t-1))$. The target series is IP.L.FD1, which is defined as IP.L.FD1 $\equiv ln(\text{IP}(t+1)) - ln(\text{IP}(t))$. The data set has been one of our benchmarks for various studies [5, 10].

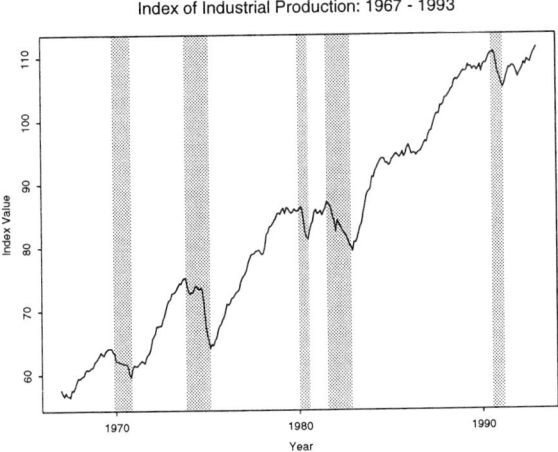

Figure 1: U.S. Index of Industrial Production (IP) for the period 1967 to 1993. Shaded regions denote official recessions, while unshaded regions denote official expansions. The boundaries for recessions and expansions are determined by the National Bureau of Economic Research based on several macroeconomic series. As is evident for IP, business cycles are irregular in magnitude, duration, and structure, making prediction of IP an interesting challenge.

Series	Description
IP	Index of Industrial Production
SP	Standard & Poor's 500
DL	Index of Leading Indicators
M2	Money Supply
CP	Consumer Price Index
CB	Moody's Aaa Bond Yield
HS	Housing Starts
TB3	3-month Treasury Bill Yield
Tr	Yield Curve Slope: (10-Year Bond Composite)-(3-Month Treasury Bill)

Table 1: Input data series. Data are taken from the Citibase database.

During the grouping procedure, measures of mutual information between all pairs of input variables are computed first. A simple histogram method is used to calculate these estimates. Then a hierarchical clustering algorithm [2] is applied to these values to group inputs. Hierarchical clustering proceeds by a series of successive fusions of the nine input variables into groups. At any particular stage, the process fuses variables or groups of variables which are closest, base on their mutual information estimates. The distance between two groups is defined as the average of the distances between all pairs of individuals in the two groups. The result is presented by a tree which illustrates the fusions made at each successive level (see Figure 2). From the clustering tree, it is clear that we can break the input variables into four groups: (IP.L.D1, DL.L.D1) measure recent economic changes, (SP.L.D1) reflects recent stock market momentum, (CB.D1, TB3.D1, Tr.D1) give interest rate information, and (M2.L.D1, CP.L.D1, HS.L.D1) provide inflation information. The grouping algorithm meaningfully clusters the nine input series.

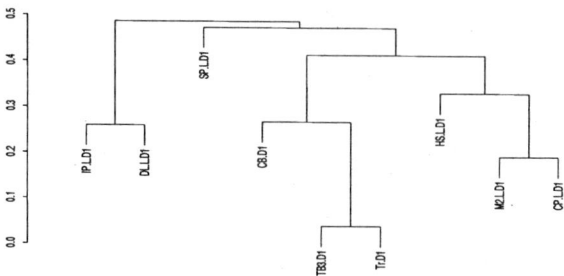

Figure 2: Variable grouping based on mutual information. Y label is the distance.

Eighteen different subsets of features can be generated from the four groups by selecting a feature from each group. Each subset is given to a committee member. For example, the subsets (IP.L.D1, SP.L.D1, CB.D1, M2.L.D1) and (DL.L.D1, SP.L.D1, TB3.D1, M2.L.D1) are used as feature sets for different committee members. A committee has totally eighteen members. Data from Jan. 1950 to Dec. 1979 is used for training and validation, and from Jan. 1980 to Dec. 1989 is used for testing. Each member is a linear model that is trained using neural net techniques.

We compare the input grouping method with three other committee member generating methods: baseline, random selection, and bootstrapping. The baseline method is to train a committee member using all the input variables. Members are only different in their initial weights. The bootstrapping method also trains a member using all the input features, but each member has different bootstrap replicates of the original training data as its training and validation sets. The random selection method constructs a feature set for a member by randomly picking a subset from the available features. For comparison with the grouping method, each committee generated by these three methods has 18 members.

Twenty runs are performed for each of the four methods in order to get reliable performance measures. Figure 3 shows the boxplots of normalized MSE for the four methods. The grouping method gives the best result, and the performance improvement is significant compared to other methods. The grouping method outperforms the random selection method by meaningfully grouping of input features. It is interesting to note that the heterogeneous committee methods, grouping and random selection, perform better than homogeneous methods for this data set. One of the reasons for this is that giving different members different input sets increases their model independence. Another reason could be that the problem becomes easier to model because of smaller feature sets.

5 Conclusions

The performance of a committee depends on both the performance of individual members and the correlational structure of errors between members. An empirical study for a noisy and nonstationary economic forecasting problem has demonstrated that committees constructed by input variable grouping outperform committees formed by randomly selecting member input variables. They also outperform committees without any input variable manipulation.

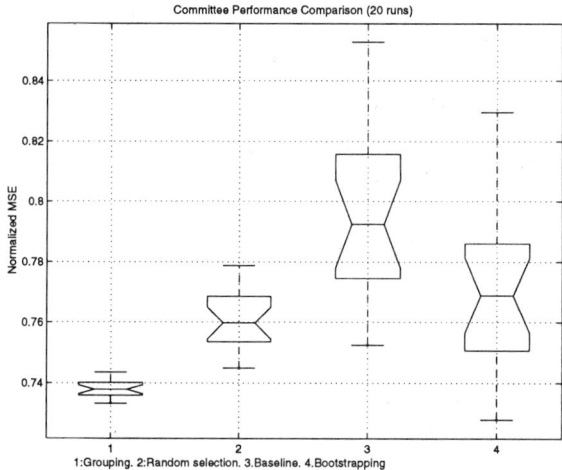

Figure 3: Comparison between four different committee member generating methods. The proposed grouping method gives the best result, and the performance improvement is significant compared to the other three methods.

References

[1] R. Battiti. Using mutual information for selecting features in supervised neural net learning. *IEEE Trans. on Neural Networks*, 5(4), July 1994.

[2] B.Everitt. *Cluster Analysis*. Heinemann Educational Books, 1974.

[3] L. Breiman. Bagging predictors. *Machine Learning*, 24(2):123–40, 1996.

[4] K.J. Cherkauer. Human expert-level performance on a scientific image analysis task by a system using combined artifical neural networks. In P. Chan, editor, *Working Notes of the AAAI Workshop on Integrating Multiple Learned Models*, pages 15–21. 1996.

[5] J. Moody, U. Levin, and S. Rehfuss. Predicting the U.S. index of industrial production. *In proceedings of the 1993 Parallel Applications in Statistics and Economics Conference, Zeist, The Netherlands. Special issue of* Neural Network World, 3(6):791–794, 1993.

[6] D. Opitz and J. Shavlik. Generating accurate and diverse members of a neural-network ensemble. In D. Touretzky, M. Mozer, and M. Hasselmo, editors, *Advances in Neural Information Processing Systems 8*. MIT Press, Cambridge, MA, 1996.

[7] Y. Raviv and N. Intrator. Bootstrapping with noise: An effective regularization technique. *Connection Science*, 8(3-4):355–72, 1996.

[8] B. E. Rosen. Ensemble learning using decorrelated neural networks. *Connection Science*, 8(3-4):373–83, 1996.

[9] K. Tumer and J. Ghosh. Error correlation and error reduction in ensemble classifiers. *Connection Science*, 8(3-4):385–404, December 1996.

[10] L. Wu and J. Moody. A smoothing regularizer for feedforward and recurrent neural networks. *Neural Computation*, 8.3:463–491, 1996.

From Coexpression to Coregulation: An Approach to Inferring Transcriptional Regulation among Gene Classes from Large-Scale Expression Data

Eric Mjolsness
Jet Propulsion Laboratory
California Institute of Technology
Pasadena CA 91109-8099
mjolsness@jpl.nasa.gov

Tobias Mann
Jet Propulsion Laboratory
California Institute of Technology
Pasadena CA 91109-8099
mann@aig.jpl.nasa.gov

Rebecca Castaño
Jet Propulsion Laboratory
California Institute of Technology
Pasadena CA 91109-8099
becky@aig.jpl.nasa.gov

Barbara Wold
Division of Biology
California Institute of Technology
Pasadena CA 91125
woldb@its.caltech.edu

Abstract

We provide preliminary evidence that existing algorithms for inferring small-scale gene regulation networks from gene expression data can be adapted to large-scale gene expression data coming from hybridization microarrays. The essential steps are (1) clustering many genes by their expression time-course data into a minimal set of clusters of co-expressed genes, (2) theoretically modeling the various conditions under which the time-courses are measured using a continious-time analog recurrent neural network for the cluster mean time-courses, (3) fitting such a regulatory model to the cluster mean time courses by simulated annealing with weight decay, and (4) analysing several such fits for commonalities in the circuit parameter sets including the connection matrices. This procedure can be used to assess the adequacy of existing and future gene expression time-course data sets for determining transcriptional regulatory relationships such as coregulation.

1 Introduction

In a cell, genes can be turned "on" or "off" to varying degrees by the protein products of other genes. When a gene is "on" it is transcribed to produce messenger RNA (mRNA) which can subsequently be translated into protein molecules. Some of these proteins are transcription factors which bind to DNA at specific sites and thereby affect which genes are transcribed and how often. This trancriptional regulation feedback circuitry provides a fundamental mechanism for information processing in the cell. It governs differentiation into diverse cell types and many other basic biological processes.

Recently, several new technologies have been developed for measuring the "expression" of genes as mRNA or protein product. Improvements in conventional fluorescently labeled antibodies against proteins have been coupled with confocal microscopy and image processing to partially automate the simultaneous measurement of small numbers of proteins in large numbers of individual nuclei in the fruit fly *Drosophila melanogaster* [1]. In a complementary way, the mRNA levels of thousands of genes, each averaged over many cells, have been measured by hybridization arrays for various species including the budding yeast *Saccharomyces cerevisiae* [2].

The high-spatial-resolution protein antibody data has been quantitatively modeled by "gene regulation network" circuit models [3] which use continuous-time, analog, recurrent neural networks (Hopfield networks without an objective function) to model transcriptional regulation [4][5]. This approach requires some machine learning technique to infer the circuit parameters from the data, and a particular variant of simulated annealing has proven effective [6][7]. Methods in current biological use for analysing mRNA hybridization data do not infer regulatory relationships, but rather simply cluster together genes with similar patterns of expression across time and experimental conditions [8][9]. In this paper, we explore the extension of the gene circuit method to the mRNA hybridization data which has much lower spatial resolution but can currently assay a thousand times more genes than immunofluorescent image analysis.

The essential problem with using the gene circuit method, as employed for immunoflourescence data, on hybridization data is that the number of connection strength parameters grows between linearly and quadratically in the number of genes (depending on sparsity assumptions) . This requires more data on each gene, and even if that much data is available, simulated annealing for circuit inference does not seem to scale well with the number of unknown parameters. Some form of dimensionality reduction is called for. Fortunately dimensionality reduction is available in the present practice of clustering the large-scale time course expression data by genes, into gene clusters. In this way one can derive a small number of cluster-mean time courses for "aggregated genes", and then fit a gene regulation circuit to these cluster mean time courses. We will discuss details of how this analysis can be performed and then interpreted. A similar approach using somewhat different algorithms for clustering and circuit inference has been taken by Hertz [10].

In the following, we will first summarize the data models and algorithms used, and then report on preliminary experiments in applying those algorithms to gene expression data for 2467 yeast genes [9][11]. Finally we will discuss prospects for and limitations of the approach.

2 Data Models and Algorithms

The data model is as follows. We imagine that there is a small, hidden regulatory network of "aggregate genes" which regulate one another by the analog neural network dynamics [3]

$$\tau_i \frac{dv_i}{dt} = g\left(\sum_j T_{ij} v_j + h_i\right) - \lambda_i v_i$$

in which v_i is the continuous-valued state variable for gene product i, T_{ij} is the matrix of positive, zero, or negative connections by which one transcription factor can enhance or repress another, and $g()$ is a nonlinear monotonic sigmoidal activation function. When a particular matrix entry T_{ij} is nonzero, there is a regulatory "connection" from gene product j to gene i. The regulation is enhancing if T is positive and repressing if it is negative. If T_{ij} is zero there is no connection.

This network is run forwards from some initial condition and time-sampled to generate a wild-type time course for the aggregate genes. In addition, various other time courses can be generated under alternative experimental conditions by manipulating the parameters. For example an entire aggregate gene (corresponding to a cluster of real genes) could be removed from the circuit or otherwise modified to represent mutants. External input conditions could be modeled as modifications to h. Thus we get one or several time courses (trajectories) for the aggregate genes.

From such aggregate time courses, actual gene data is generated by addition of Gaussian-distributed noise to the logarithms of the concentration variables. Each time point in each cluster has its own scalar standard deviation parameter (and a mean arising from the circuit dynamics). Optionally, each gene's expression data may also be multiplied by a time-independent proportionality constant.

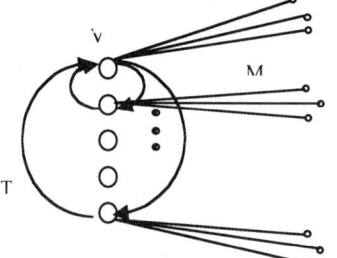

Regulatory aggregate genes (large circles) and cluster member genes (small circles).

Given this data generation model and suitable gene expression data, the problem is to infer gene cluster memberships and the circuit parameters for the aggregate genes' regulatory relationships. Then, we would like to use the inferred cluster memberships and regulatory circuitry to make testable biological predictions.

This data model departs from biological reality in many ways that could prove to be important, both for inference and for prediction. Except for the Gaussian noise model, each gene in a cluster is models as fully coregulated with every other one – they are influenced in the same ways by the same regulatory connection strengths. Also, the nonlinear circuit model must not only reflect transcriptional regulation, but all other regulatory circuitry affecting measured gene expression such as kinase-phosphatase networks.

Under this data model, one could formulate a joint Bayesian inference problem for the clustering and circuit inference aspects of fitting the data. But given the highly provisional nature of the model, we simply apply in sequence an existing mixture-of-Gaussians clustering algorithm to preprocess the data and reduce its dimensionality, and then an existing gene circuit inference algorithm. Presumably a joint optimization algorithm could be obtained by iterating these steps.

2.1 Clustering

A widely used clustering algorithm for mixure model estimation is Expectation-Maximization (EM)[12]. We use EM with a diagonal covariance in the Gaussian, so that for each feature vector component a (a combination of experimental condition and time point in a time course) and cluster α there is a standard deviation parameter $\sigma_{a\alpha}$. In preprocessing, each concentration data point is divided by its value at time zero and then a logarithm taken. The log ratios are clustered using EM. Optionally, each gene's entire feature vector may be normalized to unit length and the cluster centers likewise normalized during the iterative EM algorithm.

In order to choose the number of clusters, k, we use the cross-validation algorithm described by Smyth [13]. This involves computing the likelihood of each optimized fit on a test set and averaging over runs and over divisions of the data into training and test sets. Then, we can examine the likelihood as a function of k in order to choose k. Normally one would pick k so as to maximize cross-validated likelihood. However, in the present application we also want to reward small values of k which lead to smaller circuits for the circuit inference phase of the algorithm. The choice of k will be discussed in the next section.

2.2 Circuit Inference

We use the Lam-Delosme variant of simulated annealing (SA) to derive connection strengths T, time constants τ, and decay rates λ, as in previous work using this gene circuit method [4][5]. We set h to zero. The score function which SA optimizes is

$$S(T,\tau,\lambda) = A\sum_{it}\left(v_i(t;T,\tau,\lambda) - \hat{v}_i(t)\right)^2 + W\sum_{ij}T_{ij}^2$$
$$+ \exp[B(\sum_{ij}T_{ij}^2 + \sum_i \lambda_i^2 + \sum_i \tau_i^2)] - 1$$

The first term represents the fit to data $\hat{v}_i$. The second term is a standard weight decay term. The third term forces solutions to stay within a bounded region in weight space. We vary the weight decay coefficient W in order to encourage relatively sparse connection matrix solutions.

3 Results

3.1 Data

We used the *Saccharomyces cerevisiae* data set of [9]. It includes three longer time courses representing different ways to synchronize the normal cell cycle [11], and five shorter time courses representing altered conditions. We used all eight time courses for clustering, but just 8 time points of one of the longer time courses (alpha factor synchronized cell cycle) for the circuit inference. It is likely that multiple long time courses under altered conditions will be required before strong biological predictions can be made from inferred regulatory circuit models.

3.2 Clustering

We found that the most likely number of classes as determined by cross validation was about 27, but that there is a broad plateau of high-likelihood cluster numbers from 15 to 35 (Figure 1). This is similar to our results with another gene expression data set for the nematode worm *Caenorhabditis elegans* supplied by Stuart Kim; these more extensive clustering experiments are summarized in Figure 2. Clustering experiments with synthetic data is used to understand these results. These experiments show that the cross-validated log likelihood curve can indicate the number of clusters present in the data, justifying the use of the curve for that purpose. In more detail, synthetic data generated from 14 20-dimensional spherical Gaussian clusters were clustered using the EM/CV algorithm. The likelihoods showed a sharp peak at k=14 unlike Figures 1 or 2. In another experiment, 14 20-dimensional spherical Gaussian superclusters were used to generate second-level clusters (3 subclusters per supercluster), which in turn generated synthetic data points. This two-level hierarchical model was then clustered with the EM/CV method. The likelihood curves (not shown) were quite similar to Figures 1 and 2, with a higher-likelihood plateau from roughly 14 to 40.

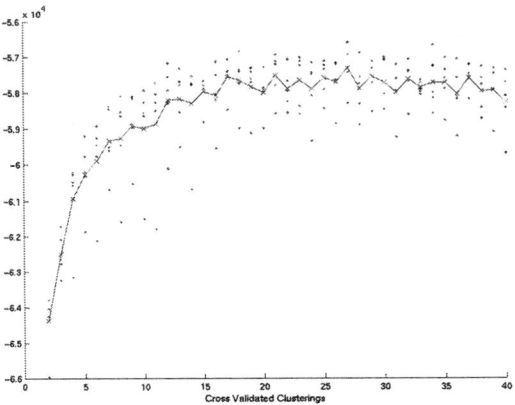

Figure 1. Cross-validated log-likelihood scores, displayed and averaged over 5 runs, for EM clustering of *S. cerevisiae* gene expression data [9]. Horizontal axis: k, the "requested" or maximal number of cluster centers in the fit. Some cluster centers go unmatched to data. Vertical axis: log likelihood score for the fit, scatterplotted and averaged. Likelihoods have not been integrated over any range of parameters for hypothesis testing. k ranges from 2 to 40 in increments of 1. Solid line shows average likelihood value for each k.

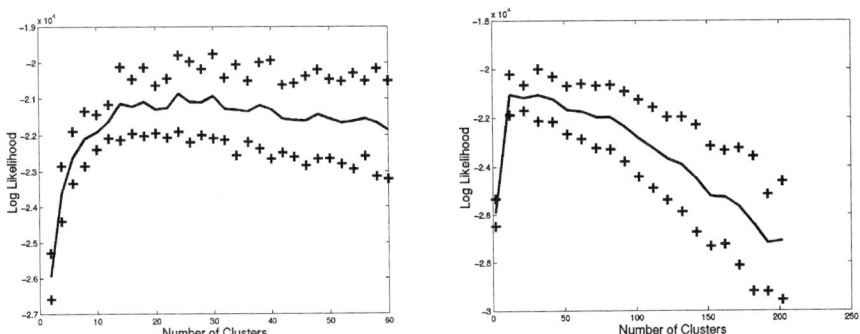

Figure 2. Cross-validated log-likelihood scores, averaged over 13 runs, for EM clustering of *C. elegans* gene expression data from S. Kim's lab. Horizontal axis: k, the "requested" or maximal number of cluster centers in the fit. Some cluster centers go unmatched to data. Vertical axis: log likelihood score for the fit, as an average over 13 runs plus or minus one standard deviation. (Left) Fine-scale plot, k =2 to 60 in increments of 2. (Right) Coarse-scale plot, k=2 to 202 in increments of 10. Both plots show an extended plateau of relatively likely fits between roughly k =14 and k =40.

From Figures 1 and 2 and the synthetic data experiments mentioned above, we can guess at appropriate values for k which take into account both the measured likelihood of clustering and the requirements for few parameters in circuit-fitting. For example choosing k=15 clusters would put us at the beginning of the plateau, losing very little cluster likelihood in return for reducing the aggregate genes circuit size from 27 to 15 players. The interpretation would be that there are about 15 superclusters in hierarchically clustered data, to which we will fit a 15-player regulatory circuit. Much more aggressive would be to pick $k=7$ or 8 clusters, for a relatively significant drop in log-likelihood in return for a further substantial decrease in circuit size. An acceptable range of cluster numbers (and circuit sizes) would seem to be $k=8$ to 15.

3.3 Gene Circuit Inference

It proved possible to fit the $k=15$ time course using weight decay $W=1$ but without using hidden units. $W=0$ and $W=3$ gave less satisfactory results. Four of the 15 clusters are shown in Figure 3 for one good run ($W=1$). Scores for our first few (unselected) runs at the current parameter settings are shown in Table 1. Each run took between 24 and 48 hours on one processor of an Sun Ultrasparc 60 computer. Even with weight decay, it is possible that successful fits are really overfits with this particular data since there are about twice as many parameters as data points.

Weight Decay W	<Score>	<Simulated Annealing Moves>/10^6	Number of runs
0	1.536 +/- 0.134	2.803 +/- 0.437	3
1	0.787 +/- 0.394	2.782 +/- 0.200	10
3	1.438 +/- 0.037	2.880 +/- 0.090	4

Table 1. Score function parameters were A=1.0, B=0.01. Annealing runs statistics are reported when the temperature dropped below 0.0001. All the best scores and visually acceptable fits occurred in W=1 runs.

The average values of the data fit, weight decay, and penalty terms in the score function for W=1 were {0.378, 0.332, 0.0667} after slightly more annealing.

There were a few significant similarities between the connection matrices computed in the two lowest-scoring runs. The most salient feature in the lowest-scoring network was a set of direct feedback loops among its strongest connections: cluster 8 both excited and was inhibited by cluster 10, and cluster 10 excited and was inhibited by cluster 15. This feature was preserved in the second-best run. A systematic search for "concensus circuitry" shows convergence towards a unique connection matrix for the 8-point time series data used here, but more complete 16-time-point data gives multiple "clusters" of connection matrices. From parameter-counting one might expect that making robust and unique regulatory predictions will require the use of more trajectory data taken under substantially different conditions. Such data is expected to be forthcoming.

4 Discussion

We have illustrated a procedure for deriving regulatory models from large-scale gene expression data. As the data becomes more comprehensive in the number and nature of conditions under which comparable time courses are measured, this procedure can be used to determine when biological hypotheses about gene regulation can be robustly derived from the data.

Acknowledgments

This work was supported in part by the Whittier Foundation, the Office of Naval Research under contract N00014-97-1-0422, and the NASA Advanced Concepts Program. Stuart Kim (Stanford University) provided the *C. elegans* gene expression array data. The GRN simulation and inference code is due in part to Charles Garrett and George Marnellos. The EM clustering code is due in part to Roberto Manduchi.

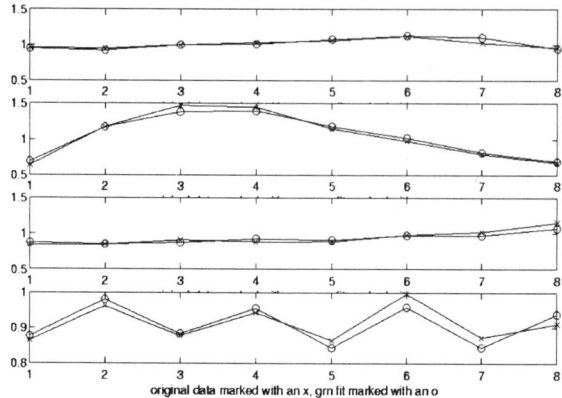

Figure 3. Four clusters (numbers 9-12) of a 15-cluster mixture of Gaussians model of 2467 genes each assayed over an eight-point time course; cluster means (shown as x) are fit to a gene regulation network model (shown as o).

References

[1] D. Kosman, J. Reinitz, and D. H. Sharp, "Automated Assay of Gene Expression at Cellular Resolution" Pacific Symposium on Biocomputing '98. Eds. R. Altman, A. K. Dunker, L. Hunter, and T. E. Klein,, World Scientific 1998.

[2] J. L. DeRisi, V. R. Iyer, and P. O. Brown, "Exploring the Metabolic and Genetic Control of Gene Expreession on a Genomic Scale". Science 278, 680-686.

[3] A Connectionist Model of Development, E. Mjolsness, D. H. Sharp, and J. Reinitz, Journal of Theoretical Biology 152:429-453, 1991.

[4] J. Reinitz, E. Mjolsness, and D. H. Sharp, "Model for Cooperative Control of Positional Information in *Drosophila* by Bicoid and Maternal Hunchback". J. Experimental Zoology 271:47-56, 1995. Los Alamos National Laboratory Technical Report LAUR-92-2942 1992.

[5] J. Reinitz and D. H. Sharp, "Mechanism of *eve* Stripe Formation". Mechanisms of Development 49:133-158, 1995.

[6] [7] J. Lam and J. M. Delosme. "An Efficient Simulated Annealing Schedule: Derivation" and "... Implementation and Evaluation". Technical Reports 8816 and 8817, Yale University Electrical Engineering Department, New Haven CT 1988.

[8] X. Wen, S. Fuhrman, G. S. Michaels, D. B. Carr, S. Smith, J. L. Barker, and R. Somogyi, "Large-Scale Temporal Gene Expression Mapping of Central Nervous System Development", Proc. Natl. Acal. Sci. USA 95:334-339, January 1998.

[9] M. B. Eisen, P. T. Spellman, P. O. Brown, and D. Botstein, "Cluster Analysis and Display of Genome-Wide Expression Patterns", Proc. Natl. Acad. Scie. USA 95:14863-14868, December 1998.

[10] J. Hertz, lecture at Krogerrup Denmark computational biology summer school, July 1998.

[11] Spellman PT, Sherlock G, Zhang MQ, et al., "Comprehensive identification of cell cycle-regulated genes of the yeast Saccharomyces cerevisiae by microarray hybridization", Mol. Bio. Cell. 9: (12) 3273-3297 Dec 1998.

[12] Dempster, A. P., Laird, N. M. and Rubin, D. B. "Maximum likelihood from incomplete data via the EM algorithm," J. Royal Statistical Society, Series B, 39:1-38, 1977.

[13] P. Smyth, "Clustering using Monte Carlo Cross-Validation", Proceedings of the 2nd International Conference on Knowledge Discovery and Data Mining, AAAI Press, 1996.

Churn Reduction in the Wireless Industry

Michael C. Mozer*+, Richard Wolniewicz*, David B. Grimes*+,
Eric Johnson*, Howard Kaushansky*
* Athene Software   + Department of Computer Science
2060 Broadway, Suite 300   University of Colorado
Boulder, CO 80302   Boulder, CO 80309–0430

Abstract

Competition in the wireless telecommunications industry is rampant. To maintain profitability, wireless carriers must control *churn*, the loss of subscribers who switch from one carrier to another. We explore statistical techniques for churn prediction and, based on these predictions, an optimal policy for identifying customers to whom incentives should be offered to increase retention. Our experiments are based on a data base of nearly 47,000 U.S. domestic subscribers, and includes information about their usage, billing, credit, application, and complaint history. We show that under a wide variety of assumptions concerning the cost of intervention and the retention rate resulting from intervention, churn prediction and remediation can yield significant savings to a carrier. We also show the importance of a data representation crafted by domain experts.

Competition in the wireless telecommunications industry is rampant. As many as seven competing carriers operate in each market. The industry is extremely dynamic, with new services, technologies, and carriers constantly altering the landscape. Carriers announce new rates and incentives weekly, hoping to entice new subscribers and to lure subscribers away from the competition. The extent of rivalry is reflected in the deluge of advertisements for wireless service in the daily newspaper and other mass media.

The United States had 69 million wireless subscribers in 1998, roughly 25% of the population. Some markets are further developed; for example, the subscription rate in Finland is 53%. Industry forecasts are for a U.S. penetration rate of 48% by 2003. Although there is significant room for growth in most markets, the industry growth rate is declining and competition is rising. Consequently, it has become crucial for wireless carriers to control *churn*—the loss of customers who switch from one carrier to another. At present, domestic monthly churn rates are 2-3% of the customer base. At an average cost of $400 to acquire a subscriber, churn cost the industry nearly $6.3 billion in 1998; the total annual loss rose to nearly $9.6 billion when lost monthly revenue from subscriber cancellations is considered (Luna, 1998). It costs roughly five times as much to sign on a new subscriber as to retain an existing one. Consequently, for a carrier with 1.5 million subscribers, reducing the monthly churn rate from 2% to 1% would yield an increase in annual earnings of at least $54 million, and an increase in shareholder value of approximately $150 million. (Estimates are even higher when lost monthly revenue is considered; see Fowlkes, Madan, Andrew, & Jensen, 1999; Luna, 1998.)

The goal of our research is to evaluate the benefits of predicting churn using techniques from statistical machine learning. We designed models that predict the probability of a subscriber churning within a short time window, and we evaluated how well these predictions could be used for decision making by estimating potential cost savings to the wireless carrier under a variety of assumptions concerning subscriber behavior.

1 THE FRAMEWORK

Figure 1 shows a framework for churn prediction and profitability maximization. Data from a subscriber—on which we elaborate in the next section—is fed into three components which estimate: the likelihood that the subscriber will churn, the profitability (expected monthly revenue) of the subscriber, and the subscriber's credit risk. Profitability and credit risk determine how valuable the subscriber is to the carrier, and hence influences how much the carrier should be willing to spend to retain the subscriber. Based on the predictions of subscriber behavior, a decision making component determines an *intervention strategy*—whether a subscriber should be contacted, and if so, what incentives should be offered to appease them. We adopt a decision-theoretic approach which aims to maximize the expected profit to the carrier.

In the present work, we focus on churn prediction and utilize simple measures of subscriber profitability and credit risk. However, current modeling efforts are directed at more intelligent models of profitability and credit risk.

2 DATA SET

The subscriber data used for our experiments was provided by a major wireless carrier. The carrier does not want to be identified, as churn rates are confidential. The carrier provided a data base of 46,744 primarily business subscribers, all of whom had multiple services. (Each service corresponds to a cellular telephone or to some other service, such as voice messaging or beeper capability.) All subscribers were from the same region of the United States, about 20% in major metropolitan areas and 80% more geographically distributed. The total revenue for all subscribers in the data base was $14 million in October 1998. The average revenue per subscriber was $234. We focused on multi-service subscribers, because they provide significantly more revenue than do typical single-service subscribers.

When subscribers are on extended contracts, churn prediction is relatively easy: it seldom occurs during the contract period, and often occurs when the contract comes to an end. Consequently, all subscribers in our data base were month-to-month, requiring the use of more subtle features than contract termination date to anticipate churn.

The subscriber data was extracted from the time interval October through December, 1998. Based on these data, the task was to predict whether a subscriber would churn in January *or* February 1999. The carrier provided their internal definition of churn, which was based on the closing of all services held by a subscriber. From this definition, 2,876 of the subscribers active in October through December churned—6.2% of the data base.

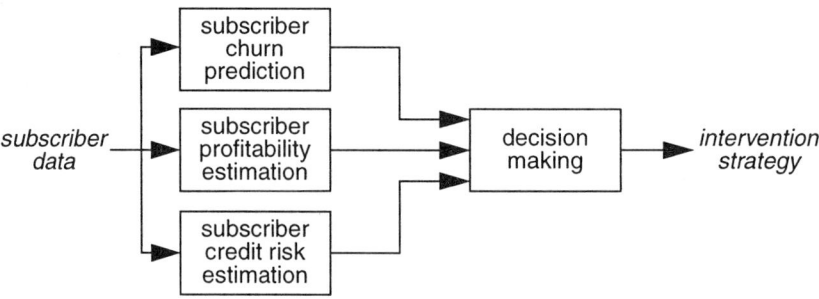

FIGURE 1. The framework for churn prediction and profitability maximization

2.1 INPUT FEATURES

Ultimately, churn occurs because subscribers are dissatisfied with the price or quality of service, usually as compared to a competing carrier. The main reasons for subscriber dissatisfaction vary by region and over time. Table 1 lists important factors that influence subscriber satisfaction, as well as the relative importance of the factors (J. D. Power and Associates, 1998). In the third column, we list the type of information required for determining whether a particular factor is likely to be influencing a subscriber. We categorize the types of information as follows.

Network. Call detail records (date, time, duration, and location of all calls), dropped calls (calls lost due to lack of coverage or available bandwidth), and quality of service data (interference, poor coverage).

Billing. Financial information appearing on a subscriber's bill (monthly fee, additional charges for roaming and additional minutes beyond monthly prepaid limit).

Customer Service. Calls to the customer service department and their resolutions.

Application for Service. Information from the initial application for service, including contract details, rate plan, handset type, and credit report.

Market. Details of rate plans offered by carrier and its competitors, recent entry of competitors into market, advertising campaigns, etc.

Demographics. Geographic and population data of a given region.

A subset of these information sources were used in the present study. Most notably, we did not utilize market information, because the study was conducted over a fairly short time interval during which the market did not change significantly. More important, the market forces were fairly uniform in the various geographic regions from which our subscribers were selected. Also, we were unable to obtain information about the subscriber equipment (age and type of handset used).

The information sources listed above were distributed over three distinct data bases maintained by the carrier. The data bases contained thousands of fields, from which we identified 134 variables associated with each subscriber which we conjectured might be linked to churn. The variables included: subscriber location, credit classification, customer classification (e.g., corporate versus retail), number of active services of various types, beginning and termination dates of various services, avenue through which services were activated, monthly charges and usage, number, dates and nature of customer service calls, number of calls made, and number of abnormally terminated calls.

2.2 DATA REPRESENTATION

As all statisticians and artificial intelligence researchers appreciate, representation is key. A significant portion of our effort involved working with domain experts in the wireless telecommunications industry to develop a representation of the data that highlights and makes explicit those features which—in the expert's judgement—were highly related to churn. To evaluate the benefit of carefully constructing the representation, we performed

TABLE 1. Factors influencing subscriber satisfaction

Factor	Importance	Nature of data required for prediction
call quality	21%	network
pricing options	18%	market, billing
corporate capability	17%	market, customer service
customer service	17%	customer service
credibility / customer communications	10%	market, customer service
roaming / coverage	7%	network
handset	4%	application
billing	3%	billing
cost of roaming	3%	market, billing

studies using both *naive* and a *sophisticated* representations.

The naive representation mapped the 134 variables to a vector of 148 elements in a straightforward manner. Numerical variables, such as the length of time a subscriber had been with the carrier, were translated to an element of the representational vector which was linearly related to the variable value. We imposed lower and upper limits on the variables, so as to suppress irrelevant variation and so as not to mask relevant variation by too large a dynamic range; vector elements were restricted to lie between −4 and +4 standard deviations of the variable. One-of-n discrete variables, such as credit classification, were translated into an n-dimensional subvector with one nonzero element.

The sophisticated representation incorporated the domain knowledge of our experts to produce a 73-element vector encoding attributes of the subscriber. This representation collapsed across some of the variables which, in the judgement of the experts, could be lumped together (e.g., different types of calls to the customer service department), and expanded on others (e.g., translating the scalar length-of-time-with-carrier to a multidimensional basis-function representation, where the receptive-field centers of the basis functions were suggested by the domain experts), and performed transformations of other variables (e.g., ratios of two variables, or time-series regression parameters).

3 PREDICTORS

The task is to predict the probability of churn from the vector encoding attributes of the subscriber. We compared the churn-prediction performance of two classes of models: logit regression and a nonlinear neural network with a single hidden layer and weight decay (Bishop, 1995). The neural network model class was parameterized by the number of units in the hidden layer and the weight decay coefficient. We originally anticipated that we would require some model selection procedure, but it turned out that the results were remarkably insensitive to the choice of the two neural network parameters; weight decay up to a point seemed to have little effect, and beyond that point it was harmful, and varying the number of hidden units from 5 to 40 yielded nearly identical performance. We likely were not in a situation where overfitting was an issue, due to the large quantity of data available; hence increasing the model complexity (either by increasing the number of hidden units or decreasing weight decay) had little cost.

Rather than selecting a single neural network model, we averaged the predictions of an ensemble of models which varied in the two model parameters. The average was uniformly weighted.

4 METHODOLOGY

We constructed four predictors by combining each of the two model classes (logit regression and neural network) with each of the two subscriber representations (naive and sophisticated). For each predictor, we performed a ten-fold cross validation study, utilizing the same splits across predictors. In each split of the data, the ratio of churn to no churn examples in the training and validation sets was the same as in the overall data set.

For the neural net models, the input variables were centered by subtracting the means and scaled by dividing by their standard deviation. Input values were restricted to lie in the range [−4, +4]. Networks were trained until they reached a local minimum in error.

5 RESULTS AND DISCUSSION

5.1 CHURN PREDICTION

For each of the four predictors, we obtain a predicted probability of churn for each subscriber in the data set by merging the test sets from the ten data splits. Because decision making ultimately requires a "churn" or "no churn" prediction, the continuous probability measure must be thresholded to obtain a discrete predicted outcome.

For a given threshold, we determine the proportion of churners who are correctly identified as churners (the *hit* rate), and the proportion of nonchurners who are correctly identified as nonchurners (the *rejection* rate). Plotting the hit rate against the rejection rate for various thresholds, we obtain an *ROC curve* (Green & Swets, 1966). In Figure 2, the closer a curve comes to the upper right corner of the graph—100% correct prediction of churn and 100% correct prediction of nonchurn—the better is the predictor at discriminating churn from nonchurn. The dotted diagonal line indicates no discriminability: If a predictor randomly classifies $x\%$ of cases as churn, it is expected to obtain a hit rate of $x\%$ and a rejection rate of $(100-x)\%$.

As the Figure indicates, discriminability is clearly higher for the sophisticated representation than for the naive representation. Further, for the sophisticated representation at least, the nonlinear neural net outperforms the logit regression. It appears that the neural net can better exploit nonlinear structure in the sophisticated representation than in the naive representation, perhaps due to the basis-function representation of key variables. Although the four predictors appear to yield similar curves, they produce large differences in estimated cost savings. We describe how we estimate cost savings next.

5.2 DECISION MAKING

Based on a subscriber's predicted churn probability, we must decide whether to offer the subscriber some *incentive* to remain with the carrier, which will presumably reduce the likelihood of churn. The incentive will be offered to any subscriber whose churn probability is above a certain threshold. The threshold will be selected to maximize the expected cost savings to the carrier; we will refer to this as the *optimal decision-making policy*.

The cost savings will depend not only on the discriminative ability of the predictor, but also on: the cost to the carrier of providing the incentive, denoted C_i (the cost to the carrier may be much lower than the value to the subscriber, e.g., when air time is offered); the time horizon over which the incentive has an effect on the subscriber's behavior; the reduction in probability that the subscriber will leave within the time horizon as a result of the incentive, P_i; and the lost-revenue cost that results when a subscriber churns, C_l.

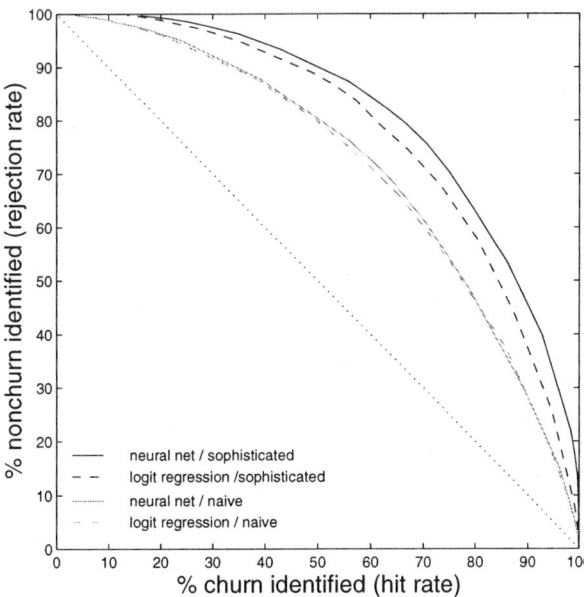

FIGURE 2. Test-set performance for the four predictors. Each curve shows, for various thresholds, the ability of a predictor to correctly identify churn (x axis) and nonchurn (y axis). The more bowed a curve, the better able a predictor is at discriminating churn from nonchurn.

We assume a time horizon of six months. We also assume that the lost revenue as a result of churn is the average subscriber bill over the time horizon, along with a fixed cost of $500 to acquire a replacement subscriber. (This acquisition cost is higher than the typical cost we stated earlier because subscribers in this data base are high valued, and often must be replaced with multiple low-value subscribers to achieve the same revenue.) To estimate cost savings, the parameters C_i, P_i, and C_l are combined with four statistics obtained from a predictor:

$N(pL,aL)$: number of subscribers who are predicted to leave (churn) and who actually leave barring intervention

$N(pS,aL)$: number of subscribers who are predicted to stay (nonchurn) and who actually leave barring intervention

$N(pL,aS)$: number of subscribers who are predicted to leave and who actually stay

$N(pS,aS)$: number of subscribers who are predicted to stay and who actually stay

Given these statistics, the net cost to the carrier of performing no intervention is:

$$net(\text{no intervention}) = [\, N(pL,aL) + N(pS,aL) \,]\, C_l$$

This equation says that whether or not churn is predicted, the subscriber will leave, and the cost per subscriber will be C_l. The net cost of providing an incentive to all subscribers whom are predicted to churn can also be estimated:

$$net(\text{incentive}) = [\, N(pL,aL) + N(pL,aS) \,]\, C_i + [\, P_i\, N(pL,aL) + N(pS,aL) \,]\, C_l$$

This equation says that the cost of offering the incentive, C_i, is incurred for all subscribers for who are predicted to churn, but the lost revenue cost will decrease by a fraction P_i for the subscribers who are correctly predicted to churn. The savings to the carrier as a result of offering incentives based on the churn predictor is then

savings per churnable subscriber =
  $[\, net(\text{no intervention}) - net(\text{incentive}) \,] / [\, N(pL,aL) + N(pS,aL) \,]$

The contour plots in Figure 3 show expected savings per churnable subscriber, for a range of values of C_i, P_i, and C_l, based on the optimal policy and the sophisticated neural-net predictor. Each plot assumes a different subscriber retention rate (= $1-P_i$) given intervention. The "25% retention rate" graph supposes that 25% of the churning subscribers who are offered an incentive will decide to remain with the carrier over the time horizon of six months. For each plot, the cost of intervention (C_i) is varied along the x-axis, and the average monthly bill is varied along the y-axis. (The average monthly bill is converted to lost revenue, C_l, by computing the total bill within the time horizon and adding the subscriber acquisition cost.) The shading of a region in the plot indicates the expected savings assuming the specified retention rate is achieved by offering the incentive. The grey-level bar to the right of each plot translates the shading into dollar savings per subscriber who will churn barring intervention. Because the cost of the incentive is factored into the savings estimate, the estimate is actually the net return to the carrier.

The white region in the lower right portion of each graph is the region in which no cost savings will be obtained. As the graphs clearly show, if the cost of the incentive needed to achieve a certain retention rate is low and the cost of lost revenue is high, significant per-subscriber savings can be obtained.

As one might suspect in examining the plots, what's important for determining per-subscriber savings is the ratio of the incentive cost to the average monthly bill. The plots clearly show that for a wide range of assumptions concerning the average monthly bill, incentive cost, and retention rate, a significant cost savings is realized.

The plots assume that all subscribers identified by the predictor can be contacted and offered the incentive. If only some fraction F of all subscribers are contacted, then the estimated savings indicated by the plot should be multiplied by F.

To pin down a likely scenario, it is reasonable to assume that 50% of subscribers can be contacted, 35% of whom will be retained by offering an incentive that costs the carrier

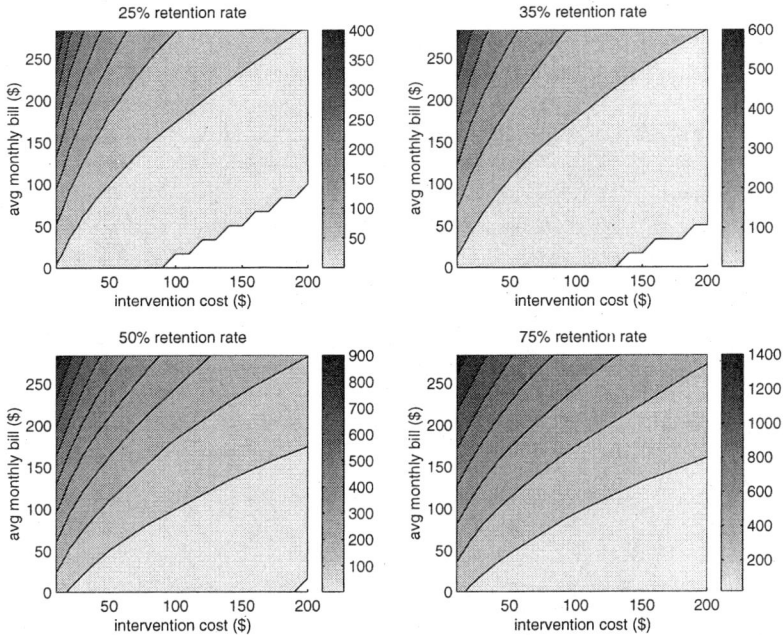

FIGURE 3. Expected savings to the carrier per churnable subscriber, under a variety of assumptions concerning intervention cost, average monthly bill of subscriber, and retention rate that will be achieved by offering an incentive to a churnable subscriber.

$75, and in our data base, the average monthly bill is $234. Under this scenario, the expected savings—above and beyond recovering the incentive cost—to the carrier is $93 based on the sophisticated neural net predictor. In contrast, the expected savings is only $47 based on the naive neural net predictor, and $81 based on the sophisticated logistic regression model. As we originally conjectured, both the nonlinearity of the neural net and the bias provided by the sophisticated representation are adding value to the predictions.

Our ongoing research involves extending these initial results in a several directions. First, we have confirmed our positive results with data from a different time window, and for test data from a later time window than the training data (as would be necessary in real-world usage). Second, we have further tuned and augmented our sophisticated representation to obtain higher prediction accuracy, and are now awaiting additional data to ensure the result replicates. Third, we are applying a variety of techniques, including sensitivity analysis and committee and boosting techniques, to further improve prediction accuracy. And fourth, we have begun to explore the consequences of iterating the decision making process and evaluating savings over an extended time period. Regardless of these directions for future work, the results presented here show the promise of data mining in the domain of wireless telecommunications. As is often the case for decision-making systems, the predictor need not be a perfect discriminator to realize significant savings.

6 REFERENCES

Bishop, C. (1995). Neural networks for pattern recognition. New York: Oxford University Press.
Fowlkes, A. J., Madan, A., Andrew, J., and Jensen, C.(1999). The effect of churn on value: An industry advisory.
Green, D. M., & Swets, J. A. (1966). *Signal detection theory and psychophysics*. New York: Wiley.
Luna, L. (1998). Churn is epidemic. Radio Communications Report, December 14, 1998.
Power, J. D., & Associates (1998). *1998 Residential Wireless Customer Satisfaction Survey*. September 22, 1998.

Unmixing Hyperspectral Data

Lucas Parra, Clay Spence, Paul Sajda
Sarnoff Corporation, CN-5300, Princeton, NJ 08543, USA
{*lparra,cspence,psajda*}*@sarnoff.com*

Andreas Ziehe, Klaus-Robert Müller
GMD FIRST.IDA, Kekuléstr. 7, 12489 Berlin, Germany
{*ziehe,klaus*}*@first.gmd.de*

Abstract

In hyperspectral imagery one pixel typically consists of a mixture of the reflectance spectra of several materials, where the mixture coefficients correspond to the abundances of the constituting materials. We assume linear combinations of reflectance spectra with some additive normal sensor noise and derive a probabilistic MAP framework for analyzing hyperspectral data. As the material reflectance characteristics are not know a priori, we face the problem of unsupervised linear unmixing. The incorporation of different prior information (e.g. positivity and normalization of the abundances) naturally leads to a family of interesting algorithms, for example in the noise-free case yielding an algorithm that can be understood as constrained independent component analysis (ICA). Simulations underline the usefulness of our theory.

1 Introduction

Current hyperspectral remote sensing technology can form images of ground surface reflectance at a few hundred wavelengths simultaneously, with wavelengths ranging from 0.4 to 2.5 μm and spatial resolutions of 10-30 m. The applications of this technology include environmental monitoring and mineral exploration and mining. The benefit of hyperspectral imagery is that many different objects and terrain types can be characterized by their spectral signature.

The first step in most hyperspectral image analysis systems is to perform a spectral unmixing to determine the original spectral signals of some set of prime materials. The basic difficulty is that for a given image pixel the spectral reflectance patterns of the surface materials is in general not known a priori. However there are general physical and statistical priors which can be exploited to potentially improve spectral unmixing. In this paper we address the problem of unmixing hyperspectral imagery through incorporation of physical and statistical priors within an unsupervised Bayesian framework.

We begin by first presenting the linear superposition model for the reflectances measured. We then discuss the advantages of unsupervised over supervised systems.

We derive a general maximum a posteriori (MAP) framework to find the material spectra and infer the abundances. Interestingly, depending on how the priors are incorporated, the zero noise case yields (i) a simplex approach or (ii) a constrained ICA algorithm. Assuming non-zero noise our MAP estimate utilizes a constrained least squares algorithm. The two latter approaches are new algorithms whereas the simplex algorithm has been previously suggested for the analysis of hyperspectral data.

Linear Modeling To a first approximation the intensities $\mathbf{X}$ $(x_{i\lambda})$ measured in each spectral band $\lambda = 1, \ldots, L$ for a given pixel $i = 1, \ldots, N$ are linear combinations of the reflectance characteristics $\mathbf{S}$ $(s_{m\lambda})$ of the materials $m = 1, \ldots, M$ present in that area. Possible errors of this approximation and sensor noise are taken into account by adding a noise term $\mathbf{N}$ $(n_{i\lambda})$. In matrix form this can be summarized as

$$\mathbf{X} = \mathbf{AS} + \mathbf{N}, \text{ subject to: } \mathbf{A}\mathbf{1}_M = \mathbf{1}_L, \quad \mathbf{A} \geq 0, \tag{1}$$

where matrix $\mathbf{A}$ (a_{im}) represents the abundance of material m in the area corresponding to pixel i, with positivity and normalization constraints. Note that ground inclination or a changing viewing angle may cause an overall scale factor for all bands that varies with the pixels. This can be incorporated in the model by simply replacing the constraint $\mathbf{A}\mathbf{1}_M = \mathbf{1}_L$ with $\mathbf{A}\mathbf{1}_M \leq \mathbf{1}_L$ which does does not affect the discussion in the remainder of the paper. This is clearly a simplified model of the physical phenomena. For example, with spatially fine grained mixtures, called *intimate mixtures*, multiple reflectance may causes departures from this first order model. Additionally there are a number of inherent spatial variations in real data, such as inhomogeneous vapor and dust particles in the atmosphere, that will cause a departure from the linear model in equation (1). Nevertheless, in practical applications a linear model has produced reasonable results for *areal mixtures*.

Supervised vs. Unsupervised techniques *Supervised* spectral unmixing relies on the prior knowledge about the reflectance patterns $\mathbf{S}$ of candidate surface materials, sometimes called *endmembers*, or expert knowledge and a series of semi-automatic steps to find the constituting materials in a particular scene. Once the user identifies a pixel i containing a single material, i.e. $a_{im} = 1$ for a given m and i, the corresponding spectral characteristics of that material can be taken directly from the observations, i.e., $s_{m\lambda} = x_{i\lambda}$ [4]. Given knowledge about the endmembers one can simply find the abundances by solving a constrained least squares problem. The problem with such supervised techniques is that finding the correct $\mathbf{S}$ may require substantial user interaction and the result may be error prone, as a pixel that actually contains a mixture can be misinterpreted as a pure endmember. Another approach obtains endmembers directly from a database. This is also problematic because the actual surface material on the ground may not match the database entries, due to atmospheric absorption or other noise sources. Finding close matches is an ambiguous process as some endmembers have very similar reflectance characteristics and may match several entries in the database.

Unsupervised unmixing, in contrast, tries to identify the endmembers and mixtures directly from the observed data $\mathbf{X}$ without any user interaction. There are a variety of such approaches. In one approach a simplex is fit to the data distribution [7, 6, 2]. The resulting vertex points of the simplex represent the desired endmembers, but this technique is very sensitive to noise as a few boundary points can potentially change the location of the simplex vertex points considerably. Another approach by Szu [9] tries to find abundances that have the highest entropy subject to constraints that the amount of materials is as evenly distributed as possible – an assumption which is clearly not valid in many actual surface material distributions. A relatively new approach considers modeling the statistical information across wavelength as statistically independent AR processes [1]. This leads directly to the contextual linear ICA algorithm [5]. However, the approach in [1] does not take into account constraints on the abundances, noise, or prior information. Most importantly, the method [1] can only integrate information from a small number of pixels at a time (same as the number of endmembers). Typically however we will have only a few endmembers but many thousand pixels.

2 The Maximum A Posterior Framework

2.1 A probabilistic model of unsupervised spectral unmixing

Our model has observations or data $\mathbf{X}$ and hidden variables $\mathbf{A}$, $\mathbf{S}$, and $\mathbf{N}$ that are explained by the noisy linear model (1). We estimate the values of the hidden variables by using MAP

$$p(\mathbf{A}, \mathbf{S}|\mathbf{X}) = \frac{p(\mathbf{X}|\mathbf{A},\mathbf{S})p(\mathbf{A},\mathbf{S})}{p(\mathbf{X})} = \frac{p_n(\mathbf{X}|\mathbf{A},\mathbf{S})p_a(\mathbf{A})p_s(\mathbf{S})}{p(\mathbf{X})} \qquad (2)$$

with $p_a(\mathbf{A})$, $p_s(\mathbf{S})$, $p_n(\mathbf{N})$ as the a priori assumptions of the distributions. With MAP we estimate the most probable values for given priors after observing the data,

$$\mathbf{A}_{\text{MAP}}, \mathbf{S}_{\text{MAP}} = \arg\max_{\mathbf{A},\mathbf{S}} p(\mathbf{A},\mathbf{S}|\mathbf{X}) \qquad (3)$$

Note that for maximization the constant factor $p(\mathbf{X})$ can be ignored. Our first assumption, which is indicated in equation (2) is that the abundances are independent of the reflectance spectra as their origins are completely unrelated: (A0) $\mathbf{A}$ and $\mathbf{S}$ are independent.

The MAP algorithm is entirely defined by the choices of priors that are guided by the problem of hyperspectral unmixing: (A1) $\mathbf{A}$ represent probabilities for each pixel i. (A2) $\mathbf{S}$ are independent for different material m. (A3) $\mathbf{N}$ are normal i.i.d. for all i, λ. In summary, our MAP framework includes the assumptions A0-A3.

2.2 Including Priors

Priors on the abundances Positivity and normalization of the abundances can be represented as,

$$p_a(\mathbf{A}) = \delta(\mathbf{A}\mathbf{1}_M - \mathbf{1}_N)\Theta(\mathbf{A}), \qquad (4)$$

where $\delta()$ represent the Kronecker delta function and $\Theta()$ the step function. With this choice a point not satisfying the constraint will have zero a posteriori probability. This prior introduces no particular bias of the solutions other then abundance constraints. It does however assume the abundances of different pixels to be independent.

Prior on spectra Usually we find systematic trends in the spectra that cause significant correlation. However such an overall trend can be subtracted and/or filtered from the data leaving only independent signals that encode the variation from that overall trend. For example one can capture the conditional dependency structure with a linear auto-regressive (AR) model and analyze the resulting "innovations" or prediction errors [3]. In our model we assume that the spectra represent independent instances of an AR process having a white innovation process $e_{m\lambda}$ distributed according to $p_e(e)$. With a Toeplitz matrix $\mathbf{T}$ of the AR coefficients we can write, $\mathbf{e}_m = \mathbf{s}_m \mathbf{T}$. The AR coefficients can be found in a preprocessing step on the observations $\mathbf{X}$. If $\mathbf{S}$ now represents the innovation process itself, our prior can be represented as,

$$p_e(\mathbf{S}) \propto p_e(\mathbf{ST}) = \prod_{m=1}^{M} \prod_{\lambda=1}^{L} p_e(\sum_{\lambda'=1}^{L} s_{m\lambda'} t_{\lambda \lambda'}), \quad (5)$$

Additionally $p_e(e)$ is parameterized by a mean and scale parameter and potentially parameters determining the higher moments of the distributions. For brevity we ignore the details of the parameterization in this paper.

Prior on the noise As outlined in the introduction there are a number of problems that can cause the linear model $\mathbf{X} = \mathbf{AS}$ to be inaccurate (e.g. multiple reflections, inhomogeneous atmospheric absorption, and detector noise.) As it is hard to treat all these phenomena explicitly, we suggest to pool them into one noise variable that we assume for simplicity to be normal distributed with a wavelength dependent noise variance σ_λ,

$$p(\mathbf{X}|\mathbf{A},\mathbf{S}) = p_n(\mathbf{N}) = \mathcal{N}(\mathbf{X} - \mathbf{AS}, \Sigma) = \prod_{\lambda=1}^{L} \mathcal{N}(\mathbf{x}_\lambda - \mathbf{As}_\lambda, \sigma_\lambda \mathbf{I}), \quad (6)$$

where $\mathcal{N}(\cdot, \cdot)$ represents a zero mean Gaussian distribution, and $\mathbf{I}$ the identity matrix indicating the independent noise at each pixel.

2.3 MAP Solution for Zero Noise Case

Let us consider the noise-free case. Although this simplification may be inaccurate it will allow us to greatly reduce the number of free hidden variables - from $NM + ML$ to M^2. In the noise-free case the variables $\mathbf{A}, \mathbf{S}$ are then deterministically dependent on each other through a NL-dimensional δ-distribution, $p_n(\mathbf{X}|\mathbf{AS}) = \delta(\mathbf{X} - \mathbf{AS})$. We can remove one of these variables from our discussion by integrating (2). It is instructive to first consider removing $\mathbf{A}$

$$p(\mathbf{S}|\mathbf{X}) \propto \int d\mathbf{A}\, \delta(\mathbf{X} - \mathbf{AS}) p_a(\mathbf{A}) p_s(\mathbf{S}) = |\mathbf{S}^{-1}| p_a(\mathbf{XS}^{-1}) p_s(\mathbf{S}). \quad (7)$$

We omit tedious details and assume $L = M$ and invertible $\mathbf{S}$ so that we can perform the variable substitution that introduces the Jacobian determinant $|\mathbf{S}^{-1}|$. Let us consider the influence of the different terms. The Jacobian determinant measures the volume spanned by the endmembers $\mathbf{S}$. Maximizing its inverse will therefore try to shrink the simplex spanned by $\mathbf{S}$. The term $p_a(\mathbf{XS}^{-1})$ should guarantee that all data points map into the inside of the simplex, since the term should contribute zero or low probability for points that violate the constraint. Note that these two terms, in principle, define the same objective as the simplex envelope fitting algorithms previously mentioned [2].
In the present work we are more interested in the algorithm that results from removing $\mathbf{S}$ and finding the MAP estimate of $\mathbf{A}$. We obtain (cf. Eq.(7))

$$p(\mathbf{A}|\mathbf{X}) \propto \int d\mathbf{S}\, \delta(\mathbf{X} - \mathbf{AS}) p_a(\mathbf{A}) p_s(\mathbf{S}) = |\mathbf{A}^{-1}| p_s(\mathbf{A}^{-1}\mathbf{X}) p_a(\mathbf{A}). \quad (8)$$

For now we assumed $N = M$.[1] If $p_s(\mathbf{S})$ factors over m, i.e. endmembers are independent, maximizing the first two terms represents the ICA algorithm. However,

---

[1] In practice more frequently we have $N > M$. In that case the observations $\mathbf{X}$ can be mapped into a M dimensional subspace using the singular value decomposition (SVD), $\mathbf{X} = \mathbf{UDV}^T$. The discussion applies then to the reduced observations $\tilde{\mathbf{X}} = \mathbf{U}_M^T \mathbf{X}$ with $\mathbf{U}_M$ being the first M columns of $\mathbf{U}$.

the prior on **A** will restrict the solutions to satisfy the abundance constraints and bias the result depending on the detailed choice of $p_a(\mathbf{A})$, so we are led to *constrained ICA*.

In summary, depending on which variable we integrate out we obtain two methods for solving the spectral unmixing problem: the known technique of simplex fitting and a new constrained ICA algorithm.

2.4 MAP Solution for the Noisy Case

Combining the choices for the priors made in section 2.2 (Eqs.(4), (5) and (6)) with (2) and (3) we obtain

$$\mathbf{A}_{\text{MAP}}, \mathbf{S}_{\text{MAP}} = \arg\max_{\mathbf{A},\mathbf{S}} \prod_{\lambda=q}^{L} \left\{ \prod_{i=1}^{N} \mathcal{N}(x_{i\lambda} - \mathbf{a}_i \mathbf{s}_\lambda, \sigma_\lambda) \prod_{m=1}^{M} p_e(\sum_{\lambda'=1}^{L} s_{m\lambda'} t_{\lambda\lambda'}) \right\}, \quad (9)$$

subject to $\mathbf{A}\mathbf{1}_M = \mathbf{1}_L, \mathbf{A} \geq 0$. The logarithm of the cost function in (9) is denoted by $L = L(\mathbf{A}, \mathbf{S})$. Its gradient with respect to the hidden variables is

$$\frac{\partial L}{\partial \mathbf{s}_m} = -\mathbf{A}^T \mathbf{n}_m \, \text{diag}(\boldsymbol{\sigma})^{-1} - f_s(\mathbf{s}_m) \quad (10)$$

where $\mathbf{N} = \mathbf{X} - \mathbf{AS}$, $\mathbf{n}_m$ are the M column vectors of **N**, $f_s(s) = -\frac{\partial \ln p_e(s)}{\partial s}$. In (10) f_s is applied to each element of $\mathbf{s}_m$.

The optimization with respect to **A** for given **S** can be implemented as a standard *weighted least squares* (LS) problem with a linear constraint and positivity bounds. Since the constraints apply for every pixel independently one can solve N separate constrained LS problems of M unknowns each. We alternate between gradient steps for **S** and explicit solutions for **A** until convergence. Any additional parameters of $p_e(e)$ such as scale and mean may be obtained in a maximum likelihood (ML) sense by maximizing L. Note that the nonlinear optimization is not subject to constraints; the constraints apply only in the quadratic optimization.

3 Experiments

3.1 Zero Noise Case: Artificial Mixtures

In our first experiment we use mineral data from the United States Geological Survey (USGS)[2] to build artificial mixtures for evaluating our unsupervised unmixing framework. Three target endmembers where chosen (Almandine WS479, Montmorillonite+Illi CM42 and Dickite NMNH106242). A spectral scene of 100 samples was constructed by creating a random mixture of the three minerals. Of the 100 samples, there were no pure samples (i.e. no mineral had more than a 80% abundance in any sample). Figure 1A is the spectra of the endmembers recovered by the constrained ICA technique of section 2.3, where the constraints were implemented with penalty terms added to the conventional maximum likelihood ICA algorithm. These are nearly identical to the spectra of the true endmembers, shown in figure 1B, which were used for mixing. Interesting to note is the scatter-plot of the 100 samples across two bands. The open circles are the absorption values at these two bands for endmembers found by the MAP technique. Given that each mixed sample consists of no more than 80% of any endmember, the endmember points on the scatter-plot are quite distant from the cluster. A simplex fitting technique would have significant difficulty recovering the endmembers from this clustering.

---

[2] see http://speclab.cr.usgs.gov/spectral.lib.456.descript/decript04.html

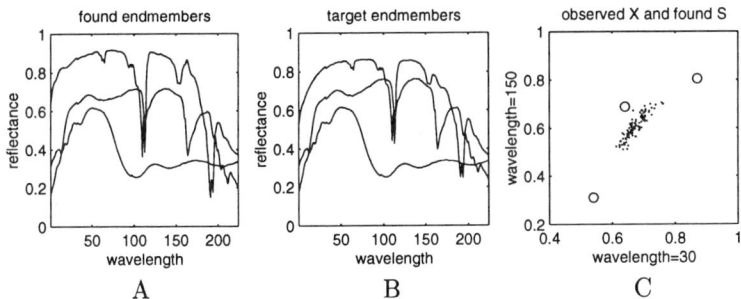

Figure 1: Results for noise-free artificial mixture. **A** recovered endmembers using MAP technique. **B** "true" target endmembers. **C** scatter plot of samples across 2 bands showing the absorption of the three endmembers computed by MAP (open circles).

3.2 Noisy Case: Real Mixtures

To validate the noise model MAP framework of section 2.4 we conducted an experiment using ground truthed USGS data representing real mixtures. We selected 10x10 blocks of pixels from three different regions[3] in the AVIRIS data of the Cuprite, Nevada mining district. We separate these 300 mixed spectra assuming two endmembers and an AR detrending with 5 AR coefficients and the MAP techniques of section 2.4. Overall brightness was accounted for as explain in the linear modeling of section 1. The endmembers are shown in figure 2A and B in comparison to laboratory spectra from the USGS spectral library for these minerals [8]. Figure 2C shows the corresponding abundances, which match the ground truth; region (III) mainly consists of Muscovite while regions (I)+(II) contain (areal) mixtures of Kaolinite and Muscovite.

4 Discussion

Hyperspectral unmixing is a challenging practical problem for unsupervised learning. Our probabilistic approach leads to several interesting algorithms: (1) simplex fitting, (2) constrained ICA and (3) constrained least squares that can efficiently use multi-channel information. An important element of our approach is the explicit use of prior information. Our simulation examples show that we can recover the endmembers, even in the presence of noise and model uncertainty. The approach described in this paper does not yet exploit local correlations between neighboring pixels that are well known to exist. Future work will therefore exploit not only *spectral* but also *spatial* prior information for detecting objects and materials.

Acknowledgments

We would like to thank Gregg Swayze at the USGS for assistance in obtaining the data.

---

[3]The regions were from the image plate2.cuprite95.alpha.2um.image.wlocals.gif in ftp://speclab.cr.usgs.gov/pub/cuprite/gregg.thesis.images/, at the coordinates (265,710) and (275,697), which contained Kaolinite and Muscovite 2, and (143,661), which only contained Muscovite 2.

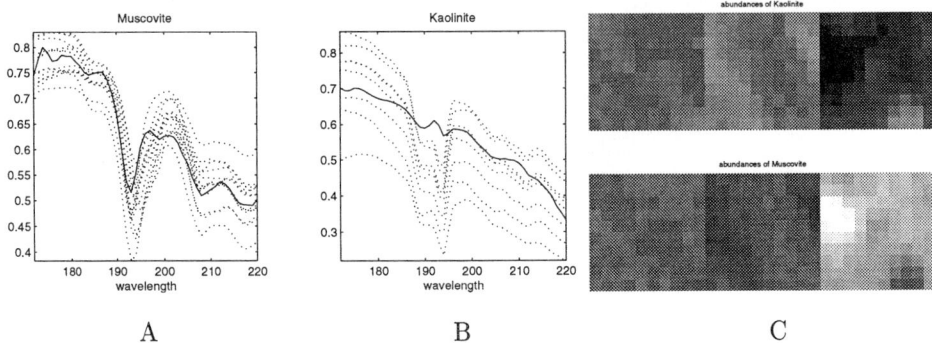

Figure 2: **A** Spectra of computed endmember (solid line) vs Muscovite sample spectra from the USGS data base library. Note we show only part of the spectrum since the discriminating features are located only between band 172 and 220. **B** Computed endmember (solid line) vs Kaolinite sample spectra from the USGS data base library. **C** Abundances for Kaolinite and Muscovite for three regions (lighter pixels represent higher abundance). Region 1 and region 2 have similar abundances for Kaolinite and Muscovite, while region 3 contains more Muscovite.

References

[1] J. Bayliss, J. A. Gualtieri, and R. Cromp. Analyzing hyperspectral data with independent component analysis. In J. M. Selander, editor, *Proc. SPIE Applied Image and Pattern Recognition Workshop*, volume 9, P.O. Box 10, Bellingham WA 98227-0010, 1997. SPIE.

[2] J.W. Boardman and F.A. Kruse. Automated spectral analysis: a geologic example using AVIRIS data, north Grapevine Mountains, Nevada. In *Tenth Thematic Conference on Geologic Remote Sensing*, pages 407–418, Ann arbor, MI, 1994. Environmental Research Institute of Michigan.

[3] S. Haykin. *Adaptive Filter Theory*. Prentice Hall, 1991.

[4] F. Maselli, , M. Pieri, and C. Conese. Automatic identification of end-members for the spectral decomposition of remotely sensed scenes. *Remote Sensing for Geography, Geology, Land Planning, and Cultural Heritage (SPIE)*, 2960:104–109, 1996.

[5] B. Pearlmutter and L. Parra. Maximum likelihood blind source separation: A context-sensitive generalization of ICA. In M. Mozer, M. Jordan, and T. Petsche, editors, *Advances in Neural Information Processing Systems 9*, pages 613–619, Cambridge MA, 1997. MIT Press.

[6] J.J. Settle. Linear mixing and the estimation of ground cover proportions. *International Journal of Remote Sensing*, 14:1159–1177, 1993.

[7] M.O. Smith, J.B. Adams, and A.R. Gillespie. Reference endmembers for spectral mixture analysis. In *Fifth Australian remote sensing conference*, volume 1, pages 331–340, 1990.

[8] U.S. Geological Survey. USGS digital spectral library. Open File Report 93-592, 1993.

[9] H. Szu and C. Hsu. Landsat spectral demixing a la superresolution of blind matrix inversion by constraint MaxEnt neural nets. In *Wavelet Applications IV*, volume 3078, pages 147–160. SPIE, 1997.

Application of Blind Separation of Sources to Optical Recording of Brain Activity

Holger Schöner, Martin Stetter, Ingo Schießl
Department of Computer Science
Technical University of Berlin Germany
{hfsch,moatl,ingos}@cs.tu-berlin.de

John E.W. Mayhew
University of Sheffield, UK
j.e.mayhew@sheffield.ac.uk

Jennifer S. Lund, Niall McLoughlin
Institute of Ophthalmology
University College London, UK
{j.lund,n.mcloughlin}@ucl.ac.uk

Klaus Obermayer
Department of Computer Science,
Technical University of Berlin, Germany
oby@cs.tu-berlin.de

Abstract

In the analysis of data recorded by optical imaging from intrinsic signals (measurement of changes of light reflectance from cortical tissue) the removal of noise and artifacts such as blood vessel patterns is a serious problem. Often bandpass filtering is used, but the underlying assumption that a spatial frequency exists, which separates the mapping component from other components (especially the global signal), is questionable. Here we propose alternative ways of processing optical imaging data, using blind source separation techniques based on the spatial decorrelation of the data. We first perform benchmarks on artificial data in order to select the way of processing, which is most robust with respect to sensor noise. We then apply it to recordings of optical imaging experiments from macaque primary visual cortex. We show that our BSS technique is able to extract ocular dominance and orientation preference maps from single condition stacks, for data, where standard post-processing procedures fail. Artifacts, especially blood vessel patterns, can often be completely removed from the maps. In summary, our method for blind source separation using extended spatial decorrelation is a superior technique for the analysis of optical recording data.

1 Introduction

One approach in the attempt of comprehending how the human brain works is the analysis of neural activation patterns in the brain for different stimuli presented to a sensory system. An example is the extraction of ocular dominance or orientation preference maps from recordings of activity of neurons in the primary visual cortex of mammals. A common technique for extracting such maps is optical imaging (OI) of intrinsic signals. Currently this is the imaging technique with the highest spatial resolution ($\approx 100\,\mu$m) for mapping of the cortex. This method is explained e.g. in [1], for similar methods using voltage sensitive dyes see [2, 3]. OI uses changes in light reflection to estimate spatial patterns of stimulus answers. The overall change recorded by a CCD or video camera is the total signal. The part of the total signal due to local neural activity is called the mapping component and it derives from changes in deoxyhemoglobin absorption and light scattering properties of the tissue. Another component of the total signal is a "global" component, which is also correlated with stimulus presentation, but has a much coarser spatial resolution. It derives its part from changes in the blood volume with the time. Other components are blood vessel artifacts, the vasomotor signal (slow oscillations of neural activity), and ongoing activity (spontaneous, stimulus-uncorrelated activity). Problematic for the extraction of activity maps are especially blood vessel artifacts and sensor noise, such as photon shot noise. A procedure often used for extracting the activity maps from the recordings is bandpass filtering, after preprocessing by temporal, spatial, and trial averaging. Lowpass filtering is unproblematic, as the spatial resolution of the mapping signal is limited by the scattering properties of the brain tissue, hence everything above a limiting frequency must be noise. The motivation for highpass filtering, on the other hand, is questionable as there is no specific spatial frequency separating local neural activity patterns and the global signal [4]).

A different approach, Blind Source Separation (BSS), models the components of the recorded image frames as independent sources, and the observations (recorded image frames) as noisy linear mixtures of the unknown sources. After performing the BSS the mapping component should ideally be concentrated in one estimated source, the global signal in another, and blood vessel artifacts, etc. in further ones. Previous work ([5]) has shown that BSS algorithms, which are based on higher order statistics ([6, 7, 8]), fail for optical imaging data, because of the high signal to noise ratio.

In this work we suggest and investigate versions of the M&S algorithm [9, 10], which are robust against sensor noise, and we analyze their performance on artificial as well as real optical recording data. In section 2 we describe an improved algorithm, which we later compare to other methods in section 3. There an artificial data set is used for the analysis of noise robustness, and benchmark results are presented. Then, in section 4, it is shown that the newly developed algorithm is very well able to separate the different components of the optical imaging data, for ocular dominance as well as orientation preference data from monkey striate cortex. Finally, section 5 provides conclusions and perspectives for future work.

2 Second order blind source separation

Let m be the number of mixtures and $\mathbf{r}$ the sample index, i.e. a vector specifying a pixel in the recorded images. The observation vectors $\mathbf{y}(\mathbf{r}) = (y_1(\mathbf{r}), \ldots, y_m(\mathbf{r}))^T$ are assumed to be linear mixtures of m unknown sources $\mathbf{s}(\mathbf{r}) = (s_1(\mathbf{r}), \ldots, s_m(\mathbf{r}))^T$ with A being the $m \times m$ mixing matrix and $\mathbf{n}$ describing the sensor noise:

$$\mathbf{y}(\mathbf{r}) = \mathbf{A}\mathbf{s}(\mathbf{r}) + \mathbf{n} \qquad (1)$$

The goal of BSS is to obtain optimal source estimates $\hat{\mathbf{s}}(\mathbf{r})$ under the assumption that the original sources are independent. In the noiseless case $\mathbf{W} = \mathbf{A}^{-1}$ would be the optimal demixing matrix. In the noisy case, however, $\mathbf{W}$ also has to compensate for the added noise: $\hat{\mathbf{s}}(\mathbf{r}) = \mathbf{W}\mathbf{y}(\mathbf{r}) = \mathbf{W} \cdot \mathbf{A} \cdot \mathbf{s}(\mathbf{r}) + \mathbf{W} \cdot \mathbf{n}$. BSS algorithms are generally only able to recover the original sources up to a permutation and scaling.

Extended Spatial Decorrelation (ESD) uses the second order statistics of the observations to find the source estimates. If sources are statistical independent all source cross-correlations

$$C^{(s)}_{i,j}(\Delta\mathbf{r}) = \langle s_i(\mathbf{r})s_j(\mathbf{r}+\Delta\mathbf{r})\rangle_{\mathbf{r}} = \frac{1}{R}\sum_{\mathbf{r}} s_i(\mathbf{r})s_j(\mathbf{r}+\Delta\mathbf{r}) \qquad , i \neq j \qquad (2)$$

must vanish for all shifts $\Delta \mathbf{r}$, while the autocorrelations ($i = j$) of the sources remain (the variances). Note that this implies that the sources must be spatially smooth.

Motivated by [10] we propose to optimize the cost function, which is the sum of the squared cross-correlations of the estimated sources over a set of shifts $\{\Delta \mathbf{r}\}$,

$$E(\mathbf{W}) = \sum_{\Delta \mathbf{r}} \sum_{i \neq j} \left((\mathbf{W} \mathbf{C}(\Delta \mathbf{r}) \mathbf{W}^T)_{i,j} \right)^2 \quad (3)$$

$$= \sum_{\Delta \mathbf{r}} \sum_{i \neq j} \langle \hat{s}_i(\mathbf{r}) \hat{s}_j(\mathbf{r} + \Delta \mathbf{r}) \rangle_{\mathbf{r}}^2,$$

with respect to the demixing matrix $\mathbf{W}$. The matrix $C_{i,j}(\Delta \mathbf{r}) = \langle y_i(\mathbf{r}) y_j(\mathbf{r} + \Delta \mathbf{r}) \rangle_{\mathbf{r}}$ denotes the mixture cross-correlations for a shift $\Delta \mathbf{r}$. This cost function is minimized using the Polak Ribiere Conjugate Gradient technique, where the line search is substituted by a dynamic step width adaptation ([11]). To keep the demixing matrix $\mathbf{W}$ from converging to the zero matrix, we introduce a constraint which keeps the diagonal elements of $\mathbf{T} = \mathbf{W}^{-1}$ (in the noiseless case and for non-sphered data $\mathbf{T}$ is an estimate of the mixing matrix, with possible permutations) at a value of 1.0. Convergence properties are improved by sphering the data (transforming their correlation matrix for shift zero to an identity matrix) prior to decorrelating the mixtures.

Note that use of multiple shifts $\Delta \mathbf{r}$ allows to use more information about the auto- and cross-correlation structure of the mixtures for the separation process. Two shifts provide just enough constraints for a unique solution ([10]). Multiple shifts, and the redundancy they introduce, additionally allow to cancel out part of the noise by approximate simultaneous diagonalization of the corresponding cross correlation matrices.

In the presence of sensor noise, added after mixing, the standard sphering technique is problematic. When calculating the zero-shift cross-correlation matrix the variance of the noise contaminates the result, and sphering using a shifted cross-correlation matrix, is recommended ([12]). For spatially white sensor noise and sources with reasonable auto correlations this technique is more appropriate. In the following we denote the standard algorithm by dpa0, and the variant using noise robust sphering by dpa1.

3 Benchmarks for artificial data

The artificial data set used here, whose sources are approximately uncorrelated for all shifts, is shown in the left part of figure 1. The mixtures were produced by generating a random mixing matrix (in this case with condition number 3.73), applying it to the sources, and finally adding white noise of different variances.

In order to measure the performance on the artificial data set we measure a reconstruction error (RE) between the estimated and the correct sources via (see [13]):

$$\mathrm{RE}(\mathbf{W}) = \mathrm{od}\left(\sum_{\mathbf{r}} \hat{\mathbf{s}}(\mathbf{r}) \mathbf{s}^T(\mathbf{r}) \right), \quad \mathrm{od}(\mathbf{C}) = \frac{1}{N} \sum_i \frac{1}{N-1} \left(\sum_j \frac{|C_{i,j}|}{\max_k |C_{i,k}|} - 1 \right) \quad (4)$$

The correlation between the real and the estimated sources (the argument to "od"), should be close to a permutation matrix, if the separation is successful. If the maxima of two rows are in the same column, the separation is labeled unsuccessful. Otherwise, the normalized absolute sum of non-permutation (cross-correlation) elements is computed and returned as the reconstruction error.

We now compare the method based on optimization of (3) by gradient descent with the following variants of second order blind source separation: (1) standard spatial decorrelation

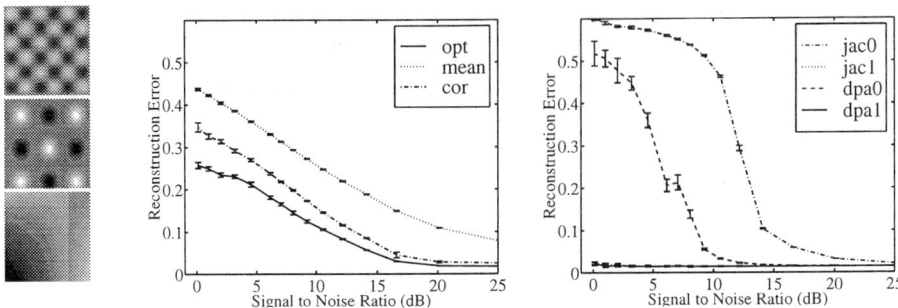

Figure 1: The set of three approximately uncorrelated source images of the artificial data set (left). The two plots (middle, right) show the reconstruction error versus signal to noise ratio for different separation algorithms. In the right plot jac1 and dpa1 are very close together.

using the optimal single shift yielding the smallest reconstruction error (opt). (2) Spatial decorrelation using the shift selected by

$$\Delta \mathbf{r}_{cor} = \mathrm{argmax}_{\{\Delta \mathbf{r}\}} \frac{\mathrm{norm}\left(\mathbf{C}(\Delta \mathbf{r}) - \mathrm{diag}\left(\mathbf{C}(\Delta \mathbf{r})\right)\right)}{\mathrm{norm}\left(\mathrm{diag}\left(\mathbf{C}(\Delta \mathbf{r})\right)\right)}., \quad (5)$$

where "diag" sets all off-diagonal elements of its argument matrix to zero, and "norm" computes the largest singular value of its argument matrix (cor). $\Delta \mathbf{r}_{cor}$ is the shift for which the cross correlations are largest, i.e. whose signal to noise ratio (SNR) should be best. (3) Standard spatial decorrelation using the average reconstruction error for all successful shifts in a 61 × 61 square around the zero shift (mean). (4) A multi-shift algorithm ([12]), using several elementary rotations (Jacobi method) to build an orthogonal demixing matrix, which optimizes the cost function (3). The variants using standard sphering and noise robust sphering are denoted by (jac0) and (jac1). cor, opt, and mean use two shifts for their computation; but as one of those is always the zero-shift, there is only one shift to choose and they are called single-shift algorithms here.

Figure 1 gives two plots which show the reconstruction error (4) versus the SNR (measured in dB) for single shift (middle) and multi-shift (right) algorithms. The error bars indicate twice the standard error of the mean ($2\times$ SEM), for 10 runs with the same mixing matrix, but newly generated noise of the given noise level. In each of these runs, the best result of three was selected for the gradient descent method. This is because, contrary to the other algorithms, the gradient descent algorithm depends on the initial choice of the demixing matrix. All multi-shift algorithms (all except opt and mean), used 8 shifts $(\pm r, \pm r)$, $(\pm r, 0)$, and $(0, \pm r)$ for each $r \in \{1, 3, 5, 10, 20, 30\}$, so 48 all together.

Several points are noticeable in the plots. (i) The cor algorithm is generally closer to the optimum than to the average successful shift. (ii) A comparison between the two plots shows that the multi-shift algorithms (right plot) are able to perform much better than even the optimal single-shift method. For low to medium noise levels this is even the case when using the standard sphering method combined with the gradient descent algorithm. (iii) The advantage of the noise robust sphering method, compared to the standard sphering, is obvious: the reconstruction error stays very low for all evaluated noise levels, for both the jac1 and dpa1 algorithms. (iv) The gradient descent technique is more robust than the Jacobi method For the standard sphering its performance is much better than that of the Jacobi method.

Figure 1 shows results which were produced using a single mixing matrix. However, our simulations show that the algorithms compare qualitatively similar when using mixing ma-

$t = 1$ sec. $t = 2$ sec. $t = 3$ sec. $t = 4$ sec. $t = 5$ sec. $t = 6$ sec. $t = 7$ sec.

Figure 2: Optical imaging stacks. The top stack is a single condition stack from ocular dominance experiments, the lower one a difference stack from orientation preference experiments (images for 90° gratings subtracted from those for 0° gratings). The stimulus was present during recording images 2-7 in each row. Two large blood vessels in the top and left regions of the raw images were masked out prior to the analysis.

trices with condition numbers between 2 and 10. The noise robust versions of the multishift algorithms generally yield the best separation results of all evaluated algorithms.

4 Application to optical imaging

We now apply extended spatial decorrelation to the analysis of optical imaging data. The data consists of recordings from the primary visual cortex of macaque monkeys. Each trial lasted 8 seconds, which were recorded with frame rates of 15 frames per second. A visual stimulus (a drifting bar grating of varying orientation) was presented between seconds 2 and 8. Trials were separated by a recovery period of 15 seconds without stimulation. The cortex was illuminated at a wavelength of 633 nm. One pixel corresponds to about 15 μm on the cortex; the image stacks used for further processing, consisting of 256×256 pixels, covered an area of cortex of approximately 3.7 mm^2.

Blocks of 15 consecutive frames were averaged, and averaging over 8 trials using the same visual stimulus further improved the SNR. First frame analysis (subtraction of the first, blank, frame from the others) was then applied to the resulting stack of 8 frames, followed by lowpass filtering with 14 cycles/mm. Figure 2 shows the resulting image stacks for an ocular dominance and an orientation preference experiment. One observes strong blood vessel artifacts (particularly in the top row of images), which are superimposed to the patchy mapping component that pops up over time.

Figure 3 shows results obtained by the application of extended spatial decorrelation (using dpa0). Only those estimated sources containing patterns different from white noise are shown. Backprojection of the estimated sources onto the original image stack yields the amplitude time series of the estimated sources, which is very useful in selecting the mapping component: it can be present in the recordings only after the stimulus onset (starting at $t = 2$ sec.). The middle part shows four estimated sources for the ocular dominance single condition stack. The mapping component (first image) is separated from the global component (second image) and blood vessel artifacts (second to fourth) quite well. The time course of the mapping component is plausible as well: calculation of a plausibility index (sum of squared differences between the normalized time series and a step function, which is 0 before and 1 after the stimulus onset) gives 0.5 for the mapping component and 2.31 for the next best one. Results for the gradient descent algorithm are similar for this data set, regardless of the sphering technique used. The Jacobi method also gives similar results, but a small blood vessel artifact is remaining in the resulting map. The cor algorithm usually gives much worse separation results. In the right part of figure 3 two es-

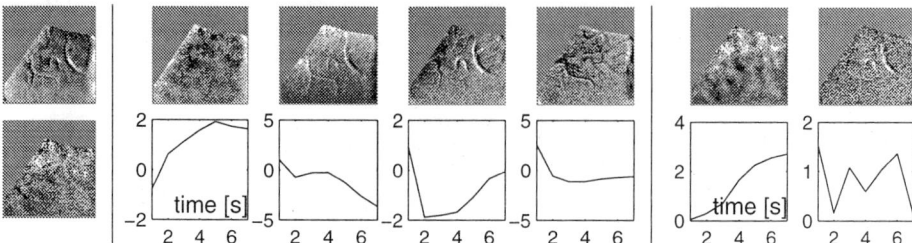

Figure 3: Left: Summation technique for ocular dominance (OD) experiment (upper) and orientation preference (OP) experiment (lower). Middle, Right: dpa0 algorithm applied to the same OD single condition (middle) and OP (right) stacks. The images show the 4 (OD) and 2 (OP) estimated components, which are visually different from white noise. In the bottom row the respective time courses of the estimated sources are given.

timated sources (those different from white noise) for the orientation preference difference stack can be seen. Here the proposed algorithm (dpa0) again works very well (plausibility index is 0.56 for mapping component, compared to 3.04 for the best other component). It generally has to be applied a few times (usually around 3 times) to select the best separation result (judging by visual quality of the separation and the time courses of the estimated sources), because of its dependence on parameter initialization; in return it yields the best results of all algorithms used, especially when compared to the traditional summation technique.

The similar results when using standard and noise robust sphering, and the small differences between the gradient descent and the Jacobi algorithms indicate, that not sensor noise is the limiting factor for the quality of the extracted maps. Instead it seems that, assuming a linear mixing model, no better results can be obtained from the used image stacks. It will remain for further research to analyze, how appropriate the linear mixing model is, and whether the underlying biophysical components are sufficiently uncorrelated. In the meantime the maps obtained by the ESD algorithm are superior to those obtained using conventional techniques like summation of the image stack.

5 Conclusion

The results presented in the previous sections show the advantages of the proposed algorithm: In the comparison with other spatial decorrelation algorithms the benefit in using multiple shifts compared to only two shifts is demonstrated. The robustness against sensor noise is improved, and in addition, the selection of multiple shifts is less critical than selecting a single shift, as the resulting multi-shift system of equations contains more redundancy. In comparison with the Jacobi method, which is restricted to find only orthogonal demixing matrices, the greater tolerance of demixing by a gradient descent technique concerning noise and incorrect sphering are demonstrated. The application of second order blind separation of sources to optical imaging data shows that these techniques represent an important alternative to the conventional approach, bandpass filtering followed by summation of the image stack, for extraction of neural activity maps. Vessel artifacts can be separated from the mapping component better than using classical approaches. The spatial decorrelation algorithms are very well adapted to the optical imaging task, because of their use of spatial smoothness properties of the mapping and other biophysical components.

An important field for future research concerning BSS algorithms is the incorporation of prior knowledge about sources and the mixing process, e.g. that the mixing has to be causal: the mapping signal cannot occur before the stimulus is presented. Assumptions about the time course of signals could also be helpful, as well as knowledge about their spatial statistics. Smearing and scattering limit the resolution of recordings of biological components, and, depending on the wavelength of the light used for illumination, the mapping component constitutes only a certain percentage of the changes in total light reflections.

Acknowledgments

This work has been supported by the Wellcome Trust (050080/Z/97).

References

[1] T. Bonhoeffer and A. Grinvald. Optical imaging based on intrinsic signals: The methodology. In A. Toga and J. C. Maziotta, editors, *Brain mapping: The methods*, pages 55–97, San Diego, CA, 1996. Academic Press, Inc.

[2] G. G. Blasdel and G. Salama. Voltage-sensitive dyes reveal a modular organization in monkey striate cortex. *Nature*, 321:579–585, 1986.

[3] G. G. Blasdel. Differential imaging of ocular dominance and orientation selectivity in monkey striate cortex. *J. Neurosci.*, 12:3115–3138, 1992.

[4] M. Stetter, T. Otto, T. Mueller, F. Sengpiel, M. Huebener, T. Bonhoeffer, and K. Obermayer. Temporal and spatial analysis of intrinsic signals from cat visual cortex. *Soc. Neurosci. Abstr.*, 23:455, 1997.

[5] I. Schießl, M. Stetter, J. E. W. Mayhew, S. Askew, N. McLoughlin, J. B. Levitt, J. S. Lund, and K. Obermayer. Blind separation of spatial signal patterns from optical imaging records. In J.-F. Cardoso, C. Jutten, and P. Loubaton, editors, *Proceedings of the ICA99 workshop*, volume 1, pages 179–184, 1999.

[6] A. J. Bell and T. J. Sejnowski. An information-maximization approach to blind separation and blind deconvolution. *Neural Computation*, 7:1129–1159, 1995.

[7] S. Amari. Neural learning in structured parameter spaces - natural riemannian gradient. In M. C. Mozer, M. I. Jordan, and T. Petsche, editors, *Advances in Neural Information Processing Systems*, volume 9, 1996.

[8] A. Hyvärinen and E. Oja. A fast fixed point algorithm for independent component analysis. *Neural Comput.*, 9:1483–1492, 1997.

[9] J. C. Platt and F. Faggin. Networks for the separation of sources that are superimposed and delayed. In J. E. Moody, S. J. Hanson, and R. P. Lippmann, editors, *Advances in Neural Information Processing Systems*, volume 4, pages 730–737, 1991.

[10] L. Molgedey and H. G. Schuster. Separation of a mixture of independent signals using time delayed correlations. *Phys. Rev. Lett.*, 72:3634–3637, 1994.

[11] S. M. Rüger. Stable dynamic parameter adaptation. In D. S. Touretzky, M. C. Mozer, and M. E. Hasselmo, editors, *Advances in Neural Information Processing Systems.*, volume 8, pages 225–231. MIT Press Cambridge, MA, 1996.

[12] K.-R. Müller, Philips P, and A. Ziehe. Jadetd: Combining higher-order statistics and temporal information for Blind Source Separation (with noise). In J.-F. Cardoso, C. Jutten, and P. Loubaton, editors, *Proceedings of the 1. ICA99 Workshop, Aussois*, volume 1, pages 87–92, 1999.

[13] B.-U. Koehler and R. Orglmeister. Independent component analysis using autoregressive models. In J.-F. Cardoso, C. Jutten, and P. Loubaton, editors, *Proceedings of the ICA99 workshop*, volume 1, pages 359–363, 1999.

Reinforcement Learning for Spoken Dialogue Systems

Satinder Singh
AT&T Labs

Michael Kearns
AT&T Labs

Diane Litman
AT&T Labs

Marilyn Walker
AT&T Labs

{baveja,mkearns,diane,walker}@research.att.com

Abstract

Recently, a number of authors have proposed treating dialogue systems as Markov decision processes (MDPs). However, the practical application of MDP algorithms to dialogue systems faces a number of severe technical challenges. We have built a general software tool (RLDS, for Reinforcement Learning for Dialogue Systems) based on the MDP framework, and have applied it to dialogue corpora gathered from two dialogue systems built at AT&T Labs. Our experiments demonstrate that RLDS holds promise as a tool for "browsing" and understanding correlations in complex, temporally dependent dialogue corpora.

1 Introduction

Systems in which human users speak to a computer in order to achieve a goal are called *spoken dialogue systems*. Such systems are some of the few realized examples of open-ended, real-time, goal-oriented interaction between humans and computers, and are therefore an important and exciting testbed for AI and machine learning research. Spoken dialogue systems typically integrate many components, such as a speech recognizer, a database back-end (since often the goal of the user is to retrieve information), and a dialogue strategy. In this paper we are interested in the challenging problem of automatically inferring a good dialogue strategy from dialogue corpora.

Research in dialogue strategy has been perhaps necessarily ad-hoc due to the open-ended nature of dialogue system design. For example, a common and critical design choice is between a system that always prompts the user to select an utterance from fixed menus (*system initiative*), and one that attempts to determine user intentions from unrestricted utterances (*mixed initiative*). Typically a system is built that explores a few alternative strategies, this system is tested, and conclusions are drawn regarding which of the tested strategies is best for that domain [4, 7, 2]. This is a time-consuming process, and it is difficult to rigorously compare and evaluate alternative systems in this fashion, much less design improved ones.

Recently, a number of authors have proposed treating dialogue design in the formalism of Markov decision processes (MDPs)[1, 3, 7]. In this view, the population of users defines the stochastic environment, a dialogue system's actions are its (speech-synthesized) utterances and database queries, and the state is represented by the entire dialogue so far. The goal is to design a dialogue system that takes actions so as to maximize some measure of reward. Viewed in this manner, it becomes possible, at least in principle, to apply the framework and algorithms of reinforcement learning (RL) to find a good dialogue strategy.

However, the practical application of RL algorithms to dialogue systems faces a number of severe technical challenges. First, representing the dialogue state by the entire dialogue so far is often neither feasible nor conceptually useful, and the so-called belief state approach is not possible, since we do not even know what features are required to represent the belief state. Second, there are many different choices for the reward function, even among systems providing very similar services to users. Previous work [7] has largely dealt with these issues by imposing a priori limitations on the features used to represent approximate state, and then exploring just one of the potential reward measures.

In this paper, we further develop the MDP formalism for dialogue systems, in a way that does not solve the difficulties above (indeed, there is no simple "solution" to them), but allows us to attenuate and quantify them by permitting the investigation of different notions of approximate state and reward. Using our expanded formalism, we give one of the first applications of RL algorithms to real data collected from multiple dialogue systems. We have built a general software tool (RLDS, for Reinforcement Learning for Dialogue Systems) based on our framework, and applied it to dialogue corpora gathered from two dialogue systems built at AT&T Labs, the TOOT system for voice retrieval of train schedule information [4] and the ELVIS system for voice retrieval of electronic mail [7].

Our experiments demonstrate that RLDS holds promise not just as a tool for the end-to-end automated synthesis of complicated dialogue systems from passive corpora — a "holy grail" that we fall far short of here[1] — but more immediately, as a tool for "browsing" and understanding correlations in complex, temporally dependent dialogue corpora. Such correlations may lead to incremental but important improvements in existing systems.

2 The TOOT and ELVIS Spoken Dialogue Systems

The TOOT and ELVIS systems were implemented using a general-purpose platform developed at AT&T, combining a speaker-independent hidden Markov model speech recognizer, a text-to-speech synthesizer, a telephone interface, and modules for specifying data-access functions and dialogue strategies. In TOOT, the data source is the Amtrak train schedule web site, while in ELVIS, it is the electronic mail spool of the user.

In a series of controlled experiments with human users, dialogue data was collected from both systems, resulting in 146 dialogues from TOOT and 227 dialogues from ELVIS. The TOOT experiments varied strategies for information presentation, confirmation (whether and how to confirm user utterances) and initiative (system vs. mixed), while the ELVIS experiments varied strategies for information presentation, for summarizing email folders, and initiative. Each resulting dialogue consists of a series of system and user utterances augmented by observations derived from the user utterances and the internal state of the system. The system's utterances (*actions*) give requested information, ask for clarification, provide greetings or instructions, and so on. The observations derived from the user's utterance include the speech-recognizer output, the corresponding log-likelihood score, the semantic labels assigned to the recognized utterances (such as the desired train departure and arrival cities in TOOT, or whether the user prefers to hear their email ordered by date or sender in ELVIS); indications of user barge-ins on system prompts; and many more. The observations derived from the internal state include the grammar used by the speech recognizer during the turn, and the results obtained from a query to the data source. In addition, each dialogue has an associated survey completed by the user that asks a variety of questions relating to the user's experience. See [4, 7] for details.

3 Spoken Dialogue Systems and MDPs

Given the preceding discussion, it is natural to formally view a dialogue as a sequence d

$$d = (a_1, \vec{o}_1, r_1), (a_2, \vec{o}_2, r_2), \ldots, (a_t, \vec{o}_t, r_t).$$

---

[1] However, in recent work we have applied the methodology described here to significantly improve the performance of a new dialogue system [5].

Here a_i is the action taken by the system (typically a speech-synthesized utterance, and less frequently, a database query) to start the ith exchange (or *turn*, as we shall call it), $\vec{o}_i$ consists of all the observations logged by the system on this turn, as discussed in the last section, and r_i is the reward received on this turn. As an example, in TOOT a typical turn might indicate that the action a_i was a system utterance requesting the departure city, and the $\vec{o}_i$ might indicate several observations: that the recognized utterance was "New York", that the log-likelihood of this recognition was -2.7, that there was another unrecognized utterance as well, and so on. We will use $d[i]$ to denote the prefix of d that ends following the ith turn, and $d \cdot (a, \vec{o}, r)$ to denote the one-turn extension of dialogue d by the turn $(a, \vec{o}, r)$. The scope of the actions a_i and observations $\vec{o}_i$ is determined by the implementation of the systems (e.g. if some quantity was not logged by the system, we will not have access to it in the $\vec{o}_i$ in the data). Our experimental results will use rewards derived from the user satisfaction surveys gathered for the TOOT and ELVIS data.

We may view any dialogue d as a trajectory in a well-defined *true* MDP M. The states [2] of M are all possible dialogues, and the actions are all the possible actions available to the spoken dialogue system (utterances and database queries). Now from any state (dialogue) d and action a, the only possible next states (dialogues) are the one-turn extensions $d \cdot (a, \vec{o}, r)$. The probability of transition from d to $d \cdot (a, \vec{o}, r)$ is exactly the probability, over the stochastic ensemble of users, that $\vec{o}$ and r would be generated following action a in dialogue d.

It is in general impractical to work directly on M due to the unlimited size of the state (dialogue) space. Furthermore, M is not known in advance and would have to be estimated from dialogue corpora. We would thus like to permit a flexible notion of *approximate* states. We define *state estimator* SE to be a mapping from any dialogue d into some space $\mathcal{S}$. For example, a simple state estimator for TOOT might represent the dialogue state with boolean variables indicating whether certain pieces of information had yet been obtained from the user (departure and arrival cities, and so on), and a continuous variable tracking the average log-likelihood of the recognized utterances so far. Then SE(d) would be a vector representing these quantities for the dialogue d. Once we have chosen a state estimator SE, we can transform the dialogue d into an $\mathcal{S}$-*trajectory*, starting from the initial empty state $s_0 \in \mathcal{S}$:

$$s_0 \to_{a_1} \text{SE}(d[1]) \to_{a_2} \text{SE}(d[2]) \to_{a_3} \cdots \to_{a_t} \text{SE}(d[t])$$

where the notation $\to_{a_i} \text{SE}(d[i])$ indicates a transition to $\text{SE}(d[i]) \in \mathcal{S}$ following action a_i. Given a set of dialogues $d_1, \ldots, d_n$, we can construct the *empirical* MDP $\hat{M}_{\text{SE}}$. The state space of $\hat{M}_{\text{SE}}$ is $\mathcal{S}$, the actions are the same as in M, and the probability of transition from s to s' under action a is exactly the empirical probability of such a transition in the $\mathcal{S}$-trajectories obtained from $d_1, \ldots, d_n$. Note that we can build $\hat{M}_{\text{SE}}$ from dialogue corpora, solve for its optimal policy, and analyze the resulting value function.

The point is that by choosing SE carefully, we hope that the empirical MDP $\hat{M}_{\text{SE}}$ will be a good approximation of M. By this we mean that $\hat{M}_{\text{SE}}$ *renders dialogues (approximately) Markovian:* the probability in M of transition from any dialogue d to any one-turn extension $d \cdot (a, \vec{o}, r)$ is (approximately) the probability of transition from SE(d) to SE$(d \cdot (a, \vec{o}, r))$ in $\hat{M}_{\text{SE}}$. We hope to find state estimators SE which render dialogues approximately Markovian, but for which the amount of data and computation required to find good policies in $\hat{M}_{\text{SE}}$ will be greatly reduced compared to working directly in dialogue space.

While conceptually appealing, this approach is subject to at least three important caveats: First, the approach is theoretically justified only to the extent that the chosen state estimator renders dialogues Markovian. In practice, we hope that the approach is robust, in that "small" violations of the Markov property will still produce useful results. Second, while

---

[2]These are not to be confused with the internal states of the spoken dialogue system(s) during the dialogue, which in our view merely contribute observations.

state estimators violating the Markov property may lead to meaningful insights, they cannot be directly compared. For instance, if the optimal value function derived from one state estimator is larger than the optimal value function for another state estimator, we *cannot* necessarily conclude that the first is better than the second. (This can be demonstrated formally.) Third, even with a Markovian state estimator SE, data that is sparse with respect to SE limits the conclusions we can draw; in a large space $\mathcal{S}$, certain states may be so infrequently visited in the dialogue corpora that we can say nothing about the optimal policy or value function there.

4 The RLDS System

We have implemented a software tool (written in C) called RLDS that realizes the above formalism. RLDS users specify an input file of sample dialogues; the dialogues include the rewards received at each turn. Users also specify input files defining $\mathcal{S}$ and a state estimator SE. The system has command-line options that specify the discount factor to be used, and a lower bound on the number of times a state $s \in \mathcal{S}$ must be visited in order for it to be included in the empirical MDP $\hat{M}_{SE}$ (to control overfitting to sparse data). Given these inputs and options, RLDS converts the dialogues into $\mathcal{S}$-trajectories, as discussed above. It then uses these trajectories to compute the empirical MDP $\hat{M}_{SE}$ specified by the data — that is, the data is used to compute next-state distributions and average reward in the obvious way. States with too few visits are pruned from $\hat{M}_{SE}$. RLDS then uses the standard value iteration algorithm to compute the optimal policy and value function [6] for $\hat{M}_{SE}$, all using the chosen discount factor.

5 Experimental Results

The goal of the experiments reported below is twofold: first, to confirm that our RLDS methodology and software produce intuitively sensible policies; and second, to use the value functions computed by the RLDS software to discover and understand correlations between dialogue properties and performance. We have space to present only a few of our many experiments on TOOT and ELVIS data.

Each experiment reported below involves choosing a state estimator, running RLDS using either the TOOT or ELVIS data, and then analyzing the resulting policy and value function. For the TOOT experiments, the reward function was obtained from a question in the user satisfaction survey: the last turn in a dialogue receives a reward of $+1$ if the user indicated that they would use the system again, a reward of 0 if the user answered "maybe", and a reward of -1 if the user indicated that they would not use the system again. All turns other than the last receive reward 0 (i.e., a reward is received only at the end of a dialogue). For the ELVIS experiments, we used a summed (over several questions) user-satisfaction score to reward the last turn in each dialogue (this score ranges between 8 and 40).

Experiment 1 (A Sensible Policy): In this initial "sanity check" experiment, we created a state estimator for TOOT whose boolean state variables track whether the system knows the value for the following five informational attributes: arrival city (denoted AC), departure city (DC), departure date (DD), departure hour (DH), and whether the hour is AM or PM (AP) [3]. Thus, if the dialogue so far includes a turn in which TOOT prompts the user for their departure city, and the speech recognizer matches the user utterance with "New York", the boolean state variable GotDC? would be assigned a value of 1. Note that this ignores the actual values of the attributes. In addition, there is another boolean variable called ConfirmedAll? that is set to 1 if and only if the system took action ConfirmAll (which prompts the user to explicitly verify the attribute values perceived by TOOT) and perceived a "yes" utterance in response. Thus, the state vector is simply the binary vector

[3] Remember that TOOT can only track its *perceptions* of these attributes, since errors may have occurred in speech recognition.

[GotAC? , GotAP? , GotDC? , GotDD? , GotDH? , ConfirmedAll?]

Among the actions (the system utterances) available to TOOT are prompts to the user to specify values for these informational attributes; we shall denote these actions with labels AskDC, AskAC, AskDD, AskDH, and AskAP. The system takes several other actions that we shall mention as they arise in our results.

The result of running RLDS was the following policy, where we have indicated the action to be taken from each state:

```
[0,0,0,0,0,0]: SayGreeting  [1,0,0,0,0,0]: AskDC   [1,0,1,0,0,0]: AskAP
[1,0,1,1,0,0]: AskDH         [0,0,0,1,1,0]: AskAP   [1,0,0,1,1,0]: AskAP
[0,1,0,1,1,0]: AskAll        [1,1,0,1,1,0]: AskAll  [1,0,1,1,1,0]: AskAP
[1,1,1,1,1,0]: ConfirmAll    [1,1,1,1,1,1]: Close
```

Thus, RLDS finds a sensible policy, always asking the user for information which it has not already received, confirming the user's choices when it has all the necessary information, and then presenting the closest matching train schedule and closing the dialogue (action Close). Note that in some cases it chooses to ask the user for values for all the informational attributes even though it has values for some of them. It is important to emphasize that this policy was derived purely through the application of RLDS to the dialogue data, without any knowledge of the "goal" of the system. Furthermore, the TOOT data is such that the empirical MDP built by RLDS for this state estimator does include actions considerably less reasonable than those chosen above from many states. Examples include confirming the values of specific informational attributes such as DC (since we do not represent whether such confirmations were successful, this action would lead to infinite loops of confirmation), and requesting values for informational attributes for which we already have values (such actions appear in the empirical MDP due to speech recognition errors). The mere fact that RLDS was driven to a sensible policy that avoided these available pitfalls indicates a correlation between the chosen reward measure (whether the user would use the system again) and the intuitive system goal of obtaining a completely specified train trip. It is interesting to note that RLDS finds it better to confirm values for all 5 attributes when it has them, as opposed to simply closing the dialogue without confirmation.

In a similar experiment on ELVIS, RLDS again found a sensible policy that summarizes the user's inbox at the beginning of the dialogue, goes on to read the relevant e-mail messages until done, and then closes.

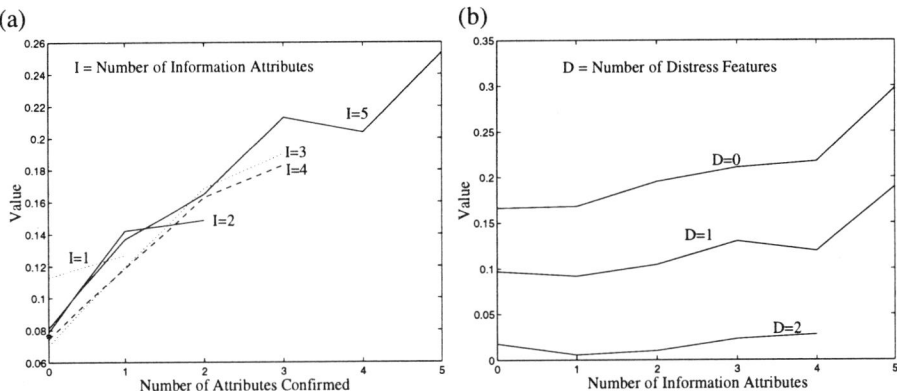

Figure 1: a) Role of Confirmation. b) Role of Distress Features (indicators that the dialogue is in trouble). See description of Experiments 2 and 3 respectively in the text for details.

Experiment 2 (Role of Confirmation): Here we explore the effect of confirming with the user the values that TOOT perceives for the informational attributes — that is, whether the trade-off between the increased confidence in the utterance and the potential annoyance to the user balances out in favor of confirmation or not (for the particular reward function we are using). To do so, we created a simple state estimator with just two state variables. The first variable counts the number of the informational attributes (DC, AC, etc.) that TOOT believes it has obtained, while the second variable counts the number of these that have been confirmed with the user. Figure 1(a) presents the optimal value as a function of the number of attributes confirmed. Each curve in the plot corresponds to a different setting of the first state variable. For instance, the curve labeled with "I=3" corresponds to the states where the system has obtained 3 informational attributes. We can make two interesting observations from this figure. First, the value function grows roughly linearly with the number of confirmed attributes. Second, and perhaps more startlingly, the value function has only a weak dependence on the first feature — the value for states when some number of attributes have been *confirmed* seems independent of how many attributes (the system believes) have been *obtained*. This is evident from the lack of separation between the plots for varying values of the state variable I. In other words, our simple (and preliminary) analysis suggests that for our reward measure, confirmed information influences the value function much more strongly than unconfirmed information. We also repeated this experiment replacing attribute confirmation with thresholded speech recognition log-likelihood scores, and obtained qualitatively similar results.

Experiment 3 (Role of Distress Features): Dialogues often contain timeouts (user silence when system expected response), resets (user asks for current context of dialogue to be abandoned and the system is reinitialized), user requests for help, and other indicators that the dialogue is potentially in trouble. Do such events correlate with low value? We created a state estimator for TOOT that, in addition to our variable I counting informational attributes, counted the number of such distress events in the dialogue. Figure 1(b) presents the optimal value as a function of the number of attributes obtained. Each curve corresponds to a different number of distress features. This figure confirms that the value of the dialogue is lower for states with a higher number of distress features.

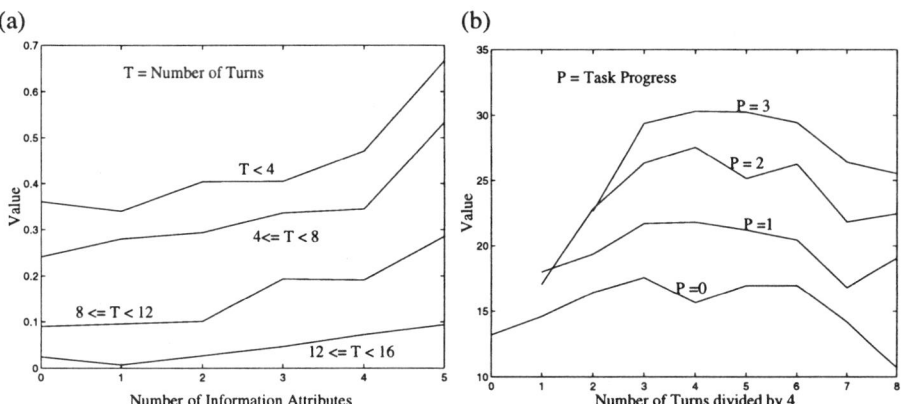

Figure 2: a) Role of Dialogue Length in TOOT. b) Role of Dialogue Length in ELVIS. See description of Experiment 4 in the text for details.

Experiment 4 (Role of the Dialogue Length): All other things being equal (e.g. extent of task completion), do users prefer shorter dialogues? To examine this question, we created a state estimator for TOOT that counts the number of informational attributes obtained (variable I as in Experiment 2), and a state estimator for ELVIS that measures "task progress" (a measure analogous to the variable I for TOOT; details omitted). In both cases, a second variable tracks the length of the dialogue.

Figure 2(a) presents the results for TOOT. It plots the optimal value as a function of the number I of informational values; each curve corresponds to a different range of dialogue lengths. It is immediately apparent that the longer the dialogue, the lower the value, and that within the same length of dialogue it is better to have obtained more attributes [4]. Of course, the effect of obtaining more attributes is weak for the longest dialogue length; these are dialogues in which the user is struggling with the system, usually due to multiple speech recognition errors.

Figure 2(b) presents the results for ELVIS from a different perspective. The dialogue length is now the x-axis, while each curve corresponds to a different value of P (task progress). It is immediately apparent that the value increases with task progress. More interestingly, unlike TOOT, there seems to be an "optimal" or appropriate dialogue length for each level of task progress, as seen in the inverse U-shaped curves.

Experiment 5 (Role of Initiative): One of the important questions in dialogue theory is how to choose between system and mixed initiative strategies (cf. Section 1). Using our approach on both TOOT and ELVIS data, we were able to confirm previous results [4, 7] showing that system initiative has a higher value than mixed initiative.

Experiment 6 (Role of Reward Functions): To test the robustness of our framework, we repeated Experiments 1–4 for TOOT using a new reward function based on the user's perceived task completion. We found that except for a weaker correlation between number of turns and value function, the results were basically the same across the two reward functions.

6 Conclusion

This paper presents a new RL-based framework for spoken dialogue systems. Using our framework, we developed RLDS, a general-purpose software tool, and used it for empirical studies on two sets of real dialogues gathered from the TOOT and ELVIS systems. Our results showed that RLDS was able to find sensible policies, that in ELVIS there was an "optimal" length of dialogue, that in TOOT confirmation of attributes was highly correlated with value, that system initiative led to greater user satisfaction than mixed initiative, and that the results were robust to changes in the reward function.

Acknowledgements: We give warm thanks to Esther Levin, David McAllester, Roberto Pieraccini, and Rich Sutton for their many contributions to this work.

References

[1] A. W. Biermann and P. M. Long. The composition of messages in speech-graphics interactive systems. In *Proceedings of the 1996 International Symposium on Spoken Dialogue.* 97–100, 1996.

[2] A. L. Gorin, B. A. Parker, R. M. Sachs and J. G. Wilpon. How May I Help You. In *Proceedings of International Symposium on Spoken Dialogue.* 57–60, 1996.

[3] E. Levin, R. Pieraccini and W. Eckert. Learning dialogue strategies within the Markov decision process framework. In *Proc. IEEE Workshop on Automatic Speech Recognition and Understanding* 1997.

[4] D. J. Litman and S. Pan. Empirically Evaluating an Adaptable Spoken Dialogue System. In *Proceedings of the 7th International Conference on User Modeling* 1999.

[5] S. Singh, M. Kearns, D. Litman, and M. Walker. In preparation.

[6] R. S. Sutton and A. G. Barto. *Reinforcement Learning: An Introduction* MIT Press, 1998.

[7] M. A. Walker, J. C. Fromer and S. Narayanan. Learning Optimal Dialogue Strategies: A Case Study of a Spoken Dialogue Agent for Email. In *Proceedings of the 36th Annual Meeting of the Association of Computational Linguistics, COLING/ACL 98* 1345–1352, 1998.

---

[4]There is no contradiction with Experiment 2 in this statement, since here we are not separating confirmed and unconfirmed attributes.

Image Recognition in Context: Application to Microscopic Urinalysis

Xubo Song*
Department of Electrical and Computer Engineering
Oregon Graduate Institute of Science and Technology
Beaverton, OR 97006
xubosong@ece.ogi.edu

Joseph Sill
Department of Computation and Neural Systems
California Institute of Technology
Pasadena, CA 91125
joe@busy.work.caltech.edu

Yaser Abu-Mostafa
Department of Electrical Engineering
California Institute of Technology
Pasadena, CA 91125
yaser@work.caltech.edu

Harvey Kasdan
International Remote Imaging Systems, Inc.
Chatsworth, CA 91311

Abstract

We propose a new and efficient technique for incorporating contextual information into object classification. Most of the current techniques face the problem of exponential computation cost. In this paper, we propose a new general framework that incorporates *partial* context at a linear cost. This technique is applied to microscopic urinalysis image recognition, resulting in a significant improvement of recognition rate over the context free approach. This gain would have been impossible using conventional context incorporation techniques.

1 BACKGROUND: RECOGNITION IN CONTEXT

There are a number of pattern recognition problem domains where the classification of an object should be based on more than simply the appearance of the object itself. In remote sensing image classification, where each pixel is part of ground cover, a pixel is more likely to be a glacier if it is in a mountainous area, than if surrounded by pixels of residential areas. In text analysis, one can expect to find certain letters occurring regularly in particular arrangement with other letters(qu, ee,est, tion, *etc.*). The information conveyed by the accompanying entities is referred to as *contextual information*. Human experts apply contextual information in their decision making [2][6]. It makes sense to design techniques and algorithms to make computers aggregate and utilize a more complete set of information in their decision making the way human experts do. In pattern recognition systems, however,

---
*Author for correspondence

the primary (and often only) source of information used to identify an object is the set of measurements, or *features*, associated with the object itself. Augmenting this information by incorporating context into the classification process can yield significant benefits.

Consider a set of N objects T_i, $i = 1, \ldots N$. With each object we associate a class label c_i that is a member of a label set $\Omega = \{1, \ldots, D\}$. Each object T_i is characterized by a set of measurements $\mathbf{x}_i \in \mathbf{R}^P$, which we call a feature vector. Many techniques [1][2][4][6] incorporate context by conditioning the posterior probability of objects' identities on the joint features of all accompanying objects, *i.e.*, $p(c_1, c_2, \ldots, c_N | \mathbf{x}_1, \ldots, \mathbf{x}_N)$, and then maximizing it with respect to $c_1, c_2, \ldots, c_N$. It can be shown that $p(c_1, c_2, \ldots, c_N | \mathbf{x}_1, \ldots, \mathbf{x}_N) \propto p(c_1|\mathbf{x}_1) \ldots p(c_N|\mathbf{x}_N) \frac{p(c_1, \ldots, c_N)}{p(c_1) \ldots p(c_N)}$ given certain reasonable assumptions.

Once the context-free posterior probabilities $p(c_i|x_i)$ are known, e.g. through the use of a standard machine learning model such as a neural network, computing $p(c_1, \ldots, c_N | \mathbf{x}_1, \ldots, \mathbf{x}_N)$ for all possible $c_1, \ldots, c_N$ would entail $(2N+1)D^N$ multiplications, and finding the maximum has complexity of D^N, which is intractable for large N and D. [2]

Another problem with this formulation is the estimation of the high dimensional joint distribution $p(c_1, \ldots, c_N)$, which is ill-posed and data hungry.

One way of dealing with these problems is to limit context to local regions. With this approach, only the pixels in a close neighborhood, or letters immediately adjacent are considered [4][6][7]. Such techniques may be ignoring useful information, and will not apply to situations where context doesn't have such locality, as in the case of microscopic urinalysis image recognition. Another way is to simplify the problem using specific domain knowledge [1], but this is only possible in certain domains.

These difficulties motivate the efficient incorporation of *partial context* as a general framework, formulated in section 2. In section 3, we discuss microscopic urinalysis image recognition, and address the importance of using context for this application. Also in section 3, techniques are proposed to identify relevant context. Empirical results are shown in section 4, followed by discussions in section 5.

2 FORMULATION FOR INCORPORATION OF PARTIAL CONTEXT

To avoid the exponential computational cost of using the identities of all accompanying objects directly as context, we use "partial context", denoted by A. It is called "partial" because it is *derived* from the class labels, as opposed to consisting of an explicit labelling of all objects. The physical definition of A depends on the problem at hand. In our application, A represents the presence or absence of certain classes. Then the posterior probability of an object T_i having class label c_i conditioned on its feature vector and the relevant context A is

$$p(c_i|x_i, A) = \frac{p(c_i, x_i; A)}{p(x_i; A)} = \frac{p(x_i|c_i, A)P(c_i; A)}{p(x_i; A)}$$

We assume that the feature distribution of an object depends only on its own class, *i.e.*, $p(x_i|c_i, A) = p(x_i|c_i)$. This assumption is roughly true for most real world problems. Then,

$$p(c_i|x_i, A) = \frac{p(x_i|c_i)p(c_i; A)}{p(x_i; A)} = p(c_i|x_i)\frac{p(c_i|A)}{p(c_i)} \frac{p(A)p(x_i)}{p(x_i; A)}$$
$$\propto p(c_i|x_i)\frac{p(c_i|A)}{p(c_i)} = p(c_i|x_i)\rho(c_i, A)$$

where $\rho(c_i, A) = \frac{p(c_i|A)}{p(c_i)}$ is called the *context ratio*, through which context plays its role. The context-sensitive posterior probability $p(c_i|x_i, A)$ is obtained through the context-free posterior probability $p(c_i|x_i)$ modified by the context ratio $\rho(c_i, A)$.

The partial-context maximum likelihood decision rule chooses class label $\hat{c}_i$ for element i such that

$$\hat{c}_i = \underset{c_i}{\operatorname{argmax}}\, p(c_i|\mathbf{x}_i, A) \qquad (1)$$

A systematic approach to identify relevant context A is addressed in section 3.3.

The partial-context approach treats each element in a set individually, but with additional information from the context-bearing factor A. Once $p(c_i|x_i)$ are known for all $i = 1, \ldots, N$, and the context A is obtained, to maximize $p(c_i|x_i, A)$ from D possible values that c_i can take on and for all i, the total number of multiplications is $2N$, and the complexity for finding the maximum is ND. Both are linear in N. The density estimation part is also trivial since it is very easy to estimate $p(c|A)$.

3 MICROSCOPIC URINALYSIS

3.1 INTRODUCTION

Urine is one of the most complex body fluid specimens: it potentially contains about 60 meaningful types of elements. Microscopic urinalysis detects the presence of elements that often provide early diagnostic information concerning dysfunction, infection, or inflammation of the kidneys and urinary tract. Thus this non-invasive technique can be of great value in clinical case management. Traditional manual microscopic analysis relies on human operators who read the samples visually and identify them, and therefore is time-consuming, labor-intensive and difficult to standardize. Automated microscopy of all specimens is more practical than manual microscopy, because it eliminates variation among different technologists. This variation becomes more pronounced when the same technologist examines increasing numbers of specimens. Also, it is less labor-intensive and thus less costly than manual microscopy. It also provides more consistent and accurate results. An automated urinalysis system workstation (The $YellowIRIS^{TM}$, International Remote Imaging Systems, Inc.) has been introduced in numerous clinical laboratories for automated microscopy. Urine samples are processed and examined at 100x (low power field) and 400x magnifications (high power field) with bright-field illumination. The $YellowIRIS^{TM}$ automated system collects video images of formed analytes in a stream of uncentrifuged urine passing an optical assembly. Each image has one analyte in it. These images are given to a computer algorithm for automatic identification of analytes.

Context is rich in urinalysis and plays a crucial role in analyte classification. Some combinations of analytes are more likely than others. For instance, the presence of bacteria indicates the presence of white blood cells, since bacteria tend to cause infection and thus trigger the production of more white blood cells. If amorphous crystals show up, they tend to show up in bunches and in all sizes. Therefore, if there are amorphous crystal look-alikes in various sizes, it is quite possible that they are amorphous crystals. Squamous epithelial cells can appear both flat or rolled up. If squamous epithelial cells in one form are detected,

Table 1: Features extracted from urine anylates images

feature number	feature description
1	area
2	length of edge
3	$\dfrac{\text{square root of area}}{\text{length of edge}}$
4	$\dfrac{\text{standard deviation}}{\text{mean}}$ of distance from center to edge
5	$\dfrac{\lambda_1}{\lambda_2}$
6	$\dfrac{\text{sum of length of two longest straight edges}}{\text{total length of edge}}$
7	$\dfrac{\text{sum of length of four longest straight edges}}{\text{total length of edge}}$
8	$\dfrac{\text{sum of length of two longest semi-straight edges}}{\text{total length of edge}}$
9	$\dfrac{\text{sum of length of four longest semi-straight edges}}{\text{total length of edge}}$
10	the mean of red distribution
11	the mean of blue distribution
12	the mean of green distribution
13	15th percentile of gray level histogram
14	85th percentile of gray level histogram
15	the standard deviation of gray level intensity
16	energy of the Laplacian transformation of grey level image

then it is likely that there are squamous epithelial cells in the other form. Utilizing such context is crucial for classification accuracy.

The classes we are looking at are bacteria, calcium oxalate crystals, red blood cells, white blood cells, budding yeast, amorphous crystals, uric acid crystals, and artifacts. The task of automated microscopic urinalysis is, given a urine specimen that consists of up to a few hundred images of analytes, to classify each analyte into one of these classes. The automated urinalysis system we developed consists of three steps: image processing and feature extraction, learning and pattern recognition, and context incorporation. Figure 1 shows some example analyte images. Table 1 gives a list of features extracted from analyte images.[1]

3.2 CONTEXT-FREE CLASSIFICATION

The features are fed into a nonlinear feed-forward neural network with 16 inputs, 15 hidden units with sigmoid transfer functions, and 8 sigmoid output units. A cross-entropy error function is used in order to give the output a probability interpretation. Denote the input feature vector as $\mathbf{x}$, the network outputs a D dimensional vector ($D = 8$ in our case) $\mathbf{p} = \{p(d|\mathbf{x})\}, d = 1, ..., D$, where $p(d|\mathbf{x})$ is

$$p(d|\mathbf{x}) = Prob(\text{ an analyte belongs to class } d| \text{ feature } \mathbf{x})$$

The decision made at this stage is

$$d(\mathbf{x}) = \underset{d}{\operatorname{argmax}}\ p(d|\mathbf{x})$$

3.3 IDENTIFICATION OF RELEVANT PARTIAL CONTEXT

Not all classes are relevant in terms of carrying contextual information. We propose three criteria based on which we can systematically investigate the relevance of the class presence. To use these criteria, we need to know the following distributions: the class prior distribution $p(c)$ for $c = 1, \ldots, D$; the conditional class distribution $p(c|A_d)$ for $c = 1, \ldots, D$

---

[1] λ_1 and λ_2 are respectively the larger and the smaller eigenvalues of the second moment matrix of an image.

and $d = 1, \ldots, D$; and the class presence prior distribution $p(A_d)$ for $d = 1, \ldots, D$. A_d is a binary random variable indicating the presence of class d. $A_d = 1$ if class d is present, and $A_d = 0$ otherwise. All these distributions can be easily estimated from the database.

The first criterion is the correlation coefficient between the presence of any two classes; the second one is the classical mutual information $I(c; A_d)$ between the presence of a class A_d and the class probability $p(c)$, where $I(c; A_d)$ is defined as $I(c; A_d) = H(c) - H(c|A_d)$ where $H(c) = \sum_{i=1}^{D} p(c = i) ln(p(c = i))$ is the entropy of the class priors and $H(c|A_d) = P(A_d = 1)H(c|A_d = 1) + P(A_d = 0)H(c|A_d = 0)$ is the conditional entropy of c conditioned on A_d. The third criterion is what we call the *expected relative entropy* $D(c||A_d)$ between the presence of a class A_d and the labeling probability $p(c)$, which we define as $D(c||A_d) = P(A_d = 1)D(p(c)||p(c|A_d = 1)) + P(A_d = 0)D(p(c)||p(c|A_d = 0))$ where $D(p(c)||p(c|A_d = 1)) = \sum_{i=1}^{D} p(c = i|A_d = 1)ln(\frac{p(c=i|A_d=1)}{p(c=i)})$ and $D(p(c)||p(c|A_d = 0)) = \sum_{i=1}^{D} p(c = i|A_d = 0)ln(\frac{p(c=i|A_d=0)}{p(c=i)})$

According to the first criterion, one type of analyte is considered relevant to another if the absolute value of their correlation coefficient is beyond a certain threshold. It shows that uric acid crystals, budding yeast and calcium oxalate crystals are not relevant to any other types even by a generous threshold of 0.10. Similarly, the bigger the mutual information between the presence of a class and the class distribution, the more relevant this class is. Ranking the analyte types in terms of $I(c; A_d)$ in a descending manner gives rise to the following list: bacteria, amorphous crystals, red blood cells, white blood cells, uric acid crystals, budding yeast and calcium oxalate crystals. Once again, ranking the analyte types in terms of $D(c||A_d)$ in a descending manner gives rise to the following list: bacteria, red blood cells, amorphous crystals, white blood cells, calcium oxalate crystals, budding yeast and uric acid crystals. All three criteria lead to similar conclusions regarding the relevance of class presence – bacteria, red blood cells, amorphous crystals, and white blood cells are relevant, while calcium oxalate crystals, budding yeast and uric acid crystals are not. (Baed on prior knowledge, we discard artifacts from the outset as an irrelevant class.)

3.4 ALGORITHM FOR INCORPORATING PARTIAL CONTEXT

Once the M relevant classes are identified, the following algorithm is used to incorporate partial context.

Step 0 Estimate the priors $p(c|A_d)$ and $p(c)$, for $c \in \{1, 2, \ldots, D\}$ and $d \in \{1, 2, \ldots, D\}$.

Step 1 For a given x_i, compute $p(c_i|x_i)$ for $c_i = 1, 2, \ldots, D$ using whichever base machine learning model is preferred (in our case, a neural network).

Step 2 Let the M relevant classes be $R_1, \ldots, R_M$. According to the no-context $p(c_i|x_i)$ and certain criteria for detecting the presence or absence of all the relevant classes, get $A_{R_1}, \ldots, A_{R_M}$.

Step 3 Let $p(c_i|x_i, A_0) = p(c_i|x_i)$, where A_0 is the null element. Incorporate context from each relevant class sequentially, i.e., for $m = 1$ to M, iteratively compute

$$p(c_i|x_i; A_0, \ldots, A_{R_{m-1}}, A_{R_m}) = p(c_i|x_i, A_0, \ldots, A_{R_{m-1}}) \frac{p(c_i|A_{R_m})p(A_{R_m})}{p(c)}$$

Step 4 Recompute $A_{R_1}, \ldots, A_{R_M}$ based on the new class labellings. Return to step 3 and repeat until algorithm converges.[2]

---
[2]Hence, the algorithm has an E-M flavor, in that it goes back and forth between finding the most

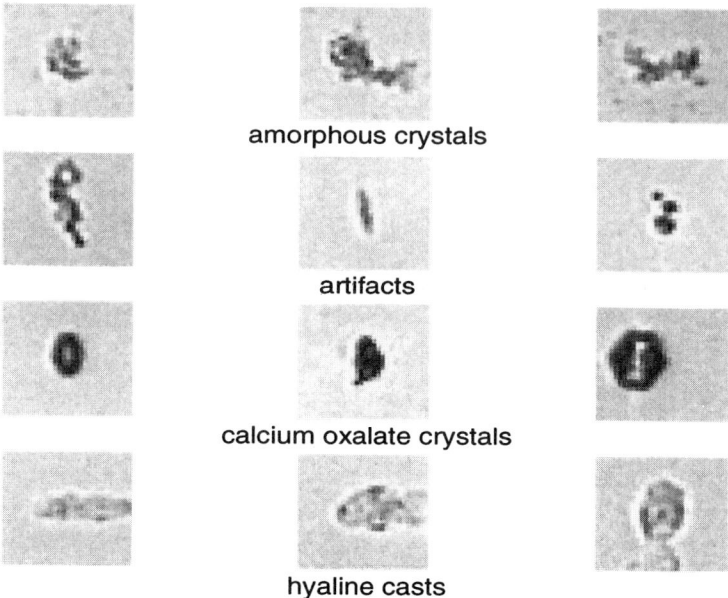

Figure 1: Example of some of the analyte images.

Step 5 Label the objects according to the final context-containing $p(c_i|\mathbf{x}_i, A_{R_1}, \ldots, A_{R_M})$, i.e., $\hat{c}_i = \mathrm{argmax}_{c_i} p(c_i|\mathbf{x}_i, A_{R_1}, \ldots, A_{R_M})$ for $i = 1, \ldots, N$.

This algorithm is invariant with respect to the ordering of the M relevant classes in $(A_1, \ldots, A_M)$. The proof is omitted here.

4 RESULTS

The algorithm using partial context was tested on a database of 83 urine specimens, containing a total of 20,276 analyte images. Four classes are considered relevant according to the criteria described in section 3.3: bacteria, red blood cells, white blood cells and amorphous crystals. We measure two types of error: analyte-by-analyte error, and specimen diagnostic error. The average analyte-by-analyte error is reduced from 44.48% before using context to 36.66% after, resulting a relative error reduction of 17.6% (Table 2). The diagnosis for a specimen is either normal or abnormal. Tables 3 and 4 compare the diagnostic performance with and without using context, and Table 5 lists the relative changes. We can see using context significantly increases correct diagnosis for both normal and abnormal specimens, and reduces both false positives and false negatives.

	without context	with context
average element-by-element error	44.48 %	36.66 %

Table 2: Comparison of using and not using contextual information for analyte-by-analyte error.

---

probable class labels given the context and determining the context given the class labels.

	estimated normal	estimated abnormal
truly normal	40.96 %	7.23 %
truly abnormal	19.28 %	32.53 %

Table 3: Diagnostic confusion matrix not using context

	estimated normal	estimated abnormal
truly normal	42.17 %	6.02 %
truly abnormal	16.87 %	34.94 %

Table 4: Diagnostic confusion matrix using context

	estimated normal	estimated abnormal
truly normal	+ 2.95 %	-16.73 %
truly abnormal	- 12.50 %	+7.41 %

Table 5: Relative accuracy improvement (diagonal elements) and error reduction (off diagonal elements) in the diagnostic confusion matrix by using context.

5 CONCLUSIONS

We proposed a novel framework that can incorporate context in a simple and efficient manner, avoiding exponential computation and high dimensional density estimation. The application of the *partial context* technique to microscopic urinalysis image recognition demonstrated the efficacy of the algorithm. This algorithm is not domain dependent, thus can be readily generalized to other pattern recognition areas.

ACKNOWLEDGEMENTS

The authors would like to thank Alexander Nicholson, Malik Magdon-Ismail, Amir Atiya at the Caltech Learning Systems Group for helpful discussions.

References

[1] Song, X.B. & Sill, J. & Abu-Mostafa & Harvey Kasdan, (1997) "Incorporating Contextual Information in White Blood Cell Identification", In M. Jordan, M.J. Kearns and S.A. Solla (eds.), *Advances in Neural Information Processing Systems 7*, 1997, pp. 950-956. Cambridge, MA: MIT Press.

[2] Song, Xubo (1999) "Contextual Pattern Recognition with Application to Biomedical Image Identification", Ph.D. Thesis, California Institute of Science and Technology.

[3] Boehringer-Mannheim-Corporation, Urinalysis Today, Boehringer-Mannheim-Corporation, 1991.

[4] Kittler, J.,"Relaxation labelling", Pattern Recognition Theory and Applications, 1987, pp. 99-108., Pierre A. Devijver and Josef Kittler, Editors, Springer-Verlag.

[5] Kittler, J. & Illingworth, J., "Relaxation Labelling Algorithms - A Review", Image and Vision Computing, 1985, vol. 3, pp. 206-216.

[6] Toussaint, G., "The Use of Context in Pattern Recognition", Pattern Recognition, 1978, vol. 10, pp. 189-204.

[7] Swain, P. & Vardeman, S. & Tilton, J., "Contextual Classification of Multispectral Image Data", Pattern Recognition, 1981, Vol. 13, No. 6, pp. 429-441.

Generalized Model Selection For Unsupervised Learning In High Dimensions

Shivakumar Vaithyanathan
IBM Almaden Research Center
650 Harry Road
San Jose, CA 95136
Shiv@almaden.ibm.com

Byron Dom
IBM Almaden Research Center
650 Harry Road
San Jose, CA 95136
dom@almaden.ibm.com

Abstract

We describe a Bayesian approach to model selection in unsupervised learning that determines both the feature set and the number of clusters. We then evaluate this scheme (based on marginal likelihood) and one based on cross-validated likelihood. For the Bayesian scheme we derive a closed-form solution of the marginal likelihood by assuming appropriate forms of the likelihood function and prior. Extensive experiments compare these approaches and all results are verified by comparison against ground truth. In these experiments the Bayesian scheme using our objective function gave better results than cross-validation.

1 Introduction

Recent efforts define the model selection problem as one of estimating the number of clusters[10, 17]. It is easy to see, particularly in applications with large number of features, that various choices of feature subsets will reveal different structures underlying the data. It is our contention that this interplay between the feature subset and the number of clusters is essential to provide appropriate views of the data. We thus define the problem of model selection in clustering as selecting both the number of clusters *and* the feature subset. Towards this end we propose a unified objective function whose arguments include the both the feature space and number of clusters. We then describe two approaches to model selection using this objective function. The first approach is based on a Bayesian scheme using the marginal likelihood for model selection. The second approach is based on a scheme using cross-validated likelihood. In section 3 we apply these approaches to document clustering by making assumptions about the document generation model. Further, for the Bayesian approach we derive a closed-form solution for the marginal likelihood using this document generation model. We also describe a heuristic for initial feature selection based on the distributional clustering of terms. Section 5 describes the experiments and our approach to validate the proposed models and algorithms. Section 6 reports and discusses the results of our experiments and finally section 7 provides directions for future work.

2 Model selection in clustering

Model selection approaches in clustering have primarily concentrated on determining the number of components/clusters. These attempts include Bayesian approaches [7,10], MDL approaches [15] and cross-validation techniques [17]. As noticed in [17] however, the optimal number of clusters is dependent on the feature space in which the clustering is performed. Related work has been described in [7].

2.1 A generalized model for clustering

Let D be a data-set consisting of "patterns" $\{d_1,..,d_v\}$, which we assume to be represented in some feature space T with dimension M. The particular problem we address is that of clustering D into groups such that its likelihood described by a probability model $P(D^T|\Omega)$, is maximized, where D^T indicates the representation of D in feature space T and Ω is the structure of the model, which consists of the number of clusters, the partitioning of the feature set (explained below) and the assignment of patterns to clusters. This model is a weighted sum of models $\{P(D^T|\Omega,\xi)|\xi \in \mathbb{R}^m\}$ where ξ is the set of all parameters associated with Ω. To define our model we begin by assuming that the feature space T consists of two sets: U - useful features and N - noise features. Our feature-selection problem will thus consist of partitioning T (into U and N) for a given number of clusters.

Assumption 1 *The feature sets represented by U and N are conditionally independent*

$$P(D^T|\Omega,\xi) = P(D^N | \Omega,\xi) P(D^U | \Omega,\xi) \tag{1}$$

where D^N indicates data represented in the noise feature space and D^U indicates data represented in useful feature space.

Using assumption 1 and assuming that the data is independently drawn, we can rewrite equation (1) as

$$P(D^T|\Omega,\xi) = \left\{ \prod_{i=1}^{v} p(d_i^N | \xi^N) \cdot \prod_{k=1}^{K} \prod_{j \in D_k} p(d_j^U | \xi_k^U) \right\} \tag{2}$$

where v is the number of patterns in D, $p(d_i^U | \xi^U)$ is the probability of d_i^U given the parameter vector ξ_k^U and $p(d_i^N | \xi^N)$ is the probability of d_i^N given the parameter vector ξ^N. Note that while the explicit dependence on Ω has been removed in this notation, it is implicit in the number of clusters K and the partition of T into N and U.

2.2 Bayesian approach to model selection

The objective function, represented in equation (2) is not regularized and attempts to optimize it directly may result in the set N becoming empty - resulting in overfitting. To overcome this problem we use the *marginal likelihood*[2].

Assumption 2 *All parameter vectors are independent.* $\pi(\xi) = \pi(\xi^N) \cdot \prod_{k=1}^{K} \pi(\xi_k^U)$

where the $\pi(...)$ denotes a Bayesian *prior* distribution. The marginal likelihood, using assumption 2, can be written as

$$P(D^T | \Omega) = \int_{\Xi^N} \left[\prod_{i=1}^{v} p(d_i^N | \xi^N) \right] \pi(\xi^N) d\xi^N \cdot \prod_{k=1}^{K} \int_{\Xi^U} \left[\prod_{i \in D_k} p(d_i^U | \xi_k^U) \right] \pi(\xi_k^U) d\xi_k^U \tag{3}$$

where Ξ^N, Ξ^U are integral limits appropriate to the particular parameter spaces. These will be omitted to simplify the notation.

3.0 Document clustering

Document clustering algorithms typically start by representing the document as a "bag-of-words" in which the features can number $\sim 10^4$ to 10^5. Ad-hoc dimensionality reduction techniques such as stop-word removal, frequency based truncations [16] and techniques such as LSI [5] are available. Once the dimensionality has been reduced, the documents are usually clustered into an *arbitrary* number of clusters.

3.1 Multinomial models

Several models of text generation have been studied[3]. Our choice is *multinomial* models using term counts as the features. This choice introduces another parameter indicating the probability of the N and U split. This is equivalent to assuming a generation model where for each document the number of noise and useful terms are determined by a probability θ^S and then the terms in a document are "drawn" with a probability (θ^n or θ_k^u).

3.2 Marginal likelihood / stochastic complexity

To apply our Bayesian objective function we begin by substituting multinomial models into (3) and simplifying to obtain

$$P(D \mid \Omega) = \binom{t^N + t^U}{t^N} \int [(\theta^S)^{t^N}(1-\theta^S)^{t^U}] \pi(\theta^S) d\theta^S \cdot$$

$$\left[\prod_{k=1}^{K} \prod_{i \in D_k} \binom{t_i^U}{\{t_{i,u} \mid u \in U\}} \right] \int \left[\prod_{u \in U} (\theta_k^u)^{t_{i,u}} \right] \pi(\theta_k^U) d\theta_k^U \cdot \quad (4)$$

$$\left[\prod_{j=1}^{v} \binom{t_j^N}{\{t_{j,n} \mid n \in N\}} \right] \int \left[\prod_{n \in N} (\theta^n)^{t_{j,n}} \right] \pi(\theta^N) d\theta^N$$

where $\binom{\cdots}{\{\ldots\}}$ is the multinomial coefficient, $t_{i,u}$ is the number of occurrences of the feature term u in document i, t_i^U is the total number of all *useful* features (terms) in document i ($t_i^U = \sum_u t_{i,u}$, t_i^N, and $t_{i,n}$ are to be interpreted similar to above but for noise features, $\binom{n}{k} = \frac{n!}{k!(n-k)!}$, t^N is the total number of all *noise* features in all patterns and t^U is the total number of all useful features in all patterns.

To solve (4) we still need a form for the *priors* $\{\pi(\ldots)\}$. The Beta family is *conjugate* to the Binomial family [2] and we choose the Dirichlet distribution (multiple Beta) as the form for both $\pi(\theta_k^U)$ and $\pi(\theta^N)$ and the Beta distribution for $\pi(\theta^S)$. Substituting these into equation (8) and simplifying yields

$$P(D \mid \Omega) = \left[\frac{\Gamma(\gamma_a + \gamma_b)}{\Gamma(\gamma_a)\Gamma(\gamma_b)} \frac{\Gamma(t^N + \gamma_a)\Gamma(t^U + \gamma_b)}{\Gamma(t^U + t^N + \gamma_a + \gamma_b)} \right] \cdot \left[\frac{\Gamma(\beta)}{\Gamma(\beta + t^N)} \prod_{n \in N} \frac{\Gamma(\beta_n + t^n)}{\Gamma(\beta_n)} \right]$$

$$\left[\frac{\Gamma(\sigma)}{\Gamma(\sigma + v)} \prod_{k=1}^{K} \frac{\Gamma(\sigma_k + |D_k|)}{\Gamma(|D_k|)} \right] \cdot \left[\prod_{k=1}^{K} \frac{\Gamma(a)}{\Gamma(a + t^{U(k)})} \prod_{u \in U} \frac{\Gamma(a_u + t_k^u)}{\Gamma(a_u)} \right]$$

(5)

where β_l and a_u are the hyper-parameters of the Dirichlet prior for noise and useful features respectively, $\beta = \sum_{n \in N} \beta_n$, $a = \sum_{u \in U} a_u$, $\sigma = \sum_k \sigma_k$ and $\Gamma()$ is the "gamma" function. Further, γ_a, γ_b are the hyper parameters of the Beta prior for the split probability, $|D_k|$ is the number of documents in cluster k and $_t U^{(k)}$ is computed as $\sum_{i \in D_k} t_i^l$. The results reported for our evaluation will be the negative of the log of equation (5), which (following Rissanen [14]) we refer to as Stochastic Complexity (*SC*). In our experiments all values of the hyper-parameters $\beta_i, a_i, \sigma_k, \gamma_a$ and γ_b are set equal to 1 yielding uniform priors.

3.3 Cross-Validated likelihood

To compute the cross validated likelihood using multinomial models we first substitute the multinomial functional forms, using the MLE found using the training set. This results in the following equation

$$P(CV^T \mid \Omega^p) = \left\{ [(\widetilde{\theta^S})^{t_{cv}^N} \cdot (1 - \widetilde{\theta^S})^{t_{cv}^U}] \prod_{i=1}^{v_{test}} p(cv_i^N \mid \widetilde{\theta^N}) \cdot \prod_{k=1}^{K} \prod_{j \in D_k} p(cv_j^U \mid \widetilde{\theta^U_{k(i)}}) \cdot p(c_k) \right. (6)$$

where $\widetilde{\theta^S}$, $\widetilde{\theta^N}$ and $\widetilde{\theta^U_{k(i)}}$ are the MLE of the appropriate parameter vectors. For our implementation of *MCCV*, following the suggestion in [17], we have used a 50% split of the training and test set. For the *vCV* criterion although a value of v = 10 was suggested therein, for computational reasons we have used a value of v = 5.

3.4 Feature subset selection algorithm for document clustering

As noted in section 2.1, for a feature-set of size *M* there are a total of 2^M partitions and for large *M* it would be computationally intractable to search through all possible partitions to find the optimal subset. In this section we propose a heuristic method to obtain a subset of tokens that are topical (indicative of underlying topics) and can be used as features in the bag-of-words model to cluster documents.

3.4.1 Distributional clustering for feature subset selection

Identifying content-bearing and topical terms, is an active research area [9]. We are less concerned with modeling the exact distributions of individual terms as we are with simply identifying groups of terms that are topical. Distributional clustering (DC), apparently first proposed by Pereira et al [13], has been used for feature selection in supervised text classification [1] and clustering images in video sequences [9]. We hypothesize that function, content-bearing and topical terms have different distributions over the documents. DC helps reduce the size of the search space for feature selection from 2^M to 2^C, where *C* is the number of clusters produced by the DC algorithm. Following the suggestions in [9], we compute the following histogram for each token. The first bin consists of the number of documents with zero occurrences of the token, the second bin is the number of documents consisting of a single occurrence of the token and the third bin is the number of documents that contain more two or more occurrences of the term. The histograms are clustered using *relative entropy* $\Delta(. \parallel .)$ as a distance measure. For two terms with probability distributions $p_1(.)$ and $p_2(.)$, this is given by [4]:

$$\Delta(p_1(t) \| p_2(t)) \equiv \sum_t p_1(t) \log \frac{p_1(t)}{p_2(t)} \qquad (7)$$

We use a k-means-style algorithm in which the histograms are normalized to sum to one and the sum in equation (7) is taken over the three bins corresponding to counts of 0,1, and ≥ 2. During the assignment-to-clusters step of k-means we compute $\Delta(p_w \| p_{c_k})$ (where p_w is the normalized histogram for term w and $p_{c_k}(t)$ is the centroid of cluster k) and the term w is assigned to the cluster for which this is minimum [13,8].

4.0 Experimental setup

Our evaluation experiments compared the clustering results against human-labeled ground truth. The corpus used was the AP Reuters Newswire articles from the TREC-6 collection. A total of 8235 documents, from the routing track, existing in 25 classes were analyzed in our experiments. To simplify matters we disregarded multiple assignments and retained each document as a member of a single class.

4.1 Mutual information as an evaluation measure of clustering

We verify our models by comparing our clustering results against pre-classified text. We force all clustering algorithms to produce exactly as many clusters as there are classes in the pre-classified text and we report the mutual information[4] (MI) between the cluster labels and pre-classified class labels

5.0 Results and discussions

After tokenizing the documents and discarding terms that appeared in less than 3 documents we were left with 32450 unique terms. We experimented with several numbers of clusters for DC but report only the best (lowest SC) for lack of space. For each of these clusters we chose the best of 20 runs corresponding to different random starting clusters. Each of these sets includes one cluster that consists of high-frequency words and upon examination were found to contain primarily *function* words, which we eliminated from further consideration. The remaining non-function-word clusters were used as feature sets for the clustering algorithm. Only combinations of feature sets that produced good results were used for further document clustering runs.

We initialized the EM algorithm using k-means algorithm - other initialization schemes are discussed in [11]. The feature vectors used in this k-means initialization were generated using the pivoted normal weighting suggested in [16]. All parameter vectors θ_k^U and θ^N were estimated using Laplace's Rule of Succession[2]. Table 1 shows the best results of the *SC* criterion, the *vCV* and *MCCV* using the feature subsets selected by the different combinations of distributional clusters. The feature subsets are coded as FSXP where X indicates the number of clusters in the distributional clustering and P indicates the cluster number(s) used as U. For *SC* and MI all results reported are averages over 3 runs of the k-means+EM combination with different initialization fo k-means. For clarity, the MI numbers reported are normalized such that the theoretical maximum is 1.0. We also show comparisons against no feature selection (NF) and LSI.

For LSI, the principal 165 eigenvectors were retained and k-means clustering was performed in the reduced dimensional space. While determining the number of clusters, for computational reasons we have limited our evaluation to only the feature subset that provided us with the highest MI, i.e., FS41-3.

Feature Set	Useful Features	SC $\times 10^7$	vCV $\times 10^7$	$MCCV$ $\times 10^7$	MI
FS41-3	6,157	**2.66**	0.61	1.32	**0.61**
FS52	386	2.8	**0.3**	**0.69**	0.51
NF	32,450	2.96	1.25	2.8	0.58
LSI	32450/165	NA	NA	NA	0.57

Table 1 Comparison Of Results

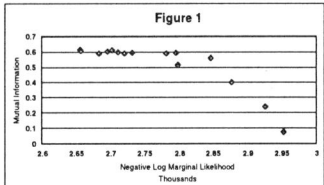
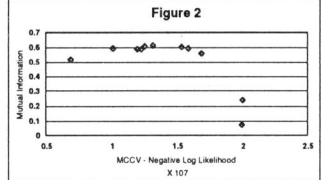

5.3 Discussion

The consistency between the MI and SC (Figure 1) is striking. The monotonic trend is more apparent at higher SC indicating that bad clusterings are more easily detected by SC while as the solution improves the differences are more subtle. *Note that the best value of SC and MI coincide.* Given the assumptions made in deriving equation (5), this consistency and is encouraging. The interested reader is referred to [18] for more details. Figures 2 and 3 indicate that there is certainly a reasonable consistency between the cross-validated likelihood and the MI although not as striking as the SC. Note that the MI for the feature sets picked by $MCCV$ and vCV is significantly lower than that of the best feature-set. Figures 4,5 and 6 show the plots of SC, MCCV and vCV as the number of clusters is increased. Using SC we see that FS41-3 reveals an optimal structure around 40 clusters. As with feature selection, both $MCCV$ and vCV obtain models of lower complexity than SC. Both show an optimum of about 30 clusters. More experiments are required before we draw final conclusions, however, the full Bayesian approach seems a practical and useful approach for model selection in document clustering. Our choice of likelihood function and priors provide a closed-form solution that is computationally tractable and provides meaningful results.

6.0 Conclusions

In this paper we tackled the problem of model structure determination in clustering. The main contribution of the paper is a Bayesian objective function that treats optimal model selection as choosing both the number of clusters *and* the feature subset. An important aspect of our work is a formal notion that forms a basis for doing feature selection in unsupervised learning. We then evaluated two approaches for model selection: one using this objective function and the other based on cross-validation.

Both approaches performed reasonably well - with the Bayesian scheme outperforming the cross-validation approaches in feature selection. More experiments using different parameter settings for the cross-validation schemes and different priors for the Bayesian scheme should result in better understanding and therefore more powerful applications of these approaches.

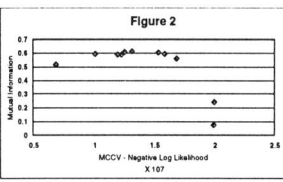

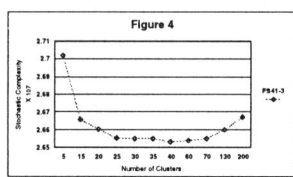

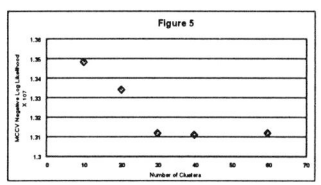

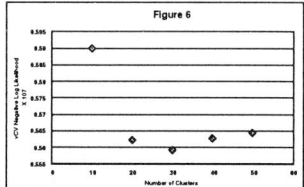

References

[1] Baker, D., et al, Distributional Clustering of Words for Text Classification, SIGIR 1998.
[2] Bernardo, J. M. and Smith, A. F. M., Bayesian Theory, Wiley, 1994.
[3] Church, K.W. et al, Poisson Mixtures, Natural Language Engineering, I(12), 1995.
[4] Cover, T.M. and Thomas, J.A. Elements of Information Theory. Wiley-Interscience, 1991.
[5] Deerwester,S. et al, Indexing by Latent Semantic Analysis,JASIS, 1990.
[6] Dempster, A.et al., Maximum Likelihood from Incomplete Data Via the EM Algorithm, JRSS, 39,1977.
[7] Hanson,R., et al, Bayesian Classification with Correlation and Inheritance, IJCAI,1991.
[8] Iyengar, G., Clustering images using relative entropy for efficient retrieval, VLBV, 1998.
[9] Katz, S.M. , Distribution of content words and phrases in text and language modeling, NLE, 2, 1996.
[10] Kontkanen, P.T. et al, Comparing Bayesian Model Class Selection Criteria by Discrete Finite Mixtures, ISIS'96 Conference, 1996.
[11] Meila, M., Heckerman, D., An Experimental Comparison of Several Clustering and Initialization Methods, MSR-TR-98-06.
[12] Nigam, K et al, Learning to Classify Text from Labeled and Unlabeled Documents, AAAI, 1998.
[13] Pereira, F.C.N. et al, Distributional clustering of English words, ACL,1993.
[14] Rissanen, J., Stochastic Complexity in Statistical Inquiry. World\ Scientific, 1989.
[15] Rissanen, J., Ristad E., Unsupervised classification with stochastic complexity." The US/Japan Conference on the Frontiers of Statistical Modeling,1992.
[16] Singhal A. et al, Pivoted Document Length Normalization, SIGIR, 1996.
[17] Smyth, P., Clustering using Monte Carlo cross-validation, KDD, 1996.
[18] Vaithyanathan, S. and Dom, B. Model Selection in Unsupervised Learning with Applications to Document Clustering. IBM Research Report RJ-10137 (95012) Dec. 14, 1998.

Learning from user feedback in image retrieval systems

Nuno Vasconcelos **Andrew Lippman**
MIT Media Laboratory, 20 Ames St, E15-354, Cambridge, MA 02139,
{nuno,lip}@media.mit.edu,   http://www.media.mit.edu/~nuno

Abstract

We formulate the problem of retrieving images from visual databases as a problem of Bayesian inference. This leads to natural and effective solutions for two of the most challenging issues in the design of a retrieval system: providing support for region-based queries without requiring prior image segmentation, and accounting for user-feedback during a retrieval session. We present a new learning algorithm that relies on belief propagation to account for both positive and negative examples of the user's interests.

1 Introduction

Due to the large amounts of imagery that can now be accessed and managed via computers, the problem of content-based image retrieval (CBIR) has recently attracted significant interest among the vision community [1, 2, 5]. Unlike most traditional vision applications, very few assumptions about the content of the images to be analyzed are allowable in the context of CBIR. This implies that the space of valid image representations is restricted to those of a generic nature (and typically of low-level) and consequently the image understanding problem becomes even more complex. On the other hand, CBIR systems have access to feedback from their users that can be exploited to simplify the task of finding the desired images. There are, therefore, two fundamental problems to be addressed. First, the design of the image representation itself and, second, the design of learning mechanisms to facilitate the interaction. The two problems cannot, however, be solved in isolation as the careless selection of the representation will make learning more difficult and vice-versa.

The impact of a poor image representation on the difficulty of the learning problem is visible in CBIR systems that rely on holistic metrics of image similarity, forcing user-feedback to be relative to entire images. In response to a query, the CBIR system suggests a few images and the user rates those images according to how well they satisfy the goals of the search. Because each image usually contains several different objects or visual concepts, this rating is both difficult and inefficient. How can the user rate an image that contains the concept of interest, but in which this concept only occupies 30% of the field of view, the remaining 70% being filled with completely unrelated stuff? And how many example images will the CBIR system have to see, in order to figure out what the concept of interest is?

A much better interaction paradigm is to let the user explicitly select the regions of the image that are relevant to the search, i.e. user-feedback at the region level. However, region-based feedback requires sophisticated image representations. The problem is that the most obvious choice, object-based representations, is difficult to implement because it is still too hard to segment arbitrary images in a meaningful way. We have argued that a better formulation is to view the problem as one of Bayesian inference and rely on probabilistic image representations. In this paper we show that this formulation naturally leads to 1) representations with support for region-based interaction without segmentation and 2) intuitive mechanisms to account for both positive and negative user feedback.

2 Retrieval as Bayesian inference

The standard interaction paradigm for CBIR is the so-called "query by example", where the user provides the system with a few examples, and the system retrieves from the database images that are visually similar to these examples. The problem is naturally formulated as one of statistical classification: given a representation (or feature) space $\mathcal{F}$ the goal is to find a map $g : \mathcal{F} \to M = \{1, \ldots, K\}$ from $\mathcal{F}$ to the set M of image classes in the database. K, the cardinality of M, can be as large as the number of items in the database (in which case each item is a class by itself), or smaller. If the goal of the retrieval system is to minimize the probability of error, it is well known that the optimal map is the Bayes classifier [3]

$$g^*(\mathbf{x}) = \arg\max_i P(S_i = 1|\mathbf{x}) = \arg\max_i P(\mathbf{x}|S_i = 1)P(S_i = 1) \qquad (1)$$

where $\mathbf{x}$ are the example features provided by the user and S_i is a binary variable indicating the selection of class i. In the absence of any prior information about which class is most suited for the query, an uninformative prior can be used and the optimal decision is the maximum likelihood criteria

$$g^*(\mathbf{x}) = \arg\max_i P(\mathbf{x}|S_i = 1). \qquad (2)$$

Besides theoretical soundness, Bayesian retrieval has two distinguishing properties of practical relevance. First, because the features $\mathbf{x}$ in equation (1) can be any subset of a given query image, the retrieval criteria is valid for both region-based and image-based queries. Second, due to its probabilistic nature, the criteria also provides a basis for designing retrieval systems that can account for user-feedback through belief propagation.

3 Bayesian relevance feedback

Suppose that instead of a single query $\mathbf{x}$ we have a sequence of t queries $\{\mathbf{x}_1, \ldots, \mathbf{x}_t\}$, where t is a time stamp. By simple application of Bayes rule

$$P(S_i = 1|\mathbf{x}_1, \ldots, \mathbf{x}_t) = \gamma_t P(\mathbf{x}_t|S_i = 1)P(S_i = 1|\mathbf{x}_1, \ldots, \mathbf{x}_{t-1}), \qquad (3)$$

where γ_t is a normalizing constant and we have assumed that, given the knowledge of the correct image class, the current query $\mathbf{x}_t$ is independent of the previous ones. This basically means that the user provides the retrieval system with new information at each iteration of the interaction. Equation (3) is a simple but intuitive mechanism to integrate information over time. It states that the system's beliefs about the user's interests at time $t - 1$ simply become the prior beliefs for iteration t. New data provided by the user at time t is then used to update these beliefs, which in turn become the priors for iteration $t + 1$. From a computational standpoint the procedure is very efficient since the only quantity that has to be computed at each time step is the likelihood of the data in the corresponding query. Notice that this is exactly equation (2) and would have to be computed even in the absence of any learning.

By taking logarithms and solving for the recursion, equation (3) can also be written as

$$\log P(S_i = 1|\mathbf{x}_1, \ldots, \mathbf{x}_t) = \sum_{k=0}^{t-1} \log \gamma_{t-k} + \sum_{k=0}^{t-1} \log P(\mathbf{x}_{t-k}|S_i = 1) + \log P(S_i = 1), \qquad (4)$$

exposing the main limitation of the belief propagation mechanism: for large t the contribution, to the right-hand side of the equation, of the new data provided by the user is very small, and the posterior probabilities tend to remain constant. This can be avoided by penalizing older terms with a *decay factor* α_{t-k}

$$\log P(S_i = 1|\mathbf{x}_1,\ldots,\mathbf{x}_t) = \sum_{k=0}^{t-1} \alpha_{t-k} \log \gamma_{t-k} + \sum_{k=0}^{t-1} \alpha_{t-k} \log P(\mathbf{x}_{t-k}|S_i = 1) + \alpha_0 \log P(S_i = 1),$$

where α_t is a monotonically decreasing sequence. In particular, if $\alpha_{t-k} = \alpha(1-\alpha)^k, \alpha \in (0,1]$ we have

$$\log P(S_i = 1|\mathbf{x}_1,\ldots,\mathbf{x}_t) = \log \gamma'_t + \alpha \log P(\mathbf{x}_t|S_i = 1) + (1-\alpha) \log P(S_i = 1|\mathbf{x}_1,\ldots,\mathbf{x}_{t-1}).$$

Because γ'_t does not depend on i, the optimal class is

$$S_i^* = \arg\max_i \{\alpha \log P(\mathbf{x}_t|S_i = 1) + (1-\alpha) \log P(S_i = 1|\mathbf{x}_1,\ldots,\mathbf{x}_{t-1})\}. \quad (5)$$

4 Negative feedback

In addition to positive feedback, there are many situations in CBIR where it is useful to rely on negative user-feedback. One example is the case of image classes characterized by overlapping densities. This is illustrated in Figure 1 a) where we have two classes with a common attribute (e.g. regions of blue sky) but different in other aspects (class A also contains regions of grass while class B contains regions of white snow). If the user starts with an image of class B (e.g. a picture of a snowy mountain), using regions of sky as positive examples is not likely to quickly take him/her to the images of class A. In fact, all other factors being equal, there is an equal likelihood that the retrieval system will return images from the two classes. On the other hand, if the user can explicitly indicate interest in regions of sky but not in regions of snow, the likelihood that only images from class A will be returned increases drastically.

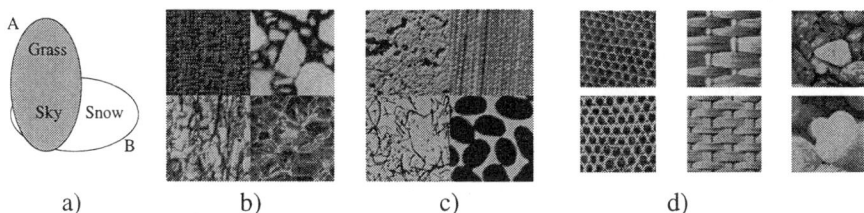

Figure 1: a) two overlapping image classes. b) and c) two images in the tile database. d) three examples of pairs of visually similar images that appear in different classes.

Another example of the importance of negative feedback are local minima of the search space. These happen when in response to user feedback, the system returns exactly the same images as in a previous iteration. Assuming that the user has already given the system all the possible positive feedback, the only way to escape from such minima is to choose some regions that are not desirable and use them as negative feedback. In the case of the example above, if the user gets stuck with a screen full of pictures of white mountains, he/she can simply select some regions of snow to escape the local minima.

In order to account for negative examples, we must penalize the classes under which these score well while favoring the classes that assign a high score to the positive examples.

Unlike positive examples, for which the likelihood is known, it is not straightforward to estimate the likelihood of a particular negative example given that the user is searching for a certain image class. We assume that the likelihood with which $\mathbf{y}$ will be used as a negative example given that the target is class i, is equal to the likelihood with which it will be used as a positive example given that the target is any other class. Denoting the use of $\mathbf{y}$ as a negative example by $\bar{\mathbf{y}}$, this can be written as

$$P(\bar{\mathbf{y}}|S_i = 1) = P(\mathbf{y}|S_i = 0). \tag{6}$$

This assumption captures the intuition that a good negative example when searching for class i, is one that would be a good positive example if the user were looking for any class other than i. E.g. if class i is the only one in the database that does not contain regions of sky, using pieces of sky as negative examples will quickly eliminate the other images in the database.

Under this assumption, negative examples can be incorporated into the learning by simply choosing the class i that maximizes the posterior odds ratio [4] between the hypotheses "class i is the target" and "class i is not the target"

$$S_i^* = \arg\max_i \frac{P(S_i = 1|\mathbf{x}_t, \ldots, \mathbf{x}_1, \mathbf{y}_t, \ldots, \mathbf{y}_1)}{P(S_i = 0|\mathbf{x}_t, \ldots, \mathbf{x}_1, \mathbf{y}_t, \ldots, \mathbf{y}_1)} = \arg\max_i \frac{P(S_i = 1|\mathbf{x}_t, \ldots, \mathbf{x}_1)}{P(S_i = 0|\mathbf{y}_t, \ldots, \mathbf{y}_1)}$$

where $\mathbf{x}$ are the positive and $\bar{\mathbf{y}}$ the negative examples, and we have assumed that, given the positive (negative) examples, the posterior probability of a given class being (not being) the target is independent of the negative (positive) examples. Once again, the procedure of the previous section can be used to obtain a recursive version of this equation and include a decay factor which penalizes ancient terms

$$S_i^* = \arg\max_i \left\{ \alpha \log \frac{P(\mathbf{x}_t|S_i = 1)}{P(\mathbf{y}_t|S_i = 0)} + (1 - \alpha) \log \frac{P(S_i = 1|\mathbf{x}_1, \ldots, \mathbf{x}_{t-1})}{P(S_i = 0|\mathbf{y}_1, \ldots, \mathbf{y}_{t-1})} \right\}.$$

Using equations (4) and (6)

$$P(S_i = 0|\mathbf{y}_1, \ldots, \mathbf{y}_t) \propto \prod_k P(\mathbf{y}_k|S_i = 0) = \prod_k P(\bar{\mathbf{y}}_k|S_i = 1)$$
$$\propto P(S_i = 1|\bar{\mathbf{y}}_1, \ldots, \bar{\mathbf{y}}_t),$$

we obtain

$$S_i^* = \arg\max_i \left\{ \alpha \log \frac{P(\mathbf{x}_t|S_i = 1)}{P(\bar{\mathbf{y}}_t|S_i = 1)} + (1 - \alpha) \log \frac{P(S_i = 1|\mathbf{x}_1, \ldots, \mathbf{x}_{t-1})}{P(S_i = 1|\bar{\mathbf{y}}_1, \ldots, \bar{\mathbf{y}}_{t-1})} \right\}. \tag{7}$$

While maximizing the ratio of posterior probabilities is a natural way to favor image classes that explain well the positive examples and poorly the negative ones, it tends to over-emphasize the importance of negative examples. In particular, any class with zero probability of generating the negative examples will lead to a ratio of ∞, even if it explains very poorly the positive examples. To avoid this problem we proceed in two steps:

- start by solving equation (5), i.e. sort the classes according to how well they explain the positive examples.
- select the subset of the best N classes and solve equation (7) considering only the classes in this subset.

5 Experimental evaluation

We performed experiments to evaluate 1) the accuracy of Bayesian retrieval on region-based queries and 2) the improvement in retrieval performance achievable with relevance feedback. Because in a normal browsing scenario it is difficult to know the ground truth for the retrieval operation (at least without going through the tedious process of hand-labeling all images in the database), we relied instead on a controlled experimental set up for which ground truth is available. All experiments reported on this section are based on the widely used Brodatz texture database which contains images of 112 textures, each of them being represented by 9 different patches, in a total of 1008 images. These were split into two groups, a small one with 112 images (one example of each texture), and a larger one with the remaining 896. We call the first group the *test* database and the second the *Brodatz* database. A synthetic database with 2000 images was then created from the larger set by randomly selecting 4 images at a time and making a 2 × 2 tile out of them. Figure 1 b) and c) are two examples of these tiles. We call this set the *tile* database.

5.1 Region-based queries

We performed two sets of experiments to evaluate the performance of region-based queries. In both cases the test database was used as a test set and the image features were the coefficients of the discrete cosine transform (DCT) of an 8 × 8 block-wise image decomposition over a grid containing every other image pixel. The first set of experiments was performed on the Brodatz database while the tile database was used in the second. A mixture of 16 Gaussians was estimated, using EM, for each of the images in the two databases.

In both sets of experiments, each query consisted of selecting a few image blocks from an image in the test set, evaluating equation (2) for each of the classes and returning those that best explained the query. Performance was measured in terms of precision (percent of the retrieved images that are relevant to the query) and recall (percent of the relevant images that are retrieved) averaged over the entire test set. The query images contained a total of 256 non-overlapping blocks. The number of these that were used in each query varied between 1 (0.3 % of the image size) and 256 (100 %). Figure 2 depicts precision-recall plots as a function of this number.

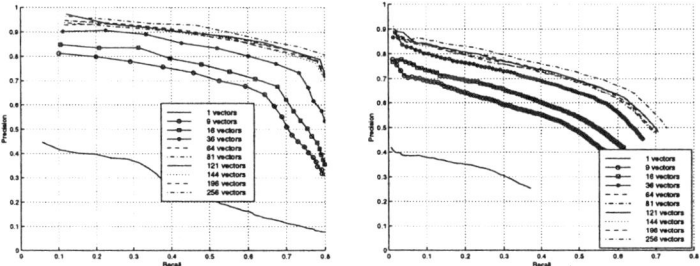

Figure 2: Precision-recall curves as a function of the number of feature vectors included in the query. Left: Brodatz database. Right: Tile database.

The graph on the left is relative to the Brodatz database. Notice that precision is generally high even for large values of recall and the performance increases quickly with the percentage of feature vectors included in the query. In particular, 25% of the texture patch (64 blocks) is enough to achieve results very close to those obtained with all pixels. This shows that the retrieval criteria is robust to missing data. The graph on the left presents similar results for the tile database. While there is some loss in performance, this loss is not dramatic - a decrease between 10 and 15 % in precision for any given recall. In fact, the results are still good: when a reasonable number of feature vectors is included in the query, about 8.5 out of the 10 top retrieved images are, on average, relevant. Once again, performance improves rapidly with the number of feature vectors in the query and 25% of the image is enough for results comparable to the best. This confirms the argument that Bayesian retrieval leads to effective region-based queries even for imagery composed by multiple visual stimulae.

5.2 Learning

The performance of the learning algorithm was evaluated on the tile database. The goal was to determine if it is possible to reach a desired target image by starting from a weakly related one and providing positive and negative feedback to the retrieval system. This simulates the interaction between a real user and the CBIR system and is an iterative process, where each iteration consists of selecting a few examples, using them as queries for retrieval and examining the top M retrieved images to find examples for the next iteration. M should be small since most users are not willing to go through lots of false positives to find the next query. In all experiments we set $M = 10$ corresponding to one screenful of images.

The most complex problem in testing is to determine a good strategy for selecting the examples to be given to the system. The closer this strategy is to what a real user would do, the higher the practical significance of the results. However, even when there is clear ground truth for the retrieval (as is the case of the tile database) it is not completely clear how to make the selection. While it is obvious that regions of texture classes that appear in the target should be used as positive feedback, it is much harder to determine automatically what are good negative examples. As Figure 1 d) illustrates, there are cases in which textures from two different classes are visually similar. Selecting images from one of these classes as a negative example for the other will be a disservice to the learner.

While real users tend not to do this, it is hard to avoid such mistakes in an automatic setting, unless one does some sort of pre-classification of the database. Because we wanted to avoid such pre-classification we decided to stick with a simple selection procedure and live with these mistakes. At each step of the iteration, examples were selected in the following way: among the 10 top images returned by the retrieval system, the one with most patches from texture classes also present in the target image was selected to be the next query. One block from each patch in the query was then used as a positive (negative) example if the class of that patch was also (was not) represented in the target image.

This strategy is a worst-case scenario. First, the learner might be confused by conflicting negative examples. Second, as seen above, better retrieval performance can be achieved if more than one block from each region is included in the queries. However, using only one block reduced the computational complexity of each iteration, allowing us to average results over several runs of the learning process. We performed 100 runs with randomly selected target images. In all cases, the initial query image was the first in the database containing one class in common with the target.

The performance of the learning algorithm can be evaluated in various ways. We considered two metrics: the percentage of the runs which converged to the right target, and the number of iterations required for convergence. Because, to prevent the learner from entering loops, any given image could only be used once as a query, the algorithm can diverge in two ways. Strong divergence occurs when, at a given time step, the images (among the top 10) that can be used as queries do not contain any texture class in common with the target. In such situation, a real user will tend to feel that the retrieval system is incoherent and abort the search. Weak divergence occurs when all the top 10 images have previously been used. This is a less troublesome situation because the user could simply look up more images (e.g. the next 10) to get new examples.

We start by analyzing the results obtained with positive feedback only. Figure 3 a) and b) present plots of the convergence rate and median number of iterations as a function of the decay factor α. While when there is no learning ($\alpha = 1$) only 43% of the runs converge, the convergence rate is always higher when learning takes place and for a significant range of α ($\alpha \in [0.5, 0.8]$) it is above 60%. This not only confirms that learning can lead to significant improvements of retrieval performance but also shows that a precise selection of α is not crucial. Furthermore, when convergence occurs it is usually very fast, taking from 4 to 6 iterations. On the other hand, a significant percentage of runs do not converge and the majority of these are cases of strong divergence.

As illustrated by Figure 3 c) and d), this percentage decreases significantly when both positive and negative examples are allowed. The rate of convergence is in this case usually between 80 and 90 % and strong divergence never occurs. And while the number of iterations for convergence increases, convergence is still fast (usually below 10 iterations). This is indeed the great advantage of negative examples: they encourage some exploration of the database which avoids local minima and leads to convergence. Notice that, when there is no learning, the convergence rate is high and learning can actually increase the rate of divergence. We believe that this is due to the inconsistencies associated with the negative example selection strategy. However, when convergence occurs, it is always faster if learning is employed.

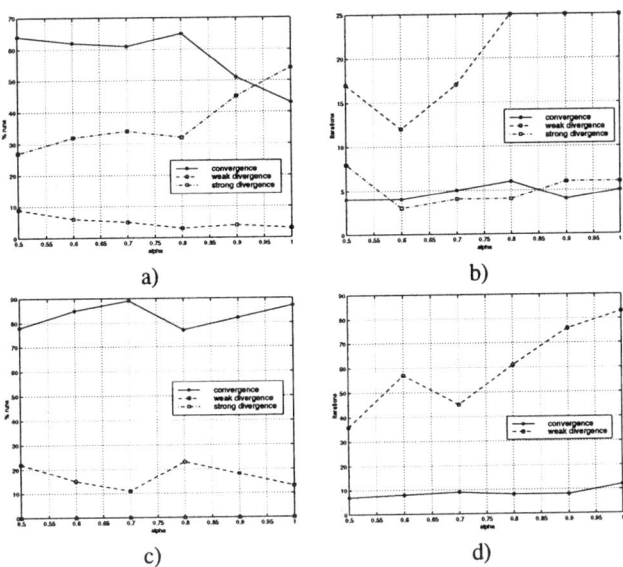

Figure 3: Learning performance as a function of α. Left: Percent of runs which converged. Right: Median number of iterations. Top: positive examples. Bottom: positive and negative examples.

References

[1] S. Belongie, C. Carson, H. Greenspan, and J. Malik. Color-and texture-based image segmentation using EM and its application to content-based image retrieval. In *International Conference on Computer Vision*, pages 675–682, Bombay, India, 1998.

[2] I. Cox, M. Miller, S. Omohundro, and P. Yianilos. PicHunter: Bayesian Relevance Feedback for Image Retrieval. In *Int. Conf. on Pattern Recognition*, Vienna, Austria, 1996.

[3] L. Devroye, L. Gyorfi, and G. Lugosi. *A Probabilistic Theory of Pattern Recognition*. Springer-Verlag, 1996.

[4] A. Gelman, J. Carlin, H. Stern, and D. Rubin. *Bayesian Data Analysis*. Chapman Hall, 1995.

[5] A. Pentland, R. Picard, and S. Sclaroff. Photobook: Content-based Manipulation of Image Databases. *International Journal of Computer Vision*, Vol. 18(3):233–254, June 1996.

Part IX
Control, Navigation and Planning

An Environment Model for Nonstationary Reinforcement Learning

Samuel P. M. Choi
pmchoi@cs.ust.hk

Dit-Yan Yeung
dyyeung@cs.ust.hk

Nevin L. Zhang
lzhang@cs.ust.hk

Department of Computer Science, Hong Kong University of Science and Technology
Clear Water Bay, Kowloon, Hong Kong

Abstract

Reinforcement learning in nonstationary environments is generally regarded as an important and yet difficult problem. This paper partially addresses the problem by formalizing a subclass of nonstationary environments. The environment model, called *hidden-mode Markov decision process* (HM-MDP), assumes that environmental changes are always confined to a small number of hidden *modes*. A mode basically indexes a Markov decision process (MDP) and evolves with time according to a Markov chain. While HM-MDP is a special case of *partially observable Markov decision processes* (POMDP), modeling an HM-MDP environment via the more general POMDP model unnecessarily increases the problem complexity. A variant of the Baum-Welch algorithm is developed for model learning requiring less data and time.

1 Introduction

Reinforcement Learning (RL) [7] is a learning paradigm based upon the framework of Markov decision process (MDP). Traditional RL research assumes that environment dynamics (i.e., MDP parameters) are always fixed (i.e., *stationary*). This assumption, however, is not realistic in many real-world applications. In elevator control [3], for instance, the passenger arrival and departure rates can vary significantly over one day, and should not be modeled by a fixed MDP.

Nonetheless, RL in nonstationary environments is regarded as a difficult problem. In fact, it is an impossible task if there is no regularity in the ways environment dynamics change. Hence, some degree of regularity must be assumed. Typically, nonstationary environments are presumed to change slowly enough such that online RL algorithms can be employed to keep track the changes. The online approach is memoryless in the sense that even if the environment ever revert to the previously learned dynamics, learning must still need to be started all over again.

1.1 Our Proposed Model

This paper proposes a formal model [1] for the nonstationary environments that repeats their dynamics in certain ways. Our model is inspired by the observations from the real-world nonstationary tasks with the following properties:

Property 1. Environmental changes are confined to a small number of *modes*, which are stationary environments with distinct dynamics. The environment is in exactly one of these modes at any given time. This concept of modes seems to be applicable to many real-world tasks. In an elevator control problem, for example, the system might operate in a morning-rush-hour mode, an evening-rush-hour mode and a non-rush-hour mode. One can also imagine similar modes for other control tasks, such as traffic control and dynamic channel allocation [6].

Property 2. Unlike states, modes cannot be directly observed; the current mode can only be estimated according to the past state transitions. It is analogous to the elevator control example in that the passenger arrival rate and pattern can only be inferred through the occurrence of pick-up and drop-off requests.

Property 3. Mode transitions are stochastic events and are independent of the control system's responses. In the elevator control problem, for instance, the events that change the current mode of the environment could be an emergency meeting in the administrative office, or a tea break for the staff on the 10th floor. Obviously, the elevator's response has no control over the occurrence of these events.

Property 4. Mode transitions are relatively infrequent. In other words, a mode is more likely to retain for some time before switching to another one. If we consider the emergency meeting example, employees on different floors take time to arrive at the administrative office, and thus would generate a similar traffic pattern (drop-off requests on the same floor) for some period of time.

Property 5. The number of states is often substantially larger than the number of modes. This is a common property for many real-world applications. In the elevator example, the state space comprises all possible combinations of elevator positions, pick-up and drop-off requests, and certainly would be huge. On the other hand, the mode space could be small. For instance, an elevator control system can simply have the three modes as described above to approximate the reality.

Based on these properties, an environment model is proposed by introducing a mode variable to capture environmental changes. Each mode specifies an MDP and hence completely determines the current state transition function and reward function (property 1). A mode, however, is not directly observable (property 2), and evolves with time according to a Markov process (property 3). The model is therefore called *hidden-mode model*. Note that our model does not impose any constraint to satisfy properties 4 and 5. In other words, the hidden-mode model can work for environments without these two properties. Nevertheless, as will be shown later, these properties can improve learning in practice.

1.2 Related Work

Our hidden-mode model is related to a nonstationary model proposed by Dayan and Sejnowski [4]. Although our model is more restrictive in terms of representational power, it involves much fewer parameters and is thus easier to learn. Besides, other than the number of possible modes, we do not assume any other knowledge about

An Environment Model for Nonstationary Reinforcement Learning

the way environment dynamics change. Dayan and Sejnowski, on the other hand, assume that one knows precisely how the environment dynamics change.

The hidden-mode model can also be viewed as a special case of the hidden-state model, or *partially observable Markov decision process* (POMDP). As will be shown later, a hidden-mode model can always be represented by a hidden-state model through state augmentation. Nevertheless, modeling a hidden-mode environment via a hidden-state model will unnecessarily increase the problem complexity. In this paper, the conversion from the former to the latter is also briefly discussed.

1.3 Our Focus

There are two approaches for RL. Model-based RL first acquires an environment model and then, from which, an optimal policy is derived. Model-free RL, on the contrary, learns an optimal policy directly through its interaction with the environment. This paper is concerned with the first part of the model-based approach, i.e., how a hidden-mode model can be learned from experience. We will address the policy learning problem in a separate paper.

2 Hidden-Mode Markov Decision Processes

This section presents our hidden-mode model. Basically, a hidden-mode model is defined as a finite set of MDPs that share the same state space and action space, with possibly different transition functions and reward functions. The MDPs correspond to different modes in which a system operates. States are completely observable and their transitions are governed by an MDP. In contrast, modes are not directly observable and their transitions are controlled by a Markov chain. We refer to such a process as a *hidden-mode Markov decision process* (HM-MDP). An example of HM-MDP is shown in Figure 1(a).

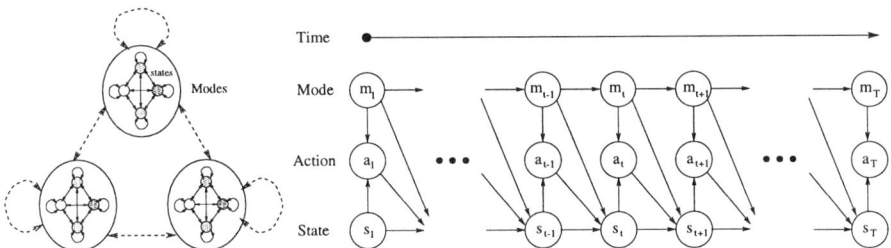

(a) A 3-mode, 4-state, 1-action HM-MDP

(b) The evolution of an HM-MDP. The arcs indicate dependencies between the variables

Figure 1: An HM-MDP

Formally, an HM-MDP is an 8-tuple $(Q, S, A, X, Y, R, \Pi, \Psi)$, where Q, S and A represent the sets of modes, states and actions respectively; the mode transition function X maps mode m to n with a fixed probability x_{mn}; the state transition function Y defines transition probability, $y_m(s, a, s')$, from state s to s' given mode m and action a; the stochastic reward function R returns rewards with mean value $r_m(s, a)$; Π and Ψ denote the prior probabilities of the modes and of the states respectively. The evolution of modes and states over time is depicted in Figure 1(b).

HM-MDP is a subclass of POMDP. In other words, the former can be reformulated as a special case of the latter. Specifically, one may take an ordered pair of any mode and observable state in the HM-MDP as a hidden state in the POMDP, and any observable state of the former as an observation of the latter. Suppose the observable states s and s' are in modes m and n respectively. These two HM-MDP states together with their corresponding modes form two hidden states (m, s) and (n, s') for its POMDP counterpart. The transition probability from (m, s) to (n, s') is then simply the mode transition probability x_{mn} multiplied by the state transition probability $y_m(s, a, s')$. For an M-mode, N-state, K-action HM-MDP, the equivalent POMDP thus has N observations and MN hidden states. Since most state transition probabilities are collapsed into mode transition probabilities through parameter sharing, the number of parameters in an HM-MDP ($N^2MK + M^2$) is much less than that of its corresponding POMDP (M^2N^2K).

3 Learning a Hidden-Mode Model

There are now two ways to learn a hidden-mode model. One may learn either an HM-MDP, or an equivalent POMDP instead. POMDP models can be learned via a variant of the Baum-Welch algorithm [2]. This POMDP Baum-Welch algorithm requires $\Theta(M^2N^2T)$ time and $\Theta(M^2N^2K)$ storage for learning an M-mode, N-state, K-action HM-MDP, given T data items.

A similar idea can be applied to the learning of an HM-MDP. Intuitively, one can estimate the model parameters based on the expected counts of the mode transitions, computed by a set of auxiliary variables. The major difference from the original algorithm is that consecutive state transitions, rather than the observations, are considered. Additional effort is thus needed for handling the boundary cases. This HM-MDP Baum-Welch algorithm is described in Figure 2.

4 Empirical Studies

This section empirically examines the POMDP Baum-Welch[1] and HM-MDP Baum-Welch algorithms. Experiments based on various randomly generated models and some real-world environments were conducted. The results are quite consistent. For illustration, a simple traffic control problem is presented. In this problem, one direction of a two-way traffic is blocked, and cars from two different directions (left and right) are forced to share the remaining road. To coordinate the traffic, two traffic lights equipped with sensors are set. The system then has two possible actions: either to signal cars from the left or cars from the right to pass. For simplicity, we assume discrete time steps and uniform speed of the cars.

The system has 8 possible states; they correspond to the combinations of whether there are cars waiting on the left and the right directions, and the stop signal position in the previous time step. There are 3 traffic modes. The first one has cars waiting on the left and the right directions with probabilities 0.3 and 0.1 respectively. In the second mode, these probabilities are reversed. For the last one, both probabilities are 0.3. In addition, the mode transition probability is 0.1. A cost of -1.0 results if

---

[1]Chrisman's algorithm also attempts to learn a minimal possible number of states. Our paper concerns only with learning the model parameters.

Given a collection of data and an initial model parameter vector $\bar{\theta}$.
repeat
$\quad \theta = \bar{\theta}$

Compute forward variables α_t.
$$\alpha_1(i) = \psi_{s_1} \qquad \forall\, i \in Q$$
$$\alpha_2(i) = \pi_i\, \psi_{s_1}\, y_i(s_1, a_1, s_2) \qquad \forall\, i \in Q$$
$$\alpha_{t+1}(j) = \sum_{i \in Q} \alpha_t(i)\, x_{ij}\, y_j(s_t, a_t, s_{t+1}) \qquad \forall\, i \in Q$$

Compute backward variables β_t.
$$\beta_T(i) = 1 \qquad \forall\, i \in Q$$
$$\beta_t(i) = \sum_{j \in Q} x_{ij}\, y_j(s_t, a_t, s_{t+1})\, \beta_{t+1}(j) \qquad \forall\, i \in Q$$
$$\beta_1(i) = \sum_{j \in Q} \pi_j\, y_j(s_1, a_1, s_2)\, \beta_2(j) \qquad \forall\, i \in Q$$

Compute auxiliary variables ξ_t and γ_t.
$$\xi_t(i,j) = \frac{\alpha_t(i)\, x_{ij}\, y_j(s_t, a_t, s_{t+1})\, \beta_{t+1}(j)}{\sum_{k \in Q} \alpha_T(k)} \qquad \forall\, i,j \in Q$$
$$\gamma_t(i) = \sum_{j \in Q} \xi_{t+1}(i,j) \qquad \forall\, i \in Q$$

Compute the new model parameter $\bar{\theta}$.
$$\bar{x}_{ij} = \frac{\sum_{t=2}^{T} \xi_t(i,j)}{\sum_{t=1}^{T} \gamma_t(i)} \qquad \delta(a,b) = \begin{cases} 1 & a = b \\ 0 & a \neq b \end{cases}$$
$$\bar{y}_i(j,k,l) = \frac{\sum_{t=1}^{T-1} \gamma_t(i)\, \delta(s_t, j)\, \delta(s_{t+1}, l)\, \delta(a_t, k)}{\sum_{l \in S} \sum_{t=1}^{T-1} \gamma_t(i)\, \delta(s_t, j)\, \delta(s_{t+1}, l)\, \delta(a_t, k)}$$
$$\bar{r}_i(j,k) = \frac{\sum_{t=1}^{T-1} \gamma_t(i)\, \delta(a_t, k)\, \delta(s_t, j)\, r_t}{\sum_{t=1}^{T-1} \gamma_t(i)\, \delta(a_t, k)\, \delta(s_t, j)}$$
$$\bar{\pi}_i = \gamma_1(i)$$

until $\max_i |\bar{\theta}_i - \theta_i| < \epsilon$

Figure 2: HM-MDP Baum-Welch Algorithm

a car waits on either side.

The experiments were run with the same initial model for data sets of various sizes. The algorithms iterated until the maximum change of the model parameters was less than a threshold of 0.0001. The experiment was repeated for 20 times with different random seeds in order to compute the median. Then the learned models were compared in their POMDP forms using the Kullback-Leibler (KL) distance [5], and the total CPU running time on a SUN Ultra I workstation was measured. Figure 3 (a) and (b) report the results.

Generally speaking, both algorithms learn a more accurate environment model as the data size increases (Figure 3 (a)). This result is expected as both algorithms are statistically-based, and hence their performance relies largely on the data size. When the training data size is very small, both algorithms perform poorly. However, as the data size increases, HM-MDP Baum-Welch improves substantially faster than POMDP Baum-Welch. It is because an HM-MDP in general consists of fewer free

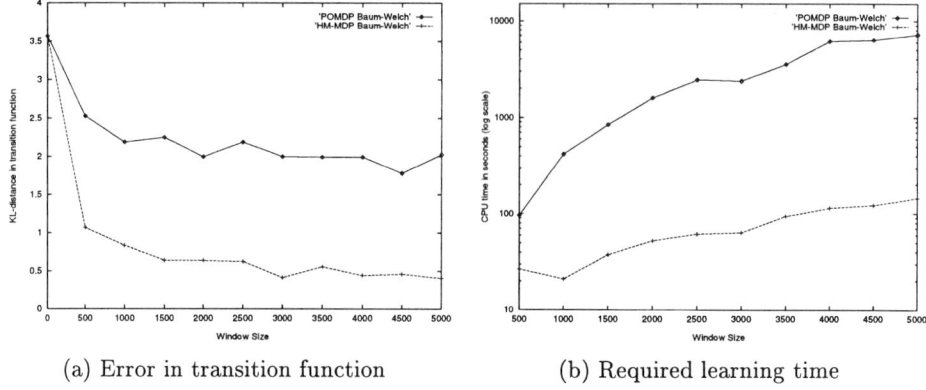

(a) Error in transition function   (b) Required learning time

Figure 3: Empirical results on model learning

parameters than its POMDP counterpart.

HM-MDP Baum-Welch also runs much faster than POMDP Baum-Welch (Figure 3 (b)). It holds in general for the same reason discussed above. Note that computational time is not necessarily monotonically increasing with the data size. It is because the total computation depends not only on the data size, but also on the number of iterations executed. From our experiments, we noticed that the number of iterations tends to decrease as the data size increases.

Larger models have also been tested. While HM-MDP Baum-Welch is able to learn models with several hundred states and a few modes, POMDP Baum-Welch was unable to complete the learning in a reasonable time. Additional experimental results can be found in [1].

5 Discussions and Future Work

The usefulness of a model depends on the validity of the assumptions made. We now discuss the assumptions of HM-MDP, and shed some light on its applicability to real-world nonstationary tasks. Some possible extensions are also discussed.

Modeling a nonstationary environment as a number of distinct MDPs. MDP is a flexible framework that has been widely adopted in various applications. Modeling nonstationary environments by distinct MDPs is a natural extension to those tasks. Comparing to POMDP, our model is more comprehensive: each MDP naturally describes a mode of the environment. Moreover, this formulation facilitates the incorporation of prior knowledge into the model initialization step.

States are directly observable while modes are not. While completely observable states are helpful to infer the current mode, it is also possible to extend the model to allow partially observable states. In this case, the extended model would be equivalent in representational power to a POMDP. This could be proved easily by showing the reformulation of the two models in both directions.

Mode changes are independent of the agent's responses. This property may not always hold for all real-world tasks. In some applications, the agent's actions might affect the state as well as the environment mode. In that case, an MDP should be used to govern the mode transition process.

Mode transitions are relatively infrequent. This is a property that generally holds in many applications. Our model, however, is not limited by this condition. We have tried to apply our model-learning algorithms to problems in which this property does not hold. We find that our model still outperforms POMDP, although the required data size is typically larger for both models.

Number of states is substantially larger than the number of modes. This is the key property that significantly reduces the number of parameters in HM-MDP compared to that in POMDP. In practice, introduction of a few modes is sufficient for boosting the system performance. More modes might only help little. Thus a trade-off between performance and response time must be decided.

There are additional issues that need to be addressed. First, an efficient algorithm for policy learning is required. Although in principle it can be achieved indirectly via any POMDP algorithm, a more efficient algorithm based on the model-based approach is possible. We will address this issue in a separate paper. Next, the number of modes is currently assumed to be known. We are now investigating how to remove this limitation. Finally, the exploration-exploitation issue is currently ignored. In our future work, we will address this important issue and apply our model to real-world nonstationary tasks.

References

[1] S. P. M. Choi, D. Y. Yeung, and N. L. Zhang. Hidden-mode Markov decision processes. In *IJCAI 99 Workshop on Neural, Symbolic, and Reinforcement Methods for Sequence Learning*, 1999.

[2] L. Chrisman. Reinforcement learning with perceptual aliasing: The perceptual distinctions approach. In *AAAI-92*, 1992.

[3] R. H. Crites and A. G. Barto. Improving elevator performance using reinforcement learning. In D. Touretzky, M. Mozer, and M. Hasselmo, editors, *Advances in Neural Information Processing Systems 8*, 1996.

[4] P. Dayan and T. J. Sejnowski. Exploration bonuses and dual control. *Machine Learning*, 25(1):5–22, Oct. 1996.

[5] S. Kullback. *Information Theory and Statistics*. Wiley, New York, NY, USA, 1959.

[6] S. Singh and D. P. Bertsekas. Reinforcement learning for dynamic channel allocation in cellular telephone systems. In *Advances in Neural Information Processing Systems 9*, 1997.

[7] R. S. Sutton and A. G. Barto. *Reinforcement Learning: An Introduction*. The MIT Press, 1998.

State Abstraction in MAXQ Hierarchical Reinforcement Learning

Thomas G. Dietterich
Department of Computer Science
Oregon State University
Corvallis, Oregon 97331-3202
tgd@cs.orst.edu

Abstract

Many researchers have explored methods for hierarchical reinforcement learning (RL) with *temporal abstractions*, in which abstract actions are defined that can perform many primitive actions before terminating. However, little is known about learning with *state abstractions*, in which aspects of the state space are ignored. In previous work, we developed the MAXQ method for hierarchical RL. In this paper, we define five conditions under which state abstraction can be combined with the MAXQ value function decomposition. We prove that the MAXQ-Q learning algorithm converges under these conditions and show experimentally that state abstraction is important for the successful application of MAXQ-Q learning.

1 Introduction

Most work on hierarchical reinforcement learning has focused on temporal abstraction. For example, in the Options framework [1, 2], the programmer defines a set of macro actions ("options") and provides a policy for each. Learning algorithms (such as semi-Markov Q learning) can then treat these temporally abstract actions as if they were primitives and learn a policy for selecting among them. Closely related is the HAM framework, in which the programmer constructs a hierarchy of finite-state controllers [3]. Each controller can include non-deterministic states (where the programmer was not sure what action to perform). The HAMQ learning algorithm can then be applied to learn a policy for making choices in the non-deterministic states. In both of these approaches—and in other studies of hierarchical RL (e.g., [4, 5, 6])—each option or finite state controller must have access to the entire state space. The one exception to this—the Feudal-Q method of Dayan and Hinton [7]—introduced state abstractions in an unsafe way, such that the resulting learning problem was only partially observable. Hence, they could not provide any formal results for the convergence or performance of their method.

Even a brief consideration of human-level intelligence shows that such methods cannot scale. When deciding how to walk from the bedroom to the kitchen, we do not need to think about the location of our car. Without state abstractions, any RL method that learns value functions must learn a separate value for each state of the world. Some argue that this can be solved by clever value function approximation methods—and there is some merit in this view. In this paper, however, we explore a different approach in which we identify aspects of the MDP that permit state abstractions to be safely incorporated in a hierarchical reinforcement learning method without introducing function approximations. This permits us to obtain the first proof of the convergence of hierarchical RL to an optimal policy in the presence of state abstraction.

We introduce these state abstractions within the MAXQ framework [8], but the basic ideas are general. In our previous work with MAXQ, we briefly discussed state abstractions, and we employed them in our experiments. However, we could not prove that our algorithm (MAXQ-Q) converged with state abstractions, and we did not have a usable characterization of the situations in which state abstraction could be safely employed. This paper solves these problems and in addition compares the effectiveness of MAXQ-Q learning with and without state abstractions. The results show that state abstraction is very important, and in most cases essential, to the effective application of MAXQ-Q learning.

2 The MAXQ Framework

Let M be a Markov decision problem with states S, actions A, reward function $R(s'|s,a)$ and probability transition function $P(s'|s,a)$. Our results apply in both the finite-horizon undiscounted case and the infinite-horizon discounted case. Let $\{M_0, \ldots, M_n\}$ be a set of subtasks of M, where each subtask M_i is defined by a termination predicate T_i and a set of actions A_i (which may be other subtasks or primitive actions from A). The "goal" of subtask M_i is to move the environment into a state such that T_i is satisfied. (This can be refined using a local reward function to express preferences among the different states satisfying T_i [8], but we omit this refinement in this paper.) The subtasks of M must form a DAG with a single "root" node—no subtask may invoke itself directly or indirectly. A *hierarchical policy* is a set of policies $\pi = \{\pi_0, \ldots, \pi_n\}$, one for each subtask. A hierarchical policy is executed using standard procedure-call-and-return semantics, starting with the root task M_0 and unfolding recursively until primitive actions are executed. When the policy for M_i is invoked in state s, let $P(s', N|s, i)$ be the probability that it terminates in state s' after executing N primitive actions. A hierarchical policy is *recursively optimal* if each policy π_i is optimal given the policies of its descendants in the DAG.

Let $V(i,s)$ be the value function for subtask i in state s (i.e., the value of following some policy starting in s until we reach a state s' satisfying $T_i(s')$). Similarly, let $Q(i,s,j)$ be the Q value for subtask i of executing child action j in state s and then executing the current policy until termination. The MAXQ value function decomposition is based on the observation that each subtask M_i can be viewed as a Semi-Markov Decision problem in which the reward for performing action j in state s is equal to $V(j,s)$, the value function for subtask j in state s. To see this, consider the sequence of rewards r_t that will be received when we execute child action j and then continue with subsequent actions according to hierarchical policy π:

$$Q(i,s,j) = E\{r_t + \gamma r_{t+1} + \gamma^2 r_{t+2} + \cdots | s_t = s, \pi\}$$

The macro action j will execute for some number of steps N and then return. Hence, we can partition this sum into two terms:

$$Q(i,s,j) = E\left\{\sum_{u=0}^{N-1} \gamma^u r_{t+u} + \sum_{u=N}^{\infty} \gamma^u r_{t+u} \bigg| s_t = s, \pi\right\}$$

The first term is the discounted sum of rewards until subtask j terminates—$V(j, s)$. The second term is the cost of finishing subtask i *after j* is executed (discounted to the time when j is initiated). We call this second term the *completion function*, and denote it $C(i, s, j)$. We can then write the Bellman equation as

$$Q(i, s, j) = \sum_{s', N} P(s', N | s, j) \cdot [V(j, s) + \gamma^N \max_{j'} Q(i, s', j')]$$
$$= V(j, s) + C(i, s, j)$$

To terminate this recursion, define $V(a, s)$ for a primitive action a to be the expected reward of performing action a in state s.

The MAXQ-Q learning algorithm is a simple variation of Q learning in which at subtask M_i, state s, we choose a child action j and invoke its (current) policy. When it returns, we observe the resulting state s' and the number of elapsed time steps N and update $C(i, s, j)$ according to

$$C(i, s, j) := (1 - \alpha_t) C(i, s, j) + \alpha_t \cdot \gamma^N [\max_{a'} V(a', s') + C(i, s', a')].$$

To prove convergence, we require that the exploration policy executed during learning be an *ordered GLIE policy*. An *ordered policy* is a policy that breaks Q-value ties among actions by preferring the action that comes first in some fixed ordering. A *GLIE policy* [9] is a policy that (a) executes each action infinitely often in every state that is visited infinitely often and (b) converges with probability 1 to a greedy policy. The ordering condition is required to ensure that the recursively optimal policy is unique. Without this condition, there are potentially many different recursively optimal policies *with different values*, depending on how ties are broken within subtasks, subsubtasks, and so on.

Theorem 1 *Let $M = \langle S, A, P, R \rangle$ be either an episodic MDP for which all deterministic policies are proper or a discounted infinite horizon MDP with discount factor γ. Let H be a DAG defined over subtasks $\{M_0, \ldots, M_k\}$. Let $\alpha_t(i) > 0$ be a sequence of constants for each subtask M_i such that*

$$\lim_{T \to \infty} \sum_{t=1}^{T} \alpha_t(i) = \infty \quad \text{and} \quad \lim_{T \to \infty} \sum_{t=1}^{T} \alpha_t^2(i) < \infty \tag{1}$$

Let $\pi_x(i, s)$ be an ordered GLIE policy at each subtask M_i and state s and assume that $|V_t(i, s)|$ and $|C_t(i, s, a)|$ are bounded for all t, i, s, and a. Then with probability 1, algorithm MAXQ-Q converges to the unique recursively optimal policy for M consistent with H and π_x.

Proof: (sketch) The proof is based on Proposition 4.5 from Bertsekas and Tsitsiklis [10] and follows the standard stochastic approximation argument due to [11] generalized to the case of non-stationary noise. There are two key points in the proof. Define $P_t(s', N | s, j)$ to be the probability transition function that describes the behavior of executing the current policy for subtask j at time t. By an inductive argument, we show that this probability transition function converges (w.p. 1) to the probability transition function of the recursively optimal policy for j. Second, we show how to convert the usual weighted max norm contraction for Q into a weighted max norm contraction for C. This is straightforward, and completes the proof.

What is notable about MAXQ-Q is that it can learn the value functions of all subtasks simultaneously—it does not need to wait for the value function for subtask j to converge before beginning to learn the value function for its parent task i. This gives a completely online learning algorithm with wide applicability.

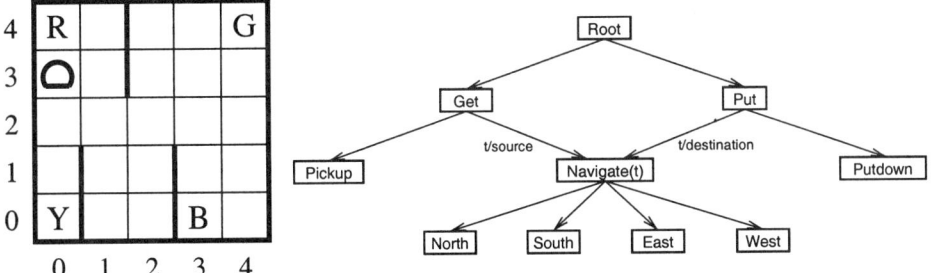

Figure 1: Left: The Taxi Domain (taxi at row 3 column 0). Right: Task Graph.

3 Conditions for Safe State Abstraction

To motivate state abstraction, consider the simple Taxi Task shown in Figure 1. There are four special locations in this world, marked as R(ed), B(lue), G(reen), and Y(ellow). In each episode, the taxi starts in a randomly-chosen square. There is a passenger at one of the four locations (chosen randomly), and that passenger wishes to be transported to one of the four locations (also chosen randomly). The taxi must go to the passenger's location (the "source"), pick up the passenger, go to the destination location (the "destination"), and put down the passenger there. The episode ends when the passenger is deposited at the destination location.

There are six primitive actions in this domain: (a) four navigation actions that move the taxi one square North, South, East, or West, (b) a Pickup action, and (c) a Putdown action. Each action is deterministic. There is a reward of −1 for each action and an additional reward of +20 for successfully delivering the passenger. There is a reward of −10 if the taxi attempts to execute the Putdown or Pickup actions illegally. If a navigation action would cause the taxi to hit a wall, the action is a no-op, and there is only the usual reward of −1.

This task has a hierarchical structure (see Fig. 1) in which there are two main sub-tasks: Get the passenger (Get) and Deliver the passenger (Put). Each of these subtasks in turn involves the subtask of navigating to one of the four locations (Navigate(t); where t is bound to the desired target location) and then performing a Pickup or Putdown action. This task illustrates the need to support both temporal abstraction and state abstraction. The temporal abstraction is obvious—for example, Get is a temporally extended action that can take different numbers of steps to complete depending on the distance to the target. The top level policy (get passenger; deliver passenger) can be expressed very simply with these abstractions.

The need for state abstraction is perhaps less obvious. Consider the Get subtask. While this subtask is being solved, the destination of the passenger is completely irrelevant—it cannot affect any of the nagivation or pickup decisions. Perhaps more importantly, when navigating to a target location (either the source or destination location of the passenger), only the taxi's location and identity of the target location are important. The fact that in some cases the taxi is carrying the passenger and in other cases it is not is irrelevant.

We now introduce the five conditions for state abstraction. We will assume that the state s of the MDP is represented as a vector of state variables. A state abstraction can be defined for each combination of subtask M_i and child action j by identifying a subset X of the state variables that are *relevant* and defining the value function and the policy using only these relevant variables. Such value functions and policies are said to be *abstract*.

The first two conditions involve eliminating irrelevant variables within a subtask of the MAXQ decomposition.

Condition 1: Subtask Irrelevance. Let M_i be a subtask of MDP M. A set of state variables Y is *irrelevant to subtask i* if the state variables of M can be partitioned into two sets X and Y such that for any stationary abstract hierarchical policy π executed by the descendants of M_i, the following two properties hold: (a) the state transition probability distribution $P^\pi(s', N|s, j)$ for each child action j of M_i can be factored into the product of two distributions:

$$P^\pi(x', y', N|x, y, j) = P^\pi(x', N|x, j) \cdot P^\pi(y'|x, y, j), \qquad (2)$$

where x and x' give values for the variables in X, and y and y' give values for the variables in Y; and (b) for any pair of states $s_1 = (x, y_1)$ and $s_2 = (x, y_2)$ and any child action j, $V^\pi(j, s_1) = V^\pi(j, s_2)$.

In the Taxi problem, the source and destination of the passenger are irrelevant to the Navigate(t) subtask—only the target t and the current taxi position are relevant.

The advantages of this form of abstraction are similar to those obtained by Boutilier, Dearden and Goldszmidt [12] in which belief network models of actions are exploited to simplify value iteration in stochastic planning.

Condition 2: Leaf Irrelevance. A set of state variables Y is *irrelevant for a primitive action a* if for any pair of states s_1 and s_2 that differ only in their values for the variables in Y,

$$\sum_{s_1'} P(s_1'|s_1, a) R(s_1'|s_1, a) = \sum_{s_2'} P(s_2'|s_2, a) R(s_2'|s_2, a).$$

This condition is satisfied by the primitive actions North, South, East, and West in the taxi task, where *all* state variables are irrelevant because R is constant.

The next two conditions involve "funnel" actions—macro actions that move the environment from some large number of possible states to a small number of resulting states. The completion function of such subtasks can be represented using a number of values proportional to the number of resulting states.

Condition 3: Result Distribution Irrelevance (Undiscounted case.) A set of state variables Y_j is *irrelevant for the result distribution of action j* if, for all abstract policies π executed by M_j and its descendants in the MAXQ hierarchy, the following holds: for all pairs of states s_1 and s_2 that differ only in their values for the state variables in Y_j,

$$\forall s' \ P^\pi(s'|s_1, j) = P^\pi(s'|s_2, j).$$

Consider, for example, the Get subroutine under an optimal policy for the taxi task. Regardless of the taxi's position in state s, the taxi will be at the passenger's starting location when Get finishes executing (i.e., because the taxi will have just completed picking up the passenger). Hence, the taxi's initial position is irrelevant to its resulting position. (Note that this is only true in the undiscounted setting—with discounting, the result distributions are not the same because the number of steps N required for Get to finish depends very much on the starting location of the taxi. Hence this form of state abstraction is rarely useful for cumulative discounted reward.)

Condition 4: Termination. Let M_j be a child task of M_i with the property that whenever M_j terminates, it causes M_i to terminate too. Then the completion cost $C(i, s, j) = 0$ and does not need to be represented. This is a particular kind of funnel action—it funnels all states into terminal states for M_i.

For example, in the Taxi task, in all states where the taxi is holding the passenger, the Put subroutine will succeed and result in a terminal state for Root. This is because the termination predicate for Put (i.e., that the passenger is at his or her destination location) implies the termination condition for Root (which is the same). This means that $C(\text{Root}, s, \text{Put})$ is uniformly zero, for all states s where Put is not terminated.

Condition 5: Shielding. Consider subtask M_i and let s be a state such that for all paths from the root of the DAG down to M_i, there exists a subtask that is terminated. Then no C values need to be represented for subtask M_i in state s, because it can never be executed in s.

In the Taxi task, a simple example of this arises in the Put task, which is terminated in all states where the passenger is not in the taxi. This means that we do not need to represent $C(\text{Root}, s, \text{Put})$ in these states. The result is that, when combined with the Termination condition above, we do not need to explicitly represent the completion function for Put at all!

By applying these abstraction conditions to the Taxi task, the value function can be represented using 632 values, which is much less than the 3,000 values required by flat Q learning. Without state abstractions, MAXQ requires 14,000 values!

Theorem 2 (Convergence with State Abstraction) *Let H be a MAXQ task graph that incorporates the five kinds of state abstractions defined above. Let π_x be an ordered GLIE exploration policy that is abstract. Then under the same conditions as Theorem 1, MAXQ-Q converges with probability 1 to the unique recursively optimal policy π_r^* defined by π_x and H.*

Proof: (sketch) Consider a subtask M_i with relevant variables X and two arbitrary states (x, y_1) and (x, y_2). We first show that under the five abstraction conditions, the value function of π_r^* can be represented using $C(i, x, j)$ (i.e., ignoring the y values). To learn the values of $C(i, x, j) = \sum_{x', N} P(x', N | x, j) V(i, x')$, a Q-learning algorithm needs samples of x' and N drawn according to $P(x', N | x, j)$. The second part of the proof involves showing that regardless of whether we execute j in state (x, y_1) or in (x, y_2), the resulting x' and N will have the same distribution, and hence, give the correct expectations. Analogous arguments apply for leaf irrelevance and $V(a, x)$. The termination and shielding cases are easy.

4 Experimental Results

We implemented MAXQ-Q for a noisy version of the Taxi domain and for Kaelbling's HDG navigation task [5] using Boltzmann exploration. Figure 2 shows the performance of flat Q and MAXQ-Q with and without state abstractions on these tasks. Learning rates and Boltzmann cooling rates were separately tuned to optimize the performance of each method. The results show that without state abstractions, MAXQ-Q learning is slower to converge than flat Q learning, but that with state abstraction, it is much faster.

5 Conclusion

This paper has shown that by understanding the reasons that state variables are irrelevant, we can obtain a simple proof of the convergence of MAXQ-Q learning

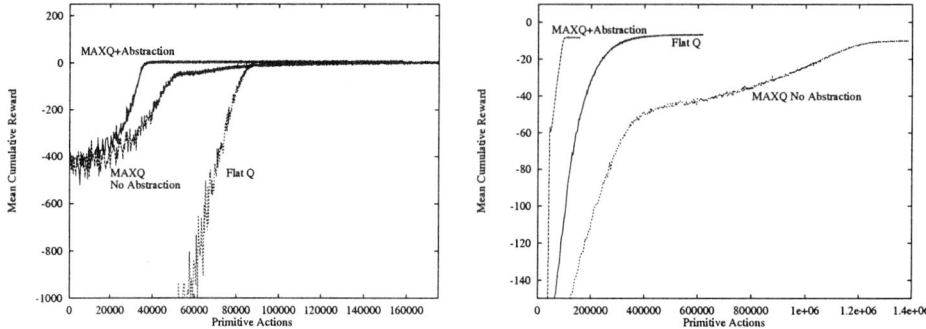

Figure 2: Comparison of MAXQ-Q with and without state abstraction to flat Q learning on a noisy taxi domain (left) and Kaelbling's HDG task (right). The horizontal axis gives the number of primitive actions executed by each method. The vertical axis plots the average of 100 separate runs.

under state abstraction. This is much more fruitful than previous efforts based only on weak notions of state aggregation [10], and it suggests that future research should focus on identifying other conditions that permit safe state abstraction.

References

[1] D. Precup and R. S. Sutton, "Multi-time models for temporally abstract planning," in *NIPS10*, The MIT Press, 1998.

[2] R. S. Sutton, D. Precup, and S. Singh, "Between MDPs and Semi-MDPs: Learning, planning, and representing knowledge at multiple temporal scales," tech. rep., Univ. Mass., Dept. Comp. Inf. Sci., Amherst, MA, 1998.

[3] R. Parr and S. Russell, "Reinforcement learning with hierarchies of machines," in NIPS-10, The MIT Press, 1998.

[4] S. P. Singh, "Transfer of learning by composing solutions of elemental sequential tasks," *Machine Learning*, vol. 8, p. 323, 1992.

[5] L. P. Kaelbling, "Hierarchical reinforcement learning: Preliminary results," in *Proceedings ICML-10*, pp. 167–173, Morgan Kaufmann, 1993.

[6] M. Hauskrecht, N. Meuleau, C. Boutilier, L. Kaelbling, and T. Dean, "Hierarchical solution of Markov decision processes using macro-actions," tech. rep., Brown Univ., Dept. Comp. Sci., Providence, RI, 1998.

[7] P. Dayan and G. Hinton, "Feudal reinforcement learning," in *NIPS-5*, pp. 271–278, San Francisco, CA: Morgan Kaufmann, 1993.

[8] T. G. Dietterich, "The MAXQ method for hierarchical reinforcement learning," in *ICML-15*, Morgan Kaufmann, 1998.

[9] S. Singh, T. Jaakkola, M. L. Littman, and C. Szpesvari, "Convergence results for single-step on-policy reinforcement-learning algorithms," tech. rep., Univ. Col., Dept. Comp. Sci., Boulder, CO, 1998.

[10] D. P. Bertsekas and J. N. Tsitsiklis, *Neuro-Dynamic Programming*. Belmont, MA: Athena Scientific, 1996.

[11] T. Jaakkola, M. I. Jordan, and S. P. Singh, "On the convergence of stochastic iterative dynamic programming algorithms," *Neur. Comp.*, vol. 6, no. 6, pp. 1185–1201, 1994.

[12] C. Boutilier, R. Dearden, and M. Goldszmidt, "Exploiting structure in policy construction," in *Proceedings IJCAI-95*, pp. 1104–1111, 1995.

Approximate Planning in Large POMDPs via Reusable Trajectories

Michael Kearns
AT&T Labs
mkearns@research.att.com

Yishay Mansour
Tel Aviv University
mansour@math.tau.ac.il

Andrew Y. Ng
UC Berkeley
ang@cs.berkeley.edu

Abstract

We consider the problem of reliably choosing a near-best strategy from a restricted class of strategies Π in a partially observable Markov decision process (POMDP). We assume we are given the ability to *simulate* the POMDP, and study what might be called the *sample complexity* — that is, the amount of data one must generate in the POMDP in order to choose a good strategy. We prove upper bounds on the sample complexity showing that, even for *infinitely large and arbitrarily complex* POMDPs, the amount of data needed can be finite, and depends only linearly on the complexity of the restricted strategy class Π, and exponentially on the horizon time. This latter dependence can be eased in a variety of ways, including the application of gradient and local search algorithms. Our measure of complexity generalizes the classical supervised learning notion of VC dimension to the settings of reinforcement learning and planning.

1 Introduction

Much recent attention has been focused on partially observable Markov decision processes (POMDPs) which have exponentially or even infinitely large state spaces. For such domains, a number of interesting basic issues arise. As the state space becomes large, the classical way of specifying a POMDP by tables of transition probabilities clearly becomes infeasible. To intelligently discuss the problem of planning — that is, computing a good strategy [1] in a given POMDP — *compact* or implicit representations of both POMDPs, and of strategies in POMDPs, must be developed. Examples include factored next-state distributions [2, 3, 7], and strategies derived from function approximation schemes [8]. The trend towards such compact representations, as well as algorithms for planning and learning using them, is reminiscent of supervised learning, where researchers have long emphasized parametric models (such as decision trees and neural networks) that can capture only limited structure, but which enjoy a number of computational and information-theoretic benefits.

Motivated by these issues, we consider a setting were we are given a *generative model*, or

---

[1] Throughout, we use the word *strategy* to mean any mapping from observable histories to actions, which generalizes the notion of policy in a fully observable MDP.

simulator, for a POMDP, and wish to find a good strategy π from some restricted class of strategies Π. A generative model is a "black box" that allows us to generate experience (trajectories) from different states of our choosing. Generative models are an abstract notion of compact POMDP representations, in the sense that the compact representations typically considered (such as factored next-state distributions) already provide efficient generative models. Here we are imagining that the strategy class Π is given by some compact representation or by some natural limitation on strategies (such as bounded memory). Thus, the view we are adopting is that even though the world (POMDP) may be extremely complex, we assume that we can at least simulate or sample experience in the world (via the generative model), and we try to use this experience to choose a strategy from some "simple" class Π.

We study the following question: How many calls to a generative model are needed to have enough data to choose a near-best strategy in the given class? This is analogous to the question of *sample complexity* in supervised learning — but harder. The added difficulty lies in the *reuse* of data. In supervised learning, *every* sample $\langle x, f(x) \rangle$ provides feedback about *every* hypothesis function $h(x)$ (namely, how close $h(x)$ is to $f(x)$). If h is restricted to lie in some hypothesis class $\mathcal{H}$, this reuse permits sample complexity bounds that are far smaller than the size of $\mathcal{H}$. For instance, only $O(\log(|\mathcal{H}|))$ samples are needed to choose a near-best model from a finite class $\mathcal{H}$. If $\mathcal{H}$ is infinite, then sample sizes are obtained that depend only on some measure of the *complexity* of $\mathcal{H}$ (such as VC dimension [9]), but which have *no dependence* on the complexity of the target function or the size of the input domain.

In the POMDP setting, we would like analogous sample complexity bounds in terms of the "complexity" of the strategy class Π — bounds that have no dependence on the size or complexity of the POMDP. But unlike the supervised learning setting, experience "reuse" is not immediate in POMDPs. To see this, consider the "straw man" algorithm that, starting with some $\pi \in \Pi$, uses the generative model to generate many trajectories under π, and thus forms a Monte Carlo estimate of $V^\pi(s_0)$. It is not clear that these trajectories under π are of much use in evaluating a different $\pi' \in \Pi$, since π and π' may quickly disagree on which actions to take. The naive Monte Carlo method thus gives $O(|\Pi|)$ bounds on the "sample complexity," rather than $O(\log(|\Pi|))$, for the finite case.

In this paper, we shall describe the *trajectory tree* method of generating "reusable" trajectories, which requires generating only a (relatively) small number of trajectories — a number that is independent of the state-space size of the POMDP, depends only linearly on a general measure of the *complexity* of the strategy class Π, and depends exponentially on the horizon time. This latter dependence can be eased via gradient algorithms such as Williams' REINFORCE [10] and Baird and Moore's more recent VAPS [1], and by local search techniques. Our measure of strategy class complexity generalizes the notion of VC dimension in supervised learning to the settings of reinforcement learning and planning, and we give bounds that recover for these settings the most powerful analogous results in supervised learning — bounds for arbitrary, infinite strategy classes that depend only on the dimension of the class rather than the size of the state space.

2 Preliminaries

We begin with some standard definitions. A **Markov decision process (MDP)** is a tuple $(S, s_0, A, \{P(\cdot|s,a)\}, R)$, where: S is a (possibly infinite) **state set**; $s_0 \in S$ is a **start state**; $A = \{a_1, \ldots, a_k\}$ are **actions**; $P(\cdot|s,a)$ gives the next-state distribution upon taking action a from state s; and the reward function $R(s,a)$ gives the corresponding rewards. We assume for simplicity that rewards are deterministic, and further that they are bounded in absolute value by $R_{\max}$. A **partially observable Markov decision process (POMDP)** consists of an underlying MDP and **observation distributions** $Q(o|s)$ for each state s, where o is the random **observation** made at s.

We have adopted the common assumption of a fixed start state,[2] because once we limit the class of strategies we entertain, there may not be a single "best" strategy in the class—different start states may have different best strategies in Π. We also assume that we are given a POMDP M in the form of a **generative model** for M that, when given as input any state-action pair (s, a), will output a state s' drawn according to $P(\cdot|s, a)$, an observation o drawn according to $Q(\cdot|s)$, and the reward $R(s, a)$. This gives us the ability to *sample* the POMDP M in a random-access way. This definition may initially seem unreasonably generous: the generative model is giving us a fully observable simulation of a partially observable process. However, the key point is that we must still find a strategy that performs well in the *partially observable* setting. As a concrete example, in designing an elevator control system, we may have access to a simulator that generates random rider arrival times, and keeps track of the waiting time of each rider, the number of riders waiting at every floor at every time of day, and so on. However helpful this information might be in *designing* the controller, this controller must only *use* information about which floors currently have had their call button pushed (the observables). In any case, readers uncomfortable with the power provided by our generative models are referred to Section 5, where we briefly describe results requiring only an extremely weak form of partially observable simulation.

At any time t, the agent will have seen some sequence of observations, $o_0, \ldots, o_t$, and will have chosen actions and received rewards for each of the t time steps prior to the current one. We write its **observable history** as $h = \langle (o_0, a_0, r_0), \ldots, (o_{t-1}, a_{t-1}, r_{t-1}), (o_t, \_, \_) \rangle$. Such observable histories, also called **trajectories**, are the inputs to strategies. More formally, a **strategy** π is any (stochastic) mapping from observable histories to actions. (For example, this includes approaches which use the observable history to track the *belief state* [5].) A **strategy class** Π is any set of strategies.

We will restrict our attention to the case of discounted return,[3] and we let $\gamma \in [0, 1)$ be the discount factor. We define the ϵ-**horizon time** to be $H_\epsilon = \log_\gamma(\epsilon(1 - \gamma)/2R_{\max})$. Note that returns beyond the first H_ϵ-steps can contribute at most $\epsilon/2$ to the total discounted return. Also, let $V_{\max} = R_{\max}/(1 - \gamma)$ bound the value function. Finally, for a POMDP M and a strategy class Π, we define $opt(M, \Pi) = \sup_{\pi \in \Pi} V^\pi(s_0)$ to be the best expected return achievable from s_0 using Π.

Our problem is thus the following: Given a generative model for a POMDP M and a strategy class Π, how many calls to the generative model must we make, in order to have enough data to choose a $\pi \in \Pi$ whose performance $V^\pi(s_0)$ approaches $opt(M, \Pi)$? Also, *which* calls should we make to the generative model to achieve this?

3 The Trajectory Tree Method

We now describe how we can use a generative model to create "reusable" trajectories. For ease of exposition, we assume there are only two actions a_1 and a_2, but our results generalize easily to any finite number of actions. (See the full paper [6].)

---

[2] An equivalent definition is to assume a fixed distribution D over start states, since s_0 can be a "dummy" state whose next-state distribution under any action is D.

[3] The results in this paper can be extended without difficulty to the undiscounted finite-horizon setting [6].

A *trajectory tree* is a binary tree in which each node is labeled by a state and observation pair, and has a child for each of the two actions. Additionally, each link to a child is labeled by a reward, and the tree's depth will be H_ϵ, so it will have about 2^{H_ϵ} nodes. (In Section 4, we will discuss settings where this exponential dependence on H_ϵ can be eased.) Each trajectory tree is built as follows: The root is labeled by s_0 and the observation there, o_0. Its two children are then created by calling the generative model on (s_0, a_1) and (s_0, a_2), which gives us the two next-states reached (say s'_1 and s'_2 respectively), the two observations made (say o'_1 and o'_2), and the two rewards received ($r'_1 = R(s_0, a_1)$ and $r'_2 = R(s_0, a_2)$). Then (s'_1, o'_1) and (s'_2, o'_2) label the root's a_1-child and a_2-child, and the links to these children are labeled r'_1 and r'_2. Recursively, we generate two children and rewards this way for each node down to depth H_ϵ.

Now for any *deterministic* strategy π and any trajectory tree T, π defines a path through T: π starts at the root, and inductively, if π is at some internal node in T, then we feed to π the observable history along the path from the root to that node, and π selects and moves to a child of the current node. This continues until a leaf node is reached, and we define $R(\pi, T)$ to be the discounted sum of returns along the path taken. In the case that π is stochastic, π defines a *distribution* on paths in T, and $R(\pi, T)$ is the expected return according to this distribution. (We will later also describe another method for treating stochastic strategies.) Hence, given m trajectory trees $T_1, \ldots, T_m$, a natural estimate for $V^\pi(s_0)$ is $\hat{V}^\pi(s_0) = \frac{1}{m} \sum_{i=1}^m R(\pi, T_i)$. Note that each tree can be used to evaluate *any* strategy, much the way a single labeled example $\langle x, f(x) \rangle$ can be used to evaluate any hypothesis $h(x)$ in supervised learning. Thus in this sense, trajectory trees are *reusable*.

Our goal now is to establish *uniform convergence* results that bound the error of the estimates $\hat{V}^\pi(s_0)$ as a function of the "sample size" (number of trees) m. Section 3.1 first treats the easier case of deterministic classes Π; Section 3.2 extends the result to stochastic classes.

3.1 The Case of Deterministic Π

Let us begin by stating a result for the special case of finite classes of deterministic strategies, which will serve to demonstrate the kind of bound we seek.

Theorem 3.1 *Let Π be any finite class of deterministic strategies for an arbitrary two-action POMDP M. Let m trajectory trees be created using a generative model for M, and $\hat{V}^\pi(s_0)$ be the resulting estimates. If $m = O\left((V_{\max}/\epsilon)^2 (\log(|\Pi|) + \log(1/\delta))\right)$, then with probability $1 - \delta$, $|V^\pi(s_0) - \hat{V}^\pi(s_0)| \leq \epsilon$ holds simultaneously for all $\pi \in \Pi$.*

Due to space limitations, detailed proofs of the results of this section are left to the full paper [6], but we will try to convey the intuition behind the ideas. Observe that for any *fixed* deterministic π, the estimates $R(\pi, T_i)$ that are generated by the m different trajectory trees T_i are independent. Moreover, each $R(\pi, T_i)$ is an unbiased estimate of the expected discounted H_ϵ-step return of π, which is in turn $\epsilon/2$-close to $V^\pi(s_0)$. These observations, combined with a simple Chernoff and union bound argument, are sufficient to establish Theorem 3.1. Rather than developing this argument here, we instead move straight on to the harder case of infinite Π.

When addressing sample complexity in supervised learning, perhaps the most important insight is that even though a class $\mathcal{H}$ may be infinite, the number of possible *behaviors* of $\mathcal{H}$ on a finite set of points is often not exhaustive. More precisely, for boolean functions, we say that the set $x_1, \ldots, x_d$ is *shattered* by $\mathcal{H}$ if every of the 2^d possible labelings of

Approximate Planning in Large POMDPs via Reusable Trajectories   1005

these points is realized by some $h \in \mathcal{H}$. The VC dimension of $\mathcal{H}$ is then defined as the size of the largest shattered set [9]. It is known that if the VC dimension of $\mathcal{H}$ is d, then the number $\Phi_d(m)$ of possible labelings induced by $\mathcal{H}$ on a set of m points is at most $(em/d)^d$, which is much less than 2^m for $d \ll m$. This fact provides the key leverage exploited by the classical VC dimension results, and we will concentrate on replicating this leverage in our setting.

If Π is a (possibly infinite) set of deterministic strategies, then each strategy $\pi \in \Pi$ is simply a deterministic function mapping from the set of observable histories to the set $\{a_1, a_2\}$, and is thus a boolean function on observable histories. We can therefore write $\text{VC}(\Pi)$ to denote the familiar VC dimension of the set of binary functions Π. For example, if Π is the set of all thresholded linear functions of the current vector of observations (a particular type of memoryless strategy), then $\text{VC}(\Pi)$ simply equals the number of parameters. We now show intuitively why a class Π of bounded VC dimension d cannot induce exhaustive behavior on a set $T_1, \ldots, T_m$ of trajectory trees for $m \gg d$. Note that if $\pi_1, \pi_2 \in \Pi$ are such that their "reward labelings" $\langle R(\pi_1, T_1), \ldots, R(\pi_1, T_m) \rangle$ and $\langle R(\pi_2, T_1), \ldots, R(\pi_2, T_m) \rangle$ differ, then $R(\pi_1, T_i) \neq R(\pi_2, T_i)$ for some $1 \leq i \leq m$. But if π_1 and π_2 give different returns on T_i, then they must choose different actions at some node in T_i. In other words, every different reward labeling of the set of m trees yields a different (binary) labeling of the set of $m \cdot 2^{H_\epsilon}$ observable *histories* in the trees. So, the number of different tree reward labelings can be at most $\Phi_d(m \cdot 2^{H_\epsilon}) \leq (em \cdot 2^{H_\epsilon}/d)^d$. By developing this argument carefully and applying classical uniform convergence techniques, we obtain the following theorem. (Full proof in [6].)

Theorem 3.2 *Let Π be any class of deterministic strategies for an arbitrary two-action POMDP M, and let $\text{VC}(\Pi)$ denote its VC dimension. Let m trajectory trees be created using a generative model for M, and $\hat{V}^\pi(s_0)$ be the resulting estimates. If*

$$m = O\left((V_{\max}/\epsilon)^2 (H_\epsilon \text{VC}(\Pi) \log(V_{\max}/\epsilon) + \log(1/\delta))\right) \tag{1}$$

then with probability $1 - \delta$, $|V^\pi(s_0) - \hat{V}^\pi(s_0)| \leq \epsilon$ holds simultaneously for all $\pi \in \Pi$.

3.2 The Case of Stochastic Π

We now address the case of stochastic strategy classes. We describe an approach where we *transform* stochastic strategies into "equivalent" deterministic ones and operate on the deterministic versions, reducing the problem to the one handled in the previous section. The transformation is as follows: Given a class of stochastic strategies Π, each with domain X (where X is the set of all observable histories), we first extend the domain to be $X \times [0, 1]$. Now for each stochastic strategy $\pi \in \Pi$, define a corresponding deterministic *transformed* strategy π' with domain $X \times [0, 1]$, given by: $\pi'(h, r) = a_1$ if $r \leq \mathbf{Pr}[\pi(h) = a_1]$, and $\pi'(h, r) = a_2$ otherwise (for any $h \in X$, $r \in [0, 1]$). Let Π' be the collection of these transformed deterministic strategies π'. Since Π' is just a set of deterministic boolean functions, its VC dimension is well-defined. We then define the *pseudo-dimension* of the *original* set of stochastic strategies Π to be $\text{pVC}(\Pi) = \text{VC}(\Pi')$.[4]

Having transformed the strategy class, we also need to transform the POMDP, by augmenting the state space S to be $S \times [0, 1]$. Informally, the transitions and rewards remain the same, except that after each state transition, we draw a new random variable r uniformly in $[0, 1]$, and independently of all previous events. States are now of the form (s, r), and we let r be an observed variable. Whenever in the original POMDP a stochastic strategy π would

---

[4]This is equivalent to the conventional definition of the pseudo-dimension of Π [4], when it is viewed as a set of maps into real-valued action-probabilities.

have been given a history h, in the transformed POMDP the corresponding deterministic transformed strategy π' is given (h, r), where r is the $[0, 1]$-random variable at the current state. By the definition of π', it is easy to see that π' and π have exactly the same chance of choosing each action at any node (randomization over r).

We are now back in the deterministic case, so Theorem 3.2 applies, with $\text{VC}(\Pi)$ replaced by $\text{pVC}(\Pi) = \text{VC}(\Pi')$, and we again have the desired uniform convergence result.

4 Algorithms for Approximate Planning

Given a generative model for a POMDP, the preceding section's results immediately suggest a class of approximate planning algorithms: generate m trajectory trees $T_1, \ldots, T_m$, and search for a $\pi \in \Pi$ that maximizes $\hat{V}^\pi(s_0) = (1/m) \sum R(\pi, T_i)$. The following corollary to the uniform convergence results establishes the soundness of this approach.

Corollary 4.1 *Let Π be a class of strategies in a POMDP M, and let the number m of trajectory trees be as given in Theorem 3.2. Let $\hat{\pi} = \arg\max_{\pi \in \Pi} \{\hat{V}^\pi(s_0)\}$ be the policy in Π with the highest empirical return on the m trees. Then with probability $1 - \delta$, $\hat{\pi}$ is near-optimal within Π:*

$$V^{\hat{\pi}}(s_0) \geq opt(M, \Pi) - 2\epsilon. \tag{2}$$

If the suggested maximization is computationally infeasible, one can search for a local maximum π instead, and uniform convergence again assures us that $\hat{V}^\pi(s_0)$ is a trusted estimate of our true performance. Of course, even finding a local maximum can be expensive, since each trajectory tree is of size exponential in H_ϵ.

However, in practice it may be possible to significantly reduce the cost of the search. Suppose we are using a class of (possibly transformed) deterministic strategies, and we perform a greedy local search over Π to optimize $\hat{V}^\pi(s_0)$. Then at any time in the search, to evaluate the policy we are currently considering, we really need to look at only a single path of length H_ϵ in each tree, corresponding to the path taken by the strategy being considered. Thus, we should build the trajectory trees *lazily* — that is, incrementally build each node of each tree only as it is needed to evaluate $R(\pi, T_i)$ for the current strategy π. If there are parts of a tree that are reached only by poor policies, then a good search algorithm may never even build these parts of the tree. In any case, for a fixed number of trees, each step of the local search now takes time only *linear* in H_ϵ.[5]

There is a different approach that works directly on stochastic strategies (that is, without requiring the transformation to deterministic strategies). In this case each stochastic strategy π defines a distribution over *all* the paths in a trajectory tree, and thus calculating $R(\pi, T)$ may in general require examining complete trees. However, we can view each trajectory tree as a small, deterministic POMDP by itself, with the children of each node in the tree being its successor nodes. So if $\Pi = \{\pi_\theta : \theta \in \mathbb{R}^d\}$ is a smoothly parameterized family of stochastic strategies, then algorithms such as William's REINFORCE [10] can be used to find an unbiased estimate of the gradient $(d/d\theta)\hat{V}^{\pi_\theta}(s_0)$, which in turn can be used to

---

[5] See also (Ng and Jordan, in preparation) which, by assuming a much stronger model of a POMDP (a deterministic function f such that $f(s, a, r)$ is distributed according to $P(\cdot|s, a)$ when r is distributed Uniform[0,1]), gives an algorithm that enjoys uniform convergence bounds similar to those presented here, but with only a polynomial rather than exponential dependence on H_ϵ. The algorithm samples a number of vectors $r^{(i)} \in [0, 1]^{H_\epsilon}$, each of which, with f, defines an H_ϵ-step Monte Carlo evaluation trial for any policy π. The bound is on the number of such random vectors needed (rather than on the total number of calls to f).

perform stochastic gradient ascent to maximize $\hat{V}^{\pi_\theta}(s_0)$. Moreover, for a fixed number of trees, these algorithms need only $O(H_\epsilon)$ time per gradient estimate; so combined with lazy tree construction, we again have a practical algorithm whose per-step complexity is only *linear* in the horizon time. This line of thought is further developed in the long version of the paper.[6]

5 The Random Trajectory Method

Using a fully observable generative model of a POMDP, we have shown that the trajectory tree method gives uniformly good value estimates, with an amount of experience linear in VC(Π), and exponential in H_ϵ. It turns out we can significantly weaken the generative model, yet still obtain essentially the same theoretical results. In this harder case, we assume a generative model that provides only *partially observable* histories generated by a *truly random* strategy (which takes each action with equal probability at every step, regardless of the history so far). Furthermore, these trajectories always begin at the designated start state, so there is no ability provided to "reset" the POMDP to any state other than s_0. (Indeed, underlying states may never be observed.)

Our method for this harder case is called the Random Trajectory method. It seems to lead less readily to practical algorithms than the trajectory tree method, and its formal description and analysis, which is more difficult than for trajectory trees, are given in the long version of this paper [6]. As in Theorem 3.2, we prove that the amount of data needed is linear in VC(Π), and exponential in the horizon time — that is, by averaging appropriately over the resulting ensemble of trajectories generated, this amount of data is sufficient to yield uniformly good estimates of the values for all strategies in Π.

References

[1] L. Baird and A. W. Moore. Gradient descent for general Reinforcement Learning. In *Advances in Neural Information Processing Systems 11*, 1999.

[2] C. Boutilier, T. Dean, and S. Hanks. Decision theoretic planning: Structural assumptions and computational leverage. *Journal of Artificial Intelligence Research*, 1999.

[3] X. Boyen and D. Koller. Tractable inference for complex stochastic processes. In *Proc. UAI*, pages 33–42, 1998.

[4] David Haussler. Decision theoretic generalizations of the PAC model for neural net and oter learning applications. *Information and Computation*, 100:78–150, 1992.

[5] L. P. Kaelbling, M. L. Littman, and A. R. Cassandra. Planning and acting in partially observable stochastic domains. *Artificial Intelligence*, 101, 1998.

[6] M. Kearns, Y. Mansour, and A. Y. Ng. Approximate planning in large POMDPs via reusable trajectories. (long version), 1999.

[7] D. Koller and R. Parr. Computing factored value functions for policies in structured MDPs. In *Proceedings of the Sixteenth International Joint Conference on Artificial Intelligence*, 1999.

[8] R. S. Sutton and A. G. Barto. *Reinforcement Learning*. MIT Press, 1998.

[9] V.N. Vapnik. *Estimation of Dependences Based on Empirical Data*. Springer-Verlag, 1982.

[10] R. J. Williams. Simple statistical gradient-following algorithms for connectionist reinforcement learning. *Machine Learning*, 8:229–256, 1992.

---

[6]In the full paper, we also show how these algorithms can be extended to find in expected $O(H_\epsilon)$ time an unbiased estimate of the gradient of the *true* value $V^{\pi_\theta}(s_0)$ for discounted infinite horizon problems (whereas most current algorithms either only converge asymptotically to an unbiased estimate of this gradient, or need an absorbing state and "proper" strategies).

Actor-Critic Algorithms

Vijay R. Konda John N. Tsitsiklis
Laboratory for Information and Decision Systems,
Massachusetts Institute of Technology,
Cambridge, MA, 02139.
konda@mit.edu, jnt@mit.edu

Abstract

We propose and analyze a class of actor-critic algorithms for simulation-based optimization of a Markov decision process over a parameterized family of randomized stationary policies. These are two-time-scale algorithms in which the critic uses TD learning with a linear approximation architecture and the actor is updated in an approximate gradient direction based on information provided by the critic. We show that the features for the critic should span a subspace prescribed by the choice of parameterization of the actor. We conclude by discussing convergence properties and some open problems.

1 Introduction

The vast majority of Reinforcement Learning (RL) [9] and Neuro-Dynamic Programming (NDP) [1] methods fall into one of the following two categories:

(a) Actor-only methods work with a parameterized family of policies. The gradient of the performance, with respect to the actor parameters, is directly estimated by simulation, and the parameters are updated in a direction of improvement [4, 5, 8, 13]. A possible drawback of such methods is that the gradient estimators may have a large variance. Furthermore, as the policy changes, a new gradient is estimated independently of past estimates. Hence, there is no "learning," in the sense of accumulation and consolidation of older information.

(b) Critic-only methods rely exclusively on value function approximation and aim at learning an approximate solution to the Bellman equation, which will then hopefully prescribe a near-optimal policy. Such methods are indirect in the sense that they do not try to optimize directly over a policy space. A method of this type may succeed in constructing a "good" approximation of the value function, yet lack reliable guarantees in terms of near-optimality of the resulting policy.

Actor-critic methods aim at combining the strong points of actor-only and critic-only methods. The critic uses an approximation architecture and simulation to learn a value function, which is then used to update the actor's policy parameters in a direction of performance improvement. Such methods, as long as they are gradient-based, may have desirable convergence properties, in contrast to critic-only methods for which convergence is guaranteed in very limited settings. They hold the promise of delivering faster convergence (due to variance reduction), when compared to actor-only methods. On the other hand, theoretical understanding of actor-critic methods has been limited to the case of lookup table representations of policies [6].

In this paper, we propose some actor-critic algorithms and provide an overview of a convergence proof. The algorithms are based on an important observation. Since the number of parameters that the actor has to update is relatively small (compared to the number of states), the critic need not attempt to compute or approximate the exact value function, which is a high-dimensional object. In fact, we show that the critic should ideally compute a certain "projection" of the value function onto a low-dimensional subspace spanned by a set of "basis functions," that are *completely determined* by the parameterization of the actor. Finally, as the analysis in [11] suggests for TD algorithms, our algorithms can be extended to the case of arbitrary state and action spaces as long as certain ergodicity assumptions are satisfied.

We close this section by noting that ideas similar to ours have been presented in the simultaneous and independent work of Sutton et al. [10].

2 Markov decision processes and parameterized family of RSP's

Consider a Markov decision process with finite state space S, and finite action space A. Let $g : S \times A \to \mathbb{R}$ be a given cost function. A *randomized stationary policy* (RSP) is a mapping μ that assigns to each state x a probability distribution over the action space A. We consider a set of randomized stationary policies $\mathbb{P} = \{\mu_\theta ; \theta \in \mathbb{R}^n\}$, parameterized in terms of a vector θ. For each pair $(x, u) \in S \times A$, $\mu_\theta(x, u)$ denotes the probability of taking action u when the state x is encountered, under the policy corresponding to θ. Let $p_{xy}(u)$ denote the probability that the next state is y, given that the current state is x and the current action is u. Note that under any RSP, the sequence of states $\{X_n\}$ and of state-action pairs $\{X_n, U_n\}$ of the Markov decision process form Markov chains with state spaces S and $S \times A$, respectively. We make the following assumptions about the family of policies $\mathbb{P}$.

(A1) For all $x \in S$ and $u \in A$ the map $\theta \mapsto \mu_\theta(x, u)$ is twice differentiable with bounded first, second derivatives. Furthermore, there exists a $\mathbb{R}^n$-valued function $\psi_\theta(x, u)$ such that $\nabla \mu_\theta(x, u) = \mu_\theta(x, u) \psi_\theta(x, u)$ where the mapping $\theta \mapsto \psi_\theta(x, u)$ is bounded and has first bounded derivatives for any fixed x and u.

(A2) For each $\theta \in \mathbb{R}^n$, the Markov chains $\{X_n\}$ and $\{X_n, U_n\}$ are irreducible and aperiodic, with stationary probabilities $\pi_\theta(x)$ and $\eta_\theta(x, u) = \pi_\theta(x) \mu_\theta(x, u)$, respectively, under the RSP μ_θ.

In reference to Assumption (A1), note that whenever $\mu_\theta(x, u)$ is nonzero we have

$$\psi_\theta(x, u) = \frac{\nabla \mu_\theta(x, u)}{\mu_\theta(x, u)} = \nabla \ln \mu_\theta(x, u).$$

Consider the average cost function $\lambda : \mathbb{R}^n \mapsto \mathbb{R}$, given by

$$\lambda(\theta) = \sum_{x \in S, u \in A} g(x, u) \eta_\theta(x, u).$$

We are interested in minimizing $\lambda(\theta)$ over all θ. For each $\theta \in \mathbb{R}^n$, let $V_\theta : S \mapsto \mathbb{R}$ be the "differential" cost function, defined as solution of Poisson equation:

$$\lambda(\theta) + V_\theta(x) = \sum_{u \in A} \mu_\theta(x, u) \left[g(x, u) + \sum_y p_{xy}(u) V_\theta(y) \right].$$

Intuitively, $V_\theta(x)$ can be viewed as the "disadvantage" of state x: it is the expected excess cost – on top of the average cost – incurred if we start at state x. It plays a role similar to that played by the more familiar value function that arises in total or discounted cost Markov decision problems. Finally, for every $\theta \in \mathbb{R}^n$, we define the q-function $q_\theta : S \times A \to \mathbb{R}$, by

$$q_\theta(x, u) = g(x, u) - \lambda(\theta) + \sum_y p_{xy}(u) V_\theta(y).$$

We recall the following result, as stated in [8]. (Different versions of this result have been established in [3, 4, 5].)

Theorem 1.

$$\frac{\partial}{\partial \theta_i} \lambda(\theta) = \sum_{x,u} \eta_\theta(x, u) q_\theta(x, u) \psi_\theta^i(x, u) \tag{1}$$

where $\psi_\theta^i(x, u)$ stands for the ith component of ψ_θ.

In [8], the quantity $q_\theta(x, u)$ in the above formula is interpreted as the expected excess cost incurred over a certain renewal period of the Markov chain $\{X_n, U_n\}$, under the RSP μ_θ, and is then estimated by means of simulation, leading to actor-only algorithms. Here, we provide an alternative interpretation of the formula in Theorem 1, as an inner product, and thus derive a different set of algorithms, which readily generalize to the case of an infinite space as well.

For any $\theta \in \mathbb{R}^n$, we define the inner product $\langle \cdot, \cdot \rangle_\theta$ of two real valued functions q_1, q_2 on $S \times A$, viewed as vectors in $\mathbb{R}^{|S||A|}$, by

$$\langle q_1, q_2 \rangle_\theta = \sum_{x,u} \eta_\theta(x, u) q_1(x, u) q_2(x, u).$$

With this notation we can rewrite the formula (1) as

$$\frac{\partial}{\partial \theta_i} \lambda(\theta) = \langle q_\theta, \psi_\theta^i \rangle_\theta, \qquad i = 1, \ldots, n.$$

Let $\|\cdot\|_\theta$ denote the norm induced by this inner product on $\mathbb{R}^{|S||A|}$. For each $\theta \in \mathbb{R}^n$ let Ψ_θ denote the span of the vectors $\{\psi_\theta^i; 1 \le i \le n\}$ in $\mathbb{R}^{|S||A|}$. (This is same as the set of all functions f on $S \times A$ of the form $f(x, u) = \sum_{i=1}^n \alpha_i \psi_\theta^i(x, u)$, for some scalars $\alpha_1, \ldots, \alpha_n$.)

Note that although the gradient of λ depends on the q-function, which is a vector in a possibly very high dimensional space $\mathbb{R}^{|S||A|}$, the dependence is only through its inner products with vectors in Ψ_θ. Thus, instead of "learning" the function q_θ, it would suffice to learn the projection of q_θ on the subspace Ψ_θ.

Indeed, let $\Pi_\theta : \mathbb{R}^{|S||A|} \mapsto \Psi_\theta$ be the projection operator defined by

$$\Pi_\theta q = \arg \min_{\hat{q} \in \Psi_\theta} \|q - \hat{q}\|_\theta.$$

Since

$$\langle q_\theta, \psi_\theta \rangle_\theta = \langle \Pi_\theta q_\theta, \psi_\theta \rangle_\theta, \tag{2}$$

it is enough to compute the projection of q_θ onto Ψ_θ.

3 Actor-critic algorithms

We view actor critic-algorithms as stochastic gradient algorithms on the parameter space of the actor. When the actor parameter vector is θ, the job of the critic is to compute an approximation of the projection $\Pi_\theta q_\theta$ of q_θ onto Ψ_θ. The actor uses this approximation to update its policy in an approximate gradient direction. The analysis in [11, 12] shows that this is precisely what TD algorithms try to do, i.e., to compute the projection of an exact value function onto a subspace spanned by feature vectors. This allows us to implement the critic by using a TD algorithm. (Note, however, that other types of critics are possible, e.g., based on batch solution of least squares problems, as long as they aim at computing the same projection.)

We note some minor differences with the common usage of TD. In our context, we need the projection of q-functions, rather than value functions. But this is easily achieved by replacing the Markov chain $\{x_t\}$ in [11, 12] by the Markov chain $\{X_n, U_n\}$. A further difference is that [11, 12] assume that the control policy and the feature vectors are fixed. In our algorithms, the control policy as well as the features need to change as the actor updates its parameters. As shown in [6, 2], this need not pose any problems, as long as the actor parameters are updated on a slower time scale.

We are now ready to describe two actor-critic algorithms, which differ only as far as the critic updates are concerned. In both variants, the critic is a TD algorithm with a linearly parameterized approximation architecture for the q-function, of the form

$$Q_r^\theta(x,u) = \sum_{j=1}^m r^j \phi_\theta^j(x,u),$$

where $r = (r^1, \ldots, r^m) \in \mathbb{R}^m$ denotes the parameter vector of the critic. The features ϕ_θ^j, $j = 1, \ldots, m$, used by the critic are dependent on the actor parameter vector θ and are chosen such that their span in $\mathbb{R}^{|S||A|}$, denoted by Φ_θ, contains Ψ_θ. Note that the formula (2) still holds if Π_θ is redefined as projection onto Φ_θ as long as Φ_θ contains Ψ_θ. The most straightforward choice would be to let $m = n$ and $\phi_\theta^i = \psi_\theta^i$ for each i. Nevertheless, we allow the possibility that $m > n$ and Φ_θ properly contains Ψ_θ, so that the critic uses more features than that are actually necessary. This added flexibility may turn out to be useful in a number of ways:

1. It is possible for certain values of θ, the features ψ_θ are either close to zero or are almost linearly dependent. For these values of θ, the operator Π_θ becomes ill-conditioned and the algorithms can become unstable. This might be avoided by using richer set of features ψ_θ^i.

2. For the second algorithm that we propose (TD(α) $\alpha < 1$) critic can only compute approximate - rather than exact - projection. The use of additional features can result in a reduction of the approximation error.

Along with the parameter vector r, the critic stores some auxiliary parameters: these are a (scalar) estimate λ, of the average cost, and an m-vector z which represents Sutton's eligibility trace [1, 9]. The actor and critic updates take place in the course of a simulation of a single sample path of the controlled Markov chain. Let r_k, z_k, λ_k be the parameters of the critic, and let θ_k be the parameter vector of the actor, at time k. Let (X_k, U_k) be the state-action pair at that time. Let X_{k+1} be the new state, obtained after action U_k is applied. A new action U_{k+1} is generated according to the RSP corresponding to the actor parameter vector θ_k. The critic carries out an update similar to the average cost temporal-difference method of [12]:

$$\lambda_{k+1} = \lambda_k + \gamma_k(g(X_k, U_k) - \lambda_k),$$

$$r_{k+1} = r_k + \gamma_k \Big(g(X_k, U_k) - \lambda_k + Q_{r_k}^{\theta_k}(X_{k+1}, U_{k+1}) - Q_{r_k}^{\theta_k}(X_k, U_k) \Big) z_k.$$

(Here, γ_k is a positive stepsize parameter.) The two variants of the critic use different ways of updating z_k:

TD(1) Critic: Let x^* be a state in S.

$$\begin{aligned} z_{k+1} &= z_k + \phi_{\theta_k}(X_{k+1}, U_{k+1}), && \text{if } X_{k+1} \neq x^*, \\ &= \phi_{\theta_k}(X_{k+1}, U_{k+1}), && \text{otherwise.} \end{aligned}$$

TD(α) Critic, $0 \leq \alpha < 1$:

$$z_{k+1} = \alpha z_k + \phi_{\theta_k}(X_{k+1}, U_{k+1}).$$

Actor: Finally, the actor updates its parameter vector by letting

$$\theta_{k+1} = \theta_k - \beta_k \Gamma(r_k) Q_{r_k}^{\theta_k}(X_{k+1}, U_{k+1}) \psi_{\theta_k}(X_{k+1}, U_{k+1}).$$

Here, β_k is a positive stepsize and $\Gamma(r_k) > 0$ is a normalization factor satisfying:

(A3) $\Gamma(\cdot)$ is Lipschitz continuous.

(A4) There exists $C > 0$ such that

$$\Gamma(r) \leq \frac{C}{1 + \|r\|}.$$

The above presented algorithms are only two out of many variations. For instance, one could also consider "episodic" problems in which one starts from a given initial state and runs the process until a random termination time (at which time the process is reinitialized at x^*), with the objective of minimizing the expected cost until termination. In this setting, the average cost estimate λ_k is unnecessary and is removed from the critic update formula. If the critic parameter r_k were to be reinitialized each time that x^* is entered, one would obtain a method closely related to Williams' REINFORCE algorithm [13]. Such a method does not involve any value function learning, because the observations during one episode do not affect the critic parameter r during another episode. In contrast, in our approach, the observations from all past episodes affect current critic parameter r, and in this sense critic is "learning". This can be advantageous because, as long as θ is slowly changing, the observations from recent episodes carry useful information on the q-function under the current policy.

4 Convergence of actor-critic algorithms

Since our actor-critic algorithms are gradient-based, one cannot expect to prove convergence to a globally optimal policy (within the given class of RSP's). The best that one could hope for is the convergence of $\nabla \lambda(\theta)$ to zero; in practical terms, this will usually translate to convergence to a local minimum of $\lambda(\theta)$. Actually, because the $TD(\alpha)$ critic will generally converge to an approximation of the desired projection of the value function, the corresponding convergence result is necessarily weaker, only guaranteeing that $\nabla \lambda(\theta_k)$ becomes small (infinitely often). Let us now introduce some further assumptions.

(A5) For each $\theta \in \mathbb{R}^n$, we define an $m \times m$ matrix $G(\theta)$ by

$$G(\theta) = \sum_{x,u} \eta_\theta(x,u) \phi_\theta(x,u) \phi_\theta(x,u)^T.$$

We assume that $G(\theta)$ is uniformly positive definite, that is, there exists some $\epsilon_1 > 0$ such that for all $r \in \mathbb{R}^m$ and $\theta \in \mathbb{R}^n$

$$r^T G(\theta) r \geq \epsilon_1 \|r\|^2.$$

(A6) We assume that the stepsize sequences $\{\gamma_k\}, \{\beta_k\}$ are positive, nonincreasing, and satisfy

$$\delta_k > 0, \ \forall k, \qquad \sum_k \delta_k = \infty, \qquad \sum_k \delta_k^2 < \infty,$$

where δ_k stands for either β_k or γ_k. We also assume that

$$\frac{\beta_k}{\gamma_k} \to 0.$$

Note that the last assumption requires that the actor parameters be updated at a time scale slower than that of critic.

Theorem 2. *In an actor-critic algorithm with a TD(1) critic,*

$$\liminf_k \|\nabla \lambda(\theta_k)\| = 0 \qquad w.p. \ 1.$$

Furthermore, if $\{\theta_k\}$ is bounded w.p. 1 then

$$\lim_k \|\nabla \lambda(\theta_k)\| = 0 \qquad w.p. \ 1.$$

Theorem 3. *For every $\epsilon > 0$, there exists α sufficiently close to 1, such that $\liminf_k \|\nabla \lambda(\theta_k)\| \leq \epsilon$ w.p. 1.*

Note that the theoretical guarantees appear to be stronger in the case of the TD(1) critic. However, we expect that TD(α) will perform better in practice because of much smaller variance for the parameter r_k. (Similar issues arise when considering actor-only algorithms. The experiments reported in [7] indicate that introducing a forgetting factor $\alpha < 1$ can result in much faster convergence, with very little loss of performance.) We now provide an overview of the proofs of these theorems. Since $\beta_k/\gamma_k \to 0$, the size of the actor updates becomes negligible compared to the size of the critic updates. Therefore the actor looks stationary, as far as the critic is concerned. Thus, the analysis in [1] for the TD(1) critic and the analysis in [12] for the TD(α) critic (with $\alpha < 1$) can be used, with appropriate modifications, to conclude that the critic's approximation of $\Pi_{\theta_k} q_{\theta_k}$ will be "asymptotically correct". If $r(\theta)$ denotes the value to which the critic converges when the actor parameters are fixed at θ, then the update for the actor can be rewritten as

$$\theta_{k+1} = \theta_k - \beta_k \Gamma(r(\theta_k)) Q_{r(\theta_k)}^{\theta_k}(X_{k+1}, U_{k+1}) \psi_{\theta_k}(X_{k+1}, U_{k+1}) + \beta_k e_k,$$

where e_k is an error that becomes asymptotically negligible. At this point, standard proof techniques for stochastic approximation algorithms can be used to complete the proof.

5 Conclusions

The key observation in this paper is that in actor-critic methods, the actor parameterization and the critic parameterization need not, and should not be chosen independently. Rather, an appropriate approximation architecture for the critic is directly prescribed by the parameterization used in actor.

Capitalizing on the above observation, we have presented a class of actor-critic algorithms, aimed at combining the advantages of actor-only and critic-only methods. In contrast to existing actor-critic methods, our algorithms apply to high-dimensional problems (they do not rely on lookup table representations), and are mathematically sound in the sense that they possess certain convergence properties.

Acknowledgments: This research was partially supported by the NSF under grant ECS-9873451, and by the AFOSR under grant F49620-99-1-0320.

References

[1] D. P. Bertsekas and J. N. Tsitsiklis. *Neurodynamic Programming.* Athena Scientific, Belmont, MA, 1996.

[2] V. S. Borkar. Stochastic approximation with two time scales. *Systems and Control Letters*, 29:291–294, 1996.

[3] X. R. Cao and H. F. Chen. Perturbation realization, potentials, and sensitivity analysis of Markov processes. *IEEE Transactions on Automatic Control*, 42:1382–1393, 1997.

[4] P. W. Glynn. Stochastic approximation for monte carlo optimization. In *Proceedings of the 1986 Winter Simulation Conference*, pages 285–289, 1986.

[5] T. Jaakola, S. P. Singh, and M. I. Jordan. Reinforcement learning algorithms for partially observable Markov decision problems. In *Advances in Neural Information Processing Systems*, volume 7, pages 345–352, San Francisco, CA, 1995. Morgan Kaufman.

[6] V. R. Konda and V. S. Borkar. Actor-critic like learning algorithms for Markov decision processes. *SIAM Journal on Control and Optimization*, 38(1):94–123, 1999.

[7] P. Marbach. *Simulation based optimization of Markov reward processes.* PhD thesis, Massachusetts Institute of Technology, 1998.

[8] P. Marbach and J. N. Tsitsiklis. Simulation-based optimization of Markov reward processes. Submitted to IEEE Transactions on Automatic Control.

[9] R. Sutton and A. Barto. *Reinforcement Learning: An Introduction.* MIT Press, Cambridge, MA, 1995.

[10] R. S. Sutton, D. McAllester, S. Singh, and Y. Mansour. Policy gradient methods for reinforcement learning with function approximation. In *this proceedings*.

[11] J. N. Tsitsiklis and B. Van Roy. An analysis of temporal-difference learning with function approximation. *IEEE Transactions on Automatic Control*, 42(5):674–690, 1997.

[12] J. N. Tsitsiklis and B. Van Roy. Average cost temporal-difference learning. *Automatica*, 35(11):1799–1808, 1999.

[13] R. Williams. Simple statistical gradient following algorithms for connectionist reinforcement learning. *Machine Learning*, 8:229–256, 1992.

Bayesian Map Learning in Dynamic Environments

Kevin P. Murphy
Computer Science Division
University of California
Berkeley, CA 94720-1776
murphyk@cs.berkeley.edu

Abstract

We consider the problem of learning a grid-based map using a robot with noisy sensors and actuators. We compare two approaches: online EM, where the map is treated as a fixed parameter, and Bayesian inference, where the map is a (matrix-valued) random variable. We show that even on a very simple example, online EM can get stuck in local minima, which causes the robot to get "lost" and the resulting map to be useless. By contrast, the Bayesian approach, by maintaining multiple hypotheses, is much more robust. We then introduce a method for approximating the Bayesian solution, called Rao-Blackwellised particle filtering. We show that this approximation, when coupled with an active learning strategy, is fast but accurate.

1 Introduction

The problem of getting mobile robots to autonomously learn maps of their environment has been widely studied (see e.g., [9] for a collection of recent papers). The basic difficulty is that the robot must know exactly where it is (a problem called localization), so that it can update the right part of the map. However, to know where it is, the robot must already have a map: relying on dead-reckoning alone (i.e., integrating the motor commands) is unreliable because of noise in the actuators (slippage and drift).

One obvious solution is to use EM, where we alternate between estimating the location given the map (the E step), and estimating the map given the location (the M step). Indeed, this approach has been successfully used by several groups [8, 11, 12]. However, in all of these works, the trajectory of the robot was specified by hand, and the map was learned off-line. For fully autonomous operation, and to cope with dynamic environments, the map must be learned online.

We consider two approaches to online learning: online EM, and Bayesian inference,

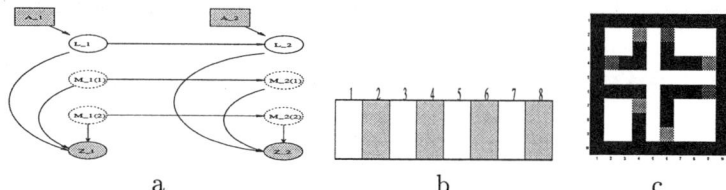

Figure 1: (a) The POMDP represented as a graphical model. L_t is the location, $M_t(i)$ is the label of the i'th grid cell, A_t is the action, and Z_t is the observation. Dotted circles denote variables that EM treats as parameters. (b) A one-dimensional grid with binary labels (white = 0, black = 1). (c) A two-dimensional grid, with four labels (closed doors, open doors, walls, and free space).

where we treat the map as a random variable. In Section 3, we show that the Bayesian approach can lead to much better results than online EM; unfortunately, it is computationally intractable, so in Section 4, we discuss an approximation based on Rao-Blackwellised particle filtering.

2 The model

We now precisely define the model that we will use in this paper; it is similar to, but much simpler than, the occupancy grid model in [12]. The map is defined to be a grid, where each cell has a label which represents what the robot would see at that point. More formally, the map at time t is a vector of discrete random variables, $M_t(i) \in \{1, \ldots, N_O\}$, where $1 \leq i \leq N_L$. Of course, the map is not observed directly, and nor is the robot's location, $L_t \in \{1, \ldots, N_L\}$. What is observed is $Z_t \in \{1, \ldots, N_O\}$, the label of the cell at the robot's current location, and $A_t \in \{1, \ldots, N_A\}$, the action chosen by the robot just before time t. The conditional independence assumptions we are making are illustrated in Figure 1(a). We start by considering the very simple one-dimensional grid shown in Figure 1(b), where there are just two actions, move right ($\rightarrow$) and move left ($\leftarrow$), and just two labels, off (0) and on (1). This is sufficiently small that we can perform exact Bayesian inference. Later, we will generalize to two dimensions.

The prior for the location is a delta function with all its mass on the first (left-most) cell, independent of A_1. The transition model for the location is as follows.

$$\Pr(L_t = j | L_{t-1} = i, A_t = \rightarrow) = \begin{cases} p_a & \text{if } j = i+1, j < N \\ 1 - p_a & \text{if } j = i, j < N \\ 1 & \text{if } j = i = N \\ 0 & \text{otherwise} \end{cases}$$

where p_a is the probability of a successful action, i.e., $1 - p_a$ is the probability that the robot's wheels slip. There is an analogous equation for the case when $A_t = \leftarrow$. Note that it is not possible to pass through the "rightmost" cell; the robot can use this information to help localize itself.

The prior for the map is a product of the priors for each cell, which are uniform. (We could model correlation between neighboring cells using a Markov Random Field, although this is computationally expensive.) The transition model for the map is a product of the transition models for each cell, which are defined as follows:

the probability that a 0 becomes a 1 or vice versa is p_c (probability of change), and hence the probability that the cell label remains the same is $1 - p_c$.

Finally, the observation model is

$$\Pr(Z_t = k | M_t = (m_1, \ldots, m_{N_L}), L_t = i) = \begin{cases} p_o & \text{if } m_i = k \\ 1 - p_o & \text{otherwise} \end{cases}$$

where p_o is the probability of a succesful observation, i.e., $1 - p_o$ is the probability of a classification error. Another way of writing this, that will be useful later, is to introduce the dummy deterministic variable, Z'_t, which has the following distribution: $\Pr(Z'_t = k | M_t = (m_1, \ldots, m_{N_L}), L_t = i) = \delta(k, m_i)$, where $\delta(a, b) = 1$ if $a = b$ and is 0 otherwise. Thus Z'_t acts just like a multiplexer, selecting out a component of M_t as determined by the "gate" L_t. The output of the multiplexer is then passed through a noisy channel, which flips bits with probability $1 - p_o$, to produce Z_t.

3 Bayesian learning compared to EM

For simplicity, we assume that the parameters p_o, p_a and p_c, are all known. (In this section, we use $p_o = 0.9$, $p_a = 0.8$ and $p_c = 0$, so the world is somewhat "slippery", but static in appearance.) The state estimation problem is to compute the belief state $\Pr(L_t, M_t | y_{1:t})$, where $Y_t = (Z_t, A_t)$ is the evidence at time t; this is equivalent to performing online inference in the graphical model shown in Figure 1(a). Unfortunately, even though we have assumed that the components of M_t are a priori independent, they become correlated by virtue of sharing a common child, Z_t. That is, since the true location of the robot is unknown, all of the cells are possible causes of the observation, and they "compete" to "explain" the data. Hence all of the hidden variables become coupled, and the belief state has size $O(N_L 2^{N_L})$.

If the world is static (i.e., $p_c = 0$), we can treat M as a fixed, but unknown, parameter; this can then be combined with the noisy sensor model to define an HMM with the following observation matrix:

$$B(i, k) \stackrel{\text{def}}{=} \Pr(Z_t = k | L_t = i; M) = \sum_j \Pr(Z_t = k | Z'_t = j) \delta(M(i), j)$$

We can then learn B using EM, as in [8, 11, 12]. (We assume for now that the HMM transition matrix is independent of the map, and encodes the known topology of the grid, i.e., the robot can move to any neighboring cell, no matter what its label is. We will lift this restriction in the 2D example.)

We can formulate an online version of EM as follows. We use fixed-lag smoothing with a sliding window of length W, and compute the expected sufficient statistics (ESS) for the observation matrix within this window as follows: $\theta_t(i, k) = \sum_{\tau = t-W : Z_\tau = k}^{t} \hat{L}_{\tau|t}(i)$, where $\hat{L}_{\tau|t}(i) = \Pr(L_\tau = i | y_{1:t})$. We can compute $\hat{L}$ using the forwards-backwards algorithm, using $\hat{L}_{t-W-1|t-1}$ as the prior. (The initial condition is $\hat{L} = \pi$, where π is the (known) prior for L_0.) Thus the cost per time step is $O(2W N_L^2)$. In the M step, we normalize each row of $\theta_t + d \times \theta_{t-1}$, where $0 < d < 1$ is a decay constant, to get the new estimate of B. We need to downweight the previous ESS since they were computed using out-of-date parameters; in addition, exponential forgetting allows us to handle dynamic environments. [1] discuss some variations on this algorithm.

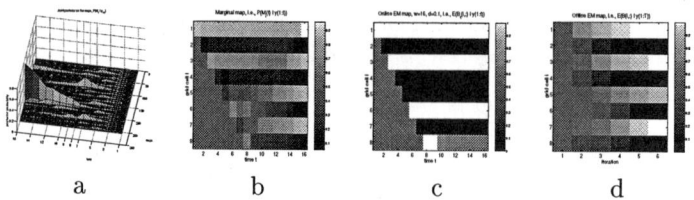

a   b   c   d

Figure 2: (a) The full joint posterior on $P(M_t|y_{1:t})$. 0 and 255, on the axis into the page, represent the maps where every cell is off and every cell is on, respectively; the mode at $t = 16$ is for map 171, which corresponds to the correct pattern 01010101. (b-d) Estimated map. Light cells are more likely to contains 0s, so the correct pattern should have light bars in the odd rows. (b) The marginals of the exact joint. (c) Online EM. (d) Offline EM.

As the window length increases, past locations are allowed to look at more and more future data, and hence their estimates become more accurate; however, the space and time requirements increase. Nevertheless, there are occasions when even the maximum window size (i.e., looking all the way back to $\tau = 0$) will perform poorly, because of the greedy hill-climbing nature of EM. For a simple example of this, consider the environment shown in Figure 1(b). Suppose the robot starts in cell 1, keeps going right until it comes to the end of the "corridor", and then heads back "home". Suppose further that there is a single slippage error at $t = 4$, so the actual path and observation sequence of the robot is as follows:

t	1	2	3	4	5	6	7	8	9	10	11	12	13	14	15	16
L_t	1	2	3	4	4	5	6	7	8	7	6	5	4	3	2	1
Z_t	0	1	0	1	1	0	1	0	1	0	1	0	1	0	1	0
A_t	-	→	→	→	→	→	→	→	←	←	←	←	←	←	←	←

To study the effect of this sequence, we computed $\Pr(M_t, L_t|y_{1:t})$ by applying the junction tree algorithm to the graphical model in Figure 1(a). We then marginalized out L_t to compute the posterior $P(M_t)$: see Figure 2(a). At $t = 1$, there are 2^7 modes, corresponding to all possible bit patterns on the unobserved cells. At each time step, the robot thinks it is moving one step to the right. Hence at $t = 8$, the robot thinks it is in cell 8, and observes 0. When it tries to move right, it knows it will remain in cell 8 (since the robot knows where the boundaries are). Hence at $t = 9$, it is almost 70% confident that it is in cell 8. At $t = 9$, it observes a 1, which contradicts its previous observation of 0. There are two possible explanations: this is a sensor error, or there was a motor error. Which of these is more likely depends on the relative values of the sensor noise, p_o, and the system noise, p_a. In our experiments, we found that the motor error hypothesis is much more likely; hence the mode of the posterior jumps from the wrong map (in which $M(5) = 1$) to the right map (in which $M(5) = 0$). Furthermore, as the robot returns to "familiar territory", it is able to better localize itself (see Figure 3(a)), and continues to learn the map even for far-away cells, because they are all correlated (in Figure 2(b), the entry for cell 8 becomes sharper even as the robot returns to cell 1)

We now compare the Bayesian solution with EM. Online EM with no smoothing was not able to learn the correct map. Adding smoothing with the maximum window size of $W_t = t$ did not improve matters: it is still unable to escape the local

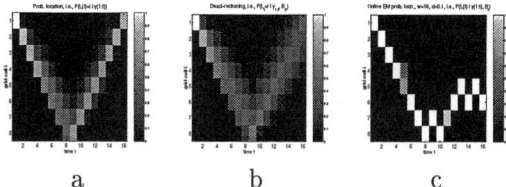

Figure 3: Estimated location. Light cells are more likely to contain the robot. (a) Optimal Bayes solution which marginalizes out the map. (b) Dead-reckoning solution which ignores the map. Notice how "blurry" it is. (c) Online EM solution using fixed-lag smoothing with a maximal window length.

minimum in which $M(5) = 1$, as shown in Figure 2(c). (We tried various values of the decay rate d, from 0.1 to 0.9, and found that it made little difference.) With the wrong map, the robot "gets lost" on the return journey: see Figure 3(c). Offline EM, on the other hand, does very well, as shown in Figure 2(d); although the initial estimate of location (see Figure 3(b)) is rather diffuse, as it updates the map it can use the benefit of hindsight to figure out where it must have been.

4 Rao-Blackwellised particle filtering

Although the Bayesian solution exhibits some desirable properties, its running time is exponential in the size of the environment. In this section, we discuss a sequential Monte Carlo algorithm called particle filtering (also known as SIR filtering, the bootstrap filter, the condensation algorithm, survival of the fittest, etc; see [10, 4] for recent reviews). Particle filtering (PF) has already been successfully applied to the problem of (global) robot localization [5]. However, in that case, the state space was only of dimension 3: the unknowns were the position of the robot, $(x, y) \in \mathbb{R}^2$, and its orientation, $\theta \in [0, 2\pi]$. In our case, the state space is discrete and of dimension $O(1 + N_L)$, since we need to keep track of the map as well as the robot's location (we ignore orientation in this paper).

Particle filtering can be very inefficient in high-dimensional spaces. The key observation which makes it tractable in this context is that, if $L_{1:t}$ were known, then the posterior on M_t would be factored; hence M_t can be marginalized out analytically, and we only need to sample L_t. This idea is known in the statistics literature as Rao-Blackwellisation [10, 4]. In more detail, we will approximate the posterior at time t using a set of weighted particles, where each particle specifies a trajectory $L_{1:t}$, and the corresponding conditionally factored representation of $P(M_t) = \prod_i P(M_t(i))$; we will denote the j'th particle at time t as $b_t^{(j)}$. Note that we do not need to actually store the complete trajectories $L_{1:t}$: we only need the most recent value of L. The approach we take is essentially the same as the one used in the conditional linear Gaussian models of [4, 3], except we replace the Kalman filter update with one which exploits the conditionally factored representation of $P(M_t)$. In particular, the algorithm is as follows: For each particle $j = 1, \ldots, N_s$, we do the following:

1. Sample $L_{t+1}^{(j)}$ from a proposal distribution, which we discuss below.

2. Update each component of the map separately using $L_{t+1}^{(j)}$ and z_{t+1}

$$\Pr(M_{t+1}^{(j)}|L_{t+1}^{(j)} = i, b_t^{(j)}, z_{t+1}) \propto \Pr(z_{t+1}|M_{t+1}^{(j)}(i)) \prod_k \Pr(M_{t+1}^{(j)}(k)|M_t^{(j)}(k))$$

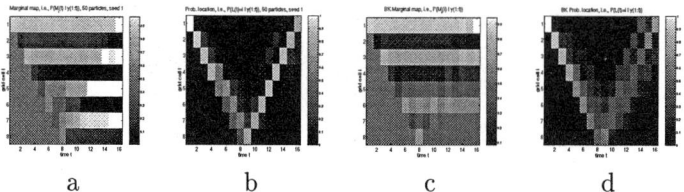

Figure 4: (a-b) Results using 50 particles. (c-d) Results using BK.

3. Update the weights: $w_{t+1}^{(j)} = u_{t+1}^{(j)} w_t^{(j)}$, where $u_{t+1}^{(j)}$ is defined below.

We then resample N_s particles from the normalised weights, using Liu's residual resampling algorithm [10], and set $w_{t+1}^{(j)} = 1/N_s$ for all j. We consider two proposal distributions. The first is a simple one which just uses the transition model to predict the new location: $\Pr(L_{t+1}|b_t^{(j)}, a_{t+1})$. In this case, the incremental weight is $u_{t+1}^{(j)} \propto P(z_{t+1}|L_{t+1}^{(j)}, b_t^{(j)})$. The optimal proposal distribution (the one which minimizes the variance of the importance weights) takes the most recent evidence into account, and can be shown to have the form $\Pr(L_{t+1}|b_t^{(j)}, a_{t+1}, z_{t+1})$ with incremental weight $u_{t+1} \propto P(z_{t+1}|b_t^{(j)})$. Computing this requires marginalizing out M_{t+1} and L_{t+1}, which can be done in $O(N_L)$ time (details omitted).

In Figure 4, we show the results of applying the above algorithm to the same problem as in Section 3; it can be seen that it approximates the exact solution very closely, using only 50 particles. The results shown are for a particular random number seed; other seeds produce qualitatively very similar results, indicating that 50 particles is in fact sufficient in this case. Obviously, as we increase the number of particles, the error and variance decrease, but the running time increases (linearly).

The question of how many particles to use is a difficult one: it depends both on the noise parameters and the structure of the environment (if every cell has a unique label, localization is easy). Since we are sampling trajectories, the number of hypotheses, and hence the number of particles needed, grows exponentially with time. In the above example, the robot was able to localize itself quite accurately when it reached the end of the corridor, where most hypotheses "died off". In general, the number of particles will depend on the length of the longest cycle in the environment, so we will need to use active learning to ensure tractability.

In the dynamic two-dimensional grid world of Figure 1(c), we chose actions so as to maximize expected discounted reward (using policy iteration), where the reward for visiting cell i is

$$H(L_t)(1 - H(M_t(i))) + (1 - H(L_t))H(M_t(i))$$

where $H(\cdot)$ is the normalized entropy. Hence, if the robot is "lost", so $H(L_t) \approx 1$, the robot will try to visit a cell which it is certain about (see [6] for a better approach); otherwise, it will try to explore uncertain cells. After learning the map, the robot spends its time visiting each of the doors, to keep its knowledge of their state (open or closed) up-to-date.

We now briefly consider some alternative approximate inference algorithms. Examining the graphical structure of our model (see Figure 1(a)), we see that it is identical to a Factorial HMM [7] (ignoring the inputs). Unfortunately, we cannot use their variational approximation, because they assume a conditional Gaussian observation model, whereas ours is almost deterministic. Another popular approximate inference algorithm for dynamic Bayes nets (DBNs) is the "BK algorithm" [2, 1]. This entails projecting the joint posterior at time t onto a product-of-marginals representation

$$P(L_t, M_t(1), \ldots, M_t(N_L)|y_{1:t}) = P(L_t|y_{1:t}) \prod_i P(M_t(i)|y_{1:t})$$

and using this as a factored prior for Bayesian updating at time $t+1$. Given a factored prior, we can compute a factored posterior in $O(N_L)$ time by conditioning on each L_{t+1}, and then averaging. We found that the BK method does very poorly on this problem (see Figure 4), because it ignores correlation between the cells. Of course, it is possible to use pairwise or higher order marginals for tightly coupled sets of variables. Unfortunately, the running time is exponential in the size of the largest marginal, and in our case, all the $M_t(i)$ variables are coupled.

Acknowledgments

I would like to thank Nando de Freitas for helping me get particle filtering to work, Sebastian Thrun for an interesting discussion at the conference, and Stuart Russell for encouraging me to compare to EM. This work was supported by grant number ONR N00014-97-1-0941.

References

[1] X. Boyen and D. Koller. Approximate learning of dynamic models. In *NIPS*, 1998.

[2] X. Boyen and D. Koller. Tractable inference for complex stochastic processes. In *UAI*, 1998.

[3] R. Chen and S. Liu. Mixture Kalman filters. *Submitted*, 1999.

[4] A. Doucet, S. Godsill, and C. Andrieu. On sequential Monte Carlo sampling methods for Bayesian filtering. *Statistics and Computing*, 1999.

[5] D. Fox, W. Burgard, F. Dellaert, and S. Thrun. Monte carlo localization: Efficient position estimation for mobile robots. In *AAAI*, 1999.

[6] D. Fox, W. Burgard, and S. Thrun. Active Markov localization for mobile robots. *Robotics and Autonomous Systems*, 1998.

[7] Z. Ghahramani and M. Jordan. Factorial Hidden Markov Models. *Machine Learning*, 29:245–273, 1997.

[8] S. Koenig and R. Simmons. Unsupervised learning of probabilistic models for robot navigation. In *ICRA*, 1996.

[9] D. Kortenkamp, R. Bonasso, and R. Murphy, editors. *Artificial Intelligence and Mobile Robots: case studies of successful robot systems*. MIT Press, 1998.

[10] J. Liu and R. Chen. Sequential monte carlo methods for dynamic systems. *JASA*, 93:1032–1044, 1998.

[11] H. Shatkay and L. P. Kaelbling. Learning topological maps with weak local odometric information. In *IJCAI*, 1997.

[12] S. Thrun, W. Burgard, and D. Fox. A probabilistic approach to concurrent mapping and localization for mobile robots. *Machine Learning*, 31:29–53, 1998.

Policy Search via Density Estimation

Andrew Y. Ng
Computer Science Division
U.C. Berkeley
Berkeley, CA 94720
ang@cs.berkeley.edu

Ronald Parr
Computer Science Dept.
Stanford University
Stanford, CA 94305
parr@cs.stanford.edu

Daphne Koller
Computer Science Dept.
Stanford University
Stanford, CA 94305
koller@cs.stanford.edu

Abstract

We propose a new approach to the problem of searching a space of stochastic controllers for a Markov decision process (MDP) or a partially observable Markov decision process (POMDP). Following several other authors, our approach is based on searching in parameterized families of policies (for example, via gradient descent) to optimize solution quality. However, rather than trying to estimate the values and derivatives of a policy directly, we do so indirectly using estimates for the probability densities that the policy induces on states at the different points in time. This enables our algorithms to exploit the many techniques for efficient and robust approximate density propagation in stochastic systems. We show how our techniques can be applied both to deterministic propagation schemes (where the MDP's dynamics are given explicitly in compact form,) and to stochastic propagation schemes (where we have access only to a generative model, or simulator, of the MDP). We present empirical results for both of these variants on complex problems.

1 Introduction

In recent years, there has been growing interest in algorithms for approximate planning in (exponentially or even infinitely) large Markov decision processes (MDPs) and partially observable MDPs (POMDPs). For such large domains, the value and Q-functions are sometimes complicated and difficult to approximate, even though there may be simple, compactly representable policies which perform very well. This observation has led to particular interest in *direct policy search* methods (e.g., [9, 8, 1]), which attempt to choose a good policy from some restricted class Π of policies. In our setting, $\Pi = \{\pi_\theta : \theta \in \mathbb{R}^m\}$ is a class of policies smoothly parameterized by $\theta \in \mathbb{R}^m$. If the value of π_θ is differentiable in θ, then gradient ascent methods may be used to find a locally optimal π_θ. However, estimating values of π_θ (and the associated gradient) is often far from trivial. One simple method for estimating π_θ's value involves executing one or more Monte Carlo trajectories using π_θ, and then taking the average empirical return; cleverer algorithms executing single trajectories also allow gradient estimates [9, 1]. These methods have become a standard approach to policy search, and sometimes work fairly well.

In this paper, we propose a somewhat different approach to this value/gradient estimation problem. Rather than estimating these quantities directly, we estimate the probability density over the states of the system induced by π_θ at different points in time. These *time slice densities* completely determine the value of the policy π_θ. While density estimation is not an easy problem, we can utilize existing approaches to density propagation [3, 5], which allow users to specify prior knowledge about the densities, and which have also been shown, both theoretically and empirically, to provide robust estimates for time slice densities. We show how direct policy search can be implemented using this approach in two very different settings of the planning problem: In the first, we have access to an explicit model of the system dynamics, allowing us to provide an explicit algebraic operator that implements the approximate density propagation process. In the second, we have access only to a generative model of the dynamics (which allows us only to sample from, but does not provide an explicit representation of, next-state distributions). We show how both of our techniques can be combined with gradient ascent in order to perform policy search, a somewhat subtle argument in the case of the sampling-based approach. We also present empirical results for both variants in complex domains.

2 Problem description

A *Markov Decision Process (MDP)* is a tuple (S, s_0, A, R, P) where:[1] S is a (possibly infinite) set of states; $s_0 \in S$ is a start state; A is a finite set of actions; R is a *reward function* $R : S \mapsto [0, R_{max}]$; P is a *transition model* $P : S \times A \mapsto \Delta_S$, such that $P(s' \mid s, a)$ gives the probability of landing in state s' upon taking action a in state s.

A stochastic policy is a map $\pi : S \mapsto \Delta_A$, where $\pi(a \mid s)$ is the probability of taking action a in state s. There are many ways of defining a policy π's "quality" or *value*. For a horizon T and discount factor γ, the *finite horizon discounted value function* $V_{T,\gamma}[\pi]$ is defined by $V_{0,\gamma}[\pi](s) = R(s)$; $V_{t+1,\gamma}[\pi](s) = R(s) + \gamma \sum_a \pi(a \mid s) \sum_{s'} P(s' \mid s, a) V_{t,\gamma}[\pi](s')$. For an infinite state space (here and below), the summation is replaced by an integral. We can now define several optimality criteria. The *finite horizon total reward with horizon* T is $V_T[\pi] = V_{T,1}[\pi](s_0)$. The *infinite horizon discounted reward with discount* $\gamma < 1$ is $V_\gamma[\pi] = \lim_{T\to\infty} V_{T,\gamma}[\pi](s_0)$. The *infinite horizon average reward* is $V_{avg}[\pi] = \lim_{T\to\infty} \frac{1}{T} V_{T,1}[\pi](s_0)$, where we assume that the limit exists.

Fix an optimality criterion V. Our goal is to find a policy that has a high value. As discussed, we assume we have a restricted set Π of policies, and wish to select a good $\pi \in \Pi$. We assume that $\Pi = \{\pi_\theta \mid \theta \in \mathbb{R}^m\}$ is a set of policies parameterized by $\theta \in \mathbb{R}^m$, and that $\pi_\theta(a \mid s)$ is continuously differentiable in θ for each s, a. As a very simple example, we may have a one-dimensional state, two-action MDP with "sigmoidal" π_θ, such that the probability of choosing action a_0 at state x is $\pi_\theta(a_0 \mid x) = 1/(1 + \exp(-\theta_1 - \theta_2 x))$.

Note that this framework also encompasses cases where our family Π consists of policies that depend only on certain aspects of the state. In particular, in POMDPs, we can restrict attention to policies that depend only on the observables. This restriction results in a subclass of stochastic memory-free policies. By introducing artificial "memory bits" into the process state, we can also define stochastic limited-memory policies. [6]

Each θ has a value $V[\theta] = V[\pi_\theta]$, as specified above. To find the best policy in Π, we can search for the θ that maximizes $V[\theta]$. If we can compute or approximate $V[\theta]$, there are many algorithms that can be used to find a local maximum. Some, such as *Nelder-Mead simplex search* (not to be confused with the simplex algorithm for linear programs), require only the ability to evaluate the function being optimized at any point. If we can compute or estimate $V[\theta]$'s gradient with respect to θ, we can also use a variety of (deterministic or stochastic) *gradient ascent* methods.

---

[1] We write rewards as $R(s)$ rather than $R(s, a)$, and assume a single start state rather than an initial-state distribution, only to simplify exposition; these and several other minor extensions are trivial.

3 Densities and value functions

Most optimization algorithms require some method for computing $V[\theta]$ for any θ (and sometimes also its gradient). In many real-life MDPs, however, doing so exactly is completely infeasible, due to the large or even infinite number of states. Here, we will consider an approach to estimating these quantities, based on a density-based reformulation of the value function expression. A policy π induces a probability distribution over the states at each time t. Letting $\phi^{(0)}$ be the initial distribution (giving probability 1 to s_0), we define the *time slice distributions* via the recurrence:

$$\phi^{(t+1)}(s') = \sum_s \phi^{(t)}(s) \sum_a \pi(a \mid s) P(s' \mid s, a) \quad (1)$$

It is easy to verify that the standard notions of value defined earlier can reformulated in terms of $\phi^{(t)}$; e.g., $V_{T,\gamma}[\pi](s_0) = \sum_{t=0}^T \gamma^t (\phi^{(t)} \cdot R)$, where $\cdot$ is the dot-product operation (equivalently, the expectation of R with respect to $\phi^{(t)}$). Somewhat more subtly, for the case of infinite horizon average reward, we have that $V_{avg}[\pi] = \phi^{(\infty)} \cdot R$, where $\phi^{(\infty)}$ is the limiting distribution of (1), if one exists.

This reformulation gives us an alternative approach to evaluating the value of a policy π_θ: we first compute the time slice densities $\phi^{(t)}$ (or $\phi^{(\infty)}$), and then use them to compute the value. Unfortunately, that modification, by itself, does not resolve the difficulty. Representing and computing probability densities over large or infinite spaces is often no easier than representing and computing value functions. However, several results [3, 5] indicate that representing and computing high-quality *approximate* densities may often be quite feasible. The general approach is an approximate density propagation algorithm, using time-slice distributions in some restricted family Ξ. For example, in continuous spaces, Ξ might be the set of multivariate Gaussians.

The approximate propagation algorithm modifies equation (1) to maintain the time-slice densities in Ξ. More precisely, for a policy π_θ, we can view (1) as defining an operator $\Phi[\theta]$ that takes one distribution in Δ_S and returns another. For our current policy π_{θ_0}, we can rewrite (1) as: $\phi^{(t+1)} = \Phi[\theta_0](\phi^{(t)})$. In most cases, Ξ will not be closed under Φ; approximate density propagation algorithms use some alternative operator $\hat{\Phi}$, with the properties that, for $\phi \in \Xi$: (a) $\hat{\Phi}(\phi)$ is also in Ξ, and (b) $\hat{\Phi}(\phi)$ is (hopefully) close to $\Phi(\phi)$. We use $\hat{\Phi}[\theta]$ to denote the approximation to $\Phi[\theta]$, and $\hat{\phi}^{(t)}$ to denote $(\hat{\Phi}[\theta])^{(t)}(\phi^{(0)})$. If $\hat{\Phi}$ is selected carefully, it is often the case that $\hat{\phi}^{(t)}$ is close to $\phi^{(t)}$. Indeed, a standard contraction analysis for stochastic processes can be used to show:

Proposition 1 *Assume that for all t, $\|\Phi(\hat{\phi}^{(t)}) - \hat{\Phi}(\hat{\phi}^{(t)})\|_1 \leq \epsilon$. Then there exists some constant λ such that for all t, $\|\hat{\phi}^{(t)} - \phi^{(t)}\|_1 \leq \epsilon/\lambda$.*

In some cases, λ might be arbitrarily small, in which case the proposition is meaningless. However, there are many systems where λ is reasonable (and independent of ϵ) [3]. Furthermore, empirical results also show that approximate density propagation can often track the exact time slice distributions quite accurately.

Approximate tracking can now be applied to our planning task. Given an optimality criterion V expressed with $\phi^{(t)}$s, we define an approximation $\hat{V}$ to it by replacing each $\phi^{(t)}$ with $\hat{\phi}^{(t)}$, e.g., $\hat{V}_{T,\gamma}[\pi](s_0) = \sum_{t=0}^T \gamma^t \hat{\phi}^{(t)} \cdot R$. Accuracy guarantees on approximate tracking induce comparable guarantees on the value approximation; from this, guarantees on the performance of a policy $\pi_{\hat{\theta}}$ found by optimizing $\hat{V}$ are also possible:

Proposition 2 *Assume that, for all t, we have that $\|\hat{\phi}^{(t)} - \phi^{(t)}\|_1 \leq \delta$. Then for each fixed T, γ: $|V_{T,\gamma}[\pi](s_0) - \hat{V}_{T,\gamma}[\pi](s_0)| = O(\delta)$.*

Proposition 3 *Let* $\theta^* = \arg\max_\theta V[\theta]$ *and* $\hat{\theta} = \arg\max_\theta \hat{V}[\theta]$. *If* $\max_\theta |V[\theta] - \hat{V}[\theta]| \leq \epsilon$, *then* $V[\theta^*] - V[\hat{\theta}] \leq 2\epsilon$.

4 Differentiating approximate densities

In this section we discuss two very different techniques for maintaining an approximate density $\hat{\phi}^{(t)}$ using an approximate propagation operator $\hat{\Phi}$, and show when and how they can be combined with gradient ascent to perform policy search. In general, we will assume that Ξ is a family of distributions parameterized by $\boldsymbol{\xi} \in \mathbb{R}^\ell$. For example, if Ξ is the set of d-dimensional multivariate Gaussians with diagonal covariance matrices, $\boldsymbol{\xi}$ would be a $2d$-dimensional vector, specifying the mean vector and the covariance matrix's diagonal.

Now, consider the task of doing gradient ascent over the space of policies, using some optimality criterion $\hat{V}$, say $\hat{V}_{T,\gamma}[\theta]$. Differentiating it relative to θ, we get $\nabla_\theta \hat{V}_{T,\gamma}[\theta] = \sum_{t=0}^T \gamma^t \frac{d\hat{\phi}^{(t)}}{d\theta} \cdot R$. To avoid introducing new notation, we also use $\hat{\phi}^{(t)}$ to denote the associated vector of parameters $\boldsymbol{\xi} \in \mathbb{R}^\ell$. These parameters are a function of θ. Hence, the internal gradient term is represented by an $\ell \times m$ Jacobian matrix, with entries representing the derivative of a parameter ξ_i relative to a parameter θ_j. This gradient can be computed using a simple recurrence, based on the chain rule for derivatives:

$$\frac{d\hat{\phi}^{(t+1)}}{d\theta}(\boldsymbol{\theta}_0) = \frac{d}{d\theta}\hat{\Phi}[\boldsymbol{\theta}_0](\hat{\phi}^{(t)}) = \frac{\partial \hat{\Phi}}{\partial \theta}(\boldsymbol{\theta}_0, \hat{\phi}^{(t)}) + \frac{\partial \hat{\Phi}}{\partial \hat{\phi}}(\boldsymbol{\theta}_0, \hat{\phi}^{(t)}) \cdot \frac{d\hat{\phi}^{(t)}}{d\theta}(\boldsymbol{\theta}_0). \quad (2)$$

The first summand (an $\ell \times m$ Jacobian) is the derivative of the transition operator $\hat{\Phi}$ relative to the policy parameters θ. The second is a product of two terms: the derivative of $\hat{\Phi}$ relative to the distribution parameters, and the result of the previous step in the recurrence.

4.1 Deterministic density propagation

Consider a transition operator Φ (for simplicity, we omit the dependence on θ). The idea in this approach is to try to get $\hat{\Phi}(\hat{\phi})$ to be as close as possible to $\Phi(\hat{\phi})$, subject to the constraint that $\hat{\Phi}(\hat{\phi}) \in \Xi$. Specifically, we define a *projection operator* Γ that takes a distribution ψ not in Ξ, and returns a distribution in Ξ which is closest (in some sense) to ψ. We then define $\hat{\Phi}(\hat{\phi}) = \Gamma(\Phi(\hat{\phi}))$. In order to ensure that gradient descent applies in this setting, we need only ensure that Γ and Φ are differentiable functions. Clearly, there are many instantiations of this idea for which this assumption holds. We provide two examples.

Consider a continuous-state process with nonlinear dynamics, where Φ is a mixture of conditional linear Gaussians. We can define Ξ to be the set of multivariate Gaussians. The operator Γ takes a distribution (a mixture of gaussians) ψ and computes its mean and covariance matrix. This can be easily computed from ψ's parameters using simple differentiable algebraic operations.

A very different example is the algorithm of [3] for approximate density propagation in *dynamic Bayesian networks (DBNs)*. A DBN is a structured representation of a stochastic process, that exploits conditional independence properties of the distribution to allow compact representation. In a DBN, the state space is defined as a set of possible assignments $\boldsymbol{x}$ to a set of random variables $X_1, \ldots, X_n$. The transition model $P(\boldsymbol{x}' \mid \boldsymbol{x})$ is described using a Bayesian network fragment over the nodes $\{X_1, \ldots, X_n, X_1', \ldots, X_n'\}$. A node X_i represents $X_i^{(t)}$ and X_i' represents $X_i^{(t+1)}$. The nodes X_i in the network are forced to be *roots* (i.e., have no parents), and are not associated with conditional probability distributions. Each node X_i' is associated with a conditional probability distribution (CPD), which specifies $P(X_i' \mid \text{Parents}(X_i'))$. The transition probability $P(\boldsymbol{X}' \mid \boldsymbol{X})$ is defined as

$\prod_i P(X'_i \mid \text{Parents}(X'_i))$. DBNs support a compact representation of complex transition models in MDPs [2]. We can extend the DBN to encode the behavior of an MDP with a stochastic policy π by introducing a new random variable A representing the action taken at the current time. The parents of A will be those variables in the state on which the action is allowed to depend. The CPD of A (which may be compactly represented with function approximation) is the distribution over actions defined by π for the different contexts.

In discrete DBNs, the number of states grows exponentially with the number of state variables, making an explicit representation of a joint distribution impractical. The algorithm of [3] defines Ξ to be a set of distributions defined compactly as a set of marginals over smaller clusters of variables. In the simplest example, Ξ is the set of distributions where $X_1, \ldots, X_n$ are independent. The parameters ξ defining a distribution in Ξ are the parameters of n multinomials. The projection operator Γ simply marginalizes distributions onto the individual variables, and is differentiable. One useful corollary of [3]'s analysis is that the decay rate of a structured $\hat{\Phi}$ over Ξ can often be much higher than the decay rate of Φ, so that multiple applications of $\hat{\Phi}$ can converge very rapidly to a stationary distribution; this property is very useful when approximating $\phi^{(\infty)}$ to optimize relative to V_{avg}.

4.2 Stochastic density propagation

In many settings, the assumption that we have direct access to Φ is too strong. A weaker assumption is that we have access to a *generative model* — a black box from which we can generate samples with the appropriate distribution; i.e., for any s, a, we can generate samples s' from $P(s' \mid s, a)$. In this case, we use a different approximation scheme, based on [5]. The operator $\hat{\Phi}$ is a stochastic operator. It takes the distribution $\hat{\phi}$, and generates some number of random state samples s_i from it. Then, for each s_i and each action a, we generate a sample s'_i from the transition distribution $P(\cdot \mid s_i, a)$. This sample $\langle s_i, a_i, s'_i \rangle$ is then assigned a weight $w_i = \pi_\theta(a_i \mid s_i)$, to compensate for the fact that not all actions would have been selected by π_θ with equal probability. The resulting set of N samples s'_i weighted by the w_is is given as input to a statistical density estimator, which uses it to estimate a new density $\hat{\phi}'$. We assume that the density estimation procedure is a differentiable function of the weights, often a reasonable assumption.

Clearly, this $\hat{\Phi}$ can be used to compute $\hat{\phi}^{(t)}$ for any t, and thereby approximate π_θ's value. However, the gradient computation for $\hat{\Phi}$ is far from trivial. In particular, to compute the derivative $\partial \hat{\Phi}/\partial \hat{\phi}$, we must consider $\hat{\Phi}$'s behavior for some perturbed $\hat{\phi}_1^{(t)}$ other than the one (say, $\hat{\phi}_0^{(t)}$) to which it was applied originally. In this case, an entirely different set of samples would probably have been generated, possibly leading to a very different density. It is hard to see how one could differentiate the result of this perturbation. We propose an alternative solution based on *importance sampling*. Rather than change the samples, we modify their weights to reflect the change in the probability that they would be generated. Specifically, when fitting $\hat{\phi}_1^{(t+1)}$, we now define a sample $\langle s_i, a_i, s'_i \rangle$'s weight to be

$$w_i(\hat{\phi}_1^{(t)}, \boldsymbol{\theta}) = \frac{\hat{\phi}_1^{(t)}(s_i)\pi_{\boldsymbol{\theta}}(a_i \mid s_i)}{\hat{\phi}_0^{(t)}(s_i)}. \tag{3}$$

We can now compute $\hat{\Phi}$'s derivatives at $(\boldsymbol{\theta}_0, \hat{\phi}_0^{(t)})$ with respect to any of its parameters, as required in (2). Let ζ be the vector of parameters $(\boldsymbol{\theta}, \boldsymbol{\xi})$. Using the chain rule, we have

$$\frac{\partial \hat{\Phi}[\boldsymbol{\theta}](\hat{\phi})}{\partial \zeta} = \frac{\partial \hat{\Phi}[\boldsymbol{\theta}](\hat{\phi})}{\partial w} \cdot \frac{\partial w}{\partial \zeta}.$$

The first term is the derivative of the estimated density relative to the sample weights (an $\ell \times N$ matrix). The second is the derivative of the weights relative to the parameter vector (an $N \times (m + \ell)$ Jacobian), which can easily be computed from (3).

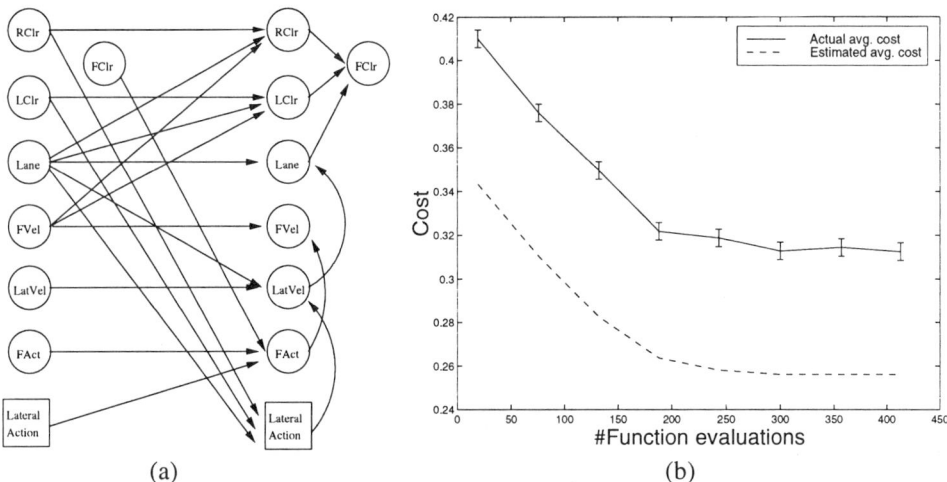

Figure 1: Driving task: (a) DBN model; (b) policy-search/optimization results (with 1 s.e.)

5 Experimental results

We tested our approach in two very different domains. The first is an average-reward DBN-MDP problem (shown in Figure 1(a)), where the task is to find a policy for changing lanes when driving on a moderately busy two-lane highway with a slow lane and a fast lane. The model is based on the BAT DBN of [4], the result of a separate effort to build a good model of driver behavior. For simplicity, we assume that the car's speed is controlled automatically, so we are concerned only with choosing the *Lateral Action – change lane* or *drive straight*. The observables are shown in the figure: *LClr* and *RClr* are the clearance to the next car in each lane (*close*, *medium* or *far*). The agent pays a cost of 1 for each step it is "blocked" by (meaning driving *close* to) the car to its front; it pays a penalty of 0.2 per step for staying in the fast lane. Policies are specified by action probabilities for the 18 possible observation combinations. Since this is a reasonably small number of parameters, we used the simplex search algorithm described earlier to optimize $\hat{V}[\boldsymbol{\theta}]$.

The process mixed quite quickly, so $\hat{\phi}^{(20)}$ was a fairly good approximation to $\hat{\phi}^{(\infty)}$. Ξ used a fully factored representation of the joint distribution except for a single cluster over the three observables. Evaluations are averages of 300 Monte Carlo trials of 400 steps each. Figure 1(b) shows the estimated and actual average rewards, as the policy parameters are evolved over time. The algorithm improved quickly, converging to a very natural policy with the car generally staying in the slow lane, and switching to the fast lane only when necessary to overtake.

In our second experiment, we used the bicycle simulator of [7]. There are 9 actions corresponding to leaning left/center/right and applying negative/zero/positive torque to the handlebar; the six-dimensional state used in [7] includes variables for the bicycle's tilt angle and orientation, and the handlebar's angle. If the bicycle tilt exceeds $\pi/15$, it falls over and enters an absorbing state. We used policy search over the following space: we selected twelve (simple, manually chosen but not fine-tuned) features of each state; actions were chosen with a softmax — the probability of taking action a_i is $\exp(\boldsymbol{x} \cdot \boldsymbol{w}_i)/\sum_j \exp(\boldsymbol{x} \cdot \boldsymbol{w}_j)$. As the problem only comes with a generative model of the complicated, nonlinear, noisy bicycle dynamics, we used the stochastic density propagation version of our algorithm, with (stochastic) gradient ascent. Each distribution in Ξ was a mixture of a singleton point consisting of the absorbing-state, and of a 6-D multivariate Gaussian.

The first task in this domain was to balance reliably on the bicycle. Using a horizon of $T = 200$, discount $\gamma = 0.995$, and 600 s_i samples per density propagation step, this was quickly achieved. Next, trying to learn to ride to a goal[2] 10m in radius and 1000m away, it also succeeded in finding policies that do so reliably. Formal evaluation is difficult, but this is a sufficiently hard problem that even finding a solution can be considered a success. There was also some slight parameter sensitivity (and the best results were obtained only with $\hat{\phi}^{(0)}$ picked/fit with some care, using in part data from earlier and less successful trials, to be "representative" of a fairly good rider's state distribution,) but using this algorithm, we were able to obtain solutions with median riding distances under 1.1km to the goal. This is significantly better than the results of [7] (obtained in the learning rather than planning setting, and using a value-function approximation solution), which reported much larger riding distances to the goal of about 7km, and a single "best-ever" trial of about 1.7km.

6 Conclusions

We have presented two new variants of algorithms for performing direct policy search in the deterministic and stochastic density propagation settings. Our empirical results have also shown these methods working well on two large problems.

Acknowledgements. We warmly thank Kevin Murphy for use of and help with his Bayes Net Toolbox, and Jette Randløv and Preben Alstrøm for use of their bicycle simulator. A. Ng is supported by a Berkeley Fellowship. The work of D. Koller and R. Parr is supported by the ARO-MURI program "Integrated Approach to Intelligent Systems", DARPA contract DACA76-93-C-0025 under subcontract to IET, Inc., ONR contract N66001-97-C-8554 under DARPA's HPKB program, the Sloan Foundation, and the Powell Foundation.

References

[1] L. Baird and A.W. Moore. Gradient descent for general Reinforcement Learning. In *NIPS 11*, 1999.

[2] C. Boutilier, T. Dean, and S. Hanks. Decision theoretic planning: Structural assumptions and computational leverage. *J. Artificial Intelligence Research*, 1999.

[3] X. Boyen and D. Koller. Tractable inference for complex stochastic processes. In *Proc. UAI*, pages 33–42, 1998.

[4] J. Forbes, T. Huang, K. Kanazawa, and S.J. Russell. The BATmobile: Towards a Bayesian automated taxi. In *Proc. IJCAI*, 1995.

[5] D. Koller and R. Fratkina. Using learning for approximation in stochastic processes. In *Proc. ICML*, pages 287–295, 1998.

[6] N. Meuleau, L. Peshkin, K-E. Kim, and L.P. Kaelbling. Learning finite-state controllers for partially observable environments. In *Proc. UAI 15*, 1999.

[7] J. Randløv and P. Alstrøm. Learning to drive a bicycle using reinforcement learning and shaping. In *Proc. ICML*, 1998.

[8] J.K. Williams and S. Singh. Experiments with an algorithm which learns stochastic memoryless policies for POMDPs. In *NIPS 11*, 1999.

[9] R.J. Williams. Simple statistical gradient-following algorithms for connectionist reinforcement learning. *Machine Learning*, 8:229–256, 1992.

---

[2]For these experiments, we found learning could be accomplished faster with the simulator's integration delta-time constant tripled for training. This and "shaping" reinforcements (chosen to reward progress made towards the goal) were both used, and training was with the bike "infinitely distant" from the goal. For this and the balancing experiments, sampling from the fallen/absorbing-state portion of the distributions $\hat{\phi}^{(t)}$ is obviously inefficient use of samples, so all samples were drawn from the non-absorbing state portion (i.e. the Gaussian, also with its tails corresponding to tilt angles greater than $\pi/15$ truncated), and weighted accordingly relative to the absorbing-state portion.

Neural Network Based Model Predictive Control

Stephen Piché	Jim Keeler	Greg Martin
Pavilion Technologies	Pavilion Technologies	Pavilion Technologies
Austin, TX 78758	Austin, TX 78758	Austin, TX 78758
spiche@pav.com	jkeeler@pav.com	gmartin@pav.com

Gene Boe	Doug Johnson	Mark Gerules
Pavilion Technologies	Pavilion Technologies	Pavilion Technologies
Austin, TX 78758	Austin, TX 78758	Austin, TX 78758
gboe@pav.com	djohnson@pav.com	mgerules@pav.com

Abstract

Model Predictive Control (MPC), a control algorithm which uses an optimizer to solve for the optimal control moves over a future time horizon based upon a model of the process, has become a standard control technique in the process industries over the past two decades. In most industrial applications, a linear dynamic model developed using empirical data is used even though the process itself is often nonlinear. Linear models have been used because of the difficulty in developing a generic nonlinear model from empirical data and the computational expense often involved in using nonlinear models. In this paper, we present a generic neural network based technique for developing nonlinear dynamic models from empirical data and show that these models can be efficiently used in a model predictive control framework. This nonlinear MPC based approach has been successfully implemented in a number of industrial applications in the refining, petrochemical, paper and food industries. Performance of the controller on a nonlinear industrial process, a polyethylene reactor, is presented.

1 Introduction

Model predictive control has become the standard technique for supervisory control in the process industries with over 2,000 applications in the refining, petrochemicals, chemicals, pulp and paper, and food processing industries [1]. Model Predictive Control was developed in the late 70's and came into wide-spread use, particularly in the refining industry, in the 80's. The economic benefit of this approach to control has been documented [1,2].

Several factors have contributed to the wide-spread use of MPC in the process industries:

1. *Multivariate Control*: Industrial processes are typically coupled multiple-input multiple-output (MIMO) systems. MIMO control can be implemented using MPC.

2. *Constraints*: Constraints on the inputs and outputs of a process due to safety considerations are common in the process industries. These constraints can be integrated into the control calculation using MPC.

3. *Sampling Period*: Unlike systems in other industries such as automotive or aerospace, the open-loop settling times for many processes is on the order of hours rather than milliseconds. This slow settling time translates to sampling periods on the order of minutes. Because the sampling period is sufficiently long, the complex optimization calculations that are required to implement MPC can be solved at each sampling period.

4. *Commercial Tools:* Commercial tools that facilitate model development and controller implementation have allowed proliferation of MPC in the process industries.

Until recently, industrial applications of MPC have relied upon linear dynamic models even though most processes are nonlinear. MPC based upon linear models is acceptable when the process operates at a single setpoint and the primary use of the controller is the rejection of disturbances. However, many chemical processes, including polymer reactors, do not operate at a single setpoint. These processes are often required to operate at different setpoints depending upon the grade of the product that is to be produced. Because these processes operate over the nonlinear range of the system, linear MPC often results in poor performance. To properly control these processes, a nonlinear model is needed in the MPC algorithm.

This need for nonlinear models in MPC is well recognized. A number of researchers and commercial companies have developed both simulation and industrial applications using a variety of different technologies including both first principles and empirical approaches such as neural networks [3,4]. Although a variety of different models have been developed, they have not been practical for wide scale industrial application. On one hand, nonlinear models built using first principle techniques are expensive to develop and are specific to a process. Conversely, many empirically based nonlinear models are not appropriate for wide scale use because they require costly plant tests in multiple operating regions or because they are too computationally expensive to use in a real-time environment.

This paper presents a nonlinear model that has been developed for wide scale industrial use. It is an empirical model based upon a neural network which is developed using plant test data from a single operating region and historical data from all regions. This is in contrast to the usual approach of using plant test data from multiple regions. This model has been used on over 50 industrial applications and was recognized in a recent survey paper on nonlinear MPC as the most widely used nonlinear MPC controller in the process industries[1].

After providing a brief overview of model predictive control in the next section, we present details on the formulation of the nonlinear model. After describing the model, an industrial application is presented that validates the usefulness of the nonlinear model in an MPC algorithm.

2 Model Predictive Control

Model predictive control is based upon solving an optimization problem for the control actions at each sampling interval. Using MPC, an optimizer computes future control actions that minimize the difference between a model of the process and desired performance over a time horizon (typically the time horizon is greater than the open-loop settling time of the process). For example, given a linear model of process,

$$y_t = -a_1 y_{t-1} - a_2 y_{t-2} + b_1 u_{t-1} + b_2 u_{t-2} \qquad (1)$$

where $u(t)$ represents the input to the process, the optimizer may be used to minimize an objective function at time t,

$$J = \sum_{i=1}^{T}((y_{t+i} - \hat{y}_{t+i})^2 + (u_{t+i} - u_{t+i-1})^2) \qquad (2)$$

where $\hat{y}_t$ is the desired setpoint for the output and T is the length of the time horizon. In addition to minimizing an objective function, the optimizer is used to observe a set of constraints. For example, it is common to place upper and lower bounds on the inputs as well as bounds on the rate of change of the input,

$$U_{upper} \geq u_{t+i} \geq U_{lower} \quad \forall \ 1 \leq i \leq T \qquad (3)$$
$$\Delta U_{upper} \geq u_{t+i} - u_{t+i-1} \geq \Delta U_{lower} \quad \forall \ 1 \leq i \leq T \qquad (4)$$

where U_{upper} and U_{lower} are the upper and lower input bounds while ΔU_{upper} and ΔU_{lower} are the upper and lower rate of change bounds. After the trajectory of future control actions is computed, only the first value in the trajectory is sent as a setpoint to the actuators. The optimization calculation is re-run at each sampling interval using a model which has been updated using feedback.

The form of the model, the objective function, the constraints and the type of optimizer have been active areas of research over the past two decades. A number of excellent survey papers on MPC cover these topics [1,2,4]. As discussed above, we have selected a MIMO nonlinear model which is presented in the next section. Although the objective function given above contains two terms (desired output and input move suppression), the objective function used in our implementation contains thirteen separate terms. (The details of the objective function are beyond the scope of this paper.) Our implementation uses the constraints given above in (3) and (4). Because we use nonlinear models, a nonlinear programming technique must be used to solve the optimization problem. We use LS-GRG which is a reduced gradient solver [5].

3 A Generic and Parsimonious Nonlinear Model

For a nonlinear model to achieve wide-spread industrial use, the model must be parsimonious so that it can be efficiently used in an optimization problem. Furthermore, it must be developed from limited process data. As discussed below, the nonlinear model we use is composed of a combination of a nonlinear steady state model and a linear dynamic model which can be derived from available data. The method of combining the models results in a parsimonious nonlinear model.

3.1 Process data and component models

The quantity and quality of available data ultimately determines the structure of an empirical model. In developing our models, the available data dictated the type of model that could be created. In the process industries, two types of data are available:

1. *Historical data:* The values of the inputs and outputs of most processes are saved at regular intervals to a data base. Furthermore, most processing companies retain historical data associated with their plant for several years.

2. *Plant tests:* Open-loop testing is a well accepted practice for determining the process dynamics for implementation of MPC. However, open-loop testing in multiple operating regions is not well accepted and is impractical in most cases even if it were accepted.

Most practitioners of MPC models have used plant test data and ignored historical data. Practitioners have ignored the historical data in the past because it was difficult to extract and preprocess the data, and build models. Historical data was also viewed as not useful because it was collected in closed-loop and therefore process dynamics could not be extracted in many cases. Using only the plant test data, the practitioner is limited to linear dynamic models.

We chose to use the historical data because it can be used to create nonlinear steady state models of processes that operate at multiple setpoints. Combining the nonlinear steady state model with linear dynamic models from the plant test data provides a generic approach to developing nonlinear models.

To easily facilitate the development of nonlinear models, a suite of tools has been developed for data extraction and preprocessing as well as model training. The nonlinear steady state models,

$$\mathbf{y}_{ss} = NN_{ss}(\mathbf{u}) \qquad (5)$$

are implemented by a feedforward neural network and trained using variants of the backpropagation algorithm [6]. The developer has a great deal of flexibility in determining the architecture of the network including the ability to select which inputs affect which outputs. Finally, an algorithm for specifying bounds on the gain (Jacobian) of the model has recently been implemented [7].

Because of limited plant test data, the dynamic models are restricted to second order models with input time delay,

$$y_t = -a_1 y_{t-1} - a_2 y_{t-2} + b_1 u_{t-d-1} + b_2 u_{t-d-2} \qquad (6)$$

The parameters of (6) are identified by minimizing the squared error between the model and the plant test data. To prevent a biased estimate of the parameters, the identification problem is solved using an optimizer because of the correlation in the model inputs [8]. Tools for selecting the identification regions and viewing the results are provided.

3.2 Combining the nonlinear steady state and dynamic models

A variety of techniques exist for combining nonlinear steady state and linear dynamic models. The dynamic models can be used to either preprocess the inputs or postprocess the outputs of the steady state model. These models, referred to as Hammerstein and Weiner models respectively [8], contain a large number of parameters and are computationally expensive in an optimization problem when the model has many inputs and outputs. These models, when based upon neural networks, also extrapolate poorly.

Gain scheduling is often used to combine nonlinear steady state models and linear dynamic models. Using a neural network steady state model, the gain at the current operating point, u_i,

$$g_i = \frac{\partial y_{ss}}{\partial u}\Big|_{u=u_i} \quad (7)$$

is used to update the gain of the linear dynamic model of (6),

$$\delta y_t = -a_1 \delta y_{t-1} - a_2 \delta y_{t-2} + v_1 \delta u_{t-d-1} + v_2 \delta u_{t-d-2} \quad (8)$$

where

$$v_1 = b_1 g_i \frac{1 + a_1 + a_2}{b_1 + b_2} \quad (9)$$

$$v_2 = b_2 g_i \frac{1 + a_1 + a_2}{b_1 + b_2}. \quad (10)$$

The difference equation is linearized about the point u_i and $y_i = NN(u_i)$, thus, $\delta y = y - y_i$ and $\delta u = u - u_i$. To simplify the equations above, a single-input single-output (SISO) system is used. Gain scheduling results in a parsimonious model that is efficient to use in the MPC optimization problem, however, because this model does not incorporate information about the *gain over the entire trajectory*, its use leads to suboptimal performance in the MPC algorithm.

Our nonlinear model approach remedies this problem. By solving a steady state optimization problem whenever a setpoint change is made, it is possible to compute the final steady state values of the inputs, u_f. Given the final steady state input values, the gain associated with the final steady state can be computed. For a SISO system, this gain is given by

$$g_f = \frac{\partial y_{ss}}{\partial u}\Big|_{u=u_f}. \quad (11)$$

Using the initial and final gain associated with a setpoint change, the gain structure over the entire trajectory can be approximated. This two point gain scheduling overcomes the limitations of regular gain scheduling in MPC algorithms.

Combining the initial and final gain with the linear dynamic model, a quadratic difference equation is derived for the overall nonlinear model,

$$\delta y_t = -a_1 \delta y_{t-1} - a_2 \delta y_{t-2} + v_1 \delta u_{t-d-1} + v_2 \delta u_{t-d-2} + w_1 \delta u_{t-d-1}^2 + w_2 \delta u_{t-d-2}^2 \quad (12)$$

where

$$w_1 = b_1 \frac{(1 + a_1 + a_2)(g_f - g_i)}{(b_1 + b_2)(u_f - u_i)} \quad (13)$$

$$w_2 = b_2 \frac{(1 + a_1 + a_2)(g_f - g_i)}{(b_1 + b_2)(u_f - u_i)} \quad (14)$$

and v_1 and v_2 are given by (9) and (10). Use of the gain at the final steady state introduces the last two terms of (12). This model allows the incorporation of gain information over the entire trajectory in the MPC algorithm. The gain at of (12) at u_i is g_i while at u_f it is g_f. Between the two points, the gain is a linear combination of g_i and g_f. For processes with large gain changes, such as polymer reactors, this can lead to dramatic improvements in MPC controller performance.

An additional benefit of using the model of (12) is that we allow the user to bound the initial and final gain and thus control the amount of nonlinearity used in the model. For practitioners who are use to implementing MPC with linear models, using gain bounds allows them to transition from linear to nonlinear models. This ability to control the amount of nonlinearity used in the model has been important for acceptance of this new model in many applications. Finally, bounding the gains can be used to guarantee extrapolation performance of the model.

The nonlinear model of (12) fits the criteria needed in order to allow wide spread use of nonlinear models for MPC. The model is based upon readily available data and has a parsimonious representation allowing models with many inputs and outputs to be efficiently used in the optimizer. Furthermore, it addresses the primary nonlinearity found in processes, that being the significant change in gain over the operating region.

4 Polymer Application

The nonlinear model described above has been used in a wide-variety of industrial applications including Kamyr digesters (pulp and paper), milk evaporators and dryers (food processing), toluene diamine purification (chemicals), polyethylene and polypropylene reactors (polymers) and a fluid catalytic cracking unit (refining). Highlights of one such application are given below.

A MPC controller that uses the model described above has been applied to a Gas Phase High Density Polyethylene reactor at Chevron Chemical Co. in Cedar Bayou, Texas [9]. The process produces homopolymer and copolymer grades over a wide range of melt indices. It's average production rate per year is 230,000 tons.

Optimal control of the process is difficult to achieve because the reactor is a highly coupled nonlinear MIMO system (7 inputs and 5 outputs). For example, a number of input-output pairs exhibit gains that varying by a factor of 10 or more over the operating region. In addition, grade changes are made every few days. During these transitions nonprime polymer is produced. Prior to commissioning these controllers, these transitions took several hours to complete. Linear and gain scheduling based controller have been tried on similar reactors and have delivered limited success.

The nonlinear model was constructed using only historical data. The nonlinear steady state model was trained upon historical data from a two year period. This data contained examples of all the products produced by the reactor. Accurate dynamic models were derived both from historical data and knowledge of the process, thus, no step tests were conducted on the process.

Excellent performance of this controller has been reported [9]. A two-fold decrease in the variance of the primary quality variable (melt index) has been achieved. In addition, the average transition time has been decreased by 50%. Unscheduled shutdowns which occurred previously have been eliminated. Finally, the controller, which has been on-line for two years, has gained high operator acceptance.

5 Conclusion

A generic and parsimonious nonlinear model which can be used in an MPC algorithm has been presented. The model is created by combining a nonlinear steady state model with a linear dynamic models. They are combined using a two-point gain scheduling technique. This nonlinear model has been used for control of a nonlinear MIMO polyethylene reactor at Chevron Chemical Co. The controller has also been used in 50 other applications in the refining, chemicals, food processing and pulp and paper industries.

References

[1] Qin, S.J. & Badgwell, T.A. (1997) An overview of industrial model predictive control technology. In J. Kantor, C. Garcia and B. Carnahan (eds.), *Chemical Process Control - AIChE Symposium Series*, pp. 232-256. NY: AIChE.

[2] Seborg, D.E. (1999) A perspective on advanced strategies for Process Control (Revisited). to appear in *Proc. of European Control Conf.* Karlsruhe, Germany.

[3] Qin, S.J. & Badgwell, T.A. (1998) An overview of nonlinear model predictive control applications. *Proc. IFAC Workshop on Nonlinear Model Predictive Control - Assessment and Future Directions*, Ascona, Switzerland, June 3-5.

[4] Meadow, E.S. & Rawlings, J.B. (1997) Model predictive control. In M. Hesnon and D. Seborg (eds.), *Nonlinear Model Predictive Control*, pp. 233-310. NJ: Prentice Hall.

[5] Nash, S. & Sofer, A. (1996) *Linear and Nonlinear Programming*. NY: McGraw-Hill.

[6] Rumelhart D.E, Hinton G.E. & Williams, R.J. (1986) Learning internal representations by error propagation. In D. Rumelhart and J. McClelland (eds.), *Parallel Distributed Processing*, pp. 318-362. Cambridge, MA: MIT Press.

[7] Hartman, E. (2000) Training feedforward neural networks with gain constraints. To appear in *Neural Computation*.

[8] Ljung, L. (1987) *System Identification*. NJ: Prentice Hall.

[9] Goff S., Johnson D. & Gerules, M. (1998) Nonlinear control and optimization of a high density polyethylene reactor. *Proc. Chemical Engineering Expo*, Houston, June.

Reinforcement Learning Using Approximate Belief States

Andrés Rodríguez [*]
Artificial Intelligence Center
SRI International
333 Ravenswood Avenue, Menlo Park, CA 94025
rodriguez@ai.sri.com

Ronald Parr, Daphne Koller
Computer Science Department
Stanford University
Stanford, CA 94305
{*parr,koller*}@cs.stanford.edu

Abstract

The problem of developing good policies for partially observable Markov decision problems (POMDPs) remains one of the most challenging areas of research in stochastic planning. One line of research in this area involves the use of reinforcement learning with belief states, probability distributions over the underlying model states. This is a promising method for small problems, but its application is limited by the intractability of computing or representing a full belief state for large problems. Recent work shows that, in many settings, we can maintain an *approximate belief state*, which is fairly close to the true belief state. In particular, great success has been shown with approximate belief states that marginalize out correlations between state variables. In this paper, we investigate two methods of full belief state reinforcement learning and one novel method for reinforcement learning using factored approximate belief states. We compare the performance of these algorithms on several well-known problem from the literature. Our results demonstrate the importance of approximate belief state representations for large problems.

1 Introduction

The Markov Decision Processes (MDP) framework [2] is a good way of mathematically formalizing a large class of sequential decision problems involving an agent that is interacting with an environment. Generally, an MDP is defined in such a way that the agent has complete knowledge of the underlying state of the environment. While this formulation poses very challenging research problems, it is still a very optimistic modeling assumption that is rarely realized in the real world. Most of the time, an agent must face uncertainty or incompleteness in the information available to it. An extension of this formalism that generalizes MDPs to deal with this uncertainty is given by partially observable Markov Decision Processes (POMDPs) [1, 11] which are the focus of this paper.

Solving a POMDP means finding an optimal behavior policy π^*, that maps from the agent's available knowledge of the environment, its *belief state*, to actions. This is usually done through a function, V, that assigns values to belief states. In the fully observable (MDP)

---
[*]The work presented in this paper was done while the first author was at Stanford University.

case, a value function can be computed efficiently for reasonably sized domains. The situation is somewhat different for POMDPs, where finding the optimal policy is PSPACE-hard in the number of underlying states [6]. To date, the best known exact algorithms to solve POMDPs are taxed by problems with a few dozen states [5].

There are several general approaches to approximating POMDP value functions using reinforcement learning methods and space does not permit a full review of them. The approach upon which we focus is the use of a belief state as a probability distribution over underlying model states. This is in contrast to methods that manipulate augmented state descriptions with finite memory [9, 12] and methods that work directly with observations [8].

The main advantage of a probability distribution is that it summarizes all of the information necessary to make optimal decisions [1]. The main disadvantages are that a model is required to compute a belief state, and that the task of representing and updating belief states in large problems is itself very difficult. In this paper, we do not address the problem of obtaining a model; our focus is on the the most effective way of using a model. Even with a known model, reinforcement learning techniques can be quite competitive with exact methods for solving POMDPs [10]. Hence, we focus on extending the model-based reinforcement learning approach to larger problems through the use of *approximate belief states*. There are risks to such an approach: inaccuracies introduced by belief state approximation could give an agent a hopelessly inaccurate perception of its relationship to the environment.

Recent work [4], however, presents an approximate tracking approach, and provides theoretical guarantees that the result of this process cannot stray too far from the exact belief state. In this approach, rather than maintaining an exact belief state, which is infeasible in most realistically large problems, we maintain an approximate belief state, usually from some restricted class of distributions. As the approximate belief state is updated (due to actions and observations), it is continuously projected back down into this restricted class. Specifically, we use *decomposed* belief states, where certain correlations between state variables are ignored.

In this paper we present empirical results comparing three approaches to belief state reinforcement learning. The most direct approach is the use of a neural network with one input for each element of the full belief state. The second is the SPOVA method [10], which uses a function approximator designed for POMDPs and the third is the use of a neural network with an approximate belief state as input. We present results for several well-known problems in the POMDP literature, demonstrating that while belief state approximation is ill-suited for some problems, it is an effective means of attacking large problems.

2 Basic Framework and Algorithms

A POMDP is defined as a tuple $< S, A, O, \mathcal{T}, \mathcal{R}, \mathcal{O} >$ of three sets and three functions. S is a set of *states*, A is a set of *actions* and O is a set of *observations*. The *transition* function $\mathcal{T} : S \times A \rightarrow \Pi(S)$ specifies how the actions affect the state of the world. It can be viewed as $\mathcal{T}(s_i, a, s_j) = P(s_j|a, s_i)$, the probability that the agent reaches state s_j if it currently is in state s_i and takes action a. The *reward* function $\mathcal{R} : S \times A \rightarrow \mathbb{R}$ determines the immediate reward received by the agent The *observation* model $\mathcal{O} : S \times A \rightarrow \Pi(O)$ determines what the agent perceives, depending on the environment state and the action taken. $\mathcal{O}(s, a, o) = P(o|a, s)$ is the probability that the agent observes o when it is in state s, having taken the action a.

2.1 POMDP belief states

A *belief state*, b, is defined as a probability distribution over all states $s \in S$, where $b(s)$, represents probability that the environment is in state s. After taking action a and observing o, the belief state is updated using Bayes rule:

$$b'(s') = P(s' \mid a, o, b) = \frac{\mathcal{O}(s', a, o) \sum_{s_i \in S} \mathcal{T}(s_i, a, s') b(s_i)}{\sum_{s_j \in S} \mathcal{O}(s_j, a, o) \sum_{s_i \in S} \mathcal{T}(s_i, a, s_j) b(s_i)}$$

The size of an exact belief state is equal to the number of states in the model. For large problems, maintaining and manipulating an exact belief state can be problematic even if the the transition model has a compact representation [4]. For example, suppose the state space is described via a set of random variables $\mathbf{X} = \{X_1, \ldots, X_n\}$, where each X_i takes on values in some finite domain $\text{Val}(X_i)$, a particular s defines a value $x_i \in \text{Val}(X_i)$ for each variable X_i. The full belief state representation will be exponential in n. We use the approximation method analyzed by Boyen and Koller [4], where the variables are partitioned into a set of disjoint clusters $\mathbf{C}_1 \ldots \mathbf{C}_k$ and belief functions, $b_1 \ldots b_k$ are maintained over the variables in each cluster. At each time step, we compute the exact belief state, then compute the individual belief functions by marginalizing out inter-cluster correlations. For some assignment, $\mathbf{c}_i$, to variables in $\mathbf{C}_i$, we obtain $b_i(\mathbf{c}_i) = \sum_{\mathbf{y} \not\in \mathbf{c}_i} P(\mathbf{c}_i, \mathbf{y})$. An approximation of the original, full belief state is then reconstructed as $b(s) = \prod_{i=1}^{k} b_i(\mathbf{c}_i)$.

By representing the belief state as a product of marginal probabilities, we are projecting the belief state into a reduced space. While a full belief state representation for n state variables would be exponential in n, the size of decomposed belief state representation is exponential in the size of the largest cluster and additive in the number of clusters. For processes that mix rapidly enough, the errors introduced by approximation will stay bounded over time [4]. As discussed by Boyen and Koller [4], this type of decomposed belief state is particularly suitable for processes that can themselves be factored and represented as a *dynamic Bayesian network* [3]. In such cases we can avoid ever representing an exponentially sized belief state. However, the approach is fully general, and can be applied in any setting where the state is defined as an assignment of values to some set of state variables.

2.2 Value functions and policies for POMDPs

If one thinks of a POMDP as an MDP defined over belief states, then the well-known fixed point equations for MDPs still hold. Specifically,

$$V^*(b) = \max_a \left[\sum_{s \in S} b(s) \mathcal{R}(s, a) + \gamma \sum_{o \in O} P(o|a, b) V^*(b') \right]$$

where γ is the discount factor and b' (defined above) is the next belief state. The optimal policy is determined by the maximizing action for each belief state. In principle, we could use Q-learning or value iteration directly to solve POMDPs. The main difficulty lies in the fact that there are uncountably many belief states, making a tabular representation of the value function impossible.

Exact methods for POMDPs use the fact that finite horizon value functions are piecewise-linear and convex [11], ensuring a finite representation. While finite, this representation can grow exponentially with the horizon, making exact approaches impractical in most settings. Function approximation is an attractive alternative to exact methods. We implement function approximation using a set of parameterized Q-functions, where $Q_a(b, \mathbf{W}_a)$ is the reward-to-go for taking action a in belief state b. A value function is reconstructed from the Q-functions as $V(b) = \max_a(Q_a(b, \mathbf{W}_a))$, and the update rule for $\mathbf{W}_a$ when a transition from state b to b' under action a with reward R is:

$$\Delta \mathbf{W}_a = \alpha(\gamma V(b') + r - Q_a(b, \mathbf{W}_a))\nabla_{\mathbf{W}_a} Q_a(b, \mathbf{W}_a)$$

2.3 Function approximation architectures

We consider two types of function approximators. The first is a two-layer feedforward neural network with sigmoidal internal units and a linear outermost layer. We used one network for each Q function. For full belief state reinforcement learning, we used networks with $|\mathcal{S}|$ inputs (one for each component of the belief state) and $\sqrt{|\mathcal{S}|}$ hidden nodes. For approximate belief state reinforcement learning, we used networks with one input for each assignment to the variables in each cluster. If we had two clusters, for example, each with 3 binary variables, then our Q networks would each have $2^3 + 2^3 = 16$ inputs. We kept the number of hidden nodes for each network as the square root of the number of inputs.

Our second function approximator is SPOVA [10], which is a soft max function designed to exploit the piecewise-linear structure of POMDP value functions. A SPOVA Q function maintains a set of weight vectors $\mathbf{w}_{a1} \ldots \mathbf{w}_{ai}$, and is evaluated as:

$$Q_a(b) = \sqrt[k]{\sum_i (b \cdot \mathbf{W}_{a_i})^k}$$

In practice, a small value of k (usually 1.2) is adopted at the start of learning, making the function very smooth. This is increased during learning until SPOVA closely approximates a PWLC function of b (usually $k = 8$). We maintained one SPOVA Q function for each action and assigned $\sqrt{|\mathcal{S}|}$ vectors to each function. This gave $O(|\mathcal{A}||\mathcal{S}|\sqrt{|\mathcal{S}|})$ parameters to both SPOVA and the full belief state neural network.

3 Empirical Results

We present results on several problems from the POMDP literature and present an extension to a known machine repair problem that is designed to highlight the effects of approximate belief states. Our results are presented in the form of performance graphs, where the value of the current policy is obtained by taking a snapshot of the value function and measuring the discounted sum of reward obtained by the resulting policy in simulation. We use "NN" to refer to the neural network trained reinforcement learner trained with the full belief state and the term "Decomposed NN" to refer to the neural network trained with an approximate belief which is decomposed as a product of marginals. We used a simple exploration strategy, starting with a 0.1 probability of acting randomly, which decreased linearly to 0.01.

Due to space limitations, we are not able to describe each model in detail. However, we used publicly available model description files from [5].[1] Table 3.4 shows the running times of the different methods. These are generally much lower than what would be required to solve these problems using exact methods.

3.1 Grid Worlds

We begin by considering two grid worlds, a 4×3 world from [10] and a 60-state world from [7]. The 4×3 world contains only 11 states and does not have a natural decomposition into state variables, so we compared SPOVA only with the full belief state neural network.

---
[1] See http://www.cs.brown.edu/research/ai/pomdp/index.html. Note that this file format specifies a starting distribution for each problem and our results are reported with respect to this starting distribution.

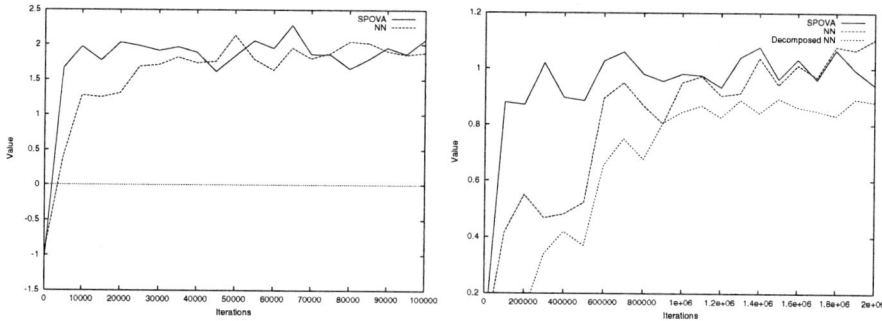

Figure 1: a) 3 × 4 Grid World, b) 60-state maze

The experimental results, which are averaged over 25 training runs and 100 simulations per policy snapshot, are presented in Figure 1a. They show that SPOVA learns faster than the neural network, but that the network does eventually catch up.

The 60-state robot navigation problem [7] was amenable to a decomposed belief state approximation since its underlying state space comes from the product of 15 robot positions and 4 robot orientations. We decomposed the belief state with two clusters, one containing a position state variable and the other containing an orientation state variable. Figure 1b shows results in which SPOVA again dominates. The decomposed NN has trouble with this problem because the effects of position and orientation on the value function are not easily decoupled, i.e., the effect of orientation on value is highly state-dependent. This meant that the decomposed NN was forced to learn a much more complicated function of its inputs than the function learned by the network using the full belief state.

3.2 Aircraft Identification

Aircraft identification is another problem studied in Cassandra's thesis. It includes sensing actions for identifying incoming aircraft and actions for attacking threatening aircraft. Attacks against friendly aircraft are penalized, as are failures to intercept hostile aircraft. This is a challenging problem because there is tension in deciding between the various sensors. Better sensors tend to make the base more visible to hostile aircraft, while more stealthy sensors are less accurate. The sensors give information about both the aircraft's type and distance from the base.

The state space of this problem is comprised of three main components. `aircraft type` — either the aircraft is a `friend` or it is a `foe`; `distance` — how far the aircraft is currently from the base discretized into an adjustable number, d, of distinct distances; `visibility` — a measure of how visible the base is to the approaching aircraft, which is discretized into 5 levels.

We chose $d = 10$, gaving this problem 104 states. The problem has a natural decomposition into state variables for aircraft type, distance and base visibility. The results for the three algorithms are shown in Figure 2(a). This is the first problem where we start to see an advantage from decomposing the belief state. For the decomposed NN, we used three separate clusters, one for each variable, which meant that the network had only 17 inputs. Not only did the simpler network learn faster, but it learned a better policy overall. We believe that this illustrates an important point: even though SPOVA and the full belief state neural network may be more expressive than the decomposed NN, the decomposed NN is able to search the space of functions it can represent much more efficiently due to the reduced number of parameters.

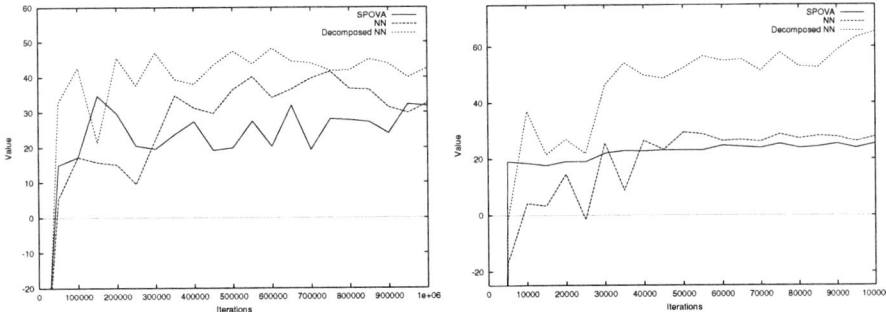

Figure 2: a) Aircraft Identification, b) Machine Maintenance

3.3 Machine Maintenance

Our last problem was the machine maintenance problem from Cassandra's database. The problem assumes that there is a machine with a certain number of components. The quality of the parts produced by the machine is determined by the condition of the components. Each component can be in one of four conditions: good — the component is in good condition; fair — the component has some amount of wear, and would benefit from some maintenance; bad — the part is very worn and could use repairs; broken — the part is broken and must be replaced. The status of the components is observable only if the machine is completely disassembled.

Figure 2(b) shows performance results for this problem for the 4 component version of this problem. At 256 states, it was at the maximum size for which a full belief state approach was manageable. However, the belief state for this problem decomposes naturally into clusters describing the status of each machine, creating a decomposed belief state with just four components. The graph shows the dominance of this this simple decomposition approach. We believe that this problem clearly demonstrates the advantage of belief state decomposition: The decomposed NN learns a function of 16 inputs in fraction of the time it takes for the full net or SPOVA to learn a lower-quality function of 256 inputs.

3.4 Running Times

The table below shows the running times for the different problems presented above. These are generally much less than what would be required to solve these problems exactly. The full NN and SPOVA are roughly comparable, but the decomposed neural network is considerably faster. We did not exploit any problem structure in our approximate belief state computation, so the time spent computing belief states is actually *larger* for the decomposed NN. The savings comes from the the reduction in the number of parameters used, which reduced the number of partial derivatives computed. We expect the savings to be significantly more substantial for processes represented in a factored way [3], as the approximate belief state propagation algorithm can also take advantage of this additional structure.

4 Concluding Remarks

We have a proposed a new approach to belief state reinforcement learning through the use of approximate belief states. Using well-known examples from the POMDP literature, we have compared approximate belief state reinforcement learning with two other methods

Problem	SPOVA	NN	Decomposed NN
3x4	19.1 s	13.0 s	
Hallway	32.8 min	47.1 min	3.2 min
Aircraft ID	38.3 min	49.9 min	4.4 min
Machine M.	2.5 h	2.6 h	4.7 min

Table 1: Run times (in seconds, minutes or hours) for the different algorithms

that use exact belief states. Our results demonstrate that, while approximate belief states may not be ideal for tightly coupled problem features, such as the position and orientation of a robot, they are a natural and effective means of addressing some large problems. Even for the medium-sized problems we showed here, approximate belief state reinforcement learning can outperform full belief state reinforcement learning using fewer trials and much less CPU time. For many problems, exact belief state methods will simply be impractical and approximate belief states will provide a tractable alternative.

Acknowledgements

This work was supported by the ARO under the MURI program "Integrated Approach to Intelligent Systems," by ONR contract N66001-97-C-8554 under DARPA's HPKB program, and by the generosity of the Powell Foundation and the Sloan Foundation.

References

[1] K. J. Astrom. Optimal control of Markov decision processes with incomplete state estimation. *J. Math. Anal. Applic.*, 10:174–205, 1965.

[2] R.E. Bellman. *Dynamic Programming*. Princeton University Press, 1957.

[3] C. Boutilier, T. Dean, and S. Hanks. Decision theoretic planning: Structural assumptions and computational leverage. *Journal of Artificial Intelligence Research*, 1999.

[4] X. Boyen and D. Koller. Tractable inference for complex stochastic processes. In *Proc. UAI*, 1998.

[5] A. Cassandra. *Exact and approximate Algorithms for partially observable Markov Decision Problems*. PhD thesis, Computer Science Dept., Brown Univ., 1998.

[6] M. Littman. *Algorithms for Sequential Decision Making*. PhD thesis, Computer Science Dept., Brown Univ., 1996.

[7] M. Littman, A. Cassandra, and L.P. Kaelbling. Learning policies for partially observable environments: Scaling up. In *Proc. ICML*, pages 362–370, 1996.

[8] J. Loch and S. Singh. Using eligibility traces to find the best memoryless policy in partially observable markov decision processes. In *Proc. ICML*. Morgan Kaufmann, 1998.

[9] Andrew R. McCallum. Overcoming incomplete perception with utile distinction memory. In *Proc. ICML*, pages 190–196, 1993.

[10] Ronald Parr and Stuart Russell. Approximating optimal policies for partially observable stochastic domains. In *Proc. IJCAI*, 1995.

[11] R. D. Smallwood and E. J. Sondik. The optimal control of partially observable Markov processes over a finite horizon. *Operations Research*, 21:1071–1088, 1973.

[12] M. Wiering and J. Schmidhuber. HQ-learning: Discovering Markovian subgoals for non-Markovian reinforcement learning. Technical report, Istituo Dalle Molle di Studi sull'Intelligenza Artificiale, 1996.

Coastal Navigation with Mobile Robots

Nicholas Roy and Sebastian Thrun
School of Computer Science
Carnegie Mellon University
Pittsburgh, PA 15213
{nicholas.roy|sebastian.thrun}@cs.cmu.edu

Abstract

The problem that we address in this paper is how a mobile robot can plan in order to arrive at its goal with minimum uncertainty. Traditional motion planning algorithms often assume that a mobile robot can track its position reliably, however, in real world situations, reliable localization may not always be feasible. Partially Observable Markov Decision Processes (POMDPs) provide one way to maximize the certainty of reaching the goal state, but at the cost of computational intractability for large state spaces.

The method we propose explicitly models the uncertainty of the robot's position as a state variable, and generates trajectories through the augmented pose-uncertainty space. By minimizing the positional uncertainty at the goal, the robot reduces the likelihood it becomes lost. We demonstrate experimentally that coastal navigation reduces the uncertainty at the goal, especially with degraded localization.

1 Introduction

For an operational mobile robot, it is essential to prevent becoming lost. Early motion planners assumed that a robot would never be lost – that a robot could always know its position via dead reckoning without error [7]. This assumption proved to be untenable due to the small and inevitable inconsistencies in actual robot motion; robots that rely solely on dead reckoning for their position estimates lose their position quickly. Mobile robots now perform position tracking using a combination of sensor data and odometry [2, 10, 5].

However, the robot's ability to track its position can vary considerably with the robot's position in the environment. Some parts of the environment may lack good features for localization [11]. Other parts of the environment can have a large number of dynamic features (for example, people) that can mislead the localization system. Motion planners rarely, if ever, take the robot's position tracking *ability* into consideration. As the robot's localization suffers, the likelihood that the robot becomes lost increases, and as a consequence, the robot is less likely to complete the given trajectory.

Most localization systems therefore compensate by adding environment-specific knowledge to the localization system, or by adding additional sensing capabilities to the robot, to guarantee that the robot can complete every possible path. In general, however, such alterations to the position tracking abilities of the robot have limitations, and an alternative scheme must be used to ensure that the robot can navigate with maximum reliability. The conventional planners represent one end of a spectrum of approaches (figure 1), in that a plan can be computed easily, but at the cost of not modelling localization performance.

At opposite end of the spectrum is the Partially Observable Markov Decision Process

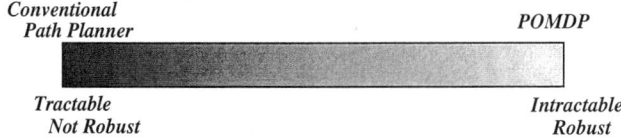

Figure 1: The continuum of possible approaches to the motion planning, from the robust but intractable POMDP, to the potentially failure-prone but real-time conventional planners. Coastal navigation lies in the middle of this spectrum.

(POMDP). POMDPs in a sense are the brass ring of planning with uncertainty; a POMDP policy will make exactly the right kind of compromise between conventional optimality considerations and certainty of achieving the goal state. Many people have examined the use of POMDPs for mobile robot navigation [5, 6, 8]. However, computing a POMDP solution is computationally intractable (PSPACE-hard) for large state systems – a mobile robot operating in the real world often has millions of possible states. As a result, many of the mobile robot POMDP solutions have made simplifying assumptions about the world in order to reduce the state space size. Many of these assumptions do not scale to larger environments or robots. In contrast, our hypothesis is that only a small number of the dimensions of the uncertainty matter, and that we can augment the state with these dimensions to approximate a solution to the POMDP.

The coastal navigation model developed in this paper represents a tradeoff between robust trajectories and computational tractability, and is inspired by traditional navigation of ships. Ships often use the coasts of continents for navigation in the absence of better tools such as GPS, since being close to the land allows sailors to determine with high accuracy where they are. The success of this method results from coast lines containing enough information in their structure for accurate localization. By navigating sufficiently close to areas of the map that have high information content, the likelihood of getting lost can be minimized.

2 Modelling Uncertainty

The problem that we address in this paper is how a mobile robot can plan in order to arrive at its goal with minimum uncertainty. Throughout this discussion, we will be assuming a known map of the environment [9]. The position, $\mathbf{x}$, of the robot is given as the location (x, y) and direction θ, defined over a space $\mathbf{X} = (X, Y, \Theta)$. Our localization method is a grid-based implementation of Markov localization [3, 5]. This method represents the robot's belief in its current position using a 3-dimensional grid over $\mathbf{X} = (X, Y, \Theta)$, which allows for a discrete approximation of arbitrary probability distributions. The probability that the robot has a particular pose $\mathbf{x}$ is given by the probability $p(\mathbf{x})$.

State Augmentation We can extend the state of the robot from the 3-dimensional pose space to an augmented pose-uncertainty space. We can represent the uncertainty of the robot's positional distribution as the entropy,

$$H(P_\mathbf{X}) = - \int_\mathbf{X} p(\mathbf{x}) \log(p(\mathbf{x})) \, d\mathbf{x} \tag{1}$$

We therefore represent the state space of the robot as the tuple

$$\begin{aligned} \mathbf{S} &= \langle x, y, \theta, H(x, y, \theta) \rangle \\ &= \langle \mathbf{x}, H(\mathbf{x}) \rangle \end{aligned}$$

State Transitions In order to construct a plan between two points in the environment, we need to be able to represent the effect of the robot's sensing and moving actions. The implementation of Markov localization provides the following equations for the tracking the robot's pose from $\mathbf{x}$ to $\mathbf{x}'$:

$$p(\mathbf{x}'|u) = \int_{\mathbf{x}} p(\mathbf{x}'|\mathbf{x}, u)p(\mathbf{x})d\mathbf{x} \qquad (2)$$

$$p(\mathbf{x}'|\mathbf{z}) = \alpha p(\mathbf{z}|\mathbf{x})p(\mathbf{x}) \qquad (3)$$

These equations are taken from [3, 12], where equation (2) gives the prediction phase of localization (after motion u), and equation (3) gives the update phase of localization (after receiving observation $\mathbf{z}$). α is a normalizing constant. We extend these equations to the fourth dimension as follows:

$$p(\mathbf{s}|u) = \langle p(\mathbf{x}|u), H(p(\mathbf{x}|u))\rangle \qquad (4)$$

$$p(\mathbf{s}|\mathbf{z}) = \langle p(\mathbf{x}|\mathbf{z}), H(p(\mathbf{x}|\mathbf{z}))\rangle \qquad (5)$$

3 Planning

Equations (4) and (5) provide a mechanism for tracking the robot's state, and in fact contain redundant information, since the extra state variable $H(\mathbf{x})$ is also contained in the probability distribution $p(\mathbf{x})$. However, in order to make the planning problem tractable, we cannot in fact maintain the probabilistic sensing model. To do so would put the planning problem firmly in the domain of POMDPs, with the associated computational intractability. Instead, we make a simplifying assumption, that is, that the positional probability distribution of the robot can be represented at all times by a Gaussian centered at the mean $\mathbf{x}$. This allows us to approximate the positional distribution with a single statistic, the entropy. In POMDP terms, we using the assumption of Gaussian distributions to compress the belief space to a single dimension. We can now represent the positional probability distribution completely with the vector $\mathbf{s}$, since the width of the Gaussian is represented by the entropy $H(\mathbf{x})$.

More importantly, the simplifying assumption allows us to track the state of the robot deterministically. Although the state transitions are stochastic (as in equation (4)), the observations are not. At any point in time, the sensors identify the true state of the system, with some certainty given by $H(p(\mathbf{x}|\mathbf{z}))$. This allows us to compress the state transitions into a single rule:

$$p(\mathbf{s}|u) = \langle p(\mathbf{x}|u), H(p(\mathbf{x}|u, \mathbf{z}))\rangle \qquad (6)$$

The final position of the robot depends only on the motion command u and can be identified by sensing $\mathbf{z}$. However, the uncertainty of the pose, $H(p(\mathbf{x}|u, \mathbf{z}))$, is a function not only of the motion command but also the sensing. The simplifying assumption of Gaussian models is in general untenable for localization; however, we shall see that this assumption is sufficient for the purpose of motion planning.

One final modification must be made to the state transition rule. In a perfect world, it would be possible to predict exactly what observation would be made. However, it is exactly the stochastic and noisy nature of real sensors that generates planning difficulty, yet the update rule (6) assumes that it is possible to predict measurement $\mathbf{z}$ at pose $\mathbf{x}$. Deterministic prediction is not possible; however, it is possible to compute probabilities for sensor measurements, and thus generate an *expected value* for the entropy based on the probability distribution of observations $\mathbf{Z}$, which leads to the final state transition rule:

$$p(\mathbf{s}|u) = \langle p(\mathbf{x}|u), E_{\mathbf{Z}}[H(p(\mathbf{x}|u, \mathbf{z}))]\rangle \qquad (7)$$

where $E_{\mathbf{Z}}[H(p(\mathbf{x}|u, \mathbf{z}))]$ represents the expected value of the entropy of the pose distribution over the space of possible sensor measurements.

With the transition rule in equation (7), we can now compute the transition probabilities for any particular state using a model of the robot's motion, a model of the robot's sensor and a map of the environment. The probability $p(\mathbf{x}|u)$ is given by a model of the robot's motion, and can be easily precomputed for each action u. The expectation term $E_{\mathbf{Z}}[H]$

can also be precomputed for each possible state s. The precomputation of these transition probabilities is very time-intensive, because it requires simulating sensing at each state in the environment, and then computing the posterior distribution. However, as the precomputation is a one-time operation for the environment and robot, planning itself can be an online operation and is (in the limit) unaffected by the speed of computing the transition probabilities.

3.1 Computing Trajectories

With the state update rule given in equation (7), we can now compute the optimal trajectory to a particular goal. We would in fact like to compute not just the optimal trajectory from the current robot position, but the optimal action from any position in the world. If the robot should deviate from the expected trajectory for any reason (such as error in the motion, or due to low-level control constraints), interests of efficiency suggest precomputing actions for continuing to the goal, rather than continually replanning as these contingencies arise. Note that the motion planning problem as we have now phrased it can be viewed as the problem of computing the optimal policy for a given problem. The Markovian, stochastic nature of the transitions, coupled with the need to compute the optimal policy for all states, suggests a value iteration approach.

Value iteration attempts to find the policy that maximizes the long-term reward [1, 4]. The problem becomes one of finding the value function, $J(\mathbf{s})$ which assigns a value to each state. The optimal action at each state can then be easily computed by determining the expected value of each action at each state, from the neighboring values. We use a modified form of Bellman's equations to give the value of state $J(\mathbf{s})$ and policy as

$$J(\mathbf{s}_i) = \max_u [R(\mathbf{s}_i) + C(\mathbf{s}, u) + \sum_{j=1}^{N} p(\mathbf{s}_j|\mathbf{s}_i, u) \cdot J(\mathbf{s}_j)] \tag{8}$$

$$\pi(\mathbf{s}_i) = \operatorname*{argmax}_u [R(\mathbf{s}_i) + C(\mathbf{s}, u) + \sum_{j=1}^{N} p(\mathbf{s}_j|\mathbf{s}_i, u) \cdot J(\mathbf{s}_j)] \tag{9}$$

By iterating equation (8), the value function iteratively settles to a converged value over all states. Iteration stops when no state value changes above some threshold value.

In the above equations, $R(\mathbf{s}_i)$ is the immediate reward at state si, $p(\mathbf{s}_j|\mathbf{s}_i, u)$ is the transition probability from state $\mathbf{s}_i$ to state $\mathbf{s}_j$, and $C(\mathbf{s}, u)$ is the cost of taking action u at state s. Note that the form of the equations is undiscounted in the traditional sense, however, the additive cost term plays a similar role in that the system is penalized for policies that take longer trajectories. The cost in general is simply the distance of one step in the given direction u, although the cost of travel close to obstacles is higher, in order to create a safety margin around obstacles. The cost of an action that would cause a collision is infinite, preventing such actions from being used.

The immediate reward is localized only at the goal pose. However, the goal pose has a range of possible values for the uncertainty, creating a set of goal states, $\mathcal{G}$. In order to reward policies that arrive at a goal state with a lower uncertainty, the reward is scaled linearly with goal state uncertainty.

$$R(\mathbf{x}_i) = \begin{cases} \tau - H(\mathbf{s}) & \mathbf{s} \in \mathcal{G} \\ 0 & \text{otherwise} \end{cases} \tag{10}$$

By implementing the value iteration given in the equations (8) and (9) in a dynamic program, we can compute the value function in $\mathcal{O}(nk_{crit})$ where n is the number of states in the environment (*number of positions* × *number of entropy levels*) and k_{crit} is the number of iterations to convergence. With the value function computed, we can generate the optimal action for any state in $\mathcal{O}(a)$ time, where a is the number of actions out of each state.

4 Experimental Results

Figure 2 shows the mobile robot, Minerva, used for this research. Minerva is a RWI B-18, and senses using a 360° field of view laser range finder at 1° increments.

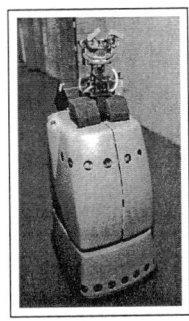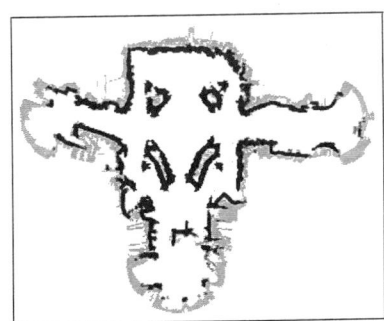

Figure 2: Minerva, the B-18 mobile robot used for this research, and an example environment map, the Smithsonian National Museum of American History. The black areas are the walls and obstacles. Note the large sparse areas in the center of the environment.

Also shown in figure 2 is an example environment, the Smithsonian National Museum of American History. Minerva was used to generate this map, and operated as a tour-guide in the museum for two weeks in the summer of 1998. This museum has many of the features that make localization difficult – large open spaces, and many dynamic obstacles (people) that can mislead the sensors.

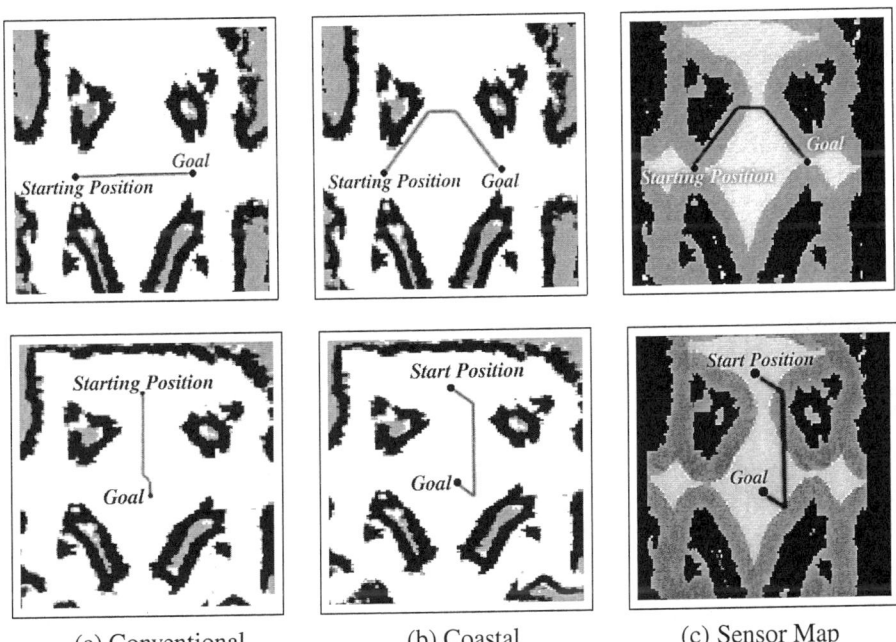

(a) Conventional   (b) Coastal   (c) Sensor Map

Figure 3: Two examples in the museum environment. The left trajectory is given by a conventional, shortest-path planner. The middle trajectory is given by the coastal navigation planner. The black areas correspond to obstacles, the dark grey areas correspond to regions where sensor information is available, the light grey areas to regions where no sensor information is available.

Figure 3 shows the effect of different planners in the sample environment. Panel (a) shows the trajectory of a conventional, shortest distance planner. Note that the robot moves directly towards the goal. Panel (b) shows the trajectory given by the coastal planner. In both examples, the robot moves towards an obstacle, and relocalizes once it is in sensor range of the obstacle, before moving towards the goal. These periodic relocalizations are essential for the robot to arrive at the goal with minimum positional uncertainty, and maximum reliability. Panel (c) shows the sensor map of the environment. The black areas show obstacles and walls, and the light grey areas are where no information is available to the sensors, because all environmental features are outside the range of the sensors. The dark grey areas indicate areas where the information gain from the sensors is *not* zero; the darker grey the area, the better the information gain from the sensors.

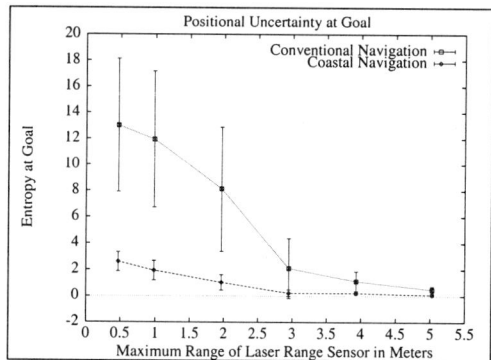

Figure 4: The performance of the coastal navigation algorithm compared to the coastal motion planner. The graph depicts the entropy of the position probability distribution against the range of the laser sensor. Note that the coastal navigation dramatically improves the certainty of the goal position with shorter range laser sensing.

Figure 4 is a comparison of the average positional certainty (computed as entropy of the positional probability) of the robot at its goal position, compared to the range of the laser range sensor. As the range of the laser range gets shorter, the robot can see fewer and fewer environmental features – this is essentially a way of reducing the ability of the robot to localize itself. The upper line is the performance of a conventional shortest-distance path planner, and the lower line is the coastal planner. The coastal planner has a lower uncertainty for all ranges of the laser sensor, and is substantially lower at shorter ranges, confirming that the coastal navigation has the most effect when the localization is worst.

5 Conclusion

In this paper, we have described a particular problem of motion planning – how to guarantee that a mobile robot can reach its goal with maximum reliability. Conventional motion planners do not typically plan according to the ability of the localization unit in different areas of the environment, and thus make no claims about the robustness of the generated trajectory. In contrast, POMDPs provide the correct solution to the problem of robust trajectories, however, computing the solution to a POMDP is intractable for the size of the state space for typical mobile robot environments.

We propose a motion planner with an augmented state space that represents positional uncertainty explicitly as an extra dimension. The motion planner then plans through pose-uncertainty space, to arrive at the goal pose with the lowest possible uncertainty. This can be seen to be an approximation to a POMDP where the multi-dimensional belief space is represented as a subset of statistics, in this case the entropy of the belief space.

We have shown some experimental comparisons with a conventional motion planner. Not only did the coastal navigation generated trajectories that provided substantial improvement of the positional certainty at the goal compared to the conventional planner, but the improvement became more pronounced as the localization was degraded.

The model presented here, however, is not complete. The entire methodology hinges upon the assumption that the robot's probability distribution can be adequately represented by the entropy of the distribution. This assumption is valid if the distribution is restricted to a uni-modal Gaussian, however, most Markov localization methods that are based on this assumption fail, because multi-modal, non-Gaussian positional distributions are quite common for moving robots. Nonetheless, it may be that multiple uncertainty statistics along multiple dimensions (e.g., x and y) may do a better job of capturing the uncertainty sufficiently. It is an question for future work as to how many statistics can capture the uncertainty of a mobile robot, and under what environmental conditions.

Acknowledgments

The authors gratefully acknowledge the advice and collaboration of Tom Mitchell throughout the development of this work. Wolfram Burgard and Dieter Fox played an instrumental role in the development of earlier versions of this work, and their involvement and discussion of this new model is much appreciated. This work was partially funded by the Fonds pour la Formation de Chercheurs et l'Aide à la Recherche (FCAR).

References

[1] R. Bellman. *Dynamic Programming*. Princeton University Press, NJ, 1957.

[2] W. Burgard, D. Fox, D. Hennig, and T. Schmidt. Estimating the absolute position of a mobile robot using position probability grids. In *AAAI*, 1996.

[3] D. Fox, W. Burgard, and S. Thrun. Active Markov localization for mobile robots. *Robotics and Autonomous Systems*, 25(3-4), 1998.

[4] R. A. Howard. *Dynamic Programming and Markov Processes*. MIT, 1960.

[5] L. Kaelbling, A. R. Cassandra, and J. A. Kurien. Acting under uncertainty: Discrete Bayesian models for mobile-robot navigation. In *IROS*, 1996.

[6] S. Koenig and R. Simmons. The effect of representation and knowledge on goal-directed exploration with reinforcement learning algorithms. *Machine Learning Journal*, 22:227–250, 1996.

[7] J.-C. Latombe. *Robot Motion Planning*. Kluwer Academic Publishers, 1991.

[8] S. Mahadevan and N. Khaleeli. Robust mobile robot navigation using partially-observable semi-Markov decision processes. 1999.

[9] H. P. Moravec and A. Elfes. High resolution maps from wide angle sonar. In *ICRA*, 1985.

[10] R. Sim and G. Dudek. Mobile robot localization from learned landmarks. In *IROS*, 1998.

[11] H. Takeda, C. Facchinetti, and J.-C. Latombe. Planning the motions of mobile robot in a sensory uncertainty field. *IEEE Trans. on Pattern Analysis and Machine Intelligence*, 16(10), 1994.

[12] S. Thrun, D. Fox, and W. Burgard. A probabilistic approach to concurrent mapping and localization for mobile robots. *Machine Learning*, 431, 1998.

Learning Factored Representations for Partially Observable Markov Decision Processes

Brian Sallans

Department of Computer Science
University of Toronto
Toronto M5S 2Z9 Canada

Gatsby Computational Neuroscience Unit[*]
University College London
London WC1N 3AR U.K.

sallans@cs.toronto.edu

Abstract

The problem of reinforcement learning in a non-Markov environment is explored using a dynamic Bayesian network, where conditional independence assumptions between random variables are compactly represented by network parameters. The parameters are learned on-line, and approximations are used to perform inference and to compute the optimal value function. The relative effects of inference and value function approximations on the quality of the final policy are investigated, by learning to solve a moderately difficult driving task. The two value function approximations, linear and quadratic, were found to perform similarly, but the quadratic model was more sensitive to initialization. Both performed below the level of human performance on the task. The dynamic Bayesian network performed comparably to a model using a localist hidden state representation, while requiring exponentially fewer parameters.

1 Introduction

Reinforcement learning (RL) addresses the problem of learning to act so as to maximize a reward signal provided by the environment. Online RL algorithms try to find a policy which maximizes the expected time-discounted reward. They do this through experience by performing sample backups to learn a value function over states or state-action pairs.

If the decision problem is Markov in the observable states, then the optimal value function over state-action pairs yields all of the information required to find the optimal policy for the decision problem. When complete knowledge of the environment is not available, states which are different may look the same; this uncertainty is called *perceptual aliasing* [1], and causes decision problems to have dynamics which are non-Markov in the perceived state.

---

[*]Correspondence address

1.1 Partially observable Markov decision processes

Many interesting decision problems are not Markov in the inputs. A partially observable Markov decision process (POMDP) is a formalism in which it is assumed that a process is Markov, but with respect to some unobserved (i.e. "hidden") random variable. The state of the variable at time t, denoted s^t, is dependent only on the state at the previous time step and on the action performed. The currently-observed evidence is assumed to be independent of previous states and observations given the current state.

The state of the hidden variable is not known with certainty, so a belief state is maintained instead. At each time step, the beliefs are updated by using Bayes' theorem to combine the belief state at the previous time step (passed through a model of the system dynamics) with newly observed evidence. In the case of discrete time and finite discrete state and actions, a POMDP is typically represented by conditional probability tables (CPTs) specifying emission probabilities for each state, and transition probabilities and expected rewards for states and actions. This corresponds to a hidden Markov model (HMM) with a distinct transition matrix for each action. The hidden state is represented by a single random variable that can take on one of K values. Exact belief updates can be computed using Bayes' rule.

The value function is not over the discrete state, but over the real-valued belief state. It has been shown that the value function is piecewise linear and convex [2]. In the worst case, the number of linear pieces grows exponentially with the problem horizon, making exact computation of the optimal value function intractable.

Notice that the localist representation, in which the state is encoded in a single random variable, is exponentially inefficient: Encoding n bits of information about the state of the process requires 2^n possible hidden states. This does not bode well for the abilities of models which use this representation to scale up to problems with high-dimensional inputs and complex non-Markov structure.

1.2 Factored representations

A Bayesian network can compactly represent the state of the system in a set of random variables [3]. A two time-slice dynamic Bayesian network (DBN) represents the system at two time steps [4]. The conditional dependencies between random variables from time t to time $t + 1$, and within time step t, are represented by edges in a directed acyclic graph. The conditional probabilities can be stored explicitly, or parameterized by weights on edges in the graph.

If the network is densely-connected then inference is intractable [5]. Approximate inference methods include Markov chain Monte Carlo [6], variational methods [7], and belief state simplification [8].

In applying a DBN to a large problem there are three distinct issues to disentangle: How well does a parameterized DBN capture the underlying POMDP; how much is the DBN hurt by approximate inference; and how good must the approximation of the value function be to achieve reasonable performance? We try to tease these issues apart by looking at the performance of a DBN on a problem with a moderately large state-space and non-Markov structure.

2 The algorithm

We use a fully-connected dynamic sigmoid belief network (DSBN) [9], with K units at each time slice (see figure 1). The random variables s_i are binary, and conditional proba-

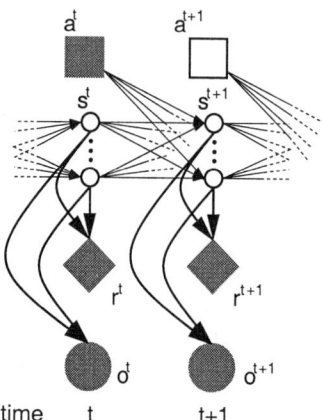

Figure 1: Architecture of the dynamic sigmoid belief network. Circles indicate random variables, where a filled circle is observed and an empty circle is unobserved. Squares are action nodes, and diamonds are rewards.

bilities relating variables at adjacent time-steps are encoded in action-specific weights:

$$P(s_i^{t+1} = 1 | \{s_k^t\}_{k=1}^K, a^t) = \sigma\left(\sum_{k=1}^K w_{ik}^{a^t} s_k^t\right) \quad (1)$$

where $w_{ik}^{a^t}$ is the weight from the ith unit at time step t to the kth unit at time step $t+1$, assuming action a^t is taken at time t. The nonlinearity is the usual sigmoid function: $\sigma(x) = 1/1 + \exp\{-x\}$. Note that a bias can be incorporated into the weights by clamping one of the binary units to 1.

The observed variables are assumed to be discrete; the conditional distribution of an output given the hidden state is multinomial and parameterized by output weights. The probability of observing an output with value l is given by:

$$P(o^t = l | \{s_k^t\}_{k=1}^K) = \frac{\exp\left\{\sum_{k=1}^K u_{kl} s_k^t\right\}}{\sum_{m=1}^{|O|} \exp\left\{\sum_{k=1}^K u_{km} s_k^t\right\}} \quad (2)$$

where $o^t \in \mathbf{O}$ and u_{kl} denotes the output weight from hidden unit k to output value l.

2.1 Approximate inference

Inference in the fully-connected Bayesian network is intractable. Instead we use a variational method with a fully-factored approximating distribution:

$$P(\mathbf{s}^t | \mathbf{s}^{t-1}, a^{t-1}, o^t) \stackrel{\triangle}{=} P_{\mathbf{s}^t} \approx \prod_{k=1}^K \mu_k^{s_k^t}(1-\mu_k)^{1-s_k^t} \quad (3)$$

where the μ_k are variational parameters to be optimized. This is the standard mean-field approximation for a sigmoid belief network [10]. The parameters μ are optimized by iterating the mean-field equations, and converge in a few iterations. The values of the variational parameters at time t are held fixed while computing the values for step $t+1$. This is analogous to running only the forward portion of the HMM forward-backward algorithm [11].

The parameters of the DSBN are optimized online using stochastic gradient ascent in the log-likelihood:

$$\mathbf{W}^{a^t} \leftarrow \mathbf{W}^{a^t} + \alpha_W \left[\mu^{t+1} - \sigma\left(\mathbf{W}^{a^t}\mu^t\right)\right] \cdot \mu^{t\top}$$

$$\mathbf{U} \leftarrow \mathbf{U} + \alpha_U \left[\nu^t - \frac{\exp\{\mathbf{U}\mu\}}{\sum_k \exp\{[\mathbf{U}\mu]_k\}}\right] \cdot \mu^{t\top} \quad (4)$$

where **W** and **U** are the transition and emission matrices respectively, α_W and α_U are learning rates, the vector μ contains the fully-factored approximate belief state, and ν is a vector of zeros with a one in the $o^{t^{th}}$ place. The notation $[\cdot]_k$ denotes the kth element of a vector (or k^{th} column of a matrix).

2.2 Approximating the value function

Computing the optimal value function is also intractable. If a factored state-space representation is appropriate, it is natural (if extreme) to assume that the state-action value function can be decomposed in the same way:

$$Q(P_{\mathbf{s}^t}, a^t) \approx \sum_{k=1}^{K} Q_k(\mu_k^t, a^t) \triangleq Q_F(\mu, a^t) \qquad (5)$$

This simplifying assumption is still not enough to make finding the optimal value function tractable. Even if the states were completely independent, each Q_k would still be piecewise-linear and convex, with the number of pieces scaling exponentially with the horizon. We test two approximate value functions, a linear approximation:

$$Q_F(\mu^t, a^t) = \sum_{k=1}^{K} q_{k,a^t}\, \mu_k = [\mathbf{Q}]_{a^t}^\top \cdot \mu \qquad (6)$$

and a quadratic approximation:

$$\begin{aligned} Q_F(\mu^t, a^t) &= \sum_{k=1}^{K} \phi_{k,a^t}\, \mu_k^2 + q_{k,a^t}\, \mu_k + b_{a^t} \\ &= [\mathbf{\Phi}]_{a^t}^\top \cdot (\mu \odot \mu) + [\mathbf{Q}]_{a^t}^\top \cdot \mu + [\mathbf{b}]_{a^t} \end{aligned} \qquad (7)$$

Where $\mathbf{\Phi}$, $\mathbf{Q}$ and $\mathbf{b}$ are parameters of the approximations. The notation $[\cdot]_i$ denotes the ith column of a matrix, $[\cdot]^\top$ denotes matrix transpose and $\odot$ denotes element-wise vector multiplication.

We update each term of the factored approximation with a modified Q-learning rule [12], which corresponds to a delta-rule where the target for input μ is $r^t + \gamma \max_a Q_F(\mu^{t+1}, a)$:

$$\begin{aligned} \phi_{k,a^t} &\leftarrow \phi_{k,a^t} + \alpha\, \mu_k^2\, E_B \\ q_{k,a^t} &\leftarrow q_{k,a^t} + \alpha\, \mu_k\, E_B \\ b_{a^t} &\leftarrow b_{a^t} + \alpha\, E_B \end{aligned} \qquad (8)$$

Here α is a learning rate, γ is the temporal discount factor, and E_B is the Bellman residual:

$$E_B = r^t + \gamma \max_a Q_F(\mu^{t+1}, a) - Q_F(\mu^t, a^t) \qquad (9)$$

3 Experimental results

The "New York Driving" task [13] involves navigating through slower and faster one-way traffic on a multi-lane highway. The speed of the agent is fixed, and it must change lanes to avoid slower cars and move out of the way of faster cars. If the agent remains in front of a faster car, the driver of the fast car will honk its horn, resulting in a reward of -1.0. Instead of colliding with a slower car, the agent can squeeze past in the same lane, resulting in a reward of -10.0. A time step with no horns or lane-squeezes constitutes clear progress, and is rewarded with $+0.1$. See [13] for a detailed description of this task.

Table 1: Sensory input for the New York driving task

Dimension	Size	Values
Hear horn	2	yes, no
Gaze object	3	truck, shoulder, road
Gaze speed	2	looming, receding
Gaze distance	3	far, near, nose
Gaze refined distance	2	far-half, near-half
Gaze colour	6	red, blue, yellow, white, gray, tan

A modified version of the New York Driving task was used to test our algorithm. The task was essentially the same as described in [13], except that the "gaze side" and "gaze direction" inputs were removed. See table 1 for a list of the modified sensory inputs.

The performance of a number of algorithms and approximations were measured on the task: a random policy; Q-learning on the sensory inputs; a model with a localist representation (i.e. the hidden state consisted of a single multinomial random variable) with linear and quadratic approximate value functions; the DSBN with mean-field inference and linear and quadratic approximations; and a human driver. The localist representation used the linear Q-learning approximation of [14], and the corresponding quadratic approximation. The quadratic approximations were trained both from random initialization, and from initialization with the corresponding learned linear models (and random quadratic portion). The non-human algorithms were each trained for 100000 iterations, and in each case a constant learning rate of 0.01 and temporal decay rate of 0.9 were used. The human driver (the author) was trained for 1000 iterations using a simple character-based graphical display, with each iteration lasting 0.5 seconds.

Stochastic policies were used for all RL algorithms, with actions being chosen from a Boltzmann distribution with temperature decreasing over time:

$$P(a^t|\mu^t) = \frac{1}{Z_B} \exp\{Q_F(\mu^t, a^t)/T\} \qquad (10)$$

The DSBN had 4 hidden units per time slice, and the localist model used a multinomial with 16 states. The Q-learner had a table representation with 2160 entries. After training, each non-human algorithm was tested for 20 trials of 5000 time steps each. The human was tested for 2000 time steps, and the results were renormalized for comparison with the other methods. The results are shown in figure 2. All results were negative, so lower numbers indicate better performance in the graph. The error bars show one standard deviation across the 20 trials.

There was little performance difference between the localist representation and the DSBN but, as expected, the DSBN was exponentially more efficient in its hidden-state representation. The linear and quadratic approximations performed comparably, but well below human performance. However, the DSBN with quadratic approximation was more sensitive to initialization. When initialized with random parameter settings, it failed to find a good policy. However, it did converge to a reasonable policy when the linear portion of the quadratic model was initialized with a previously learned linear model.

The hidden units in the DSBN encode useful features of the input, such as whether a car was at the "near" or "nose" position. They also encode some history, such as current gaze direction. This has advantages over a simple stochastic policy learned via Q-learning: If the Q-learner knows that there is an oncoming car, it can randomly select to look left or right. The DSBN systematically looks to the left, and then to the right, wasting fewer actions.

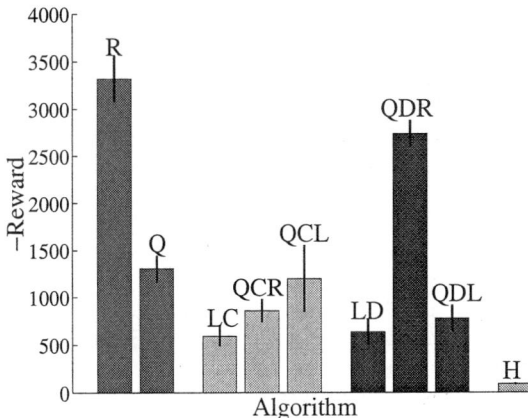

Figure 2: Results on the New York Driving task for nine algorithms: R=random; Q=Q-learning; LC=linear multinomial; QCR=quadratic multinomial, random init.; QCL=quadratic multinomial, linear init; LD=linear DSBN; QDR=quadratic DSBN, random init.; QDL=quadratic DSBN, linear init.; H=human

4 Discussion

The DSBN performed better than a standard Q-learner, and comparably to a model with a localist representation, despite using approximate inference and exponentially fewer parameters. This is encouraging, since an efficient encoding of the state is a prerequisite for tackling larger decision problems. Less encouraging was the value-function approximation: When compared to human performance, it is clear that all methods are far from optimal, although again the factored approximation of the DSBN did not hurt performance relative to the localist multinomial representation. The sensitivity to initialization of the quadratic approximation is worrisome, but the success of initializing from a simpler model suggests that staged learning may be appropriate, where simple models are learned and used to initialize more complex models. These findings echo those of [14] in the context of learning a non-factored approximate value function.

There are a number of related works, both in the fields of reinforcement learning and Bayesian networks. We use the sigmoid belief network mean-field approximation given in [10], and discussed in the context of time-series models (the "fully factored" approximation) in [15]. Approximate inference in dynamic Bayesian networks has been discussed in [15] and [8]. The additive factored value function was used in the context of factored MDPs (with no hidden state) in [16], and the linear Q-learning approximation was given in [14]. Approximate inference was combined with more sophisticated value function approximation in [17]. To our knowledge, this is the first attempt to explore the practicality of combining all of these techniques in order to solve a single problem.

There are several possible extensions. As described above, the representation learned by the DSBN is not tuned to the task at hand. The reinforcement information could be used to guide the learning of the DSBN parameters[18, 13]. Also, if this were done, then the reinforcement signals would provide additional evidence as to what state the POMDP is in, and could be used to aid inference. More sophisticated function approximation could be used [17]. Finally, although this method appears to work in practice, there is no guarantee that the reinforcement learning will converge. We view this work as an encouraging first step, with much further study required.

5 Conclusions

We have shown that a dynamic Bayesian network can be used to construct a compact representation useful for solving a decision problem with hidden state. The parameters of the DBN can be learned from experience. Learning occurs despite the use of simple value-function approximations and mean-field inference. Approximations of the value function result in good performance, but are clearly far from optimal. The fully-factored assumptions made for the belief state and the value function do not appear to impact performance, as compared to the non-factored model. The algorithm as presented runs entirely on-line by performing "forward" inference only. There is much room for future work, including improving the utility of the factored representation learned, and the quality of approximate inference and the value function approximation.

Acknowledgments

We thank Geoffrey Hinton, Zoubin Ghahramani and Andy Brown for helpful discussions, the anonymous referees for valuable comments and criticism, and particularly Peter Dayan for helpful discussions and comments on an early draft of this paper. This research was funded by NSERC Canada and the Gatsby Charitable Foundation.

References

[1] S.D. Whitehead and D.H. Ballard. Learning to perceive and act by trial and error. *Machine Learning*, 7, 1991.

[2] E.J. Sondik. The optimal control of partially observable Markov processes over the infinite horizon: Discounted costs. *Operations Research*, 26:282–304, 1973.

[3] J. Pearl. *Probabilistic Reasoning in Intelligent Systems: Networks of Plausible Inference*. Morgan Kaufmann, San Mateo, CA, 1988.

[4] T. Dean and K. Kanazawa. A model for reasoning about persistence and causation. *Computational Intelligence*, 5, 1989.

[5] Gregory F. Cooper. The computational complexity of probabilistic inference using Bayesian belief networks. *Artificial Intelligence*, 42:393–405, 1990.

[6] R. M. Neal. Probabilistic inference using Markov chain Monte Carlo methods. Technical Report CRG-TR-93-1, Department of Computer Science, University of Toronto, 1993.

[7] M.I. Jordan, Z. Ghahramani, T.S. Jaakkola, and L.K. Saul. An introduction to variational methods for graphical models. *Machine Learning*, 1999. in press.

[8] X. Boyen and D. Koller. Tractable inference for complex stochastic processes. In *Proc. UAI'98*, 1998.

[9] R. M. Neal. Connectionist learning of belief networks. *Artificial Intelligence*, 56:71–113, 1992.

[10] L. K. Saul, T. Jaakkola, and M. I. Jordan. Mean field theory for sigmoid belief networks. *Journal of Artificial Intelligence Research*, 4:61–76, 1996.

[11] Lawrence R. Rabiner and Biing-Hwang Juang. An introduction to hidden Markov models. *IEEE ASSAP Magazine*, 3:4–16, January 1986.

[12] C.J.C.H. Watkins and P. Dayan. Q-learning. *Machine Learning*, 8:279–292, 1992.

[13] A.K. McCallum. *Reinforcement learning with selective perception and hidden state*. Dept. of Computer Science, Universiy of Rochester, Rochester NY, 1995. Ph.D. thesis.

[14] M.L. Littman, A.R. Cassandra, and L.P. Kaelbling. Learning policies for partially observable environments: Scaling up. In *Proc. International Conference on Machine Learning*, 1995.

[15] Z. Ghahramani and M. I. Jordan. Factorial hidden Markov models. *Machine Learning*, 1997.

[16] D. Koller and R. Parr. Computing factored value functions for policies in structured MDPs. In *Proc. IJCAI'99*, 1999.

[17] A. Rodriguez, R. Parr, and D. Koller. Reinforcement learning using approximate belief states. In S. A. Solla, T. K. Leen, and K.-R. Müller, editors, *Advances in Neural Information Processing Systems*, volume 12. The MIT Press, Cambridge, 2000.

[18] L. Chrisman. Reinforcement learning with perceptual aliasing: The perceptual distinctions approach. In *Tenth National Conference on AI*, 1992.

Policy Gradient Methods for Reinforcement Learning with Function Approximation

Richard S. Sutton, David McAllester, Satinder Singh, Yishay Mansour
AT&T Labs – Research, 180 Park Avenue, Florham Park, NJ 07932

Abstract

Function approximation is essential to reinforcement learning, but the standard approach of approximating a value function and determining a policy from it has so far proven theoretically intractable. In this paper we explore an alternative approach in which the policy is explicitly represented by its own function approximator, independent of the value function, and is updated according to the gradient of expected reward with respect to the policy parameters. Williams's REINFORCE method and actor–critic methods are examples of this approach. Our main new result is to show that the gradient can be written in a form suitable for estimation from experience aided by an approximate action-value or advantage function. Using this result, we prove for the first time that a version of policy iteration with arbitrary differentiable function approximation is convergent to a locally optimal policy.

Large applications of reinforcement learning (RL) require the use of generalizing function approximators such neural networks, decision-trees, or instance-based methods. The dominant approach for the last decade has been the *value-function* approach, in which all function approximation effort goes into estimating a value function, with the action-selection policy represented implicitly as the "greedy" policy with respect to the estimated values (e.g., as the policy that selects in each state the action with highest estimated value). The value-function approach has worked well in many applications, but has several limitations. First, it is oriented toward finding deterministic policies, whereas the optimal policy is often stochastic, selecting different actions with specific probabilities (e.g., see Singh, Jaakkola, and Jordan, 1994). Second, an arbitrarily small change in the estimated value of an action can cause it to be, or not be, selected. Such discontinuous changes have been identified as a key obstacle to establishing convergence assurances for algorithms following the value-function approach (Bertsekas and Tsitsiklis, 1996). For example, Q-learning, Sarsa, and dynamic programming methods have all been shown unable to converge to any policy for simple MDPs and simple function approximators (Gordon, 1995, 1996; Baird, 1995; Tsitsiklis and van Roy, 1996; Bertsekas and Tsitsiklis, 1996). This can occur even if the best approximation is found at each step before changing the policy, and whether the notion of "best" is in the mean-squared-error sense or the slightly different senses of residual-gradient, temporal-difference, and dynamic-programming methods.

In this paper we explore an alternative approach to function approximation in RL.

Rather than approximating a value function and using that to compute a deterministic policy, we approximate a stochastic policy directly using an independent function approximator with its own parameters. For example, the policy might be represented by a neural network whose input is a representation of the state, whose output is action selection probabilities, and whose weights are the policy parameters. Let θ denote the vector of policy parameters and ρ the performance of the corresponding policy (e.g., the average reward per step). Then, in the *policy gradient* approach, the policy parameters are updated approximately proportional to the gradient:

$$\Delta \theta \approx \alpha \frac{\partial \rho}{\partial \theta}, \quad (1)$$

where α is a positive-definite step size. If the above can be achieved, then θ can usually be assured to converge to a locally optimal policy in the performance measure ρ. Unlike the value-function approach, here small changes in θ can cause only small changes in the policy and in the state-visitation distribution.

In this paper we prove that an unbiased estimate of the gradient (1) can be obtained from experience using an approximate value function satisfying certain properties. Williams's (1988, 1992) REINFORCE algorithm also finds an unbiased estimate of the gradient, but without the assistance of a learned value function. REINFORCE learns much more slowly than RL methods using value functions and has received relatively little attention. Learning a value function and using it to reduce the variance of the gradient estimate appears to be essential for rapid learning. Jaakkola, Singh and Jordan (1995) proved a result very similar to ours for the special case of function approximation corresponding to tabular POMDPs. Our result strengthens theirs and generalizes it to arbitrary differentiable function approximators. Konda and Tsitsiklis (in prep.) independently developed a very simialr result to ours. See also Baxter and Bartlett (in prep.) and Marbach and Tsitsiklis (1998).

Our result also suggests a way of proving the convergence of a wide variety of algorithms based on "actor-critic" or policy-iteration architectures (e.g., Barto, Sutton, and Anderson, 1983; Sutton, 1984; Kimura and Kobayashi, 1998). In this paper we take the first step in this direction by proving for the first time that a version of policy iteration with general differentiable function approximation is convergent to a locally optimal policy. Baird and Moore (1999) obtained a weaker but superficially similar result for their VAPS family of methods. Like policy-gradient methods, VAPS includes separately parameterized policy and value functions updated by gradient methods. However, VAPS methods do not climb the gradient of performance (expected long-term reward), but of a measure combining performance and value-function accuracy. As a result, VAPS does not converge to a locally optimal policy, except in the case that no weight is put upon value-function accuracy, in which case VAPS degenerates to REINFORCE. Similarly, Gordon's (1995) fitted value iteration is also convergent and value-based, but does not find a locally optimal policy.

1 Policy Gradient Theorem

We consider the standard reinforcement learning framework (see, e.g., Sutton and Barto, 1998), in which a learning agent interacts with a Markov decision process (MDP). The state, action, and reward at each time $t \in \{0, 1, 2, \ldots\}$ are denoted $s_t \in \mathcal{S}$, $a_t \in \mathcal{A}$, and $r_t \in \Re$ respectively. The environment's dynamics are characterized by state transition probabilities, $\mathcal{P}_{ss'}^a = Pr\{s_{t+1} = s' \mid s_t = s, a_t = a\}$, and expected rewards $\mathcal{R}_s^a = E\{r_{t+1} \mid s_t = s, a_t = a\}$, $\forall s, s' \in \mathcal{S}, a \in \mathcal{A}$. The agent's decision making procedure at each time is characterized by a policy, $\pi(s, a, \theta) = Pr\{a_t = a | s_t = s, \theta\}$, $\forall s \in \mathcal{S}, a \in \mathcal{A}$, where $\theta \in \Re^l$, for $l << |\mathcal{S}|$, is a parameter vector. We assume that π is diffentiable with respect to its parameter, i.e., that $\frac{\partial \pi(s,a)}{\partial \theta}$ exists. We also usually write just $\pi(s, a)$ for $\pi(s, a, \theta)$.

With function approximation, two ways of formulating the agent's objective are useful. One is the average reward formulation, in which policies are ranked according to their long-term expected reward per step, $\rho(\pi)$:

$$\rho(\pi) = \lim_{n \to \infty} \frac{1}{n} E\{r_1 + r_2 + \cdots + r_n \mid \pi\} = \sum_s d^\pi(s) \sum_a \pi(s,a) \mathcal{R}_s^a,$$

where $d^\pi(s) = \lim_{t \to \infty} Pr\{s_t = s \mid s_0, \pi\}$ is the stationary distribution of states under π, which we assume exists and is independent of s_0 for all policies. In the average reward formulation, the value of a state–action pair given a policy is defined as

$$Q^\pi(s,a) = \sum_{t=1}^\infty E\{r_t - \rho(\pi) \mid s_0 = s, a_0 = a, \pi\}, \qquad \forall s \in \mathcal{S}, a \in \mathcal{A}.$$

The second formulation we cover is that in which there is a designated start state s_0, and we care only about the long-term reward obtained from it. We will give our results only once, but they will apply to this formulation as well under the definitions

$$\rho(\pi) = E\left\{\sum_{t=1}^\infty \gamma^{t-1} r_t \,\middle|\, s_0, \pi\right\} \quad \text{and} \quad Q^\pi(s,a) = E\left\{\sum_{k=1}^\infty \gamma^{k-1} r_{t+k} \,\middle|\, s_t = s, a_t = a, \pi\right\}.$$

where $\gamma \in [0,1]$ is a discount rate ($\gamma = 1$ is allowed only in episodic tasks). In this formulation, we define $d^\pi(s)$ as a discounted weighting of states encountered starting at s_0 and then following π: $d^\pi(s) = \sum_{t=0}^\infty \gamma^t Pr\{s_t = s \mid s_0, \pi\}$.

Our first result concerns the gradient of the performance metric with respect to the policy parameter:

Theorem 1 (Policy Gradient). For any MDP, in either the average-reward or start-state formulations,

$$\frac{\partial \rho}{\partial \theta} = \sum_s d^\pi(s) \sum_a \frac{\partial \pi(s,a)}{\partial \theta} Q^\pi(s,a). \tag{2}$$

Proof: See the appendix.

This way of expressing the gradient was first discussed for the average-reward formulation by Marbach and Tsitsiklis (1998), based on a related expression in terms of the state-value function due to Jaakkola, Singh, and Jordan (1995) and Cao and Chen (1997). We extend their results to the start-state formulation and provide simpler and more direct proofs. Williams's (1988, 1992) theory of REINFORCE algorithms can also be viewed as implying (2). In any event, the key aspect of both expressions for the gradient is that their are no terms of the form $\frac{\partial d^\pi(s)}{\partial \theta}$: the effect of policy changes on the distribution of states does not appear. This is convenient for approximating the gradient by sampling. For example, if s was sampled from the distribution obtained by following π, then $\sum_a \frac{\partial \pi(s,a)}{\partial \theta} Q^\pi(s,a)$ would be an unbiased estimate of $\frac{\partial \rho}{\partial \theta}$. Of course, $Q^\pi(s,a)$ is also not normally known and must be estimated. One approach is to use the actual returns, $R_t = \sum_{k=1}^\infty r_{t+k} - \rho(\pi)$ (or $R_t = \sum_{k=1}^\infty \gamma^{k-1} r_{t+k}$ in the start-state formulation) as an approximation for each $Q^\pi(s_t, a_t)$. This leads to Williams's episodic REINFORCE algorithm, $\Delta \theta_t \propto \frac{\partial \pi(s_t,a_t)}{\partial \theta} R_t \frac{1}{\pi(s_t,a_t)}$ (the $\frac{1}{\pi(s_t,a_t)}$ corrects for the oversampling of actions preferred by π), which is known to follow $\frac{\partial \rho}{\partial \theta}$ in expected value (Williams, 1988, 1992).

2 Policy Gradient with Approximation

Now consider the case in which Q^π is approximated by a learned function approximator. If the approximation is sufficiently good, we might hope to use it in place of Q^π

in (2) and still point roughly in the direction of the gradient. For example, Jaakkola, Singh, and Jordan (1995) proved that for the special case of function approximation arising in a tabular POMDP one could assure positive inner product with the gradient, which is sufficient to ensure improvement for moving in that direction. Here we extend their result to general function approximation and prove equality with the gradient.

Let $f_w : \mathcal{S} \times \mathcal{A} \to \Re$ be our approximation to Q^π, with parameter w. It is natural to learn f_w by following π and updating w by a rule such as $\Delta w_t \propto \frac{\partial}{\partial w}[\hat{Q}^\pi(s_t, a_t) - f_w(s_t, a_t)]^2 \propto [\hat{Q}^\pi(s_t, a_t) - f_w(s_t, a_t)]\frac{\partial f_w(s_t, a_t)}{\partial w}$, where $\hat{Q}^\pi(s_t, a_t)$ is some unbiased estimator of $Q^\pi(s_t, a_t)$, perhaps R_t. When such a process has converged to a local optimum, then

$$\sum_s d^\pi(s) \sum_a \pi(s,a) [Q^\pi(s,a) - f_w(s,a)] \frac{\partial f_w(s,a)}{\partial w} = 0. \quad (3)$$

Theorem 2 (Policy Gradient with Function Approximation). If f_w satisfies (3) and is compatible with the policy parameterization in the sense that[1]

$$\frac{\partial f_w(s,a)}{\partial w} = \frac{\partial \pi(s,a)}{\partial \theta} \frac{1}{\pi(s,a)}, \quad (4)$$

then

$$\frac{\partial \rho}{\partial \theta} = \sum_s d^\pi(s) \sum_a \frac{\partial \pi(s,a)}{\partial \theta} f_w(s,a). \quad (5)$$

Proof: Combining (3) and (4) gives

$$\sum_s d^\pi(s) \sum_a \frac{\partial \pi(s,a)}{\partial \theta} [Q^\pi(s,a) - f_w(s,a)] = 0 \quad (6)$$

which tells us that the error in $f_w(s,a)$ is orthogonal to the gradient of the policy parameterization. Because the expression above is zero, we can subtract it from the policy gradient theorem (2) to yield

$$\begin{aligned}
\frac{\partial \rho}{\partial \theta} &= \sum_s d^\pi(s) \sum_a \frac{\partial \pi(s,a)}{\partial \theta} Q^\pi(s,a) - \sum_s d^\pi(s) \sum_a \frac{\partial \pi(s,a)}{\partial \theta} [Q^\pi(s,a) - f_w(s,a)] \\
&= \sum_s d^\pi(s) \sum_a \frac{\partial \pi(s,a)}{\partial \theta} [Q^\pi(s,a) - Q^\pi(s,a) + f_w(s,a)] \\
&= \sum_s d^\pi(s) \sum_a \frac{\partial \pi(s,a)}{\partial \theta} f_w(s,a). \qquad \text{Q.E.D.}
\end{aligned}$$

3 Application to Deriving Algorithms and Advantages

Given a policy parameterization, Theorem 2 can be used to derive an appropriate form for the value-function parameterization. For example, consider a policy that is a Gibbs distribution in a linear combination of features:

$$\pi(s,a) = \frac{e^{\theta^T \phi_{sa}}}{\sum_b e^{\theta^T \phi_{sb}}}, \quad \forall s \in \mathcal{S}, s \in \mathcal{A},$$

---

[1]Tsitsiklis (personal communication) points out that f_w being linear in the features given on the righthand side may be the only way to satisfy this condition.

where each ϕ_{sa} is an l-dimensional feature vector characterizing state-action pair s, a. Meeting the compatibility condition (4) requires that

$$\frac{\partial f_w(s,a)}{\partial w} = \frac{\partial \pi(s,a)}{\partial \theta}\frac{1}{\pi(s,a)} = \phi_{sa} - \sum_b \pi(s,b)\phi_{sb},$$

so that the natural parameterization of f_w is

$$f_w(s,a) = w^T\left[\phi_{sa} - \sum_b \pi(s,b)\phi_{sb}\right].$$

In other words, f_w must be linear in the same features as the policy, except normalized to be mean zero for each state. Other algorithms can easily be derived for a variety of nonlinear policy parameterizations, such as multi-layer backpropagation networks.

The careful reader will have noticed that the form given above for f_w requires that it have zero mean for each state: $\sum_a \pi(s,a)f_w(s,a) = 0$, $\forall s \in \mathcal{S}$. In this sense it is better to think of f_w as an approximation of the *advantage* function, $A^\pi(s,a) = Q^\pi(s,a) - V^\pi(s)$ (much as in Baird, 1993), rather than of Q^π. Our convergence requirement (3) is really that f_w get the relative value of the actions correct in each state, not the absolute value, nor the variation from state to state. Our results can be viewed as a justification for the special status of advantages as the target for value function approximation in RL. In fact, our (2), (3), and (5), can all be generalized to include an arbitrary function of state added to the value function or its approximation. For example, (5) can be generalized to $\frac{\partial \rho}{\partial \theta} = \sum_s d^\pi(s) \sum_a \frac{\partial \pi(s,a)}{\partial \theta}[f_w(s,a) + v(s)]$, where $v : \mathcal{S} \to \Re$ is an arbitrary function. (This follows immediately because $\sum_a \frac{\partial \pi(s,a)}{\partial \theta} = 0$, $\forall s \in \mathcal{S}$.) The choice of v does not affect any of our theorems, but can substantially affect the variance of the gradient estimators. The issues here are entirely analogous to those in the use of reinforcement baselines in earlier work (e.g., Williams, 1992; Dayan, 1991; Sutton, 1984). In practice, v should presumably be set to the best available approximation of V^π. Our results establish that that approximation process can proceed without affecting the expected evolution of f_w and π.

4 Convergence of Policy Iteration with Function Approximation

Given Theorem 2, we can prove for the first time that a form of policy iteration with function approximation is convergent to a locally optimal policy.

Theorem 3 (Policy Iteration with Function Approximation). Let π and f_w be any differentiable function approximators for the policy and value function respectively that satisfy the compatibility condition (4) and for which $\max_{\theta,s,a,i,j} |\frac{\partial^2 \pi(s,a)}{\partial \theta_i \partial \theta_j}| < B < \infty$. Let $\{\alpha_k\}_{k=0}^\infty$ be any step-size sequence such that $\lim_{k\to\infty} \alpha_k = 0$ and $\sum_k \alpha_k = \infty$. Then, for any MDP with bounded rewards, the sequence $\{\rho(\pi_k)\}_{k=0}^\infty$, defined by any θ_0, $\pi_k = \pi(\cdot,\cdot,\theta_k)$, and

$$w_k = w \text{ such that } \sum_s d^{\pi_k}(s)\sum_a \pi_k(s,a)[Q^{\pi_k}(s,a) - f_w(s,a)]\frac{\partial f_w(s,a)}{\partial w} = 0$$

$$\theta_{k+1} = \theta_k + \alpha_k \sum_s d^{\pi_k}(s)\sum_a \frac{\partial \pi_k(s,a)}{\partial \theta}f_{w_k}(s,a),$$

converges such that $\lim_{k\to\infty}\frac{\partial \rho(\pi_k)}{\partial \theta} = 0$.

Proof: Our Theorem 2 assures that the θ_k update is in the direction of the gradient. The bounds on $\frac{\partial^2 \pi(s,a)}{\partial \theta_i \partial \theta_j}$ and on the MDP's rewards together assure us that $\frac{\partial^2 \rho}{\partial \theta_i \partial \theta_j}$

is also bounded. These, together with the step-size requirements, are the necessary conditions to apply Proposition 3.5 from page 96 of Bertsekas and Tsitsiklis (1996), which assures convergence to a local optimum. Q.E.D.

Acknowledgements

The authors wish to thank Martha Steenstrup and Doina Precup for comments, and Michael Kearns for insights into the notion of optimal policy under function approximation.

References

Baird, L. C. (1993). Advantage Updating. Wright Lab. Technical Report WL-TR-93-1146.

Baird, L. C. (1995). Residual algorithms: Reinforcement learning with function approximation. *Proc. of the Twelfth Int. Conf. on Machine Learning*, pp. 30–37. Morgan Kaufmann.

Baird, L. C., Moore, A. W. (1999). Gradient descent for general reinforcement learning. *NIPS 11*. MIT Press.

Barto, A. G., Sutton, R. S., Anderson, C. W. (1983). Neuronlike elements that can solve difficult learning control problems. *IEEE Trans. on Systems, Man, and Cybernetics 13*:835.

Baxter, J., Bartlett, P. (in prep.) Direct gradient-based reinforcement learning: I. Gradient estimation algorithms.

Bertsekas, D. P., Tsitsiklis, J. N. (1996). *Neuro-Dynamic Programming*. Athena Scientific.

Cao, X.-R., Chen, H.-F. (1997). Perturbation realization, potentials, and sensitivity analysis of Markov Processes, *IEEE Trans. on Automatic Control 42*(10):1382–1393.

Dayan, P. (1991). Reinforcement comparison. In D. S. Touretzky, J. L. Elman, T. J. Sejnowski, and G. E. Hinton (eds.), *Connectionist Models: Proceedings of the 1990 Summer School*, pp. 45–51. Morgan Kaufmann.

Gordon, G. J. (1995). Stable function approximation in dynamic programming. *Proceedings of the Twelfth Int. Conf. on Machine Learning*, pp. 261–268. Morgan Kaufmann.

Gordon, G. J. (1996). Chattering in SARSA(λ). CMU Learning Lab Technical Report.

Jaakkola, T., Singh, S. P., Jordan, M. I. (1995) Reinforcement learning algorithms for partially observable Markov decision problems, *NIPS 7*, pp. 345–352. Morgan Kaufman.

Kimura, H., Kobayashi, S. (1998). An analysis of actor/critic algorithms using eligibility traces: Reinforcement learning with imperfect value functions. *Proc. ICML-98*, pp. 278–286.

Konda, V. R., Tsitsiklis, J. N. (in prep.) Actor-critic algorithms.

Marbach, P., Tsitsiklis, J. N. (1998) Simulation-based optimization of Markov reward processes, technical report LIDS-P-2411, Massachusetts Institute of Technology.

Singh, S. P., Jaakkola, T., Jordan, M. I. (1994). Learning without state-estimation in partially observable Markovian decision problems. *Proc. ICML-94*, pp. 284–292.

Sutton, R. S. (1984). *Temporal Credit Assignment in Reinforcement Learning*. Ph.D. thesis, University of Massachusetts, Amherst.

Sutton, R. S., Barto, A. G. (1998). *Reinforcement Learning: An Introduction*. MIT Press.

Tsitsiklis, J. N. Van Roy, B. (1996). Feature-based methods for large scale dynamic programming. *Machine Learning 22*:59–94.

Williams, R. J. (1988). Toward a theory of reinforcement-learning connectionist systems. Technical Report NU-CCS-88-3, Northeastern University, College of Computer Science.

Williams, R. J. (1992). Simple statistical gradient-following algorithms for connectionist reinforcement learning. *Machine Learning 8*:229–256.

Appendix: Proof of Theorem 1

We prove the theorem first for the average-reward formulation and then for the start-state formulation.

$$\frac{\partial V^\pi(s)}{\partial \theta} \stackrel{\text{def}}{=} \frac{\partial}{\partial \theta} \sum_a \pi(s,a) Q^\pi(s,a) \qquad \forall s \in \mathcal{S}$$

$$= \sum_a \left[\frac{\partial \pi(s,a)}{\partial \theta} Q^\pi(s,a) + \pi(s,a) \frac{\partial}{\partial \theta} Q^\pi(s,a) \right]$$

$$= \sum_a \left[\frac{\partial \pi(s,a)}{\partial \theta} Q^\pi(s,a) + \pi(s,a) \frac{\partial}{\partial \theta} \left[\mathcal{R}_s^a - \rho(\pi) + \sum_{s'} \mathcal{P}_{ss'}^a V^\pi(s') \right] \right]$$

$$= \sum_a \left[\frac{\partial \pi(s,a)}{\partial \theta} Q^\pi(s,a) + \pi(s,a) \left[-\frac{\partial \rho}{\partial \theta} + \sum_{s'} \mathcal{P}_{ss'}^a \frac{\partial V^\pi(s')}{\partial \theta} \right] \right]$$

Therefore,

$$\frac{\partial \rho}{\partial \theta} = \sum_a \left[\frac{\partial \pi(s,a)}{\partial \theta} Q^\pi(s,a) + \pi(s,a) \sum_{s'} \mathcal{P}_{ss'}^a \frac{\partial V^\pi(s')}{\partial \theta} \right] - \frac{\partial V^\pi(s)}{\partial \theta}$$

Summing both sides over the stationary distribution d^π,

$$\sum_s d^\pi(s) \frac{\partial \rho}{\partial \theta} = \sum_s d^\pi(s) \sum_a \frac{\partial \pi(s,a)}{\partial \theta} Q^\pi(s,a) + \sum_s d^\pi(s) \sum_a \pi(s,a) \sum_{s'} \mathcal{P}_{ss'}^a \frac{\partial V^\pi(s')}{\partial \theta}$$
$$- \sum_s d^\pi(s) \frac{\partial V^\pi(s)}{\partial \theta},$$

but since d^π is stationary,

$$\sum_s d^\pi(s) \frac{\partial \rho}{\partial \theta} = \sum_s d^\pi(s) \sum_a \frac{\partial \pi(s,a)}{\partial \theta} Q^\pi(s,a) + \sum_{s'} d^\pi(s') \frac{\partial V^\pi(s')}{\partial \theta}$$
$$- \sum_s d^\pi(s) \frac{\partial V^\pi(s)}{\partial \theta}$$

$$\frac{\partial \rho}{\partial \theta} = \sum_s d^\pi(s) \sum_a \frac{\partial \pi(s,a)}{\partial \theta} Q^\pi(s,a). \qquad \text{Q.E.D.}$$

For the start-state formulation:

$$\frac{\partial V^\pi(s)}{\partial \theta} \stackrel{\text{def}}{=} \frac{\partial}{\partial \theta} \sum_a \pi(s,a) Q^\pi(s,a) \qquad \forall s \in \mathcal{S}$$

$$= \sum_a \left[\frac{\partial \pi(s,a)}{\partial \theta} Q^\pi(s,a) + \pi(s,a) \frac{\partial}{\partial \theta} Q^\pi(s,a) \right]$$

$$= \sum_a \left[\frac{\partial \pi(s,a)}{\partial \theta} Q^\pi(s,a) + \pi(s,a) \frac{\partial}{\partial \theta} \left[\mathcal{R}_s^a + \sum_{s'} \gamma \mathcal{P}_{ss'}^a V^\pi(s') \right] \right]$$

$$= \sum_a \left[\frac{\partial \pi(s,a)}{\partial \theta} Q^\pi(s,a) + \pi(s,a) \sum_{s'} \gamma \mathcal{P}_{ss'}^a \frac{\partial}{\partial \theta} V^\pi(s') \right] \qquad (7)$$

$$= \sum_x \sum_{k=0}^\infty \gamma^k Pr(s \to x, k, \pi) \sum_a \frac{\partial \pi(x,a)}{\partial \theta} Q^\pi(x,a),$$

after several steps of unrolling (7), where $Pr(s \to x, k, \pi)$ is the probability of going from state s to state x in k steps under policy π. It is then immediate that

$$\frac{\partial \rho}{\partial \theta} = \frac{\partial}{\partial \theta} E \left\{ \sum_{t=1}^\infty \gamma^{t-1} r_t \,\middle|\, s_0, \pi \right\} = \frac{\partial}{\partial \theta} V^\pi(s_0)$$

$$= \sum_s \sum_{k=0}^\infty \gamma^k Pr(s_0 \to s, k, \pi) \sum_a \frac{\partial \pi(s,a)}{\partial \theta} Q^\pi(s,a)$$

$$= \sum_s d^\pi(s) \sum_a \frac{\partial \pi(s,a)}{\partial \theta} Q^\pi(s,a). \qquad \text{Q.E.D.}$$

Monte Carlo POMDPs

Sebastian Thrun
School of Computer Science
Carnegie Mellon University
Pittsburgh, PA 15213

Abstract

We present a Monte Carlo algorithm for learning to act in partially observable Markov decision processes (POMDPs) with real-valued state and action spaces. Our approach uses importance sampling for representing beliefs, and Monte Carlo approximation for belief propagation. A reinforcement learning algorithm, value iteration, is employed to learn value functions over belief states. Finally, a sample-based version of nearest neighbor is used to generalize across states. Initial empirical results suggest that our approach works well in practical applications.

1 Introduction

POMDPs address the problem of acting optimally in partially observable dynamic environment [6]. In POMDPs, a learner interacts with a stochastic environment whose state is only partially observable. Actions change the state of the environment and lead to numerical penalties/rewards, which may be observed with an unknown temporal delay. The learner's goal is to devise a policy for action selection that maximizes the reward. Obviously, the POMDP framework embraces a large range of practical problems.

Past work has predominantly studied POMDPs in discrete worlds [1]. Discrete worlds have the advantage that distributions over states (so-called "belief states") can be represented exactly, using one parameter per state. The optimal value function (for finite planning horizon) has been shown to be convex and piecewise linear [10, 14], which makes it possible to derive exact solutions for discrete POMDPs.

Here we are interested in POMDPs with continuous state and action spaces, paying tribute to the fact that a large number of real-world problems are continuous in nature. In general, such POMDPs are not solvable exactly, and little is known about special cases that can be solved. This paper proposes an approximate approach, the MC-POMDP algorithm, which can accommodate real-valued spaces and models. The central idea is to use Monte Carlo sampling for belief representation and propagation. Reinforcement learning in belief space is employed to learn value functions, using a sample-based version of nearest neighbor for generalization. Empirical results illustrate that our approach finds to close-to-optimal solutions efficiently.

2 Monte Carlo POMDPs

2.1 Preliminaries

POMDPs address the problem of selection actions in stationary, partially observable, controllable Markov chains. To establish the basic vocabulary, let us define:

- *State.* At any point in time, the world is in a specific state, denoted by x.

- *Action.* The agent can execute actions, denoted a.
- *Observation.* Through its sensors, the agent can observe a (noisy) projection of the world's state. We use o to denote observations.
- *Reward.* Additionally, the agent receives rewards/penalties, denoted $R \in \Re$. To simplify the notation, we assume that the *reward* is part of the observation. More specifically, we will use $R(o)$ to denote the function that "extracts" the reward from the observation.

Throughout this paper, we use the subscript t to refer to a specific point in time (e.g., s_t refers to the state at time t).

POMDPs are characterized by three probability distributions:

1. The *initial distribution*, $\pi(x) := Pr(x_0)$, specifies the initial distribution of states at time $t = 0$.
2. The *next state distribution*, $\mu(x' \mid a, x) := Pr(x_t = x' \mid a_{t-1} = a, x_{t-1} = x)$, describes the likelihood that action a, when executed at state x, leads to state x'.
3. The *perceptual distribution*, $\nu(o \mid x) := Pr(o_t = o \mid x_t = x)$, describes the likelihood of observing o when the world is in state x.

A *history* is a sequence of states and observations. For simplicity, we assume that actions and observations are alternated. We use d_t to denote the history leading up to time t:

$$d_t := \{o_t, a_{t-1}, o_{t-1}, a_{t-2}, \ldots, a_0, o_0\} \tag{1}$$

The fundamental problem in POMDPs is to devise a policy for action selection that maximizes reward. A *policy*, denoted

$$\sigma : d \longrightarrow a \tag{2}$$

is a mapping from histories to actions. Assuming that actions are chosen by a policy σ, each policy induces an expected cumulative (and possibly discounted by a *discount factor* $\gamma \leq 1$) reward, defined as

$$J^\sigma = \sum_{\tau=0}^{\infty} E\left[\gamma^\tau R(o_\tau)\right] \tag{3}$$

Here $E[\ ]$ denotes the mathematical expectation. The POMDP problem is, thus, to find a policy σ^* that maximizes J^σ, i.e.,

$$\sigma^* = \operatorname*{argmax}_{\sigma} J^\sigma \tag{4}$$

2.2 Belief States

To avoid the difficulty of learning a function with unbounded input (the history can be arbitrarily long), it is common practice to map histories into *belief states*, and learn a mapping from belief states to actions instead [10].

Formally, a *belief state* (denoted θ) is a probability distribution over states conditioned on past actions and observations:

$$\theta_t = Pr(x_t \mid d_t) = Pr(x_t \mid o_t, a_{t-1}, \ldots, o_0) \tag{5}$$

Belief are computed incrementally, using knowledge of the POMDP's defining distributions π, μ, and ν. Initially

$$\theta_0 = \pi \tag{6}$$

For $t \geq 0$, we obtain

$$\theta_{t+1} = Pr(x_{t+1} \mid o_{t+1}, a_t, \ldots, o_0) \tag{7}$$

$$= \alpha \, Pr(o_{t+1} \mid x_{t+1}, \ldots, o_0) \, Pr(x_{t+1} \mid a_t, \ldots, o_0) \tag{8}$$

$$= \alpha \, Pr(o_{t+1} \mid x_{t+1}) \int Pr(x_{t+1} \mid a_t, \ldots, o_0, x_t) \, Pr(x_t \mid a_t, \ldots, o_0) \, dx_t \tag{9}$$

$$= \alpha \, Pr(o_{t+1} \mid x_{t+1}) \int Pr(x_{t+1} \mid a_t, x_t) \, \theta_t \, dx_t \tag{10}$$

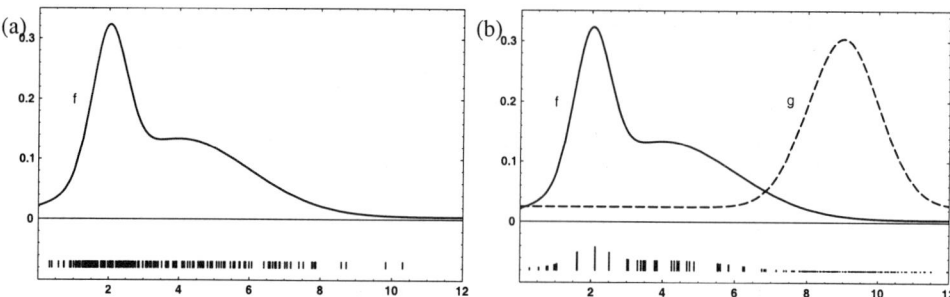

Figure 1: Sampling: (a) Likelihood-weighted sampling and (b) importance sampling. At the bottom of each graph, samples are shown that approximate the function f shown at the top. The height of the samples illustrates their *importance factors*.

Here α denotes a constant normalizer. The derivations of (8) and (10) follow directly from the fact that the environment is a stationary Markov chain, for which future states and observations are conditionally independent from past ones given knowledge of the state. Equation (9) is obtained using the theorem of total probability.

Armed with the notion of belief states, the policy is now a mapping from belief states (instead of histories) to actions:

$$\sigma : \theta \longrightarrow a \tag{11}$$

The legitimacy of conditioning a on θ, instead of d, follows directly from the fact that the environment is Markov, which implies that θ is all one needs to know about the past to make optimal decisions.

2.3 Sample Representations

Thus far, we intentionally left open how belief states θ are *represented*. In prior work, state spaces have been discrete. In discrete worlds, beliefs can be represented by a collection of probabilities (one for each state), hence, beliefs can be represented exactly. Here were are interested in real-valued state spaces. In general, probability distributions over real-valued spaces possess infinitely many dimensions, hence cannot be represented on a digital computer.

The key idea is to represent belief states by *sets of (weighted) samples* drawn from the belief distribution. Figure 1 illustrates two popular schemes for sample-based approximation: *likelihood-weighted sampling*, in which samples (shown at the bottom of Figure 1a) are drawn directly from the target distribution (labeled f in Figure 1a), and *importance sampling*, where samples are drawn from some other distribution, such as the curve labeled g in Figure 1b. In the latter case, samples x are annotated by a numerical importance factor

$$p(x) = \frac{f(x)}{g(x)} \tag{12}$$

to account for the difference in the sampling distribution, g, and the target distribution f (the height of the bars in Figure 1b illustrates the importance factors). Importance sampling requires that $f > 0 \rightarrow g > 0$, which will be the case throughout this paper. Obviously, both sampling methods generate approximations only. Under mild assumptions, they converge to the target distribution at a rate of $\frac{1}{\sqrt{N}}$, with N denoting the sample set size [16].

In the context of POMDPs, the use of sample-based representations gives rise to the following algorithm for approximate belief propagation (c.f., Equation (10)):

    Algorithm particle_filter(θ_t, a_t, o_{t+1}):
        $\theta_{t+1} = \emptyset$
        do N times:
            draw random state x_t from θ_t

sample x_{t+1} according to $\mu(x_{t+1} \mid a_t, x_t)$
　　　set importance factor $p(x_{t+1}) = \nu(o_{t+1} \mid x_{t+1})$
　　　add $\langle x_{t+1}, p(x_{t+1}) \rangle$ to θ_{t+1}
　　　normalize all $p(x_{t+1}) \in \theta_{t+1}$ so that $\sum p(x_{t+1}) = 1$
　　　return θ_{t+1}

This algorithm converges to (10) for arbitrary models μ, ν, and π and arbitrary belief distributions θ, defined over discrete, continuous, or mixed continuous-discrete state and action spaces. It has, with minor modifications, been proposed under names like *particle filters* [13], *condensation algorithm* [5], *survival of the fittest* [8], and, in the context of robotics, *Monte Carlo localization* [4].

2.4 Projection

In conventional planning, the result of applying an action a_t at a state x_t is a distribution $Pr(x_{t+1}, R_{t+1} \mid a_t, x_t)$ over states x_{t+1} and rewards R_{t+1} at the next time step. This operation is called *projection*. In POMDPs, the state x_t is unknown. Instead, one has to compute the result of applying action a_t to a belief state θ_t. The result is a distribution $Pr(\theta_{t+1}, R_{t+1} \mid a_t, \theta_t)$ over belief states θ_{t+1} and rewards R_{t+1}. Since belief states themselves are distributions, the result of a projection in POMDPs is, technically, a distribution over distributions.

The projection algorithm is derived as follows. Using total probability, we obtain:

$$Pr(\theta_{t+1}, R_{t+1} \mid a_t, \theta_t) = Pr(\theta_{t+1}, R_{t+1} \mid a_t, d_t) \qquad (13)$$

$$= \int \underbrace{Pr(\theta_{t+1}, R_{t+1} \mid o_{t+1}, a_t, d_t)}_{(*)} \underbrace{Pr(o_{t+1} \mid a_t, d_t)}_{(**)} do_{t+1} \qquad (14)$$

The term $(*)$ has already been derived in the previous section (c.f., Equation (10)), under the observation that the reward R_{t+1} is trivially computed from the observation o_{t+1}.

The second term, $(**)$, is obtained by integrating out the unknown variables, x_{t+1} and x_t, and by once again exploiting the Markov property:

$$Pr(o_{t+1} \mid a_t, d_t) = \int Pr(o_{t+1} \mid x_{t+1}) \, Pr(x_{t+1} \mid a_t, d_t) \, dx_{t+1} \qquad (15)$$

$$= \int Pr(o_{t+1} \mid x_{t+1}) \int Pr(x_{t+1} \mid x_t, a_t) \, Pr(x_t \mid d_t) \, dx_t \, dx_{t+1} \qquad (16)$$

$$= \int \nu(o_{t+1} \mid x_{t+1}) \int \mu(x_{t+1} \mid x_t, a_t) \, \theta_t(x_t) \, dx_t \, dx_{t+1} \qquad (17)$$

This leads to the following approximate algorithm for projecting belief state. In the spirit of this paper, our approach uses Monte Carlo integration instead of exact integration. It represents distributions (and distributions over distributions) by samples drawn from such distributions.

　　Algorithm particle_projection(θ_t, a_t):
　　$\Theta_t = \emptyset$
　　do N times:
　　　　draw random state x_t from θ_t
　　　　sample a next state x_{t+1} according to $\mu(x_{t+1} \mid a_t, x_t)$
　　　　sample an observation o_{t+1} according to $\nu(o_{t+1} \mid x_{t+1})$
　　　　compute $\theta_{t+1} =$ particle_filter(θ_t, a_t, o_{t+1})
　　　　add $\langle \theta_{t+1}, R(o_{t+1}) \rangle$ to Θ_t
　　return Θ_t

The result of this algorithm, Θ_t, is a sample set of belief states θ_{t+1} and rewards R_{t+1}, drawn from the desired distribution $Pr(\theta_{t+1}, R_{t+1} \mid \theta_t, a_t)$. As $N \to \infty$, Θ_t converges with probability 1 to the true posterior [16].

2.5 Learning Value Functions

Following the rich literature on reinforcement learning [7, 15], our approach solves the POMDP problem by value iteration in belief space. More specifically, our approach recursively learns a value function Q over belief states and action, by *backing up* values from subsequent belief states:

$$Q(\theta_t, a_t) \longleftarrow E\left[R(o_{t+1}) + \gamma \max_{\bar{a}} Q(\theta_{t+1}, \bar{a})\right] \tag{18}$$

Leaving open (for a moment) how Q is represented, it is easy to be seen how the algorithm **particle_projection** can be applied to compute a Monte Carlo approximation of the right hand-side expression: Given a belief state θ_t and an action a_t, **particle_projection** computes a sample of $R(o_{t+1})$ and θ_{t+1}, from which the expected value on the right hand side of (18) can be approximated.

It has been shown [2] that if both sides of (18) are equal, the *greedy* policy

$$\sigma^Q(\theta) = \underset{\bar{a}}{\operatorname{argmax}} Q(\theta, \bar{a}) \tag{19}$$

is *optimal*, i.e., $\sigma^* = \sigma^Q$. Furthermore, it has been shown (for the discrete case!) that repetitive application of (18) leads to an optimal value function and, thus, to the optimal policy [17, 3].

Our approach essentially performs model-based reinforcement learning in belief space using approximate sample-based representations. This makes it possible to apply a rich bag of tricks found in the literature on MDPs. In our experiments below, we use on-line reinforcement learning with counter-based exploration and experience replay [9] to determine the order in which belief states are updated.

2.6 Nearest Neighbor

We now return to the issue how to represent Q. Since we are operating in real-valued spaces, some sort of function approximation method is called for. However, recall that Q accepts a probability distribution (a sample set) as an input. This makes most existing function approximators (e.g., neural networks) inapplicable.

In our current implementation, nearest neighbor [11] is applied to represent Q. More specifically, our algorithm maintains a set of sample sets θ (belief states) annotated by an action a and a Q-value $Q(\theta, a)$. When a new belief state θ' is encountered, its Q-value is obtained by finding the k nearest neighbors in the database, and linearly averaging their Q-values. If there aren't sufficiently many neighbors (within a pre-specified maximum distance), θ' is added to the database; hence, the database grows over time.

Our approach uses KL divergence (relative entropy) as a distance function[1]. Technically, the KL-divergence between two continuous distributions is well-defined. When applied to sample sets, however, it cannot be computed. Hence, when evaluating the distance between two different sample sets, our approach maps them into continuous-valued densities using Gaussian kernels, and uses Monte Carlo sampling to approximate the KL divergence between them. This algorithm is fairly generic an extension of nearest neighbors to function approximation in density space, where densities are represented by samples. Space limitations preclude us from providing further detail (see [11, 12]).

3 Experimental Results

Preliminary results have been obtained in a world shown in two domains, one synthetic and one using a simulator of a RWI B21 robot.

In the synthetic environment (Figure 2a), the agents starts at the lower left corner. Its objective is to reach "heaven" which is either at the upper left corner or the lower right

---

[1]Strictly speaking, KL divergence is not a distance metric, but this is ignored here.

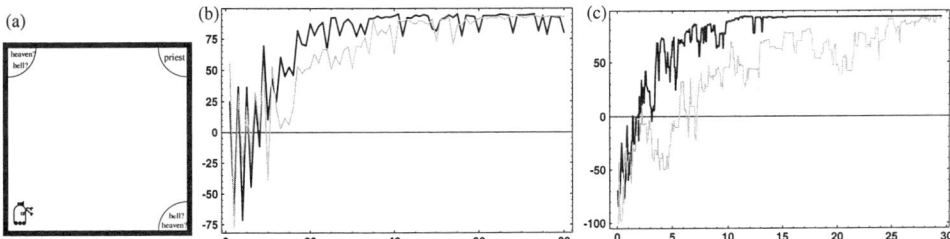

Figure 2: (a) The environment, schematically. (b) Average performance (reward) as a function of training episodes. The black graph corresponds to the smaller environment (25 steps min), the grey graph to the larger environment (50 steps min). (c) Same results, plotted as a function of number of backups (in thousands).

corner. The opposite location is "hell." The agent does not know the location of heaven, but it can ask a "priest" who is located in the upper right corner. Thus, an optimal solution requires the agent to go first to the priest, and then head to heaven. The state space contains a real-valued (coordinates of the agent) and discrete (location of heaven) component. Both are unobservable: In addition to not knowing the location of heaven, the agent also cannot sense its (real-valued) coordinates. 5% random motion noise is injected at each move. When an agent hits a boundary, it is penalized, but it is also told which boundary it hit (which makes it possible to infer its coordinates along one axis). However, notice that the *initial* coordinates of the agent are known.

The optimal solution takes approximately 25 steps; thus, a successful POMDP planner must be capable of looking 25 steps ahead. We will use the term "successful policy" to refer to a policy that always leads to heaven, even if the path is suboptimal. For a policy to be successful, the agent must have learned to first move to the priest (information gathering), and then proceed to the right target location.

Figures 2b&c show performance results, averaged over 13 experiments. The solid (black) curve in both diagrams plots the average cumulative reward J as a function of the number of training episodes (Figure 2b), and as a function of the number of backups (Figure 2c). A successful policy was consistently found after 17 episodes (or 6,150 backups), in all 13 experiments. In our current implementation, 6,150 backups require approximately 29 minutes on a Pentium PC. In some experiments, a successful policy was identified in 6 episodes (less than 1,500 backups or 7 minutes). After a successful policy is found, further learning gradually optimizes the path. To investigate scaling, we doubled the size of the environment (quadrupling the size of the state space), making the optimal solution 50 steps long. The results are depicted by the gray curves in Figures 2b&c. Here a successful policy is consistently found after 33 episodes (10,250 backups, 58 minutes). In some runs, a successful policy is identified after only 14 episodes.

We also applied MC-POMDPs to a robotic *locate-and-retrieve task*. Here a robot (Figure 3a) is to find and grasp an object somewhere in its vicinity (at floor *or* table height). The robot's task is to grasp the object using its gripper. It is rewarded for successfully grasping the object, and penalized for unsuccessful grasps or for moving too far away from the object. The state space is continuous in x and y coordinates, and discrete in the object's height.

The robot uses a mono-camera system for object detection; hence, viewing the object from a single location is insufficient for its 3D localization. Moreover, initially the object might not be in sight of the robot's camera, so that the robot must look around first. In our simulation, we assume 30% general detection error (false-positive and false-negative), with additional Gaussian noise if the object is detected correctly. The robot's actions include turns (by a variable angle), translations (by a variable distance), and grasps (at one of two legal heights). Robot control is erroneous with a variance of 20% (in x-y-space) and 5% (in rotational space). Typical belief states range from uniformly distributed sample sets (initial belief) to samples narrowly focused on a specific x-y-z location.

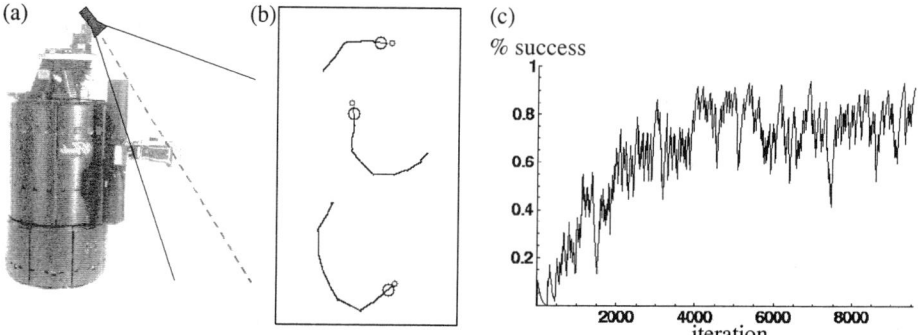

Figure 3: Find and fetch task: (a) The mobile robot with gripper and camera, holding the target object (experiments are carried out in simulation!), (b) three successful runs (trajectory projected into 2D), and (c) success rate as a function of number of planning steps.

Figure 3c shows the rate of successful grasps as a function of iterations (actions). While initially, the robot fails to grasp the object, after approximately 4,000 iterations its performance surpasses 80%. Here the planning time is in the order of 2 hours. However, the robot fails to reach 100%. This is in part because certain initial configurations make it impossible to succeed (e.g., when the object is too close to the maximum allowed distance), in part because the robot occasionally misses the object by a few centimeters. Figure 3b depicts three successful example trajectories. In all three, the robot initially searches the object, then moves towards it and grasps it successfully.

4 Discussion

We have presented a Monte Carlo approach for learning how to act in partially observable Markov decision processes (POMDPs). Our approach represents all belief distributions using samples drawn from these distributions. Reinforcement learning in belief space is applied to learn optimal policies, using a sample-based version of nearest neighbor for generalization. Backups are performed using Monte Carlo sampling. Initial experimental results demonstrate that our approach is applicable to real-valued domains, and that it yields good performance results in environments that are—by POMDP standards—relatively large.

References

[1] AAAI Fall symposium on POMDPs. 1998. See http://www.cs.duke.edu/~mlittman/talks/pomdp-symposium.html
[2] R. E. Bellman. *Dynamic Programming*. Princeton University Press, 1957.
[3] P. Dayan and T. J. Sejnowski. TD(λ) converges with probability 1. 1993.
[4] D. Fox, W. Burgard, F. Dellaert, and S. Thrun. Monte carlo localization: Efficient position estimation for mobile robots. AAAI-99.
[5] M. Isard and A. Blake. Condensation: conditional density propagation for visual tracking. *International Journal of Computer Vision*, 1998.
[6] L.P. Kaelbling, M.L. Littman, and A.R. Cassandra. Planning and acting in partially observable stochastic domains. Submitted for publication, 1997.
[7] L.P. Kaelbling, M.L. Littman, and A.W. Moore. Reinforcement learning: A survey. *JAIR*, 4, 1996.
[8] K. Kanazawa, D. Koller, and S.J. Russell. Stochastic simulation algorithms for dynamic probabilistic networks. UAI-95.
[9] L.-J. Lin. Self-improving reactive agents based on reinforcement learning, planning and teaching. *Machine Learning*, 8, 1992.
[10] M.L. Littman, A.R. Cassandra, and L.P. Kaelbling. Learning policies for partially observable environments: Scaling up. ICML-95.
[11] A.W. Moore, C.G. Atkeson, and S.A. Schaal. Locally weighted learning for control. *AI Review*, 11, 1997.
[12] D. Ormoneit and S. Sen. Kernel-based reinforcement learning. TR 1999-8, Statistics, Stanford University, 1999.
[13] M. Pitt and N. Shephard. Filtering via simulation: auxiliary particle filter. *Journal of the American Statistical Association*, 1999.
[14] E. Sondik. *The Optimal Control of Partially Observable Markov Processes*. PhD thesis, Stanford, 1971.
[15] R.S. Sutton and A.G. Barto. *Reinforcement Learning: An Introduction*. MIT Press, 1998.
[16] M.A. Tanner. *Tools for Statistical Inference*. Springer Verlag, 1993.
[17] C. J. C. H. Watkins. *Learning from Delayed Rewards*. PhD thesis, King's College, Cambridge, 1989.

Index of Authors

Abu-Mostafa, Yaser, 963
Adorján, Péter, 89
Ahuja, Narendra, 862
Amari, Shun-ichi, 192, 363
Andrieu, Christophe, 379
Attias, Hagai, 209, 386

Bakker, Rembrandt, 879
Ballard, Dana H., 3
Baram, Yoram, 694
Barber, David, 393
Barron, Andrew R., 279
Bartlett, Marian Stewart, 886
Bartlett, Peter, 512
Baxter, Jonathan, 512
Bayliss, Jessica D., 3
Beal, Matthew J., 449
Ben-Hur, Asa, 335
Bengio, Samy, 400
Bengio, Yoshua, 307, 400
Blair, Alan, 66
Bleek, Cor M. van den, 879
Boe, Gene, 1029
Bosch, Antal van den, 73
Briegel, Thomas, 407
Brown, Andrew D., 122
Brown, Edgar A., 724
Brown, Guy J., 747
Brown, Timothy X., 893
Buhmann, Joachim M., 216
Burges, Christopher J. C., 223, 244

Calabrese, Ronald L., 731
Carlile, Simon, 761, 768
Carreira-Perpiñán, Miguel Á., 414
Castaño, Rebecca, 928
Chapelle, Olivier, 230, 421
Chechik, Gal, 96
Chklovskii, Dmitri B., 103, 108
Choi, Samuel P. M., 987
Cichocki, A., 363
Coolen, A. C. C., 237
Coppens, Marc-Olivier, 879
Corderoy, Anna, 768
Cowan, Jack D., 314
Crisp, David J., 223, 244
Cristianini, Nello, 547
Csató, Lehel, 251
Cymbalyuk, Gennady S., 731

Dayan, Peter, 24
Deco, Gustavo, 10

DeWeerth, Stephen P., 724, 731
Dietterich, Thomas G., 994
Dom, Byron, 970
Donato, Gianluca, 886
Dorffner, Georg, 52, 645
Doucet, Arnaud, 379
Downs, Oliver B., 428
Duffy, Nigel, 258

Ekman, Paul, 886
Eurich, Christian W., 115

Fisher III, John W., 900
Flake, Gary William, 435
Fokoué, Ernest, 251
Frean, Marcus, 512
Freeman, William T., 673, 820
Freitas, João F. G. de, 379, 796
Frey, Brendan J., 442, 477

Gerules, Mark, 1029
Ghahramani, Zoubin, 449, 463
Ghiselli-Crippa, Thea B., 17
Giannakopoulos, Xavier, 789
Giles, C. Lee, 879
Golden, Richard M., 907
Gordon, Mirta B., 321
Graepel, Thore, 456
Grimes, David B., 935
Gyger, Stève, 710

Hager, Joseph C., 886
Hansen, Lars Kai, 265, 754
Hastie, Trevor, 540
Held, Marcus, 216
Helmbold, David, 258
Hely, Tim A., 185
Herbrich, Ralf, 456
Hermansky, Hynek, 803
Hernandez, Gerardina, 150
Hershey, John, 813
Hinton, Geoffrey E., 122, 463
Hofmann, Thomas, 914
Horn, David, 129
Howe, Nicholas R., 820
Hoyer, Patrik, 827
Husbands, Parry, 703
Hyvärinen, Aapo, 827
Højen-Sørensen, Pedro A. d. F. R., 754

Ihler, Alexander T., 900

Isbell, Jr., Charles Lee, 703

Jaakkola, Tommi, 470
Jebara, Tony, 470
Jin, Craig T., 761, 768
Johnson, Doug, 1029
Johnson, Eric, 935
Jojic, Nebojsa, 477
Jordan, Michael I., 533
Jourjine, Alexander, 775

Kabashima, Yoshiyuki, 272
Kakade, Sham, 24
Kasdan, Harvey, 963
Kaushansky, Howard, 935
Kearns, Michael, 956, 1001
Keeler, Jim, 1029
Keerthi, S. Sathiya, 631
Koch, Christof, 143
Koller, Daphne, 1022, 1036
Konda, Vijay R., 1008

Landolt, Oliver, 710
Laskov, Pavel, 484
Lee, Daniel D., 428, 491
Lee, Soo-Young, 31
Lee, Tai Sing, 834
Leventon, Michael E., 820
Levy, Nir, 129
Li, Jonathan Q., 279
Li, Song, 286
Li, Yi, 498
Li, Zhaoping, 136
Liao, Yuansong, 921
Lippman, Andrew, 977
Litman, Diane, 956
Liu, Shih-Chii, 717
Liu, Xiuwen, 38
Long, Philip M., 498
Lund, Jennifer, 949

Maass, Wolfgang, 293
Mace, C. W. H., 237
MacKay, David J.C., 428
Mann, Tobias, 928
Mansour, Yishay, 300, 1001, 1057
Manwani, Amit, 143
Margaritis, Dimitris, 505
Martin, Greg, 1029
Mason, Llew, 512
Mayhew, John E.W., 949
McAllester, David, 300, 1057
McClelland, James L., 45
McLoughlin, Niall, 949
Meila, Marina, 470
Meilijson, Isaac, 96, 129
Mel, Bartlett W., 157

Merwe, Rudolph van der, 666
Mesterharm, Chris, 519
Mika, Sebastian, 526, 561
Millman, K. Jarrod, 841
Mjolsness, Eric, 928
Moody, John, 687, 921
Movellan, Javier R., 45, 813, 886
Mozer, Michael C., 31, 80, 935
Müller, Klaus–Robert, 526, 561, 942
Mukherjee, Sayan, 659
Munro, Paul W., 17, 150
Murata, Noboru, 192
Murayama, Tatsuto, 272
Murphy, Kevin P., 1015

Nadeau, Claude, 307
Nakahara, Hiroyuki, 192
Nelson, Alex T., 666
Ng, Andrew Y., 533, 1001, 1022
Niranjan, Mahesan, 796

Obermayer, Klaus, 89, 456, 949
Ogawa, Hidemitsu, 624
Ohira, Toru, 314
Olshausen, Bruno A., 841
Onoda, Takashi, 561
Opper, Manfred, 251
Ormoneit, Dirk, 540

Parfitt, Shan, 52
Parga, Nestor, 171
Parr, Ronald, 1022, 1036
Parra, Lucas, 848, 942
Patel, Girish N., 724, 731
Pearlmutter, Barak A., 185, 435
Piché, Stephen, 1029
Piepenbrock, Christian, 89
Platt, John C., 547, 582
Poirazi, Panayiota, 157
Postma, Eric, 73

Rätsch, Gunnar, 526, 561
Rao, Rajesh P. N., 164
Rasmussen, Carl Edward, 554, 754
Renart, Alfonso, 171
Rickard, Scott, 775
Risau-Gusman, Sebastian, 321
Robinson, Tony, 796
Rodríguez, Andrés, 1036
Roitershtein, Alexander, 335
Rokni, Uri, 491
Rolls, Edmund T., 171
Rosca, Justinian, 775
Roth, Dan, 862
Roth, Volker, 568
Roweis, Sam, 782
Roy, Benjamin Van, 575

Index of Authors

Roy, Nicholas, 1043
Ruanaidh, Joseph Ó, 775
Ruppin, Eytan, 96, 129
Rusmevichientong, Paat, 575

Saad, David, 272
Sajda, Paul, 942
Sallans, Brian, 1050
Sato, Yuzuru, 314
Schaik, André van, 738, 768
Schießl, Ingo, 949
Schmitt, Michael, 328
Schneidman, Elad, 178
Schölkopf, Bernhard, 342, 526, 561, 582
Schöner, Holger, 949
Schottky, Bernhard, 251
Schouten, Jaap C., 879
Schraudolph, Nicol N., 789
Schuster, Mike, 589
Schuurmans, Dale, 596
Schwabe, Lars, 89
Schwegler, Helmut, 115
Seeger, Matthias, 603
Segev, Idan, 178
Sejnowski, Terrence J., 164, 886
Seung, H. Sebastian, 199
Shawe-Taylor, John, 342, 547, 582
Siegelmann, Hava T., 335
Sill, Joseph, 963
Simoncelli, Eero P., 855
Singer, Yoram, 610
Singh, Satinder, 956, 1057
Slonim, Noam, 617
Smith, Gavin, 796
Smola, Alexander J., 342, 526, 561, 582
Sollich, Peter, 349, 393
Sompolinsky, Haim, 491
Song, Xubo B., 963
Spence, Clay D., 848, 942
Steinhage, Volker, 568
Steinmetz, Peter N., 143
Stetter, Martin, 949
Stevens, Charles F., 103
Sugiyama, Masashi, 624
Sundararajan, S., 631
Sutton, Richard S., 1057
Sykacek, Peter, 638

Takens, Floris, 879
Tang, Akaysha C., 185
Teh, Yee Whye, 463
Tenenbaum, Joshua B., 59
Thrun, Sebastian, 505, 1043, 1064
Tiňo, Peter, 52, 645
Tipping, Michael E., 652
Tishby, Naftali, 178, 617
Tonkes, Bradley, 66
Tresp, Volker, 407

Tsitsiklis, John N., 1008

Vaithyanathan, Shivakumar, 970
Vapnik, Vladimir N., 230, 421, 659
Vasconcelos, Nuno, 977
Vicente, Renato, 272
Viola, Paul A., 900

Wainwright, Martin J., 855
Walker, Marilyn, 956
Wan, Eric A., 666
Wang, DeLiang L., 38, 747
Watanabe, Sumio, 356
Weijters, Ton, 73
Weisend, Michael P., 185
Weiss, Yair, 673
Weston, Jason, 421, 526
Wiles, Janet, 66
Wilke, Stefan D., 115
Williams, Christopher K. I., 680
Williamson, Robert C., 342, 582
Winther, Ole, 251
Wold, Barbara, 928
Wolniewicz, Richard, 935
Wong, K. Y. Michael, 286
Wu, Si, 192

Xie, Xiaohui, 199

Yang, Howard Hua, 687, 803
Yang, Ming-Hsuan, 862
Yang, Zhiyong, 869
Yeung, Dit-Yan, 987
Yu, Stella X., 834

Zemel, Richard S., 80, 869
Zhang, L.-Q., 363
Zhang, Nevin L., 987
Zhang, Tong, 370
Zibulevsky, Michael, 185
Ziehe, Andreas, 942
Zihl, Josef, 10
Zlochin, Mark, 694

Keyword Index

ν support vector machines, 244
ε-insensitive loss, 659
20 Newsgroups, 617

acoustic-to-articulatory mapping, 414
active learning, 624
actor-critic methods, 1008, 1057
adaBoost, 561
adaline learning, 286
address-event, 710
algebraic analysis, 356
analog computation, 328
analog neurons, 171
analog noise, 335
analog VLSI, 710, 724, 731, 738, 907
analytical predictions, 157
annealing, 907
anomaly detection, 470, 582
anti-Hebbian, 199
approximate inference, 442, 533, 575, 673, 1050
approximation by neural networks, 1036
approximation capabilities, 328
arcing, 561
articulatory methods, 782
artifact removal, 775
associative memory, 80, 96
asymptotic analysis, 370
asymptotic efficiency, 192
attention, 89
attention switching, 31
attractor learning, 879
attractor networks, 80
audio-visual, 813
auditory model, 747
auditory psychophysics, 761, 768
autapse, 199
autoencoders, 17
automatic relevance determination, 652
autoshaping, 24
average reward, 1057
axial locomotion, 724
axons, 108

band-pass filters, 738
bandwidth selection, 540
batch learning, 286
Bayes-optimal decision, 456
Bayesian inference, 59, 209, 251, 386, 575, 638
Bayesian learning, 265, 379, 449, 694, 977, 1015
Bayesian methods, 265, 603, 631, 652, 754, 855, 970, 977
Bayesian mixtures, 554

Bayesian models, 45, 59
Bayesian network induction, 505
Bayesian networks, 400, 505, 533
Bayesian reconstruction, 820
belief networks, 122, 575, 848, 1036
belief propagation, 272, 442, 575, 673, 1036, 1064
Bernstein's inequality, 216
bias correction, 803
bias-variance tradeoff, 265
bifurcation analysis, 731
biomedical imaging, 963
blind deconvolution, 363
blind source separation, 185, 209, 363, 386, 775, 949
Boltzmann machine, 428
boosting, 258, 300, 512, 561, 610
boundary-pair representation, 38
BP-SOM, 73
brain-computer interface, 3

capacity control, 342
causal discovery, 505
cavity method, 286
center of mass, 192
central pattern generators, 724
channel fluctuations, 143
chaotic time series, 879
character recognition, 498
churn, 935
classical conditioning, 24
classification, 251, 258, 512, 547, 638, 652, 687
clustering, 449, 477, 617, 680, 970
CNV, 3
cognitive modelling, 80
combinations, 512
combined classifiers, 547
communication, 893
complex cells, 827
computability, 335
computational auditory scene analysis, 747
computational complexity, 293, 328
computer vision, 463
concept learning, 59
condition monitoring, 582
conditional independence, 687
confidence measure, 456
context, 963
context-sensitive processing, 834
contextual influences, 136
continuity constraints, 414
control, 1029
convergence, 108
convex hulls, 244

cooperative mixture of experts, 24
cortex, 103
cortex correlation, 192
cortical dynamics, 136
cortical representation, 89
covering numbers, 370
cross validation, 307, 631, 970
cue combination, 869
cue enhancement, 869
curse of dimensionality, 400

DAGSVM, 547
data mining, 400, 935
data visualization, 687
date calculation task, 73
decision making, 935
decision trees, 300
decomposition algorithm, 484
delay, 314
delay match to sample, 171
dendrites, 108
density estimation, 279, 400, 554, 582, 659, 1022, 1036
density propagation, 1022
deterministic annealing, 216
diagnosis, 533
dialogue systems, 956
differential geometry, 694
differentiation, 435
diffusion networks, 45
digit recognition, 463
dimensionality reduction, 449, 477
directed graphs, 547
direction selectivity, 164
Dirichlet process, 554
discount factor, 893
discriminant analysis, 526
discrimination capacity, 157
distributed synchrony, 129
divergence, 108
document clustering, 970
dual estimation, 666
dynamic Bayesian networks, 122, 386, 1036, 1050
dynamic coding, 89
dynamic environments, 1015
dynamic trees, 680
dynamical systems, 724, 731, 782, 879, 900, 1029

early stopping, 286
eigenvalues, 342
electronic ear, 738
EM algorithm, 407, 477, 491, 666, 796, 848
encoding strategy, 115
energy function, 80
ensembles, 265, 921
entropy, 540
entropy minimization, 1043
entropy numbers, 342

error backpropagation, 31
error bars, 307, 349
error-correcting codes, 272
evidence, 349
evidence framework, 603
evoked potentials, 3
experimental design, 624
experts, 519
extended Kalman filter, 666
extended spatial decorrelation, 949
eye movement control, 834

face detection, 862
facial expression recognition, 886
factor analysis, 449, 477
factorial experts, 24
fast synaptic plasticity, 89
fat-shattering dimension, 547
feasible direction algorithm, 484
feature extraction, 526, 617, 900
feature grouping, 921
feature selection, 470, 687, 803, 921, 970
feature spaces, 568
feedforward neural networks, 237, 321
Feigenbaum sequence, 645
figure-ground, 38, 136
finite-memory sources, 52, 645
Fisher information, 115
Fisher kernel, 914
Fisher scoring, 407
Fisher's discriminant, 526, 568
fMRI, 754
free energy, 356
functional brain imaging, 185

Gallager codes, 272
Gaussian density, 575
Gaussian fields, 393
Gaussian mixtures, 279, 554
Gaussian network, 442
Gaussian processes, 251, 349, 603, 631, 673
gene clustering, 928
gene regulation networks, 928
generalization, 66, 230, 258, 265, 286, 307, 400, 624
generalization error inference, 307
generative models, 80, 122, 491, 827, 869
geometric convergence, 379
geometry, 244
Gestalt rules, 38
Gibbs learning, 321
Gibbs sampling, 554
Ginni index, 300
gradient methods, 258, 512, 1057
graphical models, 209, 386, 393, 400, 463, 470, 533
greedy algorithm, 279
greedy search, 300

Keyword Index

Green's function, 286

Hebbian learning, 96, 129, 150, 157, 164
hemodynamic response, 754
hidden Markov models, 209, 386, 589, 754, 782, 855
hidden Markov tree, 848
hierarchical clustering, 680
hierarchical mixtures of experts, 879
higher order statistics, 491
HIP model, 848
histogram clustering, 216
Hodgkin-Huxley neurons, 178
human learning, 59
hyperparameters, 349, 631
hyperspectral imaging, 942

ICA, 185, 209, 386, 491, 687, 703, 775, 789, 827, 886, 942, 949
ill-possed problem, 659
image basis, 886
image databases, 977
image probability, 848
image recognition, 963
image representations, 977
image statistics, 855
importance sampling, 449, 596
incremental learning, 498
independence assumption, 589
independence tests, 505
inductive bias, 66
inference, 393
infinite mixtures, 554
information coding, 178
information geometry, 914
information integration, 45
information maximization, 834
information retrieval, 914
information theory, 115, 900
inhibitory neurons, 293
input selection, 638
intersegmental coordination, 724
intracortical interactions, 136
invariant features, 526
inverse problems, 414, 782
ion channels, 178
iterative scaling, 610

Jacobi matrix, 435
joint mutual information, 687, 803

Kalman filter, 3, 24, 407
Kalman training, 666
kernel biliard, 456
kernel classifier, 603
kernel functions, 568
kernel methods, 342, 349, 498, 582, 652, 659

knowledge-based inference, 820
Kullback-Leibler risk, 279

language evolution, 66
language recognition, 335
large deviations, 216
large margin methods, 547, 561, 582
large-scale computing, 703
large-scale gene expression, 928
laser data, 879
latent class models, 914
latent variable models, 414
lateral inhibition, 293
lazy learning, 540
learning, 66
learning curves, 1001
learning derivatives, 435
learning dynamics, 237, 286
learning rate adapatation, 789
leave-one-out, 230, 421
linear classification, 370
linear functions, 519
linear programming, 561
local basis images, 886
local linear regression, 540
logistic regression, 610
loopy probability propagation, 442
lossy compression, 617
lower bounds, 293
LTP, 150
Lyapunov function, 80

machine learning, 300
macroeconomic forecasting, 921
magnetoencephalography, 185
MAP, 942
map learning, 1015
margin, 258
Markov blanket, 505
Markov chains, 379, 554, 680, 694, 754, 907
Markov decision processes, 956, 994, 1022, 1043, 1057
Markov models, 143, 335, 645, 907
match enhancement, 171
matrix momentum, 789
maximum entropy, 216, 470
maximum likelihood, 192, 265, 279, 428
MAXQ decomposition, 994
mean field methods, 10, 251, 393, 463, 533
medial axis, 136
membrane noise, 143
memory guided attention, 171
Metropolis update, 754
microprism, 710
minimal pairs, 52
minimum description length, 279
missing data reconstruction, 414
mistake bounds, 519

mistake-bound model, 498
mixture density, 848
mixture density networks, 589
mixture models, 209, 680, 855
mixture of factor analyzers, 449
mixture of Gaussians, 477, 841
model learning, 987
model order determination, 970
model selection, 216, 230, 307, 379, 449, 603, 970
model structure determination, 970
Monte Carlo methods, 143, 428, 596, 694, 907, 1064
Morris-Lecar model, 731
motion capture, 820
multi-class learning, 547
multi-class prediction, 519
multi-criteria, 893
multi-way branching, 300
multifractals, 52, 645
multinomial distribution, 400
multiplicative weights, 519
multiscale representation, 855
mutual information, 803, 813, 900

natural gradient, 363
natural image statistics, 827
natural images, 841, 855
natural language, 52
nearest neighbors, 540
neocortex, 164
network size, 328
neural activity, 754
neural communication, 724
neural network committees, 921
neural networks, 279, 694, 1029
neural oscillator, 747
neural plasticity, 150
neural population, 115
neural system models, 761
neuromorphic systems, 710, 717, 738
neuronal regulation, 96
neurons, 103
neuropsychology, 10
neuroscience, 150
noisy patterns, 31
non-identifiable models, 356
non-regular models, 356
nongaussian data, 687
nonlinear classification, 568
nonlinear discriminant, 526
nonlinear filtering, 666
nonlinear integration, 157
nonlinear principal component analysis, 879
nonminimum phase systems, 363
nonparametric density estimation, 900
nonstationary environments, 789, 987
novelty detection, 582

object recognition, 848

oculo-motor system, 710
on-line learning, 251, 498, 519, 789, 862
one-to-many mappings, 414
optical imaging, 949
optimization, 1029
orientation selectivity, 89
oscillatory correlation, 747
oscillatory networks, 724, 731
outlier, 561
overfitting, 237

P3, 3
PAC bounds, 370
parallel algorithms, 703
parameter constraints, 782
parameterized policies, 1057
parametric model, 477
parity task, 73
partially observable Markov decision processes, 987, 1001, 1015, 1022, 1036, 1050, 1064
pattern recognition, 223, 244, 862, 963
PCA, 526, 703, 886
perception, 45
perceptrons, 321, 498
perceptual organization, 38
persistent neural activity, 199
phonetic classification, 803
pixel unmixing, 942
place coding, 710
planning, 1001, 1043
policy iteration, 1057
policy search, 1022
population coding, 192, 710, 869
Potassium channels, 143
potential function, 258
power, 893
pre-attentive pop-out, 834
pre-attentive segmentation, 136
prediction trees, 645
predictive approaches, 164, 631
prepare, 393
priming, 17, 80
probabilistic inference, 533, 596
probabilistic models, 335, 349, 393, 477, 942, 1043
probability propagation, 393, 442
process control, 1029
projection learning, 624
projection pursuit regression, 540
pseudo orthogonal basis, 624
psychophysics, 45

Q-learning, 893, 994
QMR-DT, 533
quadratic programming, 484
quality of service, 893

Keyword Index

rate distortion theory, 617
rate estimation, 24
RBF networks, 279, 638
receptive field, 115
rectified Gaussian, 428
recurrent cortical networks, 89
recurrent excitation, 164
recurrent networks, 66, 164, 171, 199, 589, 717, 928
regression, 223, 484, 631, 652
regularization, 610
REINFORCE, 1057
reinforcement learning, 893, 956, 987, 994, 1001, 1008, 1036, 1050, 1057, 1064
relevance feedback, 977
reliability, 24
replica method, 237, 272
resolution, 115
resolution of singularities, 356
response latency, 185
restricted training sets, 237
reverberating circuit, 199
reversible jump MCMC, 379, 638
ridge-regression, 421
risk-sensitive applications, 456
robotic agents, 1043
robust classification, 561
robust distribution, 407
robust learning, 379
robust recognition, 31
robust regression, 407
rule extraction, 73
rules, 59

saccade planning, 834
sample complexity, 1001
sample-based inference, 1015
sampling methods, 449, 907, 1064
Sato-Bernstein's polynomial, 356
scene exploration, 834
scientific computing, 703
SDEs, 45
second-order statistics, 775
segmentation, 463
selective attention, 10, 31
semi-Markov decision process, 994
semi-Markov Q learning, 994
semiparametric models, 363
sensor fusion, 45
sequence learning, 17
sequential data, 414
Shannon's capacity, 272
shape-from-shading, 869
shape-from-texture, 869
sigmoid belief networks, 393
sigmoidal networks, 328
signal processing, 775
silicon cochlea, 738
silicon neuron, 731

similarity, 59
single-camera tracking, 820
singular point, 491
slice sampling, 428
SNoW, 862
Sodium channels, 143
soft-max property, 717
sound localization, 761, 768, 775, 813
sound separation, 747
sparse coding, 827, 841
spatial cognition, 17
spatiotemporal integration, 17
speaker/channel variability, 803
speech recognition, 589, 782
speech signal processing, 796
spike timing, 122, 129, 150, 164, 199
spiking neurons, 129, 738
stability, 363
state space model, 666, 796
stationarity, 775
statistical dependence, 803
statistical learning theory, 265
statistical mechanics, 251, 272, 321
statistically neutral tasks, 73
stochastic approximations, 1008
stochastic complexity, 356
stochastic dynamics, 694
stochastic meta-descent, 789
stochastic resonance, 178, 314
Student-t-distribution, 407
subspace identification, 796
subthreshold noise, 143
sufficient statistics, 900
superefficiency, 363
superimposed patterns, 31
supervised learning, 568, 624, 914
support vector machines, 223, 230, 244, 321, 342, 349, 421, 456, 470, 484, 498, 526, 547, 582, 603, 659
surface representation, 38
synapses, 103
synaptic plasticity, 96, 164, 199
synchrony, 813
synfire chains, 129
system identification, 1015

tag structure, 52
TAP approach, 272
task decomposition, 73
TD learning, 1008
telecommunications, 935
temporal coding, 122
temporal dynamics, 38
temporal sequences, 17
text categorization, 914
text clustering, 970
threshold circuits, 293
threshold computation, 223
time series, 150, 782

time-delay neural networks, 761
time-varying mixtures, 789
topography, 827
tracking, 820
transcriptional regulation, 928
transduction, 421, 456, 470
transformation invariance, 477
trees, 463
trigonometric polynomial space, 624
tuning curve, 115, 192
turbocode, 442, 575
two time-scale algorithms, 1008

unbiased estimation, 596
uncertain position, 1043
uncertainty, 1064
unfaithful model, 192
uniform convergence bounds, 342
uniqueness theorems, 223
universal approximators, 293, 328
unscented transformation, 666
unsupervised learning, 216, 400, 582, 841, 914, 970
urinalysis, 963

V1, 136
value functions, 1050, 1057
variable dendritic morphology, 157
variance estimate, 307
variational methods, 209, 251, 386, 393, 449, 603, 1050
VC dimension, 230, 328, 1001
vector machines, 610
virtual auditory space, 768
virtual reality, 3
visual cortex, 827, 949
visual perception, 869
visual processing, 841
visual search, 10
visual system, 185
volatility forecasting, 645
volume ratio, 456
voting methods, 512

wavelets, 855, 886
weight decay, 286, 342
weight normalization, 96
winner-take-all, 293
winner-take-all circuit, 717
Winnow, 519, 862
wireless industry, 935
wiring economy, 103, 108
working set selection, 484